current Obstetric & Gynecologic Diagnosis & Treatment

current
Obstetric & Gynecologic
Diagnosis & Treatment

4TH EDITION

Edited By

RALPH C. BENSON, MD

Professor of Obstetrics & Gynecology and
Emeritus Chairman, Department of Obstetrics & Gynecology
Oregon Health Sciences University
Portland, Oregon

With Associate Authors

Illustrated by Laurel V. Schaubert

Lange Medical Publications
Los Altos, California 94022

A Concise Medical Library for Practitioner and Student

Current Medical Diagnosis & Treatment 1982 (annual revision). Edited by M.A. Krupp and M.J. Chatton. 1113 pp.	1982
Current Pediatric Diagnosis & Treatment, 7th ed. Edited by C.H. Kempe, H.K. Silver, and D. O'Brien. 1106 pp, *illus.*	1982
Current Surgical Diagnosis & Treatment, 5th ed. Edited by J.E. Dunphy and L.W. Way. 1138 pp, *illus.*	1981
Harper's Review of Biochemistry (formerly **Review of Physiological Chemistry**), 18th ed. D.W. Martin, Jr., P.A. Mayes, and V.W. Rodwell. 614 pp, *illus.*	1981
Review of Medical Physiology, 10th ed. W.F. Ganong. 628 pp, *illus.*	1981
Review of Medical Microbiology, 15th ed. E. Jawetz, J.L. Melnick, and E.A. Adelberg. 553 pp, *illus.*	1982
Review of Medical Pharmacology, 7th ed. F.H. Meyers, E. Jawetz, and A. Goldfien. 747 pp, *illus.*	1980
Basic & Clinical Immunology, 4th ed. Edited by D.P. Stites, J.D. Stobo, H.H. Fudenberg, and J.V. Wells. 775 pp, *illus.*	1982
Basic Histology, 3rd ed. L.C. Junqueira and J. Carneiro. 504 pp, *illus.*	1980
Clinical Cardiology, 3rd ed. M. Sokolow and M.B. McIlroy. 763 pp, *illus.*	1981
General Urology, 10th ed. D.R. Smith. 598 pp, *illus.*	1981
General Ophthalmology, 9th ed. D. Vaughan and T. Asbury. 410 pp, *illus.*	1980
Correlative Neuroanatomy & Functional Neurology, 18th ed. J.G. Chusid. About 460 pp, *illus.*	1982
Principles of Clinical Electrocardiography, 11th ed. M.J. Goldman. 437 pp, *illus.*	1982
Handbook of Obstetrics & Gynecology, 7th ed. R.C. Benson. 808 pp, *illus.*	1980
Physician's Handbook, 20th ed. M.A. Krupp, L.M. Tierney, Jr., E. Jawetz, R.L. Roe, and C.A. Camargo. 774 pp, *illus.*	1982
Handbook of Pediatrics, 13th ed. H.K. Silver, C.H. Kempe, and H.B. Bruyn. 735 pp, *illus.*	1980
Handbook of Poisoning: Prevention, Diagnosis, & Treatment, 10th ed. R.H. Dreisbach. 578 pp.	1980

Lithographed in USA

Table of Contents

Preface

The basic information and most recent developments in obstetrics and gynecology are presented in concise form in this fourth edition of *Current Obstetric & Gynecologic Diagnosis & Treatment*. The book is intended for use by medical students and residents and by practicing physicians, as well as by nurses and other health professionals. Much new material has been added, and the references have been updated and expanded. Chapters or sections that have been rewritten for the new edition are those on vaginal infections, the fetus, the newborn infant, diabetes during pregnancy, and trophoblastic diseases. Substantial revisions have been made in the sections on special medical and surgical considerations in gynecology, pediatric gynecology, high-risk pregnancy, and the puerperium.

The book is available in Spanish and Portuguese translations; French, German, Italian, and Turkish translations are in preparation. An English edition for distribution in Asia is printed in Singapore, and a Middle East–African edition is produced in Beirut.

We are grateful to all of the contributing authors for their expertise and cooperation in making each chapter an integrated part of the text. Our sincere thanks go also to the many students and physicians who have offered suggestions and criticisms for this and previous editions.

Ralph C. Benson, MD

Portland, Oregon
August, 1982

Authors

Robert L. Bacon, PhD
Professor of Anatomy, School of Medicine, Oregon Health Sciences University (Portland).

David L. Barclay, MD
Clinical Professor of Obstetrics & Gynecology, University of Arkansas for Medical Sciences (Little Rock).

David E. Barnard, MD
Assistant Professor, Department of Obstetrics & Gynecology, Duke University Medical Center (Durham, North Carolina).

Ralph C. Benson, MD
Professor and Emeritus Chairman, Department of Obstetrics & Gynecology, Oregon Health Sciences University (Portland).

Hugh B. Collins, JD
Attorney at Law (Medford, Oregon).

F. Gary Cunningham, MD
Professor of Obstetrics & Gynecology, Southwestern Medical School, University of Texas (Dallas).

David N. Danforth, PhD, MD
Thomas J. Watkins Professor Emeritus of Obstetrics & Gynecology, Northwestern University Medical School (Chicago).

Russell Ramon de Alvarez, MD
Professor and Chairman Emeritus of Department of Obstetrics & Gynecology, Temple University Health Sciences Center (Philadelphia).

Albert W. Diddle, MD
Clinical Professor and Chairman Emeritus of Department of Obstetrics & Gynecology, Memorial Research Center and Hospital, University of Tennessee (Knoxville).

William J. Dignam, MD
Professor of Obstetrics & Gynecology, School of Medicine, Center for the Health Sciences, University of California (Los Angeles).

Raphael B. Durfee, MD
Professor of Reproductive Medicine, University of California School of Medicine (San Diego).

Mary Anna Friederich, MD
Clinical Associate Professor of Obstetrics & Gynecology and Psychiatry, University of Rochester School of Medicine & Dentistry (Rochester, New York).

Armando E. Giuliano, MD
Assistant Professor of Surgery and Director, Breast Clinic, University of California School of Medicine (Los Angeles).

Robert C. Goodlin, MD
Department of Obstetrics & Gynecology, University of Nebraska School of Medicine (Omaha).

Myron Gordon, MD
Professor and Chairman, Department of Obstetrics & Gynecology, The Albany Medical College of Union University (Albany, New York).

Ralph W. Hale, MD
Professor and Chairman of Department of Obstetrics & Gynecology, John A. Burns School of Medicine, University of Hawaii (Honolulu).

Lester T. Hibbard, MD
Professor of Obstetrics & Gynecology, Los Angeles County-University of Southern California Medical Center (Los Angeles).

Edward C. Hill, MD
Professor and Director, Gynecology-Oncology, University of California School of Medicine (San Francisco).

John W. Huffman, MD
Professor Emeritus of Obstetrics & Gynecology, Northwestern University Medical School (Chicago).

James M. Ingram, MD
Professor and Chairman of Department of Obstetrics & Gynecology, University of South Florida College of Medicine (Tampa).

Ernest Jawetz, MD, PhD
Professor of Microbiology and Medicine and Lecturer in Pediatrics, University of California School of Medicine (San Francisco).

Howard W. Jones, Jr., MD
Professor Emeritus of Gynecology & Obstetrics, Johns Hopkins University School of Medicine (Baltimore) and Professor of Obstetrics & Gynecology, Eastern Virginia Medical School (Norfolk).

Howard L. Judd, MD
Professor of Obstetrics & Gynecology and Director of Division of Reproductive Endocrinology, University of California School of Medicine (Los Angeles).

John L. Kitzmiller, MD
Associate Professor of Obstetrics, Gynecology, and Reproductive Sciences, University of California School of Medicine (San Francisco), and Chief, Perinatal Service, Children's Hospital of San Francisco.

Beverly L. Koops, MD
Associate Professor of Pediatrics and Director of Newborn Service, University Hospital, University of Colorado School of Medicine (Denver).

Kermit E. Krantz, MD, LittD
Professor and Chairman of Department of Gynecology & Obstetrics, Professor of Anatomy, and Associate to the Executive Vice-Chancellor for Facilities Development, University of Kansas Medical Center (Kansas City).

Daniel H. Labby, MD
Professor of Psychiatry and Medicine, Oregon Health Sciences University (Portland).

Conley G. Lacey, MD
Associate Professor and Co-Director of Gynecologic Oncology, University of California School of Medicine (San Francisco).

John M. Levinson, MD
Associate Professor of Obstetrics & Gynecology, Jefferson Medical College (Philadelphia).

Albert E. Long, MD
Clinical Associate, Stanford University School of Medicine (Stanford).

John R. Marshall, MD
Professor of Obstetrics & Gynecology, University of California School of Medicine (Los Angeles).

John S. McDonald, MD
Professor and Chairman of Department of Anesthesiology and Professor of Obstetrics & Gynecology, Ohio State University (Columbus).

Abe Mickal, MD
Professor and Emeritus Head of Department of Obstetrics & Gynecology, Louisiana State University Medical Center (New Orleans).

Ida I. Nakashima, MD
Assistant Professor of Pediatrics and Assistant Director of Adolescent Clinic, University of Colorado School of Medicine (Denver).

Kenneth R. Niswander, MD
Professor of Obstetrics & Gynecology, University of California School of Medicine (Davis).

Miles J. Novy, MD
Professor of Obstetrics & Gynecology, Oregon Health Sciences University (Portland).

April Gale O'Quinn, MD
Associate Professor, Department of Obstetrics & Gynecology, Tulane University School of Medicine (New Orleans).

Jack W. Pearson, MD
Professor, Department of Obstetrics & Gynecology, Indiana University Medical Center (Indianapolis).

Martin L. Pernoll, MD
C.J. Miller Professor and Head of Department of Obstetrics & Gynecology, Tulane University School of Medicine (New Orleans).

Keith P. Russell, MD
Clinical Professor of Obstetrics & Gynecology, University of Southern California School of Medicine (Los Angeles).

Leon Speroff, MD
Professor and Chairman of Department of Obstetrics & Gynecology, Oregon Health Sciences University (Portland).

Morton A. Stenchever, MD
Professor and Chairman of Department of Obstetrics & Gynecology, University of Washington School of Medicine (Seattle).

Richard E. Symmonds, MD
Professor and Chairman of Department of Gynecologic Surgery, The Mayo Medical School and Clinic (Rochester, Minnesota).

Howard J. Tatum, MD, PhD
Professor of Gynecology & Obstetrics, Emory University School of Medicine, and Director of Research, Family Planning Program, Emory University and Grady Memorial Hospital (Atlanta).

John L. Wilson, MD
Professor of Surgery, Stanford University School of Medicine (Stanford).

J. Donald Woodruff, MD
Richard W. TeLinde Professor of Gynecologic Pathology and Professor of Gynecology & Obstetrics, Emeritus, Johns Hopkins University School of Medicine (Baltimore).

Embryology of Structures Significant to Obstetrics & Gynecology

Robert L . Bacon, PhD

The human genitourinary system is an organ complex in which some structures that arise in close association in embryonic development assume diverse functions, and other structures that originate in widely separated areas must eventually make effective functional and structural contact. Failure particularly of the latter results in disastrous malformations in one or several portions of the system. Because of the complexity of these synchronously occurring events, the various components of the system will be described separately in the following categories: the nephroi and their ducts, the adrenal (suprarenal) glands, the gonads and their ducts, the cloaca, the urogenital sinus, and the external genitalia.

THE NEPHROI & THEIR DUCTS

The human embryo develops 3 successive sets of organs designed to remove wastes and control electrolyte balance. The **pronephros** is a system for transporting coelomic fluids; the **mesonephros** removes wastes from coelomic fluid and blood; and the **metanephros** is the definitive kidney, which excretes wastes from the circulating blood.

Pronephros

The pronephros is a functional system in embryos of many species and in a very limited number of primitive vertebrates. In humans, it is never completed either structurally or functionally, even in the embryo. This persistent vestigial structure appears to be necessary for the subsequent 2 stages of development of the excretory system. Only enough pronephros develops to set in motion the process by which the nephric duct is constructed. Approximately 7 or 8 pairs (in segments 7–14) of incompletely differentiated tubules appear in the intermediate mesoderm (between the somites and the lateral plate mesoderm), with the cephalic tubules already beginning to undergo degeneration before the caudal ones appear. The pronephros exists for about 1 week; it appears first in the third week and has degenerated by the fourth week. The duct established by fusion of the ends of these very transitory tubules persists, however, and continues to grow caudad from the future cervical (neck) region, where it originates, until it eventually fuses with the cloaca (Figs 1–1 and 1–5).

Mesonephros

The mesonephros may be a functional organ in the embryo and is structurally and functionally equivalent to the permanent excretory organ of most fish and amphibians. As the growing pronephric duct extends caudally, it apparently induces the differentiation of excretory mesonephric tubules in the tissue through which it passes. In response to this stimulus, tissue of the nephrogenic cord condenses in each segment to a cell cluster that soon becomes a hollow vesicle (Fig 1–2). The vesicle elongates and bends into an S-shaped tubule whose lateral end joins with a short outpouching of the nephric duct (Figs 1–1 and 1–3).

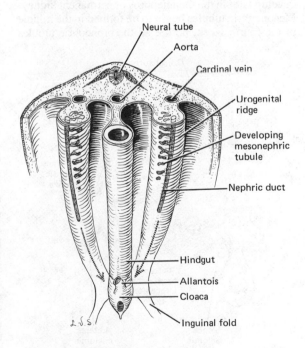

Figure 1–1. Caudad growth of the nephric duct within the urogenital ridge toward the cloaca. The tissue parallel to the duct, in which mesonephric tubules are differentiating, is the nephrogenic cord.

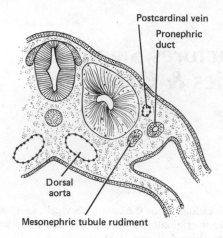

Figure 1–2. Diagrammatic section of an embryo at the level of the mesonephros in the fourth week. The rudiment of a mesonephric tubule has just developed, is still without a lumen, and is not yet connected with the nephric duct.

The medial end of each tubule thins out and surrounds a tuft of capillaries (the glomerulus) that develops at the end of a small lateral branch of the aorta (Fig 1–3). The efferent vessels from these glomeruli, after developing intimate association with the convolutions of the mesonephric tubule, empty into the cardinal system of veins (Fig 1–4). Thus is formed a simplified version of the far more complex nephron that will develop later in the metanephros or permanent kidney. Mesonephric tubules begin to be formed in the middle of the fourth week, before all the pronephric tubules

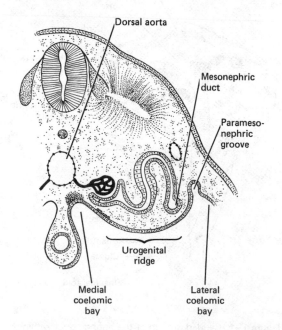

Figure 1–3. Diagrammatic section of an embryo at about 5 weeks. A glomerulus is forming, and the tubule has elongated, curved, and connected with the duct.

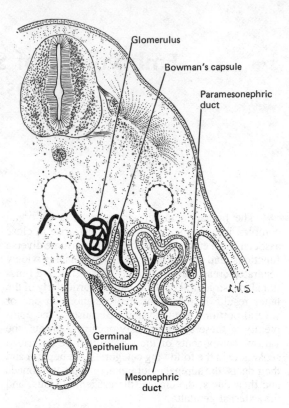

Figure 1–4. Diagrammatic section of a portion of an embryo in the sixth week. The vascular pattern is complete. The elongation and elaborate convolution of the tubule (simplified in this diagram) cause the urogenital ridge to bulge into the peritoneal cavity. The gonad will differentiate in relation to germinal epithelium facing the medial coelomic bay.

have degenerated, and first appear at about the level of T1. Thus, they overlap the pronephros both in space and in time. As with the pronephros, the processes of differentiation and regression both occur in a craniocaudal sequence. By the time most caudal tubules have developed at about somite 26, the more cephalic tubules have degenerated completely (Fig 1–5). These 2 processes occur at approximately equal rates, so that the number of mesonephric tubules remains roughly constant (30–34) and the entire organ appears to shift caudally in the embryo. Although the pronephros was segmental, with one pronephric tubule for each of the segments involved, only the most cephalic of the mesonephric tubules are segmentally arranged. Those in the lower thoracic and lumbar segments, which develop later, have 2–4 tubules with several glomeruli. At its maximum length, the mesonephros extends from the level of the heart to the future second or third lumbar segments. Shortly after the eighth week, relatively few intact mesonephric tubules still exist.

While it has been shown that the mesonephroi of the embryos of a number of mammals have the ability to eliminate phenolsulfonphthalein and ferrocyanide,

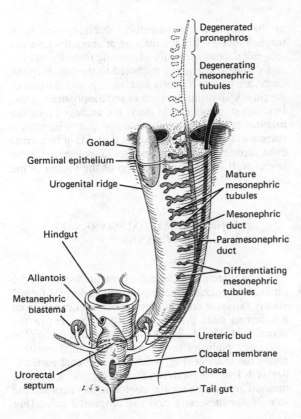

Figure 1–5. Diagram showing relations of developing gonad to mesonephric tubules and duct and relations of ureteric bud, mesonephric duct, urogenital sinus, and urorectal septum.

it is not known what functions the human mesonephros may have. Cytologic examination of the mesonephric tubules with their brush borders and readily demonstrable alkaline phosphatase, together with the remarkable electron microscopic similarities between mesonephric and metanephric tubules, suggests that the mesonephros probably is functional in the embryo.

The mesonephros itself contributes no functioning structures to the anatomy of the adult female. The degenerative process involved in removing the mesonephros includes extrusion of the glomerulus from Bowman's capsule. Most of the tubules that remain after this process is completed disappear entirely. As will be shown later, some do persist and are taken over, in the male, as efferent ductules connecting the rete testis to the epididymis. Various aberrant and vestigial vesicles, tubules, or cysts in both the male and the female may result from the persistence of mesonephric tubules at other levels. In the male, the mesonephric duct becomes the epididymis and vas deferens; in the female, a portion of the duct may persist as Gartner's duct.

Metanephros

For purposes of description and discussion, the development of the definitive kidney will be sub-

divided into collecting duct systems, excretory units, and migration.

A. Collecting Duct Systems: Shortly after attachment of the mesonephric duct to the cloaca, the metanephric diverticulum (ureteric bud) appears as a dorsal outgrowth of the duct very close to its connection to the cloaca opposite the level of the 28th somite (L4). The bud grows dorsally and cranially into the caudal end of the nephrogenic cord at the level of the 26th somite (Figs 1–5 and 1–12). The cord tissue responds to the growing tip by condensing and proliferating around it to form the metanephric blastema, which provides the cells that will form the major part of each nephron. The ureteric bud dilates to become the primitive renal pelvis and produces cranial and caudal expansions that are destined to become major calyces of the adult kidney. An additional calyx soon is added near the middle of the pelvis. Each calyx expands into 2 buds (secondary collecting tubules). Divisions continue for 12–13 generations until the fetus is 6 months old. The later generations of branching generally are dichotomous, but the third, fourth, and fifth generations may produce 3–4 buds instead of 2. While tubular divisions are continuing near the cortical surface of the metanephros, the secondary tubules enlarge and absorb the third and fourth generations of tubules, to form the minor calyces. Thus, the fifth generation tubules open into the minor calyces (expanded third and fourth generation ducts), and in view of the fact that the previous 2 generations have produced several branches instead of the usual 2, the number of collecting ducts entering a minor calyx varies widely from about 10 to about twice that number. One to 3 million collecting tubules are produced by these several generations of division.

B. Excretory Units: The excretory portion of each nephron differentiates from the blastema of nephrogenic cord tissue under the inductive action of the growing collecting duct system and passes through the same series of basic morphologic changes that characterized the development of the mesonephric tubules. An S-shaped tubule forms in the tissue cap over the end of each collecting tubule. The elongated vesicle expands, and one end thins out into a cuplike arrangement that comes to enclose a tuft of glomerular capillaries. At the other end, the vesicle joins with its collecting duct. A departure from the mesonephroslike configuration occurs when the mid portion of the S begins to grow extensively into what will be Henle's loop, which extends into the medulla of the organ. Subsequently, the 2 ends of the originally simple S elongate and become tortuous, to form the proximal and distal convoluted tubules of the adult nephron. The glomerulus and capsule remain essentially unchanged; at 2500 g (36 weeks), the glomeruli are fully developed.

C. Migration: The migration of the metanephros out of the pelvis and into the abdomen to its ultimate position (Fig 1–6) is important because deviations from the normal course of this process account for clinically significant abnormalities. Some of this mi-

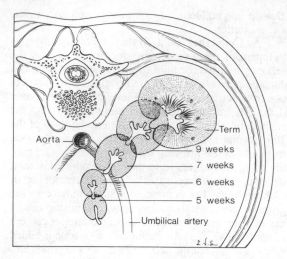

Figure 1–6. Cross-sectional diagram showing migration and rotation of the kidney. Sections of the kidney at 5 stages have been projected on one plane. (Redrawn and modified from Kelly HA, Burnam CF: *Diseases of Kidneys, Ureters and Bladder*. Appleton-Century-Crofts, 1972.)

gration is more apparent than real and is due to rapid expansion of the body wall caudal to the site of metanephric development. By the end of the 12th week, the kidney lies adjacent to the second or third lumbar vertebra. Some of this positional change is due to migration. The metanephroi, as they shift cranially, are brought close together near the midline in the angle of the aortic bifurcation. It is at this point during the seventh week, before the metanephroi have slid over the umbilical arteries out of the narrow pelvis into the more capacious abdomen, that horseshoe kidney may result if fusion occurs. Similarly, it is probable that these large vessels may act as barriers, occasionally blocking further upward migration of the metanephros. This results in pelvic kidney, with one or both organs located near the level of origin. As the normally developing kidney slides out of the pelvis over the artery, it is guided laterally by the larger developing vertebrae and muscle masses at these levels and is rotated on its long axis approximately 90 degrees, with the convex border facing laterally instead of dorsally.

Relation of Nephric Ducts to Urogenital Sinus

Enlargement of the urogenital sinus is accompanied by absorption of mesonephric ducts into its wall (Figs 1–12 to 1–15). Thus, the metanephric diverticulum—originally an outgrowth of the mesonephric duct—eventually comes to have a separate opening into the sinus. That portion of the sinus wall between the mesonephric and metanephric openings is composed of tissue derived from the ducts (trigone).

The termination of the mesonephric duct at first is superior to that of the metanephric duct (ureter). The mesonephric ducts have the same stromal investment

as the fused paramesonephric ducts, which have reached this level in the midline at about the time the urogenital sinus is rapidly expanding rostrally and laterally. The ureters, not anchored to the mesonephric ducts, are carried rostrally and laterally as the tissue of the sinus wall in this area grows and the organ expands. In contrast, mesonephric ducts are anchored near the midline to a portion of the sinus that will remain narrow as the prostatic urethra in the male or be carried even further caudally as vestiges associated with the lateral wall of the upper portion of the vagina in the female.

THE ADRENAL (SUPRARENAL) GLANDS

The adrenal (suprarenal) glands are formed by the intimate association of cell populations derived from 2 widely different origins. The medulla is derived from ectodermal cells that migrate from the crest of the neural folds (Fig 1–7). These cells follow a complex migratory pathway to arrive at their final position above the kidneys (Fig 1–8A). The adrenal cortex is derived from mesodermal cells of the coelomic mesothelium of the medial coelomic bay between the root of the mesentery and the urogenital ridge (Fig 1–8).

In the fifth week, columnar mesothelial cells proliferate and leave the coelomic epithelium to lie in the subjacent mesenchyme and differentiate into enlarged acidophilic cells (Fig 1–9A). At about the same time, clusters of future medullary cells arrive and assemble in groups closely associated with the first wave of cortical cells (Fig 1–9A). At first they are scattered on the surface or are partially within the cortical mass; they do not become truly medullary in position until later (Fig 1–9B). The initial proliferation of large acidophilic cortical cells constitutes the fetal or provisional cortex that is destined to disappear after birth. In the sixth week, a second wave of smaller, less well differentiated mesothelial cells spreads over the surface of the previously assembled glandular mass (Fig 1–9C). This second wave is destined to form the definitive cortex of the adult.

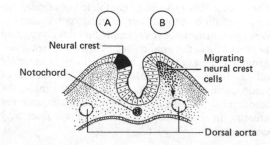

Figure 1–7. Diagrammatic section of open neural tube stage. *A:* Location of neural crest. *B:* Later stage indicating cells leaving epithelium and beginning their migration.

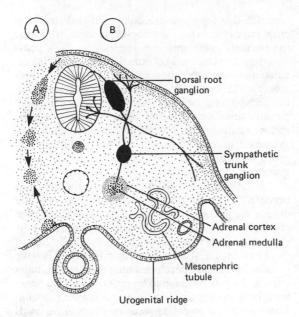

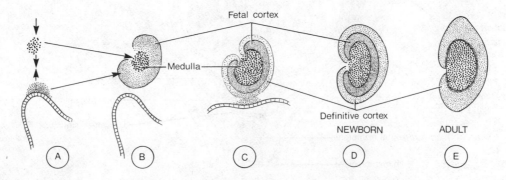

Figure 1–8. *A:* Route of migration of neural crest cells. One cluster remains near the neural tube to form the spinal ganglion; another proceeds to the location of future sympathetic trunk ganglion; and still another continues and becomes associated with cortical cells emigrating from the coelomic epithelium. *B:* Diagram of structures formed by these groups of neural crest cells.

The fetal adrenals are relatively large organs owing to the considerable size of the fetal cortex. At term they constitute about 0.2% of the body weight and are 20 times the size of those in the adult relative to body weight. Differentiation of the permanent cortex is not completed until about 3 years after birth, and it does not keep up with degeneration of the fetal cortex. As a result of this discrepancy between regression and differentiation, there is an absolute decrease in size of the adrenal glands after birth.

There is evidence that both components of the adrenal glands are functional in the fetus. The fetal cortex appears to be dependent on pituitary function during fetal life. Tumors of the fetal cortex apparently produce considerable quantities of androgens and therefore may cause pseudohermaphroditic changes in female fetuses. The medullary cells show cytochemical evidence of catecholamines, and, after the tenth week, norepinephrine and later epinephrine may be found in these cells.

As might be expected from what has just been said about the complex development of these structures, accessory medullary or cortical tissue may be found in a variety of locations. The development of this large organ in the limited space between the aorta and the urogenital ridge might lead one to predict that accessory adrenal tissue would be found near the gonads, which develop in the urogenital ridge. Accessory adrenal tissue occasionally is found in areas where it may have been carried by the migrating testis or ovary, eg, in the broad ligament of the female (accessory adrenal of Marchand) or in the scrotum of the male.

THE GONADS & THEIR DUCTS

The first indication of the developing gonad is a thickening in the coelomic epithelium on the inner surface of the urogenital ridge facing the medial coelomic bay (Figs 1–4 and 1–5). This becomes noticeable late in the fourth week. At the same time, the underlying mesenchyme condenses and the basement membrane between the epithelium and the mesenchyme disappears. The 2 cellular components become intimately mixed. Condensation of cells gives rise to the anastomosing primitive sex cords that extend from the epithelium deep into the substance of the urogenital ridge. Meanwhile, during the sixth week, the important primordial germ cells arrive after their long migration from the wall of the yolk sac near the allantois, where they first appear. They have migrated through the mesentery from the region of the hindgut to the dorsal body wall and then laterally into the developing gonad on each side. In experimental animals, if the primordial cells are removed or prevented from reaching their destination, the gonad undergoes only minimal differentiation. Thus, as with the developing

Figure 1–9. *A –E:* Stages in the migration, assembly, and differentiation of the adrenal gland.

pronephros, the primordial germ cells appear to constitute embryonic inductors. Although it has not been possible to determine this with certainty, it is currently believed that these primordial cells are the direct ancestors of the spermatozoa and ova in the adult.

This period of development of the gonad is known as the indifferent stage, because male or female gonads cannot be identified until the proliferation of the tunica albuginea, which separates the sex cords from the coelomic epithelium in the seventh week, indicates testicular development. At this time, the sex cords of the male become isolated from the coelomic epithelium, while those of the female remain in contact and continue to grow extensively.

If the gonad is to become a testis, further ingrowth and development of cortical tissue ceases, and during the eighth week the tunica albuginea isolates the 2 components. The primitive sex cords continue to grow within the medulla of the gonad and soon become less diffuse and more clearly defined as the testis cords. After its isolation from the subjacent cords by the tunica albuginea, the original germinal epithelium regresses to the typical flat squamous mesothelium. The lateral ends of the sex cords, which persist in the

medulla, develop interconnecting epithelial strands in close proximity to the mesonephric tubules, where the mesonephric glomeruli are regressing. This anastomosing network will become the rete testis, but canalization does not occur until later (in the 12th to 16th weeks). The testis cords are composed of cells probably derived from 2 origins: primordial germ cells from the allantois, and epithelial cells from the coelomic surface of the gonad. Presumably, the epithelial cells eventually become the Sertoli cells of the adult, and the primitive germ cells differentiate into the spermatogonia of the adult.

If the gonad is to become an ovary, the sex cords become subdivided and broken down into irregular groups associated with some of the primordial germ cells. These cell clusters gradually disappear, and the ovarian medulla of the newborn is essentially free of these tissues. The surface epithelium is not at this stage isolated by a highly developed tunica albuginea, however, and cords continue to be produced and to penetrate the underlying mesenchyme but not the medulla. These persistent so-called secondary or cortical cords also break down eventually, and their component cells form clusters associated with primordial germ cells

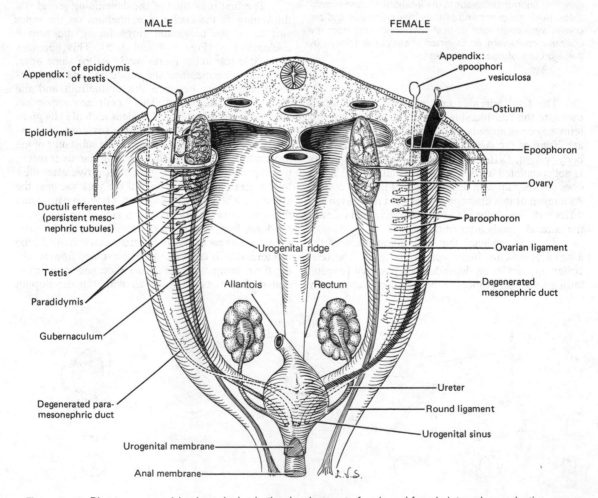

Figure 1–10. Diagram summarizing homologies in the development of male and female internal reproductive organs.

that probably become the oogonia, with the former epithelial cells making up the primordial follicles. Although a presumptive ovarian rete appears in the lateral portion of the ovary and several mesonephric tubules are present, the rete does not become patent and the mesonephric tubules are nonfunctional. They may persist, however, along with a small segment of the mesonephric duct, to become the vestigial epoophoron.

The mesenchymal substance of the genital ridge inferior to the gonad terminates caudally in the region of the future external genitalia. This strand of tissue differentiates into the gubernaculum (Fig 1–10), a structure that apparently does not grow at the same rate as the surrounding structures. The gubernaculum is thereby relatively shortened and perhaps actually contracts. The gubernaculum is involved in the process by which the gonad descends from its original high position in the abdominal cavity into the scrotum. The male gonad may carry with it remnants of the mesonephric and paramesonephric systems. Since the lower portion of the gubernaculum is made up of several strands that terminate in other areas, the male gonad occasionally may be guided to an anomalous position such as the upper thigh or prepubic region.

In the female, however, the relatively massive lateral expansions of the fused portions of the paramesonephric ducts—which are to become the uterus—attach to the gubernaculum in the angle where the paramesonephric ducts swing medially to join each other (Fig 1–10). This angle becomes the junction of the oviduct with the uterus. Thus, in the female, although the gonad descends a considerable distance, the gubernaculum is anchored at the tubo-uterine junction, and further descent of the gonad ordinarily does not occur (Fig 1–11). That portion of the gubernaculum between the ovary and the uterus is the ovarian ligament; the remainder, from the uterine attachment to the inguinal region, is the round ligament of the uterus. The course of the descent of the gonad in each sex is

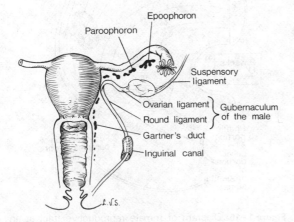

Figure 1–11. Diagram of female reproductive tract showing vestigial mesonephric structures and components of the gubernaculum.

marked by the blood vessels. The arteries arise from the aorta not far below the origin of the renal arteries; the right gonadal vein enters the vena cava at the same high level, and the left enters the left renal vein.

In the indifferent stage of sexual development, a complete set of genital duct systems is established for both sexes. That of the male is derived from the mesonephric duct, which has been discussed above. The first indication of the female duct system is the appearance in the sixth week of a groove toward the superior end of the genital ridge lateral to and parallel with the mesonephric duct (Fig 1–3). This groove becomes deeper and closes over to form a tube. The lower end of the tube grows caudally, much as the old pronephric duct did, and eventually fuses with the wall of the portion of the cloaca that is destined to become the urogenital sinus (Figs 1–5 and 1–13). The opening of the paramesonephric duct persists as the ostium of the uterine tube. The lower end of the paramesonephric duct, normally late in reaching the urogenital sinus, probably arrives at this position late in the eighth or early in the ninth week of development.

Throughout much of its length, the genital ridge is parallel to the paramesonephric duct (Fig 1–10). As these ridges are followed caudally, however, they must first swing ventrally and then medially if the lower ends of the ducts that they contain are to fuse with the portion of the cloaca that later separates from the rectum to form the urogenital sinus. As these ducts are followed caudally, they swing medially, and the originally more laterally placed paramesonephric duct finally comes to lie closest to the midline, in intimate proximity to its neighbor from the opposite side (Figs 1–10 and 1–14). Thus, the fused ends of the paramesonephric ducts are joined to the urogenital sinus in the midline dorsally. Immediately lateral to this junction are the terminations of the mesonephric duct in the wall of the same chamber.

Mesonephric Ducts

The mesonephric ducts undergo different development in the 2 sexes. If the individual is to become a male, the mesonephric duct persists and begins its typical histogenesis in the seventh week. Most of the duct is involved in the formation of the epididymis and vas deferens. From its lower portion, a new outgrowth appears that becomes a seminal vesicle (Fig 1–14), while its upper portion becomes very tortuous and does not develop an extensive muscular investment but remains as a thin-walled, highly convoluted tubule, the epididymis. The prostatic buds develop from that portion of the urogenital sinus which is to become the prostatic urethra. These buds surround and enclose the terminal portion of the mesonephric duct (Fig 1–14), which then becomes the ejaculatory duct. The most cranial portion of the mesonephric duct, superior to that part into which the efferent ductules open, persists in most instances as a small cystic structure, the appendix epididymis. From 5 to 15 mesonephric tubules persist after the degeneration of the glomeruli to connect the rete testis (which has developed from the deep

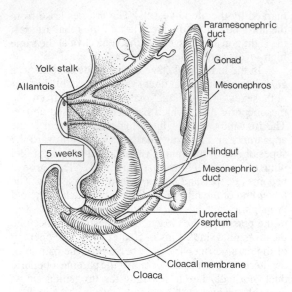

Figure 1–12. Diagrammatic left lateral view of urogenital system in relation to the hindgut at about 5 weeks. The paramesonephric duct does not appear until the sixth week but is shown here to indicate its position and downgrowth.

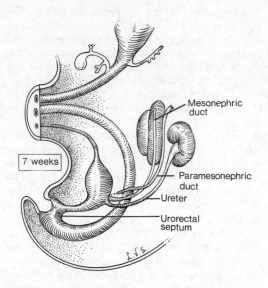

Figure 1–13. Diagrammatic left lateral view of the urogenital system in relation to gut at about 7 weeks. The paramesonephric duct is shown at a more advanced stage to demonstrate its approach to the urogenital sinus. No sexual differentiation has yet occurred.

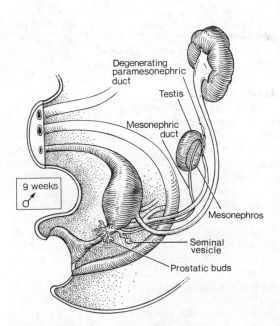

Figure 1–14. Diagram of male reproductive tract at an early stage of sexual differentiation (about 9 weeks). Although prostatic buds are shown here for emphasis, they do not reach this degree of development for several weeks.

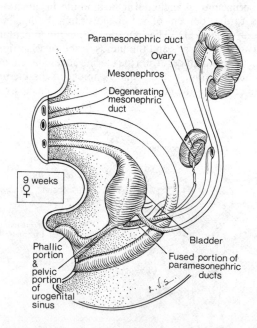

Figure 1–15. Diagram of female reproductive tract at an early stage of sexual differentiation (about 9 weeks).

ends of the sex cords of the gonad) to the mesonephric duct to form the ductuli efferentes (Fig 1–10). Above and below these persisting tubules, which ultimately have reproductive function, may lie clusters of vesicular remnants of mesonephric tubules that become the aberrant ductules and the so-called paradidymis.

If the embryo is to become a female, the main portion of the mesonephric (wolffian) duct degenerates. Portions of the lower segment of this duct occasionally persist parallel with the vagina as Gartner's duct (Fig 1–11). Cysts (Gartner's cysts) occasionally develop as enlargements of local portions of this duct. Mesonephric tubules in the neighborhood of the ovary may persist as the epoophoron or paroophoron in the mesovarium or broad ligament of the adult.

Paramesonephric Duct

The paramesonephric (müllerian) duct in the male embryo begins to regress soon after the seventh week of development (Fig 1–14). Only its upper and lower extremities persist. The former is represented in the so-called appendix testis, a small vesicular body commonly found attached to the upper pole of the testis in the adult male (Fig 1–10). The lower portion is considered to be the basis for at least a part of the prostatic utricle (vagina masculina). The prostatic tubercle (müllerian tubercle) may represent persistent tissue from the sinovaginal bulb at the point of union of the fused paramesonephric ducts with the urogenital sinus. The paramesonephric duct in the female is the precursor of the major portion of the female duct system. The more cranial portion of each paramesonephric duct forms an oviduct, and the fused caudal midline portions make up the uterus. The medial walls of the 2 paramesonephric ducts fuse into a single wall that eventually breaks down. Nevertheless, they do persist long enough to form a temporary septum in the enlarging uterus (Fig 1–10). Persistence of this septum in the adult accounts for the occasional septate uterus.

The precise origin of the vagina is uncertain. It appears to develop from proliferation of cells at the point of junction between the lower end of the fused paramesonephric ducts and the urogenital sinus. Because this junction is intimately related to the differentiation of the urogenital sinus, it will be discussed under that heading.

The precise fate of the upper end of the paramesonephric duct also is a matter of debate. It may be that the definitive ostium of the oviduct represents a new opening, with the uppermost portion of the duct becoming closed to persist as a cystic structure, the hydatid of Morgagni or appendix vesiculosa, a frequent finding in the adult.

Since this portion of the female reproductive tract is bilateral in origin, one might expect congenital malformations in which the tract has varying degrees of lateral duplication. Such anomalies vary from the simple persistence of a septum between the originally separate anlagen of the uterus to a complete double uterus—with all intervening gradations of duplication. The duct system of the female reproductive tract is closely associated with the structures that eventually become the major ligaments. Hence, it is appropriate to consider these structures here. Some of them have already been mentioned. The suspensory ligament of the ovary represents the degenerated cranial portion of the urogenital ridge. The contributions of the gubernaculum to the ligamentous structures have already been mentioned. As the urogenital ridges are followed caudally, it is apparent that they swing ventrally and medially to meet in the midline ventral to the hindgut (Fig 1–10) and that the broad ligament is a derivative of this more caudal portion of the urogenital ridge. In the embryo, the enclosed components of the female tract—eg, the paramesonephric ducts—are relatively small, and the genital ridge tissue constitutes a massive investment. As a result of the very great increase in rate of growth of the enclosed organs in comparison with the mesenchymal supportive tissue of the urogenital ridge, however, the ridge tissue itself becomes reduced to the thin broad ligament and the enclosed reproductive organs become relatively very large, so that the original ridge tissue becomes a very thin sheet supporting the large organs of the tract.

CLOACA

At the end of the third week of development, the hindgut is a caudal diverticulum of the yolk sac into the developing tail fold. A tubular evagination from the hindgut, the allantois, extends forward into the mesenchyme of the body stalk (Fig 1–12). As growth continues, the caudal end of the hindgut enlarges to become the cloaca, a common chamber into which open the gut, the allantois, and the mesonephric ducts (Fig 1–12). The dilated cloaca is in contact with ectoderm of the body surface ventral to the developing tail at the cloacal membrane. Beginning in the fourth week, a transverse crescentic fold, the urorectal septum, in the wall of the cloaca between allantois and gut grows caudally and ventrally to divide this common chamber into urogenital sinus and rectum (Figs 1–13 and 1–5). This fold or ridge passes dorsal to the termination of the mesonephric ducts, so that these tubes finally open into that portion of the cloaca which is cut off as the urogenital sinus (Fig 1–13). At 7 weeks, the septum reaches the cloacal membrane, and the separation of the 2 chambers is complete by 8 weeks (Fig 1–14). The area of fusion of urorectal septum and cloacal membrane is the primitive perineal body dividing the original cloacal membrane into urogenital and anal membranes. As mesoderm proliferates around these membranes between ectoderm and endoderm, the urogenital membrane comes to lie in a groove between 2 thickening urogenital folds, and the anal membrane lies at the bottom of the anal pit. By the eighth week, the urogenital and anal membranes break down and the internal chambers are open to the exterior.

UROGENITAL SINUS

Undifferentiated Stages

The urogenital sinus is composed of 2 parts: (1) the shallow elongated groove lying between the urogenital folds (the phallic portion), and (2) the long tubular segment (pelvic portion) that includes a dilated region (Fig 1–15). This area of widening eventually becomes the bladder, into which the mesonephric ducts open laterally. The phallic portion becomes part of the vestibule in the female and the penile urethra in the male.

Male

The pelvic portion of the urogenital sinus in the male essentially does not change from the basic pattern of the embryonic arrangement. In the tenth week, the urogenital folds fuse along their edges to enclose the penile urethra, and in the 12th week, epithelial outgrowths around the entrance of the mesonephric ducts in the lower narrow portion of the sinus below the bladder establish the prostatic anlage.

Female

The sequence of changes leading to the definitive sinus derivatives of the female are best appreciated by scanning the accompanying series of 4 sagittal diagrams of female embryos (Figs 1–15 to 1–18). The portion of the pelvic sinus below the bladder is ab-

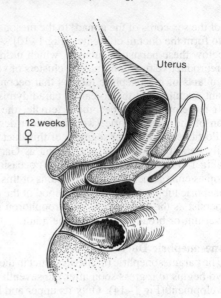

Figure 1–17. Differentiation of the urogenital sinus and fused paramesonephric ducts in the female embryo at 12 weeks. (See also Figs 1–16 and 1–18.)

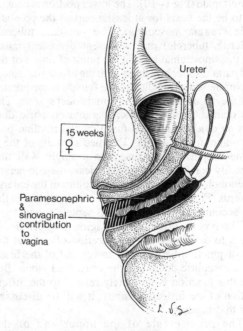

Figure 1–18. Differentiation of the urogenital sinus and fused paramesonephric ducts in the female embryo at 15 weeks. (See also Figs 1–16 and 1–17.)

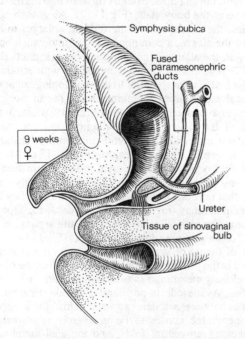

Figure 1–16. Differentiation of the urogenital sinus and fused paramesonephric ducts in the female embryo at 9 weeks. The fused ducts are still partially divided by a median septum. The sinovaginal bulbs form in the tenth week, and the urogenital sinus may contribute approximately the lower third of the vagina. (See also Figs 1–17 and 1–18.)

sorbed into the expanding vestibule to provide separate openings for vagina and urethra. The elongation of the sinovaginal bulb plays a key part in the establishment of the vagina. This structure consists of proliferating tissue from the wall of the urogenital sinus that contributes to the growing vagina and may give rise to about the lower third of this organ. The last remnant of the lower portion of this "bulb" tissue develops into the hymen.

In the adult, the line of termination of pigment on the labia minora probably represents the boundary between ectoderm of the body surface and endoderm of the urogenital sinus. Thus, cysts or tumors developing within this approximately oval area might be expected to contain at least some columnar, mucous epithelial components reminiscent of normal sinus accessories such as periurethral or Bartholin's glands. Cysts occurring within the vagina above its lower third would be more likely to be mesonephric or paramesonephric in origin. It has been suggested that some lesions outside of the pigment boundary—at least those of the labia majora—may be derivatives of the lower end of the embryonic milk line and thus potential breast tissue. These would be of ectodermal origin and should resemble sweat glands modified to varying degrees.

EXTERNAL GENITALIA

The external genitalia develop essentially as a result of mesodermal proliferation of 3 masses of tissue between the epidermis and the underlying lower portion of the urogenital sinus in the triangular region between the lower limbs and the tail (Fig 1–19). The 3 masses produce the single median genital tubercle, paired genital folds, and paired genital swellings.

From the fourth week, when local proliferation begins, until the seventh week, there are no indices of future sexual differences. As the mesoderm grows, the area of contact between epidermis and epithelium of the urogenital sinus (the urogenital membrane) becomes more deeply buried between the enlarging folds on each side. The membrane breaks down to open the urogenital sinus to the exterior, as is always the case when an intervening mesodermal layer is lacking between ectoderm and endoderm. The genital folds elon-

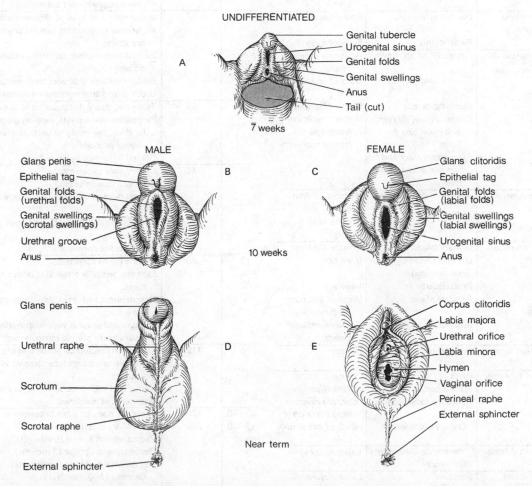

Figure 1–19. Differentiation of the external genitalia of both sexes. *A:* The external genitalia prior to sexual differentiation. *B* and *C:* External genitalia of the male and the female in the tenth week. It is difficult to diagnose sex by external inspection at this stage. *D* and *E:* External genitalia of both sexes late in gestation. In the male, the genital folds have fused to close the penile urethra, and the glans has become canalized. In the female, the genital folds have remained open to form the labia minora.

gate as a result of the growth of their mesodermal cores. Between the seventh and tenth weeks, the genital folds in the male (now urethral folds) begin to fuse (Fig 1–19B), and the sex can usually be determined by careful inspection. Nonetheless, because the genital swellings in the female are not yet large and because the genital tubercle is only now beginning to lag behind that of the male in its growth and so still projects anteriorly, many aborted fetuses of this period are

Table 1–1. Adult derivatives and vestigial remains of embryonic urogenital structures.*†

Embryonic Structure	Male	Female
Indifferent gonad Cortex Medulla	*Testis* *Seminiferous tubules* *Rete testis*	*Ovary* *Ovarian follicles* *Medulla* Rete ovarii
Gubernaculum	Gubernaculum testis	*Ovarian ligament* *Round ligament of uterus*
Mesonephric tubules	*Ductuli efferentes* Paradidymis	Epoophoron Paroophoron
Mesonephric duct	Appendix of epididymis *Ductus epididymidis* *Ductus deferens* *Ureter, pelvis, calyces, and collecting tubules* *Ejaculatory duct and seminal gland (vesicle)*	Appendix vesiculosa Duct of epoophoron Duct of Gartner *Ureter, pelvis, calyces, and collecting tubules*
Paramesonephric duct	Appendix of testis	Hydatid (of Morgagni) *Uterine tube* *Uterus*
Urogenital sinus	*Urinary bladder* *Urethra* (except glandular portion) Prostatic utricle *Prostate gland* *Bulbourethral glands*	*Urinary bladder* *Urethra* *Vagina* *Urethral* and *paraurethral glands* *Greater vestibular glands*
Müllerian tubercle	Seminal colliculus	Hymen
Genital tubercle	*Penis* *Glans penis* *Corpora cavernosa penis* *Corpus spongiosum*	*Clitoris* *Glans clitoridis* *Corpora cavernosa clitoridis* *Bulb of the vestibule*
Urogenital folds	*Ventral (under) aspect of penis*	Labia minora
Labioscrotal swellings	*Scrotum*	*Labia majora*

*Modified and reproduced, with permission, from Moore KL: *The Developing Human,* 2nd ed. Saunders, 1977.
†Functional derivatives are in italics.

Table 1–2. Developmental chronology of the human genitourinary system.*

Age in Weeks	Size (C–R)† in mm	Urogenital System
2.5	1.5	Allantois present.
3.5	2.5	All pronephric tubules formed. Pronephric duct growing caudad as a blind tube. Cloaca and cloacal membrane present.
4	5	Pronephros degenerated. Pronephric (mesonephric) duct reaches cloaca. Mesonephric tubules differentiating rapidly. Metanephric bud pushes into secretory primordium.
5	8	Mesonephros reaches its caudal limit. Ureteric and pelvic primordia distinct.
6	12	Cloaca subdividing. Pelvic anlage sprouts pole tubules. Sexless gonad and genital tubercle prominent. Paramesonephric duct appearing.
7	17	Mesonephros at peak of differentiation. Metanephric collecting tubules begin branching. Earliest metanephric secretory tubules differentiating. Bladder-urethra separates from rectum. Urethral and anal membranes rupturing.
8	23	Testis and ovary distinguishable as such. Paramesonephric ducts, nearing urogenital sinus, are ready to unite as uterovaginal primordium. Genital ligaments indicated.
10	40	Kidney able to secrete. Bladder expands as sac. Genital duct of opposite sex degenerating. Bulbourethral and vestibular glands appearing. Vaginal bulbs forming.
12	56	Uterine horns absorbed. External genitalia attain distinctive features. Mesonephros and rete tubules complete male duct. Prostate and seminal vesicle appearing. Hollow viscera gaining muscular walls.
16	112	Kidney attains typical shape and plan. Testis in position for later descent into scrotum. Uterus and vagina recognizable as such. Mesonephros involuted.
20–40 (5–10 months)	160–350	Female urogenital sinus becoming a shallow vestibule (5 months). Vagina regains lumen (5 months). Uterine glands appear (7 months). Scrotum solid until sacs and testes descend (7–9 months). Kidney tubules cease forming at birth.

*Modified and reproduced, with permission, from Arey LB: *Developmental Anatomy,* 7th ed. Saunders, 1965.
†C–R, crown-rump length.

wrongly classified as males on the basis of superficial inspection.

In the male, closure of the urethral folds along the future raphe (Figs 1–19B and 1–19D) converts the elongated phallic portion of the urogenital sinus into the penile urethra, and the genital tubercle becomes canalized to form the glans by the tunneling of an epithelial extension of the urethra. This is usually accomplished by the 12th week. The prepuce is formed later by the ingrowth of a nearly circular plate of epithelium around the tip of the glans. This plate subsequently cleaves to free a fold of tissue (the prepuce) from the surface of the glans. Formation of the male external structures is essentially completed when the genital swellings enlarge to form the scrotum. This is facilitated by the development of the processus vaginalis from the peritoneum in preparation for the later descent of the testis.

In the female, the story is simpler. The genital tubercle (the future clitoris) is slowed in its growth rate relative to the continuing expansion of the genital folds and genital swellings. Consequently, the genital tubercle becomes buried between the anterior ends of these enlarging structures. The genital folds do not fuse, and the lower portion of the urogenital sinus remains open as the vestibule (Fig 1–19E).

MALFORMATIONS

The reported incidence of the many developmental malformations of the genitourinary system varies greatly. However, it is generally accepted that the rate is probably the highest of any system in the body, as would be expected from its embryologic complexity. Autopsy studies reveal that at least 10% of individuals are born with some genitourinary anomaly, and it is generally agreed that the incidence is much higher in abortuses and stillbirths. In the first 6 days after delivery, congenital malformations of all systems account for over 14% of neonatal deaths. During the embryonic and fetal periods, death from anomalous development is probably much higher. One classic study of the structure of early human embryos recovered from women of known fertility reported on 34 embryos in the first 2 weeks of pregnancy and disclosed that 10 were so abnormal that they probably would not have survived past the end of the second week and would have been aborted by that time. It is now accepted that one-third to one-half of all fertilized eggs fail to develop to the point of implantation and are lost without the women knowing that they were pregnant. Analyses of embryos and fetuses spontaneously aborted during the first 3 months of pregnancy indicate at least a 25% incidence of chromosomal abnormalities. In light of these observations, it should be apparent that many if not most spontaneous abortions probably represent a natural process of disposal of genetically or morphologically damaged embryos.

Table 1–2 may be used to estimate the critical period for the development of malformations in the genitourinary system. For example, a teratogenic insult during the eighth week, when the paramesonephric ducts are approaching the urogenital sinus, could lead to failure of completion of this process and thus to absence of the uterus and vagina. Similarly, a teratogenic process effective during the 9- to 12-week period during which the relatively slow pairing of the paramesonephric ducts occurs could lead to failure of completion of the process and various degrees of duplication of the uterus depending upon the time at which it had its effect.

•   •   •

References

Ambrose SS, O'Brien DP III: Surgical embryology of the exstrophy-epispadias complex. *Surg Clin North Am* 1974; **54**:1379.

Dewhurst CJ: Foetal sex and development of genitalia. Pages 173–181 in: *Scientific Foundations of Obstetrics and Gynecology*. Philipp EE, Barnes J, Newton M (editors). Heinemann, 1970.

Friedrich EG: *Vulvar Disease.* Saunders, 1976.

Gardner LI: Development of the normal fetal and neonatal adrenal. Pages 460–467 in: *Endocrine and Genetic Diseases of Childhood and Adolescence,* 2nd ed. Gardner LI (editor). Saunders, 1975.

Gray SW, Skandalakis JE: The embryological basis for the treatment of congenital defects. Pages 443–664 in: *Embryology for Surgeons.* Saunders, 1972.

Jirásek JE: *Development of the Genital System and Male Pseudohermaphroditism.* Johns Hopkins Press, 1971.

McCrory WW: *Developmental Nephrology.* Harvard Univ Press, 1972.

O'Rahilly R: The embryology and anatomy of the uterus. Chap 2, pp 17–39, in: *International Academy of Pathology, Monograph No. 14.* Williams & Wilkins, 1973.

O'Rahilly R, Muecke EC: The timing and sequence of events in the development of the human urinary system during the embryonic period proper. *Z Anat Entwicklungsgesch* 1972;**138**:99.

Vaughan ED Jr, Middleton GW: Pertinent genitourinary embryology: Review for the practicing urologist. *Urology* 1975;**6**:139.

2 | Anatomy of the Female Reproductive System

Kermit E. Krantz, MD, LittD

THE ABDOMINAL WALL

Topographic Anatomy

That portion of the anterior abdominal wall that lies between the thoracic and the pelvic regions is shaped like an irregular hexagon. The top of the hexagon, marked by the sternoxiphoid process, is in the same plane as the tenth thoracic vertebra. The upper 2 sides are formed by the subcostal angle; the lower sides

extend from the lower ribs to the crest of the ilium and forward to the anterior superior iliac spines. The base is formed by the inguinal ligaments and the symphysis pubica.

The viscera and many abdominal masses tradiationally are located by dividing the anterolateral abdominal wall into regions. One line is placed from the level of each ninth costal cartilage to the iliac crests. Two other lines are drawn from the middle of the inguinal ligaments to the cartilage of the eighth rib.

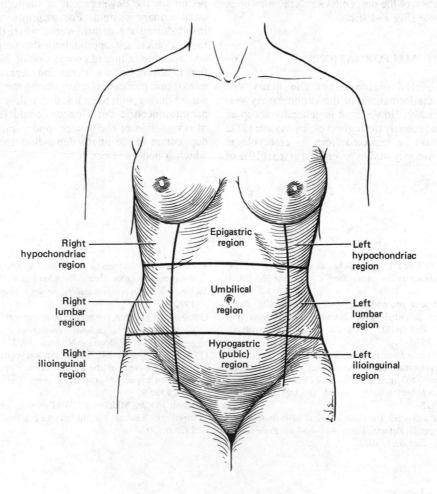

Right hypochondriac region

Epigastric region

Left hypochondriac region

Right lumbar region

Umbilical region

Left lumbar region

Right ilioinguinal region

Hypogastric (pubic) region

Left ilioinguinal region

Figure 2–1. Regions of the abdomen.

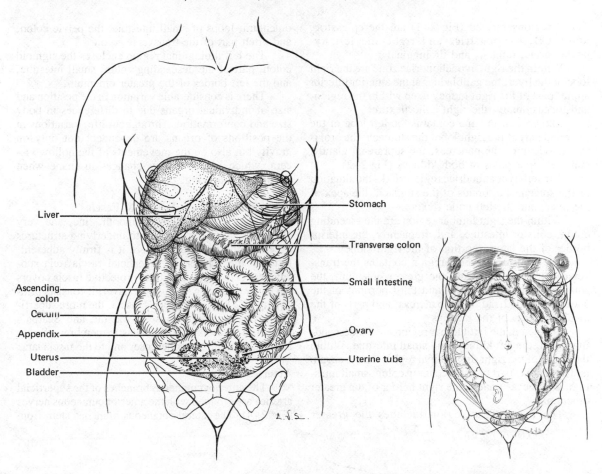

Figure 2–2. Abdominal viscera in situ. Inset shows projection of fetus in situ.

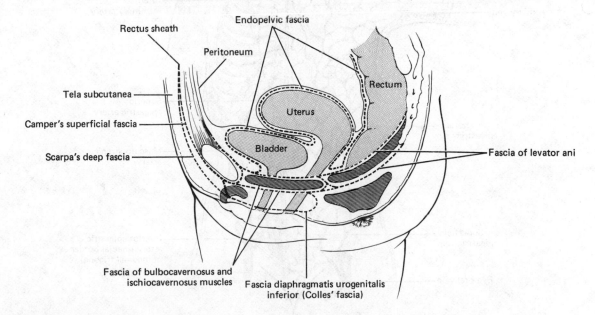

Figure 2–3. Fascial planes of the pelvis. (Modified after Netter. Reproduced, with permission, from Benson RC: *Handbook of Obstetrics & Gynecology,* 7th ed. Lange, 1980.)

The 9 regions formed (Fig 2–1) are the epigastric, umbilical, hypogastric, and right and left hypochondriac, lumbar, and ilioinguinal.

Within the right hypochondriac zone are the right lobe of the liver, the gallbladder at the anterior inferior angle, part of the right kidney deep within the region, and, occasionally, the right colic flexure.

The epigastric zone contains the left lobe of the liver and part of the right lobe, the stomach, the proximal duodenum, the pancreas, the suprarenal glands, and the upper poles of both kidneys (Fig 2–2).

The left hypochondriac region marks the situation of the spleen, the fundus of the stomach, the apex of the liver, and the left colic flexure.

Within the right lumbar region are the ascending colon, coils of intestine, and, frequently, the inferior border of the lateral portion of the right kidney.

The central umbilical region contains the transverse colon, the stomach, the greater omentum, the small intestine, the second and third portions of the duodenum, the head of the pancreas, and parts of the medial aspects of the kidneys.

Located in the left lumbar region are the descending colon, the left kidney, and small intestine. Within the limits of the right ilioinguinal region are the cecum and appendix, part of the ascending colon, small intestine, and, occasionally, the right border of the greater omentum.

The hypogastric region includes the greater omentum, loops of small intestine, the pelvic colon, and often part of the transverse colon.

The left ilioinguinal region encloses the sigmoid colon, part of the descending colon, small intestine, and the left border of the greater omentum.

There is considerable variation in the position and size of individual organs due to differences in body size and conformation. Throughout life, variations in the positions of organs are dependent not only on gravity but also on the movements of the hollow viscera, which induce further changes in shape when filling and emptying.

Skin, Subcutaneous Tissue, & Fascia

The abdominal skin is smooth, fine, and very elastic. It is loosely attached to underlying structures except at the umbilicus, where it is firmly adherent. Beneath the skin is the superficial fascia (tela subcutanea) (Fig 2–3). This fatty protective fascia covers the entire abdomen. Below the navel, it consists principally of 2 layers: Camper's fascia, the more superficial layer containing most of the fat; and Scarpa's fascia (deep fascia), the fibroelastic membrane firmly attached to midline aponeuroses and to the fascia lata.

Arteries

The anterior cutaneous branches of the superficial arteries are grouped with the anterior cutaneous nerves (Fig 2–4). The lateral cutaneous branches stem from

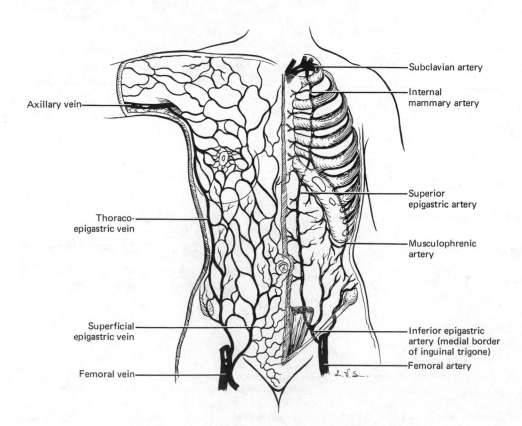

Figure 2–4. Superficial veins and arteries of abdomen.

the lower aortic intercostal arteries and the subcostal arteries. The femoral artery supplies both the superficial epigastric and the superficial circumflex iliac arteries. From its origin beneath the fascia lata at approximately 1.2 cm beyond the inguinal ligament, the superficial epigastric artery passes immediately through the fascia lata or through the fossa ovalis. From there, it courses upward, primarily within Camper's fascia, in a slightly medial direction anterior to the external oblique muscle almost as far as the umbilicus, giving off small branches to the inguinal lymph nodes and to the skin and superficial fascia. It ends in numerous small twigs that anastomose with the cutaneous branches from the inferior epigastric and internal mammary arteries. Arising either in common with the superficial epigastric artery or as a separate branch from the femoral artery, the superficial circumflex iliac artery passes laterally over the iliacus. Perforating the fascia lata slightly to the lateral aspect of the fossa ovalis, it then runs more or less parallel with the inguinal ligament almost to the crest of the ilium, where it terminates in branches within Scarpa's fascia that anastomose with the deep circumflex iliac artery. In its course, branches supply the iliacus and sartorius muscles, the inguinal lymph nodes, and the superficial fascia and skin.

Veins

The superficial veins are more numerous than the arteries and form more extensive networks. Above the umbilicus, blood returns through the anterior cutaneous and the paired thoracoepigastric veins, the superficial epigastric veins, and the superficial circumflex iliac veins in the tela subcutanea. A cruciate anastomosis exists, therefore, between the femoral and axillary veins.

Lymphatics

The lymphatic drainage of the lower abdominal wall (Fig 2–5) is primarily to the superficial inguinal nodes, 10–20 in number, which lie in the area of the inguinal ligament. These nodes may be identified by dividing the area into quadrants by intersecting horizontal and vertical lines that meet at the saphenofemoral junction. The lateral abdominal wall drainage follows the superficial circumflex iliac vein and drains to the lymph nodes in the upper lateral quadrant of the superficial inguinal nodes. The drainage of the medial aspect follows the superficial epigastric vein primarily to the lymph nodes in the upper medial quadrant of the superficial inguinal nodes. Of major clinical importance are the frequent anastomoses between the lymph vessels of the right and left sides of the abdomen.

Abdominal Muscles & Fascia

The muscular wall that supports the abdominal viscera (Fig 2–6) is composed of 4 pairs of muscles and their aponeuroses. The 3 paired lateral muscles are the external oblique, the internal oblique, and the transversus. Their aponeuroses interdigitate at the mid-

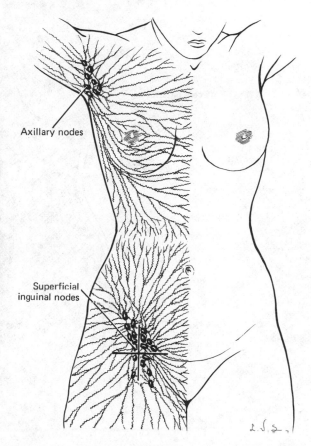

Figure 2–5. Lymphatics of abdominal wall. Only one side is shown, but contralateral drainage occurs, ie, crosses midline to the opposite side.

line to connect opposing lateral muscles, forming a thickened band at this juncture, the linea alba, which extends from the xiphoid process to the pubic symphysis. Anteriorly, a pair of muscles—the rectus abdominis, with the paired pyramidalis muscles at its inferior border with its sheath—constitute the abdominal wall.

A. External Oblique Muscle: The external oblique muscle consists of 8 pointed digitations attached to the lower 8 ribs. The lowest fibers insert into the anterior half of the iliac crest and the inguinal ligament. At the linea alba, the muscle aponeurosis interdigitates with that of the opposite side and fuses with the underlying internal oblique.

B. Internal Oblique Muscle: The internal oblique muscle arises from thoracolumbar fascia, the crest of the ilium, and the inguinal ligament. Going in the opposite oblique direction, the muscle inserts into the lower 3 costal cartilages and into the linea alba on either side of the rectus abdominis. The aponeurosis helps to form the rectus sheath both anteriorly and posteriorly. The posterior layer extends from the rectus muscle rib insertions to below the umbilicus.

C. Transversus Muscle: The transversus muscle, the fibers of which run transversely and arise from

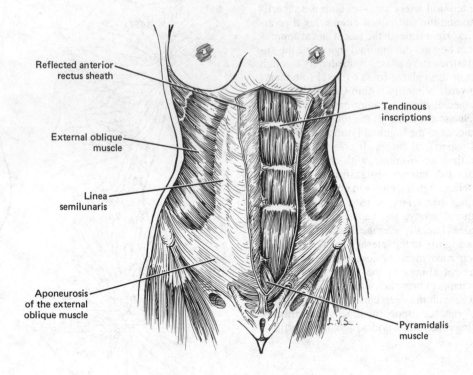

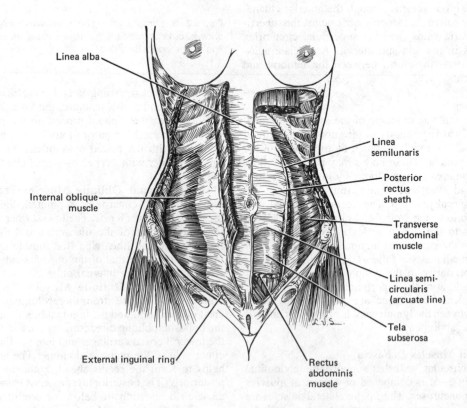

Figure 2–6. Musculature of abdominal wall.

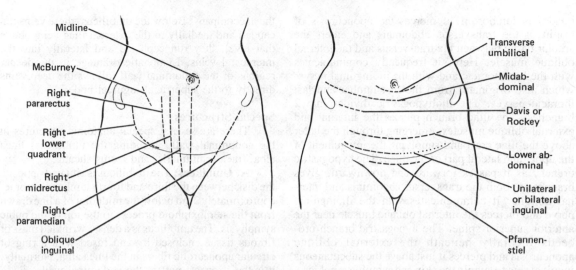

Figure 2–7. Abdominal incisions. Transverse incisions are those in which rectus muscles are cut. A Cherney incision is one in which the rectus is taken off of the pubic bone and then sewed back; the pyramidalis muscle is left on pubic tubercles.

the inner surfaces of the lower 6 costal cartilages, the thoracolumbar fascia, the iliac crest, and the inguinal ligament, lies beneath the internal oblique. By inserting into the linea alba, the aponeurosis of the transversus fuses to form the posterior layer of the posterior rectus sheath. The termination of this layer is called the arcuate line, and below it lie transversalis fascia, properitoneal fat, and peritoneum. Inferiorly, the thin aponeurosis of the transversus abdominis becomes part of the anterior rectus sheath.

D. Rectus Muscles: The rectus muscles are straplike and extend from the thorax to the pubis. They are divided by the linea alba and outlined laterally by the linea semilunaris. Three tendinous intersections cross the upper part of each rectus muscle, and a fourth may also be present below the umbilicus. The pyramidalis muscle, a vestigial muscle, is situated anterior to the lowermost part of the rectus muscle. It arises from and inserts into the pubic periosteum.

Beneath the superficial fascia and overlying the muscles is the thin, semitransparent deep fascia. Its extensions enter and divide the lateral muscles into coarse bundles.

Abdominal incisions are shown in Fig 2–7. The position of the muscles influences the type of incision to be made. The aim is to adequately expose the operative field, avoiding damage to parietal structures, blood vessels, and nerves. The incision should be so placed as to create minimal tension on the lines of closure.

Abdominal Nerves

The lower 6 thoracic nerves align with the ribs and give off lateral cutaneous branches (Fig 2–8). The intercostal nerves pass deep to the upturned rib cartilages and enter the abdominal wall. The main trunks of these nerves run forward between the internal oblique and the transversus. The nerves then enter the rectus

sheaths and the rectus muscles, and the terminating branches emerge as anterior cutaneous nerves. The iliohypogastric nerve springs from the first lumbar nerve after the latter has been joined by the communicating branch from the last (12th) thoracic nerve. It pierces the lateral border of the psoas and crosses anterior to the quadratus lumborum muscle but posterior to the kidney and colon. At the lateral border of the

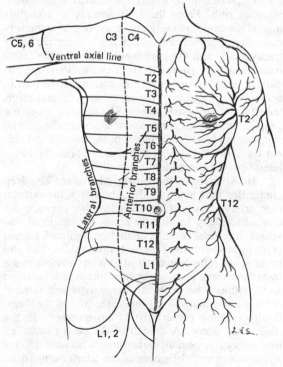

Figure 2–8. Cutaneous innervation of the abdominal wall.

quadratus lumborum, it pierces the aponeurosis of origin of the transversus abdominis and enters the areolar tissue between the transversus and the internal oblique muscle. Here, it frequently communicates with the last thoracic and with the ilioinguinal nerve, which also originates from the first lumbar and last thoracic nerves. The iliohypogastric divides into 2 branches. The iliac branch pierces the internal and external oblique muscles, emerging through the latter above the iliac crest and supplying the integument of the upper and lateral part of the thigh. The hypogastric branch, as it passes forward and downward, gives branches to both the transversus abdominis and internal oblique. It communicates with the ilioinguinal nerve and pierces the internal oblique muscle near the anterior superior spine. The hypogastric branch proceeds medially beneath the external oblique aponeurosis and pierces it just above the subcutaneous inguinal ring to supply the skin and symphysis pubica.

Abdominal Arteries

A. Arteries of the Upper Abdomen: The lower 5 intercostal arteries and the subcostal artery accompany the thoracic nerves. Their finer, terminal branches enter the rectus sheath to anastomose with the superior and inferior epigastric arteries. The superior epigastric artery is the direct downward prolongation of the internal mammary artery. This artery descends between the posterior surface of the rectus muscle and its sheath to form an anastomosis with the inferior epigastric artery upon the muscle. The inferior epigastric artery, a branch of the external iliac artery, usually arises just above the inguinal ligament and passes on the medial side of the round ligament to the abdominal inguinal ring. From there, it ascends in a slightly medial direction, passing above and lateral to the subcutaneous inguinal ring, which lies between the fascia transversalis and the peritoneum. Piercing the fascia transversalis, it passes in front of the linea semicircularis, turns upward between the rectus and its sheath, enters the substance of the rectus muscle, and meets the superior epigastric artery. The superior epigastric supplies the upper central abdominal wall; the inferior supplies the lower central part of the anterior abdominal wall; and the deep circumflex supplies the lower lateral part of the abdominal wall.

B. Arteries of the Lower Abdomen: The deep circumflex iliac artery is also a branch of the external iliac artery, arising from its side either opposite the epigastric artery or slightly below the origin of that vessel. It courses laterally behind the inguinal ligament lying between the fascia transversalis and the peritoneum. The deep circumflex artery perforates the transversus near the anterior superior spine of the ilium and continues between the transversus and internal oblique along and slightly above the crest of the ilium, finally running posteriorly to anastomose with the iliolumbar artery. A branch of the deep circumflex iliac artery is important to the surgeon because it forms anastomoses with branches of the inferior epigastric. The deep veins correspond in name with the arteries they accompany. Below the umbilicus, these veins run caudad and medially to the external iliac vein; above that level, they run cephalad and laterally into the intercostal veins. Lymphatic drainage in the deeper regions of the abdominal wall follows the deep veins directly to the superficial inguinal nodes.

Special Structures

There are several special anatomic structures in the abdominal wall, including the umbilicus, linea alba, linea semilunaris, and rectus sheath.

A. Umbilicus: The umbilicus is situated opposite the disk between the third and fourth lumbar vertebrae, approximately 2 cm below the midpoint of a line drawn from the sternoxiphoid process to the top of the pubic symphysis. The umbilicus is a dense, wrinkled mass of fibrous tissue enclosed by and fused with a ring of circular aponeurotic fibers in the linea alba. Normally, it is the strongest part of the abdominal wall.

B. Linea Alba: The linea alba, a fibrous band formed by the fusion of the aponeuroses of the muscles of the anterior abdominal wall, marks the medial side of the rectus abdominis; the linea semilunaris forms the lateral border, which courses from the tip of the ninth costal cartilage to the pubic tubercle. The linea alba extends from the xiphoid process to the pubic symphysis, represented above the umbilicus as a shallow median groove on the surface.

C. Rectus Sheath and Aponeurosis of the External Oblique: The rectus sheath serves to support and control the rectus muscles. It contains the rectus and pyramidalis muscles, the terminal branches of the lower 6 thoracic nerves and vessels, and the inferior and superior epigastric vessels. Cranially, where the sheath is widest, its anterior wall extends upward onto the thorax to the level of the fifth costal cartilage and is attached to the sternum. The deeper wall is attached to the xiphoid process and the lower borders of the seventh to ninth costal cartilages and does not extend upward onto the anterior thorax. Caudally, where the sheath narrows considerably, the anterior wall is attached to the crest and the symphysis pubica. Above the costal margin on the anterior chest wall, there is no complete rectus sheath (Fig 2–9). Instead, the rectus muscle is only covered by the aponeurosis of the external oblique. In the region of the abdomen, the upper two-thirds of the internal oblique aponeurosis splits at the lateral border of the rectus muscle into anterior and posterior lamellas. The anterior lamella passes in front of the external oblique and blends with the external oblique aponeurosis. The posterior wall of the sheath is formed by the posterior lamella and the aponeurosis of the transversus muscle. The anterior and posterior sheath join at the midline. The lower third of the internal oblique aponeurosis is undivided. Together with the aponeuroses of the external oblique and transversus muscles, it forms the anterior wall of the sheath. The posterior wall is occupied by transversalis fascia, which is spread over the interior surfaces of both the rectus and the transversus muscles, separating them from peritoneum and extending to the inguinal and lacunar ligaments. The transition from aponeurosis to fascia is usually fairly sharp, marked by a curved line called the arcuate line.

D. Function of Abdominal Muscles: In general, the functions of the abdominal muscles are 3-fold: (1) support and compression of the abdominal viscera by the external oblique, internal oblique, and transversus muscles; (2) depression of the thorax in conjunction with the diaphragm by the rectus abdominis, external oblique, internal oblique, and transversus muscles, as evident in respiration, coughing, vomiting, defecation, and parturition; and (3) assistance in bending movements of the trunk through flexion of the vertebral column by the rectus abdominis, external oblique, and internal oblique muscles. There is partial assistance in rotation of the thorax and upper abdomen to the same side when the pelvis is fixed by the internal oblique and by the external oblique to the opposite side. In addition, the upper external oblique serves as a fixation muscle in abduction of the upper limb of the same side and adduction of the upper limb of the opposite side. The pyramidalis muscle secures the linea alba in the median line.

Variations of Abdominal Muscles

Variations have been noted in all of the abdominal muscles.

A. Rectus Muscle: The rectus abdominis muscle may differ in the number of its tendinous inscriptions and the extent of its thoracic attachment. Aponeurotic slips or slips of muscle on the upper part of the thorax are remnants of a more primitive state in which the muscle extended to the neck. Absence of part or all of the muscle has been noted. The pyramidalis muscle

may be missing, only slightly developed, double, or may extend upward to the umbilicus.

B. External Oblique Muscle: The external oblique muscle varies in the extent of its origin from the ribs. Broad fascicles may be separated by loose tissue from the main belly of the muscle, either on its deep or on its superficial surface. The supracostalis anterior is a rare fascicle occasionally found on the upper portion of the thoracic wall. Transverse tendinous inscriptions may also be found.

C. Internal Oblique Muscle: The internal oblique deviates at times, both in its attachments and in the extent of development of the fleshy part of the muscle. Occasionally, tendinous inscriptions are present, or the posterior division forms an extra muscle 7–7.5 cm wide and separated from the internal oblique by a branch of the iliohypogastric nerve and a branch of the deep circumflex iliac artery.

D. Transversus Muscle: The transversus muscle fluctuates widely in the extent of its development but is rarely absent. Rarely, it extends as far inferiorly as the ligamentum teres uteri (round ligament), and infrequently it may be situated superior to the anterior superior spine. However, it generally occupies an intermediate position.

E. Other Variations: Several small muscles may be present.

1. The pubotransversalis muscle may extend from the superior ramus of the pubis to the transversalis fascia near the abdominal ring.

2. The puboperitonealis muscle may pass from the pubic crest to the transversus near the umbilicus.

3. The posterior rectus abdominis (tensor laminae posterioris vaginae musculi recti abdominis) may

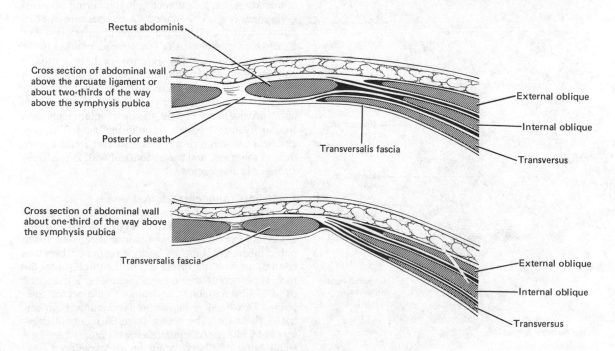

Figure 2–9. Formation of rectus sheath.

spread from the inguinal ligament to the rectus sheath on the deep surface of the rectus muscle near the umbilicus.

4. The tensor transversalis (tensor laminae posterioris vaginae musculi recti et fasciae transversalis abdominis) has appeared from the transversalis fascia near the abdominal inguinal ring to the linea semicircularis.

Hernias

A hernia (Fig 2–10) is a protrusion of any viscus from its normal enclosure, which may occur with any of the abdominal viscera, especially the jejunum, ileum, and greater omentum. A hernia may be due to increased pressure, such as that resulting from strenuous exercise, lifting heavy weights, tenesmus, or increased expiratory efforts, or may result from decreased resistance of the abdominal wall (congenital or acquired) such as occurs with debilitating illness or old age, prolonged distention from ascites, tumors, pregnancy, corpulence, emaciation, injuries (including surgical incisions), congenital absence, or poor development. Hernias are likely to occur where the abdominal wall is structurally weakened by the passage of large vessels or nerves and developmental peculiarities. Ventral hernias occur through the linea semilunaris or the linea alba. Umbilical hernias occur more frequently and can be one of three types. During early fetal development, portions of the mesentery and a loop of the intestine pass through the opening to occupy a part of the body cavity (the umbilical coelom) situated in the umbilical cord. Normally, the mesentery and intestine later return to the abdominal cavity. If they fail to do so, a congenital umbilical hernia

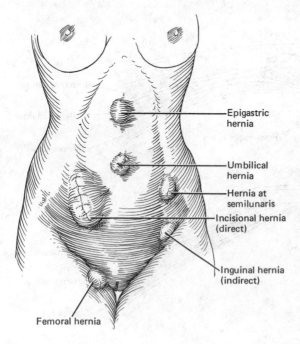

Figure 2–10. Hernia sites.

Epigastric hernia

Umbilical hernia

Hernia at semilunaris

Incisional hernia (direct)

Inguinal hernia (indirect)

Femoral hernia

results. Infantile umbilical hernias occur if the component parts fail to fuse completely in early postnatal stages. The unyielding nature of the fibrous tissue forming the margin of the ring predisposes to strangulation. Adult umbilical hernias occur frequently in females. When the hernia comes through the ring itself, it is always at the upper part.

THE INGUINAL REGION

The inguinal region of the abdominal wall is bounded by the rectus abdominis muscle medially, the line connecting the anterior superior iliac spines superiorly, and the inguinal ligament inferiorly. The region contains 8 layers of abdominal wall. These layers, from the most superficial inward, are (1) the skin, (2) the tela subcutanea, (3) the aponeurosis of the external oblique muscle, (4) the internal oblique muscle, (5) the transversus abdominis muscle (below the free border, the layer is incomplete), (6) the transversalis fascia, (7) the subperitoneal fat and connective tissue, and (8) the peritoneum. The tela subcutanea consists of the superficial fatty Camper's fascia, which is continuous with the tela subcutanea of the whole body, and the deeper membranous Scarpa's fascia, which covers the lower third of the abdominal wall and the medial side of the groin, both joining below the inguinal ligament to form the fascia lata of the thigh.

Subcutaneous Inguinal Ring

A triangular evagination of the external oblique aponeurosis, the subcutaneous inguinal ring (external abdominal ring), is bounded by an aponeurosis at its edges and by the inguinal ligament inferiorly. The superior or medial crus is smaller and attaches to the symphysis pubica. The inferior or lateral crus is stronger and blends with the inguinal ligament as it passes to the pubic tubercle. The sharp margins of the ring are attributed to a sudden thinning of the aponeurosis. In the female, the ligamentum teres uteri (round ligament) passes through this ring. The subcutaneous inguinal ring is much smaller in the female than in the male, and the abdominal wall is relatively stronger in this region.

Ligaments, Aponeuroses, & Fossae

The inguinal ligament itself forms the inferior thickened border of the external oblique aponeurosis, extending from the anterior superior iliac spine to the pubic tubercle. Along its inferior border, it becomes continuous with the fascia lata of the thigh. From the medial portion of the inguinal ligament, a triangular band of fibers attaches separately to the pecten ossis pubis. This band is known as the lacunar (Gimbernat's) ligament. The reflex inguinal ligament (ligament of Colles or triangular fascia) is represented by a small band of fibers, often poorly developed, and derived from the superior crus of the subcutaneous inguinal ring and the lower part of the linea alba. These fibers cross to the opposite side to attach to the pecten ossis pubis. The falx inguinalis or conjoined tendon is formed by the aponeurosis of the transversus abdominis and internal oblique muscles. These fibers arise from the inguinal ligament and arch downward and forward to insert on the pubic crest and pecten ossis pubis, behind the inguinal and lacunar ligaments. The interfoveolar ligament is composed partly of fibrous bands from the aponeurosis of the transversalis muscle of the same and opposite sides. Curving medial to and below the internal abdominal ring, they attach to the lacunar ligament and pectineal fascia.

Abdominal Inguinal Ring

The abdominal inguinal ring (internal abdominal ring) is the rounded mouth of a funnel-shaped expansion of transversalis fascia that lies approximately 2 cm above the inguinal ligament and midway between the anterior superior iliac spine and the symphysis pubica. Medially, it is bounded by the inferior epigastric vessels; the external iliac artery is situated below. The abdominal inguinal ring represents the area where the round ligament emerges from the abdomen. The triangular area medial to the inferior epigastric artery, bounded by the inguinal ligament below and the lateral border of the rectus sheath, is known as the trigonum inguinale (Hesselbach's triangle), the site of congenital direct hernias.

Inguinal Canal

The inguinal canal in the female is not well demarcated, but it normally gives passage to the round ligament of the uterus, a vein, an artery from the uterus that forms a cruciate anastomosis with the labial arteries, and extraperitoneal fat. The fetal ovary, like the testis, is an abdominal organ and possesses a gubernaculum that extends from its lower pole downward and forward to a point corresponding to the abdominal inguinal ring, through which it continues into the labia majora. The processus vaginalis is an evagination of peritoneum at the level of the abdominal inguinal ring occurring during the third fetal month. In the male, the processus vaginalis descends with the testis. The processus vaginalis of the female is rudimentary, but occasionally a small diverticulum of peritoneum is found passing part way through the inguinal region; this diverticulum is termed the processus vaginalis peritonei (canal of Nuck). Instead of descending, as does the testis, the ovary moves medially, where it becomes adjacent to the uterus. The intra-abdominal portion of the gubernaculum ovarii becomes attached to the lateral border of the developing uterus, evolving as the ligament of the ovary and the round ligament of the uterus. The extra-abdominal portion of the round ligament of the uterus becomes attenuated in the adult and may appear as a small fibrous band. The inguinal canal is an intermuscular passageway that extends from the abdominal ring downward, medially, and somewhat forward to the subcutaneous inguinal ring (about 3–4 cm). The canal is roughly triangular in

shape, and its boundaries are largely artificial. The lacunar and inguinal ligaments form the base of the canal. The anterior or superficial wall is formed by the external oblique aponeurosis, and the lowermost fibers of the internal oblique muscle add additional strength in its lateral part. The posterior or deep wall of the canal is formed by transversalis fascia throughout and is strengthened medially by the falx inguinalis.

Abdominal Fossae

The abdominal fossae in the inguinal region consist of the foveae inguinalis lateralis and medialis. The fovea inguinalis lateralis lies lateral to a slight fold, the plica epigastrica, formed by the inferior epigastric vessels, and just medial to the abdominal inguinal ring, which slants medially and upward toward the rectus muscle. From the lateral margin of the tendinous insertion of the rectus muscle, upward toward the umbilicus, and over the obliterated artery extends a more accentuated fold, the plica umbilicalis lateralis. The fovea inguinalis medialis lies between the plica epigastrica and the plica umbilicalis lateralis, the bottom of the fossa facing the trigonum inguinale (Hesselbach's triangle). This region is strengthened by the interfoveolar ligament at the medial side of the abdominal inguinal ring and the conjoined tendon lateral to the rectus muscle; however, these bands vary in width and are thus supportive.

Ligaments & Spaces

The inguinal ligament forms the roof of a large osseoligamentous space leading from the iliac fossa to the thigh. The floor of this space is formed by the superior ramus of the pubis medially and by the body of the ilium laterally. The iliopectineal ligament extends from the inguinal ligament to the iliopectineal eminence, dividing this area into 2 parts. The lateral, larger division is called the muscular lacuna and is almost completely filled by the iliopsoas muscle, along with the femoral nerve medially and the lateral femoral cutaneous nerves laterally. The medial, smaller division is known as the vascular lacuna and is traversed by the external iliac (femoral) artery, vein, and lymphatic vessels, which do not completely fill the space. The anterior border of the vascular lacuna is formed by the inguinal ligament and the transversalis fascia. The posterior boundary is formed by the ligamentum pubicum superius (Cooper's ligament), a thickening of fascia along the pubic pecten where the pectineal fascia and iliopectineal ligament meet. The transversalis fascia and iliac fascia are extended with the vessels, forming a funnel-shaped fibrous investment, the femoral sheath. The sheath is divided into 3 compartments: (1) the lateral compartment, containing the femoral artery; (2) the intermediate compartment, containing the femoral vein; and (3) the medial compartment or canal, containing a lymph node (nodi lymphatici inguinales profundi [node of Rosenmüller or Cloquet]) and the lymphatic vessels that drain most of the leg, groin, and perineum. The femoral canal also contains areolar tissue, which frequently condenses to form the "femoral septum." Owing to the greater spread of the pelvis in the female, the muscular and vascular lacunae are relatively large spaces. The upper or abdominal opening of the femoral canal is known as the femoral ring and is covered by the parietal peritoneum.

Arteries

In front of the femoral ring, the arterial branches of the external iliac artery are the inferior epigastric and the deep circumflex iliac. The inferior epigastric artery arises from the anterior surface of the external iliac, passing forward and upward on the anterior abdominal wall between peritoneum and transversalis fascia. It pierces the fascia just below the arcuate line, entering the rectus abdominis muscle or coursing along its inferior surface to anastomose with the superior epigastric from the internal thoracic. The inferior epigastric artery forms the lateral boundary of the trigonum inguinale (Hesselbach's triangle). At its origin, it frequently gives off a branch to the inguinal canal, as well as a branch to the pubis (pubic artery), which anastomoses with twigs of the obturator artery. The pubic branch of the inferior epigastric often becomes the obturator artery. The deep circumflex iliac artery arises laterally and traverses the iliopsoas to the anterior superior iliac spine, where it pierces the transversus muscle to course between the transversus and the internal oblique, sending perforators to the surface. It often has anastomoses with penetrating branches of the inferior epigastric via its perforators through the rectus abdominis. The veins follow a similar course.

As the external iliac artery passes through the femoral canal, which underlies the inguinal ligament, it courses medial to the femoral vein and nerve, resting in what is termed the femoral triangle (Scarpa's triangle). The femoral sheath is a downward continuation of the inguinal ligament anterior to the femoral vessel and nerve.

The branches of the femoral artery supplying the groin are (1) the superficial epigastric, (2) the superficial circumflex iliac, (3) the superficial external pudendal, and (4) the deep external pudendal. The superficial epigastric artery passes upward through the femoral sheath over the inguinal ligament, to rest in Camper's fascia on the lower abdomen. The superficial circumflex iliac artery arises adjacent to the superior epigastric, piercing the fascia lata and running parallel to the inguinal ligament as far as the iliac crest. It then divides into branches that supply the integument of the groin, the superficial fascia, and the lymph glands, anastomosing with the deep circumflex iliac, the superior gluteal, and the lateral femoral circumflex arteries. The superficial external pudendal artery arises from the medial side of the femoral artery, close to the preceding vessels. It pierces the femoral sheath and fascia cribrosa, coursing medially across the round ligament to the integument on the lower part of the abdomen and the labium majus, anastomosing with the internal pudendal. The deep external pudendal artery passes medially across the pectineus and adductor lon-

gus muscles, supplying the integument of the labium majus and forming, together with the external pudendal artery, a rete with the labial arteries.

PUDENDUM

The vulva consists of the mons pubis, the labia majora, the labia minora, the clitoris, and the glandular structures that open into the vestibulum vaginae (Fig 2–11). The size, shape, and coloration of the various structures, as well as the hair distribution, vary between individuals and racial groups. Normal pubic hair in the female is distributed in an inverted triangle, with the base centered over the mons pubis. Nevertheless, in approximately 25% of normal women, hair may extend upward along the linea alba. The type of hair is dependent, in part, on the pigmentation of the individual. It varies from heavy, coarse, crinkly hair in blacks to sparse, fairly fine, lanugo type hair in Oriental women. The length and size of the various structures of the vulva are influenced by the pelvic architecture, as is also the position of the external genitalia in the perineal area. The external genitalia of the female have their exact counterparts in the male.

Labia Majora

A. Superficial Anatomy: The labia majora are comprised of 2 rounded mounds of tissue, originating in the mons pubis and terminating in the perineum. They form the lateral boundaries of the vulva and are approximately 7–9 cm long and 2–4 cm wide, varying in size with height, weight, race, age, parity, and pelvic architecture. Ontogenetically, these permanent folds of skin are homologous to the scrotum of the male. Hair is distributed over their surfaces, extending superiorly in the area of the mons pubis from one side to the other. The lateral surfaces are adjacent to the medial surface of the thigh, forming a deep groove when the legs are together. The medial surfaces of the labia majora may oppose each other directly or may be separated by protrusion of the labia minora. The cleft that is formed by this opposition anteriorly is termed the anterior commissure. Posteriorly, the cleft is less clearly defined and termed the posterior commissure. The middle portion of the cleft between the 2 labia is the rima pudendi.

B. Deep Structures: Underlying the skin is a thin, poorly developed muscle layer called the tunica dartos labialis, the fibers of which course, for the most part, at right angles to the wrinkles of the surface, forming a crisscross pattern. Deep to the dartos layer is a thin layer of fascia, most readily recognizable in the old or the young because of the large amount of adipose and areolar tissue. Numerous sweat glands are found in the labia majora, the greater number on the medial aspect. In the deeper substance of the labia majora are longitudinal bands of muscle that are continuous with the ligamentum teres uteri (round liga-

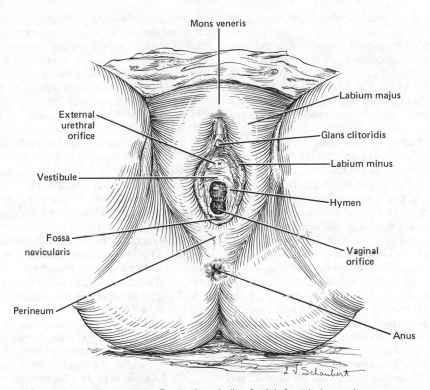

Figure 2-11. External genitalia of adult female (parous).

ment) as it emerges from the inguinal canal. Occasionally, a persistent processus vaginalis peritonei (canal of Nuck) may be seen in the upper region of the labia. In most women, it has been impossible to differentiate the presence of the cremaster muscle beyond its area of origin.

C. Arteries: The arterial supply into the labia majora comes from the internal and external pudendals, with extensive anastomoses. Within the labia majora is a circular arterial pattern originating inferiorly from a branch of the perineal artery, from the external pudendal artery in the anterior lateral aspect, and from a small artery of the ligamentum teres uteri superiorly. The inferior branch from the perineal artery, which originates from the internal pudendal as it emerges from the canalis pudendalis (Alcock's canal), forms the base of the rete with the external pudendal arteries. These arise from the medial side of the femoral and, occasionally, from the deep arteries just beneath the femoral ring, coursing medially over the pectineus and adductor muscles, to which they supply branches. They terminate in a circular rete within the labium majus, penetrating the fascia lata adjacent to the fossa ovalis and passing over the round ligament to send a branch to the clitoris.

D. Veins: The venous drainage is extensive and forms a plexus with numerous anastomoses. In addition, the veins communicate with the dorsal vein of the clitoris, the veins of the labia minora, and the perineal veins, as well as with the inferior hemorrhoidal plexus. On each side, the posterior labial veins connect with the external pudendal vein, terminating in the great saphenous vein (saphena magna) just prior to its entrance (saphenous opening) in the fossa ovalis. This large plexus is frequently manifested by the presence of large varicosities during pregnancy.

E. Lymphatics: The lymphatics of the labia majora are extensive and utilize 2 systems, one lying superficially (under the skin) and the other deeper, within the subcutaneous tissues. From the upper two-thirds of the left and right labia majora, superficial lymphatics pass toward the symphysis and turn laterally to join the medial superficial inguinal nodes. These nodes drain into the superficial inguinal nodes overlying the saphenous fossa. The drainage flows into and through the femoral ring (fossa ovalis) to the nodi lymphatici inguinales profundi (nodes of Rosenmüller or Cloquet; deep subinguinal nodes), connecting with the external iliac chain. The superficial subinguinal nodes, situated over the femoral trigone, also accept superficial drainage from the lower extremity and the gluteal region. This drainage may include afferent lymphatics from the perineum. In the region of the symphysis pubica, the lymphatics anastomose in a plexus between the right and left sides. Therefore, any lesion involving the labia majora allows direct involvement of the lymphatic structures of the contralateral inguinal area. The lower part of the labium majus has superficial and deep drainage that is shared with the perineal area. The drainage passes, in part, through afferent lymphatics to superficial subinguinal nodes; from the posterior medial aspects of the labia majora, it frequently enters the lymphatic plexus surrounding the rectum.

F. Nerves: The innervation of the external genitalia has been studied by many investigators. The iliohypogastric nerve originates from T12 and L1 and traverses laterally to the iliac crest between the transversus and internal oblique muscles, at which point it divides into 2 branches: (1) the anterior hypogastric nerve, which descends anteriorly through the skin over the symphysis, supplying the superior portion of the labia majora and the mons pubis, and (2) the posterior iliac, which passes to the gluteal area.

The ilioinguinal nerve originates from L1 and follows a course slightly inferior to the iliohypogastric nerve, with which it may frequently anastomose, branching into many small fibers that terminate in the upper medial aspect of the labium majus.

The genitofemoral nerve (L1–L2) emerges from the anterior surface of the psoas muscle to run obliquely downward over its surface, branching in the deeper substance of the labium majus to supply the dartos muscle and that vestige of the cremaster present within the labium majus. Its lumboinguinal branch continues downward onto the upper part of the thigh.

From the sacral plexus, the posterior femoral cutaneous nerve, originating from the posterior divisions of S1 and S2 and the anterior divisions of S2 and S3, divides into several rami that, in part, are called the perineal branches. They supply the medial aspect of the thigh and the labia majora. These branches of the posterior femoral cutaneous nerve are derived from the sacral plexus. The pudendal nerve, composed primarily of S2, S3, and S4, often with a fascicle of S1, sends a small number of fibers to the medial aspect of the labia majora. The pattern of nerve endings is illustrated in Table 2–1.

Labia Minora

A. Superficial Anatomy: The labia minora are 2 folds of skin that lie within the rima pudendi and measure approximately 5 cm in length and 0.5–1 cm in thickness. The width varies according to age and parity, measuring 2–3 cm at its narrowest diameter to 5–6 cm at its widest, with multiple corrugations over the surface. The labia minora begin at the base of the clitoris, where fusion of the labia is continuous with the prepuce, extending posteriorly and medially to the labia majora at the posterior commissure. On their medial aspects superiorly beneath the clitoris, they unite to form the frenulum adjacent to the urethra and vagina, terminating along the hymen on the right and left sides of the fossa navicularis and ending posteriorly in the frenulum of the labia pudendi, just superior to the posterior commissure. A deep cleft is formed on the lateral surface between the labium majus and the labium minus. The skin on the labia minora is smooth and pigmented. The color and distention varies, depending on the level of sexual excitement and the pigmentation of the individual. The glands of the labia are homologous to the glandulae preputiales (glands of Littré) of the penile portion of the male urethra.

B. Arteries: The main source of arterial supply (Fig 2–12) occurs through anastomoses from the superficial perineal artery, branching from the dorsal artery of the clitoris, and from the medial aspect of the rete of the labia majora. Similarly, the venous pattern and plexus are extensive.

C. Veins: The venous drainage is to the medial vessels of the perineal and vaginal veins, directly to the veins of the labia majora, to the inferior hemorrhoidals posteriorly, and to the clitoral veins superiorly.

D. Lymphatics: The lymphatics medially may join those of the lower third of the vagina superiorly and the labia majora laterally, passing to the superficial subinguinal nodes and to the deep subinguinal nodes. In the midline, the lymphatic drainage coincides with that of the clitoris, communicating with that of the labia majora to drain to the opposite side.

E. Nerves: The innervation of the labia minora originates, in part, from fibers that supply the labia majora and from branches of the pudendal nerve as it emerges from the canalis pudendalis (Alcock's canal) (Fig 2–12). These branches originate from the perineal nerve. The labia minora and the vestibule area are homologous to the skin of the male urethra and penis. The short membranous portion, approximately 0.5 cm of the male urethra, is homologous to the midportion of the vestibule of the female.

Clitoris

A. Superficial Anatomy: The clitoris is the

Table 2–1. Quantitative distribution of nerve endings in selected regions of the female genitalia.

	Touch			Pressure	Pain	Other Types	
	Meissner Corpuscles*	Merkel Tactile Disks*	Peritrichous Endings	Vater-Pacini Corpusclest	Free Nerve Endings	Ruffini Corpusclest	Dogiel and Krause Corpuscles‡
Mons veneris	++++	++++	++++	+++	+++	++++	++
Labia majora	+++	++++	++++	+++	+++	+++	++
Clitoris	+	+	0	++++	+++	+++	+++
Labia minora	++	++	0	++	++	++	+++
Hymenal ring	0	+	0	0	+++	0	0
Vagina	0	0	0	0	+ Occasionally	0	0

*Also called corpuscula tactus.   †Also called corpuscula lamellosa.   ‡Also called corpuscula bulboidea.

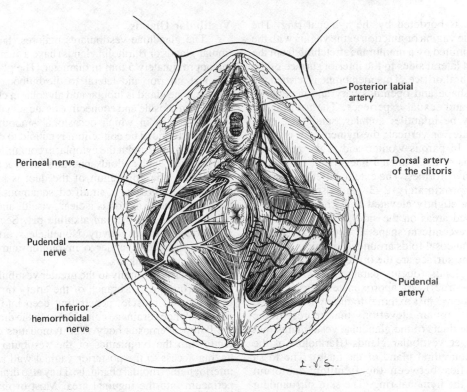

Posterior labial artery

Dorsal artery of the clitoris

Perineal nerve

Pudendal artery

Pudendal nerve

Inferior hemorrhoidal nerve

L.V.S.

Figure 2–12. Arteries and nerves of perineum.

homolog of the dorsal part of the penis and consists of 2 small erectile cavernous bodies, terminating in a rudimentary glans clitoridis. The erectile body, the corpus clitoridis, consists of the 2 crura clitoridis and the glans clitoridis, with overlying skin and prepuce, a miniature homolog of the glans penis. The crura extend outward bilaterally to their position in the anterior portion of the vulva. The cavernous tissue, homologous to the corpus spongiosum penis of the male, appears in the vascular pattern of the labia minora in the female. At the lower border of the pubic arch, a small triangular fibrous band extends onto the clitoris (suspensory ligament) to separate the 2 crura, which turn inward, downward, and laterally at this point, close to the inferior rami of the pubic symphysis. The crura lie inferior to the ischiocavernosus muscles and bodies. The glans is situated superiorly at the fused termination of the crura. It is composed of erectile tissue and contains an integument, hoodlike in shape, termed the prepuce. On its ventral surface, there is a frenulum clitoridis, the fused junction of the labia minora.

B. Arteries: The blood supply to the clitoris is from its dorsal artery, a terminal branch of the internal pudendal artery, which is the terminal division of the posterior portion of the internal iliac (hypogastric) artery. As it enters the clitoris, it divides into 2 branches, the deep and dorsal arteries. Just before entering the clitoris itself, a small branch passes posteriorly to supply the area of the external urethral meatus.

C. Veins: The venous drainage of the clitoris begins in a rich plexus around the corona of the glans, running along the anterior surface to join the deep vein and continuing downward to join the pudendal plexus from the labia minora, labia majora, and perineum, forming the pudendal vein.

D. Lymphatics: The lymphatic drainage of the clitoris coincides primarily with that of the labia minora, the right and left sides having access to contralateral nodes in the superficial inguinal chain. In addition, its extensive network provides further access downward and posteriorly to the external urethral meatus toward the anterior portion of the vestibule.

E. Nerves: The innervation of the clitoris is through the terminal branch of the pudendal nerve, which originates from the sacral plexus as previously discussed. It lies on the lateral side of the dorsal artery and terminates in branches within the glans, corona, and prepuce. The nerve endings in the clitoris vary from a total absence within the glans to a rich supply primarily located within the prepuce (Table 2–1). A total absence of endings within the clitoris itself takes on clinical significance when one considers the emphasis placed on the clitoris in discussing problems of sexual gratification in women.

Vestibule

A. Superficial Anatomy: The area of the vestibule is bordered by the labia minora laterally, by the frenulum labiorum pudendi (or posterior commissure) posteriorly, and by the urethra and clitoris anteriorly.

Inferiorly, it is bordered by the hymenal ring. The opening of the vagina or junction of the vagina with the vestibule is limited by a membrane stretching from the posterior and lateral sides to the inferior surface of the external urethral orifice. This membrane is termed the hymen. Its shape and openings vary and depend on age, parity, and sexual experience. The form of the opening may be infantile, annular, semilunar, cribriform, septate, or vertical; the hymen may even be imperforate. In parous women and in the postcoital state, the tags of the hymenal integument are termed carunculae myrtiformes. The external urethral orifice, which is approximately 2–3 cm posterior to the clitoris, on a slightly elevated and irregular surface with depressed areas on the sides, may appear to be stellate or crescentic in shape. It is characterized by many small mucosal folds around its opening. Bilaterally and on the surface are the orifices of the para- and periurethral glands (ductus paraurethrales [ducts of Skene and Astruc]). At approximately the 5 and 7 o'clock positions, just external to the hymenal rings, are 2 small papular elevations that represent the orifices of the ducts of the glandulae vestibulares majores, or larger vestibular glands (Bartholin) of the female (bulbourethral gland of the male). The fossa navicularis lies between the frenulum labiorum pudendi and the hymenal ring. The skin surrounding the vestibule is stratified squamous in type, with a paucity of rete pegs and papillae.

B. Arteries: The blood supply to the vestibule is an extensive capillary plexus that has anastomoses with the superficial transverse perineal artery. A branch comes directly from the pudendal anastomosis with the inferior hemorrhoidal artery in the region of the fossa navicularis; the blood supply of the urethra anteriorly, a branch of the dorsal artery of the clitoris and the azygos artery of the anterior vaginal wall, also contributes.

C. Veins: Venous drainage is extensive, involving the same areas described for the arterial network.

D. Lymphatics: The lymphatic drainage has a distinct pattern. The anterior portion, including that of the external urethral meatus, drains upward and outward with that of the labia minora and the clitoris. The portion next to the urethral meatus may join that of the anterior urethra, which empties into the vestibular plexus to terminate in the superficial inguinal nodes, the superficial subinguinal nodes, the deep subinguinal nodes, and the external iliac chain. The lymphatics of the fossa navicularis and the hymen may join those of the posterior vaginal wall, intertwining with the intercalated lymph nodes along the rectum, which follow the inferior hemorrhoidal arteries. This pattern becomes significant with malignancy. Drainage occurs through the pudendal and the hemorrhoidal chain and through the vestibular plexus onto the inguinal region.

E. Nerves: The innervation of the vestibular area is primarily from the sacral plexus through the perineal nerve. The absence of the usual modalities of touch is noteworthy. The vestibular portion of the hymenal ring contains an abundance of free nerve endings (pain).

Vestibular Glands

The glandulae vestibulares majores (larger vestibular glands or Bartholin glands) have a duct measuring approximately 5 mm in diameter. The gland itself lies just inferior and lateral to the bulbocavernosus muscle. The gland is tubular and alveolar in character, with a thin capsule and connective tissue septa dividing it into lobules in which occasional smooth muscle fibers are found. The epithelium is cuboid to columnar and pale in color, with the cytoplasm containing mucigen droplets and colloid spherules with acidophilic inclusions. The epithelium of the duct is simple in type, and its orifice is stratified squamous like the vestibule. The secretion is a clear, viscid, and stringy mucoid substance with an alkaline pH. Secretion is active during sexual activity. Nonetheless, after about age 30, the glands undergo involution and become atrophic and shrunken.

The arterial supply to the greater vestibular gland comes from a small branch of the artery on the bulbocavernosus muscle, penetrating deep into its substance. Venous drainage coincides with the drainage of the bulbocavernosus body. The lymphatics drain directly into the lymphatics of the vestibular plexus, having access to the posterior vaginal wall along the inferior hemorrhoidal channels. They also drain via the perineum into the inguinal area. Most of this minor drainage is along the pudendal vessels in the canalis pudendalis and explains, in part, the difficulty in dealing with malignancy involving the gland.

The greater vestibular gland is homologous to the bulbourethral gland (also known as Cowper's glands, Duverney's glands, Tiedemann's glands, or the Bartholin glands of the male). The innervation of the greater vestibular gland is from a small branch of the perineal nerve, which penetrates directly into its substance.

Muscles of External Genitalia

The muscles (Fig 2–13) of the external genitalia and cavernous bodies in the female are homologous to those of the male, although they are less well developed.

A. Bulbocavernosus Muscle: The bulbocavernosus muscle and deeper bulbus vestibuli or cavernous tissue arise in the midline from the posterior part of the central tendon of the perineum, where each opposes the fibers from the opposite side. Each ascends around the vagina, enveloping the bulbus vestibuli (the corpus cavernosum bodies of the male) to terminate in 3 heads: (1) the fibrous tissue dorsal to the clitoris, (2) the tunica fibrosa of the corpus cavernosa overlying the crura of the clitoris, and (3) decussating fibers that join those of the ischiocavernosus to form the striated sphincter of the urethra at the junction of its mid and lower thirds. The blood supply is derived from the perineal branch of the internal pudendal artery as it arises in the anterior part of the ischiorectal fossa. Deep to the fascia diaphragmatis urogenitalis inferior (Colles' fascia) and crossing between the ischiocavernosus and bulbocavernosus muscles, the pudendal ar-

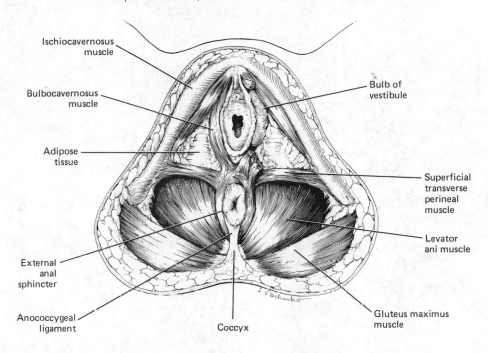

Figure 2–13. Pelvic musculature (inferior view).

tery sends 1–2 branches directly into the bulbocavernosus muscle and vestibular body, continuing anteriorly to terminate in the dorsal artery of the clitoris. The venous drainage accompanies the pudendal plexus. In addition, it passes posteriorly with the inferior hemorrhoidal veins and laterally with the perineal vein, a branch of the internal pudendal vein. The lymphatics run primarily with those of the vestibular plexus, with drainage inferiorly toward the intercalated nodes of the rectum and anteriorly and laterally with the labia minora and majora to the superficial inguinal nodes. Contralateral drainage in the upper portion of the muscle and body is evident.

B. Ischiocavernosus Muscle: The ischiocavernosus muscle and its attendant cavernous tissue arise from the ischial tuberosity and inferior ramus to the ischium. It envelops the crus of its cavernous tissue in a thin layer of muscle ascending toward and over the medial and inferior surfaces of the symphysis pubica to terminate in the anterior surface of the symphysis at the base of the clitoris. It then sends decussating fibers to the region of the upper and middle thirds of the urethra, forming the greater part of the organ's voluntary sphincter. The blood supply is through perforating branches from the perineal artery as it ascends between the bulbocavernosus and ischiocavernosus muscles to terminate as the dorsal artery of the clitoris. The innervation stems from an ischiocavernosus branch of the perineal division of the pudendal nerve.

C. Transversus Muscle: The transversus perinei superficialis muscle arises from the inferior ramus of the ischium and from the ischial tuberosity. The fibers of the muscle extend across the perineum and are inserted into its central tendon, meeting those from the opposite side. Frequently, the muscle fibers from the

bulbocavernosus, the puborectalis, the superficial transverse perinei, and occasionally the external anal sphincter will interdigitate. The blood supply is from a perforating branch of the perineal division of the internal pudendal artery, and the nerve supply is from the perineal division of the pudendal nerve.

D. Sensory Corpuscles: In the cavernous substances of both the bulbocavernosus and ischiocavernosus muscles, Vater-Pacini corpuscles (corpuscula lamellosa) and Dogiel and Krause corpuscles (corpuscula bulboidea) are present.

E. Inferior Layer of Urogenital Diaphragm: The inferior layer of the urogenital diaphragm is a potential space depending upon the size and development of the musculature, the parity of the female, and the pelvic architecture. It contains loose areolar connective tissue interspersed with fat. The bulbocavernosus muscles, with the support of the superficial transverse perinei muscles and the puborectalis muscles, act as a point of fixation on each side for support of the vulva, the external genitalia, and the vagina.

F. Surgical Considerations: A midline perineotomy is most effective to minimize trauma to vital supports of the vulva, bulbocavernosus, and superficial transverse perinei muscles. Overdistention of the vagina caused by the presenting part and body of the infant forms a temporary sacculation. If distention occurs too rapidly or if dilatation is beyond the resilient capacity of the vagina, rupture of the vaginal musculature may occur, often demonstrated by a cuneiform groove on the anterior wall and a tonguelike protrusion on the posterior wall of the vagina. Therefore, return of the vagina and vulva to the nonpregnant state is dependent upon the tonus of the muscle and the degree of distention of the vagina during parturition.

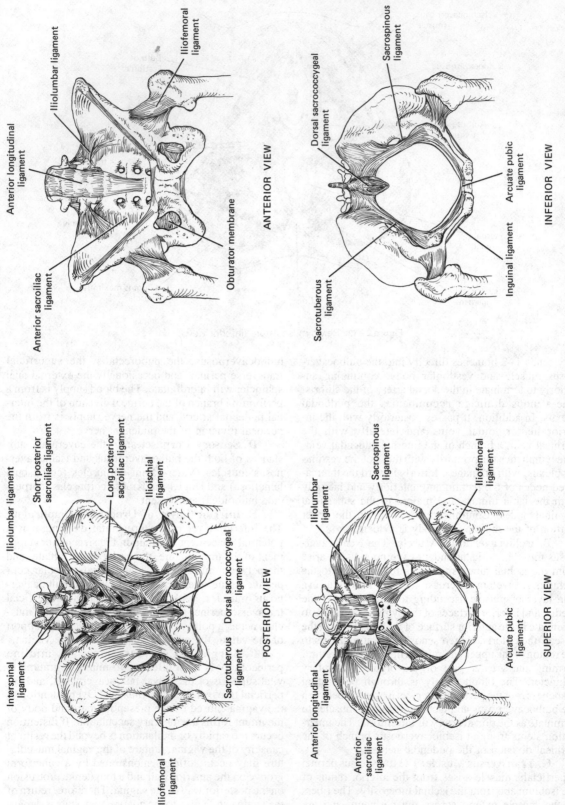

Figure 2–14. The bony pelvis. (Reproduced, with permission, from Benson RC: *Handbook of Obstetrics & Gynecology*, 7th ed. Lange, 1980.)

BONY PELVIS

The pelvis (Fig 2–14) is a basin-shaped ring of bones that marks the distal margin of the trunk. The pelvis rests upon the lower extremities and supports the spinal column. It is composed of 2 innominate bones, one on each side, joined anteriorly and articulated with the sacrum posteriorly. The 2 major pelvic divisions are the pelvis major (upper or false pelvis) and the pelvis minor (lower or true pelvis). The pelvis major consists primarily of the space superior to the iliopectineal line, including the 2 iliac fossae and the region between them. The pelvis minor, located below the iliopectineal line, is bounded anteriorly by the pubic bones, posteriorly by the sacrum and coccyx, and laterally by the ischium and a small segment of the ilium.

The Innominate Bone

The innominate bone is composed of 3 parts: ilium, ischium, and pubis.

A. Ilium: The ilium consists of a bladelike upper part or ala (wing) and a thicker, lower part called the body. The body forms the upper portion of the acetabulum and unites with the bodies of the ischium and pubis. The medial surface of the ilium presents as a large concave area: The anterior portion is the iliac fossa; the smaller posterior portion is composed of a rough upper part, the iliac tuberosity; and the lower

part contains a large surface for articulation with the sacrum. At the inferior medial margin of the iliac fossa, a rounded ridge, the arcuate line, ends anteriorly in the iliopectineal eminence. Posteriorly, the arcuate line is continuous with the anterior margin of the ala of the sacrum across the anterior aspect of the sacroiliac joint. Anteriorly, it is continuous with the ridge or pecten on the superior ramus of the pubis. The lateral surface or dorsum of the ilium is traversed by 3 ridges: the posterior, anterior, and inferior gluteal lines. The superior border is called the crest, and at its 2 extremities are the anterior and posterior superior iliac spines. The principal feature of the anterior border of the ilium is the heavy anterior inferior iliac spine. Important aspects of the posterior border are the posterior superior and the inferior iliac spines and, below the latter, the greater sciatic notch, the inferior part of which is bounded by the ischium. The inferior border of the ilium participates in the formation of the acetabulum.

The main vasculature (Fig 2–15) of the innominate bone appears where the bone is thickest. Blood is supplied to the inner surface of the ilium through twigs of the iliolumbar, deep circumflex iliac, and obturator arteries by foramens on the crest, in the iliac fossa, and below the terminal line near the greater sciatic notch. The outer surface of the ilium is supplied mainly below the inferior gluteal line through nutrient vessels derived from the gluteal arteries. The inferior branch of the deep part of the superior gluteal artery forms the

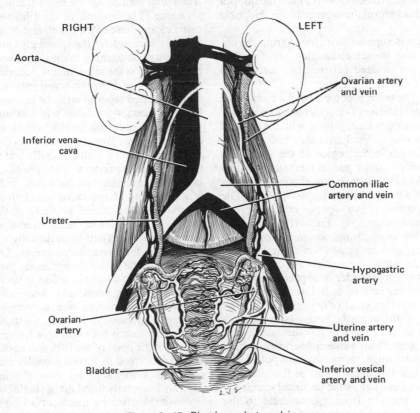

Figure 2–15. Blood supply to pelvis.

external nutrient artery of the ilium and continues in its course to anastomose with the lateral circumflex artery. Upon leaving the pelvis below the piriform muscle, it divides into a number of branches, a group of which passes to the hip joint.

B. Ischium: The ischium is composed of a body, superior and inferior rami, and a tuberosity. The body is the heaviest part of the bone and is joined with the bodies of the ilium and pubis to form the acetabulum. It presents 3 surfaces: (1) The smooth internal surface is continuous above with the body of the ilium and below with the inner surface of the superior ramus of the ischium. Together, these parts form the posterior portion of the lateral wall of the pelvis minor. (2) The external surface of the ischium is the portion that enters into the formation of the acetabulum. (3) The posterior surface is the area between the acetabular rim and the posterior border. It is convex and is separated from the ischial tuberosity by a wide groove. The posterior border, with the ilium, forms the bony margin of the greater sciatic notch. The superior ramus of the ischium descends from the body of the bone to join the inferior ramus at an angle of approximately 90 degrees. The large ischial tuberosity and its inferior portion are situated on the convexity of this angle. The inferior portion of the tuberosity forms the point of support in the sitting position. The posterior surface is divided into 2 areas by an oblique line. The lesser sciatic notch occupies the posterior border of the superior ramus between the spine and the tuberosity. The inferior ramus, as it is traced forward, joins the inferior ramus of the pubis to form the arcus pubis (ischiopubic arch).

The ischium is supplied with blood from the obturator medial and lateral circumflex arteries. The largest vessels are situated between the acetabulum and the sciatic tubercle.

C. Pubis: The pubis is composed of a body and 2 rami, superior and inferior. The body contributes to the formation of the acetabulum, joining with the body of the ilium at the iliopectineal eminence and with the body of the ischium in the region of the acetabular notch. The superior ramus passes medially and forward from the body to meet the corresponding ramus of the opposite side at the symphysis pubica. The medial or fore portion of the superior ramus is broad and flattened anteroposteriorly. Formerly called "the body," it presents an outer and an inner surface, the symphyseal area, and an upper border or "crest." Approximately 2 cm from the medial edge of the ramus and in line with the upper border is the prominent pubic tubercle, an important landmark. Below the crest is the anterior surface and the posterior or deep surface. The medial portion of the superior ramus is continuous below with the inferior ramus, and the lateral part presents a wide, smooth area anterosuperiorly, behind which is an irregular ridge, the pecten ossis pubis. The pecten pubis forms the anterior part of the linea terminalis. In front of and below the pectineal area is the obturator crest, passing from the tubercle to the acetabular notch. On the inferior aspect of the superior

ramus is the obturator sulcus. The inferior ramus is continuous with the superior ramus and passes downward and backward to join the inferior ramus of the ischium, forming the "ischiopubic arch." The pubis receives blood from the pubic branches of the obturator artery and from branches of the medial and lateral circumflex arteries.

The Sacrum

The sacrum is formed in the adult by the union of 5 or 6 sacral vertebrae; occasionally, the fifth lumbar vertebra is partly fused with it. The process of union is known as "sacralization" in the vertebral column. The sacrum constitutes the base of the vertebral column. As a single bone, it is considered to have a base, an apex, 2 surfaces (pelvic and dorsal), and 2 lateral portions. The base faces upward and is composed principally of a central part, formed by the upper surface of the body of the first sacral vertebra, and 2 lateral areas of alae. The body articulates by means of a fibrocartilage disk with the body of the fifth lumbar vertebra. The alae represent the heavy transverse processes of the first sacral vertebra that articulate with the 2 iliac bones. The anterior margin of the body is called the promontory and forms the sacrovertebral angle with the fifth lumbar vertebra. The rounded anterior margin of each ala constitutes the posterior part (pars sacralis) of the linea terminalis. The pelvic surface of the sacrum is rough and convex. In the midline is the median sacral crest (fused spinal processes), and on either side is a flattened area formed by the fused laminae of the sacral vertebrae. The laminae of the fifth vertebra and, in many cases, those of the fourth and occasionally of the third are incomplete (the spines also are absent), thus leaving a wide opening to the dorsal wall of the sacral canal known as the sacral hiatus. Lateral to the laminae are the articular crests (right and left), which are in line with the paired superior articular processes above. The lateral processes articulate with the inferior articular processes of the fifth lumbar vertebra. The inferior extensions of the articular crests form the sacral cornua that bind the sacral hiatus laterally and are attached to the cornua of the coccyx. The cornua can be palpated in life and are important landmarks indicating the inferior opening of the sacral canal (for sacral-caudal anesthesia). The lateral portions of the sacrum are formed by the fusion of the transverse processes of the sacral vertebrae. They form dorsally a line of elevations called the lateral sacral crests. The parts corresponding to the first 3 vertebrae are particularly massive and present a large area facing laterally called the articular surface, which articulates with the sacrum. Posterior to the articular area, the rough bone is called the sacral tuberosity. It faces the tuberosity of the ilium. The apex is the small area formed by the lower surface of the body of the fifth part of the sacrum. The coccyx is formed by 4 (occasionally 3 or 5) caudal or coccygeal vertebrae. The second, third, and fourth parts are frequently fused into a single bone that articulates with the first by means of a fibrocartilage. The entire coccyx may become ossified and fused with the sacrum (the sacrococcygeal joint).

The sacrum receives its blood supply from the middle sacral artery, which extends from the bifurcation of the aorta to the tip of the coccyx, and from the lateral sacral arteries that branch either as a single artery that immediately divides or as 2 distinct vessels from the hypogastric artery. The lowest lumbar branch of the middle sacral artery ramifies over the lateral parts of the sacrum, passing back between the last vertebra and the sacrum to anastomose with the lumbar arteries above and the superior gluteal artery below. The lateral sacral branches (usually 4) anastomose anteriorly to the coccyx with branches of the inferior lateral sacral artery that branch from the hypogastric artery. They give off small spinal branches that pass through the sacral foramens and supply the sacral canal and posterior portion of the sacrum.

Sacroiliac Joint

The sacroiliac joint is a diarthrodial joint with irregular surfaces. The articular surfaces are covered with a layer of cartilage, and the cavity of the joint is a narrow cleft. The cartilage on the sacrum is hyaline in its deeper parts but much thicker than that on the ilium. A joint capsule is attached to the margins of the articular surfaces, and the bones are held together by the anterior sacroiliac, long and short posterior sacroiliac, and interosseous ligaments. In addition, there are 3 ligaments (Fig 2–16), classed as belonging to the pelvic girdle itself, which also serve as accessory ligaments to the sacroiliac joint: the iliolumbar, sacrotuberous, and sacrospinous ligaments. The anterior sacroiliac ligaments unite the base and the lateral part of the sacrum to the ilium, blending with the periosteum of the pelvic surface and, on the ilium, reaching the arcuate line to attach in the paraglenoid grooves. The posterior sacroiliac ligament is extremely strong and consists essentially of 2 sets of fibers, deep and superficial, forming the short and long posterior sacroiliac ligaments, respectively. The short posterior sacroiliac ligament passes inferiorly and medially from the tuberosity of the ilium, behind the articular surface and posterior interior iliac spine, to the back of the lateral portion of the sacrum and to the upper sacral articular process, including the area between it and the first sacral foramen. The long posterior sacroiliac ligament passes inferiorly from the posterior superior iliac spine to the second, third, and fourth articular tubercles on the back of the sacrum. It partly covers the short ligament and is continuous below with the sacrotuberous ligament. The interosseous ligaments are the strongest of all and consist of fibers of different lengths passing in various directions between the 2 bones. They extend from the rough surface of the sacral tuberosity to the corresponding surface on the lateral aspect of the sacrum, above and behind the articular surface.

Ligaments

The sacrotuberous ligament, in common with the long posterior sacroiliac ligament, is attached above to

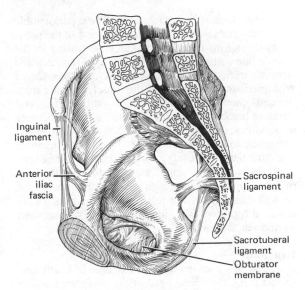

Inguinal ligament

Anterior iliac fascia

Sacrospinal ligament

Sacrotuberal ligament

Obturator membrane

Figure 2–16. Ligaments of the pelvis.

the crest of the ilium and posterior iliac spines and to the posterior aspect of the lower 3 sacral vertebrae. Below, it is attached chiefly to the medial border of the ischial tuberosity. Some of the fibers at the other end extend forward along the inner surface of the ischial ramus, forming the falciform process. Other posterior fibers continue into the tendons of the hamstrings.

The sacrospinous ligament is triangular and thin, extending from the lateral border of the sacrum and coccyx to the spine of the ischium. It passes medially (deep) to the sacrotuberous ligament and is partly blended with it along the lateral border of the sacrum.

The iliolumbar ligament connects the fourth and fifth lumbar vertebrae with the iliac crest. It originates from the transverse process of the fifth lumbar vertebra, where it is closely woven with the sacrolumbar ligament. Some of its fibers spread downward onto the body of the fifth vertebra and others ascend to the disk above. It is attached to the inner lip of the crest of the ilium for approximately 5 cm. The sacrolumbar ligament is generally inseparable from the iliolumbar ligament and is regarded as part of it.

Symphysis Pubica

The pubic symphysis is a synarthrodial joint of the symphyseal surfaces of the pubic bones. The ligaments associated with it are (1) the interpubic fibrocartilage, (2) the superior pubic ligament, (3) the anterior pubic ligament, and (4) the arcuate ligament. The interpubic fibrocartilage is thicker in front than behind and projects beyond the edges of the bones, especially on the posterior aspect, blending intimately with the ligaments at its margins. Sometimes it is woven throughout, but often the interpubic fibrocartilage presents an elongated, narrow fissure with fluid in the interspace, partially dividing the cartilage into 2 plates. The interpubic cartilage is intimately adherent to the layer of hyaline cartilage that covers the symphyseal surface of each pubic bone. The superior pubic ligament extends laterally along the crest of the pubis on each side to the pubic tubercle, blending in the middle line with the interpubic cartilage. The thick and strong anterior pubic ligament is closely connected with the fascial covering of the muscles arising from the conjoined rami of the pubis. It consists of several strata of thick, decussating fibers of different degrees of obliquity, the superficial being the most oblique and extending lowest over the joint. The arcuate ligament is a thick band of closely connected fibers that fills the angle between the pubic rami to form a smooth, rounded top to the pubic arch. Both on the anterior and posterior aspects of the joint, the ligament gives off decussating fibers that, interlacing with one another, strengthen the joint.

Hip Joint

The hip joint is a typical example of a ball-and-socket joint, the round head of the femur received by the deep cavity of the acetabulum and glenoid lip. Both articular surfaces are coated with cartilage. The portion covering the head of the femur is thicker above, where it bears the weight of the body, and thins out to a mere edge below. The pit in the femoral head receives the ligamentum teres, the only part uncoated by cartilage. The cartilage is horseshoe-shaped on the acetabulum and, corresponding to the lunate surface, thicker above than below. The ligaments are the articular capsule, transverse acetabular ligament, iliofemoral ligament, ischiocapsular ligament and zona orbicularis, pubocapsular ligament, and ligamentum teres.

A. Articular Capsule: The articular capsule is one of the strongest ligaments in the body. It is attached superiorly to the base of the anterior inferior iliac spine at the pelvis, posteriorly to a point a few millimeters from the acetabular rim, and inferiorly to the upper edge of the groove between the acetabulum and tuberosity of the ischium. Anteriorly, it is secured to the pubis near the obturator groove, to the iliopectineal eminence, and posteriorly to the base of the inferior iliac spine. At the femur, the articular capsule is fixed to the anterior portion of the superior border of the greater trochanter and to the cervical tubercle. The capsule runs down the intertrochanteric line as far as the medial aspect of the femur, where it is on a level with the inferior part of the lesser trochanter. It then runs superiorly and posteriorly along an oblique line, just in front of and above the lesser trochanter, and continues along the back of the neck of the femur nearly parallel to and above the intertrochanteric crest. Finally, the capsule passes along the medial side of the trochanteric fossa to reach the anterior superior angle of the greater trochanter. Some of the deeper fibers, the retinacula, are attached nearer the head of the femur. One corresponds to the upper and another to the lower part of the intertrochanteric line; a third is present at the upper and back part of the trochanteric neck.

B. Transverse Acetabular Ligament: The transverse ligament of the acetabulum passes across the acetabular notch. It supports the glenoid lip and is connected with the ligamentum teres and the capsule. The transverse ligament is composed of decussating fibers that arise from the margin of the acetabulum on either side of the notch. Those fibers coming from the pubis are more superficial and pass to form the deep part of the ligament at the ischium; those superficial at the ischium are deep at the pubis.

C. Iliofemoral Ligament: The iliofemoral ligament is located at the front of the articular capsule and is triangular. Its apex is attached to a curved line on the ilium immediately below and behind the anterior inferior spine; its base is fixed beneath the anterior edge of the greater trochanter and to the intertrochanteric line. The upper fibers are almost straight, while the medial fibers are oblique, giving the appearance of an inverted Y.

D. Ischiocapsular Ligament: The ischiocapsular ligament, on the posterior surface of the articular capsule, is attached to the body of the ischium along the upper border of the notch. Above the notch, the ligament is secured to the ischial margin of the acetabulum. The upper fibers incline superiorly and laterally and are fixed to the greater trochanter. The other fibers curve more and more upward as they pass laterally to their insertion at the inner side of the trochanteric fossa. The deeper fibers take a circular course and form a ring at the back and lower parts of the capsule, where the longitudinal fibers are deficient. This ring, the zona orbicularis, embraces the neck of the femur.

E. Pubocapsular Ligament: The pubocapsular ligament is fixed proximally to the obturator crest and to the anterior border of the iliopectineal eminence, reaching as far down as the pubic end of the acetabular notch. Below, the fibers reach to the neck of the femur and are fixed above and behind the lowermost fibers of the iliofemoral band, blending with it.

F. Ligamentum Teres: The ligamentum teres femoris extends from the acetabular fossa to the head of the femur. It has 2 bony attachments, one on either side of the acetabular notch immediately below the articular cartilage, with intermediate fibers springing from the lower surface of the transverse ligament. At the femur, the ligamentum teres femoris is fixed to the anterior part of the fovea capitis and to the cartilage around the margin of the depression.

Outlets of the True Pelvis

The true pelvis is said to have an upper "inlet" and a lower "outlet." The pelvic inlet to the pelvis minor is bounded, beginning posteriorly, by (1) the promontory of the sacrum; (2) the linea terminalis, composed of the anterior margin of the ala sacralis, the arcuate line of the ilium, and the pecten ossis pubis; and (3) the upper border or crest of the pubis, ending medially at the symphysis. The conjugate or the anteroposterior diameter is drawn from the center of the promontory to the symphysis pubica, with 2 conjugates recognized: (1) the true conjugate, measured from the promontory to the top of the symphysis, and

(2) the diagonal conjugate, measured from the promontory to the bottom of the symphysis. The transverse diameter is measured through the greatest width of the pelvic inlet. The oblique diameter runs from the sacroiliac joint of one side to the iliopectineal eminence of the other. The pelvic outlet, which faces downward and slightly backward, is very irregular. Beginning anteriorly, it is bounded by (1) the arcuate ligament of the pubis (in the midline), (2) the ischiopubic arch, (3) the ischial tuberosity, (4) the sacrotuberous ligament, and (5) the coccyx (in midline). Its anteroposterior diameter is drawn from the lower border of the symphysis pubica to the tip of the coccyx. The transverse diameter passes between the medial surfaces of the ischial tuberosities.

Musculature Attachments

A. Ilium: The crest of the ilium gives attachment to the external oblique, internal oblique, transversus (anterior two-thirds), latissimus dorsi and quadratus lumborum (posteriorly), sacrospinalis (internal lip, posteriorly), and tensor fasciae latae and sartorius muscles (anterior superior iliac spine) (Fig 2–17). The posterior superior spine of the ilium gives attachment to the multifidus muscle. The rectus femoris muscle is attached to the anterior inferior iliac spine. The iliacus muscle originates on the iliac fossa. Between the anterior inferior iliac spine and the iliopectineal eminence is a broad groove for the tendon of the iliopsoas muscle. A small portion of the gluteus maximus muscle originates between the posterior gluteus line and the crest. The surface of bone between the anterior gluteal line and the crest gives origin to the gluteus

medius muscle. The gluteus minimus muscle has its origin between the anterior and inferior gluteal lines.

B. Ischium: The body and superior ramus of the ischium give rise to the obturator internus muscle on the internal surface. The ischial spine provides, at its root, attachments for the coccygeus and levator ani muscles on its internal surface and for the gemellus superior muscle externally. The outer surface of the rami is the origin of the adductor magnus and obturator externus muscles. The transversus perinei muscle is attached to the lower border of the ischium. The ischial tuberosity gives rise on its posterior surface to the semimembranosus muscles, the common tendon of the biceps, and semitendinosus muscles and on its inferior surface to the adductor magnus muscle. The superior border is the site of origin of the inferior gemellus and the outer border of the quadratus femoris muscle. The superior ramus of the pubis gives origin to the adductor longus and obturator externus muscles on its anterior surface and to the levator ani and obturator internus muscles. The superior border provides attachment for the rectus abdominis and pyramidalis muscles. The pectineal surface gives origin at its posterior portion to the pectineus muscle. The posterior surface of the superior ramus is the point of attachment of a few fascicles of the obturator internus muscle. The anterior surface of the inferior ramus attaches to the adductor brevis, adductor magnus, and obturator externus muscles, and its posterior surface attaches to the sphincter urogenitalis and the obturator internus.

C. Sacrum: The pelvic surface of the sacrum is the origin of the piriform muscle. The lateral part of the fifth sacral vertebra is the point of insertion of the

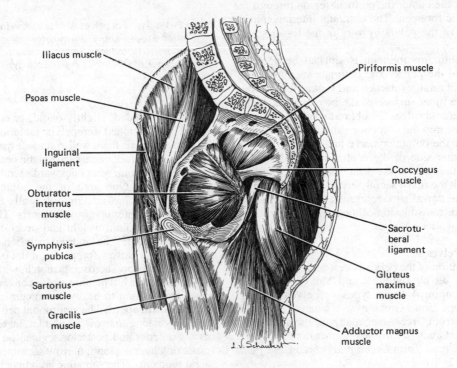

Figure 2–17. Pelvic muscles.

sacrospinalis and gluteus maximus muscles. The ala is attached to fibers of the iliacus muscle.

D. Coccyx: The dorsal surface of the coccyx is attached to the gluteus maximus muscle and the sphincter ani externus muscle. The lateral margins receive parts of the coccygeus and of the iliococcygeus muscles.

E. Greater Trochanter: The lateral surface of the greater trochanter of the femur receives the insertion of the gluteus medius muscle. The medial surface of the greater trochanter receives the tendon of the obturator externus in the trochanteric fossa, along with the obturator internus and the 2 gemelli. The superior border provides insertion for the piriformis and, with the anterior border, receives the gluteus minimus. The quadratus femoris attaches to the tubercle of the quadratus. The inferior border gives origin to the vastus lateralis muscle. The lesser trochanter attaches to the iliopsoas muscle at its summit. Fascicles of the iliacus extend beyond the trochanter and are inserted into the surface of the shaft.

Foramens

Several foramens are present in the bony pelvis. The sacrospinous ligament separates the greater from the lesser sciatic foramen. These foramens are subdivisions of a large space intervening between the sacrotuberous ligament and the femur. The piriform muscle passes out of the pelvis into the thigh by way of the greater sciatic foramen, accompanied by the gluteal vessels and nerves. The internal pudendal vessels, the pudendal nerve, and the nerve to the obturator internus muscle also leave the pelvis by this foramen, after which they then enter the perineal region through the lesser sciatic foramen. The obturator internus muscle passes out of the pelvis by way of the lesser sciatic foramen.

The obturator foramen is situated between the ischium and the pubis. The obturator membrane occupies the obturator foramen and is attached continuously to the inner surface of the bony margin except above, where it bridges the obturator sulcus, converting the latter into the obturator canal, which provides passage for the obturator nerve and vessels.

On either side of the central part of the pelvic surface of the sacrum are 4 anterior sacral foramens that transmit the first 4 sacral nerves. Corresponding to these on the dorsal surface are the 4 posterior sacral foramens for transmission of the small posterior rami of the first 4 sacral nerves.

Types of Pelves

Evaluation of the pelvis is best achieved by using the criteria set by Caldwell and Moloy, which are predicated upon 4 basic types of pelves: (1) the gynecoid type (from Greek *gyne* woman); (2) the android type (from Greek *aner* man); (3) the anthropoid type (from Greek *anthropos* human); and (4) the platypelloid type (from Greek *platys* broad and *pella* bowl) (Fig 2–18).

A. Gynecoid: In pure form, the gynecoid pelvis

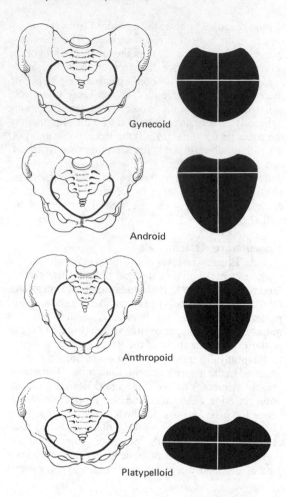

Figure 2–18. Types of pelves. White lines in the diagrams at right (after Steele) show the greatest diameters of the pelves at left. (Reproduced, with permission, from Benson RC: *Handbook of Obstetrics & Gynecology,* 7th ed. Lange, 1980.)

provides a rounded, slightly ovoid, or elliptical inlet with a well-rounded forepelvis (anterior segment). This type of pelvis has a well-rounded, spacious posterior segment, an adequate sacrosciatic notch, a hollow sacrum with a somewhat backward sacral inclination, and a Norman-type arch of the pubic rami. The gynecoid pelvis has straight side walls and wide interspinous and intertuberous diameters. The bones are primarily of medium weight and structure.

B. Android: The android pelvis has a wedge-shaped inlet, a narrow forepelvis, a flat posterior segment, and a narrow sacrosciatic notch, with the sacrum inclining forward. The side walls converge, and the bones are medium to heavy in structure.

C. Anthropoid: The anthropoid pelvis is characterized by a long, narrow, oval inlet, an extended and narrow anterior and posterior segment, a wide sacrosciatic notch, and a long, narrow sacrum, often with 6 sacral segments. The subpubic arch may be an angled Gothic type or rounded Norman type. Straight side walls are characteristic of the anthropoid pelvis, whose interspinous and intertuberous diameters are less than those of the average gynecoid pelvis. A medium bone structure is usual.

D. Platypelloid: The platypelloid pelvis has a distinct oval inlet with a very wide, rounded retropubic angle and a wider, flat posterior segment. The sacrosciatic notch is narrow and has a normal sacral inclination, although it is often short. The subpubic arch is very wide and the side walls are straight, with wide interspinous and intertuberous diameters.

The pelvis in any individual case may be one of the 4 "pure" types or a combination of mixed types. When discussing the intermediate pelvic forms, the posterior segment with its characteristics generally is described first and the anterior segment with its characteristics next, eg, anthropoid-gynecoid, android-anthropoid, or platypelloid-gynecoid. Obviously, it is impossible to have a platypelloid-anthropoid pelvis or a platypelloid-android pelvis.

Pelvic Relationships

Several important relationships should be remembered, beginning with those at the inlet of the pelvis. The transverse diameter of the inlet is the widest diameter, where bone is present for a circumference of 360 degrees. This diameter stretches from pectineal line to pectineal line and denotes the separation of the posterior and anterior segments of the pelvis. In classic pelves (gynecoid), a vertical plane dropped from the transverse diameter of the inlet passes through the level of the interspinous diameter at the ischial spine. These relationships may not hold true, however, in combination or intermediate (mixed type) pelves. The anterior transverse diameter of the inlet reaches from pectineal prominence to pectineal prominence; a vertical plane dropped from the anterior transverse passes through the ischial tuberosities. For good function of the pelvis, the anterior transverse diameter should never be more than 2 cm longer than the transverse diameter.

A. Obstetric Conjugate: The obstetric conjugate differs from both the diagonal conjugate and the true conjugate. It is represented by a line drawn from the posterior superior portion of the pubic symphysis (where bone exists for a circumference of 360 degrees) toward intersection with the sacrum. This point need not be at the promontory of the sacrum. The obstetric conjugate is divided into 2 segments: (1) the anterior sagittal, originating at the intersection of the obstetric conjugate with the transverse diameter of the inlet and terminating at the symphysis pubica, and (2) the posterior sagittal, originating at the transverse diameter of the inlet to the point of intersection with the sacrum.

B. Interspinous Diameter: A most significant diameter in the midpelvis is the interspinous diameter. It is represented by a plane passing from ischial spine to ischial spine. The posterior sagittal diameter of the midpelvis is a bisecting line drawn at a right angle from the middle of the interspinous diameter, in the same plane, to a point of intersection with the sacrum. This is the point of greatest importance in the midpelvis. It is sometimes said that the posterior sagittal diameter should be drawn from the posterior segment of the intersecting line of the interspinous diameter, in a plane from the inferior surface of the symphysis, through the interspinous diameter to the sacrum. However, this configuration often places the posterior sagittal diameter lower in the pelvis than the interspinous diameter. It is the interspinous diameter, together with the posterior sagittal diameter of the midpelvis, that determines whether or not there is adequate room for descent and extension of the head during labor.

C. Intertuberous Diameter: The intertuberous diameter of the outlet will reflect the length of the anterior transverse diameter of the inlet, ie, the former cannot be larger than the latter if convergent or straight side walls are present. Therefore, the intertuberous diameter determines the space available in the anterior segment of the pelvis at the inlet, and, similarly, the degree of convergence influences the length of the biparietal diameter at the outlet.

D. Posterior Sagittal Diameter: The posterior sagittal diameter of the outlet is an intersecting line drawn from the middle of the intertuberous diameter to the sacrococcygeal junction and reflects the inclination of the sacrum toward the outlet for accommodation of the head at delivery. It should be noted that intricate measurements of the pelvis are significant only at minimal levels. Evaluation of the pelvis for a given pregnancy, size of the fetus for a given pelvis, and conduct of labor engagement are far more important.

CONTENTS OF THE PELVIC CAVITY

The organs that occupy the female pelvis (Figs 2–20, 2–21, and 2–22) are the bladder, the ureters, the urethra, the uterus, the uterine (fallopian) tubes or oviducts, the ovaries, the vagina, and the rectum.*

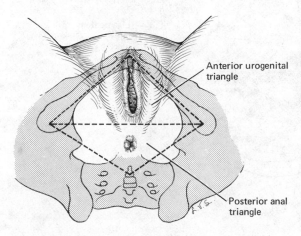

Figure 2–19. Urogenital and anal triangles.

Anterior urogenital triangle

Posterior anal triangle

*The rectum is not described in this chapter.

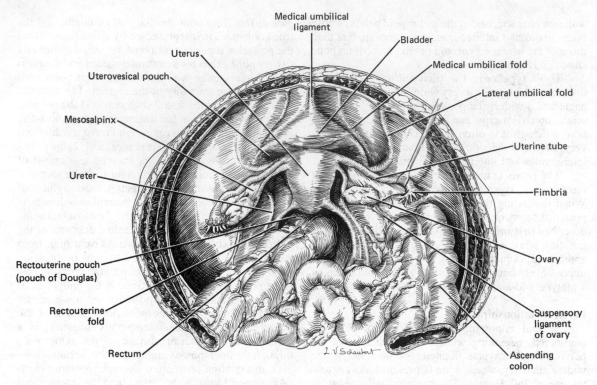

Figure 2 –20. Female pelvic contents from above.

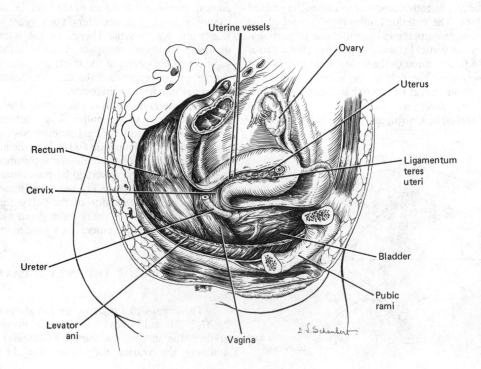

Figure 2 –21. Pelvic viscera (sagittal view).

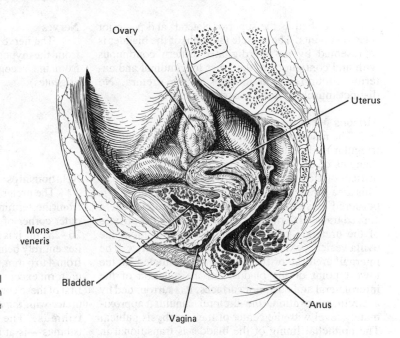

Figure 2–22. Pelvic organs (midsagittal view). (Reproduced, with permission, from Benson RC. *Handbook of Obstetrics & Gynecology,* 7th ed. Lange, 1980.)

With the exception of the inferior portion of the rectum and most of the vagina, all lie immediately beneath the peritoneum. The uterus, uterine tubes, and ovaries are almost completely covered with peritoneum and are suspended in peritoneal ligaments. The remainder are partially covered. These organs do not completely fill the cavity; the remaining space is occupied by ileum and sigmoid colon.

1. THE BLADDER

The urinary bladder is a muscular, hollow organ that lies posterior to the pubic bones and anterior to the uterus and broad ligament. Its form, size, and position vary with the amount of urine it contains. When empty, it takes the form of a somewhat rounded pyramid, having a base, a vertex (or apex), a superior surface, and a convex inferior surface that may be divided by a median ridge into 2 inferolateral surfaces.

Relationships

The superior surface of the bladder is covered with peritoneum that is continuous with the medial umbilical fold, forming the paravesical fossae laterally. Posteriorly, the peritoneum passes onto the uterus at the junction of the cervix and corpus, continuing upward on the anterior surface to form the vesicouterine pouch. When the bladder is empty, the normal uterus rests upon its superior surface. When the bladder is distended, coils of intestine may lie upon its superior surface. The base of the bladder rests below the peritoneum and is adjacent to the cervix and the anterior fornix of the vagina. It is separated from these structures by areolar tissue containing plexiform veins. The area over the vagina is extended as the bladder

fills. The inferolateral surfaces are separated from the wall of the pelvis by the potential prevesical space, containing a small amount of areolar tissue but no large vessels. This surface is nonperitoneal and thus suitable for operative procedures. Posterolateral to the region facing the symphysis, each of the inferolateral surfaces is in relation to the fascia of the obturator internus, the obturator vessels and nerve, the obliterated umbilical artery above, and the fascia of the levator ani below. Posteriorly and medially, the inferior surface is separated from the base by an area called the urethrovesical junction, the most stationary portion of the bladder.

Fascia, Ligaments, & Muscle

The bladder is enclosed by a thin layer of fascia, the vesical sheath. Two thickenings of the endopelvic fascia, the medial and lateral pubovesical or puboprostatic ligaments, extend at the vesicourethral junction abutting the levator ani muscle from the lower part of the anterior aspect of the bladder to the pubic bones. Similar fascial thickenings, the lateral true ligaments, extend from the sides of the lower part of the bladder to the lateral walls of the pelvis. Posteriorly, the vesicourethral junction of the bladder lies directly against the anterior wall of the vagina.

A fibrous band, the urachus or medial umbilical ligament, extends from the apex of the bladder to the umbilicus. This band represents the remains of the embryonic allantois. The lateral umbilical ligaments are formed by the obliterated umbilical arteries and are represented by fibrous cords passing along the sides of the bladder and ascending toward the umbilicus. Frequently, the vessels will be patent, thus forming the superior vesical arteries. The peritoneal covering of the bladder is limited to the upper surface. The reflections of the peritoneum to the anterior abdominal wall and the corresponding walls of the pelvis are sometimes described as the superior, lateral, and posterior false ligaments. The muscle (smooth) of the bladder is represented by an interdigitated pattern continuous with and contiguous to the inner longitudinal and anterior circumferential muscles of the urethra. No distinct muscle layers are apparent.

Mucous Membrane

The mucous membrane is rose-colored and lies in irregular folds that become effaced by distention. The 3 angles of the vesical trigone are represented by the orifices of the 2 ureters and the internal urethral orifice. This area is redder in color and free from plication. It is bordered posteriorly by the plica interureterica, a curved transverse ridge extending between the orifices of the ureters. A median longitudinal elevation, the uvula vesicae, extends toward the urethral orifice. The internal urethral orifice is normally situated at the lowest point of the bladder, at the junction of the inferolateral and posterior surfaces. It is surrounded by a circular elevation, the urethral annulus, approximately level with the center of the symphysis pubica. The epithelial lining of the bladder is transitional in type. The mucous membrane rests on the submucous coat, composed of areolar tissue superficial to the muscular coat. There is no evidence of a specific smooth muscle sphincter in the vesical neck.

Arteries, Veins, & Lymphatics

The blood supply to the bladder comes from branches of the hypogastric artery. The umbilical artery, a terminal branch of the hypogastric artery, gives off the superior vesical artery prior to its obliterated portion. It approaches the bladder (along with the middle and inferior vesical arteries) through a condensation of fatty areolar tissue, limiting the prevesical "space" posterosuperiorly, to branch out over the upper surface of the bladder. It anastomoses with the arteries of the opposite side and the middle and inferior vesical arteries below. The middle vesical artery may arise from one of the superior vessels, or it may come from the umbilical artery, supplying the sides and base of the bladder. The inferior vesical artery usually arises directly from the hypogastric artery—in common with or as a branch of the uterine artery—and passes downward and medially, where it divides into branches that supply the lower part of the bladder. The fundus may also receive small branches from the middle hemorrhoidal, uterine, and vaginal arteries.

The veins form an extensive plexus at the sides and base of the bladder from which stems pass to the hypogastric trunk.

The lymphatics, in part, accompany the veins and communicate with the hypogastric nodes (Table 2–2). They also communicate laterally with the external iliac glands, and some of those from the fundus pass to nodes situated at the promontory of the sacrum. The lymphatics of the bladder dome are separate on the right and left sides and rarely cross; but extensive anastomoses are present among the lymphatics of the base, which also involve those of the cervix.

Nerves

The nerve supply to the bladder is derived partly from the hypogastric sympathetic plexus and partly from the second and third sacral nerves (the nervi erigentes).

2. THE URETERS

Relationships

The ureter is a slightly flattened tube that extends from the termination of the renal pelvis to the lower outer corner of the base of the bladder, a distance of 26–28 cm. It is partly abdominal and partly pelvic and lies entirely behind the peritoneum. Its diameter varies from 4 to 6 mm, depending on distention, and its size is uniform except for 3 slightly constricted portions. The first of these constrictions is found at the junction of the ureter with the renal pelvis and is known as the upper isthmus. The second constriction—the lower isthmus—is at the point where the ureter crosses the brim of the pelvis minor. The third (intramural) constriction is at the terminal part of the ureter as it passes through the bladder wall. The pelvic portion of the ureter begins as the ureter crosses the pelvic brim beneath the ovarian vessels and near the bifurcation of the common iliac artery. It conforms to the curvature of the lateral pelvic wall, inclining slightly laterally and posteriorly until it reaches the pelvic floor. The ureter then bends anteriorly and medially at about the level of the ischial spine to reach the bladder. In its upper portion, it is related posteriorly to the sacroiliac articulation; then, lying upon the obturator internus muscle and fascia, it crosses the root of the umbilical artery, the obturator vessels, and the obturator nerve. In its anterior relationship, the ureter emerges from behind the ovary and under its vessels to pass behind the uterine and superior and middle vesical arteries. Coursing anteriorly, it comes into close relation with the lateral fornix of the vagina, passing 8–12 mm from the cervix and vaginal wall before reaching the bladder. When the ureters reach the bladder, they are about 5 cm apart. They pass through the bladder wall on an oblique course (about 2 cm long) and in an anteromedial and downward direction. The ureters open into the bladder by 2 slitlike apertures, the urethral orifices, about 2.5 cm apart when the bladder is empty.

Wall of Ureter

The wall of the ureter is approximately 3 mm thick and is composed of 3 coats: connective tissue, muscle, and mucous membrane. The muscular coat has an external circular and an internal longitudinal layer throughout its course and an external longitudinal layer in its lower third. The mucous membrane is longitudinally plicated and covered by transitional epithelium. The intermittent peristaltic action of the ureteral musculature propels urine into the bladder in jets. The oblique passage of the ureter through the bladder wall tends to constitute a valvular arrangement, but no true valve is present. The circular fibers of the intramural portion of the ureter possess a sphincterlike action. Still, under some conditions of overdistention of the bladder, urine may be forced back into the ureter.

Arteries, Veins, & Lymphatics

The pelvic portion of the ureter receives its blood supply from a direct branch of the hypogastric artery, anastomosing superiorly in its adventitia with branches from the iliolumbar and inferiorly with branches from the inferior vesical and middle hemorrhoidal arteries. Lymphatic drainage passes along the hypogastric vessels to the hypogastric and external iliac nodes, continuing up the ureters to their middle portion where drainage is directed to the periaortic and interaorticocaval nodes (Table 2–2).

Nerves

The nerve supply is provided by the renal, ovarian, and hypogastric plexuses. The spinal level of the afferents is approximately the same as the kidney (T12, L1, L2). The lower third of the ureter receives sensory fibers and postganglionic parasympathetic fibers from the Frankenhäuser plexus and sympathetic fibers through this plexus as it supplies the base of the bladder. These fibers ascend the lower third of the ureter, accompanying the arterial supply. The middle segment appears to receive postganglions of sympathetic and parasympathetic fibers through and from the middle hypogastric plexus. The upper third is supplied by the same innervation as the kidney.

3. THE URETHRA

Relationships

The female urethra is a canal 2.5–5.25 cm long. It extends downward and forward in a curve from the neck of the bladder (internal urethral orifice), which lies nearly opposite the symphysis pubica. Its termination, the external urethral orifice, is situated inferiorly and posteriorly from the lower border of the symphysis. Posteriorly, it is closely applied to the anterior wall of the vagina, especially in the lower two-thirds, where it is actually integrated with the wall, forming the urethral carina. Anteriorly, the upper end is separated from the prevesical ''space'' by the pubovesical (puboprostatic) ligaments, abutting against the levator ani and vagina and extending upward onto the pubic rami.

Anatomy of Walls

The walls of the urethra are very distensible, composed of spongy fibromuscular tissue containing cavernous veins and lined by submucous and mucous coats. The mucosa contains numerous longitudinal lines when undistended, the most prominent of which is located on the posterior wall and termed the crista urethralis. Also, there are numerous small glands (the homolog of the male prostate, para- and periurethral glands, glands of Astruc, ducts of Skene) that open into the urethra. The largest of these, the paraurethral glands of Skene, may open via a pair of ducts beside the external urethral orifice in the vestibule. The epithelium begins as transitional at the upper end and becomes squamous in the lower part. External to the urethral lumen is a smooth muscle coat composed of an outer circular layer and an inner longitudinal layer in the lower two-thirds. In the upper third, the muscle bundles of the layers interdigitate in a basketlike weave to become continuous with and contiguous to those of the bladder. The entire urethral circular smooth muscle acts as the involuntary sphincter. In the region of the juncture of the mid and lower thirds of the urethra, decussating fibers (striated in type) form the middle heads of the bulbo- and ischiocavernosus muscles and encircle the urethra to form the sphincter urethrae (voluntary sphincter).

Arteries & Veins

The arterial supply is intimately involved with that of the anterior vaginal wall, with cruciate anastomoses to the bladder. On each side of the vagina are the vaginal arteries, originating in part from the coronary artery of the cervix, the inferior vesical artery, or a direct branch of the uterine artery. In the midline of the anterior vaginal wall is the azygos artery, originating from the coronary or circular artery of the cervix. Approximately 5 branches traverse the anterior vaginal wall from the lateral vaginal arteries to the azygos in the midline, with small sprigs supplying the urethra. A rich anastomosis with the introitus involves the clitoral artery (urethral branches) as the artery divides into the dorsal and superficial arteries of the clitoris, a terminal branch of the internal pudendal artery. The venous drainage follows the arterial pattern, although it is less well defined. In the upper portion of the vagina, it forms an extensive network called the plexus of Santorini.

Lymphatics

The lymphatics are richly developed (Fig 2–23). Those of the anterior urethra drain to the vestibular plexus, the superficial inguinal nodes, the superficial subinguinal nodes, and the femoral and external iliac chain. The lymphatic drainage of the posterior urethra can be divided into 3 aspects: the anterior superior, anterolateral, and posterior. The anterior superior portion drains to the anterior bladder wall and up the lateral inferior border of the umbilical artery to the middle chain of the external iliacs. The anterolateral portion drains in several directions. Part extends to the lateral bladder wall and onto the internal chain of the external iliacs at the obturator nerve or to the hypogastrics at the bifurcation of the external and internal iliacs. Another part drains into the ischiorectal fossa and through the canalis pudendalis (Alcock's canal), following the inferior gluteal artery and obturator ar-

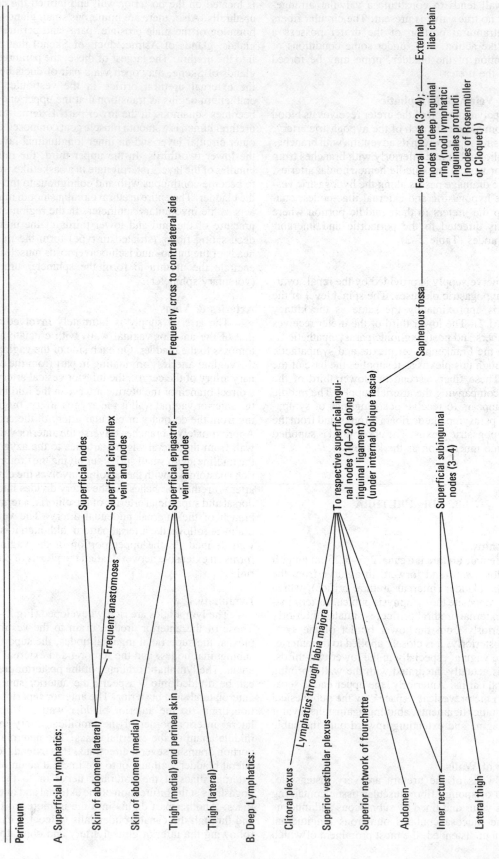

Table 2–2. Lymphatics of the female pelvis.

Perineum

A. Superficial Lymphatics:

- Skin of abdomen (lateral) → Superficial nodes
- Skin of abdomen (medial) → Superficial circumflex vein and nodes

  Frequent anastomoses

- Thigh (medial) and perineal skin → Superficial epigastric vein and nodes
- Thigh (lateral) → Frequently cross to contralateral side

B. Deep Lymphatics:

- Clitoral plexus
- Lymphatics through labia majora
- Superior vestibular plexus
- Superior network of fourchette
- Abdomen
- Inner rectum
- Lateral thigh

To respective superficial inguinal nodes (10–20 along inguinal ligament) (under internal oblique fascia)

Superficial subinguinal nodes (3–4)

Saphenous fossa → Femoral nodes (3–4); nodes in deep inguinal ring (nodi lymphatici inguinales profundi [nodes of Rosenmuller or Cloquet]) — External iliac chain

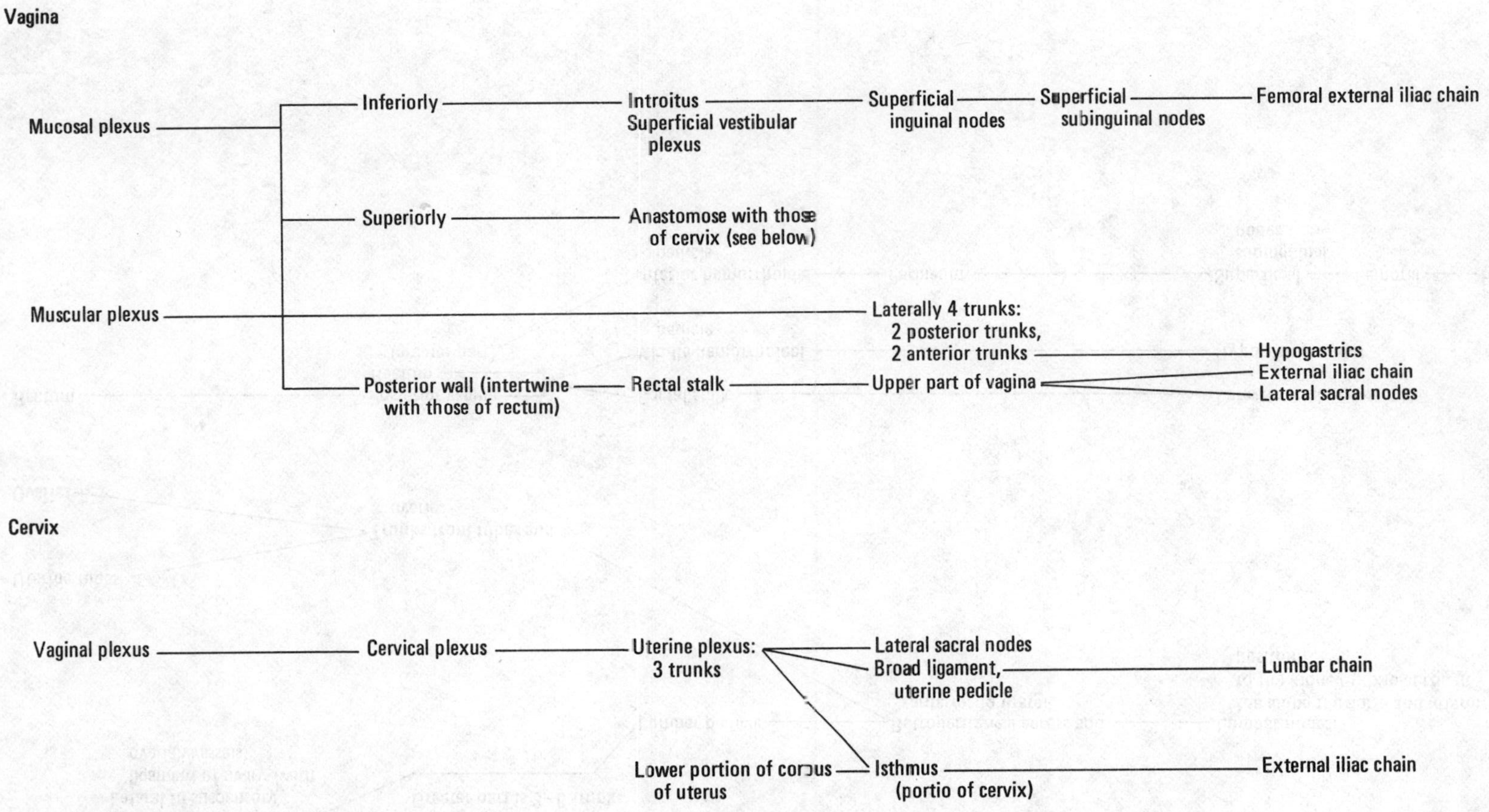

Vagina

Mucosal plexus
- Inferiorly —— Introitus, Superficial vestibular plexus —— Superficial inguinal nodes —— Superficial subinguinal nodes —— Femoral external iliac chain
- Superiorly —— Anastomose with those of cervix (see below)

Muscular plexus
- Laterally 4 trunks: 2 posterior trunks, 2 anterior trunks —— Hypogastrics, External iliac chain, Lateral sacral nodes
- Upper part of vagina
- Posterior wall (intertwine with those of rectum) —— Rectal stalk

Cervix

Vaginal plexus —— Cervical plexus —— Uterine plexus: 3 trunks —— Lateral sacral nodes, Broad ligament, uterine pedicle —— Lumbar chain
- Isthmus (portio of cervix) —— External iliac chain
- Lower portion of corpus of uterus

Table 2–2 (cont'd). Lymphatics of the female pelvis.

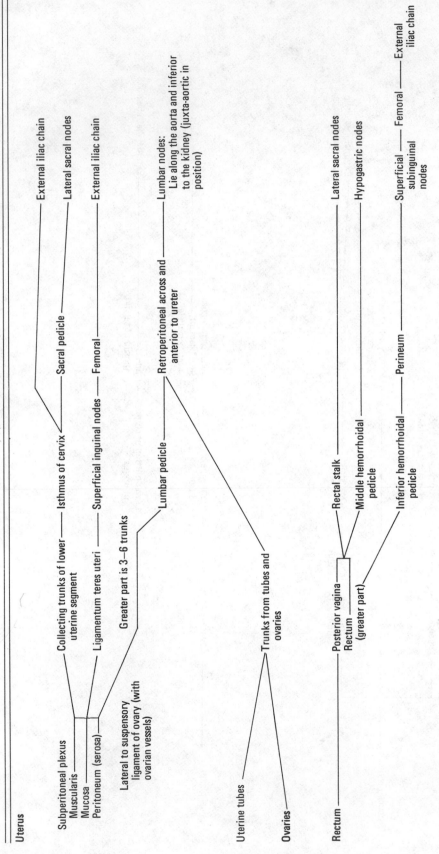

Uterus

Subperitoneal plexus
Muscularis
Mucosa
Peritoneum (serosa)

Collecting trunks of lower uterine segment —— Isthmus of cervix —— External iliac chain

—— Sacral pedicle —— Lateral sacral nodes

Ligamentum teres uteri —— Superficial inguinal nodes —— Femoral —— External iliac chain

Greater part is 3–6 trunks

Lateral to suspensory ligament of ovary (with ovarian vessels)

Lumbar pedicle —— Retroperitoneal across and anterior to ureter —— Lumbar nodes: Lie along the aorta and inferior to the kidney (juxta-aortic in position)

Uterine tubes

Ovaries

Trunks from tubes and ovaries

Rectum

Posterior vagina
Rectum (greater part)

Rectal stalk —— Lateral sacral nodes

Middle hemorrhoidal pedicle —— Hypogastric nodes

Inferior hemorrhoidal pedicle —— Perineum —— Superficial subinguinal nodes —— Femoral —— External iliac chain

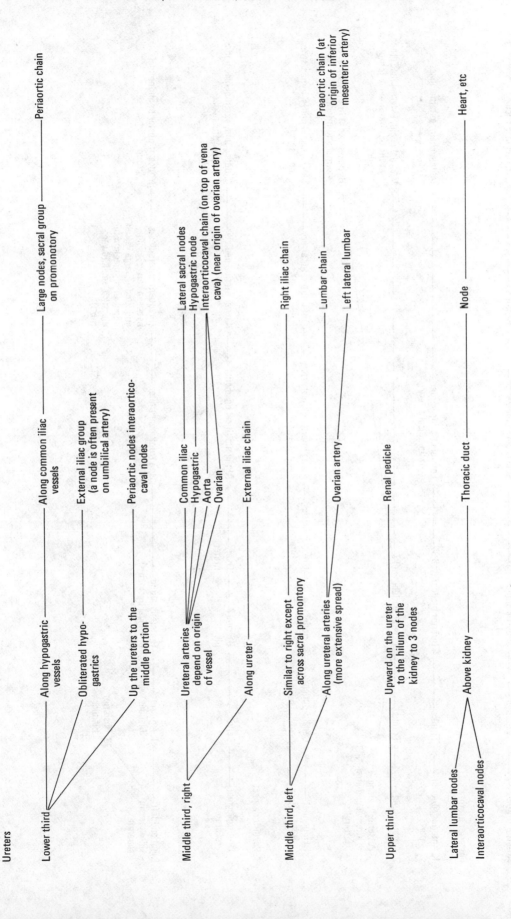

Table 2–2 (cont'd). Lymphatics of the female pelvis.

Urethra

Anterior urethra → Vestibular plexus → Superficial inguinal nodes → Femoral → Superficial subinguinal nodes → External iliac chain

Posterior urethra

1. Anterior superior part → Trunks → Interior bladder wall → Lateral inferior border of umbilical artery → Middle chain, external iliacs

2. Anterolateral → Trunks → Lateral bladder wall → Internal chain, external iliac group at the obturator nerve (obturator node)

　　Posteriorly along internal pudental artery → Hypogastrics at bifurcation of external and internal iliacs

Ischiorectal fossa → Canalis pudendalis (Alcock's canal) → 3 nodes → Greater sciatic foramen → Along inferior gluteal artery → Onto obturator artery → Lateral sacral nodes, hypogastric nodes

3. Posterior aspect

Urethrovaginal septum → Cervix → Uterine plexus → Over ureter → Along umbilical ligaments → Lower uterine pedicle → Middle chain, external iliac nodes, hypogastric nodes

Bladder

Right and left sides remain separate

1. Anterior bladder wall → (Laterally along umbilical ligaments) → One trunk near ureter → Nodes of posterior abdominal group

2. Posterior bladder wall → (Frequent anastomoses between cervix, vagina, and fundus; large vessels upper third, medium middle third, small lower third)

Table 2–3. Arterial supply to the female pelvis.

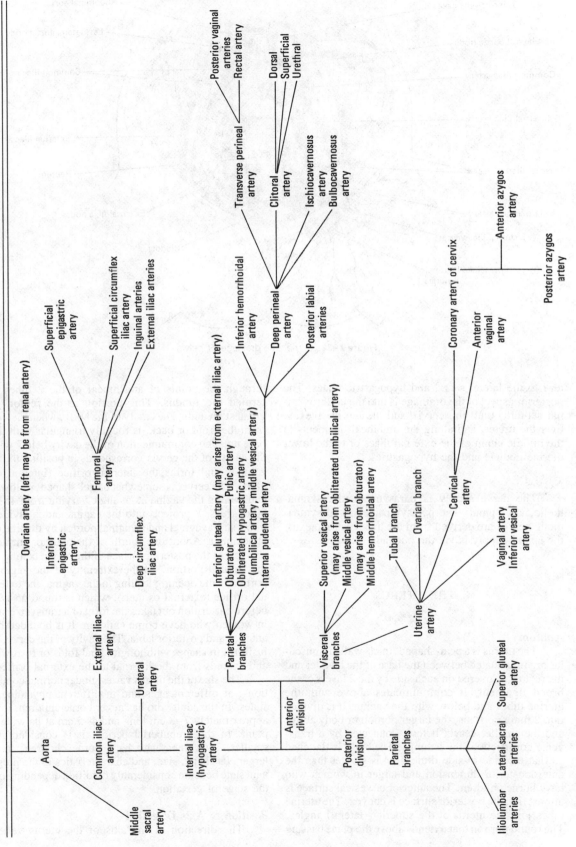

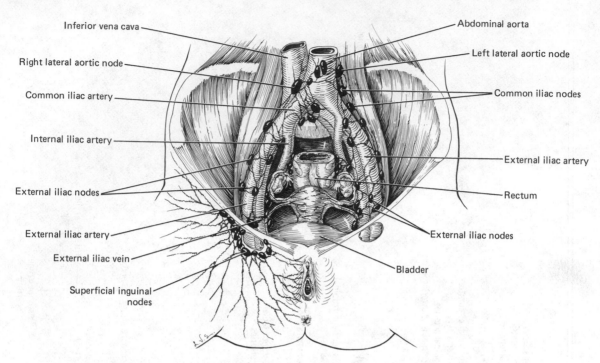

Figure 2 –23. Lymphatic drainage of pelvis.

tery to the lateral sacral and hypogastric nodes. The posterior aspect of the drainage is into the urethrovaginal septum, onto the cervix and the uterine plexus, over the ureter, and along the umbilical ligaments to the middle chain of the external iliacs or to the lower uterine pedicle and the hypogastrics.

Nerves

The nerve supply is parasympathetic, sympathetic, and spinal. The parasympathetic and sympathetic nerves are derived from the hypogastric plexus; the spinal supply is via the pudendal nerve.

4. THE UTERUS

Anatomy

The uterus is a pear-shaped, thick-walled, muscular organ, situated between the base of the bladder and the rectum. Covered on each side by the 2 layers of the broad ligament, it communicates above with the uterine tubes and below with the vagina. It is divided into 2 main portions, the larger portion or body above and the smaller cervix below, connected by a transverse constriction, the isthmus. The body is flattened so that the side-to-side dimension is greater than the anteroposterior dimension and larger in women who have borne children. The anterior or vesical surface is almost flat; the posterior surface is convex. The uterine tubes join the uterus at the superior (lateral) angles. The round portion that extends above the plane passing

through the points of attachment of the 2 tubes is termed the fundus. This portion is the region of greatest breadth. The cavity of the body, when viewed from the front or back, is roughly triangular with the base up. The communication of the cavity below with the cavity of the cervix corresponds in position to the isthmus and forms the internal orifice (internal os uteri). The cervix is somewhat barrel-shaped, its lower end joining the vagina at an angle varying from 45 to 90 degrees. It projects into the vagina and is divided into a supravaginal and a vaginal portion by the line of attachment. About one-fourth of the anterior surface and half of the posterior surface of the cervix belong to the vaginal portion. At the extremity of the vaginal portion is the opening leading to the vagina, the external orifice (external os uteri), which is round or oval before parturition but takes the form of a transverse slit in women who have borne children. It is bounded by anterior and posterior labia. The cavity of the cervix is fusiform in shape, with longitudinal folds or furrows, and extends from the internal to the external orifice.

The size of the uterus varies, under normal conditions, at different ages and in different physiologic states. In the adult who has never borne children, it is approximately 7–8 cm long and 4–5 cm at its widest point. In the prepubertal period, it is considerably smaller. In women who have borne children, it is larger. Its shape, size, and characteristics in the pregnant state become considerably modified depending on the stage of gestation.

Position & Axis Direction

The direction of the axis of the uterus varies

greatly. Normally, the uterus forms a sharp angle with the vagina, so that its anterior surface lies on the upper surface of the bladder and the body is in a horizontal plane when the woman is standing erect. There is a bend in the area of the isthmus, at which the cervix then faces downward. This position is the normal anteversion or angulation of the uterus, although it may be placed backward (retroversion), without angulation (military position), or to one side (lateral version). The forward flexion at the isthmus is referred to as anteflexion, or there may be a corresponding retroflexion or lateral flexion. There is no sharp line between the normal and pathologic state of anterior angulation.

Relationships

Anteriorly, the body of the uterus rests upon the upper and posterior surfaces of the bladder, separated by the uterovesical pouch of the peritoneum. The whole of the anterior wall of the cervix is below the floor of this pouch, and it is separated from the base of the bladder only by connective tissue. Posteriorly, the peritoneal covering extends down as far as the uppermost portion of the vagina; therefore, the entire posterior surface of the uterus is covered by peritoneum, and the convex posterior wall is separated from the rectum by the rectouterine pouch (cul-de-sac or pouch of Douglas). Coils of intestine may rest upon the posterior surface of the body of the uterus and may be present in the rectouterine pouch. Laterally, the uterus is related to the various structures contained within the broad ligament: the uterine tubes, the round ligament

and the ligament of the ovary, the uterine artery and veins, and the ureter. The relationships of the ureters and the uterine arteries are very important surgically. The ureters, as they pass to the bladder, run parallel with the cervix for a distance of 8–12 mm. The uterine artery crosses the ureter anterosuperiorly near the cervix, about 1.5 cm from the lateral fornix of the vagina. In effect, the ureter passes under the uterine artery "as water flows under a bridge."

Ligaments

Although the cervix of the uterus is fixed, the body is free to rise and fall with the filling and emptying of the bladder. The so-called ligaments supporting the uterus consist of the uterosacral ligaments, the transverse ligaments of the cervix (cardinal ligaments, cardinal supports, ligamentum transversum colli, ligaments of Mackenrodt), the round ligaments, and the broad ligaments (Fig 2–24). The cervix is embedded in tissue called the parametrium, containing various amounts of smooth muscle. There are 2 pairs of structures continuous with the parametrium and with the wall of the cervix: the uterosacral ligaments and the transverse (cardinal) ligament of the neck, the latter of which is the chief means of support and suspends the uterus from the lateral walls of the pelvis minor. The uterosacral ligaments are, in fact, the inferior posterior folds of peritoneum from the broad ligament. They consist primarily of nerve bundles from the inferior hypogastric plexus and contain pre- and postganglionic fibers and C fibers of the sympathetic lum-

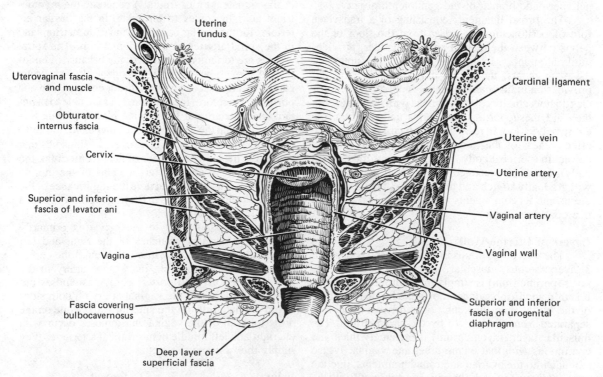

Figure 2–24. Ligamentous and fascial support of pelvic viscera. (After Netter. Reproduced, with permission, from Dunphy JE, Way LW [editors]: *Current Surgical Diagnosis & Treatment,* 5th ed. Lange, 1981.)

bar segments, parasympathetic in part from sacral components and in part from sensory or C fibers of the spinal segments.

The cardinal ligaments are composed of longitudinal smooth muscle fibers originating superiorly from the uterus and inferiorly from the vagina, fanning out toward the fascia visceralis to form, with the internal os of the cervix, the primary support of the uterus. There is a natural defect in the muscle at its sides (hilum of the uterus) and at the cervical isthmus (internal os), where the vasculature and nerve supply enter the uterus. The round ligaments of the uterus, although forming no real support, may assist in maintaining the body of the uterus in its typical position over the bladder. They consist of fibrous cords containing smooth muscle (longitudinal) from the outer layer of the corpus. From a point of attachment to the uterus immediately below that of the ovarian ligament, each round ligament extends downward, laterally, and forward between the 2 layers of the mesometrium, toward the abdominal inguinal ring that it traverses and the inguinal canal, to terminate in a fanlike manner in the labia majora and become continuous with connective tissue. The round ligament is the gubernaculum (ligamentum teres uteri), vestigial in the female. It is accompanied by a funicular branch of the ovarian artery, by a branch from the ovarian venous plexus, and, in the lower part of its course, by a branch from the inferior epigastric artery, over which it passes as it enters the inguinal ring. Through the inguinal canal, it is accompanied by the ilioinguinal nerve and the external spermatic branch of the genitofemoral nerve.

The broad ligament, consisting of a transverse fold of peritoneum that arises from the floor of the pelvis between the rectum and the bladder, provides minimal support. In addition to the static support of these ligaments, the pelvic diaphragm (levator ani) provides an indirect and dynamic support. These muscles do not actually come in contact with the uterus, but they aid in supporting the vagina and maintain the entire pelvic floor in resisting downward pressure. The effectiveness of these muscles depends on an intact perineum (perineal body, bulbocavernous muscle and body), for if it is lacerated or weakened the ligaments will gradually stretch and the uterus will descend. The uterus and its components and the vagina are, in fact, one continuous unit.

Layers of Uterine Wall

The wall of the uterus is very thick and consists of 3 layers: serous, muscular, and mucous. The serous layer (perimetrium) is simply the peritoneal covering. It is thin and firmly adherent over the fundus and most of the body, then thickens posteriorly and becomes separated from the muscle by the parametrium. The muscular layer (myometrium) is extremely thick and continuous with that of the tubes and vagina. It also extends into the ovarian and round ligaments, into the cardinal ligaments at the cervix, and minimally into the uterosacral ligaments. Two principal layers of the muscular coat may be distinguished: (1) the outer

layer, which is weaker and composed of longitudinal fibers; and (2) a stronger inner layer the fibers of which are interlaced and run in various directions, having intermingled within them large venous plexuses. The muscle layer hypertrophies with the internal os to form a sphincter. The cervix, from the internal os distally, progressively loses its smooth muscle, finally to be entirely devoid of smooth muscle and elastic in its distal half. It is, in fact, the "dead-end tendon" of the uterus, at which point, during the active component of labor, both the uterus and the vagina direct their efforts. The mucous layer (endometrium) is soft and spongy, composed of tissue resembling embryonic connective tissue. The surface consists of a single layer of ciliated columnar epithelium. The tissue is rather delicate and friable and contains many tubular glands that open into the cavity of the uterus.

Arteries

The blood supply to the uterus is from the uterine and ovarian arteries. As a terminal branch of the hypogastric artery, the uterine artery runs downward and medially to cross the ureter near the cervix. It then ascends along the lateral border of the uterus in a tortuous course through the parametrium, giving off lateral branches to both uterine surfaces. Above, it anastomoses to join with the ovarian artery in the mesometrium, which creates the main accessory source of blood. The uterine arteries within the uterus form a series of arches over the fundus, creating cruciate anastomoses with the opposite side. Branches of the arcuate arteries (radials) penetrate the myometrium at right angles to terminate in the basilar arterioles for the basilar portion of the endometrium and in the spiral arteries of the endometrium. The spiral arteries are tortuous in structure, not because of endometrial growth but because, ontogenically, an organ carries its arterial supply with it as it changes size and position. Therefore, the spiral arteries are able to maintain adequate arterial flow to the placenta while it is attached within the uterus. On the other hand, the veins of the endometrium are a series of small sinusoids that connect to the larger sinusoids of the myometrium, the latter coalescing into the larger veins of the uterine complex. It is useful here to note the significance of the muscular role of the uterus in helping to control venous bleeding during parturition.

The arterial supply to the cervix is primarily through the cervical branches of the right and left uterine arteries, which form a rete around the cervix (coronary artery), creating the azygos artery in the midline anteriorly and posteriorly. Anastomoses between this artery and the vaginal artery on both sides afford cruciate flow on the anterior wall, while on the posterior wall of the vagina anastomoses occur with the right and left middle hemorrhoidal arteries as they supply the wall and the rectum.

Veins

The veins form a plexus and drain through the uterine vein to the hypogastric vein. There are connections with the ovarian vein and the inferior epigastric by way of the vein accompanying the round ligament.

Lymphatics

Lymphatic drainage involves several chains of lymph nodes (Table 2–2). From the subperitoneal plexus, the collecting trunks of the lower uterine segment may drain by way of the cervix to the external iliac chain or by way of the isthmus to the lateral sacral nodes. Drainage along the round ligament progresses to the superficial inguinal nodes, then to the femoral, and finally to the external iliac chain. Drainage laterally to the suspensory ligament of the ovary involves the lumbar pedicle and progresses in a retroperitoneal manner across and anteriorly to the ureter, to the lumbar nodes (interaorticocaval) that lie along the aorta, and inferiorly to the kidney.

Nerves

The pelvic autonomic system can be divided into the superior hypogastric plexus (the presacral plexus and the uterinus magnus), the middle hypogastric plexus, and the inferior hypogastric plexus. The superior hypogastric plexus begins just below the inferior mesenteric artery. It is composed of 1–3 intercommunicating nerve bundles connected with the inferior mesenteric ganglia, but no ganglia are an integral part of the plexus. The intermesenteric nerves receive branches from the lumbar sympathetic ganglia.

A. Superior Hypogastric Plexus: The superior hypogastric plexus continues into the mid hypogastric plexus. The presacral nerves spread out into a latticework at the level of the first sacral vertebra, with connecting rami to the last of the lumbar ganglia. The greater part of the superior mid hypogastric plexus may be found to the left of the midline.

B. Inferior Hypogastric Plexus: At the first sacral vertebra, this plexus divides into several branches that go to the right and left sides of the pelvis. These branches form the beginning of the right and left inferior hypogastric plexus. The inferior hypogastric plexus, which is the divided continuation of the mid hypogastric plexus, the superior hypogastric plexus, the presacral nerve, and the uterinus magnus, is composed of several parallel nerves on each side. This group of nerves descends within the pelvis in a position posterior to the common iliac artery and anterior to the sacral plexus, curves laterally, and finally enters the sacrouterine fold or ligaments. The medial section of the primary division of the sacral nerves sends fibers (nervi erigentes) that enter the pelvic plexus in the sacrouterine folds. The plexus now appears to contain both sympathetic (inferior hypogastric plexus) and parasympathetic (nervi erigentes) components.

C. Nervi Erigentes: The sensory components, which are mostly visceral, are found in the nervi erigentes; however, if one takes into account the amount of spinal anesthetic necessary to eliminate uterine sensation, one must assume that there are a number of sensory fibers in the sympathetic component.

D. Common Iliac Nerves: The common iliac nerves originate separately from the superior hypogastric plexus and descend on the surface of the artery and vein, one part going through the femoral ring and the remainder following the internal iliac, finally rejoining the pelvic plexus.

E. Hypogastric Ganglion: On either side of the uterus, in the base of the broad ligament, is the large plexus described by Lee and Frankenhäuser, the so-called hypogastric ganglion. The plexus actually consists of ganglia and nerve ramifications of various sizes as well as branches of the combined inferior hypogastric plexus and the nervi erigentes. It lies parallel to the lateral pelvic wall, its lateral surface superficial to the internal iliac and its branches; the ureter occupies a position superficial to the plexus. The middle vesical artery perforates and supplies the plexus, its medial branches supplying the rectal stalk. The greater part of the plexus terminates in large branches that enter the uterus in the region of the internal os, while another smaller component of the plexus supplies the vagina and the bladder. The branches of the plexus that supply the uterus enter the isthmus primarily through the sacrouterine fold or ligament. In the isthmus, just outside the entrance to the uterus, ascending rami pass out into the broad ligament to enter the body of the uterus at higher levels—besides supplying the uterine tubes. A part of the inferior hypogastric plexus may pass directly to the uterus without involvement in the pelvic plexus.

Ganglia are in close proximity to the uterine arteries and the ureters, in the adventitia of the bladder and vagina, and in the vesicovaginal septum. The nerve bundles entering the ganglia contain both myelinated and unmyelinated elements. Corpuscula lamellosa (Vater-Pacini corpuscles) may be found within the tissues and are often observed within nerve bundles, especially within those in the lower divisions of the plexus. Both myelinated and unmyelinated nerves are present within the uterus. The nerves enter along the blood vessels, the richest supply lying in the isthmic portion of the uterus. The fibers following the blood vessels gradually diminish in number in the direction of the fundus, where the sparsest distribution occurs. The fibers run parallel to the muscle bundles, and the nerves frequently branch to form a syncytium before terminating on the sarcoplasm as small free nerve endings.

Sensory Corpuscles

Vater-Pacini corpuscles (corpuscula lamellosa) are present outside the uterus. Dogiel and Krause corpuscles (corpuscula bulboidea) appear in the region of the endocervix. They may also be found in the broad ligament along with Vater-Pacini corpuscles and at the juncture of the uterine arteries with the uterus. These corpuscles may act to modulate the stretch response that reflexly stimulates uterine contractions during labor.

The innervation of the cervix shows occasional free endings entering papillae of the stratified squamous epithelium of the pars vaginalis. The endocervix contains a rich plexus of free endings that is most pronounced in the region of the internal os. The endocervix and the isthmic portion of the uterus in the nonpregnant state both contain the highest number of nerves and blood vessels of any part of the uterus. The presence here of a lamellar type of corpuscle has already been noted.

Nerves pass through the myometrium and enter the endometrium. A plexus with penetrating fibers involving the submucosal region is present in the basal third of the endometrium, with branches terminating in the stroma, in the basilar arterioles, and at the origin of the spiral arterioles. The outer two-thirds of the endometrium is devoid of nerves.

5. UTERINE (FALLOPIAN) TUBES OR OVIDUCTS

Anatomy

The uterine tubes serve to convey the ova to the uterus. They extend from the superior angles of the uterus to the region of the ovaries, running in the superior border of the broad ligament (mesosalpinx). The course of each tube is nearly horizontal at first and slightly backward. Upon reaching the lower (uterine) pole of the ovary, the tube turns upward, parallel with the anterior (mesovarian) border, then arches backward over the upper pole and descends posteriorly to terminate in contact with the medial surface. Each tube is 7–14 cm long and may be divided into 3 parts: isthmus, ampulla, and infundibulum. The isthmus is the narrow and nearly straight portion immediately adjoining the uterus. It has a rather long intramural course, and its opening into the uterus, the uterine ostium, is approximately 1 mm in diameter. Following the isthmus is the wider, more tortuous ampulla. It terminates in a funnel-like dilatation, the infundibulum. The margins of the infundibulum are fringed by numerous diverging processes, the fimbriae, the longest of which, the fimbria ovarica, is attached to the ovary. The funnel-shaped mouth of the infundibulum, the abdominal ostium, is about 3 mm in diameter and actually leads into the peritoneal cavity, although it is probably closely applied to the surface of the ovary during ovulation.

Layers of Wall

The wall of the tube has 4 coats: serous (peritoneal), subserous or adventitial (fibrous and vascular), muscular, and mucous. Each tube is enclosed within a peritoneal covering except along a small strip on its lower surface, where the mesosalpinx is attached. At the margins of the infundibulum and the fimbriae, this peritoneal covering becomes directly continuous with the mucous membrane lining the interior of the tube. The subserous tissue is lax in the immediate vicinity of the tube. The blood and nerve supply is found within this layer. The muscular coat has an outer longitudinal and an inner circular layer of smooth muscle fibers, more prominent and continuous with that of the uterus at the uterine end of the tube. The mucous coat is ciliated columnar epithelium with coarse longitudinal folds, simple in the region of the isthmus but becoming higher and more complex in the ampulla. The epithelial lining extends outward into the fimbriae. The ciliary motion is directed toward the uterus.

Ligament

The infundibulum is suspended from the pelvic brim by the infundibulopelvic ligament (suspensory ligament of the ovary). This portion of the tube may adjoin the tip of the appendix and fuse with it.

Arteries & Veins

The blood supply to the tubes is derived from the ovarian and uterine arteries. The tubal branch of the uterine artery courses along the lower surface of the uterine tube as far as the fimbriated extremity and may also send a branch to the ligamentum teres. The ovarian branch of the uterine artery runs along the attached border of the ovary and gives off a tubal branch. Both branches form cruciate anastomoses in the mesosalpinx. The veins accompany the arteries.

Lymphatics

The lymphatic drainage occurs through trunks running retroperitoneally across and anterior to the ureter, into the lumbar nodes along the aorta, and inferior to the kidney.

Nerves

The nerve supply is derived from the pelvic plexuses (parasympathetic and sympathetic) and from the ovarian plexus. The nerves of the ampulla are given off from the branches passing to the ovary, while those of the isthmus come from the uterine branches. The nerve fibers enter the muscularis of the tube through the mesosalpinx to form a reticular network of free endings amongst the smooth muscle cells.

6. THE OVARIES

Anatomy

The ovaries are paired organs situated close to the wall on either side of the pelvis minor, a little below the brim. Each measures 2.5–5 cm in length, 1.5–3 cm in breadth, and 0.7–1.5 cm in width, weighing about 4–8 g. The ovary has 2 surfaces, medial and lateral; 2 borders, anterior or mesovarian and posterior or free; and 2 poles, upper or tubal and lower or uterine. When the uterus and adnexa are in the normal position, the long axis of the ovary is nearly vertical, but it bends somewhat medially and forward at the lower end so that the lower pole tends to point toward the uterus.

The medial surface is rounded and, posteriorly, may have numerous scars or elevations that mark the position of developing follicles and sites of ruptured ones.

Relationships

The upper portion of this surface is overhung by the fimbriated end of the uterine tube, and the remainder lies in relation to coils of intestine. The lateral surface is similar in shape and faces the pelvic wall, where it forms a distinct depression, the fossa ovarica. This fossa is lined by peritoneum and is bounded above by the external iliac vessels and below by the obturator vessels and nerve; its posterior boundary is formed by the ureter and uterine artery and vein, and the pelvic attachment of the broad ligament is located anteriorly. The mesovarian or anterior border is fairly straight and provides attachment for the mesovarium, a peritoneal fold by which the ovary is attached to the posterosuperior layer of the broad ligament. Since the vessels, nerves, and lymphatics enter the ovary through this border, it is referred to as the hilum of the ovary. Anterior to the hilum are embryonic remnants of the male and female germ cell ducts. The posterior or free border is more convex and broader and is directed freely into the rectouterine pouch. The upper or tubal pole is large and rounded. It is overhung closely by the infundibulum of the uterine tube and is connected with the pelvic brim by the suspensory ligament of the ovary, a peritoneal fold. The lower or uterine pole is smaller and directed toward the uterus. It serves for the attachment of the ligament of the ovary proper.

Mesovarium

The ovary is suspended by means of the mesovarium, the suspensory ligament of the ovary, and the ovarian ligament. The mesovarium consists of 2 layers of peritoneum, continuous with both the epithelial coat of the ovary and the posterosuperior layer of the broad ligament. It is short and wide and contains branches of the ovarian and uterine arteries, with plexuses of nerves, the pampiniform plexus of veins, and the lateral end of the ovarian ligament. The suspensory ligament of the ovary is a triangular fold of peritoneum and is actually the upper lateral corner of the broad ligament, which becomes confluent with the parietal peritoneum at the pelvic brim. It attaches to the mesovarium as well as to the peritoneal coat of the infundibulum medially, thus suspending both the ovary and the tube. It contains the ovarian artery, veins, and nerves after they pass over the pelvic brim and before they enter the mesovarium. The ovarian ligament is a band of connective tissue, with numerous small muscle fibers, that lies between the 2 layers of the broad ligament on the boundary line between the mesosalpinx and the mesometrium, connecting the lower (uterine) pole of the ovary with the lateral wall of the uterus. It is attached just below the uterine tube and above the attachment of the round ligament of the uterus and is continuous with the latter.

Structure of Ovary

The ovary is covered by cuboid or low columnar epithelium and consists of a cortex and a medulla. The medulla is made up of connective tissue fibers, smooth muscle cells, and numerous blood vessels, nerves, lymphatic vessels, and supporting tissue. The cortex is composed of a fine areolar stroma, with many vessels and scattered follicles of epithelial cells within which are the definitive ova (oocytes) in various stages of maturity. The more mature follicles enlarge and project onto the free surface of the ovary, where they are visible to the naked eye. They are called graafian follicles. When fully mature, the follicle bursts, releasing the ovum and becoming transformed into a corpus luteum. The corpus luteum, in turn, is later replaced by scar tissue, forming a corpus albicans.

Arteries

The ovarian artery is the chief source of blood for the ovary. Though both arteries may originate as branches of the abdominal aorta, the left frequently originates from the left renal artery; the right, less frequently. The vessels diverge from each other as they descend. Upon reaching the level of the common iliac artery, they turn medially over that vessel and ureter to descend tortuously into the pelvis on each side, between the folds of the suspensory ligament of the ovary into the mesovarium. An additional blood supply is formed from anastomosis with the ovarian branch of the uterine artery, which courses along the attached border of the ovary. Blood vessels that enter the hilum send out capillary branches centrifugally.

Veins

The veins follow the course of the arteries and, as they emerge from the hilum, form a well-developed plexus (the pampiniform plexus) between the layers of the mesovarium. Smooth muscle fibers occur in the meshes of the plexus, giving the whole structure the appearance of erectile tissue.

Lymphatics

Lymphatic channels drain retroperitoneally, together with those of the tubes and part of those from the uterus, to the lumbar nodes along the aorta inferior to the kidney. The distribution of lymph channels in the ovary is so extensive that it suggests the system may also provide additional fluid to the ovary during periods of preovulatory follicular swelling.

Nerves

The nerve supply of the ovaries arises from the lumbosacral sympathetic chain and passes to the gonad along with the ovarian artery.

7. THE VAGINA

The vagina is a strong canal of muscle approximately 7.5 cm long that extends from the uterus to the vestibule of the external genitalia, where it opens to the exterior. Its long axis is almost parallel with that of the lower part of the sacrum, and it meets the cervix of the uterus at an angle of 45–90 degrees. Because the cervix of the uterus projects into the upper portion, the anterior wall of the vagina is 1.5–2 cm shorter than the posterior wall. The circular cul-de-sac formed around the cervix is known as the fornix and is divided into 4 regions: the anterior fornix, the posterior fornix, and 2 lateral fornices. Toward its lower end, the vagina pierces the urogenital diaphragm and is surrounded by the 2 bulbocavernosus muscles and bodies, which act as a sphincter (sphincter vaginae). In the virginal state, an incomplete fold of highly vascular tissue and mucous membrane, the hymen, partially closes the external orifice.

Relationships

Anteriorly, the vagina is in close relationship to the bladder, ureters, and urethra in succession. The posterior fornix is covered by the peritoneum of the rectovaginal pouch, which may contain coils of intestine. Below the pouch, the vagina rests almost directly on the rectum, separated from it by a thin layer of areolar connective tissue. Toward the lower end of the vagina, the rectum turns back sharply, and the distance between the vagina and rectum greatly increases. This space, filled with muscle fibers, connective tissue, and fat, is known as the perineal body. The lateral fornix lies just under the root of the broad ligament and is approximately 1 cm from the point where the uterine artery crosses the ureter. The remaining lateral vaginal wall is related to the edges of the anterior portion of the levator ani. The vagina is supported at the introitus by the bulbocavernosus muscles and bodies, in the lower third by the levator ani (puborectalis), and superiorly by the transverse (cardinal) ligaments of the uterus. The ductus epoophori longitudinalis (duct of Gartner), the remains of the lower portion of the wolffian duct (mesonephric duct), may often be found on the sides of the vagina as a minute tube or fibrous cord. These vestigial structures often become cystic and appear as translucent areas.

Wall Structure

The vaginal wall is composed of a mucosal and a muscular layer. The smooth muscle fibers are indistinctly arranged in 3 layers: an outer longitudinal layer, a circumferential layer, and a poorly differentiated inner longitudinal layer. In the lower third, the circumferential fibers envelop the urethra. The submucous area is abundantly supplied with a dense plexus of veins and lymphatics. The mucous layer shows many transverse and oblique rugae, which project inward to such an extent that the lumen in transverse section resembles an H-shaped slit. On the anterior and posterior walls, these ridges are more prominent, and the anterior column forms the urethral carina at its lower end, where the urethra slightly invaginates the anterior wall of the vagina. The mucosa of the vagina is lined throughout by stratified squamous epithelium. Even though the vagina has no true glands, there is a secretion present. It consists of cervical mucus, desquamated epithelium, and, with sexual stimulation, a direct transudate.

Arteries & Veins

The chief blood supply to the vagina is through the vaginal branch of the uterine artery. After forming the coronary or circular artery of the cervix, it passes medially, behind the ureter, to send 5 main branches onto the anterior wall to the midline. These branches anastomose with the azygos artery (originating midline from the coronary artery of the cervix) and continue downward to supply the anterior vaginal wall and the lower two-thirds of the urethra. The uterine artery eventually anastomoses to the urethral branch of the clitoral artery. The posterior vaginal wall is supplied by branches of the middle and inferior hemorrhoidal arteries, traversing toward the midline to join the azygos artery from the coronary artery of the cervix. These branches then anastomose on the perineum to the superficial and deep transverse perineal arteries.

The veins follow the course of the arteries.

Lymphatics

The lymphatics are numerous mucosal plexuses, anastomosing with the deeper muscular plexuses (Table 2–2). The superior group of lymphatics join those of the cervix and may follow the uterine artery to terminate in the external iliac nodes or form anastomoses with the uterine plexus. The middle group of lymphatics, which drain the greater part of the vagina, appear to follow the vaginal arteries to the hypogastric channels. In addition, there are lymph nodes in the rectovaginal septum that are primarily responsible for drainage of the rectum and part of the posterior vaginal wall. The inferior group of lymphatics form frequent anastomoses between the right and left sides and either course upward to anastomose with the middle group or enter the vulva and drain to the inguinal nodes.

Nerves

The innervation of the vagina contains both sympathetic and parasympathetic fibers. Only occasional free nerve endings are seen in the mucosa; no other types of nerve endings are noted.

STRUCTURES LINING THE PELVIS

The walls of the pelvis minor are made up of the following layers: (1) the peritoneum, (2) the subperitoneal or extraperitoneal fibroareolar layer, (3) the fascial layer, (4) the muscular layer, and (5) the osseoligamentous layer (not further discussed). The anatomy of the floor of the pelvis is comparable to that of the walls except for the absence of an osseoligamentous layer.

1. PERITONEUM

The peritoneum presents several distinct transverse folds that form corresponding fossae on each side. The most anterior is a variable fold, the transverse vesical, extending from the bladder laterally to the pelvic wall. It is not the superficial covering of any definitive structure. Behind it lies the broad ligament, which partially covers and aids in the support of the uterus and adnexa.

Ligaments

The broad ligament extends from the lateral border on either side of the uterus to the floor and side walls of the pelvis. It is composed of 2 layers, anterior and posterior, the anterior facing downward and the posterior facing upward, conforming to the position of the uterus. The inferior or "attached" border of the broad ligament is continuous with the parietal peritoneum on the floor and on the side walls of the pelvis. Along this border, the posterior layer continues laterally and posteriorly in an arc to the region of the sacrum, forming the uterosacral fold. Another fold—the rectouterine fold—frequently passes from the posterior surface of the cervix to the rectum in the midline. The anterior layer of the broad ligament is continuous laterally along the inferior border with the peritoneum of the paravesical fossae and continuous medially with peritoneum on the upper surface of the bladder. Both layers of the attached border continue up the side walls of the pelvis to join with a triangular fold of peritoneum, reaching to the brim of the pelvis to form the suspensory ligament of the ovary or infundibular ligament. This ligament contains the ovarian vessels and nerves. The medial border of the broad ligament on either side is continuous with the peritoneal covering on both uterine surfaces. The 2 layers of the ligament separate to partially contain the uterus, and the superior or "free" border, which is laterally continuous with the suspensory ligament of the ovary, envelops the uterine tube.

The broad ligament can be divided into regions as follows: (1) a larger portion, the mesometrium, which is associated especially with the lateral border of the uterus; (2) the mesovarium, the fold that springs from the posterior layer of the ovary; and (3) the thin portion, the mesosalpinx, which is associated with the uterine tube in the region of the free border. The superior lateral corner of the broad ligament has been referred to as the suspensory ligament of the ovary, or infundibulopelvic ligament, because it suspends the infundibulum as well as the ovary.

Fossae & Spaces

Corresponding to the peritoneal folds are the peritoneal fossae. The prevesical or retropubic space is a potential space that is crossed by the transverse vesical fold. It is situated in front of the bladder and behind the pubis. When the bladder is displaced posteriorly, it becomes an actual space, anteriorly continuous from side to side and posteriorly limited by a condensation of fatty areolar tissue extending from the base of the bladder to the side wall of the pelvis. The vesicouterine pouch is a narrow cul-de-sac between the anterior surface of the body of the uterus and the upper surface of the bladder when the uterus is in normal anteflexed position. In the bottom of this pouch, the peritoneum is reflected from the bladder onto the uterus at the junction of the cervix and corpus. Therefore, the anterior surface of the cervix is below the level of the peritoneum and is connected with the base of the bladder by condensed areolar tissue. The peritoneum on the posterior surface of the body of the uterus extends downward onto the cervix and onto the posterior fornix of the vagina. It is then reflected onto the anterior surface of the rectum to form a narrow cul-de-sac continuous with the pararectal fossa of either side. The entire space, bounded anteriorly by the cervix and by the fornix in the midline, the uterosacral folds laterally, and the rectum posteriorly, is the rectouterine pouch or cul-de-sac (pouch of Douglas).

2. SUBPERITONEAL & FASCIAL LAYERS

The subperitoneal layer consists of loose, fatty areolar tissue underlying the peritoneum. External to the subperitoneal layer, a layer of fascia lines the wall of the pelvis, covering the muscles and, where these are lacking, blending with the periosteum of the pelvic bones. This layer is known as the parietal pelvic fascia and is subdivided into the obturator fascia, the fascia of the urogenital diaphragm, and the fascia of the piriformis. The obturator fascia is of considerable thickness and covers the obturator internus muscle. Traced forward, it partially blends with the periosteum of the pubic bone and assists in the formation of the obturator canal. Traced upward, it is continuous at the arcuate line with the iliac fascia. Inferiorly, it extends nearly to the margin of the ischiopubic arch, where it is attached to the bone. In this lower region, it also becomes continuous with a double-layered triangular sheet of fascia, the fasciae of the urogenital diaphragm, passing across the anterior part of the pelvic outlet. A much thinner portion of the parietal pelvic fascia covers the piriform and coccygeus muscles in the posterior pelvic wall. Medially, the piriformis fascia blends with the periosteum of the sacrum around the margins of the anterior sacral foramens and covers the roots and first branches of the sacral plexus. Visceral pelvic fascia denotes the fascia in the bottom of the pelvic bowl, which invests the pelvic organs and forms a number of supports that suspend the organs from the pelvic walls. These supports arise in common from the obturator part of the parietal fascia, along or near the arcus tendineus. This arc or line extends from a point near the lower part of the symphysis pubica to the root of the spine of the ischium. From this common origin, the fascia spreads inward and backward, dividing into a number of parts classified as either investing (endopelvic) fascia or suspensory and diaphragmatic fascia.

3. MUSCULAR LAYER

The muscles of the greater pelvis are the psoas major and iliacus. Those of the lesser pelvis are the piriformis, obturator internus, coccygeus, and levator ani; they do not form a continuous layer.

Greater Pelvis

A. Psoas Major: The fusiform psoas major muscle originates from the 12th thoracic to the 5th lumbar vertebrae. Parallel fiber bundles descend nearly vertically along the side of the vertebral bodies and extend along the border of the minor pelvis, beneath the inguinal ligament, and on toward insertion in the thigh. The medial border inserts into the lesser trochanter, while the lateral border shares its tendon with the iliacus muscle. Together with the iliacus, it is the most powerful flexor of the thigh and acts as a lateral rotator of the femur when the foot is off the ground and free, and a medial rotator when the foot is on the ground and the tibia is fixed. The psoas component flexes the spine and the pelvis and abducts the lumbar region of the spine. The psoas, having longer fibers than the iliacus, gives a quicker but weaker pull.

B. Iliacus: The fan-shaped iliacus muscle originates from the iliac crest, the iliolumbar ligament, the greater part of the iliac fossa, the anterior sacroiliac ligaments, and frequently the ala of the sacrum. It also originates from the ventral border of the ilium between the 2 anterior spines. It is inserted in a penniform manner on the lateral surface of the tendon that emerges from the psoas above the inguinal ligament and directly on the femur immediately distal to the lesser trochanter. The lateral portion of the muscle arising from the ventral border of the ilium is adherent to the direct tendon of the rectus femoris and the capsule of the hip joint.

Lesser Pelvis

A. Piriformis: The piriformis has its origin from the lateral part of the ventral surface of the second, third, and fourth sacral vertebrae, from the posterior border of the greater sciatic notch, and from the deep surface of the sacrotuberous ligament near the sacrum. The fiber bundles pass through the greater sciatic foramen to insert upon the anterior and inner portion of the upper border of the greater trochanter. The piriformis acts as an abductor, lateral rotator, and weak extensor of the thigh.

B. Obturator Internus: The obturator internus arises from the pelvic surface of the pubic rami near the obturator foramen, the pelvic surface of the ischium between the foramen and the greater sciatic notch, the deep surface of the obturator internus fascia, the fibrous arch that bounds the canal for the obturator vessels and nerves, and the pelvic surface of the obturator membrane. The fiber bundles converge toward the lesser sciatic notch, where they curve laterally to insert into the trochanteric fossa of the femur. The obturator internus is a powerful lateral rotator of the thigh. When the thigh is bent at a right angle, the muscle serves as an abductor and extensor.

C. Coccygeus: The coccygeus muscle runs from the ischial spine and the neighboring margin of the greater sciatic notch to the fourth and fifth sacral vertebrae and the coccyx. A large part of the muscle is aponeurotic. It supports the pelvic and abdominal viscera and possibly flexes and abducts the coccyx.

D. Levator Ani: The levator ani muscle forms the floor of the pelvis and the roof of the perineum. It is divisible into 3 portions: (1) the iliococcygeus, (2) the pubococcygeus, and (3) the puborectalis.

1. Iliococcygeus–The iliococcygeus arises from the arcus tendineus, which extends from the ischial spine to the superior ramus of the pubis near the obturator canal and for a variable distance downward below the obturator canal. Its insertion is into the lateral aspect of the coccyx and the raphe that extends from the tip of the coccyx to the rectum. Many fiber bundles cross the median line.

2. Pubococcygeus–The pubococcygeus arises from the inner surface of the os pubis, the lower margin of the symphysis pubica to the obturator canal, and the arcus tendineus as far backward as the origin of the iliococcygeus. It passes backward, downward, and medially past the urogenital organs and the rectum, inserting into the anterior sacrococcygeal ligament, the deep part of the anococcygeal raphe, and each side of the rectum. The pubococcygeus lies to some extent on the pelvic surface of the insertion of the iliococcygeus.

3. Puborectalis–The puborectalis arises from the body and descending ramus of the pubis beneath the origin of the pubococcygeus, the neighboring part of the obturator fascia, and the fascia covering the pelvic surface of the urogenital diaphragm. Many of the fiber bundles interdigitate with those of the opposite side, and they form a thick band on each side of the rectum behind which those of each side are inserted into the anococcygeal raphe.

The levator ani serves to slightly flex the coccyx, raise the anus, and constrict the rectum and vagina. It resists the downward pressure that the thoracoabdominal diaphragm exerts on the viscera during inspiration.

Pelvic Diaphragm

The pelvic diaphragm (Fig 2–25) extends from the upper part of the pelvic surface of the pubis and ischium to the rectum, which passes through it. The pelvic diaphragm is formed by the levator ani and coccygeus muscles and covering fasciae. The diaphragmatic fasciae cloaking the levator ani arise from the parietal pelvic fascia (obturator fascia), the muscular layer lying between the fasciae. As viewed from above, the superior fascia is the best developed and is reflected onto the rectum, forming the "rectal

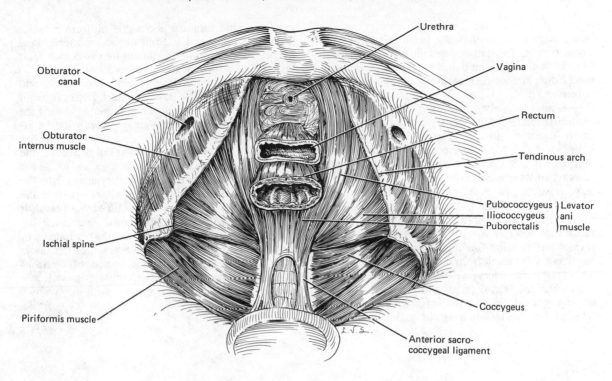

Figure 2–25. Pelvic diaphragm from above.

sheath.'' The coccygeus muscle forms the deeper portion of the posterolateral wall of the ischiorectal fossa, helping to bound the pelvic outlet. The diaphragm presents a hiatus anteriorly, occupied by the vagina and urethra. The pelvic diaphragm is the main support of the pelvic floor; it suspends the rectum and indirectly supports the uterus.

Arteries & Veins

The blood supply to the muscles lining the pelvis is primarily from branches of the hypogastric artery, accompanied by contributions from the external iliac artery. The iliolumbar branch of the hypogastric artery runs upward and laterally beneath the common iliac artery, then beneath the psoas muscle to the superior aperture of the pelvis minor, where it divides into iliac and lumbar branches. The iliac supplies both the iliacus and psoas muscles. It passes laterally beneath the psoas and the femoral nerve and, perforating the iliacus, ramifies in the iliac fossa between that muscle and the bone. It supplies a nutrient artery to the bone and then divides into several branches that can be traced as follows: (1) upward toward the sacroiliac synchondrosis to anastomose with the last lumbar artery; (2) laterally toward the crest of the ilium to anastomose with the lateral circumflex and gluteal arteries; and (3) medially toward the pelvis minor to anastomose with the deep circumflex iliac from the external iliac. The lumbar branch ascends beneath the psoas and supplies that muscle along with the quadratus lumborum. It then anastomoses with the last lumbar artery.

Another branch of the hypogastric artery, the lateral sacral artery, may be represented as 2 distinct vessels. It passes medially in front of the sacrum and turns downward to run parallel with the sympathetic trunk. Crossing the slips of origin of the piriform muscle, it sends branches to that muscle. On reaching the coccyx, it anastomoses in front of the bone with the middle sacral artery and with the inferior lateral sacral artery of the opposite side. The obturator artery usually arises from the hypogastric, but occasionally it may stem from the inferior epigastric or directly from the external iliac artery. It runs forward and downward slightly below the brim of the pelvis, lying between the peritoneum and endopelvic fascia. Passing through the obturator canal, it emerges and divides into anterior and posterior branches that curve around the margin of the obturator foramen beneath the obturator externus muscle.

When the obturator artery arises from the inferior epigastric or external iliac artery, its proximal relationships are profoundly altered, the vessel coursing near the femoral ring where it may be endangered during operative procedures. The anterior branch of the obturator artery runs around the medial margin of the obturator foramen and anastomoses with both its posterior branch and the medial circumflex artery. It supplies branches to the obturator muscles. The internal pudendal artery is a terminal branch of the hypogastric artery that arises opposite the piriform muscle and accompanies the inferior gluteal artery downward to the lower border of the greater sciatic foramen. It leaves the pelvis between the piriform and coccygeus muscles, passing over the ischial spine to enter the ischiorectal fossa through the small sciatic foramen. Then, running forward through the canalis pudendalis (Alcock's canal) in the obturator fascia, it terminates by dividing into the perineal artery and the artery of the clitoris.

Within the pelvis, the artery lies anterior to the piriform muscle and the sacral plexus of nerves, lateral to the inferior gluteal artery. Among the small branches that it sends to the gluteal region are those that accompany the nerve to the obturator internus. Another of its branches, the inferior hemorrhoidal artery, arises at the posterior part of the ischiorectal fossa. Upon perforating the obturator fascia, it immediately breaks up into several branches. Some of those run medially toward the rectum to supply the levator ani muscle. The superior gluteal artery originates as a short trunk from the lateral and back part of the hypogastric artery, associated in origin with the iliolumbar and lateral sacral and sometimes with the inferior gluteal or with the inferior gluteal and the internal pudendal. It leaves the pelvis through the greater sciatic foramen above the piriform muscle, beneath its vein and in front of the superior gluteal nerve. Under cover of the gluteus maximus muscle, it breaks into a superficial and deep division.

The deep portion further divides into superior and inferior branches. The inferior branch passes forward between the gluteus medius and minimus toward the greater trochanter, where it anastomoses with the ascending branch of the lateral circumflex. It supplies branches to the obturator internus, the piriformis, the levator ani, and the coccygeus muscles and to the hip joint. The deep circumflex iliac artery arises from the side of the external iliac artery either opposite the epigastric or a little below the origin of that vessel. It courses laterally behind the inguinal ligament, lying between the fascia transversalis and the peritoneum or in a fibrous canal formed by the union of the fascia transversalis with the iliac fascia. It sends off branches that supply the psoas and iliacus muscles as well as a cutaneous branch that anastomoses with the superior gluteal artery.

Physiology of Reproduction & Pregnancy | 3

William J. Dignam, MD

The constancy of variation is the most striking physiologic feature of the female reproductive system. At the very least, one must take into account the age of the subject, the phase of the menstrual cycle, and the presence or absence of pregnancy in the interpretation of hormone levels or biologic function. During the menstrual cycle, hormone production and the effects on target organs undergo rapid changes, particularly at the time of ovulation.

INTRAUTERINE ENDOCRINE GLAND DEVELOPMENT & FUNCTION

Gonadal development begins in utero. The direction of gonadal development is governed basically by the presence or absence of a Y chromosome (Fig 3–1). The Y-linked histocompatibility antigen (H-Y antigen) is a plasma membrane protein by which the Y chromosome directs the modification of the gonad into a testis. If this antigen is not present, the gonad develops as an ovary. If the fetal gonads develop as ovaries, they contain about 1000 **germ cells** early in gestation; this number increases by mitosis to over 500,000 during intrauterine life and falls to a level of 150–500 thousand by the time of birth. Thus, it is probable that the details of every female's ultimate menstrual and reproductive functions are foreordained during intrauterine existence. For example, in certain individuals who are destined to have dysgenetic gonads, these organs appear to be normal in early intrauterine life, but by the time of birth all or most of the primordial follicles will have disappeared.

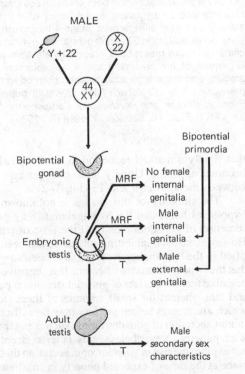

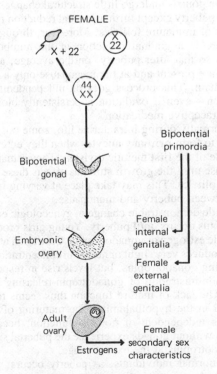

Figure 3–1. Diagrammatic summary of normal sex determination, differentiation, and development in humans. MRF, müllerian regression factor; T, testosterone or other androgen. (Reproduced, with permission, from Ganong WF: *Review of Medical Physiology,* 10th ed. Lange, 1981.)

Little is known about actual hormone production by the gonads of a developing fetus. Nevertheless, the testes secrete testosterone and müllerian regression factor, a polypeptide that acts locally to cause regression of the müllerian duct structure. If the testes are absent or not functioning, the genitalia will remain feminine in structure even in genetic male fetuses.

The pituitary and adrenal glands also function during fetal life. Mean levels of ACTH in umbilical cord plasma fall from approximately 250 pg/mL in early pregnancy to approximately 140 pg/mL at full term. The fall may be due to feedback inhibition by cortisol, since during this period cortisol in cord blood increases from very low levels to as high as 400 ng/mL. If the pituitary is absent, as in anencephaly, the adrenal glands do not develop and do not produce normal amounts of precursors for the placental synthesis of estriol. Curiously, there does not seem to be any significant relationship between these levels and the gestational age in the infant. Prolactin is present in cord blood, and the amounts vary from very low levels at the end of the second trimester to approximately 350 ng/mL at term.

PHYSIOLOGY OF THE REPRODUCTIVE TRACT FROM BIRTH TO PUBERTY

The gonads undergo little structural change from birth to puberty except further gradual reduction in the number of immature follicles. Moreover, throughout life there is a gradual reduction in the number of oocytes so that after puberty, on the average, about 34,000 are present and at the menopause only a very few remain. This process goes on independently of ovulation—even if ovulation is persistently blocked by contraceptive medication.

Normally during intrauterine life, some oogonia enlarge to form **primary oocytes** when they enter the prophase of the first meiotic division. They remain in this phase until the growth stimulus affects these particular follicles. This may take place at varying intervals between puberty and menopause.

Little demonstrable change in gynecologic endocrine status occurs until puberty. Young girls produce very little estrogen or gonadotropins. Castration at this stage produces very slight or no rise in concentration of circulating gonadotropins, but levels rise in response to the administration of gonadotropin-releasing hormone. The lack of mature function thus seems to be centered in the hypothalamus. The maturing of this center is independent of gonadal function, because children without gonads experience the pubertal surge of gonadotropins at the expected age.

In normal individuals, as puberty occurs, pulsatile or episodic secretion of gonadotropins occurs during sleep. The secretion of both FSH and LH begins gradually, but the amplitude of LH pulses is greater, so

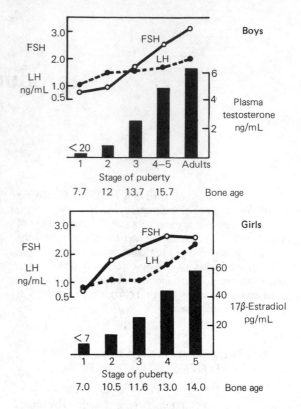

Figure 3–2. Changes in plasma hormone concentrations during puberty in boys *(top)* and girls *(bottom)*. Stage 1 of puberty is preadolescence in both sexes. In boys, stage 2 is characterized by beginning enlargement of the testes, stage 3 by penile enlargement, stage 4 by growth of the glans penis, and stage 5 by adult genitalia. In girls, stage 2 is characterized by breast buds, stage 3 by elevation and enlargement of the breasts, stage 4 by projection of the areolas, and stage 5 by adult breasts. (Reproduced, with permission, from Grumbach MM: Onset of puberty. In: *Puberty: Biologic and Psychosocial Components.* Berenberg SR [editor]. HE Stenfoert Kroese BV, 1975.)

that finally a marked reduction in the FSH/LH ratio becomes apparent. Usually these changes take place between the ages of 9 and 13 (Fig 3–2).

The stimulus for this change is not known. One hypothesis holds that the hypothalamus may prevent secretion of gonadotropins until the time of puberty. However, no such inhibiting substance has been identified in the hypothalamus. It has also been suggested that the hypothalamus may become less sensitive to the negative feedback effect of gonadal steroids at puberty and that whereas the small amounts of these steroids which are present before puberty may be sufficient to inhibit secretion of gonadotropins, such is not the case after puberty. Nevertheless, this latter concept does not explain the rise in gonadotropin secretion that takes place at the time of expected puberty in children without gonads (Fig 3–3).

The rising levels of gonadotropins are responsible for the increasing titers of estrogens that cause breast

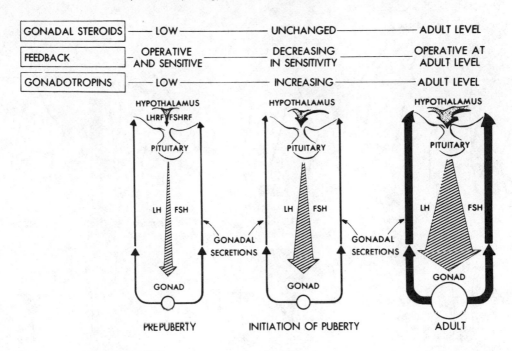

Figure 3–3. Schematic diagram of the changes in sensitivity of the hypothalamic gonadostat. In the prepubertal state, the concentration of sex steroids and gonadotropins is low; the hypothalamic ''gonadostat'' is functional but highly sensitive to low levels of sex steroids. With the onset of puberty, there is decreased sensitivity of the hypothalamus to negative feedback by sex steroids, increased release of LRF, and enhanced secretion of gonadotropins. In the negative feedback mechanism, the hypothalamus is less sensitive to feedback by sex steroids (adult set point) and adult levels of gonadotropins and sex steroids are present. (Reproduced, with permission, from Grumbach M et al [editors]: *The Control of the Onset of Puberty.* Wiley, 1974.)

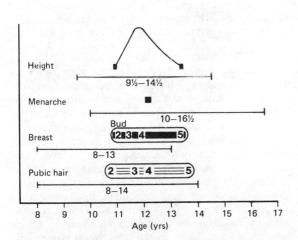

Figure 3–4. Sequence of events during adolescence in girls. At top is shown the range of ages over which the skeletal growth spurt occurs; the curve represents the average growth spurt. The other 3 ranges shown represent the *onset* of menses, breast budding, and pubic hair growth. Average age at menarche is represented by the heavy box in the second row. The numbers mounted in boxes over the ranges in the third and fourth rows refer to the stages of breast development and growth of pubic hair depicted in Fig 3–5. (Redrawn, with permission, from Tanner JM: *Growth at Adolescence,* 2nd ed. Blackwell, 1962.)

development. The growth of pubic and axillary hair may be related to increased adrenocortical function. Uterine bleeding is usually first noted about 2 years after these events. The physical changes that occur at puberty (Figs 3–4 and 3–5) have been well documented by Tanner (see references). His descriptions of these changes have been widely accepted as the standards for normal development.

MATURE REPRODUCTIVE FUNCTION

NEUROENDOCRINE REGULATION

Months or even years after vaginal bleeding begins (menarche), ovulatory menstrual cycles ensue. These are under the control of a complex neuroendocrine mechanism. While many of the details of this regulatory system are still unknown, certain inferences can be drawn from animal experiments.

The **hypothalamus** clearly plays an important role. The hypothalamus includes tissues that compose the lateral walls of the inferior portion of the third ventricle and the infundibulum. It is connected directly with the posterior lobe of the pituitary by nerves originating in the supraoptic and paraventricular nuclei

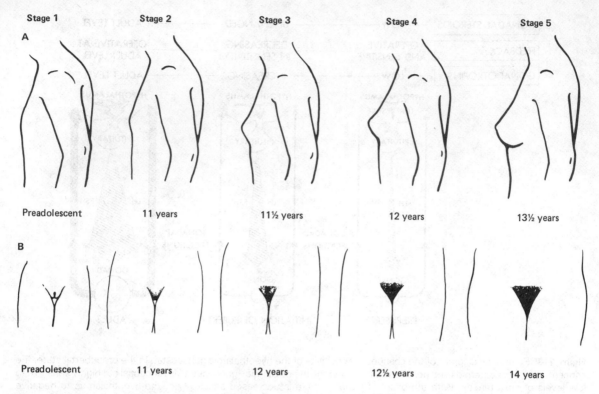

Figure 3–5. Sequence of events at adolescence in girls. Menarche may occur between ages 10 and 16½; the average age at menarche is 13. *A:* Stage 1: Preadolescent; elevation of papillae only. Stage 2: Breast bud stage (may occur between ages 8 and 13); elevation of breasts and papillae as small mounds, with enlargement of areolar diameter. Stage 3: Enlargement and elevation of breasts and areolas with no separation of contours. Stage 4: Areolas and papillae project from breast to form a secondary mound. Stage 5: Mature; projection of papillae only, with recession of areolas into general contour of breast. *B:* Stage 1: Preadolescent; normal vellus hair. Stage 2: Sparse growth along labia of long, slightly pigmented, downy hair that is straight or slightly curled (may occur between ages 8 and 14). Stage 3: Darker, coarser, more curled hair growing sparsely over pubic area. Stage 4: Resembles adult in type but covers smaller area. Stage 5: Adult in quantity and type. (Redrawn, with permission, from Tanner JM: *Growth at Adolescence,* 2nd ed. Blackwell, 1962.)

(Fig 3–6). On the other hand, there are no nerve communications between the hypothalamus and anterior lobe of the pituitary. Releasing or inhibiting hormones formed in the hypothalamus are carried from the median eminence to the anterior lobe of the pituitary in the portal vessels. The secretion of gonadotropins is under the control of gonadotropin-releasing hormone produced in the hypothalamus. A single **releasing hormone** for both gonadotropins (FSH and LH) has been chemically identified and synthesized. It is a decapeptide with the following structure:

(pyro)Glu-His-Trp-Ser-Tyr-Gly-Leu-Arg-Pro-Gly-NH₂

Evidence from animal studies suggests that there is a tonic center in the region of the ventromedial nucleus which causes release of gonadotropins sufficient to maintain estrogen production. In addition, it is likely that there is a center in the preoptic nucleus which triggers a periodic discharge of gonadotropins to stimulate ovulation. Presumably, these centers also are susceptible to other influences such as light, sleep, emotional stress, and drugs.

Gonadotropin-releasing hormone has a 2-part effect on the pituitary. Its most immediate action is to cause the discharge of stored gonadotropins from the pituitary. As releasing hormone continues to act on the pituitary, it stimulates additional synthesis and release of gonadotropins. Both of these effects are less prominent during the early follicular phase of the cycle, but as the cycle continues, the effect of releasing hormone in increasing the amount of pituitary reserve of gonadotropins becomes more prominent, due probably to the effect of increasing amounts of estradiol. As ovulation approaches, the gonadotropin-releasing effect dominates, and finally in the early luteal phase both effects are prominent until they decline before the onset of menstruation.

For the hormone prolactin, the hypothalamus provides a releasing hormone and an inhibiting hormone. In the human, it is probable that the inhibiting hormone is of major significance. It is a curious fact that synthetic thyrotropin-releasing hormone stimulates the release of prolactin as well as thyrotropin in women. However, it is improbable that thyrotropin-releasing hormone is the prolactin-releasing hormone.

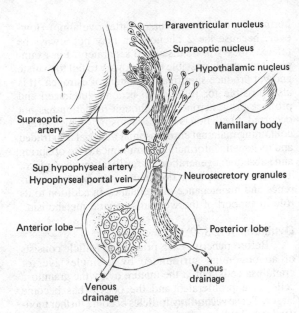

Figure 3–6. Simplified schematic reconstruction of the hypothalamus and the pituitary. (After Hansel; courtesy *International Journal of Fertility.* Redrawn and reproduced, with permission, from Schally et al: *Science* 1973;**179**:341. Copyright © 1973 by The American Association for the Advancement of Science.)

The chemical nature of the releasing hormone for prolactin is not known, but the inhibiting hormone is dopamine.

PITUITARY FUNCTION

The anterior lobe of the pituitary normally secretes many hormones. These include thyrotropin (TSH), corticotropin (ACTH), growth hormone (GH), melanocyte-stimulating hormone (MSH), follicle-stimulating hormone (FSH), luteinizing hormone (LH), and prolactin (PRL), all of which are important in reproductive physiology.

FSH and LH are produced in basophilic cells in the pituitary, whereas prolactin is produced in the acidophilic cells.

FSH, LH, and TSH are rather complex glycoproteins. All 3 have alpha and beta subunits, and the alpha subunits of all 3 are remarkably similar. The beta subunits are largely responsible for the biologic specificity. The structure of TSH is known, and the amino acid sequences of FSH, LH, and PRL have been described. Prolactin is very similar to growth hormone. Indeed, human growth hormone has lactogenic activity; however, 2 separate hormones are involved because opposite blood level responses of the 2 hormones are observed following pharmacologic manipulation (eg, the administration of levodopa causes an increase in GH but a decrease in prolactin).

The function of the posterior pituitary lobe is also important in reproductive physiology. As stated previ-

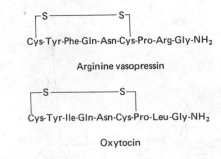

Figure 3–7. Structures of arginine vasopressin and oxytocin.

ously, the hormones of this lobe (**oxytocin** and **vasopressin**) are formed in the hypothalamus and transported to the posterior lobe within the neurons in the hypothalamohypophyseal tract. Oxytocin and vasopressin are nonapeptides with very similar structures (Fig 3–7).

Both of these hormones are stored in the posterior pituitary bound to polypeptides called neurophysins. Vasopressin (antidiuretic hormone, ADH) is mainly concerned with maintenance of proper osmolality of the plasma. Both hormones are secreted by cells in both nuclei. Oxytocin stimulates contraction of uterine smooth muscle. This hormone also causes contraction of the myoepithelial cells in the breast ductules. These effects are vital to the success of lactation and may play a role in labor.

During normal menstrual cycles, gonadotropins are secreted in a carefully regulated manner. Sensitive radioimmunoassays have made it possible to measure these and other hormones in peripheral blood at frequent intervals. FSH and LH—present in very small amounts before midcycle—begin to rise a few days before menstruation. Plasma FSH rises to a level of 5–10 mIU/mL during the first 3–5 days of the new cycle and then declines to very low levels. Both FSH and LH remain at low levels until the time of ovulation, when both hormones manifest a dynamic spurt. The plasma LH surge is most marked. It may reach a peak of even 100 mIU/mL in some patients. The entire surge lasts only 2–3 days. Similarly, plasma FSH manifests a brief surge of lesser magnitude—usually not above 40 mIU/mL. Following ovulation, both hormones again fall to levels of a few mIU/mL and remain there until a few days before the next cycle begins.

The pattern of these hormones during a normal menstrual cycle is depicted in Fig 3–8.

Prolactin is present also in the peripheral circulation during menstrual cycles. Prolactin is important in the maintenance of the corpus luteum in lower animals, particularly the rat, but its role in humans is not well understood. Prolactin levels in the peripheral circulation do not show consistent changes throughout the menstrual cycle. Interestingly, isolated determinations have failed to show significant differences between males and females. In both, the levels of prolactin in peripheral blood serum are approximately 15

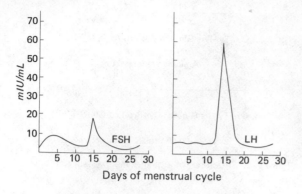

Figure 3–8. FSH and LH levels in the peripheral circulation over the course of a normal menstrual cycle.

ng/mL. During pregnancy, a level of 80 ng/mL has been recorded, and in lactating women this may rise to > 200 ng/mL.

OVARIAN RESPONSES

The endocrine changes that occur during the menstrual cycle produce marked changes in the follicles of the ovary culminating in ovulation and then the formation of a corpus luteum. There is usually a constant and recognizable relationship between ovulation and ovarian hormone production, with the greatest

hormone production occurring after ovulation. However, because the 2 phenomena may not always be related, they will be discussed separately. For example, it is entirely possible for the ovary to fail to ovulate and yet produce significant amounts of estrogen. It is also possible for follicles to become luteinized and produce progesterone even though ovulation has not occurred. Ovulation is the mechanism by which an egg containing maternal chromosomal material is extruded and its genetic information communicated to offspring and subsequent generations if fertilization takes place. Thus, hormone production makes possible the occurrence and maintenance of pregnancy in addition to its role in support of the woman's general metabolism.

Ovulation (Fig 3–9)

Before puberty, each primordial follicle consists of an oogonium surrounded by a single layer of granulosa cells, but in the mature ovary the granulosa cells have proliferated and the oocyte has become larger. These **secondary follicles** become further modified as fluid accumulates in one pool among the granulosa cells, forming the antrum of the follicle. Concomitantly, the stromal cells surrounding each follicle become modified to form the theca interna and theca externa. Capillaries are present in the theca interna but not in the granulosa layer. Under the influence of FSH and LH, a number of ovarian follicles are stimulated to increase in size. A follicle becomes ready for rupture and ovulation as the ovum, now a secondary oocyte, projects into the fluid and is covered by

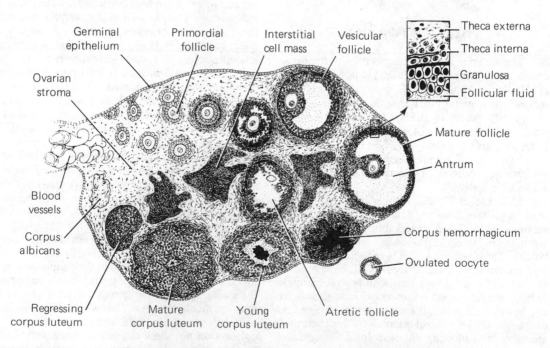

Figure 3–9. Diagram of a mammalian ovary, showing the sequential development of a follicle, formation of a corpus luteum, and, in the center, follicular atresia. A section of the wall of a mature follicle is enlarged at the upper right. The interstitial cell mass is not prominent in primates. (After Patten B, Eakin RM. Reproduced, with permission, from Gorbman A, Bern H: *Textbook of Comparative Endocrinology.* Wiley, 1962.)

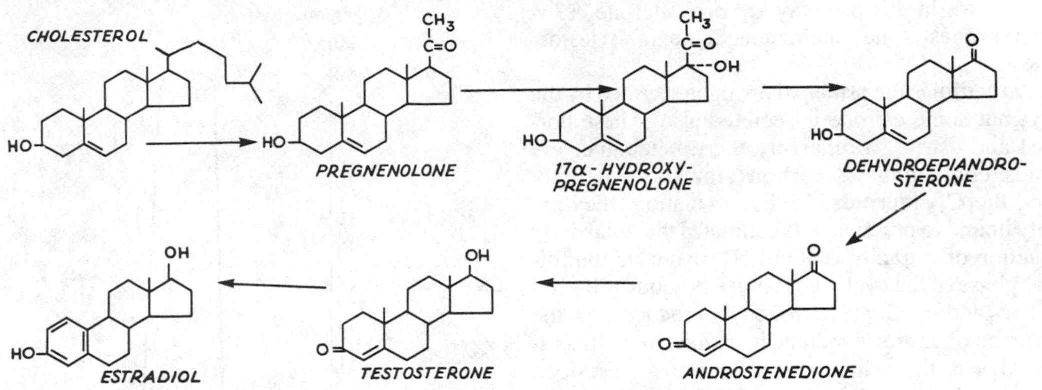

Figure 3–10. Δ^5 pathway of estrogen production.

several layers of granulosa cells, the cumulus oophorus.

The surge of LH triggers ovulation. It is not known why one particular follicle undergoes full maturation and ovulation. Nonetheless, the follicle destined for ovulation becomes large enough to protrude above the surface of the ovary, and the cells overlying that point on the ovary disintegrate, so that the follicle is exposed. It then bursts and the ovum, covered by zona pellucida and the adherent granulosa cells, the corona radiata, floats out of the follicle in the follicular fluid.

After ovulation and escape of the ovum, with its surrounding granulosa cells, the wall of the follicle collapses and capillaries grow down into the granulosa layer. The granulosa cells undergo marked hyperplasia, and the corpus luteum enlarges for a few days. The theca and granulosa cells then accumulate lipids. About 9 days after ovulation, the corpus luteum—if fertilization does not occur—begins to degenerate, and over a period of a few months, it finally becomes hyalinized to form a corpus albicans.

Those accompanying follicles that have not progressed to ovulation undergo a gradual process of hyalinization and then replacement by fibrous tissue, forming atretic follicles (atresia). New follicles soon begin to grow in preparation for the succeeding ovulation as the new menstrual cycle begins.

Hormone Production

Hormone production by the ovaries is under the control of the anterior pituitary gonadotropic hormones FSH and LH. Both FSH and LH are necessary for follicle stimulation, which results in the production of **estrogen.** The dynamic surge of LH causes ovulation, after which the corpus luteum secretes **estrogens** and **progesterone.**

Estrogens are produced predominantly by theca interna cells, but both estrogens and progesterone are produced in the luteinized granulosa cells of the corpus luteum. **Androgens** are produced predominantly in the stromal cells. The ovary can synthesize its hormones from simple compounds such as acetate and cholesterol. It is probable that during the follicular phase of the menstrual cycle estrogens are produced in the theca cells via the Δ^5 **pathway** (Fig 3–10). Specifically, the intermediates are pregnenolone, 17α-hydroxypregnenolone, dehydroepiandrosterone, androstenedione, and testosterone. In the luteal phase of the cycle, estrogens and progesterone are produced in the granulosa cells via the Δ^4 **pathway** (Fig 3–11). The

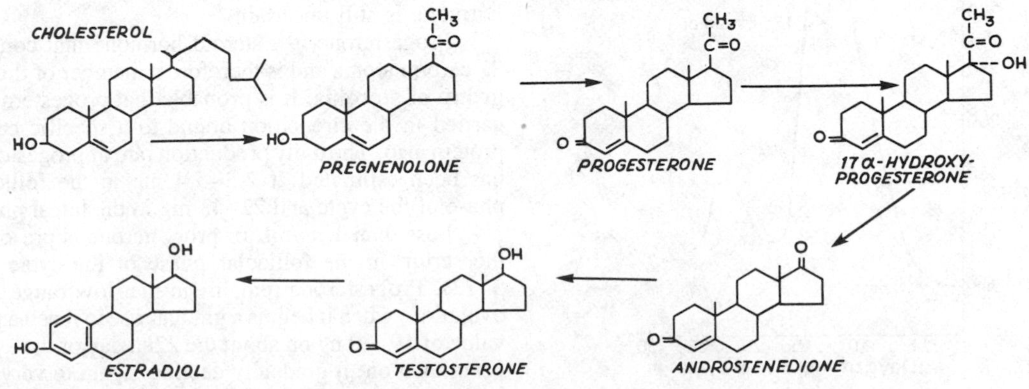

Figure 3–11. Δ^4 pathway of estrogen production.

intermediates in this pathway are progesterone, 17α-hydroxyprogesterone, androstenedione, and testosterone.

Estradiol is the principal estrogen secreted by the ovary, but some estrone is secreted also. These hormones and estriol, a relatively inert metabolite, are steroids containing 18 carbon atoms—commonly termed the C_{18} **steroids.** In the circulation, they are largely bound to proteins. It is estimated that total daily production of estradiol is about 50 μg during the follicular phase of the cycle, with a rise to about 150–300 μg at ovulation. Some estrogen is produced by the conversion of androstenedione to estrone in peripheral sites. This is the principal mechanism for estrogen production in prepubertal children and postmenopausal women.

The levels of estrogens in the peripheral circulation are closely correlated with the phase of the menstrual cycle (Fig 3–12). Early in the cycle, the level of estradiol is about 50 pg/mL of serum. This gradually rises to a peak of about 400 pg on the day preceding the LH surge, presumably just before ovulation. A second lower peak of serum estradiol occurs at about the 21st day of the cycle, whereupon the level gradually declines to the early cycle level.

The liver is the principal site of metabolism of estradiol. Estradiol is converted to estrone and estrone in turn to estriol. However, there are many intermediate estrogen metabolites, making assessment of estrogenic activity by measurement of urinary metabolites difficult because some of the metabolites are not measured by conventional methods. Estrogens are conjugated to glucuronides and sulfates for excretion. These conjugates are biologically much less active.

Progesterone is the major progestogen produced by the ovary, although other biologically active metabolites have been identified, ie, 20α-hydroxypregn-4-en-3-one and 20β-hydroxypregn-4-en-3-one.

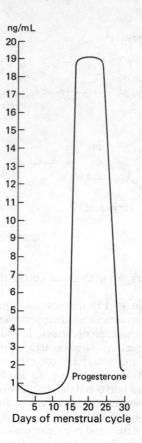

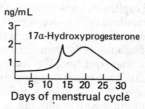

Figure 3–13. Progesterone and 17α-hydroxyprogesterone levels in peripheral circulation.

The steroid 17α-hydroxyprogesterone may be an important product of the ovary also, but its role as a hormone is still uncertain.

Progesterone is a steroid hormone that contains 21 carbon atoms and is therefore a member of the C_{21} **group of steroids.** It is probable that progesterone is carried in the circulation bound to a specific carrier protein also. The daily production rate of progesterone has been estimated at 2.3–5.4 mg in the follicular phase of the cycle and 22–43 mg in the luteal phase.

Less than 1 ng/mL of progesterone is present in the serum in the follicular phase of the cycle (Fig 3–13). Progesterone remains in that low range until ovulation, when it begins a gradual rise to reach a peak value of 10–20 ng on about the 22nd day of the cycle. From then on, it gradually declines again to very low levels at the completion of the cycle.

The level of 17α-hydroxyprogesterone is very

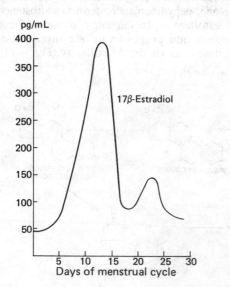

Figure 3–12. Estradiol levels in peripheral circulation.

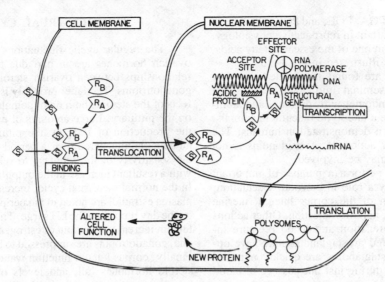

Figure 3–14. Molecular mechanism of sex steroid hormone action. The schematic representation of the subunit structure of steroid hormone receptor is based primarily on information from the progesterone receptor in the chick oviduct. It is likely, however, that the general concept applies to other steroid hormones as well. S represents steroid hormone and R_A and R_B steroid hormone receptor subunits. (Reproduced, with permission, from Chan L, O'Malley BW: Mechanism of action of the sex steroid hormones. *N Engl J Med* 1976;**294**:1322.)

low in the early part of the cycle. Just before ovulation, it rises sharply to a peak level of approximately 2 ng/mL (Fig 3–13). The level then falls again, but a second peak of about 2 ng occurs about 5 days after ovulation and is maintained for about 5 days before it falls again to initial values.

Progesterone and 17α-hydroxyprogesterone are also metabolized in the liver. Progesterone is converted to pregnanediol and conjugated, and 17α-hydroxyprogesterone is reduced to pregnanetriol. Again, the many complex forms of urinary hormone excretion products make evaluation of progestational activity by measurement of urinary metabolites an inaccurate assessment.

Androgens are produced in the ovary mainly in the stromal cells. The ovary secretes testosterone as well as dehydroepiandrosterone and androstenedione. Some of the androgen in the peripheral circulation is produced by peripheral conversion of androstenedione, produced by the adrenal cortex, to testosterone.

The daily production rate of androstenedione had been determined to be about 3.4 mg. Most of the androstenedione is produced in the adrenals, and there is very little change in circulating levels of this hormone throughout the menstrual cycle. That which is produced in the ovary may diffuse into the follicle and be aromatized to estrogens, but it is probably an important factor, along with testosterone, in causing follicular atresia. The production rate of testosterone is 0.4–1.7 mg/d. The plasma levels of androstenedione are 1.3–1.5 ng/mL, and for testosterone the corresponding levels are 0.3–0.6 ng/mL. There is a slight rise in concentration of both hormones in the peripheral circulation just before ovulation. The androgens are steroid hormones containing 19 carbon atoms and are commonly called **C_{19} steroids.**

The principal site of metabolism of androgens is the liver. Both dehydroepiandrosterone and androstenedione, as well as testosterone, are reduced primarily to androsterone and etiocholanolone. These can be measured in the urine as 11-deoxy-17-ketosteroids.

HORMONE ACTION

The protein hormones, eg, the gonadotropins, unite with specific receptors on the cell membranes of the target cells and regulate the activity of the adenylate cyclase present on the inner surface of the plasma membranes. Thus, 3'5'-cyclic adenosine monophosphate (cAMP) is formed, and this substance activates proteins that cause changes in the structure and function of the target cells.

The steroid hormones enter the target cells and react with specific protein receptors in the cytoplasm. Next, the combined steroid and receptor enters the nucleus and reacts with the chromatin, resulting in an increased production of ribonucleic acid (RNA). After processing with adenosine triphosphate (ATP), the messenger RNA moves to the ribosomes in the cytoplasm, where it causes the production of the specific proteins for which it is coded.

PROSTAGLANDINS

Prostaglandins are 20-carbon unsaturated fatty acids containing a cyclopentane ring. These hormones are divided into 3 groups according to the configuration of that ring, ie, PGA, PGE, and PGF. The latter 2 are particularly important in reproductive physiology. They are formed from one of the essential fatty acids, arachidonic acid, as illustrated in Fig 3–15.

Prostaglandins are found in a wide variety of locations, including seminal fluid, brain, nerves, most endocrine organs, endometrium, decidua, and amniotic fluid. They have a luteolytic function in animals, but this has not been demonstrated in humans. The exact mechanism of action of prostaglandins is not known, but cAMP may be involved.

Prostaglandins perform a number of important functions. They play a role in erection, ejaculation, ovulation, formation of the corpus luteum, uterine motility, parturition, and milk ejection. Other actions include platelet aggregation and blood pressure increase. Closely related prostaglandins may have opposing actions. Prostaglandins are quickly removed from the circulation during just one passage of blood through the lungs or liver.

THE MENSTRUAL CYCLE

The regular cyclic fluctuations in pituitary and ovarian hormones are in part due to the reciprocal relationships between ovarian steroids and pituitary gonadotropins. The latter probably is mediated by effects of the steroids both on hypothalamic centers and on the pituitary. Large amounts of estrogen suppress the production of FSH by the pituitary, and small amounts administered over a period of time increase the sensitivity of the pituitary to releasing hormone with a resultant increase in the output of FSH and LH. In the normal menstrual cycle, increasing amounts of plasma estradiol are noted in the peripheral circulation on the day preceding the LH surge. Then, as the corpus luteum increases its output of estrogens and progesterone, gonadotropins are suppressed to low levels again. Finally, corpus luteum function wanes. The levels of steroid hormones fall, and levels of gonadotropins begin to increase in the circulation just a few days

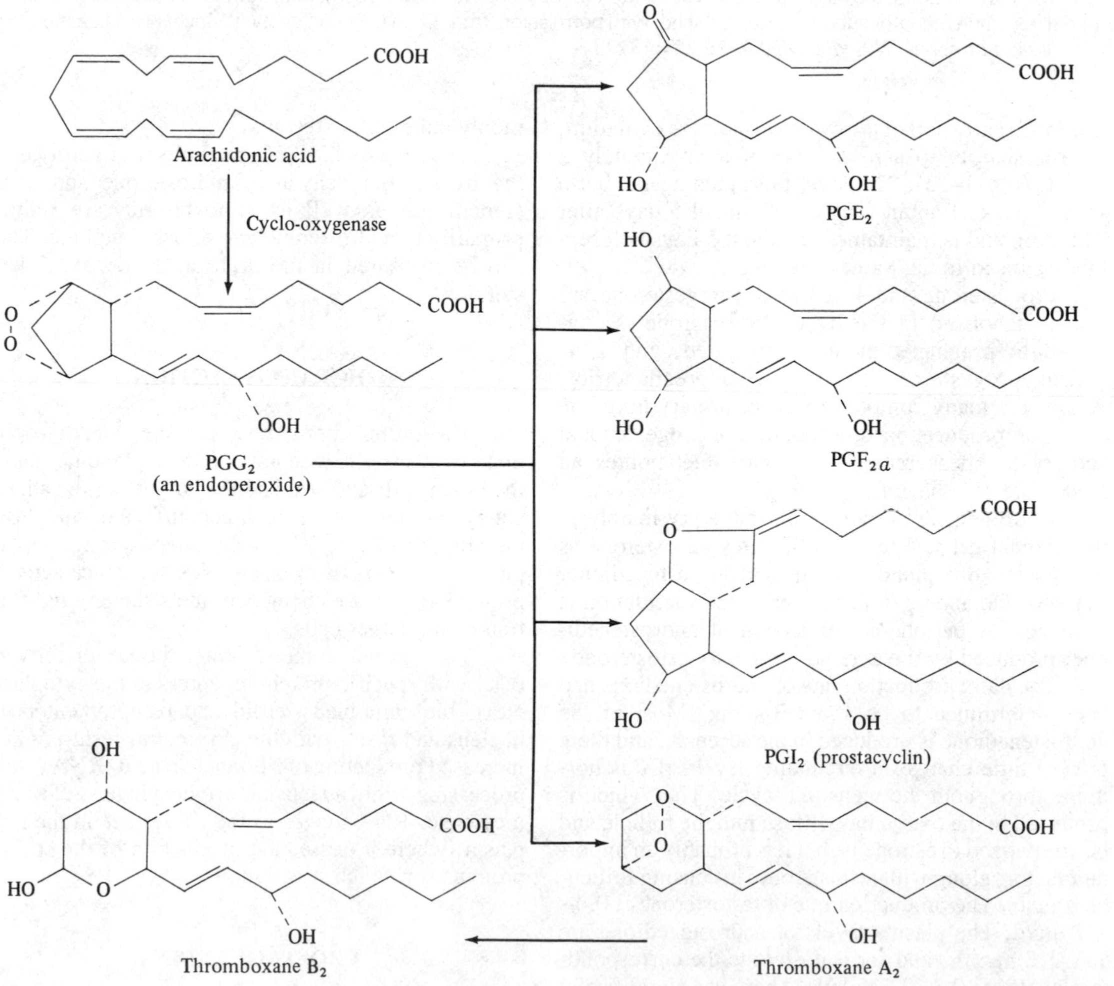

Figure 3–15. Synthesis of prostaglandins and thromboxanes from arachidonic acid. Other prostaglandins are formed from other polyunsaturated essential fatty acids. (Reproduced, with permission, from Ganong WF: *Review of Medical Physiology,* 10th ed. Lange, 1981.)

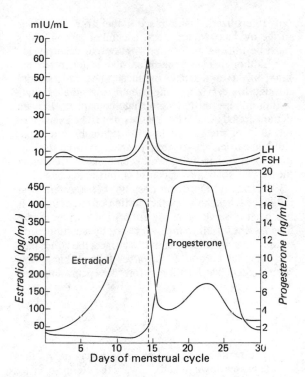

Figure 3–16. LH, FSH, estradiol, and progesterone levels in the peripheral circulation.

before menstruation. These relationships are illustrated graphically in Fig 3–16.

EFFECTS ON THE GENITAL SYSTEM

The hormone level fluctuations have obvious effects upon the **uterus, oviducts, cervix, vagina,** and **breasts.**

During the preovulatory phase of the menstrual cycle, there is a gradual increase in the thickness of the **endometrium** and the glands become more tortuous. The epithelium of the glands becomes more active and changes from simple columnar to pseudostratified with a greater number of mitoses. The stromal cells increase in number also.

At the time of ovulation, subnuclear vacuoles appear in the epithelium of the endometrium. About 4–5 days after ovulation, the nuclei descend to the base of the cells and the vacuoles migrate to the luminal border of the glands. Soon thereafter, the gland lumens show prominent amounts of secretion and the epithelial margin becomes very ragged. The stroma undergoes prominent changes in the postovulatory phase of the cycle. It becomes loose and edematous, and by 13–14 days after ovulation, it becomes infiltrated with leukocytes. The stromal cells gradually enlarge, and by the 11th–12th days after ovulation, they are predecidual in appearance.

The spiral arteries of the endometrium grow rapidly during the preovulatory phase of the cycle, and

their walls thicken during the postovulatory phase. As estrogen and progesterone levels fall rapidly in the circulation, the arteries constrict. This results in hypoxic damage to the superficial layers of the endometrium; degeneration followed by sloughing occurs with menstrual flow. It may be that prostaglandins play a role in constriction of spiral arteries. They are present in the endometrium in high concentrations at the end of the menstrual cycle and are also noted in large amounts in menstrual blood.

The epithelium of the **oviducts** contains 3 types of cells: ciliated, secretory, and intercalary or peg cells. During the preovulatory phase of the menstrual cycle, there is an increase in the number of both ciliated and secretory cells. Following ovulation, the secretory cells increase greatly in number while the ciliated cells decrease in number. The peg cells are inactive or resting cells.

The cervical mucus changes as the menstrual cycle progresses. During the preovulatory phase, the mucus is thick and tenacious. Immediately before ovulation, an outpouring of mucus with a greatly increased sodium chloride content and decreased viscosity normally occurs. These changes permit the mucus to form filaments with spaces between them that act as tracts for sperm migration. Following ovulation, the mucus again becomes thicker and decreased in amount. Hence, the conditions that favor sperm migration are present during only a few days of the menstrual cycle.

The **vaginal mucosa** also responds to the endocrine changes of the menstrual cycle. The vaginal epithelium consists of basal, parabasal, intermediate, and superficial cells. Cells that have desquamated into the vaginal fluid are mainly intermediate and superficial cells, together with a few parabasal cells. During the several days before and after ovulation, there is a marked increase in the number of superficial cells in the vaginal smear. During other phases of the cycle, the cells are predominantly intermediate cells. During the postovulatory phase of the cycle, desquamation continues with clumping and curling of cells.

OTHER EFFECTS OF OVARIAN STEROIDS

Estrogens cause retention of sodium and water, whereas large amounts of progesterone cause excretion of sodium and water. Progesterone causes a lowering of alveolar P_{CO_2}. Testosterone is converted in the peripheral tissues to dihydrotestosterone, the biologically important hormone. It causes some retention of sodium, potassium, and water.

PREGNANCY

GAMETOGENESIS & FERTILIZATION
(Fig 3–17)

Primary oogonia contain the **diploid number of chromosomes**, a total of 46. These are composed of 44 autosomes and two X chromosomes. As the oogonia divide to form primary oocytes, they divide by mitosis so that each primary oocyte also contains 46 chromosomes.

Meiosis—the division of primary oocytes to form secondary oocytes—is a much different process. Homologous chromosomes are paired before and after division, and each secondary oocyte therefore contains only 23 chromosomes, the **haploid number.** As noted above, this first meiotic division begins in utero. It is completed as the developing follicle becomes a mature graafian follicle. By this time, a thick layer of granulosa cells will have formed around the oocyte, and an acellular layer, the zona pellucida, will have developed immediately adjacent to the oocyte. The layer of granulosa cells around the zona pellucida is called the corona radiata.

With the completion of the division of the primary oocyte, 2 cells of distinctly unequal size are produced. The one that contains most of the cytoplasm is the **secondary oocyte.** The other contains very little cytoplasm and is the first polar body that disintegrates.

Just before ovulation, the secondary oocyte begins the process of division that will produce a large mature oocyte and the second polar body. It is probable that this second maturation division is accomplished only if fertilization takes place. It therefore takes place in the oviduct. Nonetheless, a number of conditions must be fulfilled before fertilization can take place.

Although many sperm are deposited in the vagina, only a few reach the oviducts. They move rapidly through the cervix and uterus and reach the oviducts within minutes or hours after intercourse. It has been demonstrated in animals that sperm must be exposed to the fluid of the genital tract—presumably the tubal fluid, in particular—in order to undergo **capacitation,** the process whereby sperm become able to penetrate the zona pellucida to accomplish fertilization.

Normally, the ovum does not become fertilized until it reaches the ampullar portion of the oviduct. It has been observed that the fimbriated portion of the tube attaches itself to the ovary and, by a combination of muscular and ciliary activity, attracts the ovum into the ampullar portion of the tube. It is probable that sperm reach that location before the ovum and wait there for its arrival.

EMBRYOGENESIS

The mature fertilized ovum is a **zygote.** As the zygote passes down the tube toward the uterine cavity, it undergoes segmentation into blastomeres. As fluid develops among the blastomeres, a **blastocyst** develops and implantation into the endometrium occurs soon thereafter. Implantation takes place about 7 days after fertilization; at that time, the fertilized ovum consists of approximately 200 cells. The blastocyst settles into the endometrium by active invasion, and about a week after implantation it is completely cov-

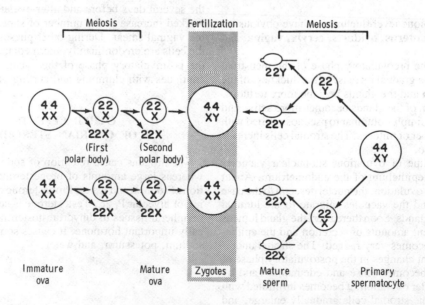

Figure 3–17. Basis of genetic sex determination. In the case of the 2-stage meiotic division in the female, 4 bodies form but only one survives as the mature ovum. In the case of the male, the meiotic division results in the formation of 4 sperms, 2 containing the X and 2 the Y chromosome. Fertilization thus produces a 44XY (male) zygote or a 44XX (female) zygote. (Reproduced, with permission, from Ganong WF: *Review of Medical Physiology,* 10th ed. Lange, 1981.)

ered by endometrium. By this time, much of the blastocyst will have differentiated into trophoblastic cells producing **chorionic gonadotropin** (hCG).

HORMONE PATTERNS IN EARLY PREGNANCY
(Fig 3–18)

During a menstrual cycle in which fertilization takes place, the pattern of circulating hormones is markedly different from that of the ordinary menstrual cycle. Progesterone, instead of falling on about the tenth postovulatory day, rises steadily until the third or fourth week of pregnancy. It falls temporarily, and after the eighth week it rises again until term. On the other hand, 17α-hydroxyprogesterone declines to very low levels. This suggests that progesterone is produced by the placenta and 17α-hydroxyprogesterone by the corpus luteum. The corpus luteum is always present in the ovary during pregnancy; however, the titers of 17α-hydroxyprogesterone suggest that it becomes much less active after pregnancy is well established. In the peripheral circulation, the level of hCG starts to rise rapidly about 10 days after spontaneous ovulation. This indicates that the embedded conceptus is already producing a tropic hormone at that early stage.

Plasma FSH falls rapidly to very low or undetect-

able levels on about the tenth postovulatory day and remains low throughout pregnancy. This indicates that the pituitary gland is relatively inactive, probably suppressed by the steroids elaborated by the corpus luteum.

HORMONE PRODUCTION BY THE PLACENTA
(Fig 3–19)

As the blastocyst invades the endometrium, maternal blood vessels are opened and lakes of maternal blood form. Placental **villi,** which form the periphery of the conceptus, may be recognized a few days after implantation. These villi consist of a core of mesenchyme covered by cytotrophoblast. Vessels are formed in the mesenchymal core of these villi very early, and circulation is present in both maternal and fetal blood vessels by about the 17th day after fertilization; thus, a true placental circulation has been established. A few of the placental villi extend through the **intervillous space** to the decidua as **anchoring villi,** but the majority of them hang free in the intervillous space to serve as structures through which exchange of materials between the maternal circulation and the fetal circulation can take place.

The placenta is not a complete endocrine organ for the production of estrogenic steroid hormones. It cannot synthesize estrogens from simple substances like acetate or cholesterol. This function requires other steroid substances as precursors. It has become customary, however, to speak of the fetoplacental unit as the source of estrogenic hormones because many of the precursors of estrogenic hormones come from the fetus.

Estrogens are produced by the syncytiotrophoblast. Estradiol is formed from both maternal and fetal dehydroepiandrosterone. Estrone is also elaborated by the placenta, but estriol seems to be a very important secretory product during pregnancy and makes up a major proportion of urinary estrogen. Estriol is also formed from precursors, including 16α-hydroxydehydroepiandrosterone, of fetal origin. Nonetheless, maternal dehydroepiandrosterone also serves as a precursor for estriol. Since the fetal precursors are such an important source of estriol, the measurement of urinary estriol has gained wide acceptance as an index of fetal welfare.

Urinary estriol values rise gradually throughout the course of normal pregnancy (Fig 3–20). Estriol is excreted in urine in amounts of 1 mg or more per 24 hours during early pregnancy, as contrasted with microgram amounts in the nonpregnant state. Urinary excretion of 30–40 mg of estriol per 24 hours is usual by the end of pregnancy.

Progesterone is synthesized and secreted by the placenta also. Precursors of fetal origin are not necessary in this instance, since the placenta can synthesize progesterone from cholesterol obtained from the maternal circulation.

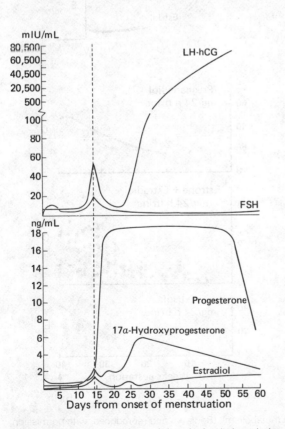

Figure 3–18. Hormones in peripheral circulation during early pregnancy.

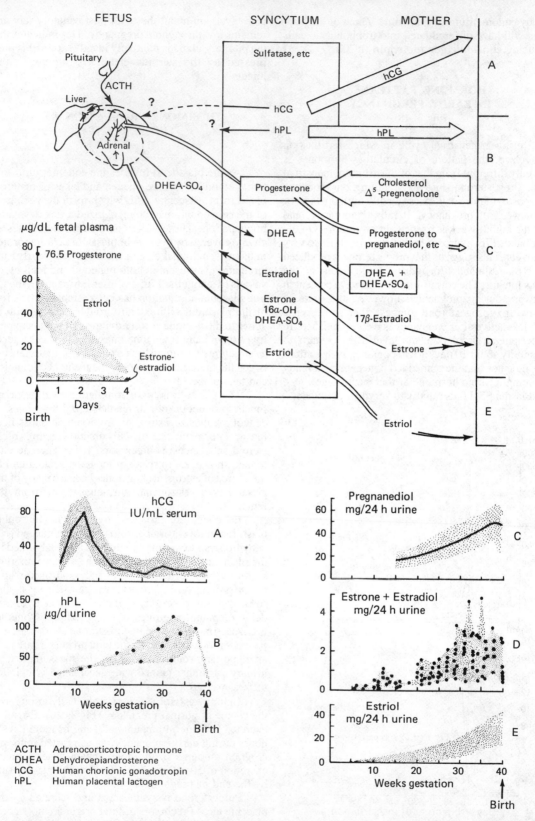

Figure 3–19. Hormones of the placenta (including intermediate metabolism). (Redrawn and reproduced, with permission, from Strauss F, Benirschke K, Driscoll SG: Placenta. In: *Handbuch der Speziellen Pathologischen Anatomie und Histologie.* Lubarsch O, Henke F. Springer-Verlag, 1967.)

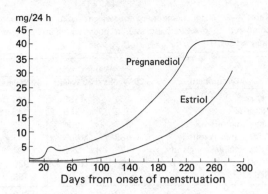

Figure 3–20. Urinary excretion of estriol and pregnanediol during pregnancy.

Plasma progesterone rises steadily during pregnancy (Fig 3–21), though the levels remain in the same range during the final 4 weeks of gestation, and some investigators have even noted a fall in the levels of progesterone before onset of labor. In the postovulatory phase of the menstrual cycle, the plasma progesterone level may be in the range of 5–10 ng/mL; by the end of pregnancy, the level may approach 150 ng/mL.

The major metabolite of progesterone is pregnanediol. Urinary excretion of pregnanediol increases gradually during pregnancy. From levels of a few milligrams per 24 hours in the luteal phase of the menstrual cycle, urinary pregnanediol rises steadily to levels of 35–40 mg/24 hours, and here again a plateau in values occurs during the last few weeks of gestation.

The hormones produced by the placenta are **chorionic gonadotropin** (hCG) and **chorionic somatomammotropin** (hCS) or **placental lactogen** (hPL). The placenta also produces a thyrotropin but not corticotropin.

Chorionic gonadotropin is a glycoprotein. Like the pituitary gonadotropins, it consists of an α and a β subunit. The α subunit seems to be identical with that of LH.

Chorionic gonadotropin is produced by the syncytiotrophoblast. It rises sharply following implantation of the fertilized ovum and reaches a peak value around the 60th–70th day of gestation. After this, it gradually falls to a lower level by about the 120th day of gestation. Normally, it remains at the lower level for the remainder of the pregnancy. Whereas chorionic gonadotropin may be present in the plasma in levels of about 0.1 IU/mL in the early days of pregnancy, it reaches peak values of approximately 120 IU/mL and then gradually falls to levels of around 20 IU/mL for the remainder of the pregnancy. hCG disappears from the circulation within 2 weeks after delivery.

The physiologic role of hCG, particularly in later pregnancy, is not known. It is apparently important for the maintenance of the corpus luteum in very early pregnancy, but after the first few weeks of gestation the corpus luteum itself is no longer essential to the maintenance of pregnancy. Recent studies suggest an immunologic role for hCG (may inhibit lymphocyte response to "foreign placenta").

Chorionic somatomammotropin (hCS) is a protein hormone that is immunologically similar to pituitary growth hormone (hGH). In some ways its metabolic activity is comparable to that of hGH. It is produced by the syncytiotrophoblast. It is detectable in the serum in very early pregnancy and rises steadily during pregnancy. From very low levels in early pregnancy, it rises to peak levels of 6–7 μg/mL at term (Fig 3–22).

hCS stimulates lipolysis, inhibits gluconeogenesis, and may have an important anabolic effect on mother and fetus. Moreover, it may be partially responsible for the diabetogenic nature of pregnancy. hCS has a synergistic action with hydrocortisone and insulin in the development of alveoli of the breast (a lactogenic effect).

Human chorionic thyrotropin (hCT) has been postulated to account for the thyroid-stimulating activity in early pregnancy and in molar pregnancy. However, some investigators believe that this activity is inherent in hCG.

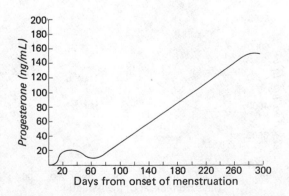

Figure 3–21. Progesterone levels in peripheral circulation during pregnancy.

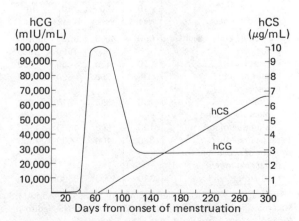

Figure 3–22. hCG and hCS levels in peripheral circulation during pregnancy.

PHYSIOLOGIC CHANGES IN PREGNANCY

General Physiologic Changes

Most of the physiologic alterations that occur during pregnancy are obligatory ones. If an organ is damaged or diseased so that it cannot respond to increased demands that may be imposed by the pregnant state, then decompensation and the symptoms and signs of impaired function will ensue.

Pregnancy is not a parasitic state. Under normal circumstances, the demands of the fetus are not met at the expense of the mother. "Eating for two" and "a tooth for every pregnancy" are fanciful sayings without basis in fact.

A. Weight Gain: (Table 3–1.) One of the most obvious changes in maternal physiology is weight gain, which somewhat exceeds that contributed by the fetus, placenta, amniotic fluid and enlarged uterus and breasts.

There is wide variation in the amount of weight gained during pregnancy, but one study showed an average of 12.5 kg (27½ lb). Of that amount, about 4.75 kg could be attributed to the fetus, placenta, and amniotic fluid. Another 1.3 kg represented the increase in weight of the uterus and breasts, and 1.25 kg could be accounted for by the increase in maternal blood volume. The remainder, 5.2 kg, would have to be explained by other phenomena. Most, if not all, of that remainder is due to increased deposition of fat. It has been suggested that this represents a readily available source of energy should the fetus require it. It is doubtful if there is any increase in maternal protein except that necessary for augmentation of the uterus, breasts, and maternal blood. Naturally, there is an added requirement for protein to supply the fetus and placenta. Approximately 500 g of protein are necessary for the uterus, breasts, and maternal blood and an additional 500 g for the fetus and placenta.

Table 3–1. Components of the average weight gained in normal pregnancy.*

	Amount (g) Gained at			
Component	10 Weeks	20 Weeks	30 Weeks	40 Weeks
Total gain of body weight	650	4000	8500	12,500
Fetus	5	300	1500	3300
Placenta	20	170	430	650
Liquor amnii	30	250	600	800
Increase of				
Uterus†	135	585	810	900
Mammary gland‡	34	180	360	405
Maternal blood	100	600	1300	1250
Total (rounded)	320	2100	5000	7300
Weight not accounted for				
(total gain minus				
total [rounded])	330	1900	3500	5200

*Reproduced, with permission, from Hytten FE, Thomson AM: Maternal physiological adjustments. In: Assali NS (editor): *Biology of Gestation.* Vol 1. Academic Press, 1968.
†Blood-free uterus.
‡Blood-free mammary glandular tissue.

Table 3–2. Water component of weight gain in pregnancy compared to measured increase in body water in 93 normal pregnancies.*

	Water Content (g)		
Component	20 Weeks	30 Weeks	40 Weeks
Fetus	264	1185	2343
Placenta	153	366	540
Liquor amnii	247	594	792
Added uterine muscle	483	668	743
Added mammary gland	135	270	304
Plasma	506	1058	920
Red cells	32	98	163
Total	1820	4239	5805
Measured Increase			
Edema			
None (47 women)	1740	4300	7500
Leg (20 women)	1810	4290	7880
Generalized (26 women)	2230	5740	10,830

*Reproduced, with permission, from Hytten FE, Thomson AM: Maternal physiological adjustments. In: Assali NS (editor): *Biology of Gestation.* Vol 1. Academic Press, 1968.

B. Water Balance: (Table 3–2). During pregnancy there is an average increase in total body water of 6.8 L in women who do not have clinically apparent edema. Again, the largest part of that gain is attributable to the fetus, placenta, amniotic fluid, uterus, breasts, and increased maternal blood volume. Until 30 weeks of gestation, all of the increased body water can be explained in this way, but, closer to term, there is also a "surplus" of extracellular fluid which amounts to 1–2 L.

C. Carbohydrate Metabolism: Pregnancy is characterized by increased amounts of circulating **insulin.** Injected insulin has a lesser effect in lowering blood glucose than during the nonpregnant state, suggesting that the increased need for insulin is due either to resistance to the effects of insulin at the level of the target cells or to increased destruction of insulin by the placenta.

D. Changes in Blood: A marked rise in **blood volume** occurs during pregnancy (Fig 3–23). The

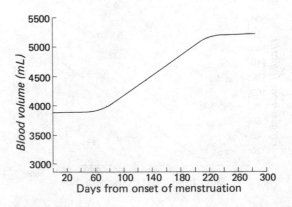

Figure 3–23. Increase in blood volume during pregnancy.

amount varies widely but averages about 1500 mL. The increased blood volume consists of an average increase of 450 mL of red cells and about 1000 mL of plasma. This increase begins during the first trimester and then gradually increases until it reaches a maximum a few weeks before term. The blood volume remains at that level until delivery.

Pregnancy normally is characterized by increased erythropoiesis. In spite of freely available iron for erythropoiesis, relatively more plasma is produced, so that normally there is a decline in hemoglobin concentration and hematocrit during pregnancy.

The increase in red cell count requires approximately 500 mg of additional iron. The fetus contains about 300 mg. Because the stored iron in the mother is only about 500 mg or less and because there is some loss of iron by excretion, exogenous sources of iron are required, particularly in late pregnancy.

In pregnancy the blood is in a **hypercoagulable state.** Plasma fibrinogen and factors VII, VIII, IX, and X are increased. However, there is a slight decrease in prothrombin time and partial thromboplastin time late in pregnancy.

Total protein concentration falls moderately in the first trimester of pregnancy and remains at that level until delivery. This is due mainly to a decrease in albumin. This change in plasma protein lowers the plasma oncotic pressure and increases the erythrocyte sedimentation rate.

Plasma lipids rise gradually during pregnancy, particularly in the second half. This is true of cholesterol, both free and esterified, phospholipids, and free fatty acids.

Serum alkaline phosphatase rises markedly, as do glutamic-oxaloacetic transaminase and lactate dehydrogenase. Serum cholinesterase is decreased during gestation.

Genital Organs

The **uterus** undergoes obvious major changes during pregnancy. It increases markedly in size, so that the capacity is increased about 500 times. This is achieved in the main by extreme hypertrophy of individual muscle cells. By the end of the fourth month, the uterus has become so large that it can be palpated above the symphysis pubica. The contractility of the uterus increases, and after the first trimester, irregular contractions may be felt by the patient and the examiner. These contractions become stronger and more frequent as term approaches.

The coiled uterine arteries gradually straighten to permit better circulation to the enlarged uterus. Uterine blood flow gradually increases during pregnancy, so that at term it is approximately 500 mL/min. This flow is greatly diminished during uterine contractions.

The **cervix** becomes very much softer and more congested as gestation progresses. These changes are apparent even in early pregnancy. There is marked hypertrophy of the endocervical glands, with a resultant increase in the amount of cervical mucus. Normally, this mucus does not form a fern pattern when it

is permitted to dry and is examined microscopically. The cervix becomes shorter (effaced) and slightly dilated as term approaches. This is particularly notable in multiparous individuals.

The **vagina** also becomes much softer and more congested. There is considerable loosening of the connective tissue to permit greater distensibility. An increased amount of glycogen in the epithelial cells normally occurs. Vaginal secretion is increased in volume, and an increased lactic acid content that causes a lowering of the pH to 4.0–6.0 is usual.

The **ovaries** are large and white, without active follicles other than the corpus luteum of pregnancy. The external surface frequently shows small irregular reddened areas that are patches of decidua.

The **oviducts** become elongated, but no hypertrophy of the muscle occurs. The epithelial lining remains low, but decidual cells may be noted here and there in the stroma. A decidual reaction may also develop on the serosal surface of the tubes.

An enormous increase in the size of the uterine and ovarian veins is characteristic of pregnancy.

Pronounced changes occur in the **breasts** also. They increase in size, and congestion is so great that breast tenderness is common in early pregnancy. Superficial veins become apparent. The breasts become more firm as a result of an increase in the alveoli. The nipples become larger, darker, and more erectile. Hypertrophy of sebaceous glands in the areolas produces small protrusions known as Montgomery's tubercles. Colostrum may be expressed after the second trimester, but this is more likely as full term approaches.

Other Endocrine Organs

A number of major changes in maternal endocrine physiology occur during pregnancy.

A. Anterior Pituitary: The pituitary gland increases in size during pregnancy and develops characteristic "pregnancy cells." The pituitary elaborates very little FSH during pregnancy, and the same is true of hGH. This markedly diminished function persists throughout pregnancy.

B. Adrenal Cortex: The increased estrogen levels in pregnancy cause a rise in **transcortin** (corticosteroid-binding globulin). This results in a large increase in bound cortisol in the circulation. There is also a small increase in the amount of free cortisol. The rate of secretion by the adrenal cortex is decreased, and the half-life of injected cortisol is prolonged. Thus, significant changes in tests of adrenal function occur during pregnancy. However, since the free cortisol is only slightly elevated, there is little evidence of hyperadrenocorticism.

C. Thyroid: The thyroid increases in size during pregnancy, and although the basal metabolic rate rises, this is not due to thyroid activity. The increased gland size is due to hyperplasia of the glandular tissue and increased vascularity. Much of the increase in basal metabolic rate is due to increased growth and oxygen consumption by the pregnant uterus, the fetus, and placenta. Estrogens also cause an increase in **thy-**

roid-binding globulin. Consequently, there is an increase in circulating **thyroid hormone** but no major increase in free thyroxine, the biologically active form of the hormone. The level increases during the second month of pregnancy, and the elevation persists until after delivery.

CARDIOVASCULAR SYSTEM

Cardiac output increases by approximately 30% during the first and second trimester and remains elevated until delivery (Fig 3–24). Some of the early studies of cardiovascular physiology in pregnancy resulted in erroneous conclusions, because they were performed with the patient supine. This resulted in pooling of blood in the lower extremities, compression of the vena cava by the pregnant uterus, and inaccurate estimations of cardiac output. There is a further increase during labor, particularly during the second stage. The increase in cardiac output is due to increased pulse rate and stroke volume.

There is no significant change in systolic blood pressure in normal pregnancy, but a slight decrease in diastolic blood pressure does occur as a consequence of decreased peripheral resistance. The pulse pressure is increased.

There is no change in **venous pressure** in the upper body, but there is a marked increase in venous pressure in the lower extremities in the supine, sitting, or standing position. Venous pressure rises from about 10 to about 30 cm of water. In some women, lying down for long periods causes decreased return of blood to the heart, decreased cardiac output, a fall in blood pressure, and edema.

The increased blood flow in pregnancy occurs mainly in the uterus, kidneys, and skin, but slight increases in blood flow to the breasts and intestines are recorded also.

The heart is displaced upward and to the left in pregnancy because of elevation of the diaphragm by the enlarging uterus. This causes left axis deviation in the ECG. Systolic murmurs are common during pregnancy over the pulmonary valve and at the apex of the heart.

THE RESPIRATORY SYSTEM

The diaphragm is elevated during pregnancy, but the ribs are flared so that there is little net change in thoracic capacity. There is a slight increase in the respiratory rate, but the **vital capacity** does not change significantly. Tidal volume is increased, so that the ventilation rate rises to about 10 L/min—an increase of more than 40%.

The lungs are somewhat compressed by the elevated diaphragm, and for this reason the **functional residual capacity** is decreased. This, together with the increased tidal volume, allows a much more effective mixing of gases so that the alveolar ventilation increases by about 65%.

The marked increase in ventilation rate results in a lowered alveolar P_{CO_2} and a decrease in blood bicarbonate. There is no change in blood pH. Oxygen consumption increases by almost 20% during pregnancy.

THE URINARY SYSTEM

There is generalized atony and dilatation of the urinary system throughout pregnancy. This results in retention of urine and susceptibility to infection.

Both **renal plasma flow** (RPF) and **glomerular filtration rate** (GFR) increase in early pregnancy and remain elevated throughout gestation (Fig 3–25). GFR may rise as much as 50%, but the plasma flow is less markedly elevated. Here again, position is very important. If the patient is standing, the GFR and RPF will be diminished. Hence, pregnant women produce less urine during the daytime and more at night. This makes urine concentration tests more difficult to evaluate during pregnancy.

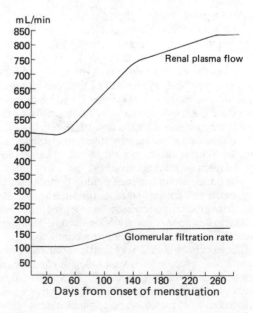

Figure 3–25. Changes in renal function during pregnancy.

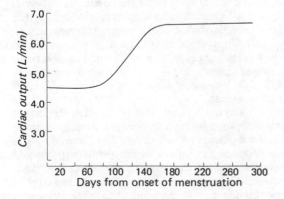

Figure 3–24. Increase in cardiac output during pregnancy.

Urea, creatinine, and uric acid are all excreted more effectively during pregnancy, so that the blood concentrations of these substances normally are lower than in the nonpregnant state.

Plasma renin and angiotensin levels are increased during pregnancy. Aldosterone production is increased owing to the effect of angiotensin II on the adrenal cortex. Although angiotensin II is a vasopressor, it is less active during pregnancy and therefore does not produce hypertension during normal pregnancy.

THE ALIMENTARY SYSTEM

The smooth muscle of the gastrointestinal system also becomes more atonic during pregnancy. Relaxation of the cardiac sphincter permits gastric contents to reach the esophagus to cause heartburn. Moreover, the gastric emptying time is prolonged. This may contribute to the nausea that often characterizes pregnancy. Acid and pepsin production are both decreased. The motility of the large bowel is diminished. The latter often explains the gaseous distention and constipation so frequently noted during pregnancy.

Liver function is apparently unchanged during gestation. There is, however, some degree of bile stasis, both in the liver and in the gallbladder. Therefore, cholestatic jaundice may occur during pregnancy, and gallstones are more common.

There are few reliable data concerning calcium metabolism during pregnancy. The amount of calcium in the term fetus is approximately 30 g. Pregnancy does not cause decalcification of teeth or bones in the mother.

There may be considerable hypertrophy of the gums, predisposing to gingivitis, probably related to the high amount of circulating estrogens.

SKIN

Pigmentation of the skin in several well-recognized areas is a common feature of pregnancy. Thus, a streak in the midline of the abdomen frequently turns dark brown, and irregular mottling of the cheeks and forehead commonly is noted. These changes may be due to increased amounts of the pigment melanin because there is an increase in melanocyte-stimulating hormone (MSH) during pregnancy.

Small, bright-red spider angiomas are commonly noted on the skin of the chest and upper extremities. They are probably related to the increased amounts of estrogen present, and, like the increased pigmentation, they subside after the pregnancy is over.

SKELETAL SYSTEM

Relaxation of the pelvic and intervertebral joints during pregnancy may explain the discomfort in the low back or extremities reported by many gravid women. It may be that these changes are due to relaxin, but the data concerning this hormone in humans are still fragmentary.

LABOR & PUERPERIUM

Human pregnancy has a mean duration of 265 days after ovulation, but considerable biologic variation is the rule. A difference of 3 weeks or more in either direction from that mean is considered abnormal and presents increased hazards to the infant.

Little is known with certainty about the factors responsible for the **initiation of labor.** Both mechanical and endocrine factors have been suggested. Thus, distention of the uterus or pressure on the cervix may be important. Endocrine factors include increased secretion of and increased uterine sensitivity to oxytocin; a decrease in the ability of progesterone to block myometrial contractility; increased levels of circulatory prostaglandins; and cortisol production by the fetal adrenals. The latter is of much interest because of the association of anencephalic fetuses with prolonged gestation.

The lack of a satisfactory assay for oxytocin has hampered efforts to clarify the role played by this hormone. Recent investigations have not been able to demonstrate changes in oxytocin levels in the peripheral circulation at the time of labor. However, it is known that women who have undergone removal of the posterior lobe of the pituitary can experience normal labor.

So many factors play a part in the initiation of labor that it is difficult to suggest a single hypothesis which combines them all. Nonetheless, evidence suggests that the fetus plays an important role in its own delivery. The fetus produces increasing amounts of cortisol as term approaches, and this acts on placental enzymes to cause a decrease in the production of progesterone along with an increase in the production of estrone and estradiol. These hormonal changes cause an increase in the production of prostaglandins by the placenta and myometrium. It may be that prostaglandins stimulate myometrial activity and cause the release of oxytocin from the maternal pituitary. The stimulation of myometrial contractility is probably due to the release of calcium from the sarcoplasmic reticulum. Next, the increased calcium activates adenosine triphosphatase (ATPase), which causes splitting of adenosine triphosphate (ATP) and initiates the action of actomyosin, the contractile protein.

With the delivery of the infant and placenta, the plasma and urine levels of chorionic gonadotropin soon fall to undetectable amounts and the levels of both estrogen and progesterone fall to very low values. This removes the inhibitory influence on the maternal pituitary gland, and prolactin and gonadotropic hormones are released into the circulation. The gonadotropins

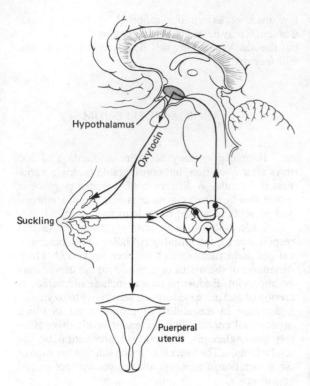

Figure 3–26. Schematic representation of postulated relation of suckling to oxytocin release and consequent contraction of myoepithelial and myometrial cells. (Redrawn from Caldeyro-Barcia R et al: *Congr Chileno Obstet Ginecol,* 1955.)

then resume the pattern characteristic of the menstrual cycle and soon demonstrate the dynamic burst of activity that characterizes ovulation. Following spontaneous abortion, this commonly occurs about 2 weeks after evacuation of the products of conception. Following term delivery, the resumption of menstruation depends on whether or not the patient lactates successfully. If lactation does not ensue, ovulation should occur about 4 weeks after delivery and menstruation about 2 weeks after that. If the patient lactates, ovulation may be postponed for months.

With the marked decrease in circulating estrogens and progesterone, stimulation of the uterus is withdrawn and the organ gradually undergoes involution. The remarkable decrease in size and weight is due to a reduction in size of individual muscle cells. The entire process takes approximately 6 weeks.

A portion of the decidua remains in the uterus following extrusion of the placenta. The decidua gradually degenerates and issues from the uterus, together with blood products, as lochia. For the first few days, a small amount of bleeding continues, causing the lochia to be red (lochia rubra). With completion of thrombosis of vessels, significant bleeding ceases and the lochia becomes yellowish (lochia alba or serosa).

The endometrium regenerates from the deeper remnants of glands that are left after the placenta has been extruded. The endometrium gradually grows in and undermines the placental site. The entire uterus is usually lined by normal endometrium about 6 weeks after delivery.

Physiologic preparation for **lactation** starts early in the pregnancy. Estrogen present in the circulation stimulates proliferation of the milk ducts, and progesterone stimulates growth of the alveoli. Chorionic somatomammotropin stimulates mammary growth and supports lactation.

Several days after delivery, the breasts become markedly hyperemic and congested. A small flow of colostrum may be noted. Colostrum contains more protein than breast milk as well as antibodies that may provide the infant with some protection against infection.

About the third day postpartum, milk production commences and the breasts become less tensely distended. The exact details of the hormonal background of lactation are not known. Steroid hormones inhibit the response of the breasts to prolactin. As they disappear from the circulation, lactation is permitted. Prolactin is also important for the continuation of lactation, but normal function of the thyroid and adrenal glands is necessary also.

Milk is removed from the breast by the suckling of the infant, and this stimulates the pituitary to release prolactin (Figs 3–26 and 3–27). Suckling, therefore, is responsible for the long-term continuation of lactation.

Once the puerperal process has been completed, regular ovulatory cycles usually supervene, and, if uninterrupted by further pregnancies, these continue until the climacteric. Many women have occasional anovulatory cycles, but these are not usually numerous until menopause approaches.

THE CLIMACTERIC

Menopause, or the cessation of menses, occurs most commonly at about age 50 in the USA, but a wide range is acknowledged. If menopause occurs before age 40, it is designated premature menopause. If bleeding occurs after age 53, one should consider it to be an abnormal sign and not menstruation. It is common for women to have some failures of ovulation for varying periods of time before menopause. A few women continue to ovulate regularly up to the time of menopause, whereupon, since there are no remaining follicles in the ovary that can be stimulated to produce hormones and bring about ovulation, menstruation ceases abruptly. Nevertheless, most women have a more gradual subsidence of the ovulatory mechanism, so that for months or years before the final cessation of bleeding they experience occasional skipped periods or episodes of irregular bleeding. The latter is occasioned by stimulation of a number of ovarian follicles and production of estrogen by these follicles, but

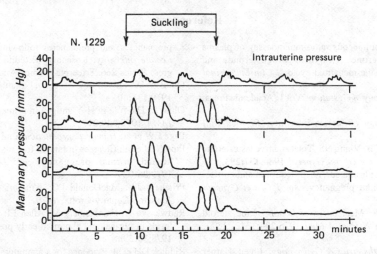

Figure 3–27. Effect of suckling on contractions of human uterus and mammary gland. Simultaneous records obtained on third day of puerperium. At end of suckling, activity of mammary gland ends abruptly, whereas that of uterus subsides more gradually. (Redrawn from Sico-Blanco Y et al: *Proc Third Uruguayan Congr Obstet Gynecol* 1960;3:283. Reproduced, with permission, from Danforth DN [editor]: *Textbook of Obstetrics and Gynecology,* 2nd ed. Harper & Row, 1971.)

because no one of them goes on to ovulation and the formation of a corpus luteum, there is no progesterone and no maturation of the endometrium to produce cyclic uterine bleeding.

In this intermediate phase between regular ovulatory menses and final menopause, the serum gonadotropins are in an intermediate range. Thus, whereas the maximum serum level of LH during a normal menstrual cycle is 100 mIU/mL—and that only very transiently at the time of ovulation—it is rarely above 10 mIU/mL during other phases of the cycle. In clearly postmenopausal women, it remains in the range of 100 mIU/mL or more, and in premenopausal women, it is frequently 50–70 mIU/mL. Clearly postmenopausal levels of FSH and LH are reached within a few months after final cessation of menses. By this time, serum estrogens are at very low levels, apparently derived from the peripheral conversion of androstenedione secreted by the adrenal cortex. Once this stage has been reached, it remains essentially unchanged and estrogen remains permanently at a very low level. After many years, the gonadotropins may gradually decline from the peak levels noted soon after menopause.

Over a period of many months or years after the estrogens reach very low levels, the genital organs undergo progressive atrophy. This varies widely from patient to patient, but, in many, obvious atrophy of the vulva, vagina, cervix, and uterus takes place. Once this state has been reached, it remains unchanged unless estrogen is administered.

After menopause, most of the estrogen produced is in the form of estrone or estrone sulfate. Postmenopausally, these hormones are not secreted by the ovaries but are produced from androstenedione generated by the adrenal cortex and converted to estrone, particularly in peripheral adipose tissue. Therefore, obese women may have greater conversion rates for these estrogens. It has been suggested that this capability may predispose obese women to the development of endometrial carcinoma. In any event, because progesterone decreases the number of estrogen receptor sites, these women may benefit from supplementary progesterone if estrogen is required for the treatment of menopausal symptoms.

● ● ●

References

Abraham GE et al: Simultaneous radioimmunoassay of plasma FSH, LH, progesterone, 17-hydroxyprogesterone, and estradiol-17β during the menstrual cycle. *J Clin Endocrinol Metab* 1972;**34**:312.

Assali NS (editor): *Biology of Gestation*. Vol 1. Academic Press, 1968.

Baird DT: Endocrinology of female infertility. *Br Med Bull* 1979;**35**:193.

Bammann BL, Coulan CB, Viang NS: Total and free testosterone during pregnancy. *Am J Obstet Gynecol* 1980;**137**:293.

Carr BR et al: Maternal plasma adrenocorticotropin and cortisol relationships throughout pregnancy. *Am J Obstet Gynecol* 1981;**139**:416.

Chan L, O'Malley BW: Mechanism of action of the steroid hormones. (3 parts.) *N Engl J Med* 1976;**294**:1322, 1372, 1430.

Danforth DN (editor): *Obstetrics & Gynecology*, 4th ed. Harper & Row, 1982.

Drake TS, Kaplan RA, Lewis TA: The physiologic hyperparathyroidism of pregnancy: Is it primary or secondary? *Obstet Gynecol* 1979;**53**:746.

Dunlop W: Renal physiology in pregnancy. *Postgrad Med J* 1979;**55**:329.

Faiman C, Reyes FI, Winter JS: Prepubertal and pubertal ovarian function. *Obstet Gynecol* 1979;**54**:161.

Fuchs F, Klopper A (editors): *Endocrinology of Pregnancy*, 2nd ed. Harper & Row, 1977.

Ganong WF: *Review of Medical Physiology*, 10th ed. Lange, 1981.

Grumbach MM et al (editors): *The Control of the Onset of Puberty*. Wiley, 1974.

Hauth JC et al: A role of fetal prolactin in lung maturation. *Obstet Gynecol* 1978;**51**:81.

Hytten FE, Leitch I: *The Physiology of Human Pregnancy*. Blackwell, 1964.

Jaffe RB et al: Physiologic and pathologic profiles of circulating human prolactin. *Am J Obstet Gynecol* 1973;**117**:757.

Liggins GC: Fetal influences on myometrial activity. *Clin Obstet Gynecol* 1973;**16**:148.

Lobo RA, Paul WL, Goebelsmann U: Dehydroepiandrosterone sulfate as an indicator of adrenal androgen function. *Obstet Gynecol* 1981;**57**:69.

Mishell DR et al: Steroid and gonadotropin levels in normal pregnancies and pregnancies following HMG therapy. In: *Female Infertility*. Rosenberg E (editor). International Congress Series 266. Excerpta Medica Amsterdam, 1973.

Odell WD: Physiology of sexual maturation. *West J Med* 1979;**131**:401.

Ohno S: The role of H-Y antigen in primary sex determination. *JAMA* 1978;**239**:217.

Page EW et al: *Human Reproduction*, 2nd ed. Saunders, 1976.

Pipe NGJ et al: Changes in fat, fat-free mass, and body water in human normal pregnancy. *Br J Obstet Gynaecol* 1979;**86**:929.

Pritchard JA, MacDonald PC: *Williams Obstetrics*, 15th ed. Appleton-Century-Crofts, 1976.

Radwanska E, Frankenberg V, Allen EI: Plasma progesterone levels in normal and abnormal early pregnancy. *Fertil Steril* 1978;**30**:398.

Riddick DH et al: Evidence for a nonpituitary source of amniotic fluid prolactin. *Fertil Steril* 1979;**31**:35.

Selenkow HH et al: Measurements and pathologic significance of human placental lactogen. In: *The Feto-Placental Unit*. Pecile A, Fenzi C (editors). Excerpta Medica Foundation, 1969.

Shome B, Parlow AF: Human follicle-stimulating hormone: First proposal for the amino acid sequence of the hormone-specific β subunit (hFSHβ). *J Clin Endocrinol Metab* 1974;**39**:203.

Shome B, Parlow AF: Human pituitary prolactin (hPRL): The entire linear amino acid sequence. *J Clin Endocrinol Metab* 1977;**45**:1112.

Sinha YN et al: A homologous radioimmunoassay for human prolactin. *J Clin Endocrinol Metab* 1973;**36**:509.

Sitteri PK, MacDonald PC: Role of extraglandular estrogen in human endocrinology. Chap 28, pp 615–629, in: *Handbook of Physiology*. Section 7. Endocrinology. Vol 2. Part 1. Greep RO, Atwood E (editors). Williams & Wilkins, 1973.

Tanner JM: *Growth at Adolescence*, 2nd ed. Blackwell, 1962.

West CP, McNeilly AS: Hormonal profiles in lactating and non-lactating women immediately after delivery and their relationship to breast engorgement. *Br J Obstet Gynaecol* 1979;**86**:501.

Winters AJ et al: Plasma ACTH levels in the human fetus and neonate as related to age and parturition. *J Clin Endocrinol Metab* 1974;**39**:269.

Yen SSC: Neuroendocrine regulation of the menstrual cycle. *Hosp Pract* (March) 1979;**15**:83.

The Placenta & Fetus | 4

Robert C. Goodlin, MD

A placenta may be defined as any intimate apposition or fusion of fetal organs to maternal tissues for the purpose of physiologic exchange. The basic parenchyma of all placentas is the trophoblast; when this becomes a membrane penetrated by fetal mesoderm, it is called the chorion.

In the evolution of viviparous species, the yolk sac presumably is the most archaic type of placentation, having developed from the egg-laying ancestors of mammals. In higher mammals, the allantoic sac fuses with the chorion, forming chorioallantoic placentas, all of which have mesodermal vascular villi. When the trophoblast actually invades the maternal endometrium (which in pregnancy is largely composed of decidua), a deciduate placenta results. In humans, maternal blood comes in direct contact with the fetal trophoblast. Thus, the human placenta may be described as a discoid, deciduate, hemochorial chorioallantoic placenta.

In the evolution of such a placenta, several major problems had to be solved: (1) The length of gestation had to be prolonged beyond one estrus or ovulatory cycle, a feat not yet accomplished by the marsupials. In higher primates, this problem was solved by trophoblastic elaboration of chorionic gonadotropin early enough to prevent the degradation of the corpus luteum. (2) The invasiveness of the trophoblast had to cease at the appropriate moment lest the maternal host be killed (as sometimes happens with choriocarcinoma). How this is accomplished is still a mystery. (3) Some mechanism had to be found to prevent the maternal tissue from immunologically rejecting the placenta, which is half paternal in origin and therefore antigenically dissimilar. The complete solution to this problem has yet to be found, but it appears that in some way the layer of trophoblast in contact with maternal blood acts as an immunologic barrier.

Development of the Human Placenta

A. Fertilization: Soon after ovulation, the endometrium develops its typical progestational pattern under the influence of progesterone from the corpus luteum. The peak of development is about a week after ovulation, which coincides with the expected time for implantation of a fertilized ovum. Pregnancy occurs when healthy spermatozoa in adequate numbers penetrate receptive cervical mucus, ascend through a patent uterotubal tract, and fertilize a healthy ovum within about 24 hours following ovulation. The spermatozoa that penetrate favorable mucus travel through the uterine cavity and the uterine tubes at a rate of about 6 mm/min. During this transit, an enzymatic change occurs that renders the spermatozoa capable of fertilizing the ovum. This process is called capacitation. The cellular union between a sperm and the egg is referred to as syngamy. The tip of the sperm head (acrosome) loses its cell membrane and probably releases a lytic enzyme that facilitates penetration of the zona pellucida surrounding the ovum.

Once the sperm head containing all of the paternal genetic material enters the cytoplasm of the ovum, a "zona reaction" occurs that prevents the entrance of a second sperm. The first cleavage occurs during the next 36 hours. As the conceptus continues to divide and grow, the peristaltic activity of the uterine tube slowly transports it to the uterus. This journey of the conceptus into the uterine cavity requires 6–7 days. Concomitantly, a series of divisions creates a hollow ball, the blastocyst, which then implants within the endometrium. The majority of cells in the wall of the blastocyst are trophoblastic; only a few are destined to become the embryo.

B. Development: Within a few hours after implantation, the trophoblast invades the endometrium and elaborates human chorionic gonadotropin (hCG), which nourishes the corpus luteum of the menstrual cycle and converts it to the corpus luteum of pregnancy. As the cytotrophoblasts (Langhans cells) divide and proliferate, they form transitional cells that are ultrastructurally more mature and a likely source of the hCG. Next, these transitional cells fuse, lose their individual membranes, and form the multinucleated syncytiotrophoblast which then ceases further mitotic division. Thus, it is the syncytial layer that becomes the front line of the invading fetal tissue, and syncytiotrophoblast is always in contact with maternal cells or plasma. Maternal capillaries and venules are tapped by the invading fetal columns to cause extravasation of maternal blood and the formation of small lakes (lacunae), the forerunners of the intervillous space.

The proliferating trophoblastic cell columns now branch to form secondary and tertiary villi. The mesoblast or central stromal core, also formed from the original trophoblast, invades these columns to form a supportive structure within which capillaries are formed. The embryonic body stalk (later to become the umbilical cord) then invades this stromal core to establish the fetoplacental circulation. This last step is most important, because if it fails to occur, the embryo will die and the avascular trophoblast may persist to form a hydatidiform mole (see below).

Where the placenta is attached, the branching villi resemble a leafy tree (the chorion frondosum), whereas that portion of the placenta covering the expanding conceptus is more smooth (chorion laeve). When the latter is finally pushed against the opposite wall of the uterus, the villi atrophy, leaving the amnion and chorion to form the 2-layered sac or fetal membranes (Fig 4–1).

About 40 days after conception, the trophoblast invades approximately 40–60 spiral arterioles, of which 12–15 may be called major arteries. Because of the pulsatile arterial pressure of blood which spurts from each of these major vessels, the chorionic plate is pushed away from the decidua to form 12–15 "tents" or maternal cotyledons. The remaining 24–45 tapped arterioles form minor vascular units that become crowded between the larger units. As the chorionic plate is pushed away from the basal plate, the anchoring villi pull the maternal basal plate up into septa that virtually surround the major cotyledons. Thus, at the center of each maternal vascular unit there is one artery that terminates in a thin-walled sac, but there are numerous maternal veins that open through the basal plate at random. Within each maternal vascular unit is the fetal vascular "tree" with the tertiary free-floating villi, the major area for physiologic exchange, acting like thousands of baffles that disperse the maternal bloodstream in many directions. A cross-sectional di-

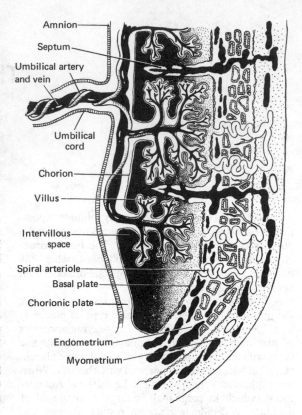

Figure 4–2. Schematic cross section of the circulation of the mature placenta. (Reproduced, with permission, from Benson RC: *Handbook of Obstetrics & Gynecology,* 7th ed. Lange, 1980.)

agram of the mature placenta is shown in Fig 4–2.

A summary of the major morphologic-functional correlations that take place in the development of the human placenta is offered in Table 4–1.

Microscopic Anatomy

The description of the finer structure of the placenta will be limited to the chorionic villus, which is the primary functioning unit. In the early placenta, 2 distinct layers of trophoblast may be seen: an inner layer of the cytotrophoblast and an outer layer of syncytiotrophoblast. In the mature placenta, only the syncytiotrophoblastic layer can be seen with the light microscope. By electron microscopy, however, scattered cytotrophoblastic cells can be seen between the syncytium and the underlying connective tissue layer. The center of the villus is filled with a loose stroma that contains a large number of fetal capillaries, spindly connective tissue cells, and a few phagocytic (Hofbauer) cells.

A diagram of the villus wall at term, viewed through the electron microscope, is shown in Fig 4–3. The outer membrane of the syncytium is thrown up into numerous microvilli that during life are constantly moving, streaming fingers of protoplasm which engulf microdroplets of maternal plasma. This process is called pinocytosis. The cytoplasm of the syncytium

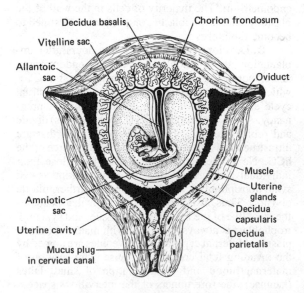

Figure 4–1. Relationships of structures in the uterus at the end of the 7th week of pregnancy. (Reproduced, with permission, from Benson RC: *Handbook of Obstetrics & Gynecology,* 7th ed. Lange, 1980.)

Table 4–1. Development of the human placenta.*

Days After Ovulation	Important Morphologic-Functional Correlations
6–7	Implantation of blastocyst.
7–8	Trophoblast proliferation and invasion. Cytotrophoblast gives rise to syncytium.
9–11	Lacunar period. Endometrial venules and capillaries tapped. Sluggish circulation of maternal blood.
13–18	Primary and secondary villi form; body stalk and amnion form.
18–21	Tertiary villi, 2–3 mm long, 0.4 mm thick. Mesoblast invades villi, forming a core. Capillaries form in situ and tap umbilical vessels which spread through blastoderm. Fetoplacental circulation established. Sluggish lacunar circulation.
21–40	Chorion frondosum; multiple anchored villi which form free villi shaped like "inverted trees." Chorionic plate forms.
40–50	Cotyledon formation: (1) Cavitation. Trophoblast invasion opens 40–60 spiral arterioles. Further invasion stops. Spurts of arterial blood form localized hollows in chorion frondosum. Maternal circulation established. (2) Crowning and extension. Cavitation causes concentric orientation of anchoring villi around each arterial spurt, separating chorionic plate from basal plate. (3) Completion. Main supplying fetal vessels for groups of second order vessels are pulled from the chorioallantoic mesenchyme to form first-order vessels of fetal cotyledons. (4) About 150 rudimentary cotyledons with anchoring villi remain, but without cavitation and crowning ("tent formation"). Sluggish, low pressure (5–8 mm Hg) flow of maternal blood around them.
80–225	Continued growth of definitive placenta. Ten to 12 large cotyledons form, with high maternal blood pressures (40–60 mm Hg) in the central intervillous spaces; 40–50 small to medium-sized cotyledons and about 150 rudimentary ones are delineated. Basal plate pulled up between major cotyledons by anchoring villi to form septa.
225–267 (term)	Cellular proliferation ceases, but cellular hypertrophy continues.

*Adapted from Reynolds SRM: *Am J Obstet Gynecol* 1966;**94**:432. (Reproduced, with permission, from Page EW, Villee CA, Villee DB: *Human Reproduction.* Saunders, 1976.)

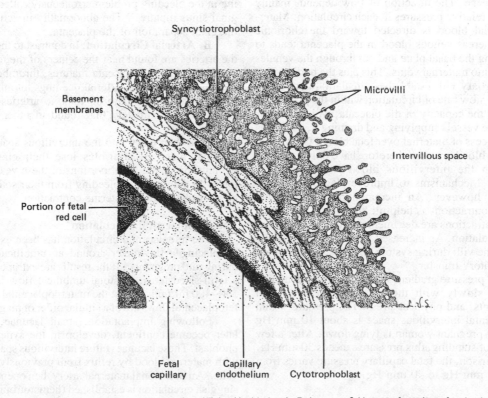

Figure 4–3. Drawing from an electron micrograph published by Verbeek, Robertson & Haust, of portion of a chorionic villus at term.

contains both rough and smooth endoplasmic reticulum, and most of the organelles, which are the mark of mature cells, elaborate protein for secretion. The cytotrophoblast is a more primitive cell specializing in growth and reproduction rather than intermediate metabolism and secretion. The protein hormones and steroids synthesized in the placenta originate in the syncytium. The trophoblast rests on 2 layers of connective tissue (basement membrane), and under this is the endothelium of the fetal capillary.

FUNCTIONS OF THE MATERNAL–PLACENTAL–FETAL UNIT

The placenta is a complex organ of internal secretion, releasing numerous hormones and enzymes into the maternal bloodstream. In addition, of course, it serves as the organ of transport for all fetal nutriments and metabolic products as well as for the exchange of oxygen and CO_2. Although mostly fetal in origin, the placenta depends almost entirely upon the maternal blood for its own nourishment.

The quantity and relative arterial pressure of the blood within different parts of the placenta vary from time to time. Nevertheless, there is little short-circuiting of blood from an arterial opening to an adjacent venous outlet because the arterial pressure of the maternal blood (60–70 mm Hg) actually causes it to be squirted into the low-pressure (20 mm Hg) intervillous space. The direction of flow depends mainly upon the relative pressures in each circulation. Maternal arterial blood is directed toward the chorionic plate, whereas venous blood in the placenta tends to flow along the basal plate and out through the venules directly into maternal veins. This plus the baffle effect of the tertiary villi establishes circulation currents.

The slow rate of circulation within the placenta is offset by the capacity of the placenta, which exceeds that of the vessels supplying and draining it, as well as by the excess of maternal over fetal blood. Changes in maternal blood pressure therefore have only a gradual effect on the intervillous blood pressure in the placenta. Mechanisms to improve placental transfer are few, however. An increased rate of rhythmic uterine contractions is helpful; but strong, prolonged labor contractions are detrimental to the placental and fetal circulation. An increased fetal heart rate tends to expand the villi during systole, and this is a minor aid in circulatory transfer.

The pressure gradient within the fetal circulation changes slowly with the mother's posture, fetal movements, and physical stress. The pressure within the placental intervillous space is about 10 mm Hg when the pregnant woman is lying down. After a few minutes of standing, this pressure exceeds 30 mm Hg. In comparison, the fetal capillary pressure varies from about 20 mm Hg to 40 mm Hg.

The Uteroplacental Circulation

The magnitude of the uteroplacental circulation is difficult to measure in women but has been estimated by a variety of methods—such as mounting an electromagnetic flowmeter about one uterine artery, using the nitrous oxide technic, or measuring the rate of disappearance of isotopes injected into the intervillous space. The consensus is that total uterine blood flow near term is 500–700 mL/min. Not all of this blood traverses the intervillous space. In pregnant sheep at term, about 85% of the uterine blood flow goes to the cotyledons and the rest to the myometrium and endometrium. One may assume that 400–500 mL of blood flow through the human placenta per minute in a patient near term who is lying quietly on her side and is not in labor.

A. Venous Circulation: Many randomly placed venous orifices can be identified over the entire decidua basalis (basal plate of the placenta).

The human placenta has no peripheral venous collecting system, a function frequently ascribed to a marginal sinus. Less than one-third of the blood drains from the placenta at its margin. A marginal sinus is not seen even in the early placenta, and subchorionic marginal lakes are not commonly found in the mature placenta. Occasionally, dilated maternal vessels are found beneath the periphery of the placenta; these have been described as wreath veins, or venous lakes. They may or may not communicate with the intervillous spaces, and their significance is still debated. Nonetheless, one of these thin-walled veins may be torn during premature marginal separation of the placenta, resulting in the bleeding problem erroneously called "marginal sinus rupture." The abnormality in actuality is marginal separation of the placenta.

B. Arterial Circulation: In contrast to the veins, the arteries are found near the centers of the maternal cotyledons. As the placenta matures, thrombosis decreases the number of arterial openings into the basal plate. At term, the ratio of veins to arteries is 2:1, which is approximately that found in other mature organs.

Near their entry into the intervillous spaces, the terminal maternal arterioles lose their elastic reticulum. Since the distal portions of these vessels are lost with the placenta, bleeding from their source can be controlled only by uterine contraction.

The Fetoplacental Circulation

The fetoplacental circulation has been estimated by placing a flowmeter around an umbilical artery during mid pregnancy. If the results are extrapolated to a term-sized fetus, the total umbilical flow is about 350–400 mL/min. Thus, the maternoplacental and the fetoplacental flows are of a similar order of magnitude.

Following implantation, small lacunae, which later become confluent, develop in the syncytiotrophoblast. These lacunae (future intervillous spaces) fill with maternal blood by reflux from previously tapped veins. An occasional maternal artery then opens, and a sluggish circulation is established (hematotropic phase of embryo).

The lacunar system is separated by trabeculae,

many of which develop buds or extensions. Within these branching projections, the cytotrophoblast forms a mesenchymal core. Later, the core is canalized, and connections are established with other potential blood vessels. The vascularized tufts are now referred to as villi.

The most extensive ramification of the villous tree occurs on that part of the chorion which is closest to the maternal blood supply (chorion frondosum). This is the site of the future placenta. Scattered villi also form over the remainder of the chorion (chorion reflexa) but soon atrophy, leaving a smooth surface (chorion laeve).

The villous system is better compared with an inverted tree rather than an inverted chandelier. The branches pass obliquely downward and outward within the intervillous spaces. This arrangement probably permits preferential currents or gradients of flow. Nevertheless, such an arrangement undoubtedly encourages intervillous fibrin deposition, commonly seen in the mature placenta.

Cotyledons (subdivisions of the placenta) can be identified early in placentation. They are separated by columns of fibrous tissue, the placental septa. Some communication between cotyledons does exist, however, via the subchorionic lake in the roof of the intervillous spaces.

Prior to labor, placental filling occurs whenever the uterus contracts (Braxton Hicks contractions). At these times the maternal venous exits are closed but the thicker-walled arteries are only slightly narrowed. When the uterus relaxes, blood drains out through the maternal veins. Hence, blood is not squeezed out of the placenta with each contraction nor does it enter the placenta in appreciably greater amounts during relaxation.

The effects of labor contractions upon maternal flow through the placenta have been studied by cineradiographic aortography in human subjects. During the height of an average first stage contraction, most of the maternal vascular units (cotyledons) are devoid of any flow and the remainder are only partially filled. Thus, intermittently—for periods of up to a minute—maternoplacental flow virtually ceases. Therefore, it should be evident that any extended prolongation of the contractile phase, as in uterine tetany from overstimulation with oxytocin, could lead to fetal hypoxia.

Aortocaval compression is a common cause of abnormal fetal heart rate during labor. In the third trimester, the contracting uterus obstructs its own blood supply to the level of L3–4 (Poseiro effect) when the mother is supine. This obstruction is completely relieved by turning the patient on her side. Although only about 30% of supine parturients will demonstrate aortocaval compression, women in labor (particularly after epidural anesthesia) should not be maintained in a supine position.

In all supine pregnant women at term, obstruction of the inferior vena cava by uterine pressure is relatively complete. However, only about 10% have inadequate collateral circulation and develop the "maternal supine hypotension" syndrome. This syndrome is characterized by decreased cardiac output, bradycardia, and hypotension. These women are likewise relieved by the lateral position. Indeed, most pregnant women near term will sleep on their side by instinct to avoid such problems.

Uterine blood flow and placental perfusion values are directly correlated with the pregnancy-related increase in maternal plasma volume. Moreover, newborn size depends upon the degree of increase in maternal plasma volume. Thus, the growth-retarded fetus is invariably associated with relative maternal hypovolemia and oligohydramnios. Uterine volume increase is closely correlated with an increased maternal plasma volume, although it is unknown whether this relationship is causal. Relative maternal hypovolemia is found in association with most complications of pregnancy, including those of pregnancy-induced hypertension, fetal growth retardation, premature labor, and various fetal anomalies.

Internal Secretions of the Placenta

The placenta produces many hormones, both steroid and polypeptide. Each of the polypeptide products has been shown to have structural homology and immunologic coreactivity with analogs from the anterior pituitary.

Human chorionic gonadotropin (hCG) is a glycopolypeptide hormone with a molecular weight of 39,000 produced in the syncytiotrophoblast. hCG is produced by normal colonic mucous cells, the liver, and perhaps the anterior pituitary gland, all in small amounts. hCG is composed of 2 subunits (α and β) which, when separated, have no biologic activity. The α subunit is nearly identical to that of human pituitary luteinizing hormone (LH), thyroid-stimulating hormone (TSH), and follicle-stimulating hormone (FSH). The β subunit of hCG is responsible for its biologic activity, and 97 of its 145 amino acids are identical with those of LH. LH and hCG have many common activities. The synthesis of β subunits is rate-limiting, and there are circulating free α subunits of hCG in maternal serum after the first trimester. hCG has been detected as early as 6 days after ovulation and has a doubling time of 2 days. After the first trimester, serum hCG declines. Umbilical blood contains only 1/800 the value of maternal blood.

hCG maintains the corpus luteum of pregnancy and stimulates progesterone and estrogen production. After the decline of the corpus luteum (after the ninth week of gestation), the function of hCG in human pregnancy is unknown. It may continue to influence placental steroidogenesis. Additional functions include promotion of steroidogenesis of the fetoplacental unit and fetal testicular secretion of testosterone. hCG is also thyrotropic, which accounts for the increased thyroid function seen in women with trophoblastic neoplasms.

Human placental lactogen (hPL), or human chorionic somatomammotropin, has structural, immunologic, and biologic similarities to both human growth hormone (hGH) and prolactin (hPL). It is synthesized by the syncytiotrophoblast of the placenta and is found in urine, amniotic fluid, and maternal serum. hPL has a serum half-life of 30 minutes and is the major protein synthetic product of the placenta, producing up to 3 g in 24 hours. Almost all of the amino acids in hPL are actual or acceptable correspondents to those in hGH. hPL secretion is apparently autonomous, correlating with no known obstetric factor other than placental size. Acute changes in maternal blood sugar levels can produce dramatic changes in maternal hPL levels.

hPL function may be a major physiologic regulator of late pregnancy with effects on fatty acid and carbohydrate metabolism. These contribute to the common relative insulin resistance of pregnancy. Low hPL values correlate positively with pregnancies complicated by hypertension and fetal growth retardation, and high hPL values correlate positively with situations associated with large placentas such as diabetes, isoimmunization, and twins. Whether hPL determinations are useful by themselves in the assessment of complications or in the management of high-risk pregnancy is debatable.

Placental Sulfatase Deficiency

Cases of placental sulfatase deficiency have been reported, all associated with healthy male infants, which suggests an X-linked recessive inheritance. Because sulfates must be removed from steroids before the placenta can metabolize them, the syndrome is characterized by extremely low maternal estriol excretions but without evidence of fetal jeopardy. There is also an associated delayed or even absent spontaneous labor. The diagnosis has been made antepartum by injecting a dehydroepiandrosterone-sulfate load into the amniotic fluid and observing no increase in maternal estrogen excretion.

PLACENTAL TRANSPORT

The placenta has a high rate of metabolism, with consumption of oxygen and sugar equal to that of the fetus. Presumably, this high requirement is for its multiple transport and biosynthesis activities. The placenta continues its functional development throughout gestation, despite the fact that it does not continue to increase in size or total DNA content. Two stages of placental growth are clearly discernible. The first stage is characterized by progressive increase in parenchymal components and terminates at approximately the 36th week of gestation. The second stage continues to term and is characterized by continued fetal growth but without any increase in placental functional tissue. During the second stage, fetuses with small placentas tend to outgrow the functional capacity of their placentas.

The primary and most important function of the placenta, of course, is the transport of oxygen and nutrients to the fetus and the reverse transfer of CO_2, urea, and other catabolites ack to the mother. The transfer of materials across the placental membrane takes place by at least 5 mechanisms: simple diffusion, facilitated diffusion, active transport, pinocytosis, and leakage.

Simple Diffusion

This is the method by which gases and other simple molecules cross the placenta. The rate of transport depends upon the chemical gradient, the diffusion constant of the compound in question, and the total area of the placenta available for the transfer. The chemical gradient, ie, the difference in concentration in the fetal and maternal plasmas, is in turn affected by the rates of flow of uteroplacental and umbilical blood. Diffusion is also the method of transfer for exogenous compounds, such as certain drugs.

The placental membrane is often referred to as a "barrier," but there are very few drugs, for example, that escape transport altogether. A few compounds, such as heparin, are of sufficiently large molecular size that minimal transfer occurs, but this characteristic is almost unique among drugs. A few compounds, such as carbon monoxide, may attach themselves so firmly to cells (in this case the hemoglobin of the maternal red cells) that there is very little left in the plasma for transport. Compounds such as histamine or epinephrine may be deaminated by placental enzymes during the transport process. With these few exceptions, the placenta rarely acts as a barrier.

The average concentration gradient for oxygen between mother and fetus is about 20 mm Hg. This seems high, but it must be remembered that even near term about 40% of the oxygen extracted from maternal blood by the uterus is utilized by the myometrium and by the placenta itself.

The mean oxygen consumption of the fetus is remarkably similar among mammals. For the sheep fetus, it is 7.1 mL/kg/min; for the cow fetus, 6.8 mL/kg/min; and for the monkey fetus, 7.0 mL/kg/min. In sheep, the oxygen consumption for the total uteroplacental mass is 14.1 mL/kg/min, so that approximately half of the total quantity of oxygen delivered to the uterus is consumed by the fetus. Of that amount, about half is accounted for by the metabolism of glucose and the balance by the catabolism of amino acids and lactate.

In general, there is an inverse relationship between the arteriovenous difference of oxygen across the umbilical to uterine circulations and the total uterine blood flow, so that oxygen consumption by the fetus remains within a narrow range despite wide changes in uterine blood flow.

Facilitated Diffusion

The prime example of a substance transported by facilitated diffusion is glucose, the major source of energy for the fetus. The transfer of glucose from mother to fetus occurs more rapidly than can be accounted for by the Fick equation that is used to calculate simple diffusion. Presumably, a carrier system operates with the chemical gradient (as opposed to active transport, which operates against the gradient) and may become saturated at high glucose concentrations. In the steady state, the glucose concentration in fetal plasma is about two-thirds that of the maternal concentration, reflecting the rapid rate of fetal utilization.

Substances of low molecular weight (less than 1000) diffuse across the placenta with ease. Thyroxine, thiamine, and many drugs, including alcohol and morphine, are in this group. Large molecules (with molecular weights more than 1000) such as blood proteins, insulin, pituitary hormones, and chorionic gonadotropin will not pass the placental barrier by diffusion.

Active Transport

When compounds such as the essential amino acids and water-soluble vitamins are found in higher concentration in fetal blood than in maternal blood — and when this difference cannot be accounted for by differential protein-binding effects — the presumption is that the placenta concentrates the materials during passage by an active transport system. In the case of selected amino acids, this has been proved in human subjects by observing that the natural L-forms are transferred with greater rapidity than the unnatural D-forms, which are simply optical isomers of identical molecular size. Thus, the selective transport of specific essential nutrients is accomplished by enzymatic mechanisms.

Pinocytosis

The electron microscope has shown pseudopodical projections of the syncytiotrophoblastic layer that reach out, as it were, to surround minute amounts of maternal plasma. These particles are carried across the cell virtually intact, to be released on the other side, whereupon they promptly gain access to the fetal circulation. Certain other proteins (ie, foreign antigens) may be immunologically rejected. This process may work both to and from the fetus, but how selective it is has not been determined. Complex proteins, small amounts of fat, and immune bodies or even viruses may traverse the placenta in this way. For the passage of complex proteins, highly selective processes involving special receptors are involved. For example, maternal antibodies of the IgG class are freely transferred, whereas other antibodies are not.

Leakage

Gross breaks in the placental membrane may occur that allow the passage of intact cells. Despite the fact that the hydrostatic pressure gradient is normally from fetus to mother, tagged red cells and white cells have been found to travel in either direction. Such breaks probably occur most often during labor, because it is at this time that fetal red cells can most often be demonstrated in the maternal circulation. This is the mechanism by which the mother may become sensitized to fetal red cell antigens such as Rh factor.

In general, those compounds that are essential for the minute-by-minute homeostasis of the fetus (oxygen, CO_2, water, sodium, etc) are transported very rapidly by diffusion. Compounds required for the synthesis of new tissues (amino acids, enzyme cofactors such as vitamins, etc) are transported by an active process. Substances such as certain maternal hormones, which may modify fetal growth and are at the upper limits of admissible molecular size, may diffuse very slowly, whereas mature proteins such as IgG immunoglobulins probably reach the fetus by the process of pinocytosis.

PATHOLOGY OF THE PLACENTA

At term, the normal placenta is a blue-red, rounded, flattened, meaty discoid organ 15–20 cm in diameter and 2–4 cm thick. It weighs 400–600 g, or about one sixth the normal weight of the newborn. The umbilical cord arises from almost any point on the fetal surface, seemingly at random. The fetal membranes arise from the placenta at its margin. In multiple pregnancy, one or more placentas may be present depending upon the number of ova implanted and the type of segmentation that occurs. The placenta is derived from both maternal and fetal tissue. At term, about four-fifths of the placenta is of fetal origin.

The maternal portion of the placenta amounts to less than one-fifth of the total placenta by weight. It is composed of compressed sheets of decidua basalis, remnants of blood vessels, and, at the margin, spongy decidua. Irregular grooves or clefts divide the placenta into cotyledons. The maternal surface is torn from the uterine wall at birth and as a result is rough, red, and spongy.

The fetal portion of the placenta is composed of numerous functional units called villi. These are branched terminals of the fetal circulation and provide for transfer of metabolic products. The villous surface, which is exposed to maternal blood, may be as much as 12 m² (130 square feet). The fetal capillary system within the villi is almost 50 km (27 miles) long. Most villi are free within the intervillous spaces, but an occasional anchor villus attaches the placenta to the decidua basalis. The fetal surface of the placenta is covered by amniotic membrane and is smooth and shiny. The umbilical cord vessels course over the fetal surface before entering the placenta.

PLACENTAL TYPES

Circumvallate (or Circummarginate) Placentas

In about 1% of cases, the delivered placenta will show a small central chorionic plate surrounded by a thick whitish ring that is composed of a double fold of amnion and chorion with fibrin and degenerated decidua in between. This circumvallate placenta may predispose to premature marginal separation and sec-

Figure 4–4. Marked circumvallate or extrachorial placenta.

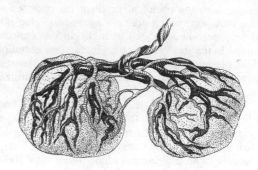

Figure 4–6. Bipartite placenta.

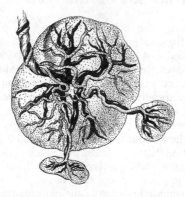

Figure 4–5. Succenturiate placenta.

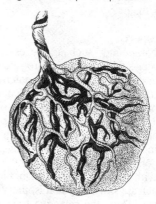

Figure 4–7. Marginal insertion or battledore placenta.

ond trimester antepartum bleeding (Fig 4–4).

This uncommon extrachorial placenta is of uncertain origin. It is associated with increased rates of slight to moderate antepartal bleeding, early delivery, and perinatal death. Older multiparas are more prone to its development. Low-birth-weight infants and extrachorial placentas seem related.

Succenturiate Lobe

Occasionally there may be an accessory cotyledon, or succenturiate lobe, with vascular connections to the main body of the placenta. A succenturiate lobe may not always deliver with the parent placenta during the third stage of labor. This leads to postpartal hemorrhage. If a careful examination of the delivered membranes reveals torn vessels, immediate manual exploration of the uterus is indicated for removal of an accessory lobe (Fig 4–5).

Bipartite Placenta

A bipartite placenta is an uncommon variety. The placenta is divided into 2 separate lobes but united by primary vessels and membranes. Retention of one lobe after birth will cause hemorrhagic and septic complications. Examine the vasculature and note the completeness of membranes of a small placenta for evidence of a missing lobe and recover the adherent portion without delay (Fig 4–6).

Marginal Insertion of Cord (Battledore Placenta)

The umbilical cord may be found inserted into the chorionic plate at almost any point, but when it inserts at the margin it is sometimes called a battledore placenta (Fig 4–7).

Placenta Membranacea

This type of placenta is one in which the decidua capsularis is so well vascularized that the chorion laeve does not atrophy and villi are maintained. Hence, the entire fetal envelope is a functioning placenta.

Placenta Accreta

In rare cases, the placenta is abnormally adherent to the myometrium, presumably because it developed where there was a deficiency of decidua. Predisposing factors include placenta previa (one-third of cases), previous cesarean (one-fourth), a prior D&C (one-fourth), and grand multiparity. The adherence may be partial or total. Rarely, the placenta may invade the myometrium deeply (placenta increta) or even perforate the uterus (placenta percreta). When attempts are made to remove a placenta accreta manually, hemorrhage may be severe. The treatment is hysterectomy.

Placenta Previa

This abnormality is discussed in Chapter 33.

PLACENTAL DISORDERS

Placental Polyps

An uninfected, retained fragment of placenta that has become enmeshed in laminar depositions of blood is called a placental polyp. Eventually, a placental polyp may become a nidus of infection or it may be responsible for late hemorrhage (over 24 hours postpartum).

Placental Infections (Placentitis)

Bacterial infection of the placenta usually involves the fetal surface, particularly the chorion and amnion near the insertion of the umbilical cord. Placentitis generally is a sequela to chorioamnionitis. A "steamy" or milky appearance of the membranes due to the presence of inflammatory cells and exudative products is characteristic of chorioamnionitis and placentitis. Perivascular leukocytic infiltration of the cord and placental fetal vessels is typical of placentitis. Focal infection involving the villi and even the decidual plate may occur. Placentitis commonly is a precursor of puerperal sepsis—a major cause of maternal mortality and morbidity. Fetal pneumonia, omphalitis, and septicemia also are serious complications associated with chorioamnionitis or placentitis.

Placental Infarcts

True infarcts of the placenta, which appear as pale firm areas containing degenerating villi and fibrin, are quite common. They result from interference with the maternal blood supply to the intervillous space. The trophoblast is dependent upon the maternal rather than the fetal blood supply so that occlusion of a maternal artery supplying a major cotyledon will result in the ischemic necrosis of a large portion of that vascular unit. This occurs more often with preeclampsia-eclampsia than during normal pregnancy. **Intervillous thrombosis** with extensive fibrin deposition is common also. When intervillous thrombosis is extensive, "placental insufficiency" and fetal growth retardation or fetal death may develop.

Placental Tumors

Except for hydatidiform mole and choriocarcinoma (see below), tumors of the placenta are rare. The only common benign tumor is a chorioangioma, which is probably a chorionic mesenchymal hamartoma. This abnormality has little clinical significance.

THE UMBILICAL CORD

The umbilical cord is a gray, soft, coiled, easily compressible structure that connects the fetus with its placenta. The average length of the umbilical cord is about 50 cm, but this is quite variable and extremes of from less than 5 to over 150 cm have been reported. The cord is 1–2.5 cm in diameter. The outer surface consists of amnion. Normally, the cord contains 2 umbilical arteries and a single umbilical vein. The

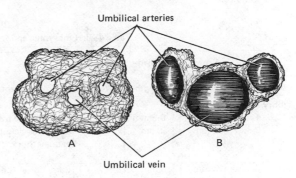

Figure 4–8. Drawings of cross sections of umbilical cord *(A)* after blood vessels are empty, and *(B)* while they are filled, as in utero. The central vein and 2 arteries occupy most of the space. (Based on photography by SRM Reynolds.)

remainder of the space is filled with a mucoid material—Wharton's jelly—which is the same as the ground substance of other body tissues. When the cut end of the cord is examined after delivery, the vessels ordinarily are collapsed (Fig 4–8A), but if a segment of cord is fixed while the vessels are distended—as they are during life—the characteristic appearance is as shown in Fig 4–8B.

Abnormalities of the Umbilical Cord

A. Velamentous Insertion: A velamentous insertion is one in which the umbilical vessels divide to course through the membranes before reaching the chorionic plate. When these vessels present themselves ahead of the fetus (vasa previa), they may rupture during labor to cause fetal exsanguination. Delicate secondary or tertiary vascular radicals supported only by the membranes pass to the placenta. Prepartal trauma to the membranes or traction on the cord during the birth process may lacerate placental arteries or veins, and fetal blood loss may be critical. Velamentous insertions occur in about 1% of placentas, and 25–50% of these infants will have structural defects. Only the testing of all episodes of painless vaginal bleeding for fetal hemoglobin (Apt test or hemoglobin electrophoresis) will allow detection of this cause of fetal distress or death.

B. Variations in Length of Cord: The normal length of the cord is 20–70 cm. With an unusually short cord, an umbilical hernia is likely, and tearing or compression of the cord or placental separation may occur. When the cord is long, encirclement of the fetus or compression of the cord is a common problem.

C. Knots in the Cord: True and false knots may occur in the cord. True knots occur in about one per 200 deliveries. If tight, true knots will cause fetal asphyxia and death.

False knots are developmental variations with no clinical importance.

D. Loops of the Cord: One or more loops of cord may be found wound about the neck in about 20% of deliveries and around the body in about 2%. Loops may involve fetal extremities also. In rare instances,

Table 4–2. Embryonic and fetal growth and development.

Fertilization Age (Weeks)	Crown-Rump Length	Crown-Heel Length	Weight	Gross Appearance	Internal Development
Embryonic stage					
1	0.5 mm	0.5 mm	?	Minute clone free in uterus.	Early morula. No organ differentiation.
2	2 mm	2 mm	?	Ovoid vesicle superficially buried in endometrium.	External trophoblast. Flat embryonic disk forming 2 inner vesicles (amnioecto-mesodermal and endodermal).
3	3 mm	3 mm	?	Early dorsal concavity changes to convexity; head, tail folds form; neural grooves close partially.	Optic vesicles appear. Double heart recognized. Fourteen mesodermal somites present.
4	4 mm	4 mm	0.4 g	Head is at right angle to body; limb rudiments obvious, tail prominent.	Vitelline duct only communication between umbilical vesicle and intestines. Initial stage of most organs has begun.
8	3 cm	3.5 cm	2 g	Eyes, ears, nose, mouth recognizable; digits formed, tail almost gone.	Sensory organ development well along. Ossification beginning in occiput, mandible, and humerus (diaphysis). Small intestines coil within umbilical cord. Pleural pericardial cavities forming. Gonadal development advanced without differentiation.
Fetal stage					
12	8 cm	11.5 cm	19 g	Skin pink, delicate; resembles a human being, but head is disproportionately large.	Brain configuration roughly complete. Internal sex organs now specific. Uterus no longer bicornuate. Blood forming in marrow. Upper cervical to lower sacral arches and bodies ossify.
16	13.5 cm	19 cm	100 g	Scalp hair appears. Fetus active. Arm-leg ratio now proportionate. Sex determination possible.	External sex organs grossly formed. Myelinization. Heart muscle well developed. Lobulated kidneys in final situation. Meconium in bowel. Vagina and anus open. Ischium ossified.
20	18.5 cm	22 cm	300 g	Legs lengthen appreciably. Distance from umbilicus to pubis increases.	Sternum ossifies.
24	23 cm	32 cm	600 g	Skin reddish and wrinkled. Slight subcuticular fat. Vernix. Primitive respiratorylike movements.	Os pubis (horizontal ramus) ossifies.
28	27 cm	36 cm	1100 g	Skin less wrinkled; more fat. Nails appear. If delivered may survive with optimal care.	Testes at internal inguinal ring or below. Talus ossifies.
32	31 cm	41 cm	1800 g	Fetal weight increased proportionately more than length.	Middle fourth phalanges ossify.
36	34 cm	46 cm	2200 g	Skin pale, body rounded. Lanugo disappearing. Hair fuzzy or woolly. Ear lobes soft with little cartilage. Umbilicus in center of body. Testes in inguinal canals; scrotum small with few rugae. Few sole creases.	Distal femoral ossification centers present.
40	40 cm	52 cm	3200+ g	Skin smooth and pink. Copious vernix. Moderate to profuse silky hair. Lanugo hair on shoulders and upper back. Ear lobes stiffened by thick cartilage. Nasal and alar cartilages. Nails extend over tips of digits. Testes in full, pendulous, rugous scrotum (or labia majora) well developed. Creases cover sole.	Proximal tibial ossification centers present. Cuboid, tibia (proximal epiphysis) ossify.

compression may cause strangulation (gangrene) of an arm or leg, or death of the fetus may ensue.

E. Torsion of the Cord: Torsion of the cord occurs counterclockwise in the vast majority of cases. If twisting is extreme, fetal asphyxia may result.

F. Single Artery: A 2-vessel cord (absence of one umbilical artery) occurs about once in 500 deliveries (6% of twins). The cause may be aplasia or atrophy of the missing vessel. The anomaly is more common in blacks than whites but is equally frequent in primiparas and multiparas. The incidence of single umbilical artery is approximately 1%, and about half of the infants will have structural defects. There is also a strong association between fetal structural anomalies and placental vascular occlusion or thrombosis. A routine examination for such vascular defects is a perinatal requirement.

THE FETUS

The human fetus is born about 9 calendar months or 40 weeks after the first day of the last menstrual period. This time span is called the "gestational age," although obviously conception cannot occur until 2 weeks after the beginning of this calculation (LMP). The 9 calendar months are divided into 3 trimesters for convenient classification of certain obstetric events. The term fetus is born 9 lunar cycles (29.53 days each) after conception, and the postconceptional age in weeks is used to denote the stage of development of the embryo.

Fetal Growth & Development

During the first 8 weeks, the term **embryo** is used to denote the developing organism because it is during this time that all of the major organs are formed (Table 4–2). After the eighth week, the word **fetus** is proper; this is a period when further growth and organ maturation occur. The loss of a fetus weighing less than 500 g (about 22 weeks of gestational age) is called an **abortion.** A fetus weighing 500–1000 g (22–28 weeks) is called **immature.** From 28–36 weeks, it is referred to as **premature.** A **term fetus** arbitrarily is defined as one that has attained 37 weeks of gestational age.

The growth of the fetus may be conveniently described in units of 4 weeks of gestational age, beginning with the first day of the last menstrual period:

8 weeks: The embryo is 2.1–2.5 cm in length and weighs 1 g, and the head comprises almost half of the bulk. The hepatic lobes may be recognized. Red blood cells are forming in the yolk sac and liver and contain hemoglobin. The kidneys are beginning to form.

12 weeks: The fetus is 7–9 cm long and weighs 12–15 g. The fingers and toes have nails, and the external genitalia may often be recognized as male or female. The volume of amniotic fluid is about 30 mL. The intestines undergo peristalsis and are capable of absorbing glucose.

16 weeks: The length is 14–17 cm and the weight about 100 g. The sex is discernible. In addition to hemoglobin F, formation of hemoglobin A begins.

20 weeks: The fetal weight is about 300 g. The fetal heart tones may often be detected by stethoscope. Fetal movements have been perceived by the mother for 2 or 3 weeks. The uterine fundus is near the level of the umbilicus.

24 weeks: Weight 600 g. Some fat is beginning to be deposited beneath the wrinkled skin. Viability is reached by the 24th week, but survival at this stage is still relatively rare.

28 weeks: Weight about 1050 g and length about 37 cm. The lungs are now capable of breathing, but the surfactant content is low; survival is possible in level 2 or level 3 neonatal centers.

32 weeks: Weight about 1700 g and length 42 cm. If born at this stage, about 5 out of 6 may survive.

36 weeks: Weight about 2500 g and length about 47 cm. The skin has lost its wrinkled appearance. The chances for survival are good.

40 weeks: The term fetus averages 50 cm in length and 3200–3500 g in weight. The fetal head has a maximal transverse (biparietal) diameter of 9.5 cm, and when it is well flexed the diameter from the brow to a point beneath the occiput (suboccipitobregmatic) is also 9.5 cm. The average fetus, therefore, requires a cervical dilatation of almost 10 cm before it can descend into the vagina.

FETAL & EARLY NEONATAL PHYSIOLOGY

There are 3 stages of fetal nutrition: (1) Absorption: Minimal quantities of tubal and uterine fluid are taken in by the fertilized ovum prior to nidation. (2) Histotrophic transfer: Strategic and waste materials are passed between the early embryo and decidua before the establishment of an effective fetal circulation. (3) Hematotrophic transfer: Anabolic and catabolic products traverse the placental barrier between the fetal and maternal circulations by both active and passive processes.

Hematology

The major items to be considered are erythropoiesis, fetal hemoglobin, the lymphoid system, and fetal immunology.

The fetal circulation is established at about 25 postconceptional days, and at that time the major sources of red cells are blood islands in the body stalk. By 10 weeks, the liver assumes the major role in erythropoiesis, but the spleen and the bone marrow gradually take over this function and, by term, the bone marrow is the source of at least 90% of the red cells. The hormone erythropoietin is produced in considerable quantities by the 32nd gestational week, but this falls almost to zero during the first week after birth—unless the infant is anemic, in which case the values are higher.

Premature as well as mature infants are polycythemic by adult standards, having red cell counts of 4–6 million/μL. The fetus also presents a relative leukocytosis, the white count being 15–20 thousand/μL at term. Macrocytic erythrocytes are typical of the entire fetal period. The life span of the fetal and adult red cell is the same—approximately 120 days.

The synthesis of hemoglobin occurs in the proerythroblast, normoblast, and reticulocyte but not in the mature red cell. The fetal hemoglobins present prior to 12 weeks are Gower I and II and Portland I. During the second and third trimesters, the main hemoglobin present in the fetus is fetal hemoglobin (Hb F). Hb F has two α and two γ globin chains, and after birth Hb F is replaced by Hb A (adult hemoglobin), which has two α and two β chains. The higher affinity of Hb F for oxygen is accentuated by 2,3-diphosphoglycerate (DPG) present in adult red cells. Fetal and maternal blood have differing oxygen saturation curves, mostly because DPG competes with oxygen for binding sites on adult cells. Fortuitously, fetal blood has a higher hemoglobin concentration and greater oxygen affinity than maternal blood. Although fetal oxygen tension is less, fetal blood is therefore able to carry an amount of oxygen comparable to that in maternal blood. The alkali resistance of Hb F makes it possible to demonstrate Hb F–containing cells in the maternal circulation.

Ferritin, the iron form essential to the production of hemoglobin, is present in the placenta as early as the first month of gestation and increases in amount through the sixth month. Ferritin appears in the fetal liver during the second and third months and may be recovered from the spleen after the fourth month. In contrast with the newborn and the adult, it is absent from the intestines. The relative amount of ferritin in the fetus does not vary significantly during normal gestation.

Circulating white cells constitute the first line of defense against pathogenic bacteria. Leukocytes appear in the fetal circulation after 2 months of gestation. Soon the thymus develops, and later the spleen. Both produce lymphocytes, a major source of the antibodies that constitute the second line of defense against harmful foreign antigens.

Antibodies are immunoglobulins (Ig) that are labeled M, G, or A according to their molecular size and carbohydrate content. IgM, the dominant antibody produced by the fetus, originates in the spleen. This immunoglobulin is most effective in mediating complement-dependent hemolysis or lysis of bacteria. Among the antigens that promote IgM formation are the AB and Rh antigens of the red cells.

IgG antibodies are of the bivalent 7S sedimentation class. In the fetus, they are transferred principally across the placenta from the maternal plasma in such quantities that in the second half of pregnancy the concentrations of IgG are about equal in the fetal and maternal plasmas. IgA production does not begin until several weeks after birth. Inasmuch as IgA is produced

in response to the antigens of enteric organisms, the newborn is particularly susceptible to intestinal infections.

The response of the fetus to antigens of maternal origin depends upon the level of immunologic competence achieved by the fetus. During the first trimester, for example, rubella virus elicits no response from the embryo, whose tissues are therefore subject to damage. Fetal and maternal tissues are no more tolerant of each other than are the tissues of 2 unrelated adults. Therefore, the lack of host-versus-graft or graft-versus-host reactions is attributable to the placental barrier.

Gastrointestinal Tract

When contrast media are injected into the amniotic fluid as early as the fourth month of gestation, they may be promptly observed within the stomach and small intestine. From this time onward, the fetus drinks considerable quantities of amniotic fluid, and this process, together with micturition, is one of the major factors controlling the volume of amniotic fluid. The full development of proteolytic activity does not develop until after birth, but the fetal gastrointestinal tract is quite capable of absorbing amino acids, glucose, and other soluble nutrients. This raises the interesting possibility of intrauterine feeding via the amniotic fluid in cases of placental insufficiency.

The degradation of red cells results in the formation of bilirubin as early as the 12th week. Nonetheless, the fetal liver has certain enzymatic deficiencies until after birth (glucuronyl transferase and UDPG dehydrogenase) that render it incapable of conjugating the bilirubin to make this catabolite water-soluble for renal clearance. The free bilirubin must be cleared by the placenta. Barbiturates will stimulate the activity of the deficient enzymes, and these drugs have been used in the perinatal period in specific cases (eg, erythroblastosis) for this purpose.

Fetal Endocrinology

The fetal **thyroid** is the first endocrine gland to develop in the fetus. As early as the fourth postconceptional week, the thyroid can synthesize thyroxine. This hormone is not necessary for fetal growth and development because small amounts of maternal thyroxine are transferred that prevent overt cretinism, but this protection is incomplete. Antithyroid drugs easily traverse the placenta and may adversely affect the fetus.

The **pancreas** develops early as an outgrowth of the duodenal endoderm, and as early as 12 weeks of gestation insulin may be extracted from the B cells of the fetal pancreas. Maternal insulin is not transferred to the fetus in physiologic quantities, and the fetus must supply whatever is needed for the metabolism of glucose. Insulin is thus the primary hormone regulating the rate of fetal growth. The B cells of the normal fetus respond poorly to hyperglycemia unless the stimulus is repeated many times, as in the fetus of a diabetic mother, when the B cells may undergo hyperplasia for the production of larger quantities of insulin. This may be why some infants of diabetic mothers grow to an excessive size or show evidences of hyperinsulinism immediately after birth. Because of its large molecular size, exogenous insulin cannot traverse the placenta.

All of the tropic hormones synthesized by the **anterior pituitary gland** are present in the fetus, although the precise role of these protein hormones in fetal growth and metabolism is not well understood. ACTH plays a vital role, however, in stimulating growth of the adrenal cortex because the tropic hormones are too large for placental transfer from the mother in significant quantities.

The fetal **adrenal cortex** consists mainly of a fetal zone that disappears about 6 months after birth. The cortex is an active endocrine organ that produces large quantities of steroid hormones, notably dehydroepiandrosterone, which is converted in the placenta to estrogens. There is evidence that the steadily increasing activity of the fetal zone of the fetal adrenal triggers the sequence of events which leads to the initiation of labor. Atrophy of the fetal adrenal (eg, anencephalic monsters) may result in marked prolongation of pregnancy. The fetal adrenal cortex is larger in premature infants when the cause of the labor is unknown than when the pregnancy is terminated by placental abruption or by physician interference.

CIRCULATORY FUNCTION IN THE FETUS & NEWBORN
(Figs 4–9 and 4–10)

Environmental changes occurring in the abrupt transition from intrauterine life to an independent existence necessitate certain circulatory adaptations in the newborn. These include diversion of blood flow through the lungs, closure of the ductus arteriosus and foramen ovale, and obliteration of the ductus venosus and umbilical vessels.

Infant circulation has 3 phases: (1) the predelivery phase, in which the fetus depends upon the placenta; (2) the intermediate phase, which begins immediately after delivery with the infant's first breath; and (3) the adult phase, which is normally completed during the first few months of life.

Predelivery Phase
The umbilical vein carries oxygenated blood from the placenta to the fetus. At the umbilicus, the vein branches and enters the liver; a small branch bypasses the liver as the ductus venosus to enter the inferior vena cava directly.

Almost all of the blood from the superior vena cava is directed through the tricuspid valve into the right ventricle, which ejects into the pulmonary trunk. Most of this relatively deoxygenated blood then passes directly through the ductus arteriosus to the descending aorta and on to the placenta. Blood from the inferior vena cava, which includes the oxygenated umbilical

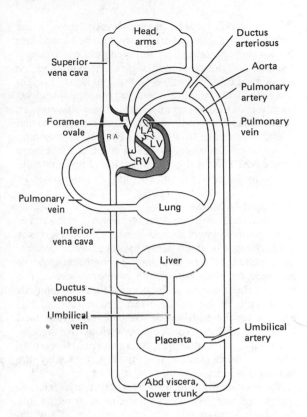

Figure 4–9. Schematic diagram of the fetal circulation. (Modified from A Rudolph.)

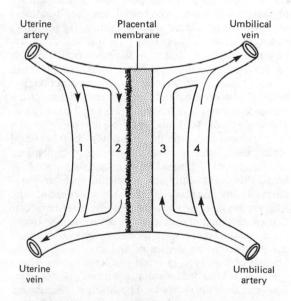

Figure 4–10. Schematic diagram of the placental circulations. (1) Shunting of maternal blood away from exchange surfaces. (2) Intervillous space. (3) Fetal capillaries of chorionic villi. (4) Shunting of fetal blood away from capillary exchange surfaces. (Modified from Metcalfe et al.)

venous blood, largely passes directly through the foramen ovale into the left ventricle to be ejected into the ascending aorta. The left ventricle ejects about one-third of the combined ventricular output of the fetus, most of which passes to the fetal head; the right ventricle, with blood of lower oxygen content, ejects mainly into the descending aorta. The aortic oxygen saturation difference is related not only to superior and inferior vena cava flow patterns but also to streaming of the umbilical venous blood as it enters the inferior vena cava. This well-oxygenated blood preferentially passes to the cerebral and coronary circulations.

Response to Stress

The fetal cardiovascular responses to stress represent a complex interplay between fetal arousal levels or state, changes in blood gases, hydrogen ion concentration, reflex effects initiated by chemoreceptor or baroreceptor stimulation, and hormonal levels. The study of these various influences in laboratory animals is difficult, as the standardized preparation (animal) must be recovered from the stress of surgery, in good health, and trained to undergo the various investigative procedures. As an example, fetal endorphin levels may modify cardiovascular responses just as may the mother's anxiety or drug level.

Superficially, the fetal hypoxemic-asphyxial response is much like the adult diving response in that they both involve selective vasoconstriction and the baroreceptor reflex, which is a primitive reflex that involves changes in heart rate, arterial and venous dilatation, and cardiac performance, is evoked by changes in mean blood pressure, and is modified by blood gas levels. The ability of some mammals to remain submerged for long periods of time remained a mystery until it was recognized that they become a "heart-brain" preparation through selective vasoconstriction. Likewise, during the fetal hypoxemic response, selective vasoconstriction diverts cardiac output to the fetal brain, heart, placenta, and adrenal gland. With widespread vasoconstriction, hypertension occurs that induces bradycardia through the baroreceptor reflex mechanism and vagal stimulation. The bradycardia is abrupt, meaning that it begins with the event and ends with the event. It is like other vagal bradycardia, such as head or uterine compression, umbilical cord compression, or even fetal grunting. A healthy fetus is usually able to tolerate such bradycardia providing that it is neither severe nor constant. The fetal asphyxial response represents depressed myocardial or central nervous system performance. Under these circumstances, even though vasoconstriction occurs, hypertension does not, and any bradycardia is gradual and delayed in onset and termination. These episodes of fetal bradycardia are termed late decelerations and are often ominous. The different mechanisms are shown in Fig 4–11.

In diving mammals, lactic acid is washed out of hypoperfused tissues after relief of the vasoconstriction. The same occurs with the hypoxic fetus, producing a brief period of acidemia after birth or after oxy-

genation. While the selective vasoconstriction provides a "heart-brain" preparation, at the same time it disturbs the preferential flow of oxygenated blood to the essential organs.

A depressed central nervous system often produces a relatively constant heart rate with lack of beat-to-beat variability. Fetal heart rate beat-to-beat variability is usually mediated through vagal stimulation resulting from activity of both higher and lower brain centers. Such central nervous system activity reflects general fetal arousal levels and is decreased when the fetus is immature, asleep, drugged, or asphyxiated. Lack of fetal heart rate variability when combined with other signs of fetal stress can likewise be an ominous sign. The fetal central nervous and cardiovascular systems respond differently to hypoxia according to gestational age.

The umbilical flow is relatively nonreactive, but the systemic and pulmonary circulation respond, when stressed, with vasoconstriction. The fetal pulmonary circulation receives a small portion of the fetal cardiac output (8–10%), and therefore it does not play a central role in the fetal cardiovascular hypoxia response. During periods of hypoxia, the reactive systemic circulation does divert more of the cardiac output to the umbilical circulation. Changes in fetal arterial pressure tend to be buffered by the fetal umbilical-placental circulation. Likewise, the decrease in fetal cardiac output seen during bradycardia is modified by the redistribution of cardiac output to vital organs such as the brain, heart, placenta, and adrenal gland, so that the baroreceptor reflex may not be as effective during fetal life. The response of the fetus to hypoxia is even more complex with chemoreceptor reflex stimulation from the aortic receptors, from the baroreceptor reflexes, and from direct myocardial depression. Fetal tachycardia may result from sympathetic nervous stimulation and from circulating catecholamines. Since the fetal capacity to respond to any one of these different stimuli varies with gestational age, arousal levels, general health, and presence of drugs and hormones, there are no universal, precise fetal heart rate responses to distress.

When the placental transfer of oxygen is inadequate, anaerobic glycolysis leads to the accumulation of excessive amounts of lactic acid in the fetus. Then, there is an associated accumulation of CO_2 and hydrogen ion (H^+). This results in decreased fetal pH. Although the maternal and fetal H^+ values maintain a relatively constant gradient, differences in the bicarbonate allow for variation in fetal pH. Thus, determination of fetal scalp pH is a useful clinical technique in the assessment of fetal well-being. During fetal distress (seriously altered homeostasis), fetal blood levels of prostaglandins, catecholamines, steroids, endorphins, and pituitary hormones are often elevated.

Intermediate Phase

At birth, 2 events occur that alter the fetal hemodynamics: (1) ligation of the umbilical cord causes an abrupt though transient rise in arterial pres-

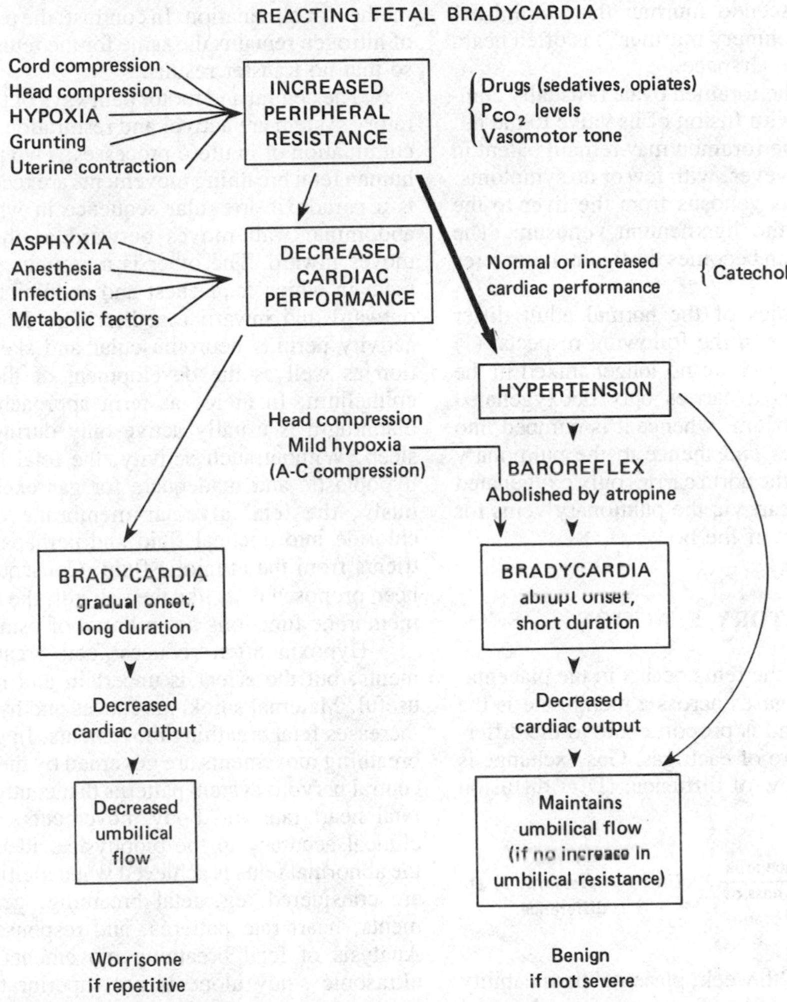

REACTING FETAL BRADYCARDIA

Figure 4–11. Proposed mechanisms of fetal bradycardia. Types of bradycardia at right may be abolished by atropine; those at left by inotropic agents. Fetal head compression, mild hypoxia, and maternal aortal caval compression may all produce direct vagal bradycardia without baroreceptor reflex. (Reproduced, with permission, from Goodlin RC, Haesslein HG: Fetal reacting bradycardia. *Am J Obstet Gynecol* 1977; **129**:845.)

sure; and (2) a rise in plasma CO_2 and fall in blood P_{O_2} help to initiate regular breathing.

With the first few breaths, the intrathoracic pressure of the newborn remains low (−40 to −50 mm Hg); after distention of the airways, however, the pressure rises to the normal adult level (−7 to −8 mm Hg). The initially high vascular resistance of the pulmonary bed is probably reduced by 75–80%. Pressure in the pulmonary artery falls by at least 60%, whereas pressure in the left atrium doubles.

In the fetus, the high resistance of the pulmonary bed causes most of the deoxygenated blood in the pulmonary artery to enter the descending aorta via the ductus arteriosus. With expansion of the lungs in the newborn, most of the blood from the right ventricle enters the lungs via the pulmonary artery. Furthermore, the increased arterial pressure reverses the flow of blood through the ductus ateriosus: Blood flows from the high-pressure aorta to the low-pressure pulmonary artery.

The increased pressure in the left atrium would normally result in backflow into the right heart through a patent foramen ovale. However, the anatomic configuration of the foramen is such that the increased pressure causes closure of the foramen by a valvelike fold situated in the wall of the left atrium.

The neonatal circulation is complete with closure of the ductus arteriosus and foramen ovale, but adjustments continue for 1–2 months when the adult phase begins.

Adult Phase

The ductus arteriosus usually is obliterated in the early postnatal period, probably by reflex action secondary to an elevated oxygen tension and the interaction of some prostaglandins. If the ductus remains open, a systolic crescendo murmur that diminishes during diastole ("machinery murmur") is often heard over the second left interspace.

Obliteration of the foramen ovale is usually complete in 6–8 weeks, with fusion of its valve to the left interatrial septum. The foramen may remain patent in some individuals, however, with few or no symptoms. The obliterated ductus venosus from the liver to the vena cava becomes the ligamentum venosum. The occluded umbilical vein becomes the ligamentum teres of the liver.

The hemodynamics of the normal adult differ from those of the fetus in the following respects: (1) venous and arterial blood are no longer mixed in the atria; (2) the vena cava carries only deoxygenated blood into the right atrium, whence it is pumped into the pulmonary arteries and thence to the pulmonary capillary bed; and (3) the aorta carries only oxygenated blood from the left heart via the pulmonary veins for distribution to the rest of the body.

RESPIRATORY FUNCTION

Gas exchange in the fetus occurs in the placenta. Diffusion transfer of gases across a membrane is the mechanism utilized and is proportionate to the difference in partial pressure of each gas. Gas exchange is measured by Fick's law of diffusion: (D = diffusion constant.)

$$\frac{\text{Amount of gas}}{\text{transferred}} = \frac{\text{Surface area}}{\text{Thickness of membrane}} \times \text{Time} \times \frac{\text{Partial pressure difference}}{} \times D$$

Until about the 12th week, placental permeability is low because of the small surface area of the placental "lake" and the early relative thickness of the trophoblastic membrane. However, from 12 to 32 weeks, the membrane thins and the surface area steadily increases. Obviously, active placental metabolism during pregnancy requires considerable oxygen, and this makes quantitation of oxygen transfer difficult.

In any event, the oxygen partial pressure (P_{O_2}) of fetal blood is less than that of maternal blood. Although this is not compatible with extrauterine life, it is adequate for the fetus because the fetus can adjust to lower oxygen tensions and can even elicit brief periods of anaerobic metabolic activity. Nevertheless, there is a higher concentration of hemoglobin in fetal blood, some of which is hemoglobin F. At birth, 20% of the hemoglobin is of the F (fetal) type. This component of red blood cells has a much greater affinity for oxygen than the so-called adult hemoglobin A, which is also normally present in red blood cells of fetuses. After delivery, the blood content of hemoglobin F diminishes, and hemoglobin F is usually not detectable after age 2½ years.

Both the P_{CO_2} and the CO_2 content of fetal blood are slightly greater than these values in the mother's blood. As a result, CO_2 tends to diffuse from fetus to mother for elimination. In contrast, the partial pressure of nitrogen remains the same for the fetus and mother, so that no transfer results.

The central and motor pathways of the fetal respiratory system are active, and respiration at birth is the culmination of in utero processes. Two main types of human fetal breathing movements are recognized. One is a paradoxic irregular sequence in which the fetal abdominal wall moves outward as the chest wall moves inward. The other is a regular, gentle movement in which fetal chest and abdominal wall move outward and inward together. The fetal respiratory activity permits neuromuscular and skeletal maturation as well as the development of the respiratory epithelium. In utero, as term approaches, the fetal diaphragm is usually active only during fetal REM sleep. Without such activity, the fetal lungs will be hypoplastic and inadequate for gas exchange. Curiously, the fetal alveolar membrane does excrete chloride into tracheal fluid and perhaps absorbs nutrients from the amniotic fluid. Consequently, it has been proposed that, like the fish gill, the fetal alveolar membrane functions as an organ of osmoregulation.

Hypoxia often reduces fetal breathing movements, but the effect is uncertain and not clinically useful. Maternal smoking reduces and hyperglycemia increases fetal breathing movements. In general, fetal breathing movements are governed by the same repeat central nervous system patterns that control changes in fetal heart rate and body movements. The greatest clinical accuracy in the biophysical identification of the abnormal fetus is achieved when multiple variables are considered, eg, fetal breathing, general movements, heart rate patterns, and response to stimuli. Analysis of fetal breathing movements by detailed ultrasonic study alone is not superior to any other antenatal assessment technique.

The first breath of the newborn normally occurs within the first 10 seconds after delivery. The first breath really is a gasp, the result of central nervous system reaction to sudden pressure and temperature change and other stimulation. With the first breath, a slight increase in P_{O_2} may activate chemoreceptors to send impulses to the central nervous system respiratory center and then to the respiratory musculature. As a result, a rhythmic but rapid breathing sequence, similar to that of the infant, usually follows. Meanwhile, amniotic fluid drains from the respiratory tree or is absorbed. If lung maturity has been achieved, good expansion and gas exchange should follow. However, if inadequate phospholipid surfactant is present (lecithin/sphingomyelin ratio < 2.0), as in the immature newborn, the surface tension at the air-fluid (membrane) interface in the alveoli will remain high, the alveoli will not expand, and respiratory distress secondary to atelectasis will promptly ensue.

With the onset of breathing, the pulmonary vascular resistance is reduced and capillaries fill with blood. Normally, the foramen ovale closes and pulmonary circulation is established.

GASTROINTESTINAL FUNCTION

The gastrointestinal tract is not truly functional until after birth because the placenta is the organ of alimentation during fetal life. Nevertheless, when a contrast medium is injected into the amniotic fluid as early as the fourth month of gestation, it may be promptly observed within the stomach and small intestine.

The full development of proteolytic activity does not develop until after birth, but the fetal gastrointestinal tract is quite capable of absorbing amino acids, glucose, and other soluble nutrients.

Meconium is produced during late pregnancy, but the amount is small. Passage of meconium in utero occurs only with asphyxia, which increases intestinal peristalsis and relaxation of the anal sphincter.

Intrahepatic erythropoiesis begins during the eighth week in the embryo, and, histologically, the liver is well developed by midpregnancy. During fetal life, the liver acts as a storage depot for glycogen and iron.

All things considered, the younger the newborn in gestational age, the poorer its liver function. Actually, reasonably complete liver function is not achieved until well after the neonatal period is passed.

Liver deficiencies at birth are many. They include reduced hepatic production of fibrinogen and coagulation factors II, VII, IX, XI, and XII.

Vitamin K stored in the liver is deficient at birth because its formation is dependent upon bacteria in the intestine. These deficiencies predispose the newborn to hemorrhage during the first few days of life.

The formation of glucose from amino acids (gluconeogenesis) in the liver and adequate storage of glucose there is not well established in the newborn. Moreover, carbohydrate-regulating hormones such as cortisol, epinephrine, and glucagon may be insufficient initially. As a consequence, neonatal hypoglycemia is common after stressful stimuli such as exposure to cold or malnutrition.

Glucuronidation is limited during the early neonatal period so that bilirubin is not readily conjugated for excretion as bile. After physiologic hemolysis of excess red blood cells in the first week after birth, or with pathologic hemolysis in isoimmunized newborns, jaundice occurs. If marked hyperbilirubinemia develops, kernicterus may ensue.

Poor metabolism of drugs by the liver in the newborn period (sulfonamides, chloramphenicol, and others) is recognized. Moreover, numerous inborn errors of metabolism (eg, galactosemia) may be diagnosed soon after birth.

Neonatal liver function gradually improves during the neonatal period and infancy, assuring proper food, freedom from infection, and a favorable environment.

Secretory and absorptive functions are accelerated after delivery. Most digestive enzymes are present, but the gastric contents are neutral at birth. Nonetheless, acidity soon develops. The initial neutrality may briefly delay the growth of bacteria in the bowel necessary for the formation of vitamin K in the intestine. The newborn can assimilate simple solutions immediately after birth but cannot digest food (milk) until after the second or third day following elimination of excessive gastric mucus.

Slow progress of milk through the stomach and upper intestine is usual during the early neonatal period. Normally, some air enters the stomach during feedings. However, pocketing of air in the upper curvature of the stomach occurs when the fetus is flat. Hence, turning of the offspring and "burping" are necessary.

Large bowel peristalsis promptly increases after delivery. The result is normal small stool frequency of 1–6 per day. Absence of stool within 48 hours after birth is indicative of intestinal obstruction or imperforate anus.

RENAL FUNCTION

The kidneys are unnecessary for fetal growth and development, as demonstrated by a rare neonate born with renal agenesis. Hence, the placenta, maternal lungs, and kidneys normally maintain fetal fluid and electrolyte balance.

The relative immaturity of the kidney even at term delivery is reflected in its limited function. The glomerular filtration of the newborn is only about 50% of that of an adult. Moreover, urine concentration and tubular resorption of sodium and phosphate are reduced also. Renal maturation continues long after delivery; in fact, the length of the proximal tubules and the diameter of the glomeruli continue to grow until adult life. Even so, considerable fluid and electrolyte variability can be managed successfully by the newborn.

With **renal agenesis** (sometimes called Potter's syndrome), there is a virtual absence of amniotic fluid. The infants have low-set ears, loose skin, flat noses, and large hands. The incidence is about one in 4000 births. If not stillborn, these infants succumb within 48 hours.

CENTRAL NERVOUS SYSTEM FUNCTION

The functional development of the human central nervous system is too complex to summarize. Nevertheless, a few clinical correlates should be mentioned. An individual's development neither begins nor ends at birth. Psychiatrists and psychologists have long recognized in utero modifying influences, and Freud stated that "each individual ego is endowed from the beginning with its own peculiar disposition and tendencies." For example, maternal anxiety levels do affect fetal development, and intrauterine stimuli determine, to a degree, the maturation of nerve cells and structural patterns of the developing brain. Maternal emotional stress can have immediate and long-term effects on fetal development, but it is unclear whether these maternal stresses have predictable effects.

Between 10 and 20 weeks of gestational age, a human fetus displays several basic motor patterns that are later integrated into specific actions. The first jerky patterns of the second trimester become the functional movement patterns that allow the fetus to move about in utero. After mid pregnancy, these motor patterns mature in a manner similar to the mature repertoire of the newborn. Clues to future central nervous system development may be found in the study of these various fetal motor patterns, and failure to progress at various stages seems to indicate subsequent cerebral dysfunction. It may be that real-time ultrasonic examination of such fetal motor patterns will allow improvement of obstetric care in certain high-risk situations.

The fetus demonstates various sleep-wake patterns throughout its development in utero. During most of its antenatal life, fetal electrocortical activity is of low voltage associated with rapid eye movements, slow fetal heart rate, and fetal breathing activity. In the third trimester, there is high-voltage activity associated with the more lively activity. Finally, near term, the fetus appears to be awake at least 30% of the time. These fetal states may be discerned by ultrasonic study of eye movements, which may be altered by drugs or maternal anxiety levels. These, in turn, affect fetal heart rate responses to stress.

The term fetus has high endorphin levels that may modify the fetal behavioral state including fetal heart rate responses. Such endorphin levels may be responsible for the primary apnea of the newborn and for the lack of fetal heart rate reactivity in otherwise normal intrapartum fetuses. The fetus probably suffers pain, as does any other individual, and high endorphin levels may limit pain and other effects of stress. The near-term fetus, then, has nearly all of the neurologic attributes of the newborn infant.

Neural Tube Defects

The occurrence of anencephaly or spina bifida is, of course, a developmental disaster. In both conditions, the concentration of alpha-fetoprotein (AFP) is increased in the amniotic fluid and in maternal serum. In theory, a suitable screening program could detect such anomalies in the mid trimester, so that pregnancy termination could be carried out. This should certainly be done in any woman who has given birth to an affected fetus previously, but to screen whole obstetric populations poses cost-benefit problems because of the rarity of the lesions. An apparently elevated serum AFP may reflect multiple gestation, an inaccurate gestational date, fetal anomaly, or fetal growth retardation. However, these suspicions should be confirmed or rejected by expertly done ultrasound studies and amniotic fluid AFP and acetylcholinesterase determinations. Acetylcholinesterase is increased in amniotic fluid in neural tube defects; there is a much lower incidence of false-positive tests than for AFP determinations.

INTRAUTERINE NUTRITION

Once the definitive placenta is formed—at about the time of appearance of the primitive streak—the embryo increases in weight in proportion to the gestational days cubed. Such a simple equation must be modified, of course, by a factor that represents the rate of nutrition, a number which varies with each mammalian species. The equation is:

$$w = a(t-36)^3$$

where w is the weight of the embryo or fetus in grams, t is the number of days from the first day of the last menstrual period, and the value of a is 0.24×10^{-6}.

Fetal Nutrition

Maternal diet among mammals is incredibly varied. For instance, the female black bear hibernates during her pregnancy, but she supplies metabolites to her fetus while neither eating nor drinking. In contrast, the pregnant guinea pig eats continuously. Obviously, forced fasting may have different effects on these different species during pregnancy.

The placenta produces both ammonia and lactate, which contribute significantly to fetal metabolism. The fetus actively synthesizes fatty acids in the liver, brain, and lung where there are special requirements for myelin and surfactin. Although fatty acids can be transported across the placenta, their oxidation does not seem to add much to the total energy economy of the fetus. The offspring regularly uses protein for oxidative metabolism. The metabolism of the human brain is very active during the perinatal period, and the brain is an obligatory consumer of glucose. Ketone bodies may partially replace glucose during periods of hypoglycemia and may also be a source of carbon for central nervous system lipids and proteins.

The placenta transports more water than any other substance. Since maternal hydrostatic and serum colloid osmotic pressures vary significantly during a normal day, unknown placental mechanisms protect the fetus against rapid shifts of water, which could cause either hydrops or dehydration. It may be that placental water transport is a passive process resulting from active solute transfer like that in the intestine.

Normally, the human fetus has a tremendous accumulation of fat of high caloric value. There are 2 components of fetal caloric intake: the building-block or accretion component and that associated with growth, or the heat production component. Starvation and protein turnover studies suggest that the fetus uses calories primarily for maintenance rather than for growth, however.

The only fetal hormone known to modify the rate of fetal growth is insulin. Fetuses with anomalies that preclude the availability of fetal growth hormone, thyroxine, adrenocortical steroids, or sex steroids achieve normal birth weights. Inasmuch as maternal insulin is not transferred to the fetus in physiologic quantities, the fetal pancreas must supply sufficient insulin for the oxidation of glucose. Under the stimulus of recurring hyperglycemia—as with maternal diabetes mellitus—the B cells of the fetal pancreas may become hyperplastic and secrete larger quantities of insulin.

Intrauterine Growth Retardation

Fetuses with intrauterine growth retardation are not a homogeneous population. Therefore, there is no broad definition of intrauterine growth retardation. Many times, intrauterine growth-retarded or small-for-gestational-age newborns are defined as weighing below the tenth percentile. We refer here only to those infants with abnormalities of development or with dysmaturity, ignoring the "small people syndrome." The cause of intrauterine growth retardation is often obscure and can involve many different factors.

Genetic factors account for approximately 40% of human newborn weight variation. Studies in humans and other mammals have shown that maternal environment is the most important determinant of newborn weight. Mating dwarfs with giants of various species, eg, ponies and horses, has shown that newborn weight is determined chiefly by the weight of the mother, whereas at puberty paternal weight is the dominant factor. Even in humans, maternal environment accounts for more similarity in birth weights of siblings than does genetic resemblance. Newborns of the same mother are more alike than those of the same father in mixed parenthood studies.

In addition to a direct relationship with the degree of maternal plasma volume expansion, many clinical factors are associated with intrauterine growth retardation, although most are also associated with relative decrease of maternal plasma volume expansion. These factors include multiple gestation; fetal, genetic, and chromosome anomalies (especially Down's and Turner's syndromes); infections such as TORCH syndrome (acronym for *to*xoplasmosis, *r*ubella, *c*ytomegalic inclusion disease, and *h*erpes simplex); and various maternal disorders including marked anemia, severe chronic asthma, cyanotic heart disease, chronic renal disease, and severe hypertension. Maternal narcotic addiction, chronic alcoholism, and anticonvulsive therapy are often associated with intrauterine growth retardation. Placental anomalies including hemangiomas, large placental infarcts, abnormal incisions to placental cords, single umbilical artery, and small placental size are likewise associated with intrauterine growth retardation. As a rule, a small fetus is associated with a small placenta, which in turn is associated with relative maternal hypovolemia and oligohydramnios. It is uncertain whether these associations are due to cause and effect. Since little is known about why plasma volume expansion occurs during pregnancy, it is difficult to propose therapy. In clinical practice, most cases of intrauterine growth retardation are without explanation, despite all the known associations with various pregnancy abnormalities.

In rodents, restriction of maternal protein and caloric intake is positively correlated with fetal size, but this does not appear to hold true for primates. Except in extreme situations, fetal size in primates is poorly correlated with inadequate maternal diet. Ligation of intraplacental blood vessels in monkeys does cause reduction in fetal weight, and this suggests that primary placental dysfunction may cause intrauterine growth retardation. In humans, growth-retarded fetuses present variable features, but many have disproportionately large heads, suggesting a sparing of fetal brain development. On the other hand, many show a proportionate decrease in all body organs, including the fetal brain.

AMNIOTIC FLUID

The origin of amniotic fluid in the first half of pregnancy presumably is the transudation of fluid from maternal plasma across the membranes that cover the placenta and the cord, because in composition the fluid is almost identical to a transudate of plasma. In the second half of pregnancy, there is a progressive admixture of fetal urine, which is hypotonic to plasma but which contains higher concentrations of creatinine, urea, and uric acid than does plasma. Accordingly, there is a progressive fall in osmolality to about 90% of plasma values and a progressive rise in the concentrations of urinary metabolites.

The volume of amniotic fluid at 10 weeks is about 30 mL; at 20 weeks 350 mL; and at 38 weeks almost 1 L. Thereafter, the volume declines, and in postmature gestations the volume may be less than 500 mL (oligohydramnios). When the volume exceeds 2000 mL, the term hydramnios is used. Amniotic fluid is of low specific gravity (about 1.008) and mild alkalinity (about pH 7.2). The amniotic fluid protects the fetus from direct injury, aids in maintaining its temperature, allows free movement of the fetus, and minimizes the likelihood of adherence of the fetus to the amniotic membrane. There is a rapid exchange of water molecules between the amniotic fluid and both fetal and maternal plasma, amounting to 300–400 mL/h, but variations in these rates are not believed to be responsible for the variations of amniotic fluid volume. Studies show that the fetus near term drinks 400–500 mL of amniotic fluid per day, which is about the same as the amount of milk consumed by a newborn infant. In order to maintain a reasonable stability of volume, the fetus must excrete about the same volume of urine into the amniotic fluid per day. If either imbibition or micturition is seriously interfered with, gross alterations of volume may occur. For example, with renal agenesis there is a virtual absence of amniotic fluid, whereas with congenital esophageal atresia severe hydramnios results. When hydramnios occurs in the presence of maternal diabetes, it is possible that episodes of fetal hyperglycemia accompanying maternal hyperglycemia result in fetal polyuria (osmotic diuresis), thus increasing the urinary contribution to amniotic fluid above the amounts of fluid swallowed.

During late pregnancy, the amniotic fluid contains increasing quantities of particulate material, including desquamated cells of fetal origin, lanugo and scalp hairs, vernix caseosa, a few leukocytes, and small quantities of albumin, urates, and other organic and inorganic salts. The calcium content of amniotic fluid is low (5.5 mg/dL), but the electrolyte concentration is otherwise equivalent to that of maternal plasma.

Meconium is ordinarily absent but is excreted by the fetus in response to episodes of hypoxia. When the fetus is reasonably mature, the fetal lungs elaborate phospholipids capable of reducing surface tension, collectively called surfactant. Some of this material gains access to the amniotic fluid, and its presence may be demonstrated by a special "shake test" (see below). When this test is positive, the fetus is judged to be sufficiently mature to escape the development of respiratory distress syndrome (hyaline membrane disease), which is thought to be due in large part to absence of pulmonary surfactant.

Amniocentesis

Amniocentesis for the purpose of obtaining samples of fluid for analysis is a relatively innocuous procedure that is being used with increasing frequency for the following purposes:

A. Determination of Fetal Maturity: The 4 constituents commonly measured are bilirubin, creatinine, lipid-staining cells, and surfactant. When a fetus has reached 37 weeks of gestational age or older, the bilirubin should have disappeared (unless the fetus has hemolytic disease); the creatinine concentration should be 1.8 mg/dL or more; at least 15% of cells should appear orange when stained with Nile blue sulfate; and tests for surfactant should be positive. Lecithin constitutes about 80% of surfactant phospholipids and phosphatidylglycerol about 10%. The presence of phosphatidylglycerol seems to improve functioning of lung surfactant and tends to reduce the likelihood of newborn respiratory distress. Phosphatidylglycerol is necessary to prevent infants of diabetic mothers from developing respiratory distress syndrome. Tests for positive phosphatidylglycerol spot on chromatographic plates are now widely available.

B. Monitoring the Severity of Hemolytic Disease: When an Rh-positive fetus is developing erythroblastosis, the severity of the anemia is closely correlated with the bilirubin concentration. The usual technique is to obtain a spectrophotometric tracing between the wave-lengths of 550 and 350 nm and then determine the deviation of the optical density (OD) at 450 nm. An illustration of such a determination is shown in Fig 4–12. In this example, the OD 450 nm peak has an OD difference of 0.069, which, if found at 37 weeks of gestation, would be an indication for immediate cesarean delivery. Further details about the management of the affected fetus are given in Chapter 36.

C. Surfactant Activity: The concentration of lecithin (phosphatidylcholine) rises abruptly at about

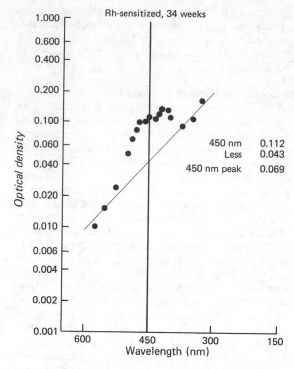

Figure 4–12. Spectrophotometric analysis of amniotic fluid and the derivation of the 450-nm peak. (Reproduced, with permission, from Westberg JA, Margolis AJ: *Am J Obstet Gynecol* 1965; 92:583.)

35–36 weeks of gestation, whereas that of another lipid, sphingomyelin, changes very little. It has been determined that when the lecithin/sphingomyelin ratio in amniotic fluid exceeds 2 there is little likelihood that the infant will develop respiratory distress syndrome.

A "shake test" has been developed that appears to be equally reliable. The test may be performed at the bedside and is based on the ability of fluids containing surfactant to form stable foam in the presence of alcohol. These tests are discussed in more detail in Chapter 28.

D. Diagnosis of Chronic Fetal Distress: When amniocentesis is done, the presence of oligohydramnios suggests chronic fetal distress, but the sign is not too reliable. Chronic distress is frequently accompanied by intrauterine growth retardation, which may be diagnosed most accurately by utilizing gray scale sonography, measuring the circumference of the fetal abdomen as well as the biparietal diameter, and measuring amniotic fluid volume. If the fetus is unable to swallow (as with anencephaly or gastrointestinal tract lesions), polyhydramnios may occur. In general, amniotic fluid volume reflects the degree of maternal plasma volume expansion. An exception is polyhydraminos due to fetal illness associated with maternal relative hypovolemia.

E. Determination of Sex: When fresh amniotic fluid is centrifuged and the cells are fixed on a slide and stained with Feulgen reagent, the presence or absence of sex chromatin (Barr bodies) may be determined. Such determinations are rarely indicated unless one is concerned with an X-linked congenital disorder.

F. Antenatal Diagnosis of Genetic Disorders: The cells from amniotic fluid may be cultured and the karyotypes studied for chromosomal disorders, or they may be studied for a variety of enzyme deficiencies that characterize some of the genetic disorders of intermediate metabolism. Details about the usefulness of this method are described in Chapter 26.

● ● ●

References

Battaglia FC, Lubchenco LO: A practical classification of newborn infants by weight and gestational age. *J Pediatr* 1967; **71**:159.

Battaglia FC, Meschia G: Fetal and placental metabolisms. *Proc Nutr Soc* 1981; **40**:99.

Beaconsfield P, Villee CA (editors): *Placenta: A Neglected Experimental Animal*. Pergamon Press, 1979.

Comparetti AM: The neurophysiologic and clinical implications of studies on fetal motor behavior. *Semin Perinatol* 1981; **5**:183.

Galbraith RS et al: The clinical prediction of intrauterine growth retardation. *Am J Obstet Gynecol* 1979; **133**:281.

Goodlin RC et al: The significance, diagnosis, and treatment of maternal hypovolemia as associated with fetal maternal illness. *Semin Perinatol* 1981; **5**:163.

Hobbins JC et al: Ultrasound in the diagnosis of congenital anomalies. *Am J Obstet Gynecol* 1979; **134**:331.

Jordaan HV, Dunn LJ: A New method of evaluating fetal growth. *Obstet Gynecol* 1978; **56**:659.

Jost A: Fetal hormones and fetal growth. *Contrib Gynecol Obstet* 1979; **5**:1.

Lauslahti K, Ikonen S: Placenta as an indicator of fetal postnatal prognosis. *Acta Obstet Gynecol Scand* 1979; **58**: 163.

Lewis P, Boylan P: Fetal breathing: A review. *Am J Obstet Gynecol* 1979; **134**:587.

Macri JN, Haddow JE, Weiss RR: Screening for neural tube defects in the United States. *Am J Obstet Gynecol* 1979; **133**:119.

Meier PR et al: Fetal protein synthesis. *Am J Physiol* 1981; **240**:E320.

Penfold P et al: Case note descriptions of the placenta: Are they worthwhile? *Br J Obstet Gynecol* 1979; **86**:337.

Pupkin MJ et al: The dehydroepiandrosterone loading test. 2. A possible placental function test. *Am J Obstet Gynecol* 1979; **134**:281.

Rudolph AM et al: Fetal cardiovascular responses to stress. *Semin Perinatol* 1981; **5**:109.

Schlueter MA et al: Antenatal prediction of graduated risk of hyaline membrane disease by amniotic fluid foam test for surfactant. *Am J Obstet Gynecol* 1979; **134**:761.

Teasdale F: Gestational changes in the functional structure of the human placenta in relation to fetal growth: A morphometric study. *Am J Obstet Gynecol* 1980; **137**:560.

Van Drie DM, Kammeraad LA: Vasa previa. *J Reprod Med* 1981; **26**:577.

5 | Gynecologic History, Examination, & Diagnostic Procedures

Albert E. Long, MD

The initial approach to the gynecologic patient and the general diagnostic procedures available for the investigation of gynecologic complaints are presented here; other aspects of the general medical examination are left to other texts. We wish to emphasize, however, that the good gynecologist is a doctor who regards each patient at every visit as a whole person and not just as an assemblage of parts, some of which are more interesting—and more apt to become cystic, cancerous, or pregnant—than others.

HISTORY

The following outline varies from the routine medical history because, in evaluating the obstetric or gynecologic patient, the setting can often be clarified if her marital, sexual, and obstetric history is obtained first. For the gynecologist, then, the following routine in obtaining the history is recommended.

Age, Marital Status, Sexual Activity, Parity

Knowledge of the patient's age is essential. Her marital status should be clearly stated, including present and past marriages and the duration and outcome of each. If the rapport between gynecologist and patient is not adequate at the first encounter to permit discussion of intimate or embarrassing subjects, the physician should sense this and defer questioning to a later interview. The process of taking the patient's obstetric history will be detailed in Chapter 27, but the parity should be recorded as part of the gynecologic evaluation. A convenient symbol for recording parity is a 4-digit code denoting the number of *t*erm pregnancies, *p*remature deliveries, *a*bortions, and *l*iving children (TPAL); eg, 2-1-1-3 means 2 term pregnancies, one premature delivery, one abortion, and 3 living children.

Chief Complaint (CC)

The patient briefly states her main complaint, eg, "pain in my right side, low down, for 3 months."

Present Illness (PI)

The chief complaint is now considered in detail. The site, duration, and intensity of the pain must be accurately described. It is often helpful in evaluating the intensity of pain to offer the patient a comparison: "Is it as bad as a labor pain?" If the patient is uncertain about the duration of the pain, the gynecologist can relate it to a memorable event: "Did you have this pain at Thanksgiving?" In investigating the nature of the present illness, the physician should ask the patient about any variation in the usual functioning of other organ systems, especially of the urinary and gastrointestinal tracts and should inquire regarding previous similar problems and their diagnosis and treatment. Other important details relate to the last pelvic examination, the LMP, and the last Papanicolaou smear. It is important for the physician to speak the patient's language: "labia" is "lip of" or "fold at the side of" the vagina, and "anus" is "rectum." Such judicious yet dignified communication with the patient in the terminology she uses helps not only to obtain an accurate history but also to establish rapport. Pleasantly for the physician, the educated patient can be conversed with straightforwardly with standard anatomic terminology.

After the physician is satisfied that all possible information concerning the present illness has been obtained, the past history should be elicited.

Past History (PH)

A. Medical: The medical history includes any significant disease that the patient may have had, especially any that may have caused significant organ damage, eg, heart disease resulting from diphtheria or rheumatic fever, salpingitis after gonorrhea. Past and present endocrinopathy is especially important to the gynecologist. Include all hospitalizations.

B. Surgical: The surgical history includes all operations, the dates performed, and associated postoperative or anesthetic complications.

C. Obstetric: The obstetric history includes each of the patient's pregnancies listed in chronologic order. The date of birth, sex, and weight of the offspring; duration of pregnancy; length of labor; type of delivery; type of anesthesia; and any complications should be included.

D. Gynecologic: The first item in the gynecologic past history is the menstrual history: age at menarche, interval between periods, duration of flow, degree of discomfort, and age at menopause. The menstrual history is often the most important clue to the diagnosis. The physician should ask about pelvic infections and take a detailed sexual history. Specific questions about sexually transmitted diseases should be asked. The patient should also be queried regarding use of contraceptives—especially oral contraceptives—and any other endocrine products. Urinary and gastrointestinal tract problems should also be included in the gynecologic history.

E. Psychiatric: The psychiatric aspect of the history may be difficult to develop because of the patient's unwillingness to reveal emotional difficulties. Later, after a more confident relationship with the physician has developed, the patient may be more ready to discuss psychiatric problems.

F. Medications (Drugs): It is important for the physician to know of any medication the patient is taking or has taken because medication may affect the diagnosis. For example, postmenopausal bleeding may be caused by estrogen therapy given to relieve the symptoms of menopause.

G. Allergies: The physician should question the patient specifically regarding possible allergic reactions to drugs, foods, pollens, etc, and ascertain the reactions produced (eg, rash, gastrointestinal upset).

H. Family: The patient's medical history should also include the state of health of relatives (parents, siblings, grandparents, offspring). Such information is significant because certain diseases such as diabetes, sickle cell anemia, and porphyria are hereditary. An increased frequency of cancer or heart disease can be expected in some women on the basis of the family history, eg, a history of breast cancer in the family puts the patient in a high-risk group.

I. Social: The social history can be an extension of earlier questions pertaining to marital and sexual history. It is helpful to know what type of work the patient does and something of her education and her community activities because some complaints are based purely upon psychoneurotic reactions to an unhappy life or to tedium (eg, the "bored housewife"). Somatic illness may be exacerbated by discontent.

J. Sexual: Sexuality is a highly important part of everyone's life. The physician should include sexual relationships in the patient's history, but this aspect of history-taking may be postponed if the present illness is not related to sexual concerns or if the patient is shy about discussing such problems. If the patient is reluctant to volunteer details about sex, the physician must decide when to broach the subject. At least half of all women are dissatisfied to some degree with their sex lives.

In taking the sexual history, the physician is saying, "I want to help you. Please talk to me. Whatever you say is confidential." The physician is a counselor who should be open-minded and not judgmental, superior, prudish, or critical. Physicians who are not comfortable dealing with their patients' sex problems should refer patients to a competent counselor for that purpose. Topics that may be covered include the following:

1. Marital status–Married? How many times? For how long? If not married, is there a current sexual relationship? Is this relationship satisfactory? If not, why not?

2. Orgasm–Always? Occasionally? Never?

3. Coital frequency–Enough? Too often?

4. Recent changes in methods–Better or worse? What is good or bad in the sexual relationship?

5. Source of sex education–Was it adequate? Is more information needed now?

6. Sex experiences–What was puberty like? Did any problems develop at that time? Premarital sex or pregnancy? Satisfaction or guilt feelings? Is there a present problem? What changes are desired?

7. Contraception–What type is being used? Is it acceptable?

PHYSICAL EXAMINATION

If the woman is referred to the gynecologist by an internist or a family practitioner, she may have already had a general physical examination. Even so, it may be indicated again at this time. A complete examination demonstrates the physician's thoroughness and establishes rapport with the patient.

A physical examination should be conducted in an environment that is aesthetically pleasing to the patient: colorful and cheerful, warm, yet reflecting the dignity and professional competence of the physician. The patient's gown and drape must be clean (ideally used once only, ie, disposable) and large enough to prevent embarrassment. All equipment must be clean and instruments sterilized between examinations. Many items in use today are disposable.

The physician's assistant should conduct the patient to the dressing area and give explicit instructions about what to take off and how to put on the gown, then take her to the examination room and drape her.

For the male physician, the assistant may remain in the examining room to assist when necessary, but whether or not she remains solely to be a chaperone depends upon local custom or legal requirements and the preference of the physician. A chaperone is not customarily or legally required today, and, considering the cost of extra personnel, most physicians do not choose to have one present for each examination. The male physician must be alertly selective in this matter and instruct his assistant to be present during the examination of an overly fearful or potentially seductive patient. If the patient wants her husband, relative, or a female friend to be present, the request should be granted unless the physician feels that some impropriety might result or the examination might be interfered with.

The gynecologic portion of the examination should include a thorough examination of the breasts and the abdomen.

Breast Examination (See Chapter 17)

First the physician inspects the breasts for size, contour, and skin conditions with the patient sitting upright with her arms at her sides. The patient then raises her arms above her head and the inspection is repeated. Nodularity or dimpling of the skin is suggestive of an underlying mass that should be further investigated. The breasts are carefully palpated with the patient supine. First, the flat hand is gently rolled over the breast so that the breast tissue can be outlined between the examining hand and the underlying ribs. The breast is then examined with the fingertips in all 4 quadrants and especially under the nipple. The axillas should also be carefully palpated.

Abdominal Examination

For this important aspect of the physical examination, the patient should be lying completely supine and relaxed; the knees may be slightly flexed and supported as an aid to relaxation of the abdominal muscles. The physician first inspects for irregularity of contour or color. Any discoloration of the umbilicus may indicate intraperitoneal bleeding. Next, the abdomen should be auscultated for intestinal activity. Auscultation should follow inspection but precede palpation because the latter may change the character of intestinal activity. The physician should next palpate the entire abdomen—gently at first, and then more firmly as indicated—and should feel for rigidity, voluntary guarding, masses, and tenderness. If the patient complains of abdominal pain, or if unexpected tenderness is elicited, the physician should ask her to indicate the point of maximal pain or tenderness *with one finger*. A painful area should be left until last for deep palpation; otherwise, the entire abdomen may be

guarded voluntarily. As a final part of the abdominal examination, the physician should carefully check for any abnormality of the abdominal organs: liver, gallbladder, spleen, kidneys, and intestines. In some instances, the demonstration of an abnormality of the abdominal muscle reflexes may be diagnostically helpful. Percussion of the abdomen should be performed to identify organ enlargement, tumor, or ascites.

PELVIC EXAMINATION

The pelvic examination is a feared procedure in the minds of many women and must be conducted in such a way as to overcome the patient's natural objections. A patient's first pelvic examination may be especially disturbing, so it is important for the physician to attempt to allay fear and to inspire confidence and cooperation. The empathic physician usually will find that by the time the history has been obtained and a painless and unembarrassing general examination performed, a satisfactory gynecologic examination will not be a problem. Relaxing surroundings, a nurse or attendant chaperone if indicated, warm instruments, and a gentle, unhurried manner with continued explanation and reassurance are helpful in securing patient relaxation and cooperation. This is especially true with the virginal patient, for whom a one-finger examination and a narrow speculum often are necessary. In some cases, vaginal examination is not possible; palpation of the pelvic structures by rectal examination is then the only recourse. If a more definitive pelvic

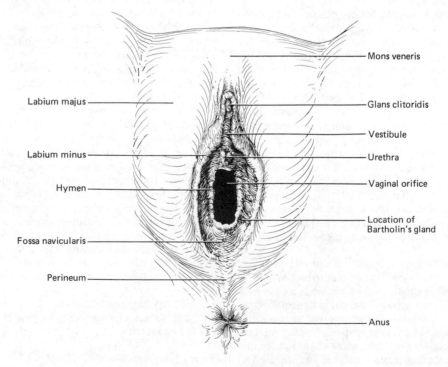

Figure 5–1. Normal external genitalia in a mature woman. (Reproduced, with permission, from Benson RC: *Handbook of Obstetrics & Gynecology,* 7th ed. Lange, 1980.)

examination is essential, it can be performed with the patient anesthetized.

External Genitalia (Fig 5–1)

The pubic hair should be inspected for its pattern (masculine or feminine), for the nits of pubic lice, for infected hair follicles, or for any other abnormality. The glans clitoridis can be exposed by gently retracting the surrounding skin folds. The clitoris is at the ventral confluence of the 2 labia; it should be no more than 2.5 cm in length, most of which is subcutaneous. The major and minor labia are usually the same size on both sides, but a moderate difference in size is not abnormal. Small protuberances or subcutaneous nodules may be either sebaceous cysts or tumors. The urethra, just below the clitoris, should be the same color as the surrounding tissue and without protuberances. Normally, Bartholin's glands can be neither seen nor felt; enlargement, therefore, may indicate an abnormality of that gland system. The area of Bartholin's glands should be palpated by placing the index finger in the vagina and the thumb outside and gently feeling for enlargement or tenderness (Fig 5–2). The perineal skin may be reddened as a result of vulvar or vaginal infection. Scars may indicate obstetric lacerations or surgery. The anus should also be inspected at this time for the presence of hemorrhoids, fissures, or irritation.

Hymen

An unruptured hymen may present in many forms (Fig 5–3), but only a completely imperforate hymen is pathologic. After rupture, it also may be seen in various forms (Fig 5–4). After the birth of several children, the hymen may almost disappear.

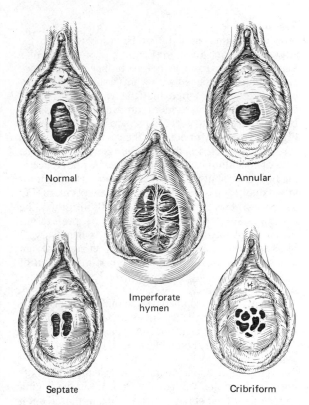

Normal   Annular

Imperforate hymen

Septate   Cribriform

Figure 5–3. Unruptured hymen.

Perineal Support

To determine the presence of pelvic relaxation, the physician spreads the labia with 2 fingers and tells the patient to "bear down" or "push all your insides out through the vagina." This will demonstrate urethrocele, cystocele, rectocele, or uterine prolapse (see Chapter 12).

Urethra

Redness of the urethra may indicate infection or a urethral caruncle or carcinoma. Skene's glands are situated below the urethra and empty into the urethra just inside the meatus. With the labia spread adequately for better vision, the urethra may be "stripped" with the finger to express discharge from the urethra or Skene's glands.

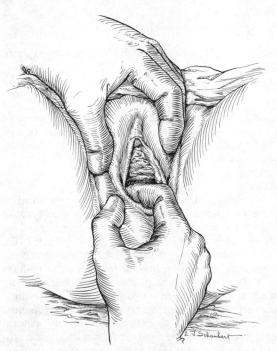

Figure 5–2. Palpation of Bartholin's glands.

Figure 5–4. Ruptured hymen (parous introitus).

Vagina

The vagina should first be inspected with the speculum for abnormalities and to obtain a Papanicolaou cytosmear before further examination. A speculum dampened with warm water but not lubricated is gently inserted into the vagina so that the cervix (Fig 5–5) and fornices can be thoroughly visualized. After the cytosmear is prepared (as illustrated in Fig 5–6; see p 91 for details), the vaginal wall is again carefully inspected as the speculum is withdrawn. The type of speculum used depends upon the preference of the physician, but the most satisfactory instrument for the sexually active patient is the Graves speculum (Fig 5–7). For the patient with a small introitus, the narrow-bladed Pederson speculum is preferable. When more than the usual exposure is necessary, 2 Sims speculums, one or both held by an assistant, are useful. To visualize a child's vagina, a Huffman or nasal speculum, large otoscope, or Kelly air cystoscope is invaluable.

Next, the vagina is palpated; unless the patient's introitus is too small, the index and middle finger of either hand are inserted gently and the tissues palpated. The vaginal walls should be smooth, elastic, and nontender.

The uterus and adnexal structures should be outlined between the 2 fingers of the hand in the vagina and the flat of the opposite hand, which is placed upon the lower abdominal wall (Fig 5–8). Gentle palpation and manipulation of the structures will delineate position, size, shape, mobility, consistency, and tenderness of the pelvic structures—except in the obese or uncooperative patient or in a patient whose abdominal muscles are taut as a result of fear or tenderness.

Cervix

The cervix is a firm structure traditionally described as having the consistency of the tip of the nose. Normally it is round and approximately 3–4 cm in diameter. Various appearances of the cervix are shown in Fig 5–5. The external os is also round and virtually closed. Multiparous women may have an os that has been lacerated. An irregularity in shape or nodularity may be due to one or more nabothian cysts. If the cervix is extremely firm, it may contain a tumor, even cancer. The cervix (along with the body of the uterus) normally is moderately mobile, so that it can be moved 2–4 cm in any direction without causing undue discomfort. (When one examines a patient, it is helpful to warn her that she will feel the movement of the uterus but that ordinarily this maneuver will not be painful.) Restriction of mobility of the cervix or corpus often follows inflammation, neoplasia, or surgery.

Corpus of the Uterus

The corpus of the uterus is approximately half the size of the patient's fist and weighs approximately 70–90 g. It is regular in outline and not tender to pressure or moderate motion. In most women, the uterus is anteposed; in about one-third of women, it is retroposed (see Chapter 12). A retroposed uterus is

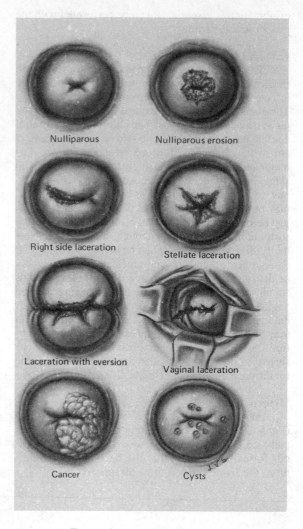

Figure 5–5. The uterine cervix: Normal and pathologic appearance.

usually not a pathologic finding. In certain cases of endometriosis or previous salpingitis, it may be that the "tipped" uterus is a result of adhesions caused by the disease process.

Adnexa

Adnexal structures (uterine tubes and ovaries) cannot be palpated in many heavy-set women because the normal tube is only about 7 mm in diameter and the ovary no more than 3 cm in its greatest diameter. In the very slender woman, however, the ovaries nearly always are palpable and, in some instances, the oviducts as well. If the relaxed patient is not obese and no adnexal structures can be palpated, one can assume provisionally that there are no abnormal enlargements. Unusual tenderness or enlargement of any adnexal structure indicates the need for further diagnostic procedures; an adnexal mass in any woman is an indication for investigation.

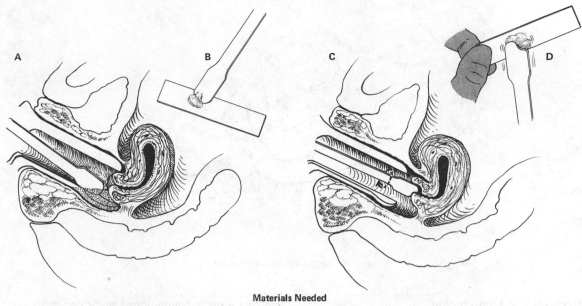

Materials Needed

One cervical spatula, cut tongue depressor, or cotton swab.
One glass slide (one end frosted). Identify by writing the patient's name on the frosted end with a lead pencil.

One speculum (without lubricant).
One bottle of fixative (75% ethyl alcohol) or spray-on fixative, eg, Pro-Fixx or Aqua-Net.

Figure 5–6. Preparation of a Papanicolaou cytosmear. *A:* Obtain vaginal pool material from posterior fornix. *B:* Place adequate drop 1 inch from end of slide, smear, fix, and dry. *C:* Obtain cervical scraping from complete squamocolumnar junction by rotating spatula 360 degrees around external os, high up the endocervical canal. *D:* Place the material 1 inch from end of slide, smear, fix, and dry. (Reproduced, with permission, from Benson RC: *Handbook of Obstetrics & Gynecology,* 7th ed. Lange, 1980.)

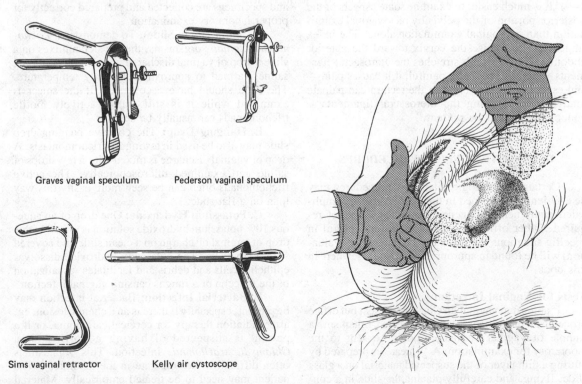

Graves vaginal speculum   Pederson vaginal speculum

Sims vaginal retractor   Kelly air cystoscope

Figure 5–7. Specula. (Reproduced, with permission, from Benson RC: *Handbook of Obstetrics & Gynecology,* 7th ed. Lange, 1980.)

Figure 5–8. Bimanual pelvic examination.

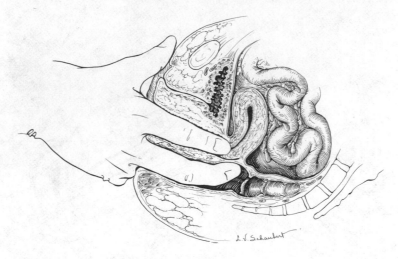

Figure 5–9. Rectovaginal examination.

Rectovaginal Examination

At the completion of the bimanual pelvic examination, a rectovaginal examination should always be performed. The well-lubricated middle finger of the examining hand should be inserted gently into the rectum to feel for tenderness, masses, or irregularities. When the examining finger has been inserted a short distance, the index finger can then be inserted into the vagina until the depth of the vagina is reached (Fig 5–9). It is much easier to examine some aspects of the posterior portion of the pelvis by rectovaginal examination than by vaginal examination alone. The index finger can now raise the cervix toward the anterior abdominal wall, which stretches the uterosacral ligaments. This is not usually painful; if it causes pain—and especially if the finger in the rectum can palpate tender nodules along the uterosacral ligaments—endometriosis may be present.

DIAGNOSTIC OFFICE PROCEDURES

Certain gynecologic diagnostic procedures may be efficiently performed in the office because complicated equipment and general anesthesia are not required. Other office diagnostic procedures useful in specific situations (eg, tests used in infertility evaluation) will be found in appropriate chapters elsewhere in this book.

Tests for Vaginal Infection

If abnormal vaginal discharge is present but office procedures do not reveal the suspected organism, a sample of vaginal discharge should be sent to the laboratory for examination. A "smear" is prepared by putting a thin layer of the suspected material on a glass slide, fixing, and carefully placing the slide in a container that is specifically designed to avoid disturbing the smeared surface of the slide; the laboratory usually provides these receptacles. A culture is obtained by applying a sterile cotton-tipped applicator to the suspect area and then transferring the suspect material to a culture medium, eg, Thayer-Martin or Transgrow. Since this is inconvenient in the physician's office, most laboratories today supply a prepackaged kit that allows the physician to put the cotton-tipped applicator into a sterile container which is then sent to the laboratory. The physician should contact the laboratory director to be certain the best materials are being used and specimens are collected and prepared correctly for proper laboratory examination.

A. Saline (Plain Slide): To demonstrate *Trichomonas vaginalis* organisms, the physician mixes on a slide a drop of vaginal discharge with 1 drop of normal saline warmed to approximately body temperature. The slide should have a coverslip. If the smear is examined while it is still warm, actively motile trichomonads can usually be seen.

B. Hanging Drop: The concave hanging drop slide may also be used in testing for trichomoniasis. A drop of vaginal discharge is mixed with a few drops of saline and examined microscopically. The active trichomonads often can be seen more easily this way than on a flat slide.

C. Potassium Hydroxide: One drop of an aqueous 10% potassium hydroxide solution is mixed with 1 drop of vaginal discharge on a clean slide and covered with a coverslip. The potassium hydroxide dissolves epithelial cells and debris and facilitates visualization of the mycelia of a fungus causing vaginal infection.

D. Bacterial Infection: Bacterial infection may be present, especially if there is an ischemic lesion, eg, after radiation therapy for cervical carcinoma, or if a patient is suspected of having gonorrhea or a *Chlamydia trachomatis* infection. This organism is often difficult to demonstrate in the laboratory. The patient may need to be treated empirically. Material from the cervix, urethra, or vaginal lesion may be smeared, stained, and examined microscopically, or the material may be cultured.

Fern Test for Ovulation

This test can be used to determine the presence or absence of ovulation or the time of ovulation.

When cervical mucus is spread upon a clean dry slide and allowed to dry in air, it may or may not assume a frondlike pattern under the microscope (sometimes seen grossly). The fern frond pattern indicates an estrogenic effect on the mucus without the influence of progesterone (Fig 5–10); thus, a nonfrond pattern can be interpreted as showing that ovulation has occurred.

Schiller Test for Neoplasia

When cancer of the cervix or vaginal mucosa is suspected, the area may be painted with Lugol's (strong iodine) solution. Any portion of the epithelium that does not accept the dye is abnormal owing to the presence of scar tissue or neoplasia. Biopsy should be performed in this area if cancer is suspected.

Sounding of the Cervix & Corpus for Patency

A standard uterine sound is 7 mm in diameter, corresponding to the diameter of the normal cervical canal. If the sound can be passed through the cervical canal without obstruction, no stricture is present. On the other hand, if the cervical canal is definitely larger than the sound, an incompetent cervical os may be present.

Many uterine sounds are calibrated so that the depth of the uterine cavity can be measured; the average uterine cavity is 7.5 cm from the external os of the cervix to the fundus of the uterine corpus. If bleeding occurs with simple passage of a sound, it may indicate the presence of endometrial cancer (Clark's test). By

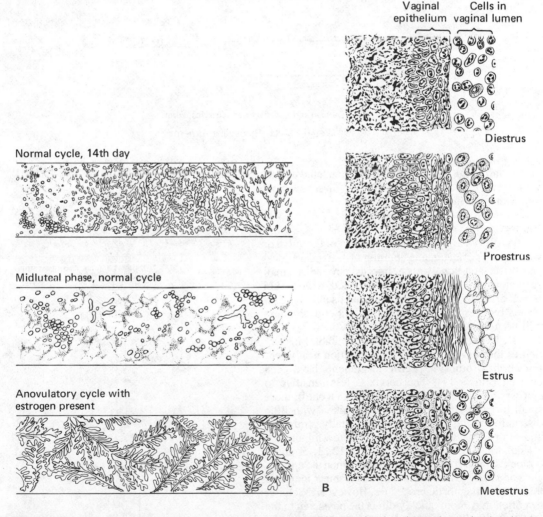

Figure 5–10. *A:* Patterns formed when cervical mucus is smeared on a slide, permitted to dry, and examined under the microscope. Progesterone makes the mucus thick and cellular. In the smear from a patient who failed to ovulate *(bottom),* there is no progesterone to inhibit the estrogen-induced fern pattern. (Reproduced, with permission, from Ganong WF: *Review of Medical Physiology,* 10th ed. Lange, 1981.) *B:* Cell changes in the vaginal wall *(left)* and type of cells found in the vaginal smear *(right)* during the estrous cycle in the rat. The vaginal smear pattern in humans is similar, but not so clear-cut. (Redrawn and reproduced, with permission, from Turner and Bagnara: *General Endocrinology,* 5th ed. Saunders, 1971.)

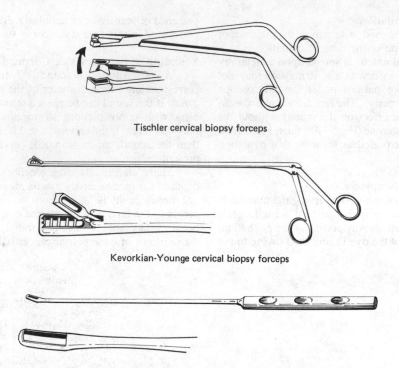

Tischler cervical biopsy forceps

Kevorkian-Younge cervical biopsy forceps

Duncan endometrial or endocervical curet

Figure 5–11. Biopsy instruments.

manipulating the sound so that it will touch the uterine walls, irregularities may be felt, eg, a submucosal tumor or a uterine septum.

Biopsy

A. Vulva and Vagina: For biopsy of the vulva or vagina, a 1–2% aqueous solution of a standard local anesthetic solution can be injected around a small suspicious area and a sample obtained with a skin punch or sharp scalpel. Bleeding can usually be controlled by pressure, but occasionally a clip or suture will be necessary.

B. Cervix: If a colposcope is available, inspection of the cervix prior to instrumentation is advised. For cervical biopsy, specific instruments have been devised (Fig 5–11). The cervix is less sensitive to cutting procedures than the vagina, so that one or more small biopsies of the cervix can be taken with little discomfort to the patient. Bleeding usually is minimal and controlled with light pressure for a few minutes. A "4-quadrant" biopsy is one taken at 12, 3, 6, and 9 o'clock. This is a common procedure when the appearance of a local lesion or a positive cytosmear indicates this further diagnostic procedure. However, a Schiller test often may more quickly direct the physician to the area that should be biopsied. The endocervix may be biopsied with a small curet (Fig 5–11).

C. Endometrium: Endometrial biopsy can be helpful in the diagnosis of ovarian dysfunction (eg, infertility) and as a screening test for carcinoma of the uterine corpus. The endometrial biopsy may be per-

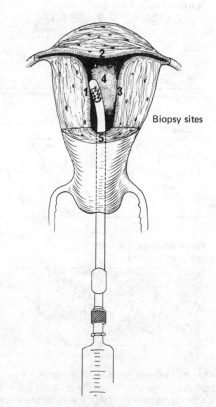

Biopsy sites

Figure 5–12. Sites of endometrial biopsy. (Reproduced, with permission, from Benson RC: *Handbook of Obstetrics & Gynecology,* 7th ed. Lange, 1980.)

formed with a cutting instrument (Fig 5–11) or by passing a hollow endometrial biopsy curet (eg, NovaK or Randall curet) (Fig 5–12) into the uterine cavity and using the suction of a syringe to aspirate fragments of endometrium into the curet. Since the procedure usually causes a cramp, the patient should be warned, and the examiner should take as few strokes of the curet as possible. Narrower biopsy curets recently have become available that cause much less discomfort but still yield an adequate tissue sample. Another approach to the collection of endometrial cellular material is the Jet Washer (Gravlee).

DIAGNOSTIC LABORATORY PROCEDURES

Routine procedures that are not discussed here but should be considered with each gynecologic investigation include a complete blood count (including differential white cell count), erythrocyte sedimentation rate (ESR), and serologic test for syphilis (STS), eg, VDRL (Venereal Disease Research Laboratory).

Urinalysis

Urinalysis should include both gross and microscopic examinations. A microscopic examination may reveal crystals or bacteria, but unless the specimen is collected in a manner that will exclude vaginal discharge, the presence of bacteria is meaningless (see below). It is often wise to ask the patient to collect her "routine" specimen 2 hours after a high-carbohydrate meal; glycosuria at that time indicates the need for a more definitive test for diabetes mellitus.

Urine Culture

Studies have demonstrated that a significant number of women (about 7%) have asymptomatic urinary tract infections. Culture and antibiotic sensitivity testing are required for the diagnosis and as a guide to treatment of urinary tract infections.

Urine cultures can be expensive; it is therefore suggested that the physician arrange with the laboratory for a "screening" culture to determine whether or not an infection is present, and then to order specific antibiotic sensitivity studies only if the screen culture is positive.* The patient who does not have a urinary tract infection thus pays only for the screening test.

Reliable specimens of urine for culture often can be obtained by the "clean catch" method: the patient is instructed to cleanse the urethral meatus carefully with soap and water, to urinate for a few seconds to dispose of urethral contaminants, and then to catch a "midstream" portion of the urine. It is essential that the urine not dribble over the labia, but this may be difficult for some patients to accomplish.

---

*This may be a matter for consultation between the physician and the laboratory pathologist. Many pathology laboratories do not offer screening examinations unless the physicians they serve insist on it.

A more reliable method of collecting urine for culture is by sterile catheterization performed by the physician or nurse. When correctly performed, catheterization rarely causes infection of the urinary tract.

Other Cultures

A. Urethral: Urethral cultures are indicated if a sexually transmitted disease is suspected.

B. Vaginal: Determining the cause of vaginal infection is usually simple, and a culture is usually unnecessary, since visual inspection or microscopic examination will usually enable the physician to make a diagnosis, eg, curdlike vaginal material that reveals mycelia (candidiasis). However, in questionable cases a culture should be obtained.

C. Cervical: As in the case of the urethra, the usual indication for a culture of cervical discharge is to find a sexually transmitted disease.

D. Endometrial Cavity: Cultures of the endometrial cavity are difficult to obtain, since inadvertent contamination is common. When infection of the endometrium is suspected, the clinical condition of the patient is usually so serious that salpingitis is a likely diagnosis. However, an endometrial culture can be obtained by passing a small sterile tube through the cervix and then passing an even smaller cotton-tipped probe through the tube.

E. Anal Cultures: For *Neisseria gonorrhoeae*.

Other Specific Tests

Specific diagnostic laboratory procedures may be indicated for some of the less common venereal diseases, eg, herpesvirus 2, lymphogranuloma venereum, and hepatitis B. These will be indicated in the discussions of the specific diseases elsewhere in this book.

Pregnancy Testing

Pregnancy testing is discussed in Chapter 27.

Papanicolaou Smear, Cervical

The Papanicolaou smear is an important part of the gynecologic examination. The frequency of the need for this test is in dispute at this time; epidemiologic statistics have led some physicians to state that for the average woman a smear test every 2 or 3 years is adequate. This is based on the observation that most cervical cancers are slow-growing. However, because rapidly growing cervical cancers are occasionally reported and because there is always a possibility of false-negative laboratory reports, most gynecologists at this time continue to advocate annual smears. Patients with a high risk of uterine, cervical, or vaginal cancer should be tested at least annually, and others, eg, "DES babies," semiannually.

The Papanicolaou smear is a screening test only; positive tests are an indication for further diagnostic procedures such as cervical biopsy or conization, endometrial biopsy, or D&C. The properly collected Papanicolaou smear can accurately lead to the diagnosis of carcinoma of the cervix in about 98% of cases at best and carcinoma of the endometrium in about 80% of cases.

The Papanicolaou smear consists of placing a film of exfoliated cells from the lower genital tract on a slide, staining, and then searching microscopically for malignant cells. The test is not as dependable as a biopsy but, if positive, indicates the need for one.

The techniques of collection may vary slightly, but the following is a common procedure.

The patient should not have douched for at least 24 hours before the examination. The speculum is placed in the vagina after being warmed and lubricated with water only. With the cervix exposed, either a cotton-tipped applicator slightly dampened with saline solution or a specially designed plastic or wooden spatula is applied to abrade the surface slightly and to pick up some of the cells from the area of the cervical os. The speculum is then maneuvered so that its posterior lip picks up some of the exfoliated cellular material lying in the posterior fornix of the vagina and is then slowly withdrawn. The cells to be examined are thus both on the applicator or spatula (from the cervix) and in the lip of the speculum (total specimen). These 2 specimens may be mixed or put on the slide separately according to the preference of the examiner. A preservative is then applied and the slide sent to the laboratory with an identification sheet including pertinent history and findings (Fig 5–6).

Papanicolaou Smear, Endometrial

Cell sampling from the endometrium for cytologic examination is not yet (1982) dependable. Several devices have recently been marketed (and one, widely advertised, removed from the market), but the dependability is probably no greater than 90% and frequently less. The procedure may be so painful for the patient in some instances that she would decline to have it repeated. It is hoped that more efficient and dependable endometrial sampling devices will be developed soon.

SPECIAL DIAGNOSTIC PROCEDURES

Amniocentesis

Amniocentesis consists of aspiration of fluid from the amniotic sac. The fluid must be collected in a dark bottle to protect against sunlight and sent promptly to the laboratory for analysis. The fetal cells found in the fluid make possible a Barr body count or a tissue culture for a chromosome karyotype determination. Amniocentesis may be performed as an office procedure. Under meticulously sterile conditions, and using local anesthesia, a long No. 18–20 needle is quickly thrust through the abdominal wall into the amniotic sac, the site of which has been previously estimated by palpation or, preferably, by ultrasonography. When the stylet of the needle is withdrawn, clear fluid emerges; a syringe is then attached and the required amount—usually not over 20 mL—of amniotic fluid is aspirated. The needle is then withdrawn and the fluid

sent to the laboratory. This procedure entails no need for bed rest, antibiotics, or other treatment for the patient; it is almost painless, does no harm to the mother, and only rarely harms the fetus. A bloody aspiration means that the position of the needle tip has been misjudged and that it is in the placental area. If clear fluid cannot be obtained, the procedure should be abandoned and attempted again no sooner than 4 days later. Amniocentesis can also be performed late in pregnancy in order to estimate fetal maturity (see Chapter 29).

Colposcopy

The colposcope (Fig 5–13) is a binocular microscope used for direct visualization of the cervix. Magnification as high as 60 × is available for research purposes, but the most popular instrument in clinical use has a 13.5 × magnification that effectively bridges the gap between what can be seen by the naked eye and by the microscope. Some colposcopes are equipped with a camera for the single or serial photographic recording of pathologic conditions.

To use the colposcope effectively, the physician needs thorough training and the opportunity for extensive experience; this, combined with the high cost of

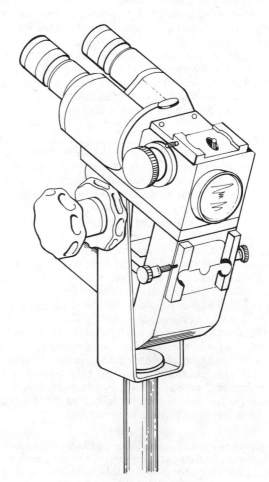

Figure 5–13. Zeiss colposcope.

the instrument, leads to the logical decision by most gynecologists not to train themselves in its use but to refer patients needing the service to an expert colposcopist in the community.

Colposcopy does not replace other methods of diagnosing abnormalities of the cervix but is instead an additional and important tool. It does not lend itself well to mass screening but is valuable in the next diagnostic step after mass screening. The 2 most important groups of patients who can benefit by its use are (1) patients with an abnormal Papanicolaou smear test and (2) the "DES babies," who may have dysplasia of the vagina or cervix (see Chapter 10).

The colposcopist is able to see areas of cellular dysplasia and vascular or tissue abnormalities not visible otherwise, which makes it possible to select areas most propitious for biopsy. Stains and other chemical agents are also used to improve visualization. The colposcope-directed biopsy decreases the number of false-negative biopsies and, frequently, the need for the conization of the cervix, which may have a high morbidity rate.

Experienced colposcopists are now able to observe cervical cellular changes over a period of time, bringing about a new approach to the management of cervical neoplasia. We are now getting reports of regression of some types of cellular changes, an observation impossible to make when our only means of observation was the histologic examination of excised tissue. This is especially important for the adolescent girl or young woman who was a "DES baby." In other instances, the progression of a pathologic state can be observed and the colposcopist can alert the physician to the need for definitive treatment (Figs 5–14, 5–15, and 5–16).

Although the colposcope was introduced in 1925, it has been only in the past decade that American physicians have undertaken the training necessary to

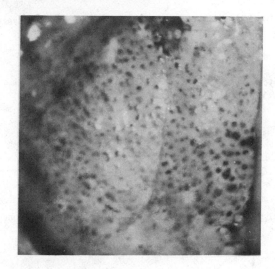

Figure 5–15. Colposcopic view showing coarse punctation of cervical dysplasia.

become proficient in its use. As we gain even more experience and as more colposcopists become trained with the instrument, we can expect even more useful applications to emerge (Fig 5–17).

Hysteroscopy

Hysteroscopy is the visual examination of the

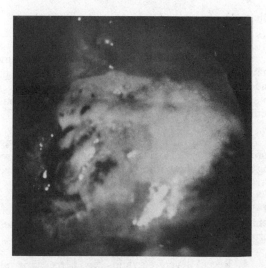

Figure 5–14. Colposcopic appearance of white epithelium in cervical dysplasia.

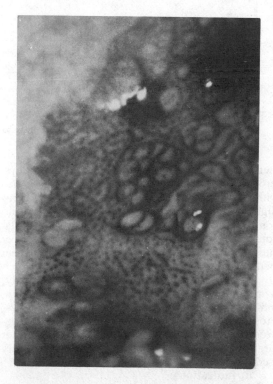

Figure 5–16. Colposcopic view showing mosaicism and coarse punctation in a patient with carcinoma in situ.

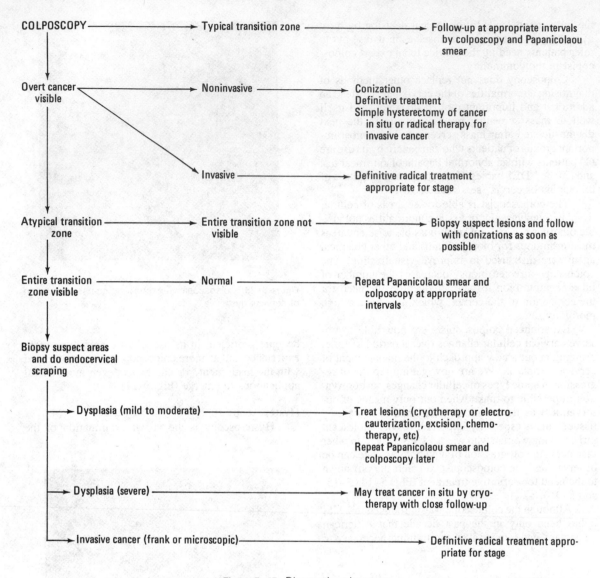

Figure 5–17. Diagnostic colposcopy.

uterine cavity through a fiberoptic instrument, the hysteroscope. In order to inspect the interior of the uterus with the hysteroscope, one must inflate the uterus slightly; this can be done with a balloon, with a solution (usually dextran), or by controlled CO_2 insufflation. If a balloon is employed, no manipulative or therapeutic procedures can be performed, so the other methods are more commonly used.

A. Anesthesia: Diazepam, 10 mg intravenously, or meperidine, 50 mg intravenously, preoperatively, and paracervical block are usually adequate if hysteroscopy is done as an outpatient procedure. If hysteroscopy is performed in conjunction with another surgical procedure, general anesthesia is commonly used.

B. Indications:

1. Infertility evaluation, eg, identification of polyps, uterine anomaly, lysis of uterine synechiae.

2. Abnormal uterine bleeding–Hysteroscopy may reveal a polyp, hyperplastic endometrium, or endometrial cancer.

3. A "lost" intrauterine device may be obvious within the uterus.

4. Uterine abnormalities, eg, arcuate uterus.

5. Amenorrhea or oligomenorrhea following curettage performed to interrupt a pregnancy or following a spontaneous abortion or postpartum hemorrhage (Asherman's syndrome).

6. Voluntary sterilization–An acceptable degree of dependability without complications has not been achieved, but the simplicity of the procedure invites further investigation.

C. Contraindications:

1. Recent severe cervicitis, eg, herpesvirus infection or pelvic inflammatory disease.

2. Possible early intrauterine pregnancy.

3. Adequacy of another method, eg, hysterosalpingography, D&C.

D. Technique: Hysteroscopy should be performed only by physicians with proper training. The tip of the instrument should be inserted just beyond the internal cervical os and then advanced slowly, with adequate distention under direct vision. Hysteroscopy is often used in conjunction with another operative procedure, eg, curettage or laparoscopy.

Small scissors have been designed specially for lysis of synechiae associated with Asherman's syndrome. To prevent re-formation of the synechiae, insert a small Foley catheter with a 3-mL bag and leave in place 5–7 days, or insert an intrauterine device for about 2 months. It is also helpful to assist endometrial regeneration by giving exogenous ovarian hormones, eg, conjugated estrogens, 0.3 mg daily, for 3 weeks each month for at least 2 cycles.

Failure of hysteroscopy may be due to cervical stenosis, inadequate distention of the uterine cavity, bleeding, or excessive mucus secretion.

E. Complications:

1. Perforation of the uterus, usually at the fundus. Unless there is damage to a viscus or internal bleeding develops, surgical repair may not be required.

2. Bleeding–This generally subsides, but fulguration following attempts to remove polyps or myomas may be required.

3. Infection–Parametritis or salpingitis, rarely noted, usually necessitates antibiotic therapy.

Culdotomy & Culdocentesis

Culdotomy consists of incising the vaginal mucosa and the cul-de-sac or pouch of Douglas through the posterior fornix of the vagina as a means of gaining entry into the peritoneal cavity. An experienced operator can do many operative procedures, eg, tubal ligation, as simple hospital procedures. This is also the operative procedure for the treatment of a pelvic abscess that, by bimanual examination, is determined to be "pointing" in the cul-de-sac.

The passage of a needle into the cul-de-sac— culdocentesis—in order to obtain fluid from the pouch of Douglas is a simple diagnostic procedure that can be performed in the office or in a hospital treatment room (Fig 5–18). The type of fluid obtained indicates the type of intraperitoneal lesion, eg, bloody with a ruptured ectopic pregnancy; pus with acute salpingitis; atypical cells (in a "button" made from a centrifuged specimen of clear fluid and examined histologically) in malignancy.

The physician should be aware of the fact that a history of salpingitis indicates the possibility of cul-de-sac adhesions with consequent intestinal perforation during either of these procedures, or during culdoscopy.

Culdoscopy

The culdoscope is an optical instrument similar to the cystoscope or laparoscope; it is used, as the name indicates, for inspection of the pelvic structures through an incision in the posterior cul-de-sac. The patient is placed in the knee-chest position, a small incision is made through the posterior fornix of the vagina into the peritoneal cavity, and the culdoscope is inserted. If necessary, CO_2 may be instilled into the peritoneal cavity through the instrument to allow the intestines to fall cephalad and permit visualization of the pelvic organs.

Culdoscopy is most commonly used to investigate infertility. Direct visualization of pelvic structures allows the culdoscopist to determine gross anatomic and pathologic conditions, eg, congenital abnormalities or the sequelae of traumatic or inflammatory processes. The culdoscope allows direct vision of tubal patency when a small Foley catheter is inserted through the cervical canal into the uterine cavity, the

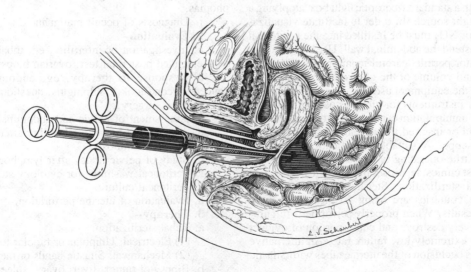

Figure 5–18. Culdocentesis.

bulb is inflated with 2 mL of sterile normal saline solution, and a nonirritating dye such as indigo carmine is injected; the culdoscopist may then observe the progress of the dye through the oviducts. The dye may flow freely or may stop at some point in either or both tubes. The tubal patency test of Rubin and the radiographic hysterosalpingogram frequently are adequate to establish tubal patency in the infertile patient; if there is uncertainty, tubal patency under direct vision by means of the culdoscope may be elected.

A technique of culdoscopic sterilization has recently been developed in which each oviduct is located with the culdoscope, grasped, and brought through the colpotomy incision into the vagina. The fimbriated extremity is ligated and excised (Kroener technique) or occluded by tantalum clips—the latter possibly allowing future reversibility. The advantages of sterilization by culdoscopy include the absence of an abdominal scar, less intraperitoneal insufflation, and the assurance that tubal patency has been obstructed by ligation more reliably than can be done by fulguration alone.

The newest laparoscopes have several advantages, however, and the laparoscope has supplanted the culdoscope in most centers. As is the case with all technical equipment, the experience and competence of the operator often outweigh the merits of the instrument and determine the procedure elected.

Laparoscopy*

Laparoscopy—alternatively called peritoneoscopy—is a transperitoneal endoscopic technique that provides excellent visualization of the pelvic structures and often permits the diagnosis of gynecologic disorders and limited surgery without laparotomy. Laparoscopy is one of the most useful of gynecologic procedures, especially for diagnostic purposes and for female sterilization.

Most basic laparoscopes are 10 mm in diameter and have a 180-degree viewing angle. The instrument has an effective length of over 25 cm and can be utilized with a standard fiberoptic light box supplying a 150-watt light source. In order to facilitate visualization, CO_2 or NO_2 must be instilled into the peritoneal cavity to distend the abdominal wall. Use of a pneumatic insufflator permits careful monitoring of the rate, pressure, and volume of the gas used for inflation. In addition to the equipment used for observation, a variety of other instruments for biopsy, coagulation, aspiration, and manipulation can be passed through a separate cannula or inserted through the same cannula as the laparoscope. A suitable modification of design provides a true operating laparoscope.

In most clinics, laparoscopy has been used largely for interval sterilization. Sterilization clinics in the developing countries are using this technique with excellent results. When properly performed, fulguration effectively destroys and cuts a portion of oviduct and has an extremely low failure rate. An alternative technique is occlusion of the uterine tubes with Silastic

bands or metal clips. Apart from its gynecologic importance, laparoscopy is being used with increasing frequency by gastroenterologists to assess liver disease and to obtain a directed percutaneous liver biopsy. Oncologists report with increasing frequency the use of laparoscopy to evaluate responses to chemotherapy and for staging of certain intra-abdominal malignancies.

Although major complications are rare, laparoscopy must be used with prudence; traditional methods of intra-abdominal diagnosis should certainly not be discarded. Laparoscopic procedures are *major* intra-abdominal operations performed through small incisions. This technique is rapidly performed, has a low morbidity rate and a short convalescence period, and is less demanding in terms of medical facilities, supplies, and personnel. It is a cost-effective outpatient procedure.

A. Indications: The indications will increase with the clinician's experience and as technical innovations permit even more complicated procedures.

1. Diagnosis–

a. Differentiation between ovarian, tubal, and uterine masses, eg, ectopic pregnancy, ovarian cyst, salpingitis, myomas, endometriosis, tuberculosis.

b. Disorders of the liver, eg, neoplasia, hepatic cirrhosis, splenomegaly.

c. Genital anomalies, eg, ovarian dysgenesis, uterine maldevelopment.

d. Ascites, eg, ovarian diseases versus cirrhosis.

e. Secondary amenorrhea of possible ovarian origin, eg, polycystic ovarian disease, arrhenoblastoma.

f. Pelvic pain, eg, possible adhesions, endometriosis, ectopic pregnancy, twisted or bleeding ovarian cyst, salpingitis, appendicitis, psychogenic pelvic pain.

g. Pelvic injuries after penetrating or nonpenetrating abdominal trauma.

h. Staging of cervical, uterine, or ovarian cancer.

i. Staging of Hodgkin's disease and the lymphomas.

j. Diagnosis of occult malignancy.

2. Evaluation–

a. Investigation of infertility, eg, tubal patency test, extended postcoital test, ovarian biopsy.

b. Response to therapy, eg, endometriosis, cancer "second-look," salpingitis, questionably successful tubal surgery.

c. Assessment of pelvic and abdominal trauma.

d. Appraisal of bowel for viability after surgery, for mesenteric thrombosis.

e. Study of pelvic nodes after lymphography.

f. Peritoneal washings for cytology study.

g. Peritoneal culture.

h. Evaluation of uterine perforation.

3. Therapy–

a. Tubal sterilization:

(1) Electrical: Unipolar or bipolar technique.

(2) Mechanical: Silastic bands or metal clips.

b. Biopsy of tumor, liver, ovary, spleen, omentum, etc.

---

*This section is contributed by John M. Levinson, MD.

c. Lysis of adhesions.

d. Fulguration of endometriosis.

e. Aspiration of small unilocular ovarian cyst or of fluid for culture.

f. Removal of extruded intrauterine device.

g. Uterosacral ligament division (denervation).

h. Removal of fetus in ectopic pregnancy.

i. Myomectomy.

j. Intraperitoneal placements of–

(1) Hydrocephalic shunt drains.

(2) Catheters for chemotherapy.

k. Placement of intraperitoneal clips as markers for radiotherapy.

l. Salpingostomy for phimotic fimbriae.

m. Removal of tuboplastic hoods or splints.

n. Ova collection for in vitro fertilization.

o. Mini-wedge resection of ovary.

B. Contraindications: *Note:* Previous intra-abdominal surgery will have been done in 15–18% of patients in large series and usually is not a contraindication to laparoscopy.

1. Absolute–Intestinal obstruction, generalized peritonitis.

2. Relative–Severe cardiac or pulmonary disease.

C. Careful explanation of the contemplated procedure must be given to each patient prior to surgery. Unless the individual is a poor operative risk, laparoscopy is usually an outpatient operation. Preparation includes no solid food for at least 8 hours prior to surgery, no liquids for more than 6 hours preoperatively, and a history and physical examination, routine blood studies, and urinalysis. Preoperative medication (eg, propiomazine, 20 mg intramuscularly, and atropine sulfate, 0.5 mg intramuscularly) should be given 1 hour before the procedure: No abdominal or perineal shaving is necessary, but skin preparation with an antiseptic is routine.

D. Anesthesia: Local anesthesia, local anesthesia with systemic analgesia, spinal or epidural block techniques, or general anesthesia with or without endotracheal intubation may be used. Acupuncture anesthesia may be effective also. Special hazards of anesthesia exist, eg, reduced diaphragmatic excursion because of the pneumoperitoneum and because the patient may be operated on in the Trendelenburg position. With adequate understanding of the physiology involved, however, effective anesthesia and laparoscopy can be accomplished safely.

Most procedures can be done with relative ease under local anesthesia. The patient is first given meperidine (Demerol), 50 mg intravenously, and diazepam (Valium), 10 mg intravenously, over a 2-minute period on the operating table. An alternative approach of fentanyl (Sublimaze), 0.1 mg (2 mL) intravenously, may be utilized to produce mild tranquilization and elevation of the pain threshold without causing anxiety or depression, which are noted occasionally with meperidine and diazepam. The patient is then positioned and prepared for surgery. A periumbilical field block with 15 mL of 1% lidocaine (Xylocaine) generally provides adequate anesthesia. Transient discomfort may be noted if the oviducts are cut with an electric current for sterilization, but this may be prevented by injection of 2% lidocaine into the oviduct just prior to that phase of the operation. By utilizing local anesthesia, patients may be ready for discharge as early as 1 hour after the operation.

E. Surgical Technique: (Figs 5–19 to 5–22.) The patient should be placed in the dorsal lithotomy

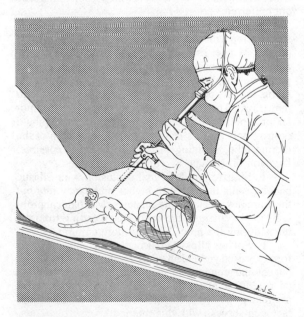

Figure 5–19. Pelvic laparoscopy with patient in Trendelenburg position.

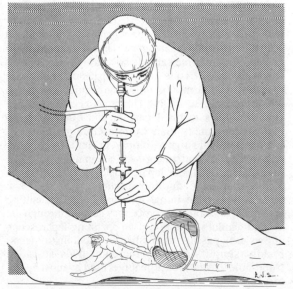

Figure 5–20. Mid abdominal laparoscopy. Patient in dorsal lithotomy position.

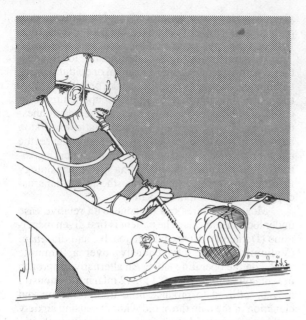

Figure 5–21. Upper abdominal laparoscopy. Patient in 10-degree reverse Trendelenburg position.

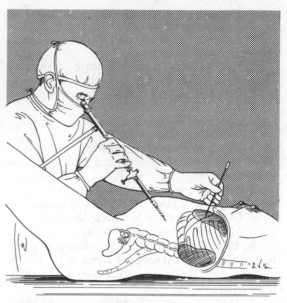

Figure 5–22. Percutaneous liver biopsy under laparoscopic guidance.

position and draped after induction of anesthesia and preparation of the abdomen and pelvic area. The bladder must be emptied by catheterization. After careful bimanual examination, a tenaculum is attached to the cervix and a tubal insufflation cannula is inserted into the cervical canal and finally fixed to the tenaculum so that it can be used as a "handle" to maneuver the uterus. A 1-cm stab wound should be made within the umbilicus through which a needle is inserted into the peritoneal cavity. Two liters of gas should then be introduced and monitored by the pneumatic insufflator. The needle is withdrawn and the laparoscopic trocar and cannula inserted. After proper abdominal entry, the trocar may be withdrawn and replaced with the fiberoptic laparoscope. The examiner manipulates the intrauterine cannula so that the pelvic organs can be observed. To test for tubal patency, methylene blue or indigo carmine solution can be injected through the intrauterine cannula. Direct observation of dye leakage attests to tubal patency and often allows a better assessment than hysterosalpingography. If intra-abdominal surgery, biopsy, or fluid aspiration is required, a second trocar with a cannula should be inserted under direct laparoscopic vision through a 5-mm transverse midline incision 8–20 cm (3–8 inches) below the initial incision. Electrical cutting forceps or an aspiration probe may be used through the second cannula. The use of an operating laparoscope allows easy passage of ancillary surgical instruments, greatly simplifying the procedure. This so-called "one-hole" technique probably is used by most operators today.

The operation is terminated by evacuating the insufflated gas through the cannula, followed by removal of all instruments and placement of a 3-0 sub-cuticular suture for wound closure. A small dressing is applied to the wound. Operating time in uncomplicated cases is about 10 minutes.

1. Sterilization–Electrical cautery, Silastic bands, and metal spring clips achieve sterilization by occluding the uterine tubes. About 1% of patients who elect to use these methods of contraception later request reversal of the procedure. Therefore, for women under age 35, techniques resulting in lesser amounts of tissue destruction limited to the mid portion of the tube are preferred.

a. Cautery (unipolar or bipolar)–Laparoscopic sterilization with an electrical cautery offers a very low pregnancy rate. Excessive tubal destruction is associated with an unacceptably high incidence of ectopic pregnancy, since it may create a tiny fistula from the uterus into the peritoneal cavity through which sperm may travel. Therefore, when using either form (unipolar or bipolar) of electrical coagulation, one should destroy only a short section of the mid portion of the uterine tube, avoiding the uterine cornu if possible. Division of the tube by cutting is not necessary.

b. Silastic bands–Tubal occlusion with Silastic bands results in a slightly higher pregnancy rate but there are fewer ectopic pregnancies. Mechanical problems in placement of the bands and bleeding from the tubes during the procedure are more common.

c. Spring clips–Tubal occlusion with the clips formerly used yielded an unacceptable pregnancy rate, but ectopic pregnancies were rare. Preliminary reports on recent modifications of the spring clip are most promising. The skill of the surgeon is an important factor in success with this method.

2. Infertility–No study of the infertile patient is complete without laparoscopic study. All secondary infertility due to a tubal sterilization should be investigated by laparoscopy to determine the possibilities and probabilities of a successful microsurgical tubal repair. In spite of a normal hysterosalpingogram, a large percentage will have tubal abnormalities apparent at the time of laparoscopy. Peritubal adhesions may be lysed with electric scissors, and salpingostomy may be accomplished. The minimal trauma of these procedures using laparoscopy and the saving of a major operative procedure are apparent. Laparoscopy should be considered for women with complaints of abnormal bleeding and pelvic pain. More liberal use of the laparoscope has led to the diagnosis of many unsuspected cases of endometriosis. Hormonal treatment of endometriosis probably should be withheld until visual or histologic confirmation of the disease is available.

3. Abdominal and pelvic pain–Laparoscopy has proved invaluable in differentiating various causes of acute and chronic pain. The technique may save the patient the necessity of a major exploration. Fluid aspiration and tissue biopsy are possible through laparoscopy. Also, pelvic and chronic intestinal disease may be differentiated. Numerous cases of chronic pain caused by intra-abdominal adhesions also have been diagnosed by laparoscopy, and relief has been obtained following resection by electric scissors.

4. Trauma–In cases of intra-abdominal trauma, laparoscopy may be utilized to exclude the need for a major abdominal operation.

5. Intra-abdominal diagnosis–Even after exhaustive studies, the possibility of intra-abdominal carcinoma may still exist. The laparoscopist, by systematically surveying the peritoneal surfaces, the bowel, the greater curvature of the stomach, the left and right lobes of the liver, the spleen, and diaphragmatic surfaces, may find the causative lesion. Intra-abdominal fluid and biopsy specimens may be removed for cytologic study. For example, in cases of suspected liver disease, a percutaneous biopsy may be performed through laparoscopic guidance (Fig 5–22). However, because tumors may lie deep within the liver or retroperitoneal structures or other structures inaccessible to the laparoscope, negative studies in a patient suspected of having intra-abdominal carcinoma may be misleading. Further exploratory laparotomy must be considered in these cases.

There is an increasing use of laparoscopy as a "second look procedure" 1 year after chemotherapy for ovarian cancer. A finding of tumor demonstrates the need for further therapy and saves the patient a major procedure. Negative findings must not be understood to rule out cancer, and a full laparotomy must be strongly considered.

6. Miscellaneous–"Missing" IUDs have been removed from the intra-abdominal cavity. Mulligan plastic hoods from tuboplasty procedures, "lost" drains, and other foreign material have been removed from the abdomen by operative laparoscopy.

F. Postsurgical Care: Patients may be sent home following full recovery from anesthesia, usually in 1–2 hours. Postoperative pain is usually minimal, and patients are discharged with a prescription for a simple oral analgesic. Patients are encouraged to resume full activity, including sexual relations, the day following surgery. Coitus is interdicted only when a D&C, therapeutic abortion, or vulvovaginal surgery has been performed concomitantly with laparoscopy. Patients should routinely be seen in the office 2 weeks postoperatively.

G. Complications: When misidentification and luteal phase pregnancies are excluded, the true failure rate for laparoscopic sterilization varies between 0.9 and 6 per 1000 sterilizations, depending in part on the technique used. This rate is similar to that of non-laparoscopic techniques. A survey conducted by the American Association of Gynecologic Laparoscopists disclosed a complication rate of 1.8:1000 with sterilization laparoscopy and 2.6:1000 with diagnostic laparoscopy. The higher incidence of complications when the instrument is used for investigation of disease is probably related to the fact that the patients are older and ill. As laparoscopists become more experienced, the incidence of complications tends to fall. Complications are infrequent when meticulous care is exercised throughout the procedure.

1. Pain–Pain may be referred from the diaphragm to the shoulder or chest due to pressure from unabsorbed gas. Using smaller volumes of gas will minimize pain. Gas is usually absorbed within hours. Mild analgesics and rest in the recumbent position should alleviate discomfort.

2. Bleeding–Insertion of a needle and trocar through the abdominal wall has inherent risks. Proper positioning of the penetrating instrument is essential.

a. Small arterial or venous bleeders usually respond to electrocoagulation or pressure with biopsy forceps. Tubal damage resulting in significant bleeding requiring laparotomy is rare.

b. Ecchymotic areas in the anterior abdominal wall or omentum need no treatment.

c. Laceration or puncture injuries of the iliac arteries or veins or of the aorta have been reported. If this is likely to have happened, immediate emergency blood replacement and laparotomy for vascular repair must be instituted.

3. Puncture injury–Injury from a trocar requires laparotomy and repair. Puncture injury to the stomach or bowel by the needle during insufflation of gas usually requires no treatment.

4. Misplacement of gas–The risk of misplacement of gas into the anterior rectus sheath is minimized by the pneumatic insufflator monitoring equipment, but on occasion it is uncertain whether or not gas has been introduced into the abdominal cavity. The ability of gas to disperse rapidly and to be absorbed through body tissues affords a safety factor.

5. Thermal burns–It was hoped that bipolar sterilization would reduce the number of thermal injuries at laparoscopy, but some still occur. With increased operator experience, the number of serious injuries with unipolar cautery has been reduced drastically. The less experienced operator should use bipolar cautery to reduce the chance of thermal injury. Burn injuries are fewer with improved equipment and operator experience.

6. Vague unexplained lower abdominal discomfort—Abdominal discomfort in the days following the procedure must be assessed with the possibility of salpingitis in mind. This is most uncommon, however. Infections of the surgical wound are exceedingly rare.

Berek JS et al: Laparoscopy for second look evaluation in ovarian cancer. *Obstet Gynecol* 1980;**58**:192.

Brenner WE: Evaluation of contemporary female sterilization methods. *J Reprod Med* 1981;**26**:439.

Chi IC et al: An epidemiologic study of risk factors associated with pregnancy following female sterilization. *Am J Obstet Gynecol* 1980;**136**:738.

Corson SL: Major vessel injury during laparoscopy. *Am J Obstet Gynecol* 1980;**138**:589.

Levinson JM: The introduction of laparoscopy in the People's Republic of China. *Del Med J* 1980;**50**:147.

Levinson JM: The role of laparoscopy in intra-abdominal diagnosis. *Del Med J* 1978;**50**:5.

Loeffer FD et al: Pregnancy after laparoscopic sterilization. *Obstet Gynecol* 1980;**55**:643.

Phillips JM et al: *The 1979 AAGL Membership Survey Presented at the Annual Meeting of the AAGL.* (November) 1980.

Phillips JM et al: *Endoscopy in Gynecology.* American Association of Gynecologic Laparoscopists, 1978.

Piver MS et al: The value of pre-therapy peritoneoscopy in localized ovarian cancer. *Am J Obstet Gynecol* 1977;**127**:288.

Radiographic Diagnostic Procedures

There are many common radiologic procedures that may be helpful in the diagnosis of pelvic conditions. The "flat film" will show calcified lesions, teeth, or a ring of a dermoid cyst and will indicate other pelvic masses by shadows or displaced intestinal loops. The use of contrast media is indicated frequently to help delineate pelvic masses or to rule out metastatic lesions: the barium enema, upper gastrointestinal series, intravenous urogram, and cystogram.

Hysterography & Hysterosalpingography

The uterine cavity and the lumens of the oviducts can be outlined by instillation through the cervix of contrast medium followed by fluoroscopic observations or film. The technique was first widely used for the determination of tubal disease as part of the investigation of the infertile woman; its use is now being extended to the investigation of uterine disease.

To determine tubal patency or occlusion, the medium is instilled through a cervical cannula; the filling of the uterine cavity and the spreading of the medium through the tubes is watched under fluoroscopy, with the radiologist taking "spot" films at intervals for subsequent more definitive scrutiny. If there is no occlusion, the medium will reach the fimbriated end of the tube and spill into the pelvis—evidence of tubal patency. This procedure will also reveal an abnormality of the uterus, eg, congenital malformation, submucous myomas, endometrial polyps.

Hysterography has been recommended as an aid in the diagnosis of the cause of abnormal uterine bleeding. The film will often demonstrate endometrial polyps, myomas, or endometrial carcinoma. If intracavitary irradiation pellets are to be used for the treatment of endometrial carcinoma, a prior hysterogram to determine the size and contour of the uterine cavity is of great benefit to the physician.

It is logical to question the advisability of hysterography in patients with endometrial carcinoma in view of the possibility of dissemination of the malignancy either through the oviducts or by intravasation. Although these complications do occur, most studies indicate that the mortality rate is no higher in patients who have had hysterography than in those who have not.

The gynecologist should consult a radiologist in each instance to gain advice on the advisability, timing, type of contrast medium to be used, and technique.

Angiography

Angiography is the radiographic demonstration of contrast medium in the blood vascular system. By demonstrating the vascular pattern of an area, tumors or other abnormalities can be delineated. This procedure is not commonly used in gynecology, since it is usually difficult to perform and uncomfortable for the patient and because ultrasonography and CT scanning usually give more information and are easier to perform.

Lymphangiography

Lymphangiography is performed by injecting contrast medium into a lymphatic vessel of the lower extremity and obtaining x-ray films as the medium advances through the pelvic and abdominal lymphatic system. It is useful in demonstrating metastasis to the lymph nodes in the pelvis or the para-aortic areas by the presence of enlarged or distorted nodes, or by filling defects indicating that nodal tissue has been replaced by tumor.

CT Scan

Although ultrasonography is the primary imaging modality in obstetrics, the radiographic technique known as CT scan (computed tomography) is playing an increasingly prominent role in gynecologic diagnosis, particularly in the evaluation of pelvic tumors.

A CT scan consists of a series of cross-sectional recordings usually taken at 1-cm intervals. Each view is the result of computer analysis of the differing ability of tissues within each "slice" to impede the passage of conventional x-rays. So that we may visualize and record this analysis, the computer translates the differences in x-ray attenuation into a gray-scale picture, which may be viewed on a television screen or radiographic film. Dense tissues, eg, bone, within a segment of the study "absorb" most of the x-rays and are depicted as light-colored, while less dense tissues appear in deeper shades of gray.

CT scan has several distinct advantages over ultrasound, even though there is radiation exposure and it is more costly. The inability of ultrasound to penetrate fatty tissue or gas make CT scan the imaging modality of choice for obese patients or those with a distended viscus such as the stomach or bowel. In addition, the presence and extent of cancer is more accurately evaluated with CT scan, particularly when there is involvement of retroperitoneal pelvic lymph nodes. The presence of lung, liver, and skeletal metastases and obstructive uropathy can be ascertained during the same CT scan.

Present techniques also permit CT-guided percutaneous "thin needle" biopsy of suspected primary or recurrent malignant masses.

Malignant invasion of the bladder or rectum may be suggested by CT scan, although this often requires cystoscopic or sigmoidoscopic verification. However, CT scan cannot demonstrate tumor nodules smaller than 1–2 cm in diameter on omental or peritoneal surfaces. In addition, soft-tissue thickening due to therapeutic radiation may be indistinguishable from small foci of tumor recurrence.

CT scan plays a limited role in the assessment of other gynecologic abnormalities. Pelvic abscesses may be demonstrated by CT scan, but most other uterine, tubo-ovarian, and cervical pathologic processes are best viewed ultrasonographically.

Pelvic Pneumography

This diagnostic technique, also called pelvic pneumoperitoneum, pneumopelvography, or gynecography, is a procedure performed by radiologists. A gas, most commonly CO_2 is instilled into the abdominal cavity through either the cul-de-sac or the abdominal wall. X-ray films are then obtained with the patient in a modified Trendelenburg position so that the upper abdominal contents fall out of the pelvis, allowing the pelvic viscera to be more clearly outlined in the film. However, since the advent of ultrasonography and laparoscopy, this procedure is rarely used.

Ultrasonography

Ultrasonography records high-frequency sound waves as they are reflected from anatomic structures. As the sound wave passes through tissues, it encounters variable acoustic densities; each of these tissues returns a different echo, depending upon the energy reflected. This echo signal, which is capable of being measured, can be converted into a 2-dimensional picture of the area under examination.

Ultrasonography is a simple and painless procedure that has the added advantage of avoiding any radiation hazard. It is especially helpful in a child, virgin, or obese woman who might otherwise be difficult or impossible to examine, although fat tends to scatter and distort sound waves, thus limiting somewhat the value of the sonogram in this instance.

The pelvis and low abdomen are scanned and recorded at regular intervals of distance, usually about 1 cm, in both longitudinal and transverse planes (Fig 5–23). Generally, the scan is performed with the blad-

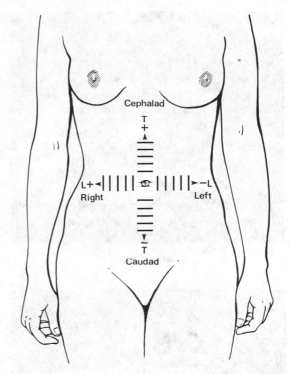

Figure 5–23. Planes of ultrasonograms.

der full; this elevates the uterus out of the pelvis, displaces air-filled loops of bowel, and provides the operator with an index of density—a sonographic "window" differentiating the pelvic organs.

Ultrasonography can be helpful in the diagnosis of almost any pelvic abnormality, since all structures, normal and abnormal, can usually be demonstrated. In most instances, a clinical picture has been developed—by history, physical examination, or both—before obtaining ultrasonograms. The scan thus often will corroborate the clinical impression, but it may also uncover an unexpected condition that the clinician should recognize. The technique is useful in many gynecologic work-ups.

A. Congenital Anomalies: Uterine or vaginal agenesis, double or bicornuate uterus, streak ovaries.

B. Foreign Bodies: The most common foreign body in the uterus is a lost IUD. Ultrasonography may be the best method to determine the unrecognized expulsion of the device; its presence if the suture has been lost or retracted; pregnancy with or without retention of the device; complete or incomplete uterine perforation; or concomitant pelvic inflammatory disease. Ultrasonography can also reveal a foreign body in a child, which often is difficult to determine by inspection or physical examination.

C. Infection: A posterior cul-de-sac abscess may be clearly demonstrated, but a fluid-filled loop of bowel, an ovarian cyst, ascites, or blood from a ruptured viscus may confuse the picture. However, the clinical history and characteristic sonographic appearance of a pelvic abscess should aid in the diagnosis.

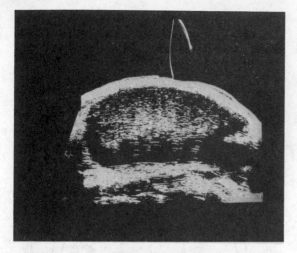

Hydatidiform mole

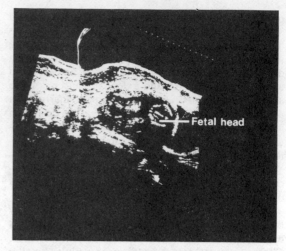

Early fetus

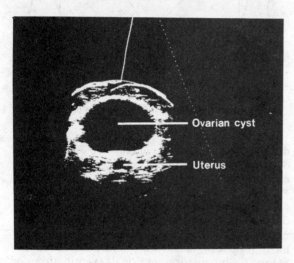

Ovarian cyst; normal uterus

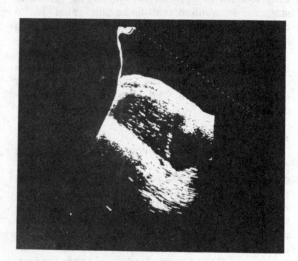

Hydatidiform mole

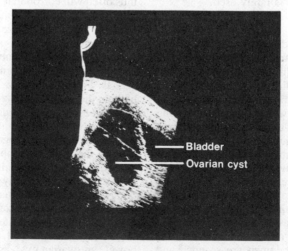

Ovarian cyst with septum; bladder

Figure 5–24. Ultrasonograms. (Courtesy of Louis Bartolucci, MD, San Francisco.)

D. Early Pregnancy: Early pregnancy may cause confusion; it may be associated with uterine myoma or ovarian tumor, or the pregnancy may be multiple or may be ectopic. Other problems include spontaneous abortion, threatened abortion, incomplete abortion, missed abortion, congenital uterine abnormality, pseudocyesis, and hydatidiform mole. In some of these, serial studies may be useful to demonstrate normal or abnormal gestational development. Ultrasonography should be employed before midtrimester amniocentesis to help the operator avoid the placenta or fetus when inserting the needle.

E. Uterine Tumors: Myomas may present a confusing picture, since their irregular or necrotic centers may suggest cancer. Ultrasonography should show the enlargement but cannot differentiate benign from malignant tumors. However, it may be possible to demonstrate endometrial carcinoma or the extension of malignancy into other pelvic sites.

F. Uterine Tube Abnormalities: Enlargement of the oviducts is usually due to infection or ectopic pregnancy; carcinoma is rare. Ectopic pregnancy usually occurs in the uterine tube, but ovarian or abdominal pregnancy may occur also. In the differential diagnosis, other abnormalities, eg, hemorrhagic corpus luteum cyst, dermoid cyst, tubo-ovarian abscess, or pregnancy in one horn of a bicornuate uterus, should be considered.

G. Ovarian Tumors: Ultrasonography can differentiate between solid and cystic tumors. A dermoid cyst often gives a distinctive pattern. A confusing picture might be produced by a pedunculated subserous myoma. Successive ultrasonograms may be desirable, because many functional ovarian cysts will regress, and solid tumors may enlarge rapidly to substantiate the clinical observation of malignancy.

H. Endometriosis: This disorder often appears on the scan as irregular collections of fluid in the pelvis. However, even with these observations, the diagnosis of endometriosis must remain suggestive or presumptive.

I. Elective Abortion: Although most elective abortions are performed by suction curettage, on occasion it may be deemed advisable to abort a patient by the amniocentesis–labor induction method. The duration of pregnancy and size of the uterine contents are the determining factors. Ultrasonography may be the best means of obtaining this information.

J. Postpartum Complications: Ultrasound may be useful in the diagnosis of several postpartum complications, eg, retained products of conception, uterine or adnexal hematoma, thromboembolism, or abscess.

Doppler Ultrasound

The frequency of sound (or light) waves depends upon the relative motion of the wave source and the observer; as an object moves, it reflects waves at slightly altered frequencies (the Doppler effect). An example is the change in pitch of a train whistle when the train is approaching or moving away. The Doppler ultrasound technique can be applied to certain body functions including blood flow and peristalsis.

The Doppler demonstration of a beating fetal heart may be recorded as early as the eighth week of pregnancy and is quite dependable by the 12th week. The technique can be helpful in the diagnosis of fetal death, multiple pregnancy, and ectopic pregnancy.

Carbon Dioxide Laser

Controlled tissue vaporization by means of the carbon dioxide laser is a new modality for the treatment of cervical, vaginal, or perineal carcinoma in situ. It also can be used for conization of the cervix for diagnosis of dysplasia or carcinoma within the cervical canal. Malignancy in situ may be as deep as 4 mm below the surface; at least another millimeter of tissue may need to be excised; and tissue damage from the thermal effect of the laser beam is approximately another millimeter; so a minimum of 6 mm of tissue should be excised in order to obtain an adequate specimen for histologic examination.

The procedure is not difficult, but training is essential. Antiseptic preparation of the vagina should be gentle, to avoid trauma to the tissue that may be examined histologically. Local anesthesia, with or without preliminary intravenous sedation, is usually adequate.

Advantages of the laser beam method of cervical conization are the following: little or no pain; a low incidence of infection, because the beam sterilizes the tissues; decreased blood loss, since the laser instrument — at a decreased energy level — is a hemostatic agent; less tissue necrosis than occurs with electrocautery (but probably the same as with excision by a sharp knife); and a decreased incidence of postoperative cervical stenosis.

Carbon dioxide lasers are expensive and are being improved continually. Rather than purchase this piece of equipment, a practitioner may wish to refer patients to a medical center where laser diagnosis and treatment are available.

THE PERIODIC HEALTH SCREENING EXAMINATION

It is now a generally accepted part of the physician's responsibility to advise patients to have periodic medical evaluations. The frequency of visits may vary from once a month to once a year depending upon the patient's problem.

The periodic health screening examination helps detect the following ailments of women that are especially amenable to early diagnosis and treatment: diabetes mellitus; urinary tract infection or tumor; hypertension; malnutrition or obesity; thyroid dysfunction or tumor; and breast, abdominal, or pelvic tumor. These conditions can be detected by a rapid review of systems, with specific questions regarding recent abnormalities or any variation in function. Determination of weight, blood pressure, and urinalysis, which can be done in minutes, may reveal variations from the previous examination. An examination of thyroid, breasts, abdomen, and pelvis, including Papanicolaou smear, should then be performed. A rectal examination is also advisable, and a conveniently packaged test for occult blood (Hemoccult) is now available and recommended for patients over 40 years of age.

The physician should also be concerned about conditions other than purely somatic ones; unless a patient's problems require the services of a psychiatrist or some other specialist, the doctor should be prepared to act as a counselor and work with the patient during a mutually agreeable time when it is possible to unhurriedly listen to her problems and give support, counsel, and other kinds of help as required.

●　●　●

References

Barbot J, Parent B, Dubuisson JB: Contact hysteroscopy: Another method of endoscopic examination of the uterine cavity. *Am J Obstet Gynecol* 1980;**136**:721.

Beck P, Gal D, Tancer ML: Silicone band sterilization with radiographic and laparoscopic evaluation. *Obstet Gynecol* 1979;**53**:698.

Brown RC et al: Accuracy of lymphangiography in the diagnosis of paraaortic lymph node metastases from carcinoma of the cervix. *Obstet Gynecol* 1979;**54**:571.

Dorsey JH, Diggs ES: Microsurgical conization of the cervix by carbon dioxide laser. *Obstet Gynecol* 1979;**54**:565.

Epley SL, Hanson JH, Cruikshank DP: Fetal injury with midtrimester diagnostic amniocentesis. *Obstet Gynecol* 1979;**53**:77.

Fleischer AC et al: Differential diagnosis of pelvic masses by gray-scale sonography. *Am J Roentgenol* 1978;**131**:469.

Golbus MS et al: Prenatal genetic diagnosis in 3000 amniocenteses. *N Engl J Med* 1979;**300**:157.

Gomel V: Laparoscopic tubal surgery in infertility. *Obstet Gynecol* 1975;**46**:47.

Gottesfeld K: Ultrasound in obstetrics and gynecology. *Semin Roentgenol* 1975;**10**:305.

Hobbins JC et al: Ultrasound in the diagnosis of congenital anomalies. *Am J Obstet Gynecol* 1979;**134**:331.

Kelly MT et al: The value of sonography in suspected ectopic pregnancy. *Obstet Gynecol* 1979;**53**:703.

Kirkpatrick RH et al: Gray scale ultrasound in adnexal thickening correlation with laparoscopy. *J Clin Ultrasound* 1979;**7**:115.

Lacey CG et al: Laparoscopy in the evaluation of gynecological cancer. *Obstet Gynecol* 1978;**52**:708.

Levinson JM: The role of laparoscopy in intra-abdominal diagnosis. *Del Med J* 1978;**50**:5.

Levitt RG et al: Computed tomography of the pelvis. *Semin Roentgenol* 1978;**13**:193.

Nash D, Haning RV Jr, Shapiro SS: The value of hysterosalpingography prior to donor artificial insemination. *Fertil Steril* 1979;**31**:378.

Persson PH, Grennert L, Gennser G: Diagnosis of intrauterine growth retardation by serial ultrasonic cephalometry. *Acta Obstet Gynecol Scand* 1978;(**Suppl 78**):40.

Phillips JM et al: *Endoscopy in Gynecology.* American Association of Gynecologic Laparoscopists, 1978.

Phillips JM et al: *Laparoscopy.* Williams & Wilkins, 1977.

Robinson JS: Growth of the fetus (ultrasonics). *Br Med Bull* 1979;**35**:137.

Rome RM et al: Observations on the surface area of the abnormal transformation zone associated with intraepithelial and early invasive squamous cell lesions of the cervix. *Am J Obstet Gynecol* 1977;**129**:565.

Sandberg EC: Benign cervical and vaginal changes associated with exposure to stilbestrol in utero. *Am J Obstet Gynecol* 1976;**125**:777.

Sanders RC, James AE Jr: *The Principles and Practice of Ultrasonography in Obstetrics and Gynecology.* Appleton-Century-Crofts, 1980.

Sciarra J, Valle R: Hysteroscopy: A clinical experience with 320 patients. *Am J Obstet Gynecol* 1977;**127**:340.

Siegler AM et al: Hysteroscopic procedures in 257 patients. *Fertil Steril* 1976;**27**:1267.

Spaulding LB et al: The role of ultrasonography in the management of endometritis/salpingitis/peritonitis. *Obstet Gynecol* 1979;**53**:442.

Sugimoto O: Diagnostic and therapeutic hysteroscopy for traumatic intrauterine adhesions. *Am J Obstet Gynecol* 1978;**131**:539.

Sweet RL et al: Use of laparoscopy to determine microbiologic etiology of acute salpingitis. *Am J Obstet Gynecol* 1979;**134**:68.

Talebian F et al: Colposcopic evaluation of patients with abnormal cervical cytology. *Obstet Gynecol* 1977;**49**:670.

Taylor KJW: *Atlas of Gray Scale Ultrasonography.* Churchill Livingstone, 1978.

Technology 1980: Physicians' annual report on diagnostic and therapeutic tools. *Contemp Obstet Gynecol* (Oct) 1979. [Special issue.]

Tovell H, Banogan P, Nash A: Cytology and colposcopy in the diagnosis and management of preclinical carcinoma of the cervix uteri: A learning experience. *Am J Obstet Gynecol* 1976;**124**:924.

Uhrich PC, Sanders RC: Ultrasonic characteristics of pelvic inflammatory masses. *J Clin Ultrasound* 1976;**4**:199.

Urcuyo R et al: Some observations on the value of endocervical curettage performed as an integral part of colposcopic examination of patients with abnormal cervical cytology. *Am J Obstet Gynecol* 1977;**128**:787.

Valle RF: Hysteroscopy in the evaluation of female infertility. *Am J Obstet Gynecol* 1980;**137**:425.

Varma TR: Ultrasound evidence of early pregnancy failure in patients with multiple conceptions. *Br J Obstet Gynaecol* 1979;**86**:290.

Wladimiroff JW, Bloemsma CA, Wallenburg HCS: Ultrasonic diagnosis of large for date infants. *Obstet Gynecol* 1978;**52**:285.

Normal & Abnormal Menstruation | 6

Leon Speroff, MD

Menstruation is bleeding and physiologic shedding of the uterine endometrium that occurs at approximately monthly intervals from menarche to menopause. It is basically a catabolic process under the control of anterior pituitary and ovarian hormones. The onset of menstruation, the **menarche,** usually occurs between 11 and 14 years of age; its termination, the **menopause,** normally occurs at 45–55 years of age. Surgery or irradiation may result in **artificial menopause** at an earlier age, and various diseases and abnormalities of the X chromosome can cause **premature menopause** (before age 40).

Menarche

The menarche is only one of the many manifestations of puberty, and its occurrence is part of the normal female growth pattern. The first sign of puberty is generally an acceleration of growth followed by the appearance of the breast buds. Pubic hair generally appears after breast development, although the sequence may be reversed; and axillary hair usually appears about 2 years after pubic hair, though in occasional cases axillary hair may be the first to appear. Menarche is a late pubertal event, occurring after the peak of the height spurt has passed.

The normal range of ages at onset of menstruation is 9.1–17.7 years in the USA, with a mean of 12.8 years. Early cycles are usually anovulatory and, therefore, irregular and occasionally heavy. Anovulatory cycles usually continue for 12–18 months. The correlation is fairly good between the ages at menarche of mothers and daughters and between sisters.

The normal menstrual cycle varies from 24 to 34 days, depending upon age and physical and emotional well-being. The usual duration of normal menstrual bleeding is 3–5 days. Normal extremes are considered to be 1–8 days. Both the duration and the amount of menstrual flow are fairly constant for any individual woman.

The amount of blood lost during normal menstruation ranges from slight spotting to 80 mL; the average is 30 mL. Loss of more than 80 mL is considered to be excessive. Menstrual blood loss can be influenced by many factors such as general state of health, specific disease, psychic upset, environment, medications, drug therapy or abuse, and the occurrence or nonoccurrence of ovulation in the preceding cycle.

Menstrual discharge contains not only blood but also endometrial debris, catabolites, prostaglandins, enzymes, cervical mucus, desquamated vaginal epithelial cells, and bacteria. Unless bleeding is excessive, clotting is prevented by a high level of fibrinolysin from the endometrium. Large clots in the vagina are evidence that the supply of fibrinolysin to prevent clotting is inadequate in relationship to the amount of uterine bleeding. However, small, fragile clots (deficient in fibrin) may accumulate in the vagina as a result of the presence of mucoproteins and glycogen. This clumping is aided by the change in pH from 7.5 in the uterine cavity to 4.0 in the vagina.

The changes in hormone levels that take place during a normal menstrual cycle are shown in Fig 6–1. During menses, the pituitary responds to low levels of estradiol by secreting FSH. This initial increase in gonadotropin is essential for follicular growth and steroidogenesis. With continued growth of the follicles, estradiol production within the follicle maintains follicular sensitivity to LH and FSH by activating FSH receptors. The combined action of LH/FSH and estradiol increases the number of LH receptors, allowing luteinization and ovulation to occur. Ovulation is triggered by the rapid rise in circulating levels of estradiol. A rise in progesterone follows ovulation along with a second rise in estradiol, forming the well-known 14-day luteal phase characterized by low FSH and LH levels. The demise of the corpus luteum, with a fall in hormone levels, allows the gonadotropins to increase again, initiating a new cycle.

A serum progesterone level greater than 3 ng/mL is presumptive evidence that ovulation and corpus luteum formation have occurred. Assay of progesterone may be used to determine the occurrence of ovulation. Other tests include secretory endometrium obtained by biopsy, biphasic basal body temperature curve, vaginal cytology, or increased urinary pregnanediol excretion.

Endometrial Changes (Figs 6–1 and 6–2)

During reproductive life, the endometrium undergoes continual cyclic changes in histologic structure. Each menstrual cycle is divided into 3 phases which can be identified by microscopic examination of

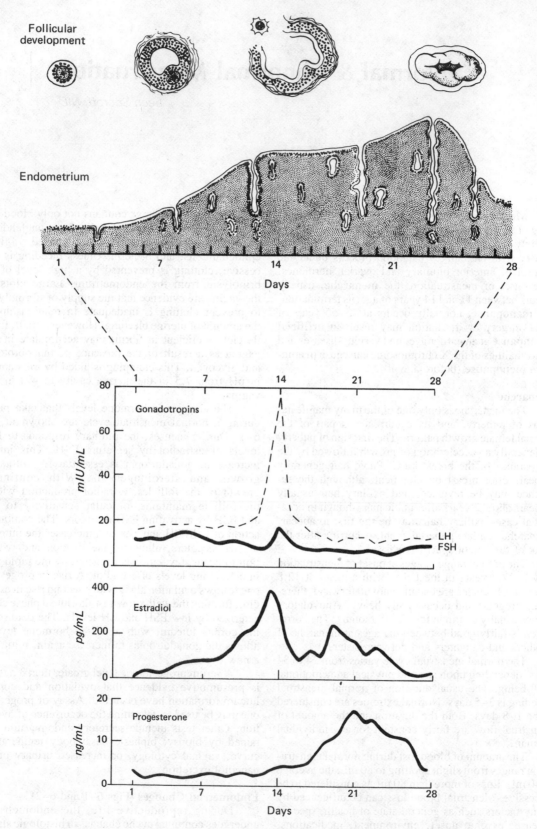

Figure 6–1. The menstrual cycle, showing pituitary and ovarian hormones and histologic changes. (Reproduced, with permission, from Meyers FH, Jawetz E, Goldfien A: *Review of Medical Pharmacology,* 7th ed. Lange, 1980.)

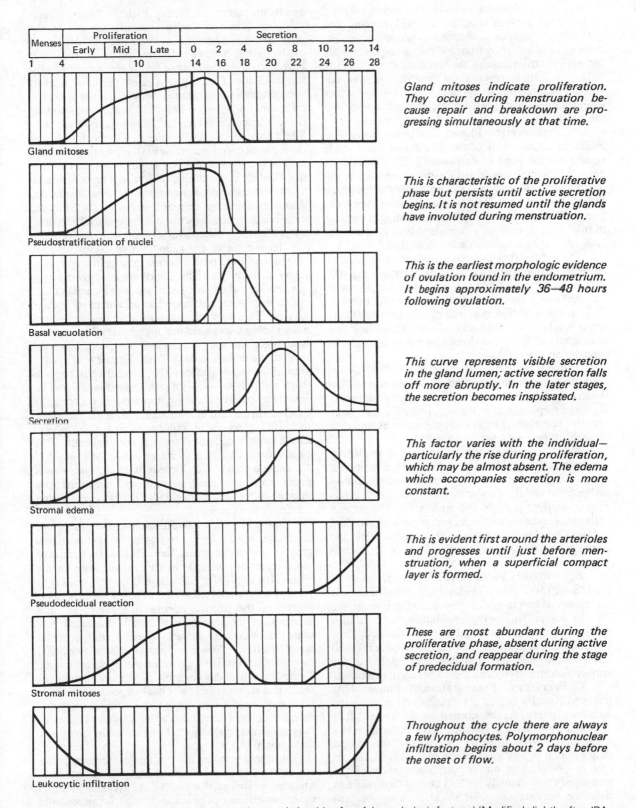

Gland mitoses indicate proliferation. They occur during menstruation because repair and breakdown are progressing simultaneously at that time.

This is characteristic of the proliferative phase but persists until active secretion begins. It is not resumed until the glands have involuted during menstruation.

This is the earliest morphologic evidence of ovulation found in the endometrium. It begins approximately 36–48 hours following ovulation.

This curve represents visible secretion in the gland lumen; active secretion falls off more abruptly. In the later stages, the secretion becomes inspissated.

This factor varies with the individual—particularly the rise during proliferation, which may be almost absent. The edema which accompanies secretion is more constant.

This is evident first around the arterioles and progresses until just before menstruation, when a superficial compact layer is formed.

These are most abundant during the proliferative phase, absent during active secretion, and reappear during the stage of predecidual formation.

Throughout the cycle there are always a few lymphocytes. Polymorphonuclear infiltration begins about 2 days before the onset of flow.

Figure 6–2. Dating the endometrium. (Approximate relationship of useful morphologic factors.) (Modified slightly after JPA Latour and reproduced, with permission, from Noyes, Hertig, and Rock: Dating the endometrial biopsy. *Fertil Steril* 1950; 1:3.)

the endometrium (usually obtained by simple biopsy). Endometrial growth is stimulated by estrogen, and glandular maturation is induced by progesterone. Estrogen produced by ovarian follicles is responsible for the proliferative phase of the menstrual cycle. Usually only one follicle reaches the graafian stage of development preparatory to ovulation, although many follicles ripen to varying degrees during the preovulatory period and then undergo degenerative atresia.

A. Proliferative Phase: The proliferative (estrogenic) endometrial phase of the menstrual cycle constitutes the stage of endometrial regrowth and reconstruction in response to the estrogen released by the developing follicles. It starts on about the fourth or fifth day of the cycle (just before the end of menstruation) and usually lasts about 10 days, ending at the time of ovulation. It may vary considerably in duration but is usually consistent with each individual.

During the first 2–3 days, surface and glandular epithelium of the denuded basal endometrium regenerates, with growth of low columnar cells whose nuclei are irregularly located and show numerous mitoses. The stroma is quite dense, and its cells have relatively large nuclei and little cytoplasm. There are few phagocytic cells. The endometrial glands are narrow, tubular, and straight.

The midproliferative phase (days 3–6) differs from the early proliferative phase only in degree. The thickness of the endometrium is materially increased. Its surface epithelium is thicker, smoother, and more regular. The glands become slightly tortuous, and their epithelium becomes pseudostratified.

The late proliferative phase ends at ovulation, approximately the 14th day of the average menstrual cycle. The endometrium becomes only slightly thicker, but cellular concentration is greater. The surface epithelium is thick and undulating. The stromal cells become more closely packed as extracellular fluid is lost. The glands become increasingly tortuous and produce a minimal secretion that does not yet contain glycogen.

B. Ovulatory Phase: Ovulation occurs on about the 14th or 15th day of a 28-day cycle. Because there is no appreciable change in the endometrium in the 24–36 hours following ovulation, one cannot distinguish microscopically between 14th- and 15th-day endometrium. Distinctive changes appear in gland cells on the 16th day and thereafter; they indicate corpus luteum activity and therefore recent ovulation.

C. Secretory (Progestational) Phase: This phase technically begins at ovulation and includes the ovulatory phase. Under normal circumstances, it is consistently 14 days in duration. (The occurrence of a "persistent corpus luteum" or a corpus luteum cyst may prolong it.) In the absence of ovulation, the secretory phase does not occur; continuation of the menstrual cycle (usually for less than 14 days) reflects only the persistence—and slight growth—of proliferative endometrium until degeneration ensues.

On the second day of the secretory phase (16th cycle day), increased tortuosity of the glands is quite apparent, there are many mitotic figures, and glycogen-laden subnuclear vacuoles appear in the glandular epithelium. (These constitute evidence that ovulation has occurred. By this time, the BBT will have risen and progesterone levels are increasing.) By the third day (17th day of cycle), the most marked vacuolization has developed. Most glandular epithelial cells contain glycogen-rich fluid in the basal portion (called "subnuclear clearing"). Mitoses now are rare. Slight stromal edema is present. On the fourth day (18th day of cycle), secretion of fluid into the glandular lumens becomes apparent. (At this time, the ovum is free-floating in the uterine cavity, so it must derive its nutrition from scant uterine fluid.) Stromal edema develops as glandular secretion increases. In addition, there is a progressive increase of endometrial vascularity as numerous dilated vessels appear in the stroma.

By the eighth day (22nd day of cycle), stromal edema reaches its peak. (Edema may facilitate implantation of the ovum.) The glands are even more tortuous, but they show less secretory activity and considerable inspissated secretion has accumulated in their lumens. This apex of secretory activity and stromal edema coincides with the highest level of corpus luteum activity and progesterone secretion. From the tenth to the thirteenth days (24th–27th days of cycle), stromal edema regresses. The stromal cells become large and polyhedral, with small round nuclei and an abundant, palely staining cytoplasm. This change is first seen in the cells around the spiral arterioles, where increased numbers of mitotic figures also appear. These stromal cells now suggest decidual cells. This final stromal change is therefore called "deciduoid," "pseudodecidual," or "predecidual." The glands then become even more tortuous, with deep serrations in their walls ("sawtooth glands"), and their secretion continues to diminish.

In the absence of fertilization and implantation, the corpus luteum begins to regress and estrogen and progesterone secretion declines. This causes a series of rapid regressive changes in the endometrium on the 13th–14th days (27th–28th days of cycle), leading to menstruation within a few days. The glands expel their secretion, the stromal edema disappears, and the thickness of the endometrium is thus decreased. Endometrial shrinkage causes increased coiling of the spiral arterioles. Moreover, withdrawal of hormonal support also results in spasm of the spiral arterioles. These 2 mechanisms combine to produce circulatory stasis and tissue ischemia. Other degenerative endometrial changes are evidenced by infiltration of polymorphonuclear neutrophils and monocytes. Tissue necrosis promptly develops to bring about the menstrual endometrial phase.

It should be noted that during the secretory phase the day-to-day morphologic changes in the endometrium are so striking that much more accurate dating of the endometrium can be accomplished by microscopic examination than is the case during the proliferative phase.

D. Menstrual Phase: The endometrial ischemia

and degenerative changes that occur at the end of the secretory phase cause tissue necrosis irregularly distributed through all endometrial layers except for the lower portion of the basalis layer of the endometrium. Tissue necrosis causes blood vessels to open, producing scattered small hemorrhages into the tissue. These enlarge and coalesce into propagating hematomas, which in turn cause shedding of the overlying endometrium and further rupture of small vessels. All this results in menstrual bleeding.

In ovulatory cycles, shedding of endometrial tissue fragments usually starts in patchy fashion about 12 hours after bleeding begins. Ordinarily, the shedding is not uniform throughout; in some areas of endometrium the processes of repair and resurfacing are already under way while others continue to bleed and shed. (The rare so-called membranous dysmenorrhea, which is undoubtedly due to an abnormally rapid and complete sequence of the above events, is associated with sudden separation of the entire secretory endometrium to produce a complete cast of the uterine cavity. The uterine contractions required to expel it are usually quite painful.) About two-thirds of the entire endometrium is lost with each ovulatory menstruation. By the time brisk flow ceases, tissue loss has occurred from most of the surface of the uterine cavity by shedding of the superficial or functionalis layer.

The pattern of menstrual bleeding is quite variable. It ranges from very heavy flow for 12–24 hours followed by scanty bleeding during subsequent days to an essentially unvarying flow throughout the period. After 4–7 days, bleeding gradually diminishes. Regional ooze in the uterine cavity is reduced by constriction and thrombosis of the remaining undamaged portions of the coiled arterioles, so that spotting finally ceases.

Clinical Phases of the Menstrual Cycle

In clinical parlance the menstrual and proliferative endometrial phases of the cycle are combined into the **preovulatory** or **follicular phase**; the **postovulatory** or **luteal phase** corresponds to the endometrial secretory phase (including the ovulatory phase).

Two of the 3 endometrial phases of the normal ovulatory menstrual cycle may vary considerably in duration. The secretory phase usually lasts 14 days. This represents the very specific life span of the normal corpus luteum. In contrast, the menstrual phase may vary from 1 to 8 days, and the proliferative phase may vary by as much as 7–8 days. In clinical terms, therefore, variation in total length of the normal and abnormal ovulatory menstrual cycle is usually the result of variation in the follicular phase.

Anovulatory Cycles

In anovulatory cycles, the maturation and differentiation of the endometrium by progesterone do not occur, and the sequence of events is therefore incomplete. The period is qualitatively similar to an ovulatory one, but minimal coiling of the spiral arterioles probably can cause only small fissures and no prop-

agating hematomas. The peeling away of the functionalis layer thus takes place only imperfectly in the proliferative or hyperplastic endometrium. Bleeding from terminal arteriolar loops occurs, but tissue loss is minimal and oliguria may result. Unless ovulation resumes, the endometrium continues to proliferate from cycle to cycle, with the result that in subsequent periods excessive bleeding from this grossly thickened tissue finally develops.

The absence of ovulation deletes the secretory phase from the anovulatory cycle. However, this does not simply shorten such a cycle to 14 days. Despite the absence of progesterone, growth stimulus continues to support the proliferative endometrium—at least for a time. Finally, the growth support is withdrawn (estrogen levels fall below the "bleeding threshold"), and the endometrial mechanisms that produce bleeding and sloughing then take place, although relatively ineffectually. This sequence of events usually results in a somewhat shortened menstrual cycle—and occasionally leads to continuous spotting.

MECHANISMS OF MENSTRUATION

Although endometrial regression is initiated by withdrawal of the sustaining influences of estrogen and progesterone following deterioration of the corpus luteum, the subsequent complex chain of events in the endometrium that causes it to break down is still incompletely understood. The following factors are involved: (1) fluctuations in ovarian and pituitary hormone levels, (2) characteristics of the endometrium (phase, receptivity to hormones), (3) activity of the autonomic nervous system, (4) vascular changes (stasis, spasm-dilatation), (5) enzymes and prostaglandins, and (6) other factors such as nutritional and emotional ones.

Hormonal Regulation

The endometrium responds directly to stimulation or withdrawal of estrogen and progesterone. In turn, regulation of the secretion of these steroids involves a well-integrated, highly structured series of activities by the hypothalamus and the anterior lobe of the pituitary. Although the ovaries do not function autonomously, they influence, through feedback mechanisms, the level of performance programmed by the hypothalamic-pituitary axis. The basic elements involved in this relationship are ovarian steroids (estrogens and progesterone), pituitary gonadotropins (FSH and LH), and releasing hormone (GnRH). The releasing hormone is elaborated by the hypothalamus to govern pituitary gonadotropin production. (For a description of the relationships between ovarian steroids and pituitary gonadotropins, see Chapter 3.)

Enzyme Factors

Cytochemical and electron microscopic studies

have shown that estrogen influences the specific endometrial localization and storage of certain hydrolytic enzymes. Estrogen also stimulates the formation of glycogen and acid mucopolysaccharides. The enzymes that accomplish this are contained in lysosomes. The acid mucopolysaccharides are easily split complexes of carbohydrates with proteins. Estrogen influences production and condensation (polymerization) of the acid mucopolysaccharides to form stromal ground substance and the so-called basement membrane. The acid mucopolysaccharides act as a gel, giving physical support to the growth and neovascularization seen in the proliferative phase of the menstrual cycle. The cyclic withdrawal of progesterone and of estrogen initiates the cellular breakdown that leads to menstruation. By the time the midluteal phase has been reached, the acid mucopolysaccharides have disappeared. Progesterone, or the decrease in estrogen, blocks acid mucopolysaccharide synthesis, and, after degradation of the acid mucopolysaccharides already formed, no more remains in the endometrial stroma. Vascular permeability is increased, and metabolites flow between cells and blood vessels to nourish the endometrium. If implantation fails to occur, progesterone production diminishes. Hormonal withdrawal is associated with increased permeability of the lysosomal envelope, possibly as a result of the change in physical consistency of the ground substance. Destructive hydrolases are released into the tissues, destroying the subcellular areas concerned with protein synthesis. Thus, the lysosomal enzymes contribute to a severe metabolic deficiency and represent an important step in the sequence of events leading to endometrial regression and bleeding.

In anovulatory cycles, the endometrium is influenced by estrogen alone—in minimal, excessive, or sustained amounts. Thus, the endometrium can range from atrophic to hyperplastic.

Vascular Factors

Vascular changes in the endometrium play a major role in menstruation. Five types of bleeding have been observed: (1) arterial bleeding with the formation of a single small hematoma; (2) arterial bleeding without hematoma formation; (3) diapedesis; (4) venous bleeding; and (5) secondary bleeding from a previously ruptured, poorly thrombosed vessel.

Blood is supplied to the endometrium by 2 types of arterioles: (1) tortuous types (**spiral, or coiled,** arterioles), which are near or surround the endometrial glands and which supply the functionalis layer or outer two-thirds of the endometrium; and (2) short, straight vessels that supply only the basalis layer or inner third of the endometrium. The basalis is not shed but remains as a reservoir of tissue for the regeneration of the stroma and superficial portions of the endometrial glands. Only the superficial coiled arterioles are involved directly in menstrual bleeding.

For the first week after the onset of menstrual bleeding, the spiral arterioles are short and relatively straight. During the period of thickening of the endometrium, they become elongated. The vessels grow more rapidly than the endometrium, however, so that they become coiled, particularly in the midportion of the functionalis.

In monkeys (and probably in humans also), just before menstrual bleeding begins, a rapid endometrial regression due to marked estrogen-progesterone depletion results in (1) buckling of the coiled arterioles in the functionalis; (2) stasis of the blood within the arteriovenous channels; (3) necrosis of the terminal arteriolar walls; (4) constriction of these arterioles within the basalis (outer third of the endometrium); and (5) periodic relaxation of and hemorrhage from these peripheral branches.

Four to 24 hours before the onset of menstruation, periodic vasoconstriction of the coiled ateriroles (every 60–90 seconds) apparently causes a type of "blanch and blush" phenomenon as relaxation follows contraction of the vessel musculature. At this time there is also considerable dehydration of the endometrium. Bleeding soon follows from localized areas throughout the endometrium.

Prostaglandins

Menstrual discharge has long been known to contain one or more muscle-stimulating substances. This oxytocic effect has been shown to be due to prostaglandins. Primary dysmenorrhea is due, at least in part, to myometrial contractions induced by prostaglandins originating in the endometrium. Endometrial production of prostaglandins is higher in the luteal phase of the cycle. With the onset of menstruation, prostaglandin levels rise even higher. Thus, the correlation of dysmenorrhea with ovulation is probably due to the higher prostaglandin production in secretory endometrium. The beneficial effect of oral contraceptives can therefore be explained by the presence of decidualized, atrophic endometrium with lower prostaglandin levels.

REPRODUCTIVE TRACT CHANGES DURING THE MENSTRUAL CYCLE

Cervical Changes

The cervical glands increase in size and secretory activity during the preovulatory phase of the cycle, paralleling the estrogen rise shown in Fig 6–2. The amount of cervical mucus secreted may normally reach as much as 60 mg by midcycle. At that time, the mucus changes from an opaque, viscid material with minimal elasticity to a clear substance of low viscosity and maximum elasticity. Penetration of midcycle cervical mucus by spermatozoa is easy compared with that of the early follicular or the late luteal phases of the cycle. Spinnbarkeit, the "stretchability" of the cervical mucus, provides a good clinical assessment of its cyclic changes. Midcycle mucus can be stretched to 8 cm—often to 10–13 cm—whereas early follicular and late luteal phase mucus can rarely be drawn out to a length of more than 1–2 cm.

The changes in cervical mucus—and the associated sperm penetrability—are determined by its chemical and physical properties. The secretion of the cervical glands contains a low-viscosity and a high-viscosity component. The low-viscosity fraction is made up of nonmucoid proteins, salts, and low-molecular-weight organic compounds (carbohydrates and lipids) that readily dissolve in water. The high-viscosity portion, which is responsible for gel formation, contains mucoglycoproteins similar to the type found in mucus secreted elsewhere in the body. The mucins consist of long macromolecular chains of polypeptides with numerous carbohydrate side links. These macromolecular aggregations join together in longitudinal fibrous structures or filaments, which then clump to form a micelle. The macromolecules responsible for the liquid properties of cervical mucus must be very flexible to allow the extensive changes in cervical mucus throughout the menstrual cycle.

The high- and low-viscosity components of cervical mucus are separated by the movement of fluid produced by ciliary activity. Cilia line the entire length of the cervical canal and beat rhythmically, thus creating oscillations in the mucus. This moves the mucus toward the external cervical os at a rate of 1–7 mm/min. At midcycle, in association with maximal estrogen levels, the high viscosity components (micelles) arrange themselves in parallel with each other to form long rods of mucus several millimeters in length. Each rod apparently comes from an individual cervical gland. By ciliary action, the low-viscosity, watery component of cervical mucus flows freely between the high-viscosity rods of mucus, which are fixed into the secreting glands. These channels of low-viscosity mucus permit maximum sperm migration during midcycle (Fig 6–3). The alkalinity of cervical mucus helps create a favorable environment for sperm survival. In the early follicular phase and the entire luteal phase, the micelles are crumpled to form a dense network which impedes sperm penetration.

When a small amount of midcycle cervical mucus is spread on a glass slide, allowed to dry, and inspected under the low-power microscope, a pattern resembling a fern is seen. This ferning pattern is caused by a property of protein which allows it to coat the surface of salt crystals. The coating prevents the crystal from following its usual growth pattern, and the dendritic crystal (fern) is formed instead. Ferning is maximal at midcycle and is associated with high estrogen levels. This "fern test" phenomenon is used as a rough qualitative test of estrogen activity. In the absence of infection or bleeding, the loss of ferning late in the cycle is also a *fair* indicator of the presence of a progesterone effect and a functioning corpus luteum.

Vaginal Changes

The vagina also responds to the hormonal changes of the menstrual cycle. Examination of daily vaginal smears shows a progressive increase in the growth of the vaginal epithelium as the menstrual cycle progresses. The epithelium contains 3 layers: parabasal; intermediate, or functional; and superficial, or cornified. During the early follicular phase, the intermediate layer thickens and the parabasal layer proliferates, its cells demonstrating numerous mitoses. Under the influence of increasing estrogen, all layers of the vaginal epithelium then become thicker, and the superficial cells are pushed farther away from the base. Hence, these cells become farther removed from their blood supply. As a result, they degenerate, cornify, and finally desquamate. Daily vaginal smears taken from the lateral vaginal wall show gradually increasing pyknosis of the nuclei and disappearance of cytoplasmic granules. At ovulation, the cytoplasm of the des-

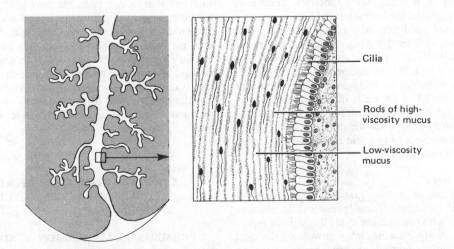

Figure 6–3. Diagrammatic representation of endocervical canal at midcyle showing cilia, rods of high-viscosity mucus, and sperm channels containing low-viscosity mucus. (Reproduced, with permission, from Davajan V, Nakamura RM, Kharma K: Spermatozoan transport in cervical mucus. *Obstet Gynecol Surv* 1970; **25**:1.)

quamated superficial cells is almost totally free of granules and the nuclei are either small, fragmented, or entirely absent. Because serial vaginal smears reflect circulating levels of estrogen, they are clinically useful in the appraisal of estrogen secretion and the identification of the phases of the menstrual cycle.

The maturation index (MI) is a method of cytohormonal evaluation obtained by means of a differential count of the 3 major cell types (parabasal, intermediate, and superficial) among the shed vaginal epithelial cells. With a good nuclear stain of properly fixed material, the parabasal, intermediate, and superficial cells usually are distinguishable. The factors that make up the maturation index are (1) strict cellular morphology, ie, cytoplasmic maturation (thick versus thin); and (2) nuclear maturation, ie, viable vesicular nuclei versus degenerate pyknotic ones. A maturation index of 0/40/60 reflects a vaginal epithelium that is shedding no parabasal cells, 40% intermediate cells, and 60% superficial cells—characteristic of the proliferative phase. As ovulation approaches, a shift to the right occurs in the maturation index. This indicates an increasing number of desquamated superficial (cornified) cells associated with an increasing estrogen level. After ovulation, estrogen drops slightly and progesterone rises. This is accompanied by exfoliation of the intermediate cells, so that the maturation index shifts toward the center number. At menstruation, a typical maturation index may be 0/70/30. Irritation, inflammation, and bleeding may change or obscure the various cell types and thus alter the interpretation or destroy the validity of the maturation index.

Other expressions of cellular maturation include the karyopyknotic index (KI), the percentage of shed squamous epithelial cells having pyknotic nuclei; and the cornification index (CI), the percentage of shed cells having pyknotic nuclei and yellow, orange, or red cytoplasm. These 2 indexes usually closely approximate the third figure of the maturation index.

The pH of the vaginal epithelium undergoes changes that parallel the hormonal changes seen in this tissue. Vaginal fluid normally is acid, with a pH of approximately 4.0 in the early follicular phase. Increasing alkalinity is noted as midcycle approaches, with a pH of 7.0–8.0 at ovulation. As the vaginal pH becomes more basic, an increasing concentration of glycogen is found in the cells of the vaginal epithelium. Although not as important for sperm transport as the preovulatory changes in the cervical mucus, these vaginal changes seem to enable more sperm to reach the cervical canal safely.

Breast Changes

Though the mammary gland normally does not secrete until lactation, it undergoes cyclic changes synchronous with the ovarian cycle throughout reproductive life. Estrogen stimulates growth of the duct system; the acinar epithelium proliferates under the influence of progesterone. Microscopic droplets of secretion are produced by the duct cells by progesterone stimulation, and this fluid collects in the ducts.

Breast swelling, tenderness, and pain experienced by many women in the 10-day period preceding menstruation may be due partially to distention of the lobules and to accumulation of slight secretion within the dilated ducts. Estrogen promotes fluid storage, however, so that premenstrual breast engorgement may be due mostly to increased hyperemia and edema of the interstitial breast tissue. During menstruation, the ducts, acini, and interstitial tissues of the breasts undergo regression, and premenstrual engorgement disappears.

SYSTEMIC CHANGES DURING THE MENSTRUAL CYCLE

During the follicular phase of the menstrual cycle, resting or basal body temperatures (BBT) taken at about the same time each morning are slightly low but relatively constant (36 °C [96.6 °F] orally or 36.6 °C [97.8 °F] rectally). (Activity, infection, inadequate sleep, and alcoholic beverages before retiring cause elevation of BBT the following morning.) These low daily BBTs reflect the hypothermic influence of estrogen. In all women, after ovulation, the rising progesterone level exerts a hyperthermic effect; BBT rises 0.5–1 degree during 24–48 hours. It remains elevated until shortly before the next menstrual period, when it again declines as the progesterone level falls. Thus is produced the biphasic BBT curve of the ovulatory menstrual cycle. It provides evidence, in any given cycle, of the formation of a corpus luteum and presumably of ovulation. In anovulatory cycles, only irregular variations in BBT occur, without any biphasic curve.

Other systemic effects seen before the time of menstruation include a slight drop in hemoglobin concentration, red cell count, and serum iron concentration. A general decrease in resistance to disease occurs at the time of menstruation, associated with a fall in the white count and a rise in the sedimentation rate. Infections and allergic reactions are more likely to occur at this time. Muscle sensitivity or hypertonicity may occur, producing irritability and agitation. Vascular alterations may cause pelvic hyperemia and increased capillary fragility with a tendency to easy bruising. Increased emotional tension is common. Headaches may occur during menses. These may be related to vascular changes and follow a pattern of "menstrual migraine"; or they may be psychogenic, of a tension type.

CLINICAL DISORDERS RELATED TO THE MENSTRUAL CYCLE

PREMENSTRUAL TENSION SYNDROME

Because of associated symptoms, the menstrual cycle exerts some influence on the general behavior and well-being of women. Most women experience minimal discomfort that does not curtail their activity. Some women, however, have one or more of a broad range of symptoms that persist for 1–10 days and usually cease abruptly or become less severe at the onset of menses (or are altered in character to become actual menstrual molimina). If the symptom complex is severe enough to disturb a woman's life pattern or impel her to seek medical relief, it is called premenstrual tension syndrome. On the other hand, some women accept such symptoms as normal manifestations of menstrual function and will reveal their occurrence only upon careful questioning.

The underlying causes of premenstrual tension syndrome are obscure. A transitory increase in water content of different body tissues seems to be the best explanation for symptoms such as weight gain, edema, bloating, and breast tenderness. A pathogenetic role has been assigned to estrogen-progesterone imbalance, excess aldosterone or ADH, allergy to progesterone, hypoglycemia, hyperprolactinemia, and psychogenic factors. Sodium and water retention are secondary to the hypovolemia produced by loss of vascular fluid into the tissues. This results in increased secretion of ADH and aldosterone and retention of sodium and water by the kidney.

Clinical Findings

The occurrence of the following symptoms differs greatly from woman to woman, but the pattern is consistent in the individual woman from cycle to cycle.

A. Behavioral Symptoms: Personality alteration may take the form of nervousness, irritability, agitation, unreasonable temper, and sleep disturbances; or fatigue, lethargy, and depression. Violent crimes committed by women and suicide among women in the reproductive age group occur with greater frequency in the week before onset of menses.

B. Neurologic Symptoms: These include headache (the most common), vertigo, syncope, paresthesias of hands or feet, and aggravation of epilepsy.

C. Respiratory Symptoms: Colds, hoarseness, allergic rhinitis, and asthma are usually worse in the week preceding onset of menses.

D. Gastrointestinal Symptoms: Abdominal bloating is almost typical of the syndrome. Less frequent symptoms are nausea and vomiting, constipation, colicky pain, and increase or decrease of appetite.

E. Miscellaneous Symptoms and Signs: These include edema, temporary weight gain, palpitations, a sense of pelvic weight, backache, oliguria, enuresis, capillary fragility (easy bruising), skin problems (acne, neurodermatitis, and exacerbations of existing dermatologic disease), breast changes (enlargement, heaviness, pain or tenderness), and eye complaints (conjunctivitis, visual changes).

Treatment

For more than 25 years, Dalton has promoted the use of progesterone by injection (100 mg daily) or by suppository (400 mg daily). Scientific evidence, however, to support this treatment is not available. There have been 2 double-blind controlled studies of progesterone therapy for premenstrual symptoms, and in both there was no significant difference between the treated and placebo groups. A review of other treatment regimens (diuretics, oral contraceptives, spironolactone, pyridoxine, bromocriptine, monoamine oxidase inhibitors) fails to reveal any clear-cut benefits.

In severe cases, empiric elimination of cyclic ovulatory hormone changes may be beneficial. This can be accomplished by intramuscular injection of a long-acting progestin such as the intramuscular-depot form of medroxyprogesterone acetate, 150 mg every 3 months. It must be remembered, however, that the placebo response may be the basis of a positive response.

MIGRAINE

Migraine is a severe paroxysmal headache, usually unilateral, associated with sensory and motor disturbances, eg, scotomas and vomiting. It may occur prior to or during menstruation. The cause is not known. There is often a positive family history. The attacks are periodic and often related to some recurring event in the patient's life, eg, the "Wednesday morning conference" or the monthly menstrual period. The frequency of headache varies greatly. True migraine headaches may be triggered by falling estrogen levels just before or during menses.

A migraine attack may be aborted, improved, or terminated by giving ergotamine tartrate or dihydroergotamine with or without caffeine. A single dose of 0.25–0.5 mg intramuscularly or 3 mg orally may suffice for some patients. Others may require two 1-mg tablets (or, with caffeine [Cafergot], 100 mg) initially and 1 tablet every 30 minutes for not more than 6 doses. If nausea and vomiting are a feature of the syndrome, it may be necessary to use rectal suppositories to ensure absorption. This medication is most likely to be effective if taken at the first sign of prodromal symptoms before onset of the headache.

Unlike the headaches associated with premenstrual tension, which disappear with the menopause, migraine often persists after menopause. Postmenopausal migraine often responds to estrogen therapy (see Chapter 25).

MASTODYNIA
(Mastalgia)

Mastodynia is pain and swelling of the breasts resulting from vascular engorgement, edema, and slight secretory engorgement of breast ducts. It represents an exaggeration of a periodic physiologic change and is a common component of premenstrual tension.

No palpable breast abnormality is usually found, but in chronic cases a cyclic, diffuse thickening of the outer edge of the breast can sometimes be noted. Inflammation and neoplasia must be considered. If mastodynia and diffuse breast nodularity persist and increase, the diagnosis may be adenosis (mammary dysplasia); excision biopsy may then be needed for definitive diagnosis.

Diuretic therapy for mastodynia during the few days that premenstrual discomfort persists generally is successful. Refractory severe premenstrual mastodynia may respond to sublingual methyltestosterone, 5 mg daily, given during the luteal phase of 2 or 3 menstrual cycles.

CYCLIC INTERMENSTRUAL PAIN
(Mittelschmerz, Ovulalgia)

Midcycle ovulatory intermenstrual pain is relatively common. Because it is often ignored by the patient or at least not reported, its true incidence is uncertain. About 25% of women experience brief discomfort at the time of ovulation. This occurs mostly in young women, particularly tense and nervous ones. Ovulation is assumed to be the cause of the discomfort because the pain does not occur in anovulatory cycles and because suppression of ovulation usually prevents it. Since bilateral oophorectomy eliminates mittelschmerz but hysterectomy and presacral neurectomy do not, the ovary is thought to be the source of the pain.

Clinically, the midcycle pain of mittelschmerz ranges from a mild, brief twinge in the lower abdomen to acute, severe, continuous abdominal pain. Occasionally the latter is mistakenly attributed to acute appendicitis or some other acute intra-abdominal disorder and unnecessary laparotomy is performed. The diagnosis is based principally on the unique nature of the pain of mittelschmerz: noncramping; nonradiating or radiating only slightly to the inner thigh; unaccompanied by nausea or vomiting; usually lasting less than 1 day; and—most importantly—occurring only at midcycle, often repeatedly but only once in any one cycle. There may be significant bleeding at the site of follicle formation. The specific characteristics of other acute intra-abdominal conditions are not present.

A further aid to diagnosis is the frequent accompanying phenomenon of "ovulation bleeding"— scanty bleeding from the cervix, mixed with cervical mucus, similar to the "bloody show" of labor. (This is caused by the brief fall in estrogen level that occurs between rupture of the follicle and development of the corpus luteum.)

In mild cases, reassurance and explanation, emphasizing the innocuous nature of the pain, usually suffice. Simple analgesics may be helpful. When the pain is frightening or disabling in severity and recurs repeatedly, ovulation should be suppressed over a period of several cycles by means of a steroid contraceptive agent. Although mittelschmerz is eliminated in the treated cycles, it often recurs when ovulation is allowed to resume. If presumed "ovulation

bleeding" becomes prolonged, or if it becomes irregular and repeated in a single cycle, it must then be regarded as metrorrhagia requiring investigation by diagnostic curettage.

VICARIOUS MENSTRUATION

Bleeding from extrauterine sites that coincides with or replaces menstruation is called vicarious menstruation. The commonest site is the nasal mucosa, which responds to estrogens with varying degrees of edema and congestion. Hypersensitive individuals may have cyclic episodes at the time of menses. Abnormality of the nasal epithelium (eg, ulceration) is often a predisposing factor.

Other areas of the body can be the source of vicarious menstruation, notably those where extrapelvic endometriosis has become implanted. Blood dyscrasias may contribute to the occurrence of this type of cyclic hormonal bleeding. Often, however, local lesions are the basic cause, and their treatment may correct the condition.

DYSMENORRHEA

Dysmenorrhea (painful menstruation) is the most common of all gynecologic complaints and the leading cause of absenteeism of women from work, school, and other activities. Because most women experience some degree of pelvic discomfort during menstruation, the term dysmenorrhea should be reserved for fairly incapacitating painful menstruation severe enough to cause the woman to seek medical help either from a physician or by self-medication with proprietary analgesics.

Classification, Causes, & Clinical Findings
Two types of dysmenorrhea are recognized: primary and secondary. **Primary dysmenorrhea** is essential, intrinsic, idiopathic dysmenorrhea not causally related to any identifiable gynecologic disorder. In **secondary** (acquired, extrinsic) **dysmenorrhea,** the pain is caused by organic pelvic disease, eg, endometriosis, salpingitis, adenomyosis, cervical stenosis, uterine myomas, or uterine malposition. Even in secondary dysmenorrhea due to extensive lesions, pain may disappear between periods. Only primary dysmenorrhea will be discussed here.

Etiology
The reported incidence of primary dysmenorrhea varies widely depending on the types of patients considered and the standards used to assess pain. The precise age at onset may be difficult to identify because menstrual discomfort may be gradually progressive. Studies of high school students indicate that about 10% of teenage girls fail to attend classes because of menstrual pain. It has been estimated that over 140 million working hours are lost annually as a result of

dysmenorrhea. Painful menses almost always follows an ovulatory cycle, and, since early postmenarcheal menstrual cycles generally are anovulatory, dysmenorrhea is uncommon in the first 1–2 years of menstrual life. On the other hand, dysmenorrhea that appears after age 20 almost always is the result of pelvic disease, eg, endometriosis.

Primary dysmenorrhea is associated with nausea in 50% of patients, vomiting in 25%, and stool frequency in 35%. The pain is usually low and crampy, recurring in waves that probably correlate with uterine contractions. The pain may be referred to the lower back, as with contractions during labor. The pain usually occurs with the onset of bleeding or just prior to bleeding and lasts a few hours to 1–2 days after the onset of flow. Absorption of prostaglandins into the uterine circulation at the time of endometrial breakdown is probably responsible for all of these symptoms.

In the past, it was felt that dilatation of the cervix was helpful. Many physicians believed also that the discomfort was entirely psychosomatic in nature. These older notions reflected a lack of knowledge of the cause. With an appreciation of the key role of prostaglandins, treatment is now more specific and more effective.

Clinical Findings

The pain of dysmenorrhea is intermittent, sharp, and cramping. It begins in the lower abdomen and radiates to the back and thighs. It usually begins with or just before the beginning of menstrual flow and reaches its peak within 24 hours. If pain of a similar character can be reproduced by passing a standard uterine sound through the internal cervical os, this suggests that the dysmenorrhea is primary. Similarly, in the absence of palpable pelvic lesions, relief of pain by paracervical anesthetic block suggests a diagnosis of primary dysmenorrhea.

Treatment

The nonsteroidal anti-inflammatory compounds are active inhibitors of prostaglandin synthesis. Treatment of dysmenorrhea with these agents is not more effective if the patient is pretreated before onset of menses. Therefore, therapy can begin with the onset of bleeding, and inadvertent drug intake during early pregnancy can be avoided.

The following agents are currently available: indomethacin, 25 mg 3–4 times daily; ibuprofen, 400 mg 3 times daily; naproxen sodium, 250 mg twice daily; and mefenamic acid, 250 mg 4 times daily. Naproxen and ibuprofen cause fewer side-effects (headaches and dizziness) than mefenamic acid. Patients may adjust their own dosages and timing of medication, experimenting to determine the most effective treatment regimen.

It has long been known that suppression of ovulation with oral contraceptives is a very effective means of preventing dysmenorrhea. Prolonged progestational treatment of endometrium reduces the prostaglandin content, and, over a period of time, the production of a relatively atrophic, decidualized endometrium is associated with low-prostaglandin menses free of pain.

With these new pharmacologic approaches, surgical therapy for dysmenorrhea should never be necessary. Primary and secondary dysmenorrhea may coexist. Treatment is worthwhile in such situations because antiprostaglandin agents may give significant relief of pain associated with pathologic problems such as endometriosis.

THE ABNORMAL MENSTRUAL CYCLE

ABNORMAL UTERINE BLEEDING

Any bleeding from the uterus that differs materially from that of the usual menstrual cycle—in frequency of occurrence or in amount or duration of flow—is abnormal. The term applies to both menstrual and nonmenstrual disturbances due to any cause. Although normal regular menstrual bleeding usually signifies the occurrence of ovulatory cycles, no pattern of uterine bleeding is of itself pathognomonic of either ovulation or anovulation.

The cause of abnormal uterine bleeding may be local or systemic, including psychogenic. The condition may represent only a disturbance of function (particularly endocrine function), or it may be the result of organic disease, either benign or malignant. At some time between menarche and menopause, almost every woman experiences one or more episodes of abnormal uterine bleeding. The blood loss itself is always annoying, often debilitating, and may even reach dangerous proportions. For these reasons, and because there may be grave etiologic implications, the prompt diagnosis and treatment of abnormal uterine bleeding are essential to the well-being of the patient.

Patterns of Abnormal Uterine Bleeding

Abnormal uterine bleeding usually conforms to one of several distinct patterns to which specific names have been given. These are described below, with mention of likely causes in each case.

A. Hypermenorrhea (Menorrhagia): (Cyclic menstrual bleeding that is excessive in amount.) The cycle may or may not be of normal length. Some use these terms to denote menstrual flow that is prolonged (more than 8 days) but not excessive in amount, but such bleeding should simply be called prolonged menstruation.

Hypermenorrhea is usually due to local lesions. Likely causes include uterine myomas, endometrial polyps, endometrial hyperplasia, adenomyosis, salpingitis, and endometritis. Prolonged menstruation often occurs following anovulatory cycles or as a result of irregular endometrial shedding.

B. Hypomenorrhea or Cryptomenorrhea: (An abnormally small amount of menstrual flow.) The bleeding may be so slight that it is called "spotting," although this term also refers to minimal bleeding from anywhere in the vulvovaginal area. A hymenal or cervical obstruction may be responsible. Uterine synechiae or endometrial tuberculosis may be found. The cycle itself may or may not be abnormal. The cause may be local, endocrine, or systemic.

C. Polymenorrhea: (Menstruallike episodes of bleeding that occur less than 21 days apart.) The bleeding may or may not be abnormal in amount. A common cause of polymenorrhea is failure of ovulation. In abbreviated ovulatory cycles, it is usually the preovulatory phase that is shortened—only rarely the postovulatory phase. The basic cause of polymenorrhea is likely to be endocrine or systemic.

D. Oligomenorrhea: (Menstruallike episodes of bleeding more than 35 days apart.) When the interval is longer than 6 months, the patient is considered to have amenorrhea. The cause of this pattern is usually endocrine or systemic; absence of ovulation is likely. The bleeding is usually also decreased in amount and duration.

E. Metrorrhagia: (Uterine bleeding at any time between menstrual periods that are essentially normal in frequency and flow—over 24 hours before onset of a period or after its presumed cessation.) The bleeding may range from slight spotting to hemorrhagic flow and from a single, short episode to bleeding that continues for days.

Metrorrhagia is more apt to be due to local disease than to endocrine or systemic disorders. It is a common early symptom of uterine malignancy, especially endometrial carcinoma, which must be ruled out by appropriate studies. Cervical erosions and polyps are characteristically associated with postcoital spotting from the trauma of coitus. "Ovulation bleeding," a single episode of spotting between menses, is quite common. In recent years, excessive or ill-advised estrogen therapy has become a fairly frequent cause of metrorrhagia (often with menorrhagia).

F. Menometrorrhagia: (Uterine bleeding that is totally irregular in frequency and duration of episodes and excessive in amount.) Bleeding from any of the conditions that cause metrorrhagia may develop into menometrorrhagia, in which the menses cannot be identified at all. Menometrorrhagia that develops quite suddenly should suggest some disorder of pregnancy such as early abortion, hydatidiform mole, or choriocarcinoma. It is also seen near the menopause in the absence of regular ovulation.

Systemic Causes of Abnormal Uterine Bleeding

Abnormal uterine bleeding may be caused by various systemic diseases and occasionally may be the first manifestation of a systemic disease. Disturbance of menstrual function is often associated with malnutrition, endocrine disturbances, debility, hematologic diseases, major metabolic disorders, or cardiac decompensation. A few examples:

The venous congestion associated with cardiac failure may cause menorrhagia. Digitalis, corticosteroid, or anticoagulant therapy may also cause menorrhagia.

Liver disease, particularly cirrhosis, may impair metabolism and excretion of estrogens, leading to endometrial hyperplasia and abnormal uterine bleeding.

Blood dyscrasias may interfere with menstrual function, particularly those that impair the blood coagulation mechanism. Thus, the thrombocytopenic diseases, eg, purpura and leukemia, frequently cause hypermenorrhea. Marked anemia, even the simple iron deficiency type, can lead to hypermenorrhea, and a vicious cycle may evolve when menorrhagia causes iron deficiency anemia. For these reasons, in all cases of abnormal uterine bleeding when no organic cause can be discerned, a reasonably complete hematologic survey should be completed before a diagnosis of unexplained dysfunctional uterine bleeding is made.

Debilitating major infections such as pneumonia or tuberculosis generally tend to cause oligomenorrhea and hypomenorrhea, sometimes progressing to total amenorrhea as debility becomes severe. (The debility of late malignancies exerts the same influence.) Early in the disease, however, infections may disturb menstrual function only enough to cause anovulation and temporary polymenorrhea and hypermenorrhea. This may also occur as a result of impairment of ovarian function by serious pelvic infections such as tuberculosis or colonic diverticulitis. Severe malnutrition may be associated with oligomenorrhea, hypomenorrhea, or amenorrhea.

Oligo-amenorrhea and amenorrhea are seen in pituitary deficiency and in most disorders of adrenocortical function.

Hyperthyroidism occasionally causes oligohypomenorrhea but in severe cases may be associated with amenorrhea. Hypothyroidism may cause anovulation, polymenorrhea, and hypermenorrhea, but severe myxedema is associated with amenorrhea. The readiness among gynecologists to prescribe thyroid hormone for patients with functional infertility or mild dysfunctional uterine bleeding even though laboratory tests show them to be euthyroid is deplored.

Psychiatric disorders may cause amenorrhea, especially if malnutrition becomes a factor as in depression or anorexia nervosa. Less severe psychic and emotional disturbances are associated with disturbances of ovulation. Sudden, severe psychic trauma may cause sudden changes in menstrual bleeding or the complete skipping of one or more periods. The amenorrhea of pseudocyesis has long been recognized.

Genital Causes of Abnormal Uterine Bleeding

Even though abnormal bleeding from the genital region usually appears to be an alteration of menstrual function, a uterine origin cannot be assumed until other sources of bleeding have been excluded. This is usually easily done by simple vulvar and vaginal speculum examination during a bleeding episode. The patient often presents at a time when bleeding is temporarily arrested. Even though the history of bleeding may strongly suggest a uterine origin, a search must be made for an extrauterine source. (Indeed, in the absence of any such findings, and with a dubious history of abnormal uterine bleeding, it is best to postpone all therapy. The patient can be instructed instead to record any bleeding—on a "menstrual card," for example—and to report for repeat examination *during* a bleeding episode.)

Urinary frequency and dysuria may be clues to a urinary tract disorder producing hematuria, which patients often mistake for vaginal bleeding. An ulcerated urethral caruncle is suggestive. Ulcerated vulvar lesions may be a source of postcoital "metrorrhagia." A blood-tinged leukorrheic discharge of severe vaginitis (bacterial, candidal, or trichomonal) may be mistaken for vaginal bleeding, especially in children, where a common cause of bloody leukorrhea is a foreign body in the vagina. General anesthesia may be required to obtain adequate vaginal inspection and examination.

Many patients report metrorrhagia after bleeding at stool. Bleeding hemorrhoids are the most common source, but more serious rectal or sigmoid lesions must not be overlooked. A fairly constant small trickle of vaginal, cervical, or uterine bleeding may collect in the vagina until relaxation of the introital muscles at urination or defecation allows its expulsion as a gush—falsely suggesting a urethral or rectal origin.

Friable or hemorrhagic lesions of the vagina may simulate metrorrhagic or menometrorrhagia. Bacterial ulcers, vaginal condylomas or hemangiomas, or vaginal carcinomas may cause bleeding.

Genital conditions that cause abnormal bleeding from the uterus may be classified according to location as follows: (1) Cervix: eversion or ectropion, polyps, pedunculated submucous myoma, acute pyogenic cervicitis, and carcinoma. (2) Uterine corpus: submucous myoma, endometritis, pathologic products of conception, uterine subinvolution, endometrial polyps, adenomyosis, sarcoma, intrauterine foreign bodies (eg, IUDs), and disturbances of normal endometrial growth, regression, and shedding. (3) Oviduct: salpingitis (including tuberculosis), neoplasms, and ectopic pregnancy. (4) Ovary: endometriosis and ovarian neoplasms, particularly hormonally functioning tumors such as granulosa or theca cell tumor.

Some specific causes of abnormal genital bleeding are more likely at certain ages. Thus, in children, the most likely source of bleeding is the vagina, as from a foreign body. At puberty, various disturbances of menarche—particularly anovulatory cycles with menorrhagia—are likely causes. In young women, abnormal uterine bleeding is most often caused by some complication of early pregnancy or by dysfunctional bleeding (see below). Constitutional diseases and specific diseases of the reproductive tract play a prominent etiologic role in the middle years of reproductive life. Late reproductive life and the menopause bring a steadily increasing likelihood of genital malig-

nancy and also recurrence of the menarcheal type of menstrual disturbance. During the postmenopausal period (see below, there is a steadily rising incidence of uterine malignancy, local reproductive tract lesions associated with involution (eg, atrophic vaginitis), and bleeding related to exogenous estrogen intake.

Dysfunctional Uterine Bleeding

Of all of the types of hormonal-endometrial relationships, the most stable endometrium and the most reproducible menstrual function, in terms of quantity and duration, is the postovulatory estrogen progesterone withdrawal bleeding response. This response is so dependable that many women over the years come to expect a certain characteristic flow pattern. Any slight deviation, eg, plus or minus 1 day in duration or some unexpected difference in napkin or tampon requirement, may be a cause for concern on the part of the patient and may require strong reassurance by the physician. The usual duration of flow is 4–6 days, but many women flow for only 2 days or as long as 8 days. While the postovulatory phase averages 14 days, there is greater variability in the duration of the proliferative phase of a menstrual cycle.

There are 3 reasons for the self-limited character of estrogen-progesterone withdrawal bleeding:

(1) It is a universal endometrial event. Because the onset and conclusion of menses are related to a precise sequence of hormonal events, the initiation of menstrual changes occurs almost simultaneously in all segments of the uterine endometrium.

(2) The endometrial tissue that has responded to an appropriate sequence of estrogen and progesterone is structurally stable. Furthermore, the events leading to ischemic disintegration of the endometrium are orderly and progressive, mediated by rhythmic waves of vasoconstriction of increasing duration.

(3) Inherent in the events that start menstrual bleeding following estrogen-progesterone stimulation are the factors involved in stopping menstrual flow. Just as waves of vasoconstriction initiate the ischemic events to provoke menses, so will prolonged vasoconstriction, abetted by the stasis associated with endometrial collapse, enable clotting factors to seal off the exposed bleeding sites. Additional and significant effects are achieved by resumed estrogen stimulation.

Most instances of anovulatory bleeding are examples of estrogen withdrawal or estrogen breakthrough bleeding. The most serious type of bleeding is secondary to sustained high levels of estrogen associated with the polycystic ovary syndrome, obesity, immaturity of the hypothalamic-pituitary-ovarian axis as in postpubertal teenagers, or late anovulation, usually involving women in their late 30s and early 40s. Unopposed estrogen induces a progression of endometrial responses in the following pattern: proliferative hyperplasia, adenomatous hyperplasia, and in some women, over the course of many years, atypia and carcinoma. In the absence of growth-limiting progesterone and periodic desquamation, the endometrium attains an abnormal height without concomitant structural support. The tissue increasingly displays intense vascularity and back-to-back glandularity but without the support of an intervening stromal matrix. This tissue is fragile and is subject to spontaneous superficial fissure formation and bleeding. As one site heals, another and then another new site of breakdown will appear.

In these instances, the usual endometrial control mechanisms are lacking. This bleeding is not a widespread phenomenon but involves random portions of the endometrium at variable times and in asynchronous patterns. The fragility of the vascular adenomatous hyperplastic tissue is responsible for this sequence, in part because of irregular stimulation in which the structural rigidity of a well-developed stroma or stratum compactum does not occur. The flow is prolonged and excessive not only because a large amount of tissue is available for bleeding but more importantly because there is a disorderly, abrupt, random, haphazard breakdown of tissue with consequent opening of multiple vascular channels. There is no vasoconstrictive rhythmicity, no tight coiling of spiral vessels, and no orderly collapse to induce stasis. The anovulatory tissue can only rely on the "healing" effects of endogenous estrogen to stop local bleeding. However, this is a vicious cycle in that this healing is only temporary and leads to certain repeat breakdown in the near future.

Treatment

The immediate objective of medical therapy in anovulatory bleeding is to retrieve the natural controlling influences missing in this tissue: universal synchronous endometrial events, structural stability, and vasomotor rhythmicity. This is accomplished rapidly and easily (but sometimes with considerable symptomatology) with combination progestin-estrogen contraceptive pills in high doses. Any of the oral combination tablets are useful. Treatment consists of giving one pill 4 times a day for 5–7 days. This 4-pills-a-day therapy is prolonged over this duration despite the anticipated cessation of flow within 12–24 hours. If flow does not clearly abate, other diagnostic possibilities (pathologic causes, eg, polyps, fibromyomas, incomplete abortion, or malignancy) should be considered by examination under anesthesia and surgical dilatation and curettage (D&C). If flow does diminish rapidly with medication, the remainder of the week of treatment should permit the evaluation of causes of anovulation, hemorrhagic tendencies, and blood or iron replacement. In addition, the week will provide time to prepare the patient for the progestin-estrogen withdrawal flow that will soon be induced. For the moment, this therapy will have induced the structural rigidity intrinsic to the compact pseudodecidual reaction. As a result, continued random breakdown of formerly fragile tissue is avoided and blood loss stopped. However, a very large quantity of endometrial tissue will remain to react to progestin-estrogen withdrawal. Consequently, the patient must be warned to anticipate a heavy and severely cramping flow 2–4 days after stopping therapy. If not prepared in this way, she will view the problem as recurrent disease or failure of hormonal therapy and will surely become a candidate for an avoidable operative D&C.

Even more reassuring than the anticipation of difficulty is the confident prophecy that this withdrawal bleeding episode, despite the pain and volume, will be self-limited (as a result of the induced vasomotor rhythmicity). Nonetheless, to ensure success, on the fifth day of flow, a low-dose cyclic contraceptive drug combination, eg, Ortho-Novum 1/50, should be initiated with three 3-week treatments interrupted by 1-week withdrawal flow intervals. The decreasing volume and pain with each successive cycle will reaffirm confidence in control mechanisms and should prevent unopposed estrogen regrowth. Early application of the progestin-estrogen combination limits growth and allows orderly regression of excessive endometrial height to normal controllable levels. If the combination is not applied, abnormal endometrial height and persistent excessive flow will recur.

In the patient not exposed to potential pregnancy in whom cyclic progestin-estrogen for 3 months has reduced endometrial tissue reservoirs to normal height, the pill may be discontinued and unopposed endogenous estrogen permitted to reactivate the endometrium. At 2-month intervals, in the absence of spontaneous (possibly postovulatory) menses, recurrence of the anovulatory status should be suspected and sustained estrogen stimulation of the endometrium assumed. Moreover, before overstimulation of the endometrium is permitted to occur, a brief course of an orally active progestin derivative should be administered, eg, medroxyprogesterone acetate (Provera), 10 mg orally daily for 10 days. Restrained reasonable flow (progesterone withdrawal flow) will occur 2–7 days after the last pill. With this therapy, excessive endometrial build-up is avoided.

Note: Not all cases of dysfunctional uterine bleeding should be treated medically with progestin therapy. In the age group over 35 years, an initial endometrial biopsy (with multiple sampling) is required. This is especially true in women age 30–50, who may have adenocarcinoma of the endometrium.

Bleeding manifestations are frequently associated with minimal (low) estrogen stimulation resulting in intermittent vaginal spotting. In this circumstance, where scanty endometrium exists, the beneficial effect of progestin treatment is of no avail because a tissue base on which the progestin may exert its organizational strengthening action is lacking. A similar circumstance also exists in the younger anovulatory patient in whom prolonged hemorrhagic desquamation leaves little residual tissue. In these instances, the appropriate therapeutic reaction is *not* the traditional operative D&C, which, although it frequently manages the acute problem, may not improve but may in fact worsen the long-range prognosis by further denuding the endometrial reserve. In such cases, high-dose estrogen therapy is recommended, eg, conjugated estrogens (Premarin), 25 mg intravenously every 4 hours until bleeding abates (up to 6 doses may be necessary).

Cessation of bleeding indicates that sufficient "healing" has been initiated. Progestin may be started at the same time.

Progestin therapy may not always be a positive controlling factor, however. Two examples in clinical practice illustrate the problems associated with progestin breakthrough bleeding: the breakthrough bleeding episodes that occur with prolonged use of birth control pills or with depot forms of progesterone derivatives. In the absence of sufficient endogenous and exogenous estrogen, the endometrium shrinks to a low height. Furthermore, it is composed almost exclusively of pseudodecidual stroma and blood vessels with minimal glands. Experience has shown that this type of endometrium is also associated with the fragility bleeding more typical of pure estrogen stimulation. The clinical history is often that of long-standing oral contraception, with marked diminution of withdrawal flow. It often happens that no bleeding will occur in the nontreatment interval. However, this is associated with intermittent, variable vaginal spotting during the month. The physician is tempted to double therapy, but this rarely succeeds because it intensifies the progestin atrophic effect. A more appropriate program in view of the condition of the endometrium is estrogen therapy, eg, ethinyl estradiol, 20 μg, or conjugated estrogen, 2.5 mg, orally daily for 10 days during and in addition to the birth control pill administration. This rejuvenates the endometrium, intermenstrual flow generally stops, and appropriate withdrawal should resume.

One problem frequently encountered is the progestin breakthrough bleeding experienced in chronic depot administration of progestin. Currently, this therapy is used not only for contraception but also in the chemotherapy of endometrial carcinoma. In the majority of these cases, continuous therapy provides control without menstrual bleeding. In the remainder, breakthrough progestin bleeding occurs. Judicious use of estrogen, then, is appropriate and effective therapy.

POSTMENOPAUSAL VAGINAL BLEEDING

Any bleeding from the genital tract that occurs more than 6 months after the last menstrual period is regarded as postmenopausal bleeding. It may vary widely in amount and duration of flow. The physician is most likely to see patients with slight bleeding at this time.

Various sites may be the source of postmenopausal vaginal bleeding, and the investigative methods outlined above should be used until a diagnosis is reached. At this age, however, certain causes of bleeding (eg, carcinoma) are much more common than in premenopausal patients. In the years before estrogen supplementation therapy came into wide use, the most frequent cause of postmenopausal vaginal bleeding was atrophic vaginitis—so-called senile vaginitis. Trauma from coitus may be a precipitating cause.

The extensive administration of estrogens to postmenopausal women has changed the pattern. Atrophic vaginitis is now being prevented in almost all cases. Exogenous estrogen administration—excessive, too continuous, or to patients with hypersensitive endometria—is now the most common cause of postmenopausal uterine bleeding. Another common cause is endometrial carcinoma. Unless the bleeding episode can be closely tied to alteration or withdrawal of estrogen dosage, it is best to assume the existence of endometrial carcinoma and perform a differential D&C.

Carcinoma of the cervix may be a cause of abnormal vaginal bleeding in postmenopausal women. However, after age 60, the ratio of endometrial to cervical carcinoma is approximately 4:1.

Like premenopausal women, postmenopausal women can bleed from any type of endometrium—proliferative, hyperplastic, or atrophic—except secretory endometrium. Endogenous estrogen production and exogenous administration determine the status of the endometrium and bleeding from it. Slight fluctuations may cause the postmenopausal patient to bleed. Rarely, an estrogen-producing functional ovarian tumor may produce cystic endometrial hyperplasia. Usually, excessive estrogen therapy is the cause of bleeding. After the menopause, proliferative or hyperplastic endometrium tends to be patchy rather than diffuse. This may be one reason for easy bleeding. On the other hand, bleeding from senile atrophic endometrium with totally inactive glands and a sparse, shrunken stroma is a puzzling clinical problem. Involutional aging changes may cause bleeding from heretofore healthy surfaces and long-quiescent lesions. Aging produces thinning of epithelial surfaces (with exposure of capillary beds), vascular fragility, varices, increased degenerative changes in tissues, and decreased local resistance to eroding infections. Not only do these factors contribute to bleeding from various epithelial surfaces—of the urethra, bladder, vulva, vagina, cervix, and endometrium—but they may also cause new bleeding from the long-standing lesions such as cervical or endometrial polyps, a urethral caruncle, or submucous myomas.

Occasionally, adenomatous hyperplasia or atypical adenomatous hyperplasia is a source of postmenopausal bleeding. The latter carries an ominous precancerous connotation because it is sometimes found coexisting with frank adenocarcinoma. In postmenopausal women, atypical adenomatous hyperplasia generally is treated by hysterectomy rather than by more conservative hormonal therapy.

Investigation of Postmenopausal Bleeding

The procedure for examination and the determination of the cause of genital bleeding in the postmenopausal woman is similar to that described for abnormal bleeding during menstrual life. Because the incidence of the various causes of bleeding is quite different in the 2 groups, however, the various investigative procedures require different emphases. The physician must search diligently for a specific cause of the bleeding. Except for exogenous estrogen intake, an organic cause is likely in postmenopausal women, since the functional disturbances associated with menstruation have subsided in this age group.

Careful inquiry about estrogen therapy or other sources of exogenous estrogen must be pressed. The physician should inquire about face and body creams and health food tablets. Patients who experience postmenopausal bleeding must discontinue all exogenous estrogen until the organic cause of bleeding has either been clearly identified (and properly treated) or eliminated, thus indicating that the exogenous estrogen is the problem. The physician must be alert for evidence of excessive estrogenic stimulation (eg, copious cervical mucus) or estrogen deficiency (eg, atrophic vaginal mucosa).

Evidence of degenerative and systemic diseases of later life that may contribute to genital bleeding must be sought.

The much greater likelihood of cancer calls for meticulous inspection of the genitalia in a search for urethral, vulvar, vaginal, or cervical carcinoma. Vaginal smears must be prepared and examined with particular care. Examination of scrapings or biopsies of suspect areas may result in the recovery of malignant cells.

The passage of a uterine sound through the cervical canal may be informative in the postmenopausal patient who is not bleeding at the time of examination and in whom no extrauterine source of bleeding has been revealed. Slight bleeding after sounding may indicate carcinoma of the endometrium or high in the cervical canal (Clark's test). Hematometra may be revealed by a gush of brownish liquid. The combination of senile cervical atresia and postmenopausal estrogen therapy may occasionally result in hematometra among postmenopausal women. In these cases, bleeding often is intermittent because the cervical canal alternately seals and opens. For such patients, the physician should proceed to diagnostic endometrial biopsy and, if indicated, a differential D&C.

Standard laboratory studies are even more important for the postmenopausal woman who is bleeding than for the premenopausal one because the tests are more likely to reveal unsuspected systemic disease of consequence.

Treatment of Postmenopausal Bleeding

A. Emergency Treatment: Emergency measures to control massive genital bleeding are rarely required for the postmenopausal woman except in the case of advanced malignancy. D&C, a necessary diagnostic measure, is also useful in the control of heavy uterine bleeding. In contrast to D&C, steroid hormonal therapy is neither diagnostic nor therapeutic.

B. Specific Treatment: Once excessive exogenous estrogen intake has been ruled out, the treatment of postmenopausal genital bleeding consists essentially of giving appropriate therapy for the specific cause. Evidence of excessive endogenous estrogen activity should suggest a functioning ovarian tumor.

Pelvic examination or perhaps laparotomy or other exploratory techniques may be necessary to make the diagnosis. The primary treatment is surgical.

Proper adjustment of estrogen therapy may require considerable ingenuity. Estrogen therapy may be indicated for the patient whose bleeding is due to postmenopausal estrogen deficiency. When friable atrophic lesions such as urethral caruncle or atrophic vaginitis are responsible, it is often worthwhile to apply local estrogen cream to obtain more rapid healing than can be achieved with oral or parenteral estrogen alone. Continued supplementation therapy may be required afterward.

Estrogens in creams and suppositories are efficiently absorbed through the wall of the vagina; hence, hormones given via this route are additive to whatever is given orally or parenterally. Therefore, if local estrogen therapy is being given, dosage by other routes must be lowered accordingly and then readjusted to proper maintenance levels when local therapy is discontinued.

AMENORRHEA

The differential diagnosis and management of amenorrhea is not difficult. Moreover, most patients with amenorrhea can be easily managed by the primary care physician. The simple scheme presented here for the differential diagnosis of amenorrhea utilizes procedures available to all physicians. This work-up should reliably localize the cause of the presenting symptom of amenorrhea. If necessary, the patient can then be referred to a specialist with the knowledge that the referral is indicated and appropriate.

DEFINITION OF AMENORRHEA

An evaluation to determine the cause of amenorrhea is indicated in the following circumstances:

(1) If menstruation has not occurred by age 14 and it is apparent that development of the secondary sex characteristics is absent or retarded.

(2) If menstruation has not occurred by age 16 even if secondary sex characteristics are developing normally.

(3) If a woman with established menses reports no menstruation for an interval of time equal to at least 3 cycles, or when amenorrhea has persisted for 6 months.

Note: The foregoing is not an all-inclusive list of the possible clinical presentations. Pregnancy must always be considered, and obvious problems such as Turner's syndrome must be recognized.

Because the work-up for the differential diagnosis of amenorrhea applies to all patients with the symptom, it is not necessary or useful to distinguish between primary or secondary amenorrhea.

THE DIAGNOSTIC WORK–UP
(Fig 6–4)

Menstruation depends on the integrity of 4 discrete compartments or systems. The diagnostic work-up can be planned so as to identify derangements of function in any of the 4, as follows (Fig 6–5):

Compartment

I Disorders of the outflow tract or uterus.
II Disorders of the ovary.
III Disorders of the anterior pituitary.
IV Disorders of the central nervous system (hypothalamus).

Step 1

Amenorrhea may be the only pertinent initial item of information, but a thorough history and physical examination often provides useful diagnostic information. In any event, adherence to the sequence of investigational steps as outlined below is essential.

There are 2 components to the initial step: assessment of the level of endogenous estrogen and measurement of the serum prolactin level. In order to determine the level of function of the hypothalamic-pituitary-ovarian axis, a course of treatment with a *pure* progestational agent (totally devoid of estrogenic activity) must be given orally or intramuscularly. A single dose of progesterone in oil (200 mg) may be administered intramuscularly, or an orally active com-

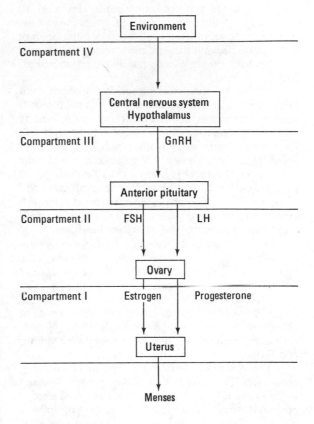

Figure 6–5. The 4 compartments involved in menstruation.

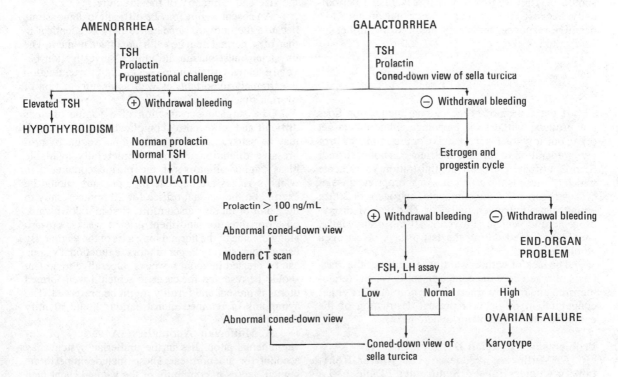

Figure 6–4. Diagnostic evaluation of amenorrhea and galactorrhea.

pound, eg, medroxyprogesterone acetate (Provera), 10 mg daily for 5 days, may be given. Other progestins, including those in oral contraceptive pills, are not appropriate because they are metabolized to estrogens and therefore do not exert a purely progestational effect.

Within 2–7 days after the conclusion of progestational medication, the patient will or will not bleed. If she bleeds, the presence of a functional uterus lined by reactive endometrium and a patent outflow tract will have been confirmed, together with a diagnosis of anovulation. In the absence of galactorrhea, and if the serum prolactin level is normal (< 20 ng/mL [< 30 ng/mL in some laboratories]), further evaluation will be unnecessary. The physician can immediately proceed to appropriate management of this problem, be it menstrual irregularity, infertility, or hirsutism.

If the serum prolactin is elevated, x-ray evaluation of the sella turcica is necessary. Regardless of the bleeding pattern or the prolactin level, the presence of definite galactorrhea requires further evaluation with x-ray. Nonetheless, a positive withdrawal bleeding response to progestational medication, the absence of galactorrhea, and a normal prolactin level together effectively rule out the presence of a pituitary tumor and further evaluation is unnecessary.

The question often arises how much bleeding constitutes a positive withdrawal response. Bleeding in any amount more than spotting is considered a positive withdrawal response. Scant spotting following progestational medication is an indication of marginal levels of endogenous estrogen. Such a patient should be followed closely and reevaluated periodically, because the marginal response may progress to a negative response, indicating the need for further investigation.

Step 2

If the course of progestational medication does not produce withdrawal bleeding, either the target organ outflow tract is inoperative or preliminary estrogen preparation of the endometrium has not occurred. Step 2 utilizes estrogen administration to indicate which of these is the problem. An appropriate dose of oral estrogen is 2.5 mg conjugated estrogens or 20 μg ethinyl estradiol given daily for 21 days. Medroxyprogesterone acetate (Provera), 10 mg orally daily, should be added during the last 5 days of estrogen administration.

The lack of withdrawal flow establishes the diagnosis of a defect in the compartment I systems (endometrium and outflow tract). These problems are either congenital in origin or represent destruction of the endometrium (Asherman's syndrome).

Problems of Müllerian Development

A. Müllerian Agenesis: The Mayer-Rokitansky-Küster-Hauser Syndrome: (Table 6–1.) After gonadal dysgenesis, lack of müllerian develop-

Table 6–1. Clinical features of müllerian agenesis.

1. Primary amenorrhea associated with congenital absence of vagina or significant hypoplasia.
2. Normal 46,XX karyotype.
3. Uterus that varies from anatomically complete to rudimentary bicornuate cords to complete absence.
4. Normal ovarian function.
5. Normal growth and development.
6. Frequent association of renal, skeletal, and other congenital anomalies.
7. Cyclic abdominal pain if a partial endometrial cavity is present.

ment is the most common cause of primary amenorrhea. These patients have an absent or hypoplastic vagina. Very rarely, the uterus may be normal but lacking a conduit to the introitus. Usually there will only be a rudimentary cordlike bicornuate uterus. If a partial endometrial cavity is present, cyclic abdominal pain may be a complaint. Because of the similarity to some types of male pseudohermaphroditism, a normal female karyotype should be documented. Ovarian function may be normal and can be established by BBT changes or by significant blood levels of progesterone. Growth and development generally are normal.

At least one-third of these patients will have an abnormal urinary tract, and about 12% will have skeletal anomalies, mostly of the spine. When the presence of a uterine structure is suspected by history or examination, ultrasound may be utilized to reveal the size and symmetry of the structure.

An absent vagina may be difficult to demonstrate because the outward appearance may be identical to that of a normal female with an intact hymen. The physician must pursue the clinical investigation beyond external visualization. Rectal digital examination is extremely important, as well as documentation of ovarian function.

The surgical construction of a vagina often is difficult and followed by complications (Fig 8–2). It may be better to produce a functional vagina by progressive dilatation. Using commercially available glass vaginal dilators (or the plastic containers in which syringes are kept sterile), pressure should be exerted on the vaginal orifice for 20 minutes daily to the point of modest discomfort, first in a downward, posterior direction and then, after 2 weeks, upward along the line of the normal long axis of the vagina. By using progressively larger dilators, a functional vagina can be created in about 6 weeks. Operative treatment should be reserved for cases in which a well-formed uterus is present and fertility might be preserved. The symptoms of retained menstruation should identify these patients.

B. Müllerian Anomalies: A variety of developmental anomalies in the müllerian system may account for amenorrhea. These include imperforate hymen, lapses in continuity of the vaginal canal, and absent portions of the uterus. The clinical problem of amenorrhea may be compounded by hematocolpos, hematometra, or hematoperitoneum. Incision and drainage should be done from below to reestablish continuity of the müllerian tract. X-ray studies may show associated lesions of the genitourinary tract.

C. Testicular Feminization: When a blind vaginal canal is encountered and the uterus is absent, testicular feminization may be the problem. The patient has testes and an XY karyotype, but there is a complete failure of virilization due to a congenital insensitivity to androgens. Transmission of this disorder is by means of an X-linked recessive gene responsible for the androgen intracellular receptor. Only those steps in sexual differentiation that require androgens fail to take place, whereas müllerian inhibition clearly does occur. This is a natural experiment that demonstrates the existence of müllerian inhibiting factor.

Clinically, the diagnosis of testicular feminization should be considered in the following circumstances: (1) a girl with inguinal hernias, because the testes are frequently only partially descended (more than half have an inguinal hernia); (2) a patient with primary amenorrhea and an absent uterus; and (3) a patient with no body hair.

Most of these patients are not seen by a physician for this problem until puberty. Except for the possible presence of an inguinal hernia, these patients appear normal at birth, and growth and development are normal also. Eventually, the breasts will be larger than normal, but actual glandular tissue is not abundant and the nipples usually are small, with pale areolas. The blind vagina may be shallow and the labia minora are usually underdeveloped. Rudimentary uterine tubes are composed of fibromuscular tissue.

The testes may be intra-abdominal but often are in the inguinal hernial sac. A high incidence of neoplasia occurs in these gonads (well over 10%). Therefore, once full development is attained after puberty, the gonads should be removed and the patient given hormonal replacement therapy. This is the only exception to the rule that gonads with a Y chromosome should be removed before puberty.

Not all of these individuals have a total absence of androgen effects. A spectrum of disorders representing varying degrees of virilization is recognized. The term incomplete testicular feminization denotes patients who have some androgen effect. Gonadectomy should not be deferred in such cases; the testes should be removed as soon as possible to avoid unwanted virilization.

Table 6–2. Clinical features of testicular feminization.

1. Primary amenorrhea associated with absent uterus and blind vaginal canal.
2. 46,XY karyotype.
3. Absent or sparse sexual hair.
4. Normal growth and development with eunuchoidal tendency.
5. Large breasts with small nipples and pale areolas.
6. Half have inguinal hernias.

Asherman's Syndrome

This syndrome refers to amenorrhea that follows destruction or elimination of the endometrium. It is usually the result of overzealous curettage postpartum or for therapeutic abortion. The result is intrauterine scarification, which may be seen as a pattern of multiple synechiae on hysterography. Treatment requires division of the synechiae by either D&C or hysteroscopy. After operation, the uterine cavity should be kept open to prevent adherence and occlusion or reestablishment of synechiae. Preoperative broad-spectrum antibiotic therapy should be continued for 10 days after surgery. A pediatric Foley catheter may be inserted and the bag filled with 3 mL of fluid. The catheter should be removed after 7 days. The patient should be treated for 6 months with high stimulatory doses of estrogen, eg, conjugated estrogens, 10 mg orally daily 3 weeks out of 4, adding medroxyprogesterone acetate, 10 mg daily, during the third week. Persistent retreatment may be necessary to restore reproductive potential.

Rarely, Asherman's syndrome may follow infectious destruction of the endometrium, eg, as a complication of genital tuberculosis. This still occurs in areas where tuberculosis remains a major public health problem.

Step 3

The patient with a competent outflow tract who fails to bleed following progestational medication may have endogenous levels of estrogen inadequate to stimulate endometrial growth. The fault may lie within compartment I (the follicles of the ovary) or compartments III and IV (the hypothalamic-pituitary axis). Step 3 is designed to rule out ovarian failure.

Step 3 involves the radioimmunoassay of gonadotropins. Since steps 1 and 2 utilized the administration of exogenous steroids, endogenous gonadotropin levels may be temporarily reduced from their true baseline concentrations. A delay of at least 2 weeks following steroid administration is therefore necessary before proceeding with step 3, the gonadotropin assay.

The results of the gonadotropin assay will fall in one of 3 categories: abnormally high, abnormally low, or within the normal range. The normal range for serum FSH is 5–30 mIU/mL and for LH 5–20 mIU/mL. One should recall that a midcycle surge of gonadotropins occurs. However, if the patient does not bleed 2 weeks after the blood sample was obtained, high levels can be interpreted as abnormal.

Amenorrhea With Elevated Gonadotropin Production

Elevated gonadotropins signify gonadal failure. With rare exceptions, FSH values over 40 mIU/mL will be found only when the supply of ovarian follicles has been exhausted. The association between a high FSH, especially when accompanied by a high LH, and ovarian failure is so reliable that further attempts to

Table 6–3. Levels of gonadotropins as determined by radioimmunoassay.

Clinical State	Serum FSH	Serum LH
Normal adult	5–30 mIU/mL, with ovulatory midcycle peak about twice base level	5–20 mIU/mL, with ovulatory midcycle peak about 3 times base level
Hypogonadotropic state: prepubertal, hypothalamic, and pituitary dysfunction	<5 mIU/mL	<5 mIU/mL
Hypergonadotropic state: postmenopausal, gonadal failure, castrate	>40 mIU/mL	>30 mIU/mL

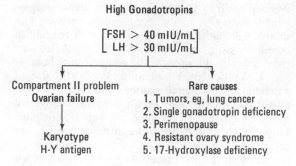

Figure 6–6. Diagnostic evaluation of amenorrhea: high gonadotropins.

document the state of the ovaries are unnecessary and unwarranted. Specifically, laparoscopy, to visualize the ovaries and to demonstrate the presence of follicles by biopsy, only exposes the patient to unnecessary anesthetic and surgical risks.

Some important exceptions to the association of ovarian failure with high gonadotropins are as follows:

(1) Rare malignant tumors, eg, carcinoma of the lung or ovarian teratoma, may produce significant amounts of gonadotropins.

(2) A rare single gonadotropin deficiency may exist. For example, a patient with an isolated deficiency of FSH will have primary amenorrhea, undetectable FSH, and a high LH level.

(3) In the perimenopausal period, gonadotropin levels begin to rise before the cessation of bleeding. An elevated FSH level will usually be noted, while LH levels remain in the normal range. It is likely that the elevated FSH levels indicate a significant reduction in the number of follicles remaining, and these may have diminished ability to produce estrogen. However, FSH may also be regulated in part by the negative feedback action of a nonsteroid substance produced by granulosa cells, a circumstance perhaps similar to the action in the male of inhibin, a peptide produced in the testicular Sertoli cells. Elevated levels of both FSH and LH appear to be conclusive evidence of ovarian failure in this age group.

(4) Resistant ovary syndrome (see below).

(5) 17-Hydroxylase deficiency in both ovaries and adrenal glands will lead to lack of development of secondary sexual characteristics with elevated gonadotropins.

Patients with an FSH value over 40 mIU/mL must have a karyotype determination to rule out the presence of a Y chromosome, which in an adult woman carries with it a 10–25% incidence of carcinoma within the gonad. Thus, all patients who have a Y chromosome in the blood karyotype must be treated by gonadectomy. It is possible that a Y-containing mosaic pattern may be present in the gonad despite the presence of a normal karyotype in the blood. Assay of the newly discovered H-Y antigen may prove to be the most reliable means of detecting cryptic testicular tissue even in the presence of a normal karyotype.

The clinical disorders in compartment II, associated with elevated gonadotropins, include Turner's syndrome, other forms of gonadal dysgenesis due to various mosaic chromosomal patterns, gonadal agenesis,* and the resistant ovary syndrome.

A. Turner's Syndrome: Accurate diagnosis of Turner's syndrome is usually possible at the first encounter with the patient. The outstanding characteristics are short stature, webbed neck, shield chest, and increased carrying angle of the arms. Coarctation of the aorta and various renal collecting system anomalies may be present also. Despite the characteristic appearance of the patient with Turner's syndrome, the diagnosis should be confirmed by karyotyping (Turner's syndrome is 45,XO).

B. Mosaicism: It is essential to rule out the presence of mosaicism because the presence of a Y chromosome in the karyotype requires laparotomy and excision of the gonads, since any testicular component may predispose to tumor formation or virilization. Only in the patient with classic complete testicular feminization should laparotomy be deferred until after puberty. Approximately 30% of patients with a Y chromosome will not develop any signs of virilization. Therefore, even the normal-appearing adult patient with elevated gonadotropins must be karyotyped to detect a silent Y chromosome so that prophylactic gonadectomy may be performed before neoplastic changes occur. As noted above, assays for H-Y antigen may prove to be more reliable in this regard than the karyotype.

Karyotyping is not necessary in older patients presenting with a complaint of amenorrhea. After age 35, elevated gonadotropins and amenorrhea are best regarded as premature menopause, and further evaluation is unnecessary. Between ages 30 and 35, the emergence of a malignant tumor in a heretofore unsuspected Y-containing karyotype is unlikely, but, to be safe, a karyotype should be performed.

C. Resistant Ovary Syndrome: Patients with resistant ovary syndrome have amenorrhea with ele-

*Very rare and not further discussed.

vated gonadotropins despite the presence of ovarian follicles. Large amounts of exogenous gonadotropins are required to produce follicular growth and estrogen production. Because of the rarity of this condition and the very low chance of achieving pregnancy even with high doses of exogenous gonadotropins, it is not worthwhile to perform a laparotomy for ovarian biopsy on patients with amenorrhea, high gonadotropins, and a normal karyotype.

Amenorrhea With Low or Normal Gonadotropin Levels

Experimental evidence indicates that hypoestrogenic patients (who show a negative withdrawal response to a progestational agent) frequently have normal circulating levels of FSH and LH as measured by radioimmunoassay, because gonadotropins produced by these amenorrheic patients have increased amounts of sialic acid in the carbohydrate portions of their molecules. Therefore, the molecules are qualitatively altered and biologically inactive. However, the antibodies used in the radioimmunoassay react with a sufficient portion of the molecule to give a normal response. The significant clinical point is that FSH and LH levels in the normal range can indicate pituitary-central nervous system failure. Extremely low or nondetectable gonadotropin levels are found rarely and then usually with large pituitary tumors or in patients with anorexia nervosa.

If the gonadotropin assay is abnormally low or in the normal range, skull x-rays should be obtained to examine the sella turcica for signs of abnormal change, to differentiate a pituitary from a central nervous system cause of amenorrhea.

In recent years, computerized axial tomography (CT scan) has largely replaced polytomography in the evaluation of the contents of the sella turcica as well as the suprasellar area.

There has been growing conservatism in the management of small pituitary tumors, because the majority of these tumors never change. We have adopted the conservative approach of close surveillance, recommending surgery only for those tumors which are already large or are growing rapidly. Hence, the initial x-ray evaluation of amenorrheic patients, with or without galactorrhea, is the coned-down view of the sella turcica to detect the presence of a large tumor. Combining this screening technique with the prolactin assay, we are able to select those few patients who require CT scan. If the serum prolactin level is greater than 100 ng/mL, or if the coned-down view of the sella turcica is abnormal, we recommend CT scan. If the CT scan rules out empty sella syndrome or a suprasellar abnormality, surgical intervention is then dictated by the patient's desires and the size of the tumor.

The above approach to the pituitary tumor implies that patients with prolactin levels less than 100 ng/mL and normal coned-down views of the sella turcica are offered a choice between bromocriptine therapy and surveillance. If surveillance is chosen, an annual prolactin level test and coned-down view are indicated to detect an emerging and slowly growing tumor. Bromocriptine therapy is recommended for patients wishing to achieve pregnancy and for those patients who have galactorrhea to the point of discomfort. Thus far, long-term therapy with bromocriptine has not been shown to produce a complete reversal of the disorder with permanent suppression of elevated prolactins and evidence of shrinkage of small tumors. Therefore, surgical intervention is not recommended when prolactin levels are below 100 ng/mL, and coned-down views of the sella turcica are normal. The prolactin level of 100 ng/mL has been determined empirically; in our experience and that of others, large tumors are most frequently associated with prolactin levels greater than 100 ng/mL.

The high incidence of pituitary tumors in patients with amenorrhea has prompted a search for a reliable method of diagnosis. These maneuvers include GnRH stimulation, TRH stimulation, and other steps to alter prolactin secretion. Expectations for the utilization of endocrine testing to discriminate between disorders of the hypothalamus and the anterior pituitary have not been realized. Tremendous variability in response is the rule, even to the degree that the patient with a pituitary tumor may or may not respond.

If the coned-down view of the sella turcica is abnormal or the prolactin level is over 100 ng/mL, further evaluation requires consultation with an endocrinologist.

HYPOGONADOTROPIC AMENORRHEA

The situation most commonly encountered is that of the patient with amenorrhea, a normal x-ray evaluation, and a normal prolactin level. This disorder has been referred to as hypothalamic amenorrhea.

Hypothalamic problems are usually diagnosed by exclusion of pituitary lesions and are the most common type of hypogonadotropic amenorrhea. Frequently, there is association with a stressful situation. A high proportion of underweight women are affected, and there is a high incidence of prior menstrual irregularities. The physician must consider such problems before prescribing hormone replacement therapy or attempting induction of ovulation in order to achieve pregnancy.

A good approach is to evaluate such patients annually after a 2-month period without hormone medication. Annual surveillance should include a prolactin assay and coned-down view of the sella turcica. Returning function may be demonstrated by the presence of a positive withdrawal response to a progestational agent. Even though a patient may not be currently interested in becoming pregnant, it is important to assure her that, at the appropriate time, treatment for the induction of ovulation will be available and that fertility usually can be achieved. Concern about fertility is often unspoken, especially in younger patients. Induction of ovulation should be carried out only for the purpose of producing a pregnancy. There is no evidence that cyclic hormone administration or induction of ovulation will stimulate the return of normal function.

Weight Loss & Amenorrhea

A special type of hypothalamic amenorrhea is associated with weight loss. Clinically, the problem covers a limited period of amenorrhea associated with a "crash" diet up to the severely ill patient with anorexia nervosa. Because the mortality rate associated with anorexia nervosa is 5–15%, it is important that attention be directed to this disorder. It is common for a physician to be the first to recognize anorexia nervosa in a patient presenting with the complaint of amenorrhea. Occasionally, a physician will evaluate and treat amenorrhea, unaware of developing anorexia nervosa.

The borderline anorectic individual often is a teenager with low body weight, amenorrhea, and hyperactivity. She may have excellent grades in school and be involved in many extracurricular activities. Amenorrhea may precede, follow, or be coincident with weight loss.

Extensive laboratory testing of these patients is unnecessary, although it is important to follow the work-up described to rule out a pathologic process. Often, a careful and gentle explanation of the relationship between amenorrhea and body weight will stimulate the patient to return to normal weight and function. Occasionally, it is necessary to see the patient frequently while she pursues a program of daily calorie-counting to break established eating habits. If progress is slow, hormone replacement therapy should be initiated. In an adult weighing less than 45 kg (100 pounds), continued weight loss requires psychiatric attention.

Amenorrhea & Anosmia

A rare condition in women is the syndrome of hypogonadotropic hypogonadism associated with anosmia. A similar syndrome in the male is hereditary and known as Kallman's syndrome. In the female, this problem is characterized by primary amenorrhea, infantile sexual development, low gonadotropin levels, a normal female karyotype, and the inability to perceive certain odors, eg, coffee or perfume. The gonads of these patients respond to gonadotropins; therefore, successful induction of ovulation with exogenous gonadotropins is likely.

POSTPILL AMENORRHEA

It had been assumed that amenorrhea could reflect the persistent suppressive effects of oral contraceptive medication or the use of the intramuscular-depot form of medroxyprogesterone acetate. It is now known that fertility is normal following discontinuance of either of these forms of contraception. Hence, this type of amenorrhea must be investigated as described, so that a serious problem will not be missed.

EXERCISE & AMENORRHEA

The problem of exercise-related amenorrhea has increased considerably over the last 10 years. In 1970, a woman jogger was a curiosity. Today, millions of women run or play competitive games, and more than one-third of high-school athletes are female. Women engaged in other forms of strenuous activity such as ballet and modern dance also have a high incidence of menstrual irregularity and amenorrhea.

Two influences appear to be critical: the level of body fat and the effect of stress. Young women who weigh less than 50 kg (115 pounds) and lose more than 5 kg (10 pounds) while exercising are the women most likely to develop the problem (Speroff and Redwine)—a relationship that supports the critical-weight concept of Frisch. The critical-weight hypothesis states that onset and regularity of menstrual function necessitate the maintenance of weight above a critical level and, therefore, above a critical amount of body fat. In actual figures, as depicted in the nomogram derived from Frisch (Fig 6–7), a loss of body weight in the range of 10–15% of normal weight for height may

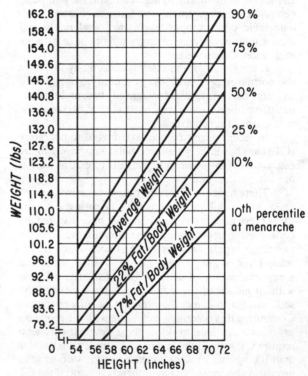

Figure 6–7. A fatness index nomogram modified from Frisch. This nomogram is useful in giving an estimate of the minimal weight necessary for a particular height in order for menstrual cycles to be restored (22% fat/body weight). However, individual variation is such that the nomogram is not infallible in predicting the return of menses for a given patient. (Reproduced, with permission, from Speroff L: Amenorrhea. In: *Office Gynecology*, 2nd ed. Glass RH [editor]. Williams & Wilkins, 1981.)

result in amenorrhea. This represents a loss of about one-third of body fat and represents a drop below a fat content of 22% of body weight. Menarche, according to Frisch, occurs when fat constitutes 17% of weight, while secondary amenorrhea occurs below 22% fat per body weight.

Women who engage in vigorous sports and other activities have about 50% less body fat than less active women of the same age and general body build. Indeed, the mean is far below the tenth percentile for secondary amenorrhea (the 22% body-fat line). The conversion of body fat to lean muscle mass can occur without discernible change in total body weight. A woman with low body weight who engages in vigorous (athletic or esthetic) activity is highly susceptible to amenorrhea. Recent studies indicate that this amenorrhea is due to hypothalamic dysfunction similar to that of anorexia nervosa.

Exercise is associated with progressively higher increases in peripheral levels of endorphins (Carr et al). Suppression of GnRH pulsatile secretion is a central feature, and this may be the result of arcuate nucleus inhibition exerted by endorphins. Therefore, physical stress (and perhaps mental stress as well) can lead to hypothalamic suppression, and this suppression is further intensified or operative in a state of low body fat.

The characteristics of exercise-related amenorrhea are strikingly reminiscent of anorexia nervosa—significant physical exercise, a need for control over the body, a striving for artistic and technical proficiency, and the consequent preoccupation with the body, together with the stressful pressures of performing and competing.

The rigidly perfectionistic girl (or boy) repeatedly threatened by overweight is highly vulnerable to an anorectic reaction. The gynecologist (or other primary care physician) may be the first to become aware of this problem, having encountered the patient because of the presenting complaint of either amenorrhea or weight loss. Physicians must be aware of this problem, because early recognition, counseling, and confidential support may intercept a progressive problem.

Simple weight gain may reverse amenorrhea. However, these patients often are unwilling to give up their exercise routines, and estrogen replacement or induction of ovulation for infertility may be necessary.

Hormone Replacement Therapy

The patient who is hypoestrogenic and who is not a candidate for induction of ovulation deserves hormone replacement therapy. This includes patients diagnosed as having gonadal failure, patients with hypothalamic amenorrhea, and postgonadectomy patients. Bone densities of these young patients are comparable to those of postmenopausal women (Klibanski et al). A reasonable schedule is the following: On days 1–25 of each month, give 1.25 mg of conjugated estrogens orally; on days 16–25, add 10 mg of medroxyprogesterone acetate orally. Beginning medication on the first of every month establishes an easily remembered routine. Menstruation generally occurs 3 days after the last dose, the 28th of each month. Rarely, estrogen dosage must be reduced because of bothersome estrogenic effects, eg, fluid retention. If the progestational agent is responsible for undesirable side-effects, the daily dose may be decreased to 5 mg.

It is useful to adopt the academic-year schedule for annual reevaluation, because many of these patients are in school. Hormone replacement therapy may be discontinued in June and reevaluation scheduled for August in countries in the northern hemisphere. If menses do not resume spontaneously, hormone replacement therapy can begin again in September.

The importance of monthly menstruation to a young girl cannot be overemphasized. Regular and visible menstrual bleeding is often a gratifying experience in the young patient with gonadal dysgenesis and serves to reinforce her sense of femininity. The estrogen dose in the replacement regimen must be high in order to achieve menstruation in a young woman, hence the use of 1.25 mg orally.

Patients with hypothalamic amenorrhea must be cautioned that replacement therapy will not protect against pregnancy in the event that normal function spontaneously returns. In the occasional patient who must have the most effective contraception possible, it is reasonable to use a low-dose oral contraceptive to provide the missing estrogen.

MENSTRUAL REGULATION

This procedure is discussed in Chapter 23.

●　　●　　●

References

Bai J et al: Drug-related menstrual aberrations. *Obstet Gynecol* 1974;**44**:713.

Blichert-Toft M et al: Treatment of mastalgia with bromocriptine: A double-blind cross-over study. *Br Med J* 1979;**1**:237.

Board JA et al: Identification of differing etiologies of clinically diagnosed premature menopause. *Am J Obstet Gynecol* 1979;**134**:936.

Carr DB et al: Physical conditioning facilitates the exercise-induced secretion of beta-endorphin and beta-lipotropin in women. *N Engl J Med* 1981;**305**:560.

Coelingh-Bennik HJT: Intermittent bromocriptine treatment for induction of ovulation in hyperprolactinemic patients. *Fertil Steril* 1979;**31**:267.

Dale E, Gerlach DH, Wilhite AL: Menstrual dysfunction in distance runners. *Obstet Gynecol* 1979;**54**:47.

Dalton K: *The Premenstrual Syndrome and Progesterone Therapy*. Heinemann, 1977.

Davajan V, Nakamura RM, Kharma K: Spermatozoan transport in cervical mucus. *Obstet Gynecol Surv* 1970;**25**:1.

Erickson GF: Normal ovarian function. *Clin Obstet Gynecol* 1978;**21**:31.

Ferenczy A, Bertrand G, Gelfand MM: Proliferation kinetics of human endometrium during the normal menstrual cycle. *Am J Obstet Gynecol* 1979;**133**:859.

Frisch RE: Food intake: Fatness and reproductive ability. Page 149 in: *Anorexia Nervosa*. Vigersky RA (editor). Raven Press, 1977.

Griffin JE et al: Congenital absence of the vagina. *Ann Intern Med* 1976;**85**:224.

Grimes DA: Estimating vaginal blood loss. *J Reprod Med* 1979; **22**:190.

Hallberg L et al: Menstrual blood loss: A population study. *Acta Obstet Gynecol Scand* 1966;**45**:320.

Heller ME, Savage MO, Dewhurst V: Vaginal bleeding in childhood: Review of 51 patients. *Br J Obstet Gynaecol* 1978; **85**:721.

Hoffman PG: Primary dysmenorrhea and the premenstrual syndrome. In: *Office Gynecology,* 2nd ed. Glass RH (editor). Williams & Wilkins, 1981.

Israel R, Mishell DR Jr, Labudovich M: Mechanisms of normal and dysfunctional uterine bleeding. *Clin Obstet Gynecol* 1970;**13**:386.

Jewelewicz R, Zimmerman E: Current management of the amenorrhea-galactorrhea syndrome. *Fertil Steril* 1978; **29**:597.

Klein SM, Garcia CR: Asherman's syndrome: A critique and current review. *Fertil Steril* 1973;**24**:722.

Klibanski A et al: Decreased bone density in hyperprolactinemic women. *N Engl J Med* 1980;**303**:1511.

Knobil E: The neuroendocrine control of the menstrual cycle. *Recent Prog Horm Res* 1980;**36**:53.

Magyar DE et al: Regular menstrual cycles and premenstrual molimina as indicators of ovulation. *Obstet Gynecol* 1979; **53**:411.

Noyes RW, Hertig AT, Rock J: Dating the endometrial biopsy. *Fertil Steril* 1950;**1**:3.

Ojeda SR et al: Recent advances in the endocrinology of puberty. *Endocr Rev* 1980;**1**:228.

Quigley ME et al: Evidence for an increased dopaminergic and opioid activity in patients with hypothalamic hypogonadotropic amenorrhea. *J Clin Endocrinol Metab* 1980;**50**:949.

Santen RJ, Ruby EB: Enhanced frequency and magnitude of episodic LH-releasing hormone discharge as a hypothalamic mechanism for increased LH secretion. *J Clin Endocrinol Metab* 1979;**48**:315.

Schwartz M, Jewelewicz R: The use of gonadotropins for induction of ovulation. *Fertil Steril* 1981;**35**:3.

Sherman BM, Koreman SG: Hormonal characteristics of the human menstrual cycle throughout reproductive life. *J Clin Invest* 1975;**55**:699.

Speroff L, Redwine DB: Exercise and menstrual function. *Phys Sports Med* 1980;**8**:42.

Speroff L et al: *Clinical Gynecologic Endocrinology and Infertility,* 2nd ed. Williams & Wilkins, 1978.

Speroff L et al: A practical approach for the evaluation of women with abnormal polytomography or elevated prolactin levels. *Am J Obstet Gynecol* 1979;**135**:896.

Warren MP: The effects of exercise on pubertal progression and reproductive function in girls. *J Clin Endocrinol Metab* 1980; **51**:1150.

Warren MP, Vande Wiele RL: Clinical and metabolic features of anorexia nervosa. *Am J Obstet Gynecol* 1973;**117**:435.

Ylikorkala O, Dawood MY: New concepts in dysmenorrhea. *Am J Obstet Gynecol* 1978;**130**:833.

Zacharias L, Rand WM, Wurtman RJ: A prospective study of sexual development and growth in American girls: The statistics of menarche. *Obstet Gynecol Surv* 1976;**31**:325.

Sex Chromosome Abnormalities; Intersex | 7

Howard W. Jones, Jr., MD

NORMAL SEXUAL DEVELOPMENT

Differentiation of the Gonad

In the 4- to 5-mm crown-rump (C–R) length embryo (about 4 weeks), a genital ridge appears as a thickening of the coelomic epithelium on the medial aspect of each mesonephros. The covering epithelium, known as germinal epithelium, is separated from the underlying mesenchyme by a basement membrane.

Another element presently appears in the form of large spherical cells with hyperchromatic vesicular nuclei. These are the gonocytes (primitive germ cells). They are interspersed in the substance of the primitive gonad. They arise from the yolk sac and hindgut endoderm and migrate to the genital ridges.

The developmental changes in the genital ridges are indistinguishable in the 2 sexes until late in the sixth week of embryonic life. In the male, the structure of the indifferent gonad begins to differentiate as a testis in the 15-mm C–R embryo (5–6 weeks), and the testis is easily recognizable as such in the 27-mm C–R embryo (about 6½ weeks). The young ovary, however, retains the structure of the primitive gonad for a longer time than does the testis. The main features of ovarian development are the persistence and increase of the superficial part, or future cortex, of the female gonadal blastema, in which primordial germ cells are situated. The deeper part, which is almost devoid of germ cells, soon becomes the ovarian medulla.

In the 20-mm C–R embryo (about 6 weeks), mesenchymal cells arrange themselves around primordial germ cells to form primordial follicles; the encapsulating cells become pregranulosa cells. The prenatal ovarian stromal cells arise from the ovarian mesenchyme, starting in the region of the hilum and later spreading peripherally into the medulla and the cortex.

Development of Male-Female Duct Systems

The müllerian ducts appear in the 10-mm C–R embryo (about 5 weeks) in either sex by invagination of the coelomic epithelium into the underlying mesenchyme of the intermediate cell mass, lateral to the cranial extremity of the wolffian ducts. In the female, the site of invagination becomes the future abdominal opening of the oviduct. At the caudal extremity of the mesonephros, the müllerian duct crosses ventrally and grows mediocaudally to meet and fuse with the duct of the opposite side. The oviducts are formed from the unfused parts of these ducts.

Fusion of the müllerian ducts is at first incomplete: for a short while, a septum separates their 2 cavities. In the 56-mm C–R embryo (about 12 weeks), the septum degenerates; this leaves a single cavity, the uterovaginal canal. The caudal tip of the canal comes in contact with the dorsal wall of the urogenital sinus, producing an elevation known as the müllerian tubercle. Proliferation of the tip of the uterovaginal canal results in the formation of a solid vaginal cord.

In the 63-mm C–R embryo (12–13 weeks), 2 sinovaginal bulbs appear in the form of bilateral posterior endodermal evaginations from the urogenital sinus close to the attachment of the wolffian ducts. These bulbs join with the caudal end of the vaginal cord to form the vaginal plate. The part of the urogenital sinus immediately cranial to the bulbs forms the urethra, while the bulbs move caudally to form the vestibule. Later in fetal life, the uterovaginal canal extends caudally and canalizes the vaginal plate, and the epithelium of the sinovaginal bulbs breaks; a communication is thus established between the urogenital sinus and the uterovaginal canal. The musculature of the female genital tract arises from the mesenchyme surrounding the müllerian ducts.

Development of the External Genitalia

The external genitalia, like other portions of the genital tract, pass through an indifferent period before specialized differentiation appears in the 50-mm C–R embryo (8–9 weeks). In the indifferent stage, they are represented by (1) a genital tubercle or phallus (primordium of the penis or clitoris); (2) a urethral groove limited laterally by 2 urethral folds; and (3) a pair of genital (scrotolabial) swellings that appear on either side of the genital tubercle.

The urogenital sinus opens into the urethral groove. The undersurface of the genital tubercle is a part of the urethral plate, which is a proliferation of sinus epithelium.

Sex differences become recognizable when the fetus measures about 50 mm C–R (8–9 weeks). In the male, the urethral folds fuse first in the pelvic region, to progressively bring the urogenital ostium from the perineum onto the genital tubercle. The fusion of the folds results in the formation of a perineal raphe extending from the anus to the urogenital ostium. The genital swellings, which now may be called scrotal swellings, have migrated toward the anus and no longer flank the base of the genital tubercle, which is differentiating as the penis.

In the female, the urethral groove remains open and becomes the vulva. The urethral folds do not fuse; instead, they form the labia minora. The genital swellings, which now may be called labial swellings, become elongated and flank the base of the genital tubercle, which is differentiating as the clitoris.

At fetal age 12 weeks, the external genitalia are definitely male or female in character.

Maturation: Changes in Puberty

Puberty—the attainment of reproductive powers—is a time of complex physiologic, psychologic, and morphologic change. The internal and external sex organs and the breasts are affected, pubic and axillary hair appears, the body contours are altered, and growth slows down. The onset of menstruation—the menarche—is the most dramatic and overt sign of female sexual maturation; its corollary in the male is the first ejaculation of sperm. Normally, puberty may begin as early as age 8 in females and age 10 in males, and it may be completed in all aspects as late as age 16 in females and age 18 in males.

The maturation of the endocrine glands in puberty is only partly understood. The initiation of estrogenic function by the ovary provides the final common impetus for most of the changes in puberty. The ovary's role in maturation is indicated by failure of important sexual changes to occur in women who lack ovaries. Nevertheless, certain manifestations of puberty do appear—notably the growth of axillary and pubic hair. This suggests adrenal androgen control; however, there must be contributory participation by ovarian hormones because body hair is scantier in women with ovarian agenesis than in normal women. The broad implication is that adrenal androgen has a role in the female maturation process, albeit a minor one.

In the final analysis, it is likely that new central nervous system functions control the changes in puberty. The pituitary itself is under the control of higher centers. It seems capable of functioning at any age as indicated by precocious development in infancy from localized intracerebral lesions.

Gonadotropins usually appear in the urine 2½ years before the menarche. Radioimmunoassay shows that the serum LH and FSH levels in infancy range from 1 to 2 mIU/mL. LH rises to adult tonic LH levels during the pubertal period, but FSH reaches adult levels much more slowly and over a longer period of time.

Serum estradiol is usually less than 3 ng/dL prior to puberty but reaches levels of 4–10 ng/dL in the adult proliferative phase just before the menarche, which occurs when the breasts are almost fully developed.

Brown's chemical method of estrogen assay reveals only traces before age 11. During the next 2–3 years, estrogen levels increase toward adult levels.

Excretion of neutral 17-ketosteroids gradually increases during puberty. In the first few days of life, values up to 3 mg/24 h may be found as a carry-over from the mother; after this time and until about age 7, values of less than 1 mg/24 h are normal. Thereafter, the excretion rate gradually rises, until at age 17–18 the normal adult value of approximately 10 mg/24 h is established.

Menarche occurs, on the average, at about age 12. It tends to be earlier with good nutrition; widely gathered information indicates that with each passing decade the age at which menarche occurs lowers by a few months.

The first few menstrual periods generally are anovulatory, ie, fertility does not begin with the menarche.

THE EXPERIMENTAL BASIS OF SEXUAL DIFFERENTIATION

The genetic determination of sex seems to be confined to controlling the sex of the gonads. Sexual differentiation of the ducts and external genitalia depends on hormonal stimuli at specific times during embryonic life. The hormonal theory of sexual differentiation is now firmly established.

Effects of Castration on Differentiation of the Genitalia

The role of the developing gonads and the differentiation of the sex ducts and external genitalia were elucidated by Alfred Jost (1947) in a series of brilliant experiments on rabbits. Castration of female fetuses in utero at various stages of pregnancy did not interfere with feminine differentiation. On the other hand, castration of male fetuses during the indifferent stage of development emphasized the primordial importance of the testis as a body sex differentiator, because no male characteristics developed; instead, the entire genital tract and external genitalia became feminine and were similar to those of the genetic females. Jost's work indicates that in the absence of a gonad, regardless of the genetic sex of the individual, the wolffian ducts will disappear; the müllerian ducts will be retained and will differentiate into oviducts, uterine horns, and the müllerian portion of the vagina; and the external genitalia will develop along female lines (Fig 7–1).

In Jost's experiments, after early removal of the testis, female organogenesis took place in the absence of any gonadal morphogenic secretion.

Under other experimental conditions, partial testicular influence can be clarified by variations in the experimental plan. Three basic experiments have been carried out: (1) removal of both testes at various stages during sexual differentiation, (2) unilateral castration at various stages, and (3) hypophysectomy.

Castration at Various Stages

Castration of the male rabbit at intervals ranging

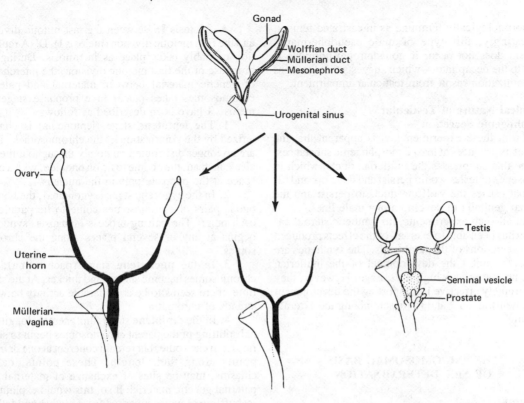

Figure 7–1. Differentiation of the sex ducts in the rabbit. **Top:** Undifferentiated condition. The female structures **(below, left)** will develop if the gonad is an ovary; the male structure **(below, right)** will develop if the gonad is a testis; and if the fetus is castrated in the indifferent stage, the female structure **(below, middle)** will develop. (Reproduced, with permission, from Jones HW Jr, Scott WW: *Hermaphroditism, Genital Anomalies and Related Endocrine Disorders,* 2nd ed. Williams & Wilkins, 1971.)

from day 19 to day 24 of intrauterine life shows that there are critical stages for each part of the genital tract during which it is delineated as masculine, for life, by the gonadal secretion. Castration before this critical stage prevents masculine organogenesis, but after this critical stage it no longer interferes with masculine differentiation even though castration is effected before sexual specialization has become morphologically obvious.

The important conclusion derived from these experiments is that the testicular impulse toward masculinity occurs during a very limited period of development and at a crucial phase. If the experimental work on rabbits can be extrapolated to human beings, the critical period for masculine differentiation should occur at approximately 30–50 mm C–R length (50–60 days of gestational age). It is noteworthy that the interstitial cells of the fetal testis seem to disappear at about the time that male organogenesis is established.

Unilateral Castration

The effect of unilateral castration in the rabbit depends on the stage of development reached at the time of operation. For example, if one testis is removed as late as day 23, the remaining testis is able to compensate and complete the sexual specialization

that had begun on the opposite (castrated) side. However, in embryos castrated early, masculine external genitalia and completely masculine organogenesis occur on the side bearing the remaining testis; the remaining testis fails to masculinize the castrated side. Thus, the wolffian duct may disappear and the müllerian duct may differentiate into a uterine horn. The result is asymmetry of the genital tract. Local control by the fetal testis at a particular time in embryonic life is also shown by grafting experiments in which a testis is implanted on one side of a feminine genital tract. In such experiments, the grafted testis is able to inhibit the development of the müllerian ducts, whereas they develop normally on the opposite (ungrafted) side.

Effect of Hypophysectomy

Decapitation of the rabbit fetus is a simplified method of hypophysectomy. Sexual abnormalities in the experimental preparation are somewhat different from those resulting from intrauterine castration. In the male, the epididymis and deferent ducts—the structures that develop in close proximity to the testes—are apparently normal, and the müllerian ducts retrogress as in normal fetuses. Nevertheless, abnormalities are found at the level of the prostate, which is rudimentary, and at the level of the external genitalia, which are morphologically feminine as in castrated fetuses. Interestingly, this type of male pseudohermaphroditism does not occur if gonadotropic hormone is given to the decapitate—which suggests that the signs of feminization result from testicular impairment.

Chemical Nature of Testicular Morphogenic Secretion

From these experiments, it is apparent that the fetal testis produces at least 2 morphogenic substances: (1) one that suppresses the müllerian ducts, which in the absence of testes would persist and develop; and (2) one that causes the wolffian ducts to persist and the external genitalia to develop along male lines.

In all such experiments, no synthetic steroid androgen has been able to exert all of the effects produced by the secretions of the fetal testis. The synthetics are unable to inhibit the development of the müllerian ducts, no matter how high the dosage. However, they are extremely effective in supporting the development of the wolffian duct and in masculinizing the external genitalia.

THE CHROMOSOMAL BASIS OF SEX DETERMINATION

Syngamy

The sex of the fetus is normally determined at the moment of fertilization. The cells of normal females contain two X chromosomes; those of normal males contain one X and one Y. During meiotic reduction, half of the male gametes receive a Y chromosome and the other half an X chromosome. Inasmuch as the female has two X chromosomes, all female gametes contain an X chromosome. If a Y-bearing gamete fertilizes an ovum, the fetus is male; conversely, if an X-bearing gamete fertilizes an ovum, the fetus is female.

Arithmetically, the situation described above should yield a male:female sex ratio of 100—the sex ratio being defined as 100 times the number of males divided by the number of females. However, for many years, the male:female sex ratio of the newborns in the white population has been approximately 105; eg, in the USA in 1973 the sex ratio of live white births was 105.7, of live nonwhite births 102.8. Apparently the sex ratio at fertilization is even higher than at birth: most data on the sex of abortuses indicate a preponderance of males.

Meiosis-Oogenesis

The final 2 nuclear divisions of the germ cells, ie, the 2 meiotic divisions, have the effect of (1) reducing the number of chromosomes from the diploid 46 to the haploid 23, so that the union of the female gamete with a male gamete will result in a zygote with a restored normal diploid chromosome number of 46 in the next generation; and (2) reshuffling the maternal and paternal genetic material, so that each individual of the next generation will be genetically unique.

A. Meiosis I: Between the last mitotic division and the first meiotic division (meiosis I), DNA replication probably takes place as in mitosis. During the prophase of the first meiotic division, the interchange of genetic material between maternal and paternal chromosomes takes place. Five prophase stages of meiosis I have been described as follows:

1. The **leptotene** stage (leptonema) is characterized by the polarization of the chromosomes. They are no longer distributed randomly throughout the nucleus; instead, they come to lie on one side, with a clear space at the opposite pole in the nucleus.

2. In the **zygotene** stage (zygonema), the homologous pairs of chromosomes come to lie parallel to each other. The pairing process (synapsis, syndesis) begins at any of several places along the chromosomes.

3. In the **pachytene** stage (pachynema), the chromosomes become shorter and thicker. At the same time, there seems to be considerable activity between strands of chromatin.

4. In the **diplotene** stage (diplonema), longitudinal splitting of the parent chromosomes begin to separate from each other but remain coherent at one or more points along their length. These points, called chiasms, may be sites of exchange of maternal and paternal genetic material; if so, this would explain the reshuffling of genes inherited from mother and father. There are at least 50 chiasms in a chromosome set.

In humans, the germ cells rest in the diplotene stage, as may be seen in fixed sections of ovary; they may remain at rest for 10–50 years. Further division in the female does not take place until ovulation.

5. **Diakinesis,** which completes the prophase, is a relatively brief stage during which the chromosomes are greatly contracted and the chiasms become terminalized. The nucleoli begin to disappear and the nuclear membrane breaks down.

Meiotic metaphase, which follows prophase, differs from mitotic metaphase in that the chromosomes are lined up on the equatorial plate of the cell in pairs instead of singly. Thus, homologous chromosomes lie side by side on the fibers of the spindle.

Anaphase is characterized by reduction of the number of centromeres and therefore of chromosomes. One of each of the 23 chromosome pairs migrates to a centriole, so that there is segregation of 23 chromosomes at each pole of the cell.

Telophase of meiosis I results in the formation of 2 cells, each of which has 23 chromosomes. It should be mentioned that while the distribution of chromatin material seems to be equal, meiosis I in the female is really an asymmetric division. The main portion of the cytoplasm remains with one of the daughter oocytes. A small polar body is extruded; it is little more than a group of 23 chromosomes.

B. Meiosis II: The second meiotic division (meiosis II) resembles mitotic division except that there are only 23 chromosomes along the equatorial axis of the cell. During this division, the centromeres divide, and each new centromere takes with it one short and one long arm of a chromosome. The migration in opposite directions along the meiotic spindle to the dispersed centrioles results in the formation of 2 cells; but, as in meiosis I, they contain unequal amounts of cytoplasm. The larger cell, which at the end of the process just described might properly be called an ovum, possesses most of the cytoplasm; the smaller contains little more than chromatin.

Conversion of the oocyte into a gamete does not occur until after ovulation and is always incomplete unless the oocyte is penetrated by a sperm. Only after fertilization can the secondary oocyte complete its division, to give rise to an ovum and the second polar body. If fertilization does not take place, the maturation of the secondary oocyte comes to an end in metaphase II.

Meiosis-Spermatogenesis

Meiosis in the male differs from meiosis in the female in 3 important respects:

(1) The process begins at puberty and continues until death.

(2) The meiotic divisions are equal. In oogenesis, as was noted, the nuclear divisions are equal, but the cytoplasmic division is unequal, so that in the female one primary oocyte gives rise to one ovum. In the male, however, the cytoplasmic divisions in both meiosis I and meiosis II are equal, with the result that one primary spermatocyte gives rise to 4 sperms.

(3) The X and Y chromosomes of the primary germ cell in the male behave quite differently in meiosis than do the two X chromosomes in the female. The X chromosomes in the female—and the autosomes as well—associate laterally during meiosis I, and chiasms are observed during the prophase of meiosis I; but in the male the association of the X and Y chromosomes is end-to-end. This biologic mechanism presumably is intended to prevent an exchange of sex-determining genetic material, for if this occurred between the X and Y chromosomes, sexual identity would be confused. There is genetic evidence, however, of an exchange of genetic material between the short arm of the X chromosome and the short arm of the Y chromosome at loci that are not concerned with sex determination but are located on X and Y chromosomes, respectively.

Abnormalities of Meiosis-Mitosis

The discussion in this section will be limited to anomalies of meiosis and mitosis that result in some abnormality in the sex chromosome complement of the embryo.

Chromosome studies in connection with various clinical conditions suggest that errors in meiosis and mitosis do indeed occur. These errors result in any of the following principal effects: (1) an extra sex chromosome, (2) a deficient sex chromosome, (3) 2 cell lines having different sex chromosomes and arising by mosaicism, (4) 2 cell lines having different sex chromosomes and arising by chimerism, (5) a structurally abnormal sex chromosome, and (6) a sex chromosome complement inconsistent with the phenotype.

By and large, an extra or a deficient sex chromosome arises as the result of an error of disjunction in meiosis I or II in either the male or the female. In meiosis I, this means that instead of each of the paired homologous sex chromosomes going to the appropriate daughter cell, both go to one cell, leaving that cell with an extra sex chromosome and the daughter cell with none. Failure of disjunction in meiosis II simply means that the centromere fails to divide normally.

A variation of this process, known as anaphase lag, occurs when one of the chromosomes is delayed in arriving at the daughter cell and thus is lost. Theoretically, chromosomes may be lost by failure of association in prophase and by failure of replication, but these possibilities have not been demonstrated.

Persons who have been found to have 2 cell lines apparently have had problems in mitosis in the very early stage of embryogenesis. Thus, if there is nondisjunction or anaphase lag in an early (first, second, or immediately subsequent) cell division in the embryo, mosaicism may be said to exist. In this condition, there are 2 cell lines; one has a normal number or an extra number of sex chromosomes and the other is deficient in a sex chromosome. A similar situation exists in chimerism, except that there may be a difference in the sex chromosome: one may be an X and one may be a Y. This apparently arises by dispermy, or by the fertilization of a double oocyte, or by the fusion, very early in embryogenesis, of 2 separately fertilized oocytes. Each of these conditions has been produced in experimental animals.

Structural abnormalities of the sex chromosomes—deletion of the long or short arm or the formation of an isochromosome (2 short arms or 2 long arms)—result from injury to the chromosomes during meiosis. How such injuries occur is not known, but the results are noted more commonly in sex chromosomes than in autosomes—perhaps because serious injury to an autosome is much more likely to be lethal than injury to an X chromosome, and surviving injured X chromosomes would therefore be more common.

The situation in which there is a sex chromosome complement with an inappropriate genotype arises in special circumstances of true hermaphroditism and XX males (see later sections).

The X Chromosome in Humans

At about day 16 of embryonic life, there appears on the undersurface of the nuclear membrane of the somatic cells of human females a structure 1 μm in diameter known as the X-chromatin body. There is genetic as well as cytogenetic evidence that this is one of the X chromosomes (the only chromosome visible by ordinary light microscopy during interphase). In a sense, therefore, all females are hemizygous with respect to the X chromosome. However, there are genetic reasons for believing that the X chromosome is not entirely inactivated during the process of formation of the X-chromatin body. In normal females, inactivation of the X chromosome during interphase and its representation as the X-chromatin body are known as the Lyon phenomenon (for Mary Lyon, British geneticist). This phenomenon may involve, at random, either the maternal or the paternal X chromosome. Furthermore, once the particular chromosome has been selected early in embryogenesis, it is always the same X chromosome that is inactivated in the progeny of that particular cell. Geneticists have found that the ratio of maternal to paternal X chromosomes inactivated is approximately 1:1.

The germ cells of an ovary are an exception to X inactivation and therefore never show an X-chromatin body. Apparently, meiosis is impossible without 2 genetically active X chromosomes. While random structural damage to one of the X chromosomes seems to cause meiotic arrest, oocyte loss, and therefore failure of ovarian development, an especially critical area necessary for oocyte development, has been identified on the long arm of the X. This essential area involves almost all of the long arm and has been specifically located from Xq13 to Xq26. If this area is broken in one of the X chromosomes as in a deletion or translocation, oocyte development does not occur. However, a few exceptions to this rule seem to have been described, and it is fair to say that for normal ovarian development 2 normal X chromosomes are required.

It is a curious biologic phenomenon that if one of the X chromosomes is abnormal it is always this chromosome that is genetically inactivated and becomes the X-chromatin body, irrespective of whether it is maternal or paternal in origin. While this general rule seems to be an exception to the randomness of X inactivation, this is more apparent than real. Presum-

ably, random inactivation does occur, but the disadvantaged cells—ie, those left with a damaged active X—do not survive. Consequently, the embryo develops only with cells with a normal active X chromosome and an inactive abnormal X chromosome which is the X chromatin in these cells.

If there are more than two X chromosomes, all X chromosomes except one are genetically inactivated and become X-chromatin bodies; thus, in this case, the number of X-chromatin bodies will be equal to the number of X chromosomes minus one. This type of inactivation applies to X chromosomes even when a Y chromosome is present, eg, in Klinefelter's syndrome.

Although the X chromosomes are primarily concerned with the determination of femininity, there is abundant genetic evidence that loci having to do with traits other than sex determination are present on the X chromosome. Thus, in the catalog of genetic disorders given in the fifth edition of *Mendelian Inheritance in Man* (McKusick, 1978), 205 traits are listed as more or less definitely X-linked. Substantial evidence for X linkage has been found for 107 of these traits; the rest are only suspected of having this relationship. Hemophilia, color blindness, childhood muscular dystrophy (Duchenne's dystrophy), Lesch-Nyhan syndrome, and glucose-6-phosphate dehydrogenase deficiency are among the better known conditions controlled by loci on the X chromosome. These entities probably arise from the expression of a recessive gene due to its hemizygous situation in males.

X-linked dominant traits are infrequent in the human. Vitamin D–resistant rickets is an example.

There is at least one disorder that is between a structural anomaly of the X chromosome and a single gene mutation. X-linked mental retardation in males is associated with a fragile site at q26, but a special culture medium is required for its demonstration. Furthermore, it has been shown that heterozygote female carriers for this fragile site have low IQ test scores.

The Y Chromosome in Humans

Just as the X chromosome represents the only chromosome visible by ordinary light microscopy in interphase, the Y chromosome is the only chromosome visible in interphase, after exposure to quinacrine compounds, by the use of fluorescence microscopy. This is a very useful diagnostic method.

In contrast to the X chromosome, essentially no traits have been traced to the Y chromosome except those having to do with testicular formation. Possession of the Y chromosome alone, ie, without an X chromosome, apparently is lethal, because such a case has never been described.

A testicular determining gene seems to express itself as a cell surface antigen—the H-Y antigen. This antigen has been found to be expressed on all Y-bearing cells in individuals with testicular development. In addition, it has been expressed in individuals without a Y chromosome but with testes—as, for example, in 46,XX males and in 46,XX true hermaphrodites.

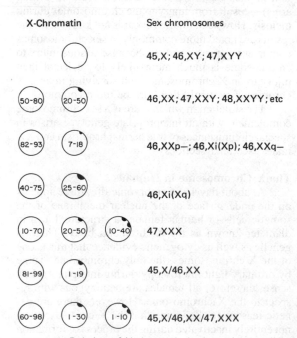

X-Chromatin			Sex chromosomes
◯			45,X; 46,XY; 47,XYY
50-80	20-50		46,XX; 47,XXY; 48,XXYY; etc
82-93	7-18		46,XXp−; 46,Xi(Xp); 46,XXq−
40-75	25-60		46,Xi(Xq)
10-70	20-50	10-40	47,XXX
81-99	1-19		45,X/46,XX
60-98	1-30	1-10	45,X/46,XX/47,XXX

Figure 7–2. Relation of X-chromatin body to the possible sex chromosome components.

At least 2 (perhaps 3) loci are required for the normal expression of the H-Y antigen. One certain locus is on the short arm of the Y; a second certain locus is on the X, probably on the short arm; and a third one may be autosomal. In addition, positivity for the H-Y antigen does not guarantee testicular development, as is evident from some cases of streak gonads. Thus, other loci for normal testicular development are required. The concept that the H-Y antigen is essential for testicular development depends upon the observation that testicular development does not seem to occur without H-Y positivity, although, as mentioned above, the opposite is true.

ABNORMAL DEVELOPMENT

OVARIAN AGENESIS–DYSGENESIS

In 1938, Turner described 7 girls 15–23 years of age with sexual infantilism, webbing of the neck, cubitus valgus, and retardation of growth. A survey of the recent literature indicates that "Turner's syndrome" means different things to different writers. After the later discovery that ovarian streaks are characteristically associated with the clinical entity described by Turner, "ovarian agenesis" became a synonym for Turner's syndrome. After discovery of the absence of the X-chromatin body in such patients, the term ovarian agenesis gave way to "gonadal dysgenesis," "gonadal agenesis," or "gonadal aplasia."

Meanwhile, some patients with the genital characteristics mentioned above were shown to have a normally positive X-chromatin count. Furthermore, a variety of sex chromosome complements have been found in connection with streak gonads. As if these contradictions were not perplexing enough, it has been noted that streaks are by no means confined to patients with Turner's original tetrad of infantilism, webbing of the neck, cubitus valgus, and retardation of growth: they may be present in girls with sexual infantilism only. Since Turner's original description, a host of additional somatic anomalies (varying in frequency) have been associated with his original clinical picture; these include shield chest, overweight, high palate, micrognathia, epicanthal folds, low-set ears, hypoplasia of nails, osteoporosis, pigmented moles, hypertension, lymphedema, cutis laxa, keloids, coarctation of the aorta, mental retardation, intestinal telangiectasia, and deafness.

For our purpose, the eponym Turner's syndrome will be used to indicate sexual infantilism with ovarian streaks, short stature, and 2 or more of the somatic anomalies mentioned above. In this context, such terms as ovarian agenesis, gonadal agenesis, and gonadal dysgenesis lose their clinical significance and become merely descriptions of the gonadal development of the person. At least 21 sex chromosome complements have been associated with streak gonads (Fig

```
45,X
46,XX
46,XY
46,XXp−
46,XXq−
46,Xi(Xp)
46,Xi(Xq)
46,XXq−?
45,X/46,XX
45,X/46,XY
45,X/46,Xi(Xq)
45,X/46,XXp−
45,X/46,XXq−
45,X/46,XXq−?
45,X/46,XX          }
45,X/46,Xi(Xq)      }
45,X/46,XX/47,XXX   }
45,X/47,XXX         }
45,X/46,XX/47,XXX        }
45,X/46,Xi(Xq)/47,XXX    }
45,X/46,XXr(X)
45,X/46,XX/46,XXr(X)
45,X/46,XXr(X)/47,XXr(X)r(X)
45,X/46,XX/47,XXX   }
45,X/46,XXq−        }
```

Figure 7–3. The 21 sex chromosome complements that have been found in patients with streak gonads.

7–3), but only about 9 sex chromosome complements have been associated with Turner's syndrome. However, approximately two-thirds of patients with Turner's syndrome have a 45,X chromosome complement, whereas only one-fourth of patients without Turner's syndrome but with streak ovaries have a 45,X chromosome complement.

Karyotype/phenotype correlations in the syndromes associated with ovarian agenesis are not completely satisfactory. Nonetheless, if gonadal development is considered as one problem and if the somatic difficulties associated with these syndromes are considered as a separate problem, one can make certain correlations.

With respect to failure of gonadal development, it is important to recall that neither the gonocytes nor the oogonia exhibit an X-chromatin body. This implies that diploid germ cells require 2 normal, active X chromosomes. This is in contrast to the somatic cells, where only one sex chromosome is thought to be genetically active, at least after day 16 of embryonic life in the human, when the X-chromatin body first appears in the somatic cells. It is also important to recall that in 45,X persons, no oocytes persist and streak gonads are the rule. From these facts, it may be inferred that failure of gonadal development is not the result of a specific sex chromosome defect but rather of the absence of two X chromosomes with the necessary critical zones.

Karyotype/phenotype correlations with respect to the somatic abnormalities are even sketchier than the correlations with regard to gonadal development. Good evidence exists, however, that monosomy for

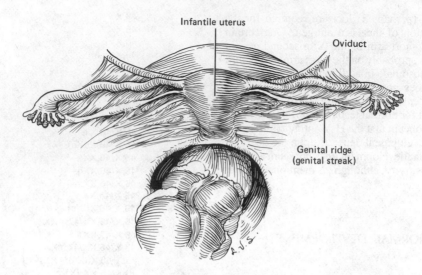

Figure 7–4. Gonadal streaks in a patient with the phenotype of Turner's syndrome. (Redrawn and reproduced, with permission, from Jones HW Jr, Scott WW: *Hermaphroditism, Genital Anomalies and Related Endocrine Disorders,* 2nd ed. Williams & Wilkins, 1971.)

the short arm of the X chromosome is related to somatic difficulties, although some patients with long-arm deletions have somatic abnormalities.

Histology of Gonadal Agenesis

The histologic findings in these abnormal ovaries in patients with gonadal streaks are essentially the same regardless of the cytogenetic background of the patient (Fig 7–4).

Fibrous tissue is the major component of the streak. It is indistinguishable microscopically from that of the normal ovarian stroma. The so-called germinal epithelium, on the surface of the structure, is a layer of low cuboid cells; this layer appears to be completely inactive.

Tubules of the ovarian rete are invariably found in sections taken from about the mid portion of the streak.

In all patients who have reached the age of normal puberty, hilar cells are also demonstrated. The number of hilar cells varies among patients. In those with some enlargement of the clitoris, hilar cells are present in large numbers. It may be that these developments are causally related. Nevertheless, hilar cells are also found in many normal ovaries. The origin of hilar cells is not precisely known, but they are associated with development of the medullary portion of the gonad. Their presence lends further support to the concept that in ovarian agenesis the gonad develops along normal lines until just before the expected appearance of early oocytes. In all cases in which sections of the broad ligament have been available for study, it has been possible to identify the mesonephric duct and tubules—broad ligament structures found in normal females.

Clinical Findings

A. Symptoms and Signs:

1. In newborn infants–The newborn with streak

ovaries often shows edema of the hands and feet. Histologically, this edema is associated with large dilated vascular spaces. With such findings, it is obviously desirable to study the buccal smear for X-chromatin bodies and to obtain a karyotype. However, some children with streak ovaries—particularly those who have few or no somatic abnormalities—cannot be recognized at birth.

2. In adolescents–The arresting and characteristic clinical findings in many of these patients is their short stature. Typical patients seldom attain a height of 1.5 m (5 ft) (Fig 7–5). In addition, sexual infantilism is a striking finding. As was mentioned above, a variety of somatic abnormalities may be present; by definition, if 2 or more of these are noted, the patient may be considered to have Turner's syndrome. Most of these patients have a negative buccal smear, and two-thirds of them have an XO sex chromosome complement. Nonetheless, normally tall patients without somatic abnormalities may also have gonadal streaks. Under these circumstances, because of mosaicism, the X chromatin bodies may be present in normal or reduced numbers. The internal findings are exactly the same as in patients with classic Turner's syndrome, however.

B. Laboratory Findings: An important finding in patients of any age—but especially after that of expected puberty, ie, about 12 years—is elevation of total gonadotropin production. From a practical point of view, ovarian failure in patients over age 15 cannot be considered as a diagnostic possibility unless the serum FSH is more than 50 mIU/mL and LH is more than 90 mIU/mL.

Other endocrine products—eg, urinary 17-ketosteroids, 17-hydroxycorticosteroids, and thyroid hormone—are present in low normal amounts. Urinary excretion of estrogens is low, and the maturation index and other vaginal smear indices are shifted well to the left.

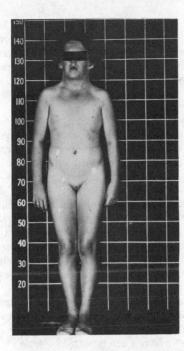

Figure 7–6. External genitalia of a patient with true hermaphroditism. (Reproduced, with permission, from Jones HW Jr, Scott WW: *Hermaphroditism, Genital Anomalies and Related Endocrine Disorders,* 2nd ed. Williams & Wilkins, 1971.)

Figure 7–5. Patient with Turner's syndrome. (Reproduced, with permission, from Jones HW Jr, Scott WW: *Hermaphroditism, Genital Anomalies and Related Endocrine Disorders,* 2nd ed. Williams & Wilkins, 1971.)

Treatment

Substitution therapy with estrogen is necessary for secondary characteristics development.

There is no known effective therapy for short stature.

The incidence of malignant degeneration is increased in the gonadal streaks of patients with a Y chromosome, as compared with normal males. Surgical removal of streaks from all patients with a Y chromosome is recommended.

TRUE HERMAPHRODITISM

By classic definition, true hermaphroditism exists when both ovarian and testicular tissue can be demonstrated in one patient. In humans, the Y chromosome carries genetic material that is normally responsible for testicular development; this material is active even when multiple-X chromosomes are present. Thus, in Klinefelter's syndrome, a testis develops with up to four Xs and only one Y. Conversely (with rare exceptions), a testis has not been observed to develop in the absence of the Y chromosome. The exceptions are found in true hermaphrodites and XX males, in whom testicular tissue has developed in association with an XX sex chromosome complement.

Clinical Findings

A. Symptoms and Signs: No exclusive features clinically distinguish true hermaphroditism from other forms of intersexuality. Hence, the diagnosis must be entertained in an infant with any form of intersexuality, excepting only those with a continuing virilizing influence, eg, congenital adrenal hyperplasia. On the other hand, firm diagnosis is possible after the onset of puberty, when certain clinical features become evident. However, the diagnosis can and should be made in infancy.

In the past, most true hermaphrodites have been reared as males because they have rather masculine-appearing external genitalia (Fig 7–6). Nevertheless, with early diagnosis, most should be reared as females.

Almost all true hermaphrodites develop female type breasts. This helps to distinguish male hermaphroditism from true hermaphroditism, because few male hermaphrodites other than those with familial feminizing hermaphroditism develop large breasts.

Many true hermaphrodites menstruate. The presence or absence of menstruation is partially determined by the development of the uterus; many true hermaphrodites have rudimentary or no development of the müllerian ducts (Fig 7–7).

B. Sex Chromosome Complements: Most true hermaphrodites have X-chromatin bodies and karyotypes that are indistinguishable from those of normal females. In contrast, a few patients who cannot be distinguished clinically from other true hermaphrodites have been reported to have a variety of other karyotypes—eg, several chimeric persons with karyotypes of 46,XX/46,XY have been identified.

In true hermaphrodites, the testis is competent in its müllerian-suppressive functions but an ovotestis may behave as an ovary insofar as its müllerian-suppressive function is concerned. The true hermaphroditic testis or ovotestis is as competent to masculinize the external genitalia as is the testis of a patient with the virilizing type of male hermaphroditism. This is unrelated to karyotype.

A clear understanding of the development of testicular tissue in the apparent absence of a Y chromosome is difficult to achieve. No evidence suggests that

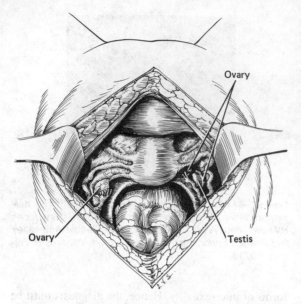

Figure 7–7. Internal genitalia of a patient with true hermaphroditism. (Redrawn and reproduced, with permission, from Jones HW Jr, Scott WW: *Hermaphroditism, Genital Anomalies and Related Endocrine Disorders,* 2nd ed. Williams & Wilkins, 1971.)

unrecognized tissue chimerism is a factor in this problem; nonetheless, abnormal crossing-over of a portion of the Y chromosome to the X, in meiosis, may explain some cases. This latter is supported by the finding of a positive H-Y antigen assay in some patients with 46,XX true hermaphroditism.

In general, the clinical picture of true hermaphroditism is not compatible with the clinical picture in other kinds of gross chromosomal anomalies. For example, very few true hermaphrodites have associated somatic anomalies, and mental retardation almost never occurs.

Treatment

The principles of treatment of true hermaphroditism do not differ from those of the treatment of hermaphroditism in general. Therapy can be summarized by stating that surgical removal of contradictory organs is indicated and the external genitalia should be reconstructed in keeping with the sex of rearing. The special problem in this group is how to establish with certainty the character of the gonad. This is particularly difficult in the presence of an ovotestis, because its recognition by gross characteristics is notoriously inaccurate and one must not remove too much of the gonad for study. In some instances, the gonadal tissue of one sex is completely embedded within a gonadal structure primarily of the opposite sex.

KLINEFELTER'S SYNDROME

This condition, first described in 1942 by Klinefelter, Reifenstein, and Albright, occurs only in apparent males. As originally described, it is characterized by small testes, azoospermia, gynecomastia, relatively normal external genitalia, and otherwise average somatic development. High levels of gonadotropin in urine or serum are characteristic.

Clinical Findings

A. Symptoms and Signs: By definition, this syndrome applies only to persons reared as males. The disease is not recognizable before puberty except by routine screening of newborn infants (see below). Most patients come under observation at 16–40 years of age.

Somatic development during infancy and childhood may be normal. Growth and muscular development may also be within normal limits. Most patients have a normal general appearance and no complaints referable to this abnormality, which is often discovered in the course of a routine physical examination or in an infertility study.

In the original publication by Klinefelter and others, gynecomastia was considered an essential part of the syndrome. Since then, however, cases without gynecomastia have been reported.

The external genitalia are perfectly formed and in most patients are quite well developed. Erection and intercourse usually are satisfactory.

There is no history of delayed descent of the testes in typical cases, and the testes are in the scrotum. Neither is there any history of testicular trauma or disease. Although a history of mumps orchitis is occasionally elicited, this disease has not been correlated with the syndrome. The testes, however, in contrast to the rest of the genitalia, are often very small (about 1.5 × 1.5 cm).

Psychologic symptoms are often present. Most studies of this syndrome have been done in psychiatric institutions. The seriousness of the psychologic disturbance seems to be partly related to the number of extra X chromosomes—eg, it is estimated that about one-fourth of XXY patients have some degree of mental retardation.

B. Laboratory Findings: One of the extremely important clinical features of Klinefelter's syndrome is the excessive amount of pituitary gonadotropin found by either urine or serum assay.

The urinary excretion of neutral 17-ketosteroids varies from relatively normal to definitely subnormal levels. There is a rough correlation between the degree of hypoleydigism as judged clinically and a low 17-ketosteroid excretion rate.

C. Histologic and Cytogenetic Findings: Klinefelter's syndrome may be regarded as a form of primary testicular failure.

Several authors have classified a variety of forms of testicular atrophy as subtypes of Klinefelter's syndrome. Be this as it may, Klinefelter believes that only those patients who have a chromosomal abnormality can be said to have this syndrome. Microscopic examination of the adult testis shows that the seminiferous tubules lack epithelium and are shrunken and hyalinized. They contain large amounts of elastic fibers. Leydig cells are present in large numbers.

Males with positive X-chromatin bodies are likely to have Klinefelter's syndrome. The nuclear sex anomaly reflects a basic genetic abnormality in sex chromosome constitution. All cases studied have had at least two X chromosomes and one Y chromosome. The commonest abnormality in the sex chromosome constitution is XXY, but the literature also records XXXY, XXYY, XXXXY, and XXXYY and mosaics of XX/XXY, XY/XXY, XY/XXXY, and XXXY/XXXXY. In all examples except the XX/XXY mosaic, a Y chromosome is present in all cells. From these patterns, it is obvious that the Y chromosome has a very strong testis-forming impulse, which can operate in spite of the presence of as many as four X chromosomes.

Thus, patients with Klinefelter's syndrome will have not only a postive X-chromatin body but also a positive Y-chromatin body.

The abnormal sex chromosome constitution causes differentiation of an abnormal testis, leading to testicular failure in adulthood. At birth or before puberty, such testes show a marked deficiency or absence of germinal cells.

By means of nursery screening, the frequency of males with positive X-chromatin bodies has been estimated to be 2.65 per 1000 live male births.

Treatment

There is no treatment for the 2 principal complaints of these patients: infertility and gynecomastia. No pituitary preparation has been effective in the regeneration of the hyalinized tubular epithelium or the stimulation of gametogenesis. Furthermore, no hormone regimen is effective in treating the breast hypertrophy. When the breasts are a formidable psychologic problem, surgical removal may be a satisfactory procedure. In patients who have clinical symptoms of hypoleydigism, substitution therapy with testosterone is an important physiologic and psychologic aid.

DOUBLE–X MALES

A few cases have been reported of adult males with a slightly hypoplastic penis and very small testes but no other indication of abnormal sexual development. These males are sterile. Unlike those with Klinefelter's syndrome, they do not have abnormal breast development. They are clinically very similar to patients with Del Castillo's syndrome (testicular dysgenesis). Nevertheless, the XX males have a positive sex chromatin and a normal female karyotype. These may be extreme examples of the sex reversal that is usually partial in true hermaphroditism. The H-Y antigen assay is positive.

Pediatric interest derives from the possible discovery of these persons by a routine buccal smear in a newborn.

MULTIPLE–X SYNDROMES

The finding of more than one X-chromatin body in a cell indicates the presence of more than two X chromosomes in that particular cell. In many patients, such a finding is associated with mosaicism, and the clinical picture is controlled by this fact—eg, if one of the strains of the mosaicism is 45,X, gonadal agenesis is likely to occur. There also are persons who do not seem to have mosaicism but do have an abnormal number of X chromosomes in all cells. In such persons, the most common complement is XXX (triplo-X syndrome), but XXXX (tetra-X syndrome), and XXXXX (penta-X syndrome) have been reported.

An additional X chromosome does not seem to have a consistent effect on sexual differentiation. The body proportions of these persons are normal, and the external genitalia are normally female. A number of such persons have been examined at laparotomy, and no consistent abnormality of the ovary has been found. In a few cases, the number of follicles appeared to be reduced, and in at least one case the ovaries were very small and the ovarian stroma poorly differentiated. About 20% of postpubertal patients with the triplo-X syndrome report various degrees of amenorrhea or some irregularity in menstruation. For the most part, however, these patients have a normal menstrual history and are of proved fertility.

Almost all patients known to have multiple-X syndromes have some degree of mental retardation. A few have mongoloid features. (The mothers of these patients tended to be older than the mothers of normal children—as is true also in Down's syndrome.) Perhaps these findings are in part circumstantial, since most of these patients have been discovered during surveys in mental institutions. The important clinical point is that mentally retarded infants should have chromosomal study.

Uniformly, the offspring of triplo-X parents have been normal. This is surprising, because theoretically in such cases meiosis should produce equal numbers of ova containing one or two X chromosomes, and fertilization of the abnormal XX ova should give rise to XXX and XXY individuals. Nevertheless, the triplo-X condition seems selective for normal ova and zygotes.

The diagnosis of this syndrome is made by identifying a high percentage of cells in the buccal smear with double X-chromatin bodies and by finding 47 chromosomes with a karyotype showing an extra X chromosome in all cells cultured from the peripheral blood. It should be noted that in the examination of the buccal smear, some cells have a single X-chromatin body. Hence, on the basis of the chromatin examination, one might suspect XX/XXY mosaicism. Actually, in triplo-X patients, only a single type of cell can be demonstrated in cultures of cells from the peripheral blood. The absence of the second X-chromatin body in some of the somatic cells may result from the time of examination of the cell (in interphase) and from the spatial orientation, which could have prevented the two X-chromatin bodies (adjacent to the nuclear membrane) from being seen. In this syndrome, the number of cells containing either one or two X-chromatin bodies is very high—at least 60–80%, as compared with an upper limit of about 40% in the normal human female.

FEMALE HERMAPHRODITISM DUE TO CONGENITAL ADRENAL HYPERPLASIA

Essentials of Diagnosis
- Female pseudohermaphroditism, ambiguous genitalia withclitoral hypertrophy, and, occasionally, persistent urogenital sinus.
- Early appearance of sexual hair; hirsutism, dwarfism.
- Urinary 17-ketosteroids elevated; pregnanetriol may be increased.
- Elevated serum 17-hydroxyprogesterone.
- Occasionally associated with water and electrolyte imbalance—particularly in the neonatal period.

General Considerations
Female hermaphroditism due to congenital adrenal hyperplasia is a clearly delineated clinical syndrome. The syndrome has been better understood since the discovery that cortisone may successfully arrest virilization.

If the diagnosis is not made in infancy, an unfortunate series of events ensues. Because the adrenals

secrete an abnormally large amount of virilizing steroid even during embryonic life, these infants are born with abnormal genitalia (Fig 7–8). In extreme cases, there is fusion of the scrotolabial folds and, in rare instances, even the formation of a penile urethra. The clitoris is greatly enlarged, so that it may be mistaken for a penis (Fig 7–9). No gonads are palpable within the fused scrotolabial folds, and their absence has sometimes given rise to the mistaken impression of male cryptorchism. Usually, there is a single urinary meatus at the base of the phallus and the vagina enters the persistent urogenital sinus as noted in Fig 7–10.

During infancy, provided there are no serious electrolyte disturbances, these children grow more rapidly than normal. For a time, they greatly exceed the average in both height and weight. Unfortunately, epiphyseal closure occurs by about age 10 years, with the result that as adults these people are much shorter than normal (Fig 7–11).

The process of virilization begins at an early age. Pubic hair may appear as early as age 2 years but usually somewhat later. This is followed by growth of axillary hair and finally by the appearance of body hair and a beard, which may be so thick as to require daily shaving. Acne may develop early. Puberty never ensues. There is no breast development. Menstruation does not occur. During the entire process, urinary 17-ketosteroid excretion is higher than would be expected at the patient's age.

Although our principal concern here is with this abnormality in females, it must be mentioned that adrenal hyperplasia of the adrenogenital type may also occur in males, in whom it is called macrogenitosomia precox. Sexual development progresses rapidly, and the sex organs attain adult size at an early age. Just as in the female, sexual hair and acne develop unusually early, and the voice becomes deep. The testes are usually in the scrotum; however, in early childhood they remain small and immature, although the genitalia are of adult dimensions. In adulthood, the testes usually enlarge and spermatogenesis occurs, allowing impregnation rates similar to that of a control population. Somatic development in the male corresponds to that of the female: As a child, he exceeds the

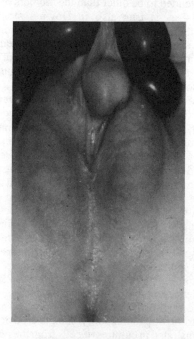

Figure 7–8. External genitalia of a female patient with congenital virilizing adrenal hyperplasia. Compare with Fig 7–9. (Reproduced, with permission, from Jones HW Jr, Scott WW: *Hermaphroditism, Genital Anomalies and Related Endocrine Disorders,* 2nd ed. Williams & Wilkins, 1971.)

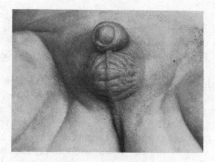

Figure 7–9. External genitalia of a female patient with congenital virilizing adrenal hyperplasia. This is a more severe deformity than that shown in Fig 7–8.

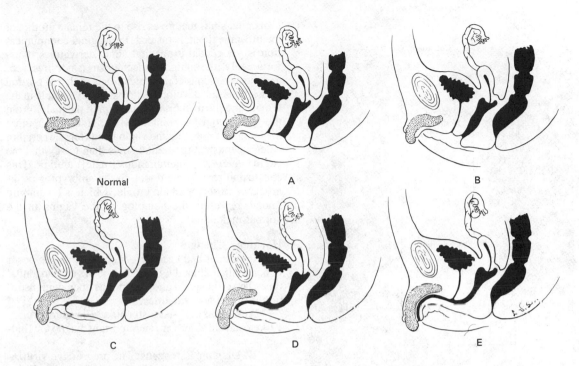

Figure 7–10. Sagittal view of genital deformities of increasing severity (A–E) in congenital virilizing adrenal hyperplasia. (Redrawn and reproduced, with permission, from Verkauf BS, Jones HW Jr: Masculinization of the female genitalia in congenital adrenal hyperplasia. *South Med J* 1970;**63**:634.)

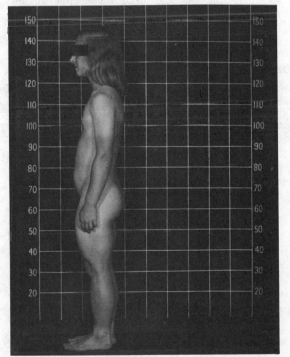

Figure 7–11. An untreated adult with virilizing adrenal hyperplasia. Note short stature and relative shortness of the extremities. (Reproduced, with permission, from Jones HW Jr, Scott WW: *Hermaphroditism, Genital Anomalies and Related Endocrine Disorders,* 2nd ed. Williams & Wilkins, 1971.)

average in height and strength, but (if untreated) as an adult he is stocky, muscular, and well below average height.

Both the male and the female with this disorder—but especially the male—may have the complicating problem of electrolyte imbalance. In infancy, it is manifested by vomiting, progressive loss of weight, and dehydration and may be fatal unless recognized promptly. The characteristic findings are an exceedingly low serum sodium level and low CO_2 combining power level and a high potassium level. The condition is sometimes misdiagnosed as congenital pyloric stenosis.

A few of these patients have hypertension in addition to virilization.

Adrenal Histology

The adrenal changes center on a reticular hyperplasia, which becomes more marked as the patient grows older. In some instances, the glomerulosa may participate in the hyperplasia, but the fasciculata is greatly diminished in amount or entirely absent. Lipid studies show absence of fascicular and glomerular lipid but an abnormally strong lipid reaction in the reticularis (Fig 7–12).

Ovarian Histology

The ovarian changes may be summarized by stating that in infants, children, and teenagers, there is normal follicular development to the antrum stage but no evidence of ovulation. With increasing age, less

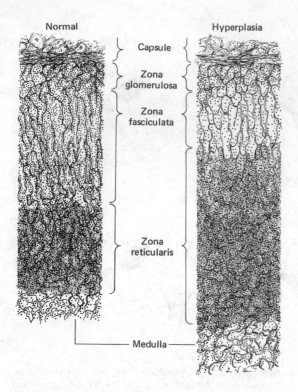

Figure 7–12. Normal adrenal architecture and adrenal histology in congenital virilizing adrenal hyperplasia. Note the great relative increase in the zona reticularis.

and less follicular activity occurs, and primordial follicles disappear. This disappearance must not be complete, however, because cortisone therapy, even in adults, usually results in ovulatory menstruation after 4–6 months of treatment.

Developmental Anomalies of the Genital Tubercle & Urogenital Sinus Derivatives

The phallus is composed of 2 lateral corpora cavernosa, but the corpus spongiosum is normally absent. The external urinary meatus is most often located at the base of the phallus (Fig 7–8). An occasional case may be seen in which the urethra does extend to the end of the clitoris (Fig 7–9). The glans penis and the prepuce are present and indistinguishable from these structures in the male. The scrotolabial folds are characteristically fused in the midline, giving a scrotumlike appearance with a median perineal raphe; however, they seldom enlarge to normal scrotal size. No gonads are palpable within the scrotolabial folds. When the anomaly is not severe (eg, in patients with postnatal virilization), fusion of the scrotolabial folds is not complete, and by gentle retraction it is often possible to locate not only the normally located external urinary meatus but also the orifice of the vagina.

An occasional patient has no communication between the urogenital sinus and the vagina. In no case does the vagina communicate with that portion of the urogenital sinus that gives rise to the female urethra or the prostatic urethra. Instead, the vaginal communication is via caudal urogenital sinus derivatives; thus, fortunately, the sphincter mechanism is not involved, and the anomalous communication is with that portion of the sinus that develops as the vaginal vestibule in the female and the membranous urethra in the male. From the gynecologist's point of view, it is much more meaningful to say that the vagina and (female) urethra enter a persistent urogenital sinus than to say that the vagina enters the (membranous [male]) urethra. This conclusion casts some doubt on the embryologic significance of the prostatic utricle, which is commonly said to represent the homolog of the vagina in the normal male.

Hormone Changes

Important and specific endocrine changes occur in congenital adrenal hyperplasia of the adrenogenital type. The ultimate diagnosis depends upon demonstration of these abnormalities.

A. Urinary 17-Ketosteroids: Elevated urinary 17-ketosteroid values are an important diagnostic finding.

B. Urinary Estrogens: The progressive virilization of female hermaphrodites caused by adrenal hyperplasia would suggest that estrogen secretion in these patients is low, and this hypothesis is further supported by the atrophic condition of both the ovarian follicular apparatus and the estrogen target organs. Actually, the determination of urinary estrogens, both fluorometrically and biologically, indicates that they are elevated.

C. Other Urinary Metabolites: The steroid metabolites in the urine of many patients with this disorder show that numerous defects in the biosynthesis of cortisol may occur. The most common defect is at the 21-hydroxylase step. Less frequent defects are at the 11-hydroxylase step and the 3β-ol-dehydrogenase step. Rarely, the defect is at the 17-hydroxylase step. Some of these abnormal metabolites are useful in diagnosis. For example, in the 21-hydroxylase defect, pregnanetriol may be abnormally elevated.

D. Serum Steroids: The development of satisfactory radioimmunoassay techniques for measuring steroids in blood serum has resulted in an increased tendency to measure serum steroids rather than urinary metabolites in diagnosing the condition and monitoring therapy. In the most common form of the disorder—21-hydroxylase deficiency—the serum 17-hydroxyprogesterone level and, to a lesser extent, the serum progesterone level are elevated. This is easily understandable when it is recalled that 17-hydroxyprogesterone is the substrate for the 21-hydroxylation step (Fig 7–13). Likewise, in the other enzyme defects, the serum steroid substrates are greatly elevated.

Pathogenesis of Virilizing Adrenal Hyperplasia

The basic defects in congenital virilizing adrenal

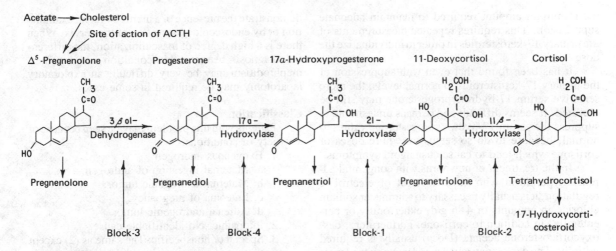

Figure 7–13. Enzymatic steps in cortisol synthesis. Localization of defects in congenital adrenal hyperplasia.

hyperplasia are one or more enzyme deficiencies in the biosynthesis of cortisol (Fig 7–13). With the reduced production of cortisol, normal feedback to the hypothalamus fails, with the result that increased amounts of ACTH are produced. This excess production of ACTH stimulates the deficient adrenal gland to produce relatively normal amounts of cortisol—but also stimulates production of abnormally large amounts of estrogens and androgens by the zona reticularis. In this overproduction, a biologic preponderance of androgens causes virilization. These abnormal sex steroids suppress the gonadotropins, so that untreated patients never reach puberty and do not menstruate.

The treatment of this disorder, therefore, consists in part of the administration of sufficient exogenous cortisol to suppress ACTH production to normal levels. This in turn should reduce the overstimulation of the adrenal, so that the adrenal will cease to produce abnormally large amounts of estrogen and androgen. The gonadotropins generally return to normal levels, with consequent feminization of the patient and achievement of menstruation.

The pathogenesis of the salt-losing type of adrenal hyperplasia involves a deficiency in aldosterone production.

Diagnosis

Hermaphroditism due to congenital adrenal hyperplasia must be suspected in any infant born with ambiguous or abnormal external genitalia. It is exceeding important that the diagnosis be made at a very early age if undesirable disturbances of metabolism are to be prevented.

All patients with ambiguous external genitalia should have an appraisal of their chromosomal characteristics. In all instances of female pseudohermaphroditism due to congenital hyperplasia, the chromosomal composition is that of a normal female.

The critical determinations are those of the urinary 17-ketosteroid and serum 17-hydroxyprogesterone levels. If these are elevated, the diagnosis must be either congenital adrenal hyperplasia or tumor. In the newborn, the latter is very rare, but in older children and adults with elevated 17-ketosteroids the possibility of tumor must be considered. One of the most satisfactory methods of making this differential diagnosis is to attempt to suppress the excess androgens by the administration of dexamethasone. In an adult or an older child, a suitable test dose of dexamethasone is 1.25 mg/45 kg (100 lb) body weight, given orally for 7 consecutive days. In congenital adrenal hyperplasia, there should be suppression of the urinary 17-ketosteroids on the seventh day of the test to less than 1 mg/24 h; in the presence of tumor, either there will be no effect or the 17-ketosteroid levels will rise.

Determination of urinary dehydroepiandrosterone (DHEA) or serum dehydroepiandrosterone sulfate (DHEAS) can also be helpful in differentiating congenital adrenal hyperplasia from an adrenal tumor. DHEA and DHEAS in patients with congenital adrenal hyperplasia may be up to 2 times normal, whereas with an adrenal tumor these metabolites are usually many times normal.

Determination of the serum sodium, potassium, and CO_2 combining power is also important to ascertain if electrolyte balance is seriously disturbed.

Treatment

The treatment of female hermaphroditism due to congenital adrenal hyperplasia is partly medical and partly surgical. Originally, cortisone was administered; today, it is known that various cortisone derivatives are at least as effective. It is most satisfactory to begin treatment with relatively large doses of cortisone for 7–10 days to obtain rapid suppression of adrenal activity. In young infants, the initial dose is about 25 mg/d intramuscularly; in older patients, 100 mg/d intramuscularly. After the output of 17-ketosteroids has decreased to a low level, the dose should be reduced to the minimum amount required to maintain adequate suppression. This requires repeated measurements of the urinary 17-ketosteroids in order to individualize the dose.

It has been found that even with suppression of the urinary 17-ketosteroids to normal levels, the more sensitive serum 17-hydroxyprogesterone may still be elevated. It seems difficult and perhaps undesirable to suppress the serum 17-hydroxyprogesterone values to normal, because to do so seems to require doses of cortisone which tend to cause cushingoid symptoms.

In the treatment of newborns with congenital adrenal hyperplasia who have a defect of electrolyte regulation, it is usually necessary to administer sodium chloride in amounts of 4–6 g/d, either orally or parenterally, in addition to cortisone. Furthermore, desoxycorticosterone acetate (Doca) usually is required initially. The dose is entirely dependent upon the levels of the serum electrolytes, which must be followed serially. Doca is conveniently supplied in the form of 125-mg pellets for subcutaneous implantation, but initial intramuscular administration in doses of 1–2 mg/d is required. After regulation is achieved and on discharge of the patient, one or 2 (rarely 5 or more) pellets may be implanted; but after the initial implantation additional Doca pellets are seldom necessary, because cortisone apparently is able to substitute for the loss of the salt-regulating hormone. In combination with cortisone, 0.05–0.2 mg of fludrocortisone may be used instead of Doca to control sodium loss.

In addition to the hormone treatment of this disorder, surgical correction of the external genitalia is usually necessary.

During acute illness or other stress, as well as during and after an operation, additional cortisone is indicated to avoid the adrenal insufficiency of stress. Doubling the maintenance dose is usually adequate in such circumstances.

FEMALE HERMAPHRODITISM WITHOUT PROGRESSIVE MASCULINIZATION

Females with no adrenal abnormality may have fetal masculinization of the external genitalia with the same anatomic findings as in patients with congenital virilizing adrenal hyperplasia. Unlike patients with adrenogenital syndrome, patients without adrenal abnormality do not have elevated levels of serum steroids or urinary 17-ketosteroids nor—as they grow older—do they show precocious sexual development or the metabolic difficulties associated with adrenal hyperplasia. At onset of puberty, normal feminization with menstruation and ovulation may be expected.

The diagnosis of female hermaphroditism not due to adrenal abnormality depends upon the demonstration of a 46,XX karyotype and the finding of normal serum steroids or normal levels of 17-ketosteroids in the urine. If fusion of the scrotolabial folds is complete, it is necessary to determine the exact relationship of the urogenital sinus to the urethra and vagina and to demonstrate the presence of a uterus by rectal examination or by endoscopic observation of the cervix. When there is a high degree of masculinization, the differential diagnosis between this condition and true hermaphroditism may be very difficult; an exploratory laparotomy may be required in some cases.

Classification

Patients with this problem may be seen because of a variety of conditions:

1. Exogenous androgen:
   a. Maternal ingestion of androgen.
   b. Maternal androgenic tumor.
   c. Luteoma of pregnancy.
   d. Adrenal androgenic tumor.
2. Idiopathic: No identifiable cause.
3. Special or nonspecific: The same as (2) except that it is associated with various somatic anomalies and with mental retardation.
4. Familial: A very rare anomaly.

MALE HERMAPHRODITISM

Persons with abnormal or ectopic testes may have external genitalia so ambiguous at birth that the true sex is not identifiable (Fig 7–14). At puberty, these persons tend to become masculinized or feminized depending upon factors to be discussed below. Thus, the adult habitus of these persons may be typically male, ie, without breasts, or typically female, with good breast development. In some instances, the external genitalia may be indistinguishable from those of a normal female; in others, the clitoris may be enlarged; and in still other instances there may be fusion

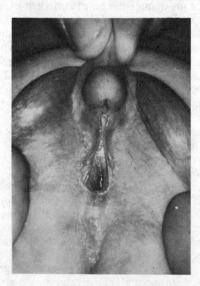

Figure 7–14. External genitalia in male hermaphroditism. (Reproduced, with permission, from Jones HW Jr, Scott WW: *Hermaphroditism, Genital Anomalies and Related Endocrine Disorders,* 2nd ed. Williams & Wilkins, 1971.)

of the labia in the midline, resulting in what seems to be a hypospadiac male. A deep or shallow vagina may be present. A cervix, a uterus, and uterine tubes may be developed to varying degrees; however, müllerian structures are often absent. Mesonephric structures may be grossly or microscopically visible. Body hair may be either typically feminine in its distribution and quantity or masculine in distribution and of sufficient quantity as to require plucking or shaving if the person is reared as a female. In a special group, axillary and pubic hair is congenitally absent. Although there is well-developed uterus in some instances, all patients so far reported have been amenorrheic—in spite of the interesting theoretic possibility of uterine bleeding from endometrium stimulated by estrogen of testicular origin. There is no evidence of adrenal malfunction. In the feminized group and, less frequently, in the non-feminized group, there is a strong familial history of the disorder. Male hermaphrodites reared as females may marry and be well adjusted to their sex role. Others, especially when there has been equivocation regarding sex of rearing in infancy, may be less than attractive as women because of indecisive therapy. Psychiatric studies indicate that the best emotional adjustment comes from directing endocrine, surgical, and psychiatric measures toward improving the person's basic characteristics. Fortunately, this is consonant with the surgical and endocrine possibilities for those reared as females, because current operative techniques can produce more satisfactory feminine than masculine external genitalia. Furthermore, the testes of male hermaphrodites are nonfunctional as far as spermatogenesis is concerned. Only about one-third of male hermaphrodites are suitable for rearing as males.

Classification

Since about 1970, considerable progress has been made in identifying specific metabolic defects that are etiologically important for the various forms of male hermaphroditism. Details are beyond the scope of this text. Nevertheless, it is important to point out that all cases of male hermaphroditism have a defect in either the biologic action of testosterone or the müllerian inhibiting factor of the testis. Furthermore, it now seems apparent that substantially all—if not all—of these defects have a genetic or cytogenetic background. The causes and pathogenetic mechanisms of these defects may vary, but the final common pathway is one of the 2 problems just mentioned; and in the adult a study of the serum gonadotropins and serum steroids, including the intermediate metabolites of testosterone, can often pinpoint a defect in the biosynthesis of testosterone. In other cases, the end organ action of testosterone may be defective. In children, the defect is sometimes more difficult to determine before the gonadotropins rise at puberty, but one may suspect a problem by observing abnormally high levels of steroids that act as substrates in the metabolism of testosterone. A working classification of male hermaphroditism is as follows:

I. Male hermaphroditism due to a central nervous system defect.
   A. Abnormal pituitary gonadotropin secretion.
   B. No gonadotropin secretion.
II. Male hermaphroditism due to a primary gonadal defect.
   A. Identifiable defect in biosynthesis of testosterone.
      1. Pregnenolone synthesis defect (lipoid adrenal hyperplasia).
      2. 3β-Hydroxysteroid dehydrogenase deficiency.
      3. 17α-Hydroxylase deficiency.
      4. 17,20-Desmolase deficiency.
      5. 17β-Ketosteroid reductase deficiency.
   B. Unidentified defect in androgen effect.
   C. Defect in müllerian duct regression (Figs 7–15 and 7–16).
   D. Familial gonadal destruction.
   E. Leydig cell agenesis.
   F. Bilateral testicular dysgenesis.
III. Male hermaphroditism due to peripheral end organ defect.
   A. Androgen insensitivity syndrome (Fig 7–17).
      1. Androgen binding protein deficiency.
      2. Unknown deficiency.
   B. 5α-Reductase deficiency.
   C. Unidentified abnormality of peripheral androgen effect.
IV. Male hermaphroditism due to Y chromosome defect.
   A. Y chromosome mosaicism (asymmetric gonadal differentiation) (Fig 7–18).
   B. Structurally abnormal Y chromosome.
   C. No identifiable Y chromosome.

DIFFERENTIAL DIAGNOSIS IN INFANTS WITH AMBIGUOUS GENITALIA

Accurate differential diagnosis is possible in most patients with ambiguous genitalia (Table 7–1). This requires a complete history of the mother's medication; an X- and Y-chromatin body determination (or, better, a complete sex chromosome study); rectal examination for the presence or absence of a uterus; several 17-ketosteroid determinations; measurement of serum steroid levels; and information about other congenital anomalies. The following disorders, however, do not yield to differentiation by the parameters of Table 7–1: (1) idiopathic masculinization, (2) the "special" forms of female hermaphroditism, (3) X chromatin body–positive true hermaphroditism, and occasionally (4) the precise type of male hermaphroditism. For these differentiations, laparotomy may be necessary for diagnosis and also for therapy.

Figure 7–15. External genitalia in male hermaphroditism. (Reproduced, with permission, from Jones HW Jr, Scott WW: *Hermaphroditism. Genital Anomalies and Related Endocrine Disorders,* 2nd ed. Williams & Wilkins, 1971.)

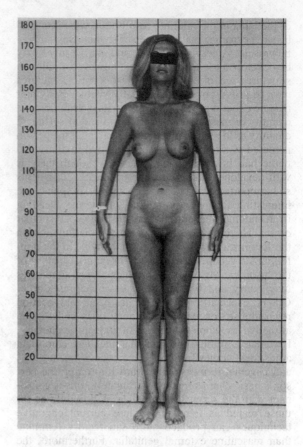

Figure 7–17. Androgen insensitivity syndrome.

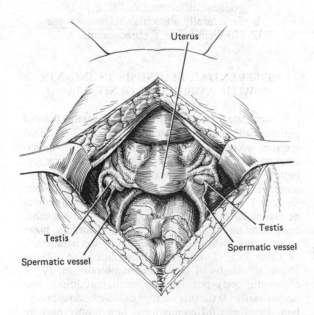

Figure 7–16. Internal genitalia of a patient whose external genitalia are shown in Fig 7–15. (Redrawn and reproduced, with permission, from Jones HW Jr, Scott WW: *Hermaphroditism, Genital Anomalies and Related Endocrine Disorders,* 2nd ed. Williams & Wilkins, 1971.)

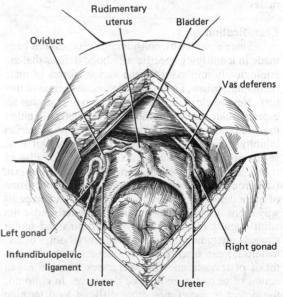

Figure 7–18. Internal genitalia in asymmetric gonadal differentiation. (Redrawn and reproduced, with permission, from Jones HW Jr, Scott WW: *Hermaphroditism, Genital Anomalies and Related Endocrine Disorders,* 2nd ed. Williams & Wilkins, 1971.)

Table 7—1. Differential diagnosis of ambiguous external genitalia.

Diagnosis	X-Chromatin	Y-Chromatin	History	Uterus	Anomalies	17-KS	Sex Chromosomes
Adrenal hyperplasia	+	−	+	+	−	E	XX
Maternal androgen	+	−	+	+	−	N	XX
Idiopathic masculinization	+	−	∓	+	−	N	XX
Special or nonspecific	+	−	−	+	−	N	XX
Female familial	+	−	+	+	+	N	XX
True hermaphroditism	+ or −	+ or −	−	+ or −	−	N	XX or other
Male hermaphroditism	−	+	+	+ or −	−	N	XY or other
Streak gonad	+ or −	+ or −	−	+	+ or −	N	XO or other

+ = positive, − = negative, N = normal, E = elevated.

THE TREATMENT OF HERMAPHRODITISM

The sex of rearing is much more important than the obvious morphologic signs (external genitalia, hormone dominance, gonadal structure) in forming the gender role. Furthermore, serious psychologic consequences may result from changing the sex of rearing after infancy. Therefore, it is seldom proper to advise a change of sex after infancy to conform to the gonadal structure or the external genitalia. Instead, the physician should exert efforts to complete the adjustment of the person to the sex role already assigned. Fortunately, most aberrations of sexual development are discovered in the newborn period or in infancy, when reassignment of sex causes few problems.

Regardless of the time of treatment (and the earlier the better), the surgeon should reconstruct the external genitalia to correspond to the sex of rearing. Any contradictory sex structures that may function to the patient's disadvantage in the future should be eradicated. Specifically, testes should always be removed from male hermaphrodites reared as females, regardless of hormone production. In cases of testicular feminization, orchiectomy is warranted because a variety of tumors may develop in these abnormal testes if they are retained, but the orchiectomy may be delayed until after puberty in this variety of hermaphroditism.

In virilized female hermaphroditism due to adrenal hyperplasia, the suppression of adrenal androgen production by the use of cortisone from an early age will result in completely female development. It is no longer necessary to explore the abdomen and the internal genitalia in this well-delineated syndrome. The surgical effort should be confined to reconstruction of the external genitalia along female lines.

Patients with streak gonads or Turner's syndrome, who are invariably reared as females, should be given exogenous estrogen when puberty is expected. Those hermaphrodites reared as females who will not become feminized also require estrogen to promote the development of the female habitus, including the breasts. In patients with a well-developed müllerian system, cyclic uterine withdrawal bleeding can be produced even though reproduction is impossible. Estrogen should be started at about age 12 and may be given as diethylstilbestrol, 1 mg/d orally (or its equivalent). In some patients, after a period of time, this dosage may have to be increased for additional breast development. In patients without ovaries who have uteri and in male hermaphrodites in the same condition, cyclic uterine bleeding can often be induced by the administration of estrogen for 3 weeks of each month. In other instances, this may be inadequate to produce a convincing "menstrual" period; if so, the 3 weeks of estrogen may be followed by 3–4 days of progestogen (eg, medroxyprogesterone acetate) orally or a single injection of progesterone. Prolonged estrogen therapy increases the risk of the subsequent development of adenocarcinoma of the corpus, so that periodic endometrial sampling is mandatory in such patients.

Reconstruction of Female External Genitalia

The details of the operative reconstruction of abnormal external genitalia are beyond the scope of this chapter. However, it should be emphasized that the procedure should be carried out at the earliest age possible so as to enhance the desired psychologic, social, and sexual orientation of the patient and also to obtain an easier adjustment by the parents. Sometimes the reconstruction can be done during the neonatal period. In any case, operation should not be delayed beyond the first several months of life. From a technical point of view, early operation is possible in all but the most exceptional circumstances.

• • •

References

Barnabei VM, Wyandt HE, Kelly TE: A possible exception to the critical region hypothesis. *Am J Hum Genet* 1981;**33**:61.

Bercu BB, Schulman JD: Genetics of abnormalities of sexual differentiation and of female reproductive failure. *Obstet Gynecol Surv* 1980;**35**:1.

Berthezène F et al: Leydig-cell agenesis: A cause of male pseudohermaphroditism. *N Engl J Med* 1976;**295**:969.

Ferguson-Smith MA: Karyotype-phenotype correlations in gonadal dysgenesis and their bearing on the pathogenesis of malformations. *J Med Genet* 1965;**2**:142.

Haseltine F, Ohno S: Mechanisms of gonadal differentiation. *Science* 1981;**211**:1272.

Jones HW Jr: A long look at the adrenogenital syndrome. *Johns Hopkins Med J* 1979;**145**:143.

Jones HW Jr, Ferguson-Smith MA, Heller RH: Pathologic and cytogenetic findings in true hermaphroditism: Report of six cases and review of 23 cases from the literature. *Obstet Gynecol* 1965;**25**:435.

Jones HW Jr, Scott WW: *Hermaphroditism, Genital Anomalies and Related Endocrine Disorders,* 2nd ed. Williams & Wilkins, 1971.

Jones HW Jr et al: The role of the H-Y antigen in human sexual development. *Johns Hopkins Med J* 1979;**145**:33.

Klinefelter HF Jr, Reifenstein EC Jr, Albright F: Syndrome characterized by gynecomastia, aspermatogenesis without a-leydigism and increased excretion of follicle-stimulating hormone. *J Clin Endocrinol* 1942;**2**:615.

McKusick VA: *Mendelian Inheritance in Man,* 5th ed. Johns Hopkins Univ Press, 1978.

Mikamo K: Prenatal sex ratio in man: Observations contradictory to the prevailing concept. *Obstet Gynecol* 1969;**34**:710.

Park IJ, Aimakhu VE, Jones HW Jr: An etiologic and pathogenetic classification of male hermaphroditism. *Am J Obstet Gynecol* 1975;**123**:505.

Park IJ, Jones HW Jr: Familial male hermaphroditism with ambiguous external genitalia. *Am J Obstet Gynecol* 1970;**108**:1197.

Turner G et al: Heterozygous expression of X-linked mental retardation and X-chromosome marker fra(X)(q27). *N Engl J Med* 1980;**303**:662.

Turner HH: A syndrome of infantilism, congenital webbed neck, and cubitus valgus. *Endocrinology* 1938;**23**:566.

Wachtel SS et al: Serologic detection of a Y-linked gene in XX males and XX true hermaphrodites. *N Engl J Med* 1976; **295**:750.

Congenital Anomalies of the Female Genital Tract | 8

Raphael B. Durfee, MD

The diagnosis of congenital anomalies of the female genital tract frequently is made by examination of the infant with ambiguous external genitalia. Anatomic abnormalities of the genital tract may be associated with other anomalies or mistaken gender identity. Obviously, sexual or obstetric difficulties will almost inevitably arise unless genital maldevelopment is diagnosed and corrected. Even if no external anomalies are identified in the newborn or young child, later gynecologic or obstetric evaluation may disclose anomalous development of the internal genitalia. Whenever urinary tract malformations are discovered during childhood, the genital tract should be examined for abnormalities also.

In any consideration of genital anomalies— especially those involving hermaphroditism or intersex —it must be remembered that the basic pattern of human development is that of the female. Sex differentiation proceeds toward "femaleness" unless it is diverted to "maleness." The stimulus involves chromosomes, androgens, and certain hypothetical inducers.

The normal development of the sex organs occurs in a definite sequence: (1) differentiation of a testis or ovary from the basic gonad; (2) development of male or female sex organs from the wolffian or müllerian systems, which are separate but coexistent in the embryo; (3) conversion of the pregenital structures of the urogenital sinus and genital tubercle to male or female; and (4) pubertal appearance of secondary sex characteristics and gametogenesis.

Sexual differentiation in relation to anomalies is better understood now because it has been shown that nuclear chromatin can be used as a histologic marker of genetic sex. In 1949, Barr identified a small, dark chromatin condensation at the periphery of the cell nucleus, mainly in neural cells. Subsequent studies disclosed that the majority of cells from females carried this mark or spot, the so-called Barr body, whereas most cells from males did not. It is likely that a single Barr body or sex chromatin spot is an X chromosome. In females, the other X chromosome, together with the autosomes, extends in a threadlike manner within the nucleus and is indistinguishable during interphase under light microscopy.

In a buccal smear stained in the conventional manner, XX females have more than 50% chromatin-positive cells, but males have less than 10% positive cells. However, the technique and experience of the investigator may influence the results of a buccal smear. Low to normal counts may occur in newborn females 14–21 days after birth. The count may also be affected by antibiotics, which lessen the size of Barr bodies, and by exogenous cortisone administration, which lowers the percentage of cells with Barr bodies.

An individual with 2 Barr bodies may be presumed to be XXX. Nonetheless, nuclear sex in questionable cases, eg, intersex, should be determined by seeking the Y chromosome, which fluoresces after quinacrine stain. If chromatin-positive cells contain Barr bodies that are unusual in number or size, a chromosome analysis or karyotype should be performed.

Embryologic studies have revealed the importance of the influence of the early testis on the development of male traits from genital primordia. Development of sex depends, therefore, upon the dynamics of the embryonic gonad as a local organizer or inducer. This induction includes stimulation of the wolffian ducts and inhibition of the müllerian system. Only testosterone will inhibit the müllerian system. Müllerian duct development in the female occurs not because of the influence of maternal hormones but as a result of the natural course of embryogenesis in the absence of testosterone.

Progress in steroid endocrinology has revealed that androgens and estrogens have common origins in the pathway from acetate → cholesterol → pregnenolone. Estrogens are produced as androgen intermediaries. Thus, the chance for development of certain abnormalities depends upon normal or abnormal metabolism.

Cellular division and chromosomal errors play important roles in the formation of anomalous sex organs. The errors in mitosis occur because of the replication of genetic material prior to division or because of the formation of an abnormal spindle. Another fault is the longitudinal splitting of the centromere and separation of the former chromatids, now chromosomes, into daughter aggregates. The process becomes abnormal when nondisjunction or chromosome division lag or both occur. If there are 2 stem lines, a mosaic is formed.

Müllerian dysgenesis is manifested by several

conditions in which genotypic and phenotypic females have congenital absence of all or part of the uterus, the uterine tubes, and the vagina; this may be vaginal aplasia, müllerian aplasia, or various combinations.

The cause of müllerian aplasia may be genetically apparent, but cytogenetic abnormalities are not usually demonstrable. Affected siblings are found in some instances, indicating that the disorders are compatible with autosomal recessive inheritance. Multiple malformation syndromes associated with müllerian aplasia include Winter's syndrome of middle ear anomalies, renal agenesis, and vaginal atresia, inherited in an autosomal recessive manner. Other autosomal recessive disorders are transverse vaginal septum and polydactyly, and longitudinal vaginal septum with hand anomalies.

Incomplete müllerian fusion producing many kinds of uterine anomalies is not rare. The pattern of inheritance does not allow for classification of the genetic pattern. Incomplete müllerian fusion may also be a part of genetically determined malformation syndromes such as the hand-foot-uterus syndrome, which is an autosomal dominant. Minor müllerian abnormalities are frequently seen with persistence of Wolffian derivatives such as Gartner's duct cysts and hydatid cysts.

The **Rokitansky-Küster-Hauser syndrome** is congenital absence of the vagina and rudimentary uterus (with bilateral muscular buds) with normal tubes and ovaries, external genitalia, and secondary sex characteristics. Normal ovarian function has been demonstrated, and apparently normal pituitary responsiveness is present as well. Spina bifida, renal agenesis, and ureteral abnormalities are also found. The defect is mesodermal and may have lethal manifestations.

ANOMALIES OF THE CLITORIS

Absence of the clitoris is the rarest of all anomalies of that organ. Duplication or splitting of the clitoris (very rare) can only be treated by plastic surgery. In extreme cases, it may be best to remove all or a portion of the clitoris.

Hypertrophy of the clitoris is uncommon save in intersex problems. Amputation may be necessary if the clitoris is very large. When removal of the clitoris is necessary, the capacity for orgasm and erotic responsiveness is apparently unimpaired.

ANOMALIES OF THE VULVA

Duplication of the entire vulva, clitoris, and labia minora and majora has been reported. As a rule, it is associated with duplication of the internal structures: vagina, uterus, bladder, and upper genitourinary tract. Numerous variations are possible with single or double parts. Most of these anomalies are exceptional, and little is known regarding the success of treatment.

ANOMALIES OF THE LABIA MAJORA

The labia majora may be hypoplastic and fail to develop normally at puberty or in adolescence. The administration of estrogen is not beneficial. Fusion of the labia majora occurs in pseudohermaphroditism. This may be associated with a penile urethra, and labial hypertrophy may simulate a scrotum. Proper diagnosis and management of the basic problem (eg, congenital adrenogenitalism) are essential.

ANOMALIES OF THE LABIA MINORA

Hypertrophy of the labia minora—bilateral or unilateral—is a fairly common congenital anomaly. If hypertrophy is extreme, surgery is indicated.

In infancy, labial adherence is a frequent problem. Application of an estrogen cream is usually curative. If true fusion has occurred, surgical separation will be required.

ANOMALIES OF THE PERINEUM

In the absence of the perineum, the anus will be imperforate or an anus vestibularis may be present. In other unusual cases, the anus may lie just posterior to the vestibule or may perforate the perineum with a thick anterior tissue layer.

A persistent cloaca may be associated with inadequate separation of the rectum from the urethra. Often, in such cases, a congenital intercommunication will be present between the urinary and genital tracts. Under the circumstances, there will be a single orifice through which pass urine and feces. The incidence of this communication is less than one in 5000 newborns with imperforate anus. The correction of imperforate anus must be accomplished promptly after delivery. Surgical separation of the urinary and intestinal tracts may require urinary or fecal diversion. Early operation is indicated, especially if upper urinary tract infection occurs. Plastic repair often yields a satisfactory result.

ANOMALIES OF THE HYMEN

The hymen may be imperforate, and this abnormality may rarely be associated with transvaginal septa. There may be one or many pinpoint perforations, and hymenal duplication may occur with or without septa. Variations from normal hymenal openings include cribriform, multiple, single small, and septate types.

Anomalies of the hymen may be associated with abnormalities of the urethra or exstrophy of the bladder. The hymen with the labia minora may cover the clitoris or may be a multifold florid projection around the vaginal and urethral orifices, obscuring both apertures.

Symptoms and signs include a tender bulging

mass in the vaginal introitus, a history of cyclic pelvic pain, urinary frequency, mild peritoneal irritation, a palpable, lower midline, tender abdominal mass, and occasional shoulder pain. Late menarche, amenorrhea, and cryptomenorrhea are not unusual. Hydrocolpos, hydrometra and mucocolpos, and mucometra have been observed; also, rarely, hydro- or mucosalpinx is seen.

The diagnosis of imperforate hymen is made at menarche on the observation of a tense, bulging hymenal membrane. This is accompanied by hematocolpos, hematometra, and spillage of blood into the peritoneal cavity. A crescentic incision should be made in the intact hymen, preferably before puberty. A longitudinal hymenal incision should be avoided lest the urethra or rectum be opened accidentally. Pinpoint perforations may be enlarged by connecting incisions. Septate hymen may be incised, and other variants of the hymenal opening may be corrected as necessary.

The patient usually recovers after a short time to allow for the onset of normal function of the reproductive tract; however, some women may continue with increasing dysmenorrhea due to endometriosis. There may be salpingitis, producing pelvic pain and infertility. Vaginal adenosis is associated with this defect.

ANOMALIES OF THE VAGINA

The vagina, which is the connection between the interior and exterior portions of the genitalia, is a frequent site of maldevelopment of the müllerian system. Vaginal abnormalies are often associated with urogenital or urorectal defects. Duplication of the rectum and sigmoid colon with congenital rectovaginal fistula can occur.

A urogenital sinus is a normal finding in the embryo, but its presence in the infant at term is abnormal.

An infinite number of variations are possible in the primary formation of the primitive endodermal cloaca. Certain of these deformities are the result of hormonal virilization, sex chromosome disorders, and genetic defects in testicular feminization. All of these patients have ambiguous genitalia.

Causes of Some Vaginal Abnormalities

Persistent fusion may cause any degree of septal partition in the craniocaudal portion of the uterovaginal canal. These anomalies vary from uterus subseptus to uterus didelphys, with a complete double vagina. In these cases, one or both of the müllerian ducts may fail to merge or may be arrested in their combination.

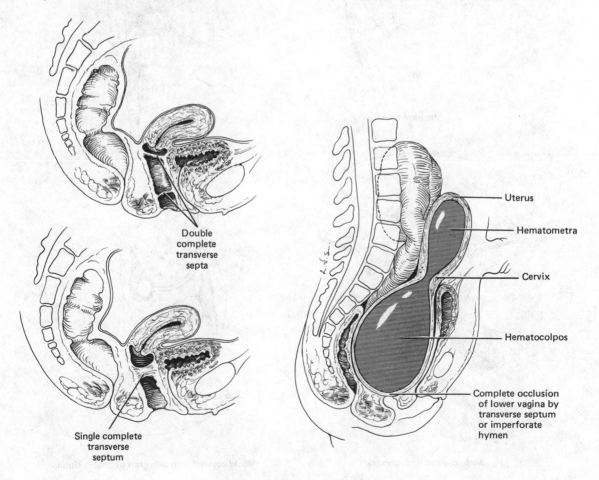

Double complete transverse septa

Single complete transverse septum

Uterus

Hematometra

Cervix

Hematocolpos

Complete occlusion of lower vagina by transverse septum or imperforate hymen

Figure 8–1. Transverse marginal septa.

Vaginal atresia or complete vaginal absence may result when the müllerian ducts migrate properly but fail to develop beyond simple epithelial cords.

Classification

A. Agenesis: Total absence.

B. Dysgenesis: Partial absence. There may be an external depression with a blind upper end or a shallow proximal vaginal depression with total obliteration of the distal portion.

C. Hypoplasia: A vaginal canal of proper length but with the caliber of the urethra may represent a persistent urogenital sinus.

D. Transverse Septa: (Fig 8–1.) Transverse vaginal septa may lie at any level and may be 1–1.5 cm thick. They are most often seen in the upper part of the vagina. Most transverse septa are lined with squamous epithelium on both sides, but some are found with columnar epithelium on the upper surface and squamous on the lower surface. Mesonephroid elements are found in the stroma of some septa and endometriosis in others. These septa arise from the vaginal plate.

E. Longitudinal Septa: Longitudinal vaginal septa may represent true duplication of the vagina, septum of mucosa only, or incomplete septum formation from either end, frequently associated with complete or partial duplication of the uterus, including the cervix. With a longitudinal vaginal septum, one side may open to a cervix and the other side may not. When a functioning double uterus and cervix are present, a

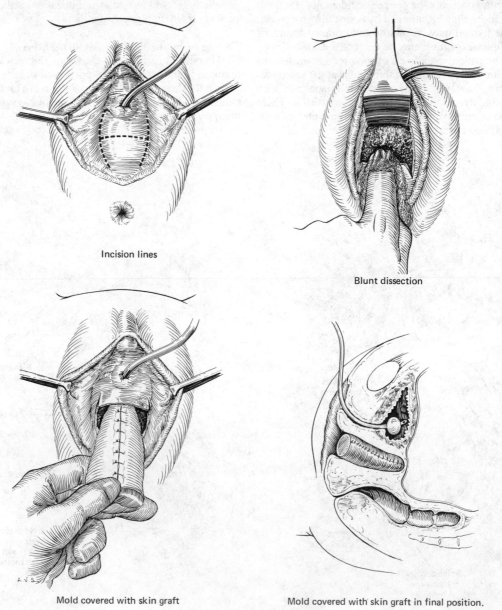

Incision lines

Blunt dissection

Mold covered with skin graft

Mold covered with skin graft in final position.

Figure 8–2. Construction of a vagina.

unilateral hematocolpos may form on the closed side. Spontaneous rupture of a vaginal septum may be the cause of abnormal bleeding in a young woman, especially when found with uterus didelphys and a unilateral imperforate vagina. If the occlusion is opened to the other side, the columnar epithelium which lines it will change to squamous by metaplasia.

F. Cysts: Congenital cysts of the vagina generally are in the deep lateral portion (Gartner's duct cysts).

G. Associated With Urinary Tract Anomalies: Anomalies of the vagina associated with abnormalities of the urinary tract are of various types. Urethral orifices may be found at any point along the anterior and lateral vaginal walls. Total absence of the anterior vaginal wall, exposing the interior of the bladder, urethra, and ureters, has been described. The urethra may present multiple abnormalities, including ectopic orifices. Exstrophy of the bladder may be present.

H. Associated With Rectal or Rectosigmoid Anomalies: Anomalies of the vagina associated with the rectum or rectosigmoid include vulvovaginal anus, vaginorectal fistula at any level, rectosigmoid fistula at any level, and absence of the rectum with a vaginosigmoidal cloaca.

Treatment

In general, total absence of the vagina or partial absence and hypoplasia of the vagina may be treated by 2 methods: (1) The area may be dissected between the urethra and the rectum and the space developed covered with a split thickness skin graft stretched over a vaginal mold (Fig 8–2). (2) When the vagina is partially occluded or when there is simply a shallow pit—the site of infolding of the urogenital sinus—the vagina may be deepened simply by local pressure using vaginal obturators.

An effective pressure technique for the correction of vaginal agenesis or stenosis using plastic dilators impressed while the patient sits on a bicycle seat stool has been devised by Ingram (Figs 8–3 to 8–7). A simple racing bicycle seat stool, just over chain height, can be purchased or constructed from the base of a metal pedestal chair. Graduated Lucite dilators, available commercially, are used to deepen the introital dimple or "soft spot" just dorsal to the urethra in patients with vaginal agenesis. A pad or girdle holds the dilator in place beneath the clothing while the patient sits on the stool, leaning forward, for several hours each day. The weight of the body presses the dilator inward. Reading, writing, or other sedentary activities may be continued during this time. There may be slight discomfort but no pain. In 4–6 weeks, an initial narrow pouch should develop. Increasing the depth and diameter of the neovagina requires larger dilators. A functional vagina usually can be created in

Figures 8–3 to 8–7 are courtesy of *The Pelvic Surgeon* (Sept) 1981;**2**:No. 6.

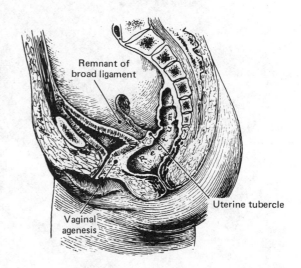

Figure 8–3. A sagittal drawing showing the anatomic situation of the majority of patients with the classic Rokitansky-Küster-Hauser syndrome—uterovaginal agenesis, a small uterine tubercle, and normally developed ovaries and oviducts.

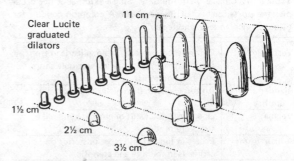

Figure 8–4. Two types of bicycle seat stools may be used.

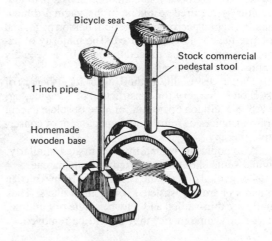

Figure 8–5. The Lucite dilators are grouped in 3 sets. The first set of 10 dilators is 1.5 cm in diameter and 1.5–10 cm in length. The second set of 5 is 2.5 cm in diameter and 3–10 cm in length. The third set of 5 is 3.5 cm in diameter and 3–10 cm in length.

Figure 8–6. Pressure is applied for at least 2 hours a day, in 15- to 30-minute intervals, by sitting on the stool with the dilator held in position.

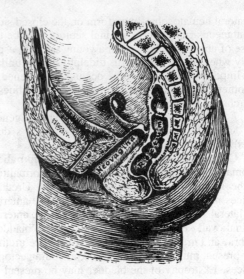

Figure 8–7. A functional vagina can be created by pressure in 5–7 months.

4–6 months. The occasional retention of a large dilator or coitus is required to maintain the vaginal dimensions. Ischemic necrosis, laceration, hemorrhage, and prolapse have not been reported. The majority of patients receptive to the procedure have been sexually responsive and orgasmic.

The success of this method makes it the therapy of first choice. Surgery for construction of a vagina, eg, the Abbe-McIndoe operation, may be obsolete except in rare instances of refusal or abandonment of conservative therapy.

A hypoplastic vagina may be treated similarly. Vaginal septa should be excised after menarche.

Congenital cysts of the vagina arise from wolffian remnants or from obstructed periurethral ducts. They usually are thin-walled and may be single or multiple. If large or symptomatic, they should be removed.

Vaginal cysts representing vaginal adenosis due to diethylstilbestrol are precursors of adenocarcinoma.

Anomalies of the vagina associated with urinary tract maldevelopment may require extensive surgical correction, especially in the case of ectopic urethra or ectopic ureters or with exstrophy of the bladder.

CLOACAL DYSGENESIS, INCLUDING PERSISTENCE OF THE UROGENITAL SINUS

The rare anomaly of cloacal dysgenesis is manifested by anatomic variants most of which are represented in Tables 8–1, 8–2, and 8–3.

Abnormal Development of the Urethra

Urethral variants may be important when endoscopy on a female child with a deep urogenital sinus is necessary. A blind sac may be found, but the true vagina usually contains a cervix.

Table 8–1. Cloacal malformations. Single external orifice occupies the posterior half of the vestibule. A common conduit for urine, cervical mucus, and feces.*

Vestibule	Deformed; flanked by labia; clitoris in front; fourchette behind; anterior vestibule short, shallow, and moist.
Bladder and/or urethra	Anterior; directed cranially and ventrally.
Vagina	Opens into the vault of cloaca; hymenlike structure present.
Anus/rectum	Enters at highest and most posterior point; orifice is in midline and stenotic.
Disposition	Lengths of urethra and vagina are inversely proportional to length of cloacal canal.

*Modified and reproduced, with permission, from Okonkwo JEN, Crocker KM: Cloacal dysgenesis. *Obstet Gynecol* 1977; 50:97.

Table 8–2. Cloacal malformation type 2. External orifices—urethra and vagina—are present. Meconium is conducted from rectum to vagina.*

Vestibule	Anatomically normal.
Bladder and/or urethra	Normal.
Vagina	May be septate or normal.
Anus/rectum	Internal in the midposterior vaginal wall.
Disposition	Anus absent from perineum.

*Modified and reproduced, with permission, from Okonkwo JEN, Crocker KM: Cloacal dysgenesis. *Obstet Gynecol* 1977; 50:97.

Table 8—3. Characteristics of other 3 types of cloacal dysgenesis.*

	Rectovestibular Fistula	**Covered Anus**	**Ectopic Anus**
Vestibule	Contains rectum, otherwise normal.	Normal.	Normal.
Urethra	Normal.	Normal.	Normal.
Vagina	Normal.		Normal.
Anus/rectum	Small, sited at the fossa navicularis.	Anus may lie at any point in the perineum between the normal site of the anus and the fourchette; anocutaneous; anovulvar.	Anus lies anterior to the normal site; function is perfect.
Disposition	Axis of rectum is craniocaudal, parallel with both vagina and urethra.	Genital folds are abnormally fused anterior and posterior to common orifice and give rise to hypertrophied perineal raphe.	Fault lies in the development of the perineum.

*Modified and reproduced, with permission, from Okonkwo JEN, Crocker KM: Cloacal dysgenesis. *Obstet Gynecol* 1977;50:97.

A persistent urogenital sinus may be deep, but in infancy it usually is no larger in diameter than the urethra. During growth in childhood, the sinus may extend to bring the urethral and vaginal orifices nearer to the introitus. The sinus may even expand at the time of puberty to resemble a vagina. Surgical correction depends upon the type and extent of the defect.

Common types of abnormal urethral development are as follows: (1) The urethral orifice may present within the vagina. (2) The urethral orifice may be abnormally anterior, near the clitoris. A double vagina may be present, with the urethra between or above the upper one. Urinary incontinence or obstruction may be associated problems. (3) The urethra may be abnormally long, convoluted, or very short, with an abnormal orifice (as noted above). (4) The urethra may be deviated to one side or the other in the presence of a double vagina.

Identification of the type of deformity is difficult. Operation may be necessary at the time of diagnosis. Multiple surgical plastic procedures may be required later for correction of complicated problems.

Urinary Tract Disorders Associated With Persistent Urogenital Sinus

These anomalies include double ureters, megaureters (single or double), absence of one ureter and kidney, pelvic kidney with abnormal ureters (unilateral or bilateral), megaureters with or without renal abnormalities, and multicystic kidneys (unilateral or bilateral) with or without anomalous ureters.

With arrest of normal evolution of the urogenital sinus or persistence of the urogenital sinus (which is the ventral portion of the cloaca *after* its separation from the rectum), malformation of the vaginal vestibule, the urethra, and the lower part of the bladder may occur.

Urorectogenital Disorders

If the cloaca remains undivided, the intestinal and urinary tracts will open into a common outlet. On the other hand, the müllerian system may be superimposed upon a closed cloaca, which then resembles a urogenital sinus—perhaps with a narrow rectal communication, a rectocloacal fistula. There may also be a rectovaginal and a rectovestibular fistula. In such cases, look for associated sacral and neurologic anomalies.

ANOMALIES OF THE CERVIX

Anomalies of the cervix are frequently the same as those of the uterus as far as absence, duplication, or hypoplasia are concerned (see next section). However, some anomalies of the cervix have been reported in which the corpus of the uterus is intact.

Congenital absence of the cervix is very rare but has been seen in cases of complete separation of the uterus in which a perfect half of the corpus, complete with oviduct and ovary, exists. The cervix is represented by a fibrous band. This anomaly is treated by plastic surgery.

Congenital shortening of the cervix with virtual absence of the vaginal portion is seen occasionally with congenital defects of the internal os. It is treated by vaginal or abdominal cerclage.

Congenital atresia of the cervix is very rare and may be associated with other genital tract anomalies. In most cases of cervical atresia the uterus is normal, but some are associated with uterine anomalies. If the endometrium and ovaries are functional, there is amenorrhea with cyclic lower abdominal pain. Findings resemble those of imperforate hymens or transverse vaginal septa, namely, hematometra, hematosalpinx, retrograde menstrual bleeding into the peritoneal cavity, and occasional great tubal enlargement. Endometriosis or adenomyosis is associated with this anomaly. Correction is accomplished by one of 3 methods: (1) creation of a uterovaginal fistula, (2) creation of a neocervical canal, or (3) total abdominal hysterectomy.

Congenital stricture, a conglutinated cervix, or increased fibrous connective elements that interfere with normal function are not treatable.

Hypertrophied endocervical folds are seen occasionally. There are excessively deep, thick transverse

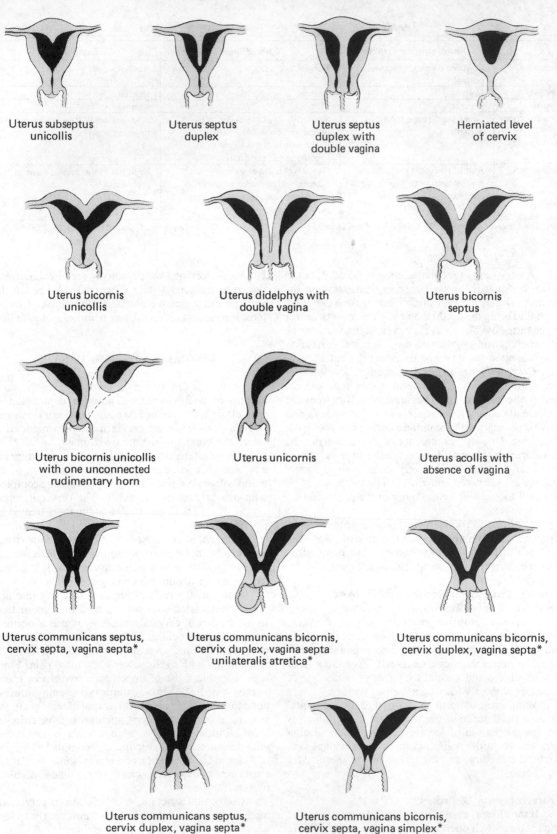

Figure 8–8. Uterine anomalies. (*Redrawn and reproduced, with permission, from Toaff R: *Obstet Gynecol* 1974;43:224.)

folds in the endocervical canal. These are sometimes arranged in a palmate manner. There may be a heavy valvular transverse fold at the upper margin of the isthmus of the cervix. There is no treatment for this condition.

Clefts, hoods, and other anomalous cervical developments occur in daughters of women who received diethylstilbestrol early in pregnancy.

ANOMALIES OF THE UTERUS

Anomalies of the uterus (Fig 8–8), including aplasia, hypoplasia, and absence, and various forms of duplication frequently are associated with congenital anomalies of the vagina and absence or duplication of portions of the urinary tract.

Subclinical or minor uterine anomalies may be an important cause of habitual abortion or premature delivery. Mild types of unicornuate and bicornuate uterus are not so obvious since they are rare. But the planifundus uterus, mildly subseptate uterus, and very mildly subseptate uterus also may be causes of infertility. Obviously, anomalous uteri are also associated with these same problems.

Classification
The following abnormalities of the uterus and cervix have been described:

(1) Complete absence, aplasia.

(2) Rudimentary maldevelopment of one or both sides. A rudimentary horn may or may not communicate with the vagina.

(3) Transverse congenital obstruction in the cervix—incomplete duplication of the cervical canal with total obstruction at the internal os.

(4) Hypoplasia, varying from a small rudimentary single uterus to one approximately two-thirds of normal size with or without oviducts and ovaries. Uterus solidaris has no cavity. A hypoplastic rudimentary horn may connect with the endometrial cavity of a unicornuate uterus on the opposite side. A rudimentary or hypoplastic uterus generally is nonfunctional.

(5) Uterus unicornis may be joined to a normal cervix or one which is obstructed.

(6) Double uterus: The following variations have been described:

a. One uterus on each side with a complete septum between.

b. One uterus on each side with a double cervix.

c. One uterus on each side with a single cervix.

d. One uterus on each side with a single cervix and vagina without connection between the 2 sides.

e. Uterus solidaris with uterus unicornis.

f. Partial uterine division: Partial double corpus with one cervix, partial uterine septum and single cervix, and arcuate or heart-shaped uterus with double cervix (rare).

. (7) Communicating uteri: The concept of communicating anomalous uteri was first described by Carrington in 1933. Since that time, several other

criteria for such anomalies have been established, by Musset and others in 1967 and by Toaff and others in 1974. There is a distinct difference in these communications in that they are usually very small and ordinarily located at the level of the internal os. Communicating uteri are usually asymptomatic except in cases in which the vagina is occluded on one or both sides.

(8) Iatrogenic congenital anomalies of the uterus: Congenital anomalies of the uterus have been discovered in several cases of young women with changes in the müllerian system associated with DES syndrome. These are distinguished by hysterosalpingography and may be classified as follows:

a. T-shaped uterus.

b. Constricting bands in the uterine cavity.

c. Synechiae.

d. Intrauterine polypoid defects.

e. Hypoplasia.

There are no significant findings on pelvic examination to indicate these changes except occasionally a small uterus and cervix. Another classification of uterine anomalies has been proposed that facilitates clinical application of management (see Buttram and Gibbons reference on p 180).

Treatment
Uterine aplasia or absence presently defies treatment, but uterine transplantation may some day be possible. Complete duplication, in which there are 2 cervices and 2 uteri—each accompanied by a tube and ovary—ordinarily requires no treatment. Other forms of uterine duplication, or septation, may require excision of one horn, especially if this is rudimentary, or bisection of the uterus with removal of the septum or the formation of a single uterus from a partial double corpus (Fig 8–9). One may discover a single uterus on each side with its own tube and ovary but with no cervix, or a single uterus without cervix. Connection of such a uterus with the vagina has been accomplished.

Whether a patient can become pregnant and carry the pregnancy to viability after correction of any particular anomaly is always a moot question. Repeated pregnancy loss is a primary indication for surgical repair of a uterine anomaly regardless of type. Uterus didelphys has the best prognosis for pregnancy to viability; septate and bicornuate uteri have the poorest prognosis for pregnancy to term. The postoperative success rate in these cases approximates 75%.

ANOMALIES OF THE UTERINE TUBES
(Fallopian Tubes, Oviducts)

Anomalies of the uterine tubes consist of the following: (1) Unilateral absence, frequently associated with uterine absence on that side. (2) Bilateral absence, most frequently seen with a rudimentary uterus or complete absence of the uterus. (3) Unilateral (occasionally bilateral) accessory small tubes, each

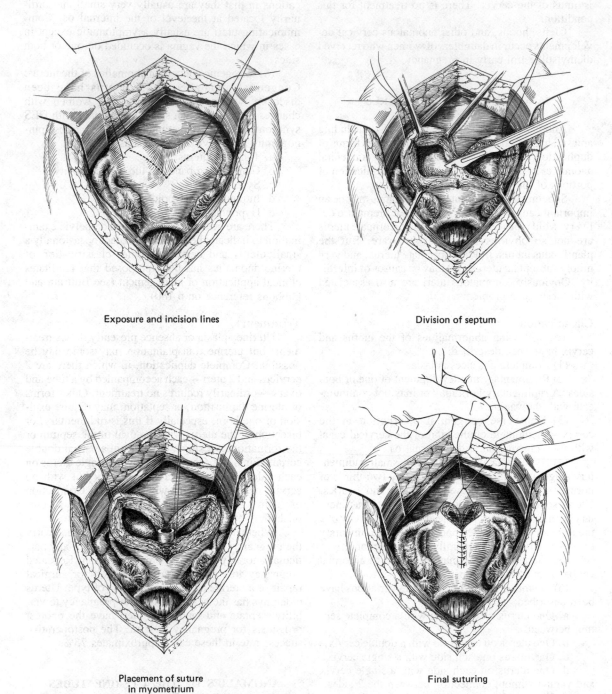

Exposure and incision lines

Division of septum

Placement of suture
in myometrium

Final suturing

Figure 8–9. Unification of bicornuate uterus.

with its fimbria, may connect with the lumen of the main tube but may be occluded in the proximal part. Accessory tubal ostia and a rare double lumen are probable variants. (4) Hypoplasia, atresia, congenital occlusion, and a complete fimbria connected to a fibrous cord extending to the uterus are all described. Hypoplasia related to the DES syndrome has been observed. (5) Segmental absence of the mid portion of the tube resembles a post–Pomeroy tubal ligation. Distal isolated fimbria in each of these conditions predisposes to distal ectopic pregnancy.

Atresia of the oviducts may be a factor in infertility or may favor ectopic pregnancy.

Most of these anomalies cannot be surgically repaired with the exception of segmental absence, which can be successfully corrected by microsurgical anastomosis if the remaining tubal tissue is at least 3 cm long at each end. If fimbria are absent with an open tubal lumen, a functioning salpingostomy can be made by microsurgery, but the prognosis is only fair for pregnancy. This prognosis is further reduced if any kind of uterine anomaly also exists. Such corrections also predispose to ectopic pregnancy.

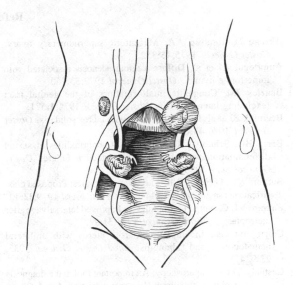

Figure 8–10. Sites of supernumerary ovaries.

ANOMALIES OF THE OVARIES

Congenital agenesis or atresia of the ovaries occurs very rarely. True agonadism but concomitant müllerian development must be considered. In most cases the oviducts are absent also. Unilateral ovarian agenesis usually is associated with absence of the oviduct and absence of the kidney, but there may be a unicornuate uterus on the affected side. Ovaries with rare or absent primary follicles result in sexual infantilism and premature ovarian failure associated with primary amenorrhea. There is no treatment.

Supernumerary ovaries are occasionally found but *always* remote from the normal ovary. They probably arise from a separate primordium, an anomalous area of the mesonephric ridge being the most likely. The possibility of arrested or anomalous migration of the germ cells is not likely. Benign teratomas and dermoid cysts of these ovaries have been found in the omentum and also retroperitoneally. Occasionally, an ovary may be split into a number of separate portions, and **accessory ovarian tissue,** usually less than 1 cm

in diameter, may be discovered in the broad ligament near the normal ovary or near the cornua of the uterus. These nodules may be mistaken for lymph nodes. Ectopic ovarian tissue may also be found near the kidney, and occasionally the ovary may be found in an unusual place, prolapsed into or included in a direct inguinal hernia, or in the retroperitoneal space. Ectopic or apparently abnormal ovarian tissue should be removed because neoplasms may develop in these foci.

Parovarian cysts are thin-walled, cystic structures in the mesosalpinx between the tube and the hilum of the ovary. They may be large or microscopic in size and single or multiple. They apparently arise in the organ of Rosenmüller, in the wolffian duct, or in a vestigial portion of the wolffian body. The blind outer extremity of the duct, when dilated, sometimes forms a cystic, pedunculated structure known as a hydatid cyst of Morgagni. If the structures are large, they may become twisted on their pedicle or may be mistaken for ovarian or tubal enlargement and should be excised. A hydatid cyst of Morgagni may cause torsion of the tube and ovary, necessitating removal of infected structures.

•   •   •

References

Abrego D, Ibrahim AA: Mesenteric supernumerary ovary. *Obstet Gynecol* 1975;**45**:352.

Amortegui AJ et al: Diffuse vaginal adenosis associated with imperforate hymen. *Obstet Gynecol* 1979;**53**:760.

Beazley JM: Congenital malformations of the genital tract (excluding intersex). *Clin Obstet Gynecol* 1974;**1**:571.

Beernink FJ et al: Uterus unicornis with uterus solidaris. *Obstet Gynecol* 1976;**47**:651.

Bercu BB, Schulman JD: Genetics of abnormalities of sexual differentiation and of female reproductive failure. *Obstet Gynecol Surv* 1980;**35**:1.

Buttram VC, Gibbons WE: Mullerian anomalies: Proposed classification (an analysis of 144 cases). *Fertil Steril* 1979;**32**:40.

Capraro VJ, Chuang JT, Randall CL: Improved fetal salvage after metroplasty. *Obstet Gynecol* 1968;**31**:97.

Carrington GL: Incomplete bipartite uterus with unilateral hematocolpos and salpingitis. *Am J Obstet Gynecol* 1933;**25**:924.

Casthely S et al: Laparoscopy: An important tool in the diagnosis of the Rokitansky-Küster-Hauser syndrome. *Am J Obstet Gynecol* 1974;**119**:571.

Farber M, Marchant DJ: Cervical atresia. (Letter.) *Obstet Gynecol* 1980;**55**:765.

Farber M, Marchant DJ: Reconstructive surgery for congenital absence of the uterine cervix. *Fertil Steril* 1976;**27**:1277.

Griffin JE et al: Congenital absence of the vagina. Mayer-Rokitansky-Küster-Hauser syndrome. *Ann Intern Med* 1976; **85**:224.

Haney AF et al: DES-induced upper genital tract abnormalities. *Fertil Steril* 1979;**31**:142.

Holloway HJ et al: Uterus didelphys with unilateral imperforate vagina: Spontaneous rupture of the vaginal septum. *Obstet Gynecol* 1980;**55**:50S.

Ingram JM: The bicycle seat stool in the treatment of vaginal agenesis and stenosis: A preliminary report. *Am J Obstet Gynecol* 1981;**140**:867.

Ingram JM: The Ingram technique for the management of vaginal agenesis and stenosis. *The Pelvic Surgeon* (Sept) 1981;**2**:1.

Ingram JM: Non-surgical technique corrects vaginal agenesis and stenosis. *Contemp Obstet Gynecol* 1982;**19**:46.

Jones H Jr: Reproductive impairment and the malformed uterus. *Fertil Steril* 1981;**36**:137.

Jones HW, Wheeless CR: Salvage of the reproductive potential of women with anomalous development of the Müllerian ducts: 1868-1968-2068. *Am J Obstet Gynecol* 1969;**104**:348.

Kaufman RH et al: Upper genital tract changes associated with exposure in utero to diethylstilbestrol. *Am J Obstet Gynecol* 1977;**128**:51.

Leverton JCS: A significant case of uterus didelphys solidus with gynatresia, adenomyosis, and pelvic endometriosis. *Obstet Gynecol* 1953;**1**:681.

Lewis BV, Brant HA: Obstetric and gynecologic complications associated with Müllerian duct abnormalities. *Obstet Gynecol* 1966;**28**:315.

Musich JR, Behrman JS: Obstetric outcome before and after metroplasty in women with uterine anomalies. *Obstet Gynecol* 1978;**52**:63.

Neves-e-Castro M et al: Lateral communicating double uteri with unilateral vaginal obstruction. *Am J Obstet Gynecol* 1976; **125**:865.

Nickerson CW: Infertility and uterine contour. *Am J Obstet Gynecol* 1977;**139**:268.

Okonkwo JEN, Crocker KM: Cloacal dysgenesis. *Obstet Gynecol* 1977;**50**:97.

Paul DJ, Lloyd TV: Hindgut duplication with recto-vaginal fistula. *Obstet Gynecol* 1979;**54**:390.

Printz LJ: The embryology of supernumerary ovaries. *Obstet Gynecol* 1973;**41**:246.

Rosenberg SM: Metroplasty for the septate uterus and reproductive failure. *Resident Staff Physician* (Dec) 1980;**26**:53.

Rowley WH: Uterine anomaly: Duplication of the uterus, three tubes and three ovaries. *Ann Surg* 1948;**127**:676.

Shane JM et al: A preliminary report on gonadotropin responsivity in the Rokitansky-Küster-Hauser syndrome. *Am J Obstet Gynecol* 1977;**127**:326.

Strassman EO: Fertility and unification of double uterus. *Fertil Steril* 1966;**17**:165.

Suidan FG, Azoury RS: The transverse vaginal septum: A clinicopathologic evaluation. *Obstet Gynecol* 1979;**54**:278.

Szlachter N, Weiss G: Distal tubal pregnancy in a patient with a bicornuate uterus and segmental absence of the fallopian tube. *Fertil Steril* 1979;**32**:602.

Thorek P et al: Simultaneous pregnancies in a fallopian tube and bicornuate uterus associated with three fallopian tubes. *Am J Surg* 1950;**79**:512.

Toaff R: A major genital malformation: Communicating uteri. *Obstet Gynecol* 1974;**43**:221.

Tompkins P: Comments on the bicornuate uterus and twinning. *Surg Clin North Am* 1962;**42**:1049.

Valentine BH, DeVere RD: Menstruation per urethram. *Br J Obstet Gynaecol* 1976;**83**:173.

Disorders of the Vulva & Vagina | 9

David L. Barclay, MD

Vulvovaginal disorders are common causes of presenting complaints in gynecologic practice, and a thorough understanding of the physiology and pathology of the lower genital tract is of great importance in their management. Many women have little knowledge about female sexual anatomy and physiology. For example, young girls often receive little or no instruction in cleansing the perineal area, and teenage girls are often misinformed about the presumed necessity for douching or the use of feminine hygiene products, which may do more harm than good.

In prepubertal girls, the absence of endogenous estrogen results in a thin vaginal epithelium deficient in glycogen. This predisposes to bacterial infection, the most common gynecologic disorder in this age group. Cancer is very rare except for the occasional occurrence of adenosis or clear cell adenocarcinoma of the vagina and cervix in the offspring of mothers who received diethylstilbestrol during pregnancy (see p 224).

During the reproductive years, the vaginal epithelium matures. However, coitus, contraceptive agents, feminine hygiene practices, and the wearing of tight, nonabsorbent, heat-retaining clothing (panty hose, etc) predispose to the development of vulvovaginal infections.

In postmenopausal patients, the level of endogenous estrogen decreases. The cells of the vaginal mucosa and vulvar skin lose glycogen, and vaginal acidity declines, resulting in fragile atrophic tissues that are susceptible to trauma and infection. The incidence of cancer of the vagina and vulva increases with age to a peak at about age 65.

The anatomy of the vulva is described on p 24. The vulvar skin is responsive to hormonal stimulation and provides a warm, moist environment exposed to urinary and fecal soiling. The first symptom of vaginal irritation is often vulvitis, which commonly results from contact with the vaginal discharge, often compounded by overlying garments made of synthetic fabrics that are heat- and moisture-retaining.

Evaluation of a patient with vulvar symptoms requires a detailed history and physical examination, including inspection of other mucosal and skin surfaces. Feminine hygiene products and contraceptives should be identified, as well as antibiotics that may alter the vaginal flora, resulting in overgrowth of *Candida albicans*. A family history of diabetes mellitus or an obstetric history of excessively large infants strongly suggests the possibility of diabetes, which also predisposes to candidiasis.

LEUKORRHEA

Although the term leukorrhea literally means a white discharge, the color may vary depending upon the cause. The most common cause of leukorrhea is a vaginal infection. Other causes range from the normal milky vaginal discharge in the premenarcheal girl to blood-tinged discharge due to cancer of the vagina or cervix. Before the menarche, there may be a scant vaginal discharge that ordinarily does not cause irritation and is not considered abnormal. Inspection of the vagina in an adolescent girl may reveal a small amount of white mucoid material in the vaginal vault which is the result of normal desquamation and accumulation of vaginal epithelial cells. Vaginal discharge in the sexually mature woman is considered abnormal if soiling of the clothing occurs, if the odor is offensive, or if irritation interferes with function.

Pathogenesis

Cervical mucus, produced chiefly in response to estrogenic stimulation, is the principal source of vaginal fluid. The vaginal mucosa normally contains no glands; however, transudation of fluid occurs in response to sexual stimulation. Stimulation by estrogen causes proliferation of the stratified squamous epithelium of the vagina. This results in desquamation of cells, which adds debris to the vaginal fluid. Maintenance of the normal environment of the vagina depends largely upon the levels of endogenous estrogen, an acid pH (3.5–4.0), and the presence of lactobacilli (Döderlein's bacilli). Any marked alteration in the normal physiology of the vagina predisposes to symptomatic leukorrhea due to a change in the flora of the vagina.

Pathologic Physiology

The pathologic physiology of leukorrhea due to vaginitis must be considered by age groups because of the influence of endogenous and exogenous estrogen and sexual activity. Under the influence of estrogens, the vaginal epithelium thickens and large quantities of glycogen are present in the epithelial cells. The collection of intraepithelial glycogen results in the production of lactic acid. This acid environment fosters the growth of a normal vaginal flora, chiefly lactobacilli and acidogenic corynebacteria. *Candida* organisms may be present but in small numbers because of the preponderance of bacteria. Normally, no trichomonads are present. Relative lack of estrogen in the premenarcheal child results in a thin vaginal mucosa that is poorly resistant to infection.

Elevated estrogen and progesterone levels during pregnancy and the use of oral contraceptives cause changes in vaginal mucosal cell metabolism that may complicate the treatment of candidiasis or trichomoniasis.

Estrogen depletion due to aging, ovariectomy, or pelvic irradiation causes atrophy of the vaginal mucosa, a reduction in glycogen content, and a decrease in the acidity of the vaginal fluid. A thin vaginal mucosa is susceptible to trauma. The bacterial population of the vagina changes from predominantly lactobacilli to a mixed flora consisting chiefly of pathogenic cocci.

Other factors that tend to decrease the acidity of the vagina are infected cervical mucus (always alkaline), menstrual fluid, and the vaginal transudate that occurs with sexual excitement. In addition, the male ejaculate is alkaline.

Although *C albicans* may be a normal inhabitant of the vagina, other types of vaginitis, eg, *Gardnerella (Haemophilus) vaginalis* vaginitis, are related to sexual activity and should be considered sexually transmitted diseases. In resistant cases, therefore, the male partner should wear a condom or undergo treatment concurrently.

Etiology

Approximately 95% of all vaginal discharges or infections are caused by *Gardnerella vaginalis, Candida albicans,* or *Trichomonas vaginalis* infections, cervicitis, and excessive but otherwise normal vaginal secretions. *G vaginalis* infection is the most common cause of a homogeneous, gray-white, malodorous vaginal discharge. The organism is not a tissue pathogen; therefore, there are no signs of irritation such as itching, burning, and soreness. The patient with symptomatic cervicitis has a mucopurulent discharge and, occasionally, intermenstrual or postcoital bleeding. Cervicitis may be caused by *Neisseria gonorrhoeae, Chlamydia trachomatis, T vaginalis,* or herpes simplex. Pruritus is a primary symptom of *Candida* vulvovaginitis; gross vaginal discharge is unusual but if present is described as curdy and white. Some patients have an excessive quantity of a physiologic gray-white, pasty, odorless, nonirritating vaginal secretion. Others have a mucoid secretion from healthy endocervical glands but with cervical ectropion or, rarely, vaginal adenosis. Symptoms of *T vaginalis* infection are quite variable and include a nonspecific (at times malodorous) discharge, itching, soreness, and spotting.

Other causes of vaginal discharge are cervical, fundal, or vaginal cancer, atrophic vaginitis, vaginitis emphysematosa, and desquamative inflammatory vaginitis. Vaginal fistulas secondary to obstetric injury, hysterectomy, Crohn's disease, or diverticulitis in older women are uncommon.

An odorous vaginal discharge from retention of a vaginal foreign body has long been recognized. Recently, however, anterior or right vaginal fornix ulcers secondary to improper insertion or placement of tampons have been reported.

A. Foreign Bodies: Foreign bodies commonly cause vaginal discharge and infection in preadolescent girls. Paper, cotton, or other materials may be placed or left in the vagina and cause secondary infection. Children may require vaginoscopic examination under anesthesia to identify or rule out foreign body or tumor high in the vaginal vault. In adults, a forgotten menstrual tampon or contraceptive device may cause malodorous leukorrhea. The diagnosis can usually be made by pelvic examination.

Improper use of vaginal tampons has recently been circumstantially and statistically related to vaginal mucosal changes, ulceration, and **toxic shock syndrome.** Biopsies from lesions have revealed embedded fibers incorporated within the granulation tissue forming the ulcer base. Differential diagnosis includes vaginal carcinoma, syphilis, trauma, herpes simplex, and granuloma inguinale. These changes are more frequent with the use of so-called super-absorbent tampons than with conventional tampons worn for the same length of time. Toxic shock syndrome affects previously healthy young women of childbearing age during an otherwise normal menstrual period. In the majority of affected women, *Staphylococcus aureus* has been isolated from the vagina, and the strains isolated produced an exotoxin called exfoliatin that causes exfoliation of the epidermis in mice. Coagulase-positive *S aureus* is not a normal inhabitant of the human vagina. However, vulvar skin has been identified as a site of colonization. In 67% of the subjects in one study, this organism was found on the labia majora.

B. Bacterial Infection: In the premenarcheal and postmenopausal hypoestrogenic vagina, a mixed bacterial flora may be expected, particularly in the presence of trauma or a foreign body. A specific diagnosis can be made only by preparation of stained smears and cultures, although culture reports may be misleading because of identification of mixed flora.

G vaginalis may be the most common cause of symptomatic bacterial vaginal infection. However, it has been suggested that the infection may be a more complex combination of *G vaginalis* and anaerobic bacteria. *G vaginalis* is a small, nonmotile, nonencapsulated, pleomorphic, gram-negative rod. The infection caused by this organism is characterized by a homogeneous, gray-white, malodorous vaginal discharge but no inflammatory response in the tissues. The odor may be due to synergism with anaerobic bacteria that produce odorous amines. *G vaginalis* is often cultured from patients with other sexually transmitted diseases and can be recovered from approximately 90% of sexual partners of infected women.

Gonorrhea is caused by *N gonorrhoeae,* a relatively fastidious gram-negative diplococcus that is naturally pathogenic only in humans. It is the most frequently reported communicable disease in the USA. Gonorrheal vulvovaginitis in children is usually transmitted by direct contact from one child to another or from an infected adult—or, infrequently, by sharing a bath towel. Gonorrhea in adolescents and adults is a sexually transmitted disease that initially may cause an acute lower genital tract inflammatory process but which, in women, may or may not be symptomatic. The preferred sites for the infection are the cervical canal, the urethra, the periurethral glands, and the anus.

The chlamydiae are obligatory intracellular microparasites once considered to be large viruses. However, a more sophisticated definition of viruses and bacteria recognizes that chlamydiae are bacterialike and definitely not viruses. Chlamydiae have a unique developmental cycle. Thus, they have been placed in their own order, the Chlamydiales. There is one genus, *Chlamydia,* and 2 species, *Chlamydia psittaci* and *Chlamydia trachomatis. C trachomatis* causes lymphogranuloma venereum, inclusion conjunctivitis, urethritis, cervicitis, salpingitis, proctitis, epididymitis, and pneumonia of newborns. Laboratory cultures for *Chlamydia* are not available to most office-based physicians. Generally, the diagnosis is exclusionary when a patient who has cervical signs suggestive of venereal disease has negative cultures for gonorrhea.

Mycoplasma hominis and *Ureaplasma urealyticum* can frequently be isolated from the human genital tract. Genital mycoplasmas colonize the urethral mucosa in men and have been implicated as causative agents in nongonococcal urethritis. In women, vaginal specimens are more likely to contain mycoplasmas than are specimens from other genital sites. *M hominis* is often isolated in association with other vaginal pathogens, but its importance is unclear. After puberty, vaginal colonization occurs primarily after sexual contact, and the incidence increases with the number of sexual partners. In women, there is no recognized vulvovaginal disorder caused by these organisms, but the organism has been related to cervicitis, salpingitis, fever after abortion, postpartum fever, premature labor, and infertility. A causal relationship has not been established.

C. Viral Infections: The DNA viruses that affect the vulva and vagina are of the herpesvirus, poxvirus, and papovavirus types. The herpesviruses that affect the lower genitalia are herpes simplex, varicella, herpes zoster, and cytomegalovirus.

Herpesvirus hominis (herpes simplex) has 2 immunologic variants, type 1 and type 2, distinguished by certain biologic differences and neutralization titrations, despite the presence of a cross-reactive antigen. In general, type 1 virus is isolated "above the waist" and type 2 "below the waist." Approximately

10–15% of genital herpes infections are caused by type 1 virus.

Cytomegalovirus, which causes no symptoms, may be cultured from the cervix. This is important because an acute but "silent" maternal infection during pregnancy may cause serious infection in the newborn.

Poxvirus causes molluscum contagiosum and vaccinia of the lower genital tract. Human papillomavirus, a papovavirus, causes the warts of condyloma acuminatum of the vulva and vagina. Vulvar condylomas are symptomatic and easily recognized, but condylomas in the vagina are often overlooked or confused cytologically with cervical or vaginal intraepithelial neoplasia. Little scientific attention has been given to vaginal condylomas. Six types of human papillomavirus have been isolated. The flat condylomas and the florid condylomas may be caused by different types. Four different types of human papillomavirus have been isolated from anorectal warts and may be responsible for morphologically different lesions, including carcinoma in situ.

D. Candidiasis: *Candida* species belong to the family Cryptococcaceae. Of the *Candida* species, *Candida albicans* most frequently causes human disease, and it has the ability to form both spores and pseudohyphae. *C albicans* is frequently a normal inhabitant of the mouth, throat, large intestine, and vagina. For propagation, the organism requires warmth and moisture; it will not grow on dry skin. Infections are thus limited mainly to mucous membranes and body folds. The many host factors controlling susceptibility are more significant in the development of a clinical infection than is the simple presence of the organism. Clinical infection occurs when the normal physiology of the vagina and vulva is disturbed by a systemic disorder (eg, diabetes mellitus), pregnancy, nondiabetic glycosuria, a diet consisting of large amounts of fruit or sugar, debilitation, corticosteroids, antibiotics, and possibly oral contraceptives. Clinical manifestations tend to be more severe just prior to menstruation, and infections become refractory during pregnancy. The ubiquitous nature of the organism allows repeated infections that may be interpreted as a chronic resistant infection. The patient's bowel is the reservoir for repeated infections.

E. Trichomoniasis: *Trichomonas vaginalis* is a unicellular flagellate protozoon. Humans are host to 3 *Trichomonas* species, but *T vaginalis,* which is found in the vagina, may be the only species that causes disease. *T vaginalis* organisms are larger than polymorphonuclear leukocytes but smaller than mature epithelial cells. Trichomoniasis is an infestation not only of the vagina but also of the lower urinary tract in both men and women. It is a sexually transmitted disease; other forms of transmission are infrequent, because large numbers of organisms are required to cause symptoms. A small number of trichomonads may occasionally be found in a patient with no symptoms, a normal vaginal pH, and normal vaginal flora. This may be interpreted as a carrier state, because most of these women have a history of symptomatic leukorrhea. High sex steroid levels, as during pregnancy, appear to promote development of refractory symptoms. The low vaginal acidity caused by menstrual blood, cervical mucorrhea, semen, and concurrent infection with *G vaginalis* encourages establishment of *T vaginalis*. The postmenopausal or premenarcheal vagina does not favor infection despite the effect of decreased acidity. Nonetheless, topical or systemic administration of estrogens may cause a subclinical infestation to become symptomatic.

F. Cervicitis: Chronic cervicitis associated with hypertrophy or eversion of the endocervical mucosa may produce a copious mucopurulent fluid. A variety of aerobic and anaerobic organisms can be cultured from cervical mucus. The alkaline cervical mucus may cause a sufficient change in vaginal pH to alter the bacterial flora, enhancing the environment for other pathogenic organisms. Herpesvirus often causes a necrotic exophytic cervical lesion that may be confused with cancer. Other causes of cervicitis are *N gonorrhoeae, C trachomatis,* and *T vaginalis.* Benign cervical polyps and cancer of the cervix are other causes of mucopurulent discharge and bleeding.

G. Atrophic Vaginitis: Prepubertal, lactating, and postmenopausal women lack the vaginal stimulation of endogenous estrogen production. The pH of the vagina is abnormally high, and the normally acidogenic flora of the vagina may be replaced by mixed flora. The vaginal mucosa is thinned, and the epithelium is thus more susceptible to both infection and trauma. Although most patients are asymptomatic, many postmenopausal women report vaginal dryness and dyspareunia. Some of the symptoms of irritation are caused by secondary infection.

H. Other Causes:

1. Cervical mucorrhea or vaginal epithelial discharge–An unusually large cervical ectropion may cause an excessive discharge of cervical mucus from normal endocervical gland cells. Vaginal adenosis may cause the same type of vaginal discharge. The discharge is mucoid and clear or slightly cloudy, but there is no itching, burning, or odor. Patients may equate the discharge with vaginal infection and seek treatment.

A gray-white, pasty discharge, which causes no irritation or odor and occasionally is quite profuse, may be caused by excessive desquamation of normal vaginal epithelial cells. Excessive but normal vaginal secretions may appear in the speculum blade as a clump or curd and be confused with a *Candida* infection. Here, the vaginal pH is normal. Microscopically, the secretions show normal bacterial flora, a heavy spread of mature vaginal squamae, and no increase in leukocytes.

2. Pinworms (*Enterobius vermicularis*)– Vaginal infestation by this organism may cause vaginitis, usually in children. The source of infection is fecal soiling of the introitus, and the result is an extremely pruritic perineal area. The parasite may be detected by pressing a strip of adhesive cellulose tape to the perineum and then adhering the tape to a slide. Microscopic examination may reveal the characteristic double-walled ova.

3. *Entamoeba histolytica*–E *histolytica* infection of the vagina and cervix is quite common in developing countries but rare in the USA. Severe involvement may resemble cervical cancer, but symptoms are chiefly due to involvement of the vulvar skin. Trophozoites of *E histolytica* may be demonstrated in wet mount preparations from the vagina or, occasionally, on a Papanicolaou smear. Because the intestinal tract is infected also, appropriate stool studies should be conducted.

4. Desquamative inflammatory vaginitis–This disorder demonstrates clinical and microscopic features of postmenopausal atrophic vaginitis but may develop in premenopausal women with normal estrogen levels. The cause is unknown. The primary complaint is discharge, vaginal soreness, and occasional spotting. The process is patchy and usually localized to the upper half of the vagina. The discharge contains many immature epithelial and pus cells not due to any identifiable cause. Synechiae may develop in the upper vagina, causing partial occlusion, and response to treatment is poor.

5. Vaginal ulcers–Most vaginal ulcers are caused by the improper use of menstrual tampons. Other causes listed previously must be excluded.

6. Vaginitis emphysematosa–This disorder is characterized by multiple gas-filled cystic structures on the vaginal and cervical mucosa. There is usually a concomitant infection by *G vaginalis, T vaginalis,* or both. The process is probably a rare manifestation of one or both infections, and the blebs disappear on eradication of these organisms.

7. Nonspecific vaginitis–Nonspecific vaginitis was defined in the past as a vaginal infection in which *C albicans, T vaginalis,* or *N gonorrhoeae* organisms were not identified. In recent years, *G vaginalis* has been considered to be the cause in many cases. More recently, it has been suggested that nonspecific vaginitis may be a complex infection process involving both *G vaginalis* and anaerobic bacteria. Other possible causes of leukorrhea or vulvovaginitis without obvious cause are allergic states, chemical irritants, cunnilingus, and possibly excessive sexual activity.

Clinical Findings

A. Symptoms and Signs: A vaginal discharge is considered abnormal by the patient if there is an increase in volume (especially if there is soiling of the clothing), an objectionable odor, or a change in consistency or color. Characteristics depend upon the cause. Secondary irritation of the vulvar skin may be minimal or extensive, causing pruritus or dyspareunia.

The patient should be examined as soon as possible after the onset of symptoms if not actively bleeding during menstruation. She should be instructed not to douche. After a clinical history is obtained, the vulva, vagina, and cervix should be thoroughly inspected. A history of previous vaginal infections may be important. The pH of secretions in the blade of the vaginal speculum should be determined, and a small amount of secretion should be placed on each of 2 glass slides. One slide should be treated with 10% potassium hydroxide and the other diluted with normal saline. A transient "fishy odor" after application of 10% potassium hydroxide is characteristic of *Gardnerella* infection. White blood cells and epithelial cells will be digested, enhancing detection of the candidal pseudohyphae and spores. Motile trichomonads may be detected under low power on the saline-diluted slide. The bacteria-covered "clue cells" of *G vaginalis* should also be sought on this slide. Next, the relative number of leukocytes should be noted and the maturity of the epithelial cells determined. Secretions from the normal vagina have few leukocytes, and the epithelial cells are mature. Patients with vaginitis or cervicitis show many white blood cells, and the presence of intermediate or basal cells indicates inflammation of the vaginal epithelium. Selective cultures may be performed for bacteria, candidiasis, and trichomoniasis.

1. Foreign bodies–(See above.) Changes in the vagina caused by improper use of vaginal tampons have been described. Symptoms of abnormal vaginal discharge and intermenstrual spotting may be secondary to drying of the vaginal mucosa, and microulceration may be detected by colposcopy. Ulcerative lesions are typically located in the vaginal fornices, and they have rolled, irregular edges with a red granulation tissue base. Regenerating epithelium at the ulcer edge may shed cells that may be interpreted as atypical, suggesting dysplasia. The lesions heal spontaneously after use of vaginal tampons is discontinued.

Toxic shock syndrome is the most serious complication of improper use of vaginal tampons. Symptoms consist of a high fever (≥ 38.9 °C [102 °F]) and may be accompanied by severe headache, sore throat, vomiting, and diarrhea. The disease may resemble viremia or meningitis. Progressive hypotension may occur and proceed to shock levels within 48 hours. Palmar erythema and a diffuse sunburnlike rash have also been described. Superficial desquamation of the palms and soles often follows within 2–3 weeks. Elevated blood urea nitrogen or oliguria may herald renal involvement. Cardiac dysfunction and central nervous system symptoms have also been reported. The syndrome has been linked to staphylococcal vaginal infection in healthy young women having an otherwise normal menstrual period. The skin rash usually disappears in 24–48 hours, but on occasion a patient will have a recurrent maculopapular, morbilliform eruption between the sixth and tenth days. Although it has been estimated that 70–80% of women in the USA use tampons, the incidence of toxic shock syndrome is only 6.2 per 100,000 menstruating women per year. Women who have had toxic shock syndrome are at considerable risk for recurrence and should not use tampons until it has been demonstrated that *S aureus* is eradicated from the vagina. This disease entity was not identified before 1974, and it appears to occur in women who wear a tampon continuously throughout the menstrual period.

2. Bacterial infections–In the premenopausal and postmenopausal patient, the hypoestrogenic vagina is susceptible to bacterial infection characterized by discharge and spotting. Inspection of the vagina will rule out a foreign body. Microscopic examination of vaginal secretions is necessary for detection of the more common causes of vaginitis and will demonstrate intermediate and parabasal epithelial cells. Bacterial cultures are usually not helpful because of the mixed flora without predominant organisms.

G vaginalis is the most common cause of bacterial vaginitis in the sexually active mature patient. The patient complains of a malodorous, nonirritating discharge, and examination reveals homogeneous, gray-white secretions with a pH of 5.0–5.5. A transient "fishy odor" may be released upon application of 10% potassium hydroxide to the vaginal secretions on a glass slide. A wet mount preparation of physiologic saline mixed with vaginal secretions should be examined under low-power and high-power objectives. There are few white blood cells and lactobacilli. The characteristic "clue cells" are identified as numerous stippled or granulated epithelial cells. This appearance is caused by the adherence of almost uniformly spaced *G vaginalis* organisms on their surfaces. The cells may be completely or only partially covered. Clumps of *G vaginalis* organisms may also be noted attached to the edges of epithelial cells or floating free in the preparation. A gram-stained smear reveals large numbers of small gram-negative bacilli and a relative absence of lactobacilli. Cultures are seldom necessary to establish a diagnosis.

Symptoms of infection by *N gonorrhoeae* may be quite severe, but up to 85% of infected female patients have no symptoms. The incidence of the disease has risen steadily, and a prevalence of 10%, detected by cervical cultures, has been reported from family planning clinics. A 2–3% prevalence has been reported in patients served by private practitioners. The gonococcus affects primarily the glandular structures of the cervix, vulva, perineum, and anus. The cervical canal, urethra, periurethral glands, and anus are the most commonly affected sites. Although clinically evident infection of the vagina is only transitory, it is the second most common site of a positive culture in infected patients who have had a hysterectomy. In acute disease, the gram-stained smear will identify the gram-negative diplococci within leukocytes, but the diagnosis must be confirmed by culture.

A nonlubricated speculum should be inserted into the vagina and the cervix inspected. A sterile moistened swab should be inserted into the endocervix and rotated. If there is excessive cervical mucus, it should be removed before the sample is taken. The swab should be rolled onto the culture medium in a Z or W pattern rather than streaked. Several culture systems providing a 5–10% CO_2 environment are available. One is a modified Thayer-Martin medium (Transgrow) dispensed in a screw-capped bottle containing 10%

CO_2. Because CO_2 is heavier than air, the bottle should be held with the mouth up or the gas will escape and compromise the microbiologic environment of the culture. Other sites for culture, in order of preference, are the urethra and rectum. It is estimated that approximately 15–20% of patients with lower genital tract infection will develop an infection of the upper genital tract.

No simple laboratory studies are available to the office-based physician for the specific diagnosis of cervicitis or urethritis caused by *C trachomatis*. The diagnosis is usually one of exclusion in a patient who has purulent cervicitis but not gonorrhea. Complement fixation tests for lymphogranuloma venereum are more accurate than the Frei skin test, which is no longer used. A titer greater than 1:28 should be expected in most infected females. The disease affects primarily the vulvar tissues. Retroperitoneal lymphadenopathy may be present. The initial lesion is a transient, painless vesicular lesion or shallow ulcer at the inoculation site. The tertiary stage of the disease, when most women are seen, is characterized by anal or genital fistulas, stricture, or rectal stenosis. The disease is uncommon in the USA but is endemic in Southeast Asia and Africa.

U urealyticum infection may be suspected as a cause of genital disease, but laboratory techniques for identification of this organism are rarely available to the practicing physician.

3. Viral infections–The DNA viruses that affect the lower genital tract are symptomatic, primarily because of involvement of the vulvar skin. Two exceptions are herpesvirus hominis and the human papillomavirus. The latter causes condylomas of the vaginal mucosa that can be confused with epithelial dysplasia. The herpesvirus may cause superficial ulcerations or an exophytic necrotic mass involving the cervix, which, in turn, causes profuse vaginal discharge. The cervix may be quite tender to manipulation and may bleed easily. The primary lesion lasts 2–6 weeks and heals without scarring. Recurrent infections may also cause cervical lesions. The virus may be isolated by culture from ulcers or ruptured vesicles. Cervical cytologic examination may reveal multinucleated giant cells with intranuclear inclusions. Approximately 83% of patients will develop antibodies to herpesvirus type 2 in a minimum of 21 days following a primary infection. Much evidence is accumulating to suggest that herpesvirus hominis is etiologically related to cancer of the cervix. (See also below under Viral Infections.)

The human papillomavirus causes condylomata acuminata of the cervix, vagina, skin of the vulva, perineum, and perianal areas. Vulvar condylomas are easily identified; those on the cervix and vaginal mucosa may not be seen with the naked eye and can be confused cytologically with cervical or vaginal intraepithelial neoplasia. The viruses are sexually transmitted, affect the same age group as other venereal diseases, and infect both partners. The exophytic or papillomatous condyloma is the typical lesion and the

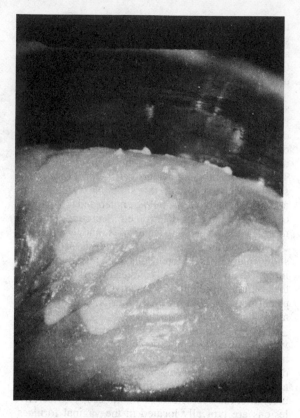

Figure 9–1. Vaginal condylomata acuminata as seen with a colposcope. × 13.

only one recognized before 1976. Since that time, other varieties have been identified in the vagina, particularly by colposcopic examination (Fig 9–1). These are the flat, the "spiked," and the inverted condyloma. The flat condyloma appears as a white lesion with a somewhat granular surface; a mosaic pattern and punctation may also be present, suggesting vaginal intraepithelial neoplasia that must be excluded by biopsy. The florid, papillomatous condyloma shows a raised white lesion with fingerlike projections often containing capillaries. Although large lesions may be seen with the naked eye, smaller ones can be identified only with the colposcope. The "spiked" condyloma presents as a hyperkeratotic lesion with surface projections and prominent capillary tips. An inverted condyloma grows into the glands of the cervix but has not been identified on the vaginal mucosa. Condylomatous vaginitis causes a rather rough vaginal surface, demonstrating white projections from the pink vaginal mucosa.

Koilocytes are superficial or intermediate cells characterized by a large perinuclear cavity that stains only faintly. They are said to be pathognomonic of human papillomavirus infection. Dyskeratocytes tend to exfoliate in dense aggregates and contain keratin or its precursors. No nuclei or inclusion bodies are seen in cells shed from human papillomavirus lesions. Careful, directed colposcopic biopsies must be taken to exclude intraepithelial neoplasia. The chief histologic difference between dysplasia and condyloma is the direction of progression of cellular atypia. In dysplasia, the dysplastic cells move toward the surface, whereas changes from condyloma progress from the epithelial surface inward toward the basal membrane.

Vaginal discharge and pruritus are the most common symptoms of florid condylomas. In addition, there may be occasional postcoital bleeding. No specific symptoms are associated with other types of condylomas. The entire lower genital tract is usually involved by subclinical or florid lesions whenever lesions are found on the vulva. Cellular immunity is lowered during pregnancy or in the diabetic or renal transplant patient, so that massive proliferation of condylomas may occur, and these are difficult to treat. Laryngeal papilloma and vulvar condylomas in infants delivered through an infected vaginal canal have been reported.

4. Candidiasis–Intense vulvar pruritus is the principal symptom of vaginal candidiasis and may interfere with normal activity. The symptoms correlate positively with the extent of vulvar erythema. A burning sensation may follow urination, particularly if there is maceration or excoriation of the skin from scratching. Widespread involvement of the skin adjacent to the labia may suggest an underlying metabolic problem, eg, diabetes. The labia minora may be erythematous, edematous, and excoriated. Typical thrush patches are uncommon in nonpregnant patients. An unpleasant odor is not a common complaint of patients with candidiasis unless secondary infection has developed. The pH of the vaginal secretions in vulvovaginal candidiasis may be relatively normal. The clinical diagnosis is based upon the clinical features of the disease as well as the demonstration of candidal mycelia. Identification of *C albicans* depends upon the finding of filamentous forms (pseudohyphae) of the organism (Fig 9–2). Vaginal wall exudate is mixed in 10–20% potassium hydroxide, placed on a cover slip, and examined microscopically. The organism may be grown on Sabouraud's or Nickerson's medium in an incubator or, less well, at room temperature.

5. *Trichomonas vaginalis* vaginitis–Trichomoniasis tends to be worse just after menstruation or during pregnancy. Persistent leukorrhea is the principal symptom of trichomoniasis with or without secondary vulvar pruritus. Leukorrhea is characteristically profuse, extremely frothy, greenish, and, in severe cases, foul-smelling. The characteristics and volume of the discharge may be altered by douching, prior medications, or duration of disease. In chronic infections, the quantity of discharge may be decreased and the color may be gray or even light green to yellow. The pH of the vagina usually exceeds 5.0. Involvement of the vulva may be limited to the vestibule and labia minora, although a profuse discharge often causes inflammation of the labia majora, perineum, and adjacent skin surfaces. The labia minora may become edematous and tender. Urinary symptoms may occur; however, burning with urination is most often associated with severe vulvitis, particularly if there has been excoriation of the skin from scratching. Gentle inspection of the vaginal mucosa with a speculum may reveal generalized vaginal erythema with multiple small petechiae, so-called "strawberry spots," which may be confused with epithelial punctation. The diagnosis is confirmed by finding characteristic motile flagellates in a wet mount preparation using physiologic saline and a drop of vaginal fluid on a slide covered with a cover slip (Fig 9–3).

Complications

A solid foreign body retained in the vagina of a child over a prolonged period may erode into the bladder or rectum. Similarly, a retained vaginal pessary in an elderly patient not only causes infection but may

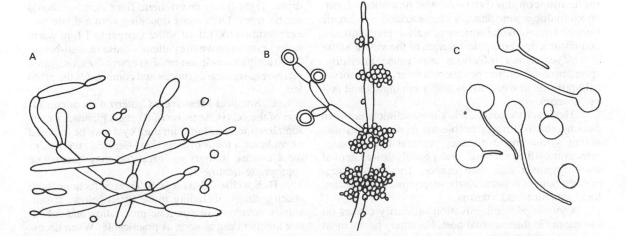

Figure 9–2. *Candida albicans.* **A:** Blastospores and pseudohyphae in exudate. **B:** Blastospores, pseudohyphae, and conidia in culture at 20 °C. **C:** Young culture forms germ tubes when placed in serum for 3 hours at 37 °C. (Reproduced, with permission, from Jawetz E, Melnick JL, Adelberg EA: *Review of Medical Microbiology,* 15th ed. Lange, 1982.)

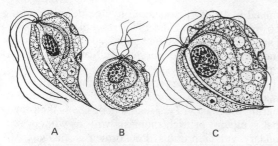

A   B   C

Figure 9–3. *Trichomonas vaginalis* as found in vaginal and prostatic secretions. *A:* Normal trophozoite. *B:* Round form after division. *C:* Common form seen in stained preparation. Cysts not found. (Reproduced, with permission, from Jawetz E, Melnick JL, Adelberg EA: *Review of Medical Microbiology,* 15th ed. Lange, 1982.)

become encrusted and erode the wall of the vagina. A spectrum of illness associated with menstrual tampon use has been described, the most severe manifestation being toxic shock syndrome.

G vaginalis vaginitis is accompanied by acute symptoms, but there may be no systemic manifestations or chronic complications. Two exceptions are puerperal morbidity and infection and septicemia after abdominal hysterectomy, with gaseous crepitation in the abdominal incision.

Gonorrheal infections cause acute lower tract symptoms, and the newborn may develop conjunctivitis by contamination during vaginal delivery. Ascending infection, with salpingitis, tubo-ovarian abscess, and peritonitis, may follow in the mother.

C trachomatis causes a purulent cervicitis that is symptomatic but unrelated to later complications. The role of the chlamydiae in upper tract infections has not been defined. It has been suggested that atypical cytologic findings are more common in patients who have a culture-proved chlamydial cervicitis. The organism is transmitted to the male urethra, causing nongonococcal urethritis. It is also responsible for inclusion conjunctivitis of the newborn. Lymphogranuloma venereum is characterized by chronic lymphadenitis, rectal stricture, vulvar elephantiasis, and chronic hypertrophic changes of the vulvar skin.

Mycoplasma infections may cause infertility, spontaneous abortion, postpartum fever, nongonococcal urethritis in men, and possibly salpingitis and pelvic abscess.

Herpesvirus infection is a major clinical problem causing the following problems: recurrent and disabling symptomatic disease, venereal transmission, infection of the newborn, and possibly lower genital tract dysplasia and even cancer. The immunosuppressed patient is particularly susceptible to refractory local infection and viremia.

Cytomegalovirus infection ordinarily causes no symptoms in the maternal host, but it may be the most common cause of congenital infection; it affects the central nervous system primarily.

The various manifestations of papillomavirus infection in humans have only recently been recognized.

Multifocal acute, commonly recurrent disease is often difficult to treat, particularly in the pregnant or immunosuppressed patient. Some varieties of papillomavirus may cause dysplasia of the lower genital tract and perianal skin. Laryngeal papilloma and vulvar condylomas in infants are caused by infection contracted during vaginal delivery.

Candida infections tend to recur and are often interpreted as chronic refractory vulvovaginitis. The organisms are particularly difficult to eradicate during pregnancy or in the immunosuppressed or diabetic patient.

Severe trichomonal vaginitis can lead to sufficient change in the epithelial surface of the cervix and vagina so that cytologic preparations may be interpreted as dysplastic. The infection must be treated and the cytologic study repeated.

Prevention

Prevention is largely a matter of patient education. The adolescent girl should be instructed in feminine hygiene. The role of douches and feminine hygiene sprays should be explained. Immediate and long-term consequences of exposure to sexually transmitted diseases should be part of the educational curriculum for all adolescents.

Treatment

A. General Measures: Coitus should be avoided until cure has been achieved—or a condom should be used, especially if there are frequent recurrences of infection. The sexual partner should be treated also if infection is repeated. Associated vulvar pruritus may be treated with local applications of corticosteroid lotion or nonoily cream. Cornstarch or talcum powder may prevent or alleviate chafing.

B. Local Nonspecific Measures: During a period of specific treatment, the external genitalia should be kept clean by gentle sponging. Dryness must be encouraged and may be accomplished with a hair dryer. Tight-fitting or synthetic fiber clothing should not be worn. Occasional douching with a dilute vinegar solution (60 mL of white vinegar to 1 L of warm water) may improve the patient's sense of well-being. This rarely causes irritation. Excessive douching often increases secretion of mucus and compounds the problem.

C. Surgical Measures: Cauterization or conization of the cervix, incision of Skene's glands, or marsupialization of a Bartholin duct cyst may be required to eradicate a focus of infection. Cervical, uterine, or tubal disease (tumors or infection) may necessitate appropriate treatment.

D. Specific Measures:* Treat infections with specific drugs, including those listed below. If sensitivity develops, discontinue medication and substitute another drug as soon as practicable. When necessary, continue treating the patient during menstruation.

---

*Gonorrhea is discussed in Chapter 15.

1. Foreign bodies–Treatment consists of complete removal of the foreign body. Local treatment with a conjugated estrogen vaginal cream, one-half applicatorful high in the vagina each evening for 7 days, is usually sufficient treatment. Rarely, specific systemic antibiotics may be administered for ulceration or cellulitis of the vagina or vulva.

Dryness or ulceration of the vagina secondary to use of menstrual tampons is transient and heals spontaneously when tampons are proscribed. Ulcers have been observed also in women who have worn tampons between menstrual periods for excessive vaginal discharge. **Toxic shock syndrome** should be suspected in any menstruating woman with a sudden onset of febrile illness. The tampon should be removed and the vagina thoroughly cleansed to decrease the inoculum of responsible organisms. Appropriate supportive measures should be instituted and a β-lactamase-resistant penicillin administered to those not allergic to the drug. Recovered patients are prone to recurrence and should discontinue use of tampons.

2. Atrophic vaginitis–In most women, an atrophic vagina is asymptomatic. Symptoms may be due to secondary bacterial infection or dyspareunia. Treatment includes intravaginal application of a conjugated estrogen cream. Because approximately one-third of the estrogen will be absorbed into the systemic circulation, such treatment is contraindicated in patients who may still have cancer of the breast or endometrium. Insertion of one-half to 1 applicatorful of cream each night for 1 week may cause breast tenderness. Maturation of the vaginal mucosa ordinarily eradicates a bacterial infection but may predispose the patient to a secondary trichomonal or bacterial vaginitis. Instillation approximately twice weekly thereafter should maintain the vaginal mucosa. If there are no contraindications, systemic estrogens may be given for associated postmenopausal symptoms.

3. Bacterial infections–

a. *G vaginalis* may be treated by orally administered medications, eg, ampicillin, cephalexin, cephradine, and tetracycline, but this therapy is only moderately successful, and it often precipitates vulvovaginal candidiasis. Although not currently approved by the FDA for this indication, metronidazole (Flagyl), 250 mg 3 times daily for 7 days for the patient and her sexual partner, has been found to be at least 95% effective. The 2-g single dose of metronidazole used for trichomoniasis is less effective for *G vaginalis* than the 7-day schedule. Topical medications such as oxytetracycline vaginal tablets and triple sulfa cream are much less beneficial than systemic therapy. Contraindications to metronidazole include certain blood dyscrasias and central nervous system diseases. An important side-effect is intolerance to alcohol. Metronidazole is contraindicated during early pregnancy and lactation. If a patient has identifiable vaginitis but few or no symptoms, treatment may be unnecessary.

b. Suspected *C trachomatis* is a diagnosis of exclusion after other etiologic diagnoses have been ruled out. The patient should be treated with tetracycline or erythromycin, 250 mg orally 4 times daily for 10 days.

If treatment of mycoplasmal infection is indicated, the tetracyclines are the most useful drugs. Demeclocycline and doxycycline are recommended. Therapeutic doses should be administered to the patient and sexual partner for 10 days.

4. Viral infections–

a. The symptoms of herpesvirus hominis infection are due to lesions of the vaginal introitus or skin of the vulva and perineum. No specific treatment for genital viral infections has been developed. Symptomatic therapy is discussed below under Viral Infections of the Vulva & Vagina.

b. Condylomas of the cervix and vagina may be treated by local caustic medication, cryotherapy, surgery, systemic therapy, or observation. Vaginal condylomas are difficult to treat, because they are usually multiple, because the mucosa readily absorbs drugs instilled into the vagina, and because the rectum or bladder may be adversely affected by vigorous treatment. Podophyllum resin in 5–25% concentrations in mineral oil, tincture of benzoin, or alcohol may be used to eliminate vulvar condylomas. However, podophyllum resin should not be used on the vagina because of systemic absorption and reported toxicity. Abortion, premature labor, and fetal death have been reported with the use of podophyllum resin during pregnancy. Although fluorouracil and bichloroacetic acid have been reported to be effective, there are insufficient data for conclusions at this time.

Surgical removal is usually compromised, because multiple small lesions, easily identified by colposcopy, may be scattered over the vaginal surface. Local excision, electrocoagulation, cryosurgery, and carbon dioxide laser vaporization have been used. Carbon dioxide laser treatment is currently the method of choice. The recurrence rate is high because of multifocal and unidentifiable disease.

Successful systemic treatment has been reported, but none can be recommended at this time. An autogenous vaccine has been prepared and administered to patients with florid lesions with reportedly good results. Because the human papillomavirus may have possible oncogenic potential, the physician may be reluctant to administer a vaccine prepared with this virus. Levamisole as a stimulant for the immune system reportedly has been effective and is undergoing further study.

In summary, there is no specific treatment for vaginal condylomas. In some clinics, they are not treated unless they are symptomatic or there is biopsy evidence of atypia for which treatment would be the same as that for vaginal intraepithelial neoplasia. Carbon dioxide laser therapy under colposcopic guidance appears to be effective treatment for isolated and symptomatic lesions.

Florid growth of vaginal condylomas during pregnancy may necessitate cesarean section to avoid bleeding and soft tissue dystocia. In addition, laryngeal papilloma of the offspring and vulvar condylomas may follow vaginal delivery. Electrocoagulation, cryotherapy, or laser therapy should be used before 32 weeks' gestation to avoid posttreatment necrosis lasting as long as 4–6 weeks.

The long-term course of untreated vaginal condylomas is unknown. In any event, spontaneous resolution occasionally occurs within 12–24 months. Use of a condom should assist in the prevention of viral transmission to sexual partners.

5. *Candida albicans* vaginitis–Treatment is limited to patients with symptoms who have *Candida* organisms present. Short-term or irregular and erratic treatment is often unsuccessful. Infection in a postmenopausal or breast-feeding woman or premenarcheal child may be an indicator of diabetes. The blood glucose in diabetics should be controlled, and complicating medications, eg, systemic antibiotics, should be discontinued. Nonabsorbent undergarments must not be worn, and self-medication and feminine hygiene products should be discontinued. The sexual partner should be examined in all instances of poor response to treatment, and intercourse should be discontinued unless a condom is used. Therapy for acute symptomatic vulvovaginitis should be modified in chronic or resistant cases.

Anti-*Candida* preparations must be applied topically to be effective. The following drugs are useful in treatment of acute vaginal candidiasis:

a. Clotrimazole 1% vaginal cream (Gyne-Lotrimin or Mycelex-G), 1 applicatorful (about 5 g) inserted high in the vaginal canal at bedtime for 7 nights. Treatment may be extended to 14 or more days in chronic, refractory cases. The cream should also be applied to the vulvar skin 3–4 times daily for pruritus. One vaginal tablet (100 mg) may be substituted for the cream; it is less messy but may be less effective. Two tablets inserted nightly 3 times may be as effective as 7 days of treatment with 1 tablet. Treatment should be continued without interruption even during menstruation. Medication is contraindicated in women who have shown hypersensitivity to any component of the preparation.

b. Miconazole nitrate, 2% (Monistat 7 Vaginal Cream), 1 applicatorful placed high in the vagina each night for 7–14 applications.

c. Patients who have demonstrated sensitivity to clotrimazole products may be treated with boric acid powder, 600 mg in a gelatin capsule. One capsule is placed high in the vagina each night for 2 weeks.

d. *Candida* vulvitis usually responds to topical applications of clotrimazole cream. If this is unsuccessful, a topical corticosteroid cream reduces the inflammatory reaction and relieves itching. Adverse reactions to topical anesthetics outweigh the possible benefits of use for relief of symptoms.

Chronic and recurring infections may be a result of decreased host immunity or reinfection. There is no uniformly successful treatment plan. It has been suggested that treatment of *C albicans* in the digestive tract would decrease the incidence of recurrence; however, controlled studies have not confirmed that suggestion. Estrogen treatment of postmenopausal pa-

tients may precipitate or aggravate recurrent candidiasis. Some studies have implicated oral contraceptives as a predisposing factor. Systemic antibiotics, particularly tetracycline, increase the number of candidal organisms in the lower bowel and vagina. Organisms in the preputial folds of the clitoris and the partner's foreskin may be a source of reinfection. Therapeutic alternatives are (1) prolonged treatment beyond the usual 7- to 14-day regimen; (2) self-medication for 3–5 days at the first evidence of symptoms; or (3) prophylactic treatment for several days before each menstrual period. Periodic examination is necessary to demonstrate that recurrent infections are in fact due to *Candida*.

6. *Trichomonas vaginalis* vaginitis–Because there are inaccessible foci of trichomonads in the urinary tracts of both sexes, a systemic agent is indicated. Most men with affected sexual partners also harbor the organism but are asymptomatic. For this reason, both partners should be treated simultaneously. Meanwhile, intercourse should be avoided unless a condom is used. Douching may temporarily remove odorous secretions and relieve symptoms. Metronidazole is the only systemic agent approved for use in the USA.

a. Metronidazole (Flagyl)–Both partners should be treated simultaneously with metronidazole, one 250-mg tablet orally 3 times daily for 7 days. A 1-day treatment regimen that may be as effective consists of administration of 2 g in 1 day in a single dose. There is controversy about the wisdom of prescribing the medication for a man if he has not been examined and apprised of the side-effects. In resistant cases, which most likely are reinfections, oral courses of metronidazole may be repeated after 4–6 weeks if the presence of trichomonads has been confirmed and the white blood cell and differential counts are normal. An undesirable side-effect is nausea or emesis with alcohol consumption. Moreover, approximately 2% of patients report the onset of nausea several hours after administration of metronidazole alone. Contraindications to metronidazole include certain blood dyscrasias and central nervous system diseases. Administration is contraindicated during early pregnancy and lactation. An oncogenic effect has been demonstrated in animals but not in humans.

b. Other drugs–Patients who develop side-effects from metronidazole may be treated with antitrichomonal suppositories (eg, Vagisec Plus [polyoxyethylene nonyl phenol, aminacrine, sodium edetate, and docusate sodium]), one inserted deep into the vagina twice daily for 2 weeks and then for at least 1 week after no organisms are identified on a vaginal smear. Although temporary relief of symptoms may be achieved, complete cure is seldom attained.

7. Cervicitis–Treatment depends upon the etiologic agent. Povidone-iodine preparations have been recommended for treatment of herpes cervicitis, but the effectiveness of this treatment is speculative. If an organism is identified, it should be treated specifically. Purulent cervicitis without an identifiable cause may be secondary to *C trachomatis* infection and can be treated with tetracycline or erythromycin. An occasional patient may require cryosurgery, cautery, or carbon dioxide laser vaporization after a premalignant or malignant lesion has been excluded by cytologic examination, colposcopy, and biopsy as needed.

8. Mucorrhea and epithelial discharge–Excessive but normal vaginal discharge from severe cervical ectropion, vaginal adenosis, or vaginal epithelial surface should be treated by reassurance. Continuous use of a vaginal tampon could be dangerous. Occasional douching may help control the discharge and relieve symptoms. Cryosurgery or carbon dioxide laser treatment of the cervix is occasionally beneficial.

9. Other causes–Pinworm and *Entamoeba histolytica* infestations of the vagina are treated specifically.

Desquamative inflammatory vaginitis in a patient with normal ovarian activity is a diagnosis of exclusion. Treatment has not been defined but has included local applications of estrogenic, antibiotic, and corticosteroid preparations.

Vaginitis emphysematosa is a manifestation of vaginitis caused by *G vaginalis* or *T vaginalis* and should be treated specifically with metronidazole.

The diagnosis of nonspecific vaginitis is seldom justified, but in an occasional patient no specific cause can be identified. Emotional factors causing psychosomatic vulvovaginitis should be considered in the history.

E. Treatment Failure: Persistent leukorrhea in spite of apparently adequate therapy requires complete reevaluation to detect recurrent or persistent disease or to establish a new diagnosis. Factors that compromise host defenses or modify the normal physiology of the vagina must be assessed. Sexual partners must be examined also.

Prognosis

An orderly approach to the diagnosis of the bacterial, candidal, or protozoal causes of leukorrhea and appropriate specific treatment when available should lead to cure. Viral infections, on the other hand, cannot be treated specifically, and the long-term serious consequences to the patient and her offspring pose significant clinical problems that cannot be resolved at this time. Improvement in laboratory technology and availability of diagnostic studies will prove or disprove the suggested roles of some currently recognized organisms and will identify others.

PRINCIPLES OF DIAGNOSIS OF VULVAR DISEASES

Pruritus

Pruritus is the most common symptom of vulvar disease. The term pruritus vulvae denotes intense itching of the vulvar skin and mucous membranes due to any cause. Specific diagnosis depends upon a thorough history, a physical examination that includes inspec-

tion of all body surfaces, and, in most instances, an adequate biopsy (Table 9–1).

Ulceration

Ulcerative lesions suggest a granulomatous sexually transmitted disease or cancer. Therefore, appropriate tests for venereal disease should be conducted along with biopsy to rule out primary or coexisting malignancy. Well-circumscribed solid tumors should be excised widely and submitted for microscopic examination. Diffuse lesions may demonstrate great histologic variability, and suitable sites for biopsies must be chosen. It is recommended that toluidine blue, 1% aqueous solution, be applied to the entire vulva and destained in 3 minutes by the application of 1% acetic acid solution. This procedure will delineate areas of epithelial hyperactivity appropriate for biopsy. A satisfactory full-thickness biopsy of the skin and tumor can be obtained with a dermatologic punch biopsy instrument under local anesthesia.

Abnormalities of Pigmentation

The color of vulvar skin or lesions depends principally upon the vascularity of the dermis, the thickness of the overlying epidermis, and the amount of intervening pigment, either melanin or blood pigments. A dystrophic lesion of the vulva may have a white appearance due primarily to a decrease in vascularity (lichen sclerosus et atrophicus) or an increase in the keratin layer (lichen simplex chronicus) which has undergone maceration from the increased moisture in the vulvar area. During the acute phase of lichen sclerosus, the vulvar skin is moderately erythematous. As the lesion matures, it becomes hyperkeratotic and develops a typical white appearance resembling cigarette paper. The epidermal thickening of neoplasia obscures the underlying vasculature and, in conjunction with the macerating effect of the moist environment, usually produces a hyperplastic white lesion. A diffuse white lesion of the vulva is also produced by loss or absence of melanin pigmentation, eg, vitiligo, a heredity disorder. Leukoderma is a localized white lesion resulting from transient loss of pigment in a residual scar after the healing of an ulcer.

A red lesion results from thinning or ulceration of the epidermis, the vasodilatation of inflammation or an immune response, or the neovascularization of neoplasia. With ulceration of the epithelium, there is loss of areas of epidermis, and the vascular dermis is apparent. Acute candidal vulvovaginitis, as seen in diabetic patients, is a typical example of vulvar erythema secondary to inflammation and the local immune response. One variety of invasive epidermoid cancer is characterized by a velvety red lesion that spreads over the vulvar skin. Psoriasis and Paget's disease are other examples of diseases that produce basically red lesions.

Dark lesions are due to an increased amount or concentration of melanin or blood pigments. These may occur after trauma. A persistent dark lesion on the vulvar skin or mucosa is usually either a nevus or a

Table 9—1. Management of vulvar lesions.

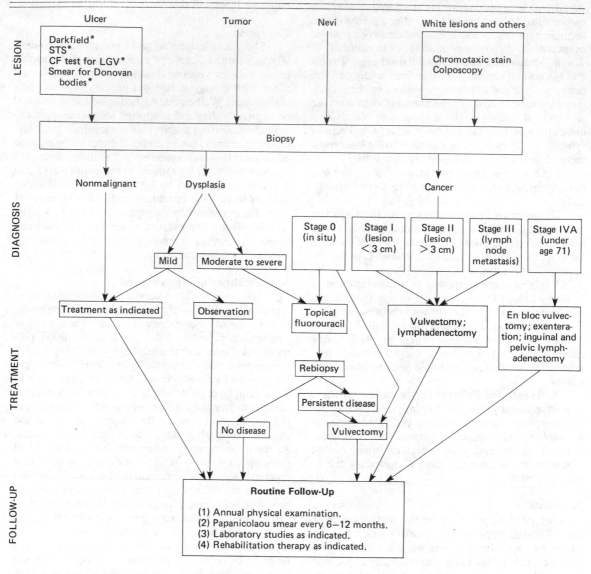

*If any tests are positive, give appropriate treatment. If ulcer does not clear, do biopsy.

melanoma. Melanosis, or lentigo, is a benign, darkly pigmented, flat lesion that must be removed by excision biopsy to exclude the possibility of melanoma. In the occasional case of carcinoma in situ of the vulvar skin, the atypical squamous cells are unable to contain the melanin pigment. As a consequence, it is concentrated in local macrophages, causing dark coloration of the tumor. Vulvar skin may darken in girls following the use of estrogen cream applied to the vulva and vagina for the treatment of vaginitis or after oral contraceptive use.

VASCULAR & LYMPHATIC DISEASES OF THE VULVA & VAGINA

The vulva and vagina have a rich vascular and lymphatic supply. These channels may undergo obstruction, dilatation, rupture, or infection or may develop tumorous lesions which are usually malformations rather than true neoplasms.

Varicosities

Varicosities of the vulva involve one or more veins. Severe varicosities of the legs and vulva may be aggravated during pregnancy. Symptomatic vulvar varices in a patient who is not pregnant are uncommon and may indicate vascular disease in the pelvis, either primary or secondary to tumor masses. Regardless of the cause, varicosities may cause considerable discomfort, consisting of pain and a sense of heaviness, and a large mass of veins may be apparent. Rupture of a vulvar varicosity during pregnancy may cause profuse hemorrhage. Acute thrombosis or phlebitis usually causes acute pain and tenderness. An examination should be performed with the patient in the standing position, which distends the veins; otherwise, the correct diagnosis may not be considered.

Treatment of vulvar and vaginal varicosities is seldom necessary, although symptoms might be quite severe during pregnancy. Support clothing such as panty hose or leotards usually provides effective support, even in pregnant patients. Operation is usually necessary only for rupture and hemorrhage, which is rare. Swelling tends to decrease considerably after the 36th week of pregnancy. Management of the pregnancy should be guided by ordinary obstetric principles. Vaginal delivery is usually advisable.

Edema

The loose integument of the vulva predisposes to edema from a variety of causes. Vascular or lymphatic obstruction may be the result of neoplasm or infection such as lymphogranuloma venereum, which can cause extensive lymphatic obstruction and gross deformity or esthiomene of the vulvar tissues. If resolution does not occur after specific antibiotic treatment, vulvectomy may be indicated.

Accidental trauma from a bicycle accident in a young girl or a blow or kick to the pudendum may cause painful swelling. An ice pack applied to the perineum after acute trauma tends to retard the development of edema; 1–2 days later, warm packs or sitz baths assist in resolution of the associated inflammation or hematoma.

Severe vulvar edema may be associated with systemic disorders that cause generalized edema, eg, congestive heart failure, nephrotic syndrome, or pre-eclampsia-eclampsia. Acute edema may be a manifestation of a systemic allergic reaction or local contact dermatitis. Dependent edema is occasionally seen in neurologic patients confined to bed.

Hematoma

The vulva has a rich blood supply, and the unusually distensible tissues often do not limit hemorrhage when a vessel is ruptured. Blunt trauma to the vulva, particularly in the pregnant patient, results in rapid development of hematoma and associated edema. An ice pack should be applied to the perineum after acute trauma. However, if a hematoma is not self-limiting and continues to expand, the area should be incised, specific bleeders ligated, and the wound packed but left unsutured. There are usually multiple bleeding sites, and ligation of individual bleeding points is ordinarily not curative. Antibiotics should be administered on an individual basis depending upon the amount of tissue trauma and contamination from the original traumatic event.

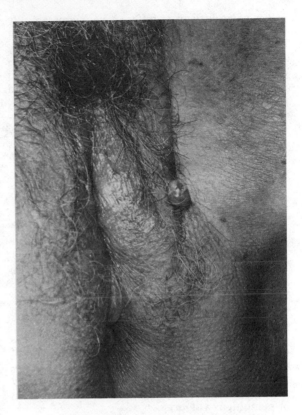

Figure 9–4. Pyogenic granuloma.

Granuloma Pyogenicum

This tumor is considered to be a variant of capillary hemangioma. It is usually single, raised, and dull red and seldom exceeds 2 cm in size (Fig 9–4). It is important because it tends to bleed easily when traumatized. Wide excision biopsy is indicated to alleviate symptoms and to rule out malignant melanoma.

Senile Hemangioma

These tumors are usually multiple small, dark blue, asymptomatic papules discovered incidentally during examination of an older patient. Excision biopsy is indicated only if they bleed repeatedly.

Hemangiomas in Children

These tumors, usually diagnosed in the first few months of life, may vary in size from small strawberry hemangiomas to large cavernous ones. They tend to be elevated and bright red or dark, depending upon their size and the thickness of the overlying skin. Those that tend to increase in size during the first few months of life are most likely to become static or regress without therapy after about age 1½.

Although most of these tumors can be observed without treatment, larger ones require dermatologic consultation regarding therapy.

Lymphangioma

Lymphangiomas are tumors of lymphatic vessels

and may be difficult to differentiate microscopically from hemangiomas unless blood cells are present within the vessels. **Lymphangioma cavernosum** may cause a diffuse enlargement of one side of the vulva and extend down over the remainder of the vulva and perineum. If the tumor is sufficiently large, it should be surgically excised. **Lymphangioma simplex** tumors are small, soft solitary or multiple nodules, usually over the labia majora. Lymphangiomas are usually asymptomatic, but on occasion an associated pruritus or formication may be intense and the involved skin must be excised.

DISORDERS OF OTHER SYSTEMS WITH VULVAR MANIFESTATIONS

Leukemia

Nodular infiltration and ulceration of the vulva and the rectovaginal septum may occur with acute leukemia.

Dermatologic Disorders

Recurrent ulcerations of the mucous membranes of the mouth and vagina may be a manifestation of **disseminated lupus erythematosus.** Bullous eruptions of apparently normal skin and mucous membrane surfaces of the vulva may be one of the first evidences of **pemphigus vulgaris.**

Contact dermatitis is an inflammatory response of the vulvar tissues to agents that may either be locally irritating or induce sensitivity upon contact. The local reaction to a systemically administered drug is termed **dermatitis medicamentosa.**

Psoriasis is a chronic relapsing dermatosis that may also affect the scalp, the extensor surfaces of the extremities, the trunk, and the vulva. The vulvar skin may be the only body surface affected, and the lesions appear typically erythematous, resembling fungal infection (Fig 9–5), but without the silver scaly crusts that occur on the other parts of the body.

An underlying adenocarcinoma may occasionally be associated with **acanthosis nigricans,** a benign hyperpigmented lesion associated with papillomatous hypertrophy. **Pseudoacanthosis nigricans** is a benign process that may appear on the skin of the vulva and inner thighs in obese and darkly pigmented individuals.

Intertrigo is an inflammatory reaction involving the genitocrural folds or the skin under the abdominal panniculus. It is common in obese patients and results from persistent moisture of the skin surfaces. An associated superficial fungal or bacterial infection may be present. The area appears either erythematous or white from maceration. Measures that promote dryness, eg, absorbent cotton undergarments and dusting with cornstarch powder, may be helpful.

Diabetes Mellitus

Diabetes mellitus is the systemic disease most commonly associated with chronic pruritus vulvae. It

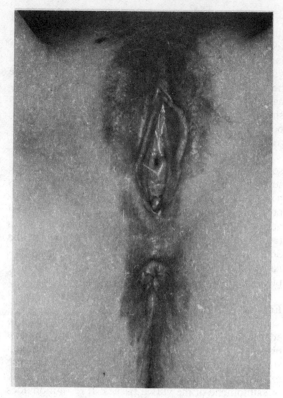

Figure 9–5. Typical lesion of psoriasis with a sharp outline and bright red surface.

has been suggested that half of diabetic women develop chronic vulvitis sufficiently characteristic to be designated **diabetic vulvitis.** The cause is a chronic vulvovaginal candidiasis. Thus, diabetes mellitus must be considered in any female who responds poorly to treatment of vulvovaginal candidiasis. Glycosuria is apparently not necessary to produce diabetic vulvitis. A 2-hour postprandial blood sugar or glucose tolerance test may be necessary to detect otherwise asymptomatic diabetes. If the condition persists without control of the systemic disorder, the skin will often undergo lichenification and secondary bacterial infection. Chronic dermatitis may develop that is compatible with lichen simplex chronicus (neurodermatitis). On occasion, bacterial infection may result in acute vulvar abscesses, chronic subcutaneous abscesses, and draining sinuses. These may be unresponsive to therapy if the diabetes is not controlled. Management of the acute phase consists of control of the metabolic disorder and specific therapy for candidiasis.

Behçet's Syndrome

Behçet's syndrome is a rare disorder of unknown cause characterized by recurrent oral and genital ulcerations. The ulcers are preceded by small vesicles or papules and last for a variable period of time. Ocular lesions begin as superficial inflammation and may proceed to iridocyclitis and even blindness. Monarticular arthritis and central nervous system symptoms are manifestations of severe disease. The syndrome may be an expression of vasculitis or perhaps of collagen disease rather than of viral infection—an earlier theory. Behçet's syndrome, together with disseminated lupus erythematosus and pemphigus, is included in the differential diagnosis of recurrent aphthous ulcers of the oral or vaginal mucosa. There is no specific therapy—only palliative treatment. Systemic corticosteroids have provided the most consistent relief. Patients with Behçet's syndrome may require consultation and long-term management by a dermatologist.

VIRAL INFECTIONS OF THE VULVA & VAGINA

Systemic viral infections in children, eg, varicella and rubeola, may involve the skin and mucosa of the vulva. The principal viruses that affect the vulva and vagina are DNA viruses, primarily of the hervesvirus, poxvirus, and papovavirus types. In adults, the principal viral infections of the lower genital tract are herpes genitalis, herpes zoster, molluscum contagiosum, condyloma acuminatum, cytomegalovirus, and vaccinia.

1. HERPES GENITALIS

Herpesvirus hominis infection of the lower genital tract (herpes genitalis) may be the most common sexually transmitted disease. It has been reported that about 10% of women seen in private practice demonstrate serologic evidence of prior exposure to the virus. The infection is acquired in early adult life with the onset of sexual activity. Approximately 85% of primary infections are secondary to herpesvirus hominis type 2, and the remainder are caused by type 1. Despite the presence of adequate humoral and cell-mediated immunity, the DNA viruses of the herpes group reactivate periodically. Between recurrent infections, the virus persists in a latent phase in sensory sacral ganglia. Type 2 virus has been recovered from the cervices of asymptomatic women and from the urethras and prostates of asymptomatic men. The risk of transmission to a sexual partner or newborn is slight in the absence of symptoms. The virus frequently is associated with other sexually transmitted diseases.

Herpetic genital infection is either primary or secondary. The incubation period of primary infection is 2–7 days. Prodromal symptoms of tingling or itching occur shortly before vesicular eruptions appear. The vesicles rapidly erode, resulting in painful ulcers distributed in small patches, or they may involve most of the vulvar surfaces (Fig 9–6). Urinary symptoms develop, eg, dysuria or even urinary retention that requires catheter drainage of the bladder. Bilateral inguinal adenopathy, fever, and malaise accompany severe infections. Herpetic cervicitis causes a profuse

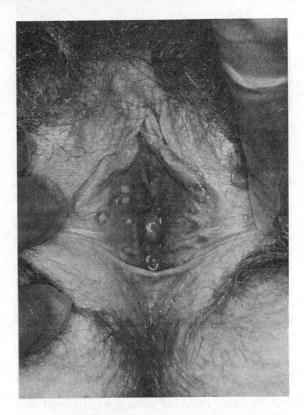

Figure 9–6. Ulcerating vesicles of herpes genitalis.

watery discharge. Rarely, disseminated infection follows a primary herpesvirus type 2 genital infection. Considering the number of women who have positive herpes antibody titers, the initial infection in some must be asymptomatic. Lesions may persist for 2–6 weeks, after which healing occurs without scarring. Virus can be recovered from vesicle fluid during the acute phase, but organisms usually cannot be recovered 2 weeks after healing of the primary lesions. Approximately 85% of patients develop antibodies to type 2 virus within 21 days of primary infection.

Type 2 virus is much more likely to cause recurrent genital disease than is type 1. Recurrent symptomatic disease is more frequent in men than in women, although clinical recurrence may not be as easily detectable in women. Approximately 50% of patients will have a recurrence within 6 months of primary infection; the median time to recurrence in women is approximately 40–45 days. Virus is usually not recoverable within 7 days after healing of recurrent lesions.

In recurrent disease, ulcers tend to be smaller, fewer in number, and confined to one area of the vulva, vagina, or cervix. Extragenital sites, such as fingers, buttocks, and trunk (eczema herpeticum), have been described. Prodromal symptoms of itching and burning at the site of future lesions and occasionally pain radiating to the back and down the legs have been reported. Inguinal adenopathy and systemic symptoms ordinarily do not recur. Healing is usually complete in 1–3 weeks. Why periodic active viral replication causes shedding of infectious virus and recurrent or reactivated clinical disease is unknown. Exogenous factors known to contribute to reactivation of herpesvirus include fever, emotional stress, and menstruation. Immunosuppressed patients are prone to develop extensive local disease and systemic dissemination. Whether frequent coitus promotes recurrent disease is unproved.

Primary infection can usually be distinguished from recurrent disease on the basis of history and clinical findings. Virus is easily recoverable from the acute lesion—if facilities for virus culture are available. Otherwise, a scraping taken from the ulcer and stained as a Papanicolaou smear often will demonstrate characteristic giant cells indicative of viral infection. Nonetheless, these may be confused with malignant cells even by a pathologist. Other cells demonstrate a homogeneous "ground-glass" appearance of cellular nuclei with numerous small intracellular, scattered basophilic particles and acidophilic inclusion bodies. Unsuspected disease is occasionally detected incidentally on a cervical or vaginal smear. An antibody titer may indicate prior exposure to the virus, and if repeated in 3 weeks, significant elevation will confirm acute infection.

An infant delivered through a birth canal with active lesions has approximately a 50% chance of developing disseminated herpesvirus infection, whereupon the mortality rate is about 50%. Of the survivors, most will suffer serious permanent central nervous system damage. If there is a prenatal history of herpes infection in the mother or her sexual partner, or if active lesions develop in either during pregnancy, cervical viral cultures should be taken weekly, starting at 34 weeks' gestation. Two negative cultures are significant. Serologic tests are unreliable, and repeat cervical vaginal cytologic studies should detect about 75% of culture-proved infections. Some have suggested that such studies are unnecessary in the absence of clinically detectable disease. However, other studies of affected infants have reported that only 30% were born to mothers with a history of genital herpes at the time of delivery. Cesarean section has been suggested if disease is detected by clinical or laboratory examination and the membranes have been ruptured for less than 4 hours. In some reviews, as many as 50% of infants were born prematurely, implicating the virus as a possible cause of premature labor. Rarely, cesarean section may fail to prevent infection in the newborn because of ascending infection, even with intact membranes, or because of viremia of primary disease. Potentially infected newborns should be isolated in the nursery. Control requires prevention or cure of sexually transmitted viral diseases.

The lesions of herpesvirus infection are self-limiting, and they heal spontaneously unless they become secondarily infected. No specific treatment has been effective in controlled studies. Photoinactivation therapy was used at one time but is now sus-

pected of having the potential to induce local cancer. Certain antiviral chemotherapeutic agents are being developed, most of them directed at enzymes specific to each virus. Acyclovir (Zovirax) is discussed on p 1003.

Treatment is symptomatic and includes good genital hygiene, loose-fitting undergarments, cool compresses or sitz baths, and oral analgesics. Local analgesics are contraindicated because they may cause severe contact dermatitis. Secondary infection may be prevented by applications of antibiotic ointments or povidone-iodine. An occasional primary infection will be sufficiently severe to require hospitalization and an indwelling catheter because of urinary retention. One cannot prevent recurrent infections. It is important to provide counseling concerning the natural history of this disease to allay undue anxiety and to avoid transmission.

Avoidance of direct contact with active lesions is one sure way to prevent spread of the disease. However, contact with an individual with subclinical disease must result in some primary infections. The general rules for prevention of dissemination are as follows: (1) Precautions are unnecessary in the absence of active lesions. (2) Small lesions situated away from the oral or vaginal orifices may be covered with adhesive or paper tape during coitus. (3) In the presence of active lesions, whether or not the partner contracts the disease depends upon previous exposure to herpes. A nonimmune partner usually will be infected. If a regular partner has had genital herpes or has not been infected after prolonged exposure, no precautions will be necessary. If a casual partner has had a history of genital herpes, a contraceptive cream or foam should be used, followed by genital cleansing with soap and water. If a partner has no past history of genital herpes, a condom should be used.

2. HERPES ZOSTER
(Shingles)

Zoster is an inflammatory disorder in which a painful eruption of groups of vesicles is distributed over an area of skin corresponding to the course of one or more peripheral sensory nerves. The causative agent is varicella-zoster virus latent for years in an individual with a history of chickenpox in childhood. The lesion is commonly unilateral and not infrequently attacks one buttock or thigh or the vulva on one side. The vesicles may rupture and crust over, although they usually dry, forming a scab that ultimately separates. The primary purposes of treatment are alleviation of pain, resolution of vesicles, and prevention of secondary infection and ulceration.

3. MOLLUSCUM CONTAGIOSUM

These benign epithelial virus-induced tumors are dome-shaped, often umbilicated, and vary in size up to

1 cm. The lesions are often multiple and are mildly contagious. The microscopic appearance is characterized by numerous inclusion bodies (molluscum bodies) in the cytoplasm of the cells. Each lesion may be treated by desiccation, freezing, or curettage and chemical cauterization of the base.

4. CONDYLOMA ACUMINATUM

Condylomata acuminata (venereal genital warts) are caused by a virus of the papovavirus group transmitted by genital contact. Papillary growths small at first tend to coalesce and form large cauliflowerlike masses that proliferate profusely during pregnancy. Management is discussed in Chapter 15.

INFESTATIONS OF THE VULVA & VAGINA*

1. PEDICULOSIS PUBIS

The crab louse *(Pthirus pubis)* is transmitted through sexual contact or from shared infected bedding or clothing. The louse eggs are laid at the base of a hair shaft near the skin. The eggs hatch in 7–9 days, and the louse must attach to the skin of the host to survive. Intense pubic and anogenital itching results. Minute pale-brown insects and their ova may be seen attached to terminal hair shafts. Treatment is with gamma benzene hexachloride (Kwell) cream, 1%, left on for 12–24 hours and then removed by washing. The treatment may be repeated in 4 days if necessary. Treat all contacts and sterilize clothing that has been in contact with the infested area.

2. SCABIES

Sarcoptes scabiei causes intractable itching and excoriation of the skin surface in the vicinity of minute skin burrows where parasites have deposited ova. The itch mite is transmitted, often directly, from infected persons. The patient should take a hot soapy bath, scrubbing the burrows and encrusted areas thoroughly. Gamma benzene hexachloride (Kwell) cream or lotion (1%) should be applied to the entire body from the neck down, with particular attention to the hands and wrists, axillas, breasts, and anogenital region. The treatment should be repeated in 24 hours but without a bath. Twenty-four hours later, a second bath should be taken and all potentially infected clothing or bedding washed or dry-cleaned. All contacts or persons in the family must be treated in the same way to prevent reinfection. Therapy should be repeated in 10–14 days if new lesions develop.

3. ENTEROBIASIS
(Pinworm, Seatworm)

Enterobius vermicularis infection is common in children. Nocturnal perineal itching is described by the patient, and perianal excoriation may be observed. Apply adhesive cellulose tape (Scotch Tape) to the anal region, stick the tape to a glass slide, and examine under the microscope for ova. Insist that the patient wash her hands and scrub her nails after each defecation. Underclothes must be boiled.

Apply ammoniated mercury ointment to the perineal region twice daily for relief of itching. Pinworms succumb to systemic treatment with pyrantel pamoate, mebendazole, or pyrvinium pamoate.

MYCOTIC INFECTIONS OF THE FEMALE GENITAL TRACT*

1. FUNGAL DERMATITIS
(Dermatophytoses)

Tinea cruris is a superficial fungal infection of the genitocrural area that is more common in men than women. The most common organisms are *Trichophyton mentagrophytes* and *Trichophyton rubrum*. The initial lesions usually are on the upper inner thighs and are well circumscribed, erythematous, dry scaly areas that coalesce. Scratching causes lichenification and a gross appearance similar to neurodermatitis. The diagnosis depends upon microscopic examination (as for *Candida*); culture on Sabouraud's medium is final proof. Treatment with 1% haloprogin or tolnaftate (Tinactin) is effective.

Tinea versicolor usually involves the skin of the trunk, although occasionally the vulvar skin is involved. The lesions are usually multiple and may have a red, brown, or yellowish appearance. The diagnostic studies are as outlined for other fungal infections. Treatment with selenium sulfide suspension (Selsun) daily for 5–7 days is usually curative.

2. DEEP CELLULITIS CAUSED BY FUNGI

Blastomycosis and **actinomycosis** are examples of deep mycoses that usually affect internal organs but may also involve the skin. Involvement of the vulvar skin in these diseases is very rare in the USA. The diagnosis is usually made by a process of exclusion of the granulomatous venereal diseases, tuberculosis, and other causes of chronic infection by laboratory means.

Treatment of blastomycosis with amphotericin B or hydroxystilbamidine is not very satisfactory. Actinomycosis can usually be treated successfully with penicillin.

---

*Trichomoniasis is discussed on p 187.

*Candidiasis is discussed on p 183.

OTHER INFECTIONS OF THE VULVA & VAGINA

1. IMPETIGO

Impetigo is caused by hemolytic *Staphylococcus aureus* or streptococci. The disease is autoinoculable and spreads rapidly to various parts of the body, including the vulva. Thin-walled vesicles and bullae develop that display reddened edges and crusted surfaces after rupture. The disease is common in children, particularly on the face, hands, and vulva.

The patient must be isolated and the blebs incised or crusts removed aseptically. Neomycin or bacitracin should be applied twice a day for 1 week. Bathing with an antibacterial soap is recommended.

2. FURUNCULOSIS

Vulvar folliculitis is due to a staphylococcal infection of hair follicles. Furunculosis occurs if the infection spreads into the perifollicular tissues to produce a localized cellulitis. Some follicular lesions are palpable as tender subcutaneous nodules that resolve without suppuration. A furuncle begins as a hard, tender subcutaneous nodule that ruptures through the skin, discharging blood and purulent material. After expulsion of a core of necrotic tissue, the lesion heals. New furuncles may appear sporadically over a period of years.

Minor infections may be treated by applications of topical antibiotic lotions. Deeper infections may be brought to a head with hot soaks, after which the pustule should be incised and drained. Appropriate systemic antibiotics are warranted when extensive furunculosis is noted.

3. ERYSIPELAS

Erysipelas is a rapidly spreading erythematous lesion of the skin caused by invasion of the superficial lymphatics by beta-hemolytic streptococci. Erysipelas of the vulva is exceedingly rare and is most commonly seen after trauma to the vulva or a surgical procedure. Systemic symptoms of chills, fever, and malaise associated with an erythematous vulvitis suggest the diagnosis. Vesicles and bullae may appear, and erythematous streaks leading to the regional lymph nodes are typical.

The patient should be placed at bed rest and given systemic (preferably parenteral) penicillin or tetracycline orally in large doses.

4. HIDRADENITIS

Hidradenitis suppurativa is a refractory infection of the apocrine sweat glands, usually caused by staphylococci or streptococci. The apocrine sweat glands of the vulva become active after puberty. Inspissation of secretory material and secondary infection may be related to occlusion of the ducts. Initially, multiple pruritic subcutaneous nodules appear that eventually develop into abscesses and rupture. The process tends to involve the skin of the entire vulva, resulting in multiple abscesses and chronic draining sinuses. Treatment early in the disease consists of drainage and administration of antibiotics based on organism sensitivity tests. Severe chronic infections may not respond to medical therapy, and the involved skin and subcutaneous tissues must be removed down to the deep fascia. This may necessitate a complete vulvectomy. The area will not heal after primary closure; therefore, the wound must be left open and allowed to heal by second intention.

5. TUBERCULOSIS
(Usually Vulvovaginal Lupus Vulgaris)

Pudendal tuberculosis is manifested by chronic, minimally painful, exudative "sores" that are tender, reddish, raised, moderately firm and nodular, with central "apple jelly"–like contents. Ulcerative, undermined, necrotic discharging lesions develop later. There is some tendency toward healing with heavy scarring. Induration and sinus formation are common in the scrofulous type of infection. Cancer and venereal disease must be ruled out and tuberculosis sought elsewhere.

Wet compresses of aluminum acetate (Burow's) solution are helpful. Systemic antituberculosis chemotherapy should be given.

VULVAR DYSTROPHIES

Vulvar dystrophies represent a spectrum of atrophic and hypertrophic lesions caused by a diverse number of stimuli that result in circumscribed or diffuse "white lesions" of the vulva. The lesions do not necessarily have a uniform microscopic appearance throughout, and there may be areas of dysplasia merging with frank cancer. Multiple biopsies are therefore necessary, and the toluidine blue test may be of assistance in delineating areas of maximum epithelial hyperactivity most suitable for biopsy. These lesions have been classified as shown in Table 9–2.

Clinical Findings

A. Hypertrophic Dystrophies: Benign epithelial thickening and hyperkeratosis may be the result of chronic vulvovaginal infections or other causes of chronic irritation. During the acute phase, as in diabetic vulvitis, the lesions may be red and moist, evidence of secondary infection. As epithelial thickening develops, the environment of the vulva causes maceration and a raised white lesion that may be circumscribed or diffuse and may involve any portion of the vulva, adjacent thighs, perineum, or perianal skin.

Table 9—2. Classification of vulvar dystrophies adopted by the International Society for the Study of Vulvar Disease.

	Clinical Features	Histologic Features
Lichen sclerosus	Pruritic, thin, parchment-like "atrophic area"; introital stenosis.	Thin, loss of rete, homogenization, inflammatory infiltrate.
Hyperplastic*	Pruritic, thick, gray or white plaques on skin or mucosa.	Acanthosis, hyperkeratosis, inflammatory infiltrate.
Mixed*	Areas compatible with both forms may be present at the same time.	(See above.)

*Atypia may accompany hyperplastic dystrophy and is graded as mild, moderate, or severe.

These lesions have been designated **lichen simplex chronicus** or **neurodermatitis.**

Either intraepithelial or invasive malignancies may appear as a circumscribed, raised white lesion of the vulvar skin or as multifocal areas of malignancy in a diffuse hypertrophic lesion. Differentiation can only be achieved by evaluating multiple biopsies. Whether or not a hypertrophic white lesion is a premalignant disorder is debatable. Patients must be reexamined periodically, and one should not hesitate to take additional biopsy specimens. Extended observation of lesser degrees of dysplasia is warranted, but excision of the more advanced lesion is indicated.

B. Atrophic Dystrophies: With aging, there is a decrease in endogenous estrogen, and atrophic changes in the vulvar skin and subdermal tissues usually occur some years after advanced atrophy of the vaginal mucous membrane. There will be contracture of the vaginal introitus, and the skin becomes thin, fragile, and easily traumatized. The chief symptoms are dysuria, pruritus, and dyspareunia.

Lichen sclerosus et atrophicus is a dermatologic disorder of unknown origin and the most common cause of an atrophic dystrophy. The vulva is the skin surface most frequently affected and may be the only one, although the skin of the back, the axillas, beneath the breasts, the neck, and the arms may be affected also. The cause is unknown. White women over age 65 are most often affected, although the disease does occur in younger women. During the acute phase, the lesion may have a reddish or purple appearance and classically involves the vulva, perineum, and perianal area in an hourglass pattern (Fig 9—7). The skin is thin, wrinkled, and has a cigarette-paper appearance. As the disease progresses, the vulvar structures contract and the labia minora blend into the labia majora. Although the process is primarily one of atrophy of the skin, areas of dysplasia and invasive cancer may develop, and suspicious areas must be biopsied (Fig 9—8). The chief symptom is intense pruritus.

Diagnosis of Dystrophic Lesions

Initial evaluation of the patient with a white lesion of the vulva must include inspection of other body

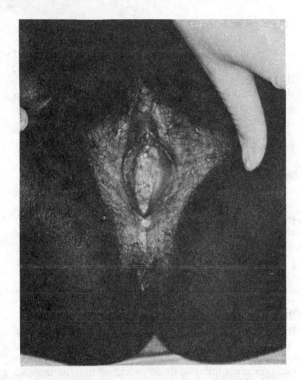

Figure 9—7. Early lesion of lichen sclerosus et atrophicus—typical hourglass configuration.

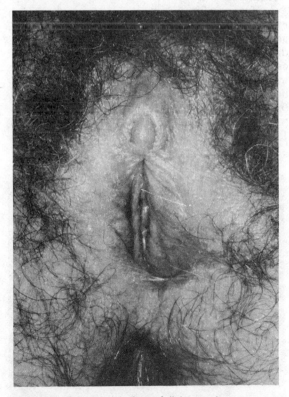

Figure 9—8. Advanced lesion of lichen sclerosus et atrophicus. The labia minora and prepuce of the clitoris have blended into the labial skin. Focal dysplasia was present in the posterior third of the right labium majus.

surfaces and a complete gynecologic examination. One or more biopsies should be taken using the toluidine blue test to assist in determining the most appropriate sites. All of these conditions are chronic; therefore, periodic reexamination is indicated, and additional biopsies should be taken of areas that appear to have changed in appearance and become particularly hypertrophic.

Pathology

Definitive diagnosis depends upon histologic examination of biopsy specimens. Characteristic microscopic findings in hypertrophic dystrophies (lichen simplex chronicus) are hyperkeratosis and acanthosis, producing thickening of the epithelium and elongation of the rete pegs. Atypical hyperplasia, or carcinoma in situ, is characterized by a pronounced degree of pleomorphism and loss of cellular polarity in the epithelium.

The microscopic appearance of lichen sclerosus et atrophicus is typical. In the well-developed lesion, there is hyperkeratosis, epithelial atrophy, and flattening of the rete pegs. Beneath the epidermis, there is a zone of homogenized collagenous tissue that is acellular and pink in appearance (Fig 9–9). Neoplastic changes are similar to those described in hypertrophic lesions.

Treatment

Hypertrophic and atrophic lesions are treated in essentially the same manner. Pruritus, dyspareunia, and urinary symptoms resulting from estrogen withdrawal respond to local applications of estrogenic creams (see section on atrophic vaginitis). Specific treatment should be administered for vaginal infections. Topical application of a corticosteroid such as 0.01% fluocinolone acetonide cream has proved helpful in hypertrophic lesions. Application of a mixture of 1% hydrocortisone and 2–3% testosterone 3–4 times

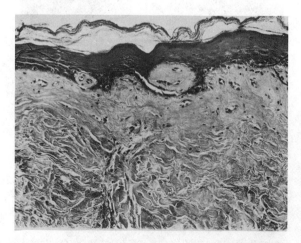

Figure 9–9. Microscopic appearance of lichen sclerosus et atrophicus characterized by hyperkeratosis, flattened epidermis, and hyalinization of the dermis.

daily has been particularly beneficial in the treatment of lichen sclerosus et atrophicus. Patients should be warned that application of excessive quantities of a testosterone preparation may cause systemic virilizing effects in addition to an increase in hair growth. If an area of dysplasia, carcinoma in situ, or invasive cancer is detected, therapy should be administered as recommended in the section on vulvar cancer (see p 208).

Prognosis

In the absence of malignant epithelial changes, the principal goal is to relieve symptoms, mainly pruritus. Symptoms are usually relieved, but a significant change in the histopathologic appearance of the skin seldom is achieved. Periodic reexamination is necessary to detect any malignant changes.

BENIGN CYSTIC TUMORS

Clinical Findings

A. Cysts of Epidermal Origin: Cysts of epidermal origin are lined with squamous epithelium and filled with oily material and desquamated epithelial cells. Epidermal inclusion cysts may result from traumatic suturing of skin fragments during closure of the vulvar mucosa and skin after trauma or episiotomy. However, most epidermal cysts arise from occlusion of pilosebaceous ducts. These cysts are usually small, solitary, and asymptomatic.

B. Sebaceous and Sweat Gland Cysts:

1. Sebaceous cysts–The occlusion of a duct to a sebaceous gland results in accumulation of sebaceous material and develops into a sebaceous cyst. These cysts are frequently multiple and almost always involve the labia majora. They are generally asymptomatic; however, acutely infected cysts may require incision and drainage.

2. Apocrine sweat gland cysts–Apocrine sweat glands are numerous in the skin of the labia majora and mons pubis. They become functional after puberty. Occlusion of the ducts results in an extremely pruritic microcystic disease called **Fox-Fordyce disease.** Chronic infection in the apocrine glands, usually with streptococci or staphylococci, results in multiple subcutaneous abscesses and draining sinuses. The condition is called **hidradenitis suppurativa.**

A diverse group of benign cystic or solid tumors of apocrine sweat gland origin present as small subcutaneous, often asymptomatic tumors. Hidradenoma and syringoma are examples of these tumors.

C. Less Common Cysts: A variety of other infrequent cystic vulvar tumors must be considered in differential diagnosis. Anteriorly, a Skene duct cyst or urethral diverticulum may be visible, suggesting a vulvar tumor. An inguinal hernia may extend into the labium majus, causing a large cystic dilatation. Occlusion of a persistent processus vaginalis (canal of Nuck) may cause a cystic tumor or hydrocele. Dilatation of müllerian duct vestiges usually produces cystic vaginal tumors; rarely, the vaginal introitus is involved.

Supernumerary mammary tissue that persists in the labia majora may form a cystic or solid tumor or even an adenocarcinoma; engorgement of such tissue in the pregnant patient can be symptomatic.

Diagnosis & Treatment

The diagnosis of small cystic structures on the vulva is ordinarily made by clinical examination or by excision biopsy, which also serves as treatment.

BARTHOLIN'S DUCT CYST & ABSCESS

Obstruction of the main duct of Bartholin's gland results in retention of secretions and cystic dilatation. The gonococcus is an important cause of obstruction. However, inspissated mucus and congenital narrowing of the duct may also be causes. Secondary infection may result in recurrent abscess formation.

A gland and duct are located deep in the posterior third of each labium majus. Enlargement in the postmenopausal patient should arouse a suspicion of cancer, and biopsy is indicated.

Clinical Findings

Acute symptoms are ordinarily the result of infection, which results in pain, tenderness, and dyspareunia. The surrounding tissues become edematous and inflamed, and a fluctuant mass usually is palpable.

Small, noninflamed cysts are asymptomatic and of little consequence unless progressive enlargement compromises the vaginal introitus or acute infection intervenes. Unless there is an extensive inflammatory process, few systemic symptoms or signs of infection are likely.

Treatment

Primary treatment consists of drainage of the infected cyst or abscess, preferably by marsupialization (Fig 9–10). Simple incision and drainage may provide temporary relief. However, the opening tends to become obstructed, and recurrent cystic dilatation and infection may result. Appropriate antibiotics should be given if considerable surrounding inflammation develops.

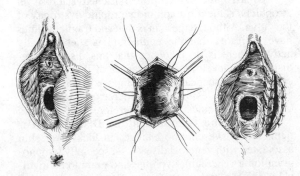

Figure 9–10. Marsupialization of Bartholin's cyst.

Prognosis

Recurrent infection resulting in cystic dilatation of the duct is the rule unless a permanent opening for drainage is established.

BENIGN SOLID TUMORS

A benign solid tumor may be an incidental finding at the time of pelvic examination, or it may be of sufficient size to interfere with function or produce symptoms due to irritation and bleeding. The diagnosis should be established by excision or biopsy. The clinical features of a representative sample of solid vulvar tumors will be described.

Acrochordon

An acrochordon is a flesh-colored, soft polypoid tumor of the vulvar skin that has been called a fibroepithelial polyp or simply a skin tag. The tumor does not become malignant and is of no importance unless the polypoid structure is traumatized, causing bleeding. Simple excision biopsy in the office is ordinarily adequate therapy.

Pigmented Nevi

Without exception, pigmented lesions of the vulva or vagina suggestive of nevi should be removed by wide excision, or a representative portion of the tumor should be biopsied to diagnose or exclude melanoma. A nevus on the vulvar skin may be flat, slightly elevated, papillomatous, dome-shaped, or pedunculated. Melanomas of the vulva are uncommon neoplasms constituting only 1–3% of vulvar cancers. They are extremely aggressive malignancies and may arise from pigmented nevi of the vulva. Adequate excision of the nevus must include 0.5–1 cm of surrounding skin and subcutaneous tissue. **Melanosis** of the vaginal mucosa or vulvar skin is a benign, flat, darkly pigmented lesion that cannot be differentiated from a nevus without histologic examination.

Leiomyoma, Fibroma, Lipoma

Tumors of mesodermal origin occur infrequently on the vulva, but they can become very large. A **leiomyoma** arises from muscle in the round ligament and appears as a firm, symmetric, freely movable tumor deep in the substance of the labium majus.

Fibromas arise from proliferation of fibroblasts and vary in size from small subcutaneous nodules found incidentally to large polypoid tumors. Large tumors often undergo myxomatous degeneration and are very soft and cystic to palpation.

Lipomas, consisting of a combination of mature fat cells and connective tissue, cannot be differentiated from degenerated fibromas except by histopathologic examination.

Small tumors can be removed under local anesthesia in the office; large ones require general anesthesia and operating room facilities. The diagnosis of sarcoma depends upon histologic examination.

Neurofibromas

These tumors are fleshy polypoid lesions and may be solitary, solid tumors of the vulva or associated with generalized neurofibromatosis (Recklinghausen's disease). They arise from the neural sheath and are usually small lesions of no consequence. Multiple disfiguring tumors of the vulva may interfere with sexual function and thus require vulvectomy.

Granular Cell Myoblastoma (Schwannoma)

This tumor is usually a solitary, painless, slow-growing, infiltrating but benign tumor of neural sheath origin, most commonly found in the tongue or integument, although about 7% involve the vulva. The usual picture is of small subcutaneous nodules 1–4 cm in greatest diameter. With increasing size, they erode through the surface and result in an ulcerative lesion that may be confused with cancer. The margins of the tumor are indistinct, and wide local excision is necessary to completely resect cells extending into contiguous tissues. The area of resection must then be periodically reexamined and secondary excision performed promptly if recurrence is suspected.

CANCER OF THE VULVA

Essentials of Diagnosis

- Occurs in postmenopausal women.
- Long history of vulvar irritation with pruritus, local discomfort, and bloody discharge.
- Early lesions may appear as chronic vulvar dermatitis.
- Late lesions appear as a lump in the labium, a large cauliflower growth, or a hard ulcerated area in the vulva.
- Biopsy is necessary to make the diagnosis.

General Considerations

Cancer of the vulva may be intraepithelial or invasive and can arise from the skin, subcutaneous tissues, urethra, glandular elements of the vulva, or the mucosa of the lower third of the vagina. Approximately 85–90% of these tumors are epidermoid cancers. Less common tumors are extramammary Paget's disease, carcinoma of Bartholin's gland, basal cell carcinoma, melanoma, sarcoma, and metastatic cancers from other sites.

Cancer of the vulva is responsible for approximately 5% of gynecologic malignancies. Whites are affected more frequently than nonwhites. Vulvar cancer is primarily a disease of postmenopausal women, with a peak incidence in the 60s. In general, the mean age of patients with carcinoma in situ of the vulva is approximately 10 years less than that for patients with invasive cancer. The number of diagnoses of intraepithelial cancer of the vulva in women in their 20s and 30s has increased remarkably in recent years coincidentally with an increase in the frequency of diagnosis of dysplasia and carcinoma in situ of the cervix. Occasionally, a vulvar cancer—usually sarcoma botryoides of the vagina or vulva—is diagnosed in a young girl.

The coincidence of carcinoma of the vulva and pregnancy is rare. Treatment can be administered during pregnancy without jeopardizing the fetus.

Considering that cancer of the vulva is a disease of a body surface readily accessible to diagnostic procedures, early diagnosis should be the rule. This is not the case, however, and a 6- to 12-month delay in reporting symptoms or discovery of a tumor is common. Physicians have been reluctant to biopsy the vulva and have often administered various forms of medical therapy for months before performing a biopsy and confirming the diagnosis. Despite the advanced age of many of these patients and the frequent finding of a moderately large tumor, the disease is usually amenable to surgical therapy. A 5-year survival rate of about 65% is reported by large centers.

Etiology

The vulvar skin is one component of the anogenital epithelium extending from the cervix to the perineum and perianal skin. The lower genital tract epithelium is of common cloacogenic origin and is responsive to endocrine stimulation. Neoplasia of the vulvar skin is often associated with multiple foci of dysplasia in the lower genital tract. The inciting agent has not been identified, but a sexually transmitted agent such as herpesvirus hominis type 2 is highly suspect.

Most patients with carcinoma of the vulva give no history of predisposing conditions. Associated disorders found most frequently with carcinoma of the vulva are obesity, hypertension, and chronic vulvar irritation secondary to diabetes mellitus, granulomatous venereal disease, or vulvar dystrophy.

A. Hypertrophic Vulvar Dystrophies: The hypertrophic vulvar dystrophies are characterized by epithelial thickening secondary to chronic irritation caused by a variety of stimuli. In some patients, there is epithelial dysplasia noted by biopsy on the first examination, and these women have a higher incidence of occurrence of invasive cancer. Long-term prospective studies have suggested an approximate incidence of neoplasia of 5% in patients who had no dysplasia at the beginning of the study period.

B. Atrophic Dystrophies: Lichen sclerosis et atrophicus is the most common atrophic dystrophy of the vulva. Although the skin is thin and fragile, studies have indicated that the epithelium is metabolically active. There is no evidence that this disorder predisposes to development of cancer of the vulva. An epidermoid cancer can be superimposed upon the basically atrophic lesion. Periodic reexamination and biopsy of suspicious areas is therefore necessary.

C. Chronic Granulomatous Disorders: Patients who have chronic changes in the vulvar skin associated with venereal disease—especially lymphogranuloma venereum, syphilis, and granuloma inguinale—have a higher incidence of cancer of the vulva (Fig 9–11). Whether or not condyloma acuminatum

Figure 9–11. Chronic hypertrophic skin changes secondary to granuloma inguinale.

predisposes to development of cancer is unclear. However, evidence from African countries suggests that it does. Vulvar condylomatosis in postmenopausal patients should be carefully differentiated from verrucous carcinoma.

D. Chronic Irritation: Persistent rubbing or scratching of the vulva because of pruritus vulvae may play a part in the development of vulvar cancer. Chronic vulvovaginal candidiasis, which is common in diabetic women, may be a predisposing factor.

E. Extramammary Paget's Disease: Paget's disease of the skin is an intraepithelial neoplasm. Reports of long-term survivals suggest that the in situ stage of the disease persists for a long time or that invasive disease is a different clinicopathologic entity. Wide excision of the lesion and thorough microscopic examination of the specimen must be performed to rule out an invasive component.

F. Pigmented Moles: All pigmented lesions of the vulvar skin and vaginal mucosa must be removed by excision biopsy to establish an early diagnosis of melanoma. A disproportionate number of melanomas in women occur on the vulva, where the disease is exceptionally virulent. Vulvar nevi are invariably of the junctional variety.

G. Irradiation: The carcinogenic potential of irradiation treatment of nonspecific pruritus vulvae or pelvic cancer has been postulated but never proved.

H. Intraepithelial Carcinoma: The frequency with which dysplasia or carcinoma in situ of the vulvar skin progresses to invasive cancer of the vulva has not been established. Careful evaluation of tissue removed for treatment of invasive epidermoid cancer will reveal an approximately 50% incidence of intraepithelial cancer in the adjacent skin.

Pathology

The gross appearance of vulvar cancer depends upon the origin and histologic type. These tumors progress by local extension and involvement of adjacent organs and, with few exceptions, by lymphatic permeation or embolism. The primary route of lymphatic spread is by way of the superficial inguinal, deep femoral, and external iliac lymph nodes (Fig 9–12). Contralateral spread may occur as a result of the rich intercommunicating lymphatic system of the vulvar skin. Direct extension to the deep pelvic lymph nodes, primarily the obturator nodes, occurs in about 3% of patients and seems to be related to midline involvement around the clitoris, urethra, or rectum or from cancer of a Bartholin gland situated deep in the substance of the labium majus. Extension of the tumor to the lower and middle third of the vagina may also allow access of tumor cells to lymph channels leading to the deep pelvic lymph nodes.

The gross and histologic appearance of the various types of vulvar cancers are as follows:

A. Epidermoid Cancer: Epidermoid cancer is by far the most common type of tumor and most frequently involves the anterior half of the vulva. In approximately 65% of patients, the tumor arises in the labia majora and minora; and in 25% the clitoris is involved. Over one-third of tumors involve the vulva bilaterally or are midline tumors. These tumors are

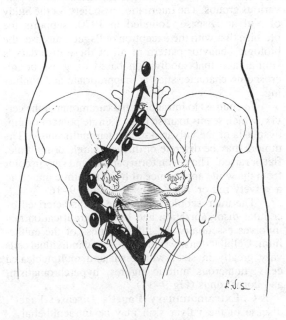

Figure 9–12. Lymphatic spread of cancer of the vulva.

most frequently associated with nodal metastases and in particular bilateral nodal metastases. Midline tumors that involve the perineum do not worsen the outlook unless they extend into the vagina or to the anus and rectum.

Epidermoid cancer of the vulva varies in appearance from a large, exophytic cauliflowerlike lesion (Fig 9–13) to a small ulcer crater superimposed on a dystrophic lesion of the vulvar skin (Fig 9–14). Ulcerative lesions may begin as a raised, flat, white area of hypertrophic skin that subsequently undergoes ulceration. Exophytic lesions may become extremely large, undergo necrosis, become secondarily infected, and cause a very unpleasant odor. A third variety arises as a slightly elevated, red velvety tumor that gradually spreads over the vulvar skin. There does not seem to be a positive correlation between the gross appearance of the tumor and either histologic grade or frequency of nodal metastases. The primary determinant of nodal metastases is tumor size.

Epidermoid cancers may be graded histologically from I to III. Grade I tumors are well differentiated, often forming keratin pearls; grade II tumors are moderately well differentiated; and grade III tumors are composed of poorly differentiated cells. The extent of underlying inflammatory cell infiltration into the stroma surrounding the invasive tumor is quite variable. The histologic grade of the tumor may be of some significance in small tumors less than 2 cm in diameter. However, the gross size of the tumor is the most significant factor in prognosis.

B. Intraepithelial Cancer: By definition, intraepithelial cancer implies full-thickness malignant change of the epidermis without invasion of the underlying dermis. Bowen's disease, erythroplasia of Queyrat, and carcinoma in situ simplex are designations previously used to divide carcinomas in situ into various groups. The International Society for the Study of Vulvar Disease, founded in 1970, supports the premise that with the exception of Paget's disease, the biologic behavior pattern of all of these disorders is similar and that subdivision based on gross or microscopic characteristics is inappropriate and confusing.

In contrast to intraepithelial carcinoma of the cervix, which seems to arise from a single point of origin, dysplasia of the vulvar skin is often multicentric. The tumors may be discrete or diffuse, single or multiple, flat or raised. They even form papules and vary in color from the white appearance of hyperkeratotic tumors to a velvety red or black (Figs 9–15 and 9–16).

The microscopic appearance is characterized by cellular disorganization and loss of stratification that involves essentially the full thickness of the epithelium. Cellular density is increased, and individual cells vary greatly in size, with giant and multinucleated cells, numerous mitotic figures, hyperchromatism, and corps ronds (Fig 9–17).

C. Extramammary Paget's Disease: Paget' disease of the vulvar skin may be intraepithelial invasive. The typical Paget cell, pathognomonic of the

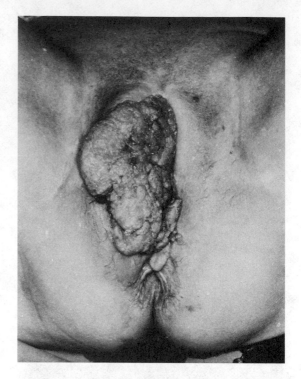

Figure 9–13. Large, exophytic epidermoid cancer of the vulva that was treated by radical vulvectomy and regional lymphadenectomy.

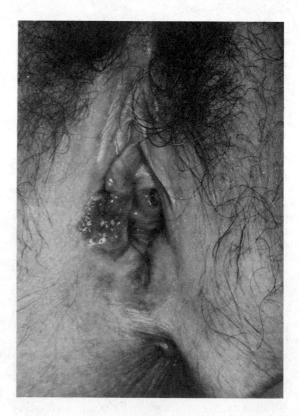

Figure 9–14. Ulcerative epidermoid cancer of the vulva.

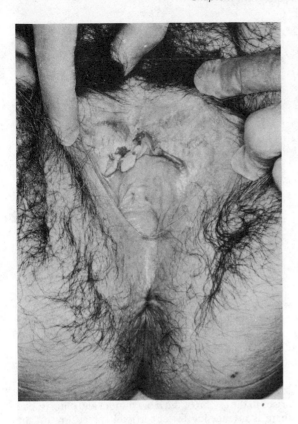

Figure 9–15. Diffuse, white carcinoma in situ of anterior vulva and clitoris.

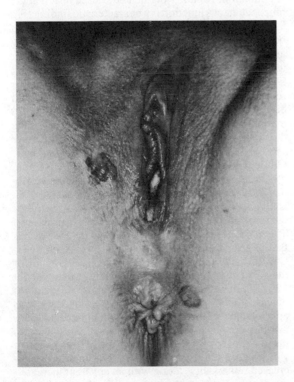

Figure 9–16. Vulvar and perianal papillary carcinoma in situ.

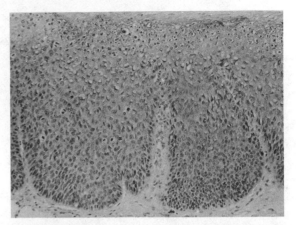

Figure 9–17. Carcinoma in situ demonstrating hyperkeratosis, acanthosis, and parakeratosis. The rete ridges are elongated and thickened, and individual cells are atypical.

disease process (Fig 9–18), apparently arises from abnormal differentiation of the cells of the basal layer of the epithelium. The appearance of malignant cells varies from that of the clear cell of the apocrine gland epithelium to a totally undifferentiated basal cell. It has been suggested that there may be an intraepithelial and an invasive variety of the disease. This theory holds that in some patients the intraepithelial stage of the disease persists for years without evidence of invasion. It is not possible to differentiate intraepithelial from potentially invasive disease in the absence of dermal invasion based upon histologic examination of the cells.

The initial lesion may be confused with a number of benign forms of chronic vulvar pruritus. The lesion appears as a pruritic, slowly spreading, velvety red discoloration of the skin that eventually becomes eczematoid in appearance with secondary maceration and development of white plaques. The lesion may spread to involve the skin of the perineum and perianal area and the adjacent skin of the thigh. The true margin

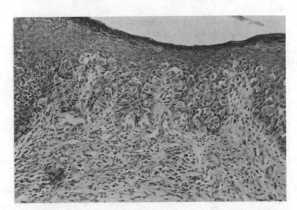

Figure 9–18. Paget's disease with typical cells in the basal layer of the epidermis.

of the disease is very difficult to determine; biopsy of normal-appearing skin adjacent to the apparent margin of the disease often reveals the presence of typical Paget's cells in the basal layer of the epidermis.

D. Carcinoma of Bartholin's Gland: Carcinoma of Bartholin's gland accounts for about 5% of vulvar cancers. Approximately half of the tumors are adenocarcinomas; the remainder are squamous or transitional cell carcinomas. About 5% of tumors represent an unusual histologic picture such as sarcoma, melanoma, or undifferentiated tumor. Adenoid cystic carcinoma is an adenocarcinoma with specific histologic and clinical characteristics.

It may be difficult by clinical examination to differentiate a tumor of Bartholin's gland or duct from a benign Bartholin duct cyst. A recurrent cyst in a postmenopausal patient must be drained and tissue from the cyst wall submitted for histologic examination. Because of the location of the lesion deep in the substance of the labium, the tumor may impinge upon the rectum and have access to lymphatic channels draining directly to the deep pelvic lymph nodes as well as the superficial channels draining to the inguinal lymph nodes.

E. Basal Cell Carcinoma: Basal cell carcinomas account for 2–3% of vulvar cancers. Most tumors are small papillomatous or elevated lesions. Some are described as pigmented tumors, moles, or simply pruritic maculopapular eruptions. These tumors arise almost exclusively in the skin of the labia majora, although an occasional one can be found elsewhere in the vulvar skin. The tumor is derived from primordial basal cells in the epidermis or hair follicles and is characterized by slow growth, local infiltration, and a tendency to recur if not totally excised. Distant metastasis via the lymphatic or blood vascular systems is unusual unless one is dealing with a basal–squamous cell tumor that has a malignant epidermoid component. Most basal cell carcinomas of the vulva are of the primordial histologic type and appear grossly as a distinct nodule on the labium majus. Other histologic varieties that may be found are the pilar, morphealike, superficially spreading, adenoid, and pigmented cell tumors.

On microscopic examination, the typical primordial type of tumor consists of nodular masses and lobules of closely packed, uniform-appearing basaloid cells with scant cytoplasm and spherical or oval dark nuclei. Peripheral margination by columnar cells is usually prominent. In larger tumor nodules, there may be areas of central degeneration and necrosis.

If a sufficiently wide local excision is not performed, there is a tendency for local recurrence, estimated to be about 20%. If a basal–squamous cell type tumor is diagnosed, appropriate therapy for invasive epidermoid cancer of the vulva should be undertaken.

F. Malignant Melanoma: About 8–11% of vulvar cancers are malignant melanomas. Since only 0.1% of all nevi in women are on vulvar skin, the disproportionate frequency of melanoma in this area may be due to the fact that nearly all vulvar nevi are of

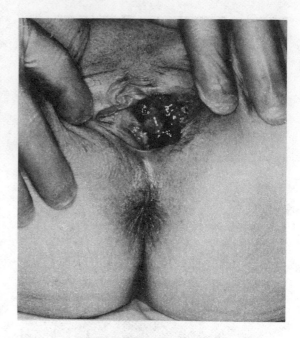

Figure 9–19. Melanoma of the vulva.

the junctional variety. This tumor most commonly arises in the region of the labia minora and clitoris, and there is a tendency for superficial spread toward the urethra and vagina. A nonpigmented melanoma may closely resemble squamous cell carcinoma on clinical examination. A darkly pigmented, raised lesion at the mucocutaneous junction is a characteristic finding (Fig 9–19); however, the degree of melanin pigmentation is quite variable, and amelanotic lesions do occur. The lesion spreads primarily through lymphatic channels, tends to metastasize early in the course of the disease, and local or remote cutaneous satellite lesions may be found. All small pigmented lesions of the vulva should be removed by excision biopsy with a 0.5- to 1-cm margin of normal skin. In the case of large tumors, the diagnosis should be confirmed by a generous biopsy.

Clinical Findings

The patient with vulvar cancer characteristically has had infrequent medical examinations. About 10% are diabetic, and 30–50% are obese or hypertensive or demonstrate other evidence of cardiovascular disease. The incidence of complicating medical illness exceeds that expected in the age group under consideration.

Invasive epidermoid cancer is a disease mainly of the seventh and eighth decades of life, though about 15% of patients are age 40 or younger. In older studies of carcinoma in situ, the average reported age was approximately 10 years younger than that recorded for patients with invasive cancer. During the last decade, the diagnosis of carcinoma in situ of the vulva in women in the third or fourth decade of life has increased remarkably, along with an apparent increased incidence of cervical neoplasia. About 20% of patients have a second primary cancer that was diagnosed prior to, at the time of, or subsequent to the diagnosis of vulvar cancer; 75% of these second primaries are in the cervix. Young patients in particular have a propensity for multicentric disease involving the entire lower genital tract.

A. Symptoms and Signs: Pruritus vulvae or a vulvar mass is the presenting complaint in over half of cases. Others will complain of bleeding or vulvar pain, whereas approximately 20% of patients in most series will have no complaints, tumor being found incidentally during routine pelvic examination. In most reported series, at least half of patients have waited 6–12 months to report symptoms or the presence of a mass. A significant number of patients, perhaps 25%, have seen a physician and received various medical treatments without benefit of a biopsy of the tumor or have undergone incomplete therapy consisting of a simple excision biopsy of an invasive tumor. The importance of performing a biopsy of any vulvar lesion cannot be overemphasized.

B. Staging: See Table 9–3.

Differential Diagnosis

The approach to the differential diagnosis of vulvar disease and exclusion of cancer depends upon an adequate biopsy. The tumor may be a diffuse white lesion, a discrete tumor, an ulcer, or diffuse papules, particularly in young women, which may not be appreciated without thorough colposcopic examination of the skin of the vulva, perineum, and perianal area.

A white lesion of the vulva must be sampled in one or more areas, using a dermatologic punch biopsy to remove a full thickness of vulvar skin. The toluidine blue test may be of value in localizing areas of epithelial hyperactivity, although dysplastic but markedly hyperkeratotic lesions do not stain well, and benign ulcers may give a false-positive stain. In the absence of epithelial dysplasia, a dystrophic lesion should be treated as recommended on p 200; however, periodic examinations and repeat biopsies are necessary.

Ulcerative lesions can be due to sexually transmitted disease such as syphilis or granuloma inguinale, pyogenic infections, a benign tumor such as granular cell myoblastoma, or viral infection such as herpes simplex or Behçet's disease.

Tumors of the vulva must be diagnosed by biopsy or excision biopsy. Isolated enlargement of a groin lymph node may require excision to establish a histologic diagnosis.

Perhaps 1–2% of young women with cervical dysplasia will be found to have multifocal disease that tends to involve the mucosa of the upper third of the vagina and the skin of the vulva, perineum, and perianal areas—the surfaces arising from a common cloacogenic origin. A spectrum of disease may be found ranging from mild dysplasia to carcinoma in situ. Involvement of skin surfaces may not be appreciated without careful inspection with and without the green colposcopy filter. The vascular pattern is often much less apparent on the vulvar skin, and the

Table 9–3. Staging of carcinoma of the vulva.*

Cases should be classified as carcinoma of the vulva when the primary site of the growth is in the vulva. Tumors present in the vulva as secondary growths from either a genital or extragenital site should be excluded from registration, as should cases of malignant melanoma. (See also carcinoma of the vagina.)

FIGO Nomenclature

Stage 0	Carcinoma in situ.
Stage I	Tumor confined to vulva—2 cm or less in diameter. Nodes are not palpable or are palpable in either groin, not enlarged, mobile (not clinically suspicious of neoplasm).
Stage II	Tumor confined to the vulva—more than 2 cm in diameter. Nodes are not palpable or are palpable in either groin, not enlarged, mobile (not clinically suspicious of neoplasm).
Stage III	Tumor of any size with (1) adjacent spread to the urethra and any or all of the vagina, the perineum, and the anus, and/or (2) nodes palpable in either or both groins (enlarged, firm, and mobile, not fixed but clinically suspicious of neoplasm).
Stage IV	Tumor of any size (1) infiltrating the bladder mucosa or the rectal mucosa or both, including the upper part of the urethral mucosa, and/or (2) fixed to the bone or other distant metastases. Fixed or ulcerated nodes in either or both groins.

TNM Nomenclature

1.1 Primary Tumor (T)
  TIS, T1, T2, T3, T4
    See corresponding FIGO stages.
1.2 Nodal Involvement (N)

NX	Not possible to assess the regional nodes.
N0	No involvement of regional nodes.
N1	Evidence of regional node involvement.
N3	Fixed or ulcerated nodes.
N4	Juxtaregional node involvement.

1.3 Distant Metastasis (M)

MX	Not assessed.
M0	No (known) distant metastasis.
M1	Distant metastasis present.
	Specify ———————————

*American Joint Committee for Cancer Staging and End-Results Reporting; Task Force on Gynecologic Sites: Staging System for Cancer at Gynecologic Sites, 1979.

lesions tend to be more hyperkeratotic. An abnormal vascular pattern is more commonly associated with a severe degree of dysplasia, carcinoma in situ, or early invasive disease. Early invasive disease in a rather extensive lesion of carcinoma in situ may be detected by identification of an area of abnormal vasculature. If dysplasia of the vulvar skin is detected in a young woman, colposcopic examination should include thorough evaluation of the cervix and upper vagina.

Complications

A. Without Treatment: It must be assumed that carcinoma in situ of the vulva will progress to invasive cancer if not treated, though there have been rare reports of postpartum spontaneous regression of multicentric, polypoid carcinoma in situ of the vulva diagnosed during pregnancy in young women. Although carcinoma in situ of the vulva is being diagnosed with increasing frequency in young women and the true biologic significance of this lesion has not been established, we are obliged to eradicate the disease if possible, using the most conservative treatment available.

Invasive cancers of the vulva progressively increase in size, encroach upon adjacent structures such as the vagina, urethra, and anus, and metastasize to the inguinal lymph nodes, which may become quite large and ulcerate through the overlying skin. Exophytic tumors can reach an exceptionally large size and become secondarily infected and necrotic, resulting in a profuse discharge and a foul odor. The enlarged inguinal lymph nodes may impinge on the lymphatic and venous drainage from the leg, resulting in chronic lymphedema and thrombophlebitis. Invasion of the base of the bladder or urethra or the rectovaginal septum can cause a fistula. Patients eventually die from hemorrhage or inanition due to locally advanced and metastatic disease.

B. With Treatment:

1. Recurrence–Carcinoma in situ of the vulva may recur at the site of excision or medical treatment, or another focus of disease may develop on the remaining vulvar or perianal skin. Periodic examinations continued indefinitely are necessary to detect a new focus of disease developing anywhere in the lower genital tract. The high incidence of a second primary tumor, particularly in the cervix, must be considered in the long-term management plan.

It is difficult to remove extramammary Paget's disease of the vulva. It has a great propensity for local recurrence, which may represent persistence of the disease or development of new disease in the remaining vulvar skin.

Local or remote persistence or recurrence of invasive cancer may be the result of undetected disease outside the treatment field or development of a new tumor. Most recurrences tend to occur within 2 years after surgery. Local recurrences may be amenable to secondary excision or radiotherapy.

2. Lymphedema–Lymphedema of varying extent occurs after a thorough deep and superficial inguinal lymphadenectomy. If edema is significant and cannot be controlled by simple measures such as elevation of the legs, a properly fitted support garment should be provided to prevent secondary changes in the skin and subcutaneous tissues. Edema from venous obstruction is uncommon and suggests a superimposed deep thrombophlebitis or recurrent tumor along the iliac or femoral veins.

Erysipelas of the lower abdomen and one or both legs is characterized by a diffuse erythematous rash over the affected superficial lymphatic that blanches with pressure, increased local heat, elevation of temperature to 39.5–40 °C (103.1–104 °F) and associated malaise and chills. Some authorities recommend a 1-year course of prophylactic penicillin or sulfonamide after a thorough lymphadenectomy.

3. Vaginal stenosis–A firm fibrotic ring will oc-

casionally develop around the vaginal introitus, particularly if vulvar cancer was associated with chronic vulvar dystrophy. Nonetheless, vaginal function is usually satisfactory, and younger women who become pregnant after vulvectomy can generally deliver vaginally with an adequate episiotomy.

4. Rectocele, cystocele, and urinary stress incontinence–Rectocele following vulvectomy can be prevented to some extent by performing a posterior colporrhaphy at the time of vulvectomy. Cystocele is usually asymptomatic if the urethrovesical angle is well supported and the hernia is not sufficiently large to cause residual urine and recurrent urinary tract infection. Permanent correction of a very large cystocele requires total vaginectomy with closure of the levator ani muscles to support the base of the bladder.

Stress urinary incontinence occasionally occurs after excision of a portion of the urethra to allow complete removal of an anterior tumor mass. Correction of the stress incontinence requires a second operative procedure, usually suprapubic urethrovesical suspension using a fascial sling.

Prevention

Because the etiologic agent causing cancer of the vulva has not been identified, specific preventive treatment is not available. Periodic gynecologic examination and excision biopsy of suspicious lesions allows early diagnosis and successful treatment. There is a place for vulvectomy in the treatment of chronic vulvar disorders that are symptomatic and have caused chronic hypertrophic changes in the vulvar skin (Fig 9–11). Chronic dystrophic lesions of the vulva must be examined periodically and biopsied when suspicious areas of epithelial thickening are detected.

Treatment

A. Surgical Measures: The primary treatment of cancer of the vulva is wide excision of the tumor and extirpation of potential routes of dissemination.

Whether the tumor is intraepithelial or invasive, the basic preoperative evaluation is the same. A complete history and physical examination should be performed, including a thorough pelvic examination, vaginal cytologic examination, endometrial biopsy if indicated, and proctoscopy. A large vulvar tumor may prevent adequate pelvic examination, and uterine bleeding may be misinterpreted as bleeding from the vulvar tumor. Therefore, a thorough pelvic examination should be performed under anesthesia, and D&C may be indicated. Other preoperative studies include chest x-ray, intravenous urogram, ECG, complete blood count, urinalysis, fasting blood sugar, and blood urea nitrogen.

Considering the incidence of complicating medical disease, a thorough medical history must be taken and additional studies ordered as indicated. Individualized cystoscopy and barium enema should be performed. Mechanical bowel cleansing is required in all cases, plus antibiotic prophylaxis if abdominoperineal resection or local excision in the perineal area is anticipated. Large tumors are necrotic and infected with aerobic and anaerobic organisms, and prophylactic antibiotic therapy beginning on the evening before and for 24 hours after surgery may be desirable. Although an attempt must be made to isolate a large necrotic tumor during the operation, it may be difficult to accomplish vulvectomy without contaminating the operative wound. For this reason, groin dissection with or without extraperitoneal pelvic lymphadenectomy should be performed before vulvectomy. At least 4 units of packed red cells should be available for transfusion. The average patient will receive 2–3 units during radical vulvectomy and lymphadenectomy.

Carcinoma in situ. The extent of involvement of the vulva, perineum, and perianal skin is defined by colposcopy. Particular attention is given to examination of the perianal skin. The cervix and upper vagina have previously been evaluated by cytologic examination and colposcopy. Circumscribed lesions may be removed by wide local excision (Fig 9–16). Extensive and diffuse hypertrophic disease should be treated by total vulvectomy. In young women, superficial multifocal disease can be treated by a "skinning" procedure in which the excised vulvar skin is replaced with a split-thickness skin graft (Fig 9–15). After either procedure, sexual function can be maintained. Nevertheless, the skinning operation results in a better cosmetic effect and preservation of the clitoris. Extension of the disease to the urethral meatus or perianal skin requires individualization of treatment with additional local excision or partial resection of the urethra.

Young women exhibiting multifocal small volume disease varying from mild dysplasia to carcinoma in situ may be treated by laser vaporization using a colposcope or operating microscope. This procedure is particularly valuable in the treatment of lesions around the clitoris and extensive perianal disease. The latter usually involves the perianal skin and does not extend onto the mucosa of the anal canal. This approach should be considered investigational, and it would appear that there is a rather high incidence of persistent or recurrent disease in the untreated skin, probably from disease not identifiable with the colposcope at the time of initial treatment.

Extramammary Paget's disease can be removed by wide local excision that ordinarily consists of a complete vulvectomy. The margins of disease often extend beyond the clinically visible erythema; for that reason, multiple punch biopsies should be taken around the periphery of the clinically apparent disease and examined by frozen section to delineate the extent of the vulvectomy incision. Careful histologic examination of the entire operative specimen is necessary to rule out areas of dermal invasion that would necessitate regional lymphadenectomy consisting of bilateral superficial and deep inguinal lymphadenectomy.

Basal cell carcinomas ordinarily occur on the skin of the labia majora. Small lesions may be removed by wide excision biopsy. Large rodent ulcers may be extensive and require deep and wide resection.

Lymphadenectomy is not indicated unless there is a squamous component in the tumor.

For **invasive cancer,** whether the tumor is an epidermoid carcinoma, malignant melanoma, sarcoma, or Bartholin's gland tumor amenable to operative removal, the basic operation is radical vulvectomy and regional lymphadenectomy. The extent of the operative procedure would be modified in the aged or medically compromised patient, in whom one might exclude the lymphadenectomy and confine the surgical procedure to removal of the primary tumor by vulvectomy. If the tumor extends anteriorly into the bladder, the involved organ must be removed by anterior exenteration with urinary diversion. If the cancer involves the rectum, abdominoperineal resection with a sigmoid colostomy is indicated.

Regional lymphadenectomy involves bilateral deep and superficial inguinal lymphadenectomy. The highest deep inguinal lymph nodes beneath the inguinal ligament must be submitted for frozen section examination. If metastatic disease is found, one should then proceed to extraperitoneal deep pelvic lymphadenectomy, which consists of removal of the common iliac, external iliac, hypogastric, presacral, and obturator lymph nodes. Bilateral pelvic lymphadenectomy may be a planned part of the primary operative procedure if there is involvement of the clitoris or urethra, when the tumor is exceptionally large, if the tumor is a melanoma or Bartholin gland tumor, or if exenteration is performed.

In most patients, regional lymphadenectomy should be performed first, followed immediately by vulvectomy. A staged procedure, ie, vulvectomy followed by lymphadenectomy at a later date, is less successful. The patient who undergoes vulvectomy for either carcinoma in situ or Paget's disease and is found to have an invasive component requires inguinal lymphadenectomy as a second procedure. In general, a patient who is not medically capable of undergoing a complete one-stage operation is not a suitable candidate for a second operation at a later date. About 80–90% of patients are candidates for operation despite the advanced age and complicating medical illness in the average patient. The principal obstacle to operative treatment is detection of metastatic disease. The primary tumor, even when very large, is seldom attached to bone and usually is resectable. The operative wound after extensive resection should be left open and allowed to heal by second intention.

Mini-dose heparin consisting of 5000 units injected deeply subcutaneously 2–3 times a day may be instituted preoperatively and continued postoperatively as prophylaxis for postoperative deep thrombophlebitis. Because deep lymphatic channels are cut, there tends to be an accumulation of lymph fluid beneath the skin flaps over the groin dissections. Therefore, suction catheters should be placed under the skin flaps bilaterally to remain in place for as long as 7 days or until there is minimal drainage from the operative site. We do not use pressure dressings, and, with few exceptions, patients are ambulatory on the first postoperative day. The primary deterrents to wound healing are accumulation of lymph fluid and wound infection. Wounds that do become infected or undergo dehiscence are cleaned twice daily with hydrogen peroxide, debrided, and packed with fine mesh gauze and unprocessed honey. Wounds are usually clean within 72 hours of open treatment and heal rapidly by second intention. A skin graft is not required.

B. Medical Treatment: Various chemotherapeutic regimens and immunotherapy, primarily the use of BCG, are being investigated for treatment of vulvar cancer. Topical fluorouracil has reportedly been used for carcinoma in situ of the vulva, particularly in young women with multicentric disease. The drug interferes with production of DNA and affects rapidly proliferating tissues, particularly tumor cells. Percutaneous absorption occurs but not enough to produce systemic toxicity. Even so, it should not be used in pregnant patients.

A concentration of 2–5% fluorouracil should be applied liberally to the vulvar skin and mucous membranes twice daily by the patient. The hands should be washed thoroughly after the application, and care should be taken to avoid contact with the eyes. Areas of epithelial dysplasia become erythematous, ulcerate, and then slowly heal. Skin surfaces that do not appear to be affected are often identified by the chemotherapeutic agent and undergo necrosis. The ulcerative phase is quite painful and disabling. After healing has occurred, biopsies must be taken to detect residual disease. Additional courses of therapy may be indicated. If this type of therapy is selected, one must exclude invasive disease with multiple biopsies prior to initiation of treatment. Long-term follow-up is required for detection of recurrent or persistent disease.

C. Irradiation: The vulvar tissues do not withstand a cancerocidal dose of irradiation; therefore, there is no place for the use of irradiation in the primary treatment of the patient amenable to surgery. Nevertheless, irradiation has proved to be useful for the treatment of unresectable locally recurrent disease. The efficacy of postoperative pelvic and groin irradiation in patients who have been found to have positive lymph nodes has not been established.

Extramammary Paget's disease or malignant melanomas do not respond to irradiation.

D. Follow-Up Measures: After the immediate postoperative period, patients should be examined every 3 months for 2 years and every 6 months thereafter. The primary purpose of reexamination is to detect recurrent disease or a second primary cancer. Patients who have been treated for extramammary Paget's disease are liable to develop cancer of the breast, and young women who have been treated for carcinoma in situ of the vulva have a particular propensity for development of multifocal dysplasia in the cervix and vagina. Malignant melanomas may recur locally or metastasize to the liver or lungs.

Prognosis

The principal prognostic factors in cancer of the vulva are the size and location of the lesion, the histologic type, and the presence or absence of regional lymph node metastases. Complete excision of epidermoid carcinoma of the vulva usually cures the primary disease process; however, one must be alert for detection of recurrent disease anywhere in the lower genital tract and the development of a second primary tumor.

An approximate 5-year survival rate of 60% should be expected after complete surgical treatment of invasive epidermoid cancer. The primary factors determining survival are tumor size and nodal metastases. With tumors less than 2 cm in diameter, the incidence of nodal metastases is 10–15%. As the tumor increases in size, the incidence of metastases increases. Several authors have reported no deaths from cancer among patients who were found to have negative lymph nodes. With nodal metastases, the 5-year cure rate varies from 15 to 30%. The worst prognosis occurs among patients who have metastases to the deep pelvic lymph nodes. Unfortunately, nodal metastases cannot be detected before operation; approximately 25% of patients who have nodal metastases do not have suspicious nodal enlargement on physical examination. In general, about 30% of patients undergoing surgery will be found to have positive lymph nodes. Involvement of contiguous organs such as the bladder or rectum increases the incidence of nodal metastases and worsens the prognosis accordingly.

Extramammary Paget's disease without evidence of dermal invasion has a great propensity for local recurrence. These patients characteristically have repeated local excisions of recurrent disease after treatment of the primary disease by total vulvectomy. Invasive disease without evidence of lymph node metastases has a favorable prognosis; however, with nodal metastases, the disease is almost invariably fatal.

Results of treatment of malignant melanoma are related to the level of penetration of the tumor into the dermis of the vulvar skin or the lamina propria of the vaginal mucosa and to the presence or absence of nodal metastases. Tumor invasion 1–2 mm into the subepithelial tissues usually results in a mortality rate (from tumor) of about 60%. Patients found to have metastases to groin lymph nodes have a 5-year survival rate of less than 15%. The most common site of recurrence is the groin.

Wide local excision of basal cell carcinoma of the vulvar skin should be curative. Some authors have reported an approximately 20% recurrence rate after local excision that may represent cases of incomplete excision.

The cure rate for adequately treated cancer of Bartholin's gland has not been established. There is a propensity for unresectable local recurrences under the pubic ramus despite a thorough primary operation.

CANCER OF THE VAGINA

Essentials of Diagnosis

- Asymptomatic: Abnormal vaginal cytology.
- Early: Painless bleeding from ulcerated tumor.
- Late: Bleeding, pain, weight loss, swelling.

General Considerations

Primary cancers of the vagina represent about 1–2% of gynecologic malignancies. About 75% are epidermoid cancers, and the remainder, in decreasing order of frequency, are adenocarcinomas, sarcomas, or melanomas. A tumor should not be considered to be a primary vaginal cancer unless the cervix is uninvolved or only minimally involved by a tumor obviously arising in the vagina. Tumors involving the vulva should be classified as vulvar cancers. Primary adenocarcinoma of the vagina should not be diagnosed unless adenocarcinoma of the endometrium has been excluded.

Since 1971, an increased incidence of clear cell adenocarcinomas of the vagina has been reported in patients aged 14–23. This tumor is usually associated with DES administration to the mother during early pregnancy. The Registry of Clear Cell Adenocarcinoma of the Genital Tract in Young Females was established in 1971 to study the clinicopathologic and epidemiologic aspects of these tumors in girls born in 1940 or later, the years during which DES was used during pregnancy.

Pathology

Primary epidermoid cancer of the vagina may be intraepithelial or invasive. Intraepithelial cancer may be an isolated tumor, but a multifocal disease is more common, and patients may have similar disease in the cervix or vulva. About 2–3% of patients develop a focus of carcinoma in situ of the upper third of the vagina after hysterectomy for treatment of carcinoma in situ of the cervix. A similar lesion may develop after irradiation therapy for invasive cervical cancer. These tumors are usually asymptomatic and detected by routine vaginal cytologic study. The lesions may be delineated by colposcopy or with Lugol's solution and a diagnosis established by directed biopsy. One must inspect the entire vagina to detect all foci of disease and obtain a biopsy specimen sufficient to rule out invasive disease. Each of these entities has a potential for progression to invasive cancer of the vagina.

Invasive epidermoid cancer of the vagina occurs in postmenopausal women, usually in the sixth or seventh decade. The tumors may be ulcerative or exophytic, usually involve the posterior wall of the upper third of the vagina, and usually are grade II or III tumors. Direct invasion of the bladder or rectum may occur. The incidence of lymph node metastases is directly related to the size of the tumor. The route of nodal metastases depends upon the location of the tumor in the vagina. Tumors in the lower third metastasize like cancer of the vulva, primarily to the inguinal lymph nodes. Cancers of the upper vagina, which is the most common site, metastasize in a manner similar to cancer of the cervix.

Melanomas and sarcomas of the vagina metastasize like epidermoid cancer, although liver and pulmonary metastases are more common and probably arise from bloodstream dissemination. Nevi rarely occur in the vagina; therefore, any pigmented lesion of the vagina should be excised and will most likely be malignant. The anterior surface and lower half of the vagina are the most common sites. Grossly, the tumors are usually exophytic and described as polypoid or pedunculated with secondary necrosis.

Sarcomas of the vagina occur in children under 5 years of age and in women in the fifth to sixth decades. Embryonal rhabdomyosarcomas replace the vaginal mucosa of young girls and consist of polypoid, edematous, translucent masses that may protrude from the vaginal introitus. Leiomyosarcomas, reticulum cell sarcomas, and unclassified sarcomas occur in older women. The upper anterior vaginal wall is the most common site of origin. The appearance of these tumors depends upon the size and the extent of disease at the time of diagnosis; an early tumor may appear as a small submucosal nodule.

Adenocarcinoma of the vagina may arise from the urethra, Bartholin's gland, the rectum or bladder, the endometrial cavity, the endocervix, or an ovary or may be metastatic from a distant site. Hypernephroma of the kidney characteristically metastasizes to the anterior wall of the vagina in the lower third. These tumors would not be primary vaginal cancers. Clear cell adenocarcinomas arise in conjunction with vaginal adenosis, which in recent years has been detected most frequently in young women with a history of exposure to DES in utero. Adenosis vaginae and adenocarcinoma do occur in sexually mature and postmenopausal women.

Clinical Findings

The mean age of women with invasive cancer of the vagina is about 55 years; carcinoma in situ patients are about 10 years younger. There is no racial predisposition. Intraepithelial cancer is usually asymptomatic, discovered by routine vaginal cytologic examination and confirmed by biopsy after delineation of the location and extent of the tumor by colposcopy. A yearly physical examination should include vaginal cytologic smear even in women who have had a hysterectomy, whether performed for invasive or intraepithelial carcinoma of the cervix or for benign disease.

Bleeding (or a bloody discharge) is the most common symptom associated with invasive vaginal cancer of any histologic type. About half of patients will report for examination within 6 months after symptoms are noted. Advanced tumors cause a vaginal discharge and vulvar pruritus; impinge upon the rectum or bladder; extend to the pelvic wall to obstruct the iliac veins; or metastasize to the lungs or inguinal lymph nodes, which enlarge and eventually ulcerate.

A diagnosis of primary cancer of the vagina can-

Table 9–4. Staging of carcinoma of the vagina.*

Preinvasive carcinoma

Stage 0	Carcinoma in situ, intraepithelial carcinoma.

Invasive carcinoma

Stage I	The carcinoma is limited to the vaginal wall.
Stage II	The carcinoma has involved the subvaginal tissue but has not extended to the pelvic wall.
Stage III	The carcinoma has extended to the pelvic wall.
Stage IV	The carcinoma has extended beyond the true pelvis or has involved the mucosa of the bladder or rectum. A bullous edema as such does not permit allotment of a case to stage IV.
Stage IVA	Spread of the growth to adjacent organs.
Stage IVB	Spread to distant organs.

*American Joint Committee for Cancer Staging and End-Results Reporting; Task Force on Gynecologic Sites: Staging System for Cancer at Gynecologic Sites, 1979.

not be established unless vaginal metastases from another source can be eliminated; therefore, a complete history and physical examination is performed, including a thorough pelvic examination, cervical cytologic examination, endometrial biopsy when indicated, complete inspection of the vagina, and biopsy of the vaginal tumor. Areas of adenosis of the cervix and upper vagina can be delineated by colposcopy. The entire cervix and vaginal tube should be stained with Lugol's iodine solution. In postmenopausal women, it may be necessary to treat the vaginal mucosa with topical estrogens for 10 days prior to application of Lugol's solution to enhance uptake of stain by normal mucosa. Careful bimanual examination with palpation of the entire length of the vagina can detect small submucosal nodules that have not been visualized during the examination.

The staging system for cancer of the vagina is outlined in Table 9–4.

Differential Diagnosis

Benign tumors of the vagina are uncommon, are usually cystic, arise from the mesonephric (wolffian) or paramesonephric ducts, and are usually an incidental finding on the anterolateral wall of the vagina (Gartner's duct cyst).

An ulcerative lesion may arise from direct trauma from a foreign object, inflammatory reaction secondary to prolonged retention of a pessary or other foreign body, or a chemical burn occasionally seen after a douche with potassium permanganate. Granulomatous venereal diseases seldom affect the vagina but may be diagnosed with appropriate laboratory studies and a biopsy.

Endometriosis that penetrates the cul-de-sac of Douglas into the upper vagina cannot be differentiated from a malignancy except by biopsy.

Cancer of the urethra, bladder, rectum, or Bartholin's gland may penetrate or extend into the vagina. Cloacogenic carcinoma is a rare tumor of the anorectal region originating from a persistent remnant of the cloacal membrane of the embryo. The tumor accounts for 2–3% of anorectal carcinomas and occurs more than twice as often in women. Although most tumors are fungating or ulcerating lesions that may penetrate into the vagina, they may present as a submucosal mass.

In decreasing order of frequency of occurrence, malignancies of the following organs or tissues of the genital tract may extend onto or metastasize to the vagina: cervix, endometrium, trophoblast, ovary, and uterine tube. Metastatic spread from a distant site is uncommon but does occur—eg, from a melanoma, a kidney, or rarely from another organ.

Biopsy establishes a histologic diagnosis. An epidermoid cancer is usually primary unless it is an extension of a tumor from the cervix, vulva, or a Bartholin gland duct. Adenocarcinoma may arise from any of the sources listed; however, the diagnosis is apparent in young girls with associated adenosis of the cervix and upper vagina in conjunction with a clear cell histologic pattern and a history of DES exposure in utero. Primary adenocarcinoma in a postmenopausal patient may not be associated with adenosis and usually arises on the anterior wall of the lower third of the vagina in close proximity to the urethra.

Treatment

The treatment of vaginal cancer may be surgical or radiologic. The treatment field must encompass the entire vaginal tumor and primary routes of dissemination. Pretreatment evaluation is the same for cancer of the vagina and of the vulva. It must be established that the tumor is primary in the vagina and that distant metastases have not occurred. Most patients are postmenopausal, which implies a higher incidence of associated medical illness to be evaluated and treated.

Treatment of either invasive or intraepithelial tumors should be individualized. Carcinoma in situ of the cervix that extends to the upper vagina can be removed with the hysterectomy specimen. It should be noted that the transition zone of the cervix extends onto the upper vagina in approximately 2–4% of patients and may be a site of recurrent disease after hysterectomy. The colposcopic biopsy must be sufficient to eliminate the possibility of early or grossly invasive disease. The upper third of the vagina is most vulnerable and almost uniformly involved; therefore, it should be completely removed if partial vaginectomy is chosen as treatment. If necessary, vaginal length may be maintained by use of a split-thickness skin graft. Intracavitary radium has proved to be satisfactory treatment. Colpostats or a specially designed (Bloedon) vaginal applicator may be used to deliver 6000–7000 rads surface dose to the vagina in approximately 72 hours. Eradication of in situ cancer with the carbon dioxide laser or intravaginal applications of fluorouracil cream are newer forms of therapy now being evaluated.

Multifocal intraepithelial disease involves the entire length of the vagina and is a special treatment problem. Irradiation of the entire length of the vagina causes stenosis and loss of vaginal function. If total vaginectomy is performed, the mucosa should be replaced with a split-thickness skin graft that maintains a functional vagina.

Carcinoma in situ or dysplasia of the vagina after irradiation for cancer of the cervix usually occurs in the upper vagina. Care should be taken to exclude coexisting recurrent or persistent invasive disease of the cervix. Because the tissues have been compromised by a therapeutic dose of irradiation, surgical excision—or even an extensive biopsy—could precipitate development of a vesicovaginal or rectovaginal fistula. Treatment is individualized, and newer forms of therapy with the carbon dioxide laser and topical application of fluorouracil cream are reportedly successful. One must always be cognizant of the multifocal nature of the disease and thoroughly evaluate the lower third of the vagina and the skin of the vulva, perineum, and perianal areas by colposcopy.

Metastatic carcinoma of the vagina originating from a primary tumor in the endometrium or cervix is a relatively common finding. The lower extent of disease is identified with a radiopaque marker, and the external irradiation field is extended to encompass the clinical limits of the disease. A vaginal cylinder or interstitial radium implant can be used to supplement the dose of irradiation derived from external therapy.

Treatment of primary invasive cancer of the vagina depends upon the location of the tumor within the vagina and the stage of the disease. Stage I or II disease in the upper vagina may be treated like cancer of the cervix. Surgical treatment would be the equivalent of radical abdominal hysterectomy, partial vaginectomy, bilateral salpingo-oophorectomy, and pelvic lymphadenectomy. Irradiation therapy should consist of approximately 4000 rads as whole pelvis external therapy, supplemented with intracavitary radium calculated to deliver a total surface dose of approximately 8000 rads in 2 applications of 48 hours each separated by 2 weeks.

Surgical therapy is not applicable to stage III or IV lesions of the upper vagina unless the tumor is confined to the midline and has invaded anteriorly into the bladder or posteriorly into the rectum, in which case an exenteration operation with removal of the involved organ might be appropriate. Most of these patients are treated by irradiation, which consists of approximately 5000 rads as whole pelvis external irradiation in 5 weeks, followed by intracavitary or interstitial radium if appropriate or additional external therapy through a treatment field which has been reduced in size and localized to the affected parametrium. A colostomy may be performed if the tumor has penetrated the rectovaginal septum.

Stage I or II tumors of the middle or lower third of the vagina may be amenable to either surgery or irradiation. Carcinoma at the introitus is treated like cancer of the vulva, utilizing radical vulvectomy, bilateral superficial and deep inguinal lymphadenectomy, and pelvic lymphadenectomy as indicated. A very small and early lesion may be treated by total vaginectomy. However, the close proximity of the bladder and the rectum often necessitates performance of an anterior or posterior exenteration. Irradiation therapy is essentially the same as that used for cancers of the upper vagina. When the lower third of the vagina is involved, the inguinal nodes must be treated as well with either irradiation, approximating 5000 rads in 5 weeks, or inguinal lymphadenectomy.

The principles of treatment of primary adenocarcinoma of the vagina are the same as those for epidermoid cancer.

Treatment of uncommon tumors such as melanoma or sarcoma is usually surgical.

Prognosis

The size and stage of the disease at the time of diagnosis are the most important prognostic indicators, assuming that surgical or irradiation therapy has been adequate. The results of treatment of carcinoma in situ are excellent, although long-term follow-up is required to detect small areas of persistent or recurrent disease or another focus of new disease in another portion of the lower genital tract. One might expect a 70–75% 5-year cure rate in stage I and II disease. In stage III disease, the cure rate is 25–30%. In stage IV disease, there are few survivors.

Melanomas—even small ones—are very malignant, and few respond to therapy. The tumor recurs locally and metastasizes to the liver and lungs. Chemotherapy and immunotherapy have been used as adjunctive treatment.

Too few sarcomas of the vagina have been reported to generate survival data; these tumors do have a propensity for local recurrence and distant metastases, and the prognosis is usually poor.

• • •

References

General

Friedrich EG: *Vulvar Disease: Major Problems in Obstetrics and Gynecology.* Vol 9. Saunders, 1976.

Gardner HL, Kaufman RH: *Benign Disease of the Vulva and Vagina.* G.K. Hall, 1981.

International Society for the Study of Vulvar Disease: New nomenclature for vulvar disease. *Obstet Gynecol* 1976; **47:**122.

Morrow CP, Di Saia PJ: Malignant melanoma of the female genitalia: A clinical analysis. *Obstet Gynecol Surv* 1976; **31:**233.

Stening M: *Cancer and Related Lesions of the Vulva.* ADIS Press Australasia Pty, 1980.

Vaginitis and Related Problems: A Symposium. The Purdue Frederick Co., 1980.

Leukorrhea

Bhattacharyya MB, Jones BM: *Haemophilus vaginalis* infection: Diagnosis and treatment. *J Reprod Med* 1980; **24:**71.

Eschenbach DA: Recognizing chlamydial infections. *Contemp Obstet Gynecol* 1980; **16:**15.

Felman YM, Nikitas JA: Nongonococcal urethritis. *JAMA* 1981; **245:**381.

Fleury FJ: Adult vaginitis. *Clin Obstet Gynecol* 1981; **24:**407.

Gardner HL: *Haemophilus vaginalis* vaginitis after twenty-five years. *Am J Obstet Gynecol* 1980; **137:**385.

Goldman P: Drug therapy: Metronidazole. *N Engl J Med* 1980; **303:**1212.

Hagar WD et al: Metronidazole for vaginal trichomoniasis: Seven-day vs single-dose regimens. *JAMA* 1980; **244:**1219.

Holmes KK: The *Chlamydia* epidemic. *JAMA* 1981; **245:**1718.

Huffman JW: Premenarchal vulvovaginitis. *Clin Obstet Gynecol* 1977; **20:**581.

Huggins GR, Preti G: Vaginal odors and secretions. *Clin Obstet Gynecol* 1981; **24:**355.

Johannisson G et al: Genital *Chlamydia trachomatis* infection in women. *Obstet Gynecol* 1980; **56:**671.

Laing FC, Shanser JD, Salmen BJ: Vaginitis emphysematosa. *Arch Surg* 1978; **113:**156.

Larsen B, Galask R: Vaginal microbial flora: Practical and theoretic relevance. *Obstet Gynecol* 1980; **55:**100S.

Maan M et al: Treatment of *Haemophilus vaginalis* vaginitis. *Obstet Gynecol* 1981; **57:**711.

McGuire LS, Guzinski GM, Holmes KK: Psychosexual functioning in symptomatic women with and without signs of vaginitis. *Am J Obstet Gynecol* 1980; **137:**600.

Monif RG, Chez RA: How to culture for gonorrhea. *Contemp Obstet Gynecol* 1980; **16:**165.

Murphy TV, Nelson JD: *Shigella* vaginitis. *Pediatrics* 1979; **63:**511.

Ostergard D: DES-related vaginal lesions. *Clin Obstet Gynecol* 1981; **24:**379.

Pheifer TA et al: Nonspecific vaginitis: The role of *Haemophilus vaginalis* and treatment with metronidazole. *N Engl J Med* 1978; **298:**1429.

Schachter J: Chlamydial infections. (3 parts.) *N Engl J Med* 1978; **298:**428, 490, 540.

Spiegel CA et al: Anaerobic bacteria in nonspecific vaginitis. *N Engl J Med* 1980; **303:**601.

Taylor-Robinson D, McCormack WM: The genital mycoplasmas. (2 parts.) *N Engl J Med* 1980; **302:**1003.

Van Slyke KK et al: Treatment of vulvovaginal candidiasis with boric acid powder. *Am J Obstet Gynecol* 1981; **141:**145.

Vaginal Tampons

Davis JP et al: Toxic-shock syndrome: Epidemiologic features, recurrence risk factors and prevention. *N Engl J Med* 1980; **303:**1429.

Friedrich EG Jr: Tampon effects on vaginal health. *Clin Obstet Gynecol* 1981; **24:**395.

Tofte RW, Williams DN: Toxic shock syndrome: Evidence of a broad clinical spectrum. *JAMA* 1981; **246:**2163.

Viral Infections

Adam E et al: Asymptomatic virus shedding after herpes genitalis. *Am J Obstet Gynecol* 1980; **137:**827.

Baggish MS: Carbon dioxide laser treatment for condylomata acuminata venereal infections. *Obstet Gynecol* 1980; **55:**711.

Dunn J et al: Immunologic detection of condylomata acuminata–specific antigens. *Obstet Gynecol* 1981; **57:**351.

Eftaiha MS et al: Condylomata acuminata in an infant and mother: Report of a case. *Dis Colon Rectum* 1978; **21:**369.

Grossman JH III et al: Management of genital herpes simplex virus infection during pregnancy. *Obstet Gynecol* 1981; **58:**1.

Guinan ME et al: The course of untreated recurrent genital herpes simplex infection in 27 women. *N Engl J Med* 1981; **304:**759.

Hain J, Doshi N, Harger JH: Ascending transcervical herpes simplex infection with intact fetal membranes. *Obstet Gynecol* 1980; **56:**106.

Hatherley LI et al: Herpesvirus in an obstetric hospital. 2. Asymptomatic virus excretion in staff members. *Surg Gynecol Obstet* 1981; **153:**132.

Hirsch MS, Swartz MN: Antiviral agents. (2 parts.) *N Engl J Med* 1980; **302:**903.

Huang ES et al: Molecular epidemiology of cytomegalovirus infections in women and their infants. *N Engl J Med* 1980; **303:**958.

Kibrick S: Herpes simplex infection at term: What to do with mother, newborn, and nursery personnel. *JAMA* 1980; **243:**157.

Menczer J et al: Herpesvirus type 2 in adenocarcinoma of the uterine cervix: A possible association. *Cancer* 1981; **48:**1497.

Michael R et al: Vaginal condylomata: A human papillomavirus infection. *Clin Obstet Gynecol* 1981; **24:**461.

Overall JC Jr: Persistent problems with persistent herpesviruses. *N Engl J Med* 1981; **305:**95.

Powell LC: Condyloma acuminatum: Recent advances in development, carcinogenesis, and treatment. *Clin Obstet Gynecol* 1978; **21:**1061.

Reeves WC et al: Risk of recurrence after first episodes of genital herpes: Relation to HSV type and antibody response. *N Engl J Med* 1981; **305:**315.

Shafeek MA, Osman MI, Hussein MA: Carcinoma of the vulva arising in condylomata acuminata. *Obstet Gynecol* 1979; **54:**120.

Tobin SM et al: Relation of herpesvirus hominis type II to carcinoma of the cervix: An animal model for the induction of long-term latency of herpesvirus hominis type II. *Obstet Gynecol* 1978; **51:**707.

Tobin SM et al: Relation of HVH-II to carcinoma of the cervix. *Obstet Gynecol* 1979; **53:**553.

Whitley RJ et al: The natural history of herpes simplex virus infection of mother and newborn. *Pediatrics* 1980;**66**:489.

Wolontis S, Jeansson S: Correlation of herpes simplex virus types 1 and 2 with clinical features of infection. *J Infect Dis* 1977;**135**:28.

Wilkins JK: Molluscum contagiosum venereum in a women's outpatient clinic: A venereally transmitted disease. *Am J Obstet Gynecol* 1977;**128**:531.

Diseases of the Vulva

Behçet's Disease: A Symposium. Elsevier North Holland, 1979.

James DG: Behçet's syndrome. *N Engl J Med* 1979;**301**:431.

Lynch PJ: Sexually transmitted diseases: Granuloma inguinale, lymphogranuloma venereum, chancroid, and infectious syphilis. *Clin Obstet Gynecol* 1978;**21**:1041.

Robboy SJ et al: Urogenital sinus origin of mucinous and ciliated cysts of the vulva. *Obstet Gynecol* 1978;**51**:349.

Tavassoli FA, Norris HJ: Smooth muscle tumors of the vulva. *Obstet Gynecol* 1979;**53**:213.

Tovell HMM, Young HW Jr: Benign diseases of the vulva: A symposium. *Clin Obstet Gynecol* 1978;**21**:955.

Young AW, Tovell HMM, Kasro S: Erosions and ulcers of the vulva: Diagnosis, incidence, and management. *Obstet Gynecol* 1977;**50**:35.

Young AW et al: Syringoma of the vulva: Incidence, diagnosis, and cause of pruritus. *Obstet Gynecol* 1980;**55**:515.

Cancer of the Vulva

Anderson JA et al: Preoperative prognosis for cancer of the vulva. *Obstet Gynecol* 1981;**58**:364.

Buscema J et al: Early invasive carcinoma of the vulva. *Am J Obstet Gynecol* 1981;**140**:563.

Davos I, Abell MR: Soft tissue sarcoma of the vulva. *Gynecol Oncol* 1976;**4**:70.

DiSaia PJ, Rich WM: Surgical approach to multifocal carcinoma in situ of the vulva. *Am J Obstet Gynecol* 1981;**140**:136.

DiSaia PJ et al: An alternate approach to early cancer of the vulva. *Am J Obstet Gynecol* 1979;**133**:825.

Friedrich EG et al: Carcinoma in situ of the vulva: A continuing challenge. *Am J Obstet Gynecol* 1980;**136**:830.

Gunn RA, Gallager HS: Vulvar Paget's disease: A topographic study. *Cancer* 1980;**46**:590.

Hart WR, Norris JH, Helwig EB: Relation of lichen sclerosus et atrophicus of the vulva to development of carcinoma. *Obstet Gynecol* 1975;**45**:369.

Kaplan AL, Kaufman RH: Management of advanced carcinoma of the vulva. *Gynecol Oncol* 1975;**3**:220.

Kaplan Al et al: Intraepithelial carcinoma of the vulva with extension to the anal canal. *Obstet Gynecol* 1981;**58**:368.

Magrina JF et al: Stage I squamous cell cancer of the vulva.

Am J Obstet Gynecol 1979;**134**:453.

Partridge EE et al: Verrucous lesions of the female genitalia. 2. Verrucous carcinoma. *Am J Obstet Gynecol* 1980;**137**:419.

Silvers DM, Halperin AJ: Cutaneous and vulvar melanoma: An update. *Clin Obstet Gynecol* 1978;**21**:1117.

Svenson EW, Montague ED: Results of treatment in transitional cloacogenic carcinoma. *Cancer* 1980;**46**:828.

Trelford JD, Deos PH: Bartholin's gland carcinoma: Five cases. *Gynecol Oncol* 1976;**4**:222.

Wilkinson EJ, Friedrich EG Jr: Multicentric nature of vulvar carcinoma in situ. *Obstet Gynecol* 1981;**58**:69.

Cancer of the Vagina

Antonioli DA, Burke L, Friedman EA: Natural history of diethylstilbestrol-associated genital tract lesions: Cervical ectopy and cervicovaginal hood. *Am J Obstet Gynecol* 1980;**137**:847.

Barclay DL: Carcinoma of the vagina after hysterectomy for severe dysplasia or carcinoma in situ of the cervix. *Gynecol Oncol* 1979;**8**:1.

Caglar H et al: Topical 5-fluorouracil treatment of vaginal intraepithelial neoplasia. *Obstet Gynecol* 1981;**58**:580.

Chirayil SJ, Tobon H: Polyps of the vagina: A clinicopathologic study of 18 cases. *Cancer* 1981;**47**:2904.

Chung AF et al: Malignant melanoma of the vagina: Report of 19 cases. *Obstet Gynecol* 1980;**55**:720.

Davos I, Abell MR: Sarcomas of the vagina. *Obstet Gynecol* 1976;**47**:342.

Herbst AL: Diethylstilbestrol and other sex hormones during pregnancy. *Obstet Gynecol* 1981;**58**:35S.

Kaufman RH et al: Upper genital tract changes and pregnancy outcome in offspring exposed in utero to diethylstilbestrol. *Am J Obstet Gynecol* 1980;**137**:299.

Ostergard DR: DES-related vaginal lesions. *Clin Obstet Gynecol* 1981;**24**:379.

Petrilli ES et al: Vaginal intraepithelial neoplasia: Biologic aspects and treatment with topical 5-fluorouracil and the carbon dioxide laser. *Am J Obstet Gynecol* 1980;**138**:321.

Piver MS et al: Postirradiation squamous cell carcinoma in situ of the vagina: Treatment by topical 20 percent 5-fluorouracil cream. *Am J Obstet Gynecol* 1979;**135**:377.

Smith WG: Invasive cancer of the vagina. *Clin Obstet Gynecol* 1981;**24**:503.

Stuart GCE et al: Squamous cell carcinoma of the vagina following hysterectomy. *Am J Obstet Gynecol* 1981;**139**:311.

Tavassoli FA, Norris HJ: Smooth muscle tumors of the vagina. *Obstet Gynecol* 1979;**53**:689.

Veridiano NP et al: Reproductive performance of DES-exposed female progeny. *Obstet Gynecol* 1981;**58**:58.

Woodruff JD: Carcinoma in situ of the vagina. *Clin Obstet Gynecol* 1981;**24**:485.

10 | Disorders of the Uterine Cervix

Edward C. Hill, MD

CERVICAL INJURIES

Lacerations

Lacerations of the cervix commonly occur during childbirth and may be a complication of both normal and abnormal delivery. Unless the cervix is routinely inspected following the completion of the third stage of labor, injury may go undetected until after it heals with one or more lacerations, even a duck-bill type of cervical deformity. Most obstetric lacerations occur on either side of the cervix at about 6 or 9 o'clock. They may vary in length from small notches less than 1 cm deep to extensive tears extending upward into the lower uterine segment. Bleeding from deep lacerations may be brisk, requiring immediate repair to control hemorrhage. The cervix should be carefully examined in every case of immediate (or delayed) postpartum hemorrhage. Examination should include not only inspection but careful palpation of the upper angle of the laceration because the visible portion may represent only the lower margin of a wound that may extend into the uterus.

A less easily recognized type of cervical laceration is the submucosal separation of the fibrous connective tissue stroma. When this occurs at the level of the internal os, an "incompetent cervix" may result.

The most important factors in the cause of obstetric lacerations of the cervix are those conditions that change the ovoid shape of the dilating cervix to an ellipsoid with resulting increased regional tension on the cervical tissues. This may occur during the delivery of unusually large babies or when the presentation is an occiput posterior or breech. Lacerations also occur when delivery is attempted before the cervix is completely dilated or effaced.

Nonobstetric lacerations of the cervix may occur during instrumental procedures, eg, D&C or radium placement. Postmenopausal atrophy, chronic inflammation, or malignant cervical disease predisposes to such iatrogenic lacerations.

Perforations

Perforation of the cervix may occur during self-induced abortion with sharp objects, eg, wires or darning or knitting needles, or inadvertently during sounding of the uterus, cervical dilatation, insertion of a radium tandem, or conization of the cervix. The urinary bladder may be injured also because of its close approximation to the anterior aspect of the cervix.

Ulcerations

Ulceration of the cervix may result from pressure necrosis due to a vaginal pessary in the vagina or a cervical stem pessary. A trophic cervical ulcer may also develop with uterine prolapse when the cervix protrudes through the vaginal introitus.

Annular Detachment

Annular detachment of the cervix is a rare complication that is the result of compression necrosis of the cervix during labor. It occurs when the external os fails to dilate and the blood supply is compromised by pressure of the fetal head. The diagnosis is made when the detached ring or portion of cervix is expelled prior to delivery of the presenting part of the fetus.

Complications of Cervical Injuries

Hemorrhage is the most immediate and serious complication of cervical laceration. Although external bleeding is usually present, intra- or extraperitoneal hemorrhage may occur when the cervical tear extends up into the uterus. The clinical picture then is that of hypovolemic shock out of proportion to visible blood loss.

Cervical incompetence results from unrecognized or improperly repaired lacerations through the internal os. Repeated or habitual abortion, which usually occurs during the second trimester of pregnancy, may be due to cervical incompetence.

CERVICITIS

Essentials of Diagnosis

- Leukorrhea—purulent discharge with a disagreeable odor.
- Vulvar-vaginal irritation (itching or burning) if associated with vaginitis.
- Red, edematous cervix.
- Tenderness on cervical motion.
- Positive laboratory studies for pathogens.

General Considerations

Acute or chronic infectious cervicitis probably is the most common gynecologic disorder, affecting more than half of all women at some time during adult life. It represents a problem of considerable complexity because of associated conditions such as ectopic columnar epithelium, cervical hypertrophy, and old, healed lacerations.

Etiology & Pathogenesis

A. Acute Cervicitis: This acute inflammatory disorder may result from direct infection of the cervix or may be secondary to a vaginal or uterine infection. The most frequent form is secondary to acute vaginal sepsis. In the USA, with the widespread use of oral contraceptives, candidiasis has become the most prevalent cause of vaginitis and cervicitis, with trichomonal vaginitis in second place. *Gardnerella vaginalis* vaginitis also involves the cervical mucosa secondarily.

Neisseria gonorrhoeae is a frequent cause of acute cervicitis and represents a direct surface infection of the endocervical mucosa by the invading gonococci. Although specific antibiotics usually destroy the gonococci, secondary invading organisms may persist for months or years as a cause of chronic cervicitis. Nonspecific infections with enterococci, streptococci, or staphylococci may accompany puerperal infection or may be associated with lacerations of the cervix or infections of the uterine corpus. Cervical infections due to *Chlamydia* are being increasingly recognized. The cervix may be the reservoir in the human for *Chlamydia*, the microorganism responsible for trachoma and inclusion conjunctivitis. Nevertheless, the absence of significant symptoms may permit the cervical infection to persist unnoticed. Rare instances of acute infection by *Corynebacterium diphtheriae* have been reported.

Viruses also may infect the cervix. Herpes simplex virus—almost always type 2—produces a transient superficial vesicular mucosal lesion that soon becomes ulcerative. A virus similar to that which causes the common wart produces condylomata acuminata (genital warts) on the cervix as well as on the vulva and in the vagina.

B. Chronic Cervicitis: This is a low-grade but often troublesome infection of the cervix that often follows acute sepsis. Nonetheless, chronic cervicitis may evolve as an indolent inflammatory condition of the cervical epithelium and stroma following abortion or obstetric delivery. This condition often is accompanied by ectopy of the cervix, or chronic cervicitis may be a sequel to injury, eg, obstetric laceration. The offending organisms usually are those of the "nonspecific" type—actually *Staphylococcus, Streptococcus*, or the coliform bacteria alone or in combination. These secondary invaders may follow an acute gonorrheal cervicitis. Some degree of chronic cervicitis exists in the majority of parous women.

Chronic cervicitis is a disorder of women of childbearing age. It is a common "incidental" pathologic diagnosis in uteri removed for other abnormalities.

Other factors in the pathogenesis of cervicitis are poor hygiene (anal-vaginal contamination), diminished resistance to infection in hypoestrogenism or hypovitaminosis, and irritation caused by foreign bodies, eg, pessaries.

Chronic cervicitis may serve as a focus of infection or cause of leukorrhea, dyspareunia, infertility, or abortion. Herpes simplex infection may even be a cause of cervical carcinoma.

Pathology

A. Acute Cervicitis: Acute cervicitis begins with surface infiltration by polymorphonuclear leukocytes. The portio vaginalis becomes red and edematous. The endocervical os "pouts," which indicates ectopy of the endocervical mucosa. The endocervix promptly becomes involved so that within 1–2 days even the remote depths of the cervix are inflamed.

As the acute process subsides, the edema lessens and the polymorphonuclear leukocytes are gradually replaced by lymphocytes and plasma cells. Irritation due to infection results in hyperfunction of the glandular epithelium, producing copious leukorrhea. Because the infected glands evacuate poorly, they become dilated, but the fibromuscular supporting framework shields the inflammatory process.

The junction between the stratified squamous cells and columnar epithelial cells is often found on the exocervix so that a portion of the cervical stroma, covered only by a single layer of columnar cells, is exposed to the vaginal bacterial flora. The existence of "endocervical" mucosa on the portio vaginalis of the cervix produces a red, granular appearance. In the past this has been called a cervical erosion—a misnomer. "Erosion" is not a proper term for cervical redness except as an acute limited denudation of the mucosquamous junction in virulent infection, following cauterization, or following radium therapy. In these circumstances, the squamous epithelium is lost for a very brief time, but it is replaced by columnar cells or squamous elements.

Cervical secretion is the result of hormonal, emotional, or irritative stimulation. The production of a thin, clear acellular cervical mucus in average amounts is of major importance in reproductive physiology. The mucous plug is a barrier to pathogenic bacteria and permits the transport of sperm to the uterine cavity. Sperm migration is hindered by infected, thick, tenacious mucus or the absence of mucus. Heavy bacterial contamination results in increased cervical viscosity and a decreased pH. Leukocytes and bacteria in the mucus result in a negative Sims-Huhner test.

B. Chronic Cervicitis: The chronic stage is characterized by diffuse or localized collections of chronic inflammatory cells in the subepithelial stroma. The clefts and tunnels of the endocervix may become occluded, with the formation of nabothian cysts that may contain small collections of purulent exudate or, with eventual resolution of infection, clear mucus.

With long-continued chronic inflammation, proliferation of the fibrous connective tissue in the cervical stroma occurs. This results in hypertrophy and elongation of the cervix. This process is most pronounced when seen in association with cervical laceration and cervical eversion.

Nabothian cysts also develop as a result of squamous metaplasia, the process by which columnar epithelium at the squamo-columnar junction is "transformed" to a stratified squamous epithelium. This process of metaplasia is a continuing, physiologic one, and it is accelerated during 3 periods of a woman's life: fetal existence, adolescence, and the first pregnancy. Metaplastic squamous cells fill in the narrow clefts near the surface. This obstructs the egress of mucus from the deeper columnar cells. To the naked eye, the presence of nabothian cysts on the portio vaginalis of the cervix indicates that this area at one time was occupied by columnar epithelium that has undergone squamous metaplasia. On gross inspection of the cervix, the nabothian cyst is the hallmark of the "transformation zone."

Clinical Findings

A. Symptoms and Signs:

1. Acute cervicitis–The primary symptom of acute cervicitis is a purulent vaginal discharge. The appearance of the discharge is most variable—often thick and creamy in the case of gonorrheal infection; foamy and greenish-white in the case of trichomonal infection; white and curdlike in candidiasis; and thin and gray in *G vaginalis* infections. Chlamydial infections often produce a purulent discharge from an angry, reddened, congested cervix. The discharge is often indistinguishable from that due to gonorrheal cervicitis.

a. Leukorrhea–In leukorrhea caused by endocervical inflammation, the characteristics vary with the menstrual cycle. In the absence of infection, the cervical mucus is thin, clear, and acellular at the time of ovulation or after moderate estrogen stimulation. Normally, in the late secretory phase, the mucus is slightly mucopurulent, and it may be tenacious and viscid.

b. Infertility–A thick, glutinous, acid, pus-laden cervical mucus is noxious to sperm and prevents fertilization.

c. Pelvic discomfort–Vulvar burning and itching may be prominent symptoms. Gonorrheal cervicitis may be accompanied by urethritis with frequency, urgency, and dysuria. If associated with acute salpingitis, the symptoms and signs will be those of pelvic peritonitis.

d. Sexual dysfunction–Constitutional symptoms do not usually occur as a result of acute cervicitis alone, but an associated parametritis may cause dyspareunia or discomfort in the lower abdomen.

e. Physical signs–Inspection of the cervix initially infected by *N gonorrhoeae* generally reveals an acutely inflamed, edematous cervix with a purulent discharge escaping from the external os. In trichomonal infection, the telltale strawberry petechiae may be visible on the squamous epithelial surface of the portio vaginalis as well as the adjacent vaginal mucosa. In candidiasis there is apt to be a white cheesy exudate which is difficult to wipe away and which, if scraped off, usually leaves punctate hemorrhagic areas.

f. Metrorrhagia–Hyperemia of the infected cervix may be associated with freely bleeding areas. Cervical ooze may account for intermenstrual (often postcoital) spotting.

g. Abortion–Cervicitis is frequently followed by endometritis, and abortion may follow.

2. Chronic cervicitis–In chronic cervicitis, leukorrhea may be the chief symptom. Although it may not be as profuse as in acute cervicitis, this discharge may also cause vulvar irritation. The discharge may be frankly purulent, varying in color, or it may simply present as thick, tenacious, turbid mucus. Intermenstrual bleeding may occur.

Associated eversion may present as a velvety to granular perioral redness or as patchy erythema due to scattered squamous metaplasia (epithelialization or epidermization). Nabothian cysts in the area of the so-called transformation zone may be seen. The Schiller test may show poorly staining or nonstaining areas. There will often be some tenderness and thickening in

Table 10–1. Pathologic features and surgical treatment of chronic cervicitis. (Modified after Hyams and Matthews.)

	Slight	Moderate	Marked	Extreme
Duration	3–12 weeks after infection or delivery	3–12 months after infection or delivery	2–5 years after infection or delivery	15–40 years after infection or delivery
Laceration	Slight	Moderate	Marked	Marked
Eversion	±	Slight	Moderate	Marked
Superficial infection	Slight	Slight	Slight	Moderate
Deep infection	0	Moderate	Moderate	Marked
Nabothian cysts	0	Few	Numerous	Numerous
Hypertrophy	0	0	Slight	Moderate
Treatment	Light cauterization or coagulation	Repeated light cauterization; cryotherapy; moderate coagulation; conization.	Cryotherapy; repeated moderate cauterization; repeated moderate coagulation; conization; perhaps trachelorrhaphy.	Cryotherapy; trachelorrhaphy; amputation of the cervix; perhaps hysterectomy.

the region of the uterosacral ligaments on pelvic examination, and motion of the cervix may be painful.

Lower abdominal pain, lumbosacral backache, dysmenorrhea, or dyspareunia occurs occasionally and is related to an associated parametritis. Infertility may be due to the inflammatory changes resulting in a tacky cervical mucus that is acid and otherwise "hostile" (toxic) to sperm. Urinary frequency, urgency, and dysuria may be seen in association with chronic cervicitis. These symptoms are related to an associated subvesical lymphangitis, not to cystitis.

Inspection of the chronically infected cervix often reveals only abnormal discharge.

a. Cervical dystocia–Fibrosis and stenosis of the cervix may follow chronic cervical infection. Delayed or incomplete dilatation of the cervix may result.

b. Laceration, eversion, and hypertrophy of the cervix may be apparent, together with nabothian cysts. Patulousness of the deeply lacerated external os often exposes the endocervical canal, which may bleed when wiped with a cotton applicator. The portio and the upper vagina usually appear normal in cervicitis.

B. Laboratory Findings:

1. Smears–Wet smear preparations of the exudate diluted with isotonic saline solution usually will demonstrate the motile flagellated *Trichomonas vaginalis* organisms when present. A similar suspension in 10% potassium hydroxide may disclose the spores and mycelia of *Candida albicans*. Yeast organisms should be cultured on Nickerson's or comparable medium. The speckled-appearing "clue cell" of *G vaginalis* is suggestive of this type of cervicitis-vaginitis. The dried mucus smear never shows the normal "fern" pattern in cervicitis.

In acute gonorrheal cervicitis, a gram-stained smear of cervical exudate may show the typical coffee-bean-shaped, paired, gram-negative, intracellular diplococci of *N gonorrhoeae*. This finding is adequate for the initiation of definitive therapy. However, one must not confuse this organism with nonpathogenic diplococci that may be found in the lower reproductive tract.

In chronic infections, the cervical mucus is thick and tenacious and contains clumps of pus cells and cervical debris.

In chronic gonococcal infections, the gram-stained smear usually fails to reveal specific pathogens. Culture on Thayer-Martin medium may be diagnostic.

2. Cultures–Culture of the material obtained from the cervix on Thayer-Martin or blood agar medium provides a positive diagnosis. Culture is essential for a definite diagnosis of gonorrhea despite a finding of intracellular diplococci. A single culture from the cervix on Thayer-Martin medium will detect *N gonorrhoeae* in 90–93% of infected women. *Chlamydia* can also be cultured, if suspected, from an infected cervix. In selected cases of chronic nonspecific cervicitis, cultures for common pathogens such as staphylococci, streptococci, and coliform organisms may be helpful. The addition of a culture

obtained from the anal canal will increase the sensitivity of diagnosis by 6–10%.

3. Cytology–Cytologic smears for malignancy usually will reflect the inflammatory component. There may be mild nuclear and cytoplasmic changes in the epithelial cells secondary to the inflammation.

4. Blood studies–In uncomplicated cervicitis not accompanied by an associated salpingitis, the white count may be normal or there may be only a slight leukocytosis and sedimentation rate elevation. In any patient with gonorrhea, syphilis must be ruled out by appropriate serologic tests.

5. Mucus studies–In patients under investigation for the cause of infertility, a postcoital examination of the cervical mucus (Sims-Huhner test) usually shows a paucity of spermatozoa, and those that are present may demonstrate poor motility and short survival times.

6. Urine–A clean-catch or catheterized urine specimen in patients with cervicitis usually contains only occasional white cells, rare or absent erythrocytes, and no casts. Culture of the urine is generally negative in urethritis and trigonitis secondary to cervicitis.

C. X-Ray Findings: In the presence of an acute cervicitis, hysterography is contraindicated. In chronic cervicitis, the introduction of a radiopaque dye (eg, Salpix) into the canal may demonstrate the hypertrophied endocervical rugae.

Differential Diagnosis

The leukorrhea of cervicitis can be distinguished from that of tension states and the physiologic outpouring of mucus at the time of ovulation by the fact that the mucus is clear and shows only rare leukocytes on microscopic examination in the latter conditions.

Rectovaginal examination should be done to distinguish the signs and symptoms of pelvic tenderness, induration, and mass formation above the cervix when discharge is noted from the cervix.

Cervicitis must be distinguished from early neoplastic processes. This may not be easy because inflammatory conditions may alter the epithelial cells to produce atypia on cytologic examination. Colposcopy is useful (see sections on cervical dysplasia and cervical cancer). Cytologic examinations of cervical scrapings as well as mucosa from endocervical aspiration and histologic examination of biopsy specimens from any suspect areas should help to distinguish chronic cervicitis from a developing cancer of the cervix. Consider also the lesions of syphilis and chancroid as well as the chronic granulomatous ulcerations of tuberculosis and granuloma inguinale.

Complications

Leukorrhea, cervical stenosis, and infertility are sequelae of chronic cervicitis. Salpingitis is common with gonorrhea and acute postabortal cervicitis. Chronic infection of the lower and subsequently the upper urinary tract may follow persistent cervicitis.

Carcinoma of the cervix usually occurs in parous

women. Examination often reveals neglected cervical lacerations and chronic infection. Nonetheless, these cannot be implicated as causes of cervical cancer.

Prevention

Acute gonorrheal cervicitis can be prevented by the avoidance of sexual contact with infected individuals or the use of a condom for protection during coitus.

The avoidance of surgical or obstetric trauma and the prompt recognition and proper repair of cervical lacerations will help to prevent the subsequent development of a chronically infected cervix.

When surgical removal of the corpus of the uterus is indicated, the cervix should be removed also if this is feasible.

Treatment

Selection of the most appropriate treatment depends upon the age of the patient and her desire for pregnancy; the severity of the cervical involvement; the presence of complicating factors (eg, salpingitis); and previous treatment.

Instrumentation and vigorous topical therapy should be avoided during the acute phase and before the menses, when ascending infection may occur.

A. Acute Cervicitis: When acute cervicitis is associated with vaginitis due to a specific organism, treatment must be directed accordingly.

Metronidazole (Flagyl) is specific for the treatment of *T vaginalis* infection. The dosage (for men and women) is 3 g orally, once only. Metronidazole is contraindicated during the first trimester of pregnancy because of possible teratogenicity.

Candidiasis may be treated topically with fungicidal preparations such as nystatin vaginal suppositories (100 mg) inserted twice daily for 10 days.

G vaginalis infection usually responds to tetracycline or ampicillin, 250 mg. Topical sulfonamide preparations, eg, Sultrin Cream, a triple sulfonamide preparation consisting of sulfathiazole, sulfacetamide, and benzoylsulfanilamide, are less effective.

See Chapter 15 for treatment of *N gonorrhoeae* infection. Chlamydial cervicitis is best treated with tetracycline, 250 mg 4 times daily for 1 week. Erythromycin should be substituted in pregnant women.

B. Chronic Cervicitis: Chronic cervicitis should be treated even if asymptomatic.

1. Medical treatment–A chronic purulent discharge from the cervical canal of an otherwise normal-appearing cervix should be cultured and sensitivity tests ordered. Antibiotic treatment should be given systemically (orally or parenterally) rather than topically because there is little justification for treating deep-seated endocervical infections, which often are unresponsive to vaginal chemotherapy.

Medical treatment should be employed initially for patients during and after the childbearing period. If the patient is unimproved after 2–3 months, minor surgical therapy is indicated.

If the uterus is retroposed, it is restored to normal

anteposition if possible and a pessary inserted. This may reduce chronic passive congestion in the cervix and corpus.

Aqueous vaginal creams of low pH are also helpful. Aci-Jel, one application after an acetic acid douche every night for 3 weeks during the interval, may be used concomitantly with endocrine and antibiotic therapy. Warm douches are of limited value.

2. Surgical treatment–Before treating cervicitis surgically, one must consider the results desired; the likelihood of postoperative bleeding, infection, stricture formation, and infertility; and the implications for vaginal delivery in future pregnancies. Cervical cauterization or office dilatation of the cervix must not be done in the premenstrual period because of the danger of ascending infection and postoperative infection, but puncture biopsy of nabothian cysts may be done at any time during the cycle.

Other surgical procedures may be employed if the canal is widely exposed by lacerations or for severe chronic cervicitis. These procedures include light electrocauterization with low-frequency current employing a nasal tip or small Post electrode, or mild electrocoagulation with a high-frequency monopolar electrode.

With electrocoagulation (and electrosurgery), both incision and coagulation are possible, and the penetration of heat and destruction of diseased gland tissue are uniform and controllable. For these reasons, most physicians prefer coagulation to cauterization, although both methods, if used with skill and restraint, will give satisfactory results. Coagulation should be done radially.

When chronic cervicitis is accompanied by an ectropion (ectopy, eversion), the most successful treatment is destruction of the involved tissues by electrocauterization or by cryosurgery.

Electrocauterization is best performed in a radial strip fashion with either a thermal or a spark-type electrocautery within a few days following the completion of a menstrual period. Because of the paucity of nerve endings carrying pain sensation from the cervix, this can be done in the office without anesthesia. It should not be performed in an acutely inflamed cervix as this may produce a spread of infection into the parametrial tissues, nor should it be done before the possibility of an early cervical cancer has been eliminated by cytologic and biopsy examinations.

Immediately after cauterization, nitrofurazone (Furacin), sulfonamide cream, or suppositories locally and daily acetic acid douches for 3–4 days may be prescribed to aid healing.

Cryosurgery destroys tissue by freezing. The refrigerants (carbon dioxide, Freon, nitrous oxide, or nitrogen—all in liquid state) are passed through a hollow probe placed in the cervical canal and against the external os. The advantages are the ease of administration and lack of discomfort as compared with thermal or electrocauterization. Moreover, postoperative bleeding and cervical stenosis are uncommon after this procedure. This treatment method has the

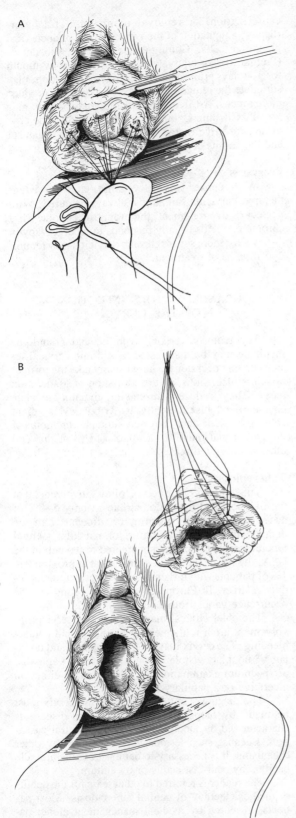

disadvantage of causing a profuse vaginal discharge for 2–3 weeks following its application.

The aim of these methods is destruction of infected tissues with subsequent healing by fibroblastic proliferation and reepithelialization. With either technique, there is a temporary increase in the amount of leukorrhea for 2–3 weeks. Anesthesia is usually unnecessary for minor surgical treatment. Complete healing may take up to 6 weeks. The cervix should be inspected again at the end of this time to be certain that healing is satisfactory. It is rarely necessary to cauterize a second time. If cauterization must be repeated, however, it should be done 1–2 months after the initial treatment to encourage healing.

Many complications of cauterization result from injudicious or overly vigorous use of the cautery. Reactivation of salpingitis may occur if treatment is given in the presence of acute cervicitis. Cervical stricture may follow deep cauterization carried high into the endocervical canal. Cauterization or freezing of a cervix that contains an unrecognized malignancy will mask the neoplastic process, resulting in further delay in its recognition and perhaps serious consequences.

On rare occasions it may be necessary to repair the lacerated cervix or remove a considerable portion of the cervix in order to eradicate a deep-seated infection. The latter requires conization (Fig 10–1) or cervical amputation (Fig 10–2) in the patient in whom it is important to preserve childbearing function. In patients with extensive chronic cervicitis who are beyond the childbearing years or who do not want more children, total hysterectomy may be the best method of management. This is particularly true when there is a second indication such as cervical dysplasia, symptomatic pelvic floor relaxation, or a need for sterilization.

Treatment of Complications

A. Cervical Hemorrhage: This may follow electrotherapy, trachelorrhaphy, or amputation of the cervix and necessitates suture and ligation of the bleeding vessels. Usually, point coagulation of bleeding areas is successful. Styptics such as negatol (Negatan) applied topically with snug vaginal packing may be helpful.

B. Salpingitis: Inflammation of the uterine tubes usually necessitates the administration of a broad-spectrum antibiotic, eg, procaine penicillin G, 1.2 million units intramuscularly daily for 3 days.

C. Leukorrhea: Discharge is usually due to persistent cervicitis caused by pyogenic organisms. In acute cases the endocervix should be cultured and suitable antibiotic treatment given. In chronic cases, retreatment of cervicitis is indicated.

D. Cervical Stenosis: The gentle passage of graduated sounds through the cervical canal at weekly intervals during the intermenstrual phase for 2–3 months following treatment will prevent or correct stenosis.

E. Infertility: Absence of cervical mucus necessary for sperm migration often causes infertility and may be due to too extensive destruction (coagulation,

Figure 10–1. Conization of the cervix.

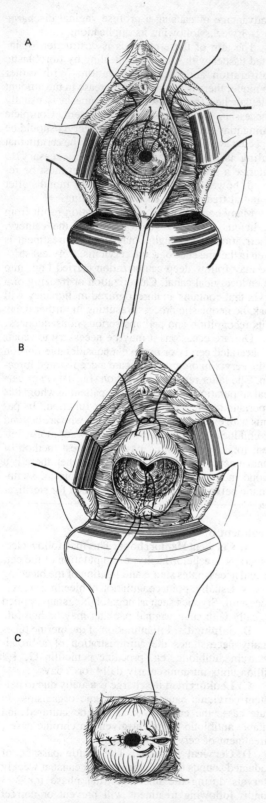

Figure 10–2. Sturmdorff trachelorrhaphy (after Ball). *A* and *B:* Cervix deeply coned (amputated if hypertrophic) and bleeding points controlled by sutures. *C:* Interrupted suture closure.

cauterization) or removal (conization, trachelorrhaphy, amputation of the cervix) of the endocervical glandular cells. Conjugated estrogenic substances (Premarin)—or equivalent—0.3 mg daily by mouth for 3–4 days prior to and on the day of ovulation, may stimulate the remaining endocervical cells to produce more mucus. Artificial insemination may be required.

F. Chronic Urinary Tract Infection: The type of anti-infective therapy depends upon the organism and the results of sensitivity tests.

Prognosis

With conservative, systemic, and persistent therapy, cervicitis can almost always be cured. With neglect or overtreatment, the prognosis is poor. Mild chronic cervicitis usually responds to local therapy in 4–8 weeks; more severe chronic cervicitis may require 2–3 months of treatment.

GRANULOMATOUS INFECTIONS OF THE CERVIX*

Tuberculosis, tertiary syphilis, and granuloma inguinale may be manifested by chronic cervical lesions on rare occasions. These usually take the form of nodules, ulcerations, or the formation of granulation tissue. They produce a chronic inflammatory exudate characterized histologically by lymphocytes, giant cells, and histiocytes. They may simulate carcinoma of the cervix and must be distinguished from this and other neoplastic diseases.

Tuberculosis

Tuberculosis of the cervix follows involvement of the oviducts and the endometrium in only 5–6% of cases, but active pulmonary disease can be documented in only one-third of patients. Genital tuberculosis is not often encountered in women in the USA, the incidence being estimated at approximately 1% of patients with inflammatory disease of the reproductive tract. In European and Asian countries, the occurrence varies from 2 to 10%.

The chief clinical manifestations of cervical involvement are a foul-smelling discharge and contact bleeding. The cervix may be hypertrophied and nodular, without any visible lesion on the portio vaginalis, or speculum examination may demonstrate either an ulcerative or a papillary lesion.

The diagnosis of tuberculosis of the cervix must be made by biopsy. Histologically, the disease is characterized by tubercles undergoing central caseation. Because such lesions may be caused by other organisms, it is necessary to demonstrate the tubercle bacillus by acid-fast stains or by culture.

The reader is referred to other texts for the details of medical therapy of genital tuberculosis. Most patients are cured by medical management alone; patients who respond poorly or who have other problems

*Syphilis and granuloma inguinale are discussed in Chapter 15.

(eg, tumors, fistulas) may require total hysterectomy and bilateral salpingo-oophorectomy after a trial of chemotherapy.

RARE INFECTIOUS DISEASES OF THE CERVIX

Lymphogranuloma venereum, a chlamydial infection, and **chancroid,** caused by *Haemophilus ducreyi,* may attack the cervix along with other areas of the reproductive tract.

Cervical **actinomycosis** may occur as a result of contamination by instruments and by intrauterine devices. The cervical lesion may be a nodular tumor, ulcer, or fistula. Prolonged penicillin or sulfonamide therapy is recommended.

Schistosomiasis of the cervix is usually secondary to involvement of the pelvic and uterine veins by the blood fluke *S haematobium.* Cervical schistosomiasis may produce a large papillary growth that ulcerates and bleeds on contact, simulating cervical cancer. In other instances, it may be found in endocervical polyps, causing intermenstrual and postcoital bleeding. An ovum can occasionally be identified in a biopsy specimen taken from the granulomatous cervical lesion. The diagnosis is usually made, however, by recovering the parasite from the urine or feces. Chemical, serologic, and intradermal tests for schistosomiasis are also available.

Echinococcal cysts may involve the cervix. Treatment consists of surgical excision.

CYSTIC ABNORMALITIES OF THE CERVIX

Nabothian Cysts

When a tunnel or cleft of tall columnar endocervical epithelium becomes sealed off, either through an inflammatory process or as a result of epidermidization (squamous metaplasia), mucous secretions become entrapped, producing a cyst of microscopic to macroscopic size. These nabothian cysts develop frequently, but only when they are so numerous that they produce marked enlargement of the cervix due to the retention of mucus are they of clinical significance. On the portio vaginalis of the cervix their presence serves as an indication that the portio was at one time the site of ectopic endocervical epithelium which has been replaced by squamous epithelium. The nabothian cyst farthest away from the external cervical os on the portio indicates the extent of the "transformation zone."

Mesonephric Cysts

Microscopic remnants of the mesonephric (wolffian) duct are often seen deep in the stroma externally in the normal cervix. Occasionally they become cystic, forming structures up to 2.5 mm in diameter lined by ragged cuboid epithelium. They may be confused with deeply situated nabothian cysts, but their location and the wolffian type cells lining the cysts serve as useful distinguishing features.

Endometriosis

Endometriosis occasionally produces small reddish or purplish cystic structures on the portio vaginalis of the cervix. These usually measure several millimeters in diameter, but cysts larger than 1 cm in diameter have occasionally been reported. Endometriosis involves the cervix primarily by implantation during delivery or surgery or by direct extension from the cul-de-sac. Biopsy showing typical endometrial glands and stroma is diagnostic. These areas of ectopic endometrium usually respond to hormonal stimuli during the menstrual cycle. Intermenstrual and postcoital bleeding, dysmenorrhea, and dyspareunia may be associated symptoms. Rarely, the lesions may resemble a cervical malignancy; hence, the diagnosis of endometriosis depends upon biopsy. Small lesions may be destroyed by cauterization, but larger ones must be excised.

Cervical Pregnancy

Cervical pregnancy is a very rare type of ectopic gestation that consists of implantation in the cervical canal below the internal os. Inasmuch as the entire product of conception must be outside (below) the uterine cavity, the available space for the developing pregnancy is extremely limited. Pelvic pain, backache, and brisk vaginal bleeding indicative of threatened or inevitable abortion generally begin in the early second trimester. Ultrasonography, demonstrating an empty uterus and a widened cervical canal with internal echoes, may be helpful. A cervical pregnancy almost never goes to viability. The hypertrophic, gaping, bleeding cervix, with degenerated tissue within the canal, may be easily mistaken for a cancer focus. If the placenta is felt within the canal, an erroneous diagnosis of placenta previa may be made. In other cases, a true cervical pregnancy may be confused with an aborted intrauterine pregnancy that had lodged within an unyielding, partially dilated cervix. In any event, hemorrhage may be exsanguinating, especially with vaginal manipulation. If evacuation of a cervical pregnancy cannot be accomplished easily and quickly, immediate total abdominal hysterectomy may be lifesaving. Successful management of cervical pregnancy by early recognition and bilateral internal artery ligation with conservation of reproductive function has been reported.

Cervical Stenosis

Cervical stenosis—of congenital, inflammatory, neoplastic, or surgical origin—may be partially or even completely occlusive. Most cases of cervical stenosis follow cauterization or coagulation of the cervix for the treatment of chronic cervicitis. Marked to complete obstruction to menstrual drainage will result in hematometra, typified by cryptomenorrhea or amenorrhea, abdominal discomfort, and a soft, slightly tender midpelvic mass.

Cautious dilatation of the cervix repeated several weeks later, when an endometrial biopsy should be done to rule out cancer, is recommended in the treatment of hematometra. The endocervical canal should receive minimal caustic therapy or electrotherapy for chronic cervicitis to avoid cervical stenosis.

Cervical Changes Related to Diethylstilbestrol Exposure in Utero

Congenital anomalies of the cervix are discussed in Chapter 8. Those related to intrauterine exposure to diethylstilbestrol (DES) deserve special consideration,

as they are encountered in about two-thirds of exposed female offspring and there are an estimated 1 million such young women in the USA alone. Although unusual cervical configurations are common in these individuals, the risk of clear cell cancer is thought to be between 0.14 and 1.4 per 1000.

The cervical changes due to DES exposure have been classified as follows (Sandberg) (Fig 10–3): (1) circular sulcus, complete or incomplete; (2) recessed area surrounding the external os; (3) portio vaginalis completely covered by columnar epithelium; (4) pseudopolyp formation due to localized, eccentric hypertrophy of endocervical tissue (not shown in illustra-

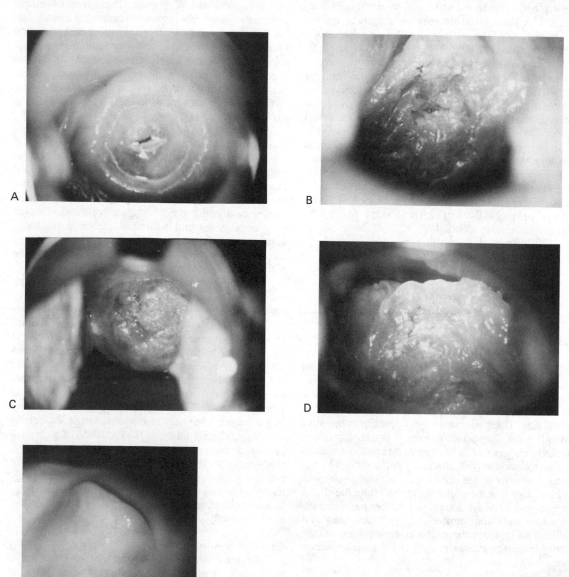

Figure 10–3. Cervical changes in women exposed to DES in utero. *A:* Circular sulcus. *B:* Central depression and ectopy. *C:* Portio vaginalis covered by columnar epithelium (ectopy). *D:* Anterior cervical protuberance (rough). *E:* Anterior cervical protuberance (smooth).

tion); and (5) and (6) anterior cervical lip protuberances, rough or smooth. These changes are often associated with certain anomalies of the vagina such as incomplete septa, fibrous bands, narrowing of the vaginal apex, and vaginal adenosis.

Preliminary studies show that some of the cervical changes associated with DES exposure may predispose to cervical incompetence in pregnancy, and an increased incidence of spontaneous abortion and ectopic pregnancies has been reported.

BENIGN NEOPLASMS OF THE CERVIX

1. MICROGLANDULAR HYPERPLASIA OF THE ENDOCERVICAL MUCOSA

Microglandular (adenomatous) hyperplasia of the endocervix, an abnormal response to the hormonal stimulus of oral contraceptive medication, may occur in occasional patients. It may also result from inflammation. Grossly, this disorder appears as exuberant granular tissue within the cervical canal, often extruding beyond the cervical os. Microscopically, it presents as a collection of closely packed cystic spaces lined by nonneoplastic columnar epithelium and filled with mucus. Grossly, adenomatous hyperplasia may be mistaken for a malignancy, but biopsy should make the distinction.

2. CERVICAL POLYPS

Essentials of Diagnosis

- Intermenstrual or postcoital bleeding.
- A soft, red pedunculated protrusion from the cervical canal at the external os.
- Microscopic examination confirms the diagnosis of benign polyp.

General Considerations

Cervical polyps are small pedunculated and often sessile or tessellated neoplasms of the cervix. Most originate from the endocervix; a few arise from the portio. They are composed of a vascular connective tissue stroma and covered by columnar, squamocolumnar, or squamous epithelium. Polyps are relatively common, especially in multigravidas over 20 years of age. They are rare before the menarche, but an occasional one may develop after the menopause. Asymptomatic polyps often are discovered on routine pelvic examination. Most are benign, but all should be removed and submitted for pathologic examination because malignant change may occur. Moreover, some cervical cancers present as a polypoid mass.

Polyps arise as a result of focal hyperplasia of the endocervix. It is not known whether this is due to chronic inflammation, an abnormal local responsiveness to hormonal stimulation, or a localized vascular congestion of cervical blood vessels. They are often

found also in association with endometrial hyperplasia, suggesting that hyperestrinism plays a significant etiologic role.

Endocervical polyps are usually red, flameshaped, fragile growths and may vary in size from a few millimeters in length and diameter to larger tumors 2–3 cm in diameter and several centimeters long. They are usually attached to the endocervical mucosa near the external os by a narrow pedicle, but occasionally the base is broad. On microscopic examination, the stroma of a polyp is composed of fibrous connective tissue containing numerous small blood vessels in the center. There is often an extravasation of blood and a marked infiltration of the stroma by inflammatory cells (polymorphonuclear neutrophils, lymphocytes, and plasma cells). The surface epithelium resembles that of the endocervix, varying from typical picket fence columnar cells to areas that show squamous metaplasia and mature stratified squamous epithelium. The surface often is thrown into folds much as is the normal endocervical mucosa.

Ectocervical polyps are pale, flesh-colored, smooth, and rounded or elongated, often with a broad pedicle. They arise from the portio and are less likely to bleed than endocervical polyps. Microscopically, they are more fibrous than endocervical polyps, having few or no mucous glands. They are covered by stratified squamous epithelium.

Metaplastic alteration is common. Inflammation, often with necrosis at the tip (or more extensively), is typical of both polyp types.

The incidence of malignant change in a cervical polyp is estimated to be less than 1%. Squamous cell carcinoma is the most common type, although adenocarcinomas have been reported. Endometrial cancer may involve the polyp secondarily. Sarcoma rarely develops within a polyp.

Botryoid sarcoma, an embryonal tumor of the cervix (or vaginal wall) resembling small pink or yellow grapes, contains striated muscle and other mesenchymal elements. It is extremely malignant.

Most polypoid structures are vascular and often infected and are subject to displacement or torsion. Discharge commonly results, and bleeding, often metrorrhagia of the postcoital type, follows.

Chronic irritation and bleeding are annoying and cause cervicitis, endometritis, and parametritis; salpingitis may develop if these are not treated successfully.

Because polyps are a potential focus of cancer, they must be examined routinely for malignant characteristics on removal.

Clinical Findings

A. Symptoms and Signs: Intermenstrual or postcoital bleeding is the most common symptom. Leukorrhea and hypermenorrhea have also been associated with cervical polyps.

Abnormal vaginal bleeding is often reported. Postmenopausal bleeding is frequently described by older women. Infertility may be traceable to cervical polyps and cervicitis.

Cervical polyps appear as smooth, red, fingerlike projections from the cervical canal and are usually about 1–2 cm in length and 0.5–1 cm in diameter. Generally they are too soft to be felt by the examining finger.

B. X-Ray Findings: Polyps high in the endocervical canal may be demonstrated by hysterography and often are a significant finding in hitherto unexplained infertility.

C. Laboratory Findings: Vaginal cytology will reveal signs of infection and often abnormal cells of Papanicolaou class II–III. Blood and urine studies are not helpful.

D. Special Examinations: Occasionally a polyp high in the endocervical canal may be seen with the aid of a special endocervical speculum. Some are found only at the time of diagnostic D&C in the investigation of abnormal bleeding.

Differential Diagnosis

Masses projecting from the cervix may be polypoid but not polyps. Adenocarcinoma of the endometrium or endometrial sarcoma may present at the external os or even beyond. Discharge and bleeding usually occur.

Typical polyps are not difficult to diagnose by gross inspection, but ulcerated and atypical growths must be distinguished from small submucous pedunculated myomas or endometrial polyps arising low in the uterus. These often result in dilatation of the cervix, presenting just within the os and resembling cervical polyps. The products of conception, usually decidua, may push through the cervix and resemble a polypoid tissue mass, but other signs and symptoms of recent pregnancy generally are absent. Condylomas, submucous myomas, and polypoid carcinomas are diagnosed by microscopic examination.

Complications

All polyps are infected, some by virulent staphylococci, streptococci, or other pathogens. Serious infections occasionally follow instrumentation for the identification or removal of polyps. A broad-spectrum antibiotic should be administered at the first sign or symptom of spreading infection.

Acute salpingitis may be initiated or exacerbated by polypectomy.

It is unwise to remove a large polyp and then do a hysterectomy several days thereafter. Pelvic peritonitis may complicate the latter procedure. A delay of several weeks or a month between polypectomy and hysterectomy is recommended.

Prevention

Because of the possible role of chronic inflammation in polyp formation, cervical ectopy and chronic cervicitis must always be treated promptly.

Treatment

A. Medical Measures: Culture and sensitivity tests of cervical discharge and appropriate therapy are indicated if infection is present.

B. Specific Measures: Most polyps can be removed in the office. This is done with little bleeding by grasping the pedicle with a hemostat or uterine packing forceps and twisting it until the growth is avulsed. Large polyps and those with sessile attachments may require electrosurgical excision and suturing. It may be wise in some cases to perform these procedures in the hospital because of the risk of hemorrhage.

If the cervix is soft, patulous, or definitely dilated and the polyp is large, surgical D&C should be done, especially if the pedicle is not readily visible. Exploration of the cervical and uterine cavities with the polyp forceps and curette may disclose multiple polyps or other important lesions.

All tissue must be sent to a pathologist to be examined for malignancy.

C. Local Measures: Warm acetic acid douches after polypectomy usually suffice to control an inflammatory reaction. Prophylactic antibiotic therapy is not usually necessary.

Prognosis

Simple removal is usually curative.

3. PAPILLOMAS OF THE CERVIX

Cervical papillomas are benign neoplasms found on the portio vaginalis of the cervix. They are composed of a central core of fibrous connective tissue and are covered by stratified squamous epithelium. These small growths usually are discovered in the course of routine pelvic examination. They present as slightly raised, papillary excrescences on the cervix. Rarely are they larger than 1 cm in diameter.

A papilloma may be confused with an exophytic squamous cell carcinoma or a single condyloma acuminatum. Although more than 95% are benign, a small number of these lesions will show anaplasia of the squamous epithelium varying from dysplasia to carcinoma in situ to invasive carcinoma.

These lesions should be surgically excised and the base treated by electrocauterization. The specimen should be examined pathologically for evidence of malignant change.

4. LEIOMYOMAS OF THE CERVIX

Because of the paucity of smooth muscle elements in the cervical stroma, leiomyomas arising primarily in the cervix are uncommon. The ratio of corpus leiomyomas to cervical leiomyomas is in the range of 12:1.

Although myomas are usually multiple in the corpus, cervical myomas are most often solitary. Grossly and microscopically, they are identical to leiomyomas arising elsewhere in the uterus.

Clinical Findings

A. Symptoms and Signs: Cervical leiomyomas are often silent, producing no symptoms, unless they become very large. Symptoms, when present, are those due to pressure on surrounding organs such as the bladder, rectum, or soft tissues of the parametrium or obstruction of the cervical canal. Frequency and urgency of urination are the result of bladder compression. Urinary retention occasionally occurs as a result of pressure against the urethra. Hematometra may develop with obstruction of the cervix.

If the direction of growth is lateral, there may be ureteral obstruction with hydronephrosis. Rectal encroachment causes constipation. Dyspareunia may occur if the tumor occupies the vagina. In pregnancy, because of their location, large cervical leiomyomas, unlike those involving the corpus, are apt to cause soft tissue dystocia, preventing descent of the presenting part in the pelvis.

Cervical leiomyomas of significant size are readily palpated on bimanual examination.

B. X-Ray Findings: A plain film may demonstrate the typical mottled calcific pattern associated with these tumors. Hysterography may define distortion of the endocervical canal. Intravenous urography may demonstrate ureteral displacement or obstruction.

Treatment

Small, asymptomatic cervical leiomyomas should be observed for rate of growth. If they become larger, they should be removed, and it may be possible to enucleate a single, small tumor via the vaginal route. However, because cervical tumors are often associated with multiple leiomyomas of the corpus, the surgical approach is usually an abdominal one and the treatment is either a multiple myomectomy or total hysterectomy, depending on the clinical circumstances and the need to preserve the uterus for childbearing.

Because of the proximity of the pelvic ureter to the cervix, this structure may be in jeopardy in any operation involving a cervical leiomyoma, and precautions should be taken to prevent its injury.

DYSPLASIA & CARCINOMA IN SITU OF THE CERVIX
(Cervical Intraepithelial Neoplasia)

Essentials of Diagnosis

- The cervix often appears grossly normal.
- Dysplastic or carcinoma in situ cells are noted in cytologic smear preparations.
- Colposcopic examination reveals coarse punctate or mosaic patterns of surface capillaries, an atypical transformation zone, and thickened "white epithelium."
- Iodine-nonstaining (Schiller-positive) area of squamous epithelium is typical.
- Biopsy diagnosis of dysplasia or carcinoma in situ.

General Considerations

Dysplasia literally means disordered growth or development. In the cervix, this term is applied to abnormal zones in which only a part of the thickness of the squamous epithelium has been replaced by abnormal cells. Dysplasia is subdivided into mild, moderate, and severe depending upon the degree of involvement of the epithelium. In severe cases, the histologic appearance resembles carcinoma in situ with the exception that a few cell layers near the surface are still capable of maturation. Carcinoma in situ exists when all of the cell layers from the basement membrane to the surface disclose an immature, disorganized pattern. Complete loss of cellular polarity is notable, and all layers show pleomorphism. The various degrees of cervical intraepithelial neoplasia, ranging from mild dysplasia to carcinoma in situ, represent a continuum in the neoplastic process. If untreated, severe dysplasia will progress to carcinoma in situ that will progress to invasive cancer in a significant number of patients.

Etiology

The field theory of the origin of squamous cell carcinoma of the cervix maintains that cancer begins in areas which have been previously altered to make them potentially neoplastic. Most cervical cancers make their initial appearance in zones of atypical or dysplastic epithelium and develop very slowly. The cause of these atypical changes in the cells is unknown. The epidemiologic factors in dysplasia are similar to those of cancer of the cervix. (See Cancer of the Cervix.)

Prevalence figures for cervical dysplasia vary from 1.2 to 3.8% in nonpregnant patients. Pregnancy may produce changes in the cervical epithelium that mimic those of cervical dysplasia. Some of these variations may be related to folic acid deficiency. Morphologically, one cannot distinguish these changes from those of true neoplasia. Of the pregnancy changes, three-fourths are involuted within 6 months postpartum with a return of the cytologic picture to normal. The incidence of true neoplastic dysplasia in pregnant women is not known. Nonetheless, dysplasia occurs in females age 15 and older, with a peak incidence in the age group from 25 to 35 years.

Pathology

On cytologic examination, the dysplastic cell is characterized by anaplasia, an increased nuclear-cytoplasmic ratio (ie, the nucleus is larger), hyperchromatism with changes in the nuclear chromatin, multinucleation, and abnormalities in differentiation.

Histologically, involvement of varying degrees of thickness of the stratified squamous epithelium is typical of dysplasia. The cells are anaplastic, hyperchromatic, and show a loss of polarity in the deeper layers as well as abnormal mitotic figures in increased numbers. Maturation of the cells is seen near the surface, however, so that the picture falls short of the changes that characterize carcinoma in situ. Benign epithelial alterations, particularly those of an inflammatory nature, as well as technical artifacts may be

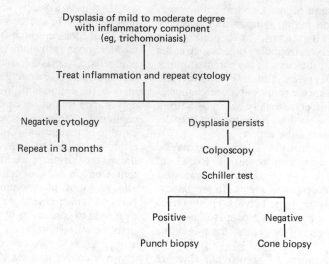

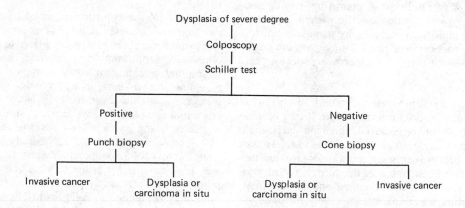

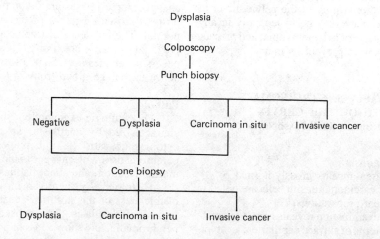

Figure 10–7. Plan for management of the abnormal cytologic smear in which there is no visible lesion.

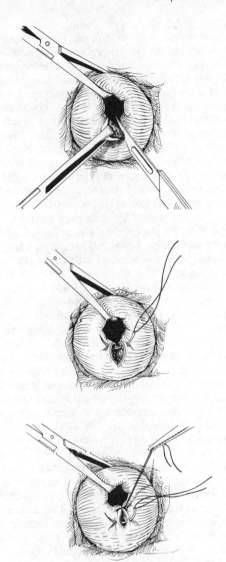

Figure 10–4. Wedge biopsy of the cervix.

mistaken for dysplasia.

Spontaneous regression, particularly of dysplasia of mild degree, occurs in a significant number of patients, so the process is reversible. In others, it appears to remain static for many years. Nonetheless, progression to carcinoma in situ and even invasive carcinoma has been observed in about one-third of patients who have been followed over long periods of time. The more severe degrees of dysplasia appear to progress to carcinoma in situ more commonly and more rapidly than those of mild degree.

It has been suggested that the various degrees of dysplasia be classified as cervical intraepithelial neoplasia (CIN) with mild dysplasia CIN I, moderate dysplasia CIN II, and both severe dysplasia and carcinoma in situ CIN III. This is because the pathologic criteria distinguishing severe dysplasia from carcinoma in situ have not been well established and

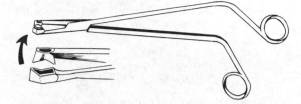

Figure 10–5. Tischler cervical biopsy forceps.

because the clinical management of both conditions is identical.

Clinical Findings

A. Symptoms and Signs: There are usually no symptoms or signs, and the diagnosis is most often based on cytologic findings in the course of a routine cervical Papanicolaou smear evaluation. Because dysplasia probably is a transitional phase in the pathogenesis of many cervical cancers, its early detection is extremely important. All postpubertal women should have a pelvic and cytologic examination at least once a year. When dysplasia is diagnosed cytologically, steps should be taken to confirm the diagnosis histologically and to determine the extent of the lesion.

B. Special Examinations: In addition to gross inspection of the cervix, the diagnostic procedures include the Schiller test, colposcopic examination, directed biopsy, endocervical curettage, and cold cone biopsy of the cervix.

1. Schiller test–The Schiller test employs the principle that normal squamous epithelium of the cervix contains glycogen, which will combine with iodine to produce a deep mahogany-brown color. Nonstaining, then, indicates abnormal squamous (or columnar) epithelium, scarring, cyst formation, etc, and constitutes a positive Schiller test. The test is not specific for cancer but merely reveals non–glycogen-containing epithelium. Immature metaplastic epithelium frequently is nonstaining.

Schiller's solution is an aqueous iodine preparation:

Iodine	0.33
Potassium iodide	0.67
Water, qs ad	120.0

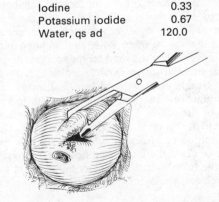

Figure 10–6. Multiple punch biopsy of cervix with Tischler forceps.

Lugol's solution is commonly used for the Schiller test as it is readily available:

Iodine	5.0
Potassium iodide	10.0
Water, qs ad	100.0

Note that Lugol's solution is over 10 times as strong as Schiller's solution. Thus, it takes less time to stain the glycogen-rich epithelium than does Schiller's solution and is a satisfactory substitute.

2. Colposcopic examination–(See Chapter 5 and illustrations there.) Colposcopy requires an instrument that allows inspection of the cervix under low-power magnification (6–40×) and an intense light source. It is especially useful in the evaluation of patients with an abnormal cytologic examination. Abnormalities in the appearance of the epithelium and its capillary blood supply often are not visible to the naked eye but can be identified by colposcopy, particularly after the application of 3% aqueous acetic acid solution. Cervical intraepithelial neoplasia produces recognizable abnormalities on the portio vaginalis of the cervix in the vast majority of patients.

Normal colposcopic findings are those of (1) original squamous epithelium; (2) transformation zone (metaplastic squamous epithelium); and (3) columnar epithelium. Abnormal findings indicative of dysplasia and carcinoma in situ are those of (1) "white epithelium" and (2) mosaicism or coarse punctate pattern of the surface capillaries. Early stromal invasion should be suspected when one finds bizarre capillaries with so-called corkscrew, comma-shaped, or spaghettilike configurations. A colposcopically directed punch biopsy of such areas should be done. Light endocervical curettage, using a small sharp curet, is worthwhile also in most cases.

Colposcopically directed punch biopsy using the Younge-Kevorkian square jaw alligator punch forceps is most revealing in the diagnosis of cervical intraepithelial neoplasia. If the squamocolumnar junction of the cervix is visible by colposcopy, the false-negative rate for colposcopically directed punch biopsy is less than 1%. Unfortunately, the transformation zone extends into the endocervical canal beyond the field of vision in 12–15% of premenopausal women and in a significantly higher percentage of postmenopausal women. When this situation exists, a cone biopsy will be required for the accurate diagnosis of intraepithelial (or invasive) neoplasia.

3. Diagnostic cone biopsy–Following expert colposcopic evaluation, diagnostic shallow cone biopsy of the cervix is indicated (1) if the lesion extends into the cervical canal beyond the view afforded by the colposcope (unsatisfactory colposcopic examination) or (2) if there is a significant discrepancy between the histologic diagnosis of the directed biopsy specimen and the cytologic examination.

Treatment

Dysplasia of mild degree (CIN I) may be managed by careful observation, with cytologic examinations repeated every 6 months in expectation of spontaneous regression. In preliminary studies, condom contraception appeared to prevent the progression of CIN and to favor regression. Controlled studies are needed for confirmation. Moderate to severe dysplasia or carcinoma in situ (CIN II or III) must be treated by eradication once careful evaluation has eliminated the possibility of coexistent invasive cancer. Moderate dysplasia can often be treated effectively in an office setting by electrocauterization, cryosurgery, or carbon dioxide laser vaporization but only after careful colposcopic evaluation and endocervical curettage have localized the process to the visible portion of the cervical portio vaginalis. Cryosurgery involves less discomfort to the patient than electrocauterization or thermal cauterization but is followed by a heavy watery discharge for 4–6 weeks. Furthermore, the rate of cell destruction falls off rapidly at a depth of 3–4 mm, so dysplasia in the deeper tunnels and crypts of the transformation zone may not be controlled. The failure rate of cryotherapy in the more severe forms of cervical intraepithelial neoplasia is about 20%. Severe dysplasia and carcinoma in situ (CIN III) are best removed by therapeutic cold cone biopsy of the cervix (Fig 10–1), although hysterectomy may be preferred if sterilization is desired or with additional indications, eg, uterine leiomyomas or dysfunctional uterine bleeding. Postoperative hemorrhage and cervical stenosis are significant complications of cold cone biopsy. Carbon dioxide laser therapy is being investigated as a therapeutic alternative to cryotherapy and cold cone biopsy. Under colposcopic visualization, the laser has the advantage of accurate control of depth of tissue destruction as well as avoidance of postcryotherapy vaginal discharge by tissue vaporization rather than necrosis. The high cost of the instrument is a disadvantage, and lack of follow-up information on sufficient numbers of treated patients makes this method experimental at present.

Recurrence of carcinoma in situ or even the development of an invasive cancer may occur many years after treatment of intraepithelial neoplasia. Following therapeutic conization, the risk of recurrent carcinoma in situ is 2–3%. After hysterectomy, 1–2% of patients develop recurrent carcinoma in situ in the vaginal apex. Careful follow-up examinations are essential for an indefinite period in all patients treated for dysplasia and carcinoma in situ regardless of the mode of therapy.

CANCER OF THE CERVIX

Essentials of Diagnosis

- Abnormal uterine bleeding and vaginal discharge.
- Cervical lesion may be visible on inspection as a tumor or ulceration; cancer within the cervical canal may be occult.
- Vaginal cytology, usually positive, must be confirmed by biopsy.

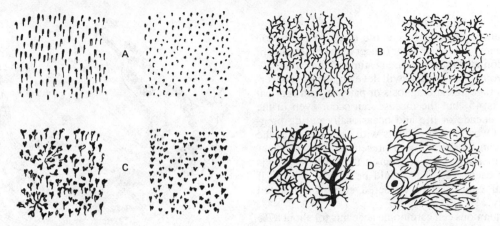

Figure 10–8. Schematic drawing of different types of terminal vessels as observed in the normal squamous epithelium. Hairpin capillaries *(A)*, network capillaries *(B)*, both found in normal states, double capillaries *(C)* seen in *Trichomonas* inflammation, and branching vessels *(D)* seen in the transformation zone.

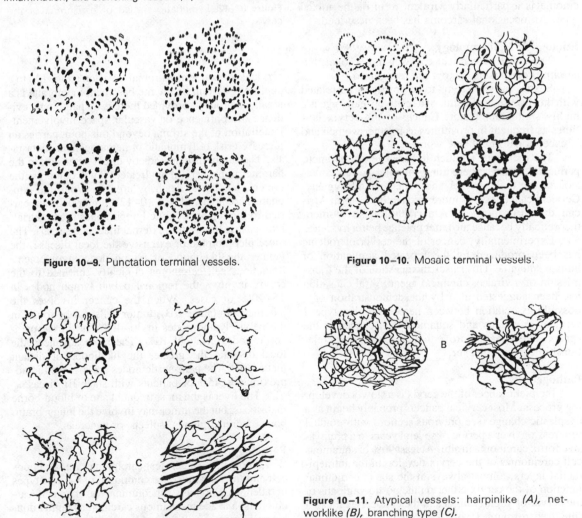

Figure 10–9. Punctation terminal vessels.

Figure 10–10. Mosaic terminal vessels.

Figure 10–11. Atypical vessels: hairpinlike *(A)*, networklike *(B)*, branching type *(C)*.

Figures 10–8 through 10–11 are reproduced, with permission, from Johannisson E, Kolstad P, Söderberg G: Cytologic, vascular, and histologic patterns of dysplasia, carcinoma in situ and early invasive carcinoma of the cervix. *Acta Radiol* [*Suppl*] (Stockh) 1966; 258.

General Considerations

Cancer of the cervix is the third most common malignancy in women after cancer of the breast and of the endometrium. It has been estimated that about 2% of all women over age 40 will develop cervical cancer. The average age at diagnosis of patients with cervical cancer is 45, but the disease can occur even in the second decade of life and occasionally during pregnancy. Over 95% of patients with early cancer of the cervix can be cured. With present methods of management, about 8000 women in the USA die of this disease each year. This could be greatly reduced if cervical cancer were detected early and treated properly.

Squamous cell carcinoma accounts for about 87% of cases and adenocarcinoma or mixed adenosquamous carcinomas for about 13% of malignant epithelial neoplasms of the cervix. The so-called glassy-cell carcinoma is a particularly virulent form of the mixed type. An occasional sarcoma has been described.

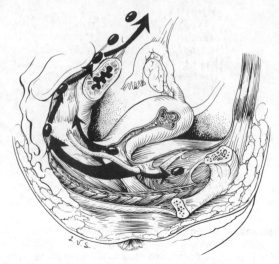

Figure 10–12. Lymphatic spread of carcinoma of the cervix.

Etiology & Epidemiology

The cause of cervical cancer is not known, but certain predisposing factors are recognized.

Sexual activity seems to be positively correlated with the disease, and coitus at a relatively early age is a highly significant factor. Cancer of the cervix is 4 times as frequent in prostitutes as in other women and is exceptional in celibate women.

The incidence is much lower in Jewish women, perhaps because of hereditary immunity or circumcision of the male partner and better genital hygiene. Cervical cancer occurs more frequently in North African than European or American Jewish women, theoretically because the latter practice better hygiene.

Experimentally, cancer of the cervix of rodents has been produced by the repeated application of human smegma. This raises the question of the transmission of a viral or chemical agent. Viral causation has been suggested also by the demonstration of a possible association between herpes simplex type 2 cervical infections and squamous cell cancer of the cervix. This does not prove that an actual causal relationship exists, however.

Pathogenesis

Incipient cancer of the cervix is a slowly developing process. Most cervical cancers probably begin as a dysplastic change (see previous section) with gradual progression over a period of several years to a preinvasive form: carcinoma in situ. At least 90% of squamous cell carcinomas of the cervix develop in the intraepithelial layers, almost always at the squamocolumnar junction of the cervix either on the portio vaginalis of the cervix or slightly higher in the endocervical canal (the transformation zone). In most instances, the preinvasive form of the disease remains static for another 7–10 years. During this time, however, it may extend over the surface to involve larger areas of squamous (and columnar) epithelium. Eventually it breaks free of its restraints and invades the subjacent

cervical stroma. Early stromal invasion (stage IA) to a depth of 1–2 mm below the basement membrane is a localized process, provided there is no pathologic evidence of confluence or vascular space involvement. Penetration of the stroma beyond this point carries an increased risk of lymphatic or hematogenous metastasis. The tumor also spreads by direct extension to the parametrium where, if not treated, it will compress the ureters, leading to death by uremia. When the lymphatics are involved (Fig 10–12), tumor cells are carried to the regional pelvic lymph nodes (parametrial, hypogastric, obturator, external iliac, and sacral). The more pleomorphic or extensive the local disease, the greater the likelihood of lymph node involvement. Squamous cell carcinoma clinically confined to the cervix involves the regional pelvic lymph nodes in 15–20% of cases. When the cancer involves the parametrium (stage IIB), tumor cells can be found in the pelvic lymph nodes in 30–40% and in the para-aortic nodes in about 10%. The more advanced the local disease, the greater the likelihood of distant metastases. The para-aortic nodes are involved in approximately 45% of patients with stage III disease.

The liver is the most frequent site of blood-borne metastasis, but the tumor may involve the lungs, brain, bones, adrenal glands, spleen, or pancreas.

Pathology

About 75% of cervical carcinomas are squamous cell and the remainder are composed of various types of adenocarcinomas, subcolumnar reserve cell carcinomas, and adenosquamous carcinomas (either double primaries or collision tumors).

A. Squamous Cell (Epidermoid) Carcinomas: Cervical squamous cell carcinomas have been classified according to the predominant cell type (Reagan and Ng): large cell nonkeratinizing, large cell keratinizing, and small cell carcinomas. The large cell nonkeratinizing variety is reputed to carry the best prognosis (68.3%), while the small cell nonkeratinizing tumor has the lowest 5-year survival rate (20%).

The most widely used classification is based on the degree of differentiation, which may be expressed more specifically as follows (Warren, Corscaden):

Well-differentiated (grade I): Squamous cells demonstrate well-defined intercellular bridges and cytoplasmic keratohyalin in the well-differentiated variety. Epithelial pearls are a common feature of this type of tumor, and mitotic figures are not too numerous—fewer than 2 mitoses per high-power field—with minimal variation in the size and shape of tumor cells.

Moderately differentiated (grade II): This is an intermediate group. Varieties of all 3 patterns may be found in the same tumor, rendering accuracy of tumor grading on the basis of degree of differentiation somewhat difficult. There are infrequent epithelial pearls, moderate keratinization, occasional intercellular bridges, 2–4 mitoses per high-power field, and moderate variation in size and shape of tumor cells.

Poorly differentiated (grade III): Poorly differentiated cancers present nests and cords of small, deeply stained cells barely resembling mature squamous epithelium. These have scant cytoplasm surrounding hyperchromatic nuclei and show little tendency to differentiation. There are no epithelial pearls, slight keratinization, no intercellular bridges, more than 4 mitoses per high-power field, often marked variation in size and shape of tumor cells, occasional small, elongated, closely packed tumor cells, and numerous giant cells.

Malignancy roughly parallels the grade: The undifferentiated variety metastasizes earlier but also responds better initially to radiation therapy. Vascular space involvement by tumor cells increases the likelihood of lymph node involvement and worsens the prognosis for survival. A marked lymphocytic response surrounding tumor cells, on the other hand, decreases the chance of lymph node spread and is associated with a somewhat better prognosis.

B. Adenocarcinoma: Adenocarcinoma of the cervix is derived from the glandular elements of the cervix. It is composed of tall, columnar secretory cells arranged in an adenomatous pattern with scant supporting stroma. A much less common adenocarcinoma is derived from the mesonephric (wolffian) duct remnants within the cervix. In these, the cells are small, cuboid, and irregular and the glandular pattern less well defined. Adenocarcinoma of the cervix usually is not diagnosed until it is advanced and ulcerative.

During pregnancy, hypertrophy and hyperplasia of the squamous and glandular elements are obvious on biopsy. However, intraepithelial as well as invasive

carcinoma may also be present. Gestational changes should not be permitted to confuse the diagnosis.

Adenocarcinoma is graded as well-differentiated, moderately well-differentiated, and poorly differentiated. However, precise classification may not be possible even after examination of numerous isolated fragments because tissue variability is marked.

C. Invasive Carcinoma: Ulceration always implies necrosis of the superficial epithelium. If extensive necrosis is present, it is imperative that biopsy be done at the margin of the ulcer to compare normal and abnormal tissue. A carcinomatous process usually has a firm, somewhat raised edge; the base of the ulcer is indurated, irregular, and granular.

A primary cancer rising elsewhere in the body may involve the cervix secondarily. The most frequent secondary malignancy of the cervix is that of carcinoma of the endometrium involving the cervix by direct extension from the corpus of the uterus (stage II). Sarcomas, choriocarcinomas, and melanomas are encountered rarely in the cervix.

Clinical Staging

It is important to estimate the extent of the disease not only as an aid to prognosis but also in order to plan treatment. Clinical staging also affords a means of comparing methods of therapy.

The International Classification adopted by the International Federation of Gynecology and Obstetrics (FIGO) is the one most widely used (Table 10–2). More recently, the so-called TNM classification, proposed by the International Union Against Cancer, has been advocated as providing a means of staging cancer in any anatomic location (Table 10–3).

Clinical Findings

A. Symptoms and Signs: Intermenstrual bleeding is the most frequent symptom of invasive cancer and may take the form of a blood-stained leukorrheal discharge, scant spotting, or frank bleeding. Leukorrhea, usually sanguineous or purulent, odorous, and nonpruritic, usually is present. A history of postcoital bleeding may be elicited on specific questioning.

Pelvic pain, often unilateral and radiating to the hip or thigh, is a manifestation of advanced disease, as is the involuntary loss of urine or feces through the vagina, a sign of fistula formation. Weakness, weight loss, and anemia are characteristic of the late stages of the disease, although acute blood loss and anemia may occur in an ulcerating stage I lesion.

Microinvasion or early stromal invasion (stage IA) causes no symptoms (preclinical carcinoma). However, as the local disease progresses, physical findings appear. Infiltrative cancer produces enlargement, irregularity, and a firm consistency to the cervix and eventually to the adjacent parametria. An exophytic growth generally appears as a friable, bleeding, cauliflowerlike lesion of the portio vaginalis. Ulceration may be the primary manifestation of invasive carcinoma, and in the early stages the change often is

Table 10–2. International classification of cancer of the cervix.*

Preinvasive carcinoma

Stage 0 Carcinoma in situ, intraepithelial carcinoma.

Invasive carcinoma

Stage I Carcinoma strictly confined to the cervix (extension to the corpus should be disregarded).

IA Microinvasive carcinoma (early stromal invasion).

IB All other cases of stage I. (Occult cancer should be labeled "occ.")

Stage II Carcinoma extends beyond the cervix but has not extended onto the pelvic wall. The carcinoma involves the vagina, but not the lower third.

IIA No obvious parametrial involvement.

IIB Obvious parametrial involvement.

Stage III Carcinoma has extended onto the pelvic wall. On rectal examination, there is no cancer-free space between the tumor and the pelvic wall. The tumor involves the lower third of the vagina. All cases with hydronephrosis or nonfunctioning kidney.

IIIA No extension onto the pelvic wall.

IIIB Extension onto the pelvic wall and/or hydronephrosis or nonfunctioning kidney.

Stage IV Carcinoma extended beyond the true pelvis or clinically involving the mucosa of the bladder or rectum. Do not allow a case of bullous edema as such to be allotted to stage IV.

IVA Spread of growth to adjacent organs (that is, rectum or bladder with positive biopsy from these organs).

IVB Spread of growth to distant organs.

*American Joint Committee for Cancer Staging and End-Results Reporting; Task Force on Gynecologic Sites: Staging System for Cancer at Gynecologic Sites, 1979. *Note:* The interpretation of the physical and microscopic findings is to some extent subjective, and the personal opinion of the examiner unavoidably influences the staging of various cases. This is especially true with stages II and III. Therefore, when the results of therapy for carcinoma of the cervix are being reported, all cases examined should be reported so that the reader can determine what series of cases in his or her own experience the data are applicable to. In reporting the results of therapy for stage II carcinoma at a given institution, the statistics for stage III should be included so that the reader may compare the reported results with a more surely comparable series of cases at another institution.

superficial so that it may resemble cervical ectopy or chronic cervicitis. With further progression of the disease, the ulcer becomes deeper and necrotic, with indurated edges and a friable, bleeding surface. The adjacent vaginal fornices may become involved next. Eventually, extensive parametrial involvement by the infiltrative process may produce a nodular thickening of the uterosacral and cardinal ligaments with resultant loss of mobility and fixation of the cervix.

B. X-Ray Findings: Pelvic lymphangiography may demonstrate involvement of the pelvic or periaortic lymph nodes. Chest x-rays are indicated routinely. A significant finding on intravenous urography in advanced cervical cancer is terminal ureteral obstruction. This produces hydroureter, hydronephrosis, and, if complete obstruction occurs, a nonfunctioning kidney.

Table 10–3. TNM classification of cancer of the cervix.

3.1 Primary tumor (T)

TIS Carcinoma in situ
See Stage 0

T1, 1a, 1b, 2a, 2b, 3a, 3b, 4
See corresponding FIGO stages

3.2 Nodal involvement (N)

NX Not possible to assess the regional nodes

N0 No involvement of regional nodes

N1 Evidence of regional node involvement

N4 Involvement of lumbo-aortic nodes

3.3 Distant metastasis (M)

MX Not assessed

M0 No (known) distant metastasis

M1 Distant metastasis present
Specify: _____

4.0 Postsurgical treatment residual tumor (R)

R0 No residual tumor

R1 Microscopic residual tumor

R2 Macroscopic residual tumor
Specify: _____

C. Laboratory Findings:

1. Vaginal smear (Papanicolaou) studies–(See p 107.) Preclinical lesions usually are initially diagnosed by cytologic examination or colposcopy (see below). Suspect or positive Papanicolaou smear calls for further investigation (see section on dysplasia); however, about 6% of cytologic smears are falsely negative.

Because of the presence of inflammatory cells and the failure of cells to shed in large numbers,

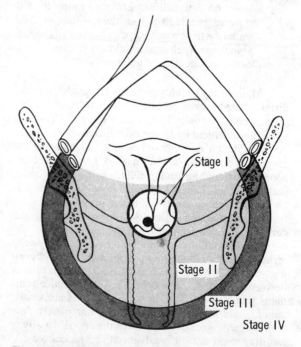

Figure 10–13. Staging of metastases of cervical cancer (corresponding to the International Federation of Gynecology and Obstetrics [FIGO] Classification; see Table 10–2).

false-negative smears are more frequent in invasive than in intraepithelial neoplasms. Moreover, in an area of invasive cancer, deficient blood supply or infection cause cytolysis. Clinical signs and symptoms suggestive of malignancy call for continued investigation even if cytologic examination is negative.

Cytologic study and biopsy of suspect areas have greatly facilitated the early diagnosis and cure of cancer of the cervix.

2. Schiller test–Aqueous solutions of iodine stain the surface of the normal cervix mahogany-brown because normal cervical epithelial cells contain glycogen. Zones of cancer within the epithelium over the cervix do not contain glycogen and remain unstained when painted with Lugol's or Schiller's iodine solutions (see p 229). Scars, erosion, eversion, cystic mucous glands, and zones of nonmalignant leukoplakia also appear pale for the same reason.

D. Special Examinations:

1. Biopsy–Punch biopsy of any Schiller-positive areas or of any ulcerative, granular, nodular, or papillary lesion will confirm the diagnosis of invasive carcinoma in most cases. Four-quadrant biopsies of the cervix or actual scalpel conization of the cervix may be required when repeated, confirmed reports of suspicious or probable exfoliated carcinoma cells are made by the pathologist.

2. Colposcopy–Early invasive carcinoma in a field of cervical intraepithelial neoplasia should be suspected when the surface capillaries are markedly irregular, appearing as commas, corkscrews, and spaghetti-shaped capillaries. Directed biopsy of these areas often will show microscopic evidence of early stromal invasion. Frank invasion frequently produces ulceration, and this is seen colposcopically as a markedly irregular surface with a waxy, yellowish surface and numerous bizarre, atypical blood vessels. Bleeding may occur also after slight irritation. Once carcinomatous invasion begins, ulceration and spotting occur. By the time sanguineous vaginal discharge or abnormal bleeding occurs, penetration of the malignancy into the substance of the cervix is certain.

Colposcopically directed punch biopsies have been useful in pinpointing the most severe epithelial change in a given cervix, and use of the colposcope, combined with light curettage of the endocervix, may avoid the need for cone biopsy in certain circumstances. Metastatic spread from a supposed in situ cancer has been reported as an extremely rare event, and this possibility must be regarded as highly unlikely. Invasive cancer, on the other hand, metastasizes frequently to adjacent organs and to the pelvic lymph nodes and less often to distant sites. Such possibilities are investigated prior to the initiation of therapy by endoscopy (cystoscopy, proctosigmoidoscopy), by x-ray studies (chest x-ray, intravenous urography, barium enema examination), and by radioisotope methods (liver and bone scans).

3. Cold cone biopsy–When the punch biopsy reveals severe dysplasia or carcinoma in situ, or when there are no suspicious areas on the portio vaginalis,

cold cone biopsy of the cervix should be performed to determine the presence or absence of invasion. This is usually performed in conjunction with a D&C, which is done after the cone biopsy has been accomplished in order to avoid denuding the cervix of malignant surface epithelium. The specimen should be properly marked, eg, with a pin or small suture, for the pathologist so that the area of involvement can be specifically localized in relation to the circumference and the upper and lower margins of the cervix.

It is a serious error to perform a cone biopsy of a lesion that is grossly suggestive of invasive cancer. This only delays the initiation of appropriate radiotherapy and predisposes the patient to serious pelvic infections in the event that radical surgery is chosen as definitive therapy. The diagnosis of such a lesion can almost always be confirmed by simple punch biopsy of the cervix. An effective instrument for this purpose is the Tischler cervical biopsy forceps (Fig 10–5).

Differential Diagnosis

A variety of lesions of the cervix may be confused with cancer. Histopathologic examination is usually definitive.

Entities that must sometimes be ruled out include the following: cervical ectopy, acute or chronic cervicitis, condyloma acuminatum, cervical tuberculosis, ulceration secondary to sexually transmitted disease (syphilis, granuloma inguinale, lymphogranuloma venereum, chancroid), abortion of a cervical pregnancy, metastatic choriocarcinoma, and rare lesions such as those of actinomycosis or schistosomiasis.

Complications

The complications of cervical cancer, for the most part, are those related to necrosis of the tumor, infection, and metastatic disease (Figs 10–12 and 10–13). There are also problems pertaining to treatment of the disease (eg, radical surgery or radiotherapy). (See Treatment, below.)

Prevention

The causes of cervical cancer are unknown. Nevertheless, chastity is associated with almost total freedom from this malignancy. Theoretically, then, carcinoma of the cervix (and penis), particularly before middle age, may be considered to be a carcinogen-induced neoplasm involving intercourse.

Prevention of morbidity and death from cervical cancer largely involves early recognition and treatment. Risk factors must be recognized, ie, early sexual experience and promiscuity or a history of cervical dysplasia. Universal cytologic screening of all postpubertal women must be continued on a regular annual basis—especially in the case of parous women in the lower socioeconomic groups and those who are sexually active. Women with cervical dysplasia should be treated by thermal or electrocautery, cryosurgery, or cone biopsy with continued careful follow-up. Personal hygiene methods that may help to prevent cervical cancer include prevention and prompt treatment of vaginitis and cervicitis, male circumcision in infancy, and precoital washing of the penis or habitual use of condoms.

Sexual abstinence, of course, is an effective though impractical prophylactic measure. Certainly the avoidance of early sexual exposure and promiscuity would be an effective measure.

Treatment: General Measures

The patient should be admitted to the hospital for thorough study and rest before therapy is begun. Vaginal, urinary, and pelvic infections should be eradicated before surgery or irradiation is initiated. Anemia must be corrected and nutrition improved. The debilitated patient should be kept in the hospital for supportive therapy during x-ray and radium treatment; if exposures are poorly tolerated, discharged patients should be readmitted.

Pain may be controlled with analgesics such as aspirin with codeine. Give diphenoxylate with atropine (Lomotil) as necessary for diarrhea. For urinary frequency and dysuria, give a bladder sedative mixture.

Plain warm water douches are permitted when necessary during x-ray therapy and after radium treatments for comfort and hygiene.

Treatment: Surgical Measures

A. Carcinoma in Situ: Carcinoma in situ is best treated by complete removal of all of the involved epithelium with an ample margin of normal epithelium. The most effective measure when reproductive function is no longer important is total hysterectomy. This may be accomplished either vaginally or abdominally, with preservation of the ovaries.

New lesions may appear at any time in these patients, whether treated by hysterectomy or by conization. Hence, follow-up utilizing periodic vaginal smears is important. Invasive carcinoma subsequently occurs in 1–2% of patients treated for carcinoma in situ. These occurrences probably can be prevented by careful follow-up.

In younger women who wish to preserve the uterus, a cone biopsy may be considered therapeutic if the following safeguards are observed:

1. Careful pathologic examination of the cone specimen must reveal an ample margin of normal columnar epithelium at the apex and squamous epithelium at the base of the cone.

2. The patient must be cooperative and return for frequent clinical and cytologic follow-up examinations (every 3 months for the first year and then every 6 months for a total of 5 years).

3. Cytologic examinations must remain consistently negative for severely dysplastic or malignant cells.

4. The cervical canal must not become stenosed, thus invalidating the cytologic sampling.

In carefully selected patients who have been subjected to colposcopic examination and endocervical curettage, cryosurgery, laser beam therapy, or electrosurgical cauterization can be used to treat areas of carcinoma in situ *localized to the exocervix*.

B. Microinvasive Carcinoma: When thorough pathologic examination of a conization specimen reveals questionable invasion or early stromal penetration to a depth of no more than 2 mm and no confluence of tumor or vascular space involvement, simple or extended hysterectomy (without lymph node or extensive ureteral or bladder dissection) should be curative. Such relatively conservative therapy is improper if the margins of the specimen are not adequate, if the tumor penetrates to a depth of more than 2 mm, if its lateral spread is greater than 4 mm, or if tumor cells are found in vascular (lymphatic or capillarylike) spaces.

C. Invasive Carcinoma: There are 2 effective methods for the treatment of invasive carcinoma: radiotherapy and radical surgery. Radiotherapy (discussed separately below) is more widely used throughout the world because it is applicable to all primary cervical cancers whereas radical hysterectomy is definitive only in stage I to stage IIA lesions. The overall 5-year cure rates for surgery and for radiotherapy in operable patients are approximately equal. The immediate complications of radiotherapy are less frequent and less severe. Irradiation may be used either as a curative or as a palliative measure.

There are specific circumstances in which the surgical approach to carcinoma of the cervix may be indicated or preferred. Radical hysterectomy may be considered in the young woman in whom preservation of the ovaries is important. Carcinoma of the cervix metastatic to the ovaries is rare in stage I–IIA patients. Moreover, because much of the ovarian blood supply is directly from the aorta, these ovaries may be detached and displaced into the abdomen during surgery without compromising the radical nature of the operation. Radical surgery may be better for patients who are poor candidates for radiotherapy (eg, those with chronic salpingitis, extensive bowel adhesions from endometriosis or previous peritonitis, diverticulitis, or ulcerative colitis); for those who cannot tolerate radiation therapy; and for those whose tumor demonstrates a poor response to radiation. Finally, surgery is the only effective method of treating cancers that persist or recur centrally following adequate radiation therapy. In such instances, pelvic exenteration is often necessary to make certain that all of the cancer has been removed.

The surgical treatment of invasive cancer of the cervix consists of one of the following: (1) extended hysterectomy without pelvic lymph node dissection (abdominal or vaginal); (2) radical hysterectomy with pelvic lymph node dissection; or (3) pelvic exenteration—anterior, posterior, or total.

1. Extended hysterectomy–Extended hysterectomy involves removal of the uterus, tubes, and ovaries together with most of the parametrial tissues and the upper vagina. Surgery involves dissection of the ureters from the paracervical structures so that the ligaments supporting the uterus and upper vagina can be removed. When the operation is done vaginally, a deep Schuchardt (paravaginal) incision is required for exposure. Extended hysterectomy is performed primarily for the removal of minimally invasive lesions (stage IA) in which the chances of lymph node involvement are extremely small. Some authorities (Navratil, Crisp) recommend this operation for more extensive disease; but others believe that it is inappropriate for the management of stage IB cancer of the cervix.

2. Radical hysterectomy and node dissection–Radical hysterectomy (Wertheim or Okabayashi) with pelvic lymph node dissection is the customary surgical procedure for invasive cancer limited to the cervix (stages I and II). This operation requires careful preoperative evaluation and preparation of the patient. The operation is technically difficult and should be performed only by those experienced in radical pelvic surgery. The so-called Wertheim operation, initiated by Clark but popularized by Meigs and modified by Okabayashi and others, involves en bloc dissection with careful removal of all of the recognizable lymph nodes in the pelvis together with wide removal of the uterus, tubes and ovaries, supporting ligaments, and upper vagina. Obviously, it involves extensive dissection of the ureters and of the bladder. The 5-year arrest rate of cervical cancer by this operation is as good as with irradiation in selected cases. Obesity, advanced age, and serious medical problems, which are likely to complicate surgery or convalescence, greatly reduce the number of candidates for elective cancer surgery. All patients and surgeons considered, the hazards of the operation exceed those of irradiation therapy, the most common serious complication being urinary tract fistula formation. Be this as it may, the Wertheim operation and pelvic lymphadenectomy are often employed as the definitive method of treatment of cancer of the cervix if (1) the patient is pregnant, (2) large uterine or adnexal tumors are present, (3) the patient has chronic salpingitis, (4) the small or large bowel adheres to the uterus, (5) the patient is under 35 years of age and demands ovarian tissue conservation, or (6) the patient refuses or abandons irradiation but is a good surgical risk.

In a small proportion of patients with cancer of the cervix treated initially with radium and x-ray, recurrence or persistence of the cancer will be noted within the cervix or vaginal vault. A Wertheim hysterectomy and lymph node resection may be indicated for good-risk patients in this group because of the serious hazards of repeated irradiation.

3. Pelvic exenteration–This operation was popularized by Brunschwig as a method of salvaging patients with central recurrences following radiotherapy (or radical hysterectomy) for cancer of the cervix. It is one of the most formidable of all gynecologic operations and requires removal of the bladder or the rectum, the vagina, and perhaps even the vulva, along with radical hysterectomy and pelvic lymph node dissection. Urinary diversion necessitates the creation of a reservoir from an isolated loop of intestine (eg, ileum), one end of which is brought through the anterior abdominal wall. A sigmoid colostomy serves for the passage of feces. Because of the high surgical morbidity and mortality rates, stringent criteria are necessary to justify these procedures. Pelvic exenteration should be reserved primarily for problems that cannot be effectively managed in any other manner. In essence, this means (1) a biopsy-proved persistence or recurrence of cervical cancer following an adequate course of radiation therapy or radical surgery in which the recurrent or persistent tumor occupies the central portion of the pelvis (without metastases) and is completely removable; and (2) a patient who is able to cope with the urinary and fecal stomas in the abdomen created by the operation. Both psychologic and physical preparation of the patient for this operation and its aftermath are of vital importance. This means making the patient's physical condition as favorable as possible by restoring good nutrition and normal blood volume, preparation of the bowel with low-residue diet and antibiotics, correction of anemia, and control of diabetes. The extent of the procedure is determined by the direction of tumor growth in the pelvis. Because of the extreme difficulties encountered in making an accurate assessment, even at the time of surgical exploration, total exenteration has been advocated as being the definitive procedure in a critical clinical situation.

D. Complications of Radical Surgery: The operative mortality rate in radical hysterectomy with pelvic lymph node dissection has been reduced to less than 1%. The most common complication is fistula formation; ureterovaginal fistula is the most frequent type, followed by vesicovaginal and rectovaginal fistulas. Modifications in technique to preserve the blood supply to the distal ureter and bladder and the use of prolonged catheter drainage of the urinary bladder (6–8 weeks) have reduced the frequency of urinary tract fistulas from 10% to less than 3%.

Other complications are urinary tract infections, lymphocysts in the retroperitoneal space, wound sepsis, dehiscence, thromboembolic disease, ileus, postoperative hemorrhage, and intestinal obstruction.

The surgical mortality rate from pelvic exenteration has been reduced from about 25% to about 2.5%. Bowel obstruction is a frequent complication. Electrolyte disturbances, leakage of urine from the urinary diversion, ureteral stricture, pyelonephritis, hemorrhage, sepsis, thromboembolism, enteric fistulas, stomal retraction, and other complications may also occur.

Treatment: Radiation Therapy

Irradiation is generally considered to be the best treatment for invasive carcinoma of the cervix. The goals of radiation therapy are (1) destruction not only of all of the tumor cells in the cervix but also of those that may lie in the parametrial tissues and the lymph nodes of the pelvis, and (2) preservation of tissues not involved in the malignancy. The amount of irradiation required to destroy cancer varies. A cancericidal dose for cervical carcinoma is about 8000 R administered over a period of 4–5 weeks.

It is impossible to administer adequate homogeneous cancericidal irradiation throughout the pelvis without damaging vital structures such as bowel, bladder, ureters, and blood vessels. The cervix can be treated intensively, however, because it has a high tolerance to radiation. The structures immediately lateral and posterior to it are damaged more easily and so must be protected from exposure to high doses. The cervix and vagina can tolerate 24,000 R, but the bladder and ureter will be seriously damaged by doses higher than 10,000 R and the bowel by doses higher than 7000–9000 R. Major blood vessels will tolerate approximately the same exposure as the intestine. Therefore, dosage is dictated both by the radiosensitivity of cancer cells and by the vulnerability of unaffected tissues. In practice, the experienced gynecologist or radiologist applies as much irradiation as possible to the cancer within a reasonable time, with particular concern for the neighboring organs.

The skilled management of cervical cancer depends more upon an understanding of the accepted principles of therapy than upon detailed familiarity with radium applicators, the many types of roentgen equipment, and other techniques employed. Radium therapy is used to destroy cancer in the cervix; external irradiation therapy is used to destroy cancer that may have progressed beyond the primary site. Both methods are employed concurrently over a period of about 5–6 weeks, although some physicians choose to start with one and some with the other.

Physicians who prefer to begin therapy with x-ray do so because they believe that the spread of cancer beyond the cervix is generally what kills the patient so that containment and destruction of cancer within the lymphatics beyond the primary lesion are the primary objectives of therapy. X-ray therapy will often (1) eradicate cervical infection, (2) control hemorrhage, and (3) reduce the size of the tumor. A further advantage is that external radiation is far less distressing to the patient early in therapy than surgery for the insertion of a radium source.

Physicians who prefer to begin therapy with radium do so in the conviction that the cancer should be treated within the cervix as soon as possible to prevent metastases. Statistical evidence for the superiority of one method over the other is equivocal.

When vaginal contractures, a cervical stump, or the patient's condition preclude radium therapy, external irradiation may be used alone. Radium alone is often used when the cancer is small and medical or surgical problems contraindicate protracted x-ray therapy.

A. Some Definitions and Basic Concepts of Radiation Therapy: Numerous methods have been developed for the radiation treatment of cervical cancer. The objective of all methods is to deliver a cancericidal dose of radiation to the involved tissues without doing irreparable damage to the normal surrounding structures. Two combined methods of delivering radiation to these tissues are commonly used; (1) intracavitary radiation, usually in the form of radium (or radioactive isotope) capsules; and (2) external radiation generated by supervoltage equipment (^{60}Co, linear accelerator, betatron). All stages of cancer may be treated by this method, and there are fewer medical contraindications to irradiation than to radical surgery.

Intracavitary radiation plays the greater role in treatment of the disease in the cervix and in the adjacent parametria. The limiting factors are the inverse square law* and the greater susceptibility of the bladder and rectal mucosa to the ionizing effects of radiation as compared with cervical tissues. Hence, external radiation must be added to eliminate cancer cells that may be more than a few centimeters away from the cervix. The 2 methods must be used in such a way as to destroy the cancer without irreparable damage to surrounding normal structures, especially the bladder and rectum. Thus, it is important to know the relative proportion of a dose of radiation that is delivered to the tumor and to the normal tissues of the pelvis. This is called dosimetry and is a function of quality, quantity, and distribution in time and in space. Consequently, certain definitions of dosages are useful:

1. Radiation energy–

a. Intracavitary radiation dosage often is roughly measured in **milligram hours,** obtained by multiplying the number of milligrams of radium (or radium-equivalent isotope such as cesium) used by the number of hours it is left in place. More useful, however, is an expression of the quantity of radiation being delivered at specific points in relation to the source. This can be calculated by taking x-ray films that will show the radiation sources and calculating isodose curves for that specific distribution. In the case of radium, these curves are based on the fact that 1 mg of radium filtered with 0.5 mm of platinum produces 8.47 R per hour at a distance of 1 cm.

b. A **roentgen (R)** is defined as the quantity of x-ray or gamma radiation such that the associated corpuscular emission (electrons) per 0.001293 g of air produces in air ions carrying one electrostatic unit (esu) of quantity of electricity of either sign.

c. A **rad** is defined as a unit of dosage that corresponds to absorption of 100 ergs per gram of any absorber.

For practical purposes, it can be assumed that the rad and the roentgen are the same. These terms are applicable to all types of radiation, whether from a generator used in external therapy, or from radium, or from a radioactive isotope applied internally.

2. Distance–The factor of distance is taken into consideration when an expression of **tumor dose** is given. In the pelvis, it is usually assumed that the bulk of the tumor is in the midplane of the pelvis. Nevertheless, because of the possibility of tumor spread laterally, a cancericidal dose of radiation must be delivered

---

*The intensity of the radiation is inversely proportionate to the square of the distance from the source.

to the side wall of the pelvis. However, the tumor dose, when measured, is usually given as that delivered to the midplane of the pelvis.

B. Specific Methods of Radiotherapy: The temporal distribution of radiation is an important consideration. In general, it is held that the more prolonged the treatment, the greater the dose required to produce a specific effect. There are essentially 2 schools of thought regarding the relationship between radiation dosage and time—the Stockholm method and the Paris method. In general, proponents of the **Stockholm method** advocate relatively high-intensity intracavitary radiation over a short period of time (2 applications of 25–28 hours at 3-week intervals). The Stockholm technique employs (1) an intrauterine tandem containing linear radium sources (no radium is left in the cervical canal), (2) metal boxes containing radium needles placed in each fornix, and (3) a box applicator applied to the cervix. Snug vaginal packing is required.

The **Paris method** involves low-dose intracavitary radium administration placed in an intrauterine tandem over a period of 8–10 days. A radium applicator is placed in each fornix; these are held by a bent spring to distend the fornices. An applicator is pressed against the cervix at the external os. Vaginal packing is employed to retain the radium.

The **Manchester method** uses a combination of the Stockholm technique and the Paris applicators by allowing some degree of flexibility in the radium applications. This method emphasizes the importance of calculating the radiation delivered to 2 precise points in the pelvis. **Point A** is defined as lying 2 cm lateral to the central canal of the cervix and 2 cm above the lateral fornix in the axis of the uterus (approximately the point where the uterine artery crosses the ureter). **Point B** lies 5 cm lateral to the central canal of the cervix and 2 cm above the lateral fornix (at the pelvic side wall). If cancer is to be destroyed without irremediable damage to normal tissues, it is necessary to deliver a cancericidal dose of radiation and still remain within the limits of a tolerable dose. A tumoricidal dose for squamous cell carcinoma of the cervix has been estimated to be 6000–7000 R given over a 6- to 8-week period.

Applicators for carrying radiation sources in tandem are available for introduction into the cervical canal and endometrial cavity. By employing paracervical applicators as well, a cross-fire is established. This is far more effective than a tandem placed in the cervix alone or radiation sources placed only in the vagina.

The optimal predetermined dosage from intracavitary radiation alone to point A is 8000 R in 144 hours. The 8000 R is delivered in 2 sessions of 2–3 days each, 2 weeks apart. (For patients over 65 years of age, the dosage usually is reduced to 6500 R.)

Radium capsules, if damaged, may leak radioactive radon gas. Because it is safer to use, [137]cesium is gradually replacing radium as a source for use in intracavitary applications.

Because of relatively high radiation exposure rates to personnel involved in the intracavitary placement of radiation sources, techniques have been developed for minimizing this exposure by the placement of unloaded applicators in the uterus and vagina, usually with the patient anesthetized. After x-ray placement films have demonstrated a satisfactory positioning of the applicators in relation to the uterine cavity, cervix, bladder, and rectum, the patient is returned to her room with the applicators in place. They are then quickly loaded with the radiation sources, minimizing the delivery time and thus the exposure to the personnel involved. This is known as "after-loading technique." Fletcher-Suit after-loading applicators are commonly used.

Currently under investigation are methods whereby exposure to medical attendants can be even further reduced through automated techniques in which the positioning of radioactive sources can be remotely controlled. Such methods will reduce radiation exposure to nurses and attendants involved in the day-by-day care of patients receiving intracavitary radiation.

The addition of external x-ray therapy augments this technique. An x-ray dose of 3000 R is given through 2 anterior and 2 posterior ports to the parametrium (point B) within 4 weeks.

C. Complications of Radiotherapy: The complications of radiotherapy can be classified according to whether they occur soon after treatment (within 2–3 weeks) or later (1 month to 5 years):

1. Immediate complications–These include castration with radiation menopause, radiation enterocolitis, radiation cystitis, and pelvic infection.

Menopausal symptoms may be controlled by the judicious use of oral estrogenic preparations. Topical hormone therapy may be useful in the patient with vaginal atrophy and dyspareunia. Diarrhea, the prominent symptom of radiation enterocolitis, is best managed with a bland diet and antiperistaltic medication (paregoric or diphenoxylate with atropine [Lomotil]). Similarly, frequency and urgency of urination, in the absence of frank bacterial infection, may be treated with a bladder sedative such as belladonna, phenazopyridine (Pyridium), flavoxate (Urispas), or a belladonna-phenobarbital preparation. Acute salpingitis following radiation therapy requires intensive antibiotic therapy and immediate removal of the involved tubes and ovaries in order to minimize the delay in continuation of radiotherapy.

2. Late complications–Cervical stricture with pyometra, vaginal stenosis and dyspareunia, radiation necrosis of the cervix, rectal ulceration, rectovaginal fistula, bladder ulceration, vesicovaginal fistula, small bowel strictures with obstruction, and enteric fistula.

The late complications are much more difficult to treat effectively and are best prevented by careful attention to dosimetry. Cervical stricture followed by pyometra may be unavoidable, but repeated cervical dilatations may keep the cervical canal patent. In some of these cases, hysterectomy may be required. Vaginal stenosis occurs less frequently in women who are sexually active and who receive estrogen supplementation following radiotherapy. The bleeding and rectal tenesmus of chronic radiation proctitis often respond to enemas containing cortisone. Bowel resection may occasionally be necessary to relieve the symptoms of chronic partial obstruction.

Fistulas are complex complications. In all cases of fistula, one should suspect recurrent carcinoma. Biopsy will usually establish the diagnosis. Repair of late radiation fistulas is exceedingly difficult because of tissue devascularization and poor wound healing. Be this as it may, techniques to overcome these handicaps (eg, gracilis muscle transplant) may be successful.

Management of Carcinoma of the Cervix in Pregnancy

Abnormal cytologic examination in pregnancy calls for immediate colposcopic evaluation. If invasive cancer can be ruled out, the pregnancy may be allowed to continue.

In situ cancer of the cervix that occurs in pregnancy is best managed by allowing the pregnancy to proceed to term. There is no contraindication to vaginal delivery. The lesion is then treated surgically by performing either a therapeutic conization or a total hysterectomy depending upon the findings and the patient's desires for further progeny.

Invasive carcinoma of the cervix in pregnancy is found more frequently in areas where routine prenatal cytologic examination is done; the incidence may be as high as 1:350 pregnancies depending upon the population sampled. As is the case with nonpregnant patients also, the principal symptom is bleeding, but the diagnosis is frequently missed because the bleeding is assumed to be related to the pregnancy rather than to malignancy. The possibility of cancer must be kept in mind. Cervical biopsy will lead to the correct diagnosis.

Radiotherapy may be used in treating invasive cancers of the cervix discovered during pregnancy. In the first trimester, irradiation therapy may be carried out with the expectation of spontaneous abortion. Deliver 6000 R of x-ray radiation of the pelvis through each of 4 ports. Concurrently, give 2 courses of intra- and paracervical radium.

In the second trimester, interruption of the pregnancy by hysterotomy prior to radiation therapy is preferred, although some advocate proceeding with treatment and ignoring the pregnancy, again awaiting spontaneous evacuation of the uterus. Another method is to place intra- and contracervical radium and then, 7–10 days later, perform an abdominal (classic) hysterotomy. Two weeks after surgery, begin 6000 R of x-ray radiation, and then give a further course of intra- and contracervical radiation during the last week of external therapy.

In the third trimester, the decision must be made whether to allow the pregnancy to proceed to viability (28–32 weeks' gestation) before performing a cesarean section and then instituting radiotherapy. In 7–10 days, begin 6000 R of external x-ray radiation and then give 2 courses of intra- and paracervical radium 1 week apart, the first during the last 7–10 days of x-ray therapy.

Radical surgery may be chosen in all 3 trimesters for stage I and IIA lesions because it simultaneously eliminates the pregnancy and the cancer.

Chemotherapy

The use of chemotherapeutic agents in the treatment of cervical carcinoma has been discouraging. This is partly because most patients who may be candidates for this type of treatment have far-advanced cancer that has already failed to respond to radical surgery or radiation therapy. As a result of the neoplastic process or because of prior therapy, there is often diminished vascularity of the pelvic tissues causing impaired pelvic vascular perfusion. Furthermore, there may be ureteral obstruction causing decreased renal function or compromised bone marrow from radiation therapy. Both of these severely limit effective chemotherapy.

Doxorubicin, cyclophosphamide, fluorouracil, and methothrexate have shown suppressive activity in squamous cell cancers of the cervix. A combination of bleomycin and mitomycin has shown some promise, and response rates of 40–45% have been demonstrated with cisplatin. Doxorubicin and methotrexate in combination have produced similar results.

At present, chemotherapy may be useful in patients with recurrent cervical cancer who cannot tolerate additional radiation therapy or surgery. Experimental protocols are being tested in which chemotherapy is added to radiation therapy as an adjuvant in the treatment of lesions with a relatively low potential for cure, eg, stages III and IV.

Palliative Care of Cervical Cancer

About half of patients cannot be cured of cervical cancer and thus are candidates for management of persistent or recurrent disease. The vast majority of these women would not benefit from pelvic exenteration operations. Eventually they develop symptoms related principally to the site and extent of the malignant disease. Ulceration of the cervix and adjacent vagina produces a foul-smelling discharge. Tissue necrosis and slough may initiate life-threatening hemorrhage. If the bladder or rectum is involved in the tissue breakdown, fistulas result in incontinence of urine and feces. Pain due to involvement of the lumbosacral plexus, soft tissues of the pelvis, or bone is frequently encountered in advanced disease. Ureteral compression leading to hydronephrosis and, if bilateral, to renal failure and uremia is a frequent terminal event.

The expert management of the patient with incurable cancer is an integral part of cancer therapy. The comfort and well-being of the patient can be considerably enhanced even though cure cannot be effected.

A foul, purulent discharge may be ameliorated by astringent douches (potassium permanganate, 1:4000) and antimicrobial vaginal creams (eg, sulfathiazole, sulfacetamide, and benzoylsulfanilamide cream [Sultrin Cream]) and nitrofurazone suppositories. Necrotic ulcers may be treated with enzymatic debridement (fibrinolysin and desoxyribonuclease, combined [bovine] ointment [Elase]), or the necrotic tissue may be removed by coating the normal vaginal mucosa with petrolatum and packing the ulcer with small cotton balls wrung out in acetone and left in place for several minutes. Occasionally, ulcerated areas will heal with the administration of high-dose estrogen therapy (diethylstilbestrol, 100 mg daily), although this may cause some nausea.

Hemorrhage from the vagina often can be controlled by packing the area with gauze impregnated with a hemostatic agent. Exposed, bleeding vessels should be ligated. Rarely, it may be necessary to ligate the hypogastric arteries on both sides to control an exsanguinating vaginal hemorrhage.

Pain relief may be afforded by the liberal use of aspirin. Codeine may be required when skeletal pain becomes worse or when the pain is visceral. Propoxyphene (Darvon or Darvon Compound) with or without codeine may be effective. Pentazocine (Talwin) is useful for relief of moderate degrees of pain.

Severe pain requires the use of more potent, addicting drugs such as morphine, hydromorphone (Dilaudid), meperidine (Demerol), alphaprodine (Nisentil), and levorphanol (Levo-Dromoran). A useful combination of drugs in terminal patients is Schlesinger's solution (morphine sulfate, 3%; ethylmorphine, 6%; and hyoscine hydrobromide, 0.02%), 5–10 drops in water every 4 hours. Tranquilizing agents, eg, chlorpromazine, often help to alleviate fear and anxiety, and when used in conjunction with nonaddictive analgesics may reduce the need for narcotic drugs.

Radiotherapy may be of great value in the relief of pain due to bony metastases or in the treatment of lesions that recur following primary surgical treatment of cervical cancer. In general, if initial therapy has been accomplished by adequate radiotherapy, re-treatment is contraindicated since it does little good and carries the potential of massive radiation necrosis.

In patients with unilateral lower abdominal, back, or extremity pain, percutaneous cordotomy or introduction of a dorsal column stimulator may provide prolonged pain relief without the use of addicting narcotic agents with their unpleasant side-effects.

The general management of incurable cancer demands that the physician maintain a sympathetic and understanding relationship with the patient. Her nutritional status and general body functions must be maintained. Anxiety, fear, and depression should be dealt with by means of friendly counseling, reassurance, and the discreet use of psychic energizing drugs. The cancer patient should be encouraged to continue her normal activities as long as she can and should be given every possible support in the effort.

Prognosis

The factors to be considered in the assessment of prognosis in cervical cancer are the following: (1) age of the patient, (2) general physical condition, (3) socioeconomic status, (4) gross features of the cancer, (5) cytologic features of the cancer, (6) histologic characteristics of the cancer, (7) the skill of the therapist, and (8) clinical staging (extent of the disease, lymph node metastases).

The age of the patient is important because the more aggressive, anaplastic tumors are more frequently encountered in young women with cervical cancer. Older individuals are more apt to harbor well-differentiated, slowly growing malignancies. This is merely a clinical impression, however, and it may not influence the ultimate prognosis significantly.

The patient's general physical condition influences survival figures in several ways. Death from intercurrent disease is more frequent in patients who have serious chronic illnesses, such as diabetes, heart disease, or kidney disease. Obesity imposes a handicap, making adequate therapy more difficult. Coincidental pelvic infection also worsens the prognosis.

Patients who are economically deprived have more advanced disease when first diagnosed and respond less well to therapy.

Exophytic or papillary tumors, ie, those with a cauliflowerlike appearance, are usually seen at an earlier clinical stage than endophytic, ulcerative, or nodular lesions, and everting cancers often are more responsive to radiotherapy.

Although more radiosensitive, the small cell carcinoma carries a poorer prognosis than the large cell, keratinizing variety. The large cell nonkeratinizing tumor falls somewhere between the two.

Tumors that demonstrate a rapid reduction in the numbers of so-called resting cells and mitotic cells with an increase in differentiating and degenerating cells on serial biopsy during radiation therapy may have a better prognosis.

The experience and skill of the therapist are of obvious importance. Stage for stage, a higher cure rate of cancer of the cervix is reported from larger treatment centers than from smaller community hospitals. Experience and dedicated interest in the care and treatment of cancer are significant factors in the outcome whether treatment is by radical surgery or radiotherapy. Precision and individualization of therapy are often necessary and may make the difference between success or failure.

Involvement of the regional lymph nodes has a profound influence on the prognosis. The external iliac nodes are the most frequently involved, followed by the obturator, common iliac, and hypogastric nodes. Small cancers less than 1 cm in diameter rarely show regional node involvement. Inverting cancers metastasize more readily than everting ones. Well-differentiated lesions appear to metastasize to the lymph nodes less frequently than poorly differentiated ones.

The more extensive the tumor, the higher the incidence of regional lymph node metastases: stage I, 15%; stage II, 30%; and stage III, 60%. The cure rate for stage I lesions when the nodes are involved by tumor is about 40% of what can be achieved if the nodes are free of cancer. There is evidence that this is true when radiation treatment is given as well as when radical surgery is used.

Although clinical staging admittedly is not precise, it is the best guide we have to the ultimate prognosis. The results of treatment stage by stage for cancer of the cervix are reported by 123 institutions from 26 countries in the *Annual Report* of the International Federation of Gynecology and Obstetrics in Stockholm. The results are equated in terms of 5-year cure rates, or those patients who are living and show no evidence of cervical cancer 5 years after the beginning of therapy. The figures below are representative results achieved in all 4 stages in cancer treatment centers where the primary method of treatment is radiotherapy.

I	II	III	IV
88.7%	42.4%	29.0%	nil
86.4	60.0	26.3	8.8%
83.9	48.3	28.6	10.0
86.6	69.9	42.5	12.8

In centers where radical surgery is used primarily for stage I of the cervix, representative reported 5-year cure rates are 87.9%, 88%, 85%, and 76.6%.

When cancer of the cervix is untreated or fails to respond to treatment, death occurs in 95% of patients within 2 years of the onset of symptoms.

Recurrences following radiotherapy are not often centrally located and thus amenable to exenteration procedures. Only about 25% of recurrences are localized to the central portion of the pelvis. The most frequent site of recurrence is the pelvic side wall. The signs and symptoms of recurrent malignant disease are (1) positive cytologic examination 2 months or more following therapy; (2) palpable tumor in the pelvis or abdomen; (3) ulceration of the cervix or vagina; (4) pain in the pelvis, back, groin, or lower extremity; (5) unilateral lower extremity edema; (6) vaginal bleeding or discharge; (7) supraclavicular lymphadenopathy; and (8) ascites.

Renal failure with uremia is the leading cause of death and almost always is the result of bilateral ureteral obstruction by the tumor. Most patients with considerable ureteral compression ultimately develop pyelonephritis, which hastens their demise. Less frequent causes of death are hemorrhage, infection, pulmonary embolism, intestinal obstruction, and liver failure.

SARCOMA OF THE CERVIX

Essentials of Diagnosis

- Abnormal vaginal bleeding or discharge.
- Fleshy polypoid tumor of the cervix.
- Biopsy diagnosis of sarcoma.

General Considerations

Pure cervical sarcomas are rare tumors arising from those elements of the müllerian duct which differentiate into various mesodermal tissues — connective tissue, cartilage, smooth muscle, skeletal muscle, etc. Most patients are postmenopausal. Mixed varieties that contain both mesodermal and epithelial elements occur also. The latter may be seen at any age but are encountered most frequently in postmenopausal women. There is no known relationship between sexual experience and sarcoma (in contrast to carcinoma of the cervix).

The pathologic diagnosis is usually based upon the basic cellular pattern. The following types are recognized: (1) leiomyosarcoma, (2) mixed mesodermal tumors (including carcinosarcoma and sarcoma botryoides), (3) stromal cell sarcoma, (4) lymphosarcoma, and (5) angiosarcoma.

These tumors may spread by direct extension or via lymphatic or hematogenous routes. Metastases appear in the lungs, brain, liver, kidney, and bone.

Clinical Findings

A. Symptoms and Signs: There are no characteristic symptoms. Some of these tumors are asymptomatic and are discovered during routine pelvic examination. In other instances, a watery, purulent, or bloody vaginal discharge may be noted, or the passage of small pieces of tissue. Eventually, with advancing disease, there are symptoms of pelvic pain, tenesmus, dysuria, weakness, weight loss, and fever.

Examination may reveal a large, grayish-pink, polypoid mass protruding from the cervix, or the cervix may be replaced by a large cluster of grapelike polyps filling the upper vagina. These masses are liable to be soft, hemorrhagic, and friable, frequently separating readily from the main tumor.

B. Laboratory Findings: Vaginal cytology may reveal sarcoma, but false-negative reports are common. Pathologic examination of a biopsy specimen taken from the tumor mass is necessary for diagnosis.

C. Special Examinations: Special studies that should be done to determine the extent of the disease include chest x-ray, intravenous urography, cystoscopy, proctosigmoidoscopy, and barium enema examination.

Treatment

Sarcomas of the cervix show a variable and generally poor response to radiation therapy. If possible, therefore, surgical removal is indicated if the disease is localized to the pelvis. This may vary from simple hysterectomy to total pelvic exenteration. Chemotherapy has not proved effective in these tumors.

Prognosis

Leiomyosarcomas that arise in cervical myomas have the best prognosis, with 5-year cure rates of more than 50%. For the remaining sarcomas, particularly those of the mixed mesodermal variety, the prognosis is very poor; most patients succumb within 2 years.

• • •

References

General

Farber M: Congenital absence of uterine cervix. *Am J Obstet Gynecol* 1975;**121**:414.

Goldstein DP: Incompetent cervix in offspring exposed to diethylstilbestrol in utero. *Obstet Gynecol* 1978; **52** (Suppl):735.

Hager JH: Comparison of success and morbidity in cervical cerclage procedures. *Obstet Gynecol* 1980;**56**:543.

Jordan JA, Singer A (editors): *The Cervix.* Saunders, 1976.

Nelson RM: Bilateral internal iliac artery ligation in cervical pregnancy: Conservation of reproductive function. *Am J Obstet Gynecol* 1979;**134**:145.

Ranade V, Palermino DA, Tronik B: Cervical pregnancy. *Obstet Gynecol* 1978;**51**:502.

Raskin MM: Diagnosis of cervical pregnancy by ultrasound: A case report. *Am J Obstet Gynecol* 1978;**130**:234.

Schmidt G, Fowler WC Jr: Cervical stenosis following minor gynecologic procedures on DES-exposed women. *Obstet Gynecol* 1980;**56**:333.

Tsukada Y et al: Microglandular hyperplasia of the endocervix following long-term estrogen treatment. *Am J Obstet Gynecol* 1977;**127**:888.

Wilkinson E, Dufour DR: Pathogenesis of microglandular hyperplasia of the cervix. *Obstet Gynecol* 1976;**47**:189.

Cervical Infections

Barlow D, Phillips T: Gonorrhea in women: Diagnostic, clinical and laboratory aspects. *Lancet* 1978;**1**:761.

Carr MC, Hanna L, Jawetz E: Chlamydial, cervicitis and abnormal Papanicolaou smears. *Obstet Gynecol* 1979; **53**:27.

Chipperfield EJ, Catterall RD: Reappraisal of Gram-staining and cultural techniques for the diagnosis of gonorrhoea in women. *Br J Vener Dis* 1976;**52**:36.

Husemeyer RP: Post-menopausal tuberculosis of the cervix: Case report and review. *Br J Obstet Gynaecol* 1977; **84**:153.

Keith L et al: Cervical gonorrhea in women using different methods of contraception. *J Am Vener Dis Assoc* 1976; **3**:17.

Klein A, Richmond JA, Mishell ER Jr: Pelvic tuberculosis. *Obstet Gynecol* 1976;**48**:99.

Nahmias AJ et al: Immunology of herpes simplex virus infection: Relevance to herpes simplex virus vaccines and cervical cancer. *Cancer Res* 1976;**36**:836.

Reid R et al: Non-condylomatous cervical wart virus infection. *Obstet Gynecol* 1980;**55**:476.

Ripa KT et al: *Chlamydia trachomatis* cervicitis in gynecologic outpatients. *Obstet Gynecol* 1978;**52**:698.

Sandberg EC: Benign cervical and vaginal changes associated with exposure to stilbestrol in utero. *Am J Obstet Gynecol* 1976;**125**:777.

Simon W: The association of herpes simplex virus and cervical cancer: A review. *Gynecol Oncol* 1976;**4**:108.

Spagna VA, Perkins RL, Prior RB: Rapid presumptive diagnosis of gonococcal cervicitis by the limulus lysate assay. *Am J Obstet Gynecol* 1980;**137**:595.

Sutherland AM: Treatment of female genital tract tuberculosis with streptomycin, PAS, and isoniazid. *Tubercle* 1976; **57**:137.

Tobin SM et al: Relation of herpesvirus hominis type II to carcinoma of the cervix: An animal model for the induction of long-term latency of herpesvirus hominis type II. *Obstet Gynecol* 1978;**51**:707.

Cervical Intraepithelial Neoplasia

Anderson MC, Hartley RB: Cervical crypt involvement by intraepithelial neoplasia. *Obstet Gynecol* 1980;**55**:546.

Averette HE et al: Diagnosis and management of microinvasive (stage 1A) carcinoma of the uterine cervix. *Cancer* 1976;**38** (Suppl 1):414.

Baggish MS: High-power–density carbon dioxide laser therapy for early cervical neoplasia. *Am J Obstet Gynecol* 1980;**136**:117.

Benedet JL et al: Colposcopic evaluation of pregnant patients with abnormal cervical smears. *Br J Obstet Gynaecol* 1977; **84**:517.

Bjerre B, Sjoberg NO, Soderberg H: Further treatment after conization. *J Reprod Med* 1978;**21**:232.

Bjerre B et al: Conization as only treatment of carcinoma in situ of the uterine cervix. *Am J Obstet Gynecol* 1976; **125**:143.

Caglar H, Delgado G: Colposcopically directed cone biopsy in the management of cervical intraepithelial neoplasia. *Obstet Gynecol* 1978;**51**:634.

Carter R et al: Treatment of cervical intraepithelial neoplasia with the carbon dioxide laser beam: Preliminary report. *Am J Obstet Gynecol* 1978;**131**:831.

Hatch KD et al: Cryosurgery of cervical intraepithelial neoplasia. *Obstet Gynecol* 1981;**57**:692.

Kaufman RH, Irwin JF: Cryosurgical therapy of cervical intraepithelial neoplasia. 3: Continuing follow-up. *Am J Obstet Gynecol* 1978;**131**:381.

Kolstad P, Klem V: Long-term follow-up of 1121 cases of carcinoma in situ. *Obstet Gynecol* 1976;**48**:125.

Masterson BJ et al: The carbon dioxide laser in cervical intraepithelial neoplasia: A five-year experience in treating 230 patients. *Am J Obstet Gynecol* 1981;**139**:565.

Ostergard DR, Nieberg RK: Evaluation of abnormal cervical cytology during pregnancy with colposcopy. *Am J Obstet Gynecol* 1979;**134**:756.

Popkin DR, Scali V, Ahmed MN: Cryosurgery for the treatment of cervical intraepithelial neoplasia. *Am J Obstet Gynecol* 1978;**130**:551.

Richardson AC, Lyon SB: The effect of condom use on squamous cell cervical intraepithelial neoplasia. *Am J Obstet Gynecol* 1981;**140**:909.

Robboy SJ et al: Squamous cell dysplasia and carcinoma in situ of the cervix and vagina after prenatal exposure to diethylstilbestrol. *Obstet Gynecol* 1978;**51**:528.

Rome RM, Urcuyo R, Nelson JH Jr: Observations on the surface area of the abnormal transformation zone associated with intraepithelial and early invasive squamous cell lesions of the cervix. *Am J Obstet Gynecol* 1977;**129**:565.

Selim MA, Vasquez H, Masri R: Indications for and experience with colposcopy in management of neoplasia of cervix. *Surg Obstet Gynecol* 1977;**145**:529.

Sevin BU et al: Invasive cancer of the cervix after cryosurgery: Pitfalls of conservative management. *Obstet Gynecol* 1979;**53**:465.

Shingleton HM, Gore H, Austin JM: Outpatient evaluation of patients with atypical Papanicolaou smears: Contribution of endocervical curettage. *Am J Obstet Gynecol* 1976; **126:**122.

Stafl A, Urlkinson EJ, Mattingly RF: Laser treatment of cervical and vaginal neoplasia. *Am J Obstet Gynecol* 1977; **128:**128.

Urcuyo R, Rome RM, Nelson JH Jr: Some observations on the value of endocervical curettage as an integral part of colposcopic examination of patients with abnormal cervical cytology. *Am J Obstet Gynecol* 1977; **128:**787.

Cancer of Cervix

Baker LH et al: Mitomycin C, vincristine and bleomycin therapy for advanced cervical cancer. *Obstet Gynecol* 1978; **52:**146.

Barber HRK et al: Vascular invasion as a prognostic factor in stage I-B cancer of the cervix. *Obstet Gynecol* 1978; **52:**343.

Berman ML et al: Operative evaluation of patients with cervical carcinoma by an extraperitoneal approach. *Obstet Gynecol* 1977; **50:**658.

Bond WH et al: Combination chemotherapy in the treatment of advanced squamous cell carcinoma of the cervix. *Clin Oncol* 1976; **2:**173.

Burghardt E, Peckel H: Local spread and lymph node involvement in cervical cancer. *Obstet Gynecol* 1978; **52:**138.

Chung CK et al: Analysis of factors contributing to treatment failures in stages IB and IIA carcinoma of the cervix. *Am J Obstet Gynecol* 1980; **138:**550.

Clarke EA, Anderson TW: Does screening by "Pap" smears help prevent cervical cancer? A case-control study. *Lancet* 1979; **2:**1.

Coppleson LW, Brown B: Prevention of carcinoma of cervix. *Am J Obstet Gynecol* 1976; **125:**53.

DiSaia PJ, Rich WM: The management of gynecologic malignancies. *J Cont Educ Obstet Gynecol* (April) 1978; **20:**13.

Guthrie D, Way S: The use of adriamycin and methotrexate in carcinoma of the cervix: The development of a safe effective regimen. *Obstet Gynecol* 1978; **52:**349.

Herbst AL et al: Analysis of 346 cases of clear cell adenocarcinoma of the vagina and cervix, with emphasis on recurrence and survival. *Gynecol Oncol* 1979; **7:**111.

Hill EC, Galante M: Radical surgery in the management of clear cell adenocarcinoma of the cervix and vagina in young women. *Am J Obstet Gynecol* 1981; **140:**221.

Iversen T, Abeler V, Kjorstad KE: Factors influencing the treatment of patients with stage IA carcinoma of the cervix. *Br J Obstet Gynaecol* 1979; **86:**593.

Kademian MT, Bosch A: Staging laparotomy and survival in carcinoma of the uterine cervix. *Acta Radiol [Ther] (Stockh)* 1977; **16:**314.

Katz HJ, Daires JNP: Death from cervix uteri carcinoma: The changing pattern. *Gynecol Oncol* 1980; **9:**86.

Kessler II: Genital herpesvirus in etiology of human cervix uteri cancer. Page 211 in: *Prevention and Detection of Cancer*. Nieburgs HE (editor). Part I: Prevention, Vol 1: Etiology. Marcel Dekker, 1977.

Kessler II: On the etiology and prevention of cervical cancer: Status report. *Obstet Gynecol Surv* 1979; **34:**790.

Kottmeier HL (editor): *Annual Report on the Results of Treatment in Gynecological Cancer*. Vol 17. FIGO, Stockholm, 1979.

Lee JKT et al: Accuracy of CT in detecting intra-abdominal and pelvic lymph node metastases from pelvic cancers. *Am J Roentgenol* 1978; **131:**675.

Lerner HM et al: Radical surgery for the treatment of early invasive cervical carcinoma (stage IB): Review of 15 years' experience. *Obstet Gynecol* 1980; **56:**413.

Miyamoto T: Drastic remission effect of a sequential combination of bleomycin and mitomycin-C (B-M) on advanced cervical cancer. *Gan To Kagaku Ryoho* 1977; **4:**273.

Miyamoto T et al: Effectiveness of a sequential combination of bleomycin and mitomycin C on an advanced cervical cancer. *Cancer* 1978; **41:**403.

Morrow CP, Townsend DE: *Synopsis of Gynecologic Oncology*. John Urley & Sons, 1981.

Morrow CP et al: Is pelvic radiation beneficial in the postoperative management of women with stage IB squamous cell carcinoma of the cervix and pelvic lymph node metastasis treated by radical hysterectomy and pelvic lymphadenectomy? *Gynecol Oncol* 1980; **10:**105.

Nelson JH, Urcuyo R: Pretreatment staging. *Cancer* 1976; **38 (Suppl 1):**458.

O'Quinn AG, Fletcher GH, Wharton JT: Guidelines for conservative hysterectomy after irradiation. *Gynecol Oncol* 1980; **9:**68.

Piver MS, Barlow JJ, Xynos FP: Adriamycin alone or in combination in 100 patients with carcinoma of the cervix or vagina. *Am J Obstet Gynecol* 1978; **131:**311.

Reagan JW, Fu YS: Histologic types and prognosis of cancers of the uterine cervix. *Int J Radiat Oncol Biol Phys* 1979; **5:**1015.

Rutledge F, Boronew RC, Wharton JT: *Gynecologic Oncology*. Wiley, 1976.

Rutledge FN et al: Pelvic exenteration: Analysis of 296 patients. *Am J Obstet Gynecol* 1977; **129:**881.

Sedlis A: Microinvasive carcinoma of the uterine cervix: A clinical pathologic study. *Am J Obstet Gynecol* 1979; **133:**64.

Thegpen T et al: Cis-dichlorodiammineplatinum (11) in the treatment of gynecologic malignancies: Phase II trials by the Gynecologic Oncology Group. *Cancer Treat Rep* 1979; **63:**1549.

Tobin SM et al: Relation of HVH-II to carcinoma of the cervix. *Obstet Gynecol* 1979; **53:**553.

Underwood PB et al: Radical hysterectomy: A critical review of twenty-two years' experience. *Am J Obstet Gynecol* 1979; **134:**889.

Urtherspoon BJ Jr et al: The role of radiation therapy in the management of the patient with IB carcinoma of the cervix. *Int J Radiat Oncol Biol Phys* 1979; **5:**1757.

Uubb MJ, Symmonds RE: Site of recurrence of cervical cancer after radical hysterectomy. *Am J Obstet Gynecol* 1980; **138:**813.

Van Nagell JR et al: The significance of vascular invasion and lymphocytic infiltration in invasive cervical cancer. *Cancer* 1978; **41:**228.

Yajima A, Noda K: The results of treatment of microinvasive carcinoma (stage IA) of the uterine cervix by means of simple and extended hysterectomy. *Am J Obstet Gynecol* 1979; **135:**685.

Disorders of the Uterine Corpus | 11

Conley G. Lacey, MD

MYOMA OF THE UTERUS
(Fibromyoma, Fibroid, Leiomyoma)

Essentials of Diagnosis

- Mass: irregular enlargement of the uterus (usually asymptomatic).
- Bleeding: hypermenorrhea, metrorrhagia, dysmenorrhea.
- Pain: from torsion or degeneration.
- Pressure symptoms: from neighboring organs (large tumors).

General Considerations

Myomas are the most common uterine tumors. They are at least 3 times more common in black than in white women. About 20% of all women over age 35 have myomas, but the majority are benign and cause no symptoms.

The common term fibroids is a misnomer when used to denote myomas. These benign tumors are composed chiefly of smooth muscle rather than fibrous tissue and should therefore be designated leiomyomas (though the term myoma is acceptable). Myomas are not a clinical problem before puberty and rarely grow after the menopause. They may occur as an isolated growth but are more likely to be multiple. They range in size from microscopic lesions to enormous masses (collections of multiple tumors) weighing more than 45 kg (100 lb). Myomas usually occur in the uterine corpus but are occasionally found in the cervix, round ligament, or broad ligament. Malignant transformation is rare, occurring in less than 0.5% of leiomyomas.

Although they are usually asymptomatic, uterine leiomyomas may cause acute symptoms requiring urgent treatment. Blood loss from these tumors can be severe. Depending upon their size and location, myomas can be challenging experiences for the gynecologic surgeon.

Pathogenesis

The cause of leiomyomas of the uterus is not known. Estrogen stimulation of susceptible fibromuscular elements has been suggested. Myomas are known to increase in size with high-dose estrogen therapy and during pregnancy. Moreover, they decrease in size and even disappear following meno-pause. Nevertheless, there is no solid evidence to suggest that estrogens cause leiomyomas.

The hypothesis that human growth hormone (hGH) is related to the development of myomas has been largely dispelled by radioimmunoassay studies of hGH in pregnant patients and in patients taking estrogens.

Pathology

Myomas are usually multiple, discrete, and spherical, or irregularly lobulated. Although myomas have a false rather than a true capsular covering, they are clearly demarcated from the surrounding myometrium and can be enucleated easily and cleanly from the surrounding tissue. On gross examination in transverse section, the tumor is buff-colored, rounded, smooth, and usually firm. Generally they are lighter in color than the myometrium.

A typical developing myoma reveals a whorled pattern of smooth muscle and fibrous connective tissue in varying proportions. The myocytes are remarkably uniform in size, and the nuclear cytoplasm gives a characteristic benign appearance. Young myomas are well vascularized; older ones are not. Telangiectasia or lymphectasia is occasionally seen. When a fresh specimen is sectioned, the myomas may project above the surface of the surrounding musculature, revealing the pseudocapsule.

A. Classification: Uterine myomas originate in the myometrium and are classified by anatomic location (Fig 11–1).

Submucous myomas lie just beneath the endometrium and tend to compress it as they grow toward the uterine lumen. They may develop pedicles and protrude fully into the cavity or even pass through the cervical canal while still attached within the corpus by a long stalk. Here they are subject to torsion or infection, conditions which must be taken into consideration before treatment.

Intramural or interstitial myomas lie within the uterine wall, giving it a variable consistency. Subserous or subperitoneal tumors may lie just at the serosal surface of the uterus or may bulge outward from the myometrium. These external tumors tend to become pedunculated. If such a tumor acquires an extrauterine blood supply from omental vessels, its pedicle may atrophy and resorb; the tumor is then said to be para-

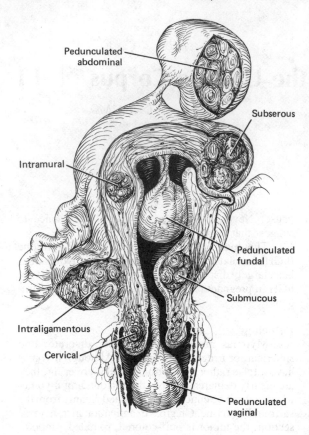

Pedunculated abdominal

Subserous

Intramural

Pedunculated fundal

Submucous

Intraligamentous

Cervical

Pedunculated vaginal

Figure 11–1. Myomas of the uterus.

sitic. Subserous tumors arising laterally may extend between the 2 peritoneal layers of the broad ligament to become intraligamentary myomas.

B. Microscopic Structure: Nonstriated muscle fibers are arranged in interlacing bundles of varying size running in different directions. Individual cells are spindle-shaped, have elongated nuclei, and are quite uniform in size. Characteristically, varying amounts of connective tissue are intermixed with the bundles of muscle cells. The tumors are sharply demarcated from surrounding normal musculature by a pseudocapsule of areolar tissue and compressed myometrium. The arterial density of a myoma is less than that of the surrounding myometrium, and the small arteries that supply the tumor are less tortuous than the adjacent radial arteries. They penetrate the myoma randomly on its surface and are oriented in the direction of the muscle bundles; thus, they present no regular pattern. One or 2 major vessels are found in the base or pedicle. The venous pattern appears to be even more sparse than the arterial pattern, but this may be in part artifactual owing to the difficulty encountered in filling the venous circulation under artificial conditions.

C. Secondary (Degenerative) Changes: Changes in myomatous tumors often create interesting histologic patterns, but these usually are unrelated to the clinical situation. There may be areas of hyalinization, liquefaction (cystic degeneration), calcification,

hemorrhage, fat, or inflammation. Whether or not leiomyosarcoma may appear as a degenerative phenomenon within a mature myoma, as is commonly stated, remains an unsettled issue. Extraordinarily cellular myomas have often been misinterpreted as sarcomas because the criteria used to differentiate myoma from sarcoma are imprecise and often subjective. Ultrastructural studies suggest that leiomyoma and leiomyosarcoma are distinct entities and that the cellular leiomyoma is merely a variety of the common leiomyoma.

1. Benign degeneration is of the following types:

a. Atrophic–Signs and symptoms regress or disappear as the tumor size decreases at menopause or after pregnancy.

b. Hyaline–Mature or "old" myomas are white but contain yellow, soft, and often gelatinous areas of hyaline change. These tumors are usually asymptomatic.

c. Cystic–Liquefaction follows extreme hyalinization, and physical stress may cause sudden evacuation of fluid contents into the uterus, the peritoneal cavity, or the retroperitoneal space.

d. Calcific (calcareous)–Subserous myomas are most commonly affected by circulatory obstruction, which causes precipitation of calcium carbonate and phosphate within the tumor. Torsion causes pain.

e. Septic–Circulatory inadequacy may cause necrosis of the central portion of the tumor followed by infection. Acute pain, tenderness, and fever result.

f. Carneous (red)–Thrombosis, venous congestion, and interstitial hemorrhage are responsible for the color of a myoma undergoing red degeneration. During pregnancy, when carneous degeneration is most common, edema and hypertrophy of the myometrium occur. The physiologic change in the myoma is not the same as in the myometrium; the resultant anatomic discrepancy impedes the blood supply, resulting in aseptic degeneration and infarction. The process is usually accompanied by extreme pain.

g. Myxomatous (fatty)–This uncommon and asymptomatic type follows hyaline and cystic degeneration.

2. Malignant transformation is a generative as opposed to a degenerative phenomenon. Leiomyosarcoma develops from a myoma with a recorded incidence of 0.1–0.5%, but the true incidence of malignant change is unknown, because most myomas are asymptomatic and consequently are never studied.

Clinical Findings

A. Symptoms: A myoma does not necessarily produce symptoms, and even very large ones may go undetected by the patient, particularly if she is obese. Symptoms from myomas depend upon their location, size, and state of preservation and whether or not the patient is pregnant.

1. Abnormal endometrial bleeding–Abnormal uterine bleeding is the most important clinical manifestation of myomas.

Bleeding from a submucous myoma is presumably due to distortion and congestion of the surrounding vessels or ulceration of the overlying endometrium. Most commonly the patient has prolonged heavy menses, but she may display any variant from the entire spectrum of abnormal bleeding. Premenstrual spotting is common, as is prolonged light staining following menses.

Minor degrees of metrorrhagia (intermenstrual bleeding) may be associated with a tumor that has areas of endometrial venous thrombosis and necrosis on its dependent surface, particularly if it is pedunculated and partially extruded through the cervical canal. Abnormal bleeding from myomas commonly produces iron deficiency anemia, which may become uncontrollable with iron therapy when the bleeding is heavy and protracted.

2. Pain–Pain is uncommon with myomas per se, but pain may result from degeneration within a tumor after circulatory occlusion or infection, twisting of the pedicle of a subserous tumor, or contractile effort of the myometrium to expel a submucous tumor from the uterine cavity. Large tumors may produce merely a sensation of heaviness in the pelvic area or perhaps the discomfort described as a "bearing down" feeling. Tumors that become impacted within the bony pelvis may press on nerves and create pain radiating to the back or lower extremities. Backache is such a common general complaint that it is usually difficult to ascribe it specifically to myoma. The pain associated with infarction from torsion or "red" degeneration can be excruciating and produces a clinical picture consistent with acute abdomen.

3. Pressure effects–Intramural or intraligamentous tumors may distort or obstruct other organs. Parasitic tumors may cause intestinal obstruction if they are large or involve omentum or bowel. Cervical tumors may cause serosanguineous vaginal discharge, vaginal bleeding, dyspareunia, and infertility. Large cervical tumors may fill the true pelvis and displace or compress the ureters, bladder, or rectum.

Compression of surrounding structures may result in urinary symptoms or hydroureter. Large tumors may cause pelvic venous congestion and lower extremity edema or constipation. Rarely, an impacted tumor may lead to urinary retention because of pressure on the urethra. A posterior fundal myoma may carry the uterus into extreme retroflexion, distorting the bladder base and causing urinary retention. This may present as intermittent overflow incontinence produced by elongation of the urethra with loss of sphincter control—a situation identical to sacculation of the uterus during early pregnancy. The condition is relieved by replacement of the uterus.

4. Infertility–Inability to conceive may be the presenting complaint. As an actual cause of infertility, myomas are uncommon, but when present they can impede conception or contribute to second trimester abortion. It is not known whether infertility is secondary to impaired sperm or ovum transport or to faulty implantation.

B. Examination: Myomas are easily discovered by routine bimanual palpation of the uterus or sometimes by simple palpation of the lower abdomen. When the cervix is pulled up behind the symphysis, large fibroids are usually implicated. The diagnosis is obvious when the normal uterine contour is distorted by one or more smooth, spherical, firm masses, but often it is not possible to be absolutely certain that such masses are part of the uterus. Insertion of a uterine sound into the endometrial cavity will help establish the diagnosis, but pregnancy must first be excluded as a cause of the uterine enlargement.

C. Laboratory Findings: Anemia may be present as a result of excessive uterine bleeding and depletion of iron reserves. Some patients display erythrocytosis. The cause is not known, but the hematocrit returns to normal levels following removal of the uterus. Some tumors (eg, hypernephroma) may produce erythropoietin, and this may be true of myomas also. However, the recognized association of polycythemia and renal disease has led to speculation that myomas may compress the ureters to cause ureteral back pressure and thus induce erythropoietin production by the kidneys. Theoretically, erythrocytosis, like other types of polycythemia, could cause excessive bleeding at operation, but this has rarely been a problem with carefully performed hysterectomy.

Leukocytosis and an elevated sedimentation rate may be present with acute degeneration or infection. Fever may also be present if the myomas are infected.

D. X-Ray Findings: Large tumors typically appear as soft tissue masses on x-rays of the lower abdomen and pelvis; however, attention is sometimes drawn to a myoma by calcification within the tumor.

Intravenous urography is indispensable in the work-up of any pelvic mass, because it frequently reveals ureteral deviation or compression and identifies genitourinary anomalies. It is essential at operation to know the anatomic position and number of ureters and kidneys.

E. Special Examinations: Hysterography or hysteroscopy may help to identify a submucous myoma in the infertile patient.

Pelvic pneumography or ultrasonography may aid in the definition of a pelvic mass in the obese patient, but these studies do not differentiate with consistent accuracy the difference between uterine and ovarian masses. Consequently, their usefulness in the evaluation of uterine leiomyomas is limited.

Laparoscopy, although usually not indicated for the evaluation of a pelvic mass, since most patients will ultimately require laparotomy, is often definitive in establishing the precise origin of the mass. In situations where exploratory laparotomy carries a high risk, as in the postmenopausal patient, laparoscopy may enable the physician to postpone major surgery temporarily or indefinitely.

Differential Diagnosis

The diagnosis of uterine myoma is not usually difficult, although any pelvic mass may be mistaken for myoma. Leiomyoma is a common preoperative diagnosis for ovarian carcinoma, endolymphatic stromal meiosis, tubo-ovarian abscess, and endometriosis. Pelvic examination with the patient anesthetized may clarify the diagnosis, particularly in obese women and those unable to relax their abdominal muscles. Tense ovarian cysts or tumors or indurated tubo-ovarian inflammatory masses may be confused with subserous myomas. Uterine enlargement due to pregnancy, cancer, adenomyosis, myometrial hypertrophy, subinvolution, congenital anomalies, or adherent adnexa, omentum, or bowel also may be erroneously attributed to myoma. Because a fetus may exist within an obviously myomatous uterus, a pregnancy test should be obtained in all women of childbearing age. Recurrent abnormal bleeding may be caused by any of the numerous conditions that affect the uterus; adenocarcinoma of the endometrium or uterine tube and uterine sarcomas are the most lethal and therefore the most important. Hyperplasia, polyps, irregular shedding, dysfunctional (nonorganic) bleeding, tubal carcinoma, ovarian neoplasms, endometriosis, adenomyosis, and exogenous estrogens or steroid hormones may all cause abnormal bleeding. The definitive diagnosis can be established by fractional D&C. This procedure should be considered essential in the work-up of any patient with abnormal bleeding or a pelvic mass who has not recently had an evaluation of her endocervical canal and endometrial cavity by curettage. Even in the presence of uterine leiomyomas, other conditions can coexist and must be ruled out before definitive surgery.

Complications

A. Myomas and Pregnancy: Although it is not known whether or not myomas in themselves impair fertility, myomectomy does improve the chance of conception in some women after other causes of infertility have been excluded. The reported incidence of pregnancy following myomectomy is somewhat higher than that achieved by infertile women who have not had this operation, including those women who have made prolonged and diligent efforts to conceive.

It is assumed that a myoma usually precedes the pregnancy during which it is discovered, but the tumor may not become apparent until the pregnancy is well established. It has not been clearly demonstrated that myomas increase the incidence of early abortion. During the second and third trimesters, myomas may increase in size from edema or hemorrhage, and degenerative changes may lead to pain and localized tenderness. Expectant management with bed rest and narcotics is virtually always successful. Once the acute episode is over, most patients can be carried to term without operation. Identification of myomas during pregnancy is sometimes difficult, but sonography can often resolve the question.

During labor, myomas may produce uterine inertia, fetal malpresentation, or obstruction of the birth canal. In general, myomas tend to rise out of the pelvis as pregnancy progresses, and vaginal delivery may be accomplished. Nevertheless, a large myoma is likely to be rather immobile, and it may become an indication for delivery by cesarean section. Myomas may interfere with effective uterine contraction immediately after delivery, and the possibility of postpartum hemorrhage must therefore be anticipated. Oxytocics must be used cautiously postpartum to avoid infarction of myomas.

B. Complications in Nonpregnant Women: Heavy bleeding with anemia is the most common severe complication of myomas. Urinary or bowel obstruction from large or parasitic myomas is less common, and malignant transformation is rare. Ureteral injury or ligation is a common complication of surgery for myomas, particularly cervical myomas. Nowhere in gynecology is surgical experience and knowledge more necessary to achieve a good outcome.

Precautions

As in all cases, estrogens must be used with caution in postmenopausal patients with leiomyomas. The dose should be the lowest necessary to control symptoms, and the size of the tumors should be closely followed with pelvic examinations every 6 months. Oral contraceptives should be used with caution in all premenopausal patients with myomas.

Treatment

Choice of treatment depends upon the patient's age, parity, pregnancy status, desire for future pregnancies, general health, and symptoms, and the size, location, and state of preservation of the leiomyomas.

A. Emergency Measures: Blood transfusions may be necessary to correct anemia. Packed red blood cells given over several days should be used for patients with chronic anemia, even though profound, because these patients have normal blood volumes and rapid transfusion of whole blood may precipitate acute heart failure. Surgery is indicated for acute torsion or intestinal obstruction caused by a pedunculated or parasitic myoma. Myomectomy is contraindicated during pregnancy, however, except for a twisted myoma that may initiate labor and result in fetal loss.

B. Specific Measures:

1. Nonpregnant women–In most instances, myomas do not require treatment, particularly if there are no symptoms or if the patient is postmenopausal. Countless women with insignificant myomas have been subjected to unnecessary hysterectomy. Countless others with ovarian cancer have been mistakenly followed for myomas. The clinical diagnosis of myoma must be unequivocal, and the patient should be examined every 6 months to detect significant growth not obvious to her and to reassure the physician that a proper diagnosis has been made. It is impossible to be precise about the size to which a myomatous uterus may be safely allowed to grow, but many gynecologists urge removal when the mass becomes larger than a pregnant uterus of 12–14 weeks' gestation. Large tumors pose difficult surgical problems of exposure and vascular control, particularly if the mass is cervical or intraligamentary and has displaced the ureter. Intramural and subserous myomas rarely require operation unless they are larger than a 12- to 14-week pregnancy or multiple or may conceal adnexal cancer. Cervical myomas larger than 3–4 cm in diameter should be removed to avoid a more difficult operative procedure in the future.

2. In pregnant women–Uterine surgery will jeopardize the fetus. If a myomatous uterus is no larger than a 6-month pregnancy by the 16th week of gestation, an uncomplicated course is probable. If a myoma—especially a cervical myoma—is the size of a 5- to 6-month pregnancy by the second month, abortion probably will occur; however, a few patients have been delivered of viable infants at term. Definitive surgery should be deferred for 5–6 months following delivery, when involution of the uterus and regression of the tumor will be complete unless pregnancy occurs again.

C. Supportive Measures: Before hysterectomy or oophorectomy, the patient should be counseled regarding the effects of the operation on menstruation, menopause, and sexual function.

D. Surgical Measures:

1. D&C and examination under anesthesia must be carried out in symptomatic nonpregnant patients to verify the diagnosis and rule out coexisting problems, especially cancer. Although there are differences of opinion about the need for routine curettage of the uterus prior to hysterectomy in the asymptomatic patient, all patients should have a cervical Papanicolaou smear and endometrial biopsy. Patients with abnormal bleeding always merit differential curettage.

2. Myomectomy–Myomectomy should be planned for the symptomatic patient who wishes to preserve fertility, but one can never be certain, before operation, that myomectomy can be accomplished easily. Occasionally, a bold surgeon has succeeded in removing a large tumor vaginally by morcellation. This potentially bloody procedure cannot be recommended, because the limited exposure prevents the surgeon from gaining adequate access to the peritoneal cavity and may preclude control of exsanguinating intraoperative hemorrhage.

3. Excision of pedunculated myoma–A pedunculated submucous myoma protruding into the vagina can sometimes be removed vaginally with a looped wire snare. This is worth trying if other tumors do not obviously require removal by abdominal hysterectomy or myomectomy. If the pedunculated myoma cannot be removed vaginally, careful biopsy should be performed to rule out leiomyosarcoma or a mixed mesenchymal sarcoma. Both of these tumors are known to protrude through the cervix in older women and may be clinically indistinguishable from an infarcted prolapsed myoma (Fig 11–2). Since infection is a real consideration in this setting, prophylactic antibiotics should be considered.

4. Hysterectomy–Uteri with small myomas may be removed by total vaginal hysterectomy, particularly if vaginal relaxation demands repair of cys-

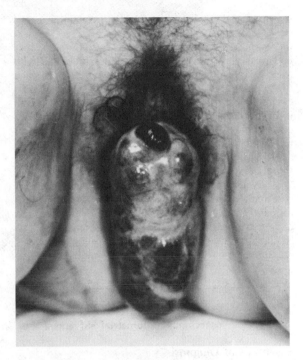

Figure 11–2. Prolapsed and partially infarcted myoma.

tocele, rectocele, and enterocele.

When numerous large tumors (especially intraligamentary myomas) are found, total abdominal hysterectomy is indicated. If the ovaries are diseased or if their blood supply has been destroyed, oophorectomy is necessary; otherwise, the ovaries should be preserved in young women. Ovaries generally are preserved in premenopausal women and removed in women after the age of 40–45, although there is no consensus about the virtue of conserving or removing them during this transitional period.

E. Radiation Therapy: Radiotherapy is effective in the rare instance of a patient who is judged to be a poor medical risk for major surgery but who is bleeding excessively from a myomatous uterus. By terminating ovarian function, it may be possible to stop the bleeding, and subsequent menopausal shrinkage of the tumors will occur. As with the hysterectomy candidate who has abnormal bleeding, preliminary curettage and microscopic examination of the endometrium are essential. External beam therapy with cobalt or the linear accelerator is preferred to intracavitary therapy because it negates the requirement for anesthesia and the technical difficulties of surgery in the midst of hemorrhage.

F. Surgical Treatment of Complications From Myomas During Pregnancy: Patients who have undergone previous multiple myomectomy, particularly if the endometrial cavity was entered, should be delivered by cesarean section. In some cases, cesarean hysterectomy is a sensible solution to the problem of myomas in a pregnant woman who wants no more children. On the other hand, although rather small myomas may increase appreciably in size during pregnancy, they usually regress after delivery. Furthermore, one must not overlook the hazards—blood loss and possible urinary tract damage—associated with removal of a huge puerperal uterus. The mere presence of myomas that were not clinically of much significance before pregnancy should not be cited as an indication for cesarean hysterectomy in the absence of compelling reasons for abdominal delivery or for removal of the uterus.

Prognosis

Hysterectomy with removal of all leiomyomas is curative. Myomectomy, when it is extensive and significantly involves the myometrium or penetrates the endometrium, should be followed by cesarean section. Recurrence of myomas following myomectomy is common, and definitive hysterectomy is often required.

SARCOMA OF THE UTERUS
(Leiomyosarcoma, Endometrial Sarcomas)

Essentials of Diagnosis

- Bleeding: intermenstrual, hypermenorrhea, postmenopausal, preadolescent.
- Mass: rapid enlargement of the uterus or of a leiomyoma.
- Pain: discomfort in the pelvis from pressure on surrounding organs.
- Malignant tissue: obtained by biopsy, D&C, or hysterectomy, confirming uterine sarcoma.

General Considerations

The uterine sarcomas, which are sometimes composed of a great variety of mesodermally derived elements—eg, bone, cartilage, fat, and striated muscle—are the subject of great histogenetic speculation and innumerable pathologic classification systems. Consequently, they are surrounded by more confusion and controversy than most gynecologic tumors. In fact, for a group of cancers that comprise only 2–3% of all corpus malignancies, they have received an inordinate degree of attention, and they occupy a disproportionate volume of controversial literature.

No common etiologic agent has been identified, but in some reports prior pelvic radiation therapy has been associated with the mixed forms of uterine sarcoma in an unexpectedly high number of cases.

Sarcomas can occur at any age but are most prevalent after age 40. They are well known as a source of hematogenous metastases, but with the exception of leiomyosarcomas, lymphatic permeation and contiguous spread are probably the most common methods of extension. Endometrial sarcomas can usually be diagnosed by endometrial biopsy or fractional D&C, but the sarcomas derived from the myometrium (leiomyosarcoma) frequently require hysterectomy to obtain adequate tissue for analysis.

There is no universal agreement on the histologic features that determine outcome, but most authorities agree that the number of mitotic figures per high-power field, vascular and lymphatic invasion, serosal extension, and in some cases degree of anaplasia are all helpful. Lack of discriminating histologic features and analytic sophistication often cause arbitrary assignment of a specific tumor to an improper category. This is regrettable, since treatment is largely predicated on correct histologic diagnosis. Historically, operation has been the favored treatment for uterine sarcomas, but there is some evidence that a combination of radiation therapy and surgery is more beneficial for patients with endometrially derived uterine sarcomas. More recently, chemotherapy has proved to be effective in treating some recurrences.

Histogenesis, Classification, & Staging

From the standpoint of clinical importance, the uterine sarcomas can be separated into 3 broad categories: leiomyosarcoma, endometrial sarcoma, and other uterine sarcomas. A brief review of the histogenesis of these tumors will help the reader to understand the conflicting literature on this subject.

Leiomyosarcoma, the most frequent sarcoma of the uterus, is thought to arise from the myometrial smooth muscle cell or a similar cell lining blood vessels within the myometrium. A less plausible explanation proposes an origin from the endometrial stromal cell, but there are almost no data to support this contention.

The endometrial sarcomas arise from undifferentiated endometrial stromal cells which retain the potential to differentiate into malignant cell lines that histologically appear native (homologous) or foreign (heterologous) to the human uterus. For purposes of classification, the endometrial sarcoma is **pure** when composed of a single cell line and **mixed** when composed of 2 or more cell lines. Because the undifferentiated stromal cells of the endometrium arise from specialized mesenchymal cells of the müllerian apparatus in the genital ridge and ultimately from the mesoderm during embryogenesis, endometrial sarcomas have been variously termed mesodermal, müllerian, or mesenchymal sarcomas. During the evolution of the nomenclature and classification of uterine sarcomas, the fundamental terms mesenchymal, mesodermal, and müllerian have been used. Despite the potential for being broadly interpreted as parent tissue for all uterine sarcomas, the terms have been interpreted by most authors to signify only the endometrial sarcomas. The origin of this confusing terminology is better understood by study of Fig 11–3, which graphically represents the histogenesis of uterine sarcomas. Table 11–1 combines the prevailing histogenetic terminology for endometrial sarcomas and depicts the various possibilities in each category. For all practical purposes, endometrial sarcomas can be divided into 2 major groups. The pure homologous tumors, ie, the stromal sarcomas, compose the smaller group, and all of the remaining tumors can be simply labeled mixed endometrial sarcomas. This latter group

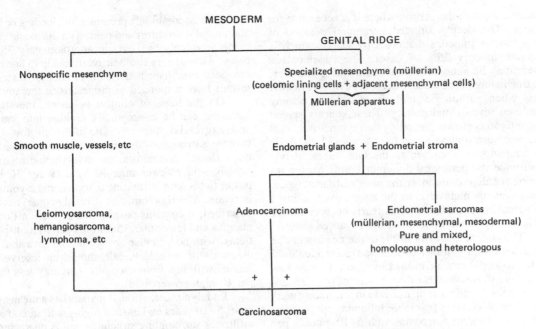

Figure 11–3. Histogenesis of uterine sarcomas.

of tumors (darkly outlined in Table 11–1), because of similar behavior and outcome, can be considered collectively. This group includes the pure heterologous tumors because, with the exception of rhabdomyosarcoma, they usually are termed carcinosarcoma.

Carcinosarcomas are a unique type of uterine cancer composed of malignant epithelium (adenocarcinoma) and one or more malignant sarcomatous elements. They make up by far the majority of mixed endometrial sarcomas.

Finally, the other uterine sarcomas (hemangiosarcoma, fibrosarcoma, reticulum cell sarcoma, lymphosarcoma, etc) are exceedingly rare, and, being indistinguishable from identical sarcomas elsewhere in the body, are not considered specialized tumors of the uterus.

There is no designated staging system for uterine sarcomas, but most authors use the FIGO system for endometrial carcinoma (Table 11–2).

Major Types of Sarcomas of Uterus

A. Leiomyosarcoma: Leiomyosarcoma is one of the more common uterine sarcomas, comprising 1–2% of all uterine malignancies. It usually occurs between ages 25 and 75, with a mean incidence at about age 50. Younger patients with this disease seem to have a more favorable outcome than postmenopausal women. Unlike the benign leiomyomas, which are much more common in blacks, leiomyosarcomas do not appear to have a true racial predilection. Leiomyomas are commonly identified in the uterus containing leiomyosarcoma, but the incidence of malignant transformation of leiomyoma is 0.5%. Only about 5–10% of leiomyosarcomas are reported to originate in a leiomyoma.

Abnormal uterine bleeding is the most common symptom, occurring in about 60% of patients; 50% describe some type of abdominal pain or discomfort; 30% complain of gastrointestinal or genitourinary symptoms; and only about 10% are aware of an abdominal mass. Occasionally, a pedunculated tumor will

Table 11–1. Classification of endometrial sarcomas. Note that the mixed and pure tumors may be of heterologous or homologous origin, but for clinical purposes the pure heterologous and mixed tumors (enclosed by heavy line) can be considered collectively.

Homologous (Tissue Native to Uterus)	Heterologous (Tissue Foreign to Uterus)
Endometrial stromal sarcomas 1. High-grade 2. Low-grade Synonyms: Endolymphatic stromal myosis Stromatous endometriosis Stromatosis **PURE** (single cell line)	Rhabdomyosarcoma (striated muscle) Chondrosarcoma (cartilage) Osteosarcoma (bone) Liposarcoma (fat) (not reported) **PURE**
Carcinosarcoma Stromal sarcoma plus adeno-carcinoma **MIXED** (multiple cell lines)	Carcinosarcoma with one or more heterologous elements Stromal sarcoma plus one or more heterologous elements Two or more heterologous elements

prolapse through the cervix, where it is accessible for biopsy. The deeply situated intramural position of most tumors impedes diagnosis by D&C, which is accurate in only 25% of cases. The Papanicolaou smear may be abnormal; more commonly, however, the true nature of the disease becomes evident after the fact, when pathologic analysis of a hysterectomy specimen reveals malignancy. These cancers spread by contiguous growth, invading the myometrium, cervix, and surrounding supporting tissues. Lymphatic dissemination is common in the late stages. Pelvic recurrence and peritoneal dissemination following resection are also common. In the more malignant types, hematogenous metastasis to the lungs, liver, kidney, brain, and bones probably occurs early but is clinically evident only in the lungs until the advanced stages.

The clinical behavior of the tumor can usually be predicted by the number of mitotic figures identified on microscopic examination. Low-grade leiomyosarcomas are those with less than 5 mitoses per 10 high-power fields, with pushing rather than infiltrating margins. The outcome is favorable following simple hysterectomy. Leiomyosarcomas with 5–10 mitoses per 10 high-power fields are considered to be of intermediate grade, but the outcome is unpredictable— usually favorable if the tumors are completely removed, but with potential to recur or metastasize. Tumors with mitosis counts greater than 10 per 10 high-power fields are highly malignant and usually lethal; less than 20% of patients whose tumors contain more than 10 mitoses per 10 high-power fields are alive at 5 years. Some authors emphasize that the mitosis count should not be the only criterion used to evaluate the aggressiveness of these tumors. An invasive pattern, particularly into the blood and lymphatic vessels and the surrounding smooth muscle, is important. By contrast, cellular characteristics such as atypia, anaplasia, and giant cells are not accurate prognosticators of aggressive potential. Clinically, the most reliable prognostic feature is stage; when the tumor has extended beyond the uterus, the outcome is uniformly fatal.

Other unusual smooth muscle tumors of the uterus such as benign metastasizing leiomyoma and intravenous leiomyomatosis should be considered low-grade leiomyosarcomas. Although they are histologically benign, they are notorious for local recurrence and can cause death by compression of contiguous *or* distant vital structures. Intravenous leiomyomatosis has been known to grow up the vena cava into the right atrium, impeding venous return and precipitating congestive heart failure. Because of their slow growth, they can frequently be controlled by repeated local excision. The metastatic lung lesions of benign metastasizing leiomyoma have disappeared following resection of the primary lesion in some cases, perhaps indicating hormone dependency.

B. Endometrial Sarcomas:

1. Stromal sarcoma–Stromal sarcoma is the rarest of the 3 major uterine sarcomas. The mean age at onset is 45 years, with a range of 30–75 years. These tumors most commonly present with bleeding or lower abdominal discomfort and pain. The diagnosis can be made accurately by D&C in approximately 75% of cases. Although no etiologic relationship to hormones has been established, a small number of metastatic lesions have responded to progesterone therapy.

On the basis of clinical behavior, the stromal sarcomas can be conceptually divided into indolent and aggressive tumors. The indolent low-grade stromal sarcomas—also referred to as stromal endometriosis, stromatosis, or endolymphatic stromal myosis—have fewer than 10 mitoses per 10 high-power fields with infiltrating margins, and myometrial invasion. A benign form, the stromal nodule, has been described; it contains pushing rather than infiltrating margins and fewer than 15 mitoses per 10 high-power fields, with no vascular or myometrial invasion. The diagnosis of stromal nodule should be reserved for lesions with low mitotic counts, certainly less than 5 per 10 high-power fields.

Endolymphatic stromal myosis has a mean age at onset 5–10 years earlier than high-grade sarcomas. It infiltrates surrounding structures and is characterized by indolent growth and a propensity to vascular invasion. It frequently presents with yellowish wormlike extensions into the periuterine vascular spaces. Under such circumstances, it may be confused grossly with intravenous leiomyomatosis previously described. It tends to recur late, sometimes after 5–10 years, and can often be controlled by repeated local excisions.

The high-grade stromal sarcomas display infiltrating margins and vascular and myometrial invasion and contain more than 10 mitoses per 10 high-power fields. These tumors are highly malignant and are associated with a poor prognosis, particularly if they extend beyond the uterus at the time of diagnosis. They spread by contiguous growth and lymphatic metastasis. Once out to the serosal surface of the uterus, they spread to the adnexa and throughout the abdomen. Distant hematogenous metastases to the lungs and liver are usually a late event.

2. Mixed endometrial sarcomas–Although taxonomically incorrect, this category includes the pure heterologous endometrial sarcomas and the mixed homologous and heterologous endometrial sarcomas, because they exhibit similar clinical behavior. They are probably the most common group of uterine sarcomas. They characteristically occur in postmenopausal women, with the exception of embryonal rhabdomyosarcoma of the cervix or vagina (sarcoma botryoides), which occurs also in infants and children. Radiation therapy may be a predisposing cause. There are many published series containing a significant number of patients with a history of pelvic radiation for benign or malignant conditions (Fig 11–4).

As with the other types, the presenting symptom is usually bleeding. Abdominal discomfort and pain or a neoplastic mass prolapsed into the vagina also occur. Since the tumors are endometrial in origin, approximately three-fourths can be diagnosed accurately by dilatation and curettage. In contrast to the other 2

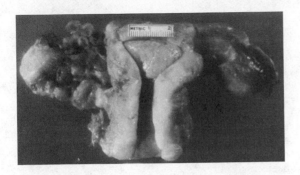

Figure 11–4. Mixed sarcoma of the uterine fundus. Prior full pelvic radiation therapy had little effect on the tumor.

major types—leiomyosarcoma and stromal sarcoma—mitotic counts are not helpful in predicting the outcome for patients with these tumors. Histologically, they are usually highly anaplastic, with many bizarre nuclei and mitotic figures. They usually contain malignant glands and heterotopic elements such as bone, striated muscle, cartilage, or fat, and are then termed carcinosarcoma. Like the high-grade stromal sarcomas, they spread by contiguous infiltration of the surrounding tissues and by early lymphatic dissemination. Hematogenous metastases are common.

The metastatic deposits are usually composed of malignant glands, but sarcomatous elements have been identified in some cases. The prognosis depends chiefly on the extent of the tumor at the time of primary surgery; there are virtually no long-term survivors if the tumor has extended beyond the confines of the uterus at the time of diagnosis.

Embryonal rhabdomyosarcoma of the cervix (sarcoma botryoides), a homolog of this group, was previously also lethal, but combination therapy utilizing surgery, radiation, and chemotherapy has considerably improved the outlook for patients with this sarcoma.

C. Other Uterine Sarcomas: Fibrosarcoma, hemangiosarcoma, reticulum cell sarcoma, hemangiopericytoma, and other esoteric and bizarre uterine sarcomas are rare. In general, they behave like the other intermediate-grade uterine sarcomas, but treatment of them must be individualized according to age, histologic type, and the patient's state of health.

Clinical Findings

A. Symptoms and Signs: Abnormal uterine bleeding is the most common manifestation of uterine sarcoma. Other recurring complaints include pelvic discomfort or pain, constipation, urinary frequency and urgency, or the presence of a mass low in the abdomen. Uterine sarcoma should be suspected in any nonpregnant woman with a rapidly enlarging uterus. Severe uterine cramps may exist if the tumor has prolapsed into the endometrial cavity or through the cervix. Pelvic examination may reveal the characteristic grapelike structures of sarcoma botryoides protruding from the cervix or the presence of velvety fronds of

endometrial stromal sarcoma in the cervical canal. A necrotic fungating mass at the vaginal apex should suggest an infarcted myoma, leiomyosarcoma, or mixed endometrial sarcoma. The uterus is usually enlarged and often soft and globular. If the cancer has involved the cervix, cul de sac, or cardinal ligaments, there may be fixation or asymmetry of the parametria. In advanced cases, inguinal or supraclavicular node metastases may be evident. Advanced uterine sarcomas may present with a large omental mass or ascites secondary to abdominal carcinomatosis.

B. Laboratory Findings: Standard laboratory evaluation of these patients should include a complete blood count and urinalysis, liver function studies (especially serum alkaline phosphatase, prothrombin time, serum lactic dehydrogenase), blood urea nitrogen, and serum creatinine. Cytologic study of tissue recovered from the endometrial cavity or endocervical canal is often positive in endometrial sarcomas but not in the more deeply situated leiomyosarcomas. Office endometrial biopsy or punch biopsy of a prolapsed vaginal mass is helpful only if positive.

C. X-Ray Findings: The chest x-ray may contain metastatic coin lesions characteristic of uterine sarcomas. Because uterine sarcomas commonly metastasize to the lung, tomograms should be considered when the routine films are negative, particularly before any radical extirpative surgery in the pelvis is performed. An intravenous urogram is indispensable in the work-up of any patient with a pelvic mass. It may reveal ureteral deviation, compression, obstruction, or anomaly and will demonstrate clearly the number and location of the kidneys and ureters. The combination of the chest x-ray and the intravenous urogram (scout film) may be used as a survey of the axial skeleton, ribs, and pelvic bones, which are the ones most frequently involved by metastases.

CT scan is not warranted routinely but may delineate enlarged retroperitoneal nodes in advanced cases. Arteriography and lymphangiography are nonspecific and expensive and should be used only for special indications.

D. Special Examinations: Pelvic ultrasound, while usually not indicated in the evaluation of palpable pelvic masses, may occasionally confirm the presence of a pelvic mass or help differentiate an adnexal from a uterine mass in the obese patient. Sigmoidoscopy should always be performed in older women, or in young women if gastrointestinal bleeding or masses suspected of being malignant are present. Cystoscopy is indicated in locally advanced disease or in the presence of gross or microscopic hematuria. Radionuclide scan has identified metastatic deposits in the liver.

Differential Diagnosis

The clinical diagnosis of uterine sarcoma is frequently overlooked. Diagnostic accuracy can be increased if the physician keeps these tumors in mind while investigating any pelvic mass. The tumor frequently does not present the classic picture of abnormal bleeding accompanied by a symmetrically enlarged soft globular uterus. It can masquerade as any condition causing uterine enlargement or a pelvic mass; of these, pregnancy, leiomyoma, adenomyosis, and adherent ovarian neoplasms or pelvic inflammatory disease are most likely to cause misinterpretation. When cytologic studies, endometrial biopsy, or fractional D&C fails to provide the diagnosis—a situation not uncommon with leiomyosarcomas—laparotomy is necessary. At laparotomy, thorough evaluation is critical to the future management of the patient with uterine sarcoma and must include inspection (where possible) and palpation of all abdominal viscera, peritoneal and mesenteric surfaces, liver, both diaphragms, and retroperitoneal structures, especially the pelvic and aortic lymph nodes. Cytologic examination of peritoneal exudate is indispensable for treatment planning; if no free fluid is present, samples may be obtained by instilling 50–100 mL of normal saline into the abdominal cavity. If a sarcoma is identified on frozen section of the hysterectomy specimen, suspicious lymph nodes should be removed. This information, gathered at the time of the initial exploration and carefully documented in the operative records, is critical for identification and staging of the neoplasm and predicting outcome.

The pathologic diagnosis is often extremely difficult and may require consultation with a gynecologic pathologist familiar with these tumors. As each cancer becomes more anaplastic, the parent cell or tissue becomes more difficult to identify histologically. Since proper treatment is predicated upon accurate histologic diagnosis, every effort should be expended to identify the cell of origin.

Complications

Severe anemia from chronic blood loss or acute hemorrhage may be present. The severity and extent of other complications from uterine sarcomas are directly related to the size and virulence of the primary tumor. A pedunculated mass may protrude into the uterine cavity or prolapse through the cervix, causing bleeding or uterine cramps as the uterus attempts to expel the tumor. Infarction with subsequent infection and sepsis may ensue. Rupture of the uterus and kidney has been reported from rapidly growing uterine sarcomas. Obstructed labor and postpartum uterine inversion secondary to endometrial sarcomas have also been noted. Extensive pulmonary metastases can produce hemoptysis and respiratory failure. Ascites is common in advanced disease with peritoneal metastases.

A wide variety of complications have been reported secondary to pressure or compression of a neighboring viscus or resulting from extension or metastases to other vital structures. Urethral elongation from stretching of the bladder over a rapidly growing mass can simultaneously produce obstruction and loss of sphincter control, with subsequent overflow incontinence. Colon compression may result in ribbon stools and eventually complete bowel obstruction. Ureteral obstruction is common, especially with recurrent pelvic sarcomas. Urinary diversion or colostomy may be required prior to treatment if life-threatening viscus obstruction is present in an untreated patient, but urinary diversion should not be performed unless there is some hope for cure or meaningful palliation, since it precludes a painless death from uremia.

Prevention

Indiscriminate use of radiation therapy for benign conditions in the pelvis should be avoided, since the possibility of an etiologic role of excess radiation exposure in the development of uterine sarcomas has not been ruled out.

Treatment

A. Emergency Measures: Hemorrhage from these tumors can be exsanguinating and requires prompt attention. When there has been acute hemorrhage, blood volume should be replaced with whole blood; patients with severe or profound anemia secondary to chronic intermittent bleeding should have blood volume replaced with packed red blood cells over a somewhat prolonged time course. Rapid replacement with whole blood in these patients can precipitate congestive heart failure.

Emergency D&C should be used only to obtain tissue for analysis. Vigorous curettage is likely to aggravate or provoke bleeding. High-dose bolus radiation is a more reliable and a safer method of controlling bleeding. Doses of 400–500 rads administered daily to the whole pelvis over 2–3 days will usually control acute hemorrhage, and this does not appreciably interfere with future management. If these measures are not successful, emergency embolization or ligation of the hypogastric arteries will sometimes control hemorrhage when hysterectomy is not indicated or not technically feasible.

B. Surgical Measures: Extirpative surgery provides the best chance of long-term palliation or cure for patients with uterine sarcomas. Surgery is the cornerstone of the treatment plan and should be the central focus of attack against these cancers.

Low-grade uterine sarcomas (some leiomyosarcomas, endolymphatic stromal myosis, intravenous leiomyomatosis), because of their propensity for isolated local spread and central pelvic recurrence, should be considered for radical hysterectomy and bilateral salpingo-oophorectomy. The benefits of this type of therapy have not been conclusively shown, but theoretically the problem of local recurrence should be improved by more radical excision of the primary tumor. Lymph node metastases in these low-grade tumors are negligible; consequently, pelvic lymphadenectomy can be reserved for patients with enlarged or suspicious nodes. Pelvic recurrences of low-grade uterine sarcomas have been successfully treated by repeated excisions of all resectable tumor. Patients have been known to survive for many years following this type of conservative treatment. Partial or complete pelvic exenteration may occasionally be useful for recurrence of indolent tumors.

The high-grade uterine sarcomas (some leiomyosarcomas, endometrial stromal sarcomas, all mixed endometrial sarcomas) display early lymphatic, local, and hematogenous metastases even when apparently confined to the uterus. For this reason, radical surgery has been abandoned in favor of simple total abdominal hysterectomy and bilateral salpingo-oophorectomy preceded or followed by adjunctive radiation therapy. The addition of radiation therapy for leiomyosarcomas, while still controversial, is being discarded by many centers because it has not improved survival and because it substantially interferes with subsequent chemotherapy. Following completion of surgery or surgery plus radiation, all of these patients should be considered for adjuvant chemotherapy.

At the time of surgical exploration, a thorough examination and evaluation of the abdominal contents must be performed and documented. Cytologic specimens and omental tissue for biopsy should be obtained, and suspicious papillations, excrescences, or adhesions should be excised for pathologic analysis. The more information obtained at the primary exploration, the less difficult will be the design of an appropriate postoperative treatment plan.

When uterine sarcomas recur in the lung and the metastatic survey is negative, unilateral isolated metastases should be excised after tomograms have ruled out other lesions not apparent on the routine chest x-ray. Considering all sources, resection of isolated sarcoma metastases to the lung carries about a 25% 5-year cure rate.

C. Chemotherapy: A number of cytotoxic agents have been evaluated for the treatment of metastatic or recurrent uterine sarcomas. Doxorubicin or dacarbazine used alone or in combination, or combinations of vincristine, cyclophosphamide, and dactinomycin have shown some activity against the sarcomas discussed here. Response rates, however, have been disappointing—10–30%, depending on the cell type. Recurrent stromal sarcoma has occasionally responded to intensive progesterone therapy. There has been very little experience with the use of progesterone in the treatment of other uterine sarcomas.

In recent years, adjuvant chemotherapy has greatly improved the treatment results, both in terms of survival and length of remission for patients with osteogenic sarcoma. This is true also for embryonal rhabdomyosarcomas of the genital tract in young children. Because of the known activity of some chemotherapeutic agents for uterine sarcoma, it is expected that prophylactic chemotherapy will improve the 5-year survival for these tumors when used in combination with surgery and radiation therapy. Such an improvement has not been demonstrated to date.

D. Radiation Therapy: When used as the only modality of treatment for uterine sarcomas, radiation has produced dismal results—very few survivors are reported in the literature following treatment with radiation therapy alone for any of the uterine sarcomas (Fig 11–4). Radiation therapy does seem to improve survival and reduce local recurrences when used in combination with surgery for the treatment of some endo-

metrial sarcomas. Collected data indicate that adjuvant radiation therapy improves the 2-year survival rate in patients with endometrial stromal sarcomas by approximately 20% and may also improve survival for the mixed endometrial sarcomas, though less convincingly. While an occasional 5-year survivor with leiomyosarcoma has been reported following radiation therapy alone, analysis of large numbers of patients from different institutions does not support its use for these tumors. Nevertheless, in advanced forms of leiomyosarcoma, radiation may prove useful for palliation and control of pelvic symptoms such as massive bleeding or pain.

Prognosis

In determining the prognosis for patients with uterine sarcomas, a constellation of factors must be simultaneously examined. Such considerations as the patient's age, state of health, and ability to withstand major surgery or radiation therapy (or both) must be evaluated. The most important clinical characteristic—and probably the overriding prognostic feature affecting the prognosis of these patients—is the stage of the disease at the time of diagnosis. In the high-grade sarcomas (leiomyosarcoma and mixed endometrial sarcoma), the presence of tumor outside the uterus at the time of diagnosis is a clear prognostic omen: fewer than 10% of patients survive 2 years. Even when the disease is apparently limited to the uterus, the prognosis is poor: 10–50% survive 5 years. In the intermediate-grade leiomyosarcomas and high-grade stromal sarcomas, the outcome is improved, with up to 80–90% of patients surviving 5 years if the disease is clinically limited to the uterus at the time of surgery. Low-grade stromal sarcomas and low-grade leiomyosarcomas have a generally favorable outcome: 80–100% of patients survive 5 years following complete excision of the uterus. Nevertheless, low-grade stromal tumors have been known to recur locally after 10–20 years, which confuses the survival statistics. Undoubtedly, these patients must be followed closely for life.

ADENOMYOSIS

Essentials of Diagnosis

- Hypermenorrhea; pre- and comenstrual dysmenorrhea.
- Diffuse globular enlargement of the uterine fundus.
- Softening of areas of adenomyosis just prior to or during the early phases of menstruation.

General Considerations

Adenomyosis is present when endometrial glands and stroma are found to be present within myometrium on pathologic examination. The condition may be entirely asymptomatic. It usually involves the posterior fundus but sometimes involves the anterior wall or cornual region. Although histologic sections often show direct continuity of ectopic endometrial islands with the mucosal surface, many foci of adenomyosis appear isolated, perhaps because their connections with the surface have been interrupted by fibrosis and advancing areas of musculature. In the more advanced degrees of adenomyosis, the uterus is diffusely enlarged and rather globular as a result of overgrowth of muscular elements.

This condition has also been called adenomyoma, which implies an isolated, distinct regional abnormality. However, a scattered, diffuse type also occurs. Neither type has a sharp limitation or pseudocapsule. The term endometriosis interna is sometimes used as a synonym, but it should be abandoned in favor of the more popular name, adenomyosis.

The cause of adenomyosis is unknown, but it occurs infrequently in nulliparas. Rapid reduction in size of a markedly distended uterus may "fold" the endometrium into the uterine wall at delivery; however, this does not explain adenomyosis when it occurs in nulliparas. By and large, it is a disorder of parous women over age 30 and often is associated with menorrhagia and increasingly severe secondary dysmenorrhea. The reported incidence of adenomyosis varies widely (8–40%) in routine sampling of surgically removed uteri. It is found in 20% of hysterectomy specimens. It causes difficulty in approximately 70% of proved cases; about 30% of cases are asymptomatic and discovered by accident. Adenomyosis is generally symptomatic at age 45–50; it is rare after the menopause. The diagnosis depends, obviously, on the diligence with which the specimens are assessed and on whether or not examples of minimal muscular invasion (adenomyosis subbasalis) are included.

Pathology

The uterine thickening produced by adenomyosis is diffuse and of uniform consistency rather than irregularly nodular (as with myomas). The fundus generally is the site of adenomyosis. It may involve either or both walls of the uterus, to create a globular mass 10–11 cm in diameter. The cut surface has a whorllike trabecular pattern, and there may be small hemorrhagic areas representing endometrial islands in which menstrual bleeding has occurred. Myomas and adenomyosis may coexist in the same specimen.

The uterus is enlarged (often symmetrically), irregularly firm, and vascular. Incision reveals coarse stippled or granular trabeculation with small yellow or brown cystic spaces containing fluid or blood. Cut surfaces appear convex and bulging and exude serum. The endometrial-myometrial juncture is often irregular, with the endometrium dipping down into the myometrium.

The microscopic pattern is one of endometrial islands scattered through myometrium. Depth of penetration can be graded, and opinion varies concerning what constitutes true adenomyosis rather than superficial extension of basal endometrium. One scheme is as follows: Grade I, or adenomyosis subbasalis, lies within the diameter of one low-power microscopic field (10×) beyond the basalis; grade II penetration extends halfway through the myometrium; and grade III lesions involve also the external half of the uterine musculature. Degrees of involvement have been described on the basis of the numbers of endometrial glands observed within one low-power field, but this is somewhat impractical owing to variations in the distribution of glandular elements from one area to another.

Myometrial hypertrophy and hyperplasia are almost invariably apparent around the endometrial islets, and phagocytosed hemosiderin occasionally may be seen in the muscularis. If the degree of involvement is marked, it may be that ectopic endometrium will show cyclic changes identical to those of normal endometrium, but in most instances the aberrant tissue appears to respond fairly well to estrogen though not to progesterone. When endometrial hyperplasia involves the mucosal layer, the same histologic pattern may be seen in the ectopic islands; invading endometrium also may participate in the decidual changes characteristic of pregnancy.

A grossly yellow specimen suggests endolymphatic stromal myosis, a low-grade stromal cell sarcoma. The stroma exceeds the glandular elements, plugs of which are found within tissue spaces and in vessels.

Pain and abnormal uterine bleeding may be caused by (1) increased vascularity of the uterus, premenstrually and intramenstrually or, (2) poor vascular control secondary to weakening of myometrial contractility by the process. Intramyometrial bleeding probably does not occur during menstruation, but blood or hemosiderin deep in the myometrium is occasionally seen later in the cycle. Ectopic glands usually resemble those in the basalis; they respond to progesterone in only about 20% of patients.

Clinical Findings

A. Symptoms and Signs: Significant degrees of adenomyosis are associated with hypermenorrhea in fully 50% of patients, and about 30% have an acquired, increasingly severe form of dysmenorrhea. However, only about 20% of women with adenomyosis are likely to have both of these classic complaints.

Despite widespread knowledge of the major symptoms of adenomyosis, this diagnosis is made correctly prior to operation in somewhat less than one-third of all instances. A recent study, however, showed that adenomyosis was the primary diagnosis in one-third of all cases of hysterectomy and that failure to make the diagnosis preoperatively was largely the consequence of failure to think of it. This oversight is not so disastrous as it may appear, because other significant lesions such as myomas, endometrial polyps, endometrial hyperplasia, endometrial carcinoma, or endometriosis generally lead to appropriate treatment.

1. Hypermenorrhea–It is claimed that even adenomyosis subbasalis may produce hypermenorrhea, usually menorrhagia, in a high proportion of cases. This would seem to invalidate the contention that increased menstrual flow results from interference with normal myometrial contraction when large areas of musculature are disrupted by numerous endometrial islands. Nevertheless, there is clearly a positive correlation between the degree of involvement (as opposed to depth of penetration), vascularity, and the occurrence of menorrhagia, whatever the precise explanation for increased bleeding may be.

2. Dysmenorrhea–Likewise, dysmenorrhea is directly related to depth of penetration and degree of involvement, and it undoubtedly results from myometrial contractions invoked by premenstrual swelling and menstrual bleeding in endometrial islands. The uterus is usually tender and slightly softened on bimanual examination done premenstrually (Halban's sign).

B. X-Ray Findings: Contrast hysterography may be diagnostic in some cases, but the yield is too low to justify routine use.

C. Special Examinations: Pelvic examination should be done just prior to or during the early phase of menstruation. Areas of adenomyosis are softened and tender as a result of the vasodilative effect of estrogen.

Differential Diagnosis

A. Submucous Myoma: Myomas are present in 50–60% of cases of adenomyosis, but the 2 disorders have different symptoms. Myomas may cause excessive and progressive menorrhagia and pain. The uterus is firm and nontender, even during menstruation, and discomfort occurs if the myoma is pedunculated and in the process of extrusion. Diagnosis is confirmed by D&C.

B. Endometrial Cancer: Diagnosed by D&C.

C. Idiopathic Hypertrophy of the Uterus: This diagnosis must be considered if menorrhagia occurs without dysmenorrhea or uterine tenderness.

D. Pelvic Congestion Syndrome (Taylor's Syndrome): Chronic complaints—often continuous pelvic pain and menometrorrhagia—should be considered in patients of hysterical personality type. In some instances, the uterus is enlarged, symmetric, and minimally softened; the cervix may be cyanotic and somewhat patulous.

E. Pelvic Endometriosis: Premenstrual and intramenstrual dysmenorrhea, adherent adnexal masses, and "shotty" cul-de-sac nodulations are typical. The disorder is associated with adenomyosis in about 15% of patients.

Complications

Chronic severe anemia may result from persistent menorrhagia.

Primary adenocarcinoma has rarely been observed in islands of aberrant endometrium within myometrium provided the surface endometrium is normal. On the other hand, endometrial adenocarcinoma is often associated with islands of malignant glands in the muscularis, but it may be impossible to determine whether there has been myometrial metasta-

sis from the primary surface tumor or development of carcinoma within a focus of adenomyosis. If the surface tumor is markedly anaplastic and the myometrial islets exhibit well-differentiated glands, it seems reasonable to conclude that the latter are not metastases.

When the stromal component of endometrium, without glands, invades the myometrium, the resulting "tumor" is referred to as endolymphatic stromal myosis, or stromatosis (see p 252). It should be pointed out that this entity is not dependent on ovarian hormonal production and therefore is not truly comparable to adenomyosis.

Prevention

There are no known measures for the prevention of adenomyosis.

Treatment

A. Hysterectomy: This is the only completely satisfactory treatment for adenomyosis and obviously the only way to establish the diagnosis with certainty. Whether the ovaries should be removed depends, as in many other situations, on the patient's age and the presence of obvious ovarian lesions or generalized pelvic endometriosis.

B. Chemotherapy: Various sex hormone regimens have been tried in women with symptoms and other findings presumed to be due to adenomyosis. Most such attempts have been totally unsuccessful. Oral contraceptives usually accentuate the pain or bleeding. A premenopausal woman in whom curettage has demonstrated no endometrial lesion or submucous myoma may be managed for an appreciable time with analgesics alone.

C. Irradiation: Theoretically, pelvic irradiation sufficient to stop ovarian hormone production will completely relieve the symptoms of adenomyosis, and such therapy might be considered in a premenopausal patient with a medical contraindication to major surgery. In actual practice, this combination of circumstances seldom arises.

Prognosis

Hysterectomy is curative.

ENDOMETRIAL CARCINOMA & HYPERPLASIA

Essentials of Diagnosis

- Bleeding: hypermenorrhea, intermenstrual or postmenopausal.
- Hyperestrogenism: conditions with possible alterations in estrogen metabolism, ie, ovarian granulosa cell tumor, polycystic ovarian syndrome, obesity, late menopause, and exogenous estrogens.
- Susceptible individuals: obese, white, diabetic, hypertensive, infertile, and nulliparous women.
- Malignant glands: identified by endometrial biopsy or fractional D&C.

General Considerations

There are approximately 49 million women over 35 years of age in the USA, and 700,000 of these women (1.4%) will develop endometrial cancer at some time during life. The peak incidence of onset is in the sixth and seventh decades, but 5% occur before age 40, and the disease has been reported in women aged 20–30. Endometrial carcinoma is now the most frequent pelvic genital cancer in women, with somewhat over 38,000 new cases expected in 1982. The incidence of endometrial cancer is rising in the USA, while that of cervical cancer is falling; the reasons are not clear, but much of the decrease in cervical cancer can be attributed to routine cytologic screening. The onset of endometrial bleeding facilitates detection in the earlier stages of disease. Consequently, the overall prognosis is considerably better than for the other major gynecologic cancers.

Ovarian cancer and cervical cancer are decidedly more lethal than endometrial carcinoma. In the USA, 38–39 thousand new cases of endometrial carcinoma are projected for 1982, but only about 3100 deaths from the disease will occur during that year. This is in contrast to carcinoma of the ovary, with 11,400 deaths and 18,000 new cases; and cervical cancer, with 7200 deaths and 16,000 new cases.

Estrogens have been implicated as a causative factor, because there is a high incidence of this disease in patients with presumed alterations in estrogen metabolism and in those who take exogenous estrogens. Classically, it affects the affluent obese, nulliparous, infertile, hypertensive, and diabetic white woman, but it can occur in the absence of all of these factors. Unlike cervical cancer, it is not related to age at first coitus, and in fact it is common in virgins. Fortunately for the victim, there is a warning; abnormal bleeding usually occurs early in the course of the disease and alerts the patient or physician to an endometrial abnormality. In the elderly patient with an obliterated endocervical canal, severe cramps from hematometra or pyometra may be the presenting symptom. In the asymptomatic patient, a fortuitous diagnosis may occur from an abnormal Papanicolaou smear, but cytologic discovery of endometrial cancer is not consistent and should not be relied on for early diagnosis. Because of the variable presence of the known prognostic criteria of histologic differentiation, stage, and depth of myometrial invasion, treatment must be individualized for each patient.

Etiology

Although the exact cause of endometrial cancer remains unknown, the argument that estrogens are somehow implicated is becoming increasingly more difficult to refute. It has been known for many years that the administration of estrogen to laboratory animals can produce endometrial hyperplasia and carcinoma. Furthermore, certain constitutional states such as diabetes mellitus, hypertension, polycystic ovary syndrome, and obesity, perhaps having in common elevated endogenous estrogen levels, are associated with a higher incidence of endometrial carcinoma. Patients receiving exogenous estrogen replacement therapy for Turner's syndrome or gonadal agenesis and patients with suspected endogenous elevations from granulosa cell tumors of the ovary are also more susceptible to endometrial carcinoma.

None of this circumstantial evidence has been sufficiently persuasive to interfere substantially with estrogen replacement therapy in this country. Recently, however, reports of case control studies and basic research investigations have supported a causal connection between estrogen administration and endometrial carcinoma.

Many studies are now available indicating a 2- to 10-fold increase in the incidence of endometrial carcinoma in women receiving exogenous estrogens. The risk of cancer is related to both the dose and the duration of exposure and diminishes with cessation of estrogens. The statistical methods and design of these investigations have been subjects of debate, but most of these studies implicate exogenous estrogens as a risk factor for the development of endometrial cancer. These conclusions are supported by basic research revealing increased conversion of androstenedione to estrone in women with recognized risk factors for endometrial cancer: advanced age, obesity, and polycystic ovary syndrome. In view of this convincing body of information, the relationship of estrogens to endometrial carcinoma clearly merits further study.

Clinical Staging (Table 11–2)

Staging of corpus carcinoma is based upon the clinical extent of disease, histologic differentiation (grade), and the presence or absence of cancer in the endocervical canal. In order to obtain enough data for treatment planning, fractional D&C is usually required

Table 11–2. Staging of carcinoma of the corpus uteri.*

Stage I	Carcinoma confined to the corpus.
IA	Length of the uterine cavity is 8 cm or less.
IB	Length of the uterine cavity is more than 8 cm. Stage I cases should be subgrouped with regard to the histologic type of the adenocarcinoma as follows:
G1	Highly differentiated adenomatous carcinoma.
G2	Moderately differentiated adenomatous carcinomas with partly solid areas.
G3	Predominantly solid or entirely undifferentiated carcinoma.
Stage II	Carcinoma has involved the corpus and the cervix but has not extended outside the uterus.
Stage III	Carcinoma has extended outside the uterus but not outside the true pelvis.
Stage IV	Carcinoma has extended outside the true pelvis or has obviously involved the mucosa of the bladder or rectum. A bullous edema as such does not permit a case to be allotted to stage IV.
Stage IVA	Spread of the growth to adjacent organs.
Stage IVB	Spread to distant organs.

*American Joint Committee for Cancer Staging and End-Results Reporting; Task Force on Gynecologic Sites: Staging System for Cancer at Gynecologic Sites, 1979.

so that the information obtained can be used in the clinical staging process. The important prognostic features of cervical involvement and histologic grade are now taken into consideration in the staging system. Although the depth of the endometrial cavity is measured for staging purposes, it has not been conclusively shown to be of value in predicting outcome. Unfortunately, depth of myometrial invasion—a far more reliable prognostic feature than uterine depth—has yet to be incorporated into the clinical system.

Seventy to 75% of endometrial carcinomas are clinically stage I at the time of diagnosis, which accounts for the relatively good overall prognosis of this disease. Ten to 15% are clinically stage II, and the remaining 10–15% are stage III and stage IV cancers.

Figure 11–5. Adenocarcinoma of the endometrium. Note the sharp demarcation of the tumor at the isthmus.

Classification

A. Endometrial Hyperplasia: The glandular hyperplasias of the endometrium are benign conditions that may produce symptoms clinically indistinguishable from early endometrial carcinoma. Because of their association with hyperestrogenic states, some of the hyperplasias, even though reversible, are considered premalignant lesions. Since endometrial hyperplasia and endometrial carcinoma present clinically as abnormal bleeding, thorough fractional curettage is always necessary when hyperplasia is present to rule out coexisting carcinoma.

1. Cystic hyperplasia–This condition occurs frequently in women at or approaching menopause, in certain anovulatory young women, in women given excessive amounts of exogenous estrogen, and in some women with rare estrogen-producing ovarian tumors. It is occasionally seen in women with endometrial polyps but is only rarely associated with endometrial adenocarcinoma and is not considered premalignant. It can, however, precede adenomatous glandular hyperplasia, considered by many to be a precursor of endometrial carcinoma. Cystic hyperplasia is often asymptomatic, being an incidental finding on the hysterectomy specimen. It may cause abnormal uterine bleeding and is reversible with progestin therapy provided the underlying hormonal stimulus to the endometrium is eliminated and carcinoma has been ruled out. It is generally estimated that endometrial carcinoma will develop in 5% or less of patients with this condition.

Histologically, the endometrium reveals large dilated endometrial glands, giving a "Swiss cheese" appearance on microscopic examination. There may be mitoses in the glands and stroma. The stroma is prominent and hyperplastic, whereas the glands are usually lined with low cuboidal epithelium.

2. Adenomatous glandular hyperplasia–This disease is considered a precursor of atypical adenomatous hyperplasia, a premalignant condition. In simple adenomatous hyperplasia, the endometrial glands are closely packed, and there is piling up of the lining cells. When the cells begin to take on a more anaplastic appearance with increased proliferation, enlarged vesicular nuclei, and altered staining charac-

teristics, the term atypical adenomatous hyperplasia is applied. When extensive, it is virtually indistinguishable from early endometrial carcinoma except by the most experienced pathologist. There is probably considerable overlap between the 2 conditions, and the final diagnosis is often based on individual judgment.

Adenomatous hyperplasia presents clinically with abnormal uterine bleeding and is reversible with progestin therapy, again provided the hormonal stimulus (estrogen) is eliminated and endometrial carcinoma has been unequivocally ruled out by fractional curettage. Young patients who wish to retain reproductive function may be treated conservatively with D&C followed by progesterone therapy provided close histologic surveillance is maintained and an estrogen-secreting ovarian tumor has been excluded. For older patients with adenomatous hyperplasia or atypical adenomatous hyperplasia, total hysterectomy and bilateral salpingo-oophorectomy is the standard treatment if exogenous estrogen administration is not the cause. When exogenous estrogens are implicated, hyperplasia will usually regress with discontinuance of estrogen following D&C. Some physicians prefer to give progesterone to accelerate endometrial atrophy, but this is not necessary. All patients require very close follow-up and repeat endometrial biopsy or curettage in 2–3 months or if abnormal bleeding recurs. It is generally estimated that 20–25% of patients with adenomatous hyperplasia and 50% of patients with atypical adenomatous hyperplasia will develop endometrial carcinoma if left untreated.

B. Endometrial Carcinoma:

1. Carcinoma in situ–There is a fine line between atypical adenomatous hyperplasia and endometrial carcinoma in situ, a term considered by many authors to be a misnomer. Since the endometrial glands are not separated from the stroma or myometrium by a continuously distinguishable landmark, it is sometimes virtually impossible to tell whether the carcinoma is "in situ" or whether some of the closely packed anaplastic glands represent invasion into the surrounding stroma. The differentiation of early cancer from atypical adenomatous hyperplasia is often made on the basis of histologic staining qualities. Endometrial carcinoma is identified by large eosino-philic, pale-staining glandular cells as opposed to normal or hyperplastic but benign endometrium, in which the glands are usually more basophilic by comparison. There is loss of polarity of the nuclei, with heaping up of the cells within the gland lumen, and nucleoli are often prominent. Intraglandular bridging and gland-in-gland formation are common features. There is often very little intervening stroma, but if the lesion is truly "in situ," there is no vascular or lymphatic invasion. The distinction between atypical adenomatous hyperplasia carcinoma in situ, and early invasive carcinoma is an extremely fine one, and even the most experienced pathologist can be misled. Since endometrial carcinoma in situ is clinically indistinguishable from early grade 1 invasive carcinoma and can only be diagnosed with confidence on the hysterectomy specimen, the separation of the 2 is unnecessary and for practical purposes can be disregarded. The discussion of endometrial carcinoma applies to both.

2. Invasive carcinoma–This tumor is characterized by obvious hyperplasia and anaplasia of the glandular elements, with invasion of underlying stroma, myometrium, or vascular spaces. As previously noted, it has been postulated that it may represent the end process of a spectrum beginning with adenomatous hyperplasia, passing through atypical adenomatous hyperplasia, and ending with frank cancer. Despite the attractiveness of this theory, only about 25% of patients with endometrial carcinoma have a history of adenomatous hyperplasia. What really happens is not known, but it is likely that endometrial cancer, while it may follow atypical hyperplasia, can develop independently of it.

In recent years, careful reevaluation of the pathologic findings and spread pattern of endometrial cancer has clarified our understanding of this disease. Pathologic differentiation (grade), depth of myometrial invasion, and cervical involvement (stage) are now recognized as extremely important prognostic features. For example, it is now known that well-differentiated (grade 1) lesions limited to the corpus (stage I) and inner third of the myometrium are almost never associated with lymph node metastases. Given the same modifiers (stage I, minimal invasion), undifferentiated lesions (grade 3) have a 30–40% incidence of pelvic node metastasis and almost a 30% incidence of aortic node metastases. Likewise, stage I cancers with deep myometrial invasion, disregarding grade and cervical involvement, again carry approximately a 30% incidence of pelvic lymph node metastasis. Since patients with lymph node metastases are at very high risk for recurrence, these pathologic features have enormous implications for treatment planning.

It is believed that the tumor remains confined to the body of the uterus for relatively long periods of time, but eventually it invades the myometrium and cervix. It may then spread to the parametria, the pelvic wall and aortic nodes, the serosa of the uterus, the ovaries, and ultimately the peritoneal surfaces. Undif-

ferentiated lesions (grade 3) may spread to the pelvic and aortic nodes while still confined to the endometrium or superficial myometrium. Hematogenous metastases to the lungs are uncommon with primary tumors limited to the uterus but do occur with recurrent or disseminated disease. In contrast to the former belief that this disease spreads primarily to the aortic lymph nodes through infundibulopelvic and broad ligament lymphatics, recent studies indicate a dual pathway of spread to the pelvic and aortic lymph nodes. The aortic nodes are rarely involved when the pelvic nodes are free of metastases, but the pelvic nodes are commonly involved when the aortic nodes are not.

Vaginal metastases occur by submucosal lymphatic or vascular metastases in approximately 10% of patients with clinical stage I disease. The concept that these metastases occur by spillage of tumor through the cervix at the time of surgery lacks convincing support. However, vaginal metastases are more frequent with higher histologic grade and with lower uterine segment or cervical involvement.

A positive peritoneal cytologic report at the time of hysterectomy is an ominous sign even when there is no other evidence of spread. Vascular and lymphatic invasion or occult ovarian metastases identified on the surgical specimen are also associated with early recurrence and a poor prognosis.

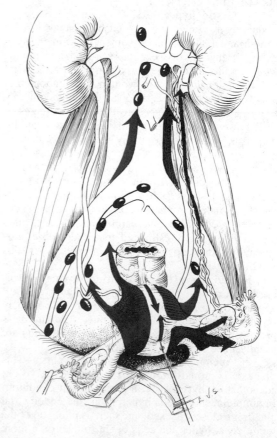

Figure 11–6. Dual lymphatic spread pattern of endometrial carcinoma.

Pathologists recognize 3 major histologic types of endometrial carcinoma: adenocarcinoma, adenoacanthoma, and adenosquamous carcinoma.

Adenocarcinoma, the most common type, is composed of malignant glands that range from very well differentiated (grade 1)—barely distinguishable from atypical adenomatous hyperplasia—to anaplastic carcinoma (grade 3). To determine stage and prognosis, the tumor is usually graded by the most undifferentiated area visible under the microscope. In the USA, adenocarcinoma comprises 70–80% of endometrial carcinomas, but this figure is higher in other countries.

Adenoacanthoma is composed of malignant glands and benign squamous metaplasia. It comprises approximately 5% of endometrial carcinomas. Although these cancers have a reputation for running a more benign course, this is probably due to the very well differentiated pattern they usually display. Grade for grade, they are probably no better or worse than other histologic types.

Adenosquamous carcinoma of the endometrium is composed of malignant glands and malignant squamous epithelium and comprises approximately 20–30% of endometrial cancers in the USA. The reason for the high incidence of adenosquamous carcinoma in this country is unknown, but there seems to be some variability in incidence from institution to institution, and the difference may be explained on the basis of pathologic interpretation. The tumor is often poorly differentiated (grade 3), which makes pathologic interpretation difficult. Because of the poor differentiation, prognosis is poorer than that of endometrial carcinoma as a whole, since the overall statistics of endometrial carcinoma are heavily weighted in favor of better-differentiated lesions.

All 3 types have identical presenting symptoms and signs, patterns of spread, and general clinical behavior. For this reason, they can be considered collectively for purposes of clinical work-up, differential diagnosis, and treatment.

Clinical Findings

A. Symptoms and Signs: Abnormal bleeding occurs in about 80% of patients and is therefore the most important warning sign of endometrial carcinoma. During the premenopausal years, the bleeding is usually described as excessive flow at the time of menstruation. However, bleeding may occur as intermenstrual spotting or premenstrual and postmenstrual bleeding. In the postmenopausal woman, intermittent spotting, described as lighter than a normal menstrual period, is more common. As a presenting symptom, hemorrhage is rare. About 20% of patients with postmenopausal bleeding have an underlying malignancy: 12–15% have endometrial carcinoma and the remainder have uterine sarcoma or cervical, vaginal, tubal, or ovarian carcinoma. Endometrial carcinoma as a cause of postmenopausal bleeding increases with age, so that after the age of 80, cancer is responsible in fully 50–60% of cases.

About 10% of patients complain of lower abdominal cramps and pain secondary to uterine contractions caused by entrapped detritus and blood behind a stenotic cervical os (hematometra). If the uterine contents become infected, an abscess develops and sepsis may supervene.

Physical examination is usually unremarkable but may reveal medical problems associated with advanced age. Speculum examination may confirm the presence of bleeding, but since it may be minimal and intermittent, blood may not be present. Atrophic vaginitis is frequently identified in these elderly women, but postmenopausal bleeding should never be ascribed to this entity without a histologic sampling of the endometrium to rule out endometrial carcinoma. Bimanual and rectovaginal examination of the uterus in the early stages of the disease will be normal unless hematometra or pyometra is present. If the cancer is extensive at the time of presentation, the uterus may be enlarged and soft and be confused with benign conditions such as leiomyoma. With very advanced cases, the uterus may be fixed and immobile from parametrial adnexal and intraperitoneal spread.

Vaginal metastases are rarely identified in early disease but are not uncommon in advanced cases or with recurrence following treatment. Ovarian metastases may cause marked enlargement of these organs.

At the time of the initial examination, the uterus should be sounded when this can be done without undue discomfort or risk of perforation. The sound is passed gently through the endocervical canal to measure not only the depth but the direction and configuration of the uterine cavity. When feasible, endocervical curettage with a small Kevorkian curet followed by endometrial biopsy may obviate the need, risk, and expense of fractional curettage.

B. Laboratory Findings: Routine laboratory findings are normal in most patients with endometrial carcinoma. If bleeding has been prolonged or profuse, anemia may be present.

Cytologic study of specimens taken from the endocervix and posterior vaginal fornix will reveal adenocarcinoma in approximately 60% of symptomatic patients. More importantly, endometrial carcinoma will be missed in 40% of symptomatic patients by routine cytologic examination. Accuracy has been greatly increased by endometrial lavage or aspiration cytologic study or biopsy, as will be discussed under special examinations. The Papanicolaou smear is nevertheless an integral part of the examination of all patients, because it will identify a small but definite percentage with asymptomatic disease. Furthermore, the presence of benign endometrial cells in the cervical or vaginal smear of a menopausal or postmenopausal woman is associated with occult endometrial carcinoma in 2–6% of cases. Thus, any woman over age 45 who shows endometrial cells on a routine cervical Papanicolaou smear requires evaluation for endometrial cancer.

Since there are no known chemical or hormonal markers to identify these patients, laboratory evaluation is limited to those tests that are both useful and economical. Routine blood counts, urinalysis, endocervical and vaginal pool cytology, chest x-ray, intravenous urography, stool guaiac, and sigmoidoscopy have proved to be useful ancillary tests in patients with endometrial carcinoma. Liver function tests, blood urea nitrogen, serum creatinine, and because of the known relationship to diabetes, a 2-hour postprandial blood glucose test are considered routine.

C. X-Ray Findings: Chest x-ray may reveal metastases in patients with advanced disease but is rarely positive in the early stages. Intravenous urography will establish the presence of a normal genitourinary system and rule out deviation or compression of the ureters by enlarged pelvic nodes or other unsuspected extrauterine spread. Barium enema is usually not necessary in a patient with a negative stool guaiac test and normal sigmoidoscopic examination but should always be performed in the patient with gross or occult gastrointestinal bleeding or symptoms.

Hysterosalpingography has been widely used in some foreign countries and in many institutions within the USA for the evaluation of endometrial carcinoma. While investigators consistently report no adverse effects from this procedure, the possibility of transtubal spread of cancer is nevertheless real. Recent studies indicate that patients with stage I disease and positive intraperitoneal cytologic specimens obtained at hysterectomy are at very high risk for recurrence. Unless the information obtained from hysterosalpingography will significantly alter the treatment plan, it should not be performed.

D. Special Examinations

1. Fractional curettage–Dilatation and fractional curettage is the definitive procedure for diagnosis of endometrial carcinoma. It should be performed under anesthesia to afford an opportunity for thorough and more accurate pelvic examination. It is carried out by careful and complete curettage of the endocervical canal followed by dilatation of the canal and circumferential curettage of the endometrial cavity. For staging purposes, an assessment of the depth of the cavity should also be performed at this time. When obvious cancer is present with the first passes of the curet, the procedure should be terminated as long as sufficient tissue for analysis has been obtained from the endocervix and endometrium. Perforation of the uterus followed by intraperitoneal contamination with malignant cells, blood, and bacteria is a common complication in patients with endometrial carcinoma and can usually be avoided by gentle surgical technique and limitation of the procedure to the extent necessary for accurate diagnosis and staging. D&C is never considered curative in these circumstances and should not be performed with the same vigor as therapeutic curettage.

2. Endometrial biopsy–This procedure is attractive because it can be performed in an outpatient setting, resulting in a substantial savings in cost. It can usually be done without anesthesia, although paracervical block is effective when necessary. Currently,

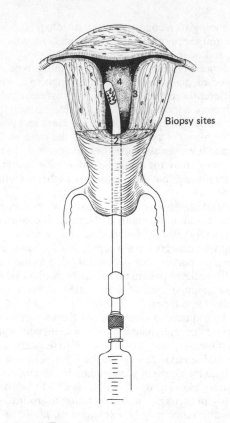

Biopsy sites

Figure 11–7. Technique of endometrial biopsy with Novak curet.

some form of negative pressure attached to an aspiration curet is the most popular method, but gentle curettage with a Kevorkian nonaspirating curet is also highly successful.

All types of endometrial biopsy are notoriously inaccurate for diagnosing polyps and will miss a significant number of cases of endometrial hyperplasia as well. Therefore, it must be emphasized that when these tests cannot be completed for technical reasons, or when the tissue obtained is insufficient for diagnosis or for accurate grading and staging of the lesion, complete fractional curettage must be performed.

a. Aspiration biopsy–This procedure is performed with a variety of aspirating or nonaspirating curets designed for easy entry into the endometrial cavity. The Novak curet (Fig 11–7) is a good example. While maintaining slight negative pressure on the syringe, the endometrial cavity is sampled, preferably in all 4 quadrants. Overall, the procedure is 80–90% accurate for the diagnosis of endometrial carcinoma when the tissue sample is adequate and when it can be successfully accomplished. It does, however, have a wide range of accuracy (between 67% and 97%), and negative findings in the symptomatic (bleeding) patient should never be considered definitive.

b. Aspiration curettage–The Vabra aspirator (Fig 11–8) is another form of endometrial biopsy technique using a 3- or 4-mm suction curet with ap-

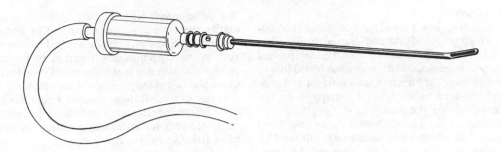

Figure 11–8. Vabra aspirator.

proximately 300–600 mm of negative pressure. To date, aspiration curettage is the most accurate outpatient method for evaluating endometrial cancer, with an overall accuracy of 95–98%. However, the range of accuracy may be as low as 80%, and various technical problems preclude completion of the procedure in about 10% of cases. In another 6–7%, the sample is considered insufficient for histologic interpretation. Consequently, negative findings in a symptomatic patient cannot be considered definitive.

3. Endometrial cytology– In recent years, several methods for obtaining endometrial cells for cytologic analysis have been introduced. These methods have in common the histologic evaluation of endometrial secretions, cells, or lavage fluid artificially introduced into the endometrial cavity. Aspirated specimens are collected in a fluid trap and sent for cytologic analysis or are directly plated out and fixed much like the routine Papanicolaou smear. Accuracy at diagnosing endometrial carcinoma can approach that of aspiration biopsy, ie, 90–95%, but the range of accuracy is wide and depends on the availability of a good endometrial cytopathologist.

Because good endometrial cytopathologic studies are not generally available, most clinicians prefer to rely on the histologic techniques of aspiration biopsy or curettage for outpatient evaluation of the uterine cavity.

It should be clear that outpatient procedures for the evaluation of endometrial carcinoma are a great advance, particularly with regard to cost. Nevertheless, their usefulness is limited, because they are unsuitable for diagnosing hyperplasia and polyps. None should be considered definitive when the findings do not unequivocally rule out endometrial cancer. Furthermore, if the tissue obtained is not suitable for grading the lesion, thorough fractional curettage must be performed. In all circumstances, endocervical disease must also be ruled out.

4. Hysteroscopy–Hysteroscopy is the technique of viewing the endometrial cavity through an optical instrument that is much like a laparoscope or cystoscope. When a liquid medium is used, as with hysterosalpingography, there is the risk of transtubal spread of cancer cells. This procedure has not proved useful for the routine evaluation of patients with en-

dometrial carcinoma but may have some utility in research settings or for the evaluation of recurrent unexplained vaginal bleeding.

5. Pelvic ultrasound–This noninvasive technique is rarely useful in the investigation of endometrial carcinoma, because the disease is usually symptomatic at an early stage. It may identify or confirm a hematometra in an obese patient or help differentiate myomas from a hematometra in the patient with an enlarged uterus.

Differential Diagnosis

Clinically, the differential diagnosis of endometrial carcinoma will generally include all the various causes of abnormal uterine bleeding. In the premenopausal or menopausal patient, complications of early pregnancy such as threatened or incomplete abortion must be high on the list; a pregnancy test will usually clarify the issue. Other causes of bleeding in this group are leiomyoma, endometrial hyperplasia and polyps, cervical polyps, and various genital or metastatic cancers. Cervical, endometrial, tubal, and ovarian neoplasms can all cause abnormal uterine bleeding. Although rare, metastatic cancers from the bowel, bladder, and breast have also been reported to cause abnormal uterine bleeding.

In the postmenopausal age group, the emphasis will be shifted to atrophic vaginitis, exogenous estrogens, endometrial hyperplasia and polyps, and various genital neoplasms. The older the patient, the more likely that her bleeding will prove to be due to endometrial cancer. In any event, the diagnosis will be evident following adequate evaluation of the endocervical and endometrial cavities. In the patient with a normal pelvic examination and recurrent postmenopausal bleeding following a recent negative D&C, tubal and ovarian cancer must be strongly considered. Patients with 2 unexplained episodes of postmenopausal uterine bleeding should undergo total hysterectomy and bilateral salpingo-oophorectomy.

Pathologically, the differential diagnosis of endometrial carcinoma is usually not difficult except in the well-differentiated forms, where the distinction from atypical adenomatous hyperplasia can be perplexing. Whenever there is doubt or disagreement, consultation with a pathologist skilled in the diagnosis of gynecologic neoplasms will usually resolve the problem.

Complications

If the patient has ignored her symptoms of bleeding over a long period of time and allowed the cancer to extensively invade the myometrium, she may present with severe anemia secondary to chronic blood loss or acute hemorrhage. If bleeding is significant and continuous, high-dose bolus radiation therapy is usually effective in slowing the hemorrhage.

The presence of a hematometra can be confirmed by sounding the uterus under anesthesia, followed by dilatation of the cervix to allow adequate drainage. When a pyometra is present, the patient may present with peritonitis or generalized sepsis, with all of the consequent complications.

Perforation of the uterus at the time of dilatation and fractional curettage or endometrial biopsy is not an uncommon problem. If the perforating instrument is large, loops of small bowel may be inadvertently retrieved through the cervical canal. A large perforation warrants laparoscopy or laparotomy to evaluate and repair the damage. If there has been significant contamination of the peritoneal cavity with blood or necrotic tumor, the patient should be treated with broad-spectrum antibiotics to prevent peritonitis. Perforation in the patient with endometrial cancer should be viewed as a major complication, since spill of tumor into the peritoneal cavity may drastically alter her prognosis.

Prevention

The constitutional and other risk factors for endometrial carcinoma are well known. Obese, diabetic, hypertensive, nulliparous women with a history of infertility or repeated D&C for abnormal bleeding certainly require close surveillance. Women with late menopause or previous pelvic radiation therapy and those taking estrogens should be under closer observation than women in the general population. Very little can be done for the constitutional risk factors other than general health measures to control diabetes and hypertension and maintain ideal body weight.

Estrogens should be prescribed only for patients with bona fide medical indications or clear symptoms of estrogen deficiency requiring replacement for continued comfortable function. They should be administered cyclically, 21–25 days each month, using the lowest dose that controls symptoms. Progesterone, 10 mg, should be added for the last 7–10 days of the cycle, because it has been shown to reduce the risk of endometrial carcinoma. The hormones should be discontinued on a slowly tapered dosage schedule as soon as the patient can tolerate it, but this is an extremely variable period of time ranging from a few months to a decade or more.

Treatment

The treatment of cancer anywhere in the body depends upon its natural history and pattern of spread. The clinician is confronted with familiar questions in each case: What is it? Where is it now or where is it most likely to be? What are its pathways of dissemination or invasion? Recent studies have done much to clarify the lymphatic spread pattern of endometrial carcinoma: Nodal metastases, vaginal recurrence, and survival have been demonstrated to be directly proportionate to the depth of myometrial invasion, degree of anaplasia, and the presence of cervical involvement. Any one of these features implies a high risk of treatment failure and recurrence. It follows that any rational treatment plan for endometrial carcinoma must take these risk factors into consideration.

Surgery and radiation therapy are the only methods of treatment that have consistently shown a high degree of success in treating this disease. It has been repeatedly demonstrated that radiation therapy can cure endometrial carcinoma in some patients, but when irradiation is used alone the survival rates have been clearly inferior to those achieved with surgery. Radiation therapy averages about a 20% lower cure rate than surgery in stage I disease. Surgery is therefore the treatment of choice whenever feasible, but some form of adjuvant therapy will be necessary in patients at high risk for metastasis. Because chemotherapy is not reliable for this purpose, radiation therapy is the clear choice for adjuvant treatment. Even though preoperative or postoperative radiation therapy in combination with surgery for stage I disease has not significantly improved 5-year survival over rates achieved by surgery alone, there is considerable evidence to support the use of adjuvant radiation therapy in this disease.

It is well known that radiation therapy alone can cure endometrial carcinoma in some patients, and when used preoperatively it will completely eradicate the primary tumor in over 50% of stage I cases. Furthermore, adjuvant radiation therapy has reduced the incidence of vaginal vault recurrence following surgery for stage I patients from an average of 3–8% to 1–3%. Also, regional radiation therapy has eliminated microscopic nodal metastases in other tumor systems, and some patients with surgically proved nodal metastases from endometrial carcinoma are now alive more than 5 years following adjuvant radiation therapy to pelvic and aortic nodes. Accordingly, in the presence of extrauterine extension, lower uterine segment or cervical involvement, poor histologic differentiation, or myometrial penetration greater than one-third the full thickness, adjuvant radiation therapy is recommended. In the absence of these findings, it is difficult to justify the risk and morbidity of any additional treatment beyond simple total abdominal hysterectomy and bilateral salpingo-oophorectomy.

A. Emergency Measures: Infrequently, the patient with endometrial adenocarcinoma may present in a critical state. When bleeding has been ignored for long periods of time, profound anemia may exist; or when blood loss is acute and massive, the patient may be in shock. Once vital signs have been stabilized and adequate blood is in reserve, emergency dilatation and fractional curettage should be performed with the utmost caution and gentleness. If the uterus is obviously full of necrotic tumor, instrumentation will only increase the bleeding. If bleeding persists following D&C, high-dosage bolus radiation therapy to the whole pelvis should be administered. Rarely, in the face of very advanced lesions, embolization of the hypogastric arteries via percutaneous selective angiography may be required to control hemorrhage before treatment can be initiated. Hysterectomy should always be considered if it can be accomplished safely without jeopardizing curative therapy.

Elderly patients may present with severe lower abdominal pain and cramping secondary to hematometra or pyometra; these complications result from endometrial carcinoma in over half of cases. When adequate blood levels of broad-spectrum antibiotics are established, the cervix should be dilated and the endometrial cavity adequately drained. In this setting, vigorous D&C is contraindicated because of the high risk of uterine perforation. If the cervix is well dilated, an indwelling drain is usually not necessary; but if sepsis is not controlled within 24–48 hours, the patient should be reexamined to ascertain cervical patency. Once the infection has completely subsided and the patient has been afebrile for 7–10 days, gentle fractional curettage should be performed if the diagnosis was not confirmed at the initial procedure.

B. Radiation Therapy: Historically, endometrial carcinoma has been treated by a variety of radiation techniques that can be conceptually divided into local and regional forms of therapy. Local therapy is performed by the application of radioactive sources into or around the tumor (or both) by the use of special containers called applicators. The purpose of therapy is to deliver a very high dose of gamma irradiation to the central portion and surface of the tumor. By applying these radioactive sources to the upper vagina and endometrial cavity, several thousand rads can be administered in a relatively short time (24–48 hours). Because of the inverse square law governing point sources of radiation, which states that the dose at any location from a point source diminishes in proportion to the inverse square of the distance from that source (dose = $1 \div$ distance^2), the dose at any significant distance from the applicators will be suboptimal. For example, the usual distance to the pelvic side wall lymph nodes from the central radium source is 5–7 cm. Consequently, the dose at the pelvic side wall will be roughly 1/25 to 1/49 of the central dose. Understandably, then, local radiation therapy alone has a sublethal effect on pelvic side wall lymphatics but is very effective against uterine and parametrial disease and against upper vaginal vault metastases. Since the uterus and cervix are removed at operation, local irradiation is mainly effective for the upper vaginal vault and immediate surrounding tissues, although it does contribute some effect to the pelvic side wall. A dose of 6000–7000 rads to the vaginal mucosa is standard.

Regional radiation therapy for pelvic cancer is administered to a large field, usually 15 × 15 cm or 16 × 16 cm, from a source external to the patient. The advantage of regional therapy is the homogeneous dose administered to the field most at risk for metastasis. In the USA, this treatment is now administered routinely with cobalt machines or linear accelerators. A dose of 5000 rads to the whole pelvis is desirable, because it should sterilize 80–90% of microscopic metastases within the field; but in elderly women, who generally tolerate radiation therapy poorly, this dose cannot always be achieved. The radiation dosage must often be reduced to alleviate gastrointestinal symptoms. When the tumor has extended beyond the uterus or is poorly differentiated, or when multiple risk factors are present, the pelvic field can be extended to include the aortic nodes, but the dose must be reduced to prevent small bowel injury.

The timing of radiation therapy in relation to surgery is a subject of considerable debate. In terms of prolonged survival or fewer complications, no statistical advantage can be demonstrated for preoperative versus postoperative therapy in stage I tumors. Theoretically, preoperative therapy should be advantageous because of its ability to destroy tumor in lymphatics and impair implantability at operation. Also, complications should be reduced because the therapy is administered to a field free of surgical adhesions and fixed loops of bowel. Evidence from the literature, however, does not support these theoretic advantages, and some studies indicate greater morbidity with preoperative than with postoperative radiation.

The advantage of primary hysterectomy is that it makes it possible to assess the peritoneal cavity and lymphatics, particularly the aortic nodes, prior to prescribing the radiation treatment plan. In this way, radiation therapy can be precisely tailored to the known extent of spread.

Nevertheless, when the risk factors of poor differentiation or cervical involvement are present, it is acceptable to administer therapy preoperatively to exploit at least the theoretic advantages. When none of the risk factors are present on the fractional curettage specimen, a simple hysterectomy and bilateral salpingo-oophorectomy may be performed. If invasion to a depth greater than one-third the myometrial thickness or other risk factors are identified during surgery or on the hysterectomy specimen, postoperative whole pelvis therapy, including the upper vagina, can be administered safely. The value of local therapy to the vaginal vault, in addition to regional whole pelvis radiation that includes the upper vagina, is unknown; but external therapy alone seems to be as effective as local vault irradiation at controlling recurrences.

When the disease involves the cervix or lower uterine segment, radiation must be administered according to the guidelines for primary cervical cancer, because the patterns of spread are similar.

If the patient is inoperable for medical reasons or the cancer is unresectable, radiation therapy is the only recourse. In this situation, combination external beam and intracavitary applications should be administered in doses at or near the tolerance level of the surrounding normal tissue.

C. Surgical Treatment: Because bleeding is usually an early sign of endometrial carcinoma, most patients present with stage I, grade 1 disease and can be adequately and completely treated by simple hysterectomy. In this situation, the results are the same whether hysterectomy is accomplished vaginally or abdominally, but the abdominal approach is superior for removal of the ovaries and for assessment of the peritoneal cavity and retroperitoneal nodes. It also permits the surgeon to obtain peritoneal washings for cytologic identification of occult spread. For these reasons, the abdominal approach is preferred except in patients with very early disease and a small uterus, in whom the risk of occult cervical involvement or deep myometrial invasion is minimal and who also have other compelling reasons for vaginal surgery. As stated previously, if risk factors are identified on the operative specimen, postoperative adjuvant radiation therapy should be administered.

For all other patients with resectable endometrial adenocarcinoma, radiation therapy in combination with surgery is the preferred treatment. This is usually accomplished by preoperative intracavitary radium or cesium applications in combination with whole pelvis radiation therapy. Simple extrafascial total abdominal hysterectomy and bilateral salpingo-oophorectomy with peritoneal washings and a thorough evaluation of the abdominal cavity and retroperitoneal nodes is the procedure of choice. Many surgeons prefer to allow 4–6 weeks to elapse between irradiation and surgery, but it seems to be unnecessary. Many treatment centers now utilize immediate surgery following preoperative radiation therapy and have noted no increase in complications. In stage I disease, initial surgery is acceptable when concomitant adnexal disease is suspected or the uterus is enlarged by leiomyomas.

Radical hysterectomy has been recommended by some, particularly for stage II tumors, but the results have been no better than with simple hysterectomy combined with radiation therapy. Furthermore, most patients are elderly or have concurrent diabetes, hypertension, or other medical problems that preclude radical surgery. Radical hysterectomy can be effective treatment, however, for patients with recurrence following treatment with radiation therapy alone or for those who have previously received therapeutic doses of pelvic radiation therapy for other pelvic cancers. The high risk of bowel or urinary tract injury in this setting must be understood and accepted by both the patient and the physician.

In many stage III patients and most patients with stage IV disease, surgery is not feasible; but when there is reason to expect cure, even pelvic exenteration may be indicated. Many patients with recurrent endometrial cancer in the central pelvis have been successfully treated by ultraradical procedures, and in some respects they are ideal candidates if life expectancy is otherwise good. With advancing age, life itself often becomes more important than reduced sexual function and diminished self-image, the unavoidable consequences of ultraradical surgery.

D. Hormone Therapy: Progesterone has been the time-honored agent for the treatment of recurrent endometrial carcinoma not amenable to irradiation or surgery. It is both safe and economical and can be administered orally or parenterally. Experience has been greatest with hydroxyprogesterone caproate (Delalutin), which must be administered parenterally. Other agents such as medroxyprogesterone acetate suspension (Depo-Provera), also administered parenterally, and megestrol (Megace), administered orally, appear to have similar effectiveness. There is an approximately 30% objective response and a further 7% arrest of recurrent disease with these drugs. The average duration of response is 20 months, and patients who respond survive more than 4 times longer than nonresponders. About 30% of responders survive 5 years; virtually all of the nonresponders die before this time. Patients who are young and have localized recurrence respond better than older patients and those with disseminated disease; well-differentiated tumors respond better than poorly differentiated ones; and patients with late recurrences respond better than those with early ones (indicating a more indolent, well-differentiated form of the disease). Because some patients do not achieve remission until after 10–12 weeks of therapy, the minimum duration of treatment should be over 3 months. Overall, about 13% of patients with recurrent disease appear to achieve long-term remissions with progesterone therapy.

While progesterones have an encouraging record in the treatment of recurrent endometrial adenocarcinoma, they are disappointing as prophylactic agents. They have not improved survival or decreased recurrence when used following definitive treatment of early stage disease.

New hormonal agents on the horizon include tamoxifen, a potent antiestrogen, which has produced a small number of responses. As with progesterone, the patients who respond generally have well-differentiated tumors and long, disease-free intervals, but many more patients need to be studied before reliable predictions about efficacy can be made.

E. Antitumor Chemotherapy: Because of the success with progesterone in the treatment of recurrent endometrial carcinoma, standard chemotherapy with cytotoxic agents has not received much interest. There are, however, many reports of small studies indicating activity by several agents. Doxorubicin (Adriamycin) is reported to have an approximately 35% overall response rate, with 25% of these responding completely. Cyclophosphamide (Cytoxan), an alkalating agent, and fluorouracil (5-FU), an antimetabolite, have both achieved about a 25% response rate in isolated small series. Cisplatin (Platinol) has proved to be very disappointing in the treatment of endometrial carcinoma.

Many studies are under way to determine the efficiency of multiple drug regimens and to evaluate the response to combination therapy using cytotoxic agents with progesterone.

F. General and Supportive Measures: When the patient presents without acute symptoms of hemorrhage or sepsis, the work-up, while it should be efficient and thorough, can be more leisurely. Patients with endometrial carcinoma are often elderly and medically feeble. They may be weak, anemic, diabetic, or hypertensive, and specific attention to these problems may be necessary before endometrial cancer can be treated.

Prognosis

Contemporary studies of the clinical, surgical, and pathologic findings in patients with endometrial carcinoma have identified subsets at greater risk for recurrence. The prognosis is proportionately worse with increasing age, higher pathologic grade and clinical stage, and greater depth of myometrial invasion. Malignant cells in the peritoneal fluid or washings are an ominous finding. Residual cancer identified in the hysterectomy specimen following preoperative radiation therapy also correlates with reduced survival.

In the USA, patients with stage I disease have an overall 5-year survival rate between 75% and 95% depending upon the source of the information. Stage I patients with poorly differentiated tumors or deep myometrial invasion have a 30–40% chance of having positive pelvic nodes. Understandably, the prognosis in these patients is markedly reduced (50–60%), reflecting inadequate treatment of high-risk patients or inability to control metastatic disease with current therapy protocols.

The overall 5-year survival rate for stage II disease is 50%, for stage III 30%, and for stage IV less than 5%. These figures underline the increasing risk for treatment failure and recurrence with increasing bulk and extension of tumor. Consequently, identification of the known risk factors by thorough preoperative and intraoperative evaluation and careful examination of the histopathologic material is vitally necessary for treatment planning.

When no risk factors are identified, conservative surgery (simple total abdominal hysterectomy and bilateral salpingo-oophorectomy) should result in corrected survivals near 100% at 5 years. The presence of risk factors mandates an aggressive approach utilizing adjuvant radiation therapy and in some instances chemotherapy as well. It is hoped that properly controlled prospective randomized studies will determine the success of such treatment.

ENDOMETRIAL POLYPS

Essentials of Diagnosis

- Bleeding—menometrorrhagic or postmenopausal.
- Examination with cytotologic study and biopsy of any visible lesion.
- Fractional D&C to rule out additional polyps or cancer.

General Considerations

The word polyp is a general descriptive term for

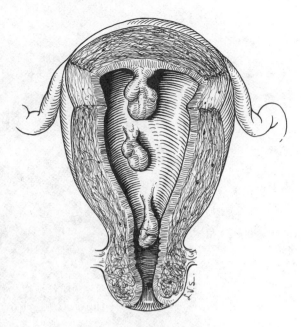

Figure 11–9. Endometrial polyps.

any mass of tissue that projects outward or away from the surface of surrounding tissues. A polyp is grossly visible as a spheroidal or cylindric structure that may be either pedunculated (attached by a slender stalk) or sessile (relatively broad-based). Polyps may undergo malignant change, and isolated endometrial carcinomas and sarcomas have been identified in solitary polyps. Benign polyps are common in the endometrial cavity at all ages but particularly at age 29–59 and have their greatest incidence after age 50. They consist of stromal cores with mucosal surfaces projecting above the level of the adjacent endometrium. Not all polypoid intrauterine structures are ordinary endometrial polyps; submucous myomas, malignant neoplasms (especially mixed sarcomas), and even retained fragments of placental tissue may grossly assume a polypoid architecture. Polyps may be single or multiple and may range in size from 1 to 2 mm in diameter to masses that fill or even distend the uterine cavity. Most polyps arise in the fundal region and extend downward. Occasionally, an endometrial polyp may project through the external cervical os and may even extend to the vaginal introitus. Postmortem examinations have shown that about 10% of uteri contain presumably asymptomatic polyps.

The histogenesis of endometrial polyps is not clear. Unresponsive areas of endometrium often remain in situ, along with the basalis, during menstrual shedding, and such an area may serve as the nidus of a polyp. However, not even the smallest polyps studied by histologic sectioning have given a wholly acceptable clue as to the precise mechanism of formation. The influence of estrogen or progesterone on the development of endometrial polyps is unknown.

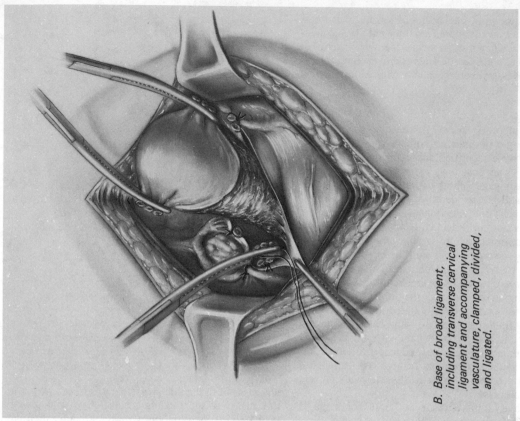

B. Base of broad ligament, including transverse cervical ligament and accompanying vasculature, clamped, divided, and ligated.

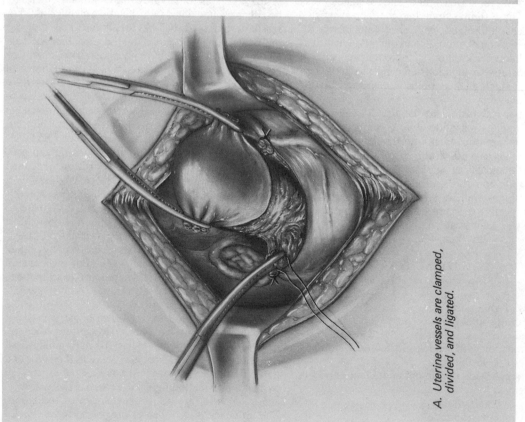

A. Uterine vessels are clamped, divided, and ligated.

Figure 11–10. Richardson technique for conservative hysterectomy.

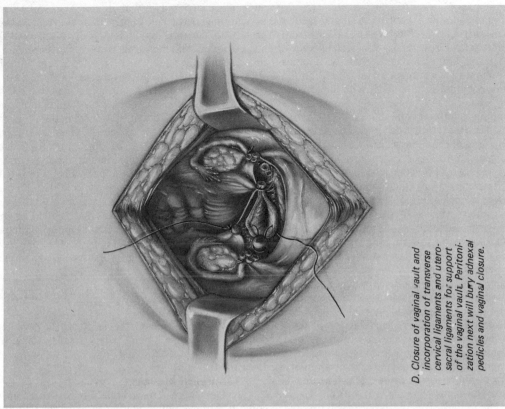

D. Closure of vaginal vault and incorporation of transverse cervical ligaments and utero-sacral ligaments for support of the vaginal vault. Peritonization next will bury adnexal pedicles and vaginal closure.

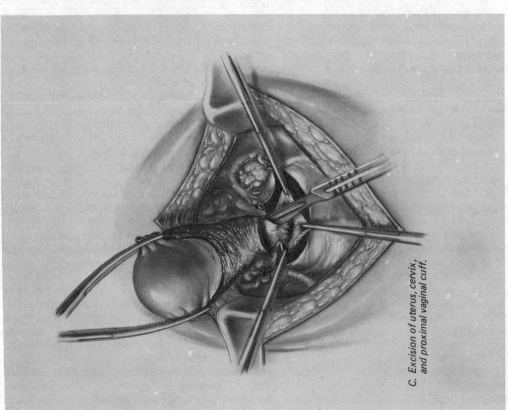

C. Excision of uterus, cervix, and proximal vaginal cuff.

Figure 11–10 (cont'd). Richardson technique for conservative hysterectomy.

Pathology

Grossly, an endometrial polyp is a smooth, red or brown, ovoid body with a velvety texture ranging from a few millimeters to several centimeters in widest diameter. A large polyp usually tapers to an obvious pedicle; a small polyp, when cut longitudinally, often presents a rather cylindric silhouette, with rounding at the distal end. Uterine polyps are of the same color as the surrounding endometrium unless they are infarcted, in which case they are dark red. The pedicle of a large polyp is likely to be attached near the apex of the endometrial cavity, but exceptions to this are common. A sectioned polyp may have a spongy appearance if it contains many dilated glandular spaces.

The microscopic pattern of a polyp is a mixture of (1) generally dense fibrous tissue—the stroma; (2) impressively large and thick-walled vascular channels; and (3) glandlike spaces, of variable size and shape, lined with endometrial epithelium. The relative amounts of these 3 components vary enormously. The surface of an intact polyp in a functioning uterus usually is covered by a layer of endometrium resembling that of the remainder of the endometrial surface, but beneath this exterior there are glandular components that are seemingly much older, and these apparently do not participate in menstrual shedding. Squamous metaplasia of the surface epithelium is not uncommon. The subsurface epithelial spaces are often compared to basal endometrial glands unresponsive to progesterone, but they tend to form bizarre shapes and become quite dilated. Hence, a fragment of polyp may be mistaken for the cystic variety of endometrial hyperplasia ("Swiss cheese" endometrium). The distal or dependent portion of a polyp may show marked engorgement of blood vessels, hemorrhage into the stroma, inflammatory cells, and perhaps ulceration at the surface.

Adenocarcinoma may develop (rarely) within an otherwise benign polyp, usually at some distance from its base or pedicle. On the other hand, a benign polyp is often found in a uterus along with areas of endometrial carcinoma. Thus, the recovery of a harmless-appearing polyp from the bleeding uterus of a postmenopausal woman is no assurance that a more serious lesion does not exist elsewhere in the cavity.

Polyps that contain interlacing bands of smooth muscle are called pedunculated adenomyomas. Generally, these have broad bases and are associated with adenomyosis of the uterus. In the same uterine cavity, endometrial polyps may coexist with pedunculated leiomyomas. In cases of hyperplasia of the endometrium, the abundant overgrowth of tissue may produce a gross pattern called **multiple polyposis,** and curettage of such lesions may suggest to the novice that he has removed a sample of adenocarcinoma because of the unexpected volume of tissue obtained.

Clinical Findings

A. Symptoms and Signs: In a uterus of normal size, a history of regularly recurring menorrhagia suggests the possibility of endometrial polyps. Presumably, a large polyp, with its central vascular component, may participate in menstrual bleeding and add greatly to the total blood loss. Polyps may be the source of minor premenstrual and postmenstrual bleeding, allegedly because the polyp's dependent tip is the first endometrial area to degenerate and the last to obtain a new epithelial covering and cease bleeding after the menstrual slough. These explanations are highly speculative, but it is true that duration and volume of menstruation often are lessened and the end points of the bleeding phase become more clear-cut by the removal of one or more endometrial polyps. In the postmenopausal woman, bleeding from polyps is usually light and is often described as "staining" or "spotting."

B. X-Ray Findings: Polyps may be evident on a hysterosalpingogram as irregularities in the outline of the uterine cavity or as filling defects. This may be a useful procedure when a polyp is suspected but has not been demonstrated by curettage.

C. Special Examinations: Hysteroscopy of the uterine cavity will demonstrate a polyp clearly when the instrument is available.

Endometrial biopsy is inadequate for complete diagnosis because a mobile polyp is easily missed.

Treatment

A. Surgical Measures:

1. Curettage–The treatment of an endometrial polyp is removal with a uterine curet or grasping forceps. A very large polyp may have to be severed at its base with a wire snare or scissors. In all cases, a fractional curettage should follow any attempt at removal of the polyp, whether it was successful or not, because of the known association of polyps and endometrial carcinoma.

Endometrial polyps generally are discovered and removed in the course of uterine curettage undertaken to diagnose and to correct endometrial bleeding of uncertain cause. An apparent polyp removed in the course of such an operation should be labeled as such, preserved separately in fixative solution, and sent to the pathology laboratory as a separate specimen, because it may prove to be the most significant portion of the total tissue sample. If it is intermingled with other curettings, there is no assurance that it will become a part of the material chosen for histologic sectioning. To avoid overlooking a polyp during curettage of the uterus, the endometrial cavity must be explored separately with a grasping forceps (such as an Overstreet polyp forceps [Fig 11–11] or a Randall stone clamp), preferably at the beginning of the curettage procedure. Despite this precaution, it is easy to leave a polyp in the uterus after curettage, only to be discovered later when a hysterectomy is performed because of persisting menorrhagia. At other times, only a portion of a polyp may be removed by curettage, and rather brisk bleeding will continue postoperatively from the residual basal portion of the lesion. The sudden occurrence of considerable bleeding in a postmenopausal woman, often accompanied by crampy uterine pain, may be the

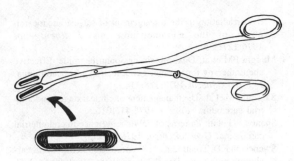

Figure 11–11. Overstreet polyp forceps.

result of infarction of a large polyp. Such bleeding episodes usually are of limited duration and are not life-threatening. Nevertheless, it is necessary to explore the uterine cavity with polyp forceps, followed by a thorough fractional D&C, to establish a firm explanation for the bleeding. If these procedures are not diagnostic, hysteroscopy may resolve the question.

A polyp that protrudes through the external cervical os is easily recognized. When one cannot be certain about the point of origin—particularly if the pedicle is lengthy and the cervix is not extensively everted due to prior obstetric lacerations—the lesion is best managed in the operating room with anesthesia, so that the cervix can be dilated and the polyp's stalk traced to its attachment on the uterine wall. Curettage should be carried out at the same time lest other polyps or additional causes of bleeding be overlooked.

2. Hysterectomy–Simple excision is adequate for a benign polyp, but, if areas of carcinoma or sarcoma are discovered, hysterectomy should be performed. In a premenopausal patient, persistence of abnormal uterine bleeding after removal of an apparently benign polyp (or some portion of it) may be an indication for hysterectomy. Uteri removed for this reason occasionally contain additional polyps, submucous myomas, or, rarely, a small area of carcinoma in a relatively inaccessible location.

Prognosis

D&C is often curative, but polyps may recur. Hysterectomy is definitive but usually unnecessary if cancer has been unequivocally ruled out.

• • •

References

Myoma of the Uterus

Babaknia A, Rock JA, Jones HW: Pregnancy success following abdominal myomectomy for infertility. *Fertil Steril* 1978;**30**:644..

Bean WJ et al: Leiomyomas of the uterus with pregnancy. *J La State Med Soc* 1976;**128**:307.

Curran JE, Maklad NF, Bouffard EV III: Ultrasonic evaluation of pelvic masses. *Australas Radiol* 1976;**20**:58.

Grossman TG, Compton AA: Recurrent premenstrual acute urinary retention due to uterine myomas. *J Reprod Med* 1978;**20**:340.

Jonas HS, Masterson BJ: Giant uterine tumors: Case report and review of the literature. *Obstet Gynecol* 1977; **50 (Suppl 1)**:2s.

Neuwirth RS, Amin HK: Excision of submucous fibroids with hysteroscopic control. *Am J Obstet Gynecol* 1976;**126**:95.

Paterson PJ: Hysteroscopy: An evaluation. *Aust NZ Obstet Gynaecol* 1976;**16**:34.

Ranney B, Frederick I: The occasional need for myomectomy. *Obstet Gynecol* 1979;**53**:437.

Underwood PB Jr et al: Endometrial carcinoma: The effect of estrogens. *Gynecol Oncol* 1979;**8**:60.

Sarcoma of the Uterus

Burns B, Curry RH, Bell ME: Morphologic features of prognostic significance in uterine smooth muscle tumors: A review of eighty-four cases. *Am J Obstet Gynecol* 1979; **135**:109.

Gallup DG, Cordray DR: Leiomyosarcoma of the uterus: Case reports and a review. *Obstet Gynecol Surv* 1979;**34**:300.

Hart WR, Billman JK: A reassessment of uterine neoplasms originally diagnosed as leiomyosarcomas. *Cancer* 1978; **41**:1902.

Hart WR, Yoonessi M: Endometrial stromatosis of the uterus. *Obstet Gynecol* 1977;**49**:393.

Kempson RL, Bari W: Uterine sarcomas. *Hum Pathol* 1970; **1**:331.

Langley FA: Malignant tumours of the uterine mesenchyme. *Clin Obstet Gynecol* 1976;**3**:425.

Lehrner LM, Miles PA, Enck RE: Complete remission of widely metastatic endometrial stromal sarcoma following combination chemotherapy. *Cancer* 1979;**43**:1189.

Perez CA et al: Effects of irradiation on mixed müllerian tumors of the uterus. *Cancer* 1979;**43**:1274.

Salazar OM, Dunne M: The role of radiation therapy in the management of uterine sarcomas. *Int J Radiat Oncol Biol Phys* 1980;**6**:899.

Yoonessi M, Hart W: Endometrial stromal sarcomas. *Cancer* 1977;**40**:898.

Adenomyosis

Dehner LP et al: Primary uterine tumors and multiple endocrine adenomatosis. *Obstet Gynecol* 1977;**49 (Suppl)**:41.

Hernandez E, Woodruff DJ: Endometrial adenocarcinoma arising in adenomyosis. *Am J Obstet Gynecol* 1980; **138**:827.

Carcinoma of the Endometrium

Antunes CMF et al: Endometrial cancer and estrogen use: Report of a large case-control study. *N Engl J Med* 1979; **300**:9.

Austin DG, Roe KM: Increase in cancer of the corpus uteri in the San Francisco-Oakland standard metropolitan statistical area, 1960–75. *J Natl Cancer Inst* 1979;**62**:13.

Ballon SC et al: Pulmonary metastases of endometrial carcinoma. *Gynecol Oncol* 1979;**7**:56.

Boronow RC: Endometrial cancer: Not a benign disease. *Obstet Gynecol* 1976;**47**:630.

Cohen CJ, Deppe G, Bruckner HW: Treatment of advanced adenocarcinoma of the endometrium with melphalan, 5-fluorouracil, and medroxyprogesterone acetate: A preliminary study. *Obstet Gynecol* 1977;**50**:415.

Cramer DW, Knapp RC: Review of epidemiologic studies of endometrial cancer and exogenous estrogen. *Obstet Gynecol* 1979;**54**:521.

Creasman WT et al: Adenocarcinoma of the endometrium: Its metastatic lymph node potential: A preliminary report. *Gynecol Oncol* 1976;**4**:239.

Gondos B, King E: Significance of endometrial cells in cervicovaginal smears. *Ann Clin Lab Sci* 1977;**7**:486.

Gusberg SB: The evolution of modern treatment of corpus cancer. *Cancer* 1976;**38**:603.

Gusberg SB, Milano C: Detection of endometrial cancer and its precursors. *Cancer* 1981;**47**:1173.

Hammond CB et al: Effects of long-term estrogen replacement therapy. 2. Neoplasia. *Am J Obstet Gynecol* 1979;**133**:537.

Hendrickson RL: Endometrial epithelial metaplasias: Proliferations frequently misdiagnosed as adenocarcinomas. *Am J Pathol* 1980;**4**:525.

Horwitz RI, Feinstein AR: Alternative analytic methods for case-control studies of estrogens and endometrial cancer. *N Engl J Med* 1978;**299**:1089.

Judd HL et al: Estrogen replacement therapy. *Obstet Gynecol* 1981;**58**:267.

Mack TM: Uterine cancer and estrogen therapy. *Front Horm Res* 1978;**5**:101.

MacKenzie IZ, Bibby JG: Critical assessment of dilatation and curettage in 1029 women. *Lancet* 1978;**2**:566.

Morrow CP, Townsend DE: *Synopsis of Gynecologic Oncology*. Wiley, 1981.

Morrow CP, Di Saia PJ, Townsend DE: The role of postoperative irradiation in the management of stage I adenocarcinoma of the endometrium. *Am J Roentgenol* 1976;**127**:325.

Muggia FM et al: Doxorubicin-cyclophosphamide: Effective chemotherapy for advanced endometrial adenocarcinoma. *J Obstet Gynecol* 1977;**128**:314.

Salazar OM et al: The management of clinical stage I endometrial carcinoma. *Cancer* 1978;**41**:1016.

Spanos WJ et al: Patterns of pelvic recurrence in endometrial carcinoma. *Gynecol Oncol* 1978;**6**:495.

Swenerton KD: Treatment of advanced endometrial adenocarcinoma with tamoxifen. *Cancer Treat Rep* 1980;**64**:805.

Thigpen JT et al: Phase II trial of adriamycin in the treatment of advanced or recurrent endometrial carcinoma: A gynecologic oncology group study. *Cancer Treat Rep* 1979;**63**:21.

Vuopala S: Diagnostic accuracy and clinical applicability of cytological and histological methods for investigating endometrial carcinoma. *Acta Obstet Gynecol Scand* 1977;(**Suppl**) **70**:1.

Weiss NS et al: Endometrial cancer in relation to patterns of menopausal estrogen use. *JAMA* 1979;**242**:261.

Welch WR, Scully RE: Precancerous lesions of the endometrium. *Hum Pathol* 1977;**8**:503.

Wharam MD, Phillips TL, Bagshaw MA: The role of radiation therapy in clinical stage I carcinoma of the endometrium. *J Radiation Oncol Biol Phys* 1976;**1**:1081.

Yoonessi M, Anderson DG, Morley GW: Endometrial carcinoma: Causes of death and sites of treatment failure. *Cancer* 1979;**43**:1944.

Endometrial Polyps

Barwick KW, LiVolsi VA: Heterologous mixed müllerian tumor confined to an endometrial polyp. *Obstet Gynecol* 1979;**53**:512.

Relaxations of Pelvic Supports | 12

Richard E. Symmonds, MD

CYSTOCELE & URETHROCELE

Essentials of Diagnosis

- Sensation of vaginal fullness, pressure, or "falling out."
- Feeling of incomplete emptying of the bladder; often stress incontinence, urinary frequency, perhaps a need to push the bladder up in order to void.
- Presence of a soft, reducible mass bulging into the anterior vagina and distending the vaginal introitus.
- With straining or coughing, increased bulging and descent of the anterior vaginal wall and urethra.

General Considerations

Descent of a portion of the posterior bladder wall and trigone into the vagina is usually due to the trauma of parturition. The stretching, attenuation, or actual laceration of the so-called pubovesicocervical fascia produced by the birth of a large baby, multiple or operative deliveries, and prolonged labors increase the possibility and degree of cystocele (Figs 12–1 and 12–2). Urethrocele (sagging of the urethra) is commonly associated with cystocele, often in women who have urinary stress incontinence. However, urethro-

cele is not a cause of urinary incontinence. Sagging of the urethra is the result of the shearing effect of the fetal head on the urethra and its attachments beneath the symphysis pubica—an occurrence that appears to be more common in women with wide gynecoid subpubic arches. A narrow android subpubic arch displaces the fetal head posteriorly, providing a measure of protection to the anterior vaginal wall and the urethra.

Cystourethrocele (simultaneous occurrence of cystocele and urethrocele) may occur in nulliparous women, apparently as a result of congenital inadequacy of the endopelvic connective tissues or fascia and of the musculature of the pelvic floor.

Although a degree of cystourethrocele is demonstrable in virtually all parous women during the childbearing years, the condition may not progress and may cause no symptoms. Treatment in such cases is not usually required until after the menopause, when the pelvic fascial and muscular supports become attenuated by slowly progressive involutional changes.

Clinical Findings

A. Symptoms: A small cystocele causes no significant symptoms, and in many cases fairly large ones cause no noteworthy complaints. A cystocele may be large enough to bulge out of the vaginal introitus, and the patient may complain of vaginal pressure or a

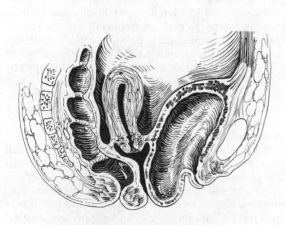

Figure 12–1. Cystocele.

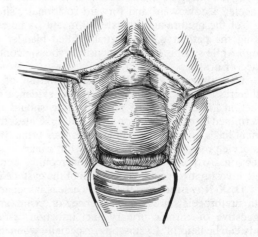

Figure 12–2. Cystocele.

protruding mass that gives her the feeling that she is "sitting on a ball." Symptoms are aggravated by vigorous activity, prolonged standing, coughing, sneezing, or straining. Relief can be obtained by rest and by assuming a recumbent or prone position.

Although urinary incontinence is the most common and most important symptom associated with cystocele, this disorder as such does not cause incontinence, and its repair does not correct stress incontinence. Stress incontinence is the result of relaxation of the musculofascial supporting tissues of the urethra. Unless special attention is directed to the urethral supports, operative correction of a large cystocele may cause rather than correct stress incontinence.

The vaginal pressure of a cystocele may be interpreted as incomplete bladder emptying and thus may lead to frequent efforts to empty the bladder. This has given rise to the popular misconception that cystocele is commonly responsible for large volumes of residual urine with accompanying problems of cystitis, trigonitis, urethritis, urinary urgency and frequency, and dysuria. It is true that a large cystocele projecting well outside the introitus is responsible for significant residual urine. This could lead to bladder infection and symptoms of inflammation. However, many patients in this category have learned through experience that complete bladder emptying can be achieved either by repeat voiding after several minutes ("double voiding") or by manually reducing the cystocele into the vagina prior to voiding. Unless the patient has significant volumes of residual urine, as demonstrated by catheterization, cystocele operations performed primarily to relieve symptoms of chronic inflammation of the urinary tract (ie, urgency, frequency, dysuria, chronic cystitis) will be unsuccessful.

B. Signs: Examination of the patient with cystocele (preferably with a full bladder) reveals a relaxed vaginal outlet with a thin-walled, rather smooth, bulging mass involving the anterior vaginal wall below the cervix. When the perineum is depressed and the patient is asked to strain, the mass descends and, depending on the degree of relaxation, distends or projects through the vaginal introitus. When there is an associated urethrocele, a downward and forward rotational "sliding" of the urethra and its external meatus is noted; asking the patient with a partially filled bladder to cough while straining may demonstrate stress incontinence of urine.

C. Laboratory Findings: Examination of a catheterized urine specimen may reveal evidence of infection. The volume of residual urine should be determined by catheterization after voiding. Unless the patient has a significant volume of residual urine, the cystocele probably is not responsible for urinary tract infection. Any urinary tract infection requires complete investigation prior to correction of the cystocele.

D. X-Ray Findings: If the cystocele is associated with urethrocele, stress incontinence, or symptoms suggestive of chronic urinary tract infection, x-ray study can be helpful. Cystoscopy, especially when the bladder has been filled with CO_2, is most helpful in

diagnosis. With contrast medium in the bladder and perhaps a metal bead chain in the urethra, anteroposterior and, especially, lateral views may demonstrate the cystocele (descent of the bladder base and trigone) and loss of the normal posterior urethrovesical angle.

Cinefluorography (without the bead chain) while voiding may reveal a patulous (funneled) proximal urethra, perhaps an occult diverticulum of the urethra or bladder, or other anomaly as a cause of urinary tract infection.

Differential Diagnosis

Tumors of the urethra and bladder are much more indurated and fixed than cystoceles.

A large urethral diverticulum may look and feel like a cystocele but usually is more lateral, sensitive, and painful; compression, as a rule, will express some purulent material from the urethral meatus.

A true bladder diverticulum is rare in the trigonal portion of the bladder. The diverticulum may appear somewhat asymmetric. Without cystoscopic or cinefluorographic study, it may go undetected.

Enterocele of the anterior vaginal wall (see below), although rare, may occur in patients who have had a hysterectomy. It can be distinguished from a cystocele by identifying the loops of intestine contained in the hernial sac. Enterocele can be demonstrated by inserting a probe inside the bladder; by vaginal palpation over the tip of the probe, one can detect the unusually thick anterior vaginal wall and perhaps note intestinal crepitation. This maneuver may also be helpful in differentiating the anterior vaginal mass produced by a previous interposition operation that interposed the uterine fundus (or just the uterine isthmus) between the bladder and the vaginal wall.

Complications

A large cystocele, perhaps in association with uterine prolapse, may lead to acute urinary retention. Recurrent urinary tract infection may occur in patients in whom bladder emptying is incomplete.

Prevention

Intrapartum and postpartum exercises, especially those designed to strengthen the levator and perineal muscle groups (Kegel), are frequently effective in improving or maintaining pelvic support. Obesity, chronic cough, straining, and traumatic deliveries must be corrected or avoided. Estrogen therapy, by maintaining the tone of pelvic musculofascial tissues after menopause, can prevent or postpone the appearance of cystocele and other forms of relaxation.

Treatment

A. Medical Measures: The patient with a small or moderate-sized cystocele requires reassurance that the pressure symptoms are not the result of a serious condition and that, even though the relaxation may progress slowly over several years, no serious illness will result. With this conservative approach, surgical correction of a cystocele is rarely indicated in a young woman still in her childbearing years who may still wish to have children. If the young woman does present with significant symptoms related to the cystocele—or with a disturbing degree of urinary incontinence—temporary medical measures may provide adequate relief until she has had all the babies she and her husband want, whereupon a definitive operative procedure can be accomplished.

1. Pessary–A vaginal pessary (Smith-Hodge, ball, bee cell) or even a tampon in the lower part of the vagina may provide adequate temporary support of the bladder and urethra and good urinary control. For the elderly patient with complicating medical factors who is therefore a poor operative risk, the temporary use of a vaginal pessary may provide relief of symptoms until her general condition has improved.

Prolonged use of pessaries, despite the utmost care, eventually leads to pressure necrosis and vaginal ulceration.

2. Exercises–In younger patients, definite improvement of pressure symptoms and of urinary control may be obtained by using Kegel isometric exercises for tightening and strengthening the pubococcygeus muscles for a period of 6–12 months. Objective evidence of improved support of the pelvic floor may be noted. Kegel exercises can be of greatest benefit when used prophylactically, beginning in pregnancy and continuing during and after the puerperium. In older patients, Kegel exercises rarely provide more than partial relief.

3. Estrogens–In postmenopausal women, inexpensive estrogen therapy (diethylstilbestrol, 0.25 mg orally daily, or equivalent) for a number of months may greatly improve the tone, quality, and vascularity of the musculofascial supports. Nevertheless, one cannot expect that severe anatomic injury (large cystocele with associated stress incontinence) will be corrected by medical measures.

B. Surgical Measures: Cystocele alone (without concomitant uterine prolapse, rectocele, or enterocele) rarely becomes large enough or causes symptoms that require operative correction. It is only when the cystocele is large, when it is responsible for urine retention and recurrent bladder infections, or when it is associated with bladder and urethral changes responsible for stress incontinence that operative repair is required.

Anterior vaginal colporrhaphy is the most effective surgical treatment for cystocele (Fig 12–3). This is often combined with vaginal hysterectomy and posterior colpoperineorrhaphy because, ordinarily, the cystocele represents only one component of a generalized relaxation of urogenital musculofascial supporting tissues. In preventing further pregnancies, hysterectomy also averts the problem of vaginal delivery, which would destroy the bladder support provided by the anterior colporrhaphy.

Obliterative vaginal operations (vaginectomy, Le Fort's operation) may effectively correct a cystocele (Fig 12–4). Unfortunately, operations of this type may not correct associated stress incontinence; in fact, traction produced by the obliterating scar tissue under the bladder neck and the urethra may actually cause or aggravate stress incontinence.

Similarly, transabdominal repair of the cystocele (along with total abdominal hysterectomy) may be elected to correct the cystocele, but urethral repair is not possible by this route. When an abdominal approach is essential for other pelvic conditions, however, a retropubic urethrovesical suspension (Marshall-Marchetti-Krantz) can be combined with abdominal cystocele repair to correct or prevent the development of stress incontinence.

Prognosis

The prognosis after anterior colporrhaphy is ex-

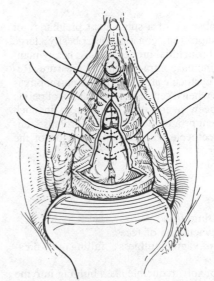

Figure 12–3. Repair of cystocele and plication of urethra for correction of stress incontinence of urine.

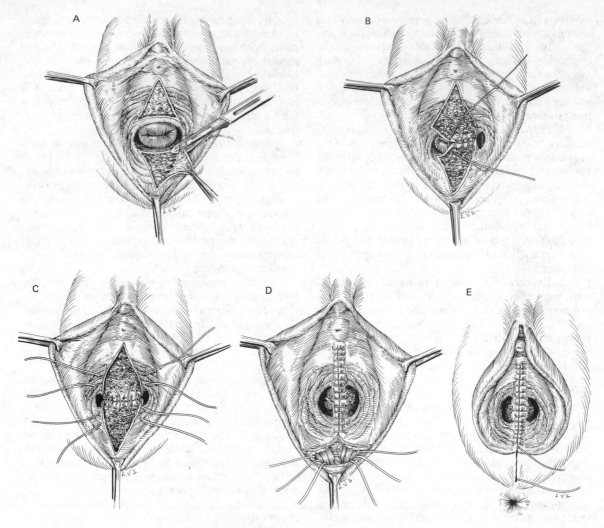

Figure 12–4. Goodall-Power modification of Le Fort operation.

cellent in the absence of a subsequent pregnancy or comparable factors (eg, constipation, obesity, large pelvic tumors, bronchitis, bronchiectasis, heavy manual labor) that increase intra-abdominal pressure. Recurrence of the cystocele after anterior colporrhaphy is rather common when a generalized relaxation of pelvic supports has been overlooked or ignored; in such cases, subsequent progression of uterine prolapse, enterocele, and rectocele will lead to disruption of the cystocele repair.

RECTOCELE

Essentials of Diagnosis

- Difficult evacuation of feces.
- Sensation of vaginal fullness ("falling out" pressure).
- Presence of soft, reducible mass bulging into the lower half of the posterior vaginal wall; frequently a flat, lacerated perineal body.

General Considerations

Rectocele is a rectovaginal hernia caused by disruption, during childbirth, of the fibrous connective tissue (rectovaginal fascia) between the rectum and the vagina (Figs 12–5 and 12–6). Some degree of damage always occurs during operative delivery—particularly of a large fetus or one presenting by the breech—and during multiple delivery. Early and adequate episiotomy reduces the amount of damage done to rectovaginal fascia and to perineal muscles by the presenting part.

Even though all multiparas have some degree of rectocele, the condition does not usually become manifest until the woman has passed the childbearing years and frequently not until several years after the menopause. This manifestation is due to the slowly progressive involutional changes in the pelvic musculofascial supporting tissues.

In addition to parturition and the inherent tone and quality of the patient's tissues, bowel habits may be an important factor in the development of rectocele.

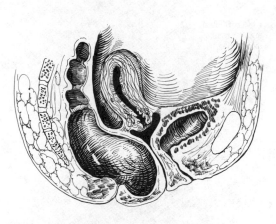

Figure 12–5. Rectocele.

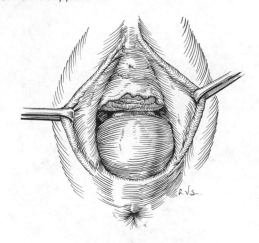

Figure 12–6. Rectocele.

Lifelong chronic constipation with straining at stool may produce—or at least aggravate—a rectocele; conversely, a rectocele produced by the trauma of parturition, by pocketing hard stool in the rectocele pouch, may aggravate chronic constipation or "mismanaged bowel syndrome." Thus, the "cause" of rectocele may be difficult to distinguish from the "effect" of rectocele.

Clinical Findings

A. Symptoms: A small rectocele, demonstrable in virtually all multiparous patients, usually causes no symptoms. With more extensive relaxation (ie, with larger rectoceles), sensations of vaginal pressure, rectal fullness, and incomplete evacuation are typical complaints. The patient may report that it is necessary to manually reduce or splint the rectocele in order to defecate. Digital extraction of hard fecal material is sometimes required. The history may include prolonged, excessive use of laxatives or frequent enemas.

B. Signs: Inspection of the area, with the patient straining and perhaps with slight depression of the perineum, discloses a soft mass bulging into the rectovaginal septum and distending the vaginal introitus. Examination (best accomplished rectovaginally, with the index finger in the vagina and the middle finger in the rectum) reveals a soft, thin-walled rectovaginal septum projecting well into the vagina. The septum may involve only the lower third of the posterior vaginal wall, but it often happens that the entire length of the rectovaginal septum is thinned out. The finger in the rectum confirms anterior sacculation into the vagina. Actually, a deep pocket into the perineal body may be noted, so that, on apposition of the finger in the rectum and the thumb on the outside, the perineal body seems to consist of nothing but skin and intestinal wall. Previously unrecognized or unrepaired perineal lacerations may have almost destroyed the normally thick and strong musculature of the perineal body. Not infrequently, this traumatic attenuation involves some or all of the anal sphincter; occasionally, there may also be a small rectovaginal (or rectoperineal) fistula. Care-

ful questioning about incontinence of feces or flatus and careful inspection of the area should disclose these associated defects.

C. X-Ray Findings: Although lateral x-ray views made after a barium enema will show the rectocele, this procedure is not essential for diagnosis. However, rectocele frequently is associated with "hemorrhoidal bleeding"; when this occurs, proctoscopic study is necessary to exclude a concomitant colonic lesion.

Differential Diagnosis

What grossly appears to be a "high rectocele," ie, one involving the entire posterior vaginal wall, may consist partially or totally of an enterocele. With the patient standing, straining, and squatting slightly, rectovaginal examination will confirm the presence of abdominal contents sliding into the enterocele sac, and bowel crepitation may be noted.

Digital examination will also disclose tumors of the rectovaginal septum (lipomas, fibromas, sarcomas) that may produce a classic "rectocele" appearance.

Treatment

Fecal impaction may require digital extraction.

A. Medical Measures: Medical management of a rectocele that is causing symptoms is usually advisable until the patient has completed her family. Increased fluid intake and correction of faulty diet and bowel habits may be beneficial. Laxatives and rectal suppositories may be required. As a temporary measure, a large vaginal pessary of the round ball or inflatable doughnut type may provide relief if the perineum is adequate to retain the device in the vagina.

B. Surgical Measures: Rectocele alone (without associated enterocele, uterine prolapse, and cystocele) seldom requires surgical management. When the rectocele becomes so large that fecal evacuation is difficult or the patient finds it necessary to manually reduce the rectocele into the vagina to expedite expulsion of feces, surgical repair is indicated.

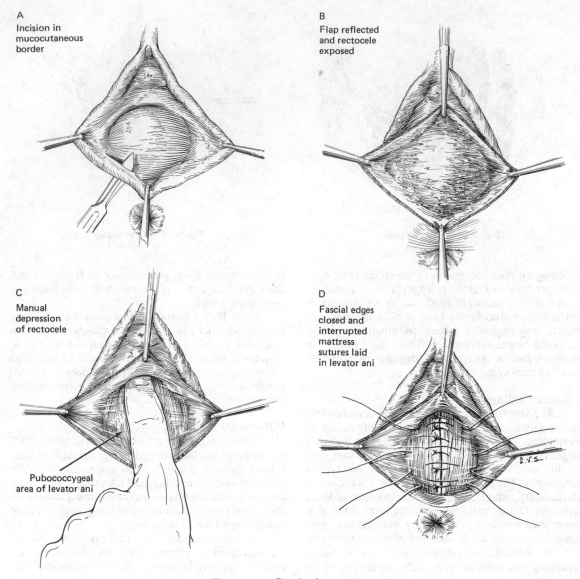

A
Incision in
mucocutaneous
border

B
Flap reflected
and rectocele
exposed

C
Manual
depression
of rectocele

Pubococcygeal
area of levator ani

D
Fascial edges
closed and
interrupted
mattress
sutures laid
in levator ani

Figure 12–7. Repair of rectocele.

Posterior colpoperineorrhaphy is usually curative. The posterior midline incision includes the perineum and the posterior vaginal wall, and it must be extended high enough to enable the surgeon to rule out the presence of an enterocele. For the latter purpose, it is frequently necessary to extend the dissection of the rectovaginal septum up to the level of the posterior vaginal fornix and to open the cul-de-sac of the peritoneum. Adequate repair includes plication of the rectovaginal fascia, excision of the redundancy of the posterior vaginal wall, and midline approximation of the levator and perineal muscles. However, overzealous perineorrhaphy should be avoided if preservation of sexual function is desirable.

Postoperative avoidance of straining, coughing, and strenuous activity is advisable. Careful instruction about diet to avoid constipation, intake of fluids, and

the use of stool-softening laxatives and lubricating suppositories is necessary to ensure permanent integrity of the rectocele repair.

Prognosis

Recurrence of rectocele after adequate colpoperineorrhaphy is uncommon if chronic constipation has been corrected, subsequent vaginal delivery is avoided, and a concomitant enterocele and uterine prolapse have not been overlooked.

ENTEROCELE

Essentials of Diagnosis

* Uncomfortable pressure and a "falling-out" sensation in the vagina.

- Associated with uterine prolapse or subsequent to hysterectomy in any age group; most common in postmenopausal women.
- Demonstration of a mass bulging into the posterior fornix and upper posterior vaginal wall.

General Considerations

Enterocele (Fig 12–8) is a herniation of the recto-uterine pouch (of Douglas) into the rectovaginal septum. This presents as a bulging mass in the posterior fornix and upper posterior vaginal wall. A similar hernial sac through the cul-de-sac, but extending posteriorly, may present through the anal canal as a rectal prolapse. Extremely large cul-de-sac hernias may present in both directions—anteriorly as an enterocele extending out through the vaginal introitus and posteriorly as a rectal prolapse out through the anal canal, creating a "saddle hernia" on both sides of the perineal body.

Enterocele may be congenital or acquired; the latter is much more common. The congenital form rarely causes symptoms. It does not appear to progress in size, and its discovery is usually incidental to hysterectomy or other procedures. The acquired form of enterocele occurs in multiparous menopausal or postmenopausal women and almost invariably is associated with other manifestations of musculofascial weakness such as uterine prolapse, cystocele, and rectocele. The trauma of many pregnancies and vaginal deliveries (perhaps breech extractions, forceps rotations), large pelvic tumors, marked obesity, ascites, chronic bronchitis, and other factors that increase intra-abdominal pressure are of etiologic importance.

Uterine prolapse is almost always accompanied by some degree of enterocele, and, as the degree of uterine descent progresses, the size of the hernial sac increases. Similarly, posthysterectomy prolapse of the vaginal vault (in a sense, an incisional hernia) usually is the result of a potential or actual enterocele that was overlooked (not repaired) at the time of hysterectomy. Rarely, after hysterectomy, the enterocele is located anterior to the vaginal vault, where it may be easily confused with ordinary cystocele.

Clinical Findings

A. Symptoms: The pelvic and abdominal symptoms produced by an enterocele are nonspecific and perhaps are actually the result of downward traction of the lower abdominal viscera. Aching discomfort frequently is described, along with the sensation of vaginal pressure and fullness commonly noted with other forms of prolapse. Gastrointestinal symptoms can rarely, if ever, be attributed to an enterocele. Peculiarly, the small bowel does not become adherent to or incarcerated in the enterocele—not even in the tight-necked hernial sac that is characteristic of the congenital type of enterocele. This effect does not apply to the thin-walled posthysterectomy enteroceles (vaginal vault prolapse), many of which contain adherent small intestine and some of which produce obstructive symptoms and even, though rarely, rupture spontaneously to eviscerate through the vagina.

B. Signs: Rectovaginal examination, especially with the patient standing, reveals a reducible thickness or bulging of the upper rectovaginal septum. After exposing the entire posterior vaginal wall (by elevating the anterior vaginal wall and cervix with a Sims retractor or a single blade of a vaginal speculum) and inserting a finger in the rectum to delineate the extent of the rectocele, one frequently can observe gradual filling and distention of the enterocele sac as the patient "strains down." With similar exposure of the posterior vaginal wall, failure of a proctoscopic light source to transilluminate the upper rectovaginal septum may suggest the presence of an enterocele. In the case of a large, thin-walled enterocele, small bowel peristalsis will be visible. Occasionally, to obtain filling of the hernial sac, it is essential to examine the patient in a standing-straining position.

C. X-Ray Findings: Lateral pelvic x-ray views obtained during barium studies of the small bowel may reveal prolapse of the ileum into the enterocele.

Differential Diagnosis

High rectocele and cystocele (when an anterior enterocele is suspected) are the most common causes of difficulty in differential diagnosis. Careful examination and palpation of the region (described above) will delineate these conditions.

Soft tumors (lipoma, leiomyoma, sarcoma) of the upper rectovaginal septum are more fixed and are nonreducible.

In obese women, a downward "sliding" of recto-sigmoid and perirectal fatty tissues may occur. This may almost exactly mimic an enterocele and may be distinguished only at operation, when the cul-de-sac of the peritoneum is found to be in a normal position, without herniation.

Prevention

Neglected, obstructed labor and traumatic delivery, which weaken uterovaginal supports, should be

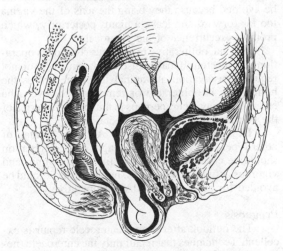

Figure 12–8. Enterocele and prolapsed uterus.

avoided. Factors that increase intra-abdominal pressure (obesity, chronic cough, straining, ascites, large pelvic tumors) should be corrected promptly. At hysterectomy (abdominal or vaginal), a diligent effort must be made to detect and repair any potential or actual enterocele.

Treatment

A. Emergency Measures: With complete eversion of the vagina by the enterocele, trophic ulceration, edema, and fibrosis of the vaginal walls may occur to such a degree that the prolapsing mass cannot be reduced. Rest in bed (with the foot of the bed elevated) and wet packs applied to the vagina will reduce edema and allow replacement of the vagina, and vaginal packing can be used to maintain reduction until local conditions permit operative correction.

Rupture of the enterocele, with evisceration of the small intestine, is managed best by prompt reduction of the prolapsing loops of small intestine followed by simple closure of the tear in the vaginal wall. Rest in bed, prophylactic broad-spectrum antibiotics, and a supporting vaginal pack (or pessary, if it can be retained) should be instituted postoperatively. Definitive repair of the ruptured enterocele can be accomplished immediately if the patient's general condition warrants. If the prolapsing bowel has become gangrenous, operation should be limited to resection of the involved segment of the bowel—in other words, definitive repair of the enterocele should be deferred until the patient's condition is less precarious.

B. Medical Measures: Many patients with large enteroceles are elderly; others are grossly obese. While the patient's general health is being improved, the prolapsing vaginal hernia can be reduced with a pessary if it can be retained. Occasionally, packing the reduced vagina with cotton tampons or gauze impregnated with medicaments (bacteriostatic, estrogenic) is more effective than using a pessary. If immediate operative correction is not essential, a rigorous program of weight reduction for several months may be extremely beneficial for the very obese patient and may increase her chance of eventually obtaining a successful repair.

C. Surgical Measures: Enterocele repair may be accomplished transabdominally. In this operation, the enterocele sac is obliterated and the uterosacral ligaments and endopelvic fascia are approximated with concentric purse-string sutures as described by Moschowitz (Fig 12–9). However, inasmuch as symptomatic enterocele almost invariably is associated with other forms of musculofascial weakness (uterine prolapse, cystocele, rectocele), a transvaginal operation provides by far the best route of repair and offers the greatest likelihood of permanent correction of the enterocele. This procedure includes excision and high ligation of the enterocele sac (a cardinal principle of any hernia repair) and approximation of the uterosacral ligaments and endopelvic fascia anterior to the rectum (floor of cul-de-sac). Concomitant vaginal hysterectomy, anterior (cystocele) and posterior (rectocele)

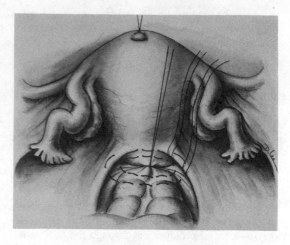

Figure 12–9. Transabdominal correction of enterocele (Moschowitz).

colporrhaphy, and perineorrhaphy greatly augment the support.

Posthysterectomy enterocele with prolapse of the vaginal vault is best managed by the transvaginal route. This procedure makes use of the same supporting tissue commonly used in ordinary vaginal hysterectomy and anteroposterior colporrhaphy (Fig 12–10).

Sometimes—not often—it is necessary to accomplish suspension of the prolapsing vaginal vault transabdominally. Because the normal vaginal axis is directed some distance posteriorly (almost horizontally when the patient is in an erect position), operative correction by any means, whether by the vaginal or the abdominal route, should restore a normal vaginal axis. This is accomplished by suspension of the vaginal apex far back on the uterosacral ligaments, the presacral fascia, or the sacrospinous ligaments. The suspension can be provided by use of nonabsorbable sutures, autogenous fascia, or prosthetic material (eg, Dacron, Teflon, or Marlex mesh). Techniques that suspend the vaginal vault from the anterior abdominal wall should be avoided because they bring the axis of the vagina too far forward and leave a hiatus posteriorly, which promotes recurrence of the enterocele.

Vaginal obliterative procedures (Le Fort's operation, vaginectomy) may be used in patients who do not require preservation of vaginal function. Unless the hernial sac is obliterated or removed, however, the enterocele may recur, perhaps in the form of a hernia of the perineum or of the ischiorectal fossa.

D. Supportive Measures: As with hernias of other types, obesity, chronic cough, and constipation should be corrected. Strenuous lifting, straining, and vigorous activity (calisthenics, bowling, etc) should be avoided for at least 6 months postoperatively.

Prognosis

The outlook after proper enterocele repair is excellent. Techniques that repair only the enterocele (neglecting the associated cystocele, rectocele, and

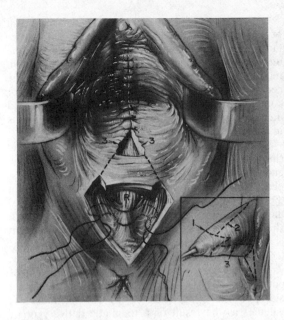
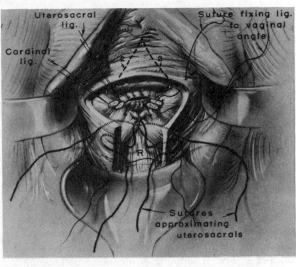

Figure 12–10. Correction of vaginal prolapse after hysterectomy. R, rectum.

uterine prolapse) and those that suspend the vaginal vault (or the intact uterus) without obliterating the hernial sac are associated with a high incidence of recurrence.

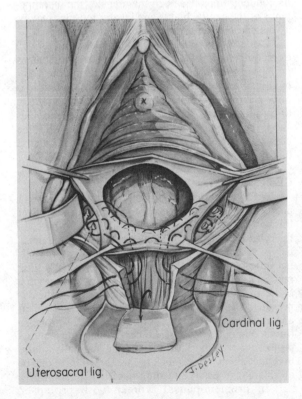

Figure 12–11. Symmonds' modification of the McCall enterocele repair (after vaginal hysterectomy and repair).

UTERINE PROLAPSE

Essentials of Diagnosis

- Firm mass in the lower vagina; cervix projecting through the vaginal introitus; vaginal inversion, with the cervix and uterus projecting between the legs.
- Sensation of vaginal fullness or pressure; lower abdominal pulling or aching; low backache.

General Considerations

Uterine prolapse (pelvic floor hernia, pudendal hernia) (Fig 12–12) is abnormal protrusion of the uterus through the pelvic floor aperture or genital hiatus. Like cystocele, rectocele, and enterocele—conditions with which it is usually associated—uterine prolapse occurs most commonly in multiparous white women as a gradually progressive result of childbirth

Table 12–1. Results of Symmonds' enterocele repair (after vaginal hysterectomy and repair) (153 patients with 89% follow-up; 68% followed 5 years or more).

Operation	No. of Patients	Result		Recurrent Prolapse	No Follow-up
		Good	Fair		
Abdominal wall suspension (fascia, silk, and Moschowitz)	22*	11	4	5	2
Vaginectomy	16	9	3	3	1
Multiple routes	8†	2	4	2	0
Vaginal repair	107‡	80	2	11	14
Total	153	102	13	21	17

*Cystocele, rectocele, or both repaired vaginally in 9.
†22 operations by vaginal, abdominal, or both routes.
‡Partial vaginectomy in 23.

injuries to the endopelvic fascia (and its condensations, the uterosacral and cardinal ligaments) and lacerations of muscle, especially the levator muscles and those of the perineal body. Uterine prolapse may also be the result of pelvic tumor; sacral nerve disorders, especially injury to S1–4 (as in spina bifida); diabetic neuropathy; caudal anesthesia accidents; and presacral tumor. Additional factors promoting uterine prolapse are (1) systemic conditions, including obesity, asthma, chronic bronchitis, and bronchiectasis; and (2) local conditions such as ascites and large uterine and ovarian tumors.

A congenital type of uterine prolapse is seen rarely in newborn infants during vigorous crying or vomiting. It is also seen occasionally in nulliparous, even virginal females with intact, strong levator muscles and a narrow genital hiatus; apparently prolapse in this case is the result of an inherent weakness of the endopelvic fascial supports of the uterus and vagina. As a rule, in uterine prolapse of the common type, symptomatic status is not reached until many years after the causative event (eg, traumatic delivery). This finding suggests that aging and involutional attenuation of the supporting structures play an important role.

A uterus that is in a retroverted position is especially subject to prolapse; with the corpus aligned with the axis of the vagina, anything increasing intra-abdominal pressure exerts a pistonlike action on the uterus, driving it down into the vagina.

Prolapse of a cervical stump (after subtotal abdominal hysterectomy) does not differ in any significant way from prolapse of an intact uterus. Admittedly, the oviducts and the utero-ovarian and round ligaments have been divided, but these structures do not contribute to the support of the cervical stump (or the uterus).

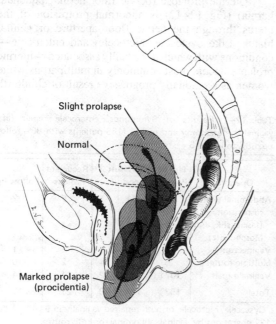

Slight prolapse

Normal

Marked prolapse
(procidentia)

Figure 12–12. Prolapse of the uterus.

The degree of uterine prolapse parallels the extent of separation or attenuation of its supporting structures. In slight intravaginal or incomplete prolapse, the uterus descends only partway down the vagina; in moderate prolapse, it descends to the introitus, and the cervix protrudes slightly beyond; and in marked or complete prolapse (procidentia), the entire cervix and uterus protrude beyond the introitus and the vagina is inverted.

The principal components of the basinlike pelvic floor are the pelvic bones (including the coccyx), the endopelvic fascia, and the levator and perineal muscles. These structures normally support and maintain the position of the pelvic viscera despite great increments of intra-abdominal pressure that occur with straining, coughing, and heavy lifting when the patient is in the erect position. The urogenital hiatus (''anterior levator muscle gap''), which permits the urethra, vagina, and anus to emerge from the pelvis, is a site of potential weakness. Attenuation of the pubococcygeal and puborectal portions of the levator muscles, whether as the result of a traumatic delivery or of involutional changes, widens the ''levator gap'' and converts this potential weakness to an actual defect. If there has been a concomitant injury or attenuation of the endopelvic fascia (uterosacral and cardinal ligaments, rectovaginal and pubocervical fascia), heightened intra-abdominal pressure gradually leads to uterine prolapse along with cystocele, rectocele, and enterocele. If the integrity of the endopelvic fascia and its condensations has been maintained, the incompetency of the genital hiatus and levator muscles may be associated only with elongation of the cervix.

Anterior and posterior vaginal relaxation, as well as incompetency of the perineum, often accompanies prolapse of the uterus. Large cystocele is more common than rectocele in prolapse because the bladder is more easily carried downward than is the rectum. Prior to the menopause, the prolapsed uterus hypertrophies and is engorged and flabby. After the menopause, the uterus atrophies. In procidentia, the vaginal mucosa thickens and cornifies, coming to resemble skin.

Clinical Findings

A. Symptoms and Signs: With mild prolapse (1 degree; cervix palpable as a firm mass in the lower third of the vagina), few symptoms can be attributed to the relaxation. With moderate prolapse (2–3 degrees; cervix visible and projecting into or through the vaginal introitus), the patient may experience a ''falling out'' sensation or may report that she is ''sitting on a ball''; of less significance may be a sensation of heaviness in the pelvis, low backache, and lower abdominal and inguinal pulling discomfort. In severe prolapse (procidentia; 4 degrees), the cervix and entire uterus project through the introitus and the vagina is totally inverted. Frequently, this large mass will have one or more areas of easily bleeding trophic ulceration.

In premenopausal women with prolapse, leukorrhea or menometrorrhagia frequently develops as a result of uterine engorgement. Infertility is often related to excessive discharge. Once well established, however, pregnancy usually continues to term. After the menopause, excessive vaginal mucus and bleeding may be due to trophic ulceration and infection of the prolapse.

Compression, distortion, or herniation of the bladder by the displaced uterus and cervix may be responsible for accumulation of residual urine, which leads to urinary tract infection, frequency and urgency, and overflow voiding. Incontinence is rare. Constipation and painful defecation occur with prolapse because of pressure and rectocele. Ease and completeness of voiding and defecation may follow manual reduction of the prolapse by the patient. Cramping and obstipation may follow intestinal constriction within a large enterocele.

B. Pelvic Examination: With the patient bearing down or straining (perhaps in a standing position), pelvic examination reveals descent of the cervix to the lower third of the vagina (mild prolapse), descent past the introitus (moderate prolapse), or descent of the entire uterus through the introitus (severe prolapse). As the uterus progressively descends, some degree of cystocele and enterocele must develop concomitantly as a result of anatomic fixation of the bladder base and of the cul-de-sac to anterior and posterior uterocervical surfaces. In fact, a supposed uterine prolapse unaccompanied by cystocele and enterocele is almost invariably the result of cervical elongation (see below).

The uterine tubes, ovaries, bladder, and distal ureters are drawn downward by the prolapsing uterus. Uterine or adnexal neoplasms and ascites associated with uterine prolapse should be noted.

Rectovaginal examination may reveal a rectocele. An enterocele may be behind and perhaps below the cervix but in front of a rectocele. A metal sound or firm catheter within the bladder may be used to determine the extent of concomitant cystocele.

Differential Diagnosis

Cervical elongation presents the most troublesome problem in differential diagnosis. The distinction is important because vaginal hysterectomy (the customary operative treatment for uterine prolapse) may be difficult when performed for cervical elongation. With cervical elongation, vaginal examination discloses that the anterior, posterior, and lateral vaginal fornices are at their customary high level and descend minimally with straining; the anterior and upper posterior vaginal walls are well supported (little or no cystocele or enterocele); and the uterine corpus remains in a relatively high and posterior position.

Cervical tumors—as well as endometrial tumors (pedunculated myoma or endometrial polyps)—if prolapsed through a dilated cervix and presenting in the lower third of the vagina, may be confused with mild or moderate uterine prolapse. Prolapse of the uterus must also be distinguished from cystocele, rectocele, uterine inversion, fecal impaction, or a large bladder stone. Myomas or polyps may coexist with prolapse of the uterus and cause unusual symptoms.

Despite the variety of possibilities, the history and physical findings in uterine prolapse are so characteristic that diagnosis is usually not a problem.

Complications

Leukorrhea, abnormal uterine bleeding, and abortion may result from infection or from disordered uterine or ovarian circulation in prolapse. Chronic decubitus ulceration may develop in procidentia, but whether or not the ulcers predispose to cancer is uncertain. Urinary tract infection is common with prolapse because of cystocele; and partial ureteral obstruction, with hydronephrosis, may occur in procidentia. Hemorrhoids result from straining to overcome constipation. Small bowel obstruction may occur within a deep enterocele.

Prevention

Prenatal and postpartum Kegel exercises to strengthen the levator muscles, early and adequate episiotomy, and avoidance of traumatic delivery tend to prevent or at least to minimize prolapse. Prolonged estrogen therapy for menopausal and postmenopausal women tends to maintain the tone and integrity of the endopelvic fascia and pelvic floor musculature.

Treatment

A. Emergency Measures: Infrequently, a patient with moderate to severe prolapse becomes pregnant. The rapidly enlarging uterus may become incarcerated within the true pelvis or, in procidentia, even outside the pelvis. It is imperative that the uterus be replaced and that the patient remain in bed until the uterus is large enough to prevent recurrence of the prolapse. An incarcerated, edematous procidentia may lead to urethral (even ureteral) obstruction, anuria, and uremia; therefore, prompt reduction of the prolapse is essential.

B. Medical Measures: A vaginal pessary (inflatable doughnut, Menge, Gellhorn, bee cell) may be used either as palliative therapy if surgical treatment is contraindicated or as a temporary measure in mild to moderate prolapse. The use of a pessary may assist in determining whether or not the rather ambiguous symptoms reported by the patient are actually produced by the uterine prolapse. In procidentia, reduction of the uterus followed by packing of the vagina to maintain uterine position may be necessary in the preoperative management of an ulcerated, infected prolapse.

In postmenopausal patients, the administration of estrogen (systemically or vaginally) will improve the tissue tone and facilitate correction of an atrophic, perhaps ulcerative, vaginitis. Ulcerated areas should be biopsied; D&C may be necessary to investigate bleeding and to rule out malignancy. Prescribe vaginal creams (eg, Aci-Jel), acetic acid douches, medicated tampons, or chemotherapy for ulceration. Treat urinary tract infection, diabetes mellitus, or cardiovascular complications appropriately. Prescribe laxatives or enemas for constipation.

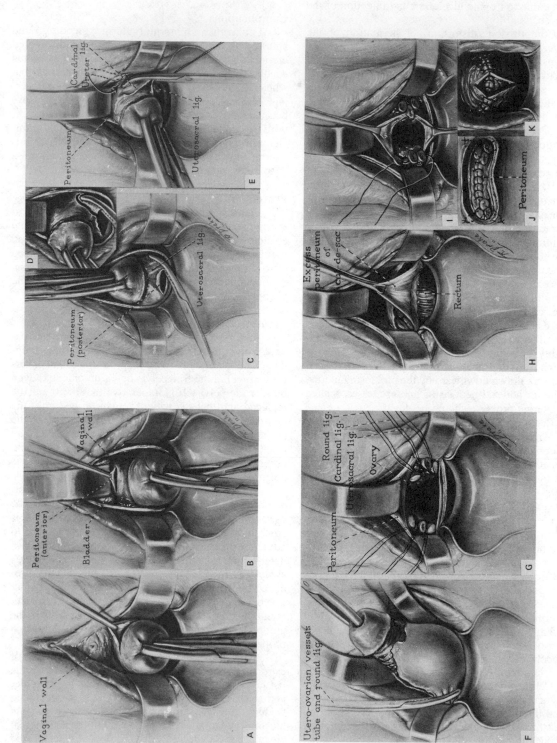

Figure 12–13. Vaginal hysterectomy for uterine prolapse.

C. Surgical Measures: Uterine prolapse may remain constant for many years or may progress very slowly, depending somewhat on the patient's age and activity. Even though one can be certain that the condition will not regress and that operation will eventually be required, its correction is not urgent, and surgical treatment should be deferred until the prolapse gives rise to significant symptoms.

Selection of a surgical approach for uterine prolapse depends on a number of variables: the patient's age, her desire for pregnancy or preservation of vaginal function, the degree of prolapse, and the presence of associated conditions (cystocele, stress incontinence, enterocele, rectocele). In general, symptoms associated with mild to moderate uterine prolapse are not severe. Thus, in the younger patient whose subsequent pregnancy may well nullify any benefits derived from an operative repair, it is customary to defer operative treatment until the childbearing years have passed or the patient has had all the babies she wants. Operations of the Manchester type were at one time recommended for the young patient with prolapse, but this procedure, which includes amputation of the cervix, has fallen into disfavor because it is associated with a high incidence of infertility and premature labor.

In young women, the pelvic floor should be restored. The Manchester-Fothergill operation is preferred if conservation of the uterus is important. Otherwise, vaginal hysterectomy with correction of hernial defects may be elected.

Most patients with uterovaginal prolapse have a composite lesion, ie, symptoms related to a moderate degree of uterine prolapse plus a moderate degree of cystocele, stress incontinence, enterocele, rectocele, and perineal relaxation. To provide good support for the vaginal vault and vaginal wall, the best surgical management consists of a composite operation. In addition to vaginal hysterectomy, the operation must include repair of actual or potential enterocele, careful anterior colporrhaphy to correct the cystocele and stress incontinence, and posterior colpoperineorrhaphy extending well up the posterior vaginal wall (Fig 12–13). If preservation of vaginal function is not important, narrowing and shortening the vagina by the removal of much of the anterior and posterior vaginal walls with the colporrhaphy, when combined with a high approximation of the levator muscles and with perineorrhaphy, will ensure the success of the operative repair. Vaginal obliterative operations (Le Fort's operation or vaginectomy) are rarely indicated or necessary; they may induce urinary incontinence, and they seldom correct an existing incontinence.

Uterine prolapse can be managed by an abdominal approach that includes total abdominal hysterectomy and the obliteration of any associated enterocele. However, this method is rather cumbersome and time-consuming; furthermore, it is permanently successful only when combined with transvaginal repair of cystocele and rectocele. Uterine suspensions—even ventrofixation of the corpus to the abdominal wall—are not effective in the treatment of prolapse.

In postmenopausal women who are sexually active, vaginal hysterectomy and repair are preferable to interposition procedures. In elderly patients, colpocleisis or colpectomy is infrequently chosen.

D. Supportive Measures: If the patient is obese, she should be encouraged to lose weight. Tight girdles and garments that increase intra-abdominal pressure and other factors (occupational or physical) that have a similar effect should be avoided or corrected.

E. Treatment of Complications: Infection of the operative area or of the urinary tract may require antibiotic therapy. Prescribe a pessary or reoperate for recurrence.

Prognosis

Vaginal hysterectomy with anteroposterior colpoperineorrhaphy provides excellent and permanent vaginal support and, if good healing occurs, preservation of vaginal function as well. Recurrent vaginal prolapse may result from generalized relaxation (unrepaired cystocele, rectocele, or enterocele) or from occupational factors such as heavy lifting or straining.

MALPOSITIONS OF THE UTERUS
("Tipped Uterus")

Significant displacement of the uterus may cause signs or symptoms such as pelvic pain, backache, menstrual aberrations, and infertility. Displacement may be lateral, anterior, or posterior. Virtually all women with symptoms that may be due to displacements are premenopausal. Almost all postpartum patients have a temporarily retroposed ("tipped") uterus.

The uterus is not a fixed organ, and the position may vary transiently as a result of pelvic inclination or prolonged sitting, standing, or lying. The body of the uterus is directed forward in 80% of women; in the remainder, it is directed backward, but fewer than 5% of these women have a bona fide complaint referable to posterior version of the uterus. Normally, the cervix is directed posteriorly in the vaginal vault in nulliparas. After parturition, the cervix is often in the vaginal axis, an attitude caused by retrodisplacement of the corpus. The cervix and uterus often are aligned following relaxation of the pelvic floor. Laxity of the transverse cervical and round ligaments accounts for a posterior deviation in uterine position. Moderate uterine prolapse is usually associated with a retroposed uterus.

Retroversion and retroflexion are more or less synonymous terms. **Retroversion** implies that the axis of the body of the uterus is directed to the hollow of the sacrum, although the cervix remains in its normal axis. If angulation of the corpus on the cervix is extreme, the term **retroflexion** is preferred. **Retrocession** implies that both the cervix and the uterus have gravitated backward toward the sacrum. Acute **anteversion** probably does not cause either obstruction to uterine

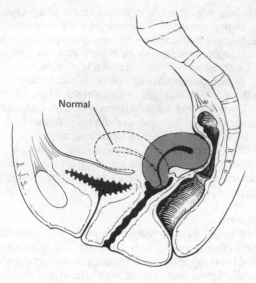

Figure 12–14. Retroflexion in an anteverted uterus.

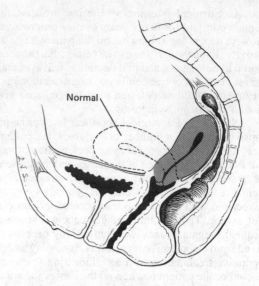

Figure 12–15. Retrocession of uterus.

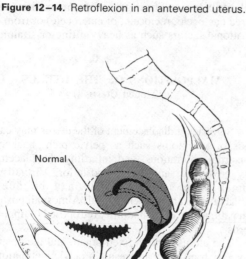

Figure 12–16. Acute anteflexion of uterus.

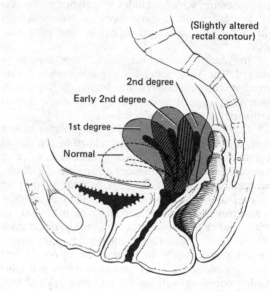

Figure 12–17. Degrees of retroversion of uterus without retroflexion.

discharge or circulatory alteration or dysmenor-rhea—a reversal of opinion of a generation or more ago. Free **dextroversion** or **levoversion** is of little clinical importance unless tumors, shortened supports, or other disorders are present.

Adherent lateral deviation of the uterus indicates primary pelvic disease (eg, salpingitis). Enlargement of the uterus, whether by pregnancy or tumor, may alter the relative position of that organ. Pelvic infections or endometriosis may obliterate the cul-de-sac. A pyosalpinx or hydrosalpinx may drag the corpus backward and downward by its weight, whereupon adhesions add restriction to cause immobility. (See Figs 12–14 to 12–17.)

The patient's complaints are not often due solely to free retroposition. Nevertheless, dysmenorrhea and menometrorrhagia may be due to utero-ovarian congestion; backache is frequently caused by similar turgescence or taut uterosacral ligaments. Prolapse of the ovaries accounts for dyspareunia in uterine retroposition. Infertility occasionally results from anterior displacement of the cervix because the ejaculate in the seminal pool in the posterior fornix does not bathe the cervix.

Constipation due to displacement of the bowel or pressure by the uterine fundus on the rectum is possible but unlikely. Bladder dysfunction secondary to malposition of the uterus rarely occurs.

Early in pregnancy, a retroposed uterus may become incarcerated, often because of adhesions; this can cause urinary retention. In addition, because adherence prevents normal uterofetal growth and development, abortion may result.

Clinical Findings

A. Symptoms and Signs: Pelvic pain, backache, abnormal menstrual bleeding, and infertility are commonly but uncritically related to malposition of the uterus. A combined abdominal and rectovaginal examination should be done to determine uterine position and to estimate the degree of misalignment of the uterus and cervix as well as the degree of adherence and tumefaction.

B. X-Ray Findings: Hysterography will reveal malposition of the uterus, especially when both anteroposterior and lateral films are obtained. Pneumoperitoneum or contrast medium within the rectum and bladder will enhance hysterography, especially when malposition is related to pelvic tumors.

C. Special Examinations: In examining a nonpregnant patient, gently insert a sterile curved uterine sound into the uterine cavity after applying a topical antiseptic to the external cervical os and distal canal. The direction of the instrument will indicate the position of the corpus.

Differential Diagnosis

A fundal myoma or ovarian tumor resting in the cul-de-sac may be mistaken for a retroposed fundus and vice versa.

Adherent retroposition of the uterus may cause the same symptoms as uterine malposition. Basically, however, the disorder may be salpingitis, endometriosis, or neoplasia.

Uterine retroposition does not usually cause backache, which is most often due to orthopedic disorders. Abnormal posture, fatigue, myositis, arthritis, and herniation of an intervertebral disk should be considered as possible causes of backache.

Prevention

Avoidance of the causes of pelvic infection and early, specific therapy when infection occurs will reduce the incidence of adherent malposition of the uterus.

Treatment

Retroposition of the uterus is now regarded as important clinically when replacement and support by a vaginal pessary relieve the symptoms. *Note:* Knee-chest exercises alone are of questionable value.

A. Emergency Measures: An incarcerated, nonadherent uterus must be surgically elevated, especially in the case of a pregnant patient who develops acute urinary retention or seems likely to abort. Rectovaginal manipulation of the corpus with the patient in the knee-chest position may facilitate restoration of uterine anteposition.

B. Specific Local Measures: In the nonpregnant patient, neither an asymptomatic retroposition nor a normally involuting retroposed puerperal uterus requires treatment. For the gynecologic patient with pelvic pain or abnormal bleeding and for the recently delivered woman with subinvolution and persistent lochia or bleeding, the uterus should be repositioned and a properly fitted vaginal pessary inserted (see below). Unless discomfort develops, permit the pessary to remain in place for 6–8 weeks and record the result. If anteversion and relief follow pessary support, no further therapy will be necessary. Reinsert the pessary after 2 months if symptoms recur.

Bimanual replacement of retrodisplaced uterus (Fig 12–18) is performed as follows: With the patient in the lithotomy position, insert one or 2 gloved fingers into the vagina, elevate the fundus, and press against the cervix. With the other hand, bring the corpus forward. Fit a vaginal pessary of the Hodge type to support the uterus in anteposition.

If this procedure is not successful, insert a pessary of the Hodge type into the posterior vaginal fornix (Fig 12–19). Have the patient sit up and then assume the knee-chest position. Apply pressure on the lateral bars

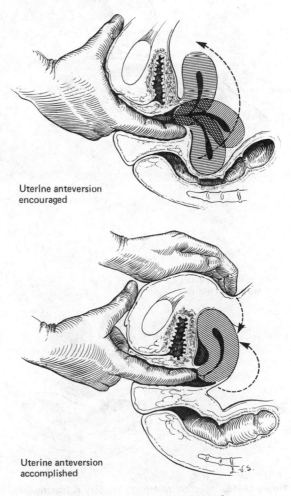

Uterine anteversion encouraged

Uterine anteversion accomplished

Figure 12–18. Bimanual replacement of uterus.

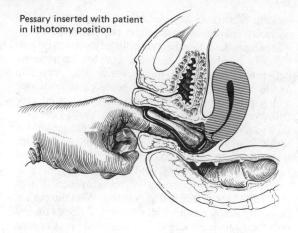

Pessary inserted with patient in lithotomy position

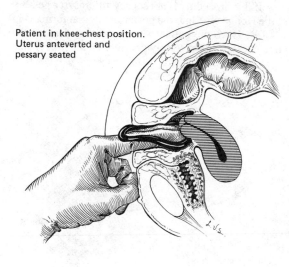

Patient in knee-chest position. Uterus anteverted and pessary seated

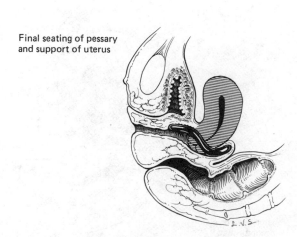

Final seating of pessary and support of uterus

Figure 12–19. Insertion of Hodge pessary if bimanual replacement of uterus is not successful.

of the pessary and displace the cervix backward while the patient coughs; the nonadherent uterus will usually fall forward. Require the patient to slip slowly into the prone position and then into the lithotomy position. Seat the pessary so as to maintain the uterus in anteposition.

C. Surgical Measures: Suspend the uterus as a primary procedure if repeated replacement of the corpus by the use of a pessary has alleviated symptoms and signs or if adherence of the uterus and prolapse of the adnexa are probable causes of disability.

Suspend the uterus as the concluding step in an operation performed to eliminate specific pelvic disease (eg, tubal plastic procedures).

D. Treatment of Complications: Occasional warm acetic acid douches or the use of vaginal creams (eg, Aci-Jel) may relieve irritation and prevent discharge caused by a vaginal pessary. (Even a well-fitted one may cause irritation.)

Prognosis

If correction of the uterine malposition follows an accurate diagnosis of symptomatic displacement, the outlook is good. It is poor if uterine suspension is done without a convincing indication.

$$\bullet \quad \bullet \quad \bullet$$

VAGINAL PESSARIES

The vaginal pessary is a prosthesis of ancient lineage, now made of rubber or plastic material, often with a metal band or spring frame. A great many types have been devised, but fewer than a dozen are basically unique and specifically helpful.

Pessaries are principally used to support the uterus, cervical stump, or hernias of the pelvic floor. They are effective because they reduce vaginal relaxation and increase the tautness of the pelvic floor structures. Little or no leverage is involved. The retrodisplaced uterus remains forward after it is repositioned and a pessary inserted because the tension produced on the uterosacral ligaments draws the cervix backward. In most cases, adequate support anteriorly and a reasonably good perineal body are required; otherwise, the pessary may slip from behind the symphysis and extrude from the vagina.

Indications & Uses
A. Obstetric:

1. To avert threatened abortion presumed to be due to marked uterine retroposition and chronic passive congestion.

2. To promote healing of trophic cervical ulceration associated with prolapse during pregnancy.

3. To relieve acute urinary retention due to retroposition of the uterus in midpregnancy.

4. To prevent or relieve postpartum subinvolution or retroversion.

5. To protect against abortion in cervical incompetence.

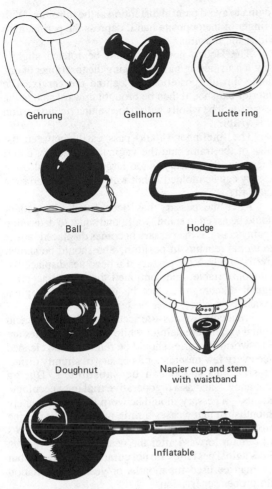

Figure 12–20. Types of pessaries.

Gehrung   Gellhorn   Lucite ring

Ball   Hodge

Doughnut   Napier cup and stem with waistband

Inflatable

Contraindications

Pessaries are contraindicated in acute genital tract infections and in adherent retroposition of the uterus.

Types of Pessaries (Fig 12–20)

A. Hodge Pessary: (Smith-Hodge, or Smith and other variations.) This is an elongated, curved ovoid. One end is placed behind the symphysis and the other in the posterior vaginal fornix. The anterior bow is curved to avoid the urethra; the cervix rests within the larger, posterior bow. This type of pessary is used to hold the uterus in place after it has been repositioned.

B. Gellhorn and Menge Pessaries: Both of these types are shaped like a collar button and provide a ringlike platform for the cervix. The pessary is stabilized by a stem that rests upon the perineum. These pessaries are used to correct marked prolapse when the perineal body is reasonably adequate.

C. Gehrung Pessary: The Gehrung pessary resembles 2 firm letter U's attached by crossbars. It rests in the vagina with the cervix cradled between the long arms; this arches the anterior vaginal wall and helps reduce a cystocele.

D. Ring Pessary: A ring pessary, either of hard vulcanite or plastic composition or the soft "doughnut" type, distends the vagina and elevates the cervix. Cystocele and rectocele are reduced considerably by a ring pessary.

E. Ball or Bee Cell Pessary: (Fig 12–21.) A hollow plastic ball or sponge rubber (bee cell) pessary functions much like a ring pessary and is used for

B. Gynecologic:

1. To treat poor-risk patients or those who refuse operation for uterine prolapse or other genitourinary hernias.

2. To serve as a preoperative aid in the healing of cervical stasis ulcerations associated with uterine prolapse.

3. To reduce cystocele or retrocele.

4. To alleviate menorrhagia, dysmenorrhea, or dyspareunia related to free uterine retroposition and adnexal prolapse.

5. To determine whether hysteropexy will relieve backache due to retroversion.

6. To control urinary stress incontinence by exerting pressure beneath the urethra or by improving the posterior urethrovesical angle.

7. To aid conception in the management of infertility, because the cervix may be displaced anteriorly, away from the posterior fornix seminal pool, or because there may be angulation of tubes or chronic passive congestion secondary to retroposition.

8. To facilitate hysteropexy by holding the uterus in position for operation.

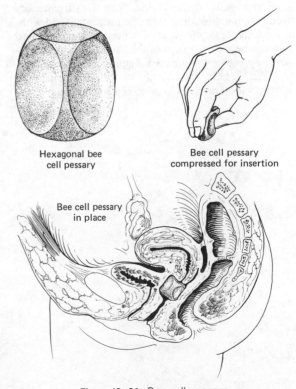

Hexagonal bee cell pessary

Bee cell pessary compressed for insertion

Bee cell pessary in place

Figure 12–21. Bee cell pessary.

similar purposes. A moderately intact perineum is necessary for retention.

F. Napier Pessary: A uterine supporter (Napier pessary) is a cup and stem arrangement supported by a belt. This device elevates the cervix and uterus and holds them in place. It is used in cases of marked prolapse when the perineum is incompetent, especially in a patient who cannot withstand an operation.

G. Inflatable Pessary: The inflatable pessary (Milex) functions much like a doughnut pessary. The ball valve is moved "up" and "down." When the ball is in the "down" position, air inflates the pessary; when in the "up" position, the air is sealed in and inflation is maintained.

Fitting of Pessaries

Pessaries that are too large cause irritation and ulceration. Those that are too small may not stay in place and may protrude. Bee cell and inflatable pessaries should be removed nightly for cleansing and to preserve the vaginal mucosa.

To determine the proper length of a pessary, pass a pair of uterine dressing forceps, using the finger as a guide, into the vagina to the top of the posterior vaginal vault. Mark the shank of the forceps at the introitus with a finger or piece of tape. Withdraw the forceps and measure the distance from the marked point to the tip of the blades. This dimension minus 1 cm is the appropriate length of the pessary. To obtain the width (assuming that an ovoid rather than a round pessary is required), introduce the forceps to about the level of the cervix and separate the handles until the blades touch the walls of the vagina. Note the distance between the handles; then close the instrument and withdraw it. Separate the handles to the distance noted and measure between the tips of the blades. This measurement represents the greatest diameter of the pessary.

The pessary should be lubricated and inserted with its widest dimension in the oblique diameter of the vagina to avoid painful distention at the introitus. With a finger of the opposite hand, depress the perineum to widen the introitus.

The Hodge pessary should be rotated slightly after it is in the vagina; then, using the forefinger of one hand, slip the posterior bar behind the cervix. The anterior bar should then be brought upward so that the pessary will be wholly within the vagina (ie, no portion of it visible).

The forefinger should pass easily between the sides of the frame and the vaginal wall at any point; otherwise, the pessary is too large. A solid vulcanite pessary can be molded in hot water and reshaped for a better fit.

After the pessary has been fitted, the patient should be asked to stand, walk, and squat to determine if pain occurs, if the pessary becomes displaced, and if the uterus remains in position. She should be shown how to withdraw the pessary if it becomes displaced or is uncomfortable, and cautioned that a contraceptive vaginal diaphragm cannot be used while a vaginal pessary is in place.

Frequent low-pressure acetic acid douches or acid vaginal creams are helpful while vaginal pessaries are being worn. Pessaries should be removed and cleaned once every few months; or a pessary of slightly different size and shape can be substituted. During pregnancy—and as a preoperative trial in gynecologic patients—a pessary should be worn for approximately 3 months. In many cases during pregnancy, if uterine retroposition is corrected with a pessary, the uterus will remain forward after the pessary is removed.

Vaginal pessaries are not curative of prolapse, but they may be used for months or years for palliation with proper supervision.

A neglected pessary may cause fistulas or favor genital infections, but it is doubtful that cancer ever occurs as a result of wearing a modern pessary.

•   •   •

References

Cystocele

Macer GA: Transabdominal repair of cystocele, a 20 year experience, compared with the traditional vaginal approach. *Am J Obstet Gynecol* 1978;**131**:203.

Nichols DH: Effects of pelvic relaxation on gynecologic urologic problems. *Clin Obstet Gynecol* 1978;**21**:759.

Wiser WL et al: Management of bladder drainage following vaginal plastic repairs. *Obstet Gynecol* 1974;**44**:65.

Enterocele

Beecham CT, Beecham JB: Correction of prolapsed vagina or enterocele with fascia lata. *Obstet Gynecol* 1973;**42**:542.

Birnbaum SJ: Rational therapy for the prolapsed vagina. *Am J Obstet Gynecol* 1973;**115**:411.

Fox PF, Kowalczyk AC: Ruptured enterocele. *Am J Obstet Gynecol* 1971;**111**:592.

Hofmeister FJ: Prolapsed vagina. (Editorial.) *Obstet Gynecol* 1973;**42**:773.

Symmonds RE et al: Posthysterectomy enterocele and vaginal vault prolapse. *Am J Obstet Gynecol* 1981;**140**:852.

Yates MJ. An abdominal approach to the repair of posthysterectomy vaginal inversion. *Br J Obstet Gynaecol* 1975;**82**:817.

Zacharin RF: Pulsion enterocele: Review of functional anatomy of the pelvic floor. *Obstet Gynecol* 1980;**55**:135.

Uterine Prolapse

Ardekany MS, Rafee R: A new modification of colpocleisis for treatment of total procidentia in old age. *Int J Gynaecol Obstet* 1978;**15**:358.

Azpuru CE: Total rectal prolapse and total genital prolapse: A series of 17 cases. *Dis Colon Rectum* 1974;**17**:528.

Chambers CB: Uterine prolapse with incarceration. *Am J Obstet Gynecol* 1975;**122**:459.

Elkin M et al: Ureteral obstruction in patients with uterine prolapse. *Radiology* 1974;**110**:289.

Lavery JP, Boey CS: Uterine prolapse with pregnancy. *Obstet Gynecol* 1973;**42**:681.

Pratt JH: Vaginal hysterectomy. In: *Complications in Obstetrics and Gynecology*. Harper & Row, 1981.

Sivanesaratnam V, Sinnathuray TA: Procidentia in the newborn. *Aust NZ J Obstet Gynaecol* 1975;**15**:60.

Wheeless CR Jr: Total vaginal hysterectomy. In: *Atlas of Pelvic Surgery*. Lea & Febiger, 1981.

Prolapse of Vaginal Vault

Feldman GB, Birnbaum SJ: Sacral colpopexy for vaginal vault prolapse. *Obstet Gynecol* 1979;**53**:399.

Langmade CF, Oliver JA, White JS: Cooper ligament repair of vaginal vault prolapse twenty-eight years later. *Am J Obstet Gynecol* 1978;**131**:134.

Zacharin RF, Hamilton NT: Pulsion enterocele: Results of an abdominoperineal technique. *Obstet Gynecol* 1980;**55**:141.

13 | Tumors of the Oviducts

Howard J. Tatum, MD, PhD

BENIGN TUMORS OF THE OVIDUCTS

Essentials of Diagnosis

- Signs and symptoms—if present—are indistinguishable from those caused by tumors of the uterus or ovary.
- Final diagnosis depends upon histologic study.
- Extension of tumors of the uterus and ovary to the oviduct should be assumed.
- Primary tumors of the oviduct are seldom diagnosed before operation.

General Considerations

Primary neoplastic tumors of the oviducts originate from cell types found in the mesonephric or müllerian ducts. Because of a common anlage, any tumor type that may be found in the uterus theoretically can be found in the oviduct. In spite of similarities between the uterus and the oviducts, the incidence of primary neoplasms of the tubes is extremely low. One explanation is that cellular mitoses seldom are found in the various tubal cell types. In contrast, mitoses are much more frequently observed in all uterine cells. Cell replication is more susceptible to abnormal change when the rate of cell division increases.

The following classification is based upon cell types found in the müllerian duct:

(1) Epithelial tumors: Adenomas, papillomas, polyps.
(2) Endothelial tumors: Hemangiomas, lymphangiomas, inclusion cysts.
(3) Mesodermal tumors: Leiomyomas, lipomas, chondromas, osteomas.
(4) Teratoid (mixed) tumors: Dermoid cysts, germinal rests, struma mülleriae, or other theoretic combinations.

All of these tumors are exceedingly rare. It is likely that most of them are so small that they cause no symptoms and are neither suspected nor diagnosed. No more than 250–300 primary benign neoplasms of the oviducts have been reported in the literature.

Pathology

The histologic picture is that of proliferative masses similar to the cells of origin—lymphatic or blood vessel endothelium, endometrium, squamous cells (in peritoneal inclusion cysts), lipoid cells, chondrocytes, osteoblasts, ectopic pancreatic tissue, etc.

Clinical Findings

Very few of these tumors cause clinical manifestations that permit identification before operation. Infertility probably is the most frequently associated condition during the reproductive years. Laparoscopy or culdoscopy may permit detection of one of these rare tumors. Hysterosalpingography may be helpful.

Differential Diagnosis

Tumors of the uterus and ovary and malignant tumors of the oviducts must be ruled out. Inflammatory diseases of the tubes must also be considered. A history of salpingitis may falsely suggest a causal relationship and conceal primary tubal neoplasm.

Complications

The only major complication other than infertility relates to torsion. This gives rise to acute pain and clinical evidence of peritoneal irritation when the tumor ruptures. Peritoneal irritation may result if the tumor is a dermoid; there may be intra-abdominal hemorrhage if a hemangioma ruptures. The acute complications are not pathognomonic of tubal neoplasm and probably will not lead to a correct preoperative diagnosis.

Treatment

Any tubal enlargement that persists must be diagnosed. In most instances, this makes surgical exploration and histologic study mandatory. Salpingectomy is the initial procedure of choice. If primary or secondary malignancy can be excluded, no further therapy usually is needed.

Prognosis

The morbidity and mortality rates are very low. The prognosis for correction of infertility (if relevant) is poor.

MALIGNANT PRIMARY TUMORS OF THE OVIDUCTS

Primary cancer of the oviduct is the least common malignancy of the female genitalia. Fewer than 1500 cases have been described in the literature to date.

The cause of tubal malignancy is not known, although in about 70% of the reported cases there is a history of chronic salpingitis. About 50% of the patients are nulliparous, which suggests that acute salpingitis earlier in life may predispose to subsequent primary malignancy in the tubes. Most patients with primary or secondary tubal cancers are postmenopausal.

Histologic evidence of a malignant lesion in the oviduct with evidence that it has not metastasized from a primary site elsewhere is the only means of making the diagnosis.

Pathology

At least 95% of all primary tubal malignancies are adenocarcinomas. The remainder are sarcomas, mixed tumors, and choriocarcinomas. The tumors are unilateral in two-thirds of cases.

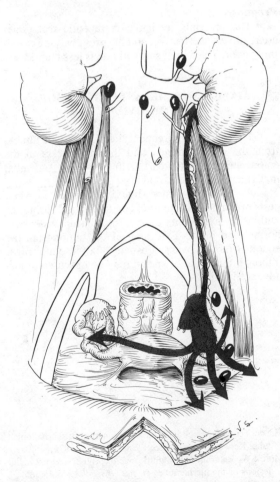

Figure 13–1. Lymphatic spread of carcinoma of the ovary and oviduct.

Carcinoma of the oviduct usually occurs in the ampullary or fimbriated portion. The tube in the area of carcinoma is rounded at first but later becomes fusiform or even sausage-shaped. The surface is glistening and red or purple; the tube is firm but not hard or nodular. In early lesions, the tumor may be an incidental finding at the time of histologic examination for a different problem. In more extensive lesions, the tube may be enlarged by the expanding tumor.

The tube contains yellow-brown grumous necrotic cancer tissue and dark brown or straw-colored sanguineous fluid. Minute bleeding points are commonly present. The fimbriated extremity is usually closed. Occasionally, the tumor mass may protrude through the fimbriated end and also become adherent to adjacent structures. The tumor may extend by direct continuity or may be disseminated to distant sites via the bloodstream or lymphatics. A diagnosis of primary carcinoma of the tube can be justified only if the cancer is limited histologically to the tube; if the tumor mass involves the ovary or the uterus as well as the tube, tubal origin can rarely be established.

The tumor usually arises from the tubal mucosa and extrudes into the tubal lumen as a papillary adenomatous growth. As the tumor mass enlarges, it distends the tube, and the tumor may protrude through the fimbriated os. The tumor usually does not invade the myosalpinx. In advanced lesions, the tumor may be found within the lymphatic channels of the tube. The normal tubal mucosa often is replaced by the adenomatous growth. Thus, if the tubal mucosa is seen to be intact and there is malignant tissue within the wall of the tube, the tumor probably is a metastatic one arising from the ovary, the uterus, or a more distant site.

Clinical Findings

A. Symptoms and Signs: Because growth and spread of carcinoma of the oviduct are often rapid, manifestations do not usually occur until the malignancy is well established. A positive vaginal cytologic examination may suggest tubal malignancy when cervical and endometrial malignancies have been ruled out by cervical conization and by thorough endometrial curettage. Irregular transcervical bleeding occurs in about half of cases, and many of these patients are postmenopausal. Hemorrhage into the tube, torsion, or pressure on the tubal mass may cause symptoms varying from lower quadrant aching to constant pain and sacral backache. Lower abdominal pain is experienced by 45–50% of patients. Intermittent serosanguineous or yellowish watery discharge, sometimes profuse, is observed in about 30% of patients. Occasionally there is an episode of sharp colicky lower abdominal pain that is followed by a reduction in size or complete disappearance of an abdominal swelling or mass and a profuse watery vaginal discharge. This complex is presumably the result of distention of the tube by fluid and sudden release of the fluid into the endometrial cavity as a consequence of intense tubal contractions. This series of events has been designated **hydrops**

tubae profluens when a nulliparous postmenopausal woman has a serosanguineous or watery discharge. In such a patient, carcinoma of the tube should be the preoperative diagnosis after cervical or endometrial carcinoma has been ruled out by colposcopic study, biopsy, and curettage.

Abdominal enlargement or intestinal obstruction is usually a late manifestation. Ascites is not often present.

On pelvic examination, a small, rounded or elongated, slightly tender pelvic mass separate from the uterus and ovary may be felt, whereas a large or infiltrating tubal cancer may be indistinguishable from these organs. However, a primary tubal cancer rarely exceeds 10 cm in diameter. An adnexal mass in a postmenopausal woman always suggests tubal or ovarian cancer.

When the tumor is primary and small, associated pelvic disease such as a large myoma may interfere with palpation of the somewhat distended oviduct. Routine examination of the oviducts should therefore be done in the course of surgery for other pelvic masses.

B. Laboratory Findings: The only helpful test is the Papanicolaou vaginal smear. A positive smear, when cervical and endometrial carcinoma have been excluded, is highly suggestive of tubal malignancy. Regrettably, most patients with tubal malignancy do not have positive Papanicolaou smears.

C. X-Ray Findings: Hysterosalpingography may be of value.

D. Special Examinations: Laparoscopy, culdoscopy, or culdotomy may be helpful. D&C will disclose only tubal cancer that has extended to the endometrium, but this may rule out an endometrial source of a positive Papanicolaou smear. Colposcopy and biopsy of the cervix should eliminate a malignant focus in the cervix.

Differential Diagnosis

In the premenopausal woman, the following must be ruled out: salpingitis, tubal pregnancy, ovarian enlargement and carcinoma, endometrial disease, hydrosalpinx, and a soft pedunculated myoma. Tubal tuberculosis often produces a highly adenomatous picture that may be mistaken for tubal cancer, particularly the papillomatous type. Unfortunately, the diagnosis usually is made during or after surgery for (1) chronic inflammatory disease, (2) ovarian tumor, or (3) an adnexal mass. It is rare to have a correct preoperative diagnosis of tubal cancer.

Complications

The principal complication of this rare disease is direct extension to adjacent structures or metastasis before the diagnosis has been made and definitive therapy provided.

Treatment

The success of treatment depends upon the type of tumor and the stage of the disease when the diagnosis is made. Except when the tumor is very small and diagnosed histologically as an incidental finding, the long-term survival rate is extremely poor. When the diagnosis has been confirmed, the treatment of choice is bilateral salpingo-oophorectomy, total hysterectomy, and postoperative irradiation. When there is direct extension to adjacent viscera (eg, the rectosigmoid), every effort should be made to resect the affected structures. Chemotherapy has been disappointing.

Prognosis

The presently available therapeutic techniques are relatively ineffective, and the prognosis is exceedingly poor. The 5-year survival rate is less than 15%.

MALIGNANT METASTATIC TUMORS OF THE OVIDUCTS

The oviduct is a frequent site of metastatic tumors from the ovary, uterus, and distant cancers in the colon, stomach, or breast. Almost 90% of all tubal malignancies are metastatic.

A secondary tumor should be suspected when nests of tumor cells are found on the serosal surface or within the myosalpinx though the adjacent mucosa is normal and intact. Extension of the tumor from the endometrium or ovary is usually via the lymphatics, although this route of spread may be obscured in far-advanced lesions.

• • •

References

Anteby SO et al: The value of laparoscopy in acute pelvic pain. *Am Surg* 1975;**181**:484.

Coutifaris B et al: Primary carcinoma of the fallopian tube. *Int Surg* 1980;**65**:83.

Kinzel GE: Primary carcinoma of the Fallopian tube. *Am J Obstet Gynecol* 1976;**125**:816.

Mason TE, Quagliarello JR: Ectopic pancreas in the Fallopian tube: Report of a first case. *Obstet Gynecol* 1976;**48**:705.

More SW, Enterline HT: Significance of proliferative epithelial lesions of the uterine tube. *Obstet Gynecol* 1975;**45**:385.

Segal S et al: Choriocarcinoma of the Fallopian tube. *Gynecol Oncol* 1975;**3**:40.

Diseases of the Ovaries | 14

J. Donald Woodruff, MD

INTRODUCTION

The diagnosis and treatment of an ovarian enlargement is one of the most significant problems facing the physician today. Little progress has been made in devising methods for differentiating the benign from the malignant neoplasm at an early stage, and the available forms of therapy have not greatly increased the salvage rates. Epidemiologic studies have not identified any high-risk populations on which to concentrate case-finding efforts.

Classification

An essential first step in the orderly investigation of a varied group of disorders is a logical system of classification. The embryologic and physiologic features of ovarian tumors are one basis for classification (Table 14–1). The histologic classification and system of staging now recommended by the International Federation of Gynecology and Obstetrics (FIGO) (Table 14–2) describes the gross extent of the neoplasm at the time of first therapy and the histopathology of the tumor. It is incomplete at present, because it categorizes only the primarily epithelial tumors; the neoplasms of germ cell origin are not included. Unfortunately, it fails to grade the malignant epithelial lesions, but even so, it is an acceptable provisional international classification.

The WHO classification is cumbersome and adds little to the FIGO grouping except the inclusion of germ cell tumors and stromal lesions.

Pathophysiology

The pathologic severity of ovarian tumors is inversely proportionate to the symptomatology. Nonneoplastic tumefactions, usually due to physiologic dysfunction or infection, are commonly symptomatic, ie, they produce pain or alterations in the menstrual cycle. True neoplasms usually are silent until they have become large enough to be palpated or have extended beyond the confines of the ovary.

Only 15–20% of all primary malignancies of the female generative system arise in the ovary. Nevertheless, ovarian cancer causes more deaths in women in the USA today than combined fatalities for all other primary pelvic malignancies (Table 14–3). Epidemiologically, ovarian neoplasia is the sixth most common

Table 14–1. Classification of ovarian tumors based on pathophysiology and embryology.

I. **Nonneoplastic lesions:**
  A. Inflammatory diseases of the ovary: Adhesive disease due to subacute or chronic infections; endometriosis or peritoneal inclusions.
  B. Nonneoplastic cysts of the ovary: Granulosa and theca lutein cysts; Stein-Leventhal ovary; diffuse or focal proliferations, eg, thecosis, cortical granulomas, luteoma of pregnancy.

II. **Ovarian neoplasia (mesothelial [stromoepithelial] tumors with or without functioning stroma):**
  A. Mesothelial tumors (primarily epithelial): Serous mucinous, endometrioid, "mesonephroid" tumors, true mesotheliomas.
  B. Mesothelial tumors (primarily stromal): Fibroadenoma, cystadenofibroma, Brenner tumor:
    1. Low functional potential.
    2. High functional potential: Granulosa–theca cell and Sertoli–Leydig cell tumors; gonadal stromal tumors with varying degrees of differentiation.
  C. Stromal (mesenchymal) tumors (of variable functional potential): Fibroma, fibromyoma, fibrothecoma, thecoma (luteoma), gonadal stromal tumors, sarcoma.
  D. Metastatic tumors and secondary malignant tumors.

III. **Germ cell tumors and associated gonadal aberrations:**
  A. Dysgerminoma (germinoma).
  B. Teratomas:
    1. Embryonal:
      a. Immature—embryoid: poorly differentiated elements.
      b. Mature—(dermoid cyst).
        Monocystic.
        Polycystic.
    2. Extraembryonal:
      a. Endodermal sinus.
      b. Polyvesicular vitelline (yolk sac).
      c. Choriocarcinoma.
    3. Dysgenetic gonad: gonadoblastoma.

IV. **Parovarian lesions:**
  A. Cysts, hydatids.
  B. "Mesonephroma," ie, metamesonephroma.
  C. Hilar cell tumor.
  D. Adrenal rest tumor.
  E. "Arrhenoblastoma."

V. **Other tumors (rarely primary in ovary):** Hemangiopericytoma, myoma, angioma, argentaffin tumor; hypernephroma.

Table 14—2. International Federation of Gynecology and Obstetrics (FIGO) classification of ovarian neoplasms.

I. Histologic classification:
  A. Serous cystomas:
    1. Serous cystadenomas, benign.
    2. Serous cystadenomas with proliferation of epithelial cells and nuclear abnormalities but without infiltrative destructive growth (low potential for malignancy).
    3. Serous cystadenocarcinomas.
  B. Mucinous cystomas:
    1. Mucinous cystadenomas, benign.
    2. Mucinous cystadenomas with proliferation of epithelial cells and nuclear abnormalities but with no infiltrative destructive growth (low potential for malignancy).
    3. Mucinous cystadenocarcinomas.
  C. Endometrioid tumors, similar to adenocarcinoma of the endometrium:
    1. Endometrioid cysts, benign.
    2. Endometrioid tumors with proliferative activity of epithelial cells and nuclear abnormalities but with no infiltrative destructive growth (low potential for malignancy).
    3. Endometrioid cyst adenocarcinomas.
  D. Mesonephric tumors:
    1. Benign mesonephric tumors.
    2. Mesonephric tumors with proliferating activity of the epithelial cells and nuclear abnormalities but with no infiltrative destructive growth (low potential for malignancy).
    3. Mesonephric cystadenocarcinomas.
  E. Concomitant carcinoma, unclassified carcinoma (tumors that cannot be allotted to one of the groups I, II, III, or IV).

II. International classification (staging):
  Stage I   Growth limited to the ovaries.
  Stage IA   Growth limited to one ovary; no ascites.
               (1) Capsule ruptured.
               (2) Capsule not ruptured.
  Stage IB   Growth limited to both ovaries; no ascites.
               (1) Capsule ruptured.
               (2) Capsule not ruptured.
  Stage IC   Growth limited to one or both ovaries; ascites present with malignant cells in the fluid.
               (1) Capsule ruptured.
               (2) Capsule not ruptured.
  Stage II   Growth involving one or both ovaries with pelvic extension.
  Stage IIA   Extension and/or metastases to the uterus and/or tubes and/or other ovary.
  Stage IIB   Extension to other pelvic tissues.
  Stage III   Growth involving one or both ovaries with widespread intraperitoneal metastases.
  Stage IV   Growth involving one or both ovaries with distant metastases.
  Special category: Unexplored cases which are thought to be ovarian carcinoma.

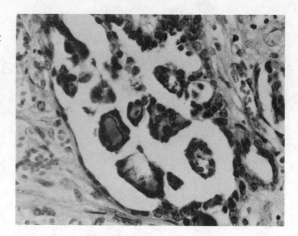

Figure 14—1. Papillary lesion with incorporated talc granules.

developing ovarian neoplasia, whereas the patient receiving oral contraceptives has a reduced incidence of such tumors. These statistics would indicate that the mesothelial inclusions produced by ovulation are of basic importance in the development of ovarian neoplasia.

With the exception of Japan, ovarian tumors are more common in industrialized countries. In the USA, the rate in whites and blacks is approximately the same. Little is known about the histogenesis of these tumors, other than that there must be a promotor and an initiator. A foreign material such as talc (Fig 14—1) or starch may serve as the promotor.

Diagnosis

The ovarian tumor represents the greatest contemporary challenge to the oncologic diagnostician, therapist, and investigator. The steps in study of the patient with an adnexal mass should include examinations sufficient to accomplish the following: (1) to evaluate carefully the general physical condition of the patient and to inspire confidence and assure the patient of her physician's concern; (2) to identify the presence or absence of urinary tract or intestinal disease; (3) to correlate the lesion with any physiologic or endocrinologic abnormalities, eg, amenorrhea, hirsutism, endometrial proliferation; (4) to determine associated karyotypic abnormalities with or without other clinical evidences of sex ambiguity; and (5) to diagnose the

malignancy and the fifth leading cause of death among women.

There is no consistent feature in the profile of the patient with ovarian cancer except for poor reproductive performance. The regularly ovulating woman with 2 or fewer pregnancies has a 2½ times greater risk of

Table 14—3. Incidences of primary invasive pelvic neoplasia in women.

Category	Cases	Deaths	Mortality Rate
Cervix	12,000	5,500	45%
Uterus	38,000	3,200	9%
"Ovary"	18,000	11,600	64%
Others		1,000	

presence of neoplasia at other sites either in the pelvic organs or at an extrapelvic site, eg, metastatic disease.

General Objectives of Treatment for Ovarian Neoplasia

Peritoneal fluid (free or from washings) should be obtained at the time of laparotomy for evaluation of cell content. Addition of heparin to the fluid will prevent coagulation of blood.

Every effort should be made to surgically excise as much neoplastic tissue as possible. Gross and microscopic analysis of all excised tissues must be meticulous. Examination of frozen sections at the time of surgery to evaluate the malignant potential of the tumor at the local site, in the abdominal cavity, and in the lymph nodes, and, on specific occasions, of the remaining "normal gonad" often will be of aid in determining the best treatment. It is important to take into consideration the patient's age in relation to the specific ovarian neoplasm (eg, conservative surgery for some ovarian tumors in the young patient). Adjunctive therapy is indicated for some specific types of lesions (eg, radiation for dysgerminoma, progesterone for endometrioid tumor). Consultants should be used if their advice and assistance offer hope to the patient of a longer and more comfortable life. The role of the gynecologist is that of primary diagnostician and therapist and physician in charge of therapy to whom the patient may turn both for care and for comfort, no matter what the outcome of therapy nor how discouraging the prognosis.

OVARIAN ENLARGEMENTS

Ovarian enlargements—cystic or solid—may occur at any age. Functional and inflammatory enlargements of the ovary develop almost exclusively during the years between menarche and the menopause. They may produce local discomfort, impairment of fertility, or, rarely, debility and death due to local problems such as intestinal or ureteral obstruction.

Diagnostic Considerations

Most neoplastic ovarian tumors produce few symptoms. Pain may be due to pulsion, traction, torsion, distention, or inflammation. The mere size of the tumor often causes a sense of pelvic weight or pressure. Rarely, a fixed, incarcerated ovarian tumor may cause severe pelvic pain, urinary retention, rectal discomfort, and bowel obstruction. Menstrual aberrations occur in only about 15% of patients with primary ovarian neoplasia.

Any palpable enlargement of the ovary in infancy or childhood is distinctly abnormal.

Precocious puberty is commonly considered to be evidence of a functioning ovarian tumor (granulosa cell or thecoma), but 90% of such problems are due to focal premenarcheal follicular ripening and thus need no surgical therapy unless they persist. Furthermore, true gonadal stromal lesions in this age group are generally benign. This is not true of the germ cell lesions.

During the menstrual years, temporary functional ovarian cysts are common; however, if they are persistent (eg, over 60 days), with normal menstrual cycles, the enlargement should be considered neoplastic. If the tumor disappears during this time, it is most likely a functional cyst. If the patient is postmenopausal, any ovarian enlargement should be investigated promptly regardless of size.

Functional cysts, eg, follicle or corpus luteum cysts, are normal transient structures related to aberrations of ovulation. They may be symptomatic and usually are unilateral. Bleeding from the hemorrhagic corpus luteum may produce acute pelvic pain, rectal tenesmus, and, on rare occasions, shock, thus simulating the picture of ruptured extrauterine pregnancy. Inflammatory ovarian disorders generally are related to salpingitis, appendicitis, or peritonitis, although even viral or parasitic infections may occur. Patients with primary malignant disease arising at an extraovarian site may develop ovarian metastases, eg, Krukenberg tumor, or the tumor may extend to the ovary, eg, from cancer of the colon.

Therapeutic Considerations

Prompt, accurate diagnosis and appropriate treatment must be the physician's goal when an ovarian enlargement is identified. The following factors must always be considered: the age of the patient, the size and persistence of the enlargement, whether one or both ovaries are involved, adherence, hormone production, neighboring irregularities, and ascites.

Severe pain, internal bleeding, or sepsis associated with ovarian enlargement requires prompt operation. Conversely, observation to confirm the persistence and to establish the character of ovarian enlargements is the best policy for questionable or asymptomatic ovarian tumors. When cancer is a reasonable possibility, operation should be carried out promptly. Once malignancy is established, definitive surgery and adjunctive therapy are mandatory if survival rates are to be improved.

Excision of some ovarian enlargements—eg, endometriosis or dermoid cysts—with preservation of the remainder of the ovary is feasible and desirable. Other benign lesions in young women, especially large cystic tumors such as cystadenomas, depending on the histopathologic features, require unilateral ovariectomy. Bisection should be avoided if at all possible, since inclusion cysts may develop at the site of incision. Furthermore, postincision adhesions may interfere with fertility.

The opposite ovary must always be inspected closely and occasionally biopsied in order to identify similar or other abnormalities in the presumably normal ovary, eg, dysgerminoma.

Tumors that are suspected of being malignant or

are of low-grade malignancy may require only removal of one ovary and tube, especially in young women who want to have children. Frozen sections should be made at the time of surgery because prompt definitive diagnosis may be possible. Nevertheless, permanent sections are mandatory for confirmation, since even the very young may have a malignant ovarian neoplasm. It is wise never to offer any definitive opinion to the family until the final sections are available, since total hysterectomy and bilateral salpingo-oophorectomy may be necessary if the tumor is highly malignant. Ovarian tumors with malignant proclivities diagnosed in the peri- or postmenopausal years are an indication for total hysterectomy and bilateral salpingo-oophorectomy.

Removal of the ovaries in a woman under 40 years of age "because she doesn't need them" or to prevent cancer is of questionable usefulness. The patient should be informed of the possible necessity for removal if unexpected pathologic conditions are found. This situation demands a careful discussion between doctor, the patient, and the patient's family. All possibilities should be presented and explained fully. The patient should be aware of future needs or problems, eg, replacement therapy or removal of the residual gonad if neoplastic potentialities exist. Undue pressure or threats should not be introduced into the discussion. After the menopause, if laparotomy is indicated for other reasons, removal of the uterus and ovaries should be elected to avoid future gynecologic problems if the patient's condition permits.

Ovariectomy (and hysterectomy) may be indicated for the palliation of estrogen-dominant (estrogen-positive receptor) metastatic breast carcinoma.

I. NONNEOPLASTIC LESIONS

INFLAMMATORY LESIONS

Adnexal enlargements of inflammatory origin are the most common of the nonneoplastic lesions. The frequency is dependent upon the social habits of the local population. Gonococcal infections of the cervix are found in routine studies of asymptomatic patients in as many as 10% of certain clinic populations. Early and adequate treatment should eliminate the frequency of residual adnexal disease; however, 5–10% of all pelvic laparotomies at the Johns Hopkins Hospital are performed as part of the treatment of a tubo-ovarian inflammatory mass. Regrettably, many of the patients are in the late second and third decades of life, and it is often inadvisable or impossible to salvage any of the internal genital organs.

The patient with such inflammatory disease often suffers from repeated bouts of lower abdominal pain, fever, and ileus, either mechanical or paralytic. Right upper quadrant pain, due to perihepatic adhesions, is a rare but well-defined result of gonococcal infection and may simulate liver or gallbladder disease. Rupture of the tubo-ovarian abscess often results in acute intra-abdominal crises, and delay in the treatment of such emergencies by hysterectomy and bilateral salpingo-oophorectomy has been associated in the past with a mortality rate approximating 90%. In the quiescent or chronic phase of such inflammatory disease, the adnexal masses often suggest the presence of a true neoplasm. Surgery may be necessary to establish the correct diagnosis.

Primary ovarian abscess and acute oophoritis are uncommon. The abscess is found primarily in the posthysterectomy patient and in previous studies was most frequently seen following vaginal hysterectomy. The classic symptom complex of the ovarian abscess consists of prolonged postoperative fever with nonspecific pelvic pain and prolonged purulent drainage from the vagina. Differential diagnosis lies between the more common tubo-ovarian inflammatory mass, a foreign body, and intestinal complications. Surgical removal of the infected ovary is the treatment of choice, since it is frequently impossible to achieve sufficient concentrations of antibiotic in the thick-walled mass to permit resolution (Fig 14–2).

Acute oophoritis, except in the vicinity of a tubo-ovarian abscess, is rare and in the past has been associated with tuberculosis. Recent studies have indicated that adnexal disease associated with the use of IUDs may represent true oophoritis and abscess formation.

Chronic adnexal disease must be differentiated from true ovarian neoplasia, particularly endometriosis and dermoid cysts, both of which are common in the third and fourth decades of life and are frequently bilateral. Nodularity in the cul-de-sac, a common finding with endometriosis, is contrasted to the diffuse thickening in the broad ligament and adjacent pelvic tissue that accompanies inflammatory disease. The

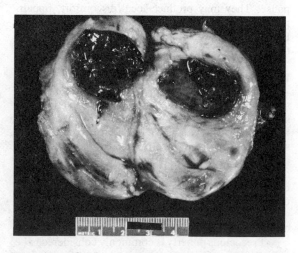

Figure 14–2. Ovarian abscess in the central core of a retained ovary.

dermoid cyst generally lies anterior to the broad ligament and is most frequently mobile. Intestinal and urinary tract disease may simulate these chronic inflammatory lesions, and adequate study should be performed to determine the status of both tracts prior to definitive therapy.

CYSTS

A cyst is a sac containing fluid or semisolid material. Ovarian cysts may develop at any time but are most common from puberty to the menopause. Many are small and clinically unimportant; however, all are potentially the sites of development of true and progressive malignant neoplasms. Ultrasonography frequently demonstrates the presence of a "2- to 3-cm" cyst. Such findings must be considered functional enlargements, since most ovaries contain cysts resulting from the inclusion of the mesothelium at the time of ovulation.

II. PHYSIOLOGIC ENLARGEMENT

FUNCTIONAL CYSTS

Follicle and corpus luteum cysts are normal transient physiologic structures.

Follicle Cysts

Follicle cysts (Fig 14–3) are common, frequently bilateral, multiple cysts that appear at the surface of the ovaries as pale blebs filled with a clear fluid. They vary

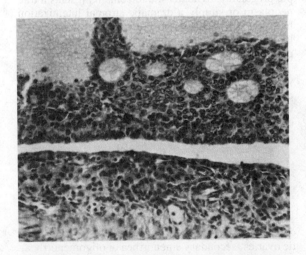

Figure 14–3. The wall of a "follicle" cyst showing the proliferating granulosa with its Call-Exner bodies (spaces) in the superior portion of the figure and the underlying luteinized theca. Note that the granulosa "pulls away" from the theca, suggesting its epithelial nature.

in size from microscopic to 4 cm in diameter (rarely larger). These cysts represent the failure of the fluid in an incompletely developed follicle to be reabsorbed. Symptoms are usually not present unless torsion or rupture with hemorrhage occurs, in which case the symptoms and signs of an acute abdomen are often present. Occasionally, such cysts are associated with an isolated menstrual abnormality such as a prolonged intermenstrual interval or short cycle. Large cysts may cause aching pelvic pain, dyspareunia, and, occasionally, abnormal uterine bleeding associated with a disturbance of the ovulatory pattern. The ovary may be slightly enlarged and tender to palpation, and the vaginal smear will often show a high estrogen level and a lack of progesterone stimulation.

Salpingitis, endometriosis, lutein cysts, and neoplastic cysts must be considered in the differential diagnosis.

Most follicle cysts disappear spontaneously within 60 days without any treatment. When symptoms are disturbing, reestablishment of the ovarian hormone cycle may be helpful. Ovulation may be simulated by 5 days of therapy with a single daily injection of progesterone in oil, 5 mg intramuscularly; or hydroxyprogesterone caproate, 1.25–2.5 mg intramuscularly. Ovulation may be induced with clomiphene citrate (Clomid), 50 mg orally daily for 5 days. However, such therapies are rarely necessary and should be avoided except in the recalcitrant case. Furthermore, ovulatory drugs are contraindicated if there is a possibility of pregnancy. Although fetal abnormalities are rare in association with progesterone therapy, one should be alert to the medicolegal aspects involved.

Any cyst that enlarges or persists longer than 60 days, particularly if a normal menstrual period intervenes, probably is not a follicle cyst.

Lutein Cysts

Two types of lutein cysts are recognized: (1) granulosa lutein, found within a corpus luteum; and (2) theca lutein, associated with hydatidiform mole, choriocarcinoma, or chorionic gonadotropin therapy.

A. Granulosa Lutein Cysts: Corpus luteum (granulosa lutein) cysts are functional, nonneoplastic enlargements of the ovary caused by the excessive accumulation of blood (corpus hemorrhagicum) during the hemorrhagic phase of the cycle and the subsequent replacement of blood by fluid, usually occurring after ovulation or during early pregnancy. They are 4–6 cm in diameter, raised, and often filled with brown serous fluid. A contracted blood clot may be found within the cavity.

Persistent corpus luteum cysts may cause local pain and tenderness and either amenorrhea or delayed menstruation followed by brisk bleeding after resolution of the cyst. They are usually readily palpable. This symptom complex simulates that associated with eccyesis and thus may demand prompt diagnostic studies in order to avoid catastrophe. A corpus luteum cyst may encourage torsion of the ovary, causing severe pain; or it may rupture and bleed, in which case laparotomy is usually required to control hemorrhage into the peritoneal cavity. Unless these acute complications develop, symptomatic therapy is all that is required. The cyst will disappear within 2 months in nonpregnant women and will gradually become smaller during the last trimester in pregnant women.

B. Theca Lutein Cysts: Theca lutein cysts range in size from minute to several centimeters in diameter. They are usually bilateral, are filled with clear straw-colored fluid, and are found in association with hydatidiform mole, choriocarcinoma, and gonadotropin or clomiphene therapy.

Abdominal symptoms are minimal. A sense of pelvic weight or aching may be described. Rupture of the cyst may result in intraperitoneal bleeding. Continued signs and symptoms of pregnancy, especially hyperemesis and breast paresthesias, are also reported.

Laboratory studies may disclose startlingly high titers of chorionic gonadotropin. Curettage should be done if there is any question of retained products of conception, a proliferative mole, or choriocarcinoma. Extrauterine pregnancy should be considered. If normal menses resume, the possibility of bilateral ovarian neoplasm (eg, dermoid cyst) must be ruled out.

Nevertheless, surgery is rarely required; the cysts disappear spontaneously following termination of the molar pregnancy, destruction of the choriocarcinoma, or discontinuation of gonadotropin therapy.

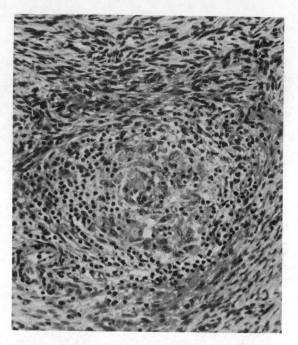

Figure 14–4. Cortical granuloma. Note the thecal proliferation around the central core.

THECOSIS

Hyperthecosis, thecomatosis, or cortical granulomas (Fig 14–4) commonly produce no gross enlargement of the ovary. Thus, the changes are demonstrable only by histologic examination of the excised gonad. These alterations may be associated with postmenopausal bleeding and endometrial hyperplasia. Both ovaries contain luteinized theca and cortical stromal cells. Actually, the true incidence of focal stromal luteinization or thecosis in the postmenopausal ovaries is unknown. Furthermore, such alterations are not the sine qua non of hormone production. It has been demonstrated that lipid and certain key enzymes are present in the large fusiform stromal cell with its metabolically active nucleus.

The arrangement of these focal luteinized stromal cells and their association with the hilar cells is interesting. In many instances, the large eosinophilic cell with its brilliant nucleolus can be traced from the hilar nerve area into the adjacent gonadal stroma. The linear arrangement is suggestive of a central core, possibly the nerve itself, as it enters the ovarian mesenchyme and may represent neural pathways and a neurohormonal mechanism by which the cell is stimulated.

Cortical Granulomas

Cortical granulomas (Fig 14–4) are a frequent finding in the ovaries of postmenopausal women. They are characterized by a central accumulation of lymphocytes surrounded by smaller stromal cells; the latter are rarely lipid-positive but may be functional.

Luteoma of Pregnancy

Extensive luteinization of the theca occurs during pregnancy because of prolonged chorionic gonadotropin stimulation. On rare occasions, overreaction may produce tumefactions that necessitate surgery. These lesions may be associated with hydramnios and multiple pregnancy. Whether the luteoma represents a true neoplasm or simply a dramatic stromal luteinization has not been determined, but the latter seems more likely. Thus, these lesions should and do regress postpartum with removal of hCG stimulation.

Of interest is the common association of maternal virilization with luteoma. In a series of 20 cases, 8 patients (40%) showed evidences of masculinization while 2 female newborns had abnormalities of the external genitalia.

POLYCYSTIC OVARIAN DISEASE
(Stein-Leventhal Syndrome, Sclerocystic Ovarian Disease)

Stein-Leventhal (polycystic ovary [PCO]) syndrome is characterized by bilaterally enlarged polycystic ovaries, secondary amenorrhea or oligomenorrhea, and infertility. About 50% of patients are hirsute, and many are obese. The syndrome affects females between the ages of 15 and 30 years. Many cases of female infertility secondary to failure of ovulation are due to polycystic ovarian disease. The disorder is pre-

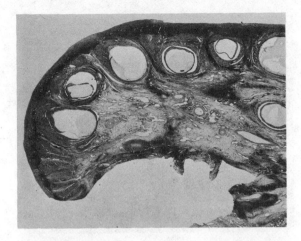

Figure 14–5. Polycystic ovary with "thickened" capsule—features of the so-called Stein-Leventhal ovary.

sumably related to hypothalamic pituitary dysfunction. However, the primary ovarian contribution to the problem has not been clearly defined.

The enlarged, "sclerocystic" ovaries with smooth, pearl-white surfaces but without surface indentations have been called "oyster ovaries." Many small, fluid-filled follicle cysts lie beneath the thick fibrous surface cortex (Fig 14–5). Luteinization of the theca interna is usually observed, and occasionally there is focal stromal luteinization.

A presumptive diagnosis of Stein-Leventhal syndrome often can be made from the history and initial examination. A normal puberty and early adolescence with reasonably regular menses are followed by episodes of amenorrhea that become progressively longer. The enlarged ovaries are identifiable on pelvic examination in about half of patients.

Urinary 17-ketosteroids are minimally elevated, but estrogen and FSH excretion are normal. Luteinizing hormone (LH) levels are elevated, and the "LH surge" is absent. Some patients have an increased Δ^4-androstenedione output; others excrete considerable amounts of dehydroepiandrosterone. Adrenocorticosteroid hormone titers are normal. BBT records and endometrial biopsies confirm anovulation.

Currently, the accepted diagnostic techniques are ultrasonography and laparoscopy. The patient is usually obese.

Adrenocortical hyperplasia or tumor is ruled out, since signs of defeminization are absent and adrenal function is normal. Dexamethasone suppression test results are negative with an adrenal tumor unless the tumor is pelvic in origin. A virilizing ovarian tumor is an unlikely diagnosis because the ovarian enlargement is bilateral and rarely do voice changes or clitoral hypertrophy occur.

Treatment varies: Hydrocortisone, 50 mg orally twice daily for 2–3 months, may be used in an attempt to induce ovulation, although only one normal cycle usually results. Clomiphene citrate (Clomid), 50–100 mg/d for 5–7 days cyclically, will be successful in inducing ovulation in most cases. In the recalcitrant case, the addition of human menopausal gonadotropin will often produce the desired ovulation. Rarely is wedge resection necessary; however, the results of such surgery have been eminently successful in restoring ovulation and fertility.

Since such patients are chronically anovulatory, the endometrium is stimulated by estrogen alone; endometrial hyperplasia, both typical and atypical, is thus more frequent in patients with polycystic ovarian disease and long-term anovulation. Well-differentiated endometrial cancer has been reported in the patient with prolonged anovulation and thus persistent estrogen stimulation. Nevertheless, many of these markedly atypical endometrial features will be reversed by large doses of progestational agents such as megestrol acetate (Megace), 40–60 mg/d for 3–4 months. Follow-up endometrial biopsy is mandatory in order to determine endometrial response and subsequent recurrence.

An interesting corollary to the polycystic ovary syndrome is the "large edematous ovary syndrome" initially reported by Sternberg. This unilaterally enlarged ovary is characterized by edematous stroma with nests of luteinized stromal cells. The classic patient is masculinized. Unilateral oophorectomy is associated with reversion of symptomatology.

III. NEOPLASTIC LESIONS

STROMOEPITHELIAL TUMORS, PRIMARILY EPITHELIAL

This large group of tumors comprises approximately 85% of all true ovarian neoplasms and includes the common mucinous, serous, endometrioid, and mesonephroid lesions, the gonadal stromal tumors with or without an epithelial element, and metastatic cancer. Except for the last-named, the epithelium of these tumors arises from a common anlage, ie, the mesothelium lining the coelomic cavity. This basic concept explains the similarity of the epithelia of the upper genital canal—endocervix, endometrium, and endosalpinx—to those found in the ovarian tumors.

It must be recognized that many so-called ovarian tumors represent intra-abdominal neoplasia with the ovary involved in the diffuse process. The validity of this thesis is demonstrated by the observation that many cases of FIGO clinical stage II disease are actually stage III in that the omentum, the peritoneum of the lateral gutters, and the dome of the diaphragm are found to be the site of tumor development. In contrast to intra-abdominal neoplasia representing common papillary lesions are intraovarian tumors characterized by mucinous lesions.

Epithelial neoplasms have not only a common cell of origin but also a common matrix, composed basically of 2 elements: an inert supporting connective tissue and the "ovarian stroma," the latter being the potentially functioning component of the gonad. All true neoplasms contain stroma; hence, all have the capacity to alter the hormonal status of the host. Thus, whether the neoplasm be a mucinous cyst, a granulosa cell tumor, or a metastatic lesion, studies have demonstrated some potential functional capability of the tumor.

Differentiated Mesotheliomas (Fig 14–6)

These epithelial neoplasms are classified on the basis of their variable histologic features and differences in growth patterns and clinical course.

Serous Tumors (FIGO Group A; Figs 14–7 to 14–11)

Serous tumors may attain a size large enough to fill the abdominal cavity, but they are usually smaller than their mucinous counterparts. Benign lesions are

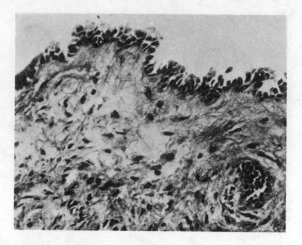

Figure 14–6. Mesothelium of the ovary. "Germinal epithelium" of the newborn. Note the "tufting" that is a classic finding in mesotheliomas.

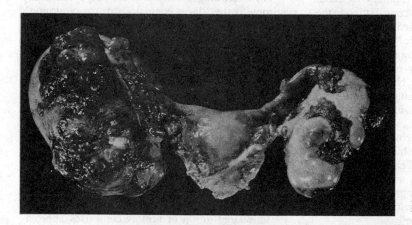

Figure 14–7. Bilateral papillary projections with satellite lesions on the serosa of uterus and tubes.

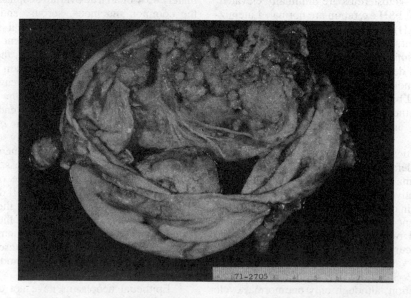

Figure 14–8. Internal papillae characteristic of the papillary serous "cystadenocarcinoma."

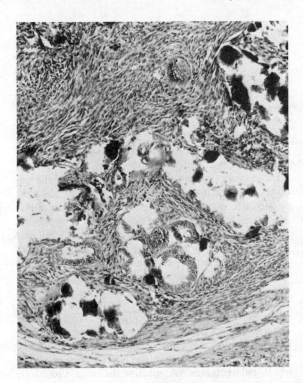

Figure 14–9. Serous tumor with well-differentiated epithelium and calcifications (so-called psammoma bodies but which probably represent foreign material).

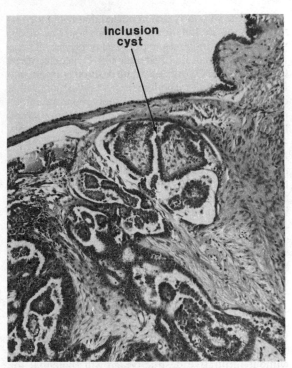

Figure 14–11. A low-grade papillary serous cystadenoma showing mesothelial budding and tubal epithelium. A small inclusion cyst without mesothelial proliferations is seen above. The patient has similar changes in small inclusions in the contralateral ovary and tubal wall.

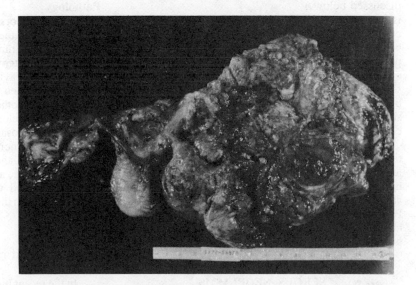

Figure 14–10. Papillary serous cystadenocarcinoma.

commonly unilocular, have a smooth surface, and contain clear yellow fluid. Proliferation of the epithelial and stromal components may produce firm areas that often are papillary cystadenomas. It is important to study these areas thoroughly, since malignancy may arise in a separate focus in these more proliferative foci. As the tumor becomes more aggressive, papillary

projections may be noted on both internal and external surfaces. The more aggressive the tumor, the poorer the prognosis. A serous tumor is serous only if it secretes clear yellow fluid. If it can perform its normal function of secreting serous fluid, the tumor is well differentiated and the prognosis is vastly improved over that for the undifferentiated tumor. Once the cell has become so poorly differentiated that it cannot perform its normal function, the tumor should be designated as undifferentiated carcinoma or mesothelioma.

The International Federation of Gynecology and Obstetrics (FIGO) divides group A serous tumors into 2 types. Type A-1 are benign serous cystadenomas that often are not adenomatous but simply represent multiple inclusion cysts. They are the most common cystic lesions of the ovary and represent approximately 40–50% of all epithelial tumors in some series. If the "simple" cysts are included, the percentage will be much higher, because peritoneal inclusions are routine findings in the ovaries of all ovulating women over the age of 35 years. These cavities of various sizes are lined by flattened mesothelium, by ciliated and secretory cells normally found in the uterine tube, or by combinations thereof.

Multiple cysts with a proliferating stroma but an epithelial lining similar to the simple cyst are generally classified as cystadenomas. The pattern tends to remain uniform from area to area although papillae may develop here and there. Nevertheless, there is no evidence of mitotic activity.

FIGO type A-2 includes serous tumors with epithelial proliferation and nuclear abnormalities but without infiltrative destructive growth (potential for malignancy). Currently, confusion surrounds these tumors, since many "low-grade" lesions merely represent mesothelial reactions to intra-abdominal irritants. Although they commonly involve the abdominal cavity diffusely, they are biologically and histopathologically benign. These mesotheliomas are discussed below.)

is generally papillary-adenomatous. The lining cells can usually be identified as similar to those seen in benign lesions. However, mitoses range from 1 to 3 per high-power field.

There may be external papillations as well as some within the cystic cavities. These lesions may become quite large, although they are generally smaller than in mucinous counterparts, perhaps because the secretory activity of the latter is greater.

Psammoma bodies—laminated, calcified particles—are present, particularly in the very low grade lesions, ie, those with one mitosis (or less than one) per high-power field. It has been suggested that these are areas of degeneration in the papillary projections. Psammoma bodies may represent foreign material that has played a part in the initiation of the proliferative process.

SEROUS NEOPLASMS
(Proliferating Lesions)

Clinical Findings

Proliferative serous tumors have been reported in all age groups. Fortunately, the low-grade neoplasms generally are found in younger patients while the anaplastic counterpart occurs more commonly in older women.

No classic symptoms are associated with the proliferating serous tumors. Many are found on routine pelvic examination. In others, the presenting symptoms include nonspecific pelvic discomfort, a palpable abdominal swelling, or ascites. Extra-abdominal disease is rarely seen in the low-grade tumor except in the terminal stages. As with all ovarian enlargements, the serous tumors must be differentiated from intestinal and urinary tract lesions. The pelvic kidney, dilatation of the ureter due to impacted stone, bladder diverticula, prolapsed intestinal neoplasm, and intestinal infections, eg, Crohn's disease, are a few of the enlargements that may simulate adnexal disease. In addition to differentiating these lesions from the true pelvic neoplasm, it is important to appreciate the possibility that the intestine may be involved in the neoplastic process arising primarily in the pelvis. Uterine tumors and salpingitis usually can be distinguished from the true ovarian neoplasms. Nevertheless, "uterine myoma" is the primary "physician diagnosis" in about one-third of all ovarian tumors. Thus, laparotomy should be performed if, because of the distortion of the pelvic architecture, ovarian neoplasm cannot be ruled out. Laparoscopy may be helpful, but laparotomy is necessary in the treatment of most adnexal enlargements. A midline incision should be made for adequate exploration.

Although the patient at risk of developing ovarian neoplasia has not been identified, several studies have recorded a high incidence of infertility; in the group of serous lesions noted above, the incidence was 27%.

Pathology

Serous tumors may attain large size but usually are smaller than their mucinous counterparts. The intricate papillary tumor often is characterized by both internal and external "treelike" proliferations and contains many cavities. The classic cell types in the well-differentiated tumor are the round or ovoid, acidophilic mesothelial variety associated with the ciliated and secretory elements characteristic of those seen in the endosalpinx. Conversely, in the poorly differentiated tumor, an individual cell type often cannot be discerned, and the classification is based strictly on the pattern, ie, a serous tumor is one that secretes serous fluid, and when component cells lose their ability to perform this function, the tumor cannot be so designated.

MUCINOUS TUMORS

In the recent literature, the term *pseudomucinous* has been superseded by the more correct designation *mucinous*. These tumors arise either as a unilateral development in a benign cystic teratoma or as mucinous metaplasia of the mesothelium.

Mucinous tumors of teratoid origin, as is true of most germ cell tumors, are found in younger patients. Malignant alteration is uncommon; however, the entire tumor must be examined thoroughly, since other

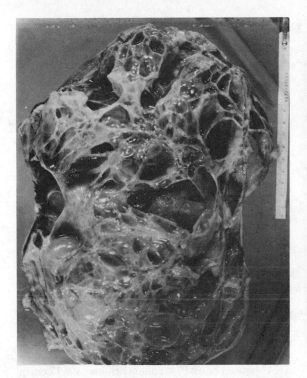

Figure 14–12. Multilocular mucinous cystadenoma of ovary.

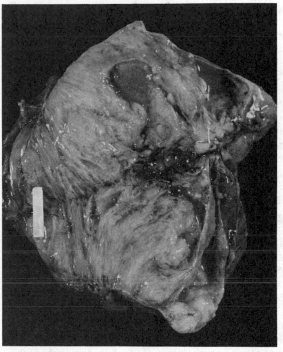

Figure 14–13. Mucinous cystadenocarcinoma; note the obvious mucinous component and the solid, more malignant areas.

teratoid elements—eg,the stroma—may be malignant. Three cases of embryonal rhabdomyosarcoma have been observed in the past 2 years, with subsequent death within 6 months. Obviously, appropriate therapy can be instituted and accurate prognosis afforded only if the correct diagnosis is made.

Mucinous tumors of heterotopic germinal epithelial origin may occur in any age group but generally develop later than the teratoid variety. Malignant mucinous tumors are less common than the serous variety, comprising approximately 8–10% of all epithelial neoplasia in our experience.

Pathology

Mucinous cysts are usually smooth-walled; true papillae, either internally or externally, are rare (as compared with the serous variety). The tumors generally are multilocular (Fig 14–12) and adenomatous; the mucus-containing locules appear blue through the tense capsule. The malignant variant may retain its mucin-secreting ability, but it may become undifferentiated (Fig 14–13). Bilateral tumor development occurs in 8–10% of all cases, whether the tumors are benign or malignant. These lesions are, in contrast to many mesothelial tumors, intraovarian in 95–98% of cases.

The internal surface is lined by tall mucinous epithelium with superficial pale blue, almost agranular cytoplasm and small, dark, basally situated nuclei as seen in the slide stained with hematoxylin and eosin stain (Fig 14–14). In compact, adenomatous areas

there is often a suggestion of stratification. Malignancy may be suspected if true papillae are demonstrated or if stratification of the cells with loss of the normal mucus production is present. When malignant, an adenocarcinoma that superficially resembles adenocarcinoma of intestinal origin may develop. More than one pattern—ie, both benign and malignant areas may be present in the same tumor. Consequently, multiple sections are necessary to deter-

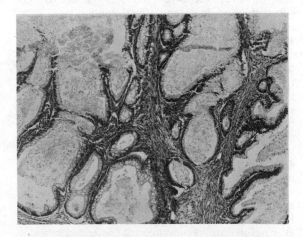

Figure 14–14. Classic mucinous cystadenoma. The lining cells are tall columnar with basally situated nuclei. (Hematoxylin and eosin stain.)

mine the true malignant potential. Finally, the stromal component of the mucinous tumors seems to be able to respond to either local or systemic stimuli and is capable of steroid production.

Clinical Findings

The mucinous tumors are the largest occurring in the human body; 15 reported tumors have weighed over 70 kg (154 lb). Consequently, the more massive the tumor, the greater the possibility that it may be mucinous. They generally are asymptomatic, and the patient is seen because of either an abdominal mass or nonspecific abdominal discomfort.

Treatment

Treatment is basically surgical. Total hysterectomy and bilateral salpingo-oophorectomy with careful staging, ie, investigating the omentum, right hemidiaphragm, lateral gutters, and pelvic and periaortic nodes, is the treatment of choice. Nevertheless, if the tumor is encapsulated and contains one or less than one mitosis per high-power field, a conservative approach may be made for the young patient desirous of maintaining fertility. In a study of 64 such lesions, 50% developed in patients under the age of 40, and the 5-year survival rate was approximately 90%. Conversely, in the more malignant lesions (those containing 2–5 mitoses in the most aggressive area), the 5-year survival rate was approximately 50%.

When tumors have extended beyond the pelvis, adjunctive chemotherapy is recommended. The various protocols are discussed below. Intraperitoneal radioisotopes, eg, chromic phosphate P 32, may be employed if only small (3- to 4-mm) fragments of tumor remain. Although this treatment was highly regarded in the past, current studies have indicated that there is poor distribution of the agent, and the delivery of large doses to the various peritoneal surfaces probably did not occur. External irradiation (cobalt or rotational) has been effective in reducing the tumor burden; however, the 5-year survival statistics do not substantiate its long-term effectiveness.

Prognosis

The results of any therapy depend upon the histology of the individual tumor and the clinical extent of the disease. Classically, the lesion with fewer mitoses is less aggressive and can often be treated in the early stages, while the converse is true for the more anaplastic lesion.

Survival depends on the biologic activity of the tumor and host resistance. Whether unilateral or bilateral, the well-differentiated lesion with less than 4 mitoses per high-power field has an excellent prognosis. If there are more than 4 mitoses in the most malignant areas, survival is reduced even in stage I disease. Interestingly, the mucinous tumor will metastasize even before local recurrence, and the secondary lesion often develops in the lungs. Since tumor grade and clinical stage seem to be closely related, careful evaluation of both factors is necessary to provide an accurate

prognosis. Adjunctive therapy is usually similar to that employed for serous lesions, although chemotherapy appears to be less effective for the mucinous variety.

ENDOMETRIOID LESIONS

Endometriosis (see Chapter 16) undoubtedly represents an "endometrioid alteration" of the mesothelium. Ovarian and peritoneal tissues may respond to hormonal or other types of stimuli to produce an endometrial type of tissue change, eg, during pregnancy (Fig 14–15).

The cause of ovarian endometrioid malignancy is unknown, but "long-term" estrogen ingestion may play a role, particularly in the patient with preexistent endometriosis.

Patients affected with functioning endometriosis are primarily in the reproductive age group. Benign endometrioid alterations of the mesothelium are seen when hormonal activity is present; malignant change may occur at any age.

Pathology

The endometrial lesions vary from microscopic in size ("powder burns") to endometriomas 10–12 cm in diameter. Dense adhesions to neighboring viscera are common.

The small, functioning bluish-purple foci are characterized by classic well-defined endometrium, ie, glands and stroma. The larger "chocolate cysts"

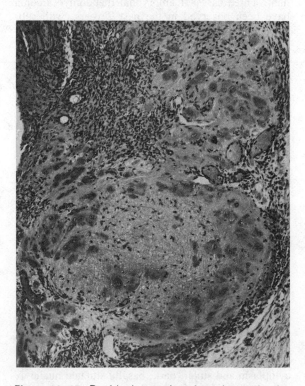

Figure 14–15. Decidual reaction just beneath the mesothelium in a patient with intrauterine pregnancy.

contain old brownish fluid, and, histologically, no definite endometrial tissue may be found. Nevertheless, the cyst lined by a nondescript, flattened epithelium beneath which is a layer of stroma composed of phagocytes filled with hemosiderin, so-called **siderophagic cyst,** is considered to be of endometrial origin. Pseudoxanthoma cells and chronic inflammatory elements with fibrosis are also recognized. Although there is a so-called endometrioid tumor of low malignant potential, its characteristics are poorly defined. These tumors may represent marked atypical hyperplasia in endometriosis or a well-differentiated carcinoma.

Cancer of the ovary that is histologically characterized by an adenoid pattern is now classified as **endometrioid carcinoma.** Nevertheless, until recently it was necessary to demonstrate benign endometriosis in the gonad with direct transition from the benign to the malignant before the diagnosis of endometrial cancer could be established. This thesis is still valid. However, if benign endometrial glands and stroma represent "metaplasia" of the coelomic epithelium, the transition can develop from this basic mesothelium without the histologic demonstration of classic endometriosis—hence the term *endometrioid* (Fig 14–16). Malignancy arising in identifiable endometriosis is less common than the adenomatoid or endometrioid variety. The degrees of anaplasia are determined, as in uterine adenocarcinoma, by the ex-

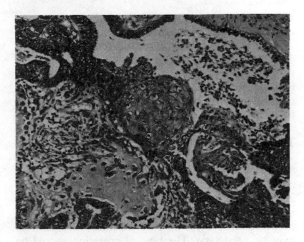

Figure 14–17. Endometrioid carcinoma showing acanthosis, a feature also characteristic of the similar lesion in the uterine cavity.

tent to which the glandular pattern is maintained. Thus, in the most undifferentiated tumor, it is practically impossible to recognize the original glands, and a diagnosis of sarcoma may be suggested. Actually, carcinosarcomas or mixed mesodermal tumors have been described as primary ovarian tumors. It is interesting to note that acanthosis, so common in intrauterine lesions (Fig 14–17), may also be found in ovarian tumors, which further documents the relationship between these histologically similar lesions. Finally, there are instances in which an apparent extension of a uterine lesion to the ovary or vice versa in reality represents an example of multifocal neoplasia. Although this association has been termed "metastatic cancer," the improved 5-year survival rate—50% in a series from the Emil Novak Ovarian Tumor Registry—suggests that many such lesions are, as noted above, multiple primary neoplasms.

Clinical Findings

The symptoms obviously are related, during the menstrual years, to the activity of the ectopic endometrium in the ovary and adjacent structures. The extent of the palpable lesion is inversely proportionate to the severity of symptoms. Pain is the most common feature, and, although pain is usually said to be typically associated with the menses, intermenstrual pain is also common. The tiny purplish foci scattered throughout the pelvis may produce incapacitating discomfort. Other symptoms include infertility and dyspareunia. Bleeding into the peritoneal cavity and adjacent tissues produces fibrosis, and scarring results in nerve irritation. In the absence of endometrial activity, the larger endometrioma may be asymptomatic.

In most cases when malignancy develops in such foci, no specific symptoms have been reported. Generally speaking, as is true of most ovarian neoplasia, the tumors are discovered on routine examination or

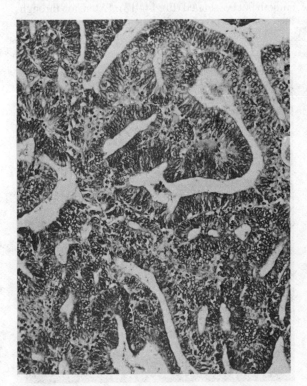

Figure 14–16. Endometrioid carcinoma as seen with high-power field. Note the tall epithelium—not a tubal type or the mucoid variety.

when the neoplasm has extended beyond the confines of the pelvic organs.

Not all "chocolate cysts" are endometrial in origin. Bleeding into any cystic cavity will eventuate in the presence of histiocytes that have phagocytosed the blood pigment, creating a "siderophagic cyst." The wall of a corpus luteum will show such a yellowish lining zone.

Treatment

The treatment of endometriosis during the menstrual years should be conservative because it commonly occurs in the third and fourth decades of life and may be relatively asymptomatic. Conversely, if a mass is present and a definite diagnosis of endometriosis cannot be confirmed by examination, operation may be necessary. The type of operation should be predicated on the age of the patient, the extent of the disease, and the interest in reproductive function.

If cancer is present in endometriosis or if adenocarcinoma of the endometrioid type is present, total ablation of the internal genital organs and affected pelvic tissues is indicated. The presence of endometriosis with cancer is usually associated with a better-differentiated lesion and thus a better prognosis.

Adjunctive therapy for the endometrioid neoplasm may consist of both radiotherapy and chemotherapy. The latter certainly should include progestational agents, particularly if progesterone receptors can be identified in the tumor cells. In general, the more differentiated the lesion histologically, the better the response to the progesterones. For poorly differentiated tumors, triple chemotherapeutic regimens may be more effective.

Prognosis

The results of all types of treatment depend on the histologic type of the tumor and the clinical stage of the disease. A wide variety of endometrioid ovarian lesions conform to the microscopic and clinical characteristics of tumors found in the endometrium. Not only well-differentiated adenocarcinomas but the most undifferentiated mixed mesodermal tumors may arise primarily in the ovary. As is true of uterine abnormalities of the latter type, the prognosis is very poor; there are no survivors in the author's series.

Of interest in this group of endometrioid cancers is the association between endometrial and ovarian tumors. These relationships demonstrate the possibility of multicentric foci of origin in the upper genital canal. In a series of 120 secondary ovarian tumors, it was found that when the primary lesion was in the endometrium the salvage rate was 50%. This survival rate suggests that the tumors are not metastatic but represent separate primary foci.

MESONEPHROID LESIONS OF THE OVARY OR CLEAR CELL CARCINOMA

Clear cell and pseudoglomerular ("hobnail") patterns in an ovarian tumor represent a specialized differentiation of the ovarian mesothelium. This conceptual approach to ovarian neoplasia again demonstrates the totipotency of the coelomic epithelium or mesothelium. Nevertheless, the general term mesothelioma is not acceptable for most epithelial lesions, because the individual histologic varieties pursue different clinical courses.

For the most part, the clear cell or mesonephroid lesion is found in patients over 40 years of age. In a study of 95 such lesions, approximately 95% were recognized in the fifth decade of life or later. They are unilateral in approximately two-thirds of cases.

Pathology

The tumor is grayish-brown, smooth, free, semisoft or cystic, and usually well encapsulated. Thin "serous" fluid fills the locules and tissue spaces, and even hemorrhagic extravasation may be found. Most tumors are 10–20 cm in diameter when first discovered.

Grossly, the mesonephroid tumors are similar to most ovarian neoplasms, with both cystic and solid components. The former may be related either to the developmental characteristics of the lesion or to degenerative changes. The external surface is usually smooth but bosselated (Fig 14–18). Extension through the capsule to involve adjacent structures occurs late.

Microscopically, there are 2 classic cell types: the

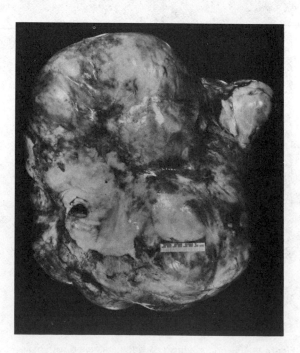

Figure 14–18. Mesonephroid carcinoma, grossly similar to many other solid ovarian cancers.

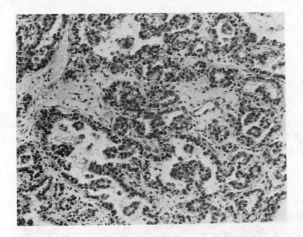

Figure 14–19. Adenomatous pattern with papillary infolding and "hobnail epithelium." In many areas, clear cells can be seen with transitions to the hobnail type.

clear cell and the irregular "hobnail" cell so characteristic of the kidney tumor, which the mesonephroid lesion simulates (Fig 14–19). Similar patterns may be found in uterine adenocarcinoma, which suggests an origin from ovarian endometriosis. Multiple cell types may be recognized in many ovarian neoplasms. Finally, direct transitions from this "coelomic epithelium" to a clear cell differentiation have been demonstrated in the earlier lesions (Fig 14–20).

Although benign mesonephroid lesions have been described, a tumor of low malignant potential has not been identified.

Clinical Findings

The symptoms of ovarian neoplasm, as is true of most other epithelial tumors, are essentially nonexistent until the tumor has reached palpable size or extension to other viscera has taken place.

The diagnosis is made by careful palpation of the pelvic contents and by studies to establish the gonadal

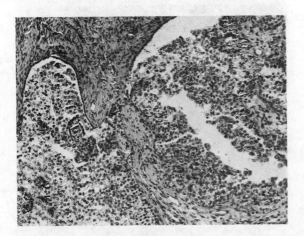

Figure 14–20. "Clear cell" or mesonephroid carcinoma arising directly from mesothelium in ovarian inclusion.

origin of the neoplasm. Obviously, in certain cases differentiation may be impossible; intestinal and urinary tract disease, with which the ovarian tumor may be confused generally, can be ruled out by appropriate studies. The "mesonephroid" tumor has been associated with hypercalcemia and hyperpyrexia more frequently than other ovarian neoplasms.

It is important to recognize that these lesions often are unilateral. In clinical stage I tumors, ie, when the lesion is confined to the ovary, the incidence of bilaterality was less than 10%. Obviously, when the tumor had spread to adjacent areas, it was difficult to determine whether the neoplasm had spread from one ovary to the other or if it had arisen in both.

Mesonephromas must be distinguished from cystadenomas and cystadenocarcinomas, clear cell kidney carcinomas metastatic to the ovary, and undifferentiated carcinomas of uncertain type. The clear cells stain faintly with periodic acid–Schiff reagent, in contrast to the striking reaction occurring in mucinous lesions. Of interest has been the association of hypercalcemia and hyperpyrexia with mesonephroid tumors. Approximately one-half of all ovarian tumors associated with elevated serum calcium have been of this variety.

Treatment

Treatment consists of surgical removal. The patients are generally over 40 years of age, and total hysterectomy and bilateral salpingo-oophorectomy is the obvious treatment of choice.

These tumors are only slightly radiosensitive. Adjunctive therapy is similar to that suggested for other ovarian neoplasms.

Prognosis

The results are dependent on the extent of the tumor at the time of initial therapy. As noted above, in spite of its size, this tumor is often confined to one ovary. The salvage rate in these cases is over 60% in the clinical stage I category; in clinical stages III and IV, the author has observed no 5-year survivors.

MESOTHELIOMA

The (true) mesothelioma occurs in the pleural cavity. It may represent simple proliferation of the mesothelial cells or a very aggressive malignancy. It is associated with asbestos. Similar tumors have been reported in the abdominal cavities of men.

Confusion has arisen over the interpretation of the benign but proliferating mesothelial lesion in the abdominal cavities of women. Many such tumors have been designated erroneously as serous lesions of low malignant potential; as a consequence, they may be over-treated.

The lesions of mesothelioma are commonly multifocal, involving many peritoneal surfaces from pelvis to diaphragm. They are characterized by papillary proliferations without mitotic activity. The classic cells

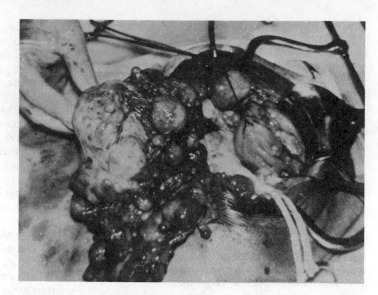

Figure 14–21. Mesothelioma of the ovary and peritoneal cavity—note the multiple nodules in the omentum. The ovaries contain small nodules of surface tumor.

are either mesothelial, ciliated, secretory, or combinations thereof. They do not appear to progress from this simple proliferative process to a more malignant variant. In a study of 154 cases followed from 2 to 40 years, there were only 2 deaths due to the lesion itself. One of these patients died of intestinal obstruction after 10 years with no effort apparently made to relieve the problem. The other died in 7 months after surgery, but she did receive radiation therapy.

Consequently, such lesions should be designated as proliferating benign intra-abdominal mesotheliomas, and an effort should be made to eliminate as much of the tumor mass as possible and to avoid complications produced by the use of adjunctive therapy. The cells are benign and thus will not be affected by irradiation or alkylating agents. However, the patient may suffer from anticancer therapy. As with endometriosis, the disease affects many surface areas and may cause intestinal or urinary tract complications, but the tumor does not metastasize.

Of interest in these lesions is the associated psammoma body. These bits of calcific material are frequently found in the lumen of the uterine tube as well as in the multiple foci of mesothelial proliferations throughout the abdomen. It is possible that they are a factor in producing the multiple sites of "tumor" formation.

In contrast to benign mesothelial proliferations are the malignant variants. The histologic patterns described for the mesothelioma seen elsewhere are classic for those noted in the pelvis and peritoneal cavity of the female: (1) stromal or fibrosarcomatous; (2) tubopapillary (papillary adenomatous); (3) mesothelial (usually papillary); and (4) mixtures of (1), (2), and (3). Many of the so-called grade 3 and 4 papillary serous tumors are really papillary mesotheliomas. These lesions make up the majority of the FIGO category "E" lesions. Since these lesions are representative of intra-abdominal neoplasia, the treatment is the same.

Diagnosis & Treatment of Mesothelial (Epithelial) Tumors

Without identification of the histopathologic and cytopathologic changes precursory to "ovarian cancer," early diagnosis of ovarian cancer is virtually impossible. Investigations of intraperitoneal cytology in the asymptomatic patient have been unrewarding. Ultrasound and radiologic techniques, including CT scan, have not helped to define the early lesion. Nevertheless, progress has been made in identifying the patient at risk, and agents such as talc have been identified that produce mesothelial proliferation. Consequently, although precursory and in situ alterations are not defined, progress in prevention and definition of the patient at risk may decrease the incidence of this distressing and destructive neoplasm.

Of major importance in treatment of the patient with ovarian cancer is thorough exploration of the entire abdominal cavity at the time of the initial opera-

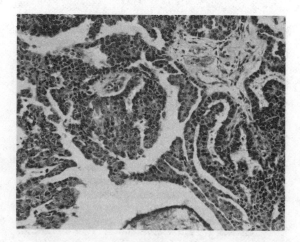

Figure 14–22. Tubopapillary lesion on the peritoneal surface. No intraovarian tumor.

tive procedure. The incision should be midline, with sufficient extension cephalad to allow for careful evaluation of the right hemidiaphragm and adjacent liver surface. The omentum should be removed if involved, or generously sampled if no gross lesion is demonstrable. The retroperitoneal nodes must be carefully palpated and biopsied if necessary. As much tumor as possible must be removed ("debulking") to increase the effectiveness of adjunctive therapy. This "tumor-reductive surgery" should eliminate as much disease as possible without jeopardizing immediate survival. Basically, the justification for such a thorough surgical survey is not only to improve prognosis but also to accurately "stage" the tumor. Recent reports demonstrate that as many as 40–45% of clinical stage IIA and B lesions are actually stage III disease.

Adjuncts to surgical extirpation of as much as possible of the "tumor burden" are irradiation and chemotherapy (either or both). Chemotherapy is currently the adjunctive treatment of choice. Single-agent treatment, usually with an alkylating agent such as melphalan, is the most widely accepted initial postsurgical treatment. Generally, a "pulse therapy regimen," ie, 5 days of therapy per month for 12 courses, followed by "second look" procedure, has been the most commonly accepted method of treatment. Response rates of 40–45%, demonstrated by reduction in residual size of tumor mass, have been achieved by such therapy. Failures or relapses have been followed by other agents, singly or in combination, eg, hexamethylmelamine, doxorubicin, and cyclophosphamide. Many other combinations are now in use. Cisplatin has been widely used in the past few years. Improvements in salvage and "quality of life" have resulted, even though the percentage of 5-year survivors has not increased significantly. Furthermore, it must be appreciated that these agents are toxic, and the combinations are more noxious than the single agents. Some of the complications that may be expected are set forth in Table 14–4.

Recently, serious complications such as nonlymphocytic leukemia have resulted in death in patients who have received alkylating agents for 2 or more years. Consequently, these patients must be monitored carefully. There is mounting evidence that if a patient has tumor progression after 6 months of treatment by one therapeutic agent, she will not respond and should be switched to other therapeutic regimens.

Radiation therapy was the prime therapeutic modality for many years, but inability to deliver effective dosages to the upper abdomen without damaging the liver or kidneys limited its usefulness. Intraperitoneal radioisotopes such as chromic phosphate are presumably effective if tumor fragments less than 5 mm in diameter remain. Although there is some doubt about the effectiveness of this treatment, the addition of external beam therapy may lead to better results in the future. The latter protocol is still experimental, and long-term results await adequate clinical trials.

STROMOEPITHELIAL TUMORS, PRIMARILY STROMAL

Stromoepithelial tumors that have a predominance of stromal components are relatively uncommon. They are interesting primarily because of the varied nature of the epithelial elements and the occasional demonstration of steroid hormone production. On the basis of this latter phenomenon, stromoepithelial tumors have been divided into 2 groups: (1) those with low functional potential (cystadenofibroma, fibrocystadenoma, Brenner tumor); and (2) those with high functional potential (granulosa–theca cell and Sertoli–Leydig cell tumors). The latter are commonly referred to as "sex cord" lesions.

1. CYSTADENOMA, FIBROCYSTADENOMA, & BRENNER TUMOR

These tumors occur most commonly in the fifth to seventh decades. They may develop at a much younger age, but, because they usually are asymptomatic, discovery may take place years later.

All types are characterized by a variety of epithelial elements in the cystic areas and by a fibrostromal component. The Brenner tumor is the best-known variety, although it simply represents squamous metaplasia in a preexisting fibroadenoma. These tumors also demonstrate the response of the stromal elements to local proliferative stimuli.

Histogenesis & Pathology

These 2 features will be discussed together because they are closely related. The Brenner tumor is a yellowish-brown, nonadherent, fibroepitheliomatous neoplasm. It is largely solid, and the cystic component, although present—as in all adenomatous tumors—usually is less prominent (Fig 14–23). Brenner tumors are usually unilateral; however, the opposite ovary often demonstrates a microscopic lesion, generally fibroma with or without "Brenner" elements. Brenner tumors represent about 1% of primary ovarian tumors.

The precursors of fibroadenomatous lesions can

Table 14–4. Toxicity of chemotherapeutic agents.

System	Drug
Hepatic toxicity	Methotrexate (especially chronic low-dose), doxorubicin
Renal toxicity	Methotrexate (especially high-dose), cisplatin
Myelosuppressive toxicity	Many agents
Peripheral neuropathy	Vincristine, hexamethylmelanine
Ototoxicity	Cisplatin
Pulmonary toxicity	Bleomycin, methotrexate, cyclophosphamide
Cardiac toxicity	Doxorubicin (acute or cumulative)

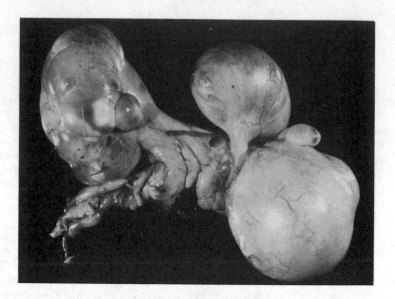

Figure 14–23. Fibrocystadenoma. Both solid "fibromatous" and cystic areas are present; the former are predominant.

be recognized in many "normal" ovaries. Isolated foci of germinal inclusions often are seen throughout the cortex of the gonad, and here the term fibroadenosis might be appropriate. In these inclusions, various degrees of squamous metaplasia may be seen as representing changes similar to those in the peritoneal inclusions known as Walthard islands (Fig 14–24). Thus, the genesis of the epithelial component of the Brenner tumor and the Walthard island relates directly to a heterotopic or metaplastic alteration of the basic mesothelium in the perisalpingeal peritoneal inclusions or in the adenomatous structures commonly seen in the ovarian cortex (Fig 14–25). In the latter, the psammoma bodies may be identified. These are typical of the low-grade papillary serous tumors and also of mesothelial inclusions associated with inflammatory

disease. Actually, the epithelium of the rete ovarii must be included as a potential site of squamous metaplasia and thus of the Brenner tumor. About 25–30% of all such lesions are found in the hilum of the ovary and may arise in the parovarian mesonephric elements. Most of these are microscopic findings.

In fibroadenomatous tumors, the stromal rather than the epithelial component is predominant. The adenomatous cystic structures are lined by typical tubal, endometrial, mucinous, mesonephroid, or mesothelial cells. As noted above, the metaplastic cell of the Brenner tumor appears squamous, with an ovoid shape, abundant light eosinophilic cytoplasm, and a pale nucleus containing finely granular chromatin.

Occasionally, the chromatin arrangement appears to divide the nucleus into 2 compartments, suggesting

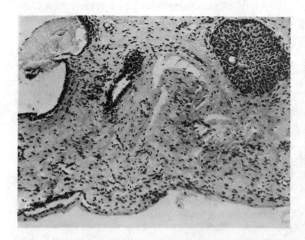

Figure 14–24. Walthard islands. Squamous metaplasia in peritubal peritoneal inclusions.

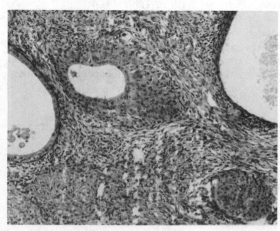

Figure 14–25. Metaplasia beginning in a fibroadenomatous tumor. Note the cystic and solid epithelial foci, with squamous metaplasia in the former.

a "coffee bean." The latter is not pathognomonic of the Brenner tumor because it is seen in metaplastic epithelium elsewhere, particularly in the endocervix. It is not known what stimulates the metaplasia that is the classic element of the Brenner tumor. The concept that mucinous lesions arise from the Brenner tumor seems inconsistent; the reverse probably is true. This simulates the common occurrence of metaplasia in mucus-secreting epithelium of the cervix.

Malignant changes in fibroadenomatous lesions are rare. The true malignant Brenner tumor is characterized by alterations that histologically simulate epidermoid carcinoma of the cervix. A preinvasive or intraepithelial variety (proliferative) and a mature epidermoid type are recognized. In a study of 10 proliferative and 37 malignant Brenner tumors, there were no deaths in the former group. Conversely, survival of women with the malignant variant was related directly to the clinical stage. No 5-year survivors were recorded if the lesion had progressed beyond the ovary. Many of the reported "malignant Brenner tumors" are actually neoplasms arising in the preexisting epithelial elements rather than in the "squamous" component of the true Brenner tumor.

Clinical Findings

Unilateral pelvic discomfort and a sense of fullness and heaviness in the lower abdomen are described. Torsion results in severe pain. Ascites or Meigs' syndrome occasionally coexists with the Brenner tumors, which may grow to 30 cm in diameter. Most tumors, however, are less than 2–3 cm in diameter, are asymptomatic, and are discovered incidentally at surgery performed for other reasons.

Feminizing or masculinizing alterations in the host have been reported in association with these lesions. The former are more common and consist largely of changes in the endometrium, as demonstrated by the finding of hyperplasia or well differentiated carcinoma, and lack of aging changes of the vaginal epithelium.

Differential Diagnosis

All adnexal enlargements must be differentiated from gastrointestinal and urinary abnormalities. Nevertheless, the solid tumor is less of a challenge than the cystic variety because the latter more commonly simulates the consistency of a urinary or an intestinal lesion.

Solid fibroadenomatous neoplasms are commonly mistaken for uterine myomas. Consequently, if a solid pelvic neoplasm is situated so that it prevents careful evaluation of the adnexa, operative removal is indicated regardless of its origin, ie, ovary or uterus.

A metastatic lesion is high on the list of ovarian tumors for which these solid neoplasms may be mistaken. If such a problem in differential diagnosis arises, search should be made for a primary malignancy elsewhere. The final diagnosis will often be made only when the tumor is studied carefully in the pathology laboratory.

Treatment

Treatment is primarily surgical, to establish the diagnosis and remove the tumor. Because most of these neoplasms are found after the menopause, hysterectomy and bilateral salpingo-oophorectomy is the procedure of choice. Adjunctive radiation may be used when the tumor is malignant.

Prognosis

Since the great majority of these tumors are benign, the prognosis is excellent. Adjunctive therapy for the malignant variety has consisted of irradiation, because the tumors simulate cervical cancer, but the 5-year survival rate has been poor. Chemotherapy has not been effective, but few cases have been so treated.

2. GRANULOSA–THECA CELL TUMORS

Lesions in this category are generally classified as one of the large groups of "functioning tumors" with masculinizing or feminizing characteristics. Nevertheless, in many instances, it is difficult to correlate the clinical findings with the histopathologic features. Thus, the various histologically identifiable lesions will be discussed individually, since, although the clinical features are usually self-evident, the prognosis depends basically on the cellular malignancy of the individual elements and the gross extent of the disease. Furthermore, it is impossible to determine the endocrine effect of the tumor by its histologic appearance.

Tumors of this type that occur before the menarche are classically associated with pseudoprecocious puberty. Early breast development, appearance of pubic and axillary hair, and vaginal bleeding make up the characteristic symptom complex. Laboratory studies may demonstrate increase in the numbers of mature, superficial cells in the vaginal cytologic specimen, increased mucoid discharge from the cervix, elevated urinary and serum estrogen levels, and varying degrees of endometrial proliferation. Epiphyseal closure must be prevented in order to permit normal growth. In other words, the "bone age" is more advanced than the chronologic age. Even though vaginal bleeding occurs, ovulation does not take place with granulosa–theca cell tumors; thus, the possibility of pregnancy does not exist. Nevertheless, such tumors are *not* the most common cause of true precocious puberty, ie, onset of menarche before age 9. Much more frequently, the transient granulosa or follicle cysts cause precocity; thus, a conservative approach is indicated. There have been no deaths recorded in the Ovarian Tumor Registry owing to granulosa–theca cell tumors found in patients younger than 14 years of age.

Granulosa–theca cell tumors during the menstrual years are heralded by amenorrhea in about 50% of cases. The increased or persistent production of estrogen "blocks" ovulation, and a pattern similar to that associated with Stein-Leventhal syndrome results. The vaginal maturation index shows a "shift to the right," with a constant predominance of superficial cells and

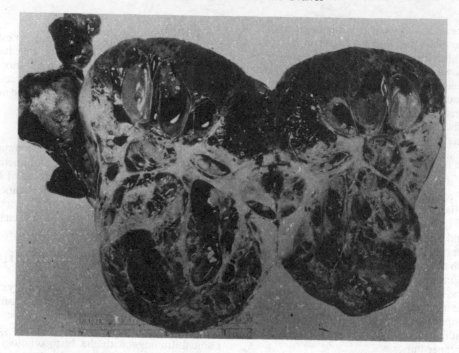

Figure 14-26. Granulosa-theca cell tumor of the ovary with focal cystic degeneration.

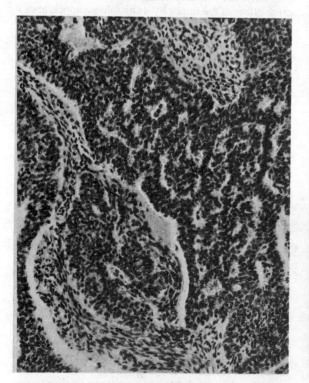

Figure 14-27. Granulosa-theca cell tumor; the trabecular and pseudoadenomatous patterns are evident in the central portions. The stromal component is clearly shown.

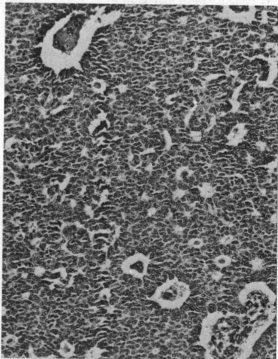

Figure 14-28. Folliculoid pattern of the granulosa cell tumor with Call-Exner bodies.

an absence of progestational changes. Similarly, the endometrium is proliferative to the point of hyperplasia, typical or atypical. The breasts may be sensitive, and fluid retention produces weight gain, nausea, gastrointestinal disturbances, and a general lack of well-being. On the other hand, tumors of this histologic type may produce few or no symptoms. Consequently, such neoplasms may be found in the pregnant patient when luteinization of the tumor cells often is noted. The "luteoma" of pregnancy is rarely the result of such a sequence of events but rather is an abnormal physiologic response of the ovary to the prolonged stimulation by chorionic gonadotropin during pregnancy.

In the postmenopausal patient, the symptoms often are similar to those of patients of comparable age who are receiving exogenous hormones. The vaginal epithelium matures, the endometrium becomes proliferative, and postmenopausal bleeding may occur. Breast soreness and fluid retention are commonly associated with granulosa-theca cell tumor.

If the stimulus that produces the endometrial hyperplasia persists, well differentiated cancer may develop. If the tumor mass becomes large, pressure symptoms may ensue. Torsion or degeneration may produce acute pain, obstipation, tympanites, and nausea and vomiting. Such tumors, interestingly, are associated with rupture and intra-abdominal hemorrhage.

When these tumors become luteinized, the alterations in the genital canal are those related to progesterone stimulation, ie, decidual reaction in the endometrium, midzone shift of the vaginal smear maturation index, and inconsistent vaginal bleeding patterns in the prepubertal, menstrual, or postmenopausal years. Breast enlargement and mastalgia are common.

Pathology

Classically, steroid-producing ovarian tumors are yellow-orange. Most of these neoplasms are less than 10–15 cm in diameter, and neoplasms found only on microscopic study have been reported. Most of the tumors are solid. However, cystic areas due to degeneration may be present (Fig 14–26).

The characteristic cell is that which lines the antrum of the developing follicle, ie, the round or slightly ovoid granulosa cell with its dark nucleus, compact chromatin, and little or no cytoplasm. This cell is seen in a variety of formations, including the macro- and microfollicular patterns (simulating the cellular arrangements in the normal follicle), the interlacing cords and strands or trabeculae (Fig 14–27), and a pseudoglandular or tubular deployment of cells. Occasionally, the "coffee bean" pattern, heretofore described as a cellular feature of the Brenner tumor, may be seen in granulosa cell tumors, thus supporting its epithelial origin. Normal mitoses are common, and the "ovumlike" Call-Exner bodies are classic (Fig 14–28). These small acellular spaces are encircled by granulosa characteristic of both neoplastic and nonneoplastic proliferations. They probably represent fluid accumulations in the actively growing tissue. Granulosa cells in the neoplastic and nonneoplastic states cannot be differentiated by tissue culture techniques. As in the normal follicle, the classic granulosa cells can become "luteinized" and thus may produce progestational alterations in the host, as previously described.

The true granulosa–theca cell tumor contains a thecal or mesenchymal component. This is the potentially functioning element in the normal gonad, but a local or systemic stimulus is required for activation. It seems possible that proliferation of the granulosa cell in the tumor, as well as in the developing follicle, may be the important factor in stimulating the theca to steroid production. Regardless of the mechanism, the classic luteinized cell is large and ovoid, with abundant cytoplasm, and a large pale nucleus suggests metabolic activity. Fat stains are frequently positive. Nevertheless, negative reactions do not rule out steroid activity.

Cellular evidence of malignancy often is difficult to evaluate. Stromal sarcomas are extremely rare. Thus, the thecal component is rarely, if ever, a serious threat. On the other hand, the granulosa component, basically an epithelial element, should always be suspect. Mitoses are common in the normal proliferating granulosa of the developing follicle. A few mitoses in a tumor should not be interpreted as evidence of serious overactivity. Similarly, tumors with well-developed cords or trabecular arrangements usually are relatively benign. Nonetheless, atypically proliferating patterns may be seen, suggesting an "undifferentiated or solid carcinoma." In almost all studies, the salvage rate has approximated 90% in mature, unequivocal granulosa cell tumors. Conversely, only a 20–25% survival rate is recorded in the patient with less well differentiated tumors. Therefore, it is reasonable to discuss the latter as solid, undifferentiated cancers because the cell type cannot be identified. This nomenclature emphasizes the poor prognosis of the nonspecific lesion. Conversely, the malignant potential of well differentiated granulosa cell tumors is overstated by the inclusion of numerous ill-defined cancers.

Differential Diagnosis

The classic symptoms should establish the presumptive diagnosis of a functioning ovarian neoplasm. It may be difficult to rule out exogenous hormone administration, since many "geriatric medications" contain a variety of hormones including estrogen, androgen, and thyroid. Similar preparations may be prescribed for a young girl with nutritional problems. Moreover, transient conditions such as persistent follicle cysts may be associated with a similar clinical picture, though the symptoms usually are self-limited. Thus, a careful history should be obtained and one must determine the consistency and general appearance of the abnormality by laparoscopy if necessary. If the patient is in the functional years, an attempt should be made to interrupt the hormone pattern with progestogen for one cycle before resorting to laparotomy. If the apparently cystic tumor does not regress within

1–2 months, surgery should be performed.

On rare occasions, tumors other than those of gonadal origin may produce steroid and thus alter the hormone pattern of the host. Adrenal tumors can exert an estrogenic or progestational effect on the endometrium and vaginal mucosa. Amenorrhea may result from pituitary or hypothalamic disorders, and thyroid dysfunction may be associated with either hypo- or hypermenorrhea.

Treatment & Prognosis

Treatment of granulosa cell tumor consists of surgical removal. These lesions may occur in the early decades of life, and, since they are bilateral in only 3–8% of cases, unilateral adnexectomy is warranted if feasible. The other gonad must be inspected thoroughly, and, if the patient has had her family or if the tumor involves both ovaries or the peritoneal structures, total hysterectomy and bilateral salpingo-oophorectomy is the procedure of choice.

If the tumor is well differentiated and confined to one ovary, no additional therapy is indicated. Nevertheless, in spite of the benign appearance of individual cells in such lesions, there are well-documented instances of recurrence as late as 15–20 years after initial therapy. These recurrences may be at an extragonadal site and may produce estrogen.

If there is extension of the neoplasm into the adjacent tissues or if the tumor lacks cellular differentiation, the postoperative therapy should be irradiation or chemotherapy.

The cure rate in well-differentiated tumors approaches 90%. Survival rates are low for patients with undifferentiated tumors regardless of treatment; however, it must be restated that the latter are *not* true granulosa cell tumors and should not be so diagnosed.

3. SERTOLI–LEYDIG CELL TUMORS & ALLIED LESIONS
(Gonadal Stromal Tumors With Tubular Differentiation; Sex Cord Tumors Including Folliculoma Lipidique; Gynandroblastoma, Arrhenoblastoma)

These rare ovarian tumors often are associated with a confusing array of features that frequently defy logical correlation of cell pattern and clinical symptomatology. Nevertheless, a basic knowledge of the histology of the gonad and its tumors will serve as an important guideline in understanding the otherwise bizarre characteristics of these lesions. The female gonad is basically a cortical structure, in contrast to the medullary male gonad. There never is a true ovarian capsule, whereas the tunica albuginea of the testis is well defined by 8–10 weeks of embryonic life. Normally, there are no sex cords in the female gonad; thus, sex-cord type tumors are expressions of pattern rather than of structure of origin.

These tumors rarely become large. They tend to be solid with a smooth capsule. The cut section (Fig 14–29) may reveal a variety of colorations, usually yellowish-brown or, if the tumor is nonfunctioning, grayish-white occasionally streaked with yellow.

Microscopically, the pattern varies strikingly depending on the type. The true Sertoli–Leydig cell

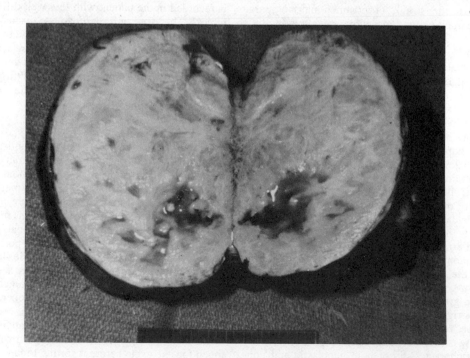

Figure 14–29. Fibrothecoma of the ovary with focal areas of cystic degeneration.

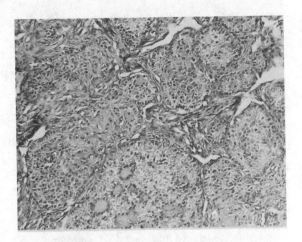

Figure 14–30. Sertoli cell tumor at the ovary (folliculoma lipidique), usually feminizing in either ovary or testes.

tumor is composed of well-developed tubular structures separated by gonadal stroma, usually with obvious luteinization, simulating the classic pattern of the testes. Germ cells are absent but, if present, should suggest an intra-abdominal testis or gonadoblastoma. Chromosome study is indicated to rule out a karyotypic abnormality.

Sertoli–Leydig cell tumors may occur at any age, and a variety of clinical manifestations may develop. Specifically, the classic Sertoli–Leydig cell tumor, the gonadal stromal lesion with tubular differentiation, and the so-called folliculoma lipidique (Fig 14–30) (or, more reasonably, the Sertoli tumor) represent neoplasms that attempt to reproduce, with more or less accuracy, the histologic components of the testes. The ability of these tumors to produce steroids seems generally unrelated to the histologic picture. Thus, a lesion composed largely of undifferentiated stroma (the previously designated "sarcomatoid" variety of arrhenoblastoma) may alter the hormone pattern of the host more strikingly than that in which the pattern closely simulates the features of the testes. Curiously, tumors in which the arrangement and cell type seem to replicate the features of the granulosa–theca cell tumor may produce masculinization of the host. Thus, because the patient's clinical profile is more important than the interesting though confusing histologic patterns, one should categorize ovarian tumors on the basis of the clinical effect—ie, masculinization, feminization, or neither—and then describe the histopathologic pattern, eg, gonadal stromal tumor with masculinization or "Sertoli cell tumor" with feminization.

If an adnexal mass is not demonstrable and the patient is masculinized, an exogenous or extragonadal source of hormone must be ruled out. Conversely, if a persistent or enlarging ovarian mass is defined, it should be removed regardless of the presence or absence of symptoms.

The Gonadal Stromal Tumor With Foci of More or Less Well Developed Tubular Structures

The cells lining the tubular structures commonly are cuboid epithelial cells, usually lower than those seen in the Sertoli–Leydig cell tumor. The cordlike arrangement of the cells will often not permit differentiation from the trabecular pattern of certain granulosa cell tumors. Actually, they may be the same because the cells of both lesions are of similar embryologic origin. Generally, the stroma is proliferative and undifferentiated, but focal "luteinization" frequently suggests Leydig or interstitial cell tumor of the testis. Stromal mitoses are not uncommon, particularly in the larger, more active elements. Nonetheless, it is rare to see more than one or 2 mitoses per high-power field, and they are usually typical of those seen in the early proliferating theca.

These patterns are classically characteristic of those seen in the so-called "arrhenoblastoma," namely: (1) the well-differentiated or "Pick's adenoma"; (2) the intermediate, composed of poorly defined tubules and gonadal stroma with foci of "interstitial cells"; and (3) the sarcomatoid or stromal tumor. Obviously, Pick's adenoma is a well-defined tubular tumor with luteinized stromal or Leydig cells. The intermediate type is well demonstrated in Fig 14–31. Such lesions are better defined as gonadal stromal tumors with varying degrees of tubular differentiation. They may be inert or may produce either androgen or estrogen. Finally, the sarcomatoid variety is a gonadal stromal tumor without identifiable tubules, and again may be steroid-producing or inert. Consequently, the term "arrhenoblastoma" simply identifies a tumor that produces an arrhenomimetic effect on the host and should be supplanted by more specific histologic identifications that will allow for better prognosis and therapy.

The classic element of the folliculoma lipidique is a tall cell with a pale cytoplasm and a small, dark

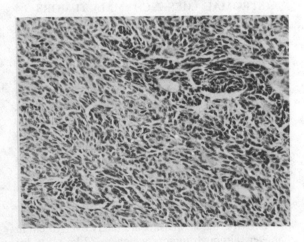

Figure 14–31. Gonadal stromal tumor. The tubular component is poorly defined.

nucleus located at the base of the cell—characteristic of the Sertoli elements in the testes. The tubules are well organized, and cellular evidence of malignancy is absent. These tumors usually are "feminizing" in both sexes.

There appears to be an association between the true Sertoli–Leydig cell tumor and Peutz-Jeghers syndrome, an autosomal dominant congenital disorder characterized by intestinal polyposis and perioral melanotic pigmentations. The folliculoid pattern with calcifications and luteinized stromal cells simulates that seen in gonadoblastoma but without germ cells.

The so-called gynandroblastoma is poorly defined. The mixture of cordlike structures, undifferentiated stroma, and the classic small dark cell of the granulosa type is not impossible, because the basic mesenchymal and "epithelial" elements of this group of tumors are of similar embryonic origin. Hence, one may expect to see many variations or combinations of the classic cells.

Treatment & Prognosis

These tumors usually pursue a benign course; malignancy develops in less than 10% of cases. Even in the more histologically aggressive lesions, the prognosis is good if the capsule is intact. They may be found in any age group but often occur in young women, and conservation of the uterus and one tube and ovary is indicated in the young patient. The contralateral ovary is the site of tumor development in approximately 5–8% of cases. Nevertheless, the opposite gonad should be investigated thoroughly. To complete the investigation, karyotyping is indicated along with x-ray and endoscopic evaluation of the intestinal canal. Karyotypes that demonstrate a Y chromosome suggest some form of dysgenesis, and the opposite gonad will frequently be abnormal, a prime site for the development of a germ cell tumor, and thus should be removed.

STROMAL (MESENCHYMAL) TUMORS
(Tumors With Variable Functional Potential, Including Fibroma, Fibrothecoma, Thecoma, and Sarcoma)

These unilateral, firm tumors often occur in postmenopausal women and represent about 5% of ovarian tumors. They arise from one or both of the basic stromal components of the ovary. There is a supporting connective tissue surrounding the vessels, lymphatics, and nerves and an undifferentiated mesenchymal component from which arises the functioning element or theca. The latter explains the endocrine potential of these lesions.

Pathology

Grossly, the neoplasms are rarely over 10 cm in diameter, although tumors weighing 22 kg (48½ lb) have been recorded. Most of these tumors are smooth, round, lobulated, and encapsulated. On cut section, they are gray-white in color with streaks of yellow thecal tissue. The more or less pure "thecomas" are yellow-orange because of the steroid-producing elements. Gritty inclusions sometimes are found.

Microscopically, fibromas and fibrothecomas are composed of both elements that make up the matrix of the ovarian cortex, ie, the supporting connective tissue and the true gonadal mesenchyme. These cells may be distinguished in most cases by the routine hematoxylin and eosin stain. The connective tissue is characterized by elongated cells containing small compact nuclei, as contrasted to the more ovoid or fusiform cells of the gonadal stromal type with their large pale nuclei, finely granular chromatin, and often prominent nucleoli.

Although pure "fibromas" develop from the supporting matrix of the so-called capsule or the perivascular or perineural connective tissue, more frequently there is an admixture of ovarian stroma (the thecalike element) and the fibrous tissue. Obviously, the opposite of the pure fibroma is the pure thecoma. In the latter, positive stains for intracellular lipid present strong circumstantial evidence of steroid production (Fig 14–32).

Degenerative changes are common, particularly in the larger tumors, and are similar to those described for uterine leiomyoma, especially hyalinization, calcification, and focal liquefaction. Malignant changes are unusual and difficult to evaluate. Mitoses are not uncommon in the proliferating fibrothecoma. In a study of these rare stromal neoplasms, it was noted that

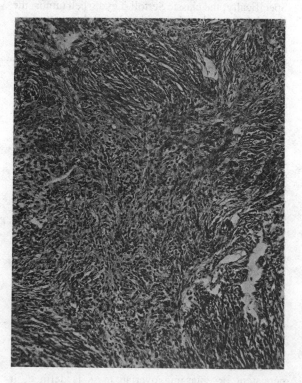

Figure 14–32. Thecoma with luteinization as noted by the increased cytoplasm in the cells of the central area.

lesions with fewer than 4 mitoses in any high-power field were associated with an excellent prognosis. In contrast, those with more than 4 mitoses were prone to local intra-abdominal recurrence. Extra-abdominal disease was not recorded.

Clinical Findings

Stromal tumors are most common in the fifth to seventh decades of life. Most are asymptomatic. Their weight may cause pedunculation of the gonad, leading to torsion, pain, and degeneration.

If a large component of the tumor is "thecal," hormone production may be sufficient to alter the biologic status of the individual. Generally, such tumors are estrogen-producing and are associated with endometrial hyperplasia or with well-differentiated cancer, particularly in the postmenopausal patient. Isolated instances of the so-called masculinizing thecoma have also been reported.

If these "fibrothecomas" develop during the menstrual years, the functioning theca may cause amenorrhea and anovulation, a symptom complex that simulates the pattern associated with granulosa–theca cell tumor or polycystic ovary syndrome. In such cases, a wide variety of endometrial proliferations associated with prolonged estrogen stimulation can be anticipated either pre- or postmenopausally.

Fibromatous tumors are associated with Meigs' (Demons-Meigs) syndrome, characterized by a solid benign tumor of the ovary and transudative hydrothorax and ascites. This symptom complex was originally reported in association with ovarian fibroma, and most cases have followed this pattern; nevertheless, other benign tumors such as struma ovarii, Brenner tumor, and thecoma have produced the classic symptom complex. Obviously, ascites may be due to malignant ovarian tumors, particularly the papillary serous neoplasms with multiple peritoneal and omental nodules. These do not qualify as cases of Meigs' syndrome, however.

In patients with this syndrome, the presenting symptoms may be abdominal distention or respiratory distress. There may be little abdominal tenderness and the tumor usually is not palpable, either because of intra-abdominal fluid accumulation or because of its small size.

The abdominal and chest fluids usually are pale straw-colored transudates containing few blood cells. Although proliferating mesothelial elements often are recognized, true malignant cells are not present. Pneumoperitoneum after paracentesis may clearly delineate the fibroma.

The mechanism responsible for the development of such large amounts of transudate in the thoracic and abdominal cavities by a relatively small benign ovarian tumor is not known. There is a direct connection between the 2 cavities through "pores" in the diaphragm or through the lymphatics.

Differential Diagnosis

Liver disease, cardiac problems, inflammatory lesions of the abdominal and thoracic structures, and a variety of malignancies must be considered in the differential diagnosis.

As with any ovarian neoplasm, the adnexal lesion must be differentiated from abnormalities of both the urinary and intestinal tracts.

Since the tumor is solid, the most common preoperative diagnosis is uterine leiomyoma. On rare occasions, if the tumor is bilateral, metastatic neoplasia should be suspected and proper preoperative studies performed in an attempt to discover a primary tumor. Although the mesenchymal tumors usually are unilateral, it is common to find foci of thecosis or adenofibromatosis in the contralateral gonad.

Treatment & Prognosis

Meigs' syndrome should be considered in every woman over 40 years of age when a relapsing unexplained pleural or peritoneal transudate is discovered.

Treatment is surgical for both diagnosis and therapy. The salvage rate with ovariectomy approaches 100%. In the younger patient, a conservative operation is in order. Since these tumors generally are found in patients 50–60 years of age, total hysterectomy and bilateral salpingo-oophorectomy is recommended. Upon removal of the fibroma, abdominal and chest fluid will usually disappear spontaneously within a week.

OVARIAN SARCOMAS

Ovarian sarcomas are rare and comprise a widely diverse group of neoplasms. They occur in various age groups depending on the histogenesis and may be classified as shown below.

Classification & Clinical Features

A. Teratoid Sarcomas: These sarcomas are found in patients under 25 years of age, and, although teratoid elements may be recognized in a majority of the cases, they are often undifferentiated, so that specific elements cannot be identified. They are asymptomatic in the early stages unless functioning teratoid elements, eg, trophoblasts, are present. The mass itself (or extensions of the tumor) produces local discomfort or evidence of other organ involvement.

The age of the patient, the rapidity of growth, and the demonstration of hormone-producing tissue should assist in establishing a presumptive diagnosis of teratoma. Nevertheless, the histopathologic diagnosis of elements such as rhabdomyoblasts or teratoid bodies is important to confirm the clinical impression and to assist in determining therapy (eg, if germ cells are present, radiation therapy should be started). However, chemotherapy offers the only hope at present for the patient with a teratoid lesion.

On rare occasions, sarcoma may develop in a preexisting benign adult or mature teratoma. Generally, these are leiomyosarcomas or fibrosarcomas. The teratoid origin may be established in some instances by identification of mature elements such as mucus-secreting epithelium in the adjacent area. In such lesions the malignancy probably arose in the smooth muscle of the gut, and the prognosis is extremely poor. Cases that we reviewed from the Ovarian Tumor Registry included no survivors.

B. Mesenchymal or Stromal Sarcomas: These tumors may be divided into (1) stromal cell sarcomas and (2) fibroleiomyosarcomas. The former are usually found in patients under 20 years of age. The histologic picture suggests that the tumors arise from the ovarian mesenchyme or stroma. In most cases, the histologic evidence of malignancy is minimal and mitoses are sparse (Fig 14–33). The prognosis is excellent if extension has not occurred at the time of initial surgery. With increased nuclear aberrations, however, the salvage rate is essentially nil. The group classified as fibroleiomyosarcoma, if, in truth, such a group exists, is found in older patients, usually over 40 years of age. In all such instances, the cellular evidence of malignancy is striking and the outcome generally is fatal, although one reported patient survived 8 years.

C. Müllerian or Paramesonephric Sarcomas: Attempts have been made to subdivide this group into mixed mesodermal tumors and carcinosarcomas. Nonetheless, as with similar lesions in the uterine fundus, this differentiation has proved to be unrealistic because the survival rates and clinical features are identical. Mixed tumors usually are diagnosed in the sixth to seventh decades of life. The initial symptom is lower abdominal pain due to extension of the tumor into the adjacent tissues.

Pathology

Grossly, these mixed mesodermal tumors rarely are large, because their local aggressive growth quickly produces pain or symptoms related to invasion of contiguous structures. Microscopically, the cellular elements vary from an irregular glandular pattern associated with abnormally proliferating stroma to the

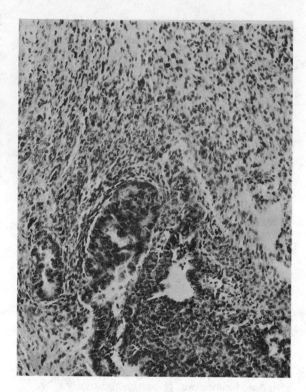

Figure 14–34. Mixed mesodermal tumor of the ovary. Both stromal and epithelial elements are malignant. (These tumors are often called carcinosarcoma.)

classic neoplasm containing cartilage, bone, or rhabdomyoblasts, in all respects similar to its counterpart in the uterine cavity (Fig 14–34). On occasion, benign endometriosis may be demonstrated in the adjacent ovary, strengthening the relationship of the tumor to the endometrium.

Treatment & Prognosis

The primary treatment for all of these lesions is operative. The salvage rate is low, even with the addition of radiation therapy or the use of chemotherapeutic agents. The exception is the tumor composed of only endometriumlike stroma. As with uterine **stromatosis,** there has been some success with the use of progestational agents in the case of primary ovarian "stromatosis," since the basic endometrial stroma may mature under the influence of such chemotherapy.

METASTATIC TUMORS

The ovary is a relatively common site of metastatic disease, particularly when the primary malignancy is in the breast or intestinal tract. These secondary ovarian cancers are challenging problems because of the marked discrepancy between the size of the primary tumor and the ovarian metastasis and because of their bizarre histologic patterns. To add to the confusion, certain lesions that develop in the ovary, al-

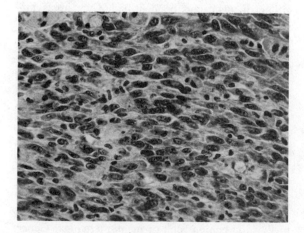

Figure 14–33. High-power magnification of a low-grade ovarian stromal sarcoma.

though previously classified as metastatic, may represent foci of malignancy developing in the upper genital canal, uterus, or uterine tube from tissues embryologically similar to the ovarian mesothelium. If surgical cases are included, about 2–4% of all ovarian neoplasms are metastatic or secondary ovarian malignancies. If autopsy material is reviewed, secondary ovarian cancer is noted in almost 10%.

Metastatic ovarian tumors are conveniently separated into 2 categories for purposes of clinical differentiation: (1) those in which the "primary" lesion has been discovered in the upper genital canal, and (2) those in which the ovarian abnormality represents either a metastatic or a secondary malignancy from some extragenital source.

Ovarian Neoplasia Associated With Other Genital Canal Malignancies

In various studies of secondary ovarian malignancy, it has been recognized that endometrial carcinoma is the most common neoplasm associated with ovarian cancer. Reviews suggest such an association in approximately 5–10% of the cases. In many instances, the ovarian tumor undoubtedly exemplifies metastatic disease, since tumor deposits are also found in the lymphatics of the hilar and adjacent area. On the other hand, there are numerous instances in which the uterine lesion is quite superficial without demonstrable myometrial or lymphatic invasion and the ovarian tumor is similarly well contained and encapsulated. Furthermore, these lesions frequently are well differentiated and follow-up has revealed a high 5-year salvage rate. In a study of 120 cases of supposedly secondary ovarian malignancies, there were 32 cases in which ovarian and endometrial lesions were associated with a 5-year salvage rate of approximately 50%, an unusual and unrealistic survival rate for true metastatic cancer.

Considering the common embryonic origin of both the ovarian mesothelium or coelomic epithelium and the endometrium, it is not surprising that tumors may arise at separate foci and thus not represent extension of metastasis. This thesis has proved to be true for tumors arising in the lower genital canal, ie, the cervix, vagina, vulva, and perianal area, where the uniform stratified epithelium covering this anogenital region frequently responds at multiple sites to a local carcinogenic stimulus.

The tubal epithelium, which is of the same embryologic origin as the epithelium lining the ovary and uterus, undoubtedly is a site where cancer may develop. The tube is often studied only superficially because of its association with the ebullient ovary. In instances where adequate investigation has been carried out, however, evidences of atypia of the tubal epithelium in association with ovarian cancer have been established. There have also been instances in which tumors have arisen at separate sites (eg, both tube and ovary) and in which the salvage rate has been better than that expected for metastatic disease. Finally, it should be recalled that the epithelial lining of many cystic ovarian tumors, particularly the common papillary serous variety, is identical with that noted in the oviduct.

Clinical Findings

The age range of patients with metastatic disease arising from a genital canal cancer is the same as that of those with the primary lesion. Endometrial cancer frequently occurs in the perimenopausal years, and the "secondary tumors" of the ovary often will thus be found in the same age group: the fifth and sixth decades. However, cancers of this type have been reported in the late third and fourth decades, as have the occasional endometrial cancers. The genesis of uterine adenocarcinoma has consistently been associated with prolonged unopposed estrogen stimulation. The same sequence of events may relate to the development of ovarian "endometrioid" cancer, but other factors are undoubtedly involved in ovarian neoplasia. There is little evidence to support the "estrogen theory" of development of these tumors.

Metastatic disease from the lower genital canal to the ovary is extremely rare, accounting for only 1–2% of cases. Furthermore, in most instances these tumors represent direct invasion into the ovary through the broad ligament rather than by lymphatic or vascular extension. This is not surprising because the lymphatic drainage from the cervix and lower genital canal avoids the ovary.

Differential Diagnosis

The presence of an adnexal tumor demands thorough study to rule out intestinal or urinary tract disease. Obviously, investigation for "primary" lesions in the genital canal other than the ovary should be carried out at the same time. The opposite of this statement is also true: When an endometrial cancer has been discovered, careful study should be instituted to eliminate the possibility that it does not represent either a second focus or an extension from the adjacent organs, particularly if a mass is present in the adnexal regions.

Pathology

A. Gross: True metastatic ovarian cancer commonly is bilateral (Fig 14–35). In cases of multicentric foci, however, this is not necessarily true. It is also important to recognize that in approximately 25% of cases of metastatic disease the ovary is not palpably enlarged. Nevertheless, if the ovarian tumor is metastatic, gross enlargement is more common.

B. Microscopic: Tumors of multicentric foci often are histologically similar, ie, the ovarian tumor and the endometrial lesion are classically adenocarcinomas rather than one of the more typical ovarian patterns (eg, papillary). Similarly, the tubal lesion, which is primarily papillary, may show the same pattern in the ovary. The more anaplastic the neoplasm, the more difficult it will be to define a specific cell type, and thus both lesions may be simply classified as undifferentiated cancer. Furthermore, in the latter

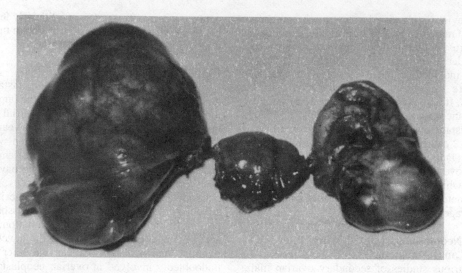

Figure 14–35. Bilateral solid metastatic cancer. In this instance, the primary tumor was in the intestinal tract and the microscopic picture is that of the Krukenberg type.

case, the tumor usually is so aggressive that it would be impossible to decide whether 2 separate foci existed at one time, since widespread invasion into the pelvic viscera is the rule.

Treatment & Prognosis

Treatment essentially consists of surgical removal. If an endometrial cancer is associated with an adnexal mass, it is important to do a D&C first, because the ovarian tumor may represent a second site of neoplasia and one must identify a functioning ovarian tumor that may produce the endometrial lesion. Moreover, the elimination of a pelvic inflammatory mass that would complicate radiation therapy is also important. Following ablation of the uterus and adnexa, the need for irradiation or chemotherapy will depend upon the extent and histologic characteristics of the neoplasm. As with most endometrial cancers, a progestogen in high doses is the chemotherapeutic agent of choice. When the tumor is confined to the pelvis, irradiation treatment probably will be beneficial.

The results depend largely on whether the ovarian tumor represents a second primary or truly a metastatic lesion. In the former instance, the prognosis is astonishingly good, with, as noted above, a 50% 5-year survival rate without tumor. On the other hand, if the ovarian lesion actually is metastatic, there will be few survivors.

IV. SECONDARY OVARIAN NEOPLASMS

METASTATIC TUMORS FROM AN EXTRAGENITAL PRIMARY MALIGNANCY

In 10% of cases of fatal malignant disease in women, the ovary is found to be secondarily involved by metastasis or extension of cancer, usually from the uterus. The gastrointestinal tract and breast are the most common primary sites of metastatic ovarian neoplasia.

Pathology

A. Gross: Metastatic tumors are bilateral in approximately 75% of cases. They often attain massive size and fill the pelvis and abdomen. Nevertheless, in about 25% of cases in which the ovaries were removed as a routine part of the treatment for breast cancer, the ovaries, although containing metastatic foci, were not grossly enlarged. These metastatic tumors generally are solid and bosselated and may be freely movable, thus superficially suggesting benign disease. On cut section the tissue usually is firm, but there may be areas of degeneration, particularly if the tumor is large. It should be noted that all metastatic tumors are not solid; if the primary is one of the mucin-producing lesions from the gastrointestinal tract, the ovarian tumor may be quite similar to the primary mucinous cystadenocarcinoma in the ovary.

B. Microscopic: The cellular details of metastatic ovarian cancer are confusing and contradictory. For example, when the primary lesion is in the breast, the patterns vary from one that accurately simulates the initial lesion to a totally undifferentiated diffuse cellular invasion of the stroma. In spite of this apparent lack of differentiation, the classic pattern is that of cells "filing in" to the stroma. It may actually be difficult to distinguish these from the stromal cells themselves because of the diffuse infiltration. The characteristic histologic feature of these lesions is the diversity of the patterns in immediately adjacent areas of the ovary. If the section from the tumor reveals a definite adenomatous pattern contiguous with a diffusely infiltrative one, metastatic disease should be high on the list of differential diagnoses. Finally, metastatic breast tumors may even suggest a lymphoma with large areas of small dark cells invading the ovarian mesenchyme. In most instances, epithelial elements can be identified in the area adjacent to these lymphoid infiltrates. In the metastatic breast tumor, it is important to identify an epithelial component in the ovary and to recognize the diverse patterns that are typical of these tumors.

As noted above, histologically, the tumor metastatic from the gastrointestinal tract may closely simulate the primary mucin-secreting adenocarcinoma of the ovary. Large locules lined by tall columnar mucin-secreting epithelium are separated by fibrous trabeculae. The epithelium may be quite well differentiated, disguising the aggressiveness of metastatic cancer. In other areas, the epithelium may become poorly differentiated, and only the occasional "signet cell" will serve to identify the tumor as one producing intracellular mucin. Thus, large areas of mucin-secreting epithelium may be associated with the diffusely infiltrative pattern more typical of the Krukenberg tumor.

The Krukenberg tumor is interesting because of its unusual histologic features and its functioning potential. It usually originates in the stomach, intestine, gallbladder, or, rarely, the breast or thyroid. Grossly, it is buff-colored, firm, solid, moderately large, lobulated, often kidney-shaped, nonadherent, and bilateral. A heavy but easily stripped capsule covers the parenchyma, which is composed of firm and softer, often minutely cystic, tissue.

Two microscopic features are diagnostic: (1) coarse, abundant, occasionally edematous stroma, and (2) islands of moderately large epithelial cells with mucin-laden or vacuolated cytoplasm and eccentrically placed, small hyperchromatic nuclei. Such cells resemble signet rings. If the tumor does not display these classic details, it is not termed a Krukenberg tumor but simply a metastatic ovarian cancer.

Clinical Findings

These neoplasms have been found in all age groups, although the great majority of patients are in the fifth to sixth decades of life.

Symptoms are often related to the primary tumor. Nevertheless, in many instances the mass of the ovarian tumor may overshadow the initial lesion. This is particularly true in cases of Krukenberg tumor. Here, the patient may complain first of the abdominal discomfort due to the tumor or ascites. Physical examination often reveals a mass filling the entire pelvis, perhaps rising to or above the umbilicus. Even

thorough study in such cases may not reveal a primary lesion, and only after histopathologic review of the neoplasm is the true nature of the tumor complex appreciated. Dyspepsia, postprandial epigastric discomfort, slight weight loss, and mild anemia may then be noted. Ascites is uncommon. On rare occasions, menorrhagia or amenorrhea may be the presenting complaint. Except for the discomfort produced by the abdominal mass, the genital canal symptoms are rarely associated with metastatic ovarian neoplasia.

Gastric washings occasionally recover cancer cells. Achlorhydria and a positive stool guaiac test for occult blood may be recorded. The x-ray appearance of the lesion in the stomach is not striking, considering the size of the ovarian tumors.

Differential Diagnosis

A most interesting aspect of metastatic ovarian tumors has been the occasional dramatic demonstration of atypical hormone activity. For example, several tumors of the Krukenberg type diagnosed during pregnancy have caused masculinization of the mother.

Bilateral solid tumors of the ovary may frequently represent metastatic lesions. Such findings on pelvic examination demand thorough study to rule out or establish the presence of a primary malignancy. The most suspicious areas must be the breast and gastrointestinal tract, particularly the stomach. The gallbladder, thyroid, pancreas, and kidneys have been reported as primary sites for metastatic ovarian cancer.

Bilateral adnexal enlargements frequently are inflammatory, but the latter are cystic and adherent. Other bilateral cystic tumors may be teratomas. Solid ovarian enlargements may represent enlarged ovaries of the Stein-Leventhal or Brenner-fibroma complex.

The term Krukenberg tumor, like most eponyms, is often misapplied. Not all metastatic tumors from the gut can be classified as Krukenberg tumors. This neoplasm has a unique infiltrative pattern and an associated heavy stromal reaction. There are primary breast tumors in which the pattern described by Krukenberg is accurately replicated, including the mucocellular nature of the infiltrating cells. Thus, in order for a lesion to qualify as a Krukenberg tumor, it should fulfill the criteria initially described by Krukenberg (Fig 14–36). The only justification for continuing to categorize certain metastatic ovarian tumors as Krukenberg tumors is the characteristic histologic picture and the unusual endocrinologic abnormalities that may be associated with such neoplasms.

The tumor represents a metastatic lesion in most instances, but the mode of spread of the neoplastic elements is controversial. Direct implantation by intraperitoneal floaters seems to be an untenable proposal in view of the intact capsule. The concept of retrograde lymphatic spread is at best a nebulous one. Vascular extension with filtering out of the tumor cells in the subcapsular channels seems to be the most acceptable explanation. The mucin-secreting epithelium at separate sites such as the ovary and gut is a rare possibility.

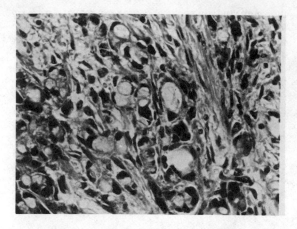

Figure 14–36. Metastatic ovarian cancer. Note the "signet cells," characteristic of the mucocellular nature of the tumor.

In light of the latter theory, it is well known that there are primary Krukenberg tumors, ie, the mucin-producing lesion of the ovary may demonstrate all of the histologic features necessary to fulfill the criteria for the diagnosis of Krukenberg tumor. If a patient survives more than 5 years without the appearance of a primary malignancy elsewhere in the intestinal tract or breast, or if she dies and thorough autopsy fails to reveal such a primary, the lesion may be considered to be a nonmetastatic Krukenberg tumor. Actually, foci of stromal infiltration suggestive of Krukenberg's tumor may be discerned in many primary mucinous carcinomas of the ovary.

Treatment

Removal of the tumor mass will in many instances afford the patient relief from local abdominal symptoms. Furthermore, the adjunctive therapy now available, particularly for breast tumors, may enable the patient to survive for some time and be relieved of the potential hormonal effect generated by the tumor. Moreover, the rare primary Krukenberg tumor may be cured by total hysterectomy and bilateral salpingo-oophorectomy. One such patient has survived for over 20 years. Consequently, it is important to perform an exploratory laparotomy with removal of the tumor to establish an accurate diagnosis and to determine the best postoperative therapeutic measures.

Chemotherapy may be palliative. Cyclophosphamide often retards the growth of solid tumors; 5-fluorouracil may suppress metastatic bowel tumors.

Quinacrine hydrochloride is a valuable agent in the control of neoplastic effusions. The drug has anti-inflammatory rather than cancericidal properties and causes surface fibrosis and adhesions that reduce fluid production. Quinacrine must be administered intraperitoneally. It is effective in limiting carcinomatous effusions originating in the ovaries, gastrointestinal system, breast, and lymphoid tissue. Fever, regional pain, nausea, and ileus are transient dose-related side-effects. Discomfort is relieved by analgesics. Bowel stasis usually is self-limited.

Intracavitary therapy requires initial trial dosage not to exceed 200 mg for peritoneal effusions. Partial evacuation of the fluid before treatment is recommended. Each 100 mg of drug should be diluted in 5 mL of effusion fluid or sterile water. The average dose of quinacrine for control of ascites of malignant origin is 400–800 mg daily for 3–5 consecutive days. For pleural effusions due to cancer, the usual dose is 200–400 mg daily for 4–5 days. The maintenance dose of quinacrine (0.2–1 g) depends upon the site and extent of cancer and the patient's tolerance.

Prognosis

The prognosis is extremely poor regardless of therapy.

V. GERM CELL TUMORS

These neoplasms may contain germ cells as the predominant component, may demonstrate an abnormal gonadal development in which the germ cell is present atypically, or may consist of mature or immature embryonic or extraembryonic elements that arise from the germ cell. A system of classification can be constructed as follows:

(1) Dysgerminoma (germinoma): Neoplasm consisting primarily of germ cells.
(2) Dysgenetic gonad (?gonadoblastoma) and allied abnormalities.
(3) Teratomas:
    (a) Mature or adult teratomas.
    (b) Immature teratomas: Embryonic or extraembryonic.
    (c) Combination of (a) and (b).

DYSGERMINOMA

This tumor, perhaps better known as a germinoma, occurs principally in young females—50% in patients 20 years of age or younger and 90% in patients under the age of 30. The seminoma, a similar tumor in the male, is also recognized in younger males. The neoplasms occur not only in the gonad but also at sites along the tract of germ cell migration, ie, the midline of the body, potentially from the coccyx to the pineal gland.

The dysgerminoma comprises approximately 1% of all germ cell tumors and 0.1% of all malignant ovarian neoplasms.

Histogenesis

In many respects, the dysgerminoma replicates the pattern seen in the primitive female gonad. The unencapsulated germ cell continues to proliferate until final encapsulation or death occurs. The nests of germ cells and associated undifferentiated stroma are routine findings in the female gonad between the embryonic ages of 6 weeks and 6 months. Consequently, the dysgenetic gonad, with its bizarre, poorly encapsulated germ cell aggregates, is a fertile field for development of dysgerminoma.

Pathology

A. Gross: The tumor is rather rubbery in consistency, smooth, rounded, thinly encapsulated, nonadherent, and brown or grayish-brown. Basically a solid neoplasm, it may show areas of softening due to degeneration. Furthermore, if it is associated with a teratoma, as it is in 3–5% of cases, the latter may develop cystic areas. Nevertheless, it should be recalled that the teratoma found in combination with a dysgerminoma usually is one that contains embryonic or immature elements and that these components are most frequently solid.

On section the surface is edematous, soft, and almost brainlike in consistency. There are no gross septa—only a tenuous connective tissue framework.

The tumors generally are unilateral. Often the lesions are quite small, measuring only 3–5 cm. Nonetheless, tumors that fill the pelvis have been recorded.

B. Microscopic: Dysgerminomas are composed of various-sized nests of germ cells separated by fibrous trabeculae (Fig 14–37). The latter are infiltrated

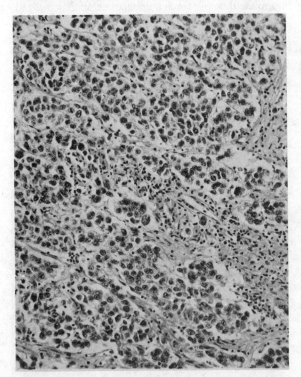

Figure 14–37. Classic histologic picture of dysgerminoma. Note nests of germ cells of various sizes separated by fibrous trabeculae.

with lymphocytes. Giant cell formation may occasionally be associated with the lymphocytic infiltrate. Anaplasia and pleomorphism may be noted, but histopathologic grading is impossible. Poor prognostic signs are rupture of the capsule, bilaterality, and periaortic node invasion.

The significance of the lymphocytes has not been established. Some investigators believe that they represent an antibody response—an attempt by the organism to prevent further proliferation. Similarly, the giant cells may indicate an immune response; nevertheless, neither of these features has proved to be of prognostic significance. Although few comments are made about the cellular components of the aggregates except for the obvious germ cell, it seems quite likely that undifferentiated stromal or "granulosa-Sertoli cell" elements are present also. This is particularly true of lesions arising from the testis, in which the Sertoli and germ cells are mixed.

Clinical Findings

The tumors generally are asymptomatic and are found either on routine examination, especially when they have reached palpable size, or when they have extended beyond the original site. In the latter instance they frequently are found in the retroperitoneum or mediastinum. Acute pain may result if the thin capsule ruptures. Weakly false-positive pregnancy tests have been reported in some cases. Malignancy must be suspected when a neoplasm grows rapidly, is firmly adherent or bilateral, or is accompanied by ascites.

On occasion, a dysgerminoma and teratoma are associated; if functioning elements are present in the latter, the host may undergo endocrinologic change. For example, trophoblast in the teratoma may produce gonadotropin and cause precocity in the child. Conversely, in the postmenarcheal girl, a positive pregnancy test may announce the functional character of the tumor elements.

In the past it has been suggested that the dysgerminoma was associated with maldevelopment of secondary sexual characteristics, with the development of a pseudohermaphrodite. In most cases, these alterations are simply expressions of the patient's age at the time the tumor usually occurs (the menarcheal years). Nevertheless, it must be appreciated that the dysgerminoma often develops in a dysgenetic gonad. Thus, the patient should be studied thoroughly to rule out any chromosomal aberration.

Other nonfunctioning ovarian tumors (eg, teratoma, cystadenoma) must be considered in the differential diagnosis.

Treatment

Ovariectomy is required. The opposite ovary should be inspected and biopsied, since minute foci of dysgerminoma elements can be discovered only by microscopic examination, which is true of 50% of bilateral lesions. If bilateral involvement is present or the tumor has spread beyond the confines of the gonad, total hysterectomy and bilateral salpingo-oophorectomy should be performed. Conversely, if the tumor is unilateral, a unilateral procedure is preferable, especially since 90% of such tumors occur in young women under 30 years of age. If metastases occur or if the tumor is bilateral or spread to other areas has occurred, radiation therapy is still effective in many cases.

Prognosis

If the dysgerminoma is unilateral and encapsulated, the salvage rate with simple unilateral adnexectomy approximates 90%. Because the tumors arise in young individuals, a conservative approach is imperative. In our recent study of 158 dysgerminomas, there was a 95% 5-year survival rate regardless of size in stage IA lesions. Obviously, when the tumor has spread beyond the confines of the gonad, occurs in an older patient, or is bilateral, more extensive surgery will be necessary. Finally, the germ cell is extremely sensitive to radiation therapy. The prognosis, with adequate irradiation, is good even when metastases have occurred. Recently, triple chemotherapy has been used effectively in patients with metastatic disease who have failed to respond to irradiation.

Reports in the literature suggest that the 70–75% 5-year salvage rate usually cited is much too high and that dysgerminoma really is much more aggressive and less responsive to therapy than is sometimes believed to be the case. One explanation of this apparent discrepancy may be failure to recognize teratoid elements in the neoplasm. Such associations are not uncommon; eg, in a study of 97 malignant teratomas, dysgerminoma was found in almost 30% of cases. Consequently, if the teratoid or immature elements are present but not diagnosed, the prognosis is poor. Furthermore, if teratoid elements are noted, radiation therapy is not the treatment of choice because teratomatas generally are radioresistant (see Teratomas, below).

DYSGENETIC GONAD & ALLIED CONDITIONS

These abnormalities usually are found in patients with karyotypic abnormalities. The dysgenetic gonad is diagnosed only if a tumor develops or if the patient is investigated because of ambiguous internal or external genitalia. Ovarian tumors arising in such situations most commonly are dysgerminomas, although teratomas are a distinct possibility.

Histologically, gonadoblastoma resembles the dysgenetic gonad in many respects. The involved gonad may be no larger than the normal ovary. Similar alterations have been noted in a "streak type" gonad, but the germ cell is the absent feature of the latter, so the "germ cell" tumor does not arise in the "XO" gonad. Thus, the critical feature of such abnormal gonads is the presence of the Y chromosome.

Classically, the gonadoblastoma is found in phenotypically normal individuals. Most of these indi-

viduals are females, but on careful analysis they regularly demonstrate karyotypic abnormalities, almost always including a Y element. In a recent case, this Y chromosomal component was found to be only a small fluorescent fragment. The patient was a previously diagnosed XO phenotypic female who had had a dysgerminoma with Sertoli cell tumor diagnosed in the contralateral ovary.

Pathology

The gonadoblastoma contains 4 key features: (1) the unencapsulated germ cell, always a potential threat as a nidus for tumor development; (2) an attempt at tubule formation, ie, cords or strands of Sertolilike cells; (3) a folliculoid pattern with nests of granulosa cells surrounding large, eosinophilic bodies; and (4) focal calcifications (Fig 14–38). The latter are occasionally demonstrable on roentgenography.

Treatment & Prognosis

Both gonads must be studied carefully; hence, bilateral adnexectomy is the operation of choice. It has been suggested that since most neoplasms, usually dysgerminomas, arise after puberty, surgery can be postponed until normal growth has been achieved. Nevertheless, 2–5% of the tumors arise prior to puberty. Thus, prompt treatment is the procedure of choice. Since malignancy arising in this context is rare, the uterus may be retained. After surgery, the phenotypic normal female can be placed on cyclic hormone therapy. Such a therapeutic approach avoids

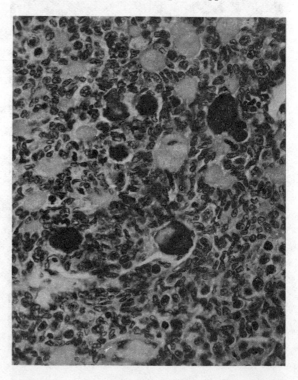

Figure 14–38. Gonadoblastoma with folliculoid pattern, focal calcifications, and concretions.

the psychologic trauma that may result from the initial diagnosis and the ultimate necessity for removal of all of the internal genitalia.

TERATOMA

The teratoma is one of the most fascinating of all neoplasms. The various elements that may make up a teratoma represent structures that arise from the fertilized egg: (1) the extraembryonic elements, primarily the trophoblast and the endoderm of the amnion; and (2) embryonic elements, mature or immature.

Incidence

Teratomas may arise either in the gonad (most common) or in the midline of the body, the areas in which the germ cell is found in embryonic life. The gonadal teratomas, which appear in the first decade of life, often are composed of immature tissues or germ cells. Extragonadal lesions that arise in the midline of the body are composed of mature elements in 60–70% of cases.

The benign cystic teratoma is quite common and comprises 12–15% of all true ovarian neoplasms. Although the varieties that occur in the first decade make up only 2–3% of all teratomas, they are the most frequent ovarian neoplasm to be found during this time of life.

Histogenesis

Most investigators regard parthenogenetic development of the tumor from the basic germ cell as the theory that is best supported by evidence. Nonetheless, the possible union of haploid cells within the mature follicle is another possible origin. Other less likely ones are a fetus in fetus (an aberrant form of twinning) and the segregation of immature cells during embryogenesis.

Pathology

The teratoma may contain either embryonic or extraembryonic elements, and the former may be either mature or immature. The mature tissues are easily recognized, eg, skin, hair, adipose and muscle tissues, bone, teeth, and cartilage. The extraembryonic elements are basically trophoblast and the endodermal sinus. The mesoblast is difficult to identify, since the cells are nonspecific. Finally, the poorly differentiated neuroblastic tissue provides the best means of demonstrating the importance of maturation. If these tumors extend beyond the ovary, they may show both differentiated and undifferentiated elements. If differentiation and excision are complete, the prognosis is excellent. Conversely, the lesion may be fatal if such maturation is poor. Thus, the malignant feature of the teratoma is well demonstrated by inability of the tissues to mature.

Clinical Findings

As is true also of most ovarian neoplasms, the teratoma is usually asymptomatic. It may become large enough to produce local pressure and vague abdominal discomfort. Menstrual irregularities are rare, and, because the teratoma is the most common true ovarian neoplasm that complicates pregnancy, infertility does not seem to be an associated problem. Very occasionally, these tumors are recognized when calcifications or teeth are identified on a routine x-ray film of the abdomen (Fig 14–39). Rarely, complications precipitate an emergency operation. Torsion, with resultant acute abdominal pain, obstipation, and vomiting, may be associated with infarction or rupture of the tumor (Fig 14–40). Discharge of the sebaceous contents into the abdominal cavity results in chemical peritonitis. A late complication may be the development of fistulas with drainage of the contents of the teratoma into the bladder, bowel, or vagina or onto the abdominal wall. Malignant change in a primarily benign cystic teratoma is uncommon. When this does

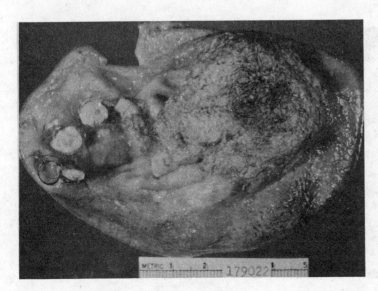

Figure 14–39. Portion of "dermoid cyst" with a section of the mandible and well-developed teeth.

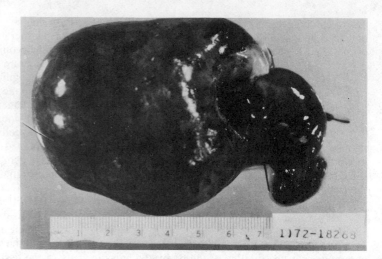

Figure 14–40. Torsion of an ovarian cyst with infarction. The histologic features of the cyst are often so distorted by the vascular occlusion that classification is impossible.

occur, it is often a squamous cell carcinoma. The incidence of malignant alteration is 0.5% at the author's institution.

Special varieties of teratoma may produce unusual symptoms. Thyroid preponderance (struma ovarii) is uncommon, although small foci of thyroid tissue are identified in 12–15% of adult teratomas. Struma ovarii may be functional and may produce classic symptoms of hyperthyroidism (Fig 14–41). Furthermore, a variety of neoplastic alterations may arise in these ovarian strumas (Fig 14–42). In addition to the thyroid lesions, the ovarian carcinoid may be of teratoid origin (Fig 14–43), and there have been instances in which the classic carcinoid syndrome has developed in association with these neoplasms even without liver metastases. If the carcinoid is bilateral, it is almost certainly metastatic, whereas the unilateral tumor is teratoid.

Treatment & Prognosis

The treatment of these tumors is surgical. Although teratoma in an adult is generally benign, it commonly occurs during the early reproductive years. Thus, it is best to resect the tumor from the ovary even though only a small amount of normal-appearing ovarian tissue can be salvaged. This fragment of capsule contains the germ cells and may be important for future reproduction. The success of conservative therapy has been repeatedly documented. Obviously, the opposite ovary should be investigated thoroughly, because bilaterality occurs in approximately 15–20% of cases. However, bisection of the contralateral gonad is to be avoided, since adhesions and inclusion cysts are the common results of trauma to the ovary. The ovaries must be palpated carefully, since more than one "dermoid" may be found in the same ovary. Nevertheless, if the tumor in one ovary is benign, a germ cell neoplasm in the other gonad is routinely of similar benign nature.

Secondary malignancy arising in a primarily benign teratoma is most commonly squamous cell carcinoma. The prognosis depends on the gross extent of

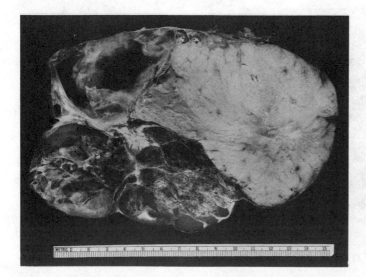

Figure 14–41. Teratoma with struma ovarii. The cystic area in the upper left is a mucinous cyst. The lower left segment is thyroid tissue. In the upper right the solid tumor shows a low-grade "fetal adenoma" of the thyroid.

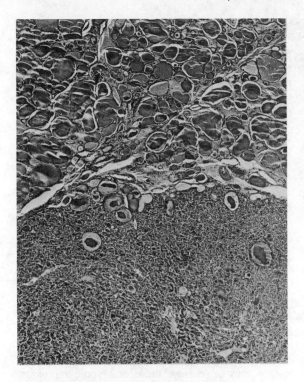

Figure 14–42. Thyroid tissue with fetal adenomatous change in an ovarian struma.

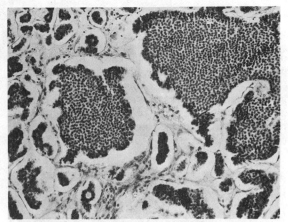

Figure 14–43. Carcinoid in the ovary.

the tumor at the time of diagnosis. Adjunctive therapy is not usually of value, although total pelvic irradiation has been the most commonly employed postoperative treatment. As is the case with most ovarian neoplasia, thoroughness of the initial surgery is most important—ie, careful evaluation of the extent of disease and removal of as much tumor as possible without jeopardizing immediate survival.

Extraembryonal teratomas almost always occur in patients in the first 2 decades of life and are usually either choriocarcinoma or one of the 2 yolk sac varieties (endodermal sinus tumor or polyvesicular vitelline tumor). They may occur in combination with other histologic patterns such as dysgerminoma or (rarely) mature or immature embryonic lesions. The biologic marker for the endodermal sinus tumor is alphafetoprotein, which may be used to identify the variety of tumor by immunoperoxidase stain of the tissue or to follow the progress of therapy by study of the protein in the serum. The usual concentration of alphafetoprotein in such lesions is 1000 ng/mL. The trophoblastic neoplasm is, as usual, identified by the levels of chorionic gonadotropin in the serum or tissue.

These lesions are always unilateral, and, since the patients are young, removal of the contralateral gonad and uterus is unnecessary. It is essential to start triple chemotherapy immediately. Generally, combination therapy with *m*ethotrexate, *d*actinomycin, and *c*yclophosphamide (MAC) has been preferred for choriocarcinoma and *v*incristine, *d*actinomycin, and *c*yclophosphamide (VAC) for the yolk sac tumor. Recently,

combination therapy with bleomycin, vinblastine, and cisplatin has been found to be an effective substitute for the VAC regimen in testicular tumors. This regimen is more toxic than VAC. The medications are given at 4- to 6-week intervals for 12 months if tolerated. Whereas there were few if any survivors in the past, recent studies have reported many 2-year survivors and a few 5-year survivors. Two normal full-term pregnancies have occurred following such rigorous therapy, indicating that conservative surgical therapy is justified.

The lesions that contain immature tissue demonstrate the importance of the ability of the tissue to mature. Immature neural tissue may be present in the ovarian tumor, and "extragonadal foci" have been recognized throughout the peritoneal cavity. Maturation at a secondary site has even occurred in some instances and the patient has survived. Everything should be done to maintain life in these patients in the hope that maturation may take place. Therefore, repeat surgery is indicated for recurrences if extra-abdominal disease is not identified. Triple chemotherapy may prolong life until the hoped-for maturation can take place.

VI. PAROVARIAN TUMORS

These tumors generally are classified as ovarian neoplasms, but it is obvious from their situation and the elements from which they arise that they represent new growths involving the gonad only secondarily. In a study of the embryonic ovary, the structures that play major roles in the genesis of these lesions can be readily identified in the parovarian region. Specifically, they are the mesonephric duct, tubules, and glomeruli, the rete ovarii, and the neural elements with their investment of specialized stroma. In combination, the latter undoubtedly represent the basic elements involved in the formation of certain tumors, many with a functional potential.

PAROVARIAN CYSTS

Parovarian cysts that lie between the tube and ovary, usually near the distal end of the broad ligament, rarely become larger than 3–4 cm in diameter (Fig 14–44). Nevertheless, on rare occasions they may grow to extreme proportions, rising to the level of the umbilicus to fill the entire pelvis. Occasionally, small cysts, or hydatids, of the parovarian type arise from the end of the tube or broad ligament.

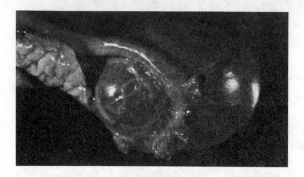

Figure 14–44. Parovarian cyst. Note the orientation of the cyst to the fimbriated end of the oviduct.

Pathology

These cysts were thought to develop from the remnants of the mesonephric system, ie, the duct and its tubules. A thorough histologic study suggests, however, that most of these tumors are paramesonephric in origin. The lining elements may be flattened as a result of pressure exerted within the cystic cavity, but where they are intact the classic cell types seen in the oviduct can be easily demonstrated. Consequently, most of these cysts represent dilated, blind accessory lumens of the tube, undoubtedly produced by the embryologic compression of the distal end between the large receding pronephros and the mesonephric body. Recognition of the tubal origin of these lesions is important because "papillae" occasionally have been thought to arise from the internal lining. Careful evaluation of such projections reveals that they are not true papillae but are actually the classic mucosal folds of the tube that have not been completely flattened by the pressure within the cyst.

Clinical Findings

These cysts are only found in postpubertal women. As with most nonmalignant cysts, these abnormalities are asymptomatic unless they reach palpable size, produce pressure symptoms, or become infarcted by torsion.

Differential Diagnosis

It may be difficult to differentiate parovarian from true ovarian cysts. Such a distinction is of academic importance because both should be treated surgically to establish the true nature of the problem.

Treatment

As with most adnexal tumors, surgical removal is of major importance to alleviate symptoms and to establish an accurate pathologic diagnosis. In the removal of these tumors, particularly if they are large, one must recall that the ureter may be buried in the posterior wall of the cyst. Furthermore, the blood supply to the tube may be jeopardized during a procedure for enucleation of the broad ligament tumor. This may necessitate removal of the tube or the ovary.

Prognosis

After removal of a parovarian cyst, the prognosis is excellent.

MESONEPHROMA
(Metamesonephroma)

Remnants of the mesonephric system may be found in sections of the broad ligament or parovarian region. The mesonephric glomerulus is characterized by a central papillary infolding with a "hobnail" epithelial lining and a clear cell component of the entering tubules. Thus, clear cell or mesonephroid lesions may arise from these embryonic remnants. Nonetheless, the genesis of most of these tumors can be explained by heterotopic alteration of the germinal epithelium or mesothelium, an origin similar to that of the other more common epithelial neoplasms of the ovary. Tumors of a similar nature have been described in the cervix and vagina. They may arise either from mesonephric or paramesonephric structures. In the author's opinion, the mesonephric and paramesonephric epithelia arise from the same basic cell, ie, the mesothelium, the only feature of importance being the biologic differentiation of these tumors. Because there are relatively few pure parovarian mesonephroid tumors, it is difficult to describe a classic picture.

Pathology

Histologically, the tumor is characterized by clear cells in the so-called Schiller pattern. The format recapitulates the mesonephric glomerulus, with papillary infolding and hobnail epithelium. The actual origin of the clear cell remains obscure. The entire picture is similar to that seen in clear cell carcinoma of the kidney, in which both the typical tall pale cells and the papillary structures are readily seen (Fig 14–45). Most epithelial tumors of the ovary arise from the basic mesothelium; thus, "clear cell" areas may be recognized in many neoplasms, especially well-differentiated ones in which cell types can be distinguished.

Clinical Findings

The clinical aspects of this lesion do not differ from those of the true ovarian tumor.

Differential Diagnosis

These solid tumors involve the ovary early. Thus,

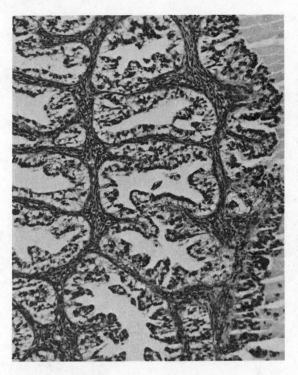

Figure 14–45. Clear cell carcinoma of the parovarian region. Origin in mesonephric or paramesonephric tissues.

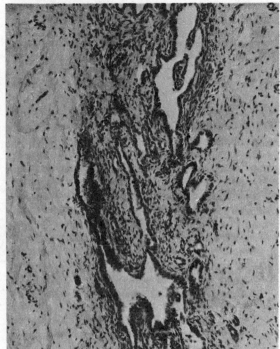

Figure 14–46. Rete ovarii. Note the intricate adenomatous pattern, the low cuboid epithelium, and the surrounding "stromal reaction."

when they have attained any appreciable size, they cannot be separated from true ovarian neoplasia. All pelvic enlargements should be studied thoroughly to rule out urinary tract or intestinal disease.

Treatment

The principal therapy, for both diagnostic and therapeutic purposes, is laparotomy. Although 60% of the mesonephroid tumors were found to be unilateral in the author's most recent series, this does not justify less than total hysterectomy and bilateral salpingo-oophorectomy. Adjunctive radiation or chemotherapy is indicated when incomplete operations are performed, ie, when tumor remains in the pelvis. These neoplasms occasionally are associated with endometriosis. Hence, progestogen treatment should be considered.

In addition to the possibility that a tumor recapitulating the features of the mesonephric glomerulus and its associated ductal system may develop in the parovarian area, there are neoplastic potentialities of the rete system. The latter are found in the hilar area of the normal adult ovary in almost all cases (Fig 14–46). The sometimes simple but often intricate retia ovarii are lined by a low, flattened cuboid epithelium. The metaplastic alterations in this epithelium with proliferations of the surrounding stroma will produce the classic picture of the Brenner tumor. Although a majority of such lesions are microscopic findings, the histologic features may justify

a diagnois of Brenner tumor. Other potential neoplastic alterations of the rete tubules and the adjacent hilar cells will be discussed later.

HILAR CELL TUMOR

These neoplasms classically occur in the peri- or early postmenopausal patient but are extremely rare and usually exert an arrhenomimetic effect on the host.

Clinical Findings

The characteristic symptoms are body and facial hirsutism, alopecia (Fig 14–47), enlargement of the clitoris (Fig 14–48), and, on rare occasions, deepening of the voice. Curiously, in some cases the endometrium is hyperplastic. The association of apparent masculinizing and feminizing features is incongruous; nevertheless, the classic large, eosinophilic "luteinized" type cell is known to produce a variety of steroids, depending on the local and systemic stimuli.

Most of these tumors occur in the early postmenopausal period, and the development may be due to stimulation and proliferation of the "hilar cells" by the elevated pituitary gonadotropins normally present after the menopause. Even in the nontumorous state, "hilar cells" are most easily recognized in the postmenopausal period, when the cells that surround the nerves become "luteinized." Similarly, it is obvious that gonadal "stromal type" cells must be present in

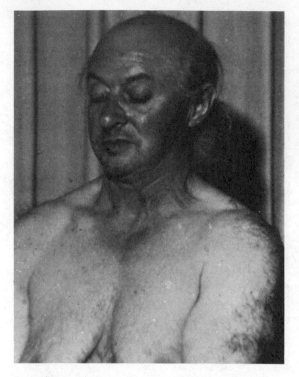

Figure 14—47. Alopecia in patient with hilar cell tumor or with other "masculinizing lesions."

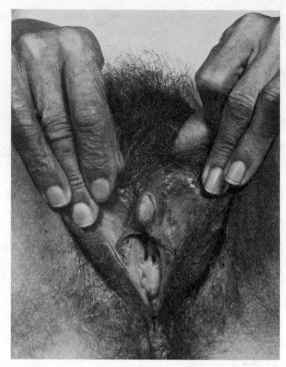

Figure 14—48. Clitoral hypertrophy in a patient with hilar cell tumor.

the area at all times because any luteinized cell, whether in the male or female gonad, needs a precursory nonluteinized mesenchymal element.

Differential Diagnosis

Differentiation of these tumors from other functioning lesions is discussed under arrhenoblastoma (see below). Until the neoplasm has been removed, the exact histologic designation may be impossible. Nevertheless, the patient's age, endometrial findings, and symptoms may be helpful in arriving at the correct diagnosis.

Pathology

These tumors usually are unilateral and rarely exceed 4–5 cm in diameter. They are brown or yellowish-brown, a feature quite characteristic of the steroid-producing lesion. The cells are large, round or ovoid, and contain abundant eosinophilic cytoplasm. The nuclei may be relatively small and dark but more classically are pale, with a prominent clear nucleolus—a classic feature of the metabolically active cell. Mitoses and other cellular evidence of anaplasia are extremely rare; only one malignant hilar cell tumor has been reported. Cytoplasmic inclusions called Reinke crystalloids—a classic structure of testicular interstitial cells—are present both in the tumor cells and in cellular aggregates surrounding the hilar nerves.

The association with hilar nerves is notable; the term sympathicotropic was at one time applied to these cells (Fig 14–49). Although a direct functional rela-

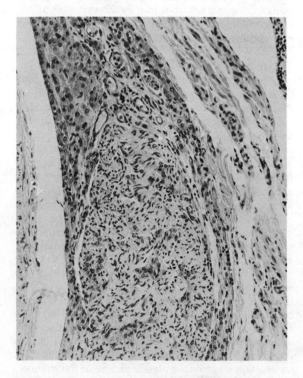

Figure 14—49. Hilar cells interspersed with the fibers of the parovarian nerves.

tionship with the nerves has been denied by most observers, studies suggest that the nerves are not simply spatially associated with the hilar cells but that they may innervate the individual hilar elements. Hilar cells may occasionally be noted in columns, making their way into the ovarian gonadal stroma. The nerves may be involved in the luteinization both of these elements and of the ovarian stroma cells.

A variety of laboratory studies, including incubation of the tissues for hormonal profile and enzyme histochemical evaluations, have demonstrated steroid production by the tumor cell.

Treatment

These patients require thorough endocrinologic study followed by surgical removal of the tumor. The tumors are almost always benign, so excision of the tumor generally is associated with feminization and long-term survival.

ARRHENOBLASTOMA

As noted previously, this term is ambiguous and refers only to a tumor that exerts a virilizing effect on the host. The amount of the "primitive mesenchyme," the extragonadal stimuli, and the local proliferants may play roles in the activity of the individual lesion. Given gonadal elements in the broad ligament, primarily perineural, and tubular structures of mesonephric origin, a combination of luteinized stromal and mesonephric elements generally constitutes the basic components of the true "arrhenoblastoma." Nevertheless, it is well known that most functioning tumors are gonadal stromal lesions and thus arise in the gonad rather than in the parovarian region.

It is difficult to present a specific clinical profile for the parovarian tumor of the "arrhenoblastoma" variety. The lesion composed of hilar cells, also a masculinizing tumor, occurs in postmenopausal patients. Neoplasms containing these "hilar cells" and tubular structures seem to be more prevalent in the menarcheal or early postmenarcheal years. Again, it must be noted that it is difficult to identify many such tumors because they are rare and because, when they attain large size, it may be impossible to identify the specific site of origin. Despite these observations, the structures from which such a tumor may arise are easily recognized in the parovarian area, and small tumors composed of these elements have been described.

Pathology

The tumors rarely attain large size. Most are 7 cm or less in greatest dimension. The cut section grossly presents a yellow or yellow-orange appearance and is solid except for rare small areas of cystic degeneration. The prominent large cells with abundant eosinophilic cytoplasm (Leydig cells) are dispersed through the tumor and separated by tubular structures of varying degrees of organization (Sertoli-like elements). Reinke

crystalloids may be aseen as cytoplasmic inclusions in the Leydig type cells, as in hilar cell tumors.

Clinical Findings

A. Symptoms and Signs: The symptoms are indicated by the term arrhenoblastoma ("male germ cell tumor"). The host is masculinized, but the degree of alteration varies according to the activity of the functioning tissues. Amenorrhea and loss of the female adipose tissues and alterations of secondary sex characteristics are the initial features of defeminization. Heterotopic hirsutism involves the shoulders, arms, legs, mid abdomen, and low back. Enlargement of the clitoris and hypertrophy of the vocal cords, definite signs of masculinization, usually develop later.

B. Laboratory Findings: Blood tests may reveal polycythemia. Thyroid function tests may be low. Urinary 17-ketosteroids are slightly to moderately increased; etiocholanolone may represent 75% of the 17-ketosteroid fraction. The dehydroepiandrosterone level is strikingly high. The estrogen, hydroxysteroid, and FSH levels are normal or minimally reduced. Most importantly, testosterone levels are increased, often to 500 ng/mL or higher.

Differential Diagnosis

The hirsutism of arrhenoblastoma must be differentiated from familial hirsutism, particularly in intensely brunet women of Mediterranean racial background; careful study should demonstrate normal plasma and urine hormone concentrations in the latter.

A variety of physiologic and pathologic conditions may result in amenorrhea with minimal alterations in body habitus, eg, mild facial and body hirsutism. These changes are characteristic of Stein-Leventhal syndrome. In many normal girls during the menarcheal years, menstrual irregularities, acne, and the appearance of scattered hairs on the chin and occasionally elsewhere on the body are commonplace. With the establishment of normal cyclic hormonal patterns, most of these temporary alterations cease.

The extraovarian adrenal tumor presents a persistent challenge. Intravenous urograms, renal scans, and aortography may assist in establishing the presence of a suprarenal mass. Adrenal corticosteroid suppression studies may identify the source of the androgen. Laparoscopy and pneumoperitoneography are diagnostic tools that assist in establishing the presence or absence of this type of tumor. Nevertheless, it may be necessary to perform exploratory surgery to establish a definitive diagnosis.

The parovarian arrhenoblastoma perhaps is the least common of all masculinizing tumors that arise in the pelvis. The age of the patient, the size of the tumor, and the clinical extent of the masculinization play a role in establishing a "tumor type" diagnosis. The well-differentiated tumor composed of hilar (Leydig) cells and mesonephric tubular structures generally occurs in the younger patient, whereas the hilar cell tumor develops postmenopausally and the gonadal stromal lesions develop during the menstrual years.

Treatment

These tumors are almost always benign and unilateral. Thus, unilateral salpingo-oophorectomy is adequate therapy in the patient who wishes to preserve her reproductive function. Obviously, for the patient with bilateral gonadal involvement who is over 35 or who no longer wishes to maintain fertility, hysterectomy and bilateral adnexectomy is the treatment of choice.

Superfluous hair should be removed and acne treated. Hormonal evaluation should be repeated after several months to guard against the possibility of recurrence.

Radiation therapy of malignant residue or recurrence is discouraging, although an occasional arrhenoblastoma is radiosensitive.

Estrogen therapy does not reverse androgenic hormone effects.

Postoperative symptoms regress in the order in which they appeared. Menses return, often within the month, and deposition of adipose tissue in the next few months. The excess fine hair falls out gradually over a longer period of time. The coarse or bristly hair remains. Clitoral enlargement and hypertrophy of the vocal cords often never regress.

Prognosis

The prognosis for patients with arrhenoblastoma actually is much better than hitherto reported. About 95% are still alive at 5 years. Persistent or recurrent tumors almost always are undifferentiated neoplasms and represent initial misdiagnosis.

ADRENAL TUMOR

Classic adrenal rests are often discovered on routine sections through the parovarian region closer to the oviduct than to the ovary (Fig 14–50). Most frequently they are incidental findings. Rarely, they may form the nidus for the development of a neoplasm.

Adrenal tumors are extremely rare and may be found at any age from 16 to 60 years. Most commonly they are associated with masculinization of the host. However, depending on which elements of the gland proliferate most extensively, they may produce other symptoms such as salt retention or paroxysmal hypertension.

The differential diagnostic features have been discussed previously. Technically, one should be able to suppress androgen from the adrenal tumor with cortisone, but one cannot depend upon the results of this test in the case of a pelvic adrenal tumor. The presence of a pelvic mass assists in establishing the diagnosis.

The most striking microscopic pathologic feature is proliferation of the cells of the reticularis and fasciculata. The classic large cells with abundant clear cytoplasm and small dark nuclei are intermingled with cells with eosinophilic cytoplasm and prominent, lighter staining nuclei (2-cell population). The latter

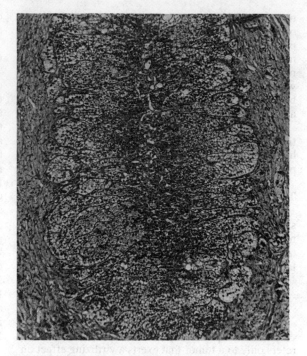

Figure 14–50. Adrenal rest showing the classic reticular and fasciculated structures.

are almost identical to the hilar cell, making differential diagnosis almost impossible. Occasional multinucleated cells are seen; but, as with the suprarenal adrenal tumors, unless extension has taken place, it is unwise to interpret such findings as malignant alterations. Because of the histologic features of the cell and positive stain for lipid, many authors have grouped these tumors together with others demonstrating the same cellular characteristics as lipoid cell tumors. Nevertheless, a specific diagnosis should be made if possible for the sake of accurate prognostication.

Although virilizing tumors obviously may arise from these adrenal rests, it must be recognized that most virilizing lesions develop from the totipotent ovarian stroma. Cells simulating the "clear" and eosinophilic varieties of stimulated "theca" are seen in the matrix of "polycystic ovary." Varying degrees of masculinization are commonly associated with the latter syndrome. Consequently, it would not be surprising to recognize a tumor composed of such elements exerting a similar effect on the host. Furthermore, because these tumors are routinely masculinizing as opposed to the varying symptomatology of the adrenal tumor in the suprarenal area, one must question whether they originate from adrenal rests.

The treatment of adrenal tumors, like that of other neoplasms in this area, is surgical excision. Since the lesions are benign, if they are encapsulated, the survival rate approximates 100% and disappearance of the arrhenomimetic symptoms is usually prompt. Of 23 cases in the Ovarian Tumor Registry, there was only one death. On the other hand, a 5-year survival rate of

65–70% is reported for the classic adrenal tumor in the adrenal area.

LYMPHOMA

Remarkably few cases of clinically significant lymphomas involving the ovary have been reported, but most patients had symptoms related to pelvic disease, thus necessitating laparotomy for positive diagnosis in most cases.

Because aggregates of lymphocytes are never found in the normal ovary, the term primary applied to an ovarian lymphoma may be improper. The great majority of patients with ovarian involvement by the lymphomatous process have an extragonadal primary. At least 20% of women dying of malignant lymphoma have ovarian involvement.

In a study of 55 cases of lymphoma from the files of the Ovarian Tumor Registry, only one patient was still living 5 years after diagnosis. All varieties of lymphoma, including Hodgkin's disease and Burkitt's tumor, have been described in the ovary. One of the major histopathologic problems was differential diagnosis. Dysgerminoma and metastatic cancer were common misinterpretations.

• • •

References

Adashi E et al: Histogenesis of the broad ligament adrenal rest. *Int J Gynaecol Obstet* 1980;**18**;102.

Anderson WR et al: Granulosa-theca cell tumors: Clinical and pathologic study. *Am J Obstet Gynecol* 1971;**110**:32.

Arey LB: Origin and form of the Brenner tumor. *Am J Obstet Gynecol* 1961;**81**:743.

Azoury RS, Woodruff JD: Primary ovarian sarcomas (43 cases from the Emil Novak Ovarian Tumor Registry). *Obstet Gynecol* 1971;**37**:920.

Barlow JJ: Abnormal estrogen responses to ACTH stimulation in the polycystic ovary syndrome. *Am J Obstet Gynecol* 1969; **103**:585.

Brooks JJ, Wheeler JE: Malignancy arising in extragonadal endometriosis. *Cancer* 1977;**40**:3065.

Czernobilsky B, Borenstein R, Lancet M: Cystadenofibroma of the ovary: A clinicopathologic study of 34 cases and comparison with serous cystadenoma. *Cancer* 1974;**34**:1971.

Decker DG, Webb MJ, Holbrook MA: Radiogold treatment of epithelial cancer of ovary: Late results. *Am J Obstet Gynecol* 1973;**115**:751.

DiSaia PJ et al: Chemotherapeutic reconversion of immature teratoma. *Obstet Gynecol* 1977;**49**:346.

Fine G et al: Mesonephroma of the ovary: A clinical, morphological and histogenetic appraisal. *Cancer* 1973;**31**:398.

Fox H, Agrawal K, Langley FA: A clinicopathologic study of 92 cases of granulosa cell tumor of the ovary with special reference to the factors influencing prognosis. *Cancer* 1975; **35**:231.

Garcia-Bunuel R et al: Luteomas of pregnancy. *Obstet Gynecol* 1975;**45**:407.

Garden AS, Best PV: Ovarian teratoma with intra-abdominal dissemination. *J Obstet Gynaecol Br Commonw* 1972; **79**:1139.

Genadry R et al: Papillary intraperitoneal proliferation: Often referred to as a papillary serous tumor of low malignant potential. *Obstet Gynecol* 1981;**58**:597.

Genadry R et al: Secondary malignancies in benign cystic teratomas. *Gynecol Oncol* 1979;**8**:246.

Gordon A, Lipton D, Woodruff JD: Dysgerminoma: A review of 158 cases from the Emil Novak Ovarian Tumor Registry. *Obstet Gynecol* 1981;**58**:497.

Greene RR: The diverse origin of Brenner tumors. *Am J Obstet Gynecol* 1952;**64**:878.

Gruenwald P: Development of the sex cords in the gonads of man and mammals. *Am J Anat* 1942;**70**:359.

Hayes D: Mesonephroid tumors of the ovary. *J Obstet Gynaecol Br Commonw* 1972;**79**:728.

Henderson WJ, Joslin CAF, Turnbull AC: Talc and carcinoma of the ovary and cervix. *J Obstet Gynaecol Br Commonw* 1971; **78**:266.

Henderson WJ & others: Analysis of particles in stomach tumours from Japanese males. *Environ Res* 1975;**9**:240.

Horton R, Neisler R: Plasma androgens in patients with the polycystic ovary syndrome. *J Clin Endocrinol Metab* 1968; **28**:479.

Ireland K, Woodruff JD: Masculinizing ovarian tumors. *Obstet Gynecol Surv* 1976;**31**:83.

Jensen RD, Morris HJ: Epithelial tumors of the ovary: Occurrence in children and adolescents less than 20 years of age. *Arch Pathol* 1972;**94**:29.

Jimerson GK, Woodruff JD: Endodermal sinus tumor. *Am J Obstet Gynecol* 1977;**127**:73.

Jimerson GK, Woodruff JD: Ovarian extraembryonal tumor. *Am J Obstet Gynecol* 1977;**127**:302.

Judd HL et al: Maternal virilization developing during a twin pregnancy: Demonstration of excess ovarian androgen production associated with theca lutein cysts. *N Engl J Med* 1973; **288**:118.

Julian CG, Woodruff JD: Biologic behavior of low-grade papillary serous carcinoma of the ovary. *Obstet Gynecol* 1972; **40**:860.

Julian CG et al: Biologic behavior of primary ovarian malignancy. *Obstet Gynecol* 1974;**44**:873.

Kurman RJ, Norris HJ: Embryonal carcinoma of the ovary. *Cancer* 1976;**38**:2420.

Kurman RJ, Norris HJ: Endodermal sinus tumor of the ovary. *Cancer* 1976;**38**:2404.

Linder D, McCau BK, Hecht F: Parthenogenic origin of benign ovarian teratomas. *N Engl J Med* 1975;**292**:63.

Masterson BJ: Multiple threat: Second primary malignancies in patients with ovarian carcinoma treated with radiation and chemotherapy. *J Kans Med Soc* 1977;**78**:282.

McArthur JW, Ingersoll FM, Worcester J: Urinary excretion of ICSH and FSH activity by women with diseases of the reproductive system. *J Clin Endocrinol Metab* 1958;**18**:1202.

Meigs JV: Pelvic tumors other than fibromas of the ovary with ascites and hydrothorax. *Obstet Gynecol* 1954;**3**:471.

Nissen ED, Goldstein AJ: Ovarian tumors with functioning stromal cells: Case report of a feminizing Brenner tumor. *Int J Gynaecol Obstet* 1973;**11**:213.

Norris HJ, Chorlton I: Functioning tumors of the ovary. *Clin Obstet Gynecol* 1974;**17**:189.

Novak ER, Woodruff JD: *Novak's Gynecologic and Obstetric Pathology: With Clinical and Endocrine Relations,* 8th ed. Saunders, 1979.

Parmley TH, Woodruff JD: The ovarian mesothelioma. *Am J Obstet Gynecol* 1974;**120**:234.

Patton WC et al: Pituitary gonadotropin responses to synthetic luteinizing hormone-releasing hormone in patients with typical and atypical polycystic ovary disease. *Am J Obstet Gynecol* 1975;**121**:382.

Piver MS, Lele S, Barlow JJ: Preoperative and intraoperative evaluation of ovarian malignancy. *Obstet Gynecol* 1976; **48**:312.

Pratt-Thomas PB et al: Proliferative and malignant Brenner tumors of the ovary. *Gynecol Oncol* 1976;**4**:176.

Robboy SJ et al: Primary trabecular carcinoid of the ovary. *Obstet Gynecol* 1977;**49**:202.

Rogers LW, Julian CG, Woodruff JD: Mesonephroid carcinoma of the ovary: A study of 95 cases from the Emil Novak Ovarian Tumor Registry. *Gynecol Oncol* 1972;**1**:76.

Roth LM: Massive ovarian edema with stromal luteinization. *Am J Clin Pathol* 1971;**55**:757.

Roth LM, Ehrlich CE: Mucinous cystadenocarcinoma of the retroperitoneum. *Obstet Gynecol* 1977;**49**:345.

Roth LM, Sternberg WH: Proliferating Brenner ovarian tumors. *Cancer* 1971;**27**:687.

Sandberg EC: The virilizing ovary. *Obstet Gynecol Surv* 1962; **17**:165.

Sandenberg HA, Woodruff JD: Histogenesis of pseudomyxoma peritonei. *Obstet Gynecol* 1977;**49**:339.

Scully RE: Gonadoblastoma: A review of 74 cases. *Cancer* 1971; **25**:1340.

Seski AG, Amirikia H: Starch granuloma syndrome. *Obstet Gynecol* 1976;**48**:605.

Spadoni LR et al: Virilization coexisting with Krukenberg tumor during pregnancy. *Am J Obstet Gynecol* 1965;**92**:981.

Spenos WJ: Preoperative hormone therapy of cystic ovarian masses. *Am J Obstet Gynecol* 1973;**116**:551.

Stern JL et al: Spontaneous rupture of benign cystic teratomas. *Obstet Gynecol* 1981;**57**:363.

Sternberg WH, Roth LM: Ovarian stromal tumors containing Leydig cells. *Cancer* 1973;**32**:940.

Stewart RS, Woodard DE: Malignant ovarian hilus cell tumor. *Arch Pathol* 1962;**73**:91.

Taylor HC Jr: Changing conceptions of ovarian tumors. *Am J Obstet Gynecol* 1940;**40**:566.

Verhoeven AT et al: Virilization in pregnancy coexisting with an (ovarian) mucinous cystadenoma: A case report and review of virilizing ovarian tumors in pregnancy. *Obstet Gynecol Surv* 1973;**28**:597.

Vogl SE, Greenwald E, Kaplan BH: The "CHAD" regimen (cyclophosphamide, hexamethylmelamine, adriamycin and diamminedichloroplatinum) in advanced ovarian cancer. *Proc Am Assoc Cancer Res and Am Soc Clin Oncol* 1979;**20**:384.

Voight JC: Carcinomatous change in ovarian endometriosis. *Int Surg* 1972;**57**:563.

Webb MJ et al: Cancer metastatic to the ovary: Factors influencing survival. *Obstet Gynecol* 1975;**45**:391.

Williamson HO, Pratt-Thomas HR: Bilateral gonadoblastoma with dysgerminoma: A case report. *Obstet Gynecol* 1972; **39**:263.

Woodruff JD, Genadry R, Parmley TH: Mucinous cystadenocarcinoma. *Obstet Gynecol* 1978;**51**:483.

Woodruff JD et al: Metastatic ovarian tumors. *Am J Obstet Gynecol* 1970;**107**:202.

Woodruff JD et al: Proliferative and malignant Brenner tumors: Review of 47 cases. *Am J Obstet Gynecol* 1981;**141**:118.

Young RC et al: Staging laparotomy in early ovarian cancer. *Proc Am Assoc Cancer Res and Am Soc Clin Oncol* 1979;**20**:399.

Younglai EV et al: Arrhenoblastoma: In vivo and in vitro studies. *Am J Obstet Gynecol* 1973;**116**:401.

Pelvic Infections | 15

F. Gary Cunningham, MD, & Abe Mickal, MD

Because of their common occurrence and often serious consequences, infections are among the most important problems encountered in the practice of gynecology. A wide variety of pelvic infections, ranging from uncomplicated gonococcal salpingo-oophoritis to septicemic shock following rupture of a pelvic abscess, confront the general physician as well as the gynecologist.

The following is a general classification of pelvic infections by frequency of occurrence:

(1) Postoperative gynecologic surgery
    (a) Cuff cellulitis and parametritis
    (b) Vaginal cuff abscess
    (c) Tubo-ovarian abscess
(2) Puerperal infections
    (a) Cesarean section (common)
    (b) Vaginal delivery (uncommon)
(3) "Pelvic inflammatory disease"
    (a) Acute salpingitis
        (i) Gonococcal
        (ii) Nongonococcal
    (b) IUD-related pelvic cellulitis
    (c) Tubo-ovarian abscess
    (d) Pelvic abscess
(4) Abortion-associated infections
    (a) Postabortal cellulitis
    (b) Incomplete septic abortion
(5) Secondary to other infections
    (a) Appendicitis
    (b) Diverticulitis
    (c) Tuberculosis

Pelvic inflammatory disease is a general term for acute, subacute, recurrent, or chronic infection of the oviducts and ovaries, often with involvement of adjacent tissues. Most infections seen in clinical practice are bacterial, but viral, fungal, and parasitic infections may occur. The term pelvic inflammatory disease is vague at best and should be discarded in favor of more specific terminology. This should include identification of the affected organs, the stage of the infection, and, if possible, the causative agent. This is especially important in view of the rising incidence of venereal disease and its complications. The ready availability of contraception and abortion, together with increasingly permissive sexual attitudes, seemingly has resulted in an increased incidence of venereal disease and pelvic infections.

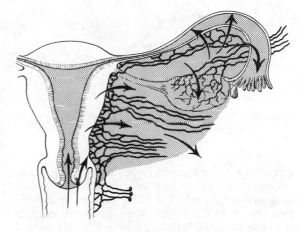

Figure 15–1. Direct spread of bacterial infection other than gonorrhea.

Proposed pathways of dissemination of microorganisms in pelvic infections are depicted in Figs 15–1 to 15–3. In Fig 15–1, dissemination is via parametrial lymphatics. These types of infections, typified by postpartum, postabortal, and some IUD-related infections, result in retroperitoneal parametrial cellulitis. In Fig 15–2, the endometrial-endosalpingeal-peritoneal

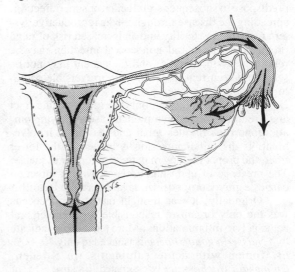

Figure 15–2. Direct spread of gonorrhea.

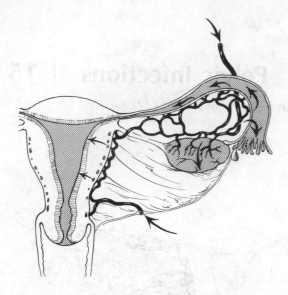

Figure 15–3. Hematogenous spread of bacterial infection (eg, tuberculosis).

spread of microorganisms is depicted; this represents more common forms of nonpuerperal "acute pelvic inflammatory disease" in which pathogenic bacteria gain access to the lining of the uterine tubes with resultant purulent inflammation and egress of pus through tubal ostia into the peritoneal cavity. These infections are represented by adnexal infection and inflammation as well as peritonitis. In rare instances, certain diseases (eg, tuberculosis) may gain access to pelvic structures by hematogenous routes (Fig 15–3).

Early recognition and treatment are mandatory. Gonorrhea, for example, is more common in single, young females of low parity. It is imperative that the diagnosis be made early so that specific therapy can be instituted to prevent damage to the reproductive system. Repeated sexual contacts with multiple partners predispose to subsequent reinfection or superinfection, spreading the disease throughout the reproductive system resulting in sterility and an increased risk of tubal pregnancy. The initial gonococcal infection may be relatively asymptomatic, and the patient may not be seen until recurrent infection with irreversible pathologic changes has taken place.

Gonorrhea involving only the lower genital tract and urethra is often asymptomatic; severe symptomatic gonorrhea implies tubal and peritoneal involvement. If the initial infection is limited to the lower tract, the proper therapy may prevent further sequelae. The presence of endosalpingitis or ovarian infection carries a graver prognosis in regard to future fertility.

Originally, it was thought that the gonococcus was the only organism responsible for nonpuerperal acute pelvic inflammations. More recent data indicate that *Neisseria gonorrhoeae* is isolated in only 40–60% of women with acute salpingitis. In Sweden, *Chlamydia trachomatis* is estimated to cause 60% of cases of salpingitis. Although direct evidence of such

infection, eg, recovery from tubal culture, is lacking in most studies done in the USA, authorities believe that this pathogen may be responsible for 20–35% of such pelvic infections. It is unclear how frequently chlamydiae alone cause salpingitis, in contradistinction to those cases in which they act in concert with other invasive microorganisms. Regardless of the initiating factors, nongonococcal pathogens that comprise the normal vaginal flora may become involved in many cases of acute salpingitis-peritonitis.

Cunningham and others have reported that 71% of nongonococcal isolates from peritoneal fluid were aerobic or anaerobic streptococci. This study also reported isolation of bacteria from aspirated peritoneal fluid from 34 of 45 women (76%). *N gonorrhoeae* was present alone or with other pathogens in 22 of the 34 specimens (65%). Chow and others reported positive cul-de-sac fluid cultures in 18 of 20 patients (90%) with acute salpingitis as compared to 8 normal patients with negative results.

If the infectious process continues, pelvic adhesions become more pronounced, and cleavage planes are lost. It becomes difficult to identify the tubes and ovaries in the inflammatory mass, which may include omental and intestinal attachments (Fig 15–4). Further progression causes tissue necrosis with abscess formation. Containment of the purulent exudate under pressure becomes impossible at certain sites, and release of pus into the peritoneal cavity occurs. This is usually at the site of an adhesion to a nearby organ, and the point of rupture can often be identified at operation. Abscess formation may be localized in either or both of the tubes and ovaries without leakage or rupture. Another possibility is accumulation of purulent material walled off in the cul-de-sac.

Recent observations have shown these infections to be polymicrobial with mixed anaerobic and aerobic bacteria. Anaerobes predominate and frequently coexist with aerobes. In some cases, aerobes alone are isolated. With further advanced disease, such as abscess formation, anaerobic organisms seem to predominate. All of these bacteria are members of the

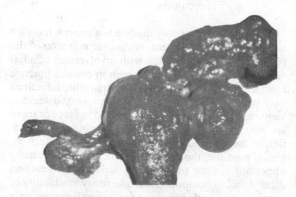

Figure 15–4. Bilateral adnexal inflammatory disease with left hydro- and pyosalpinx and acute-subacute inflammatory changes on both adnexa.

normal vaginal and endocervical flora and include *Bacteroides, Escherichia coli,* aerobic streptococci, and anaerobic cocci *(Peptostreptococcus* and *Peptococcus).* Virtually any organism indigenous to the normal vaginal or gastrointestinal flora may be isolated if specific techniques are utilized.

Many factors may account for adverse sequelae of these pelvic infections, eg, infertility, pain. Delay in initiation of treatment is associated with later symptomatology. Likewise, inadequate therapy due to improper antimicrobial selection, insufficient dosage, or inadequate duration of therapy may be responsible for subsequent problems. An inflammatory process that is allowed to continue—for whatever reason—results in anatomic derangements with adhesive attachments to nearby organs. An ovulation site in an ovary may serve as a portal of entry for extension of the infection into the ovarian stroma, and this sets the stage for formation of tubo-ovarian adhesions or abscesses.

The most important factor in diagnosis in women with pelvic infections is clinical awareness by the physician. For patients at high risk, eg, postoperative pelvic surgery, postpartum, or postabortal, fever is usually the first clue. For women without these factors, a high index of suspicion is important. If gonorrhea is suspected, a gram-stained smear of endocervical purulent material or fluid obtained by culdocentesis may be helpful. The gram-stained smear may be lifesaving in the woman now only infrequently seen with serious infection due to *Clostridium perfringens.* Except for isolation of *N gonorrhoeae* with specialized media, cultures taken from women with pelvic infections currently are not useful for clinical management. Since these infections are usually polymicrobial, sophisticated techniques are necessary for microbiologic identification. These are time-consuming, and usually, by the time the results become available to the clinician, the woman has been cured with empiric antimicrobial drug administration.

Ultrasonography has become a useful means of diagnosis of adnexal and pelvic masses. When ultrasound diagnosis is compared to laparoscopic diagnosis, it is about 70% accurate. Thickening is noted in the pelvic areas during the inflammatory process. Ultrasound has its best value in following the progression or regression of an abscess after it has been diagnosed. The borders of an abscess conform to the surrounding pelvic structures and as such do not give a well-defined border as noted in ovarian cyst. Unfortunately, x-ray films (KUB) are of little help in pelvic infections because they seldom identify pelvic masses. X-rays often identify adynamic ileus, which frequently accompanies pelvic peritonitis. Chest films are necessary to establish the condition of the lungs at the onset and to detect the presence of any concomitant or later pulmonary disease.

Complete reliance cannot be placed on the white blood count because it may be elevated, normal, or decreased in patients with moderate to severe infections.

Culdocentesis (cul-de-sac tap) may be helpful in

Table 15–1. Differential evaluation of fluid obtained by culdocentesis.

Finding	Implications for Diagnosis
Blood	Ruptured ectopic pregnancy.
	Hemorrhage from corpus luteum cyst.
	Retrograde menstruation.
	Rupture of spleen or liver.
	Gastrointestinal bleeding.
	Perforation of uterus.
Pus	Ruptured tubo-ovarian abscess.
	Ruptured appendix or viscus.
	Rupture of diverticular abscess.
	Uterine abscess with myoma.
Cloudy	Pelvic peritonitis (such as is seen with acute gonococcal salpingitis).
	Twisted adnexal cyst.
	Other causes of peritonitis: appendicitis, pancreatitis, cholecystitis, perforated ulcer, carcinomatosis, echinococcosis.

the diagnosis of suspected pelvic infection. Other conditions that may simulate infection can be ruled out by means of this simple procedure. The rectouterine pouch (of Douglas) is punctured with a long, large-bore spinal needle to obtain a sample of the contents of the peritoneal cavity. Culdocentesis is easy to perform and may be done with or without local anesthesia in the hospital or in the office. Culdocentesis is indicated whenever peritoneal material is needed for diagnosis. Cultures for aerobic and anaerobic organisms may also be obtained. Contraindications include a cul-de-sac mass or a fixed retroflexed uterus. For differential evaluation of fluid obtained by culdocentesis, see Table 15–1.

PELVIC INFLAMMATORY DISEASE

ACUTE SALPINGITIS–PERITONITIS

Essentials of Diagnosis
- Onset of lower abdominal and pelvic pain, usually following menses and associated with vaginal discharge.
- Systemic manifestations of infection: fever, lassitude, headache.
- Lower abdominal pressure and tenderness.
- Exquisite tenderness elicited on pelvic examination and movements of organs.
- Gram-negative intracellular diplococci seen on smear of cervical or periurethral gland exudates.

General Considerations
There is generally an acute onset of pelvic infection, often associated with invasion by *N gonorrhoeae* and involving the uterus, tubes, and ovaries, with varying degrees of pelvic peritonitis. In the acute

stage, there is redness and edema of the tubes and ovaries with a purulent discharge oozing from the ostium of the tube.

Clinical Findings

A. Symptoms and Signs: The insidious or acute onset of lower abdominal and pelvic pain usually is bilateral but occasionally is unilateral. There may be a sensation of pelvic pressure, with back pain radiating down one or both legs. In most cases, symptoms appear shortly after the onset or cessation of menses. There is often an associated purulent vaginal discharge.

Nausea may occur, with or without vomiting, but these symptoms may be indicative of a more serious problem (eg, acute appendicitis). Headache and general lassitude are common complaints.

Fever is not necessary for the diagnosis of acute salpingitis, although its absence may indicate other disorders, specifically ectopic pregnancy. In one study (see Westrom reference on p 359), only 30% of women with visually confirmed acute salpingitis had fever. Although standardization of criteria for diagnosis of acute salpingitis to include fever greater than 38 °C (100.4 °F) may greatly aid clinical research, such a distinction may result in many women with acute pelvic infection being erroneously diagnosed and inadequately treated.

Abdominal tenderness is often encountered, usually in both lower quadrants. The abdomen may be somewhat distended, and bowel sounds may be hypotonic. Pelvic examination may demonstrate inflammation of the periurethral (Skene) or Bartholin glands as well as a purulent cervical discharge. Bimanual examination typically elicits extreme tenderness on movement of the cervix and uterus and palpation of the parametria.

B. Laboratory Findings: Leukocytosis with a shift to the left is usually present; however, the white count may be normal. A smear of purulent cervical material may demonstrate gram-negative kidney-shaped diplococci in polymorphonuclear leukocytes. These organisms may be gonococci, but definitive cultures on selective media are advised.

Culdocentesis generally is productive of "reaction fluid" (cloudy peritoneal fluid) which, when stained, generally reveals leukocytes with or without gonococci or other organisms. Culture and sensitivity testing of organisms from culdocentesis samples may be done.

C. X-Ray Findings: X-ray examination of the abdomen may show signs of ileus, but this finding is nonspecific.

Differential Diagnosis

Acute salpingitis must be differentiated from acute appendicitis, ectopic pregnancy, ruptured corpus luteum cyst with hemorrhage, diverticulitis, infected septic abortion, torsion of an adnexal mass, degeneration of a leiomyoma, endometriosis, acute urinary tract infection, regional enteritis, and ulcerative colitis.

Complications

Complications of acute salpingitis include pelvic peritonitis or generalized peritonitis; prolonged adynamic ileus; severe pelvic cellulitis with thrombophlebitis; abscess formation (pyosalpinx, tubo-ovarian abscess, cul-de-sac abscess) with adnexal destruction and subsequent infertility; and intestinal adhesions and obstruction. More rarely, dermatitis, gonococcal arthritis, or bacteremia with septic shock may occur.

Prevention

Approximately 15% of women with asymptomatic gonococcal cervical infection will develop acute salpingitis. Detection and treatment of these women and their sexual partners should therefore prevent a substantial number of cases of gonococcal pelvic infection. Early diagnosis and eradication of minimally symptomatic disease (cervicitis, urethritis) will also usually prevent salpingitis.

Treatment

As with most female pelvic infections, the microbial etiologic agents are not readily apparent when clinical infection is diagnosed, and because of the myriad of pathogens described above, empirical therapy is given. Nonetheless, it is important that empirical therapy be given initially. The majority of women who present with acute salpingitis-peritonitis will have clinical disease of mild to moderate severity that usually responds well to outpatient antibiotic therapy. Hospitalization usually is warranted for women who appear acutely ill and especially those in whom the diagnosis of salpingitis is suspect.

A. Outpatient Therapy: (Fever of 38.5–39 °C [101.3–102.2 °F]; minimal lower abdominal findings; patient not "toxic.") These women may be treated as outpatients with antibiotics, IUD removal, analgesics, and bed rest. Two regimens recommended by the USPHS have proved effective in clinical studies: (1) Aqueous procaine penicillin G is given intramuscularly with 1 g of probenecid orally. This is followed by oral ampicillin, 500 mg 4 times daily for 10 days. (2) Tetracycline, 500 mg orally 4 times daily for 10 days. Follow-up cervical cultures for *N gonorrhoeae* should be obtained 7–14 days after completion of therapy. The patient should be referred to the city or county health department or venereal disease clinic.

B. Inpatient Therapy: (Fever > 39 °C [102.2 °F]; guarding and tenderness in lower quadrants; patient looks "toxic.") Hospitalization of these patients is necessary because intensive therapy is required and because the patient must be watched for signs of complications or deterioration. The following measures should be taken.

1. Maintain bed rest.

2. Restrict oral feeding.

3. Administer intravenous fluids to correct dehydration and acidosis.

4. Use nasogastric suction in the presence of abdominal distention or ileus.

5. No standardization of inpatient antimicrobial

therapy for women with acute salpingitis has yet been established. Symptomatic response and adverse sequelae are related to the severity of tubal inflammatory disease and the development of adnexal abscesses. USPHS guidelines for treatment of acute salpingitis include (1) aqueous crystalline penicillin G, 20 million units intravenously daily until improvement occurs (usually in 4–5 days), followed by ampicillin, 500 mg orally 4 times daily to complete 10 days of therapy; *or* (2) tetracycline, 250 mg intravenously 4 times daily until improvement occurs, followed by 500 mg orally 4 times daily to complete 10 days of therapy. Current optimal therapy for hospitalized patients usually involves combined antibiotic therapy.

The incidence of infertility even after the first episode of salpingitis is significant. Because infertility increases with the degree of inflammatory response, intensive broad-spectrum therapy should reduce complications. Thus, treatment with high doses of intravenous "second-generation" cephalosporins seems reasonable, ie, cefoxitin or cefamandole may be given in divided doses for a total of 8–12 g daily, or newer "third-generation" cephalosporins, moxalactam and cefotaxime, may be administered in doses of 6 g daily. Inclusion of therapy directed specifically at anaerobic organisms seems prudent: clindamycin, 600–1200 mg intravenously every 6 hours, or metronidazole, 15 mg/kg intravenously over 1 hour as a loading dose, followed by 7.5 mg/kg intravenously every 6 hours infused over 1 hour—in combination with other antibiotics for broad-spectrum coverage. After the patient shows clinical improvement, including return of temperature to normal, parenteral therapy can be switched to oral administration to complete a 10- to 14-day regimen.

6. Exploratory laparotomy should be performed if the abdominal symptoms persist, the clinical findings worsen, or the patient's condition deteriorates. It is better to remove an isolated adnexal abscess than await rupture, after which more extensive surgery and possibly castration is necessary.

7. Continuous evaluation by the same experienced clinician is of paramount importance to maintain accuracy and continuity of clinical observation.

Prognosis

A favorable outcome is directly related to the promptness with which adequate therapy is begun. For example, the incidence of infertility is directly related to the severity of tubal inflammation judged by laparoscopic examination. A single episode of salpingitis has been shown to cause infertility in 12–18% of women (see Westrom reference, p 359). Although tubal occlusion was demonstrated in only about 10% of these patients regardless of whether or not there had been a gonococcal or nongonococcal infection, nongonococcal infection predisposed more commonly to ectopic pregnancy and thus carried a worse prognosis for subsequent viable pregnancy. The ability and willingness of the patient to cooperate with her physician are important to the outcome of the milder cases

that are adequately treated on an outpatient basis. Follow-up care and education are necessary to prevent reinfection and complications.

RECURRENT OR CHRONIC PELVIC INFECTION

Essentials of Diagnosis

- History of acute salpingitis, pelvic infection, or postpartum or postabortal infection.
- Recurrent: Episodes of acute reinfection.
- Chronic: May be relatively asymptomatic or may provoke complaints of chronic pelvic pain and dyspareunia.
- Generalized pelvic tenderness on examination; usually less severe than with acute infection.
- Thickening of adnexal tissues, with or without hydrosalpinx (often).
- Infertility (commonly).

General Considerations

Recurrent pelvic inflammatory disease begins as does primary disease, but preexisting tubal tissue damage may result in more severe infection. Chronic pelvic infection implies the presence of tissue changes in the parametria, tubes, and ovaries. Adhesions of the peritoneal surfaces to the adnexa as well as fibrotic changes in the tubal lumen are usually present. Hydrosalpinx or tubo-ovarian "complexes" may be present. Chronic inflammatory lesions usually are secondary to changes induced by previous acute salpingitis but may represent an acute reinfection.

The diagnosis of chronic pelvic infection generally is difficult to make clinically. It has been erroneously applied to almost any cause of chronic pelvic pain.

Clinical Findings

A. Symptoms and Signs: Recurrent infection usually has the same manifestations as acute salpingitis (see above), and a history of pelvic infection can usually be obtained. Pain may be unilateral or bilateral, and dyspareunia and infertility are often reported. The patient may be febrile, with tachycardia; however, unless an acute reinfection is present, the fever is minimal. There is tenderness upon movement of the cervix, uterus, or adnexa. Adnexal masses may be present, as well as thickening of the parametria.

B. Laboratory Findings: Cultures from the cervix usually do not show gonococci unless reinfection is present. Leukocytosis may be demonstrated if active infection is superimposed on chronic changes.

Differential Diagnosis

Any patient with suspected chronic pelvic infection who presents with pelvic tenderness but without fever must be suspected of having an ectopic pregnancy. Other conditions to be considered include endometriosis, symptomatic uterine relaxation, appendicitis, diverticulitis, regional enteritis, ulcerative colitis, ovarian cyst or neoplasm, and acute or chronic cystourethritis.

Complications

The complications of chronic or recurrent pelvic infection include hydrosalpinx, pyosalpinx, and tubo-ovarian abscess; infertility or ectopic pregnancy; and chronic pelvic pain of varying degrees.

Prevention

Prompt and adequate treatment of acute pelvic infections is the essential preventive measure. Education of women in matters of sex hygiene and avoidance of venereal infection are also important.

Treatment

A. Recurrent Cases: Treat for acute salpingitis (see above). If an IUD is in place, treatment may be started, and the IUD should be removed.

B. Chronic Cases: Long-term antimicrobial administration is of questionable benefit but is worthy of trial in young women of low parity. Therapy with a tetracycline, ampicillin, or a cephalosporin, 500 mg 4 times daily for 3 weeks, may occasionally be beneficial, but changes responsible for symptoms are usually not due to active infection. Symptomatic relief can be achieved by use of analgesics such as aspirin or acetaminophen with or without codeine. Careful follow-up, preferably by the same physician, may detect serious sequelae, eg, tubo-ovarian abscess.

If the patient remains symptomatic after 3 weeks of antibiotic therapy, other causes must be considered. Consider laparoscopy or exploratory laparotomy to verify the presence of pelvic adhesions and to rule out other causes, eg, endometriosis.

If infertility is a problem, verify tubal patency by means of hysterosalpingography or laparoscopy and retrograde injection of methylene blue solution. It is important to prescribe antibiotics prior to and following either procedure because acute reinfection is not uncommon.

Total abdominal hysterectomy with bilateral adnexectomy is indicated if the disease is far-advanced and the woman is symptomatic or if an adnexal mass is demonstrated. This is usually done regardless of parity; however, in carefully selected patients of low parity, consideration may be given to resection of abscess. This procedure is questionable as most patients have bilateral tubal damage.

Prognosis

With each succeeding episode of recurrent pelvic infection, the prognosis for fertility dramatically decreases. Westrom has shown that 10% of women with one episode of acute salpingitis are involuntarily infertile. This increases to 25% and then 60% after a second and third episode, respectively. Likewise, the chances of an ectopic gestation increase with ensuing episodes of acute infection. These sequelae are undoubtedly due to chronic infection, which is the postinflammatory end result of one or multiple infections. Superimposi-

tion of acute infection on chronic disease is also associated with a higher incidence of tubo-ovarian and other pelvic abscesses.

PELVIC (CUL–DE–SAC) ABSCESS

Pelvic abscess is an uncommon complication of chronic or recurrent pelvic inflammation. It may occur as a sequela to acute pelvic or postabortal infection. Abscess formation is frequently associated with organisms other than the gonococcus, commonly anaerobic species, especially *Bacteroides*.

Any of the symptoms of acute or chronic pelvic inflammation may be present together with a fluctuant mass filling the cul-de-sac and dissecting into the rectovaginal septum. These patients usually have more severe symptoms. They may complain of painful defecation and severe back pain. The severity of symptoms is often directly proportionate to the size of the abscess, but occasionally even a large pelvic abscess may be totally asymptomatic. One woman who was admitted to the Obstetric Service with "fetal heart tones" was ultimately drained of 3000 mL of pus through a colpotomy incision.

Differential Diagnosis

The following conditions must be considered: tubo-ovarian abscess, either prolapsed or leaking into the cul-de-sac; periappendiceal abscess, ectopic pregnancy, ovarian neoplasm, uterine leiomyoma, retroflexed and incarcerated uterus, endometriosis, carcinomatosis, and diverticulitis with perforation.

Treatment

In addition to the measures outlined in the previous section, the following are required:

(1) Wide colpotomy drainage, carefully dissecting all sacculations. (The abscess usually is multiloculated.)

(2) Placement of a large catheter or drain in the abscess cavity for as long as drainage persists.

(3) Antibiotics to include probability of anaerobic as well as aerobic microorganisms: (a) Penicillin G, 20–30 million units intravenously per 24 hours, and chloramphenicol, 4–6 g intravenously per 24 hours. (b) Penicillin G, 20–30 million units intravenously per 24 hours; clindamycin, 600–1200 mg intravenously 4 times daily; and gentamicin, 5 mg/kg intravenously per 24 hours. (c) Cefoxitin, 8–12 g intravenously per 24 hours, and gentamicin or tobramycin, 5 mg/kg intravenously per 24 hours. *Caution:* Rare idiosyncratic reactions in the form of blood dyscrasias have been reported with chloramphenicol. With clindamycin, enterocolitis (diarrhea) is a complication that demands immediate cessation of use.

(4) Reevaluate abdominal findings frequently to detect peritoneal involvement.

(5) If the patient's condition deteriorates despite aggressive management, perform exploratory laparotomy. In patients with recurrent infections and loss of

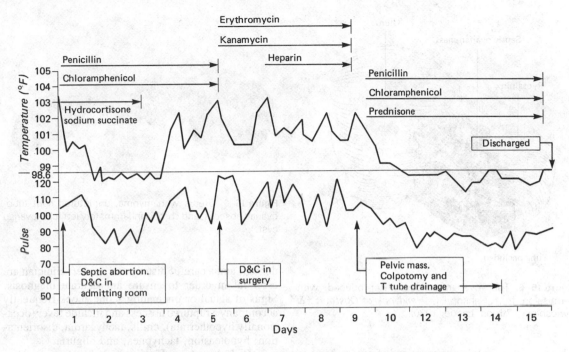

Figure 15–5. Clinical course and treatment of a typical patient with pelvic abscess.

reproductive function, total abdominal hysterectomy with bilateral salpingo-oophorectomy and lysis of adhesions offers the only cure. The patient's age and parity and the degree of involvement of the tubes and ovaries determine the extent of surgery when there is some likelihood of preservation of reproductive function. Always consider the possibility of pus in the upper abdomen.

(6) Fig 15–5 illustrates the clinical course and treatment of a typical patient with pelvic abscess. Even with adequate antibiotic therapy and heparin administration, improvement did not occur until satisfactory drainage was established.

Prognosis

With early treatment, the prognosis for the woman with a well-localized abscess is generally good. Proper drainage and antibiotic treatment are essential. Rupture into the peritoneum is a serious complication and demands immediate abdominal exploration. The prognosis for fertility is very poor following this type of abscess.

In general, the patient with a pelvic abscess, either primary or recurrent, will eventually require extirpative surgery of the internal genitalia.

TUBO–OVARIAN ABSCESS

Essentials of Diagnosis

- History of pelvic infection. May present as a complication of acute salpingitis.
- Severe lower abdominal and pelvic pain.
- Nausea and vomiting.
- Adnexal mass, usually extremely tender.
- Fever, tachycardia.
- Rebound tenderness in lower quadrants.
- Adynamic ileus.
- Culdocentesis productive of gross pus in case of rupture.

General Considerations

Tubo-ovarian abscess formation may occur following an initial episode of acute salpingitis but is usually seen with recurrent infection superimposed on chronically damaged adnexal tissue. Initially there is salpingitis with or without ovarian involvement. The inflammatory process may subside spontaneously or in response to therapy; however, the result may be anatomic derangement, with fibrinous attachments to nearby organs (Figs 15–6 to 15–8). Involvement of the adjacent ovary, usually at an ovulation site, may serve as the portal of entry for extension of infection and abscess formation.

Pressure of the purulent exudate may cause rupture of the abscess with resultant fulminating peritonitis, necessitating emergency laparotomy (Fig 15–9).

Slow leakage of the abscess may cause formation of a cul-de-sac abscess (see above). Culdocentesis into an abscess of this type will yield exudate like that of a ruptured tubo-ovarian abscess. Clinical appraisal usually will differentiate the 2 conditions, but if any doubt exists, treatment should be as specified for ruptured tubo-ovarian abscess.

Clinical Findings

A. Symptoms and Signs: The clinical spectrum may range from total absence of symptoms in a woman

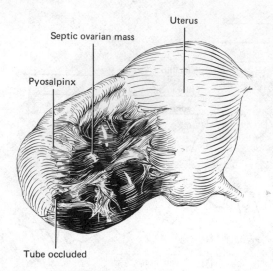

Figure 15–6. Tubo-ovarian abscess. (Reproduced, with permission, from Benson RC: *Handbook of Obstetrics & Gynecology,* 7th ed. Lange, 1980.)

Figure 15–8. Uterus with myoma, unruptured right tubo-ovarian abscess, and chronic inflammatory left tubo-ovarian cyst.

who on routine pelvic examination is found to have an adnexal mass to a moribund patient presenting with acute abdomen and septicemic shock.

The typical patient is usually young and of low parity, with a history of previous pelvic infection. No age group, however, is exempt. The usual symptoms are pelvic and abdominal pain, fever, nausea and vomiting, and tachycardia. Four-quadrant abdominal tenderness and guarding may be present. Adequate pelvic examination is often impossible because of tenderness, but an adnexal mass may be palpated. Culdocentesis usually can be performed and usually is productive of reaction fluid or gross pus.

Signs and symptoms of ruptured tubo-ovarian abscess may resemble those of any acute surgical ab-

domen, and a careful history and an alert clinician are essential in order to ensure an accurate diagnosis. Signs of actual or impending septic shock frequently accompany a ruptured abscess and include fever (occasionally hypothermia), chills, tachycardia, disorientation, hypotension, tachypnea, and oliguria.

B. Laboratory Findings: Laboratory findings are generally of little value. The white count may vary from leukopenia to marked leukocytosis. Urinalysis may demonstrate pyuria without bacteriuria.

C. X-Ray Findings: Plain films of the abdomen (KUB) usually demonstrate findings of adynamic ileus and may arouse a suspicion of adnexal mass.

D. Ultrasonography: Ultrasonography may be helpful and can be used with less complications to the patient. Ultrasound can be of great help in following the patient and detecting changes that may take place such as progression, regression, formation of pus pockets, rupture, etc.

E. Special Examinations: Culdocentesis fluid obtained in a woman with an unruptured tubo-ovarian abscess may demonstrate the same cloudy "reaction fluid" seen in acute salpingitis. With a leaking or ruptured tubo-ovarian abscess, however, grossly purulent material may be obtained.

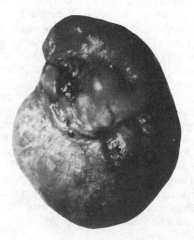

Figure 15–7. Unilateral tubo-ovarian abscess with uterine tube curled on top.

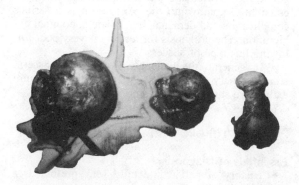

Figure 15–9. Bilateral tubo-ovarian abscess ruptured after removal.

Differential Diagnosis

An unruptured asymptomatic tubo-ovarian abscess must be differentiated from ovarian cysts or tumor, unruptured ectopic pregnancy, periappendiceal abscess, uterine leiomyoma, and hydrosalpinx.

An unruptured symptomatic tubo-ovarian abscess must be differentiated from perforation of the appendix or appendiceal abscess, perforation of a diverticulum or diverticular abscess, perforation of peptic ulcer, and any systemic disease that causes acute abdominal distress (eg, diabetic ketoacidosis, porphyria).

Complications

Unruptured tubo-ovarian abscess may be complicated by rupture with sepsis (Fig 15–10), reinfection at a later date, bowel obstruction, infertility, and ectopic pregnancy.

Ruptured tubo-ovarian abscess is a surgical emergency and is frequently complicated by septic shock, intra-abdominal abscess (eg, subphrenic abscess), and septic emboli with renal, lung, or brain abscess.

Treatment

A. Unruptured Asymptomatic Tubo-ovarian Abscess: Treatment is similar to that of chronic salpingitis: long-term antibacterial therapy and close follow-up. If the mass does not subside within 15–21 days or becomes larger, laparotomy is indicated. At exploration, total hysterectomy and bilateral adnexectomy are usually performed; however, in selected cases, unilateral salpingo-oophorectomy may be considered (see Recurrent or Chronic Pelvic Infection above).

B. Unruptured Symptomatic Tubo-ovarian Abscess: Treatment consists of immediate hospitaliza-
tion, bed rest in the semi-Fowler position, close monitoring of vital signs and urinary output, frequent abdominal examination, nasogastric suction, and intravenous sodium-containing fluids. Intensive antimicrobial therapy should be instituted and should include either clindamycin or chloramphenicol because of their specific activity against anaerobes. The following combinations, given in appropriate intravenous doses, are recommended for these severely ill patients: (1) penicillin G and chloramphenicol; (2) penicillin G plus clindamycin plus an aminoglycoside (gentamicin, tobramycin, kanamycin, amikacin); (3) cefoxitin or cefamandole plus either clindamycin or chloramphenicol; (4) moxalactam or cefotaxime with or without clindamycin or chloramphenicol.

Laparotomy is mandatory in all cases of suspected leakage or rupture as well as in all cases that do not respond to medical management.

If initial therapy is successful, the patient is kept on antibiotics (eg, oral tetracycline, 500 mg 4 times daily) for a minimum of 3 weeks and must have frequent follow-up examinations. If the abscess persists—and many do—laparotomy should be performed as indicated below. The reported incidence of surgery for clinically diagnosed, unruptured tubo-ovarian abscesses varies from 30 to 100%. On the Louisiana State University service, approximately 57% undergo surgery, and the remaining 43% seemingly respond to aggressive medical management. Similar experiences have been reported by Ginsburg et al from The John Hopkins Hospital.

C. Ruptured Tubo-ovarian Abscess: This is an acute life-threatening catastrophe requiring immediate medical therapy followed by operation. The course and treatment of a typical patient are shown in Fig 15–10. In addition to the procedures described above,

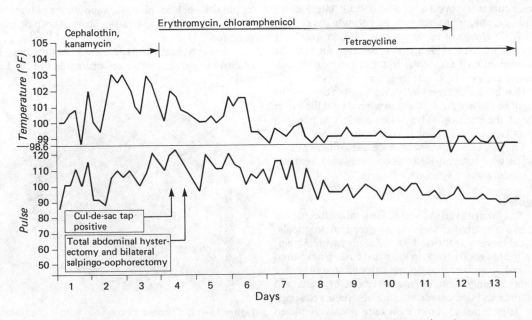

Figure 15–10. Clinical course and treatment of a patient with ruptured tubo-ovarian abscess.

the following are necessary:

1. Monitoring of the hourly urinary output with an indwelling catheter in place.

2. Monitoring of central venous pressure.

3. Administration of oxygen by mask.

4. Intravenous adrenal corticosteroids in pharmacologic doses, eg, methylprednisolone succinate, 15–30 mg/kg given as an intravenous bolus immediately. This may be repeated every 4–6 hours for 4 doses.

5. Rapid replacement of fluid and blood to maintain blood pressure and urine output greater than 30 mL per hour.

6. Rapid evaluation and preparation for immediate operation. The patient's systemic deficiencies should first be corrected by intravenous fluids and blood.

7. Surgical measures–The anesthesiologist must be completely informed of the patient's condition. A low midline incision is made to allow for cephalad extension. When the abdomen is opened, pus is obtained for aerobic and anaerobic cultures. The bowel is inspected and all loculated abscesses identified and drained. The subphrenic and subhepatic spaces are explored and loculations lysed to allow drainage of pus. Careful irrigation and suction are performed to minimize spread of infection. Total hysterectomy and bilateral salpingo-oophorectomy are usually performed; however, occasional supracervical hysterectomy is wise to expedite the operating time. The abscess wall is dissected from the adjacent structures. This is usually thick, indurated, and densely adherent to bowel, in which case it is best to dissect within the abscess wall, leaving a small portion of outer rim, rather than risk perforation of bowel wall. Careful surgical technique is necessary to avoid perforation of the bowel or ligation and transection of the ureters. The vaginal cuff is left open after a hemostatic interlocking continuous suture has been applied around the edge of the cuff. Drainage of the lower pelvis is done routinely by means of large rubber drains inserted through the open vaginal cuff after total hysterectomy or the cul-de-sac if the cervix is left in place.

Fascial drains are usually employed. They may be brought out either through a stab wound or at the lower angle of the incision. The drains are left in place as long as purulent material is recovered.

The fascia is closed with wide monofilament synthetic or wire sutures. Retention sutures may be used. The subcutaneous space is left open.

Prognosis

A. Unruptured Abscess: Generally, the patient with an unruptured abscess has an excellent prognosis. Medical therapy, followed by judicious surgical treatment, yields good results in the usual case. Unruptured localized abscesses that do not respond to aggressive medical management by improvement in signs and symptoms and decreasing size are best removed surgically. It is better to remove an unresponsive isolated abscess than to let the disease progress to ultimate rupture, requiring more extensive surgery with a strong probability of castration. Many clinically diagnosed unruptured tubo-ovarian abscesses may represent only acute salpingitis with omental and intestinal adhesions, which respond promptly to adequate antibiotic therapy. Serial ultrasound may help to identify the true unruptured tubo-ovarian abscesses. The outlook for fertility, however, is greatly reduced. The risk of reinfection must be considered if definitive surgical treatment has not been performed.

B. Ruptured Abscess: Before effective means of treating overwhelming septicemia became available and the need for immediate surgical intervention was recognized, the mortality rate from ruptured tubo-ovarian abscess was 80–90%. With modern therapeutic resources, both medical and surgical, the mortality rate should be less than 5%.

POSTOPERATIVE PELVIC INFECTIONS

Essentials of Diagnosis

- Recent pelvic surgery.
- Pelvic or low abdominal pain or pressure.
- Fever and tachycardia.
- Purulent, foul discharge.
- Constitutional symptoms: malaise, chills, etc.
- Vaginal cuff tenderness with cellulitis or abscess.

General Considerations

Patients who have had gynecologic surgery, especially hysterectomy, commonly develop postoperative infections of the remaining pelvic structures. These infections include simple cuff induration (cellulitis), infected cuff hematoma (cuff abscess), salpingitis, pelvic cellulitis, suppurative pelvic thrombophlebitis, and tubo-ovarian abscess with or without rupture.

Some typical gross specimens showing the effects of chronic pelvic disease are presented in Figs 15–11 to 15–13.

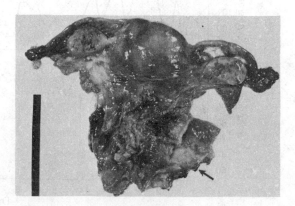

Figure 15–11. Chronic salpingitis with adhesions and thrombi in pelvic veins.

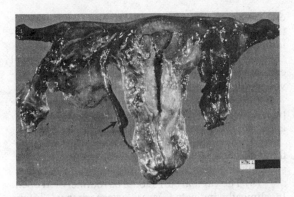

Figure 15–12. Thrombosis of pelvic veins due to chronic pelvic disease.

Figure 15–13. Bilateral chronic pelvic disease with hydrosalpinx.

The pathogenesis of posthysterectomy infection is simple and straightforward: the apex of the vaginal vault consists of crushed, devitalized tissue, and the loose areolar tissue in the parametrial areas usually oozes postoperatively. These conditions provide an ideal medium for the myriads of pathogens that normally inhabit the vagina.

The term cuff cellulitis implies that the soft tissue of the vaginal wall has been invaded by bacteria. In addition, the serum and blood at the cuff apex may become infected, resulting in an infected hematoma, which is, in essence, a cuff abscess. The infection may be forestalled at this point by establishing adequate drainage combined with antibiotic therapy. Infection may extend via lymphatic channels to the adnexa, resulting in salpingitis. Diffuse inflammatory involvement of the supporting tissue may occur, with resultant pelvic cellulitis. Pelvic veins may become involved in the infectious process, particularly if *Bacteroides* or anaerobic streptococci are predominant pathogens. Rarely, septic emboli to the lungs, brain, spleen, and elsewhere result in metastatic abscesses.

The incidence of posthysterectomy infection varies considerably with the population studied. In private patients, it is about 20–30%; in clinic patients, the rate approaches 50%.

Clinical Findings

The diagnosis of postoperative cuff infection is made clinically; laboratory studies may be useful in establishing the specific etiologic diagnosis and determining the sensitivity of the recovered bacteria to various antibiotics.

A. Symptoms and Signs: Any postoperative gynecologic patient who develops fever is considered to have pelvic infection until all other causes are ruled out. More than 90% of cases of postoperative febrile disease in these women will be due to pelvic infection. The patient usually complains of bilateral lower quadrant, pelvic, and perineal pain or pressure. She usually has tachycardia and complains of chills and malaise. Abdominal distention due to paralytic ileus is not infrequent. Urinary symptoms due to perivesical irrita-

tion are occasionally reported.

Although some investigators have stated that fever due to postoperative pelvic infection usually does not occur before the third or fourth postoperative day, it is not unusual for a patient to develop temperatures of 38.3–39.4 °C (101–103 °F) by the 24th–36th postoperative hour. It is probable that at least half of women who develop infection are febrile by the 36th hour.

The vaginal cuff is indurated and erythematous on speculum examination. Separation of the edges of the cuff usually releases a seropurulent exudate that may be foul-smelling. Manipulation of the cuff usually causes considerable pain. On bimanual examination, the cuff apex is indurated and exquisitely tender. Loculations of pus may be identified with the examining finger, especially if the disease is not manifest until the third or fourth postoperative day. In some cases in which concealed postoperative hemorrhage has occurred, a massive retroperitoneal abscess may be identified and drained.

Lymphatic extension of the infection to supporting tissues results in pelvic cellulitis, demonstrable on pelvic examination as tender induration in the parametrial areas. The infection may involve the tubes and ovaries with resultant abscess formation in unresponsive or inadequately treated patients.

The diagnosis of suppurative pelvic thrombophlebitis usually is not apparent until after the sixth postoperative day, at which time the patient continues to have hectic spiking fever with a diurnal variation of 39–40.5 °C (102.2–105 °F). The pelvic findings are usually unrevealing except for pelvic tenderness, with induration or cellulitis. Surprisingly, the woman's general health often is good unless septic embolization has occurred.

B. Laboratory Findings: Unfortunately, as previously outlined, the polymicrobial nature of these infections prohibits accurate identification of the offending microorganisms in a reasonable time period. For this reason, broad-spectrum empirical antimicrobial administration is necessary.

Serial complete blood counts usually demonstrate

leukocytosis but occasionally enable the physician to detect concealed hemorrhage, which may harbor a large pelvic abscess.

C. X-Ray Findings: Chest films are unrevealing in most cases but can be useful if pulmonary complications are suspected.

D. Ultrasonography: Pelvic sonograms may prove helpful in detecting either retroperitoneal or tubo-ovarian abscesses that develop as a complication of cuff infection.

Differential Diagnosis

The vast majority of cases of significant febrile morbidity occurring after gynecologic surgical procedures can be attributed to pelvic infection (see above). The following conditions, however, should also be considered:

Pulmonary atelectasis may become manifest within 12–36 hours after operation. This can usually be detected by auscultation and confirmed by chest x-ray. Aspiration pneumonitis must always be considered if pulmonary problems develop.

Deep vein thrombophlebitis of the lower extremities is rarely detected clinically and, when present, is seldom accompanied by significant fever. Superficial phlebitis of the upper extremity due to an indwelling venous catheter may cause significant pyrexia. Long-term (48–72 hours) infusion of intravenous antimicrobials will increase the likelihood of phlebitis. Although the routine of changing the intravenous site every 48 hours may prevent this complication, it will respond to warm soaks and anti-inflammatory agents (aspirin, indomethacin, etc) if it does develop.

Urinary tract infection may also account for the fever. Because of the liberal use of indwelling catheters in gynecologic surgery, significant bacteriuria commonly develops; however, this rarely causes fever unless acute pyelonephritis develops.

Fever from abdominal wound infection usually becomes manifest on or after the fourth postoperative day. These infections may be confused with pelvic infections which develop during this time. Examination of the abdominal wound is mandatory in all febrile cases. It may be necessary to probe the abdominal incision carefully, regardless of its appearance, especially if the pelvic examination is unrevealing.

Complications

Complications of postoperative pelvic infection include extensive pelvic or intra-abdominal abscesses, tubo-ovarian abscess with or without rupture, intestinal adhesions and obstruction, septic pelvic thrombophlebitis with metastatic abscesses, and septicemia.

Prevention

Many attempts have been made to decrease infectious morbidity following gynecologic surgical procedures. None have been uniformly successful, but the following measures may be of some help:

(1) Preoperative cleansing of the vagina for several days with douches containing bactericidal or bacteriostatic agents (eg, hexachlorophene, povidone-iodine).

(2) Preoperative insertion of antibacterial vaginal creams or suppositories, especially if cervicitis or vulvovaginitis is present.

(3) Preparation of the vagina with hexachlorophene or povidone-iodine solution just prior to surgery.

(4) Meticulous attention to hemostasis at operation and gentle handling of tissues. The use of large, strangulating hemostatic sutures should be avoided.

(5) The vaginal cuff should be routinely left open. In clinically indicated cases, extraperitoneal T tube drainage should be used.

(6) Antimicrobial prophylaxis beginning preoperatively with 2 additional doses given postoperatively (usually 6 and 12 hours) has been shown by many to significantly reduce pelvic infectious morbidity following vaginal and abdominal hysterectomy. Before using prophylaxis, one should consider the guidelines proposed by Ledger: (a) Morbidity on a specific service should be significant enough to warrant attempts to decrease it. (b) Antimicrobials of relatively insignificant toxicity but proved value should be used. (c) The first dose should be given preoperatively to ensure adequate tissue concentrations at the time of surgery. (d) Only short-term (eg, 3 doses) prophylaxis should be given. Most clinical trials of antimicrobial prophylaxis have shown that following vaginal or abdominal hysterectomy these drugs given in 3 perioperative doses significantly decreased the incidence of pelvic cellulitis. For simplicity of administration and safety, it is currently recommended that three 2-g intravenous doses of a cephalosporin be given. Cefazolin, cefamandole, and cefoxitin demonstrate dramatic lowering of pelvic infection morbidity. In otherwise uncomplicated cases, pelvic infections that develop despite administration of these drugs generally will be mild in nature. It must be emphasized that severe infections and resultant complications are not always prevented by their use, however.

(7) Severe, more advanced infections may be prevented by early diagnosis, drainage (including an open vaginal cuff), and treatment of mild infections.

Treatment

If a cuff infection is found, adequate drainage may be established by separating the apposed edges with ring forceps or some other suitable instrument. Hematomas or abscesses may also be drained in this manner. Care must be taken not to disrupt the intact peritoneum. The usual supportive measures are instituted, and antibiotic therapy is begun. These infections are generally mild and respond promptly to penicillin given intravenously in conjunction with a tetracycline or an aminoglycoside. Cefamandole and cefoxitin have proved quite valuable as single-agent therapy for these infections also. Rarely, with severely ill patients with polymicrobial or anaerobic infections, the addition of either clindamycin or chloramphenicol to these reg-

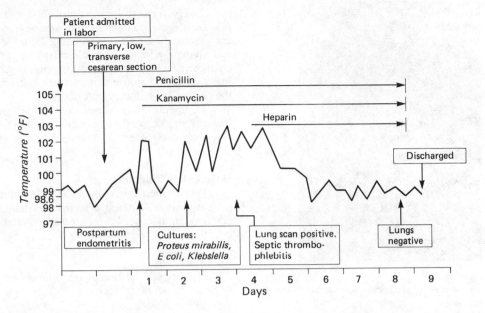

Figure 15–14. Clinical course and treatment of an obstetric patient with postoperative septic thrombophlebitis.

imens may be necessary to effect a cure.

This regimen is successful in most cases, and the patient becomes afebrile within 48–72 hours. If a large, infected pelvic hematoma has developed, more prolonged treatment will be necessary. Large hematomas may be drained and irrigated from below by means of a Foley catheter or Penrose drain introduced into the abscess cavity.

A postoperative tubo-ovarian abscess is treated expectantly as outlined in the section on unruptured tubo-ovarian abscess. If intra-abdominal rupture of a pelvic abscess or tubo-ovarian abscess is suspected, immediate laparotomy is indicated. (See section on ruptured tubo-ovarian abscess, above.)

Persistent fever and clinical signs of unresponsiveness to therapy may indicate pelvic cellulitis or septic pelvic thrombophlebitis. The latter diagnosis is generally one of exclusion after a 7- to 10-day course of antibiotics. Intermittent intravenous heparin therapy, 5000 units every 4 hours, should be given. Persistence of fever in spite of heparin therapy suggests abscess formation. Abscesses—as well as septic thrombophlebitis—are usually associated with anaerobic bacteria, and antimicrobial therapy should include clindamycin, chloramphenicol, or carbenicillin in addition to other agents effective against aerobic microorganisms.

Fig 15–14 details the course and treatment of a case of postoperative septic thrombophlebitis occurring in an obstetric patient but presenting in the same way as in a gynecologic patient.

PELVIC TUBERCULOSIS

Essentials of Diagnosis

- Infertility.
- Active or healed pulmonary tuberculosis.
- Findings by hysterosalpingography.
- Recovery of *Mycobacterium tuberculosis* from either menstrual fluid or biopsy specimen.

General Considerations

In the USA, pelvic tuberculosis is becoming a rare entity. When it does occur, it usually represents secondary invasion from a primary lung infection via the lymphohematogenous route (Fig 15–3). The overall incidence of pelvic tuberculosis in patients with pulmonary tuberculosis is approximately 5%. Prepubertal tuberculosis rarely results in infection of the female genital tract.

Once the pelvic organs become affected, direct extension to adjacent organs may occur. Older studies in the USA indicated that the oviducts were most frequently involved (90%) and the endometrium next most frequently (70%). More recent studies in Scotland, where the disease is still prevalent, showed endometrial involvement in more than 90% of cases and tubal involvement in only 5%.

Clinical Findings

A. Symptoms and Signs: The only complaint may be infertility, though dysmenorrhea, pelvic pain, and evidence of tuberculous peritonitis may also be present. Endometrial involvement may result in amenorrhea or some other disturbance of the cycle. Abdominal or pelvic pain from this infection is commonly associated with low-grade fever, asthenia, and weight

Figure 15–15. Miliary tuberculosis involving the uterus and peritoneum.

loss. The physician must keep this rare entity in mind in assessing a patient with these complaints. The diagnosis can usually be established on the basis of a complete history and physical examination, chest x-ray and lung scan, and appropriate tests such as a tuberculin (Mantoux) test, sputum smears, and sputum cultures. Tuberculosis of the female genital tract is usually secondary to hematogenous spread involving the endometrium, tubes, and ovaries. The manifestations are usually those of chronic pelvic disease and sterility. Gross ascites with fluid containing more than 3 g of protein per 100 mL of peritoneal fluid is characteristic of tuberculous peritonitis.

This entity is usually encountered in the course of a gynecologic operation done for other reasons. Although it may be mistaken for chronic pelvic inflammation, some distinguishing features usually can be found: extremely dense adhesions without planes of cleavage, segmental dilatation of the tubes, and lack of occlusion of the tubes at the ostia. If the internal genitalia are involved, with disseminated granulomatous disease of the serosal surfaces, ascites usually is present. Clinical diagnosis is difficult.

B. Laboratory Findings: The best direct method of diagnosis in suspected genital tuberculosis is detection of acid-fast bacteria by means of the Ziehl-Neelsen stain followed by culture on Lowenstein-Jensen medium. The specimen may be from menstrual discharge, from curettage or biopsy, or from peritoneal biopsy in cases where ascites is present. A rapid sedimentation rate, peripheral blood eosinophilia, and a strongly positive Mantoux test are additional evidence of tuberculous infection.

C. X-Ray Findings:

1. Chest x-ray–A chest x-ray should be taken in any patient with proved or suspected tuberculosis of other organs or tissues.

2. Hysterosalpingography–The tubal lining may be irregular, and areas of dilatation may be present. Saccular diverticula extending from the ampulla and giving the impression of a cluster of currants are characteristic of granulomatous salpingitis. Other findings that should arouse suspicion are calcifications of the periaortic or iliac lymph nodes.

D. Special Examinations: Visual inspection (laparoscopy) as well as aspiration of fluid for culture and biopsy of affected areas is possible and often diagnostic.

Differential Diagnosis

Pelvic tuberculosis should be differentiated from schistosomiasis, enterobiasis, lipoid salpingitis, carcinoma, chronic pelvic inflammation, and mycotic infections.

Complications

Sterility and tuberculous peritonitis are possible sequelae of pelvic tuberculosis.

Treatment

A. Medical Measures: Several regimens are useful. In general, 2 or 3 of the following drugs are used in various combinations and treatment schedules: isoniazid (INH), streptomycin, ethambutol, cycloserine, and rifampin. Combination therapy is used to minimize toxicity and prevent the emergence of resistant strains. Treatment should be continued for 24–36 months, since extrapulmonary tuberculosis is more difficult to eradicate.

Culture and sensitivity studies are necessary to detect variants that may be resistant to the usual combinations of tuberculostatic drugs.

B. Surgical Measures: Although the primary treatment is medical, surgery plays a role in some cases. If the diagnosis of pelvic tuberculosis is made prior to operation, medical therapy is given for 12–18 months. The ultimate indications for surgery include (1) masses not resolving with medical therapy, (2) resistant or reactivated disease, (3) persistent menstrual irregularities, and (4) fistula formation.

Prognosis

The prognosis for life and health is excellent if chemotherapy is instituted promptly, though the prognosis for fertility is poor.

SEXUALLY TRANSMITTED DISEASES

The term venereal disease, ascribed to Jacques de Bethencourt (1527), was until quite recently charged with social condemnation. The shame also was felt to contaminate, quite unfairly, those who played no part in transmission of the disease, eg, infants with congenital syphilis.

Over the years, medical philosophy turned from

censure and reluctant treatment to nonjudgmental diagnosis and specific therapy for the benefit not only of the individual patient but also of others who should be treated for or protected from the disease. Diseases such as gonorrhea and herpes simplex type 2 infection have reached epidemic proportions, attesting to the importance of the public health aspect of this problem.

The term sexually transmitted diseases is now used to denote disorders spread principally by sexual contact. These diseases are caused by organisms peculiarly adapted to growth in the genital tract. Some diseases spread by body contact but not necessarily by coitus—eg, pediculosis pubis, molluscum contagiosum—are discussed with the dermatitides rather than here.

The list of diseases traditionally thought of as venereal infections has been extended recently to include lymphogranuloma venereum, cytomegalic inclusion disease, herpes simplex type 2, and even hepatitis B. The last is not discussed further here, since nothing is known about the exact mode of transmission. Herpes genitalis is discussed in Chapter 9.

GONORRHEA

Essentials of Diagnosis

- Most affected women are asymptomatic carriers.
- Purulent vaginal discharge.
- Frequency and dysuria.
- Recovery of organism in selective media.
- May progress to pelvic infection.

General Considerations

Neisseria gonorrhoeae is a gram-negative diplococcus that forms oxidase-positive colonies and ferments glucose. The organism may be recovered from the urethra, cervix, anal canal, or pharynx. Optimal recovery of the organism is with use of Thayer-Martin or Martin-Lester (Transgrow) medium. *N gonorrhoeae* is killed rapidly by drying, sunlight, heat, and most disinfectants.

The columnar and transitional epithelium of the genitourinary tract is the principal site of invasion. The organism may enter the upper reproductive tract (Fig 15–2), causing salpingitis with attendant complications. It has been estimated that 10–17% of women with gonorrhea develop pelvic infection if untreated.

Clinical Findings

A. Symptoms and Signs:

1. Early symptoms–Most women with gonorrhea are asymptomatic. Early symptoms, when they occur, are localized to the lower genitourinary tract and include vaginal discharge, urinary frequency or dysuria, and rectal discomfort. Pharyngitis may occur after oral intercourse; acute proctitis after rectal intercourse.

2. Discharge–Pelvic examination should be complete. The vulva, vagina, cervix, and urethra may be inflamed and may itch or burn. Specimens of discharge from the cervix, urethra, and anus should be taken for culture in the symptomatic patient. A strain of purulent urethral exudate may demonstrate gram-negative diplococci in leukocytes. Similar findings in a purulent cervical discharge are less conclusively diagnostic of *N gonorrhoeae*.

3. Bartholinitis–Unilateral swelling in the inferior lateral portion of the introitus suggests involvement of Bartholin's duct and gland. In early gonococcal infections, the organism may be recovered by gently squeezing the gland and expressing pus from the duct. Enlargement, tenderness, and fluctuation may develop, signifying abscess formation. *N gonorrhoeae* is then less frequently recovered; however, the frequency of infection with other bacteria merits search for these pathogens. Spontaneous evacuation of pus often occurs if drainage by incision is not done. The infection may result in asymptomatic cyst formation.

4. Ophthalmia neonatorum may result from delivery through an infected birth canal.

5. Gonococcal vulvovaginitis in children– Gonococcal invasion of nonkeratinized membranes in young girls produces severe vulvovaginitis. This form of prepubertal vulvovaginitis is rare. Infection is commonly introduced by adults, and in such cases the physician must consider the possibility of child-molesting or battering and take appropriate steps to protect the child. The typical sign is a purulent vaginal discharge with dysuria. The genital mucous membranes are red and swollen.

B. Laboratory Findings: A presumptive diagnosis of gonorrhea can be based on examination of the stained smear; however, confirmation requires positive identification on selective media. Secretions are examined under oil immersion for presumptive identification. Gram-negative diplococci that are oxidase-positive and obtained from selective media (Thayer-Martin or Transgrow) usually signify *N gonorrhoeae*. Carbohydrate fermentation tests may be performed, but, in addition to being time-consuming and expensive, they occasionally yield other species of *Neisseria*. Cultures therefore are reported as "presumptive of *N gonorrhoeae*."

Complications

The major complication in the female is salpingitis and the complications that may arise from salpingitis (see p 339). *N gonorrhoeae* can be recovered from the cervix in about half of women with salpingitis. Asymptomatic gonorrhea may result in disseminated infection with bacteremia that usually causes arthritis and dermatitis. The arthritis is usually due to tenosynovitis, but pyoarthroses may occur. Rarely, bacteremia with *N gonorrhoeae* may cause meningitis or endocarditis.

Differential Diagnosis

Vaginitis and urethritis due to other causes may be associated with dysuria, frequency, or vaginal discharge. Once the adnexa are involved, the entities listed in the section on differential diagnosis of acute or chronic salpingitis must be considered.

A. Vaginitis and Cervicitis: Vaginal discharge and cervicitis associated with *Trichomonas vaginalis* is typically profuse, bubbly, and malodorous and frequently causes vulvar irritation with pruritus. Likewise, *Candida albicans* usually causes vulvar infection. Herpes simplex infection is associated with ulcerative lesions of the vulva and the ectocervix. *Chlamydia trachomatis* may produce purulent cervicitis identical to that caused by gonorrhea. Gram staining may be helpful in these cases.

B. Urethritis: Any of the above may cause urethritis, which also may be associated with bacterial cystitis, coital trauma, or chemical irritation.

C. Vulvovaginitis in Children: Usually this is associated with self-insertion of seemingly innocuous foreign bodies, with secondary infection with perineal flora.

Prevention

Gonorrhea is a reportable disease that can only be controlled by detecting the asymptomatic carrier and treating her and her sexual partners. All high-risk populations should be screened by routine cultures. Reexamination is mandatory to rule out reinfection or failure of therapy. The use of condoms will protect against gonorrhea.

Treatment

Note: Any patient with gonorrhea must be suspected of having syphilis also and managed accordingly.

A. Uncomplicated infections: Aqueous procaine penicillin G, 4.8 million units intramuscularly at 2 sites, with 1 g probenecid orally; *or* tetracycline, 500 mg orally 4 times daily for 5 days; *or* ampicillin, 3.5 g, or amoxicillin, 3 g, given orally with 1 g probenecid by mouth. Follow-up cultures should be obtained 3–7 days after completion of treatment. Failures are given spectinomycin hydrochloride, 2 g intramuscularly. This regimen may be given as primary therapy for the patient who is penicillin-allergic and who cannot tolerate oral tetracycline.

B. Acute salpingitis: See p 339.

Prognosis

The prognosis with prompt treatment is excellent. With recurrent attacks, infertility may result.

SYPHILIS

Essentials of Diagnosis

Primary syphilis:
- Painless genital sore (chancre) on labia, vulva, vagina, cervix, anus, lips, or nipples.
- Coitus 10–90 days before appearance of chancre (average, 21 days).
- Inguinal lymphadenopathy followed by generalized lymphadenopathy in third to sixth weeks.

- Dark-field microscopic findings positive.
- Serologic tests are positive in 25% of cases.

Secondary syphilis:
- Bilaterally symmetric papulosquamous eruption: condyloma latum, mucous patches.
- Dark-field findings positive.
- Positive serologic test for syphilis.

Syphilis of the newborn:
- History of maternal syphilis.
- Positive serologic test for syphilis.
- Stigmas of congenital syphilis (eg, x-ray changes of bone, hepatosplenomegaly, jaundice, anemia).

Tertiary syphilis:
- Saccular aneurysm of the thoracic aorta.
- Neurologic changes associated with degeneration of the posterior portion of the spinal cord.
- Gummatous lesions in any body system.
- Spinal fluid negative.
- Serologic reaction positive.

General Considerations

Syphilis is caused by *Treponema pallidum,* transmitted by direct contact with an infectious lesion. Treponemes will pass through intact mucous membranes or abraded skin. Ten to 90 days after the treponemes enter, a primary lesion (chancre) develops. The chancre persists for 1–5 weeks and then heals spontaneously. Serologic tests for syphilis are usually nonreactive when the chancre first appears but become reactive 1–4 weeks later. Two weeks to 6 months (average, 6 weeks) after the primary lesion disappears, the generalized cutaneous eruption of secondary syphilis may appear. The skin lesions heal spontaneously in 2–6 weeks. Serologic tests are almost always positive during the secondary phase. Latent syphilis may follow the secondary stage and may last a lifetime, or tertiary syphilis may develop. The latter usually becomes manifest 4–20 or more years after the disappearance of the primary lesion.

In one-third of untreated cases, the destructive lesions of late (tertiary) syphilis develop. The complications of tertiary syphilis are fatal in almost one-fourth of cases, but one-fourth never show any ill effects.

Clinical Findings

A. Symptoms and Signs:

1. Primary syphilis–The chancre (Fig 15–16) develops at the portal of entry 10–90 days (average, 21 days) after exposure. It is an indurated, firm, painless papule or ulcer with raised borders. Groin lymph nodes may be enlarged, firm, and painless. Genital lesions are not usually seen in women unless they occur on the external genitalia; however, careful examination may reveal a typical cervical or vaginal lesion. Primary lesions may occur on any mucous membrane or skin area of the body (nose, breast, perineum, etc), and darkfield examination is required for all suspect lesions. Serologic tests should be done every week for 6 weeks.

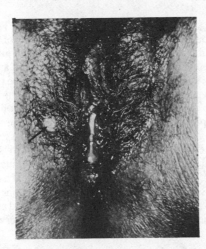

Figure 15–16. Chancre of primary syphilis (arrow).

2. Secondary syphilis–About 2 weeks to 6 months (average, 6 weeks) after the disappearance of the primary lesion, a rash develops. The typical lesions are maculopapular, follicular, or pustular. "Moth-eaten" alopecia of scalp hair in the occipital area is characteristic. Loss of the lateral third of the eyebrows may occur. Moist papules can be seen in the anogenital area and the mouth—an eruption known as condyloma latum that is diagnostic of the disease. *T pallidum* may be recovered from the lesions, and serologic tests are positive. Lymphadenopathy is an important finding; occasionally, splenomegaly is noted. Needle aspiration of enlarged lymph nodes produces fluid that is usually positive for syphilis by darkfield examination.

3. Latent syphilis–The World Health Organization has defined 2 periods: early latent, duration less than 4 years; and late latent, duration greater than 4 years. After the first year, the individual is considered noninfectious except in the pregnant woman, who can transmit syphilis to her fetus.

4. Tertiary syphilis–Neurologic, vascular, and other lesions characteristic of tertiary syphilis may be reviewed in standard textbooks.

5. Syphilis during pregnancy–The chancre is often unnoticed, insignificant, and asymptomatic, and the nonpruritic rash may be transitory. Occasionally, the primary and secondary phases may be florid and complicated by secondary infection. Pregnancy will neither alter relapses after inadequate or ill-chosen therapy nor modify latent or late syphilis.

The effect of syphilis on pregnancy and the fetus depends largely upon whether the maternal infection occurs before pregnancy, at conception, or later. As the years pass from the time the mother contracted syphilis, the likelihood of a fetus showing serologic or other evidence of syphilis diminishes despite lack of treatment. Recently, it has been shown that the spirochete may traverse the placenta and infect the fetus early in pregnancy. The previously ascribed "fetal immunity" to syphilis prior to 18 weeks of pregnancy seems therefore not to be due to placental impermeability to treponemes but rather to fetal immunoincompetence before this time. After 18 weeks, the fetus is able to mount an immunologic attack, and the resultant tissue damage from inflammatory changes may develop. The earlier in pregnancy the fetus is exposed, the more severe the fetal infection, and stillbirths may result. Infection of the mother in late pregnancy does not necessarily result in a syphilitic infant.

6. Congenital syphilis–The newborn with congenital syphilis may be undergrown, with wrinkled facies because of reduced subcutaneous fat. The skin may have a brownish (café au lait) tint. Nonetheless, the commonest lesion of early congenital syphilis in the newborn is a bullous rash, so-called **syphilitic pemphigus.** Large blebs may appear over the palms and soles and occasionally in other areas. Seropurulent fluid from these bullous lesions swarms with treponemes.

Mucositis may be noted in the mouth and upper respiratory passages of the newborn. This is identical with that of secondary syphilis in older subjects. Because of this problem, the baby may have what has been termed "syphilitic snuffles." The nasal discharge is very contagious because it contains large numbers of *T pallidum*.

The newborn may have lymphadenitis and enlarged liver and spleen. The bones usually reveal signs of osteochondritis and an irregular epiphyseal juncture (Guérin's line) on x-ray. The eyes, central nervous system structures, and other organs may reveal abnormalities at birth, or defects may develop later in untreated cases.

Any infant with the stigmas of syphilis should be placed in isolation until a definite diagnosis can be made and treatment administered.

Newborns with congenital syphilis may appear healthy at birth but often develop symptoms weeks or months later. Examine the body for stigmas of syphilis at intervals of 3 weeks to 4 months. If the mother's serologic test is positive at delivery, the baby's will also be positive. Obtain serial quantitative serologic tests of the infant's blood for 4 months. A rising titer indicates congenital syphilis, and treatment is indicated.

B. Laboratory Findings:

1. Identification of organism–*T pallidum* can usually be identified by darkfield examination of specimens from cutaneous lesions, but the recovery period of the treponeme is very brief; in most cases, diagnosis depends on the history and serologic tests. An immunofluorescent technique is now available for dried smears.

2. Serologic tests–Diagnostic tests after the primary lesion has disappeared are confined largely to serologic testing. Serologic tests become positive several weeks after the primary lesion appears.

a. Nontreponemal tests–These measure reaginic antibody detected by highly purified cardiolipin-lecithin antigen. They can be performed rapidly, relatively easily, and inexpensively. Nontreponemal tests are used principally for syphilis screening, but they are relatively specific, so they are not absolute for syphilis and false-positive reactions may occur. Nontreponemal tests currently in use are flocculation procedures that include the VDRL slide test and rapid reagin test for screening procedures in the field. These latter tests are more sensitive but less specific than the VDRL. If they are positive, the activity should be verified, and the degree of reactivity should be checked by the VDRL test. Complement fixation tests, eg, Kolmer, are no longer used in the USA.

The VDRL test (the nontreponemal test in widest use) generally becomes positive 4–6 weeks after infection, or 1–3 weeks after the appearance of the primary lesion; it is almost invariably positive in the secondary stage. The VDRL titer is usually high in secondary syphilis and tends to be lower or even nil in late forms of syphilis, although this is highly variable. A falling titer in treated early syphilis or a falling or stable titer in latent or late syphilis indicates satisfactory therapeutic progress. "False-positive" serologic reactions are frequently encountered in a wide variety of situations including collagen diseases, infectious mononucleosis, malaria, many febrile diseases, leprosy, vaccination, drug addiction, old age, and possibly pregnancy. False-positive reactions are usually of low titer and transient and may be distinguished from true positives by specific treponemal antibody tests.

b. Treponemal antibody tests–The fluorescent treponemal antibody absorption (FTA-ABS) test is the most widely employed treponemal test. It measures antibodies capable of reacting with killed *T pallidum* after absorption of the patient's serum with extracts of nonpathogenic treponemes. The FTA-ABS test has now generally replaced the *T pallidum* immobilization (TPI) test, which assays the ability of a patient's serum to immobilize live virulent spirochetes.

Differential Diagnosis

Primary syphilis must be differentiated from chancroid, granuloma inguinale, lymphogranuloma venereum, herpes genitalis, carcinoma, scabies, trauma, lichen planus, psoriasis, drug eruption, aphthosis, mycotic infections, Reiter's syndrome, and Bowen's disease.

Secondary syphilis must be differentiated from pityriasis rosea, psoriasis, lichen planus, tinea versicolor, drug eruption, "id" eruptions, perlèche, parasitic infections, iritis, neuroretinitis, condyloma acuminatum, acute exanthems, infectious mononucleosis, alopecia, and sarcoidosis.

Prevention

If the patient is known to have been exposed to syphilis, do not wait for the disease to develop to the clinical or reactive serologic stage before giving preventive treatment. Even so, every effort should be made to reach a diagnosis, including a complete physical examination, before administering preventive treatment.

In all pregnant women, a routine serologic test for syphilis should be performed at the first visit. The test should be repeated between 28 and 32 weeks of gestation. If the test is positive, attention must be given to the patient's prior serologic test and therapy (if any) for syphilis. If doubt exists as to whether or not the patient has active maternal syphilis, repeat therapy is far better than the risk of congenital syphilis in the neonate.

Syphilis is still a serious public health problem. Teaching young people about the disease and its consequences is still the best method of control. Use of a condom, together with soap and water decontamination after coitus, would prevent most cases. If a lesion develops, a physician should be notified at once. All exposed persons must be sought out and treated and the case reported to the communicable disease service in the city or state.

Treatment

A. Early Syphilis and Contacts: (Primary, secondary, and latent syphilis of less than 1 year's duration.)

1. Benzathine penicillin G, 2.4 million units intramuscularly.

2. Aqueous procaine penicillin G, 600,000 units intramuscularly daily for 8 days (4.8 million units total).

3. Tetracycline hydrochloride, 500 mg orally 4 times daily for 15 days (30 g total).

4. Erythromycin (stearate, ethylsuccinate, or base), 500 mg orally 4 times daily for 15 days (30 g total).

B. Late Syphilis: (Includes latent syphilis of indeterminate duration or more than 1 year's duration.)

1. Benzathine penicillin G, 2.4 million units intramuscularly for 3 successive weeks (7.2 million units total).

2. Aqueous procaine penicillin G, 600,000 units intramuscularly daily for 15 days (9 million units total).

3. Tetracycline hydrochloride, 500 mg orally 4 times daily for 30 days.

4. Erythromycin, 500 mg orally 4 times daily for 30 days.

C. Syphilis in Pregnancy: Treat as indicated above, except that tetracycline is not recommended. If serologic tests are equivocal (eg, possible biologic false-positive), it is better to err on the side of early treatment.

D. Congenital Syphilis: Adequate maternal treatment before 16–18 weeks prevents congenital syphilis. Treatment thereafter may arrest fetal syphilitic infection, but some stigmas may remain.

1. Benzathine penicillin G, 50,000 units/kg intramuscularly as a single injection.

2. Aqueous procaine penicillin G, 100,000 units/kg intramuscularly in divided daily doses over 10 days.

HERPES SIMPLEX

Vulvovaginal infections with this virus have assumed a primary role in sexually transmitted diseases because of frequent incapacitation from pain as well as prohibitive risks of death or morbidity to the newborn exposed to maternal lesions. These infections are discussed in Chapter 9.

TRICHOMONAS VAGINITIS

Essentials of Diagnosis

- Accounts for 20–25% cases of vulvovaginitis.
- Profuse greenish, frothy, malodorous discharge.
- Vulvar pruritus, burning, and swelling common.

General Considerations

Trichomonas vaginalis is a motile anaerobic protozoon that is frequently found in the vaginal flora of asymptomatic sexually active women. It is not known why infection with symptoms occurs, but it is transmitted during sexual contact.

Clinical Findings

A. Symptoms and Signs: Vulvovaginitis is manifested by vaginal discharge and pruritic and painful vulvar irritation. The vaginal mucosa and cervix demonstrate an inflammatory exudate, occasionally with "strawberry dots." Vulvitis is marked by erythema, pain, and edema; occasionally, the intertriginous areas of the thighs are involved.

B. Laboratory Findings: The highly motile protozoon is easily seen on a wet mount of vaginal secretions. Cultures on selective medium are commercially available but usually unnecessary.

Differential Diagnosis

Any cause of cervicitis and vulvovaginitis may simulate *Trichomonas* vaginitis.

Treatment

Metronidazole is the treatment of choice. Two regimens are effective: a 2-g dose (8 tablets of 250 mg) given at one time, or 750 mg given 3 times daily for 2 days (18 tablets). The male sexual partner should be treated simultaneously.

Metronidazole has been shown to be mutagenic (not teratogenic) in animals, so it seems wise to proscribe its use during the first trimester of pregnancy. Unfortunately, alternative treatment regimens are less effective. They include douches with povidone-iodine solution and intravaginal application of various creams.

CHLAMYDIAL INFECTIONS

Essentials of Diagnosis

- Mucopurulent cervicitis
- Salpingitis
- Urethral syndrome
- Nongonococcal urethritis in male consort
- Neonatal infections
- Lymphogranuloma venereum

General Considerations

The spectrum of genital infections caused by serotypes of *Chlamydia trachomatis* has only become recently appreciated. Chlamydiae are obligate intracellular microorganisms that have a cell wall similar to that of gram-negative bacteria. They can be grown only by tissue culture. With the exception of the L serotypes, chlamydiae attach only to columnar epithelial cells without deep tissue invasion. As a result of this characteristic, clinical infection may not be apparent. For example, infections of the eye, respiratory tract, or genital tract are accompanied by discharge, swelling, erythema, and pain localized in these areas only.

Clinical Findings

A. Symptoms and Signs: Women with cervical infection generally have a mucopurulent discharge with hypertrophic cervical inflammation. If salpingitis develops, then symptoms described above under "Acute Salpingitis-Peritonitis" become manifest.

B. Laboratory Findings: Diagnosis of *C trachomatis* using tissue culture is the most sensitive method; however, this specialized modality is not yet widely available. In infants with inclusion conjunctivitis, Giemsa stain of purulent discharge from the eye is used to identify chlamydial inclusions, but similar stained slides of exudates in adults with genital infections are only about 40% accurate in the diagnosis of these infections. Serologic methods, either the complement fixation or microimmunofluorescent test, are not totally accurate, because 20–40% of sexually active women have positive antibody titers. In fact, most women with microimmunofluorescent antibody do not have a current infection.

Differential Diagnosis

Mucopurulent cervicitis is frequently caused by *Neisseria gonorrhoeae,* and selective cultures for this organism should be performed. As discussed above, *C trachomatis* alone may cause as many as 20–35% of cases of acute salpingitis in the USA. In both cervicitis as well as salpingitis, cultures may frequently be positive for both organisms.

Complications

Adverse sequelae of salpingitis, specifically infertility due to tubal obstruction and ectopic pregnancy, are the most dire complications of these infections. Pregnant women with cervical chlamydial infection can transmit infections to their newborns; there is evidence that up to 50% of infants born to such mothers will have inclusion conjunctivitis. In perhaps 10%, an indolent chlamydial pneumonitis develops at 2–3 months of age. This pathogen may also cause otitis media in the neonate. Whether or not maternal cervical infection with *Chlamydia* causes significantly increased fetal and perinatal wastage by abortion, premature delivery, or stillbirth remains unknown.

Treatment

In most cases, *Chlamydia* can be eradicated from the cervix by oral erythromycin, tetracycline, or sulfamethoxazole given for a minimum of 14 days. Giving high doses of ampicillin has resulted in the elimination of *C trachomatis* from the cervices of women with acute salpingitis. Current studies indicate that 3–5% of pregnant women and as many as 15% of sexually active nonpregnant women have an asymptomatic chlamydial cervical infection. It is not known whether attempts to eradicate asymptomatic colonization will prevent chlamydial cervicitis, salpingitis, or neonatal infections.

LYMPHOGRANULOMA VENEREUM

Essentials of Diagnosis

- Rectal ulceration, inguinal lymphadenopathy, or rectal stricture.
- Positive complement fixation test.

General Considerations

The causative agent of lymphogranuloma venereum is one of the aggressive L serotypes of *Chlamydia trachomatis*. It is encountered more frequently in the tropical and subtropical nations of Africa and Asia but is also seen in the southeastern USA. Transmission is sexual; men are affected more frequently than women (6:1). The incubation period is 7–21 days.

Clinical Findings

A. Symptoms and Signs: (Fig 15–17.)

1. Early–Early, a vesicopustular eruption may go undetected; with inguinal (and vulvar) ulceration, lymphedema, and secondary bilateral invasion, an excruciating condition arises. Sitting or walking may

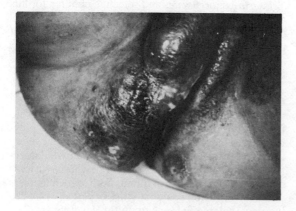

Figure 15–17. Lymphogranuloma venereum. Note involvement of perineum and spread over buttocks.

cause pain. During the inguinal bubo phase, the groin is exquisitely tender. A hard cutaneous induration (red to purplish-blue) is a notable feature. This usually occurs within 10–30 days after exposure and may be bilateral. Anorectal lymphedema occurs early; defecation is painful, and the stool may be blood-streaked.

2. Late–Later, as the lymphedema and ulceration undergo cicatrization, rectal stricture makes defecation difficult or impossible. Vaginal narrowing and distortion may end in severe dyspareunia. In the late phase, systemic symptoms—fever, headache, arthralgia, chills, and abdominal cramps—may develop.

B. Laboratory Findings: The diagnosis can be proved only by isolating *C trachomatis* from appropriate specimens and confirming the immunotype. These procedures are seldom available, so less specific tests are employed.

A complement fixation test utilizing a heat-stable antigen that is group-specific for all *Chlamydia* species is available. This test is positive at a titer of ≥ 1:16 in more than 80% of cases of lymphogranuloma venereum. If acute or convalescent sera are available, then a rise in titer is particularly helpful in making the diagnosis. Application of the microimmunofluorescent test may be useful also.

Differential Diagnosis

As with any disseminated disease, the systemic symptoms of lymphogranuloma venereum may resemble meningitis, arthritis, pleurisy, or peritonitis. The cutaneous lesions must be differentiated from those of granuloma inguinale, tuberculosis, early syphilis, and chancroid. In case of colonic lesions, proctoscopic examination and mucosal biopsy are needed to rule out carcinoma, schistosomiasis, and granuloma inguinale.

Complications

Perianal scarring and rectal strictures—late complications—can involve the entire sigmoid, but the urogenital diaphragm is rarely involved. Vulvar elephantiasis (esthiomene) produces marked distortion of the external genitalia.

Prevention

The disease is reportable. Avoiding infectious contact with a carrier is achieved by use of a condom or by refraining from coitus. Definite exposure can be treated with sulfonamides.

Treatment

A. Chemotherapy: Tetracyclines should be given orally in daily doses of 2 g for 2–4 weeks according to tolerance. If disease persists, the course should be repeated. Sulfonamide drugs are suppressive but not curative. Give in doses of 1 g 4 times daily for at least 2 weeks; then, after a rest interval of 1 week, the course is repeated. Treatment does not hasten healing but prevents secondary infections, ulcerations, and strictures.

B. Local and Surgical Treatment: Anal strictures should be dilated manually at weekly intervals. Severe stricture may require diversionary colostomy. If the disease is arrested, complete vulvectomy may be done for cosmetic reasons. Abscesses should be aspirated, not excised.

GARDNERELLA VAGINALIS VAGINITIS
(Corynebacterium Vaginale Vaginitis)

Gardnerella vaginalis (formerly designated *Corynebacterium vaginale* and *Haemophilus vaginalis*) is a small, nonmotile, nonencapsulated, pleomorphic rod that stains variably with Gram's stain. It is spread by sexual contact and, though of low virulence, causes vaginitis. The disorder may be atypical and even more troublesome when *G vaginalis* coexists with more virulent organisms.

G vaginalis infection is often overlooked. It may be suspected on the basis of the microscopic appearance of unstained exfoliated vaginal cells in a wet preparation that appears to be dusted with many small, dark particles, actually *G vaginalis* organisms. These "clue cells" are presumptive evidence of the presence of this organism. In case of mixed infection (eg, with *Candida albicans*), it may not be possible to make the diagnosis except by culture.

Specific therapy for vaginal infection caused by this organism has been neglected, owing in part to the rather innocuous symptoms reported. Standard teaching held that vaginally applied sulfonamide cream was adequate, but now this seems doubtful. Another regimen of questionable benefit is ampicillin given orally, 500 mg 4 times daily for 1 week. More recently, controlled clinical and microbiologic studies have indicated that oral metronidazole, 500 mg twice daily for 7 days, may be necessary for cure. An alternative regimen may be oral trimethoprim-sulfamethoxazole, but this has not been approved for this use in the USA.

CHANCROID
(Soft Chancre)

Essentials of Diagnosis
- Painful, tender genital ulcer.
- Culture positive for *Haemophilus ducreyi*.
- Inguinal adenitis with erythema or fluctuance.

General Considerations

Chancroid is a venereal disease characterized by a painful genital ulcer. It is infrequently seen in the USA, although it occurs more frequently in Africa, the West Indies, and Southeast Asia. The causative organism is the gram-negative rod *H ducreyi*. Exposure is usually via coitus, but accidentally acquired lesions of the hands have occurred. The incubation period is short: the lesion usually appears in 3–5 days or sooner.

Clinical Findings

A. Symptoms and Signs: The early lesion is a vesicopustule on the pudendum, vagina, or cervix. Later, it degenerates into a saucer-shaped ragged ulcer circumscribed by an inflammatory wheal. Typically, the lesion is very tender and produces a heavy, foul discharge that is contagious. A cluster of ulcers may develop.

Painful inguinal adenitis is noted in over half of cases. The buboes may become necrotic and drain spontaneously.

B. Laboratory Findings: Syphilis must first be ruled out. Clinical diagnosis is more reliable than smears or cultures, because of the difficulty of isolating this organism. If *H ducreyi* is isolated, this is diagnostic, but isolation occurs in less than one-fourth of cases. Aspirated pus from a bubo is the best material for culture.

Differential Diagnosis

Syphilis, granuloma inguinale, lymphogranuloma venereum, and herpes simplex may coexist and need to be ruled out.

Prevention

Chancroid is a reportable disease. Routine antibiotic prophylaxis is not warranted. Condoms can give protection. Soap and water liberally used are relatively effective. Education is essential.

Treatment

A. Local Treatment: Good personal hygiene is important. The early lesions should be cleansed with mild soap solution. Sitz baths are beneficial.

B. Antibiotic Treatment: Give one of the sulfonamides (eg, sulfisoxazole), 1 g orally 4 times daily for 14 days. The course may have to be repeated. Tetracycline, 500 mg orally 4 times daily for 14 days, is less effective than sulfisoxazole; however, a combination of the 2 has been recommended on the basis of experience from Vietnam.

Prognosis

Untreated or poorly managed cases of chancroid may persist, and secondary infection may develop. Frequently, the ulcers heal spontaneously. If not treated, they may cause deep scarring with sequelae in men.

GRANULOMA INGUINALE

Essentials of Diagnosis
- Ulcerative vulvitis, chronic or recurrent.
- Donovan bodies revealed by Wright's or Giemsa's stain.

General Considerations

Granuloma inguinale is a chronic ulcerative granulomatous disease that usually develops in the vulva, perineum, and inguinal regions. The disease is

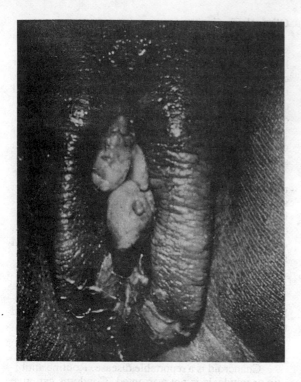

Figure 15–18. Granuloma inguinale.

almost nonexistent in the USA. It is most frequent in India, Brazil, the West Indies, some South Pacific Islands, and parts of Australia, China, and Africa. The causative organism is *Calymmatobacterium granulomatis* (Donovan body). Donovan bodies are bacteria encapsulated in mononuclear leukocytes. Transmission is via coitus. The incubation period is 8–12 weeks.

Clinical Findings

A. Symptoms and Signs: Although granuloma inguinale most often involves the skin and subcutaneous tissues of the vulva and inguinal regions, cervical, uterine, orolabial, and ovarian sites have been reported. A malodorous discharge is characteristic. The disorder often begins as a papule which then ulcerates, with the development of a beefy-red granular zone with clean, sharp edges. The ulcer shows little tendency to heal, and there are usually no local or systemic symptoms. Healing is very slow, and satellite ulcers may unite to form a large lesion. Lymphatic permeation is rare, but lymphadenitis may result when the cutaneous lesion becomes superimposed on lymphatic channels. Inguinal swelling is common, with late formation of abscesses (buboes). Granuloma inguinale may be manifested by chronic cervical lesions on rare occasions. These lesions usually take the form of redness, ulceration, or the formation of granulation tissue. They produce a chronic inflammatory exudate characterized histologically by lymphocytes, giant cells, and histiocytes. They may mimic carcinoma of the cervix and must be distinguished from this as well as other neoplastic diseases.

The chronic ulcerative process may involve the urethra and the anal area, causing marked discomfort. Introital contraction may make coitus difficult or impossible; walking or sitting may become painful. The possibility of the coexistence of another venereal disease must be considered. Spread to other areas occurs in about 7% of patients.

B. Laboratory Findings: Direct smear from beneath the surface of an ulcer may reveal gram-negative bipolar rods within mononuclear leukocytes. These are seen best in Wright-stained smears. When smears are negative, a biopsy specimen should be taken. Biopsy of the lesion generally will show granulation tissue infiltrated by plasma cells and scattered large macrophages with rod-shaped cytoplasmic inclusion bodies (Mikulicz cells). Pseudoepitheliomatous hyperplasia often is seen at the margin of the ulcer.

The diagnosis is made by demonstrating, in biopsy or smear material stained with Wright's, Giemsa's, or silver stain, large mononuclear cells containing one or more cystic inclusions containing the so-called Donovan bodies—small round or rod-shaped particles that stain purple in traditional hematoxylin and eosin preparations.

Prevention

Personal hygiene is the best method of prevention. Therapy immediately after exposure may abort the infection.

Treatment

Tetracycline is the drug of first choice. The recommended dose is 500 mg orally 4 times daily for 2–3 weeks. Occasionally, doses of 40–60 g may be used. Erythromycin or chloramphenicol, 500 mg 4 times daily for 2–3 weeks, is also effective. Penicillin is not effective.

CONDYLOMATA ACUMINATA
(Venereal Warts)

Warts are benign, virus-induced epithelial tumors caused by the human papillomavirus. These viruses belong to the virus group responsible for all human warts, which vary with their body location. In the genital region they are known as condylomata acuminata, or genital warts. These pink, elongated, pointed, soft, moist, pruritic excrescences are often seen in the vagina, on the cervix, or over the perineal region. The virus is transmitted by coitus. The lesions become especially exuberant during pregnancy. The growths may aggregate into a large mass that may even block the introitus during late delivery. Secondary infection is common. Venereal warts usually regress markedly during the puerperium and may even disappear.

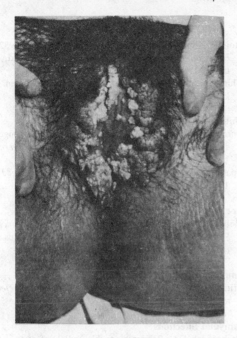

Figure 15–19. Condylomata acuminata.

The virus of condyloma acuminatum does not affect the fetus, but podophyllum resin and fluorouracil, often effective drugs during the nonpregnant state, are noxious to the fetus and therefore contraindicated during pregnancy. The gravida with condyloma acuminatum should be treated by cryotherapy, fulguration, or excision of the lesions. Improved vaginal hygiene often is beneficial. (See also Chapter 9.)

● ● ●

References

General

Cattarall RD: *A Short Textbook of Venereology: The Sexually Transmitted Diseases,* 2nd ed. English Univ Press, 1974.

Hoeprich PD (editor): *Infectious Diseases,* 2nd ed. Harper & Row, 1977.

Jones KL, Shainberg LW, Byer CO (editors): *VD.* Harper & Row, 1974.

Krupp MA, Chatton MF: *Current Medical Diagnosis and Treatment 1982.* Lange, 1982.

Ledger WJ: *Infection in the Female.* Lea & Febiger, 1977.

McCormack W: Sexually transmissible conditions other than gonorrhea and syphilis. In: *Practice of Medicine.* Wolber PGH (editor). Harper & Row, 1974.

Monif GRG: *Infectious Diseases in Obstetrics and Gynecology.* Harper & Row, 1974.

Neary MP et al: Pre-operative vaginal bacteria and postoperative infections in gynaecological patients. *Lancet* 1974;**2**:1291.

Richards RN: *Venereal Diseases and Their Avoidance.* Holt, Rinehart & Winston, 1974.

Semchyshyn S: Fitz-Hugh and Curtis syndrome. *J Reprod Med* 1979;**22**:45.

Shofield CBS: *Sexually Transmitted Diseases,* 2nd ed. Churchill Livingstone, 1974.

Stiller R: *The Love Bugs: A Natural History of the VD's.* Nelson, 1974.

Pelvic Inflammatory Disease

Chow AW et al: The bacteriology of acute pelvic inflammatory disease: Value of cul-de-sac cultures and relative importance of gonococci and other aerobic or anaerobic bacteria. *Am J Obstet Gynecol* 1975;**122**:876.

Cunningham FG et al: Evaluation of tetracycline or penicillin and ampicillin for treatment of acute pelvic inflammatory disease. *N Engl J Med* 1977;**296**:1380.

Eschenbach DA, Holmes KK: Acute pelvic inflammatory disease: Current concepts of pathogenesis, etiology and management. *Clin Obstet Gynecol* 1975;**18**:35.

Gorbach SL, Barlett JC: Anaerobic infections. *N Engl J Med* 1974;**290**:1177.

Holmes KK: The *Chlamydia* epidemic. *JAMA* 1981;**245**:1718.

Mardh PA et al: *Chlamydia trachomatis* infection in patients with acute salpingitis. *N Engl J Med* 1977;**296**:1377.

Mickal A: Management of complications of severe pelvic inflammatory disease. *J Med Liban* 1974;**27**:361.

Sweet RL: Diagnosis and treatment of pelvic inflammatory disease in the emergency room. *Sex Transm Dis* 1981;**8** (**Suppl**):156.

Sweet RL, Ledger WG: Cefoxitin: Single agent treatment of mixed aerobic-anaerobic pelvic infection. *Obstet Gynecol* 1979;**54**:193.

Sweet RL et al: Use of laparoscopy to determine microbiologic etiology of acute salpingitis. *Am J Obstet Gynecol* 1979;**134**:68.

Treharne JD et al: Antibodies to *Chlamydia trachomatis* in acute salpingitis. *Br J Vener Dis* 1979;**55**:28.

Westrom L et al: Infertility after acute salpingitis: Results of treatment with different antibiotics. *Curr Ther Res* 1979;**26** (**Suppl**):752.

Pelvic and Tubo-ovarian Abscess

Cunningham FG, Hemsell DL: Management of ruptured pelvic abscesses. *Contemp Obstet Gynecol* 1981;**18**:107.

Franklin EW III, Hevron JE Jr, Thompson JD: Management of the pelvic abscess. *Clin Obstet Gynecol* 1973;**136**:753.

Ginsburg DS et al: Tubo-ovarian abscess: A retrospective review. *Am J Obstet Gynecol* 1980;**138**:1055.

Mickal A, Sellman AH: Management of tubo-ovarian abscess. *Clin Obstet Gynecol* 1969;**12**:252.

Postoperative Pelvic Infections

Allen JL, Rampone JF, Wheeless CR: Use of a prophylactic antibiotic in elective major gynecologic operations. *Obstet Gynecol* 1972;**39**:218.

Grossman JH III et al: Prophylactic antibiotics in gynecologic surgery. *Obstet Gynecol* 1979;**53**:537.

Hemsell DL et al: Cefoxitin for prophylaxis in premenopausal women undergoing vaginal hysterectomy. *Obstet Gynecol* 1980;**56**:629.

Ledger WJ, Gee C, Lewis WP: Guidelines for antibiotic prophylaxis in gynecology. *Am J Obstet Gynecol* 1975;**121**:1038.

Pelvic Tuberculosis

Hutchins CJ: Tuberculosis of the genital tract: A changing picture. *Br J Obstet Gynaecol* 1977;**84**:534.

Klein TA & others: Pelvic tuberculosis. *Obstet Gynecol* 1976;**48**:99.

Gonorrhea

Center for Disease Control, Public Health Service: Gonorrhea: Recommended treatment schedules. *MMWR* 1979;**28**:13.

Curran JW et al: Female gonorrhea: Its relation to abnormal uterine bleeding, urinary symptoms and cervicitis. *Obstet Gynecol* 1975;**45**:195.

Gilstrap LC et al: Gonorrhea screening in male consorts of women with pelvic infection. *JAMA* 1977;**238**:965.

Holmes KK, Beaty HN: Gonococcal infections. Page 824 in: *Harrison's Principles of Internal Medicine,* 8th ed. Wintrobe MM et al (editors). McGraw-Hill, 1977.

Thin RN, Shaw EJ: Diagnosis of gonorrhea in women. *Br J Vener Dis* 1979;**55**:10.

Syphilis

Fiumara NJ, Lessell S: Manifestations of late congenital syphilis: An analysis of 271 patients. *Arch Dermatol* 1970;**102**:78.

Sparling RF: Diagnosis and treatment of syphilis. *Engl J Med* 1971;**284**:642.

Chancroid

Wilcox RR: Chancroid. Page 185 in: *Recent Advances in Sexually Transmitted Diseases.* Morton RS, Harres JRW (editors). Churchill Livingstone, 1975.

Granuloma Inguinale

Fritz GS et al: Mutilating granuloma inguinale. *Arch Dermatol* 1975;**111**:1464.

Chlamydial Infections

Eschenbach DA: Recognizing chlamydial infections. *Contemp Obstet Gynecol* 1980;**16**:15.

Grayson JT, Wang S-P: New knowledge of chlamydiae and the diseases they cause. *J Infect Dis* 1975;**132**:87.

Holder WR, Duncan WC: Lymphogranuloma venereum. *Clin Obstet Gynecol* 1972;**15**:1004.

Oriel JD et al: Chlamydial infection: Isolation of *Chlamydia* from patients with nonspecific genital infections. *Br J Vener Dis* 1972;**48**:429.

Endometriosis* | 16

James M. Ingram, MD

Endometriosis consists of the presence of functioning endometrium outside its normal site in the lining of the uterine cavity. It is usually confined to the pelvis in the region of the cul-de-sac, the ovaries, the uterosacral ligaments, and the uterovesical peritoneum, though remote sites may be affected as well.

In spite of over 80 years of research effort by many investigators, very little is known about the histogenesis of this disorder or why it does or does not respond to treatment. The major complication is infertility, but the incidence of infertility in endometriosis is variable, particularly in the early stages, so that accurate analysis of the results of treatment is difficult. Moreover, all of the studies have been done on small series of patients, and most studies have been nonrandomized and retrospective, with inadequate documentation of the location and extent of disease. Long-term follow-up reports (over 5 years) are not available.

Except for the trophoblast, endometriosis is the only example of a benign proliferative process that invades and distorts or even destroys otherwise normal organs. The rate at which proliferation and invasion occur is governed by unknown factors, and these processes are unpredictable. Therefore, the natural course of the disease in any individual patient cannot be predicted.

A high familial incidence of endometriosis, suggested earlier by random observations, has been confirmed by controlled studies. Thus, an apparently normal patient with an affected first-degree relative (sibling, offspring, parent) has about a 7% probability of developing endometriosis. Moreover, the severity of the disease and the recurrence rate are higher in a patient whose close relatives have endometriosis. Polygenic multifactorial inheritance appears to be the most likely genetic cause.

Laparoscopy has provided valuable data on the incidence of endometriosis and is mandatory for early diagnosis. Although endometriosis is still most common in white patients of higher socioeconomic status who postpone having children, laparoscopy has dispelled the notion that endometriosis is rare in other races or in the early years of reproductive life. At least 10% of Japanese women hospitalized for gynecologic symptoms had endometriosis confirmed by laparoscopy in one recent report, and endometriosis was found in 23% of black women who underwent laparoscopy for pelvic pain. Moreover, laparoscopy has disclosed that endometriosis is not uncommon in women 17–25 years of age.

Accurate clinical staging is essential for satisfactory evaluation of therapy. The most desirable components of several classification schemes have been incorporated recently into one system, which is given in Table 16–1.

Pathogenesis

Theories of the histogenesis of endometriosis fall into 3 general groups: (1) those which assume that ectopic endometrial tissue is transplanted from the uterus to a pathologic location within the peritoneal cavity by way of the uterine tubes; (2) those which suggest that ectopic endometrium develops in situ from local tissues by metaplasia; and (3) combinations of these hypotheses.

A. Transplantation Theories: Retrograde menstruation and direct implantation was proposed by Sampson in 1921 in an attempt to explain the occurrence of ectopic endometrial tissue. About half of women with patent uterine tubes who undergo surgery during menses show evidence of retrograde menstruation. This observation has been confirmed both by laparoscopy and by the finding of menstrual blood and detritus in microscopic serial step sections of oviducts removed during the menstrual period. Sampson's concept was substantiated more than 20 years later by Scott, TeLinde, and Wharton in the rhesus monkey and by Ridley's experiments demonstrating implantation of menstruum collected from the cervix in humans. The observation of bloody peritoneal fluid during repeated peritoneal dialysis indicates that retrograde menstruation occurs in the majority of cycles in many, perhaps in most, women. Retrograde menstruation must now be accepted as a common event. However, why only a minority of women develop implants in the presence of frequent retrograde flow is an unanswered question.

Iatrogenic transplantation of endometrium may occur in an abdominal incision or in other ectopic sites

---

*Adenomyosis is sometimes called "endometriosis interna" but is considered by most gynecologists and pathologists to be a distinct disease entity. It is discussed in Chapter 11.

Table 16—1. American Fertility Society Classification of Endometriosis.*

Patient's name _____

Stage I	(Mild)	1–5
Stage II	(Moderate)	6–15
Stage III	(Severe)	16–30
Stage IV	(Extensive)	31–54

Total _____

			<1 cm	1–3 cm	>3 cm
PERITONEUM	ENDOMETRIOSIS		<1 cm	1–3 cm	>3 cm
			1	2	3
	ADHESIONS		filmy	dense w/ partial cul-de-sac obliteration	dense w/ complete cul-de-sac obliteration
			1	2	3
OVARY	ENDOMETRIOSIS		<1 cm	1–3 cm	>3 cm or ruptured endometrioma
		R	2	4	6
		L	2	4	6
	ADHESIONS		filmy	dense w/ partial ovarian enclosure	dense w/ complete ovarian enclosure
		R	2	4	6
		L	2	4	6
TUBE	ENDOMETRIOSIS		<1 cm	>1 cm	tubal occlusion
		R	2	4	6
		L	2	4	6
	ADHESIONS		filmy	dense w/ tubal distortion	dense w/ tubal enclosure
		R	2	4	6
		L	2	4	6

Associated Pathology:

*From: The American Fertility Society: Classification of endometriosis. *Fertil Steril* 1979;**32**:633. Reproduced with the permission of the publisher, The American Fertility Society.

following any surgical procedure in which the uterine cavity is opened. Endometriosis may also develop in cervical or vaginal lacerations and in episiotomy incisions. Such transplantation depends upon estrogen support and is inhibited by infection. It is not known why a large inoculum of endometrium will implant readily in some women but not others.

Both Halban and, later, Javert offered the concept of "metastasis" of endometrium by lymphatic dissemination, and endometrium has been demonstrated in pelvic lymphatic channels and nodes, usually incidental to surgery for other conditions. Although lymphatic metastasis must be rare if it does occur, this avenue of spread is the best explanation for the occasional reported cases of endometriosis of the umbilicus.

Recent long-term experiments with castrated rhesus monkeys have shown that minced endometrium obtained by endometrial removal, when seeded into the peritoneal cavity of the same animal, resulted in endometrial implants that "burned out" within 12 weeks. In other ovariectomized monkeys, which were sustained by estradiol or progesterone (or both), the implants continued to grow. These findings indicate that steroids are not necessary for implantation, but hormones may be essential for continued growth of the implants.

Hematogenous (venous) spread of endometriosis has been demonstrated frequently in rabbits. In humans, vascular spread would provide a plausible explanation for the increasing numbers of reported cases of endometriosis of the pleura. Another mechanism could be the spread of endometrial implants to the pleural cavity by way of diaphragmatic "pores" or lymphatic vessels, producing a clinical entity similar to Meigs' syndrome. Metaplastic pleural change is an unlikely explanation, because 90% of the reported cases of thoracic endometriosis involved only the right lung.

B. In Situ or Metaplastic Theories: The theory of metaplasia of the coelomic epithelium, first proposed by Meyer, has been supported by Gruenwald's embryologic studies and more recently by Novak, by Meigs, and by Ranney, who have postulated that dormant immature multipotential cells of the embryonic coelomic lining, which are common in the central area of the pelvis, may persist in adult life. Certainly, during early embryonic development, small islands of coelomic epithelium do persist in the zones of formation of the limb buds and thorax. It is further postulated that under cyclic hormonal stimulation by the ovary, these cells undergo metaplasia and may form endometrial tissue. In any event, the metaplasia theory may explain the occasional implants of endometrium within the peritoneum, in the pleura, in the extremities, and even in other areas of the body.

The müllerian cell rest theory of Russell follows the same line of reasoning as the coelomic epithelium theory except that the embryonic cells are thought to be confined to the müllerian system. While this theory could explain extraperitoneal endometriosis in or along the line of the müllerian ducts, it cannot account for distant implants.

C. Combination of Transplant and In Situ Theories: Except in cases of iatrogenic transplantation, a combination of causes is probably responsible for endometriosis. From a practical point of view, a theory of retrograde flow, direct implantation, and metaplasia of coelomic epithelium is sufficient to account for endometriosis in most locations.

Pathology

A. Gross Pathologic Features: The gross pathologic appearance of endometriosis varies widely depending upon the location and extent of the disease. Typical implants are dark-blue or brownish-black cysts surrounded by a zone of fibrosis and contracture or "puckering," often adherent to surrounding structures. This puckering of adjacent tissue is pathognomonic of endometriosis and distinguishes it from other entities such as carcinoma and from other hemorrhagic cysts of the ovary.

The ovary is the most common site of implantation (approximately 50%). The cysts vary in diameter from 1 to 100 mm. Ovarian involvement is almost always bilateral. The larger cysts, filled with old dark hemolyzed blood, are often referred to as "chocolate cysts."

Other areas frequently involved are the uterosacral ligaments, the cul-de-sac, the posterior surface of the uterus and broad ligaments, the rectosigmoid colon, the round ligament, and the pelvic peritoneum overlying the bladder or lower ureters. Endometriotic foci in sites other than the ovary are usually smaller and more numerous. Thus, in the earlier stages, the lesions of endometrosis often have the appearance of "powder burns." Later, these elevated clusters of peritoneal implants become surrounded by a stellate zone of dense fibrous tissue. As the process advances, there is widespread adherence of bowel or omentum to the involved structures because of the inflammatory response secondary to repeated local hemorrhage. Periodic bleeding may occur into the surrounding tis-

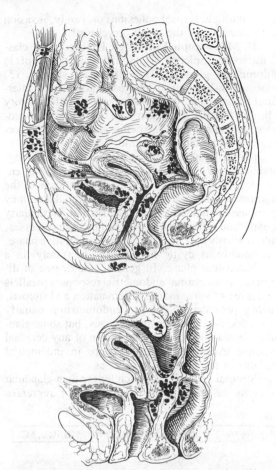

Figure 16–1. Common sites of endometrial implants (endometriosis). (Reproduced, with permission, from Dunphy JE, Way LW [editors]: *Current Surgical Diagnosis & Treatment,* 5th ed. Lange, 1981.)

sue or, by rupture of the implant, into the peritoneal cavity itself. The fibrosis often accounts for the mass of the lesion and may be considered both a result of and a limiting factor in the growth of the implants. The uterus is frequently fixed in retroversion by adhesions to the cul-de-sac and rectosigmoid colon.

Endometriosis may deeply invade the walls of the small or large bowel, the posterior vaginal wall, the bladder, or the ureters, but it rarely penetrates the mucosal surfaces of these organs. Menstrual bleeding from the gastrointestinal or urinary tract generally is the result of intense inflammation of the involved mucosa rather than actual bleeding from endometriosis that has penetrated the mucosa. Hence, endoscopy at the time of menses may reveal mucosal bleeding but not ulceration. Areas of endometriosis in the cervix, vagina, and perineum are usually deeply embedded and may be referred to as "blue-domed cysts." Most are direct mucosal implants on raw surfaces; vaginal cysts often occur as extensions from the cul-de-sac.

The appendix and small bowel are involved much less commonly than the large bowel. Obstruction is due to multiple serosal adhesions or, rarely, invasion or cicatrization of the small bowel wall.

B. Microscopic Pathologic Features: The classic microscopic picture of endometriosis consists of (1) endometrial glands, (2) endometrial stroma, (3) hemosiderin-laden macrophages, (4) old or new interstitial hemorrhage, and (5) surrounding inflammatory cells and fibrosis. If hemorrhage is recent, the phagocytes contain red cells and hemosiderin; in old hemorrhage, they contain only hemosiderin.

Glandular elements may be abundant or, in long-established or regressed disease and in stromal endometriosis, completely absent. The response of the endometrial glands to cyclic ovarian stimulation may be in phase with the uterine endometrium, particularly in early and mild disease. As the process progresses, endometriosis may be found in the proliferative phase, occasionally as cystic hyperplasia, or (rarely) in a pseudodecidual phase. In general, the degree of divergence from normal endometrial responses parallels the degree of surrounding inflammation and fibrosis. During pregnancy, ectopic endometrium usually shows decidual changes and necrosis, but some glandular elements seem to be incapable of any decidual response. Adenocarcinoma develops in endometrial implants in fewer than 1% of cases.

Stromal cells persist much longer than glandular elements as endometriosis advances or regresses

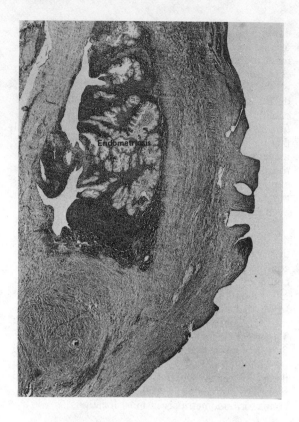

Figure 16–3. Endometriosis of ovary.

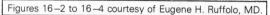

Figures 16–2 to 16–4 courtesy of Eugene H. Ruffolo, MD.

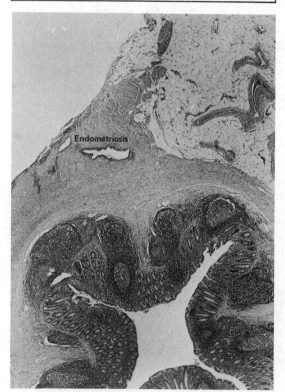

Figure 16–2. Endometriosis of appendix.

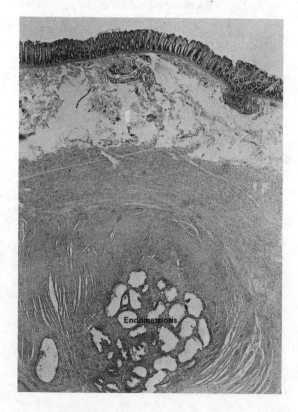

Figure 16–4. Endometriosis of colon.

("burns out"). In fact, stromal elements together with pigment-laden macrophages are the most characteristic microscopic structures in advanced disease.

Stromal endometriosis is both a clinical and histologic entity. It has also been called proliferative stromatosis or endometriosis interstitiale. The stroma is abundant, but the glandular elements are absent or sparse. The histogenesis is unknown, but it is generally accepted that endometrial stroma cannot produce glands whereas endometrial glands may produce stroma. Malignant transformation of ectopic endometrial stroma to sarcoma is not common, though a few cases have been reported.

The microscopic picture of endometriosis is variable. This is particularly true in the ovary, where atrophy due to pressure often obliterates the microscopic features so completely that in about one-third of cases no vestige of endometrial tissue can be found—only a zone of hemosiderin-filled phagocytes or pseudoxanthoma cells. In such cases, the histologic diagnosis must be presumptive, eg, "hemorrhagic cyst compatible with endometriosis." Between this latter stage and the early typical endometriosis, all degrees of histologic variation are found.

During pregnancy or hormonally induced pseudopregnancy, most endometriotic foci react by developing typical decidua. In older or larger implants, there may be only a glandular secretory response; in others, no alteration may be noted. Following delivery or hormonal withdrawal, necrosis and hemorrhage often occur followed by resolution and fibrosis of endometriotic implants.

Pathologic Physiology

The response of ectopic endometrium to hormonal stimuli depends upon numerous factors, including (1) the ratio of glandular to stromal components, (2) the size and age of the implant, (3) its location in the pelvis, (4) phases of the menstrual cycle or the duration of pregnancy, and (5) the response of adjacent tissue.

A. Bleeding: Most implants bleed during menstruation. The bleeding response is chiefly due to estrogen plus progesterone, as in ovulatory cycles. Implants on the peritoneal surfaces bleed most often into the peritoneal cavity, producing chemical irritation and adherence of adjacent organs. Egress of blood from deeply buried lesions is not always possible, so that blood may distend and infiltrate surrounding tissues. Intraperitoneal bleeding from smaller implants ceases spontaneously or is sealed off by adherence to pelvic organs, omentum, or bowel. Hemorrhage from deeper implants into surrounding tissue results in phagocytosis, slow absorption, and ultimately fibrosis. Pregnancy or pseudopregnancy exerts a beneficial effect by producing a decidual reaction. After delivery or withdrawal, a much greater degree of disorganization, resorption, and scarring generally results.

B. Pain: Pelvic pain develops for at least 3 reasons: (1) intraperitoneal hemorrhage from small implants, producing a chemical peritonitis; (2) periodic distention of overlying peritoneum by deeply embedded implants that have not ruptured intraperitoneally; and (3) traction or pulsion on both pelvic and abdominal viscera. Deep penetration dyspareunia usually is caused by tender nodular implants in the cul-de-sac and the displacement of adherent pelvic structures.

C. Dysmenorrhea: In the absence of adenomyosis, dysmenorrhea is now presumed to be due to the action of elevated levels of prostaglandins in the endometrium, producing increased uterine contractility. Substantially elevated levels of $PGF_{2\alpha}$ and PGE have been demonstrated in the endometrium and in the menstrual blood of women with both primary dysmenorrhea and with dysmenorrhea secondary to endometriosis. The inflammatory response surrounding endometrial implants is thought to produce the increased amounts of prostaglandins when endometriosis is present.

D. Infertility: In moderate or severe endometriosis, infertility may be plausibly explained on an anatomic or mechanical basis. In minimal or mild endometriosis, the mechanism of infertility remains obscure, but recent investigations have provided some insight. Infertility associated with endometriosis will be discussed with reference to mechanical factors and other factors.

1. Mechanical factors–

a. Ovaries–Adherence, with much or all of the ovary covered, often causes "trapping" of ova. In contrast, an inflammatory pseudocapsule may prevent rupture of the follicle. Moreover, cysts of large size may destroy most or all functioning parenchyma secondary to hemorrhage.

b. Oviducts–Peritubal and fimbrial implants or adhesions distort the tube and restrict its mobility. Complete occlusion is rare.

c. Peritoneum–Oozing implants or free blood may alter intraperitoneal fluid currents and divert the ovum or delay its entry into the oviduct. In other instances, the ovum may become enmeshed in a bleeding area out of range of the fimbria.

d. Uterus–Posterior fixation of the uterine fundus to cul-de-sac implants results in immobile retroversion. Thus, the cervix may be directed anteriorly so that cervical insemination may be hampered.

2. Other factors–

a. Peritoneal fluid–Recent observations of the peritoneal fluid of both women and rabbits with endometriosis have disclosed significant volume and content changes in both species. A 2- to 3-fold increase in peritoneal fluid volume is associated with endometriosis, and this increase is directly proportionate to the severity of the disease. Marked increases in PGF levels of peritoneal fluid have been observed (Schenken and Asch) in rabbits with surgically induced endometriosis. In women, significant increases in 2 of the stable products of prostaglandin endoperoxides (thromboxane B_2 and 6-keto-prostaglandin $F_{1\alpha}$) have been measured (Drake et al). Both tubal motility and rate of luteolysis could be altered by either of these compounds or their precursors. Increased numbers of peritoneal macrophages in infertile women with endometriosis, as compared with normal women, have been demonstrated as well as increased phagocytosis of sperm by the macrophages in infertile women with endometriosis (Haney et al). Also, the presence of menstruum from retrograde flow is a constant reseeding factor to reduce fertility.

b. Autoimmune response–An autoimmune response to some protein antigen present in menstrual fluid trapped in endometrial implants has been hypothesized (Weed and Holland). This is demonstrated by the deposition of complement, measured by immunofluorescence, around endometrial implants. Thus, an immune response may eventuate in infertility by interfering with sperm passage or by causing the rejection of early fertilized ova.

c. Inadequate luteal phase–The association of this defect with endometriosis was first suggested (by Grant) on the basis of studies of basal body temperature records correlated with endometrial biopsies and has been even more accurately demonstrated by measurement of decreased plasma steroids in the luteal phase of infertile patients with endometriosis (Abramson).

d. Spontaneous abortion rate–High levels of prostaglandins may play a role in the spontaneous abortion rate. When conception has occurred in the presence of endometriosis, the spontaneous abortion rate is inordinately high at 44–47% (Jones and Jones; Naples et al). Naples found that the spontaneous abortion rate dropped to about 8% after conservative surgery for endometriosis.

E. Involvement of Other Organs: Partial or complete obstruction of the small bowel is more often due to multiple serosal adhesions than to invasion and contracture of the muscularis itself. Perforation of the mucosa occurs rarely even with extensive bowel involvement. Implants around or within the wall of the ureter or bladder are commonly found, but ureteral obstruction due to endometriosis is rare.

When endometriosis is spread during surgical procedures or when it appears spontaneously in distant extrapelvic locations, the symptomatology depends upon the site and extent of the implant. Pleural implants resulting in catamenial pneumothorax or pleurisy are being recognized with increasing frequency.

Clinical Findings

A. Symptoms and Signs: The typical patient with endometriosis has traditionally been described as a tense ectomorphic white woman of relatively high socioeconomic status ("curse of the private patient") who has delayed marriage and childbearing. However, laparoscopy has demonstrated that endometriosis is common, though perhaps asymptomatic, in early menstrual life in all races.

The most common manifestation of endometriosis is pain, and the chief complication is infertility (see below and Chapter 41). "Acquired (secondary) dysmenorrhea is endometriosis until proved other-

wise" is still a valid and useful clinical aphorism. It is useful to remember the so-called 4 D's of endometriosis: dysmenorrhea, dyspareunia, dysuria, and dyschezia. The surgical history is important because cesarean section and other surgical procedures in which the uterine cavity has been opened may have initiated endometriosis. Needle tract endometriosis is becoming increasingly common with the wide use of diagnostic amniocentesis, particularly when amniocentesis is performed for genetic study in the second trimester. Prior vaginal delivery or injury to the lower genital tract should suggest the possibility of endometriosis of the lower tract. However, endometriosis may cause no symptoms, and the first indication of the disorder may be the discovery of a pelvic mass.

Meticulous evaluation of pelvic pain and bleeding is the most useful aspect of history taking when endometriosis is suspected. The pain, usually cyclic, is most severe in the premenstrual or early menstrual phase of the cycle. It is often described as "grinding." The location and referral pathways of pelvic pain frequently indicate the location of the implants.

Complaints can often be correlated with the site of ectopic endometrium as follows: (1) ovary and oviduct: infertility, profuse menses with a shortened interval; (2) cul-de-sac or ovary: deep thrust dyspareunia; (3) rectovaginal septum and colon: painful defecation, partial obstruction, rectal bleeding with menses, pain referred to sacrum or coccyx; (4) bladder: menstrual hematuria; (5) ureter: flank pain, backache, or, in advanced or total obstruction, hypertension and headache; (6) small bowel and appendix: midabdominal cramps, nausea and vomiting, worse during the days just before menses; (7) cervix, vagina, perineal area: bleeding from implants at the time of menstruation.

There is no relationship between the degree of pain and the extent of disease. Minimal endometriosis may cause excruciating pain, largely due to stretching of the peritoneum over smaller implants, and advanced disease, principally in the ovary, may be totally asymptomatic.

Acquired dysmenorrhea, a classic symptom of endometriosis, typically begins 5–7 days before menses, reaches a crescendo at about the time of maximal flow, and persists throughout the entire period and even for several more days. This is a distinctly different pattern from that of primary dysmenorrhea, in which the pain generally begins just before or at the onset of flow, reaches a crescendo within a few hours, and often subsides within 1–2 days. The pain of primary dysmenorrhea is cramplike and located in the midline, whereas the pain of endometriosis often is constant, away from the midline, in the region of the involved organs.

B. Pelvic Examination: In early endometriosis there may be no visible or palpable gynecologic findings, only tenderness to palpation of the involved areas. Endometriosis of the cervix, vagina, and external genitalia can be inspected as well as palpated and is easily confirmed by biopsy. Implants involving the uterosacral ligaments or cul-de-sac, felt as tender nodules of thickened areas, suggest endometriosis. These implants usually are nodular, firm, fixed, and discrete and are especially sensitive during menstruation. Changes in the ovary are less typical and are more difficult to distinguish from infection or tumors. Nevertheless, the ovary in endometriosis may be enlarged, cystic, and adherent and is often more tender at the lower pole. The uterus is often fixed in retroposition. Increased pain or tenderness of palpable or nonpalpable pelvic lesions just prior to and during menses is a valuable diagnostic sign. Likewise, persistent aching discomfort in the pelvis for several days after pelvic examination is strongly suggestive of endometriosis. Bidigital rectovaginal (rather than vaginal) examination is a much more accurate means of palpation of implants in the cul-de-sac and adnexal areas.

The discovery of an asymptomatic pelvic mass is often the first indication of endometriosis. An ovarian endometrioma must be distinguished from ovarian or tubal neoplasia and infection or, less commonly, from chronic ectopic pregnancy.

C. Radiologic Findings: Radiologic differentiation of endometriosis from inflammatory or malignant disease of the bowel may be required. In about half of patients with adnexal disease, the colon is involved and signs suggestive of endometriosis may be visualized in x-ray films during a barium enema study. Either constricting or nonconstricting lesions may be the result of endometriosis. Such implants on the upper, freely mobile segments of the colon are less likely to constrict the lumen than those on the rectosigmoid, where the bowel is partly extraperitoneal and more firmly attached. Partial obstruction may be influenced by at least 2 factors: (1) the endometrial tumor may impinge upon the bowel lumen, and (2) the associated inflammatory reaction may provoke spasm and eventually fibrosis with contraction and fixation.

Upper gastrointestinal studies are less useful in demonstrating endometriosis unless there is obstruction or widespread involvement. Invasion of the bowel lumen is uncommon; most obstructions are due to serosal adhesions.

D. Ultrasonography: Gray-scale ultrasonography may be extremely useful in determining the size, shape, and sites of endometriosis. Whether or not the ultrasonic resolution is adequate to differentiate endometriosis from other pelvic tumors is debated. Nonetheless, the correct diagnosis may be strongly suggested if the clinical setting is appropriate. Currently, the major value of ultrasound may be to demonstrate the extent of the disease.

E. Special Examinations: Laparoscopy has replaced culdoscopy and colpotomy for the diagnosis of endometriosis, because it provides better visualization and is associated with fewer technical problems due to cul-de-sac obliteration or implants. The 2-puncture technique of laparoscopy is essential, since it allows upward rotation of the ovaries and tubes and inspection of the entire ovary and posterior broad ligament. Confirmation of the diagnosis by biopsy is desirable.

Rectosigmoidoscopy, cystoscopy, or urography should be employed when symptoms suggest involvement of the bowel, bladder, or ureters.

When endometriosis involves less common sites such as the umbilicus, surgical scars, inguinal area, pleura, and extremities, the diagnosis must be established by excisional biopsy.

Complications

A. Infertility: Endometriosis is diagnosed in about 30% of women being studied for infertility in whom no other significant abnormalities are found. The incidence of infertility for any stage of the disorder is unknown. In general, the extent of endometriosis parallels the incidence of infertility—in contrast to the lack of correlation with degree of pain. The mechanical and other ways in which endometriosis can cause infertility are discussed above. The ancient axiom that all women with endometriosis are ovulatory has finally been disproved. Recent studies have shown that 15–20% of infertile women with endometriosis are either anovulatory or oligo-ovulatory. This group of patients poses a perplexing problem, as they require induction of ovulation, usually with clomiphine citrate. This—or any type of ovulation induction—produces surges of FSH and LH secretion, which in turn stimulates rapid growth of endometrial implants, usually in the ovary. In spite of extremely close monitoring, a portion of such patients will require laparotomy for large and persistent endometrial ovarian cysts.

B. Rupture of Endometrioma: Sudden rupture of an endometrioma is more likely to occur during pregnancy or near the end of hormonal pseudopregnancy. However, this complication may occur at any time. Rupture should be suspected in any patient with known endometriosis who presents as an acute abdominal emergency. Such a patient is usually afebrile, and the hematocrit and white blood count are often normal. There may be a chemical peritonitis due to irritation caused by blood products. The degree of rebound tenderness and peritonitis is often out of proportion to the small amount of chocolate-colored material found in the peritoneal cavity. Prompt laparotomy is indicated because the morbidity rate rises sharply with delay.

C. Intestinal Obstruction: Although intestinal obstruction due to endometriosis is not common, it is probably the most frequently overlooked cause of dynamic ileus. Complete obstruction usually arises in the small bowel and is due to adhesions rather than to invasion and blockage of the lumen. In contrast, partial rather than complete obstruction of the sigmoid colon is more common. The rectum, although often the site of endometriosis, rarely becomes obstructed owing to its large lumen.

Advanced endometriosis of the rectosigmoid colon seldom penetrates the rectal mucosa. It closely mimics primary rectal carcinoma in symptomatology, physical findings, and radiologic features. Laparotomy is often required to distinguish the 2 entities.

If endometriosis of the small or large bowel is suspected prior to surgery, adequate bowel preparation preoperatively is indicated. Preoperative bowel preparation in all patients with endometriosis is advocated by many.

Intestinal obstruction due to endometriosis must always be considered in a patient who has undergone abdominal surgery for endometriosis in which ovarian tissue was allowed to remain. Endometriosis of the appendix accounts for only about 3% of cases of gastrointestinal endometriosis.

D. Ureteral Obstruction: Although Meigs pointed out over 40 years ago that ureteral obstruction is not uncommon with endometriosis, this complication is still often overlooked. When the cardinal and uterosacral ligaments are involved with endometriosis, the ureters and kidneys are at risk, and careful and repeated urologic studies are required. The ureter may be obstructed by external pressure or—less often—may be completely engulfed by the endometrial implant. The course of progressive ureteral obstruction is usually silent and insidious. Catamenial flank pain and hematuria are the exception rather than the rule. Recurrent urinary infection is rare. Extensive or total destruction of the kidney, due to ureteral obstruction, may not be suspected until the appearance of hypertension and headache.

E. Secondary Infection of Endometrioma: This is not a common complication, but it should be considered when a patient with endometriosis develops pain, fever, a tender adnexal mass, and leukocytosis. Infected endometriomas show a strong association with tubal infection and a weak association with antecedent hysterosalpingography. Total abdominal hysterectomy and bilateral salpingo-oophorectomy may be mandated for cure. The outlook for fertility is poor even when unilateral salpingo-oophorectomy is employed.

F. Uncommon Complications: Catamenial pneumothorax or pleurisy is often associated with endometrial implants in the pleura. Bleeding and pressure symptoms from other distant implants vary with the area or organ involved.

Differential Diagnosis

Endometriosis must be distinguished principally from infection and neoplasia. The differential diagnosis includes also primary dysmenorrhea, salpingo-oophoritis, salpingitis isthmica nodosa, adenomyosis, uterine myoma, postoperative or postinfectious pelvic adhesions, and chronic ectopic pregnancy. Conversely, endometriosis must be considered in the differential diagnosis of all of the foregoing conditions.

Prevention

A. Early Marriage and Pregnancy: This conventional advice will continue to be given, but the alleged beneficial effects of pregnancy at any age have been questioned. McArthur, Ulfelder, and Ranney reporting wide variation in clinical and histologic response from patient to patient, from trimester to trimester, and in successive pregnancies in the same patient, conclude that pregnancy does not exert a consistent curative or ameliorative effect on endometriosis.

B. Pelvic Examinations: Bimanual pelvic examination during menses should be performed, but palpation must be gentle to avoid possible augmentation of menstrual reflux. For the same reason, pelvic examination under anesthesia should be done only before and not immediately after D&C.

C. Minor Gynecologic Procedures: Tubal insufflation, hysterosalpingography, surgical D&C, and procedures involving the cervix (cryosurgery, electrocautery, conization, plastic surgery) are contraindicated just prior to and during a menstrual period. Moreover, cryosurgery or cauterization must not be carried too high up the cervical canal or stenosis may develop.

D. Cervical Stenosis, Acute Anterior Angulation of the Fundus, or Uterine Retroversion: These anatomic variations are often implicated as contributing factors, but their significance is difficult to assess. Cervical stenosis, either primary or secondary to surgical procedures, may be a cause of obstruction of menstrual fluid. Cervical stenosis can be corrected by cervical dilatation. Be this as it may, there is no proof that acute anteflexion or retroversion of the uterus is associated with an increased incidence of endometriosis.

E. Adequate Drainage of Menstrual Blood: Opinion varies about what constitutes "adequate menstrual drainage," with special reference to the use of tampons. Because of a narrow vagina or small introitus, young girls may be advised to use perineal pads rather than tampons during heavy menstrual flow. Perineal pads would seem to have a logical advantage over tampons in preventing retrograde flow, but there is no proof that this is the case. The concept that coitus during the menstrual period predisposes to endometriosis has no credible evidentiary basis.

F. Avoidance of Partial Salpingectomy: The occasional development of painful endometriosis—actually endosalpingosis—from a tubal stump following partial salpingectomy has led to the recommendation that the tubal remnant be removed by wedge resection to a point within the interstitial portion of the uterus.

G. Isolation and Irrigation of the Operative Site: During uterine or tubal surgery, the operative site should be isolated by careful gauze packing. Following surgery and removal of the packs, all remaining blood and clots should be removed by sterile saline irrigation and aspiration to eliminate endometrial fragments.

H. Periodic Examination: Periodic examinations at intervals of 6–12 months should lead to earlier diagnosis and more effective therapy of endometriosis.

I. Management According to Family History: It has been suggested that women who do not have endometriosis but who have one or more affected first-degree relatives be treated by cyclic oral contraception beginning in adolescence and continuing until pregnancy is desired. The cost/benefit and benefit/risk ratios probably do not support this approach.

Classification of Endometriosis

Accurate classification or staging, by laparoscopy or laparotomy, is of paramount importance in the investigation and management of endometriosis. Various staging systems have been proposed, but the American Fertility Society (AFS [1978]) may have the most practical and accurate approach, even though the categorization is more complex than preferred by some and less detailed than desired by others (Table 16–1). In a retrospective study of conservative surgery for endometriosis (Rock et al) the AFS system correlated most accurately with the postoperative pregnancy rate.

Treatment Options in Management of Endometriosis

Treatment should be based upon the symptoms, desire for pregnancy, and anatomic extent of the disease. Therapy may consist of observation (no immediate treatment), palliation, hormone administration, or surgery.

A. Observation: The patient with endometriosis confirmed by laparoscopy who is free of pain and does not desire pregnancy needs no treatment and requires only careful reexamination at 6-month intervals. She should understand that, if the disease progresses, appropriate therapy should be employed and that this will depend upon her age and her desire to maintain reproductive function. If a strong family history of endometriosis is elicited, treatment by oral contraceptives rather than observation may be preferred.

B. Palliation:

1. Analgesics–In early endometriosis without ovarian enlargement, where pelvic pain, dysmenorrhea, or mild dyspareunia is the primary complaint and infertility is not a factor, palliative therapy is sufficient. Mild to moderate perimenstrual pain can be relieved by analgesics, eg, aspirin, 0.6 g, or aspirin with codeine, 0.03–0.06 g, every 4 hours as needed.

2. Analgesic-anti-inflammatory-prostaglandin synthetase inhibitors–Because the dysmenorrhea of endometriosis may result from elevated levels of prostaglandins in the endometrium and possibly in the peritoneal fluid, antiprostaglandin drugs are now employed widely for relief of dysmenorrhea. The long-term use of prostaglandin inhibitors may offer a future treatment modality. No studies have evaluated such long-term therapy; hence, the use of this category of drugs is restricted to periodic relief of pain.

Antiprostaglandin drugs include fenoprofen (Nalfon), 200 mg orally every 4 hours as needed; ibuprofen (Motrin), 400 mg orally 4 times daily; mefenamic acid (Ponstel), 250 mg orally 4 times daily; naproxen (Naprosyn), 500 mg orally initially followed by 250 mg every 6 hours; naproxen sodium (Anaprox), 550 mg orally, ie, 2 tablets initially and then 275 mg every 6 hours as needed; zomepirac (Zomax), 100 mg orally every 4–6 hours as needed; and aspirin, 0.6 g orally 4 times daily.

The risk imposed upon the fetus by prostaglandin synthetase inhibitors is unknown; therefore, it is best to delay administration of these drugs until the onset of menstruation.

3. Pregnancy–In spite of the doubts that have been raised about the benefits of pregnancy in endometriosis, women with endometriosis who intend to have children should be urged to become pregnant without delay (''natural hormone therapy'').

4. Infertility studies–Tubal insufflation, hydrotubation, and uterosalpingography may release tubal adhesions, kinks, and other distortions of the oviducts caused by endometriosis.

C. Endocrine Therapy: Both clinical observations and animal experiments indicate that endocrine therapy is of only temporary benefit. It is of greatest value in early endometriosis (implants $\leq$ 1 cm in diameter) in patients for whom infertility is not a primary concern. In recent years, hormonally induced pseudopregnancy has been considered to increase rather than decrease the technical problems of surgery. Similarly, pseudopregnancy in the immediate postoperative period has come into disfavor because it produces anovulation during the months when the patient who does wish to become pregnant should be experiencing the maximum benefit from the operation. Following ovariectomy for endometriosis, the benefits of exogenous estrogens in relieving menopausal symptoms far outweigh the risk of recurrence of endometriosis. If signs or symptoms of this disorder recur, estrogen should be discontinued and the problem should be reevaluated after 1–2 months.

Several trends have emerged in the use of long-term hormone treatment. The use of diethylstilbestrol or conjugated estrogens alone in large doses has been abandoned. Oral testosterone in high doses is no longer used because of virilization. In the treatment of younger women, there has been a shift away from long-acting injectable agents such as medroxyprogesterone acetate (Depo-Provera) because of the unpredictable anovulation and amenorrhea that often occur following such therapy.

The occasionally beneficial effect of hormonal pseudopregnancy is attributed to 3 factors: (1) amenorrhea due to hypothalamic pituitary suppression, (2) production of a decidualike response in the ectopic endometrium, and (3) necrosis and resorption of the decidua with resultant healing. It has been suggested that the prime benefit of pseudopregnancy may derive not from the decidual response but from the androgenic properties of the 17-norprogestogens. When the combination type oral contraceptive agents are used to produce pseudopregnancy, one should select combinations that contain the least amount of estrogen necessary to suppress ovulation and the maximum amount of progestogen available to induce a decidual reaction in the implants. Examples of such preparations are given below.

Treatment with continuous low-dose (subviriliz-ing) oral androgens (see below) appears to be gaining favor also. This mode of therapy has the dual advantage of suppressing growth of ectopic implants without preventing ovulation or menstruation.

1. Pseudopregnancy–Pseudopregnancy is achieved by administering estrogen-progestogen combinations, or progestogens alone, usually for 6–9 months. Sodium restriction or diuretics may be necessary during treatment because of fluid retention. If side-effects are troublesome, therapy may be stopped at 3–4 months. Treatment should be discontinued promptly if thromboembolic symptoms appear.

a. Estrogen-progestogens–Ovral, Demulen, and Norlestrin 2.5 all have proportionately low estrogen and high progestin formulations. The dosage is one tablet orally daily for 3 weeks, then 2 tablets daily for 3 weeks, and then 3 tablets daily for 6–9 months.

b. Progestogens–Medroxyprogesterone acetate (Provera), 10 mg orally 3 times daily, or dydrogesterone (Duphaston, Gynorest), 10 mg orally twice daily, is given for 6–9 months. Breakthrough bleeding may be disturbing but should not diminish the therapeutic effect. The same precautions are advised as with combination drugs.

2. Cyclic estrogen-progestogens–Ovral, Demulen, Norlestrin 2.5, and similar combination drugs may be used in conventional cyclic contraceptive dosage. Cyclic therapy frequently relieves dysmenorrhea, but its ability to halt or slow the progression of endometriosis is debated.

3. Androgens–Methyltestosterone, 5–10 mg orally daily, or methyltestosterone buccal Linguets, 5 mg daily, may be used for 6 months. Therapy should be discontinued promptly if virilization occurs. Moreover, if a period is overdue and pregnancy is suspected, the patient should stop the drug promptly to avoid virilization of the fetus.

4. Pseudomenopause–Danazol (Danocrine), A weak impeded androgen, has been used in the treatment of endometriosis since 1967. The action of the drug is unique—it causes marked gonadotropin inhibition with minimal overt sex hormone stimulation. The mode of action probably is interference with estrogen receptors in the hypothalamus, pituitary, ovary, endometrium, and breast. The existence of a cystoplasmic receptor protein that binds danazol has not been established. Whatever the actual mechanism, the rationale for the use of danazol is the suppression of all endogenous stimuli to the endometrium to allow spontaneous healing and atrophy of the disease.

Danazol eliminates midcycle FSH and LH peaks and decreases plasma FSH slightly. After 6–8 weeks, amenorrhea, a hypoestrogenic vaginal smear, and atrophic endometrium are produced. Relief of pain precedes objective changes in pelvic findings by 2–3 months. After discontinuation of therapy, the menses resume within 4–6 weeks, indicating a resumption of cyclic endometrial stimulation.

Posttreatment laparoscopic follow-up (Dmowski and Cohen; Biberoglu and Behrman) has shown a temporary marked regression of endometriosis. Debate persists about whether danazol reduces the size of ovarian endometriomas.

Although a recurrence rate of about 39% at 3 years has been reported, the uncorrected pregnancy rate is approximately 46%, and the corrected pregnancy rate is about 72%. This improvement is greater than can be achieved by other types of hormone therapy and compares favorably with rates attained by surgery. In general, with severe endometriosis, a combination of surgery and danazol is necessary if pregnancy is desired.

The use of danazol presents 2 major problems: it is expensive, and side-effects may be distressing. Undesirable side-effects include fatigue, depression, weight gain and edema, increased hair growth, oily skin and acne, and decreased breast size. Inadvertent administration of danazol in early pregnancy has been reported to cause female pseudohermaphroditism.

Favorable results have been obtained with danazol in doses of 200, 400, and 600 mg orally per day for 6 months in mild to moderate endometriosis. A dose of 100 mg/d has produced good temporary improvement but with a "rebound" of symptoms after the fourth month of treatment. A compromise might be 400 mg/d orally with an increase or decrease of dosage depending upon patient response. A dose of 800 mg/d orally is still recommended for severe disease. Danazol is effective as adjunctive therapy to either laparoscopic or open conservative surgery.

D. Surgical Treatment:

1. Incidental endometriosis–Small foci should be excised or destroyed by fulguration during surgery undertaken for other reasons.

2. Laparoscopic surgery–When early endometriosis is identified at laparoscopy, conservative procedures such as fulguration of implants and lysis of adhesions may be performed about half the time. Such procedures should be reserved for the experienced endoscopist, as fulguration of the bowel, ureter, and other structures may result in serious injury.

3. Conservative surgery–Laparotomy, extirpation or fulguration of implants of endometriosis, lysis of adhesions, uterine suspension, meticulous reperitonization, and, usually, appendectomy are recommended. Conservative surgery rather than hormonal therapy is the treatment of choice for women under 35 years of age with early disease who desire to have children. The fertility rate following this procedure ranges from 25 to 80%, with much better results in more recent series of patients.

About 20–50% of patients require a second operation because of progression of the disease. The patient should be fully informed of this possibility.

4. Presacral neurectomy–The efficacy of presacral neurectomy, combined with conservative surgery, is still debated. The areas innervated by the presacral nerves are mainly the uterus and the mid portions of the oviducts. Thus, if wide presacral dissection (excision of tissue between the right ureter and superior hemorrhoidal vessels) is performed, pain will be relieved only near the midline. The problems of presacral neurectomy are limited dissection, poorly controlled bleeding from the presacral vessels, postoperative adhesions, and altered bladder or bowel function. The procedure is most useful when severe pain is associated with minimal gross disease in the cul-de-sac area. A much simpler and often effective form of neurectomy is resection of 1 cm of both uterosacral ligaments.

5. Semiconservative surgery–This term is applied to procedures in which all foci of endometriosis and the uterus are removed and one or both ovaries are conserved. Though gaining increasing acceptance, it is still considered to be inadequate by many. If there are identifiable implants on the bowel, bladder, or ureter, semiconservative management should not be attempted. The patient should be warned of the possible need for reoperation.

6. Laser surgery–Currently, laser surgery is employed for vaporization of smaller ovarian and other implants (J.H. Bellina et al and M.S. Baggish, in personal communications with the author). Because of its precision control and minimal destruction of surrounding tissue, laser surgery is a promising approach to the operative treatment of endometriosis. Final evaluation must await study of long-term results.

7. Definitive surgery–Total abdominal hysterectomy, bilateral salpingo-oophorectomy, resection of peritoneal implants when feasible, and (usually) appendectomy comprise the most effective and dependable methods of surgical treatment of endometriosis. This procedure is indicated for patients over 35 years of age or for younger women who have com-

pleted their families or have advanced disease.

E. Irradiation Treatment: X-ray therapy is reserved for the exceptional patient with proved endometriosis in whom cancer has been ruled out and in whom surgery is either contraindicated or refused.

F. Treatment of Complicated or Severe Disease: Endometriosis is rarely fatal with or without treatment. However, certain complications such as rupture of an endometrioma or obstruction of bowel or ureter require prompt operative management. A complaint of scanty menstruation after total abdominal hysterectomy for endometriosis suggests the development of resectable implants of the vaginal cuff.

Prognosis

With proper hormonal or surgical treatment, the prognosis is good for relief of pain and enhancement of fertility in mild to moderate endometriosis. In most cases, hormonal therapy is temporarily effective in controlling symptoms and arresting growth but is generally less effective than surgery in increasing fertility. Because of the lack of long-term (5 years) follow-up after hormonal therapy, the permanent benefits of this management are not clearly established.

Conservative surgery by increasingly more refined techniques has offered an encouraging cure rate of 50–80% (relief of pain and correction of infertility) during the last decade. The role of semiconservative surgery with ovarian preservation has not been adequately assessed.

Definitive surgery offers good results in women over age 35 or younger women willing to sacrifice ovarian and reproductive function.

References

Biberoglu KO, Behrman SJ: Dosage aspects of danazol therapy in endometriosis: Short-term and long-term effectiveness. *Am J Obstet Gynecol* 1981;**139**:645.

Blumenkatz MJ et al: Retrograde menstruation in women undergoing chronic peritoneal dialysis. *Obstet Gynecol* 1981; **57**:667.

Chatman DL: Endometriosis and the black woman. *J Reprod Med* 1976;**16**:303.

Coleman BH, Arger PH, Mulhera CB Jr: Endometriosis: Clinical and ultrasonic correlation. *Am J Roentgenol* 1979;**132**:747.

Dizerega GE, Barber DL, Hodgen GD: Endometriosis: Role of ovarian steroids in initiation, maintenance and suppression. *Fertil Steril* 1980;**33**:649.

Dmowski WP, Cohen MR: Antigonadotropin (danazol) in the treatment of endometriosis. *Am J Obstet Gynecol* 1978; **130**:41.

Dmowski WP, Rao R, Scommegna A: The luteinized unruptured follicle syndrome and endometriosis. *Fertil Steril* 1980; **33**:30.

Drake TS et al: Peritoneal fluid thromboxane B_2 and 6-ketoprostaglandin $F_{1\alpha}$ in endometriosis. *Am J Obstet Gynecol* 1981;**140**:401.

Drake TS et al: Peritoneal fluid volume in endometriosis. *Fertil Steril* 1980;**34**:280.

Duck SC, Katayama CP: Danazol may cause female pseudohermaphroditism. *Fertil Steril* 1981;**35**:230.

Gabos P: Clomiphene citrate therapy and associated ovarian endometrial cysts. *Obstet Gynecol* 1979;**53**:763.

Goldman SM, Minkin SI: Diagnosing endometriosis with ultrasound. *J Reprod Med* 1980;**25**:178.

Grant A: Abnormal luteal function in endometriosis. *Fertil Steril* 1981;**35**:592.

Haney AF, Muscato JJ, Weinberg JB: Peritoneal fluid cell populations in infertility patients. *Fertil Steril* 1981;**35**:696.

Haney AF, Muscato JJ, Weinberg JB: Sperm phagocytosis by human peritoneal macrophages: A possible cause of infertility in endometriosis. (Abstract.) Society for Gynecologic Investigation, 1981.

Hasson HM: Electrocoagulation of pelvic endometriotic lesions with laparoscopic control. *Am J Obstet Gynecol* 1979; **135**:115.

Hibbard LT, Schumann WR, Goldstein GE: Thoracic endometriosis: A review and report of 2 cases. *Am J Obstet Gynecol* 1981;**140**:227.

Kaunitz A, Di Sant'Agnese PA: Needle tract endometriosis: An unusual complication of amniocentesis. *Obstet Gynecol* 1979; **54**:753.

Kistner WR: Endometriosis and infertility. *Obstet Gynecol* 1979; **22**:101.

Meyers WC, Kelvin FM, Jones RS: Diagnosis and surgical treatment of colonic endometriosis. *Arch Surg* 1979;**114**:169.

Moore EE et al: Management of pelvic endometriosis with low-dose danazol. *Fertil Steril* 1981;**36**:15.

Moore JG, Hibbard LT: Urinary tract endometriosis: Enigmas in diagnosis and management. *Am J Obstet Gynecol* 1979; **134**:162.

Musich JR, Behrman SJ, Menon KMJ: Estrogenic and anti-estrogenic effects of danazol administration in studies of estradiol receptor binding. *Am J Obstet Gynecol* 1981;**140**:62.

Naples JD, Batt RE, Sadigh H: Spontaneous abortion rate in patients with endometriosis. *Obstet Gynecol* 1981;**57**:509.

Prostaglandin-inhibitor analgesics. *Med Lett Drugs Ther* 1981; **23**:75.

Rock JA et al: The conservative surgical treatment of endometriosis: Evaluation of pregnancy success with respect to the extent of disease as categorized using contemporary classification systems. *Fertil Steril* 1981;**35**:131.

Schenken RS, Asch RH: Surgical induction of endometriosis in the rabbit: Effects on fertility and concentration of peritoneal fluid prostaglandins. *Fertil Steril* 1980;**34**:581.

Schmidt CL, Demopoulos RI, Weiss G: Infected endometriotic cysts: Clinical characterization and pathogenesis. *Fertil Steril* 1981;**37**:27.

Schweppe KW, Dmowski WP, Wynn RM: Ultrastructural changes in endometriotic tissue during danazol treatment. *Fertil Steril* 1981;**36**:20.

Simpson JL et al: Heritable aspects of endometriosis. Parts 1 and 2. *Am J Obstet Gynecol* 1981;**137**:327, 332.

Soules MR et al: Endometriosis and ovulation: A coexisting problem in the infertile female. *Am J Obstet Gynecol* 1976; **125**:412.

Weed JC, Holland JB: Endometriosis and infertility: An enigma. *Fertil Steril* 1977;**28**:135.

Wills JS: Radiographic features of ureteral endometriosis. *Am J Roentgenol* 1978;**131**:627.

Diseases of the Breast | 17

Armando E. Giuliano, MD, & John L. Wilson, MD

CARCINOMA OF THE FEMALE BREAST

Essentials of Diagnosis

- Higher incidence in women who have never borne children, those with a family history of breast cancer, and those with a personal history of breast cancer or dysplasia.
- Early findings: Single, nontender, firm to hard mass with ill-defined margins; nipple erosion, with or without a mass; mammography may detect cancer before development of a palpable mass.
- Later findings: Skin or nipple retraction; axillary lymphadenopathy; breast enlargement, redness, edema, pain, fixation of mass to skin or chest wall.
- Late findings: Ulceration; supraclavicular lymphadenopathy; edema of arm; bone, lung, liver, brain, or other distant metastases.

General Considerations

The breast is the most common site of cancer in women, and cancer of the breast is the leading cause of death from cancer among women in the USA. Breast cancer is the leading cause of death from all causes in women aged 40–44 and is frequent in women of all ages over 30. The probability of developing the disease increases throughout life. The mean and the median age of women with breast cancer is 60–61.

There were about 108,000 new cases of breast cancer and about 35,000 deaths from this disease in women in the USA in 1980. At the present rate of incidence, one of every 11 American women will develop breast cancer during her lifetime. Women whose mothers or sisters had breast cancer are 2 or 3 times more likely to develop the disease than controls. Risk is increased when breast cancer has occurred before menopause, was bilateral, or was present in 2 or more first-degree relatives. However, there is no history of breast cancer among female relatives in over 90% of patients with breast cancer. Single and nulliparous women have a slightly higher incidence of breast cancer than married and parous women. Women with 3 or more children have a lower incidence than women with fewer children. Menarche after age 15 and artificial menopause are also associated with a lower incidence of breast cancer, whereas early men-

arche (under age 12) and late natural menopause (after age 50) are associated with a slight increase in risk of developing breast cancer. Mammary dysplasia (cystic disease of the breast), particularly when accompanied by proliferative changes, papillomatosis, or solid hyperplasia, is associated with an increased incidence of cancer. A woman who has had cancer in one breast is at increased risk of developing cancer in the opposite breast. Women with cancer of the uterine corpus have a breast cancer risk almost double that of the general population, and women with breast cancer have a comparably increased endometrial cancer risk. In general, rates reported from developing countries are low, whereas rates are high in developed countries, with the notable exception of Japan. Some of the variability may be due to underreporting in the developing countries, but a real difference probably exists. There is some evidence that continuous administration of estrogens to postmenopausal women may result in an increased risk of breast cancer after 10–12 years.

Women who are at greater than normal risk of developing breast cancer (Table 17–1) should be identified by their physicians and followed appropriately. Screening programs involving periodic physical examination and mammography of asymptomatic women are most productive when applied to individuals at increased risk.

Growth potential of tumor and resistance of host

Table 17–1. Factors associated with increased risk of breast cancer.*

	Characteristics
Race	White vs black or Oriental
Age	Over 50
Family history	Breast cancer in mother or sister
Previous medical history	Endometrial cancer
	Mammary dysplasia
	Cancer in other breast
Menstrual history	Early menarche (under age 12)
	Late menopause (after age 50)
	Aggregate years of menstrual activity greater than 30
Marital history	Never married vs married
Pregnancy	Never pregnant
	One or 2 pregnancies vs 3 or more
	First child born after age 30

*Normal lifetime risk in white women = 1 in 11.

vary over a wide range from patient to patient and may be altered during the course of the disease. The doubling time of breast cancer cells ranges from 23 days in a rapidly growing lesion to 309 days in a slowly growing one. Assuming that the rate of doubling is constant and that the neoplasm originates in one cell, a carcinoma with a doubling time of 100 days may not reach clinically detectable size (1 cm) for 8 years. On the other hand, rapidly growing cancers have a much shorter preclinical course and a greater tendency to metastasize to regional nodes or more distant sites by the time a breast mass is discovered. Although the mean duration of life in untreated carcinoma of the breast is about 3 years, some untreated patients succumb within a few months after diagnosis, others live 4 or 5 years, and a few survive as long as 15–30 years.

Staging (Table 17–2)

The extent of disease evident from physical findings and special preoperative studies is used to determine the clinical stage of the lesion. Histologic staging is performed after examination of the mastectomy specimen. The results of clinical staging are used in designing the treatment plan, and, as shown in Table 17–2, both clinical and histologic staging are of prognostic significance.

Clinical Findings

The patient with breast cancer usually presents

Table 17–2. Clinical and histologic staging of breast carcinoma and relation to survival.

Clinical Staging (American Joint Committee)	Crude 5-Year Survival (%)
Stage I	85
Tumor < 2 cm in diameter	
Nodes, if present, not felt to contain metastases	
Without distant metastases	
Stage II	66
Tumor < 5 cm in diameter	
Nodes, if palpable, not fixed	
Without distant metastases	
Stage III	41
Tumor > 5 cm or—	
Tumor any size with invasion of skin or attached to chest wall	
Nodes in supraclavicular area	
Without distant metastases	
Stage IV	10
With distant metastases	

Histologic Staging	Crude Survival (10%)	
	5 Years	10 Years
All patients	63	46
Negative axillary lymph nodes	78	65
Positive axillary lymph nodes	46	25
1–3 positive axillary lymph nodes	62	38
> 4 positive axillary lymph nodes	32	13

Table 17–3. Initial symptoms of mammary carcinoma.

Symptom	Percentage of All Cases
Painless breast mass	66
Painful breast mass	11
Nipple discharge	9
Local edema	4
Nipple retraction	3
Nipple crusting	2
Miscellaneous symptoms	5

*Adapted from report of initial symptoms in 774 patients treated for breast cancer at Ellis Fischel State Cancer Hospital, Columbia, Missouri. Reproduced, with permission, from Spratt JS Jr, Donegan WL: *Cancer of the Breast.* Saunders, 1967.

with a lump in the breast. Clinical evaluation should assess the local lesion and must include a search for evidence of metastases in regional nodes or distant sites. After the diagnosis of breast cancer has been confirmed by biopsy, additional studies are often needed to complete the search for distant metastases or an occult primary in the other breast. Then, before any decision is made about treatment, all the available clinical data are used to determine the extent or "stage" of the patient's disease.

A. Symptoms: In taking the history, special note should be made of menarche, pregnancies, parity, artificial or natural menopause, date of last menstrual period, previous breast lesions, and a family history of breast cancer. Back or other bone pain may be the result of osseous metastases. Systemic complaints or weight loss should raise the question of metastases, which may involve any organ but most frequently the bones, liver, and lungs. The more advanced the cancer in terms of size of primary and extent of regional node involvement, the higher the incidence of metastatic spread to distant sites.

The presenting complaint in about 70% of patients with breast cancer is a lump (usually painless) in the breast (Table 17–3). About 90% of breast masses are discovered by the patient herself. Less frequent symptoms are breast pain; nipple discharge; erosion, retraction, enlargement, or itching of the nipple; and redness, generalized hardness, enlargement, or shrinking of the breast. Rarely, an axillary mass, swelling of the arm, or bone pain (from metastases) may be the first symptom.

B. Signs: The relative frequency of carcinoma in various anatomic sites in the breast is shown in Fig 17–1. Almost half of cancers of the breast begin in the upper outer quadrant, probably because this quadrant contains the largest volume of breast tissue. The high percentage in the central portion is due to the inclusion of cancers that spread to the subareolar region from neighboring quadrants. Cancer occurs 5–10% more frequently in the left breast than in the right.

Inspection of the breast is the first step in physical examination and should be carried out with the patient sitting, arms at sides and then overhead. Abnormal

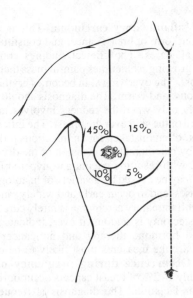

Figure 17—1. Frequency of breast carcinoma at various anatomic sites.

variations in breast size and contour, minimal nipple retraction, and slight edema, redness, or retraction of the skin are best identified by careful observation in good light. Asymmetry of the breasts and retraction or dimpling of the skin can often be accentuated by having the patient raise her arms overhead or press her hands on her hips in order to contract the pectoralis muscles. Axillary and supraclavicular areas should be thoroughly palpated for enlarged nodes with the patient sitting (Fig 17—2). Palpation of the breast for masses or other changes is best performed with the patient supine and arm abducted (Fig 17—3).

Breast cancer usually consists of a nontender,

firm or hard lump with poorly delimited margins (caused by local infiltration). Slight skin or nipple retraction is an important sign. Minimal asymmetry of the breast may be noted. Very small (1–2 mm) erosions of the nipple epithelium may be the only manifestation of carcinoma of the Paget type. Watery, serous, or bloody discharge from the nipple is an occasional early sign.

A lesion smaller than 1 cm in diameter may be difficult or impossible for the examiner to feel and yet may be discovered by the patient. She should always be asked to demonstrate the location of the mass; if the physician fails to confirm the patient's suspicions, the examination should be repeated in 1 month. During the premenstrual phase of the cycle, increased innocuous nodularity may suggest neoplasm or may obscure an underlying lesion. If there is any question regarding the nature of an abnormality under these circumstances, the patient should be asked to return after her period.

The following are characteristic of advanced carcinoma: edema, redness, nodularity, or ulceration of the skin; the presence of a large primary tumor; fixation to the chest wall; enlargement, shrinkage, or retraction of the breast; marked axillary lymphadenopathy; supraclavicular lymphadenopathy; edema of the ipsilateral arm; and distant metastases.

Metastases tend to involve regional lymph nodes (Fig 17—4), which may be clinically palpable. With regard to the axilla, one or 2 movable, nontender, not particularly firm lymph nodes 5 mm or less in diameter are frequently present and are generally of no significance. Firm or hard nodes larger than 5 mm in diameter usually contain metastases. Axillary nodes that are matted or fixed to skin or deep structures indicate advanced disease (at least stage III). Histologic studies show that microscopic metastases are present in about 30% of patients with clinically negative nodes. On the other hand, if the examiner thinks that the axillary nodes are involved, this will prove on histologic section to be correct in about 85% of cases. The incidence of positive axillary nodes increases with the size of the

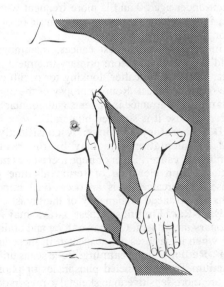

Figure 17—2. Palpation of axillary region for enlarged lymph nodes.

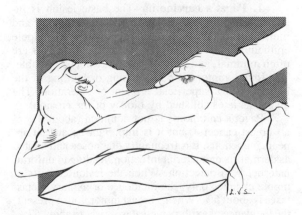

Figure 17—3. Palpation of breasts. Palpation is performed with the patient supine and arm abducted.

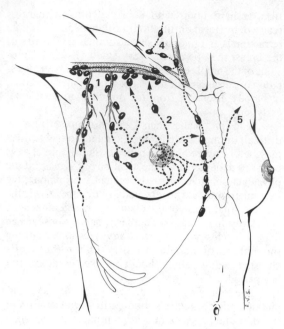

Figure 17–4. Lymphatic drainage of the breast to regional node groups. *1.* Main axillary group. *2.* Interpectoral node leading to apex of axilla. *3.* Internal mammary group. *4.* Supraclavicular group. *5.* Lymphatic channels to opposite axilla.

primary tumor and with the invasiveness of the neoplasm according to pathologic type.

Usually no nodes are palpable in the supraclavicular fossa. Firm or hard nodes of any size in this location or just beneath the clavicle (infraclavicular nodes) are suggestive of metastatic cancer and should be considered for biopsy. Ipsilateral supraclavicular or infraclavicular nodes containing cancer indicate that the patient is in an advanced stage of the disease (stage IV). Edema of the ipsilateral arm, commonly caused by metastatic infiltration of regional lymphatics, is also a sign of advanced (stage IV) cancer.

C. Special Clinical Forms of Breast Carcinoma:

1. Paget's carcinoma–The basic lesion is intraductal carcinoma, usually well differentiated and multicentric in the nipple and breast ducts. The nipple epithelium is infiltrated, but gross nipple changes are often minimal, and a tumor mass may not be palpable. The first symptom is often itching or burning of the nipple, with a superficial erosion or ulceration. The diagnosis is established by biopsy of the erosion.

Paget's carcinoma is not common (about 3% of all breast cancers), but it is important because it appears innocuous. It is frequently diagnosed and treated as dermatitis or bacterial infection, leading to unfortunate delay in detection. When the lesion consists of nipple changes only, the incidence of axillary metastases is about 5%. When a breast tumor is also present, the incidence of axillary metastases rises to about 67%, with an associated marked decrease in prospects for cure by surgical or other treatment.

2. Inflammatory carcinoma–This is the most malignant form of breast cancer and constitutes about 3% of all cases. The clinical findings consist of a rapidly growing, sometimes painful mass that enlarges the breast. The overlying skin becomes erythematous, edematous, and warm. The diagnosis should be made clinically only when the redness involves more than one-third of the skin over the breast. The inflammatory changes, often mistaken for an infectious process, are caused by carcinomatous invasion of the dermal lymphatics, with resulting edema and hyperemia. These tumors may be caused by a variety of histologic types. Metastases tend to occur early and widely, and for this reason inflammatory carcinoma is rarely curable. Radical mastectomy is seldom, if ever, indicated. Radiation and hormone therapy and anticancer chemotherapy are the measures most likely to be of value.

3. Occurrence during pregnancy or lactation–Only 1–2% of breast cancers occur during pregnancy or lactation. The diagnosis is frequently delayed, because physiologic changes in the breast may obscure the true nature of the lesion. This results in a tendency of both patients and physicians to misinterpret the findings and to procrastinate in deciding on biopsy. When the neoplasm is confined to the breast, the 5-year survival rate after radical mastectomy is about 60%. On the other hand, axillary metastases are already present in 60–70% of patients, and for them the 5-year survival rate after radical mastectomy is only 5–10%. Pregnancy (or lactation) is not a contraindication to radical or modified radical mastectomy, and treatment should be based on the stage of the disease as in the nonpregnant (or nonlactating) woman.

4. Bilateral breast cancer–Simultaneous bilateral breast cancer occurs in about 1% of cases, but there is a 5–8% incidence of later occurrence of cancer in the second breast. Bilaterality occurs more often in women under age 50 and is more frequent when the tumor in the primary breast is multicentric or of comedo or lobular type.

In patients with breast cancer, mammography should be performed before primary treatment and at regular intervals thereafter, looking for occult cancer in the opposite breast. Routine biopsy of the opposite breast may be warranted in patients with lobular breast cancer, because it is so often bilateral.

D. Laboratory Findings: A consistently elevated sedimentation rate may be the result of disseminated cancer. Liver or bone metastases may be associated with elevation of serum alkaline phosphatase. Hypercalcemia is an occasional important finding in advanced malignancy of the breast.

E. X-Ray Findings: Chest x-rays may show pulmonary metastases. CT scan of liver and brain is of value when metastases are suspected in these areas.

F. Radionuclide Scanning: Bone scans utilizing technetium Tc 99m-labeled phosphates or phosphonates are more sensitive than skeletal x-rays in detecting metastatic breast cancer. Bone scanning has not proved to be of clinical value as a routine preoperative test. The frequency of abnormal findings parallels the status of the axillary lymph nodes on pathologic examination.

G. Biopsy: The diagnosis of breast cancer depends ultimately upon examination of tissue removed by biopsy. Treatment should never be undertaken without an unequivocal histologic diagnosis of cancer. The safest course is to biopsy all suspicious masses found on physical examination and, in the absence of a mass, suspicious lesions demonstrated by mammography. About 30% of lesions thought to be definitely cancer prove on biopsy to be benign, and about 15% of lesions believed to be benign are found to be malignant. These findings demonstrate the fallibility of clinical judgment and the necessity for biopsy.

The simplest method is needle biopsy, either by aspiration of tumor cells or, preferably, by obtaining a small core of tissue with a Vim-Silverman or other special needle. This is an office procedure especially suitable for easily accessible lesions larger than a few centimeters in diameter. A negative needle biopsy should be followed by open biopsy.

The preferred method is open biopsy in the operating room under local anesthesia as a separate procedure prior to deciding upon definitive treatment. The lesion is completely excised with a significant margin at the time of biopsy when feasible. The patient need not be admitted to the hospital. Decisions on additional work-up for metastatic disease and on definitive therapy can be made and discussed with the patient after the histologic diagnosis of cancer has been established. This approach has the advantage of avoiding unnecessary hospitalization and diagnostic procedures in many patients, since cancer is found in only about 35% of patients who require biopsy for differential diagnosis of a breast lump.

As an alternative in patients for whom mastectomy is considered to be the treatment of choice in highly suspicious circumstances, the patient may be admitted directly to the hospital, where the diagnosis is made on frozen section of tissue obtained by open biopsy under general anesthesia. If the frozen section is positive, the surgeon should proceed immediately with mastectomy.

At the time of initial biopsy of breast cancer, it is important for the physician to preserve a portion of the specimen for determination of estrogen receptors.

H. Cytology: Cytologic examination of nipple discharge or cyst fluid may be helpful on rare occasions. As a rule, mammography and breast biopsy are required when nipple discharge or cyst fluid is bloody or cytologically questionable.

I. Mammography: The 2 methods of mammography in common use are ordinary film radiography and xeroradiography. From the standpoint of diagnosing breast cancer, they give comparable results.

Mammography is the only reliable means of detecting breast cancer before a mass can be palpated in the breast. Some breast cancers can be identified by mammography as long as 2 years before reaching a size detectable by palpation.

Although false-positive and false-negative results are occasionally obtained with mammography, the experienced radiologist can interpret mammograms correctly in about 90% of cases. Where mammography is employed proficiently, the yield of malignant lesions on biopsy remains around 35%. This is in spite of the fact that more biopsies are done.

Indications for mammography are as follows: (1) to evaluate the opposite breast when a diagnosis of potentially curable breast cancer has been made, and at intervals of 1–3 years thereafter; (2) to evaluate a questionable or ill-defined breast mass or other suspicious change in the breast, but only if mammographic findings will assist in determining whether or where a biopsy is to be performed; (3) to search for an occult breast cancer in a woman with metastatic disease in axillary nodes or elsewhere from an unknown primary; and (4) to screen at regular intervals a selected group of women who are at high risk for developing breast cancer (see below).

Early Detection

A. Screening Programs: A number of mass screening programs consisting of physical and mammographic examination of the breasts of asymptomatic women have been conducted with encouraging results. They are discovering more than 6 cancers per 1000 women. About 80% of these women have negative axillary lymph nodes at the time of surgery whereas, by contrast, only 45% of patients found in the course of usual medical practice have uninvolved axillary nodes. Detecting breast cancer before it has spread to the axillary nodes greatly increases the chance of survival, and about 84% of such women will survive at least 5 years.

Both physical examination and mammography are necessary for maximum yield in screening programs, since about 40% of early breast cancers can be discovered only by mammography and another 40% can be detected only by palpation. Periodic screening is now recommended for women over age 50, for those over age 40 with a history of breast cancer in mothers or sisters, and those over age 35 who have already had cancer of the breast. The usefulness of periodic mammographic screening in women without identifiable risk factors is marginal. The optimum interval between mammograms is 1 year.

B. Self-Examination: All women over 20 should be advised to examine their breasts monthly—in premenopausal women, just after the menstrual period. The breasts should be inspected initially while standing before a mirror with the hands at the sides, overhead, and pressed firmly on the hips to contract the pectoralis muscles. Masses, asymmetry of breasts, and slight dimpling of the skin may become apparent as a result of these maneuvers. Next, in a supine position, each breast should be carefully palpated with the fingers of the opposite hand. Physicians should instruct their women patients in the technique of self-examination and advise them to report at once for medical evaluation if a mass or other abnormality is noted.

Differential Diagnosis

The lesions most often to be considered in the differential diagnosis of breast cancer are the following, in order of frequency: mammary dysplasia (cystic disease of the breast), fibroadenoma, intraductal papilloma, duct ectasia, and fat necrosis. The differential diagnosis of a breast lump should be established without delay by biopsy, by aspiration of a cyst, or by observing the patient until disappearance of the lump within a period of a few weeks.

Pathologic Types

The behavior of breast cancer can be correlated with the histologic appearance of the lesion. Four types of mammary carcinoma have been identified on the basis of cellular differentiation and invasiveness (Table 17–4). Type I lesions, as exemplified by noninvasive intraductal, papillary, and lobular carcinoma, rarely metastasize (about 13% of cases have positive axillary nodes). Type II cancers, as exemplified by invasive but relatively well differentiated tumors, metastasize somewhat more frequently (about 34% positive axillary nodes). Type III and IV lesions are generally less well differentiated cancers that have a greater tendency to metastasize (55–60% positive nodes). The relative frequency of the various pathologic types (type I, 5%; type II, 15%; type III, 65%; and type IV, 15%) is such that about 80% of breast tumors are of the invasive, frequently metastasizing types. The survival rate decreases progressively with increased tendency to metastasize.

Hormone Receptor Sites

The presence or absence of estrogen receptor on tumor cells appears to be a major prognostic factor and is of paramount importance in managing patients with recurrent or metastatic disease. Patients whose primary tumor is receptor-positive have a more favorable course after mastectomy than those whose tumors are receptor-negative. Sixty percent of patients with metastatic breast cancer will respond to hormonal manipulation if their tumors contain estrogen receptor. Less than 10% of patients with metastatic, estrogen receptor-negative tumors can be successfully treated with hormonal manipulation. It is advisable to obtain an estrogen receptor assay on every breast cancer at the time of initial diagnosis. The tissue requires special handling, and the laboratory should be consulted for instructions.

Curative Treatment

Treatment may be curative or palliative. Curative treatment is advised for clinical stage I, II, and III disease (Table 17–2). Treatment can only be palliative for patients in stage IV and for previously treated patients who develop distant metastases or ineradicable local recurrence.

A. Therapeutic Options: Radical mastectomy involves en bloc removal of the breast, pectoral muscles, and axillary nodes and was the standard curative procedure for breast cancer from the turn of the century

Table 17–4. Classification of mammary carcinoma according to the cellular growth pattern. (Kouchoukos NT et al: *Cancer* 1967; 20:948.)

Type I: Rarely metastasizing (not invasive)
   1. Intraductal or comedocarcinoma without stromal invasion. Paget's disease of the breast may exist if the epithelium of the nipple is involved.
   2. Papillary carcinoma confined to the ducts.
   3. Lobular carcinoma in situ.

Type II: Rarely metastasizing (always invasive)
   1. Well-differentiated adenocarcinoma.
   2. Medullary carcinoma with lymphocytic infiltration.
   3. Pure colloid or mucinous carcinoma.
   4. Papillary carcinoma.

Type III: Moderately metastasizing (always invasive)
   1. Infiltrating adenocarcinoma.
   2. Intraductal carcinoma with stromal invasion.
   3. Infiltrating lobular carcinoma.*
   4. All tumors not classified as types I, II, or IV.

Type IV: Highly metastasizing (always invasive)
   1. Undifferentiated carcinoma having cells without ductal or tubular arrangement.
   2. All types of tumors indisputably invading blood vessels.

*Infiltrating lobular carcinoma has been moved from type II to type III because of growing experience with its metastasizing potential.

until about 10 years ago. Radical mastectomy removes the primary lesion and the axillary nodes with a wide safety margin of surrounding tissue. **Extended radical mastectomy** involves, in addition to standard radical mastectomy, removal of the internal mammary nodes. It has been recommended by a few surgeons for medially or centrally placed breast lesions and for tumors associated with positive axillary nodes because of the known frequency of internal mammary node metastases under these circumstances. **Modified radical mastectomy** (total mastectomy plus axillary dissection) consists of en bloc removal of the breast with the underlying pectoralis major fascia and all axillary lymph nodes. Some surgeons remove the pectoralis minor muscle. Others retract or transect the muscle to facilitate removal of the axillary lymph nodes. Except for preservation of the pectoralis major muscle, this procedure is of the same extent as the standard radical mastectomy. Modified radical mastectomy gives superior cosmetic and functional results compared with standard radical mastectomy. **Simple mastectomy** (total mastectomy) consists of removing the entire breast, leaving the axillary nodes intact. Limited procedures such as **segmental mastectomy** (local excision, quadrant excision, partial mastectomy) are also undergoing trials as definitive treatment for early breast cancer (eg, stage I). The proved efficacy of **irradiation** in sterilizing the primary lesion and the axillary and internal mammary nodes in properly selected cases has made radiation therapy with or without simple mastectomy (or segmental mastectomy) an option for primary treatment of certain breast cancers.

B. Choice of Primary Therapy: The extent of disease and its biologic aggressiveness are the principal determinants of the outcome of primary therapy. Clinical and pathologic staging help in assessing extent of disease (Table 17–2), but each is to some extent imprecise. Since about two-thirds of patients eventually manifest distant disease regardless of the form of primary therapy, there is a tendency to think of breast carcinoma as being systemic in most patients at the time they first present for treatment. In another 20% of patients, the disease is confined to the breast with no involvement of nearby lymph nodes or remote sites. Therefore, the extent of the primary operation, whether radical mastectomy or simple mastectomy, could at most affect the outcome in 15% of breast cancer patients.

There is presently a great deal of controversy regarding the optimal method of primary therapy of stage I, II, and III breast carcinoma, and opinions on this subject have changed considerably in the past decade. For about three-quarters of a century, radical mastectomy was considered standard therapy for this disease. The procedure was designed to remove the primary lesion, the breast in which it arose, the underlying muscle, and, by dissection in continuity, the axillary lymph nodes that were thought to be the first site of spread beyond the breast. When radical mastectomy was introduced, the average patient presented for treatment with advanced local disease (stage III), and a relatively extensive procedure was often necessary just to remove all gross cancer. This is no longer the case.

Although radical mastectomy is extremely effective in controlling local disease, it has the disadvantage of being the most deforming of any of the available treatments for management of primary breast cancer. The surgeon and patient are both eager to find therapy that is less deforming but does not jeopardize the chance for cure.

A number of clinical trials have been performed in the past decade in which the magnitude of the surgical procedure undertaken for removal of cancer in the breast and adjacent lymph nodes has been varied, with and without the use of local radiotherapy to the chest wall and node-bearing areas. The patients have further been classified according to the clinical stage of the disease.

The following are some of the points of dispute these trials should be expected to resolve: (1) Is it important to treat (ie, by surgical excision or by x-ray radiation therapy) clinically negative axillary lymph nodes, because of the microscopic deposits of tumor known to be present in 30% of such cases? (2) Is radiotherapy as effective as surgery in eradicating either gross or occult tumor in the axillary nodes? (3) Is it important to remove Rotter's nodes, the lymph nodes deep to the pectoralis major? (4) Since in 40% of cases microscopic foci of cancer are present elsewhere in the breast, is it important to remove the entire breast in addition to the segment harboring the cancer? (5) Can radiotherapy replace surgery for treating the primary tumor?

In terms of 5-year survival and local recurrence, the results of the recent trials may be summarized as follows: Survival is equal after radical mastectomy, total mastectomy plus axillary dissection, or total mastectomy plus local radiotherapy for disease in stage I, stage II, and stage III. For patients who do not have palpable axillary lymph nodes, the incidence of disseminated disease and survival are equal after total mastectomy plus radiotherapy or total mastectomy alone, but the frequency of local recurrence is much higher in the absence of radiotherapy. Local recurrence was not a clear-cut determinant of survival, however.

Therefore, in answer to the questions posed above, it can be stated that treatment of clinically negative axillary nodes does not enhance survival. In terms of survival, radiotherapy is as effective as surgical dissection for clinically positive axillary lymph nodes. Preliminary data suggest that the lymph nodes deep to the pectoralis major muscle (Rotter's nodes) do not have to be removed. Radical mastectomy gives no better survival rates than does simple mastectomy plus axillary dissection, so removal of the pectoralis muscle is unlikely to be of value in many cases.

Radiation therapy alone (without surgery) in the treatment of primary breast cancer fails to achieve local control in about 50% of cases. Small, nonrandomized studies have suggested that removal of the tumor by segmental mastectomy ("lumpectomy") combined with postoperative irradiation is as effective as mastectomy in achieving local control without diminishing long-term survival. A recent randomized study from Milan compared the results of quadrant resection, axillary dissection, and postoperative radiotherapy with those of a standard Halsted radical mastectomy. The study included only women with lesions less than 2 cm and no palpable axillary lymph nodes. There was no difference in the incidence of local recurrence or survival between the 2 kinds of treatment. Therefore, although the length of follow-up is short, it appears that small, favorable lesions may be controlled by breast-sparing techniques.

A study sponsored by the National Surgical Adjuvant Breast Project in the USA has randomized patients to treatment by segmental resection and axillary dissection, with and without radiation therapy, or to modified radical mastectomy. Patients with lesions up to 4 cm and palpable nodes are being admitted to the study. Consequently, many important questions concerning the advisability of breast-saving operations, the role of radiotherapy, and the biologic significance of multifocal lesions should be answered soon.

It is important to recognize that axillary dissection has both therapeutic and staging objectives. Although there is still some question about the inferences that can properly be drawn from the statistical analyses, the above trials suggest that radiotherapy may be as good as surgery in eradicating tumor in axillary nodes. However, since adjuvant chemotherapy is now recommended for patients with axillary node involvement, axillary dissection is increasingly important for staging purposes.

We believe that total mastectomy plus axillary dissection (modified radical mastectomy) is currently the primary procedure of choice for most patients with potentially curable carcinoma of the breast. Premenopausal patients with involvement of axillary lymph nodes should be considered for adjuvant chemotherapy. Radical mastectomy may be required for some cases of advanced local disease if the tumor invades the muscle but otherwise is no longer necessary for the average patient. Extended radical mastectomy would rarely be appropriate and could only be justified for patients with medial lesions, axillary node involvement, and no signs of more distant spread. Treatment of the axillary nodes is not indicated for **noninfiltrating** cancers, because nodal metastases are present in only 1% of such patients.

Preoperatively, full discussion with the patient regarding the rationale for mastectomy and the manner of coping with the cosmetic and psychologic effects of the operation is essential. Patients often have questions about possible alternatives to standard or modified radical mastectomy—eg, local excision, simple mastectomy, and radiotherapy—and may wish detailed explanations of the risks and benefits of the various procedures. Women with small tumors (ie, less than 2 cm) should have the option of treatment by segmental mastectomy plus axillary dissection and radiotherapy. However, patients should be cautioned that this treatment is still experimental and that its long-term results are unknown. Breast reconstruction should be discussed with the patient if this is a realistic possibility. Time spent preoperatively in ensuring the understanding of the patient and her family is well spent.

Adjuvant Therapy

Chemotherapy is now being used as adjunctive treatment of patients with curable breast cancer and positive axillary nodes, since there is a great likelihood that these patients harbor occult metastases. Overall, about 75% of such patients eventually succumb within 10 years, even though the initial therapy, either surgery or irradiation, eradicated all neoplasm evident at that time. The objective of adjuvant chemotherapy is to eliminate the occult metastases responsible for late recurrences while they are microscopic and most vulnerable to anticancer agents.

Numerous clinical trials of adjuvant chemotherapy are in progress. The most experience to date is with a regimen involving the use of cyclophosphamide, methotrexate, and fluorouracil (CMF) given in 12 monthly cycles to patients with axillary metastases who have been treated by radical or modified radical mastectomy. The results show that in premenopausal women the recurrence rate was approximately one-half that of controls, who received no adjuvant chemotherapy. No therapeutic effect has been shown in postmenopausal women, perhaps because therapy was modified so often in response to side-effects that the total amount of drugs administered was less than planned. Other trials with different agents support the value of adjuvant chemotherapy; in some cases, post-

menopausal women appear to benefit. Combinations of drugs are clearly superior to single drugs.

Hormones may also prove useful as adjuvant therapy. For example, tamoxifen has been shown to enhance the beneficial effects of melphalan mustard and fluorouracil in women whose tumors are estrogen receptor-positive. Interestingly, a good response was only seen in postmenopausal women.

Adjuvant chemotherapy can be offered confidently to premenopausal women with metastases in axillary lymph nodes and no evidence of distant disease. On the other hand, adjuvant hormonal therapy and chemotherapy must still be considered to be experimental and their use restricted to clinical trials.

Postoperative Care

A. Immediate Care: Occasional wound complications such as hematoma or serum collection under the skin flaps and necrosis of skin margins are usually easily managed. They are minimized by suction drainage of the wound and avoidance of undue tension on the skin flaps at closure by the use of a skin graft if necessary.

Active motion of the arm and shoulder on the operated side should be encouraged after the first few days, so that by 10–14 days postoperatively there is a full range of motion. Failure of the patient to cooperate or to make progress may necessitate physical therapy. The Service Committee of the American Cancer Society sponsors a rehabilitation program for postmastectomy patients called Reach for Recovery and will provide useful literature upon request. Women who have had a mastectomy may be valuable counselors for the patient before and after operation. The patient's morale is improved by provision of a temporary breast prosthesis held in place by a comfortably fitted brassiere before she leaves the hospital. She should also receive information on where to obtain a more permanent device.

B. Follow-Up Care: After primary therapy, patients with breast cancer should be followed for life for at least 2 reasons: to detect recurrences and to observe the opposite breast for a second carcinoma. Local and distant metastases occur most frequently within the first 3 years. During this period, the patient is examined every 3–4 months. Thereafter, examination is done every 6 months until 5 years postoperatively and then every 6–12 months. Special attention is given to the remaining breast, because of the increased risk of developing a second primary. The patient should examine her own breast monthly, and a mammogram should be obtained annually. In some cases, metastases are dormant for long periods and may appear up to 10–15 years or longer after removal of the primary tumor.

1. Local recurrence–Recurrence of cancer within the operative field following radical mastectomy is due to incomplete removal of tumor or involved nodes, to cutting across infiltrated lymphatics, or to spillage of tumor cells into the wound. The rate of local recurrence correlates with tumor size, the presence and number of involved axillary nodes, the histologic type of tumor, and the presence of skin edema or skin and fascia fixation with the primary. About 15% of patients develop local recurrence after total mastectomy and axillary dissection. When the axillary nodes are not involved, the local recurrence rate is 5%, but the rate is 25% when they are involved. A similar difference in local recurrence rate was noted between small and large tumors. Local recurrence is even more frequent following operations that do not include an axillary dissection or total mastectomy.

Chest wall recurrences usually appear within the first 2 years, with a peak incidence in the second year, but may occur as late as 15 or more years after radical mastectomy. Suspect nodules should be biopsied. Local excision or localized radiotherapy may be feasible if an isolated nodule is present. If lesions are multiple or accompanied by evidence of regional involvement in the internal mammary or supraclavicular nodes, the disease is best managed by radiation treatment of the whole chest wall including the parasternal, supraclavicular, and axillary areas.

Local recurrence may signal the presence of widespread disease and is an indication for bone and liver scans, determination of liver enzymes (alkaline phosphatase), posteroanterior and lateral chest x-rays, and other examinations as needed to search for evidence of metastases. When there is no evidence of metastases beyond the chest wall and regional nodes, radical irradiation for cure or complete local excision should be attempted.

2. Edema of the arm–Significant edema of the arm occurs in 10–30% of patients after radical mastectomy. When it appears in the early postoperative period, it is usually caused by lymphatic obstruction resulting from infection in the axilla. Postoperative radiotherapy to the axilla increases the incidence of arm edema. Late or secondary edema of the arm may develop years after radical mastectomy as a result of axillary recurrence or of infection in the hand or arm, with obliteration of lymphatic channels. After radical mastectomy, the lymphatic drainage of the arm is always compromised, and the extremity becomes more than normally susceptible to infection following minor injuries. The patient should be warned of this, and treatment by antibiotics, heat, rest, and elevation should be instituted promptly if infection occurs. Specific instruction should be given to the patient who has had radical mastectomy to avoid breaks in the skin of the hand and arm on the operated side and to refrain from tasks likely to cause superficial wounds and infections. Intravenous infusions and injections for inoculation and immunization should not be given in that extremity. Chronic edema is managed by elevation and by a snugly fitted elastic sleeve that is slipped over the arm from hand to shoulder. A special sleeve designed to provide intermittent compression to the entire arm may be useful in severe cases.

3. Breast reconstruction–Breast reconstruction, usually involving multiple operations and the implantation of a prosthesis, is usually feasible after standard or modified radical mastectomy. However, it should only be considered when there is a negligible likelihood of recurrence. Patients who are initially interested in reconstruction often decide later that they no longer wish to undergo the procedure.

4. Risks of pregnancy–Data are insufficient to definitely determine whether interruption of pregnancy improves the prognosis of patients who are discovered during pregnancy to have potentially curable breast cancer and who receive definitive treatment, eg, standard or modified radical mastectomy or radiotherapy. Theoretically, the increasingly high levels of estrogen produced by the placenta as the pregnancy progresses will be detrimental to the patient with occult metastases of estrogen-sensitive breast cancer. Moreover, occult metastases are present in most patients with positive axillary nodes, and treatment by adjuvant chemotherapy would be potentially harmful to the fetus. Under these circumstances, interruption of early pregnancy seems reasonable, with progressively less rationale for the procedure as term approaches. Obviously, the decision must be highly individualized and will be affected by many factors, including the patient's desire to have the baby and the generally poor prognosis when axillary nodes are involved.

Equally problematic and important is the advice regarding future pregnancy (or abortion in case of pregnancy) to be given to women of child-bearing age who have had a radical mastectomy or other definitive treatment for breast cancer. Under these circumstances, one must assume that pregnancy will be harmful if occult metastases are present. Experience shows that women with axillary metastases have a relatively poor prognosis for cure and that recurrences continue to appear for up to 10 years or longer after definitive treatment. Hence, pregnancy is generally inadvisable in this group of patients and should probably be interrupted if it occurs, at least until 5 years have passed without recurrence. Patients with stage I breast cancer who have no evidence of recurrent disease 3–5 years posttreatment are less likely to harbor occult metastases, and pregnancy is correspondingly less hazardous. In principle, the more favorable the stage and pathologic type of disease, the less the possible risk of a stimulating effect by pregnancy on occult metastases. Advice to patients should be individualized accordingly. It should be kept in mind that theoretic considerations—rather than firm clinical evidence from controlled studies—are the basis for the assumption that intercurrent pregnancy will adversely affect prognosis in patients with breast cancer.

In inoperable or metastatic cancer (stage IV disease), therapeutic abortion is usually advisable, because of the possible adverse effects upon the fetus of hormonal treatment, radiotherapy, or chemotherapy.

Prognosis

The stage and pathologic type of breast cancer are the most reliable indicators of prognosis (Table 17–2). Initial therapy also influences prognosis in potentially curable patients. As discussed above, several different treatment programs achieve approximately the same results when the disease is limited to the breast and regional nodes.

About 85% of patients with breast cancer eventually die with gross evidence of the disease. For 20 years after the initial diagnosis, the mortality rate of breast cancer patients exceeds that in age-matched controls. Thereafter, the mortality rates become parallel, even though the deaths that occur among the breast cancer patients are often directly the result of the tumor. Therefore, 5-year survival statistics do not accurately reflect the outcome of therapy.

When cancer is confined to the breast, the 5-year clinical cure rate by accepted methods of therapy is 75–90%. When axillary nodes are involved, the rate drops to 40–60% at 5 years, and by the end of 10 years, the overall clinical cure rate is only about 25%. The least favorable anatomic site for breast carcinoma is the medial portion of the inner lower quadrant. Breast cancer is probably somewhat more malignant in younger than in older women.

General

Anderson JM: Mammary cancers and pregnancy. *Br Med J* 1979;**28:**1124.

Bland KI et al: Analysis of breast cancer screening in women younger than 50 years. *JAMA* 1981;**245:**1037.

Burdick D: Rehabilitation of the breast cancer patient. *Cancer* 1975;**36:**645.

Buzdar AU et al: Management of inflammatory carcinoma of breast with combined modality approach: An update. *Cancer* 1981;**47:**2537.

Byrd BF Jr: ACS/NCI breast cancer detection demonstration projects. *Cancer* 1980;**46:**1084.

Chu AM, Wood WC, Doucette JA: Inflammatory breast carcinoma treated by radical radiotherapy. *Cancer* 1980;**45:**2730.

Cohen AM: Time for a balanced approach to the local treatment of operable carcinoma of the breast. *Surg Gynecol Obstet* 1980;**150:**891.

Devitt JE: Clinical benign disorders of the breast and carcinoma of the breast. *Surg Gynecol Obstet* 1981;**152:**437.

Donegan WL, Spratt JS: *Cancer of the Breast.* Saunders, 1979.

Duncan W, Kerr GR: The curability of breast cancer. *Br Med J* 1976;**2:**781.

Elwood JM, Moorehead WP: Delay in diagnosis and long-term survival in breast cancer. *Br Med J* 1980;**31:**1291.

Fisher B et al: The accuracy of clinical nodal staging and of limited axillary dissection as a determinant of histologic nodal status in carcinoma of the breast. *Surg Gynecol Obstet* 1981;**152:**765.

Fisher B et al: The contribution of recent NSABP clinical trials of primary breast cancer therapy to an understanding of tumor biology: An overview of findings. *Cancer* 1980;**46:**1009.

Forrest APM et al: Is the investigation of patients with breast cancer for occult metastatic disease worthwhile? *Br J Surg* 1979;**66:**749.

Fournier DV et al: Growth rate of 147 mammary carcinomas. *Cancer* 1980;**45:**2198.

Fracchia AA et al: Stage III carcinoma of the breast. *Ann Surg* 1980;**192:**705.

Hagemeister FB et al: Causes of death in breast cancer: A clinicopathologic study. *Cancer* 1980;**46:**162.

Henderson IC, Canellos GP: Cancer of the breast. (2 parts.) *N Engl J Med* 1980;**302:**17, 78.

Heuser L, Spratt JS, Polk HC Jr: Growth rates of primary breast cancers. *Cancer* 1979;**46:**1888.

Hickey RC et al: Hypercalcemia in patients with breast cancer. *Arch Surg* 1981;**116:**545.

Howe GR et al: Estimated benefits and risks of screening for breast cancer. *Can Med Assoc J* 1981;**124:**399.

Huguley CM et al: The value of breast self-examination. *Cancer* 1981;**47:**989.

Hutter RVP: The influence of pathologic factors on breast cancer management. *Cancer* 1980;**46:**961.

Kelly PT: Refinements in breast cancer risk analysis. *Arch Surg* 1981;**116:**364.

Langlands AO et al: Long-term survival of patients with breast cancer: A study of the curability of the disease. *Br Med J* 1979;**2:**1247.

Lee YTN: Bone scanning in patients with early breast carcinoma: Should it be a routine staging procedure? *Cancer* 1981;**47:**486.

Leis HP: Managing the remaining breast. *Cancer* 1980;**46:** 1026.

Letton AH et al: Five-year-plus survival of breast screenees. *Cancer* 1981;**48:**404.

Lucas FV, Perez-Mesa C: Inflammatory carcinoma of the breast. *Cancer* 1978;**41:**1595.

McDivitt RW: Breast carcinoma. *Hum Pathol* 1978;**9:**3.

Maier WP et al: A ten year study of medullary carcinoma of the breast. *Surg Gynecol Obstet* 1977;**144:**695.

Monson RR et al: Chronic mastitis and carcinoma of the breast. *Lancet* 1976;**2:**224.

Moxley JH et al: Treatment of primary breast cancer: Summary of the National Institutes of Health consensus development conference. *JAMA* 1980;**244:**797.

Mueller CB, Ames F, Anderson GD: Breast cancer in 3,558 women: Age as a significant determinant in the rate of dying and causes of death. *Surgery* 1978;**83:**123.

Mueller CB, Jeffries W: Cancer of the breast: Its outcome as measured by the rate of dying and causes of death. *Ann Surg* 1975;**182:**334.

Nealon TF Jr et al: Pathologic identification of poor prognosis stage I ($T_1N_0M_0$) cancer of the breast. *Ann Surg* 1979; **190:**129.

Nealon TF Jr et al: Treatment of early cancer of the breast ($T_1N_0M_0$ and $T_2N_0M_0$) on the basis of histologic characteristics. *Surgery* 1981;**89:**279.

Paone JF et al: Pathogenesis and treatment of Paget's disease of the breast. *Cancer* 1981;**48:**825.

Ribeiro GG, Palmer MK: Breast carcinoma associated with pregnancy: A clinician's dilemma. *Br Med J* 1977;**2:**1524.

Rosen PP et al: Epidemiology of breast carcinoma: Age, menstrual status, and exogenous hormone usage in patients with lobular carcinoma in situ. *Surgery* 1979;**85:**219.

Rosen PP et al: Lobular carcinoma in situ of the breast: Detailed analysis of 99 patients with average follow-up of 24 years. *Am J Surg Pathol* 1978;**2:**225.

Rosen PP et al: Noninvasive breast carcinoma: Frequency of unsuspected invasion and implications for treatment. *Ann Surg* 1979;**189:**377.

Scanlon EF et al: Preoperative and follow-up procedures on patients with breast cancer. *Cancer* 1980;**46:**977.

Schwartz GF, Feig SA, Patchefsky AS: Clinicopathologic correlations and significance of clinically occult mammary lesions. *Cancer* 1978;**41:**1147.

Schwartz GF et al: Multicentricity of non-palpable breast cancer. *Cancer* 1980;**45**:2913.

Stabile RJ et al: Reconstructive breast surgery following mastectomy and adjunctive radiation therapy. *Cancer* 1980;**45**:2738.

Stehlin JS et al: Treatment of carcinoma of the breast. *Surg Gynecol Obstet* 1979;**149**:911.

Urban JA: Surgical management of palpable breast cancer. *Cancer* 1980;**46**:983.

Vaitukaitis JL: Breast-cancer management: Alternatives to radical mastectomy. *N Engl J Med* 1979;**301**:326.

Valagussa P, Bonadonna G, Veronesi U: Patterns of relapse and survival following radical mastectomy: Analysis of 716 consecutive patients. *Cancer* 1978;**41**:1170.

Veronesi U et al: Inefficacy of internal mammary nodes dissection in breast cancer surgery. *Cancer* 1981;**47**:170.

Webber BL et al: Risk of subsequent contralateral breast carcinoma in a population of patients with in situ breast carcinoma. *Cancer* 1981;**47**:2928.

Westman-Naeser S et al: Multifocal breast carcinoma. *Am J Surg* 1981;**142**:255.

Wilkinson GS et al: Delay, stage of disease and survival from breast cancer. *J Chronic Dis* 1979;**32**:365.

Woods KL, Smith SR, Morrison JM: Parity and breast cancer: Evidence of a dual effect. *Br Med J* 1980;**281**:419.

Mammography

Feig SA: Low-dose mammography. *JAMA* 1979;**242**:2107.

Feig SA et al: Prognostic factors of breast neoplasms detected on screening by mammography and physical examination. *Radiology* 1979;**133**:577.

Homer MJ: Analysis of patients undergoing breast biopsy. *JAMA* 1980;**243**:677.

Roses DF et al: Biopsy for microcalcification detected by mammography. *Surgery* 1980;**87**:248.

Sibala JL et al: Computed tomographic mammography. *Arch Surg* 1981;**116**:114.

Solmer R, Goodstein J, Agliozzo C: Nonpalpable breast lesions discovered by mammography. *Arch Surg* 1980;**115**:1067.

Hormone Receptors

Bishop HM et al: Relationship of oestrogen-receptor status to survival in breast cancer. *Lancet* 1979;**2**:283.

Bloom ND et al: The role of progesterone receptors in the management of advanced breast cancer. *Cancer* 1980;**45**:2992.

Cooke T et al: Oestrogen receptors and prognosis in early breast cancer. *Lancet* 1979;**1**:995.

Gapinski PV, Donegan WL: Estrogen receptors and breast cancer: Prognostic and therapeutic implications. *Surgery* 1980;**88**:386.

Hawkins RA, Roberts MM, Forrest APM: Oestrogen receptors and breast cancer: Current status. *Br J Surg* 1980;**67**:153.

Jensen EV: Hormone dependency of breast cancer. *Cancer* 1981;**47**:2319.

Kinne DW et al: Estrogen receptor protein in breast cancer as a predictor of recurrence. *Cancer* 1981;**47**:2364.

Lesser ML et al: Estrogen and progesterone receptors in breast carcinoma: Correlations with epidemiology and pathology. *Cancer* 1981;**48**:299.

Steroid receptors in breast cancer. *Cancer* 1980;**46** (**Suppl**): 2759. [Entire issue.]

Adjuvant Chemotherapy

Adjuvant chemotherapy of breast cancer: Summary of an NIH consensus statement. *Br Med J* 1980;**281**:724.

Bonadonna G, Valagussa P: Dose-response effect of adjuvant chemotherapy in breast cancer. *N Engl J Med* 1981;**304**:10.

Caprini JA et al: Adjuvant chemotherapy for stage II and III breast carcinoma. *JAMA* 1980;**244**:243.

Cooper RG, Holland JF, Glidewell O: Adjuvant chemotherapy of breast cancer. *Cancer* 1979;**44**:793.

Rossi A et al: Multimodal treatment in operable breast cancer: Five-year results of the CMF programme. *Br Med J* 1981; **282**:1427.

Weiss RB et al: Multimodal treatment of primary breast carcinoma. *Am J Med* 1981;**70**:844.

TREATMENT OF ADVANCED BREAST CANCER

This section covers palliative therapy of disseminated disease incurable by surgery (stage IV).

Radiotherapy

Palliative radiotherapy may be advised for locally advanced cancers with distant metastases in order to control ulceration, pain, and other manifestations in the breast and regional nodes. Radical irradiation of the breast and chest wall and the axillary, internal mammary, and supraclavicular nodes should be undertaken in an attempt to cure locally advanced and inoperable lesions when there is no evidence of distant metastases. A small number of patients in this group are cured in spite of extensive breast and regional node involvement. Adjuvant chemotherapy should be considered for such patients.

Palliative irradiation is also of value in the treatment of certain bone or soft tissue metastases to control pain or avoid fracture. Radiotherapy is especially useful in the treatment of the isolated bony metastasis.

Hormonal Therapy

Disseminated disease may respond to prolonged endocrine therapy such as administration of hormones, ablation of the ovaries, adrenals, or pituitary, or administration of drugs that block hormone receptor sites (eg, antiestrogens) or drugs that block the synthesis of hormones (eg, aminoglutethimide). Hormonal manipulation is usually more successful in postmenopausal women. If treatment is based on the presence of estrogen receptor protein in the primary tumor or metastases, however, the rate of response is nearly equal in premenopausal and postmenopausal women. A favorable response to hormonal manipulation occurs in about one-third of patients with metastatic breast cancer. Of those whose tumors contain estrogen receptors, the response is about 60%. Because only 5–10% of women whose tumors do not contain estrogen receptors respond, they should not receive hormonal therapy except in unusual circumstances.

A favorable response to hormonal manipulation may be anticipated also in (1) patients with slowly growing tumors (ie, if there is a long tumor-free interval between diagnosis and the appearance of metastatic disease; (2) patients with metastases to bone and soft tissues or pleura—as opposed to visceral organs such as lung, liver, or brain; (3) very old patients; or (4) patients who have previously shown favorable responses. However, the presence of estrogen receptor protein on the tumor or metastases is the single best predictor of responsiveness. Since the quality of life during a remission induced by endocrine manipulation is usually superior to a remission following cytotoxic chemotherapy, it is usually best to try endocrine manipulation first in cases where the estrogen receptor status of the tumor is unknown. However, if the estrogen receptor status is unknown but the disease is progressing rapidly or involves visceral organs, endocrine therapy is rarely successful, and introducing it may waste valuable time.

In general, only one type of systemic therapy should be given at a time, unless it is necessary to irradiate a destructive lesion of weight-bearing bone while the patient is on another regimen. The regimen should be changed only if the disease is clearly progressing but not if it appears to be stable. This is especially important for patients with destructive bone metastases, since minor changes in the status of these lesions are difficult to determine radiographically. A plan of therapy that would simultaneously minimize toxicity and maximize benefits is often best achieved by hormonal manipulation.

The choice of endocrine therapy depends on the menopausal status of the patient. Women within 1 year of their last menstrual period are considered to be premenopausal, while women whose menstruation ceased more than a year ago are postmenopausal. The initial choice of therapy is referred to as primary hormonal manipulation; subsequent endocrine treatment is called secondary or tertiary hormonal manipulation.

A. The Premenopausal Patient:

1. Primary hormonal therapy–Bilateral oophorectomy is usually the first choice for primary hormonal manipulation in premenopausal women. It can be achieved rapidly and safely by surgery or, if the patient is a poor operative risk, by irradiation to the ovaries. Ovarian radiation therapy should be avoided in otherwise healthy patients, however, because of the high rate of complications. Oophorectomy presumably works by eliminating estrogens, progestins, and androgens, which stimulate growth of the tumor. The average remission is about 12 months.

The potent antiestrogen tamoxifen has only recently been used as an alternative to oophorectomy in the premenopausal patient. In limited trials, the response rate to tamoxifen is similar to that of oophorectomy, leading some authorities to recommend tamoxifen as the primary hormonal treatment of metastatic breast cancer in premenopausal women with estrogen receptor–positive tumors. However, only a few premenopausal patients have received tamoxifen without prior oophorectomy, and the optimal dosage remains unclear. In a study in which 40–120 mg/d was given, serum levels of estrone and estradiol were markedly

elevated, presumably due to an increased output of pituitary gonadotropins. Although 5 out of 11 women responded to tamoxifen, it appears that either escalation of the drug dosage or oophorectomy plus tamoxifen may be necessary in premenopausal patients.

Tamoxifen may eventually become the preferred primary hormonal manipulation in premenopausal women, but experience is presently insufficient to advocate tamoxifen in preference to oophorectomy. The operation is not associated with long-term endocrine dysfunction, as are adrenalectomy and hypophysectomy. Oophorectomy should definitely not be abandoned yet. Randomized trials now being conducted comparing use of tamoxifen with oophorectomy should clarify this issue.

2. Secondary or tertiary hormonal therapy– Although patients who do not respond to oophorectomy should be treated with cytotoxic drugs, those who respond and then relapse may subsequently respond to another form of endocrine treatment. The initial choice for secondary endocrine manipulation has not been clearly defined. Adrenalectomy or hypophysectomy induces regression in approximately 30–50% of patients who have previously responded to oophorectomy. In our experience, adrenalectomy is preferred, because the patient is easier to manage afterward and because there are fewer side-effects and complications. The experimental drug aminoglutethimide (Cytadren) blocks the production of adrenal hormones and may also prove useful in secondary endocrine manipulation, where androgens were previously used. The preferred treatment for the patient who has previously responded to oophorectomy and later manifests progressive disease is tamoxifen, 10 mg twice daily. This drug will induce a remission in about 30% of such patients and is clearly less toxic and troublesome than another operation or the drug aminoglutethimide.

B. The Postmenopausal Patient:

1. Primary hormonal therapy–The initial choice of therapy for postmenopausal women with metastatic breast cancer amenable to endocrine manipulation has been diethylstilbestrol (DES). A recent randomized study has shown that tamoxifen (10 mg twice daily) is as efficacious as DES but has fewer side-effects.

2. Secondary or tertiary endocrine manipulation–Patients who do not respond to primary endocrine manipulation should be given cytotoxic drugs. Postmenopausal patients who respond initially to tamoxifen and then manifest progressive disease should be given diethylstilbestrol. Alternative forms of treatment or tertiary agents include progestins (eg, megestrol acetate [Megace]) or androgens. Adrenalectomy, either surgically or with aminoglutethimide, is used for tertiary manipulation.

Chemotherapy

Cytotoxic drugs should be considered for the treatment of metastatic breast cancer (1) if visceral metastases are present; (2) if hormonal treatment is unsuccessful or the disease has progressed after an initial response to hormonal manipulation; or (3) if the tumor is estrogen receptor–negative. The most useful single chemotherapeutic agent to date is doxorubicin (Adriamycin), with a response rate of 40–50%. The remissions tend to be brief, and in general, experience with single-agent chemotherapy in patients with disseminated disease has not been encouraging.

Combination chemotherapy using multiple agents has proved to be more effective, with objectively observed favorable responses achieved in 60–80% of patients with stage IV disease. Various combinations of drugs have been used, and clinical trials are continuing in an effort to improve results and to reduce undesirable side-effects. Doxorubicin and cyclophosphamide produced an objective response in 87% of 46 patients who had an adequate trial of therapy. Other chemotherapeutic regimens have consisted of various combinations of drugs, including cyclophosphamide, vincristine, methotrexate, and fluorouracil, with response rates ranging up to 60–70%.

Malignant Pleural Effusion

This condition develops at some time in almost half of patients with breast cancer. When severe and persistent, the effusion is best controlled by closed tube drainage of the chest and intrapleural instillation of a sclerosing agent. An intercostal tube is inserted in a low interspace and placed on suction or water-seal drainage until as much fluid as possible has been removed, and 500 mg of tetracycline dissolved in 30 mL of saline are then injected into the pleural cavity through the tube, which is clamped for 6 hours. The patient's position is changed frequently to distribute the tetracycline within the pleural space. The tube is unclamped and continued on water-seal drainage until drainage has decreased to less than 60 mL in 24 hours. This will usually occur within 5–6 days if the sclerosing action of the tetracycline is effective in causing adherence of visceral to parietal pleura. Transient reaction to the tetracycline such as pleural pain or low-grade fever is treated symptomatically. Fluid reaccumulation is prevented in 50–75% of patients. The procedure may be repeated in a few weeks if fluid recurs. Tetracycline is preferable to various chemotherapeutic agents such as mechlorethamine and thiotepa that may cause nausea, vomiting, or bone marrow depression.

Asbury RF et al: Treatment of metastatic breast cancer with aminoglutethimide. *Cancer* 1981;**47**:1954.

Bisel HF: Management of locally advanced and disseminated breast cancer: Chemotherapy. *Cancer* 1980;**46**:1097.

Decker DA et al: Complete responders to chemotherapy in metastatic breast cancer. *JAMA* 1979;**242**:2075.

DiStefano A et al: The natural history of breast cancer patients with brain metastases. *Cancer* 1979;**44**:1913.

Fisher B et al: Disease-free survival at intervals during and following completion of adjuvant chemotherapy. *Cancer* 1981; **48**:1273.

Henderson IC: Less toxic treatment of advanced breast cancer. *N Engl J Med* 1981;**305**:575.

Ingle JN et al: Randomized clinical trial of diethylstilbestrol versus tamoxifen in postmenopausal women with advanced breast cancer. *N Engl J Med* 1981;**304**:16.

Karabali-Dalamaga S et al: Natural history and prognosis of recurrent breast cancer. *Br Med J* 1978;**2**:730.

Kaufman RJ: Advanced breast cancer: Additive hormonal therapy. *Cancer* 1981;**47**:2398.

Kiang DT et al: Combination therapy of hormone and cytotoxic agents in advanced breast cancer. *Cancer* 1981;**47**:452.

Legha SS, Davis HL, Muggia FM: Hormonal therapy of breast cancer: New approaches and concepts. *Ann Intern Med* 1978;**88**:69.

Legha SS et al: Complete remissions in metastatic breast cancer treated with combination drug therapy. *Ann Intern Med* 1979;**91**:847.

Legha SS et al: Response to hormonal therapy as a prognostic factor for metastatic breast cancer treated with combination chemotherapy. *Cancer* 1980;**46**:438.

Manni A, Pearson OII: Antiestrogen-induced remissions in premenopausal women with stage IV breast cancer: Effects on ovarian function. *Cancer Treat Rep* 1980;**64**:779.

McGuire W: Hormone receptors: Their role in predicting prognosis and response to endocrine therapy. *Semin Oncol* 1978; **5**:428.

Minton MJ et al: Corticosteroids for elderly patients with breast cancer. *Cancer* 1981;**48**:883.

Moseley HS et al: Endocrine ablation for metastatic breast cancer: A reappraisal of hormone receptors. *Am J Surg* 1980;**140**:164.

Powles TJ et al: Failure of chemotherapy to prolong survival in a group of patients with metastatic breast cancer. *Lancet* 1980;**1**:580.

Pritchard KI et al: Tamoxifen therapy in premenopausal patients with breast cancer. *Cancer Treat Rep* 1980;**64**:787.

Santen RJ et al: A randomized trial comparing surgical adrenalectomy with aminoglutethimide plus hydrocortisone in women with advanced breast cancer. *N Engl J Med* 1981; **305**:545.

Santen RJ, Wells SA: The use of aminoglutethimide in the treatment of patients with metastatic carcinoma of the breast. *Cancer* 1980;**46**:1066.

Schweitzer RJ: Oophorectomy/adrenalectomy. *Cancer* 1980; **46**:1061.

Stephens FO et al: Intra-arterial chemotherapy as basal treatment in advanced and fungating primary breast cancer. *Lancet* 1980;**2**:435.

MAMMARY DYSPLASIA

Essentials of Diagnosis

- Painful, often multiple, frequently bilateral masses in the breast.
- Rapid fluctuation in the size of the masses is common.
- Frequently, pain occurs or increases and size increases during premenstrual phase of cycle.
- Most common age is 30–50. Rare in postmenopausal women.

General Considerations

This disorder, also known as chronic cystic mastitis, is the most frequent lesion of the breast. It is common in women 30–50 years of age but rare in postmenopausal women, which suggests that it is related to ovarian activity. Estrogen hormone is considered a causative factor. The typical pathologic change in the breast is the formation of gross and microscopic cysts from the terminal ducts and acini. Large cysts are clinically palpable and may be several centimeters or more in diameter.

Clinical Findings

Mammary dysplasia may produce an asymptomatic lump in the breast that is discovered by accident, but pain or tenderness often calls attention to the mass. There may be discharge from the nipple. In many cases discomfort occurs or is increased during the premenstrual phase of the cycle, at which time the cysts tend to enlarge. Fluctuation in size and rapid appearance or disappearance of a breast tumor are common in cystic disease. Multiple or bilateral masses are not unusual, and many patients will give a past history of transient lump in the breast or cyclic breast pain. Pain, fluctuation in size, and multiplicity of lesions are the features most helpful in differentiation from carcinoma. However, if skin retraction is present, the diagnosis of cancer should be assumed until disproved by biopsy.

Differential Diagnosis

Pain, fluctuation in size, and multiplicity of lesions help to differentiate these lesions from carcinoma and adenofibroma. Final diagnosis often depends on biopsy. Mammography may occasionally be helpful.

Treatment

Because mammary dysplasia is frequently indistinguishable from carcinoma on the basis of clinical findings, it is advisable to biopsy suspicious lesions, which is usually done under local anesthesia. Discrete cysts or small localized areas of cystic disease may be excised. Surgery should be conservative, since the primary objective is to exclude cancer. Simple mastectomy or extensive removal of breast tissue is rarely, if ever, indicated.

When the diagnosis of mammary dysplasia has been established by previous biopsy or is practically certain, because the history is classic, aspiration of a discrete mass suggestive of a cyst is indicated. The skin and overlying tissues are anesthetized by infiltration with 1% procaine, and a 21-gauge needle is introduced. If a cyst is present, typical watery fluid (straw-colored, gray, greenish, brown, or black) is evacuated and the mass disappears. The patient is reexamined at intervals thereafter. If no fluid is obtained, if a mass persists after aspiration, or if at any time during follow-up an atypical persistent lump is noted, biopsy should be performed.

Breast pain associated with generalized mammary dysplasia is best treated by avoiding trauma and by wearing (night and day) a brassiere that gives good support and protection. Hormonal therapy is not advisable, because it does not cure the condition and has undesirable side-effects. Recently, danazol, a synthetic androgen, has been used for patients with severe pain. This treatment suppresses pituitary gonadotropins and should be reserved for the unusual, severe case.

Prognosis

Exacerbations of pain, tenderness, and cyst formation may occur at any time until the menopause, when symptoms subside. The patient should be advised to examine her own breasts each month just after menstruation and to inform her physician if a mass appears. The risk of breast cancer in women with mammary dysplasia is about twice that of women in general. Follow-up examinations at regular intervals should therefore be arranged.

Golinger RC: Hormones and the pathophysiology of fibrocystic mastopathy. *Surg Gynecol Obstet* 1978;**146**:273.

Jones BM, Bradbeer JW: The presentation and progression of macroscopic breast cysts. *Br J Surg* 1980;**67**:669.

Kline TS, Joshi LP, Neal HS: Fine-needle aspiration of the breast: Diagnoses and pitfalls: A review of 3545 cases. *Cancer* 1979; **44**:1458.

Livolsi VA et al: Fibrocystic breast disease in oral-contraceptive users: A histopathological evaluation of epithelial atypia. *N Engl J Med* 1978;**299**:381.

Minton JP et al: Caffeine, cyclic nucleotides, and breast disease. *Surgery* 1979;**86**:105.

Moskowitz M et al: Proliferative disorders of the breast as risk factors for breast cancer in a self-selected screened population: Pathologic markers. *Radiology* 1980;**134**:289.

Oluwole SF, Freeman HP: Analysis of benign breast lesions in blacks. *Am J Surg* 1979;**137**:786.

Oral contraceptive use no protection against cancer risk–associated fibrocystic breast disease. (Research findings from the NIH.) *JAMA* 1979;**241**:24.

FIBROADENOMA OF THE BREAST

This common benign neoplasm occurs most frequently in young women, usually within 20 years after puberty. It is somewhat more frequent and tends to occur at an earlier age in black than in white women. Multiple tumors in one or both breasts are found in 10–15% of patients.

The typical fibroadenoma is a round, firm, discrete, relatively movable, nontender mass 1–5 cm in diameter. The tumor is usually discovered accidentally. Clinical diagnosis in young patients is generally not difficult. In women over 30, cystic disease of the breast and carcinoma of the breast must be considered. Cysts can be identified by aspiration. Fibroadenoma does not normally occur after the menopause, but postmenopausal women may occasionally develop fibroadenoma after administration of estrogenic hormone.

Treatment is by excision under local anesthesia as an outpatient procedure, with pathologic examination of the specimen.

Cystosarcoma phyllodes is a type of fibroadenoma with cellular stroma that tends to grow rapidly. This tumor may reach a large size and if inadequately excised will recur locally. The lesion is rarely malignant. Treatment is by local excision of the mass with a margin of surrounding breast tissue.

Al-Jurf A, Hawk WA, Crile G Jr: Cystosarcoma phyllodes. *Surg Gynecol Obstet* 1978;**146**:358.

Andersson A, Bergdahl L: Cystosarcoma phyllodes in young women. *Arch Surg* 1978;**113**:742.

Browder W, McQuitty JT, McDonald JC: Malignant cystosarcoma phylloides: Treatment and prognosis. *Am J Surg* 1978;**136**:239.

Hart WR, Bauer RC, Oberman WA: Cystosarcoma phyllodes: A clinicopathologic study of twenty-six hypercellular periductal stromal tumors of the breast. *Am J Clin Pathol* 1978;**70**:211.

Pietruszka M, Barnes L: Cystosarcoma phyllodes: A clinicopathologic analysis of 42 cases. *Cancer* 1978;**41**:1974.

Rao BR et al: Most cystosarcoma phyllodes and fibroadenomas have progesterone receptor but lack estrogen receptor. *Cancer* 1981;**47**:2016.

DIFFERENTIAL DIAGNOSIS OF NIPPLE DISCHARGE

In order of frequency, the following are the commonest causes of nipple discharge in the nonlactating breast: intraductal papilloma, carcinoma, mammary dysplasia, and ectasia of the ducts. The important characteristics of the discharge and some other factors to be evaluated by history and physical examination are as follows:

(1) Nature of discharge (serous, bloody, or other).

(2) Association with a mass or not.

(3) Unilateral or bilateral.

(4) Single duct or multiple duct discharge.

(5) Discharge is spontaneous (persistent or intermittent) or must be expressed.

(6) Discharge produced by pressure at a single site or by general pressure on the breast.

(7) Relation to menses.

(8) Premenopausal or postmenopausal.

(9) Patient taking contraceptive pills, or estrogen for postmenopausal symptoms.

Unilateral, spontaneous serous or serosanguineous discharge from a single duct is usually caused by an intraductal papilloma or, rarely, by an intraductal cancer. In either case, a mass is often but not always present. The involved duct may be identified by pressure at different sites around the nipple at the margin of the areola. Bloody discharge is more suggestive of cancer. Cytologic examination of the discharge should be accomplished and may identify malignant cells, but negative findings do not rule out cancer, which is more likely in women over 50. In any case, the involved duct, and a mass if present, should be excised with an adequate margin by meticulous technique through a circumareolar incision.

In premenopausal females, spontaneous multiple duct discharge, unilateral or bilateral, most marked just before menstruation, is often due to mammary dysplasia. Discharge may be green or brownish. Papil-

lomatosis and ductal ectasia are also diagnostic possibilities. Biopsy may be necessary to establish the diagnosis of a diffuse nonmalignant process. If a mass is present, it should be removed.

Milky discharge from multiple ducts in the nonlactating breast may occur in certain syndromes (Chiari-Frommel, Argonz–Del Castillo [Forbes-Albright]), presumably as a result of increased secretion of pituitary prolactin. An endocrine work-up may be indicated. Drugs of the chlorpromazine type and contraceptive pills may also cause milky discharge that ceases on discontinuance of the medication.

Oral contraceptives may cause clear, serous, or milky discharge from a single duct, but multiple duct discharge is more common. The discharge is more evident just before menstruation and disappears on stopping the medication. If it does not and is from a single duct, exploration should be considered.

Purulent discharge may originate in a subareolar abscess and require excision of the abscess and related lactiferous sinus.

When localization is not possible and no mass is palpable, the patient should be reexamined every week for 1 month. When unilateral discharge persists, even without definite localization or tumor, exploration must be considered. The alternative is careful follow-up at intervals of 1–3 months. Mammography should be done. Cytologic examination of nipple discharge for exfoliated cancer cells may be helpful in diagnosis.

Although none of the benign lesions causing nipple discharge are precancerous, they may coexist with cancer and it is not possible to distinguish them definitely from cancer on clinical grounds. Patients with carcinoma almost always have a palpable mass, but in rare instances a nipple discharge may be the only sign. For these reasons chronic nipple discharge, especially if bloody, is usually an indication for resection of the involved ducts.

FAT NECROSIS

Fat necrosis is a rare lesion of the breast but is of clinical importance because it produces a mass, often accompanied by skin or nipple retraction, that is indistinguishable from carcinoma. Trauma is presumed to be the cause, although only about half of patients give a history of injury to the breast. Ecchymosis is occasionally seen near the tumor. Tenderness may or may not be present. If untreated, the mass associated with fat necrosis gradually disappears. As a rule, the safest course is to obtain a biopsy. When carcinoma has been ruled out, the mass should be excised.

BREAST ABSCESS

During nursing, an area of redness, tenderness, and induration not infrequently develops in the breast. In the early stages, the infection can often be reversed while continuing nursing with that breast and taking an antibiotic. If the lesion progresses to form a localized mass with local and systemic signs of infection, an abscess is present and should be drained, and nursing should be discontinued.

A subareolar abscess may develop in young or middle-aged women who are not lactating. These infections tend to recur after incision and drainage unless the area is explored in a quiescent interval with excision of the involved lactiferous duct or ducts at the base of the nipple. Except for the subareolar type of abscess, infection in the breast is very rare unless the patient is lactating. Therefore, findings suggestive of abscess in the nonlactating breast require incision and biopsy of any indurated tissue.

PUERPERAL MASTITIS

Postpartum mastitis occurs sporadically in nursing mothers shortly after they return home, or it may occur in epidemic form in the hospital. Hemolytic *Staphylococcus aureus* is usually the causative agent. Inflammation is generally unilateral, and primiparas are more often affected.

In sporadic puerperal mastitis, an acute interlobar inflammation with fever, localized pain, tenderness, and segmental erythema develops via a fissured nipple. The sepsis is neither in the acinar nor duct system, and the milk is not affected. Hence, the baby should be allowed to nurse (with a nipple shield) to prevent engorgement, which contributes to abscess formation.

Antibiotic therapy against possible penicillinase-resistant organisms (oxacillin, cephalothin, or equivalent) should be given.

In epidemic puerperal mastitis, the infection often can be traced to a carrier. The baby may acquire the pathogen orally from the mother's skin or from someone in the nursery. Epidemic puerperal mastitis is more fulminating than the sporadic type, and infection seems to follow regurgitation of small amounts of milk back into the nipple duct. Thus, the baby harbors the infective organism, which should match bacteria cultured from the milk. Prompt weaning, antibiotic therapy (as above), suppression of lactation, cold packs to the breast, and a snug brassiere to support the breasts are recommended.

If the mother begins antibiotic therapy before suppuration begins, infection can usually be controlled in 24 hours. If delay is permitted, breast abscess often results. Incision and drainage are required for abscess formation. Despite puerperal mastitis of either type, the baby usually thrives without prophylactic antimicrobial therapy.

Prevention consists of proper initial nursing procedure and breast hygiene.

Couner AE: Elevated levels of sodium and chloride in milk from mastitic breast. *Pediatrics* 1979;**63**:910.

Mahendranath D et al: Study of mastitis with special reference to antibiotic sensitivity. *Indian J Microbiol* 1976;**16**:116.

Niebyl JR, Spence MR, Parmley TH: Sporadic (nonepidemic) puerperal mastitis. *J Reprod Med* 1978;**20**:97.

Special Medical & Surgical Considerations in Gynecology | 18

Albert W. Diddle, MD

Many nongynecologic medical and surgical disorders in women are essentially the same as those seen in men. These disorders, because of either systemic or anatomically contiguous effects, may produce symptoms and signs of a gynecologic nature or may be confused with gynecologic disease. Certain medical and surgical disorders, moreover, either occur with greater frequency in women or are modified by anatomic, endocrine, and psychologic factors peculiar to women. Some medicinal agents may have different pharmacologic effects in women than in men, largely through their effects on primary and secondary sex characteristics.

The differences between women and men with respect to such matters as upbringing, social attitudes, living habits (eg, diet, smoking, drinking), occupation, recreational preferences, environmental exposure, anatomy, gonadal development, childbearing, and X-linked genetic inheritance explain the influence of sex on the incidence, severity, and prognosis in many diseases. These differences may explain why bronchogenic carcinoma, inguinal hernia, and hemophilia occur more commonly in men than in women and why varicose veins, thrombophlebitis, and urinary tract infections occur more frequently in women. It is difficult to understand, however, why diseases such as rheumatoid arthritis, systemic lupus erythematosus, and colloid goiter occur more frequently and with greater severity in women than in men.

Differences in the incidences and responses of males and females to various illnesses are summarized in Tables 18–1 to 18–5. Compared to 1975, there has been a rise in the number of destructive illnesses in proportion to diseases in general in both sexes (Tables 18–1 and 18–2). Table 18–3 concerns the higher incidences in females of disorders that affect both sexes; Table 18–4 sets forth the average life expectancy of men and women; and Table 18–5 lists sex-related adverse drug reactions in women.

That sex-related illness is influenced by the changing living habits of women is borne out by the increasingly frequent occurrence among women of what were heretofore considered to be predominantly disorders of men.

The increasing use of cigarettes by women may account for the increasing occurrence of pulmonary emphysema and bronchogenic carcinoma in women. The latter disease, which is relatively rare in nonsmok-

Table 18–1. Ten leading causes of death (both sexes, all ages) by sex in the USA. Figures in parentheses represent number of deaths per thousand.*†

Female		Male	
Heart disease	(206)	Heart disease	(299)
Cancer	(134)	Cancer	(166)
Stroke	(45)	Stroke	(66)
Accident	(44)	Accident	(50)
Suicide	(21)	Suicide	(31)
Pneumonia-influenza	(15)	Pneumonia-influenza	(21)
Hepatic cirrhosis	(12)	Hepatic cirrhosis	(17)
Diabetes mellitus	(10)	Homicide	(15)
Disease of infancy	(10)	Disease of infancy	(12)
Homicide	(9)	Bronchitis	(11)

*Some of the differences may be explained on the basis of occupation, habits, or other environmental factors. In contrast, the greater mortality rate in males from respiratory infections and vascular disease is difficult to explain. Diabetes mellitus, usually encountered in older people, is more common in women than men because of their greater longevity. Changes in modes of living undoubtedly account for the increasing number of deaths from violence.

†From: Vital Statistics of the United States, 1978.

Table 18–2. Sex differences in incidence (%) of cancer by site.*

Site	Female	Male
Breast	27	
Gastrointestinal	18	17
Colorectal	15	14
Pancreas	3	3
Genital	17	17
Uterus	13	
Ovary	4	
Prostate		17
Lung	8	22
Leukemia-lymphoma	7	8
Urinary tract	4	9
Oral	2	5
Skin	2	2
All other	15	20

*Modified from: *CA* 1981;**31**:1.

Table 18—3. Medical and surgical disorders common to both sexes but occurring more frequently in women.

Endocrine and metabolic disorders
  Simple and nodular goiter
  Hypothyroidism
  Carcinoma of the thyroid
  Osteoporosis
  Polyostotic fibrous dysplasia (Albright's syndrome in women)
  Hyperadrenocorticism (Cushing's disease)
  Adrenogenital syndrome and virilization
  Aldosteronism, primary
  Hypopituitarism (30—50% of cases associated with Sheehan's syndrome)
  Anorexia nervosa
  Diabetes mellitus, maturity onset (insulinoplethoric)
  Exogenous obesity

Neurologic disorders
  Migraine
  Myasthenia gravis
  Trigeminal neuralgia
  Sydenham's chorea

Psychiatric disorders
  Anorexia nervosa
  Phobias
  Hysteria (classic)
  Manic-depressive (affective) psychosis

Dermatologic disorders
  Acne rosacea
  Acne vulgaris(?)
  Chloasma
  Erythema nodosum

Hematologic disorders
  Iron deficiency anemia
  Autoimmune hemolytic disease
  Agranulocytosis
  Idiopathic thrombocytopenic purpura

Rheumatoid disorders
  Rheumatoid arthritis
  Systemic lupus erythematosus
  Scleroderma
  Polymyalgia rheumatica
  Sarcoidosis

"Surgical" disorders
  Femoral hernias
  Umbilical hernias (in adults)
  Cholelithiasis
  Cholecystitis
  Gallstone ileus
  Carcinoma of the gallbladder
  Varicose veins
  Thrombophlebitis
  Raynaud's disease
  Livedo reticularis
  Pulseless (Takayasu's) disease
  Cystitis
  Pyelonephritis

ers, still occurs predominantly in men, although the rate of difference is diminishing. Increased tobacco smoking by women and, perhaps, abandonment of the traditional protected role of the woman in the home may be the altered risk factors that have resulted in more coronary artery disease in women. The ratio of males to females at age 40 is still 8:1, but after age 70 the ratio changes to 1:1. The latter ratio is undoubtedly influenced by the greater longevity of women.

According to estimates by Alcoholics Anonymous (AA), the number of acknowledged alcoholic

Table 18—4. Average life expectancy is significantly higher for females than for males.* The rate is 4—5 years higher for white populations than for other races.

Average Life Expectancy			
Age (Years)	Both Sexes	Female	Male
0—1	73.3	77.2	69.5
20—25	55.0	58.7	51.4
50—55	27.6	30.5	24.6
70—75	13.1	14.7	11.1
Years Expected Life at Birth	Both Sexes	Female	Male
1910	47.3	48.3	46.3
1973	71.3	76.1	68.4
1977	73.2	77.1	69.3

*From: *Vital Statistics of the United States,* 1978.

Table 18—5. Sex-related adverse drug reactions in women.

Estrogens and oral contraceptives
  Thrombophlebitis
  Thromboembolism
  Breast enlargement and tenderness
  Edema (sodium and water retention)
  Fetal injury (masculinization of females)
  Increased breast and genital carcinogenesis
  Menstrual irregularities (from chronic use)
  Skin changes (chloasma, acne, and other disorders)
  Alopecia
  Hirsutism

Androgens
  Masculinization
  Increased libido

Clomiphene
  Multiple pregnancies
  Increased fertility
  Mittelschmerz
  Breast enlargement
  Abnormal uterine bleeding
  Hot flashes

Heparin
  Menorrhagia
  Postmenopausal bleeding
  Postpartum bleeding

Coumadin
  Excessive uterine bleeding
  Menorrhagia
  Fetal abnormalities

Other drugs*

*Countless drugs are absolutely or relatively contraindicated in pregnancy (see Chapter 29) because of their known, presumed, or possible effects on the pregnancy or the fetus.

women is on the increase. Because of the greater social stigma attached to alcoholism in women, it is possible that the proportions of problem drinkers—hidden as well as acknowledged—are the same in women as in men.

Morbidity and mortality reports validate the concept that women have greater resistance, resilience, or "staying power" than men. The increased freedom of women from past sexual stereotypes probably will influence comparative rates of illness and causes of death in the future.

SEX–RELATED PSYCHIATRIC DISORDERS

PSYCHOGENIC PELVIC PAIN

Psychogenic (functional) pelvic pain, usually chronic or recurrent, is caused by unresolved emotional conflicts. The incidence in the USA varies from 5 to 25% of gynecologic patients.

Psychogenic pelvic pain is true pain that often occurs as a manifestation of deep-seated emotional problems and may serve as a warning of a serious psychiatric disorder. The psychodynamics may be quite varied. The pain may represent an abnormal need for solicitude or gratification in the masochistic woman; resentment in the frustrated woman; anxiety in the hypochondriacal woman; guilt in the strict, introspective woman; and a psychic defense mechanism in the borderline schizophrenic woman. The type and degree of pain and the circumstances in which it appears or is intensified are also quite variable.

Pain that cannot be attributed to physical causes may result when normal physiologic impulses are exaggerated by ignorance, fear, and tension or when the perceptual threshold to disturbing stimuli is lowered. When pain occurs, the patient associates it with past or present environmental factors. Repetition of the painful sensation augments and solidifies these associations so that sensory conditioning results in pain. In her anxiety, the patient may fix her complaints on one anatomic area or organ system.

The principal emotional and personality characteristics of these women have been variously described as follows: They are egotistical, self-indulgent, and vain; demanding and independent; emotionally immature and shallow; prone to dramatize, exaggerate, and seek attention; excitable; deficient in emotional control; inconsistent in emotional reaction; and coquettish and sexually provocative but sexually fearful and often frigid. Most have an unhappy family history. Their parents and husbands have been characterized—perhaps stereotyped—as shown in Table 18–6.

There is often a history of long-standing conflict between the patient and her mother, who has failed to give the necessary love and support. The resentment and guilt created in the patient are repressed. The result

Table 18–6. Typical personality characteristics in mother, father, and husband of women with psychogenic pelvic pain.*

Mother (Often)	Father (Often)	Husband (Often)
Domineering, critical	Inadequate, repeatedly unemployed	A passive, friendly "nice guy"
Unaffectionate, cruel	Alcoholic, epileptic, brutal	Hard-working, dependable
Old-fashioned, prudish	Too serious, unaffectionate toward daughter	Less than normally demanding of coitus
A religious fanatic	A faithless woman-chaser	Subject to premature ejaculation
Complaining, chronically ill, tense	Frequently like mother	Uncomplaining, stoical, long-suffering

*Reproduced, with permission, from Benson RC: *Handbook of Obstetrics & Gynecology,* 7th ed. Lange, 1980.

is a masochistic personality with hysterical tendencies. The patient has never been able to confront her mother; her father is frequently unacceptable and therefore is rejected. Mothers with such a background frequently believe that sex is dirty and best avoided.

The woman often marries young to escape a difficult situation. The marriage is usually a dismal, loveless one, even though the woman will likely marry a kindly man unlike her father (but not a dominant, virile male). Adult life and its responsibilities thus prove unsatisfying, and the patient's sex attitudes are dominated by fear of coitus and aversion to pregnancy.

Clinical Findings

A. Symptoms and Signs: Complaints are usually multiple in number. Flank pain commonly accompanies pelvic discomfort. The patient often reports lack of gratification in intercourse, dyspareunia, leukorrhea, dysmenorrhea, dysfunctional menses, aberrations in urinary or gastrointestinal functions, backache, headache, agitation, and depressive moods. There may be signs of "pelvic congestion": persistent pelvic hyperemia, increased vaginal temperature, excessive cervical mucus in the absence of infection, and generalized pelvic sensitivity even to gentle palpation of the pelvic viscera. Short wave diathermy may accentuate the discomfort. Numerous abdominal scars may indicate polysurgery that proved to be ineffective treatment.

Although the patient complains of great pain, in about 25% of cases no physical abnormality is found; in the remainder, insignificant physical variations or minimal lesions are found. (The other extreme of pain response is illustrated by the patient who reports only slight distress despite gross organic disease.)

B. Psychiatric Evaluation: Clues to the diagnosis of psychoneurosis may include unusual attitudes and appearance (seductive dress and mannerisms, heavy make-up, etc), agitation, and rapid breathing ("acting out" the problem). A woman sensitive to minor annoyances may wear dark glasses indoors. Personification of organs or blaming certain viscera may be revealing. Psychosis may be suggested by inappropriate behavior or abnormal thought content with delusions and hallucinations. Psychiatric consultation is frequently advisable.

Complications

Surgery does not relieve the underlying distress but may actually intensify the psychiatric disorder and lead to other medical or surgical complications. On the other hand, some gynecologists condone hysterectomy with preservation of the ovaries for "pelvic congestion syndrome" in the absence of psychic illness. The trouble lies in identifying the syndrome. Until better methods of pelvic arteriography and venography are available, this treatment should be considered only with great caution and only after adequate psychogenic counseling.

Differential Diagnosis

The differentiation of functional from organic disease may be made by the process of elimination or by recognition of psychoneurosis or psychosis while investigating possible organic causes. Most patients with psychogenic pelvic pain present many characteristic features that make a direct diagnosis possible without extensive studies which themselves may tend to further fixate the patient's symptoms.

"Chronic appendicitis," adhesions, a "painful ovary," or "tipped uterus" are often suspected by physicians as possible causes of pain. Appendicitis is invariably an acute disorder, and pelvic adhesions themselves rarely cause pain. Ovarian cysts without adherence or torsion are almost never painful, and an adherent ovary is sensitive only in the second phase of the cycle. Uterine retropositions may cause specific periodic pain (dyspareunia, dysmenorrhea).

Chronic salpingitis, chronic urinary tract infection, colitis, and endometriosis must be ruled out.

A comparison of organic and psychogenic pelvic pain may be helpful in diagnosis (Table 18–7).

Table 18–7. Differentiation of organic and psychogenic pain.*

	Organic	Psychogenic
Type	Sharp, cramping, intermittent.	Dull, continuous.
Time of onset	Any time. May awaken patient.	Usually begins well after waking, when social obligations are pressing.
Radiation	Follows definite neural pathways.	Bizarre patterns or does not radiate.
Localization	Localizes with typical point tenderness.	Variable, shifting, generalized.
Progress	Soon becomes either better or worse.	Remains the same for weeks, months, years.
Provocative tests	Often reproduced or augmented by tests or manipulation, not by mood.	Not triggered or accentuated by examination but by interpersonal relationships.

*Reproduced, with permission, from Benson RC: *Handbook of Obstetrics & Gynecology,* 7th ed. Lange, 1980.

Prevention

Sex education, marriage counseling, and the early recognition and treatment of emotional illness are useful preventive measures.

Treatment

Response to treatment is often frustrating. The patient may require hospitalization for examination, observation, and treatment. Reassurance and simple symptomatic therapy are indicated. A complete history should be taken and a thorough physical examination performed. The physician must be a sympathetic, unhurried "good listener."

Once the diagnosis is established, the disorder is explained to the patient and her husband in direct, convincing terms. The patient should be provided with an acceptable explanation of psychosomatic relationships.

The physician must gain the patient's cooperation in a basic, perhaps lengthy, reorientation and reeducation program.

Narcotics, sedatives, and tranquilizers must be avoided. It is important that the patient adjust to her circumstances and solve her problem without therapeutic crutches. If simple office psychotherapy by the gynecologist or personal physician is ineffective, the patient should be referred to a psychiatrist for treatment.

When the patient is discharged from hospital care, the physician should require numerous office visits to maintain contact and ensure the continuity of therapy. Every effort must be made to assist the patient to adjust socially.

Occasional warm douches, external heat (or cold), diathermy, massage, and similar physical measures may be salutary.

Laparoscopy may be warranted in doubtful cases, but major surgery is contraindicated unless psychogenic pain can be excluded. Hysterectomy and other types of sterilizing surgery should be done only on proper indications other than pain.

Prognosis

Patients with psychogenic pelvic pain are medical "shoppers." They either refuse or interrupt treatment or are unwilling to abandon invalidism as a way of life. Often they resent the suggestion that the pain may be of psychogenic origin.

About three-fourths of patients with functional pelvic pain improve temporarily with reassurance and symptomatic therapy, but only a few derive lasting benefit from such simple measures. Over half of neurotic patients improve markedly with formal psychotherapy, and many can be cured. The prognosis in psychotic women depends upon the type and severity of the disorder.

GYNECOLOGIC BACKACHE

Backache of gynecologic origin is generally due to a well-defined pelvic disorder. It is rare before puberty and uncommon after the menopause. Multiparas are more often afflicted than nulliparas. Only about 25% of gynecologic patients who complain of backache have significant genital disease. Backache of genital origin is generally no higher than S1. Orthopedic, urologic, neurologic, or psychiatric problems account for the majority of backaches in women just as in men. Gynecologic backache may be due to any of the following causes: (1) traction or pulsion on the peritoneum or the supporting structures of the generative organs or pelvic floor (tumors, ascites, uterine prolapse); (2) inflammation of the pelvic contents: bacterial (eg, peritonitis or salpingitis) or chemical (eg, due to iodides used in salpingography or fluid from a ruptured dermoid cyst); (3) invasion of pelvic tissues or bone by tumor or endometriosis; (4) obstruction of the genital tract (cervical stenosis); (5) torsion or constriction of the pelvic viscera (ovary enmeshed in adhesions, twisted ovarian cyst); (6) congestion of internal genitalia (turgescence of the retroposed uterus, backache during menstruation); or (7) psychic tension (anxiety, apprehension). (See Psychogenic Pelvic Pain, above.)

Most cases of gynecologic backache represent referred pain, but carcinomatous extension to the spine causes direct pain. Irritation of the afferent nerves from the involved organ or abnormal nerve impulses from the site of the disorder to the back via the sympathetic nervous system are responsible. An infected, distended, or obstructed viscus may cause referred backache. Backache may also be caused by cervicitis associated with lymphangitis and by neuritis that may involve the uterosacral ligaments.

Pelvic tumors may cause pain depending upon their size and type. Tumors produce pressure, vascular engorgement, and nerve involvement. Small tumors rarely cause backache. Moderately large tumors, such as ovarian cysts 8–12 cm in diameter, or even the uterus itself in advanced pregnancy, may cause backache by exerting traction on the pelvic ligaments. Very large tumors often do not cause back pain because they tend to be immobile and may even rest upon the bones of the pelvis.

Clinical Findings
A. Symptoms and Signs: Gynecologic backache is almost invariably associated with other major signs and symptoms of pelvic disease. Fairly constant lumbosacral or sacral backache is often described with salpingitis, pelvic abscess, or twisted ovarian cyst. Discomfort is usually more pronounced on the involved side. Back pain due to endometriosis of the cul-de-sac is referred to the coccygeal region or rectum. Backache due to ovarian, renal, and ureteral lesions commonly radiates toward the inguinal region. Backache due to orthopedic and neurologic disease often radiates into the buttocks or along the distribution of the sciatic nerve. Tests may reveal faulty posture, bony deformity, muscle spasm, and spinal cord or other back injury.

Hypoesthesia, reduced reflex responses, and regional lumbar tenderness are noted on neurologic evaluation in cases of herniated intervertebral disk.

Uterine bleeding, vaginal discharge, pelvic tumor formation, prolapse of the uterus or ovaries, marked retroposition of the fundus, and similar findings may be observed.

B. Laboratory Findings: Leukocytosis and an elevated sedimentation rate may indicate infection. Vaginal cytologic examination may reveal neoplastic cells. Microscopic examination of a clean-catch urine specimen may reveal bacteriuria, pyuria, or hematuria.

C. X-Ray Findings: Anteroposterior and lateral films of the spine and pelvis often disclose a postural, degenerative, neoplastic, or other orthopedic abnormality. Myelograms are indicated to demonstrate a herniated intervertebral disk. In case x-rays are normal but the clinical data support a diagnosis of sacroiliac disease, a scanning procedure with technetium Tc 99m stannous pyrophosphate may confirm early degenerative changes.

Prevention
Many cases of gynecologic backache can be prevented by avoiding trauma in labor and delivery, repairing cervical and other obstetric lacerations immediately, properly treating cervicitis and pelvic infections, and examining women periodically so that tumors, hernias, and similar lesions can be treated early.

Treatment
A. Specific Measures: Definitive treatment of the underlying problem will usually relieve the backache.

B. Supportive Measures: The patient is placed at bed rest on a firm mattress in whatever position is most comfortable for her. Apply wet heat and diathermy to the back daily for symptomatic relief. A support provided by a broad belt or low back brace may be helpful.

Aspirin or one of the newer nonsteroidal antiinflammatory agents (eg, naproxen) may be given in pharmacologic dosages, with codeine if necessary, to control pain. A mild sedative, eg, diazepam, 2 mg orally twice daily, may be given to reduce emotional tension.

C. Local Measures: Cervicitis may respond to topical therapy (see Chapter 10).

D. Surgical Measures: Tumors, malpositions of the uterus, pelvic hernias, herniated intervertebral disk, etc, may require surgery.

Prognosis
Backache of gynecologic origin not complicated by contributing factors can usually be alleviated.

COCCYGODYNIA

Persistent pain in the region of the coccyx is a fairly common presenting complaint among women 30–50 years of age of any parity. It may be difficult to treat.

Undetermined Cause

The onset is gradual, with no history of trauma or other specific causes. The coccygeus muscles are extremely tense and tender on both sides. Pressure on the coccyx does not cause discomfort. In many cases, the pain is self-limited and disappears gradually. Brief, transrectal "stripping" or massage of the tender musculofascial structures every day for 3–4 days, together with administration of analgesics, generally brings relief.

Orthopedic Causes

A. Sacrococcygeal Arthritis, Injury, or Congenital Anomalies: Physical therapy is often helpful. Improved sitting posture—a straight-backed chair with a firm bottom—gives protection. Surgery has no place in treatment unless there is a deformity that cannot be relieved medically. Even then, surgery should be approached guardedly.

B. Lumbosacral Joint Dysfunction: Abnormal posture and mechanical irritation of the dura mater may cause pain referred to the coccyx, which may be felt during sitting but not during standing or manipulation of the coccyx. Exercises to flex the pelvis often bring relief.

Psychoneurotic Attention Fixation

Inconsistency of symptomatology and exaggerated attitudes and responses are characteristic. A fall, a "fractured coccyx" during childbirth, or a similar vaguely documented occurrence may initiate the problem. The coccyx remains sensitive, often in spite of ankylosis without deformity. Strong reassurance, suggestion, physical therapy, and prescription of analgesics should be employed. Injection of 1% lidocaine and hydrocortisone may be tried. Coccygectomy should be avoided. Patients with little or no insight into their complaint are rarely cured.

Pelvic Disorders

Endometriosis, such neoplasms as glomus tumor, and sepsis (eg, retrorectal abscess) should be sought and treated definitively.

ANOREXIA NERVOSA

Anorexia nervosa is an uncommon but serious disorder that occurs chiefly in females. It is becoming more common, presumably because psychologic problems of an existential kind, particularly for adolescents, are different now from formerly. The condition usually appears in the second and third decades of life and is manifested by an extreme neurotic aversion to food. The exact cause is unknown, but multiple factors are probably responsible. The illness appears to originate in complex psychologic problems, particularly conflicts over sexuality, aggression, and dependency that almost border on the psychotic. The patient often has a mother who is overly concerned with weight reduction and diet. The patient herself may be peculiarly sensitive about adolescent plumpness or may have a need to attract attention or escape responsibility.

There is an apparent relationship between the extreme malnutrition in anorexia nervosa and certain observed and theoretic neuroendocrine abnormalities. The serum luteinizing hormone falls as a result of hypothalamic suppression. This defect of cyclic gonadotropin release by the anterior pituitary (sparing other pituitary functions) results in ovulatory failure and decreased estrogen production.

Persistent refusal by the patient to eat adequately, even in the face of real hunger, leads to weight loss and emaciation. Deceit will be practiced in order to lose weight, including lying about having eaten, hiding uneaten food, self-induced vomiting, and purgation. Amenorrhea is the rule in women of childbearing age; it may rarely precede weight loss and may persist after weight loss has been corrected. Patients complain of intolerance to cold. Fine hair may cover the body, and the patient may actually appear hirsute. Axillary and pubic hair are normal. There may be evidence of vitamin and mineral deficiencies. Nutritional anemia is common. Gonadotropin and 17-ketosteroid levels may be low or normal.

Anorexia nervosa must be differentiated from panhypopituitarism. It should not be confused with the common striving to maintain a slender figure for innocent purposes of vanity or commonsense good health.

Treatment of women with anorexia nervosa is sometimes difficult. Care should be given in a hospital by personnel experienced in the management of this kind of patient. Emphasis is on restoration of the nutritional status. In addition, long-term psychiatric counseling is usually required. Punitive attitudes must give way to gentle but firm persuasion. The difference between the measured and predicted urine urea nitrogen for 24 hours gives the catabolic index via the following calculation:

$$\frac{(1 - \text{Net protein utilization})}{100\%} \times (\text{Dietary nitrogen intake})$$

The normal quotient is 0.5 mg plus 3 g. Below zero indicates no significant stress; 1–5, moderate stress; and above 5, severe stress calling for aggressive treatment.

The longer the illness, the poorer the outcome; the younger the patient and the smaller the initial weight loss, the better the outcome. With no treatment or inadequate treatment, 5–10% of patients die of starvation, infection, or suicide. Relapses or remissions are common. However, return of normal weight usually is accompanied by a return of emotional and physical well-being.

Table 18—8. Selected list of systemic disorders influencing normal primary and secondary sexual functions or creating problems of "special concern to women." The following includes only manifestations for which women would seek medical assistance (eg, pain, fever, weakness).

	Problem	Symptomatology
Endocrine and metabolic disorders		
Goiter (simple, nodular, neoplastic)	Cosmetic	Neck swelling
Hypothyroidism	Cosmetic	Dryness of skin, thinning of hair, brittle nails, puffiness of face and lids
	Menstruation	Menorrhagia (early), amenorrhea (late)
Hyperthyroidism	Cosmetic	Neck swelling, exophthalmos
	Menstruation	Amenorrhea
Polyostotic fibrous dysplasia (Albright's syndrome)	Cosmetic	Skin pigmentation
	Precocious puberty	
Paget's disease	Cosmetic	Head enlargement, bowed legs
Adrenocortical insufficiency (Addison's disease)	Cosmetic	Skin pigmentation, sparse axillary and pubic hair
Adrenocortical hyperfunction (Cushing's syndrome)	Cosmetic	Moon face, "buffalo" obesity, purple striae, hirsutism, chloasma
	Menstruation	Oligomenorrhea, amenorrhea
Adrenogenital syndrome	Cosmetic	Hirsutism
	Virilism	Atrophy of breasts, atrophy of genitals, clitoral enlargement
	Menstruation	Oligomenorrhea, amenorrhea
Hypopituitarism (with or without Sheehan's syndrome)	Cosmetic	Skin pallor and dryness, cachexia, loss of axillary and pubic hair
	Lack of primary and secondary sex characteristics	Libido decreased
	Menstruation	Oligomenorrhea, amenorrhea
Microadenoma of pituitary	Menstruation	Amenorrhea
Hyperpituitarism (gigantism and acromegaly)	Cosmetic	Enlargement of fingers, hands, jaw, face, tongue, and feet; teeth widely spaced, skin tough and oily, acanthosis, hyperhidrosis
	Menstruation	Amenorrhea
Diabetes mellitus	Cosmetic	Skin pigmentation, skin infections
	Pruritus vulvae	
	Pregnancy disorders	Large babies, polyhydramnios, preeclampsia, unexplained fetal loss
Hypothalamic disorders (including psychogenic)	Menstruation	Amenorrhea
Obesity, exogenous	Cosmetic	Poor body image
	Menstruation	Amenorrhea
	Decreased fertility	
Psychiatric disorders		
Anorexia nervosa (see hypopituitarism)		
Hypothalamic disorders (see above)		
Neurologic disorders		
Myasthenia gravis	Cosmetic	Ptosis, facial weakness
	Menstruation	Premenstrual weakness (generalized)
Infectious diseases		
Cytomegalic inclusion disease	Pregnancy	Fetal abnormalities of skull, nervous system, or hematopoietic system
Herpes genitalis	Pregnancy	Increased infant mortality
Coccidioidomycosis	Pregnancy	Increased maternal and infant mortality
Viral (rubella, rubeola)	Pregnancy	Fetal abnormalities (eyes, ears, central nervous system, heart, skeleton)
Toxoplasmosis	Pregnancy	Fetal abnormalities (eyes, central nervous system)
Syphilis	Pregnancy	Fetal abnormalities (any organ system)
Hematologic disorders		
Sickle cell anemia	Pregnancy	Increased maternal and infant mortality
Folic acid anemia	Pregnancy	Increased maternal and infant mortality
Iron deficiency anemia	Pregnancy	Increased maternal and infant mortality
Sports-related disorders		
(See hypothalamic disorders)	Menstruation	Excessive loss of body fat
	Temporary infertility	Oligomenorrhea, amenorrhea

MEDICAL DISORDERS

HEMORRHAGIC DISORDERS

Manifestations of the bleeding disorders may range from simple bruising to frank hemorrhage and vary in severity from almost unnoticeable to life-threatening. Apart from bleeding due to trauma, clinically significant bleeding disorders are relatively uncommon.

Etiology

Abnormal bleeding may be due to many causes, which may be classified (after Wintrobe) as outlined below. In any given patient, more than one abnormality may be involved. In some instances it is not possible to establish an etiologic diagnosis of the bleeding disorder.

A. Vascular Abnormalities: *Examples:* Trauma, infection, inflammation, neoplasms, scurvy, allergic purpura.

B. Extravascular Abnormalities: *Examples:* Senile purpura, purpura of Cushing's disease.

C. Intravascular Abnormalities:

1. Platelet abnormalities–*Examples:* Thrombocytopenic purpura, von Willebrand's disease.

2. Coagulation defects–

a. Intrinsic clotting system defects, ie, no material extrinsic to the blood is involved (eg, deficiencies of factors VIII ["classic" hemophilia], IX [Christmas disease], and XI).

b. Extrinsic clotting system defects, ie, hepatic-dependent factors—factors I, II, V, VII, and X— are involved (eg, liver disease, congenital or acquired by hypoprothrombinemia, hypofibrinogenemia).

Treatment

Patients with a bleeding diathesis should be advised against physically hazardous work, contact sports, and activities involving exposure to sharp objects. Aspirin-containing drugs, other anticoagulant drugs, and household and other industrial toxins should be avoided. Patients should be advised to inform dentists and physicians of their bleeding tendencies prior to even the most minor operative procedures.

If the correct diagnosis of the bleeding disorder is unknown and significant acute blood loss has occurred or is immediately anticipated, fresh whole blood (less than 2 days old) or frozen plasma may be given on an empiric basis. This may be required in an emergency to restore normal blood volume, correct severe anemia, and control bleeding. External hemorrhage should be controlled by local pressure or packs.

When there is a known specific bleeding or coagulation defect, specific blood components or coagulation factor concentrates may be required.

For thrombocytopenia or thrombasthenia, transfusions of fresh whole blood (less than 24 hours old) can be given. Platelet-rich plasma or platelet concentrates may be used. These latter platelet preparations are usually not advisable for the treatment of platelet deficiency in idiopathic thrombocytopenic purpura or disseminated intravascular coagulation.

Intravenous administration of 5 g of fibrinogen will usually restore fibrinogen levels in definitely es-

Table 18—9. Differential diagnosis of some bleeding disorders in women.

	Idiopathic Thrombocytopenic Purpura (ITP)	Vascular Hemophilia (von Willebrand's Disease)	Prothrombin Complex Disorders	Disseminated Intravascular Coagulation (DIC)
Clinical features				
Petechiae	++++	±	±	±
Ecchymoses	++++	+	+	+
Hemarthrosis	−	±	−	−
Postpartum or post-surgical bleeding	+	+++	++	+++
Hereditary	−	+	−	−
Laboratory findings				
Bleeding time	Increased	Increased	N	N
Coagulation time	N	N	N or increased	No clot
Clot retraction time	Increased	N	N	No clot
Prothrombin time	N	N	Increased	Increased
Partial thromboplastin time (PTT)	Only platelets abnormal	Abnormal	N	Increased
Platelet count	Decreased	N (decreased adhesiveness)	N	Decreased
Capillary fragility	Increased	±?	N	N
Treatment	Avoid aspirin and trauma. Acute: corticosteroids. Chronic: splenectomy.	Avoid aspirin and trauma. Give AHF (factor VIII) concentrates and whole blood as necessary.	Discontinue anticoagulants. Give vitamin K and whole blood as necessary (usually of no value).	Treat underlying disorder (eg, shock, sepsis). Give heparin, whole blood as necessary, and fibrinogen(?).

tablished cases of fibrinogen deficiency. Nonetheless, homologous serum jaundice may be an inescapable complication.

Frozen plasma provides all of the coagulation factors. Stored bank blood or plasma provides all of the factors except V and VIII. Concentrated factor VIII (AHF, antihemophilic factor) is available as a cryoprecipitate for use in von Willebrand's disease and the hemophilias. A concentrate of the extrinsic clotting system factors (vitamin K-dependent coagulation factors II, VII, IX and X) is commercially available (Proplex).

Phytonadione, 10–50 mg intramuscularly or intravenously—for blood or plasma—may be given to control the bleeding of prothrombin deficiency due to anticoagulant drugs or obstructive jaundice. It is not effective in hypoprothrombinemia due to intracellular hepatic disease. Hemorrhagic disease of the newborn may possibly be prevented by 0.5–1 mg phytonadione given orally, intramuscularly, or intravenously.

Patients with mild idiopathic thrombocytopenic purpura may require no treatment. Those with more marked purpura of short duration may be treated successfully with corticosteroids. Patients with known symptomatic idiopathic thrombocytopenic purpura of more than a year's duration who relapse repeatedly after corticosteroid therapy or those with severe purpura that fails to respond to corticosteroids should undergo splenectomy.

IRON DEFICIENCY ANEMIA

Iron deficiency anemia may be due to acute or chronic blood loss or to inadequate intake or malabsorption of iron. Determination of the cause may be difficult. Iron deficiency anemia is common in patients with menorrhagia. Anemia is a symptom of other disorders (eg, blood loss, gastrointestinal cancer), but it may itself produce misleading symptoms (eg, dyspnea, dysphagia) or may aggravate other disorders (eg, cardiac insufficiency). Anemic patients with or without a history of bleeding who have a red count of 1 million/μL or less and are able to ambulate should be suspected of having macrocytic, aplastic, or iron reutilization defect anemia rather than iron deficiency anemia.

Clinical Findings

Symptoms and signs include lassitude, palpitation, chronic fatigue, and pallor. Shortness of breath, tachycardia, and dysphagia may be associated with more severe degrees of anemia. The serum iron is generally less than 30 μg/dL (normal: 65–175 μg/dL), and iron stores often are severely depleted. The total iron-binding capacity is increased. The same is usually true of the reticulocyte and platelet counts. The red blood cell count seldom goes below 2.5 million/μL. Cells are microcytic in long-standing deficiency but may be normocytic in mild anemias. The bone marrow is devoid of hemosiderin and contains more nucleated red cells than usual. Iron deficiency anemia is the only type of anemia in which hemosiderin is absent in the bone marrow.

Treatment

Iron is specific. Give ferrous sulfate, 0.2 g orally, or ferrous gluconate, 0.5 g orally, 3 times daily with meals. Parenteral iron preparations are not required unless there is gastrointestinal intolerance to oral iron, defective absorption, continued blood loss, or failure to respond to oral iron therapy. The parenteral dose is 250 mg of iron for each gram of hemoglobin below normal. Medication is continued for 3–5 months after the hemoglobin reaches normal levels to elevate the iron stores. Loss of 500 mL of blood usually can be replenished by iron therapy within a month. Blood transfusions are reserved for more severe blood losses.

DISEASES OF THE THYROID

1. GOITER

Nontoxic, simple, or colloid goiter of the thyroid gland is probably the most common endocrine disorder. It has a tendency to occur endemically in certain areas of the world. The cause is unknown, although it is often associated with iodine deficiency. Deficiency of iodine or ingestion of goitrogenic substances may result in functional overactivity and growth of the thyroid. There may be symptoms of respiratory or esophageal pressure from the enlarged gland. The usual thyroid function tests are normal except in toxic nodular goiter, in which they are abnormally high. Clinically, the distinction must be made between simple goiter and a toxic or neoplastic gland. The possibility of neoplasm should be considered in the case of single nodules, especially those which increase in size or fail to subside with iodine therapy.

Treatment varies according to the size of the goiter, its configuration, duration, and the symptoms it causes. Medical treatment of simple goiter may consist of administration of iodides or medication with thyroid. Patients with nontoxic goiter may become "toxic" on large doses of iodides; presumably, synthesis and release of thyroid hormone in some of these patients are impaired. Surgical removal is reserved for enlarged glands causing pressure symptoms, those with hard single nodules, those that may be malignant, or those nodules where shrinkage of the gland is indefinite or incomplete following medical suppression therapy. One in 4–5 solitary nodules is malignant. Some goiters may regress spontaneously, and a few multinodular lesions of long standing may eventually become toxic.

2. HYPOTHYROIDISM

Deficiency of thyroid hormone may be congenital or idiopathic. It can be secondary to hypopituitarism, thyroiditis, or surgical or medical therapy to the thyroid. The congenital form is accompanied by cretinism. Hypothyroidism in the adult may cause myxedema. The prevalence of hypothyroidism is 0.6–0.8% in contrast to 1.1–1.6% for hyperthyroidism. Affected women are usually under 50 years of age. Patients with a genetic predisposition to autoimmune thyroiditis more commonly acquire hypothyroidism than do those without the genetic tendency. The illness may be confused with psychiatric disorders, cardiac disease, or blood dyscrasias.

Clinical findings may vary from minimal symptoms and signs to frank cretinism or myxedema. Children with hypothyroidism may show all degrees of dwarfism. They are often overweight and have yellowish skin and coarse features. Adult manifestations include weakness, puffy facies, thick tongue, slurred speech, hoarseness, intolerance to cold, falling scalp hair but slight general hirsutism, dry skin, brittle nails, constipation, menorrhagia (early), amenorrhea (late), anemia, cardiomegaly, heart failure, mental disturbances, and coma.

Serum thyroxine (T_4), radioiodine uptake, and other thyroid tests are low. If the patient is taking birth control drugs, this test is unreliable; Instead, the amount of free thyroxine (T_7) is the determination of choice. An elevated serum thyrotropin (TSH) level is a more sensitive marker for hypothyroidism in elderly women. TSH as measured by radioimmunoassay and serum cholesterol is always elevated. Delayed skeletal maturation is revealed by x-rays of the long bones.

Treatment

Thyroid USP or a synthetic thyroid preparation is therapeutically specific. If hypothyroidism is severe, the initial dose of medication should be small and gradually increased over a period of several days; otherwise, cardiac failure may ensue. Myxedema coma, however, requires aggressive emergency treatment; parenteral synthetic thyroid preparations and hydrocortisone may be lifesaving. If thyroid replacement therapy is initiated prior to advanced complications of the disease, the response is gratifying. Therapy must be maintained indefinitely to prevent recurrences.

3. HYPERTHYROIDISM
(Thyrotoxicosis)

Hyperthyroidism is a relatively common endocrine disorder. Its highest incidence is in women in the third or fourth decade of life. The causes of the excessive thyroid hormone production are complex and often unclear. Hydatidiform mole is a rare cause of hyperthyroidism. Ectopic production of TSH by chorionic tumors may cause asymptomatic elevation of serum thyroxine (T_4).

If untreated, hyperthyroidism is often progressive. It can lead to serious complications such as cachexia, exophthalmos, arrhythmias, congestive heart failure, and even death.

Clinical Findings

A. Symptoms and Signs: Emotional instability, hyperhidrosis, nervousness, heat intolerance, amenorrhea, palpitations, weight loss, increased appetite, fatigue, and weakness are the most frequent symptoms. Tachycardia, enlargement of the thyroid, skin changes, tremor, bruit over the thyroid, and progressive exophthalmos are common findings.

B. Laboratory Findings: The T_4 and RAI uptake are increased. Serum cholesterol is usually low.

Treatment

The use of ^{131}I has replaced surgery in the treatment of some of the thyroid diseases. For those illnesses remaining that require surgery, there is controversy about how extensive the operation should be. A solitary nodule should be evaluated initially either by punch or needle biopsy examination. If malignant, it should be removed; if not, periodic examination may be made. Cytohistologic data indicate that only one-half of patients suspected of having cancer of the thyroid actually do have cancer. Some of the advantages and disadvantages of various methods of treatment are set forth below.

A. Subtotal Thyroidectomy: (Following adequate preoperative combined propylthiouracil-iodine preparation, methimazole, carbimazole, or propranolol.)

1. Hazards of operation–Morbidity and mortality.

2. Postoperative complications–Hypothyroidism, hypoparathyroidism, exophthalmos, thyroid storm, recurrent laryngeal nerve palsy.

B. Radioiodine (^{131}I) Therapy: (*Caution: Pregnant women and nursing mothers must not receive radioactive iodine.*)

1. Posttreatment complications–Hypothyroidism, thyroid storm, ocular problems.

2. Undetected thyroid cancer.

3. Prolonged follow-up mandatory.

C. Prolonged Medical Treatment With Thiouracil and Related Drugs:

1. Drug toxicity (eg, granulocytopenia).

2. Prolonged period of active treatment necessary (6–18 months).

3. Higher incidence of recurrence.

4. Exophthalmos.

5. Use with caution in pregnancy because of effects on fetal thyroid.

OTHER ENDOCRINE & METABOLIC DISORDERS

1. NONSPECIFIC OBESITY

Susceptibility to obesity often appears early in life with an increase in the number and the size of adipose cells in the body. Adult obesity is accompanied by increase in the size but not in the number of cells. Fat accumulation is generally caused by excessive intake of food beyond body needs.

Obesity may be associated with or due to a metabolic disorder but is seldom due to hypothyroidism. Genetic factors often modify the distribution of the fat. During the pubertal period, when fat reaches or exceeds 17–20% of the body weight, the process of sexual development is triggered through the hypothalamus. Obesity early in life may give rise to earlier sexual development; in adulthood, it may be related to menstrual disturbances. Adiposity confined to the trunk with a fatty mid shoulder fullness is characteristic of Cushing's disease. Very rapid weight gain suggests a hypothalamic lesion, particularly if accompanied by visual field changes. Obese women have an increased incidence of hypertension, abnormal glucose tolerance or diabetes mellitus, and endometrial carcinoma. The death rate of grossly obese women is several times that of women of normal weight.

Reduction of caloric intake is the only practical weight loss method for the obese woman. Increased activity is desirable to "firm up," but exercise alone seldom results in a significant weight reduction. Anorexiant drugs are of limited value and often cause undesirable side-effects. Enrollment in a "weight-loss" club or psychiatric counseling with behavior modification and psychologic support by the family may provide the impetus to sustain a reduced intake of food. The intestinal (ileal) bypass operation is a drastic procedure used only for massively obese women for whom medical management has failed.

Treatment

Appetite suppressants or hormones given singly or in combination to reduce weight are either ineffective or hazardous and should not be used.

A. Diet: Obese juveniles can be difficult to treat because of psychiatric or metabolic reasons. Diet is the most important part of management. Good eating habits should be established as early as possible in the formative years. Eating unusual combinations of foods or "special" foods to promote weight loss is generally ineffective or actually harmful. Some adults, despite severe caloric restriction, fail to lose weight, perhaps in part due to idiopathic cyclic edema. This disturbance presumably consists of some derangement of the renin-angiotensin-aldosterone regulatory mechanism. Such patients excrete water readily only while lying flat.

There are a number of points to consider in the management of obesity:

1. Calories–To lose weight, it is necessary to decrease the daily caloric intake. An intake of 500 kcal/d less than the caloric requirement for sex, age, weight, and height should lead to weight loss of approximately 0.5 kg (1 lb) a week.

The number of calories per day allowed a patient who must lose weight varies with age, occupation, temperament, and the urgency of the need to lose weight. A modest reducing diet consisting of 800–1200 kcal/d is sufficient for nutritional needs.

There is no evidence that adequately supervised rapid weight loss is harmful. All diets should be calculated to maintain nitrogen balance if possible. With strict diets, ketonuria may occur; it is usually very slight after the first few days, however, and acidosis has never been observed. In addition, patients on a "diet" often will adhere more willingly when they show rapid weight loss than when the reward comes slowly.

2. Proteins–A protein intake of at least 1 g/kg should be maintained. If necessary, add protein to the low-calorie diet in the form of protein hydrolysate or casein (free of carbohydrate and fat).

Table 18–10. Low-calorie diets: Foods to be distributed into regular meals during the day.*

	800 kcal	1000 kcal	1200 kcal	1500 kcal
Breads, enriched white or whole grain†	½ slice	1 slice	2 slices	3 slices
Fruit, unsugared (½ cup)	3 servings	3 servings	3 servings	3 servings
Eggs, any way but fried	One	One	One	One
Fats and oils, butter, margarine, mayonnaise, or oil	None	3 tsp	5 tsp	6 tsp
Milk (nonfat, skimmed, or buttermilk)	2 cups	2 cups	2 cups	2 cups
Meat, fish, or poultry, any way but fried‡	4 oz	5 oz	6 oz	6 oz
Vegetables, raw (salads) (1 serving = ½ cup)	2 servings	2 servings	2 servings	2 servings
Vegetables, cooked, green, yellow, or soup (1 serving = ½ cup)	2 servings	2 servings	3 servings	3 servings
Starch, potato, etc	None	None	None	1 serving
Artificial sweeteners	As desired	As desired	As desired	As desired

*Reproduced, with permission, from Krupp MA, Chatton MJ (editors): *Current Medical Diagnosis & Treatment 1981.* Lange, 1981.
†May substitute ½ cup cooked cereal or 1 cup dry prepared cereal for 1 slice bread.
‡May substitute ½ cup cottage cheese or 3 slices (3 oz) cheddar cheese for 3 oz meat.

3. Carbohydrate and fat–To keep the calories and ketosis down, fats must be decreased. After the protein requirements have been met, the remaining calories may be supplied as half carbohydrate and half fat.

4. Vitamins and minerals–Most reducing diets are likely to be deficient in vitamins but adequate in minerals. Therefore, vitamins should be used to supply the average daily maintenance requirements during the time of weight reduction. Avoid hyperkalemia.

5. Sodium restriction–It has been shown that a normal person on a salt-free diet will rapidly lose 2–3 kg; this reduction is temporary, and the weight will return when salt is added to the diet. The same is true of the obese patient. Although an apparently dramatic effect can be obtained with salt-free diets, they are of no permanent value.

6. Starvation regimen–Total starvation is again being advocated as a weight reduction regimen. Although rapid loss of weight can be achieved by this means, the method may be hazardous. It must be carried out in a hospital with strict supervision. Several deaths have occurred. Total starvation results largely in breakdown of fat, but it may lead to excessive protein breakdown, fainting due to decrease in extracellular fluid volume because of sodium loss, and other unphysiologic results. Massive weight reduction can result in severe hepatic impairment or even fatal hepatic necrosis. Periodic total fasting to the point of producing ketonemia caused accelerated weight loss in patients who failed to lose significantly on 1000 kcal diets. Still, this accelerated weight loss is spurious and usually represents fluid loss due to ketonuria.

7. Shunt operation–Jejunoileal shunt should be considered only as a last resort to treat obese patients who weigh 2 or more times their ideal weight, who have failed to respond to all other conservative measures, and whose obesity is a hazard to their physical, psychologic, or socioeconomic well-being. The operation does result in permanent weight reduction, but it is often followed by complications, eg, hypokalemia (20%), hypocalcemia (20%), renal calculi (10%), severe arthropathy (20%), loss of libido (40–50%), impaired intestinal absorption, hepatic cirrhosis, major emotional upsets, and a high rate of reproductive mishaps. About half of these patients require rehospitalization for management of hernias and gastrointestinal or nutritional disorders. Babies born to such mothers are of low birth weight and shorter than normal. Placentas are smaller also. Oral contraception may be ineffective for these women, because of impaired intestinal absorption.

B. Medication:

1. Appetite suppressants–Amphetamines and other anorexiant drugs are not recommended for the reasons set forth above.

2. Drugs to speed up metabolism–*Note:* There is no satisfactory drug to speed up metabolism. Thyroid has little or no place in the management of obesity. The low basal metabolic rate associated with obesity merely reflects the consumption of oxygen in terms of body surface. Tests that actually measure thyroid function (eg, plasma T_3, T_4) are usually normal in obese patients.

Obese people can tolerate 0.2 g or more of thyroid per day without change in basal metabolic rate. Prolonged administration of thyroid may suppress the patient's normal thyroid secretion. Human chorionic gonadotropin exerts no physiologic antiobesity effect.

C. Exercise: Although exercise increases the energy output, extreme exercise is necessary to significantly alter weight. Playing 18 holes of an average game of golf, for instance, raises the total caloric requirements only by about 100–150 kcal. However, increase in activity is an important factor in long-range weight maintenance and for general well-being.

D. Psychologic Factors: Overeating is largely a matter of habit and may be associated with varying degrees of emotional problems. Once significant obesity has been established, many secondary psychologic reactions occur relating to altered body image and changes in interpersonal relationships. Weight reduction is therefore essential for general psychologic as well as physical well-being. Mildly or moderately obese patients often respond to simple psychologic support, encouragement, dietary management, and situational adjustments. Weight relapses occur frequently and should be dealt with in an understanding manner. Conventional psychotherapy, however, is seldom of lasting value in weight reduction in markedly obese patients. Whatever the cause, the patient must be retrained in her eating habits and educated to understand that once her weight is normal she can easily become obese again by eating more than necessary. Behavior modification therapy and self-help groups of obese patients (similar to AA for alcoholics) are effective for some patients.

Note: Sudden weight reduction in emotionally unstable persons may have severe psychic consequences, eg, anorexia nervosa, psychotic reactions.

2. HIRSUTISM & VIRILIZATION

Female hirsutism is an excessive amount of hair on the face, chest, or abdominoperineal region. This growth depends on androgenic metabolites and may occur with or without virilization. In contrast, hypertrichosis is excessive local or generalized growth of downy hair mainly over the lumbosacral area or back of the arms. Virilization is the development of secondary male characteristics, eg, clitorimegaly, deepening of the voice, increased musculature, more active sebaceous glands, excessive body hair but recession of cranial hair.

Distribution and growth of hair may be influenced by one's familial and genetic background. Approximately 40% of white women have some degree of hirsutism. They are affected more frequently than black women. The least hirsute are Asian and American Indian women. Some acquire hirsutism postmenopausally. About 5–10% of all women have excessive hair on the face, axillary regions, chest, or abdominopubic area. Of these, about 90% are hyperandrogenic.

The source of androgenic hormones is the ovaries, adrenals, or a combination of these. In some, abnormal conversion of precursor steroids by the skin, liver, lungs, or target organs to androgens is the problem. The most common cause of excessive androgen production in women is the polycystic ovary syndrome. Other causes include ovarian or adrenal androgenic tumors; adrenocortical hyperplasia; acromegaly; ingestion of phenytoin sodium, corticosteroids, diazoxide, minoxidil, cobalt, or hexachlorobenzene; and rare diseases or abnormalities, eg, congenital porphyria, Hurler's syndrome, or trisomy 18s (trisomy E) syndrome.

Most hirsute women have abnormal uterine bleeding at some time. Ovarian-adrenal dysfunction that begins at puberty often progresses unless suppressive treatment is given. Rapid masculinization at any age, particularly with a demonstrable pelvic mass, suggests the presence of an androgen-producing neoplasm. Striae, hirsutism, and obesity combined with a "buffalo hump" are signs of Cushing's syndrome. If ovulatory cycles continue, endocrinologic disease is generally not present. Moreover, if cyclic menstruation prevails with no virilization, glandular disease is unlikely.

Two kinds of hair growth are recognized: vellus hair, which is soft, unpigmented, and without a medulla, and coarse, "hard" hair with a medulla. However, if overstimulation of vellus hair follicles occurs, hirsutism may develop and persist even after the stimulus is eliminated.

Physiology

The androgens in both normal and hirsute women are dehydroepiandrosterone, dehydroepiandrosterone sulfate, androstenedione, testosterone, and dihydrotestosterone. Some hirsute women may have normal plasma levels of testosterone but produce large quantities of androstenediol. The latter and dihydrotestosterone are usually elevated in hirsute women. Normally, in the nonhirsute female, 50–70% of plasma testosterone is derived from peripheral conversion, and the remainder is produced in the ovary or adrenal. In contrast, in the hirsute woman, only about 25% of plasma testosterone is of peripheral origin, and the remaining 75% is of glandular origin. An equal amount of androstenedione and testosterone generally comes from the ovary or adrenal except at the time of ovulation. Then, the larger portion is from the ovary. Dehydroepiandrosterone and dehydroepiandrosterone sulfate are largely from the adrenal, whereas androstenedione is produced about equally by the ovary and adrenal. Dehydroepiandrosterone and dehydroepiandrosterone sulfate are partially under the control of ACTH, which is subject to variable diurnal production. Hence, determinations of serum levels of dehydroepiandrosterone and dehydroepiandrosterone sulfate should be made early in the day when the titers are maximal. The level of testosterone is not altered by the circadian cycle. In order of potency, normal serum concentrations of testosterone, androstenedione, and dehydroepiandrosterone are 40 ng/dL, 175 ng/dL, and 375 ng/dL, respectively. Testosterone is 5–10 times more potent than androstenedione, which is 20 times more potent than dehydroepiandrosterone.

The level of testosterone-estradiol–binding globulin expresses the affinity of the β globulin for testosterone. Normally, this is low, but increased amounts of circulating androgens may decrease the binding capacity. In turn, more free circulating testosterone is available for target cells to metabolize and extract. Testosterone and androstenedione are the main precursors for dihydrotestosterone, which comes primarily from peripheral conversion. In essence, most hirsute women have an elevated plasma concentration of androstenedione and testosterone and decreased testosterone-estradiol–binding globulin.

Diagnosis by Laboratory Studies

The clinical history, physical examination, and determinations of plasma androstenedione, dehydroepiandrosterone, dehydroepiandrosterone sulfate, and testosterone are usually sufficient to validate a clinical impression. Occasionally, one or more of these factors may be normal even in the presence of clinical disease; therefore, repeated analyses may be needed for diagnosis. The normal mean plasma values determined by radioimmunoassay for various androgens are listed in Table 18–11.

Approximately 70% of hirsute women with polycystic ovaries have an elevated plasma testosterone level, because the hypothalamic-pituitary-ovarian axis is altered, causing chronic anovulation. Under these circumstances, luteinizing hormone (LH) should be slightly elevated and follicle-stimulating hormone (FSH) mildly depressed. This leads to repetitious immature ovarian follicular growth because of the reduced noncyclic production of FSH. On the other hand, if the woman is obese, there may be a decrease in serum globulin binding capacity and an increase in free testosterone. Rarely, a hirsute woman may have a normal level of free testosterone even though she produces excessive androgen metabolites. Studies should be repeated in the event of inconclusive reports.

Table 18–11. Mean serum levels for androgens in women.*

Androgen	Origin (in Percent)			Serum Levels (ng/mL)
	Ovary	Adrenal	Peripheral	
Testosterone	5–20	1–30	50	0.1–0.5 (total)
Androstenedione	50	50		0.8–3.0
Dihydrotestosterone			100	0.1–0.4
Dehydroepiandrosterone	20	80		1.5–8.0
Dehydroepiandrosterone sulfate	10	90		820–3380

*Values by Radioassay Systems Laboratories.

If dehydroepiandrosterone sulfate is elevated, an androgen-producing tumor should be suspected. Currently, 4 laboratory tests are commonly employed to evaluate hirsutism in women:

(1) Urinary androgen determinations: Urinary studies will identify androgen excess but not the source. Testosterone glucuronide excretion is usually normal (and not helpful). On the contrary, the 17-ketosteroids are derived from metabolism of androgens produced by the ovaries and adrenals, and these reflect the levels of dehydroepiandrosterone, androstenedione, and testosterone. In an obese woman with striae, excretion of 20 mg or more of 17-ketosteroids in 24 hours, together with elevation of excretion of 17-hydroxysteroids, supports the diagnosis of Cushing's syndrome. If there are no clinical signs of Cushing's syndrome but corticosteroid excretion is elevated, suppression should be carried out in the hospital by giving 2 mg of dexamethasone orally 4 times a day for 5 days. The 24-hour urinary 17-ketosteroid studies studies should be repeated on the last day. Lack of suppression indicates a probable adrenocortical tumor. On the contrary, depression of the corticosteroids is consistent with adrenocortical hyperplasia.

(2) Of the serum androgen determinations discussed above, testosterone-estradiol–binding globulin is probably the most sensitive for testosterone. However, some of these determinations will direct the clinician to precise therapy.

(3) Adrenal and ovarian stimulation and suppression tests may not be consistent. Suspect a tumor rather than adrenocortical hyperplasia when ACTH stimulation, which causes hypersecretion of the corticosteroids, does not increase after 6 doses of 500 mg of metyrapone every hour are given.

(4) Catheterization of ovarian or adrenal veins for serum testosterone and androstenedione levels currently yields the most precise data. Catheterization studies are not available generally and impose a certain risk, however.

Diagnosis by Surgical & X-Ray Studies

Adjunctive laparoscopy may be valuable in the diagnosis of polycystic ovary disease or ovarian tumor, particularly if laboratory or other studies are equivocal. CT scan or digital videoangiography may eventually replace the more hazardous retrograde vascular catheterization in the verification of suspected tumors. X-ray tomographic study of the sella turcica may identify a pituitary tumor associated with abnormal stimulation of the adrenal cortex.

Treatment

Progressive hirsutism is usually reversible upon removal of a masculinizing tumor or termination of drug therapy, but the process may be only arrested in patients with adrenocortical hyperplasia or polycystic ovary disease.

Prednisone, 5 mg orally daily, may be used to suppress excessive cortisol production due to adrenocortical hyperplasia. However, one must consider the adverse effects associated with prolonged use of such medication.

Clomiphene citrate will often induce ovulation in women with polycystic ovary disease. This drug interrupts the constant production of androgens by the ovary. If conception is desired, a combination oral contraceptive, spironolactone, or medroxyprogesterone acetate may be prescribed to suppress steroidogenesis. Medroxyprogesterone acetate, 150 mg intramuscularly every 6 weeks, may be given in lieu of birth control pills if the latter are unacceptable. It will provide less intense suppression of LH than oral contraceptives, however.

In Europe, the combination of cyproterone acetate given orally from day 5 to day 25 of the menstrual cycle and estradiol-17β administered percutaneously once a month has usually prevented continued growth of hair. This regimen, not yet FDA-approved in the USA, avoids the undesirable side-effects of oral estrogens. It either causes negative feedback or diminishes LH production at the hypothalamic level. The same regimen may be effective also in normal menstruating women whose hair follicles are hypersensitive to the normal level of androgens. An undesirable effect of cyproterone acetate is the reduction of libido.

Experimental therapy with cimetidine, 300 mg orally 5 times a day for 3 months, has suppressed hair growth. However, this drug is unapproved for this purpose.

Treatment may either prevent or minimize new growth of hair, but it does not alter coarse hair already present. Removal of this hair requires plucking, shaving, or electrolysis. Androgen-suppressive therapy should be given also. A bleach may be used to make the hair less obvious. The use of cold wax periodically for epilation may result in a gradual diminution in the growth of hair. Electrolysis is costly and time-consuming, and it may cause slight scarring.

Prognosis

Any of the above procedures may be used to control hirsutism, but the problem will not be eliminated. Patients often become frustrated because improvement usually is slow, taking more than 6–12 months. Photographs taken periodically may be helpful to record therapeutic progress.

3. ALOPECIA

Excessive loss of hair can be more distressing to a woman than hirsutism. Alopecia areata may range from spotty to generalized. Systemic disease, use of various drugs, crash dieting, and psychiatric stress are generally causative. Treatment consists of removing or minimizing the cause. In the case of alopecia areata due to emotional stress, the hair will usually regrow in 6 months. Induction of allergic dermatitis by application of dinitrochlorobenzene once a week to the affected skin has met with earlier regrowth, but the reason for this result is not obvious.

4. ABNORMAL PIGMENTATION
OF SKIN

Abnormal pigmentation of the skin may be due to genetic or familial constitution or physiologic changes occurring as a result of medication or illnesses. If the skin has a bizarre or puzzling lesion, venereal diseases that may be associated with rash should be considered in the differential diagnosis. Distribution of abnormal pigmentation on the body varies greatly. Pregnancy, thyrotoxicosis, and diethylstilbestrol are well-known causes of chloasma or increased pigmentation of the nipples and linea alba. Endocrine disease may result in both generalized and localized pigmentation. Hyperpigmentation may occur with Addison's disease, hemochromatosis, adrenal tumor, or pituitary tumor. Conversely, some degree of depigmentation may exist with Addison's disease, hypogonadism, and hypopituitarism. Localized hyperpigmentation may be associated with porphyria, melanoma, drug reaction (eg, chlorpromazine, arsenic), gamma irradiation, acromegaly, fibrous dysplasia, Cushing's syndrome, and other tumors. Flushing of the cheeks occurs in myxedema; plethora may be observed in Cushing's disease.

Treatment of abnormal pigmentation is directed at the cause. Often the pigmentary changes are irreversible. Use of cosmetics may help conceal embarrassing skin pigmentation in exposed areas.

URINARY TRACT DISORDERS

NONSPECIFIC MANIFESTATIONS

Pain

Pain of urinary tract origin may be local or referred. In the former, discomfort is felt at the site of the lesion; in the latter, it is percevied away from the place of origin. In either case, pain is caused by distention of the organ or by swelling and inflammation of the adventitia surrounding the organ. If the underlying disease progresses slowly, there may be no pain.

Renal pain is usually perceived in the costovertebral angle just below the 12th rib but may be referred toward the umbilicus. It may be continuous, dull, or nagging and may be confused with radiculitis.

Ureteral pain is colicky, radiating from the costovertebral angle downward to the vulva. In general, the level of the discomfort indicates the level of ureteral obstruction that led to the symptom. For instance, acute midureteral disease will give rise to pain at McBurney's point, the site of appendiceal discomfort.

Vesical pain with overdistention of the bladder is usually felt suprapubically. It is relieved by emptying the bladder. Discomfort due to bladder infections is referred to the distal end of the urethra.

Symptoms Related to Micturition

Frequency of urination may be caused by reduced capacity of the bladder or lack of functional capacity (decreased by residual urine). These conditions may arise from infection, stones, tumors, irradiation, or foreign body. Normally, the urge to void can usually be controlled and the bladder made to hold more urine after the urge for urination occurs. This is not true in the case of vesicular inflammation. Frequency that persists both day and night (nocturia) is characteristic of infection or fibrosis of the bladder. Absence of polydipsia and nocturia indicates a habit pattern or emotional basis for day frequency.

Nocturia is commonly the result of renal disease associated with a loss of concentrating capacity, excess fluid intake, or use of diuretics. In diabetes mellitus or insipidus, polydipsia also occurs.

A continuous urge to urinate (**urgency**) is common with acute urinary infections.

Dysuria is pain or burning generally referred to the urethra during the course of urination. It may occur only at the beginning of urination, in midstream, or terminally. The most common cause is acute cystitis—seldom chronic urethritis. Urethral pain at times other than micturition is usually due to nonurinary causes.

Enuresis is uncontrolled nocturnal emptying of the bladder. It is a normal condition up to the age of 2 or 3 years, but beyond that time enuresis may reflect improper toilet training, may be a physiologic disturbance, or may be a symptom of an anatomic abnormality. Infection or a urethrovesical deformity can account for nocturnal enuresis. Enuresis after age 6 or combined with uncontrolled wetting during the day warrants a urologic survey.

Urinary incontinence may be associated with stress, may occur without stress (true incontinence), or may be due to infections, neurovesical disease (urgency incontinence), or overflow of urine. Stress incontinence occurs only when the patient is in the erect position. Treatment may be difficult and often requires urologic consulation or referral.

URINARY TRACT INFECTION

Urinary tract infections occur much more frequently in females than in males. An estimated 25% of women develop urinary tract infection some time during their life. For every decade of additional age, at least another 1% of women acquire a chronic infection. By age 70 years, about 10% of women have a chronic urinary infection. Particularly distressing is the frequency of recurrence and chronicity of infections (Table 18–12).

Various explanations have been given for the special vulnerability of females to urinary tract infections, though all are in some way unsatisfactory: (1) the shorter length of the female urethra provides easier entry of pathogens into the bladder; (2) the position of the vaginal introitus predisposes to fecal contamination; (3) the vaginal introitus serves as a reservoir for colonization of bacteria; (4) congenital structural

Table 18–12. Differential diagnosis of urinary tract infection.

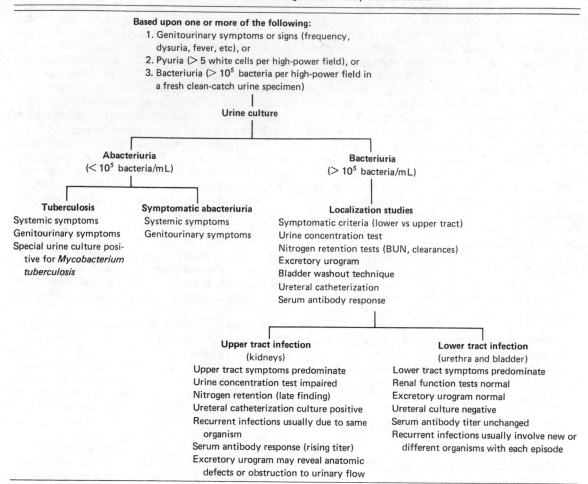

anomalies may predispose to infection; and (5) sex-related biochemical and immunologic differences in the mucosa and secretions of the genitourinary tract may be responsible.

Urinary tract infection in females may be related to poor perineal hygiene, sexual intercourse, pregnancy, urinary tract obstruction, ureteral reflux, catheterization, instrumentation, and neurogenic bladder, but in many instances the pathogenesis is equivocal. Hematogenous spread of infection to the urinary tract (bacteremia) is much less common than ascending infection.

Most urinary tract infections in women are caused by aerobic fecal organisms. *Escherichia coli* is the commonest organism found (about 75–80%), particularly with acute infection. Certain strains of *E coli* are more likely to produce infection than others. Infections may also be due to *Klebsiella, Enterobacter, Serratia, Proteus, Pseudomonas, Streptococcus faecalis*, and a wide variety of other pathogenic organisms. Recurrence of infection with the same organism (especially of the same serologic type) is regarded as a treatment failure; infection with a new organism (or another

type) implies reinfection. Persistence of infection with the same organism indicates chronicity.

The mere presence of bacteria in the urine does not signify infection of the urinary tract. Significant bacteriuria is empirically defined as 100,000 or more bacteria per milliliter of urine. This degree of bacteriuria may or may not be associated with symptoms and signs, but the potential exists for serious involvement of urinary tract tissues—urethritis, cystitis, acute papillary necrosis, pyelonephritis, perinephric abscess—and even systemic manifestations such as bacteremia and shock.

Bacteriuria greater than 10^5/mL may be suggested by a count of more than 10 bacteria per high-power field on prompt microscopic examination of freshly voided urine, and this can be verified by quantitative urine cultures. "Clean-catch" urine specimens are usually satisfactory for direct bacterial counts or quantitative cultures. Such specimens can be obtained by the following technique: The periurethral area should be carefully cleaned 4 times with a liquid soap and warm water, using soft sterile pads. The labia are then spread and the mid part of the voided stream is collected in a sterile container. Catheterization may be required to obtain urine from patients who are unable to cooperate. However, about 2% will acquire a urinary infection as a result of the procedure.

If a catheter is left indwelling 24 hours, bacteriuria will occur in 50%; in 96 hours, nearly 100% of patients will have bacteriuria. Suprapubic needle aspiration is occasionally required in infants, in equivocal cases, or in certain asymptomatic patients with pyuria.

Treatment

A. Acute Infections:

1. Initial attack–

a. Adults should receive trimethoprim, 160 mg, with sulfamethoxazole, 800 mg (Bactrim, Septra), every 12 hours, or other comparable sulfonamide; or a cephalosporin or ampicillin, 250–500 mg every 6 hours. Children should be given half the adult dosage. The duration of treatment is controversial, but 5–10 days is suggested. Tetracyclines are the drugs of choice for infections due to *Chlamydia trachomatis*.

One can anticipate that 70% of patients will be cured, 20% will relapse, and 10% will be unaffected by the above treatment.

b. If symptoms have not cleared within 4 days, reexamine the urine for possible resistant bacteria and select another drug based upon antimicrobial sensitivity of the organism.

c. Fluid intake should be adequate but not forced beyond 2 L per day, since the effectiveness of the drugs is related to their concentration in the urine. Maintain an alkaline urine by administration of oral sodium bicarbonate.

d. Obtain stained smears of the urine sediment and bacterial cultures 2 and 8 weeks after treatment is completed. If bacteriuria persists, continue treatment.

2. Recurrent attacks–

a. An antimicrobial drug selected on the basis of antimicrobial sensitivity of the cultured organism should be administered for 14–21 days.

b. If bacteriuria persists after 2 such courses of treatment with presumably appropriate drugs, perform a thorough examination to rule out organic disease of the genitourinary tract. This should include a complete physical examination, renal function tests, excretory urograms, and perhaps referral to a urologist. Functional or anatomic abnormalities (eg, obstruction, localized infection) must be corrected.

c. Recurrent urinary tract infections may occur in some patients who have no apparent evidence of associated urologic abnormalities. Catheterization and instrumentation are obvious sources of bacterial contamination of the urinary tract in women who have no history of infection. Sexual intercourse and pregnancy are known to aggravate urinary tract infection.

(1) If recurrent urinary tract infection is related to intercourse, trimethoprim-sulfamethoxazole (Bactrim, Septra) or other effective antimicrobial drug taken after intercourse may prevent reinfection. In some cases, it may be advisable to continue prophylactic use of the drug for weeks or months.

(2) Asymptomatic bacteriuria occurs in about 5% of all pregnant women. If untreated, approximately 30% of these patients develop potentially serious upper tract involvement. This is in contrast to an incidence of less than 2% in pregnant women without antecedent bacteriuria. Caution must be exercised in the selection of antimicrobial agents for use during pregnancy.

B. Chronic Infections: If bacteriuria persists despite adequate trials of therapy with several appropriate, safe antimicrobial drugs and there are no apparent functional or anatomic abnormalities of the genitourinary tract, chronic suppressive therapy may be required for months or years. The drug should be selected by antibiotic sensitivity tests.

In the absence of sensitivity tests, one may use sulfonamide, 0.5 g orally, maintaining an alkaline urine. A urinary antiseptic such as nitrofurantoin, 50 mg orally 2 times daily, is commonly used for long-term suppression; maintain an acid urinary pH (< 6.0) by use of ascorbic acid, 1 g orally 4 times daily.

Evaluation for bacteriuria (including antibiotic sensitivity testing) and of renal function should be made annually or at any time if there is significant change in the patient's clinical status. Repeated courses of specific anti-infective therapy may be required.

Avoid catheterization or instrumentation. Treat fluid and electrolyte disturbances, infection, hypertension, and regional problems that may arise.

URINARY INCONTINENCE

Urinary incontinence not associated with neurologic deficits or fistulas is involuntary loss of urine through an intact lower urinary tract. Urine may be lost even when the bladder is virtually empty. Incontinence may be spontaneous or induced, depending on the underlying cause. It generally occurs when the patient is standing or sitting and especially with increased intra-abdominal pressure or physical activity. Almost half of women have some degree of incontinence. The complaint is more common among those over 45 years of age and those who have had a vaginal obstetric delivery or pelvic surgery. About 20% of major gynecologic operations are done wholly or partially for incontinence. Preexisting incontinence as an isolated entity is uncommon. Incontinence is aggravated by pregnancy, especially after the first trimester.

Stress incontinence may be due to an anatomic defect or to detrusor dyssynergia ("unstable bladder"). In the former, the bladder base and urethra sag because of inadequate pelvic floor support. Normal intra-abdominal pressure is resisted by the bladder but not by the urethra. In detrusor dyssynergia incontinence, the bladder contracts following this stimulus, but the urethra remains uninhibited, so urine loss occurs.

The sphincteric mechanism controlling urination is a complex of muscle strands around the inferior aspect of the bladder and the upper part of the urethra.

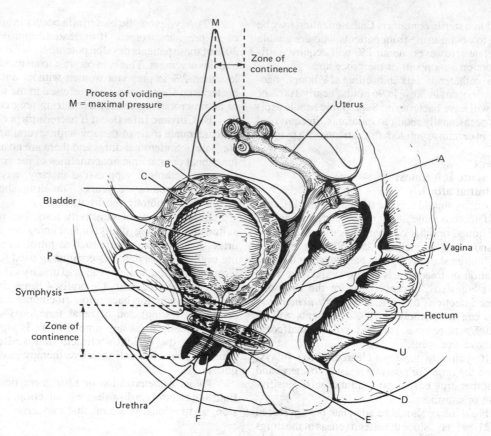

Figure 18–1. Urethrovesical musculature. *A,* cardinal ligament; *B,* detrusor muscle; *C,* bladder mucosa; *D,* constrictor urethrae membranaceae; *E,* bulbocavernous muscle; *F,* intrinsic urethral muscle; *P–U,* vesical propulsion–urethral control junction. (Redrawn after F. Netter.)

The musculature coalesces at the urethrovesical junction with other pelvic floor structures. Action is strongest at or just below the midpoint of the urethra (Fig 18–1). In repose, the involuntary vesical and circular urethral musculature closes the urethrovesical orifice to prevent leakage. When the musculature contracts, the posterior urethra opens, and funneling of the proximal urethra and lower portion of the bladder allows urine to pass through the urethra. In anatomic incontinence, intraurethral control is decreased; in detrusor dyssynergia incontinence, contractions of the bladder take place in the absence of urethral control.

Clinical Findings

It is important to determine which variety of incontinence, if not both, exists, because the 2 forms require different corrective measures. A complete history is important, but the history alone may not lead to the diagnosis. If the complaints include frequency of urination, nocturia, urgency, and urge incontinence, detrusor dyssynergia usually is present. Detrusor dyssynergia incontinence (which acounts for about 30% of all cases of incontinence) may be characterized by either reduced compliance or uninhibited contractions. Coughing, sneezing, or other physical stress may trigger leakage with either type of incontinence. Detrusor

dysfunction alone is not associated with anatomic deviations. Because the history may be misleading, urodynamic studies are important for correct diagnosis.

A. X-Ray Findings: Cystourethrograms may be abnormal in both types of incontinence. For this reason, x-ray studies are being replaced by direct urethrovesical cystometry using either water or CO_2 for differential diagnosis. With anatomic incontinence, there is a loss of the posterior urethrovesical angle. The bladder may descend below the median inferior portion of the symphysis pubica, and the proximal portion of the urethra may be widened.

B. Special Examinations:

1. Trigone (Bonney or Marchetti) test– Procaine, 2 mL of 0.5% solution or equivalent, is injected under the mucosa of the urethra at the urethrovesical junction. An Allis clamp is closed on the vaginal mucosa to the right and left of the urethra beneath the bladder neck. The site of the bulge is noted as the patient strains with the bladder full. Patients with a relaxed vesical neck and reduced posterior urethrovesical angle will lose urine when they strain or when the clamps are depressed. Urine is retained when the clamps are elevated. However, this test may be misleading if the procedure obstructs the vesical neck.

2. Direct electronic cystometry–This procedure is favored over others for differentiating bladder instability due to cystitis and nerve or muscle dysfunction. Bladder irritability may be measured by 2 provocative tests. (1) After voiding, the bladder is slowly filled with water. With a bladder catheter indwelling and the patient standing, she is asked to cough forcibly 3 times 30 seconds apart. Then she is asked to jump up and down 3 times. (2) Finally, she is placed supine, and the bladder is allowed to fill slowly until there is an urge to void. The provocative tests previously mentioned should be repeated, followed by voiding. Urethral and vesical pressures must be recorded. The volume of urine passed and the residual urine are measured also. Patients with detrusor dyssynergia never fill or empty their bladders completely, and the volume of residual urine ranges from 50 to 150 mL.

3. Urodynamics–Cystometrograms provide the essential data needed to evaluate the type of incontinence and to determine the best treatment. The procedure gives information concerning bladder capacity, irritability of the bladder musculature, and intravesical and intraurethral pressures. Evaluation of continence may be done with a microtransducer technique as represented in Figs 18–2 and 18–3. As an alternative, urethroscopic examination using water or CO_2 as a medium may be used to evaluate the urethral profile from the external to the internal meatus. Normally, the proximal urethral pressure is about 50 cm of water and the mid urethral pressure 100 cm of water. In anatomic incontinence, the pressure may be 30 cm of water or less. If the bladder neck is too mobile or opens in the absence of contraction of the bladder, anatomic incontinence exists. If uninhibited bladder contractions occur, then the bladder action is often intermittent or variable. This indicates detrusor dyssynergia. The physiologic state at rest should be compared with what happens when the patient coughs or strains. Both types of incontinence may be present.

Normally, the resting intravesical pressure after voiding is 0–5 cm of water. Ordinarily, the volume of urine may reach 500 mL with a pressure of 150 cm of water before the patient is unable to suppress the urge to urinate. With or without an anatomic defect in the urethrovesical area, the bladder capacity should be less, ie, 150–250 mL or less, with stress incontinence. The pressure may fall even to 80 cm of water or less.

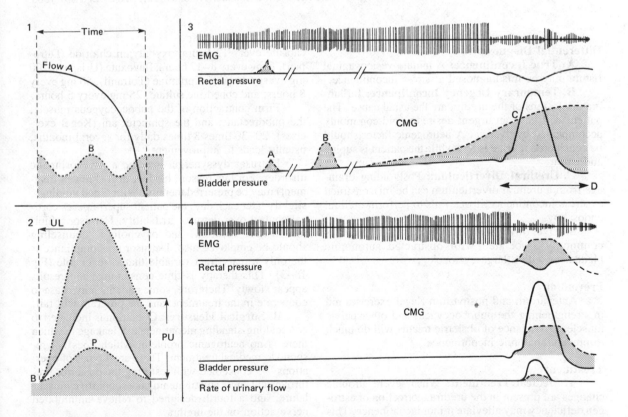

Figure 18–2. *1:* Normal urinary flow (A) and impeded flow (B). *2:* Proximal urethral pressure (P); maximal urethral pressure (PU); bladder pressure (B); urethral length (UL). *3:* Coordination of bladder pressure with rectal pressure indicates response from around bladder (A); detrusor contraction (B); rising baseline pressure indicates bladder has lost capacity as a reservoir (C); combined detrusor, abdominal, and urethral processes to voiding (D). *4:* Urethral relaxation without detrusor contraction. Stippled areas show process of voiding with Valsalva's maneuver. (Adapted from Constantinou CE: *Urol Digest* 1977; 16:13.)

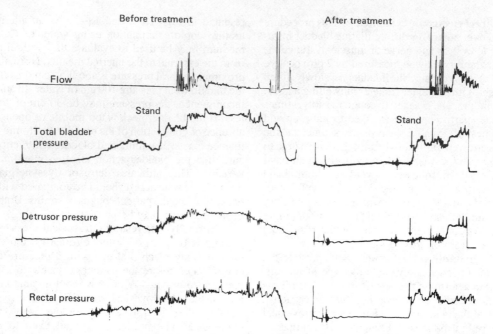

Figure 18–3. Urodynamic findings before and after bladder training. (Reproduced, with permission, from Elder DD, Stephenson TP: An assessment of the Frewen regime in the treatment of detrusor dysfunction in females. *Br J Urol* 1980; 52:467.)

Differential Diagnosis

A. True Incontinence: A minute vesicovaginal fistula may be misdiagnosed as stress incontinence.

B. Temporary Urgency Incontinence: Inflammatory lesions of the urethra are the usual cause. The patient will have an urgent desire to void commonly accompanied by dysuria. A neurogenic factor should be considered if urine is lost while the patient is supine and calm.

C. Urethral Diverticulum: Postvoiding drainage from a urethral diverticulum can be misconstrued as stress incontinence if one fails to perform urethral endoscopy.

D. Overflow Incontinence: This disorder is commonly associated with obstructed autonomic bladder or with a large cystocele.

Prevention

Antepartum and postpartum Kegel exercises aid in strengthening the pubococcygeus and other pelvic muscles. Avoidance of obstetric trauma will do much to prevent anatomic incontinence.

Treatment

A. Medical Treatment: When severe atrophic changes are present in the urethra, correction of estrogen deficiency may alleviate minor incontinence. This enhances alpha-sympathetic activity. Anticholinergic drugs or beta-adrenergic stimulants for detrusor instability give varying results. Medications currently used include propantheline (Pro-Banthine), 30 mg every 6 hours; a combination of chlorpheniramine maleate and phenylpropanolamine hydrochloride (Ornade), one capsule every 12 hours; oxybutynin chloride (Ditropan), 5 mg every 8–12 hours; flavoxate (Urispas), 200 mg every 6 hours; imipramine (Tofranil), 50 mg every 8 hours; and ephedrine sulfate, 25 mg every 6 hours.

Firm contraction of the pubococcygeus muscle, the puborectalis; and the sphincter ani (Kegel exercises), 20–30 times 3 times daily for several months, usually leads to improvement.

Detrusor dyssynergia may be a psychosomatic disorder. For this reason, bladder drill (Frewen treatment) may be preferred therapy. With timed voidings, slightly later each day, the patient superimposes cortical control over detrusor irritability. Detrusor inhibitory drugs, sedation, and psychologic counseling should be employed also. Detrusor noncompliance is the only urinary tract variable that is reversible (Fig 18–3). This therapy is time-consuming, and results appear slowly. Therefore, some patients may cease to cooperate in the treatment, and the program will fail.

B. Surgical Measures: Operation is indicated to correct long-standing incontinence or leakage in which there is no neurogenic problem, which does not respond to medical treatment. There are 4 types of operations—3 concerned with restoring the posterior urethrovesical angle and tightening the supportive musculature, and a fourth designed to relieve uninhibited nerve action on the urethra.

1. Urethroplasty and anterior colporrhaphy– This procedure is usually satisfactory in mild or moderate degrees of incontinence. The so-called pubovesical fascia and pelvic floor supports are plicated (Kelly).

2. Urethrocystopexy–The abdominal Marshall-Marchetti-Krantz operation is a suspension of the urethrovesical angle (and anterior vaginal wall). Attachment is made either to Cooper's ligament or to the retropubic fascia. This draws the bladder and urethra upward and forward. More severe cases may require this procedure.

3. Sling operations–A band of abdominal fascia or nonabsorbable ribbon is carried beneath the posterior urethra to provide support at the urethrovesical junction. The procedure may be employed for the occasional failure after urethrocystopexy.

A fixed urethra held open by a scar must be mobilized, but when the urethra is elevated, it must not be kinked. Correction of cystocele and urethrovesical displacement are necessary also. A combined abdominovaginal approach may provide a better result, but the vaginal approach usually is attempted first, since it carries less risk and highly successful.

4. Infravesical nerve resection (Ingelman-Sundberg)–This is an empiric procedure for severe detrusor dyssynergia that may be offered when other methods of treatment fail. The success rate for this operation is not encouraging.

C. Electrical Stimulation: Electronic devices (vaginal electrode) may control but do not cure incontinence. Moreover, unpleasant effects may be induced locally.

D. Mechanical Devices: Pessaries may elevate the urethrovesical junction through intravaginal pressure. They may be useful when an operation is contraindicated or when surgery is refused or has failed.

E. Postoperative Care: Prevent overdistention of the bladder postoperatively until the residual urine is less than 100 mL. This is accomplished with the use of an indwelling catheter for 3–5 days. Bethanechol chloride, 25–50 mg orally 2–3 times daily, may enhance the tone of the detrusor urinae and enhance the completion of micturition.

Prophylactic antimicrobial therapy is begun preferably by giving 500 mg of a cephalosporin intramuscularly 1 hour before the operation and repeating administration every 6–8 hours for 1–2 days postoperatively. Thereafter, trimethoprim, 160 mg, and sulfamethoxazole, 800 mg (Bactrim double strength, Septra double strength) orally, may be given every 12 hours while the catheter remains in place.

Estrogen in physiologic doses is advisable for the postmenopausal woman with atrophic genital changes unless contraindicated. It should be given for 3–4 weeks preoperatively and postoperatively.

Prognosis

Before urodynamic studies became available, the majority of patients treated surgically for urinary incontinence were cured or improved. However, of the total, approximately 20% either continued to have or acquired a more formidable problem of incontinence within 1 year postoperatively. Urodynamic studies preoperatively have identified 3 kinds of incontinence: anatomic incontinence, detrusor dyssynergia, and a combination of the 2. Detrusor instability will not improve and may worsen with the usual treatment for anatomic incontinence. Patients undergoing corrective surgery 2 or more times have a guarded prognosis with further operations because of scar formation and restriction in the urethrovesical area.

DISORDERS OF THE URETHRA

See Table 18–13 for a summary of the clinical features and treatment of the more common disorders of the female urethra. Brief descriptions of some of the

Table 18–13. Clinical features and treatment of some common disorders of the female urethra.

	Age of Patient	Symptoms	Signs	Gross Pathology	Histology	Treatment
Caruncle	Usually postmenopausal	Dysuria	Bleeding	Red, sessile growth of posterior portion of urethral orifice	Tiny blood vessels and inflammatory cells covered with epithelium	Fulgurate or excise
Thrombosed urethral vein	Older	Abrupt onset, pain	Protrusion from urethra	Bluish mass at posterior lip of urethra	Thrombosed vein	Symptomatic
Prolapse of urethral mucosa	Young child or woman with lower neuron disease	Pain	Protrusion from urethra	Angry, edematous, red	Inflamed or gangrenous	Reduce. If cannot reduce, resect.
Carcinoma	Older	Bloody discharge; may be none	Bleeding	Firm mass, sometimes ulcerative	Carcinoma	Surgical excision with dissection of regional nodes, or radiation with or without surgery
Urethral polyp	Older	Dysuria or may be none	Bleeding occasionally, or urethritis	Sessile, prolapsed lesion	Attached by pedicle	Excise or fulgurate
Urethral inflammation	Any age	Dysuria and local discomfort	No discharge	Reddened, granular, may be stenosed	Inflammation	Remove the cause; urethral dilatation if needed

less important disorders are presented in the following paragraphs. Urethral stricture, urethral caruncle, and urethral diverticulum are discussed in separate sections below.

Chronic Urethritis

Chronic urethritis often accompanies hypoestrogenism. The tissues are atrophic, dry, reddened, and hypersensitive. Urinary urgency, frequency, and stress incontinence may be present. Relief is sometimes obtained by giving conjugated estrogens, 0.3–0.625 mg orally daily 3 out of each 4 weeks; or ethinyl estradiol, 0.05 mg in a similar manner; or a small suppository containing estrogen.

Some patients with chronic urethritis not due to infection who do not respond to estrogen therapy may be treated by topical application of phenol or triamcinolone acetonide or by electrodesiccation of urethral lesions. A few patients fail to respond to any treatment; some clinicians refer to cases of this sort as "psychogenic" or "allergic" urethral syndrome.

Irradiation of the Urethra

Women treated with radiation for genital cancer may acquire some degree of urethral atrophy and chronic urethritis several months after therapy. The urethral mucosa may become ischemic, with telangiectatic areas. There may be stenosis of the canal with or without white cells in the urine. Treatment is similar to that for chronic urethritis or urethral stricture.

URETHRAL STRICTURE

Urethral stricture may be acquired or congenital. Obstetric or coital trauma most commonly predisposes to periurethral fibrosis. With voiding, there is dysuria and a slow stream. Urinary tract infection may occur as a complication. The diagnosis can be suspected by probing the urethra with graduated sounds, but cystourethrography or urethroscopy gives a more accurate diagnosis. The best treatment consists of gradual dilatation of the urethra with a 45F dilator and meatotomy.

URETHRAL CARUNCLE

A caruncle is a small reddened, sensitive fleshy outgrowth at the urethral meatus. Most caruncles represent eversion (ectropion) of the urethra or infections at the urinary meatus (or both), but vascular anomalies or benign or malignant neoplasm may also cause caruncle formation. The vast majority of caruncles are benign; persistent and progressive lesions may be cancerous. Caruncles may occur at any age, but postmenopausal women are most commonly affected.

Caruncles are categorized according to type (combined types also occur): (1) Papillary caruncles are flame-shaped and delicate, have a rich vascular supply, and are covered with stratified transitional or squamous cells. Gross infection may or may not be present. (2) Granulomatous caruncles with a wide base are inflammatory processes usually due to bacterial infection, including lymphogranuloma venereum, although they may also be caused by syphilis. (3) Vascular caruncles usually have an angiomatous pattern and are frequently infected.

Clinical Findings

A. Symptoms and Signs: A caruncle appears as a small, vividly red, sessile or flattened mass protruding from the urethral meatus. It usually bleeds, exudes, or causes pain, depending upon its cause, size, and integrity. Dysuria, frequency, and urgency are common urinary symptoms. Bleeding and leukorrhea are usually not severe except when malignant change has occurred. Dyspareunia or other types of local discomfort are frequently described, particularly during the climacteric. Malignant caruncles are firm, on a wide base, have a distinct margin, and are friable and hemorrhagic. Local ulceration, urethritis, and vulvitis may develop.

B. Laboratory Findings: Specimens for cytologic examination, bacterial smears, cultures, and biopsies should be obtained. If syphilis is suspected, darkfield examination is required; if lymphogranuloma venereum is a possibility, a Frei test or complement fixation test is indicated.

Prevention

Estrogen therapy for postmenopausal women and avoidance of local irritation will minimize formation of a caruncle.

Treatment

A. Specific Measures: Venereal disease is treated with appropriate measures. If the patient is postmenopausal and has not been receiving steroid sex hormone therapy, estrogens are applied topically (diethylstilbestrol vaginal suppositories, 0.5 mg every other night for 3 weeks) before specific therapy.

If tests are negative for malignancy and the lesion is not severely infected, light fulguration under local anesthesia, cryosurgery, or excision may be done, taking care not to produce a stricture. Repeated cryosurgery is preferable to extensive fulguration initially and may be repeated if the caruncle recurs. Topical anti-infective therapy (eg, nitrofurazone) is indicated before and after cauterization or excision.

If malignant change has occurred, radical resection or radiation therapy is required.

B. General Measures: A bladder sedative compound may be given to relieve urinary distress.

C. Treatment of Complications: The urethral meatus must be dilated after therapy if stenosis develops.

Prognosis

The prognosis is excellent in benign cases but guarded with malignant change.

URETHRAL DIVERTICULUM

Urethral diverticula are more common than formerly believed. They usually arise in the midportion of the urethra from dilatation or rupture of a paraurethral (wolffian) remnant or from an injury. They may be multiple. Approximately 10% contain stones. Not infrequently there is an associated carcinoma. Patients with urethral diverticulum usually are beyond middle age. Dysuria is usually present, and there may be a purulent urethral discharge, a deflatable paraurethral mass, vaginal pain with coitus or micturition, and terminal leakage with voiding. The diagnosis is facilitated by urethroscopy and x-ray studies using a Davis-TeLinde catheter. Sometimes the diverticulum can be palpated.

Diverticulum must be differentiated from urethrocele, midline deformity, Gartner duct cyst, and abscess of Skene's gland.

Appropriate antibiotics are given in case of infection. Aspiration of an occluded diverticulum gives prompt but only temporary relief from pain. Vaginal excision of the diverticulum is done after the inflammation subsides. Surgical treatment is generally successful unless the external urinary sphincter is involved. Urethral fistulas or stricture may occur.

DISORDERS OF THE BLADDER

1. INFLAMMATION OF THE BLADDER

Infections of the bladder generally are caused by ascent of *E coli* from the urethra. Submucosal edema, redness, and sometimes ecchymosis affect the trigone or ureteral orifices more often than other surfaces in the bladder. Symptoms may develop 24–48 hours after sexual intercourse and include dysuria, urgency, and frequency. Examination of a freshly voided urine specimen shows white blood cells, sometimes red cells, protein, and large numbers of bacteria. Treatment usually consists of administration of sulfonamide drugs. If more than 2 or 3 attacks occur within a relatively short time, a more complete urologic study, including urograms and cystoscopic study, is in order.

Interstitial ulcer (Hunner's ulcer) is a chronic disease of unknown cause. The usual symptoms are urgency, nocturia, and recurrent suprapubic pain when the bladder is full. The bladder capacity is reduced. The urine may be normal. Cystoscopic examination shows small ulcers on the anterior wall or dome of the bladder. Cauterization of the bladder or instillation of 1% silver nitrate twice a week may give relief from pain. (Instill normal saline solution within 2 minutes to counteract the action of the silver nitrate.) Symptoms frequently recur or persist for years.

Irradiation in cancericidal doses causes perivascular fibrosis, edema, and cellular necrosis. There may be symptoms of cystitis during or shortly after radiation therapy. These are generally of short duration. Six or more months after completion of radiation therapy, the bladder mucosa may show atrophic changes. Vascularity is decreased, and telangiectases may be prominent. The bladder capacity often is diminished.

Treatment of the acute phase consists of increased fluid intake and a sulfonamide drug if infection is present. Later, administration of conjugated estrogens, 0.625–1.25 mg orally, will increase vascularity and lead to epithelialization. The symptoms of frequency may persist.

2. VESICAL STONE

Stone in the bladder may not produce urinary symptoms, but some cases are associated with repeated episodes of cystitis, manifested by pus and blood in the urine. Cystoscopic examination is diagnostic. Patients with stone should be studied further to establish or rule out a diagnosis of metabolic disease associated with increased calcium excretion, uric acid, enzyme disorders, renal tubular syndromes, endocrine disorders, or upper urinary tract infection. Bladder calculi frequently can be crushed and removed through the cystoscope. Cystotomy is reserved for large stones.

URETERAL STONE

Ureteral stones are produced in the kidney and carried into the ureter by urinary flow, gravity, and peristalsis. Often they permit urinary flow and do not produce symptoms. However, they may obstruct the narrowest (ureteropelvic, midureteral, or ureterovesical) areas of the ureter to varying degrees and produce acute or chronic symptoms.

Ureteral calculi may be due to hyperparathyroidism or acute pyelonephritis, gout, or other metabolic disorders, but the origin of the stones frequently cannot be determined.

There are often no symptoms, although severe colicky or constant pain may be experienced at the level of the obstruction. Hematuria occasionally occurs. During an acute attack, the patient may be in agony and even in mild shock.

The urine should be examined for blood, pus, and crystals. Flat films of the abdomen or excretory urograms are frequently diagnostic.

Morphine may be required to control severe pain. Most stones (80%) pass spontaneously. The remainder require removal by cystoscopic manipulation or ureterolithotomy, since urinary infection, total blockage of the ureter, or uremia may develop. Periodic follow-up is recommended because renal calculi tend to recur.

OVARIAN VEIN SYNDROME

Ovarian vein syndrome is a urologic disorder in which an aberrant right ovarian vein compresses the ureter, predisposing to either pyelonephritis or hydronephrosis. Rarely are both ureters involved. Stricture of the ureter generally occurs at the level of S1, or 14 cm above the ureterovesical junction. Since most cases of pyelonephritis and hydronephrosis occur on the right side, the abnormal anatomic relationship should be considered in patients with symptoms of upper urinary tract infection.

There may be no symptoms, or right-sided pyelonephritis, or a history of vague costovertebral discomfort beginning during pregnancy. X-rays may show a persistent variation in the right kidney and ureter compared to the left. Minimal pyelocaliectasis, an atonic renal pelvis, tortuosity of the upper part of the ureter, and a constant dilatation of the mid part of the ureter down to the level of S1 become apparent in ureterograms of the patient in the Trendelenburg position.

Surgical bisection of the ovarian vein usually gives prompt relief of symptoms and signs of ureteral compression.

URINARY TRACT INJURIES FOLLOWING OBSTETRIC & GYNECOLOGIC SURGERY

Urinary fistulas and obstructions following obstetric and gynecologic surgery are usually iatrogenic. Fistulas may occur in any part of the urinary tract and result from direct or indirect injury; occlusions usually involve the ureter and occur as a result of angulation or obstruction by a suture, scarring after injury or infection, or as a complication of the treatment of pelvic malignancy. The incidence of urinary tract injury in large medical centers in the USA is about 0.8% following major gynecologic surgery and 0.08% in operative obstetrics.

Postpartum fistulas of the bladder and urethra are generally caused by extreme continued pressure of the presenting part or by instrumentation. A history of prolonged labor and operative delivery is usually present. Many fistulas are the result of poor surgical technique, hematoma formation, and infection (neglected hematoma or contaminated urinary extravasation). Deep sutures, mass ligatures, and overdistention of the bladder also cause bladder injuries and fistulas.

The ureter may be involved in fistula formation or stenosis during gynecologic surgery. Many types of fistulas may be diagnosed after operation or delivery: ureterovaginal, ureterovesical, ureteroperitoneal, ureteroenteric, vesicovaginal, vesicouterine, vesicocervical, and urethrovaginal. Some fistulas are minute; others represent loss of a major segment of the urinary tract. Strictures are confined to narrow structures, eg, the ureter and urethra. Partial or complete closure of one or both ureters may occur, but stricture of the female urethra rarely occurs postoperatively.

Clinical Findings

A. Symptoms and Signs: The symptoms depend upon the site of the injury (unilateral or bilateral), the degree of damage (partial or complete), and the direction of urine drainage (external, intraperitoneal, or retroperitoneal).

Unilateral ureteral injury usually causes flank pain, tenderness, and fever but does not alter urine volume. It may indicate constriction of the ureter, fistula, and infection. Escape of urine from the abdominal or vaginal incision indicates probable ureteral or bladder fistulas (or both). Ileus often follows urinary obstruction, extravasation, and infection. Urinary infection, especially with partial obstruction of the ureter, results in chills, fever, renal pain, and costovertebral and loin tenderness. Fever develops when a ureter to an infected kidney is ligated. In the absence of preexisting bacteriuria, complete obstruction of one ureter usually is asymptomatic. If urine leaks into the peritoneal cavity, there will be signs of free peritoneal fluid and peritoneal irritation. Progressive degeneration and necrosis of a damaged area or temporary pocketing of extravasated urine may account for delayed leakage (up to 3–4 weeks postoperatively).

Uremia ordinarily does not follow unilateral ureteral injury and intraperitoneal leakage because much of the extravasated urine is reabsorbed and excreted by the opposite kidney. Signs of perirenal or psoas abscess follow retroperitoneal extravasation of urine.

Anuria and uremia follow complete bilateral ureteral occlusion. Oliguria follows partial obstruction of both ureters, a large vesicoperitoneal fistula, or occlusion of the urethra. Dehydration, shock, lower nephron nephrosis, and congestive heart failure should be ruled out.

B. Laboratory Findings: The PSP test indicates the degree of renal tubular function. Normally, 60–70% of the dye is excreted in 2 hours; excretion of less than 50% is an indication of renal insufficiency. Passage of the dye verifies the patency of at least one ureter in cases of postoperative oliguria, provided adequate hydration and a normal blood pressure have been maintained.

C. X-Ray Findings:

1. Ureteral obstruction, fistula, or extravasation—

a. Excretory urography–The recently obstructed kidney will not excrete the contrast agent well. The clarity of the urogram may be reduced by the presence of excessive intestinal gas.

b. Retrograde urography–A ureteral catheter may be blocked by an occlusion or may be inserted easily. (A radiopaque catheter should be used so that the level of the obstruction can be observed on the film.) Injection of a contrast medium into a Braasch bulb catheter may reveal a fistula above the bulb fixed in the most distal portion of the ureter.

c. Plain film of the abdomen–This may suggest retroperitoneal extravasation of urine or psoas abscess by revealing a mass, obliteration of the psoas muscle contours, or displacement of intestinal gas.

2. Bladder fistula and extravasation–An anteroposterior scout film of the pelvis should be obtained. The bladder is filled with 50 mL of radiopaque medium such as iodopyracet or acetrizoate in 200 mL of water, and a second film is taken. The bladder is then drained and a third film obtained at once. Slight extravasation not visible in the second film may be clearly seen in the third.

3. Urethral occlusion or fistula–This may be visualized by taking lateral x-ray films promptly after injection into the urethral meatus of 5 mL of intravenous urography medium mixed with 5 mL of water.

D. Special Examinations: Passage of a urethral catheter may reveal an obstruction. Urethroscopy may expose an obstruction, perforating suture, or fistula. Cystoscopy may disclose a large vesical fistula, but direct visualization is disappointing in the identification of small fistulas. Distention of the bladder with water for cystoscopy may complicate the problem by causing gross extravasation of fluid through the defect.

1. To differentiate a ureterovaginal from a vesicovaginal fistula–

a. The bladder is distended with a solution of 5 mL of indigo carmine in 200 mL of water. In the absence of ureteral reflux (rare), a fistula will be revealed by the presence of blue fluid. Severe chronic cystitis may cause vesicoureteral reflux. When this is likely, 50 mL of an aqueous x-ray contrast medium are added to the indigo carmine solution, the bladder is filled, and an anteroposterior film of the pelvis is obtained to show backflow as well as extravasation.

b. A vaginal pack or snug menstrual tampon that has been moistened with an aqueous solution of sodium carbonate or bicarbonate is inserted. Two hundred milliliters of water containing 10 mL of methylene blue are then instilled into the bladder. The catheter is removed, avoiding any spillage that might discolor the pack, and a 1-mL ampule containing 6 mg of PSP is administered intravenously. The vaginal pack is removed in 30 minutes. If the pack is stained blue, the presumptive diagnosis is vesicovaginal fistula; if the pack is red, the defect is probably a ureterovaginal fistula; if the pack is multicolored, a ureterovesicovaginal fistula may be present.

2. Retrograde study of the urinary system–If ureteral catheters pass readily to both renal pelves and recover clear urine, ureteral injury, except perhaps a crushing injury or a small perforation, is excluded. If one of these complications seems likely, the catheter is secured in the ureter for splinting and drainage for the 10–14 days necessary for healing.

Complications

Peritonitis is the most serious complication. Anuria or oliguria may be associated with uremia and may also lead to death. Other complications are psoas or perirenal abscess, thrombophlebitis, incontinence of urine, and diarrhea. Urinary tract infection may follow obstruction, as may hydroureter, hydronephrosis, nephrolithiasis, ureterolithiasis, and marked bladder distention.

Differential Diagnosis

Some fistulas occur after irradiation, particularly radium therapy, for cancer of the cervix or the body of the uterus; some may be associated with the treatment of granulomas following pressure by a pessary, tuberculosis, lymphogranuloma venereum, and schistosomiasis. Clear, yellowish, odorless drainage from the abdominal wound may represent ascites or exudative peritoneal fluid, an antecedent of wound dehiscence. Thin, brownish discharge from an abdominal or vaginal suture line may be serum from a seroma or hematoma. In ureteral obstruction, oliguria or anuria may be due to shock, dehydration, or lower nephron nephrosis; abdominal distention may indicate dynamic ileus caused by intestinal obstruction or adynamic ileus due to peritonitis; fever may be due to an infected wound, peritonitis, or thrombophlebitis; and kidney pain and costovertebral or flank tenderness may be due to nephrolithiasis, ureterolithiasis, or pyelonephritis.

Prevention

Adequate preliminary studies of the urinary tract and full knowledge of the anatomy of the region and the pathologic features of the patient's illness are essential before surgery. The ureters should be catheterized and identified initially in all difficult cases and the wire stylet left in a ureteral catheter for identification to keep the ureter from being cut or clamped. All structures must be identified before clamping, incision, and ligation, and care must be taken so that there is no undue traction or unnecessary denudation of the ureter and the base of the bladder. Only fine absorbable sutures should be used in or around the urinary tract. Pressure is applied—rather than multiple ligatures—to control hemorrhage, and a single bleeding point sutured. The course of the ureters is traced at the completion of each abdominal operation if ureteral injury is likely. The ureter is splinted with an inlying catheter, the bladder drained with another catheter, and the area drained extraperitoneally in suspected or actual urinary tract injury.

Sufficient doses of appropriate antibiotics are utilized for treatment of infection. The experienced surgeon should personally remove ureteral catheters postoperatively if it is decided not to leave them in place.

Treatment

A. Emergency Measures: Shock, blood loss, and dehydration are treated as indicated and the bladder catheterized. If oliguria or anuria is present, a PSP test is ordered. Specific gravity should be checked and the patient weighed.

B. Specific Surgical Measures:

1. Bilateral ureteral obstruction–If both ureters are obstructed and the patient is a poor surgical risk, nephrostomy or unilateral tube ureterostomy is performed using the largest child's urethral catheter that will enter the ureter. The other kidney should not be left obstructed for more than a few days. As soon as the patient becomes a satisfactory operative risk, the second blocked kidney is relieved by nephrostomy or tube ureterostomy. Deligation alone is not satisfactory unless the suture is obvious and deligation can be performed easily. If deligation is done, a splinting catheter is inserted through a longitudinal incision several cm above the point of obstruction, passed to the kidney and bladder, brought out through the urethra, and fixed to a Foley retention catheter for 10–14 days, at which time both may be removed. The retroperitoneal area is drained through a separate lower quadrant or flank stab wound.

A gallbladder T tube can be used in lieu of a catheter as follows: (1) The cross-arm of the T is notched at the vertical segment. (2) The ureter is incised longitudinally several centimeters above the defect. (3) The tube is inserted so that the lower arm splints the point of injury. (4) The upper arm is fixed in the proximal ureter and the long arm is carried out retroperitoneally through a stab wound in the flank. (5) A drain is placed in the retroperitoneal space underlying the T tube and allowed to remain until drainage ceases (about 1 week after removal of the tube).

2. Vesicoperitoneal fistula–Laparotomy should be performed as soon as the diagnosis is established. The edges are freshened and the fistula closed without tension in 2 layers—one continuous or both interrupted. The mucosa should be avoided in suturing. The bladder is drained by cystostomy or with a Foley retention catheter and suction drainage employed for 10–14 days.

3. Vesicovaginal fistula–Local infection is treated by removing old sutures and concretions and by giving systemic antibiotics. Repair is indicated as outlined for vesicoperitoneal fistula. In general, one should wait 4 months or more after injury before attempting closure. If there are no contraindications, one may take a calculated risk in selected cases and perform earlier repair after preparation with prednisone, 10 mg 4 times daily, and massive doses of broad-spectrum antibiotics for 7 days. All but large inaccessible, immobile vesicovaginal fistulas (85–90% of total) should be closed transvaginally. The approach should be chosen on the basis of which route gives the best visualization of the defect to do the best repair.

4. Ureterovesicovaginal fistulas–These should be closed abdominally. The procedure at operation is to freshen the edges, excise scar tissue, free restrictions, and close without tension using few fine, removable nylon monofilament or silver wire interrupted mattress sutures (avoiding the mucosa).

Reimplantation of the severely damaged or severed ureter into the bladder (ureteroneocystostomy) is preferred to ureteroureterostomy on the same side. Ureteroneocystostomy should be attempted only when the proximal ureter is long enough to permit anastomosis without tension. A splinting catheter is inserted into the ureter, brought out through the urethra, and fixed to a Foley retention catheter for 10–14 days, at which time both may be removed. The bladder is drained by cystostomy or with a Foley retention catheter, and suction drainage is employed for 10–14 days.

Ligation of the damaged ureter and sacrifice of the kidney on that side is almost always contraindi-cated. A renal abscess may develop, necessitating a much more serious operation (nephrectomy) than restoration of the continuity of the urinary system. Moreover, the opposite kidney may be—or may become—grossly deficient.

Prognosis

Many ureterovaginal fistulas will heal if a ureteral catheter splint and an extraperitoneal drain are inserted promptly after the fistula is diagnosed. However, because serious, symptomatic ureteral stenosis and severe chronic urinary tract infection develop in the majority of cases, a reanastomosis procedure such as a ureteroneocystostomy, which ordinarily heals and functions well, is preferred.

Very small vesicovaginal fistulas often close spontaneously if the bladder can be kept collapsed and infection prevented.

Urethral fistulas are notoriously resistant to spontaneous closure if a urethral catheter is employed. Many heal well, however, if simply repaired and if cystostomy is used instead of a urethral catheter.

Only minor strictures of the urethra and ureter can be widened with bougie dilatation. Extensive scarring will require plastic surgery or a reanastomosis.

DISORDERS OF THE GASTROINTESTINAL TRACT & RELATED DISORDERS

ACUTE APPENDICITIS

Essentials of Diagnosis

- Anorexia; nausea and vomiting.
- Progressive mild to moderate abdominal pain.
- Localized abdominal tenderness.
- Mild fever.
- Leukocytosis with neutrophilia.

General Considerations

Appendicitis is a common acute surgical disease usually seen in patients under 30 years of age. Diagnosis is more difficult in the female than in the male, because of proximity of the diseased appendix to the internal genitalia. This is particularly true if appendicitis is associated with disorders such as acute salpingitis, ovulatory bleeding, or ectopic pregnancy. Appendicitis should be considered in the differential diagnosis of all cases of acute intra-abdominal or pelvic pain or sepsis. Appendicitis may pose a critical hazard to a gravid patient and her fetus. The enlarging uterus may obscure the diagnosis. The frequency of abortion and premature labor is increased by the disease.

If appendicitis develops in a postoperative period, there may be confusion and delay in establishing the diagnosis, with complications resulting from the delay.

Clinical Findings

A. Symptoms and Signs: Anorexia and nausea and vomiting are frequent symptoms. Early discomfort is usually periumbilical in classic appendicitis. Later in the course of the disease, pain shifts to the right lower quadrant. Tenderness at McBurney's point is aggravated by coughing or movement, and there is rebound tenderness. There may be hyperesthesia over the right lower quadrant. Rectal tenderness is common if the appendix is situated in the pelvis. Temperature elevation is generally under 38.3 °C (101 °F); a temperature of 39.5 °C (103.1 °F) or above may indicate rupture of the appendix or may alert one to a possible diagnosis other than acute appendicitis.

Retrocecal and pelvic forms of appendicitis may present minimal and atypical signs and symptoms and are frequently mistaken for simple gastroenteritis. A high index of suspicion and repeated pelvic or rectal examination may be necessary to establish the diagnosis.

Pain produced or aggravated by hyperextension of the right lower extremity may be helpful in diagnosing retrocecal appendicitis.

B. Laboratory Findings: The white count is generally elevated to 12,000–18,000/μL, with neutrophils predominating. The white count and differential count are normal in about 5–10% of patients with appendicitis.

Differential Diagnosis

Table 18–14 lists the main differential diagnostic criteria of some of the more common acute intra-abdominal disorders. Symptoms of Meckel's diverticulitis may simulate acute appendicitis so well that the correct diagnosis may not be made until the abdominal cavity is explored surgically, but pain in the left lower quadrant or both lower quadrants should suggest this lesion.

A period of observation may be required to differentiate appendicitis from simple gastroenteritis, a

Table 18–14. Differential diagnosis of acute intra-abdominal disease.

Disease	Type of Onset	Symptoms and Signs			
		Gastrointestinal Symptoms	Relationship to Menstruation	Location of Pain	Remarks
Acute appendicitis	Insidious to acute and persistent	Anorexia; nausea and vomiting.	None	Periumbilical or localized generally to right lower abdominal quadrant.	Temperature usually under 38.3 °C (101.1 °F). Leukocytosis seldom > 18,000/μL. Localized abdominal tenderness.
Ectopic pregnancy	Sudden or intermittently vague	Frequently none	Usually irregularity of recent menses	Unilateral early; may have shoulder pain after rupture.	Usually afebrile. Nonclotting blood from cul-de-sac. May be in shock. Doughy pelvic mass.
Acute pancreatitis	Acute	Anorexia; nausea and vomiting.	None	Epigastric penetrating to back.	Prostration, high serum amylase, wine-colored fluid by cul-de-sac puncture.
Ruptured corpus luteum cyst	Sudden	Seldom	May have scant uterine bleeding	Pelvic pain in region of involved adnexa.	Afebrile, normal white count, generally lasts less than 24 hours.
Torsion of tube and ovary	Sudden with change of position; then continuous.	Usually none	None	Lower quadrant of abdomen.	Pelvic mass; later, leukocytosis.
Renal colic	Sudden	Frequently nausea and vomiting	None	Costovertebral or along course of ureter.	Pyuria common with infection; red cells in urine with calculus.
Acute salpingitis	Gradually becomes worse	Diarrhea indicates pelvic abscess	Frequently begins during or following menses. Menses often abnormal.	Bilateral adnexal; later, may be generalized.	High white count, fever; masses with tubo-ovarian abscesses.
Acute cholecystitis	Insidious to acute	Anorexia; nausea and vomiting.	None	Epigastric.	Right upper quadrant tenderness; gallbladder may be palpable. Icterus indicates cholelithiasis. White count moderately elevated.
Acute gastroenteritis	Sudden	Nausea and vomiting, often with diarrhea	None	Generalized abdominal discomfort.	Dehydration. May or may not be febrile.
Cecitis	Vague to acute	Loose bloody stools, cramps	None	Right lower abdominal or generalized cramps.	History of spontaneous remissions, amebiasis.
Toxic shock syndrome	Sudden	Vomiting, diarrhea	Usually related to menses	Myalgia.	Usually with the use of vaginal tampons.

twisted tube and ovary, extrauterine pregnancy, peptic ulcer, acute salpingitis, ureteral stone, mesenteric thrombosis, or adynamic ileus.

Complications

Perforation may give rise to peritonitis or formation of an abscess. Seldom do these complications occur within the first 8–10 hours of the disease. Rarely, subphrenic abscesses or portal thrombophlebitis may occur as sequelae.

Treatment

Nothing, including antibiotics or cathartics, should be given by mouth. Enemas should be avoided. Occasional abdominopelvic and rectal examinations and other examinations may be employed to establish a definite diagnosis. Once the diagnosis of acute appendicitis is established, the appendix must be removed at once. If the appendix has ruptured, however, nasogastric suction, parenteral fluids, appropriate antibiotics, and drainage of the abscess may be the preferred course of action; the appendix should be removed later, after the acute inflammatory process has subsided.

Prognosis

Early diagnosis and treatment should yield a favorable outcome. The present mortality rate from appendicitis has been reduced to a fraction of 1%, but the problems of morbidity (eg, perforation) have not decreased correspondingly.

HERNIAS

A hernia is an evagination of peritoneum through a defect in one of its fascial or muscular coverings. The hernia consists of a sac, its contents (omentum, intestine, bladder, ovary, tube), and its investment. Hernias may be classified according to anatomic location (eg, inguinal) or cause (eg, incisional). They may be reducible or nonreducible and symptomatic or asymptomatic. An irreducible hernia is said to be incarcerated if the bowel is obstructed without interference with the blood supply; if the latter occurs, the hernia becomes strangulated or gangrenous.

Some hernias are associated with congenital defects; others are of posttraumatic or postoperative origin. Factors that contribute to hernial enlargement and advancement include strenuous physical exertion, chronic cough, chronic constipation, marked obesity, pregnancy, intra-abdominal enlargement, aging, and chronic debilitating disease.

The incidence of certain types of hernia is sex-related. Inguinal hernia is the commonest type of groin hernia in both sexes and is much more common in males than in females. Although femoral hernias are more common in females than in males, inguinal hernia is more common in females than is femoral hernia. Inguinal hernias in women are almost always of the indirect type. Umbilical hernias occur about 10 times

as often in females as in males, presumably as a consequence of multiple pregnancies, prolonged labor, obesity, or poor abdominal muscle tone.

Hernias should be repaired surgically when the patient's condition permits to relieve discomfort and to prevent the hazard of obstruction and incarceration. These latter complications require prompt surgical treatment. Emergency hernioplasty, particularly in the elderly, imposes considerably higher morbidity and mortality rates than elective hernioplasty.

INTESTINAL INJURIES IN OBSTETRIC & GYNECOLOGIC SURGERY

Surgical accidents such as laceration, incision, crushing, or puncture of the intestine may be discovered at operation or soon thereafter. Such injury is usually associated with distortion, unusual displacement of the abdominal contents, poor exposure, lack of surgical knowledge, or haste. Most operative damage occurs with pelvic tumors or chronic inflammation or after previous surgery. About 5% of gynecologic operations involve primary or secondary bowel surgery, exclusive of appendectomy.

The risk of bowel injury is increased by adherence of the intestine to the abdominal wall, dense organized adhesions, a large neoplasm, extensive infection, or endometriosis. Sharp or blunt separation may be causal in that poor differentiation of margins of adherent organs always complicates dissection. Postoperative bleeding and infection follow extensive, initially unrecognized intestinal trauma. Even if a defect is closed at surgery, it may bleed or leak later. Peritonitis, pelvic abscess, fecal fistula, evisceration, septic embolization, and death may be the sequelae.

Fever, severe anorexia, nausea and vomiting, abdominal pain, distention, tenderness, and muscle guarding develop a few days after the complicated operation. A vague abdominal mass may be outlined. Spreading sepsis, purulent or fecal drainage from the incision, or dehiscence often follows 7–10 days after surgery. The white count and erythrocyte sedimentation rate indicate an acute infectious process; anemia may be evident. X-ray studies are rarely diagnostic. Moreover, the introduction of a contrast medium may enlarge the intestinal defect.

The differential diagnosis includes incisional, urinary, or respiratory infection and intestinal obstruction.

In cases of serious surgical intestinal injury, especially those involving the colon, drainage and complete bed rest in Fowler's position must be instituted. Other measures include gastric suction, maintenance of fluid and electrolyte balance by parenteral means, replacement of blood loss, and administration of antibiotics such as penicillin and kanamycin. Enemas are contraindicated. Analgesics should be provided until bowel function is reestablished (in about 10 days).

The bowel should be inspected, bleeding controlled, and defects repaired. The suture line must be transverse—never longitudinal, or circular constriction will result. Interrupted nonabsorbable intestinal sutures are preferred.

In wounds of the serosa and the muscularis, a single row of sutures should suffice. One or 2 mattress sutures should close puncture wounds satisfactorily.

When the mucosa of the bowel has been opened, contamination of the peritoneal cavity should be assumed and spill limited by suction, laparotomy packs, and elevation of the edges of the defect. Two layers of sutures should be employed: the first in the muscularis and the second in the superficial muscularis and serosa. A Penrose type drain should be inserted through a stab incision to the site of repair.

When widespread bowel damage or its invasion by tumor is diagnosed, segmental resection, "aseptic anastomosis," and drainage should be accomplished if feasible. Repair of the bowel, proximal tube enterostomy, peritoneal drainage, and later definitive surgery may be necessary for poor-risk patients.

If intestinal obstruction or dehiscence develops, the problem must be corrected by reoperation. A "pointing" pelvic abscess should be drained transvaginally or extraperitoneally. Critical sepsis is much more likely to occur as a result of injury to the large bowel than to the small bowel.

When spreading peritonitis or large pelvic abscess develops, the prognosis is grave. In countries where amebic infestations are common, the appearance of friable ulcers in the surgical field accompanied by sepsis postoperatively should raise a suspicion of amebiasis.

PRURITUS ANI & VULVAE

Anogenital pruritus is a distressing symptom that may be due to a wide variety of local or systemic causes. It often occurs because the sensitive, moist pudendal skin is commonly exposed to irritating fecal material retained in anal recesses. It may affect women at any age, but it is most common among middle-aged women who have inadequate standards of perineal hygiene. The major causes, in approximate order of frequency, may be listed as follows:

(1) Mechanical problems: Faulty perineal hygiene, tight nonabsorbent clothing, or irritating erotic manipulation.

(2) Local proctologic, gynecologic, or urologic disease: Hemorrhoids, fissure in ano, fistula, leukorrhea, or fecal or urinary incontinence.

(3) Psychoneurosis and habit: Continued inappropriate awareness of an unpleasant sensation, often following treatment of a local anorectal condition.

(4) Infections: Dermatitis due to bacteria, fungi, yeasts, trichomonads, or intestinal parasites (particularly *Enterobius vermicularis* and *Ascaris lumbricoides*).

(5) Allergy or sensitivity reactions: Atopic eczema or contact dermatitis and, especially, deodorant sprays.

(6) Systemic diseases: Diabetes mellitus, jaundice, Hodgkin's disease, or uremia.

Pruritus is usually poorly localized; the itching is usually circumanal, often spreading over the perineum or pudendum. It may extend to or from the vaginal introitus. The perianal skin may be erythematous, excoriated, dry, moist, or bleeding; secondary chronic changes are maceration, scaling, fissuring, or lichenification. A similar dermatologic condition may also be present elsewhere (eg, fungal intertrigo, eczema). Itching may be slight to almost unbearable.

Pruritus, invariably more acute at night or during periods of inactivity, is heightened by warmth and scratching.

Treatment

Treat the problem definitively, if possible. If the cause remains obscure, treat symptomatically. Complicated forms of treatment such as x-ray, surgery, or tattooing should not be used except in specific persistent cases. Acute pruritus is much easier to relieve than chronic pruritus, which easily becomes complicated by secondary changes.

A. Specific Measures:

1. If an allergic reaction is suspected, oral antihistamines (eg, diphenhydramine) may be helpful.

2. Sedatives induce sleep and reduce the sensation of itching, but extensive use of bromides and barbiturates may cause secondary pruritus.

3. Hydrocortisone 1% lotion or cream is beneficial in idiopathic and allergic pruritus.

4. Treat local yeast or fungal infections with half-strength preparations to avoid excessive reaction.

5. Avoid topical anesthetics because sensitization and increased itching may result.

B. General Measures:

1. Keep the area clean. Use moistened toilet tissue or cloth after each bowel movement. Bland, unscented, nonmedicated soaps or mild detergents such as hexachlorophene may be employed. Carefully blot the area dry to minimize irritation.

2. Institute regular bowel habits. Soften hard stools with hydrophilic agents such as psyllium hydrophilic mucilloid (Metamucil) or dioctyl sodium sulfosuccinate (Colace and many others). Diarrhea must be controlled because watery stools accentuate anal soiling and sensitivity. Mineral oil in any form is contraindicated because the oil seals in irritants and prevents surface drying.

3. Tepid sitz baths or cool compresses of Burow's solution are soothing in acute cases.

4. Shake lotions (eg, noncarbolated calamine) or dusting powders (eg, plain talc or cornstarch) are useful as drying and protective agents.

PROCTALGIA FUGAX

Proctalgia fugax, so-called rectal spasm or rectal neuralgia, is a sudden cramping rectal pain of short duration. It is uncommon but often affects tense and introspective women. It begins without warning, ranges in intensity from marked to agonizing, and tends to recur after a few days or even after months. Its cause is not known for certain, but partial intussusception of redundant rectal mucosa is suspected. The discomfort begins low in the rectum and moves higher (perhaps combined with the urge to defecate) and is associated with sweating, agitation, and even collapse. The pain subsides gradually, leaving the patient weak and shaken.

Rectal examination readily differentiates proctalgia fugax from thrombosed hemorrhoids, fissure in ano, and abscess. The pain of factitial proctitis, which may follow intravaginal radium therapy or local treatment of acute rectal disease, is constant and is accompanied by rectal bleeding and ulceration. Sigmoidorectal obstruction causes extreme, unrelenting progressive pain and is not likely to recur. Painful disorders of the sacroiliac joint may cause diagnostic confusion but are initiated and aggravated by movement. Cauda equina lesions may cause pelvic pain but are associated with paresthesia, hypoesthesia, or weakness of the pelvic floor and sphincter muscles.

The most effective treatment consists of a combination of rectal diathermy, digital massage of the perianal muscles (Thiele's massage), and relaxation exercises. Nitroglycerin, 0.3–0.5 mg sublingually, may abort an attack. Correction of social, emotional, and related medical problems may minimize future rectal spasm. Recurrent attacks should be treated by submucosal injections of 4% phenol in 50% glycerin in water, 1 mL each at 4 points, 1 cm apart, just below the rectosigmoid junction.

HEMORRHOIDS

Hemorrhoids are anorectal varicosities caused by lax pelvic veins, venous stasis, and increased venous pressure. Many women have hemorrhoids of varying degree that often develop during pregnancy or delivery. Causes include weakness of pelvic veins (aging), increased venous pressure (portal hypertension), reduced vascular drainage of the pelvic organs (pregnancy, constipation), or rectal disease (cryptitis). Hereditary factors seem to predispose to hemorrhoids.

Inadequate perivascular support and the absence of vein valves permit reversed venous flow in the hemorrhoidal plexus. Sedentary habits, erect posture, and venous congestion and dilatation accentuate these varices. Repeated trauma to the terminal rectum and anus (eg, large or hard stool) is followed by mucosal fissures and ruptured blood vessels. Bacterial infection may develop in the venous circulation, producing periphlebitis and endophlebitis. Thrombosis or rupture of vessels often results in slough and ulceration.

Internal hemorrhoids lie above the anorectal or mucocutaneous (dentate) line and are derived from the superior and middle hemorrhoidal veins. They are usually located in the right anterior and both posterior quadrants of the rectum, are covered by thin rectal mucosa, and are innervated by autonomic nerves. External hemorrhoids develop below the mucocutaneous line and may appear in any quadrant. They are covered by skin, are supplied by the inferior hemorrhoidal vein, and are innervated by cutaneous nerves. An external hemorrhoid that has thrombosed becomes a small, coagulated perianal hematoma. Combined external and internal hemorrhoids are uncommon, but they may be serious if they involve at least one-third of the anorectal margin.

There are 3 principal symptoms: (1) Protrusion of hemorrhoids may occur suddenly after submucous rupture of veins, thrombosis, or strangulation of an internal hemorrhoid. Anal patulousness encourages prolapse of hemorrhoids. (2) Mild to severe pain is the result of constriction, edema, or strangulation of hemorrhoids. (3) Bleeding—which may be severe—may occur with mucosal laceration, venous distention, obstruction, or ulceration of prolapsed internal hemorrhoids as the result of straining or difficult defecation.(*Note:* One must never assume that hemorrhoids are the cause of gastrointestinal bleeding until careful and complete physical, proctologic, and laboratory studies have failed to reveal tumor, cancer, or other local or systemic disease.)

Prevention

Prevention includes good bowel habits, avoidance of excessive straining at stool, and prompt treatment of anorectal disorders.

Treatment

A. Asymptomatic Hemorrhoids: If there are no symptoms, no treatment is required.

B. Mild or Infrequent Symptoms: Hemorrhoidectomy should be avoided if possible. Prescribe warm sitz baths, astringent ointments or suppositories (eg, Anusol), and analgesics by mouth. Avoid the application of sensitizing local anesthetics or antibiotics. Advise the use of moist cotton or cloth instead of toilet paper, and correct faulty bowel function. The patient should cleanse irritated anal skin tags with moist cotton or cloth, dry, and powder with talc, or use a nonpetrolatum-base cleansing cream.

C. Moderate Symptoms: (Often with large, uncomplicated, internal hemorrhoids.) Treat as for mild symptoms and inject one hemorrhoid a week with 1 mL of 5% quinine and urea solution, 5% phenol in sesame oil, or 5% sodium morrhuate solution through a 22-gauge needle.

D. Severe Symptoms: (Often with large or strangulated hemorrhoids.) Plan for early hemorrhoidectomy unless thrombosis has occurred. Acutely painful, thrombosed external hemorrhoids should be incised under local anesthesia and the clot removed. For the first 24 hours after clot formation, treat as for mild symptoms.

E. During Pregnancy: Treat as for mild symptoms if possible. Injection therapy, cryosurgery, or ligation with rubber bands can be done in the second trimester. Hemorrhoidectomy should be deferred until after the puerperium if possible.

Prognosis

Hemorrhoidectomy is curative. Injection therapy is seldom curative. Use of rubber bands is simple and safe therapy for less severe hemorrhoids.

In spite of many modifications in technique, hemorrhoidectomy often is associated with discomfort, loss of work time, or need for hospitalization. Bleeding, anal stricture, or some degree of incontinence may follow.

CRYPTITIS & PAPILLITIS

Inflammation of the anal crypts and papillae causes pain and burning of brief duration with defecation. Digital and anoscopic examination reveal hypertrophic papillae and infected, often indurated crypts. Stool softeners, eg, psyllium hydrophilic mucilloid (Metamucil) or dioctyl sodium sulfosuccinate (Colace, etc), several times daily by mouth, and analgesic suppositories, eg, Anusol, after each bowel movement help greatly. A single application of 5% phenol in oil into the crypts aids resolution of the inflammation. Surgical excision of involved crypts and papillae should be considered if these measures fail.

ANAL ABSCESS

The acute stage of anal fistula should be considered to be an anal abscess unless there is evidence to the contrary. It must be drained early before the abscess points externally. Antibiotics are of limited value. Hot sitz baths and analgesics usually give symptomatic relief. Because of pain and edema, the internal orifice of a fistula generally cannot be identified; avoid drainage at this site. A few anorectal abscesses arise in the supralevator area and must be differentiated from pelvic abscess; in this instance, drainage by internal sphincterotomy is recommended—rarely through the ischiorectal fossa. Unfortunately, persistent fistulas are common.

The type of rectal pain is a clue to the source. Hemorrhoidal pain usually regresses. Pain from a fissure recurs with defecation. Pain with rectal abscess increases with time.

FISSURE IN ANO

Anorectal mucosal tears usually occur in the midline as a result of overdistention during defecation. A fissure located laterally should be investigated to rule out underlying ulcerative rectocolitis, leukemia, lymphogranuloma venereum, or other disorders. The acute fissure, although temporarily painful and perhaps associated with scant bleeding, generally heals rapidly. Bowel movements should be kept soft, preferably with hydrophilic agents such as dioctyl sodium sulfosuccinate (Colace, etc) or psyllium hydrophilic mucilloid (Metamucil). Prescription of emollient suppositories (eg, Anusol) and the application of a mild styptic such as 1% silver nitrate solution may be beneficial.

Chronic fissures are persistent; either they fail to heal or they heal and break down. They cause severe pain during and after defecation, blood in the stool or after evacuation, faulty bowel habits and constipation because of fear of pain, and eventual development of a sentinel pile, hypertrophic papillae, and anal spasm (especially painful on rectal examination). Prescribe sitz baths, analgesic suppositories, and stool softeners twice daily. Healing is often satisfactory, but excision of the sentinel pile or papilla and the fissure, preferably without suture closure, may be required. Postoperative care is similar to that after hemorrhoidectomy.

ANAL CONDYLOMAS

Anal condylomas are wartlike excrescences on the perianal skin and in the anal canal. The moist, macerated perianal epithelium is a receptive environment for condylomas, particularly when purulent discharges are present. Condylomas are not true tumors; they are the result of viral infection and are therefore autoinoculable. One must distinguish anal condylomas from condylomata lata of syphilis by means of darkfield examination or serologic tests for syphilis.

The treatment of anal condyloma consists of local application of 25% podophyllum resin in tincture of benzoin. Avoid contact with uninvolved skin. Condylomas of the anal canal are treated through the anoscope. The painted site should be dusted with talc to localize the application. Cryosurgery or electrofulguration, under local anesthesia, is effective if there are numerous lesions. Local cleanliness should be stressed.

Since anal condylomas tend to recur, the patient should be instructed to return for additional therapy if new lesions appear.

BENIGN ANORECTAL STRICTURE

Anorectal stricture, contracture, or stenosis may result from congenital maldevelopment, trauma, or infection. This is a common problem of women and may cause difficulty in achieving or completing a bowel movement, pain, bleeding, and small or ribbon-like stools. There are 3 forms: congenital, traumatic, and inflammatory.

Congenital Anorectal Stricture

Congenital anorectal stricture occurs in the newborn as a result of failure of disintegration of the anal

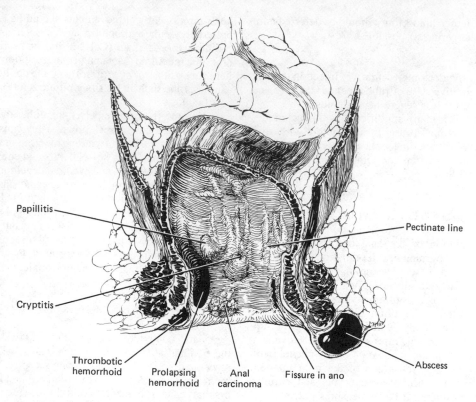

Figure 18–4. Common lesions of the anal canal. (Reproduced, with permission, from Wilson JL: *Handbook of Surgery,* 5th ed. Lange, 1973.)

plate in early fetal life. Progressive and gentle dilatation of the terminal bowel to the diameter of the little finger is often successful in resolving the problem.

Traumatic Anorectal Stricture

Traumatic anorectal stricture is acquired as a complication of surgery (eg, hemorrhoidectomy, fistulectomy) or injury that denudes the epithelium of the anal canal. It predisposes to fissure, proctitis, and fistula. It can generally be prevented by avoidance of infection and cautious postoperative digital dilatation of the anus.

In chronic cases, passage of graduated anal dilators by the patient is recommended. Correction by plastic surgery is necessary in extreme cases.

Inflammatory Anorectal Stricture

Inflammatory anorectal stricture may result from chronic infection after rectal surgery, from lymphogranuloma venereum, or from granuloma inguinale. Lymphogranuloma venereum causes early acute proctitis secondary to lymphatic spread of the organism, usually from the vagina or perineum. Perirectal mixed infection, sinus tract formation, and the growth of scar tissue cause the stricture. The Frei test and the complement fixation test are positive.

About 5% of patients with chronic proctitis and stricture due to venereal disease develop squamous cell carcinoma of the anus or rectum.

Therapy with tetracycline drugs in the initial phase of the disease is usually curative. Dilatation is helpful, but surgery to widen the stricture usually is unsuccessful. Colostomy or abdominoperineal resection may be required.

Granuloma inguinale may cause anorectal infection, fistulas, and stricture. Cellular inclusions (Donovan bodies) in a biopsy specimen indicate the presence of this venereal disorder. Treatment and prognosis are similar to those of lymphogranuloma venereum.

FISTULA IN ANO

Anal fistula is a chronically suppurating rectoperineal tract caused by tuberculosis, amebic or pyogenic infections, and obstetric trauma. A complete fistula has an internal (rectal) and one or more external (perianal) openings. An incomplete or blind fistula has an internal opening only. A blind fistulous opening above the anorectal line is called an internal fistula; below the anorectal line, an external fistula. There is usually only one rectal opening, but there may be numerous anal openings (Fig 18–5).

Over 90% of anal fistulas develop from an anal crypt, usually preceded by anal abscess. Anal fistulas are prevented from healing by persistent drainage of fecal material into or through the tract and by the activity of the sphincter and other pelvic floor muscles.

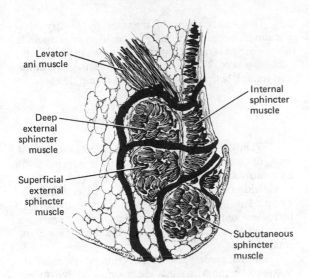

Figure 18–5. Cross section of muscles of anal wall showing usual paths of anal fistulas. (Reproduced, with permission, from Wilson JL: *Handbook of Surgery,* 5th ed. Lange, 1973.)

Pain is reported when the fistula closes temporarily and an abscess develops; drainage brings relief. Periodic soiling by fecal discharge is a common complaint. If the internal opening of a complete fistula is above the sphincter, involuntary passage of flatus may occur.

Devious sinus tracts may cause difficulty in identification of the internal opening. Injection of one part hydrogen peroxide and 2 parts methylene blue into the external openings releases oxygen by contact with the discharges. The blue dye is carried through the tract, and on anoscopic examination the colored solution can be seen to bubble from the opening. For x-ray studies, iodized oil (Lipiodol) injection may outline the fistulous tract.

Intestinal parasites should be identified by means of scrapings and treated with appropriate antiparasitic drugs.

Incision of the entire fistula with excision of all portions of the tract is the only curative treatment. Do not close with sutures, so that healing by granulation will occur. If the fistula is not totally exposed and removed, recurrence is likely. The recurrence rate is 15–25%.

Prompt and adequate treatment of proctitis usually will prevent fistula in ano.

ANAL INCONTINENCE

Anal incontinence may be a result of obstetric lacerations, anorectal operations (especially fistulectomy), and neurologic disorders involving S2–4. When incontinence is the result of trauma or a complication of surgery, operative correction is indicated after the inflammation has subsided and initial healing is complete. Most serious lacerations due to birth injury should not be repaired until about 6 months after delivery. Rectal manometry may be a useful tool to determine whether smooth or striated muscle is primarily involved in some diseases, eg, megacolon, myotonic dystrophy.

ANAL CANCER

Anal cancer, almost always of the squamous cell type, represents only 1–2% of all cancers of the colon, rectum, and anus. It appears as a slightly raised, firm, ulcerative, and slightly tender area in older women. The cause is not known, but chronic granulomatous anal lesions have been incriminated. It is frequently confused with chronic fissure in ano or bleeding hemorrhoids and treated palliatively. It may invade extensively and become difficult to cure; it extends upward into the sphincter and around the anus and metastasizes first to the inguinal glands at a relatively late stage.

Biopsy of suspicious or frankly tumorous anal lesions should be done under local anesthesia. Ample excision of very small anal cancers is sometimes feasible. Unfortunately, most malignancies are large when they are first diagnosed accurately and require abdominoperineal resection and radical groin resection.

The 5-year survival rate is for those afflicted with anal cancer is about 50%. Combined abdominal-perineal resection continues to give the most favorable outcome. Metastases to the inguinal nodes indicate a poor prognosis. Irradiation treatment is unsatisfactory, but chemotherapy may be of value.

PILONIDAL CYST SINUS

Pilonidal cysts arise from distorted hair follicles. A common site is the sacrococcygeal region. If these cysts become infected, an abscess is produced that may be confused with fistula in ano.

Simple incision and drainage and hot pack applications may suffice for the small superficial abscess. Larger abscesses may require marsupialization.

A residual sinus with many ramifications may remain if exteriorization is incomplete. The sinus tract must be excised en bloc and the normal skin edges sutured down and covered with a pressure bandage. Sutures may be removed in a week and hot sitz baths given daily until healing occurs 3–6 weeks later.

Incision may be combined with curettage and cryosurgery. This procedure improves the chance of cure and shortens the hospital stay and period of disability.

COLORECTAL CANCER

Colorectal cancer is a major cause of death due to cancer. It usually affects women 45 years of age or older but may occur in younger women. Familial polyposis, long-standing ulcerative colitis, chronic granuloma inguinale, chronic lymphogranuloma venereum, and villous adenoma of the bowel predispose to the disease. Reduced fiber and increased animal protein in the diet have been accompanied by an increased incidence of colorectal cancer. Having first-degree affected relatives increases the risk.

Patients with altered bowel action, bloody stool, and unexplained anemia or weight loss should be examined for possible colorectal cancer. Nearly two-thirds of these lesions can be identified by rectal examination or sigmoidoscopic study. Occult blood in the stool may be identified by the Hemoccult II modified guaiac test. Nearly half of positive results coincide with the diagnosis of cancer when the test is properly carried out. In any case, a positive test calls for further studies to prove or disprove the diagnosis of cancer and to locate the lesion.

Diverticulitis and bowel dysfunction disorders as well as upper tract gastrointestinal disease may enter into the differential diagnosis.

The only method of prevention is education in the formative years to inculcate the habit of including sufficient fiber in the diet. The only curative treatment is surgical resection of the lesion and the regional lymphatics. In selected cases, radiation in moderate dose makes some cancers resectable but does not appreciably add to the cure rate.

Ninety percent of colorectal cancers are operable, but only about half of afflicted patients survive 5 years. As a preventive measure, periodic sigmoidoscopic study of the colon and rectum in older patients is recommended.

PARASITIC DISEASES

BILHARZIASIS (SCHISTOSOMIASIS)

This trematode (fluke) infection is endemic in Africa and the Middle East, much of Central and South America, some of the Caribbean islands, and southern Asia. The parasites enter the body through the skin or mouth, gain access to the bloodstream, and develop into adult worms. These produce ova that frequently clog the veins of the excretory or genital organs. Pseudotubercules or papillary granulations eventually develop, followed by sloughing and discharge of ova.

Before puberty, genital bilharziasis in females is limited to the vagina and vulva. In contrast, the adult woman may harbor the parasite in the uterus, oviducts, or ovaries. The disease can be serious in the gravid patient because of partial obstruction of the ureters and ascending urinary infection.

The diagnosis is established by finding schistosome ova in the urine, vaginal discharge, stool, or tissue biopsy. Eosinophilia may reach 40%. The lesions may mimic those of cancer, tuberculosis, or venereal disease.

Treatment consists of drug therapy, dietary modifications, surgery, or all 3. Specific drugs include niridazole and sodium antimony dimercaptosuccinate, among others. The prognosis for cure is good in the early stage but poor in late stages of the disease.

AMEBIASIS

When *Entamoeba histolytica* affects the genital tract, the gastrointestinal tract usually is infected also. Symptomatic carriers of amebiasis are found worldwide but are more prevalent in parts of Africa. The parasite generally enters the body in food or drink. Increased orogenital and oral-anal sexual practices have led to a recent rise in the number of cases of amebiasis.

Internal genital amebic infection produces an offensive "anchovy paste" discharge. Friable ulcers may appear in the cervix, vagina, or perineal area and be mistaken for carcinoma, tuberculosis, schistosomiasis, or balantidiasis. The diagnosis is made by identifying the parasite in scrapings or tissue biopsy.

Genital organ or bowel surgery is contraindicated in the presence of amebic infection. If the disease is unrecognized and major surgery is done, the result may be fatal. Inadvertent administration of corticosteroids may activate a latent infection into a serious flare-up.

Treatment with diloxanide emetine, dehydroemetine, diiodohydroxyquin, metronidazole (Flagyl), chloroquine, and other drugs is individualized according to the severity of involvement and the presence or absence of concurrent bacterial infections. The outcome depends on the extent of amebic infection elsewhere in the body. The genital lesions should disappear within 2 weeks with appropriate treatment.

NERVE INJURIES IN OBSTETRICS & GYNECOLOGY

Nerve injuries during the course of obstetric or gynecologic surgical procedures may occur as a result of cutting, tearing, or external pressure. If a cut nerve cannot be reapproximated and sutured, the consequences are permanent. If repair is feasible, regeneration of a nerve and return of function may require several months. In the meantime, physiotherapy is directed to the paralyzed muscles to maintain tone and to prevent contracture of opposing unaffected muscles.

Most of these injuries can be prevented by not using certain instruments, preventing overextension of the extremities, and protecting nerves from prolonged pressure.

OBTURATOR NERVE

The obturator nerve passes downward along the lateral wall of the inner aspect of the lesser pelvis and across the obturator foramen to supply the adductor muscles of the lower extremity. Injury to the nerve may occur with radical pelvic dissection and may lead to inability to adduct the affected thigh.

SUPERFICIAL PERONEAL NERVE

The common peroneal nerve winds around the neck of the fibula and divides beneath the peroneus longus muscle into deep and superficial branches. The latter supplies the peronei muscles. Sensory fibers supply the dorsum of the ankle and contiguous sides of the third, fourth, and fifth toes. Patients anesthetized with the lateral aspect of the upper part of the leg suspended firmly against an unpadded stirrup may sustain injury to the superficial peroneal nerve. As a result, there may be sensory loss on the dorsum of the ankle and motor loss with a foot drop. During the convalescent period, the foot should be held in neutral position by a brace.

BRACHIAL NERVE

The brachial plexus supplies the muscles of the shoulder and upper extremity. Injury of the brachial nerves can occur as a result of overextension of the extremity or from pressure against the shoulderpieces used to support a patient in the Trendelenburg position. Depending on the amount of rotation and overextension of the arm, paralysis of various muscles of the upper extremity may follow. Brachial neuritis can be a painful complication.

FEMORAL NERVE

The femoral nerve passes downward between the psoas major and the iliacus muscle and behind the iliac fascia into the thigh. Motor branches supply the quadriceps femoris muscle and sensory branches to the forepart of the leg and ankle. A ddep self-retaining abdominopelvic retractor may produce enough pressure on the greater psoas muscle to initiate ischemia of the femoral nerve. Neuropathy in this instance may consist of partial loss of extensor action of the leg and loss of sensation over the forepart of the leg and ankle.

ULNAR NERVE

The ulnar nerve passes through a fibrous tunnel at the elbow. This tunnel is beneath the aponeurosis connecting the 2 heads of the flexor carpi ulnaris. Neuropathy, even ulnar palsy, may be a late complication from compression of the arm on the operating table with prolonged pressure of the cubital tunnel. The prognosis is poor. Prevention requires the avoidance of unusual or prolonged restraint.

IDIOPATHIC HYPERPYREXIA

Idiopathic hyperpyrexia is a rare (1:14,000 operations) genetic myopathy involving the neuromuscular system. It begins acutely with induction of general anesthesia. Facial flushing accompanies sudden hyperpyrexia and tonic general muscular contractions. The diagnosis may be confirmed by muscle biopsy or blood platelet bioassay which demonstrates that adenosine triphosphate is significantly decreased on exposure of platelet-rich plasma to halothane.

If hyperpyrexia is undetected during a prolonged period of anesthesia, death is the usual outcome. Early diagnosis and prompt termination of anesthesia may allow recovery. Dantrolene sodium, 1 mg/kg given intravenously to a maximum of 10 mg/kg, may aid in survival. General anesthesia is contraindicated thereafter in all patients with idiopathic hyperpyrexia.

• • •

References

Pelvic Pain

Renaer M et al: Psychological aspects of chronic pelvic pain in women. *Am J Obstet Gynecol* 1979;**134**:75.

Gynecologic Backache

Becker LA: Low back pain in family practice: A case control study. *J Fam Pract* 1979;**9**:579.

Caldwell AB, Chase C: Diagnosis and treatment of personality factors in chronic low back pain. *Clin Orthop* 1977; **129**:141.

Davis P, Lentle BC: Evidence for sacroiliac disease as a common cause of low backache in women. *Lancet* 1978; **2**:496.

Newton JR, Reading AE: An analysis of the intensity and quality of gynecological pain. *Acta Obstet Gynecol Scand* 1980;**59**:143.

Coccygodynia

Grant SR, Salvati EP, Rubin RJ: Levator syndrome: An analysis of 316 cases. *Dis Colon Rectum* 1975;**18**:161.

Anorexia Nervosa

Bistrian BR: A simple technique to estimate severity of stress. *Surg Gynecol Obstet* 1979;**148**:675.

Brown GM, Garner DM: Profile of the anorexia patient. *The Female Patient* 1979;**4**:88.

Parker JB, Blazer D, Wyrick L: Anorexia nervosa: A combined therapeutic approach. *South Med J* 1977;**70**:448.

Rohde J et al: Diagnosis and treatment of anorexia nervosa. *J Fam Pract* 1980;**10**:1007.

Hemorrhagic Disorders

Bachman F: Diagnostic approach to mild bleeding disorders. *Hematology* 1980;**17**:292.

Casciato DA, Scott JL: Acute leukemia following prolonged cytotoxic agent therapy. *Medicine* 1979;**58**:32.

Hobbs J, Wright CS: The hemolytic anemias. *Am Fam Physician* (July) 1979;**20**:83.

Nydegger UE, Miescher PA: Bleeding due to vascular disorders. *Hematology* 1980;**17**:178.

Iron Deficiency Anemia

Marx JJM: Normal iron absorption and decreased red cell iron uptake in the aged. *Blood* 1979;**53**:204.

Narasinga-Rao BS: Physiology of iron absorption and supplementation. *Br Med Bull* 1981;**37**:25.

Goiter

Crile G: Thyroid disease. *The Female Patient* 1979;**4**:74.

Miller JM, Hamburger JI, Kini S: Diagnosis of thyroid nodules: Use of fine-needle aspiration and needle biopsy. *JAMA* 1979;**241**:481.

Noguchi S, Murakami N, Noguchi A: Surgical treatment for Graves' disease: A long term follow-up of 325 patients. *Br J Surg* 1981;**68**:105.

Hypothyroidism

Capiferri R, Evered D: Investigation and treatment of hypothyroidism. *Clin Endocrinol Metab* 1979;**8**:39.

Montoro M et al: Successful outcome of pregnancy in women with hypothyroidism. *Ann Intern Med* 1981;**94**:31.

Sawin CT et al: The aging thyroid: Increased prevalence of elevated serum thyrotropin levels in the elderly. *JAMA* 1979;**242**:247.

Hyperthyroidism

Larsen PR: Hyperthyroidism. *Disease-A-Month* 1976;**22**:No. 10.

Lars-Erik H et al: Malignant thyroid tumors after iodine 131 therapy: A retrospective cohort study. *N Engl J Med* 1980; **303**:188.

Nonspecific Obesity

Bloom WH: Obesity: Medical and surgical management and mismanagement. *South Med J* 1979;**72**:1189.

Shizgal HM et al: Protein malnutrition following intestinal bypass for morbid obesity. *Surgery* 1979;**86**:60.

Straw WE: The treatment of resistant obesity. *The Female Patient* 1981;**6**:55.

Hirsutism

Kuttenn F: Oral cyproterone with percutaneous estradiol used in hirsutism. *J Clin Endocrinol Metab* 1980;**51**:1107.

Treatment of hirsutism. *Med Lett Drugs Ther* 1981;**23**:15.

Vaughn TC, Hammond CB: Diagnosing and treating the hirsute woman. *Contemp Obstet Gynecol* 1980;**15**:25.

Vigersky RH et al: Treatment of hirsute women with cimetidine. *N Engl J Med* 1980;**303**:1046.

Alopecia

Alopecia areata. (Editorial.) *Br Med J* 1979;**1**:505.

Goette DK, Odom RN: Alopecia in crash dieters. *JAMA* 1976; **235**:2622.

Rhodes EJ et al: Alopecia areata regrowth induced by *Primula obconica. Br J Dermatol* 1981;**104**:339.

Abnormal Pigmentation

Kramer KJ, Eaglestein WH: Problems in pigmentation. *J Fla Med Assoc* 1976;**63**:62.

Masu S et al: Ultrastructural studies on the development of pigmentary incontinence. *Yale J Biol Med* 1980;**53**:440.

Nordlund JJ et al: Anti-pigment cell factors and microcutaneous candidiasis. *Arch Dermatol* 1981;**117**:210.

Urinary Tract Infections

Fowler JE, Pulaski ET: Excretory urography, cystography and cystoscopy in the evaluation of women with urinary tract infections: A prospective study. *N Engl J Med* 1981; **304**:462.

Garibaldi RA et al: Meatal colonization and catheter associated bacteriuria. *N Engl J Med* 1980;**303**:316.

Nagamatsu GR: How to control the female urethritis syndrome. *The Female Patient* 1978;**3**:66.

Winick RN et al: Urine culture after treatment of uncomplicated cystitis in women. *South Med J* 1981;**74**:166.

Urinary Incontinence

Cantor TJ, Bates CP: A comparative study of symptoms and objective urodynamic findings in 214 incontinent women. *Br J Obstet Gynaecol* 1980;**87**:889.

Elder DD, Stephenson TP: An assessment of the Frewen regime in the treatment of detrusor dysfunction in females. *Br J Urol* 1980;**52**:467.

Green TH Jr: Selection of vaginal or suprapubic approach in operative treatment of urinary stress incontinence. *Clin Obstet Gynecol* 1977;**20**:881.

Hodgkinson CP, Drukker BH: Infravesical nerve resection for detrusor dyssynergia. *Acta Obstet Gynecol Scand* 1977; **56**:401.

Rud T: The effects of estrogens and gestagens on the urethral pressure profile in urinary continent and stress incontinent women. *Acta Obstet Gynecol Scand* 1980;**59**:265.

Tanagho EA: If the complaint is incontinence, determine pressure profile. *Contemp Obstet Gynecol* 1980;**15**;105.

Disorders of the Urethra

Altman BL: Treatment of urethral syndrome with triamcinolone acetonide. *J Urol* 1976;**116**:583.

Bracken RB et al: Primary carcinoma of the female urethra. *J Urol* 1976;**116**:188.

Ostergard DR: Lower urinary tract symptoms: The role of the urethra. *The Female Patient* 1979;**4**:30.

Urethral Stricture

Walther PC, Parsons CL, Schmidt JD: Direct vision internal urethrotomy in the management of urethral strictures. *J Urol* 1980;**123**:497.

Waterhouse K, Laungani G, Patil U: The surgical repair of membraneous uretheral strictures: Experience with 105 consecutive cases. *J Urol* 1980;**123**:500.

Urethral Caruncle

Drutz HP: Diagnosing conditions of the urethra. *The Female Patient* 1977;**2**:30.

Urethral Diverticulum

Lapides J: Transurethral treatment of urethral diverticula in women. *J Urol* 1979;**121**:736.

Woodhouse CRJ et al: Urethral diverticulum in females. *Br J Urol* 1980;**52**:305.

Disorders of the Bladder

Khanna OP: Disorders of micturition: Neuropharmacologic basis and results of drug therapy. *Urology* 1976;**8**:316.

Robertson JR: Q & A about urinary tract infection. *Contemp Obstet Gynecol* 1977;**2**:83.

Vitenson JH, Gabstald H, Whitmore WF: Ten thousand or more rads supervoltage irradiation to the bladder: Efficacy, sequelae and management. *J Urol* 1972;**107**:973.

Ureteral Stone

Broadus AE, Thier SO: Metabolic basis of renal-stone disease. *N Engl J Med* 1979;**300**:839.

O'Flynn JD: The treatment of ureteric stones: Report on 1120 patients. *Br J Urol* 1980;**52**:436.

Ovarian Vein Syndrome

Bellina JH: Ovarian vein syndrome: Diagnosis and management. *Contemp Obstet Gynecol* 1973;**2**:69.

Urinary Tract Injury

Clark P, Hosmane RU: Re-implantation of the ureter. *Br J Urol* 1976;**48**:31.

Davis RS, Linke CA, Kraemer GK: Use of labial tissue in repair of urethrovaginal fistula and injury. *Arch Surg* 1980;**115**:628.

Mattingly RF, Borkof HI: Acute operative injury to the lower urinary tract. *Clin Obstet Gynecol* 1978;**5**:123.

Acute Appendicitis

Kinning WK, Maull KI, Halloran LG: Postoperative appendicitis. *South Med J* 1980;**73**:732.

Murray HW, Soave R: Appendicitis with perforation: A reminder to internists. *South Med J* 1980;**73**:730.

Savrin RA et al: Chronic and recurrent appendicitis. *Am J Surg* 1979;**137**:355.

Hernias

Greenburg AG, Saik RP, Peskin GW: Expanded indications for preperitoneal hernia repair: The high risk patient. *Am J Surg* 1979;**138**:149.

Ralph DNL et al: How accurately can direct and indirect inguinal hernias be distinguished? *Br Med J* 1980;**280**:1039.

Rutledge RH: Cooper's ligament repair for adult groin hernias. *Surgery* 1980;**87**:601.

Intestinal Injuries in Surgery

Matolo NM, Cohen SE, Wolfuran EF: Effects of antibiotics on prevention of infection in contaminated abdominal operations. *Am Surg* 1976;**42**:123.

Ridley JH: Anatomical complications of pelvic gynecologic surgery. *Am Surg* 1976;**42**:706.

Pruritis Ani

Atarax (hydroxyzine). *Med Lett Drugs Ther* 1980;**11**:22.

Friend WG: The cause and treatment of idiopathic pruritus ani. *Dis Colon Rectum* 1977;**20**:40.

Sullivan ES, Garnjobst WM: Symposium on colon and anorectal surgery. Pruritus ani: A practical approach. *Surg Clin North Am* 1978;**58**:505.

Proctalgia Fugax

Cohen KD: Proctalgia fugax after coitus. (Letter.) *Med Aspects Hum Sexual* (April) 1979;**13**:113.

Sinaki M, Merritt JL, Stillwell GK: Tension myalgia of the pelvic floor. *Mayo Clin Proc* 1977;**52**:717.

Hemorrhoids

Barrios G, Khubchandani M: Urgent hemorrhoidectomy for hemorrhoidal thrombosis. *Dis Colon Rectum* 1979;**22**:159.

Marino AW et al: Symposium on anorectal surgery: Hemorrhoids. *Dis Colon Rectum* 1980;**23**:211.

Takano M: Anoderm-preserving hemorrhoidectomy. *Dis Colon Rectum* 1980;**23**:544.

Anal Abscess

Hanley PH: Anorectal supralevator abscess: Fistula in ano. *Surg Gynecol Obstet* 1979;**148**:899.

Sohn N: Patterns of rectal pain. *The Female Patient* 1979;**4**:82.

Fissure in Ano

Abcarian H: Surgical correction of chronic anal fissure: Results of lateral internal sphincterotomy vs fissurectomy-midline sphincterotomy. *Dis Colon Rectum* 1980;**23**:31.

Friend WG: Anorectal problems: Surgical incisions for complicated anal fistulas. *Dis Colon Rectum* 1975;**18**:652.

Fistula in Ano

Hanley PH: Rubber band seton in the management of abscess–anal fistula. *Ann Surg* 1978;**187**:435.

Parks AG, Gordon PH, Hardcastle JD: A classification of fistula-in-ano. *Br J Surg* 1976;**63**:1.

Parks AG, Russell WS: The treatment of high fistula-in-ano. *Dis Colon Rectum* 1976;**19**:487.

Anal Incontinence

Shafik A: A new concept of the anatomy of the anal sphincter mechanism and the physiology of defecation. 11. Anal incontinence: A technique of repair. *Dis Colon Rectum* 1981;**32**:18.

Anal Cancer

Al Jurf AS, Turnbull RB, Fazio VW: Local treatment of squamous cell carcinoma of the anus. *Surg Gynecol Obstet* 1979;**148**:576.

Key JC, Whitehead WA: Surgical treatment of carcinoma of the anus. *South Med J* 1980;**73**:131.

Pilonidal Cyst Sinus

Bascom J: Pilonidal diseases: Origin from follicles of hairs and results of follicle removal as treatment. *Surgery* 1980; **87**:567.

Gaga AA, Dutta P: Cryosurgery for pilonidal disease. *Am J Surg* 1977;**133**:249.

Pilipshen SJ et al: Carcinoma arising in pilonidal sinuses. *Ann Surg* 1981;**193**:506.

Colorectal Cancer

Ghossein NA et al: The treatment of locally advanced carcinoma of the colon and rectum by a surgical procedure and radiotherapy postoperatively. *Surg Gynecol Obstet* 1979; **148**:917.

Lipkin M: Dietary, environmental, and hereditary factors in the development of colorectal cancer. *CA* 1979;**29**:291.

Martin EW et al: Colorectal carcinoma in patients less than 40 years of age: Pathology and prognosis. *Dis Colon Rectum* 1981;**24**:25.

New screening test for colorectal cancer developed in Canada. (Editorial.) *JAMA* 1979;**242**:1005.

Infectious Disease (Metazoal)

Felman YM: Approaches to sexually transmitted amebiasis. *Bull NY Acad Med* 1981;**57**:201.

Krogstad DJ, Spencer HC Jr, Healy GR: Current concepts in parasitology: Amebiasis. *N Engl J Med* 1978;**298**:262.

Warren KS: The relevance of schistosomiasis. *N Engl J Med* 1980;**303**:203.

Nerve Injuries in Obstetrics & Gynecology

Simeone FA: Acute and delayed traumatic peripheral entrapment neuropathies. *Surg Clin North Am* 1972;**52**:1329.

Spinner M, Spencer PS: Nerve compression lesions of the upper extremity: A clinical and experimental review. *Clin Orthop* 1974;**104**:46.

Strader RP: Postoperative ulnar neuropathy. *JAMA* 1980; **243**:1233.

Hyperpyrexia During General Anesthesia

Solomons CC, McDermott N, Mahowald M: Screening for malignant hyperthermia with a platelet bioassay. *N Engl J Med* 1980;**303**:642.

Willner JH et al: Increased myophosphorylase A in malignant hyperthermia. *N Engl J Med* 1980;**303**:138.

Pediatric & Adolescent Gynecology | 19

John W. Huffman, MD

It was not fully appreciated until recent years, even by physicians, that female infants, children, and adolescents might develop the same gynecologic disorders as women. Many parents and some doctors still do not believe that inspection of the genitalia is a necessary part of the routine examination and that a complete gynecologic examination is mandatory whenever a child has symptoms of a genital disorder.

Inspection of the external genitalia during a well child examination often permits early detection of infection, labial adhesions, congenital anomalies, and even genital tumors. Women have periodic gynecologic examinations, and their daughters should be treated similarly.

Sufficient time should be spent in becoming acquainted with the child and in appraising the mother-child relationship. The questions asked depend on the patient's age and her problem. It may be that a better history can be obtained if the mother is not present during the first part of the interview so that a direct relationship can be established with the patient, particularly if she is an adolescent. This is especially true when the disorder may be sex-related. Even though a presenting complaint may ultimately prove to be of little significance, the problem should be explored thoroughly. Some conditions can be managed expeditiously after a short history and a brief examination; others may defy the diagnostic skill of the most experienced clinician.

It is essential that the young patient be approached in an unhurried and gentle manner. Children withdraw immediately when a doctor or nurse is brusque or hurried. They respond positively to a patient and kindly examiner who demonstrates interest. Older girls may be too embarrassed to cooperate at first and must be won over rather than instructed not to be "so silly." Small children who resist the examination may have been hurt during a previous medical experience. If one excludes the mother from the examining room or if the fearful parts of the examination can be deferred, the examination usually will be successful. If a child cannot cooperate, one should not attempt to examine her by force; if digital examination is essential, a general anesthetic may be necessary. The older girl usually will permit examination if she is assured that, although it may be embarrassing, it will not be unduly painful.

ANATOMIC & PHYSIOLOGIC CONSIDERATIONS

In considering the anatomy and physiology of the immature genitalia, it is well to recall that the anatomic structure of the internal and external genital organs does not necessarily establish the genetic sex of the individual. Animal experiments indicate that the gonadectomized embryo of either genetic sex will develop female genitalia and that implantation of embryonic testes into an ovariectomized female fetus will produce morphologically male genitalia. In some species, when a young male embryo is united parabiotically with an older female embryo, the testes of the former are transformed into histologically recognizable ovaries. Therefore, it would appear that the embryonic testis, at a critical time in embryonic growth, normally produces a substance that activates the development of male structures and inhibits the growth of paramesonephric (müllerian) derivatives that would persist if no testes were present.

During early infancy, the female genitalia retain the morphologic characteristics of late fetal life. The stimulating effect of maternal estrogen on the genitalia of the newborn, which was evident at birth, soon subsides. Except for a modest increase in size, there are relatively few changes in the genital organs during early childhood. The period of late childhood is one of gradually accelerating genital and somatic development. Genital growth before the menarche does not keep pace with somatic growth, however. The genitalia actually complete their maturation after the menarche and do not develop their full functional capacities until somatic maturation has created structures suitable for reproduction.

Genital changes that occur during childhood are the result of many factors. Most important are endocrine, genetic, familial, nutritional, and climatic influences. The effect of illness on genital growth varies according to the nature, severity, and duration of disease. Genital development can be adversely affected when physical growth is retarded by inadequate nutrition or medical care.

It is helpful to divide the time between birth and maturity into the following periods, each characterized by specific morphologic changes:

(1) The neonatal period, typified by marked maternal estrogen stimulation.

(2) The period of early childhood, characterized by minimal endogenous estrogen stimulation.

(3) The period of late childhood, during which augmented endogenous estrogen production is evident.

(4) The premenarcheal period, when signs of active cyclic ovarian function are present.

(5) The period of early adolescence, heralded by the menarche and characterized by periodic uterine anovulatory bleeding.

(6) The period of late adolescence, characterized by ovulatory menstruation and continued growth of the still immature uterus.

This categorization does not correspond with the usual pediatric growth span because, in the pediatric sense, childhood (during which the child is of school age) extends across 2 or more gynecologic periods. A description of these periods is presented below.

Neonatal Period

The effect of maternal estrogen on the newborn is particularly evident in the hymen, which initially is turgid and purple-red. It covers the external urethral orifice and projects from the slightly gaping vulva (Fig 19–1). In addition, the labia are soft, rounded, and full.

The thick, pink vaginal mucosa is pleated into many slack, soft folds covered by grayish-white curdlike or mucoid secretion. The former consists of cervical mucus and desquamated vaginal cells.

On the day after birth, large nucleated superficial cells are visible in the vaginal smear. They are for the most part basophilic. About the fourth day, sail- or boat-shaped epithelial cells with markedly pyknotic

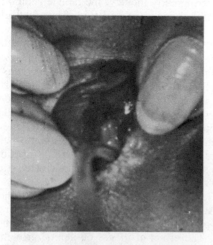

Figure 19–1. The external genitalia of a newborn female. A soft catheter has been passed through the introitus to demonstrate vaginal patency. Turgor of the vulvar tissues is a response to estrogen. (Reproduced [as are a number of other illustrations in this chapter] from Huffman JW: *The Gynecology of Childhood and Adolescence.* Saunders, 1968.)

nuclei appear in increased numbers. Also, small oval endometrial cells are present whose appearance often coincides with occult bleeding from the genital aperture. The end of the postnatal period is marked by the appearance of basal cells from the deeper layers, usually 13–24 days after delivery and rarely later than 18 days.

The cervix secretes a considerable amount of mucus which, together with exfoliated vaginal cells, coats the vulva of the newborn under normal circumstances. This discharge is important because it demonstrates that a patent tract exists distal to the cervix. The absence of mucus suggests some form of genital atresia, usually an imperforate hymen.

As a result of maternal estrogen, the fetal uterus at term is larger than it will be again until the child is 9–10 years old. The cervix is twice the size of the corpus. The uterus, which is a large organ in comparison with the other pelvic viscera, weighs about 4.2 g. In form it resembles a rounded mushroom with a large stem, the cervix, and a small cap, the corpus. The outline of the uterus is generally conical, oriented with the base downward and a depression in the apex. It lies between the symphysis pubica and pelvis because anteversion has not yet been established. The cylindric epithelium of the endocervix and the smooth squamous epithelium of the external cervix meet at the external cervical os. At this point, the squamous epithelium is often displaced by the cylindric epithelium, producing a reddened zone of "physiologic eversion."

The estrogen-induced changes in the genital organs of the newborn usually disappear in about 3 weeks, during which time the maternal hormones are excreted mainly in the urine. During the neonatal period the vagina has an acid reaction, with a pH of approximately 5.0. Vaginal cultures at this time produce a heavy growth of lactobacilli with relatively few other organisms.

Early Childhood

The period of early childhood lasts about 8 years. Its duration depends on genetic (racial) and individual characteristics. The small amounts of hormones produced by the adrenals and the ovaries are not sufficient to produce any changes in the genitalia or the secondary sex organs.

Following the excretion of maternal estrogen, the hymen and other genitalia undergo postnatal involution. The hymen is reduced to a thin, almost dry structure with a sharp edge and pinkish-red color. The smooth skin that completely covers the labia minora has the same appearance as hairless skin elsewhere on the body. The prepuce of the clitoris is hidden in the small cleft of the vulva. The mucous membrane of the introitus is pink and somewhat moist (Fig 19–2).

With postnatal involution, the vaginal epithelium becomes thinner. As a result, the vaginal mucosa appears pale, smooth, and moist. Histologically, it consists of only a few layers of epithelial cells. The withdrawal of maternal estrogen can be demonstrated on a smear at about the sixth day after birth by observation

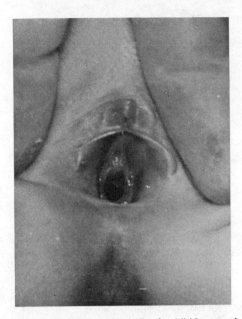

Figure 19–2. The external genitalia of a child 3 years of age.

of cells from the deeper layers of the mucous membrane. Finally, the parabasal cells become very scanty; eventually, the smaller basal cells (which have a large, centrally situated nucleus) also are found only occasionally in a cytosmear.

The vaginal reaction during this period is neutral or slightly alkaline and the vagina is almost without bacteria. A cytosmear made from what little vaginal secretion is present usually will reveal only a few epithelial cells and an occasional leukocyte. The bacterial flora varies according to the area from which the smear is taken. Secretion from near the hymenal orifice is likely to contain bacteria from the skin and the gastrointestinal tract; a cytosmear from the proximal portion of the vaginal canal will contain only occasional bacteria or vaginal cells.

The uterus of the newborn slowly regresses in size after withdrawal of the maternal hormones. Its weight decreases to half of its weight at birth by the end of the second year of life. It also becomes considerably shorter, but its main characteristic persists, ie, the large size of the cervix in relation to the size of the corpus. The corpus of the uterus flattens out from anterior to posterior to a thickness of only about 4 mm at the point of insertion of the round ligaments. The uterus remains in this form and size for several years. It gains 1 g in weight up to the eighth year of life, and only when the child is approximately 9 years old does the uterus again reach the weight of the newborn organ.

These characteristics of the child's uterus have practical significance: The small, thin corpus cannot be felt rectally or by manual palpation. The firm, roller-shaped structure discovered by touch in the pelvis is only the cervix. In describing the examination, this fact should be mentioned and the size of the cervix

estimated. At laparotomy on a female child, the operator cannot rely on inspection to determine the size and shape of the uterus. Palpation may show the uterus to be merely a strip of dense tissue in the anteromedial part of the broad ligament. If the adnexa must be removed, the operator who is unacquainted with the anatomy of the immature pelvis may cut the round ligaments, the attachments of the uterus to the pelvic wall, and may even excise a portion of the cornua of the uterus.

One of the startling changes in the child's ovary is the presence of occasional multinuclear oocytes and multiovular follicles during infancy. They virtually disappear by the time of menarche. Moreover, the cuboid cells of the surface epithelium of the ovary flatten out and come to resemble the endothelial cells of the peritoneum. In addition, the tunica albuginea becomes more dense. As the number of primordial follicles decreases, the width of the cortex is reduced. Most of the slight enlargement of the ovary during childhood is due to an increase in stroma. It has also been shown that the stroma of the ovary is not a static entity during childhood because it changes as the gonad grows. This is particularly evident when one examines the subepithelial reticular fibrils that, in infancy, lie parallel with the surface but during development alter their position to become vertical to the surface. The significance of this change is not known.

Late Childhood

Signs of sexual growth begin to appear in the external genitalia of most girls when they are 8–9 years old. The mons pubis becomes thickened. Genital hair appears first, usually as a sparse growth in the midline over the mons pubis; it gradually becomes heavier and thicker, and by the menarche it is well developed. Hair growth on the outer surfaces of the labia majora usually is not present until after menstruation has become established (see Fig 3–5).

The labia minora finally lose their thin edges to become rounded, full, and soft. The clitoris also shows a slight increase in size. An adherent clitoral prepuce may spontaneously separate as a result of augmented estrogen stimulation during the years preceding the menarche. At about this time, the urethral hillock becomes more prominent. The hymen loses its thin, almost transparent character to gradually become thicker. The hymenal orifice, which averages about 0.4 mm in diameter, increases gradually in size and measures at least 0.7 mm when evidence of estrogen stimulation is grossly visible in the vulvovaginal tissues.

Gradual deposition of fat increases the size and fullness of the labia majora. The surface of the labia soon develops fine wrinkles that become more marked during the immediate premenarcheal period. There are also signs of sebaceous gland activity before puberty. By the time of menarche, the labia majora usually are sufficiently well developed to lie in apposition and cover the vestibule.

The response of the vaginal epithelium to the

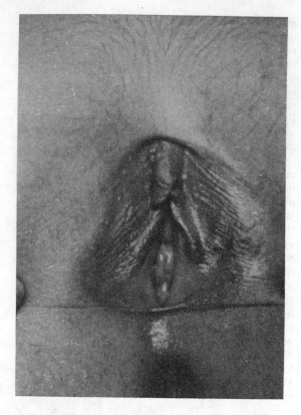

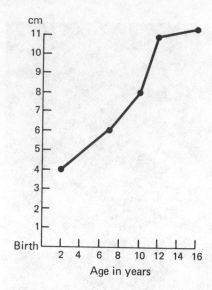

Figure 19–4. Graph showing the increasing length of the vagina from birth to maturity.

Figure 19–3. The external genitalia of a child 11 years of age. Early estrogen response is evidenced by the fuller labia, wrinkling of the vulvar mucosa, and thickening of the hymen.

onset of ovarian secretory function, demonstrable in cytosmears, occurs earlier and is more specific than that of the breasts and pudendal hair. Visible changes in vaginal structure, however, lag behind gross differentiation of the secondary sex organs.

Lengthening of the vagina is one of the first gross signs of sexual growth. During early childhood, the average length of the vaginal canal is 4.5–5.5 cm. The length averages 8 cm by the time the vagina shows

clearly defined estrogen response. At the menarche, the vagina has a length of 10.5–11.5 cm (Fig 19–4).

Vaginoscopic visualization of the upper third will show some thickening and less hyperemia of the mucosa adjacent to the cervix, although the epithelium of the distal third of the vagina, like that of the vulva, is still thin and hyperemic. These signs of beginning maturation gradually spread downward in the mucosa. Changes in vaginal cytology during late childhood usually are the first indicators of endogenous ovarian hormonal secretion.

Estrogen causes the uterus to begin to enlarge from about 6 years, and it grows rapidly during the year preceding the menarche (Fig 19–5). The body of the uterus grows more rapidly than the cervix. Normally, however, it is not until the girl is at least 10 years old that the length of the corpus equals that of the cervix. Even so, the uterus of a girl in the immediate premenarcheal period who shows every evidence of a normal estrogen secretion frequently will have a

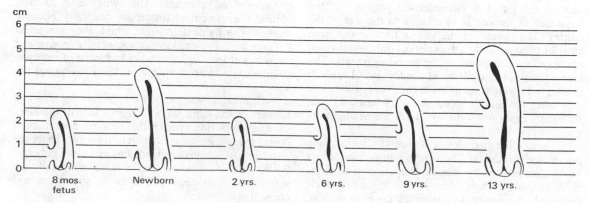

Figure 19–5. Relative increase in size of the uterus as childhood progresses.

disproportionately long cervix, typical of incomplete development. The altered shape of the uterus occurs primarily as a result of myometrial proliferation rather than of endometrial development. The endometrium does not actually participate in the growth of the uterus until menarche is impending. Before that time, there is a gradual thickening of the endometrium and a modest increase in the depth and complexity of the endometrial glands. Endometrial proliferation occurs rapidly before the first period.

The endocervical mucosa remains essentially unchanged during childhood, and it is not until menstruation that epithelial growth creates the glandular structure of the adult cervix. Again, as it was in the neonatal period, eversion of the cylindric epithelium will sometimes be found on the external cervix; this, however, is not a "congenital erosion" but an eversion of the mucosa of the endocervix.

The ovaries, heretofore spindle-shaped and elongated, gradually become larger and somewhat almond-shaped as the menarche approaches. They drop lower in the pelvis. The number of larger follicles, which are in various stages of development, increases. None of them, however, go on to ovulation. Instead, some may grow to considerable size and then regress.

Premenarcheal Period

The premenarcheal period is characterized by the effects of estrogen from the girl's own ovaries. The hymen increases in thickness; its edge, once sharp, becomes blunted, and irregularities re-form. The edges of the hymen lie together, forming a sagitally oriented convex structure that projects into the vestibule and closes off the vagina. The hymenal and vaginal mucosas are more pink and moist, indicating increased estrogen secretion. Marked thickening of the vaginal mucosa, which develops in the premenarcheal period, is also the result of estrogen production. The vaginal rugae give the vaginal lining a ruffled appearance. A multilayered pavement epithelium that is higher than in the neonatal period is formed. The cytologic picture is comparable to that seen in smears from the vagina of an anovulatory postmenarcheal girl.

The greatly increased amount of vaginal fluid that appears during the 3–12 months preceding the menarche consists largely of desquamated, adult-type intermediate and superficial epithelial cells from the vaginal mucosa. Some of the cells are cornified. Grossly, the fluid is curdlike or thick, grayish-white, odorless material that adheres to the vaginoscope or speculum. The distinctive odor of the normal adult vaginal mucus is not perceptible until after the menarche. Some mucoid secretion from the cervical and major vestibular glands may be mixed with a considerable amount of desquamated epithelium immediately before and after the menarche. The reaction of the vagina again becomes acid, with a pH usually ranging between 4.5 and 5.5. The pH serves as a rough indicator of estrogen response because it is lower as the estrogen titer rises. This index, however, lags behind the change in vaginal cytology as a measure of ovarian activity.

The copious vaginal fluid produced by girls near menarche suggests that they have an abnormal discharge. Microscopic examination of the fluid, gynecologic examination, and properly obtained cultures usually will enable the physician to assure all concerned that the patient is free of vaginal infection.

The increased secretion of estrogen during the premenarcheal period is associated with a change of the vaginal flora. Mixed cultures may still be obtained from the vaginas of girls in this age group. Nonetheless, there is a marked increase in the number of patients who have an almost pure culture of lactobacilli. Cultures from others usually show a decrease in the growth of staphylococci and coliform bacteria. This may be due to the unfavorable environment for bacterial growth created by an acid vaginal fluid, to the greater care used in obtaining cultures, or to the greater ease with which they are obtained in older women. In the author's experience, none of the cultures from premenarcheal girls who were free of vulvovaginitis contained *Trichomonas vaginalis, Gardnerella (Haemophilus) vaginalis,* mycotic organisms, or neisseriae.

Only when the secondary sex characteristics have developed and the menarche is approaching does the uterus assume its final form. The corpus attains a size equal to that of the cervix and becomes palpable. As the menarche approaches, the uterus takes on the shape of an hourglass formed of the cervix and the corpus.

The ovary, in contrast to the other internal genital organs, increases in weight constantly and grows from birth onward; nonetheless, as it grows, the number of follicles it contains becomes fewer. Ovulation normally does not occur until after several menstrual periods; rarely, ovulation will precede the first period.

Secondary sex characteristics develop during the late premenarcheal period, often rapidly. The figure, which during early childhood differed little from a boy's, becomes rounded, especially in the shoulders and hips. The pubic hair pattern assumes the characteristic triangle with the base above the mons pubis. Hair growth in the axillas appears later as a result of adrenocorticosteroid hormone stimulation.

The major vestibular (Bartholin) glands are properly included with the other genital organs. They are apparently without secretion during the neonatal and early childhood periods but begin to produce mucus just prior to menarche.

The second stage of breast development appears when the areolae become raised in a domelike fashion. The color of the areolae is dependent on individual pigment type: in blonds, pink; in brunets, brown. The third stage of development is characterized by the deposition of fat and growth of the glandular elements. As a result, the breast begins to form a cone-shaped projection. In the fifth or fully developed stage, the nipple projects above the areola and becomes erectile in response to thermal or tactile stimuli (see Fig 3–5).

Period of Early Adolescence

Early adolescence begins with the menarche and ends with the first ovulation. This interval may last only 1–2 months; it is omitted if a girl ovulates before the menarche. As a rule, this phase lasts 3–12 months.

As the first period draws near, the vulvar sebaceous glands become more active. Döderlein's bacilli replace the sparse, mixed bacteria as the predominant vaginal flora. The vaginal canal lengthens and widens. The uterus tends to become anteflexed as it develops breadth. Tubal peristalsis appears at the menarche but is not striking until ovulation occurs. The broad ligaments become wider and the pelvic recesses deepen. The internal genitalia drop lower into the true pelvis. Without specific evidence of ovulation obtained by basal body temperature or endometrial biopsy, it is impossible to determine when an adolescent girl becomes fertile. Even if she is able to produce a fertilizable ovum, she is neither sexually nor somatically mature until genital and body growth are completed; for most girls, this is about the time of the 16th birthday. Even then, she may not be psychologically mature.

GYNECOLOGIC EXAMINATION OF THE INFANT

An infant girl should have her first gynecologic examination in the delivery room or the nursery. Inspection of the external genitalia should be considered part of the routine general examination.

The general appearance of the newborn may reveal congenital anomalies or disorders that may affect her somatic and sexual growth. Moreover, the child with gonadal dysgenesis often has multiple anomalies. The newborn baby should be reexamined if she has vaginal bleeding for more than 3 days, because of the possibility of vaginal or uterine tumor.

It is not surprising that anomalies of the urinary tract and genital organs frequently occur together, considering their similarity of embryologic origin. About 65% of females with upper urinary tract malformation have genital anomalies, and approximately 30% of females with genital anomalies also have malformation of the upper urinary tract.

The general examination may disclose abnormalities that suggest a genital abnormality. Examples are the low nuchal hairline and edema of the dorsum of the hands and feet in infants with Bonnevie-Ullrich syndrome.

The infant's abdomen should be inspected and palpated; ovarian tumors, together with other types of intra-abdominal neoplasms, occasionally have been reported in newborns. Inguinal hernias infrequently are discovered at birth; nevertheless, when one is present, and particularly if there is a gonad in the hernial sac, the possibility exists that the child is a genetic male and that the gonad is a testis. An inguinal hernia must be distinguished from a cyst of the canal of Nuck, however.

Major anomalies of the external genitalia should be identified at birth or soon after. Nonetheless, the physician cannot be expected to diagnose abnormalities of the internal genitalia until later in life.

Clitoral enlargement in the newborn almost always will be associated with a persistent urogenital sinus or other anomaly. Most often the infant will have congenital adrenocortical hyperplasia, but other causes must be considered.

The hymenal orifice usually is evident when the labia are separated. If not, it can be found by gently inserting a soft rubber catheter. If there is no opening, the infant most likely has an imperforate hymen or vaginal agenesis.

As a rule, the uterus and adnexa cannot be felt on rectal examination of the newborn. Inasmuch as a considerable number of ovarian tumors in newborn infants have been reported, any palpable mass in the pelvis should be investigated further. Negative findings are valuable because they generally exclude pelvic tumors and anomalies.

Digital palpation of the anorectal canal should be part of the examination of every newborn. Passage of meconium is the best evidence of a patent gastrointestinal tract. Digital examination will reveal patency of the anorectal canal and the tone of the anal sphincter.

The infant usually urinates promptly after birth. If it does not, the nurses in the newborn nursery must be alerted to report urinary retention within 3 hours.

GYNECOLOGIC EXAMINATION OF THE PREMENARCHEAL CHILD

History

The signs and symptoms most likely to cause parents to bring a daughter to a physician for a gynecologic examination are listed in Table 19–1. With the exception of brief estrogen withdrawal bleeding from the genitalia of the newborn, all of these symptoms are reasons for examination.

Numerous symptoms that cause the mother apprehension because she fears the child has an infection

Table 19–1. Presenting symptoms in premenarcheal gynecologic patients.

Vulvar inflammations
Vulvar swellings or sores
Vulvovaginal discharge
Vulvovaginal bleeding
Anomalies of the external genitalia
Precocious or delayed sexual maturation
Abdominal pain
Rectal or urinary tract symptoms
Lower abdominal swelling
Suspected foreign body in vagina
Presumed sexual molestation

Table 19–2. Extragenital symptoms in premenarcheal gynecologic patients.

Backache
Constipation
Urinary frequency and dysuria
Headache
Neuropsychiatric disorders
Extraovarian endocrine disorders
Obesity
Masturbation
Abnormal sexual behavior

or a tumor but which are unlikely to be of genital origin are listed in Table 19–2.

Intestinal disorders, particularly constipation, often cause symptoms in little girls and may cause abdominal pain which must be differentiated from that of genital origin.

Backache is an infrequent complaint of children, but this type of pain should alert the examiner to the possibility of a serious urinary, gastrointestinal, or musculoskeletal disorder. It is rarely caused by gynecologic disease.

Abnormal sexual behavior falls within the province of the pediatric psychiatrist, but many patients will be seen first by the gynecologist or generalist. Most girls masturbate occasionally as part of their awakening sexual consciousness, and mothers usually are unnecessarily concerned about it. Abnormal sexual behavior, including abnormally frequent masturbation, is not a result of organic disease of the genitalia nor is it caused by an endocrinologic disturbance.

The disorders responsible for other presenting complaints are listed in Table 19–3. Each of them causes symptoms that are either genital or require differentiation from those caused by genital disease.

Neuropsychiatric disorders may be signaled first by a gynecologic complaint even in young children. Examples are atopic neurodermatitis in a premenarcheal girl who is under emotional tension, or sexual precocity in a child with a central nervous system lesion. Symptoms of anorectal and lower urinary tract problems often are confused with those resulting from genital disorders.

Menstruation before the ninth birthday is consid-

Table 19–3. Disorders causing gynecologic symptoms in premenarcheal patients.

Labial adhesions
Dermatologic disorders of the
    perineum and vulva
Vulvovaginal infections
Anomalies of the genitalia
Vaginal foreign bodies
Abnormal sexual maturation
Abdominal masses
Tumors of the genitalia
Intersex

ered abnormal. Evidence of ovarian activity should be present by age 12. The menarche may be delayed until age 15 without causing undue concern provided there are no other signs of endocrine or systemic disorders. Examination is indicated if the first menstrual period has not occurred by the 15th birthday.

Physical Examination

A. General Inspection: Examination begins with an evaluation of the child's general appearance, eg, body habitus, gross congenital anomalies, unusual muscular development, obesity, or abnormal skeletal growth. Nutritional deficiencies may be factors in genital disorders; eg, severe vitamin B deficiency is manifested by dermatologic disorders of the external genitalia. General uncleanliness means bad perineal hygiene, which is the commonest cause of nonspecific vulvovaginitis in little girls.

B. Breasts: The child's breasts should be inspected and palpated. Engorgement of the breasts is not uncommon in a newborn infant and is not a matter for concern. Occasionally, engorgement will be accompanied by slight secretion for a few days. The breasts usually do not begin budding until age 7–8 years. Prominence of the nipple and breast development in older girls may be the first sign of sexual precocity.

It is quite common and normal for a small, firm, flat "button" to form beneath the nipple at the start of breast growth. Fibrocystic (Schimmelbusch's) disease of the breast is not uncommon near the menarche and must be differentiated from neoplastic disease.

C. Abdomen: Inspection and palpation of the abdomen should precede examination of the genitalia. The examiner's hands must be warm. Tumors of the ovary large enough to be palpated abdominally are likely to be mistaken for other abdominal masses (eg, polycystic kidney) in children. The ovary of the premenarcheal child normally is high in the pelvis; this and the small size of the pelvic cavity tend to force ovarian tumors toward the mid abdomen above the brim of the true pelvis. If the child is ticklish, having her place one hand on or under the examiner's hand usually will overcome that difficulty. Light palpation, moving slowly from one area to the other, will elicit most information.

Inguinal hernia is less common in females than in males (about 1:10). It usually causes no discomfort. An excellent way to demonstrate an inguinal hernia is to have the child stand up and increase the intra-abdominal pressure by blowing up a rubber balloon.

D. Examination of the Genitalia:

1. External genitalia–Inspection of the external genitalia must be an integral part of the routine examination of every premenarcheal child. A gynecologic examination is necessary when a child has symptoms suggesting a genital disorder. Every girl should have a gynecologic examination when she is 8–9 years old to determine whether her secondary sex characteristics are developing normally, that her hymenal orifice is patent, and that she has a normal vagina and is producing estrogen, as evidenced by maturation of the vaginal epithelium.

Children should be permitted to sit up until the time for examination. The infant or small child should then be placed in her mother's or in a nurse's lap or on her back on the examining table. An assistant should separate the child's thighs and bring the knees upward onto the abdomen so that the examiner can inspect the perineum and vulva. A girl 4–5 years old can be examined more expeditiously if she lies in a dorsal recumbent position with her feet in the stirrups of an examining table. If the cervix cannot be found easily with the vaginoscope, the child's legs should be acutely flexed on her abdomen. The Sims position may be used for an apprehensive older girl—her face then is turned away and she cannot see what is being done. The knee-chest position is frightening to small children and uncomfortable for adolescents and is not recommended.

2. Perineum–The perineal and anal areas should be inspected next. Particular note should be taken of whether the mother has properly cleansed the child's anogenital region or if the perineal hygiene practiced by the older girl is adequate. The examiner should look for skin lesions, perineal excoriations, and ulcers or tumors.

3. Vulva and vestibule–The vulva and vestibule must be exposed by light lateral and downward pressure on each side of the perineum (Fig 19–6). The labial skin and subcutaneous tissues and the vulvar mucosa are responsive to estrogen stimulation. They lose their turgescence shortly after birth when the effect of the mother's steroid sex hormones wanes. During early childhood, the labia are flat, the labial skin smooth and pale, and the vulvar mucosa thin and slightly hyperemic. Thickening, wrinkling, and darkening of the labial integument, fullness and swelling of the labia, cornification of the vulvar mucosa, the appearance of pubic hair, and other evidences of sexual maturation normally occur when the child is 7–8 years of age. The presence of signs of hormonal stimulation in early childhood—and their absence when they should be evident—are diagnostically significant in the many endocrinopathic problems associated with precocious or delayed growth of the sexual organs. The patency of the hymenal orifice must be assured. Attention should be paid to vulvar inflammation and to any vulvar and vaginal discharge. The clitoris is normally disproportionately large during infancy, but marked enlargement is diagnostically significant. Preputial adhesions are important.

The vestibule may not be visible because of post-inflammatory adhesions between the labia minora or congenital anomalies. The former frequently are mistaken for vaginal agenesis or an imperforate hymen. A zone of inflammation below the urethral meatus may explain dysuria in a child just as in the postmenopausal woman.

In infancy and childhood, the hymenal orifice normally will admit a vaginoscope 0.5 cm in diameter. An instrument with a diameter of 0.8 cm can be used to examine most older premenarcheal girls. If the aperture is too small for an instrument to be passed without discomfort, vaginoscopy should not be attempted until the child is under general anesthesia. Persistent manipulation of the sensitive tissues without anesthesia will be traumatic and counterproductive.

4. Vagina–The Huffman vaginoscope (Fig 19–7) or a similar instrument may be used. Illumina-

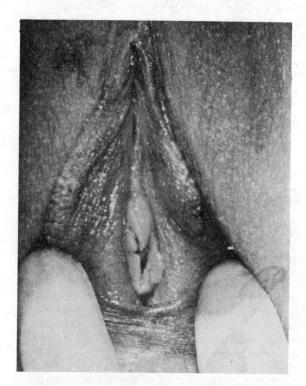

Figure 19–6. The external genitalia of a 12-year-old premenarcheal girl. The menarche occurred 2 months later.

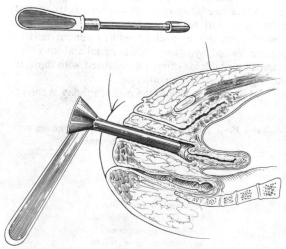

Figure 19–7. The Huffman vaginoscope being used for examination of a premenarcheal child.

tion is obtained with a head mirror or head lamp. In older girls, the Huffman long-bladed adolescent speculum is preferable to the short-bladed Graves instrument. If a vaginoscope is not available, a nasal speculum may be employed for vaginal examination in a premenarcheal child, but the blades tend to stretch the hymen painfully.

In performing vaginoscopy, it must be borne in mind that the immature vagina has a limited capacity and is relatively short and narrow; it does not acquire its adult capaciousness and pliability until after the menarche. The fornices are not formed, and the cervix is a flattened, buttonlike projection. It does not assume its adult form until near the menarche.

Cervical disorders are extremely rare before late adolescence.

The healthy vaginal mucosa in early childhood is pink, thin, and has relatively few rugae. The reaction of the scanty vaginal fluid is neutral or alkaline. In late childhood, the ovary begins to secrete increasing amounts of estrogen. As a result, the vaginal mucosa acquires a lighter and duller pink color, the rugae become more pronounced, and the now acid vaginal fluid increases in amount. The vaginal mucosa and cervix should be examined for evidence of congenital anomalies, inflammation, or tumors.

A foul-smelling, blood-streaked purulent discharge is all but pathognomonic of a foreign body. Inflammation or erosion of the cervix is extremely rare in premenarcheal children. If present, a search should be made for a foreign body. Common foreign bodies found in the vagina are bits of rolled-up ravelings of bedclothes or nightclothes or pellets of toilet tissue. Toys, erasers, beans, crayons, bobby pins, and other small objects have also been removed from children's vaginas.

5. Rectoabdominal palpation–It is impossible to do a digital vaginal examination in a child if the size of the vagina is normal for age. *Gentle* rectal digital examination can be accomplished, however, and should not cause pain. The small size of uterus and ovaries, the firmness of the abdominal wall, and the resistance most children offer to the examination render accurate intrapelvic evaluation difficult. Often it is reasonable to report negative pelvic findings in small children rather than to itemize positive findings. It can be assumed the child has no genital tumor if her uterus and ovaries are not palpable on satisfactory examination. If the presence of a pelvic tumor is suspected and is not found by rectal examination, however, gynecography or laparoscopy should be performed.

Laboratory & Other Procedures

In all cases in which there is a vulvovaginal discharge (except those in which a foreign body is found in the vagina), dry smears should be prepared for microscopic study, cultures made, and hanging drop or wet preparations examined.

A. Cultures: A sterile cotton-tipped applicator may be used for taking a culture if it is inserted through a sterile vaginoscope and if the cotton touches only the deeper part of the vagina. Forcing a dry cotton-tipped applicator through the hymenal orifice invariably picks up contaminating bacteria from the vulva. Also, the dry cotton often adheres to the vaginal rugae and causes pain. Dry cotton is not satisfactory for making wet preparations because it absorbs much of the vaginal fluid. A sterile bacteriologic platinum loop for collecting vaginal discharge is the best instrument. It does not cause pain and absorbs none of the fluid. A sterile adult glass urethral catheter may be used for the same purpose; its fenestrated end usually collects enough material for culture and smears. Occasionally, there is so little discharge in the vagina that neither of the above techniques will be satisfactory. A few drops of sterile nutrient bacteriology broth should then be injected with a sterile eyedropper through a sterile vaginoscope. After a few moments, it should be aspirated with the eyedropper and used to inoculate bacterial culture tubes. The material should be cultured for predominant organisms and *Neisseria gonorrhoeae*. Fresh wet preparations should be examined for mycotic organisms and *Trichomonas vaginalis*. Occasionally, a wet smear obtained from an older youngster who seemingly has a vaginal discharge may show an exuberant exfoliation of superficial vaginal epithelial cells, few leukocytes, and no pathogenic organisms. The proper diagnosis in such cases is excessive normal vaginal fluid, not vaginitis.

B. Vaginal Smears: Material from perineal skin scrapings or stool specimens should be examined for pinworm ova in all cases of intractable vulvovaginitis in little girls.

C. Vaginal Cytosmears: Vaginal cytosmears, stained by the Papanicolaou technique, should reveal an estrogen response of the vaginal epithelium before there is evidence of estrogen stimulation elsewhere. In rare instances in children, smears will aid in the diagnosis of genital neoplasia.

The technique of obtaining a vaginal cytosmear in children differs from that used in adults. A cotton applicator will absorb what little vaginal fluid there is and will cause the epithelium to desquamate so that a false maturation index will be obtained. Satisfactory cytosmears of the vagina can be obtained, however, if a few drops of tissue fixative solution (Mayer's albumin and glycerin solution) are injected into the vagina. After a few seconds, the solution and the vaginal cells in it should be aspirated with an eyedropper and smeared on a slide. The smear can then be processed in the same way as cytosmears from adult patients.

Examination of the exfoliated vaginal cells of a child who is 7 years old normally reveals little evidence of estrogen stimulation. A smear from a girl in early childhood is significant if it contains numerous superficial cells; these elements usually indicate either (1) that the girl will show signs of sexual precocity, (2) that she has a hormone-producing ovarian tumor, (3) that she is producing an abnormal amount of endogenous estrogen, or (4) that she has received estrogen as a result of therapy or by accident.

D. Hormone Assays: Assays of circulating hormones are occasionally indicated, eg, when there is evidence of sexual precocity, when a hormone-producing ovarian or adrenal tumor is suspected, or when virilization has occurred.

E. X-Ray Examination: X-rays are useful to demonstrate the presence of radiopaque foreign body in the vagina, to estimate bone age, to reveal the presence of an abdominal tumor, to distinguish adrenal from genital neoplasms, to demonstrate the size and shape of the internal genitalia after a pneumoperitoneum has been induced, or to outline the contour of the vaginal canal following the intravaginal instillation of a radiopaque fluid.

F. Pneumoperitoneum Roentgenography: This is of particular value in determining the state of the internal genitalia in cases of congenital adrenocortical hyperplasia, iatrogenic pseudohermaphroditism, female and male pseudohermaphroditism, and gonadal dysgenesis. The technique of pneumoperitoneum roentgenography is simple, and there is little hazard to the patient. It will often make exploratory laparotomy unnecessary. **Laparoscopy,** in the hands of one familiar with the technique in children, yields more information than gynecography. Culdoscopy is contraindicated in children because of the small size of the premenarcheal pelvis.

G. Identification of Chromosomal Sex: Study of sex chromatin (eg, Barr bodies) in buccal smears, tissue sections, and leukocytes and determination of karyotypes are essential diagnostic tools in cases of suspected gonadal dysgenesis as well as in problems of intersex.

CONGENITAL ANOMALIES

Congenital anomalies of the genitalia fall into 2 groups: those that suggest sexual ambiguity (intersex problems) and those that do not.

ANOMALIES OF THE VULVA

One of the labia minora may be considerably larger than the other, or both may be unusually large. These changes have been assumed by some—probably wrongly—to be the result of masturbation. They are most often inherited characteristics or are simple congenital anomalies.

Unusual anomalies of the vulva include bifid clitoris, which occurs in conjunction with bladder exstrophy; a caudal appendage which resembles a tail and which the infant can move; congenital prolapse of the vagina; and duplication of the vulva (see Chapter 8). The latter is ordinarily associated with duplication of the urinary and intestinal tracts and is believed to represent distorted twinning.

ANOMALIES OF THE HYMEN

The hymen has more apparent variations in structure than any other part of the female genitalia. The orifice may be very small in diameter or of the usual size. (Hymenal size is discussed in the first section of this chapter.) There may be one or more small orifices. Instead of a thin membrane, the hymenal diaphragm may be a thickened, fibrous, nonelastic, firm partition. A hymen with a single small opening may prolong the course of a vaginal infection. If the obstruction is not corrected, intravaginal treatment will be impossible. A thick median ridge separating 2 lateral hymenal orifices suggests a septate vagina.

Regardless of the age of the patient, hymenal anomalies require surgical correction if they block the escape of vaginal secretions or menstrual fluid.

Imperforate Hymen

The hymen may be a persistent portion of the urogenital membrane. It is assumed that an imperforate hymen results when the mesoderm of the primitive streak abnormally invades the urogenital portion of the cloacal membrane.

An imperforate hymen (without a mucocolpos) forms a fibrous, smooth surface between the labia minora. When a mucocolpos (Fig 19–8) develops, the membrane creates a bulging, shiny, thin protuberance. Unless a mucocolpos is diagnosed, a large mass, the distended vagina, may fill the pelvis and distort the abdominal relationships. Enlargements of this type have been mistaken for abdominal tumors, and patients have been subjected to laparotomy and even excision of the uterus and vagina, usually without a gynecologic examination having been made.

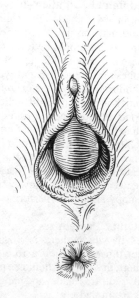

Figure 19–8. Mucocolpos in a newborn infant. (Reproduced, with permission, from Huffman JW: *The Gynecology of Childhood and Adolescence.* Saunders, 1968.)

Imperforate hymen often is not diagnosed until an adolescent girl reports primary amenorrhea and recurrent cyclic pelvic distress. Occasionally, the first symptom may be urinary retention, caused by pressure of a large hematocolpos on the bladder and urethra. Inspection of the vulva generally reveals a dome-shaped, purplish-red hymenal membrane bulging outward because of a collection of blood above it.

An imperforate hymen must be corrected. In infants, the central portion of the membrane is lifted up and snipped off. Sutures usually are not necessary.

ANOMALIES OF URETHRA & ANUS

Failure of a newborn infant to pass meconium and urine demands investigation. Passage of feces or urine through the vagina or a mixture of urine and feces suggests a fistulous communication. In such situations, either the urethra or the anus is imperforate.

Various types of major anomalies of cloacal division have been reported. Two examples involving newborns demonstrate the basic principles of treatment. In one, the short urethra empties into a urogenital sinus and a transverse vaginal septum creates a mucocolpos above the sinus. In the other, the same condition exists but there is also agenesis of the anorectal canal and communication between the rectum and the vagina.

Only broad generalizations can be offered regarding the management of urogenital anomalies of this type, because the cases seldom are alike. If there is fecal contamination of the urinary tract, it is essential that it be corrected, usually by performing a temporary colostomy. Obstruction of the urinary tract must be relieved, and this may require an initial ureterotomy or cystostomy. If the urogenital sinus cannot be used later for a urethra, a substitute may have to be created. If the vagina is obstructed, drain the mucocolpos; this is best done by incision through the perineum.

ANOMALIES OF THE VAGINA

Transverse Vaginal Septum

Transverse vaginal septa may occur at any level of the vagina (see Chapter 8) and may completely or partially occlude the vaginal canal.

An undiscovered imperforate transverse septum may lead to formation of a large mucocolpos in infancy or to cryptomenorrhea in adolescence. A diagnostic error in such a case may lead to unwarranted surgery involving the internal genitalia.

An asymptomatic complete vaginal septum in a child should be excised at some time before menarche. There are technical difficulties in performing intravaginal surgery during infancy, and it is best to wait until late childhood before attempting anything more than the establishment of vaginal drainage.

An incomplete vaginal septum discovered during childhood should not be treated until after puberty. The membrane may then be excised, together with mobilization of the ring of dense subepithelial connective tissue that usually surrounds the vagina at the level of partition.

Partial Vaginal Agenesis

Partial vaginal agenesis occurs when a large portion—almost always the distal part—of the vaginal plate fails to canalize. The cause of this uncommon anomaly is unknown. Usually, most of the vagina will be represented by a soft mass of tissue. Absence of the distal vagina should be identified when the infant is examined at birth. If the small uterus is not felt, a diagnosis of vaginal agenesis is probably justified. The parents should be told that further diagnostic procedures (see discussion of vaginal agenesis) will be necessary in late childhood.

A serious clinical problem often arises when vaginal agenesis is undiagnosed and the agenesis is limited to the lower part of the vagina. If the uterus has developed normally, it and the upper part of the vagina will fill with blood when menstruation begins. The symptoms are similar to those associated with an imperforate hymen after the menarche. Vulvar examination at this time generally reveals findings identical with those of vaginal agenesis, but rectoabdominal palpation should reveal a large, boggy pelvic mass.

Partial vaginal agenesis may occur in association with anomalies of cloacal division. In such cases, the diagnosis may be difficult.

Partial vaginal agenesis with a functioning uterus is rare. It is usually associated with hematocolpos and hematometra. Occasionally, menstrual blood will escape through the uterine tubes. The diagnosis is made when an adolescent patient presents with apparent agenesis of the vagina, a uterus palpable on rectal examination, and a history of recurrent monthly pelvic discomfort. In one case, pelvic endometriosis was discovered at laparotomy in a 14-year-old girl. Although it is impossible to specify a routine for management of such cases, retrograde flow must be stopped, usually by drainage from the uterus to the exterior vulva through a constructed vagina.

Vaginal Agenesis

With vaginal agenesis, the clitoris, labia, and urethra usually are normal. A ruffled ridge of tissue represents the hymen (Fig 19–9). Inside this circle of tissue will be an indentation. The thickened vaginal tissues between the rectum and urethra rarely are felt on rectal palpation. A uterus is seldom outlined.

Most girls with vaginal agenesis are chromatin-positive. Usually they develop normally in adolescence and have all of the usual feminine attributes except that they suffer from amenorrhea and sterility. In rare instances, vaginal agenesis may be one of the findings in a case of intersex. For this reason, a buccal smear should be obtained after the infant is several weeks old. At some time during childhood, because of the frequent association of urinary and genital tract anomalies, there should also be an evaluation of the

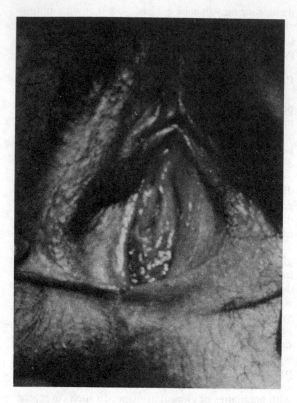

Figure 19–9. Vaginal agenesis in a girl 16 years of age.

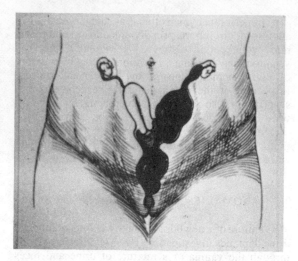

Figure 19–10. Unicornuate uterus with paramesonephric vaginal cyst.

urinary tract. The parents must be advised that further studies, particularly gynecography or laparoscopy, should be performed when the child is 8–9 years old. As a rule, gynecography will show that the uterus is absent but that the ovaries are present. An exploratory laparotomy is not indicated in these cases.

Creation of a satisfactory vagina is the objective in treatment of vaginal agenesis. The surgical procedure should be deferred until the girl is anticipating an active sexual life. Several techniques are available. Creation of a cavity by dissection, between the urethra and bladder anteriorly and the perineal body and rectum posteriorly, which is lined by a split thickness skin graft overlying a plastic or soft silicone mold, is one popular procedure. Another is an operation that utilizes the labia majora to construct a coital pouch.

SYMPTOMATIC ANOMALIES OF THE UTERUS IN CHILDREN
(Unicornuate Uterus With Paramesonephric Cyst)

A unicornuate uterus occasionally is accompanied by an anomaly of the opposite paramesonephric duct that develops in such a manner that it creates a lateral vaginal wall cyst with an endometrial lining (Fig 19–10). As a result, the cyst fills with blood at the menarche and produces a vaginal mass. The mass

either ruptures or is incised and drained. Attempts to remove cysts of this type often involve great danger to the urethra, bladder, or ureter. On the other hand, excision of a small segment of the common wall between the cyst and the vagina often provides adequate drainage. Other anomalies of the uterus are asymptomatic in childhood.

ANOMALIES OF THE OVARIES

Anomalous Ovarian Descent

An ovary may be drawn outward with the round ligament into the inguinal canal or even down into the labium majus. A firm inguinal mass, even though the external genitalia are typically feminine, should alert the examiner to the possible presence of an aberrant ovary; in a few instances it will prove to be an undescended testis of an intersex male. A buccal smear for Barr bodies should be obtained when a girl presents with an inguinal gonad. The latter should be biopsied. If an ovary is identified, it should be returned to the peritoneal cavity and the hernia repaired.

Gonadal Dysgenesis

The diagnosis of gonadal dysgenesis is difficult in premenarcheal girls who have none of the obvious stigmas of the syndrome. It may be missed unless the possible significance of the following telltale signs is borne in mind: height and weight below the third percentile, broad chests and small nipples, web neck, coarctation of the aorta, prominent epicanthal folds, nevi, and other lesser anomalies. Many patients with this clinical picture have a mosaic chromosomal constitution; they may be XX/XO and have a positive buccal smear.

The infant with gonadal dysgenesis may show other signs of the typical syndrome, ie, cutis laxa and edema of the dorsal surfaces of the hands and feet. The parents need to know what the child's medical future is likely to be. They should not be told that the buccal smear is negative but must understand that their baby has normal female organs except for impaired ovarian development; that she will need ovarian replacement therapy later; and that she can have children only by adoption.

The little girl with behavior problems, delayed menarche, and a poor scholastic record may have a genetic defect. These problems tend to become exaggerated in early teens when the girl notes that she is not developing physically like her friends. Evaluation in such a situation should not stop with the psychiatrist or the child guidance clinic. Physical examination should include examination of the genitalia and breasts, and a buccal smear for sex chromatin is indicated. Karyotyping probably will be necessary. A vaginal cytosmear to evaluate any estrogen response in the vaginal mucosa and a determination of the urinary pituitary gonadotropin titer are indicated if the patient is over 9 years of age.

INTERSEX

Intersex individuals have sufficiently ambiguous external genitalia so that the true gender cannot be immediately determined. The category also includes genetic males. (See Chapters 7 and 26.)

DISORDERS OF THE PREMENARCHEAL CHILD

VULVOVAGINITIS

Inflammatory disorders, especially those due to infections of the vulva and vagina and causing varying

Table 19–4. Etiologic classification of premenarcheal vulvovaginitis.

Nonspecific vulvovaginitis:
    Secondary to poor perineal hygiene
    Secondary to respiratory infections
    Secondary to skin infections
    Secondary to intestinal parasites
    Secondary to foreign bodies
    Secondary to urinary tract infections
    Etiology undetermined
Specific vulvovaginitis:
    Gonorrhea
    Other neisserian infections
    Mycotic infections
    Trichomoniasis
    Gardnerella (Haemophilus) vaginalis infections
    Chlamydial infections
    Exanthems
    Other specific infections, eg, pneumococcosis, diphtheria, amebiasis

---

amounts of discharge, are among the more common problems that require gynecologic evaluation. Most often the mother is concerned because she has noticed that the child has a discharge or hyperemia of the vulva. Occasionally, the youngster will complain of formication, pruritus, or dysuria. The discharge may be a scanty, serous secretion or a profuse, purulent exudate. Generally, its appearance is not diagnostic.

Pruritus is a frequent symptom of vulvovaginitis. Many of the patients have a burning sensation when urine flows over the inflamed tissues. In such cases, an erroneous diagnosis of a lower urinary tract infection may be made, especially when leukocytes are found in a voided urine specimen. As a rule, it is advisable to examine a little girl for vulvovaginitis before treatment is instituted for a bladder infection.

An etiologic classification of vulvovaginitis is shown in Table 19–4.

1. NONSPECIFIC VULVOVAGINITIS*

So-called nonspecific vulvovaginitis, in which cultures and stained smears disclose a mixed pyogenic bacterial flora without predominant organisms, is the most frequent genital disorder in premenarcheal children. Vaginal cultures may yield one or more common pathogens. Any one of a number of conditions may be responsible for the infection, eg, poor perineal hygiene, respiratory or buccal infections, infected abrasions or lacerations, foreign bodies, or infection with intestinal parasites.

Poor Perineal Hygiene

Poor perineal hygiene is failure to cleanse the perineum properly following a bowel movement. After wiping the anus, the toilet tissue may be brought forward over the vulva. Underclothing soiled with feces may also pose a problem. The organisms found in vaginal cultures include *Escherichia coli*, *Klebsiella pneumoniae*, *Enterobacter aerogenes*, and *Proteus* species—all common to the intestinal tract.

In over 20% of cases of this type of nonspecific vulvovaginitis, relief can be achieved by the use of sitz baths and by having the mother instruct the child in proper perineal hygiene. Patients with vulvovaginitis who do not respond to these simple measures usually can be cured by the intravaginal application of nitrofurazone or with broad-spectrum antimicrobial medications. One-half of an adult urethral suppository (Furacin Urethral Inserts) inserted nightly for 2 weeks is most helpful.

Respiratory Infections

The child's hands may carry infectious material to the vagina from her nose or throat. A history often is obtained of a respiratory infection preceding the vul-

---

*Vulvovaginitis due to retained foreign body is discussed in Chapter 9. Pelvic infections are discussed in Chapter 15.

vovaginal inflammation. Cultures in such cases often produce hemolytic streptococci or *Staphylococcus aureus*.

Infected Wounds

Bacteria from an infected abrasion or laceration also may be contaminants of the external genitalia. The child and her mother must be reminded that the genitalia of a healthy person may be cleaner than the hands, so that it is important to wash the hands before and after urinating.

Urinary Tract Infections

Only rarely is there any relationship between urinary tract infections and nonspecific vulvovaginitis. If the hymenal orifice is unusually patulous, contaminated urine may seep into the vagina to cause vaginitis. More often, vaginitis secondary to a urinary tract infection occurs when labial adhesions partially obstruct the vestibule and retain some urine in the vestibule and vagina.

Intestinal Parasites

Pinworm ova are excreted in the stools of infected individuals and are carried on their hands after they have touched the perianal skin. The ova may be deposited on toys, in house dust, or in playground soil, where they are picked up by a child who subsequently ingests them. They then hatch in the intestinal tract. Occasionally a worm will migrate from the anal area into the vagina, where it deposits ova. The worm often carries *E coli* and other intestinal infectious bacteria. Vulvovaginitis occurs when these organisms are introduced into the vagina. The mother may state that the child has had a low-grade vulvovaginitis for some time, with recurrent bouts of discharge and itching. Examination often reveals moderate inflammation of the vulva and vagina, perhaps with a thin, yellowish-gray mucopurulent discharge.

Other intestinal parasites, such as *Ascaris lumbricoides,* rarely invade the vagina.

The diagnosis is established by finding ova in the vaginal secretion or in smears obtained from perianal skin. Infection cannot be excluded until the laboratory reports 3 negative tests.

Children with pinworms should be treated with a single dose of pyrantel pamoate, 11 mg of base per kg orally (maximum, 1 g). An alternative safe and effective drug is piperazine citrate, given in a dosage of 75 mg/kg in 3 divided doses orally daily (maximum, 3.5 g daily) for 7 days. If a child has pinworms, it is almost certain that all other members of the family have them also. Therefore, the entire family must be treated or the patient will be reinfected.

Nonspecific vulvovaginitis secondary to intestinal parasites will recur until the child is freed of pinworms. After they have been eradicated, local treatment as described for nonspecific vulvovaginitis secondary to poor perineal hygiene should be prescribed. Reexamination for pinworms is indicated if the vulvovaginitis recurs.

Treatment of Nonspecific Vulvovaginitis

Cases that do not respond to sitz baths and improved hygiene should be treated with intravaginal medication. Oral or parenteral antibiotics almost never are indicated in the treatment of nonspecific vulvovaginitis. The inflammation, which is due to a relatively benign superficial mucosal infection, rarely affects the child's general health. It usually responds to less potent topical antimicrobial agents, eg, nitrofurazone (Furacin). It is best to reserve penicillin, sulfonamides, and other antibiotics for use against a possible serious systemic infection later.

Estrogen has been used locally in the treatment of vaginitis in children. The rationale is based on the ability of estrogen to convert the thin mucosa of the immature vagina to a thicker surface that is presumably more resistant to infection. A series of children with nonspecific vulvovaginitis who were treated with intravaginal estrogen-nitrofurazone suppositories were compared with a group who were treated with nitrofurazone alone. In most cases, the combined medication was not superior to nitrofurazone without estrogen.

Nonspecific vaginitis may be improved also by reducing the vaginal pH by instilling a lactic acid solution—1 mL of lactic acid in 250 mL of water—into the vagina. The solution may be instilled into the child's vagina twice daily with an eyedropper. For older girls, an apparatus for vaginal lavage can be made by attaching a No. 14F urethral catheter to the barrel of a 20-mL Luer-Lok syringe. Place the child supine and insert the catheter into the vagina. The barrel of the syringe serves as a funnel. Lavage is carried out twice daily.

Nonspecific vulvovaginitis secondary to respiratory or skin infection with organisms that are not susceptible to local therapy should be treated with penicillin.

2. SEXUALLY TRANSMISSIBLE DISEASES IN PREMENARCHEAL GIRLS

A premenarcheal girl may acquire any of the venereal diseases, but the mode of transmission includes both sexual and nonsexual contact with infected persons and contaminated things (Table 19–5). Physicians caring for young patients with sexually transmissible diseases must attempt to determine how the infection was transmitted, bearing in mind that newborn infants may have been exposed to pathogens in the maternal birth canal; that small children are most likely to be infected by someone or something in their home environment; and that older premenarcheal girls are at increasing risk of both voluntary and nonvoluntary sexual contact. In each case, sexual molestation—including incest—should be considered.

Gonorrhea, the most common venereal disease, may be contracted by infants and children of all ages. Prevention in newborn infants requires that all pregnant women have vaginal cultures for gonorrhea early

Table 19–5. Modes of transmission of sexually transmissible diseases during childhood.

Fetal contact with mother's infected birth canal
Sexual contact with infected individuals (voluntary or involuntary)
Genital noncoital contact
Coitus
Genitoanal
Orogenital
Digital contact by infected individuals
Manipulation of genitalia (molestation)
Touching during bathing, cleansing, diapering
Sex play
Contact with infected fomites
Bedding, clothing, towels, washcloths
Thermometers
Rectal tips
Douche syringes
Toilet seats (?)
During bathing
Two-in-a-tub
Swimming pools (?)

in the pregnancy, followed by treatment if infection is shown, and that all prepartum patients have repeat cultures during their last trimester.

The control of sexually transmissible diseases in premenarcheal girls depends upon a high degree of suspicion by physicians; on recognition that a patient who has one such disease may have another; and on early diagnosis and treatment along with identification of the mode of transmission and the source of the infection. All members of the household should be examined if a child is found to have venereal disease. Identification of the person guilty of molesting the child is often difficult because the family may not know who was responsible, or may know and be unwilling to say. Sexual partners of pubescent girls who become infected in the course of voluntary sexual activity should be identified and treated.

Although some children undoubtedly acquire infections by nonsexual contact, most little girls acquire venereal diseases through some form of sexual activity, either through sex play, fingering of the genitalia by an infected individual, or genital contact. Parents and others caring for children should realize that for many youngsters sex activity begins earlier today than they might think. Education concerning genital physiology, sexual functions, and venereal diseases should be started as soon as boys and girls enter puberty.

INJURIES TO THE GENITALIA

Most injuries to the genitalia during childhood are caused by falls. The majority are accidental, but occasionally the external genitalia are injured by kicking or beating. Many are of minor significance, but a few are life-threatening and require major surgical procedures.

Sexual trauma is relatively uncommon. Each accident presents a particular problem, and treatment must be individualized.

1. CONTUSIONS & LACERATIONS OF THE VULVA

A contusion of the vulva usually does not require treatment. Nevertheless, if the hymen has been lacerated or if there is other evidence that a sharp object may have entered the vagina, it is essential that a detailed examination be carried out to exclude intrapelvic, urethral, vesical, and rectal injuries.

A straddle type injury may cause extensive trauma to the perineum and adjacent structures. Fortunately, such accidents are relatively uncommon. General anesthesia usually is required for examination. The wound must be thoroughly but gently cleansed. After the extent of the injury has been determined, bleeding vessels must be ligated and the wound sutured. Penicillin therapy should be given if the injury is extensive or tetanus is a threat.

The treatment of serious wounds of the perineum, bowel, or bladder is based upon the principles of vaginal plastic reconstructive surgery. Knowledge of the normal anatomy of the perineum and fine surgical technique are essential. The operator should use small instruments and fine suture material. Intravenous fluid should be started before the operation is begun so that blood can be given if necessary in the operating room. Devitalized tissue must be debrided. In severe cases, broad-spectrum antibiotics should be administered postoperatively. A low-residue diet should be ordered for 5 days after the repair to restrict bowel movements if there has been a rectal injury.

Severe trauma to the external genitalia may make it impossible to perform a satisfactory primary anatomic reconstruction. Necrosis, infection, and cicatrization after the repair often distort a good repair. In such cases, the surgeon should advise the parents that additional plastic procedures may be necessary when the girl is older.

A vulvar hematoma occurs when a kick or blow ruptures blood vessels under the vulvar mucosa or perineal skin. As a result, a round, tense, ecchymotic, very tender mass is formed. If untreated, subcutaneous necrosis and rupture of the overlying skin with bleeding and perhaps infection may ensue.

A small vulvar hematoma usually can be controlled by a tight pressure dressing and an ice pack. A large hematoma or one that continues to increase in size because of continued bleeding should be incised, the clotted blood removed, the bleeding point ligated, and drainage with healing encouraged without suture closure. If the source of the bleeding cannot be found, the cavity should be packed with gauze and a firm pressure dressing applied. The pack is removed in 24 hours. Broad-spectrum antibiotics may be given prophylactically when a large hematoma is opened and for several days thereafter.

2. VAGINAL INJURIES

Lacerations of the Vaginal Wall

These are usually accompanied by vulvar injuries. Occasionally, a sharp object will strike the hymen and enter the vagina without tearing the vulvar mucosa. The hymen is almost invariably lacerated when vaginal injury occurs. Most vaginal wounds are of the lateral walls. Generally there will be relatively little blood loss, and the child will not have much pain if the damage is to the mucosa only. Usually there is very little bleeding from the hymenal injury.

Intravaginal examination is mandatory if there is vaginal trauma even though the child is not in pain and there is little bleeding. Most injuries are not serious, but there could be an extensive tear, even with peritoneal perforation, without notable symptoms for several hours after the accident. The patient must be given a general anesthetic. The examiner should inspect the wound to determine its extent. The patient must be catheterized. Difficulty in passing the catheter or recovery of bloody urine are indications for urologic study. If no urine is obtained, the bladder should be filled with sterile normal saline solution and then emptied. If the solution contains blood or is not returned, it must be assumed that the bladder has been injured. Rupture of the bladder and perforation of the peritoneum are absolute indications for exploratory laparotomy. Rectal palpation and vaginoscopy generally assure the integrity of the rectum.

Repair of vaginal injuries may be difficult in small children. Ophthalmologic instruments, very small needles, and fine absorbable suture material often make a difficult task less arduous. If the sharp object that entered the child's vagina also perforated a viscus or the peritoneum, her life is in jeopardy unless the condition is quickly diagnosed and promptly treated.

Vaginal Hematomas

Vaginal hematomas may be caused by retraction of a lacerated blood vessel when the vaginal mucosa is torn. If the vessel is small, bleeding may stop spontaneously. If bleeding does not stop, the vagina may become distended by a dark, tense tumefaction. The patient may complain of pain in the vagina, rectum, perineum, and buttocks.

If a larger vessel is torn above the level of the pelvic floor, a huge retroperitoneal hematoma may develop; it may spread upward beneath the peritoneum above the pelvic brim. The symptoms of acute retroperitoneal hematoma are intense pelvic pain, backache, unilateral lower abdominal distress, pain referred to the leg on the affected side, and signs of occult hemorrhage. A laparotomy must be performed immediately if a patient is believed to have a retroperitoneal hematoma. The pelvic peritoneum should be incised, the clot removed, the the bleeding vessel ligated. If the peritoneal cavity has been entered, laparotomy for exploration and repair is mandatory.

Sexual Molestation & Rape*

The term sexual molestation implies that the child has been subjected to noncoital sexual contact. The contact may be either digital manipulation of the girl's genitalia or the application of the male genitalia to some part of her body other than her genitalia. Rape is defined as carnal knowledge without the consent of the female or carnal knowledge of a female even with consent if the female does not have the capacity to consent because (for example) of mental deficiency, unconsciousness, or, in pediatric practice, what the law calls "infancy" (being under the statutory minimum age necessary for consent). The male need not have had an erection nor have entered the vagina. The slightest penetration is sufficient to constitute the crime of rape. As a matter of law, a boy under a certain age (usually 14) is incapable of committing the crime of rape. Molestation is rarely associated with physical trauma, but forceful entry of the immature vagina almost always causes injury.

Sexual molestation of any kind may cause the premenarcheal child acute emotional stress. However, small children often escape relatively unscathed by their experience, and it is the parents who may be most seriously concerned. Parents, relatives, and paramedical personnel should be warned specifically against suggesting to the child that something terrible has happened to her. Many young children do not understand the sexual significance of the attack. Nonetheless, for others—especially older girls—a traumatic sexual experience may have emotional consequences persisting into adulthood. Gentleness, tact, and patience are essential in treating not only the molested child but also her parents.

SEXUAL PRECOCITY

Sexual precocity is the onset of sexual maturation at any age that is 2.8 SD earlier than the norm; at present, the appearance of any of the secondary sexual characteristics before 9 years of age is considered precocious. As a rule, breast development and the growth of genital hair precede uterine bleeding by several months. In some patients, premature thelarche (Fig 19–11) or premature pubarche (Fig 19–12) may be the only signs of precocious sexual maturation; most of these girls have some acceleration of their somatic growth.

The term **true precocious puberty** is often used to differentiate premature sexual development caused by those conditions which arouse the hypothalamic-hypophyseal-ovarian axis at an abnormally early age from **pseudoprecocious puberty,** which is caused by ovarian or adrenal tumors or the action of exogenous ovarian hormones. In this context, true precocious puberty includes not only those cases associated with hypothyroidism and central nervous system disorders but also the McCune-Albright syndrome and the

*Rape is discussed in Chapter 21.

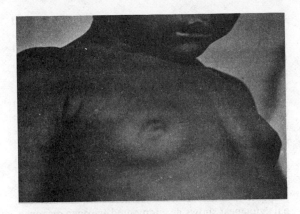

Figure 19–11. Premature thelarche in a child 5 years of age.

80–90% of all cases of sexual precocity of unknown origin. The latter are designated cryptogenic in the etiologic grouping given below. Ovulation is the best evidence that the hypothalamic-hypophyseal-ovarian axis has attained maturity. There is no way of knowing, however, how many girls with "true" sexual precocity ovulate. The number must be relatively small because, despite the relative frequency of sexual precocity, only a few of the girls have become pregnant. There are less than 25 reported cases of pregnancy in girls under 11 years of age in the world literature.

Etiology

A classification of the etiologic factors in isosexual precocity is given in Table 19–6.

A. Sexual Precocity of Intracranial Origin: Hypothalamic or pituitary disorders produce precocious genital development or function similar to that seen in children whose maturation is normal except for its prematurity; in both, ovarian follicular ripening and ovulation may occur. Most cases of sexual precocity of intracranial origin are due to lesions or tumors of the floor of the third ventricle; these lesions usually involve the posterior portion of the hypothalamus, particularly in the region of the tuber cinereum, the mammillary bodies, and the optic chiasm; congenital brain defects and encephalitis may be associated with precocious genital development as part of the clinical picture. Neurologic studies usually establish the diagnosis. McCune-Albright syndrome (Fig 19–13), in which precocious sexual development is associated with polyostotic fibrous dysplasia, areas of cutaneous pigmentation, and other endocrine disturbances, has been ascribed to congenital defects in the hypothalamus.

Some children whose sexual activity is associated with intracranial disease may have no neurologic symptoms initially. In view of the many types of intracranial disorders initiating sexual precocity, the site as well as the character of the disturbance is important.

One may explain sexual precocity produced by intracranial lesions by postulating that the posterior hypothalamus possesses the ability to inhibit the production or release of gonadotropic hormones from the anterior pituitary. Accordingly, lesions in the posterior hypothalamus may destroy a tract or inhibit some mechanism that ordinarily checks the rate of intensity

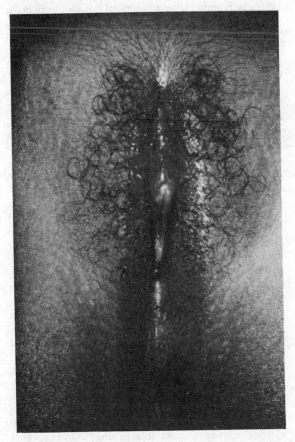

Figure 19–12. Premature pubarche in a child 4 years of age.

Table 19–6. Etiologic factors in female isosexual precocity.

Central nervous system:
Cryptogenic
Organic:
Intracranial neoplasms
Tuberous sclerosis
Congenital anomalies
Hamartomas
Encephalitis
McCune-Albright syndrome
Ovarian:
Nonneoplastic cysts
Feminizing mesenchymomas
Teratomatous choriocarcinomas
Other feminizing tumors
Adrenal feminizing tumors
Other:
Hypothyroidism
Exogenous estrogen
Other

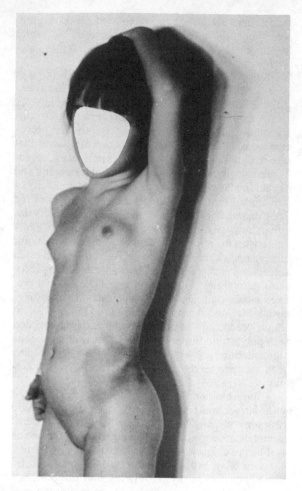

Figure 19–13. Six-and-a-half-year-old child with McCune-Albright syndrome. (Reproduced, with permission, from Huffman JW: *Gynäkologie des Kindes.* Urban & Schwarzenberg, 1975.)

associated with sexual precocity reported prior to 1930 undoubtedly were either granulosa–theca cell tumors or dysgerminomas or teratomas combined with teratomatous choriocarcinomas. Luteomas, thecomas, and other feminizing neoplasms also have been reported to be associated with sexual precocity.

In most cases of feminizing mesenchymomas in childhood, a rapid advance in body growth and bone age occurs together with the appearance of an adolescent feminine habitus, maturation of the genitalia, and enlargement of breasts. Pubic hair usually is present but less abundant than in the case of true isosexual precocious puberty. A pelvic tumor usually will be palpable. Vaginal secretion is increased, and the vaginal cytosmear shows an augmented estrogen response. Irregular genital bleeding occurs. As a rule, the rate of precocious sexual development appears to be much more rapid with estrogen-producing tumors than it is with cryptogenic isosexual puberty. The urinary excretion rate of estrogen is higher than normal for the child's age but seldom exceeds the adult level. Some granulosa cell tumors have produced tremendous amounts of estrogen, but these are the exceptions. Several luteomas, too small to palpate, have been diagnosed on the basis of pregnanediol identified in the child's urine. Still, increased pituitary gonadotropin excretion should not occur, because these tumors are ovarian. Paradoxically, in several cases of granulosa cell tumor, appreciable amounts of gonadotropin in the girl's urine have been reported. Curiously, 17-ketosteroids may be slightly elevated with ovarian feminizing tumors but not to adolescent or adult levels. Nevertheless, in these cases, ovulation and pregnancy do not occur.

Occasionally, nonneoplastic ovarian cysts of follicular origin may cause sexual precocity. Rarely, one ovary contains a large follicular cyst holding fluid high in estrogen content. Excision of such cysts has been followed by remission of precocious sexual development. Usually, however, sexual precocity will continue unabated when biopsy reveals only minor cystic changes in moderately enlarged ovaries, despite removal of portions of the gonad.

D. Other Causes of Sexual Precocity: In most instances, hormone-producing adrenal tumors cause either heterosexual precocity or a mixed type of sexual maturation. Exogenous estrogen may be obtained inadvertently from medication or other sources. Ingestion of the mother's contraceptive pills accounts for occasional cases of sexual precocity in young children. Sexual precocity has also been reported in youngsters suffering from hypothyroidism.

E. Transitory Sexual Precocity: Transient periods of precocious sexual development are uncommon but not rare. The patients in this category display accelerated development of one or more secondary sexual characteristics. Most of these children have a spurt in somatic growth; about half have breast growth; up to 45% experience vaginal bleeding; and all display a good estrogen reaction in the vaginal vault epithelium. Their precocious sexual development con-

of stimuli passing to the anterior pituitary gland. As a result, the inhibitory effect on the pituitary is removed, and its augmented production of gonadotropic substances may lead to gonadal activity and sexual maturation. In other cases, actual stimulation of the pituitary may ensue.

B. Cryptogenic Sexual Precocity: Cases of constitutional sexual precocity, which comprise 80–90% of the recorded cases, are without demonstrable cause. Constitutional precocity is included in the etiologic classification with precocity of central nervous system origin because it is probable that many of the patients may have small, unidentifiable lesions in the hypothalamus. A family history of sexual precocity can sometimes be obtained. The term cryptogenic is appropriate because it signifies that we know little about the origin of this type of precocious maturation.

C. Ovarian Tumors Causing Sexual Precocity: Much emphasis has been placed on ovarian tumors as a cause of sexual precocity, but feminizing tumors in children actually are unusual. A number of sarcomas tinues for a few months after which reversion to a normal growth pattern ensues and normal puberty occurs at the usual age.

In occasional instances, the endometrium may be exceptionally sensitive to estrogen. As a result, uterine bleeding occurs without other signs of sexual precocity. In all cases of this type observed by the author, the girls were unusually large for their age. The premature response of the endometrium in these instances is not unlike that of the breast and pubic hair (premature thelarche and pubarche).

In all such cases of premature endometrial response, gynecologic examination has failed to reveal a cause for the bleeding, and hormone assays were within normal levels for the patients' ages. Moreover, bleeding recurred periodically for a few months and then ceased spontaneously.

Girls with transitory sexual maturation or premature endometrial response should be kept under observation for several years lest they develop other unsuspected problems including genital bleeding due to other causes.

Clinical Findings

The diagnostic procedures employed in cases of female isosexual precocious development are for the purpose of determining the cause of accelerated sexual maturation. About 90% of cases are of the constitutional (essential, cryptogenic, or idiopathic) type. However, before this explanation can be accepted in any individual case, other etiologic factors must be excluded, and this may require many tests over a period of months or years.

Some children with constitutional sexual precocity begin to show signs of sexual maturation within a short time after birth; the greatest number, however, have their menarche between 7 and 8 years of age. The earlier the onset of accelerated sexual development, the more likely will the child be to start menstruating early. Sexually precocious children display accelerated growth in height, weight, and bone age; the increase in the rate of growth usually begins before the appearance of the secondary sex characteristics.

Although girls with precocious puberty are usually much taller than their age mates during early childhood, early epiphyseal closure results in short stature as adults. The earlier precocious development begins and the faster it progresses, the earlier the epiphyses close, the sooner growth is arrested, and the shorter the stature when growth ceases.

The genitalia of the little girl with sexual precocity tend to be morphologically adolescent. A vaginal cytosmear usually reveals an estrogen response in the vaginal mucosa and may even indicate ovulation. Gynecologic examination must exclude genital bleeding of other origin. Rectoabdominal palpation should indicate that the ovaries and uterus are slightly enlarged but not larger than would be expected for functioning organs of an adolescent girl. Roentgenography after pneumoperitoneum is useful for delineating the shape and size of the ovaries and uterus and may help to confirm or rule out the presence of an ovarian tumor. When there is an ovarian tumor, hormone assays should be within the range of normal for a postmenarcheal girl. Advanced bone age may be demonstrated roentgenologically. X-ray films of the sella turcica to exclude enlargement of the pituitary gland should be obtained. If the clinical evaluation, including neurologic, ophthalmologic, and laboratory studies, fails to indicate an organic cause for the developmental precocity, a diagnosis of constitutional sexual precocity may be justified.

Laparoscopy, performed by one skilled in this procedure in children, may be a substitute for exploratory laparotomy if a tumor is merely suspected.

There is no evidence that sexual precocity induces premature heterosexual activity or adversely affects reproductive potential. Intellectual development is not accelerated. Somatic and genital development parallel bone age.

Treatment

It is important that the sexually precocious child be given information regarding menstruation and menstrual hygiene. Sexual education must be started early with girls who are sexually precocious, but the manner in which the information is presented should be modified according to the child's ability to comprehend.

A. Medical Treatment: Medroxyprogesterone, 100–200 mg intramuscularly at 14-day intervals, will suppress menstruation in many girls with constitutional sexual precocity, but other signs of accelerated maturation often continue unabated.

Promising results have been reported from Europe recently in treatment of sexual precocity with cyproterone acetate, an antiandrogen with progestational properties including suppression of hypothalamic activity. Kauli and co-workers (1976) and others have reported that cyproterone suppressed signs of sexual maturation in a number of children suffering from sexual precocity.

B. Surgical Treatment: Laparotomy is necessary if a child who exhibits precocious puberty has a palpably enlarged ovary. If a follicular cyst is found, it should be excised. Preservation of the ovary usually is possible if a benign neoplasm is found.

Large, unilateral, encapsulated, mobile ovarian neoplasms in children are best treated by unilateral salpingo-oophorectomy and inspection and biopsy of the opposite ovary. The uterus and contralateral ovary should not be removed if presumably free of tumor. Ascites is not by itself a sign of malignant disease or a reason for radical surgery. A well-encapsulated, mobile granulosa cell tumor should be removed, but the opposite ovary should be preserved.

A malignant ovarian tumor requires salpingo-oophorectomy. If spread to the opposite ovary is noted, both ovaries and the uterus should be removed.

PRECOCIOUS (JUVENILE) PREGNANCY

Precocious or juvenile pregnancy is rare—only about 50 cases have been reported, but it is probable that there have been unrecorded instances. The youngest known parturient was a Peruvian girl aged 5 years, 8 months who was delivered at term of a healthy male infant weighing 2950 g by cesarean section in 1939. The girl had begun to menstruate at the age of 8 months and was impregnated before she was 5 years old. Both mother and infant survived.

In every instance, the underage mothers were sexually precocious, most having menstruated for several years before becoming pregnant. Invariably, their precocity was of the constitutional type. (Isosexual pseudoprecocity and pregnancy has never been authenticated.)

Most precocious mothers and their babies have not done so well as the Peruvian girl mentioned above. As a group, they have had an increased incidence of spontaneous abortion, preeclampsia-eclampsia, and premature labor and delivery. In the patients who were under 9 years of age, less than 50% of the labors were normal, and there was a 35% neonatal loss. Even if expert obstetric care is available, a pregnant child will have an increased risk of prepartum complications, and her labor is likely to be abnormal.

An aphorism suggests that, "The younger the child who becomes pregnant, the older the male who inseminated her." In most cases of juvenile pregnancy, the offender was either a member of the family, eg, father, brother, cousin, uncle, grandfather, or an adult family friend. Incest is more common than is generally realized, with perhaps only about 20% of cases reported to authorities. In approximately 75% of the cases investigated, there was a father-daughter relationship (Sarles, 1980).

Juvenile pregnancy per se does not increase the chance of congenital anomaly in the offspring. However, a product of incest has a greater likelihood of acquiring genetic malformations carried by recessive genes.

It is to be hoped that most little girls who become pregnant will be relieved of their tragic burden by elective abortion. If, because of legal, religious, or cultural reasons, a juvenile pregnancy is allowed to continue, the mother and fetus are at high risk, ie, dystocia should be expected, the infant may be premature, and, even if mature, the neonate may do poorly.

The underage mother (if she understands what is happening) and her family may need psychiatric counseling not only during but also after the pregnancy. Lessening the emotional, social, and medical trauma associated with such a gestation is an important task for all who assist in her care.

Emotional bonding between the mother and infant probably should be avoided, except in those societies in which premenarcheal and pubertal girls are given in marriage to mature men.

GENITAL BLEEDING DURING CHILDHOOD NOT ASSOCIATED WITH SEXUAL PRECOCITY

Three types of genital bleeding occur during childhood: (1) physiologic or estrogen-withdrawal bleeding during the neonatal period; (2) ovulatory bleeding as a sign of isosexual precocity; and (3) nonovulatory bleeding associated with isosexual precocity.

Physiologic bleeding during the neonatal period is caused by withdrawal of estrogen, the maternal hormone that stimulated the fetal genitalia during late intrauterine development. Most baby girls have some bleeding of this type, but the amount usually is very scanty. Gross physiologic genital bleeding persisting more than 10–12 days after birth requires investigation.

Genital bleeding as the result of ovulation is one of the signs of true isosexual precocity. Little girls who are sexually precocious and ovulate tend to have regular menstrual periods and to bleed more heavily than those who do not ovulate. Those whose precocity is the result of neoplastic, infectious, or inflammatory disorders (isosexual pseudoprecocity) bleed irregularly. A few with little or no premature development of any of their other secondary sexual characteristics will have a few episodes of vaginal bleeding because their endometrial receptors for estrogen are prematurely sensitive to that hormone. In contrast, some girls who display precocious maturation of certain secondary sexual characteristics do not bleed.

Vulvar pruritus due to any of several vulvar or perineal dermatologic disorders (Fig 19–14) may

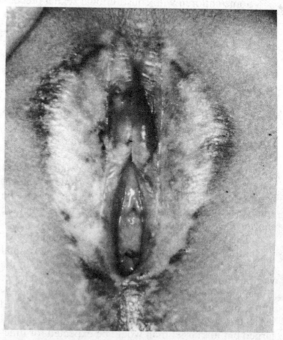

Figure 19–14. Lichen sclerosus et atrophicus of vulva of 6-year-old child. Accompanying pruritus may cause scratching that creates bleeding.

cause a child to scratch the area to the point of bleeding, which is usually scanty. The presence of blood on a child's underclothing will alarm the mother, who must be reassured.

Acute vulvovaginitis may denude the thin vulvar or vaginal mucosa, but bleeding is usually minimal. As a rule, the mucopurulent or purulent discharge will be little more than bloodstained.

A foul-smelling, purulent vaginal discharge is almost always pathognomonic of a vaginal foreign body and always requires investigation. Many things have been found in little girls' vaginas, but the most common are bits of cloth or paper. Vaginoscopy is essential to discover objects high in the vagina and to exclude other causes for bleeding. X-ray cannot be depended upon to reveal a foreign body, because many of them are not radiopaque.

An ulcerated, bleeding vaginal condyloma acuminatum may be confused with a malignant vaginal neoplasm. Condylomata acuminata, unlike most neoplasms, usually are multiple with several warty growths present on the vulva. The same is true of a prolapse of the urethral mucosa (Fig 19–15), which forms a hemorrhagic, very sensitive vulvar mass. A prolapse of the urethra is identified by the location of the urethral orifice and by the fact that the mass is separate from the vagina.

Vaginal bleeding during childhood should always alert the physician to the possibility of a genital tumor. Benign tumors of the vulva and vagina are rare in childhood, and those that do occur seldom cause bleeding. Malignant neoplasms usually bleed from necrotic or ulcerative areas that appear early in their development. Examination, including vaginoscopy, is mandatory. If a neoplasm is found, a biopsy is required for diagnosis. If the tumor is malignant, aggressive surgery combined with radiation therapy or chemotherapy offers the best chance of survival.

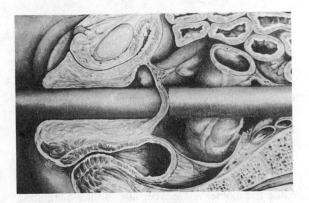

Figure 19–16. Transvaginal perforation of cul-de-sac and penetration of peritoneal cavity by a fall on a mop handle. Scanty bleeding from a hymenal tear was child's only symptom on admission.

Serious injuries may cause little bleeding while superficial ones may produce considerable blood loss. The examiner must be certain that what appears to be a minor laceration of the vulva or hymen did not cause a rectal, urethral, vesical, or cul-de-sac injury (Fig 19–16). Rectal and vaginal (including vaginoscopic) examination, catheterization, and examination of the urine for blood must be performed to be certain that occult trauma did not occur.

The victim of the battered child syndrome may have bleeding from lacerations or abrasions of the perineum, but most often kicks or blows cause contusions or hematomas that do not bleed. Sexual molestation may cause little or no bleeding, but vaginal or anal rape usually causes hemorrhage.

When it is impossible to identify the source of bloodstains (or reddish discolorations) on a youngster's underclothing, malingering must be considered. Most little girls who pretend to be ill to obtain attention are less devious, but a few discover that blood on their panties is remarkably effective. A test for hematin differentiates blood from other red stains; fresh blood is never present at the time of examination. Investigation usually uncovers a family or environmental problem that led to the make-believe illness.

GENITAL TUMORS*

Genital tumors, although uncommon, must be considered whenever a girl is found to have a chronic genital ulcer, a nontraumatic swelling of the external genitalia, tissue protruding from the vagina, a fetid or bloody discharge, abdominal pain or enlargement, or premature sexual maturation. Despite their rarity, virtually every type of genital neoplasm that has been reported in adults has also been found in girls under 14 years of age. About half of the genital tumors in children are malignant or potentially malignant.

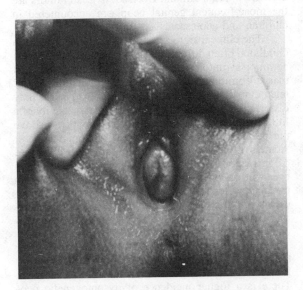

Figure 9–15. Urethral prolapse. Child aged 6 years.

*Tumors of the vagina are discussed in Chapter 9; tumors of the uterus, in Chapter 11; tumors of the ovaries, in Chapter 14.

1. TUMORS OF THE VULVA

Teratomas, hemangiomas, simple cysts of the hymen, retention cysts of the paraurethral ducts, benign granulomas of the perineum, and condylomata acuminata are representative of the benign tumors occasionally observed in children and adolescents.

Teratomas usually present as cystic masses arising from the midline of the perineum. Although a teratoma in this area may be benign, recurrence is likely unless a generous margin of healthy tissue is excised about its periphery.

Hemangiomas are not neoplastic, but they often cause the mother anxiety because of their disfiguring appearance. Capillary hemangiomas will almost invariably disappear as the child grows older. Atrophic changes begin in early childhood and are followed by gradual atrophy of the vascular components of the lesion. Excision, radiation, and radium are contraindicated. Cavernous hemangiomas, in contrast, are composed of vessels of considerable size. Injury to these may cause serious hemorrhage. For this reason, cavernous hemangiomas are best treated surgically.

Obstruction of a paraurethral duct may form a relatively large cystic mass that may distort the urethra. Recommended treatment is either marsupialization or later excision—before the childbearing age. If cysts of this type are not excised before pregnancy, they may rupture as the fetal head presses on the urethra during delivery. Thus, a urethral diverticulum or fissure may be produced.

Hymenal cysts and large **mesonephric (Gartner's duct) cysts** that block the vagina must be excised. The technical difficulties associated with excision of a large mesonephric cyst from the wall of the vagina of an infant may be considerable; a preliminary perineotomy often is helpful in providing exposure. Small cysts of mesonephric origin may be incised and drained; they do not require excision.

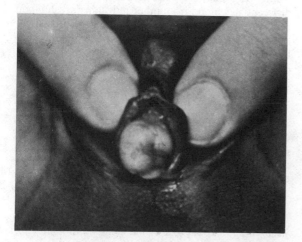

Figure 19–17. Simple vulvar or hymenal cyst arising posterior to urethra of newborn infant. (Courtesy of H Cohen et al and *Am J Dis Child.*)

Condylomata acuminata. Podophyllum resin, 5% in alcohol, may be applied to the lesions, but ointments may allow transfer of some of the irritating material to other parts of the body. Cryosurgery gives excellent results when used to remove small vulvar warts. Extensive lesions, usually seen in older girls, may require general anesthesia and fulguration or surgical excision.

2. TUMORS OF THE VAGINA & CERVIX

Most benign tumors of the vagina in children are unilocular cysts of remnants of the mesonephric duct. Squamous cell papillomas and granulation polyps of both the vagina and cervix are extremely rare in children; a few cervical papillomas have been reported.

Three types of vaginal carcinoma may appear during childhood and the early teens. Endodermal carcinoma occurs most often in young children; carcinoma arising in a remnant of a mesonephric duct (mesonephric carcinoma) occurs more often after 3 years of age; and clear cell adenocarcinoma of müllerian origin, often associated with a history of antenatal exposure to diethylstilbestrol, is encountered most frequently in postmenarcheal teenage girls.

Mixed mesodermal sarcoma of the vagina is the commonest malignant vaginal tumor in children; even so, it is very rare, most clinics having encountered only a handful of cases over many years.

The clinical features and treatment of tumors of the vagina and cervix are described in Chapters 9 and 10.

3. TUMORS OF THE OVARY

Only 1% of all neoplasms in premenarcheal children are ovarian tumors. Even so, ovarian tumors are the most frequent genital neoplasm encountered in children and adolescents.

The clinical signs presented by ovarian tumors in childhood often differ from those in adults. The 2 most common symptoms are abdominal pain and abdominal mass. Vomiting, signs of peritoneal irritation, fever, leukocytosis, and urinary frequency or dysuria may distort the clinical picture. Since the pelvic cavity of a little girl is quite small, most ovarian tumors rise above the pelvic inlet and present as an abdominal mass. Acute symptoms of severe pain, peritoneal irritation, or intra-abdominal hemmorrhage resulting from trauma (torsion, rupture, perforation) to an ovarian tumor may lead to an erroneous diagnosis of appendicitis, intussusception, or volvulus. At least one-fourth of all ovarian tumors in children elude diagnosis until they are seen at laparotomy.

Ovarian tumors of all varieties (except Brenner tumors) have been reported in premenarcheal children. Benign cystic teratomas account for at least 30%. There is a higher incidence of dysontogenetic neoplasms in children than in adolescents, and more ovarian tumors in premenarcheal girls are malignant than are ovarian tumors in adolescents and premenopausal women.

The diagnosis of an ovarian tumor in a child requires suspicion on the part of a physician. Tumors of the ovary should be considered in the differential diagnosis of most disorders causing abdominal pain or mass in a child. Pelvic (rectal) examination may be helpful if the tumor is in the pelvis but will not disclose a tumor rising above the pelvis.

Clinical features, diagnosis, and treatment of specific ovarian tumors in mature teenagers and adults are described in Chapter 14. The management of ovarian neoplasms in premenarcheal children is somewhat different from that in older patients, because the child needs continued ovarian function to complete her sexual and somatic maturation.

Conservative surgery (unilateral salpingo-oophorectomy) is justified for most premenarcheal patients with stage I cancer of the ovary provided it can be shown that the patients have no diaphragmatic or omental metastases and no extension to the para-aortic or pelvic lymph nodes and that peritoneal washings do not contain tumor cells. More radical surgery (bilateral salpingo-oophorectomy with hysterectomy) is indicated if a tumor has extended beyond the ovary, when it is a gonadoblastoma, and in some cases of dysgerminoma.

DELAYED SEXUAL MATURATION

Delayed sexual development is the absence of normal pubertal events at an age that is considered to be 2.8 SD from the mean (Styne and Grumbach, 1978). The normal sequence of events in sexual development is shown in Fig 19–18.

Most little girls will have beginning breast development by 9 years of age and menarche at 12–13. Absence of thelarche by the age of 13 and of menarche by the age of 15 are 2.8 SD from the norm. These are definitive indications of delayed sexual maturation that require investigation. However, most girls with delayed sexual development will see a physician before such obvious deviations, because of absence of breast growth. Their problems require attention not only to assuage their own and their parents' anxieties but also, and more importantly, because delayed sexual development may have serious implications for their future reproductive potential or may be the first sign of a life-threatening disorder.

Classification of Patients With Delayed Sexual Maturation

Patients with delayed sexual maturation are either **eugonadal** (with signs of ovarian function) or **hypogonadal** (with evidence of ovarian failure). Hypogonadal patients are either **hypogonadotropic** or **hypergonadotropic** depending on their gonadotropin levels. Those who have an increased secretion of go-

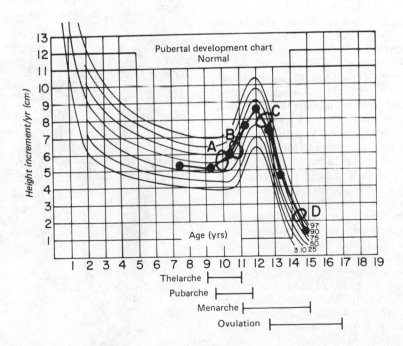

Figure 19–18. A pubertal development chart for a normally developing female adolescent. Growth data are converted to growth velocity and plotted. The growth velocity curve shows initial adolescent acceleration in growth followed by the growth spurt and subsequent deceleration. Superimposed on this curve are the following pubertal events: *A,* thelarche; *B,* pubarche; *C,* menarche; *D,* onset of ovulation. (From Reindollar RH, McDonough PG: Delayed sexual development: Common causes and basic clinical approach. *Pediatr Ann* 1981;10:178.)

Table 19–7. Classification of conditions causing delayed sexual maturation.

I. In patients with functioning gonads (eugonadism)
  A. Anatomic abnormalities
  B. Androgen insensitivity
  C. Inappropriate feedback
  D. Other causes
II. In patients with ovarian failure (hypogonadism)
  A. With decreased gonadotropin secretion (hypogonadotropism)
    1. Constitutional delay (late starters)
    2. Neoplasia
    3. Isolated deficiency of gonadotropin-releasing factor
    4. Other causes of hypothalamic-pituitary failure
  B. With increased gonadotropin secretion (hypergonadotropism)
    1. With a normal chromosomal complement
      a. 46,XX
      b. 46,XY female
    2. With an abnormal chromosomal complement
      a. Gonadal dysgenesis
        (1) 45,X
        (2) Other single cell lines
        (3) Mosaics

nadotropins are further screened for normal chromosomal complements. If one can correctly categorize the patient, as shown in Table 19–7, the diagnosis should be relatively simple.

Eugonadism

Patients with functioning ovaries and delayed sexual maturation usually consult a physician in their mid-teens because they have not menstruated. Most have well-formed female figures and developing breasts. The majority of those over the age of 12 will have pubic hair. Approximately one-fourth of the patients who present themselves because of delayed sexual maturation are eugonadal but not yet menarcheal.

Congenital anomalies of the paramesonephric (müllerian) structures are responsible for most cases in which the patients are eugonadal but fail to menstruate. The most frequent of these defects is congenital absence of the uterus and vagina, the Rokitansky-Küster-Hauser syndrome, which is also the second most frequent diagnosis in cases of delayed sexual maturation. Other anatomic causes for absence of the menarche include imperforate hymen, agenesis of the cervix, congenital noncanalization of the cervix, and partial or complete agenesis of the vagina. The uterus, usually present with this group of anomalies, may be unusually small or otherwise anomalous. Gynecologic examination establishes the diagnosis of these congenital anomalies. Their treatment is described in Chapter 8.

The possibility that an adolescent may become pregnant before she menstruates is highly unlikely but must be borne in mind when considering the causes of delayed menarche in patients with normally developed secondary sexual characteristics.

Patients with the androgen insensitivity (testicular feminization) syndrome have normal gonadal (testicular) endocrine function, develop well-formed breasts during puberty, have a female or eunuchoid habitus, and are reared as females because of the appearance of their external genitalia at birth. Their testes secrete both testosterone and the müllerian inhibitory factor that prevents embryonic development of the müllerian system, but because end-organs normally responsive to androgens are not sensitive to testosterone, male structures do not develop. The diagnosis is usually not difficult, because other members of the family may also have the syndrome (Fig 19–19). These patients have well-developed breasts, scanty pubic hair, short, blind vaginas, and an XY karyotype. Treatment is discussed on p 143.

Patients with apparent normal sexual development may have inappropriate positive feedback for luteinizing hormone surge to stimulate ovulation and a

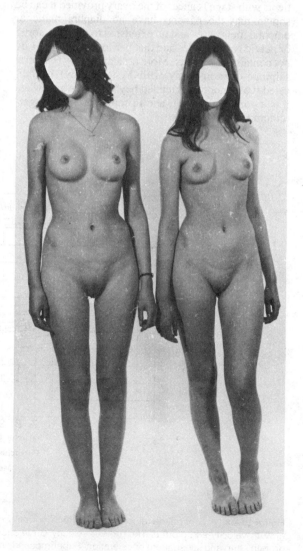

Figure 19–19. XY sisters with androgen insensitivity syndrome. (By courtesy of Prof Sir CJ Dewhurst.)

distortion of the estrogen/androgen ratio with an excess of androgen as a cause of their delayed menarche. This endocrine disturbance is encountered in adolescents with postnatal adrenogenital syndrome and polycystic ovarian disease. Excess androgen usually causes virilization, and estrogen without progesterone causes endometrial hyperplasia. Treatment of the polycystic ovary and adrenogenital syndromes are described elsewhere in this text.

Hypogonadotropic Hypogonadism

Patients in this category have normal but functionless ovaries, because the ovaries are not activated by gonadotropins. Failure of gonadotropic secretion may be the result of either hypothalamic or pituitary dysfunction.

Physiologic or constitutional delay is one of the 3 most frequent diagnoses given girls with delayed sexual maturation (Reindollar and McDonough, 1981). These adolescents are late starters whose accelerated growth and development of secondary sexual characteristics lag behind those of their peers. Frequently, there is a family history of delayed sexual development. The diagnosis is made by exclusion of other causes for delayed sexual maturation. The gonadotropin-releasing factor challenge test will differentiate constitutional delay in sexual maturation from isolated deficiency of gonadotropin-releasing factor. Reassurance is the only treatment necessary, but the patient must be kept under observation until she is having regular menstrual cycles. Occasionally, an adolescent will require hormonal replacement therapy because of psychologic distress over her condition.

Untreated congenital adrenocortical hyperplasia, hormone-producing adrenal tumors, the postnatal adrenogenital syndrome, Cushing's syndrome, untreated thyroid disorders (primary hypothyroidism, Hashimoto's thyroiditis), and protracted systemic, organic, or functional disorders may retard hypothalamic and pituitary maturation and delay sexual development.

Weight loss due to severe dieting, marked protein deficiency, and fat loss without notable loss of muscle often seen in young female athletes may also delay or suppress hypothalamic-pituitary maturation. It has been demonstrated that heroin addiction may cause amenorrhea, but its effect on sexual maturation has not been documented.

No cause for panhypopituitarism can be identified in about half of the cases. The most commonly identified cause is pituitary destruction by any one of a number of neoplastic, infectious, or inflammatory processes. The symptoms caused by the absence of the other trophic hormones generally overshadow the child's delayed sexual maturation.

A pituitary or parasellar tumor, particularly craniopharyngioma or pituitary microadenoma, should always be considered in the evaluation of a patient with delayed sexual maturation. Craniopharyngiomas are rapidly growing tumors that often develop in late childhood. Pituitary microadenomas, although slow-

growing, also may become symptomatic during puberty and interfere with sexual maturation.

Isolated deficiency of gonadotropin-releasing factor associated with intracranial anomalies that also may cause anosmia (Kallmann's syndrome or olfactory-genital syndrome) is uncommon in females. Its other symptoms are failure of sexual maturation and low gonadotropin levels. Every patient suspected of having the syndrome should be tested for sense of smell, because many have a minor degree of anosmia. All of these patients have a positive response to a gonadotropin-releasing factor challenge test. Estrogen therapy may be used to activate ovaries and cause sexual development.

Hypergonadotropic Hypogonadism

A. Patients With Normal Chromosomal Constitutions: The adolescent with ovarian failure and a normal chromosomal constitution will present with undeveloped breasts, little or no pubic hair, and an anestrogenic vaginal smear. She will be tall for her age because without ovarian steroidogenesis, the epiphyses of her long bones do not close at the normal time. Her gonadotropin titers will be elevated, and a 46,XX karyotype is expected. Her problem is one of ovarian failure due to factors other than deletion of X chromosomal material. Such causes include bilateral ovariectomy, pelvic irradiation or chemotherapy for malignant disease, bilateral mumps oophoritis, destruction of the ovaries by torsion or infection, autosomal recessive genes, or an infiltrative process that destroys the gonads. Approximately 46% of these patients will have a few ovarian follicles, and they may have a few menstrual periods. Patients with ovarian failure of this type should be treated by estrogen replacement.

The Savage syndrome (so named by Jones and De Moraes-Ruehsen, 1969, after the first patient they saw with the disorder), more properly termed the resistant ovary syndrome, is characterized by delayed menarche or primary amenorrhea, a 46,XX karyotype, hypergonadotropism, and ovaries that, despite apparently normal follicular apparatus, do not respond to endogenous gonadotropins. It is assumed that the absence of follicular receptors for gonadotropins is responsible for ovarian failure in patients with the Savage syndrome. These individuals have normally developed secondary sexual characteristics, which sets them apart from other adolescents with delayed sexual maturation, hypergonadotropic hypogonadism, and a normal chromosomal constitution. Too few patients with this syndrome have been reported to establish a protocol for treatment.

B. The XY Female: Adolescents who are being reared as girls, who have female external genitalia, intra-abdominal or ectopic malfunctioning testes, and a normal 46,XY chromosomal constitution may be XY females. Unlike those with androgen insensitivity whose testicular function is basically normal, these patients suffer from either **anatomic** or **enzymatic testicular failure.** With complete testicular failure of either type, the testes do not secrete testosterone or müllerian inhibitory factor. Adolescents with **partial testicular failure** will have ambiguous genitalia and may become virilized at puberty. The diagnosis and treatment of intersex disorders are discussed elsewhere in this book.

C. Patients With Abnormal Chromosomal Constitutions: Two intact X chromosomes are necessary for normal ovarian structure and function. Chromosomal accidents that may be associated with failure of ovarian development include loss of all of one X chromosome, deletion of part of one, or transverse division at the centromere rather than longitudinal division, leading to isochromosome formation. Mosaicism with 2 or more cell lines, one containing an abnormal chromosome, is probably more common than single cell line abnormalities.

Failure of sexual maturation is due to loss of the ovarian-determinant gene that induces ovarian formation. Somatic abnormalities that are present in many patients with gonadal dysgenesis are the result of the deletion of genetic material carried on the lost portion of the abnormal sex chromosomes. As a result, some patients with gonadal dysgenesis will have only failure of sexual maturation, whereas others will have all of the clinical features characteristic of Turner's syndrome (see p 155).

Diagnosis

The history, general and gynecologic examination, and vaginal smear will identify eugonadal patients and differentiate among those who have an anatomic cause for absent menarche, those who have the androgen insensitivity syndrome, and those with inappropriate feedback disorders. Gonadotropin assays of those who are hypoestrogenic determine which individuals secrete excessive or deficient amounts of gonadotropins.

Whether a patient who has hypergonadotropic hypogonadism has or does not have a normal chromosomal complement is determined by her karyotype. Those who are diagnosed as having hypogonadotropic hypogonadism may require more extensive testing, including skull roentgenograms, CT scans of the pituitary and sella, prolactin assays, gonadotropin-releasing factor challenge tests, and an extensive endocrinologic evaluation. A few must be followed for an extended period of time before a definitive diagnosis can be made.

●   ●   ●

References

Adelman S et al: Surgical lesions of the ovary in infancy and childhood. *Surg Gynecol Obstet* 1975;**141**:219.

Andrew D, Bumstead E: The role of fomites in the transmission of vaginitis. *Can Med Assoc J* 1975;**112**:1181.

Angeli A et al: Effect of cyproterone acetate therapy on gonadotropin response to synthetic luteinizing hormone–releasing hormone (LRH) in girls with idiopathic precocious puberty. *J Clin Endocrinol Metab* 1976;**42**:551.

Bai J et al: Drug-related menstrual aberrations. *Obstet Gynecol* 1974;**44**:713.

Bidlingmaier F, Butenandt O, Knorr D: Plasma gonadotropins and estrogens in girls with idiopathic precocious puberty. *Pediatr Res* (Feb) 1977;**11**:91.

Bloow H et al: *Cancer in Children*. Springer-Verlag, 1975.

Bramley M: Study of female babies of women entering confinement with vaginal trichomoniasis. *Br J Vener Dis* 1976;**52**:58.

Davis T: Chronic vulvovaginitis in children due to *Shigella flexneri*. *Pediatrics* 1975;**56**:41.

Dewhurst CJ: Congenital malformations of the lower genital tract. *Clin Obstet Gynaecol* 1978;**5**:250.

Dewhurst CJ: Tumors of the genital tract in childhood and adolescence. *Clin Obstet Gynecol* 1977;**20**:595.

Dungy CL et al: Hereditary hydrometrocolpos with polydactyly in infancy. *Pediatrics* 1971;**47**:138.

Escomel E: La plus jeune mère du monde. *Press Méd* 1939;**47**:875.

Frewen T, Bannotyne R: Gonococcal vulvovaginitis in prepubertal girls. *Clin Pediatr* 1979;**18**:491.

Friedrich EG Jr: *Vulvar Disease*. Saunders, 1976.

Hare M, Mowla A: Genital herpes virus infection in a prepubertal girl. *Br J Obstet Gynaecol* 1977;**89**:141.

Harris BH, Boles ET Jr: Rational surgery for tumors of the ovary in children. *J Pediatr Surg* 1974;**9**:289.

Huber A, Kalkschmid W: *Praxis der Gynäkologie im Kindes und Jungendalter*. Thieme Verlag, 1977.

Huffman JW: Endometriosis in young teen-aged girls. *Pediatr Ann* 1981;**10**:501.

Huffman JW: Gynecologic infections during childhood and adolescence. In: *Textbook of Pediatric Infectious Diseases*. Feigin R, Cherry J (editors). Saunders, 1981.

Huffman JW: Precocious motherhood. *Pediatr Ann* 1981;**10**:165.

Huffman JW: Premenarchal vulvovaginitis. *Clin Obstet Gynecol* 1977;**20**:581.

Huffman JW: Tumours of the genitalia. *Clin Obstet Gynecol* 1974;**1**:663.

Huffman JW, Dewhurst CJ, Capraro VJ: *The Gynecology of Childhood and Adolescence*, 2nd ed. Saunders, 1981.

Israel K et al: Neonatal and childhood gonococcal infections. *Clin Obstet Gynecol* 1975;**18**:143.

Jereb B et al: Ovarian cancer in children and adolescents: A review of 15 cases. *Med Pediatr Oncol* 1977;**3**:339.

Johnston FE et al: Critical weight at menarche. *Am J Dis Child* 1975;**129**:19.

Jones GS, De Moraes-Ruehsen MA: A new syndrome of amenorrhea in association with hypergonadotropism and apparently normal ovarian follicular apparatus. *Obstet Gynecol* 1969;**104**:597.

Kauli R et al: Cyproterone acetate in the treatment of precocious puberty. *Arch Dis Child* 1976;**51**:202.

Kobayashi R, Moore T: Ovarian teratomas in early childhood. *J Pediatr Surg* 1978;**13**:419.

Kurman RJ, Norris HJ: Germ cell tumors of the ovary. *Pathol Annu* 1978;**13(Part 1)**:291.

McDonough PG: Pediatric and adolescent gynecology: Menarchal delay. In: *Current Problems in Obstetrics and Gynecology.* Vol 1. Year Book, 1977.

Montagu A: *The Reproductive Development of the Female,* 3rd ed. PSG, 1979.

Nelson J et al: Gonorrhea in preschool and school-aged children. *JAMA* 1976;**236**:1359.

Pascoe DJ, Duterte BO: The medical diagnosis of sexual abuse in the premenarcheal child. *Pediatr Ann* 1981;**10**:187.

Pennington GW: The reproductive endocrinology of childhood and adolescence. *Clin Obstet Gynecol* 1974;**1**:509.

Piver MS: Management of children with unilateral ovarian malignancies. *Pediatr Ann* 1981;**10**:191.

Piver MS, Lurain J: Childhood ovarian cancers: New advances in treatment. *NY State J Med* 1979;**79**:1199.

Prader A: Delayed adolescence. *Clin Endocrinol Metab* 1975;**4**:143.

Pryse-Davies J: The development, structure and function of the female pelvic organs in childhood. *Clin Obstet Gynecol* 1974;**1**:483.

Reindollar RH, McDonough PG: Delayed sexual development. Common causes and basic clinical approach. *Pediatr Ann* 1981;**10**:178.

Rey-Stocker I: Les infections des génitaux chez le nouveau-né, l'infant et l'adolescente. *Rev Méd Suisse Romande* 1977; **97**:295.

Rogol AD, Rosen SW: LH and FSH responses to LHRH in patients with congenital anosomia and hypogonadotropic hypogonadism. In: *The LH Releasing Hormone.* Beling CG, Wentz AC (editors). Masson, 1980.

Sarles R: Incest. *Pediatr Rev* 1980;**2**:51.

Scherzer IN, Lala P: Sexual offenses committed against children. *Clin Pediatr* 1980;**19**:679.

Seidel J et al: Condylomata acuminata as a sign of sexual abuse in children. *J Pediatr* 1979;**95**:553.

Sgroi S: Pediatric gonorrhea beyond infancy. *Pediatr Ann* 1979; **8**:73.

Shalet SM et al: Ovarian failure following abdominal irradiation in childhood. *Br J Cancer* 1976;**33**:655.

Shaw R: Tests of the hypothalamic-pituitary-ovarian axis. *Clin Obstet Gynaecol* 1976;**3**:485.

Styne DM, Grumbach MM: Puberty in the male and female: Its physiologies and disorders. Page 189 in: *Reproductive Endocrinology.* Yen SSC, Jaffe RB (editors). Saunders, 1978.

Widholm O: Dysmenorrhea during adolescence. *Acta Obstet Gynecol Scand* 1979;**87**:61.

Widholm O: Genital bleeding during childhood. *Pediatr Ann* 1981;**10**:170.

Zacharias I, Rand WM, Wurtman RJ: A prospective study of sexual development and growth in American girls: The statistics of menarche. *Obstet Gynecol Surv* 1976;**31**:325.

Zuspan FP et al: Alleged rape: An invitational symposium. *J Reprod Med* 1974;**12**:133.

20 | Preoperative & Postoperative Care

Jack W. Pearson, MD

Patient attitudes toward operations are highly variable and sometimes difficult to explain. An operation is a major event in the patient's life even if the procedure is considered a minor one by the surgeon. Before recommending any diagnostic or therapeutic surgical procedure, the gynecologist must be certain that the patient understands and agrees that the benefits outweigh the risks. Operations on the reproductive organs demand particularly careful discussion with the patient. Concerns about reproductive capacity or continuation of sexual function may be uppermost in the patient's mind. The gynecologist cannot always promise to preserve fertility, since unsuspected pelvic disease may make preservation of the reproductive organs unwise. Nonetheless, the patient should be assured that her wishes will be respected if they do impose a conflict with professional judgment. Questions about continuation of reproductive function may disguise the patient's more urgent concern about sexual function. Gynecologic operations do not often prevent intercourse or interfere with sexual pleasure and gratification, but reassurance is required.

All records of prior hospitalizations should be obtained. Patients' ability to recall illnesses and surgery is notoriously inaccurate, and past records may be essential to the interpretation of present findings and may significantly influence the management plan.

It is vital that the patient and her family be thoroughly counseled so that they will recognize both the expectations and the limitations of the proposed procedure. The scope of this discussion should be incorporated into the medical record.

PREOPERATIVE CARE

GENERAL CONSIDERATIONS IN PREOPERATIVE EVALUATION

The preoperative evaluation should include, in addition to the history, physical examination, and laboratory tests, whatever may be called for in the way of consultation with the anesthesiologist and other physicians. The medical evaluation must be carried out in such a way as to identify all disorders that might complicate the operative procedure or convalescence.

History

The gynecologic history should include the menstrual history, past pregnancies, prior gynecologic disorders, and the presence of leukorrhea, vaginal bleeding, or pelvic pain.

The obstetric history should include the number and duration of pregnancies, length of labor, type of delivery, and complications.

List the dates of all operations, serious injuries, and complications if any.

The general medical history consists of a review of symptoms referable to the head, eyes, ears, nose, mouth, neck, lymph nodes, breasts, and thyroid gland as well as the cardiovascular, respiratory, gastrointestinal, and urologic systems.

The psychologic history should include emotional problems, environmental factors, and mental status.

The location, type, and severity of pain are of great importance. Note and record how the pain is induced, how it may be aggravated or relieved, and what relationship there is to effort, posture, eating, coitus, defecation, voiding, or menstruation.

Other problems of interest include bleeding tendencies, medications currently being taken, and allergies to antibiotics or other agents.

Physical Examination

The physical examination should be done in the same general sequence as the history outline. Special attention should be paid to the vaginal and combined rectovaginal examination.

Laboratory Studies

In all preoperative patients, routine laboratory procedures should include a complete blood count, serologic tests for syphilis, chest x-ray, urinalysis, and urine culture. Blood should be obtained for typing and cross-matching in case transfusions are required.

Ultrasound evaluation is of great value, particularly in obstetrics, where both Doppler techniques and imagery have helped to determine fetal maturity and rule out congenital fetal abnormalities before repeat cesarean sections are scheduled.

Fasting or 2-hour postprandial plasma glucose, bleeding and clotting studies, or erythrocyte sedimentation rate should be recorded if suggested by the initial evaluation. A Papanicolaou smear should be obtained.

Tissue biopsy, tests for endocrine function, and tests to determine causes of leukorrhea are important.

Consultations

Consultation with the anesthesiologist should be arranged well in advance of major surgery if possible. This allows for optimal selection of anesthesia for each patient with consideration for drug interactions, prior anesthetic experiences (and problems), and patient preferences, and also gives an opportunity to allay patient anxieties. Consultations with other physicians should be scheduled (1) if requested by the patient or her family, (2) if the physician feels that expert advice or assistance would in any way benefit the patient, or (3) if medicolegal problems are anticipated.

Urologic evaluation—to include cystourethroscopy, recording of residual urine, an intravenous urogram, and cystometric study—is recommended in any case of corrective bladder surgery.

In many institutions, nursing personnel from admitting services and from the operating and recovery rooms introduce themselves and their areas of responsibility with the aid of audiovisual displays to better prepare the patient emotionally as well as intellectually for the anticipated (and often dreaded) surgery.

Operative Consent

The patient or her parents or legal guardian must sign a consent form prior to surgery after the procedure has been properly explained and its risks and probable outcome and alternatives have been made clear. Permission is valid only for the procedures designated in the consent form.

Preoperative Notes

All details of the medical examination and diagnostic and therapeutic formulations must be entered in the patient's chart.

Preoperative Orders

Routine preoperative orders should cover the following:

A. Skin Preparation: Many gynecologic surgeons choose to have the skin over the operative site scrubbed with povidone-iodine the night before the procedure is to be performed and again just before surgery. It has been shown that wound infection incidence is decreased by shaving the operative site in surgery rather than the night before the procedure. When a vaginal procedure is intended or when the vagina is to be incised as in total abdominal hysterectomy, povidone-iodine douches or antibiotic suppositories or creams may be beneficial. Recent experience tends to refute this, however, and suggests that saline douches are as effective.

B. Diet: The patient should receive nothing by mouth for at least 8 hours before the operation so that the stomach will be empty at the time of anesthesia.

C. Preparation of the Gastrointestinal Tract: A cleansing enema should be ordered the night before to make certain that the examination under anesthesia will be accurate and to reduce the need for a bowel movement during the early postoperative period. Mechanical (eg, enemas until clear) or antibiotic bowel preparation (eg, neomycin) may be necessary when the nature of the disease makes the possibility of bowel injury or resection likely.

D. Sedation: A sedative-hypnotic should be prescribed to ensure restful sleep the night before the operation. Pentobarbital sodium, 100–200 mg orally (or equivalent), may be used.

E. Preanesthetic Medication: Additional preoperative medication is usually ordered by the anesthesiologist (see Chapter 30). A useful preoperative combination for most patients is morphine sulfate, 8 mg, and atropine sulfate, 0.2 mg, intramuscularly, on call to the operating room.

F. Other Medications: Special preoperative orders sometimes must be given for modification of regularly required medications such as insulin and corticosteroids. The dosage or route of administration may have to be altered.

G. Antibiotics: Preoperative or prophylactic antibiotics have been reported to be of value especially in cases of expected bowel surgery and in elective vaginal hysterectomies. The cephalosporins and metronidazole have been particularly effective in decreasing postoperative febrile morbidity.

H. Blood Transfusions: Type and cross-match the patient's blood and order enough bank blood to meet any surgical emergency. In circumstances where transfusions are not usually required, a type and screen program is clearly both clinically satisfactory and cost effective.

I. Bladder Preparations: For minor procedures, the patient voids prior to being moved to the operating room. If major pelvic surgery is planned, an indwelling Foley catheter should be anchored when the vaginal preparation is done in the operating room.

J. Douches: An antiseptic douche, eg, with povidone-iodine, is commonly prescribed prior to gynecologic operations.

DISORDERS AFFECTING OPERATIVE RISK*

1. CARDIOVASCULAR DISEASE

Any patient with significant heart disease is a high-risk surgical candidate. Careful preoperative evaluation of the lesion and the patient's functional capacity is required, and she must be observed closely during and after surgery. Many factors may adversely affect cardiovascular function postoperatively, eg, electrolyte imbalance, hypotension, severe pain, apprehension, infection, and tachycardia. If a patient presents evidence of a cardiac disorder, cardiologic consultation is usually advisable. Special attention

---

*Bleeding disorders are discussed in Chapter 33.

should be devoted to patients with a history of stroke or treatment for a cardiac condition.

Special Studies

A. Electrocardiography: Electrocardiographic studies may be of value in identifying the patient with coronary artery disease, ventricular hypertrophy, myocardial insufficiency, digitalis or other drug effect, electrolyte disturbance, or arrhythmia. An ECG probably should be obtained for all patients over 40 years of age. The ECG should serve as a baseline for subsequent studies if postoperative complications develop.

B. Central Venous Pressure: Determination of the central venous pressure may provide useful information regarding cardiovascular dynamics. In most cases, this can be obtained simply by careful attention to the aspects of the physical examination that will be affected if the central venous pressure is abnormal (eg, blood pressure, pulse, pulse pressure, heart rate, status of neck veins when supine, auscultation and percussion of chest, presence or absence of edema, size of liver). If there is a significant question, direct monitoring by means of a central venous catheter should be instituted.

Factors that tend to elevate central venous pressure include heart failure, pulmonary congestion, increased venous return due to hypervolemia or reduced peripheral resistance, and excessive intravenous administration of fluids. Low central venous pressure readings may reflect diminished venous return associated with hypovolemic shock, venous pooling, or increased peripheral resistance.

The more complicated disorders with evident marked compromise of cardiovascular status are best evaluated and followed throughout their course by use of the Swan-Ganz catheter, which accurately measures parameters such as cardiac output, central venous pressure, pulmonary wedge pressure, and atrial pressure.

Varicose Veins

Patients with large, extensive varicosities or a history of phlebitis are at risk of developing lower extremity thrombophlebitis. One may minimize this risk by discontinuance of oral contraceptives 3–4 weeks preoperatively, prevention of dehydration, early ambulation, and prompt and adequate treatment of anemia, cardiac disorders, or diabetes mellitus. Before the operation, support stockings should be worn from toe to knee (or thigh if possible). After surgery, they should be worn continuously and discarded only after full ambulation is restored. Pressure on the calf or thigh should be avoided during a long operative procedure. Postoperative leg exercises should be initiated as soon as possible to prevent phlebitis. This may be begun even before ambulation by having the patient press against a footboard whenever supine. Prophylactic administration of heparin (5000 units subcutaneously 2 hours before surgery and every 8 hours thereafter for 6 days) may be given to prevent thromboembolization in selected cases. No laboratory control is required. This regimen has been shown to decrease the incidence of deep vein thrombosis by 25–30% and fatal pulmonary embolism by almost 20%. Similarly, the empiric use of high- or low-molecular-weight dextran (1 unit on the day of surgery and 1 unit daily for the first 2 postoperative days) may prevent thrombosis.

Postoperatively, the patient should be advised to avoid prolonged sitting, eg, auto, train, or air travel, during the first month after surgery.

2. RESPIRATORY TRACT DISEASE

Acute respiratory tract infections such as pharyngitis, tonsillitis, laryngitis, pneumonitis, bronchitis, and colds are contraindications to elective surgery. If emergency surgery is necessary, inhalation anesthesia is undesirable and measures must be taken to avoid postoperative atelectasis or pneumonia. If the infection is severe, appropriate antibiotic therapy should be initiated promptly. Ampicillin often is administered until the results of cultures become available. The patient should be free of respiratory infection for 1–2 weeks before elective surgery.

Chronic pulmonary disease predisposes to serious postoperative complications. The most common disorders are chronic bronchitis, emphysema, asthma, bronchiectasis, pulmonary fibrosis, and tuberculosis. Consultation with an internist is essential, particularly if an elective procedure is planned. The risk due to bronchiectasis may be minimized by proper preoperative treatment. Asthmatic patients and those who smoke are at risk of developing pulmonary complications during or after surgery, and special care must be exercised in the management of such patients. Prolonged operations involving anesthesia or hypoventilation increase the risk of postoperative pulmonary problems. Careful evaluation, including chest x-rays and pulmonary function tests, enable the surgeon to decide when the operation may be safely undertaken.

Documentation of the presence of dentures is important especially in those individuals who will have general anesthesia and will be intubated for the operative procedure. The use of an antacid preoperatively is of great value particularly for the obstetric patient who is more apt to have a significant volume of gastric secretions in spite of fasting overnight.

3. RENAL DISEASE

Renal function should be appraised if there is a history of kidney disease, diabetes mellitus, or hypertension; if the patient is over 60 years of age; or if the routine urinalysis reveals proteinuria, casts, or red cells.

A simple screening test to measure the ability of the kidney to concentrate urine is to withhold oral fluids after supper and test the specific gravity of the urine the next morning. A specific gravity greater than 1.020 is normal.

It may be necessary to further evaluate renal function by measuring creatinine clearance, blood urea nitrogen, PSP excretion, and plasma electrolyte determinations. An intravenous urogram may also be indicated.

4. DIABETES MELLITUS

Control of diabetes is made especially difficult by the stress of operation, acute infection, anesthesia, or electrolyte imbalance. The diabetic patient must be carefully observed and promptly treated before fluid and electrolyte abnormalities, ketosis, hypoglycemia, and infection develop. Diabetics whose disease is out of control are especially susceptible to postoperative sepsis. Consultation with an internist may be considered to ensure control of diabetes before, during, and after surgery.

If the diabetes is severe, it may be necessary to admit the patient to the hospital several days before the operation for study and treatment. One may substitute crystalline insulin for long-acting insulin for tighter control.

Routine examination of the blood glucose should be performed before each meal and at bedtime to help determine diabetic control and adjust the insulin dosage.

Serum electrolyte determinations should be recorded as points of reference for postoperative management. Fasting plasma glucose should be determined prior to surgery.

Oral agents are used only infrequently. However, patients who can be controlled by diet or oral hypoglycemic agents should not be fasted for more than 8 hours before surgery. Oral treatment can often be maintained postoperatively, with supplementary 5–10% dextrose in water given slowly intravenously to prevent ketoacidosis. Blood and urine glucose determinations should be recorded postoperatively.

Insulin-dependent diabetics should be given one-half of their usual regular (crystalline and intermediate-acting) insulin dosage on the morning of the operation. Start a slow intravenous infusion of 10% dextrose in water, giving no more than 2000 mL/d. Crystalline insulin should be given every 6 hours in amounts dictated by plasma glucose determinations. Do not add the crystalline insulin directly into the intravenous dextrose container.

Neither insulin nor carbohydrate should be withheld before, during, or after surgery.

Catheterization to obtain urine specimens should be avoided if possible.

5. HYPERTHYROIDISM

A persistently rapid pulse, agitation, tremor, heat intolerance, or other manifestations of hyperthy-roidism demand careful evaluation of the thyroid status preoperatively. Consultation regarding the management of such patients should be sought before major surgery.

6. ANEMIA

Anemia diagnosed in the preoperative obstetric or gynecologic patient usually is of the iron deficiency type caused by either inadequate diet, chronic blood loss, or both. Care must be taken to differentiate iron deficiency anemia from other anemias, eg, sickle cell anemias. Iron deficiency anemia is the only type of anemia in which stained iron deposits cannot be identified in the bone marrow. Megaloblastic, hemolytic, and aplastic anemias usually are easily differentiated from iron deficiency anemia on the basis of the history and simple laboratory examinations. The diagnosis of obscure anemias may require the help of a hematologist.

Iron deficiency anemia will respond to oral or parenteral iron therapy. In emergencies or urgent cases, preoperative blood transfusions, preferably with packed red cells, may be given.

7. OTHER CONDITIONS AFFECTING OPERATIVE RISK

The Pregnant Patient

The diagnosis of early pregnancy must be considered in the decision to do elective major surgery in the female. Elective surgery generally should be postponed until after delivery. Diagnostic or evaluative procedures inherent in the proper workup for *necessary* surgery override theoretic fetal hazards in the pregnant patient. Appropriate protective measures should be taken to minimize these dangers, eg, shield the uterus from radiation during x-ray studies, use tocolytic agents to prevent premature labor, and consider possible fetal effects when pharmacologic anesthetic agents are to be employed. Hypotension and hypoxia must be meticulously avoided during anesthetic administration or surgical manipulation.

The new and more sensitive radioreceptor assay and radioimmunoassay for pregnancy are positive within 10 days of conception, before the anticipated menstrual period. This capability is important in scheduling elective surgery, especially in gynecologic procedures such as tubal ligation or hysterectomy.

The Elderly Patient

The older patient presents significant problems related to general systemic deterioration. The American Society of Anesthesiologists' class 1–5 preoperative evaluation scale has been shown to be of significant prognostic value in these patients.

Serum electrolytes must be determined in all elderly patients and any imbalances corrected by appropriate parenteral solutions. Care must be taken when administering intravenous fluids not to overload the circulation. Nutritional deficiencies should be corrected before elective surgery is undertaken in older persons. In patients who are found to be significantly deprived, total parenteral nutrition (TPN) may be required before and after surgery.

The elderly patient often requires smaller dosages of medications such as narcotics. Barbiturates should be prescribed with caution as mental confusion and uncooperative behavior often result.

Fluid intake and urinary output should be monitored carefully and the patient's daily weight recorded. Frequent change of position is essential to prevent the development of a decubitus ulcer in the older patient or in one who has been bedridden.

The Obese Patient

It is advisable to delay elective surgery until the patient loses weight. Obesity puts the patient and the hospital team at a disadvantage in avoiding morbidity. Intravenous samples are difficult to obtain, and fluid lines are difficult to maintain. The anesthesiologist experiences difficulty with induction, intubation, maintenance of anesthesia, and arousal of the patient. The surgeon must struggle for exposure, always with the risk of trauma to adjacent organs and with subsequent poor wound healing because of forced retraction of the abdominal wall. Postoperatively, nursing personnel are seriously challenged in attempting to achieve ambulation and to prevent respiratory complications and thrombotic and embolic phenomena, which are far more likely to occur in these patients than in patients of normal weight.

Drug Allergies & Sensitivities

The obstetric or gynecologic patient who is being evaluated and prepared for a major operation may receive a variety of medications. Drug allergies, sensitivities, incompatibilities, and other adverse effects must be anticipated and prevented if possible. A history of serious reaction or sickness after injection, oral administration, or other use of any of the following substances should be noted and the medication avoided: (1) antibiotic medications, (2) narcotics, (3) anesthetics, (4) analgesics, (5) sedatives, (6) antitoxins or antisera, and (7) antiseptics. Untoward reactions to other medications, foods (eg, milk, chocolate), and adhesive tape should also be noted. A personal history or strong family history of asthma, hay fever, or other allergic disorders should alert the surgeon to the possibility of drug reactions.

The Immunologically Compromised or Altered Host

A patient may be considered an immunologically compromised or altered host if her capacity to respond normally to infection or trauma has been significantly impaired by disease or therapy. Obviously, preoperative recognition and special evaluation of these patients is important.

A. Increased Susceptibility to Infection: Certain drugs may reduce the patient's resistance to infection by interfering with host defense mechanisms. Corticosteroids, immunosuppressive agents, cytotoxic drugs, and prolonged antibiotic therapy are associated with an increased incidence of superinfection by fungi or other resistant organisms. It is possible that the synergistic combination of irradiation, corticosteroids, and serious underlying disease may set the stage for clinical fungal infection. A high rate of wound, pulmonary, and other infections is seen in renal failure, presumably as a result of decreased host resistance. Granulocytopenia and diseases associated with immunologic deficiency (eg, lymphomas, leukemias, and hypogammaglobulinemia) are frequently complicated by sepsis. The uncontrolled diabetic is also observed clinically to be more susceptible to infection.

B. Delayed Wound Healing: This problem can be anticipated in certain categories of patients whose tissue repair process may be compromised. Many systemic factors have been alleged to influence wound healing; however, only a few are of clinical significance: protein depletion, ascorbic acid deficiency, marked dehydration or edema, and severe anemia.

It has been shown experimentally that hypovolemia, vasoconstriction, increased blood viscosity, and increased intravascular aggregation and erythrostasis due to remote trauma will interfere with wound healing, probably by reducing oxygen tension and diffusion within the wound.

Large doses of corticosteroids depress wound healing. This effect apparently is increased by starvation and protein depletion. Wounds of patients who have received large doses of corticosteroids preoperatively should be closed with special care to prevent disruption inasmuch as healing may be delayed.

Patients who have received anticancer chemotherapeutic agents are just as apt to require surgery as any other population group. Cytotoxic drugs may interfere with cell proliferation and may decrease the tensile strength of the surgical wound. It is wise to assume that healing may be retarded in patients receiving antitumor drugs.

Slow healing sometimes is observed in debilitated patients, ie, those with advanced cancer, renal failure, gastrointestinal fistulas, or chronic infection. Protein and other nutritional deficiencies may be major causes of poor wound repair.

Decreased vascularity and other local changes occur after a few weeks or months in tissues that have been heavily irradiated. These are potential deterrents to wound healing. Radiation therapy of 3000 R or more may be injurious to skin, connective tissue, and vascular tissue. Chronic changes include scarring, damage to fibroblasts and collagen, and degenerative changes in the walls of blood vessels. Capillary budding in granulation tissue and collagen formation are inhibited when these changes are well established. Hence, surgical wounds in heavily irradiated tissues may heal slowly or may break down in the presence of infection. Therapeutic doses of radiation, when used as a surgical adjunct, should be delayed 2–12 weeks to minimize wound complications. Technical problems in correctly timed operations for cancer are not increased by adjunctive radiotherapy in the range of 2000–4000 R. With more intense radiation (5000–6000 R), increased wound complications must be expected although these can be minimized by proper preparation and careful surgical technique. The use of retention sutures should be routine in any of the above circumstances to prevent wound dehiscence or evisceration. Either "through and through" rubber-shod retention sutures or the very effective and less disfiguring Smead-Jones closure technique will accomplish this goal.

POSTOPERATIVE CARE

The routine objectives of management during the immediate postoperative period are the patient's comfort and the prevention of complications, with greater emphasis on the latter. When prevention is unsuccessful, early recognition and treatment of the abnormality are vital. Patient cooperation and motivation can be best obtained and kept up when adequate preoperative education has been offered and all personnel exhibit positive and supportive attitudes for the patient's emotional as well as physical needs.

During the immediate postoperative period, maintenance of normal circulatory and pulmonary function should be emphasized. Vital signs should be checked frequently, so that impending shock or pulmonary obstruction can be diagnosed early. Renal function must be monitored by measuring the urinary output hourly, especially after a major procedure.

Postoperative fever is a common complication. The cause may be as simple as dehydration or as complex as infection in an obscure location. A search for the cause is mandatory before appropriate treatment is initiated. Pulmonary, urinary, and pelvic examinations are important steps in this evaluation.

Postoperative Orders

The postsurgical patient is removed to the recovery room, accompanied by the surgeon or other qualified attendant, as soon as she responds. The nurse receiving the patient should be given a verbal report of her condition in addition to an operative summary and postoperative orders. These should include the following:

A. Vital Signs: Record the blood pressure, pulse, and respiratory rate every 15–30 minutes until stable and hourly thereafter for at least 4–6 hours. Any significant change must be reported immediately. These measurements, including the oral temperature, should then be recorded 4 times a day for the remainder of the postoperative course.

B. Wound Bleeding: Watch for excessive bleeding (abdominal dressing or perineal pads). Determine the hematocrit routinely the day after major surgery and again 2 days later. An abdominal wound should be inspected daily and when the dressing is removed. Skin sutures generally are removed 3–5 days postoperatively.

C. Medications: Following major surgery, give narcotic analgesics as needed, eg, meperidine, 75–100 mg intramuscularly every 4 hours, or morphine, 10 mg intramuscularly every 4 hours.

Following minor surgery, give mild analgesics as needed, eg, aspirin, 600 mg orally every 4 hours; or codeine, 30–60 mg, with aspirin, 600 mg, orally every 4 hours. (*Caution:* the anticoagulant potential and gastric irritant effects of salicylates must be kept in mind whenever they are prescribed.)

Other medications required by the patient taken prior to surgery (insulin, digitalis, cortisone, etc) should be resumed as required.

In all major cases, ferrous fumarate, 200 mg orally twice daily, and ascorbic acid, 100 mg orally 3 times daily, may be beneficial when oral intake is established.

Prescribe a sedative, eg, pentobarbital sodium, 100 mg, to be taken at bedtime only if needed.

A recently introduced procedure for relief of postoperative discomfort is intrathecal or epidural opiate injection. Minimal dosage of less than 5 mg of morphine may allow several hours of complete pain relief without compromise of motor activity (ambulation, coughing). Respiratory depression is a hazard, however, and close monitoring of the patient is necessary.

D. Position in Bed: The patient is usually placed on her side to reduce the risk of inhalation of vomitus or mucus. Other positions desired by the surgeon should be clearly stated, eg, flat with foot of bed elevated.

E. Drainage Tubes: Connect the bladder catheter to the drainage tube and drainage bottle. Written orders for other postoperative drainage and suction catheters should be specific and clear, setting forth the degree of negative pressure desired and the intervals for measurement of drainage volume.

F. Intake and Output: Record intake and output of all fluids as well as daily weight.

G. Fluid Replacement: Administer fluids orally or intravenously as needed. In general, 3 L of a balanced crystalloid and glucose solution over a 24-hour period will suffice.

H. Diet: Offer food as desired and tolerated, when the patient is fully awake, following minor surgery. After major surgery, allow sips of tap water on the first postoperative day. Do not give ice water to the patient, because it may decrease bowel motility significantly. Give clear liquids on the second postoperative day if good bowel sounds are noted and until intestinal gas is passed. Change the diet thereafter from soft to full regular. The time needed to progress to a full diet will depend somewhat on the extent of the procedure and the duration of anesthesia.

I. Respiratory Care: Encourage deep breathing every hour for the first 12 hours and every 2–3 hours for the next 12 hours. Incentive spirometry and the assistance of a respiratory therapist may be of great value, particularly in elderly, obese, or otherwise compromised or immobilized patients.

J. Ambulation: Encourage early ambulation and bathroom privileges. If possible, require ambulation on the day of the operation after major surgery.

POSTOPERATIVE COMPLICATIONS

SHOCK

The postoperative efficiency of the circulation depends upon many factors. Some of the more important of these are blood volume, neurovascular tone, cardiac function, and adrenal secretions, eg, epinephrine, norepinephrine, and adrenocorticosteroids.

Compromise or failure of the circulation may follow excessive blood loss, major escape of vascular fluid into the extravascular compartment, marked peripheral vasodilatation, cardiac decompensation, adrenocortical failure, and pain or emotional distress. Diagnosis of the circulatory problem must be undertaken before proper treatment can be instituted. Nonetheless, because this complication may be life-threatening, it may be necessary to institute treatment with a presumptive rather than a definitive diagnosis.

Shock is present when circulatory insufficiency prevents adequate perfusion of the vital organs. Shock is most often due to acute blood loss, cardiopulmonary failure, severe infection, or severe neurogenic abnormalities. A combination of causes may be responsible. Blood loss (hypovolemia) is the most common cause of postoperative shock. The rapid loss of up to 20% of blood volume produces mild shock; loss of 20–40% produces moderate shock; and loss of over 40% produces severe shock.

General Treatment for All Types of Shock

Act quickly! Shock is an acute emergency that takes precedence over all other problems except acute hemorrhage, cardiac arrest, and respiratory failure.

Treatment should be organized to stop hemorrhage, restore fluid and electrolyte balance, correct cardiac dysfunction, maintain vital organ perfusion, and avert adrenocortical failure.

Because multiple pathologic mechanisms are in operation, there is no simple and reliable pattern of a patient's response to shock. Survival depends upon early diagnosis, correct appraisal of physiologic abnormalities, monitoring of essential parameters, and a flexible plan of therapy based upon vital signs and laboratory data.

Determine the primary cause of shock promptly. A brief history (if available) and the gross physical findings will often permit the differentiation of hemorrhagic, cardiogenic, septic, or allergic types of shock. A pelvic examination and particularly culdocentesis or paracentesis may be of inestimable value in immediately establishing the presence or absence of postoperative hemoperitoneum. Except in neurogenic shock due to fainting—a self-limiting condition that is treated by placing the patient in the recumbent position and administering stimulants—proceed with antishock measures utilizing additional therapy as required for specific problems.

A. General Antishock Measures:

1. Place the patient in a recumbent position with the foot of the bed somewhat elevated. The extreme Trendelenburg position is no longer recommended, because it may interfere with breathing. Disturb the patient as little as possible.

2. Establish an adequate airway and make certain that pulmonary ventilation is unobstructed. Administer oxygen by nasal catheter, mask, or endotracheal tube as required, especially if dyspnea or cyanosis is present.

3. Keep the patient comfortably warm with blankets. Do not apply external heat, since this will cause peripheral vasodilatation.

4. Control pain and relieve apprehension. Shock patients often have very little discomfort. When required, give a minimum effective parenteral dose of a sedative or, if imperative, morphine sulfate, 10–15 mg intravenously. (*Caution:* Narcotics are contraindicated for patients in coma, those with head injuries or respiratory depression, and pregnant women who are likely to deliver within 1–2 hours.) Avoid overdosage of sedative and narcotic drugs.

B. Fluid Replacement: The accurate determination of parenteral fluid requirements depends upon continuous clinical observation of blood pressure, temperature, pulse and respiratory rate, mental acuity, skin (color, temperature, and moisture), venous collapse, fluid intake, and urinary output. Frequent monitoring of central venous pressure and urine output and serial determination of blood pH and serum electrolytes, P_{O_2}, P_{CO_2}, and lactate are essential. Hemoglobin and hematocrit determinations are not dependable guides to blood replacement.

Obtain blood promptly for grouping, crossmatching, hematocrit, coagulation time, complete blood count, and blood chemical determinations prior to starting an infusion. If superficial veins have collapsed, puncture a large vein such as the femoral vein for temporary infusion prior to cutdown or perform percutaneous canalization of a major vessel such as the subclavian vein for central venous pressure determination.

Restore adequate blood volume immediately. The most effective replacement fluid is whole blood, especially if the hematocrit is less than 35%. However, replacement of all blood loss with whole blood may be harmful in complicated shock states. Moreover, acid-base deficits, electrolyte disturbances, or dehydration may require correction, and solutions to correct specific abnormalities, such as mannitol for osmotic diuresis, may be necessary.

Until whole blood can be procured, start intravenous crystalloid solutions (normal saline or Ringer's lactate). Also consider intravenous administration of low-molecular-weight dextran, plasma, and plasma products (see below).

Central venous pressure monitoring (or, preferably, pulmonary and wedge pressure monitoring via a Swan-Ganz catheter) should be instituted to measure the hemodynamics and to serve as a guide to treatment measures for volume expansion. This procedure also serves as a more direct route to the heart for fluid replacement and drug therapy in cases of extreme blood loss, septic shock, serious fluid and electrolyte imbalance, or when the functional capacity of the heart is precarious.

The normal central venous pressure is 8–13 cm of water. If central venous pressure is 8 cm of water or less, additional fluid replacement is essential, and large amounts of blood or other fluids may be required as judged by the initial estimate based on knowledge of fluid losses and the patient's size. If blood volume replacement establishes normal cardiac function and adequate urine production (20–30 mL/h) with a central venous pressure of 10 cm of water or less, the problem probably was hypovolemia (corrected) regardless of cause. If shock, low arterial pressure, and poor circulation persist despite a central venous pressure of 10–13 cm of water, suspect cardiac insufficiency or neurogenic or other factors.

The initial central venous pressure level provides a rough estimate of the safe infusion rate (10 cm of water = 20 mL/min; 15 cm of water = 5 mL/min). If the fluid challenge does not cause a significant rise (> 2 cm of water), the infusion may be continued. If the central venous pressure increases by > 5 cm of water, the infusion should be discontinued. Constant central venous pressure monitoring and suitable correlation with other shock parameters are required.

1. Whole blood–Blood must be correctly grouped and cross-matched for possible transfusion. In dire emergencies after initial resuscitation with crystalloids, group O, Rh-negative blood may be used cautiously without cross-matching. Treatment in cases of shock may require 4–5 L delivered rapidly under pressure to restore central venous pressure to 10–13 cm of water. Use large needles and multiple venipuncture if transfusion is urgently needed. Intra-arterial transfusion may be considered when there is marked depression of cardiac action or when citrated blood without calcium is to be used. This may reduce pulmonary vasoconstriction and myocardial depression.

2. Plasmanate (a reconstituted blood product) may be stored for emergency use and may be particularly valuable for the treatment of plasma loss, as in hemoconcentration complicating peritonitis. Hepatitis is a calculated risk (10–20% in patients receiving pooled plasma in some series).

3. Plasma expanders–Low-molecular-weight dextran (dextran 40, Rheomacrodex) is superior to regular chemical dextran because it reduces the viscosity of the blood, interferes somewhat less with blood typing, and maintains better microcirculation. Administer 1–1.5 mg/kg in 10% solution in normal saline intravenously at a rate of 20–40 mL/min, but do not give more than required to sustain the blood pressure at 85–90 mm Hg and avoid early repeated therapy. (*Caution:* Patients with cardiac or renal insufficiency may develop pulmonary edema. Dextran hypersensitivity reactions may occur.) Obtain blood samples before administering dextran because this substance may interfere with accurate blood grouping or cross-matching.

4. Saline, dextrose, mannitol solutions–Normal saline, Ringer's lactate, or 5% dextrose in saline (500–1000 mL intravenously) will expand blood volume for 1 or 2 hours—until whole blood or blood products can be administered. Mannitol, 10% in normal saline solution, 200–300 mL intravenously, may be used as an osmotic diuretic in selected patients in whom oliguria is present or impending. If ineffective initially, do not repeat mannitol.

5. Correction of bicarbonate deficit–Measures to prevent acidosis (adequate fluids, oxygen, etc) deserve first consideration. In urgent shock therapy, severe acidosis, or when hepatic function is reduced, sodium bicarbonate solution is preferred. This is available in vials containing 3.75 g (45 mEq) in 50 mL. Sodium bicarbonate should be added to 5% dextrose in water in the amount required to provide the proper correction of acidosis as indicated by serial arterial blood pH determinations (< 7.35).

6. Adjustment of electrolyte balance–Restore serum sodium, calcium, chloride, etc, to normal, using periodic blood chemistry determinations as a guide.

7. Precautions in fluid replacement–When administering fluids intravenously, care must be taken not to raise the central venous pressure to over 12–15 cm of water because the fluid volume may cause cardiac overload and pulmonary edema. Electrocardiography may provide additional information regarding cardiac status and electrolyte disturbances. A low serum potassium level or a high calcium or magnesium level can be deleterious to the myocardium. The possibility of overtaxing the heart by fluid overload during shock must be considered because the heart itself may be threatened by poor myocardial perfusion.

C. Vasoactive Drugs: Because a drop in blood pressure is the most obvious evidence of the disturbed physiology in shock, it has seemed logical to use vasopressor drugs to induce a rise in the arterial blood pressure and thus obtain better perfusion of the vital organs. The efficacy of vasopressors in the treatment of various forms of shock has been questioned. Doubt arises because increased vascular resistance in the small vessels and capillaries is a common pathophysiologic change during shock. Vasopressor drugs may intensify this alteration, which in turn could further decrease the circulation to vital organs by diversion of blood flow to other areas. This can result in decreased tissue perfusion and cellular hypoxia.

Despite these objections, vasoactive drugs may be used selectively (1) when specific pharmacologic effects are desired (eg, increased myocardial contractility); (2) when volume expanders are not available; or (3) when volume expansion and other measures are ineffective (refractory shock).

1. Dopamine (Intropin)–Dopamine is a mixed alpha- and beta-adrenergic stimulant that improves myocardial contractility and visceral (renal) blood flow. Give 200 mg in 500 mL sodium chloride injection USP at an initial rate of 2–5 μg/kg/min increasing to 20 μg/kg/min.

Other vasopressor drugs used for shock are the following:

2. Levarterenol bitartrate (norepinephrine, Levophed), a powerful vasopressor, 4–8 mg (4–8 mL of 0.2% solution) in 1 L of dextrose intravenously. Avoid extravasation (may cause tissue necrosis and gangrene). Constant supervision with regular determination of blood pressure is essential. With concentration greater than 4 mg/L, an inlying polyethylene catheter is required.

3. Isoproterenol–Isoproterenol, a beta-adrenergic stimulator, increases cardiac output by its action on the myocardial contraction mechanism and produces peripheral vasodilation. Give 1–2 mg in 500 mL of 5% dextrose in water intravenously. Because of the inotropic effect of isoproterenol, an increased incidence of cardiac arrhythmias precludes its use if the cardiac rate is greater than 120 beats per minute.

4. Metaraminol bitartrate (Aramine), a cardiotonic drug as well as a vasopressor, 2–10 mg intramus-

cularly, or 0.5–5 mg cautiously intravenously, or 15–100 mg intravenously by slow infusion in 250–500 mL of 5% dextrose solution.

5. Phenylephrine (Neo-Synephrine), a vasopressor without appreciable cardiotonic effect, 0.25–1 mg intravenously, or 5 mg intramuscularly, or by slow intravenous infusion of 100–150 mg/L of 5% dextrose solution.

D. Corticosteroids: Corticosteroids are claimed to be beneficial in shock because they support the patient in a serious stress state, decrease vascular resistance, and exert a cardiotonic effect. In septic shock, they may block intense systemic reactions to endotoxin and prevent nonspecific cellular injury.

E. Surgical Hemostasis: When operative or postoperative bleeding in the pelvis cannot be controlled by surgical ligation of individual vessels, a bilateral hypogastric artery ligation may be necessary (Fig 20–1). This procedure decreases the regional arterial pressure and thus often controls bleeding. An immediate increase in the collateral circulation follows the vessel ligation, but the force with which the blood perfuses the tissues is decreased temporarily to permit blood clotting at the operative site. Hypogastric artery ligation is relatively safe and may be lifesaving.

F. Treatment of Oliguria: All patients in shock should have frequent monitoring of urinary flow. The urine flow should be kept above 50 mL/h. Oliguria should be prevented, when possible, by adequate fluid

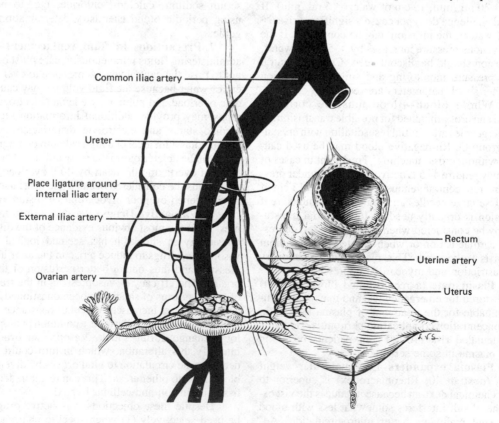

Common iliac artery

Ureter

Place ligature around
internal iliac artery

External iliac artery

Ovarian artery

Rectum

Uterine artery

Uterus

Figure 20–1. Location of ligatures for right internal iliac (hypogastric) artery ligation.

replacement. Cautious use of osmotic diuresis with mannitol, 10–25% solution in 500–1000 mL of sodium chloride injection USP intravenously, or furosemide, 20 mg (up to 200 mg if necessary) intravenously, may be required if oliguria is present or impending. If the initial mannitol fails to produce diuresis, do not repeat.

G. Treatment of Cardiogenic Shock: Treat arrhythmias, myocardial failure, cardiac tamponade, or other cardiac disturbances with appropriate medical or surgical measures. The mortality rate is unusually high in shock due to myocardial infarction. Convert arrhythmias. Digitalize for myocardial insufficiency. Relieve cardiac tamponade.

Evaluation of Antishock Therapy

Observe the patient continuously for clinical and laboratory responses to therapy. Tachycardia subsides and the skin becomes warm and dry as blood pressure returns to over 100 mm Hg.

(1) Record blood pressure, pulse rate, and respiratory rate every 15 minutes.

(2) Maintain a fluid intake and output chart, noting time and amount of replacement fluid given and measuring urine output every 30 minutes. Acute renal failure is often a sequela to untreated deep, unresponsive, or prolonged shock.

(3) Monitor central venous pressure response, especially to initial rapid infusion or transfusion, as a guide both to diagnosis (hypovolemic versus cardiogenic shock) and to subsequent treatment. Try to rapidly achieve and maintain a normal central venous pressure (8–13 cm of water). Avoid under- or over-replacement of fluids.

(4) Auscultate the chest periodically for arrhythmias, muffled heart tones, murmurs, or rales at lung bases. Obtain serial ECGs as indicated. Early medical consultation is advisable.

(5) Determine Pa_{O_2}, Pa_{CO_2}, blood pH, Na^+, K^+, and hematocrit, and blood counts serially at appropriate intervals.

Persistent or Recurrent Shock

When intensive therapy does not improve or correct shock in 30–60 minutes, or when shock recurs after treatment, consider the following causes:

A. Incompletely Corrected Blood Volume: Blood replacement may be inadequate. Very large and rapidly administered transfusions are required in severe hemorrhage or trauma. Electrolyte imbalance may be present. Persistent or recurrent bleeding (often concealed) may be responsible for failure of treatment. Other factors causing or contributing to shock may have been inadequately treated.

B. Associated Diseases: Cardiac insufficiency (myocardial failure, etc) or cerebral damage (hypoxia, thrombosis) may underlie apparent treatment failures.

1. HYPOVOLEMIC SHOCK

Shock due to blood loss may be anticipated before the full picture of vascular collapse is evident. The sympathetic nervous system reacts quickly to hypovolemia by vasoconstriction, which minimizes the fall in peripheral arterial blood pressure that may be evident later. However, the pulse rate increases, so that tachycardia may be an early sign of impending shock. The patient may soon become pale and anxious and complain of thirst. If early shock is not treated quickly, the patient's skin becomes cold, moist, and pale. The pulse becomes weak or imperceptible.

A major sign of moderate shock is oliguria or anuria. There may be a slight to significant drop in blood pressure. In severe shock, the patient shows signs of reduced cerebral perfusion: restlessness, agitation, and confusion. If the blood volume loss exceeds 50%, death usually occurs.

Persistent blood loss during the first 24 hours postoperatively is manifested early by tachycardia and relative hypotension. External (eg, vaginal) bleeding may be evident, but in many cases no definite evidence of extra- or intraperitoneal blood loss can be found at this stage. Treatment consists of whole blood replacement. Later, signs of hemoperitoneum may become manifest. Abdominal fullness may be indicative of a collection of blood. Paracentesis or culdocentesis can promptly identify this problem. Hematocrit determinations may be confusing because of hemoconcentration. Reoperation may be essential to determine the source of bleeding and to secure hemostasis.

Hemorrhagic shock in the postoperative period may mean either that blood loss during the operation was excessive, ie, the blood was not adequately replaced; or that unrecognized blood loss has continued postoperatively. It is important to make this differentiation because fluid replacement alone will be inadequate or futile if bleeding continues.

2. SEPTIC SHOCK

Septic shock, although not seen as often in obstetric and gynecologic patients as hemorrhagic shock, is apparently increasing in frequency. Since the mortality rate from septic shock is very high (40–80%), prevention and proper treatment are imperative. (See also Chapter 15.)

Frequent predisposing factors include diabetes mellitus, genitourinary tract infections, intestinal and hematologic diseases, and cancer.

Gram-negative bacilli (eg, *Escherichia coli, Proteus mirabilis*) are the most common agents of sepsis, but gram-positive bacteria (staphylococci, pneumococci, clostridia, etc) may be causative also. Although the precise pathophysiologic mechanisms have not been completely clarified, intense vasoconstriction of the capillary arterioles and venules is one of the early manifestations of septic shock. Tissue hypoxia follows, with loss of fluid into the tissues; subsequently, there is a decrease in the venous return to the heart and a decrease in cardiac output.

There is often a history of evidence of pelvic infection or traumatic delivery. Septic shock is characterized by chills, fever, tachycardia, anorexia, and occasional nausea and vomiting. Septic shock should always be suspected when a septic patient has chills associated with hypotension and when no signs of hemorrhage or other causes of shock are present. Three to 9 hours after the first shaking chill, a precipitous drop in temperature to subnormal levels often heralds disorientation, hypotension, oliguria, and cardiovascular collapse.

Susceptible patients should be observed carefully for early signs of septic shock. Prompt, early treatment of infections, including the drainage of any fluctuant abscess—especially in diabetic or debilitated patients—will decrease the risk of septic shock. If the development of septic shock is a realistic risk in any given patient, vital signs should be monitored frequently, an intravenous drip should be kept running, urinary output should be measured hourly, and baseline laboratory determinations should be obtained.

Treatment

In addition to initial general antishock measures, particular attention must be paid to the following:

A. Fluid Management: Determine central venous pressure and rapidly inject a trial volume expander such as 5% dextran (Rheomacrodex) or plasma into the catheter in the vena cava to treat hypovolemia and test cardiac reserve. Massive fluid replacement may be necessary to maintain adequate organ (especially renal) perfusion.

B. Treat Sepsis:

1. Obtain necessary specimens for culture and sensitivity studies without delay.

2. Give a "push" of diluted chloramphenicol, 1 g, penicillin G, 3 million units, and gentamicin, 100 mg (or 1.5 mg/kg), into the vena cava.

3. Give by intravenous infusion in normal saline solution: chloramphenicol, 1 g every 4 hours; penicillin G, 3 million units every 4 hours; and gentamicin, 100 mg every 8 hours for the first 24 hours.

4. Subsequent choice of antibiotics, dosage, and frequency of administration will depend on the results of culture and sensitivity studies, patient response, and assessment of renal and hepatic function.

5. Administer hydrocortisone hemisuccinate, 1 g intravenously, or dexamethasone, 40 mg intramuscularly, and repeat after 1 hour if necessary.

6. Give a vasopressor drug only for those clinical situations described on p 461.

C. Evaluate Coagulation Status: Disseminated intravascular coagulation is a frequent complication of the septic process. (See Chapter 33.)

D. Other Treatment: Correct electrolyte imbalance (usually metabolic acidosis). Treat underlying or predisposing medical problems vigorously (septic abortion, peritonitis, pyelonephritis, diabetes, etc).

Necrotic, infected tissue should be removed surgically (eg, curettage, hysterectomy).

3. ANAPHYLACTIC SHOCK

The following urgent measures must be taken immediately in the management of this critical medical emergency:

(1) Give epinephrine, 1:1000 solution, 0.1–0.4 mL in 10 mL of normal saline over a period of 3–4 minutes intravenously.

(2) Diphenhydramine or tripelennamine, 10–20 mg intravenously, may be beneficial if the response to epinephrine is not prompt and sustained.

(3) Hydrocortisone sodium succinate (Solu-Cortef), 100–250 mg intravenously over a period of 30 seconds, may be used as an adjunct to epinephrine and antihistamines. The drug may be repeated at increasing intervals (1, 3, 6, 10 hours, etc) as indicated by the clinical condition.

(4) Aminophylline injection, 0.25–0.5 g in 10–20 mL of normal saline intravenously slowly for severe bronchial spasm. The duration of action is 1–3 hours, and the drug may be repeated in 3–4 hours.

4. ANESTHESIA FOR THE SHOCK PATIENT

The choice of anesthesia for a major surgical or obstetric procedure for the patient in shock requires a specific knowledge of the pharmacology and physiology involved. Ideally, the patient should be responsive to antishock therapy before operation. If the problem is critical, a calculated risk must be taken.

Preoperative medication should consist of atropine sulfate, 0.4 mg well diluted in saline solution and given slowly intravenously. The following anesthetic methods are justified if the cause of shock has been accurately identified.

Hypovolemic Shock

Inhalation anesthesia with maximum oxygen concentration is preferable. Nitrous oxide and ethylene cause no electrolyte or metabolic impairment. Retention of CO_2 may occur with inadequate pulmonary ventilation using cyclopropane, halothane, or fluroxene. Halothane often causes uterine relaxation, and further bleeding may occur. Regional anesthetic block may result in severe, uncontrollable hypotension. In vascular (caval) obstruction by the gravid uterus, spinal or caudal anesthesia may further complicate the supine hypotensive syndrome. If this occurs, elevate the uterus; turn the patient to the semilateral position by placing a support beneath the right hip to tilt the uterus to the left; and proceed with therapy.

Cardiogenic Shock

Local infiltration with the patient in Fowler's position is recommended.

Septic Shock

Cyclopropane probably is the best anesthetic considering that vascular collapse, renal failure, and fever are present. Nitrous oxide and halothane in low concentration or minimal amounts of succinylcholine (the only muscle relaxant that is well hydrolyzed) are the second choices. (However, succinylmonocholine, produced during oliguria or anuria, may accumulate and retard dissipation of succinylcholine.)

PULMONARY & CARDIOVASCULAR COMPLICATIONS

Pulmonary complications remain one of the major hazards in the postoperative period. About 30% of postoperative deaths that occur within 6 weeks of operation are due to pulmonary complications. Postoperative problems vary with the preoperative status of the patient. Heavy smokers fall into the high-risk group because of chronic bronchitis and emphysema. Patients with excessive tracheobronchial secretions are particularly susceptible to postoperative respiratory problems. Atelectasis, bronchopneumonia or pneumonitis, aspiration, respiratory distress syndrome, and pulmonary embolism are the most frequent complications.

1. ATELECTASIS

Atelectasis is a complication of the very early postoperative period; most cases occur within the first 48 hours. Atelectasis may be massive, when a large bronchus is occluded with mucus or vomitus; or it may be patchy. Predisposing factors are chronic bronchitis, asthma, smoking, and respiratory infection.

Aspiration of stomach contents during induction of anesthesia or during postoperative vomiting may cause atelectasis (sometimes massive) and subsequent bronchopneumonia. Aged patients and those with an underlying medical complication (eg, emphysema) are more likely to have postoperative pulmonary problems. Inadequate immediate postoperative attention to deep breathing also increases the risk of subsequent pulmonary disease.

Clinical Findings

The clinical findings vary with the extent of atelectasis. With massive atelectasis, the temperature, pulse rate, and respiratory rate increase sharply. Segments of lung—sometimes entire lobes—may be dull to percussion, with breath sounds absent. Cyanosis may or may not be present. Especially in massive atelectasis, the patient may have shortness of breath. A lateral shift of the mediastinum (ie, displacement of the trachea and heart toward the atelectatic side) may occur. The x-ray findings may include patchy opacities and evidence of laterally displaced organs. Multiple small areas of atelectasis and bronchopneumonia, which often have a similar clinical picture, may com-

bine to present as a single disease process. Elevation of temperature and respiratory rate is the first sign. The patient may complain of an excess of bronchial secretions, with rhonchi and cough. Examination of the chest may detect areas of dullness to percussion, together with bronchial breathing and inspiratory rales. Patches of bronchopneumonia may be recognized on x-ray. If untreated, the disease may progressively worsen.

Pneumonitis usually is a less serious complication of atelectasis. There is gradual onset of fever and cough, but the physical findings generally are nonspecific. Early x-ray films are not diagnostic. The disease usually is effectively treated by broad-spectrum antibiotics.

Prevention

The prevention of pulmonary complications requires attention to many details.

Atropine, given before the operation, generally will reduce the quantity of tracheobronchial secretions and thus the risk of atelectasis. Care should be exercised during the operation not to permit any interference with the patient's breathing. Trendelenburg's position provides excellent exposure for the surgeon, and drainage of tracheobronchial secretions during the operation is facilitated. However, this tilted position reduces diaphragmatic movement, and aeration may be restricted. Excessive anesthesia, large doses of narcotics, pain, and abdominal distention tend to aggravate this condition.

Treatment

Once atelectasis has occurred, treatment must be vigorous.

Simple intratracheal suction at the conclusion of the operative procedure may be effective in removing mucus. Bronchoscopy may be necessary to remove a pulmonary plug. Intermittent positive pressure breathing using a nebulized combination of isoproterenol and saline solution may provide bronchial dilatation and improve pulmonary function.

Ideally, the choice of antibiotic should be based on sputum smear and culture, but ampicillin or some other broad-spectrum antibiotic may be given initially while awaiting the laboratory report.

Oxygen should be administered if breathing is labored or if cyanosis develops. Morphine and other respiratory depressants should be avoided.

In the postoperative period, the patient should be encouraged to breathe deeply and to cough up mucus. Rebreathing by means of a Bird respirator or even a paper bag should provide deeper respiratory excursions.

The preoperative administration of antibiotics may be helpful to the patient who has underlying chronic lung or bronchial disease.

An oral mucolytic agent such as saturated solution of potassium iodide may also be beneficial.

2. PNEUMONIA

Pneumonia may follow atelectasis or aspiration of vomitus or other fluid. Aspiration of nasopharyngeal secretions during or immediately following anesthesia or atelectasis may set the stage for the development of pneumonia. Abundant tracheobronchial secretions from preexisting bronchitis also predispose to this complication.

Atelectasis produces moderate fever in the first few postoperative days. If this is followed by higher temperatures, systemic toxicity, and respiratory difficulty, a presumptive diagnosis of pneumonia is justified.

If pneumonia develops, secretions become progressively more abundant and the cough becomes productive. Physical examination may reveal evidence of pulmonary consolidation, and numerous coarse rales are often present. Chest x-ray usually shows diffuse patchy infiltrates or lobar consolidation.

The treatment of pneumonia includes deep breathing and coughing. The patient should be encouraged to change position frequently. Nasotracheal suction may be used to stimulate the cough reflex. Specific broad-spectrum antibiotic therapy should be instituted and revised as indicated by subsequent cultures and sensitivity tests. In desperately weak or debilitated patients with a poor cough reflex, emergency tracheostomy may be indicated to permit adequate ventilation and bronchoscopy. Positive pressure ventilation may improve the depth of respiration and eliminate the work of breathing in extremely ill patients.

3. ASPIRATION

Aspiration is a relatively common pulmonary complication. It usually occurs in the postanesthetic period when the patient's sensorium is depressed and vital reflexes such as swallowing and coughing are absent. Aspiration of oral secretions may precipitate pneumonia, usually mild, which can be managed by vigorous therapy similar to that described for atelectasis.

A far more lethal type of aspiration pneumonia is that which occurs secondary to vomiting and inhalation of gastric contents. This can occur during induction of anesthesia in any patient who has recently eaten or in one with ileus and a stomach distended with fluid. The effects can be minimized by preoperative administration of an antacid as well as evacuation of stomach contents via nasogastric tube. Endotracheal anesthetic technique is mandatory, and, if aspiration occurs in spite of this, vigorous suctioning of the tracheobronchial tree must be accomplished. Nonetheless, severe tracheobronchitis may result from chemical injury to mucosa and secondary infection.

Antibiotic and corticosteroid therapy is advocated in the management of aspiration of gastric contents.

4. TENSION PNEUMOTHORAX

This uncommon complication is most likely to occur during the first 24–48 hours after surgery. It is marked by postoperative nausea and vomiting or coughing. It presents as acute respiratory distress with distant breath sounds on the affected side and frequently a marked mediastinal shift away from the affected side. Immediate improvement can be obtained by inserting one or more large-bore needles through the intercostal space at approximately T6-8 under local anesthesia to allow escape of air until a chest tube can be inserted.

5. ADULT RESPIRATORY DISTRESS SYNDROME (ARDS)

Respiratory distress syndrome has been recognized only in the past few years. It has many names (pump lung, shock lung, hemorrhagic lung syndrome, posttraumatic lung, fat embolism, congestive atelectasis, etc). This complication was at first thought to result only from cardiopulmonary bypass. Similar lesions are now being recognized in patients who have been in septic, hypovolemic, or cardiogenic shock or have had other types of catastrophic conditions such as massive trauma or major burns. In obstetrics, a variant of this entity has been most recently encountered as a complication of the use of tocolytic agents, particularly terbutaline.

Careful monitoring of postoperative patients with major disorders has permitted definition of the clinical syndrome. Within 24 hours of the clinical insult, the patient develops evidence of respiratory distress characterized by tachypnea and increased respiratory effort. Arterial blood gas measurements done at this time may show arterial desaturation. Chest x-ray shows diffuse, cloudy infiltrates in the lung, but—in contrast to pulmonary edema—there is no cardiac enlargement or increase in vascular markings. Lung compliance is increased, and increased effort often is required to maintain adequate tidal volume. If the P_{aO_2} is below 60 mm Hg, an endotracheal tube should be inserted and positive pressure ventilation instituted with sufficient oxygen to maintain a P_{aO_2} of 70–100 mm Hg. With prompt institution of positive pressure ventilation, the disorder usually is reversible, and gradual recovery can be expected in 3–7 days. If the insult is severe and the patient's underlying disease is not fully reversible, a progressive downhill course may result. On gross examination, the lung is hemorrhagic and resembles liver. If the patient dies within the first 24 hours, histopathologic examination reveals platelet and fibrin emboli filling the microcirculation of the lung. This is followed by congestion and then intra-alveolar hemorrhage at 24–72 hours. When death occurs between 3 and 5 days, intra-alveolar hemorrhage and hyaline membranes are the predominant features. Assuming that the patient can be carried successfully through this insult, pneumonitis will develop, so that if death occurs after an additional 5–7 days the principal changes will be those of pneumonia.

Acute pulmonary edema may result from excessive transfusion of blood or excessive administration of sodium-containing fluids. Pulmonary edema may, of course, be a complication of preexisting cardiac disease. Acute myocardial infarction may present initially as acute pulmonary edema.

Treatment

Act immediately! Obtain adequate medical consultation without delay. Any intravenous fluid should be administered at a very slow rate. Emergency treatment consists of the administration of morphine sulfate, 15–30 mg intravenously or intramuscularly every 2–4 hours, to depress pulmonary reflexes. Give oxygen (by mask) in high concentrations. A most effective and even lifesaving support technique is the use of postive end-expiratory pressure (PEEP) with endotracheal intubation. Not infrequently, adjunct paralysis with succinylcholine may be necessary to effect optimal ventilation and respiratory exchange.

Reduce blood volume by applying rubber tourniquets to the extremities with just enough pressure to obstruct the venous return. Phlebotomy may be necessary if pulmonary edema has occurred. The packed red cells should be preserved for later autotransfusion.

Digitalis should be given intravenously unless the patient has received digitalis recently. Aminophylline, 250–500 mg in 10–20 mL of normal saline solution given slowly intravenously, may also be helpful.

Except in clear-cut cases of fluid overload, diuresis is only of secondary value in the treatment of pulmonary edema.

6. CARDIAC ARREST

Cardiac arrest occurs most frequently during the induction of anesthesia, but it may also occur during the course of the operation or even in the postoperative period. Predisposing conditions include preexisting heart disease, myocardial infarction, shock, hypoventilation, airway (tracheal or pulmonary) obstruction, or drug reaction.

Clinical Findings

The signs of impending cardiac arrest are rapid fall in blood pressure and irregularity of pulse. This frequently occurs during anesthesia. Verify the diagnosis by noting the absence of pulse and heart sounds by auscultation, and *begin treatment immediately!*

Prevention

Preoperative administration of atropine and a sedative decreases the risk of cardiac arrest.

Prevent hypotension. If it does occur, immediate treatment is mandatory.

Adequate ventilation with oxygen as necessary must be maintained throughout the operative procedure.

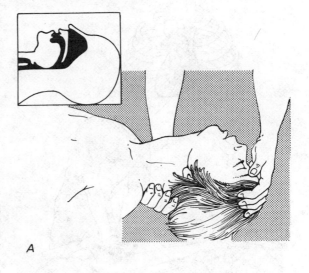

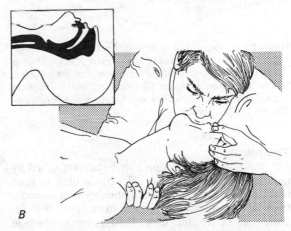

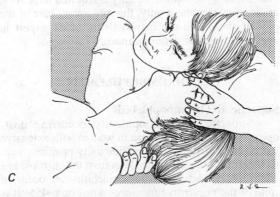

Figure 20–2. Proper performance of mouth-to-mouth resuscitation. *A:* Open airway by positioning neck anteriorly in extension. Inserts show airway obstructed when the neck is in resting flexed position and opening when neck is extended. *B:* Rescuer should close victim's nose with fingers, seal mouth around victim's mouth, and deliver breath by vigorous expiration. *C:* Victim is allowed to exhale passively by unsealing mouth and nose. Rescuer should listen and feel for expiratory air flow.

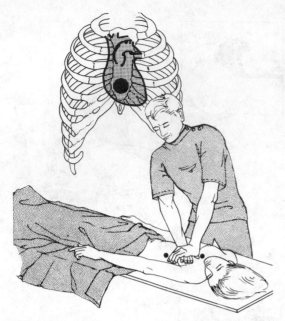

Figure 20–3. Technique of closed chest cardiac massage. Heavy circle in heart drawing shows area of application of force. Circles on supine figure show points of application of electrodes for defibrillation. (Reproduced, with permission, from Benson RC: *Handbook of Obstetrics & Gynecology,* 7th ed. Lange, 1980.)

Treatment

Pulmonary ventilation may be accomplished by mouth-to-mouth breathing (Fig 20–2) until oxygen under pressure can be given, preferably with an endotracheal tube inserted. Electrical stimulation, if available, may be helpful. Closed chest cardiac massage (Fig 20–3) is the procedure of choice in the attempt to correct the arrest; open chest massage is rarely indicated. The gynecologist usually is required to provide emergency treatment only; the subsequent care of the patient should be the responsibility of an expert in anesthesiology or cardiopulmonary medicine.

7. THROMBOPHLEBITIS

Superficial Thrombophlebitis

Superficial thrombophlebitis occurring postoperatively is most common in women with extensive varicosities of the legs. The lithotomy position, with its localized pressure on the legs from the stirrups, is a contributory factor. Thrombophlebitis can occur in spite of the preventive measures noted on p 455. It is usually recognized within the first few days after operation.

In many cases, a segment of the superficial saphenous vein becomes inflamed, manifested by redness, localized heat, swelling, and tenderness. This disorder is generally limited to the superficial veins; in such cases, pulmonary embolism is unusual.

When thrombophlebitis is diagnosed, apply warm, moist packs and elevate the extremities. Phenylbutazone (Butazolidin), 100 mg orally 3 times daily for 5 days, may aid the resolution of the process. An alternative treatment is the administration of dextran 40, 500 mL daily over a 4-hour span for 3 days. Anticoagulants are rarely indicated when only the superficial vessels are involved. As soon as clinical improvement occurs (usually in less than 48 hours), the patient may be ambulated. Prolonged bed rest predisposes to thrombophlebitis of the deep veins.

Deep Thrombophlebitis

Thrombophlebitis of the deep veins occurs most often in the calves but may also occur in the thighs or pelvis. In either case, it may be primary or an extension of more peripheral disease. Advanced age, obesity, malignancy, the postpartum state, certain drugs (eg, oral contraceptives), and anemia are predisposing factors, but the disease frequently occurs in apparently healthy patients.

A. Clinical Findings: Symptoms may be localized to the involved extremity, or there may be no symptoms or signs in the extremity. Pulmonary embolism may be the first evidence of the disease. The patient may complain of an aching pain in the leg, frank pain in the calf, or just a dull ache. There may be tenderness or spasm in the calf muscle. Examination may reveal slight swelling of the calf—so slight that it may be evident only by precise measurement of the circumference of both calves at the same level. Dorsiflexion of the foot may elicit pain in the calf (Homans' sign), and slight elevation of the temperature and pulse is frequently noted. If the disease process is in the femoral vein or in the pelvis, swelling of the extremity may be more evident and more severe. The Lowenberg cuff test, Doppler assessment of the veins proximal to the suspected site of phlebitis, with comparison of the findings in both extremities, and impedance plethysmography may afford a definitive diagnosis.

The major complication of deep thrombophlebitis is pulmonary embolism. Chronic venous insufficiency may develop as a long-term consequence of the process.

B. Treatment:

1. Medical treatment–Once the diagnosis has been made, anticoagulants should be started immediately. Heparin, which promptly prolongs the clotting time, is usually the drug of choice; it may be given either intravenously or subcutaneously. A clotting time (activated or Lee-White method) and a prothrombin time should be determined before anticoagulant therapy is started; these tests then provide a basis for interpreting the degree of anticoagulation achieved. The clotting time should be kept to 18–30 minutes (normal, 6–15 minutes). Intravenous administration of 1% protamine sulfate in saline will counteract the effect of heparin quickly on a milligram-for-milligram basis. Do not discontinue heparin earlier than 3–5 days after the disappearance of all signs and symptoms or before ambulation has been fully established and effective oral therapy has been obtained.

Prothrombin depressants such as dicumarol and warfarin are contraindicated in antepartum patients but often are started at the same time as heparin in gynecologic patients. Whereas heparin prolongs the clotting time almost immediately, the prothrombin depressants do not exert their full effect for 48–72 hours. A major advantage of the latter drugs is that they can be given orally. Hence, it is common practice to give heparin for its immediate short-term effect and to replace the heparin with prothrombin depressants for long-term treatment. The prothrombin time should be determined before therapy is begun and daily thereafter. The objective of therapy is the maintenance of prothrombin activity of 10–30%. Abnormal prolongation of the prothrombin activity or actual hemorrhage may be treated with phytonadione (Mephyton), 5–10 mg orally (or 10–40 mg intravenously if hemorrhage is severe). Oral anticoagulation is often continued empirically for 6 weeks to 3 months after initiation of therapy.

2. Local measures–Local measures in the treatment of deep thrombophlebitis include elevation of the legs to provide good venous drainage and the application of long leg gradient pressure elastic hose. When inflammation has subsided (usually within 1–2 weeks of starting therapy), walking may be permitted. The patient should be encouraged, however, to continue to elevate the legs whenever she can. Prolonged sitting and the use of constrictive garments (eg, garters) are to be avoided.

3. Surgical treatment–Thrombectomy or vena caval clipping or ligation occasionally may be indicated for persistent disease, severe swelling of the extremity, or repeated episodes of pulmonary embolism.

Septic Thrombophlebitis

The diagnosis of septic thrombophlebitis is established and effectively managed by clinical trial with heparin in conjunction with antibiotic therapy that affects both aerobic and anaerobic organisms. (See Chapter 15.)

8. PULMONARY EMBOLISM

Pulmonary embolism is a critical complication of pelvic surgery. This diagnosis should be suspected if cardiac or pulmonary symptoms occur abruptly. Cardiovascular disease, sepsis, and obesity are predisposing factors.

Pulmonary embolism is a complication of pelvic or lower extremity thrombophlebitis; nonetheless, pulmonary embolism may precede the diagnosis of peripheral vascular disease. Indeed, in some patients no evidence of thrombophlebitis can be found. It usually occurs on about the seventh to tenth postoperative days, although it may occur at any time.

The differential diagnosis includes atelectasis, pneumonia, myocardial infarction, and pneumothorax.

Clinical Findings

A. Symptoms and Signs: Patients with large emboli have chest pain, severe dyspnea, cyanosis, tachycardia, hypotension or shock, restlessness, and anxiety. If the embolus is massive, sudden death may result from acute cor pulmonale.

In patients with smaller emboli, the diagnosis is suggested by the sudden onset of pleuritic pain, sometimes in association with blood-streaked sputum. A dry cough may develop. Physical examination may reveal a pleural friction rub. In many cases, no diagnostic signs can be elicited.

B. Laboratory Findings: Moderate leukocytosis (up to 15,000/mL) occurs in 70% of cases. Serum bilirubin is often elevated and is related to heart failure rather than to hemorrhage in the lung. Elevated serum lactate dehydrogenase or serum glutamic-oxaloacetic transaminase is seen in about half of patients; both enzymes are elevated in about one-fourth of patients, and in the remainder both are within the range of normal concentration.

C. X-Ray Findings: Chest x ray may show no abnormality, or changes may be delayed 24–48 hours. In about 15% of patients, a pulmonary density is present that is sometimes (but not always) in the periphery of the lung and roughly in the shape of a triangle with its base at the lung surface. Other possible findings include enlargement of the main pulmonary artery, small pleural effusion, and elevated diaphragm. Embolism involves the lower lobes in 75% of cases, more often on the right than on the left.

D. Lung Scan: Scanning the lung fields for radioactivity after intravenous injection of radioiodinated, macroaggregated human albumin is a simple and valuable diagnostic procedure that characteristically reveals negative defects in the lung areas distal to pulmonary artery obstruction. This is a particularly useful screening technique when the chest x-ray reveals no lesions. The scan is positive because of diminished blood flow in the lung. Changes similar to those which occur with pulmonary embolism can be produced by atelectasis, pneumonia, and neoplasm; however, the clinical picture usually is sufficiently distinct in these conditions to permit differentiation from pulmonary embolism. It should be noted, however, that the scan is unreliable in pregnant or puerperal patients; angiography is of greater value in these instances.

E. Electrocardiography: The ECG may show characteristic changes of pulmonary embolism in about a third of cases. The ECG is principally of interest in differentiating pulmonary embolism from the clinically similar myocardial infarction.

F. Angiography: Pulmonary angiography should always be done before embolectomy is undertaken. It is the most reliable procedure for confirming the diagnosis and determining the location and extent of large emboli. Embolectomy is performed only on selected patients, and a definitive diagnosis is essential. Pressures measured in the right heart and pulmonary artery in conjunction with catheterization for angiography will aid in evaluating the degree of right heart failure secondary to pulmonary artery obstruction. Angiography should be preceded by a pulmonary scan; if the scan is negative, massive pulmonary embolus can be virtually ruled out and angiography should be cancelled.

Treatment

Monitor the patient constantly. Institute cardiopulmonary resuscitation measures. Treat acid-base abnormalities and shock.

Immediate treatment with heparin is indicated. It is probably better to begin heparin therapy even in the absence of a definitive diagnosis if pulmonary embolism (or myocardial infarction) is likely. Give heparin, 10,000 units intravenously every 4 hours for 6 doses, either by continuous infusion or intermittently through an indwelling catheter. If continuous infusion is used, give an initial loading dose of 10,000 units. Beginning on the second day, regulate the continuous infusion so that the Lee-White clotting time is maintained at 30–45 minutes. For intermittent injections, the clotting time should be maintained at this level about 1 hour before the next dose. Heparin therapy should be continued for 7–10 days before oral anticoagulation with a coumarin drug is introduced; this should then be continued for 6 weeks to 6 months, depending upon circumstances. Contraindications to anticoagulants in the case of pulmonary embolism are relative. Active bleeding and blood dyscrasias may be limiting factors. Severe hepatitis or renal disease often precludes the use of prothrombin depressants.

Administer oxygen in high concentration by mask, intubation, or assisted ventilation.

The patient should receive morphine or meperidine for chest pain. For severe pain, give meperidine, 50–100 mg subcutaneously or intravenously, or morphine sulfate, 8–15 mg subcutaneously or intravenously. Avoid these agents in the presence of shock. Only the intravenous route should be used in the heparinized patient.

Application of a clip to or ligation of the vena cava may be required when repeated release of thromboemboli from pelvic or leg veins occurs.

Vena cava interruption. Ligation, clipping, or plication of the vena cava should be considered when pulmonary emboli occur during anticoagulant therapy or when anticoagulants are contraindicated. Nonetheless, a minor episode of embolism during the first few days of heparinization does not necessarily mean failure of anticoagulant therapy. Vena cava interruption is not indicated unless there is a recurrence of major embolization in spite of anticoagulation at optimal therapeutic levels or unless the emboli are septic.

Embolectomy is indicated in critically ill patients with angiographic evidence of massive embolism and with persistent hypotension, severe hypoxemia, or cardiac deterioration in spite of appropriate supportive measures. It may also be considered for patients who have survived a massive embolus that continues to block the pulmonary artery, producing pulmonary

hypertension and progressive cor pulmonale. Pulmonary embolectomy requires cardiopulmonary bypass, which means that a cardiac surgeon must be available. The operation may be lifesaving, but the mortality rate is high because of the critical condition of these patients.

URINARY COMPLICATIONS

1. URINARY RETENTION

Periodic measurement of urine volume provides the most useful method of evaluating the patient's postoperative fluid balance. Except when shock or dehydration intervenes, postoperative fluid needs can be accurately gauged by an hourly—then daily—charting of urinary output.

After a minor procedure, measurement of urinary output can await natural voiding. If fluid therapy has been adequate, the patient should void by evening of the day of surgery; if she has not voided by then, bladder distention should be suspected. The patient should be encouraged to get out of bed to void. If the normal capacity of the bladder is exceeded (500 mL), serious bladder dysfunction may result. The patient may have to be catheterized if she is unable to void. Sterile technique must be employed.

Inability of the patient to void or difficulty in voiding often is due to pain caused by using the voluntary muscles to start the urinary stream. With vaginal plastic procedures or with suprapubic procedures performed to treat urinary incontinence—eg, Marshall-Marchetti-Krantz operation—sutures near the urethra or urethral edema may make voiding difficult or impossible. Continuous drainage of the bladder probably poses fewer problems than frequent intermittent catheterizations when the patient is unable to void.

It should be remembered that anxiety plays a significant role in these patients. Diazepam may be effective in management.

Treatment

A. Urethral Drainage: After a major procedure in which postoperative bleeding or operative damage to the urinary tract is a possibility, bladder drainage by means of a urethral catheter or suprapubic cystostomy tube drainage should be instituted despite the small risk of bladder infection. The catheter usually can be removed within 24–48 hours except after a vaginal plastic procedure or extended operation, either of which usually requires drainage for a longer time.

B. Suprapubic Drainage: Suprapubic drainage is preferred over urethral catheter drainage by some operators because of patient comfort, ease of care, and a reduced incidence of infection. Suprapubic drainage is illustrated in Figs 20–4 and 20–5. With the bladder distended with 200 mL of sterile water, a No. 14 or No. 16 needle or a Moskowitz trocar is inserted through the surgically prepared anterior abdominal wall approximately 2 cm above the symphysis pubica. A sterile

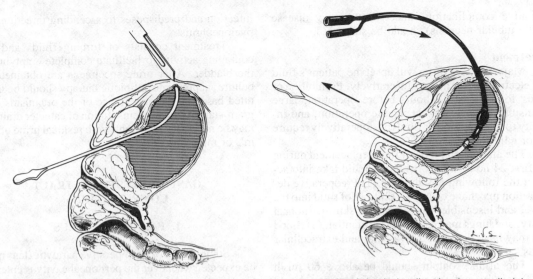

Figure 20–4. Suprapubic cystotomy. Trocar brought through incision in anterior abdominal wall and catheter pulled through incision by tie to trocar.

plastic tube or small Foley catheter is inserted through the trocar and the trocar is removed. The tube is connected to a sterile drainage bottle to provide continuous drainage. Appropriate connections in the tube keep it filled with fluid at all times as a guard against infection. The Ingram catheter may also be used to establish and maintain suprapubic bladder drainage.

2. OLIGURIA & ANURIA

Oliguria usually results from dehydration, which often can be demonstrated by diuresis following the rapid intravenous administration of 500 mL of 5% dextrose in water. Disturbances of electrolyte balance (eg, dilution syndrome) or diminished renal blood flow (cardiac failure, shock) may also cause oliguria. After these possible causes of oliguria have been eliminated, an underlying serious disorder of the urinary tract should be suspected.

Anuria must be identified promptly. It occasionally may be due to bilateral ureteral obstruction, a complication that must be considered when there is no urinary output on the operating table or during the immediate postoperative period. If an intravenous urogram fails to reveal the cause of this serious post-

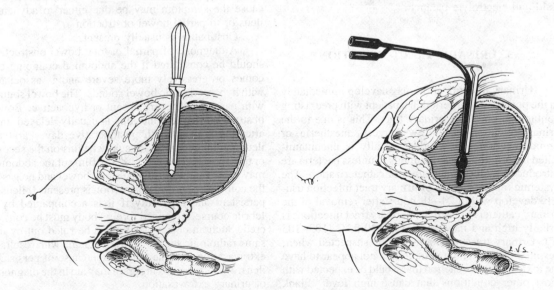

Figure 20–5. Suprapubic cystotomy. *Left:* Insertion of plastic tube through trocar previously placed in the bladder by a puncture through the abdominal skin immediately above the symphysis pubica. *Right:* Trocar has been removed and the plastic tubing has been connected to a closed drainage system.

operative complication, underlying kidney disease (acute tubular necrosis) should be suspected.

Treatment

Major surgery often will upset the patient's fluid and electrolyte balance postoperatively. Prohibition of fluids for at least 12 hours before operation, large insensible water losses during the operation, and inability to tolerate food or fluids postoperatively require major adjustments.

The amount and type of fluid replacement during the first 24 hours after operation should take into account the following possibilities: (1) Preoperative dehydration may have occurred. (2) Loss of fluid into the bowel and insensible losses from the skin, peritoneal cavity, and lungs may have been substantial. (3) Blood loss may have depleted the vascular and extracellular fluids.

The urinary output should be above 60 mL/h (1500 mL/d), and the urine specific gravity should range between 1.010 and 1.015. On the first postoperative day, at least 3000 mL of fluids should be administered intravenously. This should include 1000 mL of normal saline solution (140 mEq of sodium). The other 2000 mL should be given in the form of 5% glucose in water. Subsequent fluid requirements should be based on replacement of 1000 mL of daily insensible water loss (which is highest in febrile patients and in those exposed to heat) plus urinary output. A clinical estimate of the state of hydration can be made by noting the urinary output, moisture of the mucous membranes, and skin turgor. If the patient is unable to take fluids orally in adequate amounts after 48 hours, potassium may need to be added to the intravenous fluids after careful scrutiny of the serum electrolytes. If a major procedure has been performed, serum albumin, plasma, or whole blood may be necessary to adjust the fluid and electrolyte balance.

3. URINARY TRACT INFECTION

Urinary tract infection may develop immediately in the postoperative period in a patient with preexisting contamination of the urinary tract. This is due to the urinary retention that follows surgery, anesthesia, or immobilization. The bladder usually is uncontaminated before surgery and remains so unless bacteria are introduced by instrumentation or catheterization. The systemic manifestations of urinary tract infection usually develop within 24–48 hours after removal of the urinary catheter. Fever due to urinary tract infections is usually high and may reach 39.5–40.5 °C (103–105 °F). Urinary tract infection may be suspected when, despite high fever, the patient does not appear to have the toxic systemic reaction that would be expected with most other conditions that cause high fever. Flank tenderness may be present, suggesting pyelonephritis. Pus or bacteria are seen in the urine sediment. Residual urine, which may be present, tends to perpetuate the

infection and predisposes to ascending infection and pyelonephritis.

Treatment consists of forcing fluids and encouraging activity to facilitate complete emptying of the bladder. After urine specimens are obtained for culture, appropriate antibiotic therapy should be instituted based on the appearance of the organisms on a gram-stained smear. Reinstitution of catheter drainage may be necessary in patients with residual urine of 100 mL or more.

GASTROINTESTINAL TRACT COMPLICATIONS

1. PARALYTIC ILEUS

Some degree of postoperative paralytic ileus must be expected whenever the peritoneal cavity is entered. Gastrointestinal function in the postoperative period must be observed carefully so that ileus can be minimized. Postoperative ileus may be aggravated by food given too early. On the first postoperative day, the patient is encouraged to sip tap water (*not* ice water). On the following day, clear fluids may be taken if bowel sounds are normal. Thereafter, fluids may be taken ad lib, but solid food usually is withheld until the patient passes intestinal gas. By the fourth or fifth day, the patient is usually taking regular meals.

Clinical Findings

Nausea occurring in the immediate postoperative period may be troublesome. It may be suppressed with prochlorperazine (Compazine), 5–10 mg intramuscularly, or trimethobenzamide (Tigan), 200 mg intramuscularly. Nausea or vomiting later in the postoperative period demands diagnostic attention, because the symptom may be due either to adynamic ileus or to partial bowel obstruction.

Obstipation is usually present.

A diagnosis of partial or total bowel obstruction should be considered if the abdominal cramping becomes progressively more severe and is associated with hyperperistaltic bowel sounds. The bowel sounds with paralytic ileus are absent or hypoactive. Bowel obstruction due to adhesions is usually delayed until after the fifth or sixth postoperative day. Paralytic ileus, on the other hand, usually begins on the second or third postoperative day. X-ray films of the abdomen may show fluid levels in the small bowel and no gas in the colon when bowel obstruction is present. If ileus is persistent and especially if it is accompanied by a febrile course, a retained foreign body must be considered. Such an object usually can be ruled out by the same radiologic study. Urologic trauma with resultant extravasation of urine may be the cause of persistent ileus. An intravenous urogram may aid in the diagnosis of urinary extravasation.

Treatment

If nausea, vomiting, or abdominal distention increases or becomes severe, it may be necessary to insert a nasogastric tube into the stomach. Gastric aspiration usually reveals green to yellow fluids. The distention should lessen with this treatment; if no benefit is noted, bowel obstruction should be suspected.

Some surgeons give a mild laxative such as milk of magnesia—or a stool softener such as dioctyl sodium sulfosuccinate (Colace)—on the first to third days after operation. A tap water enema for the relief of distention probably should be deferred until the patient has passed gas or has had a small bowel movement—evidence that bowel function is returning to normal.

One may minimize the symptoms of postoperative paralytic ileus by giving the patient a pharmacologically inert wetting agent such as simethicone (Mylicon, Silain, etc) to reduce the surface tension of the intestinal mucus and thereby liberate entrapped gas. Use of sedation and a colon tube is a time-honored effective measure.

Gastrointestinal complications are most apt to occur after abdominal operations, but they may complicate other types of surgery also. In fact, any serious illness may cause malfunction of the gastrointestinal tract.

2. ACUTE GASTRIC DISTENTION

Acute gastric distention is one of the most common postoperative complications. It is caused by accumulation of air and, to a lesser extent, gastric juices in the stomach. Most patients with nausea or paralytic ileus will swallow air. If intestinal peristalsis is depressed, the swallowed gas accumulates in the stomach. As gastric distention increases, the movement of the diaphragm may be inhibited. When the patient develops hyperpnea and appears to be splinting her diaphragm, a nasogastric tube should be passed immediately and gastric aspiration continued as long as ileus persists.

3. GASTRIC DILATATION

Gastric dilatation, as opposed to gastric distention, is a grave postoperative complication that has been associated with a mortality rate as high as 50%. In gastric dilatation, the stomach is distended with fluid to such a degree that secondary hemorrhage occurs. The gastric juice becomes brown or black from the contained hemoglobin. Gastric dilatation may follow untreated gastric distention, but it often is a complication of very serious illnesses of the type associated with low cardiac output. The cause may be extra-abdominal and may be associated with such procedures as open heart surgery.

Vomiting of brown or black material means gastric dilatation or intestinal obstruction. A nasogastric tube should be passed immediately. Decompression of the stomach reverses the gastric distention and secondary bleeding and prevents aspiration. Large quantities of fluid and electrolytes usually have been lost. Shock is often present, and correction of hypovolemia is an essential part of therapy.

4. POSTOPERATIVE INTESTINAL OBSTRUCTION

Bowel obstruction may occur as a complication of any abdominal operation. It is most apt to occur as a consequence of peritonitis or generalized irritation of the peritoneal surface, resulting in varying degrees of adhesions between loops of bowel. This may be apparent after gynecologic surgery in which extensive uterine surgery, eg, myomectomy or metroplasty, has been performed. In obstetrics, it will more commonly be encountered after a classic rather than a low cervical cesarean section. Obstruction results when these adhesions trap or kink a segment of intestine. Adhesions that form within the first few weeks after surgery are rubbery and seldom compromise the circulation of the bowel. Dense, fibrous adhesions develop after 8–12 weeks, and these are more likely to entrap bowel and cause strangulation. For this reason, it is possible to treat postoperative bowel obstruction conservatively by nasogastric intubation or by the use of long intestinal tubes. Tube decompression will often result in realignment of the bowel and relief of the obstruction, or adhesions may relax sufficiently to allow spontaneous decompression. When conservative management is elected, an arbitrary period of decompression should be decided upon in advance; if the obstruction does not respond within that period (eg, 48–72 hours), reoperation is necessary.

5. CONSTIPATION & FECAL IMPACTION

A reduction in the number of bowel movements is to be expected in the early postoperative period because of low food intake and because of ileus. After gas has been passed rectally, a mild laxative (milk of magnesia, 30 mL orally) may be prescribed. A clear-water enema or rectal bisacodyl suppository is also effective.

Fecal impaction is a common cause of diarrhea in the postoperative patient. Whenever the patient develops diarrhea, digital rectal examination should be done immediately. If hard stool is encountered in the ampulla, the diagnosis of fecal impaction is verified. The condition is due to limitation of oral fluids and is especially prone to occur in elderly patients and others confined to bed. It may be aggravated by previous gastrointestinal series or barium enema with accumulation of barium in the colon.

The treatment of fecal impaction is digital disimpaction of the firm fecal masses after an oil retention enema.

WOUND COMPLICATIONS

1. HEMATOMA

Small hematomas or seromas often resolve spontaneously, but some become infected. Prevention of hematomas is best accomplished by the use of suction drainage (eg, Hemovac). Gravity or Penrose drains are far less effective in gynecologic surgery.

Insidious serous accumulations may occur either in the pelvis or under the fascia of the abdominal rectus muscle. They may be first suspected because of a falling hematocrit in association with a low-grade fever. Ultrasonography is an excellent adjunct to physical examination for diagnosis. The subrectus collection (seen most frequently after a Pfannenstiel or Maylard incision or in conjunction with a Marshall-Marchetti-Krantz procedure) may be difficult to outline clinically but is clearly delineated by ultrasound.

Drainage of the hematoma, particularly if infected, should be accomplished extraperitoneally. This is simple if it is located in the anterior abdominal wall. However, if it is in the pelvis and easy access is not available at the vaginal vault, an inguinal extraperitoneal approach may be necessary.

2. WOUND INFECTION

The frequency and degree of wound infection postoperatively depends upon skin care and preparation, the patient's nutritional status, and the patient's habits of personal hygiene.

The diagnosis of wound infection usually is made during investigation of an unexplained postoperative fever, often on about the fourth to fifth day. It is based on the physical findings of redness of the skin at the operative site and fluctuation or induration beneath. *Escherichia coli* and *Enterobacter aerogenes,* as well as staphylococci, are the pathogens most commonly cultured from infected wounds. The wound should be gently probed and cultured. If no fluid is found, a warm moist dressing should be applied and the wound reexamined 1–2 days later. If infected fluid is released, ample drainage should be provided and appropriate antibiotics ordered. Warm wet dressings should be applied constantly and the wound cleaned daily with hydrogen peroxide until definite improvement is noted. The wound should be allowed to granulate upward. A drain or gauze packing may be required to keep the skin from sealing the wound prematurely.

3. WOUND DEHISCENCE & EVISCERATION

The transverse lower abdominal incision used by many gynecologists rarely ruptures. Vertical—especially midline—incisions carry a much greater risk of breakdown. Evisceration—disruption of all layers of the abdominal wall with protrusion of the intestines through the incision—is a critical postoperative complication. The dreaded hallmark of this complication is a profuse serosanguineous discharge exuding from the abdominal incision. When the diagnosis of fascial dehiscence or evisceration is made, secondary closure must be performed immediately under general anesthesia. Interrupted nonabsorbable sutures through all layers of the abdominal wall are preferred. A broad-spectrum antibiotic should be prescribed following wound culture.

4. NECROTIC PHENOMENA

Three unusual but devastating wound complications related to ischemic phenomena should be noted. The first is the result of poor incisional planning with resultant slough of tissue if a parallel vertical incision is used rather than the excision of an old vertical scar. Necrotizing fasciitis has been described in both abdominal and perineal sites and is extremely destructive when it occurs. Pyoderma gangrenosum is of particular consequence, because it may be associated with myeloproliferative disease, eg, leukemia. All 3 conditions usually require significant (and in the latter 2, repeated) wide debridement with healing occurring by second intention.

MISCELLANEOUS COMPLICATIONS

1. NEUROLOGIC COMPLICATIONS

Peripheral neuropathies may be encountered as a direct result of surgical trauma, because of pressure from self-retaining rectractors or from a position of the patient (especially the lithotomy) in which pressure results from the operating table restraints or supports. Peroneal, femoral, obturator, genitofemoral, and sacral plexus neural impairment can result. Happily, in most instances, the disability is temporary, and recovery is the rule after several weeks. Physical therapy may be necessary during this time to assure optimal improvement.

2. ANESTHETIC COMPLICATIONS

The major anesthetic complications following inhalation anesthesia relate to the respiratory system as outlined above. Regional techniques may also pose problems ranging from disabling neurologic complications to temporary bladder dysfunction. The most common and aggravating postoperative problem with regional anesthesia is spinal headache. In most instances, headache can be avoided by the use of very small caliber needles and adequate hydration before, during, and after the procedure. Use of the so-called epidural blood patch often gives immediate relief.

3. OBSTETRIC COMPLICATIONS

Two unique and uncommon complications that must be considered in the postoperative obstetric patient with febrile morbidity are ovarian vein thrombophlebitis (see Chapter 38) and uterine dehiscence. The latter occurs exclusively following classic cesarean section and is accompanied by a course suggestive of pelvic abscess, with spiking temperatures, ileus, localized tenderness of the fundus and abdominal wall, and *a significant fixed relationship of fundus to the abdominal incision site* where it becomes adherent. Reexploration and usually hysterectomy are necessary for correction.

RELEASE FROM HOSPITAL

Every postoperative patient should have a complete physical examination (including thorough pelvic assessment) before release from the hospital. Counseling, both oral and written, should be given to assure continued optimal convalescence at home. This includes both positive and negative aspects of home care (dos and don'ts). Specific understandings should be reached and appointments made for close outpatient and office follow-up.

OUTPATIENT SURGERY

The popularity, cost-effectiveness, and demonstrated safety of outpatient surgery demand its inclusion here. It should be emphasized that one must be as conscientious and meticulous in all aspects of preoperative requirements as for inpatient care. While "ambulatory surgery" is designed for the healthy patient who is programmed for less extensive surgery, to become casual in preparation is to court disaster.

Because these patients play a more active role in the preparation and management of their surgery, the following additional elements must be considered: (1) Preoperative counseling should encompass the same information given the inpatient, but another responsible adult who will provide transportation and postoperative care for the patient must be present at the session also. (2) Emphasis should be placed on the importance of the "nothing by mouth" requirement and on the avoidance of any medications the surgeon has not prescribed or approved. Patients may otherwise take tranquilizers or other medications to "relax themselves" before surgery. (3) A pregnancy test is frequently performed routinely at the time of preoperative counseling (usually the day before surgery). (4) A hospital must be available for backup if the facility is not hospital-based, and the patient must know where to report if problems arise. This entails establishing 24-hour telephone service for access to medical advice and care.

● ● ●

References

Amstey MS, Jones AP: Preparation of the vagina for surgery: A comparison of povidone-iodine and saline solution. *JAMA* 1981;**245**:839.

Bissell S: Pulmonary thromboembolism associated with gynecologic surgery and pregnancy. *Am J Obstet Gynecol* 1977;**128**:418.

Boral LI, Henry JB: The type and screen: A safe alternative and supplement in selected surgical procedures. *Transfusion* 1977;**17**:163.

Boral LI et al: A guideline for anticipated blood usage during elective surgical procedures. *Am J Clin Pathol* 1979;**71**:680.

Brote L: Wound infections in clean and potentially contaminated surgery: Importance of bacterial and nonbacterial factors. *Acta Chir Scand* 1976;**142**:191.

Buck P, Singer A: Towards reducing operative morbidity and mortality. *Clin Obstet Gynaecol* 1978;**5**:729.

Crandon AJ et al: Postoperative deep vein thrombosis: Identifying high-risk patients. *Br Med J* 1980;**281**:343.

Dion YM et al: The influence of oral versus parenteral preoperative metronidazole on sepsis following colon surgery. *Ann Surg* 1980;**192**:221.

Dizerega G et al: Comparison of clindamycin-gentamicin and penicillin-gentamicin in treatment of post–cesarean section endomyometritis. *Am J Obstet Gynecol* 1979;**134**:238.

Djokovic JL, Hedley-Whyte J: Prediction of outcome of surgery and anesthesia in patients over 80. *JAMA* 1979;**242**:2301.

Down RHL, Whitehead R, Watts JM: Why do surgical packs cause peritoneal adhesions? *Aust NZ J Surg* 1980;**50**:83.

Doyle JF: Ligation of the internal iliac artery to control severe pelvic hemorrhage. *Ir Med J* 1975;**68**:340.

Eltringham RJ: Complications in the recovery room. *J R Soc Med* 1979;**72**:278.

Fardin P, Benettello P, Negrin P: Iatrogenic femoral neuropathy: Considerations on its prognosis. *Electromyogr Clin Neurophysiol* 1980;**20**:153.

Flynn JT et al: The early and aggressive repair of iatrogenic ureteric injuries. *Br J Urol* 1979;**51**:454.

Fox GS et al: Anesthesia for cesarean section: Further studies. *Am J Obstet Gynecol* 1979;**133**:15,

Gordon HR, Phelps D, Beauchard K: Prophylactic cesarean section antibiotics: Maternal and neonatal morbidity before and after cord clamping. *Obstet Gynecol* 1979;**53**:15.

Griffiths DA: A reappraisal of the Pfannenstiel incision. *Br J Urol* 1976;**48**:469.

Gruber UF et al: Incidences of fatal postoperative pulmonary embolism after prophylaxis with dextran 70 and low-dose heparin: An international multicentre study. *Br Med J* 1980;**280**:69.

Gustafsson LL, Feychting B, Klingstedt C: Late respiratory depression after concomitant use of morphine epidurally and parenterally. *Lancet* 1981;**1**:892.

Haeri AD et al: Effect of different preoperative vaginal preparations on morbidity of patients undergoing abdominal hysterectomy. *S Afr Med J* 1976;**50**:1984.

Hawrylyshyn PA, Bernstein P, Papsin FR: Risk factors associated with infection following cesarean section. *Am J Obstet Gynecol* 1981;**139**:294.

Helmkamp B: Abdominal wound dehiscence. *Am J Obstet Gynecol* 1977;**128**:803.

Hohl MK et al: Prevention of postoperative thromboembolism by dextran 70 or low-dose heparin. *Obstet Gynecol* 1980;**55**:497.

Holdcroft A: Outpatient preoperative assessment: The anaesthetist's view. *Ann R Coll Surg Engl* 1980;**62**:382.

Ibeziako PA, Ayeni O: Postoperative wound sepsis in obstetric and gynecologic surgery. *Int Surg* 1979;**64**:67.

Jackson P, Ridley WJ, Pattison NS: Single dose metronidazole prophylaxis in gynaecological surgery. *NZ Med J* 1979;**89**:243.

Jones TE, Newell ET Jr, Brubaker RE: The use of alloy steel wire in the closure of abdominal wounds. *Surg Gynecol Obstet* 1941;**72**:1056.

Katz J, Aidinis SJ: Complications of spinal and epidural anesthesia. *J Bone Joint Surg [Am]* 1980;**62**:1219.

Keighley MRB: Prophylactic antibiotics in surgery. *Br J Hosp Med* 1980;**23**:465.

Kunin CM: Urinary tract infections. *Surg Clin North Am* 1980;**60**:223.

Lederer DH, Van de Water JM, Indech RB: Which deep breathing device should the postoperative patient use? *Chest* 1980;**77**:610.

Ledger WJ: Prevention, diagnosis and treatment of postoperative infections. *Obstet Gynecol* 1980;**55**:203S.

Leff RG, Shapiro SR: Lower extremity complications of the lithotomy position: Prevention and management. *J Urol* 1979;**122**:138.

Luce JM: Preoperative evaluation and perioperative management of patients with pulmonary disease. *Postgrad Med* 1980;**67**:201.

McKeithen WS Jr: Major gynecologic surgery in the elderly female 65 years of age and older. *Am J Obstet Gynecol* 1975;**123**:59.

Montag TW, Mead PB: Postpartum femoral neuropathy. *J Reprod Med* 1981;**26**:547.

Mudge M, Hughes LE: The long term sequelae of deep vein thrombosis. *Br J Surg* 1978;**65**:692.

Murphy JF, Khamis B: Abdominal wound disruption following obstetric and gynaecological surgery. *Ir J Med Sci* 1978;**147**:389.

Natof HE: Complications associated with ambulatory surgery. *JAMA* 1980;**244**:1116.

Pelosi MA: Use of the radioreceptor assay for human chorionic gonadotropin in the diagnosis of ectopic pregnancy. *Surg Gynecol Obstet* 1981;**152**:149. [Reviewed, with editorial comment, in *Obstet Gynecol Surv* 1981;**36**:482.]

Petrie CR: Total parenteral nutrition: Indications and hazards in the surgical patient. *Clin Obstet Gynecol* 1976;**19**:683.

Physical methods of prophylaxis against venous thrombosis. (Editorial.) *Br Med J* 1981;**282**:1341.

Pillgram-Larsen J, Normann E, Raeder M: Skin necrosis between parallel abdominal incisions. *Acta Chir Scand* 1979;**145**:277.

Pratt JH: Common complications of vaginal hysterectomy: Thoughts regarding their prevention and management. *Clin Obstet Gynecol* 1976;**19**:645.

Quatromoni JC et al: Early postoperative small bowel obstruction. *Ann Surg* 1980;**191**:72.

Risser NL: Preoperative and postoperative care to prevent pulmonary complications. *Heart Lung* 1980;**9**:57.

Robbins JA, Mushlin AI: Preoperative evaluation of the healthy patient. *Med Clin North Am* 1979;**63**:1145.

Romano J, Safai B: Pyoderma gangrenosum and myeloproliferative disorders. *Arch Intern Med* 1979;**139**:932.

Sandusky WR: Use of prophylactic antibiotics in surgical patients. *Surg Clin North Am* 1980;**60**:83.

Schumann D: Preoperative measures to promote wound healing. *Nurs Clin North Am* 1979;**44**:683.

Segal AI, Corlett RC Jr: Postoperative bladder training. *Am J Obstet Gynecol* 1979;**133**:366.

Seligman SA: Metronidazole in obstetrics and gynaecology. *J Antimicrob Chemother* 1978;**4 (Suppl C)**:51.

Shires GT: Postoperative post-traumatic management of fluids. *Bull NY Acad Med* 1979;**55**:248.

Shy KK, Eschenbach DA: Fatal perineal cellulitis from an episiotomy site. *Obstet Gynecol* 1979;**54**:292.

Slade N: Postoperative urinary tract infections in urology and gynaecology: A review. *J R Soc Med* 1980;**73**:739.

Stanton SL, Cardozo LD, Kerr-Wilson R: Treatment of delayed onset of spontaneous voiding after surgery for incontinence. *Urology* 1979;**13**:494.

Swan HJC, Ganz W: Use of balloon flotation catheters in critically ill patients. *Surg Clin North Am* 1975;**55**:501.

Törngren S: Prophylaxis of postoperative deep venous thrombosis. *Acta Chir Scand [Suppl]* 1979;**495**:3.

Torosian M et al: Aspirin- and Coumadin-related bleeding after coronary artery bypass graft surgery. *Ann Intern Med* 1978;**89**:325.

Van Scoy RE: Prophylactic antibiotic therapy: Its use and abuse. *Clin Obstet Gynecol* 1976;**19**:721.

Webb-Johnson DC: Postoperative pulmonary complications. *Compr Ther* 1979;**5**:38.

Woods JH et al: Postoperative ileus: A colonic problem? *Surgery* 1978;**84**:527.

Wyatt GM, Spitz IIB: Ultrasound in the diagnosis of rectus sheath hematoma. *JAMA* 1979;**241**:1499.

Psychologic Aspects of Gynecologic Practice | 21

Ralph C. Benson, MD

THE SOCIAL & CULTURAL SETTING OF GYNECOLOGIC PRACTICE

Gynecology is a field of medical practice in which many of the social and attitudinal changes that have taken place in recent years in our society are perhaps more significant than in other specialties. Fundamental changes have occurred in the patient's perception of what gynecologic care should consist of and in society's perception of what gynecology as a discipline should strive to achieve to improve the welfare of women.

Virtually every culture has developed a body of folklore, taboos, and religious and civil sanctions designed to control the sexual and reproductive functions of women, and these proscriptions have been in force for generations. For example, only recently in the USA have gynecologists been free to prescribe effective contraception for any woman who asks for it or to perform therapeutic abortion as an elective method of terminating an unwanted pregnancy without medical or psychiatric indication. Many other problems still beg for solutions, eg, preservation of life of hopelessly malformed newborns and worldwide population control to preserve or improve the quality of life for the generations of the next millennium.

Our social order largely determines what the "problems" are. Gynecologists must adapt to the pressures of cultural forces on themselves individually and on their profession. If they perceive their role as partly one of problem-solver for the women who come to the office, they must understand how patients may be affected by changing attitudes and how patients perceive "what is wrong" and what their physicians can do about it.

ROLE OF THE GYNECOLOGIST IN THE CHANGING STATUS OF WOMEN

Women are demanding that more attention be paid to themselves as individuals rather than as childbearing mechanisms or the subject matter of medical and surgical textbooks. Women today are more concerned with their "health" and their special interests as women than with "sickness," which has been the medical orientation of the past. Women's self-esteem has increased, and the choice of life-styles available to them now extends beyond simply marriage and mothering.

As defined in *Dorland's Illustrated Medical Dictionary*, 26th ed, 1981, gynecology is "that branch of medicine which treats of diseases of the genital tract in women." This represents an extremely limited view of the gynecologist's role. The modern practice of gynecology is more compatible with the definition presented in *Webster's Third New International Dictionary*, 1971: "A branch of medicine that deals with women, their diseases, hygiene, and medical care." This quite properly implies that the gynecologist is a primary care physician for women, with a major role in the management of a variety of medical and psychologic problems. This is not to say, however, that the most critical area of concern in gynecologic practice is not still what it always has been—the reproductive system and specific female sexual functions.

The personality of the obstetrician-gynecologist is important in determining whether a patient will regard emotional difficulties as one kind of problem the physician can help to solve. The physician is just as much a product of the culture he or she grew up in as (for example) a younger, sexually active though unmarried patient is of her own. If the physician is clearly prejudiced, intolerant, or misinformed—or has problems in relating to sexuality or to women—the patient probably will know it and will withhold any mention of emotional problems. If the patient does offer this clinical material for examination and discussion, the physician who is not prepared to receive it in a therapeutic and nonjudgmental manner may cause even more difficulty by attempting to impose a personal (irrelevant) value system on a woman who will only be embarrassed by the effort. Therefore, the gynecologist must assess and understand his or her own attitudes about sexuality in order to deal effectively with associated psychologic problems in the patient.

The gynecologist should fulfill at least 4 distinct functions: (1) primary care physician for many women, (2) pelvic surgeon, (3) reproductive endocrinologist, and (4) sex counselor.

THE GYNECOLOGIST AS PRIMARY CARE PHYSICIAN; ROLE IN MANAGEMENT OF EMOTIONAL DISORDERS

The gynecologist as as primary care physician for women is expected to be familiar with the techniques of management of common emotional disorders. Gynecologists are medical specialists whose patients often come to them not sick but well and seeking services and advice about such things as contraceptive methods, cancer screening, and physiologic hormonal adjustments during important phases of growth, maturity, and gradual decline of gonadal function. With no pressing medical problem that must be dealt with, the gynecologist-as-primary-physician may use the visit to inquire about other problems and perhaps intervene therapeutically if the circumstances seem to be favorable. The gynecologist has access to emotional and personal data that otherwise might not be discussed. For example, in talking with a young girl seeking advice because of concerns related to puberty, the gynecologist may be able not only to give advice regarding birth control but also, by offering good counsel at an early stage in sexual life, to improve her emotional well-being throughout the period of sexual activity.

The gynecologist may be the first physician to see the patient on a continuing basis. This may help anticipate potential emotional problems which can thus be avoided or attenuated.

THE GYNECOLOGIST AS SURGEON

The psychologic aspects of gynecologic surgery are the same as those of any surgical specialty *plus* all of the special implications surrounding the reproductive system and organs of sex. Before any gynecologic operation is performed, the physician must try to understand the patient's expectations, fears, and even fantasies about the operation. In addition to the anticipated results of surgery, it is important to consider the symbolic meaning of the procedure and its ultimate psychic impact. Many operations have important effects on the body image and the patient's sense of personal validity. The effect of gynecologic surgery may be much deeper psychologically and more complicated emotionally than anatomically.

Hysterectomy or ovariectomy may leave a patient feeling less of a woman, so that loss of a basic sense of femininity and reduced libido may develop. Postoperative depression and even psychotic states are far more common following pelvic surgery than abdominal surgery. In general, the more a woman's sense of personal identity is based on ideas about femininity, menstruation, and reproductive function, the more emotionally difficult will be loss of the uterus or of ovarian function.

The gynecologic surgeon should be mindful of the emotional state, feelings, prejudices, and attitudes of the husband. Just as a woman may feel she is "no longer a woman" after reproductive function has been terminated by surgery, a man may unconsciously need to confirm his manhood periodically by fathering a child, and his wife's "castration" may cause him to have a serious emotional reaction, including impotence, depression, abusive behavior toward the wife, or even desertion of the family. The gynecologist should aid the patient and her husband to understand the operation and accept its results so that potential psychologic problems can be aborted.

THE GYNECOLOGIST AS ENDOCRINOLOGIST

The gynecologist as endocrinologist often must make difficult diagnostic decisions about which symptoms are organic and which ones are functional. There is no gynecologic endocrine disorder that does not have a psychologic component, however.

Menstruation is uniquely associated with femininity, and all cultures have peculiar folk attitudes and superstitions with regard to the menstrual cycle. Menarche is an important emotional landmark for every woman. The adolescent girl's state of mind and preparation for this important event can affect her perception of herself and her reaction to menses throughout her functional years. Menarche is a manifestation of her imminent womanhood and all that means in terms of body image and self-worth.

Menarche may require difficult adjustments during puberty and may be associated with strong emotional responses, both positive and negative. Common disturbances associated with the menstrual cycle—premenstrual tension, amenorrhea, dysmenorrhea—have been determined at various times to have both psychologic and organic causes.

A powerful determinant of success in the treatment of dysmenorrhea, for example, is the patient's personal faith in the physician and the physician's faith in the value of the treatment.

There are many organic causes of amenorrhea. Psychologic causes include sudden severe emotional trauma such as rape or the death of a loved one. Amenorrhea can occur during periods of emotional stress and can be associated with such symptoms as pseudocyesis or anorexia nervosa. Because the exact pathophysiologic mechanism of menstrual dysfunction often is not known and much of it may be psychologic, the physician's personality and rapport with the patient may be especially beneficial. This is true whether or not the physician utilizes hormones or other drugs. In the case of a psychologically determined menstrual aberration, it may take several interviews for the gynecologist to understand the cause; and in some instances, it may be necessary to refer the woman for psychiatric evaluation and treatment.

THE GYNECOLOGIST AS SEX COUNSELOR*

Many emotional problems encountered in gynecologic practice have their origins in how patients relate sexually and how they perceive themselves as sexual beings. Gynecologists are more accessible to their patients as sex counselors than other physicians because of their patients' expectations and because of the increasing recognition that sexual well-being is an important element of general health. It is impossible for a gynecologist to avoid dealing with the sexual dysfunction problems of patients. The extent of the gynecologist's involvement in such matters will of course vary depending upon the interests of the individual physician and the population group from which patients are drawn.

Because of ignorance, misinformation, or the powerful taboos and repressions surrounding sexuality, difficulties primarily due to sexual dysfunction often present as anxiety or depression, chronic pelvic pain, fatigue, insomnia, or headache. The physician should consider the possibility that these common ailments may be caused by sexual problems.

ROLE OF THE GYNECOLOGIST IN PREMARITAL COUNSELING

Counseling before marriage can be a worthwhile and satisfying aspect of preventive medicine. Premarital counseling offers a unique opportunity for the physician to deal with any fears or misunderstandings the couple may have about sexual matters and explain certain common somatic and emotional problems that may interfere with sexual fulfillment in marriage.

Men and women who request premarital counseling may be seeking reassurance that they are "doing the right thing," because they are anxious to ensure a good and enduring marriage and may have doubts about whether they are suited to marriage. The physician must identify these concerns and help the couple make a suitable decision. This does not include advice about whether to get married or not except in rare situations in which a critical or intolerable problem is present that would doom the marriage or make the couple unsuitable as parents.

The couple should be given an opportunity to talk about what they expect from marriage and any anxieties they may have about any aspect of it. The counselor should use the occasion to offer information and guidance regarding the responsibilities, needs, goals, values, and difficulties of marriage.

The physician should explore the following areas:

(1) **Courtship:** How did the couple meet, and what made them decide to get married?

(2) **Personal background:** Racial, ethnic, social, educational, cultural, family, and religious.

(3) **Family attitudes:** Will each accept the other's parents as in-laws? Will there be possible domination by one family? Are the couple financially dependent on one family, and will this persist?

(4) **Planning:** Are both individuals realistic and responsible in preparing for the wedding and for future projects, eg, buying a house? Is there an attitude of consideration, compromise, communication, and cooperation to work toward mutual goals?

(5) **Psychologic and personality factors:** Does each individual approve of and accept the other's physical and behavioral characteristics (life-style), including habits, dress, grooming, and manners?

(6) **Sex role compatibility and plans for a family:** Is there a clear understanding and agreement on sex roles? Are there possible problems regarding sexual fulfillment and parenting? Are children desired by only one partner, both, or neither?

Counseling sessions should include examination and discussion. Each of the following steps is important (not listed in order of importance):

(1) **Pelvic examination:** If the genitalia are normal, give reassurance. If not, plans should be made for correction.

(2) **Anatomy and physiology:** Include a basic discussion of male and female reproductive biology with illustrations.

(3) **Contraception:** Present an overview of contraception that is detailed enough to allow a choice of method. The advantages, disadvantages, problems and alternatives should be reviewed. Then, after a selection, make the method and materials available.

(4) **Virginity:** If the woman is a virgin, she may wish to make a decision regarding dilatation or incision of the hymen. Self-dilatation with graduated test tubes or dilators is effective if time will permit; otherwise, hymenotomy under anesthesia may be performed.

(5) **Coitus:** Include a discussion of coital physiology.

(6) **Questions:** An opportunity for asking questions should be provided, eg, the "normal" frequency of coitus. (Whatever is satisfactory to both parties is normal.)

(7) **Follow-up discussion.**

Both parties should be involved in the discussion and decision making. Ideally, an interview with and examination of the man alone should be arranged for discussion of anatomy, physiology with special reference to sex differences, and preference regarding method of contraception.

A return visit 2 months after marriage is suggested. The 2-month interval is recommended because at 4 weeks, if trouble has developed, the partners cannot admit even to themselves that there is a problem; at 6 weeks, each knows there is a problem but cannot admit it to the other; and at 8 weeks, they know they have a problem, are quite certain whose it is, and will discuss it. The physician usually can correct it.

---

*Specific aspects of sexual dysfunction in men and women are discussed in the next chapter.

THE DOCTOR–PATIENT RELATIONSHIP IN GYNECOLOGY

The doctor-patient relationship should be one which will function as required to fill the need every patient may have from time to time for a helping professional person's advice and support. Different patients have different needs, and the needs of the individual patient may change as her medical status or life situation changes over the years. Consequently, the doctor-patient relationship in gynecologic practice should be allowed to grow and change in response to events and the demands of time on the capacity to adapt to change. The doctor's relationship with the patient should be regarded as a therapeutic tool to be kept in readiness for use when needed. It may never be needed, but the patient who maintains a long relationship with her physician has a right to expect the fullest extent of the physician's help if a time of need should ever arise.

THE PATIENT INTERVIEW

The most common error in taking the history from a new patient in nonemergency circumstances is the tendency of the examiner to talk and ask questions rather than listen. It takes a while when the patient is first seen even to know what questions to ask, much less what symptoms to explore. Direct questions—the highly structured interview—often have the effect of inhibiting the patient who wishes to volunteer sensitive data, particularly in the psychosexual area of her total problem.

The examiner must be alert to nonverbal cues that may be unconscious attempts to communicate feelings about what is being said. Facial expressions, body posture and gestures, and voice quality are part of everyone's unconscious vocabulary, and no patient can be understood through a screen that blocks out a large part of the communication.

Close attention must be paid also to what the patient omits to say or passes over with rather too much haste.

After 20–30 minutes spent with the patient in a nondirective effort to understand the reason for the visit, a few specific questions may be all that is required to complete a traditional medical history. Even though in a busy practice the time may seem to be extravagant, the outlay for a good first interview is small compared with what may be wasted in a series of nonproductive office visits or laboratory tests or in an operating room performing surgery that proves not to be of significant benefit to the patient.

THE ACUTE GYNECOLOGIC EMERGENCY OR URGENT CASE

Whenever the need arises for emergency or urgent medical or surgical care, the relationship with the patient changes at once to one that requires almost total submission of the passive patient to the swift ministrations of the dominant physician. This role is often portrayed as habitual in fictional accounts of medical practice, and it may be one the physician likes best; however, just as a patient may have to be weaned from a powerful drug by tapering the dosage to nil over a short span of time, so each patient whose personal decision-making function has been taken over by a doctor acting in an emergency must gradually resume responsibility for her own emotional and physical welfare as soon as possible after the crisis has passed. Prolongation of the dominant role by the physician may easily lead to continued dependent demands after the justification for dependency has ceased to exist— even to the point of symptom formation in an unconscious attempt to sustain a relationship that has been found to be more comfortable than self-reliance. The patient recovering from surgery or regaining health after a serious illness must not be suddenly abandoned to her own devices as long as she needs her doctor's help and support; but every effort should be made to hasten her return to full health and vigor and a life without dependency on her doctor.

PSYCHOLOGIC FACTORS IN SPECIFIC TYPES OF GYNECOLOGIC PROBLEMS

Psychologic factors may be extremely important in any gynecologic symptom or organic illness. Thus, an individual patient with cancer may suffer more from the emotional impact of her disease than from the disorder itself. The clinician should appreciate the importance of psychologic factors in many gynecologic disorders and be prepared to deal with them therapeutically. In all such instances, a careful medical history, physical examination, and appropriate diagnostic studies will be required to evaluate the presence of genital, extragenital, or metabolic disease. Even when important tests are negative, they may be of psychotherapeutic value by establishing the clinician's professional thoroughness and interest in the patient as a total person.

PSYCHOLOGIC ASPECTS OF CONTRACEPTION

Contraception for Adults

The gynecologist's role in contraception is to counsel women who want fertility control and to provide effective control with the fewest possible undesirable side-effects or health hazards. The patient's religious views must be disclosed and respected and all relevant psychologic, esthetic, and economic factors properly assessed. The physician can then recommend a safe and effective method the patient can accept. The risks of any method the physician recommends should be explained, and it is useful in doing so to compare them with other risks of modern life such as driving, smoking, or flying, and, of course, the risk of becoming pregnant.

Counseling about contraception takes time in order to get to know the patient and her motivations and attitudes. It is not enough simply to know and expound the advantages and disadvantages of the methods available. The decision once arrived at is going to affect the patient's life-style and will certainly have important economic, social, and emotional consequences in the family and perhaps the community. The interview with her gynecologist in which contraception is discussed may be the most important medical event in the patient's lifetime.

Women use the various methods available for pregnancy control with success despite negative feelings they may have about the method or the necessity for contraception generally. The fear of pregnancy is both strong and realistic. In most cases, it is the patient's motivation and not the inherent effectiveness of the method chosen that determines the success or failure of contraception. However, even motivation that is strong initially may weaken as time passes—eg, if libido is lessened; if the patient becomes depressed or anxious from other causes; or if she hears one too many "horror stories" about women who have had problems while using the same or a similar method. The physician must be prepared to schedule repeat or follow-up discussions with the patient to verify continuing satisfaction and compliance with the method chosen and to recommend a change to a different method if that seems to be called for. Women who start with the pill and want to change usually ask for the IUD; if problems develop, they usually decide to use a barrier method. Eventually, when the couple have all the children they want, they choose tubal ligation for the woman or vasectomy for the man. Ideally, a good choice at the outset will prove effective and acceptable throughout the years when contraception is desired.

Contraception for Adolescents

Girls who want contraceptive advice or a prescription may be embarrassed to ask for it, and the gynecologist must be alert to such hidden agendas when a teenager seeks an appointment. The patient must be assured that her confidences will be respected. There is no legal or ethical requirement to inform the parents that a young girl has requested contraception advice.

The critical factor in success of contraception with teenagers is motivation. If the patient has decided to begin sexual activity but wants to stay in school, go on to college, get or keep a job, stay at home, postpone marriage, etc, any or all of these motives may be strong enough to ensure successful pregnancy control if the right method is chosen. Oral contraceptives are now being used more commonly by unmarried teenagers than by married women in spite of the WHO position that nonsteroidal methods are preferred for this age group. Most physicians are now willing to prescribe oral contraceptives for unmarried teenagers because

the consequences of unplanned pregnancy for these patients far outweigh the risks of adverse side-effects.

And yet the perceived risk of side-effects is a substantial factor in compliance failures after a regimen of oral contraception has been started. Weight gain and mood changes are the side-effects most often complained of. If the patient expresses concern about these or other side-effects (stroke or heart disease) at the initial interview, the physician should probably offer a different option than risk a pregnancy after a compliance failure.

In discussing the methods available, it is often useful to inquire about the quality of the patient's present relationship with a particular young man. It should be pointed out to the patient that if she "goes on the pill" and her boyfriend knows it, she may have a hard time saying no when she wants to. This conversation offers a good opportunity to suggest the many advantages of the condom over some of the forms of pregnancy control now being used by women.

PSYCHOLOGIC STRESS OF HYSTERECTOMY

Understanding the psychologic symbolism of menstruation and reproduction is basic to an appreciation of the patient's emotional reactions to hysterectomy and the stresses associated with the loss of those functions. The biologic ability to reproduce is intimately related to a woman's perception of herself as a female being. During adolescence, every girl learns to equate menstrual function with the ability to reproduce. Menstruation is thus perceived as a badge of femininity, and loss of menstrual function is regarded by many women as a deprivation of their femininity. The degree of damage this may do can be minimized by appropriate psychologic management.

The trauma of hysterectomy is greater in younger women and in those who have not established a satisfactory marriage relationship and family. Hysterectomy may have little psychologic impact on postmenopausal women who have already adjusted to the loss of the menstrual and reproductive function. Nonetheless, the menopause and climacteric mark a period when old doubts and insecurities may emerge. Consequently, this is a time when hysterectomy may cause increased psychologic stress for even relatively stable women.

Rarely must hysterectomy be proposed abruptly. Operation should be introduced as a procedure to be considered while discussing its indications. When possible, the patient's attention should be directed to the fact that conception is unlikely or impossible because of an existing pelvic disorder—not because of the proposed operation. Her attention must be gently directed to the fact that, if untreated, the disorder is or may become even more harmful to her as a woman, wife, and mother. Her positive achievements— marriage, children, a career, etc—are thereby emphasized. If ovarian function can and should be preserved, this should be explained. Such a discussion may have at least 2 psychologic benefits for the average mature woman. First, it will help to convince her that the physician is not a cold technician who is unfeelingly and autocratically trying to deprive her of a valued organ and function. Thus, a good doctor-patient relationship may develop that will be of therapeutic usefulness later. Second, the discussion may urge the patient to begin viewing the uterus with its reproductive and menstrual functions not as a prized possession but as the site of an abnormality that is or may become a danger to her personally. Because hysterectomy is seldom an emergency procedure, specific plans for the operation usually are deferred until after the first consultation. By arranging another interview, patients are allowed time to work through their natural anxieties before the decision to operate is made, and they usually experience fewer troublesome reactions postoperatively.

PSYCHOLOGIC STRESS OF STERILIZATION

Both married and single women may request sterilization, usually at the time of therapeutic abortion. It is important to determine whether or not the woman feels under pressure to submit to the procedure. Most women are aware of what is involved, but some are uncertain about making such a decision. Others may request sterilization and regret it later. Fortunately, the emotional consequences of voluntary sterilization are less damaging than when sterilization is required by medical necessity.

Many women experience feelings of guilt following the surgery. Social or religious conflicts tend to further complicate matters. It is essential that the gynecologist discuss all aspects of the operation with each woman, allowing her the opportunity to ask questions and express her feelings. It is sometimes best to postpone the surgery to allow time for mature consideration.

Postoperatively, similar discussions are equally important. A woman may not voluntarily express feelings of guilt she may have. It may be necessary for the gynecologist to broach the subject gently. If good rapport has been established, such discussions will be of tremendous benefit to the woman in alleviating concerns and in helping her adjust appropriately.

CANCER: SHOULD THE PATIENT BE TOLD?

The implication of suffering and death conveyed by the term "cancer" has made it one of the most feared diagnoses for physician and patient alike. For the patient, it carries with it not only fear of pain, wasting, and death, but also often of mutilation and social exile. The physician must use all resources as a human being in deciding whether or not to tell the patient she has cancer and just when, how, and how much to tell. The patient must be sustained in all reasonable hopes and helped to make optimal use of whatever personal resources are available in dealing with the problem. Treating the cancer patient contains perhaps the ultimate paradox of the physician's work: how to help the individual live while dying.

The experience of dying is an inevitable condition of life, and most women will not really want to be treated as if they were incapable of accepting it. Further, most women are so well informed on medical matters today that it is often impossible to conceal the diagnosis of cancer. Therefore, the patient should be told as much as she wants to know about her diagnosis and prognosis. Sometimes the family's wishes to conceal the diagnosis from the patient must be overruled, for the patient eventually may learn the truth and resent the deception. When the decision is made to tell the patient, it is the physician who should do it.

Fearsome words like "cancer," "carcinoma," and "sarcoma" should be avoided. Instead, the physician may tell the patient she has a "tumor" that may return after excision or irradiation in spite of modern treatment. However, it must be made unmistakably clear to her that many patients can be cured and that she may become worse before she gets better. The excellent methods for the control of pain that are now available should be emphasized and the horrors of chronic invalidism minimized.

There is no need to tell a pediatric gynecologic patient that she has cancer unless she has reached the age of reason. It is unfortunate that severe illness and hospitalization often are interpreted by children as a punishment for disobedience or mischief, which may, in fact, be conceived as the "cause" of the illness. Older people, too—even those who have led exemplary lives—often are unable to reject these fantasies completely.

The impact of the diagnosis of cancer on an individual patient cannot be predicted. It is best to proceed slowly, responding to requests for additional information rather than attempting a full disquisition of the estimated course and prognosis. The physician should be as optimistic as possible and never say, "Nothing can be done." Spontaneous regression does occur, and new drugs and surgical advances and improvements in irradiation techniques are being developed constantly. Something can always be done for the patient's comfort and peace of mind; spiritual progress during this critical time can be a genuine source of emotional satisfaction and consolation. Good communication and rapport between the patient, her physician, the nursing staff, and her family are essential.

Telling the patient the truth does not always mean that she will understand or accept the facts. A woman who is told she has a tumor may refuse to believe it. Similarly, a patient who is told that her tumor is benign may be certain that an awful truth is being withheld. Other women will deduce the truth from the way they are told about their illness or by mannerisms of the physician and can be spared a painstaking recital of the details. The physician must decide how good communications are with the patient, when to explain further, and when to temporize.

Every patient must be given some basis for faith and hope. There is nothing wrong with the patient's "deceiving herself" if she needs the consolation of her illusions. However, people with modest means should be prevented from impoverishing their families in futile searches for nonexistent cures. The physician must individualize and decide which false hopes are dangerous and which are useful and consoling.

The thought of suicide to avoid terminal agony and helplessness and to save the expense of prolonged hospitalization occurs to most women who are told they have cancer. Nevertheless, only a few patients with cancer actually attempt suicide. In the USA, about 2% of patients who succeed in suicide have cancer; only 5% of suicides have other types of chronic incurable illness.

Depression must not be permitted to go unnoticed or untreated. Creative opportunities should not be banished from the patient's life by her illness; existence should continue to be a rewarding experience. Many patients who are able to maintain a "brave front" while the physician is present may lapse into despondency later. Attendants and others should be asked to report occasionally on the patient's emotional status. For example, the night nurse, whom the doctor may never see, is often able to observe psychic distress more easily than the day nurse and should report any impressions regarding pain, restlessness, weeping, and other signs of tension.

The consolation of religion is the greatest source of strength and comfort for many patients in the face of suffering and impending death. The physician should be prepared to cooperate fully with the patient's religious adviser so that she will derive the greatest possible benefit from her spiritual beliefs.

The management of terminal illness requires emphasis on daily experience. The patient should not be allowed to look back with regret or forward with fear. Insofar as possible, drugs are used that do not impair the mental faculties so that reading, visiting, and entertainment still can be enjoyed.

When the end is near, heroic measures to preserve life for brief periods are seldom justified. The patient should be permitted to die with dignity.

RAPE

Common law rape is defined as unlawful carnal knowledge of a woman not the wife of the perpetrator without her consent. **Statutory rape** is defined as intercourse with a female below the legal age of consent (often 18 years) with her consent.

The typical rapist is a disturbed, compulsive, violent man who becomes sexually excited by the mortal fear of his victim. He rarely is a psychotic individual. Rape is usually motivated by a wish to terrorize and humiliate the woman and is rarely the outcome of a frustrated seduction.

Although rape is the fastest growing violent crime in the USA, fewer than 10% of rapes are reported to the police. The rapist is usually under 30 years of age and married. He may come from any level of society and often is acquainted with or related to the victim. He often has raped before and may repeat the crime.

The victim may acquire a sexually transmissible disease, may become pregnant, or may suffer physical or emotional consequences.

Rape is usually planned and generally involves a woman who does not initially fear the man. Women do not secretly want to be raped, and they do not expect, encourage, or enjoy rape. Occasionally, however, after initially consenting to intercourse, the victim may change her mind, and rape results when the man forces himself upon her.

The slightest vaginal, anal, or oral penetration, if not consented to, is sufficient to constitute the crime of rape.

General Office Procedures

The physician who first sees the alleged rape victim must take the following actions:

(1) Secure written consent from the patient, guardian, or next of kin for gynecologic examination; obtain photographs (if they are likely to reveal evidence); and release pertinent information and specimens to the authorities.

(2) Notify the police and obtain their permission to examine the patient, or await the arrival of the police physician.

(3) Obtain and record the history in the patient's own words. The sequence of events, ie, the time, place, and circumstances, must be included. Note whether the alleged victim is calm or agitated or confused (drugs, alcohol). Record whether the patient came directly to the hospital or whether she bathed or changed her clothing.

(4) Obtain appropriate tests (see below).

(5) Mark clothing for evidence.

(6) Record findings but do not issue even a tentative diagnosis lest it be erroneous or incomplete.

(7) Treat disease and psychic trauma; prevent pregnancy; counsel the patient, especially regarding her legal rights, eg, filing charges; explain subsequent therapy and follow-up as well as the prognosis.

Physical Examination

Be empathic. Begin with a statement such as, "This is a terrible thing that has happened to you. I want to help."

With witnesses present, record the general appearance, demeanor, coherence, and cooperation of the patient. Note torn, stained, or bloody clothing. Identify any lacerations or contusions (the latter may be more apparent the next day).

Search for any signs of vulvar, vaginal, or anal trauma, discharge, or bleeding. Illuminate the pudendum with an ultraviolet light (prostatic secretions are fluorescent even when dry).

Employ a water-moistened (nonlubricated) warm speculum or vaginoscope to inspect the vagina and the cervix. (If the suspected victim is a child, a general anesthetic may be required.) Prepare cervical and anal cultures for *Neisseria gonorrhoeae* in Transgrow or Thayer-Martin medium. Obtain fluid from the vulva and the posterior vaginal fornix using a cotton applicator and retain the specimens in individual corked test tubes or screw-top vials containing 2–3 mL of normal saline for police laboratory or authorized hospital laboratory tests for the following: (1) Acid phosphatase. If the reaction is strongly positive, it almost certainly indicates the presence of prostatic fluid ejaculate. (2) Blood group antigen of spermatozoa (to distinguish rape by a second individual following a recent but earlier primary, unforced act of intercourse with a partner whose blood type differs from that of the offender's). In cases in which the presence of sperm may not be decisive, this test often is critical. (3) Precipitin tests against human spermatozoa and blood. (4) Spermatozoa. Motile sperm may be seen in a wet-mount preparation. Alcohol-ether–fixed or spray-dried smears may disclose spermatozoa. (Men who have had a vasectomy may have sperm-free ejaculate, however.)

Transfer clearly labeled evidence, eg, laboratory specimens, directly to the clinical pathologist in charge or to the responsible laboratory technician, in the presence of witnesses (never via messenger), so that the rules of evidence will not be breached.

Submit marked clothing, photographs, slides, etc, to the police as evidence and obtain a written receipt.

Never commit yourself verbally or in writing to a diagnosis, even at the conclusion of the examination and the report of laboratory tests. Use terms such as "alleged victim of rape" or "suspected rape victim." The records, which may be subpoenaed, must contain any negative as well as positive evidence to determine the guilt or innocence of the accused. Whether rape has occurred or not is a legal conclusion, not a medical one.

Prevention of Rape

A. At Home: Lock doors and windows, remain in the presence of others, and avoid being "trapped" in an elevator or dark corridor.

B. Away From Home: Take a cab, avoid hitchhiking, travel on busy, well-lighted streets, walk with someone, run if followed, and lock the car.

C. Resistance: Opinion is divided on whether the rape victim should offer resistance. Many believe that the victim should scream, scratch, kick, bite, etc, when endangered. Some suggest legal self-defense methods, eg, pushing a lighted cigarette, heavy keys, or safety pin into the assailant's face, or employing karate or judo if skilled in these methods of self-defense. Other authorities recommend passive compliance to prevent serious injury or death.

D. Weapons: Carrying weapons is not the solution to the problem of rape. A woman who uses a gun,

knife, or chemical device to protect herself against rape may face a criminal concealed weapons charge. Moreover, even if the opportunity to use the weapon should arise, weapons are often ineffective or harmful to innocent persons except in the hands of trained experts such as policewomen. Brandishing a weapon may also have the effect of enraging the attacker, resulting in greater harm to the victim than would have occurred otherwise.

Treatment

A. General Measures:

1. The physician should assume a sympathetic, concerned attitude—never skeptical or cynical.

2. Avoid comments and discussion with others in the presence of the patient.

B. Medical Therapy (With the Patient's Permission):

1. Administer tetanus antitoxin if deep lacerations contain soil or dirt particles.

2. Give prophylactic aqueous penicillin G, 4.6 million units intramuscularly, to prevent syphilis and gonorrhea.

3. Prevent pregnancy by using one of the following methods:

a. Administer medroxyprogesterone (Depo-Provera), 100 mg intramuscularly, or diethylstilbestrol, 25 mg orally, twice daily for 5 days.

b. Insert an IUD (preferably one with a copper addition).

C. Surgical Measures:

1. Suture lacerations and evacuate hematomas.

2. Employ menstrual regulation to reduce the likelihood of implantation if pregnancy occurs, or—

3. Perform a D&C for prevention of pregnancy or if pregnancy develops despite hormone or other therapy (see below).

D. Follow-Up: Repeat cultures for gonorrhea 1 week later; perform a VDRL test for syphilis 6 weeks later. Perform pregnancy tests if pregnancy is a possibility. Refer the patient for psychiatric assessment and counseling if severe emotional problems persist.

Complications

Strong negative feelings by the woman, eg, humiliation, confusion, fear of retaliation, may give way to quiet anger, hatred of men, feelings of isolation or worthlessness, distrust, and fear of being raped again. This may lead to deficiencies in expressing affection or relating socially or sexually. A psychotic sequela is rare but may occur, especially in patients with a history of psychosis.

Prognosis

A. For the Patient: The prognosis is excellent if good family support and counseling by trained social workers or rape crisis center (or committee) personnel are provided.

B. For the Rapist: Despite conviction and incarceration or psychotherapy, the rapist often rapes again.

• • •

References

Abramov LA: Sexual life and sexual frigidity among women developing acute myocardial infarction. *Psychosom Med* 1976;**38**:418.

Adolescent sexuality and adolescent fertility. (Editorial.) *Lancet* 1979;**21**:129.

Battersby C: Psychological implications of mastectomy. *Aust NZ J Surg* 1981;**51**:300.

Bjornson E: Sexual response after hysterectomy-oophorectomy: Recent studies and reconsideration of psychogenesis. *Am J Obstet Gynecol* 1981;**140**:7.

Blum RW, Goldhagen J: Teenage pregnancy in perspective. *Clin Pediatr* 1981;**20**:335.

Charlton RS. Divorce as a psychological experience. *Psychiatr Ann* 1980;**10**:12.

Coulam CB: Age, estrogen and the psyche. *Clin Obstet Gynecol* 1981;**24**:203.

Curtis DM: The sequelae of female sterilization in one general practice. *R Coll Gen Practitioner* 1979;**29**:366.

Daly MJ: The emotional problems of patients encountered in the practice of obstetrics and gynecology. *Obstet Gynecol Annu* 1980;**9**:339.

Duncan SL: Ethical problems in advising contraception and sterilization. *Practitioner* 1979;**223**:237.

Edwards DW: Pelvic genital cancer: Body image and sexuality. *Front Radiat Ther Oncol* 1979;**14**:35.

Emens JM: Female sterilization. *Practitioner* 1980;**224**:1177.

Evrard JR, Gold EM. Epidemiology and management of sexual assault victims. *Obstet Gynecol* 1979;**53**:381.

Fordney DS: Dyspareunia and vaginismus. *Clin Obstet Gynecol* 1978;**21**:205.

Gitlin MJ: Psychological reactions to sterilization procedures. *Psychosomatics* 1980;**21**:10.

Gomel V: Profile of women requesting reversal of sterilization. *Fertil Steril* 1978;**30**:39.

Heath DS: The link between hysterectomy and depression. *Can J Psychiatry* 1979;**24**:247.

Hicks DJ: Rape: Sexual assault. *Am J Obstet Gynecol* 1980; **137**:931.

Horwitz MJ: A field study of the stress response syndrome: Young women after hysterectomy. *JAMA* 1979;**242**:1499.

Humphries PT: Sexual adjustment after hysterectomy. *Issues Health Care Women* 1980;**2**:1.

Jackson J: A study of hysterectomy in family practice. *J Fam Pract* 1979;**8**:723.

Jacobs TJ: Sexual aspects of dysmenorrhea. *Med Aspects Hum Sexual* (May) 1976;**10**:58.

Kantarak.S: Prevention of psychiatric disturbances following gynecological operations. *Bibl Psychiatr* 1981;**160**:84.

Katchadourian H: Adolescent sexuality. *Pediatr Clin North Am* 1980;**27**:17.

Kesselman JR: Dealing with assertive (and nonassertive) women

patients. *Pract Psychol Physicians* (May) 1976;**3**:29.

Kirkpatrick M: Woman's sexual complaints. *Med Aspects Hum Sexual* (April) 1976;**10**:118.

Kresch AJ, Borrelli-Kresch S: Sexual problems in gynecology patients: Guidelines for office practice. *Clin Obstet Gynecol* 1976;**19**:465.

Labby DH: Iatrogenic causes of sexual dysfunction. *Med Aspects Hum Sexual* (Jan) 1976;**10**:124.

Labby DH: When to refer sexual problems to a psychiatrist. *Med Aspects Hum Sexual* (Dec) 1975;**9**:79.

Mcaljsine IS: Adolescent sexuality. *Aust Fam Physician* 1980; **8**:555.

McNamara V, King, LA, Green MF: Adolescent perspectives on sexuality, contraception and pregnancy. *J Med Assoc Ga* 1979;**68**:811.

Money JW: Discussing sexual problems with your patients. *Pract Psychol Physicians* (Nov) 1975;**11**:39.

Murdoch W: Are there psychiatric grounds for terminating a pregnancy? *Cent Afr J Med* 1979;**25**:158.

Petrich JM, Holmes TH: Recent life events and psychiatric illness. *Psychiatr Ann* 1981;**11**:13.

Porter J: Pleasuring enhanced by suggestive therapy for frigidity. *Psychother Psychosom* 1978;**30**:37.

Raynal A, Kossove D: Current concepts of rape victims' management. *S Afr Med J* 1981;**31**:144.

Roeske NC: Hysterectomy and the quality of a woman's life. (Editorial.) *Arch Intern Med* 1979;**139**:146.

Rosenfeld A: The adolescent and contraception: Issues and controversies. *Int J Gynaecol Obstet* 1981;**19**:51.

Rutledge AL: Psychomarital evaluation and treatment of the infertile couple. *Clin Obstet Gynecol* 1979;**22**:255.

Smith AH: Psychiatric aspects of sterilization: A prospective survey. *Br J Psychiatry* 1979;**135**:304.

Smith DH: Psychological aspects of gynecology and obstetrics. *Obstet Gynecol Annu* 1979;**8**:457.

Spencer RF, Raft D: Identifying sexual problems disguised as somatic complaints. *Med Aspects Hum Sexual* (March) 1976; **10**:71.

Spencer RF, Raft D: Somatic symptoms of sexual conflict. *Med Aspects Hum Sexual* (June) 1976;**10**:141.

Stone CB, Judd GE: Psychogenic aspects of urinary incontinence in women. *Clin Obstet Gynecol* 1978;**21**:807.

Taymor ML: The role of counseling in infertility. *Fertil Steril* 1979;**32**:154.

Weiss L, Meadow R: Women's attitudes toward gynecologic practices. *Obstet Gynecol* 1979;**54**:110.

Wilson EA: Sequence of emotional responses induced by infertility. *J Ky Med Assoc* 1979;**77**:229.

Yalom I: Group support for patients with metastatic cancer: A randomized outcome study. *Arch Gen Psychiatry* 1981; **38**:527.

22 | Marriage, Marital Counseling, & Sex Therapy

Daniel H. Labby, MD

In most societies, marriage is still regarded as the most emotionally gratifying institution devised over the ages for enhancing the quality of life and stabilizing the social structure for the benefit of everyone involved. In the USA, over 93% of the population are or have been married. Even though 40% of marriages end in divorce, successful remarriage after divorce occurs in about half of cases.

The number of couples living together but unmarried increased 8-fold between 1960 and 1970 (from 17,000 to 143,000), and there are indications that 1980 census data will show a further increase in the number of informal living arrangements in comparable populations. Such couples usually do not want children and often desire independent careers. Parental pressure on daughters to marry early seems to have abated, and the number of women in their 20s who remain single has increased by more than 30% since 1960. Many women over age 30, regardless of marital status, now report pelvic and sexual dysfunction problems to their doctors. A satisfactory sex life seems to be an acknowledged goal of most women today.

Open and permissive marriage arrangements and co-marital sex are being explored in contemporary society as alternatives to conventional marriage. In such arrangements, each partner has the permission of the other to participate in free sexual activity outside the marriage without accountability. Since condonement is mutual, "faithlessness" does not become an issue between partners.

THE OBJECTIVES OF MARRIAGE

The complex demands of coexistence create a need for companionship and emotional security, and companionship is perceived as the principal function of the heterosexual bond. Failure to provide companionship and to satisfy mutual personal needs are the most common complaints of people seeking dissolution of marriage.

"Love" is the most common reason given by people who have decided to get married. A definition of this word that will satisfy everyone who uses it is still elusive. The very least that must be said is that love creates a genuine concern for the security, satisfaction, and welfare of the partner and a desire to fulfill his or her physical and emotional needs. Harry Stack Sullivan's definition may be as good as any: "When the satisfaction or security of another person becomes as significant to one as one's own satisfaction or security, then the state of love exists." Feeling valued and needed by one's mate allows the relationship to develop on a basis of confidence and trust. These circumstances are favorable for a healthy sex partnership leading, if both parties wish it, to procreation and parenthood.

WHAT MEN & WOMEN BRING TO MARRIAGE

Marriage is the most challenging and demanding of all relationships. It is the symbolic act of commitment that makes a union with another person permanent at least in intention. Each party in a marriage brings to it the range of life experiences and expectations derived from childhood family living as modified by individual psychosocial development. Despite widespread experimentation with alternatives to marriage, most nonmarriage relationships lack the essential element of **permanent commitment.** Some people, men as much as women, need the security of marriage and feel deprived in less well defined relationships.

The claim is often made that the best time to begin a permanent and successful marriage is in the early 20s, with the man slightly older than the woman. Recent surveys indicate that 78% of men married for 20 years who married before age 22 are still married but that 87% of men married for 20 years who married after age 22 are still married. Among women, 73% who married as teenagers are still married and 86% who married in their late 20s are still married.

It is as difficult to identify the factors that make a successful marriage as it is to predict the outcome of any other complex form of human behavior involving the interaction of 2 people over a protracted period of time under varying circumstances of stress. Compatibility between 2 people in a marriage is a function of their intelligence and early psychologic development, religious convictions, and social background, to name only a few of the more obvious determinants of compatibility. Most people starting a marriage have no idea what they must do or what to expect. Much could be done in the home or in educational programs sponsored by the schools or by community or church groups to teach young people how to choose a life companion and the kinds of problems they may have to face in family life with nobody but their spouse to help them most of the time. Contemporary experiments by young people to try out alternatives to marriage may in part be an effort to "make sure" the relationship will last before turning it into a legally binding instrument. It would be a help to any young couple contemplating marriage if a list of favorable prognostic factors for happiness in marriage could be drawn up. The following is such an attempt by G. Alport:

"Good childhood relationships with both parents, wholesome early acquiring of sexual knowledge, willingness to postpone the final marriage decision until both partners know each other thoroughly, absence of sharp differences in attitudes about matters emotionally important to both, the presence of considerable similarity in social background, openness in expression of affection and readiness to confide in the partner, good psychologic adjustment in general, and, most important, realistic awareness that marital success is based on 'friendship-love,' not the Hollywood glamour myth of perpetual romantic bliss."

TYPES OF MARRIAGE RELATIONSHIPS

Classifications of marriage relationships most often refer to the qualities of stability, vitality, and interpersonal involvement that result from the interplay of basic relationship dynamics. Two different systems of classifying marriages are given below. A physician accustomed to seeing problems according to a medical model must resist the temptation to diagnose and label marital problems in a conventional sense even though the analogy may be striking.

Marriage Classification of Cuber
Cuber defines 5 categories of marriage configuration in *ascending* order of gratification and levels of intimacy.

A. Conflict-Habituated: Communication is conducted in a style in which verbal conflict is incessant but frequently concealed from friends and family. The subject matter is of little importance. The partners are not basically hostile, argumentative, or chronically addicted to conflict outside the marriage but are habituated to this style within it.

B. Devitalized: Close sharing, identification, and deep feeling during courtship and early marriage are lost because of problems that have led to alienation. This may become apparent during parenthood, when resignation and apathy toward the marriage relationship is evident, sharing and mutual reinforcement disappear, and the partners appear to settle for gratification in other aspects of life.

C. Passive-Congenial: The passive-congenial marriage is similar to the devitalized marriage except that the relationship was never really vital in the first place, even during courtship. Feelings of disappointment and regret therefore do not surface. This low-key relationship has little color; satisfaction is found in material possessions and in a responsible but narrow range of family life. Effective intervention in this type of relationship consists of defining the dynamics and dealing with the problem openly. Such marriages have little opportunity for rehabilitation unless they are modified early.

D. Vital: In the vital marriage there is complete investment by the partners in each other, with deep mutual empathy. Cuber: "They typically spend a great deal of time together but this is not what makes them vital; it is more of the desire and the need and the successful expression of accepting, understanding association which forms the vital bond." Because their relationship is strongly empathic, they solve problems without outside help.

E. Total: Total marriages are much like vital marriages except that the "association and the psychologic investment in the mate more nearly encompasses the total needs and fulfillments of each of the spouses." This type of marriage is the rarest, and it is usually completely incomprehensible to individuals with the first 3 types of marriages described. Cuber's findings suggest that couples adjust rather early to patterns in the total marriage type and do not readily change within it.

While therapy can be built around and must include an understanding of the last type, it must be applied to fit the larger life expectations, habits, and attitudes of the couple. To suggest to a conflict-habituated couple, for example, that they should "talk things over" is to continue an already pointless procedure, since the couple is undoubtedly doing this ineffectively. A suggestion that couples in the passive-congenial or devitalized configurations spend more time together or involve themselves more deeply with each other might worsen their situation; people in these groups have probably discovered that it is best to live with a minimum of inconvenience and frustration by avoiding involvement as much as possible.

Marriage Classification by Personality Structure & Style
Marriages can be classified according to the types of personalities that come together to form the relationship. A brief characterization of some common types is presented below. (See Berman and Lief reference, p 501.)

A. Obsessive-Compulsive Husband and Hysterical Wife: The combination of a detached and aloof husband and a needy, demanding wife often makes an unhappy marriage characterized by continuing conflict. The man may be a dependent personality who has difficulty expressing feelings and may have been perceived as the "strong, silent type" during courtship. Such a man may attract—and be attracted to—a passive and sensual woman whose flirtatious mannerisms provoke exciting new thoughts in him. Her need for support and reassurance forces him into a struggle to become what he is not: a "good parent" to his wife and a source of stability and security. He often is highly organized and rational in his thinking, and her intuitive, perhaps impulsive thought patterns may be actually repellent to him. As he draws away, her demands increase, and thus the situation worsens: The good parent with the compliant child becomes the distant, rejecting parent with an angry and scornful child.

B. Passive-Dependent Husband and Dominant Wife: A man with a dependent personality may be attracted to a strong, self-reliant woman because he is in need of strength, which she has. She welcomes the relationship because of her need to control and dominate. His sense of inadequacy may lead him to alcoholism and obesity, a pattern of passive-aggressive behavior tinged with depression in reaction to what he perceives as the overly controlling woman of the house. The question of power and its abuses is the issue that becomes the ultimate focus of conflict.

C. Paranoid Husband and Depression-Prone Wife: A jealous and hostile man with unconscious doubts about his masculinity may choose a wife with low self-esteem who readily accepts blame and will take an ineffective male for a husband because it's "the best she can expect." In many cases her parents have rejected her, and she may be chronically depressed. She invests considerable energy in trying to gain approval from her husband to avoid another episode of painful rejection.

D. Depression-Prone Husband and Paranoid Wife: In the reverse of the relationship described above, the suspicious, hostile wife provides her husband with frequent excuses to remain passively depressed; this only intensifies her anger.

E. Oral-Dependent Relationship: Both partners may be immature and dependent yet competitive and demanding of love, each feeling that he or she is giving too much for what is given in return. The result may be a stormy marriage characterized by unreasonable demands, temper tantrums, and a constant search for childish forms of gratification.

F. Neurotic Wife and Omnipotent Husband: The wife may undertake a course of chronic complaining and marginal invalidism in an attempt to be comforted and cared for. The husband is outwardly strong and confident but plagued by inner feelings of inadequacy. A wife needing his care helps him to deal with these feelings by comparing himself favorably with someone even weaker than he. Since his efforts to help his wife can never be successful, he is condemned to repeated failure and eventual loss of confidence.

Though marriages may be typed, they all involve constant change and growth; as partners change, the relationship changes. Similarly, external pressures of the environment vary, and the marital state may move from one category to another. Although the relationship may be periodically fragile, it often achieves a mutually satisfactory stability. The marriage counselor

should strive to identify and cope with harmful trends in the areas of power, intimacy, and the setting of boundaries and limits.

•   •   •

These 2 contrasting systems of classification of marriage provide models for viewing total marriage configurations and their capacity to provide satisfaction, stability, and fulfillment of individual needs. If one retains a total view of the marriage as the counseling proceeds, special problems that emerge can be seen in the context of the total relationship. This facilitates the design of a therapy program individually tailored to the needs of a troubled couple.

MARITAL DYSFUNCTION & FAILURE

The success of a marriage is positively correlated with each partner's skills in forming and maintaining relationships and the validity of the original process of mate selection. Marital dysfunction or failure occurs when mutual needs are not met. When marital hopes are contaminated—by faulty communication, inability to conciliate and resolve conflicts, unsatisfactory sexual adjustment, or in other ways—a climate of mistrust develops. If the dominant mood of the marriage is negative, each partner feels rejected and the relationship may become progressively dismantled. Ultimately, each partner becomes unwilling to meet the other's needs. This occurs to some degree in the early years of most marriages, but all marriage partners must work through periods of conflict.

Problems may occur simply as a result of the physical closeness of marriage. Everyone enters marriage from the single state, which may have been unsatisfying but even so must undergo change, some of it painful, into a shared relationship with another person. Successful resolution of problems caused by unaccustomed closeness may enhance personal growth and strengthen weak areas of the personality, or the problems may cause temporary deterioration of the relationship. The most creative marriages result from a long and sometimes painful struggle to achieve harmony by perfecting the communication skills that permit resolution of conflict. Since every marriage relationship is in a constant state of evolution, every crisis is an opportunity for growth. During the problem-solving phase, the individual limits of emotional isolation must be recognized.

The precipitating causes of marital discord are different in different stages of marriage, but some occur with monotonous regularity.

Problems in the Early Years

In the early years of a marriage, incompatibilies may be based on emotional immaturity and neurotic tendencies, quarreling, money problems, the intrusion of in-laws, sexual dissatisfactions, and disparate views of role functions. During the early years of child-rearing, intimacy and sexual function may be affected by the intrusive and fatiguing demands of young children. This is an ultimate "load" test period for a marriage: The wife may consider herself primarily committed to her children's needs and have little strength left for her husband, who responds with resentment. He may also feel overworked, unappreciated, and rejected during this same period in the development of the marriage, while struggling for career success.

A wide variety of incompatibilities are common during this time, and solutions may be sought through extramarital companionship and other sexual outlets. Women's liberation, with its potential for escape from the role of housewife, may appeal to the busy and progressive mother, but the father and husband may view it both as a rejection of domestic responsibilities and as a personal threat. If this conflict is unresolved, alienation, emotional isolation, and loss of a sense of each other's needs occur to menace the marriage and the relationship model displayed to the children. The threat to the marriage at this time often causes the depressed and weeping wife to go to a physician, perhaps a gynecologist. Couples in this age group comprise a high percentage of patients in the marriage counselor's practice. Indeed, having children during the first 2 years of marriage doubles the probability of divorce, especially in marriages provoked by premarital pregnancy.

Many young couples have difficulty in establishing a satisfactory relationship with their in-laws. Years ago it was common for young married people to live with the parents on either side, but today they want their own separate domicile and the freedom to make their own decisions. The in-laws may find it difficult to accept these changing attitudes and may feel rejected. The husband's mother may resent having to share her son with another woman or may feel that the wife does not care for him properly, as she did. The wife's mother may feel that her daughter's husband is "unworthy" or not providing for her adequately. Tensions and conflicts may arise if the 2 families have different cultural or religious backgrounds; each may try to guide the couple toward its own way of life.

Carelessness in money matters can create additional problems. If the husband handles all the money, his wife may resent it. The wife will retain her self-respect and a feeling of independence if she is a wage-earner and has money to spend as she wishes.

Problems in the Middle Years

Marital problems in the middle years of the marriage are often the result of a narrowly routine life-style and increasing boredom, leading eventually to alienation and mutual dislike. Psychosomatic problems, depression, neurotic behavior, and hysteria are common symptoms during this time. Chronic disease states (eg, arthritis, obesity, cardiopulmonary and vascular disorders, and diseases of the breast, uterus, and prostate) may become a burden. These are also the tradi-

tional "dangerous years" of extramarital affairs and the desire for sexual experimentation or reassurance as the signs of fading youth begin to appear.

In the past decade, divorce among couples married for 20–24 years has increased about 28%. Moreover, a study of 100 consecutive cases of male impotence revealed many of the men to be impotent only with their wives.

Problems in the Later Years

With advancing age, marriage incompatibilities may emerge because of physical and psychologic problems as well as resentments held over from the early years of the marriage. Female menopause and male involution may be viewed as harbingers of inevitable failure of sexual function, which has devastating effects on the self-image. Emotional problems may surface that have long been suppressed for peacekeeping purposes, especially during the child-rearing period. When patience runs out, each partner is isolated and his or her frustration tolerance is exceeded. Resentment arises as a result of unmet needs for companionship and dependency. Fading physical attractiveness and recognition of failure to achieve career goals or a suitable income level, especially when retirement or job insecurity is imminent, may cause feelings of bitterness. The physical handicaps and diseases of old age, excessive use of alcohol, and undesirable side-effects of prescribed medications complicate the developing distress of a marriage. The life support systems are almost impossible to revive and present the greatest difficulties to a counselor.

THE PRESENTATION OF MARITAL DISTRESS TO THE PHYSICIAN

The wife most often initiates the search for help. If she views her personal physician as a trusted friend, she may make her first inquiries to that individual. The gynecologist may be the first marriage counselor, since a woman may take advantage of her routine pelvic examination to ask tentative questions. The sexual component of her difficulties may be her "ticket of admission." If the complaint is dyspareunia or a psychosomatic equivalent of sexual dysfunction (eg, headache, insomnia, vague aches and pains, chronic fatigue, nervousness), she may seek help from her family physician only to be referred to a gynecologist before the underlying reason—marital discord—is appreciated.

Regardless of the stated reasons, all physicians must be familiar with the proper interpretation of such complaints. As a result of the frank discussions of sexual and marital information that appear in the daily press, in magazines and books, and in general conversation, the patient may seem to be fairly well informed but is often confused. Nevertheless, her first attempt to explain her sexually oriented distress may be limited to discussion of a psychosomatic equivalent. She carefully notes the doctor's response to her first comments, looking for signs of embarrassment or uneasiness, and may "break contact" if what she sees is not reassuring.

Whether the patient's opening gambit is subtle or obvious, it is often covert, and the physician must initiate the exploration. Mace suggests that patients frequently go to a doctor about sexual problems because they see sexual activity as a bodily function and the physician as an appropriate specialist. Unfortunately, the medical model is not always adequate; though good sexual function is necessary for the maintenance of emotional well-being and, indirectly, physical health, the physician's attempts at diagnosis and therapy may be misdirected if the problem is seen only in physiologic terms. The basis of sexual dysfunction may be organic, but it is necessary to view sexual function as part of the expressive life of a patient, and, since it involves one's interaction with others, the generalization can be made that in sexual dysfunction there is no such thing as an uninvolved partner. If one partner suffers, both do.

COUNSELING THE COUPLE WITH A FAILING MARRIAGE

If signs of a deteriorating marriage are present, the physician must decide whether to offer simple sympathy and support; whether to attempt a more directive program of guidance; or whether to refer the couple to a professional counselor. Each physician must decide how much office time can realistically be set aside for management of marriage problems. Special training is necessary in order to do a good job of it, and the physician without such training should refer this class of patients to a clinic or counselor known to be reliable and professionally oriented.

The third patient in any marriage counseling situation is the marriage relationship itself. Even though the wife may present the initial complaint, it is mandatory to work with the husband as well and, overall, with the relationship they share. The common practice of utilizing men and women as co-counselors ensures adequate representation for both therapeutic points of view. Often the co-counselors obtain the marital history from each of the partners separately; in this way, the wife may tell the woman counselor things she would not tell a man, and vice versa. Conjoint counselors who are married to each other may be highly effective therapists, but sometimes their personal success may be interpreted by their patients as threatening and competitive.

STAGES IN COUNSELING THE COUPLE WITH A DYSFUNCTIONAL MARRIAGE

There are 3 recognizable periods in the process of working with a dysfunctional marriage. Each requires separate counseling strategy.

First Stage

The initial stage is characterized by a cathartic outpouring of current problems and grievances, which serves the immediate purposes of reducing tension and relieving anxiety in the presence of a caring person. Frequently, there is some withholding as a result of the intrusion of emotions that prevent clear thinking or even clear recollection of important details. However, when the counselor is regarded as a trustworthy ally, this outpouring is relatively free and uninhibited, and significant details emerge that identify the critical areas of difficulty: the chief complaints of the marriage. By listening attentively, by asking relevant questions, and by making comments in a detached and objective empathic manner, the counselor generally relieves the patient of immediate pressures and simultaneously gains useful information. This often occurs at the initial meeting with the wife, but the husband may wish to be interviewed separately or to return with his wife at the next visit. The counselor can then explore the other point of view and, if both partners are present, note the interaction between them. The preliminary period of evaluation may take several sessions but cannot be concluded until most of the critical problems have been identified. Simple suggestions for the immediate relief of marital distress are appropriate, but management of problems should be deferred until rapport has been established among the participants in the treatment alliance.

Second Stage

After sufficient information has been gathered, the counselor can assure the marital pair that their problem is understood and appreciated. The counselor's explanation of how their total situation is perceived by a professional will usually serve to identify the issues in conflict as distinct from the emotions engendered by attempts to handle them. For example, the wife may complain of difficult children or complex household demands. When the husband comes home from work, her immediate need is to let him know how tired, frustrated, and angry she is. If their discussion is focused on her feelings, he may defend himself by contrasting his fatigue and frustration with hers. Thus, the couple simply compares strong feelings of need for relief rather than dealing with the main issue of better organizing the care of the children and the management of the home. Feelings are often overwhelming and become a smokescreen covering the basic issues that need resolution. When the issues are differentiated from the feelings they engender, awareness of the realities of the marriage relationship emerges and sufficient understanding develops so that harmony can be achieved. The function of "caring" in the household may be clarified—eg, "Who cares enough about me to help me with my problem?" After a time, essential problems are identified, and interactive discussion brings about modification of the initial therapeutic suggestions. Some degree of readjustment and reestablishment of closeness in the marriage should result, diminishing feelings of alienation and estrangement.

Third Stage

The third (final) stage permits mediation of major misunderstandings because crucial misconceptions and distorted judgments will by this time be perceived more clearly. The discussions to establish effective communication and closeness should indicate whether reconciliation and a new potential for the marriage are possible or not. A variation of the inventory approach, useful at this stage, is a set of questions to be asked of each partners: What strengths did the relationship have that allowed the wedding to take place? What strengths does it still have to maintain it? What new strengths must be developed for better success? What changes must each ask of the other to enable the marriage to prosper?

Just as the principal theme of how mutual needs are or are not met in a marriage must be reviewed repeatedly during the counseling process, so also is it necessary to assess elements that represent good functioning in relationships, such as mutual esteem, caring, and basic trust. One must strive to answer the ultimate question: Will each partner be more likely to find fulfillment as an individual within this marriage or outside of it? An important principle in the field of marriage counseling states that the therapist or team of therapists is in the business of helping individuals to survive and not just marriages.

ASPECTS OF MARRIAGE IN COUNSELING

The "visible" functions of a marriage—those aspects not immediately related to love—are (1) leadership versus followership (dominance versus submission), (2) decision making, (3) problem solving, and (4) management of conflicts. These instrumental functions of a marriage allow it to continue to function, and they can be dealt with satisfactorily in counseling because they are highly specific and can be easily identified. In discussing these matters with the marriage partners, the counselor can gain insight into the communication skills of the individuals involved. The counselor may find it useful to employ such techniques as paraphrasing, interpreting, summarizing, role-playing, and role reversal, all of which the partners themselves can utilize in their private discussions between office visits.

The need for each partner to stay intact as an individual and to develop simultaneously the capacity to relate intimately to the other partner is basic in human relationships. The capacity of the marriage partners to adapt to mutual needs and to cope effectively with each other's desire for intimacy, idealization, independence, and identity constitutes one of the most sensitive indicators of the health status of the relationship.

Failure to develop an adequate sense of identity may result from uncertainty about the partner's expectations in fulfilling the role of husband or wife. Eventually, if the uncertainty persists, an adversary quality develops, and it becomes difficult to maintain autonomy while simultaneously striving to achieve intimacy. Loss of capacity for growth is the result.

In a successful marriage, each partner tends to retain a strong sense of individuality while simultaneously seeking intimacy with the other. Thus, each grows and develops individually, while together they function as a couple in close harmony. Mutual esteem in the partnership strengthens ego supports and basic trust when each maintains an idealized view of the other, while at the same time successful interaction on a day-to-day basis permits each to retain a realistic perspective. Dynamically, the result of this combination of interaction and individuality is the generation of love, creativity, and growth.

COMMITMENT & DEMANDS ON THE PHYSICIAN–COUNSELOR

Patience and commitment are basic requirements for a counselor. If rapport is established and there is opportunity for ventilation of hostilities and reduction of tension, patients will develop both a dependence on and an attachment to the counselor. It thus becomes difficult for the physician-counselor to withdraw, particularly if problems have been clearly defined and the patients feel that the counselor understands them and their situation.

The counselor must now decide whether to be totally responsible for therapy, with its demanding time commitment, or to refer the couple to a full-time marriage counselor before much more attachment develops. The time commitment in marital therapy is always heavy (several weeks to several months), since few troubled marriages can be helped quickly. Subsequent steps in treatment progressively increase the counselor's responsibility. These steps include reeducation to new insights, supportive reading, guidance in the development of better communication and interactional skills, and examination of possible alternatives for future courses of action. The counselor must also draw heavily on the guiding strength of the doctor-patient relationship to encourage patients to pursue a course of action that is both sensible and mutually beneficial.

Additionally, the physician-counselor must be aware of the extraordinary emotional energy required in marriage counseling. The patient must be protected from discouragement or despair by properly focused support. The physician must be available by telephone and at night during the hours when depression and small crises are most likely to occur. The impact of counseling work may be felt upon the counselor's own marriage, especially in the absence of special training to expect and assimilate negative assaults when anger is directed at the physician for faulty judgments or ineffective recommendations or when the situation worsens despite best efforts.

It is important for the physician-counselor to be in touch with good consultants who can accept referrals of patients who require more time or expertise than the counselor possesses. The selection of specialists has become more satisfactory with the establishment of good training programs and recognized accreditation by organizations like the American Association of Marriage and Family Therapists. Well-trained accredited counselors can be of great help whether they work individually or as team members with practitioners of obstetrics and gynecology or any medical group. Trained marriage counselors must be distinguished from self-appointed marriage counselors who are not bound by strictly enforced codes of professional ethics. Inquiries about counselors whose qualifications are in doubt should be made through local mental health clinics, family planning agencies, or university-based departments of psychology and psychiatry. Counseling activity by ministers in groups organized through church agencies is a developing resource in many local communities.

SEXUAL FUNCTION IN MARRIAGE

Ideally, when a man and a woman accept each other as lovers, their trust in one another develops sufficiently both to permit free sexual expression of individual needs and desires and to generate pleasure and mutual satisfaction. Sex and coitus need not be considered synonymous because many noncoital sexual practices (eg, kissing, embracing, manual and oral-genital contact) can provide satisfying closeness. In sexual activity, the couple has the opportunity to develop a capacity for intimacy not only physically, since there is no closer way of touching than in the acts of penetration and reception during coitus, but psychologically as well, when all the basic forces of total interaction come into play, shaped by attitudes, feelings, expectations, and past social conditioning.

Sexual interaction is one of the most highly valued common pathways that provide an opportunity for caring, being cared for, loving, and being loved. It is, however, fragile and easily threatened. Therefore, a couple's unsatisfactory or disturbed sexual behavior may be the earliest warning sign of marital difficulty. This first becomes apparent to the physician in the form of a patient's functional failure sexually or in one of its converted psychosomatic equivalents.

Mutually satisfactory sexual functioning is only one of the many adjustments to be accomplished in the normal marriage relationship, but it one of the most fundamental. Though many people with sexual experience and good communication skills do well sexually in the early phase of marriage, a good sexual relationship is more often hard-won, sometimes requiring 2–3 years to develop.

Sexual behavior is only one of the many important influences on a marriage relationship. A good premarital sex life may deteriorate after marriage; sexual function may be good after marriage but may subsequently deteriorate when the problems of living with another individual bring about unanticipated stresses; and individuals who find little satisfaction in sex before marriage and assume it will improve once intercourse is legitimized are often disappointed. Youth and inexperience, combined with uncertainties about the quality and dependability of the companionship that the partner will provide, may be prejudicial to satisfactory sexual adjustment in the early part of the marriage. The social circumstances or personal preconceptions of the marriage may indicate that the couple didn't really know each other as well as they thought they did before they were married. These include forced marriage because of pregnancy; the assumption by either partner that intercourse is dirty or sinful; a notion on the part of the wife that sex is a form of surrender without the privilege of refusal; or a notion on the part of the husband that sex is a purely physical need of his own that his wife must satisfy whether she enjoys it or not. Whether the couple lived together for an extended period before the wedding or were married after a short courtship, they may find that sex after marriage is not what they expected.

People often expect too much (or the wrong things) of sex. They may assume that, with sufficient sexual drive and urge, orgasm can always be achieved. But orgasm is only one of the things that happens during sexual intercourse. Although many satisfactions are provided by intercourse, intimacy and active loving have a special meaning in affectionate relationships, and the significance of any single sexual experience depends heavily on the symbolic meanings assigned to it at a given moment by the participants. In a truly developing relationship, the meaning of any single sexual experience is always redefined.

In exploring a couple's sexual history, attitudes acquired early in childhood should be stressed, with emphasis on the love relationships of the 2 sets of parents. For the wife, early menstrual experience may have an effect on her perception of the female role. For both, early sex education, masturbation, and fantasies indulged in or early fears about adult sex must be brought out by tactful questioning. Being comfortable with one's body and understanding early erotic feelings permit the growing person to come to terms with his or her sexuality.

Cultural and social influences have powerful effects on opinions, attitudes, and inhibitions about sex. Sex may be viewed in a context of love or of hostility or as an act "perpetrated" by one person on another. If the views of each partner are not compatible and not clarified, they will eventually cause trouble in the marriage.

The present state of sexual frankness in our culture challenges the old view that sex is to be reserved for procreation and generates an atmosphere of such permissiveness that new and often exaggerated expectations about sex are being brought to marriage. Sex is now frequently viewed as a means of meeting many needs in a marriage and is emphasized as an expression of love. Technical sexual competence requires a knowledgeable, dependable, and trusting love partner; men and women now take the view that they need not suffer in silence if their expectations of orgasm and full sexual expression are not met.

Whereas at one time the simple cultural criterion of manhood was to engage in sexual intercourse with a woman, today a man cannot claim "success" as a lover unless he is able to help her to orgasm. Whereas a woman formerly was required only to submit to the man's needs, she now considers herself a failure if she does not experience the orgasms equated today with emancipated sexual competence. The extraordinary interpersonal ramifications of sexual dysfunction in a relationship can be devastating when explicit needs inadequately met are not discussed or resolved. In addition to the risks of acceptance or rejection in sexual activity, all aspects of intimacy in the relationship are intensified either positively or negatively by the extraordinary emotional power of the sexual component.

TYPES OF SEXUAL PROBLEMS

The principal sexual problems reported in medical practice are (1) lack of female orgasm; (2) lack of desire for intercourse; (3) concern regarding the frequency of intercourse; (4) sex information on a specific problem; (5) male impotence and premature ejaculation; (6) dyspareunia, and (7) lack of affection during intercourse, regardless of the occurrence of orgasm.

All of these problems can cause marital conflict. Most of them have to do with lack of responsiveness to the partner's needs and therefore to the needs of the marriage relationship. Before a decision about therapy can be made, it must be determined whether the primary distress is simply sexual in the setting of a good marital relationship or whether—what is usually the case—it is a problem in the marital relationship with sexual manifestations. In the latter circumstance, the basic significance of the sexual symptom must be determined first in order to define the underlying feelings, personality characteristics, or neurotic needs of which the symptom is a manifestation.

Immaturity is a common difficulty in sexual adjustment. In the physician's office it may appear in the form of a complaint of exploitation and distress from a sexually demanding, hostile, and abusive spouse, whereas the spouse may simply be refusing to cater to childlike needs or childish whims. If possible, therefore, the sexual history should be obtained in the presence of both partners first and separately later. Diagnosis of the problems requires answers to basic questions of how such behavior serves the needs of the individual. A careful sexual history should also reveal what the couple has tried and found unsuccessful, the reasons for failure, and what each partner sees as the goal of therapy.

INITIATION & ONSET OF SEXUAL INTERCOURSE

Counseling should emphasize the broad range of sexual interaction rather than a stereotyped "how to" pattern of performance. Even so, after the general outlines of the relationship have been examined, the counselor needs specific information about the couple's methods of lovemaking. Such questions as who, what, when, where, and how are effective not only in gathering data but also in revealing the quality of sexual communication between the partners.

The possible questions are many and their answers—both what is said and what is unsaid—can be illuminating. Who usually makes the advances? Is it almost always the husband, or can the wife take the initiative without being considered aggressive and threatening? How sensitive is each to the other's nonverbal cues? In what circumstances does intercourse most often occur? Always at the same time of day or night and in the same place? Has the spirit of play or adventure been stifled by routine? Has it never developed? Are the partners considerate of each other? If one partner is occasionally tired and uninterested, can the other accept this without anger? What is the influence of fatigue and moods? The menstrual cycle? The stress of business or office concerns? If either partner is amorous and intercourse has not occurred recently, will the other be available? Above all, is communication forthright and open, or have pretense and secrecy come to dominate the relationship? The book by Munjack and Oziel (see p 501) contains many examples of language modeling in the asking and answering of difficult and sensitive questions of this kind.

Asking specifically about frequency of intercourse is important in order to bring out information related to possible differences in sex urge. Even if the partners are of about the same age, differences in sex drive have a critical effect on sexual function, particularly in the first few years of marriage. For men, the capacity for making love several times in a brief interval peaks in the mid teens and slowly declines thereafter. In women, maximum capacity occurs in the early 30s, though this is probably changing as the rearing of girls becomes less restrictive. However, there is always sufficient drive for both sexes to permit highly satisfactory sexual activity if other factors contributing to rapport and trust are present. Indeed, with the changing attitudes toward sex over the past 25 years, an increase in the frequency of intercourse by married couples in the USA has been documented—from a 20% increase in younger couples to as much as 90% in older ones.* However, couples requesting figures on what is "normal" or "average" are better off if simply told that whatever might be agreed to between themselves as suitable should be considered normal *for*

---

*The data are from Kinsey: Married couples up to age 25, from 134 times a year in 1948 to 154 times in 1972; couples from 36 to 45, from 75 times to 99 times; couples in the mid 50s, from 26 times a year to 49 times.

them regardless of what other couples might do or say they do.

Couples also ask what sex practices are acceptable. The best answer is that what is acceptable is whatever the partners find suitable and enjoyable. The question, however, offers a fine opportunity for sex education. Since questions usually refer to the use of a particular position, to the practice of oral or anal sex, or to the use of pornography in various forms for sexual arousal, reassurance about the acceptability of these matters is warranted, and free conversation about them permits the partners to become comfortable with concepts and practices that they might have regarded as forbidden or abnormal. Discussion also permits each to reveal what he or she has found to be the most effective in providing erotic stimulation. The matter of personal hygiene (eg, bathing, control of body odor, cleanliness of the perineum and genitalia) should be discussed at the same time in order to establish ideal circumstances for intercourse.

If a patient is troubled because her husband has suggested a sex practice of which she is uncertain or because some aspect of his behavior inhibits her sexual release, the problem should be discussed in the presence of both partners so that the doctor's response will not be left for the wife to transmit to her husband at home. Complete exploration of such topics should be conducted in a relaxed setting, with a third person serving as catalyst, mediator, or both. After the problems have been identified and possible solutions offered, the couple should be seen occasionally in follow-up visits to make certain that the guidance has been helpful and productive.

Familiarity with the details of intercourse allows the counselor to identify the inhibiting and facilitating aspects of sexual behavior. If, for example, the wife proceeds through the early stages of mounting erotic excitement and then loses her impetus before orgasm, it is crucial to discover the underlying reason. The need for an atmosphere of love and romance during foreplay, the techniques of foreplay, the differences in arousal rates between men and women, and the importance of pacing all play a role in whether the woman sustains her arousal level to and through the experience of orgasm.

PHASES OF THE SEXUAL RESPONSE CYCLE

The recognized stages of the physiologic responses to sexual arousal are described briefly below. A broader description can be found in the classic work of Masters and Johnson, *Human Sexual Response*.

Excitement Phase

Early sexual arousal in the male, whether initiated by tactile, visual, or psychic stimuli, results in engorgement and erection of the penis, with an increase in penile size and in the angle of protrusion from the body. In the woman, arousal in the excitement phase, also initiated by tactile, visual, or psychic stimuli, involves vaginal lubrication. This lubrication, previously thought to be of uterine or cervical origin, has been demonstrated by Masters and Johnson to be a "sweating reaction" of the vagina; it is probably a true transudation that continues throughout sexual excitement. Coalescence of droplets provides a lubricating film; later in the response cycle, Bartholin's glands make a small contribution. The glans clitoridis swells, often to almost double its size, as a result of engorgement, but the degree of enlargement is apparently unrelated either to the woman's capacity for sexual response or to her ability to achieve orgasm. The shaft of the clitoris also increases in diameter. Engorgement of the glans clitoridis and shaft occurs most rapidly with direct manual stimulation of them and of the mons veneris; if stimulation is by means of fantasy or by stroking the breast, these responses may be delayed.

Breast changes in the sexually aroused woman consist of erection and enlargement of the nipples and, later in the excitement phase, an increase in total size of the breasts. The labia majora, which in a resting state meet in the midline of the vagina, gape slightly and may be displaced toward the clitoris. In nulliparous women, the outer labia may also thin out and flatten against the surrounding tissue; in multiparous women, they may extend and be engorged to an exaggerated degree. The labia minora also swell. The vagina, which is in a collapsed state normally, now begins to expand in the inner two-thirds of the vaginal canal, alternating with a tendency to relax. As excitement increases, progressive distention of the vagina occurs. The vaginal walls also "tent" in response to upward and backward posterior movement of the cervix and uterus, so that the inner portion of the vagina swells dramatically. Engorgement changes the color of the vaginal wall to dark purple and causes the vaginal rugae to become smooth.

In both men and women, erotic tension causes increased muscle tone accompanied by tachycardia and blood pressure elevation. A "sex flush" begins over the upper abdomen and later spreads over the breasts as a morbilliform rash; this occurs in about 75% of women and 25% of men before orgasm. In the late phase, the man experiences shortening of the spermatic cords and retraction of the testes. The scrotum thickens and is flattened against the body.

Plateau Phase

The distinction between the excitement and the plateau phases is imprecise. Ordinarily, the penis is completely erect in the first phase. In the plateau phase, there is usually a slight increase in the diameter of the coronal ridge and, in some men, a deepening of color of the glans to reddish-purple. Progressive excitement may increase testicular size by about 50%; at this point, the man is very close to orgasm. In the late plateau phase, respiratory rate, muscle tone, pulse rate, and blood pressure changes intensify, and muscle tension increases in the buttocks and anal sphincter. A few drops of fluid may appear in the male urethra from the bulbourethral (Cowper's) gland. Although this is not semen, it can contain large numbers of active sperm, which means that impregnation and conception are possible before ejaculation.

In the woman, the "orgasmic platform" consists of engorgement and swelling of the tissues of the outer third of the vagina, which reduces its interior diameter by 30–50%, forming a grip on the penis and indicating that she is rapidly approaching orgasm. Elevation and ballooning of the inner two-thirds of the vagina increases, as does the size of the uterus (especially in multiparous women). The clitoris now erects, rises from its position over the pubic bone, and retracts into its hood, shorter by about 50%. In this position the clitoris continues to respond, either to manual stimulation or to penile thrusts. Engorgement of the labia continues until they take on a deep wine color, indicating that climax is imminent.

Orgasmic Phase

In the woman, a series of rhythmic muscular contractions of the orgasmic platform signals the onset of climax. These contractions vary in number from 3–5 to as many as 8–12 in some women. They are intense at first but subside quickly. A series of uterine contractions quickly follows, beginning in the superior portion and moving downward toward the cervix. Occasionally, rhythmic contractions in the anal sphincter occur. In the man, the rhythmic contractions stimulate a discharge in the perineal floor, particularly in the bulbocavernosus muscle. Just before orgasm, increasing tension in the seminal vesicles causes the semen to empty into the bulbous urethra. Simultaneously, the prostate begins to contract, expelling fluid and distending the bulbous portion of the urethra as semen and prostatic fluid mingle. A series of rhythmic contractions at the bulb now eject the semen with great pressure. A series of minor contractions persists in the urethra for several seconds, continuing even after complete expulsion of the semen.

Changes in pulse rate, blood pressure, and respiratory rate reach a peak and quickly dissipate, but for both the man and the woman the height of orgasm is marked by generalized muscle tension. The facial muscles tighten, and the muscles of the neck, extremities, abdomen, and buttocks are strongly contracted. There may be grasping movements by both partners, followed by clutching and even carpopedal spasm. A fleeting period of semiconsciousness occurs, in which each individual withdraws psychologically but not physically, concentrating almost solely on genital sensation, unaware perhaps of cries and uncontrollable behavior.

Resolution Phase

Muscle tension is released and engorgement subsides in the genitals and skin. The sex flush slowly fades. In the woman the nipples appear slightly prominent, but only because the swelling around them is subsiding. As the sex flush fades, slight perspiration appears. In some women, perspiration appears uniformly, and in men it occurs over the soles and palms as well; but in either case it is unrelated to the degree of muscular effort before or during orgasm.

In the woman, the clitoris promptly returns to its unstimulated state but will not reach normal size for 5–10 minutes. Relaxation of the orgasmic platform then occurs, and the diameter of the outer third of the vagina increases. Vaginal ballooning diminishes, the uterus shrinks, and the cervix descends into its normal position. The slight enlargement of the cervical canal is maintained. Total resolution time varies; as much as 30 minutes may elapse before the woman is in a truly unstimulated state.

In men, loss of erection occurs in 2 stages: In the first, most of the erectile volume is lost; the second is a refractory stage during which he is unable to be aroused again, and the remainder of the shrinkage occurs. In young men, the refractory period may be very short, but it lengthens with age. In most men it will last for several minutes; in others it may last for hours or even days.

A refractory period does not occur in women; a second orgasm or multiple orgasms are possible, and 6 orgasms are not unusual if adequate erotic excitement is maintained.

Comments on the Phases of the Sexual Response Cycle

Before offering advice and guidance, the counselor must obtain a detailed description from the couple together of their way of completing the sexual response cycle. In some cases, therapy is actually accomplished simply by taking the sexual history, for the partners then have an opportunity to explain their needs, feelings, and behavior as they review the steps of intercourse. The correction of a problem may indeed hinge on the discovery of a small misunderstanding revealed during this discussion.

The physiologic responses described are not absolute. Some individuals may not manifest all of them, and in others there may be variations in duration or sequence. It should be kept in mind also that though the basic body responses are fairly uniform, the psychologic responses to these experiences may vary widely.

The basic skill of lovemaking is pacing. Each partner must learn the optimal rate for the arousal of the other, and each must allow for physiologic differences, especially during foreplay, when the man is likely to reach a comparatively advanced state of sexual excitement sooner than the woman. Great expressive freedom is possible in this phase, and a spirit of play, adventurousness, and experimentation should be encouraged. Verbal and nonverbal communication are essential in order to permit each partner to learn the other's body responses.

During the plateau phase, the man must acquire the control necessary to sustain a high level of arousal while containing his orgasm, so that the woman can develop genital lubrication, engorgement, and clitoral sensitivity. If the husband uses manual stimulation of the clitoris to excite the woman, he must be monitored and guided by her at first, in order to learn the desired type of stroking and to be able to avoid producing unpleasant sensations.

As the orgasm phase is reached, each partner is simultaneously an observer and a participant. Fear that orgasm will not occur can prevent orgasm. Only with patience and practice, combined with honest communication, can the control skills be developed.

In the resolution phase, the couple will often relax quietly in an almost somnolent state of intimacy. Pleasure and fulfillment are combined with words of endearment and lingering tactile gestures to form a period of reaffirmation of the affectionate bond between the partners. If either partner foreshortens or neglects this phase, he or she risks nullifying the meaning of the entire experience.

THE EFFECTS OF MENSTRUATION, PREGNANCY, & AGING ON SEXUAL ACTIVITY

Coitus During Menstruation

Since there are no physiologic reasons why coitus should not take place during active menstruation, any special problems related to sex and menses are usually based on cultural taboos, socially oriented proscriptions or prejudices, or individual feelings of distaste or inferiority. It is surprising how often this matter is unresolved in a marriage. The practitioner should insist upon an open exchange of attitudes on the subject, and the partners, assured of the physiologic validity of the practice, should be encouraged to find a mutually satisfactory solution, perhaps through experimentation, that is consistent with their backgrounds and individual preferences. Some women find that their greatest desire for sex occurs just before or after the menstrual period. For couples practicing the rhythm method of contraception, intercourse at these times is common.

Coitus During Pregnancy*

Most obstetricians believe that coitus can be practiced close to the expected delivery date. Alterations in each of the 4 phases of erotic response during pregnancy are generally in the direction of intensification of sexual feelings. Breast engorgement, sensitivity, and tenderness increase as pregnancy advances, and orgasm during pregnancy in previously nonorgasmic women has been reported. Physiologically, during pregnancy, the orgasmic platform becomes more conspicuous, so that the penis is even more tightly clamped than usual and the rhythmic contractions of the platform are more pronounced. Reports that orgasm induces labor are rare. The resolution phase may be longer and less complete for the woman, and it may

*Much of the material in this section is based on research done by Masters and Johnson.

not relieve muscular tension for any significant period. Sexual desire usually returns before the postpartum visit at 4–5 weeks. Women who breastfeed their babies apparently experience return of sexual interest and responsiveness sooner than those who do not.

Obstetricians have to be ready to give sensible advice about sexual intercourse during and after pregnancy. The following points should be made:

(1) Except for women who habitually abort, there is apparently no reason to refrain from coitus during the first 3 months of pregnancy. However, because masturbation to orgasm may trigger more intense uterine contractions than those resulting from vaginal intercourse, the habitual aborter should be instructed to refrain from masturbation during the first trimester, which is in any case a critical period for her.

(2) For the average woman, there appears to be no reason to refrain from sexual activity in the second trimester.

(3) In the third trimester—especially as the expected day of delivery approaches—a few precautions are warranted. First, though infection is possible, it is unusual. Second, there is a special circumstance for a woman having her first baby: Since the baby's head engages in the cervix and descends into the main axis of the vagina, vigorous coital thrusting after descent could cause cervical trauma and possible bleeding. Intercourse should be discontinued in this circumstance. In the multiparous woman, since descent may not include engagement of the fetal head, there is less reason to prohibit intercourse. Third, orgasm occurring in late pregnancy may trigger labor, possibly because of prostaglandins in the spermatic fluid.

(4) Before the end of the third week postpartum, it is possible that the woman's physical recovery may not be complete enough for her to desire intercourse, since the episiotomy is often incompletely healed at this time and a tendency for vaginal bleeding persists. These problems are usually resolved by the end of the first month.

(5) Position during intercourse poses no problem in early pregnancy, but continued enlargement of the gravid uterus makes the side-to-side or rear-entry position more manageable and more comfortable for the woman as pregnancy progresses.

Many pregnant women seem pretty, youthful, and desirable to their husbands, but if a woman feels sexually unavailable for intercourse a problem may arise for the man that could affect the marriage. To forestall this circumstance, the counselor should inquire into the couple's feelings about the wife's giving her husband sexual pleasure by other means than vaginal intercourse. If both partners are agreeable, such practices as masturbation or oral stimulation can ward off sexual frustration on the part of the man, give pleasure to the woman in seeing the responses her attentions elicit, and allow the partners to maintain their sense of closeness until the woman again feels ready for vaginal intercourse.

Sexual Activity With Aging

Involutional changes in the vaginal tract are benefited by administration of estrogen; thus, women can have a reasonably active sex life in middle and old age. Reduced intensity of responsiveness occurs in all phases of the sexual response cycle—a lesser degree of sex and sexual excitement, less lubrication, delayed response to clitoral stimulation, and shortening of the duration of orgasm. Despite these reductions, the capacity for enjoyment of sexual activity persists. According to Masters and Johnson, "The aging human female is fully capable of sexual performance at orgasmic response levels, particularly if she is exposed to regularity of effective sexual stimulations."

In men, physical responses can diminish in intensity and duration past the age of 50; in men over 60 years of age, erection may take longer, ejaculation loses force, seminal volume diminishes, and the recovery time between separate acts of intercourse becomes longer. As with women, however, the maintenance of sexual activity depends on the individual's interest and the availability of a partner. Even the prolonged time required for erection may benefit both partners by extending the period of foreplay and allowing time for the woman's arousal. For an older man, reserving intercourse for times when he strongly feels the need to ejaculate can often result in good performance on his part and a high degree of pleasure for both partners.

For many women, the most rewarding period of their sex life may come after the years of childbearing, child-rearing, and menopause have passed, when freedom from menstruation and family responsibility (and from fear of pregnancy) may for the first time favor the development of an experimental and adventurous sex life.

SEXUAL ACTIVITY FOLLOWING MUTILATION OF THE SEXUAL SELF–IMAGE

Sexually mutilating surgical procedures (eg, hysterectomy, mastectomy) have only a temporary biologic effect on the sex urge, but the psychologic consequences can be devastating. The sexual self-image depends on the possession of healthy sex organs that can respond to the drive for union with another person who is attractive and desirable. The sexual self-image is deeply ingrained, and a feeling of sexual self-confidence is a basic human need. Therefore, surgical procedures such as hysterectomy and partial or complete mastectomy may cause a woman to feel a loss of completeness of herself. This feeling can do much psychologic damage to the woman, even if she has a thorough understanding of the medical reasons for the surgery, and if it persists it can have equally damaging effects on her husband and her marriage.

A woman's sense of feminine worthiness can be reinforced by the surgeon before surgery, when considerate preventive therapy may avoid future sexual dysfunction; by the physician who regularly takes care of her; and by her husband. All supportive and reassuring comments must be tactful, so that the whole effort does not paradoxically create fears or anxieties that had not occurred to the patient. It is useful to work with the husband so that his attitude of acceptance of his wife will be genuine and unforced. Both partners should be informed that the woman's sexual urges will return naturally with recovery from the surgery, and that devices and techniques such as a breast prosthesis or preservation of the vaginal canal for comfortable and satisfactory sexual function are available.

PRIMARY PROBLEMS OF SEXUAL FUNCTION IN WOMEN

In taking the history of a sexual complaint, the counselor should concentrate on 2 distinct areas: (1) a record of the sexual life history of the patient (including childhood), and (2) diagnosis of the specific sexual dysfunction. Mutual sexual needs and present performance should also be discussed. The interview can be conducted either by one therapist or by co-therapists working conjointly, each taking the sex history of the partners individually and privately. An excellent publication by the Group for the Advancement of Psychiatry (see references) covers the sexual interview in detail, together with methods of assessing sexual function in all age groups.

When a sexually active couple with difficulty in primary sexual function consults a physician, the partners may place inordinate emphasis on correctly practiced coitus as the ultimate goal of sexual interaction. In doing this, they disregard the entire range of physical and symbolic expressions of noncoital sex. The initial sexual history, therefore, should include an exploration of their attitudes toward the function of sex in all its dimensions, and it should be especially noted whether the noncoital aspects of sex are appreciated by the couple. Although its focus must be on the couple's primary sexual dysfunction, one of the goals of sex therapy is to create awareness of the biologic function and biologic validity of all aspects of sexuality.

The treatment described briefly here of the principal forms of sexual dysfunction should, ideally, be practiced by both partners, since sex is the only body function that requires the participation of another person for complete realization. Hence, there can be no uninvolved partner. Sexual therapy with a single person is useful (but more difficult) for those not involved in a continuing relationship.

The Nonorgasmic Woman

In the past, the sexually unresponsive woman was labeled as frigid—a pejorative term that was more accusatory than diagnostic; consequently, the more clinical expression orgasmic failure is preferred. Orgasmic failure is the most common form of sexual dysfunction in women, in curious contrast to the capacity of women for multiple orgasms.

Barriers to full sexual expression and orgasm in the woman are generally considered to have a psychologic basis in social and cultural conditioning during childhood. However, with increasing education and sexual freedom, women are discovering their own sexual responses through childhood masturbation, earlier heterosexual activity, and other investigations. Early constraints may be less operative than they were, but many women are unaware of the importance of the clitoris and, because of inhibitions, may never have learned what is erotically stimulating.

Psychologic barriers to emotional expression can be generally placed in 3 categories: (1) fear of punishment for disapproved behavior, of submission to a man, or of pregnancy; (2) hostility toward men; or (3) conflicting loves or contradictory sexual attachments, eg, strong devotion to a parental figure or unrecognized homosexual feelings. Fear, hostility, and conflict may impose crippling constraints on sexual expression.

In general, women who have learned to masturbate prior to heterosexual intercourse are more likely to achieve coital orgasm than those who have not. If a woman has never experienced orgasm, she may need instruction in how to masturbate as a necessary first step in understanding, feeling, and enjoying the sexual responses of her body. Taking into account the ideal circumstantial and psychologic requirements of women for sexual arousal, the therapist can design masturbatory exercises that the patient can teach herself. In turn, she must eventually teach her husband the techniques that will bring her to a high state of arousal. The techniques can then be transformed, with the husband's assistance, into a phase of lovemaking ultimately leading to actual intercourse and vaginal orgasm.

Although this method is usually successful, some women persist in requiring the manipulation of a partner to produce orgasm and are unable to extend this to intravaginal orgasm. An orgasm produced by manual clitoral manipulation should be considered the physiologic equivalent of one occurring during intravaginal penile intercourse. Individualization and further therapeutic effort may be required, because many women are orgasmic only during intravaginal penile intercourse.

If the woman is able to achieve orgasm through masturbation, she may find that during coitus she can reach the high plateau phase but not progress beyond it because stimulation stops before the peak of excitability is reached. If this happens, it should be recalled that the clitoris is the major focus of a woman's sensation; therefore, manual reexcitation as in foreplay may restore the woman's excitement level.

Penile thrusting provides only indirect clitoral stimulation through labial traction. Studies on the incidence of orgasm in married women have shown that about 40% "nearly always" achieve orgasm if foreplay continues for 1–10 minutes; about 50% if the foreplay period is 15–20 minutes; and about 60% if the foreplay period is longer than 20 minutes.

Even when the love relationship is secure, blocks to orgasm in intercourse may occur for many reasons (eg, anger, fatigue, anxiety). The therapist should encourage the partners to adopt a spirit of free experimentation in order to dispel individual anxieties and to produce the most joyous kind of sexual communication and release.

Vaginismus

Vaginismus is defined as an involuntary and occasionally painful spasm of the external perivaginal muscles. It is often of psychogenic origin, but it may also be associated with local infection, congenital malformation, or introital trauma. The term is most often reserved for the occlusive vaginal spasm that occurs with penile entry during coitus, but it may also occur during pelvic examination or during the insertion of a tampon.

Diagnosis requires careful evaluation if the patient attempts to avoid the examiner's fingers by moving away, crossing her legs, etc. Forcible entry should be avoided, since it only exaggerates the problem. With patience and reassurance, the physician can usually manage to insert one finger for purposes of gynecologic examination and confirmation of the diagnosis.

If the cause is psychogenic, vaginismus can be interpreted as a rejection of sex, regardless of the reasons. In such cases it is usually found that (1) the husband has some form of sexual dysfunction (eg, premature ejaculation, impotence), though whether vaginismus is the result or the cause is often unclear; and (2) there was negative early conditioning, eg, sexual assault in childhood or adolescence or austere religious proscriptions against free sexual expression.

Vaginismus of psychogenic origin can be treated by deconditioning. This begins with a demonstration of the difficulty on the examining table. Both partners should be present, and the therapist should reassure them that the spasm is beyond the woman's conscious control. If the problem is due to childhood conditioning, a patient search for the specific source may be required. If it arises from deep-seated psychologic problems, psychotherapy will be required. Occasionally, a woman will request a gynecologic examination believing that she has some physical disability, and she may have difficulty accepting the psychogenic origins of the problem until she understands her own background and sexual attitudes. An evaluation of the marital relationship should be directed particularly at her acceptance of her husband as a lover, her fear of pregnancy, or her unwillingness to do something in bed that her husband wants.

Therapy consists of reassurance and sex education. Psychotherapy in one form or another is often needed. Behavior modification therapy may be successful. Systematic desensitization or deconditioning techniques are useful. In short-term insight-directed therapy, the therapist should search for the origins of the emotional tension that precipitates vaginismus as a rejecting and self-protective conditioned reflex.

Deconditioning may be accomplished by using graduated vaginal dilators in a series of office visits. Between visits, the patient should practice dilatation below the point of pain and should be specifically instructed not to force dilatation. Her visits should continue until the dilator can be passed without pain as gradual vaginal enlargement occurs. Psychotherapy should continue during these visits. Relaxation exercises should also be taught. It is best to postpone coitus until the largest dilator can be passed with ease. At home, the husband can participate by gently inserting a well-lubricated finger intravaginally, eventually proceeding to the insertion of the erect, lubricated penis; initially, the penis should simply be held in the vagina without thrusting motions.

Although vaginismus is often associated with some alteration in orgasmic response, this is not universally true. Such women may not be sexually unresponsive, because they may achieve orgasm by other means. If so, the prognosis is better than in the primarily nonorgasmic woman. If vaginismus is related to premature ejaculation or erectile failure on the part of the husband, repeated anticipation and frustration on the part of the wife may produce recurrent pelvic congestion. Treatment for the husband's problem is then required in addition to reeducative treatment for the wife.

Dyspareunia

Intercourse may be painful for many reasons in addition to those considered in the discussion of vaginismus. Other possibilities include retroversion of the uterus, cervical tumors or polyps, cervicitis, pelvic infections, neoplasms, endometriosis, childbirth laceration of the broad ligaments, hemorrhoids, fissures, a tender episiotomy scar, kraurosis vulvae, urethral caruncle, a persistent tough hymenal remnant with vaginal stenosis, or complications of perineorrhaphy. One must determine exactly when coital pain is experienced: at intromission, during deep vaginal penetration, with penile thrusting, or during orgasm.

A common cause of dyspareunia is inadequate vaginal lubrication combined with attempted forceful insertion of the erect penis. Atrophy of the vaginal mucosa may occur after menopause and can be adequately treated with estrogen supplementation. In salpingitis, the pressure from penile thrusting will produce deep distress.

It is relatively easy to deal with the physical aspects of dyspareunia, but the emotional component must also be considered even when there is an organic basis for distress. The husband must be made to understand that his wife is not malingering. Regardless of the organic or emotional cause of the problem, it is essential to educate both partners.

When vaginismus is a predominant component of dyspareunia, some gynecologists have found it useful to invite the husband into the examining room in order to demonstrate the degree of painful vaginal spasm to both partners. The desensitizing procedure described in the previous section can then be discussed freely.

Painful intercourse may occasionally follow hysterectomy and is usually attributable to sensitive scar tissue touched by the penis, inadequate estrogen replacement following ovariectomy, and damage to a woman's sexual self-image if she believes she has lost an important component of her femininity because of the operation.

SEXUAL DYSFUNCTION IN MEN

Satisfactory sexual adjustment requires adequate function of both partners. If primary sexual failure occurs in one partner, it can produce dysfunction in the other. For example, painful intercourse in the woman can be an expression of rejection of a man who cannot achieve or sustain an adequate erection. When the man's performance is undependable because of premature ejaculation or unsustained erection, orgasmic failure can occur in the woman. Sex therapists and gynecologists must therefore manage sexual dysfunction in both partners.

Impotence

Primary impotence is a condition in which penile erection cannot be achieved under any circumstance. It may be due to organic disease, as in the case of diabetes mellitus with neuropathy—though impotence in a diabetic man is not necessarily of neurogenic origin. A variety of primary genital disorders (eg, hypogonadism with androgen failure) must also be considered. Obstructive pelvic vascular disease may retard blood flow to the penis and prevent erection. Systemic diseases (eg, anemia, tuberculosis, cancer) may contribute to functional erectile failure.

However, in over 90% of cases, impotence is secondary, ie, psychologic in origin. This can be quickly established if the man's impotence is selective, ie, if he can obtain an erection during sleep, on awakening, with sexual fantasy, or during masturbation but not under such highly specific circumstances as intercourse with his wife, even though he may be potent with an extramarital lover. He may experience erectile failure with prostitutes but not with socially acceptable or attractive women, or he may be impotent only when fatigued or when using alcohol, tranquilizing or depressant drugs, and many antihypertensive medications.

Weakening erectile capacity in the aging man is less related to age than to the availability of a cooperative partner, and the myth of impotence as a function of natural aging should be dispelled. The simple expedient of reserving intercourse for periods of ejaculatory need often is of great help to men in middle life who are anxious about their sexual performance. Depression, whether it is a primary affective psychiatric disorder or a situational reaction to impotence, must be recognized and treated. This is often difficult, because the clinical presentation may be obscure.

Once it is decided whether impotence is primary or secondary, therapy should be started. It may be an isolated problem in an otherwise good relationship, or it may be a symptom of a dysfunctional relationship between incompatible partners. If it occurs as a substitute for unexpressed anger, an opportunity for psychotherapy should be provided.

If impotence is the only problem in an otherwise good relationship, the couple's sexual techniques should be examined and modified appropriately. It may prove that adequate erection can be maintained only until intromission, when a fear of functional failure then besets the man so that he is unable to continue. The first remedial step is to request that the couple practice foreplay and noncoital arousal repeatedly, prohibiting intravaginal intercourse for the time being. If the man is relieved of the pressure to perform complete coitus, the threat of failure is removed and erectile capacity often returns. When his confidence is restored concerning his capacity to produce and maintain an erection, he should then undertake vaginal penetration and quiet containment without thrusting. At the start, the penis may alternately lose and regain its firmness while in the vagina, but it is best held intravaginally. After several occasions in which the penis is maintained erect in the vagina for a period of minutes without losing its firmness, the man should proceed to gentle, controlled thrusting interrupted by periods of rest. Repeated practice will assure competence, and often the couple will find that once the man's confidence in his erectile capacity returns, coitus can be successfully completed. Obviously, a multifaceted therapeutic procedure of this sort requires the wife's complete cooperation and a great deal of patience on the part of both husband and wife. They should be warned that recurrence is common during periods of fatigue, emotional stress, or illness but that with the technical skills they have acquired they can quickly return to satisfactory coitus.

Premature Ejaculation

The most common sexual problem in men is premature ejaculation. This has no exact counterpart in women. Complete urologic study should be done, but the cause of premature ejaculation is almost always psychogenic.

The problem is most often brought to the physician's attention by the wife, who may complain that she is slow to reach orgasm.

Functional premature ejaculation has been defined as (1) the occurrence of orgasm during foreplay and before vaginal intromission, (2) the inability to delay ejaculation after the penis is in the vagina, or (3) the achievement of orgasm and ejaculation before one wishes. It is defined by Masters and Johnson as the inability to delay ejaculation long enough for the woman to have orgasm half of the time. This last definition is perhaps more useful because it considers the wife's need as well as the husband's.

The acquisition of sufficient control in pacing sexual arousal serves the needs of both partners. Over 75% of men ejaculate within 2 minutes after vaginal entry. However, in studies relating the duration of vaginal containment of the penis to female orgasm, it was shown that when containment lasts less than 1 minute before ejaculation, about 25% of women always or nearly always achieve orgasm. About 50% of women do so if containment lasts 1–11 minutes, and approximately 65% do so if it lasts more than 11 minutes. If containment lasts at least 16 minutes before ejaculation, almost all women achieve complete orgasmic capacity.

The sexual histories of men suffering from premature ejaculation often include a history of recurrent nervous tension and stress or of early conditioning owing to hurried masturbation or intercourse due to fear of discovery. Deep-seated psychologic factors concerning relationships with women—possibly involving an overbearing and possessive mother figure—may cause a man to fear his wife, in which case he may find that premature ejaculation is a means of frustrating her sexually and therefore frustrating the mother figure he fears. Regardless of cause, in a situation in which the wife is nonorgasmic and the husband ejaculates prematurely, both partners experience great frustration.

The effects of premature ejaculation may be of insidious onset. Early in marriage, the partners may console each other with assurances that better success will come with time. This may happen but usually does not. Alienation develops when the wife feels exploited, accusing the husband of being insensitive to her sexual needs and concerned only with his own pleasure. The husband's fear that premature ejaculation will occur ensures that it will—no matter how he tries to change the pattern. He may attempt to use strong physical stimuli, such as contraction of the anal sphincter, painful pinching, or application of anesthetizing creams and lotions to the penis. All such methods are useless and frustrating, and his ultimate defense is to blame his wife for being too slow to reach orgasm.

It is the responsibility of the therapist to sort all of this out, teach the partners the known facts about the sexual response, and guide them toward the achievement of optimal pacing. If premature ejaculation goes untreated for long, the man may become impotent.

The most effective treatment method in general use today consists of having the woman masturbate the man to a point just short of ejaculation and then stop. The woman then grasps the glans between her thumb and forefinger and squeezes it almost to the point of pain; some penile stiffness will be lost. After a brief pause, the maneuver is repeated, perhaps several times as tolerated. This procedure should be done more than once in a single session, and the sessions should take place daily for several days with no attempt at intercourse. It is useful to repeat these procedures with the penis lubricated in order to condition the man to the sensation of intravaginal containment. When the man has confidence that control is possible and repeatable, masturbation is allowed to progress to intercourse, preferably with the man lying on his back and the woman straddling him. Masters and Johnson have recently recommended that at this moment the penis should be stimulated to the erect state, when it is inserted into the vagina by the woman. If loss of control is again threatened, the penis should be withdrawn and the squeezing maneuver repeated. Another variation consists of having the woman place the limp penis in the vagina so that erection can be acquired intravaginally. The penis can be withdrawn if loss of control is threatened and the squeezing maneuver repeated. If squeezing is done properly, summation stimuli are aborted and erotic stimuli terminated, preventing orgasm and ejaculation. Eventually, the male will be able to tolerate vaginal containment and, subsequently, thrusting.

A useful and effective variation, should the squeeze technique prove to be unacceptable, consists of female manual stimulation of the penis until the male feels he is close to ejaculation. Stimulation is then stopped until the sensation subsides. After a brief pause, stimulation is resumed, then stopped just before ejaculation occurs. Again, this can be practiced with the penis lubricated. Lo Piccolo suggests that the male practice this on himself by masturbation (using the squeeze or pause) preliminary to all of the above in order to reduce anxiety.

All of this is designed to teach ejaculatory control. The procedure should be successful if the woman's superior coital position is maintained for 15–20 minutes before ejaculation. Also, with this position, the husband may acquire such skill with his wife's cooperation that ejaculation can be delayed almost indefinitely, and the wife may learn to produce her own orgasm, since she is assured of a dependably controlled, erect penis. The possibilities for experimentation and free play of the imagination allow better sexual adjustment and expression.

The couple should be warned that premature ejaculation may recur from time to time and may sometimes progress to temporary impotence. Nonetheless, these techniques, once learned, can be used again. Six to 12 months may be required for optimal adjustment. Premature ejaculation is the easiest to treat successfully of the sexual problems of men. Masters and Johnson report only 4 failures in the treatment of 186 men over a period of 11 years.

• • •

References

Abse DW, Nash EM, Lovden LMR: *Marital and Sexual Counseling in Medical Practice*. Harper & Row, 1974.

Barbach LG: *For Yourself: The Fulfillment of Female Sexuality*. Doubleday, 1975.

Berman EM, Lief HI: Marital therapy from a psychiatric perspective: An overview. *Am J Psychiatry* 1975;**132**:583.

Cuber JF: Three prerequisite considerations to diagnosis and treatment in marriage counseling. Page 53 in: *Counseling in Marital and Sexual Problems: A Physician's Handbook*. Klemer RH (editor). Williams & Wilkins, 1965.

Fox AJ, Balusu L, Kinlen L: Mortality and age differences in marriage. *J Biosoc Sci* 1979;**11**:117.

Group for the Advancement of Psychiatry Committee on Medical Education: *Assessment of Sexual Function: A Guide to Interviewing*. Vol 8. (Report No. 88.) 1973. [Price $3.50. Available from the Mental Health Materials Center, 30 East 29th Street, New York, NY 10016.]

Kaplan HS: *Disorders of Sexual Desire*. Brunner/Mazel, 1979.

Kaplan HS: *The New Sex Therapy*. Brunner/Mazel, 1974.

Klemer RH (editor): *Counseling in Marital and Sexual Problems: A Physician's Handbook*. Williams & Wilkins, 1965.

Kolodny RC, Masters WH, Johnson VE: *Tetxbook of Sexual Medicine*. Little, Brown, 1979.

Leiblum SR, Pervin LA: *Principles and Practice of Sex Therapy*. Guilford Press, 1980.

Levine SB: Marital sexual function: Erectile dysfunction. *Ann Intern Med* 1976;**85**:342.

Lo Piccolo J, Lo Piccolo L: *Handbook of Sex Therapy*. Plenum Press, 1978.

Mace D: *Sexual Difficulties in Marriage*. Fortress Press, 1972.

Masters WH, Johnson VE: *Human Sexual Inadequacy*. Little, Brown, 1971.

Masters WH, Johnson VE: *Human Sexual Response*. Little, Brown, 1966.

Munjack DJ, Oziel LJ: *Sexual Medicine and Counseling in Office Practice: A Comprehensive Treatment Guide*. Little, Brown, 1980.

Otto HA: Premarital counseling. Page 258 in: *Counseling in Marital and Sexual Problems: A Physician's Handbook*. Klemer RH (editor). Williams & Wilkins, 1965.

Perkins RP: Sexual behavior and response in relation to complications of pregnancy. *Am J Obstet Gynecol* 1979;**134**:498.

Saddock BJ, Kaplan HI, Freedman AM: *The Sexual Experience*. Williams & Wilkins, 1976.

Sager CJ: *Marriage Contracts and Couple Therapy: Hidden Forces in Intimate Relationships*. Brunner/Mazel, 1976.

Sutherst JR: Sexual dysfunction and urinary incontinence. *Br J Obstet Gynaecol* 1979;**86**:387.

Vachher M, Yusof K: A psychosexual study of abortion-seeking behavior. *Med J Malaysia* 1978;**33**:50.

Vincent CE: *Sexual and Marital Health*. McGraw-Hill, 1973.

23 | Contraception & Family Planning

Howard J. Tatum, MD, PhD

I. CONTRACEPTION

Indications for Birth Control

The practice of birth control (contraception) may be desirable for many reasons, including medical contraindications, a personal desire to have no children, no children yet, or no more children, and the global problems of increasing population. The socioeconomic and environmental consequences of population density are of direct and indirect concern to everyone.

The interaction between human beings and the environment is so complex that we are unable to predict the ultimate effects of decisions now being made. The Massachusetts Institute of Technology has launched a study called the Project on the Predicament of Mankind. Its originator, Jay Forrester, has asserted that "evolutionary processes have not given us the mental skill needed to properly interpret the dynamic behavior of the systems of which we have now become a part." Accordingly, he and his associates employed a computer system to determine the outcome of several interacting factors. Fig 23–1 presents the predicted effects of changes in world population on natural resources, quality of life, capital investment, and pollution. Their conclusions include the prediction that "the quality of life will continue to decline if no curbs are placed on population, until pollution and other factors bring about their own curb on population."

Socioeconomic Indications for Birth Control

In societies where the life expectancy of children through age 12 is low, there is justification for sufficient births to ensure the maintenance of family productivity. Unfortunately, the tradition of the importance of large families persists in the USA and other countries where improvements in preventive medicine, sanitation, and medical treatment (notably antibiotics) have reduced the death rate during the first year of life and have tremendously increased survival through puberty. Therefore, the people must be convinced that spacing and limitation of births will raise the standard of living and thus make a positive contribution to the welfare of the family and the community.

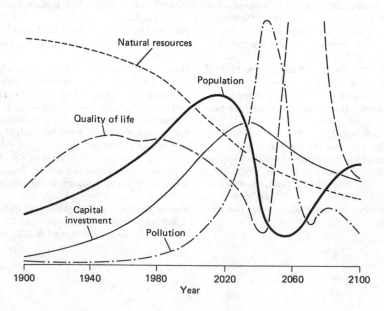

Figure 23–1. Effects of world population on natural resources, quality of life, capital investment, and pollution. (Modified from Forrester and Meadows.)

Medical Indications for Birth Control

The existence of any maternal disease that might be made worse by pregnancy is good reason for the practice of contraception. Although some maternal diseases do not preclude the possibility that a pregnancy can be tolerated and will progress satisfactorily (with appropriate medical support) to term and delivery, pregnancy does impose an additional biologic load on the maternal organism. Moreover, prevention of pregnancy is less traumatic and more acceptable than either an abortion or a full-term pregnancy and delivery. Examples of the more common diseases that may be made worse by pregnancy are heart disease, diabetes mellitus, renal disease, thyroid dysfunction, and tuberculosis.

Eugenic Indications for Birth Control

For evolutionary as well as humane and socio-economic reasons, the physician and society are responsible for discouraging conception whenever it is likely to perpetuate a seriously harmful genetic trait. To accomplish this, preventive medicine and education should be cooperatively applied to the eradication of such hereditary diseases as cerebral sphingolipidosis (amaurotic familial idiocy), Down's syndrome, sickle cell disease, Klinefelter's syndrome, and phenylketonuria.

Contraception & the Law

Contraceptives may be prescribed, demonstrated, and sold in most states of the USA without restriction. Occasionally, the law stipulates parental consent, minimum age, or relevance to marriage and parenthood. All states have family planning policies or laws.

In Scandinavia, contraceptives are sold openly. Spain and Italy have recently reversed their former strict laws against the dispensing or sale of contraceptive information and materials. In many countries the sale of birth control materials is illegal, but rarely is strict enforcement practiced.

The pros and cons of providing contraceptive information and materials to teenagers have been debated. In early 1982, a new regulation for federally funded family planning programs in the USA was proposed. If passed, the new law would require personnel at family planning facilities to notify the parent or guardian of any person under the age of 18 at least 10 working days before the clinic would provide a prescription contraceptive to the teenager. It is probable that this regulation, if it became law, would result in a major increase in teenage pregnancies and almost certainly a parallel increase in legal and illegal abortions. Because teenagers continue to be a high-risk group for illegitimacy, it is unrealistic to restrict the use of contraceptives by this group. Cutright has concluded that "access to effective medically supervised contraception and legal abortion is no more likely to encourage teenage promiscuity than denial of access has been to discourage adolescent sexual activity. The US Supreme Court has recently declared unconstitutional a New York statute that prohibited the sale of nonprescription contraceptive devices to persons under 16 years of age. Such access may, however, save many young people from traumatic out-of-wedlock pregnancies, illegitimate births, botched illegal abortions, and disastrous youthful marriages." Most physicians are in accord with these conclusions and are willing to assist teenagers by providing contraceptive advice and prescriptions within the confines of appropriate legal restraints. However, they must be careful to avoid imposing their own religious or moral views on their patients.

Opposition to Contraception

In the past, certain political groups have opposed limitation of the size of families because fewer numbers mean less political power or even military power. This philosophy now has limited appeal because it is recognized that a nation's standard of living depends to a great extent on the ratio of material goods to the number of persons who must be supported by the nation.

All faiths subscribe to the principle of family planning, but there is great variation in what is considered acceptable contraceptive practice. Roman Catholicism does not oppose birth control in principle but does oppose the use of "artificial" means to prevent conception. The "rhythm method" approved by the Roman Catholic Church is so unreliable that it must be regarded as scientifically unacceptable. Historically, Judaism has accepted the practice of contraception by the woman but not by the man. This tradition is no longer stressed in Reform Judaism.

Advising Teenage Girls About Contraception.*

Prescribing contraceptives to minors has certain legal implications that must be considered. By October 1976, 30 states and the District of Columbia had explicitly affirmed the right of persons under 18 to consent to contraceptive management, and in 1977 the US Supreme Court ruled that minors have a constitutional right of access to contraceptives.

Even so, the medical professional should not routinely dispense prescriptions for contraceptives to young teenagers. Counseling about the possible use of contraception should include a consideration of the advisability of involving the parents in the process. It is the responsibility of the medical professional to determine whether the patient has sufficient information so that she will be competent to consent on her own behalf. Documentation of the discussion with the patient and her understanding of what has been said is of legal importance. Recall that all providers of oral contraceptives and IUDs must give a copy of the appropriate FDA-approved pamphlet supplied by the manufacturer to the patient. A consent form setting forth in simple language the benefits and hazards of (and alternatives to) the specific method to be used, the patient's acknowledgment of and awareness of her right to stop

*This section is contributed by Ida I. Nakashima, MD.

using the method at any time, and an explanation of what to expect and what to do if problems develop should be signed by the patient. Such a form will serve as evidence, if needed, that counseling about use of a particular birth control method was given; that the patient appeared competent to understand what was said to her; and that she consented to receive contraceptive management in the manner specified.

As this is written, there is controversy about the physician's duty to notify parents of teenage girls' requests for prescriptions for contraceptive pills in federally supported clinics (see above).

METHODS OF CONTRACEPTION

The currently available methods of contraception may be classified as (1) "folk" methods—coitus interruptus, postcoital douche, prolongation of lactation; (2) "traditional" methods—condom, vaginal diaphragm, spermatocides (foams, creams, gels), and "rhythm"; and (3) "modern" methods—oral contraceptives, repeated injections of progestational steroids, intrauterine devices, and surgical sterilization.

COITUS INTERRUPTUS

The oldest contraceptive method is withdrawal of the penis before ejaculation. This results in deposition of the semen outside the female genital tract. It has the disadvantage of demanding sufficient self-control by the man so that withdrawal can precede ejaculation. Furthermore, if the woman fails to achieve orgasm before withdrawal, she may require additional "artificial" stimulation for adequate sexual gratification. The method probably is only slightly less effective than the conventional mechanical and chemical contraceptives. Failure may result from escape of semen before orgasm or the deposition of semen on the external female genitalia near the vagina.

POSTCOITAL DOUCHE

Plain water, vinegar, and a number of "feminine hygiene" products are widely used as postcoital douches. Theoretically, the douche serves to flush the semen out of the vagina, and the additives to the water may possess some spermicidal properties. Be this as it may, sperm have been found within the cervical mucus within 90 seconds after ejaculation. Hence, the method is very ineffective and cannot be relied upon.

PROLONGATION OF LACTATION

Women are less fertile while nursing than after weaning, and deliberate continuation of nursing after it is no longer necessary for infant nutrition has long been a widespread contraceptive method. The delay in recurrence of ovulation after delivery is due in part to hypophyseal or hypothalamic stimuli from nursing during amenorrhea. Nonetheless, the duration of suppression of ovulation is quite variable. Ovulation returns before the first postpartum menstrual cycle in about 6% of women and thus limits the success of this method. Prolonged nursing may lead to infant malnutrition if the baby is denied proper dietary supplements. In the developing countries, prolonged nursing is an essential (but poor) component of child nutrition, and the high pregnancy rates are evidence that breast feeding is not an effective method of fertility control. Pregnancy intervals for women who nursed for 1–2 years and did not use any other contraceptive method are 5–10 months longer than for women who did not nurse between pregnancies. Complementary methods such as condoms, diaphragms, or IUDs are recommended.

CONDOM

The rubber or plastic condom or contraceptive sheath serves as a cover for the penis during coitus and prevents the deposition of semen in the vagina. The advantages of the condom are that it provides highly effective inexpensive contraception and is convenient to use. It also provides some protection against venereal disease. It has the disadvantage that both partners may experience some reduction of sensation when it is used.

The condom probably is the most widely used mechanical contraceptive in the world today. It is second to oral (pill) contraception in the USA and is incorporated into most family planning programs throughout the world. Its failures are due to imperfections of manufacture (about 3 per 1000); errors of technique, such as applying the condom after some semen has escaped into the vagina; and escape of semen from the condom as a result of failure to withdraw before detumescence.

When greater contraceptive effectiveness is desired, a second method such as contraceptive vaginal jelly or foam should be used in conjunction with the condom. This will significantly reduce the chances of condom failure due to mechanical or technical deficiencies.

VAGINAL DIAPHRAGM

The diaphragm is a mechanical barrier between the vagina and the cervical canal. A contraceptive jelly or cream should be placed on the cervical side of the diaphragm before insertion. This medicament serves also as a lubricant for the insertion. Additional jelly should be introduced into the vagina on and around the diaphragm after it is securely in place. When the diaphragm is of proper size (as determined by pelvic examination and trial with fitting rings) and is used according to directions, its failure rate is no more than 2 or 3 pregnancies per 100 women per year of exposure. The diaphragm has the disadvantages of requiring fitting by a physician or a trained paramedical person and the necessity for anticipating the need for protection and having privacy for its insertion. Failures may result from improper fitting or placement and dislodgment of the diaphragm during intercourse.

Cervical caps are small cuplike diaphragms placed over the cervix. They are supposed to be held in place by "suction." To provide a successful barrier against sperm, they must fit tightly over the cervix. Because of variability in cervical size, individualization is almost essential. This greatly limits the practical usefulness of the method. Tailoring the cap to fit each cervix is almost impossible. In addition, many women are unable to feel their own cervix and thus have great difficulty in placing the cap correctly over the cervix. Because of these problems, the cervical cap has few advantages over the traditional vaginal diaphragm. Although some advocates of the cervical cap recommend that it remain in place for 1 or 2 days at a time, recent experience in the USA with toxic shock syndrome suggests that any obstruction to the normal flow of uterine and vaginal secretions for even several hours is potentially dangerous. It is doubtful that the cap in its present state of development will play an important role in contraception.

Adverse publicity concerning use of the oral contraceptive pill and IUDs has resulted in increased enthusiasm for traditional barrier contraceptives such as the condom and diaphragm. Technical improvement in these methods and the realization that they offer some protection against venereal diseases have encouraged wider use. Reduced restrictions, more advertising, and over-the-counter (nonprescription) sales of condoms have increased the use of both of these barrier methods of contraception.

SPERMICIDAL PREPARATIONS

Spermicidal vaginal jellies, creams, gels, suppositories, and foams, in addition to their killing effect on sperm, also act as a mechanical barrier to entry of sperm into the cervical canal. Many of these materials are toxic to sperm. They may be used alone or in conjunction with a diaphragm. The combination of vaginal spermicidal preparations by the woman and use of a condom by the man gives almost 100% effective contraception. Some of the foam tablets and suppositories require a few minutes for adequate dispersion throughout the vagina, and failures may result if dispersion is not allowed to occur. Infrequently, these chemical agents may irritate the vaginal mucosa and external genitalia. Conceptrol, the single-dose packaging of Delfen Cream, and probably other currently available vaginal contraceptives exert significant prophylactic effects against the common sexually transmitted organisms *Neisseria gonorrhoeae, Treponema*

pallidum, Candida albicans, and *Trichomonas vaginalis*. This factor encourages sexually active women to use a relatively effective method of contraception that also reduces the likelihood of venereal infection.

A recent study suggested a possible risk of congenital disorders in babies born to mothers who used vaginal spermicides. This report is not convincing, because, as the authors point out, there is no certainty that a spermicide was used at the time of conception. In addition, the data did not establish the existence of an integrated and well-defined set of disorders that could be linked to the use of a spermicide.

A very recent and reassuring study of the teratogenic action of nonoxynol 9–containing contraceptives in rats failed to show meaningful differences between the experimental and the control animals relevant to maternal parameters, fetal toxicity, and visceral and skeletal fetal malformations.

There was apprehension about the possibility of congenital abnormalities in babies conceived while oral contraceptives were being used. A 10-year study of the incidence of congenital defects indicated no difference between the progeny of users and nonusers of oral contraceptives in a matched control series.

"RHYTHM" METHOD

It has long been known that women are fertile for only a few days of the menstrual cycle. The rhythm method of contraception requires that coitus be avoided during the time of the cycle when a fertilizable ovum and motile sperm could meet in the oviduct. Fertilization takes place within the tube, and the ovum remains in the tube for about 3 days after ovulation; hence, the fertile period is from the time of ovulation to 2–3 days thereafter.

Accurate prediction or indication of ovulation is essential to the success of the rhythm method. The 3 means of predicting ovulation time are as follows:

(1) The **calendar method,** as described by Knaus (an Austrian) and by Ogino in Japan, predicts the day of ovulation by means of a formula based on the menstrual pattern recorded over a period of several months. Ovulation ordinarily occurs 14 days before the first day of the next menstrual period. The fertile interval should be assumed to extend from at least 2 days before ovulation to no less than 2 days after ovulation. An interval of 1–2 days of abstinence either way increases the likelihood of success.

(2) More reliable evidence of ovulation may be obtained by recording the **basal body temperature (BBT)**. The vaginal or rectal temperature must be recorded upon awakening in the morning before any physical activity is undertaken. Although it is often missed, there is a slight drop in temperature 24–36 hours after ovulation. The temperature then rises abruptly about 0.3–0.4 °C (0.5–0.7 °F) and continues on this plateau for the remainder of the cycle. The third day after the onset of elevated temperature is considered to be the end of the fertile period. For reliability,

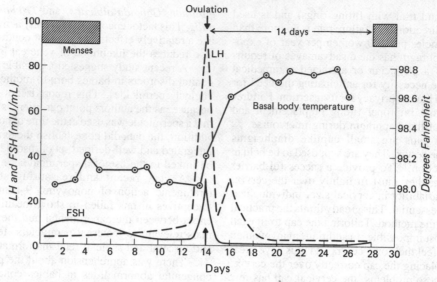

Figure 23–2. Relationship between ovulation and basal body temperature and LH and FSH surges in the normal menstrual cycle.

care must be taken by the woman to ensure that true basal temperatures are recorded, ie, that hyperthermia due to other causes does not provide misleading information.

(3) The most accurate method of determining ovulation time is to demonstrate the **luteinizing hormone (LH) peak** in serum specimens. Because of the cost and the time required for the serial measurements of LH that are essential to indicate the abrupt increment, this method is an impractical method of birth control. It is valuable in the treatment of infertility, however, when the optimal time for coitus or artificial insemination is of great importance.

Fig 23–2 shows the relationships between ovulation, BBT, serum levels of LH and FSH, and menses.

The sole advantage of the rhythm method is that it is the only contraceptive method currently sanctioned by the Roman Catholic Church. It is ineffective because it depends for its validity on a completely regular menstrual cycle. At least 20% of fertile women have enough variation in their cycles so that reliable prediction of the fertile period is impossible.

Epidemiologic studies of women using the rhythm method have suggested an increased incidence of congenital anomalies such as anencephaly and Down's syndrome among children resulting from unplanned pregnancies. Delayed fertilization has been shown in animal experiments to result in an increased incidence of aneuploidy and polyploidy in offspring, thus suggesting a possible explanation for the human fetal anomalies recently reported by Jongbloet.

Natural Family Planning; "Fertility Awareness."

Proponents of so-called natural family planning or "fertility awareness," employing the BBT temperature chart, ovulation, or sympto-thermal methods, claim that a 98% effectiveness rate was achieved for each method in a limited series in a 1980 report from the Department of Health, Education, and Welfare. However, the "use effectiveness" in this group permitted 6–10 unexpected pregnancies per 100 women years of use with the BBT method; 10–25 pregnancies with the ovulation method; and 10–15 pregnancies with the sympto-thermal method. This corresponds to an 80–90% overall effectiveness in pregnancy prevention.

Although these methods may be highly effective when used conscientiously after proper training, actual use compliance has been disappointing, especially in uneducated or poorly motivated individuals. Large-scale controlled studies on the reliability of fertility awareness methods must be completed before their practicality can be regarded as established.

ORAL HORMONAL CONTRACEPTIVES

The oral contraceptives in general use are synthetic steroids similar to the natural female sex hormones—the estrogens and progestins. These steroids are used in doses and in combinations that provide contraception by inhibiting ovulation.

Until recently there were 2 principal regimens of oral contraception: combined and sequential. In the combined method, pills containing estrogen and progestin are taken each day for 20–21 days. The sequential method, in which an estrogen pill was taken each day for 15–16 days followed by an estrogen-progestin pill each day for 5 days, has been abandoned in the USA because several studies showed a higher than normal incidence of cancer of the endometrium of the uterus in women using this method of contraception. The sequential agents are still in use outside the USA but probably will not be reintroduced here.

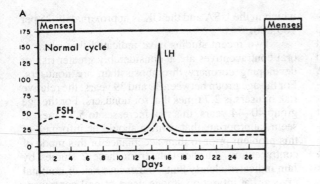

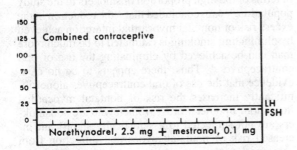

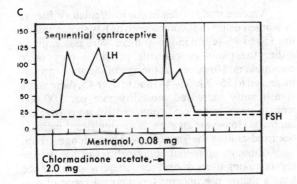

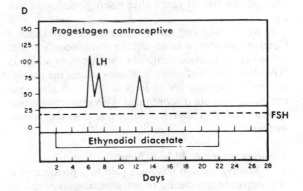

Figure 23–3. Serum levels (in mIU) of follicle-stimulating hormone (FSH) and luteinizing hormone (LH) during the menstrual cycle, with and without oral contraception. *A:* During normal cycle without medication. *B:* During a typical cycle with combined medication (see text). *C:* During a typical cycle with sequential medication (see text). *D:* During progestin-only medication. (Reproduced, with permission, from Odell WD, Moyer DL: *Physiology of Reproduction.* Mosby, 1971.)

The combined regimen is begun on the fifth day of the menstrual cycle. Withdrawal bleeding can be expected within 3–5 days after completion of the 20- or 21-day regimen. The routine is started again on the fifth day of the new cycle. Thus, the method may be described as "a 3 week on and 1 week off" pill regimen. A variation is provided by a package containing 28 pills in a specific sequence such that the first 20–21 pills contain the steroids and the last 7–8 tablets are hormonally inert. In this manner, one pill is taken each day and there is no "on" or "off" interval to be remembered.

The serum levels of FSH and LH throughout the normal menstrual cycle are shown in Fig 23–3A. During a typical cycle under the combined oral contraceptive regimen (Fig 23–3B), there is no rise during the first half of the cycle; thus, follicle growth is not initiated, ovulation does not occur, and consequently there is no FSH and LH surge. During the sequential

oral contraceptive regimen (Fig 23–3C), the estrogen stimulates LH secretion in an irregular manner. There is no concomitant early rise in FSH when progestin is added, and another LH surge usually is produced. When a progestin-only regimen (Fig 23–3D) is followed (eg, with the "mini-pill"; see below), there are multiple LH surges but no significant changes in FSH levels. For the reasons given, these oral contraceptive regimens significantly alter the physiologic hormonal balance. The mini-pill regimen causes the least derangement, but its efficacy as a contraceptive is slightly less than that of combined oral contraception. Moreover, occasional amenorrhea may occur.

Advantages

Major advantages derived from use of oral contraceptives in the USA alone include approximately 50,000 hospitalizations averted annually for conditions that include benign breast disease, retention cysts of the ovaries, and deficiency anemias. Equally striking is the estimated reduction of hospitalizations and office visits for pelvic inflammatory disease that result from the protective action of oral contraceptives and amount to 51,000 per year. Recent studies in the USA and Great Britain have shown that users of oral contraceptives have almost complete protection against ectopic pregnancies. This is estimated to prevent about 10,000 hospitalizations for this life-threatening complication annually in the USA alone.

Although there were initial concerns about oral contraceptives and carcinogenicity, recent studies have suggested that users of the combined oral contraceptives have only one-half the risk of developing endometrial cancer as do nonusers. This protection appears after 1 year of use of oral contraceptives and may persist for 10 years after discontinuation of pill use.

Recent ongoing studies at the Centers for Disease Control and several other smaller studies confirm that pill users experience a rate of ovarian cancer which is 60% that of nonpill users. In these studies, the protective effect persists for as long as 10 years after oral contraceptives are discontinued. This protective effect appears to be greater for nulliparas than for parous women.

Disadvantages & Side-Effects

Much attention has been paid to a possible relationship between the use of oral contraceptives and the incidence of thromboembolic disease, including pulmonary embolism and cerebral thrombosis. Between 1967 and 1969, reports of retrospective studies in the United Kingdom and the USA provided statistically valid data indicating that deep vein thrombosis, pulmonary embolism, and cerebral thrombosis occur 3–6 times more frequently in users of oral contraceptives than in nonusers. The mortality rate from idiopathic thromboembolic disease in the UK for women 20–34 years of age using oral contraceptives was approximately 3 per 100,000; for those 35–44 years old, 9 per 100,000. For nonusers, the incidences per 100,000 for the 2 age groups were 0.1 and 0.5, respectively. This was much lower than the maternal mortality rate in the same period. According to a 1969 study in the USA, the risk of thromboembolism was 4–5 times greater for users of oral contraceptives than for nonusers. Moreover, no correlation could be demonstrated in these studies when oral contraceptives had been discontinued at least 1 month before admission to the hospital for thromboembolism.

There is an apparent association between the use of oral contraceptives and the occurrence of postoperative deep vein thromboembolism. A recent study in the UK suggested that users have 3–4 times more risk from this surgical complication than nonusers. Although the incidence of thromboembolism is undoubtedly higher in users of oral contraceptives, their death rate—approximately 3 per 100,000—must be compared with the risk to maternal life in pregnancy and delivery (excluding deaths from illegal abortion), which in the USA and the UK is approximately 25 per 100,000.

Two recent studies have indicated that users of oral contraceptives are at considerably greater risk of developing coronary thrombosis than are nonusers. For the age group between 30 and 39 years, the relative risk of users is 2.7 times that for nonusers. For the age group 40–44 years, this risk increases to 5.7 times. It seems appropriate that women should be informed of this problem prior to their acceptance of this mode of contraception. Further data from these 2 studies by Jain indicated clearly that "the excess risk of nonfatal myocardial infarction among users of oral contraceptives observed in England and Wales can be explained in terms of the high proportion of smokers in the study population." Jain concluded that "the reduction in the excess risk of nonfatal myocardial infarction achieved by eliminating smoking is estimated to be much more than can be achieved by eliminating the use of oral contraceptives." Thus, there appears to be no clear evidence that the use of oral contraceptives alone significantly increases the risk of nonfatal myocardial infarction. In other words, women who are nonsmokers are not subjected to a statistically significant increased risk of nonfatal myocardial infarction from using oral contraceptives in contrast to women who smoke.

A recent study of deaths due to circulatory disease in women using oral contraceptives has shown that in the 15- to 25-year age group there were no deaths in either the users or controls provided they were nonsmokers. However, as the age of the study groups increased to 25–34, 35–44, and to over 45, there was a significantly increased mortality rate per 100,000 woman-years in the oral contraceptive users over the controls. However, an even more significant increase occurred among the smokers within each age group.

Although epithelial abnormalities of the uterine cervix among users of oral contraceptives were at one time a matter of concern, the preponderance of evidence indicates clearly that the use of oral contraceptives neither causes nor predisposes to the development of cancer of the cervix.

Many recent publications have indicated clearly that the use of oral contraceptives reduces significantly the incidence of benign breast diseases such as cystic mastitis.

Table 23–1 lists the currently available oral contraceptives and their contents.

The "Mini-Pill" or Nonstop Progestin

The idea of administering small daily amounts of a progestin arose when clinical experience with some of the low-dosage combination pills indicated that contraception was being provided even though ovulation was not always inhibited. Subsequent studies demonstrated that a small daily quantity of a progestin alone would provide good protection against pregnancy without suppressing ovulation. The method has the following advantages: (1) Because no estrogen is given, the side-effects attributable to the estrogen

Table 23–1. Oral contraceptive agents in use.*†

	Estrogen (mg)		Progestin (mg)	
Combination tablets				
Loestrin 1/20	Ethinyl	0.02	Norethindrone	1.0
Zorane 1/20	estradiol		acetate	
Loestrin 1.5/30	Ethinyl	0.03	Norethindrone	1.5
Zorane 1.5/30	estradiol		acetate	
Brevicon	Ethinyl	0.035	Norethindrone	0.5
	estradiol			
Lo/Ovral	Ethinyl	0.03	dl-Norgestrel	0.3
	estradiol			
Ovral	Ethinyl	0.05	dl-Norgestrel	0.5
	estradiol			
Norlestrin 1/50	Ethinyl	0.05	Norethindrone	1.0
Zorane 1/50	estradiol		acetate	
Norlestrin 2.5/50	Ethinyl	0.05	Norethindrone	2.5
	estradiol		acetate	
Demulen	Ethinyl	0.05	Ethynodiol	1.0
	estradiol		diacetate	
Norinyl 1/50	Mestranol	0.05	Norethindrone	1.0
Ortho-Novum 1/50				
Norinyl 1/80	Mestranol	0.8	Norethindrone	1.0
Ortho-Novum 1/80				
Norinyl-2	Mestranol	0.1	Norethindrone	2.0
Ortho-Novum-2				
Ovulen	Mestranol	0.1	Ethynodiol	1.0
			diacetate	
Enovid 5	Mestranol	0.075	Norethynodrel	5.0
Enovid E	Mestranol	0.1	Norethynodrel	2.5
Daily progestin tablets				
Micronor	...		Norethindrone	0.35
Nor-QD	...		Norethindrone	0.35
Ovrette	...		dl-Norgestrel	0.075

*Sequential agents have been withdrawn in the USA because of the associated occurrence of carcinoma of the endometrium in some patients.

†Reproduced, with permission, from Meyers FH, Jawetz E, Goldfien A: *Review of Medical Pharmacology,* 7th ed. Lange, 1980.

component of conventional oral contraceptives are eliminated; (2) because ovulation occurs in a high percentage of the cycles, anovulatory bleeding abnormalities are largely eliminated; and (3) the mini-pill is taken every day, ie, no special sequence of pill-taking is necessary. Norgestrel was the first mini-pill to be approved by the FDA. Clinical studies indicate that 0.35 mg of progestin per day provides good contraception while at the same time maintaining reasonably normal ovulatory cycles.

The mechanism of contraceptive action of the microdose nonstop progestins is not known. It has been suggested that the cervical mucus becomes less permeable to sperm and that endometrial activity goes out of phase, so that nidation is thwarted even if fertilization does occur. In clinical tests, the use of microdoses of progestins has resulted in a pregnancy rate of about 2–7 per 100 woman years.

Postcoital or "Morning-After" Pill

Actually, there is no morning-after pill as such. Large doses of diethylstilbestrol (25–50 mg/d for 5 days) after an isolated exposure are said to be effective in preventing pregnancy; however, if the uptake of estrogen coincides with ovulation or entrance of the ovum into the tube, transport of the ovum through the tube may be markedly accelerated. Under these conditions, fertilization may not take place; or, if fertilization has already occurred, the ovum may reach the endometrial cavity prematurely and may not achieve nidation. If coitus takes place 2–6 days before ovulation, the high doses of estrogen will effectively suppress ovulation. If coitus takes place 4 or more days after ovulation, fertilization would not take place anyway. Obviously, the use of high doses of estrogen probably will protect against pregnancy provided the estrogen is given coincident to the transport of the egg through the uterine tube or long enough before ovulation to effect suppression of ovulation.

Severe nausea and vomiting are the familiar side-effects of estrogen therapy. In instances of rape and incest, this treatment is certainly justified.

The incrimination of nonsteroidal estrogens such as diethylstilbestrol (DES) in the etiology of clear cell vaginal carcinoma of female progeny has suggested that the use of this drug as a morning-after contraceptive may be unwise. Other estrogens such as ethinyl estradiol, conjugated equine estrogens, and stilbestrol diphosphate have been used with varying degrees of success. The potential carcinogenic effect of estrogen on female progeny in later life is not relevant to the "morning-after" use of estrogens because of the very limited duration of use and the presumed resistance of the preimplanted blastocyst to drugs that may modify organogenesis. The principal side-effects associated with the use of estrogens for this purpose are bloating and the distressing nausea and vomiting that occur during the drug regimen. The reported failure rates range from 0 to 2.4%. The use of estrogens as morning-after contraceptives should not be advised unless it is understood that therapeutic abortion will be performed if pregnancy occurs.

Progestins alone or in combination with estrogens are being used as postcoital contraceptives with varying degrees of success. The most widely used progestin used alone is d-norgestrel in doses ranging from 1 mg down to 150 μg, taken within 1–8 hours following unprotected coitus. The failure rates ranged from nil with the 1-mg dose to 45% when 150 μg were used.

A more recent study utilized 2 mg of dl-norgestrel and 200 μg of ethinyl estradiol. There was one pregnancy in the series of 608 women treated in this manner (a failure rate of 0.16%).

HORMONAL CONTRACEPTION BY INJECTION

Steroid sex hormones may be injected intramuscularly to provide a depot that, depending on the drug, dosage, and formulation, may provide contraception for a month, for 6 months, or even for a year. A pure progestin may be used, or the injection may consist of a combination of a progestin with an estrogen. Most of these regimens prevent ovulation by suppression of anterior pituitary function.

The compound most widely used is medroxyprogesterone acetate (Depo-Provera). The regimen that has been most extensively evaluated consists of 150 mg every 90 days. This results in marked interference with the midcycle production of luteinizing hormone. Ovulation is suppressed, although small amounts of FSH may be produced and there may be some ovarian follicle development. Because of the marked imbalance of estrogen and progesterone produced as a consequence of pituitary suppression, the endometrium usually is atrophic, and uterine bleeding is either irregular or absent for months. Nonetheless, contraceptive effectiveness is very high. After the injections are discontinued, there may be considerable delay in reestablishment of regular ovulation and corresponding true menstrual bleeding. When fertility will return cannot be predicted, but ovulatory periods usually begin again 6–12 months after the last injection. Medroxyprogesterone acetate is currently approved for contraceptive use in over 80 countries (most recently in Sweden) but not in the USA. It is unfortunate that this very effective and safe contraceptive is being withheld from women in the USA even though early doubts about its safety have not proved to be well founded.

NONMEDICATED INTRAUTERINE CONTRACEPTIVE DEVICES

The intrauterine device (IUD or IUCD) is made of plastic or metal or a combination of these materials. It is introduced into the endometrial cavity through the cervical canal. A large variety of shapes and sizes have been tried, with varying degrees of contraceptive effectiveness.

Intrauterine devices may be classified as open or closed. They are open if they have no circumscribed aperture larger than 5 mm (through which a loop of bowel or segment of omentum could enter and be strangulated if the device were to perforate the uterus and enter the peritoneal cavity). Examples of open IUDs are the Margulies spiral, Lippes Loop, double coil, and Tatum-Zipper Copper T (Fig 23–4). The IUD Advisory Committee to the FDA recommends that closed devices should not be used if they possess the potentiality for strangulation. Examples of closed IUDs are the Gräfenberg rings, Zipper ring, Birnberg bow, Ota ring, and Hall-Stone ring (Inhiband) (Fig 23–5) and the Goldenstein ring and Silent Protector.

The IUDs are especially useful in large-scale family planning programs because they cost little and provide long-term protection. They require only a single decision by the patient and only one procedure by the physician (or a trained paramedical person such as a nurse midwife). Other advantages are that the method is independent of coitus and that fertility is restored almost immediately after the device has been removed. At the end of 1976, according to one estimate, more than 15 million women throughout the world were using the IUD.

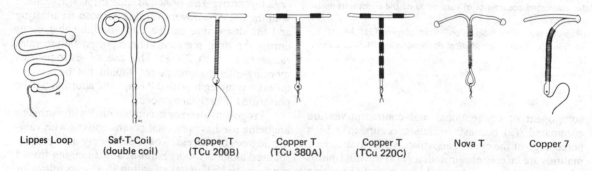

Lippes Loop · Saf-T-Coil (double coil) · Copper T (TCu 200B) · Copper T (TCu 380A) · Copper T (TCu 220C) · Nova T · Copper 7

Figure 23–4. Examples of open intrauterine contraceptive devices.

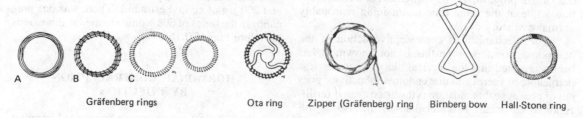

Gräfenberg rings · Ota ring · Zipper (Gräfenberg) ring · Birnberg bow · Hall-Stone ring

Figure 23–5. Examples of closed intrauterine contraceptive devices.

Mode of Action

Just how intrauterine devices act to prevent conception is not known. There is probably more than one mechanism. The most widely observed phenomenon is mobilization of leukocytes in response to the presence of the foreign body. The leukocytes aggregate around the IUD in the endometrial fluids and mucosa and, to a lesser extent, in the stroma and the underlying myometrium. It is hypothesized that the leukocytes produce an environment hostile to the fertilized ovum. In laboratory animals this leukocytic infiltration apparently is not dependent upon microbial invasion. In humans the uterine cavity sterilizes itself, usually within 2–4 weeks after the device is inserted.

Reversibility

Fertility is promptly restored when the device is expelled or removed.

Technique of Insertion (Figs 23–6 and 23–7)

It is best to insert an IUD during a menstrual period because the cervical canal is fully patent then and the patient is least likely to be pregnant. Furthermore, the endometrial cavity is more distensible at this time in the cycle, and uterine cramps, if they occur as a result of the insertion, will be less noticeable. However, insertion can be accomplished at any other time if that is desired and if it is more convenient for the patient.

After a pelvic examination has shown that the external and internal genitalia are normal, a local antiseptic is used to cleanse the cervix. A single-toothed tenaculum is then placed on the anterior lip of the cervix and gentle traction is applied. This traction tends to reduce the angle between the cervix and fundus and facilitates introduction of the uterine sound.

After the direction and depth of the uterine cavity have been determined by means of the sound, the device is inserted with the aid of the appropriate insertion tube. Most inserters are equipped with a guide that indicates the direction and the plane in which the device will lie when it emerges from the insertion tube into the cavity. Some devices, such as the Copper T, are freed within the uterine cavity by withdrawal of the insertion tube over the plunger rather than by being pushed out of the inserted tube and into the uterine cavity by the plunger, as is the Lippes Loop. This withdrawal technique reduces the chance of perforation of the uterine wall.

Most IUDs have a monofilament plastic tail or strand that extends through the cervix so that the patient can feel the thread and thus be certain the device is staying in place. Moreover, the tail facilitates removal when desired.

Complications of Insertion

There may be moderate discomfort or pain when the uterus is sounded or when the IUD is inserted. Nulliparas and nulligravidas are more likely to experience syncopal reactions than multiparous women at the time of insertion. In general, the larger the IUD, the more likely it is to cause pain. The pain and syncopal reactions are due to dilatation of the cervical canal and distention of the endometrial cavity. Paracervical anesthesia may be desirable, particularly for nulligravidas and for any woman who has a low threshold for pain. Mild analgesics may be helpful for several hours following IUD insertion.

Partial or complete perforation of the uterus is a rare complication of IUD insertion. It can be avoided by meticulous care in ascertaining the position and size of the uterus and by strict adherence to the recommended insertion procedure.

The presence of the IUD may elicit uterine cramps (an attempt by the uterus to rid itself of the device) for hours or days after insertion. With larger devices, the intensity of the cramps may require removal of the IUD.

Disadvantages & Side-Effects of IUDs

A. Pregnancy: As Table 23–2 shows, the pregnancy rate (with the device in situ) is 0.4–2.8 per 100 women in 12 months of use, depending on the device and the parity and age of the patient. If pregnancy occurs and the patient wishes it to continue, the device may be removed by traction on the plastic tail. If gentle

Table 23–2. Cumulative event rates per 100 users of representative IUDs in first year.

IUD	Pregnancy	Expulsion	Removals For		Continuation
			Bleeding or Pain	Other Medical Problems	
Lippes Loop D	1.8–2.7	7.3–9.5	9.1–11.7	2.5–3.3	77–80*
Double coil	0.4–2.8	7.5–19.3	4.0–14.7	4.0	70–88*
Copper 7 (Gravigard)	2.7	14.8	10.2	3.3	65†
Copper T (TCu 200B)‡	1.6	8.5	8.1	3.3	74†
Progesterone T (Progestasert)	0.9–2.1	2–5.8	6.4–9.5	4.5	80.2§

*Department of Medical and Public Affairs, George Washington University Medical Center: Intrauterine devices. *Popul Rep,* Series B, No. 7, pp 21–48, Jan 1975.

†Table 8 in Jain AK: Safety and effectiveness of contraceptive devices. *Contraception* 1975;**11**:243.

‡Approval of NDA by US Food and Drug Administration granted Nov 4, 1976.

§From Tatum HJ: Clinical aspects of intrauterine contraception: Circumspection 1976. *Fertil Steril* 1977;**28**:3.

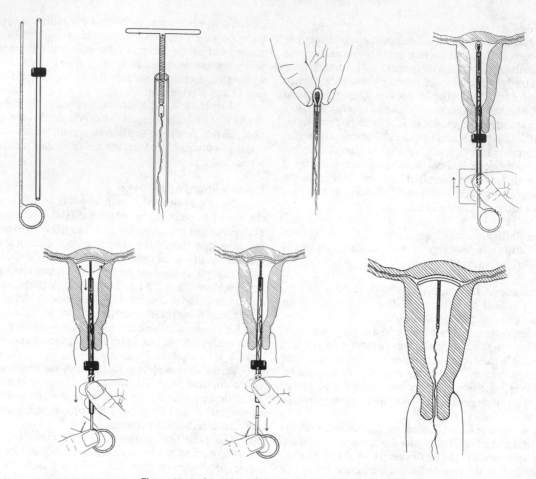

Figure 23–6. Insertion of the Tatum-Zipper Copper T.

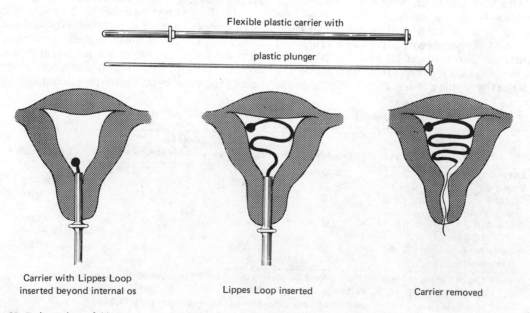

Flexible plastic carrier with

plastic plunger

Carrier with Lippes Loop
inserted beyond internal os

Lippes Loop inserted

Carrier removed

Figure 23–7. Insertion of Lippes Loop. (Reproduced, with permission, from Benson RC: *Handbook of Obstetrics & Gynecology,* 7th ed. Lange, 1980.)

traction does not effect prompt and easy removal, it is probably best to leave the device in place. However, the incidence of spontaneous abortion with a device in situ is approximately 50%, whereas the normal incidence is at least 12%. There is no increased incidence of congenital abnormalities in babies who are conceived with the IUD in utero.

B. Expulsion: Most spontaneous expulsions of IUDs occur in the first few months after their insertion—most frequently during menstruation. The incidence of expulsion varies with the stiffness, size, and shape of the device. In general, the expulsion rate is roughly proportionate to the degree of distortion of the endometrial cavity brought about by the presence of the IUD. The patient should examine herself periodically, and routinely after her menses, to be assured that the tail of the device is still present, ie, that the device is in place. If the tail cannot be felt and the patient is unaware of having expelled the device, she should see her physician. Expulsion may have gone unnoticed, or the plastic filament may have been drawn back into the cervix or endometrial cavity, or the device may have perforated the uterine wall and passed into the peritoneal cavity (< 1:1000 insertions) or the tail may have separated from the device and been expelled unnoticed. The correct explanation can be found by careful inspection or by exploration of the endometrial cavity with a sound or by x-ray. (All IUDs available in the USA are radiopaque because of their metallic components or because they have been impregnated with barium sulfate.)

After an IUD has been expelled, a similar one may be inserted. It often happens that this one will be retained.

C. Bleeding or Pain: Either or both of these problems are common causes for removal of an IUD and discontinuation of this method of contraception. As is the case with expulsions, the incidence of pain or bleeding is more or less proportionate to the degree of endometrial compression and myometrial distention brought about by the IUD. Thus, an IUD that conforms to the natural size and shape of the endometrial cavity is likely to cause less pain or bleeding than one that distorts the cavity and the uterine wall.

D. Extrauterine Pregnancy: Data from 7 recent reports on both nonmedicated and medicated IUDs indicate that there are 97 ectopic pregnancies among 2531 accidental conceptions (3.8%). Several studies have recently suggested that the chances that an accidental pregnancy occurring in an IUD user will be extrauterine in nature increase after the IUD has been used for more than 2 years. These data suggest a causal relationship between duration of use of the IUD and ectopic pregnancy. Certainly, the physician and the IUD user should be aware of the possibility of an extrauterine pregnancy even though the woman is presumably protected by an IUD. Because of these recent data on ectopic pregnancy and the IUD, a history of a previous ectopic pregnancy is a definite contraindication to the use of an IUD.

Even more disturbing is the finding by Tatum and Schmidt that micro-dose progestins, subdermal implants containing progestins, and most methods of female sterilization predispose to ectopic pregnancy if the method fails and unplanned pregnancy occurs.

Contraindications to Use of IUDs
(1) Pregnancy.
(2) Severe cervicitis or acute salpingitis.
(3) Malignant lesions of the genital tract.
(4) History of a recent class III or IV Papanicolaou smear when a definitive diagnosis has not been made and appropriate treatment has not been given.
(5) Uterine bleeding due to unknown cause.
(6) Congenital or acquired distortion of the uterine cavity such that the device cannot be easily inserted and accommodated.
(7) Acute or subacute salpingitis.
(8) Stenosis of the cervical canal.
(9) History of ectopic pregnancy.

Suitable Subjects for an IUD
(1) Any gynecologically normal woman of childbearing age who is not pregnant.
(2) Nulligravidas or nulliparas, provided the device chosen is adequate but small enough to avoid distortion of the uterine cavity.
(3) Postpartum and postabortion patients who do not have pelvic infections.

Indications for Removal of an IUD
(1) Severe uterine cramps or lower abdominal pain.
(2) Excessive and persistent uterine bleeding, either between periods or at the time of menstruation. *Note:* More than a normal amount of bleeding is not unusual during the first 3 or 4 menstrual periods after insertion. The patient should be advised that this may occur and is not a cause for alarm.
(3) Perforation of the uterus and passage of the device to an extrauterine site. The closed devices and those containing copper should be removed. Often this can be done by means of a laparoscopy or colpotomy. A special group of nonmedicated open type of IUDs should be surgically removed when intraperitoneal location has been diagnosed. They are IUDs that bear complex multifilament tails attached to them. This type of tail has wicking properties, and bacteria from the vagina have been shown to ascend these tails between the individual fibers. Intraperitoneal placement of this type of string provides added risk of infection and adhesion formation. The USFDA will in the future approve *only* those IUDs which use monofilament tails. While no IUD using a multifilament tail is currently available commercially in the USA, those which have been used are (1) the Mazjlin Spring, (2) the Dalkon Shield, and (3) the Antigon-F. The first 2

have been taken off the market, and the third has only been used experimentally.

(4) Downward displacement of the device into or partially through the cervical canal. This may reduce the degree of protection against pregnancy and may be associated with cramps and spotting or bleeding. If a portion of the device protrudes into the vagina, it may cause abrasions and lacerations of the penis.

(5) Intrauterine pregnancy. There is no evidence that the presence of an IUD causes any developmental defects in the fetus. However, the patient should be advised that her pregnancy has about a 50% chance of terminating spontaneously with an abortion. She should also be told that a successful outcome of her pregnancy would be enhanced if the IUD could be atraumatically removed early in the pregnancy. She should be advised that occasionally a pregnancy in association with an IUD will be complicated by intrauterine sepsis. There is always a risk of precipitating an abortion by any intrauterine manipulation, eg, the extraction of an IUD (even though removal may seem to be very easy and without trauma).

(6) Salpingitis of bacterial origin. Because IUDs do not prevent microbial invasion through the cervix, pelvic infection occasionally occurs in women wearing IUDs. Antibiotic treatment is usually effective and does not usually require removal of the device. While there is no proof that the presence of an IUD increases the likelihood that the patient will incur microbial endometritis or salpingitis, some recent epidemiologic studies suggest that this may be the case.

Summary

A recent, comprehensive review of intrauterine contraception (Tatum) is cited on p 531. The efficacy of currently available contraceptive methods is indicated in Table 23–3.

In a recent review of IUD safety, Jain (Table 23–4) has compared the relationship between births and deaths associated with pregnancy exposure during 1 year of use. This comparison suggests that the IUD has the best safety record, followed by pills and com-

Table 23–3. Efficacy of various methods of contraception.

Method	Pregnancy Rate Per 100 Woman-Years	One-Year Continuation Rate
Tubal closure	0.04–0.08	99%
Vasectomy	0.15	99%
Oral pills		60–82%
Combined type	0.03–0.1	60–82%
Sequential type	0.2–0.56	60–82%
Intrauterine devices (in situ)	0.8–5.8	50–92%
Lippes Loop D	1.8–2.7	77–80%
Double coil	0.4–2.8	70–88%
Copper 7 (Gravigard)	2.7	65%
Condom	7–28	
Diaphragm with jelly	4–35	
Coitus interruptus	10–38	
Postcoital douche	21–41	
Spermatocides	5–20	
Aerosol foam	N.K.–29	
Foam tablets	12–43	
Suppositories	4–42	
Jelly or cream	4–38	
Breast feeding	24–26	
Rhythm	2.4–38	

bined use of a condom and diaphragm. No other methods can be recommended that are safer and more effective.

MEDICATED INTRAUTERINE CONTRACEPTIVE DEVICES
(Metallic Copper)

The concept of using an IUD as a vehicle or carrier for an active agent evolved from development of the small self-retaining plain plastic T and the demonstration by Zipper and his associates that metallic copper placed in the uterine cavity of the rabbit provided almost perfect contraception. The rationale behind this development was modification or inactivation of the enzymatic environment of the endometrial cavity to prevent nidation. Certain enzyme systems are dependent on and sensitive to biologically active metals such as zinc, copper, silver, and iron. Of all the metals tested, zinc and copper proved to have the greatest influence upon implantation without at the

Table 23–4. Births and deaths associated with pregnancy exposure in 100,000 fertile women during 1 year (induced abortions excluded).*

Method of Contraception	Pregnancies	Births	Deaths		
			Pregnancy	Method	Total
None†	60,000	50,000	12	0	12
Condom and/or diaphragm†	13,000	10,833	2.5	0	2.5
Pills†	100	83	0	3	3
Intrauterine devices†	2190	1825	0.4	0.3	0.7

*Jain AK: Safety and effectiveness of intrauterine devices. *Contraception* 1975;11:243.

†Tietz C: Mortality with contraception and induced abortions. *Stud Fam Plann* 1969;45:6.

same time causing toxic effects such as occurred with cadmium.

Mechanism of Contraceptive Action of Intrauterine Copper

It is not known exactly how copper exerts its contraceptive effect. In most instances it does not prevent fertilization but changes the endometrial environment so that the blastocyst cannot become implanted. The contraceptive action of copper is due to a local effect—perhaps enzyme interference—rather than a systemic one.

Copper has been shown to elicit infiltration of leukocytes into the myometrium, endometrium, and uterine cavity. Leukocytic infiltration of the endometrium is an invariable finding in women wearing the Tatum copper-bearing IUD (TCu).

Safety of Copper IUDs

The increasingly widespread use of the copper IUD has generated much interest in the safety of the method. Although studies in rats have shown that some of the dissolved copper enters the systemic circulation and thus reaches many parts of the body, there is no evidence in humans that the small quantities of copper ($10–50$ $\mu g/24$ h lost from the TCu 200) result in any toxic manifestations. It should be noted that $2000–5000$ μg of copper are judged to be the minimum daily requirements of the adult human.

Pelvic Infection

The data from the Population Council indicate that the incidence of salpingitis in IUD wearers is highest during the 2 weeks following insertion. After 1 month, the incidence steadily diminishes. Until recently, the conclusion was that salpingitis occurring 1 month or more after the IUD was inserted (with the possible exception of the Dalkon Shield with its multifilament tail) is more likely due to venereal contact than to the IUD, but this is no longer accepted. Recent epidemiologic reviews have uniformly suggested that the risk of acute pelvic inflammatory disease is significantly higher in women who use IUDs than in nonusers. The most recent study by Eschenbach and associates also suggests that the relative risk of developing pelvic inflammatory disease in users compared to nonusers is higher in women who have never been pregnant than in women who have been pregnant. A similar pattern of risk has also been found with regard to the incidence of pelvic inflammatory disease and the socioeconomic status of the IUD user. It is likely that sexual mores, number of sexual contacts, and socioeconomic status have a more direct effect upon the incidence of pelvic inflammatory disease occurring during IUD use than does the parity of the wearer. These findings and those of Tatum and coworkers suggesting an increased risk of ectopic pregnancy occurring with longer duration of use of the IUD must be taken into consideration when IUDs are prescribed for women who have never been pregnant. The rate of ectopic pregnancies for women using a Copper

T IUD was found by Sivin to be less than one per 1000 years of use. These data were derived from a study of more than 35,000 women with 38,000 years of use. Based on epidemiologic data, Sivin concludes that the IUD could not have been a major factor contributing to the recent doubling of the rate of ectopic pregnancies in the USA. Venereal disease might contribute to the increased incidence of ectopic pregnancy. As is the case with oral synthetic steroids and all other contraceptive methods, the ultimate decision by the physician and the patient about which method to use must weigh the benefits against the risks. In any event, it is logical to assume that the occurrence of salpingitis and resulting infertility will usually have a more severe psychologic impact upon the never pregnant woman than upon one who has already completed her family. In addition, it should be pointed out that all currently available contraceptive methods are far safer than no contraception at all (a fact all too often overlooked or ignored).

Uterine Perforations

Two types of uterine perforations may be encountered with most types of IUDs: cervical and fundal. Both types are usually asymptomatic but require different removal procedures.

A. Cervical Perforations: Any IUD with a dependent protuberance, such as the Saf-T-Coil, Lippes Loop, Cooper 7, Copper T, Nova T, and the Progesterone T, may impinge upon one of the endocervical rugae as a result of downward displacement or partial expulsion. Repetitive uterine contractions may force this protuberance to penetrate into and occasionally through the cervical tissue and become visible in the vagina. While this perforation is usually clinically silent, the device should be removed by exerting upward pressure through the cervical canal followed by withdrawal after the dependent portion has reentered the cervical canal. The principal reason for removing the device under these circumstances is that it is no longer effective as a contraceptive device. The diameter of the dependent protuberance has little to do with the frequency with which it may perforate the cervix.

B. Fundal Perforations: Perforation of the wall of the fundus by an IUD occurs most frequently when the device is inserted after delivery and before the uterus has involuted completely. During this interval, the entire uterine wall is soft and easily damaged. Occasionally, the patient complains of sudden sharp pain on insertion. More often, there are no unusual symptoms on insertion. It is possible that some perforations begin as deep penetrations and gradually continue their migration through the uterine wall and into the abdominal cavity. Some of the IUDs in total perforations remain extraperitoneal, whereas others go into the peritoneal cavity. In most cases, a device found within the peritoneal cavity was placed there at the time of insertion.

Extrauterine location of an IUD is associated with certain complications: Contraception is no longer effective, and a *closed* device that has entered the

Table 23-5. Two-year comparisons of IUDs.*

Two-Year Rates Per 100 Women	Parous Women						Parous and Nulli-parous women		Inserted After Therapeutic Abortion	
	TCu 380	TCu 200	TCu 220	TCu 200	TCu 220	Lippes Loop D	Nova T	TCu 200	TCu 220	Lippes Loop D
Pregnancy	0.8†	5.4†	2.2†	6.0†	1.2†	3.3†	1.4†	3.6†	2.0†	4.7†
Expulsion	9.2	6.9	6.0	7.1	6.6†	10.0†	6.9	5.4	3.9†	9.3†
Removal for bleeding and pain	22.8	20.1	15.9	15.2	8.8†	12.9†	17.4	15.5	11.2	14.8
Removal for other medical problems	4.7	4.0	6.8	5.4	...	...	6.0	5.8	...	...
Continuation of use	50.5	49.9	58.5	54.6	70.2	66.6	60.2	63.6	71.6†	63.4†

*Figures from *Five Intrauterine Devices for Public Programs.* The Population Council, New York, 1979.
†Statistically significant difference.

peritoneal cavity should be removed as soon as its presence has been determined.

Copper devices such as the Copper T and Copper 7 should be removed from the peritoneal cavity as soon as is medically feasible. Because of the tissue response to the metallic copper, these devices are usually promptly enclosed by the omentum and remain fixed by adhesions.

A nonmedicated *open* IUD, such as the Lippes Loop, is much less apt to evoke tissue reactions and adhesions than a copper device. For this reason, many physicians believe that there is no medical necessity for removing them from the peritoneal cavity.

Copper T Model TCu 200B*

Clinical studies consisting of more than 42,000 insertions of the TCu 200 and more than 350,000 cycles of use have provided the data shown in Table 23-2. While clinical data indicate that there is no reduction in contraceptive effectiveness of the TCu 200 during the first 4 full years of use, the currently approved USFDA recommendation is for replacement by the end of the third year.

New Models of the Copper T IUD

Three newer models of Copper Ts have recently been shown to have better contraceptive effectiveness than the TCu 200B.

A. The Copper T 380A: This Copper T consists of the plastic T with a copper sleeve on each horizontal arm and copper wire wound around the vertical stem. The total copper surface is approximately 380 mm² (Fig 23-4). This is the most effective IUD developed by The Population Council. It has an annual pregnancy rate of less than one per 100 users per year. A 2-year comparison of the TCu 380A and the TCu 200 among parous women is shown in Table 22-5. In Population Council studies, the TCu 380 exhibited a cumulative pregnancy rate of only 1.9 per 100 users at the end of 4 years of use. Approval has not yet been requested from

*Commercially available in more than 30 countries. Approved by FDA November, 1976. Manufactured and distributed in the USA and worldwide by G.D. Searle Co. (Trade name, Tatum T^{TR} [TCu 200B].)

the FDA for this model. It has, however, been approved by the Canadian Regulatory Body and is available from several manufacturers outside the USA. Clinical data indicate that the Copper T 380A is the most effective of the copper-bearing IUDs that so far have been studied extensively.

B. The Copper T 220C: This Copper T consists of a plastic T bearing 7 pure copper collars, one each on the horizontal arms and 5 on the vertical stem (Fig 23-4). The TCu 220C is much more effective than the TCu 200 and the Lippes Loop (see Table 23-5). It is almost as effective as the TCu 380A. The copper sleeves are expected to provide contraceptive action for 20 or more years in utero. A comparison of the TCu 220C and Lippes Loop in parous women over a 2-year interval is shown in Table 23-5.

A recent WHO study indicates that the TCu 220C is more effective than the Lippes Loop when inserted immediately following therapeutic abortion (Table 23-5).

C. The Nova T-200: This modification of the TCu was developed and tested in Scandinavia. It consists of a modified plastic T bearing a coil of silver-core copper wire on the vertical stem (Fig 23-4). A 2-year comparison between the Nova T-200 and the TCu 200 is shown in Table 23-5. The silver-core wire prevents the copper coil from fragmenting segmentally and thus provides an estimated 6-10 years' more service.

Postcoital Contraception With Copper IUDs

Recent studies by Lippes and associates have shown that the TCu 200 and the Copper 7 can be used as effective postcoital methods of contraception. Approximately 300 subjects received one or the other of these 2 IUDs up to 7 days after unprotected coitus. No pregnancies occurred within the first 3 months after the insertions. The side-effects were considered to be minimal compared to those of orally administered estrogens.

Restoration of Fertility After Use of Copper T IUD

The prompt restoration of fertility among Copper T wearers after removal of the device has been established for short-term users (1-3 years). The great majority conceive within the expected interval, and full-term or premature births, stillbirths, spontaneous abortions, induced abortions, and ectopic pregnancies are within normal ranges of incidence.

Management of Accidental Pregnancy While Copper T Is Being Used

Removal of the Copper T early in pregnancy increases the chance that the pregnancy will terminate in a live full-term birth, whereas if the device is left in situ there is a better than 50% chance that the pregnancy will end in a spontaneous abortion, or, if abortion does not occur, a 19% chance that the newborn will be delivered prematurely.

Nonteratogenicity of Copper

In more than 329 pregnancies conceived while a copper IUD was in situ and allowed to progress to live birth, there has been no evidence that the incidence of congenital abnormalities is higher than normal.

Carcinogenicity of Copper IUDs

Repeated Papanicolaou smears in thousands of women using Copper 7 and Copper T IUDs have shown no alteration in the incidence of cervical cytologic abnormalities.

Present information indicates that the contraceptive effect of the Copper 7 does not diminish during the first 3 years of use. It is currently recommended that the device be removed after 3 years of use and replaced by a new one if the patient desires it.

Progestasert

The Progestasert was developed as a slow-release system of progesterone (about 65 μg/d) into the uterine cavity.

The device has the advantage of being effective for a full year. However, recent data have indicated that accidental pregnancies that occur while a Progestasert is in utero are about 6 times more likely to be ectopic than if the IUD had been nonmedicated or a copper-bearing device. It should be noted that the 6-fold increase does not result in an incidence that is higher than the 0.5 ectopic pregnancies per 100 women in 1 year considered to be the average found in unprotected women in the USA. It is anticipated that the Progestasert may be discontinued in the USA as it has been already in the United Kingdom.

THE DALKON SHIELD

Serious medical problems associated with the Dalkon Shield appeared in late 1973 when reports of septic midtrimester spontaneous abortions in women using the shield were recognized. By September of 1974 there had been 11 maternal deaths from sepsis and 209 septic abortions—all in women wearing the Dalkon Shield. The device was withdrawn from the market and will not be reintroduced without some structural modifications.

PELVIC ACTINOMYCOSIS & THE IUD

There have been many reports over the past 10 years that cervicovaginal Papanicolaou smears often are positive for *Actinomyces*. Until recently, the majority of these were found in current IUD wearers. An extensive although incomplete review of the world literature by the author on true pelvic actinomycosis involving the tubes or ovaries (pelvic inflammatory disease, PID) (as proved by histologic identification of *Actinomyces* in surgically removed tissue) identified slightly over 100 cases. Of these, about 40% were in association with multifilamented tailed IUDs (Dalkon Shield, Majzlin spring, and Birnberg bow). Based upon published data suggesting that the occurrence of pelvic actinomycosis was related somewhat directly to long-term use of an IUD, the A.H. Robins Company recommended removal of all Dalkon Shields currently in place and suggested that all IUDs be removed after 3 years of use. This latter recommendation was not supported by the USFDA IUD Advisory Panel.

Although the numbers are quite small, published reviews suggest that positive Papanicolaou smears are less frequently found in conjunction with copper-bearing IUDs than with non–copper-bearing devices.

Recent studies utilizing sophisticated staining techniques have shown that *Actinomyces* can be detected in at least 30% of all women not wearing IUDs. There seems to be agreement that *Actinomyces* is found in larger numbers on Papanicolaou smears taken from women who are using an IUD. In most, there is no clinical suggestion of pelvic disease.

The consensus at this time is that positive Papanicolaou smears should be followed up by repeat smear at least once after about 1 month. If the repeat smear is still positive, then the IUD should be removed. In the asymptomatic woman, antibiotic treatment probably is not indicated. If a repeat Papanicolaou smear taken about 1 month after the IUD has been removed is still positive, however, antibiotic therapy is recommended. Large doses of penicillin are specific for this organism. Once begun, treatment should be continued daily for at least 30 days. Subsequent therapy would depend upon the findings on Papanicolaou smears.

In the woman who has clinical evidence of salpingitis (pelvic inflammatory disease) and a positive Papanicolaou smear for *Actinomyces* (by a routine staining technique), the IUD should be removed promptly, and large doses of penicillin and perhaps broad-spectrum antibiotics should be initiated immediately. If prompt clinical improvement does not occur, definitive surgical therapy should be instituted. Extensive tubo-ovarian abscesses and generalized pelvic inflammatory disease attributable to *Actinomyces* (along with other anaerobes) must be treated by massive antibiotic therapy and by wide surgical extirpation of involved structures.

True pelvic actinomycosis is a relatively rare entity comprising only a small percentage of all types of pelvic inflammatory disease.

II. STERILIZATION

INDICATIONS

Sterilization is a permanent method of contraception available to men or women if reversible methods are undesirable or do not satisfy their requirements. Elective sterilization is rapidly becoming an acceptable means of limiting family size in all parts of the world. Voluntary sterilization is legal in all states in the USA. Close to 1 million sterilization procedures were performed on women in 1980.

SURGICAL STERILIZATION

Surgical Sterilization in Women

Ligation with or without transection or medial segmental resection of the oviducts is an effective contraceptive procedure. Although elective reanastomosis and pregnancy are possible, tubal interruption should be considered permanent. The culdoscope and laparoscope (peritoneoscope) for sectioning or fulguration of a portion of the tubes have made outpatient sterilization possible. By eliminating the need for "open" operation, mortality and morbidity rates as well as costs have been markedly reduced.

The technical aspects of the most widely used sterilization procedures are shown schematically in Figs 23–8 to 23–11.

In Table 23–6, the most common methods of female sterilization as performed by the conventional laparotomy approach are listed in order of relative effectiveness. Table 23–6 also indicates the morbidity rate associated with each method and shows whether the method can be readily accomplished as an outpatient procedure.

In Table 23–7 are listed those sterilization procedures that can be effectively performed via the minilaparotomy approach.

Table 23–8 indicates some pertinent data relevant to laparoscopic tubal occlusion.

Practical Aspects of Tubal Sterilization

As the demand throughout the world for tubal sterilization accelerates, the associated costs and medical feasibility assume major importance. The most important considerations are the safety and effectiveness of the method, the equipment and its cost, including the necessary training in its use, the types of complications that may occur and their management, and whether the procedure can be done in an outpatient facility. Perhaps the least important factor to be considered is the potential for restoration of fertility.

Summary of Practical Aspects of Sterilization

A. Transabdominal Route: This is the safest, most effective, and most practical method.

Table 23–6. Transabdominal ligation or transection and ligation.*

Method	Failure Rate (Range)	Morbidity Rate (Incidence)	Procedure Accomplished	
			Hospital	Outpatient
Uchida (Fig 22–8)	Nil	Low	+	+
Pomeroy (Fig 22–10)	0–0.4	Low	+	+
Madlener (Same as Pomeroy *except* no tubal resection)	0.3–2	Low	+	+
Fimbriectomy (Fig 22–11)	Nil	Low	+	+
Irving (Fig 22–9)	Nil	Low	+	+
Salpingectomy	0–1.9	Moderate	+	–
Cornual resection	2.8–3.2	Moderate	+	–
Simple ligation	20	Low	+	+

*Modified and reproduced, with permission, from Department of Medical and Public Affairs, George Washington University Medical Center: *Popul Rep,* Series C, No. 7, May 1976.

Table 23–7. Tubal occlusion by minilaparotomy.*

Method	Failure Rate (Range)	Morbidity Rate (Incidence)	Procedure Accomplished	
			Hospital	Outpatient
Uchida	Nil	Low	+	+
Fimbriectomy	Nil	Low	+	+
Irving	Nil	Low	+	+
Pomeroy	0–0.4	Low	+	+
Salpingectomy	0–1.9	Low	+	+
Madlener	0.3–2	Low	+	+
Simple ligation	20	Low	+	+

*Modified and reproduced, with permission, from Department of Medical and Public Affairs, George Washington University Medical Center: *Popul Rep,* Series C, No. 7, May 1976.

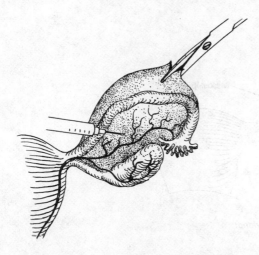

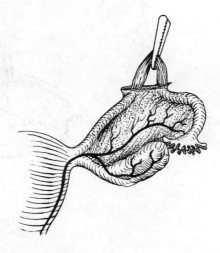

Saline with epinephrine injected below serosa, which becomes inflated locally. Muscular tube, and even blood vessels, can be separated from serosa, which is then cut open.

Muscular tube emerges through opening or is pulled out to form a U shape.

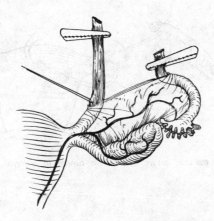

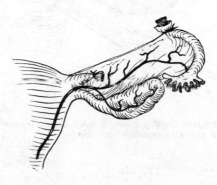

Fimbriated end is untouched, while the end leading to the uterus is stripped of serosa. This can usually be done without damaging blood vessels.

About 5 cm of muscular tube is cut away; the end is buried automatically in serosa. Fimbriated end and serosa opening are closed and tied together.

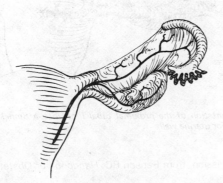

Blood supply continues normally between ovary and uterus. Hydrosalpinx or adhesion has not been noticed.

Figure 23–8. Uchida method of sterilization. (Reproduced, with permission, from Benson RC: *Handbook of Obstetrics & Gynecology,* 7th ed. Lange, 1980.)

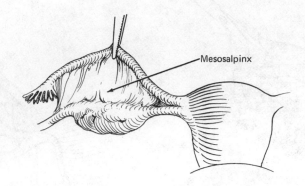

Lift and cut oviduct.

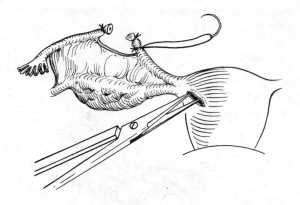

Double ligation with gut; one tie is left long for traction (special traction suture); mesosalpinx stripped back.

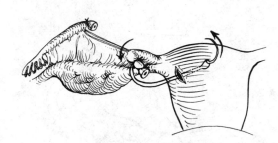

Special traction suture inserted in tunnel in anterior uterine wall.

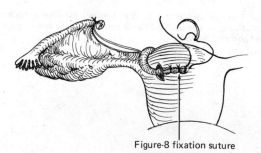

Traction suture tied and proximal tube sutured in tunnel.

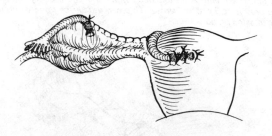

Implantation of the proximal tubal limb into a tunnel in the anterior uterine wall.

Figure 23–9. Irving method of sterilization. (Reproduced, with permission, from Benson RC: *Handbook of Obstetrics & Gynecology,* 7th ed. Lange, 1980.)

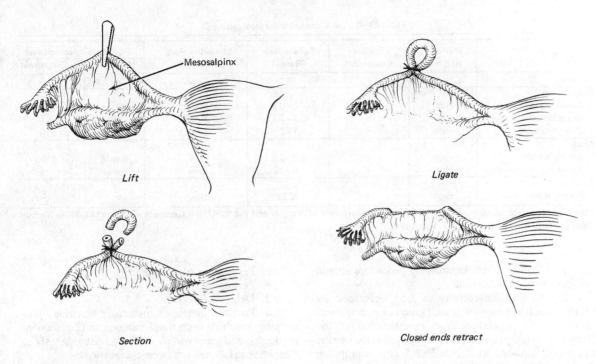

Mesosalpinx

Lift

Ligate

Section

Closed ends retract

Figure 23–10. Pomeroy method of sterilization. (Reproduced, with permission, from Benson RC: *Handbook of Obstetrics & Gynecology,* 7th ed. Lange, 1980.)

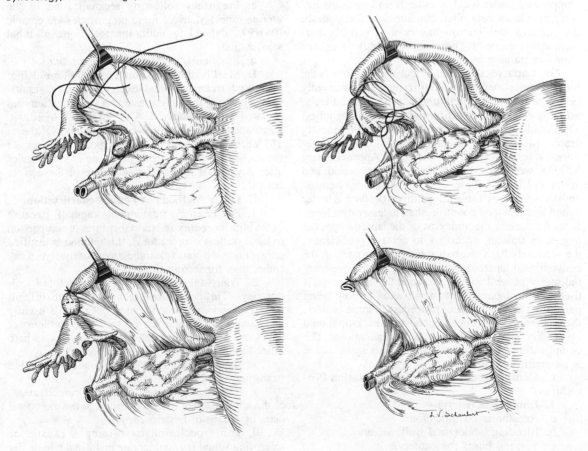

Figure 23–11. Sterilization by fimbriectomy.

Table 23—8. Tubal occlusion by laparoscopy.*

	Skill Required	Special Equipment	Failure Rate (Range)	Morbidity Rate (Incidence)	Procedure Accomplished	
					Hospital	Outpatient
Pomeroy	High	+	?	Low	+	+
Fulguration						
Coagulate and excise	High	+	0—0.6	Moderate	+	+
Coagulate and divide	High	+	0.1—2	High	+	+
Coagulate only	High	+	1—2	Low	+	+
Clips						
Spring-loaded	High	+	0.2—0.6	Low	+	+
Tantalum Hemoclips	High	+	5—18	Low	+	+
Bands						
Falope Ring	High	+	0.23	Low	+	+

*Modified and reproduced, with permission, from Department of Medical and Public Affairs, George Washington University Medical Center: *Popul Rep,* Series C, No. 7, May 1976.

1. A conventional laparotomy procedure should be performed in a hospital.

2. The minilaparotomy as first described by Osathanondh in Bangkok is well suited to an outpatient facility. The procedure is a modification of the Pomeroy technique with the innovation that the uterine fundus is directed to a small (2.5 cm) suprapubic incision by means of an intravaginal uterine manipulator (elevator). The entire procedure is readily accomplished under local anesthesia and in outpatient settings. Under controlled conditions in Bangladesh, the minilap sterilization has been effectively performed by paramedical personnel after only 6 weeks of intensive training by physicians.

B. Laparoscopy: In the USA, laparoscopy is the most popular method of sterilization. It is currently performed in a hospital under general anesthesia, utilizing electrocauterization and division of the tubes. The double entry technique is the one most frequently employed. In 1975, an estimated 547,000 sterilizations were performed in hospitals. Approximately 330,000 were done during the postpartum period, and about 217,000 of these were performed by laparoscopy. As noted in Table 22–8, this procedure is better suited to developed countries than to lesser developed areas because of the high cost of the laparoscope, the degree of training necessary to achieve proficiency, the relatively high morbidity rate as compared to the conventional laparotomy approach, and the preferential use of general anesthesia when the laparoscope is used. While laparoscopic sterilization is now being performed as an outpatient procedure in some centers, there is general agreement that hospital back-up should be readily available in case of complications. The complication most frequently requiring hospitalization is intraperitoneal bleeding.

C. Complications of Female Sterilization Procedures:

1. Immediate (early)–

a. Anesthesia complications.

b. Bleeding (abdominal wall, viscera).

c. Visceral burns (by cautery).

d. Abdominal wall burns.

e. Perforation of viscera.

f. Peritonitis.

2. Delayed (late)–

a. Possible increased menstrual bleeding, presumably resulting from tissue damage and consequent reduced blood supply to ovaries. The pathogenesis of "menorrhagia" has not been established.

b. Vague lower abdominal pain, possibly related to adhesions.

c. Pregnancy following recanalization of the uterine tubes. Many of these pregnancies are ectopic (0–65%, depending upon the technique of tubal sterilization).

d. Emotional, psychosomatic aberrations.

D. Sterilization by Yoon Tubal (Falope) Ring: Improved techniques and experience have significantly reduced the failure rate and complications associated with this method. A recent review of 10,086 cases showed 251 surgical complications. Of these, 183 were related to the technical aspects of the ring or the applicator. There were 32 pregnancies in this series after 2 years of follow-up, and none of these were ectopic.

E. Other Methods of Female Sterilization:

1. Hysterectomy (abdominal, vaginal)–Because of the high morbidity and mortality rates in comparison to tubal occlusion procedures, this method is justified *only* if there are bona fide indications for hysterectomy (other than for sterilization).

2. Transvaginal tubal ligation (culdotomy, culdoscopy)–This procedure is technically more difficult than transabdominal sterilization but there is usually less discomfort if there are no technical problems or adhesions. It is best done in a hospital, or at least where immediate hospitalization is available.

3. Experimental methods of female sterilization (transuterine tubal occlusion)–

a. Electrocoagulation, chemical cauterization, or the application of tissue adhesives to the uterotubal ostia by means of hysteroscopy.

b. Tubal occlusion by forcing a caustic or sclerosing liquid (eg, quinacrine or formaldehyde derivatives) into the proximal portion of the tube by "blind" introduction of the material into the endometrial cavity often fails. The potential complications are central nervous system excitation and tissue reactions from intra-abdominal spillage.

c. Tubal clips and rings (Table 23–8) to occlude the oviducts are being evaluated for sterilization. Tubal obstruction results from tissue strangulation, but recanalization may occur. Moreover, if pregnancy does occur, the chances are strong that it will be ectopic. Reversibility is a theoretic advantage.

F. Timing of Female Sterilization: All of the conventional sterilization procedures may be performed during the immediate puerperium, concomitantly with an induced abortion, or electively during any phase of the menstrual cycle. In general, the morbidity and the failure rates are slightly lower when the sterilization is performed as an interval procedure. However, there are obvious motivational, logistic, and practical advantages to providing sterilization services at the same time as delivery or abortion.

Male Sterilization

Partial vasectomy is the most effective means of providing reliable and permanent sterility in the male. It is estimated that about 1 million men each year since 1976 have been sterilized by this procedure in the USA alone.

The procedure (see Fig 23–12) is usually done under local anesthesia and consists of isolating the vas deferens through a small incision in the upper outer aspect of the scrotum. Next, sutures or clips are placed tightly around the vas, demarcating a 1- to 1.5-cm segment which is then excised. Finally, the ligated and fulgurated ends are tucked back into the scrotal sac. The short incision in the sac is then closed, usually with a single suture. Microscopic examination of excised segments will verify that vasal tissue was removed. An identical procedure is then performed on the other side. In order to minimize the possibility of recanalization, the cut ends may be looped and sutured in opposite directions.

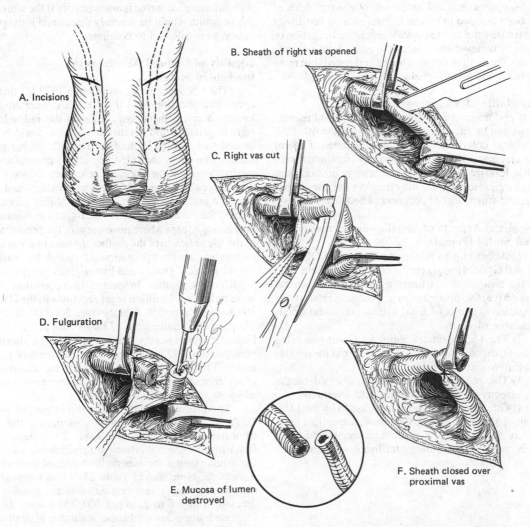

A. Incisions

B. Sheath of right vas opened

C. Right vas cut

D. Fulguration

E. Mucosa of lumen destroyed

F. Sheath closed over proximal vas

Figure 23–12. Steps in vasectomy. (Modified from a drawing by S Taft. Reproduced, with permission, from Schmidt S: Vasectomy should not fail. *Contemp Surg* 1974;4:13.)

The failure rate with this or a comparable technique is estimated to be less than 2 per 1000 males. Sterility cannot be assumed until ejaculates are found to be completely free of sperm. As long as 6 weeks (or about 15 ejaculations) may be required before all residual sperm in the distal portion of the vas have disappeared. Intercourse during the 6-week interval between surgery and the laboratory test is desirable to remove all residual sperm.

Complications following vasectomy are infrequent and usually not serious. The most frequent are bleeding (external; less frequently internal), infection (usually localized to the skin incision), suture reaction, and anesthetic reaction (rare; due to idiosyncrasy).

The only reported deaths from vasectomy have been due to tetanus in areas where routine tetanus immunization is not done. In these areas, prophylactic tetanus immunizations should precede vasectomy.

Intra-Vas Occlusive Devices for Male Sterilization

Many mechanical intra-vas occlusive devices have been devised to enhance restoration of fertility at some future time and to provide repetitive occlusion or patency whenever the man desires it. Some "do it yourself" valvelike devices have been tested, but none have been adequately evaluated.

Reversibility of Vasectomy

If restoration of fertility is desired, vasal reanastomosis can be successfully accomplished in 40–90% of cases, as determined by the reappearance of sperm in the ejaculate. However, pregnancy (functional success) is less frequent (18–60%) after reanastomosis. Microsurgical techniques may improve the rate of anatomic and functional restoration of fertility.

Medicolegal Aspects of Sterilization in the United States (Female)

(1) According to American College of Obstetricians and Gynecologists recommendations, there is no need for a hospital sterilization committee to review and approve (or disapprove) a patient's request for sterilization if she is of legal age and of sound mind, irrespective of parity.

(2) The United States Supreme Court has ruled that the husband's signature is not required for regulation of a woman's fertility.

(3) The patient must be fully informed of the risks, effectiveness, reversibility, and alternatives.

(4) Guidelines have been established by the FDA Bureau of Medical Devices that assure a specified level of safety and efficiency of the endoscopes and other devices used in performing sterilization procedures.

III. INDUCED ABORTION

Induced abortion is the deliberate termination of pregnancy in a manner which assures that the embryo or fetus will not survive. Attitudes of society toward elective abortion have undergone marked changes in the last few decades. In some situations the need for abortion is accepted by most people, but political and medical attitudes regarding induced abortion have continued to lag behind changing philosophies. Some religious concepts remain unchanged, resulting in personal, medical, and political conflicts.

About a third of the world's population live in nations that have nonrestrictive laws governing abortion. Another third live in countries having moderately restrictive abortion laws, ie, where unwanted pregnancies may not be terminated as a matter of right or personal decision but only on broadly interpreted medical, psychologic, and sociologic indications. The remainder live in countries where abortion is illegal without qualification or is allowed only if the woman's life or health would be severely threatened if the pregnancy were allowed to continue.

Legality of Induced Abortions in the United States

The US Supreme Court ruled in 1973 (1) that the restrictive abortion laws in the USA were invalid, largely because these laws invaded the individual's right to privacy; and (2) that an abortion could not be denied to a woman in the first 3 months of her pregnancy. The Court indicated that after 3 months a state might "regulate the abortion procedure in ways that are reasonably related to maternal health" and that after the fetus reaches the stage of viability (about 24 weeks) the states might refuse the right to terminate the pregnancy except where necessary for the preservation of the life or health of the mother. In spite of these clear mandates, much opposition is raised by various "right-to-life" groups and by religious groups, notably Roman Catholics. In spite of this opposition, there were more than 1 million legal abortions in the USA in 1975—in contrast to slightly over 500,000 in 1973. Thus, in 1975 there were 273 abortions per 1000 live births. It is noteworthy that one-third of the abortions performed in 1975 were on women 19 years of age or under. This emphasizes dramatically the inadequacy of sex education and the need for greater availability of adequate contraceptive methods.

The procedures currently being employed in the USA for legally induced abortions during the first trimester are relatively safe. Table 23–9 shows that first trimester legal abortions are consistently safer for the woman than if she used no birth control method and gave birth. Note also in Table 23–9 that whereas the maternal mortality rate related to births steadily increased from 5.6 to 22.6 per 100,000 women as age increased, age-related increase in number of deaths per 100,000 women per year from legal abortions was insignificant.

Table 23—9. Pregnancy-related deaths per 100,000 women per year in developed countries compared to deaths resulting from legal abortion as a means of contraception.*

Type of Birth Control	Age Groups (Years)					
	15—19	20—24	25—29	30—34	35—39	40—44
No birth control; birth related	5.6	6.1	7.4	13.9	20.8	22.6
First trimester abortion only; method related	1.2	1.6	1.8	1.7	1.9	1.2

*Adapted from Tietze C: Induced abortion: 1977 supplement (Table 11). *Rep Popul Fam Plann* 14[2nd ed. Suppl]:16, Dec 1977.

In general, the risk of death from legal abortion is lowest when performed at 8 menstrual weeks or sooner. Table 23–10 shows the relationship between the mortality rate due to legal abortion and the gestational age at the time of the procedure.

Paracervical anesthesia has replaced general anesthesia in many areas, resulting in fewer complications relevant to anesthesia. Midtrimester abortion techniques are still unsatisfactory and associated with a high mortality rate. Hysterectomy carries a far greater risk than induction of labor by amnio-infusion.

Indications

Indications for induced abortion may be categorized as maternal, paternal, fetal, social, etc. Some of the more common indications for induced abortion may be outlined as follows:

A. Obstetric: Prior major uterine injury or damage (cesarean section, myomectomy, uterine rupture, or extensive perforation), multiparity (generally considered to be more than 2 deliveries), recurrent preeclampsia-eclampsia with its multiple hazards, severe isoimmunization, older age (increased maternal risk beyond age 35).

B. Surgical: Any condition that may compromise a good previous surgical result, eg, successful closure of a vesicovaginal fistula, correction of uterine prolapse, urinary diversion procedure, kidney transplant.

C. Orthopedic: Osteogenesis imperfecta, severe kyphoscoliosis.

Table 23—10. Death-to-case rate for legal abortions by weeks of gestation (USA, 1972—1975).*

Weeks of Gestation	Deaths per 100,000 Procedures
8 weeks or less	0.7
9–10	1.9
11–12	4.1
13–15	7.5
16–20	19.6
21 weeks or more	22.9

*Adapted from Tyler CW Jr: Abortion Surveillance, 1975. Center for Disease Control, United States Department of Health, Education, and Welfare Annual Summary 1975, April 1977. [Page 36.]

D. Hematologic: Thromboembolic disorders, hemoglobinopathies, gammaglobulinopathies, clotting defects.

E. Cardiovascular: Eisenmenger's complex, tetralogy of Fallot, recurrent cardiac failure or myocarditis, systemic or pulmonary hypertension, aneurysm.

F. Pulmonary: Tuberculosis, emphysema, recurrent spontaneous pneumothorax, cystic fibrosis.

G. Urologic: Single or pelvic kidneys, chronic renal disease, neurogenic bladder.

H. Ophthalmologic: Progressive toxic goiter and retrobulbar neuritis.

I. Endocrine: Severe diabetes mellitus, pheochromocytoma, and adrenal or parathyroid hyperfunction or deficiency.

J. Gastrointestinal: Cholestatic jaundice of pregnancy, ulcerative colitis, mesenteric thrombosis.

K. Immunologic: Hypoimmune diseases, rheumatoid arthritis, systemic lupus erythematosus, polyarteritis nodosa.

L. Neurologic: Serious central nervous system diseases, grand mal epilepsy, multiple sclerosis, muscular dystrophy.

M. Congenital: Marfan's syndrome, exstrophy of bladder, Down's syndrome. Most commonly, genetic problems are associated with a fetal indication which must be evaluated carefully so that the degree of risk can be properly explained to the prospective parents. Clinics for genetic counseling are now offering expert advice about specific hereditary or familial problems. With a proper survey, the chance of the disease occurring in the offspring can be accurately assessed. Genetic indications for therapeutic abortion may include x-ray or chemical damage to the gonads, heritable metabolic diseases, chromosomal aberrations, connective tissue disorders, maternal exposure to agents harmful to the fetus, maternal disease states resulting in fetal deformity or defect, among many others. Studies on amniotic fluid or its cellular contents may reveal many genetic disorders of the fetus as early as 10–12 weeks. Rejection of one abnormal fetus may be followed by normal, acceptable offspring. On the other hand, couples fearful of a hereditary anomaly may be reassured by normal findings early in pregnancy.

N. Oncologic: Melanocarcinoma, Hodgkin's disease, leukemia.

O. Chronic infections: Systemic mycoses, persistent malaria, teriary syphilis, brucellosis.

P. Psychiatric: Intractable schizophrenia and recurrent manic-depressive psychosis. The medical profession now generally accepts the fact that a woman's mental health is as important as her physical well-being and that the preservation of her emotional health may be an adequate indication for therapeutic abortion.

Q. Paternal: Usually in part social reasons, but see also ¶M, Congenital, above.

R. Social: Mental retardation in the mother, demonstrated inability to care for children, poverty, excessive family size, rape, incest. Most of these indications are closely related to the preservation of the woman's mental health. Nonetheless, there is a growing belief that the decision to carry or not to carry a pregnancy is a basic right of every woman. Under this concept, abortion on request becomes reasonable—much like elective cosmetic surgery.

METHODS

Numerous methods are used to induce an abortion: suction or surgical curettage; induction of labor by means of intra- or extraovular injection of a hypertonic solution or other oxytocic agent; extraovular placement of devices such as catheters, bougies, or bags; hysterectomy, abdominal or vaginal; hysterotomy, abdominal or vaginal; and menstrual induction.

The method of abortion used is determined primarily by the duration of pregnancy, with due consideration for the patient's health, the experience of the physician, and the available physical facilities.

Suction Curettage

Suction curettage is the most efficient method used to terminate pregnancies of 12 weeks' duration or less. This technique has gained rapid worldwide acceptance, and about 75% of therapeutic abortions are now performed by this method in the USA. The procedure involves dilatation of the cervix by instruments or by hydrophilic laminaria tent (see below), followed by the insertion of a suction cannula of the appropriate diameter into the uterine cavity (Fig 23–13). Standard negative pressures utilized are in the range of 30–50 cm Hg (Table 23–11). Many physicians follow aspiration with light instrumental curettage of the uterine cavity, although this generally is unnecessary and may be harmful if performed too vigorously, eg, uterine synechiae may form (Asherman's syndrome) or a subsequent placenta accreta may develop.

The advantages of suction over surgical curettage are that the former empties the uterus more rapidly, minimizes blood loss, and reduces the likelihood of perforation of the uterus. However, rapid and excessive blood loss can occur if the snug cannula remains over the placental site too long. In addition, failure to recognize perforation of the uterus with a cannula may result in serious damage to other organs. Knowledge of the size and position of the uterus and the volume of the contents is mandatory for safe suction curettage. Moreover, extreme care and slow minimal dilatation

Table 23–11. Suction curettage: Factors related to duration of gestation.

Weeks of Gestation (From LMP)	Dilatation of Cervix (mm)	Size of Suction Curette (mm)	Vacuum (cm Hg)	Expected Blood Loss (mL)
1–4	4–5	4	30–40	10
5–8	8–9	8	30–40	10–30
9–10	10–11	10	40–50	30–80
11–12	12–13	12	40–50	80–200
13–14	14–15	14	50+	200–400

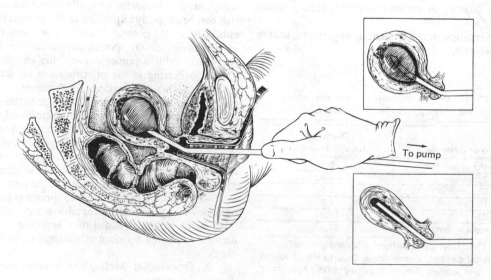

To pump

Figure 23–13. Suction method for therapeutic abortion.

of the cervix, with special consideration for the integrity of the internal os, should avoid injury to the cervix or uterus. Attention to the decrease in uterine size that occurs with rapid evacuation will help to avoid uterine injury. When performed in early pregnancy by properly trained physicians, suction curettage should be associated with a very low failure rate; the complication rate should be under 2% for infection, about 2% for excessive bleeding, and under 1% for uterine perforation. The mortality rate for suction curettage is less than 2 per 100,000 patients.

Surgical Curettage

Surgical ("sharp") curettage must be used for first trimester abortion in the absence of suction curettage equipment. This procedure is performed as a standard D&C, such as for the diagnosis of abnormal uterine bleeding or for the removal of endometrial polyps. The blood loss, duration of surgery, and likelihood of damage to the cervix or uterus are greatly increased when surgical curettage is used. At least 5% of abortions in the USA are still performed by sharp curettage.

Induction of Labor by Intra-amniotic Instillation of an Oxytocic Agent

The Japanese developed this technique for therapeutic abortion after the first trimester. The original procedure was to perform amniocentesis, aspirate as much fluid as possible, and then instill into the amniotic sac 200 mL of hypertonic (20%) saline solution. In the majority (80–90%) of cases, spontaneous labor and expulsion of the fetus and placenta would occur within 48 hours. Modifications of this technique have developed, primarily as a result of the realization that the amniotic sac need not be emptied completely—and that indeed it may be dangerous to do so—and as a result of the development of other agents that, instilled intra-amniotically, will initiate labor. Urea is used by some clinicians, but today the most commonly used agent is one of the **prostaglandins.** A prostaglandin vaginal suppository inserted at the time of expected menstruation has been reported to bring on the "menstrual period" whether the woman was pregnant or not.

It is advantageous to soften the "unripe" cervix with a laminaria tent placed in the cervix a few hours before amniocentesis is performed.

Midtrimester therapeutic abortion by this method must be done with scrupulous aseptic surgical technique, and the patient must be monitored until the fetus and placenta are delivered and postabortion bleeding is under control. The complication rate is high—up to 20% in some institutions—and the mortality rate is comparable to that of term parturition. Fortunately, because first trimester abortion is now more readily available, more women are consulting their physicians early and thus availing themselves of the much safer suction curettage.

Complications of midtrimester amniocentesis abortion can be serious. Common complications are sepsis, usually because of faulty technique; retained placenta, necessitating forceps removal or curettage and often causing hemorrhage; hemorrhage due to uterine inertia; hypernatremia, if hypertonic saline is used and is intravasated or absorbed too rapidly; and cervical laceration resulting from tumultuous labor in a patient with an "unripe" cervix.

Failure of labor to expel the products of conception necessitates either a repetition of the procedure if the membranes are still intact or oxytocin stimulation, usually by intravenous injection. If the latter procedure is chosen, it is important to limit fluid intake to 3000 mL or less per 24 hours to avoid water intoxication.

Emotional stress is an important factor for many women, since they are awake at the time of the expulsion of the fetus and the fetus is well-formed. The emotional stress is also a factor for hospital personnel—a problem impossible to avoid. Many physicians order scopolamine for the patient, to be given when delivery is imminent, to induce amnesia.

Induction of Labor With Oxytocic Agents

The use of oxytocin without an intrauterine agent invites a high failure rate, protracted delay before abortion occurs, or a liveborn fetus. It is not recommended.

Bags, Bougies, & Catheters

These methods have the disadvantages of potential trauma, infection, unpredictability, and a liveborn fetus. They are rarely used.

Hysterotomy

Abdominal or vaginal hysterotomy is a relatively simple operation. Even so, these procedures have the disadvantage of allowing delivery of a live fetus if the pregnancy is advanced. Moreover, the operation may compromise future childbearing, especially if cervical incompetence supervenes. About 1% of abortions in the USA are performed by hysterotomy.

Hysterotomy is associated with considerably higher morbidity and mortality rates than other methods of midpregnancy abortion, but it has the advantage of enabling concomitant sterilization or the treatment of preexisting pelvic disease.

Hysterectomy

Abdominal hysterectomy is feasible at or before 24 weeks of gestation without first emptying the uterus. Approximately 1% of all abortions in the USA are performed in this fashion, generally for patients who have large myomas or when sterilization is warranted.

Vaginal hysterectomy can be performed at or before 12 weeks of pregnancy without uterine evacuation—and even later if the uterus is emptied first. This technique should be used only by a physician skilled in vaginal surgery. The morbidity and mortality rates are higher than when other methods of midpregnancy abortion are used.

Menstrual Regulation

Menstrual regulation consists of aspiration of the endometrium within 14 days after a missed menstrual cycle or within 42 days after the beginning of the last menstrual period by means of a small cannula attached to a source of low-pressure suction. A syringe or other suction machine will suffice. This is a simple and safe procedure that can be readily performed in the office or outpatient clinic, usually without any anesthetic, though paracervical block can be used if necessary.

Menstrual regulation has been used extensively since 1970 and has proved to be an uncomplicated, safe, and effective method of inducing uterine bleeding that may have been delayed for one reason or another. Complications following the procedure are summarized in Tables 23–12 and 23–13.

The procedure is usually performed without a positive pregnancy test. Subsequent analyses have shown that approximately 41–73% (average, 60%) of women on whom vacuum extraction has been performed were pregnant at the time, whereas the remainder were not pregnant and therefore had an "unnecessary" procedure performed. There is general agreement among physicians who perform this procedure that the benefits far outweigh the risks.

Midtrimester Abortions

Induction of labor is the procedure of choice to

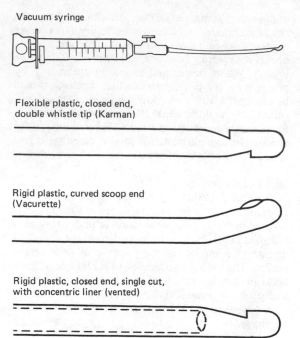

Figure 23–14. Vacuum syringe and cannulas used to perform menstrual regulation. Source: The Pathfinder Fund.

Table 23–12. Immediate complications in 12,888 women who had menstrual regulation by the vacuum aspiration technique.*

Complications	Number of Cases	Percent
Uterine perforation		
Definite	3	0.02
Suspected	1	0.01
Cervical laceration	7	0.06
Blood loss (≥ 100 mL)	51	0.40
Shock	25	0.19
Fever 38 °C (100.4 F) within 24 h	19	0.15
Pelvic infection	1	0.01
Apnea	2	0.01
Total	109	0.85

*Adapted from Laufe LE: Menstrual regulation: The method and the issues. *Stud Fam Plann* (Oct) 1977;**8**:249.

Table 23–13. Delayed complications 2–4 weeks following menstrual regulation by vacuum aspiration in 11,309 women.*

Complications	Number of Cases	Percent
Failed procedure (pregnancy test positive at follow-up visit)	111	0.98
Fever requiring antibiotics	95	0.84
Pelvic infection	90	0.80
Bleeding requiring curettage	101	0.89
Undiagnosed ectopic pregnancy	2	0.02
Total	399	3.53

*Adapted from Laufe LE: Menstrual regulation: The method and the issues. *Stud Fam Plann* (Oct) 1977;**8**:249.

terminate a pregnancy that has proceeded to 12–24 weeks. Most inductions before 1975 were accomplished by the introduction of hypertonic saline into the amniotic sac after removal of a small volume of amniotic fluid. Uterine contractions begin soon after the injection, and the labor usually continues to complete delivery of a nonviable embryo or fetus and the placenta. However, severe complications have developed with amniocentesis and hypertonic saline injection: (1) disseminated intravascular clotting; (2) hypernatremia; (3) vascular hypervolemia and heart failure; (4) myometrial necrosis if the hypertonic saline extravasates into the uterine musculature; (5) incomplete expulsion of *all* products of conception, which usually leads to uterine bleeding and requires surgical completion of the abortion; and (6) occasionally, expulsion of a live fetus.

Because of the potential toxicity of hypertonic saline, **hyperosmotic urea** (30–40%) in 5% dextrose solution is being used with considerable success. The latter procedure coupled with a slow intravenous drip of oxytocin is preferred by many at present.

Prostaglandins as Abortifacients

Prostaglandins F_2 and $F_{2\alpha}$ have been used orally, parenterally, by intra-amniotic injection, by extraovular injection, and as vaginal suppositories, alone or in combination with a laminaria tent. Intravenous oxytocin may be given if active labor is not evoked within 12 hours.

Common side-effects are severe nausea and vomiting, diarrhea, tachycardia, and substernal "pressure" and paralytic ileus.

Dilatation & Evacuation

Dilatation and evacuation during the late first trimester and early second trimester, before amniocentesis with saline or urea or prostaglandins becomes necessary, is being successfully used for abortion. Insertion of a laminaria followed in 6–8 hours by graded cervical dilatation and then a blunt curet and evacuation of tissue with forceps provides efficient and acceptably safe termination of pregnancy. The mortality rate associated with this method is reported to be lower than with saline amniocentesis.

ANESTHESIA FOR INDUCED ABORTION

Anesthesia for early transvaginal abortion can be either paracervical block or general anesthesia. Some patients are uncooperative or tense under local anesthesia, in which case the addition of parenteral sedative drugs such as alphaprodine, meperidine, diazepam, or fentanyl and droperidol (Innovar) may be useful. When general anesthesia is used, the agent should be the choice of the anesthesiologist. One advantage of general anesthesia is that the patient who is asleep is not aware of the procedure—a definite advantage for some women. Since the duration of anesthesia is short, the recovery time is rapid and smooth.

EVALUATION OF THE PATIENT REQUESTING INDUCED ABORTION

Patients give varied reasons for requesting abortion. Since in some cases the request is made at the urging of the woman's parents or in-laws, husband, or peers, every effort should be made to ascertain that the patient herself desires abortion for her own reasons. In addition, one should be certain that she knows she is free to choose among other methods of solving the problem of unplanned pregnancy, eg, adoption or single parent rearing. Help from social agencies should be made available as necessary. A complete social history, medical history, and physical examination are required. Particular attention must be given to uterine size and position; the importance of accurate calculation of the duration of pregnancy (within 2 weeks but preferably within 1 week) cannot be overstated. Routine laboratory tests should include pregnancy tests, urinalysis, hematocrit, Rh typing, serologic tests for syphilis, culture for gonorrhea, and Papanicolaou smear.

FOLLOW–UP OF PATIENTS AFTER INDUCED ABORTION

After abortion by uterine evacuation methods, human Rh_0 (D) immune globulin (RhoGAM) should be administered promptly if the patient is Rh-negative unless it is known that the male partner was Rh-negative or that the patient does not wish future pregnancies. The patient should take her temperature several times daily and report fever or unusual bleeding at once. She should avoid intercourse or the use of tampons or douches for at least 1 week. The physician should discuss with the patient the possibility that emotional depression, similar to that following term pregnancy and delivery, may occur after induced abortion. Follow-up care should include pelvic examination to rule out endo- and parametritis, salpingitis, failure of involution, or continued uterine growth. Finally, effective contraception should be made available according to the patient's needs and desires.

SEQUELAE OF INDUCED ABORTION

The Centers for Disease Control in Atlanta reported a mortality rate of 3.1 per 100,000 in the USA in 1974 for legal abortions, the rate being lowest in early abortions and higher as the duration of pregnancy increases.

Although some reports suggest that decreased fertility may occur following repeated therapeutic or elective induced abortions, the data are not convincing. Proposed causes include ascending pelvic infections, cervical or fundal damage, changes in coital frequency, and number of coital partners.

Legalization of the procedures has dramatically reduced the frequency and severity of medical and surgical problems as sequelae to early and midtrimester abortions. The reported incidence of debilitating remorse or regrets following an induced abortion has been less than 5%.

LEGAL ASPECTS OF THERAPEUTIC ABORTION

The patient must be informed regarding the nature of the procedure and its risks, including possible infertility or even continuation of pregnancy. The rights of the spouse, parents, or guardian must also be considered and permission obtained when indicated (until the individual woman's rights are clearly established).

State laws must be obeyed with special reference to residence, duration of pregnancy, indications for abortion, consent, and consultations required.

Therapeutic abortion committees have proved to be of little value. They often contribute to delay, additional cost, and harassment of the patient and can be blamed in part for the persistence of illegal abortion in some areas. In addition, birth of a malformed child or maternal sickness or death after a committee has denied abortion poses difficult questions of liability.

The United States Supreme Court's 1973 decisions on elective abortion clearly make this a matter between the physician and the patient until the stage of fetal viability (third trimester). State governments may now regulate abortion only in such a way as to protect the public health—similar to the regulation of other medical and surgical procedures.

RELIGIOUS ASPECTS
OF THERAPEUTIC ABORTION

The official Roman Catholic view is that therapeutic abortion is completely immoral and is absolutely proscribed; abortion is permitted only if incidental to saving the life of the mother, eg, removal of a cancerous organ. The official Jewish position depends on interpretation of rabbinical law, but it seems to be generally accepted by Jews that abortion may be performed for the preservation of the mother's life or physical health. The Protestant view is usually much more liberal, with several denominations recommending that therapeutic abortion be made available on request; however, some Protestant groups take the same view as the Roman Catholic Church.

POPULATION ASPECTS & INCIDENCE
OF THERAPEUTIC ABORTION

It is estimated that approximately one out of every 4 pregnancies in the world is terminated by induced abortion, making this perhaps the most common method of reproduction limitation. The most successful demonstration of population restriction in a progressive country has been in Japan, where abortion has become the principal method of birth control. In the USA, estimates of the numbers of criminal abortions performed prior to recent developments in the law ranged from 0.25 to 1.25 million a year. The number of legal abortions now being performed in this country approximates one abortion per 4 live births. In 1975, there were more than 1 million legal abortions in the USA, or 273 per 1000 live births. In 1977, there were 1 million teenage pregnancies (10% of teenage females in the USA). Of these, about 30,000 were in girls under 15 years of age. These data are resulting in greater latitude in the indications for abortion as approved by the Department of Health and Human Services.

PROVIDING THERAPEUTIC
ABORTION SERVICES

Suction curettage on an outpatient basis under local or light general anesthesia can be accomplished with a high degree of safety. The safety of outpatient abortion and the shortage of hospital beds have led to the development of single-function, "free-standing" abortion clinics in New York and other states. In addition to providing more efficient counseling and social services, these clinics have effectively reduced the cost of abortion. Many hospitals now provide "short-stay-unit" facilities, matching the efficiency of the outpatient clinics but also offering the back-up facilities of the general hospital.

NEW METHODS

Oral Contraceptive for Men

Gossypol, a pigment from the cotton plant, has been reported by Chinese physicians to be an effective male contraceptive when ingested. Local and systemic effects of this preparation are being studied by a number of investigators in China and elsewhere. Encouraging data confirm the spermicidal action of both orally and locally administered gossypol in humans and in subhuman primates. However, there are disturbing systemic effects in men that require additional pharmacologic and toxicologic study before more extensive trials in humans are carried out.

Nova T IUD

A new steroid-bearing IUD has been studied recently, the norgestrel-releasing Nova T. The initial indication is that this IUD may provide contraceptive action for 5–6 years (based upon in vitro diffusion studies). Steroid-bearing IUDs may reduce the incidence of salpingitis observed with other types of IUDs and also seen in oral contraceptive users.

Vaginal Contraceptive Ring

Vaginal delivery of contraceptive steroids was pioneered by Mishell and his associates. The most encouraging approach has been the use of silicone rubber rings impregnated with synthetic progestins that are delivered to the vaginal mucosa at a reasonably constant daily rate. Technical improvements in the delivery system and the use of newer and more potent progestins have provided encouraging data relevant to this method. A primary advantage of the vaginal contraceptive ring is that the woman herself inserts and removes it according to a predetermined schedule. The interested reader may benefit from a recent comprehensive review of the method in *Contraception* (1981;**24**:321).

• • •

References

General

Department of Medical and Public Affairs, George Washington University Medical Center: Male/female sterilization equipment: Guide to equipment selection for male/female sterilization procedures. Reingold LA et al (editors). *Popul Rep*, Series M, No. 1, Sept 1977.

New York law banning sale of nonprescription contraceptives to minors unconstitutional. *Obstet Gynecol News* (Aug 1) 1977;**12**:1.

Prolongation of Lactation

Population Information Program, The Johns Hopkins University, Family Planning Programs: Breast feeding, fertility, and family planning. *Popul Rep*, Series J, No. 24, Nov-Dec 1981.

Condom

Connell E et al: A new look at barrier contraceptives. *Contemp Obstet Gynecol* (Aug) 1977;**10**:76.

Spermicidal Preparations

Abrutyn D, McKenzie BE, Nadaskay N: Teratology study of intravaginally administered nonoxynol 9-containing contraceptive cream in rats. *Fertil Steril* 1982;**37**:113.

Cameron SM, Waller DP, Zaneveld LJD: Vaginal spermicidal activity of gossypol in the *Macaca arctoides*. *Fertil Steril* 1982;**37**:273.

Cutler JC et al: Vaginal contraceptives as prophylaxis against gonorrhea and other sexually transmitted diseases. *Adv Planned Parenthood* 1977;**12**:45.

Jick H et al: Vaginal spermicides and congenital disorders. *JAMA* 1981;**245**:1329.

Diaphragms

Loomis L, Feder HM: Toxic-shock syndrome associated with diaphragm use. (Letter.) *N Engl J Med* 1981;**305**:1585.

Tatum HJ, Connell EB: Barrier contraception: A comprehensive overview. *Fertil Steril* 1981;**36**:1.

"Rhythm" Method

Jongbloet PH: Congenital anomalies associated with unsuccessful rhythm contraception. Presented at a workshop in Arlington, Virginia, March 13-16, 1977, under the sponsorship of the Program for Applied Research on Fertility Regulation, Northwestern University.

Hormonal Contraceptives

Berger GS: The risk of post-pill amenorrhea. *Int J Gynaecol Obstet* 1977;**15**:125.

Brinton LA et al: Risk factors for benign breast disease. *Am J Epidemiol* 1981;**113**:203.

Heinonen OP et al: Cardiovascular birth defects and antenatal exposure to female sex hormones. *N Engl J Med* 1977;**296**:67.

Kaufman DW et al: Decreased risk of endometrial cancer among oral contraceptive users. *N Engl J Med* 1980;**303**:1045.

Keith L, Berger GS: The relationship between congenital defects and the use of exogenous progestational "contraceptive" hormones during pregnancy: A 20-year review. *Int J Gynaecol Obstet* 1977;**15**:115.

Newhouse ML et al: A case control study of carcinoma of the ovary. *Br J Prev Soc Med* 1977;**31**:148.

Oral contraceptives in the 1980s. *Popul Rep* Series A, No. 6, May-June 1982.

Ory H: The noncontraceptive health benefits from oral contraceptive use. *Fam Plann Perspec* 1982;**14**:182.

Petitti DB et al: Risk of vascular disease in women: Smoking, oral contraceptives, noncontraceptive estrogens, and other factors. *JAMA* 1979;**242**:1150.

Rubin GL et al: Endometrial cancer and use of oral contraceptives. Paper presented at the Epidemic Intelligence Service Conference, Atlanta, April 19, 1982.

Savolainen E et al: Teratogenic hazards of oral contraceptives analyzed in a natural malformation register. *Am J Obstet Gynecol* 1981;**140**:521.

Tietze C, Lewit S: Life-risks associated with reversible methods of fertility regulation. *Int J Gynaecol Obstet* 1979;**16**:456.

The Walnut Creek Contraceptive Drug Study: *A Prospective Study of the Side-Effects of Oral Contraceptives*. Vol 3. US Government Printing Office, 1981.

Weiss NS, Sayvetz WM: Incidence of endometrial cancer and oral contraceptive agents. *N Engl J Med* 1980;**302**:50.

Wynn V et al: Comparison of effects of different combined oral contraceptive formulations on carbohydrate and lipid metabolism. *Lancet* 1979;**2**:933.

Yuzpe AA, Lancee WI: Ethinyl estradiol and dl-norgestrel as a postcoital contraceptive. *Fertil Steril* 1977;**28**:932.

Hormonal Contraceptives by Injection

Rall HJS et al: Comparative contraceptive experience with three-month and six-month medroxyprogesterone acetate regimens. *J Reprod Med* 1977;**18**:55.

Schwallie PC, Mohberg NR: Medroxyprogesterone acetate: An injectable contraceptive. *Adv Planned Parenthood* 1977;**12**:36.

Intrauterine Contraceptive Devices

Charnock M, Chambers TJ: Pelvic actinomycosis and intrauterine contraceptive devices. *Lancet* 1979;**1**:1239.

Dashow EE, Llorens AS: Resistant gonococcal infection from an intra-uterine device. *Am J Obstet Gynecol* 1977;**129**:230.

Eschenbach DA, Harnisch JP, Holmes KK: Pathogenesis of acute pelvic inflammatory disease: Role of contraception and other risk factors. *Am J Obstet Gynecol* 1977;**128**:838.

Five Intrauterine Devices for Public Programs. The Population Council, New York, 1979.

Garcia Celso-Ramon, Rosenfeld DL: *Human Fertility: The Regulation of Reproduction*. Davis, 1977.

Hager WD, Majmudar B: Pelvic actinomycosis in women using intrauterine contraceptive devices. *Am J Obstet Gynecol* 1979;**133**:60.

Lippes J et al: Postcoital Copper IUDs. *Adv Planned Parenthood* 1979;**14**:87.

Pine L et al: Demonstration of *Actinomyces* and *Arachnia* species in cervicovaginal smears by direct staining with species-specific fluorescent-antibody conjugate. *J Clin Microbiol* 1981;**13**:15.

Sivin I: Copper T IUD use and ectopic pregnancy rates in the United States. *Contraception* 1979;**19**:151.

Sivin I, Stern J: Long-acting, more effective Copper T IUDs: A summary of US experience, 1970-1975. *Stud Fam Plann* (Oct) 1979;**10**:263.

Sivin I, Tatum HJ: Four years' experience with the TCU 380A intrauterine contraceptive device. *Fertil Steril* 1981;**36**:159.

Spence MR et al: Cytological detection and clinical significance of *Actinomyces israelii* in women employing intrauterine contraceptive devices. *Am J Obstet Gynecol* 1978;**131**:295.

Tanz A: Barrier contraception and patient guide to barrier contraception: The female patient. PW Communications, Inc., Jan 1978.

Tatum HJ: Clinical aspects of intrauterine contraception: Circumspection 1976. *Fertil Steril* 1977;**28**:3.

Tatum HJ, Schmidt FH: Contraceptive and sterilization practices and extrauterine pregnancy: A realistic perspective. *Fertil Steril* 1977;**28**:407.

WHO Special Programme of Research, Development and Research Training in Human Reproduction: *An Assessment of the Lippes Loop D and the Copper T 220C.* HRP/79.1 Rev. 1. April 1979.

Sterilization in Men

Ackerman CFS, MacIsaac SG, Schual R: Vasectomy: Benefits and risks. *Int J Gynaecol Obstet* 1979;**16**:493.

Silber SJ: Microscopic vasectomy reversal. *Fertil Steril* 1977;**28**:1191.

Sterilization in Women

Beck P, Gal D: Silicone ring technique for laparoscopic sterilization in the gravid and nongravid patient. *Obstet Gynecol* 1979;**53**:653.

Centers for Disease Control: Surgical sterilization surveillance: Tubal sterilization, 1970–1975. 1979.

Diamond E: Microsurgical reconstruction of the uterine tube in sterilized patients. *Fertil Steril* 1977;**28**:1203.

Fortier L: Minilap: A few tricks of the trade. *IPPF Med Bull* (Feb) 1977;**11(1)**:1.

Gomel V: Tubal reanastomosis by microsurgery. *Fertil Steril* 1977;**28**:59.

Hernandez IM et al: Postabortal laparoscopic tubal sterilization: Results in comparison to interval procedures. *Obstet Gynecol* 1977;**50**:356.

Hulka JF: Current status of elective sterilization in the United States. *Fertil Steril* 1977;**28**:515.

Kumarasamy T, Hurt WG: Laparoscopic sterilization with Silicone rubber bands. *Obstet Gynecol* 1977;**50**:315.

Lay CL: The new improved Silastic band for ligation of fallopian tubes. *Fertil Steril* 1977;**28**:1301.

Luwuliza-Kerunda JMM: Intraamnionic prostaglandin $F_{2\alpha}$ for termination of midtrimester abortion. *East Afr Med J* 1979;**56**:10.

Mumford SD et al: Tubal ring sterilization: Experience with 10,086 cases. *Obstet Gynecol* 1981;**57**:150.

Penfield AJ: Laparoscopic sterilization under local anesthesia: 1200 cases. *Obstet Gynecol* 1977;**49**:725.

Penfield AJ: Minilaparotomy for female sterilization. *Obstet Gynecol* 1979;**54**:184.

Penfield AJ: Minilap in a "free-standing" clinic. *Fam Plann Perspect* (March/April) 1977.

Peterson HB et al: Death following puncture of the aorta during laparoscopic sterilization. *Obstet Gynecol* 1982;**59**:133.

Poliakoff SR et al: Experience with the tubal ring for female sterilization. *Popul Rep* 1978;**2**:197.

Richart RM et al: Sterilization: Five experts compare the techniques. *Contemp Obstet Gynecol* 1977;**9**:56.

Rioux JE: Late complications of female sterilization: A review of the literature and a proposal for further research. *J Reprod Med* 1977;**19**:329.

Tatum HJ, Schmidt FH: Contraceptive and sterilization practices and extrauterine pregnancy: A realistic perspective. *Fertil Steril* 1977;**28**:407.

Uribe-Ramirez LC et al: Out-patient laparoscopic sterilization: A review of complications in 2000 cases. *J Reprod Med* 1977;**18**:103.

Medicolegal Aspects of Sterilization in the United States

Yin L: The impact of new legislation on endoscopic instrumentation. *J Reprod Med* 1977;**18**:336.

Induced Abortion

Alexander D: Prenatal detection of genetic disease by amniocentesis. *Contemp Obstet Gynecol* 1977;**10**:44.

Bracken MB: Psychosomatic aspects of abortion: Implications for counseling. *J Reprod Med* 1977;**19**:265.

Cates W Jr, Smith JC: Mortality from legal abortion in the United States, 1972–1976. In: *The Safety of Fertility Control.* Keith LG, Kent DK, Brittain JR. Springer, 1980.

Centers for Disease Control: Teenage childbearing and abortion patterns United States, 1977. *MMWR* 1980;**29**:157.

Department of Medical and Public Affairs, George Washington University Medical Center: Pregnancy termination: Cervical dilatation—A review. Ott ER et al. *Popul Rep,* Series F, No. 6, Sept 1977.

Grimes DA, Cates W Jr: The comparative efficacy and safety of intraamniotic prostaglandin $F_{2\alpha}$ and hypertonic saline for second-trimester abortion: A review and critique. *J Reprod Med* 1979;**22**:248.

Grimes DA, Cates W Jr: Complications from legally-induced abortion: A review. *Obstet Gynecol Surv* 1979;**34**:177.

Grimes DA, Ross WC, Hatcher RA: Rh immunoglobulin utilization after spontaneous and induced abortion. *Obstet Gynecol* 1977;**50**:261.

Grimes DA et al: Local versus general anesthesia: Which is safer for performing suction curettage abortions? *Am J Obstet Gynecol* 1979;**135**:1030.

Grimes DA et al: Maternal death at term as a late sequela of failed attempted abortion. *Adv Planned Parenthood* 1979;**14**:77.

Kovasznay BM et al: Intravascular spill of hyperosmolar urea during induced mid trimester abortion. *Obstet Gynecol* 1979;**53**:127.

Lee LT, Paxman JM: Legal aspects of menstrual regulation. *Stud Fam Plann* (Aug) 1977;**8**:273.

Ory HW: The health effects of fertility control. Pages 110–121 in: *Proceedings of a Symposium on Contraception: Science, Technology, and Application, May 16–17, 1978.* National Academy of Sciences, 1979.

Soderstrom RM, Haydere GE: Outpatient saline abortion: A review of 1000 cases. *Adv Planned Parenthood* 1977;**12**:98.

Tietze C: Induced abortion–1977 supplement. *Rep Popul Fam Plann* 14 (2nd ed Suppl), Dec 1977.

Contraception in the Adolescent

Greydanus DE, McAnarney E: Contraception in the adolescent: Current concepts for the pediatrician. *Pediatrics* 1980;**65**:1.

Ory HW et al: The pill at 20: An assessment. *Fam Plann Perspect* 1980;**12**:278.

New Methods

Cameron SM, Waller DP, Zaneveld LJD: Vaginal spermicidal activity of gossypol in the *Macaca arctoides. Fertil Steril* 1982;**37**:273.

Comprehensive review of the vaginal contraceptive ring. *Contraception* 1981;**24**:323. [Entire issue.]

National Coordinating Group on Male Antifertility Agents: Gossypol, a new antifertility agent for males. *Chin Med J* 1978;**4**:417.

Nilsson CG: Comparative quantitation of menstrual blood loss with a d-norgestrel–releasing IUD and a Nova-T-copper device. *Contraception* 1977;**15**:379.

Piotrow PJ et al: Intrauterine devices. *Popul Rep,* Series B, No. 3. The Johns Hopkins University, 1979.

Pösö H et al: Gossypol, a powerful inhibitor of human spermatozoal metabolism. (Letter.) *Lancet* 1980;**1**:885.

Waller DP, Zaneveld LJD, Fons HHS: In vitro spermicidal activity of gossypol. *Contraception* 1980;**22**:183.

The Borderland of Law & Medicine | 24

Hugh B. Collins, JD

NEGLIGENCE & BREACH OF IMPLIED CONTRACT

There is no essential difference between a claim that the physician was negligent and a claim that an implied contract with the patient to skillfully diagnose and treat the illness was breached. In either instance, the important underlying question is whether the physician was negligent.

Negligence in the present context is defined as failure to conform to the conduct of a reasonably prudent person under the circumstances. A reasonably prudent person is a nonexistent but perfect being who is solely a hallucination of lawyers who by custom impute understanding of him or her to the general public and whose standard of conduct decides negligence cases.

In order to be found negligent, a physician must either do something contrary to the recognized standard of good medical practice or fail to do something a physician acting in conformity with recognized standards of good medical practice would not neglect to do.

The **recognized standard of medical practice** is that degree of care and skill commonly exercised by physicians of average ability engaged in the same general type of practice in a similar locality. A general practitioner, for example, cannot be judged negligent merely because a specialist might have served the patient with greater skill and knowledge. All that is expected of the generalist is the degree of care and skill the ordinary and similarly situated reputable practitioner would exercise while engaged in this particular physician's field of practice.

The recognized standard of medical practice is an objective and subjective standard determined by custom or usage among "average" similarly situated members of the profession. What constitutes the recognized standard is, in litigation, a question of fact that can only be determined from the testimony of qualified physicians except in cases where the negligence is so grossly obvious that a layman could recognize it as such.

Thus, in order to prove that a physician was negligent, the applicable standard of medical practice recognized at that time and in that place must be determined, and it must then be proved that the physician failed to conform to that standard while rendering professional services to the patient.

Failure to make a correct (or any) diagnosis does not in itself imply negligence or cause compensable injury to the patient. It is still the law in a few states that failure to make a correct (or any) diagnosis cannot form the basis for a claim against a physician because it has not resulted in a *new* injury. In states that adhere to this rule, a physician is not liable for a delay in treatment due either to incorrect diagnosis or to failure to make any diagnosis. Liability, if any, would not arise until something the physician did caused physical harm; the physician would not be liable for giving treatment that did no harm even if such treatment did no good. Most states do allow recovery for a delay in definitive care because of negligent failure to make a correct diagnosis.

Physicians do not guarantee that their services will be curative or meliorative, and they are not responsible for failures of treatment unless the unfortunate result is due to failure to conform to the recognized standard of practice in the "community" (see below).

Where more than one method of treatment is available to the physician and both or all are within the recognized standard of medical practice, it is proper for a physician to select one such method in preference to another. The method may later prove to be a wrong one or one not favored by other practitioners, but this does not support an allegation of negligence. A physician may err in judgment or disagree with other physicians without being negligent. In other words, the law does not reject the view that "we all make mistakes." However, the difference between reasonable mistakes and unreasonable ones is important in our courts. A person who makes a reasonable mistake is acting as a reasonably prudent person and thus is free from liability for negligence. It is negligent and therefore a basis for claim of damage to make an unreasonable mistake. A physician is not liable for an honest error in judgment. The test of liability is whether the physician conformed to the recognized standard of medical practice in making the diagnosis and giving treatment.

THE "COMMUNITY" STANDARD

Formerly, professional standards were established for each individual community by the physicians practicing in that community. Today, physicians must meet the standards of physicians practicing in "the same or similar communities." Most courts now equate "community" with the nation at large.

Although it has become a legal fossil, the magic word "community" is still heard in malpractice cases. A physician called as a witness making a first visit to a given geographic area will be permitted to testify that he or she is "familiar with the standard of practice in the community" and to further testify that a given course of conduct either is or is not in accordance with that standard. Such testimony may sound incredible to the nonlawyers (and some of the lawyers) present, but the accepted fact is that the witness actually is testifying to professional usage in the country at large.

This acceptance of general national standards of medical practice rather than local standards probably is one result of the "accredited hospital." For example, the Joint Commission on Hospital Accreditation (JCHA) uniformly applies its standards without regard to geography. Some courts admit the JCHA standards as evidence of acceptable standards. Medicare has given additional impetus to this trend, involving as it does detailed administrative regulations governing the conduct of the medical staff in each participating hospital.

The courts are required to take judicial notice of the Federal Regulations and will probably apply them at least in part in establishing the standard of practice in the local jurisdiction. Certain administrative regulations promulgated by the Secretary of Health and Human Services (HHS) are required reading for any physician claiming current familiarity with the legal aspects of medical practice. The physician who does not have one already should send to HHS for a copy of HIR-10 (6/67), *Conditions of Participation; Hospitals*, containing Regulations §§405.1001 to 405.1040.

RES IPSA LOQUITUR

Res ipsa loquitur (Latin, "the thing speaks for itself") is a type of circumstantial evidence pertaining to negligence. The principle involved is that when an injury occurs through an **instrumentality or agency** under the exclusive control of another and when **as a matter of common knowledge** the injury would not ordinarily have occurred if the person in control exercised ordinary care, then—if the person in control cannot satisfactorily explain why he or she should not be held liable—the event or occurrence itself is circumstantial evidence of negligence. This principle is epitomized and emphasized in an English case in which the plaintiff, walking past the defendant's warehouse, was hit by a barrel that fell from an upper loft opening.

The principle of res ipsa loquitur has been ex-panded by some courts to include "an instrumentality, agency, or *situation*." Other courts have eliminated the requirement of exclusive control. Still other courts have eliminated the requirement of "common knowledge" and permit an inference to be based on expert testimony that the mishap will not ordinarily occur if the physician's performance conforms to recognized standards of care. The latter extension of the basic principle illustrates an unfortunate tendency to assume that an unsatisfactory result is due to negligence.

It is important that the physician possess a general understanding of the res ipsa loquitur doctrine and its various nuances. A defendant called as a witness by the plaintiff may be asked to answer questions such as the following:

Q: So what you are saying is that if it is done right, complications can be avoided?

Unthinking defendants might answer yes to that question and thereby make a *prima facie* case against themselves. Thoughtful witnesses, realizing that they do not know everything even about those things they know most about, will prefer a more accurate and less damaging answer:

A: No. At best, complications might be minimized.

To emphasize the point: A physician cannot be so expert as to be justified in categorically ruling out all possibilities that do not instantly come to mind. A witness must pay close attention to and *fully understand* each question before answering.

ASSAULT & BATTERY

Assault and battery are not the same thing. Assault is the intentional and deliberate invasion of another person's interest in freedom from apprehension of harmful or offensive bodily contacts. An assault is an incomplete attempt or an apparent attempt to touch another person in a violent or offensive manner. The utterance of threatening words does not alone constitute an assault.

Battery is the intentional invasion of another person's right to freedom from harmful or offensive bodily contacts. The intent need not be hostile and may even be friendly.

A battery may be willful and malicious, or it may be inadvertent. For example, if a surgeon with permission to operate on the right knee inadvertently operates on the left knee, battery has been committed on that patient, no matter how skillful the surgery, because permission to operate on the left knee was lacking. Such an operation would also be a negligent act, ie, failure to exercise ordinary care to avoid operating on the wrong knee.

The distinction between battery with malicious intent and inadvertent battery is important. Insurance policies usually exclude coverage for intentional acts, and insurance protection is not afforded against a claim for malicious battery.

Generally, consent is a defense against a claim of battery. An exception occurs where the law prohibits consent (eg, in instances where the battery would be a crime).

CONSENT*

A physician who renders any type of therapy without the patient's consent commits a battery for which the physician is liable in damages. Damages recoverable for a battery include compensation for any actual harm and may include punitive damages as a deterrent to such future conduct.

Where consent is disputed, the subject of the dispute is usually the nature and extent of the consent. The patient usually contends that only a specified procedure was consented to, and the physician replies that the patient gave full permission to do whatever the physician deemed appropriate. The physician should always make certain the patient has been informed and has knowingly consented to the proposed therapy. It is unlikely that the patient will be able to do so without sufficient explanation by the physician.

Consent is not subject to assignment or transfer. Consent to treatment by one physician is not consent to treatment by another. Where there is an unauthorized substitution, both physicians would be liable if a claim of battery were sustained in an action at law.

Consent is not required in cases of emergency where it is urgently necessary to proceed and the patient is incapable of intelligently giving or refusing consent. In such situations, the law presumes that consent to treat would be given. This same rule applies where, during the course of surgery, it becomes imperative to extend the procedure beyond the scope anticipated or even to perform an entirely different procedure. Nonetheless, it is questionable whether it is a defense that extension of the operation or change of operative procedure was in the patient's interest if it was *not* dictated by urgent and immediate necessity.

A true emergency, then, dispenses with the need for consent in the case of a competent adult. Authority to give or to withhold consent does not pass to the patient's spouse or next of kin. As a practical matter, some consultation with the family will make the procedure more "palatable," but, legally, a member of the family can neither give nor withhold consent in the case of an incapacitated adult any more than in the case of a conscious and competent adult.

If the patient has expressly forbidden the physician to proceed in a particular way (eg, prohibited the physician from *ever* performing a blood transfusion),

*There are statutes in some states governing consent. Arkansas: Ark Stats 82-363. Georgia: Ga Code 88-2908. Louisiana: 40 La Rev Stats 1299.40. Mississippi: Miss Code 41-41-3. Missouri: Mo Stats 431.061.

the question arises whether the physician would ever be justified in violating the patient's express instructions. The weight of judicial opinion seems to be that the physician may do so where transfusion is urgently necessary to preserve life and health. The deviation from the patient's express instructions is more acceptable in the case of an unforeseen contingency. The physician should not undertake to treat a patient who refuses permission to utilize reasonable safeguards and treatment methods. Nonetheless, in a true emergency (eg, an ectopic pregnancy), even though the patient is competent to demand assurances that the physician will forego specific standard emergency procedures, it is arguably proper to proceed with standard therapy for the emergency.

The consent to therapy of a minor must be given by a parent or closest available relative or legal guardian, but a minor of mature years can probably give consent for needed therapy. The more urgently the therapy is needed, the less maturity is required. In this shadowy area there is no "rule" upon which the physician can rely. As a practical matter, the capacity to consent is tested by hindsight, with the jurors finding the minor had the capacity to consent to those things the jurors themselves would have authorized had they been the child's guardians.

Some practical considerations enter into this problem. If it appears that the minor in fact had an adult understanding of what the proposed treatment involved, the consent may be adequate. The existence of this understanding depends on the intelligence of the minor and the degree of risk to the patient. Moreover, because litigation involving a claim of bodily injury resulting from assault and battery—as distinguished from a parent's claim for additional medical expenses and other economic loss from a bad result—would be in the name of and on behalf of the minor, such consent would be a defense in substantial mitigation of the claim for damages in those cases where the minor patient was actually benefited.

INFORMED CONSENT*

Depending upon the nature of an assault and battery, consent may be a defense to such a claim, or the offense may be such that public policy prohibits consent. Where consent is an otherwise valid defense, the

*Twenty-three states have informed consent statutes. Some constitute rules of evidence and others either completely or partially specify a standard of conduct. Alaska: AS 09.55.556. Delaware: 18 Del Code 6852. Florida: Fla Stat 768.132. Hawaii: RSH 671-3. Idaho: IC 39-4304. Iowa: ICA 147.137. Kentucky: KRS 304.40-320. Maine: 24 M 2905. Nebraska: NRS 44-2186. Nevada: NRS 41A.100. New Hampshire: RSNH 507-C:1; 507-C:2. New York: NY Pub Health 3805-d. North Carolina: NC Gen Stat 90-211.11. Ohio: ORC 2317.54. Oregon: ORS 677.097. Pennsylvania: 40 Pa Stat 1301.103. Rhode Island: RI Gen Laws 9-19-32. Tennessee: TCA 23-34141111. Texas: Tex Rev Civ Stat art. 4590 i, 6.04-.07. Utah: UCA 78-14-5. Vermont: 12 Vt Stat 1908. Washington: RCW 7.70.050. Wyoming: WS 33-340.14.

law is clear that an individual who does not know what is being agreed to cannot consent to it. "Consent," in the context of an agreement to submit to therapy, means a voluntary agreement by a person with sufficient intelligence and possessing adequate information on which to base a rational choice either to do or not do something proposed by another. *Gray v Grunnagle,* 423 Pa 144, 223 A2d 663, 669 (1966). The corollary is that one who lacks reasonable understanding of proposed medical, surgical, or diagnostic procedures cannot logically give or refuse consent. Thus the question becomes, "What constitutes reasonable understanding?" Too often, the judicial response is the question-begging assertion that "reasonable understanding is informed understanding."

Example: Patient was ill and needed treatment. Physician offered no guarantee of success but diagnosed and treated Patient with flawless care and skill. An undesirable side-effect resulted in serious permanent injury. Unable to base a claim for damages on negligence or defect in Physician's performance, Patient complains: "I did not agree to take this risk. If I had known that this result might occur, I would have refused the therapy." The legal theory underlying this complaint is "technical battery," and those who would have it upheld as actionable say it eliminates a need for expert testimony because, as was said in *Berkey v Anderson,* 1 Cal App3d 790, 82 Cal Rptr 67, 79 (1970),

> A skilled surgeon acting without consent is no less guilty of assault and battery than a bloody butcher would be.

See also *Cobbs v Grant,* 8 Cal3d 229, 104 Cal Rptr 505, 502 P2d 1 (1972).

How much disclosure is required to adequately inform the patient varies from state to state and depends on whether the underlying rationale is assault and battery or negligence. Some jurisdictions apply the standard of "reasonably prudent medical practice." Others measure the quantum of duty to disclose risks from the patient's viewpoint. The latter view was most clearly stated in *Canterbury v Spence,* 464 F2d 772 (DC Cir 1972). Courts taking the former view logically require expert testimony to establish the existence and scope of the physician's duty to inform the patient of the risks of proposed therapy. Courts taking the latter view logically hold that expert testimony is not necessary to establish the existence and scope of the physician's duty to disclose.

Since there is no uniform rule that will work in all jurisdictions, the following guidelines are suggested for the physician who wants to stay out of courtrooms and law offices:

(1) It is not necessary to warn the patient of risks that should be common knowledge or of risks that are already known to the patient.

(2) Without regard to the custom of physicians in the locality, there is a duty to warn if (a) the risk of injury inherent in the procedure is a substantial one; (b) if there are feasible alternative procedures that do not impose this particular risk or an equally grave one; and (c) if disclosure of the risk would not be detrimental to the patient. If the physician feels there is a therapeutic privilege to withhold information for the patient's own good, the reasons for doing so should be strong and well documented (ie, provable if necessary).

(3) There is a duty to disclose (a) the hazards that *commonly* occur even if the potential injury is slight, and (2) *extremely remote* risks if the possible injury is serious.

(4) Disclosure may not be withheld simply because the physician feels the patient might refuse treatment that the physician feels would be beneficial. The therapeutic privilege applies, if at all, only when a current course of therapy has reached the point of no return.

The practical problem is to prove in court that consent was given. It is easier to warn the patient in advance than it will be later to prove the patient's foreknowledge in court. Therefore, proof in the form of a detailed (as distinguished from a general pro forma) consent document is recommended.

A valuable collection of consent forms with explanatory text is Medicolegal Forms With Legal Analysis (1973), obtainable from the Office of the General Counsel, American Medical Association, 535 North Dearborn Street, Chicago, IL 60610 (single copy price: $2.50. Refer to Order No. OP–109.)

INFORMED DECISION

The doctrine of "informed consent" requires the physician to disclose to the patient the risks of the proposed treatment or procedure and the availability and risks of alternative treatments and procedures, as well as the risk of doing nothing.

A corollary doctrine is emerging from the "informed consent" cases. When it is better established, it seems likely this doctrine will be called "informed decision."

An accurate statement of the informed decision doctrine to date would be as follows: The physician has a legal duty to all patients—even apparently healthy ones—(1) to recommend diagnostic procedures and (2) to explain the possible consequences of refusal of diagnostic procedures (including those that are risk-free) designed to detect illnesses that could lead to death or serious consequences if timely action is not taken. The rationale was expressed in this way in *Keogan v Holy Family Hospital,* 24 Wash App 583, 601 P2d 1303 (1979):

> The physician's duty is to tell the patient what he or she needs to know in order to make an informed decision. The existence of an abnormal condition in one's body, the presence of a high risk of disease, and the existence of alternative diagnostic procedures to conclusively determine the presence or absence of that disease are all facts which a patient must know in

order to make an informed decision on the course which future medical care will take.

Apparently *Helling v Carey,* 83 Wash2d 514, 519 P2d 981 (1974), was the forum in which the doctrine of informed decision made its initial unequivocal appearance. A myopic patient, aged 23, was fitted with contact lenses but not tested for glaucoma. Nine years later, glaucoma was suspected and diagnosed. During the interim, she had been seen 8 times. Professional standards of ophthalmologists do not require routine pressure tests for glaucoma in patients under age 40, because the incidence of glaucoma in that age group is one out of 25,000. Because of the simplicity of the test and the seriousness of the disease if not detected, the court felt it was its duty to say what is required to protect patients under 40 from glaucoma rather than permitting ophthalmologists to follow the recognized standard of medical practice.

Next came *Truman v Thomas,* 27 Cal3d 285, 611 P2d 902 (1980), which held that a physician had not discharged his duty to his patient by repeatedly recommending a Papanicolaou smear the patient refused to take. It was held that the physician failed to discharge his duty when he failed to explain that a Papanicolaou smear might reveal the presence of cancer and failed to emphasize the devastating effects of the ailment.

Schroder v Perkel, 87 NJ 53, 432 A2d 834 (1981), held that a pediatrician who failed to diagnose cystic fibrosis in plaintiffs' *first* child was liable for the medical costs of rearing their *second* child, who also was afflicted with the disease. By negligently failing to diagnose a hereditary disease until the eighth month of the second pregnancy, the physician deprived the parents of the opportunity to choose whether to have a second child who might require prolonged and costly medical care.

STRICT LIABILITY FOR PRODUCTS

A physician who undertakes to prescribe *and furnish* medication has the same legal responsiblities as are imposed on other vendors of goods. The law holds a vendor accountable to all consumers that the product sold be reasonably fit for the purpose for which it is supplied. Lack of fitness is a "defect," and a consumer who sustains harm resulting from a defect in the product is entitled to recover from the vendor. The basis of recovery is not that the vendor failed to use reasonable care to see that the product was fit but that liability under the law attaches if the product is unfit.

Example: A vial of Miochol was supplied in surgery by the hospital's pharmacy. The vial was placed in a pan of liquid germicide containing formaldehyde for 30 minutes, then rinsed and drawn into a syringe for injection into the patient's eye. After surgery it was discovered that the Miochol had become contaminated with the formaldehyde, which had injured the eye and necessitated further corrective surgery. The hospital was held liable under the Uniform Commercial Code as a seller of goods on "an implied warranty that the good shall be fit for such purpose." *Providence Hospital v Truly,* 611 SW2d 127 (Tex Civ App [1980]).

Physicians must be aware of their legal responsibilities as sellers of goods, since insurance coverage does not include "the products hazard."

Some policies insure against "malpractice, error, or mistake." Most insurance forms in use today specify "liability arising out of professional services rendered or which should have been rendered in the practice of the insured's profession." One cannot be certain how the insurer who uses the former phrase would react when faced with a suit for the sale of a defective product. On the other hand, insurers who use the latter phrase understand that in the course of practice a physician may administer or dispense medications and that liability arising out of such administration or dispensing is covered by the professional liability policy whether or not a charge is made for the product. This coverage would probably include appliances, eg, an intrauterine device.

Any adverse reaction allegedly resulting from a defect in a pharmaceutical or appliance is potentially an action at law to recover damages under the strict liability doctrine. Most pharmaceutical companies are quick to aid and defend a physician who is sued on a complaint that their product was defective, but only if the physician has not altered the product in any way and has used it only in the manner intended by the manufacturer.

Coverage for the products hazard is commonly included in the liability form pertaining to pharmacies. The physician's insurers do not contract to insure against the hazards of a retail pharmacy business. The important distinction to be borne in mind is that a physician prescribes and administers whereas a pharmacist compounds and dispenses. Did the patient who has returned to the office for medication come so that the product can be *administered* (eg, by a parenteral route) or in order to purchase another supply of pills of the sort generally obtained at a pharmacy with or without a prescription? The physician who sells drugs (whether at wholesale or retail) is a merchant in the eyes of the law and probably in the eyes of the insurer. Even though dispensing may be allowed under the terms of a physician's license, it must be regarded as outside the scope of prudence.

STATUTES OF LIMITATION

At common law, there is no limit on the time within which an action may be commenced. The right to be free, after a given time, from exposure to litigation is conferred by legislation. These enactments are called statutes of limitations.

Such enactments are an expression of legislative policy (1) against prosecution of stale claims; (2) favoring elimination, after a reasonable time, of the difficulties that result from the need to anticipate and make provision for potential liability; and (3) to promote stability and repose in human affairs.

"Limitations" is a confused and confusing subject because the statutes vary among jurisdictions. Moreover, through "statutory construction," the courts have modified the statutes to reflect their own widely varying notions of what the legislatures should have enacted. In addition, during recent years the statutes have been repeatedly amended in legislative attempts to accommodate to judicial "construction" but preserve the policy considerations underlying the statutes.

On their face, statutes of limitation were straightforward. They established a stated interval after a cause of action arose within which to commence the action. It was generally understood that the cause of action arose at the time of the wrongful act or omission.

A major statutory amendment by judicial "construction" lies in the meaning to be given to the phrase "after the cause of action arose." Many courts have held that a cause of action cannot arise until harm becomes manifest. This definition has the effect of extending the time allowed by statutes of limitation.

The next significant extension of the statute by judicial fiat was the emergence of the "discovery rule," which states that the cause of action does not arise until the plaintiff makes—or in the exercise of ordinary care should make—certain discoveries. There has not been a consensus concerning *what* should be discovered in in order to start the statute running. Some hold it is the fact of injury or damage alone. Others hold it is the fact of injury or damage *and* that it may have resulted from a given event. Some add one or more of the following items: The plaintiff must suspect that the defendent caused the damage; the plaintiff must suspect the defendant of *culpability;* the plaintiff must reasonably know that a cause of action against the defendant exists.

Obviously, each additional item further extends the time allowed by the statute.

This problem has not occurred in any jurisdiction with a general statute prohibiting any action after the expiration of an arbitrary period following the act or omission complained of.

Where there has been any legislative reaction to the "discovery rule," it has usually been a hybrid of the "discovery" and "occurrence" rules. A typical statute will (1) define *what* constitutes "discovery"; (2) give the plaintiff a short time within which to make "discovery"; (3) specify a finite period following the act or omission complained of within which an action must be commenced or be barred; and (4) interrupt that finite period during any time which discovery was prevented by defendant's affirmative fraud or fraudulent concealment. Oregon's unique statute reads ". . . fraud, deceit *or misleading representation.*" The phrase was recently interpreted by the Oregon Court as follows in *Duncan v Augter,* 286 Ore 723, 596 P2d 555 (1979):

> The essence of the phrase is that the representation misleads the plaintiff, not that it is fraudulent or deceitful on the part of the defendant.

However, the Court distinguished therapeutic reassurance:

> Such an innocent contemporaneous representation must misrepresent something other than the careful performance or the success of the very treatment or operation whose failure is the basis of plaintiff's subsequent complaint.

The general rule is that therapeutic reassurance, whether given before, during, or after the course of treatment, does not constitute fraud and does not interrupt the running of the statute of limitations.

It is important to examine the statutes closely to determine what it is that must be "discovered." For example, in California (Code Civ Proc §340.5) and in Oregon (ORS 12.110), it is "the injury." In Washington (RCW §4.16.1), it is that "the injury or condition was caused by the wrongful act." An Illinois case, *Ilardi v Spaccapaniccia,* 53 Ill App 3d 933, 369 NE 2d 144 (1977), illustrates the distinction: *Held,* that under the Illinois statute a cause of action in medical malpractice accrues when the patient learns of the existence of the injury—not the date he or she discovers the injury is actionable. (Compare the California and Oregon statutes.)

The lessons taught by the foregoing are that the potential retrospective liability exposure has been constantly changing. This means that the physician should assemble and preserve all prior errors and omissions insurance policies and obtain copies of any that are missing; and then do what can be done to obtain additional coverage against *prior acts*.

KNOW YOUR INSURANCE COVERAGE

The 2 types of professional liability coverage presently offered to physicians are generally called **occurrence** policies and **claims made** policies. From the standpoint of the person insured, the former contract is preferable, but it is rapidly being superseded by the latter type and has almost vanished from the market.

Reading the Policy

It is difficult and confusing for a layperson to read and understand an insurance policy. An apocryphal story about a judge's instruction to a jury illustrates the point:

> Gentlemen of the jury, here on the front page the insurance company states that its policy covers everything; but here on the back page, it says it doesn't cover anything. It is for you the jury to decide which side of the policy to believe.

There is a method of reading a liability insurance policy that eliminates much of the confusion. A policy is composed of 3 parts: (1) insuring agreements, (2) exclusions, and (3) conditions. The insuring agreements describe the events against which insurance is afforded and identify the persons the insurer will protect against the consequences of those events. The exclusions are designed to eliminate from the broad terms of the insuring agreements certain events and persons the insurer does not wish to cover. The duties of the insured and the definitions of terms are encompassed within the conditions.

A liability insurance policy is more understandable if read in logical sequence. First, read the insuring agreements. Is the event one that is included within an insuring agreement, and is the person needing protection within the clause that defines "the insured"? Next, read the exclusions. Is either the person or the event excluded from coverage? If neither the event nor the person is excluded, then turn to the conditions. Has the person desiring protection met all policy conditions?

History

The difference between the occurrence policy and the claims made policy is best illustrated by a brief outline of the historical development of the "claims made" policy.

The original "claims made" coverage was developed by certain underwriters at Lloyd's, London. "Lloyd's" is not the name of an insurance company; it is a particular form of insurance written by various syndicates. The "claims made" coverage was developed to enable a syndicate to limit the term of its potential exposure to a predetermined date for closing out its particular insurance pool. The form of the contracts as it was originally conceived was not for the purpose of loss control.

Typically, the Underwriters' Certificate set forth inclusive dates on the face of the certificate and then provided, in substance, as follows:

> This insurance is to idemnify the person or persons named in the Schedule herein carrying on business under the firm name and style stated in the said Schedule (hereinafter called "the Firm" which expression shall include the aforesaid persons and any other persons who may at any time and from time to time during the subsistence of this Insurance be a partner in the Firm or any one or more of them), . . . against any claim or claims made for breach of professional duty as physicians or surgeons which may be made against them during the period set forth in the said Schedule by reason of any negligent act, error, or omission, whenever or wherever the same was or may have been committed, on the part of the Firm or their predecessors in business or persons hereafter to be employed by the Firm during the subsistence of the Insurance, in the conduct of any business conducted by or on behalf of the Firm or their predecessors in business in their professional capacity as physicians or surgeons.

The insurance afforded did not depend on the date of the error or omission giving rise to the claim. The coverage was for any claim of which the Underwriters were given notice during the time the Certificate remained in effect.

The early policies written by insurers within the United States were on an "occurrence" basis, but the insurers attempted to limit the "tail" (their term of potential exposure following expiration of the policy) by providing as follows:

> This policy applies only to negligent acts, errors, or omissions which occur during the policy period and then only if claim, suit, or other action arising therefrom is commenced during the policy or within ninety months after the end of the policy period, or if the policy period is longer than one year, within ninety months after the end of the annual period in which the negligent act, error, or omission occurred, all within the United States of America, its territories or possessions, Canada, or Newfoundland.

By this time, the actuaries had determined that the average "stringout" (time following expiration of a policy within which, on the average, some third party might make a claim) on a physician's liability policy was 7½ years. Note carefully that this time is only *average* and may be longer.

For a time the insurers had good experience with this coverage, and the form was broadened to include the best features of the "occurrence" and "claims made" forms:

> This policy applies within the United States of America, its territories or possessions, or Canada to professional services performed for others (a) during the policy period, or (b) prior to the effective date of this policy if claim or suit is brought during the policy period and providing the insured had no knowledge or could not have reasonably foreseen any circumstance which might result in a claim or suit at the effective date of the policy.

Thus, the policy was a "claims made" policy, without any retroactive time limit with respect to occurrences prior to the inception of the policy; and it was also an "occurrence" policy with respect to errors and omissions that took place during its effective date. Note also that under the "occurrence" feature there was *no subsequent time limit* on discovery.

When loss experience on physicians' coverage abruptly became adverse, the insurers did one of 3 things: (1) quit writing the coverage altogether; (2) continued to write the "broad form" coverage and hope for the best; or (3) wrote a "claims made" policy practically identical to the original Lloyd's form but with a "bedbug" endorsement excluding coverage for any act or occurrence that had taken place prior to the inception date of the policy. The latter form, in effect, relieved the insurer of the "stringout" hazard and placed that hazard entirely upon the insured.

A strict "claims made" policy affords insurance coverage for a very short time indeed, as witness the following letter: (An actual letter to a physician from The Vice President in Charge of Claims of an insurance company is paraphrased.)

> Your letter of October 17, 1976, which was routed through the A.B. Fitzhugh Company to Anson & Company, has been forwarded to us as your professional liability carrier during the period from June 27, 1973, until October 9, 1975. I must inform you that the policies involved during that interval were written on a claims made basis, which means that they provide coverage only for liability arising out of claims made during the policy period. I refer you specifically to the form attached to your policy entitled Malpractice Liability Practitioners (Claims Made Basis): "2 . . . PROVIDED ALWAYS THAT (a) such Malpractice results in a claim being made against the Assured during the period of insurance as stated in the Schedule and . . ."
>
> Since the claim in question was not presented to you until October of 1976, about one year following expiration of your coverage with this company, there would be no coverage under that policy for this loss. I would suggest that you refer the matter to your present carrier in the hope that they may provide coverage for the incident.
>
> If you have any questions concerning this matter etc . . .

A typical "claims made" policy obligates the insurer to pay a loss sustained *during the policy period* and specifies that coverage is afforded against *claims which may be made during a period scheduled in the policy*. It affords no coverage for an error or omission committed while the policy was in force but for which no claim was made and no notice of claim given until after expiration of the policy.

Retrospective Date

A modifying provision that is most desirable (but not always obtainable) reads somewhat as follows:

> This policy applies only to claims made against the insured during the policy period or during the effective date of each successive renewal of such policy.

The insurer may specially agree that the retrospective date shall be the inception date of the first in a series of "claims made" policies; however, if the insurer ceases to make renewal policies available, even a "claims made" policy with a retrospective provision does not protect the physician against the malpractice hazard. (See Prior Acts, below.)

Tail

Another desirable provision that can sometimes be added to a "claims made" policy is a provision for a "tail," which might read as follows:

> This policy applies only to claims made against the insured during the policy period, or within the 36 calendar months immediately following the expiration or termination of the policy.

Though the *average* "stringout" is 7½ years, those insurers who today can be prevailed upon to offer a tail will seldom make it longer than 3 years.

If a claims made policy is the only form of coverage available, every effort should be made to obtain the earliest possible retrospective date and the longest tail. The ideal contract—if anything about a claims made policy can be called ideal—would read as follows:

> This policy applies to any act or omission which occurs during the effective period of a policy and which was discovered during the effective period of such policy, during the effective period of any subsequent successive renewal policy, or within 36 months after the expiration of the last successive renewal policy.

When Is an Injury Sustained?

Generally speaking, an injury is "sustained" and a cause of action arises when the harm becomes manifest. This was not formerly the rule. Under the former rule, an injury was "sustained" and the cause of action arose when—for example—the sponge was left in the patient. Under the doctrines prevailing today, the injury is "sustained" and the cause of action arises when the patient starts to suffer adverse consequences or otherwise becomes aware of the oversight. (See Statutes of Limitation, above.)

With the period of insurance protection contracting and the period and amount of potential liability for an error of commission or omission concurrently expanding, the problem of obtaining adequate professional liability insurance is rapidly becoming unsolvable. The problem results from the economic consequences of inflation upon claims costs compounded by judicial amendment of statutes of limitation. Recent efforts by the medical profession to ameliorate the problem by legislation have not been properly directed at the root causes. It may be possible to alleviate the problem, but only if there is definitive restrictive legislative action returning the rules of evidence, the statutes of limitation, and the substantive law of malpractice to what was commonly understood to be the law in about the year 1950.

Prior Acts

Whether or not the insured has liability exposure for a given prior act or omission depends upon the interpretation of the statute of limitations in force not when a claim is made but at the time the physician is sued.

Whether or not the insured has liability insurance against a prior act or omission depends either upon the terms of the insurance contract at the time of the act or omission or upon the terms of the insurance contract at the time a claim is made. In some cases, it can depend on both contracts.

Whether or not the insured has insurance that is *adequate in amount* depends on the amount of *available* insurance viewed in light of current and projected inflation. The physician may have applicable insurance under an old occurrence contract, but the amount of this insurance may not be sufficient.

It now is *sometimes* possible to obtain a "claims made" policy that covers . . .

> any claim or claims first made against the insured and reported to the Company during the policy period . . .

and which excludes only those prior acts or omissions which result in a . . .

> claim arising out of any acts or omissions occurring prior to the effective date of this policy if the insured at the effective date knew or could have reasonably foreseen that such acts or omissions might be expected to be the basis of a claim or suit . . .

which contains the following condition:

> . . . provided, however, with respect to acts or omissions which occur prior to the inception date of the policy, the insurance hereunder shall apply only as excess insurance over any other valid and collectable insurance and shall then apply only in the amount by which the applicable limits of this policy exceeds the sum of the applicable limits of liability of all such other insurance. In the event that this policy is treated as excess insurance, any claims expenses allocated to it shall be included in the limit of liability . . .

and which provides that upon termination of the policy, for an additional premium (usually about 2½ times a single annual premium), the insured may purchase an Extended Reporting Endorsement which provides, in part:

> Coverage will be provided according to the applicable terms, conditions and exclusions of this policy for all claims first made after the termination of the policy period, arising out of any act or omission of the insured in rendering professional services for others in the insured's capacity as a physician and surgeon, which occurred prior to the termination of the policy period and were caused by the insured or any other person for whose acts or omissions the insured is legally responsible, and are otherwise covered by the policy.
>
> The Limit of Liability applicable to all claims first made during the Extended Reporting Period shall be the same as those shown in . . . the Declarations.

That particular policy form and endorsement will provide lifetime coverage against unknown prior acts or omissions occurring between the date the physician first entered practice and the date the underlying claims made policy was terminated and the Extended Reporting Period Endorsement was obtained.

Other forms of "claims made" policies limiting the retrospective period to the "retroactive date" as that term is defined in the policy sometimes contain a provision for the purchase of an Extended Reporting Period Endorsement upon termination of the underlying coverage with the issuing insurer. But the Extended Reporting Period Endorsement available under these forms does not provide coverage retrospective beyond the retroactive date as that term is defined in the policy.

It is important to note that prior acts coverage is applicable *only in the amount by which the applicable limit of the prior acts coverage exceeds the sum of the applicable limits of liability of all other available insurance*. This means that the physician who wishes to increase the limit of insurance for prior acts which is afforded by older occurrence policies will have to purchase both underlying claims made coverage and Extended Reporting Period Endorsement in an amount that exceeds the other applicable insurance up to the total desired amount of insurance, bearing in mind not only the limit of the other available insurance but the anticipated impact of inflation. *The old and new policies cannot be aggregated*. The physician would be insured only for the amount of applicable insurance on an older occurrence form plus the amount by which the new claims made form and Extended Reporting Period Endorsement *exceeds* the limit of the other applicable insurance.

The right to purchase an Extended Reporting Period Endorsement is a valuable one and should be carefully considered. Since available contracts vary greatly, they cannot all be discussed in this brief treatment. An insurance agent or broker should be consulted for specific details applicable to the physician's peculiar circumstances.

WITNESS FEES

An "ordinary witness" (percipient witness; fact witness) is legally entitled to the statutory witness fee plus mileage and is entitled to those amounts only if appearing under subpoena.

To what fee is an "expert witness" entitled? *Same answer!* However, the expert witness may legitimately receive compensation for special research or consultation services rendered to the attorney who engages the expert's services for these purposes.

Every person within the geographic jurisdiction of a court must obey the process of that court. When so required, a person must appear and tell what he or she knows without extraordinary compensation for appearing as a witness.

It is commonly believed, but incorrectly, that a "fact" witness testifying on the facts is required to tell what he or she knows but that an "opinion" witness need not give an opinion if he or she does not wish to do so. A witness who is required to make special preparations (eg, examination, study) to become qualified to testify in a particular case is entitled to compensation for the special work performed. A witness who is *already* prepared must appear and respond to examination with extra pay. The witness can be asked for opinions held in the past or opinions presently held. The existence of an opinion is itself a "fact."

For example, a physician managing a patient forms an opinion (the diagnosis) as a basis for therapy. The validity of this opinion is achieved by following the patient and forming other opinions (prognosis). These opinions are "past facts." The physician is not entitled to extra compensation for testifying to these facts. The doctor is in a position similar to that of a pedestrian who in testimony gives an opinion about the speed of a passing automobile.

It may happen that a person with expertise pertinent to an action will be subpoenaed without warning and asked to give an opinion. This witness must either give the opinion and the reasons for it or must explain why a valid opinion cannot be given. Not being offered a fee is not an acceptable explanation. However, the witness need not do any more than listen to the questions, examine the exhibits shown in the courtroom, and give the best answer honestly possible. There is no duty to spend time doing library research or otherwise attempting to aid the inquiry.

Imagine the result if a treating physician, attempting to retaliate for nonreceipt of an "expert" fee, were to give the history, report objective observations, deny having formed any opinion, and then testify concerning treatment administered. This would amount to a confession, under oath, to culpable negligence in undertaking to "treat" a clinical entity without any attempt to arrive at a diagnosis.

DEPOSITIONS

A deposition is a written record of testimony given before trial. Anyone giving a deposition is a witness. The term witness includes the parties to the lawsuit.

Depositions are taken in advance of a trial (1) to learn what a witness knows, (2) to bind the witness to a particular story, or (3) to preserve testimony for later use at trial.

The questions at a deposition are called interrogatories. The replies are answers or responses.

Subject to variations in the laws of various states, a deposition may be taken before any person authorized to administer oaths. The proceeding may take place (1) in the office of the witness or one of the attorneys; (2) in a courtroom or some convenient room in a courthouse; or (3) at whatever other place may have been designated or agreed upon. The proceeding is usually informal. Those in attendance at a deposition will be "the person authorized to administer oaths" (usually the court reporter doubling as a notary public), the witness, the participating attorneys, and sometimes other interested persons such as the opposing party.

The oath is administered, and the witness is then questioned as though in court.

Despite its air of informality, a deposition is just as much a judicial proceeding as is a trial. The witness is subject to the same penalties for perjury and for refusal to answer as in open court.

Attendance at a deposition may be compelled by subpoena. Additionally, under the Federal Rules of Civil Procedure and in several states, a party to the lawsuit is compelled to attend if a proper written notice has been served on the party or on the party's attorney.

Testimony by deposition has the same serious consequences as testimony at trial. Be prepared to testify appropriately. Always insist on a thorough advance consultation with the attorney responsible for safeguarding your interest. If you are a party to a lawsuit, this will be the attorney who represents you. When in any doubt about your obligations or risks, consult a "neutral" attorney of your personal choice.

Before attending a deposition, the witness should review the matter with the appropriate attorney and may have the attorney's technical assistance in formulating responses.

Witness fees at any deposition are governed by the same considerations as at trial. However, in most jurisdictions a party to the litigation (plaintiff or defendant) is entitled to no compensation, statutory or otherwise, for participating in the trial as a witness or in any other capacity. However, there is one possible exception: As a practical matter, it is harmful to a litigant's case to appear "uncooperative." Therefore, if adverse counsel asks the defendant physician to do something that takes research or study, it is best not to categorically refuse to cooperate but to defer to the defense attorney for instructions.

AVOID CROSS–LIABILITY

In the abstract, those rules by which the negligence of another is imputed to a surgeon or other physician may impose vicarious liability for any damage that occurs as a result. Briefly, these are the liability of (1) "the captain of the ship," (2) the employer for the employee, (3) the master for the loaned servant, (4) the partner for the partner, and (5) joint participants. Many courts have extended the "captain of the ship" and "joint venture" principles to hold the insured physician responsible for acts over which he or she exerts no semblance of control. This has come about apparently as a matter of judicial policy but without any statement to this effect.

In the absence of the applicability of any of the 5 categories mentioned, all courts concede in the abstract that physicians are liable only for their own errors and omissions, and the prudent physician will make every effort to keep it that way. This can be done by insisting on a clear-cut division of work and responsibility and by avoiding concurrent or overlapping functions. This is not a simple matter and must be discussed in some detail in order to make it clear.

Physicians are liable for their own culpable errors and omissions. Beginning with this established principle, the meaning of "their own culpable errors and omissions" has been extended to include the "treat together" rule as set forth in *Graddy v New York Medical College*, 19 App Div 2d 426, 243, NYS 2d 940 (1963):

> Where physicians actually participate together in diagnosis and treatment, they may each incur a liability for the negligence of the other even though a more active part in the treatment may have been taken by one of them.

The "treat together" rule acknowledges that concurrently treating physicians are not vicariously liable for each others' negligence *except* where they are acting in concert or where one or more observe but do nothing about the work-up or therapy by the other when they know or *in the exercise of ordinary care should know* that an error or omission is being or has been committed by the colleague. The realization that it is usually up to a jury to decide whether the physicians were "acting in concert" or whether one or more of them observed something which they knew or in the exercise of ordinary care should have known was erroneous makes apparent at once the wisdom of avoiding unnecessary participation with other physicians in the concurrent care of the same patient.

A physician who refers a patient to another physician may best avoid such problems by simply not seeing that patient until the second physician has referred the patient back. Admittedly, this precaution may be difficult to act on in practice. Under no circumstances should the referring physician be present at any surgical procedure, for such unrequired presence is the most notable single occasion for unnecessary liability. Unrequired hospital visits or review of the records and discussion with the physician to whom the patient has been referred to enable the referring physician to "explain" the situation to the patient or the family are imprudent. Such explanations are best left to the physician who has undertaken the management of the case. Unrequired participation invites application of the rule that if a patient suffers injury from concurring negligence of 2 or more defendants, both or all are jointly and severally liable.

An aspect of cross-liability that has been given little consideration pertains to the assistant surgeon who has no connection with the case except for the operation. The physician would clearly be liable for any erroneous affirmative act performed during the procedure and probably also for errors and omissions of others if the requisite "knew or should have known" criteria are met. The physician or the physician's employer—the hospital in the case of a resident—would be liable to indemnify the operating surgeon held liable as "captain of the ship" for the affirmative errors of an unqualified assistant. *(Maybarduk v Bustamente*, 294 So 2d 374 [Fla App 1974].)

It is in the area of "knew or should have known" that the line of separation becomes indistinct.

Two cases specifically considering the liability of one who acts as an assistant surgeon without participating in or preoperatively reviewing the diagnosis and choice of procedures, without making any surgical decisions, and without personally detecting or committing any errors during surgery, are *Wynne v Harvey*, 96 Wash 379, 165 Pac 67 (1917); and *Evans v Bernhard*, 23 Ariz App 413, 533, P2d 721 (1975). *Wynne* illustrates what ought to be the rule but what is usually obscured by overactivity on the part of the assistant surgeon and intellectual myopia on the part of the judge. Dr Harvey was employed to operate on the plaintiff. He selected Dr Clark to assist. A sponge was left in the plaintiff. After defining the duty of the assistant surgeon as being essentially ministerial and not including the removal of sponges or keeping track of them, the Court delivered the following opinion:

> Appellant Clark having had nothing to do with the sponges or mopping with them on the inside of the incision, as is shown by all the evidence . . . , it is obvious that Clark would not be liable for this negligence because of any wrongful act of his own . . . and, since the duties of an assistant are to do as directed by the chief operator, and there was no knowing that he was either directed to keep track of the sponges or that it was made his duty by custom to do so, it is apparent that, in the exercise of reasonable diligence under the circumstances, no duty devolved upon Clark to discover the sponge was not removed . . .

Contrast the attitude of the court in *Fehrman v Smirl*, 25 Wis 2d 645, 131 NW 2d 314 (1964): Dr Smirl apparently had performed surgery in a negligent manner, and it befell the jury to determine who was "captain of the ship." Predictably, the jury held that Dr Smirl was in charge and should be held liable for the negligence of Dr McDonnell. It was said in the opinion:

> To the writer of this opinion, it would appear reasonably clear from the record of the second trial that Dr McDonnell was in charge of the second operation rather than Dr Smirl. To hold that Dr Smirl (the assistant) is liable for the negligence of Dr McDonnell (the surgeon in charge) would seem to be the application of a novel doctrine of *respondeat inferior*. However, the majority of the court is persuaded that, under the circumstances of this case, Dr Smirl either was in charge of the patient or was acting jointly with Dr McDonnell. Accordingly, the court concludes that it was proper for the trial judge to instruct the jury as he did on the question of vicarious liability.

The practical problem facing a physician and the differing consequences of the choices concerning the nature and extent of participation were succinctly summed up in *Arshansky v Royal Concourse Co.*, 28 App Div 2d 986, 283 NYS 2d 646 (1967):

> A question of fact for the jury was presented as to whether the operation . . . was done properly in ac-

cordance with standard practice, and whether failure to so perform the operation was the cause of [the patient's] subsequent pain and incapacity. She was Dr Resnick's patient, and he referred her to Dr Cheifetz, who operated. The reference, in itself, would not render Dr Resnick liable . . . Dr Resnick, however, participated in the diagnosis and attended at the operation and assisted therein to a degree sufficient to present a question of fact for the jury as to his liability in connection with the alleged improper operation . . .

Just as a physician learns from the experience of others how to diagnose illness and treat patients, so may a physician learn from the experience of others how to minimize exposure to patients. Something may be learned from the misfortune that befell Dr Fabric, who examined Mrs O'Grady and reached a diagnosis. He prudently referred her to Dr Wickman, a gynecologist, who examined her and recommended right salpingo-oophorectomy. Dr. Fabric scheduled an exploratory laparotomy and acted as assistant to Dr Wickman. The trial court did not permit a jury to determine the liability of Dr Fabric for the performance by Dr Wickman of an unauthorized hysterectomy, but the appellate court in reversing and remanding for trial said, ". . . Under these circumstances, issues of material fact exist and have not been negated by the record as to whether there was a concert of action and a common purpose existing between the two doctors." (O'Grady v Wickman, 213 So 2d 321 [Fla App 1968].)

HOSPITAL STAFF COMMITTEE EXPOSURE

In *Darling v Charleston Community Memorial Hospital,* 33 Ill2d 326, 211 NE2d 253, 14 ALR3d 860 (1965), the plaintiff, after settling with his physician, sued the hospital for negligence in, among other things, permitting the physician to perform orthopedic procedures beyond his professional competence and in failing to override the practitioner in his management of the case. The plaintiff contended, and the Court agreed, that standards of The Joint Commission on Accreditation of Hospitals, state administrative regulations, and the hospital's bylaws can be considered in court as evidence of proper standards, and whether or not those standards have been met is a jury question. Juries respect standards established by reliable private or public bodies. The practical result forcast by *Darling* was that the administration must enforce compliance with accreditation standards, public administrative regulations, and hospital bylaws by all who practice on the premises.

It was held in *Joiner v Mitchell County Hospital Authority,* 12 Ga App 1, 186 SE2d 307, 51 ALR3d 976 (1971), that a hospital is liable for the consequences of incompetent treatment by a staff member if the hospital has failed to exercise care in determining his or her professional competence.

It is becoming increasingly well established that even though physicians are independent contractors, the hospital has a duty to the public to restrict the use of its facilities by independent staff physicians to those who are professionally competent and can be expected to treat their patients in full accordance with established medical practice, and that this duty is breached when the hospital either (1) fails to exercise care in determining the physician's professional competence before granting staff privileges; or (2) fails to take action against the attending physician to protect the patient when the hospital knows (or should know) that the attending physician lacks or is not exercising the necessary skill and care.

The courts have taken the initiative in establishing the standards of individual practitioners and hospitals even in remote areas. The "community" is now nationwide (see p 534). In effect, the courts have gone far toward saying that hospitals and physicians must adopt the "best" methods of professional practice, not merely average standards or those prevailing in the local community. A general summary of the judge-made law is as follows:

(1) Hospitals have a duty to supervise the competence of the medical and surgical staff, and thus have corporate responsibility for the quality of medical care rendered within the hospital.

(2) Hospitals and their governing bodies are liable for injuries resulting from negligent supervision of members of the medical and surgical staff. The hospital has assumed certain responsibilities for the care of its patients, and it must meet the standards of responsibility commensurate with this trust.

(3) If the staff negligently grants privileges to incompetent physicians, fails to supervise its members, or fails to recommend corrective action against a derelict physician prior to or upon discovery of substandard malpractice by that physician, the hospital is liable for any harm resulting therefrom.

Thus, a hospital is required to take reasonable steps to assure its patients that the physicians and surgeons to whom it grants privileges are licensed, well-trained, and qualified, both ethically and technically, to exercise those privileges in that hospital facility.

The hospital as an institution must determine the competence of applicants for staff membership and limit the grant of individual hospital privileges within the bounds of the individual's professional competence. The hospital must maintain continuing oversight to assure that the individual practitioner consistently meets acceptable standards.

Professional standards are a joint problem of hospital administration and medical staff. Therefore, medical standards and business administration cannot be separated. There is hospital liability whenever an administrator knows—or should know—that individual staff members either do not possess or are departing from acceptable standards, and the administration cannot ignore what is transpiring professionally within the hospital. *Johnson v Misericordia Community Hospital,* 99 Wis2d 708, 301 NW2d 156 (1981).

The administration initially "knows" (assesses) the individual physician's professional limitations after screening by the Credentials Committee and "knows" the quality of the physician's skills as a result of regular chart audit by the Records Committed.

Throughout 20 Code of Federal Regulations Subpart J, Conditions of Participation; Hospitals—and in particular § 405.1023—runs the theme that it is the responsibility of the administration to enforce professional standards and that it does so by appointing and disciplining *through the agency of the staff organization,* particularly the Credentials Committee.

If the hospital is liable to a patient for admitting and tolerating an incompetent physician, the next question is the corresponding liability of the physician staff through which the hospital acted. The liability of the staff to the patient is becoming identical to that of the hospital. *Corleto v Shore Memorial Hospital,* 138 NJ Super 302, 350 A2d 534 (1975), held that the hospital, its administrator, its board of directors, and the medical staff of 141 all were subject to suit for granting surgical privileges to an allegedly incompetent physician, for allowing him to perform a surgical procedure upon the plaintiff, and for allowing him to remain on the case when the situation was obviously beyond his competence.

Consideration of the hospital's problem with individual staff member incompetence is circular, in that it always returns to the *Darling* case. *Darling* held that the hospital was liable to the patient because it had permitted the surgeon of the patient's choice to use its facilities to perform a procedure that was outside the surgeon's professional competence (this was the jury's finding). How had the hospital failed? It had failed because, acting through its Credentials Committee, it had been too generous in granting of privileges. As a practical and legal matter, what recourse did the hospital have? It had a right to indemnity from the staff under the principle that one compelled to pay damages (the hospital) on account of the negligent or tortious act of another (the staff) has a right of action against the latter for indemnity. An agent (the staff) is liable to his or her principal (the hospital) for damages the latter was compelled to pay to a third person solely because of the negligent or wrongful act of the agent; it is no defense to the agent that other persons were also culpable.

The culpable surgeon had presumably received hospital privileges upon the recommendation of the staff acting through its Credentials Committee. The inference is clear that the staff and its Credentials Committee had failed in its undertaking to the hospital (1) by recommending privileges beyond the surgeon's professional ability, (2) by failing to monitor the individual staff member, and thus (3) by failing to recommend reduction of privileges as indicated.

In reallocating loss in the *Darling* case, the logical thing for the hospital to have done (at least legally speaking) would have been to tender the defense of Darling's action against it to each member of the physician staff on the theory that each member of an unincorporated association is liable for failure of the association to perform its undertakings. In this instance, the failure of the Credentials Committee and the officers of the staff was the failure of each member of the staff organization for which the staff organization and each of its members owed indemnity to the hospital.

It is, however, a gradually eroding general rule that an agent (the staff) has no liability to a third person (the patient) for failure to perform something that ought to be done by the principal (the hospital). Complete inaction by the staff (as distinguished from incompetent action) might be a defense to a suit against the staff brought by a patient (as distinguished from a demand for indemnity by the hospital). But rules change, and one cannot count on endurance of even the general rule; refer again to *Corleto* (above) and its holding that 141 staff members were exposed to suit by the patient.

In the following scenario, the foregoing concepts are summarized and carried to their logical extremes:

(1) Accrediting standards and federal regulations require that each staff member abide by hospital standards and recommendations and that the hospital appoint and police its staff according to the staff organization's recommendations.

(2) If the staff then recommends appointment or reappointment of an incompetent member or tolerates incompetent practice, then—

(3) The patient injured on hospital premises by his or her own incompetent physician can —
  (a) Sue the physician for malpractice,
  (b) Sue the hospital and its administration for allowing an incompetent physician to use its facilities, and
  (c) Sue the staff both for selecting and failing to curb an incompetent staff member.

(4) The hospital and administration may then demand indemnity from the staff for failure to perform its legal obligations in enforcing practice standards.

(5) The patient collects from the hospital, and
  (a) The hospital recoups from the staff organization, and
    (i) Those individuals in turn recoup from the individuals actually responsible for the patient's injuries.

The hospital liability insurance policy almost always extends coverage to

> . . . while acting within the scope of his duties as such, any partner, trustee, executive officer, director or stockholder. . . or any superintendent, administrator, or supervisor of the hospital or department thereof.

Some hospital policies extend coverage to staff committee members for claims arising out of the performance of committee functions but exclude claims based on or attributable to bodily injury, sickness, disease, or death of any person . . .

This exclusion would apply in a case such as *Corleto*. Discussions with selected underwriters concerning the *Corleto* problem produced a consensus that it would be "unusual" to find a hospital policy that would cover the medical and surgical staff, or even committee members, against a *Corleto* situation.

The reader should thus reflect on his or her individual exposure, as it is clear that a breach of duty to uphold professional standards among colleagues subjects each staff member to some liability toward the hospital, and the definite possibility is emerging that such failure subjects each staff member to some liability toward a complaining patient.

Menopause & Postmenopause | 25

Howard L. Judd, MD

General Considerations

According to the 1970 census of the United States, of the 104 million women in this country, 27 million were 50 years of age or older. Most of these women had had or shortly would have their last menstrual period, thus becoming postmenopausal. Statistics indicate that at age 50 a woman can expect to live another 28 years. Since this census, the population of this country has increased appreciably, and the percentage of older people has also risen. Thus, we have a large minority of our population who are without ovarian function and who live approximately one-third of their lives following ovarian failure. Consequently, it is essential that physicians caring for women have an understanding of the hormonal and metabolic changes associated with the menopause, or "change of life," and an appreciation of the potential benefits and risks of replacement therapy.

There has been some inconsistency about the meaning of certain words related to this area; however, the Comité des Nomenclatures de la Fédération Internationale de Gynécologie et d'Obstétrique has recently issued guidelines for the use of several words, and these definitions will be utilized in this chapter. The **climacteric** is the phase in the aging process during which a woman passes from the reproductive to the nonreproductive stage. The signals that this period of life has been reached are referred to as climacteric symptoms or, if more serious, as climacteric complaints (not as menopause symptomatology or menopausal complaints). **Premenopause** refers to the part of the climacteric before the menopause occurs, the time during which the menstrual cycle is likely to be irregular and when other climacteric symptoms or complaints may occur. The **menopause** is the final menstruation, which occurs during the climacteric. **Postmenopause** refers to the phase of life that comes after the menopause. It is uncertain whether this term should refer to the remainder of a woman's life or just to the period in which climacteric symptoms occur.

Etiology & Pathogenesis

A. Menopause: There are 2 types of menopause, classified according to cause.

1. Physiologic menopause–In the human embryo, oogenesis begins in the ovary around the third week of gestation. Primordial germ cells appear in the yolk sac of the embryo and by the fifth week migrate to the germinal ridge, where they undergo successive mitotic cellular divisions to give rise to oogonia, which eventually give rise to oocytes. It has been estimated that the fetal ovaries contain approximately 7 million oogonia at 20 weeks' gestation. From then until the menopause, there is a reduction in the number of germ cells. After 7 months' gestation, no new oocytes are formed. At birth, there are approximately 2 million oocytes, and by puberty this number has been reduced to 300,000. There is continued reduction of oocyte number during the reproductive years. Two general processes are responsible for this: ovulation and atresia. Nearly all oocytes vanish by atresia, with only 400–500 actually being ovulated. Very little is known about oocyte atresia. Animal studies have shown that estrogens prevent whereas androgens enhance the atretic process.

Menopause apparently occurs in the human female because of 2 processes. First, oocytes responsive to gonadotropins disappear from the ovary, and second, the few remaining oocytes do not respond to gonadotropins. Isolated oocytes can be found in postmenopausal ovaries on very careful histologic inspection. Some of them show a limited degree of development, but most reveal no sign of development in the presence of excess endogenous gonadotropins.

Because of logistic problems, it has been difficult to determine the average age at menopause currently or in the past. There may have been an increase in the age at menopause in the USA and Western Europe, but this is not clear. At this time, the average age at menopause in the USA is 49–50 years. There does not appear to be any consistent relationship between age at menarche and age at menopause. Marriage, childbearing, height, weight, and prolonged use of oral contraceptives do not appear to influence the age at menopause. Smoking, however, is associated with early menopause.

Spontaneous cessation of menses before age 40 is called **premature menopause** or **premature ovarian failure.** Cessation of menstruation and the development of climacteric symptoms and complaints can occur as early as a few years after menarche. The reasons for premature ovarian failure are unknown.

Disease processes, especially severe infections or

tumors of the reproductive tract, can occasionally damage the ovarian follicular structures so severely as to precipitate the menopause. The menopause can also be hastened by excessive exposure to ionizing radiation; chemotherapeutic drugs, particularly alkylating agents; and surgical procedures that impair ovarian blood supply.

2. Artificial menopause–The permanent cessation of ovarian function brought about by surgical removal of the ovaries or by radiation therapy is called an artificial menopause. Irradiation to ablate ovarian function is rarely used today. Artificial menopause is employed as a treatment for endometriosis and estrogen-sensitive neoplasms of the breast and endometrium. More frequently, artificial menopause is a side-effect of treatment of intra-abdominal disease; eg, ovaries are removed in premenopausal women because the gonads have been damaged by infection or neoplasia. When laparotomy affords the opportunity, elective bilateral oophorectomy is also employed to prevent ovarian cancer. For premenopausal women, this practice is still highly controversial. For postmenopausal women, it is now generally accepted as good medical practice.

B. The Premenopausal State: The decades of mature reproductive life are characterized by generally regular menses and a slow, steady decrease in cycle length. Mean cycle length at age 15 is 35 days, at age 25 it is 30 days, and at age 35 it is 28 days. This decrease in cycle length is due to shortening of the follicular phase of the cycle, with the luteal phase length remaining constant. After age 45, altered function of the aging ovary is detectable in regularly menstruating women (Fig 25–1). The mean cycle length is significantly shorter than in younger women and is attributable, in all cases, to a shortened follicular phase. The luteal phase is of similar length, and progesterone levels are not different from those observed in younger women. Estradiol levels are lower during portions of the cycle, including active follicular maturation, the midcycle peak, and the luteal phase. Concentrations of follicle-stimulating hormone (FSH) are strikingly elevated during the early follicular phase and fall as estradiol increases during follicular maturation. FSH levels at the midcycle peak and late in the luteal phase are also consistently higher than those found in younger women and decrease during the midluteal phase. Luteinizing hormone (LH) concentrations are indistinguishable from those observed in younger women. The mechanism responsible for this early rise of FSH, but not of LH, is not defined. It may result from the reduced number of oocytes still present in the older ovary. It may reflect the lower concentrations of estradiol found in these women or the absence of another ovarian factor, analogous to inhibin in the male, that would regulate FSH secretion.

The transition from regular cycle intervals to the permanent amenorrhea of menopause is characterized by a phase of marked menstrual irregularity. The duration of this transition varies greatly among women. Those experiencing the menopause at an early age

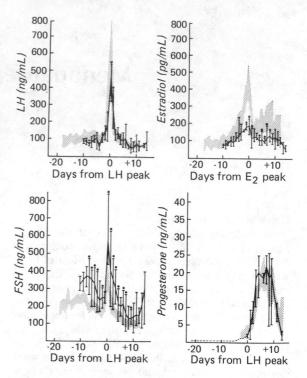

Figure 25–1. Mean and range of LH, FSH, estradiol (E_2), and progesterone levels in women with regular menstrual cycles, over age 45. Shaded area represents the mean ± 2 SEM in cycles found in young women. (Reproduced, with permission, from Sherman BM, Korenman SG: Hormonal characteristics of the human menstrual cycle throughout reproductive life. *J Clin Invest* 1975;55:699.)

have a relatively short duration of cycle variability before amenorrhea ensues. Those experiencing it at a later age usually have a phase of menstrual irregularity characterized by unusually long and short intermenstrual intervals and an overall increase of mean cycle length and variance.

The hormonal characteristics of this transitional phase are of special interest and importance. The irregular episodes of vaginal bleeding in premenopausal women represent the irregular maturation of ovarian follicles with or without hormonal evidence of ovulation. The potential for hormone secretion by these remaining follicles is diminished and variable. Menses are sometimes preceded by maturation of a follicle with limited secretion of both estradiol and progesterone. Vaginal bleeding also occurs after a rise and fall of estradiol without a measurable increase in progesterone, such as occurs in anovulatory menses. In view of the spectrum of hormonal changes observed during this transitional period, it can be postulated that residual follicles are responsible for the limited estradiol secretion that precedes episodes of anovulatory bleeding. It is not known whether ovulation actually occurs during any of these cycles. Nevertheless, the potential for conception during this time is minimal.

From these findings, it is clear that the transitional

phase of menstrual irregularity is not one of marked estrogen deficiency. During the menopausal transition, high levels of FSH appear to stimulate residual follicles to secrete bursts of estradiol. This may be followed by corpus luteum formation, often with limited secretion of progesterone. Because the episodes of follicular maturation and vaginal bleeding are widely spaced, premenopausal women may be exposed to persistent estrogen stimulation of the endometrium in the absence of regular cyclic progesterone secretion, which is thought to be related to the irregular uterine bleeding common to this period.

C. Changes in Hormone Metabolism Associated With the Menopause: (See Fig 25–2.) Following the menopause, there are major changes in androgen, estrogen, progesterone, and gonadotropin secretion, much of which occurs because of cessation of ovarian follicular activity. It is not known how soon these changes are established after the last period, but they are definitely present within 6 months.

1. Androgens–During reproductive life, the primary ovarian androgen is androstenedione, the major secretory product of developing follicles. With the menopause, there is a reduction of circulating androstenedione to approximately one-half the concentration found in young women, reflecting the absence of follicular activity. In older women, there is a circadian variation of androstenedione, with peak concentrations between 8:00 AM and noon, and the nadir occurring between 3:00 PM and 4:00 AM. This rhythm reflects adrenal activity. The clearance rate of androstenedione is similar in pre- and postmenopausal women, so the level of circulating hormone reflects production. Thus, the average production rate of androstenedione is approximately 1.5 mg/24 h in postmenopausal subjects, a rate that is one-half the rate found in premenopausal women. The source of most of this circulating androstenedione appears to be the adrenal glands, but the postmenopausal ovary continues to secrete approximately 20% of the androstenedione.

For testosterone, the mean concentration is minimally lower than the one found in premenopausal women before ovariectomy and is distinctly higher than the level observed in ovariectomized young women. There is also a prominent nyctohemeral variation of this androgen, with the highest levels occurring at 8:00 AM and the nadir at 4:00 PM. There is no difference in the clearance rate of testosterone before and after the menopause. Thus, the production rate in older women is approximately 150 μg/24 h, a rate that is only one-third lower than the rate seen in young women.

The source of circulating testosterone is more complex than that of androstenedione. After the menopause, ovariectomy is associated with a nearly 60% decrease of testosterone. There is no change of the metabolic clearance rate of the androgen with ovariectomy, so the fall in the circulating level reflects alterations of its production rate. Fourteen percent of circulating androstenedione is converted to testosterone. The small simultaneous fall of androstenedione after ovariectomy can only account for a small portion of the total decrease of testosterone. The remainder presumably represents direct ovarian secretion and is larger than the amount secreted directly by the premenopausal ovary. Large increments of testosterone have been found in the ovarian veins of postmenopausal women. These increments are greater than the ones observed in premenopausal women, which supports the hypothesis that the postmenopausal ovary secretes more testosterone directly than the premenopausal gonad. Hilar cells and luteinized stromal cells (hyperthecosis) are present in postmenopausal ovaries and have been shown to produce testosterone in premenopausal women. Presumably these cells could do the same in postmenopausal subjects. A proposed mechanism for increased ovarian testosterone production by postmenopausal ovaries is the stimulation of gonadal cells, still capable of androgen production, by excess endogenous gonadotropins, which in turn are increased because of reduced estrogen production by the ovaries. This increased ovarian testosterone secretion, coupled with a reduction of estrogen production, may in part explain the development of symptoms of defeminization, hirsutism, and even virilism occasionally seen in some older women.

For the adrenal androgens dehydroepiandrosterone and dehydroepiandrosterone sulfate, there are 60% and 80% reductions, respectively, of the levels of these hormones with age. Whether these reductions are related to the menopause or to aging has not been determined. Again, a marked circadian variation of dehydroepiandrosterone has been observed. Whether a

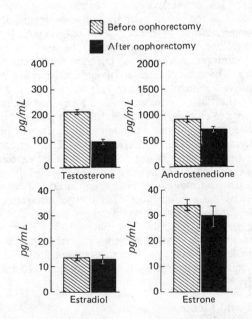

Figure 25–2. Serum androgen and estrogen levels in 16 postmenopausal women with endometrial cancer before and after ovariectomy. (Reproduced, with permission, from Judd HL: Hormonal dynamics associated with the menopause. *Clin Obstet Gynecol* 1976;1:775.)

similar rhythm is present for dehydroepiandrosterone sulfate is not known. As with younger subjects, the primary source of these 2 androgens is thought to be the adrenal glands, with the ovary contributing less than 25%. Thus, the marked decreases of dehydroepiandrosterone and dehydroepiandrosterone sulfate reflect altered adrenal androgen secretion, and this phenomenon has been called the "adrenopause." The mechanism responsible for it is not known.

In summary, there are 3 major changes in androgen metabolism with the menopause and aging: (1) reduction of androgen production by the ovary, particularly androstenedione; (2) continuation of ovarian androgen secretion, particularly testosterone; and (3) reduction in adrenal androgen secretion, particularly dehydroepiandrosterone and dehydroepiandrosterone sulfate.

2. Estrogens–Once a woman has passed the menopause, there is good clinical evidence of reduced endogenous estrogen production in most subjects. When circulating levels have been assessed, the greatest decrease is in estradiol. Estradiol concentration is distinctly lower than that found in young women during any phase of their menstrual cycle and is similar to the level seen in premenopausal women following ovariectomy. There does not appear to be a nyctohemeral variation of the circulating concentration of estradiol following the menopause. The metabolic clearance rate of estradiol is reduced by 30%. The average production rate is 12 μg/24 h.

The source of the small amount of estradiol found in older women has not been established. Direct ovarian secretion does not appear to be an important contribution. The adrenal glands appear to be the source and could contribute to the estradiol pool by either direct glandular secretion or secretion of precursor steroids, which are converted peripherally to estradiol. Investigators who have examined the concentrations of estradiol in adrenal veins have reported minimal increments, arguing against direct adrenal secretion as the major source. Both estrone and testosterone are converted in peripheral tissues to estradiol. The finding of close correlations between estradiol and estrone levels in postmenopausal subjects suggests that this conversion may account for most circulating estradiol. It is very doubtful that the low conversion of testosterone to estradiol is responsible for a substantial amount of this estrogen.

After the menopause, the circulating level of estrone is higher than estradiol and overlaps with values seen in premenopausal women during the early follicular phase of their menstrual cycle. There is a nyctohemeral variation of circulating estrone, with the peak in the morning and the nadir in late afternoon or early evening. This variation is not as prominent as observed for the androgens. In postmenopausal women, there is a 20% reduction of estrone clearance, and the average production rate is approximately 55 μg/24 h.

More is known about the source of this estrogen. Again, the adrenal gland is the major source, with minimal direct adrenal or ovarian secretion. Most estrone results from the peripheral aromatization of androstenedione. The average percent conversion is double that found in ovulatory women and can account for the total daily production of this estrogen. Aromatization of androstenedione has been shown to occur in fat, muscle, liver, kidney, brain, and the adrenal glands. Other tissues may also contribute but have not been evaluated. To what extent each cell type contributes to total conversion has not been determined, but fat cells and muscle may be responsible for only 30–40%. This conversion has been shown to correlate with body size, with heavy women having higher conversion rates and circulating estrogen levels than slender subjects.

3. Progesterone–In young women, the major source of progesterone is the ovarian corpus luteum following ovulation. During the follicular phase of the cycle, progesterone levels are low. With ovulation, the levels rise greatly, reflecting the secretory activity of the corpus luteum. In postmenopausal women, the levels of progesterone are only 30% of the concentrations seen in young women during the follicular phase. Since postmenopausal ovaries do not contain functional follicles, ovulation does not occur and progesterone levels remain low. The source of the small amount of progesterone present in older women is presumed to reflect adrenal secretion, but this matter has not been studied critically.

4. Gonadotropins–With the menopause, both LH and FSH levels rise substantially, with FSH usually higher than LH. This is thought to reflect the slower clearance of FSH from the circulation. The reason for the marked increase in circulating gonadotropins is the absence of the negative feedback of ovarian steroids, and possibly inhibin, on gonadotropin release. As in young women, the levels of both gonadotropins are not steady but show random oscillations. These oscillations are thought to represent pulsatile secretion by the pituitary. In older women, these pulsatile bursts occur every 1–2 hours, a frequency similar to that seen during the follicular phase of premenopausal subjects. Although the frequency is similar, the amplitude is much greater. This increased amplitude is thought to be secondary to increased release of the hypothalamic hormone gonadotropin-releasing hormone (GnRH) and enhanced responsiveness of the pituitary to GnRH due to low estrogen levels. Studies with rhesus monkeys suggest that the site governing pulsatile LH release is in the arcuate nucleus of the hypothalamus. The large pulses of gonadotropin in the peripheral circulation are believed to maintain the high levels of the hormones found in postmenopausal women.

Clinical Findings

A. Symptoms and Signs:

1. Reduced endogenous estrogens–

a. Reproductive tract–Alteration of menstrual function is the first clinical evidence of the climacteric, although a gradual reduction of fertility may start by age 35 and some premenopausal women complain of hot flashes. Changes in menstrual function may conform to one or more of the following patterns:

(1) Abrupt cessation of menstruation is fairly rare, because the decline of ovarian function usually proceeds slowly.

(2) The most common pattern is a gradual decrease in both amount and duration of menstrual flow, tapering to spotting only and eventually to cessation. Irregularity of the cycle appears sooner or later, with skips and delays of menses occurring.

(3) A minority of patients will have more frequent or heavier vaginal bleeding. Bleeding between periods may also occur. As mentioned earlier, the occurrence of this type of bleeding usually reflects continued follicular estrogen production with or without ovulation. However, it may also reflect organic disease, eg, atypical endometrial hyperplasia or endometrial carcinoma.

The diagnosis of permanent cessation of menses is of necessity retrospective. Amenorrhea lasting 6 months to 1 year is commonly accepted as establishing the diagnosis. Only rarely will vaginal bleeding reflecting ovarian follicular activity recur after 1 year of amenorrhea. When uterine bleeding does occur after prolonged amenorrhea, it is more suggestive of organic disease. As menstrual function declines, associated symptoms such as mastodynia, abdominal bloating, edema, headache, and cyclic emotional disturbances also subside, reflecting the decrease in ovarian estrogen secretion.

Because estrogen functions as the major growth factor of the female reproductive tract, there are substantial changes in the appearance of all of the reproductive organs. Most postmenopausal women will experience varying degrees of atrophic changes of their vaginal epithelium. The vaginal rugae progressively flatten. As the epithelium thins, the capillary bed shines through as a diffuse or patchy reddening. Rupture of surface capillaries produces irregularly scattered petechiae, and a brownish discharge may be noted. Minimal trauma with douching or coitus may result in slight vaginal bleeding. Early in the process, local bacterial invasion is likely to initiate vaginal pruritus and leukorrhea. Further atrophy of the vaginal epithelium renders its capillary bed increasingly sparse, so that the hyperemic appearance gives way to a smooth, shiny, pale epithelial surface.

There are also atrophic changes of the cervix. It usually decreases in size, and there is a reduction of secretion of cervical mucus. This may contribute to excessive vaginal dryness, which may cause dyspareunia.

Atrophy of the uterus also occurs with shrinkage of both the endometrium and myometrium. This shrinkage is actually beneficial to women who enter the climacteric with small to moderate-sized uterine myomas. Reduction in size and elimination of symptoms frequently avoids the necessity for surgical treatment. The same applies to endometriosis. With cessation of follicular activity, hormonal stimulation of the endometrium comes to an end. This tissue usually becomes atrophic and inactive, not only inside the uterus but also at ectopic sites. Hence, palpable and symptomatic areas of endometriosis generally become progressively smaller and less troublesome.

The oviducts and ovaries also decrease in size postmenopausally. Although this produces no symptoms, the smallness of the ovaries makes them difficult to palpate during pelvic examination. A palpable ovary in a postmenopausal woman must be viewed with suspicion, and the presence of an ovarian neoplasm must be considered.

The supporting structures of the reproductive organs suffer loss of tone as estrogen levels decline. Postmenopausal estrogen deficiency may lead to symptomatic progressive pelvic relaxation.

b. Urinary tract—Estrogen plays an important role in maintaining the epithelium of the bladder and urethra. Marked estrogen deficiency may produce atrophic changes in these organs similar to those which occur in the vaginal epithelium. This may give rise to atrophic cystitis, characterized by urinary urgency, incontinence, and frequency without pyuria or dysuria. Loss of urethral tone, with pouting of the meatus and thinning of the epithelium, favors the formation of a urethral caruncle with resultant dysuria, meatal tenderness, and occasionally hematuria.

c. Mammary glands—Regression of breast size during and after menopause is psychologically distressing to some women. To those who have been bothered by cyclic symptoms of chronic cystic mastitis, the disappearance of these symptoms postmenopausally is a great relief.

d. Hot flashes—The most common and characteristic symptom of the climacteric is an episodic disturbance consisting of sudden flushing and perspiration, referred to as the **hot flash** or **flush.** It has been observed in about three-fourths of women who go through the physiologic menopause or have a bilateral ovariectomy. Of those having flushes, 82% will experience the disturbance for more than 1 year and 25–50% will complain of the symptom for more than 5 years. Most women indicate that hot flashes begin with a sensation of pressure in the head, much like a headache. This increases in intensity until the physiologic flush occurs. Palpitations may also be experienced. The actual flush usually starts in the region of the head and neck and then passes to other parts of the body, often in waves over the entire body. Only a few women report that the disturbance is limited to the head, neck, and breasts. The flush is characterized as a feeling of heat or burning in the affected areas. This is followed immediately by an outbreak of sweating that affects the entire body but is particularly prominent over the head, neck, and upper chest and back. Less common symptoms include weakness, fatigue, faintness, and vertigo. The duration of the whole episode varies from momentary to as long as 10 minutes; the frequency varies from 1–2 an hour to 1–2 a week.

Because of the subjective nature of the complaint, the actual existence of hot flashes has been questioned,

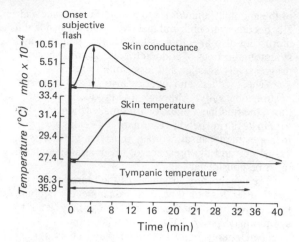

Figure 25–3. Skin conductance and temperature and core temperature changes associated with climacteric hot flushes. (Reproduced, with permission, from Tataryn IV et al: Postmenopausal hot flushes: A disorder of thermoregulation. *Maturitas* 1980;**2**:101.)

and a psychosomatic basis for the condition has been suggested. Recently, several investigators have begun to characterize the physiologic changes associated with hot flashes (Fig 25–3). The profound changes reported in these studies do indicate that some major disturbance in basic function is responsible for these events. The reports have described a prodromal period between onset of the subjective feeling and the first recordable change in physiologic function. This period may last for as long as 4 minutes. The first measurable sign of the attack is an increase in skin conductance (a measurement of perspiration). This begins an average of 45 seconds after the onset of the subjective flash, reaches its maximum by 4 minutes, and returns to baseline in 18 minutes. A rise in skin temperature (a measurement of cutaneous vasodilatation) is next, beginning an average of 90 seconds after initiation of the subjective flash. The temperature rise reaches its maximum by 9 minutes and returns to baseline by 40 minutes. The magnitude of the skin temperature rise is variable, depending on which area of the body is tested, the fingers and toes showing the greatest increases. Temperature changes on the forehead, where the symptomatic flush is experienced, are of lesser magnitude, probably because of the perspiration and evaporation that occur in this area. For the finger, the average change in temperature is about 4 °C (7.2 °F) with the maximum approximately 8 °C (14.4 °F). As heat is lost from the body by sweating and radiation, a decline in core temperature occurs. It starts about 4 minutes after the onset of the subjective symptoms and returns to baseline in about 30 minutes. The average decrease in core temperature is 0.2 °C (0.4 °F). The pulse rate increases by 13–20%. Fluctuations of the baseline ECG probably reflect changes in skin conductance. Alterations of heart rhythm and blood pressure have not been observed with symptomatic flushes.

These changes in physiologic function do not correspond identically to the subjective symptoms of the event. As mentioned previously, the subjective symptoms begin approximately 45 seconds before any recordable change and only last an average of 4 minutes. Thus, the physiologic signs continue many minutes after the subjective symptoms have ended.

Since the hot flashes occur after the spontaneous cessation of ovarian function or following ovariectomy, it has been presumed that the underlying mechanism is endocrinologic and is related to either the reduction of ovarian estrogen secretion or the enhancement of pituitary gonadotropin secretion. Low estrogen levels per se do not appear to trigger hot flashes. Prepubertal children and patients with gonadal dysgenesis have low estrogen levels but do not experience the symptom. Patients with gonadal dysgenesis do experience the symptom if they are given estrogens and the medication is then withdrawn. Thus, the presence of estrogen, followed by withdrawal, appears to be necessary for initiation of the symptom.

Hot flashes do appear to be related to gonadotropins. A close temporal association between the occurrence of flushes and the pulsatile release of LH has been demonstrated. The observation that flushes occur after hypophysectomy suggests the mechanism is not due directly to LH release (Fig 25–4). As mentioned previously, GnRH fluctuates in hypophyseal portal vein blood and is thought to be responsible for pulsatile gonadotropin release. It is likely that GnRH, or the hypothalamic factors responsible for its pulsatile release, is in some way related to the initiation of these intriguing but unpleasant symptoms.

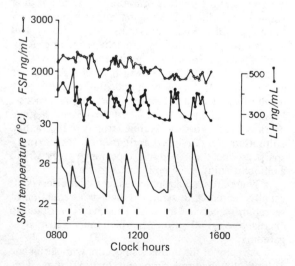

Figure 25–4. Skin temperature and LH and FSH levels in a woman with hot flushes. Note close temporal relationship between the rises in skin temperature and the occurrence of pulsatile LH release. (Reproduced, with permission, from Tataryn IV et al: LH, FSH, and skin temperature during the menopausal hot flash. *J Clin Endocrinol Metab* 1979; **49**:152.)

Estrogen has been the principal medication used to relieve hot flashes. Although the efficacy of this medication has been questioned recently, there are good randomized, prospective, double-blind, cross-over studies showing positive effects. Estrogens not only block the subjective sensation but also the physiologic changes.

e. Osteoporosis—Osteoporosis is the single most important health hazard associated with the climacteric. It is a disorder characterized by a reduction in the quantity of bone during aging without changes in its chemical composition. Loss of trabecular bone is more marked and develops earlier than loss of cortical bone, with a 50% and 5% loss of trabecular and cortical bone, respectively, occurring with aging. Loss of mineral content of bone happens in all individuals during aging, with women losing bone mass after age 30 and men after age 45–50 (Fig 25–5). In women, this reduction of bone mass is accentuated by the loss of ovarian function (Fig 25–6). Osteoporosis is more prevalent in women than men. The problem is particularly severe in women who have sustained ovariectomy early or who have gonadal dysgenesis. Bone loss appears to be rapid during the first 3–4 years after the menopause, the rate of loss being about 2.5% per year. After the rapid loss, the rate decreases to approximately 0.75% per year until death. In addition to a sexual difference, there is also a racial difference in the occurrence of symptomatic osteoporosis, with whites having the highest incidence, then Orientals, and finally blacks. Smoking is believed to enhance the development of osteoporosis. Slender women also seem more susceptible to the condition, with the classic example being a little old white woman walking hunched over and using a cane.

Loss of bone mass per se produces minimal symptoms, but it does lead to reduced skeletal strength. Thus, osteoporotic bones are more susceptible to fractures. The vertebral body is the most common site of

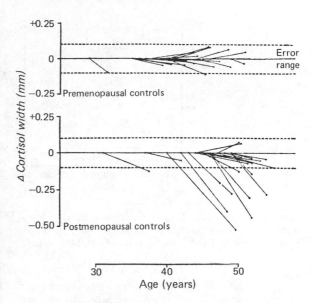

Figure 25–6. Changes in metacarpal cortical width determined by sequential measurements in pre- and postmenopausal women, age range 40–50. Note bone loss in postmenopausal women. (Reproduced, with permission, from Nordin BEC et al: Post-menopausal osteopenia and osteoporosis. *Front Horm Res* 1975;**3**:131.)

fracture, but fractures of other bones are also enhanced, including the humerus, upper femur, distal forearm, and ribs. Cross-sectional studies of white women in northern European countries have shown vertebral fractures in 25% by age 65. There is a 10-fold increase of Colles' fractures in women from age 35 to age 55 (Fig 25–7). A similar increase is not seen in men. The incidence of hip fractures also increases in women with aging, rising from 0.3 per 1000 at age 45

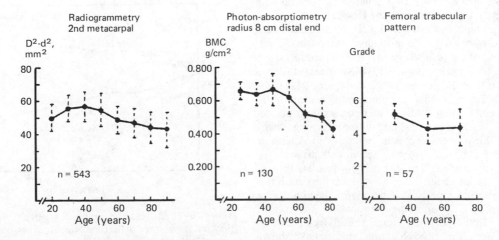

Figure 25–5. Pattern of bone changes with age in women as measured by radiogrammetry at the second metacarpal, by photon-absorptiometry at 8 cm from the distal end of the radius, and by trabecular pattern grading at the upper end of the femur. (Reproduced, with permission, from Dequeker J et al: Aging of bone: Its relation to osteoporosis and osteoarthrosis in post-menopausal women. *Front Horm Res* 1975;**3**:116.)

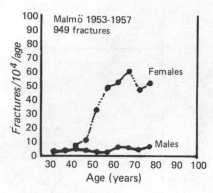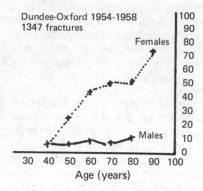

Figure 25–7. Indices of Colles' fracture in relation to age in Malmö, Dundee, and Oxford. (Reproduced, with permission, from Cope E: Physical changes associated with post-menopausal years. Page 4 in: *Management of the Menopause and Post-menopause Years.* Campbell S [editor]. MTP Press Ltd [Lancaster], 1976.)

to 20 per 1000 at age 85. Hip fractures are of great concern, and the mortality rates are high. Between 15 and 20% of patients will die because of the fracture or its complications within 3 months, and one-third will die within 6 months of the injury. Many of the remaining patients are permanently disabled and remain invalids for the rest of their lives.

The cause of climacteric osteoporosis has not been established. Most data have implicated as the underlying mechanism increased bone resorption coupled with normal bone formation. The increase in bone resorption results in a net loss of calcium of approximately 100 g between ages 50 and 70 years, or 15 mg/d. Currently, it is believed that reduction of ovarian estrogen production plays a key role in the genesis of menopausal osteoporosis. First, short-term estrogen replacement has consistently shown a reduction in parameters of bone resorption and a decrease in the loss of calcium from bone as determined by bone density measurements (Fig 25–8). Second, endogenous estrogen levels show a negative correlation with parameters of bone resorption. However, attempts to look at endogenous estrogen levels in postmenopausal women who do or do not have symptomatic osteoporosis have resulted in inconsistent findings.

Parathyroid hormone (PTH) also appears to play a central role in the genesis of the condition. PTH is the principal hormone that stimulates bone resorption. In animal and human studies, osteoporosis does not develop in the absence of PTH, thus confirming its key role in the process. To date, attempts to determine whether PTH levels are elevated in patients with osteoporosis have yielded inconsistent results. In general, levels have been found to be low or normal. If this is correct, it suggests that bone may become more sensitive to PTH after the menopause. The role of estrogen in the possibly altered sensitivity of bone to PTH is not clear. In vivo animal studies have shown that estrogens do decrease the effect of PTH on bone, but in vitro data are not convincing. These latter observations are supported by the inability of investigators to document the presence of estrogen receptors in

bone. Current beliefs concerning the mechanism of action of estrogen indicate that cytosol receptors for estrogen are obligatory for the action of the hormone on a target tissue.

If estrogen receptors are not present in bone, then estradiol must exert its action on bone resorption indirectly. Currently, 2 theories have been suggested as possible mechanisms. The first theory suggests that estrogens may act on bone by regulating the 25-dihydroxycholecalciferol-1-hydroxylase enzyme in the kidney, thus modulating the synthesis of 1,25-dihydroxycholecalciferol, the active metabolite of vitamin D. One problem with this concept is that vitamin D deficiency results in osteomalacia and not osteoporosis. The second theory suggests that estrogens may enhance calcitonin secretion. Calcitonin is a potent inhibitor of bone resorption, and enhanced secre-

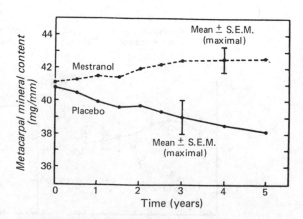

Figure 25–8. Metacarpal mineral content in postmenopausal women treated with mestranol or placebo for 5 years. Note loss of bone density in placebo but not mestranol treatment group. (Reproduced, with permission, from Lindsay R et al: Long-term prevention of postmenopausal osteoporosis by oestrogen. *Lancet* 1976; 1:1038.)

tion of this hormone could inhibit calcium loss from bone and possibly the future development of osteoporosis.

In summary, a growing body of information indicates that the climacteric, together with associated reduction of endogenous estrogens, plays a major role in the development of osteoporosis in older women. The mechanism by which estrogens exert this action has not been defined. However, osteoporosis is responsible for the most serious complications resulting from the loss of ovarian function and represents the major reason to contemplate estrogen replacement therapy.

f. Cardiovascular–In general, the incidence of death from coronary heart disease increases with age in all populations and both sexes (Fig 25–9). It is well recognized that in the USA, heart disease is less prevalent in women than men before the age of 55, and the chance of a man dying of heart disease before that age is 5–10 times greater than that of a woman. Heart disease is not only less frequent but also less severe in younger women. This sex difference is not consistent in all countries. In countries where the incidence of heart disease is high, the sex difference is marked; whereas in countries where the incidence is low, the sex difference is not apparent. In the age group between 25 and 55, the ratio of deaths from heart attacks between men and women varies from 5:1 in the USA to 2:1 in Italy, to 1:1 in Japan. The sex difference

disappears with age, so that by age 85 the ratio is unity. This change is due to a reduction in the incremental death rate in men. For each decade after age 55, there is a 2-fold increase in deaths from heart attacks in men and a 3-fold increase in women.

Two types of studies have been utilized to determine whether cessation of ovarian function is associated with increased incidence of heart disease. In the first (the Framingham study), the results of a biannual examination of nearly 3000 women for 24 years revealed that there is indeed an increased incidence of heart disease in women following the menopause that is not just age-related. Based on these studies, the impact of the menopause appears to be substantial and relatively abrupt, but worsening afterward only slowly if at all. In this study population, it was unusual to see heart disease in premenopausal women, and when present the disease was usually mild, ie, angina pectoris only. Serious heart disease, such as myocardial infarction, was not observed. In the second type of investigation, case control studies were performed comparing the degree of coronary heart disease or the incidence of myocardial infarction in women who had undergone early ovariectomy with age-matched premenopausal controls. Some of these studies revealed an increased risk of cardiovascular disease after ovarian excision, whereas other studies did not. All of these reports have been criticized because of patient selection bias, particularly the controls.

Although heart disease may increase with cessation of ovarian function, the use of replacement estrogens does not seem to decrease this risk. With large doses of estrogen, an increase of recurrent heart disease was observed in a large series of men treated with 5 mg of conjugated estrogens, whereas no reduction in deaths was noted in patients treated with 2.5 mg of the same estrogen over placebo. In postmenopausal women treated with usual replacement doses, a doubling of the incidence of coronary heart disease (angina pectoris) has been reported, although the total mortality rate did not change. The increase was in angina pectoris. The incidence of myocardial infarcts was the same as in the control population. Thus, current estrogen replacement does not seem to reduce and may actually increase the already enhanced incidence of coronary heart disease that apparently occurs with the menopause.

Several factors could be involved with the increase in heart disease associated with the menopause and estrogen therapy. These factors are known to be associated with an increased incidence of heart disease in all populations and are influenced by cessation of ovarian function, estrogen therapy, or both.

It is well recognized that increased circulating levels of cholesterol are associated with an increased risk of heart attacks. An elevation of only 40 mg/dL will increase the risk 3- to 5-fold. The menopause is associated with a rise of cholesterol of approximately 16 mg/dL. Normal replacement doses of estrogens have little effect on cholesterol, whereas higher doses will reduce the concentration.

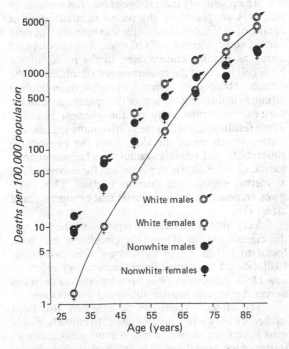

Figure 25–9. Semilog plot of mortality rates for coronary heart disease in white and nonwhite populations by sex and age in the USA in 1955. (Reproduced, with permission, from Furman RH: Are gonadal hormones [estrogens and androgens] of significance in the development of ischemic heart disease? *Ann NY Acad Sci* 1968; **149**:822.)

High triglyceride levels are also a possible risk factor for coronary heart disease. No data are available about the effect of the menopause on serum triglycerides, but it is well recognized that estrogens in normal replacement dosages will increase triglyceride concentrations.

Lipoproteins are also a risk factor for coronary heart disease. The menopause is associated with an increase of all lipoprotein fractions, with a decrease in the ratio of the high- to low-density fractions. Estrogens tend to increase the cholesterol in high-density lipoproteins and decrease it in the low-density fraction. However, estrogens have effects on the protein moiety of high-density lipoproteins as well as on just cholesterol.

Hypertension enhances the susceptibility to coronary heart disease 5-fold. After age 45, hypertension is more important than hyperlipidemia as a cause of heart disease. Hypertension practically obliterates the sex advantage in women and probably accounts for the higher vulnerability of black men and black women to heart disease at an earlier age. The menopause does not seem to be associated with a consistent change in either systolic or diastolic blood pressure. However, estrogen therapy does influence blood pressure, with small increases of both diastolic and systolic pressure usually being oberved. Occasionally, large rises will occur. To date, the use of estrogen replacement in postmenopausal women has not been associated with an increased risk of stroke.

The mechanism thought to be responsible for the increase in blood pressure with estrogen therapy involves the renin-angiotensin-aldosterone system. Estrogen stimulates hepatic synthesis and secretion of the renin substrate, resulting in enhanced production of angiotensin I and II and of aldosterone. These agents promote vasoconstriction and fluid retention, resulting in mild increases in blood pressure.

Diabetes mellitus is another risk factor for heart disease, with the risk of myocardial infarction being 2 times greater in patients with the disease. To date, no effect of the menopause on carbohydrate metabolism has been established. The actions of estrogen therapy on carbohydrate metabolism are unclear; some investigators found no effect, while others observed a decrease of glucose tolerance without an accompanying increase in insulin secretion. The alterations of carbohydrate metabolism observed with oral contraceptives appear to be related mainly to the progestins in the pills.

There are a variety of other risk factors for heart disease, including smoking, obesity, heredity, and lack of exercise. The menopause and sex hormone therapy appear to have little if any effects on these factors, in comparison to socioeconomic and cultural variables.

From this review of the risk factors for coronary heart disease, it is obvious that several are influenced by the menopause and estrogen therapy. However, the jump in the incidence of cardiovascular disease, which appears to occur with the menopause, cannot be explained by the changes recorded in any of the above-mentioned risk factors, singly or in combination. Some other feature of the climacteric must account for this increased risk. Whatever this feature may be, it must account for the fact that hysterectomy without ovariectomy apparently leads to the same risk of heart disease as bilateral oophorectomy.

g. Skin and hair–With aging, noticeable changes of the skin occur. There is generalized thinning and an accompanying loss of elasticity, resulting in wrinkling. These changes are particularly prominent in the areas exposed to light, ie, the face, neck, and hands. "Purse string" wrinkling around the mouth and "crow's feet" around the eyes are characteristic. Skin changes on the dorsum of the hands are particularly noticeable. In this area the skin may be so thin as to become almost transparent, with the details of the underlying veins easily visible.

Histologically, the epidermis is thinned, and the basal layers become inactive with age. Dehydration is typical. Reduction in the number of blood vessels to the skin is also seen. Degeneration of elastic and collagenous fibers in the dermis also appears to be part of the process of aging.

These skin changes are of cosmetic importance and have been related to the onset of the climacteric by women. It is commonly stated that women undergoing estrogen replacement look younger, and the cosmetic industry has been placing estrogens in skin creams for years for precisely this purpose.

The possibility that estrogens may have effects on skin was suggested by the recent demonstration of uptake of radiolabeled estradiol into the nuclei of both dermal and epidermal cells of mice. The radiolabeled estrogens became concentrated in the nuclei of the basal cell layers of the epidermis and fibroblasts of the dermis. There were differences in estrogen-binding affinities in different regions of the epidermis, with the perineal epidermis showing the greatest binding. These results suggest that the skin, or more specifically certain structures of the skin, have the capacity to concentrate and retain estradiol in a fashion characteristic of more classic target tissues for estrogen such as uterus, vagina, and mammary gland. This study gives credence to the hypothesis that estrogens could affect skin.

Very little work has been reported on the effect of the climacteric on skin. Skin circulation has been found to be decreased in women after castration. Radiolabeled thymidine incorporation (an index of new DNA metabolism) has been reported to decrease during the several months following ovariectomy.

The effect of estrogen on skin has also been studied by only a few investigators. In animals, estrogens have been shown to increase the mitotic rate (a reflection of growth) of skin in some studies. Estrogens appear to alter the vascularization of skin. They have also been shown to change the collagen content of the dermis, as reflected by mucopolysaccharide incorporation, hydroxyproline turnover, and alterations of the ground substance. In addition, dermal synthesis of hyaluronic acid and dermal water content are enhanced. The effects of estrogen on human skin have been studied minimally, and the reports have been conflicting. Some investigators have found epidermal atrophy after prolonged estrogen use, while others observed antiwrinkling effects secondary to thickening of the epidermis and collagen fibers. It is obvious that critical assessment of this important aspect of the menopause has yet to be performed. With the amount of estrogen-containing skin creams in current use and their potentially adverse side-effects, studies of this nature are essential.

After the menopause, most women note some change in patterns of body hair. Usually, there is a variable loss of pubic and axillary hair. Often, there is loss of lanugo hair on the upper lip, chin, and cheeks, together with increased growth of coarse terminal hairs; a slight mustache may become noticeable. Hair on the body and extremities may either increase or decrease. Slight balding occurs occasionally. All of these changes are ascribed in large part to reduced postmenopausal levels of estrogen in the face of fairly well maintained levels of testosterone.

h. Psychologic and emotional symptoms– Many women in their 40s and 50s experience changes in emotional function. These symptoms cluster around affective disorders, particularly depression. They range from mild symptoms of depression to full psychosis. Irritability, feelings of inadequacy, fits of weeping, and quickness to anger are some of the common complaints mentioned by women of this age group. There is a common belief that the climacteric may be associated with these alterations of psychologic function. This has led to the recommendation of hormone replacement therapy in older women experiencing emotional difficulties. However, the role of ovarian failure in the initiation of psychiatric disease is not clear. Stresses at the time of the menopause include adjustment to aging and forced abandonment of the maternal role, and these may lead to psychologic disturbances only coincidentally related to ovarian failure. Little information is available about psychiatric morbidity resulting from ovarian failure, and conflicting findings have been reported. There is no conclusive proof that the loss of ovarian function either enhances or causes emotional illness.

One approach to investigating the link between psychologic changes and the climacteric has been to ascertain the response of various complaints to estrogen replacement therapy. This must be carried out using a controlled, preferably double-blind study design to provide any meaningful information. The few studies that meet these criteria have suggested that estrogens may have a beneficial effect on some aspects of mental function. To date, Campbell and Whitehead have reported the largest group of patients, using a double-blind cross-over design and subjective and objective indices of psychometric function. They studied 64 patients with severe climacteric complaints for 4 months and found that 1.25 mg of conjugated estrogens daily improved memory and spirits, reduced the number and severity of hot flashes, and relieved insomnia, irritability, headaches, and anxiety. Many of these symptomatic improvements resulted from the relief of hot flashes (domino effect). However, improvement in memory and reduction of anxiety in patients without flushes suggested that estrogens have a direct tonic effect on the mental state independent of vasomotor symptoms. Sixty-one patients with less severe symptoms were studied for 1 year, and the same dose of estrogen reduced only hot flashes and insomnia and improved poor memory. Effects on mood were no greater with estrogen than placebo. Thus, it appears that estrogen replacement may influence certain aspects of brain function. Further large-scale studies are needed to critically evaluate these potentially important therapeutic effects.

2. Excess endogenous estrogens–Not all women experiencing the climacteric have symptoms of estrogen deprivation. There are subjects who have no symptoms of the climacteric or actually experience symptoms and signs of estrogen excess. These latter symptoms are usually limited to uterine bleeding, but mastodynia, abdominal bloating, edema, growth of uterine myomas, and exacerbation of endometriosis may also occur. The problems of postmenopausal uterine bleeding is of particular concern, because it may reflect the presence of endometrial hyperplasia or adenocarcinoma.

Based on a variety of evidence, it has been suggested that continuous estrogen stimulation of the endometrium, unopposed by progesterone, can lead to a progression of changes from benign proliferation to cystic hyperplasia, adenomatous hyperplasia, and varying degrees of anaplasia—including invasive adenocarcinoma. When postmenopausal patients with hyperplasia or adenocarcinoma are studied, they frequently have high levels of circulatory estrogens. Thus, the presence of hyperplastic or neoplastic endometrium suggests enhanced rather than reduced endogenous estrogen production.

As mentioned earlier, the principal source of estrogens in older women is the peripheral aromatization of circulating androgens. Thus, there are 3 mechanisms that could conceivably result in increased endogenous estrogen production: (1) increased production of precursor androgens, (2) enhanced aromatization of precursor androgens, and (3) increased production of estrogens directly. The occurrence of each has been reported and has been associated with signs of estrogen excess.

Androgen-secreting tumors are usually responsible for increases of precursor hormone production, resulting in secondary estrogen excess. Endometrial hyperplasia and adenocarcinoma have been associated with these neoplasms. These tumors include classic androgen-secreting tumors, ie, Sertoli–Leydig cell tumors, hilar cell tumors, or lipid cell tumors, or they may be so-called "nonendocrine" ovarian neoplasms. These latter tumors include Brenner tumors, benign cystic teratomas, cystadenofibromas, dysgerminomas, and Krukenberg tumors. These neoplasms are associated with ovarian stromal hyperplasia, which is thought to secrete the excess androgens. The androgens are then aromatized in peripheral tissues, leading to chronically elevated estrogens. The stromal hyperplasia is believed to result from the tumor elaborating either a gonadotropinlike substance or some type of growth factor that stimulates the surrounding stroma. To date, the substance has not been identified.

A variety of conditions are associated with enhanced peripheral aromatization. These include obesity, liver disease, and hyperthyroidism. The association of obesity and endometrial cancer has been known for years.

Granulosa-theca cell tumors of the ovary are capable of estrogen secretion directly. Numerous reports have described the presence of this tumor and endometrial cancer in the same patient.

Although the above-mentioned mechanisms have been associated with an increased risk of the development of endometrial cancer (see p 562), it must be recognized that several of these are rare and are not responsible for most cases of this tumor. The relationship of endogenous androgen and estrogen metabolism with the development of most cases of endometrial cancer is just now being defined.

Comparisons have been made between postmenopausal women who do or do not have endometrial cancer. When these comparisons have been conducted

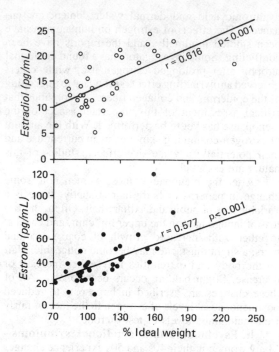

Figure 25-11. Positive correlation of estrone and estradiol levels with percent ideal weight in 35 postmenopausal women with endometrial cancer. (Reproduced, with permission, from Judd HL et al: Serum androgens and estrogens in postmenopausal women with and without endometrial cancer. *Am J Obstet Gynecol* 1980; **136**:859.)

using control subjects matched to the cancer patients for body weight, there have been no differences in androgen and estrogen levels or the conversion rate of androstenedione to estrone between the 2 groups (Fig 25-10). However, body size has always shown strong positive correlations with endogenous estrogen levels, and rates of androstenedione to estrone conversion, and it is well recognized that obese women are at greater risk of developing endometrial hyperplasia and adenocarcinoma than slender women (Figs 25-11 and 25-12). The high concentrations of endogenous estrogen found in obese subjects presumably play a role in the increased incidence of this tumor in obese older women.

3. Miscellaneous postmenopausal symptoms—More than 50 symptoms have been attributed to the endocrine changes of the postmenopausal state, but a direct cause-and-effect relationship is doubtful for many of them, and a psychogenic origin is more likely. Some of these so-called climacteric symptoms are so common that they deserve brief mention.

Symptoms possibly related to specific autonomic nervous system instability—but equally attributable to anxiety or other emotional disturbances—are paresthesias (prickling, itching, formication), dizziness, tinnitus, fainting, scotomas, and dyspnea. Symptoms clearly not of endocrine origin are weakness, fatigue, nausea, vomiting, flatulence, anorexia, constipation,

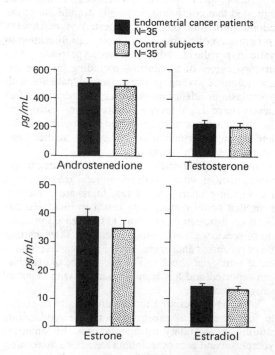

Figure 25-10. Serum androstenedione, testosterone, estrone, and estradiol levels in postmenopausal women with endometrial cancer compared with age-matched controls. No difference was observed. (Reproduced, with permission, from Judd HL et al: Serum androgens and estrogens in postmenopausal women with and without endometrial cancer. *Am J Obstet Gynecol* 1980; **136**:859.)

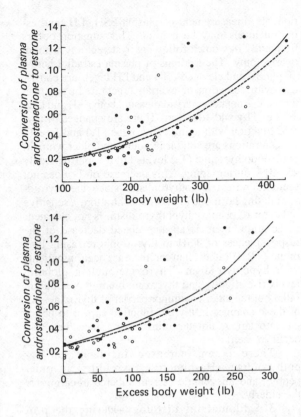

Figure 25–12. The extent of conversion of plasma androstenedione to estrone as a function of total body weight (upper panel) and excess body weight (lower panel) in postmenopausal women with endometrial cancer (●—●) and with normal endometrium (o—o). (Reproduced, with permission, from MacDonald PC et al: Effect of obesity on conversion of plasma androstenedione to estrone in postmenopausal women with and without endometrial cancer. *Am J Obstet Gynecol* 1978;**131**:448.)

diarrhea, arthralgia, and myalgia.

Many women believe erroneously that the endocrine changes accompanying menopause will produce a steady weight gain. Women do tend to gain weight at this time, but the cause is a combination of decreased exercise and possibly increased caloric intake. There may be some redistribution of body weight occasioned by the deposition of fat over the hips and abdomen. Perhaps this is partly an endocrine effect, but more likely it is the result of decreased physical activity, reduced muscle tone, and other effects of aging.

Many of the above symptoms will occasionally respond promptly to administration of estrogen. This should not mislead physicians into assuming a specific endocrine action for what is actually a placebo effect.

B. Laboratory Findings:

1. Vaginal cytologic smears–In certain laboratory animals, the degree of maturation of exfoliated vaginal epithelial cells, as revealed by stained vaginal smears, is an accurate index of estrogenic activity. When this method is applied to women, several staining techniques are available. Among the various methods of assessing the smears, the following are most commonly used: (1) The **maturation index** consists of a differential count of 3 types of squamous cells—parabasal cells, intermediate cells, and superficial cells, in that order—expressed as percentages—eg, 10/85/5. (2) The **cornification count** is the percentage of precornified and cornified cells among total squamous cells counted. This is actually a simplified maturation index, because this percentage is essentially the same as that of the superficial cells.

The assessment of exfoliated vaginal epithelial cells is influenced not only by the level of estrogenic activity but also by other hormones (particularly progesterone and testosterone), local vaginal inflammation, local medication (''hygiene''), vaginal bleeding, the presence of genital cancer, the location of the vaginal area sampled, and variations in end organ (epithelial) responses to estrogenic influence. Thus, women with identical levels of circulating estrogens may have quite different cytograms. Moreover, even with extraneous factors eliminated, the vaginal smear does not indicate absolute levels of estrogenic function; rather, it reflects the net balance of the influence on vaginal epithelium of endogenous and exogenous estrogens, androgens, and progestogens. This is well demonstrated in women taking oral combination steroid contraceptives. Despite the intake of relatively large doses of estrogen, the cornification counts are usually lower because of the concomitant effect of the progestogen.

The great variation in cytologic findings leads to the following conclusions regarding the use of smears in the clinical management of postmenopausal women: (1) The smear is only a rough measure of estrogenic status, and it may sometimes be grossly false-negative. (2) The vaginal cytogram cannot predict whether or not an individual woman is experiencing climacteric signs and symptoms, ie, it cannot be used as a ''femininity index.'' (3) The smear cannot be used as the sole guide to steroid supplementation therapy; clinical signs and symptoms are more dependable for this purpose.

2. Hormone production–For decades, the production and activity of the sex hormones has been estimated by measuring their urinary excretion, either by chemical methods or by bioassay. Today, new techniques of radioisotopic protein binding and radioimmunoassay are available for the determination of hormone levels in blood and other body fluids (Table 25–1).

a. Androgens–In premenopausal women, plasma androstenedione is approximately 1.5 ng/mL, about half of which comes from the ovary. Plasma testosterone is about 0.3 ng/mL, and it arises from ovarian and adrenal secretion and the peripheral conversion of androstenedione. Mean dehydroepiandrosterone and dehydroepiandrosterone sulfate levels are approximately 4 ng/mL and 1600 ng/mL, respectively, in samples drawn at 8:00 AM.

In postmenopausal women, the mean plasma androstenedione concentration is reduced by at least one-half to approximately 0.6 ng/mL. Plasma testos-

Table 25–1. Serum concentrations (mean ± SE) of steroids in premenopausal and postmenopausal women.

Steroid	Premenopausal (ng/mL)	Postmenopausal (ng/mL)
Progesterone	0.47 ± 0.03	0.17 ± 0.02
Dehydroepiandrosterone	4.2 ± 0.5	1.8 ± 0.2
Dehydroepiandrosterone sulfate	1600 ± 350	300 ± 70
Androstenedione	1.5 ± 0.1	0.6 ± 0.01
Testosterone	0.32 ± 0.02	0.25 ± 0.03
Estrone	0.08 ± 0.01	0.029 ± 0.002
Estradiol	0.05 ± 0.005	0.013 ± 0.001

terone levels are only slightly reduced (about 0.25 ng/mL), of which a substantial portion is derived from the postmenopausal ovary. Plasma dehydroepiandrosterone and dehydroepiandrosterone sulfate levels are decreased to mean levels of 1.8 ng/mL and 300 ng/mL in women in their 60s and 70s.

b. Estrogens–During normal menstrual life, the mean plasma estradiol fluctuates from 50 to 350 pg/mL and estrone from 30 to 110 pg/mL. These fluctuations reflect the development and involution of the follicle and corpus luteum. In postmenopausal women, cyclic fluctuations disappear. The mean estradiol level varies from approximately 13 to 25 pg/mL, with the variation being due to assay sensitivity. The mean estrone level is approximately 29 pg/mL, with a range of 20–70 pg/mL. The estradiol levels in normal, cycling young women do not overlap those observed in postmenopausal subjects. The measurement of estradiol levels below 20 pg/mL can be helpful in establishing the diagnosis of the menopause, since the fall of this estrogen is the last hormonal change associated with loss of ovarian function. There is substantial overlap of estrone levels in younger and older women, reflecting its source, ie, peripheral conversion and not direct ovarian secretion. Measurement of this estrogen is not helpful in determining the ovarian status of a patient.

c. Progesterone–In young cycling women, the mean progesterone level is approximately 0.4 ng/mL during the follicular phase of the cycle, with a range of 0.2–0.7 ng/mL. During the luteal phase, progesterone levels rise and fall, reflecting corpus luteum function, with the mean level approximately 11 ng/mL and a range of 3–21 ng/mL. In postmenopausal women, the mean progesterone level is 0.17 ng/mL. To date, no clinical use has been established for the measurement of progesterone in postmenopausal women.

d. Pituitary gonadotropins–The most striking hormonal change associated with the menopause is the enormous increase in secretion of pituitary gonadotropins. During reproductive life, the levels of both FSH and LH range from 4 to 30 mIU/mL except during the preovulatory surge, when they may exceed 50 mIU/mL and 100 mIU/mL, respectively. After the menopause, both rise to levels above 100 mIU/mL, FSH rising earlier and to greater levels than LH.

When contradictory or uncertain clinical findings make the diagnosis of the postmenopausal state questionable, measurement of plasma FSH, LH, and estradiol levels may be helpful. This situation occurs frequently in women following hysterectomy without ovariectomy. The findings of plasma estradiol below 20 pg/mL and elevated FSH and LH levels are consistent with cessation of ovarian function. In practical terms, it is not necessary to measure both FSH and LH.

e. Thyroid function–There are changes of thyroid function with aging. Thyroxine (T_4) and free T_4 concentrations are similar in young and older women, but triiodothyronine (T_3) levels fall by approximately 25–40% during aging. This decrease of T_3 does not seem to reflect hypothyroidism, since the thyroid-stimulating hormone (TSH) concentration, a sensitive indicator of primary hypothyroidism, is not elevated. In addition, there is an age-related decrease of the responsiveness of TSH to thyrotropin-releasing hormone (TRH) rather than the increase seen in patients with hypothyroidism. Thyroxine-binding globulin levels rise slightly and thyroxine-binding prealbumin falls, but the latter is a minor carrier of thyroxine. All of these changes in thyroid function appear to be related to aging, not the climacteric, since they also occur in men.

There is an increased incidence of hypothyroidism (Hashimoto's thyroiditis) in older people, and this should be remembered in caring for the elderly.

3. Endometrial histology–During the premenopausal involution, as long as menses and occasional ovulation persist, all phases of endometrial growth may be found on histologic examination of tissue taken at biopsy. After ovulation ceases, no further secretory changes are seen. After menopause, endometrial biopsy may reveal anything from a very scanty, basal, atrophic endometrium to one that is moderately proliferative. Spontaneous postmenopausal bleeding may occur in the presence of any of these patterns.

The microscopic appearance of the endometrium is apparently an unsatisfactory guide to the lack of estrogen postmenopausally. However, endometrial tissue revealing glandular hyperplasia (with or without uterine bleeding) is an indication of excessive estrogenic stimulation from either excessive endogenous estrogen production (eg, increased conversion of androgen, granulosa cell tumor) or excessive exogenous intake of estrogen.

C. X-Ray Findings: X-rays of bones, lungs, and blood vessels may show the usual changes of the aging process in the postmenopausal woman. Osteopenia and actual osteoporosis are best demonstrated by x-rays of the spine, femurs, or metacarpal bones, but variations in x-ray technique can easily give false-positive diagnoses. Only a radiologist with extensive experience can give a dependable interpretation.

Differential Diagnosis

Signs and symptoms similar to those of the climacteric can be caused by a variety of other diseases. In general, the total clinical picture is helpful in establishing the proper diagnosis. The absence of evidence of other disease will point to ovarian decline, whereas the presence of prominent features of other conditions, in the absence of other climacteric symptoms, will suggest a nonclimacteric origin. It must again be emphasized that as long as reasonably normal and regular menstrual function is present, estrogen deficiency sufficient to produce appreciable symptoms cannot exist.

A. Amenorrhea: By definition, the primary symptom of the menopause is the absence of menstruation. Amenorrhea can occur for many reasons, of which the physiologic menopause is only one. Cessation of ovarian function is by far the most common reason for amenorrhea to occur in women in their 40s or early 50s. Persistent amenorrhea in younger women may be due to premature ovarian failure but must be differentiated from other causes. Obvious features of specific disease will often suggest the proper diagnosis (eg, extreme weight loss in anorexia nervosa, galactorrhea in hyperprolactinemia, hirsutism and obesity in polycystic ovarian disease). Although the reproductive tract commonly shows evidence of lowered estrogenic activity in these and other diseases associated with amenorrhea, true vasomotor symptoms are rare. Measurement of gonadotropin concentration can be very helpful in establishing ovarian failure. If the gonadotropin levels are not elevated or the estradiol level is not below 20 pg/mL, then the entire diagnostic procedure for the elucidation of secondary amenorrhea should be undertaken.

B. Vasomotor Flushes: Several diseases can produce sensations of flushing that may be misinterpreted as hot flashes. Notable are hyperthyroidism, pheochromocytoma, carcinoid syndrome, diabetes mellitus, tuberculosis, and other chronic infections. None of these disorders produce the specific symptoms associated with the climacteric (short duration and specific body distribution). Moreover, the absence of other signs or symptoms of the climacteric will suggest further search for the cause of the flushes.

C. Abnormal Vaginal Bleeding: Prior to the menopause, irregular vaginal bleeding is expected and does not necessitate a diagnostic work-up in all cases. However, organic disease can occur at this time, and some patients require evaluation. If a woman is in her 40s or 50s and experiences an increase in cycle length and a decrease in the quantity of bleeding, menopausal involution can be presumed and endometrial sampling is not necessary. However, if the periods become more frequent and heavier or spotting between periods occurs, assessment of the endometrium should be done. Outpatient endometrial biopsy or inpatient D&C are the usual procedures. The disadvantage of the former is that it is not as accurate as D&C, and the drawbacks of the latter are greater expense and risk. If normal endometrium is found, nothing further is required. If hyperplastic or cancerous endometrium is obtained, treatment should be instituted.

It is most unusual for a woman to experience vaginal bleeding because of ovarian activity by 6 months after the menopause. Thus, postmenopausal bleeding is much more ominous and necessitates evaluation each time it occurs. The only exception to this rule is the uterine bleeding associated with estrogen replacement therapy. Other guidelines are recommended for this type of bleeding (see Treatment).

Organic disease is commonly associated with postmenopausal bleeding. Endometrial polyps may be found. If so, D&C may be therapeutic. Endometrial hyperplasia may be discovered, frequently in obese women. This can be treated by the periodic administration of progesterone or by hysterectomy. Surgery should be considered if the patient is a good surgical risk or is not reliable in taking her medications. The finding of endometrial cancer necessitates appropriate therapy depending on the stage and grade of the tumor.

D. Vulvovaginitis: Many specific vulvar and vaginal diseases (eg, trichomoniasis or candidiasis) may mimic the atrophic vulvovaginitis of estrogen deficiency. Their special clinical characteristics will usually suggest more specific diagnostic testing. When pruritus and thinning of the mucosa or vulvar skin are the only manifestations, therapeutic testing with local applications of estrogen may help to establish the diagnosis. When any whitening, thickening, or cracking of vulvar tissues is present, biopsy to rule out carcinoma is mandatory. (This can easily be accomplished under local anesthesia by using the dermatologist's skin punch.) Biopsy to rule out carcinoma is also necessary for a suspicious-looking localized vaginal lesion.

E. Osteoporosis: (See Table 25–2.) Ordinarily, the diagnosis of postmenopausal osteoporosis is made with reasonable certainty on the basis of its clinical and radiologic features together with evidence of postmenopausal estrogen deficiency of at least 2 years' duration. Occasionally, atypical manifestations may necessitate more careful differentiation from other diseases that can produce rarefaction of bone, eg, osteomalacia, multiple myeloma, osteitis deformans, metastatic cancer, and hyperparathyroidism. The measurement of serum calcium, phosphate, alkaline phosphatase, and some specific hormones or serum proteins should help to establish the proper diagnosis.

Occasionally, the pain of vertebral compression may mimic that of gastric ulcer, renal colic, pyelonephritis, pancreatitis, spondylolisthesis, acute back strain, or herniated intervertebral disk.

Prevention

Nothing can prevent the physiologic menopause (ie, ovarian function cannot be prolonged indefinitely), and nothing can be done to postpone its onset or slow its progress. However, artificial menopause can often be prevented. When ionizing radiation is used for the treatment of intra-abdominal disease, incidental ablation of ovarian function often cannot be avoided. In such cases, if an operation will serve equally well, it should be used in preference to radiation therapy in order to preserve the ovaries.

Elective removal of the ovaries to prevent ovarian cancer is frequently performed at laparotomy in pre-

Table 25–2. Selected differential diagnostic features of osteoporotic bone diseases.

Disease	X-Ray Findings	Bone Pain	Serum Ca	Serum P	Alkaline Phosphatase	Special Findings
Postmenopausal osteoporosis	Axial bone loss, particularly spine.	Pain not great. Localized to spine. Increased pain with fracture.	–	–	–	Estrogen deficiency: late ages.
Osteomalacia	Appendicular bone rarefaction; pseudofractures.	General tenderness; may be exquisite.	– or ↓	↓	↑	Gastrointestinal malabsorption (or malnutrition) muscle weakness.
Multiple myeloma	Generalized bone demineralization; occasional vertebral fractures; typical skull lesions.	Tenderness.	↑ or –	–	–	Proteinuria; Bence-Jones proteinuria, diagnostic serum electrophoresis.
Osteitis deformans (Paget's disease of bone)	Localized areas of demineralization; bony deformities; localized sclerosis of bone.	Pain may be prominent.	–	–	Greatly ↑	Bony deformities, particularly skull and lower extremities.
Metastatic cancer	Sharply localized lesions, any bone can be affected.	Local pain and tenderness.	–	–	Often ↑	History of cancer.
Hyperparathyroidism	Generalized bone demineralization, particularly phalanges and clavicles.	Generalized	↑	– or ↓	– or ↑	Renal lithiasis, high serum parathyroid hormone.

menopausal women, with deliberate acceptance of artificial menopause. This form of therapy, however, remains controversial.

Treatment

As long as ovarian function is sufficient to maintain some uterine bleeding, no treatment is usually required. As the menstrual pattern alters and symptoms commence, patients begin to seek help.

A. Counseling: Every woman with climacteric symptoms deserves an adequate explanation of the physiologic event she is experiencing in order to dispel her fears and minimize symptoms such as anxiety, depression, or sleep disturbance. Reassurance should emphasize what the climacteric is not—that contrary to anything the patient may have heard, she need not expect sudden aging or personal disasters of any sort. Specific reassurance about continued sexual activity is important.

B. Estrogen Replacement:

1. Complications–Before discussing the management of estrogen replacement, it is necessary to review the complications and contraindications of this type of therapy. These play an important role in the ultimate decision regarding treatment for all patients.

a. Cancer–The role of estrogen therapy in the development of endometrial cancer has been and continues to be one of the most highly charged issues related to the climacteric. Current concerns are based on 2 types of studies—those reporting a possible increase in the incidence of endometrial carcinoma and epidemiologic studies showing a possible association between estrogen use and endometrial cancer.

Three investigative teams have reported an increased incidence of endometrial cancer occurring in the early 1970s. Weiss and others reported data for 1969–1973 from 8 selected areas in the USA showing that the incidence rates of endometrial carcinoma increased sharply in the 1970s after many years of relative stability. This rise occurred most markedly among middle-aged women. Greenwald and others found a 68% increase in the incidence of endometrial cancer from 1960 through 1974, based on reports of the New York State Tumor Registry, one of the largest population-based cancer registries in the country. Eighty-two percent of this increase occurred during the last 5 years of the study. This increase paralleled the rise in sales of estrogens in the USA from $15,422,000 in 1962 to $82,777,000 in 1975, an increase greater than 500%. Inflation accounted for only a small part of this increase, since the price of the most commonly prescribed estrogen increased only 25% during that period. Finally, Jick and others reported data obtained from the Commission on Professional and Hospital Activities—Professional Activity Study. This bureau provides an annual projection based on an approximate 1% sample of hospital discharges in the USA. This study showed an increase of endometrial cancer from 70 per 100,000 woman years at risk in 1970 to 135 per 100,000 woman years at risk in 1975 in women 50–64 years of age. There was a drop of 27% to 102 per 100,000 woman years at risk by 1977. During the period 1975–1977 sales of estrogens were also declining in the USA.

The sharp rise described in these reports differs from the results of an earlier study by the National Cancer Institute that showed no increase for endometrial carcinoma in the USA up to 1971, which overlaps partially with the above-mentioned studies. A related study by Cramer and associates of the National Cancer Institute reaffirmed stability of the endometrial cancer incidence and indicated that the incidence of this tumor may actually be declining if figures are corrected for cancer of the uterus "unspecified." Finally, no one to date has reported an increased incidence of deaths due to this type of malignancy.

Thus, there is considerable doubt whether the reported increase in the incidence of endometrial cancer is real or not. Current attempts to relate the possible increased incidence of endometrial cancer to increased use of estrogen replacement may be a case of "post hoc ergo propter hoc," ie, the 2 may not be causally related. Therefore, examination of the epidemiologic evidence is necessary.

Seven recently published case control studies have purported to show an association between estrogen replacement and endometrial carcinoma. These reports claim that estrogen replacement therapy may be associated with a 3- to 8-fold increase in the likelihood of developing endometrial carcinoma and that this phenomenon is directly related to the duration of estrogen use and the size of dosage. The association between estrogen replacement and endometrial carcinoma seems to be independent of other risk factors or the type of estrogen used, although the increase in risk appears smaller for those women who already possessed known predisposing factors such as obesity and nulliparity. This is probably related to the fact that these women are already at risk.

These case control studies have been criticized because they were retrospective, used inappropriate controls, contained mainly early lesions, and did not have independent review of the pathologic specimens. With the exceptions of the retrospective nature of these reports and the question of appropriate controls, many of the criticisms have now been answered by subsequent studies. However, prospective studies will be necessary to substantiate the risk.

The possible association of estrogen use and the occurrence of breast cancer is a critical issue, but it has not been studied extensively. Hoover and co-workers found a significantly higher risk ratio for the occurrence of breast cancer in women who had used estrogens for 15 or more years than would be predicted by regional or national incidence figures. However, the incidence was similar to that expected for all postmenopausal women receiving estrogens regardless of duration of therapy. Further studies are urgently needed to determine if estrogen replacement may increase the occurrence of breast cancer.

b. Hypertension and myocardial infarction– Hypertension may occur or be exacerbated in some women on estrogen replacement. As mentioned previously, the mechanism thought to be responsible is increased hepatic synthesis and secretion of renin substrate, resulting in enhanced production of angiotensin I and II and aldosterone. The increase in blood pressure occurring with estrogen therapy is usually reversible with discontinuation of the medication. Although estrogen use may be associated with hypertension, it has not been related to increased risk of stroke. Hypertensive changes are seen less often in patients using estrogen replacement therapy than in those using oral contraceptives. The usual replacement therapy estrogen doses have been associated with a doubling of the

occurrence rate of some types of heart disease, although total mortality rates have not changed. The increase of heart disease is limited to the occurrence of angina pectoris. The incidence of myocardial infarction appears not to be affected by estrogen intake.

c. Gallbladder–Experimental data indicate that estrogens can induce the production of lithogenic bile. In one study, a 2.5-fold increase in the risk of surgically confirmed gallbladder disease has been reported.

d. Miscellaneous–Other side-effects of estrogen therapy include uterine bleeding from endometrial influence, excessive generalized edema, mastodynia and breast enlargement, abdominal bloating, signs and symptoms resembling those of premenstrual tension, headaches (particularly of a "menstrual migraine" type), and excessive cervical mucus. These side-effects are either dose-related or may be idiosyncratic and are managed by lowering the estrogen dosage, by substitution therapy, or by discontinuation of the medication.

2. Contraindications–Contraindications to estrogen replacement therapy include undiagnosed vaginal bleeding, acute liver disease, chronic impaired liver function, acute vascular thrombosis (with or without emboli), neuro-ophthalmologic vascular disease, and endometrial and breast carcinoma. Estrogen therapy may stimulate the growth of any malignant cells that remain after treatment of breast or endometrial carcinoma and may thus speed any recurrence of the original cancer. Therefore, it is prudent to avoid estrogen therapy for 3–5 years after the treatment of such malignancies. A history of previously treated carcinoma of the cervix is not a contraindication to estrogen therapy. Estrogens may have undesirable effects on some patients with preexisting seizures, hypertension, fibrocystic disease of the breast, uterine leiomyoma, collagen disease, familial hyperlipidemia, diabetes, migrainous headaches, chronic thrombophlebitis, and gallbladder disease. At the low dosages of estrogen recommended for replacement, increased growth of uterine myomas, endometriosis, or chronic cystic mastitis is rarely a concern.

3. Management of estrogen replacement therapy–By now it should be apparent that generalized guidelines for all patients cannot be made. The symptoms of and risk factors for each patient should be evaluated individually.

Current replacement therapy should be directed toward the relief of hot flashes and vaginal atrophy and the prevention of osteoporosis. The other suggested indications for replacement are less clearly defined and should be approached cautiously until better data are available. For hot flashes and vaginal atrophy, the severity of the symptoms is important. If the symptoms are disabling, replacement therapy should be considered; if minimal or absent, the need for treatment is reduced. Reduced body fat, white race, history of smoking, and early ovariectomy are all factors associated with an increased risk of development of symptomatic osteoporosis. Thus, an obese black woman who does not smoke may have less need for estrogen replacement to prevent osteoporosis.

The reason for therapy will also dictate how replacement should be given. Hot flashes can be treated for a finite period of time with progressive reduction in dosage. Prevention of osteoporosis with estrogen appears to require extended treatment. After 8 years of follow-up, Lindsay and co-workers found the same reduction in bone density in women treated for only the initial 4 years as that found in untreated women. If vaginal atrophy is the problem, either systemic or locally applied estrogen can be utilized.

If estrogens are given, there are certain factors that seem to influence the incidence of complications. It appears to make no difference which estrogen preparation is utilized. Synthetic estrogens, naturally occurring steroids, or nonsteroidal estrogens have all been incriminated in the genesis of side-effects, particularly endometrial cancer. Dosage is apparently an important consideration. There is reduced risk of endometrial cancer when lower amounts of medication are utilized. Duration of treatment also appears to be an important factor, with longer use associated with increased incidence of tumor formation. Data are inconsistent concerning continuous versus interrupted administration; one study reported a reduced risk with interrupted therapy, and another reported no difference between the 2 types of administration.

Sequential estrogen-progestin therapy has certain theoretic advantages over estrogen administration alone, including interruption of endometrial growth and induction of organized endometrial shedding. Progesterone also lowers the concentration of estradiol receptors in the endometrium, thus depressing estrogen stimulation, which is receptor-mediated. Progesterone also induces the formation of the enzyme 17β-dehydrogenase within endometrial cells. This enzyme converts the potent intracellular estrogen estradiol to the less potent estrone. The use of estrogens and progesterone has been shown by prospective studies to reduce the incidence of endometrial hyperplasia and by retrospective studies to reduce the incidence of endometrial cancer. There is some limited information suggesting that greater protection is provided by use of progesterone for at least 10–13 days each cycle than by shorter periods of treatment.

The use of estrogen and progesterone has been associated with a higher incidence of periodic vaginal bleeding, a condition unacceptable to some postmenopausal patients. The dosage of estrogen and progesterone can be reduced sufficiently to avoid vaginal bleeding, but the benefit of regular endometrial shedding is lost. When considering sequential estrogen-progestin administration, it must also be remembered that complications of estrogen therapy are not limited to just the effects on the endometrium. Progestin use does not prevent some of the other side-effects of estrogen, and it may add some side-effects of its own. The complications associated with oral contraceptives are examples of this. Thus, the use of sequential replacement has potential advantages but does not prevent all adverse effects of estrogen therapy.

The route of administration for hormone replacement also may contribute to the complications of replacement therapy. Oral administration of most estrogens necessitates passage of the hormone through the portal vessels and liver prior to entry into the general circulation. A portion of the estrogen is metabolized and inactivated by the liver before exposure to the rest of the body. Differential effects of estrogen on hepatic function as compared to other organ systems occur, and since the action of estrogen on liver function is responsible for many of the side-effects of the drug, this differential effect could raise the chance of complications.

Systemic therapy also has potential drawbacks. Subcutaneous implants provide constant sustained estrogen exposure, resulting in a high incidence of endometrial hyperplasia. Injections necessitate the use of large hormonal dosages to lengthen the intervals between repeat administrations. Thus, no ideal route of administration has been identified to date.

If a decision is reached to use estrogens, current recommendations are to employ conjugated equine estrogens, 0.3–1.25 mg/d, ethinyl estradiol, 0.01–0.02 mg/d, or diethylstilbestrol, 0.1–0.25 mg/d, for 3 weeks with a 1-week rest period (Table 25–3). The higher dosage of ethinyl estradiol is equivalent to the amount of mestranol utilized by Lindsay and co-workers (see above) to prevent bone loss. If the patient's uterus is still present, progestin should be added

Table 25–3. Some therapeutically useful estrogens.

Agent	Duration of Action	Available Dosage Sizes	Special Features
Oral			
Diethylstilbestrol (DES)		Tablets, 0.1, 0.25, 0.5, and 1 mg	Very low cost; frequent nausea; pigmentation of nipples, areolas, and moles.
Ethinyl estradiol		Tablets, 0.02 and 0.5 mg	Moderate cost; some nausea.
Conjugated equine estrogens		Tablets (some enteric-coated), 0.3, 0.625, 1.25, and 2.5 mg	High cost; very rare nausea.
Parenteral			
Estradiol valerate	2–3 weeks	10, 20, and 40 mg/mL (in oil for IM injection)	Certainty of absorption but peaked blood levels.
Estradiol benzoate	2–3 days	1 and 3.33 mg/mL (in oil for IM injection)	Similar to estradiol valerate.

the last 10–13 days of estrogen administration. Medroxyprogesterone acetate (Provera), 2.5–5 mg, and norethindrone acetate (Norlutate), 2.5–5 mg, are satisfactory oral progesterones for combined therapy. The need for combined estrogen-progestin therapy has not been established for patients who do not have a uterus. Larger doses of estrogen may be required to treat hot flashes, but early attempts should be made to reduce the dosage. Finally, a thorough dialogue between the patient and her physician should establish clearly in the patient's mind the therapeutic limits of estrogen replacement therapy and its advantages and disadvantages.

4. Local estrogen therapy–For a few patients who manifest slight atrophic vulvitis or vaginitis (or both) without other evidence of estrogen deficiency, local estrogen therapy may be used. It should be remembered, however, that a portion of the local estrogen is absorbed into the bloodstream, and application of large amounts can result in significant systemic effects. When atrophic vulvitis or vaginitis is severe and a rapid therapeutic response is desired while systemic therapy is being adjusted, temporary additional local application of estrogens may be used. Application of estrogen cream to a small urethral caruncle may cause it to regress. Vaginal applications may also improve urinary symptoms caused by reduced estrogen stimulation of the urethral and bladder epithelium. *Note:* Vaginal creams containing conjugated or similar estrogens are expensive. A pharmacist can compound diethylstilbestrol cheaply in a vanishing cream base (not an oily ointment) at concentrations of 0.25 or 0.5 mg/g of cream. For intravaginal use, inexpensive suppositories of diethylstilbestrol, 0.1 mg or 0.5 mg, are available.

Special Treatment Problems

A. Alternatives to Estrogen Therapy: Estrogen replacement is contraindicated in some patients, and others may want to avoid the risks of this type of therapy. Alternative medications are available for control of some of the symptoms and complaints associated with the climacteric.

For hot flashes, monthly intramuscular injections of 150 mg of medroxyprogesterone acetate have been associated with a 90% reduction of the symptom. Daily oral administration of 250 μg of dl-norgestrel also has been shown to be more effective than placebo but less efficacious than estrogen. Nonsteroid medications have also been tried. Dithiocarbamoylhydrazine, a mild tranquilizer, has been found effective in one double-blind study. Conflicting results have been reported for clonidine, an antihypertensive agent. Numerous other compounds, including vitamins E and K, mineral supplements, belladonna alkaloids in combination with mild sedatives, tranquilizers, sedatives, and antidepressants have all been used for the relief of hot flashes, but the actual effectiveness of these compounds has not been critically evaluated.

For prevention of osteoporosis, calcium supplements have been shown to significantly reduce the loss of calcium from bone. Calcium carbonate, 2.6 g, or elemental calcium, 1200 mg, appear effective. Other forms of therapy being recommended for the prevention of osteoporosis include exercise, fluorides, diphosphonates, vitamin D, calcitonin, and androgens, but these have not been assessed as critically as estrogen and calcium. For vaginal atrophy, no good substitution therapy has been devised.

B. Uterine Bleeding: If patients are given sequential estrogen and progesterone, the majority will experience some uterine bleeding. This bleeding can occur during the treatment-free interval (scheduled bleeding) or while the medications are being administered (unscheduled bleeding). Hyperplastic endometrium can develop with this type of therapy, although the incidence appears to be less than 3% if the progestational agent is given for 10 days or longer during each treatment cycle. Hyperplastic endometrium appears to occur mainly in women with unscheduled bleeding. Biopsy should be performed on these patients. If endometrial hyperplasia is present, the medications can be discontinued, or progesterone can be given each day of estrogen administration. Whichever approach is adopted, a repeat biopsy should be performed to make certain that the hyperplastic endometrium has resolved. The cost-effectiveness ratio for periodic biopsy in women who do not bleed or bleed only during the medication-free interval has not been established.

In women taking estrogen only, the incidence of endometrial hyperplasia appears to be as high as 25% after only 15 months of therapy. Hyperplasia occurs in women who do not experience vaginal bleeding, bleed only during the medication-free interval, or bleed during drug administration. Thus, serial endometrial biopsies appear to be necessary in all women receiving cyclic estrogens to determine the presence of hyperplasia. Again, estrogen withdrawal or combined estrogen-progesterone therapy may be employed to treat the hyperplasia. It is presumed, but not established, that the incidence of endometrial cancer will be reduced if the programs discussed above are instituted.

Prognosis

The prognosis for the postmenopausal woman who does not develop clinically manifest estrogen deficiency includes only the ordinary hazards of disease and aging. For the woman who does develop signs of estrogen deficiency, steroid therapy can correct physical symptoms and signs, ameliorate associated emotional disturbances, and prevent the development of major metabolic estrogen deficiency disorders. Correction of minor distressing symptoms and signs can improve the general well-being of the postmenopausal woman and help her to pursue a vigorous life. On the other hand, steroid therapy for the postmenopausal woman who does not need it serves no purpose and can cause unpleasant side-effects and impose unnecessary risks to her health.

It should be obvious to the reader that all of the questions regarding estrogen replacement therapy have not been answered. Until the risks of ovarian failure and estrogen replacement therapy have been clarified by research efforts currently in progress, it is difficult to be dogmatic about any treatment program. Newer and safer methods of treatment are being investigated. Since patients assume certain risks no matter what type of management is undertaken (treatment or nontreatment), it is imperative that the patient receive sufficient information to allow her to participate in the decision.

• • •

References

Abraham GE, Maroulis GB: Effect of exogenous estrogen on serum pregnenolone, cortisol, and androgens in postmenopausal women. *Obstet Gynecol* 1975;**45**:271.

Antunes CM et al: Endometrial cancer and estrogen use. *N Engl J Med* 1979;**300**:9.

Boston Collaborative Drug Surveillance Program, Boston University Medical Center: Surgically confirmed gallbladder disease, venous thromboembolism, and breast tumors in relation to postmenopausal estrogen therapy. *N Engl J Med* 1974;**290**:15.

Campbell S, Whitehead M: Estrogen therapy and the postmenopausal syndrome. *Clinics Obstet Gynecol* 1977;**4**:31.

Cramer DW, Cutler SJ, Christine B: Trends in the incidence of endometrial cancer in the United States. *Gynecol Oncol* 1974;**2**:130.

Cutler SJ, Young JL Jr: Third National Cancer Survey: Incidence data. Monograph 41, National Cancer Institute, Bethesda, Md, 1975. [Available from Superintendent of Documents, Washington, DC.]

Erickson GE: Normal ovarian function. *Clin Obstet Gynecol* 1978;**21**:31.

Gambrell RD Jr et al: Use of the progestogen challenge test to reduce the risk of endometrial cancer. *Obstet Gynecol* 1980; **55**:732.

Gordon T et al: Menopause and coronary heart disease. *Ann Int Med* 1978;**89**:157.

Greenwald P, Caputo TA, Wolfgang PE: Endometrial cancer after menopausal use of estrogens. *Obstet Gynecol* 1977; **50**:239.

Hammond CB et al: Effects of long-term estrogen replacement therapy. 2. Neoplasia. *Am J Obstet Gynecol* 1979;**133**:537.

Hoover R et al: Menopausal estrogens and breast cancer. *N Engl J Med* 1976;**295**:401.

Jick H et al: Replacement estrogens and breast cancer. *Am J Epidemiol* 1980;**112**:586.

Jick H et al: Replacement estrogens and endometrial cancer. *N Engl J Med* 1979;**300**:218.

Judd HL: Hormonal dynamics associated with the menopause. *Clin Obstet Gynecol* 1976;**19**:775.

Judd HL et al: Estrogen replacement therapy. *Obstet Gynecol* 1981;**58**:267.

Judd HL et al: Serum androgens and estrogens in postmenopausal women with and without endometrial cancer. *Am J Obstet Gynecol* 1980;**136**:859.

Kannel WB et al: Menopause and risk of cardiovascular disease. *Ann Intern Med* 1976;**85**:447.

Lindsay R et al: Bone response to termination of oestrogen treatment. *Lancet* 1978;**1**:1325.

Lucas WE: Causal relationships between endocrine-metabolic variables in patients with endometrial carcinoma. *Obstet Gynecol Surv* 1974;**29**:507.

MacDonald PC et al: Origin of estrogen in a postmenopausal woman with a nonendocrine tumor of the ovary and endome-

trial hyperplasia. *Obstet Gynecol* 1976;**47**:644.

Meldrum DR et al: Elevations in skin temperature of the finger as an objective index of postmenopausal hot flashes: Standardization of the technique. *Am J Obstet Gynecol* 1979;**135**:713.

Molnar GW: Body temperature during postmenopausal hot flashes. *J Appl Physiol* 1975;**3**:499.

Nordin BEC: Clinical significance and pathogenesis of osteoporosis. *Br Med J* 1971;**1**:571.

Pfeffer RI, Van den Noort S: Estrogen use and stroke risk in postmenopausal women. *Am J Epidemiol* 1976;**103**:445.

Recker RR, Saville PD, Heaney RP: Effect of estrogens and calcium carbonate on bone loss in postmenopausal women. *Ann Intern Med* 1977;**87**:649.

Rigg LA et al: Absorption of estrogens from vaginal creams. *N Engl J Med* 1978;**298**:195.

Rosenberg L et al: Myocardial infarction and estrogen therapy in postmenopausal women. *N Engl J Med* 1976;**294**:1256.

Ross GT, Vande Wiele RL: The ovaries. Pages 355–399 in: *Textbook of Endocrinology,* 6th ed. Williams RH (editor). Saunders, 1981.

Ross RK et al: A case control study of menopausal estrogen therapy and breast cancer. *JAMA* 1980;**243**:1635.

Ross RK et al: Menopausal oestrogen therapy and protection from death from ischaemic heart disease. *Lancet* 1981;**1**:858.

Ryan KJ: Estrogens and atherosclerosis. *Clin Obstet Gynecol* 1976;**19**:805.

Shahrad P, Marks R: A pharmacologic effect of estrogen on human epidermis. *Br J Dermatol* 1977;**97**:383.

Sherman BM, Korenman SG: Hormonal characteristics of the human menstrual cycle throughout reproductive life. *J Clin Invest* 1975;**55**:669.

Sitteri PK, MacDonald PC: Role of extraglandular estrogen in human endocrinology. Chap 28, pp 615–629, in: *Handbook of Physiology: Endocrinology.* 7. Vol 2 (1). Greep RO, Astwood E (editors). Williams & Wilkins, 1973.

Stern MP et al: Cardiovascular risk and use of estrogens or estrogen-progestagen combinations. *JAMA* 1976;**235**:811.

Stumpf WE, Madhabananda S, Joshi SG: Estrogen target cells in the skin. *Experientia* 1974;**30**:196.

Sturdee DW et al: Physiological aspects of menopausal hot flush. *Br Med J* 1978;**2**:79.

Tataryn IV et al: LH, FSH, and skin temperature during the menopausal hot flash. *J Clin Endocrinol Metab* 1979;**49**:152.

Vermeulen A: The hormonal activity of the postmenopausal ovary. *J Clin Endocrinol Metab* 1976;**42**:247.

Vollman RF: Page 193 in: *The Menstrual Cycle.* Saunders, 1977.

Weiss NS, Szekely DR, Austin DF: Increasing incidence of endometrial cancer in the United States. *N Engl J Med* 1976; **294**:1259.

Weiss NS et al: Decreased risk of fractures of the hip and lower forearm with postmenopausal use of estrogen. *N Engl J Med* 1980;**302**:551.

Applied Genetics & Genetic Counseling | 26

Morton A. Stenchever, MD

MENDELIAN LAWS OF INHERITANCE

TYPES OF INHERITANCE

Autosomal Dominant

In this form of inheritance it is assumed that a mutation has occurred in one gene of an allelic pair and that the presence of this new gene produces enough of the changed protein to give a different phenotypic effect. Environment must also be considered because the effect may vary under different environmental conditions. The following are characteristic of autosomal dominant inheritance:

(1) The trait appears with equal frequency in both sexes.

(2) For inheritance to take place, at least one parent must have the trait unless a new mutation has just occurred.

(3) When a homozygous individual is mated to a normal individual, all offspring will carry the trait. When a heterozygous individual is mated to a normal individual, 50% of the offspring will show the trait.

(4) If the trait is rare, most persons demonstrating it will be heterozygous. (See Table 26–1.)

Autosomal Recessive

The mutant gene will not be capable of producing a new characteristic in the heterozygous state in this circumstance under customary environmental conditions—ie, with 50% of the genetic material producing the new protein, the phenotypic effect will not be different from that of the normal trait. When the environment is manipulated, the recessive trait occasionally becomes dominant. The characteristics of this form of inheritance are as follows:

(1) The characteristic will occur with equal frequency in both sexes.

(2) For the characteristic to be present, both parents must be carriers of the recessive trait.

(3) If both parents are homozygous for the recessive trait, all offspring will have it.

(4) If both parents are heterozygous for the recessive trait, 25% of the offspring will have it.

(5) In pedigrees showing frequent occurrence of individuals with rare recessive characteristics, consanguinity is often present. (See Table 26–2.)

Table 26–1. Examples of autosomal dominant conditions and traits.

Achondroplasia
Acoustic neuroma
Aniridia
Cataracts, cortical and nuclear
Chin fissure
Color blindness, yellow-blue
Craniofacial dysostosis
Deafness (several forms)
Dupuytren's contracture
Ehlers-Danlos syndrome
Facial palsy, congenital
Huntington's chorea
Hyperchondroplasia
Intestinal polyposis
Keloid formation
Lipomas, familial
Marfan's syndrome
Mitral valve prolapse
Muscular dystrophy
Neurofibromatosis (Recklinghausen's disease)
Night blindness
Pectus excavatum
Adult polycystic renal disease
Tuberous sclerosis
Von Willebrand's disease
Wolf-Parkinson-White syndrome (some cases)

X-Linked Recessive

This condition occurs when a gene on the X chromosome undergoes mutation and the new protein formed as a result of this mutation is incapable of producing a change in phenotype characteristic in the heterozygous state. Because the male has only one X chromosome, the presence of this mutant will allow for expression should it occur in the male. The following are characteristic of this form of inheritance:

(1) The condition occurs more commonly in males than in females.

(2) If both parents are normal and an affected male is produced, it must be assumed that the mother is a carrier of the trait.

(3) If the father is affected and an affected male is produced, the mother must be at least heterozygous for the trait.

(4) A female with the trait may be produced in one of 2 ways: She may inherit a recessive gene from

Table 26–2. Examples of autosomal recessive conditions and traits.

Acid maltase deficiency
Albinism
Alkaptonuria
Argininemia
Ataxia-telangiectasia
Bloom's syndrome
Cerebrohepatorenal syndrome
Chloride diarrhea, congenital
Chondrodystrophia myotonia
Color blindness, total
Coronary artery calcinosis
Cystic fibrosis
Cystinosis
Cystinuria
Deafness (several types)
Dubowitz's syndrome
Laron's dwarfism
Dysautonomia
Fructose-1,6-diphosphatase deficiency
Galactosemia
Gaucher's disease
Glaucoma, congenital
Histidinemia
Homocystinuria
Maple syrup urine disease
Mucolipidosis I, II, III
Mucopolysaccharidosis I–H, I–S, III, IV, VI, VII
Muscular dystrophy, autosomal recessive type
Niemann-Pick disease
Phenylketonuria
Sickle cell anemia
17α-Hydroxylase deficiency
18-Hydroxylase deficiency
21-Hydroxylase deficiency
Tay-Sachs disease
Wilson's disease
Xeroderma pigmentosum

Table 26–3. Examples of X-linked recessive conditions and traits.

Androgen insensitivity syndrome (complete and incomplete)
Color blindness, red-green
Diabetes insipidus (most cases)
Fabry's disease
Glucose-6-phosphate dehydrogenase deficiency
Gonadal dysgenesis (XY type)
Gout (certain types)
Hemophilia A (factor VIII disease)
Hemophilia B (factor IX deficiency)
Hypothyroidism, X-linked infantile
Hypophosphatemia
Immunodeficiency, X-linked
Lesch-Nyhan syndrome
Mucopolysaccharidosis II
Muscular dystrophy, adult and childhood types
Otopalatodigital syndrome
Reifenstein's syndrome

sufficient to cause a change in characteristic. The following are characteristic of this type of inheritance:

(1) The characteristic occurs with the same frequency in males and females.

(2) An affected male mated to a normal female will produce the characteristic in 50% of the offspring.

(3) An affected homozygous female mated to a normal male will produce the affected characteristic in all offspring.

(4) A heterozygous female mated to a normal male will produce affected offspring in 50% of the offspring.

(5) Occasional heterozygous females may not show the dominant trait on the basis of the Lyon hypothesis. (See Table 26–4.)

Table 26–4. Examples of X-linked dominant conditions and traits.

Acro-osteolysis, dominant type
Cervico-oculo-acoustic syndrome
Hyperammonemia
Orofaciodigital syndrome I

both her mother and her father, which would suggest that the father is affected and the mother is heterozygous; or she may inherit a recessive gene from one of her parents and may express the recessive characteristic as a function of the Lyon hypothesis, which assumes that all females are mosaics for their functioning X chromosome. It is theorized that this occurs because at about the time of implantation each cell in the developing female embryo selects one X chromosome as its functioning X and that all progeny cells thereafter use this X chromosome as their functioning X chromosome. The other X chromosome becomes inactive. Since this selection is done on a random basis, it is conceivable that some females will be produced who will be using primarily the X chromosome bearing the recessive gene. Thus, a genotypically heterozygous individual may demonstrate a recessive characteristic phenotypically on this basis. (See Table 26–3.)

X-Linked Dominant

In this situation, the mutation will produce a protein that, when present in the heterozygous state, is

APPLICATIONS OF MENDELIAN LAWS

Identification of Carriers

When a recessive characteristic is present in a population, carriers may be identified in a variety of ways. If the gene is responsible for the production of a protein (eg, an enzyme), the carrier often possesses 50% of the amount of the substance present in homozygous normal persons. Such a circumstance is found in galactosemia, where the carriers will have approximately half as much galactose-1-phosphate uridyl transferase activity in red cells as do noncarrier normal individuals.

At times, the level of the affected enzyme may be only slightly below normal, and a challenge with the substance to be acted upon may be required before the carrier can be identified. An example is seen in carriers of phenylketonuria, in whom the deficiency in phenyl-alanine hydroxylase is in the liver cells and serum levels may not be much lower than normal. Nonetheless, when the individual is given a loading dose of phenylalanine orally, plasma phenylalanine levels may remain high because the enzyme is not present in sufficient quantities to act upon this substance properly.

In still other situations where the 2 alleles produce different proteins that can be measured, a carrier state will have 50% of the normal protein and 50% of the other protein. Such a situation is seen in sickle cell trait, where one gene is producing hemoglobin A and the other hemoglobin S. Thus, the individual has half the amount of hemoglobin A as a normal person and half the hemoglobin S of a person with sickle cell anemia.

Expressivity & Penetrance

These are examples of how an autosomal characteristic may not be expressed in quite the form that it ordinarily would be. With regard to expressivity, while the gene is present, the entire genome of the individual must be taken into consideration. Other genetic influences may be operating even environmental ones—that may modify the manner in which the gene expresses itself. Penetrance, on the other hand, involves the expression of a dominant gene and takes into consideration the fact that while the gene may express itself in most individuals in a similar fashion, there may be some circumstance of environment or other gene activity during the development of the individual that may modify its action so that the phenotypic factor is not seen. Thus, one could state that during embryonic development there is a requirement of some environmental factor to allow the gene to express itself and, in an occasional rare case, this may not take place. Hence, the gene is not allowed to operate at its specific time.

Incidence of Diseases With Known Inheritance Patterns

If the incidence of a particular condition known to be autosomal recessive is known in a given population, then, applying mendelian law, it is possible to calculate the number of carriers in that population. The key to this circumstance, which will prevent error, is the testing of a large number of individuals within a population to calculate the true incidence of the autosomal recessive state.

Amniocentesis as an Aid

At present, about 50–100 metabolic diseases can be diagnosed by analyzing amniotic fluid, cells from amniotic fluid, or cells obtained from amniotic fluid and grown in tissue culture. In these cases, the amount of enzyme or other specific protein present is calcu-

lated and compared to normal or carrier state values. Thus, in a pregnancy at risk for an autosomal recessive condition (ie, where both parents are afflicted with or are carriers of the condition), an affected fetus may be identified and aborted, whereas carriers and normals may be spared. In the case of a pregnancy at risk for an autosomal dominant condition (ie, one or both parents afflicted), the affected fetus may be identified and the parents offered abortion. Where there is a risk of an X-linked condition, testing may be done if a specific evaluative procedure exists; if there is no such procedure, it is possible to salvage females (unaffected) and abort males—should this be the wish of the parents.

The list of diseases that can be diagnosed by amniocentesis continues to grow larger. The greatest use of amniocentesis for prenatal diagnosis, however, is in the identification of fetuses with chromosome anomalies and neural tube defects.

POLYGENIC INHERITANCE

Polygenic inheritance is defined as the inheritance of a single phenotypic feature as a result of the effects of many genes. Most physical features in humans are determined by polygenic inheritance. Many common malformations are determined in this way also. For example, cleft palate with or without cleft lip, clubfoot, anencephaly, meningomyelocele, dislocation of the hip, and pyloric stenosis each occur with a frequency of 0.5–2 per 1000 in white populations. Altogether, these anomalies account for slightly less than half of single primary defects noted in early infancy. They are present in siblings of affected infants—when both parents are normal—at a rate of 2–5%. They are also found more commonly among relatives than in the normal population. The increase in incidence is not environmentally induced because the frequency of such abnormalities in monozygotic twins is 4–8 times that of dizygotic twins and other siblings. The higher incidence in monozygotic twins is called **concordance.**

Sex also plays a role. Certain conditions appear to be transmitted by polygenic inheritance and are passed on more frequently by the mother who is affected than by the father who is affected. Cleft lip occurs in 6% of the offspring of women with cleft lip, as opposed to 2.8% of offspring of men with cleft lip.

There are many racial variations in diseases believed to be transmitted by polygenic inheritance, so that persons of different races are more prone to certain defects than persons of other racial background. In addition, as a general rule, the more severe a defect, the more likely it is to occur in subsequent siblings. Thus, siblings of children with bilateral cleft lip are more likely to have the defect than are those of children with unilateral cleft lip.

Environment undoubtedly plays a role in polygenic inheritance, because seasonal variations alter some defects as well as variations in occurrence from place to place in the world in similar populations.

CYTOGENETICS

IDENTIFICATION OF CHROMOSOMES

In 1960, 1963, 1965, and 1971, international meetings were held in Denver, London, Chicago, and Paris, respectively, for the purpose of standardizing the nomenclature of human chromosomes. These meetings resulted in an agreed decision that all autosomal pairs should be numbered in order of decreasing size from 1 to 22. Autosomes are divided into groups on the basis of their morphology, and these groups are labeled by the letters A–G. Thus, the A group is comprised of pairs 1–3; the B group, pairs 4 and 5; the C group, pairs 6–12; the D group, pairs 13–15; the E group, pairs 16–18; the F group, pairs 19 and 20; and the G group, pairs 21 and 22. The sex chromosomes are labeled X and Y, the X chromosome being similar in size and morphology to the No. 7 pair and thus frequently included in the C group (C-X) and the Y chromosome being similar in morphology and size to the G group (G-Y) (Fig 26–1).

The short arm of a chromosome is labeled p and the long arm q. If a translocation occurs in which the short arm of a chromosome is added to another chromosome, it is written p+. If the short arm is lost, it is p-. The same can be said for the long arm (q+ and q-).

It has been impossible to separate several chromosome pairs from one another on a strictly morphologic basis because the morphologic variations have been too slight. However, there are other means of identifying each chromosome pair in the karyotype. The first of these is the incorporation of ^{3}H-thymidine, known as the autoradiographic technique. This procedure involves the incorporation of radioactive thymidine into growing cells in tissue culture just before they are harvested. Cells that are actively undergoing DNA replication will pick up the radioactive thymidine, and the chromosomes will demonstrate areas of activity. Each chromosome will incorporate thymidine in a different pattern, and several chromosomes can therefore be identified by their labeling pattern. Nonetheless, with this method it is not possible to identify each chromosome, although it is possible to identify chromosomes involved in pathologic conditions, eg D_1 trisomy and Down's syndrome.

Innovative staining techniques have made it possible to identify each individual chromosome in the karyotype and to identify small anomalies that might have evaded the observer using older methods. These involve identification of chromosome banding by a variety of staining techniques, at times with predigestion with proteolytic agents. Some of the more commonly used techniques are the following:

Q banding: Fixed chromosome spreads are stained without any pretreatment using quinacrine

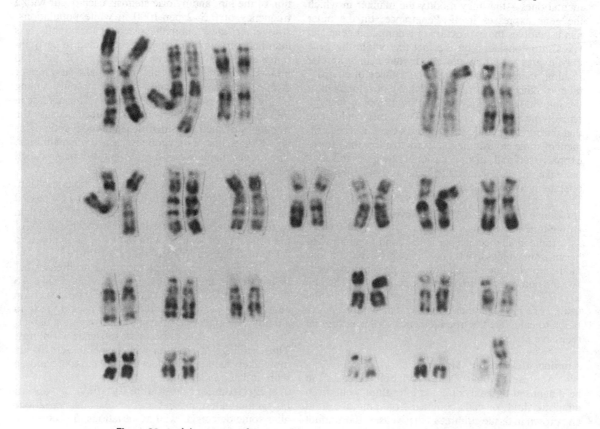

Figure 26–1. A karyotype of a normal human male demonstrating R-banding.

mustard, quinacrine, or other fluorescent dyes and observed with a fluorescence microscope.

G banding: Preparations are incubated in a variety of saline solutions using any one of several pretreatments and stained with Giemsa's stain.

R banding: Preparations are incubated in buffer solutions at high temperatures or at special pH and stained with Giemsa's stain. This process yields the reverse bands of G banding. (See Fig 26–1.)

C banding: Preparations are either heated in saline to temperatures just below boiling or treated with certain alkali solutions and then stained with Giemsa's stain. This process results in the development of prominent bands in the region of the centromeres.

CELL DIVISION

Each body cell goes through successive stages in its life cycle. As a landmark, cell division may be considered as the beginning of a cycle. Following this, the first phase, which is quite long but depends on how rapidly the particular cell is multiplying, is called the G_1 stage. During this stage, the cell is primarily concerned with carrying out its function. Following this, the S stage, or period of DNA synthesis, takes place. Next there is a somewhat shorter stage, the G_2 stage, during which time DNA synthesis is completed and chromosome replication begins. Following this comes

the M stage, when cell division occurs.

Somatic cells undergo division by a process known as **mitosis.** This is divided into 4 periods. The first is the **prophase,** during which the chromosome filaments shorten, thicken, and become visible. At this time they can be seen to be composed of 2 long parallel spiral strands lying adjacent to one another and containing a small clear structure known as the **centromere.** As prophase continues, the strands continue to unwind and may be recognized as chromatids. At the end of the prophase, the nuclear membrane disappears and **metaphase** begins. This stage is heralded by the formation of a spindle and the lining up of the chromosomes in pairs on the spindle. Following this, **anaphase** occurs, at which time the centromere divides and each daughter chromatid goes to one of the poles of the spindle. **Telophase** then ensues, at which time the spindle breaks and cell cytoplasm divides. A nuclear membrane now forms, and mitosis is complete: Each daughter cell has received chromosome material equal in amount and identical to that of the parent cell (Fig 26–2). Because each cell contains 2 chromosomes of each pair and a total of 46 chromosomes, a cell is considered to be **diploid.** Occasionally, an error takes place on the spindle, and instead of chromosomes dividing, with identical chromatids going to each daughter cell, an extra chromatid goes to one daughter cell and the other lacks that particular member. After the completion of cell division, this leads to a trisomic state (an extra dose of that chromosome) in one daugh-

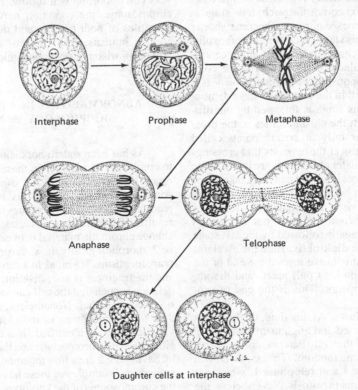

Interphase   Prophase   Metaphase

Anaphase   Telophase

Daughter cells at interphase

Figure 26–2. Mitosis of a somatic cell. (Reproduced, with permission, from Stenchever MA: *Human Cytogenetics: A Workbook in Reproductive Biology.* The Press of Case Western Reserve University, © 1972.)

ter cell and a monosomic state (a missing dose of the chromosome) in the other daughter cell. Any chromosome in the karyotype may be involved in such a process, which is known as mitotic nondisjunction. If these cells thrive and produce their own progeny, a new cell line is established within the individual. The individual then has more than one cell line and is known as a **mosaic.** A variety of combinations and permutations have been described in humans.

Germ cells undergo division for the production of eggs and sperm by a process known as **meiosis.** In the female it is known as oogenesis and in the male as spermatogenesis. The process that produces the egg and the sperm for fertilization essentially reduces the chromosome number from 46 to 23 and changes the normal diploid cell to a haploid cell, ie, a cell that has only one member of each chromosome pair. Following fertilization with the fusion of the 2 pronuclei, the diploid status is reestablished.

Meiosis can be divided into several stages. The first is **prophase I.** Early prophase is known as the **leptotene stage,** during which chromatin condenses and becomes visible as a single elongated threadlike structure. This is followed by the **zygotene stage,** when the single threadlike chromosomes migrate toward the equatorial plate of the nucleus. At this stage, homologous chromosomes become arranged close to one another to form **bivalents** that exchange materials at several points known as **synapses.** In this way, genetic material located on one member of a pair is exchanged with similar material located on the other member of a pair. Next comes the **pachytene stage** at which the chromosomes contract to become shorter and thicker. During this stage, each chromosome splits longitudinally into 2 chromatids united at the centromere. Thus, the bivalent becomes a structure composed of 4 closely opposed chromatids known as a **tetrad.** The human cell in the pachytene stage demonstrates 23 tetrads. This stage is followed by the **diplotene stage,** in which the chromosomes of the bivalent are held together only at certain points called bridges or chiasms. It is at these points that crossing-over takes place. The sister chromatids are joined at the centromere so that crossing-over can only take place between chromatids of homologous chromosomes and not between identical sister chromatids. In the case of males, the X and Y chromosomes are not involved in crossing-over. This stage is followed by the last stage of prophase, known as **diakinesis.** Here the bivalents contract and the chiasms move toward the end of the chromosome. The homologs pull apart, and the nuclear membrane disappears. This is the end of prophase I.

Metaphase I follows. At this time, the bivalents are now highly contracted and align themselves along the equatorial plate of the cell. Paternal and maternal chromosomes line up at random. This stage is then followed by **anaphase I** and **telophase I,** which are quite similar to the events in mitosis. Nevertheless, the difference is that in meiosis the homologous chromosome of the bivalent pair separate and not the sister chromatids. The homologous bivalents pull apart, one going to each pole of the spindle, following which 2 daughter cells are formed at telophase I.

Metaphase, anaphase, and telophase of meiosis II take place next. A new spindle forms in metaphase, the chromosomes align along the equatorial plate, and, as anaphase occurs, the chromatids pull apart, one each going to a daughter cell. This represents a true division of the centromere. Telophase then supervenes, with reconstitution of the nuclear membrane and final cell division. At the end, a haploid number of chromosomes is present in each daughter cell (Fig 26–3). In the case of spermatogenesis, both daughter cells are similar, forming 2 separate sperms. In the case of oogenesis, only one egg is produced, the nuclear material of the other daughter cell being present and intact but with very little cytoplasm, this being known as the **polar body.** A polar body is formed at the end of meiosis I and the end of meiosis II. Thus, each spermatogonium produces 4 sperms at the end of meiosis, whereas each oogonium produces one egg and 2 polar bodies.

Nondisjunction may also occur in meiosis. When it does, both members of the chromosome pair go to one daughter cell and none to the other. If the daughter cell that receives the entire pair is the egg, and fertilization ensues, a triple dose of the chromosome, or trisomy, will occur. If the daughter cell receiving no members of the pair is fertilized, a monosomic state will result. In the case of autosomes, this is lethal and a very early abortion will follow. In the case of the sex chromosome, the condition may not be lethal, and examples of both trisomy and monosomy have been seen in humans. Any chromosome pair may be involved in trisomic or monosomic conditions.

ABNORMALITIES IN CHROMOSOME MORPHOLOGY & NUMBER

As has been stated, nondisjunction may give rise to conditions of trisomy. In these cases, the morphology of the chromosome is not affected but the chromosome number is. Be this as it may, breaks and rearrangements in chromosomes may have a variety of results. If 2 chromosomes undergo breaks and exchange chromatin material between them, the outcome is 2 morphologically new chromosomes known as **translocations.** If a break in a chromosome takes place and the fragment is lost, **deletion** has occurred. If the deletion is such that the cell cannot survive, the condition may be lethal. Nonetheless, several examples of deleted chromosomes in individuals who have survived have been identified. If a break takes place at either end of a chromosome and the chromosome heals by having the 2 ends fuse together, a ring chromosome is formed. Examples of these have been seen in all of the chromosomes of the karyotype clinically, and generally they exhibit a variety of phenotypic abnormalities.

FIRST MEIOTIC DIVISION

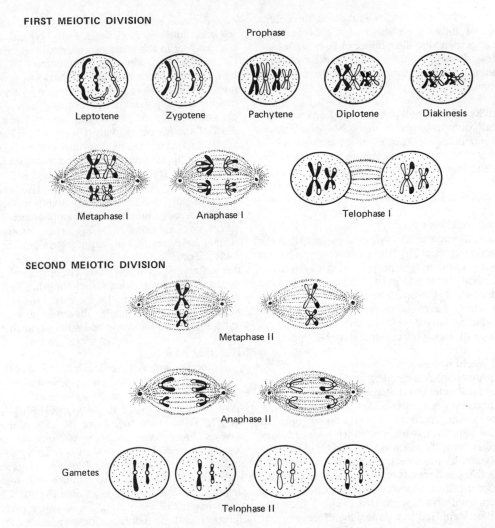

Prophase

Leptotene   Zygotene   Pachytene   Diplotene   Diakinesis

Metaphase I   Anaphase I   Telophase I

SECOND MEIOTIC DIVISION

Metaphase II

Anaphase II

Gametes

Telophase II

Figure 26–3. Meiosis in the human. (Reproduced, with permission, from Stenchever MA: *Human Cytogenetics: A Workbook in Reproductive Biology.* The Press of Case Western Reserve University, © 1972.)

At times a chromosome will divide by a horizontal rather than longitudinal split of the centromere. This leaves each daughter cell with a double dose of one of the arms of the chromosome. Thus, one daughter cell receives both long arms and the other both short arms of the chromosome. Such a chromosome is referred to as an **isochromosome,** the individual being essentially trisomic for one arm and monosomic for the other arm of the chromosome. Examples of this abnormality have been seen in humans.

Another anomaly that has been recognized is the occurrence of 2 breaks within the chromosome and rotation of the center fragment 180 degrees. Thus, the realignment allows for a change in morphology of the chromosome although the same number of genes is still present that were originally present. This is called an **inversion.** At meiosis, however, the chromosome has difficulty in undergoing chiasm formation, and abnormal rearrangements of this chromosome, leading to partial duplications and partial losses of chromatin

material, do take place. This situation may lead to several bizarre anomalies. If the centromere is involved in the inversion, the condition is called a **pericentric inversion.**

Breaks occasionally occur in 2 chromosomes, and a portion of one broken chromosome is inserted into the body of another, leading to a grossly abnormal chromosome. This is known as an **insertion** and generally leads to gross anomalies at meiosis.

METHODS OF STUDY

Sex Chromatin (X-Chromatin) Body (Barr Body)

The X-chromatin body was first seen in the nucleus of the nerve cell of a female cat in 1949 by Barr and Bertram. It has been found to be the constricted, nonfunctioning X chromosome. As a general rule, only one X chromosome functions in a cell at a given time. All other X chromosomes present in a cell may be seen as X-chromatin bodies in the resting nucleus. Thus, if one knows the number of X chromosomes, one can anticipate that the number of Barr bodies will be one less. If one counts the number of Barr bodies, the number of X chromosomes may be determined by adding one.

Drumsticks on Polymorphonuclear Leukocytes

Small outpouchings of the lobes of nuclei in polymorphonuclear leukocytes of females have been demonstrated to be the X-chromatin body in this particular cell. Hence, leukocyte preparations may be used to detect X-chromatin bodies in much the same way as buccal cells are used.

Chromosome Count

In the karyotypic analysis of a patient, it is the usual practice to count 20–50 chromosome spreads for chromosome number. The purpose of this is to determine whether mosaicism exists because if a mosaic pattern does exist, there will be at least 2 cell lines of different counts. Photographs are made of representative spreads, and karyotypes are constructed so that the morphology of each chromosome may be studied.

Banding Techniques

As previously described, it is possible after appropriate pretreatment to stain metaphase spreads with special stains and construct a karyotype that demonstrates the banding patterns of each chromosome. In this way, it is now possible to identify with certainty every chromosome in the karyotype. This is of value in such problems as translocations and trisomic conditions. Another use depends on the fact that most of the long arm of the Y chromosome is heterochromic and stains deeply with fluorescent stains. The Y chromosome may be identified at a glance, therefore, even in the resting nucleus.

APPLIED GENETICS & TERATOLOGY

CHROMOSOMES & SPONTANEOUS ABORTION

An entirely new approach to reproductive biology problems became available with the advent of tissue culture and cytologic techniques that made it possible to culture cells from any tissue of the body and produce karyotypes which could be analyzed. In the early 1960s, investigators in a number of laboratories began to study chromosomes of spontaneous abortions and demonstrated that the earlier the spontaneous abortion occurred, the more likely it was to be due to a chromosomal abnormality. It is now known that in spontaneous abortions occurring in the first 8 weeks, the fetuses have about a 50% incidence of chromosome anomalies.

A recent study by Creasy and others using banding techniques demonstrates fairly typical findings with respect to the types of abnormalities that occur. Of nearly 1000 abortuses evaluated, 30.5% had chromosome abnormalities. Of those that were abnormal, 49.8% were trisomic, suggesting an error of meiotic nondisjunction. Interestingly, although most chromosomes in the karyotype were represented, one-third of the abortuses with trisomy had trisomy 16. While this abnormality does not occur in liveborn infants, it apparently is a frequent problem in abortuses. The karyotype 45,X occurred in 23.7% of chromosomally abnormal abortuses. This karyotype occurs about 24 times more frequently in abortuses than in liveborn infants, which emphasizes its lethal nature. An additional 17.4% of chromosomally abnormal abortuses had polyploidy (triploidy or tetraploidy). These lethal conditions are seen only in abortuses except in extremely rare circumstances and are due to a variety of accidents, including double fertilization and a number of meiotic errors. Finally, a small number of chromosomally abnormal abortuses had unbalanced translocations and other anomalies.

Habitual Abortion

Couples with this problem make up about 0.5% of the population and are defined as those who have had 3 or more spontaneous abortions. Several investigators have studied groups of these couples using banding techniques and have found that 10–25% of them will have a chromosome anomaly in either the male or female partner. Those seen are 47,XXX, 47,XYY, and a variety of balanced translocation carriers. Those with sex chromosome abnormalities will frequently demonstrate other nondisjunctional events. Chromosome anomalies are thus a major cause of habitual abortion, and the incorporation of genetic evaluation into such a work-up is potentially fruitful.

CHROMOSOMAL DISORDERS

This section will be devoted to a brief discussion of various autosomal abnormalities. (Sex chromosome disorders have been dealt with in Chapter 7.) Table 26–5 summarizes some of the autosomal abnormalities that have been diagnosed. These are represented as syndromes, together with some of the signs typical of these conditions. In general, autosomal monosomy is so lethal that total loss of a chromosome is rarely seen in an individual born alive. Only a few cases of monosomy 21–22 have been reported to date. This attests to the rarity of this disorder. Trisomy may occur with any chromosome. The 3 most common trisomic conditions seen in living individuals are trisomy 13, 18, and 21. A number of cases of trisomy of various C group chromosomes have been reported sporadically. The most frequently reported is trisomy 8. Generally, trisomy of other chromosomes must be assumed to be lethal, because they do occur in abortuses but not in living individuals. To date, trisomy of

Table 26-5. Autosomal disorders.

Type	Synonym	Signs
Monosomy Monosomy 21-22		Moderate mental retardation, antimongoloid slant of eyes, flared nostrils, small mouth, low-set ears, spade hands.
Trisomy Trisomy 13	Trisomy D: The "D_1" syndrome, Edward's syndrome	Severe mental retardation, congenital heart disease (77%), polydactyly, cerebral malformations (especially aplasia of olfactory bulbs), eye defects, low-set ears, cleft lip and palate, low birth weight. Characteristic dermatoglyphic pattern.
Trisomy 18	Trisomy E: The "E" syndrome, Edward's syndrome	Severe mental retardation, long narrow skull with prominent occiput, congenital heart disease, flexion deformities of fingers, narrow palpebral fissures, low-set ears, harelip and cleft palate. Characteristic dermatoglyphics, low birth weight.
Trisomy 21	Mongolism, Down's syndrome	Mental retardation, brachycephaly, prominent epicanthal folds, Brushfield spots, poor nasal bridge development, congenital heart disease, hypotonia, hypermobility of joints, characteristic dermatoglyphics.
Translocations 15/21	Mongolism, Down's syndrome	Same as trisomy 21.
21/21	Mongolism, Down's syndrome	Same as trisomy 21.
21/22	Mongolism, Down's syndrome	Same as trisomy 21.
Deletions Short arm chromosome 4 (4p-)	Wolf's syndrome	Severe growth and mental retardation, midline scalp defects, seizures, deformed iris, beak nose, hypospadias.
Short arm chromosome 5 (5p-)	Cri du chat syndrome	Microcephaly, catlike cry, hypertelorism with epicanthus, low-set ears, micrognathism, abnormal dermatoglyphics, low birth weight.
Long arm chromosome 13 (13q-)	...	Microcephaly, psychomotor retardation, eye and ear defects, hypoplastic or absent thumbs.
Short arm chromosome 18 (18p-)	...	Severe mental retardation hypertelorism, low-set ears, flexion deformities of hands.
Long arm chromosome 18 (18q-)	...	Severe mental retardation, microcephaly, hypotonia, congenital heart disease; marked dimples at elbows, shoulders, and knees.
Long arm chromosome 21 (21q-)	...	Associated with chronic myelogenous leukemia.

every autosome except chromosome 1 has been seen in abortuses.

Translocations can occur between any 2 chromosomes of the karyotype, and a variety of phenotypic expressions may be seen after meiotic rearrangements. Three different translocation patterns have been identified in Down's syndrome: 15/21, 21/21, and 21/22.

Deletions may also occur with respect to any chromosome in the karyotype and may be brought about by a translocation followed by a rearrangement in meiosis, which leads to the loss of chromatin material, or by a simple loss of the chromatin material following a chromosome break. Some of the more commonly seen deletion patterns are listed in Table 26-5.

The most frequent abnormality related to a chromosome abnormality is Down's syndrome. Down's syndrome serves as an interesting model for the discussion of autosomal diseases. The 21 trisomy type is the most common form and comprises approximately 95% of Down's syndrome patients. There is a positive correlation between the frequency of Down's syndrome and maternal age. Babies with Down's syndrome are more often born to teenage mothers and, even more frequently, to mothers over 35. Although it is not entirely clear why this should be so, it may be that in older women, at least, the egg has been present in prophase of the first meiotic division from the time of fetal life and that, as it ages, there is a greater tendency for nondisjunction to occur, leading to trisomy. A second theory is that coital habits are more erratic in both the very young and the older mothers, and this may lead to an increased incidence in fertilization of older eggs. This theory maintains that these eggs may be more likely to suffer nondisjunction or to accept abnormal sperm. Be this as it may, the incidence of Down's syndrome in the general population is approximately 1:600 deliveries and at age 40 approximately 1:100 deliveries. At age 45, the incidence is approximately 1:40 deliveries. The other 5% of Down's syndrome patients are the result of translocations, the most common being the 15/21 translocation. Nevertheless, 21/21 and 21/22 examples have been noted. In the case of 15/21, the chance of recurrence in a later pregnancy is theoretically 25%. In practice, a rate of 10% is observed if the mother is the carrier. When the father is the carrier, the odds are less, because there may be a selection not favoring the sperm carrying both the 15/21 translocation and the normal 21 chromosome. In the case of 21/21 translocation, there is no chance for a normal child to be formed because the carrier will contribute either both 21s or no 21 and, following fertilization, will produce either a monosomic 21 or trisomic 21. With regard to 21/22 translocation, the chance of producing a baby with Down's syndrome is 1:2.

In general, other trisomic states occur with greater frequency in older women, and the larger the chromosome involved, the more severe the syndrome. Since trisomy 21 involves the smallest of the chromosomes, the phenotypic problems of Down's syndrome are the least severe and a moderate life expectancy may be anticipated. Even these individuals will be grossly abnormal, however, because of mental retardation and defects in other organ systems. The average life expectancy is much lower than for the general population.

GENETICS & CANCER

Certain families have a greater tendency to develop cancer. It is also recognized that certain cancers occur more frequently in families with notable cancer histories. Cancer of the endometrium and cancer of the breast are good examples of these. On the other hand, cancer of the cervix is a tumor that does not occur with increased frequency in women with a family history of cancer. A patient with a strong family history of cancer should be checked frequently for cancer of the endometrium and the breast.

A number of families with hereditary diseases associated with chromosome breakage have also been noted to have a high incidence of cancer. Examples of these are families with high incidences of Bloom's syndrome, Fanconi's anemia, or ataxia-telangiectasia. In addition, chromosome-breaking agents, eg, x-rays and certain viruses, seem to predispose exposed individuals to higher tumor incidences. These indirect data support a causal relationship between chromosome damage and cancer formation. Nonetheless, the exact sequence is yet to be determined.

AMNIOCENTESIS

Amniocentesis for prenatal diagnosis of genetic diseases is an extremely useful tool in the following circumstances or classes of patients:

(1) Maternal age $\geq$ 35.
(2) Previous chromosomally abnormal child.
(3) Three or more spontaneous abortions.
(4) Patient or husband with chromosome anomaly.
(5) Family history of chromosome anomaly.
(6) Possible female carrier of X-linked disease.
(7) Metabolic disease risk.
(8) Neural tube defect risk.

To date, over 50 metabolic diseases may be diagnosed prenatally by amniocentesis. In addition, it is

Table 26–6. Examples of hereditary diseases diagnosable prenatally.

Lipidoses (at least 7): Gaucher's, Tay-Sachs, Fabry's, etc.

Mucopolysaccharidoses (at least 6): Hurler's, Hunter's, etc.

Aminoacidurias (at least 11): Cystinosis, homocystinuria, maple syrup urine disease, etc.

Diseases of carbohydrate metabolism (at least 8): Glucose-6-phosphate dehydrogenase deficiency, glycogen storage disease, etc.

Miscellaneous (at least 11): Adrenogenital syndrome, Lesch-Nyhan syndrome, etc.

possible to diagnose the sex of the infant, using the X-chromatin body or fluorescent method for the Y chromosome or tissue culture and karyotypic analysis of the amniotic cells. It is also possible to diagnose a chromosome abnormality by this latter method. Before attempting amniocentesis, the patient and her husband should be told that no therapy is currently available for most of the affected infants but that, when the risk of a serious disease is present, therapeutic abortion may be a solution. Chromosome analysis of amniotic fluid cells costs about $250 in the USA, and about 3–4 weeks are required. Amniocentesis generally is carried out at the 15th to 17th weeks of gestation and is best done transabdominally. The fluid must be sent directly to the laboratory. It should not be frozen, because freezing kills the cells. Table 26–6 lists some of the conditions which can now be diagnosed prenatally by biochemical means.

OTHER TOOLS FOR PRENATAL DIAGNOSIS

Other tools useful in prenatal diagnosis of genetic problems are the following:

(1) **X-ray:** Can be useful in diagnosing structural defects as well as other selected conditions associated with defects discernible by radiologic examination.

(2) **Ultrasonography:** Useful in diagnosing structural defects including those involving the cardiovascular, renal, gastrointestinal, neuromuscular, and skeletal systems.

(3) **Fetoscopy:** Although an experimental technique, this tool not only has the potential of allowing direct visualization of the fetus but also makes possible tissue and blood sampling.

(4) **Linkage studies:** This technique utilizes the fact that 2 genes may be closely aligned on the same chromosome. Therefore, if both genes exist in a given individual, it is possible to detect the presence of one by testing for the other. Thus, indirect evidence for a defect can be ascertained even though no specific test is available for that defect. This technique is still quite experimental and has only limited potential. Nonetheless, it should be of value in certain specific problems.

GENETIC COUNSELING

While genetic counseling should generally be carried out by persons with experience in both the genetics and clinical medicine, an individual physician can play a significant role in this aspect of patient care. This role begins with the careful taking of a medical and family history. A family tree can be constructed (Fig 26–4). In doing so, it is important to systematically account for each individual in each generation in both the husband's and wife's families. Abortions should be included, as should persons who have died. When a specific diagnosis is known in the proband and the relatives are dead or otherwise not available, the physician may ask to see photographs, which may show characteristics of the suspected condition. In many cases, when the pedigree is constructed, the inheritance pattern can be determined. If this can be done, the relative risks that future progeny will be affected can be estimated. This pedigree information is also useful in discussing the case with a genetics counselor.

Single Gene Defects

If one parent is affected and the condition is caused by an autosomal dominant disorder, the chances are 1:2 that a child will be affected. If both parents are carriers of an autosomal recessive condition, the chances are 1:4 that the child would be affected and 1:2 that the child would be a carrier. Carrier status of both parents can be assumed if an affected child has been produced, or if a carrier testing program was available and both parents were discovered to be carriers by this means. Tay-Sachs disease and sickle

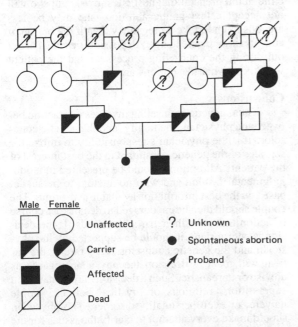

Male   Female

□ ○ Unaffected   **?** Unknown

◪ ◖ Carrier   ● Spontaneous abortion

■ ● Affected   ↗ Proband

⧄ ⦸ Dead

Figure 26–4. Pedigree showing unaffected offspring, carrier offspring, and affected offspring in a family with an autosomal recessive trait (sickle cell anemia).

cell disease detection programs are examples of the latter possibility.

When carrier testing is available and the couple is at risk, as with Tay-Sachs disease in Jewish couples and sickle cell disease in blacks, the physician should order these tests before pregnancy is undertaken, or immediately if the patient is already pregnant. When parents are carriers and pregnancy has been diagnosed, prenatal diagnostic testing is indicated if there is a test. If a physician does not know whether or not a test exists or how to obtain one, the local genetic counseling program, local chapter of the National Foundation/ March of Dimes, or state health department should be called for consultation. These sources may be able to inform the physician about new research that may have produced a prenatal test. A new test may be likely, because this area of research is very dynamic. If genetic counseling services are readily available, patients with specific problems should be referred to those agencies for consultation. It is impossible for a physician to keep track of all of the current developments in the myriad of conditions caused by single gene defects.

X-linked traits are frequently amenable to prenatal diagnostic testing. When such tests are not available, the couple has the option of testing for the sex of the fetus. If a fetus is noted to be a female, the odds are overwhelming that it will not be affected, although a carrier state may be present. If the fetus is a male, the chances are 1:2 that it will be affected. With this information, the couple can decide whether or not to continue the pregnancy in the case of a male fetus. Again, checking with genetic counseling agencies may reveal a prenatal diagnostic test that has only recently been described, or information such as gene linkage studies that may apply in the individual case.

Neural Tube Disease

Most neural tube diseases, eg, anencephaly, spina bifida, meningomyelocele, are associated with a multifactorial inheritance pattern. The frequency of their occurrence varies in different populations—eg, as high as 10 per 1000 births in Ireland and as low as 0.8 per 1000 births in the western USA. Ninety percent are index cases, ie, they occur spontaneously without previous occurrence in a family. The remaining 10%, however, are proper subjects for genetic counseling. In general, if a couple has a child with such an anomaly, the chance of producing another is 2–5%. If they have had 2 such children, the risk can be as high as 10%. However, other diagnostic possibilities involving different modes of inheritance should be considered. Siblings also run greater risks of having affected children, with the highest risk being to female offspring of sisters and the lowest to male offspring of brothers. For the couple at high risk—Irish descent, previous affected child, or sibling of an individual with an affected child—a maternal serum alpha-fetoprotein test between 16–18 weeks' gestation is indicated. If an elevation of 2.5 standard deviations above the mean or more is noted, amniocentesis for alpha-fetoprotein should be done along with a careful ultrasound study of

GLOSSARY

Alleles: Different genes that occupy the same position on homologous chromosomes and affect a similar function.

Autosomes: Chromosomes other than the sex chromosomes (X and Y).

Chromosome: Nuclear structure that contains the genes in a linear arrangement.

Chromosome number: The number of chromosomes ordinarily present in the nucleus of a somatic cell. Most animals, including humans, are diploid, meaning that the chromosomes occur in pairs. The total chromosome count in humans is 46.

Dominant characteristic: The phenotypic effect produced by a gene in the heterozygous state which is the same as that produced in the homozygous state.

Gene: Unit of genetic information; that sequence of nucleotides which forms the code for the production of specific proteins.

Genotype: The genetic makeup of the individual.

Heterozygote: An individual in whom the members of a pair of genes are dissimilar.

Homozygote: An individual in whom a pair of genes is similar.

Locus: Specific site on a chromosome occupied by a given gene.

Mutation: Alteration in genetic material, usually involving a change in the structure of the DNA molecule at a given point. This generally leads to the production of a modified protein by the mutated genetic information.

Phenotype: The appearance of the individual; the characteristic that can be observed.

Recessive characteristic: A phenotypic characteristic that is produced only in the homozygous state and not in the heterozygous state.

Sex chromosomes: The chromosomes that bear the genes that determine the sex of the individual, ie, the X (female) and the Y (male) chromosomes.

---

the fetus for structural anomalies. In questionable cases, fetal x-ray may be helpful also. Evidence for a neural tube defect noted on ultrasound or x-ray and suspected by amniotic fluid alpha-fetoprotein elevation of 3.0 standard deviations or more above the mean makes termination of pregnancy a reasonable course to follow if this is the desire of the couple.

Maternal screening of all low-risk pregnancies will not provide benefits commensurate with the costs involved.

Chromosome Abnormalities

In most parts of the USA where prenatal diagnostic screening facilities are available, it is standard policy to offer prenatal diagnostic testing to all women over age 35, because they are at greater risk than the general population for the occurrence of trisomic offspring. The risk increases with age, from roughly 1:200 for all chromosomal trisomies at age 35 to 1:20 at age 45. It is the physician's responsibility to recommend prenatal diagnostic studies in such cases and to point out the possible consequences if the studies are refused.

In the section on prenatal diagnosis, other indications for prenatal diagnostic testing have been mentioned. Individuals who are known carriers of chromosome abnormalities should certainly be offered prenatal diagnosis, since their offspring are at very high risk for an anomaly. The indication for prenatal diagnosis in the case of habitual aborters is less compelling than the others listed. This assumes that roughly half of fetuses aborted in the first trimester will have a chromosome abnormality, and that in about half of these the anomaly will consist of autosomal trisomy. If this is actually the case, one would expect that after 3 spontaneous miscarriages the mother would probably already have produced one trisomic abortion. If she has produced a trisomic abortion, she would then be in

the same category of risk as any woman who has produced a trisomic live-born child—ie, 2–5%. These possibilities should be discussed with the patient and may influence her decision about whether or not to go ahead with prenatal diagnostic studies.

Physicians have an obligation to counsel patients known to be at high risk who for that reason are reluctant to become pregnant. The patient should be informed about resources available so that she and her husband can realistically decide whether or not to conceive a child. If she is at high risk for an affected child and a prenatal diagnostic test exists but she will not accept a therapeutic abortion, she may be less anxious to undertake a pregnancy than if the option of abortion is available to her. All possibilities must be set out during the counseling process so that the patient will know what her options are.

Conclusions

Thus, genetic counseling involves interaction between the physician, the family, and the genetic counselor. It is the physician's responsibility to utilize the services of the genetic consultant in the best interest of the patient. All options should be presented in a nonjudgmental fashion and with no attempt to persuade, based on the best information available at the time. The couple should then be encouraged to decide on a course of action that suits their particular needs. If the decision is appropriate, it should be supported by the physician and the genetic counselor. Very rarely, the patient will make a decision the physician regards as unwise or unrealistic. Such a decision may be based on superstition, religious or mystical beliefs, simple naiveté, or even personality disorder. The physician should make every attempt to clarify the issues for the patient. Rarely, other resources such as family members or spiritual leaders may be consulted in strict confidence. The physician and the genetic counselor must clearly set forth the circumstances of the problem in the record, in case the patient undertakes a course of action that ends in tragedy and perhaps an attempt to blame the professional counselors for not preventing it. Fortunately, these problems occur infrequently. In most instances, the physician, genetic counselor, and couple working together can arrive at a solution in keeping with the family's best interests.

• • •

References

Barnes AC: Fetal indications for therapeutic abortion. *Annu Rev Med* 1971;**22**:133.

Bostock CJ, Summer AT: *The Eukaryotic Chromosome*. North Holland Publishing Co, 1978.

Byrd JR et al: Cytogenic findings in fifty-five couples with recurrent fetal wastage. *Fertil Steril* 1977;**28**:246.

Carr DH: Chromosome anomalies as a cause of spontaneous human abortion. *Am J Obstet Gynecol* 1967;**97**:283.

Gardner EJ: *Principles of Genetics*. Wiley, 1975.

Golbus MS et al· Prenatal genetic diagnosis in 3000 amniocenteses. *N Engl J Med* 1979;**300**:157.

Hamerton JL, Linger HP (editors): Paris Conference (1971), Supplement (1975): Standardization in human cytogenetics. *Birth Defects* 1975;**11(9)**:1. [Entire issue.]

Hsia DY-Y: The detection of heterozygote carriers. *Med Clin North Am* 1969;**53**:857.

Kajii T et al: Anatomic and chromosomal anomalies in 639 spontaneous abortuses. *Hum Genet* 1980;**55**:87.

Kosanovic M et al: Infrequent structural chromosome aberrations in women with primary amenorrhea. *Int J Fertil* 1979;**24**:68.

Levine H: *Clinical Cytogenetics*. Little, Brown, 1971

Malonsky A et al: Prenatal cytogenetic diagnosis. (3 parts.) *N Engl J Med* 1970;**283**:1370, 1441, 1498.

Menutti MT et al: An evaluation of cytogenetic analysis as a primary tool in the assessment of recurrent pregnancy wastage. *Obstet Gynecol* 1978;**52**:308.

National Institutes of Health: *Antenatal Diagnosis*. Publication No. 79-1973. National Institutes of Health, 1979.

Sant-Cassia LJ, Cooke P: Chromosomal analysis of couples with repeated spontaneous abortions. *Br J Obstet Gynaecol* 1981;**88**:52.

Smith DW et al: Polygenic inheritance of certain common malfunctions. *J Pediatr* 1970;**76**:653.

Stenchever MA: Chromosome evaluation: Clinical applications. Chapter 2 in: *Progress in Gynecology*. Vol 6. Taymor ML, Green TH (editors). Grune & Stratton, 1975.

Stenchever MA et al: Cytogenetics of habitual abortion and other reproductive wastage. *Am J Obstet Gynecol* 1977;**127**:143.

Stevenson AC, Davidson BCC: *Genetics Counseling*. Heinemann, 1971.

Stoll CG et al: Interchromosomal effect in balanced translocation. *Birth Defects* 1978;**14**:393.

Tho PT, Byrd JR, McDonough PG: Etiologies and subsequent reproductive performance of 100 couples with recurrent abortion. *Fertil Steril* 1979;**32**:389.

Tsuji K, Nakano R: Chromosome studies of embryos from induced abortions in pregnant women age 35 and over. *Obstet Gynecol* 1978;**52**:542.

27 | Diagnosis of Pregnancy & Associated Conditions

Ralph W. Hale, MD

Any physician whose patients include women in the childbearing years of life must be able to make the diagnosis of pregnancy. Late in pregnancy, the diagnosis usually is simple; early in pregnancy, it may be difficult—especially if the patient has missed only one period. The physician may be required to give an opinion about a possible diagnosis of pregnancy for various reasons. A woman who has not used contraceptive measures may wish to know as soon as possible whether or not she is pregnant in order to allay anxiety about a perhaps unwanted pregnancy; a woman who would rather have an abortion than a baby must know early so that the pregnancy can be terminated at the safest time; the infertile woman is eager to know if she has finally succeeded; the woman who wishes to enlarge her family wants to make plans; and the working woman wants to be able to make plans for maternity leave.

The physician's ability to make an accurate diagnosis of pregnancy depends upon interpreting the signs and symptoms of pregnancy, the relative importance of each, and familiarity with the available laboratory tests so that the diagnosis can be made with reasonable certainty. The physician must also be able to estimate the duration of pregnancy. A second examination should be scheduled 3–4 weeks after the initial visit. In general, it is better to postpone giving a final opinion than to make an incorrect diagnosis.

PRESUMPTIVE, PROBABLE, & POSITIVE MANIFESTATIONS OF PREGNANCY

The clinical diagnosis of pregnancy is based upon both physical signs and symptoms. These findings may be divided into presumptive, probable, and positive manifestations of pregnancy.

Presumptive Manifestations

A. Symptoms:

1. Amenorrhea–A missed period is frequently the first sign that conception has occurred, although a few women may have slight bleeding after conception—often at about the time of the usual period. However, emotional tension, chronic disease, and certain medications may also cause delayed menses, and pregnancy may occur in women who are not menstruating, eg, during lactation or after D&C.

2. Nausea and vomiting–Nausea and vomiting are common early symptoms of pregnancy, with severity ranging from queasiness or a simple distaste for food to protracted vomiting (**hyperemesis gravidarum**) necessitating hospitalization. This manifestation is called **morning sickness** because it usually occurs upon arising; however, it may occur throughout the day, and some women even report that nausea is most severe during the evening. Nausea is often precipitated by heavy cooking odors or pungent smells such as cigar smoke or diesel fumes. Psychic tension may play a role in the occurrence or severity of this disorder. Treatment consists of dietary restrictions in favor of light dry foods, small or more frequent meals, emotional support, and, rarely, antinauseant drugs. Morning sickness usually subsides by 6–8 weeks and rarely lasts more than 12 weeks. It may recur as term approaches.

3. Mastodynia–Mastodynia may be present early in pregnancy and ranges in severity from a tingling sensation to frank pain. It is caused by the influence of estrogen on the mammary ducts, the influence of progesterone on the alveolar system, and the effect of increased circulation resulting in engorgement of the breasts. The discomfort can usually be relieved by wearing a properly fitted maternity brassiere (even at night).

4. Quickening–The first perception of fetal movement generally occurs in the 18th to 20th weeks of gestation, but it has been reported as early as the 14th week in multigravidas and the 16th week in primigravidas. The sensation is first described as a "flutter," not a kick. It may be difficult for the patient to discriminate between this sensation and that produced by peristalsis. Quickening may help to determine the duration of pregnancy but by itself is unreliable as a diagnostic symptom.

5. Urinary symptoms–Bladder irritability, frequency, and nocturia frequently develop early in pregnancy. These symptoms are due to increased circulation associated with the effects of estrogen and progesterone on the bladder—combined with gradual enlargement of the uterus. Urinary tract infection must be ruled out. Later in pregnancy, the pressure of the gravid uterus upon the bladder can induce bladder symptoms.

6. Constipation–Constipation commonly occurs early and persists throughout pregnancy. Progesterone—a smooth muscle relaxant—is a major cause. Changes in dietary habits may also be a factor. As the pregnancy progresses, the heavy enlarged uterus causes displacement of bowel. Increased fluid intake, laxative foods, and stool softeners are helpful. Laxative drugs and enemas should be avoided.

7. Weight gain–Weight gain during pregnancy is also related to dietary habits. Early pregnancy is not associated with rapid weight gain; even slight weight loss may be recorded. Nonetheless, the patient who attempts to "eat for two" or eats to relieve emotional tension will gain weight rapidly and excessively.

8. Fatigue–Unexplained fatigue accompanies many pregnancies. It may occur early and persist. It is rarely incapacitating, but the patient may need additional rest and reassurance.

9. Nail signs–These may be noted as early as the sixth week. Some pregnant women complain of thinning and softening of the nails. The use of nail polish and polish removers should be discontinued. The nails should be kept short to prevent breakage.

B. Signs: The presumptive signs of pregnancy may be more specific than the symptoms, but even so they are not diagnostic. They are best understood as the reaction of an organ or system to the presence in the body of the pregnancy hormones.

1. Basal body temperature elevation–A perceptible temperature elevation for longer than 3 weeks is presumptive evidence of pregnancy in a woman who has been recording her BBT throughout several menstrual cycles.

2. Skin changes–Cutaneous manifestations are the easiest signs for the physician and the patient to recognize. The most striking, when it occurs, is chloasma—"the mask of pregnancy"—a darkening of the skin over the forehead, the bridge of the nose, and the cheek bones especially notable in dark-complexioned women. It occurs to a variable degree in most pregnant women after the 16th week. In susceptible women, excessive exposure to the sun will intensify this effect.

Other skin changes include darkening of the nipples and areolas. The **linea nigra** is a pigmented streak (darkening of the linea alba) on the lower midline of the abdomen extending from the pubis to the umbilicus. It appears about the third month in primigravidas but often earlier in multigravidas, and it is most noticeable in brunets and dark-complexioned patients. The basis for these pigmentary changes is stimulation of the melanophores by melanocyte-stimulating hormone.

Striae of the abdomen and breasts may develop also. Striae consist of separation of the underlying collagen tissue and appear as irregular scars. They are thought to be due to the action of adrenocorticosteroids and are most noticeable in patients with a fair complexion.

Occasionally, small telangiectasias will develop. These are commonly referred to as "spiders" and result from the effect of high levels of circulating estrogens.

Patients frequently complain about acne, an oily skin, and, occasionally, irregular pigmented areas on the skin.

3. Hirsutism–Increased growth of facial or body hair may occur also. This is more noticeable in women who already have abundant body hair or very dark hair. After delivery, most of the fine hair growth will gradually disappear, but coarse or bristly hair usually remains.

4. Breast changes–

a. Enlargement and vascular engorgement of the breasts occur about 6–8 weeks after conception.

b. Secondary areolas and enlargement of the circumlacteal sebaceous glands of the areolas (Montgomery's tubercles) may be noted at approximately 6–8 weeks and are presumed to be due to steroid hormone stimulation.

c. Colostrum secretion may occur after the 16th week and is caused mainly by prolactin (lactogenic hormone) and progesterone. The veins of the breasts also become more prominent as pregnancy progresses. In rare instances, secondary breasts may develop along the so-called nipple line. Lactation from these breasts rarely occurs.

5. Abdominal enlargement–Protuberance of the lower abdomen is usually evident after the 14th week.

6. Epulis–Hypertrophic gingival papillae often are seen after the first trimester of pregnancy. Unidentified hormones are probably responsible.

7. Pelvic changes–The pelvic organs undergo many changes in early pregnancy that should be perceptible to the physician. These are reliable signs but are not diagnostic even if all are present.

a. The vagina develops a bluish or purple discoloration as the pelvic vasculature becomes congested in early pregnancy. This is commonly referred to as Chadwick's sign, although Jacquemier first described it.

b. As pregnancy progresses, the patient usually will notice increased vaginal discharge—even leukorrhea—consisting of cervical mucous secretions and exfoliation of vaginal epithelial cells under the influence of increased amounts of estrogen and progesterone. The discharge is white or slightly gray, mucoid, and has a faintly musty odor. It is not associated with itching. The patient may find it necessary to wear a perineal pad, but no treatment is required. Microscopically, the navicular, clumped vaginal cells show a loss of cornification consistent with elevated circulating progesterone due to pregnancy. There are no signs of infection.

c. Cervical changes early in pregnancy consist of increasing cyanosis and a gradual softening. This bluish discoloration (Goodell's sign) is analogous to Chadwick's sign (in the vagina) and is due to increased vascularity of cervical tissue. Softening of the cervical tip (Fig 27–1) may occur as early as the fourth week. In addition, the cervical mucus of a pregnant patient loses its ability to produce a "fern pattern" upon drying; instead, a granular pattern is seen.

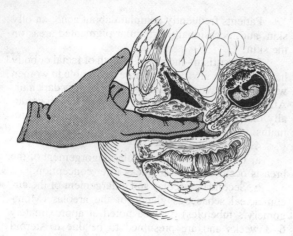

Figure 27–1. Softening of the cervix.

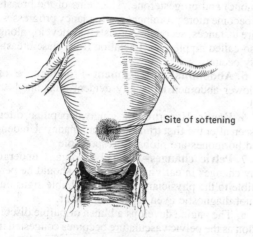

Site of softening

Figure 27–2. Ladin's sign.

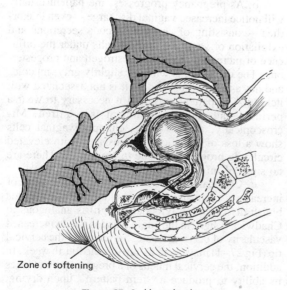

Zone of softening

Figure 27–3. Hegar's sign.

d. The uterocervical junction also undergoes changes early in pregnancy. The initial finding is a softened spot anteriorly in the midline (Ladin's sign at about the sixth week; Fig 27–2). Hegar's sign (Fig 27–3)—a widened zone of softness coupled with compressibility, resulting in a donut-shaped, slightly spongy configuration—develops next. This extremely valuable sign of pregnancy is usually noted by the sixth week. By 7 or 8 weeks, the cervix and uterus can be easily flexed at their junction (McDonald's sign).

e. The earliest change in the corpus uteri is an irregular softening of the fundus over the site of implantation (von Fernwald's sign; Fig 27–4). This usually occurs at about 4–5 weeks. If the implantation is more lateral, ie, in the cornual area, a pronounced unilateral enlargement is noted (Piskacek's sign). This may be misleading inasmuch as the examiner may confuse it with a tumor, anomalous development, or other gross abnormality of the corpus. As the pregnancy progresses, however, the corpus resumes its symmetric shape and becomes a generally enlarged and diffusely softened organ. By 10 weeks, the uterus will have enlarged to about double its nonpregnant size and will be more globular.

f. The bony and ligamentous structures of the pelvis also show changes during pregnancy. In particular, the joints develop a slight but definite relaxation. This is most noticeable in the symphysis, which may separate, sometimes to an astonishing degree, during pregnancy.

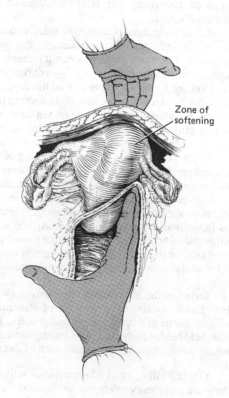

Zone of softening

Figure 27–4. Von Fernwald's sign.

Probable Manifestations

A. Symptoms: The probable symptoms of pregnancy are the same as presumptive symptoms. They are not diagnostic, either alone or in groups, but they do justify a strong suspicion of pregnancy when they occur in conjunction with probable signs.

B. Signs: The probable signs of pregnancy are related to characteristic changes in the reproductive organs and adjacent structures.

1. Abdominal enlargement–Enlargement of the abdomen in association with enlargement of the uterus is a probable sign of pregnancy. The uterus progressively enlarges from the seventh to 28th week of gestation. At about the 16th week, the patient may notice a rapid increase in abdominal size as the uterus changes from a pelvic to an abdominal organ. Changes may be less noticeable in a primigravida who still maintains good abdominal musculature. Variations in body posture also influence the type and degree of abdominal enlargement, and there is a wide variation from patient to patient.

2. Uterine contractions–As the uterus enlarges, it changes from a pear-shaped to a globular viscus and is often rotated to the right. Painless uterine contractions (Braxton Hicks sign) may be noted, and the patient may comment on or complain about a sensation of tightening and pressure. The contractions usually start about the 28th week in primigravidas but may occur earlier in succeeding pregnancies. As the pregnancy progresses, the contractions become more regular but remain relatively painless. If the patient walks or exercises, these contractions usually disappear, whereas true labor contractions increase in severity.

3. Ballottement–At 16–20 weeks, ballottement of the uterus on bimanual examination may give the impression that a floating object occupies the uterus. This is a valuable sign but is not diagnostic. A similar sign may also be elicited in the presence of uterine leiomyomas, ascites, or ovarian cysts. ·

4. Uterine souffle–Auscultation of the abdomen after the 16th week often reveals a rushing sound synchronous with the patient's pulse. It is caused by the movement of maternal blood filling the placental vessels and sinuses. The intensity may vary from a whisper to a loud rush. With anterior implantation, this sound may mask the fetal heart sounds for several months. A souffle that is synchronous with umbilical blood flow may be difficult to differentiate.

Positive Manifestations

The patient may interpret various feelings as definite evidence of pregnancy. In multigravidas, these symptoms may be very reliable. Nevertheless, there are no symptoms that are diagnostic of pregnancy.

A positive diagnosis of pregnancy must be based upon objective findings. These usually are not present until after the 16th week, but they constitute both forensic and medical proof of pregnancy.

A. Clinical Signs:

1. Fetal heart tones–Auscultation of fetal heart tones (FHTs) is the easiest method of establishing pregnancy clinically. Auscultation generally is possible in slender women after 17–18 weeks. The fetal heart rate is 120–160 beats per minute (ie, faster than the mother's) and sounds like the ticking of a watch under a pillow.

FHTs are usually best heard when the patient is in the supine position but occasionally are heard best when she lies on her side, so that the fetal back is anterior. The mother's pulse should be counted for comparison, especially when her pulse rate is about the same as that of the fetus.

Electronic devices utilizing the Doppler effect are useful in detecting FHTs and can be used to detect the heartbeat as early as the eighth week.

2. Palpation–Palpation is the other useful clinical tool in diagnosing pregnancy. After 22 weeks, the outlines of the fetus can often be felt, especially if the woman is thin or has a relaxed abdominal wall. Palpation of fetal movements is also diagnostic of pregnancy. Definite movements occur after the 18th week but may be difficult for the examiner to elicit until later. By the 24th week, it becomes easier to palpate fetal movements, and by the 28th week, it is possible to feel fetal movements in almost all pregnant women. When attempting to diagnose fetal movement, the examiner may wish to repeat the vaginal examination for confirmation of fetal activity. Fetal movements often can be felt only by vaginal examination.

B. Roentgenography: X-ray films should be avoided to protect the mother and the fetus from possible genetic damage. The bones of the fetal skeleton may begin to ossify as early as the sixth week of pregnancy, but they do not become roentgenographically apparent until the 12th–14th week. An oblique view of the lower abdomen is preferred. Because of the sacrum, pelvic bones, and bowel shadows, an anteroposterior view is usually not valuable until after the 16th week. Caution is necessary when using roentgenography as a diagnostic aid, since the fetus will receive total body radiation, which is theoretically capable of causing genetic or gonadal alterations.

C. Ultrasonography (Echography): Ultrasonography has become a valuable aid in diagnosing pregnancy. The pulsed sound waves pass through tissues of differing densities each of which returns a different echo. The echoes can be converted into a 2-dimensional picture of the area being examined. In this way, it has been possible to diagnose pregnancy at 4 weeks of gestation—even before enlargement of the uterus has taken place. A newer instrument is the real-time ultrasound, which will show fetal outline, fetal movement, and a fetal heart beat.

D. Electrocardiography: A fetal ECG can first be made by about the 12th week of pregnancy.

E. Laboratory Tests: Positive laboratory tests for pregnancy usually have been classified as probable manifestations of pregnancy. Radioimmunoassay, however, is so accurate that a positive result can be regarded as diagnostic.

1. Biologic tests–The first biologic test for pregnancy was described by Aschheim and Zondek in

1928. Urine from the patient was injected into immature mice. If a significant level of human chorionic gonadotropin (hCG) was present, the mice ovulated, and the diagnosis of pregnancy was confirmed by observing the presence of a corpus luteum. This complicated and time-consuming test was replaced by the "rabbit test," using patient's urine or serum, which was developed by Friedman and Hoffman in 1931; and the rat ovarian hyperemia test, developed by Aschheim and Zondek in 1941.

All of these tests were based upon ovarian response to anterior pituitary hormones. Mainini reported on the "frog test" in 1948 —the first test to use a male animal. It was based upon sperm ejaculation by the male frog when injected with urine containing high quantities of hCG. This test was widely used until the 1960s, when the immunologic tests became available.

2. Immunologic tests–These tests are more accurate, easier to perform, and less expensive than the biologic tests. They are based upon the finding that human chorionic gonadotropin is a polypeptide protein with antigenic properties. A number of tests are available, but all are based upon the principle of agglutination. Current tests use either direct agglutination or indirect agglutination of sensitized red cells or latex particles (Table 27–1). The tests take 2 minutes to 2 hours to complete, and either slides or test tubes may be used for the reagents. The sensitivity of these tests is variable. Some will detect as little as 700–750 IU of hCG; others require 2000–8000 IU for a positive result. It is very important that the physician be familiar with the type and sensitivity of the test used.

Immunologic pregnancy tests using the patient's urine may be influenced by proteinuria. When 1+ proteinuria is present, any of the tests may give a false-positive reaction. Chronic administration of antipsychotic tranquilizers may also cause false-positive reactions. Oral estrogen-progesterone compounds appear to have no effect upon these tests.

3. Radioimmunoassay–Radioimmunoassay for hCG is the most sensitive of all pregnancy tests. This procedure is now widely available in clinical laboratories, and when correctly performed it is virtually 100% accurate even as early as the fifth week. Radioimmunoassay can be used to measure hCG at almost any concentration. A recent advance is radioimmunoassay of the β subunit of hCG. This extremely sensitive test can diagnose pregnancy before the first missed period. It does not cross-react with luteinizing hormone and is therefore more accurate than radioimmunoassay for hCG.

Recently, a radioreceptor assay has been developed. This assay measures receptor sites by competitive binding and is the most sensitive of all the assays available, since it will measure levels of 2 mIU.

4. Home pregnancy testing–A home pregnancy testing kit for sale over the counter is now available. In clinical trials, it has been accurate in 97% of cases. It is an immunologic test and therefore subject to the same problems noted in that section plus the possibility of misinterpretation by the laity. The test is based upon detection of hCG in a first voided specimen of morning urine. A positive test consists of a dark donut-shaped ring in the test tube provided. A negative test should be repeated after 2 weeks. If the second test is negative, amenorrhea is assumed to be due to some other cause and the woman should consult her physician.

5. Hormone withdrawal test–Progesterone withdrawal bleeding is a clinical test, not a laboratory one, but it is a useful diagnostic procedure. The patient with amenorrhea is given a potent progestational drug, eg, hydroxyprogesterone caproate (Delalutin) intramuscularly or medroxyprogesterone acetate (Provera) orally. If she is not pregnant, withdrawal bleeding should occur within 7–10 days. If she is pregnant, no bleeding will follow. This test is reliable in the nonpregnant patient only if there is adequate estrogen stimulation of the endometrium and no other source of exogenous progesterone. Recently, this test has been discouraged because of the fear that it might alter embryonic development.

DIFFERENTIAL DIAGNOSIS OF SYMPTOMS & SIGNS OF PREGNANCY

Symptoms

Any symptom compatible with presumptive or probable symptoms of pregnancy may lead to an incorrect diagnosis of pregnancy. The most common causes of diagnostic error are abdominal, adnexal, and uterine masses. Emotional, endocrine, or systemic causes may also be mistaken for amenorrhea due to pregnancy.

Table 27–1. Immunologic tests for pregnancy.

Method	Materials	Results
Direct coagulation	Latex particles coated with anti-hCG + serum or urine.	Coagulation if hCG is present (pregnant).
Inhibition of coagulation	Anti-hCG + serum or urine **plus** Sensitized red cells or Latex particles coated with hCG.	Coagulation if hCG is absent (not pregnant); inhibition if hCG is present (pregnant).

A. Amenorrhea: Amenorrhea may vary from an occasional missed period to prolonged absence of menses.

1. Psychic factors–Amenorrhea is often secondary to emotional problems, including emotional shock and fear of pregnancy.

2. Endocrine factors–Amenorrhea may be related to a variety of endocrine changes, including adrenal and ovarian neoplasms, thyroid and pituitary disorders, and lactation. Menopause (permanent cessation of menses) is unusual in young women but may occur.

3. Metabolic factors–Diseases such as anemia, diabetes mellitus, malnutrition, and degenerative disorders may be associated with amenorrhea.

4. Asherman's syndrome–Obliteration of the uterine cavity following trauma or infection, usually during or after early pregnancy, is known as Asherman's syndrome. **Netter's syndrome** is a nontraumatic variant of unknown cause.

5. Systemic disease–Amenorrhea due to acute or chronic infection (eg, tuberculosis, brucellosis) or malignancy must be ruled out.

B. Nausea and Vomiting:

1. Emotional disorders–Pseudocyesis and anorexia nervosa.

2. Gastrointestinal disorders–Enteritis, peptic ulcer, hiatal hernia, appendicitis, intestinal obstruction, and "food poisoning" (contamination of foods with bacteria, toxins, allergens).

3. Acute infections–Influenza, encephalitis.

C. Mastodynia: Pain in the breast may be due to chronic or acute mastitis, chronic cystic mastitis, premenstrual tension, or pseudocyesis.

D. Urinary Frequency: Urinary frequency may reflect urinary tract infection, cystocele, diabetes mellitus, pelvic tumors, or emotional tension.

E. Quickening: A false sensation of quickening may be the result of increased peristalsis, "gas" (especially in women preoccupied with thoughts of pregnancy), abdominal muscle contractions, and shifting abdominal contents.

Signs

Most of the signs of pregnancy can also be caused by pelvic disease.

A. Leukorrhea: Leukorrhea may be due to vaginal or cervical infections, tumors, or excess cervical mucus.

B. Changes in Color of Vagina and Cervix: Color changes may occur premenstrually in the presence of exogenous progesterone, pelvic tumors, infection, and "pelvic congestion syndrome."

C. Changes in Consistency, Size, and Shape of Cervix and Uterus: The uterus is subject to numerous disorders that cause enlargement or change in shape. Leiomyomas are the most common cause of such changes. These tumors may grow at a rapid rate and thus mimic pregnancy. Leiomyomas usually are nodular and irregular, but a large solitary tumor may cause symmetric enlargement. Adenomyosis, cervical stenosis with hematometra or pyometra, and tuboovarian cysts may also distort the uterus and simulate pregnancy.

D. Enlargement of Abdomen: Abdominal enlargement may be due to obesity of rapid onset, relaxation of abdominal muscles, pelvic and abdominal tumors, ascites, or ventral abdominal hernia.

E. Nipple Discharge: Milklike secretion often persists long after delivery. Pseudolactation may be associated with estrogen-progesterone contraceptive medication, psychotropic drugs, pituitary adenomas, breast tumors, and certain disorders such as the Chiari-Frommel, Argonz–Del Castillo, and Forbes-Albright syndromes. (These abnormalities are also associated with amenorrhea.)

F. Epulis: Epulis may be due to local infection, dental calculus, or vitamin C deficiency.

G. Pseudocyesis: The patient usually has an intense desire for pregnancy and may develop classic symptoms: amenorrhea, nausea (occasionally with vomiting), urinary frequency, mastodynia, and even quickening. In most cases, she will gain weight and develop protuberance of the lower abdomen. Breast secretion resembling colostrum may occur. Examination generally reveals normal pelvic findings in a disturbed, severely psychoneurotic or psychotic woman.

Clinical & Laboratory Findings

A. Basal Body Temperature Elevation: Possible causes include a faulty thermometer and incorrect methods of taking or recording the temperature, corpus luteum cyst, and progesterone therapy.

B. Withdrawal Bleeding: This may actually be coincidental abnormal bleeding in a pregnant woman.

C. Laboratory Tests: Laboratory tests based upon elevation of gonadotropins are not usually positive until 4–6 weeks and at best are only about 98% accurate.

1. False-positive results–Inadequate safeguards against sexual stimulation or exposure of the test animal may lead to an incorrect diagnosis. Proteinuria may affect the test.

2. False-negative results–The animals may be too young or too old, or there may have been insufficient gonadotropin in the patient's test specimen, because it was obtained too early in pregnancy or because the urine sample was too dilute.

3. Incorrect interpretation of results–Incorrect interpretation may be due to the inexperience of the observer, failure to keep accurate records, or, occasionally, mixing of samples.

4. Diagnosis of early abortion–A true-positive followed by true-negative pregnancy test may indicate abortion. Very early spontaneous abortion can be diagnosed after the second week following abortion using sequential radioimmunoassay for serum hCG. It is now recognized that hCG elevation persists for only a few days in early spontaneous abortion (exclusive of hydatidiform mole or choriocarcinoma). Hence, a positive test will promptly revert to negative soon after death or separation of the trophoblast. Often the patient will have few or no symptoms of pregnancy. Hence, without these sensitive assays, an occult abortion may be regarded as merely a late or heavy period.

DURATION OF PREGNANCY & EXPECTED DATE OF CONFINEMENT

Once the diagnosis of pregnancy has been established, the physician must assess the duration of pregnancy and the expected date of confinement (EDC) or delivery. These are usually the first questions a pregnant patient asks her physician.

The gestation period in humans is variable. The usual interval from the last menstrual period (LMP) to delivery is 10 lunar months (280 days or 9 calendar months or 40 weeks). The patient will usually deliver within 2 weeks of the EDC, but only about 4% of women deliver on the exact day. An important consideration is the patient's previous obstetric history: A woman with a history of long or short gestations may have a similar termination of her current pregnancy. Multigravidas tend to have slightly longer gestations than primigravidas.

Nägele's Rule

There is no precise way to calculate the expected date of confinement (EDC), but it can be estimated by Nägele's rule: the first day of the last normal menstrual period (LNMP) is identified; 7 days are added; and 3 months are subtracted from this date. The date so derived is the EDC. (*Example:* Ms Jones had her LNMP on July 14. Her EDC is July 14 plus 7 days minus 3 months equals April 21.) This rule is based upon an ideal 28-day cycle, with ovulation occurring on the 14th day. However, not all women have 28-day cycles, and the physician must consider the length of the cycle. A woman with a 40-day cycle will obviously not ovulate on day 14 but closer to day 26, and her EDC cannot be accurately estimated by Nägele's rule. Nonetheless, in most cases, the rule does give the physician a reasonable estimate.

Height of Fundus as Measured Abdominally

As pregnancy progresses, the size of the uterus should be evaluated at each prenatal visit to determine whether or not growth is adequate. The actual size of the uterus may be difficult to determine, and most examinations involve determination of the height of the fundus uteri in the abdomen. This is carried out by using a fixed reference point—eg, the superior ramus of the pubis or the umbilicus—from which to measure the fundus.

The pregnant uterus is usually palpable at or just above the symphysis pubica at 8 weeks. By 16 weeks it is palpable midway between the symphysis and the umbilicus. The umbilicus will be reached at about 20–22 weeks.

A. Bartholomew's Rule of Fourths: Assuming that the uterus will have reached the umbilicus at 5

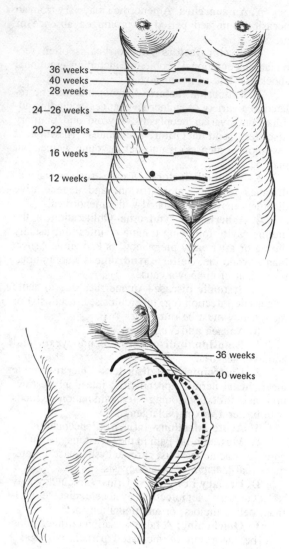

Figure 27–5. Height of fundus at various times during pregnancy.

months, the distance from the symphysis to the umbilicus is divided into 4 equal parts. As the uterus reaches each of these levels, 1 month is added. A similar procedure is carried out for the area between the umbilicus and the lower sternal border (Fig 27–5).

B. McDonald's Rule: The height of the fundus (in centimeters) is measured above the symphysis with a flexible tape (Fig 27–6). Multiplying this distance by 2 and dividing by 7 gives the approximate duration of pregnancy in lunar months. Multiplying the distance by 8 and dividing by 7 gives the duration of pregnancy in weeks. This is a useful estimate of fetal age. Unexpectedly large measurements suggest either that the date of conception is incorrect or that there is a multiple pregnancy or hydramnios. Unusually slow enlargement of the uterus suggests fetal undergrowth or abnormality or oligohydramnios, perhaps associated

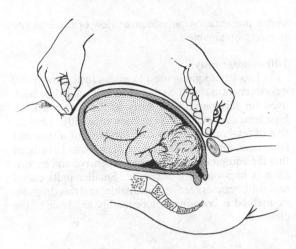

Figure 27–6. McDonald's rule.

with placental dysmaturity. Failure of the uterus to enlarge may be due to missed abortion or fetal death.

It is important that the same examiner measure the fundus whenever there is a question of uterine growth; otherwise, individual procedural differences may distort the findings.

Wide variations must be expected in the weights of fetuses during the last trimester as a result of (1) the age-weight patterns of previous offspring, (2) the slight increase in infant weight with progressive parity, and (3) hereditary traits and acquired disorders affecting infant size (eg, race, nutrition, diabetes mellitus, preeclampsia-eclampsia).

Johnson's Calculation of Fetal Weight

Estimation of fetal weight (and gestational age) is more important than estimation of uterine size. This becomes especially critical when trying to determine when to induce labor or perform cesarean section. A formula for estimating fetal weight in vertex presentation has been devised by RW Johnson (Table 27–2).

Table 27–2. Approximate duration of pregnancy according to fundal height and fetal weight.*

Weight of Fetus (g)	(lb)	(oz)	Height of Fundus† (cm)	Station‡	Duration of Pregnancy (weeks)
2100	4	9	27	Minus	34
2500	5	8	29	Minus	36
2800	6	3	30	Minus	37
3000	6	9	31	Minus	38
3150	7		32	Minus	39
3300	7	4½	33	Zero	40
3450	7	9	35	Zero to plus	43

*From Johnson RW. Reproduced, with permission, from Benson RC: *Handbook of Obstetrics & Gynecology*, 4th ed. Lange, 1971.

†Symphysis to top of fundus; see Fig 27–5.

‡Vertex presentations only.

Fetal weight (in grams) is equal to fundal measurement (in centimeters) minus n, which is 12 if the vertex is at or above the ischial spines and 11 if the vertex is below the level of the ischial spines, multiplied in either case by 155. For example, a patient with a fundal height of 30 cm whose vertex is at -2 station will have the following calculations: $30 - 12 \times 155 = 2790$ g. If the patient weighs more than 200 lb, 1 cm is subtracted from the fundal measurement. By using this calculation, an estimate within about 375 g can be obtained for 70% of newborn infants.

Quickening

Adding 22 weeks to the date when quickening is first noted in the primigravida and 24 weeks in the multigravida gives a rough estimate of the EDC.

Ultrasonography

Recent advances in the measurement of the biparietal diameter by ultrasound have been correlated with gestational age with a high degree of accuracy. The fetal skull can be measured to within 2 mm of actual size, as determined at delivery. The technique employed is based upon the knowledge that fetal growth between 20 and 30 weeks is rapid and linear. As a result, the initial measurement is taken at 20–24 weeks and a follow-up measurement at 26–30 weeks. By comparing these diameters with standard curves, the gestational age can be estimated $\pm$ 11 days with 95% confidence. These standard curves must be developed for each institution, as there are variations among institutions throughout the world. When initial measurements are performed after the 30th week or there is only one measurement, the degree of accuracy is much less.

DIAGNOSIS OF TERM PREGNANCY

When the fetus reaches that stage of development at which it has the maximum chance for extrauterine survival, "term" has been reached. Although this is usually thought of as a day, it actually refers to a period of time—a "season"—beginning with about the 37th week and extending to the 42nd week. Term is based upon the EDC as well as the other parameters of fetal growth. The fetus by this time usually weighs more than 2500 g or has the following measurements: crown to rump, 32 cm; crown to heel, 47 cm; head circumference, 33 cm; thoracic circumference, 30 cm; and occipitofrontal diameter, 11.5 cm.

As with all measurements, other factors must be considered, eg, small parents have small babies, and the mothers of large babies may be diabetic. Hence, the clinician must also rely upon other data to evaluate the stage of fetal maturity.

Clinical Findings

A. Engagement: Sometimes referred to as "lightening," engagement is descent of the fetal head into the pelvic cavity such that both parietal bones are at or below the ischial spines. When this occurs in a primigravida, delivery generally will occur within 2 weeks. Because engagement may occur suddenly, the patient is likely to report this to her physician. In the multiparous patient, engagement of the head usually does not occur before labor begins; but if it does, term probably has been reached.

B. Cervical Changes: A cervix that is completely effaced and dilated 1–2 cm is evidence that pregnancy probably has reached term. In a primigravida, noticeable effacement starts about the 36th week and may be complete by the 38th week. In a multigravida, it is unusual for complete effacement to occur prior to onset of labor, even though some dilatation may be evident.

The experienced obstetrician will be able to note changes in the position and consistency of the cervix. Early in pregnancy, the cervix is in a posterior position; as delivery approaches, it moves anteriorly. The cervix also becomes extremely soft near term.

C. Amniocentesis: Amniocentesis followed by evaluation of the fluid for creatinine, lecithin/sphingomyelin ratio, phosphatidylglycerol, exfoliated cells, etc, can also aid in establishment of the duration of pregnancy.

X-Ray Findings

A. X-Ray Visualization of Fetal Ossification Centers: X-ray films are helpful in establishing fetal age. A lateral or oblique film of the abdomen is taken at or near term while the patient is lying on the side opposite the fetal back. This helps bring the fetal extremities into a better position for determination of the distal femoral and proximal tibial ossification centers. The following possibilities exist, assuming good positioning, proper penetration, and no subject motion:

1. If no ossification centers in the extremities are seen, the patient probably is not at term.

2. If the distal femoral epiphyses are present, the fetus has reached at least 36 weeks of gestational age. However, absence of the epiphysis does not always mean the fetus has not reached this stage of maturity.

3. When the proximal tibial epiphysis is present, the fetus has reached at least 38 weeks of gestational age.

Other centers of ossification that are helpful in assessing fetal maturity are the sacrum, the calcaneus, the head of the humerus, the head of the femur, the os capitatum, and the os hamatum. Unfortunately, x-ray films normally do not reveal these bones well enough for appraisal.

Again, the physician must consider the danger of total body irradiation to the fetus before ordering this test. When other methods are available or the information sought is not essential, x-ray should be avoided.

B. Dental Calcification: Calcification appearing in the teeth can also be noted on an occasional x-ray film. Calcification begins at 4 months in the incisors and at 5 months in the molars. Unfortunately, in the vertex presentation, an adequate view of the fetal jaw is rarely obtainable.

Ultrasonography

This technique is used to assess fetal growth and development as well as fetal maturity and has been used for this purpose as early as the 13th week. A biparietal diameter of 9.8 cm or more usually is indicative of fetal maturity. No complications of ultrasound have been reported. The major drawbacks have been that the equipment is bulky and expensive and experience is important for accuracy. Smaller units called real-time scanners are now available, and this diagnostic method is becoming more readily available to the clinician.

DIAGNOSIS OF PROLONGED PREGNANCY

The diagnosis and management of prolonged pregnancy are discussed in Chapter 28.

DIAGNOSIS OF FETAL DEATH

The diagnosis of fetal death is as important as the diagnosis of pregnancy. Early in pregnancy, the most important sign of fetal death is failure of uterine growth. When a pregnancy test that was positive becomes negative on 2 subsequent occasions—in association with uterine growth suspension—the diagnosis of fetal death is likely. It should be remembered, however, that the pregnancy test measures the hormones produced by the trophoblast and that some trophoblastic tissue may remain viable for some time after the fetus has died. Certain pregnancy tests with a low sensitivity can also become negative as the pregnancy progresses due to the normal drop in chorionic gonadotropin titer. This should also be considered if a test becomes negative.

In later pregnancy, the diagnosis may be more difficult. Cessation of fetal movement is usually the first abnormal sign noted by the mother. The uterus may fail to enlarge, but it may not be possible to ascertain this until several examinations have been made. Fetal heart tones are absent even with the use of a Doppler device. The signs and symptoms of pregnancy (enlargement of the breasts, skin pigmentation, weight gain, etc) may subside. A roentgenogram of the fetus often may show evidence of fetal death: overlapping of the skull bones (Spalding's sign); gas in the fetus, especially in the circulatory system (Robert's sign); and abnormal fetal posture as evidenced by exaggeration of the spinal curvature or angulation of the spine. Most of these signs depend upon postmortem degenerative changes in the fetus. Hence, if equivocal x-ray findings are noted, further observation or a repeat examination should be performed. Amniocentesis may reveal concentrated dark-brown fluid which is diagnostic of fetal death.

The use of real-time ultrasound is a simple way to determine fetal viability. Since the machine can determine fetal movements as well as heart beat, it is virtually 100% accurate. When this technique is available, it is the procedure of choice to determine fetal viability.

Hypofibrinogenemia may develop ("dead baby syndrome") after 3–4 months. Hence, it is best to determine fibrinogen levels and accomplish delivery before the serum fibrinogen falls to below 50–200 mg/dL.

DETECTION OF PREVIOUS PREGNANCY

Occasionally the physician is called upon—for medical, legal, or other reasons—to attempt to determine if a patient has had a previous pregnancy. This diagnosis can rarely be made with certainty, but a reasonably accurate opinion often can be obtained. The appraisal is based upon the status of the reproductive organs and the changes that pregnancy generally causes. The breasts of the multiparous patient usually are less firm and more pendulous and have increased pigmentation of the areolar areas. A lax abdominal wall, with separation of the rectus muscles, may be noted. One must look for the scar of a cesarean section. Striae over the abdomen or breasts, although not diagnostic, are suggestive of prior pregnancy. The perineum may reveal the scars of a previous episiotomy or laceration. The vaginal canal may show much more relaxation than is likely in a nullipara. The external cervical os usually is transformed by delivery to a transverse slit or stellate gap as contrasted with a small, circular opening in a nulliparous patient.

● ● ●

References

Anderson SG: Real-time sonography in obstetrics. *Obstet Gynecol* 1978;**51**:284.

Anthony F, Masson GM, Wood PJ: The radioimmunoassay of a pregnancy specific β_1-glycoprotein in plasma as a pregnancy test for subfertile women. *Br J Obstet Gynaecol* 1980;**87**:496.

Cochrane WJ: Early obstetric diagnosis by diagnostic ultrasound. *Med Ann DC* 1972;**41**:148.

Derman R, Edelman DA, Berger GS: Current status of immunologic pregnancy tests. *Int J Gynaecol Obstet* 1979–1980;**17**:190.

Edelman DA et al: An evaluation of the Pregnosticon Dri-Dot test in early pregnancy. *Am J Obstet Gynecol* 1974;**119**:521.

Gal I: Risks and benefits of the use of hormonal pregnancy test tablets. *Nature* 1972;**240**:241.

Horwitz CA et al: Evaluation of a latex tube agglutination-inhibition pregnancy test: An analysis of 1776 specimens. *Am J Obstet Gynecol* 1973;**116**:626.

Isikoff SK, Civantos F, Deforge MJ: Evaluation of a new pregnancy test claiming β-subunit specificity. *Am J Clin Pathol* 1980;**74**:98.

Kosasa TS et al: Early detection of implantation using a radioimmunoassay specific for human chorionic gonadotropin. *J Clin Endocrinol* 1973;**36**:622.

Kremkau FW, Nelson LH: Diagnostic ultrasound and its obstetric applications. *Am Fam Physician* (May) 1978;**17**:148.

Landesman R, Kaye RE, Wilson KH: Menstrual extraction: Review of 400 procedures at the Women's Services, New York, New York. *Contraception* 1973;**8**:527.

Robinson ET, Barber JH: Early diagnosis of pregnancy in general practice. *J R Coll Gen Pract* 1977;**27**:335.

Sorensen S: An electroimmuno-assay of the pregnancy-specific fetal-glycoprotein (SP1) in normal and pathological pregnancies. *Acta Obstet Gynecol Scand* 1978;**57**:193.

Sullivan TF, Barg WF Jr, Stiles GE: Evaluation of a new rapid slide test for pregnancy. *Am J Obstet Gynecol* 1979;**133**:411.

28 | High-Risk Pregnancy

Martin L. Pernoll, MD

A high-risk pregnancy is one in which the mother, fetus, or newborn is or will be in a state of increased jeopardy. Altogether, a large number of conditions have been associated with high-risk pregnancy. Many of these are ultimately attributable to poverty, ignorance, and unwanted pregnancy, although the conditions may be cataloged as serious health problems, obstetric disorders, or biologic handicaps. Specific factors that involve increased risk to the mother or the baby include genetic determinants, maternal or fetal diseases, obstetric disorders, placental dysfunction, umbilical cord complications, untimely termination of intrauterine life, and the complications of labor, delivery, and neonatal existence. Broad influences associated with perinatal risk include the mother's socioeconomic status, emotional state, health, and nutrition.

Unanticipated maternal, fetal, or neonatal losses are less frequent if sustained care has been provided throughout pregnancy. However, the actual incidence of high-risk pregnancy is not known, because rigid definitions and accurate data collection are lacking. Even so, at least 20% of expectant mothers and their offspring probably are at risk. The proper identification of those at risk is mandatory in order to render timely care and thus prevent morbidity and mortality. Three-fourths of obstetric deaths (11 per 100,000 births) in the USA probably are preventable; and the perinatal mortality rate (about 20 per 1000 births), although lower than in the past, leaves little room for complacency.*

Most maternal and perinatal infant deaths may be directly ascribed to relatively few disease states. About 60% of all maternal deaths in the USA are attributable to hemorrhage, infection, or hypertensive states of pregnancy (preeclampsia-eclampsia). Most perinatal deaths not caused by congenital anomalies are associated with only 7 obstetric complications: breech presentation, placental separation, preeclampsia-eclampsia, twinning, pyelonephritis, placenta previa, and hydramnios. However, mortality data reflect only a small segment of the total spectrum of damage the baby may incur during pregnancy and delivery. In the critical period of human growth and development—from conception until 28 days after birth—any of a number of events may deprive the individual of the ability to reach maximum genetic potential.

The essential aspects of modern diagnosis and management of high-risk pregnancy may be summarized as follows:

(1) A careful history may reveal specific risk factors.
(2) The physical examination of the mother must be organized to identify or exclude risk factors.
(3) Routine maternal laboratory screening is mandatory, with special laboratory evaluation as indicated.
(4) Close and comprehensive assessment of the fetus over the entire course of the pregnancy may necessarily include special studies to ascertain fetal well-being.
(5) The effect of labor on the fetus must be assessed in order to detect distress.
(6) Selection of the method most likely to effect an atraumatic delivery decreases the likelihood of subsequent functional or growth disorder.
(7) Careful examination of the newborn immediately after delivery may reveal early signs of distress.

CLINICAL ASSESSMENT OF PERINATAL RISK FACTORS

Antenatal care provides a series of checkpoints for detection of perinatal jeopardy. Arbitrarily, these may be divided into the following: initial screening, prenatal visit screening, intrapartum screening, delivery evaluation, and postpartum evaluation.

Initial Screening History

A. Maternal Age: Maternal, fetal, and neonatal

---

*The incidence of high-risk pregnancy is sometimes correlated with perinatal mortality rates. This is only partially valid, because it ignores morbidity. Furthermore, although the higher maternal and perinatal morbidity and mortality rates of some nations or populations may be related to a less advanced stage of economic and industrial development, differences in groups at similar levels are more directly related to variations in the availability and quality of maternal and neonatal care.

risks are highest when the gravida is either very young or comparatively old for reproduction. Pregnancy is safest for the mother and offspring when the mother's age is 20–29 years. Conception under age 16 is associated with an increased perinatal death rate, and over 18% of premature deliveries occur in this age group. Currently, an increasing number of births are occurring in the adolescent age group. This group is the only age category not experiencing a decrease in birth rate. Eighteen percent of births occur to mothers under 20 years of age. The subsequent morbidity and mortality have caused this to become a pressing health problem. Conception after age 35 imposes an increased risk of genetic defects and is associated with an increased perinatal death rate. Patients 16–19 years and 30–34 years of age have some increased perinatal and maternal jeopardy.

B. Reproductive History: A high positive correlation exists between prior and subsequent reproductive failure or wastage. Overall, second pregnancies have the lowest mortality rate. The following criteria are useful in identifying those at risk.

1. Two or more previous abortions (genetic work-up of both parents may be indicated).

2. Previous stillborn infant or loss of infant in the neonatal period (knowing the duration of the gestation when death occurred may assist in determining the cause of a stillbirth).

3. Genital tract anomalies that predispose to premature delivery. The most common are incompetent cervix, cervical malformation, and uterine malformation (subseptate uterus and uterus bicornis occurring most frequently).

4. Previous premature labor or low-birth-weight infant (< 2500 g).

5. Previous excessively large infant (> 4000 g requires the exclusion of diabetes mellitus).

6. Uterine leiomyomas (5 cm or more in diameter or submucous).

7. Abnormal cervical cytology.

8. Ovarian mass.

9. Parity of 8 or more (although parity of 5 or more creates a moderate increase in risk).

10. Previous infant with isoimmunization (or ABO incompatibility).

11. Preeclampsia-eclampsia.

12. Previous infant with known or suspected genetic or familial disorders or congenital anomaly.

13. History of birth-damaged infant or need for special neonatal care.

14. Previous pregnancy terminated upon medical indications.

Additional factors that place the patient at a lesser degree of risk include previous operative delivery (cesarean section, midforceps delivery, or breech extraction), previous prolonged labor or significant dystocia, borderline pelvis, previous severe emotional problems with labor or delivery, previous uterine or cervical operations, primigravida, involuntary sterility, and pregnancy less than 3 months after the last delivery.

Table 28–1. Recurrence risks in certain high-risk pregnancies.

	Approximate Primary Occurrence Rate (%)	Approximate Recurrence Rate (%)
Preeclampsia-eclampsia	2–10	25
Abruptio placentae	1.2	10–17
Placenta previa	0.5	6
Breech presentation	3–4	14

The recurrent or continuing nature of the reproductive risk factors necessitates careful screening. Table 28–1 illustrates some risk factors that may recur in subsequent pregnancies.

C. Medical Complications of Pregnancy: Certain diseases exert a deleterious effect on pregnancy. Moreover, pregnancy may aggravate certain maternal disease processes. Gravidas with the following disorders may need referral to a high-risk clinic:

1. Chronic hypertension–Chronic hypertension is frequently associated with superimposed preeclampsia-eclampsia wherein the perinatal mortality rate is almost 25%.

2. Renal disease–Acute or chronic glomerulonephritis may be difficult to differentiate from preeclampsia-eclampsia. Pyelonephritis is most frequent in the latter part of pregnancy; if unilateral, it is more common on the right. Congenital renal disease such as polycystic kidney should be thoroughly investigated before pregnancy to guarantee adequate renal function.

3. Diabetes mellitus–All classes of diabetes are associated with increased risk. Classes of diabetes of class B or worse, which are insulin-dependent, are further associated with an increased abortion rate, an increased perinatal death rate, and a greater chance of anomalies or birth injury.

4. Heart disease–Although the New York Heart Association's classification of heart disease may not be as useful during pregnancy, it may afford a measure of changing cardiac status. Patients at severe risk include those with aortic insufficiency, pulmonary hypertension, diastolic murmur, cardiac enlargement, heart failure, abnormalities of cardiac rhythm, and those with coexisting medical complications.

5. Previous endocrine ablation.

6. Maternal malignancy (including leukemia and Hodgkin's disease).

7. Sickle cell trait or disease–These hemoglobinopathies are associated with increased rates of pregnancy wastage and premature delivery. In addition, maternal infections (most commonly pyelonephritis) and crisis pose increased risks if special attention is not given to aggressive therapy of the anemia.

8. Drug addiction, alcoholism, or heavy smoking–The abuse or misuse of various substances is often a symptom of psychic instability. Moreover, some of these habits increase fetal risk. The detrimental effect of cigarette smoking is well documented.

When the habit is excessive (over 2 packages a day) or combined with other factors (eg, hypertension or history of delivery of low-birth-weight infants), the pregnancy is considered to be at high risk. Alcoholism and drug addiction, with their potential fetal malformation syndromes, pose a special problem.

9. Pulmonary disease—A history of tuberculosis or positive protein derivative test with inflammation of more than 1 cm in diameter must be more fully investigated.

10. Thyroid disorders—Both hypothyroidism and hyperthyroidism must be investigated. Moreover, if there is a family history of cretinism or if there is evidence that the baby might be affected (eg, if radioactive iodine was inadvertently given during pregnancy), the diagnosis may be made by amniotic fluid analysis and appropriate therapy initiated. In addition, large fetal goiter may affect management of delivery.

11. Gastrointestinal or liver diseases.

12. Epilepsy (whether or not on treatment).

13. Anemia—Hematocrit < 32% or hemoglobin < 10 g/dL.

14. Other conditions—Previous injury or disease (deformity) affecting the bony pelvis, connective tissue disorders, severe nutritional deficiencies or excesses, mental retardation (IQ under 70), and emotional disturbances.

D. Exposure to Teratogens: Numerous diseases may be transmitted to the fetus in utero or may be acquired during fetal transit through the birth canal. Infections may lead to abortion, fetal death, birth of an abnormal infant, or birth of an infant who will not survive or will survive with damage. The following are some of the infections that are dangerous to the fetus or newborn: coxsackievirus infection, cytomegalic inclusion disease, herpes simplex, viral hepatitis, influenza, mumps, poliomyelitis, rubella, measles, smallpox and vaccinia, varicella, syphilis, listeriosis, mycoplasmosis, tuberculosis, and toxoplasmosis. Teratogenic drugs are listed in Table 29–2.

E. Family History: Patients must be screened for hereditary or familial factors (eg, diabetes, multiple pregnancy, hemophilia) that may pose special problems.

Physical Examination

A careful abdominal examination is helpful in the general assessment of fetal growth. Early in pregnancy, when the uterus is contained predominately in the pelvis, this can best be accomplished by estimation of the size of the uterus. Later, the physical examination must include the classic 4 maneuvers of Leopold—determinations of the lie, presentation, position, and, to some degree, station of the fetus—together with accurate measurement of fundal height and, if possible, maternal girth (Fig 31–4).

Certain findings can be correlated with an increased pregnancy hazard:

A. General Physical Examination:

1. Stature—Women under 150 cm (5 feet) tall

Table 28–2. Standard weight for women of a given height.*

Height		Weight	
ft	cm	lb	kg
4'10"	145	104	47.3
4'11"	147.5	107	48.6
5'0"	150	110	50
5'1"	152.5	113	51.4
5'2"	155	116	52.7
5'3"	157.5	118	53.6
5'4"	160	123	55.9
5'5"	162.5	128	58.2
5'6"	165	132	60
5'7"	167.5	136	61.8
5'8"	170	140	63.6
5'9"	172.5	144	65.4
5'10"	175	148	67.3
5'11"	177.5	152	69.1
6'0"	180	156	70.9

*Modified and reproduced, with permission, from Babson SG et al: *Management of High-Risk Pregnancy and Intensive Care of the Neonate,* 3rd ed. Mosby, 1975.

have a significantly increased likelihood of fetopelvic disproportion at delivery.

2. Weight—Underweight or overweight (a prepregnant weight of 20% less or more than the accepted standard of normal weight in relation to height) imposes a substantial added risk (Table 28–2).

3. Blood pressure—Hypertension of 140/90 mm Hg, or a blood pressure of more than 30 mm Hg systolic or 20 mm Hg diastolic over the previous determinations is correlated with increased risk.

4. Retinopathy—Most often due to diabetes or hypertension.

5. Breast abnormalities—Carcinoma associated with pregnancy carries a grave maternal prognosis.

6. Heart murmurs or other abnormalities (see previous section).

7. Uterine size—A uterus of a size that is inappropriate to gestational age may be due to hydramnios, tumors, multiple pregnancy, oligohydramnios, or fetal death.

8. Orthopedic problems—Deformities of the back, pelvis, or extremities may mean that the pelvis is not of a size or shape that is appropriate for vaginal delivery.

9. Venous disorders—Severe varicosities or thrombophlebitis.

B. Pelvic Examination: The pelvic examination must be planned to identify the following risk factors:

1. Genital prolapse (cervix beyond the introitus).

2. Abnormalities of the vagina or vulva that distort the birth canal (large cysts of Gartner's duct, scarring due to lymphogranuloma venereum).

3. Cervical tumors, dilatation, or prior deep lacerations of the cervix.

4. Uterine neoplasms or anomalies (including uterine contour abnormalities).

5. Adnexal tumors (more than 5 cm in diameter).

6. Bony pelvis inadequacy–

a. Inlet–Palpable sacral promontory (diagonal conjugate of < 11.5 cm).

b. Midplane–Prominent ischial spines, convergent side walls, flat sacrum.

c. Outlet–Intertuberous diameter less than 8.5 cm; narrow subpubic angle (< 90 degrees).

COURSE OF THE PREGNANCY

The entire series of antenatal visits may be regarded as an opportunity to detect abnormalities that may lead to difficulty for the mother or the baby. The frequency of visits will vary according to the patient's needs. Critical problems include hypertensive states of pregnancy, pyelonephritis, high fever, isoimmunization, diabetes mellitus, uterine bleeding, large uterus in relation to gestational age, lack of uterine growth, abnormal presentations, postmaturity (over 42½ weeks), and acute surgical problems. The physician must also be on guard to diagnose and treat viral infections, to detect early signs of malnutrition, and to combat the ill effects of the patient's indifference to the principles of health care, use of drugs, and radiation exposure.

Other specific risk factors include the need for antenatal genetic diagnosis (see Chapter 26), severe anemia (hemoglobin < 10 g/dL), unresponsive urinary tract infections, suspected ectopic pregnancy, positive gonorrhea screening, placenta previa, partial separation of the placenta, hydramnios (or oligohydramnios), thromboembolic disease, a need for physiologic maturity testing, induction of labor, and suspected fetopelvic disproportion.

PROLONGED PREGNANCY
(Postdatism)

Prolonged pregnancy, by definition, extends 294 days or more beyond the LMP, or 14 days or more beyond the conventionally accepted normal duration of pregnancy (280 days). Prolonged pregnancy occurs in 10–12% of all gestations. Perinatal mortality in prolonged pregnancy, as compared with term pregnancy, is increased 3 times at 43 weeks and 5 times at 44 weeks. Infants of primiparas with prolonged pregnancy are at greater risk than those of multiparas.

Although some neonates of prolonged pregnancies are well-developed and more mature than those born at term, others are postmature—actually dysmature. The latter have dry, cracked, wrinkled, parchmentlike skin with absent vernix caseosa and long, thin arms and legs. These neonates have a higher incidence of fetal distress and perinatal death. The normal-appearing infants do well if fetopelvic disproportion does not develop because of their increased size. A breakdown of perinatal deaths associated with prolonged pregnancy reveals that about one-third occurred antepartum, about one-half intrapartum; and about one-sixth neonatal.

When a gravida goes 2 weeks overdue, the following must be considered: (1) The pregnancy is not prolonged; there is no threat to the fetus. (2) The pregnancy is prolonged, but the placenta continues to function efficiently and there is no threat to the fetus. (3) The pregnancy is prolonged, and there is acute placental failure with threat to the fetus. (4) The pregnancy is prolonged, there has been chronic placental insufficiency, and the threat to the fetus continues.

For safe delivery of the offspring, therefore, it is important to determine whether prolonged pregnancy actually has developed and if there is any evidence of fetal jeopardy.

Verification of the LMP or a determination that it was inaccurately reported is most important to the diagnosis of prolonged pregnancy. A correlation of LMP with the estimated duration of pregnancy at 2 of the earliest obstetric examinations may lead to verification or recalculation of the EDC.

When the initial diagnosis of pregnancy was made at 20 weeks or earlier by physical examination, 3 out of the 4 following observations should place the patient in the prolonged pregnancy category: (1) 36 weeks have elapsed since the recorded positive pregnancy test; (2) 32 weeks have elapsed since the recorded FHT by Doppler instrument; (3) 24 weeks have elapsed since recorded fetal movement; (4) 22 weeks have elapsed since recorded FHT by auscultation.

Two serial ultrasound examinations and measurement of the fetal biparietal diameter should be accomplished 2 weeks apart after the 20th week. This may confirm or reestablish the EDC. However, the EDC cannot be calculated accurately in late pregnancy. This is particularly true when the initial biparietal diameter measures 9.5 cm or more (term size).

Other investigations that may support a diagnosis of prolonged pregnancy include the amniotic fluid L/S ratio, creatinine, and x-ray evidence of ossification centers.

Management

When the diagnosis of harmful prolonged pregnancy is established, the patient should be delivered. If induction (with fetal monitoring) is unsuccessful, if labor is unsatisfactory, or if fetal distress develops, proceed with cesarean section.

When the diagnosis is uncertain, additional information is required. Expectant management is indicated, with fetal monitoring by means of fetal activity determinations, weekly assessments of cervical dilatation, and serial estriol determinations.

COMPLICATIONS OF LABOR

Upon admission to the hospital or to the obstetric area, vigilant screening must be continued. It is necessary to review and exclude any preexisting factors indicative of the high-risk category. The following conditions increase the potential hazard of labor:

Hypertensive states of pregnancy
Hydramnios or oligohydramnios
Amnionitis
Premature or prolonged rupture of the membranes
Uterine rupture
Placenta previa
Abruptio placentae
Meconium staining of the amniotic fluid
Abnormal or uncertain presentations (including breech and occiput posterior positions)
Multiple gestations
Fetal weight less than 2500 g
Fetal weight over 4000 g
Fetal bradycardia
Prolapsed cord
Fetal acidosis (pH $\leqslant$ 7.2 in first stage of labor)
Fetal tachycardia (more than 30 minutes)
Shoulder girdle dystocia
Fetal presenting part not descending with labor
Evidence of maternal distress
Abnormal oxytocin challenge test
Falling estriol level
Lecithin/sphingomyelin ratio or rapid surfactant ("shake") test with results in immature or intermediate range
Fetal heart rate pattern indicative of fetal distress
Labor of more than 20 hours
Primary dysfunctional labor
Secondary arrest of dilatation
Second stage of more than 2 hours
Precipitate labor (< 3 hours)
Induction of labor

COMPLICATIONS OF DELIVERY

Delivery frequently is traumatic to the fetus. Some of the hazards are discussed below.

Maternal Analgesia & Anesthesia
The hazards of analgesia and anesthesia include inadequate placental perfusion due to hypotension caused by regional anesthesia, supine hypotensive syndrome, hypovolemic shock, or cardiac decompensation; injection of local anesthetic directly into the fetus or in such a way that it crosses the placenta rapidly; overdosage of general anesthesia; and inadequate pulmonary ventilation or oxygenation.

Trauma
Trauma to the fetus may occur secondary to the mode of delivery, including breech delivery (particularly version and extraction), difficult forceps delivery (poorly executed rotation-extraction, failed forceps, and misapplied forceps), or as a result of prolonged interval from diagnosis of fetal distress to delivery by cesarean section. (If more than 30 minutes elapse from recognition of distress to delivery, the mortality rate increases 3-fold.)

MATERNAL POSTPARTUM RISK

In the recovery room and subsequently on the postdelivery floor, the mother's vital signs, lochia, and other subjective and objective findings must be followed closely. The most common maternal risks are hemorrhage and infection.

IMMEDIATE NEONATAL EXAMINATION

The newborn usually is not attended by its own physician. It is imperative, therefore, that the physician who delivers the baby be aware of the following factors that can readily be identified by examination in the delivery room and indicate that the newborn is at risk: (1) If the Apgar score is below 7, rapid definitive treatment is urgent. (2) Abnormal birth weight (less than 2500 g or more than 4000 g). (3) Major congenital anomalies, including a single umbilical artery. (4) Pallor (anemia or shock). (5) Chilling of the newborn (must be avoided). (6) Fetal infection as indicated by hepatomegaly, jaundice, and petechiae. (7) Fetal hemorrhagic diathesis (petechiae or ecchymoses). (8) Hypoglycemia. (With blood glucose < 20 mg/dL, the symptoms often include tremors, apnea, cyanosis, and seizures.) (9) Respiratory distress syndrome (tachypnea, intercostal retraction, wheezing, grunting, often flaring of the nostrils).

NEONATAL RISK FACTORS

After the initial screening physical examination is completed in the delivery room, the infant is observed briefly and then transferred to a transitional nursery where all infants are admitted temporarily for transition care in incubators or under radiant warmers. Approximately 20% of all newborns will be at moderate risk, including (but not limited to) those with disproportionate weight, height, and gestational indices; those light for length (ponderal index less than 2.25); and those with a bilirubin over 10 mg/dL.

Approximately 5% of liveborn infants are at sufficient risk to be transferred to a neonatal intensive care unit. The reasons are many:

Fetal anomalies
Respiratory distress syndrome
Asphyxia (Apgar score less than 6 at 5 minutes)
Preterm (less than 33 weeks)
Birth weight less than 1600 g
Persistent cyanosis or suspected cardiovascular disease, including congestive heart failure and major congenital heart anomalies requiring immediate catheterization

Major congenital malformations requiring surgery

Congenital pneumonia or anomalies of the respiratory system

Convulsions

Sepsis

Hemorrhagic diathesis

Shock

Dysmaturity with meconium staining

Meconium aspiration syndrome

Severe hypoglycemia or hypocalcemia

Severe hyperbilirubinemia

Need for chromosomal analysis

Central nervous system depression for more than 24 hours

LABORATORY ASSESSMENT

1. ROUTINE SCREENING (ALL PATIENTS)

Laboratory tests are required to detect or confirm the presence of certain risk factors. All of the following studies should be initiated as early in the pregnancy as possible: hematocrit or hemoglobin, white count and differential, urinalysis, culture of urine (with sensitivities, if the bacteria count is over 10^5/mL), serologic test for syphilis, rubella screening test, blood grouping and Rh determination, screening test for antibodies (Hemantigen screening test), and Papanicolaou cervical smear and vaginal smear. In addition, the hematocrit and screening test for antibodies should be repeated in later pregnancy. In certain cases, toxoplasmosis titers, cervical cultures for gonorrhea, blood sugars, or tuberculin skin tests may be indicated.

Additionally, several nonspecific screening methods have been advocated for detection of high-risk patients. Among these, the most promising are the maternal detection and recording of fetal movements, ultrasonic screening, and human placental lactogen (hPL) assays. Ultrasound is now routinely applied in the USA and several other countries. Each of these modalities is discussed below.

2. ASSESSMENT OF PATIENTS KNOWN TO BE AT RISK

The variety and scope of methods for investigation and evaluation of each high-risk pregnancy will depend upon the specific disorder suspected or diagnosed. It is beyond the scope and intention of this chapter to discuss all of these in full; only the principal modern laboratory methods will be mentioned.

The objective of fetal monitoring is to detect fetal distress. Fetal distress may be defined as a symptom complex indicative of a critical response to stress. It implies metabolic derangements, including hypoxia and acidosis, that affect essential body functions to the point of temporary or permanent injury or death. Detection of fetal distress, short of death or permanent damage, is not easy, and current knowledge is incomplete. However, several approaches may be reasonably effective in screening for fetal distress, and the utilization of more than one method of assessment may enhance diagnostic precision. However, it must be stressed that consistency in performance and interpretation of any method of assessment by experienced personnel is of utmost importance for reliability.

Sonographic Diagnosis (Ultrasonics) (Table 28–3.)

Because the normal fetus and placenta comprise an ever-enlarging entity, various methods of evaluation have been devised in an attempt to measure growth as a function of fetal health. Until the advent of sonography, it was not possible to measure fetal growth accurately. Serial sonographic measurements of the fetal parts now provide a more precise means of determining fetal growth and obtaining other useful information.

Ultrasound has been applied clinically in several forms. The A scan produces unidirectional measurements and is useful for fetal cephalometry. The B scan provides a 2-dimensional representation. Both rely on the same principle. As a pulsed ultrasonic beam strikes a tissue interface, where densities differ, an echo is obtained. In the interval between pulses, the transducer acts as a receiver for the reflected sound. The sound is then converted into electrical energy, amplified, and recorded. Both scans have an adequate safety margin and are superior to x-ray as a means of fetal mensuration.

Ultrasound may be used for cephalometry (which is correlated with fetal weight), placental localization, volumetric appraisal of the growth of the placenta, diagnosis of molar or multiple gestation, determination of fetal placement, and detection of fetal abnormalities (anencephaly, hydrocephaly) and fetal death. Other uses include early identification of intrauterine or extrauterine pregnancy, mensuration of the uterine volume, demonstration of hydramnios or oligohydramnios, indentification of uterine or ovarian tumors, and detection of foreign bodies.

The application of real-time ultrasonic evaluation to the evaluation of fetal well-being is discussed below.

Antenatal Genetic Diagnosis

The cells or fluid contained within the amnion may be analyzed prenatally to detect a number of defects. The most common clinical indications are presented in Table 28–4. Some of the disorders now detectable are listed in Table 28–5. Because many other disorders (including cretinism) are now or soon will be detectable, when a specific case is encountered a level 3 center doing antenatal genetic diagnosis should be consulted. Only experienced personnel should undertake this procedure, which must be accomplished by a team (an obstetrician experienced in early amniocentesis, a medical genetic group with biochemical and cytogenetic expertise, a genetic coun-

Table 28—3. Ultrasonic estimation of fetal weight and maturity.*

Biparietal Diameter (cm)	Weight† g	Weight† lb/oz	Weeks of Gestation	Biparietal Diameter (cm)	Weight g	Weight lb/oz	Weeks of Gestation
1.0	NA	NA	9.0	6.0	660.4	1 8	25.5
1.1	NA	NA	9.0	6.1	737.6	1 10	26.0
1.2	NA	NA	9.5	6.2	814.8	1 13	26.0
1.3	NA	NA	10.0	6.3	892.1	2	26.5
1.4	NA	NA	10.0	6.4	969.3	2 2	27.0
1.5	NA	NA	10.5	6.5	1046.5	2 5	27.0
1.6	NA	NA	11.0	6.6	1123.7	2 8	27.5
1.7	NA	NA	11.0	6.7	1200.9	2 10	28.0
1.8	NA	NA	11.5	6.8	1278.2	2 13	28.0
1.9	NA	NA	12.0	6.9	1355.4	3	28.5
2.0	NA	NA	12.0	7.0	1432.6	3 3	29.0
2.1	NA	NA	12.5	7.1	1509.8	3 5	29.0
2.2	NA	NA	13.0	7.2	1587.0	3 8	29.5
2.3	NA	NA	13.0	7.3	1664.3	3 11	29.5
2.4	NA	NA	13.5	7.4	1741.5	3 14	30.0
2.5	NA	NA	14.0	7.5	1818.7	4	30.5
2.6	NA	NA	14.0	7.6	1895.9	4 3	30.8
2.7	NA	NA	14.5	7.7	1973.1	4 5	31.0
2.8	NA	NA	15.0	7.8	2050.4	4 8	31.7
2.9	NA	NA	15.0	7.9	2127.6	4 11	32.0
3.0	NA	NA	15.5	8.0	2204.8	4 14	32.7
3.1	NA	NA	16.0	8.1	2282.0	5	33.0
3.2	NA	NA	16.0	8.2	2359.2	5 3	33.6
3.3	NA	NA	16.5	8.3	2436.5	5 6	34.0
3.4	NA	NA	17.0	8.4	2513.7	5 8	34.6
3.5	NA	NA	17.0	8.5	2590.9	5 11	35.0
3.6	NA	NA	17.5	8.6	2668.1	5 14	35.5
3.7	NA	NA	18.0	8.7	2745.3	6	36.0
3.8	NA	NA	18.0	8.8	2822.6	6 3	36.5
3.9	NA	NA	18.5	8.9	2899.8	6 6	37.0
4.0	NA	NA	19.0	9.0	2977.0	6 8	37.4
4.1	NA	NA	19.0	9.1	3054.2	6 11	38.0
4.2	NA	NA	19.5	9.2	3131.4	6 14	38.4
4.3	NA	NA	20.0	9.3	3208.7	7 2	39.0
4.4	NA	NA	20.0	9.4	3285.9	7 3	39.0
4.5	NA	NA	20.5	9.5	3363.1	7 6	39.8
4.6	NA	NA	21.0	9.6	3440.3	7 10	40.0
4.7	NA	NA	21.0	9.7	3517.5	7 11	40.8
4.8	NA	NA	21.5	9.8	3594.8	7 14	41.0
4.9	NA	NA	22.0	9.9	3672.0	8 2	41.7
5.0	NA	NA	22.0	10.0	3749.2	8 3	NA
5.1	NA	NA	22.5	10.1	3826.4	8 6	NA
5.2	42.6	2	23.0	10.2	3903.6	8 10	NA
5.3	119.9	5	23.0	10.3	3980.9	8 13	NA
5.4	197.1	6	23.5	10.4	4058.1	8 14	NA
5.5	274.3	10	24.0	10.5	4135.3	9 2	NA
5.6	351.5	13	24.0	10.6	4212.5	9 5	NA
5.7	428.7	14	24.5				
5.8	514.9	1 2	25.0				
5.9	583.2	1 5	25.0				

*Courtesy Timothy G Lee, MD, Chief, Section of Ultrasound, Department of Diagnostic Radiology, University of Oregon Health Science Center. Reproduced, with permission, from Babson SG et al: *Management of High-Risk Pregnancy and Intensive Care of the Neonate*, 3rd ed. Mosby, 1975.

†NA = not applicable.

Table 28–4. Types of obstetric patients commonly requiring antenatal genetic diagnosis.

1. A previous child or close relative with Down's syndrome or any other chromosomal disorder.
2. Advanced maternal age (35 years or more).
3. A significant chance that a child or sibling has a severe X-linked recessive disease such as Duchenne-type muscular dystrophy.
4. A significant chance for a fetus to be affected with one of the inborn errors of metabolism now amenable to antenatal diagnosis (Table 28–5).
5. A previous child with a neural tube defect (anencephaly, hydrocephaly, or myelomeningocele).

Table 28–5. Disorders that may be detected by antenatal diagnosis.

Chromosome disorders
  Abnormalities of chromosome number, eg, trisomy 21, trisomy 18, Turner's syndrome.
  Aberrations of chromosome structure (eg, cri du chat syndrome).
X-linked disorders, eg, Duchenne muscular dystrophy, factor VIII hemophilia.
Neural tube defects, eg, anencephaly, myelomeningocele.
Inborn errors of metabolism
  Lipidoses, eg, Fabry's disease, Gaucher's disease, generalized gangliosidosis, juvenile GM gangliosidosis, Tay-Sachs disease, Sandhoff's disease, Krabbe's disease, metachromatic leukodystrophy, Niemann-Pick disease type A.
  Mucopolysaccharidoses, eg, type I (Hurler), type II (Hunter), type III (Sanfilippo A).
  Amino acid and related disorders, eg, argininosuccinicaciduria, citrullinemia, cystinuria, severe infantile maple sugar urine disease, methylmalonic aciduria responsive to vitamin B_{12}.
  Carbohydrate metabolism disorders, eg, galactosemia, glycogen storage disease types II and IV.
  Miscellaneous, eg, adenosine deaminase deficiency, congenital nephrosis, cystinosis, hypophosphatasia, I cell disease, Lesch-Nyhan syndrome, lysosomal acid phosphatase deficiency, xeroderma pigmentosum.

seling service, and the full range of professional referral services). Antenatal genetic diagnosis may be performed as early as the 12th week of gestation but is simpler at 14–20 weeks, when amniocentesis appears to carry a combined maternal and fetal risk below 0.5%.

Estriol Determinations

The biosynthesis of estriol (Fig 28–1) depends upon an intact maternal-placental-fetal unit. Only serial estriol determinations are meaningful during the latter half of pregnancy, but determinations may be obtained from either maternal plasma or urine. A normal range may indicate that the fetus is not in immediate danger; however, low or significantly decreasing estriol excretion (40% less than the mean of 3 previous values for either urinary or plasma determinations) has been associated with fetal deterioration or even impending fetal death. (Neonatal apnea, cyanosis, and neurologic abnormalities have also been associated with reduced urinary estriol excretion.)

The excretion of estriol in the maternal urine in late pregnancy is in the range of 10–40 mg/24 h, and values of 4 mg/24 h or less indicate extreme compromise or fetal death. Plasma estriols also increase in almost linear fashion in late pregnancy, and values from 30 to 40 weeks' gestation should be 5–40 ng/mL.

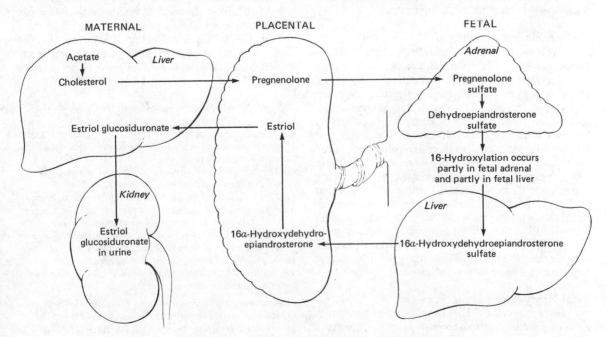

Figure 28–1. Estriol biosynthesis in late pregnancy.

For plasma estriols, obtain the serial samples at the same time of day to compensate for marked circadian variation.

Estriol values are useful in assessing the function of the maternal-placental-fetal unit, especially in diabetes, hypertension, preeclampsia-eclampsia, "placental insufficiency" (including postmaturity), and suspected fetal death. Estriol values may be decreased in the presence of isolated fetal adrenal hypoplasia and anencephaly; in patients who live at high altitudes; in patients taking penicillin (or penicillin-related antibiotics), corticosteroids, diuretics, mandelamine, probenecid, estrogens, phenazopyridine, meprobamate, phenolphthalein, cascara, senna, and glutethimide; and in anemic patients or patients with severe renal disease. In occasional women with placental sulfate deficiency, estriols may be falsely low. Estriol may be elevated in multiple pregnancy. The difficulty encountered in 24-hour collections of urine may be obviated by a shorter collection interval and utilization of the estrogen/creatinine ratio. This is probably as reliable in risk detection as the 24-hour determination of total estriol.

Other metabolites measurable in the urine are of lesser diagnostic value. Pregnanediol (the major catabolite of progesterone) has not been found to be of value in determining fetal status. Estimates of the urinary levels of chorionic gonadotropin are widely used as a pregnancy test and are valuable in following patients who are being treated for trophoblastic disease. However, this hormone, which attains peak values at 60–70 days of pregnancy and falls slowly to a relatively steady level at 100–130 days of pregnancy, has not been found prognostically useful in routine fetal evaluation. It may be abnormally high in patients with trophoblastic disease, those with multiple pregnancy, and those with isoimmunization.

Human Placental Lactogen

Fetal well-being may be reflected by human placental lactogen (hPL) levels. In a recent study of high-risk gravidas of 34 weeks' gestation or longer, 3 parameters were measured and the results compared: hPL levels, free estriol levels, and oxytocin challenge test results. There was a significant positive correlation between hPL and estriol levels. In the group with positive oxytocin challenge test results, hPL levels were lower but estriol levels were about the same. Thus, the free estriol level was not useful in predicting which patients would respond with positive oxytocin challenge results, whereas hPL levels did correlate positively with oxytocin challenge. It was concluded that one hPL measurement at about 34 weeks of gestation might be used for early identification of high-risk pregnancies. If plasma hPL is low (≤ 4 μg/mL), an oxytocin challenge test is indicated.

Fetal Heart Rate Monitoring

Fetal heart rate (FHR) monitoring as a means of assessing well-being has recently been the subject of considerable controversy. There is agreement that

heart rate monitoring is based on clinical and laboratory studies demonstrating that fetal hypoxia reliably produces changes in FHR patterns. However, these abnormal patterns may also occur in the absence of fetal distress. There is general agreement concerning the desirability of detection of the compromised fetus, because current estimates indicate that about 20% of stillbirths, 20–40% of cases of cerebral palsy, and approximately 10% of cases of severe mental retardation arise from intrapartum events leading to asphyxia. Therefore, guidelines for clinical application are necessary.

The discussion of electronic fetal monitoring conforms to the recommendations for current clinical practice set forth in the Report of the National Institute of Child Health and Human Development Consensus Development Task Force: Predictors of Intrapartum Fetal Distress: The Role of Electronic Fetal Monitoring.

A. Intrapartum Fetal Heart Rate Monitoring:
1. Auscultatory monitoring–The most widely used means of fetal assessment during labor is the head stethoscope. Even the most meticulous auscultatory monitoring is subject to considerable human error, so it must be undertaken with considerable care. There currently are 2 acceptable means of performing the evaluation. The first is auscultation of FHR every 15 minutes in the first stage and every 5 minutes in the second stage. In both instances, the auscultation is conducted for 30 seconds immediately after a contraction. The second method is that of Whitfield (Table 28–6). Both methods require adequate numbers of fully trained personnel at the bedside.

There is some evidence that auscultatory monitoring will suffice for determining the effect of labor on the fetus in situations where risk factors have not been identified. Bear in mind that intrapartum hypoxic events may occur in any pregnancy.

2. Electronic Monitoring–It must be stressed that, even when appropriately obtained and interpreted, electronic fetal monitoring only screens for

---

Table 28–6. Auscultation of fetal heart (method of Whitfield).*

(1) Count heartbeat for successive 5-second periods during and following contractions.

(2) The lowest 5-second count X 12 gives the approximate depth of bradycardia in beats per minute.

(3) The number of 5-second periods from the end of contractions to the first count of more than 10 beats—ie, a rate of over 120 beats per minute—gives a simple measure of the delay in recovery of the uteroplacental insufficiency pattern or the duration of an episode of late deceleration.

(4) Any beat-to-beat arrhythmias must be noted.

(5) The interval of observation is shortened if any bradycardia or irregularity is observed.

*Reproduced, with permission, from Whitfield CR: Clinical significance of electronic methods for monitoring the fetal heart. In: *Perinatal Medicine.* Huntingford PJ, Huter LG, Saling E (editors). Thieme-Verlag, 1969.

Table 28–7. Risk problems probably warranting electronic fetal monitoring.*

Maternal diseases predisposing to fetal problems
Hypertensive states of pregnancy
Diabetes mellitus
Isoimmunization
Premature labor
Amniocentesis
Maternal fever of any origin
Cyanotic maternal heart disease
Maternal respiratory insufficiency
Collagen diseases
History of previous stillbirth
Anemia

Uterine problems predisposing to fetal problems
Failure to progress
Uterine hypertonia or polysystole
Use of uterine relaxants
Oxytocin administration
Previous cesarean section in labor

Placenta and cord problems
Abruptio placentae
Placenta previa (external only)
Unexplained third trimester bleeding
Prolapsed cord (while awaiting cesarean or rapid vaginal delivery)
Vasa previa (while awaiting cesarean, external only)

Fetal problems
Meconium staining of amniotic fluid
Abnormal FHR by auscultation
Intrauterine growth retardation
Low or falling estriol (prior to labor)
Abnormal oxytocin challenge test prior to labor
Immature pulmonary maturity test prior to labor
Multiple gestation

*Modified after Freeman RK, Parer JT, Puttler OL: Page 70 in: *A Clinical Approach to Fetal Monitoring.* Berkeley Bio-engineering, Inc., 1974.

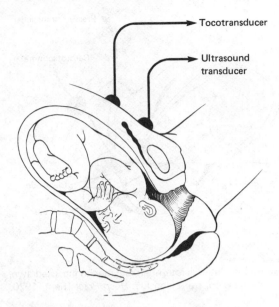

Figure 28–2. External fetal heart rate monitoring. (Redrawn, with permission, from Hon EH: *Hosp Pract* [Sept] 1970; 5:91.)

intrapartum fetal distress. It is not specifically diagnostic. Furthermore, the diagnosis of fetal distress during labor cannot be assessed by any single clinical or laboratory measurement. One must appreciate this limitation to avoid basing inappropriate clinical decisions on data derived from monitoring.

A normal FHR pattern on continuous monitoring indicates a greater than 95% probability of fetal well-being. Moreover, there is a suggestion of beneficial effect (as measured by perinatal morbidity and mortality) of electronic fetal monitoring in high-risk pregnancy. Although the specific risk factors most amenable to assessment by electronic fetal monitoring have not been detailed, the situations listed in Table 28–7 may be severe enough to warrant fetal monitoring. Currently, electronic FHR monitoring may be accomplished externally (from the maternal abdominal wall) or internally (directly from the fetus).

a. External monitoring–The external method demonstrates FHR by pulsed ultrasound (Doppler ultrasound), direct fetal electrocardiography, or phonocardiography. The last 2 may be more difficult technically than the first, especially for standard application. Therefore, the Doppler technique has enjoyed wide popularity. All 3 methods may be coupled with an external strain gauge secured over the abdomen for recording the motion of the uterus during contractions (Fig 28–2). Doppler ultrasound external monitors have a limited capability for detecting the presence or absence of irregularities, and all tracings appear to have "normal" irregularity. Also, with external monitoring, the strength of uterine contractions cannot be quantitated. However, as a screening method, its minor disadvantages are outweighed by the ease of application and the acceptance by patients and attending personnel. Certainly, if an abnormal FHR pattern is detected, direct FHR monitoring should be instituted promptly.

b. Internal monitoring–The fetal electrocardiographic impulse, obtained directly, potentially provides the greatest amount of information about FHR patterns. To accomplish this, a silver clip or screw electrode is attached directly to the fetal presenting part, either through an endoscope or by palpation. The electrocardiographic impulses are amplified and then transmitted to a cardiotachometer (Fig 28–3). The cardiotachometer uses a filter to convert the fetal electrocardiographic pattern into relatively discrete electronic impulses. Detection and counting devices then measure the interval between successive impulses. A potential that is inversely proportionate to the time between the successive impulses is computed, and this is displayed as the heart rate series.

To determine the changes in FHR evoked by the stress of uterine contractions (a period of decreased placental blood flow), it is necessary to concomitantly measure each contraction. To do this directly, a pliable

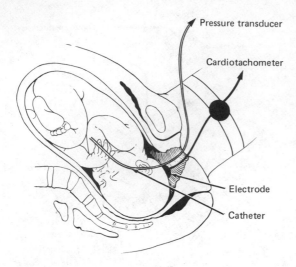

Figure 28–3. Internal fetal heart rate monitoring. (Redrawn, with permission, from Hon EH: *Hosp Pract* [Sept] 1970; 5:91.)

plastic catheter, attached to a strain gauge, is inserted through the dilated cervix into the amniotic sac to a point behind the fetal presenting part. This is accomplished by using a guide that is insinuated just beyond the lip of the cervix.

Maternal and fetal complications associated with direct electronic monitoring may occur, but the risks are low. The most frequent fetal complication is scalp abscess at the site of electrode application. Maternal complications, eg, infection, are unusual.

(1) Basal fetal heart rate–The normal FHR is 120–160 beats per minute. This rate is the average between the peaks and the depressions; it corresponds to the "average irregularity" or rapid fluctuation. Tracings of FHRs obtained from normal mature fetuses not under the influence of medications (narcotics, barbiturates, etc) show small, rapid, rhythmic fluctuations, with an amplitude of 1–8 beats per minute and a frequency of 3–10 cycles per minute. These fluctuations or irregularities are superimposed on the basal FHR. With marked immaturity, severe compromise, or anencephaly, these rapid fluctuations may be absent.

(2) Transitory changes–

(a) Decelerations–A deceleration is a transient fall in FHR in relation to a uterine contraction. The amplitude of the deceleration, in beats per minute, is the difference between the basal FHR preceding the dip and the minimum FHR recorded at the bottom of the dip. The lag time (in seconds) is the interval between the peak of the contraction and the bottom of the corresponding deceleration (Fig 28–4A). These decelerations are of 3 types: early, late, and variable.

Early deceleration (Fig 28–4B): This occurs during normal labor, particularly with ruptured membranes. Presumably, uterine contractions apply pressure to the fetal skull, and reflex bradycardia occurs at the beginning of the contraction phase. The FHR

promptly returns to normal when the contraction ends. The patterns of these decelerations are of uniform shape, and they reflect the uterine pressure curve. Rupture of the membranes is associated with an 8-fold increase in the incidence of this deceleration pattern because the fetal head is exposed to much stronger compression than when the membranes are intact. These FHR patterns are not worrisome. Babies with deviations of this type usually are born healthy. In most cases, the FHR does not fall below 100 beats per minute, and these patterns are less than 90 seconds in duration.

Late deceleration (Fig 28–4C): This is a transitory decrease in FHR that occurs after the uterus has begun to contract. The lag time is considerably greater than that of early deceleration. Like the pattern of early deceleration, the pattern of late deceleration is of uniform shape; but the FHR does not return to baseline levels until well after the uterine contraction. These changes are presumed to be caused by any of the factors that reduce uteroplacental gas exchange. Uteroplacental insufficiency may result in fetal distress, and babies with such deviations generally are born depressed. These patterns are most frequent in the range of 80–120 beats per minute, but they may occur in the range of 120–160 beats per minute. In general, the late decelerations last less than 90 seconds and are associated with a baseline FHR in the high normal or tachycardiac range. Late deceleration FHR patterns are generally associated with persistent hypoxia or fetal acidosis resulting from decreased maternal-fetal exchange. The pattern is frequently associated with high-risk pregnancies, uterine hyperactivity, and maternal hypotension.

Variable deceleration (Fig 28–4D): When the umbilical cord is compressed during contractions, changes in the FHR pattern include variable wave forms. These forms also occur at odd times during the contraction phase of the uterus. Because of the wave forms, the term variable deceleration is used. These are the most common FHR patterns associated with clinically (stethoscopically) diagnosed fetal distress. The deceleration patterns are not of uniform shape, and they vary widely in amplitude. In most cases, compression of the umbilical cord can be relieved by turning the mother from back to side or from one side to the other. Cord compression may cause transient FHRs of less than 100 beats per minute and, occasionally, of less than 50–60 beats per minute. The duration may be a few seconds or several minutes, and the decelerations usually are associated with a normal or low normal baseline FHR. Fetal acidosis does not occur unless episodes of bradycardia are frequent or prolonged.

The relationships of FHR decelerations to uterine contractions are summarized in Fig 28–5.

(b) Accelerations–Accelerations are elevations of the FHR during contractions. Accelerations are innocuous if isolated; if accelerations are associated with a lack of FHR irregularity or the development of late deceleration, the rapid heart action may be an early sign of fetal distress. However, accelerations in re-

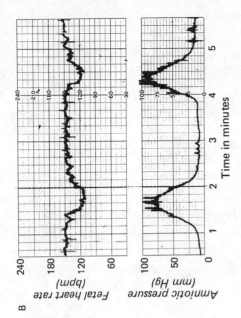

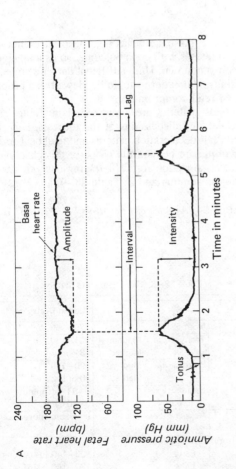

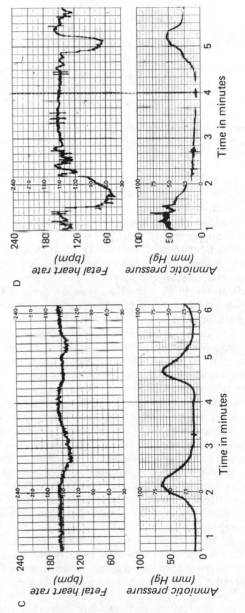

Figure 28–4. Fetal heart rate tracings. *A*: Schematic tracing. *B*: Early deceleration. *C*: Late deceleration. *D*: Variable deceleration. (Reproduced, with permission, from Babson SG et al: *Management of High-Risk Pregnancy and Intensive Care of the Neonate,* 3rd ed. Mosby, 1975.)

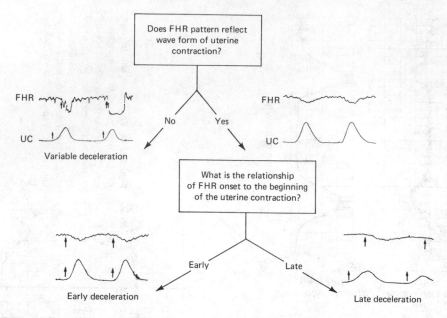

Figure 28–5. The relationship of fetal heart rate decelerations to uterine contractions. (Reproduced, with permission, from Hon EH: *An Introduction to Fetal Heart Rate Monitoring.* Postgraduate Division, University of Southern California School of Medicine, 1973.)

sponse to fetal motion may be interpreted as a sign of fetal well-being.

(3) Sustained changes–Sustained changes fall into 3 categories:

(a) Beat-to-beat variability–Beat-to-beat variability observed in normal mature fetuses is a sign of well-being, although it may be altered by a variety of medications. In the unmedicated mature fetus, if variability is absent and there is tachycardia, the absence may be ominous.

(b) Tachycardia–Tachycardia is frequently associated with extreme prematurity, maternal fever, maternal hyperthyroidism, amnionitis, use of parasympatholytic drugs, fetal hypovolemia, fetal heart failure, and fetal hypoxia. It may be an early sign of fetal distress when baseline FHR irregularity occurs late in the uterine contraction phase. When associated with prolonged variable deceleration, tachycardia indicates fetal distress, especially if irregularity is decreased.

If none of the above conditions are found, a fetal cardiac tachyarrhythmia must be considered. In such cases, a fetal ECG will aid in diagnosis of the exact type of arrhythmia and possibly alter management of the pregnancy.

(c) Bradycardia–Persistent bradycardia may indicate a congenital cardiopathy. Fixed bradycardia has not been reported in association with depression of the newborn, but it may be associated with congenital heart lesions.

(d) Sinusoidal pattern–Recently, sinusoidal FHR patterns have been reported with extreme fetal jeopardy (in association with Rh isoimmunization and fetal anemia resulting from fetomaternal transfusion).

However, this pattern has also been encountered in normal fetuses with good outcome, so its total significance is unknown. Until sufficient data are collected, the sinusoidal pattern should be viewed as a probable sign of fetal compromise.

FHR patterns are summarized in Table 28–8; more detailed discussions of the intricacies of combined FHR deceleration patterns and fetal beat-to-beat arrhythmia are beyond the scope of this chapter.* A useful organization for FHR tracing analysis and reporting is summarized in Table 28–9.

*See Hon EH: *An Atlas of Fetal Heart Rate Patterns.* Harty, 1968.

Table 28–8. Fetal heart rate patterns.

			Rate in Beats Per Minute
Basal FHR	Normal		120–160
	Tachycardia	Moderate	161–180
		Marked	181 or more
	Bradycardia	Moderate	100–119
		Marked	90 or less
	Regularity		1–8 beats/minute with 3–10 cycles/minute
Transitory FHR changes	Accelerations		Increased above basal rate
	Decelerations		
	Early		100–140 (usual range)
	Late		120–180 (usual range) (120–60 if severe)
	Variable		140–60 (usual range)

Table 28-9. FHR monitoring.

Monitor uterine activity:
Baseline tonus
Contractions: amplitude, frequency, duration
Monitor fetal heart rate:
Baseline: rate, variability
Periodic changes:
Accelerations
Decelerations: early, late, variable
Combined accelerations/decelerations
Assessment and comment

B. Antepartum Fetal Heart Rate Monitoring:
The application of knowledge relative to fetal well-being or jeopardy gained from intrapartum monitoring has afforded the opportunity to judge fetal status in the late antepartum state. Indeed, as a means of detecting the fetus at potential jeopardy, so that special care may be given, these testing methods are extraordinarily useful to clinicians.

1. Guidelines for fetal activity acceleration determinations (FAD)–The fetal activity acceleration determination is a nonstress test for gross evaluation of the uteroplacental-fetal reserve. Each determination requires simultaneous monitoring of fetal heart rate and fetal movements. It may be performed at any time in pregnancy, but interpretation at 32 weeks or earlier is somewhat theoretical, because accurate data for comparison are only now being collected and need reconfirmation.

The clinical indications include (among others) diabetes mellitus, hypertensive states of pregnancy, intrauterine growth retardation, postmaturity, a history of previous perinatal loss, and meconium-stained amniotic fluid. There are no known contraindications.

After the test and the detection of fetal movement have been explained to the mother, she is placed supine with her head elevated 30 degrees to prevent supine hypotension. Blood pressure is checked initially and then every 20 minutes and recorded on the fetal monitoring record. The baseline fetal heart rate is recorded for 10 minutes, noting rate (and variability if using the phonotransducer) and any uterine contractions. To have an acceptable fetal movement (FM), both the mother and the observer (by uterine palpation or visualization of motion of the abdominal wall) must concur that a fetal movement is occurring. The FM is then recorded on the fetal monitoring tracing. If after 10 minutes an FM has not occurred, Leopold's third and fourth maneuvers are used to stimulate the fetus. The test may be discontinued when 2 fetal movements with concurrent FADs have occurred within 20 minutes and the FADs have a regular configuration. If less than 2 fetal movements have occurred within 20 minutes, then 20 more minutes of monitoring are conducted with continued stimulation at 5-minute intervals. In the presence of a nonreactive test (the absence of FADs), an oxytocin challenge test should be initiated.

In a series of 283 patients, all with some risk factors but negative oxytocin challenge tests (see below) and no fetal distress with labor, normal newborns were delivered with Apgar scores of more than 7 at 1 and 5 minutes. The following data concerning FM and FAD in this series were collected:

FAD mean duration: 40.6 seconds with SD of 17 seconds
FAD mean amplitude: 23.3 beats per minute with SD of 6 beats per minute
FAD per patient: 3.1 per 20 minutes
Fetal movements per patient: 3.4 per 20 minutes

To be judged as **reactive,** the FAD must have a smooth, regular configuration and there must be 2 or more FADs per 20 minutes with a duration of greater than 20 seconds and more than 15 beats per minute amplitude. The **nonreactive** classification includes no fetal activity either spontaneously or with stimulation and no demonstrable fetal heart rate change in response to stimulation. The **suspicious** classification includes 3 or fewer fetal movements in 40 minutes of monitoring, with a mean duration of less than 20 seconds or longer than 60 seconds without a regular configuration. Additionally, the amplitude may be less than 15 beats per minute or not more than 30 beats per minute. If the tracing is not of sufficient quality to allow interpretation, it is classed as being **unsatisfactory.** The algorithm shown in Fig 28-6 is employed in these cases.

Recent information concerning this form of antepartum fetal heart rate monitoring strongly validates its usefulness. The test may be safely used in outpatient care and in primary screening to identify high-risk patients, and a single acceleration in response to fetal movement is sufficient to classify a fetus as reactive (thereby decreasing the monitoring time necessary for testing). The major mechanism of fetal distress the test does not identify is cord compression.

Progressive loss of baseline variability and decreasing frequency of accelerations may be early signs of fetal compromise.

The occurrence of fetal bradycardia during antepartum FHR testing (under 40 beats per minute below baseline sustained for over 60 seconds) denotes a fetus at increased risk of developing fetal distress in labor. This test should be considered abnormal, and consideration should be given to delivery of the fetus.

The false-nonreactive rate is high, and nonreactive tests require further evaluation. However, the falsely high rate may be substantially decreased by repeat testing the same day.

The nonstress test has a false-negative rate lower than that of the contraction stress test.

Whereas in a general high-risk population delivered at term the false-reactive rate (as evidenced by death or disability) is less than 1%, in postterm pregnancies the false-reactive rate may be as high at 8%.

Weekly testing may be effective for screening in some circumstances, but it is not adequate for patients

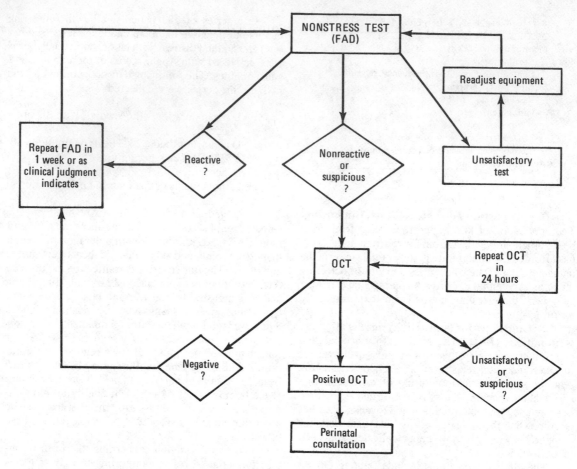

Figure 28–6. Algorithm for use in fetal activity acceleration determination (FAD). OCT, oxytocin challenge test.

with diabetes mellitus or intrauterine growth retardation. In the former group, daily screening is as effective as serum estriol determinations.

2. The contraction stress test (or oxytocin challenge test) is a means of assessing the "respiratory reserve" of the uteroplacental-fetal unit. The test consists of administering intravenous oxytocin by infusion sufficient to produce 3 contractions during a 10-minute interval, with simultaneous recording of the fetal heart rate and uterine contractions using an external electronic fetal monitor. Obviously, oxytocin is not necessary if contractions are occurring spontaneously. The test may be done as early as 32 weeks when clinically indicated.

a. Indications and contraindications–The indications include diabetes, chronic hypertension, the hypertensive states of pregnancy, intrauterine growth retardation, sickle cell disease, maternal cyanotic heart disease, postmaturity, a history of previous stillbirth, Rh isoimmunization, and meconium-stained amniotic fluid by amniocentesis.

Absolute contraindications include premature rupture of the membranes, placenta previa, incompetency of the cervix, and a cervix that has a high Bishop score (Table 28–10). Relative contraindications in-

clude previous cesarean section or a multiple gestation where the disadvantages of premature labor outweigh the advantages.

b. Procedure–A vaginal examination is performed before the procedure is done to ascertain that contraindications do not exist. The patient is placed in a supine position with the head elevated 30 degrees to prevent supine hypotension. The blood pressure is

Table 28–10. Bishop method of pelvic scoring for elective induction of labor.*†

Examination	Points		
	1	2	3
Cervical dilatation (cm)	1–2	3–4	5–6
Cervical effacement (%)	40–50	60–70	80
Station of presenting part	−1, −2	0	+1, +2
Consistency of cervix	Medium	Soft	...
Position of cervix	Middle	Anterior	...

*Modified and reproduced, with permission, from Bishop EH: Pelvic scoring for elective induction. *Obstet Gynecol* 1964; 24:66.

†Elective induction of labor may be performed safely when pelvic score is 9 or more.

checked initially and then every 20 minutes. A baseline fetal heart rate is recorded for 10 minutes, noting the rate, variability if using the microphone method, and uterine contraction pattern. (If 3 contractions with interpretable fetal heart rate are obtained during this 10-minute period, it is not necessary to give oxytocin.) Intravenous 5% dextrose in water is started, and a T connector is used to connect the oxytocin infusion. The oxytocin is started at a rate of 0.5 mU/min and doubled every 15 minutes until 3 contractions lasting 40-60 seconds are achieved within 10 minutes. More than 45 mU/min of oxytocin should not be employed. The test is discontinued after adequate contractions are established, but the recording is continued until uterine contractions diminish in frequency and intensity. The test should also be immediately discontinued if late decelerations occur, if hyperstimulation is apparent, or if prolonged bradycardia occurs. Additionally, a suspicious test is a relative contraindication to continuing. Should any of the listed ominous occurrences develop, oxytocin should be stopped, the patient turned to the left side, and oxygen administered at a rate of 6–7 L/min. For more serious hyperstimulation, amyl nitrite may be necessary.

c. **Interpretations**–A positive test suggests diminished uteroplacental reserve and indicates the need for appropriate clinical intervention. However, a positive oxytocin challenge test does not contraindicate a trial of labor with vigilant surveillance. Approximately 50% may be successfully delivered vaginally if maternal hyperoxygenation, left lateral recumbent positioning, and other precautionary steps are taken. Moreover, a positive test (late decelerations) in combination with a **latency** period of 45 seconds or more and absence of accelerations helps to predict persistent late decelerations during labor or fetal death in utero. A negative test should be repeated weekly. Tests other than negative (positive, suspicious, or unsatisfactory) may be repeated as clinically indicated.

(1) **Negative**–Uterine contractions occur with a frequency of at least 3 in 10 minutes, with no late decelerations of fetal heart rate and usually, but not necessarily, a good baseline variability and acceleration with fetal movements.

(2) **Positive**–Consistent and persistent late decelerations occur repeatedly with most (> 50%) uterine contractions, even if the frequency is less than 3 in 10 minutes. There must be no hyperstimulation. Also, but not necessarily, there may be decreased variability in FHR and absence of FHR accelerations with fetal movement.

(3) **Suspicious**–Inconsistent but definite late decelerations do not persist with most (> 50%) uterine contractions. Baseline FHR variability may be normal or decreased, and acceleration of FHR with fetal movement may be decreased or absent. It may be wise to repeat the test in 24 hours.

(4) **Unsatisfactory**–If the quality of the recording is not sufficient to ensure that no late decelerations are present, the record is classified as unsatisfactory for interpretation. Also, if the frequency of the uterine contractions achieved is less than 3 in 10 minutes, the test is not considered satisfactory for interpretation.

(5) **Hyperstimulation**–Decelerations of the fetal heart occur with uterine contractions lasting more than 90 seconds or occurring more frequently than every 2 minutes. If no periodic changes of the fetal heart are noted, in spite of uterine contractions meeting the above criteria, then the test is negative.

Oxytocin challenge testing is probably used less often nowadays for screening and more as a confirmatory examination, because of its disadvantages as a screening test. It must be performed in a hospital; it requires intravenous administration; and there are contraindications to its use. It is time-consuming (up to 120 minutes versus 12 minutes for nonstress testing), and advanced stages of fetal compromise may not demonstrate late decelerations. However, it is still appropriate for primary fetal surveillance in the postdate pregnancy and as a mechanism for risk detection when used with other tests (placental lactogen, estriol, and nonstress).

Fetal Scalp Sampling

Determining the fetal scalp blood pH may assist the obstetrician in making a diagnosis of fetal distress during the course of labor. However, the cervix must be dilated more than 2 cm and the fetal vertex well applied to the cervix. Certainly, fetal scalp sampling is easier when the vertex is low in the pelvis.

To obtain the specimen, one must insert an amnioscope and wipe the scalp clean. A silicone gel is then applied to allow a drop of blood to remain at the site of the incision. The incision is made with a special narrow blade that can penetrate no more than 1 mm. Blood is aspirated into a capillary tube and pH promptly determined. It is necessary to observe the incision carefully to be certain that bleeding stops.

If the pH is over 7.25, the fetus probably is normal; if the pH is between 7.2 and 7.24, the fetus may be somewhat compromised; and if the pH is less than 7.2, the fetus probably is severely compromised. Simultaneous maternal sampling must be employed to make certain that fetal acidosis is not secondary to maternal acidosis. When the mother is found to be acidotic, the fetus should be considered acidotic also if the scalp pH is over 0.2 pH units below that of the maternal arterial pH. Causes of maternal acidosis include muscular activity, starvation, dehydration, long first or second second stage of labor, and metabolic disease.

In interpreting fetal pH values, bear in mind that respiratory acidosis is merely an accumulation of CO_2, whereas metabolic acidosis also includes the accumulation of lactic acid from anaerobic metabolism. Fetal asphyxia combines hypercapnia, hypoxia, and metabolic acidosis. In the case of asphyxia, P_{O_2} is likely to be under 16 mm Hg and P_{CO_2} over 60 mm Hg.

Physiologic responses by the fetus to compensate for low P_{O_2} ideally include high hemoglobin concentration, high oxygen-carrying capability, an oxyhemoglobin curve shifted to the left, high oxygen saturation, increased cardiac output, and selective shunting of oxygenated blood. However, if oxygen supplies are inadequate, the fetus will revert to anaerobic metabolism.

Metabolic acidosis that is not a component of asphyxia is generally mild (pH 7.15–7.25). The most common causes of metabolic acidosis include supine hypotension, amniotomy, maternal narcosis, and transient fetal bradycardia. Because of the variability of the other components of asphyxia, the scalp pH, which is closely correlated with fetal arterial pH, may be less well correlated with Apgar score. In both term and preterm infants, a relationship has been demonstrated between pH and electronic fetal monitoring patterns, but not all fetuses with abnormal FHR patterns have acidotic pH values on sampling.

The confidence limit of fetal scalp sampling is 0.5 pH units. (Cord blood = 0.2 pH units.) However, fetal scalp sampling may produce both false abnormals or false normals. The most common causes of false abnormals (low pH with a vigorous newborn) are maternal acidosis and the variable central nervous system response of the neonate to acidosis. The usual causes of false normals (normal pH with a depressed newborn) are narcosis, infection, prematurity, asphyxia occurring after the sample was taken, neonatal airway obstruction, trauma during delivery, congenital anomalies, and incomplete recovery from asphyxia.

Indications for fetal blood sampling include the presence of meconium, FHR over 160 or less than 100, late decelerations, severe variable decelerations, and other clinical indications of fetal distress. Obvious contraindications include a fetus with possible clotting abnormalities and grossly infected amniotic fluid.

The greatest fetal complication of scalp sampling is persistent bleeding from the sample site. Hemostasis is imperative. Other risks include sampling from improper areas, deep incisions, and infection.

Subjective Fetal Movement Pattern

In a high-risk population, the fetal movement pattern as noted by the mother has been standardized as follows:

1. The gravida lies on her left side for 1 hour at any convenient time during the day.

2. She records the number of perceived fetal movements, except hiccups.

The exercise reveals fetal inactivity (lower 5% of all cases) if there are 3 or less movements per hour on 2 consecutive days. By contrast, an active fetus moves 4 or more times per hour of daily observation.

About 92% of patients will have an active fetus; there will be an approximately 97% positive correlation with antepartum FHR testing; and the test will be as accurate (in motivated patients) as antepartum FHR testing (nonstress test). In inactive fetuses, the abnormal nonstress test result is more sensitive than but not significantly different from the perceived fetal movement test. Moreover, an abnormal antepartum FHR test result coincident with fetal inactivity is highly predictive of an unfavorable outcome. Thus, observa-

tion of fetal activity in the compliant patient may be an alternative to antepartum FHR testing for the initial screening of fetal well-being. Keep in mind, however, that most fetal movements are not recognized by the mother, that this is merely a screening technique, and that motivated and well-prepared patients are likely to have better success with the technique.

Monitoring of Fetal Biophysical Activities

Observation of fetal biophysical activities yields data that may provide valuable clues to fetal well-being and risk status (see Manning et al reference). Five factors should be monitored as outlined below.

A. Fetal Breathing Movements (FBM):

1. FBM present (normal)–The presence of at least one episode of fetal breathing of at least 60 seconds' duration within a 30-minute observation period.

2. FBM absent (abnormal)–The absence of FBM or the absence of an episode of FBM of at least 60 seconds' duration during a 30-minute observation period.

B. Gross Fetal Body Movements (FM):

1. FM present (normal)–The presence of at least 3 *discrete* episodes of fetal movements within a 30-minute period. (Simultaneous limb and trunk movements are counted as a single movement.)

2. FM decreased (abnormal)–Two or less than 2 discrete fetal movements in a 30-minute observation period.

C. Fetal Tone:

1. Normal–Upper and lower extremities in position of full flexion. Trunk in position of flexion and head flexed on chest. At least one episode of extension of extremities with return to position of flexion or extension of spine with return to position of flexion.

2. Decreased (abnormal)–Extremities in position of extension or partial flexion. Spine in position of extension. Fetal movement not followed by return to flexion. Fetal hand open.

D. Qualitative Amniotic Fluid Volume:

1. Normal–Fluid evident throughout the uterine cavity. Largest pocket of fluid greater than 1 cm in vertical diameter.

2. Decreased (abnormal)–Fluid absent in most areas of uterine cavity. Largest pocket of fluid measures 1 cm or less in vertical axis. Crowding of fetal small parts.

E. Nonstress Test (NST):

1. NST-reactive (normal)–Two or more fetal heart rate accelerations of at least 15 beats per minute in amplitude and at least 30 seconds' duration associated with fetal movement in a 20-minute period.

2. NST-nonreactive (abnormal)–One or less heart rate accelerations of at least 15 beats per minute and 30 seconds' duration associated with fetal movement in a 40-minute period.

The first 4 variables are obtained by real-time B mode ultrasound. The nonstress test is conducted using Doppler external fetal heart rate monitoring. Each normal measurement is awarded a score of 2 and each abnormal measurement a score of 0, and management is based on the total score. If the score is 8–10, the test is repeated after 1 week, except in insulin-dependent diabetics and postdate patients, where the panel is repeated twice weekly. In this category, there is no indication for active intervention.

If the score is 4–6 and fetal pulmonary maturity is assured with a favorable cervix, delivery is recommended. If pulmonary maturity is immature, repeat the test after 24 hours; if there is a persistent score of 4–6, deliver 48 hours after giving glucocorticoids.

If the score is 0–2, the patient must be evaluated for immediate delivery. In cases of certain pulmonary immaturity, give glucocorticoids and deliver in 48 hours.

This technique has been found (Manning et al) to be very effective in risk detection and management. Application of several techniques may afford a more precise antenatal definition of the fetus in jeopardy.

Physiologic Maturity Testing

A. Lecithin/Sphingomyelin Ratio: According to Gluck (see reference), elucidation of the biochemistry of pulmonary surfactant (the substance that normally prevents the collapse of the alveoli with each breath) and of the timetable of its maturation in fetal life has opened the way for prenatal diagnosis of respiratory distress when premature delivery can be anticipated. Additionally, analysis of tracheal aspirates following birth of a distressed infant can provide valuable clues to prognosis.

A major component of the pulmonary surfactant is lecithin. Measurement of the amount of amniotic fluid lecithin compared to the amount of sphingomyelin has provided a practical means of evaluating maturity of the fetal lung. Mean concentrations of surface-active lecithin and sphingomyelin normally do not differ significantly until about the 30th week of pregnancy. The increase in lecithin at 35 weeks signifies that pulmonary maturity is sufficiently advanced to sustain extrauterine life with little likelihood of respiratory distress syndrome.

For measurement of the lecithin/sphingomyelin ratio, only a small amount (5 mL) of amniotic fluid is required, and the procedure can be completed in a matter of hours. Phospholipid is extracted from the amniotic fluid and evaluated by thin layer chromatography; the relative size and densities of the lecithin and sphingomyelin "spots" indicate the stage of pulmonary development at the time the test is done. In cases in which one must decide whether or not to terminate pregnancy, it is a great help to have a means of predicting respiratory distress syndrome—a major complication of neonatal life. If respiratory distress syndrome appears likely but delivery still is indicated, it is also a help to know how vigorously one must treat the newborn.

In the clinical assessment of fetal maturity, a lecithin/sphingomyelin ratio of equal to or greater than 2.0:1.0 signifies fetal maturity with no respiratory

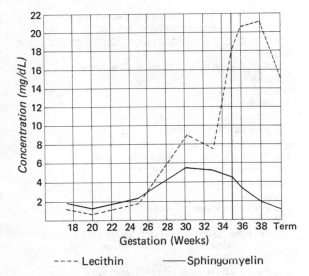

Figure 28–7. Measurement of the relationship of amniotic fluid lecithin to that of sphingomyelin has provided a practical means of evaluating maturity of the fetal lung. As shown, mean concentrations of surface-active lecithin and sphingomyelin normally do not differ significantly until about the 30th week of pregnancy; the sharp increase in lecithin at 35 weeks reflects activation of the choline incorporation pathway of lecithin synthesis and signifies that pulmonary maturity is sufficient to prevent RDS from occurring.

distress syndrome likely on delivery. A "transitional" ratio of 1.5–1.9 indicates the possibility of moderate to mild respiratory distress syndrome. A ratio of 1.0–1.49 usually reflects relative immaturity of the lung; moderate to severe respiratory distress syndrome is a distinct possibility of the infant is delivered. A ratio of less than 1.0 predicts severe respiratory distress syndrome (frequently fatal if untreated). However, it should be noted that the incidence of respiratory distress syndrome is not accurately predicted by an immature lecithin/sphingomyelin ratio.

If it is not practicable to do amniotic fluid analysis before birth, the procedure can be applied to tracheal or gastric fluid at delivery for problem cases and the lecithin/sphingomyelin ratio used in planning therapy for the newborn.

B. Rapid Surfactant Test: Clements and others described a rapid test for surfactant in amniotic fluid in 1972. This test may be performed by a technician or physician with minimal effort and equipment. It has a high degree of reproducibility. Moreover, the indication of fetal lung maturity as shown by the test is almost totally reliable. Indeed, we found that the test was more reliable in predicting fetal lung immaturity than was the lecithin/sphingomyelin ratio (Table 28–11).

These tests may prove invaluable in assessment for delivery in those conditions where judicious early delivery will increase the perinatal survival rate. Specific disorders in which they may be helpful include diabetes mellitus, hypertensive states of pregnancy, and erythroblastosis.

Table 28–11. The rapid surfactant test for assessment of fetal maturity.*

Reagents
1. 0.9% sodium chloride (9 g/L distilled water)
2. 95% ethanol

Materials
1. Centrifuge
2. Vortex mixer
3. Two 14 X 100 mm tubes
4. Two # 0 rubber stoppers
5. Two 1-mL pipettes and one 2-mL pipette
6. Test tube rack
7. Pipette bulb

Procedure
1. Immediately after drawing amniotic fluid, spin at 2000 rpm for 10 minutes to settle particulate matter.
2. From the "clear" supernatant, pipette 1 mL into one 14 X 100 mm tube (label "1:1") and 0.5 mL into the other (label "1:2").
3. Pipette 0.5 mL saline into the second tube.
4. To each tube, add 1 mL 95% ethanol; stopper, and vortex or shake for 15 seconds.
5. Immediately place the vortexed tubes upright in the test tube rack and let sit for 15 minutes.
6. A ring of bubbles completely around the meniscus at 15 minutes is a positive result. Determine fetal maturity from the following table:

Tube		Fetal Status
1:1 Dilution	**1:2 Dilution**	
Complete ring of bubbles	Complete ring of bubbles	Mature
Complete ring of bubbles	No complete ring of bubbles	Intermediate
No complete ring of bubbles	No complete ring of bubbles	Immature

*From Clements JA et al: Assessment of the risk of the respiratory-distress syndrome by a rapid test for surfactant in amniotic fluid. *N Engl J Med* 1972;**286**:1077.

C. Other Amniotic Fluid Studies: Many attempts to accurately assess fetal age (maturity) have been performed on amniotic fluid. Two such tests are summarized in Table 28–12. It is frequently useful to do amniotic fluid tests in cases of suspected intrauterine distress in order to ascertain whether meconium has been passed—an indication of stress. Similarly, fetal death may be diagnosed by the presence of a dark red-brown ("tobacco juice") amniotic fluid.

A promising new technique is the measurement of phosphatidyl-glycerol. This is obtained by bidirec-

tional thin-layer chromatography. Initial reports appear promising that it may lend a greater degree of precision to pulmonary maturity testing. Additionally, it may be of use in differentiating the preterm from the small-for-gestational-age fetus.

Radiographic Diagnosis

Because of the hazards of radiation, the necessity for x-ray in diagnosis during pregnancy must always be critically evaluated and the benefits weighed against the hazards. Theoretically, there are hazards to the maternal genetic endowment, the developing fetus (both immediate and delayed hazards), and fetal genetic potential (germ cells).

A. Chest X-ray: Because of the low diagnostic yield (1.5–2% of any pathologic process), routine chest x-ray in pregnancy is of questionable value. On the other hand, in women suspected of having cardiopulmonary disease, the slight hazard to the fetus and mother is justified by the results. If x-ray films are taken, the abdomen must be shielded to protect the ovaries and the fetus.

B. Fetograms: Attempts to determine fetal age often require numerous x-ray films. Even the most reliable criteria—x-ray studies of the distal femoral epiphysis or the proximal tibial epiphysis—are subject to great variability and inaccuracy. Less accurate indices of fetal age are the presence of fetal subcutaneous fat lines, fetal size, and bone density. The appearance of tooth buds may also give an accurate indication of fetal age. Fetograms for other reasons, such as disclosure of multiple gestation, confirmation of breech position, and detection of fetal cranial abnormalities or fetal death, are useful adjuncts to diagnosis but must be justified by clinical impression.

C. Pelvimetry: X-ray pelvimetry may provide valuable information about the feasibility of vaginal delivery. This technique allows exact measurement of all the diameters of the pelvis. Table 28–13 identifies certain critical measurements below which a pelvis must be considered inadequate (assuming the fetus to be of average size). However, pelvimetry carries with it significant hazard from radiation (mother's gonads, 2–4 R; fetus, 0.5–7 R) and therefore must not be used routinely. Important indications for x-ray pelvimetry at term are listed in Table 28–14.

D. Amniography: Amniography is the injection of water-soluble radiopaque substances into the amniotic fluid for radiographic purposes. Approximately 1 mL per gestational week of meglumine diatrizoate and

Table 28–12. Other amniotic fluid studies.

Amniotic fluid creatinine
  Before 34 weeks: none more than 2 mg/dL
  After 37 weeks: none less than 2 mg/dL; many 3–4 mg/dL
Spectrophotometric analysis (must be nonisoimmunized patient—readings at 450 nm)
  Less than 35 weeks: higher than 0.01
  At least 36 weeks: 0.00

Table 28–13. Critical measurements (diameters in cm) in x-ray pelvimetry.*

Planes	Anteroposterior	Transverse	Posterosagittal
Inlet	10	12	–
Midplane	11.5	9.5	4
Outlet	11.5	10	7.5

*Reproduced, with permission, from Hellman LM, Pritchard JA: *Williams Obstetrics,* 14th ed. Appleton-Century-Crofts, 1971.

Table 28—14. Indications for radiographic pelvimetry.

---

(1) Fetopelvic disproportion occurred in a previous pregnancy
(2) The physical examination indicates—
    (a) A diagonal conjugate of ≤ 11.5 cm
    (b) A narrow midpelvis (prominent spines and converging side walls)
    (c) A narrow intertuberous (≤ 9 cm) or decreased sum of intertuberous and posterior sagittal diameters (≤ 15 cm)
(3) A primigravida presenting at term with—
    (a) Breech presentation
    (b) Nonengagement of the fetal head
(4) Engagement of the fetal head does not occur with labor and 5 cm of cervical dilatation (in the presence of empty bowel and bladder)

---

sodium diatrizoate injection (Renografin-60) or a similar agent is used (up to 30 mL). Amniography helps to locate the placenta, may delineate abnormalities of the uterus, is useful in the diagnosis of monoamniotic twins, and outlines the fetus so that physical abnormalities (eg, hydrops fetalis) may be confirmed. The fetus soon swallows the fluid, and the gastrointestinal tract may then be visualized unless intestinal obstruction is present. It is best to take the film for outline of the fetus within 30 minutes after injection of the dye. The film for demonstration of fetal swallowing is best taken after several hours.

The injection of a hyperbaric solution into the amniotic sac adds a slight risk to the hazards of amniocentesis. Moreover, with increasingly sophisticated ultrasound, the number of indications for this procedure appears to be diminishing.

DIFFERENTIAL DIAGNOSIS

The differential diagnosis of high-risk pregnancy is relatively easy if the physician applies the definition given at the start of this chapter—"one in which the mother, fetus, or newborn is or will be in a state of increased jeopardy." Practical application of specific data should allow antenatal care to be used as a screening process, so that special care can be given to those patients whose course deviates significantly from normal. The section on clinical assessment summarizes the criteria for selection of patients for study in the high-risk clinic in one major institution.

Fortunately, every high-risk pregnancy does not result in damage. Indeed, if special care for the high-risk patient is successful, injury is unlikely. In any event, potential injury to the fetus may be preceded by fetal distress—ie, by signs to which the physician may be able to respond therapeutically).

Fetal distress (to reiterate) may be defined as a complex of signs indicating a critical response to stress. It implies metabolic derangements—notably hypoxia and acidosis—that affect the functions of vital organs to the point of temporary or permanent injury or death. Fetal distress may be acute or chronic (see below). Skillful monitoring will diagnose fetal distress (perinatal jeopardy) in at least 20% of all obstetric patients. Prompt recognition of the symptoms of fetal distress and, when necessary, decisive, well-planned intervention are imperative for the reduction of perinatal mortality and morbidity especially to prevent permanent damage to the central nervous system. Unfortunately, the diagnostic criteria for fetal distress remain unclear, and the differential diagnosis must consider many possibilities (Table 28–15).

Chronic Fetal Distress

Chronic fetal distress implies an interval of sublethal fetal deprivation that affects growth and development. The distress may be caused by a reduction of placental perfusion, by a placental abnormality, or by deficient metabolism. Decreased placental perfusion may reflect any of the following conditions in the mother: (1) vascular abnormality, as in hypertensive disease, preeclampsia-eclampsia, or diabetes with pelvic vascular complications; (2) inadequate systemic circulation, as in congenital or acquired heart disease; and (3) inadequate oxygenation of the blood, as in emphysema or by reason of residence at high altitude. Chronic fetal distress due to placental abnormality includes "premature placental aging" and diabetes mellitus. Possible fetal causes of jeopardy include multiple gestations, with possible overdistention of the

Table 28—15. Differential diagnosis of acute fetal distress.

	Normal	Possible Fetal Distress	Probable Fetal Distress	Fetal Distress
FHR in beats per minute	120–160	Possible tachycardia (probably normal)	Possible tachycardia (or normal)	Possible tachycardia (or normal) or bradycardia
Irregularity of FHR (rapid fluctuation)	Present	Present but may be decreased	Decreased or absent	Absent
Response of FHR to uterine contraction	None, or, if membranes ruptured, mild to moderate early deceleration (acceleration with stimulation)	Mild variable decelerations	Prolonged or increasingly severe variable deceleration; mild late deceleration	Severe variable deceleration, late deceleration, or combined patterns
Fetal scalp blood pH anticipated	≥ 7.25	7.20–7.24	7.20–7.24	≤ 7.20
Meconium	Usually none	Perhaps	Often present	Present
Probable fetal condition	Satisfactory	Mildly compromised	Compromised	Critical

uterus and risk of premature delivery, as well as the risk of twin-to-twin transfusion. Other fetal causes include "postmaturity," congenital anomalies, congenital infections, and erythroblastosis fetalis.

The earliest studies that make possible the diagnosis of chronic fetal distress are simple serial measurements of the height of the uterus or the patient's girth at each antenatal visit. These are at best very gross measurements of fetal growth, and it is hoped that ultrasonic measurement of the skull, thorax, and placenta will provide a more accurate means of determining chronic fetal distress. In the latter half of pregnancy, the various fetal tests outlined previously may be useful.

Acute Fetal Distress

The differential diagnosis of acute fetal distress involves 3 possibilities: possible fetal distress, probable fetal distress, and certain fetal distress (Table 28–15). Because the recommended treatment is different for each, one must consider the causes and diagnostic criteria of each. No fetal distress is present when there is absence of any abnormality of FHR or rhythm and no response to uterine contractions other than early deceleration.

A. Possible Distress: Transient acceleration of FHR, in conjunction with uterine contractions, may indicate mild cord occlusion (venous only) or slight fetal hypercapnia and hypoxia, if normal FHR variability is retained. Variable FHR decelerations in relation to uterine contractions are thought to be due to more severe cord compression. There may be violent fetal movements, and the pH of the fetal scalp blood may be slightly reduced. If the variable deceleration is transient, and not severe, permanent damage probably will not occur (Fig 28–4D).

B. Probable Fetal Distress: Lack of FHR irregularity may be associated with a number of factors (eg, fetal immaturity, effect of drugs) that do not indicate fetal distress. However, the absence of FHR irregularity may be an indication of the state of the neural mechanisms controlling the heart. For this reason, changes (decreasing variability) indicating a lessening of central nervous system control are ominous. If lack of irregularity of the FHR is coupled with acceleration in relation to uterine contractions, it is even more serious.

Prolonged or increasingly more severe variable deceleration is another warning sign. Late deceleration of the FHR, which may or may not be coupled with accelerations, is of great importance because the presumed cause of this pattern is the inability of the placenta to provide necessary exchange for normal fetal metabolism (uteroplacental insufficiency). Meconium may be passed during this fetal insult, but, unfortunately, it is gross evidence of compromise. Passing of meconium indicates neither the severity of the fetal distress nor the time of occurrence. Under these circumstances, one should expect the pH of the fetal scalp blood to be 7.10–7.24, and abnormally active fetal movements may occur.

Maternal causes of fetal distress include diverse problems such as decreased uterine blood flow (hypotension, shock, sudden heart failure), decreased blood oxygenation (hypoxia-hypercapnia), and uterine hypertonia (injudicious use of oxytocin, tetanic contractions, abruptio placentae). Placenta and cord problems include abruptio placentae, placenta previa, umbilical cord compression (knots, prolapse, or entanglement), lack of sufficient placental reserve to tolerate labor (postmaturity, premature placental aging), and ruptured vasa previa.

C. Certain Fetal Distress: If tachycardia, lack of FHR irregularity, and late FHR deceleration occur and are confirmed as an ensemble characteristic of the uterine contraction and FHR patterns, then fetal distress certainly exists. Another exceedingly critical combination is severe and prolonged variable deceleration and the development of late deceleration. If severe variable deceleration persists for 30 minutes or more or if any degree of late deceleration persists despite attempted therapy, fetal distress is present. Concomitantly, the pH will probably be 7.20 or less, and meconium most likely will be passed. Prompt treatment is mandatory (see below and Fig 28–4C).

COMPLICATIONS

Each one of the large number of high-risk states contributes to the possibility of the death or disability of the mother. It is often forgotten, however, that intrauterine life has a direct effect on the subsequent growth and development of the baby. Some notable examples of the effect of intrauterine life on subsequent development are congenital anomalies, premature birth, cerebral palsy, epilepsy, and mental retardation. A great many disease processes may occur as a direct result of alterations in this critical stage of life. Mental retardation is a major health, social, and economic problem afflicting at least 3–7% of the population of the USA, or 6–14 million persons. Mental retardation affects 10 times more persons than diabetes, 20 times more than tuberculosis, and infinitely more persons than polio. Indeed, a retarded child is born every 5 minutes—126,000 every year, according to Gold. Retarded children and adults are significantly impaired in their ability to learn and adapt to the demands of society; their custodial care costs are enormous; and these costs are exclusive of such indirect costs as public welfare expenditures and the waste of human resources. Finally, mental retardation is highly correlated with the same deficiencies in total maternal and infant care and with the same social and environmental disadvantages that are associated with elevated perinatal or infant mortality rates with a high incidence of prematurity.

Two-thirds of deaths in the first year of life are directly or indirectly associated with prematurity. The birth weight is inversely proportionate to the risk of injury to the survivor. A common denominator appears to be asphyxia and prematurity. With these insults, sequelae may include impaired intellectual development, neurologic deficiencies, defects of vision and hearing, and behavioral disorders. The arguments for prevention of the other sequelae are equally compelling.

PREVENTION

Maternal, perinatal, and infant mortality and morbidity are closely related to socioeconomic status. The chronic deprivations of poverty are serious hazards to pregnancy. For instance, it is known that chronic nutritional deprivation, even if corrected during pregnancy, may still produce low-birth-weight newborns. It is an oversimplification, however, to relate all of the perinatal hazards associated with poor socioeconomic status to nutrition. Poverty is a total life style, characterized by crowded housing, poor sanitation, neglect of basic health needs, ignorance of or indifference to health care, chronic stress, poor education, and inadequate means of maintaining personal health. Ideally, socioeconomic improvement through education, employment, and assistance would be helpful, but this goal is unlikely to be reached in the near future in any country.

Ethnic background, when separated from socioeconomic disadvantage, has little to do with maternal or perinatal salvage. In the USA, maternal and perinatal wastage among blacks occurs primarily because of low socioeconomic status, not because of genetic factors. With the exception of high-altitude residence, which is related to increased low-birth-weight babies and a greater incidence of patent ductus arteriosus, the geographic differences in maternal, perinatal, and infant mortality rates can almost always be explained in terms of affluence or poverty, education or ignorance, or availability or nonavailability of medical and other social services.

High-risk pregnancies are often pregnancies that are unplanned, accidental, unwanted, or illegitimate. Proper preconceptional, prenatal, perinatal, and postnatal care may be largely unavailable or rejected even if available. Not infrequently, emotional imbalance or ambivalence predisposes a woman to become pregnant or accompanies the pregnancy, and there may be abuse of medications, habituating substances, or illicit drugs. Many of the mothers hope their babies will die. The impact of pregnancy may overburden a precarious emotional balance, and psychosomatic illness may develop. All of these factors place both the mother and the baby in greater jeopardy.

The biologic urge for sexual gratification is so strong that irresponsible parenthood is a common problem. The best means of preventing unwanted pregnancy, then, is birth control. The medications, devices, and surgical procedures now available are negligible in cost to the individual and the community when compared with the cost of perinatal care and the social burdens of an impaired population. It has been suggested that family planning programs should give particular attention to women for whom pregnancy constitutes an increased risk, either to themselves or to their offspring. One of medicine's highest priorities should be to make *every pregnancy a wanted pregnancy*. Ultimately, this can only be accomplished by better reproductive education.

MANAGEMENT OF HIGH–RISK PREGNANCY

Three approaches to therapy must be considered: (1) elimination of unnecessary early termination of pregnancy, (2) early delivery to save the fetus, and (3) treatment of fetal distress.

Elimination of Premature Delivery

A. General Measures: The prevention of premature delivery would greatly decrease perinatal morbidity and mortality rates in the USA. Because these pregnancies most frequently involve those who neither desire them nor can afford them (ie, the young, poor, or undereducated), both general and specific means to reduce the prematurity rate must be considered. One such general plan can be outlined as follows:

1. Early pregnancy testing–This would accomplish a most difficult objective, that of providing vital information to women early in gestation. At the time of the pregnancy test, information can be given concerning the importance of early prenatal care and how to obtain good obstetric care. Alternatively, if the pregnancy is totally undesirable to the patient, information on abortion can be provided.

2. Elimination of unwanted pregnancy–This objective could best be accomplished by better sex education, family planning, and contraception.

3. Antenatal care and identification of high-risk pregnancy–Special care will be necessary for the high-risk mother or fetus, but maximum health care for the normal mother and fetus must also be maintained. Certainly, greater utilization of genetic counseling during the perinatal period will assist in identification of those at risk of being born with genetic defects so that special care can be given.

4. Development of high-risk centers–Once identification of risk patients has been accomplished, proper treatment must be instituted immediately — preferably in early pregnancy — if the fetal outcome is to be improved. Such improvement may best be accomplished by referring patients to centers where the very best medical knowledge and care are available. To accomplish this, the following will be needed in each community: (1) a center that offers complete service, training, continuing education, and data collection; (2) a cooperative, informed group of physicians, nurses, and paramedical workers; (3) rapid means of communication, not only for consultation but also for the dissemination of obstetric and gynecologic data; (4) rapid means of transportation; and (5) an ongoing public relations and community awareness program.

The Committee on Perinatal Health recommended regional development of perinatal health services, including resource analysis for patient care with designation of functional levels for hospitals from 1 (least complicated) to 3 (most complicated). The responsibilities and special services of each level are delineated. The reader is referred to this report for further information inasmuch as it will probably influence the organization of perinatal care in the foreseeable future.

5. Establishment of realistic standards of care–Once the standards of care have been established by the center and the appropriate training of workers for the community hospitals has been accomplished, the hospital requirements should be delineated and all hospitals with maternity and nursery units should be required to meet accreditation standards. Accreditation of these units should go hand in hand with requirements for continuing education so as to guarantee a consistently high level of care.

B. Specific Measures:

1. Medical correction of disease processes–Asymptomatic bacteriuria should be treated to prevent pyelonephritis. Care should be taken in the selection of antibiotics, since some of them are contraindicated in pregnancy. Anemia must be prevented or corrected.

Nutrition and vitamin and mineral supplementation should be adequate to permit maternal weight increases within normal limits.

Hypothyroidism and hyperthyroidism must be corrected, along with any other disorders amenable to treatment without hazard to the fetus.

2. Surgical correction of defects–Before pregnancy is undertaken, patients with a history of reproductive failure or wastage should receive careful, detailed study, including a hysterosalpingogram, test for cervical competency, and, perhaps, parental genetic analysis. If a surgically correctable problem is present (eg, cervical incompetency), it should be corrected before pregnancy is attempted. If cervical cerclage is done during pregnancy, it should be performed after the 12th week because of the high incidence of fetal genetic abnormality and spontaneous abortion that occurs before that time.

3. Smoking–Heavy cigarette smoking during pregnancy is associated with low-birth-weight infants and increased perinatal mortality and morbidity rates. Smoking by all pregnant women should be discouraged, and those at risk should absolutely refrain.

4. Bed rest–Bed rest is helpful in the treatment of many complications of pregnancy. Rest leads to an increased cardiac output and an increase in uterine and renal blood flow. Extended rest may be advisable for patients carrying more than one fetus. Bleeding from placenta previa or partial separation of the placenta often will subside with bed rest. Rest is also helpful in the treatment of toxemia and hypertensive disease.

5. Inhibition of labor by drugs–The intravenous administration of ethyl alcohol (9.5% solution in dextrose and water) may inhibit the release of oxytocin from the posterior pituitary. A loading dose of 15 mL/kg body weight is given intravenously over 2 hours; the maintenance dose is 1.5 mL/kg/h (one-tenth of the loading dose). Ethyl alcohol is effective only in prodromal labor or early labor; once the membranes have ruptured or the contractions have become well established, it does not quell labor.

Ritodrine is a $beta_2$-adrenergic drug that may relax the uterus in impending labor. It is FDA-approved for utilization in premature labor in the USA. If it is to be used in the management of preterm labor, the initial work-up must be careful enough to guarantee that the fetus is premature and that there are no contraindications to therapy. Initial intravenous administration is usually followed by oral therapy. The patient must be monitored rigorously, for dosage is determined by the clinical balance of uterine response and unwanted side-effects.

a. Intravenous therapy–Ritodrine for intravenous administration may be diluted with 0.9% sodium chloride solution, 5% dextrose solution, 10% dextran 40 in 0.9% sodium chloride solution, 10% invert sugar solution, Ringer's solution, or Hartmann's solution. Ritodrine, 150 mg in 500 mL of fluid, yields a final concentration of 0.3 mg/mL.

Intravenous therapy should be initiated as soon as possible after diagnosis and work-up. The usual initial dose is 0.1 mg/min, to be gradually increased (according to results) by 0.05 mg/min every 10 minutes until the desired effect is obtained, usually 0.15–0.35 mg/min. The infusion is generally continued for at least 12 hours after cessation of uterine contractions. The amount of intravenous fluid administered and the rate of administration should be monitored to avoid circulatory fluid overload. Indeed, frequent monitoring of maternal heart rate and blood pressure, fetal heart rate, and uterine contractions is required to titrate the dosage for each patient. Additionally, to minimize the risk of hypotension, the patient should be maintained in the left lateral recumbent position during the infusion and careful attention given to her hydration status.

b. Oral maintenance–Approximately 30 minutes after the termination of intravenous therapy, 10 mg of ritodrine may be given orally. For the first 24 hours of oral maintenance, the usual dosage is 10 mg every 2 hours. Thereafter, the usual dosage is 10–20 mg every 4–6 hours. Dosage depends on uterine activity and unwanted side-effects. The total daily dose of oral ritodrine should not exceed 120 mg. Treatment may be continued as long as it is deemed clinically desirable to prolong pregnancy, and recurrences of preterm labor may be treated with repeat infusion as necessary.

Symptoms of overdosage include tachycardia (maternal and fetal), palpitations, cardiac arrhythmias, hypotension, dyspnea, nervousness, tremor, and nausea and vomiting. For an excessive dose of ritodrine tablets, gastric lavage or induction of emesis is indicated. When overdosage occurs from intravenous administration, ritodrine should be discontinued. An appropriate beta-blocking agent may be used as an antidote.

Neonatal effects may include hypoglycemia and ileus. Hypocalcemia and hypotension have been reported in neonates whose mothers were treated with beta-receptor agonists.

Oral ritodrine often is associated with slight increases in maternal heart rate. Usually, there is little or no effect upon maternal systolic or diastolic blood pressure or upon fetal heart rate. Oral ritodrine may cause palpitations and tremor (10–15%), nausea and agitation (5–8%), rash (3–4%), and arrhythmia (approximately 1%).

Noncardiogenic pulmonary edema has been noted with intravenous beta-receptor agonists, and this serious complication must be carefully avoided. Hence, ritodrine should be administered only by physicians familiar with its use and capable of managing complications.

6. Use of glucocorticoids–The perinatal administration of glucocorticoids may increase the production of pulmonary surfactant and thereby decrease the incidence of respiratory distress syndrome if premature delivery is inevitable or desired. The therapy is thought to be contraindicated by the following: maternal infection, imminent delivery, hypertensive states of pregnancy, peptic ulcer disease, active tuberculosis, and viral keratitis. In the dosages used it appears safe in most other conditions. Give betamethasone (Celestone), 12 mg intramuscularly on 2 occasions 24 hours apart, if the pregnancy will be delivered prior to week 32. Before therapy is undertaken, the Ballard and Liggins references (pp 614 and 615) should be reviewed.

Early Delivery to Save the Fetus

The increasing accuracy of methods of assessment of fetal well-being (estriol determinations, fetal activity, acceleration determinations, oxytocin challenge testing, ultrasonic mensuration) and of the newborn's ability to survive in the external environment (mature rapid surfactant test or favorable lecithin/sphingomyelin ratio) is important in the solution of the obstetric dilemma: fetal loss because of prematurity versus death due to disease. When delivery for fetal salvage before the normal termination of pregnancy is necessary, patients at risk must be followed closely until the optimal time for delivery. Conditions that seem to justify such management include preeclampsia-eclampsia, isoimmunization, diabetes mellitus, placental insufficiency, oversized fetus, and fetal dysmaturity. In addition, if vaginal delivery is likely, the physician should appraise the labor closely by means of external or internal electronic monitoring of the fetus (eg, in abruptio placentae or premature rupture of the membranes). If symptoms or signs of acute fetal distress occur, labor can be terminated promptly by cesarean section.

If vaginal delivery is anticipated, great care must be taken to minimize the use of medications that might affect the fetus (eg, narcotics or barbiturates); to use anesthetic agents that do not cause maternal hypotension or otherwise reduce uterine blood flow; and to protect the fetus by (1) avoiding violent or precipitate labor, (2) denying overzealous use of oxytocin for induction or stimulation, (3) performing an adequate episiotomy before the presenting part distends the perineum, and (4) protecting the head with forceps during the perineal phase, in selected cases, to avoid sudden compression/decompression forces. Full use must be made of trained personnel to ensure the best care of the newborn.

If the delivery is to be accomplished by cesarean section, most of these criteria apply. Delivery of breech prematures of reasonable size (over 1000 g) by cesarean section may be justified because of the likelihood of trauma during breech extraction. Similarly, the fetus of excessive size is at high risk and may suffer birth injury. If the large fetus cannot be delivered safely vaginally, cesarean section is indicated.

Treatment of Fetal Intrapartum Distress

A. Specific Considerations:

1. Position of the gravida–A change of the mother's position may relieve pressure on the umbilical cord. Uterine function may also be improved with the patient in a lateral position—certainly, uterine blood flow is increased. Therefore, labor should be conducted largely with the gravida on her side.

2. Hypotension–The position change discussed above will usually correct the supine hypotensive syndrome. If this fails, shifting the uterus off of the great vessels by manual pressure may be necessary. Additional measures may include elevation of the legs, application of elastic leg bandages, and rapid administration of fluids intravenously. This will help to restore the gravida's arterial pressure and increase the blood flow in the intervillous space. If drugs are required, cardiotonics (eg, ephedrine) are preferred.

3. Decreasing uterine activity–One of the more common causes of late deceleration of the FHR is overzealous use of oxytocin. Therefore, discontinue the administration of oxytocin if stimulation is in progress. Moreover, oxytocin should not be given except by the intravenous route. Decreased uterine activity permits better placental perfusion, and the stress of violent uterine contractions will be reduced.

4. Hyperoxygenation–The administration of high concentrations of oxygen (6–7 L/min by mask) will raise the maternal-fetal P_{O_2} gradient and will increase the maternal-fetal oxygen transfer. This may be helpful when fetal hypoxia occurs.

5. Acid-base balance–Although attempts may be made to correct acid-base balance by administering sodium bicarbonate to the mother during labor, the transfer of fixed alkali is relatively slow, and treatment is therefore unlikely to be of use when given to the mother whose fetus is hypoxic and acidotic. If the acidosis is severe, the infant should be promptly delivered for primary corrective therapy. Nevertheless, if maternal acidosis is the cause of fetal acidosis, administering bicarbonate to the mother may benefit both patients.

Hypertonic glucose (usually 50 g intravenously) may be administered when there is maternal deprivation acidosis or hypoglycemia, although there may be only an indirect relationship between the level of fetal blood glucose and the base deficit.

B. Summary of Treatment: In cases of possible fetal distress, change the position of the mother, correct maternal hypotension, decrease uterine activity by stopping the administration of oxytocin, and administer oxygen at 6–7 L/min by face mask.

If the situation worsens, if the signs of probable fetal distress persist for 30 minutes, or if there is fetal distress despite conservative treatment, immediate delivery is mandatory. Obstetric judgment must dictate how the delivery will be accomplished in accordance with the presentation, station, position, dilatation of the cervix, and presumed fetal status. If cesarean section is chosen, it must be done rapidly. This implies the desirability of maintaining facilities for cesarean delivery in the labor-delivery suite and the constant availability of support services for the delivery area (ie, anesthesia, laboratory, blood bank, and neonatology). The indications for cesarean section have been broadened with its increased safety. Thus, the use of cesarean section may be justifiably increased for fetal distress, diabetes mellitus, isoimmunization, cord accidents, herpes genitalis, fetopelvic disproportion, previous uterine operation (including cesarean section), placenta previa, abruptio placentae, uterine inertia, abnormal presentations, hypertensive states of pregnancy, and maternal complications (eg, vesicovaginal fistula, invasive cervical carcinoma, and functional class IV cardiac disease).

* * *

References

Alford CA, Stagno S, Reynolds DW: Diagnosis of chronic perinatal infections. *Am J Dis Child* 1975;**129**:455.

Avery ME: Pharmacological approaches to the acceleration of fetal lung maturation. *Br Med Bull* 1975;**31**:13.

Babson SG et al: *Diagnosis and Management of the Fetus and Neonate at Risk,* 4th ed. Mosby, 1979.

Ballard P, Ballard R: Use of prenatal glucocorticoid therapy to prevent respiratory distress syndrome: A supporting view. *Am J Dis Child* 1976;**130**:982.

Bissonnette JM et al: The role of a trial labor with a positive contraction stress test. *Am J Obstet Gynecol* 1979;**135**:292.

Boddy K, Dawes GS: Fetal breathing. *Br Med Bull* 1975;**31**:3.

Bowes WA Jr et al: Fetal heart rate monitoring in premature infants weighing 1,500 grams or less. *Am J Obstet Gynecol* 1980;**137**:791.

Casalino M: Intrauterine growth retardation: A neonatologist's approach. *J Reprod Med* 1975;**14**:248.

Committee on Perinatal Health: *Toward Improving the Outcome of Pregnancy: Recommendations for the Regional Development of the Maternal and Perinatal Health Services.* National Foundation–March of Dimes, 1976.

Compton AA et al: Diurnal variations in unconjugated and total plasma estriol levels in late normal pregnancy. *Obstet Gynecol* 1979;**53**:623.

Cooper JM, Soffronoff EC, Bolognese RJ: Oxytocin challenge test in monitoring high-risk pregnancies. *Obstet Gynecol* 1975;**45**:27.

Druzin ML et al: Antepartum fetal heart rate testing. 7. The significance of fetal bradycardia. *Am J Obstet Gynecol* 1981; **139**:194.

Eastman NJ, Jackson E: Weight relationships in pregnancy. *Obstet Gynecol Surv* 1968;**23**:1003.

Freeman RK et al: Postdate pregnancy: Utilization of contraction stress testing for primary fetal surveillance. *Am J Obstet Gynecol* 1981;**140**:128.

Fujikura R, Klionsky B: The significance of meconium staining. *Am J Obstet Gynecol* 1975;**121**:45.

Gaziano EP, Hill DL, Freeman DW: The oxytocin challenge test in the management of high-risk pregnancies. *Am J Obstet Gynecol* 1975;**121**:947.

Gluck L: Pulmonary surfactant and neonatal respiratory distress. *Hosp Pract* (Nov) 1971;**6**:45.

Gratacos JA, Paul RH: Antepartum fetal heart rate monitoring: Nonstress test versus contraction stress test. *Clin Perinatol* 1980;**7**:387.

Gross TL et al: Amniotic fluid phosphatidylglycerol: A potentially useful predictor of intrauterine growth retardation. *Am J Obstet Gynecol* 1981;**140**:277.

Guilliams S, Held H: Contemporary management and conduct of preterm labor and delivery: A review. *Obstet Gynecol Surv* 1979;**34**:248.

Huddleston JF et al: Oxytocin challenge test for antepartum fetal assessment. *Am J Obstet Gynecol* 1979;**135**:609.

Hume OS: Practical management of high-risk pregnancy. *Tex Med* 1975;**71**:53.

Johnson TRB et al: Significance of the sinusoidal fetal heart rate pattern. *Am J Obstet Gynecol* 1981;**139**:446.

Keegan KA Jr, Paul RH: Antepartum fetal heart rate testing. 4. The nonstress test as a primary approach. *Am J Obstet Gynecol* 1980;**136**:75.

Keegan KA Jr et al: Antepartum fetal heart rate testing. 5. The nonstress test: An outpatient approach. *Am J Obstet Gynecol* 1980;**136**:81.

Keniston RC et al: A prospective evaluation of the lecithin/ sphingomyelin ratio and the rapid surfactant test in relation to fetal pulmonary maturity. *Am J Obstet Gynecol* 1975; **121**:324.

Khouzami VA et al: Urinary estrogens in postterm pregnancy. *Am J Obstet Gynecol* 1981;**141**:205.

Knox GE et al: Management of prolonged pregnancy: Results of a prospective randomized trial. *Am J Obstet Gynecol* 1979; **134**:376.

Lee CY, DiLoreto PC, Logrand B: Fetal activity acceleration determination for the evaluation of fetal reserve. *Obstet Gynecol* 1976;**48**:19.

Lee CY, DiLoreto PC, O'Lane JM: A study of fetal heart rate acceleration patterns. *Obstet Gynecol* 1975;**45**:142.

Lehtovirta P, Forss M: The acute effect of smoking on intervillous blood flow of the placenta. *Br J Obstet Gynaecol* 1978; **85**:729.

Liggins GC: The prevention of RDS by maternal betamethasone administration. 70th Ross Conference on Pediatric Research, Dec 1975.

Manning FA et al: Fetal biophysical profile scoring: A prospective study in 1,184 high-risk patients. *Am J Obstet Gynecol* 1981;**140**:289.

Mead P, Clapp J: The use of betamethasone and timed delivery in management of premature rupture of the membranes in preterm pregnancies. *J Reprod Med* 1977;**12**:3.

Mendenhall HW et al: The nonstress test: The value of a single acceleration in evaluating the fetus at risk. *Am J Obstet Gynecol* 1980;**136**:87.

Milunsky A: *Prevention of Genetic Disease and Mental Retardation.* Saunders, 1975.

Miyazaki FS, Miyazaki BA: False reactive nonstress tests in postterm pregnancies. *Am J Obstet Gynecol* 1981;**140**:269.

Morrison I: The elderly primigravida. *Am J Obstet Gynecol* 1975; **121**:465.

Nachtigall L et al: Plasma estriol levels in normal and abnormal pregnancies: An index of fetal welfare. *Am J Obstet Gynecol* 1968;**101**:638.

Naeye RI: Causes of perinatal mortality excess in prolonged gestations. *Am J Epidemiol* 1978;**108**:429.

Neldam S, Jessen P: Fetal movements registered by the pregnant woman correlated to retrospective estimations of fetal movements from cardiotocographic tracings. *Am J Obstet Gynecol* 1980;**136**:1051.

Parer JT, Puttler OL, Freeman RK: *A Clinical Approach to Fetal Monitoring.* Berkeley Bio-engineering, Inc., 1974.

Persson PH et al: A study of smoking and pregnancy with special references to fetal growth. *Acta Obstet Gynecol Scand* [*Suppl*] 1978;**78**:33

Phelan JP: The nonstress test: A review of 3,000 tests. *Am J Obstet Gynecol* 1981;**139**:7.

Rayburn W et al: An alternative to antepartum fetal heart rate testing. *Am J Obstet Gynecol* 1980;**138**:223.

Shields JR, Resnick R: Fetal lung maturation and the antenatal use of glucocorticoids to prevent the respiratory distress syndrome. *Obstet Gynecol Surv* 1979;**34**:343.

Sims FH, Giesbrecht E, Taylor J: Estrogen excretion in high-risk pregnancy: A comparison of two assay procedures. *Am J Clin Pathol* 1974;**62**:759.

Slomka C, Phelan JP: Pregnancy outcome in the patient with a nonreactive nonstress test and a positive contraction stress test. *Am J Obstet Gynecol* 1981;**139**:11.

Spellacy WN et al: Oxytocin challenge test results compared with simultaneously studied serum human placental lactogen and free estriol levels in high-risk pregnant women. *Am J Obstet Gynecol* 1979;**135**:917.

Tobin JOH: Herpesvirus hominis infection in pregnancy. *Proc R Soc Med* 1975;**68**:371.

Van Petten GR: Pharmacology and the fetus. Br Med Bull 31:75, 1975.

Varma TR: Prediction of fetal weight by ultrasound cephalometry. *Aust NZ J Obstet Gynaecol* 1974;**14**:83.

Varma TR: Total maternal urinary estrogen excretion and estrogen/creatinine ratio as placental function tests. *Int J Gynaecol Obstet* 1980;**18**:357.

Weingold AB: Intrauterine growth retardation: Obstetrical aspects. *J Reprod Med* 1975;**14**:244.

Weingold AB et al: Nonstress testing. *Am J Obstet Gynecol* 1980; **138**:195.

Whittle MJ et al: Estriol in pregnancy. 6. Experience with unconjugated plasma estriol assays and antepartum fetal heart rate testing in diabetic pregnancies. *Am J Obstet Gynecol* 1979; **135**:764.

Zanini B, Paul RH, Huey JR: Intrapartum fetal heart rate: Correlation with scalp pH in the preterm fetus. *Am J Obstet Gynecol* 1980;**136**:43.

Zuspan FP et al: NICHD Consensus Development Task Force Report. Predictors of intrapartum fetal distress: The role of electronic fetal monitoring. *J Reprod Med* 1979;**23**:207.

29 | Prenatal Care

Kenneth R. Niswander, MD

Prenatal care as we know it today is a relatively new development in medicine. It can be said to have originated in Boston in the first decade of this century. Before that time, the patient who thought she was pregnant may have visited a physician for confirmation of her diagnosis but did not see a physician again until delivery was imminent. The nurses of the Instructive Nursing Association in Boston, thinking that they might contribute to the health of pregnant mothers, began making house calls on all mothers registered at the Boston Lying-In Hospital for delivery. These visits were so successful that the principle behind them was gradually accepted by physicians, and our present system of prenatal care, which stresses prevention, evolved in this way.

Pregnancy is a normal physiologic event that is only occasionally complicated by pathologic processes dangerous to the health of the mother and fetus. However, even a normal pregnancy may so alter the pregnant woman's physiologic mechanisms—usually to accommodate a need of the mother or the fetus—that a hazard to one or both may result. The physician who undertakes the care of pregnant patients must be familiar with the normal changes that occur during pregnancy so that significant abnormalities can be recognized when they occur and their effects minimized.

Prenatal care should have as a principal aim the identification and treatment of the high-risk patient— the one whose pregnancy, because of some factor in her medical history or a significant development during pregnancy, is likely to have a poor outcome. (This subject is discussed further in Chapter 28.)

The purpose of prenatal care is to ensure, as far as possible, an uncomplicated pregnancy for the mother and the delivery of a live, healthy infant. There is some evidence that the mother's emotional state during pregnancy may have a direct effect on fetal outcome. Lederman et al (see references on p 629) have reported that anxiety in labor is positively correlated with plasma epinephrine levels, which in turn seem to result in abnormal fetal heart rate patterns and low Apgar scores. Similarly, Crandon (see references) measured anxiety in women in the third trimester and noted that among such women, the 5-minute Apgar score was distinctly lower.

PROCEDURES DURING THE INITIAL OFFICE VISIT

The initial office visit should be for 30–45 minutes, thus allowing sufficient time for a reasonably complete examination and discussion of any special concerns the patient may have.

Diagnosis of Pregnancy

The patient presents herself chiefly for confirmation of the diagnosis of pregnancy. The diagnosis is usually made without difficulty on the basis of the history and physical examination, although laboratory confirmation may be required (see Chapter 27).

History

A. Present Pregnancy: The interview should begin with a full discussion of the patient's current symptoms. Ideally, the patient should be encouraged to talk not only about what led her to think she might be pregnant (almost always a missed period) but also about her ideas on childbearing, sex, and marriage; her role as a woman; and what she expects of the doctor-patient relationship. Physicians who are willing to listen can learn much from their patients that will help them give better care.

1. Menstrual history–If the patient has a history of regular menses, the date of the last menstrual period (LMP) will usually give an accurate expected date of confinement (EDC) by application of Nägele's rule: count back 3 months from the first day of the LMP and add 7 days. (For example, if the LMP began July 12, the baby will be due April 19.) Forty weeks from the first day of the LMP, the pregnancy is considered to be at term.

It is important to elicit further details about the menstrual history if the intermenstrual interval has been prolonged or irregular. Because ovulation occurs about 14 days before menstruation, a 35-day menstrual interval would suggest an EDC 7 days later than that calculated by Nägele's rule. Conversely, a shorter menstrual interval would suggest an earlier EDC.

The date of an isolated act of coitus may help to establish a precise EDC. If the presumed LMP consisted of spotting only, it may simply represent implantation bleeding during pregnancy. If so, this would necessitate recalculation of the EDC from the prior period. Careful evaluation of all pertinent data from the menstrual and sexual history usually permits the physician to establish an accurate EDC. Additional information such as the date fetal heart tones were first heard with a Doppler instrument (12 weeks) or the time when fetal movement was first appreciated by the patient (16–18 weeks) may help determine a more precise EDC.

A grossly abnormal menstrual history may also point to an endocrine disturbance or some other abnormality of significance to the current pregnancy.

2. Symptoms–The common symptoms of pregnancy may be useful in helping to establish the diagnosis. Breast fullness, nipple tenderness, abdominal bloating, nausea or vomiting, frequency of urination, and lassitude or tiredness are frequently described.

B. History of Previous Pregnancy: Events of previous pregnancies frequently give clues to potential hazards during the present one. Because a poor outcome often is a recurrent event in successive pregnancies, a small percentage of pregnant women account for a disproportionately large number of obstetric complications. For each prior pregnancy, therefore, the following information should be determined.

1. Length of gestation–Was the pregnancy full-term or was delivery premature? If delivery was premature, by how long? Did the pregnancy terminate in an early abortion? If so, was D&C performed? Is there a history of mid-trimester abortion of a sort that might suggest an incompetent cervix?

2. Birth weight–Knowing the birth weights of other children can aid in evaluating the duration of prior pregnancies. Children of the same parentage tend to be of similar birth weight, which usually increases slightly with successive offspring. A discordantly small fetus in the present pregnancy may indicate an incorrect EDC or a small-for-dates fetus dangerously arrested in development. A fetus that is judged to be oversized may suggest multiple pregnancy, fetal abnormality, or an error in the determination of the EDC. A previous child of excessively large birth weight suggests the possibility of diabetes mellitus in the mother.

3. Fetal outcome–Were prior offspring normal at birth? Did they develop normally? Was any baby anemic, or was transfusion ever required? The latter suggests Rh or other isoimmunization.

4. Length of labor–Was labor spontaneous or induced? If it was induced, why? A history of a very short or very long labor should alert the obstetrician to the possible repetition of a similar event.

5. Presentation and type of delivery–Was the baby delivered vertex, breech, or face up? Was delivery spontaneous? Were forceps used, and why? Was cesarean section required, and why? Was episiotomy required? What analgesics and anesthetics were administered? Was anesthesia successful and uncomplicated?

6. Complications–

a. During pregnancy–Did the patient show any signs or symptoms of preeclampsia-eclampsia? Inquire about hypertension, proteinuria, edema, low-salt diet, hospitalization to control weight, etc. Did she have any episodes of vaginal bleeding during a prior pregnancy? Did she suffer any concurrent disease requiring medical or surgical intervention?

b. During labor–Did the patient show any evidence of preeclampsia-eclampsia during labor? Were there convulsions? Was there any unusually heavy bleeding? Did labor progress normally, or was it necessary to augment the labor? If the latter, how was it done?

c. During the postpartum period–Was there any evidence of preeclampsia-eclampsia, postpartum bleeding, or infection? How long was the patient hospitalized?

7. Nursing–Was the child breast-fed? If not, was this by choice or necessity?

C. History of Prior Illness: A standard past history should be obtained as from any nonpregnant patient.

1. Medical–Preexisting disease of the cardiovascular, endocrine, or gastrointestinal system frequently is of great importance to the physician caring for a pregnant patient. Pregnancy may aggravate such underlying disease, and, in turn, the disease may have a deleterious effect on the fetus or the mother. The combined effect of pregnancy and the disease state may be so dangerous to the mother that therapeutic abortion may be desirable.

In most instances, the diagnosis of a serious organic disease will have been made before the onset of pregnancy. Occasionally, metabolic changes induced by pregnancy are sufficient to unmask an unrecognized disease state (eg, latent diabetes mellitus) or provide clues to the development of a disease state later in life.

A record of blood transfusions is important. Rh and less common blood antigens introduced via prior maternal transfusions may produce hemolytic disease of the newborn. A history of sensitivity to drugs or other allergic disorders is obviously important for the care of the pregnant patient.

2. Surgical–Of special importance is a history of prior gynecologic surgery. Induced abortion may predispose to an incompetent cervical os or to infertility; in the latter case, the current pregnancy will be a more important one. Uterine surgery may necessitate delivery by cesarean section. Extensive repair of the pelvic floor may make cesarean section desirable.

A history of appendectomy will reassure the physician if a pregnant patient complains of pain in the right lower quadrant. Spinal surgery may contraindicate spinal or epidural anesthesia for delivery.

D. Family History: A family history of diabetes mellitus should alert the obstetrician to the possibility of this disorder, especially if a positive history is combined with a record of delivery of an unusually large or anomalous baby or of a prior fetal or neonatal death. These historical clues should prompt the physician to order a fasting blood glucose and a 2–hour postprandial plasma glucose determination at least.

A history of familial diseases is of great importance. Certain hereditary diseases can now be detected by analysis of amniotic fluid. Genetic counseling early in pregnancy may be important in the decision to abort an abnormal fetus. Genetic amniocentesis for detection of possible Down's syndrome should be encouraged in any woman 35 years of age or older and virtually demanded of a woman 40 years of age or older.

E. Social and Emotional History: The patient's social background may affect her attitude toward pregnancy, labor, and delivery and may even predict the possibility of prolonged and difficult labor. The emotional makeup (particularly tension) of the patient and her attitudes toward natural childbirth and breast feeding are significant, as are her life-style, diet, state of nutrition, and cultural background.

F. Anesthetic Preferences: Analgesia and anesthesia for labor and delivery should be discussed during prenatal visits so that a mutually agreeable plan can be developed. If the patient wishes to progress through labor—even delivery—without medication, she should be encouraged to do so and perhaps enrolled in an education-for-childbirth program.

G. Physician-Patient Rapport: More important than any detail of the history to ensure good prenatal care is the need for rapport between the patient and her physician. The physician, the nurse practitioner, or the physician's assistant must explain what is required of the patient during pregnancy and why her full cooperation is necessary. The husband should visit the office early in the course of pregnancy to learn how the pregnancy is progressing and how he can help. Lucid explanations and frank answers to all questions will promote a confident, supportive attitude on the husband's part, and this in turn will be an important source of satisfaction and support for his wife.

Physical Examination

A thorough physical examination should be performed. (*Note:* This may be the first complete examination the patient has ever had.) Items of particular importance in pregnancy are the following:

A. General Appearance: Does she have typical female contours, with wide hips and an apparently ample pelvis? Is her weight commensurate with her size, or is she markedly overweight or underweight?

B. Skin: Is she pale (anemic)? Is there evidence of jaundice? Note skin infections and other abnormalities.

C. Head and Neck: Palpate the cervical and other lymph nodes to identify possible disorders of the lymphatic system. Inspect the nasal and oral mucous membranes, bearing in mind that the hormonal changes of normal pregnancy may account for hay fever-like symptoms. The thyroid is normally slightly diffusely enlarged during pregnancy, but thyroid nodules must be investigated to rule out cancer.

D. Chest and Heart: Pulmonary rales, rubs, and rhonchi are abnormal. Note especially the presence of a heart murmur or arrhythmia. Organic murmurs must be distinguished from functional ones. A persistent cardiac irregularity may be a serious finding requiring explanation and perhaps treatment.

E. Breasts: Inspect the nipples for adequacy for breast feeding. Inverted nipples often can be everted by gentle traction. Palpate for breast nodules. Breast cancer growth may be accelerated by pregnancy.

F. Abdomen: Evaluate the tone of the abdominal wall. Poor abdominal musculature may complicate the second stage of labor by preventing adequate bearing-down efforts. Note hernias or abdominal masses and scars. Determine whether the size of the uterus is compatible with the length of gestation according to the menstrual history.

G. Extremities: Note any deformities or restriction of movement of the legs, arms, and back. Varicosities of the lower extremity may be a source of major discomfort or even embolism during pregnancy or the puerperium. Edema of the face, arms, or hands may be indicative of cardiac or renal disease or preeclampsia. Pretibial and presacral edema may be early evidence of fluid retention. Check deep tendon reflexes.

H. Pelvis: The diagnosis of pregnancy requires a careful pelvic examination.

1. Soft tissue–Any pelvic mass should be described accurately, with special regard to its relationship to the uterus or birth canal.

2. Bony pelvis–Clinical evaluation of the bony pelvis provides essential information for the conduct of labor. The astute physician will use an appraisal of pelvic capacity to identify those patients most likely to develop fetopelvic disproportion during labor.

The diameters of the inlet, the midpelvis, and the outlet should be measured. Pelvic configuration is most accurately determined by roentgenography, but x-ray pelvimetry should not be routine. Sonography can be employed at any time during pregnancy because of its safety and accuracy.

X-ray pelvimetry is contraindicated except in anticipation of fetopelvic disproportion. In any event, x-ray pelvimetry should be postponed until near term for the following reasons: (1) if the fetus is premature, one need not be concerned about a slightly small pelvis; (2) measurements of the fetal skull will be greatest near term, when the presentation and position are also important; and (3) the potential risk of radiation damage to the early fetus must be minimized. If x-ray pelvimetry is elected, the measurements are compared with average dimensions and the inlet, midpelvis, and outlet are thus evaluated. The type of pelvis (ie, gynecoid, android, anthropoid, or platypelloid) and the skull size, presentation, position, and relative size of the fetus are determined.

a. Inlet–Although the transverse diameter of the inlet cannot be measured clinically, the anteroposterior diameter or diagonal conjugate (DC) usually can be estimated accurately. For this measurement, the middle finger of the examining hand reaches for the promontory of the sacrum, and the tissue between the examiner's index finger and thumb is pushed against the symphysis pubica while the point of pressure is

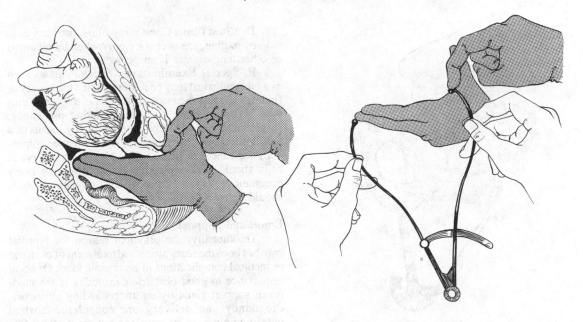

Figure 29 –1. Measurement of the diagonal conjugate (DC) (conjugata diagonalis, CD). (Reproduced, with permission, from Benson RC: *Handbook of Obstetrics & Gynecology,* 7th ed. Lange, 1980.)

noted (Fig 29–1). The distance between the tip of the examining finger and this point of pressure measures the DC of the inlet. Subtracting 1.5 cm from the DC gives a fairly satisfactory estimate of the true conjugate (conjugata vera, CV), the true anterior diameter of the pelvic inlet.

b. Midpelvis–Precise clinical measurement of the diameter of the midpelvic space is not feasible. With some experience, however, the physician can estimate this distance by noting the prominence and relative closeness of the ischial spines. If the walls of the pelvis seem to converge, if the curve of the sacrum is straightened or shallow, or if the sacrosciatic notches are unusually narrow, doubt about the adequacy of the midpelvis is justified.

c. Outlet–For clinical purposes, the outlet can be adequately estimated by physical examination. The shape of the outlet can be determined by palpating the pubic rami from the symphysis to the ischial tuberosities and noting the angle of the rami. A subpubic angle of less than 90 degrees suggests inadequacy of the outlet. The intertuberous (biischial) diameter can be accurately measured with Thoms's pelvimeter (Fig 29–2). A diameter of more than 8 cm usually is adequate for delivery of a term infant. The posterior sagittal (PS) diameter can also be measured with Thoms's pelvimeter. If the sum of the tuberischial diameter (TI) and the PS is greater than 15 cm, this usually indicates an adequate pelvic outlet. A prominent or angulated coccyx diminishes the anteroposterior diameter of the pelvic outlet (AP).

Martin's or Breisky's pelvimeter may be used to measure the distance from the inferior border of the symphysis to the posterior aspect of the tip of the sacrum, ie, the AP (normally 11.9 cm).

On rare occasions, extreme abnormality of the pelvis will preclude vaginal delivery. In the vast majority of cases, below average clinical measurements are what alert the obstetrician to the possibility of fetopelvic disproportion and, therefore, dystocia. However, an adequate trial of labor is usually the final determinant of the true adequacy of the bony pelvis.

Laboratory Tests

A. Blood Studies:

1. Serologic test for syphilis–A test for syphilis must be done early in pregnancy to aid in the preven-

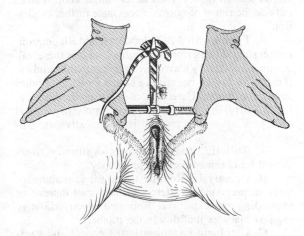

Figure 29 –2. Measurement of the biischial (BI) or intertuberous diameter (tuberischial diameter, TI) with Thoms's pelvimeter. (Reproduced, with permission, from Benson RC: *Handbook of Obstetrics & Gynecology,* 7th ed. Lange, 1980.)

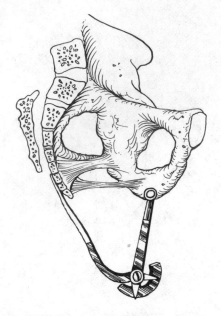

Figure 29 –3. Posterior sagittal (PS) measurements with Thoms's pelvimeter. (Reproduced, with permission, from Benson RC: *Handbook of Obstetrics & Gynecology,* 7th ed. Lange, 1980.)

tion of congenital syphilis. This test is required in all states of the USA and in many other countries. Maternal syphilis, if discovered before midpregnancy, can be treated at least to the extent of preventing congenital syphilis. The physician should repeat the test later in pregnancy if exposure to syphilis during pregnancy seems to be a possibility. Cervical and rectal cultures for gonococci may be indicated also.

2. Complete blood count–A complete blood count including hematocrit and hemoglobin determination should be recorded at the initial visit. Values outside the range of normal necessitate further evaluation.

3. Typing–An ABO blood type and Rh determination should be performed routinely unless these values are dependably known from prior reliable studies. If the patient is Rh-negative, a search for Rh antibodies should be made. Detection of other antibodies (eg, Kell, Duffy) by means of pooled antisera is good policy whether the patient is Rh-negative or Rh-positive.

4. Rubella, toxoplasmosis–Antibody titers should be obtained early in pregnancy.

B. Urinalysis: Routine urinalysis is mandatory early in pregnancy to detect urinary tract disease or impending preeclampsia. Repeated glycosuria may suggest diabetes mellitus in the mother.

C. Cytologic Examination: Cervical and vaginal Papanicolaou smears should be obtained from all pregnant patients, regardless of age, and annually from all women over age 20. In the case of obstetric patients, the first antenatal visit is a convenient time to make this test.

D. Chest films: Chest x-ray films, formerly considered routine, are necessary only when tuberculosis or other lung disease is suspected.

E. Special Examinations: Special studies such as a tuberculin test may be required when the history or findings suggest the need. Although ectropion (''erosion'') of the cervix is frequent during pregnancy, suspicious areas should be investigated by means of a Schiller test and, perhaps, cervical biopsy or colposcopy for cancer or herpesvirus. Vaginal and cervical cells should be examined microscopically in every pregnancy. Vulvar varicosities and hemorrhoids should be recorded.

Emotional Support

Traditionally, the principal reason for prenatal care has been the recognition and treatment of obstetric or medical complications of an organic kind. Of equal importance to good obstetric care today is the emotional support given by an understanding physician. Pregnancy and delivery are considered normal physiologic events by everyone but the mother. She may have many worries that should be discussed at length. Erroneous and superstitious beliefs should be dispelled. The course and conduct of labor should be discussed with the patient as soon as possible. If this is her first pregnancy she will not know what to expect; and even if she has had a baby before she may have forgotten about some of the details of labor. The patient will want to discuss the type of analgesia and anesthesia to be used, and her preferences or aversions may become apparent. The patient and her husband should be enrolled in parents' classes if available. The emotional support provided during pregnancy may make the difference between pleasant anticipation or a terrifying experience.

Printed personalized instructions for each patient are an excellent method of anticipating problems and answering questions.

SUBSEQUENT VISITS

Prenatal visits after the initial interview and examination may be brief. The patient should be seen at least once a month until the seventh month, twice a month in the seventh and eighth months, and once a week in the last month. The frequency of the visits must be increased if complications are recognized.

Office Procedures

The patient's weight should be recorded. Her blood pressure should be taken in the same position (supine or sitting) each time. The site and degree of edema, if present, should be noted.

The abdomen should be examined for the size of the uterus, the position of the fetus, fetal heart tones (by auscultation), and abnormalities in the shape and tone of the uterus. Measurements of the height of the uterus at each visit from the seventh month onward should confirm normal fetal growth.

Other areas or body systems should be examined as required.

Surgically clean vaginal examinations during pregnancy—especially near term—are not harmful and are the best means of determining the status of the cervix, the presentation, and the degree of engagement.

History

The patient should be questioned about symptoms of any kind, with particular attention to vaginal bleeding and symptoms of preeclampsia-eclampsia.

Table 29–1. Infections affecting the fetus or newborn.*

Maternal Infection	Effects on Fetus or Newborn
Specific viral infections	
Rubella	Malformations, bleeding, hepatosplenomegaly, pneumonitis, hepatitis, encephalitis
Cytomegalovirus	Microcephaly, chorioretinitis, deafness, mental retardation
Herpes simplex	Generalized herpes, encephalitis, death
Mumps	Fetal death, endocardial fibroelastosis (?), malformations (?)
Rubeola	Increased abortions and stillbirths
Western equine encephalitis	Encephalitis
Chickenpox, shingles	Chickenpox or shingles, increased abortions and stillbirths
Smallpox	Smallpox, increased abortions and stillbirths
Vaccinia	Generalized vaccinia, increased abortions
Influenza	Malformations (?)
Poliomyelitis	Spinal or bulbar poliomyelitis
Hepatitis	Hepatitis
Coxsackie B viruses	Myocarditis
Nonspecific viral infections	
Upper respiratory infections	None
Severe viral infections	Prematurity
Syphilis	Congenital syphilis
Bacterial infections	
Gonorrhea	Ophthalmitis
Acute bacterial infections	Prematurity
Tuberculosis	Congenital tuberculosis
Listeriosis	Abortions, stillbirths, septicemia, meningoencephalitis, habitual abortion (?)
Pyelonephritis	Premature labor
Protozoan infections	
Toxoplasmosis	Microcephaly, chorioretinitis, jaundice
Malaria	Low birth weight, perinatal mortality (?)

*Modified from Sever JL: Perinatal infections affecting the developing fetus and newborn. In: *The Prevention of Mental Retardation Through Control of Infectious Diseases.* Public Health Service Publication No. 1692, 1968.

Laboratory Tests

The urine should be tested at each visit for protein and reducing substances. The hematocrit determination should be repeated at about 32 weeks. If the patient is Rh-negative, Rh antibody titer should be measured early in pregnancy and again at 24 weeks; if it is greater than 1:16, the test should be repeated because amniocentesis is probably indicated. (See Chapter 4.)

Consideration of the Fetus

Maternal infections deleterious to the fetus (Table 29–1) should be prevented or, if possible, treated. X-ray radiation, teratogenic drugs, and a number of medications (Table 29–2) potentially hazardous for other reasons should be avoided. Self-medication for trivial reasons should not be allowed during the first trimester; indeed, all but the most essential drugs should be prohibited.

The physician must always bear in mind that the fetus needs caring for as well as the mother.

Preparation for Labor

As the EDC approaches, the patient should be encouraged again to discuss her concerns. If a multipara, she should be admitted to the hospital as soon as her contractions become strong, regular, or painful. If she has had children before, she probably will be admitted to the hospital when her contractions are recurring at intervals of 5–10 minutes; if she is a primigravida, she may come in sooner. The patient should be encouraged to seek her physician's advice by phone if any of the following danger signals appear during the prenatal course:

(1) Rupture of the membranes.

(2) Vaginal bleeding.

(3) Evidence of preeclampsia-eclampsia (ie, marked swelling of the hands or face, blurring of vision, headache, epigastric pain, convulsions).

(4) Chills or fever.

(5) Severe or unusual abdominal pain.

The details of what the patient can expect during labor, as well as the choice of an anesthetic, should again be reviewed briefly with the patient. The better the patient-physician rapport, the easier her labor is likely to be.

NUTRITION IN PREGNANCY

Weight Gain

Until recently, many authorities encouraged restriction of weight gain during pregnancy even to the point of recommending stringent weight reduction programs for obese patients. A weight reduction program during pregnancy, even for the obese patient, is no longer recommended. Emphasis is now placed on what the pregnant woman should eat rather than on what she should not eat. It is much easier to manage the nutrition of a pregnant patient when the positive rather than the negative factors are stressed.

Table 29–2. Risk/benefit assessment of drugs administered to pregnant women in first trimester.*

Drug	Effects Reported	Drug	Effects Reported
I. Risk outweighs benefit in first trimester			
Acetazolamide	Limb defects	Paramethadione	Multiple anomalies
Amphetamines	Transposition of great vessels, cleft palate	Phenmetrazine	Skeletal and visceral malformations
Chloroquine	Retinal damage, eighth nerve damage	Phenytoin	Multiple anomalies
Chlorpropamide	Increase of anomalies	Podophyllin (in laxatives)	Multiple anomalies
Dicumarol	Skeletal and facial anomalies, mental retardation	Serotonin	Increase of anomalies
Diethylstilbestrol	Clear cell adenocarcinoma of vagina and cervix, genital tract anomalies	Sex steroids	VACTERL syndrome
		Streptomycin	Eighth nerve damage, micromelia, multiple skeletal anomalies
Ethanol	Fetal alcohol syndrome		
Iodide	Congenital goiter, hypothyroidism, mental retardation	Tetracycline	Inhibition of bone growth, micromelia, syndactyly, discoloration of teeth
LSD	Chromosomal abnormalities, increase of anomalies	Thalidomide	Limb, auricle, eye, and visceral malformations
		Tolbutamide	Increase of anomalies
Meclizine	Multiple anomalies	Trimethadione	Multiple anomalies
Methotrexate (for psoriasis)	Multiple anomalies	Warfarin sodium	Skeletal and facial anomalies, mental retardation
II. Risk versus benefits uncertain in first trimester			
Barbiturates	Increase of anomalies	Lithium	Goiter, eye anomalies, cleft palate
Benzodiazepines	Cardiac defects	Metronidazole	None
Cannabis	Increase of anomalies	Propylthiouracil	Goiter, hypothyroidism, mental retardation
Clofibrate	None	Pyrimethamine	Increase of anomalies
Cytotoxic drugs	Increase of anomalies	Quinine	Increase of anomalies
Diazoxide	Increase of anomalies	Thiouracil	Goiter, hypothyroidism, mental retardation
EDTA	Increase of anomalies	Trimethoprim/sulfamethoxazole	Cleft palate
Gentamicin	Eighth nerve damage		
Kanamycin	Eighth nerve damage		
III. Benefit outweighs risk in first trimester			
Acetaminophen	None	Insulin	Skeletal malformations
Antacids	Increase of anomalies	Isoniazid	Increase of anomalies
Antihistamines	None	Isoproterenol	None
Bendectin	See footnote on p 625	Monoamine oxidase inhibitors	None
Chloramphenicol	None		
Clomiphene	Increase of anomalies, neural tube effects, Down's syndrome	Penicillamine	Connective tissue defect
		Penicillins	None
General anesthesia	Increase of anomalies	Phenothiazines	None
		Rifampin	Spina bifida, cleft palate
Glucocorticoids	Cleft palate, cardiac defects	Salicylates	CNS, visceral, and skeletal malformations
Haloperidol	Limb malformations	Sulfonamides	Cleft palate, facial, and skeletal defects
Heparin	None	Terbutaline	None
Hydralazine	Increase of anomalies	Theophylline	None
Idoxuridine	Increase of anomalies	Tricyclic antidepressants	CNS and limb malformations
Imipramine	CNS and limb anomalies		

*Modified and reproduced, with permission, from Howard F, Hill J: Drugs in pregnancy. *Obstet Gynecol Surv* 1979;34:643.

Teratogenicity Drug Labeling Now Required by FDA

The FDA has established 5 categories of drugs based on their potential for causing birth defects in infants born to women who use the drugs during pregnancy. By law, the label must set forth all available information on teratogenicity. The categories are as follows:

Category A: Well-controlled human studies have not disclosed any fetal risk.

Category B: Animal studies have not disclosed any fetal risk; or have suggested some risk not con-firmed in controlled studies in women; or there are no adequate studies in women.

Category C: Animal studies have revealed adverse fetal effects; there are no adequate controlled studies in women.

Category D: Some fetal risk, but benefits may outweigh risk (eg, life-threatening illness, no safer effective drug). Patient should be warned.

Category X: Fetal abnormalities in animal and human studies; risk not outweighed by benefit. *Contraindicated in pregnancy.*

Good maternal nutrition is a major determinant of normal fetal growth and development. Any gross deficiency of maternal circulation may interfere with both maternal and fetal nutrition. Obstetric patients with severe heart disease bear small babies, probably as a result of poor circulation. Placental transport mechanisms may be influenced adversely by nutritional deficiencies in the mother. The clinician should evaluate all relevant factors, including socioeconomic status and cultural habits, when considering the nutritional aspects of fetal growth and development.

Recently there has been a renewal of interest in the notion that high maternal weight gain increases mean birth weight in infants. The risk of producing an infant of low birth weight ($\leqslant$ 2500 g) is greatly increased for the patient with a small prepregnancy weight if she gains little during pregnancy. The same relationship holds for patients of higher prepregnancy weight, although the differences are less striking (Fig 29–4). The lower neonatal mortality rates of the Netherlands and Sweden as compared with the rate in the USA can probably be explained by the high incidence of low-birth-weight infants in the USA. If it is true, as has been said, that an arithmetic increase of 1% in the number of infants weighing 2500 g or less at birth is associated with an increase of 10% in mortality rate during the first week of life, the medical implications are obvious.

Evidence also suggests that lower birth weight correlates positively with lower DNA content of the placenta and, by inference, with lower DNA content of the fetal brain. In experimental animals, poor maternal nutrition may lead to permanent decrease in the number of fetal brain cells. This evidence is so con-

Table 29–3. Prenatal gain in weight.

Weeks	kg	lb	oz
6	0.2		8
8	0.5	1	
10	0.8	1	11
12	1.1	2	8
14	1.7	3	11
16	2.4	5	3
18	3.1	6	15
20	3.9	8	10
22	4.7	10	7
24	5.5	12	3
26	6.2	13	11
28	7	15	7
30	7.7	17	
32	8.4	18	8
34	9.1	20	
36	9.8	21	8
38	10.4	23	
40	10.9	24	

vincing that *severe* dietary restriction for the pregnant woman should never be undertaken. In any event, the quality of nutrition is far more important than caloric content: "Empty calories" (eg, candy, soft drinks) may be useless or even harmful.

The patient's nutritional status before conception may be as important as nutrition during pregnancy. The physician may not be able to influence the general state of the patient's nutrition, but can attempt to alter her food habits early in pregnancy.

How much weight should a pregnant woman be allowed, or encouraged, to gain? The normal mean weight gain of pregnant women eating "to appetite" is difficult to determine for many reasons—not the least of which is the fact that, in the past, few pregnant patients who were studied had been permitted to eat as much as they wanted. The average weight gain of the patient who does not have preeclampsia-eclampsia, excluding gain due to fat, is about 11 kg (24 lb) (Table 29–3). The fetus accounts for approximately one-third of this weight gain, or 3500 g. The placenta, amniotic fluid, and uterus account for 650–900 g. Increased interstitial fluid and blood volume add 1200–1800 g, respectively. Breast enlargement contributes at least 400 g. The remaining 1640 g represent principally maternal fat. It should be remembered, however, that many patients will weigh more or less than the mean without apparent ill effects.

There is no convincing evidence that excessive weight gain, whether in the form of fat or water, causes preeclampsia-eclampsia. Even Dieckmann, a vigorous advocate of dietary restriction in pregnancy, admitted that "dietetic care" did not reduce the incidence of preeclampsia or prevent eclampsia. Nevertheless, the incidence of preeclampsia-eclampsia in the USA has declined markedly, and it seems likely that better nutrition may account for at least part of this change.

Moderate weight gain is associated with the lowest incidence of low-birth-weight infants and neonatal

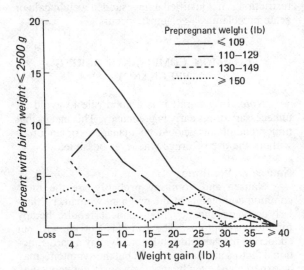

Figure 29–4. Risk of low birth weight among infants of white patients in relation to gravida's pregnancy weight and weight gain. (Reproduced, with permission, from Niswander KR et al: Weight gain during pregnancy and prepregnancy weight: Association with birth weight of term gestation. *Obstet Gynecol* 1969;33:482.)

Table 29—4. Recommended daily dietary allowance for women 18—35 years old, 162 cm (64 inches) tall, and weighing 57.5 kg (128 lb) when not pregnant. (Food and Nutrition Board, National Research Council. Revised, 1973.)

Nutrient	Nonpregnant	Increase	
		Pregnant	Lactating
Kilocalories	2000	300	500
Protein (g)	55	10	20
Vitamin A (IU)	5000	2000	3000
Vitamin D (IU)	400	None	None
Vitamin E (IU)	12	3	3
Ascorbic acid (mg)	45	15	15
Folacin* (mg)	0.4	0.4	0.2
Niacin† (mg)	14	2	4
Thiamine (mg)	1.4	0.3	0.3
Riboflavin (mg)	1.4	0.3	0.5
Vitamin B_6 (mg)	2	0.5	0.5
Vitamin B_{12} (μg)	3	1	1
Calcium (g)	0.8	0.4	0.4
Phosphorus (g)	0.8	0.4	0.4
Iodine (μg)	100	25	50
Iron (mg)	18	30—60	30—60
Magnesium (mg)	300	150	150

*Refers to dietary sources ascertained by *Lactobacillus casei* assay; pteroylglutamic acid may be effective in smaller doses.
†Includes dietary sources of the vitamin plus 1 mg equivalent for each 60 mg of dietary tryptophan.

deaths. The underweight woman with a small weight gain in pregnancy should be considered a high-risk patient. The woman who gains weight excessively will have the usual problems of obesity. Individualization seems the best course of action. Emphasis should be placed on good nutrition rather than on precise control of weight.

The daily dietary allowances recommended by the Food and Nutrition Board of the National Research Council are listed in Table 29—4. These should be considered approximations, because adult patients who are ill or underweight and young girls who have not completed their growth will require larger allowances. In any event, a pregnancy diet should include the following daily components: milk, 1 L (or quart); one average serving of citrus fruit or tomato, a leafy green vegetable, and a yellow vegetable; and 2 average servings of lean meat, fish, poultry, eggs, beans, or cheese.

The physician will be more successful as a nutrition counselor if emphasis is placed on what should be eaten rather than what should be avoided. However, one should discuss what to avoid during pregnancy when substitutes for necessary foods are the rule, eg, in the case of the teenager who subsists on soft drinks, potato chips, and hamburgers.

Supplemental Minerals & Vitamins

One liter (or quart) of cow's milk contains 1 g of calcium—approximately the recommended daily intake (1.2 g). If the patient will not or cannot drink milk, substitute sources of calcium (eg, cheese, yogurt, ice

milk, spinach) should be offered or a supplement (eg, calcium carbonate) may be prescribed. Some patients, especially American Indians and foreign-born blacks and Orientals, may have a disaccharidase deficiency which causes intolerance to lactose in milk. For these persons, protein, calcium, and vitamins must be supplied in other forms (eg, cheese, fish, fruits).

Supplemental iron is needed to prevent depletion of the maternal iron stores, especially during the latter part of pregnancy. About 30 mg of iron daily, in the form of a simple iron compound (ferrous gluconate or fumarate), provides enough iron to meet the requirements of pregnancy and protect the iron stores.

Folic acid, 1 mg/d orally, should also be given. Routine folate treatment involves little risk of central nervous system damage in women with unrecognized pernicious anemia.

Many women do not eat enough vitamin-containing foods. To make certain that the vitamin intake is adequate, half the daily recommended dietary allowances as listed in Table 29—4 should be given in the form of a supplement.

Excessive ingestion of vitamins D and A may be harmful.

The common practice of recommending prenatal vitamin supplements is not harmful in the doses usually prescribed.

Salt Restriction

Moderate amounts of salt- or sodium-containing foods are not harmful during normal pregnancy. The widespread practice of restricting sodium intake and prescribing diuretics at the same time is potentially dangerous. The requirement for sodium in pregnancy is increased slightly, and overemphasis on sodium restriction is not justified unless sudden weight gain or acute preeclampsia-eclampsia occurs.

COMMON COMPLAINTS DURING PREGNANCY

Note: In general, it is a good rule to avoid all unnecessary drugs early in pregnancy. This means that minor complaints should be managed (or endured) without the use of drugs whenever possible.

Nausea & Vomiting

Nausea and vomiting probably are the most common complaints of the pregnant woman, particularly early in pregnancy. Many patients require therapy for these symptoms. The cause is not known, but endocrine mechanisms undoubtedly play a part. Emotional factors are also involved, but the symptoms may be experienced even by women who do not know they are pregnant. There is undoubtedly a physiologic basis for the symptoms in many cases.

Typically, nausea is experienced early in the morning and abates as the day wears on. Other patients may experience nausea at any time. In severe cases, it may persist, with or without vomiting, throughout the day. Dehydration usually is not a serious concern, but in the case of persistent vomiting (hyperemesis gravidarum) hospitalization usually is necessary to correct fluid and electrolyte imbalance. With parenteral administration of fluids, rest, and sedation, most seriously ill patients improve.

Explanation, reassurance, and suggestion are the most useful remedies. If the patient can be convinced that little harm is likely to result from the complaint, she will usually feel better. Dietary changes are often helpful. Eating dry toast and jelly immediately upon arising and before the nausea begins helps some patients. Six small "dry" meals daily may be a good plan. Avoidance of disagreeable odors and rich or exotic foods is important. Mild barbiturate sedation is safe and helpful. A commonly used and effective safe antiemetic medication is Bendectin.*

Heartburn

Slowing of peristalsis and relaxation of the musculature of the gastrointestinal tract in pregnancy, due mainly to estrogen-progestin effects, may cause heartburn (pyrosis). Heartburn is due to regurgitation of gastric contents into the lower esophagus secondary to relaxation of the cardiac sphincter and reverse peristalsis. Temporary hiatal hernia is common during pregnancy and may be part of the heartburn syndrome. The symptom is most likely to occur when the patient is lying down or bending over.

Antacids containing magnesium hydroxide and aluminum hydroxide relieve heartburn for long periods. Sodium bicarbonate should be avoided, since its benefit is brief.

Because hypoacidity and reduced emptying time of the stomach are normal during pregnancy, the administration of acid (eg, glutamic acid hydrochloride, 0.3 g 3 times a day before meals) for pyrosis is effective.

Constipation

Constipation due to sluggish bowel function in pregnancy may be prevented by emphasizing fluids and laxative foods (whole fruit) and by using a stool softener such as dioctyl sodium sulfosuccinate. Mild laxatives (eg, milk of magnesia) are helpful, but purgatives (eg, castor oil) should be avoided because of the possibility of inducing labor. Mineral oil is contraindicated: It absorbs fat-soluble vitamins from the gastrointestinal tract, and lack of vitamin K is a cause of hemorrhagic disease of the newborn.

Ptyalism

Excessive salivation (sialism, ptyalism) is an in-

---

*Bendectin contains doxylamine succinate, 10 mg, and pyridoxine hydrochloride, 10 mg. Isolated reports of birth defects resulting from use of Bendectin during the first trimester have resulted in close scrutiny of its possible hazards by the FDA. Studies have been equivocal or contradictory, and continuing surveillance is indicated. The FDA is considering the insertion of a warning pamphlet in the package to alert patients to the uncertainty regarding the teratogenic potential of the drug.

frequent but troublesome complaint of pregnant women. Belladonna extract, 8–15 mg orally 4 times a day, may be tried.

Pica

Pica (cissa) is the ingestion of substances that have no value as food or are unwholesome. Common examples are clay and laundry starch. This practice probably does not derive from physiologic craving; rather, it seems to be a curious folkway and is still widespread, especially in the southeastern USA. Pica is harmful because it interferes with good nutrition by substituting nonnutritious bulk for nutritionally important foods. The necessity for good nutrition must be explained to these patients.

Abnormal Frequency of Urination

Urinary frequency is a common complaint throughout pregnancy. Vascular engorgement of the pelvis and hormonal changes are responsible for altered bladder function. Late in pregnancy, when pressure on the bladder by the enlarging uterus and the fetal presenting part decreases bladder capacity, urination becomes even more frequent.

In some cases, pollakiuria is due to urinary tract infection. Dysuria or hematuria may be signs that infection has developed and diagnostic and therapeutic measures are called for. Urinary sedative medication (eg, Urised) may be beneficial whatever the cause of pollakiuria.

Leukorrhea

Vaginal discharge increases in pregnancy because of the increased secretion of mucoid material by the hyperactive, hypertrophic spongy cervix. Reassurance and protection (pads) often are necessary.

Excessive leukorrhea accompanied by pruritus, or discoloration of the secretion, may indicate infection, which requires specific treatment (see below).

Infection

A. Trichomoniasis: *Trichomonas vaginalis* can be found in 20–30% of pregnant patients, but only 5–10% complain of leukorrhea or irritation. This flagellated, pear-shaped, motile organism can be seen under magnification when the vaginal discharge is diluted with warm normal saline solution and examined microscopically. Suspect trichomoniasis when the discharge is fetid, foamy, or greenish or when there are reddish ("strawberry") petechiae on the mucous membranes of the cervix or vagina.

Treatment is discussed on p 190. Metronidazole (Flagyl), a good trichomonacide, is contraindicated during pregnancy because its safety has not been established. Other medications may be helpful and safe during pregnancy. Acceptable antitrichomonas therapy can be given with AVC cream (aminacrine, sulfanilamide, and allantoin) or with Vagisec suppositories (dioctyl sodium sulfosuccinate, polyoxyethylene nonyl phenol, and sodium edetate).

B. Candidiasis: Although *Candida albicans* can

be cultured from the vagina in many pregnant women, symptoms occur in less than half. Symptoms when they do occur consist of severe vaginal burning and itching and a profuse caseous white discharge. Marked inflammation of the vagina and introitus may be noted. The symptoms are likely to be aggravated by intercourse, and the male partner not infrequently develops mild irritation of the penis. Topical application of miconazole nitrate in a cream base (Monistat) or nystatin (Mycostatin) by suppository usually relieves the symptoms. The infection often flares up during pregnancy, in which case re-treatment is necessary.

C. Nonspecific Infections: If irritation is obviously present but a pathogen cannot be identified, symptomatic therapy may be of value. This may include application of a cortisone cream to the vulva to alleviate itching or burning.

Varicose Veins

Varicosities may develop in the legs or in the vulva. A family history of varicosities is often present. Pressure by the enlarging uterus on the venous return from the legs is a major factor in the development of varicosities. The physician should warn the patient, early in pregnancy, of the need for elastic stockings and elevation of the legs if varices develop. Specific therapy (injection or surgical correction) usually is contraindicated in pregnancy.

The aim of therapy is to collapse the large, distended, and tortuous superficial veins but still ensure good circulation. This can be accomplished by frequent elevation of the legs or by wearing elastic stockings. Supportive pantyhose or perineal pressure pads may collapse distended vulvar veins, but this treatment is relatively unsatisfactory.

The prevention and therapy of thrombophlebitis are discussed in Chapter 38.

Hemorrhoids

Hemorrhoids are frequent in pregnancy and may cause considerable discomfort. The causes of hemorrhoids and of varicosities of the lower extremities and vulva are similar. Pregnancy precipitates the occurrence of hemorrhoidal varicosities that might otherwise not occur. Symptoms include anal swelling, pain, and bleeding. Although hemorrhoids frequently produce thrombi during pregnancy, leg varices rarely do.

An attempt should be made to replace the hemorrhoids gently, though this is rarely possible. Useful medical measures include hot sitz baths and the local application of astringent compresses. Laxatives, suppositories, and topical anesthetics may be of great help.

Surgical treatment is usually not indicated during pregnancy and is beyond the scope of this text.

Headache

Headache in pregnancy is a common, usually benign symptom. Persistent, severe headache may be a symptom of preeclampsia-eclampsia.

Most headaches in pregnancy are due to emotional tension or sinusitis. The hormones of pregnancy increase the vascularity of the nasal mucosa, and this mimics the changes caused by allergy or infection. Blockage of the sinus openings may lead to sinus congestion and sinusitis. For all of these reasons, nosebleeds frequently accompany the headaches. Treatment with nasal decongestants may relieve the symptoms.

Edema

Dependent edema due to impedance of venous return is a common but rarely serious complaint late in pregnancy. Generalized edema is seen in the hands and face and may be an ominous sign of preeclampsia-eclampsia. Edema in pregnancy is due to fluid retention under the influence of ovarian, placental, and steroid hormones. Preeclampsia-eclampsia of pregnancy must be excluded. Dependent edema should be treated only if the patient is uncomfortable. Elevation of the legs will improve the circulation, and restriction of sodium intake may retard edema formation. Diuretics (eg, thiazides, ethacrynic acid) are contraindicated and may be hazardous.

Joint Pain, Backache, & Pelvic Pressure

Although the main bony components of the pelvis (os coxae) consist of 3 separate bones, the symphysial and sacroiliac articulations permit practically no motion in the nonpregnant state. In pregnancy, however, endocrine relaxation of these joints permits some movement. The pregnant patient may develop an unstable pelvis, which produces pain. A tight girdle or a belt worn about the hips, together with frequent bed rest, may relieve the pain; however, hospitalization is sometimes necessary.

Improvement in posture often relieves backache. The increasingly protuberant abdomen causes the patient to throw her shoulders back to maintain her balance; this causes her to thrust her head forward to remain erect. Thus, she increases the curvature of both the lumbar spine and the cervicothoracic spine. A maternity girdle to support the abdominal protuberance and shoes with 2-inch heels, which tend to keep the shoulders forward, may reduce the lumbar lordosis and thus relieve backache. Local heat and back rubs may relax the muscles and ease discomfort. Exercises to strengthen the back are most rewarding.

Leg Cramps

Leg cramps in pregnancy may be due to a reduced level of diffusible serum calcium or elevation of serum phosphorus. Treatment should include curtailment of phosphate intake (less milk and nutritional supplements containing calcium phosphate) and increase of calcium intake (without phosphorus) in the form of calcium carbonate or calcium lactate tablets. Aluminum hydroxide gel, 8 mL orally 3 times a day before meals, adsorbs phosphate and may increase calcium absorption. Symptomatic treatment consists of leg massage, gentle flexing of the feet, and local heat. Tell the patient to avoid pointing the toes when she stretches her legs (eg, on awakening in the morning): this triggers a gastrocnemius cramp. She should also practice "leading with the heel" in walking.

Syncope & Faintness

Syncope and faintness are most common in early pregnancy. Vasomotor instability, often associated with postural hypotension, results in transient cerebral ischemia and pooling of blood in the legs and in the splanchnic and pelvic areas, especially after prolonged sitting or standing in a warm room. Hypoglycemia before or between meals, more common during pregnancy, may result in "lightheadedness" or even fainting.

These attacks can be prevented by avoiding inactivity and utilizing deep breathing, vigorous leg motions, and slow change of position. Encourage the patient to take 6 small meals a day rather than 3 large ones. Stimulants (spirits of ammonia, coffee, tea) are indicated for attacks due to hypotension; provide food for hypoglycemia.

Breast Soreness

Physiologic breast engorgement may cause discomfort, especially during early and late pregnancy. A well-fitting brassiere worn 24 hours a day affords relief. Ice caps are temporarily effective. Hormone therapy is of no value.

Abdominal Pain

Abdominal pain due to serious intra-abdominal disease must be ruled out. Painful contractions of the uterus—especially in the third trimester (Braxton Hicks contractions)—and round ligament tension usually yield to rest, change of position, or analgesia.

Discomfort in the Hands

Acrodysesthesia of the hands consists of periodic numbness and tingling of the fingers. (The feet are never involved.) It affects at least 5% of pregnant women. It is a brachial plexus traction syndrome due to drooping of the shoulders during pregnancy. The discomfort is most common at night and early in the morning. It may progress to partial anesthesia and impairment of manual proprioception. The condition is apparently not a serious one, but it may persist after delivery as a consequence of lifting and carrying the baby.

Carpal tunnel syndrome is characterized by paroxysms of pain, numbness, tingling, or burning in one or both hands in tissues innervated by the median nerve. It is noted occasionally in advanced pregnancy. Physiologic changes in fascia, tendons, and connective tissue in pregnancy probably tighten the carpal tunnel abnormally. Edema of the hands may trigger the syndrome. The thumb and the second and third fingers and the lateral side of the fifth finger (only) are involved. Skilled movement of the fingers is lost, and objects may be dropped inadvertently. Tapping or firm pressure on the median nerve at the wrist may cause pain, as does hyperextension or hyperflexion of the

hand. Elevation of the arms and splinting of the hand in the neutral position may help. Surgery, consisting of neurolysis of the median nerve, often is necessary for complete relief.

PERFORMANCE & HABITS

Drugs

Teratogenicity has been established for only a few drugs, but many more are still not proved to be safe for use during pregnancy. (See note on p 625 and Table 29–2.) The physician should have a good reason for prescribing any drug early in pregnancy or, indeed, during the last half of the menstrual cycle, when any fertile, sexually active woman might be pregnant.

Smoking

An increased incidence of low-birth-weight infants has been ascribed to heavy cigarette smoking by pregnant women. This effect seems to be dose-related. Smoking also increases the risk of fetal death or damage in utero. Smoking similarly increases the risk of abruptio placentae and placenta previa, each of which increases the fetal risk as well as the maternal risk of death or damage. Since there are many potentially hazardous substances in tobacco smoke, the particular one responsible for these adverse effects has not been identified. Pregnant women should be encouraged not to smoke. If quitting is too stressful, the patient should at least cut down on the number of cigarettes smoked per day.

Alcoholic Beverages

Moderate ingestion of alcohol has been thought in the past to cause no ill effects on the uterus or fetus despite the easy passage of alcohol across the placenta. Instances of newborns showing alcoholic withdrawal symptoms have been reported, but only in infants born to chronic alcoholics who drank heavily during pregnancy. Moreover, the chronic alcoholic may suffer from malnutrition, to the extent that the craving for alcohol exceeds the desire for food. Administration of alcohol (orally or parenterally) to the level of inebriation may quell prodromal labor, provided the membranes are intact.

A fetal alcohol syndrome following maternal ethanol ingestion has recently been described with an incidence varying from 1:1500 to 1:600 live births, depending apparently on variations in drinking practices. The major features include growth retardation, characteristic facial dysmorphology (including microcephaly and microphthalmia), central nervous system deficiencies, and other abnormalities (see Rosett reference). These authors have reported a dose-effect relationship, with the full-blown syndrome occurring in those who reported heavy drinking. They further noted an improved neonatal outcome when the mothers were able to reduce maternal alcohol consumption before the third trimester. They believe that counseling to reduce alcohol intake during pregnancy need not be performed by a special professional but can be integrated into routine prenatal care. Pregnant women should be encouraged to avoid alcohol intake completely during pregnancy. If this is not possible, the intake should be reduced to a minimum.

Intercourse

There has always been a suspicion that intercourse may be responsible for early abortion. Certainly, if cramps or spotting has followed coitus, it should be proscribed. There is also evidence that coitus late in pregnancy may initiate labor, perhaps because of an orgasm—uterine contraction reflex. All in all, it may be best to proscribe intercourse for patients who have had a previous premature delivery or are currently experiencing uterine bleeding.

Bathing

Bathwater does not enter the vagina. Even swimming is not contraindicated during normal pregnancy. Diving should be avoided because of possible trauma.

A woman in the last trimester of pregnancy is clumsy and has poor balance. For this reason, she should be cautioned about slipping and falling in the tub or shower.

Douching

Douching, seldom necessary, may be harmful.

Dental Care

Pregnancy has no known effect on the teeth. Dietary calcium supplementation in pregnancy is not prescribed to protect the mother's teeth (which cannot lose calcium) but to provide the fetus with enough calcium for optimal bone growth. Necessary dental fillings or extractions may be performed in pregnancy, preferably under local anesthesia.

Immunization

All pregnant women should be vaccinated against poliomyelitis if not already immune. Poliovaccine may be administered safely during pregnancy. Live virus vaccines should be avoided during pregnancy because of possible deleterious effects on the fetus.

Clothing

Loose-fitting conventional clothing often suffices until late in pregnancy, though maternity garments may be used as desired. A well-fitted bra is essential. A maternity girdle is rarely prescribed except for the relief of back pain or for abdominal weakness. Panty girdles and garters should be avoided because they interfere with circulation in the legs. Well-fitted shoes with heels of medium height are best in pregnancy.

Exercise

Exercise in moderation is acceptable during pregnancy, but the gravida should also rest an hour or 2 during the day. Dangerous sports (eg, horseback riding) and undue physical stress should be avoided.

Employment

Women who have sedentary jobs may continue to work throughout the pregnancy. Those whose employment requires physical exertion should take a leave of absence during the second trimester or seek less vigorous work. Substantial physical effort increases maternal oxygen consumption and places an increased demand on cardiac reserve that may result in decreased uterine blood flow. There are no studies as yet that prove this theory beyond doubt, but a conservative approach to the problem is recommended.

Travel

Travel (by automobile, train, or plane) does not adversely affect a pregnancy, but separation from the physician may be hazardous. For this reason, one should instruct patients with a history of abortion and those who have experienced vaginal bleeding in the course of the present pregnancy to avoid travel to distant places.

HIGH–RISK PREGNANCY

The physician should be constantly alert to identify patients whose pregnancies are at risk. Identification of such patients may be possible at the first prenatal visit (very young or very old women; women with a history of perinatal loss or with serious medical complications), during the prenatal course (delayed intrauterine growth, preeclampsia-eclampsia, third trimester bleeding), or during labor (prolonged labor, fetal distress).

PRENATAL ESTIMATION OF FETAL MATURITY

The physician will be required to estimate the length of gestation (fetal maturity) or fetal weight in many clinical situations. For example, elective repetition of cesarean section or elective induction of labor cannot be considered unless the fetus is of adequate maturity and size. Gravidas with diabetes mellitus should be delivered at a known period of gestational age to minimize the risks of low birth weight secondary to shortened pregnancy. Many methods of determining fetal maturity or size are now available to the physician (see also Chapter 28).

Abdominal Examination

Various methods of correlating fundal measurement with fetal weight may add to the accuracy of this estimation by simple abdominal palpation (with some experience). The greatest errors occur (1) with small fetuses and obese mothers and (2) with very large fetuses. In the former case, fetal weight may be overestimated by 500 g or more; in the latter instance, underestimation is common.

Ultrasonography

The biparietal diameter of the fetal skull can be determined by ultrasonic echo. Good correlation with fetal weight has been obtained by those who have expertise in sonography.

Roentgenography

X-ray examination of epiphyseal centers, especially those at the knee, correlates quite well with fetal maturity. If only the distal femoral epiphysis is seen, the pregnancy may be considered to be of 36–38 weeks' duration. If both the distal femoral and the proximal tibial epiphyses are seen, the duration is about 40 weeks. Ultrasonography is just as accurate as roentgenography and is probably safer.

Amniotic Fluid Analysis

Absence of a spectrophotometric peak at 450 nm (ie, no bilirubin present in the amniotic fluid) usually indicates fetal maturity. An amniotic fluid creatinine level of more than 2 mg/dL also indicates fetal maturity. If 20% or more of the fetal cells (presumably from fetal sebaceous glands) in the amniotic fluid stain orange with Nile blue sulfate, the infant will weigh 2500 g or more.

The most accurate method of estimating fetal maturity is based on the lecithin/sphingomyelin ratio in amniotic fluid (see Chapter 28). Phospholipids in the amniotic fluid are derived principally from the fetal lung. Lecithin biosynthesis is an index of alveolar function. When the lecithin/sphingomyelin ratio is greater than 2.0, respiratory distress syndrome, a complication of low birth weight, probably will not develop.

• • •

References

Alter BP: Prenatal diagnosis of hemoglobinopathies and other hematologic diseases. *J Pediatr* 1979;**95**:501.

Ashe JR, Schofield TA, Gram MR: The retention of calcium, iron, phosphorus and magnesium during pregnancy: The adequacy of prenatal diets with and without supplementation. *Am J Clin Nutr* 1979;**32**:286.

Atlay RD et al: Treating heartburn in pregnancy: Comparison of acid and alkali mixtures. *Br Med J* 1978;**2**:919.

Beazley JM, Swinhoe JR: Body weight in parous women: Is there any alteration between successive pregnancies? *Acta Obstet Gynecol Scand* 1979;**58**:45.

Bonebreak CR et al: Routine chest roentgenography in pregnancy. *JAMA* 1978;**240**:2747.

Chamberlain G: A reexamination of antenatal care. *J Roy Soc Med* 1978;**71**:662.

Crandon AJ: Maternal anxiety and neonatal well-being. *J Psychosom Res* 1979;**23**:113.

Edozien JC, Switzer BR, Bryan RB: Medical evaluation of the special supplemental food program for women, infants and children. *Am J Clin Nutr* 1979;**32**:677.

Emerson K Jr et al: Caloric cost of normal pregnancy. *Obstet Gynecol* 1972;**40**:794.

Fishburne JI: Physiology and disease of the respiratory system in pregnancy: A review. *J Reprod Med* 1979;**22**:177.

Galbraith RS et al: Clinical prediction of intrauterine growth retardation. *Am J Obstet Gynecol* 1979;**133**:281.

Golbus M: Teratology for the obstetrician: Current status. *Obstet Gynecol* 1980;**55**:269.

Howard F, Hill J: Drugs in pregnancy. *Obstet Gynecol Surv* 1979;**34**:643.

Jones M, Battaglia F: Intrauterine growth retardation. *Am J Obstet Gynecol* 1977;**127**:540.

Lederman E et al: Maternal psychological and physiologic correlates of fetal-newborn health status. *Am J Obstet Gynecol* 1981;**139**:956.

Leon J: High-risk pregnancy: Graphic representation of the maternal and fetal risks. *Am J Obstet Gynecol* 1973;**117**:497.

Massey EW, Cefalo RC: Carpal tunnel syndrome in pregnancy. *Contemp Obstet Gynecol* (June) 1977;**9**:39

McCalum WD, Brinkley JF: Estimation of fetal weight from ultrasonic measurements. *Am J Obstet Gynecol* 1979;**133**:195.

Morrison JC, Whybrew WJ, Bucovaz ET: The L/S ratio and "shake" test in normal and abnormal pregnancies. *Obstet Gynecol* 1978;**52**:410.

Mulvihill J, Yeager A: Fetal alcohol syndrome. *Teratology* 1976;**13**:345.

Newton RW et al: Psychosocial stress in pregnancy and its relation to the onset of premature labor. *Br Med J* 1979;**2**:411.

Niswander KR, Jackson EC: Physical characteristics of the gravida and their association with birth weight and perinatal death. *Am J Obstet Gynecol* 1974;**119**:306.

Oakes GK, Chez RA: Nutrition during pregnancy: With emphasis on overweight and underweight patients. *Contemp Obstet Gynecol* 1974;**4**:147.

Osofsky H: Relationships between nutrition during pregnancy and subsequent infant and child development. *Obstet Gynecol Surv* 1975;**30**:227.

Robinson JS: Growth of the fetus. *Br Med Bull* 1979;**35**:137.

Rosett HL, Weiner L, Edelin KC: Strategies for prevention of fetal alcohol effects. *Obstet Gynecol* 1981;**57**:1.

Sabbagha RE: Intrauterine growth retardation: Antenatal diagnosis by ultrasound. *Obstet Gynecol* 1978;**52**:252.

Schneider GT: Sexually transmissible vaginal infections in pregnancy. (2 parts.) *Postgrad Med* (Apr) 1979;**65**:177, 185.

30 | Obstetric Analgesia & Anesthesia

John S. McDonald, MD

Analgesia is the loss of perception of pain. It may be local, affecting only a small area of the body; regional, affecting a larger portion; or it may even be total. Local and regional analgesia are used in obstetrics to relieve pain associated with labor and delivery without jeopardizing the fetus. Analgesia may also be achieved by the use of hypnosis (suggestion), systemic medication, or inhalation agents.

Anesthesia is the loss of ability to perceive touch, pain, and other sensations. It may be induced by various agents and techniques. Pain relief commonly is associated with total loss of sensation by the use of **general anesthesia.** This definition is not strictly correct, however, because total loss of sensation can be accomplished in other ways. Anesthesia has long been used in obstetrics to produce total loss of sensation for vaginal as well as abdominal delivery.

The terms analgesia and anesthesia are sometimes confused in common usage. Analgesia should be used to denote those states in which loss of perception of pain only is involved and anesthesia to denote the states in which perceptions of other sensations and, especially, mental awareness are lost also. Attempts have been made to divide anesthesia into various components. Anesthesia may be considered to be composed of analgesia, amnesia, relaxation, and loss of reflex activity. Viewed in this way, analgesia can be regarded as a component of anesthesia.

ANATOMY OF PAIN

Because agreement on a definition of pain has eluded scholars for centuries, it may be academic to argue that the parturient's response to the stimuli of labor should be defined as pain. Nevertheless, one should appreciate that the "pain response" is a response of the total personality and cannot be dissected systematically and scientifically. The obstetrician is obligated to provide a comfortable or at least tolerable labor and delivery. Many patients are tense and apprehensive at the onset of labor, although there may be little or no discomfort. Success can be judged only by the patient's response.

The evolution of the pain of the first stage of labor was originally described (Cleland) as involving spinal segments T11 and T12. Subsequent research has determined that L1 is involved also (Bonica). The discomfort is associated with dilatation and effacement of the cervix. Sensory pathways that convey disturbing impulses of the first stage of labor include the uterine plexus, the inferior hypogastric plexus, the middle hypogastric plexus, the superior hypogastric plexus, the lumbar and lower thoracic sympathetic chain, and the 11th and 12th thoracic spinal segments. These impulses may be selectively interrupted at many points along this chain by local or regional nerve block.

Pain of the second stage of labor undoubtedly is produced by distention of the vagina and perineum. Sensory pathways from these areas are conveyed by branches of the pudendal nerve via the dorsal nerve of the clitoris, the labial nerves, and the inferior hemorrhoidal nerves. These are the major sensory branches to the perineum. Nevertheless, other nerves may play a role in perineal innervation: the ilioinguinal nerves, the genital branch of the genitofemoral nerves, and the perineal branch of the posterior femoral cutaneous nerves.

Although the major portion of the perineum is innervated by the 3 major branches of the pudendal nerve, innervation by the other nerves mentioned may be important in some patients. The type of pain reported may be an ache in the back or loins (referred pain, perhaps from the cervix), a cramp in the uterus (due to fundal contraction), or a "bursting" or "splitting" sensation in the distal genital canal or pudendum (due to dilatation of the cervix, vagina, and introitus).

Dystocia, which is usually quite painful, may be due to fetopelvic disproportion; tetanic, prolonged, or dysrhythmic uterine contractions; intrapartal infection; and many other causes (see Chapter 39).

Hundreds of procedures and agents have been used to assuage pain in childbirth. Every method and drug used probably has some advantage, but a perfect method has not yet been discovered and probably never will be. The following types of pain relief are in use today: (1) positive conditioning of the patient; (2) hypnosis; (3) analgesics, which raise the patient's pain threshold; (4) amnestics, which obscure the memory of pain and associated disagreeable experiences; (5) regional analgesia, which interrupts afferent pain pathways; and (6) general anesthesia, which prevents central perception of discomfort.

Ideally, obstetric deliveries today should be conducted only in maternity hospitals where equipment and specially trained personnel are available.

TECHNIQUES OF ANALGESIA WITHOUT THE USE OF DRUGS

Psychophysical Methods (See also Chapter 31.)

Essentially 3 distinct psychologic techniques have been developed as a means of facilitating the birth process and making it a positive emotional experience: "natural childbirth," psychoprophylaxis, and hypnosis. So-called natural childbirth was developed by Grantly Dick Read in the early 1930s and popularized in his book *Childbirth Without Fear*. Read's approach emphasized the reduction of tension to induce relaxation. The psychoprophylactic technique was developed by Velvovski, who published the results of his work from Russia in 1950. In Russia in the mid 1950s, it became evident that obstetric psychoprophylaxis was a useful substitute for poorly administered or dangerously conducted anesthesia for labor and delivery. This method was later introduced in France by Lamaze. Hypnosis for pain relief has achieved periodic spurts of popularity since the early 1800s and depends upon the power of suggestion.

Many obstetricians argue that psychoprophylaxis can largely eliminate the pain of childbirth by diminishing cortical appreciation of pain impulses rather than by depressing cortical function, which is what occurs with drug-induced analgesia. Relaxation, suggestion, concentration, and motivation are factors which overlap other methods of preparation in childbirth. Some of them are closely related to hypnosis.

Admittedly, these techniques may reduce anxiety, tension, and fear significantly; moreover they can provide the parturient with a valuable understanding of the physiologic changes that occur during labor and delivery. In addition, they serve as an occasion for closer understanding and communication between the patient and her spouse, who may be an important source of comfort to the patient during the stressful process of birth. If these techniques do no more than this, they deserve the commendation of the obstetrician.

Studies undertaken to assess the effectiveness of these techniques have reported widely divergent results ranging from as low as 10–20% effective to as high as 70–80% effective. It seems clear that the overall benefit is best judged by the parturient herself with validation by the observations of attendants. As is no doubt true in other aspects of medical practice where emotional overlay and subjective reporting play a role in the evaluation of specific types of therapy, the personality and enthusiasm of the doctor have a lot to do with what the patient will think and say about what has just happened. Skeptical practitioners cannot expect to accomplish very much with these techniques.

It should be obvious that none of these techniques should be "forced" on a patient even by a skillful practitioner. The patient must not be made to feel that she will have failed if she does not choose to complete her labor and delivery without analgesic medication. It must be made clear to her from the outset that she is *expected* to ask for help if she feels she wants or needs it. All things considered, these techniques should be viewed as adjuncts to other analgesic methods rather than substitutes for them.

The effectiveness of hypnosis is partially due to the well-known though incompletely understood mechanisms by which emotional and other central processes can influence one's total responses to the pain experience. Verbal suggestion and somatosensory stimulation may help to alleviate discomfort associated with the first stage of labor. In addition, hypnotic states may provide apparent analgesia and amnesia for distressing, anxiety-provoking experience. Finally, hypnotic techniques may substantially improve the parturient's outlook and behavior by reducing fear and apprehension. However, there are certain practical points to consider in regard to hypnosis because the time needed to establish a suitable relationship between the physician and patient is often more than can be made available in the course of a busy medical practice.

Psychoprophylaxis

A currently popular technique of "psychophysiologic preparation" involves educating the patient about her body functions and the physiology of labor. It emphasizes positive attitudes and stresses the need for good medical care. The goal of this technique is to use few if any drugs during the first and second stages of labor. Under optimal circumstances, it substantially reduces or even eliminates the need for narcotic drugs in the first stage of labor. When combined with certain analgesic "regional techniques" for late first stage pain relief and second stage analgesia, it approaches the ideal in management of pain relief for the childbirth experience.

TYPES OF ANALGESICS, AMNESTICS, & ANESTHETICS

Pharmacologic Aspects

A. Route of Administration: Systemic techniques of analgesia and anesthesia include both oral and parenteral routes of administration. Parenteral administration includes subcutaneous, intramuscular, and intravenous injection. Sedatives, tranquilizers, and analgesics are usually given by intramuscular injection. In some cases, the intravenous route is preferred.

The advantages of intravenous administration may be listed as follows: (1) Avoidance of variable rates of uptake due to poor vascular supply in fat or muscle. (2) Prompt onset of effect. (3) Titration of effect, avoiding the "peak effect" of an intramuscular bolus. (4) Smaller effective doses because of earlier onset of action.

The disadvantages of intravenous injection are inadvertent arterial injection and the depressant effect of overdosage. The advantage of smaller dosage overshadows the disadvantages.

$$R:NH^+ + OH^- \longrightarrow R:N + HOH$$

$$\text{Cation} \longleftarrow \text{Base}$$

$$pH = pK_a + \log \frac{\text{Base}}{\text{Cation}}$$

$$Q/T = K\left[\frac{A(C_M - C_F)}{D}\right]$$

Figure 30–1. Local anesthetics are weak bases coexisting as undissociated free base and dissociated cation. Their proportion can be calculated by means of the Henderson-Hasselbalch equation.

Figure 30–2. Fick's law. Q/T is rate of diffusion; A is the transfer surface; C_M is maternal drug concentration; C_F is fetal drug concentration; D is membrane thickness; and K is the diffusion constant of the drug.

B. Physical and Chemical Factors: Anesthetics penetrate body cells by passing a lipid membrane boundary. This membrane is not receptive to charged (ionized) drugs but is permeable to un-ionized forms of drugs. Much of the total drug transfer is dependent upon the degree of lipid solubility. Therefore, local anesthetics are characterized by aromatic rings that are lipophilic. Hence, all local anesthetics are lipid-soluble. In addition, the intermediate amine radical of a local anesthetic is a weak base that in aqueous solutions exists partly as undissociated free base and partly as dissociated cation. Fig 30–1 shows the equilibrium for such an existence and the Henderson-Hasselbalch equation, with which one can determine the proportion of the anesthetic in the charged and uncharged form. The ratio of the cation to the base form of the drug is important because the base form is responsible for penetration and tissue diffusion of the local anesthetic while the cation form is responsible for local analgesia when the drug contacts the nerve structure.

The pK_a of a drug is the pH at which equal proportions of the free base and cation form occur. Most local anesthetics used in obstetric analgesia have pK_a values ranging from 7.7 to 9.1 (Table 30–1). Since the pH of maternal blood is ≥ 7.4, the pK_a of local anesthetics is so close that significant changes in maternal and fetal acid-base balance may result in fluxes in the base versus the cation forms of the drug. For example, a rising pH will shift a given amount of local anesthetic cation to the base form, and, conversely, a fall in pH will generate more of the cationic form.

Physical factors are important in drug transfer also, eg, the molecular size of the drug. For example, drugs with molecular weights under 600 cross the placenta without difficulty, whereas those with molecular weights in excess of 1000 do not. A molecule such as digoxin (MW 780.95) has been

found to cross the ovine placenta very poorly. Molecular weights of most local anesthetics are in the 200–300 range. From the physical aspect, most local anesthetics cross the maternal-fetal barrier by simple diffusion according to Fick's law (Fig 30–2), which states that the rate of diffusion depends upon the concentration gradient of the drug between the maternal and fetal compartments and the relationship of the thickness and total surface available for transfer.

C. Placental Transfer: Factors other than the physical or chemical properties of a drug may affect its transfer across the placenta. These factors include the rate and route of drug administration and the distribution, metabolism, and excretion of the drug by the mother and fetus. Although Fick's law may appear to be a simple method of determining drug transfer, other complexities exist such as differential blood flow on either side of the placenta, volume of maternal and fetal blood, and various shunts in the intervillous space that are important determinants of the final amount of drug a fetus may receive. In addition, certain maternal disorders, eg, hypertensive cardiovascular disease, diabetes, and preeclampsia-eclampsia, may be associated with alteration of placental blood flow and may in some way affect the extent of drug distribution.

As the placenta matures, there is a progressive reduction in the thickness of the epithelial trophoblastic layer, so that the thickness of the tissue layers between the maternal and fetal compartments may be decreased 10-fold (from as much as 25 μm in early gestation to 2 μm at term in some species). As gestation progresses, the surface area of the placenta increases also. At term, these changes in physical structure tend to favor improved transfer of drugs.

Alterations in uterine blood flow may be induced by spontaneous labor, oxytocic drugs, hypotension, or aortocaval obstruction. All of these, although quite different etiologically, affect drug transfer and bring about transient reduction in intervillous space perfusion. For example, placental transfer of thiobarbiturates may be reduced by mechanical aortic compression or by reduction of end-artery perfusion secondary to a hypertonic uterine contraction. In either case, reduction in placental transfer may be expected because maternal cardiac output to the end organs, eg, the uterus, placenta, and fetus, is altered. In contrast, venous obstruction with intervillous sequestration may increase the interval over which a given drug comes in

Table 30–1. pK_as of the more commonly used local anesthetics.

Drug	Brand Name	pK_a
Bupivacaine	Marcaine	8.1
Chloroprocaine	Nesacaine	8.7
Etidocaine	Duranest	7.7
Lidocaine	Xylocaine	7.9

contact with the diffusing membrane, so that the total amount of drug transferred may be facilitated instead of reduced. At the same time, fetal cardiac output is important, since drugs that reduce it may also tend to reduce the uptake of other drugs because of depressed fetal circulation.

Placental transfer is also affected by the pH of the blood on both sides of the placenta. The pH of the blood on the fetal side of the placenta is normally 0.1–0.2 units lower than that on the maternal side. Therefore, passage of drug to the fetal unit results in a tendency for more of the drug to exist in the ionized state. Because the maternal/fetal equilibrium is established only between the *un-ionized* fraction of the drug on either side of the barrier, this physiologic differential will expedite maternal-fetal transfer of drug. With more drug in the ionized form in the fetal unit, the *new* equilibrium that arises results in a greater *total* (ionized plus un-ionized) drug load in the fetus. Because the pK_a values of commonly used local anesthetics are closer to the maternal blood pH, these agents tend to accumulate on the fetal side of the placenta. This is also true of other basic drugs such as morphine, meperidine, and propranolol. Further decreases in the fetal pH lead to additional drug entrapment in the fetus. For acidic drugs (eg, thiopental) the shift in total drug concentration is in the opposite direction, ie, toward the maternal side of the placenta.

In summary, the rate of transfer of a drug is governed mainly by (1) lipid solubility, (2) degree of drug ionization, (3) placental blood flow, (4) molecular weight, (5) placental metabolism, and (6) protein binding.

D. Fetal Distribution: After a drug deposited in the maternal compartment passes through the maternal-fetal barrier, the drug must reach the fetus and be distributed. The response of the fetus and newborn is dependent upon drug concentration in vessel-rich organs, eg, the brain, heart, and liver. Naturally, this response is similar to the mother's and depends upon the pharmacologic concentration of the drug in the vital tissues.

Placental blood is a mixture of blood already in the intervillous reservoir (this can be thought of as similar to the functional residual capacity of the lungs) and fresh blood coming from the fetus for removal of CO_2 and waste products of metabolism. Drugs being transferred from the maternal to the fetal compartment, then, are diluted before distribution to the various fetal vital organs. In fact, about 85% of the blood in the umbilical vein, which passes from the placenta to the fetus, passes through the fetal liver and then into the inferior vena cava, whereas the remainder bypasses the liver and enters the vena cava primarily via the ductus venosus. Final vena caval drug concentration is further reduced by an admixture of blood coming from the

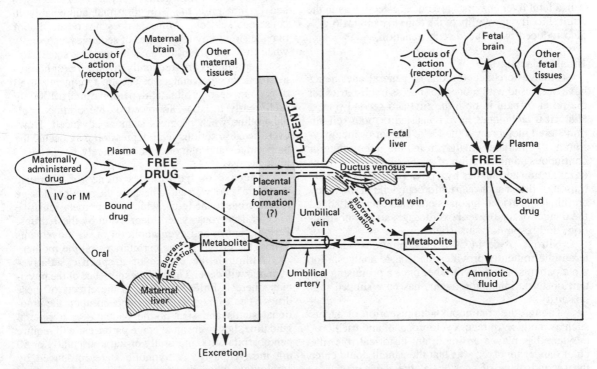

Figure 30–3. Relationship between maternal and fetal compartments and distribution of drugs between them. Drug is passed from the maternal compartment via the placenta (a partial barrier) to the fetal compartment where the principles of drug dynamics, ie, distribution, biotransformation, and excretion, determine the eventual specific organ tissue levels. One purely mechanical barrier exists between the maternal and fetal compartments that attains importance in the late first and second stage of labor—the umbilical cord, which is susceptible to partial and total occlusion. (Reproduced, with permission, from Mirkin BL: Drug distribution in pregnancy. In: *Fetal Pharmacology.* Boreus L [editor]. Raven Press, 1973.)

lower extremities, the abdominal viscera, and the upper extremities and thorax. Blood from the right atrium shunts from right to left through the foramen ovale into the left atrium, resulting in a final concentration on the left side of the heart that is only slightly lower than that in the vena cava. The amount of drug ultimately reaching a vital organ, then, is related to that organ's blood supply. Since the central nervous system is the most highly vascularized fetal organ, it receives the greatest amount of drug. Once the drug reaches the fetal liver, it may either be bound to protein or metabolized. Fetal drug uptake is increased by asphyxia in utero, which increases blood-brain barrier permeability.

The uptake of drug by fetal tissues can be very rapid after either intravenous or epidural administration. Measurable concentrations of local anesthetics have been found in fetal tissues as early as 1–2 minutes after injection. The fetal liver has been shown to metabolize drugs and numerous substrates as early as the second trimester; this ability improves to term. Lipid solubility of a drug is important in developing concentrations in certain organs with high lipid content such as the adrenal, ovary, liver, and brain.

Drug metabolism and excretion are the final features of the fetal distribution picture. Although many enzymes active in the fetal liver are capable of metabolizing drugs, there is greater susceptibility to depressant drugs, eg, narcotics and barbiturates, because fetal liver enzymes are not as effective as in the adult. Finally, the ability of the fetus to excrete drugs is also reduced by reduced renal function.

Inhalant Analgesics

Analgesic concentrations of general anesthetics have been used with moderate success in obstetrics for the relief of pain in both the first and second stages. Historical techniques have consisted of both self-administered methods via the Duke inhaler or methoxyflurane (Penthrane) Analgizer and the intermittent or continuous administration of analgesic concentrations of inhalation anesthetics by a physician. Self-administration of drugs such as trichloroethylene (Trilene) by an inhaler provided inconsistent analgesia and added the danger of inadvertent overdosage, airway obstruction, and respiratory insufficiency.

Nitrous oxide in 50% concentrations administered intermittently provides inadequate analgesia for most patients. Methoxyflurane, once a promising potent obstetric inhalation agent, has now slipped into obscurity.

Though the continuous administration of agents such as methoxyflurane, cyclopropane, and trichloroethylene has played an important historical role, the chief danger involved was that the patient could enter the second plane of anesthesia, the stage of excitement.

The use of potent inhalation anesthetics (halothane, enflurane, or isoflurane) is also practical in obstetric practice. Enflurane (Ethrane) in subanesthetic concentrations has been used safely and effectively for normal vaginal deliveries, with no detectable evidence of renal or other toxicity in mothers or newborns. Isoflurane (Forane), a new halogenated ether anesthetic agent, will most likely be used similarly. Someone who is familiar with the physicochemical features of these agents must be available; it is a mistake to allow a novice to administer these agents in the belief that no harm can be done. Administration of any potent inhalation anesthetic can result in unanticipated serious complications if adequate supervision is not available.

Since methoxyflurane, cyclopropane, and trichloroethylene all have inherent disadvantages and have fallen into disuse, only nitrous oxide (continuous), halothane, enflurane, and isoflurane are currently being used as inhalant analgesics in subanesthetic concentrations.

Sedatives (Hypnotics)

The principal use of the sedative-hypnotic drugs is to produce drowsiness. For many years, these drugs were the only ones available to reduce anxiety and induce drowsiness. The latent phase of the first stage of labor may be managed by either psychologic support alone or utilization of the sedative-hypnotic compounds. Psychologic support may at times be complemented by the use of sedatives. When properly utilized, these drugs induce tranquility and an enhanced feeling of well-being. They are poor analgesics and do not raise the pain threshold appreciably in conscious subjects. Amnesia does not occur. Labor may be slowed by large doses of sedatives, especially when they are given too early in the first stage.

Barbiturates are frequently given with (or before) a narcotic or other analgesic. The most frequently used drugs are secobarbital and pentobarbital, 100 mg orally early in labor, followed by meperidine or alphaprodine when progress is more advanced. However, because serious fetal depression may occur, the barbiturates and narcotics should rarely be given simultaneously.

The use of barbiturates alone for obstetric analgesia is not warranted because the required dosage is dangerous to the fetus, which is extremely sensitive to central nervous system depression by these drugs. Periodic apnea and even abolition of all movements outlast the effects of the barbiturates on the mother.

Although the choice of a specific sedative-hypnotic will depend upon the experience of the physician, there is little difference in the effects of these drugs. The average dose will depend upon the emotional status and size of the patient. As a general guideline, however, an average parturient will require pentobarbital, 100 mg orally or intramuscularly or 50 mg intravenously. A hypnotic state, produced by employing twice this amount, is not now recommended.

Tranquilizers & Amnestics

These drugs, used principally to relieve apprehension and anxiety, will produce a calm state. In addition, they may potentiate the effects of other sedatives and analgesics. Although an analgesic potentiating effect is often claimed for this group of agents, it has not been definitely demonstrated. Hydroxyzine (Atarax, Vistaril) and diazepam (Valium) are popular tranquilizer-amnestics. Scopolamine, which was widely popular in obstetrics in the past century, produces no analgesia but has a mild sedative and marked amnestic effect. With the advent of the new tranquilizer-amnestic drugs, there has been a gradual trend away from the use of scopolamine in labor. Although it is a potent amnestic drug, it may precipitate wild irrational behavior. Diazepam is popular for use in the first stage of labor because it has a good tranquilizing effect and because it makes it possible to reduce the dosage of analgesic. Diazepam has a long chemical half-life. Preliminary reports reveal that its use in the first stage of labor in dosages of 5–10 mg every 4 hours has no deleterious effect upon the newborn. Diazepam readily crosses the placenta and is found in significant concentrations in fetal plasma. Nevertheless, studies on mothers and newborn infants have not established a correlation between the administration of diazepam and neonatal depression. One of the primary reasons for this may be that diazepam has very little effect on cardiovascular function and, in low doses, a negligible effect upon minute ventilation. One of the controversies over this drug concerns the sodium benzoate and benzoic acid buffers found in the preparation. Both compounds are potent uncouplers of the bilirubin-albumin complex, and some investigators have suggested that the neonate may be more susceptible to kernicterus because of an increase in free circulating bilirubin. However, because injectable diazepam is effective in the treatment of human newborn seizure disorders, opiate withdrawal, and tetanus, and since it is regarded as a useful adjunct in obstetric analgesia, a study was undertaken in animals in which comparable quantities of sodium benzoate were injected to determine whether significant amounts of bilirubin would be made available to the circulation. The results supported the hypothesis that diazepam was safe in clinical neonatal medicine when used within the dosage range recommended, but little direct information is available concerning use of diazepam in human newborns. At present, diazepam is not recommended if the neonate is premature, because of the threat of kernicterus. Other potential side-effects related to the use of diazepam are fetal hypotonia, hypothermia, and a loss of beat-to-beat variability in the fetal heart rate. If diazepam can be shown to have a beneficial effect upon the mother but only a minimal effect upon the normal fetus, it will become an important drug in the management of anxiety and excitement in the first stage of labor.

Narcotic Analgesics

Systemic analgesic drugs, including narcotics, are commonly used in the first stage of labor because they produce both a state of analgesia and mood elevation. The favored drugs are codeine, 60 mg intramuscularly, or meperidine (Demerol), 50–100 mg intramuscularly or 25–50 mg (titrated) intravenously. Alphaprodine (Nisentil) is a synthetic analgesic often used in obstetrics because of its rapid action after intramuscular injection. One advantage is its shorter duration of action—about 1–2 hours, as compared with 2–4 hours for meperidine. In 40- to 60-mg increments, it is comparable to 50–100 mg of meperidine. The combination of morphine and scopolamine was once popular for its "twilight sleep" effect but is rarely used now. Nausea, vomiting, cough suppression, intestinal stasis, and diminution in frequency, intensity, and duration of uterine contractions in the early first stage of labor are common undesirable effects. Also, minimal amnesia is desired.

Morphine or comparable opiates will not interrupt premature labor. Narcotics affect the fetus adversely by depressing all of its central nervous system functions, especially the activity of the respiratory center. Gestational age, weight, trauma, and long labor enhance the susceptibility of the fetus to narcosis.

Thiobarbiturates

Intravenous anesthetics such as thiopental (Pentothal) and thiamylal (Surital) are widely employed in general surgery. However, in less than 4 minutes after injection into the mother's vein, the concentrations of the drug in the fetal and maternal blood will be equal. When a very rapid delivery is accomplished after thiopental, the baby may be so depressed that it cannot be resuscitated easily. Intravenous anesthesia should therefore not be employed as a primary agent in obstetric delivery.

Rectally Administered Drugs

This technique was used in the past before the more effective methods described here became commonplace. It is now difficult to justify the use of rectally administered agents such as ether-oil mixtures, paraldehyde, or barbiturates because other systemic or regionally administered agents can be titrated better to the patient's specific needs and have a more reliable onset of action and more predictable effect on the mother and fetus.

Uterine Relaxants

Magnesium sulfate effects a neuromuscular blocking action by antagonizing the action of Ca^{2+} on the release of acetylcholine. Its use is one of the mainstays of management of preeclampsia-eclampsia, because it causes uterine relaxation and peripheral vasodilatation by blocking the release of catecholamines from the adrenal gland. Its muscle-relaxing properties are useful in controlling muscular activity associated with convulsions. In the doses recommended, fetal well-being appears unaffected, and studies in monkeys have indicated that magnesium sulfate can even cause an increase in uterine blood flow. From an anesthetic point of view, one must recall that magnesium sulfate will potentiate the effects of both depolarizing and nondepolarizing neuromuscular blocking agents, even to the point of respiratory arrest. Administration of calcium does not completely reverse this effect, and ventilatory support may be required. Other possible potential side-effects to the mother related to the use of intravenous magnesium sulfate are hypocalcemia and anticoagulation. Fetal side-effects related to hypermagnesemia include respiratory depression, weak reflexes, lack of motor tone, and decreased sucking. Magnesium is excreted via the kidneys, and therapeutic levels are in the range of 4–7 mEq/L.

Beta-sympathomimetic drugs are also employed now to inhibit uterine activity and to increase uteroplacental perfusion. Beta₂ agonists such as terbutaline or ritodrine have been associated with minimally increased fetal risk. Maternal side-effects are related to beta₁-mediated cardiovascular stimulation. Since the glomerular filtration rate may decrease and plasma volume increase by up to 50%, the patient's fluid load must be carefully evaluated. To be effective, these drugs must increase the maternal heart rate by about 20 beats per minute as a side-effect. As long as uteroplacental perfusion is preserved, there is no increased risk for the fetus.

Potentiating Drugs

Phenothiazine drugs potentiate certain of the desirable (as well as a few of the undesirable) effects of the analgesics, amnestics, and general anesthetics.

Ketamine

The phencyclidine derivative ketamine produces analgesia and anesthesia by a dissociative interruption of afferent pathways from cortical perception. It has become a useful and widely employed adjunctive agent in obstetrics, because maternal cardiovascular status and uterine blood flow are well maintained. In low doses of 0.25–0.5 mg/kg intravenously, effective maternal analgesia results but without loss of consciousness or protective reflexes. For cesarean section, 0.4–0.5 mg/kg intravenously can be followed by 50% nitrous oxide, oxygen, and a muscle relaxant. Ketamine stimulates the cardiovascular system to maintain heart rate, blood pressure, and cardiac output and therefore is useful in complicated situations of maternal hypotension/hemorrhage. Doses greater than 1 mg/kg have been reported to increase the incidence of respiratory depression in neonates and should not be used in any situation involving fetal distress.

Inhalation Anesthetics

This group includes a number of potent agents that can often be used for major operative procedures. By far the most commonly used inhalation agents at present are nitrous oxide, enflurane, and halothane. Isoflurane will undoubtedly be added to this list in the very near future.

Other Drugs (Oxytocics, Vasopressors)

Oxytocin is used in the first and third stages of labor and preferably should be administered intrave-nously. Careful titration of dosage to achieve the desired uterine effect is necessary when this drug is used as a uterine stimulant. This is ideally achieved with some type of automated, graduated pump so that precise dosage can be achieved. For the third stage, where the aim is to provide uterine tetany to minimize blood loss, the intravenous route again is preferable. The main cardiovascular side-effect following intravenous injection of large amounts of oxytocin is hypotension due to a decrease in maternal myocardial contractility. Chemical sympathetic blockade enhances this effect. In the presence of vasospastic disease, shock can ensue. Hypotension and arrhythmias of a transient nature may also result when concentrated intravenous injections of oxytocin are used during general anesthesia, especially when halothane is employed. In general, reactions to and interactions with oxytocin can be prevented by the use of intramuscular injections or dilute intravenous solutions (10 IU/L of fluid) and slower infusion rates during labor (1–10 mIU/min).

Vasopressors are rarely indicated and are used only in cases of refractory hypotension not improved by uterine displacement, intravenous fluid administration, and elevation of the legs. When needed, ephedrine is the drug of choice, given in increments of 10–20 mg intravenously, or 25 mg intramuscularly for a more prolonged effect. Ephedrine preserves placental blood flow at doses effective in supporting maternal circulation.

General Comments & Precautions

(1) If the patient is prepared psychologically for her experience, she will require less medication. Anticipate and dispel her fears during the antenatal period and in early labor. Never promise a painless labor.

(2) Nurse anesthetists, trained by and working under the close supervision of physician anesthesiologists, generally function very well in obstetrics. They must be thoroughly indoctrinated regarding obstetric problems and must be capable of functioning efficiently whenever emergency resuscitation is required. Although nurse anesthetists are commonly restricted from instituting regional anesthetics because of legal liabilities, they are usually permitted to administer inhalation or parenteral analgesia and anesthesia.

(3) Individualize the treatment of every patient, because each one reacts differently. Unfavorable reactions occur to all drugs.

(4) Always think in terms of normal maternal-fetal physiology rather than the requests of the patient and her family. The overly demanding patient and the yielding physician are a perfect combination for tragedy.

(5) Know the drug you intend to administer. Be familiar with its limitations, dangers, and contraindications as well as its advantages.

(6) Do not render the patient unconscious in the first stage of labor. Some pain relief may be necessary, and relaxation may speed labor; but total amnesia and analgesia may be detrimental to the mother and her

infant. Mild degrees of fetal asphyxia are not easily discernible but are often harmful.

(7) Avoid injections in an area of skin infection.

(8) Spinal, caudal, and other anesthetic blocks are surgical procedures requiring scrupulous preparation and aseptic technique.

(9) All the drugs discussed in this section rapidly cross the maternal compartment and attain significant levels in the fetal compartment. In addition, most of these drugs have a central nervous system depressant effect. Although they may afford the desired effect on the mother, they may exert a mild to severe depressant effect upon the fetus or newborn. The ideal drug will have an optimal beneficial effect upon the mother and a minimal depressant effect upon the offspring. In addition, physicians in attendance should utilize small amounts of the above-mentioned drugs titrated intravenously. The fetal liver is not as efficient in drug biodegradation as the adult liver. Remembering this fact and realizing that there are other ways to effect sedation and analgesia in the first stage of labor should tend to reduce the use of these drugs in late labor. Although the reduction in use of these drugs has not been substantial as yet, the reduction in milligram dosage has been marked. This admirable trend has received impetus from physicians who realize that women properly educated in the antepartum period about the physiology and mechanics of labor require less medication.

TYPES OF REGIONAL ANALGESICS

Regional analgesia is achieved by injection of a local anesthetic (Table 30–1) around the nerves that pass from spinal segments to the peripheral nerves responsible for sensory innervation of a portion of the body. Regional nerve blocks used in obstetrics include the following: (1) lumbar epidural and caudal epidural block, (2) subarachnoid block, (3) lumbar sympathetic block, (4) spinal anesthesia, (5) paracervical block, and (6) pudendal block.

The practicality and safety of regional analgesia administered by the obstetrician-gynecologist depend upon his or her knowledge and skill as well as on the seriousness of the need for analgesia and the extent and type of operative procedure. General anesthesia and major block procedures (eg, spinal anesthesia) require continuous monitoring even when used for minor surgery. The obstetrician-gynecologist should never attempt to administer a general or an intra- or extrathecal anesthetic and then perform the delivery or surgery except in an emergency. Nonetheless, the obstetrician-gynecologist may have to assume responsibility for the management of anesthesia when a nurse anesthetist or a trainee cannot be supervised by a qualified physician.

Infiltration of a local anesthetic drug and pudendal block analgesia carry minimal risks. The hazards increase with the amount of drug employed. The safety and suitability of regional anesthesia depend upon the proper selection of the drug and the patient and the obstetrician-gynecologist's knowledge, experience, and expertise in the diagnosis and treatment of possible anesthetic and other complications.

Selection of Patient

Good candidates for regional anesthesia are healthy, mature women; poor candidates include young, emotionally unstable, or medically compromised ones, ie, those with preeclampsia-eclampsia, hypotension, or hypovolemia. Tense, fearful, psychoneurotic, or psychotic patients may require general anesthesia, and the experienced obstetrician-gynecologist should not try to persuade such women to accept regional anesthesia except for minor procedures.

Patients with severe obstetric, gynecologic, cardiac, or pulmonary disorders may do well with regional block anesthesia, but general anesthesia may be less hazardous if a prolonged procedure is anticipated. Large amounts of local anesthetics may jeopardize the patient. Moreover, the anxiety and discomfort during administration of the local anesthetic and surgery increase epinephrine secretion and O_2 consumption. This usually imposes a greater threat of cardiorespiratory decompensation than a well-managed general anesthetic.

Preparation of the Patient

The woman who is well-informed and has good rapport with her obstetrician-gynecologist generally is a calm and cooperative candidate for regional or general anesthesia. Sedatives or tranquilizers, eg, barbiturates or promazines, can be used to relieve anxiety. Nonetheless, the patient who is particularly susceptible or who receives excessive doses of barbiturates may become excited and confused, even unmanageable. Attention to detail and the addition of small amounts of narcotic intravenously in increments before and during the procedure generally produce mild euphoria and prevent these problems. On the other hand, barbiturates that increase confusion and lower pain tolerance are contraindicated when the patient is disoriented or in pain. Atropine should be given to all preoperative patients, but barbiturates and narcotics should not be given to cesarean section candidates because of possible neonatal respiratory depression, most likely in the immature or premature.

For elective surgery, the patient's stomach should be empty. Fortunately, vomiting is not a serious problem during regional anesthesia in a conscious patient in good physical condition. In contrast, if the patient is debilitated or heavily sedated, the patient may vomit and aspirate vomitus—often a critical complication. When general anesthesia is necessary—particularly when the patient has eaten recently or when a prolonged procedure is anticipated—endotracheal intubation is indicated. Preoperative medication is not used for obstetric patients.

Local Anesthetic Agents (Table 30–2)

A local anesthetic drug blocks the action potential of nerves when their axons are exposed to the medication. Precisely how this occurs is still being debated, but local anesthetic agents may act by modifying the ionic permeability of the cell membrane to stabilize its resting potential. The smaller the nerve fiber, the more sensitive it is to local anesthetics because the susceptibility of individual nerve fibers is inversely proportionate to the cross-sectional diameters of the fibers. Hence, with regional anesthesia, the patient's perception of light touch, pain, and temperature and her capacity for vasomotor control are obtunded sooner and with a smaller concentration of the drug than is the perception of pressure or the function of motor nerves to striated muscles.

Only anesthetic drugs which are completely reversible and nonirritating and which cause minimal toxicity are clinically acceptable. Other desirable properties of regional anesthetic agents include rapidity of onset, predictability of duration, and ease of sterilization. Table 30–2 summarizes the local anesthetics commonly employed in obstetrics and gynecology together with their uses and doses.

All local anesthetics have certain undesirable dose-related side-effects when absorbed systemically. Because all of these drugs are capable of stimulating the central nervous system, they may cause bradycardia, hypertension, or respiratory stimulation at the medullary level. Moreover, they may produce anxiety, excitement, or convulsions at the cortical or subcortical levels. This response simulates grand mal seizures

Table 30–3. Selection of premedication for various anesthetic agents.*

Anesthetic Agent	Barbiturates	Narcotics	Atropine or Scopolamine
Halothane	++	+	++
Methoxyflurane	++	+	++
Enflurane	++	+	+++
Local anesthetic			
Less than 200 mg procaine or lidocaine or 20 mg tetracaine	++	++	+
More than 200 mg procaine or lidocaine or 20 mg tetracaine	+++	++	+

Legend: + None or reduced dosage
            ++ Desirable
            +++ Indicated

*Modified and reproduced, with permission, from Guadagni NP: Anesthesiology. In: *Current Surgical Diagnosis & Treatment,* 3rd ed. Dunphy JE, Way LW (editors). Lange, 1977.

because it is followed by depression, loss of vasomotor control, hypotension, respiratory depression, and coma. Such an episode of indirect cardiovascular depression often is accentuated by a direct vasodilatory and myocardial depressant effect. The latter is comparable to the action of quinidine. This is why lidocaine is useful for the treatment of certain cardiac arrhythmias.

Chloroprocaine (Nesacaine) is an ester derivative that was popular in the mid 1960s but fell into disuse clinically. It recently enjoyed a resurgence in popularity primarily because of its rapid onset and short duration of action and its low toxicity to the fetus. Its physicochemical properties are imparted by the chloro substitution of the 2-position in the benzene ring of procaine. It is metabolized by plasma cholinesterase and therefore does not demand liver enzyme degradation, as do the more complex and longer acting amide derivatives. Chloroprocaine has a half-life of 21 seconds in adult blood and 43 seconds in neonatal blood. Direct toxic effects on the fetus are minimized, since less drug is available for transfer in the maternal compartment.

The potency of chloroprocaine is comparable to that of lidocaine and mepivacaine, and the drug is 3 times more potent than procaine. Its average onset of action ranges from 6 to 12 minutes and persists from 30 to 60 minutes depending on the amount used. Its use has been severely curtailed because of recent reports of toxicity that include arachnoiditis and associated neuropathies.

Bupivacaine, the amide local anesthetic, is related to lidocaine and mepivacaine but has some quite different physicochemical properties. It has a much higher lipid solubility, a higher degree of binding to maternal plasma protein, and a much longer duration of action. Since injection of bupivacaine is required only every 90–120 minutes, accumulation in maternal blood—and therefore in the fetal circulation—is not a

Table 30–2. Drugs used for local analgesia.*

	Tetracaine (Pontocaine)	Lidocaine (Xylocaine)	Bupivacaine (Marcaine)
Potency (compared to procaine)	10	2–3	9–12
Toxicity (compared to procaine)	10	1–1.5	4–6
Stability at sterilizing temperature	Stable	Stable	Stable
Total maximum dose	50–100 mg	500 mg	175 mg
Infiltration			
Concentration	0.05–0.1%	0.5–1%	0.25%
Onset of action	10–20 min	3–5 min	5–10 min
Duration	1½–3 h	30–60 min	90–120 min
Nerve block and epidural			
Concentration	0.1–0.2%	1–2%	0.5%
Onset of action	10–20 min	5–10 min	7–21 min
Duration	1½–3 h	1–1½ h	2–6 h
Subarachnoid			
Concentration	0.1–0.5%	5%	...
Dose	5–20 mg	40–100 mg	...
Onset of action	5–10 min	1–3 min	...
Duration	1½–2 h	1–1½ h	...

*Modified and reproduced, with permission, from Guadagni NP, Hamilton, WK: Anesthesiology. In: *Current Surgical Diagnosis & Treatment,* 4th ed. Dunphy JE, Way LW (editors). Lange, 1979.

problem. In addition, since bupivacaine is well bound to maternal protein, it is difficult to detect substantial levels in the fetus. In behavior studies, bupivacaine did not decrease newborn muscle tone, as do lidocaine and mepivacaine. Thus, bupivacaine is the most popular local anesthetic drug used for regional anesthesia today. However, a word of caution must be added regarding its administration. This drug has been implicated in certain cardiovascular catastrophes associated with initial drug injection. Though these catastrophes are rare and it is questioned whether they are due to true drug effect or "use error," the practitioner is well advised to inject no more than 5 mL of the drug at any one time, to wait 4–5 minutes, and then to repeat the procedure until the desired volume has been delivered.

Local Infiltration Analgesia

Local tissue infiltration of dilute solutions of anesthetic drugs generally yields satisfactory results because the target is the fine nerve fibers. Nevertheless, one must recall the dangers of systemic toxicity when large areas are anesthetized or when reinjection is required. It is good practice, therefore, to calculate in advance the milligrams of drug in the volume of solution that may be required to keep the total dosage below the accepted toxic dose.

Infiltration in or near an area of inflammation is contraindicated. Injections into these zones may be followed by rapid systemic absorption of the drug owing to the increased vascularity of the inflamed tissues. Moreover, the injection may introduce or aggravate infection.

Regional Analgesia

A. Lumbar and Caudal Peri- or Epidural: These analgesic techniques have become more popular recently, because they are well suited to obstetric anesthesia. Either a single injection may be used or multiple injections through an indwelling catheter. Patient safety is enhanced by use of the catheter technique, since smaller doses may be utilized to provide the desired effect. The "one-shot" technique invariably employs a larger volume of drug for the desired effect. The drug is administered during the latter portion of the first and all of the second stage of labor; or terminally, as a single injection just before delivery. Special training is required for both types. The advantages of caudal anesthesia are that the mother remains conscious to witness the birth, blood loss is minimal, and the vaginal and perineal structures are quite relaxed. The technique must be exact, however, and inadvertent massive (high) spinal anesthesia occasionally occurs. Undesirable reactions include the rapid absorption syndrome (hypotension, bradycardia, hallucinations, convulsions) and postpartum backache and paresthesias. The incidence of persistent occiput posterior positions is increased because the infant's head is not normally rotated on the relaxed pelvic floor; forceps rotation and delivery are therefore more often necessary. A considerable quantity of anesthetic agent must be injected: 20 mL of 1.5% lidocaine or equivalent.

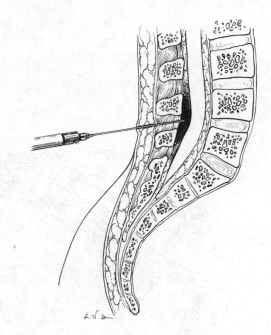

Figure 30–4. Peridural puncture and injection for caudal anesthesia.

The procedure is as follows: Inject 5 mL of a 1.5% aqueous solution of lidocaine or similar agent into the caudal canal as a test dose. If spinal anesthesia does not result after 10 minutes, assume that the solution was injected extradurally (Fig 30–4). Inject 15 mL of the anesthetic solution slowly to accomplish an adequate degree and suitable level of caudal anesthesia. This constitutes a single injection for terminal caudal anesthesia. A special caudal catheter or malleable caudal needle should be inserted and left in the caudal canal for continuous caudal anesthesia (Fig 30–5). Injections of 20 mL are required every 2–3 hours depending upon the need.

B. Saddle Block: This continues to be the most popular technique for second stage analgesia and relaxation of the perineum. Before it came to be understood that lower doses of drugs could be used effectively in the subarachnoid space in pregnancy, subarachnoid block was responsible for many maternal deaths. Subarachnoid block has been applied to obstetrics in the form of a "low spinal block" rather than a true (higher) "spinal block." Reasonably safe and effective drugs and dosages are tetracaine 1%, 4 mg, or lidocaine 5%, 50 mg.

C. Lumbar Sympathetic Block: Lumbar sympathetic block has never achieved widespread acceptance in spite of isolated enthusiastic reports. The lumbar sympathetic chain consists of bilateral ganglia extending from the first to the fifth lumbar vertebrae. They are strategically located near several vital structures including the vena cava, the aorta, and the celiac and superior hypogastric plexuses. A combination of drugs consisting of lidocaine 1%, tetracaine 0.15%, and epinephrine 1:200,000 usually is injected to effect

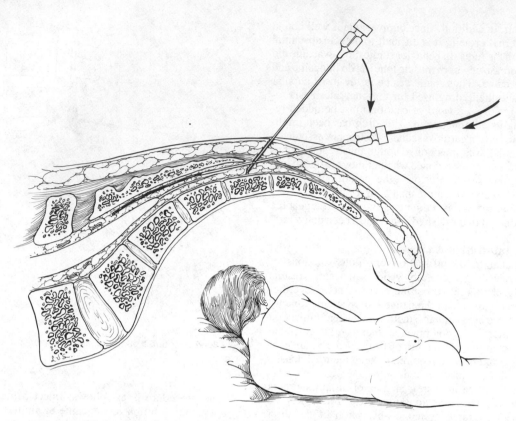

Figure 30–5. Caudal catheter in place for continuous caudal anesthesia.

prolonged blockade. If excessive volumes are utilized, extension of the effect into the proximity of the celiac and hypogastric plexuses may occur with resultant dangerous arterial hypotension. This feature, in addition to the technical nature of the block itself, is responsible for its unpopularity. Nonetheless, the block does relieve the pain of the first stage of labor effectively by interrupting the sensory pathways from the uterus and cervix. It is doubtful that lumbar sympathetic block will ever attain widespread use.

D. Spinal Anesthesia: Spinal anesthesia is currently employed to alleviate the pain of delivery and the third stage of labor. Short-acting agents (5% lidocaine, 50 mg) or long-acting drugs (1% tetracaine, 4 mg) are used. Brief or minimal spinal anesthesia is far safer than prolonged spinal anesthesia, which is not recommended for obstetric use. The advantages of spinal anesthesia are that no fetal hypoxia ensues unless hypotension occurs, blood loss is minimal, the mother remains conscious to witness delivery, no inhalation anesthetics or analgesic drugs are required, the technique is not difficult, and good relaxation of the pelvic floor and lower birth canal is achieved. Prompt anesthesia is achieved within 5–10 minutes, and there are fewer failures than with caudal anesthesia. The dosage of spinal anesthetic is small. Complications are fewer and easier to treat. Hypotension is rare with these doses. Spinal headache occurs in 5–10% of patients, however, and operative delivery is more often

required because voluntary expulsive efforts are eliminated. Drug reactions (eg, hypotension) may occur. Respiratory failure may occur if the anesthetic ascends within the spinal cord due to rapid injection or straining by the patient.

The procedure is as follows:

1. Inject 50 mg of lidocaine 5% or 4 mg of tetracaine as 1% solution with 10% glucose, or comparable drug, slowly into the third or fourth lumbar interspace between contractions. Have the patient lying on her side or sitting up. Elevate her head on a pillow immediately after the injection. Tilt the table up or down to achieve a level of anesthesia at or near the umbilicus. Anesthesia will be maximal in 3–5 minutes and will last for 1 hour or longer.

2. Obtain and record the blood pressure and respiratory rate every 3 minutes for the first 10 minutes and every 5 minutes thereafter.

3. Give oxygen for respiratory depression and mild hypotension. In addition, administer vasopressors such as ephedrine, 10–20 mg intravenously, if a marked fall in blood pressure occurs that is not responsive to intravenous fluids and lateral tilt.

E. Paracervical Block: (Fig 30–6.) Analgesia by this method is one of the most popular techniques used for first stage pain relief. Sensory nerve fibers from the uterus fuse bilaterally at the 4–6 o'clock and 6–8 o'clock positions around the cervix in the region of the cervical vaginal junction. Ordinarily, when

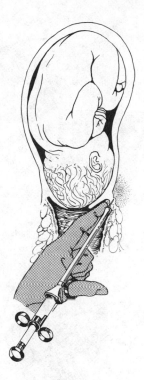

Figure 30—6. Paracervical block.

5–10 mL of 1% lidocaine or its equivalent are injected into these areas, interruption of the sensory input from the cervix and uterus promptly follows. Paracervical anesthesia is administered when the cervix is dilated 4 cm or more. It relieves pain until the presenting part reaches the lower vagina, whereupon a pudendal and perineal block or other anesthetic procedure will be required. The chief advantages of the paracervical block are simplicity, ease of administration, effectiveness, and relative safety for both the fetus and the mother.

Paracervical block has been criticized because of the occasional development of bradycardia shortly after introduction of the local anesthetic. There are many reports in the literature that place the incidence of fetal bradycardia at 8–18%. Recent work with accurate fetal heart rate monitoring associated with continuous uterine contraction patterns, however, suggests that the incidence is closer to 20–25%. Some researchers have attempted to investigate the significance of the bradycardia. One explanation is that an acid-base disturbance in the fetus does not occur unless the bradycardia lasts longer than 10 minutes and that neonatal depression is rare unless associated with delivery during the period of bradycardia. There seems to be little difference in the incidence and severity of fetal bradycardia by paracervical block between complicated and uncomplicated patients. Early Scandinavian studies suggest that paracervical block may best be reserved for uncomplicated deliveries. Other disadvantages of paracervical block include maternal trauma and bleeding, fetal trauma and direct injection,

inadvertent intravascular injection with convulsions, and short duration of the block.

Although a continuous catheter technique has been described, its acceptance has been poor. This may be partly attributed to the ease of dislodgment of the catheter. A 5- or 6-inch needle with a guide or lead shot affixed to it is used so that the point can be inserted 0.1–0.2 cm into the tissues. Inject 5 mL of a 1% aqueous solution of lidocaine (preferably) or a long-acting local anesthetic about 2 cm lateral to the cervix on both sides. If the presenting part is too far down to reach the lateral fornix easily, 5 mL injected as high as possible into each lateral vaginal wall will give considerable relief of discomfort during the second stage of labor.

The technique of paracervical block is relatively easy to master. Because it has minimal technical demands, it has continued to be a favorite approach to analgesia for the first stage of labor. Bradycardia may be a dose-related phenomenon, but use of smaller doses should substantially reduce the incidence of this complication.

F. Pudendal Nerve Block: Pudendal block, like paracervical block, has been one of the most popular of all nerve block techniques in obstetrics. The infant is not depressed, and blood loss is minimal. The technique is simplified by the fact that the pudendal nerve approaches the spine of the ischium on its course to innervate the perineum. Injection of 10 mL of 1% lidocaine on each side will achieve analgesia for 30–45 minutes about 50% of the time.

Both the transvaginal and transcutaneous methods are useful for administering a pudendal block. The transvaginal technique has important practical advantages over the transcutaneous technique. The Iowa trumpet needle guide may be used, and the operator's finger should be placed at the end of the needle guide to palpate the sacrospinous ligament, which runs in the same direction and is just anterior to the pudendal nerve and artery. It is usually very difficult to appreciate the sensation of the needle puncturing the ligament. This facet of the technique, ie, no definite end point, may make it difficult for the inexperienced individual to perform. Aspiration of the syringe for possible inadvertent entry into the pudendal artery should be accomplished, and, if no blood is returned, 10 mL of local anesthetic solution should be injected in a fanlike fashion on the right and left sides. The successful performance of the pudendal block requires injection of the drug at least 10–12 minutes before episiotomy. Often, in clinical practice, pudendal block is performed within 4–5 minutes of episiotomy. Hence, there may not be adequate time for the local anesthetic to take effect.

Completely effective pudendal blocks are often difficult to produce with regularity. Past enthusiasm for the pudendal nerve block has been due to its touted safety, ease of administration, and rapidity of onset. Disadvantages include maternal trauma, bleeding, and infection and the rare occurrence of maternal convulsions. In spite of a well-placed bilateral pudendal block, skipped areas of perineal analgesia often occur. The reason for this is that the pudendal nerve does not contribute to the entire sensory innervation of the perineum. Other perineal sensory fibers are included in the inferior hemorrhoidal nerve, the posterior femoral cutaneous nerve, and the genital branch of the genitofemoral nerve. Either lumbar epidural or caudal epidural block should eradicate pain between the T10 and S5 level for the second stage. All these nerves are denervated, since they all are derived from L1 to S5 segments.

1. Advantages and disadvantages–Enthusiasm for pudendal nerve block has been due to its safety and ease of administration and the rapidity of onset of effect. Disadvantages include maternal trauma, bleeding, and infection; rare maternal convulsions due to drug sensitivity; occasional complete or partial failure; and regional discomfort during administration.

The pudendal perineal block, like any other nerve block, demands some technical experience and knowledge of the innervation of the lower birth canal. Nevertheless, in spite of a well-placed bilateral block, skip areas of perineal analgesia may be noted. The reason for this may be that although the pudendal nerve of S2–4 derivation does contribute to the majority of fibers for sensory innervation to the perineum, other sensory fibers are involved also. For example, the inferior hemorrhoidal nerve may have an origin independent from that of the sacral nerve and therefore will not be a component branch of the pudendal nerve. In this case, it must be infiltrated separately. In addition, the posterior femoral cutaneous nerve (S1–3) origin may contribute an important perineal branch to the anterior fourchette bilaterally. In instances where this nerve plays a major role in innervation, it must be blocked separately by local skin infiltration. Two other nerves contribute to the sensory innervation of the perineum: the ilioinguinal nerve, of L1 origin, and the genital branch of the genitofemoral nerve, of L1 and L2 origin. Both of these nerves sweep superficially over the mons pubis to innervate the skin over the symphysis of the mons veneris and the labium majus. Occasionally, these nerves must also be separately infiltrated to provide optimal perineal analgesic effect. It should be apparent, then, that a simple bilateral pudendal nerve block may not be effective in many cases. For maximum analgesic effectiveness, in addition to a bilateral pudendal block, superficial infiltration of the skin from the symphysis medially to a point halfway between the ischial spines may be necessary. Thus, a true perineal block may be regarded as a regional technique.

2. Procedure–(Fig 30–7.)

a. Palpate the ischial spines vaginally. Slowly guide the needle toward each spine. Aspirate and, if not in a vessel, deposit 5 mL below each spine. This blocks the right and left pudendal nerves. Refill the syringe when necessary, and proceed in a similar manner to anesthetize the other areas specified. Keep the needle moving while injecting and avoid the sensitive vaginal mucosa and periosteum.

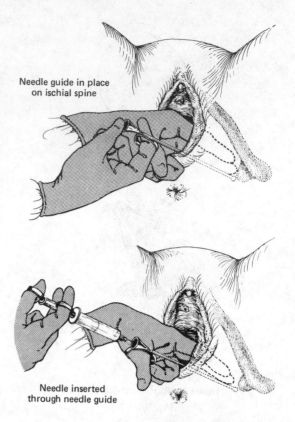

Needle guide in place on ischial spine

Needle inserted through needle guide

Figure 30–7. Use of needle guide ("Iowa trumpet") in pudendal anesthetic block. (Reproduced, with permission, from Benson RC: *Handbook of Obstetrics & Gynecology*, 7th ed. Lange, 1980.)

b. Withdraw the needle about 2 cm and redirect it toward an ischial tuberosity. Inject 3 mL near the center of each tuberosity to anesthetize the inferior hemorrhoidal and lateral femoral cutaneous nerves.

c. Withdraw the needle almost entirely and then slowly advance it toward the symphysis pubica almost to the clitoris, keeping it about 2 cm lateral to the labial fold and about 1–2 cm beneath the skin. The injection of 5 mL of lidocaine on each side beneath the symphysis will block the ilioinguinal and genitocrural nerves.

If the above procedure is not hurried and is skillfully done, there will be slight discomfort during injections only. Prompt flaccid relaxation and good anesthesia for 30–60 minutes can be expected.

Undesirable Side-Effects of Spinal or Epidural Anesthesia

Most side-effects of spinal or epidural anesthesia are secondary to the block of the sympathetic nerve fibers that accompany the anterior roots of the spinal thoracic and upper lumbar nerves (thoracolumbar outflow). Thus, many physiologic regulating mechanisms are disturbed. Most importantly, loss of motor control to the affected areas leads to local dilatation of the vasculature. The blood pressure falls as the result of loss of arterial resistance and venous pooling—assuming no compensation by change of the patient's position (eg, Trendelenburg position). Nausea and vomiting often occur at this point. Furthermore, alteration of the cardiac sympathetic innervation slows the heart rate and reduces cardiac efficiency. Epinephrine secretion by the adrenal medulla is depressed. Concomitantly, the unopposed parasympathetic effect of cardiac slowing alters vagal stimulations. As a result of these and related changes, shock follows promptly, especially in hypotensive or hypovolemic patients. Moreover, a precipitous fall in the blood pressure of the arteriosclerotic hypertensive patient is inevitable.

Fluids, oxygen therapy for adequate tissue perfusion, shock position to encourage venous return, and pressor drugs given intravenously are recommended.

So-called spinal headache due to leakage of cerebrospinal fluid through the needle hole in the dura is an early postoperative complication in up to 15% of patients. Small caliber needles (25F) decrease the incidence of headache. Therapy includes recumbent position, hydration, sedation, and, in severe cases, injection of 5 mL of the patient's fresh blood to "seal" the defect epidurally.

Rarely, spinal and epidural anesthesia have caused nerve injury and transient or permanent hypoesthesia or paresthesia. Excessive drug concentration, sensitivity, or infection may have been responsible for some of these complications. The incidence of serious complications of spinal or epidural anesthesia is considerably less than that of cardiac arrest during general anesthesia.

ANALGESIA FOR INTRAPARTUM OBSTETRICS

Analgesia for intrapartum obstetrics will be discussed from the viewpoint of both the normal obstetric patient and the patient with an obstetric complication. In addition, analgesia will be discussed for both the first and second stages of labor. Ideally, the management of analgesia for intrapartum obstetrics should be performed by the physician who has established rapport and is responsible for antepartum care. Acceptable substitutes are colleagues who are aware of a patient's personality and her problems, or perhaps even specially trained paramedical personnel who help manage patients in labor. A recent trend has been toward analgesia and not amnesia during the first 2 stages of labor. Most parturients prefer to be awake and to participate in their delivery. Admittedly, there is a wide difference in patient attitudes and personalities. These details must be tempered by experience because the patient may actually behave differently than anticipated during labor. For example, the mother who has been calm and who has accepted most minor annoyances during the antepartum period may develop anxiety or become distraught once labor begins. In such cases, mild sedation with psychologic support may be indicated.

Analgesic management in obstetrics requires some basic knowledge of the patient, including her personality and gestational problems and an assessment of the prognosis for a successful result. Therefore, although an early discussion of the types of analgesic methods available is usually desirable, it is rash to commit oneself to a definite technique at that time. Primiparous patients may respond in unexpected ways to the stress of labor. Both primiparas and multiparas may develop unforeseen complications that may make the method agreed on earlier medically unacceptable.

ANALGESIA FOR NORMAL OBSTETRICS

The overall general philosophy of management of first stage analgesia is summarized in Fig 30–8. Because most patients become more uncomfortable as labor progresses, one should plan an analgesic regimen that will adequately cover all phases of the first stage without interruption, especially between 8 and 10 cm of cervical dilatation. The parturient who has had adequate prior relief generally will be unaware of this lapse of analgesia late in labor when discomfort is maximal and contractions accentuated. Fig 30–9 shows labor data curves for patients who developed certain first stage complications. Note that an

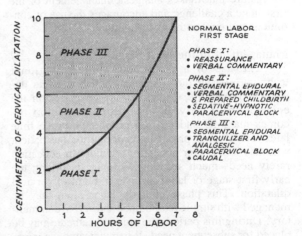

Figure 30–8. First-stage management in a primipara may be divided into 3 phases. Phase I (early labor) should be managed by simple reassurance and verbal commentary if the patient has had adequate antepartum education. Phase II may be handled by a segmental epidural block, continued reassurance, a sedative-hypnotic drug, a tranquilizer, or a paracervical block. The accentuated phase of labor (phase III) may be handled by segmental epidural block, a combination tranquilizer and analgesic, a paracervical block, or a caudal epidural block. The narrow use of reassurance and verbal commentary in conjunction with prepared childbirth methods in phase III usually results in complete relief or the development of a competitive attitude toward labor.

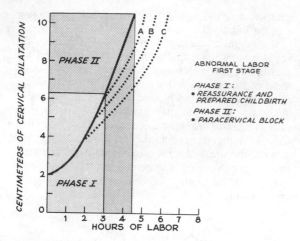

Figure 30–9. A first-stage multiparous labor is demonstrated. The physician should manage the patient with reassurance, prepare for childbirth in phase I, and decide upon paracervical block for phase II. Based upon the normal labor curve, there may be 50–70 minutes between 6 and 10 cm of cervical dilatation. Unfortunately, any patient may depart from the normal labor curve to develop a secondary delayed course designated as A, B, or C. In such cases, the paracervical block may dissipate and another first-stage analgesic technique may be necessary.

analgesic administered at 6 cm dilatation to a multipara may not last through the remainder of the first stage, although one might suppose it would suffice. This is the feature that makes analgesic management of the first stage a challenge and encourages the use of continuous regional catheter techniques.

Management of the First Stage

The use of a continuous catheter regional technique during the first stage of labor offers unequaled flexibility. Catheters may be placed in the epidural space early in labor before discomfort becomes maximal and utilized at an appropriate time later. The average primiparous or multiparous patient who has had proper antepartum childbirth education rarely needs much sedation or analgesia during the early first stage of labor prior to 5–6 cm of cervical dilatation. This phase of early labor often may be managed with simple reassurance and verbal commentary. During this period, the epidural catheter may be placed for subsequent need. When indicated, an injection of 6–8 mL of 1.5% lidocaine or 0.25% bupivacaine, for example, ordinarily will provide sensory blockade from T10 to L2. This generally will provide adequate first stage pain relief from 6 cm to complete cervical dilatation. Because this amount of sympathetic blockade rarely will result in maternal hypotension or complete motor or sensory denervation of the lower extremities, this technique may provide maximum comfort and safety to the patient and allow her to relax and observe the first stage of labor. The analgesic regimen described may be supplemented in the early portion of the first stage by sedatives or tranquilizers when indicated. For the most part, this should be adequate for most patients with uncomplicated gestation and labor. Only 90–120 mg of lidocaine are utilized for each injection, so this may be repeated when indicated during labor. Unless hypotension occurs and epinephrine is utilized, or unless a high level anesthesia develops, uterine contractions should not be affected significantly.

Epidural analgesic techniques are often not available. If this is the case, the following may be utilized for first stage pain relief: (1) systemic relief by means of a tranquilizer, sedative, or narcotic drug; and (2) paracervical block using procaine, lidocaine, or mepivacaine.

Management of the Second Stage

A. Epidural Block: If an epidural technique is utilized for first stage pain relief, it may be extended to cover the second stage. Assuming that a lumbar catheter alone is utilized, the patient may be placed in a semisitting position and 12–15 mL of 2–3% lidocaine injected for maximal sacral block of the perineum. The final level is usually between T10 and S5. This technique will suffice for most patients; only occasionally will analgesia be incomplete. The timing of second stage analgesia must be managed carefully because 10–12 minutes are required for a good sacral block to develop after the injection described above. If a caudal catheter is used, one should inject 10 mL of 2% lidocaine into the caudal epidural space; within 5–8 minutes, good sacral analgesia should be present. This technique rarely fails to produce bilateral analgesia, and its onset is more rapid. A 2% solution is preferred for the second stage for a more complete motor block of the pudendum.

B. Subarachnoid Block: Subarachnoid block may also be utilized for good second stage analgesia and muscle relaxation of the perineum. The technique may be performed with the patient in either the sitting or lateral recumbent position. The latter is preferable because it is the common position for subarachnoid block and is infinitely more comfortable for the patient. An important feature is the total amount of drug used. Four milligrams of 1% tetracaine or 50 mg of 5% lidocaine are adequate for a low spinal block of dermatomes T10–S5. One of the advantages of this technique is the rapid onset of both sensory and motor blockade. Careful attention must be paid to changes in the sensory level and blood pressure. The latter must be recorded every 2–3 minutes for the first 10 minutes to be certain that a sudden undetected hypotension does not occur. Thereafter, the blood pressure may be recorded every 5 minutes for 30 minutes.

C. Pudendal Block: Pudendal block, when performed correctly, will suffice also for second stage pain relief. As outlined above, performance of the pudendal nerve block is not as simple as many physicians believe. Inadequate perineal analgesia often occurs because of incomplete knowledge of the sensory distribution to the perineum. Nonetheless, a good bilateral pudendal block combined with superficial injection of the triangular area between the mid portion of the symphysis pubica and halfway to a line drawn to the spinous process often will effect complete perineal analgesia. In spite of this, one usually needs more analgesia for an indicated forceps delivery. If forceps extraction is necessary, it may be necessary to utilize a caudal or subarachnoid block to achieve complete perineal anesthesia.

D. Special Problems:

1. Midforceps delivery–In midforceps delivery, where careful timing may be necessary and certain specific requirements for rotation may be present, the obstetrician must choose the best analgesia for delivery. Requirements vary from patient to patient, and each situation must be considered individually. Midforceps delivery involves both rotation and traction. Hence, the anesthetic requirements must provide relaxation as well as analgesia for the perineum, lower vagina, and upper birth canal. In each instance, it is desirable to provide optimal conditions for the obstetrician to perform the anticipated procedures for delivery so that maternal and fetal trauma will be minimized. Regional analgesia with a lumbar or caudal epidural or subarachnoid block is preferable, since it provides analgesia and adequate relaxation.

2. Version extraction–One of the rare indications for version extraction today is delivery of a second twin that shows signs of fetal distress. The primary requirement for this procedure is relaxation, so that maternal and fetal trauma are minimized. The secondary requirement is for analgesia so that manipulative stresses will not stimulate movement on the mother's part. The only acceptable technique for this purpose is general anesthesia with halothane after suitable protection of the patient from the hazards of aspiration, which include antacid, 30 mL orally; adequate oxygenation; glycopyrrolate, 0.2 mg intravenously; tubocurarine, 3 mg intravenously; followed by thiopental, 200 mg intravenously; succinylcholine, 80–100 mg intravenously; and rapid intubation with cricoid pressure.

ANESTHESIA FOR THE FETUS AT RISK

Premature Labor

A. Psychoanalgesia: Familiarize the patient before labor (if possible) with a relaxing technique (Lamaze or Read) and the use of her delivery powers to reduce tension and pain (psychoprophylaxis). Establish rapport and provide emotional support. Employ reassurance and kindly direction. Use suggestion and hypnosis when feasible. Psychoprophylaxis has been most successful, but fewer than 20% of patients can be carried through labor and delivery with hypnosis alone.

B. Regional Analgesia: Conduction analgesia is usually more desirable than inhalation or parenteral analgesia. All regional blocking agents are rapidly absorbed. These agents may intoxicate the fetus when overdosage occurs, with resultant apnea and vascular collapse from medullary depression, bradycardia because of the quinidinelike effect on the myocardium, and convulsions because of cortical excitation. Those agents with the amide molecular linkage (lidocaine, mepivacaine, and prilocaine) have a stability that resists enzymatic splitting and rapidly cross the placental barrier intact. In contrast, local anesthetics with an ester bond (procaine, 2-chloroprocaine, and tetracaine) are metabolized in the plasma and placenta with only minor transfer to the fetus.

C. Paracervical Analgesia:

1. Almost immediate complete relief of pain is achieved until the presenting part distends the lower birth canal, when a pudendal block or other procedure is indicated.

a. Prepare the mucosal site 2 cm lateral to the cervix, in the vaginal fornix, with antiseptic solution.

b. Insert a 15- to 25-cm 20-gauge needle 0.3–0.5 cm into the lateral fornix using an "Iowa trumpet" (Fig 30–10). Slowly inject 5 mL of 5% lidocaine or mepivacaine just beneath the mucosa. Wait for several uterine contractions to avoid an anesthetic reaction and then inject the other side.

c. When the presenting part is deeply engaged and the fornices are blocked, inject the drug high in the lateral vaginal walls and again just beneath the mucosa (to retard absorption).

2. The anesthetic lasts about 60 minutes, yet only a minority of patients will require subsequent paracervical blocks. A temporary reduction in the intensity and duration of contractions may occur.

Figure 30–10. "Iowa trumpet" assembled.

3. Contraindications–Paracervical block should not be used if excessive uterine bleeding occurs, if vaginal or cervical sepsis is present, if a pre- or postmature infant is being delivered, or if the patient has preeclampsia-eclampsia or diabetes mellitus.

4. Complications–The complications include hematoma formation; infection; faintness, syncope, or vascular collapse from inadvertent intravenous administration, too rapid absorption, or sensitivity to the anesthetic agent; chemical lumbosacral neuritis; fetal bradycardia, acidosis, and, rarely, cardiac arrest because of rapid absorption of the drug (toxic effect).

5. Paracervical block is probably more apt to be associated with rapid drug absorption than most other techniques because of marked cervicouterine vascularity. Therefore, precautions must be taken with its use:

a. Avoid injection of an anesthetic drug directly into the maternal circulation or into fetal tissues by limiting the volume of the anesthetic agent to 5 mL on each side of the cervix and placing the drug just beneath the mucosa as a "blister."

b. Avoid paracervical block when the fetus may already be hypoxic and acidotic, as in eclamptogenic toxemia, diabetes, and possibly postmaturity.

c. Do not use paracervical anesthesia in cases of fetal heart irregularity or after meconium passage in vertex presentations.

d. Employ constant fetal heart rate monitoring in all complicated cases, especially with bradycardia.

D. Pudendal Nerve Block: The nerves supplying the lower birth canal are anesthetized by blocking the pudendal nerve at the ischial spines. Transvaginal injection is preferred. Only a spinal type needle is required, and the procedure can be carried out without assistance.

Identify the ischial spines on each side by digital examination through the elastic vagina. Then note the sacrospinous ligament across the sacrospinous notch above and posterior to the spines.

E. Lumbar Epidural Block: Continuous lumbar epidural block may be a safe method of anesthesia in the delivery of a jeopardized fetus if properly performed by well-trained personnel. It may be selected in certain maternal complications, eg, congenital or acquired heart disease, pulmonary disorders, diabetes, preeclampsia-eclampsia, hypertension, and renal or hepatic disease. It may be the best technique for premature or postmature labor, prolonged labor, or cervical dystocia. The low-dosage technique can be augmented to produce anesthesia for cesarean section.

F. Caudal Block: Epidural placement of an anesthetic solution in the caudal canal (caudal block), although it involves less risk of dural puncture, requires more medication (with attendant fetal risks), and the procedure blocks a larger nerve distribution, with the hazard of hypotension. The anesthetic may also lead to failure of spontaneous internal rotation.

G. Spinal Block: Maternal hypotension with decreased uterine blood flow is the greatest risk to the fetus when subarachnoid (spinal) block is employed. It is useful only during delivery because it often causes a temporary arrest of labor.

H. General Analgesia: General anesthetics may be useful adjuncts in certain high-risk cases. It should be recalled, however, that all general anesthetics cross the placenta and can depress the fetus. General anesthetics may be selected if regional anesthetics are contraindicated, if deep uterine relaxation is necessary, for alleviation of constriction rings, for relief of tetanic uterine contractions, or when prompt deep anesthesia is necessary.

1. Inhalation agents–

a. Halothane, a halogenated hydrocarbon, was developed in the mid 1950s and was thought to be the "perfect" agent, because it appeared to have the requisite properties of good molecular stability, nonflammability, and high potency. With time it was found to be less stable than predicted and proved also to cause myocardial sensitization and organ destruction (ie, liver toxicity) from its metabolites. In obstetrics, halothane is still the agent of choice at many centers for obtaining immediate uterine relaxation in intrapartum crises, eg, shoulder dystocia, intrauterine manipulations, and delivery in breech presentations or of a second twin. It does increase uterine bleeding because of residual vascular atony, but this can be countered by its rapid elimination and by the use of oxytocin. Only at concentrations greater than 1.5 vol% is the response of the uterus to oxytocin blocked.

b. Enflurane (Ethrane), a halogenated ether, has been safely used in subanesthetic concentrations (1 vol%) for analgesia. Reduction in both resting uterine tone and peak development of tension occurs when the drug is used in anesthetic doses but not with analgesic doses. Uterine response to oxytocin is impaired only at concentrations greater than about 2–3 vol%.

c. Isoflurane (Forane) is considered the best agent yet developed. It is a halogenated ether, as is enflurane. Isoflurane depresses uterine muscle and causes bleeding and uterine atony. However, it appears to be an excellent choice for emergent situations in which uterine relaxation is essential, since it reportedly maintains cardiac output at maximum allowable concentrations (in contrast to halothane, which decreases cardiac output). It therefore may provide uterine relaxation while maintaining uterine blood flow and maternal blood pressure.

d. Nitrous oxide is one of the most important and oldest gaseous agents used in obstetrics. In concentrations of 40%, nitrous oxide produces sufficient analgesia amnesia while preserving patient cooperation and laryngeal reflexes. Nitrous oxide has no effect on the intensity, duration, or frequency of uterine contractions. Although this agent passes easily through the placenta and into the fetal circulation, little or no depression of the newborn occurs when analgesic concentrations are used. Concentrations of nitrous oxide greater than 40% can result in an uncooperative and unconscious patient, necessitating endotracheal intubation. *Caution:* When narcotics, hypnotics, and other agents are used with nitrous oxide, they act synergistically and may result in fetal depression.

2. The parenteral anesthetics thiopental sodium (Pentothal) and thiamylal sodium (Surital) cross the placenta quickly at all anesthetic doses.

3. In the healthy preterm fetus, unless excessive dosages of thiobarbiturates are used (maternal dosage usually > 400 mg), there will be no severe central nervous system depression. If fetal acidosis is present, the likelihood of fetal depression with any anesthetic drug is greater. The possibility of cerebral depression must be kept in mind during management of all preterm fetuses, but this depression will be manifest clinically only after delivery, when the newborn's respiratory center must function independently. Before the 36th week, there is less facilitated biotransformation of all drugs. It is prudent to limit the administration of barbiturates and narcotics to the mother to an absolute minimum. If a preterm newborn has received too much barbiturate or narcotic, prompt, effective, and sustained efforts at resuscitation may be lifesaving until the respiratory center shows signs of recovery.

4. Medications to be used with caution in high-risk pregnancy of less than 36 weeks' gestation—

a. Narcotics (especially morphine).

b. Barbiturates.

c. Sedatives.

d. Tranquilizers.

e. Nonbarbiturate sedative-hypnotics (scopolamine, glutethimide).

Dysmaturity

Anesthetic drugs and techniques that may be appropriate in delivery of stressed postmature infants may be less than optimal for premature ones. Although the situations may appear similar, the postmature fetus who does poorly in utero may function quite adequately in the nursery. In contrast, the premature fetus that fares well in utero may perform poorly after delivery. The postmature fetus does present a problem in management because of decreased placental perfusion. As is true of patients with preeclampsia-eclampsia, to precipitate maternal hypotension is extremely serious as it may initiate an episode of intrapartum fetal distress. The chief threat to the postmature fetus is iatrogenic precipitation of the problems that stress the fetal oxygenator, the placenta. A secondary hazard is giving excess amounts of drugs to mothers whose fetuses are marginally oxygenated and therefore may be at risk of developing acidosis and hypoxia in utero. This additive fetal depression compounds the problem of drug dosage. The combination of a high level of drug plus hypoxia will manifest itself in the newborn. Such an infant is hypotonic, hypotensive, and prone to alveolar hypoventilation.

A. Paracervical Analgesia: Paracervical block is not recommended if the fetus is postmature, because an already marginal placental blood supply may be stressed beyond recovery if large amounts of local anesthetic precipitate bradycardia. While the bradycardia may be short-lived, it is completely unpredictable. Extended bradycardia may cause fetal acidosis, which may not be tolerated by the dysmature

fetus with already depleted uteroplacental reserves.

B. Pudendal Block: Pudendal block may be used for second stage analgesia, but the total dosage administered must be carefully controlled. Bilateral pudendal block is often performed using 10 mL of 1% mepivacaine or lidocaine bilaterally only to discover subsequently that one side of the block is ineffective. The tendency, therefore, is to repeat the injection on that side. In a short period of time, a dysmature fetus may receive high levels of drug because of a cumulative effect. This may be manifested again in the neonatal period by cerebral depression, characterized by poor muscular tone and reduced respiratory effort.

C. Lumbar Epidural Block: This regional technique is well suited to the postmature fetus, since a segmental type of lumbar epidural block usually will produce only a brief episode of hypotension or none at all. In addition, minimal amounts of drug are used. Repeated dosages may be used over several hours of labor, again taking advantage of the segmental technique, which has as its mainstay the use of a minimal amount of drug and minimal hypotension.

D. Caudal Block: The use of a caudal epidural block for first stage pain relief is not recommended when the fetus is dysmature because it is necessary to utilize considerable drug to block all the fibers which convey sensory innervation from the birth canal, cervix, and lower uterine segment to T10–L2. Therefore, the catheter tip is usually placed at S3 to obtund these upper lumbar and lower thoracic efferent fibers, and one must use at least 15 mL of drug. For this reason, it is recommended that a caudal epidural block be utilized in conjunction with the lumbar epidural block to provide only a "low caudal" for termination of the second stage and delivery. This would necessitate the use of only 4–6 mL of 2% lidocaine, which should obtund the S2–S4 fibers and provide adequate analgesia for delivery.

E. Spinal Analgesia: Subarachnoid block can be used for the second stage despite a dysmature fetus if the operator realizes that this technique must be modified to prevent hypotension and provide for analgesia of only second stage descent and delivery. This necessitates the use of a very small amount of drug, ie, 4 mg of tetracaine or 25 mg of 5% lidocaine, and careful positioning of the patient so that diffusion of the drug does not occur too far above the first sacral or fifth lumbar junction. This should leave most of the sympathetics intact and should not cause a significant fall in peripheral vascular resistance, hypotension, or hypoperfusion of the placenta, which has a restricted reserve.

F. General Analgesia: General analgesia may be used to provide for second stage pain relief during termination of the cervical stage in patients whose fetuses are dysmature. Because this, by definition, is an analgesic state, the patient will be awake and capable of managing her airway reflexes. Nonetheless, she should be afforded enough pain relief by means of nitrous oxide or subanesthetic doses of halogenated agents to withstand the possible severe discomfort of late descent and rotation of the fetal head before delivery.

Multiple Pregnancy

A. Psychoanalgesia: The psychoprophylactic technique helps to prepare the patient for the intrapartum experience. When the labor progresses normally, psychoanalgesia can effectively reduce apprehension and enhance the pleasurable aspects. It may also prepare the patient for an understanding of some of the complications of multiple pregnancy (uterine inertia in first stage of labor, uterine atony in third stage, and possible need for cesarean section) and reduce the total amount of drugs required for analgesia.

B. Regional Analgesia: Certain specialized aspects of the use of regional analgesia must be clarified before their application to patients with multiple pregnancy are discussed:

1. Paracervical analgesia–No special warnings about this technique in multiple pregnancy are required except to bear in mind that if the first twin is depressed at birth it may have received an inadvertent fetal injection, which is a complication of this technique.

2. Pudendal block–Pudendal nerve block often is preferred because it allows more spontaneous management during delivery and because the fetus or newborn is not exposed to excess drug (local anesthetic). Many are not aware that regardless of the area of injection of local anesthetic agent, the drug exposure to the fetus is similar (with the exception of subarachnoid block). Nevertheless, it is true that with the exception of local perineal injection or a low caudal (S2–4), pudendal block does allow for the most spontaneous second stage management.

3. Lumbar epidural block–This technique is quite useful as a first stage analgesic method, but only a segmental type should be utilized (T10–L2) to prevent the increased hazard of hypotension secondary to a combined large segment sympathetic block and vena cava occlusion. Ideal management here entails the use of lumbar epidural block for the first stage and low caudal for the late second stage.

4. Caudal block–This technique can be used for first and second stage pain relief, but its use in the first stage is questionable because of an increased incidence of hypotension and the hazard of uterine inertia.

In multiple pregnancy, there is a greater reduction of the epidural space because of epidural venous engorgement. Concurrently, there is a greater hazard of profound vena cava occlusion because of uterine size. This does not rule out the use of a low caudal for the late second stage and delivery as previously mentioned (lumbar epidural), but its primary use for first stage relief necessitates eradication of too many sympathetic ganglia and subsequent reduction of peripheral vascular resistance to warrant its use in lieu of the above-mentioned techniques.

5. Spinal block–The low subarachnoid block is of use during termination of the second stage for crowning, delivery, and episiotomy. With the patient's legs elevated for delivery, there is usually less of a hypotensive hazard, but it should still be considered a threat.

6. General anesthesia–General anesthetic agents (nitrous oxide, halogenated inhalant agents) may be used to afford some relief of second stage discomfort during descent of the fetal head in multiple gestations, but it must be emphasized that this is *analgesia* with the patient awake and capable of managing her own protective airway reflexes.

PREVENTION & TREATMENT OF LOCAL ANESTHETIC OVERDOSAGE

Convulsions can be prevented to a large extent by premedication, eg, pentobarbital sodium or diazepam (Table 30–3). Even so, the correct dose of any local anesthetic is the smallest quantity of drug in the greatest dilution that will provide adequate analgesia. Nonetheless, the total safe dose must be reduced appropriately in the very young, the elderly, or the medically compromised patient. Injection of the drug into a highly vascularized area, eg, the myometrium of the pregnant uterus, will result in more rapid systemic absorption than, say, injection into the skin. To prevent too rapid absorption, the operator may add epinephrine to produce local vasoconstriction and prolong the anesthetic. A final concentration of 1:200,000 is desirable, especially when a toxic amount is approached. Epinephrine is contraindicated, however, in patients with increased cardiac irritability of medical or drug origin.

The treatment of local anesthetic overdosage manifested by central nervous system toxicity (ie, a convulsion) is generally managed very effectively and without incident. However, the administrator must be aware of certain basic principles. These consist of the recognition of prodromal signs of a central nervous system toxic reaction and immediate treatment as required. A toxic central nervous system reaction to local anesthetics consists of ringing in the ears, diplopia, perioral numbness, and deep, slurred speech. As soon as any of these signs or symptoms are recognized, the patient should receive diazepam, 5 mg intravenously. An adequate airway must be maintained, and she should receive 100% oxygen, with respiratory assistance if necessary. Protection of the patient's airway and immediate injection of diazepam usually stop the convulsion immediately. In the past, succinylcholine was recommended. This drug is a potent neuromuscular relaxant which requires placement of an endotracheal tube with positive pressure ventilation. Nevertheless, recent evidence indicates that cellular metabolism is greatly increased during convulsive episodes, so that a definite increase in cellular oxygenation occurs—hence the use of a selective hypothalamic and thalamic depressant because these sites are the foci of irritation.

ANALGESIA FOR
ABNORMAL OBSTETRICS

Abnormal obstetrics may include conditions that compromise both the fetus and the mother. Analgesia management in acute and chronic fetal distress and in maternal complications such as preeclampsia-eclampsia, hypertension, heart disease, and diabetes will be discussed. Finally, the analgesic management of obstetric complications such as placenta previa, cord prolapse, abruptio placentae, and breech presentation will be considered.

Acute Fetal Distress

Acute fetal distress usually occurs intrapartum, without previously suspected fetal compromise. It may be heralded clinically by either the sudden appearance of meconium, the development of bradycardia, or a deceleration pattern detected by fetal monitoring. With continuous heart rate–monitoring equipment, a severe deceleration may be designated as variable or late. In either case, because uterine perfusion presently is correlated with blood pressure, it may be assumed that a maternal pressure fall greater than 20% of the baseline systolic figure will produce a substantial reduction in uterine perfusion. Because this will aggravate any acute intrapartum fetal distress, hypotension should be avoided. Although the incidence and degree of hypotension after sympathetic blockade can be minimized by thorough evaluation and use of the segmental technique, it may occur even in the best circumstances. With definite documentation of severe intrapartum distress, therefore, analgesic techniques should be chosen that are not associated with hypotensive sequelae. Generally, this limits regional analgesia to the segmental epidural technique. A systemic technique may be utilized, but one must recall that the systemic administration of narcotics and barbiturates may cause neonatal depression after delivery. The use of a narcotic antagonist such as naloxone (Narcan) may reverse the effect of antepartum narcotics. In addition, because paracervical block may result in bradycardia and because its significance is still not completely understood, it is best to avoid paracervical block. This usually restricts the anesthetic selection to either a small dose of intravenous tranquilizer and narcotics or to segmental epidural block.

Chronic Fetal Distress

A serious problem in anesthetic management occurs when acute intrapartum distress is superimposed upon the chronic type of fetal distress. Underlying chronic distress may be preeclampsia-eclampsia, hypertension, postmaturity, or diabetes. These disorders all reduce fetal reserve. Again, analgesic techniques that do not have hypotensive side-effects may be indicated, since the primary aim should be maintenance of uterine blood flow. Again, one's choice is limited because of postdelivery depression by narcotics and barbiturates and the unsettled role of paracervical block in fetal distress. The probable choice is between no analgesia, minimal systemic analgesia, and segmental epidural block.

Maternal Complications

A. Preeclampsia-Eclampsia: This syndrome (often called toxemia of pregnancy) is composed of the triad of hypertension, generalized edema, and proteinuria. It accounts for almost 20% of maternal deaths per year in the USA. The primary pathologic characteristic of this disease process is generalized arterial spasm. As gestation lengthens, there is a tendency toward a fluid shift from the vascular to the extravascular compartment with resultant hypovolemia—in spite of an expanded extracellular fluid space. The most significant electrolyte disturbances are those of sodium and chloride. While there is retention of both salt and water in the extracellular space, sodium and chloride values in the intravascular compartment are subnormal. This is not reflected by serum electrolyte values because of hypovolemia. Arterial spasm takes its toll via the cardiovascular system. It is estimated that nearly half of eclamptic patients who die have myocardial hemorrhages or areas of focal necrosis. Major disorders of central nervous system function probably are caused by cerebral vasospasm. It is obvious that optimal anesthetic management of these patients during the intrapartum period must include a careful preanesthetic evaluation of the cardiovascular and central nervous systems. If, after searching appraisal, the patient appears to be suffering from a mild form of the disease, one may institute almost any of the aforementioned anesthetic techniques. Nevertheless, the complications of hypotension should be avoided. Many of these patients should be medicated with magnesium sulfate so the need for substantial analgesia is reduced. Preference may be given to segmental epidural block with small increments of lidocaine following adequate fluid replacement. Adequate fluid replacement in some of these patients may necessitate the intravenous administration of 1–2 L of lactated Ringer's injection. An alternative method is administration of very small increments of narcotic to produce mild analgesia. Once again, utilization of a narcotic, which will pass the placental barrier and perhaps eventually depress the fetus, is potentially hazardous for these patients, whose infants may be primarily depressed because of their original disease process.

The physiologic changes of severe preeclampsia-eclampsia are exaggerated by regional blockade because of a restricted intravascular volume, and this may result in considerable depression of blood pressure. These patients suffer from a depressed myocardium and decreased intravascular fluid space. This, added to the reduced peripheral vascular resistance and further peripheral pooling of blood, presents a profound hypotensive potential to the obstetric anesthesiologist who wishes to use the major regional analgesic techniques. In these cases, the analgesic techniques available are limited to either systemic analgesia or paracervical block for the first stage and inhalation analgesia or pudendal block for the second stage.

B. Hemorrhage and Shock: Intrapartum obstetric emergencies demand immediate diagnosis and therapy for a favorable outcome for the mother and fetus. Placenta previa and abruptio placentae are accompanied by serious maternal hemorrhage. Aggressive obstetric management may be indicated, but superior anesthetic management will play a major role in the reduction of maternal and fetal morbidity and mortality rates. The primary threat to the mother is that of blood loss, which reduces her effective circulating blood volume and her oxygenation potential. Similarly, the chief hazard to the fetus is diminished uteroplacental perfusion secondary to maternal hypovolemia and hypotension. The perinatal mortality rate associated with placenta previa and abruptio placentae has been reported to be as low as 15–20%, but others have reported a 50–100% perinatal loss in these disorders. The overall morbidity and mortality rates for both the fetus and the mother depend upon the gestational age and health of the fetus, the extent of the hemorrhage, and the therapy given.

Good anesthetic management demands early consultation. Reliable intravenous lines should be established early. In addition, recommendations for the treatment and control of shock must be formulated. Prompt cesarean section is often indicated. A modified nitrous oxide–oxygen relaxant method of anesthesia will provide improved oxygenation for both the mother and the fetus and will have a minimal effect on the maternal blood pressure. As surgery progresses, it may be necessary to administer large volumes of warm blood, intravenous fluids, or even vasopressors when imperative. Vaginal delivery is rarely possible except after fetal death and when maternal risk is minimal. If there has been considerable blood loss, analgesia for such a procedure should not include regional techniques, which may result in substantial maternal sympathetic blockade. This restricts the choices to systemic tranquilizers or sedatives. Second stage analgesia may be achieved by pudendal block, true saddle block, or sacral caudal block.

C. Prolapse of Umbilical Cord: Umbilical cord prolapse is an acute obstetric emergency that involves a critical threat to the fetus. Often, because of confusion, irrational behavior by the medical staff may threaten the mother's life. For example, a haphazard rapid induction of anesthesia without attention to many of the essential safety details may be attempted. Naturally, prolapse of the umbilical cord is incompatible with fetal survival unless the fetal presenting part is elevated at once and maintained in that position to avoid compression of the cord. There should then be adequate time for a methodical, safe induction of anesthesia. The preferred method is the nitrous oxide–oxygen relaxant technique. Tragic errors in anesthesia may occur during such emergencies, and the anesthesiologist and obstetrician must cooperate effectively.

D. Breech Delivery: Anesthesia for breech delivery may seem to be a simple matter, but hazards to the life of the fetus and mother may develop. It is vital that the anesthesiologist be notified early in labor in order to become familiar with the situation, examine the patient, and prepare equipment for rapid induction when necessary. The anesthetic emergency usually involves rapid induction and intubation of the mother followed by adequate uterine relaxation with halothane. The primary purpose is to allow for a difficult delivery of the aftercoming head. The anesthesiologist who is not consulted until delivery of the breech has occurred cannot be expected to provide immediate safe, adequate uterine relaxation in such a brief period of time.

Compounding this problem is the lack of molding of the head of the fetus, so that the unknown midpelvis may also threaten the safety of delivery. This situation is made worse if an ill-considered attempt is made to relax and dilate the cervix with a uterine relaxant. The lower portion of the cervix is chiefly connective tissue that cannot be relaxed with any anesthetic. Cervical dilatation normally takes 1 hour for each 2 cm of dilatation, and this process cannot be accelerated even by profound myometrial relaxation with a potent inhalation anesthetic. Persistent forceful attempts at dilatation will only produce maternal trauma, possibly rupture of the lower uterine segment, with serious fetal morbidity or even death. The inhalation anesthetic technique is indicated because it provides voluntary muscular relaxation using succinylcholine and because halothane decreases uterine myometrial tone and relaxes the lower uterine segment. The optimum plan for delivery is one in which the patient is prepared for general anesthesia and prepared and draped in the usual manner for vaginal delivery. The obstetrician may wish to perform a pudendal block during descent of the breech to the introitus. When delivery to the umbilicus has occurred, the anesthesiologist may begin induction. This allows adequate time to place the endotracheal tube and begin administration of halothane 2% with oxygen 100%. Concomitantly, the obstetrician should be delivering the thorax and the upper extremities of the fetus. By this time, relaxation of both the lower uterine segment and the pelvic musculature should be adequate for delivery of the fetal head by either the Piper forceps or the Mauriceau-Smellie-Veit maneuver. This procedure has been shown to be most effective and safe for the fetus.

Because breech delivery is associated with a high perinatal mortality rate, there is a great need for excellent communication and cooperation between the obstetrician and the anesthesiologist to effect an atraumatic delivery.

E. Anesthesia for Emergency Cesarean Section: General anesthesia is the technique most suitable for the urgent cesarean section. It entails placement of an endotracheal tube with an inflated cuff to protect the patient from aspiration of gastric contents into the lung after administration of adequate barbiturate and a muscle relaxant to facilitate endotracheal intubation. Several safety measures must be taken: (1) Give 30 mL of antacid (eg, Maalox) within 15 minutes of induction. (2) Accomplish denitrogenation with 100% oxygen by tight mask fit. (3) Give atropine, 0.4 mg intravenously. (4) Give tubocurarine, 3 mg intravenously. (5) Inject thiopental, 2.5 mg/kg intravenously. (6) Apply cricoid pressure. (7) Give succinylcholine, 60–80 mg intravenously. (8) Intubate the trachea and inflate the cuff. (9) Give 6–8 deep breaths of 100% oxygen. (10) Continue to administer nitrous oxide 50% with oxygen 50%. (11) Release succinylcholine drip when indicated by slight movements of the patient's fingers or hands. The drip should be 1 mg/mL (0.1% solution).

The above steps should be instituted rapidly and with effective communication between the anesthesiologist and obstetrician, who should be scrubbing while the nurse is surgically preparing the abdomen. With this technique, anesthesia can be induced and the fetus delivered within 7–8 minutes from the time cesarean section is ordered. This technique does not cause maternal hypotension. To avoid vena cava occlusion from the heavy uterus, a wedge should be placed under the patient's right hip or the operating table rotated slightly to the left.

ANESTHESIA FOR NONOBSTETRIC COMPLICATIONS

Hypertension

Preexisting hypertensive cardiovascular disease in a pregnant woman should be differentiated from preeclampsia-eclampsia. Unlike the latter, the manifestations of hypertensive disease usually are present before the 24th week of pregnancy and persist after delivery. There is usually a long history of hypertension with superimposed proteinuria and edema. Patients with chronic hypertension should not be subjected to extensive sympathetic blockade because they may experience extreme swings in blood pressure. The untreated disease by itself may present a serious challenge to the obstetrician, and this implies a definite increase in maternal and fetal risk. As a result, analgesia for the first stage of labor should not include any technique that may cause extensive sympathetic blockade. Subarachnoid or epidural blockade of multiple sympathetic segments must be avoided because hypotensive sequelae are frequent. Perhaps the segmental epidural block may be applicable, since a minimal number of sympathetic segments are interrupted, though this remains to be proved clinically. Systemic analgesia with sedatives and tranquilizers or paracervical block may be selected for first stage pain relief, but a hazard still remains because a chronically deprived fetus exposed to a systemic depressant may suffer serious consequences during and after delivery. Second stage analgesia may be managed using either true saddle block, sacral caudal block, pudendal nerve block, or inhalation analgesia.

The double catheter technique offers all of the advantages of the other regional block procedures and minimizes most of their disadvantages. One catheter is inserted into the epidural space with its tip at the level of T12 to produce high segmental analgesia for the first stage of labor. A second catheter is placed in the sacral canal during the latent phase with its tip at the level of the third sacral vertebra. This second catheter provides analgesia for the second stage and for delivery. The dual catheter technique of epidural and caudal analgesia allows for a gradual progression of sympathetic blockade and affords much better control than a single-dose epidural or subarachnoid block alone. It is faster, and less local anesthetic agent is used, so that the risks of hypotension and other systemic side-effects are decreased. The maternal, fetal, and neonatal plasma drug concentrations are accordingly lower.

Another promising technique is the injection of opiate analgesics by either the subarachnoid or extradural route. Although this technique has not yet achieved widespread use, the logic of the approach is obvious.

Heart Disease

Pregnancy superimposed upon heart disease presents serious problems in anesthetic management. Patients with functional class I or II rheumatic or congenital heart disease usually fare well throughout pregnancy. For these patients, regional analgesia with the double catheter technique of lumbar and caudal epidural block provides ideal management of first and second stage pain relief. This avoids undesirable intrapartum problems such as anxiety, tachycardia, increased cardiac output, and the Valsalva maneuver. The lumbar epidural catheter may be activated for first stage analgesia with sensory levels of T10 through L2 segments. With the restricted epidural technique, wide variations in blood pressure usually will be avoided and adequate analgesia provided.

An important drug in the treatment of heart disease today is the potent sympathetic blocking drug propranolol. The obstetric anesthesiologist should consider patients taking therapeutic doses of propranolol to be beta-blocked pharmacologically. Both the maternal and fetal cardiovascular systems may be poorly responsive to sympathetic discharges mediating β_1 compensatory reactions to stress. As a result, positive chronotropic and inotropic responses may be sluggish. Additionally, the uterine β_2 adrenergic receptors may also be locked, rendering the uterus more responsive to exogenous oxytocin. Finally, since uteroplacental renin may also be antagonized by propranolol, and since uteroplacental renin may be vital to regulation of uterine blood flow (ie, increasing flow), one must be cautious about the delicate balance of fetal blood flow in such patients. In one reported incident, fetal distress was perhaps precipitated by such an interaction of propranolol and oxytocin.

Second stage pain relief in patients with heart disease may be managed by activation of the caudal epidural catheter with a sacral block of the second, third, and fourth fibers. Again, with a segmental sacral blockade there should not be a significant fall in blood pressure. This technique gives optimal analgesia with minimal fluctuations of blood pressure during the first and second stages of labor. It reduces patient anxiety and provides adequate conditions for forceps delivery to terminate the second stage, thereby obviating the need for bearing down (Valsalva maneuver). Patients with class III or class IV heart disease probably will tolerate only paracervical or pudendal block.

Diabetes Mellitus

Diabetes presents unique problems in management because of the hazard to the fetus. The patient with diabetes requires a detailed regimen of antepartum care that extends through the intrapartum and the neonatal period. Moreover, hypotension presents an anesthetic hazard in situations of reduced fetal reserve common to diabetes. The latent phase of labor is best managed with either psychologic support or mild sedatives or tranquilizers. The latter part of the first stage may be managed with either small intravenous doses of narcotics, paracervical block, or a combination of epidural and caudal regional techniques. If labor continues without signs of fetal distress and analgesia for the second stage is desired, one may use either local or pudendal block, saddle block, or a caudal sacral block for complete relaxation and analgesia of the lower birth canal. If a patient is allowed to undergo the stress of labor but evidence of fetal decompensation appears, operative delivery must be performed at once, with emphasis on the avoidance of hypotension. It may be best to utilize the nitrous oxide–oxygen relaxation technique to maintain normotension during induction and the immediate predelivery period.

Gastrointestinal Difficulties

Gastrointestinal nonstriated muscle has diminished tone and motility during pregnancy. Some medical gastrointestinal difficulties present special problems in management during the intrapartum period. **Peptic ulcer** often improves during pregnancy, but in some cases the disease worsens in the last trimester and causes serious problems during labor and the immediate postpartum period. Ulcer perforation and hematemesis are rare in labor. Nonetheless, good management of analgesia during delivery is necessary to decrease anxiety and apprehension.

Ulcerative colitis may become worse during pregnancy. Perinatal and maternal mortality rates are not increased because symptomatic management usually is adequate. **Regional ileitis** may also become more severe during pregnancy.

Chronic pancreatitis may be reactivated during pregnancy. **Acute pancreatitis** occasionally occurs in the third trimester. The significant laboratory values are elevated serum amylase and reduced serum calcium, along with typical symptoms of epigastric pain, nausea, and vomiting. It has been suggested that lumbar epidural block may actually decrease the severity of the pancreatitis, whether acute or an acute exacerbation of underlying chronic disease.

Sympathetic blocking techniques are not contraindicated for anesthetic management of the first and second stages of labor in these gastrointestinal

disorders that may coincide with pregnancy. It is best to alleviate anxiety and apprehension in the first stage of labor, because tension may exacerbate the disease process. Therefore, it is best to use a tranquilizer/narcotic combination early in the first stage of labor and then a combined lumbar and caudal epidural block for first and second stage management. Initially, a paracervical block may be used in the first stage followed by pudendal block for descent and delivery of the fetus for termination of the second stage. Subarachnoid block may be used to manage the second stage successfully, with use of a true saddle block obtunding chiefly the sacral fibers; but a low spinal technique may also be advantageous to relieve the uterine discomfort of contractions in the late first stage. This is done by placing the patient in a semisitting position after instilling the drug into the subarachnoid space so that a T10 level of analgesia will be attained.

Psychiatric Disorders

Most patients approaching delivery look upon the experience as one of the happiest times of their lives. However, some patients undergo severe emotional stresses during the third trimester and as delivery nears.

The obstetrician and anesthesiologist should talk openly with a psychiatric patient about problems of labor and delivery management and offer suggestions for management of discomfort so that she will have minimal emotional stress. The ideal technique is the combined use of lumbar epidural block for the first stage and lumbar or caudal epidural block for the second stage. It is best to carefully point out to the patient the reasons for choosing the technique and to review the technical points of the procedure so that she will not be alarmed when the block is attempted. These techniques are preferred because they afford early and continuous analgesia during labor and delivery.

TREATMENT OF COMPLICATIONS OF ANESTHETICS

Early Delivery

If labor terminates earlier than planned, a narcotic antagonist may reverse the depressive effect of an opiate but will intensify the barbiturate effect.

Resuscitation of the Mother*

Most anesthetic deaths are the result of 2 successive misfortunes: (1) a potentially lethal dose is given, and (2) successful resuscitation is not accomplished.

(1) Establish a patent airway (hyperextend the head; if necessary, insert a tracheal tube).

(2) Aspirate mucus, blood, vomitus, etc, with a tracheal suction apparatus. Utilize a laryngoscope for direct visualization of air passages.

(3) Administer oxygen by artificial respiration if

---

*Resuscitation of the newborn is discussed in Chapter 36.

respirations are absent or weak. If high spinal anesthesia has occurred, continue to "breathe" for the patient until paralysis of the diaphragm has dissipated.

(4) Give antihistamines intravenously (eg, diphenhydramine, 15–25 mg) and oxygen by mask for drug sensitivity (rarely indicated).

(5) Give vasopressors intravenously (ephedrine, 10–20 mg). Place the patient in the flat positive position with the feet elevated and give plasma, plasma expanders, and blood transfusion for traumatic or hemorrhagic shock.

(6) Specifically treat cardiac arrhythmias, arrest, failure, etc, if a heart disorder is the basic problem.

Spinal & Caudal Complications

Spinal or caudal reactions or complications are best averted by using the lowest effective dosage possible. Injection should be given slowly, with frequent aspiration. Unless contraindicated, vasoconstrictor drugs may be employed to reduce systemic absorption.

Untoward effects may be due to sensitivity, overdosage, or inadvertent intravascular injection. The type of reaction is unpredictable and relates to dosage, rate of absorption, and the medical status of the patient. Two types of reaction may follow systemic absorption: (1) Slow onset: stimulation leading to agitation, vertigo, blurred vision, nausea, tremors, convulsions, hypotension, and cardiovascular depression or respiratory arrest. (2) Rapid onset: depression leading to respiratory arrest, cardiovascular collapse, or cardiac arrest.

Prompt recognition and treatment are imperative: (1) Intubate the patient, maintain a patent airway, and administer oxygen. (2) Give small doses of a short-acting barbiturate, diazepam, or a muscle relaxant to control convulsions. (3) Support the circulation with vasopressor drugs as indicated. (4) Utilize external cardiac massage for cardiac arrest.

PROGNOSIS

The prognosis is excellent for mother and infant when physician anesthesiologists and obstetricians work as a team and a 24-hour anesthesiology service is available.

ANESTHESIA FOR CESAREAN SECTION

Local Analgesic Technique

Afferent innervation to the abdominal wall is via intercostal nerves T6–12 superiorly and from the upper lumbar nerves inferiorly. These nerves give off numerous branches lateral to the midline. The technique of local infiltration involves injecting along the line of the skin incision or developing a wheal of local analgesia on either side of the proposed skin incision. It may also be by intercostal block of T8–11, or paravertebral block of T12 and L1. The best needle

for achieving effective intracutaneous injections for the technique of local analgesia is a 22-gauge spinal needle. First, an intracutaneous wheal should be raised with a 25-gauge needle; a 5-cm 25-gauge spinal needle may then be used with the shaft of the needle kept parallel to the skin and a wheal raised intracutaneously as the needle is moved in the desired direction of the skin incision.

Success of these local anesthetic techniques is dependent upon technical skill, proper patient selection, and preparation. Sufficient time must be allowed for the local anesthetic to produce the desired result. Careful and gentle handling of tissues by the operator is essential.

Regional Analgesia

Lumbar epidural blockade may be utilized for cesarean section analgesia and to provide adequate analgesia for operative delivery. As mentioned, the major hazard of the regional analgesic technique is blockade of sympathetic fibers and a decrease in vascular resistance, venous pooling, and hypotension. However, this can be greatly alleviated by elevation of the patient's right hip to avoid compression of the vena cava by the gravid uterus when the patient is lying on the operating table. In addition, the anesthesiologist may rotate the operating table 15–20 degrees to the left so as to rotate the uterus away from the vena cava. This technique does demand some tactical knowledge. Moreover, the placement of the catheter in the epidural space must be guaranteed by the use of a test dose.

An excellent method is to inject the patient via a catheter, even for cesarean section, since repeated injections may be needed in prolonged procedures. Furthermore, with the use of the lumbar epidural catheter one can, with the use of a test dose, rule out the inadvertent puncture of the dura by either the needle or the catheter. After the catheter is suitably placed and taped in position, the patient should be rotated slightly out of the supine position to remove the hazard of vena cava occlusion when local anesthetic is injected as a test dose. One may use lidocaine 2% with epinephrine 1:200,000, or lidocaine 2% without epinephrine if there is cardiovascular instability. The addition of epinephrine will cause a more unstable blood pressure in the first 25–30 minutes of the lumbar epidural block. One may also utilize bupivacaine 0.5–0.75% or mepivacaine 1.5% with or without epinephrine as described for lidocaine. The total dosage for the therapeutic test is approximately 3 mL, which will be an adequate amount to ascertain whether or not inadvertent subarachnoid injection of the drug has occurred. This is followed by a therapeutic dose for analgesia of 12 mL, for a total of 15 mL of drug in the epidural space. The blood pressure is monitored every 5 minutes and the dermatome levels examined every 5 minutes for the first 20 minutes to ascertain the height and width of the analgesic block. It is usually necessary to wait only 15–20 minutes for an adequate analgesic block for incision. During this time, the patient's abdomen is surgically scrubbed and prepared and the patient draped for cesarean section. If a brief episode of hypotension should occur, the patient's legs should be elevated for a short interval and the patient given a rapid infusion of lactated Ringer's injection. In addition, the uterus must be shifted away from the vena cava. If these measures are not sufficient in relieving a brief episode of hypotension, one may utilize 10–20 mg of ephedrine intravenously followed by 25 mg intramuscularly for a mild vasopressor effect.

The subarachnoid block technique provides a regional analgesic method that has certain advantages and disadvantages in comparison to the lumbar epidural method. The advantages are the immediate onset of analgesia, so that there is no waiting for the block to become effective; and the absence of drug transmission from the maternal to the fetal compartment, because the anesthetic is deposited in the subarachnoid space in such small quantities. In addition, it may be a simpler technique to perform, since the end point is definite: the identification of fluid from the subarachnoid space. The disadvantages are a more profound and rapid onset of hypotension and more frequent nausea and vomiting, due either to unopposed parasympathetic stimulation to the gastrointestinal tract or to hypotension. Subarachnoid block is usually achieved via the paramedian or midline technique, which cannot be detailed here. The agents most commonly used for subarachnoid analgesia include tetracaine 1% (usually 6–8 mg) or lidocaine 5% (50–75 mg). As with the lumbar epidural technique, the patient is prehydrated with 500–1000 mL of lactated Ringer's injection. After the technical aspects of the procedure have been completed, the patient is placed in the supine position with the uterus displaced to the left as described above. If hypotension occurs, the legs should be elevated and the uterus pushed farther to the left to improve return of blood from the lower extremities into the circulation and increase right atrial pressure and, therefore, cardiac output. If these measures are not successful, the patient should receive ephedrine, 10–20 mg intravenously, followed by 25 mg intramuscularly to sustain a mild vasopressor effect. During a period of hypotension, the mother should receive oxygen by mask to increase oxygen delivery to the uteroplacental bed. Argument continues about whether or not regional techniques should be utilized for cesarean section in patients with either mild or moderate evidence of uteroplacental compromise. At cesarean section, a larger sympathetic and analgesic block is necessary for surgery, and this increases the incidence of maternal hypotension to cause possible fetal compromise. This argument is balanced by the thesis that there is some increased visceral blood flow, including an increased uterine and placental blood flow with sympathetic block. In any event, the prudent anesthesiologist will not utilize a technique that might increase the risk to a fetus already in a dangerous situation.

General & Local Anesthesia

Ideally, general anesthesia for cesarean section should cause the mother to be unconscious, feel no pain, and have no unpleasant memories of the procedure, while the fetus should not be jeopardized, with minimal depression and intact reflex irritability. The nitrous oxide relaxant technique for cesarean section has gained substantial popularity in the USA because it can be performed rapidly, providing safety to both the mother and the baby. Thiobarbiturates, muscle relaxants, nitrous oxide, and oxygen are the agents commonly used during the interval between induction and delivery. Currently, it is suggested that any hypotension may be too hazardous to justify regional procedures in cases of well-documented severe or moderate uteroplacental compromise. Hence, the inhalation technique is a likely choice for anesthesia in these cases.

Preoperative medication is not usually required when the patient is brought to the cesarean section room. She should have been prepared with 30 mL of antacid to offset the gastric acidity. The following procedure is suggested to prepare the patient for induction: (1) denitrogenation with 100% oxygen; (2) atropine, 0.4 mg intravenously; and (3) tubocurarine, 3 mg intravenously. This can be done during preparation and draping. Then, as the surgeon is ready to make the incision, thiopental, 2.5 mg/kg, should be injected intravenously and cricoid pressure exerted by an assistant. Immediately, succinylcholine, 60–80 mg intravenously, should be administered and intubation and inflation of the cuff performed. After 6–8 breaths of 100% oxygen, the patient should be given nitrous oxide 50% with oxygen 50% until delivery of the fetus. A 0.1% succinylcholine drip (1 mg/mL) should be administered for continued muscular relaxation if slight movements of the patient's hand or other part of the body develop. An attempt must be made to keep the induction-delivery time between 5 and 15 minutes. Five minutes are required for redistribution of barbiturate back across the placenta into the maternal compartment. After delivery of the fetus, the nitrous oxide concentration should be increased to 70% and intravenous narcotics and barbiturates injected intravenously for supplemental anesthesia.

Nitroglycerin (glyceryl trinitrate) is one of the oldest and most potent vasodilator drugs. Its primary target is smooth muscle, and its chief action is relaxation. Nitroglycerin is one of the agents of choice in preventing blood pressure elevation after tracheal intubation during cesarean section. It may be especially beneficial in patients with preinduction elevated pressures such as those with chronic hypertension or preeclampsia-eclampsia. Other agents, eg, trimethaphan or sodium nitroprusside, are also useful.

● ● ●

References

Abboud TK et al: Enflurane analgesia in obstetrics. *Anesth Analg* 1981;**60**:133.

Benedetti TJ, Gabbe SG: Shoulder dystocia: A complication of fetal macrosomia and prolonged second stage of labor with midpelvic delivery. *Obstet Gynecol* 1978;**52**:526.

Bonica JJ: *Principles and Practice of Obstetric Analgesia and Anesthesia.* Davis, 1972.

Datta S et al: Effects of maternal position on epidural anesthesia for cesarean section, acid-base status, and bupivacaine concentrations at delivery. *Anesthesiology* 1979;**50**:205.

Diaz JH, McDonald JS: Propranolol and induced labor: Anesthetic implications. *Anes Rev* 1979;**5**:29.

Friedman G, DiFazio C: Prolonged neural blockade following regional analgesia with 2-chloroprocaine. *Anesth Analg* 1980;**59**:810.

Greiss F, Still JG, Anderson SG: Effect of local anesthetic agents on the uterine vasculatures and myometrium. *Am J Obstet Gynecol* 1976;**124**:889.

Huter J, Meyer Menk W, Huter S: Placental passage of anesthetics. *J Perinat Med* 1978;**6**:223.

Jagerhorn M: Paracervical block in obstetrics: An improved injection method: A clinical and radiological study. *Acta Obstet Gynecol Scand* 1975;**54**:9.

Jouppila R et al: Segmental epidural analgesia in labour: Related to the progress of labour, fetal malposition and instrumental delivery. *Acta Obstet Gynecol Scand* 1979;**58**:135.

McDonald JS: Preanesthetic and intrapartal medications. *Clin Obstet Gynecol* 1977;**20**:447.

McDonald JS, Mateo CV, Reed EC: Modified nitrous oxide or ketamine hydrochloride for cesarean section. *Anesth Analg* 1972;**51**:975.

Moore DC et al: Chloroprocaine neurotoxicity: Four additional cases. *Anesth Analg* 1982;**61**:155.

Myers RE, Myers SE: Use of sedative, analgesic, and anesthetic drugs during labor and delivery: Bane or boon? *Am J Obstet Gynecol* 1979;**133**:83.

Nathenson G, Cohen MI, McNamara H: The effects of Na benzoate on serum bilirubin of the Gunn rat. *J Pediatr* 1975; **86**:799.

Nicholas ADG: Epidural analgesia, fetal monitoring, and condition of baby at birth with breech presentation. *Br J Obstet Gynaecol* 1975;**82**:360.

Phillips JC, Hochberg CJ, Petrakis JK: Epidural analgesia and its effects on normal progress of labor. *Am J Obstet Gynecol* 1977;**129**:316.

Ranney B, Stavage WF: The advantages of local anesthesia for cesarean section (prenatal, neonatal, and developmental comparisons). *SD J Med* 1975;**28**:23.

Ravindran R et al: Prolonged neural blockade following regional analgesia with 2-chloroprocaine. *Anesth Analg* 1980;**59**:447.

Read JA, Miller FC: The bupivacaine paracervical block in labor and its effect on quantitative uterine activity. *Obstet Gynecol* 1979;**53**:166.

Reisner L, Hochman B, Plumer M: Persistent neurologic deficit and adhesive arachnoiditis following intrathecal 2-chloroprocaine injection. *Anesth Analg* 1980;**59**:452.

Robson JE: Transcutaneous nerve stimulation for pain relief in labour. *Anaesthesia* 1979;**34**:357.

Rolbin SH et al: Anesthetic considerations for myasthenia gravis and pregnancy. *Anesth Analg* 1979;**57**:441.

Scanlon JW et al: Neurobehavioral responses and drug concentrations in newborns after maternal epidural anesthesia with bupivacaine. *Anesthesiology* 1976;**45**:400.

Singh S, Fehr P, Mirkin B: Placental transfer and pharmacokinetics of digoxin in the pregnant ewe. *Pediatr Res* 1973;**7**:318.

Skaredoff MN, Ostheimer GW: Physiologic changes during pregnancy: Effects of major regional anesthesia. *Regional Anesth* 1981;**6**:28.

Snyder SW, Wheeler AS, James FM III: The use of nitroglycerin to control severe hypertension of pregnancy during cesarean section. *Anesthesiology* 1979;**51**:563.

Toaff ME, Hezroni J, Toaff R: Effect of diazepam on uterine activity during labor. *Isr J Med Sci* 1977;**13**:1007.

31 | The Course & Conduct of Normal Labor & Delivery

Keith P. Russell, MD

Parturition is the birth process. **Labor** may be defined as a coordinated effective sequence of involuntary uterine contractions resulting in effacement and dilatation of the cervix and voluntary bearing-down efforts, all of which terminate with the expulsion of the products of conception. **Delivery** is the actual expulsion of the products of conception, including the placenta. A delivery that occurs before viability at 24 weeks of gestation is called an **abortion.** The number of weeks of gestation that determines whether a delivery is characterized as abortion rather than birth varies in different states; in California, for example, 20 weeks is the legal limit for abortion.

A **parturient** is a patient in labor. **Parity** is the state of having given birth to an infant or infants weighing 500 g or more, alive or dead. If the weight is not known, an estimated length of gestation of 24 weeks or more may be used. Thus, a patient is parous if she has given birth, whether per vagina or by cesarean section, at or beyond the 24th week of pregnancy. A **nullipara** has not delivered an offspring weighing 500 g or more or of 24 weeks' gestation or more. A **primipara** has given birth to one newborn weighing 500 g or more or at 24 weeks' gestation or more; a **multipara,** more than one. (For purposes of definition, a multiple birth is a single parous experience.)

Gravidity refers to the total number of pregnancies, including abortions, hydatidiform moles, and ectopic pregnancies as well as normal intrauterine pregnancies.

Labor is frequently divided into false and true labor. **False labor** is quite common in late pregnancy and is characterized by irregular brief contractions of the uterus accompanied by mild back or abdominal pain but lack of progress. False labor usually is inconsistent in the character of the contractions as regards time and strength, and there is no change in the cervix. The presenting part does not descend. False labor has no significance except as a frequent cause of anxiety and premature admission to the hospital. **True labor** is accompanied by a regular sequence of uterine contractions, progressively stronger and closer together, accompanied by effacement and dilatation of the cervix and, in the absence of malpresentation or fetopelvic disproportion, descent of the presenting part.

The beginning of true labor is marked by regular uterine contractions ("pains") that become more frequent and forceful and of longer duration with the passage of time.

The patient is usually aware of her contractions during the first stage. The severity of pain depends upon the fetopelvic relationships, the quality and strength of uterine contractions, and the emotional and physical status of the patient. Very few women experience no discomfort during the first stage of labor. With the beginning of true normal labor, some women describe slight low back pain that radiates around to the lower abdomen. Each contraction starts with a gradual buildup of intensity, and dissipation of discomfort promptly follows the climax. Normally, the contraction will be at its height well before discomfort is reported. Dilatation of the lower birth canal and distention of the perineum during the second stage of labor will almost always cause distress.

The tocograph, tocodynamometer, and pressure recordings with intrauterine catheters after amniocentesis or with the aid of multiple intramyometrial microballoons will reveal contraction patterns typical of normal labor; the last is a research procedure. Transcervical extraovular pressure devices are frequently used now during labor monitoring.

During the course of several days to several weeks before the onset of true labor, the cervix begins to soften and dilate. In many cases, when labor starts, the cervix is already dilated 1–3 cm in diameter. This is usually more marked in the multiparous patient, the cervix being relatively more firm and closed in nulliparous women. The average duration of the first stage of labor in primipara patients is 8–12 hours; in subsequent pregnancies, 6–8 hours. If the first stage of labor lasts longer than 12 hours or if cervical dilatation fails to advance over a period of 2 hours, this is considered abnormal. The second stage of labor varies from a few minutes to 1–2 hours. In general, if the second stage lasts 2 hours or longer, abnormal labor has developed.

The fetal membranes—a protective barrier against infection—rupture before the onset of labor in about 10% of cases (premature rupture of the membranes). At full term, 9 pregnant women out of 10 will be in labor within 24 hours after rupture of the membranes. If labor does not begin within 24 hours after rupture, the case must be considered to be complicated by prolonged premature rupture of the membranes.

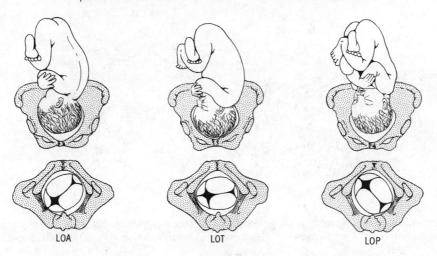

Figure 31–1. Vertex presentations. (Reproduced, with permission, from Benson RC: *Handbook of Obstetrics & Gynecology,* 7th ed. Lange, 1980.)

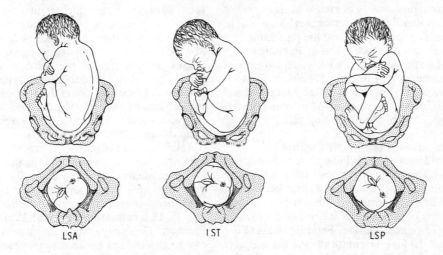

Figure 31–2. Breech presentations. (Reproduced, with permission, from Benson RC: *Handbook of Obstetrics & Gynecology,* 5th ed. Lange, 1974.)

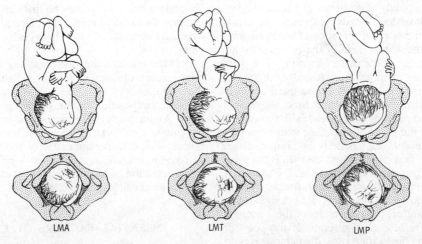

Figure 31–3. Face presentations. (Reproduced, with permission, from Benson RC: *Handbook of Obstetrics & Gynecology,* 5th ed. Lange, 1974.)

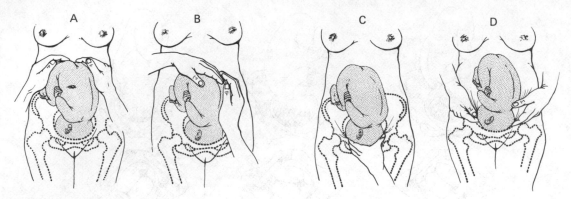

Figure 31–4. Determining fetal presentation *(A, B)*, position *(C)*, and engagement *(D)*. (The 4 maneuvers of Leopold.) (Reproduced, with permission, from Benson RC: *Handbook of Obstetrics & Gynecology*, 7th ed. Lange, 1980.)

In rare instances, actual leakage of fluid ceases in premature rupture or premature prolonged rupture of the membranes, presumably as a result of sealing off of a small "high leak" in the membranes. More often, however, drainage ceases because the presenting part descends to obstruct the free egress of amniotic fluid.

Just before the beginning of labor, a small amount of red-tinged mucus may be passed ("bloody show"). This is a plug of cervical mucus mixed with blood and is evidence of cervical dilatation and effacement and, frequently, descent of the presenting part.

Fetal Presentation, Position, & Posture

A. Fetal Presentation: Fetal presentation designates that fetal part which lies over the inlet. Under normal circumstances, about 95% of parturients have a cephalic (vertex) presentation. Breech presentation occurs in 4–5% of pregnancies at term; face, brow, or shoulder presentations are rare. **Fetal lie** refers to the relationship of the long axis of the fetus to the long axis of the mother. Fetal lie may be either longitudinal— the normal situation—or transverse, which is uncommon and usually presents serious problems of delivery. Oblique lie technically is a variant of transverse lie.

B. Fetal Position: Fetal position refers to the relationship of the point of direction of the presenting part to one of the 4 quadrants of the pelvis or to the transverse diameter of the maternal pelvis. The point of direction refers to an arbitrary (usually the lowest) portion of the presenting part. In the usual cephalic presentation with the normally flexed head, the occiput is the point of direction. If the head is deflexed, the occiput may be the point of direction; with brow presentation, the anterior fontanelle is the point of direction, whereas in face presentation the chin is the point of direction. When the breech presents, the sacrum is the point of direction. If the point of direction lies in either of the 2 posterior quadrants, it is designated as right or left posterior, but if in either of the 2 anterior quadrants it is right or left anterior. If the point of direction is in the direct transverse diameter, it is right or left transverse. Types of position are illustrated in Fig 31–1 to 31–3.

The various positions, presentations, and lies are affected by a number of factors, both maternal and fetal. Maternal factors include tumors of the uterus, congenital anomalies of the uterus, ovarian tumors, abnormalities of the maternal pelvis and lumbar spine, and extragenital factors such as pelvic kidney. Fetal factors include size of the baby, size of the fetal head—eg, hydrocephalus or anencephaly—and congenital fetal abnormalities of the bony or soft parts, eg, fetal abdominal tumors. The location of the placenta may also affect fetal position and presentation: a low-lying or centrally placed placenta over the cervical os can alter fetal lie and posture. Moreover, the amount of amniotic fluid has an indirect effect on fetal position and presentation, eg, with excessive fluid present, transverse lie is more common. Most commonly, the fetus tends to assume a position facing the placenta.

C. Determination of Fetal Presentation and Position: Generally, fetal presentation and position can be determined by abdominal examination. One abdominal examination consists of 4 maneuvers of Leopold as illustrated (Fig 31–4). In markedly obese patients or in primigravid patients with strong, tense abdominal muscles, it may be difficult to effectively perform the Leopold maneuvers. Nonetheless, vaginal or rectal examination will help to define the presenting part.

If there is any question regarding the position or presentation, ultrasonography or a plain x-ray film of the abdomen will be of help. These techniques may disclose the position of the placenta as well as the fetus. Amniography (injection of radiopaque dye into the amniotic cavity) may reveal the fetomaternal relationships. It is important in the conduct of labor and delivery to ascertain as carefully as possible the presentation, position, and posture of the fetus. Variations from normal can lead to dystocia or difficult delivery.

ESSENTIAL FACTORS OF LABOR

The progress and final outcome of labor are influenced by 4 factors called (1) the passage (the bony and soft tissues of the maternal pelvis), (2) the powers (the contractions or forces of the uterus), (3) the passenger (the fetus), and (4) the placenta. Abnormalities of any of these components, singly or in combination, may result in dystocia. The first and last are not subject to change by therapeutic manipulation during delivery; the second and third can be influenced by medications or by manual or forceps intervention.

1. THE PASSAGE

The Bony Pelvis

Variations in pelvic architecture must be carefully evaluated by the obstetrician because the progress of delivery is directly determined by the sequence of attitudes and positions the fetus must assume in its passage through the birth canal. For this reason, a reasonably accurate assessment of the pelvic architecture and the pelvic diameters is an important part of obstetric care.

The obstetrician is concerned essentially with the true rather than the false pelvis, which includes the inlet, the midpelvis, and the outlet. Modern concepts of obstetric pelvic types and their influence on the conduct of labor are based for the most part on the classic work of Caldwell and Moloy in the 1930s. The 4 basic pelvic types identified by these workers and generally adopted throughout the world are the gynecoid, android, anthropoid, and platypelloid pelvic configurations.

These designations are based essentially on the inlet configurations, but certain features of the lower true pelvis are also characteristic of each type. Most pelves are "mixed" types, the anterior segment resembling one type and the posterior segment another. The characteristics of the 4 basic pelvic types are shown in Table 31–1.

Clinical Evaluation

The capacity of the bony pelvis can be estimated accurately enough for practical purposes by careful clinical examination. Long experience in the examination of human pelves is necessary, since x-ray films and mechanical models are no substitute for the careful assessment of the characteristics of the bones of the pelvic girdle—although x-ray films may add important details. Clinical examination may have to be repeated during the course of pregnancy and even during labor if progress is unsatisfactory. It may be best to delay definitive typing and mensuration of the pelvis until shortly before term because the patient may have less discomfort late in pregnancy when the fetus has achieved maximal size.

A. Pelvic Landmarks: (See also Chapter 29.) In evaluating the course and conduct of labor, a thorough knowledge of the following pelvic landmarks and their spatial relationships is mandatory:

1. Pelvic inlet–The pelvic inlet is bounded anteriorly by the superior rami of the symphysis pubica, laterally by the iliopectineal lines, and posteriorly by

Table 31–1. Characteristics of 4 types of pelves.

	Gynecoid	Android	Anthropoid	Platypelloid
Widest transverse diameter of inlet	12.0 cm	12.0 cm	<12.0 cm	12.0 cm
Anteroposterior diameter of inlet	11.0 cm	11.0 cm	>12.0 cm	10.0 cm
Side walls	Straight	Convergent	Narrow	Wide
Forepelvis	Wide	Narrow	Divergent	Straight
Sacrosciatic notch	Medium	Narrow	Backward	Forward
Inclination of sacrum	Medium	Forward (lower 1/3)	Wide	Narrow
Ischial spines	Not prominent	Prominent	Not prominent	Not prominent
Suprapubic arch	Wide	Narrow	Medium	Wide
Transverse diameter of outlet	10.0 cm	<10.0 cm	10.0 cm	10.0 cm
Bone structure	Medium	Heavy	Medium	Medium

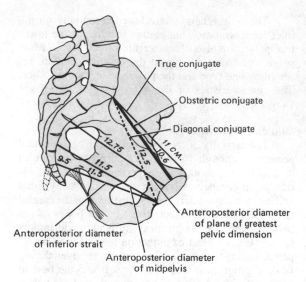

Figure 31–5. Pelvic measurements. (Reproduced, with permission, from Benson RC: *Handbook of Obstetrics & Gynecology*, 7th ed. Lange, 1980.)

the superior portion of the sacrum. Technically, the superior portion of the symphysis and the uppermost point of the sacral promontory lie just above the inlet (Fig 31–5). Thus, the anteroposterior diameter of the superior strait (**true conjugate** or **conjugata vera**) does not represent the shortest diameter. This actually lies just below the upper margin of the symphysis. The slightly shorter diameter, the **obstetric conjugate**, is the critical one through which the head must pass at this level.

The plane of the inlet, when considered as a flat surface, is inclined at an angle of about 55 degrees with the horizontal when the patient is standing. This angle is referred to as the pelvic inclination (Fig 31–5). When this angle is wide, the prognosis for satisfactory labor is better than when a narrow inclination is noted.

In actual practice, the true conjugate cannot be measured directly. For clinical purposes, however, its length is estimated indirectly by measuring the distance from the lower margin of the symphysis to the promontory of the sacrum. From this measurement— the **diagonal conjugate**—the **true conjugate** is determined by subtracting 1.5–2 cm (depending on the height and inclination of the symphysis). Normally, the true conjugate measures 11 cm or more.

The transverse diameter of the inlet is at right angles to the true conjugate and represents the greatest distance between the iliopectineal lines on either side. Unfortunately, it cannot be measured manually. The transverse diameter usually intersects the true conjugate at a point about 5 cm anterior to the sacral promontory, somewhat posterior to the true center of the inlet.

2. Midpelvis–The midpelvis is bounded anteriorly by the lower margin of the symphysis, laterally by the ischial spines, and posteriorly by the sacrum at the level of S3–S4. The midpelvis usually is the plane

of narrowest pelvic dimensions. Its normal anteroposterior diameter is about 11.5 cm, and its transverse (interspinous) diameter is approximately 10 cm.

3. Pelvic outlet–The pelvic outlet is bounded anteriorly by the subpubic arch, laterally by the ischial tuberosities, and posteriorly by the tip of the sacrum (not the coccyx). The outlet actually consists of 2 triangular planes with a common base, the latter being a line between the two ischial tuberosities. The latter measurement (intertuberous) averages 11.0 cm. The anteroposterior diameter of the outlet is 11.5–12.0 cm, while the posterior sagittal is about 7.5 cm in the average pelvis.

The side walls of the pelvis extend from the inlet at the point of the transverse diameter inferiorly and anteriorly to the lower levels of the ischial tuberosities. The side walls generally are straight; if they converge, they may limit the capacity of the midpelvis or outlet.

The axis of the pelvis refers to the curve of the birth canal (curve of Carus) as described by a line drawn through the center of each of the above planes. This line curves anteriorly as the outlet is approached (Fig 31–5).

B. Pelvic Contractions: The inlet is considered to be contracted if the anteroposterior diameter is 10 cm or less as represented by a diagonal conjugate measurement of 11.5 cm or less. Also, narrowing of the greatest transverse diameter to 11.5 cm or less or alteration of the configuration of the inlet, as revealed by x-ray, can lead to obstetric difficulty. The most common cause of inlet contraction is rickets, which affects about 7% of black women in the USA. Debilitating diseases in childhood also may lead to poor pelvic development with a generally contracted pelvis.

Midpelvic contraction generally is considered to exist when the diameter between the ischial spines is less than 9.5 cm. In addition, the capacity of the midpelvis is directly related to the posterior sagittal diameter of this plane, which normally is 5 cm. Midpelvic contracture is suggested by prominent ischial spines, converging pelvic side walls, and narrowed sacrosciatic notches.

Outlet contraction is considered to exist when the intertuberous (ischial) diameter is 8 cm or less. Contracture here, as in the midpelvis, is directly related to the posterior sagittal diameter and the subpubic arch configuration. Generally, dystocia may be expected at the outlet if the sum of the intertuberous diameter and the posterior sagittal diameter is less than 15 cm. It should be noted that the relationship between the interspinous diameter and the intertuberous diameter of a given pelvis is quite constant; outlet contraction of measurable degree is seldom seen without concomitant midpelvic contraction.

C. Prognosis for Vaginal Delivery: Pelvic (bony) dystocia may be due to the abnormalities and variations of any of the planes of the pelvis discussed above as well as to the various factors involved in size, position, presentation, and moldability of the fetal head. In addition to clinical evaluation of the pelvis, other details are helpful in prognosticating vaginal delivery in a given patient. These include data from the past obstetric history, ie, the duration and description of previous labors, the types of deliveries, and the sizes of infants born previously. A history of difficult forceps delivery, of unexplained stillbirth, of neonatal death or morbidity (particularly cerebral palsy), or of previous cesarean section after prolonged labor—each of these may suggest the possibility of pelvic contracture or relative cephalopelvic disproportion. In the primigravid patient, such factors as the age of the patient (very young or old with respect to childbearing), previous debilitating illnesses or pelvic girdle injury, nonengagement of the fetal head at term, failure to progress in labor, with primary or secondary inertia—all must be considered in the pelvic assessment.

D. Trial of Labor: In cases of borderline pelvic contraction, a trial of labor may be indicated. This must not be confused with the older concept of a "test of labor," which entailed, by definition, progression of labor to complete cervical dilatation and a period of 2 hours thereafter before deciding whether vaginal delivery was possible. This concept has no place in modern obstetrics, since many patients with significant cephalopelvic disproportion will not progress to complete dilatation or will reach this point only with serious jeopardy to both fetus and mother because of prolonged or violent labor.

No specific time limit can be imposed on the definition of trial of labor. All that is necessary is an adequate period of time in labor to provide reasonable evidence that vaginal delivery may be accomplished with safety to both mother and child. A trial of labor is often interpreted to mean 4–6 hours of good labor. If definite cervical dilatation occurs, continuing and satisfactory progress in labor should be anticipated. A definite timetable should be set up, with periodic reevaluation of all factors that might contribute to dystocia or failure of labor to progress. In general, in borderline pelvic contractions, failure to progress over a period of 4–6 hours calls for such evaluation. A complete trial of labor may occupy 6–18 hours, depending upon progress and the individual case. Nonetheless, such a trial should not be allowed to go much longer. In addition to pelvic size and configuration, fetal size and position and the character and effectiveness of uterine contractions must be assessed. The station of the fetal head, the presence or absence of molding, and the development of a fetal caput are helpful in evaluating the success of labor and the degree of disproportion.

E. X-Ray Pelvimetry: X-ray pelvimetry is a valuable adjunct in the obstetric management of patients with bony contraction of the pelvis. Be this as it may, its use must be tempered by an appreciation of the possible genetic radiation hazards involved plus the knowledge that it does not evaluate all of the numerous factors that determine the outcome of a given labor. Among these factors are the force and effectiveness of the uterine contractions, the size and malleability of the fetal head, and the presentation and position of the fetus. Other considerations involve the axis of the pelvis, the status of the fetal membranes, and the flexion of the fetal head.

X-ray films of the pelvis, desirable in specific circumstances, are not necessary in the great majority of cases. Instances in which x-ray pelvimetry may be helpful include the following:

1. Manual measurement revealing reduced diagonal conjugate (< 11.5 cm), intertuberous (ischial) diameter (< 8.5 cm), reduced posterior sagittal diameter of the outlet (< 5 cm), narrowed pubic arch, prominent ischial spines, converging pelvic side walls, or forward sacral inclination.

2. A history of difficult delivery with stillbirth, severe neonatal damage, or death in the neonatal period.

3. Unengaged fetal head at term in nulliparous patient.

4. Breech presentation in nulliparous patient.

5. Abnormal fetal presentation (face, brow, transverse).

6. Older primigravida.

7. Adolescent primigravida.

8. History of significant pelvic injury or disease.

9. Failure to progress satisfactorily in labor.

In general, an x-ray series consisting of 3 films properly taken is satisfactory for purposes of pelvimetry. These should include a lateral film with metal measuring rule included, an inlet view, and a film of the subpubic arch. The lateral film gives information about the anteroposterior diameter of the inlet and an estimation of the capacity of the posterior segment of the midpelvis and outlet. In addition, the biparietal diameter of the fetal head often can be estimated. If the film is taken with the patient standing, information about station (engagement) and position of the fetal head may also be obtained.

The inlet view reveals the shape of the pelvic inlet, with particular reference to the contour of the forepelvis. The relationships of the posterior sagittal and widest transverse diameters of this plane in order to evaluate pelvic capacity also are apparent.

The subpubic arch film, taken with the x-ray tube directed toward the symphysis (at a 45-degree angle), should reveal the intertuberous diameter, prominence of the ischial spines, extent of convergence of the side walls of the pelvis, as well as the angle and other characteristics of the subpubic arch.

X-ray pelvimetry, then, is a valuable obstetric adjunct but not a substitute for clinical judgment. A properly supervised trial of labor is justified in most patients even though a slight degree of fetopelvic disproportion may be suspected. The exact size of the infant, the efficiency of the forces of labor, and the adaptability of the fetal head to the various diameters of the pelvis often defy precise individual assessment. As with most aspects of obstetrics, the management of possible bony pelvic dystocia is a relative matter, demanding clinical judgment of the highest order in the best interests of mother and infant.

The Soft Tissues

The maternal pelvic soft tissues have an influence on the type and progress of labor. The muscles and fascia of the pelvis have been previously described in the chapter on anatomy of the pelvis. The levator ani muscles, which are the main soft tissue components of the pelvic cavity in the mid portion, consist of a pubococcygeus portion and an iliococcygeus portion. These play a role in the descent and expulsion of the fetus, since the birth canal (uterus, cervix, vagina) passes through these tissues. Also, the anatomy of the uterus and the vagina may vary the progress of labor. Occasionally, congenital malformations of these organs will obstruct labor, eg, vaginal septa or constrictions may be present. These and other vaginal abnormalities should be noted prior to the onset of labor.

Excessive rigidity or scarring of these tissues affects the flexion process as well as the resistance or nonresistance to descent of the passenger. Excessive relaxation at previous deep episiotomies with laceration of the pubococcygeal portion can presage precipitous delivery or deflexion attitudes of cephalic presentations with obstructed labor. It is these tissues that are protected by properly performed episiotomy or are overly stretched by excessive bearing-down efforts by the mother.

2. THE POWERS

The uterus remains relatively quiescent during the first half of pregnancy. Studies indicate, however, that recurrent myometrial contractions occur throughout pregnancy. These may be mild, irregular contractions that increase the intrauterine pressure only 1–5 mm Hg above the resting pressure. (The resting pressure between contractions, also called the tonus, is relatively constant throughout late pregnancy and early labor, ranging from 5 to 10 mm Hg.) As term approaches, regional activity persists, but there may be superimposed general contractions that are similar to those of normal labor. These are prodromal to true labor. With the onset of active labor, mild regional activity of the uterus disappears. Contractions become regular, stronger, and better coordinated at intervals of 2–3 minutes. In the beginning, the contractions average 20–30 mm Hg in intensity; and as labor progresses, the intensity rises to an average of about 50 mm Hg. Occasional individual contractions may peak to 100 mm Hg. The tonus or resting pressure remains at about 10 mm Hg between contractions until near the end of labor, when it may increase slightly. Since the upper part of the uterus contains many more myometrial elements than the lower portion, the usual contraction progresses through the uterus from above to below. In addition, each individual myometrial cell as it contracts does not quite regain its normal length on relaxation. This process is known as brachystasis of the uterine muscle fibers. As this mechanism progresses, an upper and a lower uterine segment are developed. Before the onset of labor, the lower uterine segment usually is thinner than the upper segment. The transition area between the 2 segments is designated the physiologic retraction ring. The lower uterine segment becomes progressively thinner as labor advances and the upper segment becomes progressively thicker. With these changes, the junction becomes more and more distinct.

Moderate obstruction is offered by the maternal soft parts even with complete dilatation of the cervix. The transverse cervical or cardinal ligaments are significant factors here, and the pubocervical fascia and uterosacral ligaments contribute also to soft tissue resistance.

3. THE PASSENGER

The diameters of the fetal head at term usually are greater than those of the body, and the head is thus the most difficult part to deliver. (In certain fetal abnormalities such as massive ascites the abdomen may be larger, but this is rare.) The fetal skull is composed of 3 major parts: the face, the vault or roof, and the base. The face and the base of the skull are composed of bones that are heavy and more or less fused. The bones of the vault are not joined. Thus, changes in shape are possible as the head passes through the pelvis and is subjected to constriction by external forces. This mechanism leads to temporary changes, defined as molding, in the general shape of the fetal head.

The vault is composed of 2 frontal bones, 2 parietal bones, and one occipital bone. They are slightly separated from one another at the sutures or margins of abutment and by wider spaces, the anterior and posterior fontanelles. The sutures and fontanelles can usually be identified by direct palpation. However, if there is excessive molding of the head or scalp edema, these landmarks may be obscured. The widest lateral diameter of the head, the biparietal diameter, averages 8.5–9.5 cm. In most cases, the head enters the pelvis with the sagittal suture line in the transverse plane of the mother's pelvis. When this suture is midway between the pubis and the sacrum, the relationship is referred to as synclitism. When the sagittal suture line deviates from the midline toward the symphysis or the sacrum, it is termed asynclitism. Asynclitism often is an indication that the pelvis is too small for descent of the fetal head, although asynclitism may be present in normal labor, particularly when the head is small. Flexion of the fetal head on the body is important in normal labor because flexion determines which diameter of the head will pass through the narrowest portion of the pelvis. In most cases, full flexion of the head is due to the pressures of the bony and soft tissues of the passage upon the fetal head as fetal descent occurs. When the head is fully flexed, the suboccipitobregmatic diameter is presented to the pelvis. This measures 9.5 cm in the average term infant. The common flexions are shown in Fig 31–6.

Gynecoid	Android	Platypelloid (flat)	Anthropoid

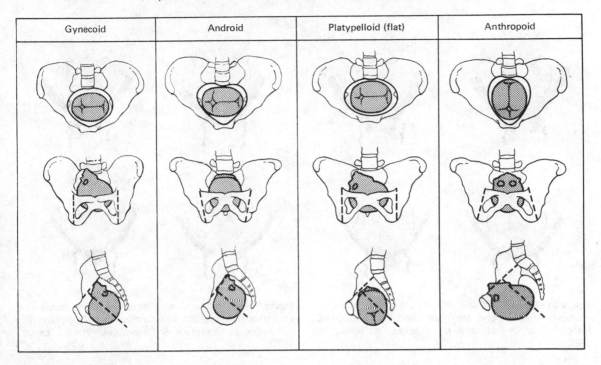

Figure 31–6. Flexions of the fetal head in the 4 major pelvic types. (Reproduced, with permission, from Danforth DN, Ellis, AH: *Am J Obstet Gynecol* 1963;**86**:29.)

4. THE PLACENTA

The placenta is a factor in labor only when it is implanted very low in the uterus. If placenta previa occurs, delivery from below may be impossible because of the likelihood of fetal and maternal hemorrhage. Cesarean section may then be mandatory.

THE COURSE OF NORMAL LABOR

Labor commonly is divided into 3 stages.

(1) The first stage begins with the onset of labor and ends when dilatation of the cervix (10 cm) is complete. This is usually the longest stage of labor and generally is longer with first pregnancies. The **average** duration of the first stage of labor in a primigravida is 8–12 hours; in a multipara 6–8 hours.

(2) The second stage of labor extends from full dilatation of the cervix to the complete birth of the baby and varies from a few minutes to several hours depending upon both fetal and maternal factors. In normal labor it usually does not exceed 2 hours.

(3) The third stage of labor is the period from the birth of the infant to delivery of the placenta. The hour immediately after delivery of the placenta, during which time the danger of postpartal hemorrhage is great, is often referred to as the fourth stage of labor; it will be considered here as part of the third stage.

During the first stage, effacement accompanies dilatation (Figs 31–7 and 31–8). It is often difficult to determine exactly when labor begins, but as a rule contractions that occur every 2–3 minutes and last 30–45 seconds result in significant dilatation or effacement of the cervix and descent of the presenting part.

The first stage of labor may be less than one hour or more than 24 hours depending upon (1) parity of the patient; (2) the frequency, intensity, and duration of uterine contractions; (3) the ability of the cervix to dilate and efface; (4) the fetopelvic diameters; and (5) the presentation and position of the fetus.

The second stage varies from a few minutes to several hours, depending upon (1) fetal presentation and position; (2) fetopelvic relationships; (3) resistance of maternal pelvic soft parts; (4) frequency, intensity, duration, and regularity of uterine contractions; and (5) efficiency of maternal voluntary expulsive efforts.

The rapidity of separation and means of delivery of the placenta determine the duration of the third stage.

MANAGEMENT OF EARLY LABOR

When the patient believes that she is in early labor, she should be carefully examined to confirm labor and to identify significant abnormalities (eg, fetopelvic disproportion, ineffectual uterine contractions). The history of the onset of contractions, the

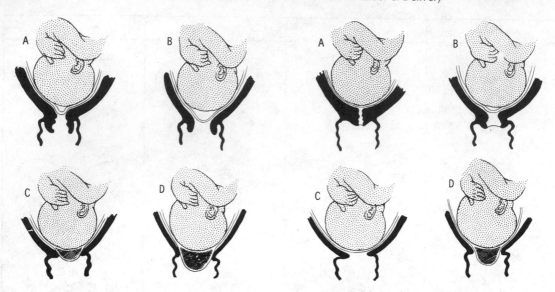

Figure 31–7. Dilatation and effacement of the cervix in a multipara. (Reproduced, with permission, from Benson RC: *Handbook of Obstetrics & Gynecology,* 7th ed. Lange, 1980.)

Figure 31–8. Dilatation and effacement of the cervix in a primipara. (Reproduced, with permission, from Benson RC: *Handbook of Obstetrics & Gynecology,* 7th ed. Lange, 1980.)

presence or absence of bleeding, the possible loss of amniotic fluid, and the fetal heart tones (FHT) and activity of the fetus should be recorded. A record of the prenatal care visits, examinations (especially pelvic measurements), laboratory reports, and any treatment given should be reviewed if it is available. The review of recent events should include not only data regarding intercurrent infections or other illnesses but also the time of the patient's last meal.

Initial Examination & Procedures

Examination of a woman in early or suspected early labor should consist of a basic evaluation of her current clinical condition. How the patient reacts to labor (eg, anxiety, tension) is also an important part of the total evaluation.

(1) Admit the patient if she has been registered in a hospital, or visit her at home if delivery at home is anticipated.

(2) Obtain a history of relevant medical details since the last examination.

(3) Record the vital signs: temperature, pulse, respiratory rate, and blood pressure. Make an appraisal of the patient's general condition together with any grossly abnormal physical findings.

(4) Obtain a clean-catch urine specimen and test for protein and glucose to establish a baseline for subsequent management of the patient.

(5) Do a brief general physical examination. Isolate the patient if infection is discovered or suspected.

(6) Examine the abdomen, noting such things as scars or evidence of old trauma. Palpate the uterus to determine the fetal presentation, engagement, position, and level of the most dependent part (Fig 31–4). Count the FHT for 1 minute with a stethoscope or

electronic instrument (eg, Doptone). (It is helpful to indicate the location of the FHT with suitable markings on the skin for the benefit of other examiners and to note rotation and descent of the fetus.)

(7) Note the frequency, regularity, intensity, and duration of the uterine contractions.

(8) If there is evidence of vaginal bleeding or loss of amniotic fluid, record the type and amount. (It is particularly important to note the color and character of the amniotic fluid, eg, the presence or absence of meconium or staining. Nitrazine indicator paper will turn to deep blue-green [alkaline] from yellow [acid] when moistened with amniotic fluid.)

(9) Vaginal or rectal examination: Aseptic vaginal examination should be done to determine the degree of dilatation and effacement of the cervix as well as any abnormalities of the soft tissues of the birth canal. Vaginal examination is preferred to rectal examination because it affords more accurate estimation of the progress of labor, dilatation and effacement of the cervix, and characteristics of the presenting part. This evaluation should identify the presenting fetal part and the station of the presenting part in relation to the level of the ischial spines (Fig 31–9). If the presenting part is at the spines, it is said to be at "zero station"; if above the spines, the distances are stated in minus figures (−1 cm, −2 cm, −3 cm, and "floating"); if below the spines, the distances are stated in plus figures (+1 cm, +2 cm, +3 cm, and "on the perineum").

(a) Dilatation of the cervical os is expressed in cm, indicating the diameter of the cervical opening. Ten centimeters constitutes full dilatation. A diameter of 6 cm or less can be measured directly; when the distance is more than 6 cm, however, it is often easier to subtract twice the width of the remaining "rim"

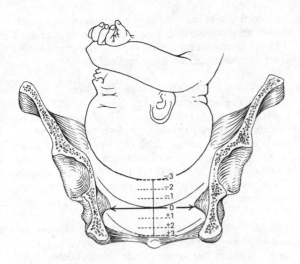

Figure 31–9. Stations of the fetal head. (Reproduced, with permission, from Benson RC: *Handbook of Obstetrics & Gynecology,* 7th ed. Lange, 1980.)

from 10 cm. For example, if a 1-cm rim is felt anteriorly, posteriorly, and laterally, this indicates 8 cm dilatation.

(b) Effacement of the cervix (Figs 31–7 and 31–8) is a process of thinning out that is accomplished before and (especially) during the first stage of labor. The cervix thins by retraction. In this manner, it "gets out of the way" of the presenting part, allowing more room for the birth process. Expression of mucus and compression aid in thinning of the cervix.

Effacement is expressed in percent from 0% (uneffaced) to 100% (cervix less than about 0.25 cm thick).

(c) The position of the presenting part can usually be confirmed by vaginal examination:

(i) Vertex presentations (Fig 31–1): The fontanelles and the sagittal suture are palpated. The position is determined by the relation of the fetal occiput to the mother's right or left side. This is expressed as OA (occiput precisely anterior), LOA (left occiput anterior), LOP (left occiput posterior), etc.

(ii) Breech presentations (Fig 31–2) are determined by the position of the infant's sacrum with respect to the mother's right or left side. This is expressed as SA (sacrum directly anterior), LSA (left sacrum anterior), LSP, etc.

(iii) Face presentations (Fig 31–3): Extension of the fetal head on the neck causes the face to be the presenting part. The chin, a prominent and identifiable facial landmark, is used as a point of reference. As with vertex presentations, the position of the fetal chin is related to the mother's pelvis, left or right side, and the anterior or posterior portion. This is expressed as RMP (right mentum posterior), etc.

(iv) Brow, bregma, or sinciput presentation is midway between flexion and extension. It usually is a temporary presentation which converts during labor to face or occiput presentation.

(v) In transverse presentations, the long axis of the body of the fetus is perpendicular to that of the mother. One shoulder (acromion) will occupy the superior strait but will be considerably to the right or left of the midline. Transverse presentations are designated by relating the child's inferior shoulder and back to the mother's back or abdominal wall. Thus, LADP (left acromiodorsoposterior) indicates that the baby's lower shoulder is to the mother's left and its back is toward her back.

(vi) Compound presentations imply prolapse of a hand, an arm, or a foot or leg complicating one of the above presentations. These special or unusual presentations are generally recorded without abbreviations.

(10) Other examinations: If there are questions about the presentation of the fetus, ultrasonograms or x-ray films of the abdomen may be helpful in determining the presence of bony abnormalities of the fetus as well as the differentiation of abnormal presentations from normal ones, eg, breech, face, compound, or transverse lie. It may be particularly difficult to determine these findings clinically in the markedly obese patient, in the gravida who is in extremely active labor with a contracting, tight uterus, or when there may be partial placental separation or abnormal uterine function. At times, although the initial physical examination may be confusing, further examination as labor progresses may help clarify the situation.

Preparation of the Patient for Labor

If the patient definitely is in early labor and therefore is to remain in the home or hospital for anticipated delivery, further preparation should be carried out.

(1) Preparation and cleansing of the pudendum should include cleansing the perineum and removal of excess labial and pubic hair. It is now customary in most obstetric services to do what is called a "miniprep" in which only the vulvar hair is removed, leaving the hair over the mons pubis. The vulva should be cleansed with a soap solution or nonirritating detergent preparation.

(2) If delivery is not imminent, the lower bowel should be emptied by means of an enema or laxative rectal suppository.

(3) The patient in mild labor should be advised to remain in bed if the membranes have been ruptured, if she is bleeding, or if a sedative has been administered.

(4) If the patient is uncomfortable or apprehensive, a barbiturate may be given, eg, secobarbital, 100 mg orally; or an antihistamine with sedative properties such as promethazine (Phenergan) may be given instead.

(5) Analgesics are helpful for the very apprehensive or agitated patient. The preferred analgesic on most services is meperidine (pethidine, Demerol), 50–75 mg intramuscularly or intravenously. To reduce the amount of analgesia needed, tranquilizers such as promethazine (Phenergan) or promazine (Sparine) may be given concomitantly to enhance the effect of the analgesic drug. Hydroxyzine hydrochloride (Vistaril) has both ataraxic and antiemetic effects. It is

useful in alleviating anxiety and tension and potentiates the effects of many analgesics, thus permitting lower doses of these agents. The usual dosage is 50 mg intramuscularly every 4–6 hours.

Analgesics should be coordinated with anesthesia (see Chapter 30). Small doses of analgesics are not injurious to the fetus and may be beneficial for the mother.

If analgesic preparations are used, they should not be administered too frequently. An interval of 2–4 hours between doses usually is advisable. Sedatives or analgesic drugs should not be given immediately before anticipated delivery because of possible depressive effects on the infant. Analgesia should not be given too early in labor because it may slow the progress of labor. This is true also if analgesia is given in excessive amounts. Drug therapy must be individualized for each patient. The progress of labor, the intensity of contractions, the pain threshold of the patient, and the presence or absence of complications—all are features in the decision whether to administer sedative or analgesic medications.

Conduction anesthesia (epidural, caudal) may be used late in the first stage of labor for analgesia and carried through delivery as anesthesia. These methods are usually reserved for the second stage of labor and delivery.

(6) Diet and fluids: Small amounts of clear liquids are permissible, but the patient should not be given solid food during labor. Gastric motility is greatly inhibited by uterine contractions, and the possibility of vomiting always involves the danger of aspiration of vomitus and respiratory complications. Small amounts of antacids may be given to prevent possible tracheal irritation in case of vomiting. If fluids are needed during prolonged labor or if dehydration exists, intravenous infusions rather than oral fluids are indicated. An indwelling, continuous intravenous drip (eg, Intracath) provides a ready means of access for medications if complications occur or for the administration of oxytocic agents if necessary for stimulation of labor. The intravenous route has an additional advantage in that the actual amount of fluid being administered can

be recorded. For the reasons given above, a continuous slow intravenous drip (5% dextrose in water at a rate of 125 mL/h) is recommended in most patients as standard procedure during labor and delivery.

Supervision of the First Stage of Labor

(1) The fetal heart tones (FHT) should be recorded every 10–15 minutes. If it is suspected that problems may arise in labor or delivery or if the patient has been categorized as "high-risk" on the basis of her obstetric history or prior examination, electronic fetal monitoring should be utilized. If the presence of complications is established or anticipated, continuous fetal heart tone monitoring will be necessary (Fig 31–10).

(2) The patient should be examined abdominally and vaginally as necessary to follow the progress of labor. Early in the uncomplicated case, such examinations may be done hourly. As labor progresses, more frequent examinations usually are required. However, too frequent vaginal or rectal examinations cause the patient discomfort and increase the incidence of intrauterine infection, particularly after rupture of the membranes. Descent of the fetus and internal rotation can often be determined by external palpation alone. Shift of the point of maximal impulse of the fetal heartbeat is a useful indication of fetal descent.

On vaginal examination, dilatation and effacement of the cervix, the station and position of the presenting part, or the presence of an abnormality should be noted, particularly if the presenting part is high. The possibility of prolapse of the umbilical cord should always be entertained. The passage of blood, amniotic fluid, or meconium should be recorded.

(3) The frequency and character of the uterine contractions, the tone of the uterus, and the general reaction of the patient in labor should be recorded periodically. Graphic display of cervical dilatation and the time elapsed provides a visual concept of the progress of labor. (Compare Figs 31–11 to 31–14.)

(4) It is important that proper perineal hygiene be maintained. Cleanse the vulvar region before and after the internal examination, after defecation and voiding, or when soiling by vaginal secretions occurs.

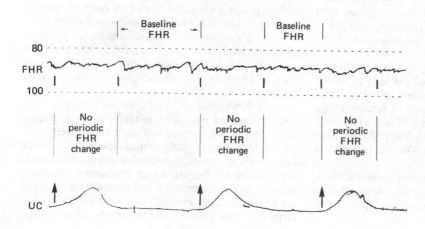

Figure 31–10. Normal FHR with average variability. UC, uterine contraction. Periodic FHR changes are, by definition, changes in FHR associated with uterine contractions. Baseline FHR is the FHR between periodic FHR changes. (Reproduced, with permission, from Hon EH: *An Atlas of Fetal Heart Rate Patterns.* Harty Press, 1968.)

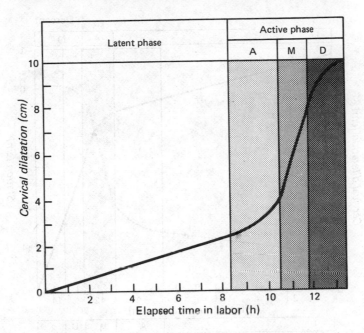

Figure 31–11. Dilatation of the cervix at various phases of labor. A, acceleration phase. M, phase of maximum slope. D, deceleration phase. (Primiparous labor.)

(5) The patient should be encouraged to void as labor progresses. This usually can be accomplished with a commode at the bedside or with a bedpan in bed. If the patient cannot void, however, she should be catheterized to prevent overdistention of the bladder. If the latter occurs, the patient may suffer from bladder atony postpartum.

Preparation for Delivery

Adequate delivery room facilities include anesthesia and resuscitation equipment and drugs as well as the sterile surgical instruments that may be needed. Drapes, sponges, and sutures should be on the delivery table. (Most delivery rooms have a standard set-up, but variations are permissible if they are in conformity with sound surgical principles.)

The patient should be transported from the labor to the delivery room on a wheeled litter with siderails. For delivery, knee crutches should be available so that the legs can be supported when the patient is in the lithotomy position. An even better procedure is to suspend the legs vertically from the feet by means of a vertical support fixed to the table. The patient's body should not be allowed to extend beyond the end of the delivery table because of the possibility of back injury.

After the patient is properly positioned on the delivery table, surgical preparation of the vulvar area should be carried out with detergent and antiseptic solution such as povidone-iodine (Betadine, Isodyne). Surgical drapes should be applied so that the legs and abdomen are covered. This procedure will ensure a surgically clean field for delivery. The physician and assistants must scrub their hands and wear masks and sterile gowns and gloves as for a major surgical procedure.

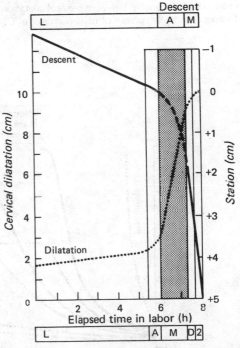

Figure 31–12. Composite mean curves for descent (solid line) and dilatation (broken line) for 389 multiparas. Intervals: L, latent. A, acceleration. M, maximum slope. D, deceleration. 2, second stage. Relationship is shown between acceleration period of descent and maximum slope of dilatation (shaded area), between latent period of descent and latent plus acceleration phases of dilatation, and between maximum slope of descent and deceleration phase plus second stage. (Redrawn and reproduced, with permission, from Friedman and Sachtleben: *Am J Obstet Gynecol* 1965;**93**:526.)

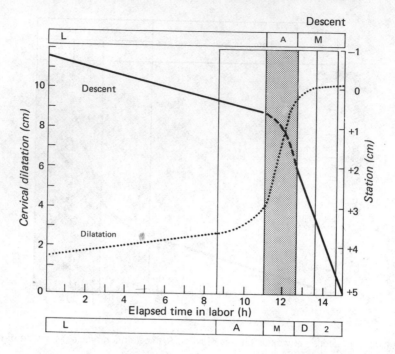

Figure 31–13. Relationship between cervical dilatation and descent of the presenting part in a primipara. L, latent phase. A, acceleration phase. M, phase of maximum slope. D, deceleration phase. 2, second stage.

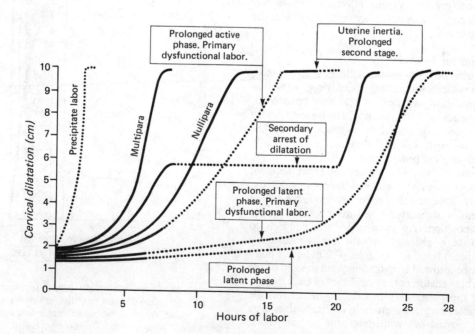

Figure 31–14. Major types of deviation from normal progress of labor may be detected by noting dilatation of cervix at various intervals after labor begins.

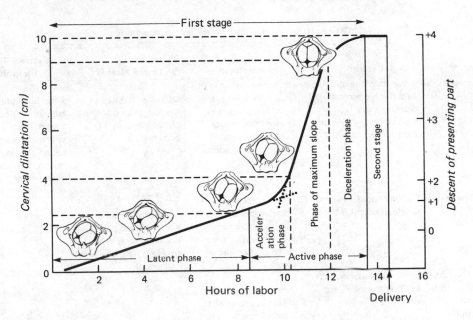

Figure 31–15. Schematic illustration of progress of rotation of OA in the successive stages of labor.

MECHANISM OF THE SECOND STAGE OF LABOR
(Tables 31–2 and 31–3; Figs 31–16 to 31–23)

Vertex Presentation

The mechanism of labor in the vertex as well as the breech presentation (see below) consists of engagement of the presenting part, flexion, descent, internal rotation, extension, and external rotation (or restitution). The mechanism of labor is dictated by the pelvic dimensions and configuration (both bony and soft parts), the size of the passenger, and the strength of the contractions. In essence, delivery proceeds along the "line of least resistance," ie, by adaptation of the smallest achievable diameters of the presenting part to the most favorable dimensions and contours of the birth canal. Particularly in the case of vertex presentations, delivery is somewhat like the passage of a rounded object through a short bent stovepipe equipped with several dampers (baffles).

The sequence of events in vertex presentation is as follows:

A. Engagement: This usually occurs late in pregnancy—in the primigravida, commonly in the last 2 weeks. In the multiparous patient, engagement usually occurs with the onset of labor. The head usually enters the superior strait in the occiput posterior position.

B. Flexion: Flexion usually is essential for passage of the smallest diameter of the head through the smallest diameter of the bony pelvis. In most cases, flexion is essential for both engagement and descent. This will vary, of course, if the head is small in relation to the pelvis or if the pelvis is unusually large. When the head is improperly flexed—or if there is significant narrowing of the pelvic strait (as in the platypelloid type of pelvis)—there may be some degree of deflex-

Table 31–2. Mechanisms of labor: vertex presentation.

Engagement	Flexion	Descent	Internal Rotation	Extension	External Rotation (Restitution)
Generally occurs in late pregnancy or at onset of labor. Mode of entry into superior strait depends on pelvic configuration; posterior occiput is most common position.	Good flexion is noted in most cases. Flexion aids engagement and descent. (Extension occurs in brow and face presentations.)	Depends on pelvic architecture and cephalopelvic relationships. Descent is usually slowly progressive.	Takes place during descent. After engagement, vertex usually rotates to the transverse. It must next rotate to the anterior or posterior to pass the ischial spines, whereupon, when the vertex reaches the perineum, rotation from a posterior to an anterior position generally follows.	Follows distention of the perineum by the vertex. Head concomitantly stems beneath the symphysis. Extension is complete with delivery of the head.	Following delivery, head normally rotates to the position it originally occupied at engagement. Next, the shoulders descend (in a path similar to that traced by the head). They rotate anteroposteriorly for delivery. Then the head swings back to its position at birth. The body of the baby is delivered next.

Table 31–3. Mechanisms of labor: frank breech presentation.

Flexion	Descent	Internal Rotation	Lateral Flexion	External Rotation (Restitution)
Hips: Engagement usually occurs in one of oblique diameters of pelvic inlet.				
	Anterior hip generally descends more rapidly than posterior, both at inlet and outlet.	Ordinarily takes place when breech reaches levator musculature. Fetal bitrochanteric rotates to anteroposterior diameter.	Occurs when anterior hip stems beneath symphysis; posterior hip is born first.	After birth of breech and legs, infant's body turns toward mother's side to which its back was directed at engagement of breech. This accommodates engagement of the shoulders.
Shoulders: Bisacromial diameter engages in same diameter as breech.				
	Gradual descent is the rule.	Anterior shoulder rotates so as to bring shoulders into anteroposterior diameter of outlet.	Anterior shoulder at symphysis and posterior shoulder is delivered first (when body is supported).	
Head: Engages in the same diameter as shoulders.				
Flexes on entry into superior strait. Biparietal occupies oblique used by shoulders. At outlet, neck or chin arrests beneath symphysis and head is delivered by gradual flexion.	Follows the shoulders.	Occiput (if a posterior) or face (if an occiput anterior) rotates to hollow of sacrum. This brings presenting part to anteroposterior diameter of outlet.		

ion if not actual extension. Such is the case with a brow (deflexion) or face (extension) presentation.

C. Descent: Descent is gradually progressive and is affected by the forces of labor and thinning of the lower uterine segment. Other factors also play a part, eg, pelvic configuration and the size and position of the presenting part. The greater the pelvic resistance or the poorer the contractions, the slower the descent.

D. Internal Rotation: Internal rotation occurs along with descent. The vertex usually rotates from the posterior to the transverse position following engagement. As the head descends, the vertex usually rotates to the anterior or posterior position. Rotation one way or the other will usually be necessary for the presenting part to traverse the plane of the ischial spines. When the vertex reaches the perineum, rotation from the posterior to the anterior position generally follows if it has traversed the spines in the posterior position. Nonetheless, the fetus may present in a persistent posterior position.

E. Extension: Extension follows extrusion of the head beyond the introitus, with the occiput beneath the symphysis pubica.

F. External Rotation: External rotation (restitution) follows delivery of the head when it rotates to the position it occupied at engagement. Following this, the shoulders descend in a path similar to that traced by the head to expulsion. The shoulders rotate anteroposteriorly for delivery. As this occurs, the head swings back to its position at birth. Following these maneuvers, the body, legs, and feet are delivered.

Breech Presentation

The mechanism of labor varies for breech presentations. The hips usually engage in one of the oblique diameters of the pelvic inlet. As descent occurs, the anterior hip generally descends more rapidly than the posterior hip both at the inlet and the outlet. Internal rotation occurs when the breech reaches the levator muscles and the fetal bitrochanteric diameter rotates to the anteroposterior diameter. Lateral flexion occurs when the anterior hip stems beneath the symphysis; this allows the posterior hip to be born first. The infant's body turns toward the mother's side to which its back was directed at engagement. This allows accommodation for engagement of the shoulders. Hence, the bisacromial diameter engages in the same diameter as the breech. There is gradual descent. The anterior shoulder rotates so as to bring the shoulders into the anteroposterior diameter of the outlet just as did the fetal trochanteric diameter. The anterior shoulder then follows lateral flexion to appear beneath the symphysis and the posterior shoulder is delivered first as the body is supported. The head in breech presentation tends to engage in the same diameter as the shoulders. It flexes on entry into the superior strait and the biparietal diameter occupies the oblique used by the shoulders. Descent occurs following the path of the shoulders, and internal rotation occurs to the hollow of the sacrum.

MANAGEMENT OF THE SECOND
STAGE OF LABOR
(Vertex Delivery)

Spontaneous delivery of the fetus presenting by the vertex is divided into 3 phases: (1) delivery of the head, (2) delivery of the shoulders, and (3) delivery of the body and legs. The second stage of labor begins when the cervix is fully dilated. The obstetrician should be alert to the imminence of delivery following complete dilatation of the cervix. However, this stage may last as long as 1–2 hours.

Delivery should be anticipated when the presenting part reaches the pelvic floor. This may be sooner if the patient is a multipara or if labor is progressing rapidly.

Preparations for delivery should be made as noted above. When the presenting part distends the perineum, anesthesia may be administered. Pudendal block or induction of general anesthesia may be performed at this time. If conduction anesthesia is being used (epidural, caudal, or spinal), it is usually administered in the late first stage or in the second stage as previously noted.

Episiotomy is carried out when delivery is imminent. Median episiotomy is preferred in most cases. If the perineum is short or if there are contraindications to a median episiotomy, mediolateral episiotomy may be performed. Bleeding should be controlled by hemostats. In the case of a breech, the episiotomy should be very generous so as not to impede delivery of the aftercoming head.

Distention of the perineum may be accentuated by voluntary efforts by the patient, by forceps, or with a vacuum extractor. Between uterine contractions the presenting part tends to recede slightly, but "crowning" occurs when the head is visible at the vaginal introitus and the widest portion (biparietal diameter) of the head distends the vulva just prior to its delivery.

In all cases, delivery should be controlled so as to prevent forceful, sudden expulsion or extraction of the baby. Central nervous system damage to the offspring can be caused by sudden precipitous birth; a controlled delivery should prevent fetal and maternal injury. Thus, as the head advances, its progress should be controlled by pressure applied laterally beneath the symphysis, and flexion of the head should be maintained, when necessary, by pressure over the perineum. The speed of delivery should be slowed as necessary to avoid pudendal lacerations or unexpected extrusion of the fetal head. Sudden marked variations in intracranial pressure may cause cerebral hemorrhage.

Gentle, gradual delivery is desirable. The perineum may be drawn downward with 2 fingers to allow the head to clear the perineal body. Do not insert the fingers into the birth canal or anus to facilitate delivery at this time; trauma or infection may occur. Pressure applied from the coccygeal region upward (modified Ritgen maneuver [Fig 31–19]) will extend the head at the proper time and thereby protect the perineal musculature.

Episiotomy is done when the infant's head begins to distend the introitus.

Delivery of the Head (Figs 31–16 to 31–21)

In vertex presentations, the forehead appears first (after the vertex) and then the face and chin. The neck appears next. The umbilical cord is around the baby's neck in about 15–20% of deliveries. Fortunately, the cord is rarely tight enough to cause fetal hypoxia. It should be loosened cautiously and pulsations checked. If the cord is pulsating well, there is no need to hasten delivery. Gently slip the cord over the infant's head. If this cannot be done easily, doubly clamp the cord with forceps, cut between the forceps, and proceed with the delivery. Once the head has been delivered, the infant's airway should be cleared by pressure on the trachea and nose. Wipe fluid from the nose and mouth and then aspirate the nasal and oral passages with a soft rubber suction bulb or with a small catheter attached to a DeLee suction trap.

Before external rotation (restitution), which occurs next, the head is usually drawn back toward the perineum. This movement precedes engagement of the shoulders, which are now entering the pelvic inlet. From this time on, support the infant manually and facilitate the mechanism of labor.

Do not hurry! If the strength of contractions seems to wane, be patient—labor will continue. Once the airway is clear, the infant can breathe and is in no immediate danger.

Following delivery of the head, gentle traction should be exerted on it downward or posteriorly; this aids progression of the anterior shoulder beneath the symphysis. The forward shoulder will gradually appear. Next, the head should be lifted upward to aid delivery of the posterior shoulder. If it becomes necessary to expedite delivery of the shoulders, the posterior arm of the fetus may be delivered by inserting the fingers into the vagina to bring the arm down across the baby's chest and out of the introitus. Traction on the head should be gentle to avoid excessive stretching. Do not hook a finger into the axilla to deliver a shoulder as it may cause brachial plexus injury (Erb or Duchenne), hematoma of the neck, or fracture of the clavicle.

Delivery of the Shoulders (Figs 31–22 and 31–23)

Delivery of the shoulders should be slow and gradual; the shoulders should be rotated if necessary to the anteroposterior diameter of the outlet.

Elevate the head toward the mother's symphysis for release of the posterior shoulder; this is often easily done and should be tried.

Depress the head toward the mother's coccyx to bring out the anterior shoulder.

In vertex presentations, a hand may present after the head. This need not obstruct delivery of the shoulders. Merely sweep the baby's hand and arm over its face, draw the arm out, and deliver the other shoulder as outlined above.

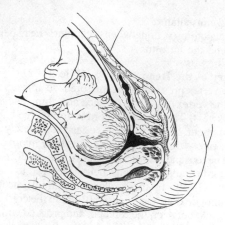

Figure 31–16. Engagement of LOA. (Reproduced, with permission, from Benson RC: *Handbook of Obstetrics & Gynecology,* 7th ed. Lange, 1980.)

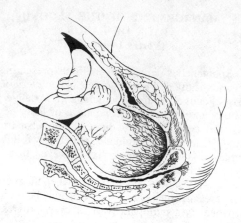

Figure 31–17. Descent in LOA position. (Reproduced, with permission, from Benson RC: *Handbook of Obstetrics & Gynecology,* 7th ed. Lange, 1980.)

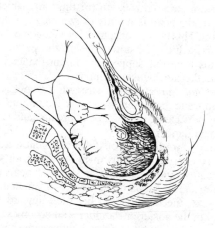

Figure 31–18. Anterior rotation of head. (Reproduced, with permission, from Benson RC: *Handbook of Obstetrics & Gynecology,* 7th ed. Lange, 1980.)

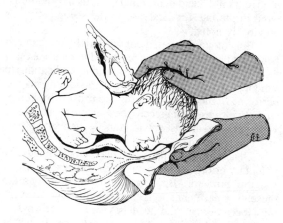

Figure 31–19. Modified Ritgen maneuver. (Reproduced, with permission, from Benson RC: *Handbook of Obstetrics & Gynecology,* 7th ed. Lange, 1980.)

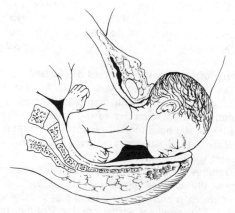

Figure 31–20. Extension of head. (Reproduced, with permission, from Benson RC: *Handbook of Obstetrics & Gynecology,* 7th ed. Lange, 1980.)

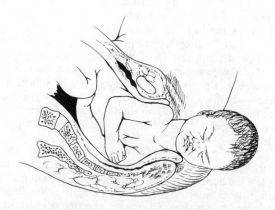

Figure 31–21. External rotation of head. (Reproduced, with permission, from Benson RC: *Handbook of Obstetrics & Gynecology,* 7th ed. Lange, 1980.)

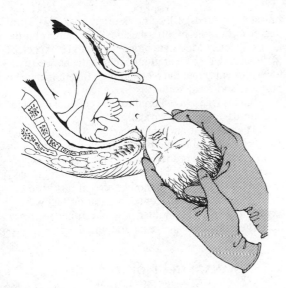

Figure 31–22. Delivery of anterior shoulder. (Reproduced, with permission, from Benson RC: *Handbook of Obstetrics & Gynecology,* 7th ed. Lange, 1980.)

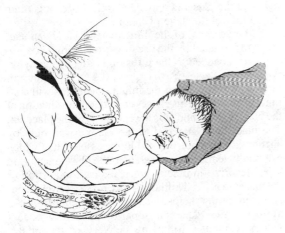

Figure 31–23. Delivery of posterior shoulder. (Reproduced, with permission, from Benson RC: *Handbook of Obstetrics & Gynecology,* 7th ed. Lange, 1980.)

Caution: Avoid undue pressure and traction on the neck and shoulders in order to prevent injury to the brachial plexus and large vessels.

Delivery of the Body & Extremities

The body and legs should be delivered gradually by easy traction after the shoulders have been freed.

Immediate Care of the Infant

As soon as the infant is delivered, it should be held with the head lower than the body (no more than 15 degrees) to facilitate drainage by gravity of accumulated mucus and bronchial secretions in the airways. Record the Apgar rating at 1 minute and at 5 minutes. The air passages should be cleared by means of a soft rubber bulb syringe. Place the baby on a wheeled stand or tray the height of the delivery table or slightly lower. If it is below the level of the placental insertion, blood will drain readily from the placenta and cord to the newborn. This will amount to 30–90 mL before the cord is clamped or the placenta separates. Resuscitation measures must be instituted immediately if there is evidence of cardiorespiratory distress. The baby should be placed under radiant heat or in a heated newborn care cart to preserve body heat. Cooling of the infant should be avoided at all times.

Some physicians place the child on the mother's abdomen. This contaminates the sterile field, however, and the baby is not secure there. Furthermore, with the baby on the mother's abdomen blood may drain from the baby into the cord and placenta.

The body temperature of the newborn must be maintained by radiant heat from above to avoid chilling. The cord must be clamped and cut as soon as its pulsations cease (or sooner if the infant is premature or distressed or if erythroblastosis is probable). The umbilical cord should be examined to identify the number of vessels. Two arteries and one vein are normal.

Apply a sterile cord clamp, cord tie of umbilical tape, or a rubber band just distal to the skin edge at the cord insertion at the umbilicus. Cover the cord stump with a dry gauze dressing held by a belly band, preferably of elastic material. It is best to clamp the umbilical cord approximately 1 cm from the skin reflection. Wipe the eyelids with moist cotton. Next, 1 drop of 1% aqueous silver nitrate must be instilled into each eye. The medication must be freshly prepared or expressed from commercial wax "pearls" which maintain the safe concentration. (Penicillin ophthalmic ointment is as effective as silver nitrate against gonococci and pneumococci and costs about the same, but the law in some jurisdictions calls for silver nitrate.) Excessive silver nitrate should be washed out with sterile saline after about 30–60 seconds.

A general physical examination is next in order, and any gross abnormalities or congenital malformations are noted in the record. Record also the weight, total length, crown-rump length, shoulder circumference, head circumference, and cranial diameters.

It is imperative that proper identification be affixed in the form of a necklace or bracelet before the newborn is transferred from the labor room to the nursery, and this must be verified by checking with the mother's identification.

When feasible, the mother should be given the infant to hold or even to nurse. The infant is then transferred to the nursery for further observation and care.

Immediate Care of the Mother Postpartum

Following delivery of the placenta (described below), the perineum, vagina, and cervix must be inspected thoroughly for lacerations, hematomas, or extension of episiotomy incisions. The cervix may be examined by manual retraction of the vaginal walls for visualization or by placement of a self-retaining retractor. The cervix should be examined circumferentially and any significant lacerations noted. Lacerations longer than 1 cm should be repaired at this time with interrupted absorbable sutures. The mattress type suture, tied not too tightly because of cervical edema, should ensure hemostasis and healing. Lacerations of the vaginal vault must be sought and repaired also. Hematomas greater than 3 cm in diameter should be excised and drained and deep mattress sutures placed for control of bleeding. Following inspection of the cervix and the vaginal vault, a temporary pack may be placed in the vagina to maintain a clear field of visualization during the episiotomy repair.

The extent of laceration of the birth canal may be designated roughly in degrees (Fig 31–24): (1) In first degree lacerations, only mucosa or skin (or both) is damaged. Bleeding is usually minimal. (2) Second degree lacerations include tears of the mucosa or skin (or both) plus disruption of the superficial fascia and the transverse perineal muscle. (The sphincter ani

muscle is spared.) Bleeding is often brisk. (3) Third degree lacerations involve the above structures plus the anal sphincter. Moderate blood loss is to be expected. (4) Fourth degree lacerations include the above structures plus entry into the rectal lumen. Bleeding may be profuse, and fecal soiling is inevitable.

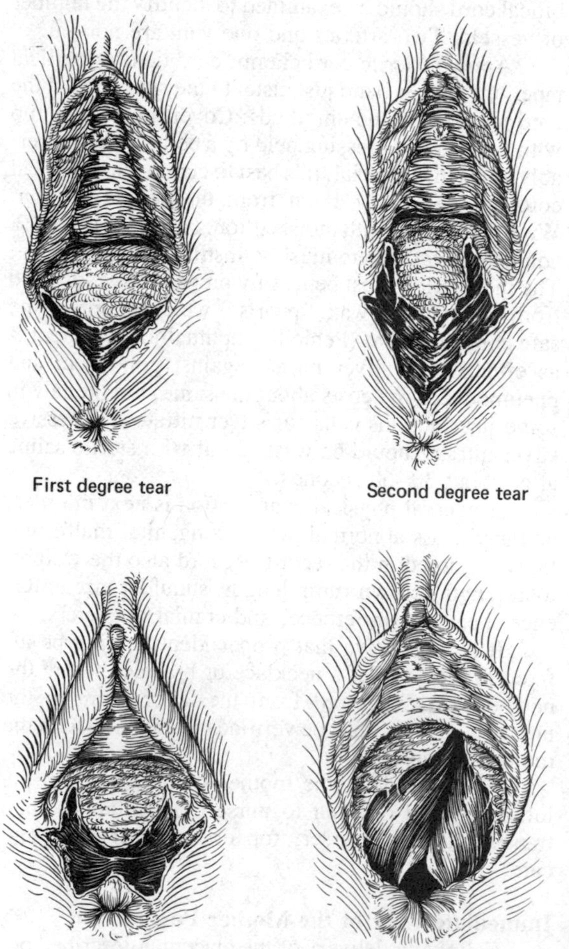

Sulcus lacerations, urethral and cervical damage, etc, are designated specifically.

The administration of oxygen to the mother after delivery of the infant but before the cord is clamped is of no value if one is attempting to increase the oxygenation of the infant's blood. Little or no oxygen can reach the baby from the mother after it has been delivered because of placental separation. However, oxygen given to the mother may aid in her recovery from the effects of analgesia and anesthesia.

MANAGEMENT OF THE THIRD STAGE OF LABOR

The third or placental stage of labor extends from the delivery of the infant's body to delivery of the placenta. Because the hour immediately following delivery of the placenta may be a critical one, it is often called the fourth stage of labor.

Management of the third stage of labor can usually be facilitated by the use of oxytocic drugs (oxytocin), 10 IU added to the infusion bottle; or methylergonovine maleate (Methergine), 0.2 mg intramuscularly. After delivery of the infant, the uterus will continue to contract. This causes considerable reduction of the placental site and aids in separation of the placenta. The placenta is attached to the uterine wall only by anchor villi and thin-walled blood vessels, all of which eventually tear. In some instances the placental margin separates first; in others, when the central portion of the placenta is freed initially, there may be retroplacental bleeding that helps to shear the placenta from the uterine wall. Placental separation usually occurs within 5 minutes following delivery of the infant. There may be incomplete or gradual separation of the placenta, however, due to uterine relaxation, minimal retroplacental bleeding, or placental or uterine abnormalities that lead to fibrosis and firm attachment of the placenta to the uterine wall. Extensive placental attachment is known as placenta accreta and may be partial or total. When the placenta separates incompletely, it may allow retroplacental blood sinuses to remain open, so that severe blood loss may result. Moreover, the presence of the placenta in the uterus may prevent contraction of the uterus, thus allowing considerable blood loss during the third stage. Normal placental separation is indicated by a firmly contracting and rising uterine fundus.

Uterine anomaly or tumor, a second undelivered fetus, feces, a tumor, and lacerations of the birth canal can mimic many of the signs of normal placental separation. There is a palpable and visible prominence above the symphysis (if the bladder is empty) and a slight gush of blood from the vagina.

First degree tear

Second degree tear

Third degree tear

Complete tear

Figure 31–24. Perineal tears. (Reproduced, with permission, from Benson RC: *Handbook of Obstetrics & Gynecology,* 7th ed. Lange, 1980.)

As the uterus contracts and becomes smaller, it changes in shape from discoid to globular. The umbilical cord, which is still attached to the placenta, becomes longer as the placenta descends. When the placenta is ready for expulsion or extraction, it will present at the cervical os and may even dilate the cervix slightly. Palpation of the placenta should be done per vaginam and not by rectal examination. If digital palpation of the placenta cannot be accomplished and only the cord is felt, the placenta probably has not separated. Do not attempt to pull on the cord until it is completely detached, or uterine inversion may occur. Do not knead the fundus and use the uterus as a piston to expel the placenta. This **Credé maneuver** may be traumatic, leading to hemorrhage or to inversion of the uterus, which is further compounded by shock and infection. As the placenta passes from the uterus into the vagina, it may present by either the fetal surface or the maternal surface of the placenta. These have been termed the Schultze and Duncan mechanisms, respectively, but such designations are archaic and without significance. The mechanism preferred for the recovery of the placenta is the Brandt-Andrews maneuver (Fig 31–25), in which pressure is placed abdominally just above the symphysis to elevate the uterus into the abdomen and at the same time express the placenta into the vagina. Gentle cord traction will then help to guide the placenta out of the birth canal.

The placenta must be carefully inspected to make certain that there are no missing cotyledons and that the membranes have been totally recovered. Occasionally, the membranes tear off and will remain attached to the endometrium. In such cases, manual exploration of the uterus, using gauze over the fingers, may dislodge and remove the retained products of conception. Some physicians perform this maneuver routinely in all cases to make certain that retained fragments will not be overlooked. One may also employ a gauze sponge held in a ring forceps to carefully swab the interior of the uterus.

The uterus should be palpated and elevated at completion of the third stage of labor. Firm compression of the uterus may express clots and stimulate the corpus to contract. This reduces total blood loss. If there is persistent bleeding from a flaccid uterus, gentle massage and oxytocics may be employed as necessary during repair of the episiotomy and in the immediate postpartum period. When there is excessive bleeding, it is always important to have an intravenous route available for administration of blood and other fluids and such drugs as may be required. For this purpose, a large-bore needle (16 or 18 gauge) should be indwelling for emergency therapy.

Complications of Third Stage of Labor

Uterine inertia may be followed after delivery of the infant by uterine atony. This occurs in prolonged labor, polyhydramnios, multiple pregnancy, myomas of the uterus, heart disease, traumatic delivery, hemorrhage and excessive analgesia, and cessation of stimulation after anesthesia and delivery.

Anticipation of conditions that may lead to uterine atony and aids to combat this will avoid complications during the third stage of labor.

Failure of placental separation and expression may be due to any of the following causes:

A. Uterine Abnormalities: Anomalies of the uterus or cervix may cause restriction and retention of the placenta. Weak, ineffectual uterine contractions do not constrict the placental site sufficiently to force

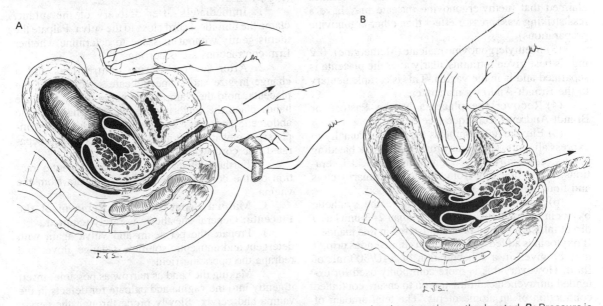

Figure 31–25. Brandt-Andrews maneuver. *A:* Traction is exerted on the cord as the uterus is gently elevated. *B:* Pressure is exerted between the symphysis and the uterine fundus, forcing the uterus upward and the placenta outward, as traction on the cord is continued.

separation. Uterine ring formation, tetanic contractions, or closure of the cervix may trap the placenta.

B. Placental Abnormalities: Increased uteroplacental cohesion or partial or complete placenta accreta may create an unusually firm uteroplacental union. Abnormalities of placentation at term include the following: (1) Low-lying placenta (placenta previa); (2) cornual implantation of the placenta, or nidation in a separate portion of a subseptate or arcuate uterus; (3) succenturiate lobe; and (4) placenta accreta, complete (about one in 8000 deliveries) or partial (about one in 4000 deliveries).

C. Mismanagement of the Third Stage of Labor: Manipulation of the fundus before separation of the placenta stimulates tetanic, not rhythmic fundal contractions. Administration of parenteral ergot preparations too early or too late causes sustained uterine or cervical contractions that may trap the placenta. Improper anesthetic management (especially deep general anesthesia) may depress uterine motility and prevent contractions.

Obstetric Procedures That Minimize Complications During the Third Stage

The following procedures will usually prevent entrapment of the placenta and conserve blood:

(1) Give oxytocin (Pitocin, Syntocinon), 5 IU (0.5 mL) intramuscularly, immediately after delivery of the infant.

(2) Another method utilizes the intravenous injection of 0.2 mg of methylergonovine maleate (Methergine) or equivalent with delivery of the anterior shoulder. This is not recommended because some ergot products may cause sudden dangerous hypertension plus entrapment of the placenta as a result of marked cervicouterine contraction (although it is sometimes claimed that methylergonovine maleate may have a less striking vasopressor effect than other ergonovine preparations).

(3) Methylergonovine maleate (Methergine), 0.2 mg, is best given intramuscularly after the placenta is separated and is in the vagina. This is complementary to the Brandt-Andrews maneuver.

(4) Recover the placenta by the Pastore or Brandt-Andrews technique (see below).

(5) Elevate and compress the uterus manually to express all clots. (Clots may form when brisk bleeding occurs, especially from vaginal and cervical lacerations. Slight bleeding from the uterus ordinarily clots and liquefies to pass finally as fluid blood.)

(6) Another procedure is to give the synthetic oxytocin intravenously. Not more than 2–3 units as a direct infusion should be administered in this manner. If oxytocin is added to a continuous intravenous drip, it may be given in a concentration of 5 IU/500 mL of fluid. However, this is more commonly used for extended intravenous administration to ensure continued contraction of an atonic uterus. The total amount of fluids administered should always be monitored to avoid overhydration.

(7) If bleeding continues and intravenous fluids have not been started, insert a No. 16 or No. 18 needle into a large vein and administer 5 IU (0.5 mL) of oxytocin in 1 L of 5% glucose in water. Have cross-matched blood available.

(a) Examine the lower genital tract for lacerations.

(b) Explore the uterus without anesthesia, if possible, for retained products of conception and rupture of the uterus.

(8) Give a second dose of methylergonovine maleate, 0.2 mg intravenously.

(9) Repair lacerations quickly.

Techniques of Recovery of the Placenta

A. Pastore Technique:

1. Stand to the patient's left and elevate the fundus with the fingers of the right hand.

2. If the placenta separates, massage the fundus gently; otherwise, leave it alone until contractions occur.

3. Place the left hand flat over the abdomen with the fingers superior to the symphysis.

4. When contractions occur and the placenta separates, squeeze the fundus gently and push it downward slightly with the right hand.

5. Prevent the fundus from entering the pelvis by holding the left hand above and behind the symphysis. The placenta can be felt to slide beneath the hand through the lower uterine segment into the cervix or vagina.

6. Lift the fundus upward to leave the placenta free in the vagina.

7. Extract the placenta from the vagina by gentle cord traction.

B. Brandt-Andrews Technique (Modified): (Fig 31–25.)

1. Immediately after delivery of the infant, clamp the umbilical cord close to the vulva. Palpate the uterus gently without massage to determine whether firm contractions are occurring.

2. After several uterine contractions and a change in size and shape indicate separation of the placenta, hold the clamp at the vulva firmly with one hand, place the fingertips of the other hand on the abdomen, and press between the fundus and symphysis to elevate the fundus. If the placenta has separated, the cord will extrude into the vagina.

3. Further elevate the fundus, apply gentle traction on the cord, and deliver the placenta from the vagina.

C. Manual Separation and Removal of the Placenta: General anesthesia is rarely required.

1. Prepare the perineum and vulva again with detergent and antiseptic solution. Change gloves and redrape the operating field.

2. Making the hand as narrow as possible, insert it gently into the vagina and palpate for defects in the vagina and cervix. Slowly probe through the cervix with the fingers, taking care not to lacerate or forcefully dilate the canal. (Moderately deep anesthesia may be required.)

3. Locate the placenta and separate it if this can be done easily. Do not attempt to force separation against unusual resistance (placenta accreta).

4. Palpate the fundus for defects or tumors.

5. Remove the hand, grasping the completely separated placenta, or leave the placenta in the uterus if it is firmly adherent. Hysterectomy will probably be required in the latter case.

Treatment of Complications

When hemorrhage is due to hypofibrinogenemia, replace blood loss and restore the normal clotting mechanism (see p 715). Fibrinogen should only be given on specific indication, as it has a definite risk of subsequent hepatitis. *Caution:* Never operate until the coagulation mechanism is restored to normal. If the patient continues to bleed excessively, prepare for hysterectomy. In most instances, packing the uterus is only a temporary expedient. One cannot insert enough packing, and the pack may hold the sinuses open rather than closed.

Blood replacement is almost always inadequate. Estimates are often only half or less than half of the actual loss. Using skin color, pulse, respiration, blood pressure, central venous pressure, patient response, etc, as guides, replace blood loss and treat shock.

In certain cases of postpartum hemorrhage, conservative measures will not prevent death, whereas timely hysterectomy may be lifesaving. Fortunately, these cases are rare. If, after correction of the blood coagulation defect, the patient continues to bleed excessively, hysterectomy is indicated—even in a primipara—preferably under balanced light general anesthesia. Do not give spinal or—unless in combination with another agent—thiopental anesthesia, since these types of anesthesia tend to cause hypotension and prolonged depression of vital functions.

Consider uterine (and often vaginal) packing in the following cases: (1) Gross cervical laceration when sufficient assistance for repair is not immediately available. (2) Rupture of the uterus while waiting for an operating room in which to do a laparotomy. (3) Cases of placenta previa after placental extraction when bleeding continues from blood vessels in the lower uterine segment that are not collapsed even when the fundus is well contracted. (4) When it is necessary to retain a uterus replaced after inversion. (5) When it is necessary to temporarily control paravaginal and vulvar hematomas. (6) After evacuation of a large hydatidiform mole.

In general, packing can be avoided by the proper use of intravenous oxytocics, elevation and gentle massage of the uterus, and proper management of the third stage of labor.

AIDS TO NORMAL DELIVERY

EPISIOTOMY (PERINEOTOMY); REPAIR OF EPISIOTOMY & LACERATIONS

Episiotomy consists of making a pudendal incision to widen the vulvar orifice and permit easier passage of the fetus. Episiotomies are necessary in most first deliveries and even in many cases in multigravid women.

Normal Labor & Delivery

The advantages of episiotomy are that it prevents perineal lacerations, relieves compression of the fetal head, and shortens the second stage of labor by removing the resistance of the pudendal musculature. Furthermore, a surgical incision can be repaired more successfully than a jagged tear.

Episiotomy is indicated (1) when a tear is imminent, (2) in most forceps and breech deliveries, and (3) to facilitate delivery of a premature infant.

Types of Episiotomy (Fig 31–26)

The tissues incised by an episiotomy are (1) skin and subcutaneous tissues, (2) vaginal mucosa, (3) the urogenital septum (mostly fascia, but also the transverse perineal muscles), (4) intercolumnar fascia or the superior fascia of the pelvic diaphragm, and (5) the lowermost fibers of the puborectalis portions of the levator ani muscles (if the episiotomy is mediolateral and deep).

A. Median: This is the easiest episiotomy to accomplish and to repair and is certainly the most bloodless. It consists of incising the median raphe of the perineum almost to the anal sphincter. The disadvantage of this procedure is the occasional accidental

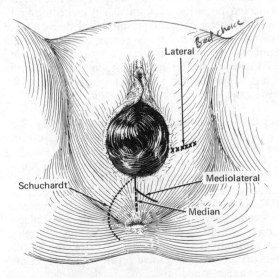

Figure 31–26. Types of episiotomy. (Reproduced, with permission, from Benson RC: *Handbook of Obstetrics & Gynecology,* 7th ed. Lange, 1980.)

extension of the incision through the sphincter (third degree laceration) or through the sphincter and into the lumen of the rectum (fourth degree laceration).

B. Mediolateral: The mediolateral incision is widely used in operative obstetrics because of its safety. Incise downward and outward in the direction of the lateral margin of the anal sphincter. The choice of a right or left incision depends upon the position of the presenting part and the surgical facility of the operator in repairing an oblique defect. A right mediolateral episiotomy widens the introitus slightly more (on the right) than a left mediolateral episiotomy does if the infant presents in an LOA, LOP, LSA, LMA, or any position in which the small parts are to the right. This is particularly important in forceps delivery and when the infant is large because it relieves stretch where the tension is greatest, thereby preventing lacerations. It also avoids the extension of an episiotomy when placed on the opposite side.

Bilateral mediolateral episiotomies are not recommended, since they cause excessive blood loss, marked discomfort during healing, and an ultimately unsatisfactory anatomic result.

C. Schuchardt Incision: This is a maximally extended mediolateral episiotomy that is carried deep into one vaginal sulcus and is curved downward and laterally part way around the rectum. Although rarely required, it is of great help in the difficult delivery of a large head, a restricted decomposition of a breech, and in the correction of shoulder dystocia. It is also employed in vaginal surgery requiring wide exposure.

D. Lateral: Lateral episiotomy affords very little relaxation of the introitus, is associated with profuse bleeding, and is difficult to repair. This incision has no merit and has been all but abandoned.

Timing of the Episiotomy

Episiotomy should be done when the head begins to distend the perineum, immediately preceding application of forceps, and just prior to breech extraction (or internal podalic version of a second twin). The slight reduction in blood loss that is achieved by delaying episiotomy until after forceps insertion and articulation is less important than a satisfactory application of the blades and a good episiotomy repair.

Repair of Episiotomy & Lacerations (Fig 31–27)

Episiotomy repair is actually a fascial repair and not merely the suture of muscle. Ligate freely bleeding points, using No. 000 chromic or plain catgut sutures. It is preferable to wait until the placenta is recovered before repairing the defect, since this limits blood loss and leads to the best possible surgical result. If speed is important, however, the deep sutures should be placed but not tied before delivery of the placenta; complete the suturing after expulsion or extraction of the placenta and inspection and repair of the cervix and upper vaginal canal.

Interrupted or continuous suture or a combination of both may be used if catgut is chosen. Chromic catgut, No. 000, is usually selected. Carefully reap-

proximate the edges of the divided muscles and fascia, using either interrupted or continuous sutures beginning at the inner aspect or the apex of the defect. Avoid mass ligatures and tension on sutures; do not tie the sutures too tightly, or pain will occur later. In general, buried sutures cause less discomfort than those tied over the skin.

Employ a continuous suture to reapproximate the vaginal mucosa from the apex of the defect to the hymenal ring. Close the perineal skin with a subcutaneous suture, using the long strand left from the vaginal mucosa repair. It is preferable to bury the closing knot in the incision, not at the hymenal ring. This may reduce the amount of scar tissue and prevents tenderness and dyspareunia.

Interrupted, removable nonabsorbable sutures, such as No. 00 silkworm gut, are occasionally used

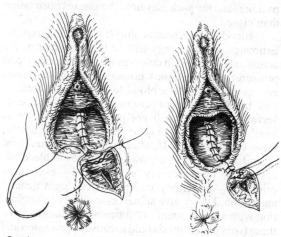

Continuous suture of mucosa with inverted suture of perineal musculature

Mucosal suture continued in skin and tied with inverted suture

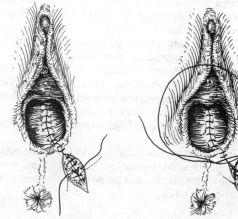

Closure of levator ani and perineal musculature

Skin closed subcutaneously

Figure 31–27. Episiotomy repair. (Reproduced, with permission, from Benson RC: *Handbook of Obstetrics & Gynecology,* 7th ed. Lange, 1980.)

when a rapid closure is desired or a grossly infected wound is to be repaired.

In fourth degree laceration repairs, close the rectal wall with fine interrupted catgut sutures tied within the lumen of the bowel. Reapproximate the ends of the rectal sphincter with interrupted catgut sutures, preferably in the perimuscular fascia rather than the friable muscle itself. Then suture lacerations in the more superficial structures.

Recovery Period

The mother should remain in the delivery or recovery room for at least 1 hour after delivery of the placenta. Observe her vital signs and note her reactions. Record the blood pressure and the pulse rate, force, and rhythm every 15 minutes, or oftener if necessary.

Support the uterine fundus and massage it gently and frequently to maintain firm contraction. Express clots occasionally and estimate blood loss.

Be alert to complaints of severe perineal pain suggestive of hematoma formation. A rapid pulse and increasing hypotension indicate impending shock, usually due to continued or excessive blood loss. Severe headache and hyperreflexia may precede eclampsia.

Do not release any patient to ward or room care until her condition is sufficiently improved and stable to permit convalescent status.

USE OF OXYTOCICS

Oxytocics are employed after delivery to reduce blood loss and to prevent subinvolution of the uterus and the spread of endometritis. Two principal products are used: the ergot preparations and oxytocin (natural or synthetic).

Oxytocin (Pitocin, Syntocinon—nearly pure oxytocin) is used in doses of 0.5 mL (5 IU of extract) with or immediately after delivery of the infant and repeated in the same dose following recovery of the placenta. *Caution:* Never use posterior pituitary extract (Pituitrin) because it contains vasopressin, which is capable of causing sudden hypertension, coronary occlusion, and asthmatic crises.

Methylergonovine maleate (Methergine), 0.2 mg intramuscularly, may be given immediately after the placenta is delivered. *Caution:* Do not administer this drug to patients with preeclampsia-eclampsia because of its slight pressor effect. Avoid intravenous administration (unless diluted in 50 mL or more of fluid) for fear of hypertensive reactions and cardiovascular accidents.

OUTLET FORCEPS
(Elective Outlet Forceps)

Outlet forceps are employed to extend the head and to guide the fetus beneath the symphysis and over the perineum. An outlet forceps is employed only when the vertex is on the perineum and extension is beginning.

Outlet forceps are used in the following circumstances: (1) When spontaneous expulsion is inhibited by analgesic or anesthetic drugs. Caudal or spinal anesthesia diminishes the patient's voluntary expulsive efforts. Outlet forceps are used in the majority of these cases. (2) When uterine inertia delays or prevents delivery of an infant whose vertex is distending the perineum. (3) When fetal distress is discovered during the late second stage. (4) When laceration of the introitus is likely. In such cases, prophylactic episiotomy is also utilized.

Caution: Outlet forceps delivery, like any surgical procedure, is safe only in skilled hands. An experienced obstetrician can reduce fetal and maternal mortality and morbidity by outlet forceps delivery. In the hands of an inexperienced physician, the outlet forceps has the opposite result. The availability of outlet forceps delivery does not justify shortening the second stage by means of low- or midforceps extraction.

INDUCTION OF LABOR

Induction of labor by medical or surgical means usually should be performed only upon specific indications. Elective induction or induction for minor or controversial reasons ("meddlesome midwifery") often increases maternal and fetal mortality and morbidity. The decision to induce labor implies that the indications are present for the patient to be delivered within 24 hours and termination of pregnancy should be pursued by all available means until the fetus is delivered successfully. This means that if labor cannot be induced easily by relatively safe procedures, a more dangerous procedure will be required. Unless the reason for inducing labor in the first place was a logical and acceptable one, the physician risks an accusation of malpractice or, at best, bad professional judgment for having started on a course that led to avoidable difficulties. X-ray or ultrasonography studies are useful before elective induction, as are fetal maturity studies such as the lecithin/sphingomyelin ratio and the creatinine concentration of the amniotic fluid.

Indications

Indicated induction of labor, especially in the treatment of abnormal pregnancy (preeclampsia-eclampsia, pyelonephritis), usually reduces maternal and fetal mortality and morbidity. The following indications for induction of labor are valid in 5–8% of pregnancies.

(1) Maternal infections (pyelonephritis, diverticulitis), which often fail to resolve and are likely to become more severe unless pregnancy is interrupted.

(2) Uterine bleeding with partial placental separation or partial placenta previa.

(3) Preeclampsia-eclampsia that is unresponsive or only temporarily responsive to therapy.

(4) Diabetes mellitus.

(5) Renal insufficiency.

(6) Premature rupture of the membranes after the 37th week.

(7) Previous precipitate delivery in a woman who cannot be transported quickly to a hospital.

(8) Marked polyhydramnios.

(9) Placental insufficiency (dysmaturity).

(10) Isoimmunization (erythroblastosis).

Contraindications

(1) Cephalopelvic disproportion.

(2) A floating or deflected vertex, or an unfavorable presentation (including breech and multiple pregnancy).

(3) A firm, closed, uneffaced posterior cervix. (A vaginal examination must be performed before induction so that ''ripeness'' of the cervix can be confirmed.)

(4) Previous cesarean section, hysterotomy, or extensive myomectomy.

(5) Maternal cardiac disease (functional class III or IV).

(6) Grand multiparity (more than 5 pregnancies) for fear of uterine rupture with oxytocin.

Dangers of Induction of Labor

A. For the Mother: In many cases, induction of labor exposes the mother to more distress and discomfort than judicious delay and subsequent vaginal or cesarean delivery. The following hazards must be borne in mind: (1) emotional crisis (fear and anxiety); (2) failure of induction and subsequent attempts to institute labor or to deliver the fetus; (3) uterine inertia and prolonged labor; (4) tumultuous labor and tetanic contractions of the uterus, causing premature separation of the placenta, rupture of the uterus, and laceration of the cervix; (5) intrauterine infection; (6) postpartum hemorrhage; (7) hypofibrinogenemia; and (8) amniotic fluid embolization.

B. For the Fetus: An induced delivery exposes the infant to the risk of prematurity if the EDC has been inaccurately calculated. Violent labor or trauma in delivery may result in damage due to hypoxia or physical injury. Prolapse of the cord and infection may follow amniotomy.

Methods of Induction of Labor

A. Medical Methods:

1. Oxytocin–Parenteral administration of a very dilute solution of oxytocin is the most effective medical means of inducing labor. (*Note:* Ergot preparations cause sustained contractions and must not be used before delivery for any reason. Posterior pituitary extract [Pituitrin] should never be used because of the vasoconstricting and antidiuretic effect of the vasopressin it contains.) Oxytocin exaggerates the inherent rhythmic pattern of uterine motility, which often becomes clinically evident during the last trimester and increases as term is approached.

The dosage of oxytocin must be individualized.

The administration of oxytocin is really a biologic assay: the smallest possible effective dose must be determined for each patient and then utilized to initiate labor.

Note: Constant observation by qualified attendants (preferably the physician) is required if this method is used.

The intravenous route is preferred. (Intramuscular administration of oxytocics may be dangerous.)

It is the physician's responsibility (not the nurse's) to determine that the correct amount of oxytocin has been added to the infusion bottle and that a given number of drops per minute will deliver a specific oxytocin dose in milliunits (mU) per minute.

In most cases, it is sufficient to add 0.1 mL of oxytocin (1 unit, Pitocin, Syntocinon) to 1 L of 5% dextrose in water (1 mU/mL). Thus, each 1 mL of solution will contain 1 mU of oxytocin.

Begin induction or augmentation at 1 mU/min, preferably with an infusion pump or other accurate delivery system.

Increase oxytocin arithmetically by 2-mU increments—1, 3, 5, etc, mU/min—at 15-minute intervals.

When contractions of 50–60 mm Hg (internal monitor pressure) or 40–60 seconds (on the external monitor) occur at 2.5- to 4-minute intervals, the oxytocin dose should not be increased further.

Caution: Sparteine sulfate (Actospar, Tocosamine) should never be used antepartum. This is an unpredictable and very dangerous oxytocic drug (tetanic contraction, uterine rupture, fetal asphyxia are possible complications).

2. Mechanical methods–Reflex hyperactivity of the uterus occurs after intestinal and ureteral hyperactivity. (Patients with colitis or pyelonephritis complicating pregnancy often develop uterine contractions that lead to premature labor.) This is the basis for the use of enemas and purges for the induction of labor, but this method is often unsuccessful and is not recommended.

B. Surgical Methods:

(1) Amniotomy is the easiest and surest way to induce labor. Release of amniotic fluid shortens the muscle bundles of the myometrium; the strength and duration of the contractions are thereby increased and a more rapid contraction sequence follows. Amniotomy causes few complications and is not painful.

The membranes should be ruptured at the internal os with a hook or other sharp instrument. Make no effort to strip the membranes, and do not displace the head upward to drain off amniotic fluid. Keep the patient in bed in Fowler's position after amniotomy so that drainage of fluid can occur. Anticipate labor within 6 hours if the patient is at term.

(2) Drainage of the hindwaters with a Drew-Smythe S-shaped metal catheter is an effective induction technique. Much amniotic fluid may be drawn off without releasing the forewaters and without seriously dislodging the presenting part. A breech presentation can often be accommodated in this way. Cautious

insertion of the catheter is required in order to avoid the placenta and to prevent perforation of the uterine wall.

(3) Stripping of the membranes (alone) is not recommended, since it is unpredictable, increases maternal morbidity, may lead to bleeding from a low-lying placenta, may cause rupture of the membranes and prolapse of the cord with a high presenting part, and is painful.

(4) A bougie or Voorhees bag has been used in the past—inserted through the cervix into the uterus as a foreign body and dilator that causes the uterus to contract and expel it along with the uterine contents. This method is *not recommended,* since it displaces the presenting part, is traumatic to the cervix, and increases the risks of infection.

C. Hypertonic Solutions: Transuterine injection of hypertonic (irritating) solutions into the amniotic cavity is dangerous to the fetus and is not sanctioned for induction of labor except after fetal death in utero.

THE ENDOCRINE BASIS FOR ONSET OF LABOR

Many theories have been proposed over the years to explain the sequence of events that culminate in labor and delivery. A consideration of several of the more plausible theories suggests that the mother, the fetus, and the placenta all contribute to the maintenance of pregnancy and that the removal of certain restraints finally triggers progressively more forceful periodic uterine contractions that terminate in delivery.

Early pregnancy apparently is maintained by estrogen and progesterone produced initially by the corpus luteum of pregnancy. After about the eighth week, however, this function is transferred largely to the placenta. The fetal progesterone contribution is negligible, as evidenced by only a slight decline in the level of this hormone with sudden fetal death. In contrast, the fetus produces considerable estrogen, and a sharp reduction in total estrogen occurs with fetal demise.

Estrogen, cortisol, and prostaglandin appear to have an excitatory effect on the uterus, whereas progesterone has an inhibitory effect.

In sheep experiments, Liggins demonstrated a slow fall in plasma progesterone beginning several days before onset of labor at term, and at the same time a significant rise in estradiol-17β and prostaglandin F$_{2\alpha}$ was noted. These events have been correlated with a definite increase in fetal cortisol production. Actually, early labor in the ewe can be initiated by an infusion of ACTH or cortisone into the fetus. In contrast, fetal hypophysectomy or adrenalectomy will

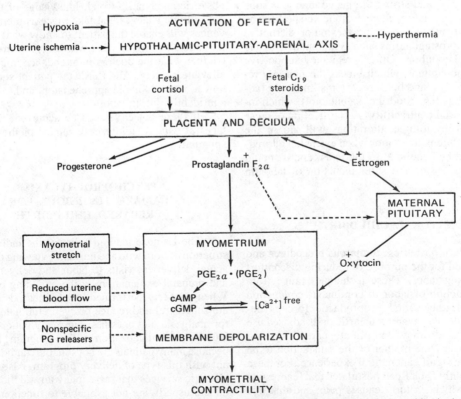

Figure 31–28. A schematic representation of the sequence of endocrine events that occur in parturition in the sheep and in several other mammalian species. Although substantial data exist to support most of the relationships, the importance of these mechanisms and their ultimate application to primates requires documentation. PG, prostaglandin. (Courtesy of Miles J. Novy, MD.)

delay labor. Admittedly, an actual surge of cortisol has not been demonstrated in the human fetus, but the possible extrapolation to the human is intriguing. In the ewe, at least, the fetus may signal its own release.

Another hypothesis, that of Csapo, holds that altered placental function may activate the labor mechanism by releasing the uterus from a "progesterone block" effect. Csapo theorizes that the placenta, the major site of progesterone production, inhibits uterine activity by its local effect, thus preventing labor. However, as the uterus approaches its capacity—ie, a term-sized fetus, polyhydramnios, or multiple pregnancy—or when, for example, it is stimulated by oxytocin, progesterone control is finally lost and the musculotonic property of estrogen plus that of intra-uterine prostaglandin sets the labor sequence in motion.

The sudden fetal contribution of cortisol and estrogen may be a reaction to stress—an appealing notion supported by clinical evidence. Nevertheless, with fetal death, pregnancy may continue for weeks. Hence, the fetus is not indispensable for parturition, but perhaps the placenta is.

With poor uteroplacental circulation (eg, abruptio placentae or eclampsia), the gravida often goes into premature labor, presumably because of the loss of placental "control." In another instance, when the membranes are ruptured, the uterine capacity is reduced suddenly, and strong uterine contractions soon ensue. Here, circulatory changes, followed perhaps by prostaglandin release, may be the major disruptive factors. Antiprostaglandins such as indomethacin may quell or delay labor. Other pregnancy-supportive drugs include ethanol, which blocks the pituitary release of oxytocin, and beta$_2$ receptor-stimulating (adrenergic) drugs (eg, ritodrine, salbutamol), which inhibit myometrial contractility. A clarification of these and related physiologic alterations will aid in the avoidance of premature labor when extension of pregnancy would be beneficial to the fetus, and it should also facilitate easier and safer induction of labor in selected cases.

"NATURAL CHILDBIRTH"

In modern obstetrics, numerous procedures and drugs are used for the purpose of reducing discomfort and shortening labor. These techniques range from elective induction of labor to continuous conduction analgesia-anesthesia and prophylactic forceps delivery. Admittedly, overenthusiastic or ill-advised use of such methods may complicate parturition and perhaps "cheat" the mother of the satisfaction to be gained from a significant natural experience. For these reasons, Grantly Dick Read postulated that fear results in tension, which, in turn, causes pain, and that this can retard the progress and intensify the discomforts of labor and delivery.

Natural childbirth programs are popular in current obstetric practice. Properly utilized, these require the adequate preparation of the patient and her husband so that both will understand the nature and progress of labor and delivery. In addition, they must be apprised of the actual delivery procedure and the physical appearance and reactions of the infant. Properly performed, natural childbirth usually calls for the father to be an active participant and aide during parturition rather than simply an observer. This in turn requires his full understanding and assistance in timing contractions, aiding in breathing mechanisms and relaxing techniques used by the patient, and giving emotional support.

Natural childbirth has come to mean different things to different people, and there are some erroneous concepts that should be explained. One widespread notion that must be corrected is that "natural" childbirth means "painless" delivery. Even the most enthusiastic adherents of natural childbirth do not claim this. Nor does natural childbirth necessarily mean drugless labor—although lower doses of medications usually are employed. Natural childbirth is an attempt to make labor easier through the elimination of fear and tension. It is based on the perfectly valid premise that labor is easier for women who are self-assured, relaxed, and cooperative. This can be accomplished in 3 ways. First, the main prerequisite is complete confidence in the obstetric team; the presence of able, dedicated attendants is an effective obstetric anodyne. Second, knowledge of the natural physiologic changes that take place as pregnancy advances will enable the patient to know what to expect; an understanding of what will transpire in labor, including what the doctors in attendance must do, will alleviate anxiety. And third, the patient should learn how to relax, to avoid apprehension, and to cooperate confidently during labor.

If these objectives can be achieved, the advantages of natural childbirth or related methods will be apparent.

PSYCHOPROPHYLAXIS: LAMAZE TECHNIQUE FOR PREPARED CHILDBIRTH

The Lamaze method calls for the individual instruction of both wife and husband, viewing of films of actual deliveries, visits to labor and delivery rooms, and prenatal explanation by the attending physician. When properly performed, these methods generally are successful and reduce or even eliminate the need for analgesia and anesthesia in many patients. There must be individualization in this program, however, because many patients are not suitable candidates or do not wish this type of delivery program. Also, on large obstetric services that serve many unwed mothers, the fathers usually are not available to function as assistants at the time of labor and delivery.

The psychoprophylaxis program of preparation for childbirth emphasizes body-building exercises, relaxation, breathing techniques, and comfort aids. It has been successful in alleviating tension and pain during labor. A trained "teacher" (often a nurse or midwife) assists the patient in physical education and relaxation procedures. Exercises such as sitting in "tailor" fashion, squatting, and abdominal and pelvic floor muscle contractions are employed. Relaxation concentrates on muscle groups and includes contraction and relaxation on command. Breathing techniques involve chest (not abdominal) breathing. The patient uses her intercostal muscles, but the diaphragm is relaxed. In abdominal breathing, the diaphragm tenses with uterine contractions, so that it may actually press down on the uterus and interfere with relaxation.

During the first stage of labor the patient uses slow, deep chest breathing. Rapid, shallow breathing and panting are recommended just before full dilatation of the cervix ("transition phase"), immediately prior to the phase of voluntary expulsive efforts.

During the second stage of labor, pushing alternates with panting. The patient sits in the tailor position, holding her flexed knees. This allows her to brace during bearing-down efforts. Panting between the contractions helps in the relaxation phase.

Comfort aids include light massage of the back, pressure on the sacrum, and lying "on the side of the occiput."

This preparation for childbirth generally requires 6–8 weeks of practice sessions. The patient's self-confidence and her ability to cope with the labor process are improved by such a program, which is especially popular in western Europe and in Russia as "psychoprophylaxis."

The Leboyer method of "natural childbirth," a modification of the Lamaze concept, calls for birth of the infant in a darkened room free of bright lights and immediate immersion of the infant in a tepid tub to simulate the fetal state, followed by stroking or gently massaging the infant as it adjusts to its extrauterine environment. There is then emphasis on immediate "bonding" with the mother by means of cuddling and stroking of the newborn by the mother, plus putting the infant to breast while the mother is still on the delivery table.

Both of the methods discussed above call for husband (or mate) participation in the antenatal training and in the delivery process. The husband participates as an active member of the supporting team—a participant in the birth process rather than simply an observer. He is educated in the process of labor and delivery and assists the patient in her breathing and relaxing exercises. He is present in the delivery room during the actual birth and is encouraged to hold and caress the newborn.

Fears that husband participation would lead to increased puerperal and neonatal infections have been largely eliminated by requiring aseptic conditions for the husband, including proper gowning and handwashing techniques. Similarly, concerns over the possibility of the husband fainting or interfering and presenting an obstacle when emergencies arise have been eliminated by providing him with proper prelabor and predelivery instruction and education, including viewing films of childbirth. Thus, "childbirth education" is an important component of family-centered maternity care. The concept of family-centered maternity care is a logical extension of the natural childbirth principles exemplified by the Lamaze and Leboyer methods. This concept extends the father's participation throughout the postpartum and nursing periods in the hospital and includes rooming-in of the infant with the mother. It calls again for teaching and education in aseptic techniques and contagious disease prevention measures, including proper gowning and handwashing procedures. The ultimate goal is a strongly bonded family unit as well as a healthy one, with all of the advantages of modern obstetric care.

● ● ●

References

Baxi LV, Petrie RH, James LS: Human fetal oxygenation following paracervical block. *Am J Obstet Gynecol* 1979;**135:**1109.

Coats PM et al: A comparison between midline and mediolateral episiotomies. *Br J Obstet Gynaecol* 1980;**87:**408.

Collea JV, Chein C, Quilligan EJ: Randomized management of term frank breech presentation: Study of 208 cases. *Am J Obstet Gynecol* 1980;**137:**235.

Collea JV et al: The randomized management of term frank breech presentation: Vaginal delivery vs. cesarean section. *Am J Obstet Gynecol* 1978;**131:**186.

Evrard JR, Gold EM, Cahill TF: Cesarean section: Contemporary assessment. *J Reprod Med* 1980;**24:**147.

Fliegner JRH: Third stage management: How important is it? *Med J Aust* 1978;**2:**190.

Flynn AM et al: Ambulation in labour. *Br Med J* 1978;**2:**591.

Gregoriou O et al: Prolactin levels during labor. *Obstet Gynecol* 1979;**53:**630.

Hughey MJ, McElin TW, Young T: Maternal and fetal outcome of Lamaze-prepared patients. *Obstet Gynecol* 1978;**51:**643.

Jouppila P et al: Effect of induction of general anesthesia for cesarean section on intervillous blood flow. *Acta Obstet Gynecol Scand* 1979;**58:**249.

Jouppila R et al: Segmental epidural analgesia in labour: Related to the progress of labour, fetal malposition and instrumental delivery. *Acta Obstet Gynecol Scand* 1979;**58:**135.

Kelso IM et al: An assessment of continuous fetal heart rate monitoring in labor: A randomized trial. *Am J Obstet Gynecol* 1978;**131:**526.

Liggins GC: Foetal participation in the physiological controlling mechanisms of parturition. In: *Foetal and Neonatal Physiology.* Comline J et al (editors). Cambridge Univ Press, 1973.

Liggins GC: Initiation of parturition. *Br Med Bull* 1979;**35:**145.

Mann LI, Gallant JM: Modern management of the breech delivery. *Am J Obstet Gynecol* 1979;**134:**611.

McDonald JS: Preanesthetic and intrapartal medications. *Clin Obstet Gynecol* 1977;**20:**447.

Modanlow HD et al: Macrosomia: Maternal, fetal and neonatal implications. *Obstet Gynecol* 1980;**56:**35.

Myers RE, Myers SE: Use of sedative, analgesic, and anesthetic drugs during labor and delivery: Bane or boon? *Am J Obstet Gynecol* 1979;**133:**83.

Nelson NM et al: A randomized clinical trial of the Leboyer approach to childbirth. *N Engl J Med* 1980;**302:**655.

O'Driscoll K et al: Active management of labour: Care of the fetus. *Br Med J* 1977;**2:**1451.

Parry-Jones E: The use of obstetric forceps in the active management of labour. *Clin Obstet Gynecol* 1975;**2:**221.

Powell OH, Melville A, Mackenna J: Fetal heart rate acceleration in labor: Excellent prognostic indicator. *Am J Obstet Gynecol* 1979;**134:**36.

Stewart P: Patients' attitudes to induction and labour. *Br Med J* 1977;**2:**749.

Tepperman HM, Beydonn SN, Abdul-Karim RW: Drugs affecting myometrial contractility in pregnancy. *Clin Obstet Gynecol* 1977;**20:**423.

Weber T, Hahn-Pederson S: Normal values for fetal scalp tissue pH during labor. *Br J Obstet Gynaecol* 1979;**86:**728.

Williams RM, Thom MH, Studd JW: A study of the benefits and acceptability of ambulation in spontaneous labor. *Br J Obstet Gynaecol* 1980;**87:**122.

Wood C, Walker A, Yardley R: Acceleration of the fetal heart rate. *Am J Obstet Gynecol* 1979;**134:**523.

Yudkin P et al: A retrospective study of induction of labour. *Br J Obstet Gynaecol* 1979;**86:**257.

COMPLICATIONS OF PREGNANCY
Raphael B. Durfee, MD

SPONTANEOUS ABORTION

Essentials of Diagnosis
- Terminated, retained pregnancy with vaginal bleeding.
- Suprapubic pain and uterine cramping.
- Disappearance of symptoms and signs of pregnancy and negative pregnancy test suggest pregnancy loss.

General Considerations

Abortion is termination of pregnancy before 24 weeks of gestation or before the fetus becomes viable. Early abortion occurs before the 12th week; late abortion occurs in the interval between 12 and 24 weeks. At least 12% of all pregnancies end in spontaneous abortion. About 75% of abortions occur before the 16th week, and most of these occur before the eighth week. Subclinical (undiagnosed) spontaneous abortion is an established entity that if included in the above would increase the reported incidence of abortion. However, the true frequency of occult pregnancies associated with subclinical spontaneous abortion is unknown.

Pathology

Spontaneous abortion generally occurs 1–3 weeks after the death of the embryo or fetus. Missed abortion is the exception.

In spontaneous early abortion, hemorrhage into the decidua basalis occurs. Necrosis and inflammation appear in the region of implantation. The pregnancy becomes partially or entirely detached and is, in effect, a foreign body in the uterus. Uterine contractions and dilatation of the cervix result in expulsion of most or all of the products of conception.

There are distinct patterns of spontaneous abortion. The amniotic sac and contents may be evacuated with the chorion and decidua; the embryo may be expelled, with rupture of the amniotic sac and passage of the fetus alone; or the entire pregnancy and the decidua may be passed intact.

In cases of missed abortion, there may be partial organization of the blood clot surrounding the conceptus. This results in the formation of a fleshy, nodular, dark red mass called a carneous or blood (Breus) mole.

Etiology

At least 80% of spontaneous abortions are due to ovular defects. In these, hydropic degeneration is a common finding. This alteration may be due to an abnormal germ cell or accidental injury to the developing embryo. Maternal factors account for only about 15% of spontaneous abortions.

A. Ovular Factors: Many abortuses show characteristics of hydatidiform mole, but many pregnancies are expelled so early that deficiencies cannot be accurately determined. Ovular factors that cause spontaneous abortion, most often in the first trimester, include the following:

1. First trimester–

a. Gross anomaly of the chromosome structure, most commonly X-monosomy, trisomy, and polyploidy.

b. Abnormal formation of the placenta, eg, hypoplastic trophoblast.

c. Localized anomaly of the embryo.

d. Congenital absence of the embryo or of the chorionic cavity.

2. Second trimester–The major fetal causes of abortion are syphilis and shallow circumvallate implantation of the placenta. Erythroblastosis and other fetal anomalies are less frequently responsible.

B. Maternal Factors: Maternal factors cause spontaneous abortion more frequently in the second trimester. Representative problems are as follows:

1. Systemic disease–

a. Maternal infections, eg, herpes simplex virus type 2, rubella, T strain mycoplasma infections, toxoplasmosis, and cytomegalic inclusion disease. Syphilis is a rare cause, and brucellosis is a questionable cause of human abortion.

b. Endocrine disorders, eg, hyper- or hypothyroidism.

c. Cardiovascular-renal hypertensive disease.

2. Protein and vitamin undernutrition.

3. Immunologic disorders, eg, incompatibility due to ABO, Rh, Kell, or other less common factor systems. Mixed lymphocyte cultures indicate a depressed response in the mothers in cases of habitual abortion—an influence of paternal factors in the fetal tissues.

4. Toxic factors such as thalidomide, folic acid antagonists, anticoagulants, lead poisoning, maternal hypoxia.

5. Uterine defects–

a. Congenital anomalies that distort or reduce the size of the uterine cavity.

b. Uterine tumors, particularly submucous or intramural myomas.

c. Uterine malposition, especially with retroflexed incarceration.

d. Previous scarring of the uterine wall following myomectomy, unification procedures, or cesarean section.

e. Asherman's syndrome of uterine synechia formation.

f. Anatomic or functional incompetence of the uterine cervix as a result of previous pregnancies and lacerations, causing second trimester abortion. Uterine anomalies may be responsible for first or second trimester abortion.

g. Uterine stimulation, which may cause onset of abortion, most likely an aftereffect of orgasm.

6. Psychic or emotional causes of abortion are speculative. There is no valid evidence to support the concept that abortion may be induced by psychic stimuli such as fright, grief, anger, or anxiety.

C. Trauma:

1. Direct–Local injury to the pregnant uterus, especially penetrating wounds or steering wheel or seat belt injury in midtrimester pregnancy.

2. Indirect–Examples are surgical trauma, eg, removal of an ovary containing the corpus luteum of pregnancy, total body irradiation greater than 3000 R, and electric shock (lightning or power line contact).

Clinical Findings

Threatened abortion is not a disease entity. The previable pregnancy may be in jeopardy, but pregnancy continues. The cervix remains closed, although slight bleeding or cramping may be noted.

A. Symptoms and Signs: The clinical classification of abortion is as shown below. Any of the following types may be septic.

1. Inevitable abortion–Pain and bleeding with an open cervix indicate impending abortion, and the expulsion of the uterine contents is imminent. Abortion is inevitable when 2 or more of the following are noted: (1) moderate effacement of the cervix, (2) cervical dilatation greater than 3 cm, (3) rupture of the membranes, (4) bleeding for more than 7 days, (5) persistence of cramps despite narcotic analgesics, and (6) signs of termination of pregnancy. Fever and generalized pelvic discomfort indicate infection. Retained tissue is evidenced by continued bleeding, a patulous cervix, and an enlarged, boggy uterus.

2. Incomplete abortion–(Fig 32–1.) This is a disorder in which the products of conception have partially passed from the uterine cavity. Cramps are usually present but may not be severe. Bleeding generally is persistent and is often severe enough to constitute frank hemorrhage.

3. Complete abortion–(Fig 32–2.) Complete abortion is identified by cessation of pain and brisk bleeding after the entire conceptus has been passed.

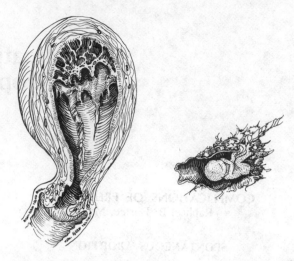

Figure 32–1. Incomplete abortion. *At right:* Product of incomplete abortion. (Reproduced, with permission, from Benson RC: *Handbook of Obstetrics & Gynecology,* 7th ed. Lange, 1980.)

Slight bleeding may continue for a short time. When complete abortion is impending, the symptoms of pregnancy often disappear and sudden bleeding begins, followed by cramping. The fetus and the placenta may be expelled separately. When the entire conceptus has been expelled, pain ceases but slight spotting persists. It is important that the conceptus be very carefully examined for completeness and trophoblastic disease.

4. Missed abortion–See p 688.

5. Induced abortion is accomplished for therapeutic or elective termination of pregnancy. (See Chapter 41.)

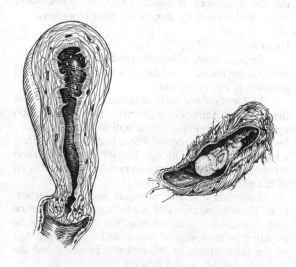

Figure 32–2. Complete abortion. *At right:* Product of complete abortion. (Reproduced, with permission, from Benson RC: *Handbook of Obstetrics & Gynecology,* 7th ed. Lange, 1980.)

B. Laboratory Findings:

1. Pregnancy tests may be equivocal or negative.

2. Urine– Commercial pregnancy tests are negative or equivocally positive. A stained smear of centrifuged sediment should reveal epithelial cells similar in form and staining properties to those seen in vaginal smears.

3. Blood–If significant bleeding has occurred, blood studies will indicate anemia. If infection is present, the count will be elevated (12–20 thousand). The sedimentation rate, already elevated by pregnancy, increases with infection and anemia. hCG radioimmunoassay serum tests are approximately 90% accurate in predicting first trimester abortion. In such cases, the hCG ratio is well below normal.

4. Hormones–With the possible exception of hypothyroidism, only the most extreme deficiencies in hormone secretion ever cause abortion. Elevated blood and urine hormone levels in pregnancy are almost always physiologic. (1) Chorionic gonadotropin: This hormone is produced by the cytotrophoblast (Langhans' cells). It is present in the urine in diminished amounts in failing pregnancy and is absent after pregnancy ceases. (2) Estrogen: The greatest source of estrogen is the trophoblast; a small amount is secreted by the ovary. A falling blood or urine estrogen titer may signify impending abortion. (3) Progesterone: During the first trimester, the principal source of progesterone is the corpus luteum. Thereafter, the principal source is the chorioplacental system. Pregnanediol (the major catabolite of progesterone) drops precipitously in abortion.

5. Vaginal smears–The incidence of spontaneous abortion is related directly to the percentage of karyopyknotic cells in the vaginal smear obtained from the upper lateral vaginal wall. The karyopyknotic index (KI) is the number of karyopyknotic cells per 100 exfoliated cells counted. A normal KI is ≤ 10; the incidence of abortion in patients whose KI is > 10 is approximately 20%. Theoretically, progestogen hormone therapy may benefit patients with a "poor" KI index who are threatening to abort; however, it may not benefit patients who display the symptoms and signs of abortion but who have a "good" KI index. Proof of the value of such therapy is awaited. When estrogen is inadequately opposed by progestogen, the cornification index (CI) increases as well as the KI.

C. X-Ray Findings: X-rays are of no value in the diagnosis of early abortion. In advanced missed abortion, x-rays may reveal a distorted fetal skeleton and intravascular gas in the fetus. Ultrasonography using the gray scale can be helpful.

Differential Diagnosis

Ectopic pregnancy is the probable cause of menstrual abnormality, unilateral pelvic pain, uterine bleeding, and a tender adnexal mass. Membranous dysmenorrhea is characterized by cramps, bleeding, and passage of endometrial casts. Decidua and villi are absent; amenorrhea does not occur. Hyperestrogenism in the nonpregnant woman causes abnormal uterine bleeding.

Hydatidiform mole usually ends in abortion before the fifth month. Theca lutein cysts, when present, cause bilateral ovarian enlargement; the uterus may be unusually large. Bloody discharge may contain hydropic villi.

Other entities that may be confused with abortion include extruding pedunculated myoma and cervical neoplasia (polyps, carcinoma, etc).

Complications

Severe or persistent hemorrhage during or following abortion may be life-threatening. Obviously, the more advanced the gestation, the greater the likelihood of excessive blood loss. Sepsis develops most frequently after criminal or self-induced abortion but may occur also in women who are sexually active immediately following abortion. Perforation of the uterine wall may occur during D&C because of the soft and vaguely outlined uterine wall and may be accompanied by injury to the bowel and bladder, hemorrhage, infection, and fistula formation.

Death may result from salpingitis, peritonitis, septicemia, intravascular coagulation, or septic shock. Thrombophlebitis and septic embolization may also occur. Anaerobic bacteria are frequently responsible.

Choriocarcinoma is a rare complication of abortion. Multiple pregnancy with the loss of one fetus and retention of another is possible also. The sequelae of infection, eg, salpingitis and intrauterine synechias or infertility, are other complications of abortion.

Prevention

Cerclage closure of an incompetent cervix (Fig 32–3) is effective in prevention of midtrimester abortion.

Many abortions can be prevented by study and treatment of maternal disorders before pregnancy; by early obstetric care, with adequate treatment of maternal disorders such as diabetes and hypertension; and by protection of pregnant women from industrial hazards to health and from exposure to rubella or other infectious diseases.

Treatment

Successful management of abortion depends upon early diagnosis. Every patient should receive a general physical (including pelvic) examination, and a complete history should be taken. Laboratory studies should include cultures of cervical mucus to determine pathogens in case of infection, antibiotic sensitivity tests, blood typing and cross-matching, and a complete blood count. Endocrine deficiency should be determined by appropriate tests.

If abortion has occurred after the first trimester, the patient should be hospitalized. In all cases, give oxytocics, eg, oxytocin, 1 mL per 500 mL of 5% dextrose in water intravenously, or 0.5 mL intramuscularly every 30 minutes for 2–4 doses, to contract the uterus and limit blood loss and aid in the expulsion of

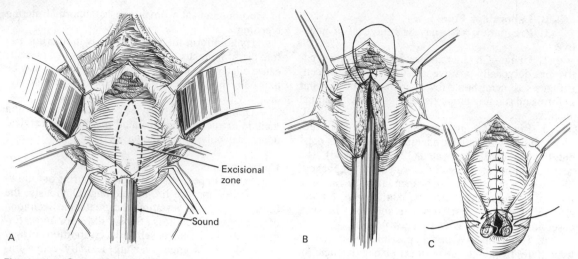

Figure 32–3. Correction of cervical incompetence in the nonpregnant patient (after Ball). *A:* Bladder displaced upward, exposing cervicouterine junction. *B:* Reapproximation of cervicouterine junction. *C:* "Crown suture" mucosal closure. (Modified and reproduced, with permission, from Benson RC: *Handbook of Obstetrics & Gynecology,* 7th ed. Lange, 1980.)

clots and tissues. Ergot preparations, which contract the cervix as well as the uterus, should be given only if the diagnosis of complete abortion is certain. Give antishock therapy, including blood replacement, to prevent collapse after hemorrhage.

Place the patient at bed rest and give sedatives to allay uterine irritability and limit bleeding. Coitus and douches are contraindicated.

D&C should be performed for possible retained tissue. (Start an oxytocin intravenous drip prior to surgery to avoid uterine perforation.)

A. Threatened Abortion: Place the patient at bed rest, forbid intercourse, and observe the patient's progress. Mild sedatives may be helpful. If bleeding continues, hospitalization is indicated.

Blood should be cross-matched and grouped in case transfusion is necessary. Drug therapy is generally ineffective in preventing abortion because so many of these uncertain pregnancies are abnormal. Progestogens, even if they prevent abortion, may cause the fetus to be masculinized. Moreover, these drugs increase the incidence of missed abortion, and an abnormal pregnancy, even a hydatidiform mole, may be retained.

The prognosis is good when all abnormal signs and symptoms disappear and when resumption of the progress of pregnancy is apparent. Real-time ultrasonography is helpful in the management of threatened abortion by detecting fetal movement. This prognostic sign is most reliable after 7 weeks' gestation.

B. Inevitable and Incomplete Abortion: Evacuate the uterus promptly. Suction D&C is effective. Type and cross-match for possible blood transfusion if bleeding is brisk or if the initial hemoglobin is less than 10 g/dL. Administer 5% dextrose in normal saline intravenously with 10 units of oxytocin.

Examination should be both manual and by speculum. Tissue at the external os should be removed with sponge forceps and examined by a pathologist.

When completeness of abortion is in doubt, D&C should always be accomplished.

Use a sharp curet to ensure complete removal of all tissue after suction curettage, but do not do a vigorous "total curettage" or uterine synechias (Asherman's syndrome) may result.

The prognosis for the mother is good if the retained tissue is promptly and completely evacuated.

C. Complete Abortion: The patient should be observed for further bleeding. All products of conception must be thoroughly examined for completeness and characteristics. The prognosis is excellent when all products of conception have been removed and when proliferative mole or choriocarcinoma can be ruled out.

Treatment of Complications

Uterine perforation is manifested by signs of intraperitoneal bleeding, rupture of the bowel or bladder, or peritonitis. Exploratory laparotomy may be necessary.

Pelvic thrombophlebitis and septic emboli are critical sequelae. Consider antibiotics, anticoagulants, ligation of the internal iliac and ovarian veins, and clipping or ligation of the vena cava.

MISSED ABORTION

Missed abortion implies that the pregnancy has been retained for 2 months or more following death of the fetus. Any of the causes of abortion may be responsible, but missed abortion usually does not occur until the pregnancy has advanced into the second trimester. A uterine anomaly, eg, a rudimentary horn, may be discovered. Why the patient does not expel the pregnancy is unknown, but exogenous long-acting progestogens given to prevent pregnancy loss may be responsible. It is possible that normal progestogen production by the placenta continues while the estrogen levels fall, which in some cases reduces uterine contractility.

Clinical Findings

A. Symptoms and Signs: Missed abortion is manifested by loss of symptoms of pregnancy and decrease in uterine size. The embryo or fetus has been dead at least 1 month, but no tissue is passed. BBT is not elevated. There may be a brownish vaginal discharge but no fresh bleeding. Pain or tenderness is unlikely. A bizarre configuration of fetal bones may be seen on x-ray. Ultrasonography is effective in following a pregnancy suspected of being a missed abortion. The cervix remains firm and closed, and no adnexal abnormality can be identified.

B. Laboratory Findings: Pregnancy tests are negative. In midtrimester abortion, the plasma fibrinogen level is abnormally low.

Differential Diagnosis

Missed abortion must be differentiated from continued pregnancy inaccurately dated and from pelvic tumor without pregnancy.

Treatment

The patient should be carefully reexamined 2–4 weeks following the suspected diagnosis. If there is evidence of a seriously reduced fibrinogen level, infection, or anemia, the uterus should be evacuated. Induction of labor with oxytocin given intravenously may be effective. The value of high-dosage estrogen is initially uncertain. If bleeding or hypofibrinogenemia develops, intravenously administered fibrinogen may be required. Hysterotomy should be considered after 2–3 months when attempts to empty the uterus fail.

Dilute prostaglandin given intravenously will usually cause evacuation of the uterus. Concentrated glucose or saline injection to induce labor in missed abortion may be ineffectual and hazardous; the injection of physiologic saline, covered with an antibiotic, is very effective in producing uterine contractions.

Prognosis

The prognosis for the mother is good. Serious complications are uncommon.

RECURRENT (HABITUAL) ABORTION

Recurrent, or habitual, abortion is defined as the sequential loss of 3 or more previable pregnancies. It is a clinical and not a pathologic diagnosis. It occurs in about 0.4% of all pregnancies and is usually due to recurrent factors rather than accidental causes. Although the pattern of pregnancy loss may be similar from one pregnancy to another, the causes may be different.

The pathologic findings in most cases of recurrent abortion include congenital anomalies, hydrops fetalis, abnormal placenta, implantation of the placenta in the lower third of the uterine cavity, and failure of a decidual response in the endometrium.

The most common causes of recurrent abortion are hormonal abnormalities (eg, hypothyroidism), genetic disorders (eg, trisomy), and acute or chronic maternal diseases (eg, viral infections) and disorders. Anatomic contributing factors include uterine abnormalities (congenital anomalies, hypoplasia, myomas) and incompetence of the cervix. Physiologic factors include corpus luteum malfunction (eg, repeated phase defect). Blood group incompatibility is also a common cause of recurrent abortion.

Recurrent abortions may be placed in 3 categories: (1) Consistent early pregnancy loss suggests a lethal anomaly, and such anomalies imply that the abortion was inevitable from nidation. (2) If the abortuses are normal in recurrent abortion, endometrial or reproductive organ defects are implied. (3) If both early and late abortuses are found, both embryonic and uterine factors must be investigated.

Certain highly emotional women may have recurrent abortions, but whether psychic factors are capable of causing abortion is still debated. Nutritional deficiencies such as protein starvation and avitaminosis may cause recurrent abortion.

Clinical Findings

A. Symptoms and Signs: Any of the abortion states may occur, including septic complications. In instances of midtrimester abortion, the findings of incompetence of the cervix should be considered.

1. Evidence of previous trauma, eg, deep lateral cervical lacerations.

2. Partial or complete amputation of the cervix.

3. A cervix that will not resist increasing sizes of an olive-tipped sound at the level of the internal os to No. 16–18F. (Best demonstrated at the time of removal of the sound from the endometrial cavity.) If an olive-tipped sound is not available, the easy passage of a No. 16–18F cervical dilator through the nonpregnant cervix will make the diagnosis.

4. Congenital abnormality of the cervix or uterus.

5. History of previous surgery, eg, cervical myomectomy, vaginal cesarean section or Dührssen's incision, traumatic or difficult forceps delivery, forceful or multiple D&Cs.

6. A history of 2 or more abortions in the second trimester without pain, cramps, or bleeding, with sudden spontaneous rupture of the membranes and passage of the fetus. Such a history is highly suggestive of incompetence of the internal cervical os.

7. Shortening, softening, and dilatation of the cervix late in the first trimester or early in the second trimester.

B. Laboratory Findings: The routine work-up should include hemoglobin determination, white count and differential, serologic antibody titers, VDRL testing, blood typing of the patient and the father for Rh and ABO compatibility, and tests of thyroid function.

Urinary pregnanediol should be measured during early pregnancy. Obtain uterine cultures for T strain mycoplasmas.

C. X-Ray Findings: There may be x-ray evidence of cervical incompetence by hysterogram or with double balloon catheter (in nonpregnant patients).

Differential Diagnosis

The differential diagnosis is the same as outlined above for spontaneous abortion in the first or second trimester, plus the additional possibility of cervicovaginal fistula.

Complications

The complications of recurrent abortion include excessive blood loss and retention of placental tissue followed by sepsis; increased trauma to an already damaged cervix or internal cervical os; emotional disorders, including acute situational anxiety or depression; rupture of the lower uterine segment; and amputation of the cervix.

Prevention

Prevention of recurrent abortion requires thorough study of possible etiologic factors followed

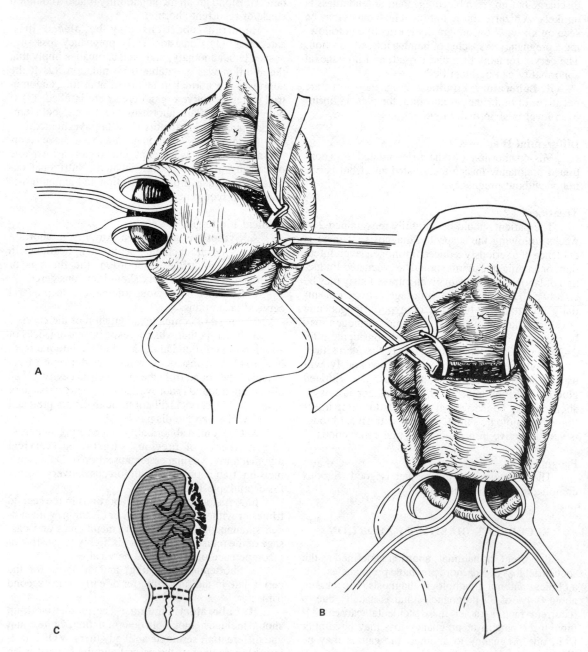

Figure 32-4. Cerclage of the cervix (Shirodkar) with incompetent os in pregnant patient.

by definitive treatment when one or more factors are found or suspected: (1) Verify the fact that the patient truly has had recurrent abortions; she may have had anovulatory cycles. (2) Cytogenetic studies are indicated in both partners if a previous pregnancy has been associated with fetal malformation. Studies should include routine blood examination, total thyroid examination, and endometrial biopsy for endometrial abnormalities or corpus luteum deficit (third and 25th days). Use BBT and serum progesterone determinations as indicated. (3) Determine the menstrual cycle by counting back from the next bleeding date. (4) Use hysterosalpingography and pelvic pneumography as indicated, looking for uterine malformations. (5) Check for positive titers of cytomegalic inclusion disease or toxoplasmosis. (6) Treat the couple with tetracycline for T mycoplasma *(Ureaplasma urealyticum)* vaginitis for 10–14 days. Use progesterone vaginal suppositories. (7) At 14 weeks, do cytogenetic evaluation of the fetus by amniocentesis.

Treatment

A. Medical Treatment: The management of recurrent abortion consists of ensuring a proper dietary intake, with thyroid or other hormonal supplements as indicated (but not diethylstilbestrol or other estrogens), and establishment of a therapeutic supportive relationship between physician and patient.

B. Surgical Treatment: Surgical measures include correction of obvious abnormalities of the genital tract (eg, removal of myomas) and repair of an incompetent cervix.

1. Trachelorrhaphy (eg, Lash operation) consists of removing a wedge from the anterior segment of the cervix, with closure to correct the incompetence. *Note:* This procedure cannot be performed during pregnancy.

2. Cervical cerclage may be performed using nonabsorbable heavy suture or tape at 3 months or more of gestation. This may be done by the McDonald method or by a double mattress suture (Würm procedure). The easiest and best method (Shirodkar) uses Dacron tape instead of fascia lata (Fig 32–4).

3. Insertion of a Smith-Hodge pessary or an inflatable donut-shaped pessary may provide adequate protection against abortion associated with cervical incompetence.

4. Transabdominal cerclage may be employed in unusual cases, eg, cervical amputation, deep cervical-uterine lacerations, or congenital shortening of the cervix.

Prognosis

Measures designed to correct problems responsible for recurrent abortion frequently will result in a viable pregnancy.

SEPTIC ABORTION

Septic abortion is manifested by an odorous discharge from the vagina and cervix, pelvic and abdominal pain, marked suprapubic tenderness, signs of peritonitis, tenderness upon movement of the uterus or cervix, fever of 37.8–40.6 °C (100–105 °F)—though hypothermia often heralds or accompanies endotoxic shock (see below)—and jaundice due to hemolysis or oliguria secondary to septicemia. Trauma to the cervix or upper vagina may be recognized if there has been a clumsy attempt to induce an abortion.

Obtain a complete blood count, urinalysis, culture of discharge from the uterus, blood cultures, chest x-ray for diagnosis of septic emboli, and abdominal x-ray for diagnosis of perforation of the uterus or uterine foreign body. Serum or plasma sodium, chloride, and potassium and arterial blood pH should be recorded.

Treatment

Give massive doses of a broad-spectrum antibiotic in large doses, but individualize in the presence of a specific sensitivity reaction.

Give whole blood transfusion as required, preferably of freshly drawn blood, and intravenous 5% glucose in water with 10 units of oxytocin through a No. 18 needle. Determine central venous pressure and urinary output. Periodic estimations of blood volume and blood gas analysis may be essential for successful management.

Abdominal hysterectomy should be considered when clostridia are the causative organisms, when uterine perforation has occurred, or when the patient responds after being in septic shock. Vena caval clipping and ovarian vein ligation may be indicated when repeated septic pulmonary embolization occurs.

Treatment of septic shock is discussed on p 463.

D&C should be done, but hysterectomy may have to be carried out if sepsis fails to respond adequately to treatment.

Disseminated intravascular clotting is discussed in Table 18–9.

EXTRAUTERINE PREGNANCY
(Ectopic Pregnancy)

An extrauterine pregnancy (ectopic pregnancy, heterotopic pregnancy, eccyesis) is one in which a fertilized ovum implants in an area other than the uterine cavity. At least 90% of extrauterine pregnancies occur in a uterine tube, and more than half of these are on the right side. The incidence is about one per 100 pregnancies, and over 75% are diagnosed before the 12th week of gestation. Ectopic pregnancy may occur at any time from menarche to menopause, but 40% occur in women between ages 20 and 29. There are more ectopic pregnancies in "infertile" women, in those in lower socioeconomic groups, and in women who have had a previous ectopic pregnancy. Women

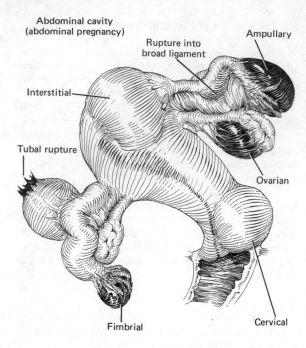

Figure 32–5. Sites of ectopic pregnancies. (Reproduced, with permission, from Benson RC: *Handbook of Obstetrics & Gynecology,* 7th ed. Lange, 1980.)

who have been treated for salpingitis or have had tuboplasty are more prone to tubal ectopic pregnancy. Patients with intrauterine devices have an increased incidence, especially with the Progestasert.

Classification

Ectopic pregnancy may be classified as follows:

(1) Tubal: isthmic, ampullary, fimbrial, interstitial, bilateral, distal with segmental absence of the tube.

(2) Uterine: cornual, angular, in a uterine diverticulum, in a uterine sacculation, in a rudimentary horn, intramural.

(3) Cervical.

(4) Intraligamentous.

(5) Ovarian: tubo-ovarian, abdomino-ovarian (secondary abdominal pregnancy).

(6) Abdominal: primary, secondary, abdomino-ovarian, tuboabdominal.

(7) Associated with hysterectomy: following total or subtotal hysterectomy, in a uterine tube, in a prolapsed uterine tube (fimbria), in the vesicovaginal space, in a cervical stump. All of these are very rare.

(8) Combined with intrauterine pregnancy, also known as compound.

Etiology

The causes of ectopic pregnancy include conditions that either prevent or impede passage of a fertilized ovum through the uterine tube.

A. Tubal Factors: Tubal factors that interfere with the progress of the fertilized ovum are adherent folds of tubal lumen due to inflammation, developmental abnormalities of the tube (congenital diverticula, accessory ostia, or atresia), previous tubal surgery (plastic tubal repair, tubal ligation, conservative treatment of unruptured rub tubal pregnancy), extrinsic adhesions (after peritonitis, kidney transplants, diverticulitis), pelvic tumors, endometriosis, excessive length or tortuosity, physiologic failure such as tubal spasm or inadequate peristalsis, and problems associated with intrauterine devices.

B. Ovarian Factors: Ovarian factors that may result in the development of an ectopic pregnancy are fertilization of an unextruded ovum, transmigration of the ovum, and abnormal early implantation.

C. Others: Other factors include tubal abortion and subsequent implantation, the proclivity of a fertilized ovum to implant in an unusual area, endometriosis, and any form of intraperitoneal bleeding.

Pathology

One important aspect of ectopic pregnancy is the lack of resistance or response of tissues into which the developing ovum is abnormally implanted. There may be little or no decidual reaction and minimal defense against permeating trophoblast. The trophoblast invades the blood vessels to cause local hemorrhage. In tubal pregnancy, distention and thinness of the tube predispose to rupture. There may be serious effects from invasion of vital organs in case of abdominal pregnancy. The invasive characteristics of trophoblast resemble those of carcinoma. In any event, the embryo rarely survives the initial hemorrhage.

In the tube, intracapsular or extracapsular rupture may occur, and the pregnancy may be aborted from the tube. Extracapsular rupture occurs when the villous ovum erodes through the tubal wall. In intracapsular rupture, the embryo, fluid, and blood are expelled from the fimbriated ostium of the tube after rupture of the amniotic and chorionic membranes.

Bleeding may cease temporarily after either extracapsular or intracapsular rupture, but the embryo rarely survives. In occasional cases, pregnancy may continue if an adequate portion of the placental attachment is retained or if secondary implantation occurs elsewhere.

Generally, an abdominal pregnancy is primary; very rarely, it may be secondary to a tubal rupture or abortion with the trophoblast maintaining its tubal attachment or the entire ovum implanting again at another site. The incidence of abdominal pregnancy is one per 15,000 pregnancies; the fetal mortality rate is about 90%.

The corpus luteum of pregnancy continues only as long as there is viable trophoblastic tissue. The uterus enlarges slightly and is softened because of the added circulation and the decidual reaction in the endometrium. There may be endometrial separation and uterine bleeding when the ectopic pregnancy terminates and separates; only in interstitial ectopic nidation is there drainage of blood from the tube through the uterus, cervix, and vagina.

Endometrial Changes & Vaginal Bleeding

In tubal ectopic pregnancy, bleeding is of uterine origin and is caused by endometrial involution and slough of the superficial tissues—largely decidua. Atypical changes in the endometrium occasionally are suggestive but not diagnostic of ectopic pregnancy. The **Arias-Stella reaction** consists of great variation in nuclear size, numerous mitoses in atypical areas, nuclear hypertrophy, focal enlargement of cells of the glands, loss of cell boundaries and "stacking" of gland cells, increase in quantity of cytoplasm, disappearance of lumens of glands owing to cellular hypertrophy, vacuolization and loss of cellular polarity, and nuclear lobulation and frothy appearance of cytoplasm. The reaction probably is due to hormonal overstimulation. In some respects, the Arias-Stella reaction may even resemble endometriosis.

Occasionally, endometrial tissue may be passed as a so-called decidual cast. Superficial secretory endometrium usually is present, but no trophoblastic cells.

Termination of the Pregnancy

This occurs in various ways depending on the site of implantation.

A. Tubal: A tubal pregnancy may terminate by abortion or missed abortion, extratubal rupture into the broad ligament, or intratubal rupture leading to tubal abortion or formation of hematosalpinx or pelvic hematocele. Pregnancy may proceed to an advanced stage with or without rupture but rarely to viability.

B. Interstitial, Angular, Cornual: Since the pregnancy begins in the portion of the tube that crosses the myometrium, the fate of the gestation resembles that of intrauterine pregnancies that implant in the cornu or near to it. In these 3 types, the pregnancy may rupture into the uterine cavity; the uterine wall may divide, causing severe local destruction to the myometrium; or the rupture may be directed into the broad ligament or directly into the peritoneal cavity. An angular ectopic pregnancy may carry to term, since the nidation point is just inside the uterine cavity. This is a serious, potentially lethal form of ectopic pregnancy that often requires hysterectomy as an emergency procedure. Occasionally, these pregnancies may abort into the uterine cavity.

C. Cervical: A cervical pregnancy may rupture into the cervical canal, may go directly into the vagina, and rarely may rupture into the base of the broad ligament, with an intra-abdominal complication of hematoma formation.

D. Abdominal: Abdominal pregnancy may rupture into the peritoneal cavity, into the retroperitoneal space, or into a vital organ. The pregnancy may form an unrecognizable mass (adipocere), or an intraperitoneal abscess may be formed from infected fetal parts, or a lithopedion may be the end result. The pregnancy may continue to an advanced stage.

E. Ovarian: Ovarian pregnancy usually ruptures into the peritoneal cavity but may dissect into the folds of the ovarian ligament or form a lithopedion. An ovarian pregnancy almost never reaches viability.

F. Combined: The tubal pregnancy may abort or rupture and the uterine pregnancy may abort, terminate prematurely, or continue to term. A bilateral tubal pregnancy may abort or rupture on both sides—not always simultaneously. Both pregnancies never continue to viability.

G. Times of Rupture at Various Sites in the Tube: Isthmic rupture often occurs at 6–8 weeks, ampullary rupture at 8–12 weeks, and interstitial rupture at about 4 months depending upon such factors as the size of the uterus and whether or not trauma occurs.

Clinical Findings

A. Symptoms and Signs: No specific symptoms or signs are pathognomonic of ectopic pregnancy, but a combination of findings may be suggestive. Ectopic pregnancy should be suspected when bleeding or pain occurs within the first 1–8 weeks after the missed period. Regardless of site, the ectopic pregnancy may be acute (ruptured), chronic (threatened or atypical), or unruptured.

The following symptoms and signs are present in 75% of cases:

1. Secondary amenorrhea due to increasing chorionic gonadotropin.

2. Uterine bleeding following failure of pregnancy, irrespective of its situation.

3. Pelvic or lower abdominal pain due to rupture of the amniotic-chorionic sac, with local bleeding, or bleeding with an enlarging pregnancy, pulsion, or traction. Pain may be exquisitely severe on palpation or slight movement of the cervix and uterus.

4. Subdiaphragmatic pain or sharp shoulder pain, with extensive intra-abdominal bleeding.

5. Palpation of a cul-de-sac or adnexal mass that represents the conceptus, hematoma from placental separation or host organ, adherence of bowel and omentum, infection, crepitating clotted blood, or combinations of these. The mass usually is boggy and poorly delineated.

6. Pregnancy changes in the uterus are not correlated with the duration of an advanced ectopic pregnancy.

7. Leukocytosis or slight fever.

8. "Fixed abdominal tenderness" on turning the patient (a positive **Adler sign**).

B. Laboratory Findings: Pregnancy tests are not useful in ectopic pregnancy because they are positive in only 35–40% of cases and, in any event, do not identify the site of pregnancy. Furthermore, negative tests do not exclude an aborted ectopic pregnancy with hematoma.

1. Blood—Anemia often develops suddenly and may be severe as a result of intraperitoneal bleeding. The icterus index may be elevated in chronic cases. The white count is elevated if infection is present. Serum amylase may be as high as 1600 Somogyi units/dL (normal, 80–180 units) if narcotics have not been given. Reticulocytosis (due to bleeding) is present; reticulocytes may be increased to 2.2%.

Hematin is detected by spectroscopy in peripheral blood 2 days after 100 mL or more of blood accumulate intraperitoneally.

2. Urine–Urine urobilinogen is elevated, indicating decomposition of blood. Slight porphyrinuria is present with hematocele and hemoperitoneum, but this finding may also be noted with twisted ovarian cyst.

C. X-Ray Findings: Hysterosalpingography may permit a diagnosis of tubal pregnancy, but the procedure is extremely dangerous, because the injected fluid may rupture the tube or aggravate bleeding. It will not identify an abdominal pregnancy. A flat film (AP) with pneumoperitoneum or pneumocolon may disclose a mass, fluid level (after rupture), or fetal bones. Arteriography may define ectopic pregnancy but is impractical to employ routinely.

D. Special Examinations: Several procedures are helpful in diagnosing ectopic pregnancy:

1. Careful pelvic examination under anesthesia.

2. Culdocentesis, which may reveal free blood in the cul-de-sac. Blood recovered by culdocentesis is evidence of hemoperitoneum if red cell rouleaux are absent; if red cells are crenated; if blood is dark and viscid and contains small clots; or if blood is noncoagulable (having already clotted and liquefied). If the hematocrit of blood from the cul-de-sac aspirate is 15% lower than the peripheral hematocrit, the sample probably is blood from a ruptured ovarian cyst. This will not apply to unruptured tubal pregnancy, however. Culdoscopy is rarely used.

3. Laparoscopy has specifically improved the diagnosis of ectopic pregnancy, especially the early and the unruptured. Its use also eliminates ectopic pregnancy from the difficult differential diagnosis of acute abdominal pain. Abdominal visualization may identify an early tubal abortion, and, while extensive intra-abdominal bleeding may preclude its actual use, the presence of a flowing bloody abdominal tap with a Verres needle still leads to definitive treatment. Simple paracentesis is not indicated.

4. Quantitative serum hCG tests every 48 hours show a doubling in value in normal pregnancy. If an hCG value is significantly lower than this figure, suspect ectopic pregnancy or spontaneous abortion.

5. D&C, which may exclude intrauterine pregnancy. The Arias-Stella reaction should reinforce a presumptive diagnosis of ectopic pregnancy. A normal intrauterine pregnancy may be interrupted by curettage, however. D&C and endometrial biopsy may disclose decidual endometrium (without chorionic villi). If trophoblast is recovered, uterine pregnancy is established. Inadequate, degenerated tissue will be obtained after 4–5 days of continued bleeding. A steroid sex hormone shift, as reflected by vaginal smears, may indicate abortion, but the site of pregnancy will not be identified.

6. Posterior colpotomy, which will give much information and may even permit removal of an early tubal or unruptured tubal pregnancy.

7. Exploratory laparotomy, which is the final and most specific diagnostic procedure. It will establish the presence or absence of ectopic (but not cervical) pregnancy. Frequent use of minilaparotomy for treatment of early ruptured or aborted tubal pregnancy and for unruptured tubal cases is the present trend. Laparotomy is indicated (1) when the presumptive diagnosis of ectopic pregnancy has been made but culdotomy does not permit adequate exposure for removal of the conceptus; (2) when an acute abdominal emergency necessitates investigation; or (3) when a definite diagnosis of tubal disease has been made by laparoscopy.

8. Ultrasonography is successful in making a diagnosis of ectopic pregnancy; however, false-negative findings do occur. The most frequent source of error is misdiagnosis of a corpus luteum cyst in early pregnancy.

Differential Diagnosis (Table 32–1)

About 50 pathologic conditions may be confused with extrauterine pregnancy. The most common of these are appendicitis, salpingitis, ruptured corpus luteum cyst or ovarian follicle, uterine abortion, twisted ovarian cyst, and urinary tract disease.

Complications

Hemorrhage is the major cause of maternal death in untreated ruptured ectopic pregnancy; without surgery, a ruptured ectopic pregnancy may result in exsanguination and death.

Chronic salpingitis often follows neglected ruptured tubal ectopic pregnancy. Infertility or sterility develops in many patients who have undergone surgery for extrauterine pregnancy. Intestinal obstruction and fistulas may develop after hemoperitoneum and peritonitis.

Prevention

Treat salpingitis early and vigorously; perform D&C promptly for incomplete abortion; and avoid adhesions at surgery. Early diagnosis of unruptured tubal pregnancy will obviate later extensive surgery. Most forms of ectopic pregnancy other than tubal are not preventable.

Treatment

The treatment of ectopic pregnancy in general is considered here, and specific therapeutic measures are presented in the following sections devoted to extrauterine pregnancy at specific sites.

A. Emergency Treatment: Immediate surgery is indicated when the diagnosis of ectopic pregnancy is made. Transfusion with whole blood as soon as possible is indicated when the patient is in shock. If bleeding is extensive, a large needle should be inserted into a vein and blood should be given under pressure. It should be warmed if possible to prevent chilling. Administer antishock measures as indicated, ie, keep the patient comfortably warm, give oxygen, and apply moderately snug tourniquets around the upper legs.

B. Surgical Treatment: Rapid entry into the abdomen should be accomplished; control of hemorrhage

Table 32–1. Differential diagnosis of ectopic pregnancy.

	Ectopic Pregnancy	Appendicitis	Salpingitis	Ruptured Corpus Luteum Cyst	Uterine Abortion
Pain	Unilateral cramps and tenderness before rupture.	Epigastric, periumbilical, then right lower quadrant pain; tenderness localizing at McBurney's point. Rebound tenderness.	Usually in both lower quadrants, with or without rebound.	Unilateral, becoming general with progressive bleeding.	Midline cramps.
Nausea and vomiting	Occasionally before, frequently after rupture.	Usual. Precedes shift of pain to right lower quadrant.	Infrequent.	Rare.	Almost never.
Menstruation	Some aberration; missed period, spotting.	Unrelated to menses.	Hypermenorrhea or metrorrhagia, or both.	Period delayed, then bleeding, often with pain.	Amenorrhea, then spotting, then brisk bleeding.
Temperature and pulse	37.2–37.8 °C (99–100 °F). Pulse variable: normal before, rapid after rupture.	37.2–37.8 °C (99–100 °F). Pulse rapid: 99–100.	37.2–40 °C (99–104 °F). Pulse elevated in proportion to fever.	Not over 37.2 °C (99 °F). Pulse normal unless blood loss marked, then rapid.	To 37.2 °C (99 °F) if spontaneous; to 40 °C (104 °F) if induced (infected).
Pelvic examination	Unilateral tenderness, especially on movement of cervix. Crepitant mass on one side or in cul-de-sac.	No masses. Rectal tenderness high on right side.	Bilateral tenderness on movement of cervix. Masses only when pyosalpinx or hydrosalpinx is present.	Tenderness over affected ovary. No masses.	Cervix slightly patulous. Uterus slightly enlarged, irregularly softened. Tender with infection.
Laboratory findings	White cell count to 15,000/μL. Red cell count strikingly low if blood loss large. Sedimentation rate slightly elevated.	White cell count 10,000–18,000/μL (rarely normal). Red cell count normal. Sedimentation rate slightly elevated.	White cell count 15,000–30,000/μL. Red cell count normal. Sedimentation rate markedly elevated.	White cell count normal to 10,000 /μL. Red cell count normal. Sedimentation rate normal.	White cell count 15,000/μL if spontaneous; to 30,000/μL if induced (infection). Red cell count normal. Sedimentation rate slightly to moderately elevated.

can be lifesaving. Careful, fast exploration of the abdominal cavity should be done at once, for the bleeding may be from a site other than the adnexa. Remove products of conception, clots, and free blood, exposing the area of nidation. If the pregnancy is advanced, do not disturb an adherent placenta but leave it in situ. Do not insert drains. If necessary, give an autotransfusion, using the patient's own citrated and filtered blood; this may be lifesaving if no other blood is available. It must be remembered that only fresh blood should be used and also that this is primarily a volume expander, since such blood is low in hemoglobin content. Stimulant general anesthesia should be used; avoid depressants such as regional blocks or thiopental.

C. Supportive Treatment: If symptoms and signs of infection are present, give broad-spectrum antibiotics; prescribe oral or intravenous iron therapy, or both, and order a high-protein diet with vitamin and mineral supplements as soon as the patient is on oral intake.

Prognosis

Another tubal pregnancy will occur in about 10% of cases treated. Infertility develops in approximately half of patients who have undergone surgery for the treatment of an ectopic pregnancy. Of these, about 30% become sterile. Normal pregnancies are achieved in about half of patients who have one ectopic pregnancy. The maternal mortality rate due to ectopic pregnancy in the USA is 1–2%; the perinatal mortality rate is almost 100%.

1. TUBAL ECTOPIC PREGNANCY
(Not Including Interstitial Type)

Tubal pregnancy is the most common form of ectopic pregnancy, and for this reason the terms tubal pregnancy and ectopic pregnancy are frequently taken to be synonymous. Delivery of a viable fetus is exceptional. In the past 5 years, the incidence of tubal ectopic pregnancy has increased more than 50% owing to the following factors: epidemic salpingitis treated with antibiotics; tubal infection related to the IUD, especially the Progestasert; microscopic tubal surgery of all kinds; conservative management of the tube with preservation of an organ that still retains the causative factor; the timing of artificial insemination and natural methods of contraception, which may lead to fertilization of a late ovum; an increased number of tubal ligations with increased failures; and abnormal atretic tubes related to the DES syndrome. The incidence of tubal ectopic pregnancy is higher in black women than in white women.

Figure 32—6. Tubal pregnancy. (Modified from a drawing by Ashworth.)

Etiology

Conditions and contributing factors that may lead to tubal pregnancy may be listed as follows:

Acute or chronic salpingitis

Peritubular adhesions or tumor with fixation of the tube

Congenital anomalies such as accessory tubes

Infantile tubal development or abnormal length

Functional failure with poor peristalsis or tubal spasm

Endosalpingosis

Endometriosis

Postperitonitis inflammatory reaction

Inhibition of ciliary action

Microsurgical plastic surgery of the tube, including anastomosis, fimbrioplasty, salpingostomy, and reimplantation

Tubal sterilization procedures: electrocoagulation, fimbriectomy, Pomeroy

Clinical Findings

A. Acute Tubal Rupture: (40% of tubal ectopic pregnancies.) A history of abnormal menstruation and infertility is present in about 60% of cases, with scanty persistent vaginal bleeding in 80%. Sharp abdominal or pelvic pain is present, an adnexal mass is felt, and signs of peritoneal irritation with shoulder pain and backache are found. There is a falling blood pressure, hemoglobin, and hematocrit and classic symptoms of hemorrhagic shock with weakness, thirst, profuse perspiration, "air hunger," and oliguria. Coma and narrowing pulse pressure are ominous signs. Complications of acute tubal rupture may be life-threatening.

B. Chronic Tubal Rupture: (60% of tubal ectopic pregnancies.) When the point of rupture is small and bleeding slow, the symptoms generally are vague and inconclusive.

C. Unruptured Tubal Pregnancy: (2% of tubal ectopic pregnancies.) This may be suspected if there is a history of amenorrhea, with symptoms and signs of early pregnancy, scanty dark vaginal bleeding, and discomfort in the affected adnexal area, especially when the uterus is moved. The diagnosis should be more clear when a definite tender, slightly fixed mass is felt, particularly when the ovary can be felt separately on the same side.

Treatment

See general treatment discussion above.

When the tube is grossly enlarged or distorted (as in pregnancy of more than 3 months' duration), clamp the tube from the fimbrial end inward and then on the uterine side. Excision of the cornu with removal of the tube is preferred to cornual resection to prevent repeat ectopic pregnancy and endosalpingitis of the stump. The ovary should be conserved if possible.

Conservative surgery may be done in some cases of missed tubal abortion or completed tubal abortion. Under certain conditions, nonoperative management of tubal pregnancy may be successful. Elements of risk can be minimized by persistent, careful observation. In certain cases of early tubal abortion, the contents can be gently milked out of the distal end of the tube. A salpingostomy will permit removal of any remaining tubal contents and allow ligation of bleeding points. In some instances, a polyethylene splint may be left in place in the tubal lumen. Marsupialization may improve tubal function at a later date. This should be followed by postoperative hydrotubation. When the opposite tube is absent or diseased beyond repair, conservative operations are more strongly indicated than otherwise.

Separation of adhesions or correction of tubal disease on the other side may be indicated if the patient has had only minor bleeding and is not in shock. Reimplantation of a tube should not be done at this time.

2. INTERSTITIAL ECTOPIC PREGNANCY

In interstitial pregnancy, the fertilized ovum implants in the portion of the uterine tube that traverses the uterine wall. This type of ectopic pregnancy occurs in 2–4% of all pregnancies, most frequently in multiparas 25–35 years of age. It may occur following previous salpingectomy. The nidation site may be in the uterointerstitial (inner) portion, the true interstitial (middle) portion, or the tubointerstitial (outer) portion.

Etiology

Descent of the fertilized ovum through the tube proceeds at a reduced rate through the interstitial portion, and the ovum may be arrested here. This is often due to obstruction of the tubal lumen or failure of the transport mechanism. The question of increased incidence of interstitial pregnancy associated with the use of IUDs is not settled. The following factors influence the formation of obstruction or interfere with passage of the gamete:

(1) Developmental anomalies, eg, partial atresia, accessory tube, or diverticula.

(2) Intra-abdominal fertilization, with a developing morula too large for the tubal lumen.

(3) Pelvic infections, eg, salpingitis, ciliary destruction, and interference with tubal peristalsis and perisalpingitis and parametritis, which cause adhesions, edema, and fibrosis.

(4) Peritubal adhesions, with kinking or angulation of the tube from pelvic surgery, endometriosis, previous ectopic pregnancy, and ovarian or other pelvic tumors.

(5) Adjacent uterine tumor such as intramural or subserous myomas, which often occlude or impair the tubal lumen in the interstitial area.

(6) An endometriumlike transformation of the tubal epithelium, which may encourage implantation.

(7) Interstitial pregnancy in the stump of a tube previously removed either for a previous tubal ectopic pregnancy or other adnexal disease.

Course of the Disease

The tubal epithelium becomes eroded by the trophoblast, and the myometrium is invaded. The muscle is destroyed by infiltration in the area of least resistance. The gestational sac is composed of serosa, a small amount of connective tissue, and thinned uterine muscle lying in the posterior-superior part of the involved cornu. The pregnancy has thus become intramural and extracanalicular.

The embryo or fetus may die at any stage of development as a result of periovular hemorrhage. If the fetus dies early, the tissues generally are absorbed.

Rupture of the uterine wall is the most frequent outcome until the 10th–14th weeks. The duration of pregnancy seems to depend upon the nidation site: (1) Implantation in either the utero- or tubointerstitial area favors early rupture. No living children have been reported with interstitial pregnancy. (2) Implantation in the middle third or true interstitial portion prolongs the gestation somewhat.

Occasionally, the pregnancy will abort into the uterine cavity if the implantation is in the uterointerstitial area.

A lithopedion may be formed with rupture.

Clinical Findings

A. Symptoms and Signs: The manifestations are generally nonspecific, with the usual signs of early normal intrauterine pregnancy. Intermittent, recurrent, sharp abdominal pain occurs at 4–6 weeks. Sudden abdominal pain is followed by collapse.

Localized tenderness occurs over the affected cornu.

Vaginal bleeding occurs in only about 25% of cases.

Pelvic examination may reveal uterine findings compatible with early uterine pregnancy and a palpable mass in the area of pregnancy with a broad base extending outward **(Baart de la Faille's sign).** This mass will be softer than the uterus and may be very sensitive.

Unruptured interstitial pregnancy may be diagnosed by ultrasonography, but laparoscopy is a much more effective procedure in that visualization of the pathologic process is almost unimpeded.

Diagnostic findings at surgery **(Ruge-Simon syndrome)** are displacement of the uterine fundus to the opposite side, elevation of the involved cornu, and rotation of the uterus on its long axis.

In addition to the tube, the round and ovarian ligaments will be lateral to the sac.

Manipulation of the uterus may make the cornual mass more apparent, or the administration of oxytocin may cause it to contract and stand out more prominently.

B. Laboratory Findings: There are no characteristic laboratory findings except those that occur following rupture with massive intraperitoneal hemorrhage. Pregnancy tests usually are positive.

Differential Diagnosis

Interstitial pregnancy must be differentiated from tubal ectopic pregnancy near the uterus, cornual pregnancy, angular pregnancy, cornual myoma, cornual abscess, pregnancy in one horn of a bicornuate uterus, large endometrioma at the uterotubal junction, and endosalpingosis. Angular pregnancy should be differentiated from interstitial pregnancy by laparoscopy, because such a pregnancy can carry to term. Angular pregnancy forces the round ligament to lie lateral to the mass, which is not the case with interstitial pregnancy.

Complications

Rupture is a catastrophic event because massive hemorrhage, shock, and early maternal death may follow, especially if the uterine artery is lacerated. The uterine wall below the tubal insertion is the most frequent site of rupture, and this may extend down into the uterine vasculature and cause extensive uterine damage. The ovarian circulation may be involved also, and the pregnancy may be extruded intra- or extraperitoneally.

Prevention

Interstitial pregnancy may recur in cases of previous salpingectomy with cornual resection; hence, this procedure does not ensure against recanalization. Excision of the cornual area with careful—preferably double—peritonization is the procedure of choice. The round ligament may be brought over and sutured for reinforcement.

Treatment

A. Emergency Measures: Management of shock due to hemorrhage, as in any other case, requires rapid massive blood replacement, perhaps intraarterial administration.

B. Surgical Measures: Once the diagnosis is

made—either before or after rupture—immediate laparotomy is required. Simple wedge resection, reconstruction of the uterine wall, and salpingectomy may be the best procedure. Preservation of the ovary should be attempted if feasible. The extent of surgery depends upon the degree of damage to the uterus and adnexa. Total abdominal hysterectomy and unilateral salpingo-oophorectomy on the affected side may be necessary. In the severely shocked patient, a supracervical hysterectomy may be lifesaving. A conservative, extensive, prolonged uterine reconstruction is ill-advised in a patient with massive hemorrhage.

Prognosis

The prognosis for viability of the fetus is nil. The reconstructed uterus may rupture during a subsequent pregnancy, and delivery after uterine repair or reconstruction should be by elective cesarean section, with careful exploration of the area following placental removal. Consider the possibility of placenta accreta in the region of repair.

The prognosis is good for the mother if adequate blood transfusion and early surgery are accomplished, but poor if shock is deep and occurs early after rupture or if treatment is delayed. The mortality rate in interstitial pregnancy is 2–3%; following a previous salpingectomy, it is about 7%.

3. ABDOMINAL ECTOPIC PREGNANCY

Abdominal pregnancy is rare, occurring in approximately one per 15,000 live births. It is a matter of debate whether most abdominal pregnancies are primary or are secondary to a tubal ectopic gestation. Abdominal pregnancy seems to occur in older women of low parity, but endometriosis is rarely reported.

In secondary abdominal pregnancy, the primary site of the gestation may have been tubal, ovarian, or even uterine.

The pregnancy usually develops normally if the implantation sites provide sufficient blood supply to the placenta. Discomfort, genitourinary symptoms, and actual pain are the rule as the pregnancy progresses. If undiagnosed and untreated, the fetus will die and suppurate, with abscess formation; form a true lithopedion or calcified fetus; develop into an adipocere; or result in undetermined retention of bony fetal parts with absorption of soft tissues. Massive intra-abdominal hemorrhage may ensue, or fetal parts may extrude through the rectum, bladder, or vagina; or an abdominal fistula may form.

Clinical Findings

A. Symptoms and Signs: Abdominal pregnancy may be suspected in relation to bizarre pregnancy symptoms, ie, a history suggestive of tubal rupture or abortion; a pregnancy complicated by unusual gastrointestinal symptoms; fetal movements that are very marked or painful; easy palpation of the fetal parts and movement; pregnancy described by a multipara as

"different"; false labor near term (a small uterus may be felt in the pelvis by examination early in the pregnancy); high-lying fetus in abnormal presentation—often transverse; displacement of a firm, long cervix; palpation of fetal parts through the vaginal fornix; or a palpable placental mass and an unusually loud vascular souffle.

B. X-Ray Findings: The fetus rides high in the abdomen over the maternal spine in the lateral view. Ultrasonography is useful in making a diagnosis of abdominal pregnancy and also in following regression in the size of a retained placenta associated with abdominal pregnancy. Amniography may indicate a bizarre fetal relationship, and arteriography should indicate abnormal positioning of the uterine and placental vessels. The fetal skeleton is unusually clear in relation to maternal organs.

Differential Diagnosis

Differential diagnosis usually concerns intrauterine or abdominal pregnancy. Give oxytocin; if uterine contractions can be felt, abdominal pregnancy is ruled out. The same is true if the fetus can be felt through the cervical canal.

Complications

Most complications are related to preoperative intra-abdominal hemorrhage or the postoperative course after removal of the fetus. Reoperation may be necessary because of obstruction, abscess, fistula, or bleeding.

Treatment

Treatment consists of immediate surgical removal of the fetus and membranes and ligation of the cord near the placenta. The placenta should only be removed when the operator is absolutely certain that total hemostasis can be accomplished (very rare). The abdomen should be closed without drainage except in the presence of infection. If the placenta is allowed to remain, methotrexate or dactinomycin in full antitumor dosage may be given to destroy the trophoblast and speed resorption of the placenta.

Prognosis

The maternal mortality rate is approximately 10%. About 50% of fetuses are alive at surgery, but only about 20% survive.

4. COMBINED & COMPOUND EXTRA-& INTRAUTERINE ECTOPIC PREGNANCY

Combined intrauterine and extrauterine pregnancy means the existence of simultaneous pregnancies. Compound intrauterine and extrauterine pregnancy is superposition of the intrauterine pregnancy on the extrauterine one. It may be classified according to the duration of gestation. Along with the general increase in incidence of tubal ectopic pregnancies there has been an increase in heterotopic pregnancies well above that previously reported—at present 1:2600 pregnancies. A history of spontaneous or elective abortion with subsequent persistent pain should be examined by means of ultrasonography or laparoscopy for concomitant tubal pregnancy. Multiparas are more commonly affected. A compound pregnancy of the extra- and intrauterine type is one in which a normal intrauterine pregnancy occurs when an ectopic pregnancy has died, ruptured, or resolved. Approximately 10% of complicated pregnancies are of this type.

The tubal pregnancy may terminate early and the intrauterine pregnancy be lost at the same time, or the tubal pregnancy may terminate early and the intrauterine pregnancy may remain intact. Both pregnancies may go to viability, but the uterine pregnancy may abort and the tubal pregnancy may rupture later.

Clinical Findings
If the patient gives a history compatible with ectopic pregnancy but presents with a large, soft uterus and accentuated symptoms and signs of pregnancy, she may have a combined pregnancy. Unusual abdominal pain in the presence of spontaneous abortion or profuse uterine bleeding with signs of peritoneal irritation should suggest combined pregnancy. An enlarged uterus beyond the size usually anticipated with an ectopic pregnancy—or the presence of a palpable adnexal mass and 2 corpora lutea seen at exploratory laparotomy—is suggestive of combined pregnancy. A history of an ectopic pregnancy may also be helpful in diagnosis. Colpotomy, culdoscopy, or laparoscopy may assist in the diagnosis of tubal plus uterine pregnancy. Ultrasound may be an aid to diagnosis.

Differential Diagnosis
Consider retained products of conception, salpingitis, myoma, twisted ovarian cyst, or acute appendicitis. Rarely is the correct diagnosis made prior to surgery.

Complications
Massive intra-abdominal hemorrhage with shock often occurs. There may also be excessive bleeding from the uterus, with simultaneous spontaneous uterine abortion. A normal intrauterine pregnancy may be removed by an ill-timed diagnostic D&C.

Treatment
The treatment is the same as for ruptured or unruptured ectopic pregnancy with an intrauterine pregnancy. If possible, the intrauterine pregnancy should be preserved, but if abortion is inevitable or incomplete, a D&C must be done as soon as possible to avoid blood loss.

If 2 living premature fetuses are diagnosed, immediate hospitalization and treatment should be arranged. Delivery by abdominal laparotomy and cesarean section may be indicated. If the placenta remains in situ, the mother may be given methotrexate following the surgery.

Prognosis
The maternal mortality rate is about 1%; most fetuses of a uterine pregnancy will survive following removal of a concomitant ectopic pregnancy.

5. OTHER UNCOMMON ECTOPIC PREGNANCIES

Multiple Tubal Ectopic Pregnancy
This is similar to tubal ectopic pregnancy, with the possible addition of bilateral palpable, tender adnexal masses.

Treatment should be as conservative as possible, and the tube should be preserved when feasible; nonetheless, successive coexistent tubal pregnancies have been recorded that required bilateral salpingectomy with or without abdominal hysterectomy.

Cornual Pregnancy
Cornual pregnancy is one in which nidation has occurred in one side of a double or septate uterus or in one horn of a bicornuate uterus. The term cornual pregnancy is sometimes used as a synonym for interstitial or angular pregnancy.

Abnormal contour of the early pregnant uterus should suggest a uterine anomaly. Unusual discomfort and tenderness may be described. Failure of engagement of the presenting part in a primigravida or a palpable uterine mass adjacent to the pregnancy (may be the other horn or the other uterus) may be noted.

Cesarean section or abdominal hysterectomy may be necessary, especially when the placenta separates prematurely.

Pregnancy in a Uterine Diverticulum
Uterine diverticula are rare, and a pregnancy within one is exceptional. It resembles abdominal pregnancy or a uterine saccular pregnancy.

Delivery by abdominal laparotomy and hysterotomy is usually necessary.

Pregnancy in a Uterine Sacculation
Saccular pregnancy, because of the thin wall, suggests an abdominal pregnancy except that the pregnancy is not high in the abdomen and there are no gastrointestinal symptoms.

Removal of the pregnancy must be by incision through the saccular wall. This may not be a true cesarean section, even if at term. Abdominal hysterotomy is the best term to describe such an evacuation.

Angular Pregnancy
In this case, the conception becomes implanted in the angle of the uterus just inside the uterotubal attachment on the side of the uterine cavity. This is often over the tubal ostium.

The symptoms may differ from normal uterine pregnancy either at the time of spontaneous abortion or labor and delivery. Diagnosis usually is made following delivery, with manual removal of the placenta, or at cesarean section.

Angular pregnancy may present as a painful, tender sacculation of the uterus; vaginal bleeding may be present.

Manual removal of the placenta during the third stage of labor may be required. Curettage for bleeding after incomplete abortion may identify the placental site.

Pregnancy in a Rudimentary Horn

It is most difficult to make this diagnosis before surgery. However, the condition is most hazardous to maternal life because pregnancy frequently progresses into the mid trimester or later and delivery is possible only by abdominal surgery. Rupture of such a pregnancy usually occurs and is accompanied by serious intraperitoneal hemorrhage.

Surgical exploration in case of rupture and hemorrhage should be immediate. A viable infant may be delivered by cesarean section. Total excision of the abnormal horn is advised. Total hysterectomy is occasionally necessary.

Intramural Pregnancy

This diagnosis is almost never made prior to termination of the pregnancy; however, unruptured intramural pregnancies have been described. Irregular development of the uterine mass and abnormal or persistent pain and tenderness may point to an abnormal gestation. The definitive diagnosis may be made on pathologic examination at which an incomplete or absent decidua basalis is found and occasionally placenta percreta or accreta. Intramural pregnancy is defined as a gestation separate from the uterine tubes or uterine cavity that is surrounded by the myometrium. Uterine wall rupture occurs in the area of the pregnancy. In some cases, the uterine cavity is intact; in others, the uterine cavity is involved; and rarely, rupture may occur next to the pregnancy and not involve the cavity.

Treatment consists of surgical removal of the pregnancy with reconstruction of the area of rupture. It may be possible to detach the tissue mass without entering the uterine cavity. If damage is severe, total hysterectomy may be necessary; but subtotal hysterectomy has been performed in the presence of massive hemorrhage with extensive tissue damage and a patient in severe shock.

Intraligamentous Pregnancy

Clinical findings are similar to those of an abdominal pregnancy. The patient may be hospitalized several times before the diagnosis is made. The uterus is usually displaced to the opposite side. If the pregnancy persists, the mass may become palpable abdominally and occasionally may be detected by pelvic or rectovaginal examination.

Immediate surgical removal is required under emergency conditions.

Cervical Pregnancy

A large, dark, highly vascularized cervix with bleeding or extrusion of dark tissue through the external os will be noted. There may be backache or dysuria, and abdominal pain is described. Distention of the cervix and dilatation of the external os is thought to be the source of the low abdominal pain.

The diagnosis is suggested clinically by continuous bleeding after amenorrhea; a soft and disproportionately enlarged cervix equal to or greater than the uterine corpus (an hourglass effect); a tight internal cervical os and a patulous external cervical os; and a dilated, thin-walled cervical canal with histologic evidence of the products of conception. Diagnosis may be made by ultrasonographic demonstration of a characteristic cervical enlargement. The differential diagnosis is from cervical phase uterine abortion, cervical abortion, placenta previa, and uterine or cervical cancer.

Immediate surgery is indicated as soon as the diagnosis is suspected. Hemorrhage may be massive and sometimes fatal. Ligation of the hypogastric arteries or the cervical branches of the uterine arteries may be effective in controlling excessive bleeding. Curettage of the endocervix and endometrium may stop the heavy bleeding. Sutures and Gelfoam or gauze packing may be necessary. Packing of the endometrial cavity, dilated cervical canal, and vagina with gauze for counterpressure may control bleeding. If tissue damage or necrosis is great, hysterectomy will be necessary. Amputation of the cervix is not recommended. The prognosis for the mother is grave.

Ovarian Pregnancy

Ovarian pregnancy cannot be diagnosed on the basis of clinical signs. In fact, a careful examination by a pathologist is the only way a diagnosis of true ovarian ectopic pregnancy can be made. Ovarian twin pregnancy is a rarity, as is tubal triplet pregnancy, but unilateral twin pregnancy in the tube is more common. Pain and cramps, a pelvic mass, symptoms of early pregnancy, and vaginal bleeding are the most common findings.

The incidence of ovarian to tubal ectopic pregnancy with intrauterine devices is 1:9, compared to 1:150 in the general population.

Treatment is surgical removal. Sacrifice of the ovary and occasionally the tube is usually necessary. Excessive blood loss will require all of the usual supportive measures.

Pregnancy Subsequent to Hysterectomy

The pregnancy follows the course of a tubal ectopic gestation if nidation takes place in the tube. The gestation may develop as an abdominal pregnancy when the implantation is in the abdominal cavity.

Clinical findings are those of a postoperative and rapidly growing intra-abdominal tumor and ectopic pregnancy.

Laparotomy is the treatment of choice. Surgical excision of the ectopic pregnancy is required.

TROPHOBLASTIC DISEASES
April Gale O'Quinn, MD, & David E. Barnard, MD

Essentials of Diagnosis

- Uterine bleeding in first trimester.
- Absence of fetal heart tones and fetal structures.
- Rapid enlargement of the uterus; uterine size greater than anticipated by dates.
- hCG titers greater than expected for gestational age.
- Expulsion of vesicles.
- Hyperemesis.
- Theca lutein cysts.
- Onset of preeclampsia in the first trimester.

General Considerations

Gestational trophoblastic neoplasms include the tumor spectrum of hydatidiform mole, invasive mole (chorioadenoma destruens), and choriocarcinoma. They arise from fetal tissue within the maternal host and are composed of both syncytiotrophoblastic and cytotrophoblastic cells. In addition to being the first and only disseminated solid tumors that have proved to be highly curable by chemotherapy, they elaborate a unique and characteristic tumor marker, human chorionic gonadotropin (hCG).

Hydatidiform mole is the most common gestational trophoblastic neoplasm. Its incidence varies worldwide from 1:125 deliveries in Mexico and Taiwan to 1:1500 deliveries in the USA. The incidence is higher in women under 20 and over 40 years of age, in patients of low economic status, and in those whose diets are deficient in protein and folic acid. Molar pregnancy occurs in 1% of subsequent gestations in women with a history of mole.

Hydatidiform mole should be suspected in any woman with bleeding in the first half of pregnancy, passage of vesicles, hyperemesis gravidarum, or preeclampsia-eclampsia with onset before 24 weeks. Absent fetal heart tones and a uterus too large for the estimated duration of gestation on physical examination support the diagnosis. Ultrasonography, amniography, and repeated hCG determinations are necessary to establish a firm diagnosis of hydatidiform mole.

Invasive mole is reported in 10–15% of patients who have had primary molar pregnancy. Although considered a "benign" neoplasm, invasive mole is locally invasive and may produce distant metastases.

Choriocarcinoma is rare, reported in 2–5% of all cases of gestational trophoblastic neoplasia. The incidence in the USA is 1:40,000 pregnancies, but it is higher in the Orient. Choriocarcinoma is thought to follow hydatidiform mole in 50% of cases. One-fourth follow term pregnancy, and the remainder occur following abortion.

A generalization worth repeating is that any woman presenting with bleeding or a tumor in any organ who has a recent history of molar pregnancy, abortion, or term pregnancy should have at least one hCG assay to be sure that metastatic gestational tropho-blastic neoplasia is not the cause. This is important, for the cure rate of properly treated metastatic gestational trophoblastic neoplasia is approximately 90%.

Etiology & Pathogenesis

Gestational trophoblastic tumors arise in fetal rather than maternal tissue. Cytogenetic studies have demonstrated that true moles are usually (perhaps always) euploid and sex chromatin–positive 46,XX; transitional moles are usually trisomic; and partial moles are triploid. In 1978, Kajii reported that all chromosomes in true moles are paternal in origin. The development of an ovum under the influence of a sperm nucleus requires the absence or inactivation of the ovum nucleus and the presence of a diploid sperm or the duplication of its chromosomes. This provides important insight into the pathogenesis of gestational trophoblastic neoplasms, because this process results in a homozygous conceptus with a propensity for altered growth.

To date, hydatidiform mole has been considered to be derived from extraembryonic trophoblasts. Histologic similarities between molar vesicles and chorionic villi support the view that one is derived from the other. However, detailed morphologic study of a hysterectomy specimen containing an intact molar pregnancy presents a new concept regarding genesis of hydatidiform mole as a transformation of the embryonic inner cell mass at a stage just prior to the laying down of endoderm. At this stage in embryogenesis, the inner cell mass has the capability of developing into trophoblasts, ectoderm, and endoderm. If normal development is interrupted, such that the inner cell mass loses its capacity to differentiate into embryonic ectoderm and endoderm, a divergent developmental pathway is created. This pathway may then result in formation of trophoblasts (from the inner cell mass) that develop into cytotrophoblasts and syncytiotrophoblasts with sufficient differentiation to produce extraembryonic mesoderm, giving rise to molar vesicles with loose primitive mesoderm in their villous core. In contrast, choriocarcinoma is less well differentiated and, lacking this capability, is composed of only cytotrophoblasts and syncytiotrophoblasts.

Thus, the ultimate cause of gestational trophoblastic disease may be genetic. Nonetheless, there are interesting clinical correlates, some of which are mentioned above. Additionally, evidence indicates that the distribution of ABO blood groups in women with gestational trophoblastic neoplasms and their sexual partners differs from that of the general population. The most remarkable findings are that group A women impregnated by group O men have an almost 10 times greater risk of developing choriocarcinoma than group A women with group A partners and that women with group AB have a relatively poor prognosis. A study of the ABO blood groups of children resulting from pregnancies with subsequent choriocarcinoma revealed fewer instances than expected in which the child was ABO-incompatible with its mother. The leukocytes of these children frequently showed antigenic differences from the mothers' cells. Although these antigens are regarded as strong transplantation antigens, they seem notably weaker than the ABO factors—evidence that choriocarcinoma is able to grow and to kill in spite of the immune response it evokes.

Pathology

Three distinct forms of gestational trophoblastic neoplasia are recognized: hydatidiform mole, invasive mole (chorioadenoma destruens), and choriocarcinoma.

A. Hydatidiform Mole: Hydatidiform mole is an abnormal pregnancy characterized grossly by multiple grapelike vesicles filling and distending the uterus (Fig 32–7), usually in the absence of an intact fetus. Most hydatidiform moles are recognizable on gross examination, but some are small and may seem to be ordinary abortuses.

A blighted ovum, with an embryo or amniotic sac but little or no trophoblastic hyperplasia, appears to be a progenitor of the true or complete mole and accordingly has been termed a transitional mole. Molar transformation of portions of the placenta in a second or third trimester pregnancy constitutes a partial or incomplete mole. The fetus is usually stillborn.

Microscopically, moles may be identified by 3 classic findings: edema of the villous stroma, avascular villi, and nests of proliferating syncytiotrophoblastic or cytotrophoblastic elements surrounding villi (Fig 32–8). The likelihood of malignant sequelae is in-

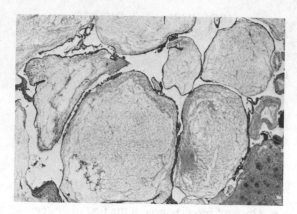

Figure 32–8. Photomicrograph of hydatidiform mole characterized by well-developed but avascular villi with stromal edema and minimal trophoblastic proliferation.

creased in patients whose trophoblastic cells show increased proliferation and anaplasia. Although histologic study of the trophoblast provides some basis for predicting a benign or malignant course for the mole, the correlation is not absolute, and it is essential to obtain accurate, sensitive gonadotropin assays in all patients who have had hydatidiform moles.

B. Invasive Mole (Chorioadenoma Destruens): Invasive mole is a hydatidiform mole that invades the myometrium or adjacent structures. It may totally penetrate the myometrium and be associated with uterine rupture and hemoperitoneum (Fig 32–9). The microscopic findings are the same as in hydatidiform mole (Fig 32–10). Since adequate myometrium is rarely obtained at curettage, the diagnosis is made by histologic study less frequently now than formerly, because fewer hysterectomies are performed in patients with trophoblastic disease. Metastatic lesions may contain invasive mole, but most will

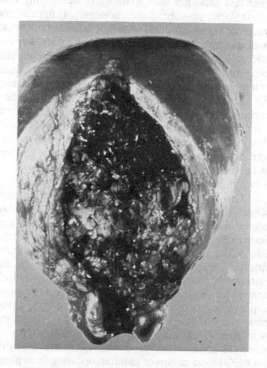

Figure 32–7. Hysterectomy specimen with anterior wall incised, displaying typical miliary, clear, "grapelike" vesicles filling the uterine cavity. Hysterectomy was performed as primary treatment for molar gestation.

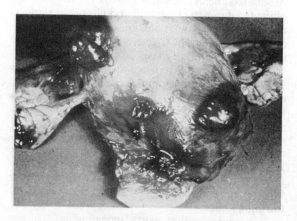

Figure 32–9. Hysterectomy specimen showing invasive mole penetrating the myometrium and serosal surface of the uterus that resulted in life-threatening intraperitoneal hemorrhage.

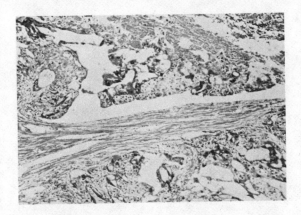

Figure 32–10. Photomicrograph of invasive mole. The pattern of hydatidiform mole is maintained with avascular villi and stromal edema, but they are deep within the utorine wall, interspersed among smooth-muscle bundles.

be choriocarcinoma regardless of the morphologic features of the uterine tumor.

C. Choriocarcinoma: Choriocarcinoma is a pure epithelial tumor composed of syncytiotrophoblastic and cytotrophoblastic cells. It may accompany or follow any type of pregnancy. Histologic examination discloses no villi but sheets or foci of trophoblasts on a background of hemorrhage and necrosis. A histopathologic diagnosis of choriocarcinoma in any site is an indication for prompt treatment after confirmation by gonadotropin excretion measurements. Assessment of trophoblastic tissue following or accompanying pregnancy may be difficult because of the histologic similarity of the trophoblastic pattern in very early human pregnancy and in choriocarcinoma. The entire specimen must be processed for histologic study when curettage is done, because specimens may reveal only small, isolated areas of choriocarcinoma. Careful search usually discloses the villous pattern in the tissue of early normal pregnancy.

Choriocarcinoma may also arise from ectopic pregnancy. In confusing situations, hCG testing may clarify the diagnosis and document the need for therapy.

Clinical Findings

A. Symptoms and Signs: Abnormal uterine bleeding, usually during the first trimester, is the most common symptom, occurring in over 90% of patients with molar pregnancies. Three-fourths of patients with bleeding have this symptom before the end of the third month of pregnancy. Only one-third of patients have profuse vaginal bleeding. In over 80% of cases, the first evidence of hydatidiform mole is the passage of vesicular tissue.

Nausea and vomiting, frequently excessive but at times difficult to distinguish from similar complaints normally occurring in pregnancy, have been reported to occur in 14–32% of patients with hydatidiform mole. Ten percent of patients with molar pregnancies

have nausea and vomiting severe enough to require hospitalization.

Disproportionate uterine size is the most common sign of molar gestation. About half of patients have excessive uterine size for gestational date, but in one-third the uterus is smaller than expected.

Multiple theca lutein cysts causing enlargement of one or both ovaries occur in 15–30% of women with molar pregnancies. In about half of the cases, both ovaries are enlarged and may be a source of pain. Involution of the cysts proceeds over several weeks, usually paralleling the decline of hCG level. Operation is indicated only if rupture and hemorrhage occurs or if the enlarged ovaries become infected. Patients with associated theca lutein cysts appear to have a greater likelihood of developing malignant sequelae of gestational trophoblastic neoplasia.

Preeclampsia in the first trimester or early second trimester—an unusual finding in normal pregnancy—has been said to be pathognomonic of hydatidiform mole, although it occurs in only 10–12% of those patients.

Hyperthyroidism from production of thyrotropin by molar tissue occurs in up to 10% of patients with hydatidiform mole. The manifestations disappear following evacuation of the mole. An occasional patient may require brief antithyroid therapy.

B. Laboratory Findings: A most important characteristic of gestational trophoblastic neoplasms is their capacity to produce human chorionic gonadotropin (hCG). This hormone may be detected in serum or urine in virtually all patients with hydatidiform mole or malignant trophoblastic disease. Careful monitoring of hCG levels is necessary for diagnosis, treatment, and follow-up in all cases of trophoblastic disease.

The amount of hCG found in the serum or excreted in the urine correlates closely with the number of viable tumor cells present. Various studies indicate that one tumor cell produces about $5 \times 10^{-5}–5 \times 10^{-4}$ IU of hCG in 24 hours. Thus, a patient excreting 10^6 IU of hCG in 24 hours has about 10^{11} viable tumor cells. At the point at which hCG is lost in the background of normal pituitary LH levels, there may remain $10^5–10^6$ viable tumor cells.

The usefulness of a gonadotropin assay depends upon the level of the patient's hCG titer and the sensitivity of the test. As many as 25% of patients with malignant trophoblastic disease have been found to have urinary hCG concentrations that are elevated but below the value detectable by urinary pregnancy tests. The most sensitive immunologic pregnancy test detects concentrations of hCG no lower than 200 IU/L. Most require hCG concentrations greater than 500–1000 IU/L of urine to give a positive result. Biologic pregnancy tests measure hCG levels in the range of 3000–5000 IU. Therefore, a negative pregnancy test in the postmole patient is of no value in accurately assessing the course of the disease. A more sensitive bioassay or radioimmunoassay that will measure down to the basal pituitary range must be used.

Because hCG and LH have identical alpha chains,

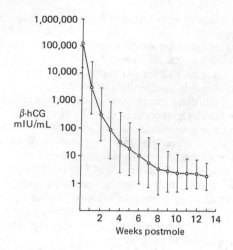

Figure 32–11. Normal post–molar pregnancy regression curve of serum β-hCG measured by radioimmunoassay. Vertical bars indicate 95% confidence limits. (Reprinted, with permission from The American College of Obstetricians and Gynecologists, Schlaerth et al: Prognostic characteristics of serum human chorionic gonadotropin titer regression following molar pregnancy. *Obstet Gynecol* 1981; 58:478.)

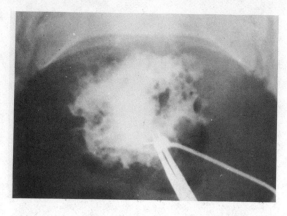

Figure 32–12. Amniogram of uterus with classic radiologic "honeycomb" appearance of unevacuated hydatidiform mole after intrauterine injection of radiopaque dye.

most tests do not differentiate between the 2 hormones. This is true of all biologic assays, immunoassays utilizing agglutination of particles, and radioimmunoassays utilizing agglutination of intact molecules of hCG. Therefore, a "normal" hCG titer is in the range of 20–30 IU (the pituitary level of LH). However, the beta chains of hCG and LH are not the same. A specific beta subunit assay for hCG is available that allows precise hCG determinations to a level approaching zero. With functioning gonads, a woman excretes less than 4 IU of hCG in 24 hours. It is in these lower ranges of gonadotropin excretion that specific assay for the beta subunit of hCG has been most useful.

The rate and constancy of the decline in hCG titer are important also. Using the serum β-hCG radioimmunoassay, a normal post–molar pregnancy hCG regression curve based on weekly determinations in patients undergoing spontaneous remission has been constructed (Fig 32–11). This provides a reference with which random or serial values can be compared. In most instances, the hCG values exhibit a progressive decline to normal (< 1 mIU/mL) within 14 weeks following evacuation of a molar pregnancy. If metastases are detected or if the hCG titer rises or plateaus, it must be concluded that viable tumor persists.

C. X-Ray Findings: Because of its universal availability, transabdominal amniocentesis combined with amniography may be used to confirm the presence of hydatidiform mole. The uterus should be at or beyond 14 weeks in size, so that it is palpable above the symphysis pubica, allowing the bladder to be safely avoided when a needle is inserted into the uterine cavity. If amniotic fluid can be withdrawn after the needle is introduced, a diagnosis of pregnancy is pre-

sumed; radiopaque dye should not be injected in such cases, since there is a small risk that the hyperosmolar contrast media may induce premature labor. When little or no amniotic fluid is obtained on aspiration of the uterine cavity, radiopaque dye should be injected. The diagnosis of hydatidiform mole can be made by x-ray demonstrating the characteristic honeycomb pattern produced by the dispersion of dye around the vesicles (Fig 32–12).

D. Special Examinations: The simplicity, safety, and reliability of ultrasonography make it the diagnostic method of choice for patients with suspected molar pregnancy. In a molar pregnancy, the characteristic ultrasound pattern includes multiple echoes formed by the interface between the molar villi and the surrounding tissue without the presence of a normal gestational sac or fetus (Fig 32–13). This study should be done in any patient who experiences bleeding in the first half of pregnancy and has a uterus greater than 12 weeks' gestational size. Even when the uterus is smaller or when an equivocal amniogram is

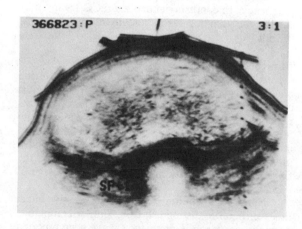

Figure 32–13. A gray-scale ultrasonogram depicting the typical intrauterine multiple-echo pattern of hydatidiform mole.

present, ultrasonography may be very specific in differentiating between a normal pregnancy and hydatidiform mole.

Differential Diagnosis

Gestational trophoblastic disease must be distinguished from normal pregnancy. Ultrasonography is useful, and quantitative urinary hCG levels afford another means of differentiation. In general, urinary hCG values greater than 500,000 IU/24 h are usual with molar pregnancies, in contrast to normal pregnancy values below 100,000 IU/24 L.

Complications

The maternal/fetal barrier contains leaks large enough to permit passage of cellular and tissue elements. Trophoblastic deportations to the lungs are frequent and have totally unpredictable manifestations, including spontaneous regression. A dramatic, life threatening complication of molar pregnancy in patients with uterine enlargement beyond 16 weeks' gestational size is a syndrome of acute pulmonary insufficiency characterized by sudden onset of dyspnea, often with cyanosis. Symptoms usually begin within 4–6 hours after evacuation. Historically, the syndrome has been attributed to massive deportation of trophoblasts to the pulmonary vasculature, but the most likely cause may be pulmonary edema secondary to cardiac dysfunction and excessive fluid administration. Nevertheless, massive fatal pulmonary embolization by gross deportation of villous tissue masses may occur, as documented by postmortem examination.

Treatment

A. Hydatidiform Mole:

1. Evacuation—When the diagnosis has been confirmed, molar pregnancy should be terminated.

Suction curettage is the method of choice. It is safe, rapid, and effective in nearly all cases. Intravenous oxytocin should be started after a moderate amount of tissue has been removed. Suction curettage should be followed by gentle sharp curettage, and tissue from the decidua basalis should be submitted for pathologic study. Suction curettage can be safely accomplished even when the uterus is as large as in a 28-week pregnancy. Blood loss usually is moderate, but precautions should be taken for massive transfusion. When a large hydatidiform mole (> 12 weeks in size) is evacuated by suction curettage, a laparotomy setup should be readily available, since hysterotomy, hysterectomy, or bilateral hypogastric artery ligation may be necessary if perforation or hemorrhage occurs.

Before the use of suction curettage, hysterectomy was frequently used for patients with uteri beyond 12–14 weeks in size. Hysterectomy remains an option for good surgical candidates not desirous of future pregnancy and for older women (who are more likely to develop malignant sequelae). If theca lutein cysts are encountered at hysterectomy, the ovaries should remain intact, because regression to normal size will occur as the hCG titer diminishes. Hysterectomy does not eliminate the need for careful follow-up and hCG testing, although the likelihood of metastatic disease following hysterectomy for gestational trophoblastic disease is low (3.5%).

Hysterotomy is no longer a method of choice in typical cases. The higher incidence of malignant disease following hysterotomy is probably attributable to greater uterine enlargement in patients selected for this therapy. Current recommendations restrict hysterotomy to cases complicated by hemorrhage.

Prostaglandin induction is being studied for evacuation of molar pregnancy. Oxytocin induction and intra-amniotic instillation of prostaglandin or hypertonic solutions (saline, glucose, urea, etc) are no longer considered useful for this purpose.

2. Prophylactic chemotherapy—Prophylactic dactinomycin therapy may be appropriate for patients with large uteri or in whom poor follow-up is anticipated. Caution is needed, since several deaths due to toxicity have been reported.

3. Surveillance following molar pregnancy—Regardless of method of termination, close follow-up with serial hCG titers is essential for every patient because of the 15% incidence of malignant disease (10% for invasive mole and 5% for choriocarcinoma). Three-fourths of patients with malignant nonmetastatic trophoblastic disease and half of patients with malignant metastatic disease develop these tumors as sequelae to hydatidiform mole. In the remainder, disease arises following term pregnancy, abortion, or ectopic pregnancy.

Several clinical features of hydatidiform mole are recognized as having a high association with malignant trophoblastic neoplasia. In general, at diagnosis, the larger the uterus, the higher the hCG titer; and the shorter the gestation, the greater the risk for malignant gestational trophoblastic disease. The combination of theca lutein cysts and uterine size excessive for gestational age is associated with an extremely high risk (57%) of malignant sequelae.

These patients should be given oral contraceptives for contraception and to suppress pituitary gonadotropin excretion, thus making the differentiation between hCG and LH easier.

Following evacuation of hydatidiform mole, the patient should have serial β-hCG determinations at weekly intervals until serum hCG declines to nondetectable levels (<5 mIU/mL by β-hCG radioimmunoassay) on 2 successive assays. If titer remission occurs spontaneously within 14 weeks and without a titer plateau, the β-hCG titer then should be repeated monthly for at least 1 year before the patient is released from close medical supervision. Thereafter, the patient may enter into a regular gynecologic care program.

Gynecologic examination should be done 1 week after evacuation, at which time blood may be taken for the first postevacuation hCG titer. Estimates of uterine size and adnexal masses (theca lutein cysts) and a careful search of the vulva, vagina, urethra, and cervix should be made for evidence of genital tract metastases. Unless symptoms develop, the examination should be repeated at 4-week intervals throughout the observation period.

Chest x-ray should be obtained prior to evacuation and at 2- to 4-week intervals thereafter until spontaneous remission is confirmed, then at 3-month intervals during the remainder of the surveillance period.

A patient who has entered into spontaneous remission with negative titers, examinations, and chest x-rays for 1 year and who is desirous of becoming pregnant may terminate contraceptive medication. Successful pregnancy is usual, and complications are similar to those of patients in the general population.

Therapy for progressive gestational trophoblastic neoplasia after delivery of a hydatidiform mole is usually instituted because of an abnormal hCG regression curve. While the hCG titer usually returns to normal within 1–2 weeks after evacuation of a hydatidiform mole, it should be normal by 8 weeks. The most critical period of observation is the first 4–6 weeks postevacuation. Few patients whose hCG titers are normal during this interval will require treatment. Approximately 70% of patients achieve a normal hCG level within 60 days postevacuation.

In the past, therapy was recommended if the hCG titer remained elevated at or beyond 60 days after termination of molar pregnancy. However, current data suggest that an additional 15% of patients demonstrate a continuous decline in titers and ultimately achieve normal titers without treatment. About 15% of patients who have elevated titers at 60 days postevacuation demonstrate a rising or plateauing titer. Nearly half of these patients have histologic evidence of choriocarcinoma, and the rest have invasive mole.

Delayed postevacuation bleeding is uncommon after molar pregnancy, but it signifies the presence of invasive mole or choriocarcinoma and is invariably attended by an enlarging uterus and abnormal hCG regression pattern. On pelvic examination, the enlarged uterus may have the characteristics of an intrauterine pregnancy. Curettage is effective in stopping the bleeding, although little intracavitary tissue will be present in most of these cases.

In summary, the indications for initiating chemotherapy during the postmolar surveillance period are (1) β-hCG levels rising for 2 successive weeks or constant for 3 successive weeks; (2) β-hCG levels elevated at 15 weeks postevacuation; (3) rising β-hCG titer after reaching normal levels; and (4) postevacuation hemorrhage. Too, treatment should be instituted whenever there is a tissue diagnosis of choriocarcinoma. However, histologic confirmation is unnecessary, because the presence of metastasis is a sufficient justification for chemotherapy.

B. Malignant Gestational Trophoblastic Neoplasia: Once the diagnosis of malignant trophoblastic disease has been established, obtain an accurate history and perform a physical examination, including pelvic examination. Most patients have an enlarged uterus, and ovarian enlargement due to theca lutein cysts is common. Sites of metastasis must be sought, especially in the lower genital tract. Obtain a chest x-ray, intravenous urogram, and liver scan. The CT scan is now the diagnostic procedure of choice for brain metastasis; however, evaluation of the ratio of serum hCH to the concentration of hCG in cerebrospinal fluid may be helpful. Carefully consider the baseline hematologic counts as well as hepatic and renal function, which may be critical in the risk and monitoring of drug toxicity.

After sites of metastases or of abnormal function have been identified, the patient's desires for preservation of reproductive function are known, and the disease has been categorized as nonmetastatic or metastatic, specific therapy should be started.

1. Nonmetastatic gestational trophoblastic disease–Trophoblastic disease confined to the uterus is the most common malignant lesion seen in gestational trophoblastic neoplasia. The diagnosis is usually made during follow-up after evacuation of molar pregnancy. If there is no evidence of spread outside the uterus, histologic examination may be important, for nonmetastatic choriocarcinoma is a more serious condition than nonmetastatic hydatidiform mole. Therapy for patients with nonmetastatic malignant trophoblastic disease includes (1) single-agent chemotherapy; (2) combined chemotherapy and hysterectomy, with surgery done on the third day of drug therapy if the patient does not wish to preserve reproductive function and her disease is known to be confined to the uterus; and (3) intra-arterial infusion of chemotherapeutic agents in selected cases.

Single-agent chemotherapy using methotrexate or dactinomycin has demonstrated clear-cut superiority over the protocols (Table 32–2). The therapeutic efficacy of the 2 drugs is apparently equivalent, but dactinomycin is favored by some because it is less toxic. Methotrexate is contraindicated in the presence of hepatocellular disease or when renal function is impaired. Each treatment cycle should be repeated as soon as normal tissues (bone marrow and gastrointestinal mucosa) have recovered, with a minimum 7-day window between the last day of one course and the first day of the next one.

During treatment, weekly β-hCG titers and complete blood counts should be obtained. Before each course of therapy, liver and renal function assessments should be done. At least one course of drug therapy should be given after the first normal β-hCG determination. The number of treatment cycles necessary to induce remission is proportionate to the magnitude of the β-hCG concentration at the start of therapy. An average of 3 or 4 courses of single-agent therapy is required. After remission has been induced and treatment is completed, β-hCG assays should be obtained monthly for 12 months.

Methotrexate with leucovorin calcium* rescue has also been used to treat nonmetastatic trophoblastic disease (Table 32–3). This regimen requires hospitalization or daily outpatient visits. Blood counts are obtained on each day of methotrexate administration, and

*Formerly called citrovorum factor or folinic acid.

Table 32–2. Single-agent chemotherapy.

A. Methotrexate, 0.4 mg/kg/d IV or IM,

or

Dactinomycin, 10–12 μg/kg/d IV.

1. Give either one in 5-day course.
2. Repeat cycle with minimum interval of 7–10 days as toxicity allows.
3. Oral contraceptive agents, if not contraindicated.

B. Continue repeated chemotherapy cycles until—
1. One course after a negative β-hCG titer.
2. Remission, defined as 3 consecutive normal weekly β-hCG titers.

Switch to alternative drug if—
   a. Titer rises (10-fold or more).
   b. Titer plateaus at an elevated level.
   c. New metastasis appears.

C. Laboratory values: Obtain daily during treatment cycle, weekly, or as indicated between treatment cycles. Take β-hCG titers weekly until remission induction. Do not begin or continue a course of chemotherapy if—
1. White blood count < 3000/μL.
2. Granulocytes < 1500/μL.
3. Platelets < 100,000/μL.
4. BUN, SGOT, SGPT, bilirubin significantly elevated.

D. Other toxicity mandating postponement of chemotherapy:
1. Severe stomatitis or gastrointestinal ulceration.
2. Febrile course (usually present only with leukopenia).

E. Follow-up program:
1. β-hCG titer weekly until 3 consecutive normal titers; monthly β-hCG titers for 12 months thereafter; then β-hCG titers every 2 months for 12 additional months or every 6 months indefinitely.
2. Physical examination including pelvic examination and chest x-ray monthly until remission is induced; at 3-month intervals for 1 year thereafter; then at 6-month intervals indefinitely.
3. Continue contraception for minimum of 1 year after remission induction.

therapy is deferred if white blood cell and platelet counts are low.

Excellent results have been achieved with alternating sequential courses of dactinomycin and methotrexate (Table 32–4). This regimen avoids the cumulative toxicity of methotrexate and may retard the development of resistance.

Surgery combined with chemotherapy for patients with nonmetastatic gestational trophoblastic disease who do not desire future pregnancy is being evaluated.

Table 32–3. Methotrexate–leucovorin calcium rescue chemotherapy for nonmetastatic trophoblastic neoplasia.*

Therapy	Time	Interval
Complete blood count; platelet count, SGOT	8 AM	Day 1, 3, 5, 7
Methotrexate, 1 mg/kg IM	4 PM	Day 1, 3, 5, 7
Leucovorin calcium, 0.1 mg/kg IM	4 PM	Day 2, 4, 6, 8

*Modified from Goldstein et al, 1978.

Table 32–4. Alternating sequential chemotherapy.*

Methotrexate, 15–30 mg/d IV daily for 5 days
Dactinomycin, 0.5 mg/kg IV daily for 5 days

The drugs are given sequentially and alternately as soon as the oral and hematologic toxicity from the preceding drug has subsided.

*Modified from Smith, 1973.

2. Metastatic gestational trophoblastic disease–Therapy in metastatic disease depends on multiple factors that characterize patients as good-prognosis or poor-prognosis patients (Table 32–5). Therapy is based on this initial categorization as well as on factors governing selection of techniques (Table 32–6).

Table 32–5. Categorization of gestational trophoblastic neoplasia.

A. **Nonmetastatic disease:** No evidence of disease outside uterus.
B. **Metastatic disease:** Any disease outside uterus.
   1. **Good-prognosis metastatic disease—**
      a. Short duration (< 4 months).
      b. Urinary hCG < 100,000 IU/24 h or serum β-hCG < 40,000 mIU/mL.
      c. No metastasis to brain or liver.
      d. No significant prior chemotherapy.
   2. **Poor-prognosis metastatic disease—**
      a. Long duration (> 4 months).
      b. Urinary hCG > 100,000 IU/24 h or serum β-hCG > 40,000 mIU/mL.
      c. Metastasis to brain or liver.
      d. Unsuccessful prior chemotherapy.
      e. Gestational trophoblastic neoplasia following term pregnancy.

Table 32–6. Selection of therapy in metastatic trophoblastic disease.

A. **Good Prognosis:**
1. Single-agent methotrexate or dactinomycin chemotherapy.
2. Alternating sequential single-agent chemotherapy.
3. Methotrexate with leucovorin calcium rescue chemotherapy.
4. Delayed hysterectomy if residual resistant disease in uterus.
5. Combination chemotherapy.
6. Arterial infusion chemotherapy.

B. **Poor Prognosis:**
1. Combination chemotherapy (MAC [see Table 32–7]).
2. Whole brain irradiation to 3000 rads and/or whole liver irradiation to 2000 rads given over 10–14 days concomitantly with chemotherapy.
3. Delayed hysterectomy if residual resistant disease in uterus, and surgical "debulking" resection of isolated accessible resistant metastasis in pelvis, lung, brain.
4. Other multiple-agent chemotherapeutic regimens (MBP [see Table 32–8] or VBP [see Table 32–9]).
5. Arterial infusion chemotherapy.
6. Single-agent chemotherapy.

a. Good-prognosis patients–Patients can be expected to respond satisfactorily to single-agent chemotherapy if (1) metastases are confined to the lungs or pelvis *and* (2) urine hCG excretion is below 100,000 IU/24 h or serum β-hCG levels are below 40,000 mIU/mL at the onset of treatment *and* (3) therapy is started within 4 months of apparent onset of disease.

The most common site of metastasis is the lung. When a patient develops pulmonary metastases and elevation of hCG titer, choriocarcinoma is a more likely cause than metastatic mole. Invasive mole may also metastasize to the lungs, and hydatidiform mole has occasionally been reported to metastasize to the chest. Probably any form of metastasis (even benign deportation) should suggest metastatic trophoblastic disease.

In these patients, single-agent chemotherapy is almost uniformly successful. The complete remission rate in this group of patients has been 100%. Methotrexate is considered the drug of choice. Ideally, treatment is given every other week, because tumor regrowth becomes significant after treatment gaps of 2 weeks or longer. Once negative titers have been achieved, an additional course is administered. If resistance to methotrexate occurs, manifested either by rising or plateauing titers or by the development of new metastases—or if negative titers are not achieved by the fifth course of methotrexate—the patient should be given dactinomycin.

The advantage of single-agent chemotherapy is that it is less toxic and its toxicity is less apt to be irreversible than is the case with multiple-agent chemotherapy.

There is a tendency to approach the treatment of these patients too lightly, probably because of the "good-prognosis" (low-risk) designation. But failure of drug therapy does occur in about 10% of cases, and meticulous care by physicians familiar with these problems is necessary for good results.

b. Poor-prognosis patients–"Poor-prognosis" patients are those with (1) serum β-hCG titers greater than 50,000 mIU/mL or urinary hCG levels greater than 100,000 IU/24 h *or* (2) disease diagnosed more than 4 months after molar pregnancy *or* (3) brain or liver metastases *or* (4) prior unsuccessful chemotherapy *or* (5) onset following term gestation. These patients present a serious challenge. Many have been previously treated with chemotherapy and have become resistant to that treatment while accumulating considerable toxicity and depleting bone marrow reserves. Prior unsuccessful chemotherapy is one of the worst prognostic factors.

Generally, these patients require prolonged hospitalization and many courses of chemotherapy. They often need specialized care and other life-support measures, including hyperalimentation, antibiotics, and transfusions to correct the effects of marrow depression.

Central nervous system involvement, particularly brain metastasis with focal neurologic signs suggestive of intracranial hemorrhage, is common in choriocarcinoma. Since patients with brain or liver metastases are at great risk of sudden death with hemorrhage from these lesions, it is now standard practice for the therapy plan of these patients to include immediate institution of whole-brain or whole-liver irradiation concomitantly with combination chemotherapy. It is uncertain whether radiation therapy exerts its beneficial effect by destroying tumor in combination with drug therapy or by preventing fatal hemorrhage and thus keeping the patient alive until remission with chemotherapy can be achieved.

Cerebral metastasis should be treated over a 2-week period with radiation given in a dosage of 300 rads daily, 5 days a week, to a total organ dose of 3000 rads. Whole-liver irradiation is usually accomplished over 10 days to attain a 2000-rad whole-organ dose given at a rate of 200 rads daily, 5 days a week.

The standard treatment regimen is with triple-agent MAC (*m*ethotrexate, d*a*ctinomycin, and *c*hlorambucil or *c*yclophosphamide) chemotherapy (Table 32–7). These drugs are employed in 5-day intermittent courses repeated every 12–14 days, depending on toxicity. The same tests must be employed to detect toxicity as are used when single-agent chemotherapy is given, but monitoring must be even more careful because of the possibility of combined toxicity.

Treatment of malignant trophoblastic disease must be continued with repeated courses of combination chemotherapy until β-hCG titers return to non-

---

Table 32–7. Combination (MAC) chemotherapy.

A. Methotrexate, 10–15 mg/d IV or IM
        and
   Dactinomycin, 10–12 μg/kg/d IV
        and
   Chlorambucil, 8–10 mg/d by mouth, or cyclophosphamide, 3–5 mg/kg/d IV.
   1. Given in 5-day courses.
   2. Repeat cycles with minimum interval of 10–14 days, as toxicity allows.
   3. Oral contraceptive agents, if not contraindicated.
B. Continue repetitive chemotherapy cycles until—
   1. Three courses after negative β-hCG titers.
   2. Remission, defined as 3 consecutive normal weekly β-hCG titers.
Switch to alternative combination drug regimens if—
   a. Titer rises.
   b. Titer plateaus after 2 courses of MAC.
   c. Increasing metastatic disease is evident.
C. Laboratory values: Same as outlined in Table 32–2.
D. Complications:
   1. Severe stomatitis or gastrointestinal ulceration.
   2. Severe bone marrow suppression is major morbidity.
   3. Mortality rate 10–15%.
E. Follow-up program: Same as outlined in Table 32–2 except continue contraception for minimum of 2 years after remission induction.
F. Liver and/or brain metastasis require emergent radiation to a whole-organ dose of 2000 and 3000 rads, respectively, delivered in 10–14 days concomitantly with chemotherapy.

Table 32—8. Modified Bagshawe protocol (MBP) for poor-prognosis trophoblastic disease.*

Day	Hour	Drug	Dose
1	6 AM	Hydroxyurea	500 mg orally
	12 NOON	Hydroxyurea	500 mg orally
	6 PM	Hydroxyurea	500 mg orally
	7 PM	Dactinomycin	200 μg IV
	12 MID-NIGHT	Hydroxyurea	500 mg orally
2	7 AM	Vincristine	1.0 mg/m² IV
	7 PM	Methotrexate	100 mg/m² IV
		Methotrexate	200 mg/m² infused over 12 hours
		Dactinomycin	200 μg IV
3	7 PM	Dactinomycin	200 μg IV
		Cyclophosphamide	500 mg/m² IV
		Leucovorin calcium	14 mg IM
4	1 AM	Leucovorin calcium	14 mg IM
	7 AM	Leucovorin calcium	14 mg IM
	1 PM	Leucovorin calcium	14 mg IM
	7 PM	Leucovorin calcium	14 mg IM
		Dactinomycin	500 μg IV
5	1 AM	Leucovorin calcium	14 mg IM
	7 PM	Dactinomycin	500 μg IV
6		No treatment	
7		No treatment	
8	7 PM	Cyclophosphamide	500 mg/m² IV
		Doxorubicin	30 mg/m² IV

Wait 7—14 days for recovery and repeat cycles as toxicity allows.

*As currently used at the Southeastern Regional Center for Trophoblastic Disease.

Table 32—9. VBP chemotherapy for poor-prognosis trophoblastic disease.

Drug	Dose	Interval
Vinblastine	0.2 mg/kg IV	Day 1 and 2
Bleomycin	30 units IV	Weekly × 12
Cisplatin	20 mg/m² IV infusion	Day 1, 2, 3, 4, 5

Repeat cycle every 3 weeks for 3—4 cycles

*Modified from Einhorn and Donahue, 1977.

Two regimens are effective in management of MAC treatment failures: (1) The modified Bagshawe multidrug protocol (Table 32–8) and (2) Einhorn's regimen of vinblastine, bleomycin, and cisplatin (Table 32–9). These multiple-agent combinations appear to be effective adjuncts to MAC in resistant cases. Another drug protocol occasionally employed in resistant cases is methotrexate infusion.

In resistant cases, adjunctive measures along with chemotherapy may include hysterectomy, resection of metastatic tumors, or irradiation of unresectable lesions.

Prognosis

The prognosis for hydatidiform mole following evacuation is uniformly excellent, though surveillance is needed as outlined in the text. The prognosis for malignant nonmetastatic disease with appropriate therapy is also quite good, since almost all patients are cured. Over 90% of patients have been able to preserve reproductive function, but first-line therapy failed in 6.5% of patients with nonmetastatic disease. In one large reported series, no deaths from toxicity occurred and only one patient died of the disease.

Prognostic factors in malignant metastatic disease are set forth in the discussion of treatment. In poor-prognosis metastatic disease, the best results are with chemotherapy plus concurrent radiation therapy, with 87% or more achieving remission. This has been accomplished not only with newer chemotherapeutic regimens but also with an aggressive multimodal approach. Deaths from toxicity have decreased considerably. Recurrence, when it happens, is usually in the first several months after termination of therapy but may be as late as 3 years.

detectable levels. Complete remission is documented only after 3 consecutive weekly normal β-hCG titers have been achieved. It is recommended that all high-risk patients receive at least 3 courses of triple-agent chemotherapy after β-hCG titers have returned to normal. After remission is achieved, follow-up is the same as for hydatidiform mole and nonmetastatic or good-prognosis disease.

If the hCG titer rises or plateaus after 2 courses of MAC chemotherapy or if the patient fails to achieve a normal titer after 4–5 courses of MAC, an alternative method of therapy should be used. If toxicity is too severe, a less intensive regimen should be considered.

• • •

References

Complications of Pregnancy

Anderson SG: Management of threatened abortion with real-time sonography. *Obstet Gynecol* 1980;**55**:259.

Block MF, Rahhal DK: Cervical incompetence: A diagnostic and prognostic scoring system. *Obstet Gynecol* 1976; **47**:279.

Braunstein GD et al: First-trimester chorionic gonadotropin measurements as an aid in the diagnosis of early pregnancy disorders. *Am J Obstet Gynecol* 1978;**131**:25.

Braunstein GD et al: Subclinical spontaneous abortion. *Obstet Gynecol* (July) 1977;**50(Suppl)**:41S.

Cava EF, Russell WM: Intramural pregnancy with uterine rupture. *Am J Obstet Gynecol* 1978;**131**:214.

Chandra P et al: Unruptured interstitial pregnancy. *Obstet Gynecol* 1978;**52**:612.

Clark JFJ, Jones SA: Advanced ectopic pregnancy. *J Reprod Med* 1975;**14**:30.

Danforth DN: Discussion of uterine sacculation. *Am J Obstet Gynecol* 1963;**87**:511.

De Cherney A, Kase N: The conservative management of unruptured ectopic pregnancy. *Obstet Gynecol* 1979; **54**:451.

Franklin EW, Zeiderman AM: Tubal ectopic pregnancy: Etiology and obstetric and gynecologic sequelae. *Am J Obstet Gynecol* 1973;**117**:220.

Gitstein S et al: Early cervical pregnancy: Ultrasonic diagnosis and conservative treatment. *Obstet Gynecol* 1979;**54**:758.

Goldstein A, Dumars KW, Kent DR: Prenatal diagnosis of chromosomal and enzymatic defects. *Obstet Gynecol* 1976;**47**:503.

Graber CD et al: *T mycoplasma* in human reproductive failure. *Obstet Gynecol* 1979;**54**:558.

Gustavii B: Missed abortion and uterine contractility. *Am J Obstet Gynecol* 1978;**130**:18.

Hallatt JG: Ectopic pregnancy associated with intrauterine device: Study of 70 cases. *Am J Obstet Gynecol* 1976; **125**:754.

Harter CA, Benirschke K: Fetal syphilis in the first trimester. *Am J Obstet Gynecol* 1976;**124**:705.

Jansen RPS, Elliott PM: Angular intrauterine pregnancy. *Obstet Gynecol* 1981;**58**:167.

Jouppila P et al: Early pregnancy failure: Study by ultrasonic and hormonal methods. *Obstet Gynecol* 1980;**55**:42.

Kadar N et al: A method of screening for ectopic pregnancy and its indications. *Obstet Gynecol* 1981;**58**:162.

Kajii T, Ferrier A: Cytogenetics of aborters and abortuses. *Am J Obstet Gynecol* 1978;**131**:33.

Kalchman GG, Meltzer RM: Interstitial pregnancy following homolateral salpingectomy. *Am J Obstet Gynecol* 1966; **96**:1139.

Kalfayan B, Gundersen JH: Ovarian twin pregnancy. *Obstet Gynecol* 1980;**55**:25S.

Kelly RW et al: Delayed hemorrhage in conservative surgery for ectopic pregnancy. *Am J Obstet Gynecol* 1979;**133**:225.

Lauritsen JG, Grunnet N, Jensen OM: Materno-fetal ABO incompatibility as a cause of spontaneous abortion. *Clin Genet* 1975;**7**:308.

Lawson TL: Ectopic pregnancy: Criteria and accuracy of ultrasonic diagnosis. *Am J Roentgenol* 1978;**131**:153.

Mahajan RC et al: Toxoplasmosis: Its role in abortion. *Indian J Med Res* 1976;**64**:797.

Mashiach S et al: Nonoperative management of ectopic pregnancy. *J Reprod Med* 1982;**27**:133.

McArdle CR: Failed abortion in a septate uterus. *Am J Obstet Gynecol* 1978;**131**:910.

McCausland A: High rate of ectopic pregnancy following laparoscopic coagulation failures. *Am J Obstet Gynecol* 1980;**136**:97.

Metz KGP, Mastroianni L: Tubal pregnancy distal to complete tubal occlusion following sterilization. *Am J Obstet Gynecol* 1978;**131**:911.

Nelson DM: Bilateral internal iliac artery ligation in cervical pregnancy: Conservation of reproductive function. *Am J Obstet Gynecol* 1979;**134**:145.

Ohel G, Katz M: Lactic dehydrogenase measurement in chronic ectopic pregnancy. *Am J Obstet Gynecol* 1979; **135**:149.

Orr JW et al: False negative oxytocin challenge test associated with abdominal pregnancy. *Am J Obstet Gynecol* 1979; **133**:108.

Poland BJ, Dol FJ, Styblo C: Embryonic development in ectopic human pregnancy. *Teratology* 1976;**14**:315.

Poland BJ, Yuen BH: Embryonic development in consecutive specimens from recurrent spontaneous abortions. *Am J Obstet Gynecol* 1978;**130**:512.

Rantakyla P et al: Ectopic pregnancy and the use of intrauterine device and low dose progestogen contraception. *Acta Obstet Gynecol Scand* 1977;**56**:61.

Richards SR et al: Heterotopic pregnancy: Reappraisal of incidence. *Am J Obstet Gynecol* 1982;**142**:928.

Robinson HP: The diagnosis of early pregnancy failure by sonar. *Br J Obstet Gynaecol* 1975;**82**:849.

Rust JA Jr, Botte JM: Curved Allis (tonsil) forceps technic in Shirodkar operation. *Obstet Gynecol* 1967;**30**:438.

Simpson JL et al: Parental chromosomal rearrangements associated with repetitive spontaneous abortions. *Fertil Steril* 1981;**36**:584.

Tatum HJ, Schmidt FH, Jain AK: Management and outcome of pregnancies associated with the Copper T intrauterine contraceptive device. *Am J Obstet Gynecol* 1976;**126**:869.

Taylor P, Cumming D: Combined laparoscopy and minilaparotomy in the management of unruptured tubal pregnancy. *Fertil Steril* 1979;**32**:521.

Valle RF, Sabbagha RE: Management of first trimester pregnancy termination failures. *Obstet Gynecol* 1980;**55**:625.

Weathersbee PS: Early reproductive loss and the factors that may influence its occurrence. *J Reprod Med* 1982;**25**:315.

Wolf GC, Thompson NJ: Female sterilization and subsequent ectopic pregnancy. *Obstet Gynecol* 1980;**55**:17.

Zuspan FP: Second trimester abortion. *J Reprod Med* 1976; **16**:47.

Trophoblastic Diseases

Bagshawe KD: *Choriocarcinoma: The Clinical Biology of the Trophoblast and Its Tumours.* Williams & Wilkins, 1969.

Bagshawe KD: Risk and prognostic factors in trophoblastic neoplasia. *Cancer* 1976;**38**:1373.

Bagshawe KD: Treatment of trophoblastic tumors. *Ann Acad Med* 1976;**5**:273.

Brewer JI, Halpern B, Torok EE: Gestational trophoblastic disease: Selected clinical aspects and chorionic gonadotropin test methods. *Curr Probl Cancer* 1979;**3**:1.

Curry SL et al: Hydatidiform mole: Diagnosis, management, and long-term follow-up of 347 patients. *Obstet Gynecol* 1975;**45**:1.

Fuller AF, Schiff I, Knapp RC: Immunity, trophoblast, and trophoblastic neoplasia. *Clin Obstet Gynecol* 1977;**20**:681.

Goldstein DP: Prevention of gestational trophoblastic disease by use of actinomycin D in molar pregnancies. *Obstet Gynecol* 1974;**43**:475.

Goldstein DP et al: Methotrexate with citrovorum factor rescue for gestational trophoblastic neoplasms. *Obstet Gynecol* 1978;**51**:93.

Hammond CB, Parker RT: Diagnosis and treatment of trophoblastic disease. *Obstet Gynecol* 1970;**35**:132.

Hammond CB et al: Treatment of metastatic trophoblastic disease: Good and poor prognosis. *Am J Obstet Gynecol* 1973;**115**:451.

Hertig AT, Mansell H: Tumors of the female sex organs. 1. Hydatiform mole and choriocarcinoma. In: *Atlas of Tumor Pathology*. Armed Forces Institute of Pathology, Washington DC, 1956.

Kajii T, Ohama K: Androgenetic origin of hydatidiform mole. *Nature* 1977;**268**:633.

Lewis JL: Treatment of metastatic gestational trophoblastic neoplasms: A brief review of developments in the years 1968 to 1978. *Am J Obstet Gynecol* 1980;**136**:163.

Li MC: Trophoblastic disease: Natural history, diagnosis, and treatment. *Ann Intern Med* 1971;**74**:102.

Miller JM Jr, Surwitt EA, Hammond CB: Choriocarcinoma following term pregnancy. *Obstet Gynecol* 1979;**53**:207.

Morrow CP et al: Clinical and laboratory correlates of molar pregnancy and trophoblastic disease. *Am J Obstet Gynecol* 1977;**128**:424.

Ross GT et al: Sequential use of methotrexate and actinomycin D in the treatment of metastatic choriocarcinoma and related trophoblastic diseases in women. *Am J Obstet Gynecol* 1965;**93**:223.

Schlaerth JB, Morrow CP, DePetrillo AD: Sustained remission of choriocarcinoma with cis-platinum, vinblastine, and bleomycin after failure of conventional combination drug therapy. *Am J Obstet Gynecol* 1980;**136**:983.

Surwitt EA et al: A new combination chemotherapy for resistant trophoblastic disease. *Gynecol Oncol* 1979;**8**:110.

Twiggs LB, Morrow CP, Schlaerth JB: Acute pulmonary complications of molar pregnancy. *Am J Obstet Gynecol* 1979;**135**:189.

Vassilakos P, Riotton G, Kajii T: Hydatidiform mole: Two entities. A morphologic and cytogenetic study with some clinical considerations. *Am J Obstet Gynecol* 1977;**127**:167.

Weed JC Jr, Hammond CB: Cerebral metastatic choriocarcinoma: Intensive therapy and prognosis. *Obstet Gynecol* 1980;**55**:89.

Yamashita K et al: Human lymphocyte antigen expression in hydatidiform mole: Androgenesis following fertilization by a haploid sperm. *Am J Obstet Gynecol* 1979;**135**:597.

Yen S, MacMahon B: Epidemiologic features of trophoblastic disease. *Am J Obstet Gynecol* 1968;**101**:126.

33 | Complications of Labor & Delivery*

Lester T. Hibbard, MD

CAUSES OF THIRD TRIMESTER HEMORRHAGE

In 5–10% of pregnancies, bleeding occurs during the third trimester that requires careful evaluation to determine its source. Hemorrhage may be due either to local, nonobstetric abnormalities of the lower birth canal or to obstetric causes, many of which are dangerous and potentially lethal. In the USA, hemorrhage is the major cause of obstetric deaths and is a serious threat to the fetus. Blood dyscrasias may also contribute to either obstetric or nonobstetric hemorrhage.

Etiology

Local nonobstetric disorders such as eversions, polyps, varices, and tumors of the vagina and cervix rarely produce severe bleeding and, with the exception of invasive carcinoma, present no threat.

Extrusion of the cervical mucus plug ("bloody show") is sometimes accompanied by sufficient bleeding to create confusion and concern.

Maternal hemorrhage from the placental site is the principal source of significant obstetric hemorrhage. Among the causes of placental hemorrhage are placenta previa, premature separation of the placenta, "ruptured marginal sinus" (rupture of the peripheral portion of the intervillous space), and circumvallate placenta.

Rupture of the uterus may result in extensive maternal hemorrhage, but most of the blood loss may be concealed.

Although almost all of the blood loss from placental accidents is maternal, some fetal loss is also possible, particularly if the substance of the placenta is traumatized. Bleeding from vasa praevia is the only cause of pure fetal hemorrhage. Fortunately, this is rare. If fetal bleeding is suspected, the presence of nucleated red cells in the vaginal blood may be seen or the presence of fetal hemoglobin may be confirmed by elution techniques.

The one important blood dyscrasia causing obstetric hemorrhage is disseminated intravascular coagulation, which results in depletion of fibrinogen, platelets, and other clotting factors. Obstetric complications that can produce this syndrome include prema-

ture separation of the placenta, preeclampsia-eclampsia, prolonged retention of a dead fetus, and amniotic fluid embolus.

Hospital Procedure

The only safe approach to diagnosis is to hospitalize the patient without delay and without having done a preliminary vaginal or rectal examination. In the presence of vaginal bleeding, careful speculum examination is almost free of risk and often gives valuable information, whereas rectal examination is both dangerous and futile. Such an examination outside of a hospital is extremely hazardous because of the possibility of provoking an uncontrollable, catastrophic hemorrhage.

On admission, the patient's vital signs should be checked and a careful abdominal examination done to determine the approximate duration of gestation, fetal size, presentation, position, and whether the presenting part is engaged or not. The fetal heartbeat should be auscultated and the uterus evaluated for tenderness, resting tone, and contractions. Since the need for transfusion may become acute, a blood sample should be sent immediately for typing and cross-matching, and an infusion should be started through an 18-gauge needle.

If the patient is in active labor and the presenting part is unquestionably engaged, there is no merit in delaying vaginal examination. Both a speculum and a manual vaginal examination should be done. If possible, the membranes should be ruptured. The diagnosis will probably be either "bloody show" or partial premature separation of the placenta.

If the patient is in labor with an unengaged presenting part, manual vaginal or rectal examination must be delayed until blood for possible transfusion becomes available. Instead, only a careful speculum examination should be done to rule out local causes of bleeding and to observe, if possible, cervical dilatation and the condition of the membranes. If the speculum examination establishes that labor is advanced and the membranes are bulging with no visible placenta, manual examination is no longer contraindicated. On the other hand, if the presenting part subsequently descends into the pelvis, vaginal examination is indicated.

If the patient is not in labor and there is nothing to

---

*Shock and cardiac arrest are discussed in Chapter 20.

suggest a major placental separation or uterine rupture, the patient should be observed at bed rest until after cross-matching of blood is completed. Careful vaginal speculum examination should then be done to rule out local causes of bleeding. In about 90% of cases, third trimester bleeding will subside within 24 hours.

Assuming that the fetus is mature (over 37 weeks gestational age), the next step should be sterile manual vaginal examination in the operating room readied for possible cesarean section ("double set-up") to rule out placenta previa and determine whether or not the pregnancy should be terminated.

If the fetus is not mature, the patient should be treated expectantly unless additional complications appear, eg, continuing bleeding, fetal distress, labor, or spontaneous rupture of the membranes. Local lesions may be ruled out by speculum examination, and ultrasonography or x-ray placentography is helpful to identify the site of placental implantation.

If placenta studies signify a high placental implantation and bleeding stops, manual vaginal examination is indicated prior to discharge (see section on placenta previa for management of low placental implantation).

The management of disseminated intravascular coagulation is discussed under placental separation and shock (see below and Chapter 20).

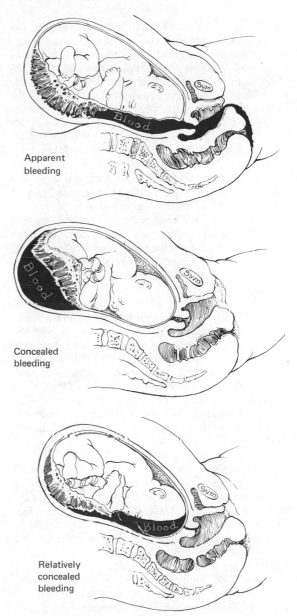

Figure 33–1. Types of premature separation of the placenta. (Redrawn and reproduced, with permission, from Beck AC, Rosenthal AH: *Obstetrical Practice,* 7th ed. Williams & Wilkins, 1957.)

PREMATURE SEPARATION OF THE PLACENTA
(Abruptio Placentae, Ablatio Placentae, Accidental Hemorrhage)

Essentials of Diagnosis
- Abdominal (uterine) pain usually present.
- Uterus usually irritable and tender; may be spastic.
- Hemorrhage may be visible or concealed.
- Evidence of fetal distress may or may not be present depending on the severity of the process.

General Considerations

Two principal forms of premature separation of the placenta may be recognized depending upon whether the resulting hemorrhage is external or concealed (Fig 33–1). In the **concealed** form (20%), the hemorrhage is confined within the uterine cavity, the detachment of the placenta from its bed may be complete, and the complications are often severe. In the **external** form (80%), the blood drains through the cervical os, the placental detachment is more likely to be incomplete, and the complications are fewer and less severe. Hemorrhage from an incompletely detached placenta may sometimes be concealed by intact membranes, in which case it is said to be **relatively concealed.** Occasionally, the placental detachment involves only the margin or placental rim. Here, the most important complication is the possibility of premature labor.

Approximately 30% of cases of third trimester bleeding are due to placental separation, with the initial hemorrhage usually encountered after the 26th week. Placental separation in early pregnancy cannot be distinguished from other causes of abortion. About 50% of separations occur before the onset of labor, and 10–15% are not diagnosed before the second stage of labor.

Etiology

The causes of placental separation are often difficult to ascertain. One mechanism is local vascular injury that results in vascular rupture into the decidua basalis, bleeding, and hematoma formation. The hematoma shears off adjacent denuded vessels, producing further bleeding and enlargement of the area of separation. Another mechanism is initiated by an abrupt rise in uterine venous pressure transmitted to the intervillous space. This results in engorgement of the venous bed and the separation of all or a portion of the placenta. Conditions predisposing to vascular injury and known to be associated with an increased incidence of placental separation are preeclampsia-eclampsia, chronic hypertension, diabetes mellitus, and chronic renal disease. Factors that predispose to a disturbed vascular equilibrium and the possibility of passive congestion of the venous bed in response to an abrupt rise in uterine venous pressure are compression of the vena cava by the gravid uterus, which impedes venous return, vasodilatation secondary to shock, compensatory hypertension as a result of aortic compression, and the paralytic vasodilatation of conduction anesthesia.

Mechanical factors causing premature separation are rare (1–5%). They include transabdominal trauma, sudden decompression of the uterus such as with the delivery of a first twin or rupture of the membranes in hydramnios, or traction on a short umbilical cord.

Placental separation is more common among multiparous women and has a tendency to recur. Poor nutrition also appears to be a factor, but an association between abruptions and specific nutritional deficiencies, eg, ascorbic or folic acid, has not been clearly established.

Pathophysiology

As previously mentioned, concealed hemorrhage is more likely to be associated with a complete placental detachment. If the placental margins remain adherent, a central placental separation may result in hemorrhage that infiltrates the uterine wall. Uterine tetany follows. Occasionally, extensive intramyometrial bleeding results in uteroplacental apoplexy—the so-called Couvelaire uterus, a purplish, copper-colored, ecchymotic, indurated organ that all but loses its contractile power because of disruption of the muscle bundles.

In the more severe cases of separation, there may be a clinically significant amount of disseminated intravascular coagulation associated with depletion of fibrinogen and platelets as well as other clotting factors. The mother may then develop a hemorrhagic diathesis that is manifested by widespread petechiae, active bleeding, hypovolemic shock, and failure of the normal clotting mechanism. In addition, fibrin deposits in small capillaries (along with the hypoxic vascular damage of shock) can result in potentially lethal complications, including acute cor pulmonale, renal cortical and tubular necrosis, and anterior pituitary necrosis (Sheehan's syndrome).

The likelihood of fetal hypoxia and fetal death depends upon the amount and duration of placental separation and, in severe cases, the loss of a significant amount of fetal blood.

Clinical Findings

A. Symptoms and Signs: In general, the clinical findings correspond to the degree of separation. With marginal separation there may be a limited amount of external bleeding (50–150 mL) that can be either bright or dark depending upon the rapidity of its appearance. There is no uterine tenderness, minimal uterine irritability, and no evidence of fetal distress. Premature labor can occur but is not likely unless the membranes also rupture.

About 30% of separations are small, produce few or no symptoms, and usually are not noted until the placenta is inspected.

B. Laboratory Findings: The degree of anemia will probably be considerably less than the amount of blood loss would seem to justify because changes in hemoglobin and hematocrit are delayed during acute blood loss until secondary hemodilution has occurred. A peripheral blood smear may show a reduced platelet count; the presence of schistocytes, suggesting intravascular coagulation; and fibrinogen depletion with release of fibrin split products. If serial laboratory determinations of fibrinogen levels are not available, the clot observation test is a simple but invaluable bedside procedure. A venous blood sample is drawn every hour, placed in a clean test tube, and observed for clot formation and clot lysis. Failure of clot formation within 5–10 minutes or dissolution of a formed clot when the tube is gently shaken is proof of a clotting deficiency that is almost surely due principally to a lack of fibrinogen and platelets. More sophisticated studies (eg, plasma protamine paracoagulation test for soluble fibrin monomer complex; partial thromboplastin time) are most helpful if they are available on an emergency basis.

Treatment

A. Emergency Measures: If the patient exhibits clinical findings that become progressively more severe or if a major placental separation has already occurred as manifested by hemorrhage, uterine spasm, or fetal distress, an acute emergency exists.

As the first step toward delivery and in an effort to minimize the possibility of disseminated intravascular coagulation or amniotic fluid embolus, the membranes should be artificially ruptured to release as much amniotic fluid as possible. Internal monitoring will provide useful information about uterine tonus and contractions as well as the status of the fetus.

At the same time, blood should be drawn for laboratory studies and at least 4 units of blood made ready for possible transfusion. An infusion apparatus with an 18-gauge needle or cannula is advisable. A solution of lactated Ringer's injection should be administered, and additional antishock measures should be instituted as necessary. (See Shock, Chapter 20.)

B. Expectant Therapy: Expectant therapy is appropriate when the fetus is immature, bleeding is not extensive, and uterine irritability is absent or minimal. The presumptive diagnosis, if placenta previa can be ruled out, is probably a small marginal placental separation. The patient should be hospitalized, typed and cross-matched, and observed for a period of 24–48 hours until one is certain that further placental separation is not occurring, premature labor is not likely, and placenta previa is not present.

C. Vaginal Delivery: An attempt at vaginal delivery is indicated if the degree of separation appears to be limited, assuming the fetus can be monitored for signs of fetal distress. When placental separation is extensive but the fetus is dead or of dubious viability, vaginal delivery is also indicated unless hemorrhage is rapid and uncontrollable.

Induction of labor with an oxytocin infusion (see p 679) should be instituted if active labor does not begin shortly after amniotomy. In practice, augmentation is not often needed because the uterus usually is already excessively irritable. If the uterus is extremely spastic, uterine contractions cannot be clearly identified unless an internal monitor is used, and the progress in labor must be judged by observing cervical dilatation. Progress in labor is usually so rapid that forceps are not needed to shorten the second stage of labor. Paracervical and pudendal block anesthesia are recommended. Conduction anesthesia is to be avoided in the face of significant hemorrhage because profound, persistent hypotension may result.

D. Cesarean Section: The indications for cesarean section are both fetal and maternal. Abdominal delivery should be selected whenever delivery is not imminent for a fetus with a reasonable chance of survival who exhibits persistent evidence of distress. Cesarean section is also indicated if conditions are not favorable for rapid delivery, in the face of progressive or severe placental separation, if the fetus is in good condition. This includes most nulliparous patients with less than 3–4 cm of cervical dilatation. Maternal indications for cesarean section are uncontrollable hemorrhage from a contracted uterus or uterine apoplexy as manifested by hemorrhage with secondary relaxation of a previously spastic uterus.

Complications

A. Defibrination Syndrome: The mother must be continuously monitored well into the postpartum period for evidence of a clotting deficiency (see Laboratory Findings). There may be depletion not only of fibrinogen but also of platelets and of factors II, V, VIII, and X. Treatment will depend not only upon the demonstration of hematologic deficiencies but also on the amount of active bleeding and the anticipated route of delivery.

1. Fresh whole blood–Fresh whole blood, although often difficult to obtain, is superior for treating clotting deficiencies and replacing blood loss because all the necessary factors will be present.

2. Bank blood–Bank blood is satisfactory for replacing blood loss, but unless it was recently drawn it may not contain sufficient clotting factors to counteract severe depletion.

3. Cryoprecipitate packs–Cryoprecipitate packs contain all the necessary labile coagulation factors and are free of hepatitis B virus.

4. Platelets–During active bleeding, the transfusion of platelets is often the best practical means of counteracting a clotting deficiency. A platelet pack contains about 20% fewer platelets than 1 unit of fresh blood.

5. Fibrinogen–Fibrinogen is rarely indicated and should be reserved for those cases with demonstrated fibrinogen depletion associated with *active* hemorrhage which has not responded to other available measures including fresh blood, bank blood, and platelets. *Do not administer fibrinogen solely on the basis of laboratory tests.* In the absence of active bleeding, fibrinogen deficiency may be corrected spontaneously in a matter of hours. To administer fibrinogen under these circumstances is both unnecessary and likely to make matters worse because the excess fibrinogen may be converted to fibrin emboli. The best source of fibrinogen other than fresh blood is a cryoprecipitated preparation. Concentrated plasma can also be used. Quadruple strength plasma contains about 4.4 g of fibrinogen per unit. The initial dose of fibrinogen is 4–6 g, but as much as 20–24 g may be required depending upon the response.

6. Heparin–The prophylactic administration of heparin to block conversion of prothrombin to thrombin (and thereby reduce the consumption of coagulation factors) has been successfully employed in the management of the defibrination associated with fetal death ("dead fetus syndrome"). The value of heparin in the treatment of acute placental separation has not been clearly established, however. If employed, heparin may complicate a subsequent operative procedure because of the likelihood of hematoma formation unless the heparin effect is vitiated by administration of protamine sulfate.

The safest regimen if heparin is used is to give 2000 units intravenously and repeat every 3–4 hours until platelet counts and fibrinogen levels begin to rise. However, heparin should be given before the patient receives other blood products.

7. Fibrinolysins–Aminocaproic acid (Amicar) should *not* be given. This drug will complicate the problem by interfering with the mechanism of fibrinolysis.

8. Preparation for surgery–If cesarean section is indicated, materials to control a clotting deficiency must be on hand before an operation is undertaken and treatment with coagulants should be under way if a clotting deficiency is already present. Although preoperative control of a clotting deficiency before surgery is started is desirable, a rapid rate of blood loss may require earlier intervention. In rare instances, removal of an extensively damaged uterus has been necessary to control hemorrhage—or even the clotting deficiency.

B. Acute Cor Pulmonale: Acute cor pulmonale is always a possibility because of emboli in the pulmonary microcirculation as a result of either defibrination or the escape of amniotic cellular debris into maternal veins. The most important aspect of the immediate treatment of this life-threatening complication is the use of a volume respirator.

C. Renal Cortical and Tubular Necrosis: The possibility of renal cortical or tubular necrosis must be considered if oliguria persists after an adequate blood volume has been restored. An attempt should be made to improve renal circulation and promote diuresis by increasing fluid volume (with the aid of central venous monitoring) and the administration of a 50-mL intravenous bolus of 20% mannitol. If oliguria or anuria persists, renal necrosis is probable and fluid intake and output must be carefully monitored. Continuing impairment of renal function may require peritoneal dialysis or hemodialysis.

D. Transfusion Hepatitis: The risk of posttransfusion hepatitis has been reduced an estimated 25–40% by hepatitis antigen (HAA) screening tests. However, there is no evidence that prophylactic gamma globulin will reduce either the incidence or the severity of hepatitis.

E. Uterine Apoplexy: Extensive infiltration of the myometrial wall with blood may result in loss of myometrial contractility. If, as a result, bleeding from the placental bed is not controlled, hysterectomy may be necessary. If future childbearing is an important consideration, bilateral ligation of the ascending branches of the uterine arteries should be accomplished before resorting to hysterectomy. Not only will blood flow be reduced, but the relative ischemia produced may result in a satisfactory contraction of the damaged uterus. (If ligation of the uterine vessels proves ineffective, bilateral ligation of the hypogastric arteries, reducing arterial pressure within the uterus to venous levels, may effect hemostasis.) Following ligation of either the uterine or hypogastric arteries, collateral circulation should be adequate to preserve uterine function, including subsequent pregnancies.

Prognosis

External or concealed bleeding, excessive blood loss, shock, nulliparity, a closed cervix, absence of labor, and delayed diagnosis and treatment are unfavorable prognostic factors. Maternal mortality rates ranging from 0.5 to 5% are currently reported from various parts of the world. Most women die of hemorrhage (immediate or delayed) or cardiac or renal failure. A high degree of suspicion, early diagnosis, and definitive therapy should reduce the maternal mortality rate to 0.5–1%.

Reported fetal mortality rates range from 50 to 80%. In about 20% of cases, no fetal heartbeat can be heard on admission to the hospital, and in another 20% fetal distress is noted early. In cases in which transfusion of the mother is urgently required, the fetal mortality rate will probably be at least 50%. Liveborn infants have a high rate of morbidity resulting from predelivery hypoxia, birth trauma, and the hazards of prematurity (40–50%).

PLACENTA PREVIA

Essentials of Diagnosis

- Spotting during first and second trimesters.
- Sudden, painless, profuse bleeding in third trimester.
- Initial cramping in 10% of cases.

General Considerations

In placenta previa, the placenta is implanted in the lower uterine segment within the zone of effacement and dilatation of the cervix (Figs 33–2 and 33–3), thus constituting an obstruction to descent of the presenting part. Placenta previa is encountered in approximately one in 200 births; about 90% of patients will be parous. Among grand multiparas the incidence may be as high as one in 20. Placenta previa may also be involved in up to 5% of spontaneous abortions, although its presence usually is not recognized.

Etiology

The cause of placenta previa is not known, but possible etiologic factors include scarred or poorly vascularized endometrium in the corpus, a large placenta, and abnormal forms of placentation such as succenturiate lobe or placenta diffusa. A large placenta probably accounts for the observation that the incidence of placenta previa is doubled in multiple pregnancy. A low cervical cesarean section scar triples the incidence of placenta previa. Another contributory factor is an increased average surface area of a placenta implanted in the lower uterine segment, possibly because these tissues are less well suited for nidation.

Bleeding in placenta previa may be due to any of the following causes: (1) Mechanical separation of the placenta from its implantation site, either during the formation of the lower uterine segment, during effacement and dilatation of the cervix in labor, or as a result of intravaginal manipulation. (2) Placentitis. (3) Rupture of poorly supported venous lakes in the decidua basalis that have become engorged with venous blood.

Classification (Figs 33–4 and 33–5)

A number of different clinical classifications of placenta previa have been proposed, all of which are based on the relationship of the placenta to the cervix either prior to the onset of labor or at various stages of cervical effacement and dilatation. For example, prior to the onset of labor, placenta previa may be classified as **complete** if it covers the entire internal cervical os, **partial** if the os is incompletely covered, **marginal** if its edge reaches the rim of the os, and **lateral** (or low-lying) if it can be palpated beyond and above the os. On the other hand, as effacement and dilatation take place, these relationships change.

As a practical matter, a precise clinical classification of placenta previa is not of great importance unless vaginal delivery is required. If the fetus is viable, as is usually the case, abdominal delivery is preferred for all types of placenta previa with the possible exception of

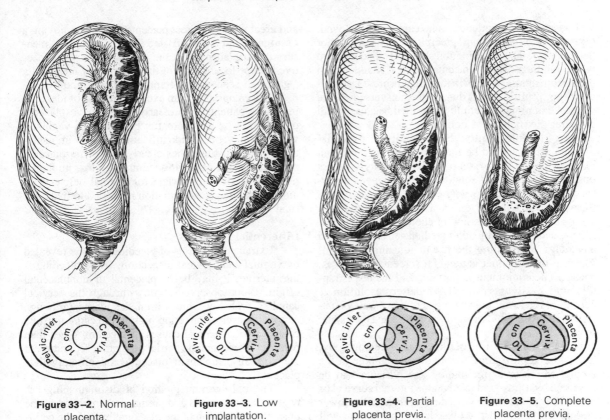

Figure 33–2. Normal placenta.

Figure 33–3. Low implantation.

Figure 33–4. Partial placenta previa.

Figure 33–5. Complete placenta previa.

those cases in which the placental edge is at least 2–3 cm removed from an undilated internal cervical os.

Diagnosis

Every patient suspected of placenta previa should be hospitalized before vaginal (or rectal) examination, and at least 3 units of cross-matched blood should be at hand. Unless these precautions are taken, there is always the danger that vaginal manipulation may provoke an uncontrollable, fatal hemorrhage.

A. Symptoms and Signs: Painless hemorrhage is the cardinal sign of placenta previa. Although spotting may occur during the first and second trimester of pregnancy, the first episode of hemorrhage usually begins at some point after the 28th week and is characteristically described as being sudden, painless, and profuse. Clothing or bedding is soaked by an impressive amount of bright red, clotted blood, but the blood loss usually is not extensive, seldom produces shock, and is almost never fatal. In about 10% of cases there is some initial pain because of coexisting placental abruption, and spontaneous labor may be expected over the next few days in 25% of patients. In a small minority of cases, bleeding will be less dramatic or will not begin until after spontaneous rupture of the membranes or the onset of labor. A few nulliparous patients even reach term without bleeding, possibly because the placenta has been protected by an uneffaced cervix.

1. Abdominal findings–The uterus usually is soft, relaxed, and nontender. A high presenting part cannot be pressed into the pelvic inlet. The infant will be presenting as an oblique or transverse lie in about 15% of cases. No evidence of fetal distress is likely unless there are complications such as hypovolemic shock, abruption, or a cord accident.

2. Speculum examination–A carefully performed speculum examination to rule out local causes of bleeding carries almost no risk of provoking further hemorrhage. Generally, the cervix is congested and patulous, with clotted blood within the os.

3. "Limited" vaginal examination–One always is tempted to do a limited vaginal examination with the exploration confined to palpation of the vaginal fornices to learn if there is an intervening bogginess between the fornix and presenting part. While this procedure probably is relatively safe, it is also apt to be inaccurate and not worth even the minimal risk. Rectal examination is both useless and dangerous.

4. Sterile vaginal examination–Before attempting a vaginal examination that includes digital probing of the cervical canal, 2 conditions must be met: (1) Preparations must be complete before the examination is undertaken for transfusion and delivery, including delivery by cesarean section ("double set-up"). (2) Unless complications make the examination an urgent necessity, the time selected must be propitious for delivery should hemorrhage from the examination make delivery necessary. The examination should proceed from inspection to palpation of the fornices and then to digital exploration of the cervical canal.

Unless extreme gentleness and care are employed, digital examination can precipitate a rapid, major hemorrhage. The examination should be discontinued when the diagnosis of placenta previa is made. When the circumstantial evidence for placenta previa is sufficient (eg, profuse hemorrhage plus transverse lie), the vaginal examination should be omitted because it will not alter the method of delivery.

B. Placentography: Prior to vaginal examination, an effort should be made to confirm or rule out placenta previa by means of placentography—unless immediate delivery is either desirable or made necessary by hemorrhage, labor, or fetal distress. An ultrasonic scan utilizing either a linear real-time or a static scanner is the method of choice, because it is at least as accurate as any other method and has the added advantage of avoiding the use of ionizing radiation. The real-time scanner is ideal for screening purposes, because the equipment is portable and the test is rapidly and easily performed. If better resolution is needed or the lower uterine segment is not well visualized, a real-time study can be supplemented by a static scan.

In the interpretation of ultrasonic placentography, it must be kept in mind that during the middle of the second trimester of pregnancy, the placenta will be observed by ultrasound to cover the internal cervical os about 30% of the time. With development of the lower uterine segment, most of these low implantations will be carried to a higher station. The point to remember is that an early ultrasonic diagnosis of placenta previa will require the confirmation of an additional study before definitive action is taken. A second source of error is a blood clot in the lower uterine segment that can be mistaken for placenta if the test has not been carefully performed.

Other methods of placentography that yield useful results—if ultrasonic equipment is unavailable—are soft tissue radiography utilizing lateral recumbent and erect views, indirect placentography employing a cystogram and air insufflated into the rectum to measure the displacement of the presenting part, radioactive isotope localization of the placenta by means of a "gamma" scan, amniography, and aortography.

Placentography is an excellent means of identifying those patients who clearly do not have placenta previa and who can thereafter be examined vaginally with impunity; but the identification of a low implantation seldom distinguishes clearly between a placenta previa requiring cesarean section and a low implantation that is still appropriate for vaginal delivery. In most cases, pelvic examination is needed to make the final decision.

Differential Diagnosis

Extrauterine causes of bleeding may be revealed by vaginal and cervical inspection. If the bleeding is intrauterine, it may be of placental or nonplacental origin. Blood observed to flow through the cervical canal is probably from within the uterus (although cervical cancer or infection high in the canal must be considered). Placental causes of bleeding other than placenta previa include partial premature separation of the normally implanted placenta and circumvallate placenta.

The only certain method of distinguishing between placenta previa and premature separation of the placenta is palpation of the placenta through the cervical os. One cannot distinguish premature separation of the margin of the placenta before delivery and inspection of the placenta.

Complications

A. Maternal: Maternal hemorrhage, shock, and death may follow severe antepartum bleeding resulting from placenta previa. Death may also occur as a result of intrapartum and postpartum bleeding, operative trauma, infection, or embolism.

Premature separation of a portion of a placenta previa occurs in virtually every case and causes excessive external bleeding without pain; however, complete or wide separation of the placenta before full dilatation of the cervix is not common. Rupture of the lower uterine segment may follow version.

Intrapartum and postpartum endometritis, parametritis, and peritonitis commonly occur following placentitis.

Placenta previa accreta is a rare but serious abnormality in which the sparse endometrium and the myometrium of the lower uterine segment are penetrated by the trophoblast in a manner similar to placenta accreta higher in the uterus.

B. Fetal: Prematurity (gestational age less than 36 weeks) due to placenta previa is the major cause of fetal death, accounting for 60% of perinatal deaths. The fetus may die as a result of intrauterine asphyxia or birth injury. Fetal hemorrhage due to tearing of the placenta occurs with vaginal manipulation and especially upon entry into the uterine cavity at cesarean section done for placenta previa. About half of these

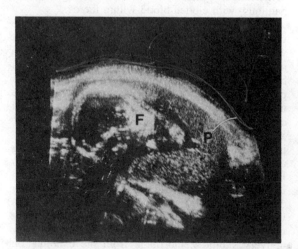

Figure 33–6. Ultrasonogram showing central placenta previa. The placenta (P) is clearly shown implanted on the lower uterine segment. F, fetus.

cesarean babies lose some blood. Fetal blood loss is directly proportionate to the time that elapses between laceration of a cotyledon and clamping the cord.

Treatment

The type of treatment given depends upon the amount of uterine bleeding, the duration of pregnancy and viability of the fetus, the degree of placenta previa, the presentation, position, and station of the fetus, the gravidity and parity of the patient, the status of the cervix, and whether or not labor has begun. The patient must be admitted to the hospital to establish the diagnosis and ideally should remain in the hospital once the diagnosis is made. Two or more units of bank blood should be typed, cross-matched, and ready for transfusion. Be prepared to replace twice as much blood as the estimated loss.

A. Expectant Therapy: Great gains in fetal survival can be achieved by postponing delivery. If possible, the baby should not be delivered before the 36th week. If severe hemorrhage occurs between 37 and 40 weeks, consider emptying the uterus. Earlier in pregnancy, a more conservative program is recommended, including repeated transfusions to replace blood loss and the occasional use of tocolytic agents for threatened premature labor. Maturity is a prime requisite for fetal survival.

Seventy-five percent of cases of placenta previa are now terminated by cesarean section at 36–40 weeks.

In selecting the optimal time for delivery, tests of fetal maturation are invaluable, particularly the lecithin/sphingomyelin ratio. Once adequate maturation is assured, the additional benefits to be realized from procrastination must be weighed against the danger of subsequent major hemorrhage.

Because of the costs of hospitalization, patients with a presumptive diagnosis of placenta previa are sometimes sent home after their condition has become stable under ideal, controlled circumstances. Such a policy is always a calculated risk in view of the unpredictability of further hemorrhage.

B. Delivery:

1. Vaginal delivery–Vaginal delivery is usually reserved for patients with a low-lying implantation and a cephalic presentation or a greater degree of placenta previa when there is little or no prospect of salvaging the fetus. If vaginal delivery is elected, the membranes should be artificially ruptured prior to any attempt to stimulate labor (oxytocin given before amniotomy is likely to cause further bleeding). Although prolapse of the cord during amniotomy is a risk, this probably will not occur if the patient is placed in the Fowler position during slow drainage. Tamponade of the presenting part against the placental edge usually reduces bleeding as labor progresses.

If labor does not follow rupture of the membranes within 6–8 hours, cautious stimulation with intravenous oxytocin (Pitocin, Syntocinon), 5 units (0.5 mL) in 1 L of 5% glucose, may be given at a rate of 1–2 mL/min (or better given by an infusion pump).

Because of the possibility of fetal hypoxia either due to placental separation or to a cord accident (as a result of either prolapse or compression of low insertion of the cord by the descending presenting part), internal fetal monitoring should be employed. If equipment is not available, the fetal heart should be auscultated at 5- to 10-minute intervals during active labor and more frequently if active bleeding occurs. If fetal distress develops, a rapid cesarean section should be performed unless vaginal delivery is imminent.

Deliver the patient in the easiest and most expeditious manner as soon as the cervix is fully dilated and the presenting part is on the perineum. For this purpose, a vacuum extractor is particularly valuable because it expedites delivery without risking rupture of the lower uterine segment. Operative vaginal manipulations such as forceps rotation, breech extraction, and version should be avoided because of the danger of uterine rupture.

2. Cesarean section–Cesarean section is preferable for most cases of placenta previa. Unless the conditions for vaginal delivery are particularly favorable, a cesarean section is decidedly safer for the fetus and probably no more hazardous for the mother.

Hypovolemic shock should be corrected by intravenous fluids and blood before the operation is started; not only will the mother be better protected, but a jeopardized fetus will also recover more quickly in utero than if born while the mother is still in shock.

The choice of anesthesia depends upon current and anticipated blood loss. A combination of rapid induction, endotracheal intubation, succinylcholine, and nitrous oxide is a suitable way to proceed in the presence of active bleeding.

The choice of operative technique is of importance because of the placental location and the development of the lower uterine segment. If the incision passes through the site of placental implantation, there is a strong possibility that the fetus will lose a significant amount of blood—even enough to require subsequent transfusion. With posterior implantations of the placenta, a low transverse incision may be best if the lower uterine segment is well developed. Otherwise, a classic incision may be required to secure sufficient room and to avoid incision through the placenta.

Preparations should be made for care and resuscitation of the infant if it becomes necessary. In addition, the possibility of blood loss should be monitored in the newborn if the placenta has been incised. A fall in hemoglobin to 12 g/dL within 3 hours or to 10 g/dL within 24 hours requires urgent transfusion.

In a small percentage of cases, hemostasis in the placental bed will not be satisfactory because of the poor contractility of the lower uterine segment. Mattress sutures or packing may be required; and if a placenta previa increta (see p 725) is found, hemostasis will only be obtained by a total hysterectomy.

Puerperal infection and anemia are the most likely postoperative complications.

Prognosis

A. Maternal: With antibiotics, a blood bank, expertly administered anesthesia, and cesarean section, the maternal prognosis in placenta previa is excellent. The abandonment of hazardous vaginal maneuvers such as version and the hydrostatic bag, the recognition of the dangers of injudicious vaginal and rectal examinations, and the hospitalization of mothers at risk have virtually eliminated the principal maternal hazard, hypovolemic shock.

B. Fetal: The perinatal mortality rate associated with placenta previa in most medical centers has been 15–20%, or at least 10 times that of normal pregnancy. Although premature labor, placental separation, cord accidents, and uncontrollable hemorrhage cannot be avoided, the mortality rate can be reduced by half if ideal obstetric and newborn care is given.

PROLAPSE OF THE UMBILICAL CORD

Essentials of Diagnosis

- Violent fetal activity.
- Fetal bradycardia during contraction.
- Visualization or palpation of cord on vaginal examination.

General Considerations

Prolapse of the umbilical cord can be classified (Fig 33–7) as (1) **occult prolapse,** in which the cord lies over the face or head of the fetus but cannot be felt on internal examination; (2) **forelying cord,** in which the cord precedes the presenting part, is held within intact membranes, and can usually be palpated through the membranes if the cervix is patulous; and (3) **complete prolapse,** in which the cord descends past ruptured membranes into the vagina, often through the vaginal introitus. A forelying cord or an occult prolapse risks intermittent compression of the cord with resulting fetal hypoxia and possible permanent brain

damage or even death due to anoxia. Complete cord prolapse, unless expeditiously managed, greatly increases the fetal risks as well as the possibility of severe maternal trauma if an emergency vaginal delivery is attempted.

Obstetric factors favoring prolapse of the umbilical cord include the following: (1) abnormal presentation (breech, shoulder, face, brow, transverse, compound), (2) multiple pregnancy, (3) premature rupture of the membranes prior to engagement of the vertex or breech, (4) contracted pelvis (fetopelvic disproportion) or distorting pelvic tumor, (5) hydramnios, (6) low implantation of the placenta, and (7) abnormally long cord (over 75 cm).

The incidence of complete prolapse of the cord is about one in 200 advanced pregnancies, but the incidence of occult prolapse is unknown. Some degree of occult prolapse is quite common, since in about half of monitored labors there are one or more episodes of a heart rate pattern consistent with a tentative diagnosis of cord compression. In most monitored labors this phenomenon is temporary, particularly if the patient is shifted into a different position.

Clinical Findings

Compression of the cord sufficient to produce fetal hypoxia often causes violent fetal activity, obvious to the patient and even to the observer.

If the fetus is in good condition, the typical auscultatory finding is marked bradycardia that develops rapidly during contraction and is followed by rapid recovery when the contraction ends.

A sterile vaginal examination will confirm the finding of a complete prolapse and may confirm the presence of occult prolapse.

During monitored labor, variable deceleration patterns suggest cord compression. The diagnosis is reinforced if those patterns are not eliminated by a change of the patient's position and can be confirmed by blood gas analysis or scalp vein samples demonstrating evidence of metabolic acidosis.

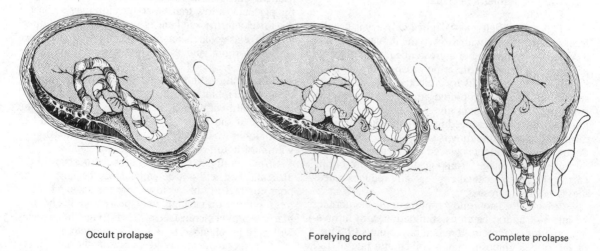

Occult prolapse   Forelying cord   Complete prolapse

Figure 33–7. Types of prolapsed cords.

Prevention

Iatrogenic prolapse during artificial rupture of the membranes can usually be avoided by either deferring the procedure until the presenting part completely fills the pelvic inlet or by careful needling of the membranes followed by a slow, controlled release of amniotic fluid should amniotomy be required when the presenting part is high.

If the membranes rupture spontaneously while the patient is under observation, prompt vaginal examination should be done to rule out prolapse, particularly if the presentation is other than cephalic.

If the presenting part does not completely fill the pelvis, occult cord prolapse can best be detected by internal fetal monitoring.

Treatment

A. Emergency Treatment: Unless immediate delivery is feasible or the fetus is known to be dead, the patient with complete prolapse should be placed in either the knee-chest or deep Trendelenburg position (the former is preferable), and upward manual pressure should be exerted through the vagina to lift and maintain the presenting part away from the prolapsed cord. While reposition of the cord within the uterine cavity can be attempted, such maneuvers are rarely successful and carry a risk of additional fetal hypoxia if delivery is further delayed. Both the patient's position and vaginal support of the presenting part are continuously maintained until anesthesia is being induced. The mother should also be given oxygen by mask.

B. Delivery:

1. Vaginal delivery–Vaginal delivery should not be attempted unless it can be completed without undue trauma to either the fetus or the mother. Measures such as forcible manual dilatation of the cervix, version and extraction, and incision of a thick undilated cervix must be condemned because the risk is far greater than is the case with cesarean section. Whether or not vaginal delivery is feasible depends upon the time of delivery as judged by parity, the feasibility of rapid cesarean section if needed, the quality of labor progress, cervical dilatation and presentation, and the maturity and immediate condition of the fetus. In borderline situations (26–29 weeks' gestation), the advantage of salvaging premature infants is also a factor.

2. Abdominal delivery–When the prospects for vaginal delivery are unfavorable or doubtful, emergency cesarean section is preferred. Select an intravenous or rapid inhalation anesthetic and an incision long enough to permit rapid entry and unimpeded delivery. Preparations for resuscitation should be complete.

C. Expectant Therapy: In the event of occult prolapse prior to the second stage of labor, it may be possible to relieve compression (and the prolapse) by shifting the patient to a lateral position or to a lateral Trendelenburg position. If this is achieved, labor may be permitted to continue as long as the fetus can be monitored by means of an internal fetal monitor and, when indicated, sampling of scalp vein blood.

Complications

Resuscitation of the newborn infant may be complicated by metabolic acidosis, prematurity, and birth trauma. The principal maternal complications of rapid vaginal delivery are lacerations of the birth canal, ruptured uterus, and uterine atony due to anesthesia. In any event, blood should be typed and cross-matched for either vaginal or abdominal delivery.

Prognosis

A. Fetal: Partial cord compression for less than a 5-minute period may not be harmful. Complete occlusion for the same period or partial occlusion for a longer time will almost surely cause death or significant central nervous system damage.

B. Maternal: The puerperium may be complicated by infection or anemia due to excess blood loss as a result of attempts to replace the cord and the trauma of delivery.

POSTPARTUM HEMORRHAGE

Essentials of Diagnosis

- Steady vaginal bleeding.
- Sudden gush after passage of placenta that obstructed cervical os.

General Considerations

Postpartum hemorrhage is defined as the loss of 500 mL or more of blood following delivery of the fetus. This definition is arbitrary and not completely satisfactory for 3 reasons: (1) Careful measurements of blood loss at the time of delivery suggest that the average blood loss is much greater than usually estimated. (2) An arbitrary figure does not allow for the fact that blood volume is related to body size and that a small woman with a smaller blood volume cannot tolerate a given blood loss as well as a large woman. A more useful definition of postpartum hemorrhage would be blood loss greater than 1% of body weight (eg, for a 50-kg woman, 500 mL of blood). (3) Blood loss is seldom measured accurately in obstetric practice. Ideally, blood loss should be estimated by weight.

About 5–8% of obstetric patients suffer serious postpartum blood loss, and postpartum hemorrhage is a leading cause of maternal death. Although postpartum hemorrhage usually occurs early (within 24 hours), late hemorrhage (24 hours to 4 weeks) can be severe and may require rehospitalization, transfusion, and even operation.

Etiology

The 3 most common causes of postpartum hemorrhage are (1) uterine atony, (2) laceration of the birth canal, and (3) retained placental fragments or membranes.* In addition, mismanagement of the third stage of labor may result in hemorrhage due to prolapse

---

*Ruptured uterus as a cause of postpartum hemorrhage is discussed on p 735.

of the uterus in the birth canal, retention of a partially separated placenta, or even uterine inversion.

Another consideration is disseminated intravascular coagulation with depletion of fibrinogen and platelets, an obstetric complication that results in a clotting deficiency. Among the complications that predispose to disseminated intravascular coagulation are premature separation of the placenta, preeclampsia-eclampsia, amnionitis, and amniotic fluid embolus.

Less common causes of hemorrhage are ruptured varices, inadequate hemostasis of an episiotomy repair, placenta accreta or increta (particularly in association with placenta previa), and hematologic disorders such as thrombocytopenia.

Of particular importance is hematoma resulting from laceration of paravaginal blood vessels. The hematoma usually forms adjacent to an ischial spine and, if not controlled, expands downward to the vulva and rectum (Fig 33–8). Other hematomas originating in the vulvar area are less extensive.

Delayed postpartum hemorrhage can be due to retention of membranes and placental fragments or to postpartum endoparametritis. Hemorrhage occurring after discharge from the hospital probably is due to subinvolution of the placental site, a retained placental fragment, or the injudicious use of hormones to suppress lactation.

Clinical Findings

A. Hemorrhage Occurring From the Time of Delivery to Separation of the Placenta: Episiotomy, perineal or vaginal lacerations, and rupture of varices are usually accompanied by a steady ooze of dark red blood. Cervical lacerations cause a free flow of bright red (arterial) blood. Incomplete separation of the placenta or partial placenta accreta causes loss of dark red blood in spurts with uterine manipulation or fundal contraction.

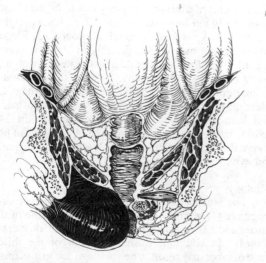

Figure 33–8. A paravaginal hematoma formed in the infralevator space and extending to vulvar and rectal areas. (After Melody.)

B. Hemorrhage Occurring From the Time of Separation to Expression of the Placenta: A separated placenta lying free within the uterine cavity can cover the cervical canal and interfere with the normal contractions of the uterus. Bleeding continues, and blood is trapped temporarily. When the placenta finally is expelled or extracted, an accumulation of large blood clots is released suddenly.

C. Hemorrhage Following Recovery of the Placenta: Atony of the uterus causes steady, persistent bleeding, with additional gushes during uterine contractions. Prolapse of the uterus into the pelvis can be associated with a profuse continuous flow of blood not related to uterine contractions. Lacerations of the birth canal—particularly lacerations of the uterus—cause continuous hemorrhage, principally of arterial blood.

Complications

Complications include puerperal infection, anemia, and embolism.

Prevention

Faulty technique in management of the third stage of labor contributes substantially to blood loss. Expression of the placenta should be delayed until separation has been confirmed, and the Credé maneuver must be avoided. Timely manual removal of a partially separated placenta can also save considerable blood.

Predisposing factors to placental hemorrhage require vigilance. Among these factors that should be recognized are overdistention of the uterus by hydramnios or multiple pregnancy, desultory labor, prolonged labor, oversedation, deep general anesthesia, amnionitis, placental separation, a potential clotting deficiency, anemia, and a history of a previous retained or adherent placenta. Additional blood loss associated with operative vaginal or abdominal delivery must be anticipated also. When the risk of postpartum hemorrhage is increased, the following preventive measures should be instituted:

(1) If the patient is in active labor, start an infusion of 5% glucose in water through a No. 18 needle or vein cannula.

(2) Immediately after the birth of the fetus, add oxytocin (2–3 units/dL) to the infusion bottle. (Avoid injecting a bolus of oxytocin into the tubing.)

(3) After the third stage of labor, give an intramuscular injection of methylergonovine maleate (Methergine), 0.2 mg. Intravenous injection of this drug involves some risk of precipitous elevation of blood pressure unless the injection is given slowly and with care.

(4) Elevate the fundus out of the pelvis until it remains firm.

(5) Observe the patient in the delivery recovery room for at least 1 hour after delivery and until vital signs are stable.

Treatment

A. Emergency and Specific Measures:

1. Initial emergency care–Inspect the vagina

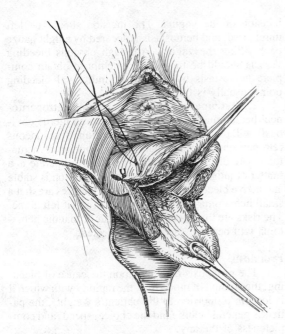

Figure 33–9. Repair of cervical lacerations. (After Edgar.)

and cervix carefully for lacerations and palpate the lower uterine segment for rupture (most likely to be found at the lateral angles). Repair all lacerations promptly (Fig 33–9).

2. Incomplete separation of the placenta or partial placenta accreta accompanied by uterine bleeding–If bleeding is slight, wait a reasonable time to permit the placenta to separate. If bleeding is profuse, remove the placenta manually (without additional anesthesia, if possible), using the ulnar edge of the gauze-covered hand from above downward to avoid perforation of the uterus (Fig 33–10).

3. Delay in expression of separated placenta– Express the placenta when the signs of separation indicate that it is free. Do not delay recovery of the placenta until perineal repair is complete. Use the Pastore or Brandt-Andrews technique for placental recovery.

4. Atony of the uterus–Hold the uterus out of the pelvis and massage the fundus. If bleeding is profuse, give 30 units of oxytocin in an intravenous infusion. Intracervical injection of 10 units of oxytocin or 0.5–1 mg of prostaglandin $F_{2\alpha}$ intramuscularly is also effective. If atony persists, proceed immediately to bimanual compression with massage as shown in Fig 33–11.

B. Prolapse of the Uterus Into the Pelvis: Lift the uterus and support the fundus. Elevate the cervix and uterus with gauze on a sponge stick if necessary.

C. Profuse Atonic Hemorrhage Not Responding to Massage or Oxytocin:

1. Occlude the aorta by transabdominal compression against the sacral promontory and lower lumbar spine until blood replacement is available.

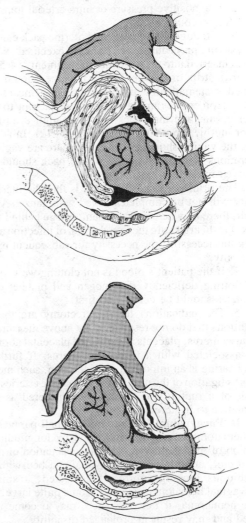

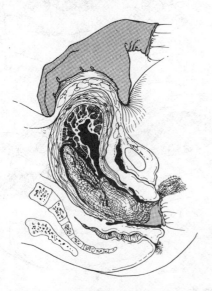

Figure 33–10. Finger and gauze curettement of uterus.

Figure 33–11. Bimanual compression of uterus.

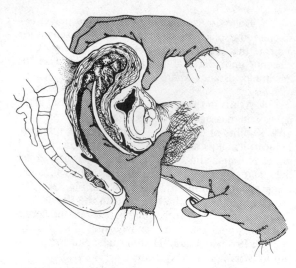

Figure 33–12. Packing the uterus with forceps.

2. Use positive pressure or intra-arterial transfusions for profound shock.

3. Although rarely needed, a uterine pack can be a livesaving procedure when properly executed. With a hand inserted into the lower uterine segment, a 4.5-m (5-yard) strip of 10-cm (4-inch) gauze should be packed systematically into the fundus by means of packing forceps beginning on one cornu, passing to the other cornu, and then back and forth until even the lower uterine segment is filled (Fig 33–12). In addition, the vagina should be packed if there are vaginal lacerations or hematomas. A vaginal pack should be removed in 8–12 hours.

The principal risk of packing is that the uterine cavity will not be completely filled with gauze. As a result, there may be concealed hemorrhage behind the pack. Further risks are the introduction of infection and when unsuccessful, the necessity for subsequent hysterectomy.

4. If the patient's blood is not clotting well, rule out clotting deficiency. Fibrinogen and platelet deficiencies should be considered first.

5. The indications for hysterectomy are those conditions that do not respond to the above measures: ruptured uterus, placenta accreta, and placental abruption associated with a Couvelaire uterus. If further childbearing is an important consideration, such measures as ligation of the uterine or hypogastric arteries or repair of a rupture site should be considered as an alternative to hysterectomy.

D. Paravaginal Hematoma: A small paravaginal hematoma can be easily treated by longitudinal incision of the lateral vaginal wall, evacuation of the blood clot, and closure of the hematoma bed with a continuous locking suture. If untreated, a small paravaginal hematoma is apt to become quite large. A large hematoma, if not evacuated, may become infected and may result in prolonged disability.

A large paravaginal hematoma extending to the vulva or rectum can also be evacuated through a linear incision of the vagina. The incision should be left unrepaired, and hemostasis is secured by a tight gauze pack filling the vagina. Although obvious bleeding vessels should be ligated, an attempt to obtain complete hemostasis by ligature of individual bleeding points usually is futile.

E. Retroperitoneal Hematoma: Retroperitoneal hematoma associated with ruptured uterus obviously will require operative intervention. Spontaneous retroperitoneal hematomas and postoperative hematomas are different. Here the decision to operate is a matter of judgment. If the patient's condition is stable and active bleeding has stopped, the chances are that a small hematoma will be slowly absorbed if left alone. The risks are that bleeding will recur or that the hematoma will become secondarily infected.

Prognosis

The prognosis depends upon the cause of bleeding, the amount of blood lost, the rapidity with which it is lost (in proportion to the patient's weight), the patient's general health, and the choice, speed, and completeness of therapy.

Maternal mortality and morbidity rates rise in direct proportion to the amount of blood lost. A febrile puerperium is 4 times more likely to occur after postpartum hemorrhage (without blood replacement) than following normal termination of the third stage of labor.

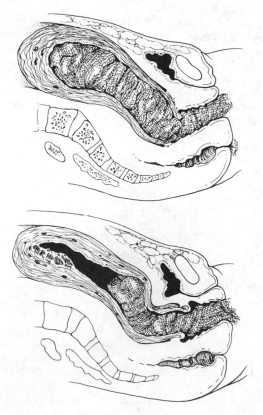

Figure 33–13. Correct (above) and incorrect (below) packing of the uterus.

RETAINED & ADHERENT PLACENTA

A common complication of delivery is a delay in completion of the third stage of labor, often accompanied by excessive blood loss, due to either a retained or an adherent placenta. Since spontaneous detachment of the placenta should occur in 90% of patients within 15 minutes and 95% of patients within 30 minutes, any further delay in its delivery should be considered to be due to retention, ie, it is free but still within the uterus, or adherence.

Etiology

The causes of placental retention are partial separation of a normally implanted placenta or entrapment of a partially or completely separated placenta by a uterine constriction ring at the junction of the upper and lower uterine segments. An adherent placenta is due either to the absence of all or part of the normal cleavage plane at the site of placental attachment or to an actual placental invasion of the myometrial wall (placenta accreta, increta, or percreta). A number of factors favor placental retention: (1) Improper management of the third stage of labor, including massage of the uterine fundus (Credé maneuver) prior to placental separation and administration of ergot preparations before expulsion of the placenta. (2) Impairment of the uterine contractions necessary for expulsion because of either prolonged labor, excessive medication, or profound anesthesia. (3) Tetanic uterine contractions that often produce a constriction. (4) Uterine abnormalities that favor retention, particularly a subseptate or bicornuate uterus. (5) Abnormalities of placentation such as cornual implantation. In addition, a succenturiate lobe may be overlooked unless the placental vessels and membranes are inspected carefully. Factors that favor placental adherence include previous endometritis, submucosal tumors, uterine scars, low implantation, and placental malformations such as an extrachorionic placenta. Among the operative procedures that increase the risk of abnormal placental attachment are cesarean section, myomectomy, vigorous curettage, and previous manual removal of a placenta.

Since trophoblastic tissue is normally invasive, an occasional unusual degree of placental penetration of the uterus should not be surprising, but fortunately this is rare (1:12,000 deliveries). This phenomenon is categorized according to the depth of penetration:

(1) Placenta accreta (rare): Slight penetration of the myometrium in areas of deficient, sparse, or absent decidua with invasion of the myometrium by chorionic villi. A dense fibrous area is formed by the fusion of Nitabuch's layer and Rohr's stria accompanied by hyalinization of the neighboring myometrium. Because there is no cleavage plane, forceful separation results in lacerations of the uterine wall and myometrial sinusoids. Profuse hemorrhage is likely because of the large vessels exposed and the poor contractility of the underlying myometrium. Placenta accreta is more likely to be partial than complete.

(2) Placenta increta (very rare): Deep penetration of the myometrial wall. There is no possible plane of cleavage and removal is impossible.

(3) Placenta percreta (exceptional): The trophoblast penetrates through the uterine wall, even into the bladder, to produce hemorrhage and rupture of the uterus.

Clinical Findings*

An adherent or penetrating placenta cannot be readily diagnosed prior to an attempt at manual removal. The clinical picture will resemble that of a retained placenta which remains completely or partially attached. Significant hemorrhage usually does not occur prior to attempts at manual removal.

The differential diagnosis is between placental retention, an adherent placenta which can successfully be manually separated and removed, and degrees of placental penetration that make successful separation impossible. Unfortunately, the diagnosis of penetration is seldom appreciated before overly zealous efforts at removal have resulted in uterine rupture or a major hemorrhage—even exsanguination.

Prevention

An important measure to prevent an adherent or penetrating placenta (as well as Asherman's syndrome) is to refrain from removing the basilar endometrium by forceful curettage at the time of a diagnostic or therapeutic D&C. Prevention of the complications of placental penetration rests upon recognition of factors that predispose to this condition and on a certain amount of caution and restraint whenever a cleavage plane cannot be found at the time of manual removal of the placenta.

Treatment

A. Emergency Measures: Make no further attempts to separate the placenta. Make certain that continuing infusion with an 18-gauge needle or cannula is established. Type and cross-match at least 3 units of blood (or more if there is active bleeding). Prepare the patient for immediate laparotomy under general anesthesia. If hemorrhage is brisk, a temporary uterine pack may be effective in controlling blood loss until an operation can be performed.

B. Surgical Treatment: Hysterectomy is almost always indicated. If the placenta is implanted in the fundus, either subtotal or total hysterectomy is essential if the placenta has penetrated the lower uterine segment—as is true in about 15% of cases—because lesser operations do not control hemorrhage from the lower uterine segment which is supplied by both cervical branches of the uterine arteries and vaginal arteries. About 3% of cases of placenta previa are associated with placenta accreta, and failure to control hemorrhage from the lower uterine segment accounts for most maternal deaths associated with placenta previa.

---

*See Delivery of the Placenta, Chapter 31, for the diagnosis, prevention, and management of a retained placenta.

C. Conservative Therapy: If the patient insists that she wants to have more children, preservation of the uterus may be attempted in the following circumstances: (1) If the bleeding provoked by manipulations has been minimal and the placenta left in situ will be resorbed and the endometrium restored (unlikely). Severe infection and hemorrhage are the risks. (2) If the disorder is discovered at the time of cesarean section and bleeding can be controlled by suturing and packing following placental morcellation. (3) If it is understood that a subsequent pregnancy will be terminated by cesarean section and hysterectomy if, as is probable, placenta accreta or increta recurs.

INVERSION OF THE UTERUS

Essentials of Diagnosis

- Sudden agonizing pelvic pain.
- Feeling of fullness extending into the bladder.
- Signs of shock.
- Brisk vaginal bleeding (not invariable).
- Depressed or absent fundus in the abdomen.
- Presence of inverted fundus at the vaginal introitus.

General Considerations

An inverted uterus is one that is partially or completely turned inside out. Partial inversion is herniation of the uterine fundus into the uterine cavity. Complete inversion is extrusion of the entire corpus through the cervix, into or beyond the vagina. This condition usually occurs immediately following delivery, but inversion may also occur during the puerperium. In rare instances, inversion may develop in the nonpregnant uterus—eg, when a pedunculated myoma is in the process of extrusion. Either partial or complete inversion can be acute or chronic and spontaneous or induced.

Although puerperal inversion of the uterus occurs in only about one per 15,000 deliveries, familiarity

with its diagnosis, causes, prevention, and emergency treatment will minimize the potential severe complications of this unfortunate accident.

Spontaneous acute puerperal inversion is due to straining by the patient after delivery or the weight of the infant on the cord and placenta (eg, when delivery is spontaneous and precipitous with the patient in a standing position and unattended). Induced acute puerperal inversion is the result of (1) traction on the cord before placental separation, (2) severe "kneading" of the fundus (vigorous Credé maneuver to induce placental separation and expulsion), (3) excessive pressure on the uterine fundus (Kristeller maneuver), (4) delivery of an infant with a short cord or one that has been shortened by coiling, (5) separation and extraction of an adherent placenta done manually in haste, or (6) when multiple pregnancy or hydramnios delivers rapidly.

Chronic puerperal inversion is due to the same causes as acute induced puerperal inversion, but it is not recognized until 1 month or more after delivery.

Clinical Findings

Acute complete inversion causes sudden agonizing pain combined with an explosive sensation of "fullness" extending downward into the vagina. Most patients exhibit some degree of neurogenic shock, and over half will have brisk bleeding with additional hypovolemic shock. Death often results from exsanguination.

Bimanual examination is necessary. Abdominally, the depressed fundus or absent corpus is revealed by gross "dimpling" or a craterlike depression (Fig 33–14). Vaginally, complete inversion is manifested by the presence of a large bleeding mass within the vagina or outside the introitus, often with the placenta attached. In partial inversion, a cup-shaped mass can be palpated just above or bulging through the cervix.

Differential Diagnosis

Even though the findings in uterine inversion are distinctive, the unexpected is liable to be confusing and a false diagnosis—eg, "fibroid" or "hematoma"—may be made unless a careful examination is done.

Complications

The complications of inversion include shock, hemorrhage, infection, paralytic ileus, intestinal obstruction, anemia, embolization, and in some cases sterility.

Prevention

Induced inversion can be prevented by proper management of the third stage of labor. Do not pull on the cord unless the placenta has separated; do not push on the fundus or use the Credé maneuver; do not place a pad or roll beneath the abdominal binder postpartum; and do not leave the patient until the uterus is contracted and rounded.

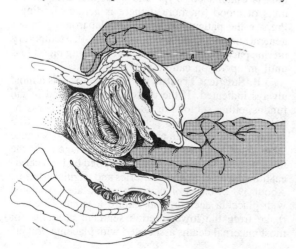

Figure 33–14. Partial inversion of the uterus.

Treatment

A. Manual Replacement:

1. Early replacement–If inversion is recognized early before the inverted corpus is trapped, replacement often can be accomplished by manual compression and insertion (Fig 33–15). At the same time, blood transfusion and intravenous fluids should be started to counteract neurogenic and hypovolemic shock. Type and cross-match at least 2 units of whole blood. The fist should remain within the uterine cavity until the corpus is well contracted by oxytocics to prevent recurrence of inversion.

2. Late replacement–If early replacement proves impossible, avoid further manipulations until shock has been corrected by fluids, plasma, or whole blood. Avoid ergot preparations until replacement has been completed. Deep general anesthesia (eg, halothane) may be required to relax the uterus. Leave the placenta attached, compress the fundus in the anteroposterior diameter, and apply countertraction with a ring forceps applied to the anterior cervical lip. Epinephrine, 1:1000, 0.3–0.6 mL intramuscularly, may relieve uterine spasm. As soon as replacement is complete, discontinue anesthesia and retain a fist within the uterine cavity as described above. Do not employ a uterine pack but rather rely on oxytocics to keep the uterus well contracted.

3. Surgical replacement–If correction is not accomplished easily and quickly by manipulation, immediate surgery is mandatory.

a. Haultain technique (transabdominal)–Incise the posterior wall of the inverted uterus, withdraw the fundus with towel clamps placed hand-over-hand, and suture the uterine wall.

b. Spinelli technique (transvaginal)–Transsect the cervix anteriorly, replace the fundus from below, and suture the cervix.

c. Küstner technique (transvaginal)–Incise through the cervix posteriorly, replace the fundus, and repair the cervix.

4. Hysterectomy–Chronic inversion of the uterus may be treated by hysterectomy.

B. Antibiotics: Postoperatively, administer broad-spectrum antibiotics, replace blood, fluid, and electrolytes, and decompress the stomach with a nasogastric tube.

Prognosis

If manual replacement is accomplished early without anesthesia, the results are uniformly good. Otherwise, manual replacement is successful in about 75% of cases. If the patient is not properly prepared for anesthesia or surgery, the mortality rate will be approximately 30%. It is unlikely that inversion will recur in succeeding pregnancies if good obstetric care is given.

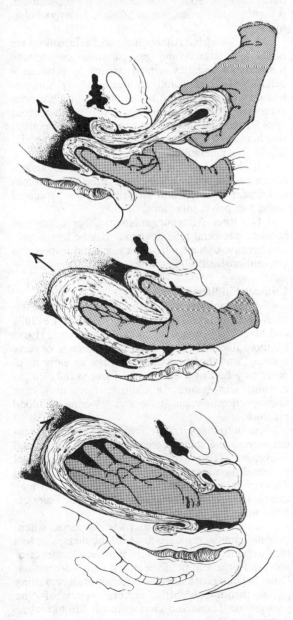

Figure 33–15. Replacement of inverted uterus.

PUERPERAL SEPSIS

Essentials of Diagnosis

- Fever in late afternoon or early evening.
- Tender, boggy uterus.
- Parametrial pain and thickening.
- Foul-smelling lochia.

General Considerations

Puerperal sepsis is any postpartum infection of the genital tract complicating labor or delivery. (Postabortal infection, another type of puerperal sepsis, is not included in this discussion.) The various manifestations of puerperal sepsis include cellulitis of the perineum or vagina, endometritis, parametritis, salpingo-oophoritis, pelvic thrombophlebitis, peritonitis, septic embolization, septic shock, infected hematomas, or wound abscess.

While the true incidence of puerperal sepsis is

almost impossible to determine, it constitutes a major component of infection encountered in the postpartum period. The standard definition of febrile puerperal morbidity is an oral temperature of 38 °C (100.4 °F) or more on any of the first 10 postpartum days, excluding the first 24 hours. If one adds those patients not fulfilling the standard definition but who are treated with systemic antibiotics, it can be estimated that 5–15% of postpartum patients have some type of infection and that many of these are due to puerperal sepsis.

The most important factor contributing to puerperal sepsis is poor operative technique. Before the necessity for aseptic procedure was recognized, puerperal sepsis was primarily a contagious disease resulting from inadvertent contamination of the birth canal, usually by beta-hemolytic streptococci. With the introduction of antibiotics, blood transfusion, and improved anesthesia, the margin of safety against accidental infection has increased greatly, but some of the gain has been offset by careless practices.

Puerperal sepsis has become an endogenous infection associated with impairment of host defense mechanisms, now involving different bacterial pathogens from just beta-hemolytic streptococci. The major technical factors currently are disregard of aseptic principles, obstetric trauma, and the greatly expanded use of procedures that increase the risk of infection, eg, fetal monitoring or cesarean section. The bacterial pathogens involved include numerous aerobic gram-negative organisms as well as a multitude of anaerobic organisms formerly thought to be nonpathogenic.

Pathophysiology

Puerperal myoparametritis usually involves 2 or more microorganisms, and at least three-quarters of polymicrobial infections include anaerobic species. The characteristics of commonly encountered bacterial infections are as follows:

A. Hemolytic Streptococci: Hemolytic streptococci rapidly penetrate the uterine wall, producing few local signs but eventually resulting in peritonitis with a minimal inflammatory response. The infection spreads quietly but relentlessly. Paralytic ileus may follow, and pelvic structures can become matted into a massive cellulitis; or septic emboli from focal myometrial abscesses may feed a prolonged and debilitating septicemia. Convalescence is prolonged, and death may occur. Opportunities to drain a well-localized abscess are few.

B. Aerobic and Anaerobic Streptococci: These infections are encouraged by local trauma associated with devitalized tissue. The microorganisms are nurtured in sequestered collections of blood, with a gradual spread into thrombosed vessels and then into pelvic veins to produce a localized pelvic thrombophlebitis. Before the introduction of antibiotics, septic emboli were a likely consequence.

C. Gram-Negative Aerobic Bacteria: These are the most common cause of amnionitis that occasionally is followed by the rapid development of endo- and parametritis, peritonitis, septicemia, and septic shock.

These organisms may be part of the mixed flora identified in pelvic abscesses.

D. Anaerobic Bacteria: The anaerobes produce infections that are slow to develop but are often widespread and slow to resolve. Anaerobes commonly invade tissues damaged by trauma or by a primary aerobic infection. Extensive pelvic cellulitis and multiple abscess formation complicate both antibiotic therapy and surgical drainage. Progression to septic thrombophlebitis and septic embolization is more likely to occur with these organisms than with any other group.

E. Staphylococcal Infections: Staphylococcal infections tend to remain localized to endometrial and parametrial tissues. Rarely, a virulent infection produces multiple septic foci from which the bloodstream is continuously inoculated to produce an overwhelming sepsis.

F. Clostridia: Although clostridial infections are rare, both tetanus and gas gangrene can invade traumatized and devitalized tissues to produce a cellulitis that is comparatively localized but is nonetheless devastating because of the release of circulating exotoxins. The toxin of tetanus involves the nervous system, whereas that of gas gangrene produces massive hemolysis with acute tubular necrosis and anuria. Septic shock may also occur.

It should be recalled that clostridial organisms which do not produce the above clinical syndromes and appear to possess little virulence are also a frequent finding in pelvic infections.

G. Other Microorganisms: Other organisms produce puerperal infections that may be less important because of their infrequency or rapid response to conventional antibiotic therapy.

Clinical Findings

A. Symptoms and Signs: The first manifestations of a puerperal infection almost always are chills and fever, but the first significant temperature rise is far more likely to occur in the late afternoon or early evening, and the opportunity to make an early diagnosis may be lost if attention is focused only on the morning temperature. In addition, there may be a disproportionate rapid pulse and lowering of blood pressure.

Early findings include foul lochia, a boggy, tender uterus, and some degree of parametrial pain and thickening. There may also be evidence of retained placental membranes or inadequate drainage through the cervical canal. Evidence of local infection may exist in the perineum, paravaginal tissues, or a surgical incision.

An anaerobic infection can be suspected whenever the clinical response to antibiotic therapy is less than expected, and particularly if there is evidence of abscess formation, tissue necrosis, or gas formation. Other indicators of anaerobic infection are a coexisting pelvic thrombophlebitis, culture reports of "no growth" or "a mixed bacterial growth" from routine cultures, or the recovery of foul-smelling pus.

B. Laboratory Findings: The white blood count and differential count may be difficult to interpret because leukocytosis with an increased percentage of immature cells frequently occurs during labor and in the postpartum period in women who do not have infections. Although a moderate to marked leukocytosis is usual, gram-negative organisms may be associated on one day or another with a normal or low white count, and the only significant finding then will be a marked shift to the left.

Blood cultures and cultures of the lochia may be positive for pathogenic aerobic bacteria, but a search for anaerobic bacteria will almost surely be unproductive unless anaerobic cultures are properly collected and processed in the microbiologic laboratory without delay.

Cultures should always be taken because information on antibiotic sensitivity will be needed if the response to therapy is unsatisfactory.

C. X-Ray Findings: Roentgenologic studies of advanced infections sometimes identify gas formation in soft tissues. Unless there is coexisting obvious evidence of intravascular hemolysis, a diagnosis of gas gangrene is highly unlikely. All of the anaerobic pathogens are capable of producing gas.

Complications

With inadequate response to treatment, the clinical picture often includes peritonitis, pelvic abscess, abdominal abscess, pelvic thrombophlebitis, septic emboli, and septic shock.

Puerperal sepsis may be a progressive disease with many complications. Rare sequelae include intrahepatic or subhepatic abscess, cerebral abscess, cardiac infections, emphysema, and femoral thrombophlebitis ("milk leg"). Rarely, infection secondary to pudendal or paracervical anesthesia may spread along fascial planes to produce bizarre infections including abscess formation in a retroperitoneal space or around the hip joint capsule. Complications of therapy include pseudomembranous enterocolitis, "respiratory lung," and hemorrhage secondary to anticoagulation. Prolonged infection can lead to severe nutritional deficiencies.

Following recovery, permanent sterility is likely and residual chronic pelvic infection may require hysterectomy.

Differential Diagnosis

Examination of the febrile patient should include a search for *all* common causes of postpartum fever:

A. Breast Engorgement: Inflammation is obvious, but fever usually subsides promptly after local therapy is instituted. Persistent fever in the immediate postpartum period is never due to breast engorgement.

B. Mastitis: Mastitis usually appears in nursing mothers after they have been released from the hospital. The common organism is a coagulase-positive *Staphylococcus aureus*. Oral semisynthetic penicillins (eg, oxacillin, nafcillin, cloxacillin, or dicloxacillin) should be given. In most cases, discontinuation of

nursing will not be necessary. If abscess formation requires rehospitalization, the mother should be isolated in an area away from the maternity unit.

C. Urinary Tract Infection: This is the most common cause of fever requiring specific therapy. It is often complicated by urinary retention, which is aggravated by anesthesia, postpartum diuresis, and episodes of bladder overdistention. Most of the pathogenic organisms recovered are drug-sensitive, and clinical response usually is satisfactory to commonly employed urinary antibiotics, eg, sulfisoxazole and the nitrofurantoins. Sulfonamide drugs are contraindicated if the mother is nursing, because of the possibility of drug transmission and hyperbilirubinemia in the baby. Therapy should be continued for at least 10 days and followed by a 4-week screening culture.

D. Thrombophlebitis: Superficial thrombophlebitis is easily diagnosed by the findings of local erythema and tenderness and induration of superficial veins. Although anticoagulant therapy is not essential, it is advisable nevertheless because of the danger of a coexisting deep thrombophlebitis.

Deep thrombophlebitis of the femoral veins during the postpartum period carries an increased risk of pulmonary embolism. Anticoagulant therapy should not be withheld in patients with only minimal pain and tenderness, because embolization is more likely to occur when the inflammatory reaction is less severe.

Pelvic thrombophlebitis is almost impossible to distinguish from coexisting parametritis or salpingo-oophoritis on the basis of physical findings. Nonetheless, thrombophlebitis may be suspected if the patient's response to appropriate antibiotics is unsatisfactory as evidenced by a continuing febrile course after 48 hours of antibiotic medication. The diagnosis of thrombophlebitis is most likely if septic embolization occurs, and anticoagulant therapy should be added to the antibiotic regimen at this point.

E. Respiratory Complications: Respiratory complications are an infrequent cause of puerperal morbidity. When pneumonia or atelectasis is suspected, x-ray films of the chest should be obtained and proper treatment instituted.

Prevention

(1) Observe good aseptic technique. Reliance on antibiotics to control carelessly introduced infections cannot be justified.

(2) Minimize obstetric trauma. Injured, devitalized tissues encourage anaerobic infection.

(3) Avoid prolonged labor and frequent vaginal examinations, which lead to chorioamnionitis.

(4) If it becomes necessary to perform a cesarean section, administer antibiotics to patients at high risk for infection, eg, patients whose membranes have been ruptured more than 6 hours. Give intravenous penicillin plus gentamicin or cefamandole in therapeutic doses 1 hour before surgery, and continue treatment for 48 hours. Operative technique should be scrupulous, including packing of the pelvic gutters, meticulous hemostasis, and lavage.

Treatment

A. General Measures: Obtain both aerobic and anaerobic cervical and blood cultures. For the latter, proper collection and disposition are critical.

Strict isolation is necessary only if the causative microorganisms appear to be beta-hemolytic streptococci. For other infections, unit isolation is adequate.

Place the patient at bed rest in the semi-Fowler position.

Establish adequate drainage from the uterine cavity by gently dilating the cervical canal with sponge forceps and removing any membranes that are visible. (This is an excellent time to recover a forgotten sponge from the vagina.)

Severe infection accelerates metabolic processes and thus the utilization of nutrients, leading specifically to the depletion of folic acid (which can be replaced easily) or even general depletion which may require hyperalimentation if oral intake is inadequate.

B. Specific Measures:

1. Anticoagulants–Anticoagulants should be given for pelvic thrombophlebitis. Heparin is the anticoagulant drug of choice initially. Regulation of dosage is better accomplished by the utilization of partial thromboplastin times than by the Lee-White bleeding time. As long as the immediate response is satisfactory, treatment should be given for 10–14 days. If there is evidence of pulmonary embolization, anticoagulant therapy should be continued for at least 3 months.

2. Antibiotics–Give penicillin G, 5 million units intravenously initially, or erythromycin if penicillin allergy exists, plus kanamycin, gentamicin, or tobramycin.

3. Resistant infection or positive identification of anaerobic species–The most likely organism is *Bacteroides fragilis,* which usually responds well to clindamycin (600 mg intravenously every 6 hours) or chloramphenicol (1 g intravenously every 6 hours). Other antibiotic choices are lincomycin, carbenicillin, and cefoxitin.

C. Surgical Measures for Severe Infections: Vein ligation or clipping of the vena cava prevents propagation of septic emboli, but these operations are only necessary if there is evidence of recurrent embolization despite vigorous antibiotic and anticoagulant therapy.

In the event of a progressive unresponsive infection or a ruptured abscess, hysterectomy combined with bilateral salpingo-oophorectomy and extensive pelvic drainage probably will be necessary.

An upper abdominal infection, particularly a subdiaphragmatic or intrahepatic abscess, may require surgical drainage.

Tetanus is a rare complication that probably cannot be cured unless the pelvic nidus of infection is surgically excised shortly after the first symptoms appear. Unfortunately, operation often is delayed well beyond this point.

Puerperal gas gangrene can be arrested only by vigorous antibiotic therapy and debridement of necrotic tissues. Since the infection often is located in the uterus, curettage may suffice, but in advanced disease hysterectomy may be required. Nevertheless, the prospect for salvage of unaffected ovaries is reasonably good. The results of hyperbaric oxygen therapy have been disappointing. The risk of oxygen toxicity probably outweighs the benefits.

Prognosis

Maternal death attributable to puerperal sepsis currently is estimated to be less than 0.02%, primarily because of the recent dramatic reduction in deaths due to infected abortion as a consequence of the introduction of elective abortion. The incidence of postpartum infertility probably is low, but the incidence of sterility following elective therapeutic abortion is unknown. The infant's prognosis depends chiefly on the time elapsed between the introduction of an antepartum infection and delivery. After several hours of clinically recognized amnionitis, the infant's chances steadily diminish.

CHORIOAMNIONITIS

During normal pregnancy, the uterine contents are protected from ascending infection by the cervical mucous plug and intact membranes. Further protection is obtained from an as yet unspecified amniotic fluid inhibitory factor that appears during the second trimester and increases until the last weeks of pregnancy. This factor exerts a bacteriostatic effect up to 36 weeks, and then it combines with zinc to give a limited bactericidal effect that varies among individual patients. Once the membranes have ruptured, these protective mechanisms are lost, and the risk of chorioamnionitis increases with the passage of time. Chorioamnionitis contributes substantially to postpartum and neonatal sepsis.

Etiology

Spontaneous premature rupture of the membranes, followed by a prolonged latent period before the onset of labor, often is basic to the development of chorioamnionitis. During this period, proliferation of vaginal pathogens is encouraged by the alkalinity of the leaking amniotic fluid. Concomitantly, bacteria inevitably ascend through the cervical canal into the uterine cavity. This spread is accelerated by repeated vaginal or rectal examinations. After the membranes have been ruptured for 24 hours, about three-fourths of undelivered women will have intrauterine bacterial contamination, and almost one-fifth of newborns will have bacteremia. Other causes of chorioamnionitis during labor are cervicitis or vaginitis in the presence of intact but devitalized membranes; previous cerclage; and, more rarely, infection following diagnostic amniocentesis. Viral infections, eg, with herpesvirus, may invade along the same route.

Pathophysiology

Escherichia coli is the organism most commonly recovered in chorioamnionitis, although most aerobic and anaerobic bacteria as well as other microorganisms often cause chorioamnionitis, salpingitis, peritonitis, or infection in newborns. Beta-hemolytic streptococci may cause premature labor also, and anaerobic bacteria should be suspected if the amniotic fluid has a foul odor. Despite protective components, amniotic fluid contaminated by ascending bacteria is capable of supporting bacterial growth. If the fluid contains meconium, bacterial propagation is considerably enhanced. Infection of the chorion, amnion, placental fetal vessels, and umbilical cord often follows. These developments may or may not be associated with significant symptomatology. If the maternal vasculature is penetrated, however, maternal septicemia may result, with septic shock or consumption coagulopathy the critical sequela. Other complications of postpartum sepsis, eg, pulmonary embolism, are also possible. The fetus may develop intra-alveolar pneumonia from aspirated amniotic fluid, or infection may develop from bacteremia derived from placentitis or omphalitis.

Diagnosis

The treatment of chorioamnionitis may be hampered by the lack of clear-cut diagnostic criteria. The most predictive findings are ruptured membranes, leukocytosis, and maternal fever. Fetal or maternal tachycardia, uterine tenderness, and malodorous amniotic fluid also support the diagnosis. The observation of bacteria in an otherwise unremarkable amniotic fluid suggests chorioamnionitis and is more reliable than the finding of white blood cells. If the mother has sepsis, blood cultures should be drawn from at least 2 puncture sites to demonstrate aerobic or anaerobic organisms. Cultures of the cervix or amniotic fluid are rarely helpful, because of the many bacterial contaminants that confuse the interpretation.

Treatment

If the fetus is small (less than 2000 g) and further fetal maturation is desirable, premature rupture of the membranes may be managed expectantly by hospitalization, bed rest, and careful monitoring for signs of infection. Unnecessary vaginal or rectal examinations should be avoided. Prophylactic antibiotics are ineffective, because blanket coverage of all of the potentially pathogenic microorganisms is impossible. If infection ensues, labor should be induced.

When the fetus is more mature and premature rupture of the membranes occurs, the patient should be hospitalized. If spontaneous labor does not ensue within 12 hours, labor should be induced.

Once a presumptive diagnosis of chorioamnionitis is made, delivery must be effected in a reasonably short period of time, ie, before maternal or fetal infection becomes well established. While vaginal delivery is preferable, factors favoring cesarean section include slow progress of labor, fever, or evidence of fetal distress. In probable chorioamnionitis, the mother may be treated with ampicillin, an antibiotic that is effective against the most likely predominant microorganism, ie, *E coli*. When an anaerobic infection is suspected, combination drug therapy, eg, clindamycin and gentamicin, is preferred. If a severe infection is present and abdominal delivery becomes necessary, extraperitoneal section can be considered. Upon delivery, the oropharynx and trachea of the newborn infant should be carefully aspirated to remove infected meconium and mucus in order to avoid neonatal pneumonia. Antibiotics given to the mother during labor do not cross the placenta in sufficient amounts to protect the fetus from infection.

Complications

Septicemia in the mother is occasionally followed by septic shock (see Chapter 20). Consumption coagulopathy may also occur (see Chapter 33). In the postpartum period, parametritis may develop and further spread of infection to produce pelvic peritonitis, abscess formation, or septic thrombophlebitis may ensue. Occasionally, a patient with sepsis unresponsive to antibiotic therapy will require hysterectomy and extensive pelvic drainage. These patients may develop a secondary anaerobic infection, often with *B fragilis*, which grows readily in devitalized tissues. If delivery is by cesarean section, wound infection often follows.

AMNIOTIC FLUID EMBOLUS

Amniotic fluid embolization into the maternal circulation is a rare but frequently fatal complication of labor. About half of the patients die rapidly, and half of those who survive the initial insult die within hours. This syndrome is typically encountered in an older multipara at term in hard labor with ruptured membranes. Contributing factors may be placental separation, a dead fetus, or the presence of excessive particulate matter in the amniotic fluid, including meconium. Treatment is complicated and often ineffective.

Etiology

A bolus of amniotic fluid can pass into the maternal circulation, either through the placental site or by way of lacerations of the cervical or myometrial surfaces, to produce embolic blockage of pulmonary vessels or, possibly, a vasospastic anaphylactoid reaction. As a result, there is a decrease in left ventricular cardiac output associated with peripheral vascular collapse, pulmonary hypertension, right heart failure, and pulmonary edema. Accompanying anoxemia may lead to convulsions and coma. These problems often are further complicated by hemorrhage due to decreased uterine tone and by disseminated intravascular coagulation triggered by the thromboplastic action of amniotic fluid.

Diagnosis

A presumptive diagnosis is reasonable if cardiovascular collapse associated with severe cyanosis, dyspnea, and pulmonary edema occur suddenly during or shortly after the end of labor. Chest pain is rarely present, but there may be a preceding chill, coughing, sweating, and convulsions or coma. If the patient survives the initial insult, a clotting deficiency, uterine atony, and secondary hemorrhage often follow. Other causes of shock and acute collapse must be considered. Time permitting, an ECG may show right heart strain, or a lung scan may show areas of perfusion defect. The diagnosis can be confirmed (and treatment expedited) by the demonstration of fetal squamae and lanugo hair in blood aspirated from the right heart. Undoubtedly, some patients exhibiting uterine atony or disseminated intravascular coagulation without pulmonary symptoms have also suffered an infusion of amniotic fluid.

Prevention

Because of the rarity of amniotic fluid embolus, its occurrence is unpredictable. Avoidance of hyperstimulation of the uterus, particularly in the presence of a dead fetus, clearly reduces the risk. Oxytocic agents that increase uterine tonus, such as sparteine sulfate or prostaglandins, magnify the risk. Other procedures that have been implicated as a cause of amniotic fluid embolus are amniocentesis in the presence of hydramnios and excessive stripping of the membranes.

Treatment

Treatment must necessarily be vigorous and rapid for relief of pulmonary arteriolar spasm, uterine hypotonia, hypovolemic shock, and coagulation failure. Pulmonary edema should be treated with positive pressure oxygen therapy, morphine, and periodic vascular restriction with tourniquets on the extremities. Aminophylline and intravenous corticosteroids (eg, 1000 mg hydrocortisone) may relieve the pulmonary arteriolar spasm. Rapid digitilization is advisable. Blood replacement may be required, but transfusion must be administered with care in view of the cardiopulmonary complications. Fluid administration is greatly assisted by the placement of a central venous or Swan-Ganz vascular catheter. Uterine atony not responding to oxytocics can sometimes be controlled by a uterine pack. Hemorrhage due to a clotting defect must also be corrected (see Abruptio Placentae).

ASPIRATION PNEUMONIA

A woman giving birth is particularly vulnerable to aspiration pneumonia because of delayed gastric emptying time. Aspiration may or may not be recognized at the time of birth, but symptoms are usually manifested within 12 hours of the insult by the onset of fever associated with tachypnea, hypoxemia, hypercapnia, and other evidences of respiratory distress. Bronchoscopy is useful to remove large food particles but is of limited value in removing aspirated fluid. X-ray findings include diffuse, cloudy, patchy infiltrates that may be confused with atelectasis or pulmonary embolus.

Effective measures to prevent aspiration pneumonia—particularly if birth is by section—include oral antacids before anesthetic induction, the introduction of an endotracheal tube, and close observation during the recovery period. Treatment includes 100% oxygen administered by positive pressure, bronchodilators, antibiotics, and corticosteroids. The best initial antibiotic is probably penicillin, but additional antibiotics effective against anaerobic bacteria are sometimes necessary: Intravenous aminophylline is probably the best bronchodilator. Steroids in pharmacologic doses appear to be of benefit in reducing the inflammatory reaction produced by vomitus.

PREMATURE RUPTURE OF THE MEMBRANES

Spontaneous rupture of the membranes prior to the onset of labor is a significant problem if the fetus is premature or, in the case of a mature fetus, whenever the latent period is unduly prolonged.

Etiology

The cause of rupture usually is not known, although contributory factors such as cervical incompetence or hydramnios can be identified.

Diagnosis

Minimize vaginal examinations to reduce the risk of chorioamnionitis. Expose the posterior vaginal fornix by means of a sterile speculum, and test the pH of pooled fluid with nitrazine paper (amniotic fluid has a pH of 7–7.25). As an alternative, a sample of fluid may be air-dried on a slide and examined for a fern pattern. If no free fluid is found, place a dry pad under the patient's hips, and observe for subsequent leakage.

Management

Differences of opinion regarding details of management are recognized, but the following recommendations have been helpful:

A. Estimated Gestational Age ⩾ 36 Weeks; Fetal Weight ⩾ 2500 g: Although there is a 90% expectation of spontaneous labor within 24 hours, whenever the latent period exceeds 8–12 hours, induction by means of an oxytocin infusion is indicated to minimize the risk of infection.

B. Estimated Gestational Age ⩾ 34–36 Weeks; Fetal Weight 2000–3000 g: Induction as above is probably indicated. Some may prefer to wait 16–24 hours in the expectation of accelerated lung surfactant production.

C. Estimated Gestational Age 26–34 Weeks; Fetal Weight 500–2000 g: Management should be based on diagnostic amniocentesis. If there is evidence of lung maturation (mature lethicin:sphingomyelin ratio) or amnionitis (bacteria in amniotic fluid), labor should be induced. If the lecithin:sphingomyelin ratio is in the immature range and there is no evidence of amnionitis, the patient should be maintained at bed rest, with vital signs taken every 4 hours and white blood count daily. Adrenocorticosteroid drugs for lung maturation may be beneficial, eg, betamethasone sodium phosphate, 6 mg, or the equivalent, intramuscularly, repeated once within 24 hours. If leakage of fluid stops and the patient remains afebrile, without evidence of increasing uterine irritability, she may be allowed to walk, and then dismissed with the admonition that vaginal douches and coitus must be avoided and with instructions to monitor her temperature. If amnionitis develops, pregnancy must be terminated.

D. Estimated Gestational Age < 26 Weeks; Fetal Weight Less Than 500 g: Once the diagnosis is firmly established, the pregnancy should be terminated, because there is no hope for salvaging the fetus.

PREMATURE LABOR

Preterm (premature) birth is the single largest problem in obstetrics, because of high morbidity and mortality rates. In some hospitals, at least 80% of perinatal deaths are associated with prematurity. Moreover, a premature birth involves a large commitment of time and money with no guarantee that even a surviving infant will be normal. For these reasons, every effort must be made to inhibit premature labor, when reasonable, and to conduct labor and delivery in the least traumatic fashion when inhibition of labor is either contraindicated or impossible.

Diagnosis

The diagnosis of prematurity or premature labor is always imprecise. In assessing prematurity, a menstrual history of less than 37 weeks is more reliable as evidence and more important to the outcome than an estimated fetal weight of less than 2500 g. A single set of ultrasonic measurements of biparietal and anteroposterior truncal diameters is of limited value in assessing fetal age, particularly when employed to distinguish between a premature and a mature fetus, but a series may be most revealing.

The criteria for a presumptive diagnosis of premature labor are as follows: (1) regular uterine contractions occurring at intervals of 10 minutes or less, with a duration of at least 30 seconds; or (2) progressive cervical effacement and dilatation observed over a period of 30–60 minutes, or a cervix that is well effaced and dilated at least 2 cm on the patient's admission to the hospital.

Extended observation is undesirable, because the effectiveness of therapy diminishes as labor advances.

Inhibition of Labor

A. Patient Selection:

1. Indications for tocolysis–

a. An apparently healthy fetus.

b. Gestation between 20 and 34 weeks (or up to 37 weeks, if good neonatal care is not available).

c. Cervical dilatation 4 cm or less.

d. Intact membranes. (This criterion may be waived in occasional cases requiring more time to accelerate fetal lung maturation with adrenocorticosteroid drugs.)

2. Contraindications to the use of tocolytic agents–

a. A disease that specifically contraindicates their use.

b. Uncorrected fetal distress.

c. Obstetric complications requiring early delivery, eg, abruptio placentae, placenta previa with major hemorrhage, severe preeclampsia-eclampsia, hemolytic disease, and hydraminos.

d. Chorioamnionitis.

e. Bulging membranes.

B. Methods: About half of patients suspected of being in premature labor will respond to bed rest, mild sedation, and avoidance of pelvic examinations. Rapid hydration with lactated Ringer's injection to inhibit oxytocin release may be helpful. If a tocolytic agent is needed, the following may be considered:

1. Beta-adrenergic agents–Beta-mimetic adrenergic agents act directly on beta receptors (β_2) to relax the uterus and uterine vessels. Their use is limited by dose-related major cardiovascular side-effects including pulmonary edema; adult respiratory distress syndrome; elevated systolic and reduced diastolic blood pressure; and both maternal and fetal tachycardia. Other dose-related effects are decreased serum potassium and increased blood glucose, plasma insulin, and lactic acidosis. Maternal medical contraindications to the use of beta-adrenergic agents include cardiac disease, hyperthyroidism, uncontrolled hypertension, or pulmonary hypertension; asthma requiring sympathomimetic drugs or corticosteroids for relief; uncontrolled diabetes; and chronic hepatic or renal disease. Commonly observed effects during intravenous administration are palpitations, tremors, nervousness, and restlessness.

a. Ritodrine–The patient should be prehydrated with lactated Ringer's injection and placed on her left side to ensure adequate venous return to the heart. Prepare to monitor maternal blood pressure, pulse, urinary output and fetal heart rate. Start an infusion of normal saline containing 0.5 mg of ritodrine per mL, infuse 0.2 mL/min, and increase by 0.1-mL increments every 10 minutes to a maximum of 0.7 mL/min. Maintain at the lowest effective rate for 12 hours. One-half hour before infusion is to be stopped, start the patient on oral ritodrine, 10 mg every 2 hours for 24 hours followed by 20 mg every 4–6 hours until the 36th week of pregnancy.

In most cases, side-effects can be controlled by reducing the rate of infusion. Adverse effects requiring discontinuation are persistence of maternal heart rate over 150, a fetal heart rate over 200, systolic pressure over 180, or diastolic pressure below 40. Intravenous fluids should be administered with care to avoid circulatory overload.

b. Terbutaline–Although not approved in the USA, terbutaline has been used elsewhere as a tocolytic agent. The mode of action is similar to that of ritodrine, and the precautions and contraindications are the same. A bolus of 250 μg followed by 10–80 μg/min until labor stops may be effective. The drug is then administered subcutaneously, 2.5–5 mg every 2–4 hours for 12 hours. Oral maintenance therapy requires 5 mg every 4–6 hours. Intravenous terbutaline may not be as easily controlled as ritodrine and is more costly.

c. Isoxsuprine–Isoxsuprine also is not approved in the USA for tocolysis and has a narrow therapeutic range. The optimal intravenous dose is 0.25–0.5 mg/min for an 8- to 12-hour period. The maintenance dose is 5–20 mg intramuscularly or orally every 3–6 hours.

2. Magnesium sulfate–Magnesium sulfate has not been approved for use as a tocolytic drug. Nonetheless, although considerably less effective than ritodrine or terbutaline, magnesium sulfate is less likely to cause serious side-effects (respiratory and cardiac depression) and is probably the best alternative if beta-mimetic drugs are contraindicated or toxic. A loading dose of 40 mL of a 10% solution (given slowly intravenously) should be followed by a maintenance infusion of a 2% solution at a rate of 100 mL/h until labor stops. Test the patient's reflexes periodically for magnesium overdosage. Calcium gluconate solution given intravenously is the antidote.

3. Ethyl alcohol–The effectiveness of ethyl alcohol is presumably due to oxytocin inhibition. It has not been approved for use as a tocolytic agent in the USA. Whatever success can be achieved with this agent may be negated by the necessity for prolonged administration and close supervision, as well as a plethora of undesirable side-effects. These include inebriation, headache, nausea and vomiting, urinary incontinence, coma, and lactic acidosis. A reasonable loading dose is 7.5 mg/kg given intravenously over 2 hours, followed by a maintenance dose of 1.5 mL/h.

4. Progesterone–Progesterone is still an experimental tocolytic drug. It is ineffective once labor is established.

5. Antiprostaglandins–Prostaglandin inhibitors are effective, but they may cause premature closure of the fetal ductus arteriosus. These drugs are still experimental and are not recommended as tocolytics.

If cervical dilatation reaches 5 cm, the treatment should be considered a failure and abandoned. If labor resumes after a period of quiescence, treatment may be reinstituted using the same or a different drug.

C. Results of Tocolytic Therapy: The results of tocolytic therapy are difficult to judge because of the lack of well-controlled studies. It is estimated that labor was halted for 72 hours or more in at least 70% of patients who received ethyl alcohol and in 90% who received ritodrine.

Ritodrine is credited with reducing the neonatal death rate in one series from 13% to 5% and the incidence of respiratory distress from 20% to 11%. Fifty-eight percent of the infants had a birth weight in excess of 2500 g, and no adverse long-term effects

have been observed over a 2-year period. Further confirmation is awaited.

Conduct of Labor and Delivery

Small premature infants should be delivered in a hospital equipped for intensive neonatal care whenever possible, because transfer following birth is deleterious. Premature breech infants weighing less than 1500–2000 g are generally delivered by cesarean section. If the presentation is cephalic, vaginal birth is preferred in the absence of fetal distress—with the possible exception of occasional cases in which a long labor is anticipated because of an unfavorable cervix.

Every effort should be made to avoid fetal hypoxia and intraventricular hemorrhage. Adequate hydration should prevent maternal acidosis. Internal fetal monitoring and scalp sampling for blood pH should be done if hypoxia is suspected. Sedative and analgesic drugs in reduced dosages should be used sparingly. Paracervical block should be avoided because of adverse fetal effects.

Inhalation anesthesia should not be used for delivery. Conduction anesthesia (particularly epidural) is the best choice because it provides maximum relaxation of the birth canal and reduces the risk of trauma. Pudendal block anesthesia is also satisfactory if the pelvic floor and perineum are pliable or relaxed. A generous episiotomy should be made to further reduce the risk of injury. Delivery can be aided by forceps with a short cephalic curve (eg, Tucker-McLean forceps) serving as a sort of helmet to protect and guide the fetal head over the perineum. Before clamping the cord, wait 45–60 seconds—while holding the neonate below tabletop level—to ensure that adequate blood is being received from the placental circulation.

If a cesarean section is indicated, the decision to operate is based on maturity of the fetus and prognosis for survival. In borderline cases, good criteria on which to base a decision are lacking. The problem is further complicated by the physician's inability to reliably estimate the weight of the premature fetus.

When performing a cesarean section, it is important to make certain that the uterine incision is adequate for extraction of the fetus without delay or unnecessary trauma. This often requires a vertical incision when the lower uterine segment is incompletely developed.

In managing the premature newborn infant, the avoidance of heat loss is of critical importance. When birth follows the unsuccessful use of parenteral tocolytic agents, keep in mind the potential residual adverse effects of these drugs. Beta-adrenergic agents may cause neonatal hypotension, hypoglycemia, hypocalcemia, and ileus. Magnesium sulfate may be responsible for respiratory and cardiac depression. Alcohol produces lactic acidosis and hyperglycemia. In addition, oral maintenance doses of a beta-adrenergic agent can produce hypoglycemia in the newborn.

RUPTURED UTERUS

Rupture of the pregnant uterus is a potential obstetric catastrophe and a major cause of maternal death. The incidence of uterine rupture is approximately one in 1500 deliveries.

Complete rupture includes the entire thickness of the uterine wall and, in most cases, the overlying serosal peritoneum. Occult or incomplete rupture is a term usually reserved for dehiscence of a uterine incision from previous surgery. Such defects are usually asymptomatic unless converted to complete rupture during the course of pregnancy or labor.

Complete ruptures usually occur during the course of labor. One notable exception is the scar of a classic cesarean section (or hysterotomy) that typically ruptures during the third trimester before term and before the onset of labor. Other causes of rupture without labor are placenta percreta, invasive mole, choriocarcinoma, and cornual pregnancy.

Complete ruptures may be classified as traumatic or spontaneous. Traumatic ruptures occur most commonly as a result either of improper administration of an oxytocic agent or an inept attempt at operative vaginal delivery. The most dangerous oxytocic agents are those that increase uterine tonus, eg, sparteine sulfate, any of the prostaglandins, or ergot preparations. Sparteine sulfate and prostaglandins given to induce labor must be administered with extreme care; and ergot preparations are contraindicated either until the anterior shoulder is born or until the third stage of labor. Breech extraction through an incompletely dilated cervix is the type of operative vaginal delivery most likely to produce uterine rupture. Other maneuvers that impose some risk of rupture—unless expertly performed under proper conditions—are internal podalic version and extraction, difficult forceps, destructive operations, and maneuvers to relieve shoulder dystocia. Tumultuous labor, excessive fundal

pressure or violent bearing down efforts, and neglected obstructed labor may also be responsible for rupture of the uterus. Causes of obstructed labor include contracted pelvis, fetal macrosomia, brow or face presentation, hydrocephalus, or tumors involving the birth canal. Direct violence to the abdomen is a rare cause of rupture but is occasionally encountered in automobile accidents, particularly if the victim was wearing a lap type seat belt.

Spontaneous rupture is somewhat of a misnomer because most such patients either have a uterine scar or give a history compatible with previous trauma that may have resulted in permanent uterine damage. Previous uterine surgery includes both classic and low cervical section, intramural or submucous myomectomy, resection of the uterine cornu, metroplasty, and trachelectomy. Other operative procedures that may have damaged the uterus are vigorous curettage, induced abortion, and manual removal of the placenta. In contrast, some patients give no history of surgery but may be suspected of having a weakened uterus because of multiparity. Such patients are particularly at risk if they have an old lateral cervical laceration that could extend to involve a uterine artery.

Clinical Findings of Complete Uterine Rupture

There are no reliable signs of impending uterine rupture, although the sudden appearance of gross hematuria is suggestive.

Prior to the onset of labor, a beginning rupture may produce local pain and tenderness associated with increased uterine irritability and, in some cases, a small amount of vaginal bleeding. Premature labor may follow. As the extent of the rupture increases, there will be more pain, more bleeding, and perhaps signs of hypovolemic shock. Exsanguination prior to surgery is unlikely because of the reduced vascularity of scar tissue, but the placenta will be completely separated and the fetus extruded partially or completely into the abdominal cavity.

Rupture of a low cervical scar usually occurs during labor, but clearly identifiable signs and symptoms are often lacking. Thus, it is quite possible that labor will progress to the vaginal birth of an unaffected infant. Even so, the rupture may lacerate a uterine artery, producing exsanguination, or the fetus may be extruded into the abdominal cavity. If a defect is palpated in the lower uterine segment following vaginal delivery, laparotomy will be necessary to assess the damage. Laparotomy is mandatory if continuing hemorrhage is present.

The classic findings of spontaneous rupture during labor are suprapubic pain and tenderness, cessation of uterine contractions, disappearance of fetal heart tones, recession of the presenting part, and vaginal hemorrhage—followed by the signs and symptoms of hypovolemic shock and hemoperitoneum. X-ray examination might confirm an abnormal fetal position or extension of the fetal extremities. Hemoperitoneum can easily be confirmed by paracentesis.

Uterine rupture due to obstetric trauma is usually

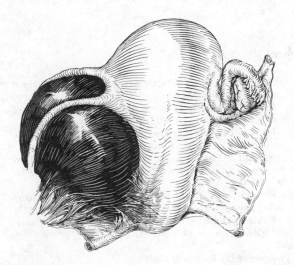

Figure 33–16. Rupture of lower uterine segment into broad ligament.

not diagnosed until after the infant's birth. The clinical picture depends on the site and extent of rupture. Unfortunately, valuable time is often lost because the rupture was not diagnosed at the time of the initial examination. Whenever a newly delivered patient exhibits persistent bleeding or shock, the uterus must be carefully reexamined for signs of a rupture that may have been difficult to palpate because of the soft, irregular tissue surfaces. Whenever an operative delivery is performed—especially if the past history includes events or problems that increase the likelihood of uterine rupture—the initial examination of the uterus and birth canal must be diligent.

Complications

The complications of ruptured uterus are hemorrhage, shock, postoperative infection, ureteral damage, thrombophlebitis, amniotic fluid embolus, disseminated intravascular coagulation, pituitary failure, and death. If the patient survives, infertility or sterility may result.

Prevention

Most of the causes of uterine rupture can be avoided by good obstetric assessment and technique. Probably the most common error in judgment leading to rupture is underestimation of fetal weight, resulting in traumatic delivery. The most common technical error is the poorly supervised administration of oxytocin during labor. A frequent deficiency in operative technique is poor closure of a cesarean section incision. To maximize the prospects for good wound healing in the low cervical operation, the uterine incision is best closed with interrupted sutures followed by a continuous inverting suture in the periuterine fascia—rather than closure with a locking suture, which may strangulate the wound edges and interfere with healing.

Treatment

Hysterectomy is the preferred treatment for most cases of complete uterine rupture. Either total hysterectomy or the subtotal operation can be employed, depending on the site of rupture and the patient's condition. The most difficult cases are lateral ruptures involving the lower uterine segment and a uterine artery with hemorrhage and hematoma formation obscuring the operative field. These patients may be better served by ligation of the ipsilateral hypogastric artery for hemostasis, thus avoiding the risk of ureteral drainage by blind suturing at the base of the broad ligament. If there is a question of ureteral occlusion by a suture, it is best to perform cystotomy to observe the bilateral appearance of an intravenously injected dye, eg, indigo carmine. If doubt still exists, a retrograde ureteral catheter should be passed upward through the cystotomy wound.

If childbearing is important and the risks—both short- and long-term—are acceptable to the patient, many ruptures can be repaired.

In long-neglected and badly infected cases, survival may be improved by limiting the surgical procedure to repair of the rupture and by antibiotic therapy.

Occult ruptures of the lower uterine segment encountered at repeat section may be treated by freshening the wound edges and secondary repair, but the newly repaired incision will probably be weak.

Prognosis

The maternal mortality rate ranges from 10 to 40%, and deaths are about equally divided among oxytocic augmentation of labor, delivery trauma, and previous obstetric or surgical uterine scars. Only about 25% of delivered patients who die are correctly diagnosed at the time of the initial postdelivery vaginal examination. The perinatal mortality rate exceeds 50%.

• • •

References

Premature Separation of the Placenta

Huisjes HM et al: Perinatal mortality and late sequelae in children born after abruptio placentae. *Eur J Obstet Gynecol Reprod Biol* 1979;**9**:45.

Knab DR: Abruptio placentae: An assessment of the time and method of delivery. *Obstet Gynecol* 1978;**52**:625.

Odendaal HJ: Clinical and haematological problems associated with severe abruptio placentae. *S Afr Med J* 1978;**54**:476.

Paterson MEL: The etiology and outcome of abruptio placentae. *Acta Obstet Gynecol Scand* 1979;**58**:31.

Shu G: Pathogenesis and management of uterine inertia complicating abruptio placentae with consumption coagulopathy *Am J Obstet Gynecol* 1977;**129**:164.

Placenta Previa

Brenner WE et al: Characteristics of patients with placenta previa and results of expectant management. *Am J Obstet Gynecol* 1978;**132**:180.

Cotton DB et al: The conservative aggressive management of placenta previa. *Am J Obstet Gynecol* 1980;**137**:687.

Hill DJ, Beischer NA: Placenta previa without antepartum hemorrhage. *Aust NZ J Obstet Gynaecol* 1980;**20**:21.

Naeye, RL: Placenta previa: Predisposing factors and effects on the fetus and surviving infants. *Obstet Gynecol* 1978;**52**:521.

Rizos N et al: Natural history of placenta previa ascertained by diagnostic ultrasound. *Am J Obstet Gynecol* 1979;**133**:287.

Wexler P, Gottesfeld KR: Early diagnosis of placenta previa. *Obstet Gynecol* 1979;**54**:231.

Prolapse of the Umbilical Cord

Ekweinpu CC: Cord prolapse through a fenestration in a cesarean section scar. *East Afr Med J* 1979;**54**:692.

Kleinschmidt R et al: Practical significance of umbilical cord complications in the management of labor. *Zentralbl Gynaekol* 1975;**97**:722.

Tejani NA et al: The association of umbilical cord complications and variable decelerations with acid-base findings. *Obstet Gynecol* 1977;**49**:159.

Postpartum Hemorrhage

Brisden PRS, Clark AD: Postpartum haemorrhage after induced and spontaneous labor. *Br Med J* 1978;**2**:855.

Howie PC: Blood clotting and fibrinolysis in pregnancy. *Postgrad Med J* 1979;**55**:362.

Moir DD: Ergometrine or oxytocin? Blood loss and side effects at spontaneous vertex delivery. *Br J Anaesth* 1979;**51**:113.

Redman CW: Coagulation problems in human pregnancy. *Postgrad Med J* 1979;**55**:367.

Weekes LR: Five year study of postpartum hemorrhage: Queen of Angels Hospital 1973–1977. *J Natl Med Assoc* 1979;**71**:829.

Retained and Adherent Placenta

Kitchen DH: Placenta accreta, percreta, and praevia accreta. *Aust NZ J Obstet Gynaecol* 1978;**18**:238.

Malvern J, Campbell S, May P: Ultrasonic scanning of the puerperal uterus following secondary postpartum hemorrhage. *J Obstet Gynaecol Br Commonw* 1973;**80**:320.

Read JA et al: Placenta accreta: Changing clinical aspects and outcome. *Obstet Gynecol* 1980;**56**:31.

Inversion of the Uterus

Feheng K: Acute inversion of the uterus. *Int Surg* 1977;**62**:100.

Gudgeon CW: Inversion of the uterus: Replacement without general anesthesia. *Med J Aust* 1979;**2**:434.

Lee WK et al: Acute inversion of the uterus. *Obstet Gynecol* 1978;**51**:144.

Watson P et al: Management of acute and subacute puerperal inversion of the uterus. *Obstet Gynecol* 1980;**55**:12.

Puerperal Sepsis

DePalma RT et al: Identification and management of women at high risk for pelvic infection following cesarean section. *Obstet Gynecol* [*Suppl*] 1980;**55**:185.

Gall SA et al: Intravenous metronidazole or clindamycin with tobramycin for therapy of pelvic infections. *Obstet Gynecol* 1981;**57**:51.

Gibbs RS: Clinical risk factors for puerperal infection. *Obstet Gynecol* [*Suppl*] 1980;**55**:78.

Pond DG et al: Comparison of ampicillin with clindamycin plus gentamicin in the treatment of postpartum uterine infection. *Can Med Assoc J* 1979;**120**:533.

Chorioamnionitis

Bobbit JR, Ledger WJ: Amniotic fluid analysis: Its role in maternal and neonatal infection. *Obstet Gynecol* 1978;**51**:56.

Gibbs RA et al: Management of acute chorioamnionitis. *Am J Obstet Gynecol* 1981;**136**:799.

Naeye RI, Peters RC: Amniotic fluid infection leading to perinatal death. *Pediatrics* 1978;**61**:171.

Woods DL et al: Antibacterial activity of amniotic fluid. *S Afr Med J* 1979;**55**:1059.

Amniotic Fluid Embolus

Morgan M: Amniotic fluid embolus. *Anaesthesia* 1979;**34**:20.

Schaerf RH, deCampo T, Civetta JM: Hemodynamic alterations and rapid diagnosis in a case of amniotic fluid embolus. *Anesthesiology* 1977;**46**:155.

Wasser WG et al: Nonfatal amniotic fluid embolism. *Mt Sinai J Med* 1979;**46**:388.

Aspiration Pneumonia

Hester JB et al: Pulmonary acid aspiration syndrome: Should prophylaxis be routine? *Br J Anaesth* 1977;**49**:595.

Toung T et al: Aspiration pneumonia: Beneficial and harmful effects of positive-end expiratory pressure. *Surgery* 1977;**82**:279.

Wolfe JE et al: Effects of corticosteroids in the treatment of patients with gastric aspiration. *Am J Med* 1977;**63**:719.

Suppression of Premature Labor

Barden T et al: Ritrodrine hydrochloride: A betamimetic agent for use in preterm labor I and II. *Obstet Gynecol* 1980;**56**:1.

Brown SM et al: Terbutaline sulfate in the prevention of recurrence of premature labor. *Obstet Gynecol* 1981;**57**:22.

Caritas SN et al: Pharmacologic inhibition of preterm labor. *Am J Obstet Gynecol* 1979;**133**:557.

Guilliams S, Held B: Contemporary management and conduct of preterm labor and delivery: A review. *Obstet Gynecol Surv* 1979;**34**:248.

Niebyl JR et al: The pharmacologic inhibition of premature labor. *Obstet Gynecol Surv* 1978;**33**:507.

Wallace RL, Herrick CN: Amniocentesis in the evaluation of premature labor. *Obstet Gynecol* 1981;**57**:483.

Rupture of the Uterus

Golan A et al: Rupture of the pregnant uterus. *Obstet Gynecol* 1980;**56**:549.

Mokgokang EM, Marivate M: Treatment of ruptured uterus. *S Afr Med J* 1976;**50**:1621.

Schrinsky DC, Benson RC: Rupture of the pregnant uterus: A review. *Obstet Gynecol Surv* 1978;**33**:217.

Spaulding LB, Gallup DG: Current concepts of management of rupture of gravid uterus. *Obstet Gynecol* 1979;**54**:437.

Taylor MB, Cumming DC: Spontaneous rupture of a primigravid uterus. *J Reprod Med* 1979;**22**:168.

Premature Rupture of the Membranes

Eggers TR et al: Premature rupture of the membranes. *Med J Aust* 1979;**1**:209.

Johnson JWC et al: Premature rupture of the membranes and prolonged latency. *Obstet Gynecol* 1981;**57**:547.

Lavery JP et al: Effects of meconium on the strength of chorioamniotic membranes. *Obstet Gynecol* 1980;**56**:711.

McVicar J, Chordia SKS: Premature rupture of the membranes before the 38th week of pregnancy. *Br J Clin Pract* 1978;**32**:249.

Miller JM: Premature rupture of the membranes: Material and neonatal morbidity related to betamethasone and antibiotic therapy. *J Reprod Med* 1980;**25**:173.

34 | Preeclampsia-Eclampsia & Other Gestational Edema-Proteinuria-Hypertension Disorders (GEPH)

Russell Ramon de Alvarez, MD

Hypertension in pregnant patients may represent either of the following: (1) The development of a significant rise of blood pressure during pregnancy in a previously normotensive woman. Hypertensive disorders caused by gestation represent components or combinations of the **gestational edema–proteinuria–hypertension complex (GEPH),** classified in Table 34–1. (2) The occurrence of pregnancy in a patient with prepregnant essential hypertension, cardiovascular hypertensive disease, or renal hypertensive disease, ie, the hypertensive disease existed prior to pregnancy. This represents **hypertension complicated by pregnancy (HCP).**

For many decades, these disorders have been called the **toxemias of pregnancy;** the term **gestational hypertensive disorders** is preferable. The term toxemia is an unfortunate misnomer because it implies what is not true—that a toxin circulating in the blood is the cause of these disorders.

The term **eclamptogenic toxemia** is sometimes used to denote **preeclampsia** and **eclampsia.** Eclampsia actually is the most fulminating degree of preeclampsia, characterized by convulsions in addition to the other signs and symptoms of preeclampsia. This spectrum is best referred to as **preeclampsia-eclampsia.** Although the 2 forms of the disorder differ substantially in clinical manifestations and prognosis, the treatment is essentially the same.

Principal Diagnostic Criteria

A. Hypertension: Average systolic/diastolic blood pressure values (in mm Hg) for nonpregnant females are 103/70 at age 10; 120/80 at age 20; 123/82 at age 30; 126/84 at age 40; and 130/86 at age 50. Adult nonpregnant women are considered to be "normotensive" (ie, not hypertensive) with a systolic blood pressure less than 140 mm Hg or a diastolic blood pressure less than 90 mm Hg (or both). There is some variation with age, race, physiologic state, dietary habits, and heredity. Techniques of measurement must be standardized also.

A diagnosis of hypertension can be made only after several separate measurements. Early detection of hypertension in pregnant patients is best achieved by meticulous measurement and recording of blood pressure at each prenatal visit. At subsequent visits, a careful review should be made of these serial blood

pressures; trends and actual elevations become readily apparent when recorded graphically (Table 34–1). There are no proven means of predicting which patients will or will not develop a gestational hypertensive disorder.

Analysis of serial blood pressure measurements as a basis for a diagnosis of hypertension is particularly important in pregnancy, when physical activity, psychologic stress or other stimuli, and endocrine influences often produce circulatory alterations that give rise to transient elevations of arterial blood pressure.

A consistent elevation of diastolic pressure usually warrants a diagnosis of clinical hypertension. Hypertension in pregnant women exists if one or more of the following is present: (1) a systolic pressure of 140 mm Hg or more; (2) a rise of 30 mm Hg or more above the patient's prepregnant systolic level; (3) a diastolic pressure of 90 mm Hg or more; (4) a rise of 15 mm Hg or more above the prepregnant diastolic level. (Comparable criteria for mean arterial pressure are 105 mm Hg or more *or* a rise of 15 mm Hg or more.) Data from over 50,000 pregnancies* have shown that before the 19th week of pregnancy a maternal blood pressure as low as 125/75 mm Hg can have ominous implications if it represents a substantial rise above the prepregnant level.

B. Edema: Edema (excessive accumulation of fluid in tissues) may be either intracellular or only extracellular, ie, in the vascular channels or interstitial spaces. For therapeutic purposes, edema can be viewed primarily as the result of abnormal retention of sodium and water.

C. Proteinuria: Proteinuria is defined as the presence of protein in the urine in concentrations of 300 mg/L or more in a 24-hour collection or 1 g/L or more in a random daytime urine specimen.

Special Problems of Diagnosis

A. Preeclampsia and Eclampsia: Preeclampsia is defined as the occurrence of hypertension (as defined above during pregnancy in the absence of other causes of elevated blood pressure) in combination with generalized edema (including face, neck, and upper

*The Collaborative Project on Neurological Disorders and Blindness, conducted by the Toxemia Task Force of the National Institutes of Health.

Table 34–1. Classification of gestational edema, proteinuria, and hypertension (GEPH).

I. Gestational transient) *E*dema (GEPoHo): Thighs and above.

II. Gestational (transient) *P*roteinuria (GEoPHo):
   A. Twenty-four-hour collections: > 300 mg/L.
   B. Random collections: > 1 g/L (1–2+) in 2 or more specimens obtained 6 hours apart by the clean-catch or catheter method.

III. Gestational (transient) *H*ypertension (GEoPoH):
   A. Mild:
      1. Blood pressure rise of ≥ 30 mm systolic or ≥ 15 mm diastolic, but < 60/30 rise.
      2. If previous blood pressure not known (so that a rise cannot be calculated): Blood pressure of ≥ 140 systolic or ≥ 90 diastolic, but < 170 systolic or 110 diastolic.
   B. Severe:
      1. Blood pressure rise of ≥ 60 mm systolic or ≥ 30 mm diastolic.
      2. If previous blood pressure not known (so that a rise cannot be calculated): Blood pressure of ≥ 170 systolic or ≥ 110 diastolic.

IV. Preeclampsia (GEoPH, GEPoH, GEPH).†

V. Eclampsia: Tonic-clonic convulsions (5% of patients with preeclampsia develop eclampsia).

VI. Preeclampsia-eclampsia (GEPH) superimposed on pregestational hypertension complicated by pregnancy (HCP).

*Gestational *E*dema, *P*roteinuria, and *H*ypertension = GEPH. Specific designation of each one of these disorders is clarified by indicating the absence (indicated by o) or presence of 1 or more of the signs as noted below.

   GEPoHo: Gestational edema, no proteinuria, no hypertension.
   GEoPHo: Gestational proteinuria, no edema, no hypertension.
   GEoPoH: Gestational hypertension, no edema, no proteinuria.
   GEoPH: Preeclampsia (proteinuria and hypertension; no edema).
   GEPoH: Preeclampsia (edema and hypertension; no proteinuria).
   GEPH: Preeclampsia (edema, proteinuria, and hypertension.

†Preeclampsia has traditionally been classified as mild or severe:
   A. Mild:
      1. Blood pressure: ≥ 30/15 mm rise; ≥ 140/90 but < 170/110; or a mean arterial blood pressure of 105 mm or 20 mm rise.
      2. Proteinuria: < 5 g/24 h.
      3. Urine output: > 500 mL/24 h.
      4. Edema: Generalized, but no pulmonary edema or anasarca.
   B. Severe:
      1. Blood pressure: ≥ 170/110; ≥ 60/30 rise, or mean arterial blood pressure of 130 mm, or 40 mm rise.
      2. Proteinuria: > 5 g/24 h.
      3. Urine output: < 500 mL/24 h.
      4. Edema: Massive, generalized; pulmonary edema or anasarca present.

However, if a mother, a fetus, or a newborn infant dies as a result of preeclampsia, it makes no difference whether the degree of the disorder is classified as mild or severe. Because practically all modern and detailed analyses of obstetric data now indicate that preeclampsia is a significant cause of prematurity, perinatal mortality and morbidity, maternal death, and related complications, all forms of preeclampsia should be considered severe. Therefore, any traditional classification that differentiates between mild and severe preeclampsia should be abandoned.

extremities), or proteinuria, or both. When arterial hypertension due to some other disease such as essential hypertension, renal disease, or diabetes mellitus is already present, additional elevation of blood pressure (by the criteria described above) plus edema or proteinuria justifies a diagnosis of superimposed preeclampsia. In both instances, the presence of convulsions or coma warrants the diagnosis of eclampsia. The fact that preeclampsia-eclampsia may be superimposed upon underlying cardiovascular or renal disease does not justify inclusion of the latter in the classification as a hypertensive disorder *of* pregnancy (GEPH), although all such conditions would appear in any listing of hypertensive disorders *in* pregnancy (HCP).

B. Chronic Hypertensive Cardiovascular Disease (Essential Hypertension): It may be difficult to determine whether a patient's hypertension antedates her pregnancy or derives from it if she is first examined after the 20th week of pregnancy. The diagnosis of hypertension unrelated to pregnancy can be made by careful serial evaluations of cardiovascular and renal status during the first 3 months after delivery. Blood pressure elevation that persists for more than 6 weeks after delivery is due to hypertensive disease, because the toxemias usually subside by this time and always—by definition—within 3 months after delivery. (See further discussion under Differential Diagnosis, p 745.)

Classification

Table 34–1 presents a classification of hypertensive states during pregnancy. It must be emphasized that edema alone, or proteinuria alone, or hypertension alone does not justify a diagnosis of preeclampsia. The physician who treats these disorders must have a thorough knowledge of cardiovascular problems (especially hypertension and heart failure), chronic edema and other disturbances of fluid and electrolyte balance, kidney disease, blood disorders, and convulsive disorders. If the primary physician responsible for obstetric care of the patient does not have this knowledge, appropriate consultation or referral is mandatory.

Incidence

The frequency of hypertensive disorders in pregnancy is illustrated in Table 34–2. The overall incidence in obstetric patients in the USA is about 5%.

The following conditions are associated with a higher incidence of preeclampsia-eclampsia:

(1) Primigravidity: There is a higher incidence of toxemia among primigravidas as compared with multiparas, and 65% of cases of preeclampsia-eclampsia occur during the first pregnancy. This incidence is increased even more if the primigravida is young (under 17) or older (over 35).

(2) Multiple pregnancy: The likelihood of preeclampsia-eclampsia increases progressively with the number of fetuses.

(3) Vascular diseases, especially essential hypertension, vascular or hypertensive renal diseases, diabetes mellitus.

Table 34—2. Final diagnoses among 1204 patients initially admitted to hospital with a diagnosis of toxemia of pregnancy.*

Diagnosis	Number	Percentage
No toxemia (8%)	97	8.0
Gestational hypertensive disorders (75.5%)		
Preeclampsia	775	64.4
Eclampsia	21	1.7
Gestational (transient) hypertension (mild)	55	4.6
Gestational (transient) hypertension (severe)	13	1.1
Gestational (transient) edema	32	2.7
Gestational (transient) proteinuria	12	1.0
Hypertensive diseases in pregnancy (15.75%)		
Essential hypertension	87	7.2
Essential hypertension with superimposed mild preeclampsia	51	4.2
Essential hypertension with superimposed severe preeclampsia	21	1.7
Malignant hypertension	6	0.5
Kimmelstiel-Wilson disease	3	0.25
Renal hypertension (1.9%)		
Chronic glomerulotubular nephritis	11	0.95
Acute glomerulotubular nephritis	3	0.25
Chronic pyelonephritis	8	0.7
Pseudopreeclampsia (0.75%)		
Lupus erythematosus, nephrotic syndrome, hyperuricemia, pheochromocytoma	9	0.75

*Author's series. The final diagnosis in each of the 1204 patients was based upon analysis of clinical, laboratory, and research data during the prenatal, intrapartum, and early postpartum courses and during subsequent follow-up 3 and 6 months after delivery. Each patient was admitted with a clinical diagnosis of "toxemia."

(4) **Polyhydramnios,** when it accompanies any of the other conditions that predispose to preeclampsia-eclampsia (most often, multiple pregnancy).

(5) **Hydatidiform mole** predisposes to preeclampsia-eclampsia, and the disease often becomes manifest before the 20th week of pregnancy.

(6) **Dietary deficiencies, severe malnutrition:** Protein deficiencies and probably water-soluble vitamin deficiencies may belong in this category, but there is no convincing proof that specific deficiencies are responsible.

(7) **Familial tendency:** Whether this apparent predisposing factor is genetic or environmental is disputed.

Etiology

The cause of preeclampsia-eclampsia remains unknown. Important areas of suspicion in the past have been protein and other metabolic disturbances, interference with hormonal activity or metabolism by the developing placenta, idiosyncratic features of vascular reactivity, nutritional deficiencies (including protein, calories, sodium, vitamins, and minerals), and smoking. Recent attempts to implicate uteroplacental ischemia have been popular, but this theory is still being examined. Girls delivered of mothers with gestational hypertensive disorders have significantly higher mean blood pressures at age 7 years than girls in the total population. Longer term evaluation by Chesley of daughters and even granddaughters of women who have had eclampsia reveals a higher rate of gestational hypertension in these familial groups.

Pathology

Pathologic changes attributed to preeclampsia-eclampsia are as follows:

A. Blood Vessels: Abnormal vasospasm occurs with preeclampsia-eclampsia. When secondary hypoxia develops, hemorrhage or necrosis may develop in the placenta and other organs.

B. Placenta: Histologic changes in the placenta in acute preeclampsia-eclampsia suggest premature aging. In addition, syncytial degeneration, paravillous hyaline deposition, and congestion of the villous space ensue. Further villous degeneration follows diminution of maternal blood flow to the placenta.

Degeneration and thrombosis of the spiral arterioles in the decidua lead to necrosis of the decidua and hemorrhage into the surrounding tissue.

Grouped early necrosed villi, or red infarcts, appear grossly as darker areas surrounded by light-colored, spongy, normal placental tissue. When a large, laminated clot forms beneath the decidual plate, however, the clot may become a zone of extensive intravillous thrombosis that may lead to premature placental separation.

Areas of placental necrosis are present in about 60% of patients with preeclampsia-eclampsia. However, the histopathologic findings in the placenta do not correlate well with the severity of the disease.

C. Kidney: Unique glomerular changes are characteristic. Swelling of endothelial cells and the deposit of amorphous material in their cytoplasm produce enlargement and swelling of the glomerular capillaries. Thus, the capillary tuft becomes enlarged, but the lumens of the capillaries become narrowed, so that ischemia is striking; interstitial cells between the capillaries proliferate; and the capillary tuft crowds the entire glomerulus. In severe cases, the entire tuft may appear to be vacuolated. With such changes, reduction of glomerular blood flow and glomerular filtration is apparent. The renal tubules usually show varying degrees of tubular necrosis or nonspecific abnormalities secondary to ischemia together with proteinaceous material within the tubular lumens. Interstitial edema generally is secondary to cellular damage.

Complete repair of these lesions usually occurs rapidly after delivery, but occasional patients may develop permanent vascular glomerular damage after eclampsia. Even in those with apparent clinical and laboratory resolution of preeclampsia-eclampsia, electronmicroscopy of the nephron 1 year later reveals persistence of vacuoles that may be of etiologic significance.

In rare cases, severe renal vascular spasm and ischemia may produce extensive arterial thrombosis and infarction resulting in bilateral renal cortical necrosis, which often is fatal.

D. Blood: Disseminated intravascular coagulation may be associated with preeclampsia-eclampsia because of patchy (but often extensive) premature separation of the placenta that initiates progressive consumption coagulopathy. Fibrin microthrombi affect distant organs, most frequently the precapillary renal arterioles. This may lead to local necrosis and hemorrhage. Needle liver biopsies have demonstrated fibrin thrombi in the hepatic periportal system of women who have survived eclampsia. Vascular occlusive damage to the pituitary or hypothalamus may follow acute preeclampsia-eclampsia.

E. Liver: Significant liver damage may occur in eclampsia and in some cases of severe preeclampsia.

The characteristic liver lesion of eclampsia is lobular periportal hemorrhagic necrosis. The necrosis may extend toward the center of the hepatic lobule. The surrounding blood sinuses may be compressed; in other areas, extravasation may occur and fibrin clots may form, especially at the bases of the liver cell columns. These changes are the result of thrombosis in hepatic arterioles—particularly extensive in the small vessels of the periportal system.

F. Brain: Although cerebral edema does occur, it is estimated that small cerebral hemorrhages may affect almost 20% of women with acute preeclampsia-eclampsia. The pons, basal ganglia, and subcortical areas are most often involved.

G. Heart: Subendothelial hemorrhages may discolor the heart in preeclampsia-eclampsia. Fibrin thrombi, focal necrosis, and hemorrhage may also be noted in the myocardium. These patients may develop alterations in the conducting system.

H. Lungs: Almost every patient dying of eclampsia will have pulmonary edema and severe diffuse hemorrhagic bronchial pneumonia.

Pathophysiology

Although numerous abnormalities of physiologic mechanisms occur in patients with preeclampsia-eclampsia, their etiologic role is unclear.

A. Hypertension: Hypertension in preeclampsia is characteristically labile. This probably reflects a demonstrable sensitivity in arteriolar response to pressor amines and peptides of endogenous origin.

Actually, no pressor agent has been found to account for the hypertension that occurs during pregnancy. Renin has been incriminated on theoretic grounds. However, patients with preeclampsia have lower plasma renin levels than are recorded during normal pregnancy in spite of the presence of high concentrations of uterine renin and reninlike enzymes late in pregnancy. On the other hand, renal vein renin may be somewhat higher in occasional patients with preeclampsia than in normal gravidas at the same period of gestation. Moreover, levels of other pressor agents (vasopressin, epinephrine) are not high in preeclampsia-eclampsia. Be this as it may, the arterioles are abnormally sensitive to even normal amounts of angiotensin II (and other vasoconstrictor

agents) in preeclampsia-eclampsia. This sensitivity disappears after delivery.

Sodium retention has been considered as an inciting agent. Even in normal pregnancy, there is considerable sodium retention. This is much greater in preeclampsia when clinical edema and obvious water retention occur. Nevertheless, because marked sodium and water retention can occur in pregnancy without hypertension—and because preeclampsia can occur without significant salt and water retention—it is unlikely that sodium retention alone is the etiologic factor in the production of hypertension.

Other agents that may play a role in preeclampsia include the catecholamines and prostaglandins. The levels of the catecholamines epinephrine and norepinephrine may be above normal in some patients. Prostaglandins are normally produced in the placenta, and the presence of prostaglandin E or I in increased concentration in normal pregnancy may reduce the vasoconstriction produced by angiotensin II. A reduction of these prostaglandins of placental origin in preeclampsia may account for the exaggerated vasoconstriction due to angiotensin II.

Still to be adequately explored is the role of the steroid sex hormones in control of blood pressure during pregnancy, because estrogen, progesterone, or other metabolites may sensitize blood vessels to unidentified pressor substances.

The **roll-over test** has only a slight predictive value in identifying women who will develop preeclampsia. If the pregnant woman's diastolic blood pressure rises by 20 mm Hg or more when she turns from a lateral recumbent to a supine position, then she has a propensity to develop preeclampsia late in pregnancy. This may be due to the altered angiotensin II metabolism when women predisposed to hypertension lie supine.

B. Edema: Edema is common and perhaps even normal during pregnancy. It may be that there is more than one cause of pregnancy edema. Excessive sodium chloride ingestion, hypoproteinemia, mechanical pressure on the leg veins, increased venous pressure, vasopressors, and hormones must all be considered.

Some patients with eclamptogenic toxemia become markedly edematous and remain so until other signs of the disorder subside.

Weight gain alone may be less useful in predicting preeclampsia than a combination of weight gain plus initial blood pressure or weight gain plus a rise of blood pressure between the 20th and 30th weeks of pregnancy. Nonetheless, a sudden gain of weight of 1 kg (2.2 lb) or more in a week or 3 kg (6.6 lb) or more in a month should alert the physician to the possibility that preeclampsia-eclampsia may be developing. On the other hand, failure to gain weight may indicate poor fetal growth and impending fetal death.

C. Sodium Retention: With the physiologic increase in blood volume in pregnancy and with fetal growth, there is commensurate sodium retention. In preeclampsia, the capacity to excrete sodium is impaired beyond what can be accounted for by a decrease

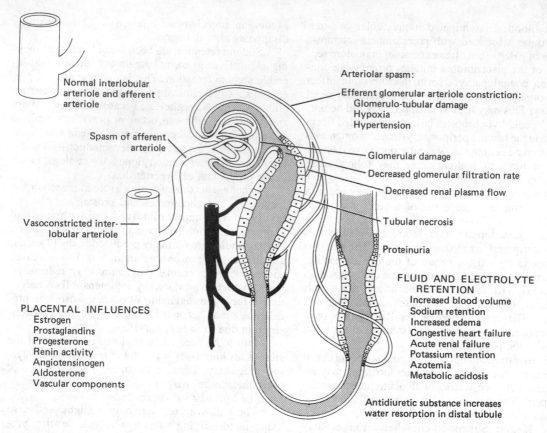

Figure 34–1. The nephron in preeclampsia-eclampsia. Note vasoconstriction of interlobular arterioles and afferent arterioles and effects produced. (Redrawn, with permission, from de Alvarez RR: Managing hypertension in pregnancy. *The Female Patient* [April] 1979;3:78.)

in glomerular filtration rate. Aldosterone secretion increases as normal pregnancy progresses. Aldosterone levels, however, are not demonstrably different in normal pregnancy from levels in women who go on to develop preeclampsia. Furthermore, aldosterone levels decline when preeclampsia occurs. Increased sensitivity to the vasoactive action of ADH on renal circulation may contribute to salt and water retention. Little is known about the contribution of other steroid hormones to the mechanisms of sodium retention.

Careful metabolic studies have shown that patients with preeclampsia given low-sodium diets develop negative sodium balance to the point of hyponatremia requiring the administration of salt. With a high-sodium diet, the positive balance becomes even greater. Salt and water retention persists until a few days following delivery, when spontaneous diuresis occurs. Two conclusions follow: (1) Extra salt intake may be harmless to most normal pregnant women. However, in some instances, additional salt intake may not only contribute to rapid weight gain and increased edema but also may be lethal to the preeclamptic patient and her fetus. (2) Electrolyte metabolism in mild preeclampsia is altered in a manner similar to that in normal pregnancy.

Therefore, normal pregnancy and preeclampsia differ in this regard only in degree.

D. Proteinuria: In proteinuria of preeclampsia-eclampsia, the protein excreted is principally albumin and, in lesser amounts, globulin. These proteins pass through the glomerulus into the urine more rapidly and in larger quantities than can be reabsorbed in the proximal tubules because of glomerular or tubular damage.

Proteinuria alone, independently of hypertension, is associated with increased perinatal mortality rates (Table 34–3). Moreover, proteinuria of preeclampsia-eclampsia accompanies hypertension. It is known that the greatest loss of protein occurs when

Table 34–3. Fetal death rates (per 100,000 pregnancies) for diastolic pressure–proteinuria combinations.*

Diastolic Pressure Maxima	Proteinuria Maxima					
	None	Trace	1+	2+	3+	4+
< 65	15.0	13.8	6.0	–	–	–
65–74	9.0	7.8	4.8	33.0	42.0	–
75–84	6.0	7.8	6.0	19.2	–	–
85–94	9.0	9.0	24.0	–	22.2	–
95–104	19.2	58.0	27.0	55.9	115.2	143.0
105+	19.8	28.2	63.0	69.0	124.8	118.0

*Author's data.

renal involvement is advanced. Proteinuria is a common manifestation of many diseases of the kidney.

Among the proteins lost in the urine is angiotensinase, which inactivates angiotensin II. Thus, in spite of the gradual increase of angiotensinase levels after the 20th week of pregnancy, the loss of angiotensinase in the urine may reduce the rate of inactivation of angiotensin II and contribute to hypertension.

E. Cerebral Function: Cerebral blood flow is normal in preeclampsia but is reduced during the coma of eclampsia. Cerebral dysrhythmia is common in preeclampsia and is manifested as hyperreflexia. Increased vascular resistance in the brain may account for the dulled sensorium of preeclamptic patients. Eclamptogenic convulsions are caused by abnormal stimulation of motor areas of the brain and often begin as localized twitching. The stimuli are derived from acute vasospasm resulting in cerebral ischemia. Bizarre generalized convulsions may reflect extensive cerebral edema or hemorrhage. The coma probably is produced by edema, hypoxia, or biochemical alterations of the central nervous system.

F. Ophthalmic Function: Central nervous system dysfunction may cause visual disturbances that accompany preeclampsia. Scotomas are usually manifestations of extensive primary, generalized vascular disease; they are not commonly reported by patients with preeclampsia-eclampsia alone. Hypertensive retinopathy may cause arteriolar spasm, ischemia, edema, and, rarely, retinal detachment. The most frequently reported finding is arteriolar spasm, which first produces constrictions of the arterioles, in segmental fashion. These spindle-shaped distortions usually are located in the first half of the retinal arteriole near the optic disk. An arteriolar spasm may reduce the normal ratio of vein-arteriole diameter from 3:2 to 3:1 or more. The firmly contracted arteriolar spasm accounts for arteriovenous "nicking" and endothelial vasculopathy.

Edema of the retina occurs almost as frequently as spasm of the arterioles. This edema presents as a mirror-like reflection of light from the ophthalmoscope; it constitutes an early sign of preeclampsia. Retinal hemorrhages and exudates may develop rarely during eclampsia and advanced preeclampsia; they are usually manifestations of pronounced hypertension. Even though these ocular changes may clear completely, these patients should be evaluated at least annually after the pregnancy for evidence of essential hypertension or renal disease.

Retinal detachment is a rare and potentially serious ocular complication of preeclampsia-eclampsia. Daily ophthalmoscopic examinations may be rewarded by the diagnosis of this and other ophthalmic disorders. If the macula is detached, the prognosis is poor. Papilledema always suggests malignant hypertension or intracranial disease. The finding of any funduscopic abnormality always mandates immediate ophthalmologic consultation. Fortunately, eye changes during pregnancy are usually completely reversible, and normal vision should return in 3 weeks or less. Permanent blindness rarely follows preeclampsia or eclampsia; when it does, it is almost always due to primary disorders unrelated to the pregnancy.

Clinical Findings

The signs of preeclampsia are insidious in onset. It is of the utmost importance that regular visits to a physician for prenatal care start early in pregnancy for the prevention, early detection, and treatment of preeclampsia. The achievement of this goal depends upon education of the public as well as the medical profession.

A. Preeclampsia:

1. Symptoms and signs—Hypertension is the most significant primary sign of preeclampsia. The diastolic blood pressure is more reliable than the systolic because it is less susceptible to extrinsic influences. Any repeated or constant elevation of the diastolic pressure of 15 mm Hg or more above the prepregnancy level must be regarded as hypertension. This is also true of elevations of 30 mm Hg or more of systolic pressure. Nevertheless, readings are dependable only when obtained under relatively basal conditions. Such elevation of blood pressure, when not accompanied by either of the other 2 cardinal signs of preeclampsia (edema and proteinuria), suggests that the clinical complication is imminent. The diagnosis is confirmed when hypertension is accompanied by edema or proteinuria. The same is true of persistent elevation of diastolic pressure to 90 mm Hg or more in a patient without prior hypertension.

Diastolic blood pressure levels of 110 mm Hg and systolic levels of 180 mm Hg are frequently encountered in severe preeclampsia, but systolic levels over 200 mm Hg are rare. These usually reflect the presence of essential hypertension.

The cardiovascular components of preeclampsia-eclampsia, especially increased peripheral vascular resistance, may compromise cardiac reserve seriously.

Sudden excessive weight gain is a common first sign of impending or actual preeclampsia. It often develops before the hypertension appears. A gain of more than 1 kg (2.2 lb) in a week or 3 kg (6.6 lb) in a month is generally regarded as significant. Gradual increases of weight of up to 0.25–0.5 kg (0.5–1 lb) per week are normal in pregnancy; the weight gain in preeclampsia (or just before it becomes overt) usually is sudden because it is due almost entirely to retention of fluid. The gain may be noted even before the generalized edema of preeclampsia becomes apparent. As the actual disease becomes manifest and progresses, gains of as much as 5 kg (11 lb) per week frequently occur. When significant edema and proteinuria exist in the absence of hypertension, subsequent and significant elevation of blood pressure is possible or imminent.

Ordinarily, edema is first noted in the lower legs, and a small degree of this is normal in many normal pregnant women. As fluid retention progresses to imminent or frank preeclampsia, however, the patient is likely to note puffiness around the eyes and tightness of finger rings, particularly on arising in the morning.

Examination then demonstrates pitting edema, present over the sacrum and deep over the pretibial surfaces.

Headache, either frontal or occipital, is the principal symptom of preeclampsia-eclampsia. The frequency and severity of headache increase as preeclampsia worsens. Constant severe headache is a warning of an impending convulsion.

In the late stage of preeclampsia, the development of epigastric pain may signal the imminence of convulsions. Its cause is not clear.

Patients with liver disorders rarely manifest significant hepatic insufficiency, because of hepatic reserve and regeneration even during the height of eclampsia. Nevertheless, right upper quadrant pain and intrahepatic hemorrhage may occur with rupture of the capsule, followed by intraperitoneal bleeding—an acute surgical emergency.

2. Laboratory findings–Protein usually appears in the urine after the hypertension of preeclampsia becomes manifest. Proteinuria is always an important finding, even in trace amounts. The amount varies greatly, but, when careful determination reveals more than 300 mg/L in a 24-hour collection or more than 1 g/L in a random sample of urine, this is significant proteinuria. Proteinuria is usually the last of the 3 major signs of preeclampsia to appear.

Oliguria is common, and anuria may develop. Hyaline and granular casts may occur but do not commonly appear in the urine of the patient with eclamptogenic toxemia. Epithelial casts, isolated renal cells, and red blood cells may also be seen.

Blood chemistry determinations should be performed to assess renal function and changes characteristic of eclampsia. In eclampsia, about 75% of patients show laboratory evidence of altered liver function. If the patient recovers, hepatic dysfunction is extremely rare. One of the characteristic changes is an unusual elevation of serum uric acid concentration as a result of diminished renal clearance.

Cryofibrinogen appears in the circulating blood of pregnant women, but much more of this partially polymerized fibrinogen is present during preeclampsia-eclampsia. Cryofibrinogenemia also occurs with disseminated intravascular coagulation. After delivery, however, the cryofibrinogenemia rapidly disappears.

In the presence of disseminated intravascular coagulation, the components of blood coagulation in plasma are depleted.

3. Other examinations–The retinal changes of preeclampsia are described above. The patient will have no eye complaints except in the most severe cases, when blurring of vision or scotomas develop. However, retinal edema and arteriolar changes may be seen on ophthalmoscopic examination early in the development of preeclampsia-eclampsia.

In severe preeclampsia, hyperreflexia may be an important sign because its progressive increase implies the threat of imminent convulsions. It is therefore important in the management of the patient with preeclampsia to test the deep tendon reflexes at intervals. Increasing hyperreflexia often is accompanied by apprehension, restlessness, and excitability.

B. Eclampsia: When the cardinal signs of acute preeclampsia worsen and headache, epigastric pain, marked visual disturbances, or hyperreflexia appears, severe preeclampsia exists and eclampsia may be imminent. The diagnosis of eclampsia is warranted only for patients who have preeclampsia and then develop convulsions or coma. This supports the concept that preeclampsia and eclampsia are progressive gradations of the same pathologic process.

Eclamptic convulsions are rarely preceded by an aura. Epigastric pain or tightness in the chest may be premonitory symptoms. Often the first sign is a fixed stare and turning of the head to one side. The pupils are usually dilated. Muscular twitchings of the mouth and face mark the **stage of invasion** of the convulsion, which lasts only a few seconds.

The **stage of contraction** lasts not more than 30 seconds. Simultaneous contraction of all muscles produces opisthotonos, distortion of the face, protrusion of the eyes, clenching of the jaws and hands, and extension of the limbs.

The sequence then passes quickly into the **stage of convulsion,** which lasts approximately 1 minute. The convulsive phase may manifest itself as a single abnormal contraction of voluntary muscles or as a series of paroxysmal contractions of muscle groups. Thus, it is important that observers not overlook or minimize a single episode. The convulsive movements usually are obvious, and they may be accompanied by exaggerated smooth muscle activity, eg, vomiting or fecal or urinary incontinence. Suddenly, all the muscles of the body begin to contract and relax in clonic fashion, so violently that the patient may injure herself. The face is suffused and the eyes bloodshot. A foam, sometimes bloody, issues from the mouth; when it does, it is important to determine whether pulmonary edema is present. The jaws open and close so violently that protection against biting the tongue is essential. The diaphragm becomes immobile, and death by respiratory arrest may seem imminent. As the clonic contractions gradually subside, the patient draws a long, stertorous breath, resumes respiration, and usually lapses into coma. In some cases, coma may be due to profound acidosis or hyperosmolality (particularly when the patient has been overtreated with hyperosmolar agents).

The entire ictal episode may include only a single convulsion, especially if it occurs late in labor or during the puerperium. In mild cases there are usually 1–2 convulsions; in severe ones, 20 or more. In rare instances, seizures follow one another so closely that the patient appears to be having one continuous convulsion.

The duration of coma varies greatly. The obstetrician must rule out other causes of coma, eg, drug abuse or iatrogenic overdosage with narcotics, sedatives, and other medications. If convulsions do not occur too frequently, the patient may regain consciousness between them. Amnesia for the convulsion is an invariable feature. In severe cases, coma is continuous between convulsions, and coma progressively deepens in terminal cases. Only rarely do coma and death follow a single convulsion.

In eclampsia, the immediate cause of death may be pulmonary edema, central nervous system hemorrhage, or cardiac failure. Death several days after convulsions may be caused by aspiration pneumonia, liver failure, stroke, or acute renal failure.

The blood pressure usually is markedly elevated in eclampsia. Increases of at least 60 mm Hg systolic and 30 mm Hg diastolic are to be expected. Nevertheless, in a rare patient (usually young and with a normally low pressure), the entire eclamptogenic episode may transpire without the systolic pressure ever reaching 140 mm Hg or the diastolic pressure 90 mm Hg. This is where eclampsia occurs in patients with a "normal" blood pressure; it is therefore important to know what the blood pressure was before pregnancy or during the first trimester of pregnancy.

Infections (eg, pulmonary, urinary) may produce fever. In the absence of infection, a third of patients will have a temperature elevated to at least 38.5 °C (101.3 °F). A temperature of 39.5 °C (103.2 °F) or higher is a serious prognostic sign.

Respirations are usually rapid and stertorous during the coma of eclampsia. Such hyperventilation may cause serious respiratory alkalosis. In severe eclampsia, cyanosis often develops. Pulmonary edema is a serious complication of eclampsia, frequently developing shortly before death. Cyanosis, tachycardia, and hypotension are typical of the terminal stage. Convulsions may progressively decline and cease completely just before death. In other instances, death due to cerebral hemorrhage may occur suddenly.

In antepartum eclampsia, labor usually begins shortly after the onset of convulsions. As a rule, its progress is so rapid that vigorous and skillful management is required. Convulsions during labor tend to accelerate its course. After delivery, the coma of eclampsia may last from a few hours to several days. As the patient regains consciousness, she may be disoriented, irrational, and belligerent and must be managed accordingly.

In some cases, labor does not begin after the onset of convulsions. If the seizures cease, the patient may regain consciousness and be much improved. When this state persists for more than 1 day, the condition is called **intercurrent eclampsia.** Some regard this as a form of arrested or reversed eclampsia. However, most patients with this problem will continue to have hypertension, proteinuria, or edema (though the degree may be less), so that the clinical picture is suggestive of a return to preeclampsia rather than to normal. Moreover, these patients frequently develop convulsions again. Such recurrent convulsions are likely to be more severe, and death is an even greater threat. The danger of such a relapse must be recognized, but one may gain time during this phase of intercurrent eclampsia to institute proper treatment and delivery.

The first evidence of recovery from eclampsia often is an increase in urinary output. Proteinuria and edema may then subside over a period of several days. Normal blood pressure may not be established until at least 2 weeks after delivery.

After coma clears, 1–2% of patients with eclamptogenic toxemia note dimness of vision. This usually lasts less than a week. Even patchy hemorrhagic retinitis or partial retinal detachment has a good prognosis for recovery.

In the recovery period after eclampsia, about 5% of patients develop acute postpartum toxic psychosis. This problem seems to be extremely rare with current management, suggesting that the "psychoses" are probably due to prolonged overmedication. Unless the patient has a history of significant mental illness, the prognosis is good. Rarely, cerebral hemorrhage may cause permanent neurologic damage. Impaired cerebral function, paralysis, and pituitary necrosis are rare sequelae.

Coagulation Defects & Anticoagulation

Coagulation defects may occur in occasional patients with hypertensive disorders of pregnancy. Coagulopathy may be manifested as disseminated intravascular coagulation; as thrombosis in the legs, pelvis, brain, or mesentery; or as embolization.

Coagulation defects may be initiated by placental abruption, amniotic fluid embolism, gram-negative sepsis, primary heart disease, or chronic pulmonary disease, all of which may occur as complications of any pregnancy. Premature separation of the placenta, however, occurs with increased frequency in patients with preeclampsia-eclampsia. Moreover, disseminated intravascular coagulation develops more often in patients with abruptio placentae than in normal gravidas. Thus, disseminated intravascular coagulation that follows placental abruption in eclampsia has been incorrectly interpreted to be a manifestation of the hypertensive disorder itself. This misinformation has led some physicians to treat eclampsia with heparin. Since preeclampsia-eclampsia does *not* cause coagulation defects, heparin is *not* a part of the treatment of these gestational hypertensive disorders per se. The indications for the use of heparin and other anticoagulant drugs in the preeclamptic or eclamptic patient are the same as in any other obstetric patient.

Differential Diagnosis

A. Chronic Hypertensive Vascular Disease: When essential hypertension is complicated by pregnancy, it often is mistaken for preeclampsia. Final differentiation depends upon the persistence of the hypertension—transient in preeclampsia-eclampsia, permanent in essential hypertension. Whether or not hypertension is present prior to or early in pregnancy, its persistence for more than 3 months postpartum establishes the diagnosis of chronic hypertensive vascular disease.

Hypertension recorded before the 20th week of pregnancy (except in the case of hydatidiform mole) is almost certainly due to essential hypertension. On the

Table 34–4. Differential diagnosis of essential hypertension and preeclampsia.

Features	Essential Hypertension	Preeclampsia
Onset of hypertension	Before pregnancy; during first 20 weeks of pregnancy	After 20th week of pregnancy (exception: trophoblastic tumors)
Duration of hypertension	Permanent. Hypertension persists beyond 3 months postpartum	Hypertension usually absent at 6 weeks postpartum; always by 3 months postpartum
Family history	Often positive	Usually negative; may be positive
Past history	Recurrent "toxemia"	Psychosexual problems common
Age	Usually older	Generally teenage, early 20s
Parity	Usually multigravida	Usually primigravida
Habitus	May be thin or brachymorphic	Usually eumorphic
Retinal findings	Often arteriovenous nicking, tortuous arterioles, cotton wool exudates, hemorrhages	Vascular spasm, retinal edema; rarely, protein extravasations
Proteinuria	Often none	Usually present (see definition); absent at 6 weeks postpartum

other hand, if a patient who manifests signs and symptoms of acute preeclampsia is first seen late in pregnancy, a tentative diagnosis of underlying essential hypertension must be entertained pending definitive studies 6–12 weeks after delivery. Preeclampsia superimposed upon essential hypertension carries a grave prognosis for both mother and infant and is more difficult to manage than preeclampsia alone. The features that may aid in the differentiation of these disorders are listed in Table 34–4.

B. Primary Renal Disease: Only thorough diagnostic study can differentiate primary renal disease from toxemia of pregnancy. The initial case history may reveal prior episodes of upper urinary tract infection or conditions that might be sequelae of underlying renal disease, eg, late abortion, premature delivery, or atypical "toxemia" in prior pregnancies. Proper laboratory tests are required for definitive diagnosis.

An important first step is examination of a clean-catch midstream urine specimen. Pyuria and bacteriuria (more than 10^5 organisms/mL) indicate urinary tract infection. Renal function tests (eg, creatinine clearance) may demonstrate diminished function, but this may be masked by the normally increased glomerular filtration rate during pregnancy. Indeed, after the 20th week of pregnancy, renal function tests that give normal (nonpregnant) values suggest the possibility of underlying renal damage except in the presence of preeclampsia, when they are consistently depressed. In perplexing cases, renal biopsy should be considered.

1. Acute glomerulonephritis–The signs and symptoms of acute glomerulonephritis are similar to those of preeclampsia. Therefore, acute glomerulonephritis is diagnosed correctly more often in early pregnancy than in late pregnancy. A correct differential diagnosis is important, because even brief episodes of acute glomerulonephritis of mild degree may result in spontaneous abortion or premature delivery and because the disease may be aggravated by pregnancy itself. If the disorder is severe or lasts more than 2 weeks, interruption of pregnancy may be advisable. Nonetheless, further pregnancies are not contraindi-

cated after healed acute glomerulonephritis unless severe renal damage has occurred.

Like preeclampsia, acute severe glomerulonephritis can be complicated by pulmonary edema, acute renal failure, or hypertensive encephalopathy.

Signs and symptoms similar to those of acute glomerulonephritis may occur in a variety of diseases, eg, subacute infective endocarditis and the collagen diseases, especially disseminated lupus erythematosus.

2. Chronic glomerulonephritis–Patients with chronic glomerulonephritis generally are asymptomatic for years, the only evidence of the disease being proteinuria and the abnormal components of the urinary sediment seen in acute glomerulonephritis.

When hypertension becomes a feature of chronic glomerulonephritis, pregnancy tends to exacerbate the disease and to accelerate deterioration of renal function. The disorder may then resemble preeclampsia. The most valuable differential diagnostic signs are hematuria, retinal hemorrhages and exudates, and abnormalities of urinary sediment. With clinically mild disease, elevated levels of blood urea nitrogen and creatinine or the presence of lipidemia or hypoproteinemia may be suggestive. Not infrequently, the differential diagnosis must be made by renal biopsy when there is urgent need to select therapy and assess prognosis.

The prognosis for the pregnant patient with chronic glomerulonephritis depends upon the degree of hypertension and renal impairment. As with acute glomerulonephritis, the perinatal mortality rate is high. Continuation of the pregnancy may greatly increase renal damage, so that interruption often is the best treatment. This is particularly true when hypertension is severe and when azotemia develops.

3. Nephrosis–The fact that nephrosis is rarely diagnosed in pregnancy probably reflects the lack of a satisfactory definition or the inability of the physician to recognize it. The nephrotic syndrome is characterized by gross edema, massive proteinuria (over 5 g/24 h), hematuria, impaired renal function, and a distinctive urinary sediment that contains oval doubly

Table 34—5. Differential diagnosis of nephrosis and preeclampsia.

	Nephrosis	Preeclampsia
Onset	Any trimester	After 20 weeks (exception: trophoblastic tumors)
Proteinuria	Massive	Variable (as defined)
Edema	Usually marked	Variable
Hypertension	Commonly absent	Present
Hematuria	Usually microscopic	Absent
Serum cholesterol	Greatly elevated	Same as normal pregnancy
Hypoproteinemia	Marked	Decreased below normal pregnancy
Alpha- and beta-globulins	Decreased	Increased
Glomerular filtration rate	Decreased, normal, or increased	Decreased
Urinary sediment	Usually oval, doubly refractile fat bodies, fatty casts, waxy casts	Absent

refractile fat bodies and fatty and waxy casts. Nephrosis may develop in the course of a variety of diseases, including acute glomerulonephritis, diabetes mellitus, the collagen disorders, syphilis, malaria, and thrombosis of the renal vein. In any of these, pregnancy may be a clinical "complication." Pregnancy may worsen the nephrotic syndrome (1) by thromboembolization caused by increased fibrinogen or decreased antithrombin, or (2) by infection resulting indirectly from hypogammaglobulinemia. Pregnancy does not usually further impair renal function, however, so interruption of pregnancy is rarely indicated.

Differential diagnosis of nephrosis from preeclampsia usually can be established presumptively by the criteria outlined in Table 34—5. When a definitive diagnosis is essential, renal biopsy usually is required. Generally, this shows a thickened glomerular membrane, lipid deposits in endothelial cells, hyaline material and red blood cells in Bowman's capsule, and degeneration of the tubular epithelium in nephrosis. If the biopsy shows obliteration of capillary loops by glomerular hyalinization or if hypertension, marked renal insufficiency, or uremia develops, prompt termination of pregnancy must be considered to avert further kidney damage.

C. Convulsive Disorders: Convulsions are paroxysmal alterations of central nervous system function, usually sudden in onset and commonly involving or followed by changes in the state of consciousness.

Convulsions may be produced by many disorders other than eclampsia, and most of these can coexist with pregnancy. Consider any of the following: grand mal or petit mal epilepsy, chronic renal failure, organic brain damage, central nervous system tumors, hypoglycemia, hypocalcemia (of parathyroid or renal origin), and hemolytic crisis of sickle cell anemia. The most important aspect of care is correct diagnosis.

Ruptured intracranial aneurysm and subarachnoid hemorrhage should be suspected in any case of convulsion occurring in a pregnant woman or one who has recently given birth if there is a history of sudden severe headache, neck stiffness, and nausea and vomiting. Immediate neurosurgical consultation is mandatory. Meanwhile, if spinal fluid obtained by lumbar puncture reveals the presence of bloody or xanthochromic fluid, the diagnosis of subarachnoid hemorrhage is confirmed, and neurosurgical consultation is in order. Of special concern in recent years is the production of convulsions by acute or chronic abuse of drugs such as LSD and amphetamines. Convulsions may also be caused by water intoxication from excessive therapeutic hydration or by the low sodium syndrome induced by therapeutic abuse of diuretics. Acute poisoning by various agents may cause convulsions, eg, strychnine, phosphorus, or nitrobenzol. The differentiation of eclampsia from other causes of convulsions in pregnancy is not usually difficult. Other causes of convulsions in pregnancy almost always are accompanied by other distinctive manifestations and are usually *not* accompanied by marked edema or proteinuria, though hypertension is not uncommon.

D. Coma: Most descriptions of the terminal clinical course of patients who have died consist of familiar phrasing such as the following: "The patient experienced a gradual downhill course, eventually continuing into convulsions, coma, and death." Since convulsions and coma are common features in the patient with eclamptogenic toxemia, it is important that the obstetrician be familiar with some of the other clinical possibilities that must be differentiated from eclampsia. Among the causes that must be considered in the pregnant patient are the following:

1. Alcoholism—Coma not deep, hyperpnea, pupils dilated and equal, blood alcohol 200 mg/dL or more.

2. Acidosis (diabetic; metabolic)—Gradual onset, Kussmaul breathing, skin dry, dehydration, hyperglycemia in diabetes, electrolyte imbalance.

3. Azotemia—Deep coma, acute renal failure, chronic renal disease.

4. Cranial trauma—Local evidence of injury, bloody cerebrospinal fluid, positive skull x-ray.

5. Drug intoxication—Personality problems, cyanosis, muscle twitching, sluggish reflexes. Identify drug by study of gastric contents or specific testing.

6. Epilepsy—History, sudden onset, vital signs and blood pressure usually normal.

7. Hypoglycemia—Acute onset, sweating, nausea and vomiting, abdominal pain, low plasma glucose.

8. Stroke—Usually over age 35 but may be very young; history of cardiovascular disease or hypertension; hemiplegia, unequal pupils.

9. Syncope—Sudden onset, emotional crises, initial bradycardia.

E. Pheochromocytoma: Pheochromocytoma is a relatively rare catecholamine-producing tumor that arises from the chromaffin cells of the sympathoadrenal system, usually in the adrenal gland but also along the sympathetic nervous chain in aberrant, sometimes multiple locations. The catecholamine secretion produces hypertension of a fluctuating, paroxysmal type, although rarely it may be sustained.

Because of the hypertension and headache, pheochromocytoma may be confused temporarily with preeclampsia, but its other striking manifestations help to clarify the diagnosis promptly. Especially indicative is the extreme sweating, which occurs only in pheochromocytoma (that of hyperthyroidism is much less). In addition, the wide fluctuations of blood pressure, postural hypotension (in 70% of cases), paradoxic response to autonomic blocking agents, elevated basal metabolic rate, abnormal glucose tolerance, high hematocrit, and rapid progressive weight loss help to differentiate this problem from preeclampsia. Elevated levels of plasma and of urinary catecholamines are diagnostic of pheochromocytoma.

F. Other Disorders: Other conditions that may be confused with gestational hypertensive disorders include poisoning, lupus erythematosus, gout, hyperaldosteronism, hypoglycemia, alkalosis, Cushing's syndrome, and coarctation of the aorta. Until the diagnosis is clarified, these problems are categorized as pseudopreeclampsia, since their clinical manifestations may simulate those of preeclampsia or eclampsia.

Prevention

In the past half-century, good prenatal care has become available to more and more women. This has contributed to lowering the incidence of preeclampsia-eclampsia to less than 2% of patients seeking early and adequate prenatal care. The features of obstetric management responsible for this great improvement must embrace all of the possible etiologic factors, because the relative importance of individual ones is unknown. The important aspects of obstetric care are visits to the physician at least monthly for the first 6 months of pregnancy for urinalysis and evaluation of blood pressure, weight, and possible edema. These observations should be repeated every 2 weeks in the seventh and eighth months of pregnancy and every week in the last month. In addition to watching carefully for signs and symptoms of preeclampsia at these visits, the physician should be alert for evidence of other medical, surgical, or obstetric diseases.

Prevention of preeclampsia-eclampsia probably depends ultimately upon the maintenance of good nutrition, optimal water and electrolyte balance, and emotional stability. These subjects are discussed more fully in Chapter 29 and elsewhere in this text.

General Considerations in Treatment

The objectives of the treatment of preeclampsia are (1) to prevent eclampsia, (2) to reduce vasospasm, (3) to avoid vascular accidents (central nervous system, renal, ophthalmic), and (4) to ensure delivery of a normal live baby. These objectives may be accomplished by measures designed to correct or at least stabilize altered physiology and by termination of

pregnancy at the optimal time. Early in the third trimester, a compromise between these 2 modalities may be unavoidable, and attempts may be made to postpone delivery until the fetus is mature enough to survive outside the uterus. On the other hand, when preeclampsia worsens rapidly despite therapeutic efforts, it may be necessary to terminate pregnancy to protect the mother, accepting as unavoidable the almost certain neonatal loss.

A. Home Care: All patients with preeclampsia require hospitalization. Some may be managed in an intermediate care nursing unit. No case of preeclampsia should be considered to be mild.

As a rule, all patients with GEPH should be hospitalized for control and investigation, since convulsions can occur suddenly despite good supervision. Eclampsia in the home setting—or even delay in admitting the patient with preeclampsia to the hospital—greatly increases the chances of maternal or fetal death.

The patient, if sent home from the hospital, should be examined at least twice a week by the physician or nurse practitioner to note any change in her condition that might require rehospitalization. It is essential that she (and persons caring for her at home) be properly warned regarding ominous signs or symptoms: edema, headache, visual disturbances, undue irritability or hyperreactivity, poor sleep, decreased urinary output, epigastric pain.

B. Hospital Care: Patients with overt preeclampsia must be hospitalized at once. This applies also to any patient who simply develops hypertension of 150/100 mm Hg or more or proteinuria of 1 g/24 h or more. Patients with lesser degrees of hypertension should be hospitalized without hesitation if, in addition, they develop any of the following: proteinuria of 1+ or more, increasing edema, decreased renal clearances (creatinine/urate), oliguria or anuria, persistent or severe headache, blurred vision, nausea and vomiting, epigastric pain. Hospital facilities are needed for the treatment and further investigation of all these features.

C. Principles of Management: The principles of the management of preeclampsia and of eclampsia are as follows:

1. Treatment to correct specific manifestations—

a. Reduction of nervous system irritability.

b. Reduction of hypertension.

c. Correction of water imbalance, acid-base imbalance, and other types of electrolyte disorder or abnormality.

d. Prevention or termination of convulsions.

e. Prevention or treatment of fetal or placental complications.

2. Differential diagnosis and treatment of other (coincidental) conditions.

3. Obstetric choices—

a. Whether, when, and how to induce labor.

b. Method of delivery after spontaneous labor.

c. Election of cesarean section.

Emergency Treatment

Because eclampsia is the final stage of preeclampsia, treatment of the latter takes on added importance in the prevention of convulsions. Convulsions can almost always be avoided if the patient receives proper management early enough in the course of the disease. Nevertheless, one must always be prepared for the occurrence of fulminant convulsions.

Next to acute hemorrhage, control of convulsions presents the most hazardous and one of the most startling emergencies in obstetrics. All preeclamptic patients should be in the hospital with an intravenous line in place to provide access for emergency transfusion. The principal consideration during the convulsive phase of eclampsia is to assure a patent airway. Adequate oxygenation must then be provided. This may be accomplished in most patients (after placing the patient in the Trendelenburg position) by simple manipulation and extension of the head, neck, and mandible and by suctioning the mouth and pharynx. If this does not suffice, oxygenation may be attempted with a nasopharyngeal or an oropharyngeal airway, an esophageal obturator airway, oral or nasal endotracheal intubation, or even tracheostomy. Of great concern is the possibility of aspiration of gastric contents. Anesthesiologists and some obstetricians have experience in the use of cuffed endotracheal tubes to provide reasonable protection against aspiration. The patient should be treated by the most experienced physician available.

Once the airway is secured, breathing must be maintained. Spontaneous respiration and oxygenation should be confirmed by arterial blood gas studies. Oxygenation by a self-inflating resuscitation bag may be required. Seizures increase oxygen consumption and can reduce available oxygen, especially to the maternal brain. Hypoxemia causes anaerobic metabolism. This results in lactic acid production and metabolic (lactic) acidosis in mother and fetus.

During the hospital management of the patient with eclamptogenic toxemia, a cart or tray with materials and equipment for dealing with eclamptogenic seizures or with acute renal failure must always be instantly available. A list of drugs and supplies that should be at the bedside of an eclamptic or preeclamptic patient appears in Table 34–6. Electronic equipment for both maternal and fetal monitoring is mandatory. Examinations should include frequent measurements of blood pressure, auscultation of the chest, testing of tendon reflexes, observation for hyperactivity or trend toward coma, and evaluation of fetal heart tones, fetal measurements by ultrasound, and uterine contractions. Digitalization may be required if signs of impending congestive heart failure develop. Administration of oxygen may be needed by a patient with tachycardia, cyanosis, pulmonary edema, or reduced pulse pressure. Supervision of fluid intake and output should be the responsibility of a single individual. Intubation or tracheostomy may be required for laryngotracheal obstruction. If shock develops, it may be necessary to monitor central venous pressure or to

Table 34–6. Drugs and equipment for the treatment of patients with eclampsia.

Drugs
Magnesium sulfate—(2 ampules), 10 mL/ampule (5 g, 50%) 500 mg (4 mEq) per mL
Sodium bicarbonate—50 mL (7.5%) = 44.6 mEq
Hydralazine—(5 ampules), 20 mg/ampule
Heparin sodium—(10 mL), 5000 USP units/mL
Diazepam—(2 mL), 5 mg/mL
Chlordiazepoxide—(5 mL), 20 mg/mL
Epinephrine 1:1000 (1 mg/mL)
Atropine sulfate—0.4 mg/0.5 mL
Atropisol, 1% (mydriatic)
Sterile water ampules
Sterile normal saline ampules
Calcium gluconate, 10% (1 g/10 mL) 10 mL = 97 mg (4.8 mEq) Ca^{2+}
Phenytoin—(2 mL), 50 mg/mL
Propranolol—(tablets), 40 mg
Intravenous barbiturates

Supplies	
Needles—2-inch and 3-inch (22-, 20-, 18-gauge)	Tourniquet
Padded tongue blade	Syringes—50-mL, 10-mL, 2-mL
Airway	Reflex hammer
Cut-down	

institute intermittent positive pressure breathing. Central venous pressure lines are reserved for the patient in shock; these procedures are unnecessary or overly aggressive for standard management.

At all times, the physician must render treatment based upon the individual patient's requirements—no matter how much they diverge from standard criteria—rather than rely blindly upon a set pattern of management.

Treatment of Preeclampsia-Eclampsia

A. Environmental Management: Many patients hospitalized with a gestational hypertensive disorder or even hypertension complicated by pregnancy become normotensive after 5–7 days of bed rest. It is this group that should be carefully evaluated before discharge from the hospital in order not to overlook diagnoses such as latent chronic hypertensive disease, latent renal disease, collagen diseases, pheochromocytoma, and other diseases of which lability of blood pressure may be the most prominent sign.

In the hospital, the patient with preeclampsia should be kept alone in a single room. Her eyes should be shielded from strong light, the room must be quiet, and other stimuli should be minimized for fear of precipitating a convulsion. However, the room must be lighted well enough to permit good observation of the patient. The necessary examinations and special tests should be done at judicious intervals—4 times daily and as needed—with a minimum of disturbance to the patient.

No visitors other than the husband or other close relative should be allowed, and visits should be only long enough to give the patient emotional reinforcement without tiring her. If visits disturb the patient, they should be curtailed or forbidden. The patient with eclampsia should be treated similarly with the exception that she should not be left unattended at any time; hence, a special nurse is required for her care.

For the patient with eclampsia, complete restriction to bed in a lateral or lateral recumbent position is essential, and bed rails must be in place. This is also true for the patient with preeclampsia, although, if her disease is stabilized or improving and adequate precautions for measuring urinary output are present, she may be allowed the use of a commode in her room. Bathroom privileges should be forbidden until she is no longer under sedation or under the influence of other drugs that will affect her sensorium. To aid in the observation of fluid balance, a special bed scale may be used in the patient's room.

B. Diet: For the patient with preeclampsia, the diet should be neutral ash and high-protein (100 g/d or more), with a caloric intake of approximately 1600 kcal/d. Excess alkaline ash in the diet predisposes to edema enhanced by vasoconstriction. In the presence of massive edema, salt intake should be restricted to less than 0.5 g/d.

C. Fluids and Electrolytes: Initial intake of fluid should be based upon the need to combat dehydration. Once this is corrected, further fluid intake should be guided by observation of fluid balance. Therefore, a careful record of fluid intake and output is essential. An indwelling catheter should be used as necessary to measure urine output.

During the first 24 hours, the patient should receive a challenge of at least 1500 mL of fluid if she is dehydrated or if significant hypovolemia has been measured. Thereafter, if she is not dehydrated, daily intake of fluid should approximate the amount of urinary output in the previous 24 hours plus 1000 mL. (In acute renal failure, total fluid intake should not exceed 500 mL.) Intake of fluids should be oral, if possible. When it must be parenteral, 5% dextrose in water may be used. At the same time, volume control and osmotic pressure should be monitored. While it is true that blood volume in normal pregnancy is greater than in the nonpregnant state, it must also be remembered that blood volume in preeclampsia is reduced when compared to normal pregnancy at the same duration of pregnancy. If plasma colloidal osmotic pressure is reduced in the preeclamptic patient, colloid fluid infusion or even blood transfusion may be required. Maintenance of proper water balance is imperative in order to prevent water intoxication, dehydration, hyponatremia, or pulmonary edema.

Initial evaluation of the patient's condition requires a record of electrolyte intake and output for the first 24 hours. Thereafter, electrolyte intake is based upon serum electrolyte determinations made every 3 days. Serum creatinine and blood urea nitrogen should be determined to provide criteria for possible dialysis.

When a patient with preeclampsia becomes hyponatremic, intake of sodium ion is not harmful but actually beneficial. When hyponatremia is the result of water excess, total fluid intake should be reduced.

D. Medications:

1. Sedatives–For mild cases, the sedative of choice is phenobarbital, 60 mg orally 3 times daily. In more severe cases, phenobarbital is best given intramuscularly as phenobarbital sodium in a dosage of 250 mg every 6 hours. Diazepam (Valium) may be substituted in doses of 5 mg intravenously or 10 mg intramuscularly every 2 hours. These agents should be administered in large enough doses—and continued for a long enough time—to obtain adequate sedation and control hyperreflexia.

For fulminating eclamptogenic convulsions, thiopental or diazepam may be used intravenously to temporarily control the seizures, but not until an adequate airway and oxygenation have been achieved. Diazepam, the preferred drug, should be given intravenously for its rapid effect.

Diazepam may be administered just prior to delivery. Consequently, the neonate may exhibit lethargy and sluggish body heat regulation, necessitating monitoring during its first 24–36 hours.

If thiopental is used, the dose should be individualized (approximately 4 mg/kg) and administered intravenously with all of the cardiorespiratory considerations used for general anesthesia.

Thiopental may cause maternal laryngospasm on initial administration and neonatal respiratory depression if given late during labor.

2. Magnesium sulfate as anticonvulsant– Magnesium sulfate by injection has been used successfully for many years in the treatment of preeclampsia and eclampsia. This drug also exerts deleterious effects (eg, it increases retention of sodium) and is toxic even at slight overdosage. For these reasons, the physician who uses this drug must be thoroughly familiar with its effects on the mother and fetus, its correct dosage and routes of administration, and the signs and management of overdosage.

The greatest value of magnesium sulfate is as a sedative and an anticonvulsant. Magnesium ion will prevent convulsions at a serum level of 1.67 mmol/L or more. However, at a serum level of 4.17–5 mmol/L, reflexes—particularly knee jerks—disappear; at levels of 5–6.25 mmol/L, respirations are slowed or absent; and at levels above 6.25 mmol/L, cardiac arrest may occur. Consequently, a repeat parenteral dose of magnesium sulfate is contraindicated by any of the following findings: (1) absent or very sluggish knee jerks, (2) respiratory rate below 16/min, or (3) urinary output less than 100 mL in the preceding 4 hours. (Similarly, marked slowing of respiration or hyporeflexia in the newborn infant of a mother who has been receiving magnesium sulfate suggests the possibility of a toxic serum level of magnesium. In such instances, exchange transfusion to the newborn may be necessary.)

Intramuscular administration of magnesium sulfate USP (hydrated $MgSO_4 \cdot 7H_2O$) is still a safe and satisfactory means of delivering large volumes of the drug in effective and tolerable doses. However, it has recently been shown that an initial bolus of 4 g intravenously in patients with normal or borderline renal function produces a significant reduction in the knee-jerk reflex, reduced urinary output, and slight reduction of the respiratory rate. These functions must be monitored and adjusted during the continuous intravenous administration of the drug. One should employ a continuous calibrated Harvard-type pump, infusing at a rate of about 1 g/h as needed. In this way, one can control the dosage and determine more rapidly the onset of action of the drug and assess its effects.

The important features of magnesium sulfate administration are to start the drug early during the course of eclampsia or advanced preeclampsia; to maintain an adequate dose; and to monitor serum levels in the mother in order to anticipate fetal and early neonatal serum concentrations.

Intravenous calcium is the specific antidote for a toxic level of serum magnesium (whether from overdosage or unexpected reduction of urinary output). Therefore, a 20-mL vial of 10% calcium gluconate solution should be kept at the bedside.

3. Antihypertensive drugs–In treating severe preeclampsia or eclampsia, almost all medications are administered parenterally. Oral antihypertensive preparations have no place in the management of these acute problems.

a. Hydralazine (Apresoline)–Hydralazine is an effective antihypertensive agent. The size of the dose and the interval between doses are based upon the response of the patient's blood pressure and urinary output. Intravenous hydralazine is the antihypertensive drug of choice in the hypertensive disorders of pregnancy. The indications for initial use are evidence of acute renal failure and marked elevations in blood pressure (usually systolic blood pressure about 200 mm Hg and diastolic blood pressure of 120 mm Hg or above). However, the objective is not to reduce the blood pressure to or by any specific figure, and one must take care not to produce precipitate drops in blood pressure, since shock will occur if the pressure falls too suddenly to "normal" values. In addition to its peripheral action, hydralazine also has a central blocking effect on sympathetic vasomotor (vasopressor) impulses. It usually does not produce the profound hypotension obtained with many of the newer central blocking agents but possesses sufficient potency to reduce blood pressure satisfactorily and to increase renal perfusion and urinary output—effects that are obviously desirable in the oliguric patient with preeclampsia-eclampsia. Hydralazine should not be administered to patients with or suspected of having systemic lupus erythematosus. Hydralazine should not be injected by bolus but through a Y-tube drip Buretrol in concentrations of 20 mg/dL of dextrose in water. In general, the administration of hydralazine is titrated against hourly urinary output as a reflection of renal perfusion. Hydralazine increases cardiac output, increases renal blood flow (and possibly placental blood flow), often produces pronounced tachycardia, and exerts a direct vasodilator effect on peripheral arterioles.

b. Propranolol–Propranolol, a beta-adrenergic receptor blocking agent, is given in conjunction with hydralazine to oppose its cardiac effects. This beta blockade decreases not only the heart rate but also the contractility of cardiac muscle, accounting for a reduction of about 18–20% in cardiac output while preventing the reflex tachycardia induced by hydralazine. Propranolol also probably inhibits the release of renin, which, in turn, produces angiotensin vasoconstrictive activity. Propranolol should not be used alone in the pregnant hypertensive patient but should be utilized to counteract the increased cardiac output induced by hydralazine. However, propranolol may have a theoretic advantage as a pharmacologic approach toward regulating renin-angiotensin-induced hypertension.

c. Diazoxide (Hyperstat)–Diazoxide, a powerful vasodilator, has limited application in the management of hypertensive encephalopathy and other hypertensive crises in toxemic patients. The rapid intravenous administration of 300 mg of diazoxide will produce immediate vasodilatation and reduction in blood pressure. The drug is not without significant problems, since it enhances the retention of sodium and water, inhibits insulin release (and therefore should not be given to diabetics), elevates blood uric acid, and increases serum free fatty acids (aggravating any already existing metabolic acidosis).

Since diazoxide is reserved principally for acute situations, continued antihypertensive synergy may be sustained with methyldopa, 250 mg intravenously every 6 hours.

d. Other antihypertensive agents–Several other hypotensive agents that have been studied in the management of patients with eclamptogenic toxemia still have some advocates but have not been generally accepted for use. Both the great number of unrefined alkaloids of *Veratrum viride* and recently purified veratrum alkaloids have been used for many years, but their effects are unpredictable. They are also undesirable because they decrease urinary output. Rauwolfia alkaloids (reserpine) exert their hypotensive effect on the postganglionic sympathetic fibers. Although reserpine has been useful in other hypertensive diseases, it has not proved particularly effective in preeclampsia-eclampsia.

Ganglionic blocking agents such as guanethidine (Ismelin) are little used in obstetrics; they produce such extreme, sudden reduction of blood pressure that they probably are unsafe for standard use.

Monoamine oxidase inhibitors have received some attention but have not been accepted for use in obstetrics.

4. Diuretics–Routine administration of diuretics to normal pregnant women as a means of controlling weight gain or sodium balance can only be condemned. *Diuretics do not prevent preeclampsia or* *eclampsia.* The indication for diuretics in preeclampsia and eclampsia is limited to mobilizing edema fluid, just as they are used to mobilize extracellular fluid in renal disease and congestive heart failure. Unfortunately, none of the diuretic agents yet available are consistently effective in removing excess extracellular fluid without disturbing electrolyte balance.

The most satisfactory diuretic agents in preeclampsia-eclampsia are the thiazides. They inhibit reabsorption of sodium ion in the renal proximal tubule, producing (because of the ion exchange conditions in the distal tubule) increased excretion of both sodium and potassium as well as water. Toxicity and other undesirable effects of the thiazides are minimal. Nevertheless, prior to their use and during their administration, determinations of blood chemistry must be made frequently enough to detect and to avoid hyponatremia, hypokalemia, alkalosis, decreased carbohydrate intolerance, arrhythmias, and accumulation of purine metabolites. Postpartum vascular collapse can result from prolonged and excessive thiazide therapy.

Diuretic management of the excess water and sodium retention that frequently accompanies preeclampsia commonly starts with the administration of chlorothiazide, 50 mg orally twice a day, and ample water for the first 24 hours, if the patient is able to take oral medication. When parenteral administration is required, 250–500 mg of chlorothiazide intravenously every 8–12 hours may be given.

Because of its great potency and rapidity of diuretic action, ethacrynic acid (Edecrin) may be preferred to the thiazides, particularly when acute pulmonary edema is present or imminent. This drug can increase sodium excretion enormously—to as much as 25% of the glomerular filtered load. Associated with this sodium excretion is a marked increase in excretion of chloride, potassium, and water. The oral dose is 50–200 mg daily, but only rarely should a single dose exceed 50 mg because of this agent's remarkable natriuretic and diuretic effects. Repeat doses are usually given at 12-hour intervals. Ethacrynic acid may be given intravenously in doses of 10–50 mg; the smaller dose is preferable. In using this diuretic agent, one must be alert to complications from excessive loss of electrolytes and water: hypovolemia, hypotension, hyponatremia, hypochloremia, hypokalemia, and even metabolic alkalosis.

Furosemide (Lasix) is more potent than ethacrynic acid. Chloride, sodium, and potassium are excreted much as with ethacrynic acid. The oral dose is 40–200 mg/d. Furosemide may be administered intravenously, but the same monitoring precautions must be observed as for ethacrynic acid.

5. Plasma expanders–Expanders of plasma volume do have a place in treatment, but only where there is volume depletion. The diagnosis of preeclampsia or eclampsia does not always mean that hypovolemia is present. Consequently, it is important to make certain that these patients do not receive hyperosmolar preparations empirically or automatically to evoke volume expansion unless blood volume has been measured. When these preparations were first marketed, their indiscriminate use in preeclampsia-eclampsia resulted in acute pulmonary edema and even death in patients with already overstressed circulatory and cardiopulmonary dynamics, particularly where acute renal failure was imminent or actually present.

Recall that overly aggressive use of other treatment measures (intravenous fluids, hydralazine, analgesics, central venous pressure or respiratory tract catheterization or intubation) may lead to fulminating pulmonary edema.

E. Delivery: Regardless of the severity of the disease, most patients with preeclampsia must be delivered electively, since awaiting spontaneous labor usually is too dangerous. It is always desirable to choose the least traumatic method. Elective delivery will be required only occasionally for patients with eclampsia because labor usually begins spontaneously shortly after the onset of convulsions.

The delivery of every patient with preeclampsia-eclampsia presents a major challenge: The metabolic problems are great enough, but the likelihood of concurrent or subsequent cardiac, renal, pulmonary, or cerebral impairment must also be considered. Predelivery therapy must be judiciously balanced between over- and undertreatment and must attempt to control nervous system irritability, hypertension, water and electrolyte imbalance, and impaired renal function in order to bring the patient into the best possible condition for delivery.

If treatment of preeclampsia does bring about satisfactory improvement—and if greater fetal maturity is required—the pregnancy may be allowed to continue under careful management. This should include not just one test but all tests of fetal well-being, fetoplacental function, amniocentesis, and ultrasonic examination to evaluate fetal status. When elective delivery is finally undertaken, it should be accomplished by the most conservative appropriate means, with fetal monitoring.

If preeclampsia fails to improve within 24–48 hours in response to medical management, elective delivery becomes mandatory. Induction of labor should be undertaken by rupture of the membranes or by medical means (intravenous oxytocin). In most cases, delivery should be assisted by low forceps to shorten the stress of the second stage of labor on the vascular and central nervous systems—unless labor is progressing so rapidly and easily in a multipara that little is to be gained thereby. Anesthesia for delivery should usually be by pudendal block or local infiltration, but well-controlled epidural anesthesia may be ideal for calming the patient, for helping to lower the blood pressure, and for increasing uterine and renal blood flow. Spinal anesthesia must be avoided because of the danger of sudden, severe hypotension.

Cesarean section may be the method of choice in the following circumstances: (1) In women with obstetric complications (and complications of labor) that would indicate cesarean section for the non-toxemic patient. (2) In women with preeclampsia-eclampsia who have been brought into optimum condition for delivery (a) if vaginal examination reveals conditions totally unfavorable for the induction of labor, (b) if labor does not begin promptly after attempted induction, or (c) if survival of a preterm infant is likely. Elective cesarean section may be lethal for a patient with continuing convulsions or for one who is in coma; neurologic consultation should be sought. Delivery by elective cesarean section may be considered when convulsions or coma has been absent for a period of at least 12 hours.

Prognosis

Reported maternal and fetal morbidity and mortality rates for GEPH vary considerably throughout the world, probably largely as a result of inadequate definitions, inaccurate diagnoses, lack of uniformity in collection of medical statistics, inaccurate census reports, and unreliable registration of national vital statistics. It is important to recognize that maternal and fetal death rates due to the hypertensive disorders of pregnancy in the USA, even today, are grossly under-reported.

Sepsis, hemorrhage, and preeclampsia-eclampsia still are the 3 major causes of maternal deaths and obstetric morbidity. Thirty years ago, the maternal mortality rate from eclampsia was about 20%. This has been lowered significantly since then, but even now 5-10% of patients with eclampsia in the USA die because of the disorder.

A few obstetric services, some of which are in hospitals with large publicly supported patient loads, report few or no maternal deaths from eclampsia. This may reflect excellent patient care, but one must also consider that such obstetric departments may not include in their statistics patients dead on arrival, moribund patients who die within 12 hours after admission, or patients who die on other services in the hospital.

In a report of one of the largest series of eclampsia (2164 patients) in recent times, Agüero in Venezuela cites an insignificant decline in the maternal death rate over a 37-year period (10.6% in 1939 to 8.8% in 1976). Cesarean section played a prominent role in this high maternal mortality rate, especially when the sole indication for cesarean section was eclampsia or cerebral hemorrhage. The overall perinatal mortality rate was 136 per 1000 live births.

The Orient and the Middle East lead the world in maternal mortality rates for eclampsia. The rate for the British Isles is 5 per 100,000; for the USA, 6 per 100,000; and for Canada, 7 per 100,000. Deaths from preeclampsia alone are rare.

Gestational hypertensive disorders also account for a large share of the overall fetal mortality rate, but specific data are almost impossible to obtain because of diagnostic uncertainties. Acceptance of the revised and more specific nomenclature in Table 34-1 should help to minimize confusion in diagnosis and statistical reporting.

The recurrence of preeclampsia in a subsequent pregnancy is rare. Also rare are long-term sequelae from the preeclamptic attack. If hypertension or renal damage persists or is diagnosed in a subsequent pregnancy, it probably is the result of a preexisting underlying vascular or renal disorder, not the episode of preeclampsia. Long-term follow-up coupled with technologic and surgical advances may reveal disease not suspected at the time of pregnancy, eg, aneurysm of the renal artery, fibromuscular hyperplasia, and renal artery stenosis 15-30 years after the episode of eclampsia. The only continuing factor seems to be a hereditary predisposition to preeclampsia in daughters of women who have had the disorder.

The occurrence of a gestational hypertensive disorder greatly increases the perinatal mortality rate. Prompt delivery will improve fetal and neonatal salvage, but the immature fetus is at great hazard in such circumstances. The perinatal mortality rate may be as high as 20%, especially when delivery occurs before the 36th week of gestation.

In an attempt to assess definitive influences of the hypertensive disorders of pregnancy on the fetus or the newborn, only the perinatal mortality rate provides a quantitative approach. The occurrence of proteinuria or significant elevations of blood pressure during pregnancy are important factors in increasing fetal and neonatal death rates. Whether these same individual factors or the preeclampsia contribute to mental retardation has not been determined with certainty. Although there is no definite evidence at present that GEPH causes mental retardation, the ongoing evaluation of long-term survivors in the Collaborative Project through the seventh year of life (and even longer) may provide the answer.

The fetal prognosis in eclampsia is always grave, although the perinatal mortality statistics are improving. Early in this century, it was customary to terminate the pregnancy of a patient with eclampsia as quickly as possible in an attempt to cure the disorder. This practice produced such a high maternal mortality rate that it was then replaced by an extremely conservative attitude, and operative delivery became the method of last resort. This in turn again increased the perinatal mortality rate.

In accomplishing delivery 12 hours or more after convulsions have ceased and after the cardiovascular and pulmonary status has stabilized, the current, practically standardized method—not actually a compromise—is again lowering the perinatal mortality rate and further reducing maternal mortality rates.

●　　●　　●

References

Agüero O, Aure M, Alezard L: Eclampsias fatales. *Revista de Obst y Gin de Venezuela* 1977;**37**:447.

Andersen WA, Harbert GM Jr: Conservative management of preeclamptic and eclamptic patients: A reevaluation. *Am J Obstet Gynecol* 1977;**129**:260.

Arias F, Zamora J: Antihypertensive treatment and pregnancy outcome in patients with mild chronic hypertension. *Obstet Gynecol* 1979;**53**:489.

Benedett TJ et al: Hemodynamic observations in severe preeclampsia with a flow-directed pulmonary artery catheter. *Am J Obstet Gynecol* 1980;**136**:465.

Cavanagh D et al: Experimental hypertension in the pregnant primate. *Am J Obstet Gynecol* 1977;**128**:75.

Chesley LC: *Hypertensive Disorders in Pregnancy.* Appleton-Century-Crofts, 1978.

Chesley LC: Proposal for classification. Pages 249–268 in: *Blood Pressure, Edema and Proteinuria in Pregnancy: Proceedings of the Toxemia Task Force, National Institutes of Health.* Friedman EA (editor). AR Liss, 1976.

Cunningham FG, Pritchard JA: Hematologic considerations of pregnancy-induced hypertension. *Semin Perinatol* 1978;**2**:29.

Curet LB, Olson RW: Evaluation of a program of bed rest in the treatment of chronic hypertension of pregnancy. *Obstet Gynecol* 1979;**53**:336.

de Alvarez RR: Effect of blood pressure and proteinuria on perinatal mortality. Pages 168–192 in: *Blood Pressure, Edema and Proteinuria in Pregnancy: Proceedings of the Toxemia Task Force, National Institutes of Health.* Friedman EA (editor). AR Liss, 1976.

de Alvarez RR: Preeclampsia, eclampsia, and other hypertensive disorders of pregnancy. Chapter 30 in: *Obstetrical Practice.* Aladjem S (editor). Mosby, 1980.

de Alvarez RR, Welt SI: Hypertension complicated by pregnancy. Chapter 71 in: *Textbook of Obstetrics & Perinatology.* Iffy L, Kaminetzky H (editors). Wiley, 1981.

Friedman EA: Effect of blood pressure on perinatal mortality. Pages 123–154 in: *Blood Pressure, Edema and Proteinuria in Pregnancy: Proceedings of the Toxemia Task Force, National Institutes of Health.* Friedman EA (editor). AR Liss, 1976.

Gant NP et al: A study of angiotensin II pressor response throughout primigravid pregnancy. *J Clin Invest* 1973;**52**:2682.

Grunfeld J, Ganeval D, Bournerias F: Acute renal failure in pregnancy. *Kidney Int* 1980;**18**:179.

Hiel LM: Metabolism of uric acid in normal and toxemic pregnancy. *Mayo Clin Proc* 1978;**53**:743.

Lawson J: Current views on the management of eclampsia. *Clin Obstet Gynecol* 1977;**4**:707.

Lieberman BA et al: The possible adverse effect of propranolol on the fetus in pregnancies complicated by severe hypertension. *Br J Obstet Gynaecol* 1978;**85**:678.

Lim YL, Walters WAW: Haemodynamics of mild hypertension in pregnancy. *Br J Obstet Gynaecol* 1979;**86**:198.

MacGillivray I: Sodium and water balance in pregnancy hypertension. *Clin Obstet Gynecol* 1977;**4**:549.

Naeye RL, Friedman EA: Causes of perinatal death associated with gestational hypertension and proteinuria. *Am J Obstet Gynecol* 1979;**133**:8.

Neutra R, Neff R: Fetal death in eclampsia. 2. Effects of nontherapeutic factors. *Br J Obstet Gynaecol* 1975;**82**:390.

Phelan JP: Enhanced prediction of pregnancy-induced hypertension by combining supine pressor test with mean arterial pressure of middle trimester. *Am J Obstet Gynecol* 1977;**129**:387.

Porapakkham S: An epidemiologic study of eclampsia. *Obstet Gynecol* 1979;**54**:26.

Scott JR, Beer AE, Stastny P: Immunogenetic factors in preeclampsia and eclampsia. *JAMA* 1976;**235**:402.

Sibai BM, Lipshitz J, Anderson GD: Reassessment of intravenous magnesium sulfate therapy in preeclampsia-eclampsia. *Obstet Gynecol* 1981;**57**:199.

Sommer DG et al: Hepatic rupture with toxemia of pregnancy: Angiographic diagnosis. *Am J Roentgenol* 1979;**132**:455.

Tribe CR et al: A renal biopsy study in toxemia of pregnancy. *J Clin Pathol* 1979;**32**:681.

Wardle EN: Preeclamptic toxemia: A reappraisal. *Nephron* 1978;**20**:241.

Wightman H, Hebbard BM, Rosen M: Perinatal mortality and morbidity associated with eclampsia. *Br Med J* 1978;**2**:235.

Zuspan TP, O'Shaughnessy R: Chronic hypertension in pregnancy. Page 11 in: *Year Book of Obstetrics and Gynecology 1979.* Year Book, 1979.

Multiple Pregnancy | 35

Ralph C. Benson, MD

Twins produced from a single ovum are said to be monozygotic, or identical ("true" twins); those produced from separate ova are dizygotic or fraternal ("false" twins). Monozygotism is random, ie, does not fit any discernible genetic pattern; dizygotism has hereditary determinants.

In North America, dizygotic twinning occurs about once in 83 conceptions and triplets about once in 8000 conceptions. Multiple pregnancy is most common in blacks, least common in Orientals, and of intermediate occurrence in whites. Slightly more than 30% of twins are monozygotic; nearly 70% are dizygotic. There is a lesser preponderance of males in twins than in singletons. The incidence of maternal morbidity and mortality is much higher in multiple pregnancy than in single pregnancy because of medical and obstetric complications. The perinatal mortality rate of twins is 3–4 times higher—and for triplets much higher again—than in the case of singletons as a result of prematurity and associated difficulties. The antepartum diagnosis of multiple pregnancy is made in only about 75% of cases, and often late—which is regrettable, because untimely early delivery contributes to fetal jeopardy. Much can be done for the mother and the offspring if treatment is given early.

About 75% of twins are of the same sex. Both twins are males in about 45% of cases and both females in about 30%.

A racial or familial propensity for twinning increases the likelihood of dizygotic pregnancy, but monozygotic pregnancy is not predictable.

Twinning is suggested by a relatively large uterus for dates; greater-than-expected maternal weight gain; increased fetal activity; multiplicity of fetal parts; more than one fetal heartbeat; at least 2 fetal electrocardiographic complexes; and 2 or more fetuses as shown by ultrasonography or roentgenography. Maternal hypochromic normocytic anemia and, in many cases, preeclampsia-eclampsia are often problems in multiple pregnancy.

Twinning is associated with greatly increased perinatal mortality and morbidity rates (prematurity, hypoxia, trauma, anomalies), especially for monozygotic twins; and increased maternal morbidity (hemorrhage, infection).

It is estimated that at least two-thirds of multiple pregnancies end in a single birth; the other embryo is lost with bleeding, is absorbed within the first 10 weeks of pregnancy, or becomes mummified (fetus papyraceus).

Pathogenesis

Monozygotic twinning occurs in about 2.3–4 per 1000 pregnancies in all races. The rate is remarkably constant and is not influenced by heredity, age of the mother, or other factors. The frequency of dizygotic twinning varies from 1.3 per 1000 in Japan to 49 per 1000 in Western Nigeria. The rate in the USA is about 12 per 1000. Dizygotic twinning probably is inherited as a recessive autosomal trait via the female descendants of mothers of twins. Height and weight have a positive influence on twinning, but the rate does not vary among social classes. Blood groups O and A are more prevalent in white mothers of twins than in the general population, for unknown reasons. The father's genetic endowment has little or no influence on the incidence of monozygotic or dizygotic twinning.

The number of fertilized ova and the timing of division (symmetric or asymmetric) determine the number of offspring.

Many dizygotic twins are born early in the birth order, but twins are born most frequently to older multiparas. Parity does not influence the incidence of twinning. The rate of dizygotic twinning of women in the general population peaks between 35 and 40 years of age and then declines sharply. In contrast, white

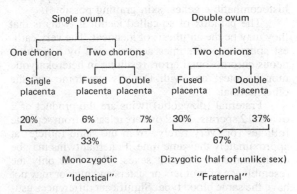

Figure 35–1. Placental variations in twinning. (After Potter. Reproduced, with permission, from Benson RC: *Handbook of Obstetrics & Gynecology,* 7th ed. Lange, 1980.)

women who are dizygotic twins or who are siblings of dizygotic twin mothers have a higher twinning rate among their offspring than women from the general population. In women who are twins or daughters of twins, the twinning rate peaks at about age 35, at which time it plateaus until almost age 45 and then declines. Black women, whether or not they are twins or siblings of twins, have a prolonged incidence of dizygotic twinning from 35 to 45 years of age. Although delayed menopause has been suggested as an explanation, the reverse seems to be the case.

Dizygotic twinning is more frequent among women who become pregnant soon after cessation of long-term oral contraception. It is theorized that this may be a reflection of high "rebound" gonadotropin secretion. Dizygotic twins are more common among unwed than wed mothers of the same age. High fertility (polyovulation) is associated with multiple pregnancy. Excessive production of pituitary gonadotropins, relatively high frequency of coitus, and inability of one graafian follicle to inhibit others have been postulated as reasons for a greater frequency of dizygotic twinning. Undernutrition appears to be a reductive factor. Women who conceive late in an ovulatory cycle have a greater chance of multiple pregnancy, perhaps owing to ovular "overripeness."

Induction of ovulation with human pituitary gonadotropin in previously infertile patients has resulted in many multiple pregnancies—even the gestation of septuplets and octuplets. The estrogen analog clomiphene citrate (Clomid) increases the occurrence rate of dizygotic pregnancy to about 5–10%.

Monozygotic twins, always derived from a single fertilized ovum, may develop differently depending upon the time of preimplantation division.

Identical (monozygotic) twins, which result from the fertilization of a single ovum by a single sperm, are always of the same sex. Nevertheless, they are not mirror images of one another (one left-handed, the other right-handed, etc), and their fingerprints differ. Normally, monozygotic twins have the same physical characteristics (skin, hair, and eye color and body build) and the same genetic features (blood characteristics: ABO, M, N, haptoglobin, serum group; same histocompatible genes: skin grafting possible).

The paradox of so-called identical twins is that they may be the antithesis of identical. The very earliest splits are sometimes accompanied by a simultaneous chromosomal error, resulting in heterokaryotic monozygotes, one with Down's syndrome and the other normal.

Fraternal (dizygotic) twins are the product of 2 ova and 2 sperms. The 2 ova are released from separate follicles (or, very rarely, from the same follicle) at approximately the same time. Fraternal twins may be of the same or different sexes. They bear only the resemblance of brothers or sisters and may or may not have the same blood type. Significant differences usually can be identified after a time.

Other kinds of twinning are theoretically possible in humans. Dispermic mosaicism may result from fertilization of 2 ova that have not been independently released but, instead, have developed from the same oocyte. Another possibility is the fertilization of one ovum by 2 sperms. (Such twinning, if it does occur in humans, should lead to mosaicism of one individual rather than to the formation of "identical" twins.) Twinning of discordant twins may be explained by meiotic abnormalities, including polar body twinning, delayed implantation of the embryo, retarded or arrested intrauterine development, or superfetation.

Monozygotic triplets result from repeated twinning (also called supertwinning) of a single ovum. Trizygotic triplets develop by individual fertilization of 3 simultaneously expelled ova. Triplets may also be produced by the twinning of 2 ova and the elimination of one of the 4 resulting embryos.

Quadruplets, similarly, may be monozygotic, paired dizygotic, or quadrizygotic, ie, they may arise from 1 to 4 ova.

Superfecundation is the fertilization of 2 ova, released at about the same time, by sperm released at intercourse on 2 different occasions. The rare cases in which the fetuses are of disparate size or skin color and have blood groups corresponding to those of the mother's 2 male partners lend credence to (but do not conclusively validate) this possibility.

Superfetation is the fertilization of 2 ova released in different menstrual cycles. This is virtually impossible in humans, because the initial corpus luteum of pregnancy would have to be suppressed to allow for a second ovulation about a month later.

A traditional approximation of the frequency of occurrence of multiple pregnancies is as follows:

Twins	1:80
Triplets	$1:80^2 = 1:6400$
Quadruplets	$1:80^3 = 1:512,000$
Etc	

The relative number of females increases considerably as the number of fetuses increases in multiple births.

Pathologic Factors Associated With Twinning

A. Maternal Pathologic Factors: Although the blood volume is increased in multiple pregnancy, maternal anemia often develops because of greater demand for iron by the twins. However, prior anemia, poor diet, and malabsorption may precede or compound iron deficiency during multiple pregnancy. Respiratory tidal volume is increased, but the woman pregnant with twins often is "breathless." Marked uterine distention and increased pressure on the adjacent viscera and pelvic vasculature are typical of multiple pregnancy. Lutein cysts and even ascites are the result of abnormally high levels of chorionic gonadotropin in occasional multiple pregnancies.

Placenta previa develops because of the large size of the placenta or placentas.

B. Fetal Pathologic Factors: Each twin and its placenta generally weigh less than the newborn and placenta of a singleton pregnancy after the 30th week, but near term the aggregate weight is almost twice that of a singleton.

The placenta and membranes of monozygotic twins may vary considerably, depending on the time of initial division of the embryonic disk. Variations are as follows:

1. Division prior to the morula stage and differentiation of the trophoblast (fifth day) results in separate or fused placentas, 2 chorions, and 2 amnions. (This process grossly resembles dizygotic twinning and accounts for almost one-third of monozygotic twinning.)

2. Division after differentiation of the trophoblast but before the formation of the amnion (fifth to tenth days) yields a single placenta, a common chorion, and one amnion. (This accounts for about two-thirds of monozygotic twinning.)

3. Division after differentiation of the amnion (tenth to 14th days) results in a single placenta, one (common) chorion, and one (common) amnion. This is rare. Thus, at least 13% of monozygotic twins are dichorionic, and approximately 10% of dichorionic twins are monozygotic.

Placentation is of help only in zygosity determinations in twins with monochorionic placentas because these are always monozygotic. Almost 20% of all twins and about 5% of all monozygotic twins are monoamniotic. Placental forms (single, fused, or double) do not aid in determining zygosity in individual twin pairs, because any of these forms may be found in mono- or dizygotic twins.

At delivery, the membranous "T" septum or dividing membrane of the placenta between the twins must be inspected and sectioned for evidence of the probable type of twinning (Fig 35–2). Monozygotic twins have a transparent (thin) septum made up of 2 amniotic membranes only (no chorion and no decidua). Dizygotic twins have an opaque (thick) septum made up of 2 chorions, 2 amnions, and intervening decidua.

A monochorionic placenta can be identified by stripping away the amnion or amnions to reveal a single chorion over a common placenta. In virtually every case of monochorionic placenta, vascular communications between the 2 parts of the placenta can be identified by careful dissection or injection. In contrast, dichorionic placentas (of dizygotic twinning) only rarely have an anastomosis between the fetal blood vessels.

Normal twins that differ considerably in birth weight commonly have diamniotic-dichorionic placentas. This suggests independent intrauterine growth of co-twins. The converse is true of twins with fused diamniotic-dichorionic placentas.

Low-birth-weight monochorionic twins are the rule rather than the exception. Low birth weight in the various types of multiple pregnancy probably is evidence of growth retardation due to inadequate nutrition. This is at least partially responsible for the much higher early neonatal mortality rate of newborns from multiple births.

The incidence of serious congenital anomalies is about 3 times greater in multiple than in single pregnancies. The abnormalities are almost all found in monozygotic twins. This may be due to overcrowding in utero, competition by the placenta for uterine surface (circulation), or the circumstances that led to twinning.

In a collaborative project, 18% of twins had malformations: 15% single and 3% multiple, contributed by monozygotic twins. This was true for both major and minor malformations. Abnormalities were higher in black than white twins. Twins had more malformations of the central nervous system, musculoskeletal system, ears, respiratory system, cardiovascular system, and alimentary tract but fewer malformations of the genitourinary system and skin than singletons.

Conjoined or Siamese twins result from incomplete segmentation of a single fertilized ovum between the eighth and the 14th days; if cleavage is further postponed, incomplete twinning (2 heads, one body)

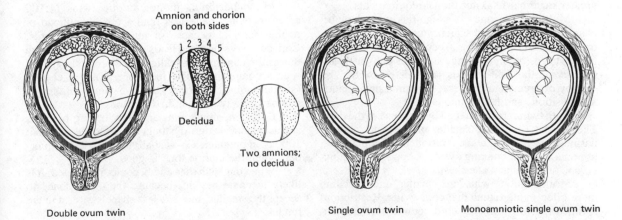

Amnion and chorion
on both sides

Decidua

Two amnions;
no decidua

Double ovum twin   Single ovum twin   Monoamniotic single ovum twin

Figure 35–2. Amniotic membranes of twins. (Reproduced, with permission, from Benson RC: *Handbook of Obstetrics & Gynecology,* 7th ed. Lange, 1980.)

may occur. Lesser abnormalities are also noted, but these occur without regard to specific organ systems. Conjoined twins are described by site of union; pygopagus (at the sacrum—the most common conjunction); thoracopagus (at the chest); craniopagus (at the heads); and omphalopagus (at the abdominal wall). Curiously, conjoined twins usually are female. Recently, numerous conjoined twins have survived separation.

Fetus papyraceus (fetus compressus) is a small, blighted, mummified fetus usually discovered at the delivery of a well-developed newborn. This occurs once in 17–20 thousand pregnancies. Several possibilities are plausible. Perhaps, months before, a dizygotic twin died, its amniotic fluid was resorbed (or lost), and the enlarging amniotic sac of the surviving fetus compressed the dead fetus against the placenta or the uterine wall. Or the twins may have been monozygotic monochorionic, with interplacental vascular anastomoses; one twin died early, and the other survived.

A fetus acardiacus is a parasitic fetus without a heart. This monster is a monozygotic twin that was the donor of blood transmitted through placental anastomoses to its stronger, more fortunate co-twin. In addition to failure of the heart to develop, the growth and development of the entire body of the fetus acardiacus is distorted and rudimentary. Inexplicably, the cord may be attached to almost any part of the maldeveloped, diminutive fetus. In contrast, the other twin may appear to be normal, usually larger than average.

Velamentous insertion of the cord occurs in about 7% of twins but in only 1% of singletons.

Two-vessel cords occur more frequently in monozygotic twins than in singletons. Whether this is due to primary aplasia or is the result of secondary atrophy is not known.

Pathophysiology of Twinning

The cardiovascular, respiratory, gastrointestinal, renal, and musculoskeletal systems are especially subject to stress in multiple pregnancy, and there are greater maternal-fetal nutritional requirements.

Multiple pregnancy is a high-risk pregnancy because of the increased frequency of maternal anemia, urinary tract infection, preeclampsia-eclampsia, hemorrhage (before, during, and after delivery), and uterine inertia. The fetus is jeopardized by the frequency of premature delivery, abnormal presentation and position, and hydramnios.

Both twins are threatened by prolapse of the cord. The second (often the smaller of the pair) may be harmed by premature separation of the placenta, hypoxia, constriction ring dystocia, operative manipulation, or prolonged anesthesia.

Monozygotic twins are smaller and succumb more often in utero than dizygotic twins. Restriction, competition for nutrition, cord compression and entanglement, prematurity, and operative delivery are responsible for a significant part of the perinatal mortality rate in multiple pregnancy.

A single (monochorionic) placenta probably is less competent than a fused (dichorionic) placenta; as a consequence, more disease processes are noted, often as a result of placental vascular problems, in connection with the former than with the latter. Inequities of the placental circulation in one area (marginal insertion, partial infarction or thinning) may deprive or destroy one fetus while the other thrives.

In growth-retarded human fetuses, the brain and heart seem to be relatively less affected than the liver or peripheral musculature. Because the limits of placental growth and function are finite, hormone alterations may develop to trigger early labor. A large pregnancy with small newborns often results in premature delivery. In any event, retarded fetal growth has a small but lasting effect on postnatal physical and possibly mental development.

The most serious problem with monochorionic placentas is local shunting of blood—also called twin-to-twin transfusion syndrome, cross-transfusion, the "third circulation," or intrauterine parabiosis. This occurs because of vascular anastomoses to each twin, established early in embryonic life, probably by random growth. The possible communications are artery-to-artery, vein-to-vein, and combinations of these. Artery-to-vein communication is by far the most serious; it is most likely to cause twin-to-twin transfusion (if not relieved by a rare vein-to-artery return). In uncompensated cases, the twins, though genetically identical, differ greatly in size and appearance. The **recipient** twin will be plethoric, edematous, and hypertensive. Ascites and kernicterus are likely. The heart, liver, and kidneys will be enlarged (glomerulotubal hypertrophy). Hydramnios follows fetal polyuria. Although ruddy and apparently healthy, the recipient twin with hypervolemia may die of congenital heart failure during the first 24 hours after birth. The **donor** twin will be small, pallid, and dehydrated (growth retardation, malnutrition, hypovolemia). Oligohydramnios will be present. Severe anemia, due to chronic blood loss to the other twin, may lead to hydrops and heart failure.

Monochorionic, monoamniotic twins (1:100 cases of twins) have less than a 50% likelihood of double survival because of tangled, twisted cords. Cord compression often leads to fetal hypoxia or death unless the abnormality is diagnosed promptly and rescue accomplished. The incidence of 2-vessel cord (single umbilical artery) is 4–5 times higher in monozygotic twins than in singletons.

Collision, impaction, and interlocking of twins are accidental. Such dystocia occurs once in about 1000 twin pregnancies—usually early in the birth order, when the uterine tone is good.

When one twin dies and becomes macerated, it is likely to come second, because the uterus tends to accept the smaller, more or less shapeless form in the fundus.

Clinical Findings

A. **Symptoms and Signs:** All of the common

annoyances of pregnancy are more troublesome in multiple pregnancy. The effects of multiple pregnancy on the patient include earlier and more severe pressure in the pelvis, nausea, backache, varicosities, constipation, hemorrhoids, abdominal distention, and difficulty in breathing. A ''large pregnancy'' may be indicative of twinning (distended uterus). Fetal activity is greater and more persistent in twinning than in single pregnancy. The median weight of twins at birth is just over 2270 g in the USA. Male infants weigh slightly more than females.

Considering the possibility of multiple pregnancy is essential to early diagnosis. If one assumes that all pregnancies are multiple ones until proved otherwise, physical examination alone will identify most cases of twinning before the second trimester.

Maternal bleeding in the first trimester may indicate spontaneous abortion. However, the dead fetus may be one of twins as demonstrated by real-time ultrasonography (one anechoic or hypo-echoic amnionic sac and one normal sac).

Manual diagnosis of twinning is possible in over 75% of cases. The following signs should alert the physician to the possibility or definite presence of multiple pregnancy:

1. Excessive maternal weight gain that is not explained by edema or obesity.

2. Polyhydramnios, manifested by uterine size out of proportion to the calculated duration of gestation. This condition is almost 10 times more common in multiple pregnancy.

3. Outline or ballottement of more than one fetus.

4. Multiplicity of small parts.

5. Uterus containing 3 or more large parts.

6. Simultaneous recording of different fetal heart rates, each asynchronous with the mother's pulse and with each other and varying by at least 8 beats per minute. (The fetus can be irritated mechanically, by pressure or displacement, to accelerate its heart rate.)

7. Palpation of one or more fetuses in the fundus after delivery of one infant.

B. Laboratory Findings: The vast majority of multiple pregnancies can be identified by radioimmunoassay for placental lactogen (hPL) with confirmation by ultrasonography or roentgenography. A single hPL value significantly above 3 μg/mL before 25 weeks' gestation, above 4 μg/mL at 25–30 weeks' gestation, or above 8 μg/mL after the 30th week indicates the probable presence of multiple pregnancy. However, variability is significant, so that the assay cannot substitute for clinical assessment of the pregnant uterus.

In multiple pregnancy, the mother's urinary chorionic gonadotropin, estriol, and pregnanediol titers are elevated. In addition, her mean serum values for cystine and leucine aminopeptidase, oxytocinase, and alkaline phosphatase are elevated above those of single pregnancy. Unfortunately, none of these determinations is augmented so greatly or noted early enough to be helpful in the diagnosis of plural pregnancy.

In twin pregnancies not accompanied by neural tube defects, the maternal serum α-fetoprotein (AFP) level will average twice the median level for singleton pregnancies, from about the third to the sixth month of gestation. With neural tube defects, the AFP level will be considerably higher.

The hematocrit, hemoglobin, and red cell count usually are considerably reduced, but blood volume is increased. Maternal anemia is common in plural pregnancy, beginning in the second trimester, when the fetal demand for iron increases beyond the mother's ability to assimilate iron.

C. Ultrasonography and X-Ray Findings: Ultrasonography is preferred to avoid unnecessary x-ray exposure of mother and fetuses. Twin pregnancy has been diagnosed by ultrasonography as early as the tenth week. Either modality will reveal the number of fetuses and their presentation in plural pregnancy after the 20th week. Both twins will present by the vertex in almost half of cases. One will be a vertex and the other a breech in slightly more than 33% of cases (Fig 35–3). Both fetuses will be breech presentations in 10% of cases, and almost that many will be single (or double) transverse presentations. Vertex presentation occurs 10 times more often in multiple pregnancy than in single pregnancy.

Approximately 70% of first twins present by the vertex. Breech presentation occurs in slightly more than 25%.

D. Electrocardiographic Findings: Electrocardiography by means of electrodes placed on the mother's abdomen in midline positions may be used to diagnose multiple pregnancy after the 20th week. Individual fetal electrocardiographic patterns will be superimposed upon the mother's. During the last 2 months of pregnancy, breech and vertex presentation can also be determined with great accuracy: If the baby's cardiac axis is similar to the mother's, both R waves will be in the same direction and the fetus must

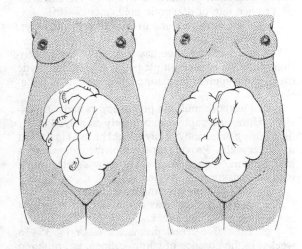

Figure 35–3. *Left:* Both twins presenting by the vertex. *Right:* One vertex and one breech presentation. (Reproduced, with permission, from Benson RC: *Handbook of Obstetrics & Gynecology,* 7th ed. Lange, 1980.)

be a breech. The R waves are in the opposite direction if the presentation is vertex.

Differential Diagnosis

Multiple pregnancy must be distinguished from the following conditions:

A. Single Pregnancy: Inaccurate dates may give a false impression of the duration of the pregnancy, and the fetus may be larger than expected. However, only one fetus can be palpated and one fetal heart heard.

B. Polyhydramnios: Either single or multiple pregnancy may be associated with excessive accumulation of fluid. Careful examination may distinguish one or more fetuses. Use ultrasonography or obtain x-ray films if the number and normality of the fetuses are still undetermined in the last trimester.

C. Abdominal Tumors Complicating Pregnancy: Fibroid tumors of the uterus, when present in great numbers, are readily identified. Ovarian tumors are generally single, discrete, and harder to diagnose.

D. Complicated Twin Pregnancy: If one dizygotic twin dies early in pregnancy and the other lives on, the dead fetus may become flattened and mummified (fetus papyraceus; see above). Its portion of a fused placenta will be pale and atrophic, but remnants of 2 sacs and 2 cords may be found. If one twin dies in late pregnancy, considerable enlargement of the uterus will persist, although the findings on palpation may be unusual and only one fetal heart will be heard. The living fetus generally will present first.

Amniography should reveal a single or double amniotic cavity.

Prevention

A. Of Multiple Pregnancy: Avoid the use of human pituitary gonadotropin to induce ovulation until the proper dosage has been established. Clomiphene citrate induction of multiple ovulation increases the occurrence rate of dizygotic pregnancy 5–10%.

B. Of Complications of Multiple Pregnancy:

1. Maternal–

a. Cervical cerclage has no place in the prevention of early birth in multiple pregnancy, but tocolytic drugs may suppress premature labor and extend gestation.

b. Diagnose multiple pregnancy as early as possible. Ultrasonography can be safely employed at any time during pregnancy; x-ray should be used in the last trimester only. Provide iron supplementation and a high-protein, high-vitamin diet; allow ample weight gain and ensure good hygiene.

c. Schedule more frequent antenatal visits.

d. Encourage the gravida to take frequent rest periods after the 24th week.

e. Treat threatened premature labor (< 35–36 weeks) in the absence of complications, eg, ruptured membranes or bleeding, with ritodrine or a comparable drug. (See p 612.)

f. All patients with multiple pregnancy should be delivered in a well-equipped hospital by an experienced physician who has adequate assistance with a pediatrician in attendance.

2. Fetal–

a. Identification of multiple births before the second trimester should result in better support and better fetal nutrition. Early arrangements should be made for delivery in a perinatal center.

b. Obtain ultrasonography late in pregnancy to determine the status of the fetuses. The risk of fetal abnormality in twins is more than double that in singleton pregnancy.

c. Monitor the fetuses carefully.

d. Use psychoprophylaxis; keep analgesia and general anesthesia to a minimum; employ local anesthesia.

e. Immaturity, trauma of manipulative delivery, and associated asphyxia are the major preventable causes of morbidity and mortality in twins, especially the second twin.

f. Convert the second twin to vertex by external (not internal) version immediately after delivery of the first twin, if feasible.

g. Deliver the second twin as soon as possible after rupture of the second sac.

h. Do a cesarean section during labor or promptly after diagnosis of monoamniotic twins. If cesarean section is not possible, deliver the second twin immediately after the first.

i. In cases of antepartum bleeding or hydramnios, try to delay the delivery until twins weigh at least 2500 g each. Increased rest periods during the second trimester may avoid premature labor.

j. Insist that pediatric care be given by specially trained personnel.

Treatment

A. Delivery: An assistant—scrubbed, gowned, and gloved—should always be present at the delivery of a patient with multiple pregnancy. During the latter part of the first stage of labor and continuing until the third stage is completed, give 1 L of 5% glucose in water through a No. 16 or No. 18 needle. Blood or specific medication, if indicated, should be administered without delay. The patient's blood should be typed and cross-matched, and several units of blood should be available in the delivery room for emergency transfusion.

Note: Do a cesarean section for accepted obstetric reasons. Multiple pregnancy itself is not an indication, but malpresentation, disproportion (eg, conjoined twins), or monoamniotic twins (diagnosed by amniography) are, especially for *low-birth-weight* babies.

The recommended procedure for delivery of twins is as follows:

1. Admit the patient to the hospital at the first sign of labor, significant bleeding, or leakage of amniotic fluid.

2. Limit analgesia drastically during labor. Infants often are premature, and operative intervention may be necessary. Use pudendal block anesthesia if

possible, since spinal, intravenous, deep intravenous, and deep inhalation anesthesia may be dangerous. Give oxygen to the mother by face mask during the second stage of labor.

Supplementary anesthesia for delivery of the second twin or manual removal of the placenta may be necessary.

3. If the first fetus presents by vertex or breech, deliver it in the usual manner. Avoid a difficult forceps or rapid breech extraction. The umbilical cord should be clamped promptly to prevent the second twin of a monozygotic pregnancy from partially exsanguinating through the first cord. The cord should be cut as far outside the vagina as possible. The cord then can hang loose to permit vaginal examination or manipulation. This also eliminates inadvertent cord traction on the placenta.

If the second fetus is in transverse presentation, do an external version and a slow, gentle extraction when the cervix is close to full dilatation. If the breech presents, anticipate engagement and progress toward an assisted breech delivery. In any case, make a deep episiotomy incision to minimize constriction of the head.

Tag and label (A and B) the twins and the cords attached to the placenta.

4. Do not give oxytocin or ergot products after the birth of the first twin. Reduction of the uteroplacental circulation will jeopardize the second twin.

5. Perform a vaginal examination immediately after delivery of the first infant to ascertain the presentation of the second infant, the presence of a second sac, and the possibility of cord prolapse or entanglement.

6. Within minutes after the birth of the first twin, bring the second into a longitudinal presentation (preferably vertex) by abdominovaginal manipulation. Cautiously rupture the membranes to allow a slow loss of fluid while the presenting part is being pressed into the inlet by an assistant.

If there is no second amniotic sac (monoamniotic monozygotic twins), deliver the second twin at once to prevent cord entanglement, asphyxia, or premature separation of the placenta. About 50% of such second twins die if delivery is not rapidly and skillfully accomplished.

Encourage a vertex presentation to progress, with the next few contractions, toward spontaneous delivery or prophylactic forceps delivery. If the breech is presenting, proceed with an assisted breech delivery.

If the second twin cannot be brought in easily as a vertex, plan delivery as a breech. If descent is delayed, version and extraction within about 5 minutes after rupture of the second amniotic sac is better than procrastination or a difficult forceps delivery.

Cautiously administer dilute oxytocin intravenously, to stimulate uterine contractions when uterine inertia becomes a problem.

7. Manage the third stage of labor with care. Administer oxytocin (Pitocin), 1 mL intravenously, immediately after delivery of the second twin; con-

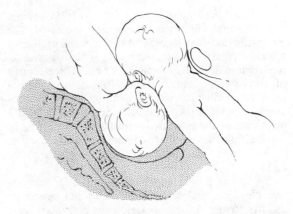

Figure 35–4. Locked twins. (Reproduced, with permission, from Benson RC: *Handbook of Obstetrics & Gynecology,* 4th ed. Lange, 1971.)

tinue the intravenous oxytocin drip. Elevate but do not massage the fundus until after the uterus contracts and expels the separated placenta; then give an ergot preparation such as ergonovine maleate (Methergine), 0.1 mg intravenously, and gently massage and elevate the fundus for 15–30 minutes. If separation of the placenta is delayed or bleeding is brisk, separate and extract the placenta manually.

8. In the case of locked twins (Fig 35–4), the patient should be placed under deep anesthesia. Have an assistant support the twin already partially delivered as a breech. Push both hands upward out of the pelvis, rotate both fetuses, and then try to deliver the first. If this cannot be done, elevate the partially delivered twin, establish an airway, and protect the cord. When the undescended twin dies, decapitate it, deliver the first twin, and then deliver the body and head of the dead twin. In most instances, both fetuses will die if the physician takes time to do a cesarean section.

B. General Measures: Maintain optimal weight gain during pregnancy: ideal weight for height and build plus approximately 11–13 kg. Try to prevent anemia, preeclampsia-eclampsia, and vaginal infections; if they do occur, treat them early.

Reduced activity and prolonged rest periods (with the patient lying down) after the 24th week (or whenever the diagnosis is made) may limit the incidence of prematurity in multiple births and, therefore, the high incidence of perinatal morbidity and mortality in this gestational period.

C. Treatment of Complications: Preeclampsia-eclampsia, premature labor and delivery, etc, are managed as outlined elsewhere in this book. If dystocia occurs, obtain x-ray films to rule out malpresentation or conjoined twins. Explore the cervical canal and the lower uterine segment vaginally for soft tissue dystocia.

Complications

A. Maternal Complications: The frequency of spontaneous abortion of at least one of several fetuses is increased in plural pregnancy (at least 1:35). Premature labor and delivery are also greatly increased. The overdistended uterus seems, at last, to reach its limit of tolerance, and the result is uterine contractions, premature rupture of the membranes, or both. Three-fourths of all multiple pregnancies result in delivery before term. Stillbirth occurs twice as often among twin as among singleton pregnancies. Most twins are born 3 weeks before the estimated date of confinement. Early cervical dilatation and effacement and inadequacy of the placenta to meet fetal needs are possible causative factors.

Placenta previa may be responsible for antepartum bleeding, malpresentation, or unengagement of the first fetus. A large placenta (or placentas) and, perhaps, fundal scarring or tumor may lead to low implantation of the placenta.

Hypochromic normocytic anemia is 2–3 times more common in multiple pregnancy than in single pregnancy. Thus, anemia may be a sign of plural pregnancy. A greater need for iron must be met, even at the mother's expense.

Urinary tract infection is at least twice as frequent in multiple pregnancy as in single-fetus pregnancy owing to increased ureteral dilatation secondary to higher serum progesterone and uterine pressure on the ureters.

Preeclampsia-eclampsia occurs about 3 times as often in multiple pregnancy as with a singleton. Uterine distention, impairment of the uteroplacental circulation, and nutritional deficiencies have been postulated as causes.

A thinned uterine wall, secondary to unusually large uterine contents, is associated with hypotonic uterine contractions and a longer latent stage of labor. Prolonged labor is uncommon in multiple pregnancy, however, because rupture of the membranes generally is followed by improvements in the uterine contraction pattern.

If the amniotic sac of the second twin ruptures before that of the first and if the cord prolapses, cesarean section usually is indicated. Otherwise, allow labor to proceed.

Premature separation of the placenta may occur antepartum, perhaps in association with preeclampsia-eclampsia or with rupture of the first bag of waters and the initiation of strong uterine contractions, or after the delivery of the first twin. Careless traction on the first cord may encourage early partial separation of the placenta.

When there are 2 separate placentas, one of them may deliver immediately after the first twin. Although the second twin may not be compromised, it is best to proceed with its delivery, both for its protection and to conserve maternal blood.

Operative intervention is more likely in multiple pregnancy because of increased obstetric problems such as malpresentation, prolapsed cord, and fetal distress.

Uterine atony often is accompanied by excessive loss of blood postpartum owing to inability of the overdistended uterus to contract well and remain contracted after delivery.

B. Fetal Complications:

1. Antepartum complications–Fetal death is about 3 times more common in multiple than in single pregnancy. Death may be due to cord compression, placental disorders, or developmental anomalies. The greatest hazard from cord compression is cord entanglement of monozygotic twins with only one amniotic sac. Developmental anomalies and polyhydramnios are common in monozygotic twins. Almost twice as many monozygotic as dizygotic twins die in the perinatal period. Attrition is even greater for triplets, quadruplets, etc.

2. Intrapartum complications–These are the most common causes of fetal loss in multiple pregnancy. Delivery 1 month before term is due to premature labor, often secondary to premature rupture of the membranes, which occurs in about 25% of twin, 50% of triplet, and 75% of quadruplet pregnancies. Abnormal and breech presentation, circulatory interference by one fetus with the other, and operative delivery all increase fetal loss. Prolapse of the cord occurs 5 times more often in multiple than in single pregnancy. Premature separation of the placenta before delivery of the second twin may cause death of the second twin by hypoxia. One twin may obstruct the delivery of both fetuses; in locked twins (Fig 35–4), the first is always a breech and the second a vertex presentation. The heads become impacted in the pelvis, and one or both fetuses may die despite operation. Conjoined twins may be undetected before labor. Dystocia often occurs, and the twins may die during attempts at vaginal delivery.

3. Postpartum complications–Regardless of the cause, delivery before 33 weeks' gestational age (< 2000 g) is extremely hazardous for the newborns. Such premature infants account for more than 75% of the neonatal deaths in multiple pregnancies.

The mortality rates for infants weighing less than 2000 g are approximately the same in twins and singletons: about 30%. Although the complications in multiple gestations are much greater, the slowing of fetal growth in the last trimester gives twin fetuses the advantage of increased maturity for weight. If we could delay delivery in cases of multiple birth until the fetuses achieve a weight of even 2000–2250 g, the overall mortality rate would be reduced at least 8 times. Perhaps as important, the chance of residual damage in survivors and the cost of intensive care would be greatly diminished.

It is urgent for an experienced physician to be present for resuscitation and stabilization of each infant born at high risk. Unfortunately, most multiple-birth newborns who were delivered before the 34th week and were referred to a neonatal center for care were undiagnosed before birth. Survival depends upon obstetric and pediatric difficulties and their solution. Delivery before the 36th week is twice as frequent in twin pregnancies as in single pregnancies. Intracranial injury is more common in premature infants—even those delivered spontaneously—and often leads to death in the neonatal period.

Treatment of twins involved in cross-transfusion is as follows:

a. Donor twin–Replace blood to correct fluid and electrolyte imbalance.

b. Recipient twin–Phlebotomize until normal venous pressure is restored; administer digitalis.

Prognosis

A. Maternal: The maternal mortality rate in multiple pregnancy in the USA is only slightly higher than in single pregnancy. A history of previous dizygotic twins increases the likelihood of subsequent multiple pregnancy 10-fold. Hemorrhage is about 5 times as frequent in plural as in single pregnancies. The probability of abnormal presentation and of operative delivery and its complications is increased in multiple pregnancy. Premature rupture of the membranes and premature labor, often with a long prodromal phase, are a common occurrence in multiple pregnancy.

Almost 50% of twins weigh 2500 g or less, but the majority of these are of 36 weeks' gestational age or more. A gravida with a multiple pregnancy has about 5 times the likelihood of having a morbid (febrile, complicated) course as an average patient of the same parity with a single fetus.

B. Fetal: Hydramnios is 5 times as frequent in multiple as in single pregnancies, principally because of fetal abnormality.

"Unlike sex, generally unlike outcome" applies to twins. The greatest loss occurs when both twins are of the same sex; and male pairs succumb more readily than female pairs.

Perinatal mortality and morbidity rates are increased in multiple pregnancy, mainly because of prematurity and the complications of labor and delivery. Preeclampsia-eclampsia and other disorders may further jeopardize the fetuses.

The best outlook is for both twins to present by the vertex. Twins and other multiple fetuses delivered by spontaneous means do better than those extracted by forceps or after version.

The critical weight level for survival of twins is about 2500 g. If twins weigh more than this at birth, the likelihood that they will live approximates that of a singleton of about the same gestational age.

The perinatal death rates (per 1000) for single and multiple pregnancy are as follows: singletons, 39; twins, 152; triplets, 309; and quadruplets, 509. The rates are proportionately higher for quintuplets, etc.

First twins have about a 3% greater chance of survival than second twins. Breech presentation of the second twin carries a higher mortality and morbidity rate. Internal podalic version is especially dangerous. Hypoxia and trauma of operative delivery are the primary causes of death of the second twin. Central nervous system disease and hyaline membrane disease are frequently diagnosed in a surviving second twin.

Dystrophy noted at birth is associated with a slower weight gain during extrauterine life. A twin whose birth weight is less than 20% of that of its partner will not gain as rapidly and may never catch up with the other in weight and height.

The larger monozygotic twin's IQ is likely to be higher than that of the smaller twin if the weight difference is more than 300 g at birth.

The female twin of a female-male pair that survives cross-transfusion is not sterile (like a bovine freemartin).

Concordance of placental examination, clinical comparisons, and hematologic and serologic tests provides presumptive evidence of monozygotic twinning. The total probability of diagnosis of zygosity is over 95% using ABO, MNSs, Rh, Kell, Kidd, Duffy, and Lewis A and B antigens. Actual proof, however, requires successful skin grafting or organ transplantation.

• • •

References

Austin E et al: The antepartum diagnosis of conjoined twins. *Pediatr Surg* 1980;**15**:332.

Cetrulo CL, Ingardia CJ, Sbarra AJ: Management of multiple gestation. *Clin Obstet Gynecol* 1980;**23**:533.

Crane JP, Tomich PG, Kopta M: Ultrasonic growth patterns in normal and discordant twins. *Obstet Gynecol* 1980;**55**:678.

Doig JR, Svensen TC: Conjoined twins. *Aust NZ J Obstet Gynaecol* 1978;**18**:215.

Duncan SLB, Ginz B, Waliab H: Use of ultrasound and hormone assays in the diagnosis, management, and outcome of twin pregnancy. *Obstet Gynecol* 1979;**53**:367.

Ekwemper CC: Continuation of abdominal pregnancy complicated by preeclampsia 3 weeks after birth of an extrauterine twin. *Int J Gynaecol Obstet* 1979;**16**:324.

Finberg HJ, Birnholz JC: Ultrasound observations in multiple gestation with first trimester bleeding. *Radiology* 1979;**132**:137.

Genetic amniocentesis in twin pregnancies. (Editorial.) *Br Med J* 1979;**2**:1455.

Gerbie ES et al: Genetic amniocentesis in twin gestations. *Am J Obstet Gynecol* 1980;**138**:169.

Grennert L et al: Zygosity and intrauterine growth of twins. *Obstet Gynecol* 1980;**55**:684.

Hafez ESE: Physiology of multiple pregnancy. *J Reprod Med* 1978;**12**:88.

Haney AF, Crenshaw MC Jr, Dempsey PJ: Significance of biparietal diameter differences between twins. *Obstet Gynecol* 1978;**51**:609.

Itzkowic D: A survey of 59 triplet pregnancies. *Br J Obstet Gynaecol* 1979;**86**:23.

James WH: Gestational age in twins. *Arch Dis Child* 1980;**55**:281.

Jarvis GJ: Diagnosis of multiple pregnancy. *Br Med J* 1979;**2**:593.

Keith L et al: The Northwestern University multihospital twin study. 1. A description of 588 twin pregnancies and associated pregnancy loss. *Am J Obstet Gynecol* 1980;**138**:781.

Livenko KJ et al: Sonar cephalometry in twins: A table of biparietal diameters for normal twin fetuses and a comparison with singletons. *Am J Obstet Gynecol* 1979;**135**:727.

Livingston JE, Poland BJ: A study of spontaneously aborted twins. *Teratology* 1980;**21**:139.

MacGillivray I: Twin pregnancies. *Obstet Gynecol Annu* 1978;**7**:135.

MacLean AB et al: Successful triplet pregnancy following renal transplantation. *Scott Med J* 1980;**25**:320.

Manlan G, Scott KE: Contribution of twin pregnancy to perinatal mortality and fetal growth retardation: Reversal of growth retardation after birth. *Can Med Assoc J* 1978;**118**:365.

Medaris AL et al: Perinatal deaths in twin pregnancy–5-Year analysis of statewide statistics in Missouri. *Am J Obstet Gynecol* 1979;**134**:413.

Naeye RJ et al: Twins: Causes of perinatal death in 12 United States cities and one African city. *Am J Obstet Gynecol* 1978;**131**:267.

Panayiotis G, Grunstein S: Extramembranous pregnancy in twin gestation. *Obstet Gynecol* 1979;**53 (Suppl)**:34S.

Persson PH et al: On improved outcome of twin pregnancies. *Acta Obstet Gynecol Scand* 1979;**58**:3.

Powers WF, Miller TC: Bed rest in twin pregnancy: Identification of a critical period and its cost implications. *Am J Obstet Gynecol* 1979;**134**:23.

Record RG, Armstrong E, Lancashire RJ: A study of the fertility of mothers of twins. *J Epidemiol Community Health* 1978;**32**:183.

Rosenberg HK, Spackman TJ, Chait A: The Dominican Republic conjoined twins: Ischiopagus, tetrapus, omphalopagus. *Am J Roentgenol* 1978;**130**:921.

Schenker JG et al: Quintuplet pregnancies. *Eur J Obstet Gynaecol Reprod Biol* 1980;**10**:257.

Simon R: Statistical methods for evaluating pregnancy outcome in patients with Hodgkin's disease. *Cancer* 1980;**45**:289.

Spellacy WM, Buhi WC, Birk SA: Human placental lactogen levels in multiple pregnancies. *Obstet Gynecol* 1978;**52**:210.

Tamby RRL, Salmon Y: Salbutamol therapy for prevention of prematurity in twins. *Med Sci Clin Med* 1978;**6**:91.

Terasaki PI et al: Twins with two different fathers identified by HLA. *N Engl J Med* 1978;**299**:590.

The Newborn Infant | 36

Beverly L. Koops, MD

Anticipation of high-risk neonatal situations, prevention of their occurrence, and provision of sensitive, family-centered care to all newborn infants, normal and abnormal, are the goals of today's neonatal health care providers. The attitudes and perspectives commensurate with these goals have been founded on a relatively new area of knowledge and skills and embodied in a subspecialty of pediatrics called **neonatology.** As neonatology has become more complex and highly subspecialized, the need for careful decision making and cooperation with health care providers to the pregnant couple has become increasingly clear. The goals of perinatal/neonatal medicine are to decrease perinatal and neonatal mortality and morbidity. Health care professionals who advocate this perinatal/neonatal perspective have developed a regionalized network of maternal and newborn care. They believe that pregnant and newborn patients, entering at any point in the care system, must have access to whatever level of health services they need.

During the past few years, neonatal services have been divided into 3 levels of infant care (low-risk care, level 1; intermediate care, level 2; and intensive care, level 3) and 2 levels of obstetric services (a "regular" or low-risk service and a high-risk service).

The low-risk level 1 nurseries are usually for full-term infants and often function as "rooming-in" units. The major tasks of level 1 personnel are to encourage the development of good parenting skills, to assist and monitor the infant in adjusting to extrauterine life, and to initiate screening tests for various acute and congenital problems such as hypoglycemia, phenylketonuria, and hypothyroidism. Level 1 units should have excellent delivery room and treatment area facilities, so that infants with unexpected problems in the delivery room or nursery can be cared for briefly and their conditions stabilized in preparation for transport to level 2 or level 3 units.

Level 2 nurseries are for sick and convalescent newborn infants, including most preterm infants above 32 weeks in gestational age or 1500 g in birth weight. Most infants with intrauterine growth retardation or infants of diabetic mothers can be cared for in these units. These nurseries rarely attempt to treat infants requiring arterial catheterization, specialized respiratory care, or intubation, but they do care for infants requiring intravenous infusions, management of infections, and a variety of metabolic problems.

Level 3 nurseries care for sick infants regardless of their size, gestational age, or severity of illness. In general, these nurseries treat infants during the acute phase of a critical illness. Infants with chronic intensive care problems (eg, those who need central alimentation, tracheostomy care, etc) usually remain in level 3 units. Once the condition of the infants has improved sufficiently, they are discharged to a level 2 nursery closer to their homes.

The major responsibility for optimal care rests with primary health care providers who see, examine, and evaluate patients and who are the first to plan management of pregnancy, delivery, and postpartum care for mother and infant. When risks or problems are recognized, appropriate care may be provided at the primary care level, or consultation and referral to centers with secondary or tertiary care services may be arranged.

This chapter discusses the newborn care that is appropriately delivered in community health care centers and the interrelationships of primary, secondary, and tertiary services within the regional system. More detailed discussion of newborn illnesses and care techniques may be found in the pediatric and neonatal references listed at the end of this chapter.

PREDICTION OF PREGNANCY OUTCOME

Earlier chapters have included discussions of factors that may be anticipated to increase the risk of poor pregnancy outcome—repeated pregnancy loss, previous premature delivery, multiple gestation, maternal hypertension, infection, and many others. Identification of these risk factors guides physicians and nurses toward appropriate observation and monitoring of a current pregnancy. They also serve as a data bank upon which to base decisions about how delivery should be accomplished and what specialist personnel should be present in the delivery room in order to ensure the best outcome for the infant.

An important example of this type of planning is one based on estimates of birth weight and length of gestation (Fig 36–1). These 2 predictors place the infant into the categories of large-, appropriate-, or small-for-gestational-age and preterm, term, or post-term. Establishing the category is important in caring for an infant, because one can thereby anticipate mor-

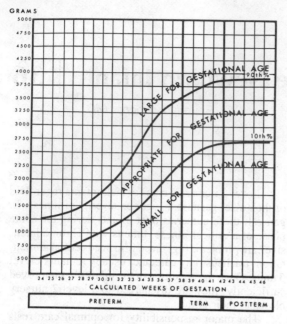

Figure 36–1. Classification of newborn infants by birth weight and calculated gestational age, from Colorado data. (Reproduced, with permission, from Battaglia FC, Lubchenco LO: *J Pediatr* 1967;**71**:160.)

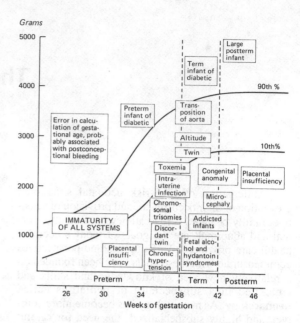

Figure 36–2. Conditions associated with intrauterine growth and their relation to birth weight and gestational age. (Reproduced, with permission, from: Lubchenco LO: *The High Risk Infant.* Saunders, 1976.)

tality risk and potential neonatal problems. For example, infants who are born extremely preterm usually require vigorous resuscitation and immediate intensive care upon delivery; they are best delivered in a center that provides high-risk care 24 hours a day.

Normal intrauterine growth leading to term delivery results in a baby with the best chance of an excellent outcome. Deviations from normal intrauterine growth patterns represent reliable and sensitive criteria for identifying newborns who are at risk. Fig 36–2 shows conditions that affect the fetus and are associated with predictable deviations from normal intrauterine growth patterns.

Large-for-gestational-age (LGA) infants are most commonly at risk of birth injury, birth asphyxia, hypoglycemia, and selected birth defects. Small-for-gestational-age (SGA) infants may have severe intrapartum asphyxia, nutritional deprivation, mechanical trauma during labor and delivery, and congenital infections or defects. Premature infants are susceptible to metabolic derangements, respiratory distress, central nervous system hemorrhage, and infection, all associated with immature functioning of organ systems. Postmature infants are typically depleted of oxygen and nutritives during the intrapartum events, resulting in asphyxia, meconium aspiration, hypoglycemia, and polycythemia in the immediate newborn period. Those infants who are born at term, ie, 38–41 weeks of gestation, have the lowest predicted mortality rate (Fig 36–3). These data were developed from neonatal mortality rates for infants delivered at the tertiary center (rather than transported) during the

years 1958–1969, which was before the era of intensive neonatal care. Given the aggressive perinatal approach to delivery and neonatal resuscitation of all birth weight and gestational age groups, prevention or early treatment of neonatal problems noted above, and current tools for fetal monitoring and neonatal care (including the ventilator, alarming monitor, blood gas analyzer, and transport incubator), mortality rates have changed dramatically. Deaths are now rare among LGA, SGA, and postmature infants. The death rate of premature infants has been markedly reduced at all gestational ages, and the limit of viability is now near 25 weeks of gestation and 700 g birth weight.

Classification of neonatal mortality rates by birth weight and gestational age is a concept that can quickly be put to practical use by every medical center where infants are delivered. As shown in Fig 36–4, the Oregon mortality rate of 13:1000 and the Colorado mortality rate of 23:1000, during the same years of service, were in fact closely similar when corrected for birth weight and gestational age. Furthermore, it was shown that although risk factors of race, altitude, multiple gestation, and financial status were associated with neonatal birth weight and gestational age, they were not causes of death. Each hospital should review its own neonatal mortality statistics, so that decisions about upgrading services and about referring or accepting perinatal or neonatal patients can be made rationally.

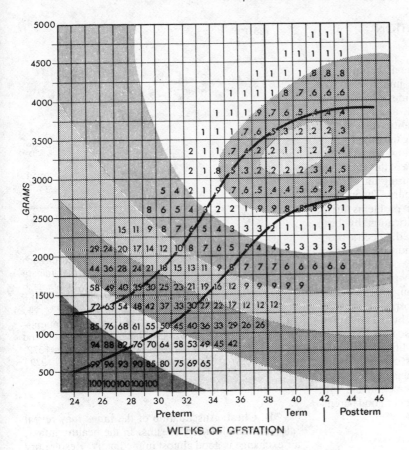

Figure 36–3. Neonatal mortality risk by birth weight and gestational age. The interpolated data, expressed in percentage, are based on mathematical fit from original data on University of Colorado Medical Center newborns, 1 July 1958 to 1 July 1969. (Reproduced, with permission, from Lubchenco LO et al: *J Pediatr* 1972; **81**:814.)

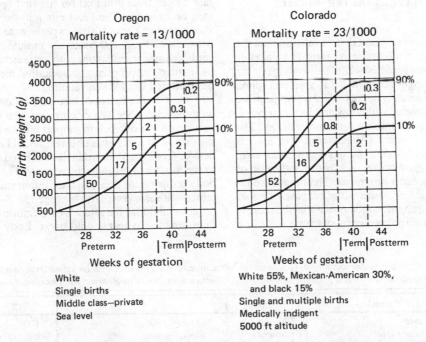

Figure 36–4. Although the overall neonatal mortality rate for Oregon is 13 per 1000 live births and for Colorado the rate is 23 per 1000, the mortality rates by birth weight and gestational age are essentially the same in the 2 populations. Therefore, the distribution of births in the Oregon population must include more term infants who are appropriate for gestational age. (Reproduced and adapted, with permission, from Behrman RE, Babson GS, Lessell R: Fetal and neonatal mortality risks by gestational age and weight. *Am J Dis Child* 1971; **121**:486.)

PHYSICAL EXAMINATION

The physical examination of the newborn should be appropriate for the age of the infant. The first examination should be performed immediately after birth, usually in the delivery room, and is aimed at identifying life-threatening abnormalities that require immediate attention and at evaluating the infant's ability to adjust to extrauterine life. A thorough or "complete" examination is not appropriate at this time. The second examination may be done during the "transition" period, which may last 1–4 hours. The infant is observed but not disturbed unless problems arise. Weight, measurements, and classification by birth weight and gestational age are recorded. Specific problems that are likely to occur, as indicated by these parameters, may be investigated. The complete examination, or third evaluation, is ideally performed after 12–24 hours and should be thorough. The fourth evaluation is done at the time of hospital discharge. The discharge examination may be brief and is performed in the presence of the mother so that she and the examiner may assess the infant's condition and discuss the findings. Considerable effort is currently being expended to find ways of evaluating the infant with the least disturbance to mother-child interaction and with the least disruption to the development of good parenting patterns.

THE INFANT
IMMEDIATELY AFTER BIRTH

Evaluations

A. Apgar Score: Immediate evaluation of the newborn at 1 and 5 minutes after birth is a valuable routine procedure (Table 36–1). The newborn in the best condition (Apgar score 8–10) is vigorous, pink, and crying. A moderately depressed baby (Apgar score 5–7) appears cyanotic, with slow and irregular respirations, but has good muscle tone and reflexes. The severely depressed infant (Apgar score 4 or less) is limp, pale or blue, apneic, and has a slow heart rate. The 5-minute Apgar score is a better indicator of neonatal and long-term prognosis. The premature infant may have a lower Apgar score because of lesser muscle tone and strength, which means that the score is of much less value for predicting outcome.

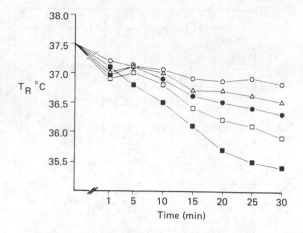

Figure 36–5. Mean deep body temperatures (T_R) of each group during the first 30 minutes of life. T_R is on the ordinate and minutes postdelivery on the abscissa. ■ wet infants in room air; □ dry infants in room air; ● wet infants under the radiant heater; △ dry infants wrapped in a blanket; ○ dry infants under the radiant heater. (Reproduced, with permission, from Dahm LS, James LS: Newborn temperature and calculated heat loss in the delivery room. *Pediatrics* 1972; **49**:504. Copyright American Academy of Pediatrics 1972.)

B. Chest: Auscultation of the lungs may reveal rales with the first few breaths. In the healthy infant, air exchange is good almost immediately. Respiratory rate ranges from 30 to 60 for the first few hours and may be irregular. The heart rate may be variable but should remain above 100 beats per minute and stabilize between 120 and 160 beats per minute. Satisfactory cardiopulmonary adjustment to extrauterine life must be assured. Appropriate resuscitative measures must be instituted early when required.

C. Temperature: At birth, the infant's skin must be toweled dry because evaporative heat loss is enormous, and it is difficult to support body temperature if the skin is wet. A radiant heater should be used in the delivery room until the infant is stable and can be given to the mother or taken to the nursery (Fig 36–5). The body temperature of a newborn infant must be maintained within a very narrow range (36.5–37.3 °C) in order to minimize the infant's own caloric expenditure in responding to heat or cold stress. Body temperature

Table 36–1. Infant evaluation at birth (Apgar score).* One minute and 5 minutes after complete birth of infant (disregarding cord and placenta), the following objective signs should be observed and recorded.

Points	0	1	2
1. Heart rate	Absent	Slow (<100)	>100
2. Respiratory effort	Absent	Slow, irregular	Good, crying
3. Muscle tone	Limp	Some flexion of extremities	Active motion
4. Response to catheter in nostril (tested after oropharynx is clear)	No response	Grimace	Cough or sneeze
5. Color	Blue or pale	Body pink; extremities blue	Completely pink

*Reproduced, with permission, from Apgar V: *JAMA* 1958;**168**:1985.

will fall precipitously in a cool environment unless adequate precautions are taken. As cooling occurs, the infant becomes cyanotic—first in the hands and feet, then in the face, and finally over the entire body—and may develop grunting respirations and retractions.

D. Skin: Cyanosis of the peripheral portions of the extremities is common for a short time after birth. The presence of persistent cyanosis, pallor, petechiae, ecchymoses, or plethora requires further investigation. Pallor in the newborn infant may indicate possible acute hemorrhage into the maternal circulation, perhaps caused by a tear in a placental vessel. Ecchymoses of the skin, particularly in preterm infants following breech vaginal deliveries, may be a manifestation of extensive hemorrhage into the deep muscles of the back or buttocks, which may be severe enough to cause shock. In all cases of suspected hemorrhage, prompt expansion of blood volume should be achieved by means of placental blood, albumin, Plasmanate, or some other appropriate colloid solution. Blood volume expansion should be done with care; infusion of blood products and large volumes of solutions are not without risk. However, except for infectious or hypoxic shock, few conditions occur in the newborn infant at delivery that are likely to be confused with acute blood loss. Jaundice at birth is a grave finding and requires immediate evaluation.

E. Abdomen: The abdomen should be soft and somewhat scaphoid immediately after birth. As the bowel fills with gas, the abdomen becomes more full. Abdominal organs are easily palpated during this period. A marked and persistent scaphoid abdomen suggests diaphragmatic hernia with some abdominal contents within the chest. A distended abdomen may suggest organomegaly, ascites, or bowel obstruction.

F. General Appearance: Sex, physical growth parameters, and neurologic maturity should be noted in relation to gestational age. Malformations, deformations, asymmetric movements, or other evidence of birth injury should be observed.

Fetal Adnexa

A. Amniotic Fluid: The color, appearance, and estimate of volume of amniotic fluid should be noted. Normal amniotic fluid at term is a light straw color, usually slightly turbid with vernix and other debris. Yellow color suggests bilirubin, usually secondary to hemolytic disease in the fetus. Bright red fresh blood or chocolate-colored old blood pigments may be present. Meconium may discolor fluid dark green or greenish-yellow, and chunks of meconium may be present. Excessive fluid volume may occur when the upper gastrointestinal tract is obstructed or when fetal swallowing is deficient (as with anencephaly). Scanty fluid occurs with certain fetal anomalies (renal agenesis, urinary obstruction) and ruptured membranes.

B. Umbilical Cord:

1. Gross appearance–Cord diameter varies greatly, depending chiefly on the amount of Wharton's jelly present. The cord of term infants with small placentas is likely to be thin and stained yellow. Meconium staining of the cord indicates prior fetal distress. The cord is usually inserted concentrically on the placenta. When the insertion is velamentous, arising away from the placental margin and supported only by the amnion, there is increased risk of fetal hemorrhage during delivery. Velamentous insertions of the cord occur commonly in multiple births.

2. Length–A very short cord is uncommon but can result in abruptio placentae or rupture of the cord. A very long cord (75 cm or more) may loop around the body or neck, resulting in a relatively short cord during delivery. Loops about the neck are rarely a cause of asphyxia.

3. Single umbilical artery–The vessels of the umbilical cord are best observed in a freshly cut section at birth. Normally, 2 arteries and one vein are present. A single artery is present in approximately 1% of births. The incidence rises to 5–6% in twins. The twin with a single umbilical artery is often significantly smaller than the twin with 2 arteries. A single umbilical artery is considered a congenital vascular malformation. Associated congenital abnormalities, especially of the cardiovascular, gastrointestinal, or urinary systems, may be present, although the incidence of associated anomalies is not high enough to justify special diagnostic tests in the absence of any specific clinical signs.

4. Prolapsed cord–Prolapsed umbilical cord with compression during labor causes acute fetal distress. This is an obstetric emergency, and prompt treatment is necessary if the life and welfare of the baby are to be preserved. Perinatal mortality with prolapsed umbilical cord is about 35%.

C. Placenta: In general, the weight of the placenta is related to the weight of the baby. The average placenta weighs about 500 g. Small placentas result from local disease in the placenta (infarction) or systemic disease in the mother (severe hypertension or chronic vascular disease). The infant is small and undernourished. Before delivery, these infants may have suffered chronic hypoxia and may tolerate labor stress poorly. After delivery, they may become hypoglycemic. The presence of congenital anomalies or chronic infection should be suspected if the infant is small but the placenta is of normal size.

Large placentas occur with large normal babies, with infants of diabetic mothers, in Rh isoimmunization, and in chronic intrauterine infection.

Careful examination of the placenta and membranes in multiple births can often differentiate single ovum and multiple ovum twinning. In single ovum twins, two-thirds will show one placenta, one chorion, and a double or single amnion. The remainder will have 2 placentas (sometimes fused), 2 chorions, and 2 amnions—the same as double ovum twins.

THE INFANT DURING THE FIRST FEW HOURS AFTER BIRTH

During the first few hours after birth, the normal baby progresses through a fairly predictable sequence of events, recovering from the stress of delivery and adaptation to extrauterine life. The baby neither requires nor easily tolerates the handling involved with a complete physical examination. However, a considerable portion of the physical examination and evalua-

tion of the newborn can be based on careful observation of the infant. This is especially important during the birth recovery period in order to identify early—but without excessive handling—the infant who is at increased risk of developing problems. Observation of abnormal findings such as hypotension, pallor, cyanosis, plethora, jaundice, birth injury, respiratory distress, abdominal distention, hyperactivity, abnormal birth recovery period, or discrepant clinical estimation of gestational age requires early, more detailed

Table 36—2. Assessment of gestational age.*†

	0	1	2	3	4	5
Neuromuscular maturity						
Posture						
Square window (wrist)	90°	60°	45°	30°	0°	
Arm recoil	180°		100°–180°	90°–100°	< 90°	
Popliteal angle	180°	160°	130°	110°	90°	< 90°
Scarf sign						
Heel to ear						
Physical maturity						
Skin	Gelatinous, red, transparent	Smooth, pink; visible veins	Superficial peeling and/or rash; few veins	Cracking, pale area; rare veins	Parchment, deep cracking; no vessels	Leathery, cracked, wrinkled
Lanugo	None	Abundant	Thinning	Bald areas	Mostly bald	
Plantar creases	No crease	Faint red marks	Anterior transverse crease only	Creases anterior two-thirds	Creases cover entire sole	
Breast	Barely perceptible	Flat areola; no bud	Stippled areola; bud, 1–2 mm	Raised areola; bud, 3–4 mm	Full areola; bud, 5–10 mm	
Ear	Pinna flat; stays folded	Slightly curved pinna; soft; slow recoil	Well-curved pinna; soft; ready recoil	Formed and firm; instant recoil	Thick cartilage; ear stiff	
Genitals (male)	Scrotum empty; no rugae		Testes descending; few rugae	Testes down; good rugae	Testes pendulous; deep rugae	
Genitals (female)	Prominent clitoris and labia minora		Majora and minora equally prominent	Majora large; minora small	Clitoris and minora completely covered	

*Maturity rating.

Score	5	10	15	20	25	30	35	40	45	50
Weeks	26	28	30	32	34	36	38	40	42	44

†Reproduced, with permission, from Klaus MH, Fanaroff AA: *Care of the High-Risk Neonate.* Saunders, 1973.

evaluation. The nurses caring for the infant play a vital role in observing and evaluating the infant during this period. (See below for description of the complete physical examination, and pp 779 ff for routine care of the newborn during this period.)

Birth Recovery Period

Desmond has described the physical findings associated with the postnatal adjustment in normal infants.

A. First Stage: For 30–60 minutes after delivery, the infant is active, with eyes open and alert and muscle tone increased. The heart and respiratory rates are rapid, and transient rales may be heard. Bowel sounds are absent. The infant may drool or vomit mucus. There is usually some fall in body temperature. Respirations may be accompanied by flaring of the alae nasi, costal retractions, and grunting.

B. Second Stage: Between about 30 minutes and 2 hours, there is a decrease in heart and respiratory rates; motor activity declines; and the infant falls asleep.

C. Third Stage: After about 2 hours, the infant arouses. There again is an increase in heart rate, vasomotor instability, and irregular respirations with rest periods. Oral mucus is present. Bowel sounds appear, and meconium is passed. The infant gradually stabilizes, and by 6–12 hours may begin to demand feedings.

Recognition of an abnormal birth recovery period may be an important clue to underlying disease. Significant deviation from the basic sequence of events may result from a variety of influences. The preterm infant's response is prolonged. Infants with low Apgar scores show an initial delay in the first stage but may then recover rapidly. Drugs administered to the mother, birth trauma, and disease in the newborn may alter the birth recovery events.

Clinical Estimation of Gestational Age

The onset of the mother's last menstrual period is the basic information from which the period of gestation is calculated. During pregnancy, observations of increasing fundal height, onset of fetal movement, detection of fetal heart beat, and certain laboratory tests aid in determining the degree of maturity of the fetus.

It is possible to estimate the gestational age of the infant by examination after birth, since fetal physical characteristics and neurologic development progress in a predictable fashion with increasing gestational age. Table 36–2 itemizes the clinical criteria used in determining gestational age and outlines the physical and neurologic findings observed in the infant born at various gestational ages. This is a shortened version of the Dubowitz estimate of clinical gestational age. It takes only 5–10 minutes and is usually adequate. The detailed examination is presented in many pediatric textbooks. The examination for gestational age requires very little manipulation of the infant yet gives important data for assessing gestational age. Each

physical characteristic is given a score from 0 to 5. Similarly, selected neurologic characteristics are examined that reflect the infant's muscle tone and strength. These are also scored from 0 to 5. The total score achieved on this "maturity rating" is correlated with the clinical gestational age given in the table. Discrepancies in maturation between the physical and neurologic characteristics often reflect a problem in intrauterine growth.

The clinical findings may be altered when intrauterine growth is altered. For example, infants with intrauterine growth retardation due to undernutrition may show the following:

(1) Diminished growth or absence of breast tissue and, in the female, diminished labia majora.

(2) Loss of vernix and desquamation of the skin prior to term.

(3) Meconium staining of the skin and nails due to fetal distress with bowel evacuation.

(4) Weight is affected first, followed by decreased growth in length and, in severe undernutrition, head circumference.

(5) Neurologic examination is least affected and is usually appropriate for the actual gestational age.

COMPLETE NEWBORN PHYSICAL EXAMINATION

A complete physical examination should be done on each newborn within 24 hours after delivery. However, it should be delayed until the baby has stabilized following birth because of the infant's limited tolerance to handling during the birth recovery period (see above). Careful observation for abnormal findings during this time by the physician and nursing staff will identify those infants who require earlier, more detailed examination and evaluation.

A rigid sequence for doing various parts of the newborn physical examination is not necessary. It may not be possible to complete the entire examination at one time, in which case the balance can (and must) be finished later. The goal is to provide a complete record of the newborn that will contain essential information for reference if problems develop in the nursery or later in the infant's life. Parts of the examination require a quiet infant. Usually, the infant can be quieted sufficiently by being given a pacifier or by being held by the examiner or the parent.

There are distinct advantages in having the mother present and assisting the examination: (1) Her participation with the examiner in this intimate evaluation of her baby can enhance the development of the normal mother-baby relationship. (2) Her response and involvement with the baby can be observed, allowing early identification of problems in mothering that may exist. (3) She can be reassured immediately about minor variations in normal findings. (4) The meaning and plan for evaluation of significant abnormal findings can be discussed, allowing early involvement with the sick baby.

When abnormal findings are observed, they must be documented and a plan for evaluation developed. In caring for the newborn, it is crucial that abnormal findings be reevaluated at frequent intervals. Changes in physical findings such as heart murmurs can occur rapidly.

(1) Observation: Observation is particularly important in the newborn examination. A major portion of the information gathered will be obtained by patient, careful observation of the infant before it is handled and during various stages of activity. The usual order is to observe the infant generally and then to concentrate on specific areas for more detailed observation.

(2) Auscultation: Listen to the heart, lungs, abdomen, and head when the baby is quiet. Be alert for any asymmetry in breath sounds.

(3) Palpation and manipulative procedures: These must be timed in order to obtain reliable information but without disturbing the infant to such a degree that valid observations cannot be made. Adequate palpation of the abdomen and portions of the neurologic examination must be done with the infant quiet; examination of the mouth, throat, and ears can be done adequately even in an actively crying infant.

General Appearance & Evaluation

A. Vital Signs and Physical Measurements: These may be obtained from the nurse's record or during the course of the examination. It is usually not advisable to make these observations first, since the baby will become fussy. The heart rate for a normal newborn infant ranges from 120 to 160 beats per minute. The respiratory rate may be as high as 60 per minute within the first 1–2 days of life but settles to a normal range of 25–40 per minute. Normal blood pressures are related to size and postnatal age of the infant (Fig 36–6). Blood pressure should be determined in both upper and lower extremities using the Doppler method and a cuff that covers two-thirds of the extremity. Length, weight, and head circumference are measured and plotted on the intrauterine growth charts related to gestational age (Fig 36–7).

B. Appearance: The general appearance, maturity, nutritional status, presence of abnormal facies or body deformities, and state of well-being are noted. Before the baby is disturbed, observe the resting position (which frequently reflects the position assumed in utero), quality of respirations, color, and character of sleep pattern. While the baby is being undressed, observe its response to handling and general muscle tone and mottling. The usual quieting response upon being picked up and held may be demonstrated after undressing.

Specific Observations

A. Skin:

1. Color and appearance–The skin becomes erythematous for a few hours after birth, then fades to its normal appearance. The presence of **jaundice** and age at onset of jaundice should be noted. **Peripheral cyanosis** (acrocyanosis) is commonly present, particu-

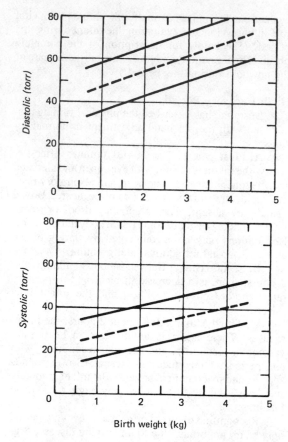

Figure 36–6. Aortic blood pressure during the first 12 hours of life in infants with birth weights of 610–4220 g. (Reproduced, with permission, from Versmold HT et al: *Pediatrics* 1981; **67**:607. Copyright American Academy of Pediatrics 1981.)

larly when extremities are cool. **Generalized cyanosis** is an important observation requiring immediate evaluation.

Pallor may be due to acute blood loss at the time of delivery or to gastrointestinal bleeding from a variety of causes or may be iatrogenic, particularly in the preterm infant who has had multiple samples of blood drawn for blood chemistry and blood gas measurements. Even so-called microchemistries can lead to appreciable blood loss in infants weighing less than 1200 g. The amount of blood withdrawn each time for sampling should be recorded. **Plethora** suggests polycythemia, which may lead to hyperviscosity syndrome. It occurs frequently in infants of diabetic mothers, small-for-gestational-age babies, and twins who have received a twin-twin transfusion. **Vernix caseosa,** a whitish, greasy material, normally covers the body of the fetus, decreasing in amount as term approaches. It is usually present in body creases of term infants but may be completely absent on a postterm infant. **Dry skin,** with cracking and peeling of the superficial layers, is common in infants who are postterm or who have had intrauterine growth retarda-

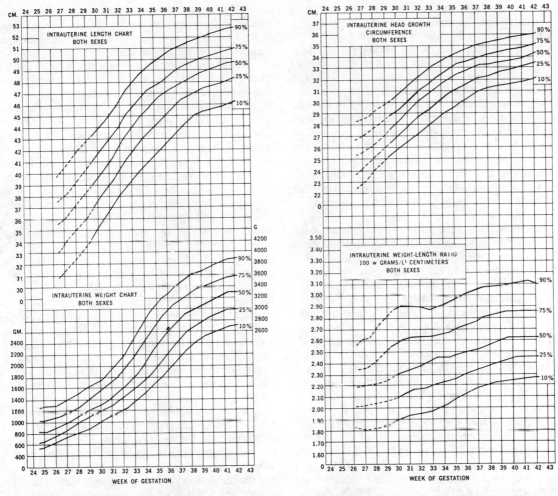

Figure 36–7. Intrauterine growth charts, from Colorado data. These values are lower than those reported by others. (Reproduced, with permission, from Lubchenco LO et al: *Pediatrics* 1966;37:403.)

tion. Normal skin is present underneath. **Edema** may be generalized (usually indicating serious renal, cardiac, or other systemic disease) or localized (dorsum of extremities in Turner's disease, eyelids with acute conjunctivitis). **Meconium staining** of the umbilical cord, vernix, nails, and skin suggests prior fetal distress. The **preterm infant's skin** is more translucent and may be covered with fine lanugo hair.

2. Skin lesions–Many lesions are present on the skin of normal newborns and must be differentiated from significant skin disease. **Mongolian spots**— bluish-black areas of pigmentation over the back and buttocks—are seen with more frequency in dark-skinned races. **Capillary hemangiomas** are common over the occiput, eyelids, forehead, nares, and lips. These lesions tend to decrease in size and intensity as the child grows. A few **petechiae** may be seen over the presenting part. Numerous or fresh petechiae should suggest thrombocytopenia. **Milia** are the small, yellowish-white papular areas over the nose and face. **Erythema toxicum** is characterized by an evanescent

rash with lesions in different stages—erythematous macules, papules, or small vesicles containing eosinophils—that spread to a variable extent over the skin, more commonly on the trunk. It occurs with decreasing frequency in preterm infants.

Staphylococcal or streptococcal infection of the skin in preterm babies may resemble erythema toxicum, a diagnosis that should always be made with caution in preterm infants.

B. Head: Note size, shape, symmetry, and general appearance of the head. **Molding** of the presenting part due to pressures during labor and delivery causes transient deformation of the head. **Head circumference** measurement may be affected by molding and should be repeated at discharge. **Caput succedaneum** is an area of edema over the presenting part that extends across suture lines. This differentiates it from a **cephalhematoma**, bleeding into the subperiosteal space on the surface of a skull bone (most commonly the parietal), which is circumscribed by the borders of the individual skull bone. The quantity of blood draining into a cephalhematoma can be significant in contributing to anemia appearing soon after birth and in causing early hyperbilirubinemia.

Normally, the size of the **anterior fontanelle** varies from 1 to 4 cm in any direction; it is smaller when the sutures are overriding. It is soft, pulsates with the baby's pulse, and becomes slightly depressed when the baby is upright and quiet. The **posterior fontanelle** is less than 1 cm in diameter. A **third fontanelle,** a bony defect along the sagittal suture in the parietal bones, may be present. The sutures may feel open to a variable degree or may be overriding. These findings are usually of no clinical importance as isolated findings. **Craniosynostosis** presents as a ridge along one or more sutures and is associated with increasing cranial deformity.

Increased intracranial pressure in the newborn is associated with increasing head circumference and a full anterior fontanelle. **Skull fractures** resulting from birth trauma may be linear or depressed and may be associated with the common cephalhematoma.

Transillumination—the degree of light transmitted through the head—should be done in any baby suspected of having neurologic disease. The procedure is done in a completely dark room after the examiner's eyes have become dark-adapted. The circle of light extending beyond the flange of the transillumination flashlight should be no more than 1.5 cm in term or up to 2 cm in preterm infants. Excessive light transmission occurs when diminished brain tissue is present, such as that observed with collection of subdural fluid, hydrocephalus, or brain atrophy.

Computerized tomography (CT) and ultrasound scans in preterm infants may reveal subependymal, intraventricular, or other intracerebral hemorrhage during the first few days of life even in the absence of physical signs or symptoms. For this reason, all newborn infants with gestational ages less than 35 weeks should have a CT or ultrasound scan at 7–10 days of age. If hemorrhage into the ventricles or brain has occurred, or if a scan was not done, ultrasonography of the brain is indicated at 10–21 days of age to rule out progressive hydrocephalus. Increasing head circumference is an extremely late sign and cannot be used to predict whether an infant had a hemorrhage. In addition, any infant with neurologic symptoms or neurologic disorders, such as seizures or meningitis, should also have a CT scan and ultrasound testing for clarification of brain insults.

C. Face: The general appearance and symmetry of the face are observed. **Odd facies** are often associated with specific syndromes and should alert the examiner to search for other abnormalities. Localized swelling, ecchymoses, or asymmetry of movement may result from birth pressure or the use of forceps during delivery. **Facial nerve palsy** is observed when the baby cries; the unaffected side of the mouth moves normally, giving a distorted facial grimace. When injury is more extensive, the eyelid will remain partially open on the affected side. Facial edema can be marked following a face presentation and can be severe enough to cause airway obstruction. Careful evaluation of fluid intake and output for 24–48 hours is in order for infants with facial edema, because they are prone to dilutional hyponatremia.

D. Eyes: The eyes of each newborn should be examined carefully at least once during the nursery stay—preferably before silver nitrate prophylaxis is given, since periorbital edema and conjunctivitis may make examination difficult following the procedure. This is particularly important when eye disease or head trauma is suspected. An ophthalmologist should be available for consultation, since loss of vision may result from delay in proper diagnosis and treatment.

Eye examination should include evaluation of the periorbital structures, nerve function, anterior orbital structures, and light reflex. In infants of less than 38 weeks' gestational age, the remnant of the pupillary membrane may be used as an adjunct determination of gestational age. If indicated, an ophthalmoscopic examination through dilated pupils may be done after examination has ruled out the presence of glaucoma or anterior chamber hemorrhage. Mydriatic and cycloplegic ophthalmic drops, in concentrations not exceeding 0.2% cyclopentolate and 1% phenylephrine, may be instilled to obtain good pupillary dilatation. Side-effects of the drugs or the examination include vagal slowing of the heart, cold stress on the infant, and acceleration of the heart rate beyond 180 beats per minute.

The eyes are usually open, and the infant is alert for the first 30 minutes; then the eyes tend to be closed during sleep for the next few hours. The baby will open its eyes when awake, especially when picked up in a semidark room. The baby will look toward a light and may focus briefly on the examiner's face. The size, shape, and position of the eyes and the presence of epicanthal folds are noted. Eyelid swelling and some conjunctival discharge are frequent after instillation of silver nitrate, but the possibility of infection must always be considered. **Eyelid movement** is observed. Occasional **uncoordinated eye movements** are common, but persistent irregular movements (nystagmus, eye deviation) are abnormal. **Acute dacryocystitis** associated with swelling and redness along the course of the lacrimal duct may become apparent in the newborn period. Corneal or lens **opacities** and **pupil size** can be observed with an ordinary flashlight. **Iris** abnormalities, such as Brushfield spots and colobomas, are noted. **Anterior chamber hemorrhage** may occur following eye trauma during birth but may not be apparent for several hours. A fluid level of blood will form when the baby is upright. **Congenital glaucoma** must be recognized early to preserve vision. The cornea is large (> 11 mm) and is often cloudy as a result of edema. Photophobia is common. Enlargement of the entire eye is a late finding.

Chorioretinitis may occur as a result of congenital toxoplasmosis, cytomegalic inclusion disease, rubella, or herpesvirus hominis infection. Small **retinal hemorrhages** are commonly observed in normal newborns, but more extensive hemorrhage is indicative of trauma or bleeding disorder. **Tumors** are rare in the newborn; retinoblastoma must be considered if the light reflection is grayish-yellow or absent or if strabismus or a dilated pupil is noted. Orbital hemangiomas may displace the eye in the orbit.

E. Nose: The shape and size of the nose are noted. Deformities may be due to in utero pressure, but many congenital syndromes are associated with abnormal nose configuration. Nasal discharge, noisy breathing, or complete obstruction to breathing may be present, suggesting choanal atresia or other nasal abnormality. When nasal obstruction is present, the infant may become cyanotic or apneic, since about one-third of term infants are obligatory nasal breathers. Nasal obstruction from mucous discharge can occur in those infants born with an upper respiratory tract infection acquired as a viral infection in utero. Flaring of the alae nasi occurs with increased respiratory effort.

F. Ears: Malformed or malpositioned (low-set or rotated) ears are often associated with other congenital abnormalities, especially of the urinary tract. The amount of cartilage in the pinnas is related to maturity. The **tympanic membranes** may be visualized with careful examination. Fluid may be present behind the drum for the first few hours.

Otitis media occurs fairly frequently in the neonatal period, particularly in preterm infants, in those with deformities of the palate, or in those who have been intubated for long periods of time (particularly with nasotracheal intubations). A careful examination of the eardrums should be made whenever sepsis or other infection is suspected.

Congenital deafness may be detected by standardized hearing screening tests in the newborn period. There are 2 important new tools for accurate auditory testing in the newborn period. One involves electrical monitoring of infant movement in response to a loud sound stimulus repeated over several hours. The second method is brain stem–evoked response audiometry in which sound stimuli are presented to one or both ears and the electrical responses in the brain stem are monitored from 3 scalp electrodes. Abnormal responses are indicative of conductive or sensorineural hearing loss, and immediate referral and treatment of these infants is indicated.

G. Mouth: Observe the lips and mucous membranes for pallor and cyanosis. The membranes should be moist in a normally hydrated infant. **Epithelial pearls** or retention cysts are noted on the gum margins and at the junction of the soft and hard palates. **Natal teeth** may be present—usually soft incisors—and may need to be removed in order to avoid the risk of aspiration. **High-arched palate** may be present as an isolated finding or may be associated with abnormal facies. **Cleft lip and palate** should be noted. Most newborns have relatively small **mandibles** that cause no problem. When the mandibles are very small, as in Pierre Robin syndrome, difficulty in breathing may occur when the tongue blocks the airway as it falls back against the pharynx. In the prone position, the baby usually has less respiratory difficulty. Some **drooling**

of mucus is common in the first few hours after birth; excessive drooling occurs with esophageal atresia. The **tonsils** and **adenoids** are quite small in newborns.

H. Neck: Position, symmetry, range of motion, and muscle tone are noted. **Webbing** of the neck suggests Turner's syndrome. Enlargement of the **thyroid** may occur in the newborn and must be evaluated. **Sinus tracts** may be seen as remnants of branchial clefts. **Torticollis** due to shortening or spasm of one sternocleidomastoid muscle may occur when there is hemorrhage or fibrosis in the body of the muscle. A persistent **tonic neck reflex,** assumed spontaneously and maintained by the infant, may be caused by brain damage. A very **short neck** may be associated with cervical vertebral abnormalities.

I. Vocalization: Note character of the **cry.** A high-pitched cry suggests brain damage. A hoarse cry results from inflammation or edema of the larynx or vocal cord paralysis. A whining "cat's cry" occurs with the syndrome of partial deletion of the short arm of chromosome 5. A weak cry may be a general sign occurring in a sick infant. A delay in vocalizing the cry after the baby appears to be crying is noted in congenital hypothyroidism.

Expiratory grunting occurs with respiratory distress due to many causes—notably the respiratory distress syndrome. **Inspiratory stridor** is associated with partial obstruction of the upper airway during inspiration such as occurs with the soft, collapsible tracheal structures of congenital stridor.

J. Thorax: Note shape, symmetry, position, and development of the thorax, nipples, and breast tissue. Determine the respiratory pattern and the character of the respirations.

Absent **clavicles** permit unusual anterior movement of the shoulders. Fracture of the clavicle is detected by tenderness and crepitus at the fracture site and limited movements of that arm. After a few days, callus is formed and the deformity can be easily visualized and felt. **"Fullness" of the thorax** due to increased anteroposterior diameter occurs with overexpansion of the lungs. Note asymmetry in expansion of the 2 sides or retractions during inspiration in the subcostal, intercostal, xiphoid, and suprasternal areas. These signs indicate pulmonary disease, airway obstruction, or air leaks.

K. Lungs: Auscultation of newborn lungs reveals bronchovesicular or bronchial breath sounds. Fine rales may be present during the first few hours. When there is a pneumothorax or pneumomediastinum, the breath sounds and heart sounds may be distant and the percussion sound may be hyperresonant. Decreased air entry and expiratory grunting are noted in respiratory distress syndrome. A chest x-ray must be obtained when abnormal lung findings are suspected because of the limited usefulness of physical findings alone in evaluation of respiratory disease.

L. Heart and Vascular System: When the cord is clamped and breathing begins, major adjustments occur within the circulation. Placental circulation is interrupted and pulmonary circulation becomes a major route of blood flow. Fetal shunts (patent ductus, foramen ovale) close and normal extrauterine circulation will be established. These changes occur uneventfully in the normal infant.

In the presence of heart disease or great vessel abnormality, these events often precipitate cardiovascular decompensation, which becomes evident in the newborn period. Early recognition is important.

General findings that suggest heart disease include growth failure, tachypnea, cyanosis, and shock. Determine **heart size** and the intensity and location of the **cardiac impulse** by palpation. **Heart sounds** are evaluated. If murmurs are present, their timing, duration, and intensity are determined. **Femoral pulse, heart rate and rhythm,** and **blood pressure** (flush or ultrasonic methods) are determined. Further evaluation may require chest x-ray, ECG, echocardiogram, and other specialized diagnostic techniques.

M. Abdomen: The abdomen will appear slightly scaphoid at birth but will become more protuberant as the bowel fills with gas. The abdominal organs are most easily palpated soon after birth, before the bowel becomes distended. A markedly scaphoid abdomen associated with respiratory distress suggests the presence of a diaphragmatic hernia. These are generally on the left side. An **omphalocele** may be present at birth; sometimes it may be small and may be included in the cord clamp if not recognized. **Umbilical hernias** are common and usually cause no difficulty. **Absence of abdominal musculature** or "prune belly" may occur in association with severe urinary tract abnormalities.

Abdominal distention may occur with **intestinal obstruction** or **paralytic ileus** in an infant with peritonitis or generalized sepsis. Palpation of the abdomen for organs or masses should be done with a light touch. The spleen tip is felt from the patient's right side and is sometimes 2–3 cm below the left costal margin. The liver usually is palpable 1–2 cm below the right costal margin. The lower poles of both kidneys should be felt. Abdominal muscle rigidity and apparent abdominal tenderness should be evaluated.

The outline of a distended **bladder** may be seen above the symphysis and may be felt as a ballottable mass in the lower abdomen. Contraction of bladder muscles with voiding often occurs with palpation.

Superficial veins may appear prominent over the abdominal wall with or without pathologic conditions.

The **umbilical cord** begins drying within hours after birth, becomes loose from the underlying skin by 4–5 days, and falls off by 7–10 days. Occasionally, a granulating stump remains that heals faster if treated with silver nitrate cauterization.

N. Genitalia: Male and female genitalia show findings characteristic of gestational age (Table 36–2). In most term male infants, the scrotum is pendulous, with rugae completely covering the sac. The testes have completely descended. The size of the scrotum and the penis varies widely in individual normal infants. The foreskin is adherent to the glans.

In females, the labia majora at term completely cover the labia minora and clitoris. A hymenal ring may be visible as a protruding tab of tissue. During the first few days after birth, a white mucous discharge that may contain blood issues from the vagina. Occasionally, a thin septum produced by fusion of the labia minora covers the vagina. The fusion is easily disrupted with a blunt probe.

O. Anus and Rectum: Observe anatomy and muscle tone of the anus. **Patency** should be checked if meconium has not been passed; use a soft catheter or little finger—not a rectal thermometer or other rigid object. **Irritation** or **fissures** may occur after the immediate newborn period. A firm **meconium plug** may be present.

"Meconium plug" syndrome may occur in the newborn with hard meconium producing total intestinal obstruction. These infants generally appear well, despite marked abdominal distention. Once the plug is passed, the distention is rapidly relieved and does not recur except when it results from the abnormal meconium that occurs in **cystic fibrosis.**

P. Extremities and Back: The arms and legs should be relatively symmetric in anatomy and function. Obvious **major abnormalities** of the extremities include absence of a bone, clubfoot, fusion or webbing of digits, or missing parts. **Hip dislocation** is suspected when there is limitation of abduction of the hips or when a click can be felt when the femur is pressed downward and then abducted. The legs may be unequal in length, and extra skin folds in the affected thigh are seen. **Palsies** involving the extremities are recognized when there are limited movements of the extremities, especially if only one is involved. **Fractures** may present with the same findings; in addition, swelling and crepitation are felt. Note the size and shape of the hands and feet. Deformities are frequent with **chromosomal abnormalities.**

The back is observed for curvature, spinal defects such as meningomyelocele, and dimples or defects overlying the lower lumbar spine.

Q. Neurologic Examination: The neurologic behavior of the newborn has become more clearly understood in recent years. Certain test items and observations on muscle tone are useful in assessing gestational age, since normal neurologic development follows a predictable course (Table 36–2).

Other items, described below, are those traditionally associated with abnormal central nervous system function (Prechtl and Beintema), and still others (Brazelton) attempt to test higher centers of central nervous system function. These authors stress the importance of testing the infant during specific awake-asleep states. A guide to the items applicable in each of the neurologic examinations is detailed in Table 36–3.

1. Traditional neurologic examination–Head circumference, sutures, fontanelles, and presence of cephalhematoma have been described, and evidence of jaundice, plethora, cyanosis, and sepsis are included in a neurologic examination because of the potential association with central nervous system pathology (eg, kernicterus, meningitis, alteration of central nervous system circulation and oxygen supply). Facial palsies

Table 36—3. Neurologic examinations of the newborn. The first describes evaluation of normal neurologic development; the second is the classic neurologic examination for central nervous system disease; and the third extends the evaluation to include study of higher central nervous systems centers and to elucidate individual behavior.

(1) NORMAL NEUROLOGIC DEVELOPMENT (Estimate of gestational age.) (From Dubowitz & others.)	(2) ABNORMAL CENTRAL NERVOUS SYSTEM FUNCTION (From Prechtl & Beintema.)	(3) FUNCTION OF HIGHER CENTRAL NERVOUS SYSTEM CENTERS AND BEHAVIOR (From Brazelton.)
Muscle tone	**Muscle tone**	**Response decrements**
Resting posture	Resting posture and recoil	Visual
Recoil of extremities	Opisthotonos versus frog position	Auditory
Horizontal suspension	Hypertonic versus hypotonic	Tactile
Vertical suspension	Flopping hand and foot	**Orientation:** visual
Heel to ear	Unequal tone	Inanimate
Popliteal angle	Pull to sit	Animate
Scarf sign	Spontaneous movements	**Orientation:** auditory
Neck extensors ⎫	Lack of or excessive	Inanimate
Neck flexors ⎬ pull to sit	Fisting	Animate
Body extensors ⎭	Tremors → seizures	**General behavior (tone, irritability, spontaneous motor behavior, maturity)**
Standing	Passive movement	Level of consciousness
Reflexes	**Reflexes**	Initial state
Suckling	Moro Hand grasp	Predominant state
Rooting	Knee jerk Plantar grasp	Alertness
Grasp	Ankle clonus Tonic neck	Lability of state
Crossed extension	Biceps Crawling	Rapidity of build-up
Automatic walk	Suck and root Babinski	**Specific behavior**
Moro	**Eyes**	Cuddliness
Tonic neck	Strabismus, nystagmus	Consolability
Neck righting	Abnormal movements	Hand-to-mouth
Pupillary	Setting sun	Self-quieting
Glabellar tap	Doll's eyes	Smiles
Babinski	Corneal reflex	Lability of state
Magnet	Ophthalmologic examination	Lability of skin color
Flexion angles	**Face**	Rapidity of build-up
Ankle	Expression	**Reflexes**
Wrist (square window)	Facial palsies	Defensive movements
	Cry	
	High-pitched	
	Skull	
	Sutures	
	Fontanelles	
	Cephalhematoma	
	Other	
	Jaundice Abdominal	
	Plethora distention	
	Cyanosis Skin turgor	

and ocular disorders also have been described.

Some observations are made while the infant is completely undisturbed; some involve minimal handling; and some can only be made by observing responses to specific stimuli. The infant should not be too hungry or too sleepy. Because a prolonged examination may exhaust the infant or cause irritability, the examination may have to be done in parts.

a. General observations—Paucity of **spontaneous movements** may be as important as abnormal movements. Discordant movements of one limb or of one side, hyperactivity, opisthotonos, athetoid movements, and movements ranging from tremors or jerks to frank convulsions may be seen in the infant with central nervous system damage. Brief seizures may present as momentary cessation of movements in a crying infant. Continuous chewing or sucking movements, protrusion of the tongue, and frequent yawning are other abnormal movements.

Resting position is observed without disturbing the infant. **Asymmetry** of the skull, face, jaw, or extremities may result from intrauterine pressures. The infant may be passively "folded" into the position of comfort assumed in utero.

b. Muscle tone—Test recoil of the extremities. Extend the legs and then release; both legs return promptly to the flexed position in the term infant. Extend arms alongside the body; upon release, there is prompt flexion at the elbows in the term infant. The amount of flexion and extension around joints is further tested at the neck, trunk, shoulders, elbows, wrists, hips, knees, and ankles.

Another means of testing for tone is the passivity test. As the wrist is moved sharply back and forth, the hand flops for a brief period and then the infant resists the movement and holds the hand or wrist firm. Normal term infants show approximately as much flopping as resistance to this maneuver.

A general impression of hypotonia or hypertonia can be gained from this testing. The **hypertonic** baby is usually jittery and startles easily; the fists are tightly closed, the arms in tight flexion, and the legs stiffly extended. The **hypotonic** or **lethargic** infant is "floppy" and has little head control. The extremities fall to the bed loosely when picked up and released. Recoil of arms and legs to the flexed position after being extended helps determine tone as well as gestational age.

c. Rooting reflex—The rooting reflex occurs so early in gestation that its absence in a viable baby should cause concern. However, the rooting reflex is strongest when the infant is hungry and may disappear after feeding. The reflex is elicited in 4 areas: at both corners of the mouth and on the upper and lower lips at the midline. The mouth opens or the head turns toward the side of the stimulus.

d. Sucking reflex—The sucking reflex can be obtained by placing a finger in the baby's mouth and noting the vigor of the movements and the amount of suction produced. A hypertonic or irritable infant makes biting rather than sucking movements.

e. Traction response: Head flexion and extension—The infant is pulled gently to a sitting position by traction on the hands and wrists. In the term infant, there is at first a head lag and then active flexion of the neck muscles, so that the head and chest are in line when the infant reaches the vertical position. The head is maintained in the upright position for a few seconds and then falls forward. The infant will then raise its head again, either spontaneously or following a slight stimulus such as stroking the upper lip.

f. Grasp reflex—

(1) Fingers—When the palm is stimulated with a finger, the infant's fingers will close on it. A term infant's grasp should be strong enough that the infant can be lifted from the table by holding onto the examiner's finger.

(2) Toes—Pressing the ball of the foot elicits a definite and prompt toe flexion.

g. Biceps, triceps, knee, and ankle tendon reflexes—These are best elicited with the finger rather than a percussion hammer. The infant must be relaxed.

h. Ankle clonus—Normally present in the newborn; sustained clonus is abnormal.

i. Incurvation of the trunk—The infant is lifted up and held over the hand in a prone position. The amount of flexion of the head and body is noted for an additional estimate of tone. The incurvation reflex is obtained by stroking or applying intermittent pressure with the finger parallel to the spine, first on one side and then the other, watching for a movement of the pelvis to the stimulated side.

j. Righting reaction—When the infant is lifted from the table vertically, the legs will usually flex. If the soles of the feet then touch the table, the infant will respond with the righting reflex, ie, first the legs will extend, then the trunk, and then the head.

k. Placing—The baby is held vertically, its back against the examiner and one leg restrained. The other leg is moved forward so that the dorsum of the foot touches the edge of the examining table. The baby will flex the knee and bring the foot up as though trying to step onto the table.

l. Automatic walking—Following the preceding tests, the ability to perform automatic walking movements is evaluated. The baby is inclined forward to begin automatic walking. When the sole of one foot touches the table, the infant tries to right itself with that leg and the other foot flexes. As the next foot touches the table, the reverse action occurs. Term infants will walk on the entire sole of the foot, whereas preterm infants often walk on their toes.

m. Moro (startle) reflex—When eliciting the Moro response, observe the arms, hands, and cry. The arms show abduction at the shoulder and extension of the elbow, followed by adduction of the arms in most infants. The hands show a prominent spreading or extension of the fingers. Any abnormality in the movements should be noted, such as jerkiness or tremor, slow response, or asymmetric response. A cry follows the startle and should be vigorous. The nature of the cry is important—absent, weak, high-pitched, or excessive.

The Moro reflex may be elicited in several ways:

(1) While holding the baby's hands, lift the body and neck (but not the head) off the examining table and quickly let go.

(2) While holding the infant with one hand supporting the head and the other the body, allow the head to drop a few centimeters rather suddenly.

(3) While holding the infant in both hands, lower both hands rapidly a few centimeters so that the infant experiences a sensation of falling.

(4) If the baby is quiet in the bassinet, lift the head of the bassinet a few centimeters and let it drop.

2. The Brazelton examination—This behavioral assessment of the newborn is presented as a research tool with an elaborate scoring system and, when it is used as such, observer reliability must be established. However, items in the examination lend themselves to routine application. (See Table 36–3.)

The various tests and observations are all done in relation to specific states. The infant should pass through all 6 states during the examination, including quiet sleep, active sleep, drowsy alertness, active alertness, animated alertness, and the irritable or crying awake state.

During the testing, observations on lability of state, skin color, rapidity of build-up, self-quieting activity, startle responses, irritability, and spontaneous movements are noted and recorded.

a. Response decrements—Visual (flashlight), auditory (rattle and bell), and tactile (pinprick) stimuli are presented repetitively to the infant in states 1, 2, or

3. The response to each is noted and the time of the decrement noted.

b. Orientation (state 4)–The infant's ability to orient to and attend to visual stimuli (animate and inanimate) is tested, and orientation to auditory stimuli is noted. Again, animate and inanimate sounds are presented.

c. Behavior–Cuddliness is defined as molding of the body of the infant to the examiner and can be elicited in the arms or by placing the infant over the shoulder. Consolability is scored on the number of ways necessary to quiet the infant, ranging from the examiner's face, voice, hand on belly, to holding, rocking, and finally a pacifier. Self-quieting activity is observed when the infant has reached state 6. The infant may not be able to remain quiet at all or may only be quiet for brief periods. The infant may have the capacity to be quiet for sustained periods. Associated with self-quieting is hand-to-mouth facility, which may range from brief swipes to thumbsucking.

d. Defensive movements–In this part of the examination, the observer tests the infant's ability to remove a cloth placed over the face.

THE DISCHARGE EXAMINATION

Since the complete examination has already been performed, only supplemental observations need be made at discharge, eg, rechecking a heart murmur, vital signs, and growth. The infant should be examined at the mother's bedside, and she should be given ample opportunity to raise questions. The physician should check the late appearance of medical problems such as jaundice, infection, skin rashes, etc, and be aware of maternal behavior that may affect care of the infant. Plans for medical follow-up are made at this time.

NORMAL NEWBORN

CARE OF THE NORMAL NEWBORN

Immediately After Delivery

Certain routines must be performed after delivery to make certain that the infant is adapting smoothly to extrauterine life and that there are no immediate life-threatening problems.

A. Nasopharyngeal Suction: Gentle suctioning of the mouth and throat with a bulb syringe is done during or immediately after delivery to remove mucus or blood and to clear the airway of obstructive debris.

B. Breathing: Occasionally, a baby needs help in establishing ventilation. A short period of assistance with bag, mask, and oxygen is often the only therapy necessary. Mild respiratory depression in a full-term infant is most likely the result of anesthetics or analgesics given to the mother.

C. Apgar Scoring: Determined at 1 and 5 minutes (Table 36–1).

D. Maintenance of Body Temperature: Every effort should be made to prevent a fall in body temperature. This is especially important in cool, air-conditioned delivery rooms. Evaporative heat loss from wet skin and radiant heat loss into the cool environment can be excessive unless special precautions are taken. The baby should be wiped dry, wrapped in a warm blanket, and placed in a warm environment until it is stabilized and able to maintain its temperature well.

E. Stomach Tube: Passing an orogastric tube should *not* be routine. Stimulation of the posterior pharynx and esophagus may cause bradycardia and apnea. Therefore, if the procedure is required, it should be done in the nursery after the baby has stabilized. An exception is a delivery complicated by polyhydramnios, when it is important to rule out the possibility of a tracheoesophageal fistula by passing a soft rubber catheter into the stomach.

F. Eye Prophylaxis: Routine eye prophylaxis against gonorrheal infection must be done as defined by local health codes. One percent silver nitrate is instilled carefully into each eye so that the conjunctival surface is adequately bathed in the solution. Single-dose vials are preferred. The eyes are not irrigated with water or saline. This procedure is best done after the initial awake period rather than in the delivery room.

G. Identification: Bands are placed on the ankle and wrist before the baby is removed from the delivery area.

H. Cord Blood Collection: At least 10–20 mL of clotted cord blood in 2 tubes should be collected. One tube is used for blood typing, Coombs testing, serologic examination, and other tests that may be needed. The other tube should go to the nursery with the infant and be kept in a refrigerator, where it will be available if other tests are required as the baby is further evaluated. This second tube should be retained for 7 days or should go with the baby if transferred to another nursery for care.

I. Mother-Baby Relationship: Important aspects of developing mother-baby relationships optimally occur in the delivery area. Therefore, the mother and the father should be given time to see, touch, and explore the infant. If the baby is ill or cold, this must be a brief contact. If the baby is well, the mother may wish to hold the swaddled infant while she is still on the delivery table.

J. Transfer to Nursery: If the nursery is adjacent to the delivery area, the baby may be carried, adequately protected from chilling. For the premature infant, specially designed transport incubators are available for use when the nursery is far removed from the delivery area by time or distance. In addition to heat, these special incubators provide for visibility, easy access to the infant, complete monitoring, and oxygen administration.

In the Transitional Nursery Area

An area or room in the nursery should be designated for admission of newborns from the delivery room for careful observation during the birth recovery period. All newborns should be admitted to this area except sick babies or those at high risk, who are admitted directly to the special care nursery. All babies are potentially at risk, and most of those who will become sick during their nursery stay can be identified in the first few hours after birth by careful observation and evaluation. The nursery staff play a vital role during this time in evaluating the infant and identifying those who require special attention.

A. Data Compilation and the Medical Record: Begin the newborn record with the calculated gestational age, birth weight, length, and head circumference. The medical record should be designed to relate to problems that the baby presents as well as to record the data required for the infant's care and for evaluation of the nursery service activities.

B. Classification: Determine the baby's newborn classification based on birth weight and gestational age (Fig 36–1), identifying all those outside the low-risk, term, appropriate-for-gestational-age group.

C. Prognosis: An estimate of the mortality risk based on birth weight and gestational age is then made. In general, infants with a 10% or greater chance of dying, based on these criteria, should be placed in a special care nursery. Other factors that may contribute to the risk of a particular newborn must also be considered in determining the level of care that should be given. Examples of these additional factors include maternal hypertension, drug therapy, diabetes, Rh sensitization, bleeding, infection, and previous neonatal deaths.

D. Examination: The appropriate examination at this time includes a review of the maternal and immediate perinatal history, noting whether fetal monitoring was done and, if so, whether results were normal; clinical estimation of gestational age; evaluation of vital signs and pulmonary and cardiac status, including routine blood pressure measurement; and notation of factors that may influence the baby's course. A careful review of potential drug exposure must be made.

E. Birth Recovery Period: The sequence of events related to birth recovery and deviations from normal pattern are noted. Abnormal symptoms or signs that may suggest developing problems should be noted. Findings that are unimpressive by themselves may acquire significance if observed and recorded objectively. A checklist of significant observations can be picked up by careful reading of the nurse's notes.

F. Temperature Control: After delivery and until the baby has stabilized, the body temperature may be labile. Cooling should be avoided, since it will delay the normal cardiovascular adjustments required of the infant after birth. Radiant heat devices or incubators are ideal for this purpose in the transitional nursery area. For premature or low-birth-weight infants, it is very important to conserve the baby's calorie and oxygen requirements for growth rather than to consume them for temperature maintenance. Therefore, guidelines for starting and adjusting the environ-

mental temperature by birth weight and age of the baby are valuable in the nursery (Table 36–4).

G. Vitamin K: Phytonadione, 1 mg intramuscularly, should be given routinely to every newborn as part of the admission procedure to the nursery.

H. First Urine and Stool: Time must be noted. If these events have not occurred prior to transfer to the general care nursery, a special note must be made. The normal infant will pass stool and urine within 24–48 hours of age.

I. Care and Feeding: After the baby stabilizes, usually in 2–6 hours after delivery, it can be bathed, dressed, and fed. Normal babies tolerate bathing and dressing with little difficulty.

J. Physician Responsibility: The physician responsible for the care of the newborn reviews the history and neonatal course and performs a complete physical examination after the baby is stable, preferably before 24 hours of age. The physician is notified of any significant abnormalities that have been identified before the expected visit to allow for immediate early evaluation of the problem.

Continued Care in the Level 1 Nursery

Although a registered nurse will supervise the area, the bulk of the day-to-day care in a level 1 nursery may be given by personnel at lower professional levels who are trained in the care of newborns. The emphasis is on well baby care, enhancing successful mother-baby relationships, feeding, and teaching care techniques. However, the staff must be continually alert for any significant evidence of illness that may require evaluation.

A. Admission: The staff should review the baby's history and immediate postnatal events in order to be aware of any problems.

B. Duration of Stay: Following an uncomplicated perinatal course, mother and baby may stay in the hospital for 3 days (up to 7 days following cesarean section). Some families request discharge within the first 1–2 days after delivery. They think that a "rooming–in" experience in their own home will benefit the bonding process and decrease hospital expenses. However, follow-up by public health nurses within 1–2 days and clinic visits within 7–10 days should be arranged and agreed to by the family. Early discharge is accompanied by definite risk of delay in detecting problems: breast feeding is not established; the severity of "physiologic" jaundice cannot be evaluated; and subtle symptoms of illness may not be recognized before discharge.

C. Adapting Nursery Activity to Needs of Mother and Child: The life situation of the mother and the family is important in their acceptance of the newborn baby. Favorable conditions exist when the mother is married, the child is wanted at this time, there is some financial security, and the parents themselves are emotionally mature. Even when these favorable factors are operative, however, there may be adverse factors that interfere with satisfactory adjustment. Problems in pregnancy, a difficult delivery,

Table 36—4. Neutral thermal environmental temperatures.[*]

Age and Weight	Starting Temperature[†] (C)	Range of Temperature (C)	Age and Weight	Starting Temperature[†] (C)	Range of Temperature (C)
0—6 hours			**72—96 hours**		
Under 1200 g	35.0	34.0—35.4	Under 1200 g	34.0	34.0—35.0
1200—1500 g	34.1	33.9—34.4	1200—1500 g	33.5	33.0—34.0
1501—2500 g	33.4	32.8—33.8	1501—2500 g	32.2	31.1—33.2
Over 2500 (and > 36 wk)	32.9	32.0—33.8	Over 2500 (and > 36 wk)	31.3	29.8—32.8
6—12 hours			**4—12 days**		
Under 1200 g	35.0	34.0—35.4	Under 1500 g	33.5	33.0—34.0
1200—1500 g	34.0	33.5—34.4	1501—2500 g	32.1	32.0—33.2
1501—2500 g	33.1	32.2—33.8	Over 2500 (and > 36 wk)		
Over 2500 (and > 36 wk)	32.8	31.4—33.8	4—5 d	31.0	29.5—32.6
12—24 hours			5—6 d	30.9	29.4—32.3
Under 1200 g	34.0	34.0—35.4	6—8 d	30.6	29.0—32.2
1200—1500 g	33.8	33.3—34.3	8—10 d	30.3	29.0—31.8
1501—2500 g	32.8	31.8—33.8	10—12 d	30.1	29.0—31.4
Over 2500 (and > 36 wk)	32.4	31.0—33.7	**12—14 days**		
24—36 hours			Under 1500 g	33.5	32.6—34.0
Under 1200 g	34.0	34.0—35.0	1501—2500 g	32.1	31.0—33.2
1200—1500 g	33.6	33.1—34.2	Over 2500 (and > 36 wk)	29.8	29.0—30.8
1501—2500 g	32.6	31.6—33.6	**2—3 Weeks**		
Over 2500 (and > 36 wk)	32.1	30.7—33.5	Under 1500 g	33.1	32.2—34.0
36—48 hours			1501—2500 g	31.7	30.5—33.0
Under 1200 g	34.0	34.0—35.0	**3—4 weeks**		
1200—1500 g	33.5	33.0—34.1	Under 1500 g	32.6	31.6—33.6
1501—2500 g	32.5	31.4—33.5	1501—2500 g	31.4	30.0—32.7
Over 2500 (and > 36 wk)	31.9	30.5—33.3	**4—5 weeks**		
48—72 hours			Under 1500 g	32.0	31.2—33.0
Under 1200 g	34.0	34.0—35.0	1501—2500 g	30.9	29.5—32.2
1200—1500 g	33.5	33.0—34.0	**5—6 weeks**		
1501—2500 g	32.3	31.2—33.4	Under 1500 g	31.4	30.6—32.3
Over 2500 (and > 36 wk)	31.7	30.1—33.2	1501—2500 g	30.4	29.0—31.8

[*]Reproduced, with permission, from Klaus M, Fanaroff A: The physical environment. Chap 3, p 68, in: *Care of the High-Risk Neonate.* Saunders, 1973.

[†]Starting temperature is the first environmental temperature the baby should be placed in.

birth of an abnormal or premature infant, and development of maternal or infant illness are a few such factors. The nursing staff should understand the needs of the mother and child and show their willingness to meet these needs. The following suggestions will help (see also Parent-Baby Relationship, below): (1) Become acquainted with the mother and father—before delivery if possible. (2) Show an interest in the total family unit. (3) Visit the mother daily while she is in the hospital and be attentive to her expressed anxieties. (4) Institute flexible schedules of feeding, especially for mothers who are breast feeding. (5) Institute flexible schedules for the amount of time the baby and mother spend together. (6) Examine the infant in the mother's presence. Above all, it is important that *both* physicians and nurses respect the diversity of lifestyles and approaches to parenting. The health care team should *assist* the parents and infant, not *dictate* any particular approach to the family. Parents should not be made to feel guilty if they do not choose to use rooming-in nursery arrangements, natural childbirth, or breast feeding. Criticism is often implied when parents do not choose the same approach to childbirth

and infant care that the health care team would, despite the fact that different approaches to parenting and family life are equally compatible with development of a healthy child.

D. Rooming-In: The optimal family-centered program is the rooming-in situation with mother and baby together in the room under the supervision of an understanding and helpful nurse, with unrestricted visiting by the father or other supportive persons. The mother can get instruction in caring for the baby as she watches her baby being examined, and her questions about the significance of findings can be answered as they arise. Continued help and encouragement from well-trained nurses for the mother who is breast feeding are very helpful. Rooming-in may be continuous in a separate unit or modified, using existing postpartum and nursery facilities. Close cooperation between obstetric and pediatric and nursing personnel is essential.

E. Screening for Disease: Since nearly all babies in the USA are born in hospitals, an excellent opportunity exists to screen mother and baby for disease that may not become manifest during their stay in the hospital. Some of these tests can be routine, and some are required by law:

1. Blood type and direct Coombs test to identify potential blood group incompatibilities.

2. Serologic test for syphilis.

3. Elevated serum phenylalanine (causing phenylketonuria); α-keto acids, valine, isoleucine, and leucine (causing maple syrup urine disease); and homocystine (causing homocystinuria).

4. Thyroid function tests, eg, T_4 and TSH, which are more commonly abnormal in premature infants.

5. Galactosemia.

6. Sickle cell and other hemoglobinopathies.

7. Other tests have been recommended in some screening programs, eg, G6PD deficiency, IgM, indirect Coombs, histidinemia, adenosine deaminase deficiency.

The major problems in all screening programs consist of the time delay of 2–6 weeks between sample collection and reporting of results to health care personnel, locating families and obtaining compliance for recall testing, providing follow-up treatment and counseling, and determining the long-term efficacy and cost benefits of this approach in alleviating or preventing rare diseases.

F. Preparation for Discharge:

1. Perform a physical examination—preferably with the mother in attendance—and discuss the care of the cord, circumcision, genitalia, etc, as the baby is examined.

2. Make sure the mother has mastered and understands the reasons for procedures for caring for the baby. Give her ample opportunity to discuss questions she may have.

Now that infants are being discharged from the nursery earlier and parents are assuming more of the medical care of the newborn at home, it is important to explain to parents the need to observe the infant for jaundice. They should be prepared to bring the infant to their physician as soon as significant signs or symptoms are noted. It is not unusual for infants discharged early from nurseries to have jaundice that goes unrecognized until bilirubin levels exceed 15–20 mg/dL. Parents should be taught to look for poor feeding, lethargy, excessive yawning, and yellow skin extending down the trunk and extremities. Newborns with heart murmurs must be watched for poor color, vomiting, poor feeding, and sweating.

3. Give feeding instructions and a suggested formula. Careful attention to preparation of the formula is essential, since improperly prepared formula is dangerous to the infant. If coupons or food stamps are used to obtain formula, this—as well as a visit from a public health nurse—should be arranged before discharge.

4. Vitamin and iron supplementation may be required. Most proprietary infant formulas contain adequate vitamins. If breast milk is used exclusively and the mother's diet is inadequate, supplementation with vitamins A, C, and D is recommended. Fluoride supplementation is indicated if there is no fluoride in the local water.

5. Give an appointment to the physician's office or clinic in 10–14 days for well baby care or specific problem follow-up.

6. Make sure the parents know whom to call if they have questions or if problems develop.

7. Check identification of baby and of person accepting responsibility for the infant at time of discharge.

PARENT–BABY RELATIONSHIP*

Mothers' feelings for their newborn infants may vary over a range extending from strong feelings of love and protection to complete rejection. Many factors that affect a woman's capacity for mothering are ingrained, ie, dependent on her genetic endowment, her relationship with her own parents, and cultural practices. Other factors include her marital status, financial situation, and attitudes about the pregnancy. Obstetric and nursery routines and attitudes of hospital personnel also affect the mother's ability to relate to her child. The separation of mother and baby at birth and during much of the postnatal period is probably the most arbitrary and potentially harmful of current postnatal practices.

Development of Maternal Attachment to the Infant

The mother's emotional attachment to the baby begins early in pregnancy. If the fetus or newborn dies, she will go through a process of mourning, even following an early abortion. During the early months she may be preoccupied with the certainty of the diagnosis of pregnancy. Fetal movements are the first concrete evidence that she is truly going to have a baby. These movements are usually pleasant and associated with considerable fantasy. At this time, the parents often decide on a choice of names for the baby.

Behavior After Birth

The mother's initial thoughts at the moment of birth are usually, "Is my baby all right?" and, "Is it a boy or a girl?" The answer may provoke profound expressions of joy or, at times, withdrawal and tears.

---

*In the first 2 editions of this book the title of this section was "mother-baby relationship." The authors and editor understand that the baby's relationship with its father is also an important source of gratification and emotional nourishment, and that young fathers today are perhaps closer to their infant sons and daughters than was customary in former times when men worked harder and longer and perhaps turned aside from "child care" as inappropriate to their masculine role. It is certainly true that men are more likely nowadays than formerly to present themselves with babe in arms in the well baby clinic because the wife is working or going to law school. In the text that follows we will make occasional references to the father's role. For the present, however, and for some time to come, it is probably true that the mother is the main person in the infant's life for the first few years or so.

When the mother is given the opportunity in the delivery room to hold her infant, she will regard it with tenderness, tending to concentrate on the eyes. Klaus and Kennel have observed a pattern of examination and touching that the mother follows when the nude infant is presented to her at about 1 hour of age. She usually begins with fingertip touching of the extremities and proceeds to palm contact of the trunk within a few minutes. There is noticeable attention paid to the infant's eyes.

Both the mother and the infant may go through a stage of wakefulness during the first hour after birth. The baby is wide-eyed, alert, and responsive. The mother's wakefulness may persist until she has held and fed the baby. It is as though the birth process is not finished until she has cared for her child. Following this period of wakefulness, both the mother and the infant fall into a deep sleep lasting several hours.

Implications for Hospital Care of Mother & Infant

If these observations give some insight into the needs of the mother and baby, then the routines of delivery and nursery care must be reoriented. Prolonged separation of mother and baby and rigidity of schedules and routine activities in the postnatal areas may be playing a significant negative role in development of normal mother-baby relationships.

Guidelines to Provide Optimal Parent-Baby Relationships

(1) The mother's comfort and access to her baby are of prime importance.

(2) The physician or other health professional responsible for the baby's care should talk with the parents—preferably together—at least once a day.

(3) If the baby is ill, it is important to explore the parents' understanding of the baby's illness and its causes. They should be prepared for the baby's appearance and for the equipment used in the special care nursery before visiting the infant. An informed individual must be present to answer questions and give support. Physical contact with the baby should be allowed whenever possible.

(4) The physician and nurse should not overburden the parents with details or concerns of care and prognosis during the early period. Optimism about prognosis is essential whenever possible. The parents are developing an important relationship with the infant during this time that should not be interrupted by needless anxieties.

(5) The teenage mother, especially when unmarried, will need compassionate attention and teaching to help her become attached to her baby and assume the responsibilities of motherhood.

The Sick Infant

Occasionally an infant has a grave illness or serious congenital anomaly requiring immediate management. If the difficulty has been anticipated, the problems will have been prepared for prior to delivery.

If the occurrence is unexpected, the following will be helpful:

(1) A prompt survey of the seriousness of the condition and decisions about immediate treatment are urgently required. Additional help or immediate transfer to the nursery may be required.

(2) The parents will sense the seriousness of the situation. An absent cry and increased activity around the baby cannot be disguised. A word to the parents that indicates there is a problem and that the baby's welfare is being considered first is vital. Some indication of the type of trouble should be given, eg, "He has a defect of his spine," or "She has difficulty breathing."

(3) If the baby is likely to die or must be removed from the room immediately, they should be told these facts and be assured that someone will return soon to report what is happening.

(4) Should the parents see a sick or deformed infant? Yes, for many reasons. Even a glimpse of the infant will prevent a grossly exaggerated imaginary picture from forming in their minds. If possible, they should be allowed to see and touch their infant in order to complete the perinatal experience. If the appearance of the infant is gruesome, the parents will require preparation plus added support and understanding. If the infant dies, it is especially important that they see the infant so that they will be able to accomplish the mourning process. These comments also apply when a stillbirth has occurred.

(5) No emotionally charged comments should be made to the parents. Decisions involving long term outcome and disposition should be postponed.

(6) The parents will go through a period of shock and disappointment, often associated with feelings of guilt, and will require understanding and emotional support from health professionals during the succeeding days and weeks.

(7) Early separation of infants from their parents, prolonged hospitalization, and socioeconomic problems of parents are common associated problems in extremely premature births. The increased risks of abuse, neglect, and dysfunctional parenting have been well documented for these surviving infants.

Genetic Counseling

The likelihood of genetic defects reappearing in future pregnancies need not be considered or discussed immediately after the birth of an abnormal child. At some point in the following weeks, the perceptive physician will recognize the parents' need for additional information and will offer genetic counseling. Sufficient information is available about most defects to allow satisfactory assessment of the chance of recurrence of an abnormality. Interested and informed concern by the physician will aid the parents in arriving at realistic plans for future pregnancies.

Relinquishing an Infant

Although pregnancy in the unmarried does not carry the same social stigma as in the past, there is still much misunderstanding about the emotional aspects of the adoption process in such cases. Relinquishment of the baby should be presented to pregnant women carrying an unwanted child as an acceptable alternative. They should be aware of the current favorable adoption statistics showing that infants will almost certainly be placed in appropriate homes. Another popular belief is that "the mother does not want to see or hear about the child"; that "she does not want to become attached to it"; or that "she might change her mind." However, since the mother already has related to the fetus early in pregnancy, special feelings cannot be avoided when she relinquishes the infant for adoption. If she can see and touch the baby, the experience of pregnancy and delivery can be completed rather than forever shrouded in uncertainty, denial, and fantasy, because the mother can work through her feelings more easily. Predelivery counseling is desirable, including informed discussion of expected emotional reactions after delivery. The process of delivery and immediate handling by the mother may be the same as for the mother who is keeping her baby.

The *earliest possible* placement of the infant in a permanent adoptive home is best for the new parents and for the baby.

FEEDING OF THE NEWBORN

Feeding schedules in newborn nurseries have tended to be fairly rigid, primarily for the convenience of the staff. The result has been that some babies are awake and hungry for long periods and others must be awakened to be fed, and neither is optimal from the baby's point of view. "Demand feeding"—allowing the baby to eat when awake and hungry—usually leads to optimal intake and eventual establishment of a "schedule" that will be both satisfying to the baby and reasonable for the family. Initiating demand feeding in the nursery is entirely feasible and most easily done with a modified or continuous rooming-in program where the mother can respond to the baby's needs with ease.

What, When, & How Much to Feed?

The first water feeding should be offered as the birth recovery period is ending and the baby appears hungry, which is normally at 3–6 hours of age. The baby should appear actively hungry and should have normal bowel sounds and no abdominal distention. When these conditions are met, the first feeding of sterile water may be given.

One water feeding is usually sufficient to make certain that feedings are well tolerated. Full-strength milk formula (approximately 20 kcal/oz) or breast feedings can then be given. Ready-to-use formulas rather than concentrates are recommended for use in the nursery, since they provide a maximum of convenience and safety.

The initial feeding may consist of a few swallows

or several ounces. As feedings are established, the baby should be allowed to regulate the volume and frequency of feedings so long as fluid and caloric requirements are met. By the third day the baby should receive a minimum of 100 mL/kg/d and will soon thereafter start taking about 120 kcal and 180 mL/kg/d or more, allowing for hunger satisfaction and optimal growth.

Methods of Feeding

A. Bottle Feeding: Most commercial bottles and nipples are satisfactory. If the nipple hole needs to be enlarged, this can easily be done with a hot needle. For premature or debilitated babies, a soft nipple with easy flow (cross-cut hole) is required.

B. Breast Feeding: (See also below.) When a mother wants to nurse her infant, success or failure is related to the amount of factual information given her and the emotional support of physician and nurses. The staff can share the role of listening, giving factual data, and encouraging the mother to continue nursing long enough to overcome occasional problems she may have in establishing lactation. Having a nurse present when the mother first attempts to feed, providing explanation of physiologic processes, and making her physically comfortable will assure success.

A variable amount of breast engorgement occurs on about the third day after delivery. The engorgement may interfere with nursing because the infant is unable to grasp the nipple. A nipple shield may be used to reduce the areolar engorgement and to draw out the nipple. The infant may then nurse directly from the breast. Prolonged use of the shield interferes with complete emptying of the breasts. Nipple soreness is minimized if the nursing time is kept to approximately 5 minutes during the prelactation period until milk flow is established. Only a bland ointment should be used on the nipples.

The mother should be forewarned that her infant will seem to become more hungry about the fourth or fifth day and will want to nurse more frequently. This behavior lasts only 1–2 days. The baby will then return to a less frequent feeding schedule.

The mother who wishes to nurse a premature, sick, or debilitated infant may be successful if given some additional suggestions. She must empty her breasts several times a day with a mechanical pump or by manual expression to maintain lactation until her infant is able to nurse from the breast. The healthy premature infant will begin breast feeding at 36–40 weeks' gestation. If the baby does not empty the breast, milk production can be increased if the mother pumps the breast after feedings. She may have insufficient milk for a few days, and a supplement immediately following feeding will be necessary until supply increases.

C. Gavage Feeding: Intermittent gavage feeding should be used when the baby has a weak sucking and swallowing reflex or tires easily. Gavage feeding can be done safely with minimal handling. However, in a sick infant with danger of abdominal distention, regurgitation, and aspiration, gavage feeding has the same risk as nipple feeding.

D. Intravenous Fluids: Intravenous fluids are always required in preterm babies, in very low birth weight infants, and in any critically ill infant. The fluids are given primarily to ensure adequate hydration and electrolyte intake. Infants who cannot take oral or gavage feedings should be transferred to a level 2 or level 3 center immediately, because management of glucose, electrolyte, and fluid balances requires constant instrument and laboratory monitoring. A multivitamin preparation, as well as protein and lipid, should be added by the fifth day if feedings have not yet been started.

1. BREAST FEEDING

Advantages & Disadvantages of Breast Feeding

A. Advantages: Breast feeding has been encouraged mainly for its psychologic advantages, economy, and asepsis. The composition of human milk is ideal for most infants. Recent information on the quality and function of lipozyme and IgA in colostrum has caused renewal of interest in its anti-infectious properties. Breast-fed infants are not as likely to become obese as are formula-fed infants. There are fewer allergic problems in breast-fed infants. Nursing is of benefit to the mother in the postpartum period because it is associated with vigorous contraction of the uterine musculature and speeds the return of that organ to normal size and position.

B. Disadvantages and Contraindications: Absolute contraindications to breast feeding are few, eg, tuberculosis in the mother and the presence of maternal drugs, including phenylbutazone, antithyroid medicines, and certain anticancer agents. (See also Chapter 37, p 832.)

Management of Breast Feeding

It is important to understand that very few women are unable to nurse their infants. The mother should know that breast milk may look "weak or dilute," but if the infant is not satisfied the problem is one of supply and not quality. Her fluid intake, especially milk, should exceed 2 L/d. It is essential that she understand that milk production can be increased by frequent nursing and that the supply of milk lags behind the infant's demand for approximately 24 hours. She should know that if she substitutes supplementary feedings for nursing—especially in the first weeks after birth—the supply of milk will decrease. Many working mothers find it possible to nurse their infants once milk production is well established. However, it is likely that a woman who breast feeds less than 5 times a day will stop effective lactating within about 1–2 months.

Technique of Nursing

A. Breast Preparation Before Delivery: It is thought by some that nipple soreness can be minimized by preparation of the breasts prior to delivery. The method recommended is as follows: Cup one breast from below with the palm of the hand and, with a soft washcloth, rub the nipple 4 or 5 times. Then gently pull the nipple several times. This can be done once or twice daily.

B. Preparation for Nursing: A daily bath is all that is necessary for cleanliness of the breasts. When nursing, the mother should assume a comfortable position either lying down or sitting in a rocking or upright chair.

C. Nursing the Infant: The infant should be fed when signs of hunger appear and should be offered both breasts at each feeding for maximum milk production. The infant usually nurses for about 10 minutes on the first side, completely emptying this breast, and then finishes the feeding on the opposite breast.

The rooting reflex is stimulated by touching the infant's cheek with the nipple (not pushing the mouth toward the breast). It is important to help the infant grasp the whole areola and to have the nipple well back in the infant's mouth.

The breast may need to be held away from the infant's nostrils once sucking begins.

After a minute or two of nursing, the letdown reflex occurs and the infant may have difficulty swallowing the rapidly flowing milk. The letdown affects both breasts simultaneously.

After nursing, the infant usually releases the nipple. If not, suction should be broken by gently opening the infant's mouth before removing the breast. Burping the infant following feeding is usually done, but breast-fed infants do not swallow as much air as bottle-fed infants.

Colostrum

Colostrum is a yellow, alkaline breast secretion that may be present in the last few months of pregnancy and for the first 2–4 days after delivery. It has a higher specific gravity (1.040–1.060); a higher protein, vitamin A, and mineral content; and a lower carbohydrate and fat content than breast milk.

Colostrum contains antibodies that may play a part in the immune mechanism of the newborn. It has a laxative action and is an ideal natural starter food.

Transmission of Nutrients, Drugs, & Toxins in Breast Milk

Virtually all nutritives, drugs, and toxins are transmitted through breast milk to the infant. Foods eaten by the mother may cause increased gas or stool changes in the infant. Minerals and vitamins are usually adequate in breast milk if the mother's dietary intake is well balanced. Drugs and toxins do diffuse into milk, and some are concentrated there by active secretion of the mammary gland. However, except for those drugs mentioned above, this is rarely a reason to discourage breast feeding. If the mother's intake of any drug is excessive, toxicity may be produced in the child.

2. INFANT FORMULAS

A variety of satisfactory prepared formulas are available commercially (Table 36–5). Cow's milk and evaporated milk formulas are not now recommended because of the relatively high osmotic load, the low content of linoleic acid, the poor availability of the iron content, and the greater danger of preparation error. Table 36–6 shows the schedule of milk feedings for infants up to 1 year of age.

Preparation of the Formula

A ready-to-use formula is preferred because it prevents contamination and mixing errors. Milk con-

centrates are less expensive; if they are used, the physician should make certain that the formulas are diluted correctly and that caloric needs are being met. An infant generally does not need more than 1 quart of milk per day.

Sterilization of bottles and formulas is not usually necessary. In most city homes, the opened can is stored in the refrigerator and each bottle is diluted as required, using warm tap water. Bottles and nipples are washed in soap and water, rinsed, and dried. Where the water supply may not be clean, boiled water should be used. In situations where cleanliness is more difficult to maintain, powdered milks should be used and dissolved in boiled water.

Table 36–5. Normal and special infant formulas.

Formula	Calories/dL	Carbohydrate Type	% of Calories	g/dL	Protein Type	% of Calories	g/dL	Fat Type	% of Calories	g/dL	Ca:K Ratio	Osmolality/Renal Solute (mosm/kg/L)
Enfamil 20	68	Lactose	40	7.0	Casein (cow's milk)	10	1.5	Soy oil, coconut	50	3.7	1.2:1	290/110
Enfamil 24	80	Lactose, sucrose	45	9.2	Casein	10	2.2	MCT,* corn oil, coconut	45	4.1	2:1	355/130
Isomil 20	68	Corn syrup, sucrose	40	6.8	Soy	12	2.0	Coconut, soy oil	48	3.6	1.3:1	250/126
Lofenalac	68	Corn syrup, tapioca	52	8.8	Hydrolyzed casein	13	2.2	Corn oil	35	2.7	1.3:1	454/130
Nutramigen	68	Tapioca, sucrose	52	8.8	Hydrolyzed casein	13	2.2	Corn oil	35	2.6	1.3:1	493/130
Portagen	68	Corn syrup, sucrose, lactose	44	7.7	Sodium caseinate	14	2.3	MCT,* corn oil, lecithin	42	3.3	1.3:1	236/150
Pregestimil	68	Glucose, corn syrup, tapioca	52	8.8	Hydrolyzed casein	13	2.2	MCT,* corn oil	35	2.8	1.3:1	496/130
Similac 20	68	Lactose	40	7.2	Casein (cow's milk)	10	1.6	Coconut, soy oil	50	3.6	1.3:1	290/108
Similac 60/40	68	Lactose	44	7.6	Lactalbumin, casein	9	1.6	Coconut, corn oil	47	3.5	2:1	260/92
Similac LBW 24	81	Lactose, polycose	40	8.5	Nonfat cow's milk	10	2.5	MCT,* coconut, soy oil	50	4.5	1.3:1	290/ —

*MCT = medium chain triglycerides.

Table 36–6. Schedule of milk feedings for infants up to 1 year of age.*

Age (months)	0	1	2	3	4	5	6	7	8	9	10	11	12
Calories (kcal) per day†	130–100/kg (60–45/lb)						110–100/kg (50–45/lb)				100–90/kg (45–40/lb)		
Fluid per day (mL)	130–200/kg (2–3 oz/lb)					130–165/kg (2–2½ oz/lb)				130/kg (2 oz/lb)			
Number of feedings per day‡	6 or 7			4 or 5				3 or 4				3	
Ounces per feeding	2½–4	3½–5	4–6	5–7	6–8	7–9							

*Modified and reproduced, with permission, from Silver HK, Kempe CH, Bruyn HB: *Handbook of Pediatrics*, 13th ed. Lange, 1980.

†The larger amount should be used for the younger infant.

‡Will vary somewhat with individual babies.

SPECIAL CARE OF THE
HIGH–RISK INFANT

PERINATAL RESUSCITATION

Anticipation

It is no longer adequate to begin resuscitation of the newborn after delivery; instead, the entire sequence of decisions made by obstetricians, pediatricians, and family physicians throughout the course of labor and delivery must be seen as significantly affecting the condition of the infant at birth. Parturition and the many endocrine and cardiovascular changes it induces in the mother and infant begin sometime before uterine contractions actually start. However, attention focuses most closely on the time of labor, when synchronous cervical dilatation and uterine contractions lead to delivery of the infant. Labor constitutes a stress that is perfectly normal and well tolerated by the full-term, healthy infant delivered after an uncomplicated pregnancy. However, the stress of labor and delivery may cause marked fetal distress in pregnancies having one or more complications, eg, intrauterine growth retardation.

For this reason, it is important to emphasize preplanning for delivery by the entire health care team. The plan not only considers the optimal time and mode of delivery (ie, vaginal versus cesarean section) that would minimize fetal and maternal complications but also considers what level of care will be required by the mother and infant. The latter evaluation determines which hospital in the community will be used for delivery. Increasing emphasis is being placed on determining the best setting for delivery before the birth takes place so that the parents can be informed that delivery is anticipated, for example, at a level 3 perinatal center. This contrasts with the past practice of delivery at any community hospital followed by transport of a critically ill infant to some referral nursery.

Effective preplanning based on multiple assessments of gestational age and maturity can virtually eliminate the complication of elective delivery of a preterm infant who subsequently develops iatrogenic hyaline membrane disease.

Intrapartum Resuscitation

In high-risk pregnancies the obstetrician must continuously assess the condition of the fetus through measurements of maternal blood pressure, maternal acid-base status, oxygenation of the mother, intrauterine pressure recordings, instantaneous fetal heart rate recordings, and occasional scalp pH measurements. Any fall in maternal blood pressure is reflected in a fall in uterine blood flow and potential uterine and fetal hypoxia. This accounts for attempts to avoid maternal hypotension by infusing isotonic salt solutions or colloid into the mother or by placing the mother on her side to avoid pressure from the gravid uterus upon the inferior vena cava, which would reduce return of blood to the right side of the heart. Oxygen tension in the most highly oxygenated blood of the fetus, ie, the umbilical venous blood, tends to equilibrate with uterine *venous* P_{O_2}, not with maternal arterial P_{O_2}. When oxygen in high concentration is given to the mother, her arterial P_{O_2} rises to very high levels, but the P_{O_2} in the uterine vein does not and increases to a much smaller extent. This increase in uterine vein P_{O_2} leads to a small but very important increase in umbilical venous P_{O_2}. Since the oxygen affinity of fetal blood is greater than that of adult blood and since the human fetus functions on the steep part of its oxygen dissociation curve, the small change in oxygen tension effects a very large change in oxygen content in the umbilical venous blood. This is why oxygen therapy is used when there is any evidence of fetal distress.

Obstetric Management at Delivery

Because unexpected complications at delivery can develop in the form of prolapse of the umbilical cord, unexpected dystocia of a head or shoulder, etc, it is important—particularly at medical centers where a choice can be made—that the most experienced obstetrician be available for the delivery of high-risk infants. One very useful procedure, performed by the obstetrician immediately after delivery of the infant, is the drawing of umbilical artery and umbilical venous blood samples into heparinized 1-mL syringes for blood gas analysis. These laboratory results often reflect the degree of longevity of in utero fetal hypoxia.

Whenever meconium-stained amniotic fluid is noticed at delivery, the obstetrician should deliver the head of the infant and then suction the nasopharynx, using a catheter and a DeLee trap before the shoulders are delivered and the thorax expands. This simple procedure has markedly reduced the incidence of severe meconium aspiration pneumonitis. The pediatrician should visualize the vocal cords; if meconium is on them, the infant should be intubated and the trachea suctioned until no meconium returns. Only after suctioning is completed should positive-pressure bagging and resuscitation be given.

Resuscitation of the Newborn Infant

The flow chart presented in Fig 36–8 shows the resuscitation procedures for newborn infants according to the severity of the neonatal depression shown at delivery. A few general comments apply to all infants. A physician skilled in the mechanics of resuscitation and in the evaluation of depressed infants of any weight or gestational age should be present for the delivery of every high-risk infant. In multiple pregnancies, there should always be one physician present for each infant. The knowledge of the attending physician should encompass technical skills in airway management and the ability to recognize clinical signs of impending shock. Ideally, a staff nurse from the neonatal intensive care unit should be present at the delivery of a high-risk infant. This enables the high-risk obstetrics nurse to concentrate exclusively upon the care of the mother. In addition, nurses from intensive care units are familiar with all the equipment and

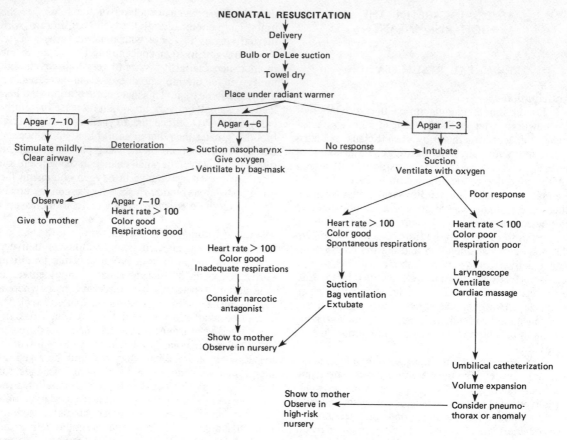

Figure 36–8. Flow diagram for neonatal resuscitation. (Modified and reproduced, with permission, from Lemons JA, Battaglia FC: Resuscitation of the newborn. Pages 811–814 in: *Current Therapy 1977*. Conn HF [editor]. Saunders, 1977.)

procedures required for support of the circulation and other procedures in high-risk infants. At medical centers with residency training programs, the physician and nursing staff should be supplemented by pediatric house staff members who assist in resuscitation for both training and service purposes.

The basic approach to resuscitation should center on adequate oxygenation and temperature support of the infant. It should ensure that these needs are met promptly and should de-emphasize pharmacologic management. The mechanics of resuscitation are far more important than the use of any pharmacologic agents, including sodium bicarbonate. All newborn infants, even the low-risk, full-term newborn infant, require adequate temperature support at delivery. In addition, every delivery suite should have adequate lighting and a gentle suction source for aspiration of the oro- or nasopharynx. Temperature support of the infant requires that a radiant heat source be provided. Precautions must be made to ensure that the skin is dry, to reduce evaporative heat loss and to provide a neutral thermal environment. Swaddling the infant in specially designed materials that reduce radiant, evaporative, and convective heat loss is a useful additional

safeguard. Adequate resuscitation of a newborn infant involves clearing the airway, establishing adequate ventilation, and providing circulatory support. The latter may require cardiac massage.

When volume expansion is required, give 10 mL/kg of 5% albumin, or Plasmanate, or unmatched O-negative whole blood.

Prognosis

An aggressive approach to the early identification of high-risk pregnancies, transport of mothers prior to delivery to a level 3 center, and presence of high-risk teams at the delivery have markedly reduced mortality rates of very-low-birth-weight infants. Further improvement in outcome of high-risk pregnancies will result from prevention of premature delivery and the development of effective intermediate community-based maternal and neonatal care centers. In addition, the prevention or prompt treatment of severe asphyxia will result in improved prognosis for that condition, which is reviewed in a later section of this chapter.

THE PRETERM INFANT

Infants born prematurely make up the major portion of newborns who are at increased risk. (For definitions and classification, see the early sections of this chapter.) Gestational age and birth weight correlate well with mortality risk (Fig 36–3).

Physiologic Handicaps Due to Prematurity

The increased risk due to prematurity is largely due to the functional and anatomic immaturity of various organs. Some of the more important examples are as follows:

(1) Weak sucking, swallowing, gag, and cough reflexes, leading to difficulty in feeding and danger of aspiration.

(2) Pulmonary immaturity and a pliable thorax, leading to hypoventilation and hypoxia with respiratory and metabolic acidosis.

(3) Decreased ability to maintain body temperature.

(4) Limited ability to excrete solutes in urine.

(5) Increased susceptibility to infection.

(6) Limited iron stores and rapid growth, leading to later anemia.

(7) Tendency to develop rickets due to rapid growth with diminished intake of calcium and vitamin D.

(8) Nutritional disturbances secondary to feeding difficulties and limited absorption of fat and fat-soluble vitamins.

(9) Immaturity of some metabolic processes, which influences the metabolism of certain nutrients and drugs as well as maintenance of normal homeostasis.

Care of the Preterm Infant

A. Delivery Room: See Perinatal Resuscitation on p 787 for resuscitation procedures for preterm infants.

B. Care in Nursery: Infants born at 36–38 weeks' gestation may need only general nursery care, stabilizing uneventfully after birth and going home with the mother. The more premature infant will require special care in either a level 2 or level 3 nursery.

Recently, there has been a tendency to care for small, preterm, or growth-retarded infants under open radiant heaters instead of in incubators because it is more convenient for nurses and doctors to examine infants and adjust tubes and equipment. However, easy accessibility introduces the risk of infection from contact with hospital personnel, whereas incubator care tends to remind the staff of the need for scrupulous hand washing and other such isolation procedures. Another of the disadvantages of the open radiant heater is the increased evaporative water losses and increased caloric requirements that may occur, particularly in very low birth weight infants; occasionally, very low birth weight infants may require more than 175 mL/kg/d of free water intake to prevent hypertonicity secondary to dehydration. Thus, incubator care still has some advantages over open radiant heaters. The incubators should be set to maintain skin temperature at 36–37°C (96.8–98.6°F). This generally requires an air temperature of 32–36°C (89.6–96.8°F) (see Table 36–4). The larger and more mature the infant, the lower the incubator temperature required to achieve a neutral thermal zone with minimal oxygen consumption.

Satisfactory incubators may be either servocontrolled or manually controlled. The use of manually controlled incubators for temperature regulation encourages observation of the infant's thermal stability and increases the chances that elevations of body temperature will be noted more readily. Humidification of the incubator environment by the addition of water is no longer routine because the inspired air, supplemented with oxygen, has often already been warmed and humidified and because there is concern that the high humidity within the incubator may encourage the growth of hydrophilic organisms (eg, *Pseudomonas*) on the inner surfaces, thus predisposing to infections with these organisms.

C. Transfer From Incubator to Bassinet: The premature infant who is swaddled and able to maintain body temperature without added environmental heat is placed in an open bassinet. This usually may be done when the infant reaches 1800–2000 g. Body temperature should be monitored to be sure normal temperature is maintained. This step represents one more reduction in the level of support the infant requires.

Examination

Evaluation and diagnostic procedures are done gently and carefully. The infant may not tolerate excessive handling well, so that the thoroughness of the examination may have to be tempered by a practical consideration of the infant's condition. Careful observation will provide much information, diminishing the amount of handling needed for the physical examination. Whenever possible, procedures should be done without removing the infant from the incubator, and they should be done within the nursery environment.

The advent of relatively noninvasive techniques for monitoring physiologic variables in infants has greatly reduced the amount of manipulation and handling required for care. Doppler techniques for measuring arterial blood pressure and transcutaneous electrodes for measuring continuous arterial P_{O_2} have reduced the need for long-term umbilical artery catheterization along with its complications and the need for arterial punctures in infants. Finally, continuous P_{O_2} recordings using transcutaneous electrodes are of great help in recognizing specific events that trigger hypoxia in particular infants and in following infants with long-term oxygen dependence.

Growth of Preterm Infant

In order to monitor the growth, hydration, and nutrition of preterm infants, standard postnatal growth curves can be used to which further data are added. Each day the infant's weight, total water intake (in mL/

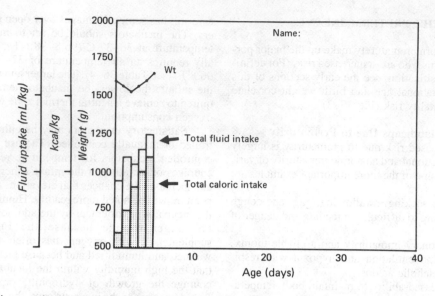

Figure 36–9. A convenient method of presenting a summary of hydration, nutrition, and body weight in newborn infants.

kg/d), and total caloric intake (kcal/kg/d) are plotted on the same graph (Fig 36–9).

Nutrition

In feeding premature infants of any size, the goal is not only to achieve adequate caloric intake but also to balance the intake of carbohydrates, amino acids, and fats. The general principles, which often require extensive modifications, are as follows:

A. Carbohydrates: Premature infants will require intravenous or intra-arterial infusion of 10% glucose at a rate sufficient to provide approximately 7 mg/kg/min. The rate can then be increased or decreased as required in a particular infant to maintain a blood glucose level greater than 40 mg/dL and under 120 mg/dL. When lactose-containing milk feedings are begun, they will provide additional carbohydrate in the form of lactose, which is rapidly taken up by the newborn liver and converted to glucose and glycogen.

B. Amino Acids: Amino acids can be given intravenously to infants using any one of the commercially available protein hydrolysates. However, whenever possible, one should provide amino acids as protein contained in milk feedings. Infants will tolerate a wide range of protein intakes, and it is not clear at this time whether there are any advantages to increasing protein intake substantially above 2 g/kg/d. Human breast milk or modified cow's milk formulas with high whey/curd ratios are the preferred feedings in very low birth weight infants.

C. Fats: Fat ingestion appears important in establishing normal postnatal liver and gastrointestinal function. Formulas with mixtures of medium-chain triglycerides and complex fats should be used. When the introduction of milk feedings has been markedly delayed in newborn infants, essential fatty acid intake must be assured.

Supplements

A. Vitamins: For infants receiving adequate amounts of breast milk or a proprietary formula, controversy exists about the need for vitamin supplements. It is our policy to give vitamin D and intravenous or oral calcium during the first few days to weeks of life to prevent rickets. In addition, for infants of less than 35 weeks' gestation, we recommend 50 mg of vitamin C, 25 IU of vitamin E, and 50 μg of folate daily. Phytonadione (vitamin K_1, AquaMephyton), 1 mg intramuscularly, is given on admission to the nursery. If oral intake of milk is not adequate, the vitamin K is repeated once weekly.

When infants receive only intravenous or intra-arterial fluids during the first few days of life, a water-soluble multivitamin preparation should be added to the fluids to ensure adequate intake of water-soluble vitamins. This must include vitamin B_{12}.

B. Iron: Infants with birth weight less than 1800 g need supplemental iron, since their iron stores at birth are limited and there is rapid growth with an increase in red cell mass during the first year of life. Oral iron supplementation is begun after 38 weeks' gestation in these infants, when the risk of hemolytic anemia of the premature has passed.

C. Trace Metals: Zinc and copper deficiencies have been reported in premature infants and in infants with short bowel or malabsorption syndromes.

Discharge

Discharge from the hospital usually occurs when the infant weighs 2000–2500 g and is eating well and coexistent medical problems have resolved or are sufficiently improved. In the nursery, the parents are encouraged to visit the infant frequently and help care for and feed their child. A social worker or visiting nurse may be very helpful in aiding the mother to care for the infant and in helping to solve the special problems related to prolonged mother-infant separation, disease, or handicaps.

Follow-Up Care

Long-term follow-up care is especially important for infants discharged from level 2 or level 3 nurseries because of the high incidence of significant handicaps occurring later. In recent follow-up studies, 10–20% of surviving infants who had birth weights less than 1500 g later had physical problems, neurologic difficulties, visual impairment, deafness, learning and perceptual problems, or mental retardation. Early recognition of these handicaps and appropriate treatment when indicated will improve outcome. The effects of family characteristics and socioeconomic status on psychomotor achievements of high-risk infants must be remembered during follow-up. Family-structured rehabilitation programs for the handicapped infant are necessary.

MULTIPLE BIRTHS

Twinning occurs in about one out of 90 pregnancies. The incidence of twins increases with the mother's age and parity. There is a familial tendency toward dizygotic twinning.

Dizygotic twinning occurs with increased frequency following the use of drugs, eg, clomiphene, which induce ovulation and which may be used in the treatment of infertility. Twins may develop from a single ovum (monozygotic, identical) or from 2 ova (dizygotic, fraternal).

About one-third of twins are of the single ovum type. About one-third of identical twins have a double placenta, amnion, and chorion. However, if the partition between the twins consists of 2 layers of transparent amnion without an intervening chorion, a diagnosis of monozygotic twinning can be made with certainty. Similarly, if the twins are of opposite sexes, the diagnosis of dizygotic twins is made with certainty.

Intrauterine Growth

The fetal growth pattern in multiple pregnancy differs from that of a single fetus. Intrauterine growth retardation occurs at a given total weight of all fetuses regardless of the number. Thus, intrauterine growth retardation appears in each fetus later in gestation in triplets than in quadruplets and still later in twins. In addition, the greater the number of fetuses, the earlier in pregnancy labor will occur, ie, triplets tend to be delivered earlier than twins. Thus, infants in multiple pregnancies are more likely to be affected by problems of preterm delivery and intrauterine growth retardation than are singletons. Discordant twins, whose birth weights differ markedly (by at least 20% or more), often are found in association with twin-twin transfusion syndrome and are more common when there is a single chorion, as in monozygotic twins. The larger, plethoric twin tends to be much more ill than the

anemic, smaller one when twin-twin transfusion syndrome occurs, perhaps because hypervolemia and hyperviscosity may contribute to the symptoms in the larger twin.

Complications of Multiple Births

A. Preterm Delivery: Pregnancy is usually several weeks shorter with twins.

B. Polyhydramnios: Ten times more common.

C. Preeclampsia and Eclampsia: Three times more common.

D. Placenta Previa: More frequent, presumably from increased placental mass.

E. Abruptio Placentae: May occur with second twin placenta due to reduction in size of uterus following delivery of the first twin.

F. Presentation: Breech and other abnormal presentations are more frequent.

G. Duration of Labor: Usually not much longer, though uterine contractions after delivery may be poor, with subsequent bleeding.

H. Prolapse of the Cord: Seven times more frequent than in single deliveries because of abnormal presentations and rupture of the second twin's membranes when unengaged.

Prognosis

The morbidity and mortality risks in multiple births are greater than with single births. More secondborn twins die than firstborn twins.

Follow-up studies of twins for later growth and development are conflicting, with some studies supporting a continued discrepancy in size of the 2 twins into adulthood and other studies being unable to demonstrate persistent differences in developmental size from those recorded in single births.

BIRTH INJURY

Injuries to the infant resulting from the birth process fall into 4 general categories.

(1) Hemorrhage: Bleeding into the central nervous system may result from birth trauma or birth asphyxia. Cephalhematoma or bruising of the skin is rarely of clinical significance. Damage to abdominal organs with internal bleeding or hematuria may become apparent if the newborn develops signs of shock.

(2) Fracture: Skull fracture may occur but usually requires no specific treatment unless it is depressed, in which case neurosurgical decompression is required. Fracture of the clavicle or humerus may be noted first because of diminished movement in the affected extremity.

(3) Nerve injury: Injury to branches of the brachial plexus may result from difficult delivery of the shoulder or aftercoming head. This injury is associated with diminished movement or abnormal position of the affected extremity. Phrenic nerve injury may cause asymmetric respiratory movement. Facial nerve injury is indicated by asymmetry of the mouth on the affected side when the infant cries.

(4) Asphyxia: Birth asphyxia is an important cause of neonatal death or long-term disability. With identification of high-risk pregnancies, fetal monitoring during labor of those at risk, and optimal decisions about mode of delivery, the frequency of this important preventable cause of perinatal morbidity should be significantly reduced.

Prognosis

Hemorrhage and asphyxia are discussed further below (p 801). It is important not to overlook fracture and nerve injury, so that further injury and pain can be reduced by careful observation and handling. These injuries usually resolve with time, although they may interfere with the smooth adaptation of the infant to normal care and feedings. Long-term sequelae are uncommon, but the infants should be followed closely, and early physical therapy may be very helpful in preventing contractures and maintaining joint mobility. If the nerve damage leaves permanent disability, continued therapy is important.

DISEASES SPECIFICALLY OF THE NEWBORN

RESPIRATORY DISEASES

1. APNEA

Apnea is defined as cessation of respiration for 20 seconds or longer and is accompanied by cyanosis and bradycardia. It must be distinguished from **periodic breathing** (see below), in which the apnea is brief (usually less than 10 seconds) and is not accompanied by cyanosis or bradycardia.

Apnea is often a sign of serious significance in the newborn. Apnea can occur at any time during the neonatal period, particularly in very immature infants. Generally, the appearance of severe apneic episodes in a previously well preterm baby signals the onset of some other serious illness (eg, meningitis, sepsis, intracranial hemorrhage), but in some instances, apnea apparently unassociated with any metabolic problem or illness may occur. Virtually any serious illness may precipitate apneic episodes. For this reason, apneic attacks require a thorough evaluation of the infant's condition, with particular attention directed to any infection or central nervous system disorder as a possible cause of the attacks. Severe apneic attacks in a previously well infant may be an indication for an electroencephalogram, because seizures in the newborn may present as apnea only. Apneic episodes in infants with neonatal seizures will often stop when seizures are controlled and successfully treated with anticonvulsants. If idiopathic apneic episodes are frequent, an oral loading dose of theophylline, 5 mg/kg,

can be given. A blood level reading should be obtained 2 hours after administration of the loading dose, at which time the drug level is likely to be at its peak. A maintenance dose is adjusted on the basis of blood level readings but is generally in the range of 1–2 mg/kg every 8 hours, given orally.

2. PERIODIC BREATHING

Periodic breathing is common in newborn and young infants. It is usually not clinically significant, but in some infants, most commonly prematures, prolonged respiratory pauses may be associated with cyanosis and bradycardia. It then becomes a major problem for diagnosis and management. Reports suggest that irregular respiratory patterns may be due to changes in respiratory drive or effective respiratory timing. Stimulation of laryngeal chemoreceptors may result in slowing or cessation of respiration. Finally, careful monitoring has revealed that active and quiet sleep states may not develop normal cycling and regulation in some premature and term infants.

Follow-up data on these infants have not yet defined the relationship between periodic breathing of prematurity and subsequent clinically significant apnea in young infants.

3. RESPIRATORY DISTRESS

A number of diseases involving the respiratory system as well as other systems can present a clinical picture similar to respiratory distress syndrome in the newborn. The symptom complex consists of expiratory grunting and retractions of the chest wall, accompanied by varying degrees of cyanosis, increased respiratory rate, and decreased volume of inspired air. Because of the variety of diseases that can cause respiratory distress, it is important to give careful consideration in each case to all possibilities. Appropriate diagnostic procedures include a careful history, physical examination, cultures, and chest x-ray.

Respiratory distress syndrome (RDS, hyaline membrane disease) occurs chiefly in preterm infants. It is characterized by decreased or absent pulmonary surfactant. The lungs show decreased compliance, widespread atelectasis, and injury to the parenchyma. Cellular debris and plasma exudate accumulate in the alveolar ducts, forming the membrane seen at autopsy.

Clinical Findings

A. Symptoms and Signs: Retractions and expiratory grunting begin soon after birth and become progressively more severe over the next few hours. Decreased air exchange, cyanosis, and increasingly rapid breathing occur as the disease progresses. Symptoms increase in severity until 24–48 hours of age, when the disease reaches its peak. If the course is progressive, death from ventilatory insufficiency occurs in 2–3 days; but if there is gradual improvement in ventilation, the infant is likely to recover. With careful management begun early in the course of the disease, the mortality rate will be about 10–15% or less.

B. Laboratory Findings: Studies will reflect the degree of ventilatory insufficiency: acidosis, CO_2 retention, and lowered oxygen tension. Pulmonary function studies show lowered compliance, decreased lung volume, and reduced effective pulmonary blood flow.

C. X-Ray Findings: Chest x-ray usually reveals a characteristic "ground glass" appearance. The lungs are hypoexpanded, and air bronchograms are prominent.

Prevention & Prediction

Because pulmonary immaturity is a primary factor in the development of respiratory distress syndrome, every effort should be made to avoid preterm deliveries. Meticulous prenatal care should be provided for mothers known to be at risk; this includes mothers with diabetes, multiple gestation, isoimmunization, a history of preterm deliveries, a previous baby with respiratory distress syndrome, and elective termination of pregnancy.

Differential Diagnosis

Respiratory distress may be due to disorders with increased or normal pulmonary expansion, hilar infiltrates, and rales and rhonchi and include **congenital bacterial pneumonias, "wet lung" syndrome, transient tachypnea** of the newborn, and **amniotic fluid aspiration or meconium aspiration.** Wheezing may be present. The chest x-ray shows a slightly enlarged heart and streaky infiltrates radiating from the hilum of the lung following the general pattern of the lymphatic and venous drainage of the lung. The peripheral lung fields are clear. Areas of infiltrate and atelectasis may be present. Although some of the diseases in this category are quickly diagnosed (eg, hyperviscosity syndrome with the help of a hematocrit determination), congenital bacterial pneumonias and "wet lung" syndrome cannot be easily diagnosed. For this reason, infants in whom a tentative diagnosis of "wet lung" syndrome has been made should be treated with antibiotics until bacterial infection is clearly ruled out.

Disorders with normal lung expansion, relatively clear lung fields, and marked hypoxemia are most commonly associated with **persistent fetal circulation.** Any congenital heart lesion with inadequate pulmonary blood flow will also have these findings. Occasionally, **"shock lung"** following a severe hypoxic and hypotensive episode will also have these signs. More commonly, however, shock lung has a clinical spectrum comparable to that of "wet lung" syndrome.

Treatment

Early recognition is imperative. Infants with severe respiratory distress require special care. Those in attendance must be aware of the potential need for an early decision to transfer the infant to a newborn center. The infant is placed in an incubator in order to maintain a normal body temperature. Humidity should be adequate (60–80%), but mist is not necessary.

Supplemental oxygen administration is needed for infants whose arterial oxygen tensions fall below 50–60 mm Hg. Cyanosis does not provide an accurate indication of arterial oxygen levels and cannot be used as a guide for continued oxygen therapy. The use of equipment to maintain an ambient oxygen concentration at less than 40% is not recommended, because this amount of oxygen may be both toxic to the retinas (arterial P_{O_2} levels may exceed 100 mm Hg) and at the same time too low to satisfy the oxygen requirement of an infant with respiratory distress. The concentration being delivered into the incubator or hood should be monitored by an oxygen analyzer located near the infant's nose. This level of inspired oxygen should be measured and recorded each time a blood gas sample is drawn. Whenever an infant has respiratory distress, blood gases must be monitored accurately. Arterial oxygen should be maintained at 60–70 mm Hg.

Arterial oxygen tension determinations may be done from the descending aorta or the temporal, brachial, or radial arteries. Values from blood obtained from a warmed heel are not reliable. Recently, the use of indwelling arterial lines and transcutaneous oxygen analyzers, which give continuous readouts of arterial oxygenation, have shown the rapid and marked swings with handling, suctioning, and simply observing the infant.

If blood gas measurements are not available, oxygen supplementation may be administered in concentrations just high enough to relieve cyanosis. However, because of the special risk of retrolental fibroplasia and other toxic effects of oxygen administration, the infant should be transferred for care where blood gas measurements are available. Infants with gestational ages of less than 36 weeks who have received oxygen therapy should have a careful eye examination for evidence of retrolental fibroplasia before discharge. The development of retrolental fibroplasia is directly related to increased arterial oxygen tensions in the susceptible premature infant. Therefore, careful monitoring of arterial P_{O_2} is required to avoid this complication and yet provide adequate oxygenation. The pathogenesis of retrolental fibroplasia includes retinal vessel dilatation, proliferation into the vitreous, hemorrhage, and fibrosis. This process may spontaneously regress, or it may continue to complete retinal detachment.

A second organ injured by administration of oxygen in high concentrations is the lung. Prolonged exposure to high ambient oxygen concentrations will produce bronchopulmonary dysplasia. Since this condition is caused by exposure of the surface of the respiratory tract to high concentrations of inspired oxygen rather than by a high arterial P_{O_2} it may to some extent be unavoidable in those infants with severe hyaline membrane disease who require high oxygen concentrations to ensure acceptable arterial oxygen tension. Positive pressure ventilation with high oxygen concentrations increases the risk of pulmonary damage.

If the infant cannot achieve adequate oxygenation in the oxygen-enriched atmosphere—or if CO_2 retention and acidosis are present as a mark of progressive respiratory failure—respirator support should be used. The infant may need no more than continuous positive airway pressure to keep the alveoli open and decrease the work of breathing. If this is insufficient, positive pressure ventilation should be given. This may be done by hand-bagging or by using an infant ventilator. The infant must be attended constantly until respiratory stabilization has been achieved and maintained.

General supportive care is crucial in avoiding iatrogenic complications or other problems. Hypothermia should be avoided, since this will increase the infant's oxygen requirements. An infusion of 10% glucose with appropriate sodium intake provided as $NaHCO_3$ should be given because infants with hyaline membrane disease almost invariably demonstrate combined respiratory and metabolic acidosis. The quantities of water and sodium required will vary depending upon the size and maturity of the infant; general guidelines have been given above. Frequently, infants severely ill with respiratory distress may require circulatory support with intravenous infusion of colloid or red blood cells. However, expansion of circulating blood or plasma volume should not be confused with expansion of extracellular volume caused by the increased administration of sodium and water. Expansion of extracellular volume should be avoided.

If infection cannot be ruled out as a cause of the respiratory distress, appropriate cultures and antibiotic treatment are indicated.

Prognosis

With the advent of ventilators and continuous positive air pressure devices, the mortality rate from acute respiratory failure in newborns has been notably reduced. For example, in hyaline membrane disease, it has decreased from 75% to 25%. In addition, the long-term outcome is normal for both pulmonary and developmental well-being.

HEART DISEASE

The incidence of congenital heart disease is about 1% of the population. The most important clues to the presence of heart disease are cyanosis and congestive heart failure. Cyanosis due to heart disease may be difficult to distinguish from pulmonary disease. Poor feeding, tachypnea, and hypoxemic spells may suggest primary cardiac failure.

Signs & Symptoms of Heart Failure in the Newborn

Heart failure in the newborn infant may be difficult to recognize because the signs and symptoms are not the same as in older infants. The infant in early failure will show only an increased heart and respiratory rate, excessive weight gain, and, perhaps, irritability. With increasing failure, sweating, anxiety, and poor feeding occur. Auscultation of the lungs rarely reveals evidence of pulmonary edema. Abnormal heart sounds and murmurs often are not diagnostic. X-ray examination may show the heart to be enlarged, but in newborn infants minimal cardiac enlargement is difficult to determine, particularly if there is a large thymus shadow. Assessing heart size by physical examination is even more difficult.

Increasing liver size is an important finding. An enlarged or enlarging liver, in the absence of other disease, is good evidence of heart failure. Liver size should be followed as a means of evaluating the effectiveness of treatment.

Peripheral edema is frequent in preterm babies but it is rarely a sign of heart failure. When it does occur as a result of heart failure, it is a late and ominous sign. In general, peripheral edema reflects excessive sodium and water intake rather than heart failure.

Diagnosis

If the history, physical examination, and chest x-ray suggest cardiac disease, early consultation with a pediatric cardiologist is indicated. Further work-up may include electrocardiography, echocardiography, and cardiac catheterization and angiography. **Electrocardiography** is important in determining axis and atrial or ventricular dilatation or hypertrophy. **Echocardiography,** a new and powerful noninvasive tool requiring little manipulation of the infant, enables physicians to safely perform serial examinations of critically ill infants. It has been useful in assessing the strength of myocardial contractions, facilitating the early diagnosis of various congenital anomalies of the heart, and providing an estimate of left atrial size. If structural abnormalities are suspected, **cardiac catheterization** may be indicated.

Treatment

Treatment of congestive heart failure of whatever cause consists of restricting water intake to the amount of evaporative losses and eliminating sodium intake. If water restriction is coupled with complete sodium restriction, hyponatremia will not result even if potent diuretics are used. This regimen can be instituted along with a single dose of furosemide and digitalization of the infant. After 12–24 hours, water and sodium intake may then be increased, with the degree of water and sodium administered depending upon the clinical course of the infant.

Surgical palliation or correction of anatomic defects of the heart and great vessels is now widely available. The procedures call for sophisticated anesthetic and surgical capabilities and should only be performed in centers with experienced personnel.

Prognosis

Without proper care, over 50% of infants with congenital heart disease will die before 1 year. With good medical and surgical management, the prognosis for life is primarily related to the complexity of the anatomic or functional defect. Morbidity is due to failure to thrive and uncontrolled heart failure.

Congenital heart disease may be complicated by severe spells of cyanosis, hypoperfusion, and cardiac arrest. These should be prevented or responded to rapidly in order to avoid possible irreversible brain damage.

OTHER DISEASES & DISORDERS IN THE NEWBORN

METABOLIC DISORDERS

1. HYPOGLYCEMIA

Diagnosis

In normal infants at birth the blood glucose level is the same as or slightly lower than that of the mother. During the hours after delivery, the blood glucose level decreases (rarely below 30–40 mg/dL), and by 6–12 hours of age it stabilizes at 50–80 mg/dL. Blood glucose levels below 30 mg/dL are considered abnormal in the newborn period.

Etiology

Hypoglycemia is frequent in 2 extremes of altered intrauterine nutrition: the infant of the diabetic mother, who is well nourished, with abundant glycogen and fat stores; and the infant with intrauterine growth retardation, who is undernourished, with minimal glycogen and fat deposits. In addition, hypoglycemia is associated with Beckwith's syndrome, erythroblastosis fetalis, nesidioblastosis, leucine sensitivity, glycogen storage disease, and galactosemia. Hypoglycemia may occur in any sick infant and is frequent after birth asphyxia.

Clinical Signs

Manifestations of hypoglycemia in the newborn may be mild and nonspecific: lethargy, poor feeding, regurgitation, apnea, and twitching. As symptoms become more severe, the baby develops pallor, sweating, cool extremities, and prolonged apnea and convulsions. In all clinical conditions in which hypoglycemia is likely to occur, it is important to follow the blood glucose concentration closely; administration of intravenous glucose may be necessary to maintain acceptable blood levels initially. Careful blood glucose measurements are again indicated at the time the infant is weaned to milk feedings, since milk feedings decrease the glucose intake and the infant must switch to gluconeogenesis. Thus, hypoglycemia may reappear in the susceptible infant at the time of weaning from continuous intravenous infusion to milk feedings.

Prognosis

The clinical significance of hypoglycemia in the newborn is not clear inasmuch as low plasma glucose levels are frequently found in newborns who have few apparent symptoms. However, certain cells, including those of the brain and lung parenchyma, rely on glucose as the primary metabolic substrate. Severe and prolonged hypoglycemia is known to cause progressive, irreparable brain damage; the effect of less severe hypoglycemia is not known.

Infants of Diabetic Mothers

Pregnancy in a woman with controlled diabetes seems to present no special problems to the fetus until about the 28th week. The fetus may then show differing patterns of intrauterine growth, ie, it may (1) grow more rapidly, associated with an increase in fat and glycogen deposition and growth in length, probably secondary to a hyperinsulin state; (2) continue to show normal intrauterine growth, most commonly occurring in mothers under good control; or (3) show intrauterine growth retardation, presumably due to placental insufficiency, occurring in mothers with severe diabetes and vascular complications.

Infants of diabetic mothers have physical characteristics compatible with their gestational age even though they may be quite large. The typical appearance is that of a large, fat, plethoric baby.

Treatment

Management consists first of anticipating the problems mentioned above. The baby should receive special care until it is evaluated and has stabilized. Hypoglycemia is usually transient; the plasma glucose often returns to normal levels by 6 hours of age and the infant responds well to oral feedings. Continuous intravenous administration of 10% glucose in water may be required, and this should be the initial therapy if the baby is sick and does not tolerate oral feedings. If the hypoglycemia is refractory, the glucose may be increased to a 12.5% concentration and more rapid infusion rates. Higher glucose concentrations should not be used because of the excessive insulin secretion that would be stimulated. Inadvertent interruption of intravenous glucose solutions in babies with hypoglycemia should be considered a medical emergency, since reactive hypoglycemia may be severe.

Infants With Intrauterine Growth Retardation

The fetus with chronic intrauterine malnutrition will be born with diminished stores of glycogen and fat. Hypoglycemia is likely to occur during the first few hours and may continue over a period of days.

The small-for-gestational-age infant with hypoglycemia and a very high hematocrit (central venous hematocrit > 62%) is likely to show the most severe clinical signs of hypoglycemia, presumably reflecting a reduction in glucose delivered to the brain. A small exchange transfusion with fresh frozen plasma should be given to reduce the hematocrit and correct the hypoglycemia.

Treatment

Early oral or gavage feedings with glucose in water or milk may suffice in cases of transient, mild hypoglycemia. Management of more severe hypoglycemia (< 30 mg/dL) should include intravenous administration of 10% glucose in water to maintain blood glucose concentrations above 30 mg/dL. A 15% glucose solution may be required, but higher concentrations should be avoided. Serial measurements of plasma glucose levels are essential in order to determine the adequacy of treatment.

2. HYPERBILIRUBINEMIA

Clinical Course

Jaundice is the most frequent clinical problem in the neonatal period. The age at onset, the degree of jaundice, and the condition of the baby are important observations in determining the cause and significance of the elevated level of bilirubin in the blood.

When red blood cells break down, the iron and protein are stored and reused. However, the porphyrin ring is reduced to bilirubin (unconjugated, indirect) in the reticuloendothelial cells and is then transported to the liver, bound to albumin. In the liver, the bilirubin is conjugated mainly to bilirubin diglucuronide (conjugated, direct) and excreted through the biliary ducts to the gut. In the intestine, it would normally be converted to urobilinogen by bacterial action. However, since the newborn intestine is sterile, conjugated bilirubin excreted in the bile can be hydrolyzed back to bilirubin and reabsorbed if the bowel contents are not evacuated.

The degree of jaundice that develops will depend upon the rate of red cell breakdown (bilirubin load), the rate of conjugation, the rate of excretion, and the amount of bilirubin reabsorbed from the intestine. In normal term infants, red blood cells have an average life span of about 100 days; therefore 1% of the cells are removed from the circulation every day. The average capacity of the liver to conjugate bilirubin in the first few days of life approximately equals the bilirubin load, since about half of infants will show laboratory evidence of a significant rise in bilirubin levels and about one-third show clinical jaundice. Jaundice tends to occur first in the head and neck. As the unconjugated bilirubin concentration increases, more of the body appears jaundiced; jaundice involving most of the body surfaces including the palms and soles occurs only with markedly elevated bilirubin concentration.

Etiology

A. Increased Rate of Hemolysis: (All patients in this category have an increased unconjugated bilirubin concentration and an increased reticulocyte count.)
1. Patients with positive Coombs test (this category includes all patients with isoimmunization, including ABO incompatibility, Rh incompatibility, etc).

2. Patients with negative Coombs test.
   a. Abnormal red cell shapes, including spherocytosis, elliptocytosis, pyknocytosis, stomatocytosis.
   b. Red cell enzyme abnormalities: glucose 6-phosphate dehydrogenase deficiency, pyruvate kinase deficiency.

B. Decreased Rate of Conjugation: Unconjugated bilirubin elevated, reticulocyte count normal.
1. Immaturity of bilirubin conjugation ("physiologic jaundice").
2. Congenital familial nonhemolytic jaundice (inborn errors of metabolism affecting glucuronyl transferase system and bilirubin transport).
3. Breast milk jaundice?

C. Abnormalities of Excretion or Reabsorption: Conjugated and unconjugated bilirubin elevated, Coombs test negative, reticulocyte count normal.
1. Hepatitis–Viral, parasitic, bacterial, toxic.
2. Metabolic abnormalities–
   a. Galactosemia.
   b. Glycogen storage diseases.
   c. Infant of diabetic mother.
   d. Cystic fibrosis.
3. Biliary atresia.
4. Choledochal cyst.
5. Obstruction at ampulla of Vater (annular pancreas).
6. Sepsis.
7. Gastrointestinal obstruction—structural or functional.

Diagnosis of Bilirubin Toxicity

Serum levels of indirect bilirubin should be determined periodically on all jaundiced infants because of the special dangers of neurosensory hearing loss and kernicterus. Guidelines for suggested bilirubin levels for exchange transfusion based on birth weight and clinical course of the infant are shown in Table 36–7.

More recent tests have become available in the laboratory that allow determination of unbound bilirubin, albumin-binding capacity, and albumin saturation. These tests may prove to be much better predictors of bilirubin toxicity. Follow-up studies based on these tests have not yet been completed.

Treatment of Hyperbilirubinemia

Specific recommendations for management depend upon the cause of jaundice and are discussed in detail in neonatal textbooks. Double-exchange transfusion of the infant's estimated blood volume is indicated as soon as possible after birth in infants with severe Rh sensitization and in all infants whose serum bilirubin levels approach the toxic range (Table 36–7). For infants who can tolerate manipulation of the gastrointestinal tract, early milk feedings and glycerin suppositories have been shown to decrease the serum bilirubin level, presumably by enhancing early evacua-

Table 36—7. Serum levels of indirect bilirubin and exchange transfusions.*†

Birth Weight (g)	Serum Bilirubin Level for Exchange Transfusion (mg/dL)	
	Normal Infants‡	Abnormal Infants§
< 1,000	10.0	10.0**
1,001–1,250	13.0	10.0**
1,251–1,500	15.0	13.0
1,501–2,000	17.0	15.0
2,001–2,500	18.0	17.0
> 2,500	20.0	18.0

*Reproduced, with permission, from American Academy of Pediatrics: Page 95 in: *Standards and Recommendations for Hospital Care of Newborn Infants,* 6th ed. American Academy of Pediatrics, 1977. Copyright American Academy of Pediatrics, 1977.

†These guidelines have not been validated.

‡There have been case reports of basal ganglion staining at levels considerably lower than 10 mg.

§Normal infants are defined for this purpose as having none of the problems listed below.

**Abnormal infants have one or more of the following problems: perinatal asphyxia, prolonged hypoxemia, acidemia, persistent hypothermia, hypoalbuminemia, hemolysis, sepsis, hyperglycemia, elevated free fatty acids or presence of drugs that compete for bilirubin binding, signs of clinical or central nervous system deterioration.

tion of gut contents, including bilirubin. Appropriate supportive care is indicated for all infants; in those with hemolytic processes, weekly follow-up of hematocrit and reticulocyte count is necessary up to 4 months.

In addition to exchange transfusion, the most important therapeutic modality is phototherapy. Light energy enhances the degradation of unconjugated bilirubin in the skin to colorless by-products that are apparently nontoxic. Certain important routines must be followed whenever phototherapy is used:

(1) Phototherapy should be used only when significant unconjugated (indirect) hyperbilirubinemia is present; its use with elevated conjugated (direct) bilirubin levels is contraindicated ("bronze baby syndrome"). It is begun when the bilirubin is approximately 4 mg/dL below the exchange level.

(2) The etiologic basis for jaundice must always be sought.

(3) Bilirubin levels must be determined serially while the infant is receiving phototherapy; skin jaundice is not a reliable indicator of serum bilirubin levels.

(4) The indication for exchange transfusion and other methods of management of neonatal jaundice is not changed by phototherapy.

(5) The eyes should be protected from intense light by appropriate patching. The patch must be applied carefully and should be removed at regular intervals to examine the eyes; conjunctivitis and corneal abrasion are the main hazards. The patch should be removed and phototherapy discontinued when the parents visit, to encourage eye-to-eye contact.

(6) The use of phototherapy or an open radiant heater (or both) produces considerable evaporative water losses in infants. It is customary to increase free water intake during phototherapy by about 25% and to follow urine flow rates and specific gravities carefully in order to readjust fluid intake as required. An increase in the evaporative water loss may be associated with an increase in caloric requirements. This may constitute an additional nutritional problem in certain instances in which nutrition has been inadequate for other reasons. Phototherapy also increases gastrointestinal transit time and may interfere with the absorption of drugs administered orally.

(7) Electrical and mechanical safety of the phototherapy unit must be assured.

Prognosis

Regardless of cause, bilirubin causes damage when it passes from the serum into the basal ganglion cells of the brain and the inner hair cells of the cochlea. Neurosensory hearing loss is the most common sequela of excessive serum bilirubin. Kernicterus is less common, but it refers to the clinical syndrome and pathologic changes in the central nervous system secondary to deposition of unconjugated bilirubin in certain nuclei of the brain. Depending on gestational age, the risk of kernicterus becomes significant at serum bilirubin levels of 10–20 mg/dL. Certain factors predispose to the development of kernicterus at lower serum levels. These factors mainly result in decreased albumin-binding capacity for bilirubin (acidosis, low albumin levels, sulfonamide administration, elevated free fatty acid, etc).

The infant with kernicterus initially has severe hyperbilirubinemia, usually secondary to erythroblastosis but in some cases associated with jaundice due to other causes. There is a fairly sudden onset of lethargy and poor feeding; a weak or incomplete Moro reflex; a weak, high-pitched cry; and opisthotonos. In premature infants, slowed respiratory rate and apneic periods may be prominent findings. Apnea, respiratory arrest, and convulsions characterize the terminal episode. Infants who survive have severe motor impairment, including hypotonia, spasticity, and athetosis. Mental retardation is less severe. Fortunately, kernicterus has become extremely rare as techniques for monitoring newborn infants have improved. Kernicterus can be prevented by close monitoring of unconjugated bilirubin concentrations and the initiation of appropriate treatment in jaundiced infants.

HEMATOLOGIC DISORDERS

1. BLEEDING DISORDERS

The most common causes of bleeding in the newborn are vascular accidents, clotting deficiencies (vitamin K-dependent factors being the most common), thrombocytopenia, and disseminated intravascular coagulation.

Hemorrhagic Disease of the Newborn (Hypoprothrombinemia)

Vitamin K–dependent clotting factors (factors II, VII, IX, X) are normal at birth but decrease within 2–3 days. In vitamin K–deficient infants, these levels may be very low, resulting in prolonged bleeding times. Bleeding may occur into the skin or gastrointestinal tract, at the site of injection or circumcision, or at internal sites. Small amounts of vitamin K are sufficient to correct the clotting factor defects unless liver function is immature in a very sick or premature infant. All newborns should receive 1 mg of vitamin K intramuscularly on admission to the nursery.

Blood in Vomitus or Stool

Swallowing maternal blood during delivery is not uncommon. If enough has been ingested, the baby may vomit bright red or dark blood or may pass stool containing dark or bright red, fresh-appearing blood. Clinical evidence of acute blood loss is lacking, but a transient rise in blood urea nitrogen may occur. Blood of maternal origin may be differentiated from infant blood by testing for fetal hemoglobin, which is resistant to alkali denaturation: a small amount of red bloody stool or vomitus is mixed with 5–10 mL of water and centrifuged. To 5 parts of pink supernatant, add 1 part 0.25 N sodium hydroxide. If fetal hemoglobin is present, the solution stays pink; if adult hemoglobin is present, it becomes brown.

Gastrointestinal bleeding in the newborn may be due to trauma, peptic ulcer, duplication of bowel, Meckel's diverticulum, intussusception, volvulus, hemangioma or telangiectasis of the bowel, polyp, rectal prolapse, anal fissure (a common cause of a small amount of blood in the stool in infants), infection (salmonellae, shigellae), systemic bleeding disorders (particularly hemorrhagic disease of the newborn), and tumors.

If blood is of maternal origin, no treatment is needed. If bleeding is of fetal origin, treat as for acute blood loss with blood transfusions and supportive care and then proceed with diagnosis and treatment of the underlying disease. The most common intrinsic cause of bloody vomitus is a gastric ulcer, which seldom causes massive bleeding and perforation. The bleeding generally can be managed with frequent oral milk feedings alone. If blood loss has been significant but transfusion is not necessary, iron supplementation may be required during the first few months.

2. ANEMIA

Acute blood loss before or during delivery can occur into the maternal circulation or the amniotic sac, into a twin fetus in the twin-twin transfusion syndrome, or into the vagina. Acute blood loss after delivery may be external (gastrointestinal, circumcision site, umbilical stump) or internal (fracture site, cephalhematoma, central nervous system or pulmonary hemorrhage, soft tissue hematoma, injured internal organ). Anemia may be secondary to hemolysis (isoimmunization, acquired hemolytic disease, red cell metabolic abnormalities) or to congenital aplastic or hypoplastic anemia.

The degree of bleeding, which may occur at many sites during delivery (including muscle and skin), is frequently underestimated. In general, whenever there is serious doubt about the extent of bleeding in the fetus, the infant's blood volume should be expanded with plasma expanders or whole blood.

If severe anemia is chronic or due to acute hemolysis, transfusion may have to be done with sedimented red cells, using small volume exchange transfusions to avoid overloading the vascular space.

3. POLYCYTHEMIA

Unusually high hematocrits are seen in newborn infants infrequently in some pediatric services and in as many as 5% of all births in others. Polycythemia results in increased blood viscosity, particularly when the hematocrit exceeds 70%. A peripheral hematocrit of 70% is an indication for performing a venous hematocrit. If the venous hematocrit is greater than 65%, hyperviscosity is commonly present. The cause of polycythemia is not always apparent. Known causes include fetofetal transfusions in twins, leaving one twin anemic and the other plethoric. It is often seen in small-for-gestational-age infants but frequently occurs in the infant of the diabetic mother as well.

Hyperviscosity decreases effective perfusion of the capillary beds of the microcirculation and increases the work load of the heart. Clinical manifestations include an enlarged heart, pulmonary perihilar infiltrates, tachypnea, oxygen dependency, priapism, and central nervous system signs ranging from increased jitteriness to overt seizures.

Treatment is recommended for symptomatic infants. Acute symptoms, particularly poor feeding, lethargy, and poor peripheral perfusion, may be dramatically improved. More serious symptoms of hyperviscosity associated with ischemia of the kidneys (glomerular damage) and bowel (necrotizing enterocolitis) may be avoided. Treatment for asymptomatic infants is still controversial.

Treatment consists of administering a small isovolumetric exchange transfusion using plasma or Plasmanate as the donor fluid. Phlebotomy alone should not be done, because it reduces the hematocrit slowly and because it reduces circulating blood volume, which may cause hypotension. In asymptomatic infants, simple hydration, orally or intravenously, may help resolve the condition more quickly.

GASTROINTESTINAL DISEASES

1. TRACHEOESOPHAGEAL FISTULA & ESOPHAGEAL ATRESIA

Findings secondary to these defects may present soon after birth and must be recognized early in order to minimize morbidity and allow earlier treatment. Atresia of the upper esophagus is associated with excessive salivation; choking and aspiration are likely to occur. Tracheoesophageal fistula will lead to aspiration of stomach secretions. Sump pump drainage in the proximal esophageal pouch and early gastrostomy placement are essential in order to minimize the danger of aspiration. Thus, early surgical consultation is imperative. Diagnosis based on the findings noted above usually can be made before the first feeding.

Determination of abnormal anatomy is usually made on clinical grounds. X-ray demonstration of the upper pouch should be done with a radiopaque catheter in place. Instillation of radiopaque dye is no longer recommended because of the danger of aspiration and the certainty of diagnosis on plain film and clinical grounds. If the abdomen remains scaphoid and no bowel gas is seen on x-ray up to 24 hours, there is no associated tracheoesophageal fistula.

When fistula is present alone, the diagnosis may be difficult to confirm. Careful evaluation must be done in any baby who has respiratory symptoms, particularly coughing, choking, and cyanosis associated with feeding. The differential diagnosis includes pharyngeal muscle weakness, vascular rings, and esophageal diverticula.

Treatment varies depending upon the type of lesion and the degree of abnormality present. Frequent or continuous gentle suctioning of the upper pouch and pharynx will minimize tracheal aspiration of saliva. Generally, gastrostomy is performed early and the fistula ligated at that time. If the ends of the esophagus are close enough, primary anastomosis may be done. If they are too far apart for a direct anastomosis, the upper pouch is exteriorized. After a sufficient period of growth, during which time the infant is fed through the gastrostomy, a primary repair of the esophagus is made.

Careful attention to fluid, electrolyte, and caloric requirements, as well as infection, is important during preparation for surgery and in the postoperative period. Associated congenital anomalies, particularly vertebral, anal, cardiac, renal, and limb, may coexist. Evaluation for these should be made prior to surgery.

2. INTESTINAL OBSTRUCTION

A newborn infant with abdominal distention and vomiting must be suspected of having intestinal obstruction.

High intestinal obstruction will present soon after birth with vomiting of nonbilious secretions if the obstruction is proximal or, more commonly, bile-containing secretions if the obstruction is distal to the ampulla of Vater. Every newborn with bile-stained vomitus must be evaluated for the presence of anatomic or functional obstruction. Dilatation of the proximal gut is usually evident on physical examination.

Obstruction of the lower intestinal tract may result from abnormal bowel function or abnormal meconium. A meconium plug, meconium ileus (with abdomen full of doughy loops of bowel), and Hirschsprung's disease are among the problems associated with delayed or abnormal stooling patterns in the newborn period.

The level of intestinal obstruction can usually be determined and the decision whether or not to undertake surgery can usually be made by careful review of the history and physical examination. A plain film of the abdomen is frequently all that is needed to confirm the clinical impression.

Immediate treatment consists of placing a soft, large-bore, red rubber catheter into the stomach and instituting intermittent mechanical suction. This will prevent further distention and decrease the risk of viscus perforation. The baby's temperature, vital signs, urine output, and electrolyte status should be monitored frequently. The baby should receive nothing by mouth, and intravenous fluids should be begun. Additional colloid or crystalloid fluids may be needed prior to surgery if the baby is dehydrated or in shock.

Additional work-up should be done only when needed to clarify the diagnosis or to aid in planning surgery. Unnecessary studies put the baby through needless procedures and delay definitive treatment. The baby may tolerate surgery better soon after birth than later. Needless delay must be avoided when vascular supply to the bowel may be compromised. Again, careful attention to the baby's needs in preparation for surgery and during the postoperative period is important.

Surgery may consist of definitive repair of the abnormality or may be palliative, ie, decompression of the bowel followed later by repair of the primary lesion. Total parenteral nutrition (TPN) may be a useful adjunct to care in the preoperative and postoperative periods.

3. OTHER ABDOMINAL SURGICAL CONDITIONS

Appendicitis & Meckel's Diverticulum

These disorders may occur in the newborn period and always present difficult diagnostic problems. The infant will show general symptoms of illness and may have abdominal distention, decreased bowel sounds, and constipation. Fever and leukocytosis may not be present. Careful examination of the abdomen will usually show localizing findings of peritonitis. The appendix is often ruptured at the time of diagnosis. Meckel's diverticulum may present with sudden gastrointestinal bleeding.

Omphalocele

Omphalocele will be present at birth and requires immediate surgical consultation. Part or all of the intestine, as well as the liver and spleen, may be visible through the sac. In addition to the preoperative medical care detailed in the section on intestinal obstruction, sterile saline gauze packs and an occlusive plastic bandage should be used to cover the wound. Transport to a level 3 care center must be done without delay. Other anomalies, particularly of midline structures (brain and heart) should be ruled out.

Gastroschisis

Gastroschisis is a congenital defect of the abdominal wall that results in herniation of all or part of the abdominal organs into the amniotic sac. Because the bowel is exposed to amniotic fluid for a prolonged time during the gestation, it will be edematous, thickened, malrotated, and shortened. Preoperative care consists of all the procedures noted above as well as cultures and antibiotics. Postoperatively, bowel function returns slowly, and central alimentation is lifesaving.

Necrotizing Enterocolitis

This illness of the newborn infant most commonly occurs in the sick premature baby and the hyperviscous term baby. The pathogenesis includes infectious necrosis of an ischemic bowel wall. Infants present with abdominal distention, vomiting, positive Hematest or grossly bloody stools, and pneumatosis intestinalis on x-ray. Medical management consists of suction-decompression, septic work-up and antibiotics, and aggressive blood pressure support. Metabolic acidosis and hyperkalemia are ominous signs of necrosing tissue. Early surgical consultation is indicated in all cases.

Ruptured Abdominal Viscera

A ruptured abdominal viscus will present with peritonitis and pneumoperitoneum if the stomach or bowel is perforated. Rupture of a solid viscus presents with hemoperitoneum, anemia, and shock.

Pneumoperitoneum

Pneumoperitoneum may occur spontaneously, particularly in very immature infants. The rupture is often in the large bowel along the hepatic flexure. In contrast to the findings of necrotizing enterocolitis, the bowel is entirely normal except for the perforation. Depending on when the perforation occurs, postoperative complications may be minimal, since the bowel contents are often sterile.

Pneumoperitoneum may also result from dissection by air along the mediastinum and through the diaphragm next to the esophagus, with rupture into the peritoneal cavity. This complication develops in infants receiving positive pressure ventilation with the respirator set at relatively high pressures. With positive pressure ventilation, air may accumulate rapidly in the peritoneal cavity, and continuous drainage of air from the peritoneum may be required to allow adequate movement of the diaphragm. Although the accompanying pneumomediastinum or pneumothorax is generally obvious, it occasionally may be inapparent.

Diaphragmatic Hernia

This congenital malformation consists of herniation of abdominal organs into the hemithorax (most commonly left) because of a defect in the diaphragm. Infants present in the delivery room with severe respiratory distress, cyanosis, and failure to respond to oxygen and mask-bag ventilation. Associated findings are a shift of the heart tones to the right and a scaphoid abdomen, because herniated abdominal contents are located in the left thoracic cavity. Increased respiratory distress develops as the intestinal contents fill with gas; this may be made worse by resuscitation efforts with bag and mask. Successful management depends on early recognition, decompression of the stomach and intestine with continuous suction, appropriate supportive care (ventilatory support via endotracheal tube; circulatory support via volume and pharmacologic agents), and urgent surgical correction of the defect. Associated "hypoplasia" of the lung often complicates the postoperative period and is the most important threat to survival.

GENITOURINARY DISORDERS

The most common causes of renal failure in premature and full-term newborn infants are asphyxia and shock. The other renal problems that may be encountered in the nursery are infections and anomalies.

1. RENAL FAILURE

The normal urine output of a newborn infant is 1–2 mL/kg/h. After a severe intrapartum or neonatal asphyxial insult, there may be 2–3 days of anuria or oliguria, followed by polyuria and then gradual recovery. If glomerular damage has occurred, the urine will contain protein and red blood cells. If the damage is primarily tubular, the problems will be abnormal urine flow rates and electrolyte imbalances. If the insult is due to hypotension or prerenal failure, treatment should be early colloid administration followed by restriction of fluids to insensible losses plus urine output replacement. The baby should be weighed every 8–12 hours and given time to recover. Excessive fluid administration will lead to pulmonary edema, accumulation of extravascular water, and congestive heart failure. Hyperkalemia may lead to cardiac arrhythmias and death and must be aggressively treated with intravenous calcium, bicarbonate, continuous insulin and glucose infusion, or cation-exchange resin enemas. Serial measurements of urine and serum electrolytes and osmolalities will be extremely useful in determining fluid and electrolyte management.

Another problem of the very low birth weight infant is glucosuria with obligate water and sodium losses and rapid dehydration. Therefore, we recommend that infants weighing less than 1200 g be started on 5% dextrose solutions.

2. URINARY TRACT INFECTIONS

Infants with prolonged jaundice, failure to thrive, and vomiting must be considered for urinary tract infection. In the premature infant, this may be part of a generalized sepsis, whereas in the full-term infant, it is more commonly associated with an anomaly of the urinary tract.

3. URINARY TRACT ANOMALIES

The incidence rate of functionally significant anomalies of the kidneys or excretory tracts in newborn infants is around 0.8%. In infants who seem to be well, over 90% of these anomalies can be detected by careful abdominal palpation. Abnormal abdominal masses in the newborn must be diagnosed; in descending order of frequency, they are hydronephrosis, cystic kidney, renal artery or renal vein thrombosis, neuroblastoma, and Wilms' tumor. In infants with oligohydramnios and anuria, renal agenesis must be suspected. Syndromes with multiple anomalies or chromosomal abnormalities frequently include congenital renal abnormalities.

4. ABNORMAL EXTERNAL GENITALIA

Ambiguous or frankly abnormal external genitalia must be evaluated immediately after delivery. Any questions about sex assignment must be resolved before the baby goes home, since the family's perception of the infant's sex is the single most important factor in the development of sex orientation of the individual in later life.

The child should be examined carefully for other anomalies. Buccal smear for chromosomal study and measurement of urinary 17-ketosteroids and pregnanetriol should be done within the first 72 hours. The maternal history of drug exposure, illnesses during pregnancy, and dietary habits should be reviewed. Other studies may include intravenous urography and perhaps even exploratory laparotomy with gonadal biopsies.

Infants with ambiguous genitalia who also have adrenogenital syndrome are genetically female. Male infants with adrenogenital syndrome may elude diagnosis until symptoms appear as a result of severe electrolyte imbalance with hyponatremia and hyperkalemia leading to shock, dehydration, and death within 3–14 days. Infants with a family history of adrenogenital syndrome can sometimes be salvaged by careful early electrolyte monitoring. Hypertension is a threat in the non-salt-losing form of adrenogenital syndrome. With early diagnosis and recognition of the enzymatic defect underlying adrenogenital syndrome, appropriate treatment can be instituted to help these children lead relatively normal lives but of course with no hope of procreation.

Male infants with abnormal genitalia must not be circumcised because the foreskin tissue may be required for surgical repair of the abnormality at a later date.

BRAIN & NEUROLOGIC DISORDERS

Brain damage in newborn full-term infants is usually due to physical trauma at birth or to perinatal asphyxia; congenital anomalies and infections of the central nervous system are the next most common causes. Most of the brain damage due to trauma or asphyxia is preventable, primarily through improved obstetric care and, secondarily, through improved neonatal care immediately following delivery.

1. PROLONGED & SEVERE HYPOXIA

Clinical Findings

Intrauterine hypoxia causes brief tachycardia in the fetus and increased fetal movement, followed by depression and bradycardia. Meconium may be passed into the amniotic fluid and subsequently aspirated. At delivery, the infant is hypotonic, cyanotic, and pale and makes little or no respiratory effort. The Apgar score is less than 3.

Hypoxia causes a redistribution of cardiac output, with the brain and the heart receiving increased blood flow, whereas the lung and certain other organs have markedly decreased blood flow even with relatively moderate degrees of hypoxia. If hypoxia is severe, other organs such as the skin, muscle, and gastrointestinal tract also have reduced blood flow and become underperfused with blood of low oxygen content. This state leads to an increasingly severe metabolic acidosis. Active resuscitation is indicated, and prolonged assisted ventilation may be necessary. After a variable period, the infant may make spontaneous respiratory efforts and gradually establish spontaneous respirations. A high-pitched, irritable cry; absent or poor Moro reflex; diminished or absent deep tendon reflexes; decreased muscle tone; and retinal hemorrhages are common.

By the second day of life, reflexes become hyperactive. There may be less spontaneous activity and a weak sucking reflex. The infant may remain hypotonic, become increasingly hypertonic with opisthotonos and spasticity, or regain normal tone and flexion posture. Recovery in the following days may be limited, gradual, or complete. It has been shown that in the infant, the brain stem is selectively more vulnerable than the cerebral cortex to anoxia. This may explain the types of disorders seen in severe asphyxia, ie, pinpoint pupils; absence of cough and gag reflexes; cranial nerve palsies; and disorders of muscle tone, temperature control, and regulation of breathing.

Trauma that may result in subarachnoid or cerebral hemorrhage is usually associated with a history of difficult delivery, often precipitous or breech. The baby may appear well after birth, but within a few hours develops clinical findings of irritability, increased muscle tone, high-pitched cry, respiratory distress, decreased or absent Moro and sucking reflexes, increased or asymmetric muscle tone, twitching, retinal hemorrhages, and dilated pupils. Convulsions may occur. Anemia and shock will occur if bleeding has been of sufficient volume. If bleeding is mild and does not recur, symptoms will begin to improve. The degree of permanent neurologic damage will depend on the extent and location of the injury.

Treatment

The infant who has sustained an injury to the central nervous system requires special care and observation. Good supportive care can reduce the risk of additional injury from hemorrhage, hypoglycemia, hypocalcemia, or aspiration pneumonia. This may include ventilatory and circulatory support until the extent of brain damage can be determined. A precise prognosis is often not possible in the first days of life and should be made with caution. Periodic reassessment and reevaluation are often needed. This should be explained to the parents. Parents need to know *and believe* that the physician and the rest of the health care team will continue to provide support, advice, and assistance during the difficult days of diagnosis and decision making.

Lumbar puncture, CT scanning, and ultrasonography are valuable adjuncts to the clinical examination in determining the extent of the insult and the onset of complications, specifically hydrocephalus.

Prognosis

The behavioral abnormalities that asphyxiated infants have in the immediate newborn period have been correlated with long-term sequelae. These include difficulty in feeding (which necessitates gavage), cyanotic or apneic spells, lethargy, seizures, temperature instability, high-pitched cry, and persistent vomiting. The recovery of muscle tone during the first few days of life in asphyxiated newborns has also been helpful in predicting outcome. Infants with behavioral abnormalities and hypotonia tend to have high mortality and morbidity rates, whereas those with increased or normal tone and normal behaviors may have only slight motor handicaps or be completely normal. In general, premature infants have a greater capacity to withstand severe hypoxic insults and recover than do full-term infants. Infants who suffer acute intrapartum or neonatal cardiorespiratory arrest have a high mortality risk, but if resuscitation leads to spontaneous breathing by 30 minutes, the morbidity risk is, surprisingly, as low as 25%.

2. CONVULSIONS

Clinical Findings

Seizures occurring at the time of delivery or very shortly thereafter in the newborn infants of full-term, uncomplicated pregnancies are rare and should raise the possibility of intrauterine cerebral hemorrhage, pyridoxine dependency, or intoxication with local anesthetics. Some of the causes of neonatal seizures are listed in Table 36–8.

Treatment

Phenobarbital is an excellent anticonvulsant in the newborn, giving a good anticonvulsive effect at doses that do not cause respiratory depression. For status epilepticus, give 5–10 mg/kg intravenously and repeat in 30 minutes until seizures are controlled or a total dose of 15 mg/kg has been given. Maintenance phenobarbital doses of 5–10 mg/kg/24 h should then be given. Serum levels of the drug may need to be checked at intervals to determine the optimal dosage. If breakthrough seizures occur, diazepam (Valium) may be given in a dose of 0.1–0.3 mg/kg intravenously. However, this drug may exacerbate respiratory depression and it has a half-life of around 15 minutes, so it has limited usefulness. Phenytoin (Dilantin) may be added in a dose of 5–15 mg/kg/24 h for more prolonged seizure control.

In all infants, diagnosis and treatment of the underlying cause of seizures is preferred. For seizures due to metabolic disorders, improvement may be dramatic and the need for anticonvulsants alleviated. For infants who have had central nervous system hemorrhage or infection, resolution of the insult must be achieved before the seizures can be controlled. When structural abnormalities of the brain or genetic diseases are the cause, lifelong drug therapy must be anticipated.

Prognosis

Long-term follow-up studies of children who had neonatal seizures have shown that the outcome depends principally upon the cause. Thus, newborn infants with hypocalcemic seizures have a very good prognosis. On the other hand, infants with seizures due to anoxia or congenital anomalies have a poor prognosis. Infants with seizures associated with intracerebral hemorrhage or infection have a variable future. Long-term neurologic handicaps and seizure disorders are well predicted by abnormal electroencephalograms in the first 1–3 weeks of life.

3. CENTRAL NERVOUS SYSTEM HEMORRHAGE OF THE PRETERM INFANT

Prior to 35 weeks of gestation, the premature brain has an immature vascular bed in the germinal matrix. Thus, the premature infant is susceptible to subependymal hemorrhage with rupture of blood into the ventricles and extension into the cerebral cortex.

Table 36—8. The causes of neonatal seizures.*

Metabolic
  Asphyxia
  Alkalosis
  Hypocalcemia
  Hypomagnesemia
  Hypoglycemia
  Hyponatremia
  Water intoxication
  Hypernatremia
Intracranial hemorrhage
  Traumatic asphyxia
  Birth trauma (subdural and subarachnoid)
  Intraventricular hemorrhage, dissecting subependymal
    hemorrhage, prematurity
  Asphyxia, consumption coagulopathy, secondary
    hemorrhagic disease
  Hemorrhagic disease of the newborn (vitamin K
    deficiency)
  Arteriovenous malformations
Infections
  Meningitis
  Encephalitis
  Abscess or subdural empyema
  Rubella encephalitis
Genetic
  Familial neonatal convulsions
  Neurodermatoses, neurofibromatosis, incontinentia
    pigmenti, tuberous sclerosis
  13/15 trisomy
Miscellaneous
  Narcotic withdrawal
  Compression head injury without hemorrhage
  Neoplasm

Hyperbilirubinemia
Pyridoxine deficiency
Pyridoxine dependency
Neurolipidoses
Organic acidurias
Galactosemia
Hyperammonemia
Aminoacidopathies

Berry aneurysms (with coarctation of aorta)
Battered baby syndrome (subdural and subarachnoid)
Hypernatremic dehydration
Thrombocytopenia (drugs to mother; mother with
  idiopathic thrombocytopenic purpura; consumption coagulopathy and disseminated intravascular
  coagulation; rhesus hemolytic disease; intrauterine
  infection)
Idiopathic subarachnoid hemorrhage

Congenital toxoplasmosis
Cytomegalic inclusion disease
Septicemia with disseminated intravascular coagulation
Gastroenteritis (biochemical)

Congenital cerebral malformations and dysplasias
Alpers' cortical degeneration of infancy
Degenerative disease (Gaucher's, Krabbe's leukodystro-
  phy, Niemann-Pick disease)

Ectodermal dysplasia with hyperpyrexia
Exogenous toxins (eg, hexachlorophene)

*Adapted and reproduced, with permission, from Brown JK: Convulsions in the newborn period. *Dev Med Child Neurol* 1973;**15**:823.

Clinical Findings

In the past, autopsy studies have shown that premature infants dying between 3 and 7 days of age often had extensive central nervous system hemorrhage, and this was interpreted to mean a uniformly fatal disease. Recent investigators have reported that nearly 30% of infants with birth weights less than 1500 g will have hemorrhages, and two-thirds of these will be asymptomatic. The peak incidence of hemorrhage occurs in infants born before 32 weeks of gestation. Factors that appear to increase the likelihood of hemorrhage are male sex, ventilatory support, coagulation disorders in the infant, and neonatal transport.

Treatment

It is important to diagnose the extent of hemorrhage by obtaining an ultrasound or a CT scan during the third to seventh days of life. If ventricular dilatation with blood is present, serial ultrasound examinations of the brain should be done at weekly intervals. In mild hemorrhages, the blood will resolve and no further ventricular dilatation will occur. In hemorrhages where intraventricular dilatation is marked, some may remain static but others will show progressive hy-

drocephalus. Research is currently under way to determine if serial lumbar puncture, aggressive osmotic diuresis, or early ventriculoperitoneal shunting is the therapy of choice.

Prognosis

One-year follow-up of survivors has shown a good outcome in infants who did not have ventricular dilatation or progressive hydrocephalus. However, the outcome was less favorable in infants who were not shunted until the hydrocephalus was recognized by increasing head circumference, ie, at 1–3 months of age. Infants with extensive hemorrhage involving the cerebral cortex usually had early clinical symptoms and significant motor handicaps at follow-up.

4. CONGENITAL ANOMALIES

Perhaps the most heartrending problem in the newborn nursery is the birth of an infant with a severe defect. What was anticipated as a happy event suddenly becomes a devastating experience. The defect and uncertainty about the infant's immediate needs and long-term prognosis cause the parents to feel loss of control over their own lives and the infant's. At these times, parents need honest and sensitive direction from their health care providers, so that the best possible care is given to their infant and the decision-making process becomes a basis for reestablishing control in their lives.

Diagnosis

Maternal, obstetric, and family history may be contributory and should always be taken. Particularly helpful in the history are problems of polyhydramnios, oligohydramnios, previous birth defects in the family, and the mother's sense during her pregnancy that something was wrong. Antepartum diagnosis using ultrasound or amniocentesis may be extremely valuable to the pediatric staff in preparing for the resuscitation, diagnostic procedures, and surgery that may be necessary within the immediate newborn period. Delivery of these infants at a level 3 care center may be critical to their survival.

Most birth defects, however, occur in full-term infants and are unexpected. Early recognition, stabilizing care, transport to an intensive care center, and specific diagnostic tests and surgery may be instrumental to the intact survival of infants with significant congenital heart disease, metabolic disorders, and surgically correctable lesions.

It is important to recognize certain defects on the first day of life, so that specific care can be initiated. Examples are cleft lip, cleft palate, hip dislocation, and clubfoot as well as the more life-threatening problems associated with myelomeningocele and chromosomal disorders.

Treatment

Specific attention to an infant's congenital anomaly in the nursery will often prevent complications and enhance long-term outcome. Successful treatment of hip dislocation may be accomplished with splinting and banding if initiated in the nursery. Special methods of feeding the infant with cleft lip or palate can help avoid regurgitation, aspiration, inflammation of nasal mucosa, and poor nutrition and growth. The work-up and diagnosis of ambiguous genitalia and the determination of the child's sex are critical for care and for parent bonding. Consultation with appropriate medical, psychiatric, and surgical subspecialists should be done within the first few hours to days of life, depending on the urgency of the problem and the clinical course of the infant. In all cases, both special and routine care arrangements must be clearly planned with the parents prior to nursery discharge.

One role of the primary physician is the repeated explanation to the parents of the problem and of the recommended therapy as new findings, test results, and consultations become available. The family will absorb and process the information at its own pace. Many families will handle well the stress of an abnormal infant and their own emotional reactions, simply with the counseling of a professional person whom they trust and with their own natural support systems. If psychologic or social needs are not being met, the primary caretaker may be the key person in assisting families to seek and accept more expert help.

Prognosis

Mortality rates vary depending on the individual anomalies. Deaths of infants with anomalies either in utero or during the newborn period demand professional follow-up and counseling of the parents for at least 3–12 months. Late infant deaths, ie, between 28 days and 1 year, often occur in infants with birth defects. Families should be prepared for this possibility and should be allowed to choose whether the infant dies at home or in the hospital whenever death can be anticipated. The emotional support these families require calls for committed caretakers.

The long-term outcome of infants who survive with major congenital anomalies is dependent upon the medical nature of the problem and the family's emotional ability to cope with the infant. Intensive support and subspecialty care offer infants increasingly better chances for corrective treatment. Ancillary professionals such as physical therapists, occupational therapists, developmental psychologists, and visual and auditory specialists are increasingly more interested in and capable of treating the newborn to 3-year-old child. The family's ability to find and utilize an appropriate program for the child is greatly enhanced by a close working relationship between the primary physician and subspecialists or therapists. The goals are to provide the child with the optimal environment to reach full potential and to allow the parents and siblings to enjoy guilt-free, satisfying lives.

INFECTIONS IN THE NEWBORN

1. GENERAL APPROACH

The fetus and newborn are unusually susceptible to generalized, sometimes overwhelming infection. The symptoms may be deceptively mild until the infection is far advanced, making early recognition and treatment difficult. Immunoglobulin G (IgG) is transferred from the mother to the fetus, providing passive protection against some infections. Antibodies to gram-negative organisms are contained in the IgM fraction, which is not transferred to the fetus. Many gram-negative bacteria produce hemolysins that increase the rate of hemolysis of red blood cells, resulting in hyperbilirubinemia. Other toxins may be produced that cause systemic and cellular injury.

The newborn infant is also highly susceptible to parasitic and viral infections because of an immature cellular immune system and unusual modes of organism entry. Organisms may infect the infant in several ways: in utero, through hematogenous spread from the placenta; by colonization during passage through the birth canal; and through fresh wounds, such as the cut surface of the umbilical cord, the circumcision site, or a scalp electrode site.

Hospital Precautions

Because of this susceptibility to infection, the nursery is a place where traffic must be monitored and controlled. All persons entering the nursery who will handle infants, including physicians, nurses, laboratory technicians, parents, students, etc, must wash their hands for 3 minutes with germicidal soap and put on a clean gown. This procedure should be repeated between each infant that is handled. If a person has a lip herpes or any type of infected wound, it must be covered by a mask, gloves, or bandage to prevent spread to the infant. People with systemic illnesses, such as viral upper respiratory infections and diarrhea, must be rigorous about hand washing or be restricted from the nursery. If a specific bacterial organism is cultured from an infected person, appropriate antibiotic treatment is required for 24–48 hours before returning to the nursery, even if there are no symptoms of infection.

If a newborn infant is considered infectious at birth based on clinical signs or obstetric history, specific orders must be written for handling of the infant, bed linens, waste products, etc. Since many of these infants are very sick, they should be placed in the nursery where monitoring, observation, and treatment are immediately available. Isolation in a remote area is rarely indicated; if the infant is put in room isolation, appropriate nursing coverage must be arranged. For most infants, the appropriate precautions are careful hand washing, gowning during care, disposing of diapers and linens separately, and, if necessary, gloving while handling. Guidelines for specific infections are outlined in references listed below.

Diagnosis

A. History: Maternal and obstetric histories are essential for early diagnosis of congenital neonatal infections. Maternal illnesses known to be associated with a high probability of neonatal infection include maternal urinary tract infection, amnionitis, prolonged rupture of amniotic membranes, genital herpes, gonorrhea, syphilis, vaginal streptococcosis, maternal tuberculosis, hepatitis, and systemic viral or bacterial illness in the third trimester, especially when it results in premature labor and delivery.

If the mother is ill at the time of delivery, uterine cultures and cultures of the placenta may help reveal the causative organism of her newborn's infection. Additional data of value to the infant's caretakers include previous positive cultures, laboratory reports, and antibiotic treatments the mother has received.

B. Laboratory Findings: The white blood cell and differential counts are useful in the early diagnosis of infection; elevation in number of band forms occurs early. Extremely low granulocyte counts, particularly in the first 24 hours of life, are an ominous sign and should always be regarded as indicating overwhelming infection until proved otherwise. Serial white counts are often useful in managing the individual infant, because they may reflect improvement or deterioration in condition. Platelet counts below $200,000/\mu L$ may also indicate infection and correlate positively with a localized or systemic consumptive coagulopathy.

Treatment

Early diagnosis, supportive care, and specific therapy are essential for effective management of neonatal infections. The infant frequently cannot tolerate oral feedings, and intravenous fluids must be given to maintain normal water, glucose, and electrolyte status. Accurate records of body weight, intake, urine output, and gastrointestinal fluid losses must be kept. Careful attention to these measurements and hourly changes in fluid administration may be necessary in the first few days when the infection is not yet controlled. Shock must be treated with blood volume expanders and, rarely, with pharmacologic agents, eg, adrenocorticosteroids. In the debilitated or neurologically depressed infant, ventilatory support may be necessary.

Prognosis

The long-term outcome of neonatal infections is related to the extent and location of the insult and the etiologic organism. The mortality and morbidity rates are very high in neonatal infections, as noted below; therefore, prevention or early recognition and treatment are major goals in this area of newborn medicine. In all survivors of congenital or neonatally acquired infection, careful follow-up and early therapy for specific motor, mental, neurologic, visual, and auditory deficiencies are clearly of utmost benefit in minimizing sequelae.

2. SPECIFIC INFECTIONS

Bacterial Sepsis

The most common bacterial organisms infecting newborn infants are group B beta-hemolytic streptococci and *Escherichia coli*. However, many other gram-negative and gram-positive bacteria have been proved by positive blood cultures to cause neonatal sepsis. Even organisms that are usually nonpathogenic in older children may cause clinical disease in the newborn infant. If bacterial infection is suspected, the work-up should include 2 blood cultures, suprapubic aspiration or bladder catheterization for urine culture, and lumbar puncture for cerebrospinal fluid culture. The spinal fluid should be analyzed for elevation of white blood cell count, especially the neutrophils; elevation of protein concentration; and abnormally low glucose concentration. Surface cultures or histologic examination of the umbilical cord, external ear, or stomach contents are not worthwhile unless obtained within 1 hour of birth. Diagnosis is certain if one or more blood cultures are positive. In addition, infection may be clinically diagnosed or ruled out by the infant's course even when cultures are negative.

Treatment at the outset should cover both gram-positive and gram-negative organisms, using ampicillin and an aminoglycoside for their individual and synergistic effects. Specific drug dosages and schedules are given in many pediatric textbooks. For infants less than 5–7 days old, adequate antibiotic treatment may be achieved by parenteral dosages at 6- to 8-hour intervals depending on the drug. Seventy-two hours after cultures are obtained, the diagnosis of neonatal infection should be ruled out or established. Antibiotics are discontinued, changed because of the organism isolated, or continued for 10 days as appropriate. In severe or unresponsive infections, repeat cultures and assays of serum antibiotic levels are indicated. Hospital observation of the infant for 2–3 days after antibiotics are stopped is necessary to make certain the infection does not recur. Negative blood cultures obtained at least 24 hours after antibiotics are discontinued confirms the adequacy of treatment.

The mortality rate in neonatal sepsis as reported by several large institutions is 15–30%. The morbidity rate is 20–30% and includes mental retardation, developmental delays, motor handicaps, and hearing loss.

Pneumonia

The respiratory system of an infant may be infected in utero, during passage through the birth canal, or during the first months of life. The most serious illness in this organ system is pneumonia. The diagnosis of pneumonia may be suspected in infants with tachypnea, cyanosis, and retractions. Blood gas determinations will show respiratory distress with hypoxia and, in serious cases, progressive evidence of respiratory failure with hypoxia, hypercapnia, and acidosis. In addition to blood cultures, a deep tracheal aspirate should be obtained for culture and Gram's stain. A chest film should be obtained to look for infiltrates, atelectasis, and pleural effusion. Repeat films should be obtained to follow the progression and resolution of pneumonia.

Treatment includes ventilatory support if respiratory failure occurs, appropriate antibiotics, and percussion, drainage, and suction therapy as frequently as needed to keep the airways clear of secretions.

The outcome in group B streptococcal and listerial pneumonia varies from a fulminating course leading to death within hours in 50% of cases to a slow but complete recovery. In survivors of neonatal pneumonia, recovery to normal pulmonary function is anticipated, since the infant can entirely regenerate normal lung tissue.

Meningitis

The diagnosis of meningitis is suspected when one sees irritability in an infant with symptoms of sepsis. Localizing physical findings may include a bulging anterior fontanelle or meningeal irritation with opisthotonos and convulsions, but more commonly newborn infants may respond to central nervous system infection with little if any localizing findings.

Laboratory findings include cerebrospinal fluid containing over 150 mg/dL of protein, less than 30 mg/dL of glucose, and over 25 white blood cells/μL. CT scans and ultrasound scans are important tests for detecting early cerebral edema and late problems of encephalomalacia, hydrocephalus, or brain abscess.

Treatment should include general supportive care and specific therapy with antibiotics effective against both gram-positive and gram-negative organisms until the etiologic agent is identified. Treatment is continued for a minimum of 3 weeks and until lumbar punctures show completely normal spinal fluid and negative cultures.

The mortality rate for neonatal meningitis remains near 50% in spite of antibiotic therapy and intensive supportive care. It is higher with gram-negative organisms and appears to correlate positively with high cerebrospinal fluid protein levels. Long-term follow-up studies of survivors have suggested that approximately 10% have severe sequelae requiring institutionalization, 30% fall below accepted norms on psychometric assessment, and 60% have electroencephalographic abnormalities with or without seizures. Some children have difficulties with speech and perceptual motor function.

Urinary Tract Infection

Newborn infants with symptoms of infection may have a focus of infection in the urinary tract. This is especially true of a urinary tract anomaly or an infection beginning later than 72 hours after birth. Septicemia, abnormal fistulous connections between the bowel and the urinary tract, patent urachus, vesicovaginal fistula, or other structural anomaly of the urinary tract associated with obstruction will predispose to urinary tract infection.

A specimen taken by means of suprapubic aspiration is desirable for examination and culture. Colony counts of about 10,000 organisms per milliliter of urine in a clean, freshly voided specimen—or any colonies in a suprapubic tap—should be considered evidence of infection. Jaundice is common in pyelonephritis in the newborn infant. Other diagnostic procedures such as intravenous urography, cystography, renal scanning, and ultrasonography may be needed to demonstrate congenital anomalies or obstruction of the urinary tract.

Treatment with antibiotics should be continued until the urine is normal and cultures are negative. An infant with documented urinary tract infection must be followed for a long time with repeated urine cultures to be sure that infection does not recur after therapy is discontinued. Underlying urinary tract anomalies and obstruction make recurrence or continued chronic infection more likely, and they may require surgical correction.

Osteomyelitis & Bacterial Gastroenteritis

These disorders are rare in newborns but may occur in infants requiring invasive manipulation or those exposed to cases of endemic or epidemic diarrhea.

Omphalitis

A normal umbilical cord stump will mummify and separate at the skin level. Saprophytic organisms occasionally cause a small amount of purulent material to form at the base of the cord. Other organisms may colonize and cause infection, especially *E coli,* streptococci, and staphylococci.

Omphalitis is a potential danger when umbilical vessels are catheterized for administration of intravenous fluids or exchange transfusion. Strict aseptic technique and immediate removal of catheters at the first sign of any complication are important.

Signs include redness and edema of the skin around the umbilicus, including cellulitis. Serosanguineous or purulent discharge indicates progress of the infection. Systemic reaction occurs as infection becomes more severe. Culture of skin around the cord base and blood cultures should be done.

Treatment is with appropriate antibiotics for gram-positive and gram-negative organisms until the cause is specifically identified, and the antibiotics are continued until all evidence of disease has disappeared and blood cultures are negative.

Local therapeutic measures should also be used and include drying the base of the cord thoroughly with absolute ethanol swabs, swabbing the area with one of the surgical soaps containing an organic iodide, or applying bacitracin.

Since staphylococcal epidemics in nurseries often begin with an outbreak of several apparently minor infections of the skin in infants, even relatively minor infections should receive aggressive treatment and should stimulate a review of hand-washing techniques among nursery personnel.

The extent of infection into omphalic vessels determines the prognosis. Septic thrombophlebitis can lead to hepatic abscess, generalized septicemia, and portal vein thrombosis.

Congenital Syphilis

The diagnosis must be suspected from the maternal history, since the infants are usually asymptomatic and term. A test of IgM-fluorescent antibody specific for syphilis is positive from the infant's serum. Darkfield examination of cerebrospinal fluid is positive for treponemes. X-rays of the long bones should be done. Cure is possible with adequate penicillin therapy. Good outcome depends on recognition and treatment of the infection in the neonatal period before symptoms appear. Otherwise, sequelae in infants, particularly involving the central nervous system, may be severe.

Gonococcal Infection

If the mother is infected, this organism will colonize in an infant during passage through the birth canal. Therefore, obstetric diagnosis, by serum testing and histologic positive vaginal discharge, should be communicated to the infant's caretakers. Cord blood and a repeat serum sample from the infant in 6–12 weeks should be tested for specific antibody titer.

Prophylactic eye care at birth usually prevents conjunctivitis and keratitis, but a common presentation of neonatal disease is copious purulent drainage from the eyes at 5–7 days; these infants require readmission for parenteral antibiotic therapy.

Tuberculosis

Tuberculosis is another common infection of mothers that poses a serious threat to newborn infants immediately after birth. If the mother is diagnosed as having active tuberculosis based on symptoms and a positive chest x-ray, the infant must be separated from her completely and cared for by someone else until she is no longer excreting organisms (usually 6 months). It is much more common to have an asymptomatic but skin test–positive mother. These mothers should be placed on drug therapy, and the infants should be followed carefully with skin tests for several months. The key to appropriate care is meticulous arrangement of follow-up plans.

Cytomegalovirus Infection

Congenital cytomegalovirus infection usually follows an apparently normal pregnancy and delivery, although the mother may have symptoms similar to those of infectious mononucleosis. In severe infection, the infant is acutely ill at birth with signs of multiple organ involvement. The infant tends to be small for gestational age and to have a disproportionately small head circumference. Central nervous system signs include symptoms of meningoencephalitis and later development of muscle weakness or spasticity. Chorioretinitis has been observed. Mental retardation accompanies the severe form.

In the milder infection, the infant may have jaundice, petechiae, feeding difficulties, irritability, muscle weakness, spasticity, and hepatosplenomegaly.

IgM in cord blood is usually elevated. Cerebrospinal fluid is abnormal—with elevated protein and white cell count—and epithelial cells in the urine show inclusion bodies. Cytomegalovirus may be cultured from the urine, saliva, and cerebrospinal fluid. Skull x-rays may show periventricular calcification. Paired sera at birth and at 6 weeks will show a rising or persistent cytomegalovirus antibody titer in the infant. Infants with congenital cytomegalovirus may excrete the virus for several years. Therefore, follow-up is indicated to detect late onset of sequelae and to determine by repeat urine culture when the organism has cleared.

Rubella

Congenital rubella infection occurs as a result of rubella infection in the mother during pregnancy. The earlier in pregnancy the disease occurs, the more severely affected the fetus is likely to be—particularly during the first trimester.

The incidence of major anomalies—some of which may not be apparent immediately at birth—has has been estimated to range from 20% to 60%. Therefore, it is essential that the rubella titer in a pregnant woman be determined. Vaccination is recommended prior to reproductive age.

Rubella should be considered in an infant with thrombocytopenia with petechiae or purpura, hepatitis, microcephaly, congenital heart disease (patent ductus arteriosus is the most common lesion), low birth weight for gestational age, cataracts, hepatosplenomegaly, myocarditis, and interstitial pneumonia. X-rays show characteristic longitudinal radiolucent areas in the distal metaphyses of long bones. Cultures of the infant's nasopharynx, throat secretions, and stool are usually positive, often for several weeks after delivery. Antibody titers, liver function tests, and long bone x-rays are needed.

No specific treatment is available. The prognosis is variable, depending on the degree of involvement of various organs. The highest incidence of severe involvement occurs with infection soon after conception. In these children, sequelae include mental retardation, behavioral disorders, and sensory handicaps. Nearly one-third have visual impairment because of cataracts, glaucoma, or retinitis. However, the most widespread problem in survivors, even with late-gestation infections, is hearing loss. In spite of these problems, up to 90% of survivors have been well adjusted socially and well integrated into work or school settings.

Herpes

Congenital or neonatal infection with herpesvirus hominis is now commonly recognized. Infant infection is usually secondary to genital infection in the mother, primarily with type 2 herpesvirus hominis. The spectrum of infection in the infant may extend from subclinical, with apparent recovery, to generalized multiple organ involvement and death. Skin vesicles are common and are sometimes present at birth. Central nervous system, eye, and generalized visceral involvement occurs frequently. Later handicaps are common in survivors, particularly when the central nervous system is affected.

The diagnosis is made by virus culture from maternal and infant lesions and by demonstrating inclusion bodies and positive fluorescent antibodies in cytologic preparations of cells from the margins of skin lesions. A rising antibody titer in the infant is confirmatory.

Treatment is supportive. Idoxuridine has been given with variable results. Isolation techniques should be instituted to minimize spread to personnel or other susceptible infants. If the mother is clinically well, it is best to have the infant room-in with her in a private room.

Prevention may be attempted by cesarean delivery when maternal genital lesions are present, thus avoiding fetal contact with the lesions during delivery. This is effective only if the cesarean section is done within 4 hours after rupture of membranes. The prognosis is guarded.

Other Viral Infections

Echoviruses, coxsackieviruses, myxoviruses, and a variety of other viruses may cause congenital infection. They should be considered when meningoencephalitis, pneumonia, myocarditis, hepatitis, cataracts, or other unexplained disease is present.

Varicella may occur in a fetus or newborn if the mother develops the disease during pregnancy. The infant will develop clinical disease—usually typical skin vesicles—after the usual incubation period of 2–3 weeks. The clinical course is usually modified in the infant, presumably by passive antibodies from the mother. The disease is contagious while active lesions are present.

Infants born to mothers who are positive for hepatitis B antigen are at high risk of becoming positive over the first several months of life. The illness is characterized by hepatomegaly, prolonged or recurrent jaundice, poor appetite, and failure to thrive. The best treatment is prevention, and it is recommended that these exposed infants get high-titer hepatitis B immune globulin within 72 hours of birth and every 6 weeks up to 6 months of age.

3. INFECTIONS DUE TO OTHER CAUSES

Toxoplasmosis

Toxoplasmosis is caused by the parasite *Toxoplasma gondii*. The clinical features of congenital toxoplasmosis closely resemble those of cytomegalic inclusion disease with a similar spectrum of degree of involvement. More severe clinical disease is associated with intrauterine growth retardation, microcephaly or hydrocephaly, microphthalmia, chorioretinitis, calcifications in skull x-rays, thrombocytopenia, and jaundice.

Diagnosis is confirmed by antibody titers that rise or persist in the infant. IgM in cord blood is usually elevated. The organism may be cultured, but this must be done in a laboratory with small animal or tissue culture capabilities, because *Toxoplasma* organisms are obligate intracellular parasites.

Treatment is difficult and controversial and beyond the scope of this book. Because cats may shed mature oocysts infectious for humans, pregnant women should avoid handling cats or cat litter.

Many infants affected at birth die during the neonatal period. Those who survive are usually handicapped, with mental retardation, convulsions, neuromuscular disease, poor vision, and microcephaly or hydrocephaly.

Chlamydia

Chlamydia has been implicated as the cause of significant conjunctivitis in the newborn. It may also cause systemic infection, particularly pneumonia, but the data are not yet conclusive.

Mycoplasma

Mycoplasma species are known to cause abortions and mid trimester losses, but their importance as infectious agents in surviving newborns is not certain.

INFANTS OF ADDICTED MOTHERS

1. NARCOTICS

Clinical Findings

Withdrawal symptoms occur in about two-thirds of infants born to mothers who are addicted to heroin, methadone, or related drugs. Symptoms consist primarily of increased tremors, irritability and hyperactivity, hypertonicity, sweating, yawning, sneezing, excessive hunger and salivation, nasal stuffiness, and regurgitation. More severely affected infants may have vomiting, diarrhea, respiratory distress, and convulsions. This clinical picture of increased activity— often frantic behavior—is typical enough to suggest the diagnosis even though a history of drug abuse had not been elicited prior to delivery. Infants may be small for gestational age. Confirmation can be obtained by doing a screening test for drug excretory products on the urine of mother or infant.

Treatment

Observe carefully for onset and progression of symptoms. Give no specific treatment until symptoms develop.

With onset of significant irritability, tremors, and hyperactivity, sedation is required. Phenobarbital, 8–12 mg/kg/d in divided doses every 4–6 hours, is recommended because of its safety and predictability of effect. The dose may need to be increased cautiously to provide adequate control of symptoms, but respiratory depression must be avoided. Phenobarbital blood levels should be obtained in infants treated near the limits of the therapeutic range, since phenobarbital plasma clearances in newborn infants vary considerably from one infant to another. Continue dose until withdrawal symptoms subside—a few days or several weeks—and then gradually decrease the dose. In addition to sedation, swaddling the infant and using a pacifier may help control the excessive activity, allowing the infant to rest between feedings.

Prognosis

The prognosis is good for the immediate health of the infant. Careful evaluation of the family unit must be made in each case. The infant may be cared for by the mother, but continued interest and long-term support by the health team and the mother's active involvement with a drug treatment program are essential. Otherwise, arrangements for care of the infant by temporary placement must be considered.

Long-term outcome of these infants is somewhat more worrisome. The distribution of growth in all parameters is skewed downward in follow-up studies of preschool children born to heroin-addicted mothers. Furthermore, they have been rated as more difficult behavior problems, and they have increased perceptual and organizational problems compared to control children born to nonaddicted mothers in equally high-risk social and drug environments.

2. ALCOHOL

Clinical Findings

Recently, it has become clear that alcohol, when used during pregnancy, is an important teratogen. In mothers with chronic alcoholism, there is an increased probability of fetal wastage and fetal alcohol syndrome. In fully manifest cases, these infants have severe intrauterine growth retardation, postnatal growth and developmental delays, short palpebral fissures, joint anomalies, and heart defects. In mothers who drink moderately, ie, 1–2 oz of absolute alcohol daily, there is a 10–20% incidence of anomalies, mental deficiency, and growth retardation.

Treatment

Supportive care may be required in the immediate newborn period for infants of chronic alcohol users. More commonly, they will have the typical problems of small-for-gestational-age infants, ie, hypoglycemia, polycythemia, and hyperviscosity. These problems should be anticipated and prevented.

Prognosis

Infants who have features of the fetal alcohol syndrome at birth are very likely to show long-term sequelae. Growth deficiencies occur in all children, and the degree of mental deficit correlates with the severity of dysmorphism at birth. Hyperactivity adds to the school problems. The severity of outcome is not influenced by socioeconomic background or educational opportunities.

3. NICOTINE

Clinical Findings

Maternal smoking has been conclusively associated with decreased birth weight at every gestational age after 30 weeks, and it appears to follow a dose-response curve. With more detailed questioning, investigators have found that light smoking as well as heavy smoking, defined as less or more than 10 cigarettes per day, is associated with increased perinatal death. The increased rate of fetal death has been attributed to anoxia and prematurity. The physiologic responses to anoxia in smokers' infants are increased placental-to-fetal weight ratios, increased carboxyhemoglobin levels, and a shift of the oxygen dissociation curve to the left. The differences in placental morphology and implantation may account for the increased incidences of bleeding, abruptio placentae, placenta previa, and premature rupture of membranes in smokers.

Treatment

Treatment consists of prevention. Infants of mothers who stop smoking completely during the last 3 months of pregnancy have no increased risk of perinatal death on that basis.

Prognosis

The Brazelton Assessment Scale in newborn infants of smoking mothers reveals decreased responses to auditory stimuli. Preliminary results of follow-up for 5 years have shown an increase in postneonatal deaths, hospital admissions, physical and mental impairments, and respiratory and skin diseases in children of smoking compared to nonsmoking mothers.

• • •

References

General

Assali NS (editor): *Pathophysiology of Gestation.* 3 vols. Academic Press, 1972.

Avery GB (editor): *Neonatology: Pathophysiology and Management of the Newborn.* Lippincott, 1981.

Battaglia FC, Meschia G, Quilligan EJ: *Perinatal Medicine.* Vol 2. Mosby, 1978.

Committee on Perinatal Health: *Toward Improving the Outcome of Pregnancy: Recommendations for the Regional Development of Perinatal Health Services.* National Foundation–March of Dimes, 1976.

Kempe CH, Silver HK, O'Brien D (editors): *Current Pediatric Diagnosis and Treatment,* 7th ed. Lange, 1982.

Klaus MH, Fanaroff AA: *Care of the High-Risk Neonate,* 2nd ed. Saunders, 1979.

Schaffer AJ, Avery ME: *Diseases of the Newborn,* 4th ed. Saunders, 1977.

Standards and Recommendations for Hospital Care of Newborn Infants, 6th ed. American Academy of Pediatrics, 1977.

Prediction of Pregnancy Outcome

Hack M, Fanaroff AA, Merkatz IR: The low-birth-weight infant: Evolution of a changing outlook. *N Engl J Med* 1979;**301**:1162.

Harris TR, Isaman J, Giles HR: Improved neonatal survival through maternal transport. *Obstet Gynecol* 1978;**52**:294.

Koops BL, Harmon RJ: Studies on long-term outcome in newborns with birth weights under 1500 grams. In: *Advances in Behavioral Pediatrics,* Vol 1. Camp BW (editor). JAI Press, 1980.

Pape KE et al: The status at two years of low birth weight infants born in 1974 with birth weights of less than 1001 grams. *J Pediatr* 1978;**92**:253.

Schechner S: For the 1980s: How small is too small? *Clin Perinatol* 1980;**7**:135.

Intrauterine Growth Patterns

Lubchenco LO: *The High Risk Infant.* Saunders, 1976.

Physical Examination

Brazelton TB: *Neonatal Behavioral Assessment Scale.* Spastics International Medical Publications. Heinemann, 1973.

Dubowitz LMS, Dubowitz V: *Gestational Age of the Newborn: A Clinical Manual.* Addison-Wesley, 1977.

Prechtl HFR: *The Neurological Examination of the Full-Term Newborn Infant,* 2nd ed. Spastics International Medical Publications. Heinemann, 1977.

Smith DW: *Recognizable Patterns of Human Malformations.* Saunders, 1976.

Solomon LM, Esterly NB: *Neonatal Dermatology.* Saunders, 1973.

Care of the Normal Newborn

Frankenburg WK, Camp BW: *Pediatric Screening Tests.*
Thomas, 1975.

Hunter RS et al: Antecedents of child abuse and neglect in premature infants: A prospective study in a newborn intensive care unit. *Pediatrics* 1978;**61**:629.

Illingsworth RS: *The Development of the Infant and Young Child: Normal and Abnormal,* 7th ed. Churchill Livingstone, 1980.

Klaus M, Kennel JH: *Maternal-Infant Bonding: The Impact of Early Separation or Loss on Family Development.* Mosby, 1976.

Lozoff B et al: The mother-newborn relationship: Limits of adaptability. *J Pediatr* 1977;**91**:1.

Feeding of the Newborn

Appelbaum RM: The obstetrician's approach to the breasts and breastfeeding. *J Reprod Med* 1975;**14**:98.

Barness LA et al: Nutritional needs of low-birth-weight infants. *Pediatrics* 1977;**60**:519.

Barness LA et al: Vitamin and mineral supplement needs in normal children in the United States. *Pediatrics* 1980; **66**:1015.

Catz C, Giacoia GP: Drugs and breast milk. *Pediatr Clin North Am* 1972;**19**:151.

Dallman PR: Iron, vitamin E, and folate in the preterm infant. *J Pediatr* 1974;**85**:742.

Fomon SJ et al: Recommendations for feeding normal infants. *Pediatrics* 1979;**63**:52.

Hambracus L: Proprietary milk versus human breast milk in infant feeding. *Pediatr Clin North Am* 1977;**24**:17.

Quinby GE et al: Parenteral nutrition in the neonate. *Clin Perinatol* 1975;**2**:59.

Raiha NC et al: Milk protein quantity and quality in low-birth-weight infants. 1. Metabolic responses and effects on growth. *Pediatrics* 1976;**57**:659.

Sinclair JC et al: Supportive management of the sick neonate: Parenteral calories, water, electrolytes. *Pediatr Clin North Am* 1970;**17**:793.

Special Care of the High-Risk Infant

Berkowitz RL: High-risk pregnancy. *Clin Perinatol* 1980; **7**:227.

Bowes WA Jr: Results of the intensive perinatal management of very low birth weight infants (500–1500 grams). Pages 331–335 in: *Preterm Labor.* Anderson A et al (editors). Royal College of Obstetrics and Gynecology, 1978.

Carson BS et al: Combined obstetric and pediatric approach to prevent meconium aspiration syndrome. *Am J Obstet Gynecol* 1976;**126**:712.

Cunningham MD, Smith FR: Stabilization and transport of severely ill infants. *Pediatr Clin North Am* 1973;**20**:359.

Desmond MM et al: The very low birth weight infant after discharge from intensive care: Anticipatory health care and developmental course. *Curr Probl Pediatr* 1980;**10**:1.

Sell EJ: *Follow-up of the High-Risk Newborn: A Practical Approach.* Thomas, 1980.

Respiratory Disease

Gregory GA: Respiratory care of newborn infants. *Pediatr Clin North Am* 1972;**19**:311.

Huch R et al: Transcutaneous P_{O_2} monitoring in routine management of infants and children with cardiorespiratory problems. *Pediatrics* 1976;**57**:681.

Krouskop RW, Brown EG, Sweet AY: The early use of continuous positive airway pressure in the treatment of idiopathic respiratory distress syndrome. *J Pediatr* 1975; **87**:263.

Thibeault DW, Gregory GA: *Neonatal Pulmonary Care.* Addison-Wesley, 1979.

Cardiac Diseases

Graham TP, Bender HW: Preoperative diagnosis and management of infants with critical congenital heart disease. *Ann Thorac Surg* 1980;**29**:272.

Lees MH, Sunderland CO: Heart disease in the newborn. Chap 39, pp 619–628, in: *Heart Disease in Infants, Children, and Adolescents,* 2nd ed. Moss AJ et al (editors). Williams & Wilkins, 1977.

Sahu DJ, Friedman WF: Difficulties in distinguishing cardiac from pulmonary disease in the neonate. *Pediatr Clin North Am* 1973;**20**:293.

Stark J: Analysis of factors which might improve the survival rate of infants with congenital heart disease. *Prog Pediatr Surg* 1979;**13**:131.

Metabolic Disorders

Bowman JM: Neonatal management. Pages 200–239 in: *Modern Management of the Rh Problem.* Queenan JT (editor), Harper & Row, 1977.

Cashore WJ et al: Clinical application of neonatal bilirubin-binding determinations: Current status. *J Pediatr* 1978; **93**:827.

Cockington RA: A guide to the use of phototherapy in the management of neonatal hyperbilirubinemia. *J Pediatr* 1979;**95**:281.

Fisher DA, Klein AH: Thyroid development and disorders of thyroid function in the newborn. *N Engl J Med* 1981; **304**:702.

Hematologic Disorders

Hathaway WE, Bonnar J: *Perinatal Coagulation.* Grune & Stratton, 1978.

Oski FA, Naiman JL: *Problems in the Newborn,* 2nd ed. Saunders, 1972.

Gastrointestinal Disorders

Gryboski J: *Gastrointestinal Problems in the Infant.* Saunders, 1975.

Lilly JR et al: *Pediatric Surgery: Case Studies.* Medical Examination Publishing Co, 1978.

Genitourinary Disorders

Leake RD: Perinatal nephrobiology: A developmental perspective. *Clin Perinatol* 1977;**4**:321.

Brain & Neurologic Disorders

Brann AW Jr, Dykes FD: The effects of intrauterine asphyxia on the full term infant. *Clin Perinatol* 1977;**4**:149.

Brown JK et al: Neurological aspects of perinatal asphyxia. *Dev Med Child Neurol* 1974;**16**:567.

Johnson ML, Rumack CM: Ultrasonic evaluation of the neonatal brain. *Radiol Clin North Am* 1980;**18**:117.

Mizrahi EM, Dorfman LJ: Sensory evoked potentials: Clinical applications in pediatrics. *J Pediatr* 1980;**97**:1.

Pape KE, Wigglesworth JS: *Haemorrhage, Ischaemia and the Perinatal Brain.* Spastics International Medical Publications, 1979.

Rose AL, Lombroso CT: Neonatal seizure states. *Pediatrics* 1970;**45**:404.

Volpe JJ: Neonatal intraventricular hemorrhage. *N Engl J Med* 1981;**304**:886.

Infections

McCracken GH, Nelson JD: *Antimicrobial Therapy for Newborns.* Grune & Stratton, 1977.

Remington JR, Klein JO: *Infectious Diseases of the Fetus and Newborn Infant.* Saunders, 1976.

Infants of Addicted Mothers

Bryan EM, Nicholson E: Congenital syphilis. *Clin Pediatr* 1981;**20**:81.

Clarren SK, Smith DW: The fetal alcohol syndrome. *N Engl J Med* 1978;**298**:1063.

Cooper LZ: Congenital rubella in the United States. Pages 1–22 in: *Infections of the Fetus and Newborn Infant.* Krugman S (editor). Year Book, 1975.

Gardner P, Breton S, Carlos DG: Hospital isolation and precaution guidelines. *Pediatrics* 1974;**53**:663.

Gardner P, Oxman MN, Breton S: Hospital management of patients and personnel exposed to communicable disease. *Pediatrics* 1975;**56**:700.

Hanshaw JB et al: School failure and deafness after "silent" congenital cytomegalovirus infection. *N Engl J Med* 1976; **295**:468.

Little RE: Moderate alcohol use during pregnancy and decreased infant birth weight. *Am J Public Health* 1977; **67**:1154.

Lumicao GG, Heggie AD: Chlamydial infections. *Pediatr Clin North Am* 1979;**26**:269.

Meyer MB, Tonascia JA: Maternal smoking, pregnancy complications, and perinatal mortality. *Am J Obstet Gynecol* 1977;**128**:494.

Naeye RL: Abruptio placentae and placenta previa: Frequency, perinatal mortality and cigarette smoking. *Obstet Gynecol* 1980;**55**:701.

Neumann LL, Cohen SN: The neonatal narcotic withdrawal syndrome: A therapeutic challenge. *Clin Perinatol* 1975; **2**:99.

Rantakallio P: The effect of maternal smoking on birth weight and the subsequent health of the child. *Early Hum Dev* 1978;**2**:371.

Rothstein P, Gould JB: Born with a habit: Infants of drug-addicted mothers. *Pediatr Clin North Am* 1974;**21**:307.

Tennes K, Blackard C: Maternal alcohol consumption, birth weight and minor physical anomalies. *Am J Obstet Gynecol* 1980;**138**:774.

Wilson GS et al: The development of preschool children of heroin-addicted mothers. *Pediatrics* 1979;**63**:135.

Birth Defects

Duff RS: Counseling families and deciding care of severely defective children: A way of coping with "Medical Vietnam." *Pediatrics* 1981;**67**:315.

Fost N: Counseling families who have a child with a severe congenital anomaly. *Pediatrics* 1981;**67**:321.

Lewis E: Mourning by the family after a stillbirth or neonatal death. *Arch Dis Child* 1979;**54**:303.

Speck WT, Kennell JH: Management of perinatal death. *Pediatrics in Review* 1980;**2**:59.

37 | The Puerperium

Miles J. Novy, MD

The puerperium is the period of adjustment after pregnancy and delivery when the anatomic and physiologic changes of pregnancy are reversed and the body returns to the normal nonpregnant state. The time required for these changes varies with each organ system. In addition, there are the alterations that occur because of complications of labor or delivery or the administration of exogenous drugs and hormones. Disease states specific to pregnancy and the puerperium may occasionally be life-threatening. It is therefore important to consider the interaction of the anatomic and physiologic changes of the puerperium with preexisting medical and surgical complications of pregnancy. Finally, initiation of new behavior patterns, eg, nursing the baby, may modify the course of involution and may profoundly affect the patient's attitude.

Less is known about the changes that occur during the puerperium than about those occurring during the 9 months of pregnancy. The postpartum period has been arbitrarily divided into the **immediate puerperium**—the first 24 hours after parturition—when acute postanesthetic or postdelivery complications may occur; the **early puerperium,** which extends until the first week postpartum; and the **remote puerperium,** which includes that period of time required for involution of the genital organs. Traditionally, the latter period has extended through the sixth week postpartum, a practice that may have originated in biblical times.*

The reproductive organs return to virtually the normal state by 6 weeks after delivery, and a majority of nonlactating women resume menstrual cycles at this time or soon thereafter.

ANATOMIC & PHYSIOLOGIC CHANGES DURING THE PUERPERIUM

Uterine Involution

The uterus increases markedly in size and weight during pregnancy (about 11 times the nonpregnant weight) but involutes rapidly after delivery. Estrogens, progesterone, and the chronic stretching of muscle induced by the enlarging fetus exert synergistic effects on the synthesis of actomyosin and collagen. Progesterone alone is not a prominent cause of myometrial hyperplasia, but estrogen stimulates both uterine hyperplasia and hypertrophy. Withdrawal of the steroid sex hormones of pregnancy increases the activity of uterine collagenase and the release of proteolytic enzymes. At the same time, macrophages migrate into the endometrium and myometrium. Involution of the uterus after delivery occurs chiefly as a result of a decrease in myometrial cell size.

Immediately following delivery, the uterus weighs about 1 kg and its size approximates that of a 20-week pregnancy (at the level of the umbilicus). At the end of the first postpartum week, it normally will have decreased to the size of a 12-week gestation to be just palpable at the symphysis pubica (Fig 37–1). Ultrasonography can be used to measure length and width of the uterine cavity. During the first week, there is a 31% decrease in uterine area; during the second and third weeks, a 48% decrease; and subsequently, an

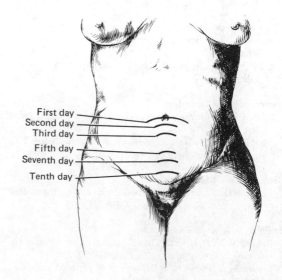

First day
Second day
Third day
Fifth day
Seventh day
Tenth day

Figure 37–1. Involutional changes in the height of the fundus and the size of the uterus during the first 10 days postpartum.

---

*For medicolegal purposes, some states classify a maternal death as one related to obstetric causes occurring within 90 days of delivery.

18% decrease. The observed changes in uterine area are mainly due to changes in uterine length, since the transverse diameter remains relatively constant during the puerperium. Uterine involution is nearly complete by 6 weeks, at which time the organ weighs less than 100 g. The rapid catabolism of uterine tissue postpartum is demonstrated by a release of approximately 20 g of nitrogen and an increase in the urinary excretion of creatinine and urea. The increase in the amount of connective tissue and elastin in the myometrium and blood vessels and the increase in numbers of cells are permanent to some degree, so that the uterus is slightly larger following pregnancy.

Because of the decreased volume of the uterus following expulsion of the fetus and placenta, myometrial force and intrauterine pressures are higher in the early puerperium than they are before delivery. Myometrial contractions that can develop pressures of 150 mm Hg or more have been recorded. These contractions (referred to as afterpains) are less disturbing than the contractions of labor, however, because no cervical dilatation or stretching of the perineal floor occurs. Afterpains occur during the first 2–3 days of the puerperium and are more common in multiparas than in primiparas. Such pains are accentuated during nursing as a result of oxytocin release from the posterior pituitary. During the first 12 hours postpartum, uterine contractions are regular, strong, and coordinated (Fig 37–2). The intensity, frequency, and regularity of contractions decrease after the first postpartum day as involutional changes proceed.

Changes in the Placental Site

Following delivery of the placenta, there is immediate contraction of the placental site to a size less than half the diameter of the original placenta. This contraction causes constriction and permits occlusion of underlying blood vessels. It also accomplishes hemostasis and presumably leads to endometrial necrosis. Initially, the placental site is elevated and somewhat ragged and friable in appearance. Involution occurs by means of the extension and downgrowth of marginal endometrium and by endometrial regeneration from the glands and stroma in the decidua basalis. Endometrial regeneration is completed by the end of the third postpartum week except at the placental site, where regeneration is usually not complete until 6 weeks postpartum. In the disorder termed **subinvolution of the placental site,** complete obliteration of the vessels in the placental site fails to occur. Patients with this condition have persistent lochia and are subject to brisk hemorrhagic episodes. Curettage reveals partly obliterated hyalinized blood vessels.

Lochia rubra is the blood-tinged uterine discharge which includes shreds of tissue and decidua. It is termed **lochia serosa** after a few days when it becomes serous and paler. During the second postpartum week, the lochia becomes thicker, mucoid, and yellowish-white **(lochia alba),** coincident with a predominance of leukocytes and degenerated decidual cells. During the fourth week postpartum, the lochial secretions cease as healing nears completion. Although the lochia provides a good culture medium for the growth of microorganisms, the bactericidal properties of the uterine granulation tissue ensure a virtually sterile uterine cavity if adequate drainage is available. A mild chronic cellular infiltrate of leukocytes persists in the myometrium for as long as 4

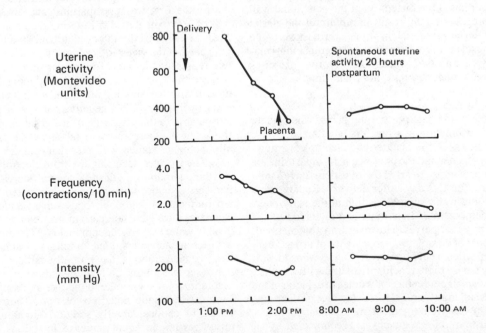

Figure 37–2. Uterine activity during the immediate puerperium *(left)* and at 20 hours postpartum *(right).* (Adapted from Hendricks CH et al: *Am J Obstet Gynecol* 1962;83:890.)

months postpartum. These findings must be taken into account if pelvic surgery during the puerperium is contemplated.

Changes in the Cervix, Vagina, & Muscular Walls of the Pelvic Organs

The cervix gradually closes during the puerperium; at the end of the first week, it is little more than 1 cm dilated. The external os is converted into a transverse slit, thus distinguishing the parous woman who delivered vaginally from the nulliparous woman or from one who delivered by cesarean section. Colposcopic examination soon after delivery may reveal ulceration, ecchymosis, and laceration. Complete healing and reepithelialization occur 6–12 weeks later. Stromal edema and round cell infiltration and the endocervical glandular hyperplasia of pregnancy may persist for up to 3 months. Cervical lacerations heal in most uncomplicated cases, but the continuity of the cervix may not be restored, so that the site of the tear may remain as a scarred notch.

After vaginal delivery, the overdistended and smooth-walled vagina gradually returns to its antepartum condition by about the third week. Thickening of the mucosa, cervical mucus production, and other estrogenic changes may be delayed in a lactating woman. The torn hymen heals in the form of fibrosed nodules of mucosa, the **carunculae myrtiformes.** Two weeks after delivery, the uterine tube reflects a hypoestrogenic state marked by atrophy and partial deciliation of the epithelium.

The voluntary muscles of the pelvic floor and the pelvic supports gradually regain their tone during the puerperium. Tearing or overstretching of the musculature or fascia at the time of delivery predisposes to genital hernias. Overdistention of the abdominal wall during pregnancy may result in rupture of the elastic fibers of the cutis, persistent striae, and diastasis of the rectus muscles. Involution of the abdominal musculature may require 6–7 weeks, and vigorous exercises are not recommended until after that time.

Urinary System

In the immediate postpartum period, the bladder mucosa is edematous as a result of labor and delivery. Overdistention of the bladder and incomplete emptying of the bladder and the presence of residual urine are common problems. Nearly 50% of patients have a mild proteinuria for 1–2 days after delivery. Radiographic examination in the supine position in the early puerperium demonstrates hypotonia and dilatation of the ureters and renal pelves. However, most women will show partial or complete disappearance of urinary tract dilatation when standing erect. Those who do not, generally have a higher incidence of urinary tract infections. In a small percentage of women, dilatation of the urinary tract may persist for 3 months postpartum. Significant renal enlargement may persist for many weeks postpartum. Pregnancy is accompanied by an estimated increase of about 25–50% in renal plasma flow and glomerular filtration rate. These values return

to normal or less than normal during the puerperium, but the exact length of time required for these changes has not been determined. There is usually a close correlation between renal blood flow and cardiac output, and it is reasonable to expect that changes in these functions should parallel one another during the puerperium as well. The hormonal changes of pregnancy (high steroid levels) also contribute to the increase in renal function, and the diminishing steroid levels after delivery may partly explain the reduced renal function during the puerperium. The renal glycosuria induced by pregnancy disappears, and the creatinine clearance is generally normal at the end of the first week postpartum. The blood urea nitrogen rises during the puerperium: At the end of the first week postpartum, values of 20 mg/dL are reached, compared with 15 mg/dL in the late third trimester.

Fluid Balance & Electrolytes

The total water gain during pregnancy is about 8.5 L; 6.5 L are gained extracellularly and 2 L intracellularly. Two-thirds of the extracellular fluid gain are distributed to maternal tissues and the other one-third is distributed to the intrauterine contents. Of the 4 L gained by maternal tissues, 1.5 L are found in the expanded plasma and red cell volumes and 2.6 L in the interstitial space.

As a result of insensible water losses, an average decrease in maternal weight of 5.5 kg (12 lb) occurs during labor and after delivery of the infant and placenta and the loss of amniotic fluid. The average patient may lose an additional 4 kg (9 lb) during the puerperium as a result of excretion of the fluids and electrolytes accumulated during pregnancy.

There is an average net fluid loss of at least 2 L during the first week postpartum, and an additional loss of approximately 1.5 L during the next 5 weeks. Measurements of the thiocyanate and sodium spaces indicate that the water losses in the first week postpartum represent a loss of extracellular fluid. A negative balance must be expected of slightly more than 100 mEq of chloride per kilogram of body weight lost in the early puerperium. This negative balance is probably attributable to the discharge of maternal extracellular fluid. The puerperal losses of salt and water are generally larger in women with preeclampsia-eclampsia.

The changes occurring in serum electrolytes during the puerperium indicate a general increase in the numbers of cations and anions as compared with antepartum values. Although total exchangeable sodium decreases during the puerperium, the relative decrease in body water exceeds the sodium loss. The diminished aldosterone antagonism due to falling plasma progesterone concentrations may partially explain the rapid rise in serum sodium. Cellular breakdown due to tissue involution may contribute to the rise in plasma potassium concentration noted postpartum. The mean increase in cations, chiefly sodium, amounts to 4.7 mEq/L, with an equal increase in anions. Consequently, the plasma osmolality rises by 7 mOsm/L at the end of the first week postpartum. In keeping with the chloride shift, there is a tendency for the serum chloride concentration to decrease slightly postpartum as serum bicarbonate increases.

Metabolic & Chemical Changes

Elevated estrogen levels and the anti-insulin effects of placental lactogen in pregnancy lead to a decrease in glucose tolerance, an increase in fat mobilization, and a rise in plasma lipids, which become maximal during the third trimester. Plasma cholesterol increases by about 50%, while plasma triglyceride concentrations triple. All of the major lipoproteins participate in these changes, but pregnancy results in an increased low-density lipoprotein (LDL) to high-density lipoprotein (HDL) ratio. Total fatty acids and nonesterified fatty acids return to nonpregnant levels on about the second day of the puerperium. Both cholesterol and triglyceride concentrations decrease significantly within 24 hours after delivery, and this change is reflected in all lipoprotein fractions. Plasma triglycerides continue to fall and approach nonpregnant values 6–7 weeks postpartum. By comparison, the decrease in plasma cholesterol levels is slower; LDL cholesterol remains above nonpregnant levels for at least 7 weeks postpartum. Lactation does not influence lipid levels, but, in contrast to pregnancy, the postpartum hyperlipidemia is sensitive to dietary manipulation.

Insulin resistance is a characteristic feature of pregnancy, as demonstrated by higher circulating levels of insulin in normal women and increased insulin requirements in diabetic pregnant women. Although the B cell sensitivity (insulin response) to a glycemic stimulus is substantially increased in normal late pregnancy, the A cell sensitivity (glucagon suppression) is unaffected by pregnancy. Progesterone, estrogen, cortisol, and placental lactogen have been suggested as the responsible factors. Since cellular insulin receptors are not decreased, the insulin resistance of pregnancy must be due to a postreceptor mechanism.

During the early puerperium there is a tendency for blood glucose concentrations (both fasting and postprandial) to fall below the values seen during pregnancy and delivery. This fall is most marked on the second and third postpartum days. Accordingly, the insulin requirements of diabetic patients are lower. Reliable indications of the insulin sensitivity and the blood glucose concentrations characteristic of the nonpregnant state can be demonstrated only after the first week postpartum. Thus, a glucose tolerance test performed in the early puerperium may be interpreted erroneously if nonpuerperal standards are applied to the results.

The concentration of free plasma amino acids increases postpartum. Normal nonpregnant values are regained rapidly on the second or third postpartum day and are presumably a result of reduced utilization and an elevation in the renal threshold.

Enzyme Changes

Certain enzymes increase during pregnancy (eg,

diamine oxidase, oxytocinase, and alkaline phosphatase). Diamine oxidase values fall to one-tenth of the antepartum levels on the third day postpartum and to nonpregnant values after 10–14 days. Peak levels of heat-stable alkaline phosphatase of placental origin are observed during labor (10–15 King-Armstrong [KA] units). The half-life of the isoenzyme in maternal blood is about 48–72 hours, so that levels around 5 KA units are achieved on the fifth postpartum day. Hepatic sulfobromophthalein (Bromsulphalein; BSP) storage capacity is increased 2-fold in late pregnancy, while the maximal tubular excretory rate is decreased. However, BSP retention in serum may remain in the normal range, because hepatic clearance is increased as a result of the relative hypoalbuminemia of pregnancy. These changes in BSP metabolism are probably estrogen-related and revert to normal soon after delivery. Serum alkaline phosphatase of hepatic origin returns to nonpregnant levels by the third week postpartum. Serum glutamic-oxaloacetic transaminase (SGOT) and serum glutamic-pyruvic transaminase (SGPT) are unchanged in normal pregnancy and the puerperium unless there is hepatocellular injury. As a result of the muscular activity of labor, creatine phosphokinase and lactic dehydrogenase activities may be elevated in maternal blood for several days after delivery. Lipoprotein lipase activity is increased during pregnancy and returns to nonpregnant levels by 10 days postpartum. Pregnancy-associated proteins believed to be of placental origin disappear from blood within a few days after delivery. Alpha-fetoproteins and oxytocinase can be detected in plasma for many weeks postpartum, suggesting that they are not solely of placental origin.

Cardiovascular Changes

A. Blood Coagulation: The concentrations of factors I, VII, VIII, IX, and X increase gradually during pregnancy. The production of both prostacyclin (PGI_2), an inhibitor of platelet aggregation, and thromboxane A_2, an inducer of platelet aggregation and a vasoconstrictor, is increased during pregnancy and the puerperium. Possibly, the balance between thromboxane A_2 and PGI_2 is shifted to the side of thromboxane A_2 dominance during the puerperium, since platelet reactivity is increased at this time. Rapid and dramatic changes in the coagulation and fibrinolytic systems occur after delivery (Table 37–1). A decrease in the platelet count occurs immediately after separation of the placenta, but a secondary elevation occurs in the next few days together with an increase in platelet adhesiveness. The plasma fibrinogen concentration begins to decrease during labor and reaches its lowest point during the first day postpartum. Thereafter, rising plasma fibrinogen levels reach prelabor values by the third or fifth day of the puerperium. This secondary peak in fibrinogen activity is maintained until the second postpartum week, after which the level of activity slowly returns to normal nonpregnant levels during the following 7–10 days. A similar pattern occurs with respect to factor VIII and plasminogen. Circulating levels of antithrombin III are decreased in

Table 37–1. Changes in blood coagulation and fibrinolysis during the puerperium.*

	Time Postpartum				
	1 Hour	1 Day	3–5 Days	1st Week	2nd Week
Platelet count	↓	↑	↑↑	↑↑	↑
Platelet adhesiveness	↑	↑↑	↑↑↑	↑	0
Fibrinogen	↓	↓	↑	0	↓
Factor V		↑	↑↑	↑	0
Factor VIII	↓	↓	↑	↑	↓
Factors II, VII, X		↓	↓	↓↓	↓↓
Plasminogen	↓	↓↓	0	↓	↓
Plasminogen activator	↑↑↑	↑↑	0		
Fibrinolytic activity	↑	↑↑	↑↑	↑	
Fibrin split products	↑	↑↑	↑↑		

*The arrows indicate the direction and relative magnitude of change compared with late third trimester or antepartum values. Zero indicates a return to antepartum but not necessarily nonpregnant values. (Prepared from the data of Manning FA et al: *Am J Obstet Gynecol* 1971;**110**:900; Bonnar J et al: *Br Med J* 1970;**2**:200; Ygge J: *Am J Obstet Gynecol* 1969;**104**:2; Shaper AG et al: *J Obstet Gynaecol Br Commonw* 1968;**75**:433.)

the third trimester of pregnancy and in women taking estrogens for postpartum lactation suppression. Patients with a congenital deficiency of antithrombin III (an endogenous inhibitor of factor X) have recurrent venous thromboembolic disease, and a low level of this factor has been associated with a "hypercoagulable state."

The fibrinolytic activity of maternal plasma is greatly reduced during the last months of pregnancy but increases rapidly after delivery. In the first few hours postpartum, an increase in plasminogen activator activity develops, together with a slight prolongation of the thrombin time and a significant rise in fibrin split products. These changes gradually reverse themselves, and nonpregnant values return after 3–5 days postpartum. According to current concepts, the fibrinolytic system is in dynamic equilibrium with the factors that promote coagulation. Thus, after delivery, the increased plasma fibrinolytic activity coupled with the consumption of several clotting factors suggests a large deposition of fibrin in the placental bed. Because of the continued release of fibrin breakdown products from the placental site, the concentration of fibrin split products continues to rise even after the spontaneous plasma fibrinolytic activity decreases. Increased levels of soluble fibrin monomer complexes are observed during the early puerperium as compared to 3 months postpartum.

The increased concentration of clotting factors normally seen during pregnancy can be viewed as teleologically important in providing a reserve to compensate for the rapid consumption of these factors during delivery and in promoting hemostasis after par-

turition. Nonetheless, extensive activation of clotting factors together with immobility, sepsis, or trauma during delivery may set the stage for later thromboembolic complications (see Chapter 20). The secondary increase in fibrinogen, factor VIII, or platelets (which remain well above nonpregnant values in the first week postpartum) also predisposes to thrombosis during the puerperium. The abrupt return of normal fibrinolytic activity after delivery may be a protective mechanism to combat this hazard. A small percentage of puerperal women who show a diminished ability to activate the fibrinolytic system appear to be at high risk for the development of postpartum thromboembolic complications.

B. Blood Volume Changes: The total blood volume normally decreases from the antepartum value of 5–6 L to the nonpregnant value of 4 L by the third week after delivery. One-third of this reduction occurs during delivery and soon afterward and a similar amount is lost by the end of the first postpartum week. Some variation is expected if lactation is permitted. The hypervolemia of pregnancy may be viewed as a protective mechanism that allows most women to tolerate considerable loss of blood during parturition. The quantity of blood lost during delivery will generally determine the blood volume and hematocrit during the puerperium. Normal vaginal delivery of a single fetus entails an average blood loss of about 400 mL, whereas cesarean section leads to a blood loss of nearly 1 L. If total hysterectomy is performed in addition to cesarean section, the mean blood loss increases to approximately 1500 mL. Delivery of twins and triplets entails blood losses similar to those of operative delivery, but a compensatory increase in maternal plasma volume and red blood cell mass is observed during multiple pregnancy.

Dramatic and rapid readjustments occur in the maternal vasculature after delivery, so that the response to blood loss during the early puerperium is different from that occurring in the nonpregnant woman. Delivery leads to obliteration of the low-resistance uteroplacental circulation and results in a 10–15% reduction in the size of the maternal vascular bed. Loss of placental endocrine function also removes a stimulus to vasodilatation.

A declining blood volume with a rise in hematocrit is usually seen 3–7 days after vaginal delivery (Fig 37–3). In contrast, serial studies of patients after cesarean section indicate a more rapid decline in blood volume and hematocrit and a tendency for the hematocrit to stabilize or even decline in the early puerperium. Hemoconcentration occurs if the loss of red cells is less than the reduction in vascular capacity. Hemodilution takes place in patients who lose 20% or more of their circulating blood volume at delivery. In patients with preeclampsia-eclampsia, resolution of peripheral vasoconstriction and mobilization of excess extracellular fluid may lead to a significant expansion of the vascular volume by the third postpartum day. Occasionally, there will be a patient who sustains minimal blood loss at delivery. In such a patient, marked hemo-

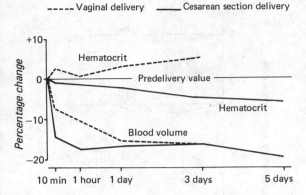

Figure 37–3. Postpartum changes in hematocrit and blood volume in patients delivered vaginally and by cesarean section. Values are expressed as the percentage change from the predelivery hematocrit or blood volume. (From the data of Ueland K et al: *Am J Obstet Gynecol* 1968; **100**:42; Ueland K, Hansen J: *Am J Obstet Gynecol* 1969; **103**:8.)

concentration may occur in the puerperium, especially if there has been a preexisting polycythemia or a considerable increase in the red cell mass during pregnancy.

C. Hematopoiesis: The red cell mass increases by about 30% during pregnancy, while the average red cell loss at delivery is approximately 14%. Thus, the mean postpartum red cell mass level should be about 15% above nonpregnant values. The sudden loss of blood at delivery, however, leads to a rapid and short-lived reticulocytosis (with a peak on the fourth postpartum day) and moderately elevated erythropoietin levels during the first week postpartum.

The bone marrow in pregnancy and in the early puerperium is hyperactive and capable of delivering a large number of young cells to the peripheral blood. Prolactin may play a minor role in bone marrow stimulation.

A striking leukocytosis occurs during labor and extends into the early puerperium. In the immediate puerperium the white blood cell count may be as high as 25,000/μL, with an increased percentage of granulocytes. The stimulus for this leukocytosis is not known, but it probably represents a release of sequestered cells in response to the stress of labor.

The serum iron level is decreased and the plasma iron turnover is increased between the third and the fifth days of the puerperium. Normal values are regained by the second week postpartum. The shorter duration of ferrokinetic changes in puerperal women compared to the duration of changes in nonpregnant women who have had phlebotomy is due to the increased erythroid marrow activity and the circulatory changes described above.

Most women who sustain an average blood loss at delivery and who have had iron supplementation during pregnancy show a relative erythrocytosis during the second week postpartum. Since there is no evidence of increased red cell destruction during the puer-

perium, any red cells gained during pregnancy will disappear gradually according to their normal life span. A moderate excess of red blood cells after delivery, therefore, may lead to an increase in iron stores. Iron supplementation is not necessary for normal postpartum women if the hematocrit or hemoglobin concentration 5–7 days after delivery is equal to or greater than a normal predelivery value. In the late puerperium, there is a gradual decrease in the red cell mass to nonpregnant levels as the rate of erythropoiesis returns to normal.

D. Hemodynamic Changes: The hemodynamic adjustments in the puerperium depend largely on the conduct of labor and delivery, eg, maternal position, method of delivery, mode of anesthesia or analgesia, and blood loss. Cardiac output increases progressively during labor in patients who have received only local anesthesia. The increase in cardiac output peaks immediately after delivery, at which time it is approximately 80% above the prelabor value. During a uterine contraction there is a rise in central venous pressure, arterial pressure, and stroke volume—and, in the absence of pain and anxiety, a reflex decrease in the pulse rate. These changes are magnified in the supine position. Only minimal changes occur in the lateral recumbent position because of unimpaired venous return and absence of aortoiliac compression by the contracting uterus (Poseiro effect).

Caudal anesthesia modifies the progressive rise in cardiac output during labor and reduces the absolute increase probably caused by limiting pain and anxiety observed immediately after delivery. In relation to prelabor values, stroke volume and cardiac output increase and bradycardia occurs (Fig 37–4). Central

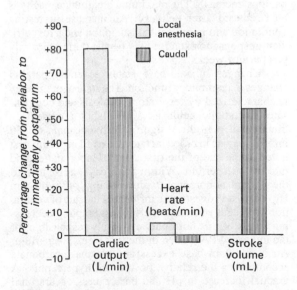

Figure 37–4. Maternal hemodynamic adjustments in the immediate puerperium expressed as a percentage change from prelabor values. The effects of local and caudal anesthesia on cardiac output, heart rate, and stroke volume are compared. (From Metcalfe J, Ueland K: *Prog Cardiovasc Dis* 1974; **16**:363.)

venous pressure also increases. The major factors accounting for these changes are related to alterations in blood volume and hematocrit described earlier.

The hemodynamic effects of uterine contractions are avoided when cesarean section delivery is performed prior to the onset of labor. Nonetheless, the rise in cardiac output noted in the immediate puerperium still occurs. Major fluctuations in blood pressure, cardiac output, heart rate, and stroke volume occur during cesarean section delivery under subarachnoid block or balanced general anesthesia. Extradural anesthesia without epinephrine provides hemodynamic stability during cesarean section and only a small rise in cardiac output after delivery, suggesting that this would be the preferred mode of analgesia in patients with heart disease.

Although major hemodynamic readjustments occur during the period immediately following delivery, there is a return to nonpregnant conditions in the early puerperium. An average increase in cardiac output of approximately 13% occurs after delivery and persists for about 1 week. A more prolonged increase in maternal cardiac output is anticipated in the presence of lactation.

Respiratory Changes

Observations of pulmonary function in the early puerperium indicate that this is an abnormal period. The functions that change most rapidly are those influenced by alterations in abdominal contents and thoracic cage capacity. Lung volume changes in the puerperium are compared with those occurring during pregnancy in Figure 37–5. The residual volume increases, but the vital capacity and inspiratory capacities decrease. The maximum breathing capacity is also reduced after delivery. An increase in resting ventilation and in oxygen consumption and a less efficient response to exercise may persist during the early postpartum weeks.

Changes in acid-base status generally parallel changes in respiratory function. The state of pregnancy is characterized by respiratory alkalosis and compensated metabolic acidosis, while labor represents a transitional period. A significant hypocapnia (< 30 mm Hg), a rise in blood lactate, and a fall in pH are first noted at the end of the first stage of labor and extend into the puerperium. Within a few days, a rise toward the normal nonpregnant values of P_{CO_2} (35–40 mm Hg) occurs. Progesterone influences the rate of ventilation by means of a central effect, and rapidly decreasing levels of this hormone are largely responsible for the increased P_{CO_2} seen in the first week postpartum. An increase in base excess and plasma bicarbonate accompanies the relative postpartum hypercapnia. A gradual increase in pH and base excess occurs until normal levels are reached at about 3 weeks postpartum.

The resting arterial P_{O_2} and oxygen saturation during pregnancy are higher than in nonpregnant women. During labor, the oxygen saturation may be depressed, especially in the supine position, probably

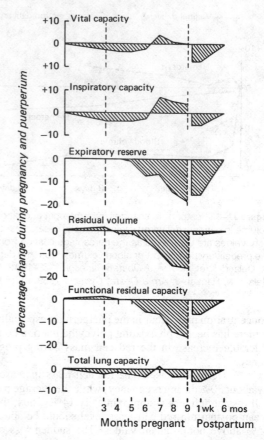

Figure 37–5. Alterations in lung volumes during pregnancy and 1 week and 6 months postpartum. (Modified after Cugell DW et al: *Am Rev Tuberc* 1953;**67**:568.)

as a result of a decrease in cardiac output and a relative increase in the amount of intrapulmonary shunting. However, a rise in the arterial oxygen saturation to 95% is noted during the first postpartum day. An apparent oxygen debt incurred during labor extends into the immediate puerperium and appears to depend upon the length and severity of the second stage of labor. Many investigators have commented on the continued elevation of the basal metabolic rate for a period of 7–14 days following delivery. The increased resting oxygen consumption in the early puerperium has been attributed to mild anemia, lactation, and psychologic factors.

Pituitary-Ovarian Relationships

The plasma levels of placental hormones decline rapidly following delivery. Human placental lactogen has a half-life of 20 minutes and reaches undetectable levels in maternal plasma during the first day after delivery. Human chorionic gonadotropin (hCG) has a mean half-life of approximately 9 hours. The concentration of hCG in maternal plasma falls below 1 IU/mL within 48–96 hours postpartum and falls below 100 mIU/mL by the seventh day. Follicular phase levels of immunoreactive LH-hCG are reached during the second postpartum week. Standard urinary pregnancy tests based on inhibition of a latex agglutination reaction are usually negative at 1 week after normal delivery. Highly specific and sensitive radioimmunoassays for the beta subunit of hCG indicate virtual disappearance of hCG from maternal plasma between days 11 and 16 following normal delivery. The regressive pattern of hCG activity is slower after first trimester abortion than it is after term delivery and even more prolonged in patients who have had a suction curettage for molar pregnancy. In the latter patients, the elimination curve of hCG is influenced both by storage of the hormone in tissues or theca lutein cysts and by continued production of hCG by viable trophoblast.

Plasma levels of estrogens and progesterone also decline rapidly after delivery. Within 3 hours after

removal of the placenta, the plasma concentration of estradiol-17β falls to 10% of the antepartum value. The lowest levels are reached by the seventh postpartum day (Fig 37–6). Plasma estrogens do not reach follicular phase levels (> 50 pg/mL) until 19–21 days postpartum in nonlactating women. The return to normal plasma levels of estrogens is somewhat delayed in lactating women. The postpartum urinary excretion patterns of estrone, estradiol, and estriol parallel the progressive fall in plasma estrogens. The onset of breast engorgement on days 3–4 of the puerperium coincides with a significant fall in the urinary estrogens and supports the view that high estrogen levels suppress lactation.

The metabolic clearance rate of progesterone is high, and, as with estradiol, the half-life is calcu-

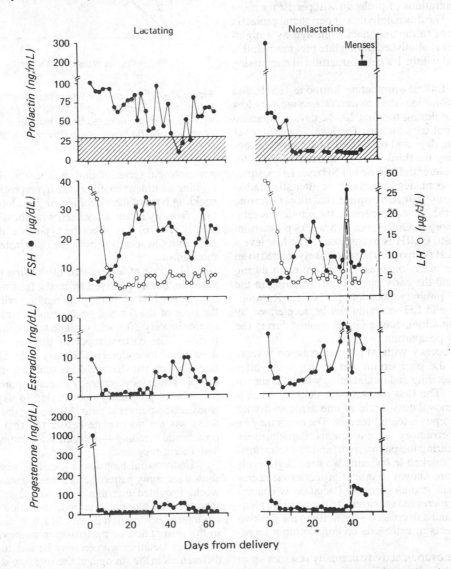

Figure 37–6. Serum concentrations of prolactin, FSH, LH, estradiol, and progesterone in a lactating and nonlactating woman during the puerperium. The hatched bars for the prolactin data represent the normal nongravid range. To convert the FSH and LH to milli-International units per milliliter, divide the FSH values by 2 and multiply the LH values by 4.5. (From Reyes FI, Winter JSD, Faiman C: *Am J Obstet Gynecol* 1972;**114**:589.)

lated in minutes. By the third day of the puerperium, the plasma progesterone concentrations are below luteal phase levels (< 1 ng/mL).

Prolactin levels in maternal blood rise throughout pregnancy to reach concentrations of 200 ng/mL or more. After delivery, prolactin declines in erratic fashion over a period of 2 weeks to the nongravid range in nonlactating women (Fig 37–6). In women who are breast-feeding, basal concentrations of prolactin remain above the nongravid range and increase dramatically in response to suckling. As lactation progresses, the amount of prolactin released with each suckling episode declines. If breast feeding occurs only 1–3 times each day, serum prolactin levels return to normal basal values within 6 months postpartum; if suckling takes place more than 6 times each day, high basal concentrations of prolactin will persist for more than 1 year. The diurnal rhythm of peripheral prolactin concentrations (a daytime nadir followed by a nighttime apogee) is abolished during late pregnancy but is reestablished within 1 week postpartum in nonnursing women.

Serum follicle-stimulating hormone (FSH) and luteinizing hormone (LH) concentrations are very low in all women during the first 10–12 days postpartum whether or not they lactate. The levels increase over the following days and reach follicular phase concentrations during the third week postpartum (Fig 37–6). There is a preferential release of FSH over LH postpartum during spontaneous recovery or after stimulation by exogenous gonadotropin-releasing hormone (GnRH). In the early puerperium, the pituitary is relatively refractory to GnRH, but 4–8 weeks postpartum the response to GnRH is exaggerated. The low levels of FSH and LH postpartum are most likely related to an insufficiency of endogenous GnRH secretion during pregnancy and the early puerperium, resulting in the depletion of pituitary gonadotropin stores. Resumption of FSH and LH secretion can be accelerated by administering a long-acting GnRH agonist during the first 10 days postpartum.

The frequency with which menstruation is reestablished in the puerperium and in the weeks after delivery in lactating and nonlactating women is shown in Fig 37–7. The first menses after delivery usually follows an anovulatory cycle or one associated with inadequate corpus luteum function. The ovary may be somewhat refractory to exogenous gonadotropin stimulation during the puerperium, and this refractoriness is more marked in lactating women. High levels of prolactin are known to inhibit progesterone secretion by human granulosa cells. Lactation is characterized by an increased sensitivity to the negative feedback effects and a decreased sensitivity to the positive feedback effects of estrogens on gonadotropin secretion.

Because ovarian activity normally resumes upon weaning, either the suckling stimulus itself or the raised level of prolactin is responsible for the suppression of pulsatile gonadotropin secretion. Hyperprolactinemia may not account entirely for the inhibition of

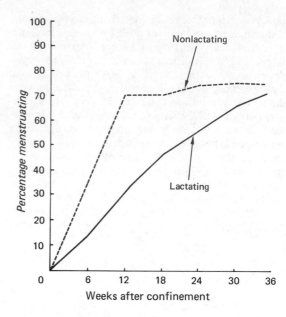

Figure 37–7. Frequency at which menstruation is reestablished in the puerperium in lactating and nonlactating multiparous women. (Adapted from Sharman A: *Reproductive Physiology of the Post-partum Period.* Livingstone, 1966.)

gonadotropin secretion during lactation, since bromocriptine treatment abolishes the hyperprolactinemia of suckling but not the inhibition of gonadotropin secretion. Sensory inputs associated with suckling (if sufficiently intense) may affect the hypothalamic control of gonadotropin secretion by some other neuroendocrine mechanism.

The time of appearance of the first ovulation is variable, but it is delayed by breast feeding. Approximately 10–15% of nonnursing mothers will ovulate by the time of the 6-week postpartum examination, and approximately 30% will ovulate within 90 days postpartum. The earliest reported time of ovulation as determined by endometrial biopsy is 33 days postpartum. Patients who have had a first trimester abortion or ectopic pregnancy generally ovulate sooner after termination of pregnancy (as early as 14 days) than do women who deliver at term. Moreover, the majority of these women do ovulate before the first episode of postabortal bleeding—in contrast to women who have had a term pregnancy.

Endometrial biopsies in lactating women do not show a secretory pattern before the seventh postpartum week. Provided that nursing is in progress and that menstruation has not returned, ovulation before the tenth week postpartum is rare. Much of the variability in the resumption of menstruation and ovulation observed in lactating women may be due to individual differences in the strength of the suckling stimulus and to partial weaning (formula supplementation). This emphasizes the fact that suckling is not a reliable form of birth control. Since the period of lactational infertility is relatively short in Western societies, some form of contraception must be used if pregnancy is to be avoided.

Other Endocrine Changes

Pregnancy is associated with an increase in the number of pituitary lactotropic cells at the expense of the somatotropic cell types. Thus, growth hormone secretion is depressed in late pregnancy and the early puerperium. The rapid disappearance of placental lactogen and the low levels of growth hormone after delivery lead to a relative deficiency of anti-insulin factors in the early puerperium. It is not surprising, therefore, that low fasting plasma glucose levels are noted at this time and that the insulin requirements of diabetic patients usually drop after delivery. When the relative hyperinsulinism and hypoglycemia of pregnancy return to the nonpregnant range at 6–8 weeks postpartum, a paradoxic decline in fasting glucagon levels is found. Since the early puerperium represents a transitional period in carbohydrate metabolism, the results of glucose tolerance tests may be difficult to interpret.

The evaluation of thyroid function is also difficult in the period immediately after birth because of rapid fluctuations in many indices. Characteristically, the plasma thyroxine and other indices of thyroid function are highest at delivery and in the first 12 hours thereafter. A decrease to antepartum values is seen on the third or fourth day after delivery. Reduced available estrogens postpartum lead to a subsequent decrease in circulating thyroxine-binding globulin and a gradual diminution in bound thyroid hormones in serum. Serum concentrations of thyroid-stimulating hormone (TSH) are not significantly different postpartum from those of the pregnant or nonpregnant state. Administration of thyroid-releasing hormone (TRH) in the puerperium results in a normal increase in both TSH and prolactin, and the response is similar in lactating and nonlactating patients. Because pregnancy is associated with some immunosuppressive effects, hyperthyroidism or hypothyroidism may recur postpartum in autoimmune thyroid disease. Failure of lactation and prolonged disability may be the result of hypothyroidism postpartum. In Sheehan's syndrome of pituitary infarction, postpartum cachexia and myxedema are seen secondary to anterior hypophyseal insufficiency.

Plasma concentrations of corticosteroids rise progressively during pregnancy, increase further during labor, and decline postpartum. Most of the rise during pregnancy is due to the parallel increase in the cortisol-binding globulin (CBG), resulting in little actual increase in the effective concentration of free cortisol. Plasma 17-hydroxycorticosteroids increase from a concentration of 4–14 μg/dL of blood before pregnancy to 20–30 μg/dL at 40 weeks' gestation. A 2- to 3-fold increase is seen during labor. Antepartum values are regained on the first day postpartum and are followed by a progressive decline. A return to normal nonpregnant cortisol and 17-hydroxycorticosteroid levels is seen at the end of the first week postpartum.

The excretion of urinary 17-ketosteroids is elevated in late pregnancy as a result of an increase in androgenic precursors from the fetoplacental unit and the ovary. An additional increase of 50% in the amount of excretion occurs during labor. Excretion of 17-ketosteroids returns to antepartum levels on the first day after delivery and to the nonpregnant range by the end of the first week. The mean levels of testosterone during the third trimester of pregnancy range from 3 to 7 times the mean values for nonpregnant women. The elevated levels of testosterone decrease after parturition in parallel with the gradual fall in sex hormone-binding globulin (SHBG). Androstenedione, which is poorly bound to SHBG, falls rapidly to nonpregnant values by the third day postpartum. Conversely, the postpartum plasma concentration of dehydroepiandrosterone sulfate (DHEAS) remains lower than that of nonpregnant women, because its metabolic clearance rate continues to be elevated in the early puerperium. Persistently elevated 17-ketosteroids or androgens during the puerperium are an indication for investigation of ovarian abnormalities. Plasma renin and angiotensin II levels fall during the first 2 hours postpartum to levels within the normal nonpregnant range. This suggests that an extrarenal source of renin has been lost with the expulsion of fetus and placenta.

There is little direct information about the puerperal changes in numerous other hormones, including ACTH, aldosterone, oxytocin and vasopressin, parathyroid hormone, calcitonin, and others. More research should be done on these important endocrine relationships in the puerperium.

COMPLICATIONS DURING THE PUERPERIUM

Postpartum Complications

A. Postanesthetic Problems: Serious and acute obstetric and postanesthetic complications often occur during the few hours immediately following delivery. The patient should therefore be transferred to a recovery room where she can be constantly attended and where observation of bleeding, blood pressure, pulse, and respiratory change can be made every 15 minutes for at least 1–2 hours after delivery or until the effects of general or major regional anesthesia have disappeared. Upon return to the patient's room or ward, the patient's blood pressure should be taken and the measurement repeated every 12 hours for the first 24 hours and daily thereafter for several days. Preeclampsia-eclampsia, infection, or other medical or surgical complications of pregnancy may require more prolonged and intensive postpartum care.

The most common respiratory complications that follow general anesthesia and delivery are airway obstruction or laryngospasm and vomiting with aspiration of vomitus. Bronchoscopy, tracheostomy, and other related procedures must be done promptly as indicated. Hypoventilation and hypotension may follow an abnormally high subarachnoid block. Because serum cholinesterase activity is lower during labor and the postpartum period, hypoventilation during the early puerperium may also follow the use of large amounts of succinylcholine during anesthesia for cesarean section. Brief postpartum shivering is commonly seen after completion of the third stage of labor and is no cause for alarm. The cause is unknown, but it may be related to loss of heat or it may be a sympathetic response. Subcutaneous emphysema may make its appearance postpartum after vigorous bearing down efforts. Most cases resolve spontaneously.

Hypertension in the immediate puerperium is most often due to excessive use of vasopressor or oxytocic drugs. It must be treated promptly with a vasodilator. Chlorpromazine, 5–15 mg slowly intravenously, usually reduces the blood pressure.

Postanesthetic complications that manifest themselves later in the puerperium include post-subarachnoid puncture headache, atelectasis, renal or hepatic dysfunction, and neurologic sequelae.

Postpuncture headache is usually located in the forehead, deep behind the eyes; occasionally, the pain radiates to both temples and to the occipital region. It usually begins on the first or second postpartum day and lasts for 1–3 days. Because new mothers frequently develop various types of headache, the correct diagnosis is essential. An important characteristic of post-spinal puncture headache is increased pain in the sitting or standing position and significant improvement when the patient is supine. The mild form is relieved by aspirin or other analgesics. Headache is due to leakage of cerebrospinal fluid through the site of dural puncture into the extradural space. It is advisable to supplement the daily oral intake of fluids with at least 1 L of 5% glucose in saline intravenously. Administration of 7–10 mL of the patient's own blood into the thecal space at the point of previous needle insertion will "patch" the leaking point and relieve the patient in the great majority of cases. Subdural hematoma is a rare complication of chronic leakage of cerebrospinal fluid and resultant loss of support to intracranial structures.

A small percentage of women who develop headaches during this time also show symptoms of meningeal irritation. Headache due to aseptic chemical meningitis is not relieved by lying down. Lumbar puncture reveals a slightly elevated pressure and an increase in spinal fluid protein and white blood cells but no bacteria. Symptoms usually disappear 1–3 days later, and the spinal fluid returns to normal within 4 days with no sequelae. Treatment is conservative and includes supportive measures, analgesics, and fluids.

Neurologic problems in the puerperium sometimes follow traumatic childbirth, eg, injury to the femoral nerve caused by forceps when the patient was in the lithotomy position. Such complications are rarely bilateral, which aids in the differential diagnosis of a spinal cord lesion. Evidence of more serious neurologic sequelae following regional or general anesthesia for delivery requires consultation with the anesthesiologist and a neurologist.

B. Postpartum Hemorrhage: After the third stage of labor, the uterus must be palpated frequently to make certain that the fundus remains firmly contracted and that no excessive vaginal bleeding occurs. Estimates of blood loss are imprecise, especially when clots are passed, but the loss of more than 300 mL of blood constitutes excessive loss and, traditionally, if more than 500 mL are lost, postpartum hemorrhage is said to have occurred. Lack of clotting or clot formation indicates a coagulation defect. Puerperal inversion of the uterus is an obstetric emergency associated with hemorrhage and shock. Immediate recognition and prompt manual replacement will ensure a normal postpartum course.

If uterine atony develops, the fundus should be elevated and massaged to stimulate uterine contractions. Compression of the uterus with the hand placed on the abdomen and a fist in the vagina with anteflexion of the uterus may be necessary to control the bleeding. Methylergonovine (Methergine), 0.2 mg intramuscularly (or its equivalent), should be administered unless contraindicated (as in cardiac or hypertensive patients). Start an oxytocin (Pitocin, Syntocinon) intravenous drip of 10–20 units in 1 L of 5% dextrose in water using a large-bore needle. If needed, blood transfusion should be given early before shock occurs. Prostaglandin $F_{2\alpha}$ ($PGF_{2\alpha}$), 0.25–1 mg injected directly into the myometrium, is highly effective as a hemostatic agent in controlling postpartum hemorrhage. A 20-mg prostaglandin E_2 suppository placed in the posterior vaginal fornix can be used to treat persistent postpartum uterine atony. When the degree of postpartum bleeding is significant but not serious enough to warrant immediate exploration of the uterine cavity, ultrasonic evaluation may differentiate retained placental tissue and blood clots from an empty uterus. When bleeding cannot be controlled, the patient should be returned to the delivery room for inspection of the birth canal. It may be necessary to suture lacerations, remove placental fragments, pack the uterus, or perform bilateral internal iliac artery ligation or even hysterectomy to control hemorrhage. An effective alternative approach to the control of pelvic hemorrhage consists of angiographic localization of the specific bleeding vessel and transcatheter embolization with Gelfoam fragments. The complications of labor and delivery that lead to postpartum hemorrhage and the specific management of these problems are discussed in Chapter 33.

C. Postpartum Infections: Febrile morbidity in the puerperium is defined as a temperature elevation of 38 °C (100.4 °F) or more occurring after the first 24 hours postpartum on 2 or more occasions that are not within the same 24 hours. The most frequent causes of fever in the postpartum period are infections of the genital tract, urinary tract, and breasts. Cesarean section presents a much higher risk of postpartum infection and subsequent death or morbidity. The risk of death from cesarean section is estimated to be 4 times greater than that from vaginal delivery. Prolonged labor, rupture of the membranes, and chorioamnionitis increase the risk of postpartum uterine infection.

Fever during the puerperium must be regarded as resulting from genital tract infection unless evidence to the contrary is found. The most common pathogens in puerperal infection are anaerobic nonhemolytic streptococci, coliform bacteria, *Bacteroides,* and staphylococci. Because of improved obstetric care, there has been a reduced incidence of beta-hemolytic streptococcal infection. Genital tract colonization with *Mycoplasma hominis* is detected in almost 40% of lower socioeconomic group patients and in about 20% of higher income patients. Peripartum tissue invasion by *M hominis* (as determined by antibody titer rise) is commonly associated with moderate fever and minimal or no physical findings in colonized women who lack protective antibody. Chlamydiae are associated with approximately 25% of the uterine infections that occur from 48 hours to 6 weeks postpartum among patients who deliver vaginally. Mycoplasmas are sensitive to tetracycline or lincomycin; chlamydiae are sensitive to tetracycline or erythromycin. A low-grade fever on the second or third postpartum day commonly results from retention of the lochia or a saprophytic infection of retained fragments of fetal membranes. There may be a delay in uterine involution, but the pulse rate generally remains normal. Resolution of the fever follows improved uterine drainage after the administration of oxytocic agents or removal of free placental fragments from the cervical os. Infection in uterine fibroids is unusual, but when it occurs it tends to be in the early puerperium. After delivery, the blood supply to fibroids is greatly diminished, and they tend to undergo ischemic degeneration.

1. Endometritis–The majority of patients with puerperal infection have endometritis. On the third postpartum day, the temperature often rises to 38.8–39.4 °C (102–103 °F) and remains elevated. Associated signs and symptoms are tachycardia, uterine tenderness, and malaise. The lochia is often profuse and has a foul odor. The infection may spread to the parametrium and pelvic peritoneum. Paralytic ileus may be an associated problem. In puerperal sepsis caused by group A or B beta-hemolytic *Streptococcus,* the lochia may be scanty and free of odor, but rapid lymphatic spread of the infection, bacteremia, and toxicity are a classic sequence. The most striking clinical signs include the onset of uterine tenderness and an abrupt temperature elevation to 38.8 °C (102 °F) or higher within the first 24 hours after delivery. Serious late complications of pelvic peritonitis include abscess formation, pelvic thrombophlebitis, disseminated intravascular coagulation, septic shock, and subsequent infertility.

Aseptic technique during labor and the early puerperium and the avoidance of trauma during delivery will reduce the incidence of puerperal infection. Isolation precautions are appropriate. Intrauterine cultures and blood cultures should be obtained and treatment with broad-spectrum antibiotics instituted until more specific therapy can be selected on the basis of bacteriologic studies. Patients who do not respond to an initial antibiotic regimen of ampicillin or penicillin and an aminoglycoside (kanamycin, gentamicin) or a cephalosporin should be reexamined for the presence of anaerobic organisms, eg, *Bacteroides*. The most common combinations of drugs for treating anaerobes are an aminoglycoside and clindamycin, penicillin and chloramphenicol, and an aminoglycoside and metronidazole. Treatment of postpartum endometritis or parametritis includes bed rest in the semi-Fowler position, hydration with intravenous fluids, decompression of the bowel, and maintenance of electrolyte balance.

2. Urinary tract infections–Urinary tract infections occur during the puerperium in about 5% of patients. Most are caused by coliform bacteria. Symptoms of acute cystitis usually develop on the first or second postpartum day, often following urinary retention, instrumentation, or trauma to the bladder. Operative delivery and vaginal or vulvar lacerations may interfere with normal micturition. Predisposing factors include prolonged labor, administration of a large volume of intravenous fluid, and conduction anesthesia. On the first postpartum day, 17% of patients have asymptomatic bacteriuria (> 100,000 colonies/mL). Spontaneous resolution of bacteriuria occurs in three-fourths of these women by the third postpartum day, the most appropriate time to obtain a clinically meaningful urine culture. A patient with bacteriuria during pregnancy is at higher risk of developing this complication than patients with negative urine cultures.

Upper urinary tract infection characteristically develops on the third or fourth postpartum day and is manifested by chills, spiking fever, costovertebral angle tenderness, and frequently nausea and vomiting. Diagnosis must be confirmed by urinalysis and a culture, colony count, and bacterial sensitivity study of an uncontaminated urine specimen. Treatment consists of a high fluid intake, good drainage of urine, and appropriate antibiotic therapy. If the patient does not improve, urinary tract obstruction should be suspected. All patients who have had a puerperal urinary tract infection should have urine cultures repeated at the 4- or 6-week postpartum visit.

Other Medical Complications in the Puerperium

The patient with a preexisting medical or surgical illness that complicates pregnancy requires special attention during the puerperium. Women with pulmonary disease, especially those with an obstructive component, are at increased risk of developing atelectasis and pneumonia, partly as a result of impaired diaphragmatic motion after delivery. Careful attention to pulmonary toilet and avoidance of both heavy sedation and dehydration will reduce the incidence of pulmonary complications.

Before optimal management of pregnant cardiac patients became available, most maternal cardiac deaths occurred postpartum. After the stress of labor and delivery, patients with severe mitral stenosis may develop pulmonary edema in the immediate or early puerperium, when there are significant shifts in extracellular and intravascular fluid volumes. In patients with rheumatic heart disease, cardiac and extracardiac factors such as ectopic beats, tachycardia, upper respiratory infection, emotional upset, and anemia can so affect the patient's condition in the span of 24 hours as to precipitate congestive heart failure. Factors predisposing to the development of thrombophlebitis or pulmonary embolism pose additional hazards to the cardiac patient during the puerperium. Routine antibiotic prophylaxis against endocarditis is not necessary at normal delivery but is probably indicated after abortion, cesarean section, or manual removal of the placenta.

The immediate and early puerperium are especially hazardous for the patient with cyanotic congenital heart disease and pulmonary hypertension (eg, Eisenmenger's syndrome). Systemic hypotension and metabolic and respiratory acidosis may lead to exaggeration of a right-to-left shunt or to reversal of a left-to-right shunt. Death characteristically occurs during labor or within the first 10 days postpartum. Deterioration is characterized by increasing cyanosis and deterioration of cardiovascular function. Treatment must concentrate on the prevention of contributing factors such as blood loss, hypoxemia, pulmonary irritants, venous pooling, spinal anesthesia, and sepsis.

It is pertinent to emphasize here that the interaction of other medical illnesses with pregnancy and the puerperium is not entirely predictable. Papular and herpetiform eruptions and idiopathic jaundice precipitated by pregnancy characteristically improve after the first week postpartum. On the other hand, aggravation of the following conditions may occur during the puerperium: myasthenia gravis, sarcoidosis, ulcerative colitis, rheumatoid arthritis, and the collagen diseases. In asthma and allergic manifestations, the pattern observed during pregnancy tends to reverse itself during the puerperium. These observations provide the basis for the clinical impression that a state of relative hypoadrenocorticism exists in the early puerperium. Corticosteroid therapy initiated during pregnancy for the management of collagen disorders should be continued and the dosage probably increased during the puerperium to reduce the hazards of exacerbations.

A. Postpartum Cardiomyopathy: Postpartum cardiomyopathy is a disorder of the heart muscle of unknown cause that presents clinically with the onset of cardiac failure. This serious, even critical complication is seen most commonly in older multiparous women without evidence of prior heart disease and in women who have had preeclampsia-eclampsia or a multiple pregnancy, but the syndrome can follow stillbirths and even early abortions. Pathologically, there are focal degeneration and fibrosis of muscle fibers with mural thrombi but without coronary artery disease. Catheter studies have demonstrated low-output cardiac failure with dilated, poorly contracting ventricles, pulmonary and systemic hypertension, and absence of significant pericardial effusions. The

majority of patients with postpartum cardiomyopathy develop this disorder in the first month postpartum, but it may occur as late as 3–5 months postpartum. In about 7% of reported cases, onset of the disorder has been noted in the last month of pregnancy. Postpartum cardiomyopathy should be considered in the differential diagnosis of a patient without preexisting evidence of heart disease who develops moderate respiratory distress and chest pain with signs of left heart failure postpartum. A holosystolic murmur indicating mitral insufficiency and evidence of cardiomegaly on chest x-ray should aid in excluding other causes of these symptoms.

Postpartum cardiomyopathy responds to digitalis and the conventional management of pulmonary edema. Anticoagulation is recommended to minimize pulmonary and systemic emboli. Extended bed rest accelerates the rate of recovery. Patients whose heart size returns to normal within 6 months have a good prognosis and may resume their normal activity; those who want more children should be advised that they are likely to have recurrences of the disorder in subsequent pregnancies.

B. Postpartum Hemolytic Uremia: The syndrome of postpartum hemolytic uremia has been recently described. Renal failure due to intrarenal intravascular coagulation is associated with a microangiopathic hemolytic anemia. Most of the patients have an uncomplicated pregnancy and delivery, but in a few cases there has been a mild preexisting preeclampsia. A brief influenzalike illness has also been described. Cases of postpartum hemolytic uremia differ from other cases of this disorder in that the patient is reasonably well for a period of 1–10 weeks following childbirth before renal failure becomes apparent. The pathogenesis is obscure, but the condition may be similar to thrombotic thrombocytopenic purpura. It is hypothesized that an antecedent infection triggers either the generalized Shwartzman reaction or the formation of an antigen-antibody complex which circulates and produces immune complex glomerulonephritis and subsequent intravascular coagulation.

The patient may present with nausea, vomiting, dyspnea, cyanosis, a bleeding tendency, oliguria or anuria, convulsions, and abdominal and back pain. Prompt diagnosis is essential if treatment is to be successful. Helpful laboratory studies include tests for intravascular coagulation and fibrinogen degradation products. Intravenous heparin (approximately 20,000 units/d with appropriate controls) should be instituted, although heparin therapy is not uniformly successful. Although the cause of hemolytic-uremic syndrome remains undetermined, some cases are associated with a marked decrease in plasma antithrombin III. Since heparin increases the turnover rate of antithrombin, the administration of heparin to antithrombin III–deficient patients may therefore paradoxically increase the risk of thrombosis. Common supportive measures include digitalis, transfusion, and drug therapy for hypertension, hyperkalemia, and hyperuricemia. Immunosuppressive therapy is ineffective and potentially harmful.

Dipyridamole is advocated in combination with aspirin or prostacyclin infusion as in other disorders involving rapid platelet destruction. Plasma exchange (plasmapheresis with plasma infusions) may be dramatically beneficial. Renal biopsy should be postponed because of the danger of hemorrhage at the biopsy site. Despite treatment of this disorder with hemodialysis, the prognosis is poor.

C. Postpartum Eclampsia: Eclampsia occurs before labor in about 25% of reported cases, during labor in approximately 50%, and postpartum in the remaining 25%. The onset of postpartum convulsions usually occurs near delivery and declines progressively with each 12-hour postpartum period. After 48 hours, the disorder is rare. Although uncommon, late postpartum eclampsia can occur up to 14 days postpartum. It has been postulated that retained placental fragments play a role in some patients with late postpartum convulsions and that these patients require curettage for management. The eclamptic patient must be differentiated from those with any of the following conditions: epilepsy; metabolic, infectious, or hypertensive diseases; space-occupying central nervous system lesions; and cerebrovascular accidents. Some patients with late postpartum eclampsia do not manifest any signs or symptoms of preeclampsia in the antenatal or intrapartum periods and thus are not treated prophylactically. Other patients develop late postpartum seizures in spite of intrapartum and early postpartum magnesium sulfate therapy (see Chapter 34). At present, it is difficult to identify those patients who need prolonged therapy.

D. Postpartum Psychosis: Although postpartum psychosis is not a specific entity distinct from other major diagnostic categories of mental illness, the onset of psychiatric symptoms soon after delivery may be acute and dramatic. The postpartum reaction syndrome includes a spectrum of psychiatric disorders (schizophrenia, manic-depressive psychosis, psychoneuroses, and depression). Affective disorders are by far the most common. Early symptoms include withdrawal, paranoia, and refusal to eat. Depression may soon alternate with manic behavior. During these mood swings, patients may harm themselves or their infants. Nonetheless, mothers should be kept in contact with their babies whenever possible. Childbirth and its attendant stress is seen as the precipitating event that leads to the exacerbation of an underlying or latent disorder. The woman who feels unloved, is involved in a discordant marital relationship, or did not want the baby is at a higher risk for postpartum depression. Emotional support and physical assistance from family, friends, and medical personnel during pregnancy, delivery, and the puerperium are important preventive measures. Psychotherapy holds a prominent place in management. The usual drugs and supportive treatment appropriate to the patient's disorder should be given—phenothiazines for schizophrenia, mood-elevating drugs and other appropriate therapy for depression, and sedatives for manic states. Vitamin B_6 supplementation has no place in the prevention or treatment of postpartum depression. On rare occasion, puerperal psychosis associated with folic acid deficiency will respond to appropriate therapy. The prospect of recovery from postpartum mental illness is good, although in some studies the risk of recurrence after subsequent pregnancy and delivery has been 10–20%.

Surgical Complications

Surgical problems during the puerperium mainly concern complications of labor and delivery such as hemorrhage, wound infections and dehiscence, uterine rupture and inversion, urinary tract injuries, and thrombophlebitis (see Chapter 33). Surgical complications are more common with cesarean section or operative delivery. Postpartum surgical problems may also follow adjunctive surgery such as sterilization procedures performed at delivery or soon thereafter. Certainly, the increased vascularity and edema of pelvic tissues predispose to a higher incidence of postoperative bleeding from ligated vascular pedicles.

The mild adynamic ileus commonly seen after labor and delivery predisposes to gastrointestinal complications in the puerperium. Dramatic distention of the cecum and colon may follow cesarean section. Mechanical obstruction must be ruled out if bowel problems do not respond to nasogastric tube decompression.

Appendicitis may occur less frequently postpartum than during pregnancy. Torsion of the spleen or rupture of a splenic aneurysm, or ovarian artery aneurysm, while rare, do occur in the puerperium. Cholecystectomy, not usually recommended during pregnancy, may be required in the puerperium for serious gallbladder disease. The acute surgical abdomen is particularly dangerous in the early puerperium because there is a tendency to attribute symptoms such as pain and vomiting to the recent delivery and the stretched abdominal muscles do not respond normally to peritoneal irritation.

Management of venous thrombosis and thrombophlebitis is discussed in Chapter 20. Although rare, pregnancy and the puerperium predispose to ovarian and cerebral venous thrombosis and the Budd-Chiari syndrome (hepatic vein thrombosis).

CONDUCT OF THE PUERPERIUM

All patients will benefit from 3–5 days of hospitalization after delivery. Nonetheless, increasing hospital costs and shortage of obstetric beds have reduced the duration of the traditional lying-in period. Most women can now return home safely 3 days after normal vaginal delivery if proper instructions are given. Earlier discharge may be unwise, especially for the unselected primiparous patient. Selected mothers and infants who have had uncomplicated labors and deliveries may be discharged safely 24 hours postpartum if discharge criteria are met and follow-up care is provided. Optimal care includes daily visits by a perinatal nurse practitioner through the fourth postpartum day.

Emotional Reactions

Several basic emotional responses occur in almost every woman who has given birth to a normal baby. A woman's first emotion is usually one of extreme relief followed by a sense of happiness and gratitude that the new baby has arrived safely. A regular pattern of behavior occurs in the human mother immediately after birth of the infant. Touching, holding, and grooming of the infant under normal conditions rapidly strengthen maternal ties of affection. However, not all mothers react in this way, and some may even feel detached from the new baby. Such feelings are usually temporary and should not give rise to anxiety. In the first few days after delivery, the mother may experience feelings of inadequacy and depression, commonly referred to as postpartum blues. Evidence suggests that rooming-in during the hospital stay reduces maternal anxiety and results in more successful breast feeding.

Prematurity or illness of the newborn delays early intimate maternal-infant contact and may have an adverse effect on the rapid and complete development of normal mothering responses. Stressful factors during the puerperium, eg, marital infidelity or the loss of friends as a result of the necessary confinement and preoccupation with the new baby, may leave the mother feeling unsupported and may interfere with the formation of a maternal bond with the infant. When a baby dies or is born with a congenital defect, the obstetrician should tell the mother and father about the problem together, if possible. The baby's normal healthy features and potential for improvement should be emphasized, and positive statements should be made about the present availability of corrective treatment and the promises of ongoing research. A photograph of the deceased newborn can be a solace to the parents after the infant has been buried. During the puerperium, the obstetrician has an important opportunity to help the mother whose infant has died work through her period of mourning or discouragement and to assess abnormal reactions of grief that suggest a need for psychiatric assistance. Pathologic grief is characterized by the inability to work through the sense of loss within 3–4 months, with subsequent feelings of low self-esteem.

Ambulation & Rest

The policy of early ambulation after delivery benefits the patient. Early ambulation provides a sense of well-being, hastens involution of the uterus, improves uterine drainage, and lessens the incidence of postpartum thrombophlebitis. After the second postpartum day, the patient may be out of bed as desired, but early ambulation does not mean return to normal activity or work. Rest is essential after delivery, and the demands on the mother should be limited to allow for adequate relaxation and adjustment to her new responsibilities. It is helpful to set aside a few hours each day for rest periods. Many mothers do not sleep well for several nights after delivery, and it is surprising how the day is occupied with the care of the newborn. Sedatives such as secobarbital, 100 mg orally, or flurazepam (Dalmane), 30 mg orally, at bedtime as necessary, will generally ensure a good night's rest.

Diet

A regular diet is permissible as soon as the patient regains her appetite and is free from the effects of analgesics and anesthetics. Protein foods, fruits, vegetables, milk products, and a high fluid intake are recommended, especially for nursing mothers. However, even lactating women probably require no more than 2600–2800 kcal/d. It may be advisable to continue the daily vitamin-mineral supplement during the early puerperium.

Care of the Bladder

Most women will empty the bladder during labor or will have been catheterized at delivery. Even so, serious bladder distention may develop within 12 hours. A long and difficult labor or a forceps delivery may traumatize the base of the bladder and interfere with normal voiding. In some cases, overdistention of the bladder may be related to pain or spinal anesthesia. The marked polyuria noted for the first few days postpartum causes the bladder to fill in a relatively short time. Hence, obstetric patients require catheterization more frequently than most surgical patients. The patient should be catheterized every 6 hours after delivery if she is unable to void or empty her bladder completely. Intermittent catheterization is preferable to an indwelling catheter because the incidence of urinary tract infection is less. However, if the bladder fills to more than 1000 mL, at least 2 days of decompression by a retention catheter is usually required to establish voiding without significant residual urine. If the catheter is left in the bladder for more than 12 hours, bacteriuria is likely. Prophylaxis may include urinary acidifying agents, but urine cultures are necessary to ascertain the nature of the invading organism. Therapy should be instituted with sulfisoxazole, ampicillin, or another appropriate antibiotic.

Bowel Function

The mild ileus which follows delivery, together with perineal discomfort and postpartum fluid loss by other routes, predisposes to constipation during the puerperium. Obstruction of the colon by a retroverted uterus is a rare complication during the puerperium. If an enema was given before delivery, the patient is unlikely to have a bowel movement for 1–2 days after childbirth. Milk of magnesia, 15–20 mL orally on the evening of the second postpartal day, usually will stimulate a bowel movement by the next morning. If not, a rectal suppository such as bisacodyl or a small tap water or oil retention enema may be given. Less bowel stimulation will be needed if the diet contains sufficient roughage. Stool softeners such as dioctyl sodium sulfosuccinate may ease the discomfort of early bowel movements. Hemorrhoidal discomfort is a frequent complaint postpartum and usually responds to conservative treatment with suppositories and sitz baths. It is rarely necessary to treat hemorrhoids surgically postpartum unless there is extensive thrombosis.

Laxatives, enemas, and a diet with ample roughage are contraindicated in the early puerperium in the patient who has had suture repair of severe childbirth lacerations. Phenolphthalein, senna, and jalap laxatives should not be used if the patient is nursing because slight contamination of breast milk may occur.

Bathing

As soon as the patient is ambulatory, she may take a shower. Sitz or tub baths after the second postpartum day are probably safe if the tub is clean, because bath water will not gain access to the vagina unless it is directly introduced. Most patients prefer showers to tub baths because of the profuse flow of lochia immediately postpartum. Vaginal douching is contraindicated in the early puerperium.

Care of the Episiotomy

The perineal area should be gently cleansed with plain soap at least once or twice a day and after voiding or defecation. If the pudendum is kept clean, healing should occur rapidly. Dry heat applied to the perineum with an infrared lamp for 20 minutes 3 times daily should relieve local discomfort and promote healing. Some obstetricians recommend cool sitz baths for relief of perineal pain. Episiotomy pain is easily controlled by simple analgesics. The use of sanitary napkins should be avoided during the first day after delivery. Ointments and anesthetic solutions have little value.

The episiotomy or repaired pudendal lacerations should be inspected daily. A vaginal or rectal examination should be performed only if a hematoma or infection seems likely and then using aseptic technique. Episiotomy wounds rarely become infected, which is remarkable when one considers the difficulty of avoiding contamination of the perineal area. In the event of sepsis, local heat and irrigation should cause the infection to subside. Appropriate antibiotics may be indicated if an immediate response to these measures is not observed. In rare instances, the wound should be opened widely and sutures removed for adequate drainage. Necrotizing fasciitis is a rare but serious complication of episiotomy incision extension caused by anaerobic bacteria. When cleaned, secondary closure of the wound may be attempted, even though only a minority of such closures heal well. Perineorrhaphy may be required several weeks later if there has been considerable distortion of the normal tissue relationships.

Oxytocic Agents

Administration of oxytocic agents beyond the immediate puerperium should be limited to those patients who have specific indications such as postpartum hemorrhage or endometritis. The routine use of ergot preparations such as methylergonovine maleate (Methergine), 0.2 mg orally every 6 hours for extended periods of time, is of questionable value in hastening uterine involution. Potential disadvantages include interference with normal lactation as a result of inhibition of prolactin release and the possibility of ergot poisoning if prolonged therapy is permitted.

Postpartum Immunization

A. Prevention of Rh Isoimmunization: The postpartum injection of Rh_0 (D) immune globulin* will prevent sensitization in the Rh-negative woman who has had a fetal-to-maternal transfusion of Rh-positive fetal red cells. The risk of maternal sensitization rises with the volume of fetal transplacental hemorrhage. The usual amount of fetal blood that enters the maternal circulation is less than 0.5 mL. The usual dose of 300 μg of Rh_0 (D) immune globulin is in excess of the dose generally required because 25 μg of RhoGAM per milliliter of fetal red cells is sufficient to prevent maternal immunization. If neonatal anemia or other clinical symptoms suggest that a large transplacental hemorrhage has occurred, the amount of fetal blood in the maternal circulation can be estimated by the Kleihauer-Betke smear and the amounts of RhoGAM to be administered can be adjusted accordingly. An alternative to the acid-elution smear is the D^u test, which will detect 20 mL or more of Rh-positive fetal blood in the maternal circulation.

Rh_0 (D) immune globulin is administered after abortion without qualifications or after delivery to women who meet all of the following criteria: (1) the mother must be Rh_0 (D)–negative without Rh antibodies; (2) the baby must be Rh_0 (D)- or D^u-positive; and (3) the cord blood must be Coombs-negative. If these criteria are met, a 1:1000 dilution of Rh_0 (D) immune globulin is cross-matched to the mother's red cells to ensure compatibility and 1 mL (300 μg) is given intramuscularly to the mother within 72 hours after delivery. If the 72-hour interval has been exceeded, it is advisable to give the globulin rather than withhold it, for it may still protect against sensitization. Rh-immune globulin should also be given after delivery or abortion when serologic tests of maternal sensitization to the Rh factor are questionable. *Caution:* Do not inject the infant. Do not give intravenously.

The average risk of maternal sensitization after abortion is approximately half the risk incurred by full-term pregnancy and delivery; the latter has been estimated at 11%. Even though mothers have received Rh_0 (D) immune globulin, they should be screened with each subsequent pregnancy, since occasional failures are related to inadequate Rh_0 (D) immune globulin administration postpartum or an undetected very low titer in the previous pregnancy.

B. Rubella Vaccination: A significant number

---

*Trade names include D-Immune, Gamulin Rh, HypRho-D, and RhoGAM.

Rest on the elbows and knees, keeping the upper arms and legs perpendicular to the body. Hump the back upward. Contract the buttocks and draw the abdomen in vigorously. Relax, breathe deeply.

Lie flat on the back with the knees and hips flexed. Tilt the pelvis inward and contract the buttocks tightly. Lift the head while contracting the abdominal muscles.

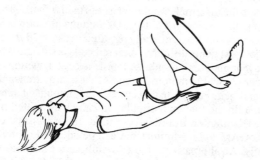

Slowly flex the knee and then the thigh on the abdomen. Lower the foot to the buttock. Straighten and lower the leg to the floor.

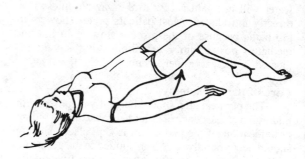

Lie flat on the back with the arms at the sides. Draw the knees up slightly. Arch the back.

Raise first the right and then the left leg as high as possible. Keep the toes pointed and the knee straight. Lower the leg gradually, using the abdominal muscles but not the hands.

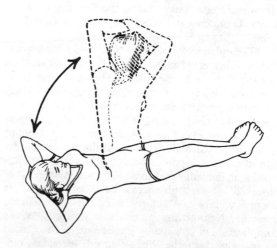

Lie flat on the back with the arms clasped behind the head. Then sit up slowly. (If necessary, hook feet under furniture.) Slowly lie back.

Figure 37–8. Recommended postpartum exercises. Exercises to strengthen the muscles of the back, pelvic floor, and abdomen are advocated but should be postponed for approximately 3 weeks after delivery. This allows the abdominal muscles to partially regain their original length and tone and prevents undue patient fatigue. The patient should begin with a single exercise that is performed 5 times and repeated twice daily. On subsequent days, additional exercises are added sequentially. Strengthening of the back and abdominal muscles will correct lordosis and the diastasis of the rectus muscles and improve posture. (Reproduced, with permission, from Benson RC: *Handbook of Obstetrics & Gynecology,* 5th ed. Lange, 1974.)

of women of childbearing age have never had rubella. When tested by the hemagglutination inhibition method, 10–20% of women are seronegative (titer of 1:8 or less). Women who are susceptible to rubella can be vaccinated safely and effectively with a live attenuated rubella virus vaccine (RA 27/3 strain) during the immediate puerperium. Seroconversion occurs in approximately 90% of women vaccinated postpartum. The puerperium appears to be the ideal time for vaccination because it avoids the risk of inadvertently vaccinating a pregnant woman. Although there have been no reports of human fetal malformations due to the vaccine virus, the theoretic possibility of teratogenicity exists. Since the attenuated virus is not communicable, nursing mothers need not be excluded from an immunization program. Vaccinated patients should be informed that transient side-effects (arthralgia or rash) are common and that contraception for 2 months postpartum is mandatory. Since Rh_0 (D) immune globulin may contain rubella antibodies, there has been some concern that these may prevent successful vaccination against rubella. However, it has been shown that the serologic response to rubella vaccination in the puerperium was satisfactory even when anti-D immunoglobulin was given shortly before vaccination. On the other hand, it has been shown that a blood transfusion can prevent successful rubella vaccination if it is performed soon after the transfusion.

Discharge Examination & Instructions

Before the patient's hospital discharge, the breasts and abdomen should be examined. The degree of uterine involution and tenderness should be noted. The calves and thighs should be palpated to rule out thrombophlebitis. The characteristics of the lochia are important and should be observed. The episiotomy wound should be inspected to see whether the sutures are healing satisfactorily. A blood sample should be obtained for hematocrit or hemoglobin determination. Unless the patient has an unusual pelvic complaint, there is little need to perform a vaginal examination. Occasionally, a sponge may be left in the vagina at delivery, but with proper technique this should not occur. The obstetrician should be certain that the patient has had a bowel movement, is voiding normally, and is physically able to assume her new responsibilities at home.

The patient will require some advice on what she is allowed to do when she arrives home. Hygiene is essentially the same as practiced in the hospital, with a premium on cleanliness. Upon discharge from the hospital, the patient should be instructed to rest for at least 2 hours during the day, and her usual household activities should be curtailed. She should not take over her full household duties for at least 3 weeks; thereafter, most normal activities can be resumed. She may climb up and down stairs, but walking or riding outdoors should be minimized during the first 2 weeks. She should avoid carrying heavy packages or doing taxing household chores for about 3–4 weeks after delivery. It is inadvisable for the patient to return to

work until 5–6 weeks after delivery. Generally, sports and athletic activities may be resumed after the postpartum evaluation (see below).

The patient who has had frequent prenatal visits to her obstetrician may feel cut off from the doctor during the interval between discharge and the first postpartum visit. She will feel reassured in this period of time if she receives thoughtful advice on what she is allowed to do and what she can expect when she arrives home. She should be instructed to take her temperature at home twice daily and to notify the physician or nurse in the event of fever, vaginal bleeding, or back pain. At the time of discharge, the patient should be informed that she will note persistent but decreasing amounts of vaginal lochia for about 3 weeks and possibly a small period during the fourth or fifth week after delivery. A consultation with the pediatrician before the first postpartum visit with the obstetrician will be helpful.

Postpartum Exercises

Exercises to strengthen the muscles of the back, pelvic floor, and abdomen are advocated, but strenuous ones should be postponed until approximately 3 weeks after delivery. This allows the abdominal muscles to partially regain their original length and tone and prevents undue patient fatigue. The recommended forms of postpartum exercises are illustrated in Fig 37–8. The patient should begin with a single exercise performed 5 times and repeated several times daily. On subsequent days, additional exercises are added sequentially. Strengthening of the back and abdominal muscles will correct lordosis and diastasis of the rectus muscles and will improve posture.

Contraception & Sterilization

The immediate puerperium has long been recognized as a convenient time for the performance of tubal ligation. Parous women should be informed of the availability of postpartum sterilization during their prenatal visits. Despite the increasing success rate of microsurgical tubal reanastomosis, the permanence of tubal ligation should be emphasized. Sterilization is not recommended in young women of low parity or when the outcome of the pregnancy is in doubt and survival of the infant is not assured. Postpartum tubal ligation can be done easily and rapidly through a small midline or periumbilical incision immediately after delivery and does not prolong hospitalization. Laparoscopic sterilization is not advisable in the immediate puerperium because of increased pelvic vascularity and the large size of the fundus.

Coitus is best postponed until after the postpartum visit and examination. This period of abstinence is considered excessive by most couples, but abstinence should be practiced for at least 2–3 weeks. Nonetheless, contraceptive methods should be discussed prior to hospital discharge and the patient advised of the relative risks of conception, depending on whether she is nursing or not (see Chapter 23). During lactational amenorrhea, the pregnancy rate is approximately 8%; however, once menstruation has resumed, the rate rises to 36% despite continued lactation. The earliest reported time of ovulation as determined by endometrial biopsy is 33 days postpartum in nonlactating women and 49 days in lactating women. Contraceptive advice should take into account the possibility that conception may occur as early as the second or third week after abortion or ectopic pregnancy.

The use of vaginal foam, condom, or both may be prescribed until the postpartum examination. Fitting of a diaphragm is not practical until involution of the reproductive organs has taken place. The use of oral contraceptives in the immediate puerperium in the nonlactating woman is avoided by many obstetricians to allow time for the hypothalamic-pituitary axis to recover from the prolonged suppression of pregnancy. However, no firm data exist showing that immediate postpartum institution of oral contraceptives leads to an increased incidence of postpill amenorrhea. In view of the hypercoagulable state postpartum, it is advisable to postpone oral contraceptive therapy until 2 weeks after delivery.

The intramuscular injection of a long-acting progestin such as medroxyprogesterone acetate (Depo-Provera), 50-200 mg, provides effective contraception for the lactating woman for a 3- to 6-month period without provoking maternal thromboembolism or decreasing milk yield. However, questions relating to prolonged amenorrhea or the inconvenience of irregular bleeding limit the usefulness of this method. Oral contraceptives containing less than 50 μg of mestranol are also satisfactory contraceptives for the nursing mother, since the effect on decreasing milk volume is minimal. The extent of mammary transfer of ethinyl estradiol is small. After the daily administration of 50 μg of ethinyl estradiol to the mother, the concentration in milk is below the practical detection limit of the radioimmunoassay (15 pg/mL). It has been estimated that the baby ingesting about 600 mL of milk per day would receive about 0.02% of the estrogen dose to the mother. A combination pill containing 20 μg of ethinyl estradiol and 1 mg of norethindrone acetate (Loestrin) or one with 0.35 mg of norethindrone (Micronor) may be especially useful in this instance.

Insertion of an intrauterine device during the immediate puerperium has been advocated in some clinics as a means of providing birth control to a large number of women in lower socioeconomic groups who may not return to the hospital postpartum. Although this practice appears to be safe, the cumulative rates for pregnancy, expulsion, and removal because of side-effects are highest within 2-4 weeks postpartum. The immediate puerperium is not the optimal time for insertion of an intrauterine device if the patient will return for a postpartum visit.

Postpartum Examination

At the postpartum visit—4 to 6 weeks after discharge from hospital—the patient's weight and blood pressure should be recorded. Most patients will retain about 60% of any weight in excess of 11 kg (24 lb) that was gained during pregnancy. A suitable diet may be prescribed if the patient has not returned to her approximate prepregnant weight. If the patient was anemic upon discharge from the hospital or has been bleeding during the puerperium, a complete blood count should be determined. Persistence of uterine bleeding demands investigation and definitive treatment.

The breasts should be examined and the adequacy of support, abnormalities of the nipples or lactation, and the presence of any masses should be noted. The patient should be instructed concerning self-examination of the breasts. A complete rectovaginal evaluation is required.

Profuse vaginal discharge is usually not present at 4–6 weeks postpartum unless there is an associated vaginitis, which will generally respond to specific treatment. Nursing mothers may show a hypoestrogenic condition of the vaginal epithelium. Prescription of a vaginal estrogen cream to be applied at bedtime should relieve local dryness and coital discomfort without the side-effects of systemic estrogen therapy. The cervix should be inspected and a Papanicolaou smear obtained. When minimal cervicitis or eversion is present, mild acetic acid douches or application of an antibiotic vaginal cream (eg, Sultrin Triple Sulfa Cream) may be all that is necessary. If there is persistent eversion of the squamocolumnar junction, the patient should return for treatment by cervical cauterization or cryotherapy.

The episiotomy incision and repaired lacerations must be examined and the adequacy of pelvic and perineal support noted. Bimanual examination of the uterus and adnexa is indicated. Most patients have some degree of retrodisplacement of the uterus at the postpartum examination that may soon correct itself.

Asymptomatic retroposition of the uterus is not regarded as an abnormal condition. If pain, abnormal bleeding, or other symptoms are present, a vaginal pessary may be inserted as a trial procedure to encourage anteversion of the fundus. However, pessary support for long periods of time is not recommended. In the absence of pelvic disease, uterine retrodisplacement rarely if ever requires surgical correction. If marked uterine descensus is noted or if the patient develops stress incontinence, symptomatic cystocele, or rectocele, surgical correction should be considered. Hysterectomy or vaginal repair is best postponed for at least 3 months after delivery to allow maximal restoration of the pelvic supporting structures.

The patient may resume full activity or employment if her course to this point has been uneventful. Once again, the patient should be advised regarding family planning and contraceptive practices. A further gynecologic and cytologic examination is desirable about 6 months after delivery. The rapport established between the obstetrician and the patient during the prenatal and postpartum periods provides a unique opportunity to establish a preventive health program in subsequent years.

LACTATION

PHYSIOLOGY

The mammary glands are modified exocrine glands that undergo dramatic anatomic and physiologic changes during pregnancy and in the immediate puerperium. Their role is to provide nourishment for the newborn and to transfer antibodies from mother to infant.

During the first half of pregnancy, proliferation of alveolar epithelial cells, formation of new ducts, and development of lobular architecture occur. Later in pregnancy, proliferation declines, and the epithelium differentiates for secretory activity. At the end of gestation, each breast will have gained approximately 400 g. Factors contributing to increase in mammary size include hypertrophy of blood vessels, myoepithelial cells, and connective tissue; deposition of fat; and retention of water and electrolytes. Blood flow is almost double that of the nonpregnant state.

The mammary gland has been called the mirror of the endocrine system, because lactation depends upon a delicate balance of several hormones. An intact hypothalamic-pituitary axis is essential to the initiation and maintenance of lactation. Lactation can be divided into 3 stages: (1) mammogenesis, or mammary growth and development; (2) lactogenesis, or initiation of milk secretion; and (3) galactopoiesis, or maintenance of established milk secretion (Table 37–2). Estrogen is responsible for the growth of ductular tissue and alveolar budding, whereas progesterone is required for optimal maturation of the alveolar glands. Glandular stem cells undergo differentiation into secretory and myoepithelial cells under the influence of prolactin, growth hormone, insulin, cortisol, and an epithelial growth factor. Although alveolar secretory cells actively synthesize milk fat and proteins from mid pregnancy onward, only small amounts are released into the lumen. However, lactation is possible if pregnancy is interrupted during the second trimester.

Prolactin is an obligatory hormone for milk production, but lactogenesis also requires a low estrogen environment. Although prolactin levels continue to rise as pregnancy advances, placental sex steroids block prolactin-induced secretory activity of the glandular epithelium. Therefore, lactation is not initiated until plasma estrogens, progesterone, and human placental lactogen (hPL) fall after delivery. Progesterone inhibits the biosynthesis of lactose and α-lactalbumin; estrogens impede the release of milk secretions into the alveolar lumen. hPL may also exert a prolactin-antagonist effect through competitive binding to alveolar prolactin receptors.

The maintenance of established milk secretion requires periodic suckling and the actual emptying of ducts and alveoli. Growth hormone, cortisol, thyroxine, and insulin exert a permissive effect. Prolactin is required for galactopoiesis, but high basal levels are not mandatory, because prolactin concentrations in the nursing mother decline gradually during the late puerperium and approach that of the nonpregnant state. However, if a woman does not suckle her baby, her serum prolactin concentration will return to nonpregnant values within 2–3 weeks. If the mother suckles twins simultaneously, the prolactin response is about double that when one baby is fed at a time, illustrating an apparent synergism between the number of nipples stimulated and the frequency of suckling. The mechanism by which suckling stimulates prolactin release probably involves the inhibition of dopamine, which is thought to be the hypothalamic prolactin-inhibiting factor (PIF).

Stimulation of the nipples by suckling or other physical stimuli evokes a reflex release of oxytocin from the neurohypophysis. The release of oxytocin is mediated by afferent fibers of the fourth to sixth intercostal nerves via the dorsal roots of the spinal cord to the midbrain. The paraventricular and supraoptic neurons of the hypothalamus make up the final afferent pathway of the milk ejection reflex. The central nervous system modulates the release of oxytocin; stress or fear may inhibit the letdown reflex, whereas the cry of an infant may provoke it. Oxytocin levels may rise during orgasm, and sexual stimuli may trigger milk ejection.

SYNTHESIS OF HUMAN MILK

Milk is secreted by apocrine (with pinching-off of the cellular apex) and porous merocrine (with no change in cellular morphology) processes. The principal carbohydrate in human milk is lactose. Glucose metabolism is a key function in human milk production, because lactose is derived from glucose and galactose; the latter originates from glucose 6-phosphate. A specific protein, α-lactalbumin, catalyzes lactose synthesis. This rate-limiting enzyme is inhibited by progesterone during pregnancy. Prolactin and insulin, which enhance the uptake of glucose by mammary cells, also stimulate the formation of triglycerides. Fat synthesis takes place in the endoplasmic reticulum. Most proteins are synthesized de novo in the secretory cells from essential and nonessential plasma amino

Table 37–2. Multihormonal interaction in mammary growth and lactation.

Mammogenesis	Lactogenesis	Galactopoiesis
Estrogens	Prolactin	↓ Gonadal hormones
Progesterone	↓ Estrogens	Suckling (oxytocin, prolactin)
Prolactin	↓ Progesterone	Growth hormone
Growth hormone	↓ hPL (?)	Glucocorticoids
Glucocorticoids	Glucocorticoids	Insulin
Epithelial growth factor	Insulin	Thyroxine and parathyroid hormone

Arrows signify that lower than normal levels of the hormone are necessary for the effect to occur.

acids. The formation of milk protein and mammary enzymes is induced by prolactin and enhanced by cortisol and insulin.

Mature human milk contains 7% carbohydrate as lactose, 3–5% fat, 0.9% protein, and 0.2% mineral constituents expressed as ash. Its energy content is 60–75 kcal/dL. About 25% of the total nitrogen of human milk represents nonprotein compounds, eg, urea, uric acid, creatinine, and free amino acids. The principal proteins of human milk are casein, α-lactalbumin, lactoferrin, IgA, lysozyme, and albumin. Milk also contains a variety of enzymes that may contribute to the infant's digestion of breast milk, eg, amylase, catalase, peroxidase, lipase, xanthine oxidase, and alkaline and acid phosphatase. The fatty acid composition of human milk is rich in palmitic and oleic acids and varies somewhat with the diet. The major ions and mineral constituents of human milk are Na^+, K^+, Ca^{2+}, Mg^{2+}, Cl^-, phosphorus, sulfate, and citrate. Calcium concentrations vary from 25 to 35 mg/dL and phosphorus concentrations from 13 to 16 mg/dL. Iron, copper, zinc, and trace metal contents vary considerably. All of the vitamins except vitamin K are found in human milk in nutritionally adequate amounts. The composition of breast milk is not greatly affected by race, age, or parity and does not differ between the 2 breasts unless one is infected.

Colostrum, the premilk secretion, is a yellowish alkaline secretion that may be present in the last months of pregnancy and for the first 2–3 days after delivery. It has a higher specific gravity (1.040–1.060); a higher protein, vitamin A, immunoglobulin, and sodium and chloride content; and a lower carbohydrate, potassium, and fat content than mature breast milk. Colostrum has a normal laxative action and is an ideal natural starter food.

Ions and water pass the membrane of the alveolar cell in both directions. Human milk differs from milk of many other species by having a lower concentration of monovalent ions and a higher concentration of lactose. The aqueous phase of milk is isosmotic with plasma; thus, the higher the lactose, the lower the ion concentration. The ratio of potassium to sodium is 3:1 in both milk and mammary intracellular fluid. Because milk contains about 87% water and lactose is the major osmotically active solute, it follows that milk yield is largely determined by lactose production.

IMMUNOLOGIC SIGNIFICANCE OF HUMAN MILK

The neonate is immunologically immature, and maternal antibody will bolster the infant's defenses against infection. The transfer of IgG is accomplished during fetal life chiefly by active transport across the placenta. All classes of immunoglobulins are found in milk, but IgA comprises 90% of immunoglobulins in human colostrum and milk. The output of immunoglobulins by the breast is maximal in the first week of life and declines thereafter as the production of milk-

specific proteins increases. Lacteal antibodies against enteric bacteria and their antigenic products are largely of the IgA class. IgG and IgA lacteal antibodies provide short-term systemic and long-term enteric humoral immunity to the breast-fed neonate. IgA anti-poliomyelitis virus activity present in breast-fed infants indicates that at least some transfer of milk antibodies into serum does occur. However, maternal lacteal antibodies are absorbed systemically by human infants for only a very short time after birth. Long-term protection against pathogenic enteric bacteria is provided by the adsorption of lacteal IgA to the intestinal mucosa. In addition to providing passive immunity, there is evidence that lacteal immunoglobulins can modulate the immunocompetence of the neonate, but the exact mechanisms have not been described. For instance, the secretion of IgA into the saliva of breast-fed infants is enhanced in comparison with bottle-fed controls.

Breast milk also contains more than 100,000 blood cells per milliliter, most of which are leukocytes. The total cell count is even higher in colostrum. In human milk, the leukocytes are predominantly mononuclear cells and macrophages. Both T and B lymphocytes are present. The immunologic value of the lymphoid and reticuloendothelial cells in human milk is yet to be clarified, but data from animal experiments indicate that maternal lymphocytes can be incorporated into the suckling's tissues and function in a variety of immunologic contexts. In humans, the evidence is circumstantial and is based on the transfer of tuberculin sensitivity to infants from their tuberculin-positive mothers and on the greater histocompatibility between mother and infant compared with that between father and infant. Finally, sensitized T lymphocytes and other immunocompetent cells in mammary secretions may protect the breast itself against bacterial colonization.

Elements in breast milk other than immunoglobulins and cells have prophylactic value against infections. The marked difference between the intestinal flora of breast-fed and bottle-fed infants is due to a dialyzable nitrogen-containing carbohydrate (bifidus factor) that supports the growth of *Lactobacillus bifidus* in breast-fed infants. The stool of bottle-fed infants is more alkaline and contains predominantly coliform organisms and *Bacteroides* sp. *L bifidus* inhibits the growth of *Shigella* sp, *Escherichia coli*, and yeast. Human milk also contains a nonspecific antimicrobial factor, lysozyme (a thermostable and acid-stable enzyme that cleaves the peptidoglycans of bacteria), and a "resistance factor," which protect the infant against staphylococcal infection. Lactoferrin, an iron chelator, exerts a srong bacteriostatic effect on staphylococci and *E coli* by depriving the organisms of iron. Both C3 and C4 components of complement are found in human milk. Unsaturated vitamin B_{12}-binding protein in milk renders the vitamin unavailable for utilization by *E coli* and *Bacteroides*. Finally, interferon in milk may provide yet another nonspecific anti-infection factor.

Human milk may also have prophylactic value in childhood food allergies. During the neonatal period, permeability of the small intestine to macromolecules is increased. Secretory IgA in colostrum and breast milk reduces the absorption of foreign macromolecules until the endogenous IgA secretory capacity of the newborn intestinal lamina propria and lymph nodes develops at 2–3 months of age. Protein of cow's milk can be highly allergenic in the infant predisposed by heredity. The introduction of cow's milk-free formulas (Table 36–5) has considerably reduced the incidence of milk allergy. Thus, comparative studies on the incidence of allergy, bacterial and viral infections, severe diarrhea, necrotizing enterocolitis, tuberculosis, and neonatal meningitis in breast-fed and bottle-fed infants support the concept that breast milk fulfills a protective function.

ADVANTAGES & DISADVANTAGES OF BREAST FEEDING

For the Mother

A. Advantages: Breast feeding is economical, and it is emotionally satisfying to most women. It helps to contract the uterus and accelerates the process of uterine involution in the postpartum period. It promotes mother-infant bonding. According to epidemiologic studies, breast feeding may help to protect the suckled breast against cancer.

B. Disadvantages and Contraindications: Regular nursing restricts activities and may be perceived by the mother as an inconvenience. In cultures in which nursing in public is commonplace, nursing is less inconvenient. Twins can be nursed successfully, but few women are prepared for the first weeks of almost continual feeding. Cesarean section may necessitate modifications of early breast-feeding routines. Difficulties such as nipple tenderness and mastitis may develop. There are few absolute contraindications other than breast cancer. Augmentation mammoplasty with silicone implants should not affect breast feeding, but reduction mammoplasty involving nipple autotransplantation severs the lactiferous ducts and precludes nursing.

For the Infant

A. Advantages: Breast milk is digestible, available at the right temperature, and free of bacterial contamination. The composition is ideal, it has anti-infectious properties, and there are fewer allergy problems in breast-fed infants. Breast-fed infants are not so likely to become obese as are formula-fed babies. Suckling promotes infant-mother interactions and bonding.

B. Contraindications: Absolute contraindications to breast feeding are breast cancer; active pulmonary tuberculosis in the mother; severe mastitis; or maternal intake of antithyroid medications, cancer chemotherapeutic agents, or certain other drugs (Table 37–3). Hepatitis B antigen has been found in breast milk, but transmission by this route is unlikely to occur. Breast feeding is not usually possible for the weak, ill, or very premature infant or for the infant with cleft palate, choanal atresia, or phenylketonuria.

ANTENATAL PREPARATION FOR BREAST FEEDING

Patient education and the decision to breast-feed should ideally be accomplished in the prenatal period. The first step in patient education is to explain to the mother the advantages and disadvantages of nursing the infant. The next step is instruction in preparation techniques.

The attitudes of the mother and those about her are especially important. If she regards breast feeding as abnormal, unclean, or embarrassing, no amount of persuasion or antenatal preparation will influence the outcome, particularly if she is compelled to nurse. In contrast, a woman who has a very strong desire to breast-feed her baby may succeed even if her breasts are small and the nipples poorly protractile. Antenatal discussion of the patient's desire is most important. In some cases, the maternal instinct does not become strong until after the baby is born. A woman may have no inclination toward breast feeding during pregnancy, but she may change her mind after delivery. The patient who is antagonistic to the idea of breast feeding—especially if she has been unsuccessful in the past—should be assured that she will not be obliged to breast-feed after her present delivery. This may eliminate a major source of anxiety and guilt.

Although many methods of preventing breast and nipple problems have been advocated, the majority of women have never used any type of antenatal breast preparation. No convincing evidence exists that successful lactation depends on the application of this cream or that lotion. Moreover, it is doubtful whether one can "toughen" the skin of the nipples successfully, although tenderness may be reduced by washing and by the application of hydrous lanolin or similar unguents. Alcohol, benzoin tincture, and other drying agents should not be used on the nipples, because they remove natural skin oils and may do more harm than good by causing irritation and fissures. Support of the enlarged breast is important to prevent "sagging" following pregnancy.

Flat or inverted nipples the baby cannot grasp may cause failure of nursing. Gentle traction by the patient may elevate the nipples during the latter part of pregnancy, but some nipple protraction during gestation should be expected even without special manipulation. Nipple shields worn under a brassiere during the last trimester have been recommended for retracted nipples.

Regular gentle manual expression of colostrum during the final weeks of pregnancy may be of value in the initiation of lactation. Emptying the breasts during the puerperium is beneficial, and the patient may learn the technique before painful engorgement occurs.

Table 37–3. Transmission of drugs and toxins in breast milk.

	Drug Transfer to Milk	Drug-Induced Neonatal Problem	Comment re Use in Nursing Women
Anticoagulants			
Dicumarol	Very slight	...	Acceptable
Warfarin (Coumadin)	Traces	...	Acceptable
Phenindone (Hedulin)	?Significant	Bleeding.	Contraindicated
Antihypertensive diuretics			
Guanethidine (Ismelin)	Minimal	...	Acceptable
Propranolol (Inderal)	Minimal	...	Acceptable
Chlorthalidone (Hygroton)	Significant	Diuresis.	Contraindicated
Chlorothiazide (Diuril)	Significant	Thrombocytopenia.	Contraindicated
Antimicrobials			
Chloramphenicol (Chloromycetin)	Significant	Induction of "gray disease" in neonate. Bone marrow suppression.	Contraindicated
Metronidazole (Flagyl)	Significant	Blood dyscrasias. Neurologic disorders.	Contraindicated
Penicillins, aminoglycosides	Moderate	...	Safe
Tetracycline	?Significant	Permanent discoloration of teeth.	Contraindicated
Sulfonamides	Varies with product	G6PD anemia or kernicterus with Rh or ABO incompatibility.	Use with caution
Nalidixic acid (NegGram)	Significant	G6PD anemia.	Contraindicated
Pyrimethamine	Significant	Vomiting, marrow suppression. Thrombocytopenia.	Contraindicated
Quinine	Significant	Thrombocytopenia occasionally.	Use with caution
Chloroquine	None	...	Safe
Antithyroid Drugs			
^{131}I and other radioactive products	Very significant	Permanent athyreosis.	Contraindicated
Thiouracils	Significant	Hypothyroidism.	Contraindicated
Drugs affecting central nervous system			
Alcohol	Slight	Sedative, pseudo–Cushing's disease.	May use in small amounts occasionally
Chloral hydrate	Minimal	...	Safe
Meprobamate	4 × plasma level	Sedation.	Contraindicated
Diazepam (Valium)	Moderate	Sedation.	Use judiciously
Lithium	1/3–1/2 plasma level	Hypotonia, hypothermia, cyanosis, ECG changes.	Contraindicated
Phenothiazines	?Significant	Drowsiness.	Use cautiously
Phenobarbital	?Significant	Hepatic microsomal enzymes produced.	Minimal dosage safe
Phenytoin (Dilantin)	Minimal	...	Safe
Propoxyphene (Darvon)	Minimal	...	Safe
Aspirin	?Significant	Altered platelet function.	Safe in small doses
Morphine	Significant	Narcotic addiction.	Contraindicated
Methadone	Significant	Narcotic addiction.	Contraindicated
Heroin	Significant	Narcotic addiction.	Contraindicated
Codeine	Minimal	...	Safe
Caffeine	Moderate	Irritability.	Avoid excessive doses
Nicotine (tobacco smoking)	?Significant	...	?Safe
Hormones			
Insulin	None	...	
Corticotropin	None	...	Safe
Ephedrine	None	...	Safe
Thyroxine	Slight to moderate	...	Safe
Oral contraceptives	?Significant	Gynecomastia in males. ?Carcinogenic.	Probably safe
Laxatives			Contraindicated
Phenolphthalein	Significant	Loose stools.	Safe in small doses
Cascara sagrada	Significant	Loose stools.	Safe in small doses

A popular method of manual expression consists of 2 movements. The first is compression of the whole breast between the hands, starting at the margins and continuing inward as far as the areola. Firm pressure is maintained throughout this movement, which is repeated 10 times. Its object is to move colostrum from the finer into the larger ducts and the lacteal sinuses. The second movement is designed to empty the sinuses. The latter are pinched sharply and repeatedly between the thumb and forefinger of one hand while the breast is held firmly in the other hand. Success in expelling colostrum depends on the direction in which the force of the pinch is applied. The force must be directed somewhat backward, toward the center of the breast, rather than toward the base of the nipple.

PRINCIPLES & TECHNIQUES OF BREAST FEEDING

The interrelationships of mother, father, baby, and environment (including the medical personnel who care for mother and baby in the prenatal and postnatal periods) influence the nursing experience. Consideration must be given to (1) the mother's attitude toward nursing and her emotional status, breast anatomy, and general health; (2) the father's interest; (3) conditions in the home; and (4) the baby's maturity, normality, weight, vigor, and appetite. Each case must be managed individually, using the guidelines outlined below.

In the absence of anatomic or medical complications, the timing of the first feeding and the frequency and duration of subsequent feedings largely determine the outcome of breast feeding. Infants and mothers who are able to initiate breast feeding in 1–2 hours after delivery are more successful than are those whose initial interactions are delayed for several hours. Suckling has a propitious oxytocic effect, and colostrum is good for the newborn. Unfortunately, feeding may be delayed by hospital routine or custom. Lactation is established most successfully if the baby remains with the mother and she can feed it on demand for adequate intervals throughout the first 24-hour period. The initial feeding should last 5 minutes at each breast in order to condition the letdown reflex. At first, the frequency of feedings may be very irregular (8–10 times a day), but after 1–2 weeks a fairly regular 4- to 6-hour pattern will emerge. When the milk "comes in" abruptly on the third or fourth postpartum day, there is an initial period of discomfort caused by vascular engorgement and edema of the breasts. The baby does not nurse so much by developing intermittent negative pressure as by a rhythmic grasping of the areola; the infant "works" the milk into its mouth. Little force is required in nursing, because the breast reservoirs can be emptied and refilled without suction. Nursing mothers notice a sensation of drawing and tightening within the breast at the beginning of suckling after the initial breast engorgement disappears. They are thus conscious of the milk ejection reflex, which may even cause milk to spurt or run out.

Some women expend a great deal of emotion on the subject of breast feeding, and a few are almost overwhelmed by fear of being unable to care for their babies in this way. If attendants are sympathetic and patient, however, a woman who wants to nurse usually can do so. Attendants must be certain that the baby "fixes" on (actually over) the nipple and the areola so as to feed properly without pain to the mother (Fig 37–9).

The baby should nurse at both breasts at each feeding, because overfilling of the breasts is the main deterrent to the maintenance of milk secretion. Nursing at only one breast at each feeding inhibits the reflex that is provoked simultaneously in both breasts. Thus, nursing at alternate breasts from one feeding to the next may increase discomfort due to engorgement and reduce milk output. It is helpful for the mother to be taught to empty the breasts after each feeding; a sleepy baby may not have accomplished this. The use of supplementary formula or other food during the first

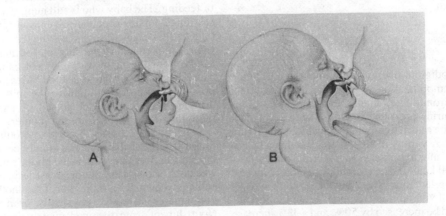

Figure 37–9. Mechanism of suckling in the neonate. *A:* Tongue moves forward to draw nipple in as glottis still permits breathing. *B:* Tongue moves along nipple, pressing it against palate with glottis closed. Ductules under the areola are compressed, and milk flow begins. The cheeks fill the mouth and provide negative pressure.

6–8 weeks of breast feeding can interfere with lactation and should be avoided except when absolutely necessary. The introduction of an artificial nipple, which requires a different sucking mechanism, will weaken the sucking reflex required for breast feeding. Some groups such as the La Leche League recommend that other fluids be given by spoon or dropper rather than by bottle.

In preparing to nurse, the mother should (1) wash her hands with soap and water, (2) clean her nipples and breasts with water, and (3) assume a comfortable position in, preferably, a rocking or upright chair. If the mother is unable to sit up to nurse her baby because of painful perineal sutures, she may feel more comfortable lying on her side. A woman with large pendulous breasts may find it difficult to manage both the breasts and the baby. If the baby lies on a pillow, the mother will have both hands free to guide the nipple.

Each baby nurses differently; however, the following procedure is generally successful:

(1) Allow the normal newborn to nurse at each breast on demand or approximately every 3–4 hours, for 5 minutes per breast per feeding the first day. Over the next few days, gradually increase feeding time to initiate the letdown reflex, but do not exceed 10–15 minutes per breast. Suckling for longer than 15 minutes may cause maceration and cracking of the nipples and thus lead to mastitis.

(2) Compression of the periareolar area and expression of a small amount of colostrum or milk for the baby to taste may stimulate it to nurse.

(3) Try to keep the baby awake by moving or patting, but do not snap its feet, work its jaw, push its head, or press its cheeks.

(4) Place the nipple well back in the baby's mouth so that it rests against the palate and the baby can compress the periareolar area with its jaws. The breast should be held away from the baby's nostrils.

(5) Before removing the infant from the breast, gently open its mouth by lifting the outer border of the upper lip to break the suction.

After nursing, gently wipe the nipples with water and dry them.

MILK YIELD

The prodigious energy requirements for lactation are met by mobilization of elements from maternal tissues and from dietary intake. Physiologic fat stores laid down during pregnancy are mobilized during lactation, and the return to prepregnant weight and figure is promoted. A variety of studies suggest that a lactating woman should increase her normal daily food intake by 600 kcal/d. The recommended daily dietary increases for lactation are 20 g of protein; a 20% increase in all vitamins and minerals except folic acid, which should be increased by 50%; and a 33% increase in calcium, phosphorus, and magnesium. There is no evidence that increasing fluid intake will increase milk volume. Fluid restriction also has little effect, because urine output will diminish in preference to milk output.

With nursing, average milk production on the second postpartum day is about 120 mL. The amount increases to about 180 mL on the third postpartum day and to as much as 240 mL on the fourth day. In time, milk production reaches about 300 mL/d.

A good rule of thumb for the calculation of milk production for a given day in the week after delivery is to multiply the number of the postpartum day by 60. This gives the approximate number of milliliters of milk secreted in that 24-hour period.

Assuming that all goes well, sustained production of milk will be achieved by most patients after 10–14 days. A yield of 120–180 mL per feeding is common by the end of the second week. When free secretion has been established, marked increases are possible; a wet nurse can often suckle 3 babies successfully for weeks.

Early diminution of milk production often is due to failure to empty the breasts because of weak efforts by the baby or ineffectual nursing procedures; emotional problems, such as aversion to nursing; or medical complications, eg, mastitis, debilitating systemic disease, Sheehan's syndrome. Late diminution of milk production results from too generous complementary feedings of formula, emotional or other illness, and pregnancy.

Adequate rest is essential for successful lactation. Sometimes it is difficult to ensure an adequate milk yield if the mother is working outside the home. If it is not possible to rearrange the nursing schedule to fit the work schedule or vice versa, it may be necessary to empty the breasts manually or by pump. The Loyd-B-Pump is a simple hand-triggered pump easy to carry in a large handbag. The Egnell Breast Pump is a larger, more sophisticated, and costlier piece of equipment for use on the maternity floor. Milk output can be estimated by weighing the infant before and after feeding. If there has been a bowel movement during feeding, the baby should be weighed before the diaper is changed.

The baby's behavior, sleep periods, and the character of its stools are the best measures of success of feeding. The baby who is still hungry at the end of a session of nursing should be given water and should be patted to expel gas. It should also be fed earlier the next time. Supplementary feeding of formula should be reserved for the baby who does not gain weight because it cannot get enough food. Measures that are popularly supposed to improve the milk supply (eg, drinking beer, eating rich foods) probably do little more than relax or reassure the mother.

It may be necessary to substitute bottle feeding for breast feeding if the mother's supply continues to be inadequate (less than half of the infant's needs) after 3 weeks of effort; if nipple or breast lesions are severe enough to prevent pumping; or if the mother is either pregnant or severely (physically or mentally) ill. Nourishment from the inadequately lactating breast can be augmented with the Lact-Aide Nursing Trainer, a device that provides a supplemental source of milk via a plastic capillary tube placed beside the breast and suckled simultaneously with the nipple. Disposable plastic bags serve as reservoirs, and the supplemental milk is warmed by hanging the bag next to the mother. The Lact-Aide supplementer has also been used to help nurse premature infants and to reestablish lactation after untimely weaning due to illness. Further study is needed to evaluate the safety of galactagogues, eg, chlorpromazine and metoclopramide. The long-term success of breast feeding is increased by a structured home support system of postnatal visiting by allied health personnel or experienced volunteers.

DISORDERS OF LACTATION

Painful Nipples

Tenderness of the nipples, a common symptom during the first days of breast feeding, generally begins when the baby starts to suck. As soon as milk begins to flow, nipple sensitivity usually subsides. If maternal tissues are unusually tender, dry heat may help between feedings. Nipple shields should be used only as a last resort, since they interfere with normal sucking. Glass or plastic shields with rubber nursing nipples are preferable to shields made entirely of rubber.

Nipple fissures cause severe pain and prevent normal letdown of milk. Local infection around the fissure can lead to mastitis. Unless the fissures heal, lactation will fail. The application of vitamin A and D ointment or hydrous lanolin, which do not have to be removed, is often effective. Benzoin tincture is a traditional remedy for cracked nipples, but this gummy substance may occlude the nipple ducts and should not be used. Dilute silver nitrate is much too irritating to be recommended. To speed healing, the following steps are recommended. Apply dry heat for 20 minutes 4 times a day with a 60-watt bulb held 18 inches away from the nipple. Conduct prefeeding manual expression. Begin nursing on the side opposite the fissure with the other breast exposed to air to allow the initial letdown to occur atraumatically. Apply expressed breast milk to nipples and let it dry on between feedings. If necessary, use a nipple shield while nursing, and take aspirin with or without codeine just after nursing. On rare occasions, it may be necessary to stop nursing temporarily on the affected side and to empty the breast either manually or by gentle pumping. If a painful fissure persists or recurs despite therapy, the success of breast feeding is remote, and suppression of lactation is indicated.

A cause of chronic severe sore nipples without remarkable physical findings is candidal infection. Prompt relief is provided by topical nystatin cream. Thrush or candidal diaper rash or maternal candidal vaginitis must be treated as well.

Engorgement

Engorgement of the breasts occurs in the first week postpartum and is due to vascular congestion and accumulation of milk. The primiparous patient and the patient with inelastic breasts are more prone to engorgement. Vascularity and swelling increase on the second day after delivery; the areola or breast may become engorged. Prepartum breast massage and around-the-clock demand feedings help to prevent engorgement in these patients. When the areola is engorged, the nipple is occluded and proper grasping of the areola by the infant is not possible. With moderately severe engorgement, the breasts become firm and warm, and the lobules may be palpable as tender, irregular masses. Considerable discomfort and, often, a slight fever can be expected, and the patient may become frustrated and tearful. All this is a threat to milk production.

Mild cases may be relieved by aspirin or other analgesics, cool compresses, and partial expression of the milk before nursing. In severe cases, administer hypnotics, and have the patient empty the breasts manually. The patient should support the breast with her fingers and with her thumbs distally and massage gently toward the areola. When the peripheral lobules have been softened, areolar expression is carried out. Hand pumps exert negative pressure only on the areola and must be accompanied by massage of the distal lobules. The Egnell mechanical pump simulates the stroking action of the infant's tongue. Oxytocin—by injection or intranasally—to augment the milk letdown reflex may help certain patients with engorged breasts. Nevertheless, persistent engorgement carries a poor prognosis, and suppression of lactation may be necessary.

Mastitis

Mastitis occurs most frequently in primiparous nursing patients and is usually caused by coagulase-positive *Staphylococcus aureus*. High fever should never be ascribed to simple breast engorgement alone. Inflammation of the breast seldom begins before the fifth day postpartum. Most commonly, symptoms of a painful erythematous lobule in an outer quadrant of the breast are noted during the second or third week of the puerperium. Inflammation may occur with weaning when the flow of milk is disrupted, or the nursing mother may acquire the infection during her hospital stay, and it is then transmitted to the infant. Many infants harbor an infection and, in turn, infect the mother's breast during nursing. Neonatal streptococcal infection should be suspected if mastitis is recurrent or bilateral. In a recent series of breast abscesses, 70% of the infants had furunculosis. Prevention of breast infection requires meticulous breast hygiene. If a fissure of the nipple develops, a nipple shield should be tried in order to allow nursing to continue. Infection may be limited to the subareolar region but more frequently involves an obstructed lactiferous duct and the surrounding breast parenchyma. If cellulitis is not properly treated, a breast abscess may develop. When only mastitis is present, it is best to prevent milk stasis by continuing breast feeding (unless fissures are present) or by using a breast pump. Apply local heat, provide a well-fitted brassiere, and institute appropriate antibiotic treatment. Cephalosporins, methicillin sodium, and cloxacillin sodium are the antibiotics of choice to combat penicillinase-producing bacteria. The dosage of cloxacillin is 500 mg every 6 hours for 1–3 days until symptoms subside and then 250 mg every 6 hours for a total of 10 days.

Pitting edema over the inflamed area and some degree of fluctuation are evidence of abscess formation. It is necessary to incise and open loculated areas and provide wide drainage. In contrast to mastitis, continuing breast feeding is not recommended in the presence of a breast abscess.

Miscellaneous Complications

A galactocele, or milk-retention cyst, is caused by the blockage of a milk duct. Diagnosis may be made by mammography. The cyst may be aspirated but will fill up again. It can be removed surgically under local anesthesia without discontinuing nursing. Sometimes the infant will reject one or both breasts. Strong foods such as beans, cabbage, turnips, broccoli, onions, garlic, or rhubarb may cause aversion to milk or neonatal colic. A common cause of nursing problems is maternal fatigue.

Transmission of Drugs in Breast Milk

The benefits of prescribing drugs for the breast-feeding mother must be weighed against the potential hazards of the drug to the infant. As a general rule, administration of a drug immediately after the infant suckles will result in a lower concentration of the substance in the milk at the next feeding. Drugs that can be given in a single daily dose should be taken just prior to the infant's longest sleep period. The quantity of a drug that will be ingested by a breast-fed neonate can be estimated if one knows the concentration of the drug in the breast milk. Infants take an average of 165 mL/kg/d of milk. The maximal daily drug dose ingested can be calculated as peak milk level × 165 mL/kg/d.

The physicochemical determinants of the rate of passage of a drug into milk are pK_a and lipid solubility (oil/water partition coefficient). Compounds that exist primarily in the ionized form at physiologic pH diffuse slowly into milk, as do compounds which are extensively protein-bound. Highly lipid-soluble drugs pass more rapidly into milk than do more water-soluble ones. For the most part, drugs are transported more efficiently across the placenta than into breast milk.

Drugs that may have an adverse effect on lactation include oral contraceptive steroids, ergot derivatives, and pyridoxine (vitamin B_6) in large doses. Drugs that may have an adverse effect on the breast-fed infant when taken by the mother include anticancer agents; certain antimicrobials such as chloramphenicol, metronidazole, nitrofurantoin, and sulfonamides; antithyroid drugs such as propylthiouracil and methimazole; and diazepam and other tranquilizers in protracted use. Heparin does not appear in milk and is safe to use during lactation. The safety of thiazide diuretics is controversial. The excretion characteristics and compatibility with breast feeding of various pharmacologic compounds are given in Table 37–3.

INHIBITION & SUPRESSION OF LACTATION

Despite a recent upsurge in breast feeding in Western countries, there are many women who will not or cannot breast-feed and others who fail in the attempt. Supervised lactation inhibition is desirable in the event of fetal or neonatal death as well. Approximately half of parturients are candidates for postpartum lactation suppression.

The oldest and simplest method of suppressing lactation is to stop nursing, to avoid nipple stimulation, to refrain from expressing or pumping the milk, and to bind the breasts snugly for 48–72 hours. Ice bags and analgesics are helpful. Patients who receive no medication will complain of breast engorgement (45%), pain (45%), and leaking breasts (55%). Although the breasts will become considerably engorged and the patient may experience discomfort, the collection of milk in the duct system will suppress its production, and resorption will occur. After approximately 2–3 days, engorgement will begin to recede, and the patient will be comfortable again.

A variety of naturally occurring and synthetic estrogens used alone or in combination with an androgenic hormone are effective in suppressing lactation. Antiestrogenic compounds, eg, clomiphene (100 mg orally daily for 5 days), will also inhibit lactation postpartum, probably by reducing prolactin secretion. Estrogens probably suppress galactopoiesis at the level of breast tissue, since estrogens stimulate rather than inhibit prolactin release. Estrogenic compounds have been shown to be superior to placebo in relieving breast engorgement and milk leakage. However, rebound lactation has been noted in some patients 8–10 days after cessation of estrogen therapy.

Diethylstilbestrol and ethinyl estradiol are the cheapest estrogens used to inhibit lactation. A typical diethylstilbestrol regimen calls for 10 mg 3 times a day on the first day, 5 mg 3 times a day on the second and third days, 5 mg twice a day on the fourth and fifth days, and 5 mg once a day on the sixth and seventh days—for a total of 90 mg in 7 days. Quinestrol (5 mg orally) is effective as a lactation suppressant; so is chlorotrianisene (Tace) in a dosage of 72 mg orally twice a day for 2 days. The rebound secretion of milk is perhaps less marked with single-dose therapy than with the week-long course of oral estrogens. When estrogen preparations are used alone, lactation can be suppressed and painful breast engorgement prevented in approximately 75% of patients.

The possibility that estrogen therapy during the puerperium may increase the incidence of venous thromboembolism is supported by certain retrospective studies, but not all groups of patients are equally affected. Specifically, the risk of thromboembolic disease is not increased in women under 25 years of age who have had a normal delivery, but it is increased 10-fold in women over 35 years who have had a cesarean section and received estrogens. Although estrogens probably are not contraindicated in most normal patients, their use for lactation suppression should be discouraged, because other pharmacologic methods are safer and more effective.

Combinations of estrogen and androgen have been used in order to improve the effect of estrogens alone. The most successful regimen is to inject intramuscularly the following after the first stage of labor: 3 mL of a solution containing (in oil, per milliliter) 90 mg of testosterone enanthate and 4 mg of estradiol valerate. This procedure prevents symptoms in 90% of patients. Despite the speculation that such hormone combinations might lead to virilization, this or other undesirable side-effects have not been observed, and this medication is not associated with significant thromboembolic risk in the young patient who has delivered vaginally.

Lactation suppression by inhibiting prolactin secretion with synthetic ergot alkaloids such as bromocriptine (Parlodel) is safe and highly effective both immediately postpartum and after lactation has been established. Bromocriptine is a specific dopamine receptor agonist that has a direct action on the anterior pituitary lactotropes to inhibit prolactin secretion. Because it accelerates the natural postpartum fall in prolactin, it suppresses both lactogenesis and galactopoiesis. Bromocriptine is, on physiologic grounds, the most logical medication to use, but it requires prolonged therapy and is not without unpleasant side-effects. The recommended dosage is 2.5 mg orally twice daily for 2 weeks after vital signs have stabilized, beginning no sooner than 4 hours after delivery. A substantial minority of patients complain of nasal congestion, mild constipation, nausea, headache, dizziness, and postural hypotension. In the event of side-effects, the daily dose can be halved. Recent reports suggest that oral tablets of prostaglandin E_2 (2 mg every 6 hours on the fourth and fifth days postpartum) are effective inhibitors of milk secretion and breast engorgement. The mechanism of action is not known, but a PGE_2-induced decrease in prolactin may be mediated by hypothalamic dopaminergic neurons.

INAPPROPRIATE LACTATION

Galactorrhea refers to the inappropriate and persistent mammary discharge of a fluid that is usually milky or clear but may be yellow or even greenish in color. It may involve both breasts or just one breast. Even minimal galactorrhea should be evaluated in a nulliparous woman and, if at least 12 months have passed since the last pregnancy, in a parous woman. Amenorrhea does not necessarily accompany galactorrhea.

The differential diagnosis of galactorrhea syndrome is complex (see Chapter 6) because many factors influence prolactin secretion. Inappropriate lactation is frequently present in both sexes with acromegaly and, more rarely, with myxedema. In some forms of hypothyroidism, hypothalamic TRH is produced in excess and acts as a prolactin-releasing factor. Galactorrhea may occur after thoracoplasty, cervical spinal lesions, herpes zoster, or excessive nipple stimulation by activating the afferent neural arc. Abnormal lactation occurs rarely with estrogen-secreting adrenal tumors, corpus luteum cysts, and choriocarcinoma. Occasionally, fluid leakage from the breast will occur after discontinuation of oral contraceptives.

A variety of drugs (phenothiazine derivatives, benzodiazepines, butyrophenones, methyldopa, and tricyclic antidepressants) can deplete hypothalamic dopamine levels or block dopamine receptors, thereby stimulating prolactin release. Several eponyms have been applied to the galactorrhea syndromes—inappropriate lactation with intrasellar tumor (Forbes-Albright), antecedent pregnancy with persistent galactorrhea (Chiari-Frommel), and galactorrhea in the absence of previous pregnancy (Ahumada-del Castillo). Regardless of clinical circumstances, persistent galactorrhea demands a serum prolactin assay and polytomographic recording of the sella turcica to exclude pituitary adenoma.

• • •

References

Anatomy and Physiology of the Puerperium

Baird DT et al: Failure of estrogen-induced discharge of luteinizing hormone in lactating women. *J Clin Endocrinol Metab* 1979;**49**:500.

Dawood MY et al: Oxytocin release and plasma anterior pituitary and gonadal hormones in women during lactation. *J Clin Endocrinol Metab* 1981;**52**:678.

Graeff H et al: Amount and distribution pattern of soluble fibrin monomer complexes during the early puerperium. *Am J Obstet Gynecol* 1976;**124**:21.

Hornnes PJ, Kuhl C: Plasma insulin and glucagon responses to isoglycemic stimulation in normal pregnancy and postpartum. *Obstet Gynecol* 1980;**55**:425.

Howie PW et al: The relationship between suckling-induced prolactin response and lactogenesis. *J Clin Endocrinol Metab* 1980;**50**:670.

Keye WR, Jaffe RB: Changing patterns of FSH and LH response to gonadotropin releasing hormone in the puerperium. *J Clin Endocrinol Metab* 1976;**42**:1133.

McNeilly AS: Prolactin and the control of gonadotrophin secretion in the female. *J Reprod Fertil* 1980;**58**:537.

Moore P et al: Insulin binding in human pregnancy: Comparisons to the postpartum, luteal and follicular states. *J Clin Endocrinol Metab* 1981;**52**:937.

Pipkin FB, Oats JJN: Sequential changes in the human renin angiotensin system following delivery. *Br J Obstet Gynaecol* 1978;**85**:821.

Potter JM, Nestel PJ: The hyperlipidemia of pregnancy in normal and complicated pregnancies. *Am J Obstet Gynecol* 1979;**133**:165.

Sheehan KL, Yen SSC: Activation of pituitary gonadotropic function by an agonist of luteinizing hormone–releasing factor in the puerperium. *Am J Obstet Gynecol* 1979;**135**:755.

Van Rees D, Bernstine RL, Crawford W: Involution of the postpartum uterus: An ultrasonic study. *J Clin Ultrasound* 1981;**9**:55.

Ylikorkala O, Viinikka L: Thromboxane A$_2$ in pregnancy and puerperium. *Br Med J* 1980;**281**:1601.

Complications of the Puerperium

Brandt P, Jerpersen J, Gregersen G: Postpartum haemolytic-uraemic syndrome treated with antithrombin-III. *Nephron* 1981;**27**:15.

Davidson NM, Parry EHO: Peri-partum cardiac failure. *Q J Med* 1978;**47**:431.

Eschenbach DA, Wager GP: Puerperal infections. *Clin Obstet Gynecol* 1980;**23**:1003.

Filker R, Monif GRG: The significance of temperature during the first 24 hours postpartum. *Obstet Gynecol* 1979;**53**:358.

Hertz RH, Sokol RJ, Dierker LRJ: Treatment of postpartum uterine atony with prostaglandin E$_2$ vaginal suppositories. *Obstet Gynecol* 1980;**56**:129.

Kincaid-Smith PS, Fairley KF: The changing spectrum of acute renal failure in pregnancy and the post-partum period. *Contrib Nephrol* 1981;**25**:159.

Lee CY, Madrazo B, Drukker BH: Ultrasonic evaluation of the postpartum uterus in the management of postpartum bleeding. *Obstet Gynecol* 1981;**58**:227.

Platt R et al: Infection with *Mycoplasma hominis* in postpartum fever. *Lancet* 1980;**2**:1217.

Sibai BM et al: The late postpartum eclampsia controversy. *Obstet Gynecol* 1980;**55**:74.

Sugrue D et al: Antibiotic prophylaxis against infective endocarditis after normal delivery: Is it necessary? *Br Heart J* 1980;**44**:499.

Watson P, Besch N, Bowes WA: Management of acute and subacute puerperal inversion of the uterus. *Obstet Gynecol* 1980;**55**:12.

Yabu Y et al: Postpartum recurrence of hyperthyroidism and changes of thyroid-stimulating immunoglobulins in Graves' disease. *J Clin Endocrinol Metab* 1980;**51**:1454.

Conduct of the Puerperium

Edgar WM, Hambling MJ: Rubella vaccination and anti-D immunoglobulin administration in the puerperium. *Br J Obstet Gynaecol* 1977;**84**:754.

Freda VJ et al: Prevention of Rh hemolytic disease: Ten years' clinical experience with Rh-immune globulin. *N Engl J Med* 1975;**292**:1014.

Fuller WE: Family planning in the postpartum period. *Clin Obstet Gynecol* 1980;**23**:1081.

Kowalski K: Managing perinatal loss. *Clin Obstet Gynecol* 1980;**23**:1113.

Mabray CR: Postpartum examination: A reevaluation. *South Med J* 1979;**72**:1433.

Lactation

Anderson PO: Drugs and breast feeding. *Semin Perinatol* 1979;**3**:271.

Aono T et al: Augmentation of puerperal lactation by oral administration of sulpiride. *J Clin Endocrinol Metab* 1979;**48**:478.

Jelliffe DB, Jelliffe EFP: "Breast is best": Modern meanings. *N Engl J Med* 1977;**297**:912.

Kochenour NK: Lactation suppression. *Clin Obstet Gynecol* 1980;**23**:1045.

Lawrence RA: *Breast-Feeding: A Guide for the Medical Profession.* Mosby, 1980.

McNeilly AS: Effects of lactation on fertility. *Br Med Bull* 1979;**35**:151.

Nasi A et al: Inhibition of lactation by prostaglandin E$_2$. *Clin Exp Obstet Gynecol* 1979;**6**:255.

Pitt J: Breast milk and the high-risk baby: Potential benefits and hazards. *Hosp Pract* (May) 1979;**14**:81.

Pittard WB, Bill K: Immunoregulation by breast milk cells. *Cell Immunol* 1979;**42**:437.

Platzker ACD, Lew CD, Stewart D: Drug "administration" via breast milk. *Hosp Pract* (Sept) 1980;**15**:111.

Salariya EM, Easton PM, Cater JI: Duration of breast-feeding after early initiation and frequent feeding. *Lancet* 1978;**2**:1141.

Vorherr H: Pregnancy and lactation in relation to breast cancer risks. *Semin Perinatol* 1979;**3**:299.

Wenlock RW: Birth spacing and prolonged lactation in rural Zambia. *J Biosoc Sci* 1977;**9**:481.

West CP, McNeilly AS: Hormone profiles in lactating and nonlactating women immediately after delivery and their relationship to breast engorgement. *Br J Obstet Gynaecol* 1979;**86**:501.

Medical & Surgical | 38
Complications During Pregnancy

Ralph C. Benson, MD

DERMATOLOGIC PROBLEMS

Many physiologic changes that occur during pregnancy are manifested in the skin. Some skin disorders occur only with pregnancy, and others are merely temporally associated with pregnancy. Pregnancy has an ameliorating effect on a few skin disorders, and a larger number are aggravated by pregnancy. The response is unpredictable in many cases. Pregnancy is generally reported as having a beneficial effect on acne, psoriasis, and seborrheic dermatitis and to aggravate adenoma sebaceum, pyogenic granuloma, candidal vulvovaginitis, acne vulgaris (early in pregnancy), scleroderma, erythema multiforme, dermatitis herpetiformis, granuloma inguinale, condyloma acuminatum, pemphigus, and neurofibromatosis. Dermatologic problems whose response to pregnancy is unpredictable include atopic dermatitis, lupus erythematosus, sarcoidosis, and herpes simplex.

Normal changes require little more than explanation and reassurance. Abnormal conditions, however, may pose serious problems in diagnosis and treatment.

SKIN CHANGES PECULIAR TO PREGNANCY

Chloasma (Melasma, Melanoderma, "Mask of Pregnancy")

Chloasma is a roughly symmetric, sharply demarcated area of confluent yellowish to dark brown skin pigmentation over the temples, forehead, nose, and malar prominences that develops in at least two-thirds of white women during late pregnancy and sometimes with oral contraceptive therapy. Brunets and women with dark complexions are usually more susceptible.

Chloasma is induced by ultraviolet light and is the result of increased production and central, perinuclear aggregation of cytoplasmic melanin pigment granules in the dermal cells. It is apparently a response to an increase of melanocyte-stimulating hormone during well-established pregnancy. However, predisposition as well as high levels of estrogen and progestogen seem to be essential to the changes.

The patient should be instructed to avoid direct sunlight if possible or to use a sunscreen preparation.

Cosmetics should be of the nonallergenic type. No perfumed preparations should be used on the face lest photosensitization occur. In severe cases, combination oral contraceptives postpartum may prolong melasma.

Treatment is unreliable, but hydroquinone cream 2% (Eldoquin) applied nightly or Eldopaque used on bright sunny days may speed the clearing of chloasma. However, dermatitis, hyperpigmentation or leukoderma may follow use of these medications.

Erythema Palmare

Erythema palmare is characterized by diffuse reddish mottling of the palms and suffused skin over the thenar and hypothenar eminences and the fleshy portions of the tips of the fingers. It occurs in over 50% of pregnant women. Genetic predisposition and hyperestrogenism may be responsible.

No treatment is necessary. The erythema disappears about 1 week after delivery.

Vascular Spiders (Angiectids, Spider Angiomas)

Very small, stellate or branched, slightly raised, faintly pusating (arteriolar) telangiectactic points, most notable in the skin of the neck, thorax, face, and arms (in that order), may develop during the second or third trimester of pregnancy in many patients. These "spiders" are abnormally large end-arterioles of the skin. A vascular defect and high levels of estrogen reportedly cause these asymptomatic abnormalities, which fade slowly during the late puerperium but rarely disappear completely.

Opaque creams may conceal vascular spiders in exposed areas. Electrodesiccation with a fine needle applied to the center of the spider will neatly destroy persistent punctate points. No anesthesia is necessary, and the cosmetic result is good.

Striae Gravidarum ("Stretch Marks")

Striae gravidarum are irregular, linear, pink to purple, slightly depressed, finely wrinkled stripes in the skin of the lower abdomen, buttocks, breasts, thighs, and upper arms. They often appear during the last half of pregnancy. Striae develop in the vast majority of white women but are uncommon in blacks or Orientals. They may occur without pregnancy as a result of rapid development of obesity or with hyperadrenocorticism.

Weakening of collagenous or elastic fibers together with loss of ground substance in the subdermal tissues in a predisposed patient are the responsible factors. Striae probably are secondary to enhanced activity and secretion of adrenocortical hormones. Although stretching of the skin may influence distribution of the striae, it is not the cause.

Striae fade during the puerperium and finally appear as thin silver scars. There is no treatment. The normal obstetric patient can be reassured that the marks have no adverse medical connotation.

Gingivitis & Epulis

Nonspecific gingivitis often develops after the third to fourth months of pregnancy. Hyperemia, hypertrophy, bleeding, and tenderness may be so marked as to suggest scurvy. Estrogen stimulation causes selective increased vascularity and connective tissue proliferation. Secondary infection may be responsible for the inflammation. Epulis can become an area of trauma and is comparable to pyogenic granuloma, which may be especially troublesome during pregnancy.

Treat infections and avitaminosis and remove dental calculus and other pathologic factors.

The gingivitis of pregnancy and small nodules of epulis disappear spontaneously 1–2 months after delivery.

Noninflammatory Pruritus of Pregnancy (Spangler)

Idiopathic papular pruritic dermatitis of pregnancy, a rare generalized eruption of 3- to 5-mm crimson papules, may appear at any time during pregnancy. It is associated with abnormally high chorionic gonadotropic hormone but low cortisol levels and presumably a high perinatal mortality rate. This disorder must be differentiated from noninflammatory cholestasis of pregnancy, which is not papular. Systemic corticosteroid therapy may be beneficial. Occasionally, fetal deaths have been ascribed to this disorder. Symptomatic treatment with preparations such as trimeprazine (Temaril) is indicated.

Prurigo of Pregnancy (Besnier's Prurigo)

Prurigo of pregnancy refers to the gradual appearance in the midtrimester of small, closely aggregated, pruritic papules of unknown cause. They appear on the extensor surfaces of the extremities and across the upper back, spreading slowly to the chest and abdomen. There is no maternal or fetal toxicity from this disorder.

Topical antipruritic medications and mild sedation are helpful. The rash usually disappears within 1 week after delivery, leaving small pigmented areas.

Hair Growth & Loss During Pregnancy & the Puerperium

The rate of hair growth and its distribution are unpredictable during pregnancy. Generally, the growing or anagen hairs increase markedly in number and hair loss decreases with pregnancy. Gravid women have increased, fine lanugo hairs on the face, arms, and legs and over the trunk, similar to that of patients who have received prolonged corticosteroid therapy. These changes probably are due to increased ACTH and adrenocorticosteroid secretion and augmented ovarian androgen production in response to chorionic gonadotropin stimulation during pregnancy.

Anagen hairs are far outnumbered by telogen or resting hairs after delivery. There is diffuse hair loss 2–3 months following delivery, undoubtedly the result of endocrine and metabolic alterations. The **telogen effluvium** is similar to hair loss that occurs after a critical infection or serious emotional crisis. Assuming that there are no significant health problems, a complete reconstitution of hair growth should occur within 6 months after delivery. Hair gain or loss is unrelated to the number of pregnancies.

Reassurance and attention to hygiene, especially proper care of the scalp and hair, are important. Correction of metabolic aberrations (eg, hypothyroidism, anemia) and elimination of emotional stress are essential.

Herpes Gestationis

Herpes gestationis probably is a hyperimmune reaction, as evidenced by marked eosinophilia, but it certainly is not caused by the herpesvirus. The disorder complicates about 1:4000 gestations. It is characterized by a chronic polymorphous pruritic rash and systemic symptoms. It usually develops after the fifth month of pregnancy, but flares often occur immediately postpartum or premenstrually for up to 6 months.

The skin changes generally begin as a periumbilical, patchy erythema, associated with itching or burning. Groups of vesicles and bullae soon appear. Partially encrusted exudative areas are typical. The generalized lesions heal with local hyperpigmentation.

One must differentiate herpes gestationis from other pruritic disorders that may occur during pregnancy, eg, impetigo herpetiformis, dermatitis herpetiformis, erythema bullosum, drug reactions, and allergies.

Herpes gestationis may be relieved by prednisone, 10–30 mg orally daily in divided doses (or equivalent).

The maternal prognosis is good. Spontaneous cure 6–8 weeks postpartum is the rule. The perinatal mortality rate may reach 30%. Transient lesions similar to the mother's have been described in the newborn. Herpes gestationis may recur in or skip subsequent pregnancies.

Pruritic Urticarial Papules & Plaques of Pregnancy

This newly described, intensely pruritic cutaneous eruption of late pregnancy is of unknown origin. Symptoms include numerous erythematous urticarial papules and myriads of minute plaques. These lesions appear in the third trimester first on the abdomen and spread to involve the thighs and, at times, the buttocks and arms; the face is never involved. Biopsy specimens from the lesions have no immunofluorescent features and are not specifically diagnostic, but biopsy aids in the differential diagnosis, which includes herpes gestationis, prurigo gravidarum, and papular dermatitis of pregnancy. Biopsy specimens from the lesions should reveal deposits of complement in the region of the basement membrane with immunofluorescent staining. High blood levels of IgG and C3 and, occasionally, IgA are typical. Corticosteroid therapy is moderately helpful, and the dermatitis improves rapidly after delivery. Months later, occasional patients have slight itching of the hands—a few during menses. The fetus is not threatened, and the neonate will be free of skin abnormalities. Because of the small number of patients followed thus far, the risk of recurrence of the disorder in subsequent gestations is uncertain.

SKIN DISORDERS THAT MAY OCCUR DURING PREGNANCY

Impetigo Herpetiformis

Impetigo herpetiformis is an uncommon but extremely serious dermatosis, usually associated with well-established pregnancy. The cause is unknown, but it may be either a variant of psoriasis with marked systemic symptoms or an extensive pyoderma complicating dermatitis herpetiformis.

Small grouped pustules on an inflammatory base first appear in the intertriginous areas and on the mucous membranes. The eruption soon spreads to produce extensively exudative, bleeding, crusted areas of denudation over the abdomen, chest, and flexor surfaces of the arms and legs. Itching is minimal. Chills, fever, nausea, tetany, and pain often precede death of the fetus, mother, or both. The fetus is not marked by the dermatitis.

Adrenal corticosteroids, calcium and vitamin D, and supportive therapy, including soothing baths or lotions, may be lifesaving. Interruption of pregnancy has been reported to be beneficial.

Dermatitis Herpetiformis

This rare recurrent, persistent, occasionally pruritic or painful polymorphous eruption has no known cause, but an autoimmune reaction is suspected. It may erupt during pregnancy. The fetus is unaffected. The disease may be differentiated from herpes gestationis on the basis of histologic and immunologic criteria. Treatment during pregnancy is symptomatic only.

Erythema Multiforme

This inflammatory dermatitis, which is a symptom complex of herpes simplex in some cases, may have its onset during pregnancy. Patients are not very ill, but a low-grade fever and leukocytosis often accompany the red, vesicopustular, maculopapular rash that appears over the extensor surfaces of the extremities. A vesicomucosal eruption may develop in the mouth, throat, or vagina. Mucosal lesions often show concentric rings of various colors, eg, "erythema iris," but this is seen more often in nonpregnant than in pregnant patients. Spontaneous resolution can be anticipated following delivery. Meanwhile, symptomatic relief should be provided. The fetus will show no skin lesions in erythema multiforme.

Stevens-Johnson Syndrome

This rare disorder is characterized by mucocutaneous lesions similar to those of erythema multiforme but with severe constitutional symptoms. It is a severe, often fatal disease, in contrast to the usual erythema multiforme. The cause is unknown, but an allergic reaction to sulfonamides, penicillin, or other drugs may be responsible in some cases. Stevens-Johnson syndrome usually begins abruptly with sore mouth and throat, malaise, a high fever, and tachycardia followed by a vesicobullous eruption of the skin and mucous membranes and arthralgia. An intense conjunctivitis then develops. Bronchopneumonia and blindness due to corneal ulcerations may be complications. The mortality rate is 8–10%.

Treatment consists of adrenocorticosteroids, antibiotics to the conjunctiva and vagina, antihistaminics, and application of soothing soaks such as Burow's solution. The prognosis must be guarded; fetal death often occurs, and partial vaginal obstruction by synechiae may ensue if the patient survives.

Neurofibromatosis (Recklinghausen's Disease)

Pregnancy has a severely aggravating effect on this autosomal dominant hereditary disorder. Café au lait spots and myriads of new cutaneous (and other) nodules may appear during pregnancy; fibromas already present usually increase in size. Pelvic fibromas may become so large or numerous that they cause soft tissue dystocia at term. Other complications involve tumors of the central nervous system or mediastinum and sarcomatous degeneration.

No medical therapy is feasible. Therapeutic abortion and sterilization may be warranted.

Pemphigus

Pemphigus is a rare, chronic bullous dermatitis. It is aggravated by pregnancy and is often fatal. The cause is not known. The onset is insidious. Crusted lesions of the palms, superficial ulceration of the tongue, and acute conjunctivitis are typical. Bullae may develop anywhere over the body, and raw surfaces then coalesce so that extensive areas are often denuded. The patient generally has eosinophilia and leukocytosis. Relative adrenal insufficiency may be suspected, and with secondary infection fever is common. There have been reports of bullous eruptions on the newborn, and an increased perinatal mortality rate is associated with maternal pemphigus. Intensive corticosteroid and broad-spectrum antibiotic treatment is recommended.

CARDIOVASCULAR COMPLICATIONS

HEART DISEASE

Congenital heart disease has now surpassed rheumatic carditis as a complication of pregnancy in the USA. Syphilitic carditis rarely occurs. The reported incidence of heart disease varies from 0.5 to 2% of obstetric patients.

Heart disease is a major cause of maternal death, but maternal and perinatal mortality rates are only slightly increased if the disability is minimal. With marked degrees of cardiac disease, the maternal death rate is 1–3% and the perinatal mortality rate may reach 50% even in large medical centers.

Functional Classification of Heart Disease*

For practical purposes, the functional capacity of the heart is the best single measurement of cardiopulmonary status:

Class I: Ordinary physical activity causes no discomfort.

Class II: Ordinary activity causes discomfort and slight disability.

Class III: Less than ordinary activity causes discomfort or disability; patient is barely compensated.

Class IV: Patient decompensated; any physical activity causes acute distress.

Eighty percent of obstetric patients with heart disease have lesions that do not interfere seriously with their activities (classes I and II) and usually do well. About 85% of deaths ascribed to heart disease complicating pregnancy occur in patients with class III or IV lesions (20% of all pregnant patients with heart disease). Nevertheless, much can still be done to improve the prognosis for the mother and her baby in these unfavorable circumstances.

Pathologic Physiology

The effects of pregnancy on circulatory and respiratory function (Table 38–1) produce both symptoms and physical signs which mimic those of heart disease.

The presence of any of the following symptoms may occur in the absence of heart disease: pedal edema, breathlessness at rest or with exertion, including orthopnea and paroxysmal nocturnal dyspnea, palpitations, and fatigue.

Similarly, the presence of any of the following signs may occur in the absence of heart disease: sinus tachycardia, atrial premature beats, ventricular premature beats, split pulmonary second sound, widened pulse pressure, systolic (but not diastolic) murmurs, rales, abnormal electrocardiogram with axis shift or abnormal T waves, and x-ray evidence of cardiomegaly (usually with elevation of the diaphragm) or

*New York Heart Association, 1964.

Table 38–1. Effect of pregnancy on maternal circulatory and respiratory functions.*

Function	Change
Heart rate	Slow increase of 10 beats/min from 14 to 30 weeks. Rate maintained at this level to 40 weeks.
Arterial blood-pressure	Systolic unchanged until the 30th week. Diastolic slightly reduced (period of maximum pulse pressure).
Venous blood-pressure	Arms: No change. Legs: Gradual marked increase between 8 and 40 weeks.
Cardiac output	Increase of 30–50% by the 20th week is maintained until 32nd week, then slight decline.
Total body water	Increased between 10 and 40 weeks.
Plasma and blood volume	Rise of 25% between 12 and 32 weeks; slight decline to 40 weeks.
Red cell mass	Augmented 10–15% between 8 and 40 weeks.
Vital capacity	Rises 15% by the 20th week; decline of 5% by 40 weeks.
Oxygen consumption	Increased 15% between 16 and 40 weeks.
Circulation time	Decreases from 13 to 11 seconds by 32nd week; returns to 13 seconds by 40th week.

*Reproduced, with permission, from Benson RC: *Handbook of Obstetrics & Gynecology,* 7th ed. Lange, 1980.

prominence of the pulmonary conus. Diagnosis may require serial examinations throughout the pregnancy.

Three major burdens on the heart are associated with pregnancy: Cardiac output is increased by more than one-third; the pulse rate is accelerated by about 10 beats per minute; and blood volume expands by about 25%. These unavoidable stresses must be considered in an appraisal of the patient's ability to undergo pregnancy, delivery, and the puerperium.

In addition to these unavoidable physiologic burdens, there are medical liabilities that are avoidable or can be treated, eg, anemia, obesity, hyperthyroidism, myxedema, infection, and emotional and physical stresses. The peaks of physical stress occur at about the 32nd week of pregnancy and during labor.

Youth, adequate functional cardiac reserve, stability of the cardiac lesion, and an optimistic, cooperative attitude are important assets that do much to improve the cardiac patient's chances for a successful confinement. Good antenatal care and help at home are essential features of the total medical program. The physician must help the pregnant cardiac patient to avoid overburdening the heart. Unnecessary stresses must be eliminated or drastically curtailed so that the patient's good qualities will tip the scales favorably to preserve health and avoid cardiac disaster.

Labor, delivery, and the early puerperium impose the following physiologic burdens on the maternal heart:

A. During Labor and Delivery: Cardiac patients generally tolerate labor well.

1. A rise in pulse rate with the beginning of each

contraction. This is the reaction of the heart to intermittent work.

2. Slowing of the pulse at the end of each contraction.

3. Return of the pulse to the resting level between contractions.

4. Intermittent increase of oxygen consumption with uterine contractions, approaching that of moderate to severe exercise.

5. Tachycardia during the second stage may result from distention of the right atrium and ventricle by blood from the uterus and from the effect of straining.

B. During the Puerperium:

1. A slight increase in cardiac output occurs for about 1 week after delivery. Elimination of the placenta, contracture of the uterus, and reduction of the pelvic circulation suddenly makes more blood available to the heart.

2. Decrease in the plasma volume (hematocrit increase) for 12 hours after delivery is due primarily to readjustments in venous pressure. A second marked decrease in plasma volume persists for 7–9 days together with a reduction in the amount of total body water during the same period. These changes are due to postpartum diuresis.

Treatment

A cardiologist should be in attendance. Determine the functional class of the cardiac disorder before the third month if possible and again at 7–8 months. Restrict physical activity to necessary duties only, using fatigue as the limiting factor. Make certain that the patient obtains assistance with essential household duties (child care, laundry, cleaning, and marketing). Help the patient and her family to understand the medical problem, and allay her anxieties. Periods of maximal cardiac stress occur from 14 to 32 weeks, during labor, and particularly during the immediate postpartum period. Especially good rapport and medical control must be maintained at these times.

Stable or inactive heart disease, such as mitral stenosis, mitral insufficiency, mitral valve replacement, and congenital defects require serial observations of functional cardiac status. In addition, stable valvular or septal lesions will require antibiotic prophylaxis to prevent implantation of bacteria on scarred endocardial surfaces (infective endocarditis). Bacteremia following dental extractions or during urinary tract infections and active labor justifies antibiotic protection initiated before these procedures (or when the problem is diagnosed) and continued for 3–10 days.

Rheumatic myocarditis or valvular disease that has been inactive in the past 3 years can be reactivated by streptococcal infections. Low-dosage oral penicillin daily throughout pregnancy usually will prevent reactivation of rheumatic fever and myocarditis.

The incidence of active rheumatic or viral myocarditis has increased recently. Mycoarditis and infective endocarditis have appeared in drug users. Recognition of febrile disease or maladies with changing murmurs may alert the clinician to these entities.

Treatment with rest and salt restriction as in the nonpregnant state is indicated. The use of digitalis and steroids is controversial and must be individualized.

Peripartum cardiomyopathy, which until now has been classified as a nonspecific entity, either has increased in incidence or is being recognized with greater frequency. The appearance of classic symptoms and signs of heart failure with cardiac enlargement by x-ray, occasionally at term and usually early in the postpartum period, may establish the diagnosis. Severe restriction of activity is mandatory, possibly with additional corticosteroid therapy.

A. Medical Measures: Correct anemia, hyperthyroidism, and obesity as indicated. Treat cardiac complications such as congestive failure, pulmonary edema, infective endocarditis, and arrhythmia as in the nonpregnant patient. Prevent and treat preeclampsia-eclampsia. Treat all infections specifically, promptly, and vigorously. Intercurrent respiratory, gastrointestinal tract, or urinary tract infections can be serious. Restrict sodium intake and use diuretics, but not to the point of hyponatremia. Avoid hypokalemia.

B. Obstetric Measures:

1. Prevent complications of labor, delivery, and the puerperium.

2. Administer full doses of analgesics as necessary, but do not give scopolamine, since it may cause excitement and overactivity.

3. Delivery should be under local or regional anesthesia if possible. Administer oxygen freely during labor and in the early puerperium, when tachycardia, dyspnea, and chest pain are most severe.

4. Shorten the terminal stage of labor by elective low forceps delivery to spare the patient the effort of bearing down in the second stage. Do not intervene too early, however, or lacerations, excessive blood loss, and shock may occur.

5. Manage the third stage of labor carefully to limit postpartum bleeding. Do not administer ergot preparations (to avoid a drug pressor effect), and give oxytocin cautiously if necessary after delivery to prevent (or treat) uterine atony.

6. Lower the patient's legs promptly after delivery to reduce drainage of blood into the general circulation.

7. Anticipate the possibility that some women who have experienced no cardiac symptoms during pregnancy or labor sometimes go into shock or acute cardiac failure immediately after delivery owing to the sudden engorgement of the splanchnic vessels. Treat for hypovolemic shock and acute cardiac failure if these develop.

8. A Class I or II patient may nurse if she wishes.

9. Prescribe cautious, brief, early ambulation for patients with class I–III functional disability provided the medical course is otherwise uncomplicated. Class I patients may be sent home at the same time as patients without complications.

10. Patients with class II–IV functional disability should remain in the hospital after delivery until the

cardiovascular function is stable. Class IV patients must remain in bed for as long as necessary to recover from the effects of labor and delivery.

11. Before discharge, make certain that the patient is returning to a favorably controlled home situation where adequate rest in a nonstressful milieu will be possible. Recommend contraception and discuss sterilization, particularly for class II–IV patients.

C. Surgical Measures:

1. Therapeutic abortion may be indicated in 5–8% of cases of heart disease complicating pregnancy. The decision to abort is not based upon the presence of any specific lesion but on a thorough evaluation of the patient's total life situation, including the type and severity of the heart disease, other medical illnesses, and religious and emotional factors. Patients who have had cardiac failure in a previous pregnancy will usually have failure again with another pregnancy and so should be aborted if this is acceptable. Abortion is seldom beneficial after the fourth month but may be considered (see Chapter 23). Of course, there are risks in abortion, too, that cannot be disregarded.

2. If the cardiac lesion is severe enough to warrant abortion and if surgical treatment is not available and there is little prospect that therapeutic advances will alter the situation favorably, sterilization is indicated. If the patient is not sterilized, strict pregnancy prevention must be employed.

3. Mitral valvotomy is indicated only in patients with severe mitral valve stenosis who also have insufficient myocardial reserve to withstand the stress of pregnancy, even with ideal supportive therapy. In general, patients who have had cardiac decompensation in a previous pregnancy will again develop heart failure. Mitral valvotomy can be performed during the fourth, fifth, or sixth month of pregnancy with excellent results and should be considered in this group.

Open heart surgery for cyanotic heart disease should be considered with some urgency. Open heart surgery for congenital septal defects should be considered if the shunt is large or if pulmonary hypertension is present. Cardiac catheterization is justified in this group when cardiac surgery is seriously contemplated.

Open heart surgery is a danger for the fetus because of hypoxia despite a well-functioning heart-lung bypass.

4. Cesarean section is not recommended for the pregnant cardiac patient unless it is performed for primarily obstetric reasons. The contractions of labor contribute to the progressive obliteration of the placental arteriovenous shunt and thereby protect the heart from the abrupt overload of the surgical obliteration of the shunt. A woman who can withstand a major operation can undergo vaginal delivery.

Prognosis

The maternal and fetal prognosis in heart disease complicating pregnancy depends upon the severity of the heart disorder, the availability of medical and obstetric care, medical and surgical complications, the patient's emotional, socioeconomic, and environmen-

tal status, and local policy regarding therapeutic abortion and sterilization. Although rheumatic heart disease is not exacerbated by successive pregnancies, the increased load of pregnancy and care of an infant by a cardiac patient frequently will worsen the patient's clinical status.

Congenital heart disease with **pressure load,** without shunt (including idiopathic hypertrophic subaortic stenosis, aortic stenosis, coarctation of the aorta, and pulmonary stenosis), is associated with hemodynamic problems, including heart failure and syncope, and an increased incidence of fetal death and of babies with congenital anomalies.

Congenital heart disease with **volume load** (left-to-right shunts, including patent ductus arteriosus, interatrial septal defect, interventricular septal defect, and congenital mitral insufficiency) is usually tolerated well. However, if the shunt is large or if pulmonary hypertension is present, the added arteriovenous shunt of the placenta may be sufficient to increase the hemodynamic burden and produce heart failure. A large interatrial septal defect shunt may be reversed by pulmonary hypertension produced by respiratory infection, pulmonary emboli, or asthma, especially during labor or in early postpartum hours, and may cause cyanosis and death.

Congenital heart disease with **hypoxia,** including cyanotic heart disease with right-to-left shunt and pulmonary hypertension (Eisenmenger's syndrome), as in tetralogy of Fallot or transposition of the great vessels or pulmonary hypertension with large interatrial septal defects, implies a high incidence of maternal and fetal death. Surgery produces the best result in this group but does not eliminate the risk of childbearing.

The maternal mortality rate for all types of heart disease is 0.5–3% in large medical centers in the USA, and heart disease accounts for 5–10% of all maternal deaths.

The perinatal mortality rate (including fetal deaths due to therapeutic abortion) largely depends upon the functional severity of the mother's heart disease:

Mother's Functional Disability	Perinatal Mortality Rate
Class I	About 5%
Class II	10–15%
Class III	About 35%
Class IV	Over 50%

The incidence of congenital defects is greater among infants delivered of women with congenital and syphilitic heart disease than among those delivered of women with normal hearts, but rheumatic and other types of heart disease do not increase the incidence of fetal anomalies.

CARDIAC ARREST*

Cardiac arrest is cessation of heart action as a result of acute myocardial hypoxia or alteration in conduction. Ventricular standstill (asystole) and ventricular fibrillation are the immediate causes. Cardiac arrest occurs most commonly during induction of anesthesia and during operative surgery or instrumental delivery. Cardiovascular disease increases the risk of cardiac arrest; hypoxia and hypertension are contributory causes. Cardiac arrest may follow shock (hypovolemia or another type), hypoxia, airway obstruction, excessive anesthesia, drug administration or drug sensitivity, vagovagal reflex activity, myocardial infarction, air and amniotic fluid embolism, and heart block.

Cardiac arrest occurs about once in 800–1000 operations and is apt to occur during minor surgical procedures as well as during major surgery. It occurs about once in 10,000 obstetric deliveries—usually operative, complicated cases. Fortunately, it is possible to save up to 75% of patients when cardiac arrest occurs in the well-equipped operating or delivery room.

Clinical Findings

Premonitory signs (especially during induction of anesthesia, intubation or extubation, moving the patient, deep or prolonged anesthesia, hypoxia or hypotension with vagotonic effect) consist of irregular cardiac rhythm, bradycardia, and sudden or marked hypertension. Cyanosis (difficult to perceive in black women), absence of a palpable pulse in a major artery (aorta, carotid, femoral), absence of heart sounds over the precordium, and dilatation of the pupils are diagnostic of cardiac arrest. Emergency treatment should not be withheld for electrocardiographic confirmation of the diagnosis. (See Figs 20–2 and 20–3.)

Prevention

Ensure a constant, generous oxygen supply during induction of anesthesia and throughout surgery and delivery.

Avoid undesirable vagal effects: (1) Give atropine routinely before surgery or delivery. (2) Give atropine, 0.5–0.6 mg intravenously, for bradycardia, atrioventricular dissociation, or atrioventricular nodal rhythm. (3) Avoid placing extensive traction on the viscera during surgery or on the fetus during delivery. (4) Do not administer vasopressors such as epinephrine or ephedrine during trichloroethylene anesthesia.

Treat excessive blood loss or hypotension promptly and effectively.

VARICOSE VEINS

Varicosities are usually a problem of the multipara and may cause severe complications. They are

---

*A fuller discussion, including emergency management, is given in Chapter 20.

caused by congenital weakness of the vascular walls; increased venous stasis in the legs owing to the hemodynamics of pregnancy; extensive collateral circulation in the pelvis; inactivity and poor muscle tone; and obesity, since the excessive tissue mass requires increased circulation, and fatty infiltration of connective tissue impairs vascular support.

Serious phlebothrombosis and thrombophlebitis or embolization often complicate the puerperium but are uncommon during pregnancy when pulmonary emboli are rare.

The vulvar, vaginal, and even the inguinal veins may be markedly enlarged during pregnancy. Damaged vulvovaginal vessels give rise to hemorrhage at delivery.

Large vulvar varices cause pudendal discomfort. A vulvar pad wrapped in plastic film, snugly held by a menstrual pad belt or T-binder and elastic leotards, gives relief.

Anticoagulants may be required in acute thrombophlebitis. Heparin is preferred to dicumarol, since it does not cause fetal damage, is more easily controlled, and is not excreted in the milk. Fortunately, whether anticoagulants are administered before or during labor, increased bleeding from the uterus is not common, since efficient mechanical compression of the myometrial vessels prevents excessive blood loss despite increased blood coagulation time. Cervical, vaginal, and perineal lacerations may bleed more briskly if the patient has received heparin or dicumarol.

Injection treatment of varicose veins during pregnancy is futile and hazardous. Varicose veins secondary to causes other than pregnancy, eg, deep vein thrombosis, congenital arteriovenous fistula, are difficult to control.

Vascular surgery can be performed during the first or second trimester, but vein stripping is best delayed until after the puerperium. In all other respects, management is the same as in nonpregnant women.

PREVENTION & TREATMENT OF ESSENTIAL HYPERTENSION COMPLICATED BY PREGNANCY (HCP)

Hypertensive disease may be "essential" (vascular); it may be of renal or endocrine origin; or it may be a feature of preeclampsia. It may be difficult to determine whether or not hypertension in a pregnant woman precedes or derives from the pregnancy if she is not examined until after the 20th week and there is no reliable medical history. Preeclampsia often is superimposed upon hypertensive disease, but the signs of preeclampsia-eclampsia do not persist for more than 6 weeks after parturition. In questionable cases, the patient should be treated as having had preeclampsia, so that cardiovascular, renal, or other appropriate studies can be performed 3 months after delivery.

Pregnant women with probable hypertensive disease require antihypertensive drugs only if the diastolic pressure is sustained at or above 110 mm Hg. One should strive to keep the diastolic pressure between 90 and 100 mm Hg. However, if the pressure is over 110 mm Hg, do not attempt to lower it quickly by more than 25%. Diuretic drugs should be avoided, since they reduce the effectiveness of other antihypertensive agents and may be harmful to the fetus.

If the hypertensive patient is under medical treatment when she registers for antenatal care, one may continue the antihypertensive medication and withdraw the diuretic agent. For initiation of treatment, it is best to admit the patient to the hospital for assessment. If she is near term, one may begin with hydralazine, 25 mg orally daily, and increase the dosage as indicated. If the response is unsatisfactory or if the patient is not near term, give methyldopa, 250 mg orally twice daily, again increasing in divided doses as needed to as much as 2 g daily.

Therapeutic abortion may be indicated in cases of severe hypertension during pregnancy. If pregnancy is allowed to continue, the risk to the fetus must be assessed periodically in anticipation of early delivery.

Maternal indications for early delivery include the following: (1) suddenly developing, poorly controlled or persistently high blood pressure (approximately 180/120); (2) severe, unresponsive superimposed preeclampsia; (3) marked proteinuria (≥ 3 g/d) or oliguria (≤ 800 mL/d); and (4) encephalopathy, retinal detachment, cardiac decompensation, or premature separation of the placenta. Fetal indications for premature delivery are (1) marked fetal growth retardation as noted by sequential ultrasonography, or (2) fetal distress demonstrated by significantly reduced fetal activity determination (FAD) or positive oxytocin challenge test (OCT).

Induction of labor by artificial rupture of the membranes is much preferred over oxytocin stimulation—often a cause of excessive fluid retention. Careful fetal monitoring is mandatory throughout labor. Cautious augmentation of labor may be useful. However, if the cervix is unfavorable, if labor is desultory, if malpresentation (eg, single footling breech) is diagnosed, or if fetal distress develops, cesarean section must be accomplished without delay.

Avoid heavy sedation during labor. Insert a retention catheter, and record urinary protein content and output hourly. Employ epidural or pudendal block anesthesia whenever possible. Spinal anesthesia is hazardous, because of the danger of sudden hypotension. Parenteral ergot medications are contraindicated because of their pressor effect.

Maternal complications (stroke, cardiac failure, etc) require definitive medical therapy. Neonatal problems such as respiratory distress syndrome usually necessitate pediatric consultation and specific treatment.

Combination oral contraceptive drugs are contraindicated, because they may increase hypertension or worsen the basic disorder causing hypertension. Intrauterine contraceptive devices may cause increased bleeding, and barrier methods may not be adequately protective. Therefore, sterilization should be offered to women with progressive or serious hypertensive disease who are still fertile.

The incidence of severity of preeclampsia and the increased perinatal mortality rate associated with hypertensive syndromes are reduced only slightly by long-term drug therapy. Nonetheless, with proper management, the prognosis for the hypertensive mother and her offspring is good.

NEUROLOGIC DISEASES

The effect of neurologic disease on pregnancy is rarely critical. Neurologic diseases that are aggravated by pregnancy include chorea gravidarum (Sydenham's chorea), severe nonspecific polyneuritis, and herniation of an intervertebral disk.

HEADACHES

The patient with a constant throbbing or "splitting" headache, either frontal, sincipital, or occipital and usually bilateral, should be examined for generalized edema, hypertension, and proteinuria, which may indicate preeclampsia. Tension headaches, functional in origin, are likely to occur for the first time during pregnancy or to be severely exacerbated by pregnancy. Tension headaches are much more common than vascular (migraine) type headaches.

Headache is most disturbing during the first and third trimesters. Emotional tension is the most common cause; consider anxiety, uncertainty, and similar psychic causes when headache is migrainous, band type, occipital, or more or less constant. Refractive errors and ocular imbalance are not caused by normal pregnancy, but the pregnant woman tends to be sedentary and may read or sew more despite "eyestrain." Hormonal stimulation causes vascular engorgement of the nasal turbinates, and the resultant congestion contributes to sinusitis and headache. The belief that pituitary swelling during normal pregnancy causes headache is without foundation.

PSEUDOTUMOR CEREBRI

Pseudotumor cerebri—actually acute cerebral edema—is a rare disorder of unknown cause that may seriously complicate pregnancy. The signs and symptoms basically result from increased intracranial pressure, ie, severe bitemporal headaches—worse with bending or straining—tinnitus, nausea, vomiting, and greatly diminished vision. These problems may begin at any time in pregnancy. Loss of visual acuity (even blindness) and bitemporal papilledema, occasionally with retinal hemorrhage, are typical findings. Greatly increased opening lumbar spinal fluid pressure will be noted, but cerebrospinal fluid tests should be normal. Cerebral tomography, angiography, or pneumoencephalography will be negative. Unless there is evidence of cardiovascular-renal disease or preeclampsia-eclampsia, the patient will be normotensive.

Central nervous system tumor or preeclampsia must be considered in the differential diagnosis. Great confusion may occur if the latter is an associated problem or if pseudotumor cerebri is overlooked. Neurologic consultation should be obtained. However, treatment basically consists of repeated spinal taps to relieve symptoms when necessary. Diuretic therapy is of doubtful value for pseudotumor cerebri and may be harmful to the fetus.

Pseudotumor cerebri is a self-limited entity. Cerebral decompression will relieve headache and will restore normal vision unless extensive retinal hemorrhage or detachment has occurred. The pregnancy will be unaffected. Pseudotumor cerebri alone is not an indication for early delivery or cesarean section. Recurrence of pseudotumor cerebri with or without pregnancy is unlikely.

CHOREA GRAVIDARUM

Sydenham's chorea that recurs or develops for the first time in young women during pregnancy is believed by many to be a form of encephalitis. Although very rare and becoming rarer, it may be a serious complication of pregnancy. It usually appears early after the first missed period and, curiously, it vanishes following termination of pregnancy. The fetus is unaffected. Treatment is similar to that of Sydenham's chorea in the nonpregnant patient.

EPILEPSY

Convulsive seizures may be associated with disturbed physiology: edema, alkalosis, fluid and electrolyte imbalance, cerebral hypoxia, hypoglycemia, or hypocalcemia. Recurrent attacks of grand mal or petit mal epilepsy and psychomotor seizures may occur.

Epilepsy has no demonstrable effect on the clinical course of pregnancy. This is fortunate, because the incidence of epilepsy is rather high (1:1000 gestations). Although a woman with idiopathic epilepsy has about one chance in 40 of having an epileptic child, it is doubtful that epilepsy is hereditary. What is more likely is that epilepsy may result from developmental problems or from birth trauma. In any event, the effect of pregnancy on epilepsy cannot be predicted.

The differential diagnosis of epilepsy versus eclampsia may be difficult. An accurate past history of seizures in the nonpregnant state is most helpful in the diagnosis of epilepsy. The burden of proof is on the physician who claims that convulsions in the third trimester of pregnancy do not indicate eclampsia.

If preeclampsia-eclampsia can be ruled out, grand mal seizures generally can be controlled by slow intravenous administration of 2.5% sodium amobarbital or 10 mL of 50% magnesium sulfate. Rapidly administered intravenous sodium amobarbital may cause fatal pulmonary edema and right heart failure, because of vascular instability of patients with severe preeclampsia or eclampsia.

Phenytoin (Dilantin) may be toxic to the fetus. Other sedative drugs that are safer for the offspring include phenobarbital, diazepam (Valium), and chlordiazepoxide (Librium).

Therapeutic abortion is not medically indicated for epilepsy, because this disorder may or may not constitute a problem during pregnancy.

SUBARACHNOID HEMORRHAGE OR "STROKE"

More than three-fourths of spontaneous subarachnoid hemorrhages are due to rupture of a silent congenital intracranial "berry" aneurysm, usually of the circle of Willis. The remainder follow bleeding from cerebral angiomas or cerebral thrombosis. Stroke may complicate preeclampsia-eclampsia. Usually a "silent" aneurysm ruptures at the peak of blood volume early in the third trimester, but a few occur during labor. For this reason, ergot preparations should not be given intravenously.

The symptoms of subarachnoid hemorrhage include nausea, vomiting, paralysis, convulsions, and coma. Sudden death occurs in 2–5% of patients, and the subsequent mortality rate is about 40%. Recurrent episodes of intracranial hemorrhage occur in one-third to one-half of patients.

The treatment after antepartum rupture of a cerebral aneurysm has often been cesarean section to avoid significant shifts in blood pressure and to avoid the strain of labor in the hope of circumventing further intracranial hemorrhage. Nevertheless, cesarean section has not reduced the maternal mortality rate nor has it prevented secondary hemorrhages during the puerperium. Therefore, cesarean section is not indicated except for obstetric reasons. If an aneurysm is diagnosed during pregnancy, prompt neurosurgery should be accomplished. Pregnancy is not contraindicated subsequent to operation for the correction of aneurysms.

MYASTHENIA GRAVIS

Pregnancy causes relapses of myasthenia gravis even during the first few weeks following a missed period or later in pregnancy; the first 2 weeks postpartum may be the most critical. Increased oral or parenteral doses of neostigmine will be needed at these times. Edrophonium chloride (Tensilon), 2–3 mg intravenously, may be used as a test dose for patients under treatment to distinguish between myasthenic crisis (improves) and overtreatment (no change). Many patients are better during pregnancy and require less medication or go into remission during pregnancy.

There is no demonstrable effect of myasthenia gravis on pregnancy. Labor is not affected; certainly, uterine inertia is not more common in women with myasthenia gravis. Certain drugs, including magnesium sulfate, aminoglycoside antibiotics, and ester-type local antibiotics, should be avoided.

One should employ amide-type local obstetric infiltration anesthesia. Do not give scopolamine because it may mask overdosage with anticholinergic drugs. Tubocurarine should not be given during general anesthesia, since breathing problems may result.

Transient neonatal myasthenia gravis has been reported in 20–30% of infants born to mothers with myasthenia gravis. Neostigmine therapy will confirm the diagnosis and benefit the newborn. Spontaneous recovery after 1–8 weeks should be anticipated.

MULTIPLE SCLEROSIS

The cause of this disorder is unknown. The incidence is 2–3 per 1000 pregnancies. The dominant pathologic feature is patchy demyelinization of the brain and spinal cord.

Pregnancy cannot be implicated in the onset of multiple sclerosis. Hence, exacerbations and remissions must be coincidental. Certainly, it cannot be shown that hormone changes, fluid and electrolyte variations, or the so-called hypercoagulability of the blood during pregnancy influences the development or the course of multiple sclerosis. For this reason, therapeutic abortion is not medically indicated. However, because pregnancy imposes an additional burden on the woman for the care of the child, early therapeutic abortion in severe cases may be warranted. Whenever interruption on such an indication is accomplished, sterilization should be effected also.

Multiple sclerosis does not affect the course of labor. Spinal anesthesia should be avoided when spinal cord disease is present. Vaginal delivery is preferred.

Pregnancy is not contraindicated after a remission of several years.

PITUITARY DYSFUNCTION

Important anatomic and physiologic changes in the anterior pituitary are associated with pregnancy. During normal pregnancy, the anterior pituitary enlarges to twice its normal size, but it resumes its normal dimensions 6–8 weeks postpartum. The enlargement is due mainly to an increase in the number of eosinophil cells during pregnancy, but basophil cells also are more numerous in pregnancy. During pregnancy, a transitional or so-called pregnancy cell can be identified in the anterior pituitary. This element, perhaps specific for pregnancy, may be a chromophobe or chromophil variant. Although chorionic gonadotropin (hCG) levels are high, pituitary gonadotropin production is suppressed during pregnancy.

Few changes normally occur in the posterior pituitary during pregnancy. Oxytocin, which can influence the contractility of the uterus during labor and is responsible for the milk letdown reflex during lactation, is stored in and released from the posterior pituitary.

Tumors or gross disorders of the pituitary are rarely associated with pregnancy, since severe pituitary disease, eg, chromophobe adenoma, is a common cause of female infertility. Other pituitary endocrine problems may have their onset during pregnancy (eg, diabetes insipidus, Chiari-Frommel syndrome, and acromegaly). Intrapartum or postpartum complications are responsible for Sheehan's syndrome and prolonged postpartum amenorrhea.

Postpartum Anterior Pituitary Necrosis (Sheehan's Syndrome, Hypophyseal Cachexia)

Postpartum anterior pituitary necrosis and hypopituitarism occur in about 15% of survivors of hypovolemic shock, usually associated with postpartum hemorrhage.

After delivery, rapid hypophyseal involution occurs with sharp curtailment of its vascularity. Added to this, postpartum hemorrhage and vasomotor collapse may cause an extreme reduction in pituitary circulation.

It has been estimated that if about half of anterior lobe function is eliminated, significant gonadotropin depletion will result, but essentially all adrenocortical function is lost when over 75% of the gland is destroyed.

Sheehan's syndrome is characterized by reduced or absent secretions of the pituitary, leading to a deficiency in thyroid, adrenocortical, and ovarian functions. The degree of deficiency depends upon the extent of pituitary necrosis and subsequent regeneration. One of the first diagnostic observations following convalescence from hemorrhage and shock is failure of lactation. Decreased breast size, loss of pubic and axillary hair, genital atrophy, and, in severe cases, myxedema complete the picture. Subsequent amenorrhea is the rule. Most patients tire very easily and are apathetic or even cachectic.

Classic instances of Sheehan's syndrome may not be difficult to diagnose, but lesser degrees of pituitary failure often pose problems. Many of the latter patients function fairly well despite extended ill health. Oligomenorrhea and occasional ovulation may be noted. A serious accident, sepsis, or an unanticipated pregnancy in these women may cause a sudden acute adrenal crisis. Vaginal dryness and irritation are common. Weight change is slight in mild cases, but in severe cases cachexia may be striking. Premature aging is notable in chronic Sheehan's syndrome.

Laboratory studies may show a decrease in the production of one or more of the pituitary hormones. In patients with minimal dysfunction, tests of reserve function are employed.

Treatment involves replacement therapy depending upon the severity of the deficiency. Thyroid supplementation generally will be required, but this must be given with caution if serious hypoadrenocorticism exists, or an adrenal crisis may be precipitated. Hydrocortisone, 12.5–25 mg orally daily, together with increased sodium chloride intake, should relieve the adrenal deficiency. Diethylstilbestrol, 0.5 mg orally daily (or equivalent), will be beneficial. A high-protein diet with ample carbohydrates should be prescribed.

The prognosis depends upon the degree of pituitary deficiency. Reasonably good health is likely with proper supplements. Although infertility is usual, pregnancy may occur. With careful management, it should be possible to deliver a normal baby.

THYROID DISEASES

Changes in Maternal & Fetal Thyroid Function in Pregnancy

The thyroid gland undergoes diffuse hyperplasia during pregnancy. This is thought to be due to changes in iodide metabolism rather than increased secretory activity. During pregnancy, iodide excretion is increased because of the increased glomerular filtration rates and transport across the placenta to meet requirements.

Under the stimulation of estrogen, thyroxine-binding globulin concentration increases gradually during early pregnancy, reaching a plateau or rising only slowly after 10–12 weeks. This results in increasing levels of circulating thyroxine (T_4) and triiodothyronine (T_3), the thyroid hormones. The unbound or free levels of T_4 and T_3 are not significantly altered, and the utilization of these hormones peripherally is unchanged. Plasma levels of thyroid-stimulating hormone (TSH) are also normal.

The fetal thyroid is unable to synthesize thyroid hormones during the first trimester. Iodine uptake by the fetal thyroid can be demonstrated after 13 weeks, and the synthesis of mono- and diiodotyrosines begins at that time. Gradually, more T_4 and T_3 are produced, and the levels at term are similar to those of the mother. Immediately following delivery, the levels of T_4 temporarily increase in the infant.

T_4 is poorly transported across the placenta to the fetus from the maternal circulation. When infused intravenously at term, cord levels in the fetus are less than 5% of those found in the fetal circulation. T_3 can be demonstrated to cross the placenta in 50% of women when 300 μg/d or more are administered to the mother. When infused intravenously at term, fetal cord levels may reach 25% of those in the maternal circulation.

The Assessment of Thyroid Function During Pregnancy

The critical assessment of thyroid function is somewhat more difficult in the pregnant woman. Early in pregnancy, women often complain of sleepiness and constipation, which may suggest mild hypothyroidism. Later in pregnancy, the increase in cardiac output, oxygen consumption, and heat production may suggest mild hyperthyroidism.

Although thyroid function is not significantly altered in pregnancy, there may be marked changes in tests of function. As noted above, there is an increase in the binding proteins for the thyroid hormones. This results in an increase in the circulating levels of T_4 when measured as serum T_4. In order to obtain an estimate of the available T_4 or free T_4, it is necessary to have an index of the binding activity. Some laboratories perform measurements of T_4-binding globulin; however, in most laboratories an estimate may be obtained by measuring the red cell or resin T_3 uptake. Since more of the added radioactive T_3 is bound to plasma protein, less is free to be taken up by red cells or resin. The values for this test are therefore lower than in nonpregnant women. Typically, T_4 levels are elevated and T_3 uptake is reduced in normal pregnant women. An estimate of the free T_4 can be obtained by calculating the T_4 index:

T_4 (μg/dL) $\times$ T_3 uptake (%) $\div$ 100 = T_4 index
Example: T_4 16.5 μg/dL (slightly elevated for non-pregnant patient); T_3 uptake 20% (slightly below normal for nonpregnant patient):
16.5 $\times$ 20 $\div$ 100 = 3.3 (which is normal)

The normal range of values for the T_4 index is unchanged in pregnancy. The radioactive ^{123}I uptake and scans cannot be performed during pregnancy, since the radioactive iodine is taken up by the fetal thyroid and may damage it.

DISORDERS OF THYROID FUNCTION

Hypothyroidism

In pregnant patients with undiagnosed hypothyroidism or inadequately treated hypothyroidism, there appear to be increased numbers of stillbirths, abortions, premature deliveries, and major anomalies. Studies on the offspring of patients treated with thyroid hormone but having lower than normal levels of T_4 indicate that at age 4 they score lower on tests of speech, vocabulary, intelligence, and fine motor performance. It is therefore exceedingly important to detect and adequately treat hypothyroidism. If the indications for treatment in patients taking this hormone are inadequate or unclear, stopping treatment to restudy the patient should be delayed until after delivery.

Measurements of radioactive T_3 uptake are useful in confirming the diagnosis of suspected hypothyroidism and assessing the adequacy of replacement therapy. If the values obtained in these studies are borderline, measurement of circulating TSH levels is helpful. If replacement therapy is incomplete or if mild hypothyroidism exists, TSH levels should be elevated above the normal range of 3–10 ng/mL.

Goiter

Goiter occurs in a small percentage of women and is particularly common in low-iodide regions. In addition to iodine deficiency, goiters result from inborn errors of metabolism of the thyroid hormones. The majority of euthyroid goiters are thought to be due to latent, genetically transferred mild defects of hormone synthesis that require an increase in stimulation by TSH to achieve a normal secretory output.

In euthyroid patients whose glands are less than twice normal in size, treatment is not required. An attempt may be made to reduce the size of larger glands by full thyroid replacement therapy. If this is unsuccessful and the gland is sufficiently large to be cosmetically unacceptable or cause tracheal or esophageal obstruction, surgery is indicated.

Enlargement of the thyroid gland may also be due to autoimmune thyroiditis. The finding of various antithyroid antibodies supports this diagnosis.

Hyperthyroidism

Hyperthyroidism affects about one in 1500 pregnant women. Although hyperthyroidism may be well tolerated by the mother, it is associated with an increase in the frequency of premature labor and delivery, postpartum hemorrhage, and hypertensive disorders. If hyperthyroidism is untreated, large stores of thyroid hormone in the gland may be released during a period of stress or delivery, causing thyroid storm.

The clinical diagnosis of hyperthyroidism is suggested by the presence of weight loss, unexplained diarrhea, heat intolerance, tachycardia, flushing, excessive perspiration, and the presence of a fine tremor. The typical eye signs of Graves' disease or exophthalmos may also be present. A thyroid nodule or small goiter may be present. The diagnosis can usually be confirmed by the finding of an elevated level of T_4 and T_3 uptake for pregnancy. The thyroid index is usually above 6.3. In mild instances, the values may be at the upper limits of normal and the diagnosis difficult to confirm. In such patients, the lack of a TSH response to the infusion of 200 μg of thyroid-releasing hormone (TRH) will confirm the diagnosis. In some patients, T_3 but not T_4 levels are elevated. The diagnosis can be made in these patients by measuring T_3 by radioimmunoassay.

The treatment of thyrotoxicosis during pregnancy is complicated by the fact that radioactive iodine, iodides, antithyroid drugs, and adrenergic blocking agents, all of which are useful, cross the placenta into the fetus, and radioactive iodine cannot be given to a pregnant woman. The treatment of thyrotoxicosis in pregnancy usually consists of bringing the signs and symptoms under control by administration of propylthiouracil or methimazole. Treatment is started with relatively large doses of the drug, eg, 100–150 mg of propylthiouracil every 6 hours or 50–100 mg of methimazole daily until symptoms abate. The dose should then be reduced to the lowest possible level for maintenance until delivery. If the maintenance dose is 150 mg or less of propylthiouracil (or equivalent) per day, goiters are uncommon in the fetus. However, they may occur when larger doses are required. During this period, hypothyroidism should be avoided and the patient maintained in the euthyroid state. The concomitant use of T_4 is not required. The use of iodides for a few days if thyroidectomy is contemplated during the second trimester has been recommended. However, chronic use for the control of symptoms can damage the fetal gland.

The resemblance of the signs and symptoms of hyperthyroidism to the effects of catecholamines has led to the use of drugs such as reserpine, guanethidine, and propranolol to control its manifestations. Phenobarbital appears to be as effective as the first 2 drugs and is probably safer during pregnancy. The chronic use of propranolol may not be safe during pregnancy, because it may cause fetal growth retardation. Therefore, its use should be restricted to the control of severe tachycardias or during thyroid storm.

Surgery, preferably done at the end of the second trimester, can be considered in patients with recurrent disease, in those with continued enlargement of the gland on medical therapy, or for the convenience of the patient when an excellent thyroid surgeon is available. Radioactive iodine is contraindicated during pregnancy since it is also taken up by the fetal thyroid.

After delivery, surgery and other more definitive forms of therapy or continuation of medical therapy can be used in the treatment of these patients.

Nodules

Single nodules of the thyroid gland in young women may be a serious problem. Ten to 25% of these are due to thyroid cancer. Papillary and follicular tumors are the most common and are very low-grade malignancies.

In nonpregnant patients, a scan is ordinarily carried out after the administration of radioactive iodine. If the nodule is nonfunctioning (cold), the chance of malignancy is higher. However, such patients may be treated by suppression with replacement doses of thyroxine. During pregnancy, radioactive iodine scans cannot be performed, as noted above. However, fluorescence scans can be done. A collimated source of americium 241 is focused on the gland from the side. The radiation excites the orbital electrons of ^{127}I, causing them to emit x-rays that can be detected by a fluorescent screen.

During pregnancy, it is appropriate to administer maximum tolerable amounts of thyroid extract or T_4 to such patients. If suppression causes a reduction in the size of the nodule, this therapy is continued throughout the remainder of the pregnancy. If the nodule does not change or continues to grow, it should be surgically removed.

PARATHYROID DYSFUNCTION

The major function of the parathyroid glands is to mediate calcium and phosphorus metabolism. Bone is the principal repository of these substances, and parathyroid hormone is responsible for their deposit and release. Moreover, parathyroid hormone is the principal factor in control of renal excretion of phosphate. In health, parathyroid hormone maintains normal levels of calcium and phosphorus in the plasma and in extracellular fluids.

Hypoparathyroidism is marked by hypocalcemia. This is associated with an increased deposition of calcium and phosphorus in bone. Augmented renal tubular reabsorption of phosphate ultimately results in hyperphosphatemia.

Hyperparathyroidism causes demineralization of bone, hypercalcemia, and hypercalciuria. Concomitantly, abnormal amounts of phosphate are passed in the urine, resulting in hypophosphatemia.

Pregnancy normally induces a slight (secondary) hyperparathyroidism. Severe, chronic hyperparathyroidism causing osteitis fibrosa cystica is rare during pregnancy except in patients with long-standing renal disease. The most serious symptoms of parathyroid dysfunction during pregnancy are muscle cramps and hypoparathyroid tetany. Tetany usually is associated with a deficiency of calcium or excess of phosphate (eg, due to intake of calcium phosphate prenatal mineral supplement tablets) or lack of vitamin D and parathyroid hormone. In established hypoparathyroidism, hypocalcemia is observed during pregnancy as a dilutional phenomenon, but there will be a normal hypocalcemia due to a decrease in binding albumin. The requirements for vitamin D and calcium in hypoparathyroidism are usually greater in pregnant than in nonpregnant women.

Tetany may follow infection or the hypocalcemia that sometimes occurs during lactation or may be seen during the latter months of pregnancy if calcium supplements are inadequate. Hyperventilation during labor may precipitate tetany.

Tetany of the newborn is unusual in breast-fed infants, but it may occur transiently if phosphate intake of the infant is excessive, eg, if too much cow's milk is given or as a result of relative hypoparathyroidism in the neonatal period.

Patients with severe hyperparathyroidism may be candidates for therapeutic abortion if their renal function is severely impaired as a consequence of nephrocalcinosis and pyelonephritis. Considerable bone demineralization is rare.

The treatment of moderate or severe hyperparathyroidism during pregnancy requires prompt parathyroidectomy before a severe metabolic crisis occurs. Administration of calcium gluconate, 10–20 mL of 10% solution rapidly intravenously, and 50 mL of a similar substance as a slow drip should correct tetany. Tetany of the newborn may occur in infants born to women with hyperparathyroidism. This disorder also responds to intravenous calcium gluconate.

Hypoparathyroidism, generally secondary to unintentional ablation of the parathyroid glands during thyroidectomy, may cause serious problems during pregnancy. Prior to therapy, hypoparathyroid patients also have decreased phosphorus excretion, associated with high serum levels of that ion, and a concomitant reduction in serum calcium. Obstetric patients with hypoparathyroidism have muscular irritability and tetany. Occasionally, spontaneous abortion, fetal death, or premature labor may be caused by severe undiagnosed or undertreated hypoparathyroidism. Administration of 50–200 thousand units of vitamin D_2 per day and calcium lactate orally together with the elimination of milk and cheese from the diet is most effective therapy. The offspring of mothers with undertreated or poorly treated hypoparathyroidism may be affected by tetany. This is especially true of prematures, who normally tend toward hypocalcemia. Infants respond quickly to oral therapy with calcium gluconate solution.

BREAST COMPLICATIONS

BREAST CANCER

In the first and second trimesters, the usual radical or modified radical operation combined with postoperative radiotherapy, if evidence of spread is recognized, should be performed. In the third trimester, we believe that pregnancy should be terminated at viability by induction of labor or cesarean section if the uterus is nonreactive, and then breast surgery performed. Radiotherapy may be required in more extensive cases. Lactation generally is avoided on general principles.

After successful treatment of cancer of the breast, pregnancy should be proscribed for at least 3 years.

PULMONARY COMPLICATIONS

Upward displacement of the diaphragm by pressure of the pregnant uterus, especially with the patient supine, is compensated in part by broadening of the chest and thoracic rather than abdominal breathing. Moderate diaphragmatic excursions are maintained during pregnancy, but costal breathing is evoked to maintain increased respiratory efficiency, especially during labor.

An increase of about 10% in the respiratory rate during late pregnancy together with an approximately 45% augmentation of tidal volume increases the minute ventilation by about 50%. Respiratory center hypersensitivity or compensation for slight acidosis may theoretically explain these changes. Oxygen and CO_2 exchange are increased during pregnancy, as one would expect in this hypermetabolic state.

Most normal pregnant patients display slight dyspnea at rest, but this is more apparent with exercise. This "breathlessness" is a progesterone effect. While this tendency toward labored breathing may be expected, abnormalities or disease processes that can further embarrass respiration (eg, emphysema, polyhydramnios, anemia) should be identified and treated when possible.

PULMONARY TUBERCULOSIS

If a positive skin reaction to tuberculin is the diagnostic criterion, about 20% of the adult population can be said to be affected. The incidence of active infection is much lower depending upon geographic and socioeconomic factors. Pulmonary tuberculosis has been diagnosed in slightly less than 2% of pregnant women in the USA by chest x-ray screening. The diagnosis is best made using a 35.5 × 43 cm (14 × 17 inch) x-ray film. X-ray studies should be reserved for patients with a positive tine test.

Pulmonary tuberculosis has no specific effect on pregnancy, and congenital tuberculosis is rare. Most cases of pulmonary tuberculosis in infants are due to postdelivery exposure to tuberculosis.

Neither pregnancy nor the puerperium can be linked with the onset of tuberculosis in a cause and effect sequence, and pregnancy does not predispose to infection with tuberculosis. The natural history of the disease is one of exacerbations and remissions. In most cases, pregnancy is merely incidental.

A positive diagnosis of tuberculosis may take time, but a correct interpretation is urgent. If the patient has been delivered and a serious possibility of tuberculosis exists, the highly susceptible newborn must be separated from the mother.

The management of the pregnant patient with tuberculosis requires the collaboration of the pulmonary physician and the obstetrician. The treatment of tuberculosis includes rest (physical and emotional), hospitalization if the disease is moderate or advanced, and chemotherapy. (The reader is referred to other texts for details.)

In numerous studies of drugs considered to be effective against pulmonary tuberculosis—isoniazid, ethambutol, rifampin, and streptomycin—only streptomycin was shown to be dangerous to the fetus (ototoxic). Thus, for active mild to moderate pulmonary tuberculosis, the Centers for Disease Control recommends isoniazid in combination with ethambutol. If the disease is extensive or seriously progressive, rifampin may be added. Streptomycin should not be used in the treatment of the tuberculous gravida unless rifampin is contraindicated or proves to be unsatisfactory.

Therapeutic abortion is not medically indicated for pregnant women with pulmonary tuberculosis who

are receiving isoniazid, ethambutol, or rifampin, except in very unusual circumstances.

The obstetric routine for the antepartum patient must include an ample diet for normal weight gain. Rest is important, and assistance in the care of other children or for household duties is recommended.

BRONCHIAL ASTHMA

Asthma is an acute respiratory disorder in which recurrent attacks of wheezing, expiratory dyspnea, cough, and mucoid sputum are notable. About 1–2% of people in the USA have bronchial asthma. Familial susceptibility, environmental exposure, respiratory infections, and psychogenic factors must all be considered in the evaluation of an asthmatic patient. Half of these individuals give a family history of allergy (rhinitis, asthma, eczema, urticaria).

The incidence of bronchial asthma in obstetric patients is only 0.5–1%. The effect of pregnancy on asthma is unpredictable; the effect of asthma on pregnancy is more definite. The incidence of abortion, premature labor, and maternal deaths is probably not increased in asthmatics who receive proper medical care. However, the pregnant patient with severe asthma may present extremely serious problems if there is marked impairment of respiratory function or medical complications. Acute complications of asthma include physical exhaustion, progressive hypoxemia or hypercarbia, atelectasis, pneumothorax, pneumomediastinum, pulsus paradoxus, and drug hypersensitivity reactions. Chronic complications are pulmonary emphysema and cor pulmonale.

The wheezing of asthma must be distinguished from that due to bronchitis, obstructive emphysema, congestive heart failure, and pulmonary embolism. In bronchial asthma there is a history of recurrent acute attacks of wheezing, dyspnea, cough, and tenacious mucoid sputum. In addition to a careful medical history and physical examination, chest x-rays should be obtained. In severe asthma it is often necessary to perform pulmonary function studies and to measure blood electrolytes and blood gases.

Two phases of treatment of bronchial asthma are recognized: therapy of the acute attack and interim therapy to prevent or minimize subsequent attacks.

Treatment of an Acute Attack

In general, treatment should be directed at the asthma without special consideration of the pregnancy. Known allergens should be eliminated when possible. Give reassurance and tranquilizers for apprehension. Treat respiratory infections with antibiotics. Mist or steam inhalations may help loosen tenacious mucus.

A. Status Asthmaticus or Severe Attack in Epinephrine-Responsive Patient: Hospitalize the patient and obtain medical consultation. Administer aminophylline, 0.25–0.5 g in 30 mL of sterile saline *slowly* intravenously and follow with a continuous intravenous infusion of 0.9 mg/kg/h. Give hydrocortisone sodium succinate (Solu-Cortef) or equivalent, 100–200 mg intravenously every 2–4 hours as necessary. Start the patient on prednisone, 20 mg orally 4 times daily. Give oxygen freely by mask or nasal catheter; intermittent positive pressure breathing may be required. Correct dehydration and electrolyte disturbances by giving adequate intravenous fluids. If the patient fails to improve clinically with the above measures and there is evidence of progressive hypoxemia and hypercapnia, intubation and controlled ventilatory assistance may be required.

Note: Sedatives should not be used in patients with severe asthma.

B. Mild or Moderate Attacks of Asthma: Epinephrine is the drug of choice.

1. Epinephrine injection (1:1000), 0.2–0.5 mL subcutaneously. For moderately severe attacks, repeat every 1–2 hours.

2. Epinephrine inhalation (1:1000) or isoproterenol inhalation (1:200 in aqueous solution) or nebulizer, one or 2 inhalations every 30–60 minutes as necessary, may suffice for mild attacks.

3. If the attack is not controlled by epinephrine or isoproterenol, give aminophylline, 0.25–0.5 g in 10–20 mL saline slowly intravenously. Aminophylline may also be given rectally in solution or as suppositories.

4. Ephedrine sulfate or hydrochloride, 25–50 mg orally, 2–3 times daily with or without a barbiturate, may relieve mild attacks. Oral theophylline is also useful.

5. Phenobarbital, 30 mg orally 3–4 times daily, may be used to counteract overstimulation by bronchodilator drugs. Heavy sedation should be avoided.

Interim Therapy

Identify responsible allergens and treat appropriately. Eliminate or reduce emotional tensions. Treat respiratory infections with antibiotics. Cromolyn sodium inhalations have proved useful in preventing recurrent attacks in some patients, but their use in pregnancy is not approved.

Early therapeutic abortion is warranted only in patients who have severe asthma or perhaps those with a history of severe exacerbations during pregnancy.

Morphine should be avoided in the treatment of obstetric patients with asthma because it may induce bronchospasm. Meperidine (Demerol), 50–100 mg intramuscularly, usually will relieve bronchospasm.

Epinephrine and ephedrine should be used cautiously in patients with preeclampsia-eclampsia because of the pressor effect of these drugs.

Corticotropins are contraindicated in patients with antepartum bleeding because of possible shock and in those with preeclampsia-eclampsia because these medications cause hypertension and fluid retention.

Vaginal delivery is best for asthmatic patients unless obstetric indications demand cesarean section. Paracervical and pudendal or epidural block are preferable to general—especially inhalation—obstetric anesthesia for asthmatic patients to avoid hypertensive or respiratory side-effects. If inhalation anesthesia must be given, cyclopropane may be a satisfactory choice.

The outlook for the fetus and mother is good except in complicated cases, when pregnancy may have to be terminated to save the mother's life.

HEMATOLOGIC DISORDERS

ANEMIA

Physiologic and pathologic changes in the mother during pregnancy make the determination of anemia difficult. Not only do blood values during pregnancy differ from those in the nonpregnant patient, but these factors also vary with the course of the pregnancy. If deficiencies of a significant degree are noted, the patient is anemic and specific therapy is indicated.

In every evaluation of clinical and laboratory data, the following questions must be answered: (1) Is anemia present? (2) Is there evidence of iron deficiency? (3) Are megaloblasts present in the blood smear? (4) Are there signs of hemolysis? (5) Is there bone marrow deficiency?

1. IRON DEFICIENCY ANEMIA

Iron deficiency must be considered in all cases of anemia of uncertain cause, regardless of cell morphology. Inquire about a history of blood loss or dietary inadequacy. A stool guaiac test will demonstrate occult gastrointestinal bleeding. A stained smear of bone marrow should be examined for hemosiderin, which is always absent in iron deficiency but is present in normal or increased amounts in all other anemias. Only in iron deficiency is the serum iron low and the total iron-binding capacity elevated.

Iron deficiency anemia in women is usually due to blood loss resulting from excessive menses, postpartum hemorrhage, or iron deprivation from previous pregnancies. Iron deficiency anemia occurs in at least 20% of pregnancies in the USA. About 95% of pregnant women with anemia have the iron deficiency type. Pregnancy increases the woman's iron requirements because an increase of about 30% in total blood volume is necessary to meet the needs of the enlarged uterus and augmented vascular system. However, this increase does not include all blood components in proportionately equal amounts. For example, the increase in plasma volume is greater than the increase in red cell mass. This difference is probably due to hemodilution.

These changes will be reflected in the laboratory studies. If the plasma volume increased considerably more than the red cell mass, an apparent "physiologic" anemia of pregnancy will be evident, because hematocrit and hemoglobin concentrations are low. Nonetheless, when the hemoglobin is less than 12 g/dL or the hematocrit reading is less than 35%, true anemia exists.

The increase in red cell mass that develops during pregnancy requires additional iron to supply the increased numbers of erythrocytes. The result is a temporary loss of 0.5–0.7 g of available iron from storage, but this loss is returned to iron deposits postpartum.

Fetal iron derived from the mother and the iron lost in blood at the time of delivery and in the postpartum period average 0.4–0.5 g per pregnancy. Repeated pregnancies, especially when there is a short interval between, may result in a severe iron deficiency. Many women, anemic before pregnancy, never "catch up" during or after delivery.

A normal diet contains 12–15 mg of iron, or approximately 6 mg of iron per 1000 kcal, of which 5–10% (0.6–1.5 mg) is absorbed. (However, more iron is absorbed in iron deficiency anemia.) Because less than 1 mg of iron is excreted normally per day, normal persons are in positive iron balance. Chronic bleeding of as little as 2–4 mL of blood per day may lead to negative iron balance and iron deficiency anemia. Unfortunately, there is no way to estimate iron reserves while the hemoglobin determinations remain within the normal range. If the hemoglobin is reduced, however, the iron stores are depleted.

Clinical Findings

A. Symptoms and Signs: The symptoms may be vague and of long standing. Pallor, easy fatigability, palpitations, tachycardia, and dyspnea are reported.

B. Laboratory Findings: The hemoglobin may fall to as low as 3 g/dL, but the red cell count is rarely below 2.5 million/μL. The red cells usually are small (microcytic) and hypochromic, although in approximately 20% of adults the red cells are of normal size and nearly normochromic. The reticulocyte and platelet counts are normal or high. The white count is normal. Serum iron is usually below 30 μg/dL (normal is 90–150 μg/dL); total iron-binding capacity is elevated to 350–500 μg/dL (normal is 250–350 μg/dL). Percent saturation is 10% or less.

Differential Diagnosis

One must distinguish iron deficiency anemia from other hypochromic microcytic anemias (eg, anemia of infection, hemoglobinopathy, and anemia with intramedullary hemolysis).

Complications

Dysphagia, angina pectoris, or congestive failure may develop as a result of marked iron deficiency anemia in predisposed patients. Severe iron deficiency anemia is associated with definitely increased perinatal morbidity and mortality rates.

Prevention

Because so many women are iron deficient, oral iron should be administered to all patients during pregnancy and for at least 1 month following delivery. If iron is given prophylactically, the great majority of patients will maintain a hemoglobin concentration greater than 12 g/dL.

Treatment

Iron is curative for this type of anemia. Prompt, adequate treatment is necessary, but transfusions are rarely required.

A. Oral Iron Therapy: Maximum absorption is about 25 mg/d. Give 3 times daily after meals: ferrous sulfate, 0.2 g, or ferrous gluconate, 0.3 g. Oral iron should be continued for 3 months after hemoglobin values return to normal in order to replenish iron stores.

B. Parenteral Iron Therapy: The indications for parenteral administration are intolerance or refractoriness to oral iron (poor absorption); intestinal disease precluding the use of oral iron; continued blood loss; and the need to replace depleted iron stores when oral iron fails. Parenteral iron should be given only in the amounts necessary to correct the deficiency. Calculate the total dosage as follows: 250 mg for each gram of hemoglobin below normal. (Normal in women is 12–16 g/dL.)

Iron dextran injection (Imferon) for intramuscular use contains 5% metallic iron (50 mg/mL). Give 50 mg (1 mL) immediately and 100–250 mg intramuscularly twice a week until the total dosage has been given. Inject deeply with a 2-inch needle into the upper outer quadrant of the buttock, using the "Z" technique (pulling the skin and superficial musculature to one side before inserting the needle) to prevent leakage of the solution and tattooing of the skin. Imferon may also be given intravenously in doses of 250–500 mg. A test dose of 0.5 mL should be given first; if the patient experiences no adverse effects such as urticaria, nausea, or headache, the entire amount may be given over 3–5 minutes. Excessive dosage beyond the calculated need may cause hemosiderosis.

Prognosis

Signs and symptoms of anemia will clear with correction of anemia. Improvement following the use of parenteral iron therapy is usually only slightly more rapid than with oral medication.

2. FOLIC ACID DEFICIENCY ANEMIA
(Megaloblastic Anemia of Pregnancy)

Megaloblastic anemia of pregnancy is caused by folic acid—not vitamin B_{12}—deficiency. This disorder is most common in multiparas over age 30. The reported incidence varies from 1:200 to 1:40 deliveries. Folic acid deprivation is most common where dietary resources are inadequate, although some women on apparently adequate diets may be deficient. Curiously, only a small percentage of women with low serum folic acid levels have megaloblastic anemia.

Folic acid deficiency anemia follows malnutrition and is often associated with alcoholism or protracted vomiting. It may be associated with multiple pregnancy or preeclampsia-eclampsia and may accompany sprue or sickle cell disease. It often occurs in epileptic patients who have received prolonged primidone (Mysoline), phenytoin (Dilantin), or barbiturate medication.

Clinical Findings

A. Symptoms and Signs: Lassitude, progressive anorexia, mental depression, and nausea are the principal complaints. Pallor often is not marked. Glossitis, gingivitis, vomiting, and diarrhea often occur. There are no abnormal neurologic findings.

B. Laboratory Findings: Folic acid deficiency results in hematologic findings similar to those of true pernicious anemia (vitamin B_{12} deficiency), which is very rare in the pregnancy age group. With folic acid lack, blood changes appear sooner. The hemoglobin may be as low as 4–6 g/dL. The red blood cell count may be less than 2 million/μL in severe cases. Extreme anemia often is associated with leukocytopenia and thrombocytopenia. The mean corpuscular volume is normal or increased. The peripheral white blood cells are hypersegmented. The bone marrow is hyperplastic and megaloblastic. Free gastric hydrochloric acid is present in normal amounts. Serum iron values are high, and serum vitamin B_{12} levels are normal.

Complications

Give folic acid, 5–10 mg/d orally or parenterally, until a hematologic remission is achieved. Megaloblastic anemia of pregnancy does not usually respond to vitamin B_{12} even in large doses. Administer iron orally or parenterally (or both) as indicated. Prescribe a high-vitamin, high-protein diet. Transfusions are rarely necessary except when anemia is extreme, especially if the patient is near term.

Therapeutic abortion and sterilization are not indicated for megaloblastic anemia.

Prognosis

Megaloblastic anemia during pregnancy is not apt to be severe unless it is associated with systemic infection or preeclampsia-eclampsia. If the diagnosis is made at least 4 weeks before term, treatment can often raise the hemoglobin to normal or nearly normal levels. The outlook for mother and baby is good if there is adequate time for treatment. Spontaneous remissions usually occur after delivery. Anemia usually recurs only when the patient becomes pregnant again.

3. APLASTIC ANEMIA

Aplastic anemia is rare, but it may be devastating during pregnancy. The anemia may be a toxic sequela to ingestion of drugs such as chloramphenicol, phenylbutazone, mephenytoin, or alkylating chemotherapeutic agents. Hair dyes, insecticides, and cleaning fluids may be implicated also. In about half of cases, the cause cannot be identified.

The rapidly developing anemia causes pallor, fatigue, and tachycardia. Pancytopenia is usually present.

The red cell count may be less than 1 million/μL, and the cells usually are slightly macrocytic. A low reticulocyte count may be noted, although variability is the rule. The white cell count may be less than 2000/μL and the platelet count less than 30,000/μL. The icterus index is usually low. The bone marrow is fatty, with few red cells, white cells, or megakaryocytes. Hemosiderin is present in normal amounts on a stained smear.

In hypersplenism, the marrow is hyperactive and the spleen is large. In myelofibrosis, the spleen and liver are enlarged; bizarre red cells and leukocytosis are to be expected; the platelet count often is normal or elevated; and the marrow is fibrotic rather than fatty. The diagnosis of aleukemic leukemia or lymphosarcoma requires special marrow stains.

Fetal death or premature labor may ensue. Infection or hemorrhage may be the terminal event for the mother.

Treatment, in addition to discontinuing exposure to the toxic agent (if known), consists of giving prednisolone (or equivalent corticosteroid), 10–20 mg orally 4 times daily, and transfusions of fresh packed red cells as necessary. Platelet-rich fresh blood may check abnormal bleeding. Treat infection with appropriate antibiotics, but do not give antibiotics prophylactically.

Severe bone marrow depression carries about a 50% threat of death due to hemorrhage or infection within weeks or months. Partial or complete remissions do occur, however.

4. DRUG–INDUCED HEMOLYTIC ANEMIA

Drug-induced hemolytic anemia often occurs in individuals with inborn errors of metabolism. Blacks are frequently affected, and glucose-6-phosphate dehydrogenase deficiency in erythrocytes and other tissues is the most common cause. Catalase and glutathione deficiency is associated with this disorder. The trait is X-linked and of intermediate dominance. While it is far more common in American black males, at least 2% of American black females are afflicted also. Moreover, the fetus may also suffer from this disorder.

The red cell count and morphology are normal until challenged by a noxious drug. Over 40 substances toxic to susceptible people are recognized, including sulfonamides, nitrofurans, antipyretics, analgesics, sulfones, water-soluble vitamin K, and uncooked fava beans. Viral or bacterial infections and diabetic acidosis may cause red cell hemolysis in the absence of a "bad" drug.

Specific laboratory tests to identify susceptible

individuals include a glutathione stability test and a cresyl blue dye reduction test.

Discontinuation of the drug or elimination of the toxic material generally leads to recovery.

5. SICKLE CELL DISEASE
(Sickle Cell Anemia)

Sickle cell disease is a dominant heritable disorder of individuals almost always of black African ancestry. Abnormal hemoglobins may result from altered genes. It is theoretically possible to inherit one or 2 abnormal hemoglobins (eg, hemoglobin S) from one or both parents. Heterozygous carriers have mixtures of normal and sickle (S) hemoglobin in their red cells. These individuals have the **sickle cell trait** but few or no problems. Homozygous persons have a double gene problem: only hemoglobin S in their red cells. They have **sickle cell disease** or **sickle cell anemia.**

Homozygous patients often are tall and slender with long, spindly legs. Many will have had sickle cell crises in childhood or adolescence, but some have no ill effects until adult life. Persistent scleral icterus is usual. A crisis is manifested by attacks of abdominal, head, joint, or bone pain lasting for hours or days.

Two screening tests are in common use: (1) The sodium metabisulfite test uses 1 drop of fresh 2% reagent mixed on a slide with 1 drop of the patient's blood; sickling of most red blood cells will occur in a few minutes. Sodium metabisulfite is a strong reducing agent, and the deoxygenated red blood cells become distorted as their hemoglobin becomes insoluble. (2) Sickledex Test is a simple solubility test that does not require a microscope; sodium dithionite is the reducing agent, and saponins and phosphate buffers are the precipitating agents. When 0.2 mL of blood is mixed with 2 mL of the reagent, a clear tube indicates normal blood and a cloudy tube hemoglobin S.

Sickle cell anemia must be differentiated from other hemoglobinopathies (eg, sickle cell–hemoglobin C or D disease, sickle cell–thalassemia, and sickle cell–persistent fetal hemoglobin syndrome) by hemoglobin electrophoresis, sickle cell test, and fetal hemoglobin determination. The sickle cell test does not differentiate between sickle cell anemia (homozygous disorder) and sickle cell trait (heterozygous state). In sickle cell anemia, the red blood count is always low. However, the finding of a low hemoglobin with a normal red blood count in a black patient with a positive sickle cell preparation is not diagnostic of sickle cell anemia but rather suggests iron deficiency anemia plus sickle cell trait.

The bone marrow shows erythroid hyperplasia, with the red cell count relatively higher than the white count. Hemosiderin is present on a stained smear of bone marrow. The indirect bilirubin test is usually elevated, and some plasma hemoglobin elevation should be expected. The specific gravity of the urine is fixed at about 1.010, and hemosiderinuria may be identified. The bones may reveal cortical thinning and diffuse osteoporosis with thickening of trabecular markings on x-ray films.

Bone and joint pains may resemble rheumatic fever. A rigid, tender abdomen may suggest an acute surgical problem, but persistence of normal bowel sounds may be a helpful differentiating sign. Headache, convulsions, and paralysis due to cerebral thrombosis may be mistaken for eclampsia. The spleen is not enlarged in women with sickle cell anemia but may be in other hemoglobinopathies.

Complications include hematuria, pyelonephritis, leg ulcers, bone infarction, osteomyelitis, myocarditis, and cholelithiasis. An aplastic crisis may follow a severe infection.

Symptomatic therapy is required. For sickle cell anemia during pregnancy, consider exchange transfusion and bring the hemoglobin to 1–10 g/dL in the third trimester. Bed rest and analgesics are helpful. Sodium bicarbonate (3.5 mEq/kg/h intravenously) or 5% glucose with 0.45% sodium chloride intravenously may relieve pain. Elimination of infection and transfusion—often replacement transfusion—are required for aplastic crisis.

Pregnancy has a worsening effect on sickle cell disease. Almost half of these pregnancies are complicated by anemia (often with folic acid and iron deficiency overlay), pyelonephritis, thrombosis, and bone and joint pain. (Iron and folic acid supplements should be given to all pregnant patients with sickle cell disease.) The maternal mortality rate may be as high as 5–10%. Cesarean section should be done on obstetric indications.

The risk to the fetus is increased considerably because of the complications, although the offspring will suffer no specific adverse effects.

Avoidance of pregnancy—by sterilization if necessary—is indicated. Oral contraceptives are contraindicated in patients with sickle cell disease, because they may induce thromboembolic phenomena.

HEMORRHAGIC DISORDERS

The incidence, types, diagnosis, and treatment of hemorrhagic disorders complicating pregnancy are in most respects the same as in nonpregnant women. Anemia due to blood loss, postpartum hemorrhage, and development of bleeding diseases in the infant may have a significant influence on the morbidity and mortality rates of both mother and infant.

Idiopathic thrombocytopenic purpura, when it has its onset during pregnancy, may be very serious. The maternal death rate in this condition is 1–2%, but the fetal death rate may be as high as 20%. If the mother fails to respond adequately to medical measures, including corticosteroids and blood transfusions, a splenectomy may be necessary. In early pregnancy, particularly, surgery may produce abortion. Cesarean section should be elected for obstetric reasons only.

Hypofibrinogenemia may occur in cases of

abruptio placentae, amniotic fluid embolism, and intrauterine retention of a dead fetus. Bleeding in such instances may be very severe and requires emergency administration of fresh whole blood cryoprecipitate or human fibrinogen USP, 5–20 g intravenously (see p 715).

Circulating anticoagulants of unknown origin, presumably immunologic, may cause hemorrhagic manifestations some time after delivery. Treatment is symptomatic and supportive.

THALASSEMIA
(Cooley's Anemia)

The term thalassemia refers to a group of hereditary hemolytic microcytic anemias that occasionally complicate pregnancy. Thalassemia major is the homologous—and thalassemia minor the heterologous—form of the disorder. The defect lies in reduced synthesis of one of the globin chains characterized by abnormal amounts of certain hemoglobins, eg, A, B, C, H, or S. The specific abnormality can be identified by electrophoresis. The severity of the anemia varies with the type of hemoglobin abnormality. In β-thalassemia, the beta hemoglobin chains are defective but the alpha chains are normal; in α-thalassemia, the reverse is true. The unbalanced synthesis results in precipitation of the normal chains. This leads to premature disruption of the red blood cells.

Five percent to 15% of Greeks, Italians, Iranians, Sardinians, and Cypriots and some Chinese persons have thalassemia, and about 0.5% of infants born to such individuals are homozygous for this potentially fatal disease. In the USA, there are at least 1000 cases of thalassemia leading to almost 50 deaths per year.

Among the hemoglobinopathies, thalassemia includes a variant with 2 alpha chains altered, and sickle cell anemia typifies a variant with 2 beta chains altered. Thalassemia results from diminished rates of production of one of the globin chains, whereas sickle cell disease is caused by a changed beta globin amino acid sequence that impairs the oxygen-transport potential of hemoglobin. Orientals (in contrast to Europeans) with thalassemia have a deficiency in alpha globin production.

Thalassemia is not apparent in neonates because fetal hemoglobin ($\alpha_2\gamma_2$) contains no beta globin chains. However, fetal hemoglobin production terminates suddenly at birth, and hemoglobin A ($\alpha_2\beta_2$) production becomes predominant, so that by the time the infant is 6–10 months old, fetal hemoglobin normally accounts for only 2–3% of red blood cell hemoglobin. However, at about 1 year of age, a baby with defective beta globin production usually begins to show signs of thalassemia, despite the presence of some compensatory fetal hemoglobin.

If beta chains are absent, excess alpha chains form tetramers that precipitate within red blood cell precursors in the bone marrow to cause hemolysis. Thus, the blood of thalassemia patients reveals microcythemia, hypochromia, poikilocytosis, and erythroblastosis.

During the formative years, in some individuals with severe anemia and hemolysis, erythropoietic bone marrow hypertrophies and distorts bone, resulting in curious facies.

In spite of blood transfusions, victims of severe thalassemia often die in their late teens or early twenties because of congestive heart failure secondary to chronic iron overload, often associated with liver failure, hypoadrenocorticism, diabetes mellitus, or splenomegaly.

Women with β-thalassemia minor have mild to moderate persistent anemia and weakness and lassitude. Their red blood cells are smaller than normal and are variable in size and shape. However, the cells have a normal or slightly elevated hemoglobin content. Similar blood findings are found in one of the parents.

During pregnancy, generous iron supplements, particularly parenteral iron administration, must be denied. Such treatment will not improve the anemia and may lead to hemosiderosis and its complications. Rarely, transfusions may be necessary to maintain the hemoglobin above 9 g/dL. The fetus is not directly harmed by thalassemia minor, and mothers with this disorder have a normal life expectancy.

Antenatal diagnosis of some hemoglobinopathies, including β-thalassemia, is now possible by fetoscopy, fetal blood sampling, and column chromatography at 18–20 weeks' gestation. As little as 1 μL of blood may be sufficient. Fetal risk (about 5–10%) depends on the skill of the operator.

The diagnosis of fetal α-thalassemia can be made by DNA analysis in amniotic fluid cells obtained by amniocentesis for evidence of alpha globin gene deletion, which is the cause of this disorder.

LEUKEMIA, LYMPHOMA, & HODGKIN'S DISEASE

Leukemia, lymphoma, and Hodgkin's disease, disorders of unknown origin, are uncommon complications of pregnancy. The incidence of myelocytic leukemia is 5–6 times that of the lymphocytic type. The frequency of chronic myelogenous leukemia is 3 times that of the acute type.

Lymphoma and Hodgkin's disease usually are chronic disorders, whereas most lymphatic leukemias are acute. While the chronic variety may persist for years, patients with acute leukemia die within a few months following onset.

Pregnancy has no specific effect on leukemia, lymphoma, or Hodgkin's disease. Consequently, the patient should receive good obstetric care and specific treatment of the cancer, assuming that treatment does no harm to the pregnancy.

The debilitating effect of leukemia on the mother is the main problem and is dependent upon the type and stage of the disease and the duration of pregnancy. Normochromic, normocytic anemia occurs in leukemia and Hodgkin's disease. Moderate thrombocytopenia and marked leukocytosis must be expected. Bleeding and premature delivery are very common. The perinatal mortality rate is very high. Several cases of possible transfer of leukemia or Hodgkin's disease to offspring have been reported, but these are exceptional.

Little can be done for the patient with acute leukemia, but much can be done for the comfort of the patient with chronic leukemia, lymphoma, or Hodgkin's disease. Radioisotopes must be avoided during pregnancy, but local radiation therapy to the liver, spleen, or lymphatic masses may be given provided the uterus is shielded from radiation. Irradiation, antimetabolite drugs, and alkylating agents are hazardous to the fetus, especially during the first trimester. Therapeutic abortion may be indicated if extensive specific therapy of the cancer is indicated.

COMPLICATIONS INVOLVING THE GASTROINTESTINAL TRACT, LIVER, BILIARY TRACT, & PANCREAS

Despite the major psychogenic overlay in hyperemesis gravidarum and capricious food choices of many women during pregnancy, obvious physiologic alterations (eg, the greatly enlarging uterus) and many less apparent changes (eg, altered capacity for glucose absorption) require explanation for proper diagnosis and treatment.

Stomach

Upward displacement of the stomach to cause widening of the hiatus of the diaphragm during late pregnancy allows herniation of the stomach in about 20% of patients. Delayed gastric emptying time and decreased gastrointestinal motility may become a problem in advanced pregnancy. Gastroesophageal eructation is common. Hydrochloric acid secretion is reduced. It is believed that pregnancy reduces gastric mucosal responsiveness. Pepsinogen production is increased slightly, but there is no augmentation of intrinsic factor (needed for vitamin B_{12} absorption).

Small Bowel

Certain functions of the small bowel are changed by pregnancy. Absorption of iron is reduced, and glucose absorption is decreased so that delayed return to normal blood glucose levels should be expected after an oral glucose tolerance test load.

Large Bowel

The motility of the colon is markedly reduced, but its absorptive capacity is unchanged by pregnancy. Thus, the fluid content of feces is further limited by delay in evacuation, constipation may become a problem, and hemorrhoids often develop.

Liver

No specific gross or microscopic anatomic changes in the liver have been demonstrated during normal pregnancy. However, liver function tests still leave much to be desired. Even a battery of assessments will not appraise the many functions of the liver well enough to establish a good comparison between pregnant and nonpregnant patients. Nonetheless, the following laboratory test variations due to pregnancy are recognized: (1) Serum alkaline phosphatase is elevated from the 12th week until 6 weeks postpartum. (2) The cephalin flocculation test is positive in about 10% of pregnant women. (3) The thymol turbidity test is positive in almost 15% of pregnant women. (4) Serum globulin and albumin values are decreased. (5) α_2-Globulin and β-globulin levels are increased during pregnancy. (6) Serum cholesterol rises about 60% from the 16th to the 32nd weeks of pregnancy, when it reaches a plateau. After delivery, it falls to normal levels.

Tests that are unchanged during pregnancy include those for serum glutamic-oxaloacetic transaminase, serum lactate dehydrogenase, and serum bilirubin levels. The BSP excretion test probably is not affected.

GASTROINTESTINAL DISORDERS

Hyperemesis Gravidarum

Vomiting of pregnancy—including hyperemesis gravidarum, its most pernicious form—affects many pregnant women in the USA. About two-thirds of these are primiparas. Most cases are very mild. Intractable uncompensated vomiting can be fatal, but therapeutic abortion is justified only in extreme cases.

There are no proved causes of vomiting of pregnancy. Psychically unstable women whose established reaction patterns to stress involve gastrointestinal disturbances often are affected. However, pregnant women who do not know that they are carrying a multiple pregnancy or hydatidiform mole often have severe vomiting. A markedly elevated hCG titer has been postulated as the cause.

Dehydration leads to fluid and electrolyte complications, particularly acidosis. Starvation causes hypoproteinemia and hypovitaminosis. Jaundice and hemorrhagic diatheses secondary to vitamin C and B complex deficiency as well as hypoprothrombinemia lead to bleeding from mucosal surfaces. The embryo or fetus may die in utero, and the patient sometimes succumbs to irreversible metabolic alterations or to visceral involvement.

In most cases, despite the severity of subjective complaints, there are few or no signs of nutritional deficiency.

In severely ill patients, hemoconcentration is reflected in a relative elevation of hemoglobin, red blood cells, and hematocrit. There may be a slight increase in white blood cells and a shift to the left of the differential count, with increased numbers of eosinophils and band forms.

Ketone bodies (acetone) will be found in the urine, which is usually concentrated. Slight proteinuria (trace to 1+) is a frequent finding.

In very ill patients, depletion of the serum proteins and alkali reserve is common. If the patient is oliguric, the blood urea nitrogen, serum sodium, and serum potassium may be elevated.

No specific abnormality is typical of hyperemesis. Nevertheless, one must search for possible hiatal hernia, peptic ulcer, or gastric carcinoma.

Periodic ophthalmoscopic evaluation may reveal retinal hemorrhage or detachment, which are unfavorable prognostic signs.

For the patient with **slight to moderate nausea and vomiting** of pregnancy, provide reassurance and relieve any fears related to pregnancy, ensure rest, and reduce the patient's work load. Prescribe sedation, eg, phenobarbital, 30–60 mg orally or rectally 2–3 times daily. Attempt to identify and resolve problems and conflicts.

For **severe nausea and vomiting** (hyperemesis gravidarum), hospitalize the patient in a quiet, cheerful, well-ventilated single room. Insist upon complete bed rest without bathroom privileges and record fluid intake and output accurately until improvement occurs. Give antiemetics (eg, dicyclomine hydrochloride [Bendectine] or chlorpromazine [Thorazine]) and protracted, moderate sedation, rectally or parenterally. Allow no visitors—not even the husband—until vomiting ceases and the patient is eating. Inform the family of the rationale of therapy and enlist their cooperation. Report to the husband daily regarding his wife's progress. Encourage the patient, emphasizing an early, complete recovery.

Permit nothing by mouth for the first 48 hours. Provide adequate parenteral fluids, electrolytes, carbohydrates, and protein by means of 10% glucose in water intravenously (2000 mL) and 5% in normal saline (1000 mL) daily, with potassium added, plus vitamins; and, if the serum proteins are depleted, intravenous amino acid preparations, eg, Amigen, 500 mL twice daily. (Blood transfusion should be used only if the patient is markedly anemic.) Vitamins—especially B complex, C, and K—should be added to the infusion. Many injectable B complex preparations are available to which ascorbic acid and vitamin K can be added.

Nasogastric tube feeding of a well-balanced liquid baby formula by slow drip should be instituted if the patient cannot retain food by mouth after 48 hours. If she responds to the above regimen after 48 hours, prescribe a dry diet in 6 small feedings daily with clear liquids 1 hour after meals.

If severe vomiting recurs before the patient is discharged from the hospital, parenteral therapy must be repeated from the beginning. Readmission to the hospital may be necessary.

Obtain medical and psychiatric consultation if the patient's condition deteriorates despite therapy. Delirium, blindness, tachycardia at rest, jaundice, anuria, and hemorrhage are ominous manifestations of severe organ toxicity; therapeutic abortion may be required in order to save the patient's life.

Vomiting of pregnancy usually is self-limited, and the prognosis is good. However, severe hyperemesis gravidarum may be a serious threat to the life of the mother and the fetus.

Hiatal Hernia

Hiatal hernia, or partial rupture of the stomach or esophagus (or both) through the diaphragm, develops in about 15% of obstetric patients as a result of increased intra-abdominal pressure during pregnancy and progressive enlargement of the uterus. These women have a weakened or congenitally widened crus of the diaphragm. Hiatal hernia occurs more often in multiparas and older or obese women.

Persistence of nausea and vomiting beyond mid pregnancy and progressive pyrosis, eructation, and regurgitation of food and acid contents during recumbency are typical findings. The sensation of substernal pressure may be severe and is relieved by erect posture but aggravated by lying down.

Many patients with pyrosis actually may have hiatal hernia. X-ray films after a barium swallow should show upward protrusion of the stomach with this abnormality. Erosive esophagitis or peptic ulcer may accompany hiatal hernia.

Conservative treatment usually is adequate to carry the patient through pregnancy and delivery. Prescribe a bland diet, antispasmodics, antacids, and sedatives, and caution the patient against lying down or exercising immediately after eating or drinking. Prevent unnecessary increases in intra-abdominal pressure by prescribing laxatives for constipation, by restricting lifting and straining, and by the use of low forceps delivery so that the patient will not have to bear down during the second stage of labor. The patient should sleep in a semireclining position. Obese women should be encouraged to reduce.

Postpartum surgery should be considered only if the symptoms are persistent and marked. The great majority of hiatal hernias disappear soon after delivery, and the relief of symptoms usually is dramatic.

Peptic Ulcer

Peptic ulcer is less common in women than in men and is not commonly diagnosed during pregnancy. An ulcer may occur or recur during pregnancy, but patients with known peptic ulcer usually improve during pregnancy. Postpartum flare-ups may develop.

Why such improvement frequently occurs is speculative. Nonetheless, willing acceptance of pregnancy, reduced gastric hydrochloric acid production, and lessened gastrointestinal motility seem to have an ameliorating effect on peptic ulcer.

Diagnosis and treatment during pregnancy is the same as for the nonpregnant person.

Heartburn

Heartburn (pyrosis or "acid indigestion") results

from gastroesophageal regurgitation. In late pregnancy, this may be aggravated by displacement of the stomach and duodenum by the uterine fundus.

A. Neostigmine Bromide (Prostigmin): Give 15 mg orally 3 times daily as necessary to stimulate gastrointestinal secretion and motility.

B. Acidifying Agents: Glutamic acid hydrochloride, 0.3 g 3 times daily before meals. (Hydrochloric acid solutions damage the teeth.) Avoid antacids during early pregnancy because gastric acidity is already low at this time.

C. Other Measures: Hard candy, hot tea, and changes of posture are helpful. In late pregnancy, antacids containing aluminum hydroxide gel to reduce gastric irritation are beneficial.

Constipation

Bowel sluggishness is common in pregnancy. It is due to suppression of smooth muscle motility by increased steroid sex hormones and pressure upon and displacement of the intestines by the enlarging uterus. Constipation frequently causes hemorrhoids and aggravates diverticulosis and diverticulitis.

A. General Measures: Stress good bowel habits. The patient should attempt to have an evacuation at the same time every day. The diet should consist of bulk foods, including roughage (unless contraindicated by gastrointestinal intolerance), laxative foods (citrus fruits, apples, prunes, dates, and figs), adequate cereal fiber (whole grain flour, bran), and a liberal fluid intake. Encourage exercise (walking, swimming, calisthenics).

B. Medical Treatment: To soften the stool, give bulk laxatives and "smoothage" agents that are neither absorbed by nor irritating to the bowel. By accumulating fluid volume, they increase peristalsis. Dioctyl sodium sulfosuccinate (Colace, Doxinate) has a detergent action; psyllium hydrophilic mucilloid (Metamucil) a hydrophilic one.

Prescribe mild laxatives such as cascara sagrada fluid extract, milk of magnesia, or phenolphthalein in more severe cases.

Avoid purges for fear of inducing labor. Do not prescribe mineral oil, since it prevents absorption of fat-soluble vitamins when administered in large amounts.

Hemorrhoids

Straining at stool and bearing down at delivery often exacerbate hemorrhoids, especially in women prone to varicosities. For these reasons, it is best to prevent or treat constipation early and to spare the patient from having to strain during the second stage of labor by using elective low forceps delivery with episiotomy when feasible.

For treatment, see discussion in Chapter 18.

Injection treatments to obliterate hemorrhoids during pregnancy are contraindicated. They may cause infection and extensive thrombosis of the pelvic veins and are rarely successful because of the great dilatation of many vessels.

Abdominal Pain

Intra-abdominal alterations causing pain during pregnancy include the following:

A. Pressure: Pelvic heaviness—a sense of "sagging" or "dragging"—is due to the weight of the uterus on the pelvic supports and the abdominal wall. Frequent rest periods in the supine or lateral recumbent position and a maternity girdle are recommended.

B. Round Ligament Tension: Tenderness along the course of the round ligament (usually to the left) during late pregnancy is due to traction on this structure by the uterus with rotation of the uterus and change of the patient's position. Local heat and treatment as for pain due to pressure are effective.

C. Flatulence, Distention, and Bowel Cramping: Large meals, fats, gas-forming foods, and chilled beverages are poorly tolerated by pregnant women. Mechanical displacement and compression of the bowel by the enlarged uterus, hypotonia of the intestines, and constipation predispose to gastrointestinal distress. Correct and simplify the diet, and reduce food intake at any one meal. The patient should maintain regular bowel habits; mild laxatives are prescribed when indicated. Recommend regular exercise and frequent change of body position.

D. Uterine Contractions: Braxton Hicks contractions are a normal phenomenon that may be distressing to nervous women. The onset of premature labor must be considered when forceful contractions develop, but if contractions remain infrequent and brief, the danger of early delivery is not significant. Analgesics (eg, acetaminophen) and sedatives (eg, phenobarbital, alcohol) may be of value. Codeine is rarely required.

E. Intra-abdominal Disorders: Pain due to obstruction or inflammation involving the gastrointestinal, urinary, nervous, or vascular system must be diagnosed and treated specifically.

F. Uterine or Adnexal Disease: Consider and treat pathologic pregnancy, eg, premature separation of the placenta, and tubal or ovarian disease appropriately.

G. Appendicitis: See p 878.

VIRAL HEPATITIS
(Infectious or Epidemic Hepatitis)

Infectious hepatitis affects females of all ages. The manifestations of epidemic hepatitis may be more severe and prolonged when the disease occurs in advanced pregnancy. Acute yellow atrophy of the liver may be a terminal phase of this disorder. When infectious hepatitis develops during the first trimester, the likelihood of fetal anomalies is increased about 2-fold. The incidence of abortion is not increased, but the frequency of fetal anomalies and premature delivery is.

Treatment consists of supportive medical measures as for the nonpregnant patient. Avoid operative obstetric intervention. Anesthetics, analgesics, and sedatives may be hepatotoxic. A low plasma pro-thrombin concentration may lead to hemorrhage, which should be treated with oral or parenteral vitamin K. No major surgical procedures should be performed unless the need is great. Therapeutic abortion is almost never advisable. The maternal and fetal risks are low if adequate nutrition is maintained.

Terminate pregnancy only in case of impending or actual hepatic coma. Deterioration may justify cesarean section if the infant is viable.

Administration of immune human serum globulin (gamma globulin), 0.01–0.03 mL/kg body weight, intramuscularly, to all contacts may prevent or reduce the severity of viral hepatitis. Transfusions increase the risk of viral hepatitis. Do not allow a pregnant patient to lose too much weight during periods when hepatitis is prevalent in the community (usually in the winter). Malnutrition may make the patient more susceptible to viral hepatitis.

Assuming good obstetric care and nutrition, the maternal mortality rate is approximately the same as that of nonpregnant women with viral hepatitis.

It is wise to allow at least 6 months to elapse between hepatitis and subsequent pregnancy. During this interval there must be no clinical abnormality related to liver dysfunction and no alterations in the BSP excretion, total blood proteins, serum albumin and globulin, A/G ratio, cephalin flocculation, thymol turbidity, alkaline phosphatase, and serum trans-aminase. All tests should be done in the same laboratory and repeated at 2 months, 4 months, and 6 months after delivery and early during the next pregnancy.

BILIARY TRACT DISORDERS

Cholelithiasis

Biliary colic is more common in pregnant than in nonpregnant women. Cholelithiasis and cholecystitis are responsible for biliary colic, but the exact sequence is still unclear. It is probable that during pregnancy increased amounts of cholesterol in the bile, altered bile salts, biliary stasis, and sepsis are responsible. Certainly, gallstones are more frequently diagnosed in women of advanced parity than in nulliparas of the same age and background. Smaller stones, particularly those that become impacted in the cystic duct, are most likely to cause biliary colic. Although gallstones generally are asymptomatic, even mild cholecystitis may trigger acute biliary colic. Biliary calculi and acute inflammation of the gallbladder are almost always coexistent.

Acute Cholecystitis

Acute cholecystitis occurs in about 1:4000 pregnancies. It is more common in older gravidas, during late pregnancy, and in those who have had previous attacks.

Displacement or compression of the extrahepatic biliary system by the enlarged pregnant uterus may interfere with circulation and drainage of the gallblad-der. This often predisposes to acute cholecystitis. Chemical and bacterial inflammation of the gallblad-der and duct system lead to empyema, perforation of the gallbladder, and peritonitis.

Rule out pyelonephritis and acute appendicitis. (The appendix is rotated high and to the right by the enlarging fundus during pregnancy.) The major obstet-ric complication to be considered in the differential diagnosis is premature separation of the placenta, but in this disorder discomfort is well localized to the uterus.

The patient should receive nothing by mouth, but fluid and electrolyte balance must be maintained. Broad-spectrum antibiotic therapy, eg, cephalothin (Keflin), 500 mg intravenously 4 times daily, is pru-dent therapy. Meperidine (Demerol), 50–100 mg in-tramuscularly every 4 hours for pain, and atropine, 0.4 mg intramuscularly every 4 hours as an antispasmodic, are helpful. The attack should subside within 36–48 hours in most cases of cholecystitis.

If the patient fails to respond, if jaundice develops (common duct stone), or if peritonitis (rupture of gallbladder) ensues, surgery may be lifesaving. Cholecystostomy usually is the operation of choice. Because of inadequate operative exposure due to the enlarged uterus and the risk of spread of sepsis during pregnancy, cholecystectomy generally must be de-ferred until after delivery.

Abortion and cesarean section are not medically indicated for acute cholecystitis. However, fever and stress of surgery may precipitate premature labor and delivery.

RECURRENT JAUNDICE
(HEPATIC CHOLESTASIS)
OF PREGNANCY

Cholestatic or recurrent jaundice of pregnancy is an uncommon disorder of successive gestations caused by an inherited error of liver metabolism. Estrogen apparently provokes hepatic excretory insufficiency and may be a distressing and confusing complication of pregnancy.

Cholestatic jaundice of pregnancy is charac-terized by itching, gastrointestinal complaints, and jaundice. The disorder occurs during the last trimester of pregnancy, but symptoms disappear within 2 weeks following delivery. Most determinations of liver disease are only slightly elevated, but cephalin floccu-lation and thymol turbidity tests are normal in this disorder.

The diagnosis of cholestatic jaundice of preg-nancy requires the exclusion of other liver disorders (viral hepatitis, drug toxicity) and of cholecystitis. A history of jaundice during a previous pregnancy or with oral contraceptives is diagnostically helpful.

Treatment is symptomatic. Ion exchange resin and absorption of bile salts will diminish jaundice and itching. However, the phenothiazines frequently employed to relieve itching are contraindicated because these drugs will intensify the jaundice. The offspring is rarely affected except in severe cases, when chronic fetal distress may develop. If labor intervenes before recovery, the fetus should be carefully monitored.

Abortion is not indicated, but early delivery may be warranted. The disorder should be managed with careful fetal surveillance, although urinary estriol levels are poorly predictive of fetal compromise in this disorder.

Combination oral contraceptives will activate cholestatic jaundice, but progestogen alone should be well tolerated. Cholestatic jaundice invariably affects all advanced pregnancies in susceptible women.

ACUTE FATTY LIVER OF PREGNANCY

Acute fatty liver of pregnancy is a devastating, rare disorder of uncertain origin. It may be the chief manifestation of some unidentified multisystem disorder. Malnutrition, occupational exposure to toxic chemicals, and drug ingestion (tetracyclines, alcohol) during the last trimester have been studied as possible causes.

Severe nausea and vomiting, hematemesis, abdominal pain, jaundice, stupor, and progressive hepatic insufficiency are typical findings. The differential diagnosis includes toxic or viral hepatitis, cholestatic liver dysfunction, cholecystitis, and pancreatitis.

If a cause cannot be identified and treated, supportive management is all that can be offered. The outlook is poor in any case. Most neonates are stillborn, and about 85% of women with the disorder die, most of them early in the puerperium. Disseminated intravascular coagulation or renal failure is often the immediate cause of death. The prognosis is most favorable in cases where organs other than the liver are relatively unaffected.

REGIONAL ENTERITIS
(Crohn's Disease)

Nonspecific granulomatous ileocolitis is most uncommon in obstetric patients. The cause is unknown, but serious psychogenic factors can be identified in most patients with this diagnosis. Most cases complicating pregnancy represent reactivation of previous nonspecific enteritis. The perinatal mortality rate is increased relative to the severity of the disorder.

The symptoms include diarrhea, abdominal pain, tenderness over the ileum or colon, and low-grade fever. X-ray findings include mucosal irregularities, ulceration, stiffening of the bowel wall, and luminal constriction of the terminal ileum. Laboratory tests reveal no specific pathogens.

Antibiotic and supportive therapy are recommended. Operation should be deferred until after delivery unless perforation, hemorrhage, or other

emergency demands intervention. Psychotherapy may be invaluable, particularly in cases where the pregnancy is unwanted or where emotional assets and support are limited. Interruption of an early pregnancy may be justified when pregnancy exacerbates regional enteritis or when a fulminating case defies medical treatment. Later in pregnancy, interruption rarely is helpful and may even compromise the patient, especially when a bowel resection is necessary. Cesarean section should be accomplished only for obstetric reasons. The prognosis is best for patients who develop the disorder late in pregnancy or in the puerperium. Counseling regarding contraception and sterilization is a must for patients with regional enteritis.

DIABETES MELLITUS*

Diabetes mellitus is a term used to denote at least 2 major types of disorders of carbohydrate, lipid, and protein metabolism. Type I, insulin-dependent diabetes, is usually of juvenile onset and is associated with deficiency of insulin secretion, so that ketoacidosis is likely if exogenous insulin is withheld. Pathogenesis of type I diabetes is multifactorial, with genetic predisposition (family history and HLA type), and may be associated with viral infections and autoimmune responses of the islet cells (insulitis and antibodies to islet cells). Type II diabetes is non–insulin-dependent, since elevated serum insulin levels are often found. This disorder has a strong hereditary component and usually develops in adults who are overweight. It is unclear whether hyperinsulinism or obesity develops first. Excess insulin can contribute to excess triglyceride synthesis in adipose tissue, and obesity is characterized by decreased number or affinity of insulin receptors. The state of insulin resistance explains the glucose intolerance and probably leads to further hypertrophy of the islets of Langerhans and to hyperinsulinism.

The effects of deficiency of secretion or activity of insulin on carbohydrate metabolism are 2-fold. There is underutilization of glucose by skeletal muscle, adipose tissue, and the liver, which results in postprandial hyperglycemia. With insulinopenia, hepatic glycogenolysis and gluconeogenesis is excessive, and overproduction of glucose contributes to hyperglycemia in the postabsorptive period (between meals). When hyperglycemia exceeds the renal threshold for glucose reabsorption, glycosuria can result in osmotic diuresis and total body water and electrolyte depletion.

The metabolic derangement of lipid metabolism associated with diabetes (insulin lack, perhaps glucagon excess) is excessive lipolysis and enhanced ketogenesis. Increased mobilization of free fatty acids from adipose tissue leads to increased plasma levels of free fatty acids. These are oxidized at an accelerated rate to the ketone acids β-hydroxybutyrate and

*This section is contributed by John L. Kitzmiller, MD.

acetoacetate in the liver cells in poorly controlled diabetes. Excessive ketonemia leads to metabolic acidosis. Insulin deficiency also results in increased reesterification of free fatty acids to triglycerides within liver cells, with increased hepatic production and decreased peripheral clearance of very low density lipoproteins.

Insulin deficiency also results in diminished uptake of amino acids by skeletal muscle, decreased protein synthesis, and proteolysis. In poorly controlled diabetes, protein breakdown leads to increased urinary excretion of nitrogen, even negative nitrogen balance. As a result of reduced uptake of amino acids by muscle, blood levels of the branched-chain amino acids leucine, isoleucine, and valine increase, and alanine and glycine, released by muscle, contribute to hepatic gluconeogenesis.

Hormone & Fuel Balance During Normal Pregnancy

Pregnancy produces major changes in the homeostasis of all metabolic fuels, which, in turn, affect the management of diabetes. Plasma concentrations of glucose in the postabsorptive state decline as pregnancy advances, because of increasing placental uptake of glucose and a probable limitation on hepatic glucose output. Therefore, fasting hypoglycemia is more common during pregnancy. Gluconeogenesis could be limited by a relative lack of the major substrate alanine. The plasma concentration of alanine has been shown in some studies to be lower during pregnancy, probably as a result of placental uptake and a restraint on proteolysis. Although fat deposition is accentuated in early pregnancy, lipolysis is enhanced by human placental lactogen (hPL) later in gestation, and more glycerol and free fatty acids are released in the postabsorptive state. Ketogenesis is thus accentuated in the postabsorptive state during pregnancy, probably secondary to increased provision of substrate free fatty acids and hormonal effects on the maternal liver cells.

The balance of metabolic fuels is also different in the fed state during pregnancy. Despite hyperinsulinism in normal pregnancy, the disposal of glucose is impaired, producing somewhat higher maternal blood levels. The contrainsulin effects of gestation have been related to hPL, progesterone, and cortisol. The disappearance in plasma of administered insulin is not greater during pregnancy, despite the presence of placental insulin receptors and degrading enzymes. Glucagon is well suppressed by glucose during pregnancy, and secretory responses of glucagon to amino acids are not increased above nonpregnant levels. After meals, more glucose is converted to triglyceride in pregnant compared with nonpregnant animals, which would tend to conserve calories and enhance fat deposition. Insulin resistance during pregnancy does not seem to extend to the lipogenic and antilipolytic effects of the hormone.

Classification of Diabetes During Pregnancy

Diabetic pregnant women have been classified on the basis of duration and severity of diabetes (Table 38–2). A classification system (White) was originally used for prognosis of perinatal outcome and to determine obstetric management. Because perinatal mortality has declined dramatically for many reasons in women in all classes, the system is now used mainly to

Table 38–2. Classification of diabetes during pregnancy (Priscilla White).

Class	Characteristics	Implications
Glucose intolerance of pregnancy	So-called gestational diabetes; abnormal glucose tolerance during pregnancy; postprandial hyperglycemia during pregnancy.	Diagnosis before 30 weeks' gestation is important to prevent macrosomia; treatment with diabetic pregnancy diet adequate in calories to prevent maternal weight loss. Goal is fasting plasma glucose < 105 mg/dL, 2-hour postprandial plasma glucose < 120 mg/dL. If insulin is necessary, manage as in classes B, C, and D.
A	Chemical diabetes diagnosed before pregnancy; managed by diet alone; any age at onset.	Management same as for gestational diabetes.
B	Insulin treatment necessary before pregnancy; onset ≥ age 20; duration < 10 years.	Some endogenous insulin secretion may persist; insulin resistance at the cellular level in obese women; fetal and neonatal risks equivalent to classes C and D, as is management.
C	Onset at age 10–20, or duration 10–20 years.	Insulin-deficient diabetes of juvenile onset.
D	Onset before age 10, or duration > 20 years, or chronic hypertension (not preeclampsia), or benign retinopathy (tiny hemorrhages).	Fetal macrosomia or intrauterine growth retardation possible; so-called retinal microaneurysms may progress during pregnancy, then regress after delivery.
F	Diabetic nephropathy with proteinuria.	Anemia and hypertension common; proteinuria increases in third trimester, declines after pregnancy; fetal intrauterine growth retardation common; perinatal survival about 85% under optimal conditions; bed rest necessary (class T—post–renal transplant—outlook is good).
H	Coronary artery disease.	Serious maternal risk.
R	Malignant proliferative retinopathy.	Neovascularization; risk of vitreous hemorrhage or retinal detachment; laser photocoagulation is useful; abortion usually not necessary; route of delivery is controversial.

describe and compare populations of diabetic pregnant women. However, certain characteristics of patients are still pertinent. The risk of complications is minimal in gestational diabetics (glucose intolerance of pregnancy) well controlled by diet alone, and they may be otherwise managed as normal pregnant women. Class B women, whose insulin dependence is of recent onset, will probably have residual islet B cell function, and control of hyperglycemia may be easier than in class C or D patients; however, fetal and neonatal risks are generally equivalent. Finally, the most complicated and difficult pregnancies occur in women with renal, retinal, or cardiovascular disease.

The hormonal and metabolic effects of pregnancy increase the tendency to both hypoglycemic reactions and ketoacidosis. The amount of insulin required to maintain good control will probably increase dramatically throughout pregnancy. Polyhydramnios is common in diabetic pregnant women and may lead to premature delivery. Fetal distress may develop in the third trimester, especially if diabetic control has been inadequate. Careful fetal monitoring must be used to prevent stillbirths. The high incidence of fetal macrosomia (birth weight > 90th percentile for gestational age) increases both the potential for difficult vaginal delivery and the primary cesarean section rate. In contrast, fetal intrauterine growth retardation may occur in women with diabetic vascular disease. The risk of congenital malformations is increased in infants of diabetic mothers, as is the risk of respiratory distress syndrome, macrosomia, hypoglycemia, hyperbilirubinemia, hypocalcemia, and poor feeding in the neonate. However, these problems are limited to the special care nursery, and childhood development is usually normal. Despite these possible complications of pregnancy, diabetic women now have a 96–98% chance of survival of a healthy child in some centers if they adhere to a program of careful management and surveillance.

Glucose Intolerance of Pregnancy

The hormonal and metabolic changes of pregnancy result in the diagnosis of glucose intolerance during the second half of gestation in 2–3% of pregnant women. Criteria for diagnosis are given in Table 38–3. It is unclear whether glucose intolerance of pregnancy results from inadequate insulin response to carbohydrate load, from excessive resistance to the action of insulin, or from both. Once the diagnosis has been made, the patient should be placed on a diabetic diet modified for pregnancy, ie, 30–35 kcal/kg ideal weight; 50–60% carbohydrate, 20–25% protein, and 20% fat. Calories are distributed over 3 meals and 3 snacks. The goal of therapy is not weight reduction but prevention of both fasting and postprandial hyperglycemia. If postprandial plasma glucose values are consistently above 120 mg/dL, it is necessary to determine if the "hyperglycemia" will persist on the same diet given in the hospital. If the diet fails to prevent hyperglycemia, insulin therapy is begun, and the patient is managed as if insulin-dependent.

Table 38–3. Diagnosis of glucose intolerance during pregnancy.

Indications for screening

All gravidas

  or

All gravidas overweight* or > 25 years of age

  plus

Gravidas with glycosuria; a history of diabetes in parents, siblings, aunts, or uncles; or a history of stillbirth or macrosomic infant.

Screen with glucose loading test

50 g of glucose by mouth at 20 and 28 weeks' gestation; if whole blood or plasma glucose exceeds 112 or 130 mg/dL, respectively, gravida should have a glucose tolerance test.

Oral glucose tolerance tests†

100 g of glucose by mouth

	Fasting	1 h	2 h	3 h
Plasma or serum glucose† (mg/dL)	> 105	> 190	> 165	> 145
(Glucose oxidase method)	(100)	(180)	(160)	(140)

Test is abnormal if 2 of 3 postprandial values are elevated above values listed. Glucose should not be given if fasting blood is > 130 mg/dL.

*< 5 ft 5 in, > 150 lb in first trimester; > 5 ft 5 in, > 180 lb in first trimester.

†Criteria of National Diabetes Data Group (NIH). (See *Diabetes* 1979;**28**:1039.)

The treatment of all glucose-intolerant women with an arbitrary amount of insulin should reduce the incidence of macrosomia; however, this benefit must be balanced against the unknown risk of producing insulin antibodies in women who may well need insulin therapy later in life. The new "pure" insulins may obviate this problem. Follow-up studies indicate that approximately 40% of women with glucose intolerance during pregnancy will develop overt diabetes in 10–20 years. This has been used to justify the term "gestational diabetes." Nevertheless, many of these women will not develop diabetes, especially if they maintain ideal body weight. These women are currently, and perhaps unfairly, labeled as diabetics during pregnancy. Glucose intolerance of pregnancy seems a more appropriate diagnosis.

Insulin Management

The goal of insulin therapy during pregnancy is to prevent both fasting and postprandial hyperglycemia and to avoid debilitating hypoglycemic reactions. The level of glucose control that will yield the least maternal and perinatal morbidity has not yet been established. However, one should aim for fasting plasma glucose levels below 120 mg/dL and postprandial levels below 160 mg/dL. Self-monitoring of capillary blood glucose at home with glucose oxidase strips and portable reflectance colorimeters has proved a reliable means of helping patients monitor the course of therapy. Since hemoglobin A_{1c} (Hb A_{1c}) correlates with mean daily capillary blood glucose over a few weeks during pregnancy, sequential measurement of Hb A_{1c} (normal range 5–6%) will provide another

Table 38–4. Illustration of use of home blood glucose monitoring to determine insulin dosage during pregnancy.

Self-Monitored Capillary Blood Glucose		Insulin Doses
Fasting blood glucose	148 mg/dL	14 units regular, 28 units intermediate
1 h after breakfast	206 mg/dL	
1 h after lunch	152 mg/dL	
1 h after supper	198 mg/dL	9 units regular, 10 units intermediate
2–4 AM	142 mg/dL	

Suggested changes based on pattern of blood glucose values over 2–3 days: slight increases in presupper intermediate insulin to control fasting blood glucose next day, in morning regular insulin to control postbreakfast glucose, and in presupper regular insulin to control postsupper hyperglycemia. Dose of morning intermediate insulin is adequate to control early afternoon blood glucose. When dose of presupper intermediate insulin is increased, patient should test to detect and prevent nocturnal hypoglycemia. One-hour postprandial testing is advised to detect the probable peaks of glycemic excursions. Patient should also test when symptoms of hypoglycemia appear.

indicator of long-term control. Yet, because insulin dosage must be frequently adjusted up or down during the metabolically dynamic state of pregnancy, capillary blood glucose must be measured several times each day to assist in the "fine-tuning" of insulin management.

Most pregnant insulin-dependent patients will require at least 2 injections of about a 1:2 mixture of regular and intermediate insulin each day in order to prevent fasting and postprandial hyperglycemia. The usual practice is to give two-thirds of the insulin before breakfast and one-third before supper (Table 38–4). More stringent regimens of administering regular subcutaneous insulin 4–6 times each day or continuously with a portable insulin pump are under investigation.

Hypoglycemic reactions are more frequent and sometimes more severe in early pregnancy. Therefore, patients must keep glucagon on hand, and a member of the household must be instructed in the technique of injection. Hypoglycemic reactions have not been associated with fetal death or congenital anomalies.

Fetal Development & Growth

Major congenital anomalies are those which may severely affect the life of the individual or require major surgery for correction. The incidence of major congenital anomalies in infants of diabetic mothers is 6–12%, compared with 2% in infants of a nondiabetic population. While perinatal deaths due to stillbirth and respiratory distress syndrome have declined in pregnancies complicated by diabetes, the proportion of fetal and neonatal deaths ascribed to congenital anomalies has risen to 50–80%. The types of anomalies most common in infants of diabetic mothers and their presumed time of occurrence during embryonic development are listed in Table 38–5. It is apparent that any intervention to reduce the incidence of major congenital anomalies must be applied very early in pregnancy. For unknown reasons, the incidence of anomalies is highest in infants delivered of diabetic mothers with vascular disease. The additional finding that the excess risk of anomalies is associated with the group of diabetic women with elevated Hb A_{1c} early in pregnancy suggests that poor diabetic control is related to the risk of major congenital anomalies in infants of diabetic mothers. Protocols of rigid, early diabetic management are being evaluated to determine whether the incidence of congenital anomalies can be reduced.

Ultrasonography in the first half of pregnancy may detect neural tube defects (anencephaly, meningomyelocele) that occur with a higher than normal incidence in infants of diabetic mothers. The physician should also screen all insulin-dependent pregnant women for elevated serum alpha-fetoprotein levels at 14–16 weeks' gestation to detect other cases of neural tube defects. Later in pregnancy, sophisticated ultrasonographic examinations may detect congenital heart defects or other anomalies.

An initial ultrasonographic examination at about 16 weeks confirms the dating of gestation, and subsequent examinations at 26 and 36 weeks measure fetal growth. Many of these infants are large for dates, ie, macrosomic infants with increased body fat and glycogen stores, increased length, and increased abdomen-to-head or thorax-to-head ratios. The hypothesis that fetal macrosomia resulted from the causal chain of maternal hyperglycemia → fetal hyperglycemia → fetal hyperinsulinemia → fetal macrosomia has long

Table 38–5. Congenital malformations in infants of diabetic mothers.[*]

	Ratio of Incidences Diabetic vs Control Group	Latest Gestational Age for Occurrence (Weeks After Menstruation)
Caudal regression	252	5
Anencephaly	3	6
Spina bifida, hydrocephalus, or other central nervous system defects	2	6
Cardiac anomalies	4	
Transposition of great vessels		7
Ventricular septal defect		8
Atrial septal defect		8
Anal/rectal atresia	3	8
Renal anomalies	5	
Agenesis	6	7
Cystic kidney	4	7
Ureter duplex	23	7
Situs inversus	84	6

[*]Modified and reproduced, with permission, from Kucera J: Rate and type of congenital anomalies among offspring of diabetic women. *J Reprod Med* 1971;7:61; and Mills JL, Baker L, Goldman AS: Malformations in infants of diabetic mothers occur before the seventh gestational week: Implications for treatment. *Diabetes* 1979;28:292.

been debated. Excess insulin increases fetal glycogen and fat deposition. Macrosomic infants of diabetic mothers have significantly higher concentrations of C peptide in their cord sera (representing endogenous insulin secretion) than do infants of diabetic mothers of birth weight appropriate for gestational age. The determinants of fetal hyperinsulinemia throughout pregnancy may not be simply maternal hyperglycemia, however. Other metabolic substrates that cross the placenta and are insulinogenic, eg, branched-chain amino acids, may play a role in fetal macrosomia.

The degree of maternal glycemia is related to birth weights of infants of diabetic mothers adjusted for gestational age. This suggests that prevention of maternal hyperglycemia throughout pregnancy may reduce the incidence of macrosomia. Pilot studies of highly selected patients have shown this to be the case in many but not all instances. The metabolic and nutritional determinants of birth weights of infants of diabetic mothers other than maternal glucose are under study.

Polyhydramnios is an excess volume of amniotic fluid (> 1000 mL, often > 3000 mL). It may cause severe discomfort or premature labor and is most often associated with fetal macrosomia. The excess volume of amniotic fluid was not related to the concentration of glucose or other solutes in amniotic fluid or to excess fetal urine output as measured by change in bladder size by means of ultrasonography in one study. Additional possible factors in causation of polyhydramnios in diabetic pregnancies include fetal swallowing, decidual and amniotic fluid prolactin, and yet unknown determinants of the complicated multicompartmental intrauterine transfer of water. However, diuretics do little to mobilize excessive amniotic fluid.

In contrast to fetal macrosomia, the fetus of a woman with diabetes of long duration and vascular disease may suffer intrauterine growth retardation. This problem is apparently related to inadequate uteroplacental perfusion. All body diameters may be below normal on ultrasonographic measurements; oligohydramnios is common; and after 30 weeks' gestation, maternal plasma or urinary estriol levels are usually below the 95% confidence limits for stage of gestation.

Obstetric Management

Not long ago, the incidence of apparently sudden intrauterine fetal demise in the third trimester of diabetic pregnancies was at least 5%. Since the risk increased as pregnancies approached term, preterm delivery was instituted but risk of neonatal death from respiratory distress syndrome increased. Curiously, the cause of stillbirth was usually not obvious. The risk was greater with poor diabetic control, and the incidence of fetal death exceeded 50% with ketoacidosis. Some instances of fetal demise were associated with preeclampsia, which formerly was a common complication of diabetic pregnancy. Today, the incidence of preeclampsia in pregnant diabetics is only slightly above that in nondiabetic pregnant women. Fetal death

was also associated with pyelonephritis, which is now largely prevented by screening for and treating asymptomatic bacteriuria. Other than these known risk factors, one can speculate that fetal distress was related to (1) a combination of relative fetal hypoxia and hyperglycemia, (2) severe hypoglycemia (although there is no clinical evidence for this), or (3) fetal myocardial dysfunction.

In the past decade, conceptual and technologic advances have permitted the application of several techniques to detect fetal distress and prevent stillbirth. The infrequency of fetal movement as noted in fetal activity determinations (FAD) may indicate fetal jeopardy. More quantitative studies of fetal activity patterns using ultrasonography are under investigation. The rationale for the use of estriol assays and continuous monitoring of the fetal heart rate (FHR) as measures of fetal well-being is discussed on p 603. A nonreactive nonstress test (FAD) may be suspicious and should be followed promptly by a contraction stress test. Daily monitoring of serum or 24-hour urinary estriol is necessary so as not to miss the rapid decline to below 40% of the recent mean level exhibited by a fetus in distress. If the estriol and FHR tests remain normal, the pregnancy may continue to term. Both tests have a definite false-positive rate. Therefore, one should not depend on only one assessment to diagnose fetal distress. Diagnostic specificity is increased by using both tests. True fetal jeopardy is reflected by both low or falling estriol levels and an abnormal FHR pattern.

Insulin-dependent diabetic patients are usually admitted to the hospital at 36 weeks' gestation or earlier for fetal monitoring and careful control of diabetes. However, women achieving very good control (fasting blood glucose about 100 mg/dL, 1-hour postprandial blood glucose < 150 mg/dL) with home blood glucose monitoring probably have no excess risk of fetal distress and may not require antepartum admission to the hospital.

Unless maternal or fetal complications arise, the goal for the termination of pregnancy should be 38 weeks or even later, in order to reduce neonatal morbidity from preterm deliveries. Before the delivery decision is made, fetal pulmonary maturity should be determined. The standard test for pulmonary maturity is the lecithin/sphingomyelin (L/S) ratio, in which a value greater than 2 indicates a low risk for respiratory distress syndrome. However, in pregnancies complicated by diabetes, most authors have reported a false-positive rate of 6–12% with L/S values between 2 and 3. The reason for the discrepancy is unknown, but the lowest risk for respiratory distress syndrome is attained by delaying delivery (if possible) until L/S reaches a supranormal ratio greater than 3.5. The false-negative rate for L/S ratios of 1.5–2.0 is at least 50% in nondiabetic pregnancies (ie, delivery occurs within 72 hours but respiratory distress syndrome does not develop). Other amniotic fluid assays, eg, desaturated phosphatidylcholine or phosphatidylglycerol, may have greater diagnostic specificity, but they are yet to be tested in large numbers of diabetic pregnant women.

Once fetal lung maturity is likely, the route of delivery must be selected based on the usual obstetric indications. If the fetus seems large on clinical and ultrasonographic examination ($\geq$ 4300 g), primary cesarean section probably should be performed because of the possibility of shoulder dystocia. Otherwise, labor induction is reasonable, because maternal and peripartum risks are less following vaginal delivery. Once labor is under way, continuous FHR monitoring with scalp pH backup measurements must be performed.

Traditional insulin management for labor and delivery has been to give only one-third to one-half the prepregnancy dose in the morning. The diabetic parturient may be unusually sensitive to insulin after delivery, and insulin shock is possible if delivery occurs sooner than anticipated. Protocols for continuous low-dose intravenous insulin administration during labor or prior to cesarean delivery are being appraised to determine whether stringent control of blood glucose will reduce the incidence of intrapartum fetal distress and neonatal metabolic problems. A cord blood glucose level at delivery correlates positively with the slightly higher maternal levels, and there does not seem to be an upper limit on placental transfer of glucose. During labor, maternal plasma glucose can usually be kept below 120 mg/dL with 1–2 units of regular insulin and 7.5 g of dextrose given intravenously every hour. If cesarean section is necessary, insulin management is similar, and infants do equally well with general, spinal, or epidural anesthesia. Nonetheless, the anesthesiologist should be cautioned against the administration of copious glucose-containing intravenous solutions.

Neonatal Morbidity

Planning for the care of infants of diabetic mothers should begin prior to delivery, with participation by the neonatologist in decisions about timing and management of delivery. The pediatrician must be in attendance to know of antenatal problems, to assess the need for resuscitation, and to determine major congenital anomalies.

Infants of diabetic mothers have an increased risk of respiratory distress syndrome compared with infants of matched nondiabetic mothers. Possible reasons include abnormal production of pulmonary surfactant or connective tissue changes leading to decreased pulmonary compliance. The relationship of fetal metabolic characteristics to pulmonary abnormalities in the environment of maternal diabetes is not yet clear. However, in recent years, the incidence of respiratory distress syndrome has declined from 24% to 5%, probably related to use of the L/S ratio and delivery of most infants at term (see above). The diagnosis of respiratory distress syndrome is based on clinical signs (grunting, retractions, respiratory rate > 60/min), typical findings on chest x-ray (diffuse reticulogranular pattern and air bronchograms), and an increased oxygen requirement (to maintain the P_{aO_2} at 50–70 mm Hg) for more than 48 hours with no other identified cause of respiratory difficulty (heart disease, infection). Survival of infants with respiratory distress syndrome has dramatically improved as a result of advances in ventilation therapy.

Hypoglycemia is common in the first 48 hours after delivery and is defined as blood glucose below 30 mg/dL regardless of gestational age. The symptomatic infant may be lethargic rather than jittery, and hypoglycemia may be associated with apnea, tachypnea, cyanosis, or seizures. Hypoglycemia has been related to elevated fetal insulin levels during and after delivery. Nevertheless, infants of diabetic mothers may also have deficient catecholamine and glucagon secretion, and the hypoglycemia may be related to diminished hepatic glucose production and oxidation of free fatty acids. The neonatologist attempts to prevent hypoglycemia in "well" infants with early feedings of 10% dextrose in water by bottle or gavage by 1 hour of age. If this is not successful, treatment with glucagon injections or intravenous dextrose solutions is indicated. Rigid control of diabetes to prevent fetal hyperglycemia may reduce the incidence of neonatal hypoglycemia. Long-term sequelae of episodes of neonatal hypoglycemia are uncertain, but follow-up studies suggest that some offspring of diabetic mothers are neurologically impaired.

Other frequent problems in infants of diabetic mothers include hypocalcemia (< 7 mg/dL), hyperbilirubinemia (> 15 mg/dL), polycythemia (central hematocrit > 70%), and poor feeding. Further investigation is necessary to determine the cause of these problems. Better control of the maternal diabetic state in the future should reduce their incidence.

PANCREATITIS

Pancreatitis is rare in pregnant women. The cause is unknown, although many have been postulated. Pancreatitis may occur in association with alcoholic excess, hyperthyroidism, hyperlipemia (often after oral contraceptive use), or vasculitis, or during cortisone or thiazide therapy. Pregnancy does not alter the course of pancreatitis, and pregnancy is not influenced by the disorder.

The chief symptom of acute pancreatitis is abrupt onset of severe, steady epigastric pain radiating through to the back—often after a heavy meal or alcohol intake. A previous mild attack may be described. Premonitory symptoms often include vague gastrointestinal discomfort for 1–2 days. Epigastric tenderness without guarding, rigidity, or rebound is usual. Slight abdominal distention without bowel sounds may be expected. Fever, tachycardia, hypotension, pallor, and shock may be noted. Mild jaundice is common, but a palpable upper abdominal mass is rare.

Serum amylase is greatly elevated within 24 hours, returning to normal by the third day. Leukocytosis, hyperglycemia, glycosuria, and perhaps proteinuria may develop. Serum bilirubin blood urea nitrogen, and serum alkaline phosphatase are usually elevated.

X-ray may disclose gallstones or a "sentinel loop" of gas-distended small bowel in the left upper quadrant. These are suggestive but not diagnostic of pancreatitis.

The differential diagnosis must consider common duct stone or the rare perforated peptic ulcer with elevated serum amylase. Other problems with similar symptoms are mesenteric thrombosis, renal colic, acute cholecystitis, and intestinal obstruction.

Treatment includes meperidine (Demerol) or pentazocine (Talwin) for pain and atropine sulfate, 0.4–0.6 mg subcutaneously, as an antispasmodic. The patient should receive nothing by mouth; fluids and electrolytes given intravenously may be necessary. Antibiotics are reserved for septic complications.

Early surgical consultation should be requested. Conservative measures during pregnancy are preferred, and surgery is warranted only when the diagnosis is in doubt.

Severe pancreatitis or operation may precipitate premature labor and delivery. Pancreatitis may recur, but chronic pancreatitis will develop in only about 10% of acute cases. Diabetes mellitus is a rare complication.

RENAL & URINARY TRACT PROBLEMS

Pregnancy causes anatomic changes in the urinary system such as dilatation of the ureters and collecting system. This is due primarily to the effect of estrogen and secondarily to pressure of the presenting part in advanced pregnancy. There is no ureteral hypotonicity, however, if one uses a closed system for recording. Dextroversion and dextrorotation of the uterus cause more dilatation of the right than of the left ureter. Sporadic vesicoureteral reflux occurs in many pregnant patients, possibly as a result of shortening of the ureter in the bladder wall, which reduces the normal valve effect.

Assessment of Renal Function

Many problems complicate renal testing during pregnancy. These include endocrine factors such as increased secretion of cortisol, renin, thyroid hormones, growth hormone, and somatomammotropin. Moreover, renal function varies depending upon the total blood volume and the patient's posture and physical activity. Sodium intake and aldosterone cause augmentation of serum sodium. Carbohydrates and corticosteroids increase serum glucose levels.

The glomerular filtration rate (GFR) is increased by about 50% during pregnancy, and a return to normal nonpregnant levels occurs during the early puerperium. The renal plasma flow (RPF) is also increased by approximately 25% by the end of the second trimes-

ter. After this, there is a fall of RPF to control levels in the last trimester and a drop below nonpregnant levels in the early puerperium. A return to normal nonpregnant levels should occur after 2 months.

The actual filtration rate (GFR/RPF) is moderately increased during pregnancy. It gradually peaks near term and returns to prepregnancy levels in the puerperium. Consequently, there is a decrease in NPN, BUN, serum creatinine, and serum uric acid.

Renal function seems to be slightly better during the night when the patient is supine. Moreover, better function is likely when the individual is lying on her left side, which is the best position for laboratory studies.

Sodium and water retention, especially during late pregnancy, is due to increased levels of corticosteroids and aldosterone, together with increased tubular absorption of water, venous congestion, and hypersensitivity to vasopressin. All this contributes to edema, which appears first in the lower extremities. In preeclampsia-eclampsia, endogenous angiotensin II is increased and renin and aldosterone levels are reduced.

Diuretics should be avoided during pregnancy and especially during renal evaluation. Potent diuretics are dangerous because they may cause hypokalemia and hyponatremia, particularly in patients on diets or when salt is restricted. Vasopressin may cause oliguria.

Postural changes alter renal function, and pelvic venous congestion is increased by pressure of the pregnant uterus on the vena cava. Moreover, oxytocin has a slight antidiuretic component (vasopressin) and, when administered in large quantities, may cause water intoxication.

Occasional obstetric patients may have slight orthostatic proteinuria. In testing for orthostatic proteinuria, empty the bladder, require the patient to remain supine until the next voiding, and then allow her to assume the erect posture and ambulate until she voids again. To fulfill the criteria for orthostatic proteinuria, the patient must have proteinuria only while erect. (Normal is < 1 g protein per day, assuming a normal urinary sediment.)

Urinary Screening Procedures*

First visit: Obtain a medical and obstetric history and perform a complete physical examination. Do a qualitative urinalysis and complete blood count.

Subsequent visits: Every 4 weeks through the 28th week; every 2 weeks through the 36th week; and weekly thereafter. The blood pressure, weight, and results of urinalysis should be recorded as well as any unusual symptoms or signs.

If the specific gravity is < 1.020, repeat in the morning after fluid restriction. If the specific gravity is still < 1.020, the patient probably has tubular disease.

If the protein content of the urine is > 1 g/24 hours, persistent proteinuria is almost always patho-

*This is the routine recommended by the American College of Obstetricians and Gynecologists.

logic (even prolonged orthostatic proteinuria). The predominant protein in urine is globulin (not albumin), in contrast with serum. The electrophoretic pattern may be diagnostic and prognostic, but vaginal fluid contamination must be avoided in the collection of urine.

One should seek to (1) prevent infection and preeclampsia-eclampsia; (2) properly select and time the method of delivery; (3) utilize special diagnostic methods after necessary consultation; (4) evaluate the patient after the puerperium; and (5) provide contraceptive counseling.

SOLITARY KIDNEY

A solitary kidney may be the result of developmental aberration or surgery. A single kidney may be abnormally developed (eg, fused) or it may be placed low, perhaps even within the true pelvis. A second, small, virtually functionless kidney may not be disclosed by traditional diagnostic tests. Anatomic and functional hypertrophy of the remaining kidney usually occurs, and this increase in size and capacity is considerably augmented by pregnancy.

There is no medical contraindication to pregnancy provided the function of a solitary kidney is good. Even successful renal transplantation has not prevented pregnancy in the limited number of cases available thus far.

A pelvic kidney may cause soft tissue dystocia; pressure by the presenting part or trauma from forceps application must be avoided. Renal compression may seriously damage the only functional remaining kidney. A cesarean section may be warranted in these cases and when previous successful surgery has been done for congenital anomalies.

PYELONEPHRITIS

Pyelonephritis may be extremely serious for the pregnant patient. There is an increased incidence of pyelonephritis in primiparas and those who have difficult labors, women with sickle cell disease, and women with diabetes mellitus. Catheterization and dehydration (diuretics) contribute to the incidence of urinary infection. A raised serum antibody titer to enterococci probably indicates prior urinary tract infections. Nephrolithiasis or structural damage to the urinary tract predisposes to the development of pyelonephritis. Antibacterial therapy is discussed below and on pp 404–405.

URINARY SYMPTOMS

Urinary frequency, urgency, and stress incontinence are quite common, especially in advanced pregnancy. They are due to reduced bladder capacity and the pressure of the presenting part upon the bladder.

Suspect urinary tract disease, especially infection, if dysuria or hematuria is reported.

When urgency is particularly troublesome, the patient should avoid tea, coffee, spices, and alcoholic beverages. Bladder sedatives are available in various forms. Hyoscyamine, 0.125 mg 3 times daily (or similar preparation), may be beneficial.

URINARY TRACT INFECTION

The urinary tract is especially vulnerable to infections during pregnancy, because the altered secretions of steroid sex hormones and the pressure exerted by the gravid uterus upon the ureters and bladder cause hypotonia and congestion and predispose to ureterovesical reflux and urinary stasis. The trauma of labor and delivery and urinary retention after delivery may initiate or aggravate urinary tract infection. *Escherichia coli* is the offending organism in the majority of cases.

Asymptomatic bacteriuria occurs in about 5% of all pregnant women. Intercurrent pyelonephritis can be expected in approximately 30% of these patients if prophylactic treatment is not given, whereas urinary tract infection will develop in only 1–2% of pregnant women without antecedent bacteriuria. Symptomatic urinary tract infection is responsible for a considerable increase in the incidence of premature labor and delivery. Whether or not asymptomatic bacteriuria is associated with premature delivery is a debatable issue at present.

If urine culture reveals more than 100,000 colonies per mL, treat with a broad-spectrum antibiotic (eg, ampicillin) for 2 weeks. If repeat culture 1 month after therapy is started again discloses significant infection, sensitivity tests and appropriate re-treatment for a similar period are indicated. Continuous therapy (eg, sulfisoxazole, 0.5 mg orally 4 times daily) may be necessary during pregnancy. We have not found this to be harmful even to premature neonates.

Patients with asymptomatic or symptomatic bacteriuria during pregnancy require investigation after the puerperium. The majority will be found to have important upper urinary tract abnormalities.

Almost 10% of pregnant women suffer from urinary tract infection. Serious antepartum infection occurs in 5–8% of pregnant women. An additional 5% develop urinary tract infections after delivery. Chronic pyelonephritis, a major cause of death in older women, often follows recurrent acute urinary tract infections during successive pregnancies. Urinary tract infection increases the likelihood of premature delivery and perinatal mortality.

The diagnosis should be based upon stained smear and culture of a catheterized or clean-catch specimen of urine. An acid-fast stain of the urinary sediment should be performed if tuberculosis is suspected. Sensitivity tests to determine responses to the various anti-infective agents are desirable. Bacillary infection should be treated initially with sulfisoxazole, 2 g orally immediately and then 1 g 4 times daily; or nitrofurantoin, 100 mg orally 4 times daily. If cocci are present, give procaine penicillin G, 1 million units intramuscularly immediately and then 600,000 units intramuscularly twice daily. Mixed infections may be treated with cephalexin (Keflex), 250 mg orally 4 times daily. Change to other drugs as dictated by the results of laboratory studies. Do not give tetracyclines to pregnant women, since the offspring are apt to develop yellow deciduous teeth of poor quality. Chloramphenicol may cause pediatric problems also.

For urgency and frequency, give hyoscyamine, 0.125 mg 3–4 times daily as necessary (or similar preparation).

Force fluids and alkalinize the urine with sodium bicarbonate. Give analgesics, laxatives, and antipyretic drugs as indicated.

Three successive negative urine cultures taken at weekly intervals are necessary before the patient can be considered "cured."

If urine cultures are not available, a stained smear of the centrifuged sediment of a catheterized or clean-catch specimen may be examined for bacteria each week for 3 weeks. If no bacteria or pus cells are seen and the patient is asymptomatic, she is presumed to be cured.

If obstruction is present, it may be necessary to employ urethral or ureteral catheterization. Ureteral obstruction usually resolves after delivery, but if it is permanent, surgical repair may be required. If response to chemotherapy and ureteral catheterization is inadequate, nephrostomy is indicated, particularly during the second trimester and prior to fetal viability. Induce labor at term by amniotomy. Consider therapeutic abortion if there is no response to medical and surgical therapy when the mother's life is in jeopardy.

Routine urinalysis during pregnancy must include microscopic examination and stain for bacteria (and cultures) to discover asymptomatic bacteriuria.

Avoid urethral catheterization whenever possible; when catheterization is necessary, sterile technique is imperative. Eradicate genital and urinary tract infections promptly. Study and treat patients before or early in pregnancy when there is evidence or a history of a previous urinary tract infection, especially during gestation. Even if a "cure" is achieved, suppressive long-term antibiotic therapy continued throughout pregnancy and the puerperium is warranted.

If initial treatment proves ineffective, the patient should be thoroughly studied by a urologist.

URETEROLITHIASIS

Symptomatic urinary calculus is common during pregnancy. Causes include chronic urinary tract infection, hyperparathyroidism, congenital or familial cystinuria or oxaluria, gout, and obstructive uropathy. Physiologic hydroureter and pyelectasis develop during the second and third trimesters in response to high levels of steroid sex hormones and slight ureteral compression by the enlarging uterus. These tend to dislodge small renal stones, and this causes severe ureteral colic and hematuria. The incidence of ureterolithiasis is about one per 3000 pregnancies.

Sudden agonizing pain in the costovertebral angle and flank with radiation to the lower quadrant and vulva, urinary urgency, and hematuria (initially without pyuria or fever) are characteristic of ureteral stone. X-ray films rarely reveal a small stone, but intravenous urography may demonstrate partial obstruction. (The pregnant uterus should be shielded during roentgenography.)

Symptomatic therapy with hypnotics and antispasmodics, together with forced fluids, is indicated. Paravertebral or epidural block may be useful for relief of pain and to relax the spastic ureter. Most ureteral stones are painfully passed in the urine; others become impacted. Retrograde catheter manipulation may free the stone and permit it to pass, or the stone may be extracted transurethrally. If such efforts are unsuccessful, and if severe pain persists with the development of progressive hydronephrosis, the stone should be removed by extraperitoneal urethrolithotomy irrespective of the patient's obstetric status.

GLOMERULONEPHRITIS

An initial attack of acute glomerulonephritis is rare during pregnancy; most obstetric problems relating to glomerulonephritis involve transitional chronic forms of the disease. There is no convincing evidence that pregnancy aggravates glomerulonephritis.

Infertility, abortion, premature delivery, fetal death in utero, premature separation of the normally implanted placenta, and placental dysmaturity occur with greater frequency in women with glomerulonephritis than in normal women. Nephritis causes hypertension, predisposes to preeclampsia-eclampsia, and is associated with a high incidence of perinatal death and disease.

The medical treatment of glomerulonephritis in pregnancy is the same as if the patient were not pregnant. Adrenocortical steroids may be harmful, and antibiotics are ineffective. Therapeutic abortion may be justified for acute, severe exacerbations of glomerulonephritis with renal insufficiency.

Glomerulonephritis may be an indication for cesarean section when placental dysmaturity or preeclampsia-eclampsia occurs.

ACUTE RENAL FAILURE

Acute renal failure is the diagnosis when the urinary output is less than 100 mL in a 6-hour period even after corrective measures (eg, correction of dehydration or hypovolemia) have been taken. Acute renal failure may result from insufficient blood flow through the glomeruli, damaged glomeruli or tubules, obstruction to the collecting system, or ureteral occlusion. The incidence of acute renal failure during pregnancy is about one per 4000 deliveries, and either the mother or the offspring may die.

Oliguria may result from shock, dehydration, electrolyte imbalance, intravascular hemolysis, preeclampsia-eclampsia, primary renal parenchymal disease, renotoxic substances, blockage by stones and crystals, surgical damage to the ureter, and excessive oxytocin administration.

The predisposing causes include septic abortion, premature separation of the placenta, placenta previa, administration of nephrotoxic drugs, hypertensive vascular disorders, blood transfusion reactions, and dehydration.

Uremia is rarely a threat for 2–3 days after the kidneys fail to eliminate water and catabolic products. Nevertheless, metabolic acidosis occurs after the carbonic acid-bicarbonate buffer system fails. Hyperkalemia develops from acidosis and cellular breakdown, red blood cell disintegration, and tissue necrosis. The complications are renal or extrarenal infection, anemia, stomatitis, parotitis, and urinary tract infection.

Treatment

Treatment (prior to dialysis or diuresis) includes the following:

A. Emergency Measures: Treat the causative problem (eg, shock due to hemorrhage).

B. Surgical Measures: Determine the central venous pressure and eliminate infected products of conception.

C. Routine Measures: Maintain fluid and electrolyte balance. Prescribe a high-carbohydrate diet (no protein). Limit fluids to the amount allowing weight loss of 250 g/d (assuming a room temperature of approximately 22–23 °C (71.6–73.4 °F). Do not give prophylactic antibiotics, but treat infection with antibiotic drugs that are without renal toxic effects (eg, penicillin). Avoid catheterization because of the danger of infection.

D. Dialysis: Dialysis is indicated if serum potassium is ≥ 7 mEq/L or serum sodium is ≤ 130 mEq/L; if CO_2 combining power is ≤ 13 mEq/L; or if blood urea nitrogen is ≥ 220 mg/dL.

DISORDERS OF ADRENOCORTICAL FUNCTION

Hyperfunction of the adrenal cortex occurs in Cushing's syndrome, Cushing's disease, adrenogenital syndrome, and hyperaldosteronism. In contrast, disorders due to hypoadrenocorticism include Addison's disease and the syndrome following withdrawal of cortisone after extended administration. The basic threat is infection or shock, either of which may be fatal.

CUSHING'S SYNDROME & CUSHING'S DISEASE (Hyperadrenocorticism)

Cushing's syndrome is a symptom complex characterized by buffalo hump obesity, easy bruisability, hirsutism, purple striae, and acne. These patients often are emotionally unstable. Osteoporosis, hypertension, and glycosuria are common. The disease is characterized by an elevation in the secretion of cortisol and results in elevated serum and urinary excretion of this hormone and its metabolites (17-hydroxycorticosteroids). Cushing's syndrome is caused by an adrenocortical tumor or hyperplasia.

Cushing's disease, a disorder with symptoms similar to those of Cushing's syndrome, is caused by anterior pituitary basophilic adenoma or a preponderance of actively secretory basophilic cells that stimulate the adrenal cortex to hyperfunction. In either case, excessive function of the adrenal cortex is the basic problem. Special x-ray studies may reveal a pituitary tumor, hyperplasia, or neoplasia of either the anterior pituitary or the adrenal cortex.

Anovulation and oligomenorrhea or amenorrhea usually accompanies hyperadrenocorticism, whatever its cause may be. For this reason, pregnancy rarely is complicated by this disorder. Patients often first seek the advice of an obstetrician because of their amenorrhea, frequently believing that they are pregnant. If pregnancy should occur, the major hazard is serious, even critical, hypertension. Infection and osteoporosis may be complications also.

One can suppress adrenocortical hyperplasia by cortisone or its analogs. Unfortunately, drug suppression of pituitary hyperfunction or an adrenal tumor is impossible. If pituitary disease is diagnosed, hypophyseal irradiation or surgery may be curative. Removal of an adrenal tumor or bilateral adrenalectomy for diffuse cortical hyperplasia may be necessary even during pregnancy. Although these are formidable procedures, they have been carried out successfully during gestation. Adequate maintenance doses of cortisone or hydrocortisone will be essential in any event. At term, management would be similar to that of the patient with Addison's disease.

The maintenance of normal electrolyte balance is most important during the stress of labor and delivery. Hemorrhage and shock must be assiduously avoided in patients with definite or suspected hyperadrenocorticism. Because these patients overreact to medications, analgesics and anesthetic agents should be used in minimal doses. Pudendal block is a wise choice for delivery inasmuch as hypotension must be avoided. Gradual reduction of cortisone therapy to a maintenance dose by the end of the first week postpartum is feasible, barring infection or other complications.

The risk of premature labor and delivery is increased in severe hyperadrenocorticism, and major surgery is also a threat to mother and offspring. Nonetheless, adequate cortisone therapy during and after any operation will increase the likelihood of a favorable outcome. Corticosteroids do not predispose to nor aggravate preeclampsia-eclampsia, and these drugs are not teratogenic for the human fetus.

PHEOCHROMOCYTOMA

Pheochromocytomas are uncommon chromaffin cell tumors 90% of which are in the adrenal medulla. Ectopic tumor sites include the para-aortic sympathetic nerve chain, the ovary, and the mediastinum. Pheochromocytomas release epinephrine or norepinephrine (or both) to cause episodic or sustained hypertension and related distressing symptoms. This tumor is rare during pregnancy but must be considered in the diagnosis of every patient with "toxemia" of pregnancy, because pheochromocytomas are often lethal for the mother or offspring. Early diagnosis and proper medical and surgical treatment are mandatory.

The classic triad of palpitations, headache, and sweating occur simultaneously—what one would expect from an injection of epinephrine. Other symptoms are nervousness, agitation, and apprehension. Additional signs include pallor and subsequent flushing. In such cases, poor weight gain (or weight loss) during pregnancy may be attributed to hyperthyroidism, or diabetes mellitus may be suspected because of increased blood glucose.

About 95% of pheochromocytomas in adults are benign. Symptomatology may persist even after excision of the typical reddish-brown, vascular, firm, microcystic tumor (average weight about 100 g), because approximately 10% are bilateral or extend beyond the adrenal.

Laboratory tests are essential for diagnosis. Screening involves analysis of the urine for 3-methoxy-4-hydroxymandelic acid (vanillylmandelic acid, VMA) and metanephrine. If these substances are identified in significant amounts, urinary assay for epinephrine and norepinephrine should be done. When the level of epinephrine is elevated, the tumor is probably in the adrenal; if norepinephrine is secreted, the tumor is likely to be in an extra-adrenal site. Glycosuria and hyperglycemia are supportive laboratory findings.

Contrary to former opinion, suppression or excitation tests are rarely essential for diagnosis. Moreover, they may be very dangerous. Nevertheless, if laboratory findings are equivocal, the glucagon test is the safest method of stimulation, and the phentolamine (Regitine) suppression test is the least hazardous suppression test. If a hypertensive crisis develops, phentolamine, 5 mg slowly intravenously, is both diagnostic and therapeutic.

Immediately after the presumptive diagnosis is made, antihypertensive therapy should be instituted—before ancillary determinations or surgery is attempted.

CT scan is the best and safest method of diagnosis. Only about 1 rad (plus scatter radiation) is delivered to the fetus at each "cut" of the scan. This is acceptable, considering the seriousness of the disorder. Standard x-ray films of the abdomen, intravenous urography, and traditional tomography, even with shielding, usually expose the fetus to much more radiation and are less efficient diagnostically. Angiography should be avoided if possible, because it may precipitate a hypertensive crisis and because it delivers a considerable amount of radiation to the fetus.

Ultrasonography may reveal a suprarenal tumor or displacement of the kidney, but the resolution is greatly inferior to what can be achieved with CT scan.

The differential diagnosis must include all of the hypertensive disorders that complicate pregnancy—hyperthyroidism, acute anxiety attacks, or carcinoid.

Complications of pheochromocytoma generally are those related to hypertension: stroke, cardiac decompensation due to myocardial infarction, ventricular arrhythmia, and renal failure. Prolonged general vasoconstriction due to an excess of catecholamines may foster hypovolemia. Thus, after removal of the tumor, marked hypotension must be avoided in order to prevent vascular collapse. Intravenous fluids are required to augment the reduced blood volume.

Treatment

A. Medical Treatment: Administer alpha-adrenergic blocking agents as soon as the biochemical diagnosis is made. This should help restore blood volume and should limit the danger of a severe attack and associated serious complications. Phenoxybenzamine (Dibenzyline) is the preferred drug, because of its prolonged action. Begin cautious therapy with 10 mg orally every 8 hours and increase the dosage as allowed by postural hypotension and faintness until all of the signs of catecholamine excess have disappeared and blood volume is clinically normal. The drug has a cumulative effect, but as much as 100–150 mg/d may be required.

Propranolol (Inderal), a beta-blocking drug, is useful when cardiac arrhythmia or marked tachycardia ensues. To avoid a hypertensive crisis, propranolol should be administered only after an alpha-blocking drug has become effective.

Sedatives and tranquilizers are helpful in controlling the severe anxiety that is a feature of pheochromocytoma.

B. Surgical Treatment: Extirpation of the tumor is curative, but in therapeutically responsive patients—especially those in the third trimester—palliative medical therapy may occasionally be given until after delivery, when surgery should be easier. In acute cases, if the fetus is definitely viable, cesarean section followed by ablation of the tumor should be accomplished.

During operation, central venous pressure recording and constant electrocardiographic monitoring are essential. Phentolamine or nitroprusside and propranolol should be at hand to treat sudden hypertension or cardiac arrhythmia. The possibility of multiple small tumors usually requires at least bilateral adrenal exploration.

Prognosis

Untreated or inadequately treated gravidas with pheochromocytoma often die. Effective management has reduced the operative mortality rate drastically. Extreme variations in the pregnant patient's blood pressure, especially hypotension, pose a grave threat to the fetus, and this accounts for the continuing high perinatal mortality and morbidity rates.

ORTHOPEDIC COMPLICATIONS

POSTURAL BACKACHE

Backache is the most common orthopedic problem of the pregnant woman. Most cases of back pain during pregnancy are caused by mechanical problems and postural changes. The considerable distention of the abdomen and decreased abdominal muscle tone, especially during late pregnancy, necessitate realignment of the spinal curvatures. The normal lumbosacral curve is increased, therefore, and a compensatory curvature in the cervicodorsal region is necessary to maintain balance. Large breasts and a stoop-shouldered posture will further increase both dorsal and lumbar curvatures, often to the point of backache. In the young, well-muscled woman, the changes may be well tolerated, but in an older woman, especially one with a back disorder, poor posture, or a faulty sense of balance, backache is even more likely. Naturally, all this will be worse in patients with an exaggerated lateral curvature, prior neurologic disease, or old fracture.

Backache may be a problem of individuals who have abnormal spinal architecture and posture, such as those with scoliosis, excessive lordosis, spondylolisthesis, or congenital anomalies of the back.

Backache is a common complaint of patients with lordosis, which may be caused by abdominal relaxation, pendulous abdomen, and large, unsupported breasts, as well as an associated slouching posture. A compensatory dorsal "round back," jutting head, and slight hip and knee flexion are typical. Thus, the ligamentous and muscular structures of the mid and lower spine are stressed.

Return to more normal back curvatures following delivery is favored by bed rest on a firm mattress. Elevation of the upper part of the body by a mechanical bed aggravates the disorder. Sudden increased demands on the postpartum patient—the new baby, additional household duties necessitating stooping, bending, lifting—all a part of the return to active home life, may precipitate or aggravate backache.

RHEUMATIC DISORDERS

RELAXATION OF THE PELVIC JOINTS
(Pregnancy Pelvic Arthropathy)

Slight relaxation of the pelvic joints, the result of increased circulating steroid sex hormones and relaxin, is normal during pregnancy. The degree of relaxation is variable, but considerable separation of the pubis and instability of the sacroiliac joint, causing pain and difficulty in walking, occur occasionally. Obesity and multiple pregnancy contribute to the disability of pelvic arthropathy. About one patient in 100 suffers from pelvic joint pain and about one in 1500 is seriously incapacitated.

Joint relaxation is progressive in most obstetric patients during the second trimester and the early part of the third trimester. Undue mobility persists until after delivery. Return to normal joint stability following parturition may require several months.

Exaggerated elasticity of connective and collagen tissue in response to the hormones of pregnancy is presumed to occur in pelvic arthropathy. However, the extent of disability is not always directly related to the degree of play in the joints concerned.

Pain in the sacroiliac and pubic joints on standing, walking, and turning may be extreme. With the index finger in the vagina and the thumb above the symphysis, the examiner can feel abnormal movement of the pubic bone when traction is placed on one of the patient's legs while the other thigh is held firmly. X-ray evidence of separation of the pubic bone of more than 2 cm is abnormal. X-rays of the patient's pelvis, one taken while she is standing on the right leg and another while she is supported by the left, will usually reveal the magnitude of pelvic joint relaxation.

Prolonged sacroiliac backache may be a sequela to sacroiliac arthropathy of pregnancy.

Treatment consists of limitation of activities, analgesics, and a sturdy fitted girdle that gives support by snug encirclement of the sacrum, symphysis, and greater trochanters. The girdle may be required during the antepartum period and for 3–4 weeks postpartum. Orthopedic surgery to secure the symphysis is rarely required. Cesarean section should be performed only for obstetric reasons.

To prevent prolonged disability, every precaution must be taken to avoid exaggerated positions, marked traction, and sudden movement of the patient while she is under general anesthesia during delivery.

RHEUMATOID ARTHRITIS

Rheumatoid arthritis occurs rarely during pregnancy, but it may be extremely serious, especially during the puerperium.

Pregnancy suppresses rheumatoid arthritis. In general, patients with this disease are considerably improved during the last trimester, presumably because of an elevated titer of corticosteroids. Following delivery, however, and for as long as 2–4 months thereafter, there is a likelihood of serious relapse and rapid progression of the disease. For obscure reasons, lactation appears to prolong the remission. The fetus is never adversely affected.

Treatment is directed toward reduction of inflammation and pain, preservation of joint function, and prevention of deformity. Adequate diet, rest, analgesic drugs, and physical therapy are the mainstays of treatment. Pregnancy is not a contraindication to corticosteroids and other drugs used in the treatment of rheumatoid arthritis, although they should be employed with due caution during the first trimester.

The prognosis is unpredictable but generally poor. The offspring will be unaffected by the mother's disorder.

SYSTEMIC LUPUS ERYTHEMATOSUS

Systemic lupus erythematosus affects principally women and develops most frequently during the childbearing years. It is a rare but often extremely serious complication of pregnancy. About 500 cases of systemic lupus erythematosus during pregnancy have been reported in the past 10 years.

Pregnancy does not influence the disease in any consistent or predictable way. In over half of patients with systemic lupus erythematosus, the disease remains unchanged, and in a few cases it improves during pregnancy; but increase in the number and severity of exacerbations may occur during pregnancy and the puerperium. In contrast with nonpregnant patients with acute systemic lupus erythematosus, the probability of an exacerbation may be 3 times greater in the first half of pregnancy and twice as great in the second half. Flare-ups during the puerperium occur 6–7 times more frequently than during the nonpregnant period.

Neither the disease itself nor its treatment with corticosteroids commonly reduces the incidence of conception. Spontaneous abortion, usually before the 14th week, occurs in about 20% of patients with acute systemic lupus erythematosus. The incidence of premature labor and delivery, preeclampsia-eclampsia, and phlebitis is also increased.

Cardiac insufficiency is often a critical problem, but progressive renal failure is the most frequent contributory cause of death in pregnant women with systemic lupus erythematosus.

Fetal anomalies and growth retardation of the fetus are not increased because of systemic lupus erythematosus or corticosteroid therapy. Fetal adrenal insufficiency due to maternal corticosteroid therapy is rarely a problem.

Admit the patient to a hospital promptly, since extensive investigation of the gravida's cardiorenal status and appropriate treatment of acute systemic lupus erythematosus are important. Patients must avoid overactivity and exposure to the sun and other sources of ultraviolet light. Pigmented emollient cosmetic lotions that are opaque to ultraviolet light may be applied over the face lesions. Analgesics and physical therapy may be given for musculoskeletal discomfort.

Corticotropin and the corticosteroids may relieve the symptoms and reduce the number and intensity of the acute exacerbations. There is no agreement about whether the corticosteroids should be given only to treat acute attacks or whether they should be administered for maintenance therapy also.

Prednisone, 30–50 mg (or equivalent) daily orally in 4 divided doses, may be required for the treatment of an acute attack. After improvement has occurred, gradual reduction to withdrawal or to a maintenance dose of about 10 mg/d may be employed for a prolonged period during pregnancy and the puerperium.

Pregnancy rarely exacerbates systemic lupus erythematosus so severely that therapeutic abortion is justified. Employ cesarean section for clear-cut obstetric indications only.

The maternal mortality rate is approximately 20% and the perinatal mortality rate about 30% in acute disseminated systemic lupus erythematosus. The mortality rates in chronic systemic lupus erythematosus depend upon the duration and severity of the disease.

Adrenocorticosteroid therapy before or during pregnancy probably does not influence the number of patients going to term or the fetal outcome.

THROMBOEMBOLIZATION

The term thromboembolization denotes all vascular occlusive processes, including thrombophlebitis, phlebothrombosis, and embolization of venous clots to the lung. Thromboembolization occurs in 0.5% of patients who have been delivered vaginally, but the incidence increases to 1–2% of patients who have sustained cesarean section. Clinically, about 10% of emboli appear to be of pelvic origin, and about 30% of all autopsies on women reveal pelvic vascular thrombosis. The onset of thromboembolization may be 1 day to 1 month following delivery or surgery. Despite the serious implications, and with the exception of a massive pulmonary embolism, thromboembolization generally is a successfully treatable disorder.

Vascular clotting develops mainly because of circulatory stasis, infection, vascular abnormality (eg, the enlarged ovarian veins during pregnancy), and increased coagulability of the blood postpartum. Heavy smoking, obesity, varices, heart disease, preeclampsia-eclampsia, prolonged labor, anemia, hemorrhage, and malignancy increase the likelihood of thromboembolization. Induced abortion, operative delivery (especially cesarean section), and postpartum or postoperative pelvic infection often are initiating incidents.

The pathogenesis usually relates to infection, hematoma formation, or birth canal lacerations—especially those of serious degree. Septic emboli in women usually are from the uterine, ovarian, or iliac veins. Suppurative emboli almost always involve the lung, but secondary abscesses may occur in the brain or the heart, or a mycotic aneurysm may even develop in one of the great vessels. Thrombi develop as often in the veins on the right side of the body as on the left.

Phlebothrombosis is a bland, initially loosely adherent, noninflammatory vascular clot that usually causes incomplete occlusion of the vein.

Thrombophlebitis is clotting that results from bacterial inflammation of the vein. The clot generally is firmly adherent to the vein wall and usually occludes the lumen. Nonetheless, a bland clot may extend proximally from the tip of an infected clot.

In septic thrombophlebitis, partial liquefaction of the infected thrombus allows showers of bacteria-laden emboli to fly off into the venous circulation.

Initial damage to a vein occurs as a result of bacterial invasion, usually by streptococci, staphylococci (both aerobic and anaerobic), or enterococci. Pathogenic organisms spread by direct extension along the intima or in the perivascular lymphatics. The clotting process is initiated concomitantly. Bacterial invasion of the clot soon occurs. Fragmentation of the clot causes emboli to be released into the venous circulation.

The symptoms of thrombophlebitis include pain, high spiking fever with chills, and tachycardia. A tender, swollen leg or pelvic pain may be noted. A cordlike, sensitive large vein (eg, the femoral or popliteal) or a pelvic mass often can be identified. The lochia may be abnormal. Blood cultures generally are positive at the height of the temperature elevation.

OVARIAN VEIN THROMBOPHLEBITIS

Ovarian vein thrombophlebitis may follow spontaneous as well as operative deliveries. The onset generally is on the second or third postpartum day. There may be right or left anterior upper quadrant and flank pain, muscle guarding, and ileus. Nausea and vomiting are uncommon. Occasional adnexal thickening may be noted, but mass formation is rare. Leukocytosis may be reported, but urinalysis will be negative.

The differential diagnosis involves appendicitis, pyelonephritis, hematoma formation, adnexal cellulitis, degenerative myoma, and torsion of the adnexa.

If the likelihood of ovarian vein thrombophlebitis is strong, give heparin and defer definitive surgery for approximately 48 hours to note possible improvement. If improvement occurs, surgery probably will be unnecessary.

Surgery is indicated if (1) medical management fails, (2) septic emboli occur during medical therapy, or (3) medical therapy is contraindicated. Surgery involves ligation of the major venous tributaries from the pelvis (eg, vena cava, ovarian veins). A transabdominal approach may be used, or management may consist of retroperitoneal partial occlusion of the vena cava with a caval clip or ligation of the vena cava. Vena caval clipping is followed by less disabling edema, fewer leg ulcers, and fewer recurrences of embolization than vena caval ligation.

If appendicitis cannot be excluded and operation is done only to find ovarian vein thrombophlebitis, ligation of both ovarian veins should be done regardless of whether involvement is unilateral or bilateral. Thrombectomy is preferred, but one should clip or ligate the vena cava if the thrombus extends into the lumen and cannot be readily removed. Administer heparin and a broad-spectrum antibiotic.

AMNIOTIC FLUID EMBOLISM

Amniotic fluid embolism, a rare but generally lethal complication of late labor, is characterized by unexpected orthopnea, cyanosis, and profound shock. The disorder is caused by the sudden entrance of a considerable amount of amniotic fluid and detritus through a rupture of the membranes into the maternal venous circulation. Embolic occlusion of pulmonary venules results in pulmonary intravascular coagulation and uterine hemorrhage secondary to defibrination of blood. The mother and fetus often succumb even with prompt, heroic therapy.

The mother, frequently an older multipara with large uterine veins, will invariably have had ruptured membranes and forceful uterine contractions. The fetus, often large, may cause obstructed drainage from below so that amniotic fluid under pressure can pass through a rent in the membranes to gain entrance into the uterine circulation via placental sinusoids. This type of embolus often occurs in cases of partial separation of the placenta, laceration or partial rupture of the uterus, or even during cesarean section.

A definitive diagnosis can only be made at autopsy when fetal squamae, vernix, and meconium are identified in the fine pulmonary vasculature. Nonetheless, a presumptive diagnosis may be tenable in nonfatal cases of sudden respiratory distress, collapse, and uterine hemorrhage. In the differential diagnosis one must consider aspiration of gastric contents, massive collapse of the lung, and myocardial infarction. These conditions do not include coagulopathy, however.

Treatment of amniotic fluid embolus includes oxygen by face mask or tent; antishock therapy, including hydrocortisone intravenously; application of tourniquets to the extremities to limit right ventricular strain of cor pulmonale; fibrinogen, 5 g intravenously diluted in 100 mL of saline; and transfusion of fresh whole blood.

ACUTE ABDOMINAL EMERGENCIES

The accurate diagnosis of serious abdominal disorders during pregnancy is difficult for several reasons: (1) The enlarging uterus distorts the typical anatomic relationships of the nonpregnant state, eg, the appendix is displaced upward and backward. (2) The distended abdomen makes palpation difficult so that adnexal tumors (for example) are concealed. (3) Muscle guarding as a reaction to inflammation is reduced before and after delivery so peritonitis is obscured. (4) Normal discomforts of pregnancy and delivery obscure symptoms of visceral disease, eg, the pain that may accompany sliding internal hernia. (5) Obstetric problems must be differentiated from nonobstetric conditions, eg, abruptio placentae versus volvulus.

In general, elective surgery should be avoided during pregnancy, but it is necessary to operate promptly if a definite or probable diagnosis of an acute surgical disorder is made.

APPENDICITIS

Acute appendicitis occurs in about one out of 1200 pregnancies and is an extremely serious complication. Rupture of the appendix occurs 2–3 times more often than in nonpregnant women with appendicitis. Maternal perinatal mortality and morbidity rates are greatly increased when appendicitis is complicated by peritonitis.

Increased vascularity of the pelvis, augmented lymphatic drainage, and higher levels of corticosteroids make appendicitis more severe during pregnancy, and rupture seems to occur more rapidly. Patients who have had previous attacks are more likely to develop acute appendicitis during pregnancy, possibly due to prior kinking or adhesion formation. Most attacks occur during the first 6 months, with decreasing incidence in the last trimester, during labor, and in the puerperium. The basic problem with acute suppurative appendicitis is the development of gangrene and peritonitis.

During gestation, the appendix is carried high, to the right, and often posteriorly, away from McBurney's point, by the enlarging uterus. This disturbs the assumed intestinal relationships. Fundal displacement of the omentum and the presence of the enlarged uterus make walling off of an appendiceal abscess difficult. The uterus generally becomes the median wall of the abscess; uterine contractions may be induced by inflammation; and abortion or premature labor and delivery often ensues. The sudden decrease in the size of the uterus with delivery, together with manipulation, may lead to the spread of peritonitis.

Differential Diagnosis

The differential diagnosis includes diverticulitis, parasitic infections of the intestines, cecitis, epiploic appendagitis, neoplasm, twisted ovarian cyst, mesenteric adenitis, urinary tract infection, and Meckel's diverticulitis. Nausea and vomiting of pregnancy may confuse the issue.

Clinical Findings

A. First Trimester: The site of pain and of point tenderness is slightly above and to the side of McBurney's point.

B. Second Trimester: The site of pain and of point tenderness is high and toward the right flank.

C. Third Trimester: The symptoms are completely atypical. One must maintain a high level of suspicion for appendicitis in order not to miss the diagnosis.

Treatment

Appendectomy is essential before rupture. Antibiotic therapy prior to rupture is of doubtful value; after rupture, it may be lifesaving. Therapeutic abortion is never indicated in appendicitis. If drainage is necessary, drains should be placed transabdominally, never transvaginally.

Prognosis

The maternal mortality rate increases to almost 10% in the third trimester and is about 15% when acute appendicitis occurs during labor. The perinatal mortality rate is about 10% with unruptured appendicitis but approximately 35% with peritonitis.

ACUTE ORGANIC INTESTINAL OBSTRUCTION

Acute organic intestinal obstruction, or dynamic ileus, is a rare but serious complication of pregnancy. Dynamic ileus generally involves the small intestine, particularly the ileum. Major exciting causes are band adhesions and external hernias. Less common causes are volvulus, intussusception, internal hernias, granulomatous processes, and neoplasms, in about that order. Large bowel obstruction is very rare during pregnancy. With either small or large bowel obstruction, undue delay in diagnosis and the attendant hazards of infection and fluid and electrolyte imbalance critically increase maternal and fetal morbidity and mortality rates.

The enlarging uterus itself will not cause intestinal obstruction, but adhesions secondary to previous abdominal surgery, endometriosis, or peritonitis often will. Mechanical bowel obstruction becomes more likely (1) when the uterus becomes an abdominal viscus (after 16 weeks), (2) when the presenting part engages (after 38 weeks), (3) when uterine contractions occur or frank labor develops, or (4) when early postpartum uterine involution occurs. Any woman with a well-established pregnancy who has an abdominal scar and who develops severe abdominal pain, acute nausea, and vomiting must be evaluated for intestinal obstruction. Distention is not essential for the diagnosis.

Clinical Findings

A. Symptoms and Signs: Colicky abdominal pain in the periumbilical area becomes more constant, severe, and diffuse as distention develops. Vomiting, initially of a reflex nature associated with waves of pain, finally becomes fecal. Borborygmi and consciousness of intestinal movement, obstipation, weakness, profuse perspiration, and anxiety usually are present. The patient is restless and changes position frequently in an attempt to relieve pain. A shocklike state with sweating, tachycardia, and dehydration may develop. Abdominal tenderness may be absent to moderate and generalized, but there will be no signs of peritoneal irritation. Fever may be absent or low-grade. A tender hernia may be present. Abdominal distention may be localized with an isolated loop but usually is generalized. The higher the obstruction, the less the distention; the longer the duration of obstruction, the greater the distention. Audible and visible peristalsis, peristaltic rushes with pain paroxysms, and high-pitched tinkles may be present.

B. Laboratory Findings: With dehydration, expect hemoconcentration. Leukocytosis may be absent or mild. Vomiting often causes electrolyte imbalance.

C. X-Ray Findings: Abdominal x-ray films reveal gas-filled loops of bowel, and the gas does not progress downward on serial x-rays. Fluid levels may be visible. If there is small bowel obstruction, no gas will be seen in the colon after an effective enema.

Complications

Anoxic changes occur initially as a result of volvulus, external or internal hernia, band obstruction of the closed loop type, and intussusception.

Treatment

A. Small Bowel Obstruction: Conservative supportive therapy (eg, fluid and electrolyte replacement and mild sedation) may be cautiously pursued if the patient rapidly improves with bowel decompression after the passage of a long, weighted intestinal tube. If the tube will not progress beyond the pyloric sphincter in 3–4 hours, or if the patient does not respond to general measures after 6–8 hours, exploratory laparotomy is mandatory.

Corrective intestinal surgery should be carried out without regard to the uterus, which rarely compromises even an extensive small bowel operation.

B. Large Bowel Obstruction: Because this generally is a closed loop obstruction, surgery is urgent. A transverse colostomy is indicated if a tumor of the left colon is discovered. Early in pregnancy, resection of a malignancy in 2–4 weeks is feasible. Although a calculated risk, delay until viability may be reasonable, whereupon cesarean section or cesarean hysterectomy and colectomy may be accomplished.

OVARIAN TUMORS

NONNEOPLASTIC OVARIAN CYSTS

Most asymptomatic ovarian cysts less than 6 cm in diameter are functional, nonneoplastic enlargements (eg, cystic corpora lutea of pregnancy), which generally can be managed conservatively. Removal of a corpus luteum of pregnancy more than 3 weeks after the last menstrual period probably will not terminate the pregnancy because by this time the placenta will be producing adequate estrogen and progestogen.

Occasionally with multiple pregnancy, hydatidiform mole, or choriocarcinoma, bilateral theca lutein cysts develop as a result of the unusually high level of human chorionic gonadotropin. These cystic ovaries may exceed 10 cm in diameter and often are tender but nonadherent. Rarely, torsion or leakage and bleeding may necessitate laparotomy. Theca lutein cysts will regress. Therefore, surgery is contraindicated except for such emergencies.

OVARIAN NEOPLASMS

Ovarian neoplasms, most of which are cystic or semisolid (eg, dermoid cysts and serous or mucinous cystadenomas), are larger than 6 cm in diameter when discovered during pregnancy. The majority are initially "silent" nonfunctional tumors and probably were present before pregnancy. Ovarian neoplasms are diagnosed in about one in 2000 pregnancies. Only 2–3% of these will be malignant, however.

An increased frequency of complications of ovarian neoplasm occur during pregnancy. These include torsion, rupture, hemorrhage, suppuration, and dystocia secondary to nonengagement of the fetal presenting part.

Ovarian tumors complicate pregnancy because of (1) delay in diagnosis and palliation of possible malignant neoplasms; (2) torsion, suppuration, rupture, or chemical peritonitis or intraperitoneal spread of the tumor; and (3) obstruction of the birth canal.

Differential Diagnosis

A. During the First Trimester: An unruptured corpus luteum cyst may suggest a tubal pregnancy. Torsion or rupture of an ovarian cyst must be distinguished from an ectopic pregnancy or a hemorrhagic corpus luteum. A pedunculated myoma may pass for a solid ovarian tumor.

B. During the Second Trimester: Acute adnexal problems may simulate acute appendicitis, ureteral stone, or pyelonephritis. An adnexal mass may resemble a pelvic kidney, the rudimentary horn of a bicornuate uterus, or a uterine tumor.

C. During the Third Trimester: In addition to the above, consider degeneration of a uterine myoma, rupture of an endometrial cyst, abruptio placentae, and rupture of the uterus. Late in pregnancy, large ovarian cysts may be confused with polyhydramnios or multiple pregnancy.

Treatment

All persistent ovarian neoplasms larger than 6 cm in diameter in premenopausal women should be removed. Nevertheless, if the patient is pregnant, the decision about when to operate will depend upon the duration of pregnancy; whether the persistent tumor is symptomatic, adherent or free, solid, or cystic; and whether it is probably malignant or probably benign.

About three-fourths of all ovarian tumors are diagnosed during the first trimester, often at the initial pelvic examination. The remainder are diagnosed during later pregnancy or the puerperium. After the fourth month, the ovaries are drawn up out of the true pelvis and an ovarian tumor may be felt abdominally. Curiously, however, occasional sizable neoplasms may go unrecognized, even in women of moderate build, only to be identified at cesarean section or postpartum, when the abdominal wall is relaxed.

During early pregnancy, the removal of ovarian neoplasms larger than 6 cm in diameter should be deferred until after the third or fourth month, when the risk of spontaneous abortion is minimal, unless acute symptoms demand immediate intervention. On the other hand, if the neoplasm is solid, bilateral, adherent, or associated with ascites, cul-de-sac nodulation, or other findings indicating the probable presence of cancer, surgery is indicated without delay.

If a cystic tumor is identified in the second trimester of pregnancy and is asymptomatic, it may be best to defer operation until near term. Asymptomatic tumors of moderate size, particularly the unimpacted type, generally do not interfere with labor and vice versa. Removal should be accomplished early in the puerperium to avoid an intra-abdominal complication.

Conservation of residual ovarian tissue may be possible in the case of benign tumors, eg, dermoid cyst or fibroma. The opposite ovary must be inspected, incised, or biopsied to make certain that the tumor is not bilateral. Salpingectomy should be avoided if possible. Torsed ovarian cysts must not be untwisted prior to clamping the pedicle, or fatal pulmonary embolization may occur.

Definite malignancy that is spreading must be treated radically with total hysterectomy, bilateral salpingo-oophorectomy, and possible later radiation therapy.

There is no evidence that estrogen or progestogen will protect against abortion in patients who require ovariectomy. Routine postoperative care and strong reassurance are recommended.

INFECTIOUS DISEASES*

Any severe systemic maternal infectious disease may cause abortion, fetal death, or premature labor

*Syphilis and cytomegalovirus infections are discussed in Chapter 15.

and delivery. Septicemia or an unfavorable reaction to medical therapy may be the immediate cause. While undergrowth of the fetus may occur during chronic or debilitating maternal infectious disorders (eg, amebiasis or malaria), fetal abnormalities occur only in a relatively small number of diseases, the most common being syphilis, rubella, cytomegalic inclusion disease, and toxoplasmosis.

EXANTHEMATOUS DISEASES
(Table 38–6)

Most exanthematous or contagious rash-producing diseases are caused by viruses disseminated by oral contact or respiratory droplet spread. Viremia ensues and the fetus is invaded via the placenta. Abortion or premature labor and delivery may result from hyperpyrexia; fetal death often follows septicemia.

The virulence of the virus, the patient's immune status, and the stage of fetal development determine the effect on the mother and fetus. Active fetal immunity is deficient for most agents, but passive immunity (eg, vaccination with killed rubeola virus) may be beneficial.

Rubella (German Measles)

Rubella, generally a mild, brief illness for the mother, is extremely teratogenic for the fetus. Many infants are abnormal or maldeveloped if the mother contracts rubella during the first trimester of pregnancy. Excluding patients affected during epidemics, the risk of congenital anomalies occurring during the first 3 months of pregnancy varies from 50% (first month) to 10% (third month). After the first trimester, the danger of anomaly is slight.

Fetal defects include cataracts, congenital heart

Table 38–6. Exanthematous diseases in pregnancy.*

Disease	Effect of Disease on Pregnancy	Effect of Disease on Offspring
Variola (smallpox)†	Abortion, premature delivery frequent; postpartal hemorrhage, maternal mortality increased.	May be born with pocks.
Rubeola (measles)	Abortion; premature labor if disease is severe.	May be born with rash.
Varicella (chickenpox)	Severe, disseminated epidemic type may be fatal to mother due to necrotizing angiitis.	Virulent infection may cause fetal death in utero. Neonate may be born with pocks.
Rubella (German measles)	Occasional early abortion.	Congenital anomalies if disease occurs during first trimester.

*Reproduced, with permission, from Benson RC: *Handbook of Obstetrics & Gynecology,* 7th ed. Lange, 1980.
†For all practical purposes, smallpox has been eradicated as a public health problem.

disease, deafness, and mental retardation. It may take 1–2 years to be certain of the seriousness of infant defects.

Prophylactic immune human serum globulin (gamma globulin) may prevent the rash but not the viremia of rubella, even when given before exposure to the disease. Therefore, although gamma globulin may obscure a sign (rash) that the gravida has been exposed to a teratogenic agent, the virus will still be a significant threat to the fetus. An expectant mother might therefore be denied a therapeutic abortion as a result of having received gamma globulin.

If a woman develops German measles in the first trimester of pregnancy, the importance of therapeutic abortion is invariably raised. Many insist that even a 10–15% risk of a seriously damaged fetus is justification for interruption of pregnancy. However, this does mean sacrificing 9 normal fetuses out of 10 fetuses at risk in order to prevent the unwanted survival of one abnormal infant. Moreover, the malformations may be so slight that good health and function and a normal life span are possible.

Attenuated rubella virus vaccine will confer active immunity for a prolonged but uncertain period. Susceptibility to rubella can be demonstrated by the absence of specific serum hemagglutinating antibody. Because the vaccine can infect the fetus, immunization should be carried out in women only if pregnancy can be excluded and avoided for at least 2 months after vaccination. This may require a negative pregnancy test—or administration of vaccine during a menstrual period or immediately after childbirth—and effective contraception. Reaction to the vaccine may include mild fever, soreness at the site of injection, and arthralgia. Spread of the virus to others after vaccination is not a problem.

POLIOMYELITIS

Poliomyelitis is caused by a specific virus that affects pregnant women with slightly greater frequency than nonpregnant women of comparable age and socioeconomic status. The disease is still a serious threat in underdeveloped areas, but it is almost nonexistent where widespread immunization is practiced. About two-thirds of women who contract poliomyelitis during pregnancy are 20–29 years of age, and the majority are parous. Poliomyelitis has a most unfavorable effect on pregnancy and the puerperium. Early therapeutic abortion should be considered.

Poliomyelitis is more serious during pregnancy. Moreover, the perinatal mortality rate is increased, generally as a result of untimely termination of pregnancy. Occasional congenital anomalies have been ascribed to this virus. The fetus may be infected prior to or during delivery.

Curiously, both paralytic and nonparalytic poliomyelitis occur more often in pregnancy at 3–5 months and 8–9 months. Bulbar poliomyelitis, the most serious type, is most likely to develop during late pregnancy. All in all, maternal and fetal loss is greatest during the last trimester.

Poliomyelitis may cause paralysis of the intercostal and abdominal muscles as well as the diaphragm. The enlarged uterus reduces maternal ventilation even when the patient is in a respirator. Hence, delivery near term, often by elective cesarean section, may enhance the efficiency of mechanical (tank) ventilation of the mother.

Emergency treatment of the pregnant woman with acute bulbar poliomyelitis may require tracheostomy, endotracheal suction, positive pressure oxygen-helium administration, catheter drainage of the bladder, and antibiotics to combat respiratory or other infection.

In the poliomyelitis patient, the contractions of the first stage of labor are normally efficient. Operative delivery generally is required, however, because of limited or absent voluntary bearing down efforts during the second stage.

The incidence of spontaneous abortion is increased when poliomyelitis affects the patient early in pregnancy. If the fetus survives, it may be small but otherwise unaffected, or it may have flaccid paralysis.

Viral cultures of the newborn's stools during the first or second day and again 1–2 weeks later may help distinguish pre- from postnatal poliomyelitis.

Pregnancy complicated by poliomyelitis carries a maternal mortality rate at least 5–10% higher than that of otherwise normal pregnancy. The later in pregnancy the disease occurs, the greater the maternal and perinatal mortality and morbidity rates.

MALARIA

Malaria may cause abortion or premature labor and delivery. The infants of mothers with malaria are often smaller than average. Approximately 10% of infants born of women with demonstrable parasites in their blood will have plasmodia in cord blood films.

Malaria may cause infertility; it also complicates pregnancy. For unknown reasons, malarial relapses often occur during pregnancy. A renewal of attacks is common during the puerperium or after hemorrhage and infection.

Labor is frequently prolonged and hazardous for obstetric patients with malaria. These women become fatigued sooner, and operative delivery is required more often. The parasite is not transmitted in the milk, but lactation should be discouraged in women with clinical evidence of malaria. The severity of maternal malaria is reflected in the stillbirth rate, which rises as pregnancy approaches term, and the vitality of newborns that do survive is temporarily reduced.

Chloroquine, 1 g orally immediately and 0.5 g in 6 hours followed by 0.5 g daily for 2 days, is effective against all forms of malaria. Unfortunately, this drug may cause fetal retinal damage and (rarely) death.

LISTERIOSIS

Maternal listeriosis may be responsible for abortion and fetal disease or death depending upon the severity of the infection and the duration of pregnancy. Encephalitis and granulomatosis of the newborn are described also. Pregnant women suffering from a septic form of this disease transmit the infection to the fetus either transplacentally or by exposure of the fetus to the organisms in the lower genital canal during the birth process.

In the mother, listeriosis causes slight temperature elevations and general malaise. The parasite may also be responsible for vaginitis, urinary tract infection or enteritis, and, rarely, meningitis.

A diagnosis of listeriosis during pregnancy is difficult but can be made upon repeated clinical examination, complement fixation or fluorescent antibody tests, and bacterial cultures of leukorrheic discharges or urine or stool specimens. A positive complement fixation test in high dilution is almost invariably present in an acute maternal infection. Gram-positive rods should be sought in the meconium of the newborn to diagnose listeriosis early.

Treat the mother and child with large doses of penicillin or erythromycin.

TOXOPLASMOSIS

Toxoplasmosis, a multisystem disease caused by the protozoon *Toxoplasma gondii,* is a serious threat to the fetus. Cats who hunt rodents that harbor the parasite excrete the infective oocytes in the feces. Human inoculation follows hand-to-mouth contact after disposal of cat litter or after ingestion of rare meat from cattle or sheep put to graze in contaminated fields. Cytologic evidence of *T gondii* infection is present in almost 25% of women in the USA, most being chronic cases.

Parasitemia results in fetal infection, especially during acute gestational toxoplasmosis. The threat of involvement of the offspring is far more likely and serious in acute *T gondii* infections that begin during pregnancy. Thus, cats are undesirable as pets for pregnant women. However, transmission of the disease also occurs even in asymptomatic chronic cases, when trophozoites are released into circulation.

Toxoplasmosis clinically resembles cytomegalic inclusion disease in the mother and the infant. Both disorders are responsible for significant perinatal mortality and morbidity rates. Severe toxoplasmosis is associated with growth retardation, microcephalus or hydrocephalus, microphthalmia, chorioretinitis, central nervous system calcification, thrombopenia, jaundice, and fever.

The Sabin-Feldman dye test and the indirect immunofluorescent test are diagnostic. Both tests are positive 2–3 weeks after infection and remain positive for years. Thus, unless one can obtain sequential tests, an acute infection cannot be distinguished from a chronic one. Recent *T gondii* infection is probable if the titer of the dye test has increased 8 times or more or if the indirect immunofluorescent antibody titer rises 4-fold or more when a 2-fold dilution of both acute and chronic convalescent sera are tested at the same time.

The diagnosis of toxoplasmosis in a newborn is supported by an elevated concentration of cord blood serum IgM. Culture of the organism in experimental animals is possible but difficult.

Routine antenatal screening for antibodies to *T gondii* should be accomplished; if negative, repeat tests during pregnancy are recommended.

Treatment of toxoplasmosis during pregnancy is problematic. Pyrimethamine currently is the first choice drug against *T gondii.* However, this drug may be teratogenic, especially during the first trimester. Sulfonamide therapy is effective, but the drug must be discontinued prior to delivery, and exchange transfusion of the newborn may be necessary to avoid kernicterus. This may occur because sulfonamides have a greater albumin-binding affinity than bilirubin, which may rise after delivery to critical levels. Even so, the newborn may be treated with pyrimethamine if folinic acid is given to reduce the toxicity of the drug.

Developmental delay or neurologic damage due to congenital toxoplasmosis is not affected by treatment, although progression of the disease can be controlled by therapy. Regrettably, encysted (intramuscular) forms of *T gondii* cannot be eradicated by any therapy and may cause recrudescence of the disease.

Cats should be avoided by pregnant women. Meat should be well cooked.

LOWER EXTREMITY DISCOMFORT

LEG CRAMPS

Cramping or "knotting" of the muscles of the calves, thighs, or buttocks may occur suddenly after sleep or recumbency after the first trimester of pregnancy. For unknown reasons, it is less common during the month prior to term. Sudden shortening of the leg muscles by "stretching" with the toes pointed precipitates the cramp. It is theorized that cramps are due to reduction in the level of diffusible serum calcium or increase in the serum phosphorus level (or both). This follows excessive dietary intake of phosphorus in milk, cheese, meat, or dicalcium phosphate, diminished calcium intake, or impaired calcium absorption. Fatigue and sluggish circulation in the extremities are contributory factors.

Treatment
   A. Immediate Treatment: Require the patient to stand barefooted on a cold surface (eg, a tiled bathroom floor). Rub and "knead" the contracted, painful muscle. Passively flex the foot to lengthen the calf muscles. Apply local heat.

B. Preventive and Definitive Treatment:

1. Reduce dietary phosphorus intake temporarily by limiting meat to one serving daily and milk to 1 pint daily. Discontinue dicalcium phosphate and other medications containing large amounts of phosphorus.

2. Eliminate excess phosphorus by absorption with aluminum hydroxide gel, 0.5–1 g orally in liquid or tablet form with each meal.

3. Increase the calcium intake by giving calcium lactate, 0.6 g (or equivalent) orally 3 times daily before meals. Even larger doses may be required if the absorption of calcium from the intestinal tract is impaired.

4. Instruct the patient in how to walk with the toes pointed forward but leading with the heel.

5. Vibratory shaking of the legs from foot to hip each night before retiring may reduce leg cramps.

ANKLE SWELLING

Edema of the lower extremities not associated with preeclampsia-eclampsia develops in two-thirds of women in late pregnancy. Edema is due to sodium and water retention as a result of ovarian, placental, and adrenal steroid hormones and the normally increased venous pressure in the legs. Varicose veins may be familial. They develop from venous congestion, prolonged sitting or standing, and elastic garters and panty girdles.

Treatment is largely preventive and symptomatic, since nothing can be done about the level of the pregnancy hormones. The patient should elevate her legs frequently and sleep in a slight Trendelenburg position. Clothing that interferes with venous return should not be worn.

Avoid excessive salt intake. Diuretics should not be used, since they may be harmful to the fetus. Provide elastic support for varicose veins (see p 847).

● ● ●

References

Dermatologic Problems

Bakan P: Allergy and pregnancy and birth complications. *Ann Allergy* 1977;**38**:54.

Caruthers JA et al: Immunopathological studies in herpes gestationis. *Br J Dermatol* 1977;**96**:35.

Harrington CI, Bleehen SS: Herpes gestationis: Immunopathological and ultrastructural studies. *Br J Dermatol* 1979;**100**:389.

Lawley TJ et al: Pruritic urticarial papules and plaques of pregnancy. *JAMA* 1979;**241**:1696.

Salvatore MA, Lynch PJ: Erythema nodosum, estrogens and pregnancy. *Arch Dermatol* 1980;**116**:557.

Wade TR, Wade SI, Jones HE: Skin changes and diseases associated with pregnancy. *Obstet Gynecol* 1978;**52**:233.

Cardiovascular Complications

Birch GE: Heart disease and pregnancy. *Am Heart J* 1977;**93**:104.

Ciraulo DA, Markovitz A: Myocardial infarction in pregnancy associated with coronary artery thrombus. *Arch Intern Med* 1979;**139**:1046.

Etheridge MJ, Pepperell RL: Heart disease and pregnancy at the Royal Women's Hospital. *Med J Aust* 1977;**2**:277.

Gleicher N et al: Eisenmenger's syndrome and pregnancy. *Obstet Gynecol Surv* 1979;**34**:721.

Gothard JWW: Heart disease in pregnancy. The anesthetic management of a patient with prosthetic heart valves. *Anesthesia* 1978;**33**:523.

Hibbard LT: Maternal mortality due to cardiac disease. *Clin Obstet Gynecol* 1975;**18**:27.

Laird-Meeter K et al: Cardiocirculatory adjustments during pregnancy: An echocardiographic study. *Clin Cardiol* 1979;**2**:328.

Limet R et al: Cardiac valve prostheses, anticoagulation and pregnancy. *Ann Thorac Surg* 1977;**23**:337.

Lumley J, Owen R, Morgan M: Amniotic fluid embolism. *Anaesthesia* 1979;**34**:33.

Lutz DJ et al: Pregnancy and its complications following cardiac valve prostheses. *Am J Obstet Gynecol* 1978;**131**:460.

Oakley GD et al: Management of pregnancy in patients with hypertrophic cardiomyopathy. *Br Med J* 1979;**1**:1749.

Pitts JA: Eisenmenger's syndrome in pregnancy: Does heparin prophylaxis improve the maternal mortality rate? *Am Heart J* 1977;**93**:321.

Taguchi K: Pregnancy in patients with a prosthetic heart valve. *Surg Gynecol Obstet* 1977;**145**:206.

Neurologic Diseases

Aita JF: Myasthenia gravis and pregnancy. *Nebr Med J* 1977;**62**:8.

Coroscio JT, Pellmar M: Pseudotumor cerebri: Occurrence during the third trimester of pregnancy. *Mt Sinai J Med NY* 1978;**45**:539.

Grimes HD, Brooks MH: Pregnancy in Sheehan's syndrome: Report of a case and review. *Obstet Gynecol Surv* 1980;**35**:481.

Jarvis GJ, Crompton AC: Neurofibromatosis and pregnancy. *Br J Obstet Gynaecol* 1978;**85**:844.

Luboshitzky R, Dickstein G, Barzilai D: Bromocriptine-induced pregnancy in an acromegalic patient. *JAMA* 1980;**244**:584.

Ohry A et al: Sexual function, pregnancy and delivery in spinal cord injured women. *Gynecol Obstet Invest* 1978;**9**:281.

Thyroid Diseases

Bolan P, Frury MI: Pregnancy in untreated hypothyroidism. *Irish J Med Sci* 1979;**148**:10.

Cheron RG, Marais HJ, Selenkow HA: Thyroid function and dysfunction. *Compr Ther* 1978;**4**:64.

Harada A et al: Comparison of thyroid stimulators and thyroid hormone concentrations in the sera of pregnant women. *J Clin Endocrinol Metab* 1979;**48**:793.

Levy CA et al: Thyrotoxicosis and pregnancy: Use of preoperative propranolol for thyroidectomy. *Am J Surg* 1977;**133**:319.

Montgomery DAD: Thyroid disease in pregnancy. *Ulster Med J* 1979;**48**:69.

Potter JD: Hypothyroidism and reproductive failure. *Surg Gynecol Obstet* 1980;**150**:251.

Parathyroid Dysfunction

Drake TS, Kaplan RA, Lewis TA: The physiologic hyperparathyroidism of pregnancy. Is it primary or secondary? *Obstet Gynecol* 1979;**53**:746.

Reitz RE et al: Calcium, magnesium, phosphorus and parathyroid hormone relationships in pregnancy and newborn infants. *Obstet Gynecol* 1977;**50**:701.

Salem R, Taylor S: Hyperparathyroidism in pregnancy. *Br J Surg* 1979;**66**:648.

Taylor J et al: Hyperparathyroidism during pregnancy and neonatal hypocalcemia. *Surg Forum* 1976;**27**:82.

Breast Complications

Conner AE: Elevated levels of sodium and chloride in milk from mastitic breast. *Pediatrics* 1979;**63**:910.

Stone DA: Carcinoma of the breast in women under 30 and during pregnancy. *J Am Osteopath Assoc* 1979;**79**:91.

Zinns JS: The association of pregnancy and breast cancer. *J Reprod Med* 1979;**22**:297.

Pulmonary Complications

Fishburne JI: Physiology and disease of the respiratory system in pregnancy: A review. *J Reprod Med* 1979;**22**:177.

Hernandez E, Angell CS, Henson JWC: Asthma in pregnancy: Current concepts. *Obstet Gynecol* 1980;**55**:739.

Leontic EA: Respiratory disease in pregnancy. *Med Clin North Am* 1977;**61**:111.

Snider DE Jr et al: Treatment of tuberculosis during pregnancy. *Am Rev Respir Dis* 1980;**122**:65.

Hematologic Disorders

Alter BP: Prenatal diagnosis of hemoglobinopathies and other hematologic diseases. *J Pediatr* 1979;**95**:501.

Blattner P, Dar H, Nitowsky HM: Pregnancy outcome in women with sickle cell trait. *JAMA* 1977;**238**:1392.

Bloomfield RD, Suarez JR, Malangit AC: The placenta: A diagnostic tool in sickle cell disorders. *J Natl Med Assoc* 1978;**70**:87.

Charache S et al: Management of sickle cell anemia in pregnant patients. *Obstet Gynecol* 1980;**55**:407.

Cotter KP: Haematological changes in pregnancy. *Practitioner* 1978;**220**:289.

Dickinson FT: Sickle-cell hemoglobin C disease in pregnancy: Report of a case with review of the literature. *J Am Osteopath Assoc* 1980;**79**:591.

Jenkins DT, Wishart MM, Schenberg C: Serum ferritin in pregnancy. *Aust NZ J Obstet Gynaecol* 1978;**18**:223.

Jennings JC: Hemoglobinopathies in pregnancy. *Am Fam Physician* (Jan) 1977;**15**:104.

Knispel JW et al: Aplastic anemia in pregnancy: A case report, review of the literature and reevaluation of management. *Obstet Gynecol Surv* 1976;**31**:523.

Mintz U, Moohr JW, Ultmann JE: Hemolytic anemias during pregnancy and in the reproductive years. *J Reprod Med* 1977;**19**:243.

Morrison JC, Wiser WL: Use of prophylactic partial exchange transfusion in pregnancies associated with sickle cell hemoglobinopathies. *Obstet Gynecol* 1976;**48**:516.

Sicuranza BJ et al: Thalassemia minor: Cause of complications in pregnant black and Hispanic women. *NY State J Med* 1978;**78**:1691.

Simon R: Statistical methods for evaluating pregnancy outcomes in patients with Hodgkin's disease. *Cancer* 1980;**45**:2890.

Ssebabi ECT, Bulwa FM: Sickle cell trait anemia in pregnancy. *East Afr Med J* 1977;**54**:258.

Thomas RM, Skalicka AE: Successful pregnancy in transfusion-dependent thalassemia. *Arch Dis Child* 1980;**55**:572.

Complications Involving the Gastrointestinal Tract, Liver, Biliary Tract, & Pancreas

Aranson M: Appendicitis during pregnancy: Ten year review at Maine Medical Center. *J Maine Med Assoc* 1979;**70**:341.

Atlay RD et al: Treating heartburn in pregnancy: Comparison of acid and alkali mixtures. *Br Med J* 1978;**2**:919.

Babaknia A et al: Appendicitis during pregnancy. *Obstet Gynecol* 1977;**50**:40.

Bolen JW et al: Pancreatitis in pregnancy. *Va Med* 1977;**104**:237.

Boyle JM, McLeod ME: Pancreatic cancer presenting as pancreatitis of pregnancy: Case report. *Am J Gastroenterol* 1978;**70**:371.

Breen KJ et al: Idiopathic acute fatty liver of pregnancy. *Gut* 1970;**11**:822.

Cano RI et al: Acute fatty liver of pregnancy: Complication by disseminated intravascular coagulation of pregnancy. *JAMA* 1975;**231**:159.

Coughlan BM, O'Herlihy C: Acute intestinal obstruction during pregnancy. *J R Coll Surg Edinb* 1978;**23**:175.

Gomez A, Wood MacD: Acute appendicitis during pregnancy. *Am J Surg* 1979;**137**:180.

Hasselgren PO: Acute pancreatitis in pregnancy: Report of two cases. *Acta Chir Scand* 1980;**146**:297.

Hatfield AK et al: Death from extrahepatic acute fatty liver of pregnancy. *Am J Dig Dis* 1972;**17**:167.

Hey VMF: Gastro-oesophageal reflex in pregnancy: A review article. *J Int Res* 1978;**6 (Suppl 1)**:18.

Hill LM et al: Small bowel obstruction in pregnancy: A review and report of 4 cases. *Obstet Gynecol* 1977;**49**:170.

Hughes RO, O'Mullane NM, Pratt IT: Acute pancreatitis and vitamin K deficiency in pregnancy. *Br J Obstet Gynaecol* 1978;**85**:634.

Infled DS, Borkowf HI, Varma RR: Chronic persistent hepatitis and pregnancy. *Gastroenterology* 1979;**77**:524.

Johnston WG, Baskett TF: Obstetric cholestasis: A 14 year review. *Am J Obstet Gynecol* 1979;**133**:299.

Khuroo MS, Datta DV: Budd-Chiari syndrome following pregnancy: Report of 16 cases, with roentgenologic, hemodynamic and histologic studies of the hepatic outflow tract. *Am J Med* 1980;**68**:113.

Laatikainen T, Ikonen E: Serum bile acids in cholestasis of pregnancy. *Obstet Gynecol* 1977;**50**:313.

McComb P, Laimon H: Appendicitis complicating pregnancy. *Can J Surg* 1980;**23**:92.

McKay AJ, O'Neill J, Imrie CW: Pancreatitis, pregnancy and gallstones. *Br J Obstet Gynaecol* 1980;**87**:47.

Mistra PS et al: Idiopathic intrahepatic cholestasis of pregnancy: Report of an unusual case and review of the recent literature. *Am J Gastroenterol* 1980;**73**:54.

Soules MR et al: Nausea and vomiting of pregnancy: Role of human chorionic gonadotropin and 17-hydroxyprogesterone. *Obstet Gynecol* 1980;**55**:696.

Steven MM, Buckley JD, Mackay IR: Pregnancy in chronic active hepatitis. *Q J Med* 1979;**48**:519.

Tew WL et al: Perforated duodenal ulcer in pregnancy with double survival. *Am J Obstet Gynecol* 1976;**125**:1151.

Van Thiel DH et al: Heartburn of pregnancy. *Gastroenterology* 1977;**72**:666.

Wands JR: Viral hepatitis and its effect on pregnancy. *Clin Obstet Gynecol* 1979;**22**:301.

Willoughby CP, Truelove SC: Ulcerative colitis and pregnancy. *Gut* 1980;**2**:469.

Diabetes Mellitus

Cassar J et al: Simplified management of pregnancy complicated by diabetes. *Br J Obstet Gynaecol* 1978;**85**:585.

Horwat M et al: Diabetic retinopathy in pregnancy: A 12 year old prospective study. *Ophthalmology* 1980;**64**:398.

Jackson WP, Coetzee EJ: Glycosuria as an indication for glucose tolerance testing during pregnancy. *S Afr Med J* 1979;**56**:921.

Johnston GP: Pregnancy and diabetic retinopathy. *Am J Ophthalmol* 1980;**90**:519.

Martin TR, Allen AC, Stinson D: Overt diabetes in pregnancy. *Am J Obstet Gynecol* 1979;**133**:275.

Mestman JH: Outcome of diabetes screening in pregnancy and perinatal morbidity in infants of mothers with mild impairment in glucose tolerance. *Diabetes Care* 1980;**3**:447.

O'Sullivan JB: Establishing criteria for gestational diabetes. *Diabetes Care* 1980;**3**:437.

Rovers GD et al: Maximal tolerated insulin therapy in gestational diabetes. *Diabetes Care* 1980;**3**:489.

Silfen SL, Wapner RJ, Gabbe SG: Maternal outcome in class H (ischemic heart disease) diabetes mellitus. *Obstet Gynecol* 1980;**55**:749.

Skyler JS et al: Blood glucose control during pregnancy. *Diabetes Care* 1980;**3**:69.

Steel JM, Gray RS, Clarke BF: Obstetric history of diabetics: Its relevance to the aetiology of diabetes. *Br Med J* 1979;**1**:1303.

Renal & Urinary Tract Problems

Bear RA: Pregnancy in patients with chronic renal disease. *Can Med Assoc J* 1978;**118**:663.

Coe FL, Parks JH, Linaheimer MD: Nephrolithiasis during pregnancy. *N Engl J Med* 1978;**298**:324.

Cumming DC, Taylor PJ: Urologic and obstetric significance of urinary calculi in pregnancy. *Obstet Gynecol* 1979;**53**:505.

Greenfeld JP, Ganeval D, Bournerias F: Acute renal failure in pregnancy. *Kidney Int* 1980;**18**:179.

Harris HE, Thomes VI, Hui GW: Postpartum surveillance for urinary tract infection: Patients at risk of developing pyelonephritis after catheterization. *South Med J* 1977;**70**:1273.

Harris RE: The significance of eradication of bacteriuria during pregnancy. *Obstet Gynecol* 1979;**53**:71.

Jones WA, Correa RJ Jr, Ansell JS: Urolithiasis associated with pregnancy. *J Urol* 1979;**122**:333.

Lattanzi DR, Cook WA: Urinary calculi in pregnancy. *Obstet Gynecol* 1980;**56**:462.

Leppert P et al: Antecedent renal disease and outcome of pregnancy. *Ann Intern Med* 1979;**90**:747.

Marwood RP: Anuria in pregnancy. *Br Med J* 1978;**2**:931.

Mattingly RF, Borkowf HS: Clinical implications of ureteral reflex in pregnancy. *Clin Obstet Gynecol* 1978;**21**:863.

Middleton AW Jr, Middleton GW, Dean LK: Spontaneous renal rupture in pregnancy. *Urology* 1980;**15**:60.

Peyser MR et al: Late follow-up in women with nephrosclerosis diagnosed at pregnancy. *Am J Obstet Gynecol* 1978;**132**:480.

Rehn M, Nilsson CG, Hankkamaa M: Significant bacteriuria in the puerperium: A prospective study of the risk factors. *Ann Clin Res* 1980;**12**:112.

Taylor J et al: Focal sclerosing glomerulopathy with adverse effects during pregnancy. *Arch Intern Med* 1978;**138**:1695.

Trebbin WM: Hemodialysis and pregnancy. *JAMA* 1979;**241**:1811.

Whalley PJ et al: Short-term versus continuous antimicrobial therapy for asymptomatic bacteriuria in pregnancy. *Obstet Gynecol* 1977;**49**:262.

Zacur HA et al: Renal disease in pregnancy. *Med Clin North Am* 1977;**61**:89.

Disorders of Adrenocortical Function

Burgess GE III: Alpha blockade and surgical intervention of pheochromocytoma in pregnancy. *Obstet Gynecol* 1979;**53**:266.

Durham JA: A noradrenaline secreting pheochromocytoma complicating pregnancy. *Aust NZ J Obstet Gynaecol* 1979;**17**:53.

Keegan GT et al: Pregnancy complicated by Cushing's syndrome. *South Med J* 1976;**69**:1207.

Ping WW et al: Pheochromocytoma in pregnancy. *Aust NZ J Obstet Gynaecol* 1977;**17**:108.

Shroff CP, Deodhar KP: Bilateral adrenal pheochromocytoma with pregnancy. *Aust NZ Obstet Gynaecol* 1980;**20**:185.

Sukenik S et al: Successful control of phaeochromocytoma in pregnancy: Case report. *Eur J Obstet Gynaecol Reprod Biol* 1979;**9**:249.

Svigos JM, Strasburg ER: Pheochromocytoma and pregnancy: A case report. *S Afr Med J* 1977;**52**:496.

Orthopedic Complications

Gilstrap LC III: Osteomyelitis and pregnancy: Case report. *Milit Med* 1976;**141**:468.

Kelsey JL et al: Pregnancy and the syndrome of herniated lumbar intervertebral disc: An epidemiological study. *Yale J Biol Med* 1975;**48**:361.

Ovarian Tumors

DiOrio J Jr, Lowe LC: Hemangioma of the ovary in pregnancy: A case report. *J Reprod Med* 1980;**24**:232.

Karpathios S et al: Ovarian neoplasms and pregnancy. *Int Surg* 1977;**62**:80.

Infectious Diseases

Brann AW et al: Perinatal herpes simplex virus infections. *Pediatrics* 1980;**66**:147.

Freedman IJ, Mennati MT, Schwarz RH: Obstetrical management of maternal *Listeria*. *Diagn Obstet Gynecol* 1980;**2**:157.

Griffiths PD, Campbell-Benzie A, Heath RB: Prospective study of primary cytomegalovirus infection in pregnant women. *Br J Obstet Gynaecol* 1980;**87**:308.

Hensleigh PA, Glover DB, Cannon M: Systemic Herpesvirus hominis in pregnancy. *J Reprod Med* 1979;**22**:171.

Herrimann KI et al: Subclinical congenital rubella infection associated with maternal rubella vaccination in early pregnancy. *J Pediatr* 1980;**96**:869.

Jones JE Jr, Harris RE: Diagnostic evaluation of syphilis during pregnancy. *Obstet Gynecol* 1979;**54**:611.

Kinghorn GR: Genital warts: Incidence of associated genital infections. *Br J Dermatol* 1978;**99**:405.

Lee TJ, Sparling PF: Syphilis: An algorithm. *JAMA* 1979;**242**:1187.

Leinikki P et al: Epidemiology of cytomegalovirus infections during pregnancy and infancy: A prospective study. *Scand J Infect Dis* 1978;**10**:165.

Solomon F et al: Case of listeriosis in pregnancy with fetal survival. *Eur J Obstet Gynecol* 1978;**8**:103.

Stray-Pedersen B, Lorentzen-Styr AM: The prevalence of *Toxoplasma* antibodies among 11,736 pregnant women in Norway. *Scand J Infect Dis* 1979;**11**:159.

Ueda K et al: Congenital rubella syndrome: Correlation of gestational age at time of maternal rubella with type of

defect. *J Pediatr* 1979;**94**:763.

Welch JP: Prevention of congenital rubella. *Can Med Assoc J* 1977;**117**:151.

Other Disorders

Devoe LD, Taylor RL: Systemic lupus erythematosus in pregnancy. *Am J Obstet Gynecol* 1979;**185**:473.

Dystocia | 39

Myron Gordon, MD

Dystocia (abnormal or difficult labor) is an umbrella diagnosis for a variety of conditions, clinical events, and physical states that may affect the course of labor and delivery. One or more of the following factors may be involved: abnormal or inefficient uterine activity (work), fetopelvic disproportion, and abnormal fetal position, posture, or structure. Dystocia is also a retrospective diagnosis of prolonged labor or labor exceeding 18–24 hours.

The incidence of dystocia in labor is unknown, because the diagnosis depends on the outcome of the delivery. If the delivery is accomplished spontaneously and without incident, the presence of dystocia may be overlooked. On the other hand, dystocia may be the diagnosis in more than 40% of primary cesarean sections.

Types of Dystocia

Classically and pragmatically, dystocia has been classified under 3 general headings: the passage, the powers, and the passenger.

(1) The passage may be inadequate because of pelvic contraction at the inlet or the outlet or because of soft tissue dystocia. The latter may occur with a very pendulous abdomen or large ventral hernia; a neoplasm, such as a benign cystic teratoma of the ovary or the occasional cervical fibroid blocking the birth canal; cervical rigidity or cervical dystocia; or an unyielding perineum, attributable to scarring from a posterior perineorrhaphy, to lymphogranuloma venereum, or to marked vulvar edema. Of the 2 types of pelvic dystocia, soft tissue dystocia is rare, but bony pelvic contraction dystocia is common.

Abbreviations Used in This Chapter	
AP	Anteroposterior (diameter)
APM	Anteroposterior diameter of midplane
APO	Anteroposterior diameter of outlet
CD	Diagonal conjugate (conjugata diagonalis)
IS	Interspinous diameter
IT	Intertuberous diameter
OA	Occiput anterior (L, left; R, right)
OC	Obstetric conjugate
OP	Occiput posterior (L, left; R, right)
OT	Occiput transverse (L, left; R, right)
PSO	Posterior sagittal diameter of the outlet

(2) The contractions (powers) may be hypotonic, hypertonic, or dystonic uterine contractions.

(3) The passenger may cause dystocia because of excessive size (infant weight > 4000 g); abnormal presentation; fetal maldevelopment, as in hydrocephalus, large benign cystic hygroma, or, occasionally, abdominal tumor; or, very rarely, locked or conjoined twins.

PELVIC DYSTOCIA

Pelvic dystocia is abnormal labor in which delay or arrest of progress is caused by an abnormality of the bony pelvis. With rare exceptions, the abnormality is one of size or shape.

Etiology

The most common cause of bony pelvic dystocia is small size; the next is abnormal shape. There are many other rare causes, eg, tuberculosis of the spine with associated kyphotic pelvis. Nutritional deficiencies may produce rachitic or osteomalacic changes. Trauma may cause deformities. Weight bearing and the effect of upward pressure from the femurs, when abnormal, may cause some distortion.

Incidence

The incidence of pelvic dystocia cannot be specified because of the variety of definitions. Even if the contracted pelvis is used as the standard, there is no consensus. In Kiel, Germany, the incidence of contracted pelvis has been reported as about 7% and as 13–15%, depending on the author. In India, it has been reported as 7–8%; in China, almost 4%; in New York City, 3–4%. In Baltimore, it is 11% among blacks and 3% among whites. Pelvic dystocia varies with the age of the patient, being more common at extremes of age.

GROWTH & DEVELOPMENT OF THE PELVIS

The pelvis of the newborn consists of scant bone but considerable cartilage. The innominate bone, as such, is absent. The ilium, pubis, and ischium are connected only by cartilage. The vertebral column is almost vertical and lacks the lumbar curve. The prom-ontory of the sacrum is much higher than in the adult, and the sacrum is straight longitudinally but has a greater transverse curvature. The pelvic inlet is pro-portionately narrower and has an anthropoid shape. The pubic rami are short, and the pubic arch is more acute than in the adult.

The transition from the fetal to the adult female pelvis depends upon the following factors: (1) hor-mones, (2) hereditary traits, (3) weight bearing, (4) nutrition.

Effects of Weight Bearing

From the time the child begins to stand and then to walk, increasing weight affects the pelvis as follows:

(1) The sacrum is pushed downward and forward so as to place the promontory at a lower level, closer to the symphysis pubica. This has the apparent effect of shortening the pelvis anteroposteriorly and enlarging it transversely.

(2) The sacrum is bowed longitudinally. This bowing pivots around the third sacral segment. The thrust of the femurs from below helps to arch the sacrum.

(3) The transverse concavity of the sacrum is flat-tened anteriorly. The innominate bone rotates laterally to widen the pelvis anteriorly.

If the child never walks, the pelvis retains its in-fantile characteristics despite growth and ossification.

Effects of The Femurs

The thrust of the femurs from below, combined with body weight from above, produces the longitudi-nal curve of the sacrum and pushes the sacrum back-ward. This has the effect of rotating the sacrum on its longitudinal axis at the third sacral segment so that the promontory of the sacrum is brought forward and the tip of the sacrum is directed posteriorly. Sufficient pressure is applied to the pubic bones to increase the subpubic angle and widen the pubic arch. An added force in preventing excessive width of the pelvic cavity is the cohesiveness of the pubic bones. The combina-tion of all these factors flattens the anterior portion of the pelvis, converting the anterior segment of the pel-vis from the infantile, anthropoid shape to a gynecoid (or platypelloid) shape.

Effects of Nutrition

Normal bone growth is not achieved without good nutrition, particularly vitamin D, calcium, and phos-phorus. Vitamins and minerals in adequate amounts are necessary for optimal female pelvic shape and size. The height of an adult female reflects nutritional as well as genetic influences. A tall woman usually has a large pelvis, which is likely to be gynecoid or an-thropoid in configuration. A short woman is likely to have a small pelvis, with brachypellic or platypellic characteristics. Poor calcium and phosphorus metabo-lism is reflected in the excessive flattening of the pelvic inlet that is typical of the rachitic pelvis. This pelvic deformity is becoming rare.

Hormonal & Hereditary Influences

There are many differences between the adult male and female pelvis. Generally speaking, the male pelvis is heavier in texture and structure and thus is bulkier; the female pelvis, in comparison, seems fragile and light. The external measurements of the pelvis are comparatively greater in the woman. The depth of the male pelvis is comparatively greater than that of the female, but the cavity is smaller from the inlet to the outlet. Just the opposite is true of the female pelvis. The pubic arch is narrower in the man, and this brings the ischial tuberosities closer together. The male pelvic inlet usually is triangular; that of the female is more rounded, with a wider posterior seg-ment and a flatter anterior segment.

The width of the posterior segment of the inlet affects the size and shape of the sacrosciatic notch. When the posterior segment of the inlet is wide, the sacrosciatic notch is wide, as in the female pelvis. When the posterior segment of the inlet is narrow, as in the male pelvis, the sacrosciatic notch is narrow. The ischial spines are sharp and close together in men; they are usually blunt and farther apart in women.

On pelvic examination, palpation of the woman's sacrum usually shows its anterior surface to be smooth, however, if the woman's pelvis has android charac-teristics, the anterior surface of the sacrum is irregular. The sacrum inclines backward in women; in men, the tip of the sacrum is much closer to the symphysis pubica and the ischial tuberosities. The foramen ob-turatum is narrow and ovoid in men but rounded in women. The sacrospinous ligaments (easily examined by vaginal or rectal examination) are, in women, soft, long, and somewhat thin; in men, they are firm, thick, and short. In brief, the female pelvis is graceful and rounded, and the male pelvis is angular and rough.

What the endocrine contributions are to these sexual differences and what the genetic contributions are is not clear, but many believe that the sex hormones play a major role. Whatever the mechanism, it is certain that the female pelvis has the greater capacity for lateral growth, which is essential to the develop-ment of a rounded, broad pelvic cavity.

Size of the Pelvis

Attempts to determine pelvic capacity have been based on measurements. In the past when ante-partum pelvic examination was interdicted, only external measurements were used. They were the interspinous, intercrestal, and intertrochanteric distances and the external conjugate (Baudelocque's diameter: the ex-ternal distance from sacrum to symphysis pubica). The first 3 of these measurements were used in attempts to determine pelvic shape and transverse capacity; the external conjugate diameter was thought to reflect the anteroposterior diameter.

Subsequently, when internal pelvic examination was allowed, the opportunity arose to more accurately determine the anteroposterior diameter of the inlet vaginally, by measuring the diagonal conjugate (CD), defined as the distance from the promontory of the sacrum to the underborder of the symphysis pubica. The standard of pelvic contraction was a CD of 11.5 cm or less. The obstetric conjugate (OC) was estimated to be 1.5 cm less than the CD, thus, an OC of 10 cm or less was considered evidence of contracted pelvis.

Additional measurements to be considered are the intertuberous, the posterior sagittal of the outlet, and the anteroposterior of the outlet.

The intertuberous diameter (IT) and the posterior sagittal diameter of the outlet (PSO) are measured externally and have been used to estimate pelvic capacity at the outlet. If the external measurements are compared with x-ray measurements, the variation is considerable. For these reasons, one usually cannot depend upon clinical measurements alone in making decisions about the management of a patient with dystocia. Undoubtedly more exact, radiographic measurement has not been universally useful in predicting dystocia and this modality has some risk for mother and fetus.

Roentgenography is most accurate in delineating bony landmarks, assessing configuration, and obtaining measurements. Most of the available techniques have a gross error of no more than 3%, which is acceptable in clinical obstetrics. As many as 20 roentgenographic measurements have been suggested as helpful aids in assessing the pelvic capacity; practically speaking, however, only 4 diameters are required. These are the anteroposterior and transverse diameters of the inlet and the outlet.

Normal ranges of these measurements are as follows: for the AP, > 10 cm; for the transverse diameter of the inlet, > 12 cm; for the IS, > 9.5 cm; and for the APO, > 11.5 cm.

X-Ray Pelvimetry

A. Methods: Numerous roentgenographic methods of pelvimetry have been devised, and several are widely used. Table 39–1 lists some of the more common methods and the advantages and disadvantages of each.

B. Indications: Because of the dangers of radiation, x-ray pelvimetry should be used judiciously. It is of value in the following circumstances:

1. Uterine dysfunction.
2. Lack of descent of the presenting part, with or without uterine inertia.
3. Abnormal presentations, eg, breech, face, or brow.
4. The need to determine engagement. The lateral view is of particular value.
5. Intention to use oxytocin for induction or stimulation of labor.
6. Previous cesarean section when anticipating vaginal delivery.
7. Previous pelvic injury due to trauma or disease.

Determination of Fetal Head Size

Accurate measurement of fetal head size before delivery is still not possible. X-ray studies for this

Table 39–1. Methods of pelvimetry in common use.

Method	Advantages	Disadvantages
Thoms's isometric	Pelvic shape can be seen; ischial spines clear.	Assumption that plane of the inlet is always same height from film. May be moderate error in TI and IS.
Colcher-Sussman isometric	Simplicity; easiest of all.	IS usually inaccurate and obscured. TI not very accurate. Shape cannot be seen.
Caldwell-Moloy stereoscopic	Accuracy; pelvis seen in 3 dimensions.	Complicated technique. Stereoscopic vision sometimes difficult to maintain by many.
Ball pelvicephalometric	Prognostic of fetopelvic relationships.	Questionable accuracy in determining the volume of fetal head and pelvis; prognosis therefore questionable.
Javert-Steele	Shape seen; accurate; no calculation necessary.	No standing films. Symphysis occasionally obscured.
Hodge stereoscopic and isometric	Advantage of combined methods.	Too many films. Complicated technique. Stereoscopic vision needed.

purpose give approximations that may be off the mark by 5–10%. Ultrasonography reduces the margin of error in most cases to an acceptable 2%—and without radiation.

Pelvic Shape

Turner, in 1885, first described the pelvis according to its shape at the inlet, using a brim index. He classified pelves as (1) dolichopellic, in which the OC almost equals or actually exceeds the transverse diameter; (2) platypellic, in which the transverse diameter greatly exceeds the OC; and (3) mesatipellic, in which the transverse diameter exceeds the OC but not by as much as the platypellic type. This is an anthropomorphic view of the pelvic inlet, not an obstetric one.

Later, Thoms added a fourth classification, the brachypellic, in which the relationship between the anteroposterior diameter and the transverse diameter falls between that of the platypellic and the mesatipellic. He found this classification of 4 types to be useful in the clinical practice of obstetrics. More recently, Caldwell and Moloy used Turner's basic concept but changed the names. The dolichopellic pelvis became the anthropoid, the mesatipellic became the gynecoid, and the platypellic became the platypelloid. In place of Thoms's fourth classification, which depended upon the length of the OC, Caldwell and Moloy introduced a fourth type based on female pelves with male characteristics. They called these pelves android. Table 39–2 describes this classification. (See also p 36.) (*Note:* The various shapes, as well as the characteristics of these shapes, are not necessarily seen in pure form.)

Table 39—2. Pelvic types. (After Caldwell and Moloy.)

	Gynecoid	Android	Anthropoid	Platypelloid
Inlet	Rounded or slightly heart-shaped. Ample anterior and posterior segments.	Wedge-shaped or rounded triangle. Posterior segment wide, flat; anterior narrow, pointed.	Anteroposterior ovoid with length of anterior and posterior segments increased. Transverse diameter reduced.	Transverse ovoid; increased transverse. AP diameter of both segments reduced.
Sacrum	Curved, average length.	Straight with forward inclination.	Normally curved, but long and narrow.	Curved, short.
Sacrosciatic notch	Medium width	Narrow	Wide, shallow.	Slightly narrowed
Inclination of the sacrum	Neutral backwards	Anteriorly	Posteriorly	Posteriorly
Side walls (AP view; "lateral bore")	Straight, divergent, or convergent.	Usually convergent	Often straight	Straight or divergent
Interspinous diameter	Wide	Shortened	Shortened	Increased
Pubic arch	Curved	Straight	Slightly curved	Curved
Subpubic angle	Wide	Narrow	Narrow	Wide
Intertuberous diameter	Wide	Shortened	Often shortened	Wide

The transverse diameter of the inlet divides the pelvis into a posterior segment and an anterior segment. The posterior segment is of greater importance in contributing to pelvic shape than the anterior segment. Each segment may be classified as to type, eg, the posterior segment may be gynecoid and the anterior segment android. All combinations except the anthropoid and platypelloid combinations are possible, ie, there are 10 possible variants of the basic shapes.

Among pelves of normal size, the gynecoid pelvis is the most desirable for childbirth (Table 39—3) because it will accept with ease the occiput anterior (OA), occiput transverse (OT), and occiput posterior (OP) presentations, either at the inlet or the outlet. The anthropoid pelvis at the inlet accepts the OP and OA best, but the OT is an abnormal position for this pelvis unless the pelvis is large. The OP may not rotate at the lower pelvis when the shape is anthropoid; indeed, rotation may be contraindicated and dangerous to the fetus in some instances. With the platypeloid pelvis, the OT is the best position and the OA is less acceptable than the OP. Rotation of the OT does not usually occur until the head is coming through the perinum with the platypelloid pelvis. The android pelvis accepts the OA poorly; the OP fits the inlet better. The OP, however, may have difficulty rotating at the lower level, and rotation must occur for the fetus to be delivered. The OT is the better position because rotation can occur at the lower level with greater case than the OP.

Table 39—3. Pelvic shape and fetal position.

Shape	Good Position*	Poor Position
Anthropoid	OP, OA	OT
Gynecoid	OA, OT, OP	—
Platypelloid	OT	OA, OP
Android	OT, OP	OA

*At inlet.

Clinical Classification of Pelves

Many attempts at clinical classification of pelves have been made by obstetricians over the past few centuries. Some of these systems of classification were based not only on size and shape but also on various disease entities and genetic defects that are now seldom seen, and for this reason these clinical classifications are outdated. The rachitic pelvis is no longer an important cause of pelvic dystocia, and tuberculosis of the spine, which results in a kyphoscoliotic pelvis, is extremely rare. Abnormalities of the pelvis resulting from genetic defects (eg, Nägele's pelvis, Robert's pelvis) are so rare that an obstetrician who has delivered thousands of women will not have seen one. The most common defect is smallness due to genetic, nutritional, or unknown causes.

Mechanism of Labor in Relation to Pelvic Shape

The classic movements of the head of the fetus through the pelvis in a vertex presentation are descent accompanied by flexion, internal rotation, extension, and external rotation, whether the vertex presentation is OA, OT, or OP. The head begins to enter the inlet in a semiflexed position, so that a longitudinal diameter between the occipitofrontal and suboccipitobregmatic diameters is presented at the superior strait. The plane that is formed by this longitudinal diameter and the biparietal diameter is oval, not circular, as is the largest plane when the head is well flexed. Because the shape of the pelvic inlet in a gynecoid pelvis is essentially round, the head in a semiflexed position will not meet resistance to descent as long as the pelvis is large enough.

The most common position at the beginning of labor is the OT, with the sagittal suture of the fetus not occupying the middle of the pelvic inlet (synclitism) but lying somewhat anterior to it (posterior asynclitism). The force of the uterine contraction allows the anterior parietal bone to slip behind the symphysis pubica while the posterior parietal bone remains relatively stationary against the sacrum; this corrects the posterior asynclitism.

As descent proceeds, the head continues to flex until the chin is on the chest and engagement is completed, ie, the suboccipitobregmatic-biparietal plane of the head has descended below the transverse diameter of the inlet. This plane is circular. At this time the head is asynclitic, with the sagittal suture in the posterior half of the pelvis (anterior asynclitism).

Flexion is accomplished by meeting soft tissue resistance from below and by the force of the uterine contractions from above. The uterine force is partially transmitted to the buttocks of the fetus and along the vertebral column (which the fetus straightens during the contraction from the relaxed, curved position) to the base of the skull. Here the force, acting as a fulcrum, is applied to the short arm of the lever (the occipital portion of the fetal head) in the same direction as the force, while the long arm of the lever (the portion of the head from the vertebral column to the brow) is moving in the opposite direction; thus, flexion is increased.

As cervical dilatation progresses, the head descends to the tip of the sacrum and the ischial spines. At this time, the anterior parietal bone is the portion of the head most easily palpated vaginally. The uterus during contraction now assists in rotation of the body anteriorly, and this aids in the rotation of the fetal head anteriorly when it reaches the pelvic floor. The greater length of the APO compared with the transverse diameter also encourages anterior rotation of the head. Furthermore, the pelvic canal has a rather sharp bend anteriorly, and this forces the fetus to bend on its own axis. While the head is rotating, there is also lateral forward flexion, so that the anterior asynclitism is corrected. During this process the soft tissues (lower uterine segment and cervix) play an ever more minor role. Nonetheless, the soft tissue effect is to direct the axis along which the fetal head will descend through the pelvis—ie, anteriorly or posteriorly—and this varies with each patient. The anterior rotation (clockwise or counterclockwise, depending upon whether the occiput is right or left) is completed when the sagittal suture is in the midline of the pelvis anteroposteriorly. At this time, the perineal floor, the anterior curve of the pelvic canal, and the forces from above continue to extend the head as it progresses through the perineum. This phase is called extension, along with the maneuver of expulsion. Once the head is delivered, it rotates 90 degrees back to the transverse position or 145 degrees to the posterior position—a rotation that depends on the relationship of the shoulders to the inlet, not on the position of the head. At this time, the head tends to reassume its normal relationship with the trunk, ie, with the face looking anteriorly and at right angles to the shoulders. This is called external rotation. After external rotation has occurred, the shoulders are delivered. Usually, the anterior shoulder comes into view beneath the symphysis with the force of the uterine contraction. With further force from above, the posterior shoulder is delivered by anterior flexion of the trunk of the fetus.

If the pelvis is anthropoid, there may be some differences in the mechanism of labor because the OT is not the usual position. The OP is common. The mechanism differs from that of the OT in that flexion may not be complete until a later stage of descent; also, anterior rotation proceeds through 145 degrees rather than 45 degrees or 90 degrees. The OP position may be maintained throughout the entire birth process, and internal rotation to the anterior may not occur. This is particularly true when the transverse diameter is narrow, the ischial spines are close together, and there is no divergence of the side-walls of the pelvis at the lower levels. Under these circumstances, internal rotation to the anterior is contraindicated. When the transverse diameter is too narrow for internal rotation to occur, damage to the fetus by intracranial hemorrhage may result if rotation is insisted upon.

In the platypelloid pelvis, the head usually enters as an OT and maintains this position because the APO is shorter, restricting the head from rotating anteriorly until the perineum is bulging or the head is actually passing over the perineal body.

In the android pelvis, if the position is OP, descent and flexion can occur in the same fashion. However, internal rotation to the OA may occur in the midpelvis, before the vertex reaches the pelvic floor, depending upon the pelvic capacity and the anterior inclination of the sacrum when funneling of the pelvis is present. Descent in the OP position is frequently difficult unless active rotation is accomplished before the vertex reaches the pelvic floor.

MIDPELVIC–OUTLET DYSTOCIA

Anatomically, the pelvis is divided into an inlet, a midplane, and an outlet. In the management of a patient with dystocia, such a division is impractical, because it is difficult to determine where the midpelvis ends and the outlet begins. Furthermore, the midplane, as usually defined, involves a larger anteroposterior diameter (APM) when a smaller one (APO) at the outlet is within 1–2 cm of it. It is much simpler to look at dystocia as an inlet problem or an outlet problem. This may seem unorthodox, because the IT usually has been considered the transverse diameter of the outlet.

For our purpose, the plane of the outlet will be defined by 2 diameters: (1) transversely by the distance between the ischial spines (IS), and (2) by the APO. The latter is measured from the lower and inner border of the symphysis pubica to the anterior end of the sacrum (Fig 39–1). With these points as references, cephalopelvic disproportion at the outlet may be defined as the inability of the biparietal-suboccipitobregmatic plane of the fetal head to traverse the IS-APO plane of the pelvis. Engagement at the outlet occurs when this plane of the fetal head is below the plane of the outlet. The outlet plane imposes the last bony constriction on the descent of the fetal head.

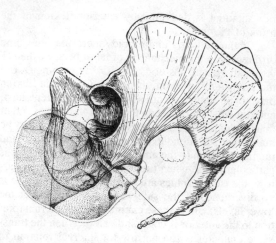

Figure 39–1. The biparietal diameter of the head lies in the IT, and it also lies outside the pelvic cavity.

Once the AP diameter of the outlet has been negotiated, the AP restriction is gone, and only soft tissue may obstruct the descent of the fetal head. A narrow pubic arch (Fig 39–2) will force the fetal head posteriorly, but there will be no bony constriction, because the end of the sacrum will have been negotiated. By the time the fetal head has passed the outlet, the presenting part will distend the perineum; therefore, the diagnosis of outlet disproportion must be made clinically, ie, without the aid of x-ray pelvimetry.

Clinical Findings & Diagnosis

The course of the first stage of labor in a patient with outlet dystocia often is unremarkable. Labor progresses without difficulty to full dilatation of the cervix, with the vertex 1–2 cm below the spines. It is at

this point that dystocia begins to develop. Progress in the second stage of labor is delayed even though the patient may be having adequate uterine contractions. The normal fetal descent through the pelvis is delayed, and the presenting part remains at the same level in spite of strong contractions. There may also be increased molding and caput formation. This is the time when the patient must be reevaluated to determine the cause of dystocia. Reassessment of the pelvis may reveal sharp spines and a narrowed interspinous dimension as well as a short AP diameter of the inlet. This is best determined by rectal examination. X-ray pelvimetry is indicated to confirm the initial impression. An IS of less than 9.5 cm and an APO of 11.5 cm should be suspect. Mengert's areas are of more practical value if borderline contraction is less than 85% of normal (100% = 125).

Differential Diagnosis

In many cases, one cannot be sure that contracted pelvic outlet, however firmly diagnosed, is the only cause—or even the main cause—of lack of descent in the second stage of labor. The 4 reasons for delayed progress in the second stage of labor are as follows:

(1) Uterine impetus or voluntary bearing-down effort insufficient to accomplish further descent of the presenting part or to bring about rotation of the fetal head.

(2) Abnormal position, eg, an occipitotransverse presentation in an anthropoid pelvis. Descent is thwarted by the incompatible pelvic shape.

(3) Soft tissue dystocia. The levator ani muscle may not be relaxed. This is often the case in obese patients with android pelves.

(4) Outlet contraction.

Complications

Many of the complications discussed below under Inlet Dystocia may also occur when the inlet is normal but the outlet is contracted. Uterine inertia may develop during the first or second stage of labor. Prolongation of labor, if it occurs, is more frequent in the second stage. Amnionitis is less common with outlet dystocia than with inlet dystocia. During delay in the second stage of labor, the lower uterine segment may become attenuated; if so, it may rupture. Treatment should be instituted long before rupture is imminent. Necrosis of the anterior wall of the vagina and the posterior wall of the bladder may follow; this often results in a vesicovaginal fistula if the labor is allowed to continue for a long time.

Abnormal presentations are not as common with outlet dystocia as with inlet dystocia. When midforceps are used, deep lateral lacerations of the vagina or lacerations of the cervix may occur, and avulsion of the cervix is an occasional complication. Lacerations of the perineum, with or without episiotomy, are even more common. With median episiotomy, extension through the transverse perineal muscles and into the rectum may result. With mediolateral episiotomy, lacerations through the sphincter or into the rectum are not

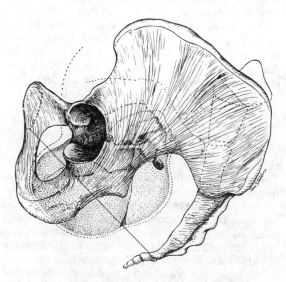

Figure 39–2. The biparietal diameter of the fetus is at the level of the APO, or in the pelvic outlet.

as frequent, but local hemorrhage is. In some instances, the laceration may extend around the rectum and literally lift it from its attachment laterally and posteriorly.

The fetus is at greater risk in outlet dystocia than in inlet dystocia. Prolongation of the second stage of labor, irrespective of outlet contraction, is dangerous, because placental transfer seems to become deficient and the fetus is at increased risk of hypoxia. Also, as the second stage lengthens, there may be progressive molding of the fetal head and even greater caput formation. Caput formation is not harmful to the fetus, but the fullness may confuse the physician about the actual station of the presenting part. Increased molding of the head can cause intracranial hemorrhage. The injudicious use of forceps, usually with an incorrect application, may also be a cause of postnatal complications.

Prevention

Outlet dystocia, like inlet dystocia, could be totally prevented only by recourse to cesarean section for all patients, before or during the first stage of labor; but this is, of course, an impossible absolute. However, there are ways to prevent outlet dystocia in certain cases of abnormal presentation (see Treatment).

For the dangers of premature induction of labor in outlet dystocia, see Inlet Dystocia, below.

Treatment

A. General Considerations: Supportive therapy with fluids and maintenance of a proper biochemical balance are just as important in outlet dystocia as in inlet dystocia. For the general care of the patient during labor and its complications, see pp 896 ff.

B. Vertex Presentation: In outlet dystocia (unlike inlet dystocia), engagement at the outlet cannot be determined without carrying out therapy at the same time. Engagement at the outlet should mean that the largest plane of a well-flexed fetal head is engaged, ie, the suboccipitobregmatic-biparietal plane has passed both the ischial spines and the APO. When this has occurred, the presenting part not only will be on the perineum but will be "bulging" or actually delivering.

Since perinatal mortality and morbidity rates are increased when the forceps (or the vacuum extractor) are used above the perineum—ie, use of midforceps—attempts to determine the cause of the outlet dystocia by such methods as trial forceps are not recommended. Midforceps should be abandoned and replaced by cesarean section in the management of outlet dystocia. If the presenting part is on the perineum, the use of low forceps, if easily completed, is acceptable practice.

When arrest of descent occurs during the second stage with the presenting part above the perineum, before beginning the cesarean section and after anesthesia is given, check the descent of the presenting part. When the musculature of the outlet has been relaxed under anesthesia, the presenting part may have descended to the perineum, allowing an atraumatic outlet forceps delivery.

If cesarean section is selected, one should remember that the fetal head is engaged, and there may have been molding. Prior to opening the uterus, the fetal head should be gently displaced upward by using the palm of the hand, so that the pressure exerted can be distributed over a wide area. Attempts at disengagement of the head must be suspended while a uterine contraction is occurring. This procedure will aid the operator in delivering the head through the incision in the lower uterine segment. It may be necessary also to have an assistant apply pressure vaginally while one delivers the head abdominally. If the presenting part cannot be pushed well up, it may be impossible to deliver the head through a transverse incision. An inverted T incision in the upper segment may be necessary in order to deliver the fetus by breech extraction.

C. Abnormal Presentations: If, during labor, an abnormal presentation is detected and x-ray pelvimetry reveals a contracted outlet, labor should be terminated by cesarean section—the only satisfactory method. The method described above for the vertex presentation will not adequately manage the breech, face, or brow presentation or the transverse lie.

D. Multiparity: Outlet dystocia occurs more often in white multiparas than in dark-skinned multiparas. Moreover, outlet dystocia is uncommon in primigravidas of any race. Infants often increase in size with increasing parity; hence, the risk of the infant's being too large for a contracted outlet is increased. Other causes of outlet dystocia, such as soft tissue obstruction, abnormal positions, and inadequate uterine forces, can occur in any patient at any time.

E. Common Pitfalls:

1. Insistence upon vaginal delivery after a prolonged second stage, with the head 1–2 cm below the spines, without knowing the outlet is contracted.

2. Application of forceps without knowing whether or not engagement of the fetal head has occurred.

3. Use of oxytocin in the second stage of labor without recognizing contracted outlet or abnormal position.

4. Improper application of forceps; improper use of traction.

INLET DYSTOCIA

Cephalopelvic Disproportion & Engagement
(Fig 39–3)

One of the major concepts in dystocia of pelvic origin is expressed by the term "cephalopelvic disproportion." Various definitions have been assigned to this important concept. Because of its importance in management of the patient and the welfare of both the mother and the fetus, it must be defined precisely.

A theoretic definition is clinically useful. The initial definition will apply principally to the 3 varieties of vertex presentation. Cephalopelvic disproportion,

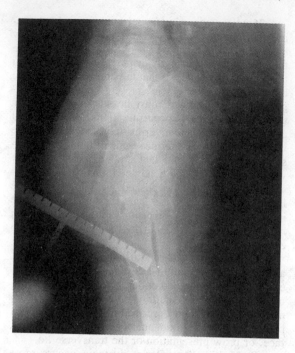

Figure 39–3. AP contraction at the inlet. OC = 9.8 cm and TI = 12.8 cm. There is sacralization of the fifth lumbar vertebra. The sacrum is flat and slightly forwardly inclined. Cephalopelvic disproportion is present. The x-ray was taken with the membranes ruptured and almost full dilatation of the cervix. The OA vertex is floating.

in its purest form, is lack of engagement of the fetal head when the cervix is fully dilated and the membranes have been ruptured. This definition assumes there has been effective labor. In order to further clarify cephalopelvic disproportion, we must define "engagement." When the cervix is fully dilated, the head is usually well flexed. In order for an engagement to have occurred in a well-flexed head, the biparietal-suboccipitobregmatic plane of the head must have descended below the transverse diameter of the inlet. When the transverse diameter of the inlet has been negotiated, the OC will also have been negotiated because the OC is never nearer to the outlet than the transverse diameter of the inlet. The OC is usually 0.5–2 cm superior to the transverse diameter of the inlet.

Cephalopelvic disproportion can occur at the midpelvis or the outlet despite an adequate inlet. A short transverse diameter is more often a cause of inlet disproportion than is a short AP diameter. The diagnosis of engagement can be accurately determined by means of a standing lateral x-ray film. Traditionally, engagement is said to occur when the presenting part is felt on pelvic examination to be level with the ischial spines.

It would be fortunate if all pelves were of the same depth. The depth of the pelvis varies from 8 to 15 cm, with an average of 12 cm. Most pelves fall within the range of 10–13 cm. If the exact depth of the pelvis is

not known, accepting engagement of the head when it is level with the spines is frequently misleading. The pelvis may be shallow, or there may have been so much molding and caput succedaneum formation that the fetal scalp may appear at the vulva without engagement having occurred. Thus, the clinical diagnosis of engagement is difficult and inexact. The membranes must be ruptured, because, if the amniotic sac is intact, trapped fluid discourages descent. Rupturing the membranes under these circumstances, even though it involves the risk of prolapse of the umbilical cord, usually solves the problem, and rapid descent of the head may follow with good uterine contractions.

In cases of contracted pelvis, the cervix may prevent the head from descending. If the cervix is high at the beginning of labor, descent may be late and may be delayed until the cervix has become almost fully dilated.

Clinical Findings & Diagnosis

In many patients with contracted pelves, labor is normal, with progression to full cervical dilatation and normal descent of the presenting part. In other patients, certain clinical findings may indicate that difficulty is likely. On pelvic examination, the following are suspicious indices: (1) A sacrum that cannot be reached, a wide sacrosciatic notch, and sharp ischial spines indicate a possible transversely contracted pelvis. (2) A forwardly inclined sacrum and a shortened APO, with or without sharp spines, indicate possible contraction of the outlet. (3) An easily reached sacrum indicates probable AP contraction of the inlet.

Typically, in a case of contracted inlet with a vertex presentation, the patient begins labor with the presenting part floating or dipping into the pelvic cavity. If labor progresses normally, 8–9 cm of cervical dilatation may be reached, with the membranes bulging before the presenting part has descended. If the membranes should rupture at this time, the presenting part may not descend farther or may descend to a point only 1–2 cm above the spines.

Initial and term clinical reevaluation of the patient is indicated in order to determine fetal size, fetal presentation, descent of the presenting part, caput and molding of the fetal head, effacement (or edema) and dilatation of the cervix, and pelvic size and shape. X-ray pelvimetry is indicated in order to corroborate the clinical findings. In this way the presentation can be verified, the size and shape of pelvic cavity can be assessed, and the descent of the presenting part can be determined. X-ray films may show that the pelvis is contracted in one or both diameters; that the presenting part, although well flexed, has not traversed the pelvic inlet; and that engagement has not occurred. The clinical and x-ray findings fulfill the definition for cephalopelvic disproportion. If the uterine contractions were to continue in the usual manner late in the first stage and early in the second stage of labor, the fetus would be subject to increasing hypoxia and probable intracranial hemorrhage. The lower uterine segment would become increasingly long, thin, and fragile. Sooner or later it would rupture, followed by formation of a tight Bandl retraction ring.

All labors do not follow the course just outlined. Most commonly, the uterine contractions become weak and farther apart, producing uterine inertia rather early in labor at 4–7 cm of cervical dilatation. Rupture of the membranes does not improve the labor. The cause must be determined. The same clinical and x-ray findings will be found when pelvic dystocia is present.

Differential Diagnosis

Uterine inertia is the most common problem with which cephalopelvic disproportion due to contracted pelvis may be confused. Failure to recognize that both may occur at the same time may be catastrophic. Abnormal presentations at the inlet without pelvic contraction may cause dystocia such as occurs when a large plane of the fetal head attempts to negotiate the pelvic inlet, eg, the occipitofrontal diameter in a "military" attitude and the occipitomental in a brow presentation. A face presentation or a compound presentation may confuse the diagnosis. Rarely, there may be marked asynclitism of the fetal head, so that the ear, rather than the parietal bone, is the presenting part. On reexamination, some other cause of dystocia may be determined, such as a tumor blocking the birth canal, a fetal anomaly (eg, hydrocephalus), or macrosomia.

Anticipating Dystocia; Vaginal or Cesarean Delivery; Effects on the Fetus

In order to predict whether delivery will be accomplished vaginally or by cesarean section, the obstetrician requires as much data as can be assembled including the dimensions of the OC and the transverse diameter of the inlet; the shape of the inlet; the fetal position and the degree of head flexion; the exact fetal head size and the dimensions of the effective plane of the fetal head; the fetal weight; the character of the uterine contractions and the progress of effacement; the dilatation of the cervix; and the state of the membranes (intact or ruptured). Even if all of this information is available, a prediction may not survive the test of events.

Other factors that affect the decision to deliver vaginally or by cesarean section are not so well documented. If the fetal position does not correspond well with the shape of the pelvis (eg, an occiput transverse presentation in an anthropoid pelvis), cesarean section will be more likely. The same is true when the fetus is large. If the patient develops uterine inertia, the need for cesarean section is increased because the combination of oxytocin stimulation and contracted pelvis can be disastrous to the fetus and the mother. If the presentation is abnormal (eg, face or brow), the need for cesarean section is increased. The ultimate decision depends upon evaluation of all of the factors; a judgment cannot be made without having adequate information about the passenger, the passage, and the powers (contractions).

The outlook for the fetus is good with proper management. This assumes that there are no accompanying problems that could endanger the infant, eg, erythroblastosis fetalis, placenta previa, or other complications not pertinent to inlet dystocia. The fetus should be at no greater risk than if there were an easy labor and a simple vaginal delivery.

Complications

The most common complication of inlet dystocia is secondary uterine inertia. Occasionally, the contractions are so inefficient that cervical dilatation and effacement proceed slowly and prolonged labor can be anticipated. The definition of the term prolonged labor must take into account the stage of labor, the parity of the patient, and the presence or absence of definitive dystocia. It is fallacious to assume that at some specified number of hours after onset of labor the process should be considered "prolonged." Each patient must be individually evaluated. If the membranes are intact, a detailed evaluation of the patient is not mandatory until appropriate cervical dilatation has been attained: 3 cm in a primigravida, 4 cm in a multigravida. The latent phase of labor is seldom complicated unless the membranes have been ruptured. Amnionitis is a risk, though the risk is not as great as if premature rupture of the membranes had occurred. With premature rupture of the membranes and inlet dystocia, the risk of amnionitis is increased.

Two complications should never occur if adequate medical care is available. The first is rupture of the uterus. If cephalopelvic disproportion is associated with prolongation of the second stage of labor, the lower uterine segment will become very thin and friable. With proper management, this complication is preventable. The same is true of the risk, during a prolonged second stage, of soft tissue necrosis of the anterior vaginal wall, which may result in vesicovaginal fistula.

A frequent complication of inlet contraction is abnormal presentation. This problem must be handled individually. When a malpresentation occurs, the incidence of dystocia increases regardless of pelvic size.

When the pelvic inlet is not well filled by the presenting part, prolapse of the cord may occur when the membranes rupture. If amnionitis is present, the fetus is at increased risk of pneumonia or septicemia, either in utero or during the neonatal period. Prolongation of labor and traumatic operative delivery can result in intracranial hemorrhage and give rise to significant neurologic deficits. In such cases, early cesarean section should be considered.

Prevention

There is no way of preventing inlet dystocia except by doing a cesarean section on all patients prior to labor. The physician must rely, therefore, on early signs indicating that difficulty may occur. This concern may even be aroused when the patient is seen for the first time. If, on pelvic examination, the sacral promontory can be easily reached, shortening of the OC may be present. If the ischial spines are sharp and close together, there may be constriction of the transverse diameter of the inlet. A wide sacrosciatic notch accentuates the possibility of transverse contraction. A history of difficult labor, possibly associated with large size of the infant, should raise this suspicion. As pregnancy reaches term, a floating presenting part or abnormal presentation (eg, transverse lie or face presentation) may presage pelvic dystocia.

Traditionally, attempts to determine disproportion before labor have involved pressing with the palm of one hand over the vertex just above the symphysis pubica while the other hand presses on the fundus in an attempt to force the head into the pelvic inlet. In a variation of this maneuver, the left index finger is held in the patient's rectum to determine the relationship of the rest of the vertex to the interspinous diameter as fundal pressure is applied with the examiner's right hand. If the head slips behind the symphysis and seems to descend into the pelvic cavity, disproportion is unlikely. If the head seems to override the symphysis and bulge above the pubic bone at the onset of labor, disproportion is suggested but not proved. A floating head in an elderly primigravida is suspect, yet will require a cesarean section because of inlet dystocia only 15% of the time. A significant number of primiparas require cesarean section for inlet dystocia if the head is unengaged at the onset of labor. However, a floating head at the onset of labor does not necessarily indicate impending difficulty in labor.

X-ray pelvimetry prior to onset of labor rarely permits diagnosis of cephalopelvic disproportion or inlet dystocia. With a normal-sized infant (2500–4000 g) and a markedly contracted pelvis the fetus can be safely delivered vaginally in about 70% of cases. Occasionally, a transverse lie may be converted into a vertex presentation by external version, and inlet dystocia may thereby be prevented. The use of the same maneuver to convert a breech presentation into a vertex presentation may have the same preventive effect.

Treatment

A. General Considerations: All patients in true labor should receive fluids intravenously both to maintain adequate hydration and to keep a vein open for use in emergencies. Patients should be carefully observed throughout labor, with particular attention given to cervical dilatation, cervical effacement, the descent of the presenting part, and early recognition of any abnormality. There should be steady progress of cervical dilatation, and the presenting part should descend within a reasonable period of time in accordance with the Friedman curve (Fig 31–15). If there is any significant deviation from normal, the patient should be reevaluated with respect to the presenting part, position of the fetus, estimated weight of the fetus, caput formation, status of the membranes, effacement or edema of the cervix, pulse rate, body temperature, fetal heart rate, and uterine contractions. If uterine inertia develops and labor becomes prolonged, fetal hypoxia can be determined by obtaining the pH of the fetal scalp blood (in vertex presentation). The size of

the pelvis should be appraised by x-ray examination; this will determine accurately the critical measurements and the engagement or lack of engagement of the fetal head.

B. Vertex Presentation: In a vertex presentation, spontaneous onset of labor is desirable. Repeated observations and evaluations as noted above should be started. No decision regarding pelvic dystocia should ever be made during the latent phase of labor; this judgment is reserved for the accelerated phase. During the latent phase of labor while the membranes are still intact, active interference should be avoided. If this phase becomes prolonged and distressing to the patient, rest and morphine are the treatment of choice. Morphine either may convert an abnormal uterine contractile pattern to normal, so that cervical effacement and dilatation will occur, or may stop uterine contractions temporarily. If the membranes have been ruptured and cephalopelvic disproportion is not a factor, stimulation of uterine contraction is indicated. According to Friedman, 85% of cases in the latent phase can be terminated by this method. If true inertia develops and the presenting part is not engaged at the pelvic inlet on clinical evaluation, x-rays should be obtained in order to determine whether or not pelvic contraction is present. If contracted pelvis is diagnosed, no further labor should be permitted and cesarean section should be performed at once.

If x-ray pelvimetry films reveal the pelvis to be adequate and if the "fit" of the fetal head into the pelvis appears normal, oxytocin stimulation may be used to overcome uterine inertia.

If the progress of labor has been normal in terms of time, if full cervical dilatation has been attained, if the membranes have ruptured, and if spontaneous descent of the presenting part to the lower portion of the pelvis has occurred, then vaginal delivery should be anticipated. Vaginal delivery is possible in over 75% of cases of contracted inlet when there is a vertex presentation and the infant is of normal size at term. If complete cervical dilatation has been reached but the presenting part has not descended into the pelvic cavity (no obvious engagement), immediate cesarean section is necessary. If the descent is difficult to assess because of molding and caput formation—and one should remember that in many cases the head is not engaged even when it is level with the spines—lateral pelvimetric films should be obtained in order to determine whether or not engagement has occurred. After the vertex has engaged, descent can be expected during the second stage; without engagement, immediate cesarean section is required.

If almost full dilatation has been attained and the membranes are intact, the membranes should be ruptured, using the "double set-up" technique (preparations completed for an immediate cesarean section), because of possible prolapse of the umbilical cord. Instead of tearing the membranes, remove the fluid slowly by needle puncture. After the fluid has been evacuated, the fetal head may descend into the pelvis. If it does, it will do so after a few uterine contractions.

If it does not descend promptly, cesarean section will be required. Under this regimen, one can prove cephalopelvic disproportion, the indication for surgical delivery.

If labor becomes desultory early in labor or in midlabor, the indication for cesarean section is uterine inertia with contracted pelvis.

C. Occiput Posterior (OP) Presentation: This presentation is likely to cause particular problems at the inlet. One of these is a relationship termed "poor pelvic drive." In the OA and OT positions, the force of the uterine contraction follows the fetal vertebral column, which is usually at right angles to the pelvic inlet; thus, the force is directed into the pelvic cavity. In some posterior positions (notably the direct OP), the vertebral column of the fetus is parallel to that of the mother. As the head attempts to enter the inlet, normal flexion is difficult to achieve because the vertebral column is far posterior in the uterine cavity and the force of uterine contraction tends to extend the head. At the same time, the line of force is directed toward the symphysis pubica, where it is dissipated. The fetus presenting OP has a tendency to remain stationary (ie, does not descend), and secondary uterine inertia is a common complication.

If extension continues, the posterior vertex assumes a sincipital position, ie, the head is at a right angle to the vertebral column (military attitude) rather than in flexion (attitude of subjection). The longer (AP) diameter of the head now attempts to engage the inlet and meets resistance because of the larger diameter (ie, the biparietal-occipitofrontal). Correction may be possible during labor by placing the patient in the knee-chest position. Because uterine inertia usually intervenes and because oxytocin should not be used to treat this abnormality, cesarean section is warranted.

D. Multiparity: The multipara with contracted pelvis has been called the "dangerous multipara." There is no such thing as a "tried pelvis" in any pregnancy: Each combination of fetus and pelvis, in a given patient, must be considered a complete, identifiable, and unique combination. The patient may have a markedly contracted pelvis and yet deliver several term offspring vaginally. Suppose, for example, that a patient with an OC of 9.6 cm and a transverse diameter of 12.5 cm has had 3 previous vertex presentations, all of which were occipitotransverse and in all of which the infants were term-sized. In a subsequent pregnancy, a fetus weighing 3400 g causes cephalopelvic disproportion. The use of oxytocin in this instance may cause uterine rupture, or the fetus may sustain an intracranial hemorrhage. A multipara with contracted pelvis with or without an abnormal presentation is a dangerous patient, because the obstetrician has been lulled into a sense of security for the reason that the woman has been delivered vaginally with success previously.

E. Common Pitfalls:

1. Failure to recognize uterine inertia early enough results in delay in management.

2. The use of oxytocin to treat uterine inertia in contracted pelvis frequently results in intracranial hemorrhage in the fetus.

3. Assuming that engagement has occurred when the presenting part is level with the spines may result in a difficult mid or high forceps delivery, with fetal damage.

4. Internal podalic version and breech extraction is a hazardous procedure.

5. The concept of a "tried pelvis" in the multipara is erroneous.

SOFT TISSUE DYSTOCIA

Soft tissue dystocia may be defined as any anatomic abnormality, other than bony, that causes delay in labor. The causes may be congenital anomalies, tumors, infection from previous operative procedures, or prior injury.

Soft tissue dystocia is uncommon. Some of the causes are becoming rarer because of better obstetric practice and improvements in the prevention and treatment of disease. The incidence of congenital anomalies has remained unchanged.

Congenital Anomalies

A. Bicornuate Uterus: The bicornuate uterus is a frequent cause of abnormal presentations—particularly the breech and the transverse lie—owing to the abnormal configuration of the intrauterine cavity. It is also a frequent cause of retention of the placenta during the third stage of labor. The diagnosis of bicornuate uterus occasionally may be made during pregnancy by noting the characteristic indentation of the fundus of the uterus. The diagnosis can readily be made manually after termination of the third stage of labor, when the uterine cavity can be felt easily and accurately.

This uterine abnormality cannot be prevented. Anomalies of the urinary tract are a frequent association and should be considered in all patients with bicornuate uterus. Treatment depends in large part on the abnormal presentation. If a congenital anomaly interferes with the containment of pregnancy beyond the second trimester or the early part of the third trimester, an operation to develop a uterine cavity of more nearly normal shape and size may be helpful. A unification operation (usually for a double uterus) is an example (see p 178).

B. Vaginal Septum: This congenital anomaly is due to the incomplete resorption of the vaginal cell core early in the embryonic stage of fetal growth. The septum usually is longitudinal, but it may be transverse (see p 172). The longitudinal septum will be in the midline and may extend the entire length of the vaginal canal (as with a double uterus), or it may be incomplete. During labor, the septum usually will be pushed aside; seldom will it cause delay in the descent of the presenting part, but it may be lacerated and bleed copiously. The transverse septum not only is uncommon but also may be difficult to recognize. It is frequently located in the vault of the vagina and has a small opening in the center. It may be close enough to the cervix to be confused with the cervical os. During labor, full dilatation may be reached without recognition, with a resultant delay in descent during the second stage. In some instances, the cervix dilates satisfactorily; more often, cruciate incisions are necessary to relieve the obstruction.

C. Conglutination of the External Os: Whether this condition is the result of previous injury or is a congenital anomaly is not certain. When seen in a nullipara, it is probably congenital. It may be described as a very small opening of the external os of the cervix, which remains undilated during labor. The cervix will become completely effaced with the full development of the lower uterine segment, so that on pelvic examination one may assume that full dilatation has occurred. On speculum examination, a dimplelike structure may be seen at the top of the vagina. If pressed with the finger, the dimple may begin to dilate and then go to full dilatation in a very short time. Occasionally, it will be necessary to do a hysterostomatomy to fully dilate the cirvix.

Previous Injury

A. Pendulous Abdomen: An obese woman who has had numerous pregnancies often develops a wide diastasis recti, and in subsequent pregnancies the uterus may extrude between the rectus muscles. The abdominal wall then gives so little protection that the uterus may become anteflexed and a pendulous abdomen results. The anteflexion and relaxation may be drawn forward during a uterine contraction to prevent descent of the presenting part into the pelvic cavity. In such cases, the force will be directed posteriorly against the sacrum. This problem may be solved simply by using an abdominal binder; uterine contraction will then direct the head into the pelvic cavity and vaginal delivery will be encouraged.

B. Cervical Injury: Injury to the cervix may be of several types. Deep lacerations of the cervix may have occurred during a previous delivery; some of these may even have extended into the lower uterine segment. Many heal without incident; however, in a subsequent labor, a laceration may recur and extend again into the lower uterine segment, causing uterine rupture.

In some cases, a previously healed laceration may prevent normal dilatation of the cervix, because the cervix is rigid. This causes labor to be prolonged. With sufficient uterine contractions, the cervix may suddenly lacerate and abrupt delivery occur.

C. Previous Operative Procedures: Operative procedures may result in tissue distortion sufficient to cause dystocia. Patients who have had an extensive cystocele or rectocele repair may require cesarean section, interdicting labor, to avoid breakdown of the repair. A previous **myomectomy** may endanger the integrity of the uterus during labor, and cesarean section may be desirable to prevent uterine rupture. Prior **conization of the cervix,** particularly when it has been done with the cautery, may cause cervical dystocia, cervical adhesions, and cervical scarring. Very rarely, previous abdominal operative procedures may cause adhesions to the uterus, with retroflexion or anteflexion and **fixation of the uterus.** During pregnancy, this may lead to **sacculation of the uterus,** which will require operative interference later in pregnancy. Previous cesarean section cannot in itself be considered a cause of dystocia. The lower segment incision is safer than the upper segment incision, which is more likely to rupture during pregnancy or labor.

D. Infection: The most common infectious disease causing dystocia is **lymphogranuloma venereum.** As this disease progresses, gross scar tissue forms in the perineum, and this tissue resists dilatation during the second stage of labor. More than one episiotomy may be necessary if the fetal head is to pass the perineum. The rectum often is involved, and a stricture that includes the rectovaginal septum may result. The vagina may not dilate at the stricture; in that case, rupture through the scar tissue may result in a rectovaginal fistula. If the rectal stricture lies above the perineal body, passage of the fetus through the birth canal should not be permitted; instead, cesarean section is indicated.

E. Tumors: It is fortunate that in the childbearing years most tumors are uncommon, benign, and amenable to treatment. However, malignancies do occur.

1. Carcinoma of the cervix is not uncommon during the childbearing years. Stage I carcinoma of the cervix is occasionally diagnosed during pregnancy. During labor, cervical laceration is a serious complication because of bleeding and possible metastasis. The treatment of invasive carcinoma of the cervix diagnosed late in pregnancy is delivery by cesarean section and prompt radiation therapy. In special cases, radical cesarean hysterectomy and lymphadenectomy may be warranted.

2. Myomas of the uterus are commonly seen but seldom cause dystocia. Myomas may be a rare cause of uterine inertia. Even cervical myomas seldom obstruct labor because, during the formation of the lower uterine segment, the cervix retracts and the tumor is often drawn out of the true pelvis. Submucous myomas may prevent pregnancy. If pregnancy does occur, they may predispose to placenta accreta. If a patient has had a previous myomectomy, she is at risk of rupture of the uterus. Rupture during labor may be prevented by cesarean section.

3. Tumors of the ovaries are not often seen during pregnancy. They usually are benign cystic teratomas. Dermoids may not be recognized during pregnancy because they remain abdominal throughout gestation and do not often cause dystocia. They are subject to twisting and infection during pregnancy. They may prolapse behind the uterus, occupy the cul-de-sac, and prevent descent of the presenting part. The diagnosis of a tumor previa can be made on vaginal examination by palpating the cystic ovarian mass in the cul-de-sac with the presenting part above. If the patient is in early labor, the knee-chest position may be used in an at-

tempt to dislodge the ovarian tumor and shift it above the presenting part, but this usually fails. The preferred treatment in obstructive cases is cesarean section and removal of the tumor. Wedge biopsy of the opposite ovary is important because cystic teratomas often are bilateral.

Other tumors (eg, dysgerminomas) are occasionally diagnosed. Tumors with malignant potential should be removed and the pregnancy managed as a separate entity.

Other Causes

When a multipara enters labor with the presenting part in the oblique position, suspect a **full bladder.** The bladder may fill the pelvic inlet and prevent descent of the presenting part as the cervix dilates. Emptying the bladder should correct the abnormal lie and allow descent.

Occasionally, **cervical edema** occurs in labor when the cervix is caught between the presenting part and the symphysis. The problem frequently solves itself as the head descends farther into the pelvic cavity. However, it is advisable, when the cervix is almost fully dilated, to reduce the obstruction by gently pushing the cervix over the head if possible. If the edema persists, necrosis and avulsion of the cervix may result.

Vulvar edema is rare. It is sometimes seen in patients with chronic heart failure and occasionally in severe preeclampsia-eclampsia. In either case, the head usually is delivered without serious difficulty.

FETAL DYSTOCIA

Fetal dystocia is abnormal labor caused by an unusual presentation of the fetus or by maldevelopment or excessive size of the fetus. The fetal enlargement may be due to macrosomia (excessive overall growth) or to excessive local growth.

Etiology

The following abnormal presentations may be associated with dystocia: sincipital, breech, face, brow, transverse lie, and compound. Occiput transverse (OT) and occiput posterior (OP) presentations are considered normal if transient, but if persistent they may cause dystocia.

Large size of the fetus (> 4000 g) may be due to heredity, diabetes mellitus, maternal obesity, generalized fetal edema, erythroblastosis, or high parity of the mother. In many instances, shoulder dystocia (see p 924) is an accompanying problem. A relative fetopelvic disproportion may be a critical factor.

Fetal anomalies—hydrocephalus and other types of local enlargement—may be due to urinary retention, liver tumors, or meningomyelocele.

Incidence

The OT is one of the commonest presentations at term, and yet it may cause dystocia in the lower pelvis,

as a transverse arrest. The OP presentation is less common but is more often the cause of dystocia because of the common failure of internal rotation of the OP to the OA position. The sincipital (military) attitude is still less common (less than 1% of cases at term) but may cause dystocia at the inlet. The breech presentation is that of 4% of fetuses weighing more than 500 g, but at term it is the presentation in fewer than 2% of all deliveries. In most instances, the breech presentation is not a cause of dystocia; but when it is, the infant may be critically jeopardized. The face presentation occurs once in approximately 500 deliveries and frequently causes dystocia. The brow presentation occurs about once in 1000 deliveries and invariably causes dystocia if the infant is at term. The transverse lie occurs once in 250 pregnancies and always causes dystocia at term. Compound presentation is less frequent; and, curiously, it does not often cause dystocia. Macrosomia (fetal size > 4000 g) occurs in 5% of deliveries. The large size causes shoulder dystocia and cephalopelvic disproportion. Congenital anomalies occur rarely; when they do, dystocia generally is associated with regional enlargements

Pathogenesis

Typically, labor with the macrosomic fetus is similar to that in which cephalopelvic disproportion is present. Uterine inertia may be an early complication, although initially the labor may be normal. In some instances, labor progresses normally until the head is delivered; shoulder dystocia then becomes apparent.

In regional enlargement, dystocia usually does not occur until the region of fetal distortion reaches the inlet.

Treatment

A. Midpelvic and Deep Transverse Arrest: The OT is the most common fetal position, and in most instances it does not complicate labor. In the normal pelvis it seldom is a cause of inlet dystocia unless the baby is large. The head usually rotates from the OT to the OA position in the lower pelvis and is delivered by extension as it comes over the perineum. However, on occasion, due either to an incompatibility between the fetal position and the pelvic shape or to insufficient powers, there may be midpelvic transverse arrest or deep transverse arrest when the arrest occurs above the perineum. There will be little fetal distress unless the second stage of labor is prolonged. The occiput may descend to 1–2 cm below the ischial spines, where neither further descent nor rotation occurs despite seemingly normal uterine contractions. If arrest occurs closer to the perineum, it is called deep transverse arrest.

After the physician has determined by x-ray pelvimetry that the pelvis is normal and that engagement has occurred, the patient can be delivered by forceps. The head may be rotated manually or by forceps to the OA position. After rotation, delivery should be completed in the usual manner. In a platypelloid pelvis, however, rotation is not the procedure of choice; instead, apply the forceps to the OT and exert downward traction after having done an episiotomy. As the head descends, allow the pelvic architecture to determine when the head should rotate to the anterior position. In some platypelloid pelves, the occiput cannot rotate to the anterior and delivery must be accomplished in the OT position. This is more likely to happen when the APO is contracted and the lower pelvis is wide.

Transverse arrest cannot be prevented. Early diagnosis is the key to treatment. During labor, there should be frequent monitoring of the fetal heart and, when necessary, sampling of fetal scalp blood to detect the acidosis that signifies fetal hypoxia. One should not delay if there is lack of progress during the second stage. If the pelvis is adequate and uterine inertia is the apparent cause of arrest, oxytocin drip stimulation may solve the problem by improving the quality of uterine contractions. The outlook for both the mother and the fetus should be excellent under these circumstances. When the second stage is prolonged, the fetus is at greater risk of hypoxia.

B. Occiput Posterior (OP) Presentation: The OP presentation, although less frequently encountered than the OT, causes dystocia more commonly. In many pelves, as descent occurs, the head in the OP position is not as well flexed as is the case in the OT or OA position because of the angle between the lumbar vertebrae and the pelvic cavity. Because the fetal vertebral column lies directly on the maternal vertebral column in a direct OP presentation, some extension must occur if the head is to enter the pelvic cavity. A larger plane of the fetal head is commonly used as the head descends; therefore, delay may occur. In most instances, however, labor is of normal duration, and rotation to the OA position occurs without prolongation of the second stage of labor. When delay does occur, it is usually late in the first stage of labor (from 7–8 cm to full dilatation of the cervix) because of the lack of rotation. The lack of rotation may be due to an incompatibility between the pelvic shape and the fetal position or to insufficient uterine force. An OP presentation is easily determined by pelvic examination when there is delay in descent. With each uterine contraction there may be slight rotation or slight descent, but between contractions the head reverts to its original position. With subsequent contractions, further progress stops. It is at this point that a reevaluation of the patient is indicated, to be certain that the pelvic capacity and shape will accommodate the OP. Proper treatment may then be instituted. If the pelvis is normal but the uterine contractions are too weak, oxytocin should be infused, and, with pushing efforts with each contraction, rotation to the OA or OP position may occur. The head may descend to the perineum as an OP, depending upon pelvic shape. If the head does not descend to the perineum in a reasonable period of time during the second stage, cesarean section should be done. If the presenting part descends to the perineum, delivery may then be accomplished (1) by forceps rotation to the anterior position and then reapplication of the forceps followed by traction and delivery, or (2)

by manual rotation to the anterior position followed by the application of forceps. It is wise to rotate 180 degrees rather than 90 or 135 degrees: there will be less chance of reverting to the original position during the interval between rotation and the application of the forceps.

A preferred method is to apply the forceps to the OP and exert traction. If descent occurs, apply traction intermittently. If the head rotates directly to the OP position, deliver as such. If, as descent occurs, the head begins to rotate, rotation should be allowed until the OA position is reached; then the forceps should be reapplied and delivery completed as an OA. It is unwise to make a firm prior decision about the method of delivery in an OP presentation. Rotation should never be attempted in a contracted anthropoid pelvis without attempting forceps delivery as an OP initially.

A satisfactory maternal and fetal outcome can be expected. It goes without saying that judicious traction, care, deliberation, and accuracy of forceps application are essential to any operative vaginal delivery.

The type of operative delivery just described carries with it risks of lateral sulcus tears, cervical lacerations, and extension of episiotomies. After delivery, there should be a complete inspection of the vaginal canal, including the cervix, the lateral sulci, and the perineum, so that any unintentional lacerations can be repaired.

C. Sincipital (Military) Attitude: (Fig 39–4.) It is normal for the fetus in vertex presentation to be poorly flexed or not flexed at all as it enters the pelvic inlet. This is the sincipital attitude—also called the military attitude because the fetal head is in the same relationship to its chest as that of a soldier standing at attention. This fetal position may cause dystocia in several ways. If the head flexes with the onset of uterine contractions, there will be no difficulty. This is the usual circumstance when the occiput is in the anterior portion of the pelvis. When, however, the occiput is in the posterior part of the pelvis or slightly toward the transverse, there may be difficulty. The head may not flex at all; in that case, the large occipitofrontal-biparietal plane is the critical plane for engagement, and the bregma presents. On pelvic examination, the anterior fontanelle can be felt as easily as the posterior fontanelle. There may be sufficient increase in the relative size of the fetal head in its relationship to the pelvis to prevent the head from descending. With labor, the head may extend to a brow presentation.

There is no satisfactory primary method for treating the patient so that safe and successful vaginal delivery can be assured. One must wait and assess what labor can accomplish. If the head flexes, one can expect conversion to the occiput followed by vaginal delivery. If the military attitude remains unchanged, the head may descend to the mid pelvis and uterine inertia may develop. Stimulation of labor is contraindicated for the abnormal presentation; instead, cesarean section is the procedure of choice. If there is conversion to the brow presentation, it is expedient to deliver by cesarean section.

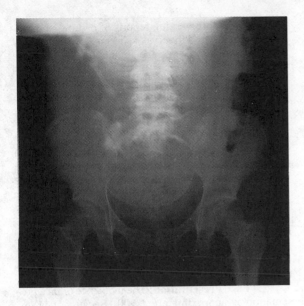
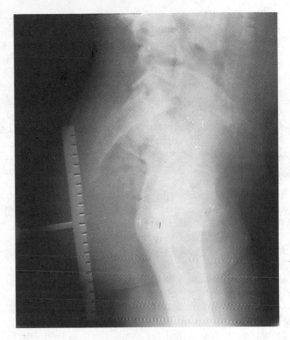

Figure 39–4. Sincipital (military attitude) presentation (AP view) and asynclitism (lateral view) in a transversely contracted pelvis. OC = 11.5 cm, TI = 10.5 cm. The IS measures only 7.9 cm, with an adequate APO of 11.0 cm.

D. Breech Presentation: The overall incidence of breech presentation is about 3% in newborns weighing more than 1000 g. As term approaches, the incidence falls to about 2%. The breech is more likely to produce dystocia than is the vertex when, in either case, the pelvis and the fetus are of normal size. With the breech, delay of onset of labor after premature rupture of the membranes is a common problem, for undetermined reasons. The use of oxytocin to induce labor after premature rupture of the membranes carries little risk and may actually decrease fetal loss in cases of vertex presentation; but the use of oxytocin for any reason in cases of breech presentation increases the risk to the fetus. This danger makes management of the patient with premature rupture of the membranes more difficult. Abdominal delivery of the breech baby should be considered if labor does not ensue within a reasonable time after premature rupture of the membranes. As is true of other methods of elective induction of labor, induction with oxytocin carries a higher risk of perinatal loss. It is also advisable not to use oxytocin during labor.

Because the circumference of the shoulders in the premature infant is smaller than that of the head, it is not uncommon for the head to be trapped by the cervix. When there is delay in delivery of the aftercoming head, one should immediately ascertain whether or not the cervix is preventing the head from descending. The head should not be forcibly extracted through the cervix because of the danger of intracranial hemorrhage or tentorial tears, which may kill or severely injure the infant. In order to more easily deliver the head, hysterostomatomy (Dührssen's incisions) can be done.

One incision at 10 or 2 o'clock on the circumference of the cervix may permit the cervix to accommodate the aftercoming head, and the operator will be able to complete the delivery without difficulty. This method of management is not recommended unless a cesarean section cannot be done or the fetus is dead. Labor should then be allowed to continue and terminate spontaneously.

Delivery of the aftercoming head by the use of forceps has certain advantages. During spontaneous delivery of the fetal head or delivery by means of the Bracht maneuver, the Mauriceau-Smellie-Veit maneuver, or the Prague maneuver, it is not possible to control the speed with which the head is delivered. This complicates delivery of the aftercoming head in 2 ways: (1) a tentorial tear or (of less danger) a falx tear may occur; and (2) hemorrhage into the subarachnoid space (without laceration) of the dura mater may result. The risk is particularly great when the head is small and fragile, as in the premature infant. With the use of forceps, the aftercoming head can be deliberately and slowly brought through the introitus under control. This avoids a sudden release of intracranial pressure, which often occurs when the head "pops out" when other methods of delivery are used. The incidence of intracranial damage can be reduced if forceps are used judiciously in the delivery of the aftercoming head for both the premature and the term infant.

The maternal complications are those of any labor in which there is inertia or operative delivery. The fetus is at greater risk because the aftercoming head traverses the pelvic cavity so much more rapidly. The perinatal death rate is higher than in vertex deliveries, but not all of the increase is attributable to breech presentation alone. In fetuses weighing over 1000 g in breech presentation, the prematurity rate is 4 times as great as in vertex presentation; placenta previa occurs 6 times and abruptio placentae 3 times as often; the incidence of congenital anomalies may be as high as 6%; and the fetus is at greater risk if oxytocin is used. Fetal death occurs prior to onset of labor more often in breech presentation than in other types of presentation. Injuries peculiar to breech delivery are brachial nerve injury, spinal injury (particularly in the region of the neck), and the intracranial damage described above. If deliberation, care, and gentleness are used in the operative maneuvers in breech delivery, injury should occur rarely if at all. More frequent resort to cesarean section, rather than oxytocin, in solving dystocia problems will also reduce the risks of perinatal death and postnatal morbidity. The high incidence of prematurity, which is related to the greatest fetal and neonatal loss, has yet to be solved.

The multipara and her fetus may be at greater risk than the primigravida and her fetus for 2 reasons: (1) prolapse of the umbilical cord is more frequent in multiparous births; and (2) the obstetrician usually feels safer with the multipara because she has delivered without difficulty before, ie, there is a tendency to observe her progress less carefully and perhaps fail to anticipate problems or treat them adequately as they arise. A more liberal use of cesarean section in breech presentations is warranted.

External version is one method of preventing breech presentation. This maneuver may be tried between the 32nd and 36th weeks of gestation. After 36 weeks, it becomes increasingly difficult because of the tightness of the uterus and the size of the fetus. The best time for external version is the 32nd to 34th weeks. External version should be done gently, without anesthesia, while listening frequently to the fetal heart. The maneuver should be stopped if the fetal heart slows or the mother complains of pain.

Rotation cannot always be done. It is more difficult when there is a frank breech with extended legs. The full or the footling breech is easier to rotate. Even if the maneuver is successful, the fetus may rotate spontaneously back to the breech. There are widely divergent opinions about the success rate and usefulness of rotation.

According to Berendes, the greater incidence of neurologic defects in later life in infants delivered by breech over those delivered by vertex is due to lower birth weight, shorter gestational age, congenital anomalies, late presentation to the obstetrician for prenatal care (in the third trimester), and vaginal delivery under regional anesthesia. Because of the greater perinatal loss and neurologic sequelae, some contemporary obstetricians deliver breeches by cesarean section. With or without the current preference of many couples for smaller families, it is realistic to place more emphasis on the quality of life. At this time, the neurologic sequelae following cesarean section are un-

known. There are varying reports of neurologic problems in vaginal delivery of infants presenting by breech and vertex when the infants are of the same weight. Because of these unknowns, other obstetricians use the following criteria for vaginal delivery: (1) The fetus is presenting as a frank breech with an estimated fetal weight of not more than 3500 g and not less than 1500–2000 g; (2) the patient has an adequate pelvis as determined by x-ray pelvimetry; (3) there is normal labor, and oxytocin will not be used; and (4) there are no major obstetric complications. If these criteria are observed, one can anticipate a favorable vaginal delivery with no increase in perinatal loss or morbidity. Manzke, in a review of infant morbidity following breech delivery, concluded that "the prognosis for development of those children born through the vagina . . . is on the whole *marginally* less favorable than that for children . . . who were delivered by cesarean section."

E. Face Presentation: The incidence of face presentation is approximately 1:500. Because it is uncommon, it is not a major factor in dystocia. Indeed, many fetuses in face presentation can be delivered vaginally without difficulty. The anencephalic fetus almost always delivers as a face presentation, and the birth is easy except for occasional difficulty during delivery of the shoulders. The face usually enters the pelvic cavity as an anterior or transverse face presentation, rotates to the direct anterior during the latter part of the first stage of labor or early in the second stage, and then delivers by flexion of the head, with the chin beneath the symphysis. Many fetuses can be delivered as term-sized infants without difficulty if the pelvis is adequate. The major dystocia problems are the posterior face presentation (see below) and the occurrence of uterine inertia. Therapy is the same as for other abnormal presentations, ie, oxytocin should not be used, and delivery should be by cesarean section.

With proper management, a face presentation should not entail greater risk to the fetus or newborn than the more common occiput presentation. There is no known method of preventing face presentation.

F. Posterior Face Presentation: (Fig 39–5.) Lack of rotation and uterine inertia are the major dystocia problems with the posterior face presentation. The posterior face cannot be delivered as such, and rotation or conversion to a less formidable presentation is hazardous; therefore, cesarean section should be done. This is better than a difficult vaginal procedure, which may produce a fetal injury.

G. Brow Presentation: The brow presentation is very rare: its incidence is about 1:1500. It may evolve during labor by extension of a sincipital attitude or flexion of the face presentation, or it may be primary. Because the occipitomental diameter—ie, the longest diameter—is the AP diameter of the head in a brow presentation, it usually is best to perform a cesarean section unless the infant is small. The pelvis must be large if a term-sized infant is to negotiate the pelvis in this position. The brow presentation is frequently associated with uterine inertia; and, because of the rela-

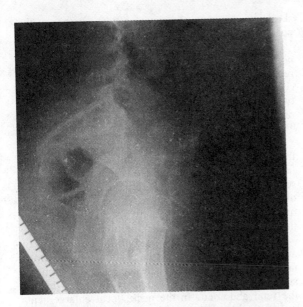

Figure 39–5. An uncommon posterior face presentation. X-ray taken in very early labor (primary face presentation). The inlet is borderline, OC = 10.6 cm and TI = 11.9 cm. Impossible to deliver vaginally.

tively large head diameter that must engage in the pelvis, oxytocin should never be used if uterine inertia does develop.

II. Transverse Presentation: The transverse presentation—more commonly termed the transverse lie—occurs once in every 250 deliveries. Like other abnormal presentations, the transverse lie may be associated with abnormal shape of the uterine cavity (eg, bicornuate uterus); a low-lying or fundally implanted placenta; a relaxed anterior abdominal wall; twins; polyhydramnios; and, in prematurity, instances in which the fetus is converting from the breech to the vertex presentation, or vice versa, and the membranes rupture. Because of the obvious incompatibility of the transversely positioned fetus and the pelvic cavity, dystocia is inevitable. With labor, full dilatation of the cervix may be attained with the membranes intact. Eventually the fetus will be jammed into the pelvic inlet, with or without prolapse of an arm. Small fetuses have been known to shift spontaneously from the transverse lie to the breech presentation, but this is very rare; and, if it should occur, the shift may seriously injure the small premature infant.

Because of the dystocia and the high perinatal mortality rate with vaginal delivery, the method of choice is in almost all cases cesarean section, which should be accomplished as soon as rupture of the membranes occurs or at the onset of labor. However, if the diagnosis is made prior to labor or early in labor, external version may be attempted, preferably to the vertex presentation. If this is successful, one should hold the fetus over the inlet until the head becomes fixed into the pelvic inlet lest the transverse lie recur. If a patient of low parity is seen late in labor, even with

the cervix fully dilated and the membranes intact, cesarean section is preferable to internal podalic version and breech extraction.

As stated above, the preferred treatment in almost all cases of transverse lie is cesarean section. As a result of improvements in the intensive care of the newborn, small infants delivered by cesarean section are at less risk than formerly. Vaginal delivery by internal version is particularly lethal to a small infant. Internal podalic version is dangerous because the transverse diameter of the lower uterine segment must be rapidly and greatly increased, which may rupture the uterus. There is risk of prolapse of the cord when the membranes rupture unless the thorax or arm of the fetus is filling the pelvic inlet.

The outlook is good if transverse lie is treated conservatively, ie, by cesarean section. Indeed, perinatal loss should be associated only with the incidence of prematurity and undetected early prolapse of the umbilical cord.

It is difficult to deliver a transversely presenting fetus through a transverse incision in the lower uterine segment. A vertical incision should be used. Moreover, the incision should be made where it will be easy to reach the lower extremities because in most instances delivery must be accomplished by breech extraction. More often than not, classic cesarean section is required. Transverse lie is one of the few conditions in which classic cesarean section may be the procedure of choice.

When a neglected transverse lie is recognized and the uterus is infected, cesarean hysterectomy may be the procedure of choice.

I. Compound Presentation: The incidence of compound presentation is about 1:800. The most common types are vertex presentation complicated by prolapse of a hand or foot and breech presentation complicated by prolapse of an arm alongside the buttocks. Compound presentation is more common in instances of (1) prematurity, (2) relaxed anterior abdominal wall, and (3) a pelvic inlet large enough to accept both the head and the extremities. In most instances, labor proceeds normally and without difficulty. It is useless to attempt to replace the prolapsed extremity because the prolapse invariably recurs. The prolapsed extremity may become edematous, but swelling will dissipate within a few days after delivery. The marked edema and, occasionally, nerve pressure may paralyze the extremity, but usually not permanently.

Cesarean section is occasionally necessary, but the indication for cesarean section generally is an accompanying maternal problem. Perinatal losses must be expected because of the high incidence of prematurity and, to a lesser extent, because of trauma to term infants delivered vaginally.

J. Macrosomia: Excessively large infants are not common: Only 5% of infants weigh more than 4000 g at birth, and only 0.05% weigh more than 4500 g. In most instances, excessive size causes no difficulty as long as the pelvis is large enough. Genetic factors, nutritional stimulation, and metabolic diseases may be responsible for oversized fetuses. Larger babies are born to tall women and obese women. Maternal diabetes mellitus is commonly related to large size of infants; thus, any patient who has been delivered of a large infant should be tested for this disorder. Occasionally, an erythroblastotic fetus is sufficiently anasarcic to cause dystocia.

The large baby may cause dystocia at the inlet, with cephalopelvic disproportion, and at the outlet, with shoulder dystocia. When dystocia occurs at the inlet, the condition is the reverse of the cephalopelvic disproportion of contracted pelvis: The large head cannot be satisfactorily accommodated by a pelvis of normal size. Or the disproportion may result in uterine inertia, so that cesarean section is required. The greatest risk to the infant, under these circumstances, is the administration of oxytocin by the physician who assumes that the pelvic cavity is normal but underestimates the size of the baby. (As mentioned above, physicians commonly underestimate the weight of large babies and overestimate the weight of small babies.) The oxytocin corrects the uterine inertia, but the fetal head still cannot negotiate the inlet.

K. Shoulder Dystocia: This common problem is encountered about once in 750 deliveries. It is discussed in Chapter 40. The incidence of shoulder dystocia for fetuses weighing more than 4000 g is no more than 1:50. When it does occur, it can be a problem for both the baby and the obstetrician. Typically, the delivery of the head may not progress normally in that there is resistance to slipping the vulvar and perineal tissues over the head. At this moment, in normal deliveries, the neck is usually visible; with shoulder dystocia, it is not. Rotation of the fetus to permit the shoulders to engage in another diameter is recommended.

L. Local or Regional Macrosomia: Regional macrosomia usually is due to congenital anomalies. The most common of these is **hydrocephalus,** in which cephalopelvic disproportion is a common problem whether the presentation is vertex or breech. The cause usually is not known. The diagnosis may be suspected on abdominal examination because hydramnios is commonly associated with hydrocephalus. X-ray examination is indicated in order to determine whether or not a congenital bony anomaly of the fetus coexists. On pelvic examination, when the cervix is sufficiently dilated, the sutures of the fetal skull will be found to be widely separated. Because of the extreme softness of the skull, the diagnosis of breech presentation may be incorrectly made. Even on x-ray examination, the diagnosis is not always easily made because of the marked thinning of the skull.

The course of labor may be normal in a vertex presentation, but more frequently uterine inertia complicates labor. The treatment of choice in the vertex is to insert a needle through the suture to tap the fluid. The fluid flows rapidly until the pressure is reduced; then it flows more slowly. With successive uterine contractions and further release of fluid, the size of the skull is reduced so that eventually it engages at the pelvic inlet and the fetus can be delivered vaginally.

In breech presentation, labor usually proceeds normally until, with delivery of the shoulders, mild resistance is encountered. When the base of the skull comes into view, insert a needle into the suture between the occipital bones. Fluid will be evacuated rapidly because of the sustained pressure on the head. The aftercoming head can soon be delivered.

The purpose of this procedure is not to kill the fetus but to reduce the head size sufficiently so that the fetus can be delivered without resorting to cesarean section. In many instances, the baby is born alive but dies soon after birth. This procedure is acceptable to most religious groups. When hydrocephalus is mild, it may not recur for a considerable time after birth.

Enlargement of the fetal abdomen because of an enlarged bladder may be the result of stenosis of the urethral valve or stricture. Unusual abdominal tumors, such as those of the liver or kidney, may also distend the fetal abdomen. In the neck, local enlargements may be produced by **meningomyelocele** and **hygroma.** These anomalies may cause dystocia because of the expansion of the neck to a size greater than that of the head. It may be necessary to drain the cystic masses in order to deliver the fetus.

M. Anencephaly: Most congenital anomalies do not cause dystocia. However, one of the common reasons for face presentation is anencephaly, in which the skull plates are completely missing. Dystocia involving the head does not occur, but there may be some delay after delivery of the head before the cervix is dilated sufficiently to permit delivery of the shoulders, which have a greater circumference than the head.

N. Twinning Problems: Double monsters such as Siamese twins are very rare. They may have to be managed with on-the-spot ingenuity.

Locked twins are also rare. As the first twin descends—in breech presentation—the head of the second twin descends alongside the thorax of the first twin. Obstruction occurs because the chest of the first twin and the head of the second twin cannot enter the pelvic inlet at the same time. Even more rarely, the fetuses may both be in the vertex presentation; if so, the head of the first twin is extended and the head of the second twin is caught in the hollow of the neck, between the chin and the thorax of the first twin. The dystocia occurs before delivery of the head, and labor is arrested. In locked twins of the first type, destruction of one infant may be necessary; in the second type, cesarean section solves the problem of dystocia.

UTERINE DYSTOCIA

Uterine dystocia may be defined as any abnormality of the contractile pattern of the uterine musculature that prevents the normal progress of labor.

Normal Labor

Normal labor (outlined here for purposes of comparison) consists of 3 concomitant processes:

(1) There is a regular progression of uterine contractions: from those that are weak, far apart, and of short duration, commonly occurring early in labor, to those that are closer together, of greater intensity, and of longer duration.

(2) There is effacement of the cervix, accompanied by progressive dilatation of the cervix over a reasonable period of time. Fig 31–15 shows Friedman's curve of cervical dilatation, which is divided into a latent (prodromal) phase and an active (dilatation) phase. The latent phase of labor may be described as that period of time during which the rather weak uterine contractions produce effacement of the cervix as the only major ensuing event. There must be continuity of uterine contractions between the latent phase and the active phase of labor. During the active phase, dilatation of the cervix progresses rapidly, from 3–4 cm to 9–10 cm, to terminate the first stage of labor.

At this point, cervical dilatation reaches its maximum; the second stage begins; and only a short time elapses until the baby is delivered. This progress, when graphed, produces the typical S-shaped curve of labor that Friedman characterizes as normal. Two important points must not be misinterpreted: (a) the latent phase of labor must not be confused with lack of progress or with uterine inertia, and (b) delay in the active phase should not be interpreted as lack of progress within normal limits. The latter is a frequent misinterpretation in patients with dystocia.

(3) There is progress in the descent of the presenting part through the pelvic cavity. Descent of the presenting part does not occur during the latent phase of labor, and very little descent is likely during the early part of the active phase. A more rapid descent is accomplished when the cervix has become dilated to 5–7 cm and when the membranes have ruptured.

These 3 events—progress of uterine contractions, progress of effacement and dilatation of the cervix, and progress of the descent of the presenting part—constitute normal labor. *Any deviation from this pattern must be considered dystocia, and immediate attempts must be made to identify the cause so that adequate therapeutic measures may be instituted.*

The normal pattern of uterine contractility during labor is as follows: Contractions are initiated simultaneously and bilaterally, near each uterine horn. The contractions increase in intensity as they spread mesiad and caudad in unison. Characteristically, the contractile pattern reaches its maximum first in the fundus of the uterus, next in the portio of the uterus, and then in the lower uterine segment, and the contractions are most intense in the fundus and less intense along a gradient extending toward the internal os. Given these findings, the pattern may be more precisely defined as consisting of 2 simultaneous contractions, one in each longitudinal half of the uterus, acting in a peristaltic manner and progressing toward the cervix.

Abnormal Labor

Using a multichannel recording of myometrial activity, several types of abnormal contractility can be identified: (1) peristaltic uterine contraction; (2) an asymmetric pattern, in which the 2 halves of the uterine musculature are contracting unequally; (3) reverse peristalsis, in which the contraction begins in the lower portion of the uterus and spreads upward with decreasing intensity; (4) segmental tetanic contraction, as in the constriction ring; (5) uniform tetanic contraction, in which the entire musculature contracts to produce a squeezing effect; and (6) a normal pattern that is too weak to be effective.

These abnormalities may be further classified as (1) hypotonic, in which the contractions are weaker than normal and thus ineffective; (2) hypertonic, in which the contractions are excessive in intensity and duration, with little if any diastole; and (3) dystonic, as in asymmetric contraction or reverse peristalsis.

Hypotonic labor, or uterine inertia, usually accompanies some type of relative or absolute dystocia, as in cases of abnormal presentation, contracted pelvis, or other incompatibility between the passage and the passenger. Sometimes, however, there is no such disparity and the cause of uterine inertia is undetermined. It may occur with too early administration of an analgesic, overdistention of the uterus, twinning, macrosomia, and hydramnios.

Hypertonic uterine contractions are most commonly seen in association with abruptio placentae and with excessive use of oxytocin and least commonly with obstructed labor.

Dystonic labor may be a misnomer except for constriction ring dystocia. In this rare condition, there is a continuous and excessive contraction around a small area of the fetus' body—usually the neck but sometimes the abdomen. This is the only type of dystocia contraction that occurs during labor. More commonly, it occurs during prelabor, when the uterine contractions are painful but unproductive of substantial cervical change. It is frequently associated with emotional tension (fear, anxiety) and, perhaps, fatigue.

Hypotonic labor is the most common problem. Hypertonic labor is less common. Occasionally, normal uterine contractions become excessive and precipitous labor ensues, sometimes with complications for mother and fetus. Dystonic labor is very common during prelabor but is rare during true labor.

1. HYPOTONIC LABOR

Typically, hypotonic labor develops as follows: A patient begins labor normally, with increasing intensity and duration of contractions. Concomitantly, there is shortening of the interval between contractions associated with gradual dilatation of the cervix. After an indefinite interval, labor appears to slacken and then to stop; as a result, cervical dilatation ceases. In some instances, irregular, nagging contractions continue; in other cases, contractions do not stop but progress does. It is at this point that the diagnosis of uterine inertia

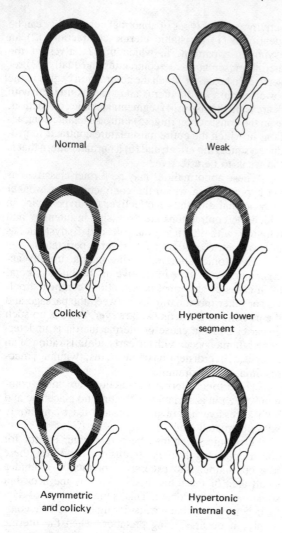

Normal   Weak

Colicky   Hypertonic lower
                          segment

Asymmetric   Hypertonic
and colicky   internal os

Figure 39–6. Normal and dysfunctional uterine contraction types. (After Jeffcoate.) Black, strong contraction; shaded, slight contraction; white, atonic areas. (Reproduced, with permission, from Benson RC: *Handbook of Obstetrics & Gynecology,* 7th ed. Lange, 1980.)

should be made and its cause determined if possible. The diagnosis is simple in that the characteristics just described are almost invariably present. To find the cause and therefore to institute correct therapy, reevaluation of the patient is necessary. Is the fetus larger than it had been thought to be? What are the presentation and the size and shape of the pelvis by x-ray pelvimetry? Does pelvic examination confirm lack of further effacement and dilatation of the cervix?

If the situation is not reappraised at this time, delay in termination of labor will result, with the complications common to prolonged labor. Amnionitis is an ever-present threat. For the fetus, septicemia or intrauterine pneumonia (or both) may follow. If the amnionitis is intensively treated with appropriate antibiotics and if delivery is not delayed for too long, the infection may not spread to the maternal tissues. With

delay, the sepsis may spread to the decidua and, by the lymphatic route, to the pelvic structures. The fetus may succumb to hypoxia.

Differential Diagnosis

Few conditions can be confused with uterine inertia. Because there has been cervical dilatation, false labor can be ruled out. If the cervix is soft and moderately effaced, cervical dystocia can be ruled out: In cervical dystocia, the cervix is firm and effacement is difficult to achieve. In dystonic uterine contraction, the labor pains are colicky; in uterine inertia, the contractions are weak and cause little discomfort.

Prevention

There is no known way to prevent uterine inertia, but there are adequate methods of therapy.

Treatment

The treatment of uterine inertia is relatively simple. If there is an abnormality of the passage or the passenger, including abnormal presentation, cesarean section is the preferred treatment.

If no reason for the uterine dystocia can be found after reevaluation of the patient by abdominal examination, x-ray examination, and pelvic examination, oxytocin stimulation is the procedure of choice. Uterine musculature varies remarkably in its response to oxytocin. Early in pregnancy, large doses may be required for an adequate response. As term approaches, smaller doses are needed. After the onset of labor, minuscule doses may reactivate a lagging uterine musculature to normal activity. Thus, the dosage must be accurately titrated. Intravenous administration is the procedure of choice, with a pump delivery system of milliunits of oxytocin per minute. If a pump is unavailable, a simple procedure is to add a 0.1-mL ampule (1 unit) of oxytocin to 1000 mL of 5% dextrose solution in water. Allow the fluid to drip, counting the drops per minute to deliver 1–2 mU/min. The dose can be calculated moderately well, but the method is not as accurate as using a pump, which permits the dosage to be accurately determined and the rate of injection to be accurately varied. The response of the uterus to oxytocin cannot be predicted. If the uterus responds immediately, the initial dose need not be increased throughout the remainder of labor. When the uterine inertia has been corrected and normal labor resumes, it is preferable to continue with a very small dose of oxytocin throughout the rest of labor so that uterine inertia will not recur. If oxytocin stimulation does not improve the uterine contractions within a short time, the chance of successful therapy is minimal. When contractions of 50–60 mm Hg (internal monitor pressure) or 40–60 seconds (on the external monitor) occur at 2- to 3-minute intervals, the oxytocin dose should not be increased further. If therapy is continued without improvement, complications detrimental to both the mother and the fetus may result; therefore, the labor should be terminated by cesarean section.

Oxytocin is contraindicated in the following situations: (1) normal labor; (2) dystonic labor, both in prelabor and in cases of constriction ring dystocia; (3) abnormal presentation; (4) contracted pelvis or other pelvic abnormality; (5) previous uterine surgery, eg, cesarean section or myomectomy; (6) overdistention of the uterus, as with hydramnios, large fetus, or twins; (7) fetal distress; (8) patients of high parity (over para 4); and (9) older patients (over 35 years).

If oxytocin stimulation is not used carefully, severe complications may arise: (1) A tetanic contraction may be induced, and this may cause fetal distress or fetal death. Observations of the fetal heart tones throughout the period of oxytocin stimulation and continuous observation of the type of uterine contractions are imperative during oxytocin stimulation. (2) Precipitous labor may develop, and the fetus may be damaged by intracranial hemorrhage. (3) If oxytocin is used in obstructed labor or in cases of relative disproportion, it may not only subject the fetus to hypoxia and intracranial hemorrhage but may also rupture the uterus. This is especially true in patients of high parity.

Oxytocin, when given judiciously, will convert an abnormal pattern of uterine contractility to a normal pattern. Its use requires constant observation by a physician who is aware of all the possible complications of oxytocin use. Oxytocin is one of the most important therapeutic agents in obstetrics, but it can also be the most lethal.

Other drugs that stimulate uterine contractions are available. These include the ergot derivatives. They should never be used prior to delivery of the fetus because they induce a prolonged tetanic contraction (not the rhythmic contractions induced by oxytocin). Sparteine sulfate is effective, but its use in labor is unpredictable; tetanic contractions may occur because the dosage cannot be easily controlled.

Rupture of the membranes can be effective in encouraging the return to normal labor in cases of uterine inertia. It is most effective when the cervix is dilated to 4 cm or more and when the membranes bulge with a uterine contraction. If the membranes are artificially ruptured, it is mandatory that labor be terminated within a reasonable time. Prolapse of the cord is a possible complication. The best way to prevent this catastrophe is to avoid rupturing the membranes unless the presenting part is engaged. Recent statistical evidence indicates that rupture of the membranes usually does not speed labor, but there are cases in which it is helpful.

The outlook in uterine inertia should be good for both the mother and the baby if therapy as outlined above has been given. If uterine inertia is not treated, fetal distress and fetal death are likely and the risk of maternal infection and fatigue is heightened. If the patient is given oxytocin under adverse circumstances, she may suffer uterine rupture and the fetus may be damaged by intracranial hemorrhage and hypoxia. If the patient is treated by cesarean section, the mother and infant should do well.

2. HYPERTONIC LABOR

Problems associated with hypertonic dystocia are abruptio placentae, the hazards of oxytocin stimulation, and obstructed labor. Hypertonic dystocia is much less common than uterine inertia, and many instances could be avoided, because excessive oxytocin stimulation is always iatrogenic. Obstructed labor occurs only in neglected patients. When the contractions are hypertonic, there is little relaxation between the pains. The tonus of the uterus is so great that the organ is almost boardlike at the height of contraction. The contraction lasts much longer than usual; in fact, it may seem continuous. After only a short period of hypertonic contractions, the fetal heart may be depressed—an indication of fetal distress. This may progress to loss of fetal heart tones. Depending on the stage, the termination of labor may be so precipitous as to produce lacerations of the birth canal or uterus. The fetus may be at risk of intracranial hemorrhage or death.

The goal of therapy is a return to normal labor. Uterine contractions can be slowed by discontinuing the oxytocin drip. The fetal heart should be monitored and oxygen given. The patient should be prepared for immediate delivery, particularly if the progress of labor has been rapid. A general anesthetic may be lifesaving if long-acting oxytocin, ergonovine maleate, or methylergonovine maleate has been given accidentally during labor. With abruptio placentae, there is no way to cope with the tetanic contraction except by delivery. If the uterus is hypertonic because of disproportion or obstructed labor, cesarean section is the only solution.

3. DYSTONIC DYSTOCIA

During true labor, the most characteristic type of dystonic dystocia is constriction ring dystocia. The more common type of dystonic contraction is caused by emotional tension and is usually noted at the beginning of cervical effacement and dilatation, during "preliminary labor," "prelabor," "latent labor," or "the latent phase of labor." The uterine contractions are uncoordinated. The patient is more uncomfortable at each contraction than the intensity or duration of the contraction would seem to justify. There is little change in cervical dilatation and effacement.

Dystonic dystocia is more common among primigravidas, and the patient appears extremely worried. Misinterpretation by the obstetrician may influence the therapy in that the pregnancy may be terminated because of lack of progress before the patient has actually entered into labor. Onset of labor is not established in the primigravida until the cervix has been dilated 3 cm; in the multigravida, at least 4 cm. With dystonic uterine contractions, the cervix is usually no more than a fingertip or 2 cm dilated. The patient usually will react favorably to 15 mg of morphine or 100 mg of meperidine. After morphine therapy, it is not uncommon for the uterine contractions to become regular and more intense and for cervical dilatation and effacement to begin. The patient should be more comfortable when the abnormal uterine contractions have been converted by the narcotic to the normal rhythmic type of contraction necessary to the normal progress of labor.

Constriction ring dystocia is characterized by segmental constriction of the uterus. The constriction is almost continuous. It usually forms late in labor. Typically, there is lack of progress, even though the uterine contractions seem to be unchanged. Diagnostic observations are as follows: (1) On manual examination, the patient begins to feel pain before the observer can palpate a uterine contraction, and she continues to feel pain after the observer no longer feels the contraction. This is the reverse of normal uterine contractions; in the latter, the observer feels the beginning of the contraction before the patient expresses any discomfort. (2) At the height of the contraction, the presenting part recedes instead of being impelled downward. (3) The cervix is loose, flabby, and not tightly applied to the presenting part.

The constriction ring frequently is around the neck of the fetus; at times, it may be around the abdomen. It is difficult to feel the constriction, vaginally or abdominally. The complications are fetal hypoxia (followed by fetal death), prolongation of labor, and maternal infection. Therapy is not always satisfactory. Occasionally, magnesium sulfate given intravenously will relax the ring. Epinephrine, 1:1000, 0.15 mL intramuscularly, may relieve the constriction briefly. Amyl nitrite is sometimes effective. However, no drug is dependable. When sedation or a muscle relaxant is not effective, cesarean section is indicated. At cesarean section, the ring must be incised before the fetus can be removed. If constriction ring dystocia occurs at full dilatation of the cervix, there will be a prolonged second stage and a trial of forceps will fail.

• • •

References

Ang LT: Compound presentation following external version. *Aust NZ J Obstet Gynaecol* 1978;**18**:213.

Benedetti TJ, Gable SG: Shoulder dystocia: A complication of fetal macrosomia and prolonged second stage of labor with mid pelvic delivery. *Obstet Gynecol* 1978;**52**:526.

Collea JV et al: The randomized management of term frank breech presentation: Vaginal delivery vs cesarean section. *Am J Obstet Gynecol* 1978;**131**:186.

Friedman EA: *Labor, Clinical Evaluation and Management,* 2nd ed. Appleton-Century-Crofts, 1982.

Friedman EA: The therapeutic dilemma of arrested labor. *Contemp Obstet Gynecol* (March) 1978;**11**:34.

Goldenberg RL, Nelson KG: The premature breech. *Am J Obstet Gynecol* 1977;**127**:240.

Golditch IM, Kirkman K: The large fetus: Management and outcome. *Obstet Gynecol* 1978;**52**:26.

Holmberg NG: The influence of the bony pelvis in persistent occiput posterior position. *Acta Obstet Gynecol Scand* [*Suppl*] 1977;**66**:49.

Kelly KM et al: The utilization and efficacy of pelvimetry. *Am J Roentgenol* 1975;**125**:66.

Manzke H: Morbidity among infants born in breech presentation. *J Perinat Med* 1978;**6**:127.

Merrill BS, Gibbs CE: Planned vaginal delivery following cesarean section. *Obstet Gynecol* 1978;**52**:50.

Moolgooker AS, Ahamed S, Payne PR: A comparison of different methods of instrumental delivery based on electronic measurements of compression and traction. *Obstet Gynecol* 1979; **54**:299.

Quilligan EJ, Zuspan FP: *Operative Obstetrics,* 4th ed. Appleton-Century-Crofts, 1982.

Rudich JP, Cheynier JM, Cheynier-Auget C: Les dystocies de démarrage et leur traitement par un beta sympatho-mimétique. *J Gynecol Obstet Biol Reprod* 1978;**7**:87. [English abstract.]

Schlensker KH, Enderer-Steinfort G, Bolte A: Die äussere Wendung des Feten aus Beckenendlage in Schädellage am Schwangerschaftsende. *Geburtshilfe Frauenheilkd* 1978; **38**:744. [English abstract.]

Steer CM: *Moloy's Evaluation of the Pelvis in Obstetrics,* 3rd ed. Plenum, 1975.

Operative Delivery | 40

David N. Danforth, PhD, MD

The term operative delivery denotes any obstetric procedure in which active measures are taken to accomplish delivery. The procedures, which should be used only upon clear indications, are often major ones whose success depends not only on the skill with which they are used but also on the proper timing of their use. Obstetric catastrophes are more apt to occur as a result of intervention than from lack of it. If left to proceed unhindered, natural processes will resolve most obstetric difficulties; in the remaining cases, the obstetrician must know when, in the interests of mother or baby, intervention is both safe and indicated, and what available procedures will give the best result.

In former years, the ability to perform difficult vaginal delivery was an essential part of obstetric practice. In earlier editions of this book, the nuances of operative vaginal delivery were considered in detail, as were the complex and sometimes difficult methods for dealing with the complications often encountered. This is no longer appropriate, for in current practice one mark of a skilled obstetrician is the ability to *avoid* difficult vaginal delivery. However, the obstetrician should have sufficient knowledge and experience to be able to intervene vaginally when indicated and to perform the obstetric operation that is safest for mother and baby. This chapter considers the obstetric operations in modern use that should be within the competence of the obstetrician. Those who require greater detail should consult older references listed at the end of the chapter.

FORCEPS OPERATIONS

The obstetric forceps is an instrument designed to extract the baby's head. It is used either to expedite delivery or to overcome or correct certain abnormalities in the cephalopelvic relationship that interfere with advancement of the head in labor.

The primary functions of the forceps are **traction** (either for assistance in the terminal phase of labor or to deal with arrest of the head) and **rotation** (in cases in which there is no disproportion but the head presents with an unfavorable diameter).

Forceps delivery may be indicated in the interests of mother or baby, and when properly performed it may be lifesaving.

Abbreviations Used in This Chapter	
AP	Anteroposterior (diameter)
OA	Occiput anterior (L, left; R, right)
OP	Occiput posterior (L, left; R, right)
OT	Occiput transverse (L, left; R, right)
SA	Sacrum anterior (L, left; R, right)
SP	Sacrum posterior (L, left; R, right)
ST	Sacrum transverse (L, left; R, right)
DSA	Direct sacrum anterior
DSP	Direct sacrum posterior
FHT	Fetal heart tones

THE OBSTETRIC FORCEPS

The obstetric forceps consists of 2 matched parts that articulate, or "lock." Each part is composed of a **blade, shank, lock,** and **handle** (Fig 40–1). Each blade is so designed that it possesses 2 curves: the

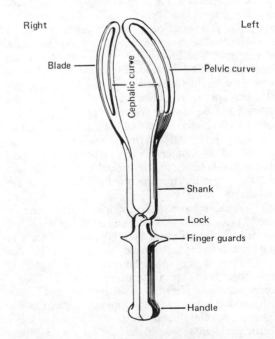

Figure 40–1. DeLee modification of Simpson forceps. (Reproduced, with permission, from Benson RC: *Handbook of Obstetrics and Gynecology*, 7th ed. Lange, 1980.)

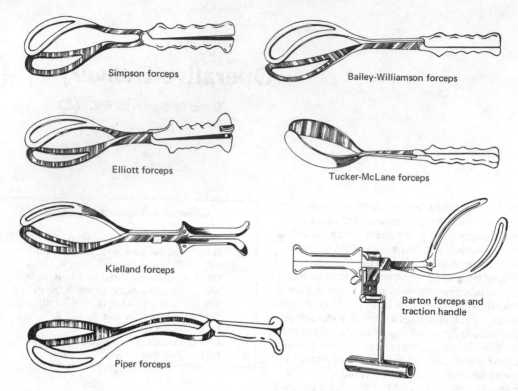

Figure 40–2. Commonly used forceps. (Reproduced, with permission, from Benson RC: *Handbook of Obstetrics and Gynecology,* 7th ed. Lange, 1980.)

cephalic curve, which permits the instrument to be applied accurately to the sides of the baby's head; and the **pelvic curve,** which conforms to the curved axis of the pelvis. The tip of each blade is called the **toe.**

The **front** of the forceps is the concave side of the pelvic curve. The blades are referred to as **left** and **right** according to the side of the mother's pelvis on which they lie after application. According to the **rule of the forceps,** the handle of the left blade is held in the left hand and the blade is applied to the left side of the mother's pelvis; the handle of the right blade is then held in the right hand and inserted so as to lie on the right side of the mother's pelvis. When the blades are inserted in this order, the right shank comes to lie atop the left so that the forceps articulate or lock as the handles are closed.

Physicians have made modifications in one or more of the 4 basic parts ever since forceps were first invented. Although more than 600 kinds of forceps have been described, only a few are currently in use.

Obstetric forceps may be divided into 2 groups: classic forceps and special forceps (Fig 40–2). Classic forceps are those with the usual cephalic and pelvic curves and English lock; the Simpson forceps is the prototype. Special forceps are those designed to solve specific problems; those in modern use are the Piper, Kielland, and Barton forceps.

INDICATIONS & CONDITIONS FOR FORCEPS DELIVERY

In each of the following indications for forceps delivery, it should be emphasized that cesarean section is an alternative procedure that may or may not be appropriate under the prevailing circumstances. Recognizing the inherent risk of cesarean section, the obstetrician must decide which operation, vaginal delivery or cesarean section, will be safer for mother and baby.

Prophylaxis

The principle of prophylactic forceps was first enunciated by DeLee in 1920. Although it instantly provoked bitter denunciation as "meddlesome midwifery," it is now generally accepted that when the perineum and coccyx offer the only resistance to delivery, the use of episiotomy and outlet forceps is indeed prophylactic because the fetal head is spared unpredictable stress—especially compression against the perineum. The second stage of labor is significantly shortened, greatly minimizing the patient's physical discomfort. The repair of a cleanly incised wound rather than of a jagged, macerated laceration facilitates healing and recovery of the pelvic floor and perineal structures. Episiotomy is the most frequently performed obstetric operation; prophylactic forceps is next most common.

Dystocia

In the second stage of labor, a period of 30 minutes or more when labor fails to progress or a second stage lasting 2 hours or more is usually an indication for operative delivery. Good judgment is necessary to decide whether forceps delivery or cesarean section is indicated.

A. Uterine Inertia: Uterine inertia may account for both failure to progress and prolongation of the second stage of labor. In such cases, oxytocin must be used with great caution. Disproportion must be excluded. If the conditions for forceps delivery have not been met, cesarean section may be appropriate. Uterine inertia may also be responsible for failure of the head to rotate to the anterior position. In such cases, artificial rotation is usually not difficult, but the obstetrician must decide whether cesarean section is safer.

B. Faulty Cephalopelvic Relationships: Despite contractions of good quality, arrest may occur in the following circumstances: (1) if an unfavorable diameter of the head presents to the pelvis (eg, OA in a flat pelvis); (2) if the position is such that the head cannot negotiate the pelvic curve (eg, certain cases of OP); or (3) if cephalopelvic disproportion exists. In the latter case, molding of the head may overcome minor degrees of disproportion and permit the head to advance without injury. After 1–2 hours of good voluntary bearing down in the second stage, the infant must be delivered, and the physician must determine whether vaginal delivery by forceps is safe and appropriate or whether true disproportion requiring cesarean section for delivery is present.

Maternal & Fetal Indications for Forceps Delivery

Maternal and fetal indications for forceps delivery include circumstances in which continuation of the second stage of labor would constitute a significant threat to the mother or the baby. Forceps delivery in such cases should impose no additional risk on either. In many such cases, cesarean section is preferable.

A. Maternal Indications: The second stage should be shortened in cases of exhaustion, severe cardiac or pulmonary problems accompanied by dyspnea, and intercurrent debilitating illness.

B. Fetal Indications: The primary fetal indication for terminating the second stage prematurely is fetal distress, as manifested by (1) fetal heart tones (FHT) with a rate of less than 100 or more than 160 beats per minute, late deceleration patterns, or gross irregularity; (2) excessive fetal movements; or (3) the passage of meconium-stained amniotic fluid in cephalic presentation. In many of these cases, cesarean section is preferable to forceps delivery.

Conditions for Forceps Delivery

The use of forceps is permissible only when *all* of the following conditions prevail, regardless of the urgent need for delivery.

(1) **The cervix must be fully dilated.** Extraction of the head through an incompletely dilated cervix invariably produces ragged, bleeding tears that may extend as high as the broad ligament of the uterus. The uterine supports may be damaged also, thus setting the stage for later prolapse. In extraordinary emergency, forceps may be applied inside a cervix dilated more than 8 cm, with Dührssen's incisions (see p 937) made before traction is applied.

(2) **The membranes must be ruptured.** Forceps are not useful before the membranes rupture. Furthermore, if the membranes are intact and forceps are used, they will slip, and traction upon the membranes may detach the edge of the placenta.

(3) **The head must be engaged (preferably deeply) to a station below +2.** Engagement means that the biparietal diameter of the fetal head has passed the plane of the inlet. If the head is not molded, the tip of the vertex, at the time of engagement, is at 0 station; in extreme molding with a large caput succedaneum, the scalp may be almost at the introitus when the biparietal diameter is still at the level of the inlet. The higher the station of the head, the greater the likelihood of serious damage to mother or baby. One should not apply forceps if the sinciput can be felt above the symphysis.

(4) **The head must present correctly.** All vertex presentations and all face presentations with chin anterior are suitable. Neither brow presentation nor face presentation with chin posterior is suitable for application of forceps. One may apply forceps to the aftercoming head in breech presentation provided the head is engaged and is in the occiput anterior position.

(5) **There must be no significant cephalopelvic disproportion.** In the case of a "tight fit," one may advance the head provided that only moderate traction is needed; it is severely damaging to use extreme force to drag the head past significant bony resistance.

(6) **The bladder should be empty.** The bladder should be drained by catheterization before forceps are used.

It is to be emphasized that merely meeting the foregoing conditions does not justify forceps delivery. A specific indication for the application of forceps must be present, and the timing of the procedure is of vital importance. Countless obstetric disasters have resulted from the untimely or too early use of forceps and from the employment of forceps when another mode of delivery would have been preferable.

CLASSIFICATION & DEFINITIONS OF FORCEPS DELIVERIES

No classification of forceps delivery will be acceptable to all obstetricians. Nevertheless, a workable classification is essential to permit comparison of the results and the relative difficulties encountered with the procedures. One reasonable and useful classification (Danforth) is the following.

Outlet forceps is the application of forceps when the scalp is or has been visible at the introitus (without the need to separate the labia), the skull has reached the pelvic floor, and the sagittal suture is in the anteroposterior diameter of the pelvis. (In outlet forceps, the perineum and coccyx offer the only resistance to delivery.)

Low forceps is the application of forceps when the skull has reached a station of +3 (at or immediately above the pelvic floor) and the sagittal suture is in the anteroposterior or an oblique diameter of the pelvis.

Mid forceps is the application of forceps when the head is engaged but has not reached a station of +3 or the occiput has not rotated as far as the anterior oblique diameter.

High forceps is the application of forceps at any time prior to engagement of the head. This erstwhile common practice has been abandoned because of the dire injuries that it almost always inflicts on both mother and baby. If the biparietal diameter has not passed through (below) the inlet, forceps delivery is contraindicated.

The foregoing definitions refer only to the station of the head at the time the operation is begun. Three additional definitions apply to special circumstances:

Prophylactic forceps is the use of outlet forceps (not low or mid forceps) and episiotomy in order to prevent injury to the fetal head and pelvic floor and to reduce maternal stress.

Failed forceps denotes an unsuccessful attempt at forceps delivery and abandonment of this effort in favor of cesarean section (or, in former years, craniotomy and delivery of a dead or severely damaged infant).

Trial forceps is tentative, cautious traction with forceps with the intent of abandoning attempts at forceps delivery if undue resistance is encountered. Since there is also the intent to deliver with forceps if feasible, the term trial forceps is appropriate.

CHOICE & APPLICATION OF FORCEPS

The results of forceps delivery depend far more on the judgment and skill of the operator than on the selection of any particular instrument. Certain instruments clearly are preferable to others for particular problems, however, and it is important to know exactly what is to be accomplished and which instrument is safest and most effective for the specific difficulty encountered. The forceps used most frequently are shown in Fig 40–2. It is important that the obstetrician in training become familiar with all of the standard instruments. Additionally, the obstetrician must settle upon one instrument for outlet forceps; one instrument for traction in the OA position; one instrument for rotation from the OP position; one instrument for traction and rotation in the OT position; and one instrument for application to the aftercoming head.

(1) **For outlet forceps,** in which no significant traction is needed, either the Tucker-McLane or the Wrigley instrument is preferable. The Tucker-McLane

forceps has the advantage of overlapping shanks, which do not spread and extend the episiotomy as the head is brought through the introitus. The disadvantage is that the blades may not fit the head well, especially if there is heavy molding. If any significant traction is exerted, the fetal cheeks may be marked or cut over the zygoma.

(2) **For traction to the OA** (or in one of the oblique anterior positions), the Simpson forceps or one of its modifications (DeLee-Simpson or Elliot) is often used. If applied correctly and if traction is made in the proper diameter of the pelvis, considerable force may usually be applied without fetal injury. Moreover, the Simpson and DeLee-Simpson instruments generally cannot be locked or articulated properly except when they are applied accurately—unlike the Tucker-McLane forceps, which usually can be locked regardless of the accuracy of their application.

(3) **For rotation from the OP to the OA,** many obstetricians prefer either the Tucker-McLane or the Luikart forceps. The Kielland forceps is also applicable for rotation from posterior to anterior.

(4) **For transverse arrest,** either the Barton or the Kielland forceps is applicable.

(5) **For application to the aftercoming head,** the Piper forceps is preferred by American obstetricians. The long-shanked classic forceps is also applicable.

Two methods of application are available:

(1) **Cephalic application** denotes the deliberate and accurate application of the forceps to the sides of the baby's head in a line from the chin to a point between the anterior and posterior fontanelles, somewhat closer to the posterior than the anterior. Cephalic application is possible in OA, OT, OP, face presentation with chin anterior (see Fig 40–3), and for the aftercoming head.

(2) **Pelvic application** is made by applying the blades and locking the forceps, by force if necessary, without reference to the position of the head. This application in modern obstetrics is condemned because it imposes dangerous (even lethal) stresses that the fetal head can rarely withstand. If a proper cephalic application cannot be made, some other method of management is mandatory.

PREPARATION OF THE PATIENT FOR FORCEPS DELIVERY

The lithotomy position is required, and the buttocks should extend 5 cm beyond the end of the table. Some means should be available to move the knees forward easily as the head crowns in order to reduce the stress on the perineum and to prevent extension of the episiotomy. The clamps holding the stirrups may be loosened (which can be awkward and time-consuming), or assistants can support the legs and move them when necessary. The latter method is preferred and requires the presence of 2 scrubbed assistants.

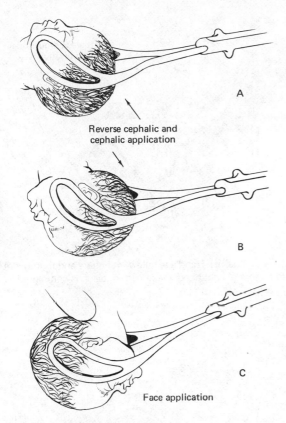

Reverse cephalic and
cephalic application

Face application

Figure 40–3. Forceps correctly applied along occipitomental diameter of head in various positions of the occiput. *A:* Occiput posterior. *B:* Occiput anterior. *C:* Mentum anterior. (Reproduced, with permission, from Benson RC: *Handbook of Obstetrics and Gynecology,* 7th ed. Lange, 1980.)

If conduction anesthesia is to be used, it must be administered prior to the foregoing steps in delivery. If inhalation anesthesia, pudendal block, or local infiltration is to be used, it should not be administered until after the preliminary examination has been made and all is in readiness for delivery. An appropriate and effective anesthetic is essential to the performance of any forceps delivery.

Because forceps delivery is an operative procedure, surgical aseptic and antiseptic conditions must be maintained. The vulva and perineum are cleansed with soap and water and sprayed or painted with an antiseptic solution. Sterile drapes are applied, and the bladder is catheterized with a rubber catheter.

The Preliminary Examination

Before any other steps are taken, a careful examination must be made to determine the following:

(1) The **position of the fetal head** is usually easily determined by first locating the lambdoid sutures and then determining the direction of the sagittal suture. The posterior fontanelle is readily evident after the 3 sutures running into it are identified. If the most accessible fontanelle is found to have 4 sutures running

into it, it is the anterior fontanelle and the position is almost surely OP. In the presence of marked edema of the scalp or caput succedaneum, both sutures and fontanelles may be masked, and position can then be determined only by feeling an ear and then noting the direction of the pinna.

(2) The **station of the fetal head** is determined by noting the relationship of the tip of the vertex to the ischial spines. In labor that proceeds swiftly without complication, such a determination is usually accurate. When the first or, especially, the second stage is prolonged and is further complicated by marked molding and a heavy caput, this relation may suggest a false level of the head in the pelvis. If the head can be felt above the symphysis, forceps should not be used.

(3) The **adequacy of the pelvic diameters** of the midpelvis and outlet can be determined by noting the following: (a) the prominence of the spines, the degree to which they shorten the transverse diameter of the midpelvis, and the amount of space between the spine and the side of the fetal head; (b) the contour of the accessible portion of the sacrum and the amount of space posterior to the head; and (c) the width of the subpubic arch. This kind of appraisal is not needed or feasible in outlet forceps, but for indicated low forceps or midforceps it is essential to know whether the AP or the transverse diameter is the shorter so that the biparietal diameter can be brought through it.

FORCEPS DELIVERY: POSITION OCCIPUT ANTERIOR (OA)

An episiotomy is an essential part of almost all forceps deliveries. It usually is made after the preliminary examination but before the application for forceps.

The method of forceps delivery in OA is shown in Figs 40–4 through 40–7. The legends should be given special attention. This technique is applicable to both outlet forceps and midforceps delivery when the head is in the direct OA position or in one of the oblique diameters.

The operator should be seated in front of the patient, and all maneuvers should be made carefully and slowly.

Application of Forceps

The left handle is held between the thumb and fingers of the left hand, and, by means of 2 or 3 fingers of the right hand, the blade is guided to its correct position on the left side of the fetal head. This is repeated with the right hand and right blade, using the fingers of the left hand to guide the blade. The handles are depressed slightly before locking in order to place the blades properly along the optimal diameter of the fetal head.

Articulation of Forceps

The forceps are so designed that if the application is accurate they should lock easily as the handles are

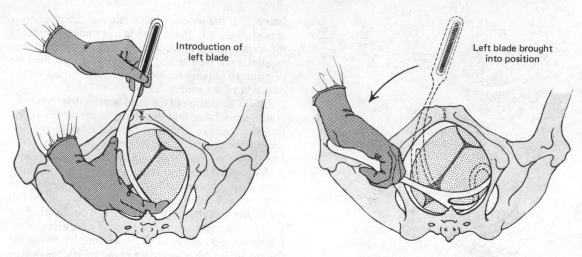

Figure 40–4. Introduction of left blade (left blade, left hand, left side of pelvis). Handle is held with fingers and thumb, not clenched in hand. Handle is held vertically. Blade is guided with fingers of right hand. Placement of blade is completed by swinging handle down to horizontal plane.

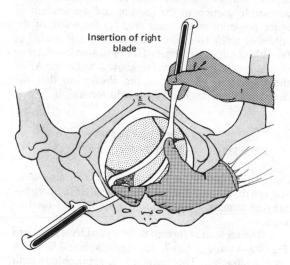

Figure 40–5. Introduction of right blade (right blade, right hand, right side of pelvis). The left blade is already in place. The handle is grasped with the fingers and thumb, not gripped in the whole hand. The handle is held vertically.

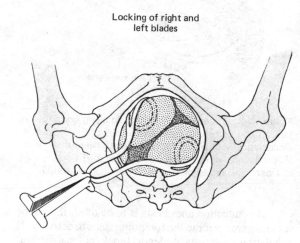

Figure 40–6. Both blades introduced. The 2 handles are brought together or locked. If application is correct, handles lock precisely, without force.

Figures 40–4 through 40–7 are reproduced, with permission, from Benson RC: *Handbook of Obstetrics and Gynecology,* 7th ed. Lange, 1980.

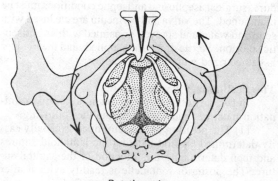

Rotation prior to traction

Figure 40–7. Traction on forceps. Some prefer to place fingers of right hand in crotch of instrument to facilitate traction. If heavier traction is needed, no more force should be used than can be exerted by flexed forearms.

closed. If the handles are askew, or if any force is needed to achieve precise articulation, the application is faulty and the position must be checked again by noting the relation of each blade to the lambdoid suture. If simple manipulation of the blades does not permit easy articulation, the forceps should be removed, the position verified (by feeling an ear if necessary), and the blades reapplied correctly.

Traction

Different obstetricians hold forceps for traction in different ways. The author's preference is to grasp the crossbar of the handle between the index and middle fingers of the left hand from underneath (DeLee-Simpson forceps) and to insert the middle and index finger of the right hand in the crotch of the instrument from above. Traction is made only in the axis of the pelvis along the curve of the birth canal. No more force is applied than can be exerted by the flexed forearms; the muscles of the back must not be used, and it is dangerous to brace the feet against the table. If this degree of traction is needed, the cause may be either cephalopelvic disproportion or an error in evaluation of the wide and narrow pelvic diameters. The obstetrician should reassess the possibility of successful vaginal delivery.

During normal labor, the head is relieved of pressure between uterine contractions; during a contraction the pressure increases gradually, is sustained at its maximum for 15–30 seconds, and wanes gradually. Similarly, traction upon the forceps should also be applied gradually, sustained at its maximum intensity for not more than 25 seconds, and released gradually. When traction ceases, the handles are separated slightly and the head is allowed to recede at will. Traction is resumed after 15–20 seconds.

Delivery of the Head

As the head begins to distend the perineum, both the amount and the direction of traction must be altered. The farther the head advances, the less the resistance offered both by the pelvis and by the soft parts; hence, only minimal traction should be applied as the head is about to be delivered. Actually, unless traction is controlled carefully, the head will "jump" over the coccyx and cause extension of the episiotomy.

The head negotiates the final portion of the pelvic curve by extension, and the physician should simulate this movement by elevating the handles of the forceps more and more as the head crowns (Fig 40–8). If the forceps are allowed to remain in place throughout delivery of the head, the handles will have passed the vertical plane as delivery of the head is completed. It is preferable to remove the forceps as the head crowns in the reverse order of their application by first disarticulating the forceps and then raising the right handle until the blade is delivered. The left blade is then removed in similar fashion. Early removal of the forceps is less important when a mediolateral episiotomy is used, because minor degrees of extension do not matter. When a median episiotomy is

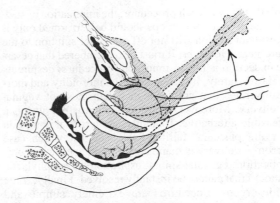

Figure 40–8. Upward traction with low forceps. As head extends, handles are raised until they pass the vertical. Little force is needed. One hand suffices; the other hand may support the perineum. (Reproduced, with permission, from Benson RC: *Handbook of Obstetrics & Gynecology*, 7th ed. Lange, 1980.)

performed, early removal of the forceps reduces the size of the spheroid that must pass through the introitus and thus reduces the likelihood of extension. After removal of the forceps, the head may recede; but if the forceps have not been removed too soon the head can be delivered readily by slight fundal pressure and the Ritgen maneuver (Fig 31–19).

The Use of Forceps When Anterior Rotation Is Not Complete

If it is necessary to intervene when the sagittal suture has passed the transverse plane of the pelvis but has not reached the exact anterior position, the physician may obtain a precise cephalic application by "wandering" the appropriate blade of the forceps toward the parietal bone that lies farthest anteriorly and inserting the other blade a little more posteriorly than is done in the direct OA position. For example, if the position is ROA, the left blade is inserted on the left side of the pelvis as though the position were OA; the blade is wandered anteriorly by placing the tips of the right index and middle fingers under the heel of the blade. Using this point as a fulcrum, the physician swings the blade into the correct position on the head by gentle lever motions of the handle. The right blade usually can be inserted directly into its correct position, but if it skips toward the right lateral aspect of the pelvis it can be wandered posteriorly in a similar manner.

MIDFORCEPS DELIVERY

Several series of cases have demonstrated increased morbidity, with lowered Apgar ratings and increased neurologic deficits, among newborns delivered by midforceps. Although it is not possible to gauge the skill and experience of those who performed the midforceps operations or the indication or degree of difficulty of each procedure, the implication of such studies is that midforceps should be performed only if cesarean section will not offer a better solution to the problem. However, it must be remembered that cesarean section is not an innocuous procedure; despite its relative safety, it carries maternal morbidity and mortality rates that are far higher than those of vaginal delivery. Moreover, cesarean section is not always a feasible alternative. Examples are terminal abruption of the placenta, failing fetal heart (in which case prompt delivery is mandatory), or an anesthetic complication (eg, total spinal, aspiration, or anaphylactic shock) that cannot be instantly resolved. Finally, some midforceps procedures are extremely simple and atraumatic, far more so than cesarean section; it should be within the obstetrician's competence to recognize such cases and to perform such midforceps operations when they can be accomplished easily and safely. The obstetrician should be able to avoid the trap of having to perform a difficult and traumatic vaginal delivery that might have been avoided with forethought and preparation.

Conduct of the Second Stage

The lower the head at the time delivery begins, the less chance of injury to mother and baby. Also, the deeper the head is in the birth canal, the greater the likelihood of spontaneous rotation of the occiput to the anterior. Accordingly, the conduct of the second stage of labor is of special importance.

A. Bladder: Because a full bladder can impede the second stage of labor, it should be emptied whenever it can be felt abdominally.

B. Dehydration: Most labors are now conducted with an infusion running, which usually prevents dehydration. If dehydration occurs, it can lead to decelerative patterns in the FHT, maternal exhaustion, and ineffective voluntary effort.

C. Voluntary Efforts: The patient's voluntary efforts may not be crucial if the pelvis is large and the baby is small. In contrast, if there is borderline disproportion ("tight fit"), strong voluntary effort may be essential for safe delivery. Accordingly, anything that impairs the patient's ability to bear down (eg, heavy systemic analgesia or conduction anesthesia used too early) should be avoided. In cases in which voluntary effort is needed, the delivery table should be equipped with handles the patient may pull on while straining, and the knees should be flexed far back on the abdomen so the axis of uterine force is directly into the inlet. Most patients will bear down more effectively if they take 2 or 3 deep breaths of a nitrous oxide-oxygen mixture (50/50) at the beginning of each contraction; these simple expedients may make the difference between an easy low forceps delivery and a difficult midforceps delivery.

D. Uterine Contractions: Uterine contractions during the second stage normally occur at 2-minute intervals. The contractions are of strong intensity and last 45–50 seconds. A delay in the interval between contractions or in their duration or intensity causes inertia that may be sufficient to delay or even stop progress. The management of second stage inertia is quite different from that in the first stage because the use of oxytocin carries a much greater risk during the second stage (see Chapter 33). An infusion pump designed to administer exact amounts of oxytocin at a preselected rate is essential (a drip should not be used). In addition, during the second stage the infusion should be started at a rate of 0.5 mU/min. This may be increased by 0.5 mU/min at 5-minute intervals, but the rate must not exceed 4 mU/min. If the desired result has not been achieved within 30 minutes, the infusion should be abandoned and other steps taken to accomplish delivery.

E. Length of the Second Stage: The length of the second stage is determined basically by the effectiveness of the contractions and the rate of progress. An active second stage should be terminated after 1–2 hours because of the increasing danger of uterine rupture or constriction ring dystocia. A slower second stage may be permitted to proceed for a longer period under careful observation as long as progress is being made. This second circumstance is unusual, however, and in most cases it is wise to follow the rule of intervening after 2 hours. Operative assistance is also advised if there is lack of progress for 30 minutes or more.

F. Anesthesia: Anesthesia that is satisfactory for outlet forceps delivery in most cases is satisfactory for midforceps delivery also. The only exception is an occasional OP presentation in which the head and shoulders must be rotated artificially. Unless the anesthetic is sufficiently deep to relax the uterus, the body of the infant will be held so tightly that rotation may be impossible. Inhalation anesthesia is usually preferable; on occasion, halothane may be required.

G. Cephalopelvic Relationships: A knowledge of variations in pelvic architecture and their effect on the mechanism of labor is essential for the proper performance of any midforceps delivery. As a rule, the midpelvis and outlet can be evaluated by digital examination during or before labor. However, if the adequacy of these diameters is questionable or if the head does not readily engage, x-ray pelvimetry may be helpful if the obstetrician is experienced in interpreting the films and if the technique includes a direct view to show inlet shape and a standing lateral and a subpubic arch film (Fig 40–9). The mechanism of labor that is typical of each of the pure pelvic types is diagrammed in Fig 40–9. Because most pelves are of mixed type, combinations of these mechanisms usually are encountered.

Two facts are important in appraising and predicting the mechanism of labor: (1) The biparietal diameter is the shortest diameter of the head; therefore, it is this diameter that should be directed through the narrowest diameter of the pelvis. (2) The occiput tends to rotate to the widest, most ample portion of the pelvis at any given level. Regardless of the position at which arrest occurs, it is essential that the area of greatest narrowing be determined, either by palpation or by a trial of traction or both, and that the biparietal diameter of the head be brought through it safely.

Midpelvic Arrest, Position Occiput Anterior

In the presence of uterine contractions of good quality and adequate voluntary effort, arrest in the anterior position most commonly results from the combination of slight transverse narrowing of the midpelvis (caused by either prominent spines or converging side walls) and a slightly forward lower sacrum. Usually, classic forceps are applied to the OA and traction applied as outlined above. If undue resistance is encountered, the head may be elevated slightly, rotated by the forceps to an oblique diameter, and traction repeated. If marked resistance is again encountered, the forceps should be removed and both the position and the pelvic features reevaluated. Cesarean section should be selected in almost all cases of arrest in the anterior or oblique position if heavy resistance is encountered on traction.

Midpelvic Arrest, Position Occiput Posterior

As shown in Fig 40–9, an anthropoid pelvis predisposes to the posterior mechanism of labor. In about 70% of cases, an effective second stage results in spontaneous rotation of the occiput to the anterior position and an uneventful delivery. In the remaining cases, the head arrests in the posterior position. In the OP position, the choice of an appropriate method of delivery depends on the configuration of the pelvis.

A. Delivery in the Occiput Posterior Position, Face to Os Pubis: This is the customary method of delivery in the monkey, in which the classic anthropoid pelvis is typical. When the sacrum flares widely posteriorly and the head is low in the pelvis, the pelvic floor may offer the only resistance to delivery. In such cases, it is entirely appropriate to make a wide episiotomy, apply classic forceps to the head in the posterior position (Fig 40–3), and deliver the fetus face to os pubis if there is no significant resistance. On the other hand, if there is resistance the head must be rotated to the anterior position before extraction.

B. Rotation to the Anterior Position and Midforceps Delivery: When the head is in the anterior position, it must negotiate the terminal portion of the pelvic curve by extension; when it is in the posterior position, however, the chin is already flexed on the thorax as much as possible and cannot advance unless, as in the monkey, there is virtually no terminal pelvic curve. Not more than 20% of the cases of arrest in the OP position can be safely delivered simply by traction without rotation. In at least 80% of cases, the head must be rotated to the anterior position. If the arrest occurs at or above station +2, cephalopelvic disproportion is almost surely the cause, and delivery should be by cesarean section. However, if the head is well molded, advanced as far as possible by the patient's voluntary effort, and deeply engaged, rotation is almost invariably not only feasible but very easily accomplished. It is emphasized that rotation, either

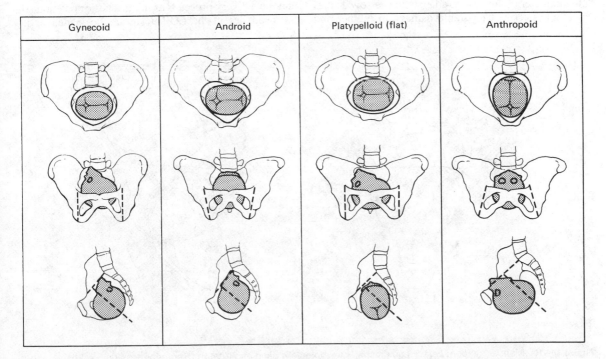

Figure 40–9. Diagrammatic representation of 4 parent pelvic types (Caldwell-Moloy) and influence of characteristic pelvic variations on mechanism of labor. (Reproduced, with permission, from Danforth DN, Ellis AH: *Am J Obstet Gynecol* 1963; 86:29.)

manually or by forceps, is an essential skill required of all obstetricians.

Artificial rotation to the anterior is required in 2 circumstances:

1. In the patient whose sacrum curves slightly forward, ample space for rotation at the level of arrest exists if the side walls are straight or divergent. If uterine force is sufficient, the occiput should rotate spontaneously away from the forward lower sacrum, and the baby will be delivered in the manner described for the anterior position. The cause of this type of arrest is uterine inertia or inadequate voluntary effort. Rotation in this circumstance is rarely difficult and can usually be facilitated by gently inserting the tips of the fingers of one hand onto the posterior fontanelle against the lambdoid suture that is on the same side as the baby's back. Elevating the head slightly and moving the lambdoid suture toward the side of the baby's back generally will move the head to the anterior position. Delivery may then be accomplished by application of classic forceps as in the anterior position.

2. In the presence of a slightly forward lower sacrum *and* transverse narrowing of the midpelvis (due to prominent spines or converging side walls), arrest in the posterior position is inevitable, regardless of the effectiveness of uterine forces or voluntary effort, because there is an insufficient transverse diameter to permit the longer anteroposterior dimension of the head to rotate through it. Generally, artificial rotation will be needed, and it usually must be done *above* the level of arrest. A "spiral extraction" has no place in the management of this problem, since it forces the long diameter of the head to adapt to the narrow diameter of the pelvis. Irreparable damage to mother and

baby may result. There are 2 techniques of rotation: manual and forceps. Manual rotation usually is preferred by obstetricians who have a relatively small, narrow hand; forceps rotation generally is selected if the hand is large or the fingers short. Both techniques are acceptable and widely used. It is important to master one or the other and use it exclusively unless some unusual problem should require a variant.

C. Manual Rotation: The rotation maneuver described by W.C. Danforth perhaps is most widely used (Fig 40–10). Anesthesia must be sufficient to relax the uterus for this maneuver. The right hand is used regardless of whether the head is to be rotated to the right or to the left. Working on the assumption that the position is ROP, the operator introduces the right hand into the vagina. With the fingers spread widely, the thumb is directed posteriorly in the pelvis and the fingers anteriorly; the head is grasped with the entire hand and turned to the occiput anterior position. It is important that the left (external) hand assist in this maneuver by applying pressure on the shoulder through the lower part of the mother's right abdomen. If necessary, the head may be elevated slightly to gain a little more space, but it should not be disengaged. The head is rotated slightly beyond the exact anterior position to allow for the tendency of the presenting part to slip back. The right thumb is now withdrawn from the vagina, leaving the fingers in contact with the side of the infant's face to prevent the head from rotating back to the posterior position. The left blade of the forceps is introduced in the usual manner, using the fingers in the vagina as a guide. The right blade is then introduced, and the delivery proceeds as in the anterior position. If the head lies in the LOP position, the maneuver is

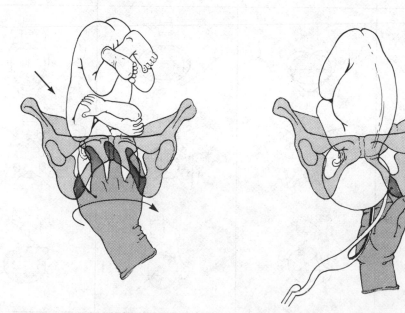

Figure 40–10. Manual rotation. *Left:* Head grasped by whole right hand and rotated to anterior position. Left hand (upper arrow) pushes shoulder toward woman's left, aiding rotation. *Right:* Anterior rotation complete. Right hand maintains head in anterior position while left blade of forceps is applied. (Redrawn and reproduced, with permission, from Danforth WC: *Am J Obstet Gynecol* 1932; **23**:360.)

reversed, although the right hand is still used. The use of the right hand always makes it possible to introduce the left blade first and obviates the need to readjust the handles for locking, as would be necessary if the right blade were introduced first.

D. Forceps Rotation: Forceps rotation is maligned in many texts on the grounds that it is likely to produce high vaginal tears and severely damage the baby, but if it is performed skillfully, deliberately, and with knowledge of what must be accomplished, it is safe, effective, and extremely simple. Many experienced obstetricians prefer it to manual rotation because of its simplicity and safety.

In all operations in which the head is rotated by means of forceps, the operator must clearly understand the movements of the forceps within the birth canal. If any classic forceps with the standard pelvic curve is held horizontally and the instrument rotated while keeping the handles in the same axis, the tips of the blades will describe an arc. Causing the handles to describe a wide arc, however, makes it possible to rotate the forceps so that the tips of the blades remain in the same place (Fig 40–11). The operator who performs a forceps rotation must constantly be aware of the position of each portion of the entire forceps blade and must cause the handles to describe a sufficiently wide arc so that the blades will not deviate from the axis of the pelvis or the space available in the birth

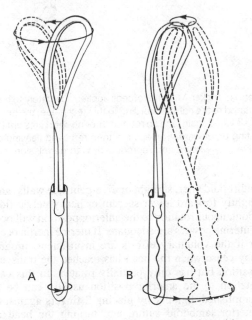

Figure 40–11. Action of forceps in rotation of head in occiput posterior. *A:* Incorrect technique. If handles are merely turned in same axis, tips of blades swing widely, making rotation impossible and damaging soft parts. *B:* Correct technique. Handles are first elevated and then describe wide arc, tips of blades remaining at approximately same point, and blades remaining in same axis throughout rotation. (Redrawn and reproduced, with permission, from Douglas RG, Stromme WG: *Operative Obstetrics,* 2nd ed. Appleton-Century-Crofts, 1976.)

canal. Most maternal and fetal injuries result from failure to observe this maxim.

Many techniques of forceps rotation have been described, and several are *not* recommended either because the author has personally found them awkward or because the chance of injury to mother and baby seems to be excessive. Included in this category are (1) the modern concept of the Scanzoni maneuver, which implies spiral extraction followed by reapplication of the forceps; (2) DeLee's key-and-lock maneuver; (3) Kielland rotation from the posterior; and (4) Bill's rotation.

The preferred technique is the **Stillman maneuver,** a procedure evolved by trial and error in a difficult case in which standard methods of rotation had failed. The steps in the Stillman rotation are as follows (Fig 40–12).

1. The Tucker-McLane forceps (or equivalent) is placed by an accurate cephalic application with the pelvic curve of the forceps toward the infant's face.

2. The head is pushed upward gently in the birth canal for a distance of 1–3 cm above the level of arrest, or until an outpouring of amniotic fluid occurs, suggesting that the head has been elevated sufficiently to permit easy rotation.

3. While the head is held at this slightly higher level, the handles of the forceps are elevated so as to center the blades in the birth canal in the axis they will occupy throughout the rotation.

4. When the handles are raised and the head is held at this slightly higher level, the operator moves the handles through an arc of 15–30 degrees *only;* this causes the head to rotate an equivalent amount. As the head rotates it tends to descend slightly, returning to the level of arrest.

5. The head is again elevated above the level of arrest from its new position and again rotated through a short arc of 15–30 degrees, during which time it tends to advance again to the former level of arrest. The operator repeats the maneuver, swinging the handles widely, until the position reaches OA. When the rotation is completed, the handles will point toward the floor. Slight traction is then made to fix the head in its new position.

6. The left blade of the rotating forceps, now lying on the *right* side of the mother's pelvis, is removed and replaced by the right blade of the DeLee-Simpson forceps. Next, the right blade of the rotating forceps is removed and replaced by the *left* blade of the DeLee-Simpson (or similar) forceps. (Both blades of the rotating forceps should not be removed at once. If the operator leaves one blade in place at all times, the head will be prevented from rotating back to the posterior position.)

7. Because the right blade of the DeLee-Simpson forceps has been applied first, the handles must be positioned for locking. This done, the extraction is accomplished by intermittent traction as though the position initially had been OA.

The foregoing steps in the rotation should be carried out slowly, deliberately, with the utmost gen-

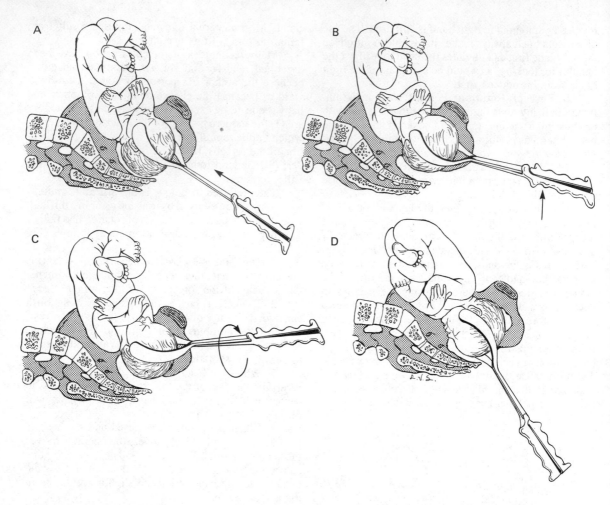

Figure 40–12. Forceps rotation of head in occiput posterior position. *A:* Tucker-McLane forceps applied accurately to head. Head elevated in axis of birth canal. *B:* Handles elevated and *(C)* rotated to the right. According to this technique, the head is rotated only through a short arc (during which it advances slightly), elevated again, and so rotated through short arcs until the anterior position is reached. *D:* Rotation complete, handles pointing downward. Forceps are then removed (leaving one blade in place) and replaced by DeLee-Simpson forceps for delivery. (Redrawn and reproduced, with permission, from Danforth DN: *Am J Obstet Gynecol* 1953; **65**:120.)

tleness. The procedure should require only about 1 minute. The operator's grip on the handles should be sufficiently delicate so that any resistance, however slight, will be perceived immediately. If resistance occurs at any point in the rotation or if the FHT indicate fetal distress, the head should be returned immediately to its original posterior position and rotation carried out in the opposite direction. During the various steps in the rotation, an assistant should direct the anterior shoulder across the abdomen as described for manual rotation.

Midpelvic Arrest, Position Occiput Transverse

Transverse arrest may result either from failure of the uterine forces of contraction or from borderline cephalopelvic disproportion. It occurs most frequently in the following situations:

A. En Route to the Anterior From a Primary Occiput Posterior Position: In the presence of an anthropoid inlet, straight or divergent side walls, and a slightly forward lower sacrum or heavy pelvic floor, spontaneous rotation to the anterior position will occur if uterine powers are adequate. If uterine inertia occurs or if the voluntary efforts are insufficient, progress may cease when the head has reached the transverse position but has only partially rotated. In this case, rotation to the anterior position usually can be accomplished digitally by placing 2 fingers against the anterior lambdoid suture and turning the head anteriorly beneath the symphysis.

If this cannot be achieved and there is sufficient room behind the head in the hollow of the sacrum, classic forceps often can be applied easily to the head in the transverse position. The blade that is to lie anteriorly (the left blade in right occiput transverse, the right blade in left occiput transverse) is introduced to the proper side of the mother's pelvis and wandered anteriorly; the opposite blade then is introduced posteriorly, the forceps are locked, and the head is rotated to the anterior position and extracted.

A third means of dealing with this problem is to rotate the head (pressure against the lambdoidal suture usually suffices) back to the posterior position, which can be done with remarkable ease, and then to employ either forceps or manual rotation and delivery as outlined above.

Kielland forceps may be used by those experienced in their use, but in this particular situation any of the solutions mentioned above is preferable. The "classic" application of Kielland forceps is shown in Fig 40–13. An alternative method of application is to introduce the blade that is to lie anteriorly on the lateral side of the mother's pelvis and to "wander" it anteriorly until it comes into position over the parietal bone.

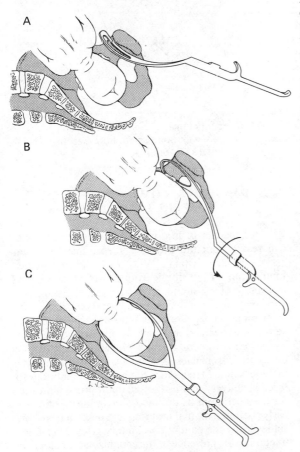

Figure 40–13. Classic application of Kielland forceps. *A:* Introduction of first blade (in this case, *left* blade, since position is ROT). *B:* Concavity of blade looks upward, and tip of blade is rotated toward patient's right (as shown by arrow) through arc of 180 degrees until blade lies in contact with head. *C:* Instrument applied, right blade having been introduced posteriorly. Note that buttons point toward occiput. (Redrawn and reproduced, with permission, from WC Danforth. In: *Obstetrics and Gynecology.* Curtis AH [editor]. Saunders, 1933.)

B. En Route to the Anterior From a Primary Transverse Mechanism: In a gynecoid pelvis, the customary mechanism of labor is engagement and descent in the transverse position, followed by flexion of the head and rotation to the anterior position as the result of slight transverse narrowing of the midpelvis and the normal tendency of the occiput to rotate away from the pelvic floor. If the AP at the outlet and lower midpelvis is normal, rotation to the anterior position and extraction are indicated. Sometimes this can be accomplished digitally. If not, manual rotation or application of classic or Kielland forceps to the head in the transverse position is appropriate.

C. Flat Pelvis, Primary Transverse Mechanism: According to the classic mechanism of labor in the flat pelvis, the head engages in the transverse position and advances through the midpelvis in the transverse position without anterior rotation. If the lower sacrum will permit, anterior rotation may occur on the pelvic floor; if the lower sacrum is also forward, the head actually may be born in the transverse position. In this instance, the pelvic curve will be negotiated by *lateral* flexion of the head.

In the management of transverse arrest of this type, rotation to the anterior and extraction from the anterior position are specifically contraindicated because they would bring the long AP of the head through the shortened AP of the pelvis. The head must be advanced in the transverse position and allowed to rotate to the anterior position only when it has reached a level at which the anteroposterior diameters are favorable. The Barton forceps (Figs 40–14 and 40–15) is preferred for cases of transverse arrest in which the head must be advanced in the transverse position. The Kielland forceps may also be used in this situation, although the application of traction is more difficult and less precise. Application of the Kielland and the Barton forceps is shown in Figs 40–13 and 40–14. The technique of rotation and delivery with the Barton forceps is shown in Fig 40–15.

Like the Kielland forceps, the Barton forceps should be reserved for those who have experience in their use and are able to predict with confidence that delivery can be safely and easily accomplished by this means. Also, as with Kielland forceps, the position of Barton forceps in the obstetrician's armamentarium is daily becoming more tenuous: If the choice is offered, most problems for which these forceps are really needed are preferably dealt with by cesarean section. The method of application of Barton forceps is shown in Fig 40–14. Traction is made with the head in the transverse position and is continued until the occiput is felt to rotate to the anterior. When the anterior rotation is achieved, the head has passed the area of major obstruction and little force is needed; the traction bar is removed and, with the handles pointing toward one maternal thigh or the other, the delivery is accomplished by continued slight traction.

Forceps Delivery in Face Presentation

If the chin is anterior, the same indications, conditions, and stipulations apply for forceps delivery as in the OA position. The classic forceps are applied to the occipitomental diameter of the head (Fig 40–3), and elevating the handles as the head advances causes the chin to stem under the symphysis, and the occiput emerges posteriorly.

If the chin is posterior, rotation of the chin to the anterior position sometimes occurs spontaneously as labor progresses. If not, it is virtually impossible to accomplish artificial rotation safely. Extraction with the chin in the posterior position will almost surely kill the baby regardless of how small it is or how large the pelvis is. Forceps delivery is contraindicated, and cesarean section is required.

Forceps Delivery in Brow Presentation

An average-sized fetal head cannot enter even a large pelvic inlet when the brow presents. Some brow presentations will convert to an occiput presentation spontaneously during the first stage of labor or can be converted to either occiput or face presentation, in which case labor should be managed accordingly. If a brow presentation fails to convert to a favorable position (chin anterior or occipital presentation) or cannot be converted readily, the infant must be delivered by cesarean section.

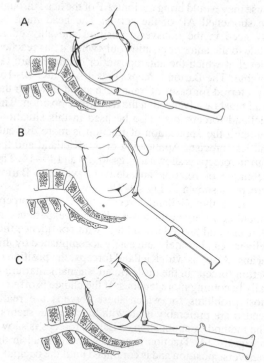

Figure 40–14. Application of Barton forceps for advancement of head in transverse position. *A:* Introduction of anterior hinged blade posteriorly, behind head. *B:* Anterior blade has been wandered to position over anterior parietal bone. *C:* Posterior blade introduced, forceps locked. The traction bar, as shown in Fig 40–2, is now affixed to facilitate traction in the proper pelvic diameter. (Redrawn and reproduced, with permission, from Barton LJ, Caldwell WE, Studdiford WE: *Am J Obstet Gynecol* 1928; **15**:16.)

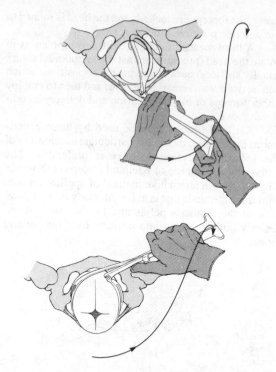

Figure 40–15. Completion of rotation using Barton forceps for advancement of head in transverse position. (Redrawn and reproduced, with permission, from Bachman C: *Surg Gynecol Obstet* 1927; **45**:805.)

DANGERS & COMPLICATIONS OF FORCEPS DELIVERIES

All manner of injuries to both mother and baby can result from the use of forceps, many of them serious and some fatal. With regard to the mother, injuries range from simple extension of the episiotomy to rupture of the uterus or vesicovaginal fistula. The baby may sustain transient facial paralysis, irreparable intracranial damage, or other injuries. Almost all of the serious injuries and many of the minor ones inflicted by obstetric forceps result from errors in judgment rather than from lack of technical skill. Such errors include failure to recognize the essential conditions for forceps delivery and lack of an appropriate indication for the operation, as outlined above; intervention too early, before maximal molding and descent have been achieved by the patient's voluntary efforts; relentless traction in the presence of unrecognized cephalopelvic disproportion; errors in diagnosis of the position of the head, with consequent application of forceps to the wrong diameter; and an incomplete knowledge of the architecture of the particular pelvis in question, with an attempt to advance the head in the wrong pelvic diameter.

Fortunately, most physicians who care for obstetric patients quickly develop respect for the operation of forceps delivery and an intuitive knowledge of when and how a patient can be delivered most safely. It is also essential that physicians be able to admit an error in judgment and resort to cesarean section when confronted with a forceps delivery of unusual difficulty.

THE VACUUM EXTRACTOR

The vacuum extractor, or ventouse, introduced by Malmström in 1954, is designed to assist delivery by the application of traction to a suction cup attached to the fetal scalp. The instrument has been widely used with good reported results in some countries. In the USA, the vacuum extractor has never been accepted as a substitute for obstetric forceps.

The ventouse gains its purchase by pulling the scalp into a specially designed cup whose diameter at the rim is smaller than that above the rim; a consequence is distortion of the scalp into the somewhat grotesque caput succedaneum, called a "chignon," which, at least hypothetically, could lead to serious injury to the scalp and to the delicate cranial and intracranial tissues of the fetus. The data from continental Europe, the United Kingdom, Australia, and other areas in which the instrument is used extensively attest to its safety, provided the instrument is used correctly. The instrument lacks the precision of forceps and disregards the finer details of pelvic architecture as well as the mechanism of labor—all essential and traditional parts of skillful forceps delivery. Moreover, the instrument is somewhat cumbersome,

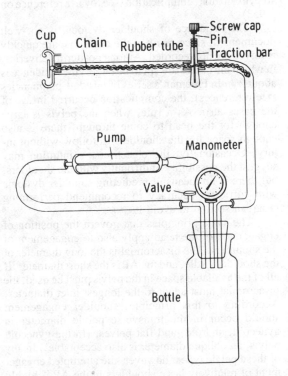

Figure 40–16. Modified Malmström vacuum extractor. (Reproduced, with permission, from Benson RC: *Handbook of Obstetrics & Gynecology.* 7th ed. Lange, 1980.)

and 6–8 minutes are normally required for application of the suction cup to the scalp.

The ventouse, as designed by Malmström, has the following components: a specially designed suction cup, a hose connecting the suction cup to a suction pump with intervening trap bottle and manometer, and a chain inside the hose that connects the suction cup to a crossbar for traction. The design of the cup, smaller at the rim than above the rim, permits the scalp to be anchored in the peripheral reaches of the cup. Three sizes (40 mm, 50 mm, and 60 mm) are available.

Two important modifications of the device have simplified its use: In the original model, negative pressure was attained by a hand pump; an electric pump is reported to be more efficient and easier to use. Bird's modification of the suction cup (Fig 40–17) permits far more efficient traction and also eliminates the need to thread the chain through the hose.

The largest cup that can be easily introduced is selected and is positioned to cover the posterior fontanelle so that the sagittal and lambdoid sutures are symmetrically palpable at the cup's periphery. Negative pressure is induced at a rate of 0.2 kg/cm² per 2 minutes until a negative pressure of 0.6 kg/cm² is attained, an elapsed time of about 6–7 minutes. (The slow increments of induction of negative pressure have as their primary purpose the even and complete filling of the cup by the fetal scalp. Achieving the correct pressure rapidly, in case of emergency, evidently has no deleterious fetal effects, but the cup is more apt to slip off, and a higher negative pressure, eg, 0.8 kg/cm² may be required.)

Once the cup has been applied, traction is made intermittently, coincident with uterine contractions and supplemented by the mother's bearing down efforts as needed. The direction of traction is determined with due attention to the pelvic curve of Carus, depending on the station of the head at the time, and it should be perpendicular to the cup to prevent the cup from slipping off the scalp. Traction should be sustained and even throughout the uterine contraction and should be discontinued between contractions. The procedure should be considered to have failed if the head is not delivered after 5 such tractions made over the course of about 15 minutes; in such a case, cesarean section is the preferable recourse, since failure of vacuum extraction implies cephalopelvic disproportion. The cup should not be allowed to remain in place for more than 30 minutes, because of the possibility of damage to the scalp.

Anesthesia requirements are usually less than for forceps delivery; pudendal block usually suffices, and in many cases no anesthesia may be needed, or local infiltration of the perineum may be sufficient.

Several studies have compared neonatal results by type of delivery—spontaneous vacuum extraction, forceps, or cesarean section. In the study reported by Greis et al (see references), neither perinatal mortality nor serious traumatic complications were attributable to vacuum extraction if the instrument was used judiciously. Apgar scores were similar in each of the

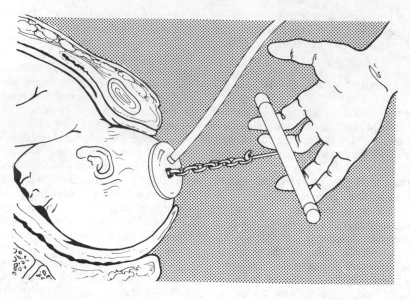

Figure 40–17. Bird's modification of Malström's vacuum extractor.

groups. Except for the incidence of "chignon," skin bruises and lacerations were less frequent in the group delivered by vacuum extraction than in the group delivered by forceps. Cephalhematoma can be expected in a high percentage of babies delivered by vacuum extraction, but unlike the customary cephalhematomas, they tend to vanish in 2–5 days.

Complications due to vacuum extraction are usually attributed to improper use, ie, failure to recognize the circumstances in which it is contraindicated, overlong or incorrectly applied traction, use of excessive negative pressure, overlong application of the suction cup to the scalp, and failure to prevent cervical or vaginal tissue from entering the cup.

Use of the ventouse is obviously contraindicated in the presence of cephalopelvic disproportion; in breech, brow, or face presentation; or if the head of a single fetus is not engaged in the pelvis. It should not be used if the membranes are intact. The propriety of its use in preterm delivery is unsettled.

The technique has been used successfully for delivery of a second twin in preference to version and extraction or cesarean section. Those who are experienced in its use find it to be suitable in occiput posterior presentations: If the interspinous diameter is wide, spontaneous rotation to the anterior usually occurs as the head is advanced. Attempts to rotate the head by turning the instrument usually fail, because the cup either detaches or turns only on the scalp.

The trend is away from forceps delivery. As more and more cesarean sections are performed in order to avoid forceps delivery, the very real risks of cesarean section will become more apparent; also, fewer obstetricians will gain the skills that are essential to the performance of forceps delivery. The vacuum extractor may gain acceptance as a means of avoiding both forceps delivery and, in some cases, cesarean section.

SOME SPECIAL CONSIDERATIONS IN DIFFICULT DELIVERIES

SHOULDER DYSTOCIA

Impaction of the fetal shoulders occurring after delivery of the head in vertex presentation is a formidable, even fatal, complication (see Swartz reference on p 953).

The incidence of shoulder dystocia is not well documented, since many of the cases that are quickly resolved are not recorded. Among postterm deliveries, in which the babies are apt to be larger, the incidence is about 2%. In Freeman's series of postdate pregnancies (see references), the complication occurred in 2% of the cases also. As a rule, when the pelvis is large enough for the head to come through, there is also enough space for the shoulders to follow without injury. Occasionally, the obstetrician's intuition may suggest the possibility of difficulty with the shoulders, but there is no means of predicting shoulder dystocia with sufficient accuracy to recommend performing cesarean section to avoid it.

The same principles that govern the position of engagement of the head apply also to engagement of the shoulders. The bisacromial is the long diameter of the shoulder girdle, and the AP is the short diameter. If all of the available space in the pelvis must be used, the bisacromial must adapt to the longest inlet diameter. According to this principle, shoulder engagement should occur in the transverse pelvic diameter in gynecoid, android, and flat pelves. (In the gynecoid pelvis, an oblique diameter is also acceptable.) In any of these pelvic types, however, the attempted engagement of relatively large shoulders in the AP is highly unfavorable and predisposes to shoulder impaction; the posterior shoulder usually advances past the sacral promontory into the upper midpelvis, but the anterior shoulder overhangs the upper margin of the symphysis and cannot advance. These relationships are less important when the pelvis is of ample size and the shoulder girdle is not overly large. They are of vital importance if the relationships are such that the shoulders can pass only by utilizing the optimal diameters of the inlet.

In the inlet of the anthropoid pelvis, engagement of the shoulders with the bisacromial diameter in the direct AP axis is the rule; hence, in this type of pelvis, shoulder dystocia is rare.

Diagnosis

Shoulder dystocia should be anticipated when the newborn's head appears to be obese, with chubby cheeks and a double chin. The diagnosis is confirmed when a combination of gentle depression of the head and moderate fundal pressure fails to cause the anterior shoulder to stem beneath the symphysis. Only one such effort, continued for no more than 4–5 seconds, is required to confirm the diagnosis. This maneuver is a diagnostic one and is *not* to be used therapeutically.

Treatment

If the first attempt to deliver the anterior shoulder fails, it is highly imprudent to repeat the maneuver. When the head is subjected to sharp lateral flexion or moved downward in a jerky manner, great tension is put upon the brachial plexus and Erb's palsy may result. The obstetrician should immediately execute the following steps in an orderly sequence. General anesthesia is desirable if it can be induced immediately.

(1) The hand is passed upward along first the anterior and then the posterior aspect of the baby to note any fetal tumor or anomaly that might cause obstruction. If none is found, the middle finger is placed in the posterior axilla and the heaviest possible traction is made in an effort to advance the posterior shoulder; it is difficult to exert enough traction in this fashion to do any damage. If the posterior shoulder can be advanced more deeply into the hollow of the sacrum, a little more room will be provided, and the combination of strong fundal and suprapubic pressure and *gentle* depression the head may then be fruitful.

(2) If step 1 fails, the operator identifies the clavicle and with 2 fingers exerts lateral pressure on the anterior aspect of the posterior shoulder in an effort to move the shoulders to an oblique diameter of the pelvis. *Simultaneously,* the abdominal hand should attempt to move the anterior shoulder in the opposite direction (Morris maneuver). When the bisacromial diameter has been dislodged from the AP diameter, fundal pressure alone may result in advancement of the anterior shoulder. If this does not occur, the shoulder may deliver as the result of heavy fundal and suprapubic pressure and *gentle* downward pressure on the head. If rotation to the oblique diameter fails, an attempt should be made to bring the bisacromial diameter to the direct transverse.

(3) If step 2 fails, the "screw principle" of Woods is used. This is a variant of Lovset's maneuver for delivery of the shoulders in breech presentation; since the posterior shoulder is already engaged at a relatively low level in the pelvis, rotation of this shoulder to the anterior (through an arc of 180 degrees) causes it to stem beneath the symphysis anteriorly in a manner similar to that encountered when one disengages a screw. Assisted by fundal pressure with the opposite hand as needed (*not* by an assistant), 2 vaginal fingers press firmly on the anterior aspect of the posterior shoulder, causing it to swing upward around the periphery of the pelvis to and past the 12 o'clock position and, usually, to stem beneath the symphysis. By means of rotation in the opposite direction accompanied by fundal pressure, the formerly impacted shoulder, now in the hollow of the sacrum, is moved to the anterior position and, usually, is easily delivered.

(4) If step 3 fails, the operator's hand passes into the uterus posteriorly and brings down the entire posterior arm by flexing the elbow, looping a finger around the forearm (called triggering), and delivering it. The anterior shoulder usually follows without incident. This maneuver is highly effective, but it may also result in uterine rupture and other serious lacerations of the maternal soft parts. Accordingly, if the baby is dead, this step is omitted, and the operator proceeds immediately to step 5.

(5) Cleidotomy (see p 952) is the ultimate solution for cases of shoulder dystocia that cannot be dealt with by the aforementioned measures.

BREECH PRESENTATION & DELIVERY

A breech presentation is one in which the caudal pole of the fetus is the presenting part (Fig 40–18).

(1) **Frank breech** (about 65% of cases). The thighs are acutely flexed and the legs are extended upward along the anterior aspect of the baby's trunk.

(2) **Full breech** or **complete breech** (about 10% of cases). The thighs are flexed on the abdomen but the knees are also flexed so that the baby assumes a cross-legged sitting posture.

(3) **Footling breech** or **incomplete breech** (about 25% of cases). One or both feet are lowermost, designated, respectively, as single or double footling breech.

The sacrum is the point of reference in breech presentation regardless of whether the breech is frank, full, or footling. As in vertex presentations, position is defined as the relation of the point of reference to one of the 4 quadrants or to the transverse or anteroposterior diameter of the pelvis. Accordingly, 8 possible positions are recognized: right sacrum anterior (RSA), transverse (RST), and posterior (RSP); left sacrum anterior (LSA), transverse (LST), and posterior (LSP); and direct sacrum anterior (DSA) and posterior (DSP) (Fig 40–19).

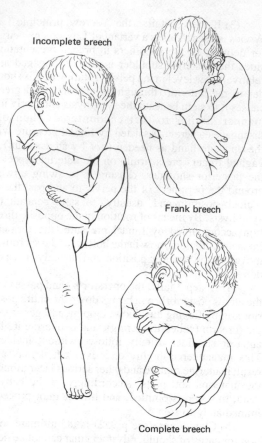

Incomplete breech

Frank breech

Complete breech

Figure 40–18. Types of breech presentations. (Reproduced, with permission, from Benson RC: *Handbook of Obstetrics & Gynecology,* 7th ed. Lange, 1980.)

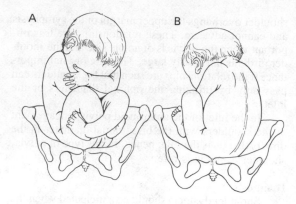

A   B

Figure 40–19. Breech presentation. *A:* Right sacrum posterior (RSP) position. *B:* Left sacrum anterior (LSA) position. (Redrawn and reproduced, with permission, from Bumm E: *Grundriss zum Studium der Geburtshilfe.* Bergmann, 1922.)

It is usually impossible to identify a specific cause for a given case. Factors predisposing to breech presentation include the following:

(1) Accommodation of the large pole of the baby to the more commodious portion of the uterus. In the case of a premature infant, the head is the larger pole and tends to occupy the fundus; in the term infant, the breech is the larger pole and tends to occupy the fundus unless this space is compromised, eg, by cornual implantation of the placenta or by septate or bicornuate uterus. Certain fetal anomalies, eg, hydrocephalus or large congenital goiter, may also predispose to breech presentation because of the tendency of the larger fetal pole to occupy the fundus.

(2) Extension of the legs of the fetus, as in frank breech, may so immobilize (splint) the body as to discourage the spontaneous change from breech to vertex presentation that usually occurs during the seventh or eighth month.

(3) Increased uterine tone and relative oligohydramnios during later pregnancy may also impede spontaneous version to a cranial presentation. These factors are regarded by some as the commonest cause of breech presentation at term.

(4) Other predisposing causes that have been

proposed include advanced multiparity, placenta previa, polyhydramnios, contracted pelvis, and pelvic tumor; however, more recent studies have shown that the incidence of breech presentation is *not* increased by any of these complications.

The incidence of breech presentation correlates directly with fetal weight and, consequently, with the duration of pregnancy. In babies weighing approximately 1000 g, the incidence is approximately 23%; at a weight of 1500 g, about 12%; at 2000 g, about 8%; and at 3000 g or more, approximately 3%.

Dangers of Breech Presentation

A. To the Mother: In breech presentation, the presenting part does not accurately conform either to the lower uterine segment or to the pelvis. Premature rupture of the membranes may result and predispose to intrapartum and postpartum infection. Failure of the presenting part to conform to the contours of the lower uterine segment may result in uterine incoordination and consequent prolonged labor with its attendant risks. The need for vaginal manipulations (some of them difficult) is much greater in breech presentation. Such manipulations predispose to laceration of the perineum, vagina, cervix, and lower uterine segment and cause hemorrhage and infection.

B. To the Baby: The neonatal death rate directly attributable to breech delivery is 4–5 times that of vertex presentations. There is no good estimate of the number of babies who survive delivery but suffer either immediate or late sequelae. The incidence of cord prolapse is high, especially in footling and full breech. In vertex presentation, molding of the head is gradual, occurring sometimes over the course of hours; in breech presentation, molding is abrupt, subjecting the delicate supporting tissues of the aftercoming head to sudden and often violent stresses. Intracranial hemorrhage is the most frequent cause of death in breech delivery. Injuries that can occur include laceration of the tentorium and falx of the cerebellum, broken neck, and injury to the brachial and cervical plexuses. The umbilical cord is necessarily compressed during engagement and delivery of the shoulders and head. Heretofore, it was maintained that failure to deliver the head within 5 minutes of the appearance of the umbilicus at the vulva would result in irreparable fetal asphyxia. Although this is an important danger, it is not sufficiently great that haste should overtake caution in the delivery of the shoulders or head; most deliveries can be completed within 5 minutes, but if problems are encountered they should be approached deliberately, gently, and without any stipulation of time.

The above-listed dangers of breech delivery to the mother and baby are not overstated and are reflected in all large series of cases.

Prevention of Breech Presentation

The hazard of breech delivery is so great that any attempt to prevent it should be commended. External cephalic version has enjoyed some popularity because, theoretically at least, if breech presentation is diagnosed during late pregnancy—but prior to onset of labor—the outlook for the baby is greatly improved if the presentation is converted so that the head presents instead of the breech. This conversion can usually be accomplished (if the uterus is not too irritable and if the amount of amniotic fluid is adequate) by placing the patient in a Trendelenburg posture of 30 degrees, sprinkling the abdomen liberally with powder, moving the breech upward in the patient's abdomen, and shifting it toward the iliac fossa on the side of the back while the other hand displaces the head toward the opposite flank. The version is completed gradually and slowly, and the baby is held in its new position for 5 minutes after the cephalic presentation is achieved.

The attempt must be abandoned immediately if any resistance is encountered or if there is any significant change in FHT, which must be monitored as the version progresses. Hazards include separation of the placenta, rupture of the uterus, and even the tying of knots in the umbilical cord.

There is no uniformity of opinion about the propriety of external cephalic version. Many cases of breech presentation encountered at 36–38 weeks of gestation revert spontaneously to cephalic presentation without artificial conversion. Nicholson J. Eastman, the leading obstetrician of his day, believed that those in whom the version is done easily enough to inflict no damage are the very ones in which spontaneous version would have occurred had the version not been done. He was satisfied also that enough babies who had been turned reverted later to breech presentation so that the final incidence of breech was affected little or not at all. Among modern writers, Morley and Ranney believe the procedure to be clearly indicated in all cases in which it is feasible, and in the course of considerable experience they encountered few significant complications. The question continues to be moot: Casual inquiry among many obstetricians suggests that most prefer not to perform external version and, if breech presentation persists, to deal with it

in the manner that seems most appropriate when the patient is admitted in labor.

The Mechanism of Labor in Breech Presentation

There are 3 distinct and mutually exclusive mechanisms in breech delivery: the mechanism of the breech, the mechanism of the shoulders, and the mechanism of the head (Fig 40–20). Constant awareness of each mechanism is essential to the proper performance of breech delivery. (Indeed, the quickest way to appraise an obstetrician's technical competence is to watch the performance of a breech delivery.) Each of the mechanisms follows the same rules that obtain for vertex presentation: At each level, the shortest fetal diameters traverse the shortest diameters of the pelvis. Also, in each mechanism the pelvic curve must be negotiated.

A. The Mechanism of the Breech: The transverse (bitrochanteric) diameter of the fetus is the longer and the AP the shorter. In a gynecoid pelvis, the breech characteristically engages with the sacrum anterior, and the bitrochanteric diameter of the fetus is in the transverse diameter of the pelvis. The buttocks descend either in this position or in one of the oblique diameters until they encounter the levator muscles and sacrum. At this level internal rotation occurs, the anterior hip rotating beneath the symphysis. The remainder of the pelvic curve is now negotiated by lateral flexion of the spine. The anterior hip then passes beneath the os pubis, followed by the posterior hip. The shoulders now begin to engage (also in the transverse position), and, as they do so, the back rotates anteriorly and the breech advances with the back stemming beneath the os pubis.

B. The Mechanism of the Shoulders: The shoulders enter the pelvis with the bisacromial diameter in the transverse diameter of the inlet. Ideally, and in most cases, the arms are folded across the chest. As the shoulders advance into the pelvis they rotate into either an oblique diameter or the AP of the pelvis, the anterior shoulder stemming beneath the os pubis. The anterior shoulder is born first, followed by the posterior shoulder.

C. The Mechanism of the Head: The head begins to engage in the transverse or an oblique position at the time the shoulders reach the hollow of the sacrum. The head descends in this position, rotating to the OA position at the level of or just above the pelvic floor. The head negotiates the pelvic curve by increasing flexion, with the occiput finally stemming beneath the symphysis as the forehead, nose, mouth, and chin are born.

The 3 mechanisms outlined above refer to uncomplicated totally spontaneous delivery, in a patient with a normal gynecoid pelvis of adequate size, in which no unusual turns must be made to negotiate narrow diameters. It should be evident, however, that the mechanism of labor in breech presentation is both complex and hazardous and that total spontaneous breech delivery imposes risks that can be avoided by

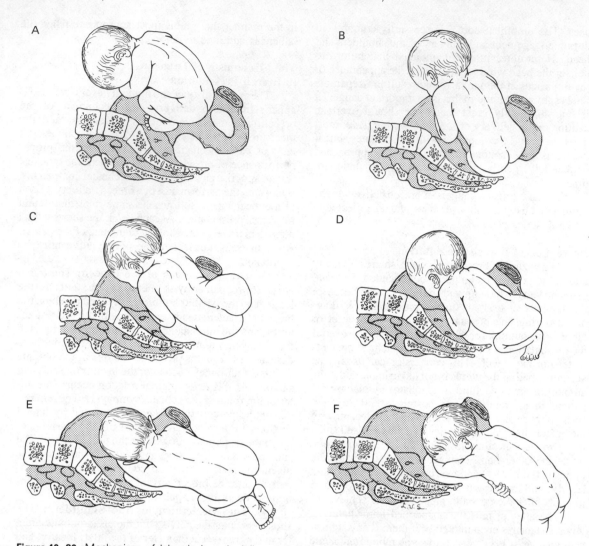

Figure 40–20. Mechanism of labor in breech delivery. **A:** Mechanism of breech delivery. RST at the onset of labor; engagement of the buttocks usually occurs in the oblique or transverse diameter of the pelvic brim. **B:** Early second stage. The buttocks have reached the pelvic floor and internal rotation has occurred so that the bitrochanteric diameter lies in the AP diameter of the pelvic outlet. **C:** Late second stage. The anterior buttock appears at the vulva by lateral flexion of the trunk around the symphysis pubica. The shoulders have not yet engaged in the pelvis. **D:** The buttocks have been born, and the shoulders are adjusting to engage in the transverse diameter of the brim. This movement causes external rotation of the delivered buttocks so that the fetal back becomes uppermost. **E:** The shoulders have reached the pelvic floor and have undergone internal rotation so that the bisacromial diameter lies in the AP diameter of the pelvic outlet. Simultaneously, the buttocks rotate anteriorly through 90 degrees. This is called **restitution.** The head is engaging in the pelvic brim and the sagittal suture is lying in the transverse diameter of the brim. **F:** The anterior shoulder is born from behind the symphysis pubica by lateral flexion of the delivered trunk. (Redrawn and reproduced, with permission, from Llewellyn-Jones D: *Fundamentals of Obstetrics and Gynecology.* Vol 1. Faber & Faber, 1969.)

judicious assistance at the critical stages. Any or all of the "normal" mechanisms in breech presentation can be altered at any stage, and in the several pelvic types each of the 3 breech mechanisms is influenced by pelvic variations in the same manner as for vertex presentation. The exact kind of assistance to be given requires precise knowledge of the normal mechanism and of the deviations that result from variations in pelvic configuration and from abnormal attitudes of the baby.

Diagnosis of Breech Presentation

There are no symptoms that may lead one to suspect breech presentation, nor are there any characteristic signs on inspection. Nonetheless, a breech presentation can be confirmed in the following ways:

A. Palpation: All but 4–5% of breech presentations can be diagnosed by the 4 maneuvers of Leopold (see Fig 31–4): (1) The firm, round, ballotable head is felt in the fundus; (2) the back and small parts are identified laterally, as in vertex presentation; (3) the softer and often ill-defined breech is felt over the inlet; and (4) the cephalic prominence is not defined. The Pawlik grip that is used for the third maneuver may now be applied to the fundus to confirm the presence of the head. Of the maneuvers mentioned above, ballottement of the head in the fundus is the most characteristic finding in breech presentation; however, failure of ballottement does not rule out breech presentation, for the sign cannot be elicited if the head is firmly flexed on the chest or if the quantity of amniotic fluid is reduced.

B. Auscultation: In breech presentation, the FHT are best heard over the back at or above the level of the umbilicus.

C. Vaginal Examination: The presenting part is irregular and lacks the hard, rounded symmetry of vertex presentation. (The irregular presenting part of breech presentation must also be distinguished from face presentation and from anencephaly; the abdominal examination should help in this distinction. An x-ray film is definitive.) The examiner gently introduces a finger through the cervix and sweeps it around the periphery of the presenting part. The hard sacrum is found on the side of the back, and a sulcus on the opposite side—or the feet in the case of full or footling breech. Efforts to define the genitalia, anus, and buttocks are imprudent; these areas can be easily injured, and no information about them is needed at the time of diagnosis.

D. X-Ray: X-ray studies will confirm a breech presentation and also provide the information needed to complete the diagnosis: the size and attitude of the baby, the degree of extension of the fetal head, and the position of the legs. It also eliminates face presentation and monstrosity as possible diagnoses.

Formerly, x-ray pelvimetry was an essential part of the evaluation of a patient with breech presentation; more recently, some physicians have insisted that it is not useful for this or for any other purpose. This is unfortunate, for their conclusions are based on the use of x-ray techniques that cannot provide the information that is needed. As noted earlier, the minimal essentials for useful x-ray pelvimetry are (1) three films—a direct view of the inlet to visualize inlet shape, a standing (not recumbent) lateral view, and a film to show the subpubic arch, the splay of the sidewalls, and the prominence of the ischial spines; and (2) an informed obstetrician or radiologist (preferably the former) who is able to read the films accurately, ie, to evaluate the significance of any areas of narrowing and to interpret the nuances of the mechanism of labor. If vaginal delivery is contemplated, proper x-ray pelvimetry should be part of the preliminary workup.

E. Ultrasound: The biparietal diameter (in this case, the outer skull diameter should be reported) can be measured in breech presentation with reasonable accuracy. If this measurement is more than 9.5 cm, it is usually wise to deliver by cesarean section. If the biparietal diameter is 9.5 cm or less and no other factors suggest the desirability of cesarean section, the adequacy of the pelvis should be determined by x-ray

pelvimetry; if the pelvis is found to be unfavorable, cesarean section should be elected.

In some cases, ultrasonography can lead to suspicion of extension of the fetal head. This should be confirmed by abdominal x-ray.

Differential Diagnosis

Breech presentation must be distinguished from face presentation; fetal anomalies, such as anencephaly presenting by the vertex; shoulder presentation; and compound presentation, eg, hand and foot, or foot and head. The foot can be distinguished from a hand by the prominence of the heel and the hand from a foot by the flexibility of the fingers as opposed to the toes.

Careful vaginal examination (not rectal examination) may rule out the foregoing possibilities. Nevertheless, the digital manipulations that are needed may be sufficiently vigorous to cause injury to the fetal soft parts (the eyes in face presentation, the genitalia or anus in breech). X-ray is usually needed for definitive and complete diagnosis and is preferably performed immediately.

Terminology of Breech Delivery

The following definitions are set forth in *Obstetric-Gynecologic Terminology,* prepared by the Committee on Terminology of the American College of Obstetricians and Gynecologists:

In **spontaneous breech delivery** the entire body is born spontaneously without traction or other manipulation or assistance except support of the trunk. **Partial breech extraction** is spontaneous delivery to the umbilicus and extraction of the remainder of the baby. **Total breech extraction** is extraction of the entire body of the infant.

The term spontaneous breech delivery means just what it seems to mean. The terms partial breech extraction and total breech extraction are not so exact, because they do not indicate the manner of delivery of the head; moreover, the latter term does not indicate the means by which the breech is delivered. Two terms preferred by the author and used by most obstetricians in practice are **assisted breech delivery,** in which manual aid is used in the delivery of the legs, shoulders, or head and the delivery is performed without the need for the operator's hand to enter the uterine cavity; and **breech extraction** (''breaking up the breech,'' decomposition of the breech), in which a frank breech is converted to a double footling breech to complete delivery of the legs and pelvis.

In either assisted breech delivery or breech extraction, the head may be delivered by forceps or by manual assistance. If only the hands are used in assisted breech delivery, the term assisted breech delivery is sufficient and the procedure needs no further description. If forceps are applied to the aftercoming head in either assisted breech extraction or breech delivery, a statement to this effect is added; if the head is delivered manually after breech extraction, this is noted as part of the terminology of the procedure.

Admission Evaluation

At the time of admission, a tentative decision must be made about whether vaginal delivery is feasible and safe or if cesarean section is preferable. An x-ray of the abdomen should be taken both to verify the breech presentation and to rule out extension of the fetal head. As noted in the preceding section, ultrasonography and x-ray pelvimetry may be needed to complete the evaluation.

In some services, the hazard of breech delivery is considered to be so great that all breeches are delivered by cesarean section. More recently, there is a trend toward selection of cases, vaginal delivery being selected for those that qualify as extremely favorable. The importance of this trend is that in appropriate cases it eliminates the maternal hazards of cesarean section.

A. Favorable Factors: In general, the following obstetric factors are considered favorable for vaginal delivery:

1. Gestational age of more than 36 or less than 38 weeks. (If the baby is too small, the head will be larger than the breech and may be trapped in the cervix; if too large, the difficulty is obvious.)

2. Estimated fetal weight of more than 2500 or less than 3175 g.

3. The presenting part at or below station −1 at the onset of labor.

4. The cervix soft, effaced, and dilated more than 3 cm.

5. Ample gynecoid or anthropoid pelvis. (The head will enter the pelvis in the anterior position.)

6. A history of a previous breech delivery of a baby weighing more than 3175 g or a previous vertex delivery of a baby weighing more than 3630 g.

B. Unfavorable Factors: In general, the following obstetric factors are considered to be unfavorable for vaginal delivery:

1. Gestational age of more than 38 weeks.

2. Estimated fetal weight of more than 3175 g.

3. Presenting part at or above station −2.

4. Cervix firm, incompletely effaced, and less than 3 cm dilated.

5. No history of prior vaginal delivery, or history of difficult vaginal delivery.

6. Android or flat pelvis. (The head may enter the pelvis in the transverse position, requiring artificial rotation before it can engage.)

7. Footling or full breech presentations, because they predispose to cord prolapse.

8. Hyperextension of the fetal head (an x-ray diagnosis) is extremely unfavorable and is an indication for cesarean section.

The presence of any one of the aforementioned unfavorable factors should strongly suggest the desirability of delivery by cesarean section. The Zatuchni-Andros breech score can be a tentative guide but fails to consider some of the most important conditions.

Early Management of Labor in Breech Presentation

A. Electronic Fetal Monitoring: Electronic fetal monitoring should be continued throughout labor to alert the obstetrician to cord prolapse or other cause of fetal distress. Failing this, the fetal heart should be auscultated no less frequently than every 10 minutes during the first stage of labor and after every contraction in the second stage.

B. Rupture of the Membranes: In footling or full breech, the membranes should not be ruptured artificially during the first stage of labor; vaginal examination is done immediately after spontaneous rupture to rule out cord prolapse and also to reevaluate pelvic relationships. In frank breech the membranes may be ruptured provided the breech fills the pelvis and has reached a station of +1 or below.

C. Induction of Labor: Induction of labor is contraindicated in footling and full breech; if immediate termination of pregnancy is essential, it should be done by cesarean section. In frank breech, labor may be induced for a medical or obstetric indication provided all of the conditions for induction are present (see p 679) and provided the conditions for vaginal delivery are extremely favorable.

D. Conduct of the First Stage of Labor: The conduct of the first stage is similar to that of vertex presentation except that (1) special vigilance is needed to identify the moment the membranes rupture, (2) the fetal heart requires continuous monitoring, and (3) systemic analgesia must be used in minimally effective amounts. General anesthesia may be needed for delivery, and its depressing effect on the baby is compounded if full doses of meperidine or other systemic analgesics have been used. Lumbar epidural block (from T12 to L4) is applicable in the first stage. Continuous caudal anesthesia is not applicable (with the possible exception of the small premature), because the bearing-down efforts of the second stage are impeded.

E. Conduct of the Second Stage of Labor, Prior to Delivery: The conduct of the second stage of breech presentation is similar to that of vertex presentation except that cesarean section should be considered if, after 1 hour of good voluntary effort, the breech has not yet descended to the pelvic floor. In modern obstetrics, no one should deliberately undertake a difficult breech delivery; cesarean section should be elected.

F. Trial and Test of Labor: A **test of labor** (2 hours of good voluntary effort in the second stage, with ruptured membranes) is not applicable in breech presentation; a decision about whether vaginal delivery is feasible should be made long before a full test could be completed. A **trial of labor** in footling or full breech often is retrospective in the sense that cesarean section will have been selected either because of uterine inertia or failure of the cervix to dilate normally during the course of labor. In frank breech, the same reasons for cesarean section apply as in footling or full breech; moreover, the pelvic relationships may appear favorable at the beginning of labor, but as the breech advances in the pelvis it may become evident that there is less space than originally anticipated. In such cases the term trial of labor is applicable, and cesarean section should be elected.

G. Oxytocin Stimulation in Breech Presentation: Most obstetricians consider it unwise to employ oxytocin stimulation in breech presentation, and if uterine inertia intervenes cesarean section is usually selected. However, if there is some reason why cesarean section is not wholly appropriate and if the conditions for vaginal delivery are extremely favorable, an oxytocin infusion may be used. The infusion should be started at a rate of 0.5 mU/min, increasing at very small increments. The indications, contraindications, and admonitions are the same as for vertex presentation. Special vigilance is needed in full and footling breech because of the constant hazard of cord prolapse.

Special Considerations in Preparation for Breech Delivery

A. The Predelivery Examination: If it is anticipated that the breech will be born spontaneously to the level of the umbilicus and if progress is being made in that direction, the predelivery examination is omitted. On the other hand, if intervention is likely before this point is reached, the examination is essential. Its chief purpose is to confirm that the cervix is completely dilated and *retracted* high in the pelvis; although the breech (especially in the premature or in footling breech) may pass the cervix without incident, the shoulders or head will surely be trapped by an incompletely dilated cervix. The position of the fetal sacrum must also be verified and a final evaluation made of the wide and narrow diameters of the mother's pelvis.

B. Anesthesia: The selection of anesthesia depends on the anticipated technique of delivery. A breech extraction (breaking up the breech) requires a general anesthetic that will relax the uterus. Ether or halothane is applicable. If the breech is to be expelled spontaneously or with manual assistance, pudendal block and local infiltration of the perineum are appropriate. Single injection caudal anesthesia, or extension of a prior lumbar epidural to S2–4, is also effective if administered when the breech distends the perineum. In most cases, the patient can be encouraged to advance the breech so it can be delivered without the need for extraction. In some cases, the same anesthesia used for spontaneous delivery of the breech will also suffice for delivery of the shoulders and head. However, for every breech delivery, because supplementary general anesthesia is often needed, either an inhalation anesthesia apparatus or an intravenous system should be ready for the instant administration of intravenous (or inhalation) anesthesia as soon as the umbilicus is born. Thiopental may be administered as a hypnotic dose (150–200 mg). With either thiopental or inhalation anesthesia, the use of succinylcholine chloride is desirable; it has no effect on the uterus but reduces the amount of general anesthetic needed.

C. Assisting Personnel: A breech delivery requires the intense and undivided attention of the obstetrician and therefore demands the presence of a trained assistant who should have been instructed in advance, preferably using a mannikin, in what is expected. The assistant must be shown exactly how moist, warm towels are to be applied to the baby's back after delivery of the pelvis; the specific manner in which the arms and trunk are to be supported after delivery of the shoulders; and the precise manner in which suprapubic pressure is to be applied if needed. In addition, the anesthesiologist should be informed of the obstetrician's intentions and probable requirements.

D. Position on the Delivery Table: The patient should be positioned in the lithotomy position as for vertex delivery. Some of the crucial maneuvers require traction toward the floor, and a bed is not suitable; in an emergency, the patient may be placed across the bed with her buttocks at the edge of the mattress, the legs being supported by assistants. The bladder should be catheterized and the vulva, perineum, thighs, and lower abdomen prepared as for vertex delivery.

E. Episiotomy: It is impossible to estimate in advance the amount of space that will be needed for delivery of the infant, and it is awkward to make or enlarge an episiotomy after the delivery is begun. Accordingly, *a generous episiotomy should be the first step in delivery.*

Delivery of the Breech

A. Spontaneous Delivery: It is desirable that the breech be born spontaneously to the level of the umbilicus if there is no indication for extraction. This is especially important in the premature infant because there is no other means of assuring maximum dilatation and retraction of the cervix and lower uterine segment. (In footling or full breech, the mere appearance of the feet through the vulva is not an indication to proceed with delivery, for the cervix may be only partly dilated; rather, it is important to wait for the feet, legs, *and buttocks* to advance through the introitus even though an extended wait may be required.) After delivery of the buttocks, the back normally rotates to the anterior as the shoulders begin to engage. A loop of cord should now be advanced to avoid the shock accompanying traction on the umbilicus.

B. Assisted Delivery:

1. In footling breech, no problem should be encountered and assistance will be unnecessary if the normal mechanism of labor occurs and the back rotates to the anterior as the buttocks advance. In contrast, if the back should rotate posteriorly, the shoulders will engage with the sternum anterior, which may cause great difficulty in delivery of both the shoulders and the head. Consequently, the obstetrician must make certain that the back rotates to the anterior after the buttocks appear.

2. In frank breech, if the buttocks distend the perineum and cannot be expelled, traction should be created by placing the index finger of the right hand in the anterior groin (Fig 40–21). (Inserting more than one finger may dislocate the hip.) This procedure is very tiring, and it is difficult to exert sufficient traction to dislodge the breech using one hand alone. Additional force should be exerted by grasping the right wrist with the left hand. When the posterior groin is accessible, the left index finger may be placed therein

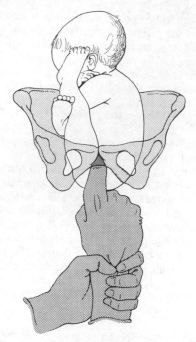

Figure 40–21. Delivery of breech with one finger in the groin. The wrist is supported with the other hand. When the posterior groin is accessible, the index finger of the other hand is placed in it to complete delivery of the breech. (Redrawn and reproduced, with permission, from Greenhill JP: *Obstetrics,* 12th ed. Saunders, 1960.)

and delivery of the breech should be completed easily. The back now rotates (or is rotated) to the anterior. The extended legs still lie within the vagina; they must be disengaged by *upward and outward pressure in the popliteal fossa,* causing the knee to flex and the hip to hyperflex, with the foot emerging laterally (Fig 40–22). A common and serious error by the uninitiated is the attempt to flex the knee in the wrong direction. This may result in fracture of the femur.

C. Breech Extraction (Decomposition or Breaking Up the Breech):

1. Indications–This is one of the most difficult and hazardous of obstetric maneuvers. It is usually reserved for (1) the requirement for instant vaginal delivery; and (2) cases in which, for whatever reason, one is already committed to vaginal delivery and cesarean section is not appropriate or feasible. Breech extraction was formerly considered appropriate for delivery of a second twin, but cesarean section is now preferred. The operation of breech extraction should always be avoided if cesarean section is a reasonable alternative.

2. Technique–The uterus *must* be relaxed. This operation may be impossible to accomplish if the uterus is tight. Deep inhalation anesthesia is required. The entire hand (the right hand if the baby's back and sacrum are to the mother's right; the left hand if they are to the mother's left) should be introduced into the vagina, and the breech should be displaced sufficiently

so that the hand can be passed through the cervix into the uterine cavity. The anterior thigh must be identified and abducted laterally, to cause the knee to flex (Pinard's maneuver) (Fig 40–23).

Flexion should be increased by pressure in the popliteal fossa with the index finger and the middle finger triggered over the lower leg. The foot should be grasped between the index and middle fingers and drawn through the introitus. If this is not too difficult, the other leg may be similarly delivered. If both feet can be delivered, the buttocks now rest in the hollow of the sacrum; if only the anterior leg was delivered, the bitrochanteric diameter usually lies in the AP diameter of the mother's pelvis. In either case, traction and rotation should now be applied simultaneously in such a manner that the breech will advance and the back will rotate to the anterior (Fig 40–24). If only the anterior leg has been delivered, the other leg must be disengaged from the vagina as outlined under assisted delivery of the breech.

3. Complications–Entanglement of the cord may be avoided by noting the position of the cord before the first foot is brought down and disengaged if necessary. Fracture of the lower leg or femur may result, respectively, from too vigorous an effort to bring down the foot inside an incompletely relaxed uterus or from attempts to flex the knee in the wrong direction after delivery of the buttocks. Advancement of the trunk with the back posterior is dangerous principally because of the abnormal mechanism it imposes on both shoulders and head. It results from failure to carry out the rotation maneuver noted above. This problem sometimes may be corrected by Piper's maneuver, in which, under deep anesthesia, the baby's body is lubricated and pushed backward in the birth

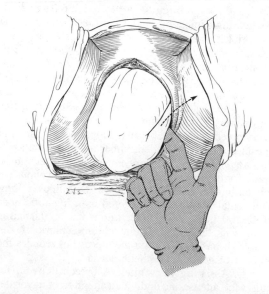

Figure 40–22. Flexion and abduction of thigh to deliver extended leg. (Redrawn and reproduced, with permission, from Llewellyn-Jones D: *Fundamentals of Obstetrics and Gynecology.* Vol 1. Faber & Faber, 1969.)

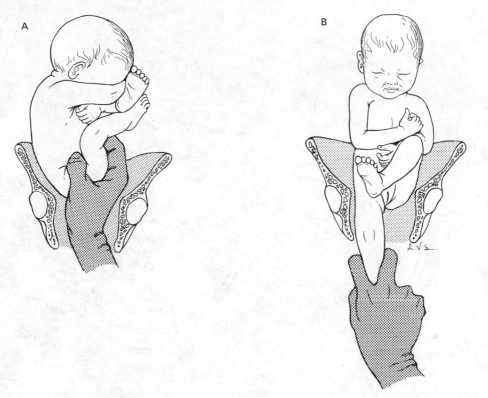

Figure 40–23. Extraction of breech. *A:* Abduction of thigh and pressure in popliteal fossa causing knee to flex and foot to become accessible. *B:* Delivery of leg by traction on foot. (Redrawn and reproduced, with permission, from Benson RC: *Handbook of Obstetrics & Gynecology,* 6th ed. Lange, 1977.)

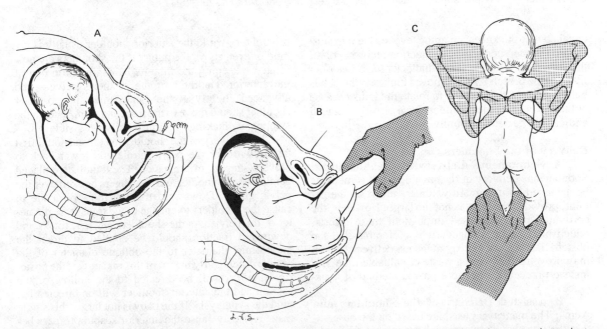

Figure 40–24. Extraction of breech. *A:* Buttocks brought to hollow of sacrum. *B:* Traction on anterior leg causes buttocks to advance and rotate into direct AP diameter of pelvis. Continued downward traction causes the back to rotate anteriorly. *C:* Further downward traction causes the shoulders to engage in the transverse diameter of the inlet. (Redrawn and reproduced, with permission, from Caldwell WE, Studdiford WE: A review of breech deliveries during a 5-year period at the Sloane Hospital for Women. *Am J Obstet Gynecol* 1929; **18**:623.)

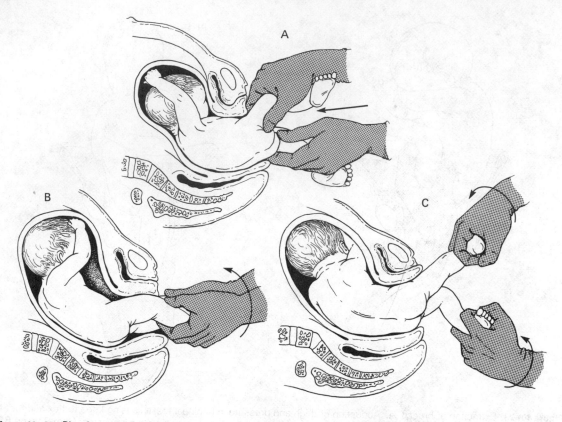

Figure 40–25. Piper's method of dealing with sacrum posterior that results from permitting the breech to advance too far without rotation. *A* and *B:* Fetus is pushed back until buttocks are in hollow of sacrum, causing shoulders to disengage. *C:* Rotation accomplished by traction on anterior leg, as in Fig 40–26B. (Redrawn and reproduced, with permission, from Piper EG, Bachman C: The prevention of fetal injuries in breech delivery. *JAMA* 1929; **92**:217.)

canal so that the knees are at the level of the introitus; rotation is then performed by traction and rotation of the legs (Fig 40–25). If the buttocks have been delivered, the breech *must* be moved higher in the pelvis before any attempt is made to rotate the fetus because at the lower level the shoulders have already engaged and cannot be rotated simply by turning the hips.

Delivery of the Shoulders

A. Spontaneous Delivery of the Shoulders: Spontaneous delivery of the shoulders can sometimes be achieved by maximum voluntary effort by the patient, provided the baby is not too large. However, the cord may be compressed throughout these efforts, which often are prolonged. It is preferable that the obstetrician not attempt spontaneous delivery, which may prove fruitless and a waste of valuable time, but instead proceed at once to a proved method of assistance.

B. Assisted Delivery of the Shoulders and Arms: The maneuvers used are based on the observation that the shoulders approach the inlet in the transverse diameter and that as they engage they rotate either to the AP or an oblique diameter. At the time of this rotation, the posterior shoulder, because of the inclination of the inlet, will have passed the sacral promontory while the anterior shoulder usually is behind or even above the pubis. If the shoulders are now rotated—keeping the infant's back always in one of the anterior quadrants of the mother's pelvis—and advanced slightly at the same time, the posterior shoulder should move to the front and stem beneath the symphysis, making the arm readily accessible.

For delivery of the shoulders, a towel should first be thrown over the pelvic girdle and lower back to prevent slipping of the hands. The thumbs are placed parallel to one another and the fingers hooked over the pelvic girdle. Downward traction must be made to cause the shoulders to engage in the transverse diameter of the pelvis. As the shoulders engage, rotary and downward traction should be applied to direct the bisacromial diameter to the oblique diameter of the mother's pelvis. By means of this maneuver, the posterior shoulder will be directed to the hollow of the sacrum and the anterior shoulder will be directed behind the symphysis. If the baby is not large, this single maneuver may cause the anterior scapula to pass beneath the symphysis, signifying that the anterior shoulder has passed the level of the inlet and that the anterior arm can now be delivered. (It is important that no effort be made to deliver the anterior arm until the angle of the scapula is seen; the attempt invariably will

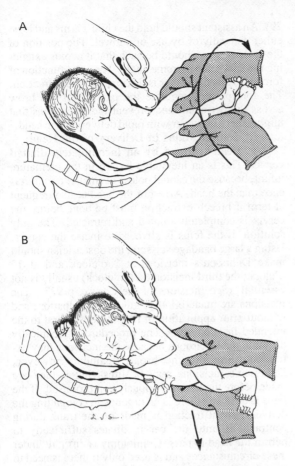

Figure 40–26. Assisted delivery of shoulders, Løvset's maneuver. *A:* Shoulders engaged, posterior (right) shoulder at lower level in pelvis than anterior shoulder. *B:* Rotation of trunk causing posterior shoulder to rotate to anterior and stem beneath symphysis. (Redrawn and reproduced, with permission, from Løvset J: Shoulder delivery by breech presentation. *J Obstet Gynaecol Br Commonw* 1937; 44:696.

be futile, and the effort wastes time.)

If the baby is large, the first rotation will merely bring the anterior shoulder behind the symphysis and the arm will not be accessible. In this case, downward traction and rotation in the opposite direction cause the posterior shoulder—which is at a lower level in the pelvis—to rotate to the anterior and to stem beneath the symphysis (Løvset's maneuver) (Fig 40–26). The arm can now be delivered either by hooking the fingers in the antecubital fossa (fingers parallel to the humerus) or, as recommended by Potter, by pushing the lateral aspect of the scapula toward the fetal spine and under the symphysis, causing the arm and shoulder to deliver immediately. By applying downward traction, the trunk is now rotated to the opposite oblique diameter, moving the posterior shoulder to the anterior at a lower level, causing the scapula to appear, and making the arm accessible. According to this technique, each shoulder will be delivered as an anterior shoulder.

An alternative method is preferred by the author when the first scapular angle (assume it is the right) has stemmed beneath the symphysis. The operator's right hand is inserted laterally so that the fingers hook the humerus and upper forearm. With the operator's left hand grasping the breech, the body is now turned clockwise through a 90-degree angle to the opposite oblique diameter; simultaneously, the operator's right hand causes the baby's right arm to be swept downward over the chest to deliver posteriorly. As a result of this movement, the left scapula appears beneath the symphysis and the left arm is delivered either laterally or, if space is insufficient, by repeating the maneuver in a counterclockwise direction so the arm can be delivered posteriorly as was done with the first arm.

The priorities for the various shoulder maneuvers are not entirely clear. Potter and Løvset were both prominent in recommending delivery of the shoulders one at a time, anterior first, and converting the second (posterior) shoulder to the anterior for delivery. The Potter maneuver refers only to scapular pressure to effect delivery of the anterior arm after the scapular angle has been brought beneath the symphysis. The alternative method described above was used by W.C. Danforth beginning in the early 1930s, but no description of it can be found.

Delivery of the Head

Cerebral and spinal cord injuries attributable to breech delivery are sustained at the crucial point of delivery of the head. In all maneuvers concerned with delivery of the head, it is of vital importance that *no* traction be applied to the shoulders and that there be *no* hyperextension of the neck. If there is no cephalopelvic disproportion, the aftercoming head engages in the OT position in gynecoid, android, and flat pelves. In the anthropoid pelvis, if the back is anterior, the head engages in the direct OA position. For this reason, and also because the pelvic diameters increase with advancing station, the anthropoid pelvis allows easier breech delivery.

A. Assisted Delivery of the Head: As a rule, the head engages spontaneously as the shoulders are delivered. If the position is OT at the inlet, spontaneous rotation usually occurs as the head advances toward the hollow of the sacrum. Many maneuvers have been recommended; the 2 most commonly used are those of Wigand and of Mauriceau-Smellie-Veit. These are illustrated in Figs 40–27 and 40–28. One or the other may be tried, but forceps should be applied if the head does not quickly advance *without* traction. Most obstetricians prefer to apply forceps at once, without a trial of either of these maneuvers.

B. Forceps Delivery of the Aftercoming Head: The Piper forceps was designed specifically to solve this problem and is preferred. Forceps should be immediately available and opened on the scrub table for each breech delivery. The conditions for application of forceps to the aftercoming head are the same as for forceps application in vertex presentations: The cervix must be fully dilated and the head must be fully en-

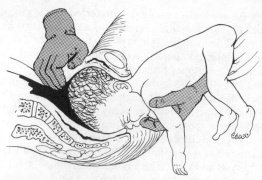

Figure 40–27. Wigand maneuver for delivery of head. Fingers of left hand inserted into infant's mouth or over mandible; right hand exerting pressure on head from above. (Modified and reproduced, with permission, from Benson RC: *Handbook of Obstetrics & Gynecology,* 7th ed. Lange, 1980.)

gaged in the pelvis and must present correctly. The OA presentation is ideal, and an oblique anterior presentation is acceptable. OT presentation is not desirable. Posterior presentations are unsatisfactory, but the application of forceps should be attempted.

1. Indications–If the baby is in danger, it is best to apply forceps immediately. It is entirely proper to apply forceps electively without any attempt to use the Wigand or Mauriceau-Smellie-Veit maneuver. Equally acceptably, the obstetrician may try the Wigand maneuver if the breech and shoulders cause no problem and the baby's condition is good. If the maneuver is not immediately successful, forceps should be applied.

2. Technique–The technique consists of aiming the blades of the forceps from below directly at the sides of the head without rotating the blades (Fig 40–

29). An assistant should hold the child's arms and legs, either manually or by use of a towel. The position of the child's trunk should be such that it avoids extending the neck at an extreme angle. The chief function of forceps in this maneuver is flexion rather than traction. The forceps also regulate the passage of the brow across the perineum and prevent the lacerations that might otherwise occur with rapid delivery of the head.

C. Complications in Delivery of the Head:

1. Head trapped by an incompletely dilated cervix–This is an inevitable hazard in the premature infant, because the caudal pole is of smaller circumference than the head. Arrest of the head is also frequent at term if breech extraction must be done before the cervix is completely dilated and retracted. The only solution, if the fetus is alive, is to incise the cervix. Using a large bandage scissors, the obstetrician should make Dührssen's incisions at 2 o'clock and at 10 o'clock; the third incision (at 6 o'clock) usually is not essential. (See Incisions of the Cervix, p 937.) The incisions are made blindly, guided by palpation, and without prior application of ring forceps lateral to the intended incision sites. The procedure is technically difficult and hazardous because the incisions may extend upward into the broad ligament; however, Dührssen's incisions may be lifesaving if they are made before the fetus is seriously compromised. If the fetus is dead and there is no urgency in completing the delivery, slight traction is made on the trunk during contractions until the cervix dilates sufficiently to permit the head to pass. Craniotomy is difficult under these circumstances and is used only if there is need to complete the delivery at once.

2. Head trapped by spasm of the lower uterine segment–This is one of the hazards of conduction anesthesia, in which uterine tone may be increased, or of tedious labor, in which excessive irritability of the

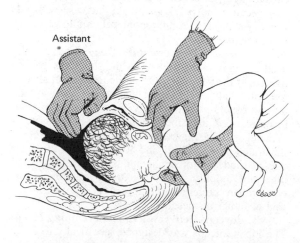

Figure 40–28. Mauriceau-Smellie-Veit maneuver for delivery of head. Fingers of left hand inserted into infant's mouth or over mandible; fingers of right hand curved over shoulders. Assistant exerts suprapubic pressure on head. (Reproduced, with permission, from Benson RC: *Handbook of Obstetrics & Gynecology,* 7th ed. Lange, 1980.)

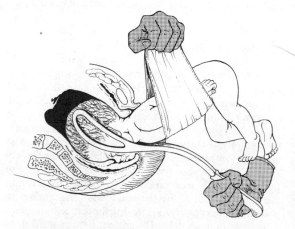

Figure 40–29. Application of Piper forceps, employing Savage's towel sling support. Forceps are introduced from below, left blade first, aiming directly at intended positions on sides of head. (Reproduced, with permission, from Benson RC: *Handbook of Obstetrics & Gynecology,* 7th ed. Lange, 1980.)

INCISIONS OF THE CERVIX
(Dührssen's Incisions)

Dührssen's incisions are those made in the cervix to enlarge the birth canal and make certain that the opening is adequate for delivery. Such incisions have a limited place in modern obstetrics but may be lifesaving if immediate delivery is mandatory and the cervix offers the *only* obstruction to delivery.

The incisions are made (1) when death will result from fetal distress unless delivery is accomplished within minutes, and (2) when the aftercoming head is trapped by an incompletely dilated cervix. In all cases of breech presentation, and especially in the case of the premature infant, the unmolded head may be larger than the breech, and the cervix, although dilated sufficiently to accommodate the breech, may trap the aftercoming head. This is less likely to occur if the cervix has been drawn upward as high as it will go and the breech is allowed to deliver spontaneously to the umbilicus. The possible need for cervical incision should be anticipated in all cases of breech presentation in which early intervention and delivery are necessary during the second stage.

In vertex presentation, Dührssen's incisions are safe only if the following conditions are rigidly observed: (1) The cervix must be partially effaced and dilated more than 6 cm. (2) The head must be engaged to a station of not less than +3. (3) There must be no impediment to delivery except the cervix, and, after incision, easy delivery by outlet or low forceps must be feasible. (4) There must be a clear requirement for delivery more quickly than could be accomplished by cesarean section.

Cervical incisions may be dangerous if all of the foregoing conditions do not obtain. When the head is not deeply engaged, the cervical incisions may extend even into the broad ligament as the head is advanced. In some cases, failure of the cervix to dilate may be the result of midpelvic obstruction that prevents the head from fitting well into the cervix; in such a case, the cervical incisions are only the beginning of an extremely difficult and hazardous delivery.

Classically, Dührssen's incisions are made at 2, 6, and 10 o'clock. If the head is low enough and the cervix is dilated more than 6 cm, the 2 anterior incisions usually will suffice. Some prefer to make the incisions laterally (eg, at 3 and 9 o'clock) at the site where spontaneous lacerations are most apt to occur; others prefer "southeast and southwest." The exact site is unimportant as long as it is accessible and the incisions avoid the anterior cervical quadrant. The cervix should not be clamped before it is cut; bleeding at this stage is usually minimal, and the clamps only get in the way. With the middle finger placed inside the cervix and the index finger apposed on the external aspect of the cervix, the incision is made blindly using bandage scissors. The incision should stop short of the vaginal reflection.

After delivery, the incisions are closed by grasping the edges with sponge forceps and placing interrupted sutures at least 1 cm from the edge of the incisions. It is preferable not to place sutures in the cervical mucosa. A suture should be placed at the exact apex of the incision to control subsequent bleeding; posterior and lateral retractors are most helpful in accomplishing this step. If the apex cannot be visualized, a suture should be placed at the highest accessible point, and, using this for traction, sutures should be placed at successively higher points until the apex is reached.

---

uterus results. Arrest is diagnosed by passing the hand upward through the lax cervix until the constriction is encountered. Deep general anesthesia will be needed to relax the uterus, but if the induction requires more than 2 minutes it will be too late. Give thiopental and succinylcholine at once through the intravenous catheter. Administer halothane in concentrations of up to 2% immediately. If feasible, the cord should be protected from compression until the uterus relaxes.

3. Occiput posterior presentation–This rarely occurs if the delivery has been properly conducted from the outset, because the head necessarily engages as an OA if the back faces upward after delivery of the breech. In the case of nuchal arms, the posterior arm usually can be freed without incident, but if the anterior arm is not accessible the shoulders may have to be counterrotated, sternum upward, before the arm can be released; posterior engagement of the occiput should then follow. If the midpelvis and outlet are large enough, rotation to the OA sometimes can be accomplished after the shoulders have been delivered. The child should be grasped as for the Mauriceau-Smellie-Veit maneuver and the trunk and head caused to rotate *as a single unit* (the neck will be broken if only the trunk or thorax is turned). If this fails, Piper forceps must be applied to the occiput posterior, the infant's feet carried upward toward the mother's abdomen, and the head extracted. If the head extends and the chin lodges behind the symphysis, the Prague maneuver is indicated, in which the operator's left hand is slipped posteriorly along the infant's back to its neck; the fingers are hooked over the shoulders and gentle traction is made, supplemented by suprapubic pressure in the axis of the birth canal. The infant's body must be elevated in an arc high over the mother's abdomen and the occiput eased out over the perineum. OP is an unusual and unfortunate complication of breech delivery. Craniotomy should be elected if the baby does not survive the necessary manipulations, or if the fetus cannot be delivered using one of the aforementioned techniques.

4. Hydrocephalus–Hydrocephalus is commonly associated with breech presentation. If it is diagnosed before labor, withdrawal of cerebrospinal fluid by transabdominal encephalocentesis can reduce the size of the head sufficiently that vaginal delivery may occur without incident. If this is not feasible, the breech and shoulders should be delivered according to standard procedure. The back should be rotated to the direct anterior position and the skin incised over the 2 highest spinous processes that can be readily palpated. Laminectomy should be performed by incising the laminae on either side. The tip of a uterine dressing forceps should be introduced into the opening in the spinal canal and forced upward into the cranial cavity. The forceps should then be rotated to enlarge the tract. Pressure on the head from above will cause the cerebrospinal fluid to drain, and the decompressed head should advance without incident.

VERSION

Version is an obstetric operation whose purpose is to change the position of the fetus with reference to the mother in order to achieve a more favorable position for delivery. The maneuver is termed **cephalic** or **podalic** version, according to the pole of the fetus that is brought into presentation. Three kinds of version are recognized: (1) **External cephalic version** (see p 927) uses external manipulations to convert a breech presentation to a vertex. (2) **Internal podalic version** employs intrauterine manipulations to convert a cephalic presentation to a breech. (This designation is not entirely accurate, because assistance by the external hand is an integral part of the procedure.) (3) **Combined (internal and external) version (Braxton Hicks version)** is similar to internal podalic version except that it is usually conducted with 2 fingers through a partially dilated cervix. This operation has no place in modern obstetrics.

General Considerations

The indications for external cephalic version are outlined on p 927. Internal podalic version is all but obsolete, and the indications have become quite narrow. Formerly, version was considered an appropriate recourse in transverse and oblique presentations, arm prolapse, posterior chin presentation, persistent brow presentation, high or unengaged occiput posterior presentation, failed forceps, and, indeed, most conditions of the mother or baby for which prompt delivery was indicated. Among the patients so managed, the incidence of uterine rupture was high, and the perinatal results were poor. Version is now virtually outmoded in the management of any of the problems mentioned above, and with rare exceptions they should be dealt with by cesarean section. Some texts suggest that version may be applicable in the patient with transverse lie if the membranes are intact, the cervix fully dilated, and the pelvis of proved adequacy; it is the author's conviction that any patient in labor with transverse lie should be delivered by cesarean section, regardless of whether the baby is alive or dead and irrespective of how favorable the outlook for vaginal delivery may appear to be.

The only modern indication for internal podalic version is delivery of a second twin, and even this indication requires qualification. In delivery of the second twin, version was formerly considered the method of choice, but it is now apparent that the chances for fetal survival are better if the head of the second twin can be directed into the pelvis for subsequent delivery as a vertex. Version should be reserved for cases in which the head cannot be caused to engage immediately and in which cesarean section is not feasible.

Despite the precarious status of podalic version in modern obstetrics, the technique is one that the obstetrician must be prepared to use in the extraordinary case for which it may be needed.

Technique

The technique of internal podalic version is as follows: With the uterus relaxed under deep general anesthesia, the presenting part should be displaced and the hand introduced into the uterus on the side of the fetus's abdomen to grasp the feet. As the feet are drawn

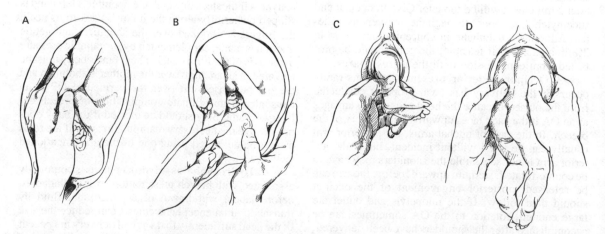

Figure 40–30. Version and extraction. *A:* Feet are grasped. *B:* Baby is turned; hand on abdomen pushes head toward uterine fundus. *C:* Feet are extracted. *D:* Torso is delivered. From this point onward, procedure is same as for uncomplicated breech delivery. (Reproduced, with permission, from EL DeCosta. In: *Textbook of Obstetrics and Gynecology,* 3rd ed. Danforth DN [editor]. Harper & Row, 1977.)

into the vagina, the external hand must move the head toward the fundus. When the version is completed, delivery is conducted as for footling breech presentation.

Complications & Prognosis

When the indications for version and extraction were more liberal (before 1950), the maternal mortality rate attributed to the operation accounted for almost 5% of all maternal deaths. The deaths were predominantly due to rupture of the uterus and its complications. No accurate appraisal can be made of the perinatal mortality rate; reports vary from 5 to 25%. Cerebral hemorrhage and asphyxia were frequently listed in the death certificates. In infants who survived, fractures, dislocations, epiphyseal separation, and neurologic deficits occurred with some regularity.

COMPOUND PRESENTATION

Compound presentation is a rare presentation in which a hand or a foot prolapses or presents together with the presenting part, which may be either the breech or the head. The most common variety is a hand alongside the presenting head. This usually is an unimportant complication because the presenting part will generally be well into the lower uterine segment and inlet, and the prolapsed extremity tends either to remain in the same position or to slide upward as the presenting part advances. Nonetheless, some cases of compound presentation are variants of transverse lie, with the head or breech off to one side and the extremity prolapsed from the opposite side. In these instances, cord prolapse is a major hazard. If the extremity cannot be replaced in the uterus by the most gentle manipulations and if the presenting part cannot be caused to enter the pelvis, delivery should be accomplished as for transverse lie, ie, by immediate cesarean section. During the preparations for cesarean section, the examiner's hand should remain in the vagina to protect the cord in the event of prolapse.

CESAREAN SECTION

The term cesarean section denotes the delivery, after 28 weeks' gestation, of fetus, placenta, and membranes through an incision in the abdominal and uterine walls. This definition excludes the obsolete operation of vaginal cesarean section, in which transvaginal access to the fetus is achieved by incising the anterior lip of the cervix and lower uterine segment. The term also excludes the operation involving the recovery, through an abdominal incision, of a fetus lying free in the abdominal cavity after secondary implantation or uterine rupture.

The transabdominal delivery of a previable baby is sometimes called a miniature cesarean section; the correct term is abdominal hysterotomy.

The first cesarean section performed on a patient is known as primary cesarean section; subsequent ones are referred to as secondary, tertiary, etc, or simply as repeat cesarean section.

An elective cesarean section is one that is performed before the onset of labor or before the appearance of any complication that might constitute an urgent indication.

Historical Note

Historians agree that the term "cesarean section" has nothing to do with the birth of Julius Caesar. It has been suggested that the term is derived from the *lex caesarea*, a decree said to have continued under the rule of the Caesars from the time of Numa Pompilius (715–672 BC) requiring that before burial of the mother the child be removed from the uterus of any woman dying in late pregnancy. Certain historians also disapprove of this derivation. The term probably derives from the Latin word *caedere*, "to cut" (past participle *caesum*, "cut").

The first documented operation on a living patient (who died on the 25th postoperative day) was done in 1610. The first successful cesarean section in the USA was done in a cabin near Staunton, Virginia, in 1794; both mother and baby survived.

In early cesarean sections, no sutures were placed in the uterus, and sepsis was likely in those who survived the initial hemorrhage from the open uterine sinuses. Two reports, in 1876 and 1882, did much to lower the mortality rate, which theretofore had varied from 50 to 85%. The first, by Porro, concerned a patient in whom the corpus uteri was excised because of uncontrollable hemorrhage from the uterine wound. He sutured the cervix into the lower angle of the incision for drainage. Although the operation was extremely formidable, it provided a means of controlling hemorrhage; in addition, it prevented the later development of metritis and parametritis that led so often to peritonitis and death.

The second report, by Sänger, emphasized the desirability of suturing the uterine defect before closing the abdomen. In the latter part of the 19th century, the advent of anesthesia and aseptic surgical techniques resulted in a further reduction of the mortality rate. The term Porro operation is still used inaccurately (although with decreasing frequency) to designate the procedure of cesarean section–hysterectomy; the Sänger operation is now known as classic cesarean section, in which the uterine incision is made in a longitudinal direction through the corpus uteri.

The lower uterine segment or low cervical cesarean section was designed, performed, and recommended by Osiander in 1805 but gained no recognition until 1906, when Frank recalled Osiander's operation and made the first of many modifications. The place of this operation in modern obstetrics was largely established by DeLee's repeated emphasis upon its safety and relative lack of immediate and late sequelae as compared with the Sänger incision. DeLee's enthusiasm was not greeted by universal accord, and criticism arose from high places. In 1919, J. Whitridge Williams, responding to DeLee's thesis, declared that when "the old-fashioned, conservative (classic) operation is properly done, the danger of a weakened scar is very slight, and the probability of rupture remote." Williams' opinions have proved to be in error.

Before the advent of antibiotics, it was recognized that after the membranes had been ruptured for 10–12 hours, the performance of cesarean section imposed a great threat of intractable sepsis; indeed, with each hour that passed, the hazard increased by almost geometric progression. Accordingly, it soon became an all but inviolable rule that cesarean section was forbidden for any patient in whom the membranes had been ruptured for more than 12 hours and that, regardless of the problem, delivery was to be accomplished vaginally. This policy saved the lives of many women, but in cases of cephalopelvic disproportion it also imposed a need for craniotomy, sometimes upon the living baby.

Today, refinements in surgical technique, asepsis, antibiotic therapy, blood transfusion, and anesthesia have reduced but not eliminated the risk of cesarean section. The attainment of good results requires appropriate surgical and perinatal conditions and full knowledge of the possible consequences of deviating from the principles upon which this major operation is based.

General Considerations

In the past 15 years, the cesarean section rate has steadily increased from about 5% to 15%. Most of this is due to increasing avoidance of midforceps and vaginal breech delivery and, as a result of fetal monitoring, to greater awareness of serious fetal distress. Also, an increase in the primary cesarean section rate is followed by a greater number of repeat cesarean sections in subsequent years.

Cesarean section is not to be taken lightly, and unless the indications are unmistakable one should pause to consider its risks versus its benefits. The maternal mortality rate associated with cesarean section varies in different series from 4 per 10,000 to 8 per 10,000. In one series, the risk of death from cesarean section was found to be 26 times greater than with vaginal delivery. Ledger observed that the most seriously ill of all postpartum patients with hospital-acquired infections are those who have been monitored by internal leads and come to cesarean section. As to the fetal effects, it is clear that cesarean section is far preferable to a difficult vaginal delivery, but there is no conclusive proof that very liberal use of cesarean section has done anything to improve the mental performance or reduce the incidence of neurologic deficits of children or adults in our population.

Indications

Cesarean section is employed in cases in which vaginal delivery either is not feasible or would impose undue risk on mother or baby. Some of the indications are clear and absolute (eg, central placenta previa, obvious cephalopelvic disproportion); others are relative. In some cases, fine judgment is needed to determine whether cesarean section or vaginal delivery would be better.

It is not possible to prepare a complete list of indications, for there is hardly an obstetric complication that has not been dealt with by cesarean section. The following indications are most frequent.

A. Cephalopelvic Disproportion: Cases in which the head is too large to come through the pelvis should be managed by cesarean section. The term contracted pelvis is sometimes listed as an indication; this is not a precise designation because a small baby can sometimes negotiate a small pelvis, just as a large pelvis may be inadequate for a very large baby.

Extreme cases of cephalopelvic disproportion can sometimes be identified before the onset of labor, whereas in others a trial or test of labor is required. A **test of labor** is defined as 2 hours of good voluntary effort in the second stage of labor with ruptured membranes. If the baby cannot be safely delivered vaginally by this time, cesarean section is elected. In a **trial of labor** this conclusion is reached either prior to full dilatation of the cervix or before 2 hours of the second stage have elapsed.

Test of labor is now a rarity. Fetal monitoring is used in cases of possible disproportion, and evidence of fetal distress almost always appears before the test can be completed. If the head fails to descend at an appropriate rate, cesarean section is usually the proper course.

Inlet disproportion can often be diagnosed with reasonable accuracy by x-ray pelvimetry and cephalometry. In the primigravida, it can be suspected if the patient begins labor with the fetal head unengaged; in a significant number of such patients, the head will fail to engage and cesarean section will be indicated.

Midpelvic disproportion may be suspected if the AP diameter is short, the ischial spines very prominent, and the baby large. Cesarean section should be selected, usually after a trial of labor, if the head can still be felt above the symphysis or if the vertex fails to advance beyond station +2. A trial of forceps may or may not be necessary to make this decision.

Outlet disproportion usually requires a trial of forceps before one can decide definitely that safe vaginal delivery is not possible. In general, x-ray pelvimetry and digital examination are unsatisfactory for assessment of the outlet.

B. Uterine Inertia: Uterine inertia (either primary or secondary to abnormal fetal positions) is a common indication for cesarean section. A partogram, preferably using Studd's stencil, can be extremely helpful in evaluating the course of labor and in bringing instant attention to the appearance of uterine inertia. If the cervix fails to dilate at a rate of 1 cm/h, one should recognize the possibility of dysfunctional labor. As noted elsewhere in this book, many of these cases are resolved by oxytocin infusion, but if not, cesarean section is appropriate.

C. Placenta Previa: If expectant treatment is not

suitable because the pregnancy has proceeded beyond 36 weeks or because bleeding from the uterus is severe, cesarean section should be performed if the placenta is found on "double set-up examination" (examination done with preparations made for either vaginal or cesarean delivery) to cover more than 30% of the external os. The double set-up examination should be omitted and cesarean section performed immediately if the symptoms of placenta previa are unmistakable or if unremitting bleeding produces impending or actual hypovolemic shock. Vaginal examination in such cases only worsens the bleeding and delays delivery. If it should happen that placenta previa is not confirmed at cesarean section, a meticulous search must be made for obscure sites of bleeding from vaginal or cervical lesions. Evaluation and treatment of the problem will be much simpler after the baby has been delivered.

D. Premature Separation of the Placenta: In *all* cases of definite abruptio placentae the membranes should be ruptured at once, regardless of the intended method of delivery, the degree of separation, or the development of shock. In **moderate abruption** (ie, separation of more than one-fourth but less than two-thirds of the placental surface), cesarean section should be selected (1) if fetal distress occurs; (2) if effective labor does not immediately follow rupture of the membranes; or (3) if vaginal delivery is unlikely to occur within 2 hours. In **severe abruption** (separation of more than two-thirds of the placental surface), cesarean section should be selected only (1) if the baby is still alive; (2) if effective labor does not immediately follow rupture of the membranes; or (3) if vaginal delivery cannot be anticipated within 2 hours.

E. Malposition and Malpresentation: Posterior chin position and transverse lie in labor are in themselves indications for cesarean section; attempts to convert these positions to favorable ones are almost invariably futile and may be damaging. Brow presentation during labor warrants cesarean section unless a cautious attempt at conversion to an occipital or anterior chin position is successful. Shoulder presentation and compound presentation are variants of transverse lie and, with few exceptions, are best managed by cesarean section.

F. Preeclampsia-Eclampsia: Medical management is of course an integral part of the treatment of preeclampsia-eclampsia, but the definitive treatment is delivery. If induction of labor is not feasible, the solution is cesarean section.

G. Fetal Distress: Fetal monitoring both before labor (nonstressed and stressed techniques) and during labor has disclosed fetal problems that would not otherwise be evident and, consequently, has increased slightly the number of cesarean sections performed for the indication of fetal distress or fetal jeopardy.

H. Cord Prolapse: This complication must be treated by the most expeditious method. If the conditions are such that immediate vaginal delivery would be hazardous to the mother or the baby, the patient should be placed in the Trendelenburg position, the cord protected by the index and middle fingers inside the cervix between the head and the uterine wall, and cesarean section should be performed without changing this position or altering the digital protection of the cord.

I. Diabetes, Erythroblastosis, and Other Threatening Conditions: In such conditions as diabetes, Rh incompatibility, or postterm pregnancy, fetal welfare is usually monitored by nonstress or stress testing (oxytocin challenge test) or by estriol studies. If the well-being of the fetus seems compromised, it should be decided, first, *when* to deliver, and second, *how* to deliver the fetus. For the most part, a nonreactive nonstress test followed by a positive oxytocin challenge test (late deceleration of fetal heart tones) is an indication for delivery by cesarean section. If the challenge test is negative (no late deceleration of fetal heart tones) but estriol levels are falling, induction of labor may be appropriate if the conditions for induction are extremely favorable. The membranes should be ruptured and oxytocin stimulation begun if needed. Cesarean section should be employed if vaginal delivery cannot be anticipated within a reasonable time. If the delay involved in induction of labor cannot be justified or if conditions are unfavorable, immediate cesarean section should be chosen. It is usually fruitless to attempt to induce labor without rupturing the membranes simply in order to avoid a total commitment. The induction is either appropriate or it is not. If it is, one should proceed by the most effective means; if it is not, no attempt should be made.

J. Carcinoma of the Cervix: Cesarean section followed by definitive treatment is indicated when invasive carcinoma of the cervix is diagnosed after 28 weeks of gestation. If it is diagnosed before the fetus becomes viable, there is general agreement that the disease should be dealt with either by radical hysterectomy or by external radiation and radium therapy. External radiation of this order is damaging to the conceptus, and abortion usually follows; if it does not, the pregnancy should be terminated.

Colposcopy is applicable in pregnancy, and, indeed, its accuracy may be enhanced by the physiologic cervical eversion of pregnancy. If preinvasive carcinoma of the cervix is diagnosed by this means and directed biopsy—or by primary biopsy—the consensus is to permit vaginal delivery (unless there is another indication for cesarean section) and, 3 months after delivery, to repeat such studies as may be needed for definitive staging and treatment.

K. The X Factor: In addition to the absolute indications for cesarean section, there are also relative indications which, considered separately, might not warrant this mode of delivery but which taken together do constitute a valid indication. Eastman, in referring to postmaturity, termed these "X" factors: Cesarean section would not be indicated because of postmaturity alone or because of X alone, but it could be indicated because of postmaturity plus X. X might stand for such factors as elderly primigravida, prior infertility problem, ruptured membranes but patient not in labor, or diabetes.

L. Cervical Dystocia: In former years, failure of the cervix to dilate properly was considered to be invariably due to incoordinate uterine action. In fact, most cases do result from uterine inertia, but some are the result of cervical scarring following deep cauterization or conization, and some occur following failure of the connective tissue mechanisms normally responsible for effacement of the cervix. Although the presence of an additional X factor is often useful in electing cesarean section in cases of cervical dystocia, cesarean section—in the absence of an X factor—may be appropriate for the patient whose cervix remains rigid and fails to dilate more than 3–4 cm despite strong, frequent first stage uterine contractions.

M. Previous Uterine Incision: A previous uterine incision such as a myomectomy or prior cesarean section may weaken the uterine wall or predispose to rupture if labor is permitted. The outmoded but entrenched maxim—"Once a cesarean, always a cesarean"—has many supporters. There is now ample evidence, however, that many uterine scars are indeed firm and that many patients who have had a prior uncomplicated cesarean section can be delivered easily and with less hazard vaginally than by repeat cesarean section. In general, post-cesarean section patients who are suitable candidates for vaginal delivery are (1) those whose operation was of the low cervical (not classic) type; (2) those who begin labor before the estimated date of confinement; and (3) those who enter the labor suite with the head well engaged and the cervix soft, anterior, effaced, and dilated at least 3 cm. In such cases it is entirely appropriate to rupture the membranes and await progress. One should be prepared for immediate cesarean section if there is delay or other abnormality of labor or if vaginal bleeding, pain, etc, indicate rupture of the scar. In general, elective repeat cesarean section is indicated (1) for those whose first cesarean section was done because of cephalopelvic disproportion; (2) for those whose labor is likely to be long and tedious (eg, when the patient enters the hospital with ruptured membranes, a high presenting part, and an uneffaced, rigid cervix); (3) for those who have had a prior classic cesarean section or myomectomy (unless a short, easy labor and an uncomplicated vaginal delivery can be confidently predicted); (4) for those who, after viability is reached, experience persistent pain in the region of the uterine incision; and (5) for those who are 1 week overdue with a baby estimated to be at term. Following the above rules, the first pregnancy of one of the author's patients was delivered by cesarean section, the second vaginally, the third by cesarean section, and the fourth and fifth vaginally. The first cesarean section was done because of preeclampsia; in the other pregnancies, the decision about mode of delivery was made either at term or after admission to the hospital. More recently, the practice of planned vaginal delivery in selected cases after one low cervical cesarean section is gaining popularity. Its purpose, of course, is to avoid if possible the inherent risks of cesarean section. Since most cesarean section scars, if they are going to rupture, do so prior to the onset of labor, the author prefers to make no decision about mode of delivery until late in pregnancy, when the obstetric status can be properly evaluated, or until the patient is admitted in labor; at this time, the route of delivery is selected that will be safest and easiest for both mother and baby. If vaginal delivery is allowed to proceed, alert surveillance is essential, since some cesarean section scars do rupture during labor. In the Merrill and Gibbs series, 3 scars ruptured in labor among 526 such patients.

The major hazard in the performance of elective repeat cesarean section is miscalculation of dates with consequent delivery of a premature baby. Amniocentesis with estimation of surfactant in amniotic fluid is a definitive method of ascertaining fetal age. Serial ultrasound scans during pregnancy (at 15–18 weeks, then at 20–22 weeks, and again at 26–30 weeks) can be helpful in verifying fetal maturity. Such scans are of course essential in determining a reasonable date for repeat cesarean section if the menstrual dates are uncertain or if the timing of the pregnancy is uncertain—for example, because of oral contraception or amenorrhea prior to conception.

N. Other Indications: Unusual and infrequent indications for cesarean section include tumor obstructing the birth canal, a prior extensive vaginal plastic operation, severe heart disease or other debilitating condition in which vaginal delivery would impose a greater threat than cesarean section, and herpes genitalis.

Contraindications

The major contraindication to cesarean section is absence of an appropriate indication. Pyogenic infections of the abdominal wall, an abnormal fetus, a dead one, and lack of appropriate facilities or assistants have been suggested as contraindications. In each instance, the hazard of performing an indicated operation in the face of an alleged contraindication must be weighed against the possible consequence of not performing it.

Preparation for Cesarean Section

A. Ultrasound Scan: If serial scans were not done earlier in pregnancy, a scan is desirable prior to nonemergent operations to determine the position and size of the baby, to rule out gross abnormality or twins, and to determine the location of the placenta.

B. Timing: The low cervical technique, which is preferred for almost all cesarean sections, is simpler to perform if the lower uterine segment changes of early labor have developed and the bladder fold of peritoneum has advanced upward; hence, for elective repeat cesarean section, it may be desirable to await the onset of labor. The wait will also ensure that the baby has attained maximum development before delivery. As to the time of day, no operation should be deliberately undertaken during off hours if it can be safely deferred until full staff and full laboratory facilities are available.

C. Blood for Transfusion: Except in extraordinary emergency (when more may be needed), 2 units of matched blood should be at hand before surgery.

D. Preoperative Preparation: Preoperative sedatives should be avoided. A clear antacid (eg, 15 mL of 0.3 M sodium citrate in 20% syrup) should be given 1 hour before operation to minimize the effects of aspiration if it should occur during anesthesia. An intravenous 18-gauge needle should be in place and 5% dextrose in water running before the operation begins. A Foley catheter should be in place, and 5 mL of indigo carmine should have been instilled in the bladder to facilitate the recognition of any bladder injury. Surgical preparation (shaving, antisepsis, enema) is the same as for any other abdominal surgical procedure.

Procedural Details

A. Prophylactic Antibiotics: In patients who are at minimal risk for infection, prophylactic antibiotics are not recommended prior to cesarean section. Such patients include those having repeat cesarean section and those in whom vaginal examination is not done after admission to the hospital.

Women at risk for infection include those with premature rupture of the membranes, prolonged labor, invasive methods of monitoring, and trial or failed forceps. If the membranes are ruptured longer than 12 hours, there is a likelihood of chorioamnionitis, and therapeutic antibiotics should be used. In other cases, prophylactic antibiotics are appropriate and have been found to reduce significantly the incidence of postcesarean morbidity. One regimen employs cefazolin (Ancef, Kefzol) and cephalothin (Keflin). Give cefazolin, 1 g intramuscularly on call to the operating room; and cephalothin, 2 g intravenously at 6, 12, and 24 hours after the preoperative dose of cefazolin. Aerobic and anaerobic cultures should be taken of the uterine cavity, preferably from a dry area, before delivery of the placenta.

B. Anesthesia: General anesthesia (thiopental induction, nitrous oxide with succinylcholine chloride) is usually preferred if it can be anticipated that the baby will be delivered within 4–5 minutes. Lumbar epidural or spinal anesthesia may be used if a longer interval is likely or, in an emergency, if the patient has eaten within 4–6 hours of the onset of labor. The chief objection to spinal anesthesia is that the uterus is relatively tight, and delivery of the baby may be more difficult; also, hypotension is not uncommon, and the pressor agents used to control it may compound the tendency to fetal asphyxia by constriction of the uterine arteries. (See also Chapter 30.)

C. Position on the Table: Placing the patient in the Trendelenburg position at an angle of 25–30 degrees may be extremely helpful during dissection of the bladder fold and disengagement of the fetal head. If the head is deeply engaged, upward pressure from below by an assistant may be needed.

Tilting the patient slightly to the left moves the uterus to the left of the midline and minimizes pressure on the inferior vena cava.

D. Abdominal Incision: There is difference of opinion regarding the abdominal incision. An increasing number of obstetricians use the transverse incision with or without transection of the rectus muscles because wound dehiscence and postoperative incisional hernia are rare and because the cosmetic result is usually better. Others, including the author, prefer the midline suprapubic incision because it is much quicker, and the exposure for expeditious delivery and dealing with uterine bleeding (by hysterectomy if needed) is usually better.

E. Uterine Incision: Before the uterine incision is made, laparotomy pads that have been soaked in warm saline and wrung out should be placed on either side of the uterus to catch the spill of amniotic fluid. The degree of dextrorotation should also be determined by noting the position of the round ligaments so that the uterine incision will be centered. Torsion should not be corrected; instead, access to the midline should be obtained by retraction of the abdominal wall to the patient's right.

F. Heavy Bleeding: Heavy bleeding from large sinuses in the uterine incision usually can be controlled with large T clamps, but lesser bleeding points should be left to be controlled when closure sutures are placed. It is unwise to routinely place a palisade of clamps on the uterine wall because, even though this may seal the bleeders temporarily, they may begin to bleed again after the patient is in the recovery room.

G. Suture of the Uterine Incision: Swaged needles cause less bleeding and are useful for placing sutures in the uterine wall. The entire thickness of the myometrium should be closed, and no harm is done if the deep sutures include the endometrium.

H. Encountering the Placenta: If the placenta is encountered beneath the uterine incision, the operator must try to avoid perforating it or serious fetal bleeding may result. A way should be found around the placenta and the membranes then ruptured.

I. Delivery: The operator delivers the baby and then separates and extracts the placenta. After delivery of the placenta, oxytocin should be administered. Oxytocin should be given by intravenous drip (10 units in 1000 mL of 5% dextrose in water) at a rate sufficient to maintain a firm contraction. If the operation was performed before the onset of labor, a finger should be passed through the cervix to be sure it is sufficiently open for drainage of lochia and the glove on that hand then immediately discarded to prevent contamination of the incision.

Types of Cesarean Section

The types of cesarean section in modern use are (1) classic cesarean section, (2) low cervical cesarean section, (3) cesarean hysterectomy, and (4) extraperitoneal cesarean section. The last, designed for use in infected or potentially infected patients, was introduced before the modern era of antibacterial agents and blood transfusion. The procedure is more time-consuming and may not be effective in preventing spillage into the peritoneal cavity, because the peritoneum often is perforated even by the expert. Although the operation was virtually discarded more

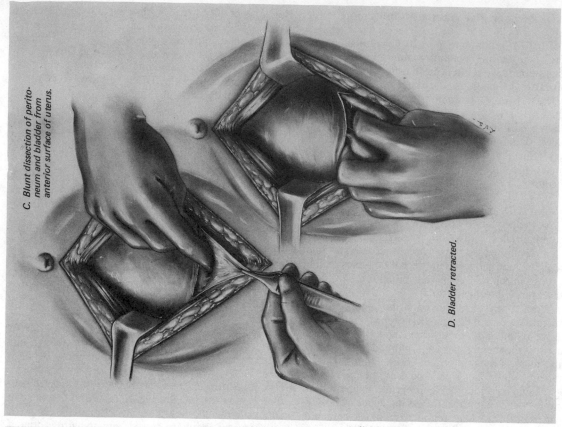

C. Blunt dissection of peritoneum and bladder from
anterior surface of uterus.

D. Bladder retracted.

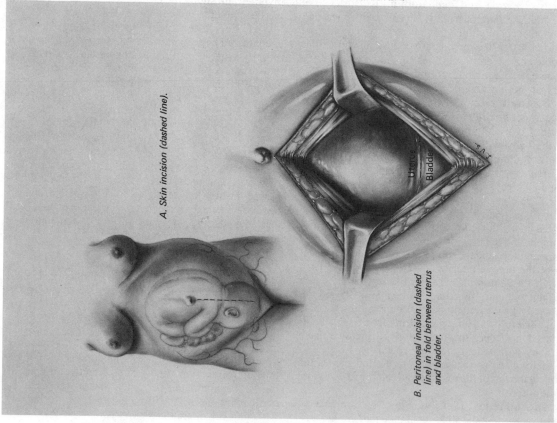

A. Skin incision (dashed line).

B. Peritoneal incision (dashed
line) in fold between uterus
and bladder.

Figure 40–31. Cesarean section.

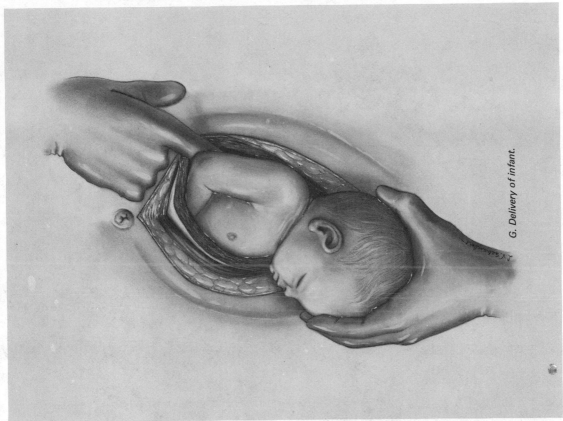

G. Delivery of infant.

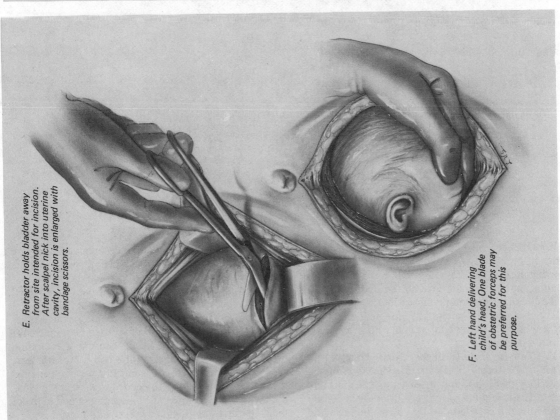

E. Retractor holds bladder away from site intended for incision. After scalpel nick into uterine cavity, incision is enlarged with bandage scissors.

F. Left hand delivering child's head. One blade of obstetric forceps may be preferred for this purpose.

Figure 40–31 (cont'd). Cesarean section.

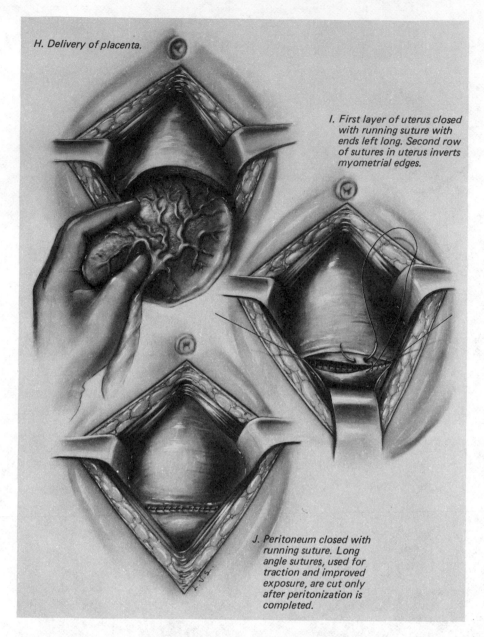

H. Delivery of placenta.

I. First layer of uterus closed
with running suture with
ends left long. Second row
of sutures in uterus inverts
myometrial edges.

J. Peritoneum closed with
running suture. Long
angle sutures, used for
traction and improved
exposure, are cut only
after peritonization is
completed.

Figure 40–31 (cont'd). Cesarean section.

than 20 years ago, the question has recently been raised whether it might not be applicable for the potentially infected patient. The data are still too meager for evaluation, and at present most obstetricians will perform cesarean hysterectomy if the uterus is frankly infected; if it is only potentially infected, they will prefer low cervical cesarean section with therapeutic antibiotic coverage.

A. Classic Cesarean Section: This is the simplest to perform. It is also associated with the greatest loss of blood, and it leaves a scar that may rupture in a subsequent pregnancy. Moreover, a loop of small bowel may adhere to the uterine incision and predispose to intestinal obstruction. The currently ac-

cepted indications for classic cesarean section are placenta previa (because the incision in the corpus usually will avoid the low-lying placenta) and transverse lie (in which better access to the baby is provided by the Sänger incision). Some prefer the low cervical operation for both of these conditions, however.

Classic cesarean section may also be preferred if there is need for extreme haste, because it offers the quickest means of delivering the baby. Nonetheless, the hazards of this procedure must be weighed against the additional minute or so needed to dissect the bladder away from the lower uterine segment and to make the transverse semilunar low cervical incision.

In performing the classic procedure, a vertical

incision is made in the corpus; a scalpel is used to enter the uterine cavity; and the incision is enlarged with bandage scissors. Since the incision is relatively high in the uterus, the head is rarely accessible. Accordingly, the feet are grasped and brought through the incision. The remainder of the delivery is accomplished using the several maneuvers appropriate to breech delivery, as outlined elsewhere in this chapter. After removal of the placenta and membranes, the uterine defect may be repaired with 3 layers of chromic catgut, No. 0 for the 2 deeper layers and No. 00 for the superficial suture to coapt the serosal edges. In placing the superficial layer, a "baseball" stitch minimizes bleeding from the cut edges: Each suture enters the myometrium on the cut surface, emerging on the serosal surface about 5 mm from the edge, and is so continued side-to-side for the length of the incision.

B. Low Cervical Cesarean Section: (Lower uterine segment cesarean section or cervical cesarean section.) The confused terminology of this procedure is understandable: Before labor, when the cervix is closed, uneffaced, and located at about the level of the ischial spines, a transverse uterine incision (which is made 2–3 cm superior to the symphysis pubica) necessarily is made in the lower uterine segment; when the cervix is fully dilated and retracted, the anterior lip is just superior to the symphysis and the incision just superior to the symphysis is through the cervix. When the operation is performed after the onset of labor but before full dilatation, there is no indication whether the incision is made in the cervix proper or in the lower uterine segment—a detail of only academic interest.

The steps in the operation are shown in Fig 40–31. The bladder fold of peritoneum is picked up with tissue forceps and incised transversely. By means of finger dissection through the loose areolar tissue, the bladder is separated from the anterior aspect of the uterus inferiorly for a distance of 3–4 cm. The bladder is held away from this denuded area by a specially designed bladder retractor, and a transverse incision about 2 cm long is made through the anterior uterine wall. The membranes are preferably left intact, but no real damage follows if they should be inadvertently ruptured. Using bandage scissors, the operator enlarges the transverse incision in a crescent-shaped path that extends superiorly at the lateral extremities so as to avoid the uterine vessels. If it can be readily accomplished, the baby's face is now rotated into the incision, and the left blade of the DeLee cesarean section forceps or the Simpson forceps is introduced and applied to one side of the head. Using this blade as a vectis and combining it with moderate fundal pressure, the operator can usually deliver the baby's head with ease; if not, the second blade may be applied. If the face cannot be easily rotated into the incision, the head should be turned to the OA position and delivered using one or both blades of the forceps, as above. On occasion, with considerable molding and deep engagement, a vertex delivery may be difficult, in which case the feet must be brought down and delivery accomplished as in classic cesarean section.

The transverse semilunar incision is preferred by most obstetricians. In former years a longitudinal incision, usually extending into the corpus uteri superiorly, was more popular.

The uterine incision generally is repaired using 2 layers of No. 0 chromic catgut. (It is helpful, in gaining exposure for subsequent steps, to leave the first suture long at each end of the incision. These function as lifting sutures, and they should not be cut until the peritonization is completed.) The peritoneal reflection is sutured either to the superior peritoneal flap or to the anterior uterine wall just superior to the uterine incision. With involution, the uterine incision moves downward into the pelvis. Slight seepage through the incision usually is confined to the retroperitoneal spaces.

Complications & Prognosis

The major factors affecting healing of the uterine incision are hemostasis, accuracy of apposition, quality and amount of suture material, and avoidance of infection and tissue strangulation. Unfortunately, little information about the integrity of a particular scar in a subsequent pregnancy is gained by inquiry as to the presence or absence of postoperative infection and the location of the incision.

In a later pregnancy, pain in the area of the scar may suggest dehiscence. About half of all ruptures of uterine scars occur before the onset of labor. The incidence of rupture is about 1–2% of classic scars and about 0.5–1% in cases of low cervical cesarean section. Rupture of the classic scar is usually catastrophic, occurring suddenly, totally, and with partial or total extrusion of the fetus into the abdominal cavity. Shock due to internal hemorrhage is a prominent sign. Rupture of the low cervical scar is usually more subtle and is characterized principally by pain and occasionally by evidences of slower internal bleeding. Some ruptures are entirely silent, and, during repeat cesarean section, myometrial fenestrations covered only by visceral peritoneum may be noted.

A. Maternal Morbidity and Mortality Rates: Average maternal morbidity and mortality rates after cesarean section suggest that the risk from the operation per se is very small. Some large series with no postoperative deaths have been reported. In other series, mortality rates have ranged from 40 to 80 per 100,000 cases. In general, it is reasonable to conclude that the risk of death following cesarean delivery is at least twice the risk following vaginal delivery. Such figures are difficult to interpret, however, because of the great variability of indications and complications. Even in the most favorable cases there are variable factors, including spill of amniotic fluid and blood into the peritoneal cavity; ease or difficulty of delivering the baby through the uterine incision; amount of incisional bleeding; and patient response to anesthesia. Factors contributing heavily to postoperative complications are prior internal monitoring, prolonged rupture of the membranes, unsuccessful prior efforts at vaginal delivery, hemorrhage, uterine rupture, and countless other obstetric problems that may have compromised the patient and for which emergency cesarean section was performed.

The longer the operative procedure, the greater the likelihood of postoperative complications. As Victor Bonney noted in an early edition of his classic *Gynecological Surgery,* "An operation rapidly yet correctly performed has many advantages over one technically as correct, yet laboriously and tediously accomplished."

Disasters following cesarean section are rare. Some are clearly not preventable. Others are due directly to faulty surgical technique, especially lack of attention to hemostasis, inept or ill-chosen anesthesia, inadequate blood replacement or transfusion of mismatched blood, and mismanagement of infection.

B. Perinatal Morbidity and Mortality Rates: Perinatal problems are as difficult to assess as maternal ones. Data suggest clearly that spontaneous vaginal delivery in the uncomplicated multipara is less hazardous for the baby than repeat elective cesarean section and that if cesarean section is performed, regional anesthesia for elective cesarean section appears to be less noxious than general anesthesia.

The first conclusion will be acceptable to most; spontaneous vaginal delivery is usually the most "normal" of births, whereas repeat cesarean section may entail time-consuming procedures such as dissection of an adherent bladder, aspiration of amniotic fluid during attempts at delivery, fetal hypoxia if the placenta is encountered beneath the prior incision, and the occasional need for version to accomplish delivery. There is less general agreement on the greater safety of regional anesthesia. The author has abandoned the use of spinal anesthesia in favor of thiopental and nitrous oxide with succinylcholine for cesarean section because of its ease and safety and lack of effect on the baby. Nevertheless, if it is anticipated that more than 4 minutes will be required to deliver the baby, spinal anesthesia is preferable because general anesthesia will then depress the baby.

Elective Procedures Coincidental to Cesarean Section

A. Appendectomy: Appendectomy can be performed at the time of cesarean section if the appendix is immediately accessible and if the patient is not or has not been at risk because of such factors as prolonged operating time, prior transfusion, preeclampsia-eclampsia, potential or actual infection, etc.

B. Myomectomy: Myomectomy is permissible at the time of cesarean section only if the tumor is pedunculated. Extracting intramural tumors can provoke intense and uncontrollable bleeding. Also, myomas almost invariably regress after pregnancy; indeed, even large myomas are sometimes not palpable 3 months after delivery.

C. Tubal Ligation: This procedure is usually offered the patient at the time of the third cesarean section; it may be performed at an earlier delivery if the physician is convinced that the patient and her husband

have adequately considered the matter and have reached a firm decision. If a Pomeroy sterilization procedure is done, the fimbriated end of the tube must first be identified (the round ligament has been mistaken for the tube) and the operation performed *at the junction of the mid and outer thirds of the tube.* If it is done closer to the uterus, where the mesosalpinx is shorter, the tube may recanalize. This error accounts for many of the pregnancies following sterilization at cesarean section.

Cesarean Hysterectomy

A major indication for this operation is inability to stop bleeding from the uterine incision. A second important indication, formerly more common than at present, is a potentially infected—membranes ruptured for more than 12 hours—or frankly infected uterus. Other indications are rupture of the uterus in which repair is impractical, placenta accreta, uterine hemorrhage from uncontrollable atony, and large uterine myomas.

Enthusiasm for cesarean hysterectomy as a means of sterilization has waned. Most now agree that the procedure is much too formidable for this purpose alone; postpartum tubal ligation is far less hazardous and is highly effective if done properly.

The superiority of total over subtotal hysterectomy has been amply demonstrated, and it is now accepted that the cervix should be removed in all cases unless this would impose undue risk or serious technical problems. At the time of cesarean section, it is also preferable to remove the cervix if the patient's condition is good and if there is no contraindication to prolonging operating time by 10–15 minutes. Supravaginal hysterectomy should be performed if it is desirable to terminate the operation quickly.

The technical aspects of hysterectomy at the time of cesarean section do not differ basically from those of hysterectomy in the nonpregnant patient except that all structures and cleavage planes are highly vascular and the tissues are friable. At least 2 units of matched blood must be at hand. In one study, blood replacement was needed in 98% of the indicated cesarean hysterectomies and in 66% of the elective sterilization group; two-thirds of the patients in the elective group received an average of 1.6 units of blood.

Postmortem Cesarean Section

Chassar Moir describes the delivery of a second twin, inadvertently overlooked at postmortem cesarean delivery of the first baby 20 minutes earlier, that survived and was discharged from the hospital, apparently in good condition, 14 days later. This case must be unique because of the long interval between the mother's death and delivery of the second infant. No mention is made of any neurologic sequelae.

Postmortem cesarean section is a difficult problem for the following reasons:

(1) The possibility of litigation is introduced if the operation *is* done without informed consent of the next of kin (usually an impractical detail in these circum-

stances), or if it *is not* done in the interests of the baby.

(2) The definition of legal death is not yet fully established, but most agree that in the adult, irreversible brain damage results after 5 minutes or more of total anoxia. There is inconclusive evidence that the fetal brain may be more resistant to hypoxia than that of the adult. The prospects for a healthy baby depend to a certain extent on whether the mother's death was instantaneous or whether she was moribund for an extended period.

Regardless of how quickly the operation is done after the mother's death, the outlook for the baby is bleak. Jeffcoate, the preeminent Liverpudlian obstetrician-gynecologist, commented that some "continue to report with misplaced pride the delivery by postmortem caesarean section of babies which have suffered so much cerebral anoxia whilst in utero that they are permanantly crippled mentally and physically as well as being motherless. Indeed, from personal experience of several cases, I question the propriety and wisdom of postmortem caesarean section under any circumstances." Arthur has reviewed the subject and suggests that with modern life-support systems, the outlook for the baby may be immeasurably improved if the operation can be performed when death is imminent but has not yet occurred.

DESTRUCTIVE OPERATIONS

In industrialized parts of the world, destructive operations are virtually obsolete and are almost never performed. In developing countries, they continue to be an essential part of obstetric practice; many women with obstructed labor remain "in the bush" until long after the baby has died and until they themselves are moribund. This book is used in such areas, and it is necessary to make note of the detail of destructive operations. Those who must acquire skill in these techniques are urged to consult the references at the end of this chapter.

All destructive operations present a degree of danger to the mother, and some are decidedly more hazardous than cesarean section. Accordingly, the following maxims must be stringently observed.

(1) No destructive operation should be undertaken unless it can be performed with greater safety to the mother than cesarean section and unless the alternative of cesarean section has been considered and rejected in favor of vaginal delivery.

(2) The presence of a dead baby is clearly *not* a contraindication to cesarean section if vaginal delivery would entail greater risk.

In the reported experience in underdeveloped countries, many patients are first seen with established obstruction after many hours in the second stage of labor; infection, exhaustion, and imminent or actual uterine rupture are not unusual. Some patients are at the point of death, and in many patients immediate

delivery is imperative. Among this group of flagrantly neglected patients, destructive operations are preferred if the baby is dead ("craniotomy is generally both easier and quicker than cesarean section"), and the obstetricians in these areas have attained great skill in their use. The techniques described here are largely those of Lawson, Lister, and Morris. Fortunately, only a few will ever have occasion to use them, but each obstetrician must know the best means of dealing with such problems, and the necessary instruments must always be available.

The embryotomy set should consist of the following instruments (Figs 40–32 and 40–33): Simpson cutting perforator, Blond-Heidler thimble and decapitating wire, Braun-Jardine-DeLee hook, heavy long-handled scissors (eg, Dubois), and 4 heavy 20-cm Ochsner clamps or Morris bone forceps.

A cranioclast, although obsolete for craniotomy, may be useful in retrieving a decapitated head. It should therefore be part of the set.

The following operations are included among destructive procedures: craniotomy, decapitation, cleidotomy, and evisceration.

CRANIOTOMY

In its obstetric context, craniotomy refers to perforation of the fetal skull and evacuation of part of its contents for the purpose of reducing the size of the head.

Impaction of the Forecoming Head in Neglected Labor

Cesarean section should be employed if the baby is living or if uterine rupture is suspected. If the baby is dead, the cervix is fully dilated, the uterus is intact, and conditions are such that cesarean section is not appropriate, craniotomy should be performed. The technique is as follows:

Classic forceps are first applied to steady the head during perforation. An accessible central area is selected; it makes no difference whether the perforation is made through a suture, a fontanelle, or a bone plate. While an assistant holds the head steady, the point of the Simpson perforator is pushed through the skull to the depth of the shoulder of the blade. (During the perforation it is essential that the fingers of the opposite hand fix the point of the instrument so that it will not glance off the skull.) The handles are squeezed, opening the blades for a distance of 2–5 cm. The instrument is then closed, rotated 90 degrees, and again opened. The entire instrument is now inserted into the center of the head up to the level of articulation of the 2 blades. With the blades widely separated, the cranial contents and septa are fragmented by rotating the instrument to and fro. Cerebral tissue escapes after removal of the perforator, and 4 Ochsner or Morris clamps are applied to the edges of the hole, the obstetric forceps are removed, and the head is delivered by traction on the clamps.

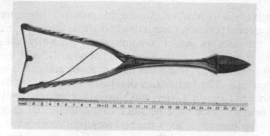

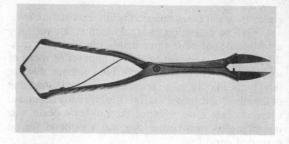

Simpson cutting perforator

Crossbar at end of handles locks instrument and must be released to permit blades to be opened

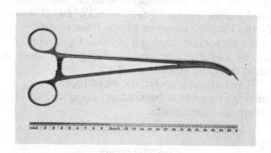

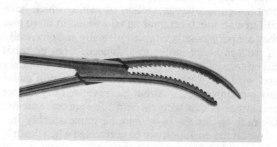

Morris bone forceps

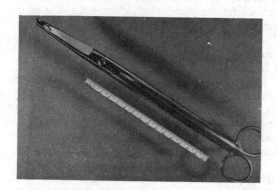

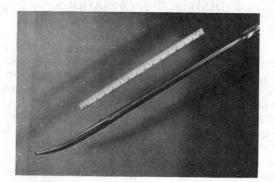

Cleidotomy scissors

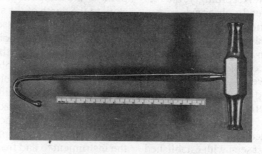

Braun-Jardine-DeLee decapitation hook

Figure 40—32. Embryotomy instruments.

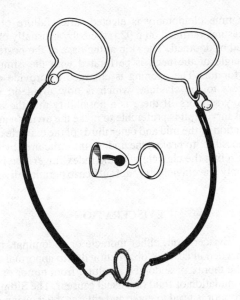

Figure 40–33. Blond-Heidler thimble and saw. Metal balls at ends of wire are to engage thimble for application around neck (see text) and metal handles for sawing. (Redrawn and reproduced, with permission, from Roques FW, Beattie J, Wrigley AJ: *Midwifery by Ten Teachers*. Arnold, 1961.)

Note that the cranioclast is not used. Those with most experience in destructive operations consider the instrument to be unwieldy, dangerous to the mother, unnecessary, and obsolete for its intended purpose.

Impaction of the Aftercoming Head

After delivery of the arms, the head is firmly fixed by traction on the trunk. An accessible portion of the skull is selected, either the occiput or the lambdoid suture behind an ear, and the same steps are followed as though the head presented. If it is needed, extraction of the head is accomplished with a Braun-Jardine-DeLee hook inserted through the opening in the head, the point of the instrument being directed toward the foramen magnum.

Hydrocephalus

In cases of hydrocephalus in the forecoming head, simple perforation usually allows the escape of enough amniotic fluid so that the decompressed head can be readily delivered by traction to the edges of the perforation by Ochsner clamps. In cases of hydrocephalus in the aftercoming head, the problem may be solved by withdrawal of cerebrospinal fluid by transabdominal encephalocentesis. If not, after delivery of the shoulders, knife laminectomy is performed over the highest readily accessible thoracic vertebra. A uterine dressing forceps is introduced through the spinal canal directly into the head, twisted to and fro to enlarge the opening, and the head is readily advanced by traction on the trunk as soon as sufficient decompression has occurred (Fig 40–34).

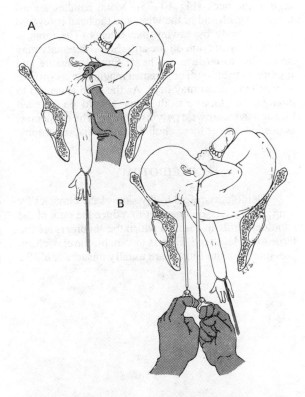

Figure 40–35. *A:* Introducing the Blond-Heidler saw. The thimble is worn on the thumb of the hand introducing the saw and is readily transferred to the middle finger of the same hand curving over the fetal neck and slipping into the loop on the thimble. The thimble carrying the saw is thus transferred from the operator's digit in front of the neck to the digit behind it. *B:* The saw in position. When the operator's hand is withdrawn, the saw glides up over the neck of the fetus and sawing can begin. (Redrawn and reproduced, with permission, from Roques FW, Beattie J, Wrigley AJ: *Midwifery by Ten Teachers*. Arnold, 1961.)

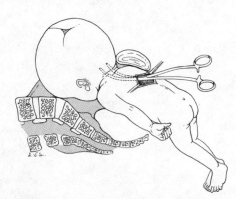

Figure 40–34. Craniotomy on aftercoming hydrocephalic head. Uterine dressing forceps inserted into head through laminectomy incision. (Redrawn and reproduced, with permission, from Danforth DN: *Am J Obstet Gynecol* 1947; 54:694.)

DECAPITATION

Decapitation is appropriate in some cases of neglected transverse lie and shoulder presentation. It may also be useful in certain cases of locked twins. In one of Lister's cases, the aftercoming head of twin A (dead) was obstructed by the forecoming head of twin B (alive); the body of the breech was removed by decapitation, the head pushed upward into the uterine cavity, and a live twin B delivered by forceps.

If an arm is prolapsed, a long tape is tied to the wrist so the arm will not be lost in subsequent maneuvers.

For decapitation, the Blond-Heidler saw—as Lawson notes—"has superseded clumsy hooks and scissors." The decapitating wire is attached to the Blond-Heidler thimble, which is placed on the left thumb. The thumb and fingers then encircle the neck, which is held as low as possible in the pelvis by traction on the arm. The left middle finger engages the ring attached to the thimble, and the wire, which is protected except for 7.5–10 cm at its center, is pulled around the neck (Fig 40–35). Metal handles are attached to each end of the wire, and the head is severed from the body by sawing movements. The trunk is delivered by traction on the arm. Some ingenuity may be needed to retrieve the head. Fundal pressure and traction in the mouth or foramen magnum may suffice; a large tenaculum may help. As the head is caused to engage, the biparietal diameter should be directed through the narrowest pelvic diameter. The cranioclast is needed only if there should be inlet disproportion.

CLEIDOTOMY

Cleidotomy refers to division of the clavicles by long, heavy scissors in order to reduce the bulk of the shoulder girdle in cases in which the shoulders are too large to be delivered. Efforts to "snap" the clavicle by pressure with the fingers are usually unsuccessful. By the time cleidotomy is elected, after failure of the measures outlined on p 925, the baby is usually either dead or doomed. The skin at the base of the posterior triangle of the neck is perforated with the Simpson perforator. The opening is enlarged to provide easy access to the clavicle, which is now dividedd with heavy scissors. If there is a possibility that the baby will survive, it is preferable to make the division at the junction of the mid and outer thirds of the clavicle and, if possible, to protect the underlying structures by first encircling the clavicle with the index finger. Division of only one clavicle may not suffice to permit delivery.

EVISCERATION

Evisceration, either thoracic or abdominal, may be needed in cases of obstruction due to abnormal size of the thorax or abdomen resulting from tumor or the accumulation of fluid (the usual causes). The Simpson perforator is used to make and enlarge the incision and to break up the viscera, which are then extracted manually.

AFTERCARE

After any destructive operation it is imperative that the vagina, cervix, and lower uterine segment be explored immediately for evidence of laceration or rupture. In neglected patients, the quickest and least traumatic means of repair offers the best chance of survival. In uterine rupture, bleeding is controlled with one or 2 layers of suture, and, if the scar will be unfit for subsequent pregnancy, tubal ligation is performed; hysterectomy is rarely required unless the rupture is so extensive that repair is impractical.

In all neglected cases, the bladder requires particular attention because of the possibility of pressure necrosis. A catheter is left in place for 10 days. A fistula, if present, is repaired 3 months after delivery.

●   ●   ●

References

Forceps Delivery

Bachman C: The Barton obstetric forceps: A review of its use in 55 cases. *Surg Gynecol Obstet* 1927;**45**:805.

Barton LJ, Caldwell WE, Studdiford WE: A new obstetric forceps. *Am J Obstet Gynecol* 1928;**15**:16.

Chiswick ML, James DK: Kielland's forceps: Association with neonatal morbidity and mortality. *Br Med J* 1979;**1**:7.

Danforth DN: The mechanism of normal labor. Chapter 30 in: *Obstetrics and Gynecology*, 4th ed. Danforth DN (editor). Harper & Row, 1982.

Danforth DN: A method of forceps rotation in persistent occiput posterior. *Am J Obstet Gynecol* 1953;**65**:120.

Danforth DN, Ellis AC: Midforceps delivery: A vanishing art? *Am J Obstet Gynecol* 1963;**86**:29.

Danforth WC: Forceps. Chap 43, p 319, in: *Obstetrics and Gynecology*, Vol 2. Curtis AH (editor). Saunders, 1933.

Danforth WC: The treatment of occiput posterior with special reference to manual rotation. *Am J Obstet Gynecol* 1932; **23**:360.

Das K: *Obstetric Forceps. Its History and Evolution*, Mosby, 1929.

DeLee JB: The prophylactic forceps operation. *Am J Obstet Gynecol* 1920;**1**:34.

Friedman EA, Sachtleben MR: Station of the fetal presenting part. 6. Arrest of descent in nulliparas. *Obstet Gynecol* 1976;**47**:129.

Hughey MJ, McElin TW, Lussky R: Forceps operations in perspective. 1. Midforceps rotation operations. *J Reprod Med* 1978;**20**:253.

Laufe LE: *Obstetric Forceps*, Harper & Row, 1968.

Shoulder Dystocia

Benedetti TJ, Gabbe SG: Shoulder dystocia: A complication of fetal macrosomia and prolonged second stage of labor with midforceps delivery. *Obstet Gynecol* 1978;**52**:526.

Freeman RK et al: Postdate pregnancy: Utilization of contraction stress testing for primary fetal surveillance. *Am J Obstet Gynecol* 1981;**140**:128.

Golditch IM, Kirkman K: The large fetus. *Obstet Gynecol* 1978;**52**:26.

Hardy AE: Birth injuries of the brachial plexus: Incidence and prognosis. *J Bone Joint Surg* [*Br*] 1981;**63**:98.

Morris WIC: Shoulder dystocia. *J Obstet Gynaecol Br Emp* 1955;**62**:302.

Swartz DP: Shoulder girdle dystocia in vertex delivery. *Obstet Gynecol* 1960;**15**:194.

Woods CE: A principle of physics as applicable to shoulder delivery. *Am J Obstet Gynecol* 1943;**45**:769.

Vacuum Extractor

Baggish MS: Vacuum extraction. Chapter 87 in: *Textbook of Obstetrics and Perinatology*. Iffy L, Kamininetzky HA. Wiley, 1981.

Bird GC: Modification of Malmström's vacuum extractor. *Br Med J* 1969;**3**:526.

Chalmers JA: *The Ventouse: The Obstetric Vacuum Extractor*. Year Book, 1971.

Greis BJ, Bieniarz J, Scommegna A: Comparison of maternal and fetal effects of vacuum extraction with forceps or cesarean deliveries. *Obstet Gynecol* 1981;**57**:571.

Leijon I: Neurology and behaviour of newborn infants delivered by vacuum extraction on maternal indication. *Acta Paediatr Scand* 1980;**69**:625.

Breech Delivery

Alexandropoulos KA: Importance of breech delivery in pathogenesis of brain damage: End results of long term follow-up. *Pediatrics* 1973;**12**:248.

Ballas S, Toaff R, Jaffa AJ: Deflexion of the fetal head in breech presentation: Incidence, management and outcome. *Obstet Gynecol* 1978;**52**:653.

Behrman SJ: Fetal cervical hyperextension. *Clin Obstet Gynecol* 1962;**5**:1018.

Caldwell WE, Studdiford WE: A review of breech deliveries during a five year period at the Sloane Hospital for Women. (2 parts.) *Am J Obstet Gynecol* 1929;**18**:623, 720.

Collea JV et al: The randomized management of breech presentation: Vaginal delivery vs. cesarean section. *Am J Obstet Gynecol* 1978;**131**:186.

Cruikshank DP, Pitkin RM: Delivery of the premature breech. *Obstet Gynecol* 1977;**50**:376.

DeCrespigny LJC, Pepperell RJ: Perinatal mortality and morbidity in breech presentation. *Obstet Gynecol* 1979;**53**:141.

Hibbard T, Schumann WR: Prophylactic external version in obstetric practice. *Am J Obstet Gynecol* 1973;**116**:511.

Karp LE et al: The premature breech: Trial of labor or cesarean section? *Obstet Gynecol* 1979;**53**:88.

Llewellyn-Jones D: Chapter 38 in: *Fundamentals of Obstetrics and Gynaecology*. Vol 1: *Obstetrics*. Faber & Faber, 1969.

Lovset J: Shoulder delivery by breech presentation. *J Obstet Gynaecol Br Emp* 1937;**44**:696.

Mann LI, Gallant JM: Modern management of the breech delivery. *Am J Obstet Gynecol* 1979;**134**:611.

Morley GW: Breech presentation: A 15 year review. *Obstet Gynecol* 1967;**30**:745.

Myerscough PR: *Munro Kerr's Operative Obstetrics*, 9th ed. Baillere, Tindall, & Cassell, 1977.

O'Leary JA: Vaginal delivery of the term breech. *Obstet Gynecol* 1979;**53**:331.

Piper EB, Bachman C: The prevention of fetal injuries in breech delivery. *JAMA* 1929;**92**:217.

Ranney B: Gentle art of external cephalic version. *Am J Obstet Gynecol* 1973;**116**:239.

Savage JE: Management of the fetal arms in breech extraction: A method to facilitate application of Piper forceps. *Obstet Gynecol* 1954;**3**:55.

Woods JR Jr: Effects of low-birth-weight breech delivery on neonatal mortality. *Obstet Gynecol* 1979;**53**:735.

Version

Chapman K: Internal version: Review of 118 cases. *J Obstet Gynaecol India* 1967;**17**:368.

Potter MG: The pitfalls of podalic version and extraction. *Am J Obstet Gynecol* 1939;**37**:675.

Rosensohn M: Internal podalic version at New York Lying-In Hospital (1932–1950). *Am J Obstet Gynecol* 1954;**68**:916.

Dührssen's Incisions

Danforth DN: Discussion of paper by Carrow L: Cervical incisions in present-day obstetrics. *Am J Obstet Gynecol* 1960;**79**:563.

Cesarean Section

Arthur RK: Postmortem cesarean section. *Am J Obstet Gynecol* 1978;**132**:175.

Brocke-Utne JG et al: Advantages of left over right lateral tilt for cesarean section. *S Afr Med J* 1978;**54**:489.

Evrard JR, Gold EM: Cesarean section and maternal mortality in Rhode Island: Incidence and risk factors, 1965–1975. *Obstet Gynecol* 1977;**50**:594.

Evrard JR, Gold EM: Cesarean section: Risk/benefit. *Perinat Care* 1978;**2**:4.

Flaksman FJ, Vollman RH, Benfield DG: Iatrogenic prematurity due to elective termination of the uncomplicated pregnancy: A major perinatal health care problem. *Am J Obstet Gynecol* 1978;**132**:885.

Gall SA: The efficacy of prophylactic antibiotics in cesarean section. *Am J Obstet Gynecol* 1979;**134**:506.

Hertz RH et al: Clinical estimation of gestational age: Rules for avoiding preterm delivery. *Am J Obstet Gynecol* 1978; **131**:395.

Jeffcoate N: Medicine versus nature. *J R Col Surg Edinburgh* 1976;**21**:263.

Ledger WJ: Hospital-acquired obstetric infections. Chapter 10 in: *Infections in the Female.* Lea & Febiger, 1977.

Mann LI, Gallant J: Modern indications for cesarean section. *Am J Obstet Gynecol* 1979;**135**:437.

Merrill BS, Gibbs CE: Planned vaginal delivery following cesarean section. *Obstet Gynecol* 1978;**52**:50.

Morewood GA, O'Sullivan MJ, McConney J: Vaginal delivery after cesarean section. *Obstet Gynecol* 1973;**42**:589.

NIH Consensus Development Task Force: Statement on cesarean childbirth. *Am J Obstet Gynecol* 1981;**139**:902.

Perlo M, Curet LB: The effect of fetal monitoring on cesarean section morbidity. *Obstet Gynecol* 1979;**53**:354.

Petitti D, Olson RO, Williams RL: Cesarean section in California—1960 through 1975. *Am J Obstet Gynecol* 1979; **133**:391.

Phelin JP, Pruyn SC: Prophylactic antibiotics in cesarean section: A double blind study of cefazolin. *Am J Obstet Gynecol* 1979;**133**:474.

Speert H: Cesarean section. (Historical highlights.) Page 11 in: *Obstetrics and Gynecology,* 4th ed. Danforth DN (editor). Harper & Row, 1982.

Studd J: Partograms and nomograms of cervical dilatation in management of primigravid labour. *Br Med J* 1973;**4**:451.

Destructive Operations

Borno RP et al: Vaginal frank breech delivery of an hydrocephalic fetus after transabdominal encephalocentesis. *Am J Obstet Gynecol* 1978;**132**:336.

Lawson JB: Obstructed labor. *J Obstet Gynaecol Br Commonw* 1965;**72**:877.

Lawson JB: Tropical obstetrics. Chapter 26 in: *Combined Textbook of Obstetrics and Gynaecology.* MacGillivary I, Macnaughton MC (editors). Churchill Livingstone, 1976.

Lister UG: Obstructed labor: A series of 320 cases occurring in four years in a hospital in southern Nigeria. *J Obstet Gynecol Br Commonw* 1960;**67**:188.

Morris WIC: Embryotomy. Page 603 in: *Combined Textbook of Obstetrics and Gynecology,* 8th ed. Baird D (editor). Churchill Livingstone, 1969.

Infertility | 41

John R. Marshall, MD

Infertility is defined as failure to conceive after 1 year of regular coitus without contraception. **Subfertility** is a synonymous term. **Sterility** is total inability to conceive. **Fecundity** is the capacity to participate in production of a child. The term **fecundability** has been coined to denote the probability of conception. Infertility may be classified as **primary,** when there is no history of pregnancy having occurred, or **secondary,** when inability to conceive occurs after one or more successful pregnancies.

Approximately 15% of couples in the USA are infertile, and about 1–2% are sterile. Infertility is becoming an increasingly more serious medical and social problem. Because of the widespread availability of abortion for unwanted pregnancy, fewer infertile couples have the alternative of adoption available to them. In addition, the current prevalence of venereal disease causes infertility in an increasing number of women.

Infertility is a disorder of couples, and both partners must be evaluated. The man is responsible in about 30% of cases, the woman in approximately 40% of cases, and both in the remainder.

Fecundability is strongly influenced by the ages of the parties, the frequency of coitus, and the duration of sexual activity without contraception. In women, fecundability is maximal at about age 24; at age 24–30, there is a slight decline, and after age 30 the decline is quite rapid. Fecundability in women under 18 years of age is roughly half that of women age 24. In men, fecundability is also maximal at age 24–25. Coital frequency of about 4–5 times a week is associated with maximal fecundability. The longer the couple have been trying to produce a child without success, the greater the progressive decline in the conception rate. This decline is independent of the age of the parties or the frequency of coital exposure.

A thorough diagnostic work-up should identify one or more causes of infertility in about 90% of couples. Appropriate therapy will result in pregnancy in about 40% of couples treated. Thus, there is good reason to undertake diagnostic evaluation and initiate proper therapy.

There are 3 main purposes of an infertility evaluation: (1) to determine the cause of infertility; (2) to arrive at a prognosis, which has important psychologic implications; and (3) to serve as the basis for therapy.

PSYCHOLOGIC ASPECTS OF INFERTILITY

Because of her psychosocial upbringing in our society, the woman usually assumes initial responsibility for failure to produce a child and is usually the first to seek medical care. In contrast, the man may demonstrate his inability to face the possibility of being infertile by avoiding examination.

A number of feelings are common to infertile patients. Initially, these may be surprise, denial, and isolation, followed by anger, guilt, depression, and even grief. With appropriate resolution of these reactions, the condition may be accepted, but it is essential that the therapist recognize the powerful emotional impact of the realization that one is unable to produce offspring. Too frequently, the couple are simply left uninformed. After a thorough infertility evaluation, the therapist should carefully and honestly counsel the couple concerning their chances for conception. Too often the evaluation lacks such a definitive statement, and the uncertain patients are left with no clear idea of their possibility to conceive. Such uncertainty may be worse than knowing they will not be able to produce a child.

Infertility has important effects on sexuality, self-image, and self-esteem, for men as well as women. Some women may regard childbearing as the ultimate expression of their biologic identity as women, and there is no doubt that some men regard fathering children as the supreme affirmation of their masculinity. Being confronted with the knowledge that they are unable to produce a child may thus have psychologic consequences for one or both partners that reach deeper than simple childlessness and absence of the nurturing function to affect their concepts of themselves as valid human beings.

Additional problems may arise during the evaluation period. Having intercourse according to the schedule prescribed by the doctor may remove desirable spontaneity in lovemaking. Moreover, the knowledge that intercourse may involve a subsequent post-coital examination may result in impotence. Excessive preoccupation with a basal body temperature chart can make married life unnecessarily tedious. The physician must take care to maintain and support the relationship between the husband and wife regardless of the type of infertility therapy being used.

DIAGNOSIS OF CAUSES OF INFERTILITY

Possible causes of infertility are outlined in Table 41–1. However, such a classification may not be applicable in clinical practice, and a more clinically useful functional classification of the causes of infertility is presented in Table 41–2. The functional classification is more helpful because it is correlated with the testing procedures used in the evaluation of infertility.

FUNCTIONAL CLASSIFICATION OF CAUSES OF INFERTILITY

Time

Contrary to popular opinion, unprotected intercourse, even during the preovulatory period, does not usually result in conception. In couples who do not use contraception, about 25% of women will be pregnant in the first month, at least 60% in 6 months, about 75% in 9 months, 80% in a year, and approximately 90% in 18 months. When all conditions for conception are ideal, 42% of menstrual cycles result in no conception, 16% produce abortive ova, and 42% produce normal fertilized ova. If the woman misses her period, her chances of having a normal pregnancy are 72%, and the chance of aborting is 28%. However, since not all of these abortions cause clinically recognizable symptoms, several such episodes may occur before the woman has a viable pregnancy. Since the woman is "at risk" for conception only if coitus occurs during her fertile period, only those months in which there has

Table 41–2. Functional classification of causes of infertility.

Time	Transport
Timing of coitus	Male
Frequency of coitus	Coital
Semen	Female
Sperm	Cervical transport failure
Other components of ejaculate	Uterine transport failure
	Tubal transport failure
Ova	**"Incubator" (endometrial dysfunction)**
Growth and development of viable ova	
Ovulation	**Other problems**
Implantation	Generalized endocrine disorders
Adequacy of corpus luteum	Systemic diseases (eg, diabetes mellitus)

been adequate coital exposure can be included in an assessment of infertility.

Semen

In order for conception to occur, the man must produce a sufficient number of normal, motile spermatozoa in an ejaculate made up of appropriate secretions from the accessory genital glands.

Ova

Conception cannot occur without ovulation of an oocyte that is successfully implanted and then supported by an adequately functioning corpus luteum.

The hormonal events associated with follicular maturation, ovulation, and corpus luteum formation have profound effects on the entire female reproductive system. Fertility is possible only when all parts of this system function so that hormone production is suitable and consistent, follicles develop and mature, ovulation occurs regularly, and optimal conditions exist for the support of a fertilized ovum, eg, adequate corpus luteum, appropriate site of implantation.

Transport

Transport mechanisms of spermatozoa and semen

Table 41–1. Causes of infertility.

	General	Developmental	Endocrine	Genital Disease
Female	Dietary disturbances, severe anemias; anxiety, fear, etc (hypothalamus)	Uterine absence, hypoplasia, uterine anomalies, gonadal dysgenesis	Pituitary failure, thyroid disturbances, adrenal hyperplasia, ovarian failure, polycystic disease	Pelvic inflammation, tuberculosis, tubal obstructions, endometriosis, myoma and polyps, cervicitis, vaginitis, venereal disease
Male	Fatigue, excess smoking, alcohol, excess coitus, fear, impotence	Undescended testis, testicular germinal aplasia, hypospadias, Klinefelter's syndrome	Pituitary failure, thyroid deficiency, adrenal hyperplasia	Mumps orchitis, venereal disease, prostatitis
Female and Male	Marital maladjustments, sex problems, ignorance (timing, douching, sperm leakage), low fertility index, immunologic incompatibility			

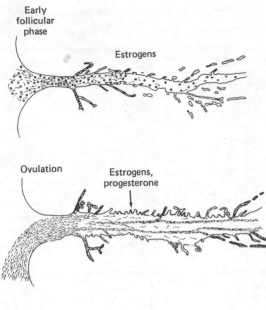

Early
follicular
phase

Estrogens

Ovulation

Estrogens,
progesterone

Luteal
phase

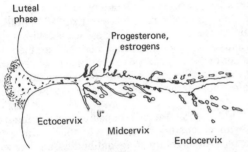

Progesterone,
estrogens

Ectocervix

Midcervix

Endocervix

Figure 41–1. Pattern of sperm transport through the cervical canal. During midcycle, the spermatozoa travel in strands of cervical mucus. During the luteal phase, sperm transport in the uterus is greatly inhibited, and during the follicular phase, a few sperm are found with leukocytes. (Modified and reproduced, with permission, from Hafez ESE: Sperm transport. In: *Progress in Infertility,* 2nd ed. Behrman SJ, Kistner RW [editors]. Little, Brown, 1975.)

in human reproduction are complex. Spermatozoa and seminal fluid must both traverse the accessory reproductive ducts of the male and be appropriately ejaculated from the penis. Coitus must occur so that the semen is deposited in or near the cervix. In the female, initial transport of sperm occurs in the cervical mucus, which is profoundly altered by the presence or absence of estrogens and progesterone (Fig 41–1). Immunologic incompatibilities may be manifested as abnormalities of cervical transport.

Uterine transport of sperm is a poorly understood phenomenon. The oviduct transports sperm toward the ovary while simultaneously moving ova in the opposite direction. This function is easily disturbed by an antecedent infection with resulting adhesions or by inflammatory processes such as endometriosis.

The "Incubator"

In virtually all pregnancies carried to term, the endometrial cavity serves as the "incubator" of the fertilized ovum. Endometrial infections or an inability of the endometrium to respond appropriately to endocrine stimulation of the ovary may result in infertility. Distortion of the endometrial cavity by submucous myomas, synechiae, or congenital uterine anomalies is an uncommon cause of infertility but a frequent cause of spontaneous abortion in the first trimester.

Other Problems

Generalized endocrine disorders, eg, hypothyroidism or severe adrenocortical hyper- or hypofunction, may result in infertility. In most of these disorders, associated anovulation causes infertility. Systemic diseases such as severe or poorly controlled diabetes are associated with decreased fertility, often for reasons that are not clearly understood.

THE DIAGNOSTIC EVALUATION

Because infertility involves both the man and the woman, both should be present at the initial visit. The man can contribute valuable information to the medical history, and his participation acquaints him with the problem and increases his involvement and concern. Subsequent evaluation proceeds separately but simultaneously with both the woman and the man.

During the course of an infertility evaluation, it is frequently difficult to correlate data accumulated from multiple simultaneous evaluations. Summarizing these data on a Summary Work Sheet using the subject headings given in Table 41–2 with abnormal findings entered in red has several advantages: Abnormal findings are easily recognized and rarely forgotten; blank spaces indicate that no information has been obtained and that further tests are required; and the headings recall to memory the necessary areas for evaluation. The evaluation is not complete until data have been obtained about each of the possible problem areas.

In the woman, evaluation should begin with a thorough history and physical examination. The history should include the duration and type of infertility, coital frequency, menstrual pattern, duration and frequency of flow, premenstrual molimina, and any past history of vaginal discharge, cervicitis and associated treatment, pelvic infections, surgery, or accidents, as well as general physical condition, illnesses, allergies, drug intake, or significant family history. During the physical examination, special attention should focus on secondary sex characteristics: body contour, hair distribution, breast development, and external and internal genitalia.

Baseline laboratory studies should consist of a serologic test for syphilis, blood count, sedimentation rate, urinalysis, serum TSH by radioimmunoassay to rule out hypothyroidism, and other specific tests to rule out suspected systemic disease.

In the man, the evaluation should begin with semen analysis, preferably at least 2 samples. In the presence of a normal semen analysis, most other abnormalities of the man are probably inconsequential, and no further evaluation is necessary. However, if the semen analysis is abnormal, further evaluation is in order. Since a specific cause for an abnormal semen analysis can be identified in over half of infertile men and since many of the specific problems are treatable, thorough evaluation is warranted.

The history should record mumps orchitis, diabetes mellitus, herniorrhaphy, and exposure to x-rays or toxic substances (eg, lead, iron, zinc, copper). Men who lead sedentary indoor lives, are markedly obese, are subject to high environmental temperatures, or who wear tight underclothing may have abnormal spermatogenesis resulting from interference with the thermoregulatory mechanism of the scrotum. The history should also include the duration of the infertility and the pattern and frequency of coitus.

Physical examination should note the existence of systemic disease and endocrinopathy; the presence of secondary male sex characteristics, varicocele, or hydrocele; and congenital abnormalities such as hypospadias or cryptorchidism.

Initial laboratory examination should consist of a serologic test for syphilis, complete blood count, sedimentation rate, urinalysis, examination of the prostatic secretion for prostatic inflammation, and serum TSH by radioimmunoassay. Additional examination of the testicular and pituitary endocrine function, including testicular biopsy, may be warranted.

Evaluation of Semen

The semen specimen should be obtained by masturbation or coitus interruptus into a clean, well-rinsed dry jar or disposable plastic container. Three to 5 days should have elapsed between the day of collection and the last ejaculation. Because semen specimens vary, the initial evaluation should always be based on the analysis of 2 specimens obtained in a 1- to 2-week interval. Little reliance can be placed on a single sample, particularly if it is abnormal. At least 2 and frequently 3–4 samples should be examined before the physician reaches a conclusion. The sample should be delivered to the laboratory within 1 hour after collection and should not have been cooled or warmed. The entire ejaculate should be contained in the specimen jar.

The most important elements of the semen analysis are the number, motility, and morphology of the spermatozoa and certain chemical analyses of the seminal plasma. Normal values are given in Table 41–3.

There is a strong correlation between the likelihood of subsequent pregnancy and the percentage of normal sperm, the percentage of live sperm (Fig 41–2), and sperm counts. Sperm counts below 10 million/mL or total sperm counts below 25 million per ejaculate are frequent in infertile men. When pregnancy rates are related to semen analyses, sperm counts between 5 and 60 million or total sperm counts

Table 41–3. Recommendations for standards in semen analysis.

Parameter	Recommendation/Normal Value
Abstinence	5 (3–7) days
Collection	Masturbation (coitus interruptus)
Volume	2–6 mL
Viscosity	Full liquefaction within 60 minutes
Sperm density	40–250 million/mL
Sperm motility	
Progressive	Good—very good
Quantitative	First hour ≥ 60%; 2–3 hours ≥ 50%
Vitality	≤ 35% dead cells
Sperm morphology	≥ 60% with normal configuration
Acid phosphatase	25,000–60,000 IU/mL
Zinc	90–250 μg/mL
Fructose	150–600 mg/dL

between 25 and 200 million are associated with a pregnancy rate of 50%, whereas sperm counts over 60 million or total sperm counts over 200 million per ejaculate are associated with pregnancy rates of greater than 70%. Sperm counts of less than 12.5 million motile sperms per ejaculate are associated with a significantly decreased pregnancy rate. If the other elements of the semen analysis are normal, a total sperm count of greater than 12.5 million per ejaculate can therefore not be considered a significant cause of infertility.

Three to 5% of men demonstrate autoimmunization with circulating antibodies to their own spermatozoa. Autoagglutinating antibodies are present

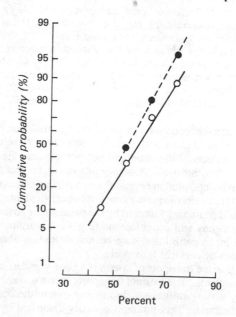

Figure 41–2. Cumulative probability of pregnancy in relation to the percent normal (o——o) and live (●——●) spermatozoa. (Reproduced, with permission, from Eliasson R: Parameters of male infertility. In: *Human Reproduction.* Hafez ESE, Evans TN [editors]. Harper & Row, 1973.)

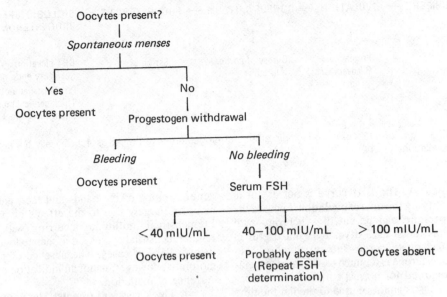

Figure 41–3. Flow chart for determining presence or absence of oocytes

when clumping of spermatozoa is noted on semen analysis, whereas autoimmobilizing antibodies are revealed by poor motility of sperm. Autoimmunization arises from obstruction of the vas deferens, inflammatory prostatitis, orchitis, or testicular biopsy. However, about one-third of cases have no recognizable cause. The presence of agglutinating antibodies decreases the pregnancy rate by about one-half; the presence of immobilizing antibodies carries a much poorer prognosis.

Evaluation of Ova

A. Presence of Oocytes: Without oocytes, ovulation, and normal corpus luteum function, pregnancy is impossible.

Fig 41–3 presents a flow chart that can be used to determine the presence or absence of oocytes. Spontaneous menses or progestogen withdrawal bleeding without prior administration of exogenous estrogen suggests the presence of oocytes, because each of these requires the prior presence of estrogen to effect endometrial proliferation (Fig 41–4). In most women of childbearing age, if this estrogen comes from endogenous sources but not from an estrogen-producing tumor, it will arise from the ovarian follicles, each of which contains an oocyte. If bleeding does not occur upon progestogen withdrawal, measurement of serum FSH is indicated. Concentrations of less than 40 mIU/mL clearly indicate the presence of oocytes. Concentrations of 40–100 mIU/mL indicate the absence of oocytes with 95% accuracy. Concentrations of more than 100 mIU/mL indicate a lack of oocytes

with virtual certainty. Ovarian biopsy to document the presence or absence of oocytes is usually unnecessary.

B. Ovulation: Ovulation is defined as the release of a ripened oocyte from the ovarian follicle. Assuming that the endometrium is capable of responding to estrogen, amenorrhea clearly indicates anovulation. Oligomenorrhea and eumenorrhea can be either ovulatory or anovulatory.

Indicators of ovulation are shown in Fig 41–5. Only indirect indicators are practical. Mittelschmerz, although present in less than 5% of patients, is a reasonably reliable indicator of ovulation. Measurement of serum concentrations of progesterone on 3 alternate days during the midluteal phase is an effective but expensive indication of ovulation.

The following biologic effects of progesterone are clinically important in evaluating ovulation.

1. Basal body temperature–The basal body temperature (BBT) is that temperature obtained immediately upon awakening every morning and before any activity has occurred (Fig 41–6). It should be measured with a special BBT thermometer. The luteal phase rise, which is usually slightly greater than 0.3 °C (0.6 °F) and which accounts for the biphasic nature of the curve, is due to the secretion of progesterone by the corpus luteum. The biphasic pattern almost always indicates ovulation; a monophasic pattern can occur with either ovulation or anovulation. Ten to 20% of monophasic curves will occur in ovulatory women. The retrospective examination of the recording for an entire month enables the physician to identify the presence or absence of ovulation and of a short luteal phase

ENDOMETRIUM + ESTROGEN + PROGESTOGEN WITHDRAWAL → BLEEDING

Figure 41–4. Relationship of menses to endometrium, estrogen, and progestogen withdrawal.

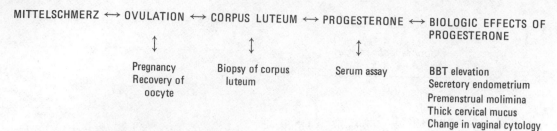

Figure 41–5. Indicators of ovulation. The biologic effects of progesterone are most useful clinically but are only indirect indicators of ovulation.

(less than 10 days). The BBT curve is not useful in precisely identifying the time of ovulation, because the shift in temperature can be out of synchrony with ovulation by as much as 3 days. It is not useful in identifying inadequate corpus luteum function, because less progesterone is required to shift the temperature than is required for normal corpus luteum function. The BBT also cannot be used to predict the time for coitus for conception; it can only indicate in retrospect when coitus should have occurred in order for conception to have taken place.

2. Secretory endometrium–Progesterone exerts a profound effect upon the character of the endometrium in the proliferative and secretory phases. By examining a midluteal phase endometrial biopsy, a pathologist can determine within ±2 days the day in the cycle on which the endometrium was obtained.

3. Premenstrual molimina–Premenstrual molimina (those signs and symptoms which indicate that a period is imminent, eg, bloating, cramping,

acne, swelling of the hands and feet, emotional tension) are largely due to the effects of progesterone. Premenstrual molimina occurring with reasonably regular menstrual cycles are associated with ovulation in over 95% of cases. The absence of premenstrual molimina, however, is not an indication of the nonoccurrence of ovulation.

4. Thick cervical mucus–The prompt development of thick cervical mucus following a flow of clearly identifiable estrogen-stimulated mucus can be useful in pinpointing the time of ovulation, particularly when the development of the mucus is plotted on a menstrual calendar.

5. Vaginal cytology–Although progesterone exerts clearly recognizable changes on the exfoliated cells of the vaginal mucosa, the interpretation of such changes is best done by a competent cytologist working with a set of serial smears.

C. Corpus Luteum Function: After ovulation has occurred, the corpus luteum is responsible for the

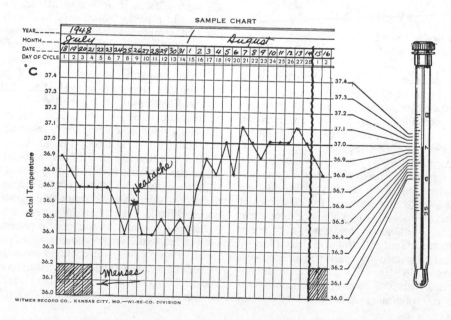

Figure 41–6. BBT recording. The temperature (oral, vaginal, or rectal) must be taken immediately upon awakening every morning before any activity whatever. The thermometer is allowed to remain in place for at least 5 minutes and the recording is made immediately. This procedure must be continued over a period of at least 3 cycles in order to obtain an accurate chart. (Courtesy of Witmer Record Co.)

production of estrogen and progesterone. Without adequate corpus luteum function, the chances for establishment and maintenance of pregnancy are markedly diminished. Two types of inadequate corpus luteum function have been identified:

1. Short luteal phase—A short luteal phase is one lasting less than 8 days. It is identifiable in retrospect by BBT changes or by daily serum progesterone measurements. It may occur spontaneously, and its relationship to infertility is unknown.

2. Inadequate corpus luteum—The inadequate corpus luteum is defective in progesterone production. It is an uncommon cause of infertility and is more commonly associated with habitual abortion. An inadequate corpus luteum may be diagnosed by multiple serum progesterone values that fall below the normal range or by an endometrial biopsy performed on the 26th day of the menstrual cycle which shows that endometrial development is out of phase by 2 or more days. The abnormality must be confirmed in a subsequent cycle. Moreover, unless the finding is consistent and repetitive, an inadequate corpus luteum cannot be considered as a primary cause of infertility.

Evaluation of Transport

A. Male Transport: This is evaluated by semen analysis (see p 958) and by physical examination.

B. Coital Transport: Coital transport is evalu-

Table 41–4. Postcoital test procedure.

1. Schedule the test for time of peak spontaneous cervical mucus flow or give exogenous estrogen to induce mucus flow if spontaneous and reasonably regular ovulation does not occur.
2. Require at least 2 days of ejaculatory abstinence before the test.
3. Proscribe douches for 24 hours before coitus and the use of vaginal creams or lubricants during coitus.
4. Time coitus to occur the night before or the morning of the postcoital test.
5. Expose the cervix with a speculum; gently wipe away excess mucus from the portio. Leave clear, shiny mucus in the internal os.
6. Remove sample of cervical mucus from cervical canal using a polyethylene catheter attached to a syringe. (After drawing mucus into the catheter, it is helpful to clamp the catheter close to the mucus with a clamp.)
7. Expel mucus from the catheter onto a glass slide. (Recall that mucus from the tip of the catheter is from deeper in the cervical canal and that mucus closer to the syringe is from the external os.)
8. Note amount of mucus. (Mucus column in the catheter should be at least 2 cm long.)
9. Note spinnbarkeit ("stretchability"). (Spinnbarkeit strand should be at least 6 cm long.)
10. Cover mucus on a slide with a coverslip and examine microscopically using both low- and then high-power objectives. (There should be at least 2 normal, motile sperms per high-power field in the mucus from near the internal os. In most normal tests there will be more than 5 normal motile sperms per high-power field. Very few white cells and no red cells should be present.)

Table 41–5. Interpretation of abnormal findings in postcoital test.

Finding	Cause
Thick yellow mucus with poor spinnbarkeit	Test performed at inappropriate time of cycle
Inadequate amount of clear mucus	Insufficient estrogen stimulation
	Inadequate number of mucus-secreting glands, eg, following cervical conization
Multiple white cells	Cervicitis
No sperm	Azoospermia
	Failure of male transport
	Failure of coital transport
Inadequate number of motile sperm	Oligospermia
	Inadequate cervical mucus
	Immunologic incompatibility

ated by a postcoital test such as the Sims-Hühner test, which is an excellent screening test and which should be required in every infertility evaluation. A normal postcoital test signifies normal sperm production, normal male transport, normal coital technique, and normal cervical transport. However, an abnormal test cannot identify a specific abnormality. The precise diagnosis must be obtained by comparing the results of the postcoital test, semen analysis, in vitro tests of sperm–cervical mucus interaction, further tests of the cervix, and additional immunologic tests.

The steps in performing a postcoital test are detailed in Table 41–4. The interpretation of abnormal findings is shown in Table 41–5.

C. Female Transport:

1. Cervix—Cervical transport is best evaluated by a postcoital test and careful examination of the cervix. If postcoital examination results are normal, cervicitis and cervical ectropion are unlikely causes of infertility.

Male-female immune reactions resulting in infertility are frequently (not always) manifested in an abnormal postcoital test. A normal semen analysis and a consistently poor postcoital test suggest the need for immunologic evaluation.

Semen contains many proteins that can be highly antigenic. In some women these are absorbed from the genital tract and result in the development of either circulating or tissue-bound antibodies (Fig 41–7). The antibodies are of 3 types: precipitating, agglutinating, or immobilizing. With subsequent coitus, these antibodies can adversely affect sperm. However, the specific role of these immunologic reactions in the genesis of infertility remains controversial.

The specific tests required to evaluate these problems must include suitable control mechanisms and should be precisely performed and carefully interpreted. Patients thought to be infertile because of immunologic causes should be referred to a specialist for evaluation.

2. Uterine and tubal transport—Uterine and tubal transport are always examined simultaneously. None of the currently available tests can investigate

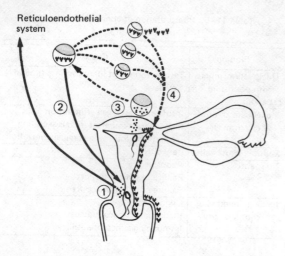

Figure 41–7. The sequence of events in the immune mechanism. (1) Primary response. As a result of sperm invasion, the reticuloendothelial system produces large, 19S-containing lymphocytes. (2) These migrate to site of invasion. (3) The secondary response is activated by macrophages stimulating large lymphocytes to produce small lymphocytes, which (4) migrate to uterus, cervix, and vagina. (Reproduced, with permission, from Behrman SJ: The immune response and infertility. In: *Progress in Infertility,* 2nd ed. Behrman SJ, Kistner RW [editors]. Little, Brown, 1975.)

actual transport function; instead, they only provide information about gross anatomy, ie, tubal patency or appearance. It is generally assumed that if the uterus and tubes are patent and appear normal, their function is satisfactory. Since this is not necessarily true, some cases of infertility are undoubtedly associated with undiagnosed tubal disease. Scarring and tubal adhesions are the major causes of transport infertility in women. Disorders that may affect fertility, in order of increasing severity, are illustrated in Fig 41–8 and include (1) minimal tubal distortion from peritubal adhesions, (2) phimosis of the fimbria, (3) hydrosalpinx with occlusion of the fimbria, (4) cornual block, and (5) dense periovarian and tubal adhesions.

Tubal transport function may be evaluated by means of 3 techniques (Fig 41–9). None is ideal and each carries a different risk and cost. The more costly and hazardous tests, eg, laparoscopy, should be performed only after other parts of the infertility study have been completed.

a. Uterotubal CO$_2$ insufflation (Rubin's test)—This test is a safe office procedure, though not as useful for diagnosis or treatment as formerly thought. It should be performed during the early follicular phase. A special uterotubal insufflator that provides a kymographic recording of pressure is recommended. CO$_2$ should be insufflated into the endometrial cavity using a special olive-tipped cannula. Tubal patency is

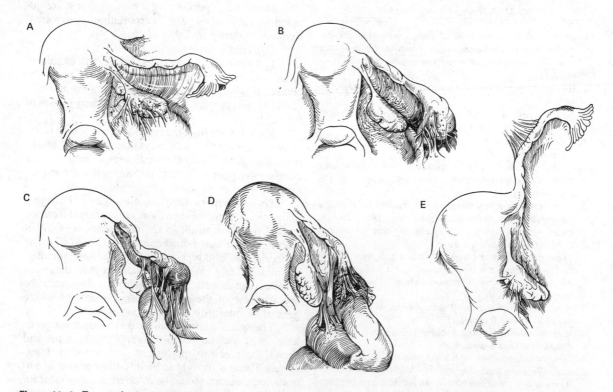

Figure 41–8. Types of tubo-ovarian distortion producing infertility. *A:* Ovarian adhesions to broad ligament. *B:* Adhesions blocking fimbriated end of tube. *C:* Tubo-ovarian adhesions following ruptured appendix. *D:* Peritoneal blockage. *E:* Functional block due to fixation of tube and ovary. (Reproduced, with permission, from Patton GW, Kistner RW: Surgical reconstruction of the oviduct. In: *Progress in Infertility,* 2nd ed. Behrman SJ, Kistner RW [editors]. Little, Brown, 1975.)

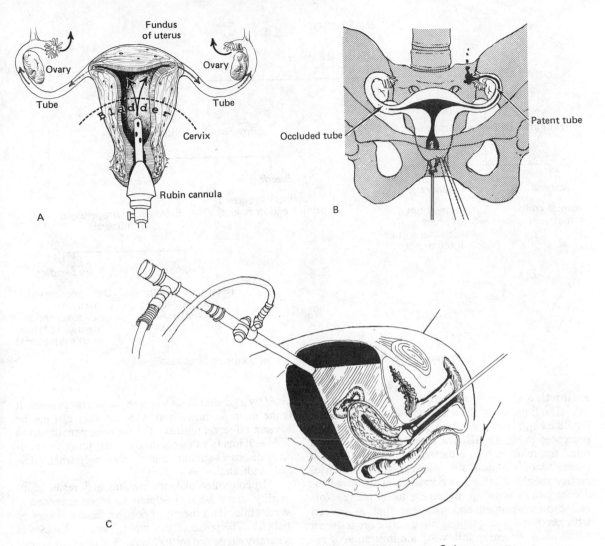

Figure 41–9. *A:* Tubal insufflation (Rubin test). *B:* Hysterosalpingogram. *C:* Laparoscopy.

best confirmed by the kymographic record, but it is also suggested by auscultation of the escaping gas or by identification of subsequent pneumoperitoneum, usually manifested by shoulder pain when the patient assumes the upright position. This test shows only blockage or patency; at best it can only indicate that one tube must be patent or that both are obstructed.

b. Hysterosalpingogram–A hysterosalpingogram may be obtained by instilling a liquid radiographic contrast medium into the endometrial cavity and tubes and observing the shadow of this material by means of image intensification or x-ray films. It permits examination of the internal surfaces of the uterus and tubes for anatomic abnormalities. Results are misinterpreted in about 25% of cases. The best sign of tubal patency is the crescent-shaped collections of dye spillage that appear between loops of small bowel. Hysterosalpingograms may be done without anesthesia in the outpatient department.

c. Laparoscopy with dye instillation–Laparoscopy with dye instillation shows not only whether the tubes are patent or blocked but also enables the physician to perform a direct examination of the peritoneal surfaces of the internal reproductive organs and to identify endometriosis as well as adhesions.

Laparoscopy usually is performed in the hospital under general anesthesia. The laparoscope should be inserted through a small periumbilical incision into the peritoneal cavity, which has previously been insufflated with 2–3 liters of CO_2. An accessory probe is frequently introduced through the lower anterior abdominal wall to facilitate manipulation of the viscera. After the peritoneal surfaces of the pelvis and pelvic organs have been examined, a liquid solution containing visible dye may be instilled through the endocervix, endometrial cavity, and tubes. Spillage of dye through the fimbria indicates tubal patency.

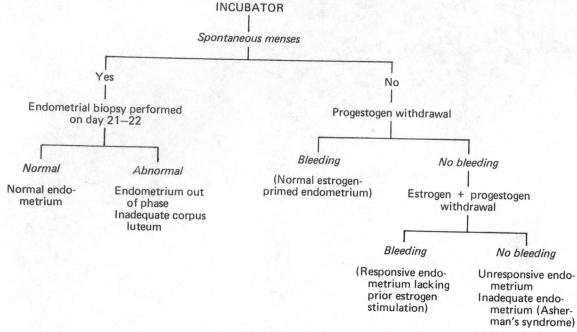

Figure 41–10. Assessment of function of uterus as "incubator."

Evaluation of the "Incubator"

The function of the uterus as "incubator" of the fertilized egg is evaluated according to the flow chart presented in Fig 41–10. The physician should keep in mind the relationships indicated in Fig 41–4. In the presence of spontaneous menses, an endometrial biopsy should differentiate normal from abnormal endometrium or show an inadequate luteal phase. Normal estrogen-primed endometrium, such as is seen with persistent anovulation, bleeds after progestogen withdrawal. Bleeding following administration of estrogen and withdrawal of progestogen indicates responsive endometrium that has been lacking prior estrogen stimulation. If no bleeding occurs following adequate estrogen therapy and progestogen withdrawal, the endometrium is unresponsive or is present in insufficient quantity. The latter state is found with endometrial adhesions (Asherman's syndrome) and is most often associated with a history of a previous pregnancy complicated by endometritis or vigorous surgical curettage.

All endometrial abnormalities probably cannot be identified using the procedures outlined above. Many enzymes present in the endometrium are necessary to assure the supply of nutriments to the developing blastocyst. Defects of these enzyme systems are associated with infertility, but at present clinically useful tests to detect such abnormalities are not available.

The interior of the endometrial cavity can be evaluated using the hysteroscope; however, the indications for this procedure are not yet clearly defined.

Evaluation of Other Problems

Subclinical hypothyroidism is not usually recognized by a general history and physical examination. It is the major common endocrine disorder that has an adverse effect on fertility. The measurement of serum TSH will identify this condition. Tests for other endocrine disorders should be performed only when clinically indicated.

Uncontrolled diabetes mellitus may result in infertility, and a 2-hour postprandial blood sugar test is worthwhile when there is a positive family history of diabetes. The possibility of other systemic diseases is generally suggested by the history and physical examination.

SCHEDULING THE EVALUATION

On the first visit, virtually all infertility patients should undergo the same general history, physical examination, laboratory studies, and psychologic assessment. A thorough explanation of the proposed evaluation should also be provided.

The Man

The next several visits on the part of the man are for the purpose of semen analyses. If these are abnormal, subsequent visits probably will be required to complete the appraisal.

The Woman

The procedures during subsequent visits on the part of the woman are determined by her ovulatory status. The timing of various tests for the ovulatory

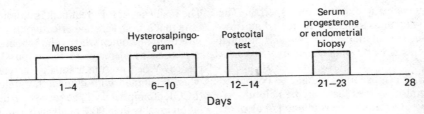

Figure 41–11. Optimal time in cycle for indicated tests. (Reproduced, with permission, from Abu FS, Marshall JR: The infertile couple. *Continuing Education* [March] 1977:58.)

woman is indicated in Fig 41–11. Testing may begin at any time in the woman's cycle, and the tests are then obtained sequentially. Thus, a patient who is in the early follicular phase should have a hysterosalpingogram immediately. The postcoital test for the next visit is scheduled for the next preovulatory period, and corpus luteum function is evaluated in the following luteal phase. For patients who are seen later in the cycle, the physician simply begins with the first appropriate test and then proceeds sequentially through the remainder.

Oligo-ovulatory and anovulatory patients should first receive progesterone, 100–200 mg in oil intramuscularly, in an attempt to induce progesterone withdrawal bleeding. After progesterone withdrawal, a hysterosalpingogram should be obtained, and the patient should then take estrogen, 1.25 mg of conjugated estrogen daily or its equivalent, for 10 days. A postcoital test is then performed near the end of estrogen administration, and bleeding is induced by progestogen withdrawal, eg, medroxyprogesterone acetate, 10 mg/d orally for 7 days.

If a schedule such as the one above is used, the major aspects of an infertility evaluation should not require more than 4–6 weeks. If an abnormality is found, additional testing may be required.

THERAPY

There is no general therapy for infertility. Specific therapies must be aimed at specific identified causes. This section can only provide an overview of treatment measures.

PROBLEMS OF TIME

Optimal Time for Conception

Couples frequently do not understand their inability to conceive immediately upon desire. Their failure carries important psychologic implications, and they may seek medical help. If, upon brief history, no readily identifiable cause of inability to conceive is found, eg, amenorrhea, the couple should be instructed in reproductive physiology, told about the importance of adequate coital exposure during the woman's fertile period, and counseled to return if they are still unsuccessful after 6 months.

Coital Frequency & Timing

A coital frequency of roughly every other day during the fertile period (3–4 days) results in maximal fertility. Identification of the woman's fertile period is of benefit, particularly for those couples who may feel that they cannot sustain the recommended coital frequency for an entire cycle.

In women with reasonably regular cycles, the fertile period can be estimated from its relationship to the next menstrual flow. This requires about 6 months' past experience with the length of the cycle as well as calculations that consider both the mean and the variables of the cycle. The calculations are relatively simple but are time-consuming and bothersome. The use of a mechanical calculator (Ovuguide, manufactured by Reproduction Research Laboratory, Westport, Connecticut) may be helpful. In women with a preovulatory cervical mucus flow, the mucus flow usually will identify the fertile period.

PROBLEMS OF SEMEN

Sperm

Azoospermia secondary to lack of gonadotropins is remedied by administration of human menopausal gonadotropins (hMG). There is no treatment for azoospermia associated with elevated serum concentrations of follicle-stimulating hormone and due to congenital anomalies or chromosomal abnormalities.

Oligospermia is generally not due to gonadotropin insufficiency but can be a manifestation of varicocele, which may be responsible for up to 15% of cases of male infertility. Ligation of the involved spermatic vein has resulted in improved semen quality in 70% and pregnancy in 53%. Better results are obtained when the preoperative sperm counts are greater than 10 million/mL.

Although administration of thyroid is specific and highly effective therapy for hypothyroidism, thyroid hormone is of no value in idiopathic oligospermia. The rebound phenomenon associated with the administration of testosterone is ineffective. Other hormonal therapies are generally not valuable and may be harmful.

Patients with oligospermia should be counseled regarding general measures that may be helpful. Patients should avoid excessive consumption of alcohol, tobacco, and caffeine and should refrain from excessive coitus. They should obtain adequate sleep and regular exercise. An adequate diet that includes weight reduction for the obese patient is recommended. Men should avoid excessive and prolonged exposure of the scrotum to heat by avoiding hot baths, jockey shorts, or prolonged sitting in a hot environment.

Seminal Fluid

Treatment of acute and chronic infection in the accessory sex organs can exercise a beneficial effect in the treatment of infertility.

There is no known effective therapy for infertility due to autoimmunity.

PROBLEMS OF OVA

Lack of Oocytes

There is no known therapy for the lack of oocytes.

Anovulation

Anovulation and oligo-ovulation may be treated by the induction of ovulation, as shown in Fig 41–12.

The mainstay of this treatment is clomiphene citrate, a drug that is both safe and effective. It will not improve infertility in women who ovulate spontaneously unless it is used as a treatment for corpus luteum insufficiency. When used in gradually increasing doses and when combined with human chorionic gonadotropin (hCG), clomiphene will be successful in inducing ovulation in more than 90% of all anovulatory and infertile women who show evidence of a good level of estrogen secretion by the ovary.

Sequential administration of human menopausal gonadotropin (hMG) and human chorionic gonadotropin (hCG) is effective in inducing ovulation in almost all other patients who have oocytes. Therapy with these medications is difficult, expensive, and hazardous and should be reserved for specialists.

Corpus Luteum Abnormalities

Therapy for short luteal phase is not known to be necessary or effective.

Therapy for inadequate luteal phase must be precisely timed during the ovulatory cycle because inappropriate timing may have profound adverse effects, and it must be started before the missed period of pregnancy if implantation is to be maintained. An accurate basal body temperature recording is essential and provides a useful chart for managing all types of therapy.

Progesterone is the principal agent for treatment of corpus luteum insufficiency. It should be started 3 days after the basal body temperature rise and should be administered in physiologic doses, ie, 25 mg suppositories twice daily, or 12.5 mg in oil intramuscularly, daily for 2 weeks. Suppositories are the preferred

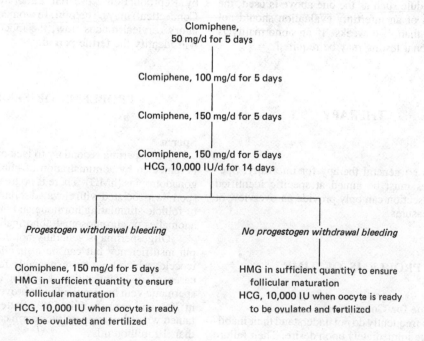

Clomiphene,
50 mg/d for 5 days

Clomiphene, 100 mg/d for 5 days

Clomiphene, 150 mg/d for 5 days

Clomiphene, 150 mg/d for 5 days
HCG, 10,000 IU/d for 14 days

Progestogen withdrawal bleeding

Clomiphene, 150 mg/d for 5 days
HMG in sufficient quantity to ensure
  follicular maturation
HCG, 10,000 IU when oocyte is ready
  to be ovulated and fertilized

No progestogen withdrawal bleeding

HMG in sufficient quantity to ensure
  follicular maturation
HCG, 10,000 IU when oocyte is ready
  to be ovulated and fertilized

Figure 41–12. Treatment plan for anovulatory infertility. (Modified and reproduced, with permission, from Marshall JR: Induction of ovulation. *Clin Obstet Gynecol* 1978;21:147.)

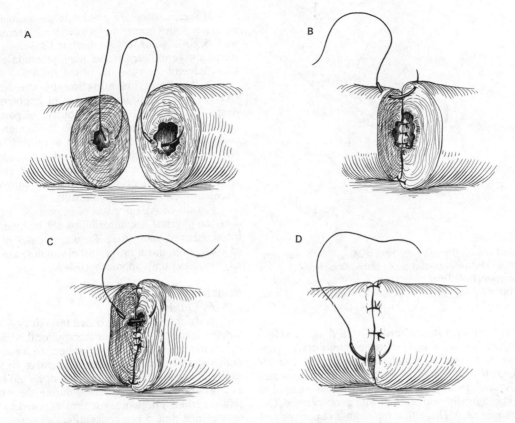

Figure 41–13. Technique for 2-layer reanastomosis of vas deferens which is best performed using 16–25 × magnification. The smaller lumen is about 0.33 mm in diameter. The anastomosis should be water-tight and is achieved using 9-0 nylon sutures. (Reproduced, with permission, from Silber SJ: Vasectomy and its microsurgical reversal. *Urol Clin North Am* 1978;**5**:575.)

treatment. However, they are not commercially available and must be specially prepared. Synthetic progestational agents should not be used.

hCG can stimulate progesterone production in the normal corpus luteum. However, in some cases of inadequate corpus luteum, hCG may not stimulate progesterone production. If the cause of the inadequate corpus luteum is inadequate FSH in the antecedent follicular phase, clomiphene citrate may be effective therapy.

If pregnancy occurs, treatment should be continued with injections of 17α-hydroxyprogesterone caproate, 125 mg intramuscularly twice weekly; progesterone suppositories should also be continued until at least the 12th week of pregnancy, when placental production of progesterone is well under way.

PROBLEMS OF TRANSPORT

Male Transport

Hypospadias may be surgically repaired with good results. Most blockage of male transport occurs in the vas deferens secondary to prophylactic vasec-tomies. A number of surgical procedures have been developed to reanastomose the vas deferens. Success is determined by the site of the obstruction, the duration of the obstruction, the reaction of the surrounding tissue secondary to the previous vasoligation, meticulous surgical technique, and diligent postoperative care. The success rate ranges from 0 to 85%. The highest success rates are associated with microsurgical techniques (Fig 41–13). Congenital obstruction and aplasia of the vas deferens are usually much more difficult to repair and are associated with a lower success rate.

Coital Transport

Coital transport problems are managed by education and counseling regarding coital techniques. Success is the rule. It should be pointed out to the couple that orgasm is not required for conception.

Male impotence is occasionally a cause of coital infertility. Eighty-five to 90% of male impotency has psychogenic causes; less than 2% is organic in origin.

A. Artificial Insemination: Although it is used to treat problems other than those arising from coital transport, artificial insemination will be discussed here.

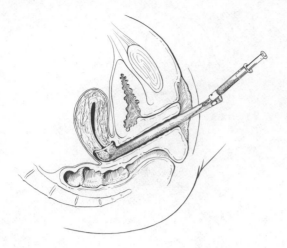

Figure 41–14. Artificial insemination using the cervical cup. (Modified and reproduced, with permission, from Davajan V, Nakamura RM: The cervical factor. In: *Progress in Infertility,* 2nd ed. Behrman SJ, Kistner RW [editors]. Little, Brown, 1975.)

1. Artificial insemination by a donor (AID)– AID involves numerous important philosophic, psychologic, religious, legal, and technical considerations. It is primarily indicated in a physiologically and psychologically normal woman who is married to a psychologically normal man with azoospermia. The advantages of AID are that the mother conceives and bears the child and that the child more closely resembles at least one of the parents than is the case with adoption. Legal problems are fewer than those that may occur with adoption. However, physicians should be thoroughly familiar with any legal regulations concerning AID in their areas.

The donor should be as closely matched to the husband as possible in physical appearance and genetic background and should be carefully screened for physical health, including the absence of venereal disease. Either fresh or frozen semen may be used. It should be remembered that both types of semen can transmit gonorrhea.

Insemination is performed during the immediate preovulatory period as determined by cervical mucus flow or another suitable indicator. Generally, at least 2 inseminations should be performed about 48 hours apart. The donor sperm can be introduced into the uterine cavity, the endocervical canal, the vagina, or a cervical cup (Milex Products, Chicago) placed against the cervix (Fig 41–14). The results using the vaginal or cup technique are at least as good as those obtained from the endocervical or intrauterine methods. No advantage arises from mixing cervical mucus with the donor specimen.

When AID using fresh semen is performed in the preovulatory period in women who have negative infertility evaluations, the pregnancy rate is at least as good as that which occurs with natural coitus. Pregnancy rates with AID using frozen semen are generally 50–70% of those with fresh semen.

If spermatozoa are present in the husband's semen, any coitus occurring between the 2 inseminations will deposit some of the husband's semen in the woman's genital tract and may preclude absolute knowledge of the paternity of the child.

2. Artificial insemination by the husband (AIH)–AIH is indicated in cases of impotence, hypospadias, physical incompatibility, oligospermia, and low seminal plasma volume. The semen can be deposited intracervically or into a cervical cup. If oligospermia is the indication for this procedure, insemination with the first portion of the ejaculate, which usually contains most of the spermatozoa (split ejaculate), tends to improve results.

Results of AIH in cases of impotence, hypospadias, or physical incompatibility are comparable to those obtained using AID. Results in cases of oligospermia, even those using split ejaculates, are generally poor and only approach 10%.

Female Transport
  A. Cervix:
    1. Immunologically based infertility–Condom therapy is the most effective therapy for this disorder. In this treatment, a condom must be used for all coitus until the sperm antibody titer is negative or significantly lowered. Thereafter, a condom should be used except when intercourse occurs during the woman's fertile period. The woman is thus exposed to semen only at that time when conception can occur. About two-thirds of women will demonstrate a significant decrease in antibody titer after 3–6 months of restrictive condom therapy. Of those who develop lower antibody titers, about one-half will become pregnant, whereas only 15% of those whose titers remain high will conceive. Agglutinating antibodies are associated with a better prognosis than are immobilizing antibodies.

    2. Insufficient cervical mucus–Insufficient or inadequate cervical mucus should be treated by the preovulatory administration of estrogen, which should begin on about the eighth or tenth day of the cycle. Doses can be increased every other day until a sufficient outpouring of clear, watery, slippery mucus is noted. In most patients this gradually increasing administration of estrogen in the preovulatory period will not inhibit ovulation. Estrogen should be continued until the basal body temperature rises.

In some patients, particularly those who have had previous conization, cauterization, or cyrosurgery of the cervix, there may be an insufficient number of cervical glands to produce an adequate quantity of mucus even with the aid of estrogen therapy. Attempts to treat these women with donor instillation of cervical mucus remain experimental.

  B. Uterus: Endometrial cavity adhesions (Asherman's syndrome) are best treated by careful dilatation of the endocervix and endometrial cavity, gentle endometrial curettage, and insertion of an IUCD followed by administration of large doses of estrogen, eg, conjugated estrogen, 2.5 mg orally daily. The

IUCD should remain in place for 3–6 months, during which time the endometrium should regenerate throughout the newly recreated endometrial cavity.

C. Tubes:

1. Scarring–The major cause of tubal infertility is scarring secondary to prior infection or endometriosis. The only effective treatment is operation, and surgical procedures must be specifically tailored to separate the adhesions and relieve the scarring. Operations are generally classified as follows: (1) salpingolysis, separation of adhesions around the tubes; (2) fimbriolysis, separation of sealed but essentially normal fimbria; (3) salpingoplasty, plastic reconstruction of a severely damaged tube; (4) uterotubal implantation; and (5) tubal resection and anastomosis.

Both macrosurgical and microsurgical (up to 20 × magnification with up to 9-0 sutures) techniques have been used for these procedures. Although definitive comparative studies have not yet been performed, it appears that better results are obtained with microsurgical techniques.

a. Salpingolysis–Approximately 30–40% of infertility operations require only separation of peritubal or periovarian adhesions or the excision of minimal endometriosis. Of these cases, 40–50% of patients will conceive, and approximately one-half will carry their pregnancies to term.

b. Fimbriolysis–The technique is illustrated in Fig 41–15. Pregnancy should occur in 5–40% of patients undergoing this operation, and about one-half of these pregnancies should proceed to live births. Ectopic pregnancies are relatively common.

c. Salpingoplasty–Salpingoplasties may be performed on patients with hydrosalpinx and more severe tubal disease. Some authors advocate the use of a Silastic fimbrial prosthesis (Rock-Mulligan hood) to cover the newly formed tubal ostium and prevent secondary adhesions. Removal of the prosthesis requires a second surgical procedure, often a laparotomy. Pregnancy and live birth rates are similar to those following fimbriolysis.

Available data suggest that intraoperative administration of high-molecular-weight dextran may be beneficial in decreasing postoperative adhesions and increasing the subsequent pregnancy rate.

d. Uterotubal implantation–Uterotubal implantation (Fig 41–16) is used in obstruction at the uterotubal junction. The procedure usually involves insertion of a tubular prosthesis that may be subsequently removed through the cervix. The pregnancy rate after this type of surgery is about 40%; about half of these will be full-term intrauterine pregnancies.

e. Midsegment reconstruction–Tubal resection and anastomosis are most often performed following a midsegment tubal ligation. The procedure is illustrated in Fig 41–17. About 50% of patients will conceive, and, again, about one-half will deliver full-term infants. Electrocautery tubal ligations are more difficult to repair satisfactorily because there is usually more extensive tubal damage.

2. Endometriosis–Endometriosis often causes

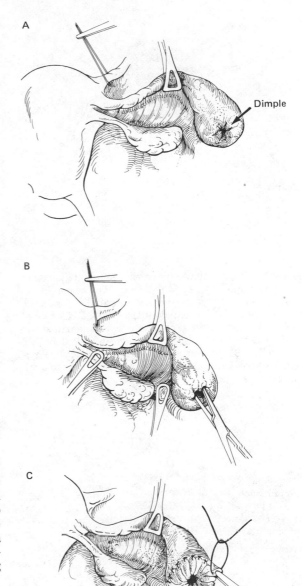

Figure 41–15. Fimbriolysis for partial occlusion of the oviduct. *A:* Hydrosalpinx. *B:* Fimbria teased open. *C:* Fimbria sutured to tubal serosa. (Reproduced, with permission, from Patton GW, Kistner RW: Surgical reconstruction of the oviduct. In: *Progress in Infertility,* 2nd ed. Behrman SJ, Kistner RW [editors]. Little, Brown, 1975.)

scarring, but even minimal endometriosis without scarring can also diminish fertility. When endometriosis is present, the chances for pregnancy are about 50% of normal.

Endometriosis with severe scarring should be treated surgically. Endometriosis without significant scarring may be treated hormonally, using an estrogen, a progestogen, a combination of estrogen and progestogen, or an antigonadotropin. The last 3 are the most

A

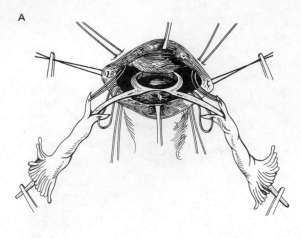

B

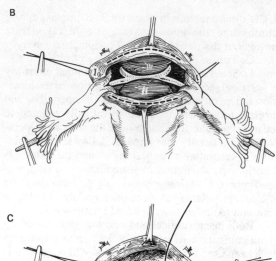

C

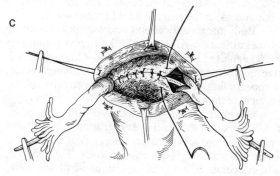

Figure 41–16. Uterotubal implantation showing method of insertion of prosthesis. *A:* Prosthesis well seated in the uterine cavity. *B:* Mersilene flap sutures tied. Incisions made in posterior and anterior uterine wall. *C:* Closure of deep myometrium over prosthesis with interrupted sutures. (Reproduced, with permission, from Patton GW, Kistner RW: Surgical reconstruction of the oviduct. In: *Progress in Infertility,* 2nd ed. Behrman SJ, Kistner RW [editors]. Little, Brown, 1975.)

A

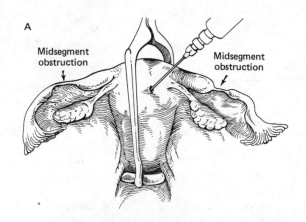

Midsegment obstruction

Midsegment obstruction

B

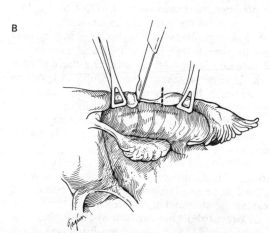

C

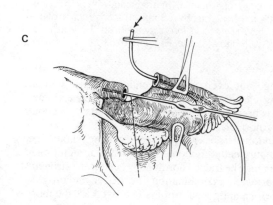

Figure 41–17. Midsegment anastomosis for occlusion of the oviduct. *A:* Transuterine lavage reveals distention of isthmic portion. Arrows indicate midsegment obstruction. *B:* The tube is placed on slight tension with Babcock clamps. The point of obstruction is excised. Care is taken not to enter the mesosalpinx. *C:* Lacrimal duct probe into isthmic portion. Polyethylene tubing through distal portion of oviduct (arrow). (Reproduced, with permission, from Patton GW, Kistner RW: Surgical reconstruction of the oviduct. In: *Progress in Infertility,* 2nd ed. Behrman SJ, Kistner RW [editors]. Little, Brown, 1975.)

commonly used treatments at present.

Two progestogens, medroxyprogesterone acetate and dydrogesterone, are useful in the treatment of endometriosis. The more popular, medroxyprogesterone acetate (Provera), 30 mg/d orally for 90 days, has resulted in improvement or remission in more than 90% of cases. Patients are anovulatory while on therapy, but 25% have breakthrough bleeding. About 45% of infertile patients become pregnant, and approximately 90% of infertile women whose partners are of normal fertility subsequently conceive. Ovulation promptly returns following termination of therapy.

Dydrogesterone (Duphaston), 5 mg twice daily for 9 months, has resulted in 90% of patients being free of symptoms. Approximately 45% of infertile women conceive. It is interesting to note that therapy does not disturb normal ovulation.

Combination treatment with estrogen and progestogen uses gradually increasing doses of oral contraceptive formulations to create a pseudopregnancy. Treatment initially consists of one tablet per day; this dose should be doubled when breakthrough bleeding occurs and then doubled again if breakthrough bleeding recurs. Therapy should be continued for 9 months. Eighty-five percent of patients show improvement, but less than one-half of them conceive.

Antigonadotropin therapy with danazol, 800 mg/d orally for 6 months, has resulted in marked improvement in 87% of cases. Because of its high cost, however, it is generally used only in patients who have not shown improvement after therapy with other hormones or in those who can afford this medication.

The progestogens are probably effective because of the marked decidual reaction with gradual necrosis and absorption that they seem to induce in the ectopic endometrium.

In Vitro Fertilization

In women with irreparable tubal obstruction, the only hope for pregnancy is by some technique that bypasses that obstruction. The recent development of techniques for obtaining oocytes from mature follicles, for fertilizing the oocytes in vitro, and then for placing the zygote in the uterus has opened a new era in the treatment of these women and in human reproductive biology. However, present success rates are abysmally low, and the specter of major chromosomal or congenital abnormalities, as well as the difficult ethical questions concerning experimentation on the living human zygote, remain unanswered. These concerns have caused the US government—at least temporarily—to ban use of federal funds for experimentation with in vitro fertilization. Although the successes have caused much excitement in the lay press and among patients, in vitro fertilization remains strictly experimental and probably will not be suitable for general clinical use for several years.

PROBLEMS OF THE "INCUBATOR"

Infection

Tuberculous endometritis is frequently associated with infertility and should be treated using standard antituberculosis therapy. Because the main effects of pelvic tuberculosis related to reduced fertility are in the oviducts, the resulting pregnancy rate is very low.

Chronic nonspecific endometritis is sometimes diagnosed on endometrial biopsy. The precise relationship of chronic endometritis to infertility is not clearly understood, and there is no specific therapy.

Anatomic Abnormalities

Congenital anomalies and uterine myoma generally do not result in infertility but may cause repeated first trimester abortions. Good results usually follow appropriate surgery.

OTHER PROBLEMS

Treatment of the other endocrine or systemic diseases associated with infertility is specific for the underlying disease.

● ● ●

References

Behrman SJ, Kistner RW (editors): *Progress in Infertility,* 2nd ed. Little, Brown, 1975.

Hafez ESE, Evans TN (editors): *Human Reproduction: Conception and Contraception,* Harper & Row, 1973.

Howards SS, Lipschultz LI (editors): Symposium on male infertility. *Urol Clin North Am* 1978;**5**:433.

Lamb EJ: Prognosis for the infertile couple. *Fertil Steril* 1972; **23**:320.

Lenton EA, Weston GA, Cooke ID: Long-term follow-up of the apparently normal couple with a complaint of infertility. *Fertil Steril* 1977;**28**:913.

Marshall JR: Induction of ovulation. *Clin Obstet Gynecol* 1978; **21**:147.

Menning BE: *Infertility: A Guide for the Childless Couple.* Prentice-Hall, 1977.

Moghissi KS: The function of the cervix in fertility. *Fertil Steril* 1972;**23**:295.

Moghissi KS et al: Homologous artificial insemination: A reappraisal. *Am J Obstet Gynecol* 1977;**129**:909.

Siegler AM, Kontopoulos V: An analysis of macrosurgical and microsurgical techniques in the management of the tuboperitoneal factor in infertility. *Fertil Steril* 1979;**32**:377.

Smith KD, Rodriguez-Rigau LJ, Steinberger E: Relation between indices of semen analysis and pregnancy rate in infertile couples. *Fertil Steril* 1977;**28**:1314.

Zukerman Z et al: Frequency distribution of sperm counts in fertile and infertile males. *Fertil Steril* 1977;**28**:1310.

42 | Emotional Aspects of Pregnancy

Mary Anna Friederich, MD

Emotional factors are of great importance during pregnancy and the puerperium. Some physicians possess a high degree of skill in dealing with their patients' psychologic problems; many others do not. The emotional aspects of obstetric practice have only recently been included in most standard textbooks and medical school instruction. Unfortunately, much of the literature on this subject deals mainly with the conscious fears that patients may experience, and therapy is discussed as if all that is required is simple reassurance and explanation of the effects of childbearing. If the doctor-patient relationship is mentioned, it is only to emphasize the importance of the patient's confidence in her obstetrician.

Some of what is known about the psychodynamics of human gestation will be reviewed here, and criteria will be offered that will help to identify psychologic high-risk patients. Prevention and management will be discussed, including the aspects of routine prenatal care that tend to favor a smooth progress through pregnancy and delivery and into a stabilized relationship with the baby and other members of the family.

MOTIVATIONS FOR PREGNANCY

Before one considers the stresses of pregnancy, it is important to understand what the couple brings to the pregnancy and to have some background information about why a given pregnancy occurs when it does. The almost universal availability of effective contraception means that for the first time in history men and women are able to decide when pregnancies shall occur, yet many pregnancies are still not consciously planned. Thus, there is a continuing need for pregnancy interruption.

Some psychologic settings are apparently inducive to procreation. The physician who understands these emotional goals and the meaning of "having a child" to a particular couple at a particular time can often help patients to plan pregnancies that are based on "good reasons" and perhaps avoid some that are unconsciously motivated by bad ones.

For example, the need to become pregnant may be quite different from the need to continue the pregnancy and to have and raise a child. Couples who feel inadequate as men or women may need to conceive a child in order to demonstrate their biologic validity. Once the point is made, however, they may lose interest in having a child and may request an abortion. A woman may need to become pregnant and carry to term in order to fulfill certain fantasies arising from loneliness. However, such a person may be unable to cope with the reality of child rearing and in time give up the child by adoption or neglect. A teenage girl who feels lonely and unloved may want a child to love and care for. Her fantasy is that by becoming a mother she will be in charge of her life—grown up ("happily ever after")—with a life companion who will love her and respond to her needs.

Pregnancy is commonly used as a defense against grief and loneliness when death or some other form of separation from significant family members or friends occurs. A suitable example is the couple who loses a child through illness or accident. In contrast, a military man who impregnates his wife just prior to going to war may unconsciously want to leave her with a child. The woman may turn to him for comfort and solace prior to separation without a conscious desire for a child. A child so conceived may be viewed as a substitute for the absent lover, with the result that the child may have less opportunity to develop to his or her full potential because of the intervening responsibility to satisfy the mother's needs.

There is a tendency for pregnancy to occur at a time of change in circumstances such as moving, changing jobs, etc. For many women, child rearing is a familiar and satisfying role—the thread of continuity running through their lives from their own childhood into adult life. Often they will conceive children at a time of life change rather than accept a new role that is unfamiliar and perhaps more difficult.

The ideal motivation for pregnancy, of course, is the need of a mature couple to produce and rear a child as a reflection of their own mutual love and expression of their ability to provide a home in which a child can grow to healthy adulthood. Often a child represents immortality to the parents. As people grow older, they may have a need to think of themselves as living on in future generations. This universal hope is given expression in many different religions.

PREGNANCY AS
A DEVELOPMENTAL CRISIS

Pregnancy is one of a chain of events in a person's development from birth to death. Part of the definition of crisis (Webster) is "an emotionally significant event or radical change of status in a person's life." Crises may also be considered as situations that block the usual patterns of action and call for new ones. In any event, pregnancy is a developmental crisis from which there is no return. A woman who has become pregnant or a man who has fathered a child can never be the same afterward.

The way in which an individual responds to a crisis will depend on his or her past development and the social setting of the crisis. Each parent must relive his or her own childhood during pregnancy in order to achieve freedom from some of the conflicts that inevitably occur in the course of growth and development in a human family. Much of this takes place at the unconscious level and is reflected in reports of "moodiness" during pregnancy. Feelings of sadness and depression occur at times of most intense unconscious effort to "work through" a previous family conflict. Women usually welcome the opportunity to talk about themselves and their families to an empathic professional person either individually or in a group setting. Men also need this review of their past experiences in order to father a child without undue conflicts. Despite wide recognition of the importance of these factors, little attention has been paid to them. Nonetheless, prenatal classes allowing couples to share their own past experiences in child rearing under professional guidance will be most helpful to the couple during pregnancy.

PSCYCHODYNAMIC FEATURES OF
STRESS IN PREGNANCY
& THE PUERPERIUM

The Elements of Stress

Pregnancy and the puerperium are periods of psychologic stress for all women, though some women experience minimal emotional discomfort during this time, and for many it may be the happiest time of life. The clinician must attempt to evaluate the patient's response to her condition not only to offer help if it is needed but also because her emotional state often has adverse effects on her physical well-being.

The physiologic requirements of uncomplicated pregnancy may overtax the somatic reserve of a woman with a preexisting organic disorder, and in such cases pregnancy may be a threat to the patient's health. Even manifestly healthy women may have physical and emotional problems during pregnancy, ranging from relentless abdominal enlargement to disarrangements of career and social activities. The pregnant patient may wonder whether the new baby will create problems in family relationships, with the burden of the change falling upon her.

Conception places the woman in the role of a giver much more than it does the man. Any event that so profoundly affects an individual's present and future life situation may be viewed as a potential threat to eventual adjustment. The clinical manifestations will depend upon the degree of stress and the efficiency of the individual's adaptive processes. These in turn relate to the circumstances of her past and present life.

Normal Adaptive Processes

There are 4 "tasks" each pregnant woman must perform to mother her offspring (Ballou). She must develop a sense of (1) her own mother; (2) her husband; (3) herself; and (4) her unborn child. Men must work through similar concepts to become good fathers.

One learns mothering or fathering best from one's own mother or father. The pregnant woman's relationship with her mother is a dynamic one that undergoes continuing change from infancy through childhood growth and development and the adolescent period. It will continue to be modified well into the middle and older years. A woman must make a conscious effort during pregnancy, with counseling help if needed, to appreciate her mother as a good, giving person who has provided emotional support and physical care. If she fails in this primary task, she may fail to think of herself as a good, giving, satisfying mother to her own child.

The pregnant woman who contemplates her relationship with her mother must reexamine her feelings of dependency and learn to tolerate and even to enjoy them. Unless this is done, the new baby's total dependency may be intolerable. This emotional reconciliation with the idea of dependency may be expressed as enjoyment in being with her mother and sharing pregnancy and child-rearing experiences. In contrast, women with unresolved anger toward their mothers may misinterpret their offers of advice or help as hostile attacks. Physicians or nurses are often unconsciously perceived by patients as "father figures" or "mother figures." They can be helpful to a pregnant woman in her reconciliation with her own mother or father. It is not essential for the woman to assume the characteristics of her own mother, but she must come to terms with the kind of mother she herself had before she can decide what kind of mother she should be. Occasionally, the physician or nurse may serve as a model in lieu of the patient's own mother. Thus, building a more adult "sense" of her own mother during pregnancy will further the process of emotional maturation.

The pregnant woman's relationship with her husband changes throughout pregnancy. Little has been said about his role during pregnancy itself, although his role during labor and delivery has been the subject of extended comment. The husband may functionally represent both his wife's mother and her father during this time (Ballou). Mates are often chosen because they resemble parents in some ways, and certain of these similarities may be emphasized during pregnancy. A supportive husband can help his wife resolve ambivalent feelings about her mother by protecting her from conflict with her mother and by accepting unresolved maternal dependency. Moreover, the pregnant woman may look to her husband as she once did to her father—eg, for compliments or reassurance about her appearance when she feels unattractive. Being both surrogate father and surrogate mother may be a heavy burden for a man who must also deal with identity conflicts involving his own parents. During his wife's pregnancy, he must discover in himself a dependent, hitherto denied feminine aspect. For some men, this is threatening and disruptive at a time when maximum fortitude is needed. A man may hesitate to behave in a paternally strong and masculine way toward his wife if he unconsciously equates this as unacceptable competition with the image of his own father. Such a husband may react punitively—eg, by forcing his wife to cook dinner when she has nausea of pregnancy. Or the husband may simply be preoccupied with his own emotional development at a time of increased demands for support from his wife as she works through hers. The obstetrician who appreciates these forces can help by offering support and counseling to both the husband and the patient.

The major developmental task for the pregnant woman may be to learn to feel like a mother and function as one. She must develop her unique inherent capacity for mothering. After she acquires mastery of that role, the accompanying sense of competence and effectiveness will then extend to other aspects of her life. The experience should make her a better person as well as a better mother.

The psychologic adaptation to pregnancy varies at different times during the course of pregnancy. Early in pregnancy, most women report that the pregnancy seems unreal to them, ie, they cannot believe they are pregnant. This denial mechanism helps them to gradually assimilate the changes that are going on within so they will not have to deal with all of the changes at once. It also allows for interruption of pregnancy by abortion if the woman does not want a child. The most common and most successful adaptive process is **identification**, ie, the woman unconsciously absorbs the concept of pregnancy into her own ego. She perceives the pregnancy as an essential part of herself, and the implication of this is nonthreatening. Identification is an effective adaptive reaction because what is perceived and accepted as an integral part of oneself is not as threatening as something that is perceived as a foreign body. The identification is associated with an introversion of interests that varies in degree and is manifested in different ways. A woman who has made this adjustment will talk about "my pregnancy" but rarely "the pregnancy" or "it." On the other hand, women who are seeking an abortion will usually show by choice of words that they have not accepted the pregnancy as part of themselves.

A well-adjusted woman who has enjoyed her work and social activities may become less interested in these things when she is pregnant. She may prefer to remain at home and may tend to eat more than before. She may be introspective but has not yet focused emotionally upon a baby as much as upon "my pregnancy." She often spends time talking with other women about her pregnancy. She may actively seek out her own mother in order to hear about mother's pregnancies. In this way she usually can identify more fully with her mother.

Finally, one must consider the normal symptoms of pregnancy, most of which relate to body functions and are brought repeatedly to mind. This does not imply that the symptoms are emotional in origin, but psychologic components are often present. The perceptive physician will note that the patient in early pregnancy talks about her symptoms with interest and in a conversational rather than a complaining manner.

As pregnancy progresses, the patient may experience a change in her emotional focus. She may begin to feel intellectually and emotionally that the pregnancy truly consists of a separate individual with a potential of its own. At about 18 weeks, she begins to feel fetal movements and the physician hears the fetal heart tones.

Fantasies about the baby are an important adaptive device during the second trimester. Although most women are quite secretive about their daydreams, the gratification thus derived often helps them adjust to the continuing stresses of pregnancy and to prepare for the giving role that will impose its greatest demands during the puerperium.

The focus of attention changes from "my pregnancy" to "the baby," and this attitude is reflected in interest in layettes, choice of name, and indecisiveness about whether to knit blue or pink booties—regardless of how many have already been knitted. The physician may be asked if it is possible to predict the sex of the baby. Discussions of growth and development and interest in the fetal heartbeat do more than inform. They feed fantasy and help the woman focus on the baby as an entity.

As term nears, attitudes and interests are in sharp contrast to those noted during the first trimester. The woman becomes impatient with maternity clothes and her ever-enlarging abdomen and hopes she will be "early." Even women who have enjoyed their pregnancies are often eager to "get it over with" at this stage. The fantasy life has begun to pall and is no longer an adequate source of ego gratification as the patient's interests turn outward again. She looks forward to delivery because she is eager to have a real baby in place of the imagined one. These psychologic shifts help to prepare the adequately adjusted woman for the discomfort of labor and the assumption of postpartum maternal responsibilities.

Most women welcome the onset of labor because of the nagging physical discomforts of the last trimester and their eagerness to have the baby in arms. Some women prefer being at home in familiar surroundings for early labor; others are so anxious that they need the support of the hospital at an early stage. Almost all women are concerned about the safety of the baby during labor. For some, fetal monitoring may be reassuring; for others, it may only increase their anxiety to hear or see the fetal heart tracings as they vary with contractions.

Women with problems in prior pregnancies, particularly fetal losses, will respond most favorably to the fetal monitor. They will view the monitor as a protector, as an aid in communication with the nurse and obstetrician, as evidence that the fetus is alive and well, or as an aid to increasing the involvement of their husbands in sharing the labor experience. Other women will view the monitor as a competitor, feeling that the husband or staff hover about the monitor rather than about them. The monitor may be viewed as a mechanical monster causing distress and discomfort or enforced immobility. It may increase anxiety due to variations in the fetal heart rate. Some women are concerned that the scalp electrode may injure the baby. It is important to talk about the monitor in a positive fashion, both prenatally and in the labor room prior to its use.

Women who need to be in control during labor look upon modern technology as depriving them of their dignity. Modern obstetrics faces the dilemma now of a growing demand for home deliveries at a time when modern technology is making childbirth safer for both mother and baby. This demand reflects women's great sensitivity to the ambience during labor and delivery and their need to be treated with concern and humaneness. It also reflects the needs of certain women to deny the frightening aspects of labor and delivery that concern everyone, men as well as women. All women are anxious about labor and delivery. Nevertheless, there is evidence that those who can talk and dream about this in advance may have fewer complications.

At delivery, the obstetrician and the obstetric nurse are in the best position to notice how the mother—and father if present—accept the newborn. Their first remarks and first expression of feelings will reflect their true feelings toward the child. For example, some women will cry with disappointment at the sex of the child, yet quickly seal this over and appear happy by the time they reach the postpartum floor. Recent studies indicate that mother-child bonding goes on within the first few minutes to hours after delivery. If a mother holds the child skin to skin, this makes a long-term difference in mother-child interaction. In some studies, this bonding has favorably influenced motor and verbal development of the child well into the third year of life.

Kennell and Klaus, who introduced the concept of maternal-infant bonding, view the immediate postpartum period as a "sensitive period" though not necessarily a critical one for mother and baby. Other investigators are attempting to learn more about the long-term consequences for childhood development of this initial mother-infant interaction. Although little is known about father-child interaction at the time of delivery, many fathers present at the time of delivery report that they feel more involved with the child as well as its mother. Sharing the birth experience may influence the father's attitude toward sharing child care tasks. The couple's interaction at this crucial time will help the physician understand how the couple will interact in the raising of this child. Such data may be helpful in later counseling of the couple.

The puerperium may be a period of psychologic stress for many women. The mother is now faced with the need to provide primary care for a helpless and demanding other person. She is not always able to correctly interpret squalled messages from the baby, especially during the early days and weeks of postnatal life, when the rewards of having a smiling and crooning happy baby to show off and play with are not yet offered. Transient or chronic fatigue is a common problem. Fatigue lowers the psychologic reserve and leads to irritability. If the husband becomes the target of her vexation, a source of needed support may be temporarily lost at a time when it is most needed. If anger is internalized, depression may develop ("postpartum blues").

Breasts that are full and tender are a painful annoyance, and the unfamiliar and often frustrating nursing routine may provoke tears of discouragement. Complete dependency of the infant on the mother is a responsibility that may be burdensome at first. Explanation, demonstration of nursing and child care procedures, and reassurance will help to minimize the feeling of dejection that is common during this period.

A brief episode of mild depression may develop about 1 month after delivery, when personal sacrifices and the drudgery of daily routines have taken much of the glamor out of motherhood. Feelings of resentment toward the baby and the husband are often present. Additional household help, a cooperative and understanding attitude on the part of the husband and the physician, and adequate reassurance usually will prevent serious depression.

In rare instances, the period following the puerperium is too stressful to be borne, and in these cases psychotic behavior may serve as an avenue of escape. Such cases always represent long-standing emotional problems jolted into overt psychosis by the triggering mechanism of pregnancy, labor, and motherhood. It might be said that childbirth does not cause postpartum psychosis so much as it destroys habitual defenses against psychosis. Even in psychologically healthy women, the stress of the puerperium may occasionally lower the psychologic reserve and result in mild and transient depression.

Determinants of Stress

The magnitude of the psychologic stress of pregnancy and the puerperium and the success of adaptation depend upon the woman's past and current life experiences and her reactions to them. Acceptance of a capacity for mothering as a natural element of every woman's biologic endowment is a normal part of psychosexual development. This implies a willingness to accept the giving role as well as the physical discomfort and other sacrifices that pregnancy and motherhood impose on every woman. However, every woman retains the need to receive as well as give, to be secure in her husband's affections and her life situation, and to be confident in her relationships with the professional men and women who will care for her during this important period of her life.

Diagnosis of Stress Reactions in Pregnancy & the Puerperium

The physician who takes care of obstetric patients has the responsibility of identifying, early in prenatal care, those women who are unable to withstand the stresses they must undergo and those with existing problems that they cannot verbalize. Patients who are able to discuss their emotional difficulties may present problems of management but not of diagnosis.

The psychologic high-risk patient may be identified by one or more of the following items in the medical history:

(1) Ambivalent identification with the mother; strong repudiation of the mother; a dread of becoming like her mother—more ominous in a grown woman than a pregnant teenager.

(2) Major episodes of psychologic distress related to pregnancy in the patient's mother or sisters.

(3) Major emotional problems during or after a previous pregnancy.

(4) Severe or prolonged somatic symptoms without apparent organic cause in a previous pregnancy; extravagant terms ("ghastly," "stormy") used to describe a previous labor which was normal by usual criteria.

(5) Failure to act out mother roles in early childhood; seldom played with dolls, avoided baby-sitting; extended "tomboy" phase.

(6) Current life situation that appears to offer little psychologic support; unwed girl or woman rejected by family and without other supporting interpersonal relationships; woman confined to household role with disinterested husband or other major marital or situational difficulties.

Signs of existing emotional problems include the following:

(1) Failure to exhibit normal adaptive devices; failure to accept the reality of pregnancy; persistent (beyond 10–12 weeks) use of terms or expression of attitudes indicating that pregnancy is unwanted; persistent (beyond 14–20 weeks) failure to show interest in baby; failure to anticipate termination of pregnancy as term approaches.

(2) Major sustained mood changes or repeated, rapid mood swings; striking changes in sleep patterns.

(3) Severe, prolonged, or multiple somatic symptoms with no organic cause shown by diagnostic study.

Severe emotional problems that develop after delivery embrace a variety of psychiatric problems of which schizophrenia is probably the most common. The onset of overt illness may occur at any time including the first postpartum day. In most cases, the onset of

symptoms is during the first 2 weeks (median: fourth or fifth postpartum day). Symptoms and signs consist of confusion, often associated with marked uncertainty and indecision; disorientation, usually in time but sometimes in space; déjà vu sensations; and feelings of hopelessness, despair, and depression.

Transient mood changes (irritability, crying) are signs of lesser degrees of puerperal emotional stress that occur in otherwise stable women and do not herald psychologic collapse. Uncertainty and confusion are not pervasive; disorientation, daydreaming, and detached states are not seen. Fatigue is realistic—if someone else takes care of the baby, the mother can sleep and awakes refreshed. Despite this, early malignant signs of severe emotional problems in the puerperium should not be casually dismissed as "normal postpartum blues."

Treatment of the Emotionally High-Risk Patient

Brief informal psychotherapy and the administration of appropriate psychotropic drugs suffice for most patients. If there are signs of psychosis and unremitting depression or severe anxiety, prompt psychiatric referral is indicated. After the patient adjusts well enough to get by, consideration may be given to more prolonged insight-oriented psychotherapy.

MANAGEMENT OF EMOTIONAL PROBLEMS IN PREGNANCY & PUERPERIUM

Antenatal Period

Psychiatric advice should be obtained for pregnant women whose history indicates that they are psychologic high-risk patients. Referral to a psychiatrist is essential when signs of a major disorder are first noted during the puerperium. The primary physician rarely can repair major personality defects or deal directly with deep-seated conflicts during the course of prenatal care. However, effective prevention or treatment of the minor emotional problems of a large majority of patients is possible within the context and demands of a busy obstetric practice.

The cornerstone of effective psychotherapy is the doctor-patient relationship, and the manner in which this relationship is utilized by the clinician must be emphasized.

Most women exhibit dependent needs during pregnancy. All patients must feel that they can rely on the physician's medical and technical competence. The fact that a patient returns to the same obstetrician or obstetric group in subsequent pregnancies indicates that she has found satisfaction in the relationship and approves of the way she has been treated. What is sometimes forgotten is that the pregnant patient needs to be told that she too is "doing a good job" and that the doctor is interested in her as an individual with whom to engage in the pursuit of important goals. Throughout the months of gestation, the patient obtains reassurance from displays of professional interest in her and in the developing fetus. During labor, normal dependent needs are satisfied by the periodic examinations and encouragement that characterize good intrapartum nursing care. Routine obstetric care has psychotherapeutic value, and this must be understood if the obstetrician's program is to be improved and altered to meet individual needs.

To foster a doctor-patient relationship that only fulfills dependent needs is only a part of the plan. The objective should be to utilize the dependency relationship to increase the woman's acceptance of her biologic endowment and to help her acquire a realistic confidence in her own ability to fulfill her potential. In other words, by fulfilling normal dependent needs, the clinician gains the patient's confidence, then uses this confidence to increase her reliance in herself. Specific suggestions include the following:

(1) Provide important factual instruction. This has special psychologic value if it is given by the physician or someone the physician designates. Group instruction classes conducted by experienced personnel have great value for some patients. This is superficial but positive group psychotherapy.

(2) Emphasize the natural and normal nature of pregnancy. This means that the patient should not be burdened with arbitrary restrictions on her activities or given unnecessary medications. (Many obstetricians routinely prescribe multivitamin preparations without knowing either the recommended daily intake or the content of their own prescriptions.) Brief statements that cite specific normal findings are of value.

(3) Recognize and encourage normal adaptive aids. It is of greater therapeutic value to listen for a few minutes as a patient talks about her symptoms than it is to reach for a prescription pad. In many cases she is not really complaining but only wants to talk about her feelings. During the second and third trimester, the doctor-patient exchange should include comments on normal intrauterine development, and the patient should be encouraged to listen to the fetal heart and to palpate the bony and soft parts. Ultrasonography gives the couple a chance to "see" the baby in utero and helps enrich their fantasy life and fosters early bonding to the infant. Unpublished data from England show that this is useful in encouraging compliance with good prenatal care, eg, giving up smoking, drinking, or using other recreational drugs that may harm a developing fetus. If the couple is having difficulty accepting the idea of a new baby or is unable to perceive the fetus as a separate individual, ultrasound examination might enhance prenatal fetal bonding and solve problems of inadequate nurturing before they arise.

(4) Manipulate the patient's environment so as to lessen realistic stress and provide needed support. Specific measures will vary with individual patients, but the father is of critical importance. His continued display of affection and interest in both the patient and baby is essential. His attendance at prenatal classes and his presence during labor or delivery should be encouraged as a way of demonstrating his interest and concern. Some men have little curiosity about the biology of pregnancy and may find the details of labor and delivery upsetting or distasteful. They should be allowed to show their love and desire to help, which is often deep and sincere, in other ways. Some do so naturally and intuitively; others require counseling by the physician. Indeed, with the increasing number of fathers who are encouraged to attend their wives in labor, it is paradoxic to observe how infrequently they are invited to be present at prenatal examinations when they may talk with the obstetrician.

Factual information about labor and delivery is now widely disseminated among laymen. However, generations of biologically uninformed women have done well in labor and become good mothers. Information about the role played by a supportive doctor-patient relationship and the interpersonal support of the husband and family help many women achieve greater confidence in their own biologic capability.

Intrapartum Period

Intrapartum psychologic difficulties are seldom experienced by a patient who has entered labor reasonably confident about herself and her obstetrician. With or without analgesia, such a patient is prepared to accept the inevitable discomfort because "it's worth it." If the delivery is spontaneous, the patient's confidence can be increased just by being congratulated by her doctor for having delivered the baby herself. Even if an operative delivery is necessary, the patient still does most of the work involved in labor. Reinforcement should still be employed; appropriate self-reliance is a valuable asset during the puerperium.

The emotions of a woman in labor profoundly influence her reactions to pain and discomfort. It may be her first experience in a hospital, and it is important that the surroundings be compatible, homelike, and restful. A tour of the maternity area of the hospital prior to labor as well as an introduction to some of the hospital staff will help decrease the fears that may attend the prospect of hospitalization. The couple will probably be apprehensive, and a warm, friendly welcome by the hospital staff is important. The atmosphere and attitudes created by the staff play a prominent part in influencing the behavior of a woman in labor. Most women respond to sympathetic understanding and kindness.

Emotional support must be given during the prenatal period and especially during labor. A woman in labor is undergoing one of life's basic experiences, and support must be given to prevent it from becoming traumatic and devastating. If it is traumatic, it may have an adverse effect on the mother's attitude toward her new infant and on her postpartum recovery and may contribute toward "postpartum blues."

A woman in labor needs companionship and should not be left alone or isolated. If left alone, she may fear that the baby will be born suddenly and the call button will not be answered promptly. She should be assured that if she sleeps she will be supervised closely.

It is important that the woman in labor be attended by nurses who are empathic in their responses to her feelings and suffering. Encouragement, reassurance, and an explanation of the progress being made are of great value at this time. The mere presence of the nurse is not enough; support must be demonstrated by actions and by words of encouragement and praise, to which women in labor respond magnificently.

Very often the father is with the mother during labor and can give this emotional support; however, they both may find labor and delivery distressing and disturbing. Some men may be unable to be present at this critical time for other reasons. Under these circumstances, the attitude of the nursing staff is of even greater importance.

Puerperium

Clinicians should vary the time of their hospital rounds to include times when patients are nursing or have just finished nursing. During nursing, observation and not discussion is the prime objective. Upon entering the room, the doctor should encourage the mother to continue feeding the baby and watch her for a short time. The verbal exchange should be kept light so that the patient will be minimally distracted from the experience of feeding her baby. Advice and instruction are offered only if the patient's questions or obvious difficulties indicate some urgency; otherwise, she should be congratulated for doing well. The observer should note the mother's demeanor (relaxed or tense, calm or excited), her behavior toward the baby (cuddling, maternal cooing or talking, stroking or petting the child), and her techniques (appropriate burping). Observations can also be made during patient rounds that are timed to the postfeeding period. It is at this time that many patients will benefit maximally from special advice, given according to individial need. If suggestions have already been given, these may be repeated if it seems that reinforcement is needed.

Observations by experienced nursery and obstetric nurses are another source of valuable information. Indeed, the nursing staff is in the best position to encourage mother-child interaction by being supportive of the mother, reassuring her, and teaching her about baby care. The success of breast feeding by a primigravida often depends upon the support she receives from the nurses.

Instructions given at the time of hospital discharge should not be routine for all patients but must be modified by estimates of the particular needs of the individual and her family. Such appraisals are of clinical value even though they may be imprecise by scientific standards.

The experienced multigravida with a record of success in taking care of newborn babies is not likely to have any significant difficulties if her health is still good and there have been no adverse changes in her situation at home.

Unnecessarily restrictive instructions may aggravate the problems of even a reasonably stable woman who has not yet acquired an adequate sense of self-confidence. A patient who has more confidence in an overly authoritative clinician and medical discipline than in her own common sense generally follows strict instructions. Psychologic reserves should not be further stressed during the puerperium by restrictions that impose more sacrifices. There is no reason why a physically normal woman of average stability should be confined to her home, let alone restricted to a single floor, even during the early puerperium. Nor should she be restricted to a shower if she prefers a tub. She should resume intellectual, social, or other activities at her own pace. A couple should not arbitrarily defer coitus in deference to the calendar without considering the state of the perineum and their own mutual desires. In some instances, the husband-wife or mother-child relationship may be unnecessarily strained during a period when such relationships should be strengthened. Women should be assured that it is normal to feel irritated by a problem posed by the newborn and to want to get away for a short time—to the theater, to dinner at a restaurant, to the office or library.

Different estimates of psychologic needs are appropriate for a patient who appears somewhat unstable yet manageable. She may benefit most from instructions that are quite different in a psychologic sense. It is likely that the patient who has been overly dependent throughout pregnancy and the early puerperium will continue to feel insecure after hospital discharge. If she seems indecisive, very specific instructions should be given; the advice should be based more upon psychologic than biologic considerations. (For example, a woman might be instructed to take her iron tablets at specific times rather than 3 times a day.) The pediatrician should be alerted to her needs, and the patient should be required to telephone at specific times of the day if questions arise. This reduces the number of phone calls, especially of the type that might seem trivial to the clinician who is unfamiliar with (or unsympathetic to) the dependency needs many women have during this time.

By these devices the clinician attempts to be as supportive as possible during a limited but difficult time; moreover, this can be done within the limits of a demanding practice. A properly instructed husband often is able to reinforce postpartum advice during his wife's periods of indecisiveness. Consequently, it is often desirable to give postpartum advice in writing to an overly dependent or indecisive patient in the presence of the husband.

While all patients may benefit from some household help during the early puerperium, assistance may be particularly valuable for those women who adjusted poorly during the pregnancy. It is important, however, that special consideration be given to the person who will provide the help. Near relatives with whom the patient has felt competitive, especially a mother, may create or intensify psychologic problems. The help should bolster the patient's ego by removing some of the physical load and the need for routine decision making so she can focus her attention and reserves on neonatal care and baby-oriented decisions. Conflicting advice from relatives and friends, especially to insecure patients, should be avoided.

Still different estimates of psychologic support during the puerperium are appropriate for a patient who has been identified as a high psychologic risk. If psychiatric consultation has not been obtained, the patient's ability to cope should be observed by an experienced person who can visit the home periodically, at least during the first 2 weeks. In most areas, a Visiting Nurse Association provides such a resource. The physician should tell these people what information is desired and what instructions have been given the patient. If such visits must continue beyond 2 weeks, it may be wise to see the patient at the end of 2–3 weeks rather than wait for the postpartum visit at 6 weeks.

SOME SELECTED PROBLEMS OF PSYCHOLOGIC IMPORTANCE DURING PREGNANCY & THE PUERPERIUM

Libido Changes

According to Masters and Johnson, normal pelvic turgescence heightens sexual tension during pregnancy. As a result, most pregnant women experience increased sexual desire, particularly during the second trimester. Hence, orgasm may be achieved more easily and more often during pregnancy—occasionally in previously nonorgasmic women. Paradoxically, whereas detumescence following orgasm may be slower, the period of satiation may be shorter. Nonetheless, the frequency of coitus may not be increased, tempered as it is by fear of compromising the pregnancy. Actually, most women report a decline in frequency of intercourse during late pregnancy.

Problems may result from a significant variation in the libido of either partner, especially early in pregnancy, if the other's sexual desires remain unchanged.

A reduction in libido probably is associated with a general inversion of the mother's interests, and couples should be reassured that the change is transient so that it will not be unduly magnified. Such reassurance is more apt to be accepted, and therefore effective, if it is accompanied by a simple explanation reinforced by an appropriate analogy. One such comparison is the decrease or loss of normal sexual drive men often experience during periods of preoccupation with business or professional problems. Among couples who have established a strong sexual relationship, it is usually adequate to give this reassurance to the patient, who can then effectively transmit it to her husband. In other instances, effective consultation in the office with both husband and wife may be necessary.

Decreased male libido during pregnancy may be due to an unconscious feeling that a pregnant woman is an improper object of sexual desire. Such men seldom complain, and their drives are usually expended on their businesses or in increased athletic activity. Others may fear that coitus may jeopardize the pregnancy.

The result may be that the woman believes she has lost her husband's affection because of her pregnancy. What she misses is the kissing, fondling, and hugging that she associates with affection, though her husband may associate them with sexual desires he no longer experiences as he did before the pregnancy. In most instances, simple explanation to the husband will enable him to show his affection for his pregnant wife and keep the marriage warm and happy during what should be a happily remembered time for both partners.

Hyperemesis Gravidarum

Anorexia and varying degrees of nausea and vomiting are extremely common during early pregnancy and may be in part a physiologic response. However, when vomiting interferes with the patient's metabolism (dehydration, weight loss, ketonuria, electrolyte imbalance) and organic causes are excluded by reasonable diagnostic study, it usually can be assumed that the symptom is emotional in origin. Hyperemesis may be a classic example of expression of a neurotic conflict along physiologic pathways. However, it is not necessarily correct to assume that the pregnancy and the baby are unwanted just because the patient experiences severe vomiting at this time. The mother and father usually have ambivalent feelings about the pregnancy. A woman may report varying degrees of nausea with successive pregnancies. Those gestations with the most nausea often come at a time in the woman's life when she is not quite ready for a child, either because of her own psychologic needs or for social reasons. Nonetheless, relatively few women use excessive nausea as a reason for requesting abortion.

The high success rate of drugless therapy for hyperemesis gravidarum indicates that psychosocial factors are important in this symptom complex. The woman often needs to be hospitalized not only to treat the dehydration, ketonuria, and electrolyte imbalance but also to totally change her environment (at least temporarily) and to reduce whatever secondary gain she is receiving from the symptoms. Hospitalization allows the physician and nurses to spend more time with the woman in order to learn more about her motivations for the pregnancy, her own upbringing, her relationship with her husband, and her current life stresses. While learning about these, the professional staff should be developing a deeper relationship with the woman while allowing her to ventilate her feelings. This and isolation in the hospital from some of the patient's current life stresses may be all that is necessary to relieve many of the psychic pressures that contribute to the nausea. Frequently, this will tide her over until the physiologic stresses that cause nausea in early pregnancy have passed.

Prenatal Diagnosis of Fetal Defects

Prenatal diagnosis of fetal defects is becoming an increasingly important part of obstetric practice. It requires a team effort in which the obstetrician, genetic counselor, and ultrasonographer must cooperate and communicate effectively. Genetic counseling centers play a large role in distributing information and facilitating the parents' decision-making process. The obstetrician, however, is usually the person to whom the parents look for support and guidance. The coping mechanisms of parents presented with a possibility (or certainty) of having a defective baby may begin with a **first stage** of denial, followed by shock. They may appear calm only because they are unable to integrate information about the problem when the diagnosis is first presented to them. A second meeting should be scheduled so that the **second stage** of cognitive awareness, characterized by severe anxiety, can be dealt with. At this time, the physician can discuss plans and alternatives, since the couple is now motivated to seek relief from anxiety. Intellectual coping devices soon give way to underlying hostility and anger in the **third phase.** ("Why me?" "Why us?") Either party may direct feelings of anger at the other, at the physician, or even at the personnel at the genetic counseling center.

The **final phase** in the coping process is the phase of depression and withdrawal, characterized by sadness and a need for support from the physician. The couple may want the physician to make all of the important decisions, which of course the physician must not do.

Some couples decide to continue a pregnancy even though there is almost no chance of having a normal baby. Others demand termination of the pregnancy even though the chances of having a normal baby are statistically quite good. Some couples are interested in prenatal disease detection even though they would never even consider abortion, feeling perhaps that by knowing in advance what the problem will be, they will have more time to prepare for it. The couple should not be made to feel that because they have been referred for prenatal diagnosis they must have an abortion, nor should they be denied prenatal diagnosis if they indicate that they are not interested in abortion.

Abortion after diagnosis of fetal defect may be far more traumatic than the usual induced abortion for an unplanned pregnancy. Blumberg et al report that 92% of mothers undergoing elective abortion after diagnosis of a genetic defect suffered postabortion depression and guilt feelings. The obstetrician must be aware of what the couple undergoing fetal diagnostic studies might be feeling, so they can be offered appropriate support along with technical and scientific advice and expertise.

Infant Feeding

Much has been written about the physical and psychologic advantages of breast feeding to the mother and her infant. It may be helpful to mention some psychologic details that may be overlooked.

The advantages of breast feeding do not apply to women who have strong feelings against it or whose husbands have such feelings. The desire to avoid breast feeding may be an isolated phenomenon unrelated to the woman's ability to mother an infant. Women who elect to bottle-feed their babies can enjoy considerable fondling and body contact with the baby nonetheless. Some do so instinctively; others if the importance of fondling and body play is discussed with them.

Women who are undecided about which method of infant feeding they prefer will usually choose the method that best suits their needs after a discussion with the doctor. In part their choice is determined by their social and educational status. In the USA, breast-feeding mothers are usually from the higher socioeconomic groups and have more than a high school education. Their choice is also determined by their own past rearing and is largely an unconscious decision. Women must achieve gratification from breast feeding in order to be successful at it. It is unwise for the physician to try to persuade a woman to breast-feed. If pressed, she may comply for a few days in the hospital but soon gives up in despair at home, claiming that her milk "dried up." Unfortunately, women must now leave the hospital by the third or fourth postpartum day—hardly long enough for the support and help that is often needed with the often painful start of breast feeding. Community groups of mothers who have successfully breast-fed are often good referral sources for the mother who is breast feeding for the first time.

Adequate feeding instructions are of obvious importance whether the patient has elected to breast- or bottle-feed her baby. One detail frequently overlooked is the dictum that newborns are not all alike, ie, some are "suckers" and others are "chewers." The chewers can be managed by letting them work on a finger before being put to breast.

Rooming-In

The advantages of rooming-in are many. For the newborn, the likelihood of infection probably is reduced by the elimination of care by multiple hospital personnel. Feeding is usually timed to the baby's individual needs, and better physical care (dryness, warmth) is likely if the mother is experienced or adequately instructed. For the mother, rooming-in affords better assurance that she will become truly familiar with her newborn and confident about its care before hospital discharge. Questions that might otherwise remain unanswered can be dealt with as the need arises. Patients who elect rooming-in require no expensive equipment and reduce the demands on the newborn nursery and its personnel. In some institutions, a flexible variation of rooming-in permits mothers to send the baby back to the nursery for rest periods.

The disadvantage of rooming-in is that some women already feel confident about being able to take care of the baby and need rest more than anything else.

A contributing factor to postpartum depression is the feeling of insecurity in handling the new baby. The stay in the hospital is so short that there is little opportunity for the mother to change diapers or bathe the infant under supervision unless she is rooming-in. Although prenatal classes are attended by many mothers, bathing a live infant is quite a different matter.

Each new mother must be supervised in bathing and caring for her baby before leaving the hospital. Many new mothers are afraid to handle the baby because it is so "fragile." Many have no help when they go home and must fend for themselves.

PSYCHOLOGIC PROBLEMS RELATED TO SPONTANEOUS ABORTION

Chromosomal abnormalities and defective placentation are responsible for the vast majority of spontaneous abortions. There is no convincing evidence that emotional factors can cause abortion.

A personality profile has been described by a few clinicians of women who exhibit the syndrome of habitual abortion without apparent organic cause. The profile includes such traits as an unusual degree of dependency, a high degree of suggestibility, and an inability to express hostility. Nevertheless, the role of emotional factors in the genesis of habitual abortion is difficult to assess.

The traits described are difficult to quantitate, especially in the absence of reliable psychologic testing. Reported studies seldom include the evaluation of possible chromosomal or placentation abnormalities, are retrospective in nature, and do not include satisfactory controls. Because current knowledge does not establish a definite cause in most patients who habitually abort, individual clinicians will continue to have

their own opinions about the role of emotional factors. With respect to psychologic management, however, the isolated spontaneous abortion may be more traumatic than is generally appreciated, especially for a patient who has not yet established her reproductive ability. Strong reassurance giving data derived from investigative studies is often helpful. A simple way of explaining what may happen is to say that normal men may ejaculate a small number of abnormal sperms and normal women may discharge an occasional immature or abnormal ovum, and that if an abnormal sperm unites with a normal ovum, or vice versa, an abnormal pregnancy ensues that "nature" rejects by the device of spontaneous abortion. Emphasis should be on the element of chance and the basic normality of the couple, with reassurance that the mishap was not related to anything they did or did not do.

The pregnant woman who appears unduly dependent, meek, and suggestible will require a very dependent doctor-patient relationship regardless of whether her history justifies the diagnosis of habitual abortion without apparent cause. Once such a relationship is established, attempts should be made to use it to increase the patient's confidence in herself, though it may not be successful until after the 16th week of gestation if the patient has a history of habitual abortion. Occasionally, the dependent needs of an individual patient may be so great that they cannot be fulfilled by the obstetrician. In such cases, psychiatric assistance may prove helpful.

● ● ●

References

Asch SS, Rubin LJ: Postpartum reactions: Some unrecognized variations. *Am J Psychiatry* 1974;**131**:870.

Bahna SL, Bjerkedal T: Course and outcome of pregnancy in women with neuroses. *Acta Obstet Gynecol Scand* 1974; **53**:129.

Ballou JW: *The Psychology of Pregnancy, Reconciliation and Resolution.* Lexington Books, 1978.

Blumberg BD, Golbus MS, Hanson KH: The psychological sequelae of abortion performed for a genetic indication. *Am J Obstet Gynecol* 1975;**122**:799.

Burstein I, Kinch R, Stern L: Anxiety, pregnancy, labor, and the neonate. *Am J Obstet Gynecol* 1974;**118**:195.

Colman AD, Colman LL: Pregnancy as an altered state of consciousness. *Birth and Family* 1973;**1**:7.

Falicov CJ: Sexual adjustment during first pregnancy and postpartum. *Am J Obstet Gynecol* 1973;**117**:991.

Flapan M: A paradigm for the analysis of childbearing motivations of married women prior to birth of the first child. *Am J Orthopsychiatry* 1969;**39**:3.

Frommer E, O'Shea G: Antenatal identification of women liable to have problems in managing their infants. *Obstet Gynecol Surv* 1974;**29**:185.

Heymans H et al: Fears during pregnancy: An interview study of 200 postpartum women. *Isr J Med Sci* 1975;**11**:1219.

Jackson LG: Prenatal genetic counseling. In: *Psychosomatic Obstetrics and Gynecology.* Youngs DD, Ehrhardt AA (editors). Appleton-Century-Crofts, 1980.

Kennell JH, Klaus M: *Maternal-Infant Bonding: The Impact of Early Separation or Loss on Family Development.* Mosby, 1976.

Kennell JH, Trainer MA, Klaus MV: Evidence for a sensitive period in the human mother. *Ciba Found Symp* 1975; **33**:187.

Klaus MH et al: Maternal attachment: Importance of the first postpartum days. *N Engl J Med* 1972;**286**:460.

LaBarre M: Emotional crises of school-age girls during pregnancy and early motherhood. *J Am Acad Child Psychiatry* 1972;**11**:537.

Light HK, Solheim JS, Hunter GW: Satisfaction with medical care during pregnancy and delivery. *Am J Obstet Gynecol* 1976;**125**:827.

McDonald RL: The role of emotional factors in obstetrics: A review. *Psychosom Med* 1968;**30**:222.

Miller WB: Psychological vulnerability to unwanted pregnancy. *Fam Plann Perspect* 1973;**5**:199.

Nadelson C: Normal and special aspects of pregnancy. *Obstet Gynecol* 1973;**41**:611.

Nilsson A et al: Parental relations and identification in women with special regard to paranatal emotional adjustment. *Acta Psychiatr Scand* 1971;**47**:57.

Psychosomatic aspects of Ob-Gyn practice. *Contemp Obstet Gynecol* (Oct) 1974;**4**:45.

Ringler NM et al: Mother-to-child speech at two years: Effects of early postnatal contact. *J Pediatr* 1975;**86**:141.

Rosenwald GC, Stonehill MW: Early and late postpartum illnesses. *Psychosom Med* (March-April) 1972;**34**:129.

Samko MR, Schoenfeld LS: Hypnotic susceptibility and the Lamaze childbirth experience. *Am J Obstet Gynecol* 1975; **121**:631.

Solberg DA, Butler J, Wagner NN: Sexual behavior in pregnancy. *N Engl J Med* 1973;**288**:1098.

Starkman JN, Youngs DD: Reactions to electronic fetal monitoring. In: *Psychosomatic Obstetrics and Gynecology.* Youngs DD, Ehrhardt AA (editors). Appleton-Century-Crofts, 1980.

Starkman M: Fetal monitoring: Psychologic consequences and management recommendations. *Obstet .Gynecol* 1977; **50**:500.

Uddenberg N et al: Nausea in pregnancy: Psychologic and psychosomatic aspects. *J Psychosom Res* 1971;**15**:269.

Wilson JG et al: Prognosis of postpartum mental illness. *Compr Psychiatry* 1972;**13**:305.

Wingate C, Kapp IT: The relationship of the manifest content of dreams to duration of childbirth in primiparas. *Psychosom Med* 1977;**34**:313.

Maternal & Perinatal Statistics | 43

Martin L. Pernoll, MD

Statistical data may seem onerous and difficult to assimilate unless one realizes the absolute necessity of their proper use as a weapon against death and disability. Statistical analysis offers a measure of the effectiveness of medical care. The techniques of adequate recording, processing, recovery, and utilization of data should be as familiar to the practitioner as prescription writing. In this chapter we shall define and discuss some maternal and perinatal statistical concepts that are often useful in the practice of obstetrics and gynecology.

According to the National Center for Health Statistics, life expectancy for everyone in the USA has risen since 1971, most notably in the past 3 years. In 1971, life expectancy was 74.6 years for women and 67 years for men. In 1977, life expectancy rose to 77.1 years for women and 69.3 years for men (73.2 years for the overall population). Currently (1978 data), the overall life expectancy in the USA is 73.3 years. Nonwhites of both sexes still have a lower life expectancy (68.8 years) than whites (73.8 years).

The overall death rate in 1980 in the USA was 8.9 per 1000 population—an increase of 2.3% over 1979. The reduction in the infant death rate was offset by a higher death rate for persons aged 65 years or older. The total number of deaths during 1980 was 1,986,000, and the excess of births over deaths added 1,612,000 persons to the population of the USA during that year.

Diseases of the heart (> 332,000 cases) and malignant diseases (> 179,000 cases) caused almost two-thirds of the deaths that occurred in 1979.

Despite an 85% 5-year cure rate in favorable cases, breast cancer is still the leading cause of death due to cancer in women. When there is spread to the axillary nodes, the survival rate declines to 56%.

The uterus and cervix are the sites of 13% of cancers but account for only 5% of deaths in women due to cancer, whereas ovarian cancer, only 4% of the total, accounts for 6% of deaths in women due to cancer.

Over the past 50 years, the number of deaths due to breast cancer has remained constant, while deaths due to cancer of the uterus and cervix have declined—by 57% in the last 30 years. Ovarian cancer, responsible for an increasing number of deaths in the past, has been a lesser problem since 1960.

Sites of cancer leading to death in women that have remained constant include the esophagus, kidney, mouth, and skin. There has been a decrease in cancers of the bladder, colon and rectum, liver, and stomach in women. A slight increase in the frequency of deaths due to leukemia and pancreatic cancer has moderated, but there has been a startling increase in the incidence of lung cancer in women since 1965. This has been attributed to cigarette smoking.

FERTILITY RATES

The fertility rate is the number of births per 1000 women between the ages of 15 and 44 years (inclusive), calculated on a yearly basis. It is a more accurate means of comparing the reproductive behavior of different population groups than the birth rate (number of births per 1000 total population). Over the last 40 years, the fertility rate in the USA has varied from 66.4 to 122.9. The latest fertility rate of 66.4 (1978) demonstrates a continuation of the low rates in recent years. However, the number of births is currently rising. For example, in 1980 there were 3,598,000 births, compared to 3,149,000 in 1975. This is due to the greater number of women in the reproducing age group. The sociologic factors that influence these rates are beyond the scope of this limited discussion. It may be useful, however, to have data available concerning a given population for purposes of planning obstetric and neonatal care facilities and personnel training and for making informed decisions concerning the practice of obstetrics, pediatrics, or neonatology.

The marriage rate, which has risen each year since 1977, was 10.9 per 1000 population in 1980; there were 2,413,000 marriages. The divorce rate was 5.3 per 1000 population; there were 1,182,000 divorces in 1980.

The average number of lifetime births to be expected by women 18–24 years of age has remained stable during the last 5 years at approximately 2.2 births per married woman. The expected number of lifetime births was 2.9 per married woman of the same age group in 1967 and 2.4 in 1971.

The equilibrium level of fertility in the USA is approximately 2.1 children per woman. This level has existed for some time (with slight fluctuations) in many western European countries and in Japan.

Almost 70% of the women who were married for the first time between 1965 and 1969 were 21 years of age or younger. The proportion dropped to 60% from 1975 to 1979. More than 55% of first-born children in the latter half of the 1960s were born to women under 21 years of age. A decade later, this proportion has fallen to 47%. Moreover, the longer a woman delays having children, the less likely she is to have one. Nearly 90% of childless wives aged 25–29 years and married for less than 2 years expect to have children. Fewer than 70% of childless wives in this age group married for 5 or more years expect to have children. It may be anticipated that as many as 25–30% of women in the USA may complete their childbearing years without giving birth. However, these data must be interpreted carefully, because there is a recent trend for older women to have children.

MATERNAL MORTALITY RATES

A maternal death is the death of any woman, from any cause, while pregnant or within a certain interval after termination of pregnancy, irrespective of the duration or site of the pregnancy. Although the interval after termination of pregnancy may be variously defined by different states and countries, the majority accept 42 days. For statistical evaluation, it is necessary to divide the 42 days after pregnancy into 2 periods:

Period I: 1–7 days after termination of pregnancy.

Period II: 8–42 days after termination of pregnancy.

Maternal deaths are classified into 3 broad etiologic groupings: **Direct maternal death** (formerly obstetric mortality) is a death resulting from obstetric complications of the pregnant state, labor, or puerperium or from intervention, omission of necessary treatment, incorrect treatment, or combinations of these causes. **Indirect maternal death** is an obstetric death resulting from previously existing disease or disease that developed during pregnancy, labor, or the puerperium. It is not directly due to obstetric causes but is aggravated by the physiologic effects of pregnancy. **Nonmaternal death** is an obstetric death resulting from accidental or incidental causes not related to the pregnancy or its management.

The **maternal death rate** is the number of maternal deaths (direct, indirect, or nonmaternal) per 100,000 births for any specified period. Maternal deaths from all causes and particularly from obstetric causes have become less common. The currect obstetric (direct maternal) mortality rate in the USA is approximately 9.9 per 100,000 births (1978). One of the major etiologic factors in the marked reduction of maternal mortality rates (since 1930, over a 30-fold decrease) has been the improved health care systems for pregnant patients. Nonetheless, some obstetric patients still die of preventable disorders.

One of the most important contributing factors may be that modern obstetric care is not equally distributed. Individuals of lower socioeconomic status who receive less than adequate prenatal care have a consistently higher mortality rate.

Many other factors may be correlated with maternal mortality rates. Increased maternal age carries an increased risk of death in pregnancy. The mortality hazard rises steadily after 30 years, and for those over age 45 it is approximately 9 times that of women 20–24 years of age. Increasing parity is also associated with increased risk.

MATERNAL MORBIDITY

Maternal morbidity may be defined as an elevation of body temperature, after the first 24 hours following delivery, above 38 °C (100.4 °F) on 2 occasions 24 hours apart, within 10 days postoperatively or postpartum. This usually is expressed as a percentage of total patients in each group and may be used to compare operative problems or puerperal infection in different institutions, or in the same institution, over a period of time. Unfortunately, it expresses only the infection parameter of morbidity, and morbidity may occur from many causes (eg, hemorrhage, atelectasis, embolization, or nervous system damage). Nevertheless, because of the seriousness of puerperal infection and the simplicity and sensitivity of body temperature recording, it is still widely used.

Puerperal infection is most often due to anaerobic infections (in at least three-fourths of cases), and the most common of these is streptococcal infection. Other common organisms include *Escherichia coli* and staphylococci. Virulent clostridial and *Bacteroides* infections are less common (under 6% of all cases) but are of great seriousness when they do occur. The puerperal morbidity rate should not exceed 2%.

PREGNANCY

Pregnancy (gestation) is the maternal condition of having a developing fetus in the body. The human conceptus from fertilization through the eighth week of pregnancy is termed an **embryo;** from the eighth week until delivery, it is a **fetus.** For obstetric purposes, the duration of pregnancy is based on **gestational age:** the estimated age of the fetus calculated from the first day of the last (normal) menstrual period (LMP), assuming a 28-day cycle. Gestational age is expressed in completed weeks. This is in contrast to **developmental age (fetal age),** which is the age of the offspring calculated from the time of implantation.

The term **gravid** is a general one meaning pregnant, and **gravidity** is the total number of previous pregnancies (normal or abnormal). **Parity** is the state of having given birth to an infant or infants weighing 500 g or more, alive or dead. In the absence of known weight, an estimated duration of gestation of 20 completed weeks or more (calculated from the first day of the LMP) may be used. From the practical clinical viewpoint, a fetus is considered viable when it has reached a gestational age of 23–24 weeks and a weight of 600 g or more. However, only very rarely will a fetus of 20–23 weeks weighing 500–600 g or less survive, even with optimal care. With regard to parity, a multiple birth is a single parous experience.

LIVE BIRTH

Live birth is the complete expulsion or extraction of a product of conception from the mother, irrespective of the duration of pregnancy, which, after such separation, breathes or shows other evidence of life (eg, beating of the heart, pulsation of the umbilical cord, or definite movements of the involuntary muscles) whether or not the cord has been cut or the placenta detached. An infant is a live-born individual from the moment of birth until the completion of 1 year of life.

In the most recent nomenclature, a **preterm infant** is defined as one born at any time through the 37th completed week of gestation (259 days). Unfortunately, for the purposes of evaluation of statistical data, this definition does not specify that there are great differences among fetuses in this group. Therefore, it is useful to preserve the classification by weight or duration of gestation still used by many. Using the latter system, an **abortion** is the expulsion or extraction of all (complete) or any part (incomplete) of the placenta or membranes, without an identifiable fetus or with a fetus (alive or dead) weighing less than 500 g. In the absence of known weight, an estimated duration of gestation of under 20 completed weeks (139 days) calculated from the first day of the LMP may be used.

An **immature fetus** weighs 500–1000 g and has completed 20 to less than 28 weeks of gestation. A **premature infant** is one with a birth weight of 1000–2500 g and a duration of gestation of 28 to less than 38 weeks. A **low-birth-weight infant** is any live-born infant weighing 2500 g or less at birth. An **undergrown** or **small-for-date infant** is one that is significantly undersized (< 2 SD) for the period of gestation. A **mature infant** is a live-born infant who has completed 38 weeks of gestation (and usually weighs over 2500 g). A **postmature infant** is one that has completed 42 weeks or more of gestation (Fig 43–1). The **postmature syndrome** is characterized by prolonged gestation, sometimes an excessive-size fetus (see below), and diminished placental capacity for sufficient exchange, associated with cutaneous and nutritional changes in the newborn infant.

A fetus or infant of **excessive size** is one that is larger than the gestation would indicate or that at the time of birth weighs over 4500 g. Significantly increased morbidity and mortality rates may be associated with the relative dystocia created by the large fetus. About 10% of newborn infants are oversized (over 4000 g), and 2% are of "excessive" size (over 4500 g). With better nutrition and heavier infants, there has not been a commensurate increase in maternal pelvic dimensions. Excessive fetal size should be suspected in large multiparous or obese mothers, those with diabetes mellitus, or those whose weight gain during pregnancy has been greater than anticipated.

The untimely termination of pregnancy constitutes one of the major problems of perinatal care. The factors that lead to the initiation of labor and the subsequent termination of pregnancy remain unknown. This is the case for both late termination and premature termination (discussed in the section on neonatal mortality rates, p 987). A prolonged pregnancy is a gestation that has advanced beyond 2 SD from the mean and with a duration of ≥ 42½ weeks (297 days). The perinatal mortality rate at 43 weeks is twice that at 39–42 weeks. The fetus probably develops a relatively restricted placental exchange capability, leading to an increased intrauterine death rate.

Each of the above terms is numerically expressed by a rate per 1000 births over a given interval.

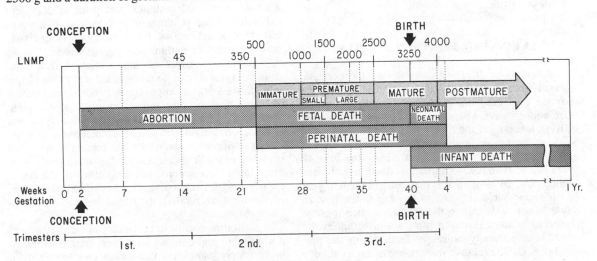

Figure 43 –1. Graphic display of perinatal nomenclature.

BIRTH RATE

During 1980, the birth rate in the USA rose 4% over 1979 to a rate of 16.2 live births per 1000 population or 69.2 live births per 1000 women aged 15–44 years. This rise reflects both a continued growth in the number of women of childbearing age and an increase in the childbearing rate. During 1980, the number of births reached 3,598,000. Moreover, this number is expected to increase by slightly over 1% annually until 1985.

NEONATAL INTERVAL

The neonatal interval is from birth until 28 days of life. During this interval, the infant is referred to as a **newborn infant.** The interval may be divided into 3 periods:

Neonatal period I: birth through 23 hours, 59 minutes.

Neonatal period II: 24 hours of life through 6 days, 23 hours, 59 minutes.

Neonatal period III: 7th day of life through 27 days, 23 hours, 59 minutes.

PERINATAL INTERVAL

The perinatal interval is the span of fetal and neonatal life. It is an important concept because many of the stresses and hazards that affect the fetus have either a direct or an indirect effect in the neonatal period. An arbitrary division of authority (between obstetrician and pediatrician) and attention only to the product of conception at birth may be hazardous and unwarranted. The perinatal interval of life may be divided into 2 periods:

Perinatal period I: 28 weeks of completed gestation to the first 7 days of life.

Perinatal period II: 20 weeks of gestation through 27 days of life.

PERINATAL MORTALITY RATES

Jeopardy to life is greater during the perinatal interval than at any subsequent time. Current data indicate that Yankauer's estimates from New York were conservative when he indicated that the number of lives lost during the 5-month period from the 20th week of gestation to the seventh day after birth is almost equal to the number lost during the next 40 years of life. Table 43–1 illustrates death rates by age in the USA. Of those deaths occurring in the first year of life, approximately 70% will occur in the first 28 days. If one adds this to the fetal loss, then it is the period of greatest threat to life for a given interval.

There are many causes of death during the prenatal period. The relative importance of each can only be assessed in the context of overall mortality rates and

Table 43–1. USA death rates by age (per 100,000 population).*

Age	1978 (Estimated)	1977 (Final)	Percent Difference
Less than 1 year	1417.0	1485.6	−4.6
1–4 years	66.9	68.8	−2.8
5–14 years	34.7	34.6	0.3
15–24 years	120.3	117.1	2.7
25–34 years	136.8	136.2	0.4
35–44 years	239.2	247.5	−3.4
45–54 years	610.3	620.7	−1.7
55–64 years	1414.2	1434.9	−1.4
65–74 years	3018.1	3055.6	−1.2
75–84 years	7161.0	7181.9	−0.3
85 and over	14,679.1	14,725.9	−0.3
All ages	882.3	878.1	0.5

*Monthly Vital Statistics Report: An Annual Summary for the United States, 1978. National Center for Health Statistics, US Department of Health, Education, & Welfare, Vol 27, No. 13, August 13, 1979.

appraisal of those factors that present the greatest hazard to the fetus and infant. It is important to note that fetal deaths occurring after the 20th week of pregnancy account for about half of all perinatal deaths.

FETAL DEATH

Fetal death is the cessation of fetal life prior to complete expulsion or extraction, irrespective of the duration of pregnancy. It is expressed as a rate per 1000 births. **Early fetal death** is abortion (see definition above). Generally, an **early abortion** occurs before 16 weeks of gestation and a **late abortion** occurs from the 16th through the 20th week, although there is considerable variation for these definitions. **Intermediate fetal death** occurs when the pregnancy has progressed for 20–28 weeks. **Late fetal death** is death after 28 weeks of gestation and prior to complete expulsion of the products of conception. With carefully applied definitions, the accuracy of comparisons between states or nations will be improved.

In nearly half of all intermediate or late fetal deaths, no cause can be determined. Of those deaths with defined causes, approximately 60% are placental and umbilical in origin (eg, infection, cord compression, prolapsed cord, placental abruption, placenta previa, circumvallate placenta, placental insufficiency). Approximately 20% are related to maternal obstetric or medical diseases, and approximately 10% are related to congenital malformations of the fetus. Nearly 7% are related to diseases of the fetus (eg, erythroblastosis fetalis); the remaining 3% are due to other causes.

Stillbirths decline as the quality of care before and during labor and delivery improves. Identification of high-risk pregnancies so that special care can be given is essential to minimize fetal deaths (see Chapter 28).

NEONATAL MORTALITY RATES

A neonatal death is the death of a baby during the first 28 days of life. Rates are expressed in deaths per 1000 live births. If the infant has survived the fetal stage, the neonatal mortality rate is inversely proportionate to birth weight. Each year, 7–8% of all live births in the USA occur prematurely. Thus, prematurity is clearly one of the chief contributing factors in death and disease during the neonatal period. Because low-birth-weight infants comprise the largest identifiable group not only in neonatal but perhaps also in perinatal morbidity and mortality, the major causes of prematurity must be briefly mentioned.

In most cases, no definite cause is found. Approximately 20% of premature deliveries are the result of early onset of labor secondary to premature rupture of the membranes.

Pregnancies complicated by the hypertensive states of pregnancy have twice the incidence of premature labor as compared with uncomplicated pregnancies of similar duration. Patients with chronic hypertensive vascular disease have twice the prematurity

Table 43–2. Live births and neonatal deaths by weight groups, Oregon, 1978.*

Total	
All live births	38,386.0
Neonatal deaths	296.0
Deaths per 1000	7.7
Percentage of immature births in total births	5.3
Less than 1000 g	
Live births	144.0
Neonatal deaths	117.0
Deaths per 1000	812.5
1001–2500 g	
Live births	1873.0
Neonatal deaths	93.0
Deaths per 1000	49.7
2501 g and over	
Live births	36,368.0
Neonatal deaths	86.0
Deaths per 1000	2.4

*Oregon State Health Division, Vital Statistics Section.

Table 43–3. Causes of infant death in the USA.*

Cause	Rate per 1000 1980 (est)	Live Births 1973	Percent Change
Congenital anomalies	2.7	2.9	−6.9
Asphyxia of newborn (unspecified)	0.5	1.7	−70.6
Immaturity (unqualified)	1.1	1.7	−35.3
Influenza and pneumonia	0.1	1.1	−90.9
Birth injuries	0.2	0.6	−66.7
Gastrointestinal diseases	0.1	0.2	−50.0
Other diseases of early infancy	4.1	5.6	−26.8
All other causes	3.9	3.8	2.6
Total infant deaths	12.5	17.7	−29.4
Neonatal deaths	8.5	13.0	−34.6
Postneonatal deaths	4.0	4.8	−16.7

*Monthly Vital Statistics Report: An Annual Summary for the United States, 1980. National Center for Health Statistics, US Department of Health and Human Services, Vol 29, No. 13, 1980.

rate of normal pregnant women.

Table 43–2 illustrates the relationship between size and neonatal survival. These data are for a predominantly white (< 4% nonwhite) population of North European ancestry. Data of this type are vital in the assessment of the quality of neonatal care available in various regions, districts, and specific hospitals.

INFANT MORTALITY RATES

Infant death is death between delivery and 1 year of age. The infant mortality rate is inversely related to age. Over 70% of all infant deaths occur before 28 days of life, and over 60% before 7 days of life. The major causes of death in infants in the USA are listed in Table 43–3.

During 1980, the infant mortality rate in the USA continued to decline to a record low of 12.5 deaths per 1000 live births. This reduction in the death rate occurred primarily in infants under 28 days of age. Deaths of infants under 1 year of age totalled 45,000 during 1980.

• • •

•   •   •

References

Babson SG et al: *Management of High Risk Pregnancy and Intensive Care of the Neonate,* 4th ed. Mosby, 1979.

De Crespigny LJC, Pepperell RJ: Perinatal mortality and morbidity in breech presentation. *Obstet Gynecol* 1979;**53**:141.

Evrard JR, Gold EM: Cesarean section and maternal mortality in Rhode Island: Incidence and risk figures, 1965–1975. *Obstet Gynecol* 1977;**50**:594.

Fox AJ, Bulusu L, Kinlen L: Mortality and age differences in marriage. *J Biosoc Sci* 1979;**11**:117.

Gabbe SG et al: Current patterns of neonatal morbidity and mortality in infants of diabetic mothers. *Diabetes Care* 1978; **1**:335.

Haesslein HC et al: Delivery of the tiny newborn. *Am J Obstet Gynecol* 1979;**134**:192.

Hughes EC (editor): *Obstetric-Gynecologic Terminology.* Davis, 1972.

Low JA et al: Intrapartum fetal asphyxia: Preliminary report in regard to long-term morbidity. *Am J Obstet Gynecol* 1978; **130**:525.

Low JA et al: Intrauterine growth retardation: Preliminary report of long-term morbidity. *Am J Obstet Gynecol* 1978;**130**:534.

Monthly Vital Statistics Report: An Annual Summary for the United States, 1980. National Center for Health Statistics, US Department of Health and Human Services. Vol 29, No. 13, 1980.

Neutra RR et al: Effect of fetal monitoring on neonatal death rates. *N Engl J Med* 1978;**299**:324.

Oregon Public Health Statistics Report for Calendar Year 1978. Vital Statistics Section, Oregon State Health Division, 1979.

Paul RH, Koh KS, Monfared AH: Obstetric factors influencing outcome in infants weighing from 1,001 to 1,500 grams. *Am J Obstet Gynecol* 1979;**133**:503.

Tietze C, Lewitt S: Mortality and fertility control. *Int J Gynaecol Obstet* 1977;**15**:100.

Wightman H, Hibbard BM, Rosen M: Perinatal mortality and morbidity associated with eclampsia. *Br Med J* 1978;**2**:235.

Williams RL, Hawes WE: Cesarean section, fetal monitoring and perinatal mortality in California. *Am J Public Health* 1979; **69**:864.

Appendix:
Antimicrobial Chemotherapy

Ernest Jawetz, MD, PhD

ANTIMICROBIAL CHEMOTHERAPY

Microbial infection has always been a threat to obstetric or surgical procedures. Sepsis has either delayed or prevented successful results and has often resulted in death of the patient. Conversely, localized infections of many types—ranging from simple pus collections to infected prosthetic heart valves—have required surgery for cure. The major step in the control of infectious complications of obstetric and gynecologic surgery was the concept of antisepsis, sterilization of instruments, and asepsis. The second was the development of drugs that could be used for the cure of systemic microbial infections.

Antimicrobial drugs are effective adjuncts but not panaceas. Antimicrobial drugs never are a substitute for sound surgical technique, but they can be of help in the management of local infections and may be lifesaving in systemic disseminated infections. Improper application of antimicrobials not only fails to cure the patient but may contribute significantly to patient morbidity and mortality. Widespread improper administration of antimicrobials favors the emergence of drug-resistant organisms, enhances the risk of hospital infections, dangerously sensitizes the population, and carries the risk of serious direct toxic effects.

PRINCIPLES OF SELECTION OF ANTIMICROBIAL DRUGS

Antimicrobial drugs are used on a very large scale, and their proper use gives striking therapeutic results. On the other hand, they can create serious complications and should therefore be administered only upon proper indication.

Drugs of choice and second-line drugs are presented in Table 1.

The following steps merit consideration in each patient.

A. Etiologic Diagnosis: Formulate an etiologic diagnosis based on clinical observations. Microbial infections are best treated early. Therefore, the physician must attempt to decide on clinical grounds (1) whether the patient has a microbial infection that can probably be influenced by antimicrobial drugs, and (2) the most probable pathogen responsible ("best guess").

B. "Best Guess": Select a specific antimicrobial drug on the basis of past experience (personal or in the literature). Based on a "best guess" about the probable cause of the patient's infection, the physician should choose a drug that is likely to be effective against the suspected microorganism

C. Laboratory Control: Before beginning antimicrobial drug treatment, obtain meaningful specimens for laboratory examination to determine the causative infectious organism and, if desirable, its susceptibility to antimicrobial drugs.

D. Clinical Response: Based on the clinical response of the patient, evaluate the laboratory reports and consider the desirability of changing the antimicrobial drug regimen. Laboratory results should not automatically overrule clinical judgment. The isolation of an organism that reinforces the initial clinical impression is a useful confirmation. Conversely, laboratory results may contradict the initial clinical impression and may force its reconsideration. If the specimen was obtained from a site normally devoid of bacterial flora and not exposed to the external environment (eg, blood, cerebrospinal fluid, pleural fluid, joint fluid), the recovery of a microorganism is a significant finding even if the organism recovered is different from the clinically suspected etiologic agent and may force a change in antimicrobial treatment. On the other hand, the isolation of unexpected microorganisms from the respiratory or genital tract, gut, or surface lesions (sites that have a complex flora) must be critically evaluated before drugs are abandoned that were judiciously selected on the basis of an initial "best guess."

E. Drug Susceptibility Tests: Some microorganisms are fairly uniformly susceptible to certain drugs; if such organisms are isolated from the patient, they need not be tested for drug susceptibility. For example, pneumococci, group A hemolytic streptococci, and clostridia respond predictably to penicillin. On the other hand, some kinds of microorganisms (eg, coliform gram-negative rods) are sufficiently variable in their response to warrant drug susceptibility testing whenever they are isolated from a significant specimen.

Antimicrobial drug susceptibility tests may be done on solid media as "disk tests," in broth tubes, or

Table 1. Drug selections, 1981–1982.

Suspected or Proved Etiologic Agent	Drug(s) of First Choice	Alternative Drug(s)
Gram-negative cocci		
Gonococcus	Penicillin[1], ampicillin, tetracycline[2]	Spectinomycin, cefoxitin
Meningococcus	Penicillin[1]	Chloramphenicol, sulfonamide
Gram-positive cocci		
Pneumococcus *(Streptococcus pneumoniae)*	Penicillin[1]	Erythromycin[3], cephalosporin[4]
Streptococcus, hemolytic groups A, B, C, G	Penicillin[1]	Erythromycin[3], cephalosporin[4]
Streptococcus viridans	Penicillin[1] plus aminoglycoside(?)	Cephalosporin, vancomycin
Staphylococcus, nonpenicillinase-producing	Penicillin[1]	Cephalosporin, vancomycin
Staphylococcus, penicillinase-producing	Penicillinase-resistant penicillin[5]	Vancomycin, cephalosporin
Streptococcus faecalis (enterococcus)	Ampicillin plus aminoglycoside	Vancomycin
Gram-negative rods		
Acinetobacter (Mima-Herellea)	Gentamicin	Minocycline, amikacin
Bacteroides (except *B fragilis*)	Penicillin[1] or chloramphenicol	Clindamycin
Bacteroides fragilis	Clindamycin, cefoxitin	Metronidazole, chloramphenicol
Brucella	Tetracycline plus streptomycin	Streptomycin plus sulfonamide[6]
Enterobacter	Gentamicin or amikacin	Chloramphenicol
Escherichia		
Escherichia coli sepsis	Gentamicin or kanamycin	Cephalosporin, ampicillin
Escherichia coli urinary tract infection (first attack)	Sulfonamide[7] or TMP-SMX[8]	Ampicillin, cephalosporin[4]
Haemophilus (meningitis, respiratory infections)	Chloramphenicol	Ampicillin, TMP-SMX[8]
Klebsiella	Cephalosporin or gentamicin	Chloramphenicol
Legionella pneumophila (pneumonia)	Erythromycin	Tetracycline
Pasteurella (Yersinia) (plague, tularemia)	Streptomycin or tetracycline	Sulfonamide[6], chloramphenicol
Proteus		
Proteus mirabilis	Penicillin or ampicillin	Kanamycin, gentamicin
Proteus vulgaris and other species	Gentamicin or amikacin	Chloramphenicol, tobramycin
Pseudomonas		
Pseudomonas aeruginosa	Gentamicin plus carbenicillin	Polymyxin, amikacin
Pseudomonas pseudomallei (melioidosis)	Tetracycline	Chloramphenicol
Pseudomonas mallei (glanders)	Streptomycin plus tetracycline	Chloramphenicol
Salmonella	Chloramphenicol or ampicillin	TMP-SMX[8]
Serratia, Providencia	Gentamicin, amikacin	TMP-SMX[8] plus polymyxin
Shigella	Ampicillin or chloramphenicol	Tetracycline, TMP-SMX[8]
Vibrio (cholera)	Tetracycline	TMP-SMX[8]
Gram-positive rods		
Actinomyces	Penicillin[1]	Tetracycline
Bacillus (eg, anthrax)	Penicillin[1]	Erythromycin
Clostridium (eg, gas gangrene, tetanus)	Penicillin[1]	Tetracycline, cephalosporin[4]
Corynebacterium	Erythromycin	Penicillin, cephalosporin
Listeria	Ampicillin plus aminoglycoside	Tetracycline
Acid-fast rods		
Mycobacterium tuberculosis	INH plus rifampin or ethambutol[9]	Other antituberculosis drugs
Mycobacterium leprae	Dapsone, clofazimine	Amithiozone, rifampin
Mycobacteria, atypical	Ethambutol plus rifampin	Rifampin plus INH
Nocardia	Sulfonamide[6]	Minocycline
Spirochetes		
Borrelia (relapsing fever)	Tetracycline	Penicillin
Leptospira	Penicillin[1]	Tetracycline
Treponema (syphilis, yaws)	Penicillin[1]	Erythromycin, tetracycline
Mycoplasma	Tetracycline	Erythromycin
Chlamydia trachomatis, Chlamydia psittaci	Tetracycline, sulfonamide[6]	Erythromycin, chloramphenicol
Rickettsiae	Tetracycline	Chloramphenicol

[1] Penicillin G is preferred for parenteral injection; penicillin V for oral administration. Only highly sensitive microorganisms should be treated with oral penicillin.

[2] All tetracyclines have similar activity against microorganisms and comparable therapeutic activity and toxicity. Dosage is determined by the rates of absorption and excretion of different preparations.

[3] Erythromycin estolate is the best-absorbed oral form but carries greatest risk of hepatitis.

[4] Cefazolin, cephapirin, cephalothin, cefamandole, and cefoxitin are parenteral cephalosporins; cephalexin and cephradine the best oral forms.

[5] Parenteral nafcillin or oxacillin. Oral dicloxacillin, cloxacillin, or oxacillin.

[6] Trisulfapyrimidines and sulfisoxazole have the advantage of greater solubility in urine over sulfadiazine for oral administration; sodium sulfadiazine is suitable for intravenous injection in severely ill persons.

[7] For previously untreated urinary tract infection, a highly soluble sulfonamide such as sulfisoxazole or trisulfapyrimidines is the first choice. TMP-SMX[8] is acceptable.

[8] TMP-SMX is a mixture of 1 part trimethoprim plus 5 parts sulfamethoxazole.

[9] Either or both.

in wells of microdilution plates. The latter method yields results expressed as MIC (minimal inhibitory concentration), and the technique can be modified to permit MBC (minimal bactericidal concentration) determination. In some infections, the minimal inhibitory concentration or minimal bactericidal concentration permits a better estimate of the amount of drug required for therapeutic effect in vivo.

Disk tests usually indicate whether an isolate is susceptible or resistant to drug concentrations achieved in vivo with conventional dosage regimens, thus providing valuable guidance in selecting therapy. When there appear to be marked discrepancies between test results and clinical response of the patient, the following possibilities must be considered:

1. Failure to drain a collection of pus or to remove a foreign body.

2. Failure of a poorly diffusing drug to reach the site of infection (eg, joint cavity, pleural space) or to reach intracellular phagocytosed bacteria.

3. Superinfection in the course of prolonged chemotherapy. After suppression of the original infection or of normal flora, a second type of microorganism may establish itself against which the originally selected drug is ineffective.

4. Emergence of drug-resistant mutants from a large microbial population.

5. Participation of 2 or more microorganisms in the infectious process of which only one was originally detected and used for drug selection

F. Adequate Dosage: To determine whether the proper drug is being used in adequate dosage, a serum assay can be performed. If an adequate dose of a proper drug is being employed, the serum should be markedly bactericidal in vitro. In infections limited to the urinary tract, the antibacterial activity of urine can be estimated.

G. Duration of Antimicrobial Therapy: Generally speaking, effective antimicrobial treatment results in reversal of the clinical and laboratory parameters of active infection and marked clinical improvement within a very few days. Treatment may, however, have to be continued for varying periods to effect cure.

To minimize untoward reactions from drugs and the likelihood of superinfection, treatment should be continued only as long as necessary to eradicate the infectious agent.

H. Adverse Reactions: The administration of antimicrobial drugs is commonly associated with untoward reactions. These fall into several groups. (1) Hypersensitivity: The most common reactions are fever and skin rashes. Hematologic or hepatic disorders and anaphylaxis are rare. (2) Direct toxicity: Most common are nausea, vomiting, and diarrhea. More serious toxic reactions are impairment of renal, hepatic, or hematopoietic functions or damage to the eighth nerve. (3) Suppression of normal microbial flora and "superinfection" by drug-resistant microorganisms, or continued infection with the initial pathogen through the emergence of drug-resistant variants.

I. Oral Antibiotics: The absorption of oral penicillins, tetracyclines, lincomycins, etc, is impaired by food. Therefore, these oral drugs must be given between meals.

J. Intravenous Antibiotics: When an antibiotic must be administered intravenously (eg, for life-threatening infection or for maintenance of very high blood levels), the following cautions should be observed:

(1) Give in neutral solution (pH 7.0–7.2) of isotonic sodium chloride (0.9%) or dextrose (5%) in water.

(2) Give alone without admixture of any other drug in order to avoid chemical and physical incompatibilities (which can occur frequently).

(3) Administer by intermittent (every 2–6 hours) addition to the intravenous infusion to avoid inactivation (by temperature, changing pH, etc) and prolonged vein irritation from high drug concentration, which favors thrombophlebitis.

(4) The infusion site must be changed every 48 hours to reduce the chance of superinfection.

Oliguria, Impaired Renal Function, & Uremia

Oliguria, impaired renal function, and uremia have an important influence on antimicrobial drug dosage, since most of these drugs are excreted—to a greater or lesser extent—by the kidneys. Only minor adjustment in dosage or frequency of administration is necessary with relatively nontoxic drugs (eg, penicillins) or with drugs that are detoxified or excreted mainly by the liver (eg, erythromycins or chloramphenicol). On the other hand, aminoglycosides (gentamicin, tobramycin, amikacin, etc), tetracyclines, and vancomycin must be drastically reduced in dosage or frequency of administration if toxicity is to be avoided in the presence of nitrogen retention. The administration of particularly nephrotoxic antimicrobials such as aminoglycosides to patients in renal failure should be guided by direct, frequent assay of drug concentration in serum.

ANTIMICROBIAL DRUGS

PENICILLINS

The penicillins are a large group of antimicrobial substances, all of which share a common chemical nucleus (6-aminopenicillanic acid) that contains a β-lactam ring essential to their biologic activity. All β-lactam antibiotics inhibit formation of microbial cell walls. In particular, they block the final transpeptidation reaction in the synthesis of cell wall mucopeptide (peptidoglycan), and they activate autolytic enzymes in the cell wall. These reactions result in cell death.

Antimicrobial Activity

The initial step in penicillin action is the binding

of the drug to cell receptors, at least some of which are enzymes involved in the cross-linking of peptide side chains (transpeptidation reactions). Gram-positive organisms have far more such receptors than do gram-negative organisms. After penicillins have attached to receptors, peptidoglycan synthesis in inhibited, because the activity of transpeptidation enzymes is blocked. The final bactericidal action is the removal of an inhibitor of the autolytic enzymes in the cell wall, which activates the enzymes and results in cell lysis. Organisms that are defective in autolysin function are inhibited but not killed by β-lactam antibiotics. Organisms that produce β-lactamases (and other similar enzymes) are resistant to some penicillins because the β-lactam ring is broken and the drug inactivated. Only organisms that are actively synthesizing peptidoglycan (in the process of multiplication) are susceptible to β-lactam antibiotics. Nonmultiplying organisms or those lacking cell walls (L forms) are not susceptible but may act as "persisters."

One million units of penicillin G equal 0.6 g. Other penicillins are prescribed in grams. A blood level of 0.01–1 μg/mL of penicillin G or ampicillin is lethal for a majority of susceptible microorganisms. Most β-lactamase–resistant penicillins are 5–50 times less active.

Penicillins can be arranged into groups:

1. Highest activity against gram-positive organisms but susceptible to hydrolysis by β-lactamases, eg, penicillin G, benzathine penicillin.

2. Relatively resistant to β-lactamases but of lower activity against gram-positive organisms and inactive against gram-negative ones, eg, nafcillin, methicillin.

3. Relatively high activity against both gram-positive and gram-negative organisms but destroyed by β-lactamases (penicillinases), eg, ampicillin, amoxicillin, carbenicillin, ticarcillin.

4. Stable to gastric acid and suitable for oral administration, eg, penicillin V, cloxacillin, ampicillin.

Resistance

Resistance to penicillins falls into several categories:

1. Production of β-lactamases, eg, by staphylococci, gonococci, *Haemophilus,* coliform organisms.

2. Lack of penicillin receptors; impermeability of outer layers to penicillins so that they cannot reach receptors, eg, metabolically inactive bacteria.

3. Failure of activation of autolytic enzymes in the cell wall; "tolerance," eg, in staphylococci, *Streptococcus faecalis.*

4. Cell wall–deficient (L) forms or mycoplasmas, which do not synthesize peptidoglycans.

Absorption, Distribution, & Excretion

After parenteral administration, absorption of most penicillins is complete and rapid. After oral administration, only a portion of the dose is absorbed (from 1/20 to 1/3, depending upon acid stability, binding to foods, and the presence of buffers). In order to minimize binding to foods, oral penicillins should not be preceded or followed by food for at least 1 hour.

After absorption, penicillins are widely distributed in body fluids and tissues. With parenteral doses of 3–6 g (5–10 million units) per 24 hours of any penicillin injected by continuous infusion or divided intramuscular injections, average serum levels of the drug reach 1–10 units (0.6–6 μg) per mL.

In many tissues, penicillin concentrations are equal to those in serum. Lower levels are found in the eyes and central nervous system. However, with active inflammation of the meninges, as in bacterial meningitis, penicillin levels in the cerebrospinal fluid exceed 0.2 μg/mL with a daily parenteral dose of 12 g. Thus, pneumococcal and meningococcal meningitis may be treated with systemic penicillin G and *Haemophilus* meningitis with intravenous ampicillin, and there is no need for intrathecal injection. Penetration into inflamed joints is likewise sufficient for treatment of infective arthritis caused by susceptible organisms.

Most of the absorbed penicillin is rapidly excreted by the kidneys into the urine—90% by tubular secretion. Tubular secretion can be partially blocked by probenecid (Benemid), 0.5 g every 6 hours by mouth, to achieve higher systemic levels.

Renal excretion of penicillin results in very high levels in the urine. Thus, systemic daily doses of 6 g of penicillin may yield urine levels of 500–3000 μg/mL—enough to suppress not only gram-positive but also many gram-negative bacteria in the urine (provided they produce no β-lactamase).

Indications, Dosages, & Routes of Administration

The penicillins are by far the most effective and the most widely used antimicrobial drugs. All oral penicillins must be given 1 hour away from mealtimes to reduce binding and acid inactivation. Blood levels of all penicillins can be raised by simultaneous administration of probenecid, 0.5 g every 6 hours orally (10 mg/kg every 6 hours).

A. Penicillin G: This is the drug of choice for infections caused by pneumococci, streptococci, meningococci, non-β-lactamase–producing staphylococci and gonococci, *Treponema pallidum* and many other spirochetes, *Bacillus anthracis* and other gram-positive rods, clostridia, *Listeria,* and *Bacteroides* (except *Bacteroides fragilis*).

1. Intramuscular or intravenous–Most of the above-mentioned infections respond to aqueous penicillin G in daily doses of 0.6–5 million units (0.36–3 g) administered by intermittent intramuscular injection every 4–6 hours. Much larger amounts (6–50 g daily) can be given by intermittent addition (every 2–4 hours) to an intravenous infusion in serious or complicated cases. Sites for such intravenous administration are subject to thrombophlebitis and superinfection and must be rotated every 2 days and kept scrupulously aseptic. In enterococcal endocarditis, an aminoglycoside is given simultaneously with large doses of a penicillin.

2. Oral–Penicillin V is indicated only in minor infections (eg, of the respiratory tract or its associated structures) in daily doses of 1–4 g (1.6–6.4 million units). Oral administration is subject to too many variables to be relied upon in seriously ill patients.

B. Benzathine Penicillin G: This penicillin is a salt of very low water solubility. It is injected intramuscularly to establish a depot that yields low but prolonged drug levels. An injection of 2.4 million units intramuscularly once a week for 1–3 weeks is satisfactory for treatment of early syphilis. An injection of 1.2–2.4 million units intramuscularly every 3–4 weeks provides satisfactory prophylaxis for rheumatics against reinfection with group A streptococci. There is no indication for using this drug by mouth. Procaine penicillin G is another repository form for maintaining drug levels for up to 24 hours. For highly susceptible infections, 600 thousand units intramuscularly are usually given once daily. For uncomplicated gonorrhea, give 4.8 million units of procaine penicillin G intramuscularly once with probenecid, 1 g orally.

C. Ampicillin, Amoxicillin, Carbenicillin, Ticarcillin: These drugs differ from penicillin G in having greater activity against gram-negative bacteria, but, like penicillin G, they are destroyed by penicillinases.

Ampicillin can be given orally in divided doses, 2–3 g daily, to treat urinary tract infections with coliform bacteria, enterococci, or *Proteus mirabilis*. It is ineffective against *Enterobacter* and *Pseudomonas*. In *Salmonella* infections, ampicillin, 3–6 g daily orally or intravenously, can be effective in suppressing clinical disease (alternative to chloramphenicol in acute typhoid or paratyphoid) and may eliminate salmonellae from some chronic carriers. Ampicillin is more effective than penicillin G against enterococci and may be used in such infections in combination with an aminoglycoside. Amoxicillin is similar to ampicillin but is better absorbed. Bacampicillin can be given orally every 12 hours (400–800 mg) to achieve an effect comparable to ampicillin given every 6 hours.

Carbenicillin is more active against *Pseudomonas* and *Proteus,* but resistance emerges rapidly. A combination of carbenicillin, 12–30 g/d, with gentamicin is suggested in *Pseudomonas* sepsis. Indanyl carbenicillin, 2–4 g orally, can be given in some urinary tract infections. Hetacillin is converted in vivo to ampicillin and should not be used. Ticarcillin resembles carbenicillin, but the dose is lower (200–300 mg/kg/d intravenously).

D. Penicillinase-Resistant Penicillins: Cloxacillin, nafcillin, and others are relatively resistant to destruction by β-lactamase. The only indication for the use of these drugs is infection by β-lactamase-producing staphylococci.

1. Oral–Oxacillin, cloxacillin, dicloxacillin, or nafcillin may be given in doses of 0.25–0.5 g every 4–6 hours in mild or localized staphylococcal infections (50–100 mg/kg/d for children). Food markedly interferes with absorption.

2. Intravenous–For serious systemic staphylococcal infections, nafcillin, 6–12 g, is administered intravenously, usually by injecting 1–2 g during 20–30 minutes every 2 hours into a continuous infusion of 5% dextrose in water or physiologic salt solution. The dose for children is nafcillin, 50–100 mg/kg/d.

Adverse Effects

The penicillins undoubtedly possess less direct toxicity than any other antibiotics. Most of the serious side-effects are due to hypersensitivity.

A. Allergy: All penicillins are cross-sensitizing and cross-reacting. Any preparation containing penicillin may induce sensitization, including foods or cosmetics. In general, sensitization occurs in direct proportion to the duration and total dose of penicillin received in the past. Skin tests with penicilloyl-polylysine, with alkaline hydrolysis products (minor antigen determinants), and with undegraded penicillin can identify many hypersensitive individuals. Among positive reactors to skin tests, the incidence of subsequent immediate penicillin reactions is high. Although many persons develop IgG antibodies to antigenic determinants of penicillin, the presence of such antibodies is not correlated with allergic reactivity (except rare hemolytic anemia). A history of a penicillin reaction in the past is not reliable; however, in such cases the drug should be administered with caution— ie, have available an artificial airway, 1% epinephrine in a syringe, running intravenous fluids, and competent personnel standing by; or a substitute drug should be given.

Allergic reactions may occur as typical anaphylactic shock, typical serum sickness type reactions (urticaria, fever, joint swelling, angioneurotic edema, intense pruritus, and respiratory embarrassment occurring 7–12 days after exposure), a variety of skin rashes, oral lesions, fever, nephritis, eosinophilia, hemolytic anemia and other hematologic disturbances, and vasculitis. The incidence of hypersensitivity to penicillin is estimated to be 3–5% among adults in the USA. Acute anaphylactic life-threatening reactions are fortunately very rare (0.05%). Ampicillin produces skin rashes (mononucleosislike) 3–5 times more frequently than other penicillins, but some ampicillin rashes are not allergic. Methicillin and other penicillins can induce interstitial nephritis.

B. Toxicity: Since the action of penicillin is directed against a unique bacterial structure, the cell wall, it is virtually without effect on animal cells. The toxic effects of penicillin G are due to the direct irritation caused by intramuscular or intravenous injection of exceedingly high concentrations (eg, 1 g/mL). A rare patient receiving more than 50 g of penicillin G daily parenterally has exhibited signs of cerebrocortical irritation as a result of the passage of large amounts of penicillin into the central nervous system. With doses of this magnitude, direct cation toxicity (Na$^+$, K$^+$) can also occur. Potassium penicillin G contains

1.7 mEq of K$^+$ per million units (2.7 mEq/g), and potassium may accumulate in the presence of renal failure. Carbenicillin contains 4.7 mEq of Na$^+$ per gram—a risk in heart failure.

Large doses of penicillins given orally may lead to gastrointestinal upset, particularly nausea and diarrhea. These symptoms are most marked with oral ampicillin or amoxicillin. Oral therapy may also be accompanied by luxuriant overgrowth of staphylococci, *Pseudomonas, Proteus,* or yeasts, which may occasionally cause enteritis. Superinfections in other organ systems may occur. Carbenicillin and ticarcillin may damage platelet function, cause bleeding, or result in hypokalemic alkalosis.

CEPHALOSPORINS

Cephalosporins and cephamycins are compounds related to penicillins. In place of 6-aminopenicillanic acid they have a nucleus of 7-aminocephalosporanic acid. Their mode of action is similar to that of penicillins, there is limited cross-allergenicity, and they are relatively resistant to inactivation by β-lactamases. New semisynthetic derivatives are appearing in profusion. Cefotaxime and moxalactam are now marketed, and cefuroxime and cefoperazone are in clinical trials; their individual advantages are not well established.

Antimicrobial Activity

Cephalosporins and cephamycins inhibit the final transpeptidation of bacterial cell wall peptidoglycan. They are relatively resistant to inactivation by β-lactamases. The cephalosporins are bactericidal in vitro in concentrations of 1–20 μg/mL for most gram-positive bacteria except *Streptococcus faecalis* and in concentrations of 5–30 μg/mL for many gram-negative bacteria, excluding *Pseudomonas, Acinetobacter, Serratia,* and *Proteus.* Cefamandole and cefoxitin have somewhat greater activity against the latter aerobic gram-negative organisms and also against some anaerobic bacteria. There is at least partial cross-resistance between cephalosporins and β-lactamase–resistant penicillins; methicillin-resistant staphylococci are thus also resistant to cephalosporins. The principal differences among the cephalosporins and the cephamycins lie more in their pharmacokinetics and cost-effectiveness than in their microbiologic activity or toxicity.

Absorption, Distribution, & Excretion

Cephalothin, cefazolin, cephapirin, cefamandole, and cefoxitin are not significantly absorbed from the gut. After parenteral injection, they are distributed widely, and 40–80% of the drugs in serum are protein-bound. Concentrations in synovial fluid, central nervous system, and cerebrospinal fluid are low after parenteral injection. Thus, cephalosporins should not be used in meningitis. Excretion of cephalosporins is primarily by tubular secretion into the urine and, to a lesser extent, into bile. Urine levels may reach 200–

1000 μg/mL. Cephalexin, cephradine, and cefaclor are somewhat better absorbed from the gut; therapeutic levels are reached after oral doses.

Indications, Dosages, & Routes of Administration

A. Oral: Cephalexin, cefaclor, or cephradine, 0.5 g orally 4 times daily (50 mg/kg/d), can be used in urinary or respiratory tract infections due to organisms susceptible to this drug. Urine levels reach 50–500 μg/mL.

B. Intravenous: Cephalothin or cephapirin is given as a 1- or 2-g bolus every 4–6 hours into a continuous drip (50–100 mg/kg/d). This results in serum levels of 2–20 μg/mL, 50–65% of it protein-bound. Such treatment is often adequate for bacteremic infections caused by gram-negative organisms or staphylococci.

Cefazolin, 1 g every 6 hours intramuscularly or intravenously, gives the highest cephalosporin blood levels (20–50 μg/mL) but is more strongly protein-bound (85%). Cefamandole or cefoxitin, 1–2 g intravenously into a drip every 4–6 hours (50–150 mg/kg/d), gives serum levels of 20–40 μg/mL, with 60–70% protein binding. These drugs are all used for similar indications, but susceptibility varies among different strains of gram-negative bacteria. None of the drugs are appropriate for central nervous system infections.

C. Intramuscular: Cefazolin, 0.5–1 g every 4 hours, provides adequate levels for treating less ill patients for the same indications or for surgical (24-hour) prophylaxis. Cephapirin, 1 g every 4–6 hours, is equivalent, although producing somewhat lower levels in serum.

Adverse Effects

A. Allergy: Cephalosporins are sensitizing, and a variety of hypersensitivity reactions occur, including anaphylaxis, fever, skin rashes, granulocytopenia, and hemolytic anemia. Cross-allergy also exists with penicillins and can produce the same hypersensitivity reactions. Perhaps 6–18% of penicillin-allergic persons are also hypersensitive to cephalosporins.

B. Toxicity: Local pain after intramuscular injection, thrombophlebitis after intravenous injection. Cephaloridine can cause renal damage with tubular necrosis and uremia and should not be used.

ERYTHROMYCIN GROUP
(Macrolides)

The erythromycins are a group of closely related compounds that inhibit protein synthesis and are bacteriostatic or bactericidal against gram-positive organisms—especially pneumococci, streptococci, and corynebacteria—in concentrations of 0.02–2 μg/mL. Chlamydiae, mycoplasmas, *Legionella,* and *Campylobacter* are also susceptible. Activity is enhanced at alkaline pH.

Erythromycins are the drugs of choice in corynebacterial infections (diphtheroid sepsis, erythrasma), in respiratory, genital, or ocular chlamydial infections, or in pneumonia caused by mycoplasmas or *Legionella*. They are useful as substitutes for penicillin in persons with streptococcal and pneumococcal infections who are allergic to penicillin.

Dosages

A. Oral: Erythromycin base, stearate, succinate, or estolate, or troleandomycin, 0.5 g every 6 hours (for children, 40 mg/kg/d).

B. Intravenous: Erythromycin lactobionate or gluceptate, 0.5 g every 12 hours.

Adverse Effects

Nausea, vomiting, and diarrhea may occur after oral intake. Erythromycin estolate or troleandomycin can produce acute cholestatic hepatitis (fever, jaundice, impaired liver function) because of hypersensitivity. Most patients recover completely.

TETRACYCLINE GROUP

The tetracyclines are a large group of drugs with common basic chemical structures, antimicrobial activity, and pharmacologic properties. Microorganisms resistant to one tetracycline show cross-resistance to all tetracyclines.

Antimicrobial Activity

Tetracyclines are inhibitors of protein synthesis and are bacteriostatic for many gram-positive and gram-negative bacteria. They are strongly inhibitory for the growth of mycoplasmas, rickettsiae, chlamydiae, and some protozoa (eg, amebas). Equal concentrations of all tetracyclines in blood or tissue have approximately equal antimicrobial activity. However, there are great differences in the susceptibility of different strains of a given species of microorganism, and laboratory tests are therefore important. Because of the emergence of resistant strains, tetracyclines have lost some of their former usefulness. *Proteus* and *Pseudomonas* are regularly resistant; among coliform bacteria, *Bacteroides,* pneumococci, staphylococci, and streptococci, resistant strains are increasingly common.

Absorption, Distribution, & Excretion

Tetracyclines are absorbed somewhat irregularly from the gut. Absorption is limited by the low solubility of the drugs and by chelation with divalent cations, eg, Ca^{2+} or Fe^{2+}. A large proportion of orally administered tetracycline remains in the gut lumen, modifies intestinal flora, and is excreted in feces. Of the absorbed drug, 40–80% is protein-bound in the blood. With full systemic doses (2 g/d), levels of active drug in serum reach 2–10 μg/mL. Tetracyclines are specifically deposited in growing bones and teeth, bound to calcium.

Absorbed tetracyclines are excreted mainly in bile and urine. Up to 20% of oral doses may appear in the urine after glomerular filtration. Urine levels may be 5–50 μg/mL or more. With renal failure, doses of tetracyclines must be reduced or intervals between doses increased. Up to 80% of an oral dose appears in the feces.

Demeclocycline, methacycline, minocycline, and doxycycline are well absorbed from the gut but are excreted more slowly than others, leading to accumulation and prolonged blood levels. Renal clearance ranges from 9 mL/min for minocycline to 90 mL/min for oxytetracycline.

Indications, Dosages, & Routes of Administration

At present, tetracyclines are the drugs of choice in cholera, mycoplasmal pneumonia, and in infections with chlamydiae or rickettsiae. They may be used in various susceptible bacterial infections and in amebiasis.

A. Oral: Tetracycline hydrochloride and oxytetracycline are dispensed in 250 mg capsules. Give 0.25–0.5 g orally every 6 hours (for children, 20–40 mg/kg/d). In acne vulgaris, 0.25 g once or twice daily for many months is prescribed by dermatologists. Tetracycline hydrochloride, 2 g/d orally for 5 days, can cure acute gonorrhea. Tetracycline is also the drug of choice in genital chlamydial infections (urethritis, cervicitis, and pelvic inflammatory disease), but erythromycin is preferred during pregnancy.

Demeclocycline and methacycline are long-acting tetracyclines available in capsules containing 50 or 150 mg. Give 0.15–0.3 g orally every 6 hours (for children, 12–20 mg/kg/d). Doxycycline and minocycline are available in capsules containing 50 or 100 mg or as powder for oral suspension. Give doxycycline, 100 mg every 12 hours on the first day and 100 mg/d for maintenance. Give minocycline, 200 mg for the first dose and then 100 mg every 12 hours.

B. Intramuscular or Intravenous: Several tetracyclines (eg, rolitetracycline) are formulated for intramuscular or intravenous injection. Give 0.1–0.5 g every 6–12 hours to individuals unable to take oral medication.

Adverse Effects

A. Allergy: Hypersensitivity reactions with fever or skin rashes are uncommon.

B. Gastrointestinal Side-Effects: Gastrointestinal side-effects—especially diarrhea, nausea, and anorexia—are common. These can be diminished by reducing the dose or by administering tetracyclines with food or carboxymethylcellulose, but sometimes they force discontinuance of the drug. After a few days of oral use, the gut flora is modified so that drug-resistant bacteria and yeasts become prominent. This may cause functional gut disturbances, anal pruritus, and even enterocolitis with shock and death.

C. Bones and Teeth: Tetracyclines are bound to calcium deposited in growing bones and teeth, causing fluorescence, discoloration, enamel dysplasia, deformity, or growth inhibition. Therefore, tetracyclines should not be given to pregnant women or to children under 6 years of age.

D. Liver Damage: Tetracyclines can impair hepatic function or even cause liver necrosis, particularly during pregnancy, in the presence of preexisting liver damage, or with doses of more than 3 g intravenously.

E. Kidney Damage: Outdated tetracycline preparations have been implicated in renal tubular acidosis and other renal damage. Tetracyclines may increase blood urea nitrogen when diuretics are administered.

F. Other: Tetracyclines, principally demeclocycline, may induce photosensitization, especially in blonds. Intravenous injection may cause thrombophlebitis, and intramuscular injection may induce local inflammation with pain. Minocycline causes vestibular reactions (dizziness, vertigo, nausea) in 30–60% of cases after doses of 200 mg daily. Demeclocycline inhibits antidiuretic hormone.

CHLORAMPHENICOL

Chloramphenicol is a potent inhibitor of bacterial protein synthesis that inhibits the growth of many bacteria and rickettsiae in concentrations of 0.5–10 μg/mL. Resistant mutants that produce an enzyme which inactivates the drug are present in most susceptible species. There is no cross-resistance with other drugs.

After oral administration, chloramphenicol is rapidly and completely absorbed. Administration of 2 g/d orally to adults results in blood levels of 5–10 μg/mL. In children, chloramphenicol palmitate, 50 mg/kg/d orally, is hydrolyzed in the gut to yield free chloramphenicol and gives a blood level of 10 μg/mL. Chloramphenicol succinate, 25–50 mg/kg/d intramuscularly or intravenously, yields free chloramphenicol by hydrolysis and gives blood levels comparable to those achieved by oral administration. After absorption, chloramphenicol is widely distributed to all tissues, including the central nervous system and cerebrospinal fluid. It penetrates cells readily. About 50% of drug in the serum is protein-bound. Chloramphenicol is metabolized either by conjugation with glucuronic acid in the liver or by reduction to inactive arylamines. In hepatic insufficiency, the drug may accumulate to toxic levels. Only 10% of active drug is excreted by glomerular filtration in the urine.

Because of its potential toxicity, chloramphenicol is at present a possible drug of choice in obstetrics and gynecology for (1) occasional gram-negative bacteremia or (2) *Bacteroides* or other anaerobic infections.

In serious systemic infection, the dose is 0.5 g orally every 4–6 hours (for children, 30–50 mg/kg/d) for 7–21 days. Similar amounts are given intravenously.

Adverse Effects
Nausea, vomiting, and diarrhea occur infre-

quently. The most serious adverse effects pertain to the hematopoietic system. Adults taking chloramphenicol in excess of 50 mg/kg/d regularly exhibit disturbances in red cell maturation after 1–2 weeks of blood levels above 25 μg/mL. There are anemia, rise in serum iron concentration, reticulocytopenia, and the appearance of vacuolated nucleated red cells in the bone marrow. These changes regress when the drug is stopped and are not related to the rare aplastic anemia.

Serious aplastic anemia is a rare consequence of chloramphenicol administration and represents a specific, probably genetically determined individual defect. It is seen more frequently with either prolonged or repeated use. It tends to be irreversible and fatal. It is estimated that fatal aplastic anemia occurs 13 times more frequently after the use of chloramphenicol than as a spontaneous occurrence. Hypoplastic anemia may be followed by the development of leukemia.

Chloramphenicol is specifically toxic for newborns. Because they lack the mechanism for detoxification of the drug in the liver, the drug may accumulate, producing the highly fatal "gray syndrome" with vomiting, flaccidity, hypothermia, and collapse.

AMINOGLYCOSIDES

Aminoglycosides are a group of bactericidal drugs sharing chemical, antimicrobial, pharmacologic, and toxic characteristics. At present, the group includes streptomycin, neomycin, kanamycin, amikacin, gentamicin, tobramycin, sisomicin, netilmycin, and others. All these agents inhibit protein synthesis in bacteria by attaching to and inhibiting the function of the 30S subunit of the bacterial ribosome. Resistance is based on (1) a deficiency of the ribosomal receptor (chromosomal mutant); (2) the enzymatic destruction of the drug (plasmid-mediated transmissible resistance of clinical importance) by acetylation, phosphorylation, or adenylylation; or (3) a lack of permeability to the drug molecule or failure of active transport across cell membranes. The last-named form of resistance can be chromosomal (eg, streptococci are relatively impermeable to aminoglycosides), or it may be plasmid-mediated (clinically significant resistance among gram-negative enteric bacteria). Anaerobic bacteria are often resistant to aminoglycosides because transport across the cell membrane is an oxygen-dependent energy-requiring process.

All aminoglycosides are more active at alkaline than at acid pH. All are potentially ototoxic and nephrotoxic, though to different degrees. All can accumulate in the presence of renal failure; therefore, dosage adjustments must be made in uremia.

Aminoglycosides are used most widely against gram-negative enteric bacteria or when there is a suspicion of sepsis. In the treatment of bacteremia or endocarditis caused by fecal streptococci or by some gram-negative bacteria, the aminoglycoside is given together with a penicillin to enhance permeability and facilitate the entry of the aminoglycoside. Aminoglycosides are selected according to recent susceptibility patterns in a given area or hospital until susceptibility tests become available on a specific isolate. All (positively charged) aminoglycosides and polymyxins are inhibited in blood cultures by sodium polyanetholesulfonate and other polyanionic detergents. Some aminoglycosides (especially streptomycin) are useful as antimycobacterial drugs.

Streptomycin is the oldest of the aminoglycosides, and its pharmacologic properties are very well known. Neomycin is now limited to topical use, and kanamycin is used mainly in small children. Among the newer aminoglycosides, tobramycin, gentamicin, and amikacin are well well established, whereas there is less experience with sisomicin, netilmycin, and others.

General Properties of Aminoglycosides

Because of the similarities of the aminoglycosides, a summary of properties is presented briefly before each drug is taken up individually for a discussion of its main clinical uses.

A. Physical Properties: Aminoglycosides are water-soluble and stable in solution. If they are mixed in solution with β-lactam antibiotics, they may form complexes and lose some activity.

B. Absorption, Distribution, Metabolism, and Excretion: Aminoglycosides are well absorbed after intramuscular or intravenous injection but are not absorbed from the gut. They are distributed widely in tissues and penetrate into pleural, peritoneal, or joint fluid in the presence of inflammation. They enter the central nervous system to only a slight extent after parenteral administration. There is no significant metabolic breakdown of aminoglycosides. The serum half-life is 2–3 hours; excretion is mainly by glomerular filtration. Urine levels are 10–50 times higher than serum levels. Aminoglycosides are removed effectively but somewhat irregularly by hemodialysis.

C. Dose and Effect of Impaired Renal Function: In persons with normal renal function, the dose of kanamycin or amikacin is 15 mg/kg/d; that for gentamicin or tobramycin is 3–7 mg/kg/d, usually injected in 3 equal amounts every 8 hours.

In persons with impaired renal function, excretion is diminished and there is a danger of drug accumulation with increased side-effects. Therefore, if the interval is kept constant, the dose has to be reduced, or the interval must be increased if the dose is kept constant. Nomograms have been constructed relating serum creatinine levels to adjustments of treatment regimens. One widely used formula uses a multiplication factor (kanamycin or amikacin = 9, gentamicin = 8, tobramycin = 6) times the serum creatinine value (mg/dL) to give the interval between doses in hours. However, there is considerable variation in aminoglycoside levels in different patients with similar creatinine values. Therefore, it is highly desirable to monitor drug levels in blood whenever possible to avoid severe toxicity when renal functional capacity is rapidly changing.

D. Adverse Effects: All aminoglycosides can cause varying degrees of ototoxicity and nephrotoxicity. Ototoxicity can present either as hearing loss (cochlear damage) that is noted first with high-frequency tones, or as vestibular damage, evident by vertigo, ataxia, and loss of balance. Nephrotoxicity is evident with rising serum creatinine levels or reduced creatinine clearance.

In very high doses, aminoglycoside can be neurotoxic, producing a curarelike effect with neuromuscular blockade that results in respiratory paralysis. Neostigmine can be an antidote to this reaction. Rarely, aminoglycosides cause hypersensitivity and local reactions.

1. STREPTOMYCIN

This drug has been used longer than any other aminoglycoside, and many organisms have developed resistance. The principal indications for streptomycin at present are (1) plague and tularemia and (2) endocarditis or sepsis caused by *Streptococcus faecalis* and perhaps some other streptococci, where it is used in conjunction with a penicillin. The dose is 0.5 g intramuscularly every 6–8 hours. As a precaution against excessive toxicity, streptomycin should not be given together with other aminoglycosides.

2. KANAMYCIN–NEOMYCIN

These drugs are very similar; there is complete microbial cross-resistance. Neomycin is used only topically, whereas kanamycin is sometimes used intramuscularly, particularly in infants, in a dose of 15 mg/kg/d. Neomycin ointment (1–5 mg/g) can be applied to surface lesions of mixed flora. In preparation for elective bowel surgery, neomycin or kanamycin is given in a dosage of 1 g orally every 4–8 hours for 1–2 days to reduce intestinal flora. The same can be done in hepatic coma to reduce ammonia intoxication.

These drugs should never be used for peritoneal or pelvic postoperative irrigation, because respiratory arrest may result.

3. AMIKACIN

Amikacin is a semisynthetic derivative of kanamycin. It is relatively resistant to several of the enzymes that inactivate gentamicin and tobramycin and therefore can be employed against some microorganisms resistant to these drugs. However, bacterial resistance due to impermeability to amikacin is increasing. Many gram-negative enteric bacteria—including many strains of *Proteus, Pseudomonas, Enterobacter,* and *Serratia*—are inhibited by 1–20 μg/mL of amikacin in vitro. After the injection of 500 mg amikacin intramuscularly every 12 hours (15 mg/kg/d), peak levels in serum are 10–30 μg/mL. Some infections caused by gram-negative bacteria resistant to gentamicin respond to amikacin. Central nervous system infections require intrathecal or intraventricular injection of 1–10 mg daily.

Like all aminoglycosides, amikacin is nephrotoxic and ototoxic (particularly for the auditory portion of the eighth nerve). Its levels should be monitored in patients with renal failure.

4. GENTAMICIN

Gentamicin is a widely used aminoglycoside antibiotic. In concentrations of 0.5–5 μg/mL, gentamicin is bactericidal not only for staphylococci and coliform organisms but also for many strains of *Pseudomonas, Proteus,* and *Serratia.* Enterococci are resistant. With doses of 3–7 mg/kg/d, serum levels reach 3–8 μg/mL. Gentamicin may be synergistic with carbenicillin against *Pseudomonas.* However, the 2 drugs cannot be mixed in vitro because they inactivate each other. Sisomicin resembles the C1a component of gentamicin.

Indications, Dosages, & Routes of Administration

Gentamicin is used in severe infections caused by gram-negative bacteria. Included are sepsis, infected burns, pneumonia, and other serious infections due to coliform organisms, *Klebsiella-Enterobacter, Proteus, Pseudomonas,* and *Serratia.* The dosage is 3–7 mg/kg/d intramuscularly (or intravenously) in 3 equal doses for 7–10 days. In urinary tract infections caused by these organisms, 0.8–1.2 mg/kg/d is given intramuscularly for 5–10 days. It is necessary to monitor renal, auditory, and vestibular functions and to reduce the dosage or lengthen the interval between doses if renal function declines. About 2–3% of patients develop vestibular dysfunction and loss of hearing when peak serum levels exceed 10 μg/mL. Serum concentrations should be monitored by laboratory assay. For infected burns or skin lesions, creams containing 0.1% gentamicin are used. Such topical use should be restricted in hospitals to avoid favoring the development of resistant bacteria. In meningitis due to gram-negative bacteria, 1–10 mg of gentamicin have been injected daily intrathecally or intraventricularly in adults. However, in neonatal meningitis the benefit of either of these routes is in doubt, and intraventricular gentamicin is toxic.

5. TOBRAMYCIN

Tobramycin is an aminoglycoside that greatly resembles gentamicin in antibacterial activity and pharmacologic properties and exhibits partial cross-resistance. Tobramycin may be effective against some gentamicin-resistant gram-negative bacteria, especially *Pseudomonas.* A daily dose of 3–5 mg/kg is given in 3 equal amounts intramuscularly at intervals

of 8 hours. In uremia, the suggested dose is 1 mg/kg intramuscularly every (6 × serum creatinine level [in mg/dL]) hours. However, blood levels should be monitored. Tobramycin may be less nephrotoxic than gentamicin; their ototoxicity is similar.

SPECTINOMYCIN

This is an aminocyclitol antibiotic, related to the aminoglycosides. Its sole indication is for the treatment of penicillin-resistant gonorrhea or gonorrhea in a penicillin-hypersensitive person. One injection of 2 g produces blood levels of 100 μg/mL. This produces pain at the injection site and occasional nausea or fever. The cure rate may be 90–95%.

POLYMYXINS

The polymyxins are a group of basic polypeptides bactericidal for most gram-negative bacteria except *Proteus* and especially useful against *Pseudomonas.* Only 2 drugs are used: polymyxin B sulfate and colistin (polymyxin E) methanesulfonate.

Polymyxins are not absorbed from the gut. They are distributed in some tissues after parenteral injection, but they do not reach the central nervous system, cerebrospinal fluid, joints, or ocular tissues unless injected locally. Blood levels usually do not exceed 1–4 μg/mL. Polymyxins are excreted into the urine (colistin more rapidly than polymyxin B), where concentrations of 25–300 μg/mL may be reached. Excretion is impaired in renal insufficiency.

Indications, Dosages, & Routes of Administration

With the availability of other drugs, polymyxins are now only rarely indicated in serious infections due to gram-negative bacteria resistant to aminoglycosides. Polymyxins may be synergistic with trimethoprim-sulfamethoxazole against *Serratia.*

A. Intramuscular: The injection of polymyxin B is painful. Therefore, colistimethate, which contains a local anesthetic and is more rapidly excreted in the urine, is given intramuscularly, 2.5–5 mg/kg/d, for urinary tract infection.

B. Intravenous: Instead of gentamicin, polymyxin B sulfate, 2.5 mg/kg/d, can be injected by continuous intravenous infusion in gram-negative bacterial sepsis.

C. Intrathecal: In cases of confirmed *Pseudomonas* meningitis, administer polymyxin B sulfate, 2–10 mg once daily for 2–3 days and then every other day for 2–3 weeks.

D. Topical: Solutions of polymyxin B sulfate, 1 mg/mL, can be applied to infected surfaces; injected into joint spaces, intrapleurally, or subconjunctivally; or inhaled as aerosols. Ointments containing 0.5 mg/g polymyxin B sulfate in a mixture with neomycin or bacitracin are often applied to infected skin lesions.

Solutions containing polymyxin B, 20 mg/L, and neomycin 40 mg/L, can be used for continuous irrigation of the bladder with an indwelling catheter and a closed drainage system. Purulent exudates inactivate polymyxins.

Adverse Effects

The toxicities of polymyxin B and colistimethate are similar. With the usual blood levels there are paresthesias, dizziness, flushing, and incoordination. These disappear when the drug has been excreted. With unusually high levels, respiratory arrest and paralysis can occur. This can be reversed by calcium gluconate. Depending upon the dose, all polymyxins are nephrotoxic. Kidney function must be monitored and the regimen adjusted as necessary.

SULFONAMIDES

Since 1935, more than 150 different sulfonamides have been marketed. The increasing emergence of sulfonamide resistance (eg, among streptococci, meningococci, and shigellae) and the higher efficacy of other antimicrobial drugs have drastically curtailed the number of specific indications for sulfonamides as drugs of choice. The present indications for the use of these drugs can be summarized as follows:

(1) First (previously untreated) infection of the urinary tract: Many coliform organisms, which are the most common causes of urinary infections, are still susceptible to sulfonamides.

(2) *Chlamydia trachomatis* infections of genital tract and eye: Sulfonamides may suppress clinical activity, particularly in acute infections, but they are probably less effective than tetracyclines and erythromycins.

(3) Parasitic diseases: In combination with pyrimethamine, sulfonamides are used in toxoplasmosis. In combination with trimethoprim, sulfonamides are sometimes effective in falciparum malaria.

(4) Bacterial infections: Sulfonamides may be drugs of choice in nocardiosis. In underdeveloped parts of the world, sulfonamides, because of their availability and low cost, may still be useful for the treatment of pneumococcal or staphylococcal infections, bacillary (*Shigella*) dysentery, and meningococcal infections. In most developed countries, sulfonamides are not the drugs of choice for any of these conditions because sulfonamide resistance is widespread.

Dosages & Routes of Administration

A. Oral: For systemic disease, the soluble, rapidly excreted sulfonamides (eg, sulfadiazine, sulfisoxazole) are given in an initial dose of 2–4 g (40 mg/kg) followed by 0.5–1 g (10 mg/kg) every 4–6 hours. Trisulfapyrimidines USP may be given in the same total doses. Urine must be kept alkaline.

For urinary tract infections (first attack, not previously treated), trisulfapyrimidines, sulfisoxazole, or another sulfonamide with equally high solubility in urine is given in a dose of 2–4 g daily. Following one course of sulfonamides, resistant organisms usually prevail. Simultaneous administration of a sulfonamide, 2 g/d orally, and trimethoprim, 400 mg/d, orally may be more effective in urinary, respiratory, or enteric tract infections than sulfonamide alone.

Sulfasalazine (salicylazosulfapyridine), 6 g/d, has been given in ulcerative colitis. The drug is split in the gut into sulfapyridine and salicylate. The latter has anti-inflammatory effects.

Long-acting sulfonamides (eg, sulfamethoxypyridazine) have a significantly higher rate of toxic effects than the short-acting sulfonamides.

B. Intravenous: Sodium sulfadiazine and other sodium salts can be injected intravenously in 0.5% concentration in 5% dextrose in water, physiologic salt solution, or other diluent in a total dose of 6–8 g/d (120 mg/kg/d). This is reserved for comatose individuals or those unable to take oral medication.

Adverse Effects

Sulfonamides produce a wide variety of side-effects—due partly to hypersensitivity, partly to direct toxicity—that must be considered whenever unexplained symptoms or signs occur in a patient who may have received these drugs. Except in the mildest reactions, fluids should be forced, and—if symptoms and signs progressively increase—the drugs should be discontinued. Precautions to prevent complications (below) are important.

A. Systemic Side-Effects: Fever, skin rashes, urticaria; nausea, vomiting, or diarrhea; stomatitis, conjunctivitis, arthritis, exfoliative dermatitis; hematopoietic disturbances, including thrombocytopenia, hemolytic (in G6PD deficiency) or aplastic anemia, granulocytopenia, leukemoid reactions; hepatitis, polyarteritis nodosa, vasculitis, Stevens-Johnson syndrome; psychosis; and many others.

B. Urinary Tract Disturbances: Sulfonamides may precipitate in urine, especially at neutral or acid pH, producing hematuria, crystalluria, or even obstruction. They have also been implicated in various types of nephritis and nephrosis. Sulfonamides and methenamine salts should not be given together.

Precautions in the Use of Sulfonamides

(1) There is cross-allergenicity among all sulfonamides. Obtain a history of past administration or reaction. Observe for possible allergic responses.

(2) Keep the urine volume above 1500 mL/d by forcing fluids. Check urine pH—it should be 7.5 or higher. Give alkali by mouth (sodium bicarbonate or equivalent, 5–15 g/d). Examine fresh urine for crystals and red cells every 2–4 days.

(3) Check hemoglobin, white blood cell count, and differential count every 3–5 days to detect possible disturbances early.

TRIMETHOPRIM

This folate antagonist may act together with sulfonamides or alone. Trimethoprim, 100 mg orally every 12 hours, is effective in urinary tract infections. Intravenous forms of trimethoprim-sulfamethoxazole are approved for use in *Pneumocystis* pneumonia or some (*Serratia* sp) gram-negative bacteremias. Trimethoprim-sulfamethoxazole mixtures, one-half tablet daily or 1 tablet 3 times weekly, can be effective chemoprophylaxis for recurrent urinary tract infections. The side-effects of trimethoprim resemble those of the sulfonamides.

SPECIALIZED DRUGS AGAINST GRAM–POSITIVE BACTERIA

1. BACITRACIN

Systemic administration of bacitracin has been abandoned because of its severe nephrotoxicity.

2. LINCOMYCIN & CLINDAMYCIN

These drugs resemble erythromycin (although different in structure) and are active against gram-positive organisms (except enterococci) in concentrations of 0.5–5 μg/mL. Lincomycin, 0.5 g orally every 6 hours (30–60 mg/kg/d for children), or clindamycin, 0.15–0.3 g orally every 6 hours (10–40 mg/kg/d for children) yields serum concentrations of 2–5 μg/mL. The drugs are widely distributed in tissues. Excretion is through the bile and urine. The drugs are alternatives to erythromycin as substitutes for penicillin. Clindamycin is effective against most strains of *Bacteroides* and is a drug of choice in anaerobic infections, sometimes in combination with an aminoglycoside. Seriously ill patients are given clindamycin, 600 mg (20–30 mg/kg/d) intravenously during a 1-hour period every 8 hours. Success has also been reported in staphylococcal osteomyelitis. These drugs are ineffective in meningitis.

Common side-effects are diarrhea, nausea, and skin rashes. Impaired liver function and neutropenia have been noted. If 3–4 g are given rapidly intravenously, cardiorespiratory arrest may occur. Bloody diarrhea with pseudomembranous colitis has been associated with clindamycin administration and has caused some fatalities. This appears to be due to a necrotizing toxin produced by *Clostridium difficile*. This organism is clindamycin-resistant and increases in the gut with the selection pressure exerted by administration of this drug. The organism is sensitive to vancomycin, and the colitis rapidly regresses during oral treatment with this drug.

3. METRONIDAZOLE

Metronidazole is an antiprotozoal drug used for trichomonal and amebic infections. It also possesses striking antibacterial effects in anaerobic infections, in which the dose is 500–750 mg orally 3 or 4 times daily. In trichomoniasis, give 2 g orally once or 250 mg orally 3 times daily for 10 days. Similar dosage regimens appear to be effective also in *Gardnerella (Haemophilus)* vaginitis. Metronidazole may also be effective for preparation of the colon before bowel surgery, although it is not approved for this purpose because of its possible carcinogenic effect.

Adverse effects including stomatitis, nausea, diarrhea, and vestibular reactions may occur with prolonged use of higher dosages.

4. VANCOMYCIN

Vancomycin is bactericidal for most gram-positive organisms, particularly staphylococci and enterococci, in concentrations of 0.5–10 μg/mL. Resistant mutants are very rare, and there is no cross-resistance with other antimicrobial drugs. Vancomycin is not absorbed from the gut. It is given orally (2 g/d) only for the treatment of antibiotic-associated enterocolitis. For systemic effect, the drug must be administered intravenously, and for meningitis intrathecally. After intravenous injection of 0.5 g over a period of 20 minutes, blood levels of 10 μg/mL are maintained for 1–2 hours. Vancomycin is largely excreted into the urine. In the presence of renal insufficiency, the half-life may be up to 8 days. Thus, only one dose of 0.5–1 g may be given every 4–8 days to a uremic individual undergoing hemodialysis.

The only indications for vancomycin are serious staphylococcal infection or enterococcal endocarditis untreatable with penicillins. Vancomycin, 0.5 g 4 times daily orally, is very effective in enterocolitis. Vancomycin, 0.5 g, is injected intravenously over a 20-minute period every 6–8 hours (for children, 20–40 mg/kg/d). Against streptococci, synergism with an aminoglycoside can occur.

Vancomycin is irritating to tissues; chills, fever, and thrombophlebitis sometimes follow intravenous injection. Vancomycin is sometimes ototoxic and (perhaps) nephrotoxic.

URINARY ANTISEPTICS

Urinary antiseptics exert antimicrobial activity in the urine but have little or no systemic antibacterial effect. Their usefulness is limited to urinary tract infections.

1. NITROFURANTOIN

Nitrofurantoin is bacteriostatic and bactericidal for both gram-positive and gram-negative bacteria in urine. The activity of nitrofurantoin is greatly enhanced at pH 5.5 or lower. The drug has no systemic antibacterial activity.

The average daily dose in urinary tract infections is 100 mg orally 4 times daily (for children, 5–10 mg/kg/d), taken with food.

Oral nitrofurantoin often causes nausea and vomiting. Hemolytic anemia occurs in G6PD deficiency. Hypersensitivity may produce skin rashes and pulmonary infiltration. In uremia, there is virtually no excretion of nitrofurantoin into the urine and no therapeutic effect.

2. NALIDIXIC ACID & OXOLINIC ACID

Nalidixic acid inhibits many gram-negative bacteria in the urine but has no effect on *Pseudomonas*. In susceptible bacterial populations, resistant mutants emerge fairly rapidly. Nalidixic acid has no systemic antibacterial action.

The dose in urinary tract infections is 1 g orally 4 times daily (for children, 30–60 mg/kg/d). Adverse reactions include nausea, vomiting, skin rashes, drowsiness, visual disturbances, central nervous system stimulation, and, rarely, increased intracranial pressure with convulsions.

Oxolinic acid has similar activity and indications.

3. METHENAMINE MANDELATE
(Mandelamine)
& METHENAMINE HIPPURATE

These are salts of methenamine and mandelic acid or hippuric acid. The action of the drug depends on the liberation of formaldehyde and of acid in the urine. The urinary pH must be below 5.5, and sulfonamides must not be given at the same time. The drug inhibits a variety of different microorganisms except those (eg, *Proteus*) that liberate ammonia from urea and produce strongly alkaline urine. The dosage is 2–6 g orally daily.

4. ACIDIFYING AGENTS

Urine with a pH below 5.5 tends to be antibacterial. Many substances can acidify urine and thus produce antibacterial activity. Ammonium chloride, ascorbic acid, methionine, and mandelic acid are sometimes used. The dose has to be established for each patient by testing the urine for acid pH with test paper at frequent intervals.

SYSTEMICALLY ACTIVE DRUGS IN URINARY TRACT INFECTIONS

Many antimicrobial drugs are excreted in the urine in very high concentration. For this reason, low and relatively nontoxic amounts of aminoglycosides and polymyxins can produce effective urine levels. Many penicillins and cephalosporins can reach very high urine levels and can thus be effective in urinary tract infections.

ANTIFUNGAL DRUGS

Most antibacterial drugs have no effect on yeasts and fungi. Others (eg, amphotericin B) are used relatively effectively in some systemic mycotic infections but are difficult to administer because of toxicity. New imidazoles promise to be both effective and relatively nontoxic. Miconazole 2% cream has been used in vaginal candidiasis. Ketoconazole can be given orally, 200–400 mg once daily, preferably with food. It is well absorbed, reaches serum levels of 2–4 μg/mL, and is degraded in tissues, thus requiring no renal or biliary excretion. It has a dramatic therapeutic effect on chronic mucocutaneous candidiasis, vaginal candidiasis, and some systemic mycoses. Adverse effects are mild, with nausea, headache, skin rashes, and occasional elevations in transaminase levels.

• • •

ANTIMICROBIAL DRUGS USED IN COMBINATION

Indications

Possible reasons for employing 2 or more antimicrobials simultaneously instead of a single drug are as follows:

(1) Prompt treatment in desperately ill patients suspected of having a serious microbial infection. A good guess about the most probable 2 or 3 pathogens is made, and drugs are aimed at those organisms. Before such treatment is started, it is essential that adequate specimens be obtained for identifying the etiologic agent in the laboratory. Gram-negative sepsis and peritonitis of uncertain cause are important diseases in this category at present.

(2) To delay the emergence of microbial mutants resistant to one drug in chronic infections by the use of a second or third non–cross-reacting drug. The most prominent examples are miliary tuberculosis, tuberculous meningitis, and chronic active tuberculosis of any organ with large microbial populations.

(3) Mixed infections, particularly those following massive trauma. Each drug is aimed at an important pathogenic microorganism.

(4) To achieve bactericidal synergism (see below). In a few infections, eg, enterococcal sepsis, a combination of drugs is more likely to eradicate the infection than either drug used alone. Unfortunately, such synergism is unpredictable, and a given drug pair may be synergistic for only a single microbial strain.

Disadvantages

The following disadvantages of using antimicrobial drugs in combinations must always be considered:

(1) The surgeon may feel that since several drugs are already being given, everything possible has been done for the patient. This attitude leads to relaxation of the effort to establish a specific diagnosis. It may also give the surgeon a false sense of security.

(2) The more drugs are administered, the greater the chance for drug reactions to occur or for the patient to become sensitized to drugs.

(3) Unnecessarily high cost.

(4) Antimicrobial combinations usually accomplish no more than an effective single drug.

(5) On very rare occasions, one drug may antagonize a second drug given simultaneously. Antagonism resulting in increased morbidity and mortality has been observed mainly in bacterial meningitis when a bacteriostatic drug (eg, tetracycline or chloramphenicol) was given with a bactericidal drug (eg, penicillin or ampicillin). However, antagonism is usually overcome by an excess dose of one of the drugs in the pair and is therefore a very infrequent problem in clinical therapy.

Synergism

Antimicrobial synergism can occur in at least 3 types of situations. Synergistic drug combinations must be selected by complex laboratory procedures.

(1) Sequential block of a microbial metabolic pathway by 2 drugs. Sulfonamides inhibit the use of extracellular para-aminobenzoic acid by some microbes for the synthesis of folic acid. Trimethoprim or pyrimethamine inhibits the next metabolic step, the reduction of dihydro- to tetrahydrofolic acid. The simultaneous use of a sulfonamide plus trimethoprim is effective in some bacterial infections (eg, urinary tract, enteric) and in malaria. Pyrimethamine plus a sulfonamide is used in toxoplasmosis.

(2) One drug may greatly enhance the uptake of a second drug and thereby greatly increase the overall bactericidal effect. Penicillins enhance the uptake of aminoglycosides by enterococci and some gram-negative bacteria. Thus, a penicillin plus an aminoglycoside may be essential for the eradication of enterococcal *(Streptococcus faecalis)* infections, particularly sepsis or endocarditis or gram-negative sepsis in compromised hosts. In a like manner, carbenicillin plus gentamicin may be synergistic against some strains of *Pseudomonas*. Polymyxins are synergistic with trimethoprim-sulfamethoxazole (or rifampin) against *Serratia* sp, and flucytosine is synergistic with amphotericin B against *Cryptococcus*.

ANTIMICROBIAL CHEMOPROPHYLAXIS IN SURGERY

A major portion of all antimicrobial drugs used in hospitals is employed on surgical services with the stated intent of "prophylaxis." The administration of antimicrobials before and after surgical procedures is sometimes viewed as "banning the microbial world" both from the site of the operation and from other organ systems that suffer postoperative complications. Regrettably, the provable benefit of antimicrobial prophylaxis in surgery is much more limited.

Several general features of "surgical prophylaxis" merit consideration.

(1) In clean elective surgical procedures (ie, procedures during which no tissue bearing normal flora is traversed, other than the prepared skin), the disadvantages of "routine" antibiotic prophylaxis (allergy, toxicity, superinfection) generally outweigh the possible benefits.

(2) Prophylactic administration of antibiotics should generally be considered only if the expected rate of infectious complications approaches or exceeds 5%. An exception to this rule is the elective insertion of prostheses (cardiovascular, orthopedic), where a possible infection would have a catastrophic effect.

(3) If prophylactic antimicrobials are to be effective, a sufficient concentration of drug must be present at the operative site to inhibit or kill bacteria that might settle there. Thus, it is essential that drug administration begin some hours before operation.

(4) Prolonged administration of antimicrobial drugs tends to alter the normal flora of organ systems, suppressing the susceptible microorganisms and favoring the implantation of drug-resistant ones. Thus, antimicrobial prophylaxis should last only 1–3 days after the procedure to prevent superinfection.

(5) Systemic antimicrobial levels usually do not prevent wound infection, pneumonia, or urinary tract infection if physiologic abnormalities or foreign bodies are present.

In major surgical procedures, the administration of a "broad-spectrum" bactericidal drug from just before until 1 day after the procedure has been found effective. Thus, cefazolin, 1 g intramuscularly given 2 hours before gastrointestinal, gallbladder, or orthopedic operations and again at 2, 10, and 18 hours after the end of the operation, results in a demonstrable lowering of the risk of deep infections at the operative site. Similar reasoning applies to hysterectomy and cesarean section. In cardiovascular surgery, antimicrobials directed at the commonest pathogens are begun just prior to the procedure and continued for 2 or 3 days thereafter. While this prevents drug-susceptible organisms from producing endocarditis, pericarditis, or similar complications, it may favor the implantation of drug-resistant bacteria or fungi.

Other forms of surgical prophylaxis attempt to reduce normal flora or existing bacterial contamination at the site. Thus, the colon is routinely prepared not only by mechanical cleansing through cathartics and enemas but also by the oral administration of poorly absorbed drugs (eg, neomycin, 1 g, plus erythromycin base, 0.5 g, every 6 hours) for 1–2 days before operation. In the case of a perforated viscus resulting in peritoneal contamination, immediate treatment with an aminoglycoside, a penicillin, or clindamycin reduces the impact of seeded infection. Similarly, grossly infected compound fractures or war wounds benefit from a penicillin or cephalosporin plus an aminoglycoside. In all these instances, the antimicrobials tend to reduce the likelihood of rapid and early invasion of the bloodstream and tend to help localize the infectious process—although they generally are incapable of preventing it altogether. The surgeon must be watchful for the selection of the most resistant members of the flora, which tend to manifest themselves 2 or 3 days after the beginning of such "prophylaxis"—which is really an attempt at very early treatment.

In all situations where antimicrobials are administered with the hope that they may have a "prophylactic" effect, the risk from these same drugs (allergy, toxicity, selection of superinfecting microorganisms) must be evaluated daily, and the course of prophylaxis must be kept as brief as possible.

Topical antimicrobials have limited usefulness.

ANTIVIRAL CHEMOPROPHYLAXIS & THERAPY

Several compounds can suppress replication of influenza virus and the development of viral disease.

Amantadine hydrochloride, 200 mg orally daily for 2–3 days before and 6–7 days after influenza A infection, reduces the incidence and severity of infection. It is effective prophylaxis during outbreaks of influenza A but may induce insomnia and dizziness. In patients with renal insufficiency, amantadine may accumulate and produce toxic effects.

Idoxuridine, 0.1% solution or 0.5% ointment, effectively suppresses herpesvirus replication in corneal infections, but it has no effect on skin or mucous membrane lesions. Idoxuridine is ineffective in the treatment of genital (type 2) herpes infections.

Vidarabine (adenine arabinoside), 3% administered topically, is very effective in herpetic keratitis. Vidarabine, 10–15 mg/kg/d intravenously, is the least toxic and the most promising systemic drug for herpesvirus infections, including encephalitis, and disseminated zoster. Vidarabine can also suppress viremia in chronic active hepatitis. However, if serious neurologic sequelae are to be avoided, vidarabine treatment must be started early, before the onset of coma in encephalitis. The toxic effects of vidarabine may be more significant than was formerly believed. However, the topical application of vidarabine to skin or mucous membrane lesions of herpes simplex or zoster has no demonstrable beneficial effect.

Methisazone, 2–4 g/d orally, can inhibit the growth of smallpox or vaccinia viruses if administered within 1–2 days after exposure to these viruses.

Photodynamic inactivation has been widely used as topical therapy for skin and mucous membrane lesions caused by herpes simplex. Controlled clinical studies have failed to show a significant benefit from this treatment, and there is experimental evidence that it may induce neoplastic changes. There is thus no justification for its use.

Acyclovir (acycloguanosine) inhibits replication of herpesviruses in infected cells. When given intravenously (15 mg/kg/d), acyclovir is effective in controlling disseminating herpesvirus infections in immunocompromised patients; it can also markedly reduce pain and extent of lesions in primary genital herpes infections of women. Use in neonatal herpes is in clinical trial.

Topical acyclovir ointment (5% in polyethylene glycol) (Zovirax) applied several times daily can limit pain and virus shedding and reduce healing time in *primary* genital herpes infections. In *recurrent* herpetic lesions, the effect is minimal or questionable. Topical or systemic acyclovir has no effect on the frequency or severity of herpetic recurrences. Acyclovir-resistant herpesviruses emerge readily in patients receiving the drug and may be spread from them by contact. Topical or intravenous acyclovir produces few and mild side-effects.

INFECTIONS INVOLVING THE FEMALE GENITAL TRACT

The obstetrician-gynecologist is often confronted with infections—sometimes classic, often complex—which originate in or involve the female genital tract. Many of these are of polymicrobial etiology from the bowel, skin, or vagina; others begin as specific sexually transmitted diseases; and still others as complications of pregnancy or surgery.

NORMAL FLORA OF THE FEMALE GENITAL TRACT

Soon after birth, aerobic lactobacilli appear in the vagina and persist for weeks or even months, associated with an acid pH. They are replaced by a mixed flora with a neutral pH during childhood and adolescence. At puberty, lactobacilli reappear in large numbers and are important in maintaining acid pH by liberating organic acids from carbohydrates. If such lactobacilli are suppressed by antimicrobial drugs, yeasts and undesirable bacteria increase markedly and may cause inflammation. After menopause, the lactobacilli diminish, and a mixed flora returns.

The normal vaginal flora often includes organisms which are potential pathogens: clostridia, group B streptococci, enterococci, anaerobic streptococci (*Peptostreptococcus*), staphylococci, *Bacteroides* and other anaerobic rods, gram-negative aerobic bacteria (*E coli* and others), *Gardnerella (Haemophilus) vaginalis*, and *Listeria* species. The vaginal introitus may contain a heavy flora resembling that of the perianal area. This may be a source of recurrent vaginal or urinary tract infections.

INFECTIOUS AGENTS COMMONLY SEXUALLY TRANSMITTED OR PASSED FROM MOTHER TO NEWBORN

During the past 2 decades, there has been a marked increase in the incidence of sexually transmitted diseases, so that they are now among the most prevalent infections even in developed countries. All of the infectious agents listed below can produce asymptomatic or symptomatic infections; 2 or more are commonly present simultaneously; for control, it is essential to treat both sexual partners.

Neisseria gonorrhoeae enter mucous membranes of the genital tract, pharynx, or eye and spread from the vagina to the urethra, cervix, and rectum, giving rise to mucopurulent discharges in the acute phase. They may progress to produce salpingitis, pelvic inflammatory disease, tubo-ovarian abscess, bacteremia, arthritis, and other manifestations. Gonococci can be transmitted to the newborn, producing ophthalmia. For diagnosis and management, see Chapter 15.

Chlamydia trachomatis are intracellular parasites resembling gram-negative bacteria. They produce nongonococcal urethritis, vaginitis, cervicitis, salpingitis, and occasionally peritonitis. Chlamydial cervicitis is commonly asymptomatic but serves as a source of infection for the sexual partner or a newborn, in whom conjunctivitis or pneumonitis occurs. Drugs of choice are erythromycin for the pregnant woman and newborn or tetracycline for the nonpregnant female and her male partners.

Gardnerella (Haemophilus) vaginalis is commonly associated with vaginitis characterized by a malodorous (amine) discharge containing many "clue cells" on microscopic examination. The organisms can be part of the normal flora, but the mode of transmission, although not definitely established, is probably sexual contact. Metronidazole is the most effective drug available (see Chapter 9).

Syphilis *(Treponema pallidum)* may produce local or systemic lesions but is frequently asymptomatic and the primary lesion obscure (cervix). Early infection can be eradicated by penicillin (or tetracycline) treatment of gonorrhea, but serologic testing is mandatory for all pregnant women to avoid possible transmission to the fetus. (See Chapter 15.)

Mycoplasmas *(Ureaplasma urealyticum* and others) are often present in the vagina, cervix, and urethra. They infrequently produce symptomatic infection in the female, but asymptomatic infection may be associated with spontaneous abortion or premature delivery. Leukorrhea due to mycoplasmas is best treated with one of the tetracyclines.

Trichomonas vaginalis is a common cause of vaginitis (see Chapter 9). It is diagnosed by microscopic examination of the leukorrheal exudate for characteristic motile organisms. The patient and her sexual partner are best treated with metronidazole.

Toxoplasma gondii, a protozoon, and rubella virus produce systemic infections with no special genital tract involvement in the adult. However, both agents can infect the fetus in utero with potentially grave consequences. All prepubertal females should receive rubella vaccine to prevent infection during pregnancy (see Chapter 38). *Toxoplasma* infection of the newborn is occasionally treated with trimethoprim-pyrimethamine.

Herpes simplex virus (herpesvirus hominis) commonly produces primary genital infection as a sexually transmitted disease. About 80% of primary lesions are asymptomatic, but the remainder cause vulval and vaginal ulcerations, with severe pain and fever. Thereafter, the virus is carried for life in dorsal (sensory) ganglia, and recurrences with genital mucocutaneous lesions are common. Herpesvirus type 2 accounts for 90% of recurrent herpesvirus shedding from cervical or from vulvar lesions. It is an important cause of neonatal infection intrapartum, sometimes with disastrous consequences. Prevention rests on repeated cultures of the cervix or vagina for virus late in pregnancy. If suggestive lesions or virus are found during the last 2–4 weeks of gestation, cesarean section must be considered. Disseminated or central nervous system infection of the newborn is sometimes treated with vidarabine with some saving of life. However, a high proportion of surviving neonates have permanent neurologic damage. No practical antiviral treatment for recurrent herpes in the mother is yet available. (See p 1003.)

Cytomegalovirus can be transmitted by sexual contact and also by blood transfusion. Rarely, it causes symptomatic involvement of the adult genital tract. It may manifest itself as hepatitis, "mononucleosis," or pneumonia, especially in immunocompromised patients. The infected pregnant woman can transmit cytomegalovirus to the fetus with resulting microcephaly, cerebral calcifications, chorioretinitis, or hepatosplenomegaly. It is estimated that 4500 children are born each year in the USA with cytomegalovirus infections of lesser severity, which, however, may result in neurologic impairment or neurosensory defects.

Other sexually transmitted infections include chancroid *(Haemophilus ducreyi),* granuloma inguinale *(Calymmatobacterium granulomatis),* genital warts, or condyloma acuminatum (human papillomavirus), and candidiasis *(C albicans).* Also transmitted in the course of sexual contact are pubic lice and scabies mites.

SOFT TISSUE PELVIC INFECTIONS

These are usually polymicrobial infections attributable to members of the genital tract flora that often find favorable conditions for tissue invasion. A majority of them are anaerobes, and the following conditions encourage anaerobic infections: disorders involving reduced oxygen tension, especially the presence of necrotic tissue; impairment of local blood supply or tissue damage by toxins, primary aerobic infections. Among the factors that contribute to the development of such conditions are cancer and irradiation (creating necrotic tissue), vascular insufficiency (local or systemic, creating poor perfusion), trauma (surgical, intrapartum, abortion), foreign bodies (IUD), primary infection (gonococcal salpingitis), and cervical obstruction or stenosis (favors retention of sloughed tissue or secretions). Thus, a mixed predominantly anaerobic infection is established.

The commonest organisms that participate in such infections are gram-negative anaerobes (*Bacteroides* and related organisms), gram-positive anaerobes (peptostreptococci, peptococci, clostridia), and gram-negative aerobes (*E coli* and other enteric bacteria, which may be found in the vagina). The last-named group is encountered most often in sepsis with positive blood cultures.

Clinical signs suggestive of polymicrobic anaerobic infections typically include tissue necrosis, abscess formation, putrid odor, presence of gas in tissues, and a chronic course. None of these, however, are invariably present or diagnostic. A high index of suspicion should lead the gynecologist to obtain appropriate specimens from a central area of the lesion. These must be processed with appropriate methods that should detect various anaerobic as well as aerobic organisms. Meanwhile, the clinician must initiate provisional treatment on the assumption that a polymicrobial anaerobic infection may be present. This includes both attention to the removal of necrotic products by drainage, debridement, or resection and the administration of antimicrobial drugs. Initial therapy often utilizes a combination of drugs, including ampicillin, clindamycin or cefoxitin, and tobramycin or amikacin. The microorganisms that are isolated in culture often represent only a part of the complex flora which participated in the infection; thus, culture results cannot regularly predict the response to therapy.

Some illustrative examples are given below.

Postpartum febrile endometritis or chorioamnionitis is usually managed with the same drugs directed toward gram-negative enteric aerobes (aminoglycosides), anaerobic streptococci (a penicillin), and *Bacteroides* (clindamycin or cefoxitin), although good evidence pointing to a single etiologic organism may be lacking. In infected abortion, the cornerstone of treatment is curettage to eliminate any possible retained tissue, plus systemic drugs (as above) unless blood cultures point to a different infecting organism (see Table 1 for drugs of choice).

In salpingo-oophoritis, the initial infecting organisms may be gonococci or chlamydiae. However, anaerobes frequently appear later and contribute to abscess formation. A ruptured abscess always requires immediate operative intervention in addition to selected systemic antimicrobials. By contrast, gonococcal or chlamydial salpingitis treated early with full systemic doses of a tetracycline may respond in 48–72 hours and require no surgery.

Vaginal—and, less frequently, abdominal—hysterectomy may be followed by postoperative infections, many of which can be prevented by brief perioperative antimicrobial drug prophylaxis. Cefazolin or other cephalosporins are preferred. For established pelvic postoperative infections, nafcillin or vancomycin (aimed at β-lactamase–producing staphylococci) is often added initially to clindamycin (for the treatment of anaerobes) and an aminoglycoside (to destroy gram-negative aerobic enteric bacteria). Clinical response and cultures from involved sites must guide later possible changes in drug choice.

•   •   •

References

General

Bauer AW et al: Antibiotic susceptibility testing by a standardized single disc method. *Am J Clin Pathol* 1966; **45**:493.

Bennett WM et al: Drug therapy in renal failure. *Ann Intern Med* 1980;**93**:62.

Gall SA: The efficacy of prophylactic antibiotics in cesarean section. *Am J Obstet Gynecol* 1979;**134**:506.

Garibaldi RA et al: Factors predisposing to bacteriuria during indwelling urethral catheterization. *N Engl J Med* 1974; **291**:215.

Garrod LP, Lambert HP, O'Grady F: *Antibiotic and Chemotherapy*, 4th ed. Churchill Livingstone, 1973.

Hunt TK, Alexander JW, Burke JF: Antibiotics in surgery. *Arch Surg* 1975;**110**:148.

Kaplan EL et al: Prevention of bacterial endocarditis. (AHA Committee Report.) *Circulation* 1977;**56**:139A.

Klein RS, Berger SA, Yekutiel P: Wound infection during the Yom Kippur War: Observations concerning antibiotic prophylaxis and therapy. *Ann Surg* 1975;**182**:15.

Meyers FH, Jawetz E, Goldfien A: *Review of Medical Pharmacology*, 7th ed. Lange, 1980.

Rahal JJ: Antibiotic combinations: The clinical relevance of synergy and antagonism. *Medicine* 1978;**57**:179.

Roberts JM, Homesley HD: Low-dose carbenicillin prophylaxis for vaginal and abdominal hysterectomy. *Obstet Gynecol* 1978;**52**:83.

Stone HH et al: Antibiotic prophylaxis in gastric, biliary, and colonic surgery. *Ann Surg* 1976;**184**:443.

Storring RA et al: Oral non-absorbed antibiotics prevent infection in acute non-lymphoblastic leukaemia. *Lancet* 1977; **2**:837.

Thadepalli H, Gorback SL, Keith L: Anaerobic infections of the female genital tract: Bacteriologic and therapeutic aspects. *Am J Obstet Gynecol* 1973;**117**:1034.

Vosti KL: Recurrent urinary tract infections: Prevention by prophylactic antibiotics after sexual intercourse. *JAMA* 1975;**231**:934.

Penicillins & Cephalosporins

Border WA et al: Antitubular basement-membrane antibodies in methicillin nephritis. *N Engl J Med* 1974;**291**:381.

Brown CH et al: The hemostatic defect produced by carbenicillin. *N Engl J Med* 1974;**291**:265.

Itskovitz J et al: Effect of prophylactic antibiotics on febrile morbidity following cesarean section. *Obstet Gynecol* 1979;**53**:162.

Murray BE, Moellering RC: Cephalosporins. *Annu Rev Med* 1981;**32**:559.

Neu HC: Comparative studies of cefoxitin and cephalothin: An overview. *Rev Infect Dis* 1979;**1**:144.

Rudolph AH, Price EV: Penicillin reactions among patients in venereal disease clinics: A national survey. *JAMA* 1973; **223**:499.

Tetracyclines

Barza M, Schiefe RT: Antimicrobial spectrum, pharmacology, and therapeutic use of antibiotics. 1. Tetracyclines. *Am J Hosp Pharm* 1977;**34**:49.

Aminoglycosides

Love LJ et al: Randomized trial of empiric antibiotic therapy with ticarcillin in combination with gentamicin, amikacin, or netilmicin in febrile patients with granulocytopenia and cancer. *Am J Med* 1979;**66**:603.

McCormack WM, Finland M: Spectinomycin. *Ann Intern Med* 1976;**84**:712.

Meyer RD: Patterns and mechanisms of emergence of resistance to amikacin. *J Infect Dis* 1977;**136**:449.

Neu HC: Tobramycin, an overview. *J Infect Dis* 1976;**134 (Suppl)**:S3.

Sarubbi FA, Hull JH: Amikacin serum concentrations: Prediction of levels and dosage guidelines. *Ann Intern Med* 1978; **89**:612.

Siber GR et al: Pharmacokinetics of gentamicin. *J Infect Dis* 1975;**132**:637.

Metronidazole

Goldman P: Metronidazole. *N Engl J Med* 1980;**303**:1212.

Willis AT et al: Metronidazole in prevention and treatment of *Bacteroides* infections after appendicectomy. *Br Med J* 1976;**1**:318.

Vancomycin

Cook FV, Farrar WE: Vancomycin revisited. *Ann Intern Med* 1978;**88**:813.

Specialized Drugs Against Gram-Positive Bacteria

Swenson RM et al: Clindamycin in infections of the female genital tract. *Obstet Gynecol* 1974;**44**:699.

Other

Bennett JE: Chemotherapy of systemic mycoses. (2 parts.) *N Engl J Med* 1974;**290**:30, 320.

Corey L et al: A trial of topical acyclovir in genital herpes simplex virus infections. *N Engl J Med* 1982;**306**:1313.

Graybill JR, Drutz DJ: Ketoconazole. *Ann Intern Med* 1980; **93**:921.

Hirsch MS, Swartz MN: Antiviral drugs. (2 parts.) *N Engl J Med* 1980;**302**:903, 949.

Kaufman RH et al: Treatment of genital herpes simplex infection with photodynamic inactivation. *Am J Obstet Gynecol* 1979;**132**:861.

Lohr JA et al: Prevention of recurrent urinary tract infections in girls. *Pediatrics* 1977;**59**:562.

Rubin RH, Swartz MN: Trimethoprim-sulfamethoxazole. *N Engl J Med* 1980;**303**:426.

Whitley RJ et al: Herpes simplex encephalitis: Vidarabine therapy and diagnostic problems. *N Engl J Med* 1981; **304**:313.

Conversion of Inches to Centimeters

Inches	Centimeters	Inches	Centimeters
10	25.4	20½	52.1
10½	26.7	21	53.3
11	27.9	21½	54.6
11½	29.2	22	55.9
12	30.5	22½	57.2
12½	31.8	23	58.4
13	33.0	23½	59.7
13½	34.3	24	61.0
14	35.6	24½	62.2
14½	36.8	25	63.5
15	38.1	25½	64.8
15½	39.4	26	66.1
16	40.6	26½	67.4
16½	41.9	27	68.7
17	43.2	27½	69.9
17½	44.4	28	71.1
18	45.7	28½	72.4
18½	47.0	29	73.7
19	48.3	29½	74.9
19½	49.5	30	76.2
20	50.8	30½	77.5

Apothecary Equivalents

Metric		Approximate Apothecary Equivalents		Metric		Approximate Apothecary Equivalents	
30	g	1	oz	25	mg	3/8	gr
6	g	90	gr	20	mg	1/3	gr
5	g	75	gr	15	mg	1/4	gr
4	g	60	gr	12	mg	1/5	gr
3	g	45	gr	10	mg	1/6	gr
2	g	30	gr	8	mg	1/8	gr
1.5	g	22	gr	8	mg	1/10	gr
1	g	15	gr	5	mg	1/12	gr
0.75	g	12	gr	4	mg	1/15	gr
0.6	g	10	gr	3	mg	1/20	gr
0.5	g	7½	gr	2	mg	1/30	gr
0.4	g	6	gr	1.5	mg	1/40	gr
0.3	g	5	gr	1.2	mg	1/50	gr
0.25	g	4	gr	1	mg	1/60	gr
0.2	g	3	gr	0.8	mg	1/80	gr
0.15	g	2½	gr	0.6	mg	1/100	gr
0.12	g	2	gr	0.5	mg	1/120	gr
0.1	g	1½	gr	0.4	mg	1/150	gr
75	mg	1¼	gr	0.3	mg	1/200	gr
60	mg	1	gr	0.25	mg	1/250	gr
50	mg	3/4	gr	0.2	mg	1/300	gr
40	mg	2/3	gr	0.15	mg	1/400	gr
30	mg	1/2	gr	0.12	mg	1/500	gr
				0.1	mg	1/600	gr

Conversion of Pounds and Ounces to Grams*

Pounds \ Ounces	0	1	2	3	4	5	6	7	8	9	10	11	12	13	14	15
0	—	28	57	85	113	142	170	198	227	255	283	312	340	369	397	425
1	454	482	510	539	567	595	624	652	680	709	737	765	794	822	850	879
2	907	936	964	992	1021	1049	1077	1106	1134	1162	1191	1219	1247	1276	1304	1332
3	1361	1389	1417	1446	1474	1503	1531	1559	1588	1616	1644	1673	1701	1729	1758	1786
4	1814	1843	1871	1899	1928	1956	1984	2013	2041	2070	2098	2126	2155	2183	2211	2240
5	2268	2296	2325	2353	2381	2410	2438	2466	2495	2523	2551	2580	2608	2637	2665	2693
6	2722	2750	2778	2807	2835	2863	2892	2920	2948	2977	3005	3033	3062	3090	3118	3147
7	3175	3203	3232	3260	3289	3317	3345	3374	3402	3430	3459	3487	3515	3544	3572	3600
8	3629	3657	3685	3714	3742	3770	3799	3827	3856	3884	3912	3941	3969	3997	4026	4054
9	4082	4111	4139	4167	4196	4224	4252	4281	4309	4337	4366	4394	4423	4451	4479	4508
10	4536	4564	4593	4621	4649	4678	4706	4734	4763	4791	4819	4848	4876	4904	4933	4961
11	4990	5018	5046	5075	5103	5131	5160	5188	5216	5245	5273	5301	5330	5358	5386	5415
12	5443	5471	5500	5528	5557	5585	5613	5642	5670	5698	5727	5755	5783	5812	5840	5868
13	5897	5925	5953	5982	6010	6038	6067	6095	6123	6152	6180	6209	6237	6265	6294	6322
14	6350	6379	6407	6435	6464	6492	6520	6549	6577	6605	6634	6662	6690	6719	6747	6776
15	6804	6832	6860	6889	6917	6945	6973	7002	7030	7059	7087	7115	7144	7172	7201	7228
16	7257	7286	7313	7342	7371	7399	7427	7456	7484	7512	7541	7569	7597	7626	7654	7682
17	7711	7739	7768	7796	7824	7853	7881	7909	7938	7966	7994	8023	8051	8079	8108	8136
18	8165	8192	8221	8249	8278	8306	8335	8363	8391	8420	8448	8476	8504	8533	8561	8590
19	8618	8646	8675	8703	8731	8760	8788	8816	8845	8873	8902	8930	8958	8987	9015	9043
20	9072	9100	9128	9157	9185	9213	9242	9270	9298	9327	9355	9383	9412	9440	9469	9497
21	9525	9554	9582	9610	9639	9667	9695	9724	9752	9780	9809	9837	9865	9894	9922	9950
22	9979	10007	10036	10064	10092	10120	10149	10177	10206	10234	10262	10291	10319	10347	10376	10404

*Reproduced, with permission, from Babson SG et al: *Management of High-Risk Pregnancy and Intensive Care of the Neonate*, 3rd ed. Mosby, 1975.

Index